OLD ENGLAND:

A PICTORIAL MUSEUM

OF

REGAL, ECCLESIASTICAL, MUNICIPAL, BARONIAL, AND POPULAR ANTIQUITIES.

EDITED

BY CHARLES KNIGHT.

PORTLAND HOUSE
NEW YORK

Originally published by James Sangster & Co,
Paternoster Row, London, 1847

This 1987 edition is published by Portland House,
distributed by Crown Publishers, Inc.,
225 Park Avenue South, New York,
New York 10003.

ISBN 0 517 63184 9

Printed and bound in Italy
by Milanostampa - Farigliano (CN)
h   g   f   e   d   c   b   a

CONTENTS OF VOLUME I.

BOOK I.

BEFORE THE CONQUEST.

BOOK II.

THE PERIOD FROM THE NORMAN CONQUEST TO THE DEATH OF KING JOHN. A.D. 1066—1216.

BOOK III.

THE PERIOD FROM THE ACCESSION OF HENRY III. TO THE END OF THE REIGN OF RICHARD II. A.D. 1216—1399.

BOOK IV.

THE PERIOD FROM THE ACCESSION OF HENRY IV. TO THE END OF THE REIGN OF RICHARD III. A.D. 1399—1485.

ILLUMINATED ENGRAVINGS OF OLD ENGLAND.

⁎ Some of these Engravings are described at the pages to which they are respectively assigned in the following list. Others are not so described, although they are placed with reference to the general subject to which they belong. Where such description is not found in the text, we here subjoin a more particular notice of the Engraving.

BRERETON Hall, in Cheshire, was built in the reign of Elizabeth, by Sir William Brereton; and it is said that the queen herself laid the foundation stone. The founder appears to have liberally used the beautiful art of staining glass in the decoration of his mansion. In many of the windows were the various bearings of the principal Cheshire families, some of which still remain. But the greatest object of curiosity in this mansion, an object indeed of historical interest, was the painted window, of which we have given a faithful copy in the illuminated engraving. This window, we know not for what cause, was some years ago removed to Aston Hall, in Warwickshire. It has had the advantage of being described and engraved in Ormond's ' History of Cheshire ;' and a most beautiful and elaborate series of coloured fac-similes, the size of the originals, was executed by Mr. William Fowler, and published in 1808. From these our engraving is copied. Two of the figures represent Leofwine and Leofric, Saxon earls of Mercia. The other figures exhibit the seven Norman earls of Chester. The first earl, Hugh, surnamed Lupus, came into England with the Conqueror, who gave to him and his heirs the county of Chester, to hold as freely by him with the sword as he (William) held by the crown. He died in 1103. Richard, the son of Hugh, was the second earl. He was drowned in returning from Normandy in 1120. Dying without issue, he was succeeded by his cousin, Randolph de Meschines, the third earl, who died in 1129. The fourth earl, Randolph, surnamed de Gernonijs, took part with the Empress Maud and her son Henry, and he, with Robert Earl of Gloucester, made King Stephen prisoner at Lincoln in 1141. He died by poison in 1158. Hugh, surnamed Cyveliok, from the place in Wales where he was born, was the fifth earl; he died in 1180. Randolph, surnamed Blundeville, was the sixth earl. He was a brave, and what was more unusual for a baron, a learned man, having compiled a treatise on the Laws of the Realm. He lived in great honour and esteem in the reigns of Henry II., Richard I., John, and Henry III. He fought in the Holy Land with Cœur-de-Lion, and was the founder of the abbey of Delacroix in Staffordshire and of the Grey Friars at Coventry. He died in 1233, having held the earldom fifty-three years. Although married three times, he had no issue; but was succeeded by his nephew John, surnamed Le Scot. Upon his death without issue, in the twenty-second of Henry III., 1238, the King "thought it not good to make a division of the earldom of Chester, it enjoying such a regal prerogative; therefore, taking the same into his own hands, he gave unto the sisters of John Scot other lands, and gave the county palatine of Chester to his eldest son." (Ormerod.) John le Scot was therefore the last independent Earl of Chester. From that time the eldest sons of the sovereigns of England have been Earls of Chester from the day of their birth.

In the painted window it will be observed that each figure is placed within an arch. Each arch in the original window is seventeen inches in height, and about eight in width between the columns. The arches are struck from two centres, and have a keystone on which is represented a grotesque head under a basket of fruit. It will of course suggest itself to the reader that this window, being in all probability executed in the time of Elizabeth, cannot be received as a perfectly faithful representation even of the costume of these redoubted vice-kings of the county palatine. Upon this point Ormerod has the following remarks: "The style of the architecture is of the era of Elizabeth, but an erroneous idea prevails as to the high antiquity of these figures, and as to their having been the identical representations of the earls which formerly graced the windows of Chester Abbey." To correct this idea the county historian refers to a rude drawing in the Harleian MS. 2151, which shows the character of that ancient glass. But he adds, "It is, however, not unlikely that the figures may have been copied from paintings, stained glass, or monkish illuminations, of considerable antiquity; though the paintings themselves were most probably executed for the decoration of the newly-erected Hall of Brereton at the close of the sixteenth century."

The furniture of the ancient halls and castles of England was for the most part peculiarly suited to the size and structure of the apartments in which it was placed. Much of it was of oak, boldly and richly carved, in a manner exceedingly appropriate to the beautiful Gothic style of the windows, the panelling of the walls, and the decorations of the mantel-pieces and ceilings. The massy sideboard, or court-cupboard, as it is sometimes called, is one of those grand pieces of old Gothic furniture, of which, besides the one at Warwick Castle represented in our coloured engraving, there are still many specimens remaining in the old baronial apartments of England.

THE parish church of Stratford-upon-Avon is a large and handsome structure, of the usual cross-form, with a central tower surmounted by a spire. The chancel, of which the coloured engraving exhibits a view from the south door, showing Shakspere's monument on the north wall, is a fine specimen of late perpendicular architecture; the west end of the nave, the north porch, the piers, arches, and clerestory, are also perpendicular, but of earlier date; the tower, transept, and some parts of the nave, are early English: the ancient arches of the tower have been strengthened by underbuilding them with others of perpendicular character. Some of the windows have portions of good stained glass. Shakspere was buried on the north side of the chancel: his monument on the north wall must have been erected previous to 1623, when his works were first published, for Leonard Digges, in the verses prefixed to that first edition, thus addresses the departed poet :—

> Shakespeare, at length thy pious fellows give
> The world thy works : thy works by which outlive
> Thy tomb thy name must : when that stone is rent,
> And time dissolves thy Stratford monument,
> Here we alive shall view thee still. This book,
> When brass and marble fade, shall make thee look
> Fresh to all ages.

The sculptor of the monument was Gerard Johnson. It consists of a bust of Shakspere with the body to the waist, under an ornamented arch between two Corinthian columns which support an entablature, above which are the arms and crest of Shakspere in bold relief, surmounted by a sculptured skull. Below the figure are the following Latin and English verses :—

> Judicio Pylium, genio Socratem, arte Maronem,
> Terra tegit, populus mœret, Olympus habet.
>
> Stay, passenger, why goest thou by so fast?
> Read, if thou canst, whom envious death hath placed
> Within this monument—Shakspeare, with whom
> Quick nature died ; whose name doth deck this tomb
> Far more than cost ; sith all that he hath writ
> Leaves living art but page to serve his wit.
> Obiit Ano. Dni. 1616, ætatis 53, die 23 Apr.

Mr. Britton in 1816 published 'Remarks on Shakspeare's Monumental Bust,' in which is the following passage :— " The bust is the size of life ; it is formed out of a block of soft stone, and was originally painted over in imitation of nature. The hands and face were of flesh colour, the eyes of a light hazel, and the hair and beard auburn ; the doublet, or coat, was scarlet, and covered with a loose black gown, or tabard, without sleeves ; the upper part of the cushion was green, the under half crimson, and the tassels gilt. Such appear to have been the original features of this important, but neglected or insulted bust. After remaining in this state above one hundred and twenty years, Mr. John Ward, grandfather to Mrs. Siddons and Mr. Kemble, caused it to be repaired, and the original colours preserved, in 1748, from the profits of the representation of Othello. This was a generous and apparently judicious act, and therefore very unlike the next alteration it was subjected to in 1793. In that year Mr. Malone caused the bust to be covered over with one or more coats of white paint, and thus at once destroyed its original character, and greatly injured the expression of the face."

THE chantry, or oratory, represented in the illuminated engraving, is a detached building, separated from the chapel by an open screen. It is a beautiful work of art, and the groined ceiling is especially rich and elegant.

Between pages 250 and 251

11. METHLEY HALL . . . .

METHLEY Hall, or Methley Park, in the West Riding of Yorkshire, seven miles south-east from Leeds, is the seat of the Saviles, Earls Mexborough, which family have held the manor for several centuries. The original manor-house was built by Sir Robert Waterton, in the reign of Henry IV.; but after the manor became the property of the Saviles, the old house was pulled down, and the present magnificent mansion erected on its site by Sir John Savile, Baron of the Exchequer, with additions by his son Sir Henry Savile, in a handsome and uniform style. Of this building only the hall and the back part of the house remain: the far-famed gallery with its armorial bearings in painted glass no longer exists; it has given place to the present front part of the mansion, which is of no great magnificence without, but contains some very fine apartments, one of which, with its beautiful painted ceiling and pendent ornaments, its antique furniture, rich carving, and lofty mullioned windows, is exhibited in our coloured engraving.

12. MORRIS DANCE . . . . "

THE coloured engraving which is given as a title to the first volume of 'Old England' is the representation of an ancient window of stained glass, formerly in the house of George Tollett, Esq., of Betley, in Staffordshire, which has been conjectured by Mr. Douce, from certain peculiarities of costume, to have been executed in the time of Edward IV. The six interior lozenges on which we have engraved the title of our work are vacant in the original. The figures on the other lozenges represent the performers of a Morris Dance round a May-pole, from which are displayed a St. George's red cross and a white pennon. Immediately below the May-pole is the character who manages the pasteboard hobby-horse, who, from the crown which he wears, and the richness of his attire, appears to represent the King of May; while, from the two daggers stuck in his cheeks, he may be supposed to have been a juggler and the master of the dance. Beneath the King of May is Maid Marian, as the Queen of May; with a crown on her head and attired in a style of high fashion, her coif floating behind, her hair unbound and streaming down her waist, and holding in her hand an emblematic flower. Margaret, eldest daughter of Henry VII., when married to James, King of Scotland, appeared thus, wearing a crown and with her hair hanging down her back. Of the other characters some are obvious enough, but others are conjectural. The left-hand figure at the top is the court fool, with his cockscomb cap and his bauble. The first figure to the right is supposed to represent a Spaniard, and the next a Morisco or Moor, both men of rank, in rich dresses, with the long outer sleeves hanging loose like ribbons, a fashion once prevalent in England as well as on the Continent. Beneath the Morisco is the instrumental per-former, with his pipe and tabor; below him, the lover or paramour of Maid Marian; and under him the friar, in the Franciscan habit. The King of May is the supposed representative of Robin Hood; the Queen of May, of his favourite Marian; and the friar, of his chaplain Friar Tuck. Passing by Marian, we have the inferior fool furnished with his bib; above him, the representative of the clown or peasant; and next above, the franklin or gentleman. The dresses are curiously appropriate to the characters.

Between pages 378 and 379

OLD ENGLAND.

ADVERTISEMENT.

One of the most picturesque descriptions in the most picturesque of poets,—that in 'The Faery Queen' of the old man who

"things past could keep in memory,"

shows him sitting in a chamber which "seemed ruinous and old," but whose walls were "right firm and strong." Such are the Antiquities of a great Nation. They may appear "worm-eaten and full of canker-holes," but they are teeming with life, and will be fresh and beautiful as long as civilization endures. When the knights who looked on the old man of Spenser had perused his "antique Registers," and had traced his wondrous legends up to the time of the British kings who

"entombed lie at Stonehenge by the heath,"

one of them bursts forth into this noble apostrophe :—

"Dear Country! O how dearly dear
Ought thy remembrance and perpetual band
Be to thy foster-child, that from thy hand
Did common breath and nouriture receive!
How brutish is it not to understand
How much to her we owe, that all us gave;
That gave unto us all whatever good we have!"

Such is the just effect upon every generous mind of the study of the "ancient records" of our native land. The richest treasures that we have derived from a long line of ancestors are our antiquities. They carry us back to dim periods that have bequeathed to us no written explanation of the origin and the uses of their indestructible monuments. *Vast mounds, gigantic temples, mystic towers,* belong to ages not of barbarism, but of civilization different from our own. These are succeeded by *the remains of the great Roman conquerors of the world,* who bestowed upon Britain their refinements and their learning. Our *Anglo-Saxon Arts and Sciences* have left indelible traces, in written descriptions and pictorial representations snatched from the spoils of time; and in some architectural remains of early piety which have escaped the ravages of the Dane. Gradually the *influences of Christianity* are spread over the land; and the great connecting links between the past and the present rise up, in the glorious *Ecclesiastical edifices* that we are now at length learning to look upon with love and admiration—to preserve and to restore. But there are also monuments scattered through the country of the antagonist principles of brute force and military dominion. The *Feudal Times* have left us their impressive memorials, in *Baronial Castles* and crumbling Fortresses,—in the *Weapons and Armour* of their haughty Chieftains. These are succeeded by the *venerable Palaces* and *Mansions* which belonged to the age of early *constitutional Government,* when the *Law* allowed comfort to be studied in conjunction with security. To this age belong the monuments of *Civic Power,*

—the *Halls of Guilds* and *Companies;* and, more important still, the splendid seats of liberal *Education,* our *Endowed Schools and Colleges.* Amidst all these instructive though silent chronicles of the past, in which England is richer than any other country, have grown up the infinitely-varied peculiarities of *the middle classes,* during five centuries in which they have formed the strength of the nation; and these are preserved in numberless evidences of their *modes of life, public and domestic.* These things are surely of the deepest interest even to millions who speak the language of "old England," scattered through every quarter of the habitable Globe. The Antiquities of England are the Antiquities of North America and of Australia,—of mighty continents and fertile islands where the descendants of the Anglo-Saxon have founded "new nations." They are of especial interest to every dweller in the father-land. These "remnants of History which have casually escaped the shipwreck of time" (so Bacon defines Antiquities) are amongst the best riches of the freight of knowledge—not merely curiosities, but of intrinsic value.

We propose to open to all ranks of the people, at the cheapest rate, a complete view of the REGAL, ECCLESIASTICAL, BARONIAL, MUNICIPAL, and POPULAR ANTIQUITIES OF ENGLAND, by the publication of the largest collection of Engravings, with explanatory letterpress, that has ever been devoted to this important branch of general information. Our work is addressed to the People; but the knowledge which it seeks to impart will be as scrupulously accurate as if it were exclusively intended for the most critical antiquary. To be full and correct it is not necessary to be tedious and pedantic. That knowledge will be presented, for the most part, in a chronological order; and thus our work will be a *Companion and a Key to every English History.* The Engravings will embrace the most remarkable of our *Buildings* from the earliest times—Druidical Remains, Cathedrals, Abbeys, Churches, Colleges, Castles, Civic Halls, Mansions: *Sepulchral Monuments* of our Princes and Nobles: *Portraits* of British Worthies, and representations of the localities associated with their names: *Ancient Pictures* and *Illuminations* of Historical Events: the *Great Seals* and *Arms* of the Monarchy: *Coins* and *Medals: Autographs:* and, scattered amongst these authentic memorials of the rulers of the land, and of those who sat in high places, the fullest Pictorial indications of the *Industry,* the *Arts,* the *Sports,* the *Dresses,* and the *Daily Life* of the People.

The Forty Coloured Engravings which will form a portion of the work will consist of *Fac-Similes of Elaborate Architectural Drawings,* made expressly for this publication, and forming in themselves a most interesting series of Picturesque Antiquities.

✱✱✱ The Border represents the following objects :—at the top, Stonehenge, from the Salisbury side ; on the left hand—Roman Pharos, Dover ; Keep, Kenilworth Castle ; the Duke's House, Bradford ; Boar-hunt : on the right hand—Pevensey Castle : Bastion, and Tower of Cathedral, Canterbury ; Caius Gate of Honour, Cambridge ; Tomb of Queen Elizabeth , at the foot, South Terrace and Round Tower, Windsor Castle.

OLD ENGLAND.

BOOK I.

CHAPTER I.—THE BRITISH PERIOD.

ARUM Plain—the Salisbury Plain of our own day—an elevated platform of chalk, extending as far as the eye can reach in broad downs where man would seem to have no abiding place, presents a series of objects as interesting in their degree as the sands where the pyramids and sphinxes of ancient Egypt have stood for countless generations. This plain would seem to be the cradle of English civilization. The works of man in the earliest ages of the world may be buried beneath the hills or the rivers; but we can trace back the labours of those who have tenanted the same soil as ourselves, to no more remote period than is indicated by the stone circles, the barrows, the earth-works, of Salisbury Plain and its immediate neighbourhood.

The great wonder of Salisbury Plain,—the most remarkable monument of antiquity in our island, if we take into account its comparative preservation as well as its grandeur—is Stonehenge. It is situated about seven miles north of Salisbury. It may be most conveniently approached from the little town of Amesbury. Passing by a noble Roman earth-work called the Camp of Vespasian, as we ascend out of the valley of the Avon, we gain an uninterrupted view of the undulating downs which surround us on every side. The name of *Plain* conveys an inadequate notion of the character of this singular district. The platform is not flat, as might be imagined; but ridge after ridge leads the eye onwards to the bolder hills of the extreme distance, or the last ridge is lost in the low horizon. The peculiar character of the scene is that of the most complete solitude. It is possible that a shepherd boy may be descried watching his flocks nibbling the short thymy grass with which the downs are everywhere covered; but, with the exception of a shed or a hovel, there is no trace of human dwelling. This peculiarity arises from the physical character of the district. It is not that man is not here, but that his abodes are hidden in the little valleys. On each bank of the Avon to the east of Stonehenge, villages and hamlets are found at every mile; and on the small branch of the Wyly to the west there is a cluster of parishes, each with its church, in whose names, such as Orcheston Maries, and Shrawston Virgo, we hail the tokens of institutions which left Stonehenge a ruin. We must not hastily conclude, therefore, that this great monument of antiquity was set up in an unpeopled region; and that, whatever might be its uses, it was visited only by pilgrims from far-off places. But the aspect of Stonehenge, as we have said, is that of entire solitude. The distant view is somewhat disappointing to the raised expectation. The hull of a large ship, motionless on a wide sea, with no object near by which to measure its bulk, appears an insignificant thing: it is a speck in the vastness by which it is surrounded. Approach that ship, and the largeness of its parts leads us to estimate the grandeur of the whole. So is it with Stonehenge. The vast plain occupies so much of the eye that even a large town set down upon it would appear a hamlet. But as we approach the pile, the mind gradually becomes impressed with its real character. It is now the Chorea Gigantum—the Choir of Giants; and the tradition that Merlin the Magician brought the stones from Ireland is felt to be a poetical homage to the greatness of the work.

Keeping in view the ground-plan of Stonehenge in its present state (Fig. 1), we will ask the reader to follow us while we describe the appearance of the structure. Great blocks of stone, some of which are standing and some prostrate, form the somewhat confused circular mass in the centre of the plan. The outermost shadowed circle represents an inner ditch, a vallum or bank, and an exterior ditch, *m, n.* The height of the bank is 15 feet; the diameter of the space enclosed within the bank is 300 feet. The section *l* shows their formation. To the north-east the ditch and bank run off into an avenue, a section of which is shown at *p.* At the distance of about 100 feet from the circular ditch is a large gray stone bent forward, *a,* which, in the dim light of the evening, looks like a gigantic human being in the attitude of supplication. The direct course of the avenue is impeded by a stone, *b,* which has fallen in the ditch. A similar single stone is found in corresponding monuments. In the line of the avenue at the point marked *c* is a supposed entrance to the first or outer circle of stones. At the points *d* near the ditch are two large cavities in the ground. There are two stones *e,* and two *o,* also near the ditch. It is conjectured by some, that these formed part of a circle which has been almost totally destroyed. The centre of the enclosed space is usually denominated the temple. It consists of an outer circle of stones, seventeen of which remain in their original position; and thirteen to the northeast, forming an uninterrupted segment of the circle, leave no doubt as to the form of the edifice. The restored plan of Dr. Stukeley (Fig. 2) shows the original number of stones in this outer circle to have been thirty; those shadowed on the plan are still remaining. The upright stones of the outer circle are 14 feet in height, and upon the tops of them has been carried throughout a continuous impost, as it is technically called, of large flat stones of the same width. This has not been a rude work, as we see in the structures called cromlechs, where a flat stone covers two or three uprights, without any nice adjustment: but at Stonehenge sufficient remains to show that the horizontal stones carefully fitted each other, so as to form each an arc of the circle; and that they were held firmly in their places by a deep mortice at each end, fitting upon the tenon of the uprights. This careful employment of the builder's art constitutes one of the remarkable peculiarities of Stonehenge. The blocks themselves are carefully hewn. It is not necessary to add to our wonder by adopting the common notion that the neighbouring country produces no such material. The same fine-grained sand stone of which the greater number of the masses consists, is found scattered upon the downs in the neighbourhood of Marlborough and Avebury. The stones of the second circle are, however, of a different character; and so is what is called the altar-stone, marked *f* on the ground-plan. Of the inner circle, enclosing a diameter of 83 feet, which appears to have consisted of much smaller stones without imposts, but about the same in number as the outer circle, there are very few stones remaining. There is a single fallen stone with two mortices *g,* which has led to the belief that there was some variation in the plan of the second circle, such as is indicated by the letter *a* on the restored plan. Within the second circle were five distinct erections, each consisting of two very large stones with an impost, with three smaller stones in advance of each: these have been called trilithons. That marked *h* in the ground-plan is the largest stone in the edifice, being 21 feet 6 inches in height. The two trilithons marked *i* are nearly perfect. The stones of the trilithon *k* are entire; but it fell prostrate as recently as 1797. The external appearance which the whole work would have if restored, is shown in the perspective elevation (Fig. 3). The internal arrangement is exhibited in the section (Fig. 4). The present appearance of the ruin from different points of view is shown in Figs. 5 and 6.

The description which we have thus given, brief as it is, may appear somewhat tedious; but it is necessary to understand the

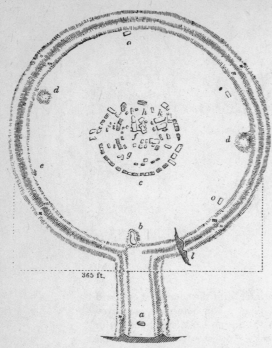

1.—Ground-Plan of Stonehenge in its present state.

5.—Stonehenge.

6.—Stonehenge.

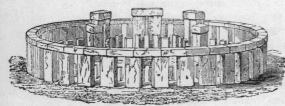

3.—Stonehenge.—Perspective Elevation restored.

4.—Stonehenge: section 1 to 2 (Restored Plan, Fig. 2), 105 feet.

7.—Druidical Circle at Darab.

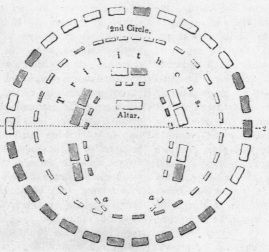

2.—Stonehenge.—Restored Plan.

8.—Druidical Stone in Persia.

4

were the Druids the instructors of youth, but the preservers and disseminators of science, the proclaimers of an existence beyond this finite and material world—idolaters, but nevertheless teaching something nobler than what belongs to the mere senses, in the midst of their idolatry. We give entire what Cæsar says of the religious system of this remarkable body of men :—

"It is especially the object of the Druids to inculcate this—that souls do not perish, but after death pass into other bodies : and they consider that by this belief more than anything else men may be led to cast away the fear of death, and to become courageous. They discuss, moreover, many points concerning the heavenly bodies and their motion, the extent of the universe and the world, the nature of things, the influence and ability of the immortal gods; and they instruct the youth in these things.

"The whole nation of the Gauls is much addicted to religious observances, and, on that account, those who are attacked by any of the more serious diseases, and those who are involved in the dangers of warfare, either offer human sacrifices or make a vow that they will offer them; and they employ the Druids to officiate at these sacrifices ; for they consider that the favour of the immortal gods cannot be conciliated unless the life of one man be offered up for that of another : they have also sacrifices of the same kind appointed on behalf of the state. Some have images of enormous size, the limbs of which they make of wicker-work, and fill with living men, and setting them on fire, the men are destroyed by the flames. They consider that the torture of those who have been taken in the commission of theft or open robbery, or in any crime, is more agreeable to the immortal gods; but when there is not a sufficient number of criminals, they scruple not to inflict this torture on the innocent.

"The chief deity whom they worship is Mercury; of him they have many images, and they consider him to be the inventor of all arts, their guide in all their journeys, and that he has the greatest influence in the pursuit of wealth and the affairs of commerce. Next to him they worship Apollo and Mars, and Jupiter and Minerva; and nearly resemble other nations in their views respecting these, as that Apollo wards off diseases, that Minerva communicates the rudiments of manufactures and manual arts, that Jupiter is the ruler of the celestials, that Mars is the god of war. To Mars, when they have determined to engage in a pitched battle, they commonly devote whatever spoil they may take in the war. After the contest, they slay all living creatures that are found among the spoil; the other things they gather into one spot. In many states, heaps raised of these things in consecrated places may be seen : nor does it often happen that any one is so unscrupulous as to conceal at home any part of the spoil, or take it away when deposited : a very heavy punishment with torture is denounced against that crime.

"All the Gauls declare that they are descended from Father Dis (or Pluto), and this, they say, has been handed down by the Druids : for this reason, they distinguish all spaces of time not by the number of days, but of nights; they so regulate their birth-days, and the beginning of the months and years, that the days shall come after the night."[*]

The precise description which Cæsar has thus left us of the religion of the Druids—a religion which, whatever doubts may have been thrown upon the subject, would appear to have been the prevailing religion of ancient Britain, from the material monuments which are spread through the country, and from the more durable records of popular superstitions—is different in some particulars which have been supplied to us by other writers. According to Cæsar, the Druids taught that the soul of man did not perish with his perishable body, but passed into other bodies. But the language of other writers, Mela, Diodorus Siculus, and Ammianus Marcellinus, would seem to imply that the Druids held the doctrine of the immortality of the soul as resting upon a nobler principle than that described by Cæsar. They believed, according to the express statement of Ammianus Marcellinus, that the future existence of the spirit was in another world. The substance of their religious system, according to Diogenes Laertius, was comprised in their three precepts—to worship the gods, to do no evil, and to act with courage. It is held by some that they had a secret doctrine for the initiated, whilst their ritual observances were addressed to the grosser senses of the multitude; and that this doctrine was the belief in one God. Their veneration for groves and of oak and for sacred fountains was an expression of that natural worship which sees the source of all good in the beautiful forms with which the earth is clothed. The sanctity of the mistletoe, the watch-fires of spring and summer and autumn, traces of which observances still remain amongst us, were

* Cæsar de Bell. Gall., lib. vi.   Our translation is that of the article "Britannia," in the Penny Cyclopædia.

tributes to the bounty of the All-giver, who alone could make the growth, the ripening, and the gathering of the fruits of the earth propitious. The sun and the moon regulated their festivals, and there is little doubt formed part of their outward worship. An astronomical instrument found in Ireland (Fig. 10) is held to represent the moon's orbit and the phases of the planets. They worshipped, too, according to Cæsar, the divinities of Greece and Rome, such as Mars and Apollo : but Cæsar does not give us their native names. He probably found ascribed to these British gods like attributes of wisdom and of power as those of Rome, and so gave them Roman names. Under the church of Notre Dame, at Paris, were found in the last century two bas-reliefs of Celtic deities, the one Cernunnos (Fig. 11), the other Hesus (Fig. 12), coresponding to the Roman Mars. Other writers confirm Cæsar's account of their human sacrifices. This is the most revolting part of the Druidical superstition. The shuddering with which those who live under a pure revelation must regard such fearful corruptions of the principle of devotion, which in some form or other seems an essential part of the constitution of the human faculties, produced this description of Stonehenge from the pen of a laborious and pious antiquary, Mr. King :—"Although my mind was previously filled with determined aversion, and a degree of horror, on reflecting upon the abominations of which this spot must have been the scene, and to which it even gave occasion, in the later periods of Druidism, yet it was impossible not to be struck, in the still of the evening, whilst the moon's pale light illumined all, with a reverential awe, at the solemn appearance produced by the different shades of this immense group of astonishing masses of rock, artificially placed, impending over head with threatening aspect, bewildering the mind with the almost inextricable confusion of their relative situations with respect to each other, and from their rudeness, as well as from their prodigious bulk, conveying at one glance all the ideas of stupendous greatness that could be well assembled together." And yet the "determined aversion and degree of horror" thus justly felt, and strongly expressed, might be mitigated by the consideration that in nations wholly barbarous the slaughter of prisoners of war is indiscriminate, but that the victim of the sacrifice is the preserver of the mass. If the victims once slain on the Druidical altars were culprits sacrificed to offended justice, the blood-stained stone of the sacred circle might find a barbarous parallel in the scaffold and the gibbet of modern times. Even such fearful rites, if connected with something nobler than the mere vengeance of man upon his fellows, are an advance in civilization, and they are not wholly inconsistent with that rude cultivation of our spiritual being which existed under the glimmerings of natural impulses, before the clear light of heaven descended upon the earth.

We stand without the bank of Stonehenge, and we look upon the surrounding plains, a prospect wide as the sea. We walk along the avenue previously noticed which extends for the third of a mile on the north-east. It then divides into two branches, the northward of which leads to what is called the cursus. This is a flat tract of land, bounded on each side by banks and ditches. It is more than a mile and five furlongs in length. Antiquaries have not settled whether it was a more recent Roman work or an appendage to the Druidical Stonehenge. At either extremity of the cursus are found what are called barrows. The southern branch of the avenue runs between two rows of barrows. On every side of Stonehenge we are surrounded with barrows. Wherever we cast our eyes we see these grassy mounds lifting up their heads in various forms (Fig. 18). Some are of the shape of bowls, and some of bells; some are oval, others nearly triangular; some present a broad but slight elevation of a circular form, surrounded by a bank and a ditch (Figs. 19, 20, 21, and 22). The form of others is so feebly marked that they can be scarcely traced, except by the shadows which they cast in the morning and evening sun. This is the great burial-place of generations long passed away. Spenser tells us, according to the old legends, that a long line of British kings here lie entombed. Milton, in his History, relates their story, "Be it for nothing else but in favour of our English poets and rhetoricians." The poets had used these legends before Milton collected them. If the old kings were here buried, though their very existence be now treated as a fable, they have wondrous monuments which have literally survived those of brass and stone. Unquestionably there were distinctions of rank and of sex amongst those who were here entombed. Their graves have been unmolested by the various spoilers who have ravaged the land; and, what is more important to their preservation, the plough has spared them, in these chalky downs which rarely repay the labours of cultivation. But the antiquary has broken into them with his spade and his mattock, and he has established their sepulchral character, and the peculiarities of their sepulture. Sir

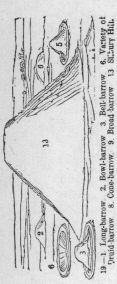

18.—*a*. Long Barrow. *b*, *c*. Druid Barrows. *d*. Bell shaped Barrow. *e*. Conical Barrow. *f*. Twin Barrow.

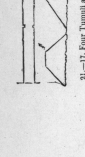

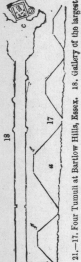

20.—Remains of Old Sarum.

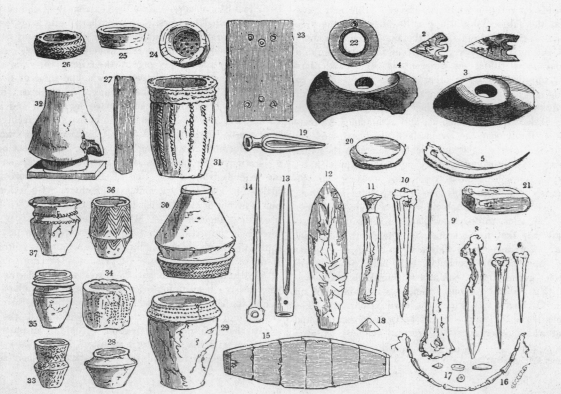

1. ⎫
2. ⎭ Flint Arrow-Heads.
3. ⎫
4. ⎭ Celts.
5. Weapon.
6. Pin. ⎫
7. Arrow-Heads. ⎬ Of Bronze.
8. Dirk or Knife. ⎭
9. Spear-Head.
10. Lance-Head.
11. Brass Knife in sheath, set in stag's-horn handle.
12. Flint Spear-Head.
13. Ivory Tweezers.
14. Ivory Bodkin.
15. Amber Ornament.

16. Necklace of Shells.
17. Beads of Glass.
18. Ivory Ornament.
19. Nippers.
20. Stone for Sling.
21. Stone to sharpen bone.
22. Ring Amulet.
23. Breastplate of Blue Slate.
24. Incense Cup.
25. Ditto.
26. Ditto.
27. Whetstone.
28 to 32. Urns.
33 to 37. Drinking-Cups.

8

25.—General View of Abury—restored.

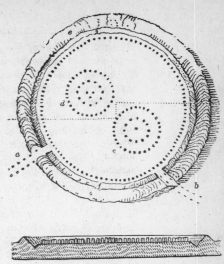

26.—Abury. Plan and Section.

29.—Arch-Druid in his full Judicial Costume.

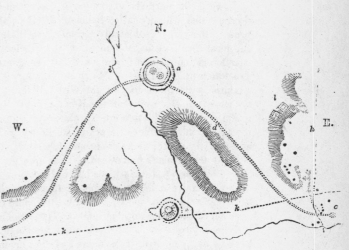

27.—Abury. Extended Plan.

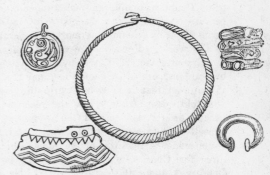

30.—Ornaments and Patterns of the Ancient Britons.

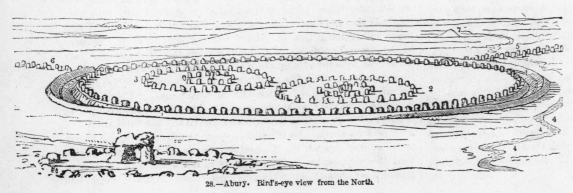

28.—Abury. Bird's-eye view from the North.

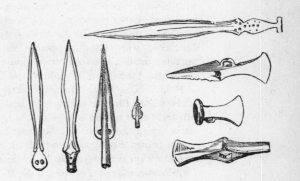

31.—British Weapons of bronze, in their earliest and improved state.

Richard Colt Hoare, who devoted a life to the examination of the antiquities of Wiltshire, justly says: " We must not consider every barrow as a mere tumulus, or mound, loosely or fortuitously thrown up: but must rather view them as works of evident design, and executed with the greatest symmetry and precision." These remarkable monuments contain not only the bones and the ashes of the dead, but various articles of utility and ornament, domestic utensils, weapons of war, decorations of the person, perhaps insignia of honour (Figs. 13 and 14), the things which contributed to comfort, to security, and to the graces of life (Fig. 24). Mela says that the Druidical belief in a future state led the people to bury with the dead things useful to the living. The contents of these barrows indicate different stages of the arts. In some there are spear-heads and arrow-heads of flint and bone (Fig. 16); in others brass and iron are employed for the same weapons. In some the earthen vessels are rudely fashioned, and appear to have been dried in the sun; in others they are of regular form, as if produced by the lathe, and are baked and ornamented. But whatever be the difference in the comparative antiquity of these barrows, it is a remarkable fact that in those of South Wiltshire, which have nearly all been explored, nothing whatever has been discovered which could indicate that this mode of sepulture was practised after the Roman dominion had commenced in Britain. The coins of the conquerors of the world are not here to be looked for.

Towards the northern extremity of that extensive range of chalky downs which, whether called Salisbury Plain or Marlborough Downs, present the same geological character, we find the seat of one of the most remarkable monuments of the ancient inhabitants of this island. About a mile to the north of the great road from Bath to London is the village of Abury or Avebury. A traveller unacquainted with the history of this little village, lying in its peaceful obscurity on the banks of the Kennet, out of the common way of traffic, might walk through it almost without noticing the vast blocks of stone which lie scattered at very irregular distances amongst its ploughed fields, or stand, as if defying time and man, close by the farmer's homestead. Year after year has their number been diminished; so that if we had only now begun to judge of the whole from its remaining parts, the great temple of Abury might have appeared to the incredulous eye little more than the imaginative creation of confiding antiquarianism. Upon the neighbouring downs there are large blocks of stone lying here and there, and seeming perhaps as symmetrically arranged as the remains of Abury. The shepherds call them the Grey Wethers, a name which implies that they have an affinity to natural objects. Man, indeed, has not disturbed their rest since they were thrown on these downs like pebbles cast by the Titans. The land upon which the Grey Wethers lie is too barren for culture; but the soil of Abury rendered the great Druidical temple an incumbrance upon its fertility. For two centuries we can trace the course of its destruction. Gibson describes it as " a monument more considerable in itself than known to the world. For a village of the same name being built within the circumference of it, and, by the way, out of its stones too, what by gardens, orchards, enclosures, and the like, the prospect is so interrupted that it is very hard to discover the form of it." The good old gossip Aubrey saw the place in 1648, and Charles the Second desired him to write an account of it in 1663. The King himself went to see it in that year; and perhaps we can have no better evidence than this of the remarkable character of the structure; for Charles, we imagine, would be as sceptical as Edie Ochiltree* about the existence of circles, and avenues, and altarstones, and cromlechs, whose plan could be indicated only by a few crumbling sand-stones. Gibson, continuing his very brief notice of Abury, says, " It is environed by an extraordinary *vallum*, or rampire, as great and as high as that at Winchester; and within it is a graff (ditch or moat) of a depth and breadth proportionable. . . . . The graff hath been surrounded all along the edge of it with large stones pitched on end, most of which are now taken away; but some marks remaining give liberty for a conjecture, that they stood quite round." In Aubrey's time, sixty-three stones, which he describes, were standing within the entrenched enclosure. Dr. Stukeley made a minute examination of Abury, from 1720 to 1724. His work, ' Abury, a Temple of the British Druids,' was published in 1743. King says, " In Dr. Stukeley's time, when the destruction of the whole for the purpose of building was going on so rapidly, still forty-four of the stones of the great outward circle were left, and many of the pillars of the great avenue: and a great cromlech was in being, the upper stone of which he himself saw broken and carried away, the fragments of it alone making no less than twenty

* "Prætorian here, Prætorian there, I mind the biggung o't."—Scott's *Antiquary.*

good cartloads." In 1812, according to Sir Richard Hoare, only seventeen of the stones remained within the great enclosure. Their number has been since still further reduced. The barbarism of the Turks, who burned the marble monuments of Greece for lime, may find a parallel in the stone-breakers of Abury, and in many other stone-breakers and stone-defacers,—the beautifiers as bad as the destroyers,—in our own country, and almost in our own day.

Dr. Stukeley, who brought to the study of these early antiquities something similar to the genius by which a naturalist can discover the structure of a fossil animal by the formation of a tooth or a claw, has given us some very complete plans for the restoration of Abury; and although he has been sometimes held to be enthusiastic and credulous, there is such sound foundation for his conjectures in this particular case, that antiquarians are pretty well agreed to speak of Abury, as it was, upon his authority. His admiration of this monument is, as we might expect, somewhat exaggerated. Aubrey said, " These antiquities are so exceedingly old that no books do reach them; I can affirm that I have brought this temple from utter darkness into a thin mist." But Stukeley endeavours to bring the original structure of the building into the clear light of day; and to describe it as perspicuously as if the ground-plans of the Arch-Druid architect were lying before him. We may smile at this; but we must not forget that the elements of such an erection are very simple. No one doubts about the great circular vallum and ditch which surround the principal work. It was there when Aubrey wrote; it remains to this day, however broken and obscured. The plan (Fig. 26) exhibits this bank e with the ditch f: immediately within the ditch was a circle of stones, dotted on the plan. This circle is stated to have been composed of a hundred stones, many from fifteen to seventeen feet in height, but some much smaller, and others considerably higher, of vast breadth, in some cases equal to the height. The distance between each stone was about twenty-seven feet. The circle of stones was about thirteen hundred feet in diameter. The inner slope of the bank measured eighty feet. Its circumference at the top is stated by Sir Richard Hoare to be four thousand four hundred and forty-two feet. The area thus enclosed exceeds twenty-eight acres. Halfway up the bank was a sort of terrace walk of great breadth. Dimensions such as these at once impress us with notions of vastness and magnificence. But they approach to sublimity when we imagine a mighty population standing upon this immense circular terrace, and looking with awe and reverence upon the religious and judicial rites that were performed within the area. The Roman amphitheatres are petty things compared with the enormous circle of Abury. Looking over the hundred columns, the spectators would see, within, two other circular temples, marked c and d; of the more northerly of these double circles some stones of immense size are still standing. The great central stone of c, more than twenty feet high, was standing in 1713. In 1720 enough remained decidedly to show their original formation. The general view (Fig. 25) is a restoration formed upon the plan (Fig. 26). Upon that plan there are two openings through the bank and ditch, a and b. These are connected with a peculiarity of Abury, such as is found in no other monument, of those called Celtic, although near Penrith a long avenue of granite stones formerly existed. At these entrances two lines of upright stones branched off, each extending for more than a mile. These avenues are exhibited in the plan (Fig. 27). That running to the south and south-east d, from the great temple a, terminated at e, in an elliptical range of upright stones. It consisted, according to Stukeley, of two hundred stones. The oval thus terminating this avenue was placed on a hill called the Hakpen, or Overton Hill. Crossing this is an old British track-way h. Barrows, dotted on the plan, are scattered all around. The western avenue c, extending nearly a mile and a half towards Beckhampton, consisted also of about two hundred stones, terminating in a single stone. It has been held that these avenues, running in curved lines, are emblematic of the serpent-worship, one of the most primitive and widely extended superstitions of the human race. Conjoined with this worship was the worship of the sun, according to those who hold that the whole construction of Abury was emblematic of the idolatry of primitive Druidism. The high ground to the south of Abury within the avenues is indicated upon the plan (Fig. 27.) Upon that plan is also marked f, a most remarkable monument of the British period, Silbury Hill, of which Sir R. Hoare says, " There can be no doubt it was one of the component parts of the grand temple at Abury, not a sepulchral mound raised over the bones and ashes of a king or arch-druid. Its situation, opposite to the temple, and nearly in the centre between the two avenues, seems in some degree to warrant this supposition." The Roman road k from Bath to London passes close under Silbury Hill, diverging from the usual straight line instead of being cut through this colossal mound. The bird's-eye view (Fig. 28) exhibits the restoration of Abury and its neighbourhood somewhat more clearly. 1 is the circumvallated bank, 2 and 3 the inner temples, 4 the river Kennet, 5 and 6 the avenues, 7 Silbury Hill, 8 a large barrow, 9 a cromlech.

Silbury Hill (Fig. 32) is the largest artificial mound in Europe. It is not so large as the mound of Alyattes in Asia Minor, which Herodotus has described and a modern traveller has ridden round. It is of greater dimensions than the second pyramid of Egypt. Stukeley is too ardent in the contemplation of this wonder of his own land when he says, " I have no scruple to affirm it is the most magnificent mausoleum in the world, without excepting the Egyptian pyramids." But an artificial hill which covers five acres and thirty-four perches; which at the circumference of the base measures two thousand and twenty-seven feet; whose diameter at top is one hundred and twenty feet, its sloping height three hundred and sixteen feet, and its perpendicular height one hundred and seven feet, is indeed a stupendous monument of human labour, of which the world can show very few such examples. There can be no doubt whatever that the hill is entirely artificial. The great earth-works of a modern railway are the results of labour, assisted by science and stimulated by capital, employing itself for profit; but Silbury Hill in all likelihood was a gigantic effort of what has been called hero-worship, a labour for no direct or immediate utility, but to preserve the memory of some ruler, or lawgiver, or warrior, or priest. Multitudes lent their aid in the formation; and shouted or wept around it, when it had settled down into solidity under the dews and winds, and its slopes were covered with everspringing grass. If it were a component part of the temple at Abury, it is still to be regarded, even more than the gathering together of the stone circles and avenues of that temple, as the work of great masses of the people labouring for some elevating and heart-stirring purpose. Their worship might be blind, cruel, guided by crafty men who governed them by terror or by delusion. But these enduring monuments show the existence of some great and powerful impulses which led the people to achieve mighty things. There was a higher principle at work amongst them, however abused and perverted, than that of individual selfishness. The social principle was built upon some sort of reverence, whether of man, or of beings held to preside over the destinies of man.

It requires no antiquarian knowledge to satisfy the observer of the great remains of Stonehenge and Abury, that they are works of art, in the strict sense of the word—originating in design, having proportion of parts, adapted to the institutions of the period to which they belonged, calculated to affect with awe and wonder the imagination of the people that assembled around them. But there are many remarkable groups of immense stones, and single stones in various parts of England, which, however artificial they may appear, are probably wholly or in part natural productions. Some of these objects have involved great differences of opinion. For instance, the Rock of Carnbré, or Karn-bré, near Truro, is held by Borlase, in his 'Antiquities of Cornwall,' to be strewed all over with Druidical remains. He says, " In this hill of Karn-bré, we find rock-basins, circles, stones erect, remains of cromlechs, cairns, a grove of oaks, a cave, and an inclosure, not of military, but religious, structure; and these are evidences sufficient of its having been a place of Druid worship; of which it may be some confirmation, that the town, about half a mile across the brook, which runs at the bottom of this hill, was anciently called Red-drew, or, more rightly, Ryd-drew, i. e., the Druid's Ford, or crossing of the brook."

The little castle at the top of the hill is called by Borlase a British fortress (Fig. 33); and in this point some antiquaries are inclined to agree with him. But they for the most part hold that his notions of circles, and stones erect, and cromlechs, are altogether visionary; and that the remarkable appearances of these rocks are produced by the unassisted operations of nature. It is certain, however, that about a century ago an immense number of gold coins were discovered on this hill, which bear no traces of Roman art; and which, having the forms of something like a horse and a wheel impressed upon them, Borlase thinks allude to the chariot-fighting of the British, being coined before the invasion of Cæsar. Davies in his 'Mythology and Rites of the British Druids,' considers them to be Druidical coins; the supposed horse being a mystical combination of a bird, a mare, and a ship,—" a symbol of Kêd or Ceridwen, the Arkite goddess, or Ceres of the Britons." It is unnecessary for us to pursue these dark and unsatisfactory inquiries. We mention them to point out how full of doubt and difficulty is the whole subject of the superstitions of our British ancestors. But wherever we can find distinct traces of their work, we discover something far above the conceptions of mere barbarians—great

monuments originating in the direction of some master minds, and adapted by them to the habits and the feelings of the body of the people. The Druidical circles, as we have shown, are not confined to England or Scotland. On the opposite shores of Brittany the great remains of Carnac exhibit a structure of far greater extent even than Abury. " Carnac is infinitely more extensive than Stonehenge, but of ruder formation; the stones are much broken, fallen down, and displaced; they consist of eleven rows of unwrought pieces of rock or stone, merely set up on end in the earth, without any pieces crossing them at top. These stones are of great thickness, but not exceeding nine or twelve feet in height; there may be some few fifteen feet. The rows are placed from fifteen to eighteen paces from each other, extending in length (taking rather a semicircular direction) above half a mile, on unequal ground, and towards one end upon a hilly site. When the length of these rows is considered, there must have been nearly three hundred stones in each, and there are eleven rows: this will give you some idea of the immensity of the work, and the labour such a construction required. It is said that there are above four thousand stones now remaining." (Mrs. Stothard's 'Tour in Normandy and Brittany.') It is easy to understand how the same religion prevailing in neighbouring countries might produce monuments of a similar character; but we find the same in the far East, in lands separated from ours by pathless deserts and wide seas. So it is with those remarkable structures, the Round Towers of Ireland; which were considered ancient even in the twelfth century. Many of these towers are still perfect. They are varied in their construction, and their height is very different; but they all agree in their general external appearance, tapering from the base to a conical cap or roof, which forms the summit. They are almost invariably found close to an ancient Christian church; which is accounted for by the fact that the sites of pagan worship were usually chosen by the early missionaries for rearing a holier structure, which should reclaim the people from their superstitious reverence, to found that reverence upon the truths which were purifying the lands of classic paganism. The Round Tower of Donoughmore (Fig. 35) is one of these singular monuments. " The only structures that have been anywhere found similar to the Irish Round Towers are in certain countries of the remote East, and especially in India and Persia. This would seem to indicate a connexion between these countries and Ireland, the probability of which, it has been attempted to show, is corroborated by many other coincidences of language, of religion, and of customs, as well as by the voice of tradition, and the light, though faint and scattered, which is thrown upon the subject by the records of history. The period of the first civilization of Ireland then would, under this view, be placed in the same early age of the world which appears to have witnessed, in those Oriental countries, a highly-advanced condition of the arts and sciences, as well as flourishing institutions of religious and civil polity, which have also, in a similar manner, decayed and passed away." ('Pictorial History of England.') The same reasoning may be applied to the Druidical circles, of which the resemblances are as striking, in countries far removed from any knowledge of the customs of aboriginal Britons.

About seven miles south of Bristol is a small parish called Stanton Drew. The name is held to mean the Stone Town of the Druids. Stukely was of opinion that the Druidical monument at this place was more ancient than Abury. The temple is held to have consisted of three circles, a large central circle, and two smaller ones. Of the larger circle five stones are still remaining; and of the smaller ones still more. Stanton Drew was described in 1718, by Dr. Musgrave, and afterwards by Stukeley. The stones had suffered great dilapidation in their time; and the process of breaking them up for roads has since gone forward with uninterrupted diligence. They are very rude in their forms, as will be seen by reference to the engraving (Fig. 34). That marked a is singular in its ruggedness. The stone b inclines towards the north, and its present position is supposed to be its original one: in its general appearance of bending forward, it is not unlike the single stone in the avenue at Stonehenge. The stone c differs greatly from the others, in being square and massive. The largest stone, d, is prostrate; it is fifteen feet and a half in length. The engraving represents not the circular arrangement, but remarkable separate stones, of which e is at a considerable distance from either of the circles. The largest stones are much inferior in their dimensions to those at Stonehenge and Abury. The smaller ones lie scattered about at very irregular distances; and it certainly requires a great deal of antiquarian faith to find the circles which are traced with such infallible certainty by early and recent writers. It is very different with Abury and Stonehenge. The country people have their own traditions about

32.—Silbury Hill, in Wiltshire.

35.—Round Tower at Donoughmore.

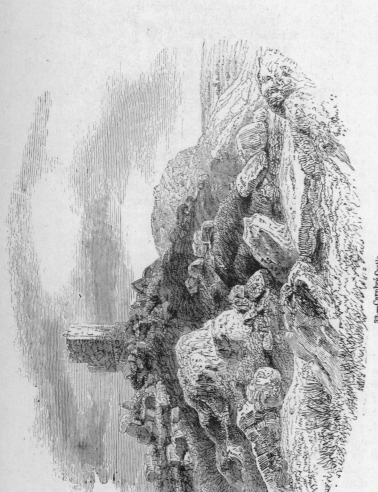

33.—Carnbré Castle.

34.—Stones at Stanton Drew.

12

36.—Kit's Coty House, near Aylesford, Kent.

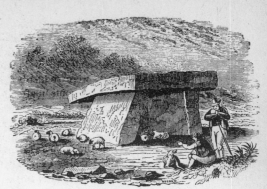

37.—Kit's Coty House.

38.—Kit's Coty House.

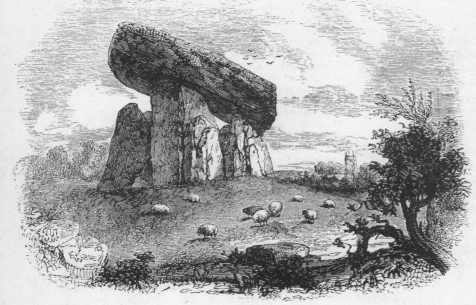

39.—Trevethy Stone.

40.—Cromlech at Plas Newydd, Anglesey.

41.—Constantine Tolman, Cornwall.

42.—Wayland Smith's Cave.

13

these remains. They call them, "the wedding;" holding that, as a bride and bridegroom were proceeding to their espousals, surrounded by pipers and dancers, the whole party, for what crime we are not informed, were suddenly turned into stone. The theories of the learned are in some matters almost as difficult to be received as the traditions of the vulgar. King says of the remains of Stanton Drew, "There are stones cautiously placed nearly on each side of the meridian, two at the one end for a sort of observer's index, and two at the other, as if designed for leading sites to direct the eye to certain points in the heavens, equally distant, a little to the east and west of the south: and so in like manner, two to the east, and one on the west side for an index, as if to observe the rising of certain stars and planets." Superstition, we apprehend, settles these matters much more easily than science. There were formerly three huge upright stones near Kennet, not far from Abury, which Dr. Plot held to be British deities. The country people had a readier explanation of their use: for they called them from time immemorial 'the Devil's Coits.' They could be playthings, it might be readily imagined, for no other busy idler. But the good folks of Somersetshire, by a sort of refinement of such hackneyed traditions, hold that a great stone near Stanton Drew, now called 'Hackell's Coit,' and which formerly weighed thirty tons, was thrown from a hill about a mile off by a mortal champion, Sir John Hautville. It is remarkable, though perhaps natural, that there is generally some superstitious notion associated with these monuments of a dim antiquity. We shall have presently to speak of the singular erection near Maidstone, called Kit's Coty House. Near this supposed cromlech are some large stones, scattered about a ploughed field. A coachman, who was duly impressed with the claims of Kit's Coty House to notice, told us, as the climax of the extraordinary things connected with it, that no one had ever been able to count the stones in that field, so that it was impossible to say what was their exact number. In the neighbourhood of Stanton Drew, they have a variation of this belief which does not go quite so far. They simply hold that it is wicked to attempt to count the stones.

The remains of Druidical circles are so similar in their character that a minute description of any other than the most remarkable would be tedious and uninteresting to the general reader. We shall content ourselves, therefore, with pointing out those of chief importance, which may either recompense the visit of the traveller, or lead the student of British antiquities to more careful inquiries.

Camden, who made an exact survey of Cumberland in 1599, thus describes a celebrated British monument near Penrith: "At Little Salkeld there is a circle of stones, seventy-seven in number, each ten foot high: and before these, at the entrance, is a single one by itself, fifteen foot high. This the common people call Long Meg, and the rest her daughters; and within the circle are two heaps of stones, under which they say there are dead bodies buried. And indeed it is probable enough that this has been a monument erected in memory of some victory." It is held by later antiquaries that Camden was in error in considering this to have been a monument of some victory, and that it is an undoubted Druidical circle. It is not of the grandeur of Stonehenge and Abury, for none of the stones exceed ten feet in height. There is another circle of stones within a mile and a half of Keswick. Near that bleak and dreary region, between Penrith and Kendal, called Shapfells, was, some thirty years ago, another remarkable Druidical monument; but upon the inclosure of the parish of Shap the stones were blown up by gunpowder, and were converted into rude fences. At Arbelows, about five miles from Bakewell, in Derbyshire, is a Druidical circle, which, according to King, "there is great reason to think, notwithstanding its mutilated appearance in its present ruined state, was once a regular structure very nearly of the same kind with that of Stonehenge." In Oxfordshire, about three miles north-west of Chipping Norton, are the remains of a circle of small rude stones, the highest of which is not more than five feet above the ground. There appears to be little doubt of this circle belonging to the early British period; though Camden and others hold it to be the monument of a Danish victory. The description which Camden gives of these Rollrich or Rowldrich stones is very curious: "A great monument of antiquity: a number of vastly large stones placed in a circular figure, which the country people call Rolle-rich-stones, and have a common tradition that they were once men and were turned into stones. They are irregular, and of unequal height, and by the decays of time are grown ragged and very much impaired. The highest of them, which lies out of the ring towards the east, they call The King, because they fancy he should have been King of England if he could have seen Long Compton, a village which is within view at a very few steps farther. Five larger

stones, which on one side of the circle are contiguous to one another, they pretend were knights or horsemen, and the other common soldiers." About five miles from Aberdeen in Scotland are the remains of a circle of large stones and smaller stones. At Stennis in the Orkney Islands a circle is described where some of the stones are twenty feet high.

The Druidical circles in their uniformity of character present the indubitable evidence that they were symbolical of the mysteries of the prevailing religion of the country. They were essentially religious edifices. They were probably, at the same time, what the Icelandic writers call Doom rings, or Circles of Judgment. That these monuments, in association with religious rites and solemn decisions, had a deep influence upon the character of our rude forefathers, we cannot reasonably doubt. They were a bold and warlike race, an imaginative race, not placing the sole end of existence in the consumption of the fruits of the earth, but believing in spiritual relations and future existences. Degrading as their superstitions might be, and blind their notions of the future, their belief was not a mere formal and conventional pretence; it was a principle operating upon their actions. We have the express testimony of an ancient poet to this effect of the old worship of this land. Lucan, in a noble passage in the first book of the Pharsalia, addresses the Druids in the well known lines beginning "Et vos babaricos." The translation of Rowe is generally quoted: but it appears to us that the lines are rendered with more strength and freedom by Kennett, who translated the poetical quotations in Gibson's edition of Camden's 'Britannia:'

"And you, O Druids, free from noise and arms,
Renew'd your barbarous rites and horrid charms.
What Gods, what powers in happy mansions dwell,
Or only you, or all but you can tell.
To secret shades, and unfrequented groves,
From world and cares your peaceful tribe removes.
You teach that souls, eas'd of their mortal load,
Nor with grim Pluto make their dark abode,
Nor wander in pale troops along the silent flood,
But on new regions cast resume their reign,
Content to govern earthy frames again.
Thus death is nothing but the middle line
Betwixt what lives will come, and what have been.
Happy the people by your charms possess'd!
Nor fate, nor fears, disturb their peaceful breast.
On certain dangers unconcern'd they run,
And meet with pleasure what they would not shun;
Defy death's slighted power, and bravely scorn
To spare a life that will so soon return."

In reading this remarkable tribute to the national courage of our remote ancestors, let us not forget that this virtue, like all other great characteristic virtues of a community, was based upon a principle, and that the principle, whatever might be its errors, rested upon the disposition of man to believe and to reverence. Those who would build the superstructure of national virtue upon what they hold to be the more solid foundation of self-interest, may, we conceive, create a restless, turmoiling, turbulent democracy, astute in all worldly business, eager for all sensual gratifications, exhibiting the glitter of wealth plating over vice and misery; confident in their superiority; ignorant of the past, careless of the future; but they will raise up no high-minded, generous, self-devoting people; no people that will distinguish between liberty and anarchy; no thoughtful, and therefore firm and just, people; no people that will produce any great intellectual work, whether in art or in literature: no people that will even leave such monuments behind them as the Stonehenge and Abury of the blind and benighted Druids.

The high road from Rochester to Maidstone presents several of those rich and varied prospects which so often in England compensate the traveller for the absence of the grander elements of picturesque beauty. Here, indeed, are no mountains shrouded in mist or tipped with partial sunlight; but the bold ridges of chalk are the boundaries of valleys whose fertility displays itself in wood and pasture, in corn-lands, and scattered villages. If we look to the north, the broad Medway expands like a vast lake, with an amphitheatre of town and hill-fort, which tell at one and the same time the history of the different warfare of ancient strength and of modern science. When we have ascended the highest point of the ridge, we again see the Medway, an attenuated stream, winding amidst low banks for many a mile. The hill of chalk is of a sufficient height to wear an aspect of sterility; it has some of the bleak features of a mountain-land. The road lies close under the brow of the hill, with a gentle slope to the village of Aylesford—an histori-cal village. Not far from the point where the Aylesford road intersects the high road is the remarkable monument called Kit's Coty House (Fig. 36). Unlike most monuments of the same high antiquity, it remains, in all probability, as originally constructed. It was described two hundred and fifty years ago by the antiquary Stow, and the description is as nearly exact as any that we could write at the present hour: "I have myself, in company with divers worshipful and learned gentlemen, beheld it in anno 1590, and it is of four flat stones, one of them standing upright in the middle of two others, inclosing the edge sides of the first, and the fourth laid flat across the other three, and is of such height that men may stand on either side the middle stone in time of storm or tempest, safe from wind and rain, being defended with the breadth of the stones, having one at their backs on either side, and the fourth over their heads." In one point the description of Stow does not agree with what we find at the present day: "About a coit's cast from this monument lieth another great stone, much part thereof in the ground, as fallen down where the same had been affixed." This stone was half buried in 1773, when Mr. Colebrooke described the monument; it is now wholly covered up. The demand of a few square feet for the growth of corn, in a country, with millions of acres of waste land, would not permit its preservation. Is this Kit's Coty House something different from other ancient monu-ments, either in its site or its structure? Let us see how Camden, writing at the same period as Stow, describes an erection in Caer-marthenshire, in the parish of Trelech: "We find a vast rude chech, or flat stone somewhat of an oval form, about three yards in length, five foot over where broadest, and about ten or twelve inches thick. A gentleman, to satisfy my curiosity, having em-ployed some labourers to search under it, found it, after removing much stone, to be the covering of such a barbarous monument as we call Kist-vaen, or Stone-chest; which was about four foot and a half in length, and about three foot broad, but somewhat narrower at the east than west end. It is made up of seven stones, viz., the covering stone already mentioned, and two side stones, one at each end, and one behind each of these, for the better securing or bolstering of them; all equally rude, and about the same thickness, the two last excepted, which are considerably thicker." The dimensions of Kit's Coty House are thus given in Grose's 'Antiqui-ties:' "Upright stone on the N. or N.W. side, eight feet high, eight feet broad, two feet thick; estimated weight, eight tons and a half. Upright stone on the S. or S.E. side, eight feet high, seven and a half feet broad, two feet thick; estimated weight eight tons. Upright stone between these, very irregular; medium dimensions, five feet high, five feet broad, fourteen inches thick; estimated weight, about two tons. Upper stone, very irregular, eleven feet long, eight feet broad, two feet thick; estimated weight, about ten tons seven cwt.' Holland, the first translator of Camden's 'Bri-tannia,' gives a description of Kit's Coty House, which includes his notion, which was also that of Camden, of the original purpose of this monument. "Catigern, honoured with a stately and solemn funeral, is thought to have been interred near unto Aylesford, where under the side of a hill, I saw four huge, rude, hard stones erected, two for the sides, one transversal in the middest between them, and the hugest of all, piled and laid over them in manner of the British monument which is called Stonehenge, but not so arti-ficially with mortice and tenants." The tradition to which Holland refers is, that a great battle was fought at Aylesford, between the Britons commanded by Catigern, the brother of Vortimer, and the Saxon invaders under Hengist and Horsa: in this battle the Saxons were routed, but Catigern fell. An earlier writer than Holland, Lambarde, in his 'Perambulations of Kent,' 1570, also describes this monument in the parish of Aylesford as the tomb of Catigern: "the Britons nevertheless in the mean space followed their victory (as I said) and returning from the chace, erected to the memory of Catigern (as I suppose) that monument of four huge and hard stones, which are yet standing in this parish, pitched upright in the ground, covered after the manner of Stonage (that famous sepul-chre of the Britons upon Salisbury Plain), and now termed of the common people here Citscotehouse." Antiquaries have puzzled themselves about the name of this Kentish monument. Kit, ac-cording to Grose, is an abbreviation of Catigern, and Coty is Coity, coit being a name for a large flat stone; so that Kit's Coty House is Catigern's House built with coits. Lambarde expressly says, 'now termed of the common people here Citscotehouse." The fa-miliar name has clearly no more to do with the ancient object of the monument than many other common names applied to edifices belonging to the same remote period. No one thinks, for example, that the name of 'Long Meg and her daughters,' of which we have

spoken, can be traced back even to the Saxon period. The theory of the earlier antiquaries that the monuments which we now gene-rally call Druidical belong to a period of British history after the Christian era, and commemorate great battles with the Saxons or the Danes, is set at rest by the existence of similar monuments in distant parts of the world; proving pretty satisfactorily that they all had a common origin in some form of religious worship that was widely diffused amongst races of men whose civil history is shrouded in almost utter darkness. Palestine has its houses of coits as well as England. The following description is from the travels of Cap-tains Irby and Mangles: "On the banks of the Jordan, at the foot of the mountain, we observed some very singular, interesting, and certainly very ancient tombs, composed of great rough stones, resembling what is called Kit's Coty House in Kent. They are built of two long side stones, with one at each end, and a small door in front, mostly facing the north: this door was of stone. All were of rough stones apparently not hewn, but found in flat frag-ments, many of which are seen about the spot in huge flakes. Over the whole was laid an immense flat piece, projecting both at the sides and ends. What rendered these tombs the more remarkable was, that the interior was not long enough for a body, being only five feet. This is occasioned by both the front and back stones being considerably within the ends of the side ones. There are about twenty-seven of these tombs, very irregularly situated." These accomplished travellers call these Oriental monuments tombs, but their interior dimensions would seem to contradict this notion. The cause of these narrow dimensions is clearly pointed out; the front and back stones are considerably within the ends of the side ones. Kit's Coty House (Figs. 37, 38) has no stone that we can call a front stone; it is open; but the back stone has the same peculiarity as the Palestine monuments; it is placed considerably within the side ones. The side stones lean inwards against the back stone; whilst the large flat stone at top, finding its own level on the irre-gular surfaces, holds them all firmly together, without the mortice and tenon which are required by the nicer adjustment of the super-incumbent stone upon two uprights at Stonehenge. It is evident that the mode of construction thus employed has preserved these stones in their due places for many centuries. The question then arises, for what purpose was so substantial an edifice erected, hav-ing a common character with many other monuments in this coun-try, and not without a striking resemblance to others in a land with which the ancient Britons can scarcely be supposed to have held any intercouse? It is maintained that such buildings, called cromlechs, were erected for the fearful purpose of human sacrifice. "For here we find in truth a great stone scaffold raised just high enough for such a horrid exhibition, and no higher; and just large enough in all its proportions for the purpose, and not too large, and so contrived as to render the whole visible to the greatest multitude of people; whilst it was so framed and put together, though super-stitiously constructed only of unhewn stones in imitation of purer and more primeval usages, that no length of time nor any common efforts of violence could destroy it or throw it down." This is King's description of what he believes to have been the terrible use of Kit's Coty House. The situation of this monument certainly renders it peculiarly fitted for any imposing solemnity, to be per-formed amidst a great surrounding multitude. But it does appear to us that a stone scaffold, so constructed, was of all forms the most unfitted for the sacrifice of a living victim, to be accomplished by the violence of surrounding priests. Diodorus says of the Druids of Gaul, "Pouring out a libation upon a man as a victim, they smite him with a sword upon the breast in the part near the diaphragm, and on his falling who has been thus smitten, both from the manner of his falling and from the convulsions of his limbs, and still more from the manner of the flowing of his blood, they presage what will come to pass." King accommodates Kit's Coty House to this descrip-tion; arguing that the top of the flat stone was a fitting place for these terrible ceremonies. The notion seems somewhat absurd; the extreme dimensions of the top stone are not more than eleven feet in any direction; a size in itself unsuited enough for such a display of physical force. But this narrow stone is also shelving; it is about nine feet from the ground in front, and seven feet at the back, having a fall of two feet in eleven feet. King says, "And yet the declivity is not such as to occasion the least danger of any slipping or sliding off." The plain reader may possibly ask what at any rate is to prevent the victim falling off when he receives the fatal blow; and wonder how the presage described by Diodorus is to be collected from the manner of his falling, when he must infallibly slide down at the instant of his fall. We must in truth receive the Roman accounts of the sacrificial practices of the ancient Druids with some suspicion. Civilized communities have

46.—Kilmarth Rocks, as seen from the South-east.

43.—Harold's Stones, Trelech, Monmouthshire.

45.—Coronation Chair. Beneath the seat is the "Stone of Destiny."

47.—The Cheesewring, as seen from the North-west.

44.—Hare Stone, Cornwall.

-48.—Hugh Lloyd's Pulpit.

16

49.—Huts in a Cingalese Village.

55.—Welsh Pigsty.

50.—Gaulish Huts.—From the Antonine Column.

56.—The Druid Grove.

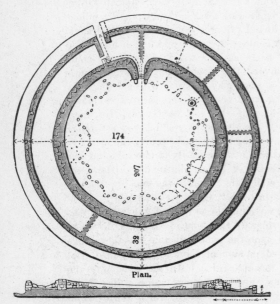

51.—Plan and Section of Chun Castle.

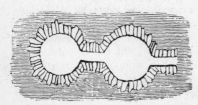

53.—Plan of Chambers on a Farm twelve miles from Ballyhendon.

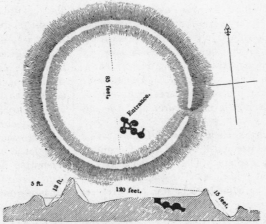

54.—Ground-plan and Section of the Subterranean Chamber at Carrighill.

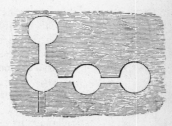

52.—Plan of Chambers at Ballyhendon.

No. 3.

17

a natural tendency to exaggerate the horrors of superstitious observances amongst remote nations that they call barbarous. The testimony is too strong to admit of a doubt that human sacrifice did obtain amongst the ancient Britons; but it can scarcely be believed that the practice formed so essential a part of their worship as to call for the erection of sacrificial altars throughout the land. Kit's Coty House is by some called a cromlech (or flat stone resting upon other stones), by which name is now generally understood an altar of sacrifice; but by others it is called a kist-vaen (or stone-chest), being, as they hold, a sepulchral monument. The Isle of Anglesey, anciently called Mona, was the great strong-hold of Druidism, whilst the Romans had still a disturbed possession of the country. Tacitus, describing an attack upon Mona, says that the British Druids "held it right to smear their altars with the blood of their captives, and to consult the will of the gods by the quivering of human flesh." At Plas Newydd, in the Isle of Anglesey, are two cromlechs (Fig. 40); and it is believed that these remains confirm the account of Tacitus, and that they were the altars upon which the victims were sacrificed. Near Liskeard, in Cornwall, in the parish of St. Clear, is a cromlech called Trevethy Stone, Trevedi being said to signify in the British language a place of graves (Fig. 39). In the neighbourhood of Lambourn, in Berkshire, are many barrows, and amongst them is found the cromlech called Wayland Smith (Fig. 42.) The tradition which Scott has so admirably used in his 'Kenilworth,' that a supernatural smith here dwelt, who would shoe a traveller's horse for a "consideration," is one of the many superstitions that belong to these places of doubtful origin and use, a remnant of the solemn feelings with which they were once regarded. In Cornwall there are many cromlechs and kist-vaens described by Borlase. They are numerous in Wales, and some are found in Ireland. In the county of Louth there is one which bears the name of the Killing Stone; and this is held by King to be a decisive proof of its original use. But, although we may well believe that the horrid practice of human sacrifice was incidental to the Druidical worship, we are not to collect from the Roman writers that it constituted the chief part of the Druidical system. It is clear that there were many high and abstract doctrines taught under that system; and that the very temples of the worship were symbolical of certain principles of belief. Whether the cromlechs or kist-vaens were used for sacrifice, it has been thought that the stone-chests, at least, were symbolical of one of the great traditions of mankind which was widely diffused; and which therefore exhibited itself in the outward forms of sacred places amongst divers nations. The form of an ark or chest is prevalent in all the ancient religions of the world. A recent writer says, "On careful deliberation, and considering that the first tabernacles and constructed temples are to be taken as commentaries on the stone monuments of more ancient date, we are disposed to find an analogy between the kist-vaen, or stone-chest, and the ark, or sacred chest, which we find as the most holy object in the tabernacle and temple of the Hebrew, as well as in the Egyptian and some other heathen temples." (Kitto's 'Palestine.') The ark of Noah, the cradle of the post-diluvian races, was thus symbolized. In this point of view we can understand how the same form of building shall be found on the banks of the Jordan and on the banks of the Medway. It is a curious fact that the Bards, who were the direct successors of the Druids, and who continued to preserve some of their mysterious and initiatory rites after the Druidical worship was suppressed by the Romans, have distinct allusions to the ark, or stone-chest, in which the candidate for admission to the order underwent a probationary penance. The famous Welsh bard, Taliesen, gives a remarkable description of this ceremony, which is thus translated by Davies: "I was first modelled into the form of a pure man, in the hall of Ceridwen, who subjected me to penance. Though small within my chest, and modest in my deportment I was great. A sanctuary carried me above the surface of the earth. Whilst I was enclosed within its ribs, the sweet Awen rendered me complete: and my law, without audible language, was imparted to me by the old giantess, darkly smiling in her wrath; but her claim was not regretted when she set sail." Davies adds, "Ceridwen was, what Mr. Bryant pronounces Ceres to have been, the genius of the ark; and her mystic rites represented the memorials of the deluge."

There are remains of the more ancient times of Britain whose uses no antiquarian writers have attempted, by the aid of tradition or imagination, satisfactorily to explain. They are, to a certain extent, works of art; they exhibit evidences of design; but it would appear as if the art worked as an adjunct to nature. The object of the great Druidical monuments, speaking generally, without reference to their superstitious uses, was to impress the mind with something like a feeling of the infinite, by the erection of works of such large proportions that in these after ages we still feel that they are sublime, without paying respect to the associations which once surrounded them. So it would appear that those who once governed the popular mind sought to impart a more than natural grandeur to some grand work of nature, by connecting it with some effort of ingenuity which was under the direction of their rude science. Such are the remains which have been called Tolmen; a Tolman being explained to be an immense mass of rock placed aloft on two subjacent rocks which admit of a free passage between them. Such is the remarkable remain in the parish of Constantine in Cornwall: "It is one vast egg-like stone thirty-three feet in length, eighteen feet in width, and fourteen feet and a half in thickness, placed on the points of two natural rocks, so that a man may creep under it' (Fig. 41.) There appears to be little doubt that this is a work of art, as far as regards the placing of the huge mass (which is held to weigh seven hundred and fifty tons), upon the points of its natural supporters. If the Constantine Tolman be a work of art, it furnishes a most remarkable example of the skill which the early inhabitants of England had attained in the application of some great power, such as the lever, to the aid of man's co-operative strength. But there are some remains which have the appearance of works of art, which are probably, nothing but irregular products of nature,—masses of stone thrown on a plain surface by some great convulsion, and wrought into fantastic shapes by agencies of dripping water and driving wind, which in the course of ages work as effectually in the changes of bodies as the chisel and the hammer. Such is probably the extraordinary pile of granite in Cornwall called the Cheesewring, a mass of eight stones rising to the height of thirty-two feet, whose name is derived from the form of an ancient cheese-press (Fig. 47). It is held, however, that some art may have been employed in clearing the base from circumjacent stones. Such is also a remarkable pile upon a lofty range called the Kilmarth Rocks, which is twenty eight feet in height, and overhangs more than twelve feet towards the north (Fig. 46.) The group of stones at Festiniog in Merionethshire, called Hugh Lloyd's pulpit (Fig. 48), is also a natural production. But there are other remains which the antiquaries call Logan, or Rocking-stones, in the construction of which some art appears decidedly to have been exercised. Cornwall is remarkable for these rocking-stones. Whether they were the productions of art or wholly of nature, the ancient writers seem to have been impressed with a due sense of the wonder which attached to such curiosities. Pliny tells of a rock near Harpasa which might be moved with a finger (placed no doubt in a particular position) but would not stir with a thrust of the whole body. Ptolemy, with an expression in the highest degree poetical, speaks of the Gygonian rock, which might be stirred with the stalk of an asphodel, but could not be removed by any force. There is a rocking-stone in Pembrokeshire, which is described in Gibson's edition of Camden's 'Britannia,' from a manuscript account by Mr. Owen; "This shaking stone may be seen on a sea-cliff within half a mile of St. David's. It is so vast that I presume it may exceed the draught of an hundred oxen, and it is altogether rude and unpolished. The occasion of the name (Y maen sigl, or the Rocking-stone) is for that being mounted upon divers other stones about a yard in height is so equally poised that a man may shake it with one finger so that five or six men sitting on it shall perceive themselves moved thereby." There is a stone of this sort at Golcar Hill, near Halifax in Yorkshire, which mainly lost its rocking power through the labours of some masons, who, wanting to discover the principle by which so large a weight was made so easily to move, hewed and hacked at it until they destroyed its equilibrium. In the same manner the soldiers in the civil wars rendered the rocking-stone of Pembrokeshire immoveable after Mr. Owen had described it; but their object was not quite so laudable as that of the masons who sought to discover the mystery of the stone of Golcar Hill. The soldiers upset its equipoise upon the same principle that they broke painted glass and destroyed monumental brasses; they held that it was an encouragement to superstition. In the same way the soldiers of Cromwell threw down a famous stone called Men-amber, in the parish of Sithney, in Cornwall, which a little child might move; and it is recorded that the destruction required immense labour and pains. Some few years ago one of these famous rocking-stones, on the coast of Cornwall, was upset by a ship's crew for a freak of their officers; but the people, who had a just veneration for their antiquities, insisted upon the rocking-stone being restored to its place: it was restored; but the trouble and expense were so serious, that the disturbers went away with a due sense of the skill of those who had first poised these mighty masses, as if to assert the permanency of their art, and to show that all that is gone before us is not wholly barbarous. It is a curious fact that the tackle which was used for the restoration of this rocking-stone, and which was applied by military engineers, broke under the weight of the mass which our rude forefathers had set up. The rocking-stones which are found throughout the country are too numerous here to be particularly described. They are in many places distinctly surrounded by Druidical remains, and have been considered as adjuncts to the system of divination by which the priesthood maintained their influence over the people.

In various parts of England, in Wales, in Ireland, and in the Western Islands of Scotland, there are found large single stones, firmly fixed in the earth, which have remained in their places from time immemorial, and which are generally regarded with some sort of reverence, if not superstition, by the people who live near them. They are in all likelihood monuments which were erected in memory of some remarkable event, or of some eminent person. They have survived their uses. Written memorials alone shine with a faint light through the darkness of early ages. The associations that once made these memorials of stone solemn things no longer surround them. When Jack Cade struck his sword upon London Stone, the act was meant to give a solemn assurance to the people of his rude fidelity. The stone still stands; and we now look upon it simply with curiosity, as one of the few remains of Roman London. Some hold that it had "a more ancient and peculiar designation than that of having been a Roman Milliary, even if it ever were used for that purpose afterwards. It was fixed deep in the ground; and is mentioned so early as the time of Æthelstan, king of the West Saxons, without any particular reference to its having been considered as a Roman Milliary stone." (King.) If this stone, which few indeed of the busy throngs of Cannon-street cast a look upon, were only a boundary-stone, such stones were held as sacred things even in the times of the patriarchs: "And Laban said to Jacob, Behold this heap and behold this pillar, which I have cast betwixt me and thee; this heap be witness, and this pillar be witness, that I will not pass over this heap to thee, and that thou shalt not pass over this heap and this pillar unto me, for harm." (Genesis, c. xxxi., v. 51, 52.) In the parish of Sancred, in Cornwall, is a remarkable stone called the Hare Stone (hare or hoar meaning literally border or boundary), with a heap of stones lying around it (Fig. 44). It is held that these stones are precisely similar to the heap and the pillar which were collected and set up at the covenant between Jacob and Laban, recorded in the Scriptures with such interesting minuteness. It is stated by Rowland, the author of 'Mona Antiqua,' that wherever there are heaps of stones of great apparent antiquity, stone pillars are also found near them. This is probably too strong an assertion; but the existence of such memorials, which, King says, "are, like the pyramids of Egypt, records of the highest antiquity in a dead language," compared with the clear descriptions of them in the sacred writings, leaves little doubt of the universality of the principle which led to their erection. A heap of stones and a single pillar was not, however, the only form of these stones of memorial. At Trelech, in Monmouthshire, are three remarkable stones, one of which is fourteen feet above the ground, and which evidently formed no part of any Druidical circle. These are called Harold's Stones (Fig. 43). Near Boroughbridge, in Yorkshire, are some remarkable stones of similar character, called the Devil's Arrows. The magnitude of these stones of memorial was probably sometimes regulated by the importance of the event which they were intended to celebrate; but their sacred character in many cases did not depend upon their size, and their form is sometimes unsuited to the notion that they were boundary stones, or even monumental pillars. The celebrated stone which now forms the seat of the coronation chair of the sovereigns of England is a flat stone, nearly square. It formerly stood in Argyleshire, according to Buchanan; who also says that King Kenneth, in the ninth century, transferred it to Scone, and enclosed it in a wooden chair. The monkish tradition was, that it was the identical stone which formed Jacob's pillow. The more credible legend of Scotland is, that it was the ancient inauguration-stone of the kings of Ireland. "This fatal stone was said to have been brought from Ireland by Fergus, the son of Eric, who led the Dalriads to the shores of Argleshire. Its virtues are preserved in the celebrated leonine verse:—

Ni fallat fatum, Scoti, quocunque locatum
Invenient lapidem, regnare tenentur ibidem.

Which may be rendered thus:—

Unless the Fates are faithless found,
And Prophet's voice be vain,
Where'er this monument be found
The Scottish race shall reign."

Sir Walter Scott, in his graceful style, gives us this version of his country's legend. The stone, as the youngest reader of English history knows, was removed to Westminster from Scone, by Edward I.; and here it remains, as an old antiquarian has described it, "the ancientest respected monument in the world; for, although some others may be more ancient as to duration, yet thus superstitiously regarded are they not." (Fig. 45.) The antiquity of this stone is undoubted, however it may be questioned whether it be the same stone on which the ancient kings of Ireland were inaugurated on the hill of Tara. This tradition is a little shaken by the fact that stone of the same quality is not uncommon in Scotland. The history of its removal from Scone by Edward I. admits of no doubt. A record exists of the expenses attending its removal; and this is the best evidence of the reverence which attached to this rude seat of the ancient kings of Scotland, who, standing on it in the sight of assembled thousands, had sworn to reverence the laws, and to do justice to the people.*

———

Of the domestic buildings of the early Britons there are no remains, if we except some circular stone foundations, which may have been those of houses. It is concluded, perhaps somewhat too hastily, that their houses were little better than the huts of the rude tribes of Africa or Asia in our own day (Fig. 49). In the neighbourhood of Llandaff were, in King's time, several modern pig-sties, of a peculiar construction; and he held that the form of these was derived from the dwellings of the ancient Britons (Fig. 55). This form certainly agrees with the description which Strabo gives of the houses of the Gauls, which he said were constructed of poles and wattled work, of a circular form, and with a lofty tapering roof. On the Antonine column we have representations of the Gauls and the Gaulish houses, but here the roofs are for the most part with domes (Fig. 50). Strabo further says, "The forests of the Britons are their cities; for, when they have enclosed a very large circuit with felled trees, they build within it houses for themselves and hovels for their cattle. These buildings are very slight, and not designed for long duration." Cæsar says, "What the Britons call a town is a tract of woody country, surrounded by a vallum and a ditch, for the security of themselves and cattle against the incursions of their enemies." The towns within woods were thus fortresses; and here the Druidical worship in the broad glades, surrounded by mighty oaks, which were their natural antiquities, was cultivated amidst knots of men, held together by common wants as regarded the present life, and common hopes with reference to the future (Fig. 56). A single bank and ditch, agreeing with Cæsar's description, is found in several parts of the island. There is such an entrenchment in the parish of Cellan, Cardiganshire, called Caer Morus. We shall presently have to speak of the ramparted camps, undoubtedly British, which are found on commanding hills, exhibiting a skill in the military art to which Cæsar bore testimony, when he described the capital of Cassivellaunus as admirably defended both by nature and art. But we here insert a description of Chun Castle, in Cornwall, to furnish a proof that the skill of the ancient Britons in building displayed itself in more important works than their wattled huts: "It consists of two circular walls, having a terrace thirty feet wide between (Fig. 51). The walls are built of rough masses of granite of various sizes, some five or six feet long, fitted together, and piled up without cement, but presenting a regular and tolerably smooth surface on the outside. The outer wall was surrounded by a ditch nineteen feet in width: part of this wall in one place is ten feet high, and about five feet thick. Borlase is of opinion that the inner wall must have been at least fifteen feet high; it is about twelve feet thick. The only entrance was towards the south-west, and exhibits in its arrangement a surprising degree of skill and military knowledge for the time at which it is supposed to have been constructed. It is six feet wide in the narrowest part, and sixteen in the widest, where the walls diverge, and are rounded off on either side. There also appear indications of steps, up to the level of the area within the castle, and the remains of a wall which, crossing the terrace from the outer wall, divided the entrance into two parts at its widest end. The inner wall of the castle incloses an area measuring one hundred and seventy-five feet north and south, by one hundred and eighty feet east and west. The centre is without any indication of buildings; but all around, and next to the wall, are the remains of circular inclosures, supposed to have formed the habitable parts of the

* The Coronation Chair, the seat of which rests upon this stone of destiny, is also represented in the illuminated engraving which accompanies this portion of our work. It is a fac-simile of a highly-finished architectural drawing, and is printed in oil colours from twelve separate plates, so united in the printing as to produce a separate outline, and to give all the various tints of the original.

60.—Woad. (Isatis Tinctoria.)

Side View.

Foreshortened View showing the end

57.—Ancient British Canoes—Found at North Stoke, Sussex.

58.—British Coracles.

61—Gaulish Costume.

59.—British Pearl Shells.   Natural size
Duck fresh-water Pearl Mussel (Anodon Anatinus).   b. Swan ditto (Anodon Cygneus)

62.—Gaulish Costume.

63.—Gaulish Costume.

20

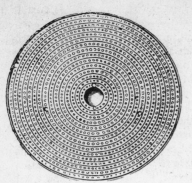

66.—Shield in the Meyrick Collection.

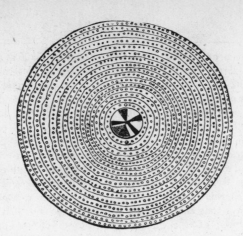

67.—Circular British Shield.

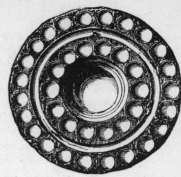

65.—Shield in the British Museum.

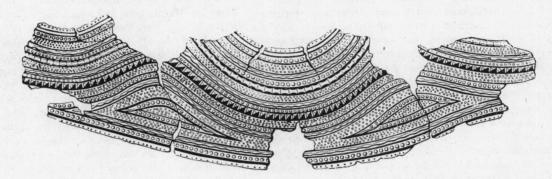

64.—Remains of a British Breast-plate, found at Mold.

68.—Ancient British Coins.

69.—Group of Ring Coins.

castle. They are generally about eighteen or twenty feet in diameter, but at the northern side there is a large apartment thirty by twenty." ('Pictorial History of England.')

That the Britons were agriculturists, using the term in a larger sense than applies to the cultivation of small patches of land by solitary individuals, we may reasonably infer from some remarkable remains that are not uncommon in these islands. Tacitus, in his account of the manners of the Germans, says, "the Germans were accustomed to dig subterraneous caverns, and then to cover them with much loose mould, forming a refuge from wintry storms, and a recepticle for the fruits of the earth: in this manner the rigour of the frost is softened." Tacitus also says that these caverns are hiding-places for the people upon the irruption of an enemy. Such pits were common to the ancient people of the East, and are found in modern times in other European countries. There is a singular cavern of this sort at Royston, in Hertfordshire, which was discovered in the market-place of that town in 1742. Kent has several such pits. Hasted, the topographer of that country, describes many such in the heaths and fields and woods near Crayford. He says that at the mouth, and thence downward, they are narrow, like the tunnel or passage of a well; but at the bottom they are large and of great compass, so that some of them have several rooms, one within another, strongly vaulted, and supported with pillars of chalk. Camden has given a rude representation of two caverns near Tilbury in Essex, "spacious caverns in a chalky cliff, built very artificially of stone to the height of ten fathoms, and somewhat straight at the top. A person who had been down to view them gave me a description of them." The chambers in the caverns, which Camden depicts, consist either of a large space, with semicircular recesses, or of two chambers, each with three semicircular recesses connected by a passage. The universality of the practice is shown in the caves which were discovered in Ireland, in 1829, which are described in the 'Transactions of the Antiquarian Society of London,' vol. xxiii. (Figs. 52, 53, and 54.) There can be little doubt of the use of such caves. Diodorus Siculus expressly says that the Britons laid up their corn in subterranean repositories. There are other remarkable remains whose purposes do not seem quite so clear. These are artificial pits of a conical form. At the top of the Combe Hills, near Croydon, in Surrey, is a pit of this sort, minutely described by King. An early antiquarian, John Leland—who peregrinated England and Wales in the time of Henry VIII., and whose descriptions, whenever he entered into detail, are so curious that we sigh over his usual brevity, and wish that he were as prolix as the travellers of our own age—thus described similar pits near Caernarvon: "There be a great number of pits made with hand, large like a bowl at the head, and narrow in the bottom, overgrown in the swart with fine grass, and be scattered here and there about the quarters where the head of Kenner river is, that commeth by Caire Kenner. And some of these will receive a hundred men, some two hundred. They be in the Black Mountain." ('Itinerary,' vol. viii. folio 107, a.)

Of a later period than that to which we are referring are probably the very singular caves of Hawthornden. Beneath the rock on which Drummond and Jonson sat, looking out upon the delicious glen whose exquisite beauties would seem the natural abodes of peacefulness and innocence, are the hiding-places of remote generations. Long galleries and dreary caverns cut in the rock, are peopled by tradition with the brave and the oppressed hiding from their enemies. Here we are shown the king's bedchamber; and another cave, whose walls are cut into small recesses of about a foot square, was the king's drawing-room. He was here surrounded by ample conveniences for arranging the petty treasures of his solitude. Setting these traditions aside, we may reasonably conclude that the caves of Hawthornden were at once hiding-places and storehouses: and it is not carrying our fancies too far to believe that the shelved cavities of the rock were receptacles for food, in small portions—the oatmeal and the pulse that were thus preserved from worms and mildew.

The primitive inhabitants of all sea-girt countries are fishermen. It is impossible not to believe that the people of Britain, having at their command the treasures of wide æstuaries and deep rivers, were fishermen to a large extent. The Britons must always have been a people who were familiar with the waters. The Severn and the Wye have still their coracles. Little boats so peculiar in their construction that we may readily conceive them to belong to a remote antiquity. Gibson, the translator and best editor of Camden, has described these boats upon the Severn: "The fishermen in these parts use a small thing called a coracle, in which one man being seated will row himself with incredible swiftness with one hand, while with the other he manages his net, angle, or other fishing-

tackle. It is of a form almost oval, made of split sally-twigs interwoven (willow-twigs), round at the bottom, and on that part which is next the water it is covered with a horse-hide. It is about five feet in length and three in breadth, and is so light that, coming off the water, they take them upon their backs and carry them home." Such, we may conclude, were the fishing-boats of our primitive ancestors (Fig 58). Some of the Roman writers might lead us to believe that the Britons had boats capable of distant navigation; but this is doubted by most careful inquirers. But the light boats which were peculiar to the island were certainly of a construction well suited to their objects; for Cæsar, in his history of the Civil War, tells us that he had learnt their use in Britain, and availed himself of boats of a similar formation in crossing rivers in Spain. These were probably canoes, hollowed out of a single tree. Such have been found, from seven to eight feet long, in morasses and in the beds of rivers, at very distant parts of the country—in Dumfries and in the marshes of the Medway. In 1834 a boat of this description was discovered in a creek of the river Arun, in the village of North Stoke, Sussex (Fig. 57). In draining the Martine Mere, or Marton lake, in Lancashire, eight canoes, each formed of a single tree, were found sunk deep in the mud and sand. The pearl-fishery of Britain must have existed before the Roman invasion, for Suetonius says that the hope of acquiring pearls was a main inducement to Cæsar to attempt the conquest of the country. The great conqueror himself, according to Pliny, the naturalist, dedicated to Venus a breast-plate studded with British pearls, and suspended it in her temple at Rome. In a later age the pearls of Caledonia were poetically termed by Ausonius the white shell-berries. Camden thus describes the pearls of the little river Irt in Cumberland: "In this brook the shell-fish, eagerly sucking in the dew, conceive and bring forth pearls, or, to use the poet's words, shell-berries. These the inhabitants gather up at low water; and the jewellers buy them of the poor people for a trifle, but sell them at a good price. Of these, and such like, Marbodæus seems to speak in that verse,

'Gignit et insignes antiqua Britannia baccas.'
('And Britain's ancient shores great pearls produce.')"

The British pearls were not found in the shells of the oyster, as is often thought, but in those of a peculiar species of mussel (Fig. 59). The oysters of Britain, celebrated by Pliny and Juvenal after the Roman conquest, contributed, we may reasonably suppose, to the food of the primitive inhabitants.

The dresses of the inhabitants of Britain before the Roman invasion are not, like those of the people of ancient Egypt, and other countries advanced in the practice of the imitative arts, to be traced in painting or sculpture. In Roman statues we have the figures of ancient Gauls, which give us the characteristic dress of the Celtic nations: the braccæ, or close trowsers, the tunic, and the sagum, or short cloak (Figs. 61, 62, 63). The dye of the woad was probably used for this cloth, as it was to colour the skins of the warriors stripped for battle (Fig. 60). It is difficult to assign an exact period to their use of cloth in preference to skins. It is equally difficult to determine the date of those valuable relics which have been found in various places, exhibiting a taste of symmetry and nice workmanship in the fabrication of their weapons, offensive and defensive, and the ruder decorations of their persons. Such are the remains of a golden breast-plate found at Mold, in Flintshire now in the British Museum (Fig. 64). Such are the shields (Figs. 65, 66, 67), of one of which (Fig. 67) Sir Samuel Meyrick, its possessor, says, "It is impossible to contemplate the artistic portions without feeling convinced that there is a mixture of British ornaments with such resemblances to the elegant designs on Roman works as would be produced by a people in a state of less civilization." Torques, or gold and bronze necklaces composed of flexible bars, were peculiar to the people of this country. Of all these matters we shall have further to speak in the next chapter—the Roman Period. There also we may more properly notice the great variety of British coins, of which we here present a group (Fig. 68). Ring-money, peculiar to the Celtic nations, undoubtedly existed in Ireland previous to the domination of the Romans in Britain. Although Cæsar says that the ancient Britons had no coined money, there is sufficient probability that they had their metal plates for purposes of currency, such being occasionally found in English barrows. The Ring-money (Fig. 69) has been found in great quantities in Ireland, of bronze, of silver, and of gold. The rings vary in weight; but they are all exact multiples of a standard unit, showing that a uniform principle regulated their size, and that this was determined by their use as current coin. The weapons of the ancient Britons show their acquaintance with the casting of metals. Their axe-heads, called Celts, are composed of ten parts of copper and one of tin (Figs. 70 and 71); their spear-heads, of six parts of copper and one of tin. Moulds for spear-heads have been frequently found in Britain and Ireland (Figs. 72 and 73).

There are no remains of those terrible war-chariots of the Britons which Cæsar describes as striking terror into his legions. King, who labours very hard to prove that the people who stood up not only with undaunted courage, but military skill, against the conquerors of the world, were but painted savages, considers that the British war-chariot was essentially the same as the little low cart which the Welsh used in his day for agricultural purposes (Fig. 74). The painters have endeavoured to realize the accounts of the Roman writers, with more of poetry, and, we believe, with more of truth (Fig. 75).

But if the chariots have perished,—if the spears and the axe-heads are doubtful memorials of the warlike genius of the people,—not so are the mighty earth-works which still attest that they defended themselves against their enemies upon a system which bespeaks their skill as well as their valour. The ramparted hill of Old Sarum, with terrace upon terrace rising upon its banks and ditches, and commanding the country for miles around, is held not merely to have been a Roman station, or a British station after the Romans, but a fortified place of the people of the country, even in the time of the great Druidical monuments which are found scattered over the great plain where this proud hill still stands in its ancient majesty. The Roman walls, the Saxon Towers, the Norman cathedral which have successively crowned this hill, have perished, but here it remains, with all the peculiar character of a British fortress still impressed upon it (Fig. 23). Such a fortress is the Herefordshire beacon (Fig. 76), which forms the summit of one of the highest of the Malvern hills, and looks down upon that glorious valley of the Severn which, perhaps more than any other landscape, proclaims the surpassing fertility of 'Old England.' Such is in all likelihood the castellated hill near Wooler, in Northumberland, which rises two thousand feet above the adjacent plain, with its stone walls, and ditches and crumbling cairns. It was in these hill-forts that the Britons so long defied the Roman power; and one of them (near the confluence of the Coln and Teme, in Shropshire) is still signalised by the name of one of the bravest of those who fought for the independence of their country—Caer-Caradoc, the castle of Caractacus (Fig. 77). The Catter-thuns of Angus (Forfarshire) are amongst the most remarkable of the Caledonian strongholds. They are thus described by Pennant, in his 'Tour in Scotland:'—"After riding two miles on black and heathy hills, we ascended one divided into two summits; the higher named the White, the lower the Black Catter-thun, from their different colour. Both are Caledonian posts; and the first of most uncommon strength. It is of an oval form, made of a stupendous dike of loose white stones, whose convexity, from the base within to that without, is a hundred and twenty-two feet. On the outside, a hollow, made by the disposition of the stones, surrounds the whole. Round the base is a deep ditch, and below that, about a hundred yards, are vestiges of another that went round the hill. The area within the stony mound is flat; the greater axis or length of the oval is four hundred and thirty-six feet; the transverse diameter, two hundred. Near the east side is the foundation of a rectangular building; and on most parts are the foundations of others small and circular; all which had once their superstructures, the shelter of the possessors of the post. There is also a hollow, now almost filled with stones, the well of the place. The literal translation of the word Catter-thun is Camp-town." The vitrified forts of Scotland are so mysterious in their origin and their uses, some holding them to be natural volcanic productions, others artificial buildings of earth, made solid by the application of fire, without cement, that we may safely omit them in this notice of the British period.

In speaking of those ancient works in these islands which were constructed upon a large scale for the defence of the country and for the accommodation of the people, it is difficult to define the precise share of the ancient Britons in their construction, as compared with the labours of successive occupants of the country. Old Sarum, for example, has the characteristics of a work essentially different from the camps and castles of Roman origin. But the Romans, too wise a people to be destroyers, would naturally improve the old defences of the island, and adapt them to their own notions of military science. So, we imagine, it would have been with what we are accustomed to call the four great Roman Ways. The old chroniclers record that King Dunwallo (called also Moliuncius or Mulmutius) "began the four highways of Britain, the which were finished and perfited of Belinus his son." This is the Mulmutius whose civilizing deeds are thus described by Spenser:—

"Then made he sacred laws, which some men say
Were unto him reveal'd in vision;
By which he freed the traveller's highway,
The Church's part, and ploughman's portion,
Restraining stealth and strong extortion;
The gratious Numa of Great Britainy:
For, till his days, the chief dominion
By strength was wielded without policy:
Therefore he first wore crown of gold for dignity."

Camden, who naturally enough has a disposition, from the nature of his learning, to hold that the civilization of Britain began from the Roman conquest, laughs to scorn the notion of the great highways being made before the Romans:—"Some imagine that these ways were made by one Mulmutius, God knows who, many ages before the birth of Christ: but this is so far from finding credit with me, that I positively affirm they were made from time to time by the Romans. When Agricola was Lieutenant here, Tacitus tells us, that 'the people were commanded to carry their corn about, and into the most distant countries: not to the nearest camps, but to those that were far off and out of the way.' And the Britons (as the same author has it) complained, ' that the Romans put their hands and bodies to the drudgery of clearing woods and paving fens, with stripes and indignities to boot." And we find in old records, ' In the days of Honorius and Arcadius, there were made in Britain certain highways from sea to sea.' That they were the work of the Romans, Bede himself tell us: "The Romans lived within that wall (which, as I have already observed, Severus drew across the island) to the southward; as the cities, temples, bridges and highways made there, do plainly testify at this day.'" But in these quotations there is nothing to prove that there were not roads in Britain before the Romans. That the more ancient roads were not the magnificent works which the Romans afterwards constructed we may well believe; but, on the other hand, it is impossible to imagine that a people accustomed to military movements were without roads. The local circumstances also belonging to the great Druidical monuments, such as Stonehenge and Abury, indicate with sufficient clearness that they were not solely constructed with reference to the habits of a stationary population, but that they were centres to which great bodie of the people resorted at particular seasons of solemnity. We may take, therefore, the statements of the old chroniclers with regard to the more ancient and important of the highways as not wholly fabulous. Robert of Gloucester, in his rude rhyme, has told us as much as is necessary here to say about them :—

"Faire weyes many on ther ben in Englonde;
But four most of all ther ben I understonde,
That thurgh an old kynge were made ere this,
As men schal in this boke aftir here tell I wis.
Fram the South into the North takith Erminge-strete.
Fram the East into the West goeth Ikeneld-strete.
Fram South-est to North-west, that is sum del grete,
Fram Dover into Chestre goeth Watlyng-strete.
The ferth of thise is most of alle that tilleth fram Tateneys.
Fram the South-west to North-est into Englondes ende
Fosse men callith thilke wey that by mony town doth wende.
Thise four weyes on this londe kyng Belin the wise
Made and ordeined hem with gret fraunchise."

We have thus hastily presented a sketch, imperfect in the details, but not without its impressiveness if regarded as exhibiting the solemn picture of man struggling to comprehend the Infinite through clouds and darkness—we have thus attempted to group the memorials of ages which preceded the Roman domination in 'Old England.' We look back upon these earliest records of a past state of society with wonder not unmixed with awe, with shuddering but not with hatred :—

"Yet shall it claim our reverence, that to God,
Ancient of Days! that to the eternal Sire
These jealous ministers of law aspire,
As to the one sole fount whence wisdom flow'd,
Justice, and Order. Tremblingly escaped,
As if with prescience of the coming storm,
That intimation when the stars were shaped;
And still, 'mid yon thick woods, the primal truth
Glimmers through many a superstitious form
That fills the soul with unavailing ruth."

WORDSWORTH.

70.—Celt.

76.—The Herefordshire Beacon.

71.—Celt.

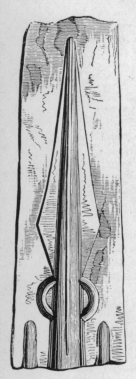

72.—Spear-Mould.

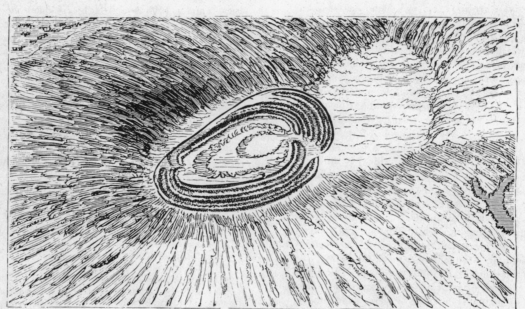

77—British Camp at Caer-Caradoc.—From Roy's Military Antiquities.

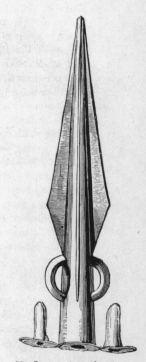

73.—Spear as it would have come from the Mould.

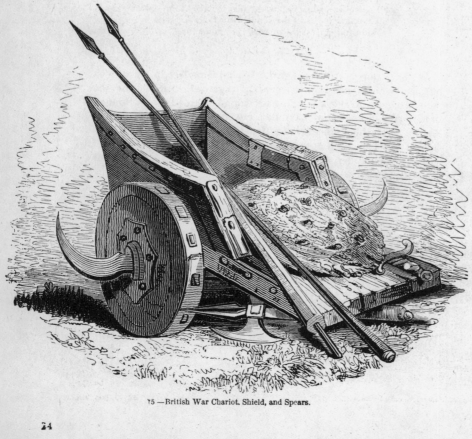

75—British War Chariot, Shield, and Spears.

74.—Welsh Agricultural Cart.

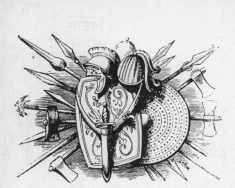

80.—British and Roman Weapons.

79.—Symbols of Rome.

81.—Captive wearing the Torque.

85.—Roman Eagle.

86.—Prow of a Roman Galley.

87.—Country near Dover.

88.—Dover Cliffs.

83.—Julius Cæsar. From a Copper Coin in the British Museum.

82.—Roman General, Standard-Bearers, &c.

84.—Julius Cæsar.

CHAPTER II.—THE ROMAN PERIOD.

HE inland part of Britain, says Cæsar, "is inhabited by those who, according to the existing tradition, were the aborigines of the island; the sea-coast, by those who, for the sake of plunder or in order to make war, had crossed over from among the Belgæ, and in almost every case retained the names of their native states from which they emigrated to this island, in which they made war and settled, and begun to till the land. The population is very great, and the buildings very numerous, closely resembling those of the Gauls: the quantity of cattle is considerable. . . . . . The island is of a triangular form, one side of the triangle being opposite Gaul. One of the angles of this side, which is in Cantium (Kent), to which nearly all vessels from Gaul come, looks toward the rising sun; the lower angle looks towards the south. . . . . Of all the natives, those who inhabit Cantium, a district the whole of which is near the coast, are by far the most civilized, and do not differ much in their customs from the Gauls." With these more civilized people Cæsar negotiated. They had sent him ambassadors and hostages to avert the invasion which they apprehended; but their submission was fruitless. In the latter part of the summer of the year 55 B.C. (Halley, the astronomer, has gone far to prove that the exact day was the 26th of August), a Roman fleet crossed the Channel, bearing the infantry of two legions, about ten thousand men. This army was collected at the Portus Itius (Witsand), between Calais and Boulogne. Eighty galleys (Fig. 86) bore the invaders across the narrow seas. As they neared the white cliffs which frowned upon their enterprise (Figs. 87, 88, 90), Cæsar beheld them covered with armed natives, ready to dispute his landing. The laurelled conqueror (Figs. 83, 84), who, according to Suetonius, only experienced three reverses during nine years' command in Gaul, would not risk the Roman discipline against the British courage, on a coast thus girt with natural defences. It is held that the proper interpretation of his own narrative is, that he proceeded towards the north; and it is considered by most authorities that the flat beach between Walmer Castle and Sandwich was the place of his disembarkation. It was here, then, that the British and Roman weapons first came into conflict (Fig. 80). But the captains and the standard-bearers marched not deliberately to the shore, as they are represented on the Column of Trajan (Fig. 82). The cavalry and the war-chariots of the active Britons met the invader on the beach: and whilst the soldiers hesitated to leave the ships, the standard-bearer of the tenth legion leaped into the water, exclaiming, as Cæsar has recorded, "Follow me, my fellow-soldiers, unless you will give up your eagle to the enemy: I, at least, will do my duty to the republic and to our general!" (Fig. 85.) The Romans made good their landing. The symbols of the great republic were henceforward to become more familiar to the skin-clothed and painted Britons (Fig. 79); but not as they were they to be bound with the chain of the captive (Fig. 81). The galleys in which the cavalry of Cæsar were approaching the British shores were scattered by a storm. This calamity, and his imperfect acquaintance with the country and with the coast, determined the invader to winter in Gaul. It is a remarkable fact that Cæsar was ignorant of the height to which the tide rises in these narrow seas. A heavy spring-tide came, and his transports, which lay at anchor, were dashed to pieces, and his lighter galleys (Figs. 93, 94, 95), drawn up on the beach, were swamped with the rising waves. This second disaster occurred within a few hours of the conclusion of a peace between the invader and the invaded. That very night, according to Cæsar, it happened to be full moon, when the tides always rise highest—"a fact at the time wholly unknown to the Romans." The Britons, with a breach of confidence that may almost be justified in the case of the irruption of a foreign power into a peaceful land, broke the treaty. Cæsar writes that they were signally defeated. But the invader hastily repaired his ships; and set sail, even without his hostages, for the opposite shores, where his power was better established.

Cæsar, early in the next year, returned to a conflict with the people whose coast "looks towards the rising sun." He came in a fleet of eight hundred vessels; and the natives, either in terror or in policy, left him to land without opposition. The flat shores of Kent again received his legions; and he marched rapidly into the country, till he met a formidable enemy in those whom he had described as "the inland people," who "for the most part do not sow corn, but live on milk and flesh, and have their clothing of skins." Cæsar himself bears the most unequivocal testimony to the indomitable courage of this people. The tribes with whom Cæsar came into conflict were, as described by him, the people of Cantium, inhabitants of Kent; the Trinobantes, inhabitants of Essex; the Cenimagni, inhabitants of Norfolk, Suffolk, and Cambridge; the Segontiaci, inhabitants of parts of Hants and Berks; the Ancalites, inhabitants of parts of Berks and Wilts; the Briboci, inhabitants of parts of Berks and the adjacent counties; the Cassi, conjectured to be the inhabitants of Cassio hundred, Herts.* Cæsar, after various fortune, carried back his soldiers in the same year to Gaul. He set sail by night, in fear, he says, of the equinoctial gales. He left no body of men behind him; he erected no fortress. It is probable that he took back captives to adorn his triumph. But the Romans, with all their national pride, did not in a succeeding age hold Cæsar's expedition to be a conquest. Tacitus says that he did not conquer Britain, but only showed it to the Romans. Horace, calling upon Augustus to achieve the conquest, speaks of Britain as "intactus," (untouched); and Propertius, in the same spirit, describes her as "invictus," (unconquered). There is, perhaps, therefore, little of exaggeration in the lines which Shakspere puts into the mouth of the Queen in 'Cymbeline:'

> Remember, Sir, my liege,
> The kings your ancestors; together with
> The natural bravery of your isle, which stands
> As Neptune's park, ribbed and paled in
> With rocks unscaleable, and roaring waters;
> With sands that will not bear your enemies' boats,
> But suck them up to the top-mast. A kind of conquest
> Cæsar made here; but made not here his brag
> Of came, and saw, and overcame: with shame
> (The first that ever touch'd him) he was carried
> From off our coast, twice beaten; and his shipping
> (Poor ignorant baubles!) on our terrible seas,
> Like egg-shells mov'd upon their surges, crack'd
> As easily 'gainst our rocks.

We have thus narrated very briefly the two descents of Cæsar upon Britain; because, from the nature of his inroad into the country, no monuments exist or could have existed to attest his progress. But it is not so with the subsequent periods of Roman dominion. The great military power of the ancient world may be here traced by what is left of its arms and its arts. Camden has well described the durable memorials of the Roman sway: "The Romans, by planting their colonies here, and reducing the natives under the rules of civil government—by instructing them in the liberal arts, and sending them into Gaul to learn the laws of the Roman empire,—did at last so reform and civilize them by introducing their laws and customs, that for the modes of their dress and living they were not inferior to the other provinces. The buildings and other works were so very magnificent, that we view the remains of them to this day with the greatest admiration; and the common people will have these Roman fabrics to be the works of giants." We proceed to a rapid notice of the more important of these monuments.

* See Maps of the Society for the Diffusion of Useful Knowledge.

In that curious record, in old French, of the foundation of the Castle at Dover, which we find in Dugdale's 'Monasticon,' we are told that when Arviragus reigned in Britain, he refused to be subject to Rome, and withheld the tribute; making the Castle of Dover strong with ditch and wall against the Romans, if they should come. The old British hill-forts and cities were not works of regular form, like the camps and castles of the Romans; and thus the earliest remains of the labours of man in Dover Castle exhibit a ditch and a mound of irregular form, a parallelogram with the corners rounded off, approaching to something like an oval. Yet within this ditch are the unquestionable fragments of Roman architecture, still standing up against the storms which have beaten against them for nearly eighteen centuries (Fig. 89). We may well believe, therefore, that the statement of the chronicler is not wholly fabulous when he said that a British king strengthened Dover Castle; and that the Romans, as in other cases, planted their soldiers in the strongholds where the Britons had defied them. Be this as it may, the Roman works of Dover Castle are among the most interesting in the island, remarkable in themselves, suggestive of high and solemn remembrances. Toil up the steep hill, tourist, and mount the tedious steps which place you on the heights where stands this far-famed castle. Look landward, and you have a prospect of surpassing beauty, not unmixed with grandeur; look seaward, and you may descry the cliffs of France, with many a steamboat bringing in reality those lands together which dim traditions say were once unsevered by the sea. Look not now upon the Norman keep, for after a little space we will ask you to return thither; but wind round the slight ascent which is still before you, till you are at the foot of the grassy mound upon which stand the ruined walls which attest that here the Romans trod. That octagonal building, some thirty or forty feet high, and which probably mounted to a much greater height, was a Roman pharos, or lighthouse. Mark the thickness of its walls, at least ten feet! see the peculiarity of its construction, wherever the modern casing, far more perishable than the original structure, will permit you. The beacon-fires of that tower have long been burnt out. They were succeeded by bells, which rung their merry peals when kings and lord-wardens came here in their cumbrous pageantry. The bells were removed to Portsmouth, and the old tower was unroofed. Man has taken no care of it; man has assisted the elements in its destruction. But its builders worked not for their own age alone, as the moderns work. Its foundations are laid in clay, and not upon the chalk. The thin flat bricks, which are known as Roman tiles, are laid in even courses, amidst intermediate courses of blocks of hard stalactitical concretions which must have been brought by sea from a considerable distance. Some of the tiles are of a peculiar construction having knobs and ledges as if to bind them fast with the other materials. In the true Roman buildings the uniformity of the courses, especially where tiles are used, is most remarkable. Such is the case in this building: "With alternate courses formed of these and other Roman tiles, and then of small blocks of the stalactitical incrustations, was this edifice constructed, from the bottom to the top; —each course of tiles consisting of two rows; and each course of stalactites, of seven rows of blocks, generally about seven inches deep, and about one foot in length. Five of these alternate courses, in one part, like so many stages or stories, were discernible a few years ago very clearly."—(King.) When the poor fisherman of Rutupiæ (Richborough) steered his oyster-laden bark to Gesoriacum (Boulogne), the pharos of Dover lent its light to make his path across the Channel less perilous and lonely. At Boulogne there was a corresponding lighthouse of Roman work; an octagonal tower, with twelve stages of floors, rising to the height of one hundred and twenty-five feet. This tower is said to have been the work of Caligula. It once stood a bowshot from the sea; but in the course of sixteen centuries the cliff was undermined, and it fell in 1644. The pharos of Dover has had a somewhat longer date, from the nature of its position. No reverence for the past has assisted to preserve what remains of one of the most interesting memorials of that dominion which had such important influences in the civilization of England. The mixed race in our country has, in fact, sprung from these old Romans; and the poetical antiquary thus carries us back to the great progenitors of Rome herself: "Whilst," says Camden, "I treat of the Roman Empire in Britain (which lasted, as I said, about four hundred and seventy-six years), it comes into my mind how many colonies of Romans must have been transplanted hither in so long a time; what numbers of soldiers were continually sent from Rome, for garrisons; how many persons were despatched hither, to negotiate affairs, public or private; and that these, intermarrying with the Britons, seated themselves here, and multiplied into families: for, 'Wherever' (says Seneca) 'the Roman conquers

he inhabits.' So that I have ofttimes concluded that the Britons might derive themselves from the Trojans by these Romans (who doubtless descended from the Trojans), with greater probability than either the Arverni, who from Trojan blood styled themselves brethren to the Romans, or the Mamertini, Hedui, and others, who upon fabulous grounds grafted themselves into the Trojan stock. For Rome, that common mother (as one calls her), challenges all such as citizens—

"Quos domuit, nexuque pio longinqua revinxit."
("Whom conquer'd, she in sacred bonds hath tied.")

The old traditions connected with Dover Castle, absurd as they are, are founded upon the popular disposition to venerate ancient things. The destruction of ancient things in this country, during the last three centuries, was consummated when a sceptical, sneering, unimaginative philosophy was enabled, in its pride of reason, to despise what was old, and to give us nothing that was beautiful and venerable in the place of what had perished. Lambarde thus writes: "The Castle at Dover, say Lydgate and Rosse, was first built by Julius Cæsar, the Roman Emperor, in memory of whom they of the Castle keep till this day certain vessels of old wine and salt which they affirm to be the remain of such provisions as he brought into it." The honest topographer adds, with a beautiful simplicity, "As touching the which, if they be natural and not sophisticate, I suppose them more likely to have been of that store which Hubert de Burgh laid in there." Now Hubert de Burgh lived three hundred and fifty years before Lambarde; and we are inclined to think that even his vessels of old wine might have stood a fair chance of being tapped and drunk out during the troublesome times which elapsed between the reign of John and the reign of Elizabeth. But yet it were vain of us to despise this confiding spirit of the old writers. We have gained nothing in literature or in art, perhaps very little in morals, by calling for absolute proof in all matters of history; and by fancying that, if we cannot have a clear microscopic bird's-eye view of the past, we are to turn from its dimly-lighted plains, and its misty hills losing themselves in the clouds, as if there were nothing soothing and elevating in their shadowy perspective. There must be doubt and difficulty and uncertainty in all that belongs to very remote antiquity:—

"Darkness surrounds us; seeking, we are lost
On Snowdon's wilds, amid Brigantian coves,
Or where the solitary shepherd roves
Along the plain of Sarum, by the Ghost
Of Time and Shadows of Tradition crost,
And where the boatman of the Western Isles
Slackens his course to mark those holy piles
Which yet survive on bleak Iona's coast.
Nor these, nor monuments of eldest fame,
Nor Taliesin's unforgotten lays,
Nor characters of Greek or Roman fame,
To an unquestionable Source have led;
Enough—if eyes that sought the Fountain-head
In vain, upon the growing Rill may gaze."
Wordsworth.

This is wisdom—a poet's wisdom, which has sprung and ripened in an uncongenial age. But if we seek the "growing Rill," we shall not gaze upon it with less pleasure if we have endeavoured, however imperfectly and erringly, to trace it to the "Fountain-head."

Close by the pharos are the ruins of an ancient church (Fig. 89). This church, which was in the form of a cross, was unquestionably constructed of Roman materials, if it was not of Roman work. The tiles present themselves in the same regular courses as in the pharos. The latter antiquarians are inclined to the belief that this church was constructed of the materials of a former Roman building. It appears exceedingly difficult to reconcile such a belief with the fact that Roman walls, wherever we find them in this country, are almost indestructible. The red and yellow tiles at Richborough, for example, of which we shall have presently to speak, are embedded as firmly in the concrete as the layers of flint in a cliff of chalk. The flints may be removed with much greater ease from the chalk than the tiles from the concrete. The whole forms a solid mass which tool can hardly touch. It would have been no economy, we believe, of labour or of material to have pulled down such a Roman building, to erect another out of its ruins; although, indeed, the building may have been destroyed, and another building of new materials may have been put together upon the principles of Roman construction. Such considerations ought to induce us not lightly to reject the traditions, which have come down to us through the old ecclesiastical annalists, of a very early Christian church, some say the first Christian church, having been erected within the original Roman, or earlier than Roman, hill-fort in Dover Castle. Little is left of this interesting ruin of some Christian church: and

E 2

92.—Roman Eagle.

89.—Roman Lighthouse, Church, and Trenches in Dover Castle.

93.—Roman Galley.

96.—Roman Standard Bearer.

91.—Roman Church in Dover Castle.

97.—Roman Soldiers.

94.—Roman Galley.

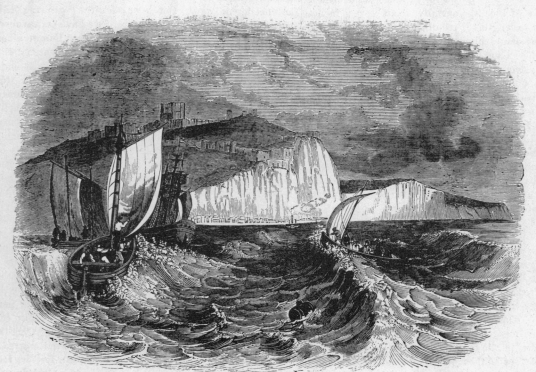

90.—Dover Cliffs.

95.—Roman Galley.

98.—Plan of Richborough.

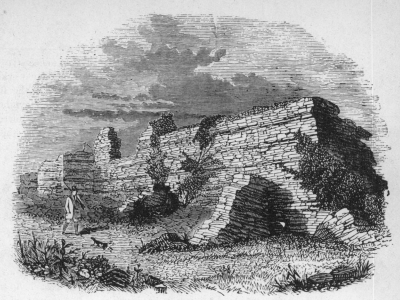

100.—North Wall of Richborough

102.—Bronze found at Richborough.

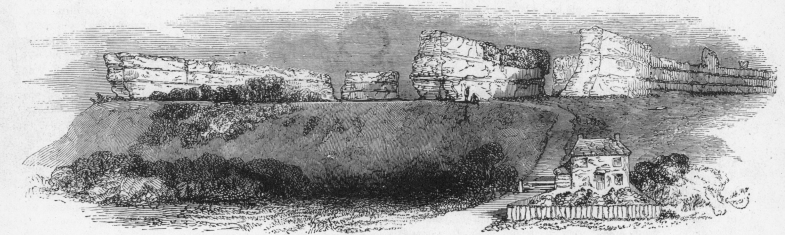

99.—Richborough. General View, from the East.

101.—Plan of the Platform and Cross, Richborough.

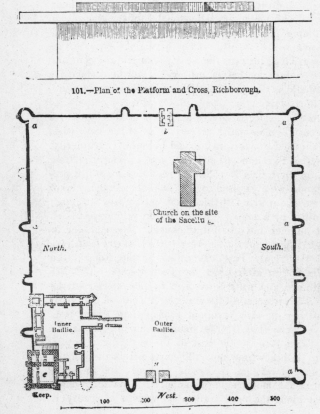

104.—Plan of Porchester Castle, Hants.

103.—Ruins of Ancient Church of Reculver.

that little has been defaced by the alterations of successive centuries (Fig. 91). But here is a religious edifice of Roman workmanship, or built after the model of Roman workmanship, in the form dear to the Christian worship, the primitive and lasting symbol of the Christian faith. It is held by some, and perhaps not unreasonably, that here stood the Prætorium of the Roman Castle—the elevated spot for state display and religious ceremonial, the place of command and of sacrifice. It is held, too, that upon such a platform was erected the Sacellum, the low buildings where the eagles which led the Roman soldiers to victory were guarded with reverential care. Such buildings, it is contended, might grow into Christian churches. It is difficult to establish or to disprove these theories; but the fact is certain that in several of the undoubted Roman castles, or camps, is a small building of cruciform shape, placed not far from the centre of the enclosure. At Porchester (Fig. 104) and at Dover these buildings have become churches. The chronicle of Dover Castle says (see Appendix, No. 1, to Dugdale's Account of the Nunnery of St. Martin), "In the year of grace 180, reigned in Britain Lucius. He became a Christian under Pope Eleutherius, and served God, and advanced Holy Church as much as he could. Amongst other benefits he made a church in the said castle where the people of the town might receive the Sacraments." The chronicler then goes on to tell us of "Arthur the Glorious," and the hall which he made in Dover Castle; and then he comes to the dreary period of the Saxon invasion under Hengist, when "the Pagan people destroyed the churches throughout the land, and thrust out the Christians." The remaining part of this history which pertains to the old church in the castle is told with an impressive quaintness: "In the year of grace 596, St. Gregory, the Pope, sent into England his cousin St. Augustine, and many other monks with him, to preach the Christian faith to the English. There then reigned in Kent Adelbert (Ethelbert), who, through the Doctrine of St. Augustine, became a Christian with all his people; and all the other people in the land so became through the teachers which St. Augustine sent to them. This Adelbert had a son whose name was Adelbold (Eadbald), who, after the death of his father, reigned; and he became a Pagan, and banished the people of Holy Church out of his kingdom. Then the Archbishop of Canterbury, Laurence, who was preacher after St. Augustine, fled with others out of the land. But St. Peter appeared to him, and commanded that he should go boldly to the king and reprove him for his misdeeds. He did so, and by the grace of God the king repented and became devout to God and religious. This Adelbold ordained twenty-two secular canons in the castle to serve his chapel, and gave them twenty and two provenders (means of support). The said canons dwelt in the castle a hundred and five years, and maintained a great and fine house there, and went in and out of the castle night and day, according to their will, so that the serjeants of the king which guarded the castle could not restrain them." The canons, it would appear from this record, conducted themselves somewhat turbulently and irregularly during these hundred and five years, till they were finally ejected by King Withred, who removed them to the church of St. Martin, in the town of Dover, which he built for them. A fragment of the ruins of the town priory is to be seen near the market-place in Dover. This ejectment is held to have happened in the year 696. If the story be correct, the church within the castle must have been erected previous to the end of the seventh century. It might have been erected at a much earlier period, when many of the Roman soldiers of Britain were converts to the Roman faith; and here, upon that commanding rock which Matthew Paris called "Clavis et Repagulum totius Regni," the very key and barrier of the whole kingdom, might the eagles have vailed before the emblems of the religion of peace (Figs. 92, 96), and the mailed soldiers have laid down their shields and javelins (Fig. 97) to mingle in that common worship which made the Roman and the Barbarian equals.

It was a little before the commencement of a glorious corn-harvest that we first saw Richborough. Descending from the high fertile land of the Isle of Thanet, we passed Ebbefleet, the spot in Pegwell Bay where tradition says Hengist and Horsa landed, to carry war and rapine into the country. The coast here wears an aspect of melancholy dreariness. To the east we looked back upon the bold cliff of Ramsgate; to the west, upon the noble promontory of the South Foreland. But all the land space between these two extremities of the bay is a vast flat, drained in every direction by broad ditches, amidst which, in propitious seasons, thousands of sheep find a luxuriant though coarse pasture. At low-water the sea retires many furlongs from this flat shore; and then the fisherboy fills his basket with curious shells, which are here found

in great variety. When the tide has ebbed, a narrow stream may be traced for a long distance through the sand, which, when the salt wave has receded, still fills the little channel into which it empties itself from its inland source. This is the river Stour, whose main branch, flowing from Ashford by the old Roman Castle of Chilham, and onward to Canterbury, forms the boundary of the Isle of Thanet on the south-west; and making a sudden bend southerly to Sandwich, returns again in a northerly direction to empty itself into its sea-channel in Pegwell Bay. The road crosses the peninsula which is formed by this doubling of the river. At about a mile to the west is a gentle hill crowned with a large mass of low wall. At the distance of two or three miles we distinctly see that this is some remarkable object. It is not a lofty castle of the middle ages, such as we sometimes look upon, with tower and bastion crumbling into picturesque ruin; but here, on the north side, is a long line of wall, without a single aperture, devoid alike of loophole or battlement, and seemingly standing there only to support the broad masses of ivy which spread over its surface in singular luxuriance. We take boat at a little ferry-house, at a place called Saltpans. Leland, when he went to Richborough three hundred years ago, found a hermit there; and he says, "I had antiquities of the heremite, the which is an industrious man." So say we of the ferryman. He has small copper coins in abundance, which tell what people have been hereabout. He rows us down the little river for about three-quarters of a mile, and we are under the walls of Richborough Castle (Fig. 99). This is indeed a mighty monument of ages that are gone. Let us examine it with somewhat more than common attention.

Ascending the narrow road which passes the cottage built at the foot of the bank, we reach some masses of wall which lie below the regular line (Plan 98). Have these fallen from their original position, or do they form an outwork connected with fragments which also appear on the lower level of the slope? This is a question not very easy to decide from the appearance of the walls themselves. Another question arises, upon which antiquarian writers have greatly differed. Was there a fourth wall on the south-eastern side facing the river? It is believed by some that there was such a wall, and that the castle or camp once formed a regular parallelogram. It is difficult to reconcile this belief with the fact that the sea has been constantly retiring from Richborough, and that the little river was undoubtedly once a noble estuary. Bede, who wrote his 'Ecclesiastical History' in the beginning of the eighth century, thus describes the branch of the river which forms the Isle of Thanet, and which now runs a petty brook from Richborough to Reculver: "On the east side of Kent is the Isle of Thanet, considerably large; that is, containing, according to the English way of reckoning, six hundred families, divided from the other land by the river Wantsumu, which is about three furlongs over, and fordable only in two places, for both ends of it run into the sea." Passing by the fragments of which we have spoken, we are under the north (strictly north-east) wall—a wondrous work, calculated to impress us with a conviction that the people who built it were not the petty labourers of an hour, who were contented with temporary defences and frail resting-places. The outer works upon the southern cliff of Dover, which were run up during the war with Napoleon at a prodigious expense, are crumbling and perishing, through the weakness of job and contract, which could not endure for half a century. And here stand the walls of Richborough, as they have stood for eighteen hundred years, from twenty to thirty feet high, in some places with foundations five feet below the earth, eleven or twelve feet thick at the base, with their outer masonry in many parts as perfect as at the hour when their courses of tiles and stones were first laid in beautiful regularity. The northern wall is five hundred and sixty feet in length. From the eastern end, for more than two-fifths of its whole length, it presents a surface almost wholly unbroken. It exhibits seven courses of stone, each course about four feet thick, and the courses separated each from the other by a double line of red or yellow tiles, each tile being about an inch and a half in thickness. The entrance to the camp through this north wall is very perfect, of the construction marked in the plan. This was called by the Romans the Porta Principalis, but in after times the Postern-gate. We pass through this entrance, and we are at once in the interior of the Roman Castle. The area within the walls is a field of five acres covered, when we saw it, with luxuriant beans, whose green pods were scarcely yet shrivelled by the summer sun. Towards the centre of the field, a little to the east of the postern-gate, was a large space where the beans grew not. The area within the walls is much higher in most places than the ground without; and therefore the walls present a far more imposing appearance on their outer side. As we pass along the north wall to its western extremity, it becomes much more broken and dilapidated; large fragments having fallen from the top, which now presents a very irregular line. (Fig. 100.) It is considered that at the north-west and south-west angles there were circular towers. The west wall is very much broken down; and it is held that at the opening (Plan 98) was the Decuman gate (the gate through which ten men could march abreast). The south wall is considerably dilapidated; and from the nature of the ground is at present of much less length than the north wall. Immense cavities present themselves in this wall, in which the farmer deposits his ploughs and harrows, and the wandering gipsy seeks shelter from the driving north-east rain. One of these cavities in the south wall is forty-two feet long, as we roughly measured it, and about five feet in height. The wall is in some places completely pierced through; so that here is a long low arch, with fifteen or eighteen feet of solid work, ten feet thick, above it, held up almost entirely by the lateral cohesion. Nothing can be a greater proof of the extraordinary solidity of the original work. From some very careful engravings of the external sides of the walls, given in King's 'Munimenta Antiqua,' we find that the same cavity was to be seen in 1775.

Of the early importance of Richborough we have the most decisive evidence. Bede, eleven hundred years ago, speaks of it as the chief thing of note on the southern coast. Writing of Britain, he says, " On the south it has the Belgic Gaul; passing along whose nearest shore there appears the city called Rutubi Portus, the which port is now by the English nation corruptly called Reptacester: the passage of the sea from Gesoriacum, the nearest shore of the nation of the Morini, being fifty miles, or, as some write, four hundred and fifty furlongs." Camden thus describes the changes in the name of this celebrated place: " On the south side of the mouth of Wantsum (which they imagine has changed its channel), and over against the island was a city, called by Ptolemy, Rhutupiæ; by Tacitus, Portus Trutulensis, for Rhutupensis, if B. Rhenanus's conjecture hold good; by Antoninus, Rhitupis Portus; by Ammianus, Rhutupiæ statio; by Orosius, the port and city of Rhutubus; by the Saxons (according to Bede), Reptacester, and by others Ruptimuth; by Alfred of Beverley, Richberge; and at this day Richborrow: thus has time sported in varying one and the same name." It is unnecessary for us here to enter into the question whether Rhutupiæ was Richborough, or Sandwich, or Stonor. The earlier antiquaries, Leland, Lambarde, Camden, decide, as they well might, that the great Roman Castle of Richborough was the key of that haven which Juvenal has celebrated for its oysters (Sat. iv), and Lucan for its stormy seas (lib. vi.). Our readers, we think, will prefer, to such a dissertation, that most curious description of the place which we find in Leland's 'Itinerary'—a description that has been strangely neglected by most modern topographers: " Ratesburgh, otherwise Richeboro, was, or ever the river of Sture did turn his bottom or old canal, within the Isle of Thanet; and by likelihood the main sea came to the very foot of the castle. The main sea is now off of it a mile, by reason of woze (ooze) that hath there swollen up. The site of the old town or castle is wonderful fair upon a hill. The walls, the which remain there yet, be in compass almost as much as the Tower of London. They have been very high, thick, strong, and well embattled. The matter of them is flint, marvellous and long bricks, white and red after the Britons' fashion. The cement was made of sea-sand and small pebble. There is a great likelihood that the goodly hill about the castle, and especially to Sandwich-ward, hath been well inhabited. Corn groweth on the hill in marvellous plenty; and in going to plough there hath, out of mind, been found, and now is, more antiquities of Roman money that in any place else of England. Surely reason speaketh that this should be Rutupinum. For besides that the name somewhat toucheth, the very near passage from Clyves, or Cales, was to Ratesburgh, and now is to Sandwich, the which is about a mile off; though now Sandwich be not celebrated because of Goodwin Sands and the decay of the haven. There is a good flight shot off from Ratesburgh, towards Sandwich, a great dike, cast in a round compass, as it had been for fence of men of war. The compass of the ground within is not much above an acre, and it is very hollow by casting up the earth. They call the place there Lytleborough. Within the castle is a little parish-church of St. Augustine, and an hermitage. I had antiquities of the hermit, the which is an industrious man. Not far from the hermitage is a cave where men have sought and digged for treasure. I saw it by candle within, and there were conies (rabbits). It was so strait, that I had no mind to creep far in. In the north side of the Castle is a head in the wall, now sore defaced with weather. They call it Queen Bertha Head. Near to that place, hard by the wall, was a pot of Roman money found."

In the bean-field within the walls of Richborough there was a space where no beans grew, which we could not approach without trampling down the thick crop. We knew what was the cause of that patch of unfertility. We had learnt from the work of Mr. King, who had derived his information from Mr. Boys, the local historian of Sandwich, that there was, " at the depth of a few feet, between the soil and rubbish, a solid regular platform, one hundred and forty-four in length, and a hundred and four feet in breadth, being a most compact mass of masonry composed of flint stones and strong coarse mortar." This great platform, " as hard and entire in every part as a solid rock," is pronounced by King to have been " the great parade, or Augurale, belonging to the Prætorium, where was the Sacellum for the eagles and ensigns, and where the sacrifices were offered." But upon this platform is placed a second compact mass of masonry, rising nearly five feet above the lower mass, in the form of a cross, very narrow in the longer part, which extends from the south to the north (or, to speak more correctly, from the south-west to the north-east), but in the shorter transverse of the cross, which is forty-six feet in length, having a breadth of twenty-two feet. This cross, according to King, was the site of the Sacellum. Half a century ago was this platform dug about and under, and brass and lead, and broken vessels were found, and a curious little bronze figure of a Roman soldier playing upon the bagpipes (Fig. 102). Again has antiquarian curiosity been set to work, and labourers are now digging and delving on the edge of the platform, and breaking their tools against the iron concrete. The workmen have found a passage along the south and north sides of the platform, and have penetrated, under the platform, to walls upon which it is supposed to rest, whose foundations are laid twenty-eight feet lower. Some fragments of pottery have been found in this last excavation, and the explorers expect to break through the walls upon which the platform rests, and find a chamber. It may be so. Looking at the greater height of the ground within the walls, compared with the height without, we are inclined to believe that this platform, which is five feet in depth, was the open basement of some public building in the Roman time. To what purpose it was applied in the Christian period, whether of Rome or Britain, we think there can be no doubt. The traveller who looked upon it three centuries ago tells us distinctly, " within the Castle is a little parish-church of St. Augustine, and an hermitage." When Camden saw the place, nearly a century after Leland, the little parish-church was gone. He found no hermitage there, and no hermit to show him antiquities. He says, " To teach us that cities die as well as men, it is at this day a cornfield, wherein when the corn is grown up one may observe the draughts of streets crossing one another, for where they have gone the corn is thinner. . . . Nothing now remains but some ruinous walls of a square tower cemented with a sort of sand extremely binding." He also says that the crossings of the streets are commonly called St. Augustine's Cross. There is certainly more confusion in this description of crossings as one cross. To us it appears more than probable that the " little parish-church of St. Augustine," which Leland saw, had this cross for its foundation, and that when this church was swept away—when the hermit who dwelt there, and there pursued his solitary worship, fell upon evil times—the cross, with a few crumbling walls, proclaimed where the little parish church had stood, and that this was then called St. Augustine's Cross (Fig. 191). The cross is decidedly of a later age than the platform; the masonry is far less regular and compact. Camden, continuing the history of Richborough after the Romans, says, " This Rutupiæ flourished likewise after the coming in of the Saxons, for authors tell us it was the palace of Ethelbert, king of Kent, and Bede honours it with the name of a city." The belief that the palace of Ethelbert was upon this commanding elevation, so strengthened by art, full no doubt of remains of Roman magnificence, the key of the broad river which allowed an ample passage for ships of burthen from the Channel to the estuary of the Thames, is a rational belief. But Lambarde says of Richborough, " Whether it were that palace of King Ethelbert from whence he went to entertain Augustine, he that shall advisedly read the twenty-fifth chapter of Beda his first book shall have just cause to doubt; forasmuch as he showeth manifestly that the king came from his palace into the Isle of Thanet to Augustine, and Leland saith that Richborough was then within Thanet, although that since that time the water has changed its old course and shut it clean out of the island." This is a refinement in the old Kentish topographer which will scarcely outweigh the general fitness of Richborough for the palace of the Saxon king. The twenty-fifth chapter of Bede is indeed worth reading " advisedly;" but not to settle this minute point of local antiquarianism. We have given Bede's description of the Isle of Thanet, in which island, he says, " landed the servant of our Lord, Augustine, and his com-

107.—Walls and Gate, Pevensey.

108.—Walls, Pevensey.

105.—General View of the Ruins of Pevensey Castle.

109.—Supposed Saxon Keep, Pevensey.

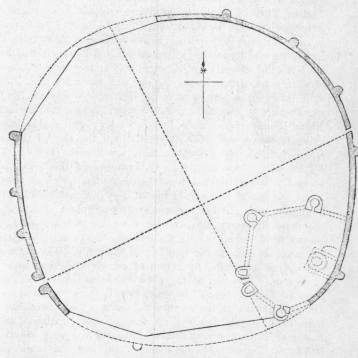

106.—Plan of Pevensey Castle.

110.—Sally-port, Pevensey.

111.—Norman Keep, Pevensey.

112.—Interior of Norman Tower, Pevensey.

115.—Rome—a fragment after Piranesi.

114.—Conflict between Romans and Barbarians. From the Arch of Trajan.

116.—Roman Victory.

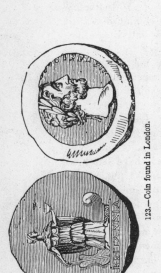

123.—Coin found in London.

113.—The Thames at Coway Stakes.

—The earliest figure of Britannia on a Roman Coin.

117.—Augustus.

119.—Coin of Claudius, representing his British Triumph. From the British Museum.

121.—Coin of Cunobelinus.

120.—Coin of Claudius. Actual size. Gold. Weight 122 Grains. In Brit. Mus

118.—Claudius.—From a Copper Coin in the British Museum.

No. 5.

panions, being as it is reported near forty men." The king, according to Bede's narrative, hearing of their arrival, and the nature of their mission, ordered them to stay in the island, where they should be furnished with all necessaries. "Some days after, the king came into the island, and, sitting in the open air, ordered Augustine and his companions to be brought into his presence. For he had taken precaution that they should not come to him in any house, according to the ancient superstition, lest, if they had any magical arts, they might at their coming impose upon and get the better of him. But they came furnished with divine virtue, not with disabolical, bearing a silver cross for their banner, and the image of our Lord and Saviour painted on a board, and, singing the litany, offered up their prayers to the Lord for their own, and the eternal salvation of those to whom they were come. Having, pursuant to the king's commands, after sitting down, preached to him and all his attendants there present the Word of Life; he answered thus : 'Your words and promises are very taking, but in regard that they are new and uncertain, I cannot approve of them, forsaking that which I have so long followed with the whole English nation. But because you are come from far into my kingdom, and, as I conceive, are desirous to impart to us those things which you believe to be true, and most beneficial, we will not molest you, but rather give you favourable entertainment, and take care to supply you with your necessary sustenance ; nor do we forbid you by preaching to gain as many as you can to your religion.' Accordingly he gave them a dwelling-place in the city of Canterbury, which was the metropolis of all his dominions, and pursuant to his promise, besides allowing them their diet, permitted them to preach." This memorable transaction, told with such touching simplicity a little more than a century after its occurrence, by the illustrious monk of Jarrow, imparts a far deeper interest to this locality than its Roman memorials.

John Twyne, a celebrated antiquarian who lived in the sixteenth century, says, "There be right credible persons yet living that have often seen not only small boats but vessels of good burden to pass to and fro upon the Wantsum, where now the water, especially towards the west, is clean excluded; and there be apparent marks that Sarr, where they now go over, was a proper haven." Those who have traversed the low country which lies between Reculver and Sandwich—a task not very easily to be accomplished unless the pedestrian can leap the broad ditches which drain the marsh—will readily comprehend how, in the course of eighteen centuries, the great estuary may have dwindled into a petty rill. There is nothing in the nature of the country to prevent one believing that a large arm of the sea cut off the Isle of Thanet from the mainland of Kent, and that this channel, in the time of the Romans, formed the readiest passage from the coast of Gaul to London. The late Mr. John Rickman has well described the course of communication between the Continent and Britain :—"The Roman roads in Kent deserve notice as having been planned with an intention of greater scope than (within my knowledge) has been ascribed to them. The nearest and middle harbour of access from Gaul was evidently Dover ; but whenever the wind was unfavourable for a direct passage, further recourse became desirable, and from Lemanis (Lymne, near Hythe) and Ritupæ (Richborough, near Sandwich) branch roads were made, joining the Dover road at Canterbury ; so that a dispatch-boat, by sailing from the windward port, or steering for the leeward of these three ports, could seldom fail of a ready passage to or from the Continent ; and especially it is remarkable that the prevailing south-west wind (with this advantage) permitted a direct passage from Gessoriacum or Itius (Boulogne or Witsand) to Ritupæ, in effect to London ; the Wantsum channel then and long after existing within the Isle of Thanet to Regulbium (Reculver) on the Thames, being that by which early navigation was sheltered in its access to the British metropolis. Indeed the first paragraph of the Itinerary of Antoninus gives the reputed distance from Gessoriacum to Ritupæ, as if more important or more in use than the shorter passage to Dover." ('Archæologia,' vol. xxviii.) With this explanation we can comprehend the advantage of the Roman position at Reculver. Through this broad channel of the Wantsum the Roman vessels from Boulogne sailed direct into the Thames, without going round the North Foreland ; and the entrance to the estuary was defended by the great Castle of Richborough at the one end, and by the lesser Castle of Reculver at the other. The Roman remains still existing at Reculver are less interesting than those at Richborough, chiefly because they are of less magnitude and are more dilapidated. Very close to the ruins of the ancient church, whose spires were once held in such reverence that ships entering the Thames were wont to lower their top sails as they passed (Fig. 103), is an area, now partly under the plough and partly a kitchen garden. It is somewhat elevated above the surrounding fields ; and, descending a

little distance to the west of the ruined church, we are under the Roman wall, which still stands up on the western and southern sides with its layers of flat stone and concrete, defying the dripping rain and the insidious ivy. The castle stood upon a natural rising ground, beneath which still flows the thread-like stream of the river Stour or Wantsum. Although it was once the key of the northern mouth of the great estuary, it did not overhang the sea on the northern cliff, as the old church ruin now hangs. When the legions were here encamped, it stood far away from the dashing of the northern tide, which for many generations has been here invading the land with an irresistible power. Century after century has the wave been gnawing at this cliff ; and, as successive portions have fallen, the bare sides have presented human bones, and coins, and fragments of pottery, and tessellated pavements, which told that man had been here, with his comforts and luxuries around him, long before Ethelbert was laid beneath the floor of the Saxon church, upon whose ruins the sister spires of the Norman rose, themselves to be a ruin, now preserved only as a sea-mark. Reculver is a memorable example of the changes produced in a short period of three centuries. Leland's description of the place is scarcely credible to those who have stood beneath these spires, on the very margin of the sea, and have looked over the low ruined wall of the once splendid choir, upon the fishing-boats rocking in the tide beneath :— "Reculver is now scarce half a mile from the shore." In another place—"Reculver standeth within a quarter of a mile or a little more from the sea-side. The town at this time is but village-like ; sometime where as the parish church is now was a faire and a great abbey, and Brightwald, Archbishop of Canterbury, was of that house. The old building of the church of the abbey remaineth, having two goodly spiring steeples. In the entering of the choir is one of the fairest and the most ancient cross that ever I saw, nine feet, as I guess, in height ; it standeth like a fair column." Long ago has the cross perished, with its curiously-wrought carvings and its painted images ; and so has perished the "very ancient book of the Evangeles," which Leland also describes. The Romans have left more durable traces of their existence at Reculver than the ministers of religion, who here, for centuries, had sung the daily praises of Him who delivereth out of their distress those "that go down to the sea in ships, and occupy their business in great waters." The change in names of places sometimes tells the story of their material changes. The Regulbium of the Romans became the Raculfcester of the Saxons, cester indicating a camp ; that name changes when the camp has perished, and the great abbey is flourishing, to Raculf-minster ; the camp and the abbey have both perished, and we have come back to the Latin Regulbium, in its Anglicized form of Reculver. Some fiercer destruction even than that which swept away the abbey probably fell upon the Roman city. Gibson, speaking of the coins and jewellery which have been found at various times at Reculver, says, "These they find here in such great quantities that we must needs conclude it to have been a place heretofore of great extent, and very populous, and that it has one time or other underwent some great devastation, either by war or fire, or both. I think I may be confident of the latter, there being many patterns found of metals run together." The antiquities of Regulbium are fully described in the elegant Latin treatise of Dr. Battely, 'Antiquitates Rutupinæ,' 1711.

After the Romans had established a permanent occupation of Britain, the defence of the coast was reduced to a system. Wherever the Romans conquered, they organized, and by their wise arrangements became preservers and benefactors. It is generally supposed that Richborough and Reculver were Roman forts as early as the time of Claudius, but that other castles on the coast were of later date, being for defence against the Saxon pirates of the third century. At this period there was a high military officer called Comes Littoris Saxonici per Britanniam, the Count of the Saxon Shore in Britain. He was the commander of all the castles and garrisons on the coast of Norfolk, of Essex, of Kent, of Sussex, and of Hampshire. These coasts formed the Saxon Shore. Sir Francis Palgrave thinks that the name was derived from the Saxons having already here made settlements. Others believe that the Saxon Shore was so called from its being peculiarly exposed to the ravages of the Saxons, to resist whom the great castles which stood upon this shore were built or garrisoned. These castles were nine in number ; and, although in one or two particulars there are differences of opinion as to their sites, the statement of Horsley is for the most part admitted to be correct.

On the Norfolk coast there were two forts. Branodunum (Brancaster, about four miles from Burnham Market) overlooked the marshes. The station is well defined by the remains which are constantly dug up. Gariannonum (Burgh, in Suffolk, situated at the junction of the Waveney and the Yare) is a noble ruin. Two engravings of its walls will be found at page 36 (Figs. 129, 130). These walls, which are almost fourteen feet high and nine thick, inclose on three sides an area forming nearly a regular parallelogram, six hundred and forty-two feet long by four hundred feet broad. The western boundary is now formed by the river Waveney, it being supposed, and indeed almost proved by a very ancient map, that the west side of the station was once defended by the sea. If there was ever a west wall, which is much to be doubted, it has now entirely disappeared. The east wall is almost perfect, as shown in our engravings. The north and south walls are in great part ruinous. We transcribe from the ' Penny Cyclopædia ' a brief description of these walls, written by an architect who visited the place, and surveyed it with great care :—" The whole area of the inclosure was about four acres and three-quarters. The walls are of rubble masonry, faced with alternate courses of bricks and flints : and on the tops of the towers, which are attached to the walls, are holes two feet in diameter and two feet deep, supposed to have been intended for the insertion of temporary watch-towers, probably of wood. On the east side the four circular towers are fourteen feet in diameter. Two of them are placed at the angles, where the walls are rounded, and two at equal distances from the angles ; an opening has been left in the centre of the wall, which is considered by Mr. King to be the Porta Decumana, but by Mr. Ives the Porta Prætoria. The north and south sides are also defended by towers of rubble masonry. The foundation, on which the Romans built these walls was a thick bed of chalk lime, well rammed down, and the whole covered with a layer of earth and sand, to harden the mass and exclude the water : this was covered with two-inch oak plank placed transversely on the foundation, and over this was a bed of coarse mortar, on which wa roughly spread the first layer of stones. The mortar appears to be composed of lime and coarse sand, unsifted, mixed with gravel and small pebbles or shingle. Mr. Ives thinks they used hot grouting, which will account for the tenacity of the mortar. The bricks at Burgh Castle are of a fine red colour and a very close texture—they are one foot and a half long, one foot broad, and one inch and a half thick."

In Essex there was one fort, Othona (Ithanchester, not far from Malden), over which the sea now flows.

In Kent there were four castles thus garrisoned and commanded : Regulbium (Reculver), Ritupæ (Richborough), Dubræ (Dover), and Lemanæ (Lymne). The remains of this last of the Kentish fortresses are now very inconsiderable. Leland, however, thus describes it :—" Lymme, hill of, or Lyme, was some time a famous haven, and good for ships, that might come to the foot of the hill. [The river Limene, or Rother, formerly ran beneath the hill.] The place is yet called Shipway and Old Haven ; farther, at this day the Lord of the Five Ports keepeth his principal court a little by east from Lymme Hill. There remaineth at this day the ruins of a strong fortress of the Britons hanging on the hill, and coming down to the very foot. The compass of the fortress seemeth to be ten acres. The old walls are made of Britons' bricks, very large, and great flint, set together almost indissolubly with mortars made of small pebble. The walls be very thick, and in the west end of the castle appeareth the base of an old tower. About this castle in time of mind were found antiquities of money of the Romans. There went from Lymme to Canterbury a street fair-paved, whereof of this day it is called Stony Street. It is the straightest that ever I saw, and toward Canterbury-ward the pavement continually appeareth for four or five miles." Such is Leland's account, three centuries ago, of a ruin which since that period has more rapidly perished from the subsidence of the soil upon which it stands. Lambarde, who wrote half a century after Leland, says of Lymme, " They affirm that the water forsaking them by little and little, decay and solitude came at the length upon the place." There is the gate-house of a later building than the Roman walls still remaining, built of large bricks and flints, as the tower of the neighbouring church is built. These may contain some of the ancient materials.

Anderida, the sea-fort of Sussex, is held by some to be Hastings, by others to be East Bourn. It is not our purpose to enter upon any controversial discussion of such matters ; but it appears to us that Pevensey, one of the most remarkable castles in our country, which the Roman, and the Saxon, and the Norman, had one after the other garrisoned and fortified,—the ruins of each occupier themselves telling such a tale of " mutability " as one spot has seldom told,—was as likely to have been the Anderida of the Saxon shore, as Hastings and East Bourn, between which it is situated.

Be that as it may, we proceed briefly to describe this remarkable ruin. The village of Pevensey is about equidistant from Bexhill and East Bourn. The approach to it from either place is as dreary as can well be imagined, over a vast marsh, with nothing to relieve the prospect seaward but the ugly Martello towers, which on this coast are stuck so thick that a second William of Normandy would scarcely attempt a landing. They now guard the shore, not against Williams and Napoleons, but against those who invade the land with scheidam and brandy. Rising gently out of this flat ground we see the Castle of Pevensey. It is, with very slight differences, situated exactly as Richborough is situated—a marsh from which the sea has receded, a cliff of moderate height rising out of the marsh. a little stream beneath the cliff. Here, as at Richborough, have the Roman galleys anchored ; sheltered by the bold promontory of Beachy Head from the south-west gales, and secured from the attacks of pirates by the garrison who guarded those walls. We ascend the cliff from the village, and enter the area within the walls at the opening on the east (Plan 106). The external appearance of the gate by which we enter is shown in Fig. 107. This is held to have been the Prætorian Gate. The external architecture of the gate and of the walls has evidently undergone great alteration since the Roman period. In some parts we have the herring-bone work of the Saxon, and the arch of the Norman ; but the Roman has left his mark indelibly on the whole of these external walls, in the regular courses of brick which form the bond of the stone and rubble, which chiefly constitute the mighty mass. The external towers, which are indicated on the plan, are quite solid : some of these have been undermined and have fallen, but others have been carefully buttressed and otherwise repaired in very modern times (Fig. 108). Having passed into the area by the east gate, we cross in the direction of the dotted line to the south-western or Decuman Gate. This is very perfect, having a tower on each side. Going without the walls at this point, and scrambling beneath them to the south, we can well understand how the fort stood proudly above the low shore when the sea almost washed its walls. The ruin on this side is highly picturesque, large masses of the original wall having fallen (Fig. 105). On the north side was a few years since a fragment of a supposed Saxon keep, held to be an addition to the original Roman Castrum (Fig. 109). But the most important and interesting adaptation to another period of the Roman Pevensey is the Norman keep, the form of which is indicated on the Plan 106, at the south-east, and which was evidently fitted upon the original Roman wall so as to form the coast defence on that side. We purposely reserve any minute description of this very remarkable part of the ruin for another period. The ponderous walls of the Roman dominion are almost merged in the greater interest of the moated keep of the Norman conquest. It will be sufficient for us here to present engravings of the Norman works (Figs. 110, 111, 112), reserving their description for another Book. The area within the Roman walls of Pevensey is seven acres. The irregular form of the walls would indicate that here was a British stronghold before the Roman castle.

The one Roman sea-fort of Hampshire, Portus Adurnus (Portsmouth), offers a striking contrast to the decay and solitude which prevail, with the exception of Dover, in all the other forts of the Saxon shore.

———

In noticing the two descents of Cæsar upon Britain (page 26) we said, " From the nature of his inroad into the country, no monuments exist, or could have existed, to attest his progress." But there is a monument, if so it may be called, still existing, which furnishes evidence of the systematic resistance which was made to his progress. Bede, writing at the beginning of the eighth century, after describing with his wonted brevity the battle in which Cæsar in his second invasion put the Britons to flight, says, " Thence he proceeded to the river Thames, which is said to be fordable only in one place. An immense multitude of the enemy had posted themselves on the farthest side of the river, under the conduct of Cassibelan, and fenced the bank of the river and almost all the ford under water with sharp stakes, the remains of which stakes are to be there seen to this day, and they appear to the beholders to be about the thickness of a man's thigh, and being cased with lead, remain immoveable, fixed in the bottom of the river." Camden, writing nine centuries after Bede, whose account he quotes, fixes this remarkable ford of the Thames near Oatlands: " For this was the only place in the Thames formerly fordable, and that too not without great difficulty, which the Britons themselves in a manner pointed out to him [Cæsar]; for on the other side of the river a strong body of the British had planted themselves, and the bank

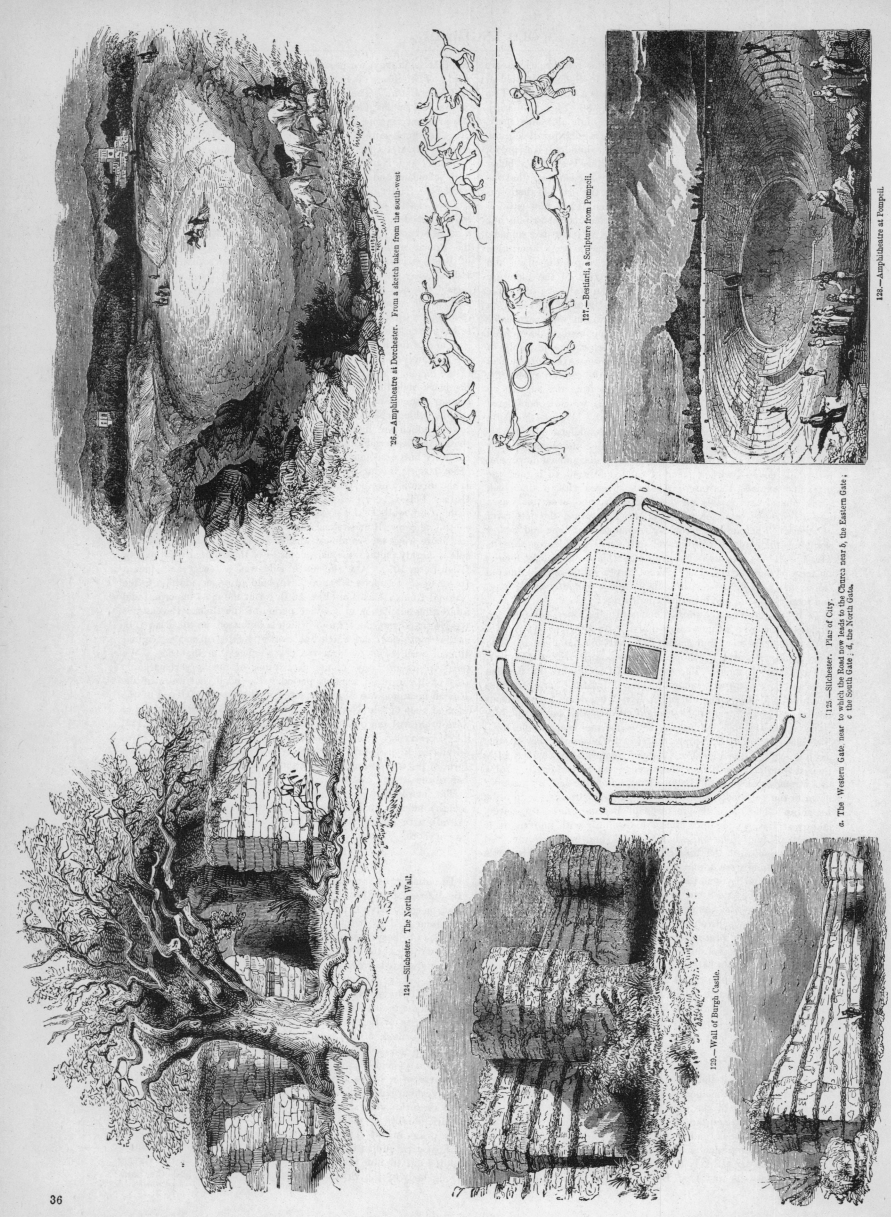

126.—Amphitheatre at Dorchester. From a sketch taken from the south-west.

127.—Bestiarii, a Sculpture from Pompeii.

128.—Amphitheatre at Pompeii.

125.—Silchester. Plan of City.

a. The Western Gate, near to which the Road now leads to the Church near b, the Eastern Gate; c, the South Gate; d, the North Gate.

124.—Silchester. The North Wall.

129.—Wall of Burgh Castle.

130.—Wall of Burgh Castle.

131.—Wall of Severus, on the Sandstone Quarries, Denton Dean, near Newcastle-upon-Tyne

133.—Roman Citizen.

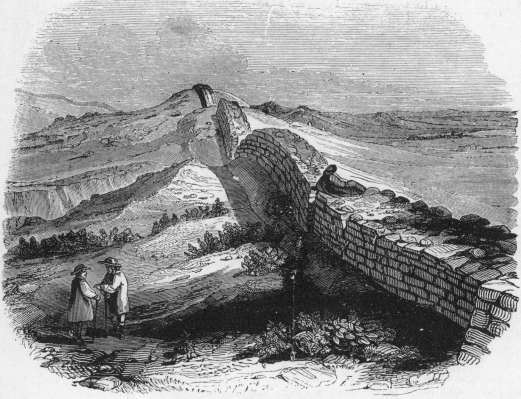

132.—Wall of Severus, near Housestead, Northumberland.

134.—Tomb of a young Roman Physician.

136.—Roman Soldier.

137.—Roman Highway on the Banks of the Tiber.

135.—Roman Image of Victory.

37

itself was fenced with sharp stakes driven into the ground, and some of the same sort were fastened under water." Camden here adopts Cæsar's own words: "Ripa autem erat acutis sudibus præfixis munita, ejusdemque generis sub aqua defixæ sudes flumine tegebantur" ('De Bell. Gal.' lib. v.). Our fine old topographer is singularly energetic in fixing the place of Cæsar's passage: "It is impossible I should be mistaken in the place, because here the river is scarce six foot deep; and the place at this day, from those stakes, is called Coway Stakes; to which we may add that Cæsar makes the bounds of Cassivelan, where he fixes this his passage, to be about eighty miles distant from that sea which washes the east part of Kent, where he landed: now this ford we speak of is at the same distance from the sea; and I am the first, that I know of, who has mentioned, and settled it in its proper place." It is a rational belief of the English antiquaries that there was a great British road from Richborough to Canterbury, and thence to London. Cæsar's formidable enemy, Cassivelaunus, had retreated in strong force to the north bank of the Thames; and Cæsar speaks of the river as dividing the territories of that chieftain from the maritime states. If we look upon the map of England, we shall see how direct a march it was from Canterbury to Oatlands near Walton, without following the course of the river above London. Crossing at this place, Cæsar would march direct, turning to the north, upon the capital of Cassivelaunus,—Verulam, or Cassiobury. Our engraving (Fig. 113) represents the peaceful river gliding amidst low wooded banks, disturbed only by the slow barge as it is dragged along its stream. At the bend of the river are to this hour these celebrated stakes. They were minutely described in 1735, in a paper read to the Society of Antiquaries, by Mr. Samuel Gale: "As to the wood of these stakes, it proves its own antiquity, being by its long duration under the water so consolidated as to resemble ebony, and will admit of a polish, and is not in the least rotted. It is evident from the exterior grain of the wood that the stakes were the entire bodies of young oak-trees, there not being the least appearance of any mark of any tool to be seen upon the whole circumference, and if we allow in our calculation for the gradual increase of growth towards its end, where fixed in the bed of the river, the stakes, I think, will exactly answer the thickness of a man's thigh, as described by Bede; but whether they were covered with lead at the ends fixed in the bottom of the river, is a particular I could not learn; but the last part of Bede's description is certainly just, that they are immoveable, and remain so to this day.' Mr. Gale adds, that since stating that the stakes were immoveable, one had been weighed up, entire, between two loaded barges, at the time of a great flood.

Gibson, the editor of Camden, confirms the strong belief of his author that at Coway Stakes was the ford of Cæsar, by the following observations:—"Not far from hence upon the Thames is Walton, in which parish is a great camp of about twelve acres, single work, and oblong. There is a road lies through it, and it is probable that Walton takes its name from this remarkable vallum." Mr. Gale, in his paper in the 'Archæologia,' mentions "a large Roman encampment up in the country directly southward, about a mile and a half distant from the ford, and pointing to it." Here he imagines Cæsar himself entrenched. When we consider that the Romans occupied Britain for more than four centuries, it is extremely hazardous to attempt to fix an exact date to any of their works. Encampments such as these are memorials of defence after defence which the invader threw up against the persevering hostility of the native tribes, or native defences from which the Britons were driven out. For ninety-seven years after the second expedition of Cæsar, the country remained at peace with Rome. Augustus (Fig. 117) threatened an invasion; but his prudence told him that he could not enforce the payment of tribute without expensive legions. The British princes made oblations in the Capitol; and, according to Strabo, "rendered almost the whole island intimate and familiar to the Romans." Cunobelinus (Fig. 121), the Cymbeline of Shakspere, was brought up, according to the chroniclers, at the court of Augustus. Succeeding emperors left the Britons in the quiet advancement of their civilization, until Claudius (Fig. 118) was stirred up to the hazard of an invasion. In the sonorous prose of Milton—"He, who waited ready with a huge preparation, as if not safe enough amidst the flower of all his Romans, like a great Eastern king with armed elephants marches through Gallia. So full of peril was this enterprise esteemed as not without all this equipage and stronger terrors than Roman armies, to meet the native and the naked British valour defending their country." (Fig. 114.) The genius of Roman victory inscribed the name of Claudius with the addition of Britannicus (Fig. 116). The coins of Claudius still bear the symbols of his British triumphs (Figs. 119, 120). But

the country was not yet wholly won. Then came the glorious resistance of Caractacus, which Tacitus has immortalized. Then came the fierce contests between the Roman invaders and the votaries of the native religion, which the same historian has so glowingly described in his account of the attack of Suetonius upon the island of Mona:—"On the shore stood a line of very diversified appearance; there were armed men in dense array, and women running amid them like furies, who, in gloomy attire, and with loose hair hanging down, carried forth torches before them. Around were Druids, who, pouring forth curses and lifting up their hands to heaven, struck terror by the novelty of their appearance into the hearts of the soldiers, who, as if they had lost the use of their limbs, exposed themselves motionless to the stroke of the enemy. At last, moved by the exhortations of their leader, and stimulating one another to despise a band of women and frantic priests, they make their onset, overthrow their opponents, and involve them in the flames which they had themselves kindled. A garrison was afterwards placed among the vanquished; and the groves consecrated to their cruel superstitions were cut down." Then came the terrible revolt of Boadicea or Bonduca,—a merciless rising, followed by a bloody revenge. Beaumont and Fletcher have well dramatized the spirit of this heroic woman:—

> "Ye powerful gods of Britain, hear our prayers!
> Hear us, ye great revengers! and this day
> Take pity from our swords, doubt from our valours;
> Double the sad remembrance of our wrongs
> In every breast; the vengeance due to these
> Make infinite and endless! On our pikes
> This day pale Terror sit, horrors and ruins
> Upon our executions; claps of thunder
> Hang on our armed carts; and 'fore our troops
> Despair and Death. Shame beyond these attend 'em!
> Rise from the dust, ye relics of the dead,
> Whose noble deeds our holy Druids sing:
> Oh, rise, ye valiant bones! let not base earth
> Oppress your honours, whilst the pride of Rome
> Treads on your stocks, and wipes out all your stories!"
>   BONDUCA.

The Roman dominion in Britain nearly perished in this revolt. Partial tranquillity was secured, in subsequent years of mildness and forbearance, towards the conquered tribes. Vespasian extended the conquests; Agricola completed them in South Britain. His possessions in Caledonia were, however, speedily lost. But the hardy people of the North were driven back in the reign of Antoninus Pius. Then first appeared on the Roman money the graceful figure of Britannia calmly resting on her shield (Fig. 122), which seventeen centuries afterwards has been made familiar to ourselves in the coined money of our own generation. Let us pause awhile to view one of the great Roman cities which is held to belong to a very early period of their dominion in England.

In 1837 a plan was exhibited to the Society of Antiquaries, reduced from a survey made in 1835, by students of the senior department of the Royal Military College at Sandhurst, of a portion of the Roman road from London to Bath. The survey commences close by Staines; at which place, near the pillar which marks the extent of the jurisdiction of the city of London, the line of road is held to have crossed the Thames. Below Staines, opposite to Laleham, there are the remains of encampments; and these again are in the immediate neighbourhood of the ford at which Cæsar crossed the Thames. All the country here about, then, is full of associations with the conquerors of the world; and thus, when the "contemplative man" is throwing his fly or watching his float in the gentle waters between Staines and Walton, he may here find a local theme upon which his reveries may fruitfully rest. The more active pedestrian may follow this Roman road, thus recently mapped out, through populous places and wild solitudes, into a country little traversed in modern times; but, like all unhackneyed ways, full of interest to the lover of nature. The course of the road leads over the east end of the beautiful table-land known as Englefield Green; then through the yard of the well-known Wheatsheaf Inn, at Virginia Water; and, crossing the artificial lake, ascends the hill, close by the tower called the Belvidere. In Windsor Park the line is for some time lost; but it is extremely well defined at a point near the Sunning Hill road, where vast quantities of Roman pottery and bricks have been discovered. It continues towards Bagshot, where, at a place called Duke's Hill, its westerly direction suddenly terminates, and it proceeds considerably to the northward. Here, in 1783, many fragments of Roman pottery were discovered. The Roman road ascends the plain of Easthampstead, sending out a lateral branch which runs close to well-known places within the ancient limits of Windsor Forest, called Wickham Bushes and Cæsar's Camp. We remember this vast sandy region before it was covered with fir plantations; and in these solitary hills, where the eye for miles could rest upon nothing but barren heath, we have listened with the wonder of boyhood to the vague traditions of past ages, in which the marvels of history are made more marvellous. Cæsar's Camp is thus described by Mr. Handasyd, in a letter to the Society of Antiquaries, in 1783:—"At the extremity of a long range of hills is situated a large camp, known by the name of Cæsar's Camp, which is but slightly noticed by Dr. Stukeley, nor is any particular mention made of it in any account I have hitherto seen. In it is a hollow, which has a thick layer of coarse gravel all round it, and seems to have been made to contain rain water. At not half a mile from the camp stand a vast number of thorn bushes, some of a very large size (known by the name of Wickham Bushes), bearing on their ragged branches and large contorted stems evident marks of extreme age, yet in all probability these are but the successors of a race long since extinct. The inhabitants of the neighbourhood have a tradition that here formerly stood a town, but that Julius Cæsar, whom they magnify to a giant (for stories lose nothing by telling), with his associates laying the country waste, the poor inhabitants were obliged to fly, and seek an asylum in the valley beneath." As we proceed along the road approaching Finchhampstead, we find the object of our search, sometimes easily traced and sometimes continuously lost, bearing the name of the Devil's Highway. At length the line crosses the Loddon, at the northern extremity of Strathfieldsaye (Strathfield being the field of the Strat, Street, or Road), the estate which a grateful nation bestowed upon the Duke of Wellington; through which park it passes till it terminates at the parish church of Silchester. This is the line which the students of the Military College surveyed.* The survey has gone far to establish two disputed points—the situation of the Roman *Pontes*, and whether Silchester should be identified with *Vindonum* or *Calleva*. A very able correspondent of the Society of Antiquaries, Mr. Kempe, thus observes upon the value of the labours of the students of the Military College:—"The survey has effected a material correction of Horsley, for it shows that the station *Pontes*, which he places at Old Windsor, and for which so many different places have been assigned by the learned in Roman topography, must have been where the Roman road from London crossed the Thames at Staines. . . . . The line of road presents no place for the chief city of the Attrebates until it arrives at the walls of Silchester. Is this, then, really the *Calleva* Attrebatum? The distance between Pontes and Calleva, according to the Itinerary [of Antoninus], is twenty-two miles; by the Survey, the distance between Staines and Silchester is twenty-six; a conformity as near as can be required, for neither the length of the Roman mile nor the mode of measuring it agreed precisely with ours." Having led our reader to the eastern entrance of this ancient city, we will endeavour to describe what he will find there to reward his pilgrimage. Let us tell him, however, that he may reach Silchester by an easier route than over the straight line of the Roman Highway. It is about seven miles from Basingstoke, and ten from Reading: to either of which places he may move more rapidly from London, by the South Western or the Great Western Railway.

If we have walked dreamingly along the narrow lanes whose hedge-rows shut out any distant prospect, we may be under the eastern walls of Silchester before we are aware that any remarkable object is in our neighbourhood. We see at length a church, and we ascend a pretty steep bank to reach the churchyard. The churchyard wall is something very different from ordinary walls—a thick mass of mortar and stone, through which a way seems to have been forced to give room for the little gates that admit us to the region of grassy graves. A quiet spot is this churchyard; and we wonder where the tenants of the sod have come from. There is one sole farmhouse near the church; an ancient farmhouse with gabled roofs that tell of old days of comfort and hospitality. The church, too, is a building of interest, because of some antiquity; and there are in the churchyard two very ancient Christian tombstones of chivalrous times, when the sword, strange contradiction, was an emblem of the cross. But these are modern things compared with the remains of which we are in search. We pass through the churchyard into an open space, where the farmer's ricks tell of the abundance of recent cultivation. These may call to our mind the

* An account of this survey is very clearly given in the 'United Service Journal' for January, 1836. Knowing something of the country, we have reversed the order of that description, leading our readers from Staines to Silchester, instead of from Silchester to Staines.

story which Camden has told:—"On the ground whereon this city was built (I speak in Nennius's words) the Emperor Constantius sowed three grains of corn, that no person inhabiting there might ever be poor." We look around, and we ask the busy thatchers of the ricks where are the old walls; for we can see nothing but extensive corn-fields, bounded by a somewhat higher bank than ordinary,—that bank luxuriant with oak, and ash, and springing underwood. The farm labourers know what we are in search of, and they ask us if we want to buy any coins—for whenever the heavy rains fall they find coins—and they have coins, as they have been told, of Romulus and Remus, and this was a great place a long while ago. It is a tribute to the greatness of the place that to whomsoever we spoke of these walls and the area within the walls, they called it *the city*. Here was a city, of one church and one farmhouse. The people who went to that church lived a mile or two off in their scattered hamlets. Silence reigned in that city. The ploughs and spades of successive generations had gone over its ruins; but its memory still lived in tradition; it was an object to be venerated. There was something mysterious about this area of a hundred acres, that rendered it very different to the ploughman's eye from a common hundred acres. Put the plough deep as he would, manure the land with every care of the unfertile spots, the crop was not like other crops. He knew not that old Leland, three hundred years ago, had written, "There is one strange thing seen there, that in certain parts of the ground within the walls the corn is marvellous fair to the eye, and, ready to show perfecture, it decayeth." He knew not that a hundred years afterwards another antiquary had written, "The inhabitants of the place told me it had been a constant observation amongst them, that though the soil here is fat and fertile, yet in a sort of baulks that cross one another the corn never grows so thick as in other parts of the field" (Camden). He knew from his own experience, and that was enough, that when the crop came up there were lines and cross lines from one side of the whole area within the walls to the other side, which seemed to tell that where the lines ran the corn would not freely grow. The lines were mapped out about the year 1745. The map is in the King's Library in the British Museum. The plan which we have given (Fig. 125) does not much vary from the Museum map, which is founded on actual survey. There can be no doubt that the country-people of Camden's time were right with regard to these "baulks that cross one another." He says, "Along these they believe the streets of the old city to have run." Camden tells us further of the country-people, "They very frequently dig up British [Roman] tiles, and great plenty of Roman coins, which they call Onion pennies, from one Onion, whom they foolishly fancy to have been a giant, and an inhabitant of this city." Speaking of the area within the walls, he says, "By the rubbish and ruins the earth is grown so high, that I could scarcely thrust myself through a passage which they call Onion's Hole, though I stooped very low." The fancy of the foolish people about a giant has been borne out by matters of which Camden makes no mention. "Nennius ascribes the foundation of Silchester to Constantius, the son of Constantine the Great. Whatever improvements he might have made in its buildings or defences, I cannot but think it had a much earlier origin: as the chief fastness or forest stronghold of the Segontiaci, it probably existed at the time of Cæsar's expedition into Britain. The anonymous geographer of Ravenna gives it a name which I have not yet noticed, Ard-*oneon*; this is a pure British compound, and may be read *Ardal-Onion*, the region of Einion, or Onion" ('Archæologia,' 1837). It is thus here, as in many other cases, that when learning, despising tradition and common opinion, runs its own little circle, it returns to the point from which it set out, and being inclined to break its bounds finds the foolish fancies which it has despised not always unsafe, and certainly not uninteresting, guides through a more varied region.

By a broader way than Onion's Hole we will get without the walls of Silchester. There is a pretty direct line of road through the farm from east to west, which nearly follows the course of one of the old streets. Let us descend the broken bank at the point *a* (Fig. 125.) We are now under the south-western wall. As we advance in a northerly direction, the walls become more distinctly associated with the whole character of the scene. Cultivation here has not changed the aspect which this solitary place has worn for centuries. We are in a broad glade, sloping down to a ditch or little rivulet, with a bold bank on the outer side. We are in the fosse of the city, with an interval of some fifty or sixty feet between the walls and the vallum. The grass of this glade is of the rankest luxuriance. The walls, sometimes entirely hidden by bramble and ivy,—sometimes bare, and exhibiting their peculiar construction,—sometimes fallen in great masses, forced down by the roots of

144.—Hadrian.
From a Copper Coin in the British Museum.

143.—Old Walls of Rome.

146.—Antoninus Pius.
From a Copper Coin in the British Museum.

139.—Restoration of the Roman Arch forming Newport Gate, Lincoln.

145.—Copper Coin of Hadrian, from one in the British Museum.

140.—Roman Arch forming Newport Gate, Lincoln, as it appeared in 1792.

141.—Remains of a Roman Hypocaust, or Subterranean Furnace, for Heating Baths, at Lincoln.

142.—Ancient Arch on Road leading into Rome.

147.—Copper Coin of Antoninus Pius, commemorative of his victories in Britain, from one in the British Museum.

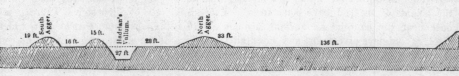

138.—Profile of the Roman Wall and Vallum, near the South Agger Port Gate.

North. South.

Section and Wall of Severus.

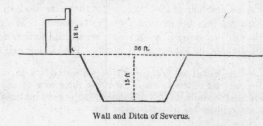

Wall and Ditch of Severus.

40

148.—Part of a Roman Wall; the Site of the Ancient Verulam, near St. Alban's.

149.—Part of the Roman Wall of London excavated behind the Minories.

150.—London Stone.

151.—Duntocher Bridge.

152.—Bronze Patera. View 1.

153.—Bronze Patera. View 2.

154.—Bronze Patera. View 3.

156.—Pig of Lead, with the Roman Stamp.

155.—Pig of Lead, with the Roman Stamp.

157.—Pig of Lead, with the Roman Stamp.

mighty trees, which have shared the ruin that they precipitated,—sometimes with a gnarlèd oak actually growing out of their tops,—present such a combination of picturesqueness as no pencil can reach, because it can only deal with fragments of the great mass. The desolation of the place is the most impressive thing that ever smote our minds with a new emotion. We seem alone in the world; we are here amidst the wrecks of ages; tribes, whose names and localities are matters of controversy, have lived here before the Romans, for the Romans did not form their cities upon such a plan. The Romans have come here, and have mixed with the native people. Inscriptions have been found here: one dedicated to the Hercules of the Segontiaci, showing that this place was the Caer Segont of the Britons; another in honour of Julia Domna, the second wife of the Emperor Severus. Splendid baths have been dug up within the walls: there are the distinct remains of a forum and a temple. In one spot so much coin has been found, that the place goes by the name of Silver Hill. The city was the third of British towns in extent. There is an amphitheatre still existing on the north-eastern side of the wall, which tells us that here the amusements of ancient Rome were exhibited to the people. History records that here the Roman soldiers forced the imperial purple upon Constantine, the rival of Honorius. The monkish chroniclers report that in this city was King Arthur inaugurated. And here, in the nineteenth century, in a country thickly populated,—more abundant in riches, fuller of energy than at any other period,—intersected with roads in all directions,—lies this Silchester, which once had its direct communications with London, with Winchester, with Old Sarum, the capital doubtless of a great district,—here it lies, its houses and its temples probably destroyed by man, but its walls only slowly yielding to that power of vegetable nature which works as surely for destruction as the fire and sword, and topples down in the course of centuries what man has presumed to build for unlimited duration, neglected, unknown, almost a solitary place amidst thick woods and bare heaths. It is an ingenious theory which derives the supposed Roman name of this place from the great characteristic of it which still remains: "The term Galleva, or Calleva, of the Roman Itineraries, appears to have had the same source, and was but a softened form of the British *Gual Vawr*, or the Great Wall; both names had their root perhaps in the Greek χάλιξ (silex), whence also the French *Caillon* (a pebble). *Sile-chester* or Silchester is therefore but a Saxonizing, to use the term, of *Silicis Castrum*, the Fortress of the Flint or Wall, by the easy metonymy which I have shown." ('Archæologia,' 1837.) The striking characteristic of Silchester is the ruined wall, with the flourishing trees upon it and around it, and the old trees that have grown up centuries ago, and are now perishing with it. This is the poetry of the place, and the old topographers felt it after their honest fashion. Leland says, "On that wall grow some oaks of ten cart-load the piece." Camden says, "The walls remain in good measure entire, only with some few gaps in those places where the gates have been; and out of those walls there grow oaks of such a vast bigness incorporated as it were with the stones, and their roots and boughs are spread so far around, that they raise admiration in all who behold them." (Fig. 124.)

> "High towns, fair temples, goodly theatres,
> Strong walls, rich porches, princely palaces,
> Large streets, brave houses, sacred sepulchres,
> Sure gates, sweet gardens, stately galleries,
> Wrought with fair pillars and fine imageries "—

ye are fallen. Fire has consumed you; earth is heaped upon you; the sapling oak has sprung out of the ashes of your breathing statues and your votive urns, and having flourished for five hundred years, other saplings have rooted themselves in your ruins for another five hundred years, and again other saplings are rising—so to flourish and so to perish. Time, which has destroyed thee, Silchester, clothes thee with beauty. "Time loves thee:"

> "He, gentlest among the thralls
> Of Destiny, upon these wounds hath laid
> His lenient touches."

Mr. John Rickman, speaking of Silchester, "the third of British towns in extent," says, "that the Romanized inhabitants of the last-named town were distinguished by their cultivated taste, is testified by the amphitheatre outside the walls, one of the few undisputed relics of that kind in Britain." ('Archæologia,' vol. xxviii.) Whether the presence of the inhabitants of Silchester at the brutal games of the Romans be any proof of their cultivated taste may be reasonably questioned; but the existence of the amphitheatre is an evidence that the Roman customs were here established, and that the people had become habituated to them. The amphitheatre at Silchester is situated without the walls, to the north-east. There can be no doubt about the form and construction of this relic of antiquity. We stand upon a steep circular bank covered with trees, and descend by its sloping sides into an area of moderate dimensions. Some describers of this place tell us that the seats were ranged in five rows, one above the other. Earlier, and perhaps more accurate observers, doubt whether seats were at all used in these turfy amphitheatres. "It is well known that the Romans originally stood at games, till luxury introduced sitting; and it is observable, that the Castrensian amphitheatres in general preserve no signs of subsellia, or seats; so that the people must have stood on the grassy declivity. I saw no signs of seats in that of Carleon, nor in the more perfect one near Dorchester, as Stukeley has also observed. Nor do I recollect that any such have been discovered in any other Castrensian amphitheatre, at least in our island, where they seem to have been rather numerous." (Mr. Strange, in 'Archæologia,' vol. v.) The very perfect amphitheatre at Dorchester is much larger than that of Silchester, Stukeley having computed that it was capable of containing twenty-three thousand people. The form, however, of both amphitheatres is precisely similar (Fig. 126). Their construction was different. The bank of the amphitheatre at Silchester is composed of clay and gravel; that at Dorchester of blocks of solid chalk. These were rude structures compared with the amphitheatres of those provinces of Rome which had become completely Romanized. Where the vast buildings of this description were finished with architectural magnificence, the most luxurious accommodation was provided for all ranks of the people. Greece and Britain exhibit no remains of these grander amphitheatres, such as are found at Nismes and at Verona. The amphitheatre of Pompeii, though of larger dimensions than the largest in England, Dorchester, appears to have been constructed upon nearly the same plan as that (Fig. 128.) Some bas-reliefs found at Pompeii indicate the nature of the amusements that once made the woods of Silchester ring with the howlings of infuriated beasts and the shouts of barbarous men (Fig. 127).

The Roman Wall—the Wall of Agricola—the Wall of Hadrian—the Wall of Severus—the Picts' Wall—the Wall, are various names by which the remains of a mighty monument of the Romans in England are called by various writers. William Hutton, the liveliest and the least pedantic of antiquarians, who at seventy-eight years of age twice traversed the whole length of the Roman Wall, denominates it "one of the grandest works of human labour, performed by the greatest nation upon earth." From a point on the river Tyne, between Newcastle and North Shields, to Boulness on the Solway Frith, a distance of nearly eighty miles, have the remains of this wall been distinctly traced. It was the great artificial boundary of Roman England from sea to sea; a barrier raised against the irruptions of the fierce and unconquerable race of the Caledonians upon the fertile South, which had received the Roman yoke, and rested in safety under the Roman military protection. The *Wall*, speaking popularly, consists of three distinct works, which by some are ascribed to the successive operations of Agricola, of Hadrian (Figs. 144, 145), and of Severus. The Wall of Antoninus (Figs. 146, 147), now called Grimes Dyke, was a more northerly intrenchment, extending from the Clyde to the Forth; but this rampart was abandoned during subsequent years of the Roman occupation, and the boundary between the Solway Frith and the German Ocean, which we are now describing, was strengthened and perfected by every exertion of labour and skill. Hutton may probably have assigned particular portions of the work to particular periods upon insufficient evidence, but he has described the works as they appeared forty years ago better than any other writer, because he described from actual observation. We shall, therefore, adopt his general account of the wall, before proceeding to notice any remarkable features of this monument.

"There were four different works in this grand barrier, performed by three personages, and at different periods. I will measure them from south to north, describe them distinctly, and appropriate each part to its proprietor; for, although every part is dreadfully mutilated, yet, by selecting the best of each, we easily form a whole; from what is, we can nearly tell what was. We must take our dimensions from the original surface of the ground.

"Let us suppose a ditch, like that at the foot of a quickset-hedge, three or four feet deep, and as wide. A bank rising from it ten feet high, and thirty wide in the base; this, with the ditch, will give us a rise of thirteen feet at least. The other side of the bank sinks into a ditch ten feet deep, and fifteen wide, which gives the north side of this bank a declivity of twenty feet. A small part of the soil thrown out on the north side of this fifteen feet ditch, forms a bank three feet high and six wide, which gives an elevation from the bottom of the ditch of thirteen feet. Thus our two ditches and two mounds, sufficient to keep out every rogue but he who was determined not to be kept out, were the work of Agricola.

"The works of Hadrian invariably join those of Agricola. They always correspond together, as beautiful parallel lines. Close to the north side of the little bank I last described, Hadrian sunk a ditch twenty-four feet wide, and twelve below the surface of the ground, which, added to Agricola's three-feet bank, forms a declivity of fifteen feet on the south, and on the north twelve. Then follows a plain of level ground, twenty-four yards over, and a bank exactly the same as Agricola's, ten feet high, and thirty in the base; and then he finishes, as his predecessor began, with a small ditch of three or four feet.

"Thus the two works exactly coincide; and must, when complete, have been most grand and beautiful. Agricola's works cover about fifty-two feet, and Hadrian's about eighty-one; but this will admit of some variation.

"Severus's works run nearly parallel with the other two; lie on the north, never far distant; but may be said always to keep them in view, running a course that best suited the judgment of the maker. The nearest distance is about twenty yards, and greatest near a mile; the medium, forty or fifty yards.

"They consist of a stone wall eight feet thick, twelve high, and four the battlements; with a ditch to the north, as near as convenient, thirty-six feet wide and fifteen deep. To the wall were added, at unequal distances, a number of stations, or cities, said to be eighteen, which is not perfectly true; eighty-one castles, and three hundred and thirty castelets, or turrets, which, I believe, is true: all joining the wall.

"Exclusive of this wall and ditch, these stations, castles, and turrets, Severus constituted a variety of roads, yet called Roman roads, twenty-four feet wide, and eighteen inches high in the centre, which led from turret to turret, from one castle to another; and still larger and more distant roads from the wall, which led from one station to another, besides the grand military way before mentioned, which covered all the works, and no doubt was first formed by Agricola, improved by Hadrian, and, after lying dormant fifteen hundred years, was made complete in 1752.

"I saw many of these smaller roads, all overgrown with turf; and when on the side of a hill, they are supported on the lower side with edging stones.

"Thus Agricola formed a small ditch, then a bank and ditch, both large, and then finished with a small bank.

"Hadrian joined to this small bank a large ditch, then a plain, a large mound, and then finished with a small ditch.

"Severus followed nearly in the same line, with a wall, a variety of stations, castles, turrets, a large ditch, and many roads. By much the most laborious task. This forms the whole works of our three renowned chiefs."

Eleven hundred years before the persevering Hutton began his toilsome march along the Roman Wall, Bede had described it as "still famous and to be seen . . . . . eight foot in breadth and twelve in height, in a straight line from east to west, as is still visible to the beholders." Bede resided in the neighbourhood of the Wall, and he notices it as a familiar object would naturally be noticed—as incidental to his narrative. The dimensions which he gives are, however, perfectly accurate, as Gibson has pointed out. Long before Bede noticed the Wall the Romans had quitted the country; and this great barrier was insufficient to protect the timid inhabitants of the South against the attacks of their Northern invaders, "who, finding that the old confederates were marched home, and refused to return any more, put on greater boldness than ever, and possessed themselves of all the North, and the remote parts of the kingdom to the very Wall. To withstand this invasion the towers are defended by a lazy garrison, undisciplined, and too cowardly to engage an enemy, being enfeebled with continual sloth and idleness. In the meanwhile the naked enemy advance with their hooked weapons, by which the miserable Britons are pulled down from the tops of the walls and dashed against the ground." This is the description of Gildas, our most ancient historian, who lived in the sixth century. Generations passed away; new races grew up on each side of the Wall; and there, for another long period of strife, was the great scene of the Border feuds between the English and the Scotch. It is no wonder that the traces of the Wall in many places should be almost obliterated; or that the fair cities and populous stations which, under the Roman dominion, existed along its line, should have left only fragmentary remains of their former greatness. And yet these remains are most remarkable. House-steads, which is about the centre of the work, is held to

have been the eighth station, Borcovicus: and the fragments of antiquity here discovered have commanded the admiration of all antiquarian explorers. Gibson, who surveyed a portion of the Wall in 1708, here saw seven or eight Roman altars which had been recently dug up, and a great number of statues. Alexander Gordon, whose 'Itinerarium Septentrionale' was published in 1726, describes House-steads, "so named from the marks of old Roman buildings still appearing on that ground," as "unquestionably the most remarkable and magnificent Roman station in the whole island of Britain." He says, amidst his minute descriptions of statues and altars, "It is hardly credible what a number of august remains of the Roman grandeur is to be seen here to this day; seeing in every place where one casts his eye there is some curious Roman antiquity to be seen, either the marks of streets and temples in ruins, or inscriptions, broken pillars, statues, and other pieces of sculpture, all scattered along this ground." When Hutton surveyed the Wall, he found one solitary house upon the site of the Roman City; and in this lone dwelling a Roman altar, complete as in the day the workman left it, formed the jamb which supported the mantel-piece, "one solid stone, four feet high, two broad, and one thick." The gossiping antiquary grows rhetorical amidst the remains of Borcovicus:—"It is not easy to survey these important ruins without a sigh; a place once of the greatest activity, but now a solitary desert: instead of the human voice is heard nothing but the wind." Some of the statues and inscriptions found at House-steads and other parts of the Roman Wall now form a portion of the beautiful collection of Roman antiquities in the Newcastle Museum (Figs. 133, 134, 135, and 136). Of these the Roman soldiers and the Victory are rudely engraved in Gordon's book. The appearance of the Wall at House-steads is shown in Fig. 132; and this engraving suggests a conviction of the accuracy of Camden's description of the Wall:—"I have observed the track of it running up the mountains and down again in a most surprising manner." The massive character of the works is well exhibited at the sandstone-quarries at Denton Dean, where the wall, whose fragment is five feet high, has only three courses of facing-stones on one side and four on the other. Blocks of stone of such dimensions must of themselves have formed a quarry for successive generations to hew at and destroy (Fig. 131). There is a pretty tradition recorded by Camden, which offers as good evidence of the Roman civilization as the fragments of their temples and their statues. The tomb of a young Roman physician is amongst the antiquities of the Newcastle Museum; and our old topographer tells us, "One thing there is which I will not keep from the reader, because I had it confirmed by persons of very good credit. There is a general persuasion in the neighbourhood, handed down by tradition, that the Roman garrisons upon the frontiers set in these parts abundance of medicinal plants for their own use. Whereupon the Scotch surgeons come hither a-simpling every year in the beginning of summer; and having by long experience found the virtue of these plants, they magnify them very much, and affirm them to be very sovereign." The general appearance of the Roman Wall and Vallum is exhibited in Fig. 138. This was delineated by John Warburton, from a portion of the wall near Halton-Chesters, in 1722. A little farther beyond this point Hutton was well repaid for his laborious walk of six hundred miles, by such a satisfactory view of the great Roman work, that the admiration of the good old man was raised into an enthusiastic transport, at which the dull may wonder, and the unimaginative may laugh, but which had its own reward. With this burst of the happy wayfarer we conclude our notice of "that famous wall which was the boundary of the Roman province." "I now travel over a large common, still upon the Wall, with its trench nearly complete. But what was my surprise when I beheld, thirty yards on my left, the united works of Agricola and Hadrian, almost perfect! I climbed over a stone wall to examine the wonder; measured the whole in every direction; surveyed them with surprise, with delight; was fascinated, and unable to proceed; forgot I was upon a wild common, a stranger, and the evening approaching. I had the grandest works under my eye of the greatest men of the age in which they lived, and of the most eminent nation then existing; all which had suffered but little during the long course of sixteen hundred years. Even hunger and fatigue were lost in the grandeur before me. If a man writes a book upon a turnpike-road, he cannot be expected to move quick; but, lost in astonishment, I was not able to move at all."

The Wall of Antoninus, or Grimes Dyke, to which we have already referred, was carried across the north of Britain, under the direction of Lollius Urbicus, the legate of Antoninus Pius, about the year A. D. 140. It is noticed by an ancient Roman writer as a turf wall; and although its course may be readily traced, it has, from the nature of its construction, not left such enduring remains

G 2

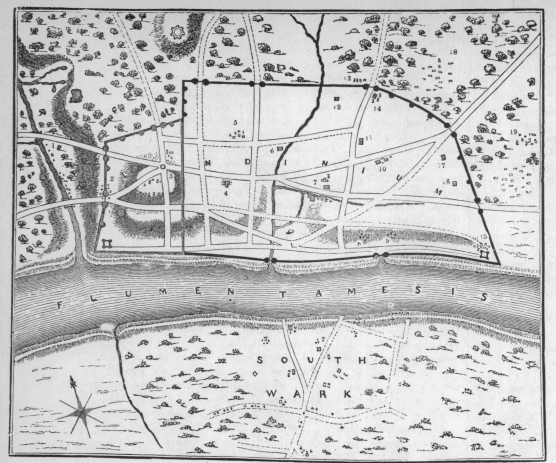

158.—Plan of Roman London.

159.—Roman Bath, Strand Lane.

165.—Coin and Fragment.

160.—Sepulchral Stone found at Ludgate.

161.—Tessellated Pavement.

162.—Bronze Statues found in the Thames.

163.—Vases, Lamps, &c., found after the Great Fire

164.—Roman Antiquities found on the Site of St. Paul's Cross

166.—Urns, Vases, Key, Bead, and Fragment of Pottery, found in Lombard Street 1785.

167.—Altar of Apollo, and Vases.

1 Bronze Spear-Head.
2 Bronze Dagger.
3 Iron Knife.
4 Bronze Lance-Head.
5 Iron Lance-Head.
6 Celt.
7 Bronze Lance-Head.
8 Bronze Celt.
9 Ivory Arrow-Head.
10 Iron Boss of a Shield.
11 Bronze Buckle.
12 Iron Crook.
13 Iron Ring.
14 Plated Iron Stud.
15 Bronze Pin.
16 } Bronze Pins with Ivory Handles.
17 }
18 } Bronze Ornaments.
19 }

20 Amulet.
21 Gold Box.
22 } Gold Ornaments.
23 }
24 Amber and Bead Necklace.
25 Gold Breastplate.
26 Patera.
27 Ivory Bracelet.
28 Drinking Cup.
29 Incense Cup.
30 }
31 } Drinking Cups.
32 }
33 } Double Drinking Cup.
34 }
35 }
36 } Urns.
37 }
38 Druidical Hook for gathering
   the Sacred Mistletoe.

168.—Roman-British Weapons, Ornaments, &c.

169.—Roman Vessels, &c., found in Britain.

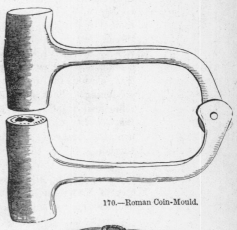

170.—Roman Coin-Mould.

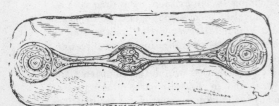

171.—Metal coating of an ancient Roman-British Shield, found in the bed of the river Witham, and now in the Meyrick Collection.

173.—British Coin of Carausius.
From a unique Gold Coin in the British Museum.

172.—Constantine the Great.
From a Gold Coin in the British Museum.

as the Wall of Severus. The Wall of Antoninus connected a line of Roman forts; and these were necessarily built of substantial materials. Duntocher Bridge, on the line of this wall, was long popularly considered to have been a Roman work; but it has been more reasonably conjectured to have been a very ancient work, constructed out of materials found on the line of the wall (Fig. 148). The military way in some places runs parallel with Grimes Dyke. The ditch itself presents in some places a wonderful example of the Roman boldness in engineering. At a part called Bar Hill, Gordon describes "the fossa running down in a straight line from the top of the hill in such a magnificent manner as must surprise the beholder, great part of it being cut through the solid rock, and is of such a vast breadth and depth, that when I measured it it was no .ess than forty feet broad and thirty-five feet deep." The surprise of Mr. Gordon was before the age of railways: the time may perhaps arrive when the deep cuttings and tunnellings through the solid rock in the nineteenth century shall be compared with the Roman works of the second century, by new races of men who travel by other lines or with different mechanism. But, however obscure may then be the history of our own works, it is quite certain that we shall have left our traces upon the earth; some consolation, though small, to balance the reflections which are naturally suggested when we look upon the ruins of populous cities and mighty defences, and consider how little we know of their origin, of the people who built them, and of the individual life that was once busy in these solitary places.

We have described, rapidly and imperfectly, some ancient places now buried in deep solitude, which were once filled with many people who pursued the ordinary occupations of human industry, and who were surrounded with the securities, comforts, and elegancies of social life. Great changes have necessarily been produced in the revolution of two thousand years. Hume, in his ' Essay of the Populousness of Ancient Nations,' says, " The barbarous condition of Britain in former times is well known, and the thinness of its inhabitants may easily be conjectured, both from their barbarity, and from a circumstance mentioned by Herodian, that all Britain was marshy, even in Severus's time, after the Romans had been fully settled in it above a century." In process of time the marshes were drained; the population of the hills, as in the case of Old Sarum, descended into the plains. The advantages of communication located towns upon the banks of rivers, which were restrained within deep channels by artificial bounds. London thus grew when the Thames was walled out of the low lands. So probably York, when the Ouse became tributary to man, instead of being a pestilent enemy. When the civilizers taught the original inhabitants to subdue the powers of nature to their use, the sites of great towns were fixed, and have remained fixed even to our own day, in consequence of those natural advantages which have continued unimpaired during the changes of centuries. The Romans were the noblest of colonizers. They did not make their own country rich by the exhaustive process which has been the curse of modern colonization. They taught the people their own useful arts, and they shared the riches which they had been the instruments of producing. They distributed amongst subdued nations their own refinements; and in the cultivation of the higher tastes they found that security which could never have resulted from the coercion of brutal ignorance. Tacitus says of Agricola, the great colonizer of England, "That the Britons, who led a roaming and unsettled life, and were easily instigated to war, might contract a love of peace and tranquillity by being accustomed to a more pleasant way of living, he exhorted and assisted them to build houses temples, courts, and market-places. By praising the diligent, and reproaching the indolent, he excited so great an emulation amongst the Britons, that after they had erected all those necessary edifices in their towns, they proceeded to build others merely for ornament and pleasure, such as porticoes, galleries, baths, banqueting-houses, &c." Many of the still prosperous places of England, even at the present day, show us what the Romans generally, if not especially Agricola, did for the advancement of the arts of life amongst our remote forefathers. Lincoln is one of these cities of far-off antiquity—a British, a Roman, a Saxon city. Leland says, " I heard say that the lower part of Lincoln town was all marsh, and won by policy, and inhabited for the commodity of the water. . . . It is easy to be perceived that the town of Lincoln hath been notably builded at three times. The first uilding was on the very top of the hill, the oldest part whereof inhabited in the Britons' time was the northest part of the hill, directly without Newport gate, the ditches whereof yet remain, and great tokens of the old town-walls taken out of a ditch by it, for all the top of

Lincoln Hill is quarry-ground. This is now a suburb to Newport Gate." And there at Lincoln stills stands Newport Gate—the Roman gate,—formed by a plain square pier and a semicircular arch (Figs. 139, 140). The Roman walls and the Roman arches of Lincoln are monuments of the same great people that we find at Rome itself (Figs. 142, 143). At Lincoln too are the remains of such baths as Agricola taught the Britons to build (Fig. 141). The Newport Gate of Lincoln, though half filled up by the elevation of the soil, exhibits a central arch sixteen feet wide, with two lateral arches. Within the area of the Roman walls now stand the Cathedral and the Castle, monuments equally interesting of other times and circumstances. At Lincoln, as at all other ancient places, we can trace the abodes of the living in the receptacles for the dead. The sarcophagi, the stone coffins, and the funereal urns here found, tell of the people of different ages and creeds mingled now in their common dust.

A fragment of Roman wall still proclaims the site of the ancient Verulam (Fig. 149). Camden says, "The situation of this place is well known to have been close by the town of St. Albans. . . . . Nor hath it yet lost its ancient name, for it is still commonly called Verulam; although nothing of that remains besides ruins of walls, chequered pavements, and Roman coins, which they now and then dig up." The fame of the Roman Verulam was merged in the honours of the Christian St. Albans; and the bricks of the old city were worked up into the church of the proto-martyr of England. Bede tells the story of the death of St. Alban, the first victim in Britain of the persecution of Diocletian, in the third century, with a graphic power which brings the natural features of this locality full before our view: " The most reverend confessor of God ascended the hill with the throng, the which decently pleasant agreeable place is almost five hundred paces from the river, embellished with several sorts of flowers, or rather quite covered with them; wherein there is no part upright, or steep, nor anything craggy, but the sides stretching out far about, is levelled by nature like the sea, which of old it had rendered worthy to be enriched with the martyr's blood for its beautiful appearance."

> "Thus was Alban tried,
> England's first martyr, whom no threats could shake:
> Self-offered victim, for his friend he died,
> And for the faith—nor shall his name forsake
> That Hill, whose flowery platform seems to rise
> By Nature decked for holiest sacrifice."
>
> WORDSWORTH.

In the time of Aubrey, some half-century later than that of Camden, there were "to be seen in some few places some remains of the walls of this city." Speaking of Lord Bacon, Aubrey says, " Within the bounds of the walls of this old city of Verulam (his lordship's barony) was Verulam House, about a half mile from St. Alban's, which his lordship built, the most ingeniously-contrived little pile that ever I saw." It was here that Bacon, freed, however dishonourably, from the miserable intrigues of Whitehall, and the debasing quirks and quibbles of the Courts, laid the foundations of his ever-during fame. Aubrey tells us a story which is characteristic of Bacon's enthusiastic temperament:— " This magnanimous Lord Chancellor had a great mind to have made it [Verulam] a city again; and he had designed it to be built with great uniformity; but fortune denied it to him, though she proved kinder to the great Cardinal Richelieu, who lived both to design and finish that specious town of Richelieu, where he was born, before an obscure and small village." Fortune not only denied Bacon to found this city, but even the "ingeniously-contrived little pile," his gardens, and his banqueting-houses, which he had built at an enormous cost, were swept away within thirty years after his death: " One would have thought," says Aubrey, " the most barbarous nation had made a conquest here." To use the words of the philosopher of Verulam himself, " It is not good to look too long upon these turning wheels of Vicissitude, lest we become giddy."

York, the Eboracum of the Romans, was one of the most important of these British cities. Its Roman remains have very recently been described by a learned resident of this city:—" One of the angle-towers, and a portion of the wall of Eboracum attached to it, are to this day remaining in an extraordinary state of preservation. In a recent removal of a considerable part of the more modern wall and rampart, a much larger portion of the Roman wall, connected with the same angle-tower, but in another direction, with remains of two wall-towers, and the foundations of one of the gates of the station, were found buried within the ramparts; and excavations at various times and in different parts of the present city have discovered so many indubitable remains of the fortifications of Eboracum, on three of its sides, that the conclusion appears to be fully warranted that this important station was of a rectangular form, corresponding very nearly with the plan of a Polybian camp, occupying a space of about six hundred and fifty yards, by about five hundred and fifty, enclosed by a wall and a rampant mound on the inner side of the wall, and a fosse without, with four angle-towers, and a series of minor towers or turrets, and having four gates or principal entrances, from which proceeded military roads to the neighbouring stations mentioned in the 'Itinerary' of Antonine. Indications of extensive suburbs, especially on the south-west and north-west, exist in the numerous and interesting remains of primeval monuments, coffins, urns, tombs, baths, temples, and villas, which from time to time, and especially of late years, have been brought to light. Numberless tiles, bearing the impress of the sixth and ninth legions, fragments of Samian ware, inscriptions, and coins from the age of Julius Cæsar to that of Constantine and his family, concur, with the notice of ancient geographers and historians, to identify the situation of modern York with that of ancient Eboracum." ('Penny Cyclopædia,' vol. xxvii.)

And well might York have been a mighty fortress, and a city of palaces and temples; for here the Roman emperors had their chief seat when they visited Britain; here Severus and Constantius Chlorus died; here, though the evidence is somewhat doubtful, Constantine the Great was born.

Bath, a Roman city, connected by great roads with London and with the south coast, famous for its baths, a city of luxury amongst the luxurious colonizers, has presented to antiquarian curiosity more Roman remains than any other station in England. The city is supposed to be now twenty feet above its ancient level; and here, whenever the earth is moved, are turned up altars, tessellated pavements, urns, vases, lachrymatories, coins. Portions of a large temple consisting of a portico with fluted columns and Corinthian capitals, were discovered in 1790. The remains of the ancient baths have been distinctly traced. The old walls of the city are held to have been built upon the original Roman foundations. These walls have been swept away, and with them the curious relics of the elder period, which Leland has thus minutely described:—"There be divers notable antiquities engraved in stone that yet be seen in the walls of Bath betwixt the south gate and the west gate, and again betwixt the west gate and the north gate." He then notices with more than ordinary detail a number of images, antique heads, tombs with inscriptions, and adds, "I much doubt whether these antique works were set in the time of the Romans' dominion in Britain in the walls of Bath as they stand now, or whether they were gathered of old ruins there, and since set up in the walls, re-edified in testimony of the antiquity of the town." Camden appears to have seen precisely the same relics as Leland saw, "fastened on the inner side of the wall between the north and west gates." These things were in existence, then, a little more than two hundred years ago. There have been no irruptions of barbarous people into the country, to destroy these and other things of value which they could not understand. We had a high literature when these things were preserved; there were learned men amongst us; and the writers of imagination had that reverence for antiquity which is one of the best fruits of a diffused learning. From that period we have been wont to call ourselves a polite people. We are told that since that period we have had an Augustan age of letters and of arts. Yet somehow it has happened that during these last two centuries there has been a greater destruction of ancient things, and a more wanton desecration of sacred things, perpetrated by people in authority, sleek, self-satisfied functionaries, practical men, as they termed themselves, who despised all poetical associations, and thought the beautiful incompatible with the useful—there has been more wanton outrage committed upon the memorials of the past, than all the invaders and pillagers of our land had committed for ten centuries before. The destruction has been stopped, simply because the standard of taste and of feeling has been raised amongst a few.

It is inconsistent with our plan to attempt any complete detail of the antiquities of any one period, as they are found in various parts of the kingdom. To accomplish this, each period would require a volume, or many volumes. Our purpose is to excite a general spirit of inquiry, and to gratify that curiosity as far as we are able, by a few details of what is most remarkable. Let us finish our account of the Roman cities by a brief notice of Roman London.

A writer whose ability is concurrent with his careful investigation of every subject which he touches, has well described the circumstances which led to the choice of London as a Roman city, upon a site which the Britons had peopled, in all likelihood, before the Roman colonization:—

"The spot on which London is built, or at least that on which the first buildings were most probably erected, was pointed out by nature for the site of a city. It was the suspicion of the sagacious Wren, as we are informed in the 'Parentalia,' that the whole valley between Camberwell Hill and the hills of Essex must have been anciently filled by a great frith or arm of the sea, which increased in width towards the east; and that this estuary was only in the course of ages reduced to a river by the vast sand-hills which were gradually raised on both sides of it by the wind and tide, the effect being assisted by embankments, which on the Essex side are still perfectly distinguishable as of artificial origin, and are evidently works that could only have been constructed by a people of advanced mechanical skill. Wren himself ascribed these embankments to the Romans; and it is stated that a single breach made in them in his time cost 17,000*l.* to repair it—from which we may conceive both how stupendous must have been the labour bestowed on their original construction, and of what indispensable utility they are still found to be. In fact, were it not for this ancient barrier, the broad and fertile meadows stretching along that border of the river would still be a mere marsh, or a bed of sand overflowed by the water, though left perhaps dry in many places on the retirement of the tide. . . . . . The elevation on which London is built offered a site at once raised above the water, and at the same time close upon the navigable portion of it—conditions which did not meet in any other locality on either side of the river, or estuary, from the sea upwards. It was the first spot on which a town could be set down, so as to take advantage of the facilities of communication between the coast and the interior presented by this great natural highway." ('London,' vol. i. No. IX.)

The walls of London were partly destroyed in the time of Fitz-Stephen, who lived in the reign of Henry II. He says, " The wall of the city is high and great, continued with seven gates, which are made double, and on the north distinguished with turrets by spaces. Likewise on the south London hath been enclosed with walls and towers; but the large river of Thames, well stored with fish, and in which the tide ebbs and flows, by continuance of time hath washed, worn away, and cast down those walls." Camden writes: " Our historians tell us that Constantine the Great, at the request of Helena, his mother, first walled it [London] about with hewn stone and British bricks, containing in compass about three miles; whereby the city was made a square, but not equilateral, being longer from west to east, and from south to north narrower. That part of these walls which runs along by the Thames is quite washed away by the continual beating of the river; though Fitz-Stephen (who lived in Henry the Second's time) tells us there were some pieces of it still to be seen. The rest remains to this day, and that part toward the north very firm: for having not many years since [1474] been repaired by one Jocelyn, who was Mayor, it put on, as it were, a new face and freshness. But that toward the east and the west, though the Barons repaired it in their wars out of the demolished houses of the Jews, is all ruinous and going to decay." The new face and freshness that were put on the north wall by one Jocelyn the Mayor, have long since perished. A few fragments above the ground, built-in, plastered over, proclaim to the curious observer, that he walks in a city that has some claim to antiquity. It was formerly a doubt with some of those antiquarian writers who saw no interest in any inquiry except as a question of dispute, whether the walls of London were of Roman construction. A careful observer, Dr. Woodward, in the beginning of the last century, had an opportunity of going below the surface, and the matter was by him put beyond a doubt. He writes:—" The city wall being upon this occasion, to make way for these new buildings, broke up and beat to pieces, from Bishopgate, onwards, S.E. so far as they extend, an opportunity was given of observing the fabric and composition of it. From the foundation, which lay eight feet below the present surface, quite up to the top, which was in all near ten foot, 'twas compiled alternately of layers of broad flat bricks and of rag-stone. The bricks lay in double ranges; and each brick being about one inch and three-tenths in thickness, the whole layer, with the mortar interposed, exceeded not three inches. The layers of stone were not quite two foot thick of our measure. 'Tis probable they were intended for two of the Roman, their rule being somewhat shorter than ours. To this height the workmanship was after the Roman manner; and these were the remains of the ancient wall supposed to be built by Constantine the Great. In this 'twas very observable that the mortar was, as usually in the Roman works, so very firm and hard, that the stone itself as easily broke and gave way as that. 'Twas thus far from the foundation upwards nine foot in thickness." The removal of old houses in London is still going on as in Woodward's time; and more important excavations have been made in our own day, and at the

174.—Atrium of a Roman House.

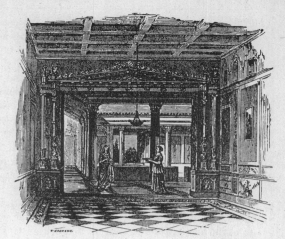

175.—Room of a Roman House. Restoration from Pompeii.

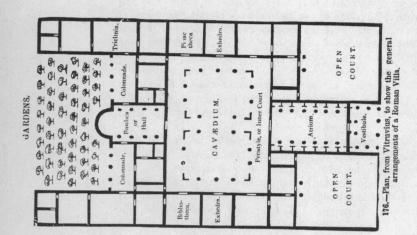

176.—Plan, from Vitruvius, to show the general arrangements of a Roman Villa.

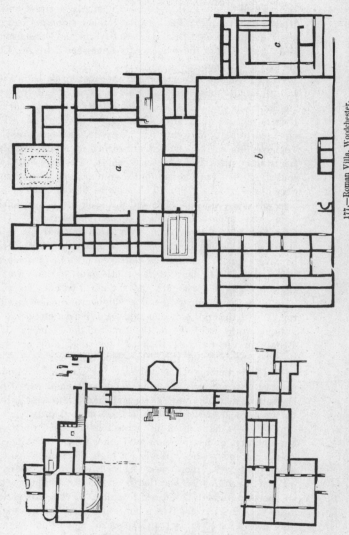

177.—Roman Villa, Woodchester.

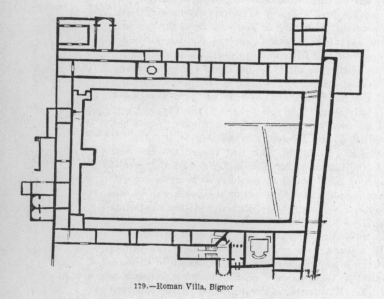

179.—Roman Villa, Bignor

178.—Roman Villa, Great Witcombe, Gloucestershire.

180.—Room of a Roman House. Restoration from Pompeii.

181.—Atrium of a Roman House. Restoration from Pompeii.

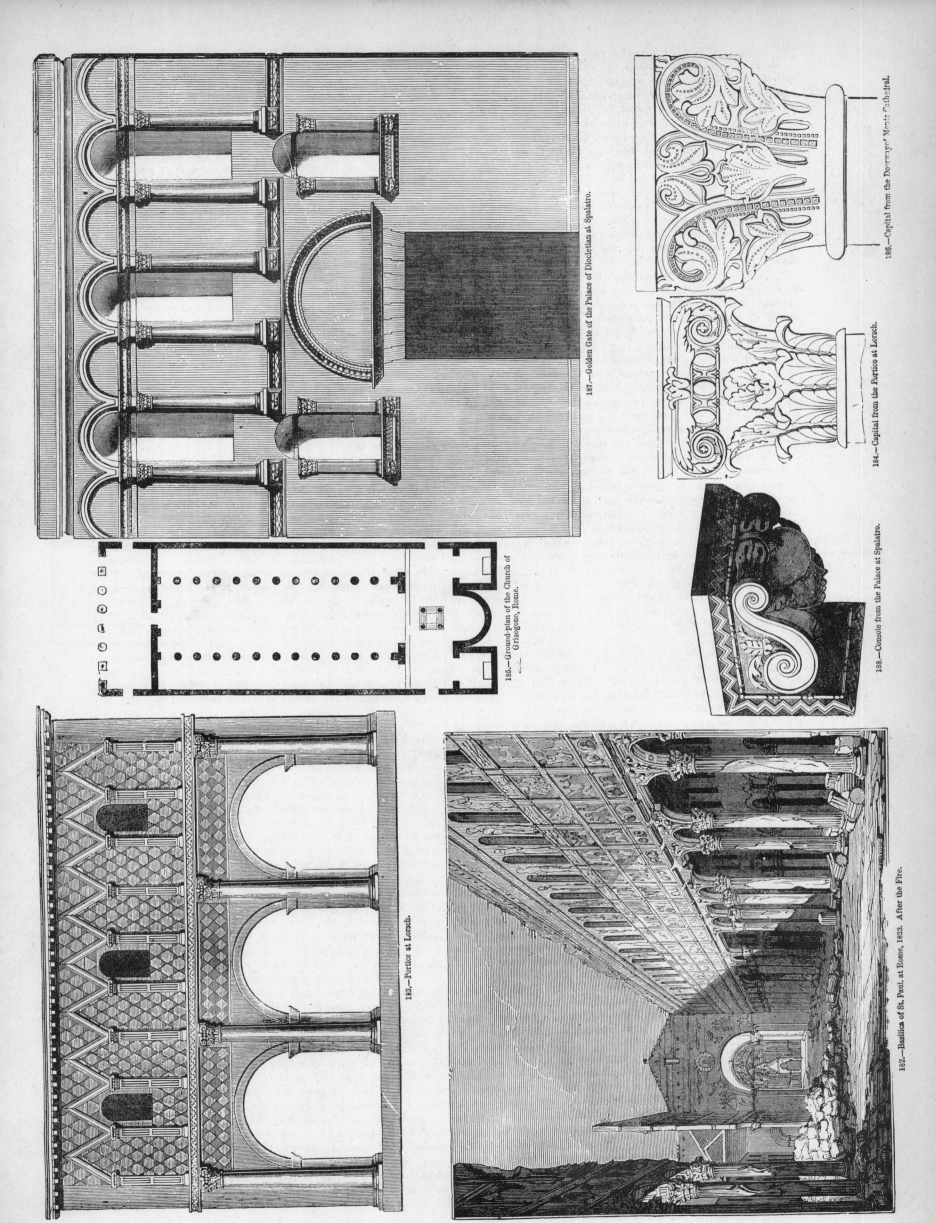

187.—Golden Gate of the Palace of Diocletian at Spalatro.

186.—Capital from the Doorway, Montz Cathedral.

184.—Capital from the Portico at Lorsch.

188.—Console from the Palace at Spalatro.

185.—Ground-plan of the Church of Grisogono, Rome.

183.—Portico at Lorsch.

182.—Basilica of St. Paul, at Rome, 1823. After the Fire.

very hour in which we are writing. Close by St. Paul's, in the formation of a deep sewer, the original peat-earth, over which probably the Thames once flowed before man rested his foot here, has been dug down to. In such excavations the relics of age after age have turned up. The Saxon town lies above the Roman; and the Norman above the Saxon; but when the spade and the pickaxe have broken against some mass solid as the granite rock, then the labourer knows that he has come to a building such as men build not now, foundations that seem intended to have lasted for ever, the Roman work. Woodward described the Wall as he saw it in Camomile Street in 1707. Mr. Craik, the writer whom we have recently quoted, has recorded the appearance of the Wall as he saw it in 1841, laid bare for the works of the Blackwall Railway.

"Beneath a range of houses which have been in part demolished, in a court entering from the east side of Cooper's Row, nearly opposite to Milbourne's Almshouses, and behind the south-west corner of America Square, the workmen, having penetrated to the natural earth—a hard, dry, sandy gravel—came upon a wall seven feet and a half thick, running a very little to the west of north, or parallel to the line of the Minories; which, by the resistance it offered, was at once conjectured to be of Roman masonry. When we saw it, it had been laid bare on both sides, to the height of about six or seven feet, and there was an opportunity of examining its construction, both on the surface and in the interior. The principal part of it consisted of five courses of squared stones, regularly laid, with two layers of flat bricks below them, and two similar layers above—the latter at least carried all the way through the wall—as represented in the drawing (Fig. 150). The mortar, which appeared to be extremely hard, had a few pebbles mixed up with it; and here and there were interstices, or air-cells, as if it had not been spread, but poured in among the stones. The stones were a granulated limestone, such as might have been obtained from the chalk-quarries at Greenhithe or Northfleet. The bricks, which were evidently Roman, and, as far as the eye could judge, corresponded in size as well as in shape with those described by Woodward, had as fine a grain as common pottery, and varied in colour from a bright red to a palish yellow. A slight circular or oval mark—in some cases forming a double ring—appeared on one side of each of them, which had been impressed when the clay was in a soft state." ('London,' Vol. I. No. ix.)

A peculiarity in the construction of a portion of the ancient wall of London was discovered during some large excavations for sewerage, between Lambeth Hill and Queenhithe, in 1841. The wall in this part measured in breadth from eight to ten feet. Its foundation was upon piles, upon which was laid a stratum of chalk and stones; then a course of ponderous hewn sandstones, held together by the well-known cement; and upon this solid structure the wall itself, composed of layers of rag and flint, between the layers of Roman tiles. The peculiarity to which we allude was described to the Antiquarian Society by Mr. Charles Roach Smith:—"One of the most remarkable features of this wall is the evidence it affords of the existence of an anterior building, which from some cause or other must have been destroyed. Many of the large stones above mentioned are sculptured and ornamented with mouldings, which denote their prior use in a frieze or entablature of an edifice, the magnitude of which may be conceived from the fact of these stones weighing in many instances upwards of half a ton. Whatever might have been the nature of this structure, its site, or cause of its overthrow, we have no means of determining." The undoubted work of fourteen or fifteen centuries ago is something not to be looked upon without associations of deep and abiding interest; but when we find connected with such ancient labours more ancient labours, which have themselves been overthrown by the changes of time or the vicissitudes of fortune, the mind must fall back upon the repose of its own ignorance, and be content to know how little it knows.

In the year 1785 a sewer, sixteen feet deep, was made in Lombard Street. Sewers were not then common in London, and Sir John Henniker, speaking of this work, says, " A large trench has been excavated in Lombard Street for the first time since the memory of man." In making this excavation vast quantities of Roman antiquities were discovered, which are minutely described and represented in the eighth volume of the 'Archæologia.' Amongst other curiosities was found a beautiful gold coin of the Emperor Galba. The coin came into the possession of Sir John Henniker, who thus relates the circumstances under which it was found :—"The soil is almost uniformly divided into four strata; the uppermost, thirteen feet six inches thick, of factitious earth; the second, two feet thick, of brick, apparently the ruins of buildings; the third, three inches thick, of wood-ashes, apparently the remains of a town built of wood,

and destroyed by fire; the fourth, of Roman pavement, common and tessellated. On this pavement the coin in question was discovered, together with several other coins, and many articles of pottery. Below the pavement the workmen find virgin earth." ('Archæologia,' vol. viii.) In 1831 various Roman remains were found in the construction of a sewer in Crooked Lane, and in Eastcheap. There, at a depth of about seventeen feet, were found the walls of former houses covered with wood-ashes, and about them were also found many portions of green *molten* glass, and of red ware discoloured by the action of fire. Mr. A. J. Kempe, who communicates these discoveries to the Society of Antiquaries, adverts to the wood-ashes found in Lombard Street in 1785; and he adds, " Couple this with the circumstances I have related, and what stronger evidence can be produced of the catastrophe in which the dwellings of the Roman settlers at London were involved in the reign of Nero? The Roman buildings at the north-east corner of Eastcheap afforded a curious testimony that such a conflagration had taken place, and that London had been afterwards rebuilt by the Romans. Worked into the mortar of the walls were numerous pieces of the fine red ware, blackened by the action of an intense fire."

The circumstances recorded certainly furnish strong evidence of a conflagration and a rebuilding of the city; but the fact recorded in 1785, that under the wood-ashes was a coin of Galba, is evidence against the conflagration having taken place in the time of Nero, whom Galba succeeded. Mr. Kempe has fallen into the general belief that when Londinium was abandoned to the vengeance of Boadicea, its buildings were destroyed by a general conflagration. This was in the year A. D. 61. The coin of Galba under the wood-ashes would seem to infer that the conflagration was at a later date, in connection with circumstances of which we have no tradition. The short reign of Galba commenced A. D. 68. But be this as it may, here, seventeen feet under the present pavement of London, are the traces of Roman life covered by the ashes of a ruined city, and other walls built with the fragments of those ruins, and over these the aggregated rubbish of eighteen centuries of inhabitancy. The extent of Roman London, of the London founded or civilized, burnt, rebuilt, extended by the busiest of people, may be traced by the old walls, by the cemeteries beyond the walls, and by the remains of ancient relics of utility and ornament constantly turned up wherever the soil is dug into to a sufficient depth. Look upon the plan of this Roman London (Fig. 158). The figures marked upon the plan show the places where the Romans have been traced. 1. Shows the spot in Fleet Ditch where vases, coins, and implements were found after the Great Fire of 1666. In many other parts were similar remains found on that occasion (Fig. 163). On the plan, 2 shows the point where a sepulchral stone was found at Ludgate, which is now amongst the Arundel Marbles at Oxford (Fig. 160). In the plan, 3 marks the site of St. Paul's, where many remains were found by Sir Christopher Wren, in digging the foundation of the present Cathedral—the burial-place of " the colony when Romans and Britons lived and died together" (Fig. 164). At the causeway at Bow Church, marked 4, Roman remains were found after the Great Fire. At Guildhall, marked 5, tiles and pottery were found in 1822. In Lothbury, in 1805, digging for the foundation of an extended portion of the Bank of England, marked 6, a tessellated pavement was found, which is now in the British Museum. Other tessellated pavements have been found in various parts of London, the finest specimens having been discovered in 1803, in Leadenhall Street, near the portico of the India House, (Fig. 161). The spot in Lombard Street and Birchin Lane, where, previous to the discoveries in 1785 already mentioned, remains had been found in 1730 and 1774, is marked 7 on the plan. Some of these remains are represented in Fig. 166. In 1787 Roman coins and tiles were found at St. Mary at Hill, close by the line of the Thames, marked 8. In 1824, near St. Dunstan's in the East, on the same line, marked 9, were pavements and urns found. In Long Lane, marked 10, a pavement has been found; also a tessellated pavement in Crosby Square, marked 11; a pavement in Old Broad Street, marked 12; a tessellated pavement in Crutched Friars, marked 16; a pavement in Northumberland Alley, marked 17. Sepulchral monuments have been found within the City wall, as in Bishopsgate, in 1707, marked 14; and in the Tower, in 1777, marked 15. But the great burial-places, especially of the Christianized Romans, were outside the wall; as at the cemetery beyond Bishopsgate, discovered in 1725, marked 13; that in Goodman's Fields, marked 19, found in 1787; and that at Spitalfields, marked 18, discovered as early as 1577. The old London antiquary, Stow, thus speaks of this discovery: " On the east side of this churchyard lieth a large field, of old time called Lolesworth, now Spitalfield, which about the year 1576 was broken up for clay to make brick; in the digging whereof many earthen pots called Urnæ were found full of ashes, and burnt bones of men, to wit of the Romans who inhabited here. For it was the custom of the Romans to burn their dead, to put their ashes in an urn, and then to bury the same with certain ceremonies, in some field appointed for that purpose near unto their city. . . . . . There hath also been found (in the same field) divers coffins of stone, containing the bones of men; these I suppose to be the burials of some special persons, in time of the Britons or Saxons, after that the Romans had left to govern here. Moreover there were also found the skulls and bones of men without coffins, or rather whose coffins (being of great timber) were consumed. Divers great nails of iron were there found, such as are used in the wheels of shod carts, being each of them as big as a man's finger, and a quarter of a yard long, the heads two inches over."

The plan thus detailed indicates the general extent of Roman London. Within these limits every year adds something to the mass of antiquities that have been turned up, and partially examined and described, since the days when Stow saw the earthern pots in Spitalfields. Traces of the old worship have at various times been found. A very curious altar was discovered fifteen feet below the level of the street in Foster Lane, Cheapside, in 1830. Attention has recently been directed to a supposed Roman bath in Strand Lane, represented in Fig. 159 (See 'London,' Vol. II.). But the bed of the Thames has been as prolific as the highways that are trampled upon, in disclosing to its excavators traces of the great colonizers of England. Works of high art in silver and in bronze were found in 1825 and 1837, embedded in the soil over which the river has been rolling for ages. In the southern bank of the Thames evidences have recently been discovered that parts of Southwark contiguous to the river were occupied by the Romans, as well as the great city on the opposite bank. Mr. Charles Roach Smith, in a paper read to the Society of Antiquaries in 1841, says, "The occurrence of vestiges of permanent occupancy of this locality by the Romans, is almost uninterrupted from the river to St. George's Church in the line of the present High Street." Mr. Smith is decidedly of opinion that a considerable portion of Southwark formed an integral part of Londinium, and that the two shores were connected by a bridge. Mr. Smith holds, "First, that with such a people as the Romans, and in such a city as Londinium, a bridge would be indispensable; and, secondly, that it would naturally be erected somewhere in the direct line of road into Kent, which I cannot but think pointed toward the site of Old London Bridge, both from its central situation, from the general absence of the foundations of buildings in the approaches on the northern side, and from discoveries recently made in the Thames on the line of the old bridge." The bronzes, medallions, and coins found in the line of the old bridge, which have been dredged up by the ballast-heavers from their position, and the order in which they occur, strongly support the opinion of Mr. Smith. The coins comprise many thousands of a series extending from Julius Cæsar to Honorius; and Mr. Smith infers "that the bulk of these coins might have been intentionally deposited, at various periods, at the erection of a bridge across the river, whether it were built in the time of Vespasian, Hadrian, or Pius, or at some subsequent period, and that they also might have been deposited at such times as the bridge might require repairs or entire renovation."

The shrewd observer and sensible writer whom we have quoted has a valuable remark upon the peculiar character of the Roman antiquities of London:—"Though our Londinium cannot rival, in remains of public buildings, costly statues, and sculptured sarcophagi and altars, the towns of the mother-country, yet the reflective antiquary can still find materials to work on,—can point to the localities of the less obtrusive and imposing, but not less useful, structures—the habitations of the mercantile and trading population of this ever-mercantile town. The numerous works of ancient art which have yet been preserved afford us copious materials for studying the habits, manners, and customs of the Roman colonists; the introduction and state of many of the arts during their long sojourn in Britain, and their positive or probable influence on the British inhabitants. This is, in fact, the high aim and scope of the science of antiquities—to study mankind through their works."

It is in this spirit that we would desire to look at the scattered antiquities of 'Old England,' to whatever period they may belong. Whenever man delves into the soil, and turns up a tile or an earthen pot, a coin or a weapon, an inscription which speaks of love for the dead, or an altar which proclaims the reverence for the spiritual, in some form, however mistaken, we have evidences of antique modes of life, in whose investigation we may enlarge the narrow bounds of our own every-day life. Those who have

descended into the excavated streets of the buried Pompeii, and have walked in subterranean ways which were once radiant with the sunshine, and have entered houses whose paintings and sculptures are proofs that here were the abodes of comfort and elegance, where taste displayed itself in forms which cannot perish, —such have beheld with deep emotion the consequences of a sudden ruin which in a few hours made the populous city a city of the dead. But when we pierce through the shell of successive generations abiding in a great city like London, to bring to light the fragments of a high state of civilization, crushed and overthrown by change and spoliation, and forgotten amidst the trample of successive generations of mankind in the same busy spot, the eye may not so readily awaken the mind to solemn reflection; but still every fragment has its own lesson, which cannot be read unprofitably. It is not the exquisite art by which common materials for common purposes were moulded by a tasteful people, that can alone command our admiration. A group of such is exhibited in Fig. 169. That these are Roman is at once proclaimed by their graceful forms. But mingled with these are sometimes found articles of inferior workmanship and less tasteful patterns, which show how the natives of the Roman colony had gradually emulated their arts, and were passing out of that state when the wants of life were supplied without regard to the elegancies which belong to an advanced civilization (see Fig. 168). The Romans put the mark of their cultivated taste as effectually upon the drinking-cups and the urns of the colonized Britons, compared with the earlier works of the natives, as the emperor Hadrian put his stamp upon the pigs of lead which were cast in the British mines, and which may still be seen in our national Museum (Figs. 165, 166, 167). The bronze patera, or drinking-bowl, found in Wiltshire, marked with the names of five Roman towns on its margin, was a high work of Roman-British art (Figs. 152, 153, 154). The metal coating of an ancient Roman-British shield, found in the bed of the river Witham, belongs to a lower stage of the same art (Fig. 171). The British coin of Carausius (Fig. 173), of which a unique example in gold is in the British Museum, and the coin of Constantine the Great in the same collection (Fig. 172), each probably came out of the Roman coin-mould (Fig. 170). After years of contest and bloodshed, the Roman arts became the arts of Britain; and when our Shakspere made Iachimo describe the painting and the statuary of Imogen's chamber, though the description might be an anachronism with regard to Cymbeline, it was a just representation of the influence of Roman taste on the home-life of Britain, when the intercourse of the countries had become established, and the peaceful colonization of those whose arts always followed in the wake of their arms, had introduced those essentially Roman habits, of which we invariably find the relics when in our ancient cities we come to the subsoil on which the old Britons trod.

A writer on early antiquities, Mr. King, to whom we have several times referred, has a notion that the private dwellings of the Romans, especially in this island, were not remarkable for comfort or elegance, to say nothing of magnificence: "In most instances a Roman Quæstor, or Tribune, sitting here in his toga on his moveable sella, or wallowing on his triclinium, on one of those dull, dark, and at best ill-looking works of mosaic, did not, after all, appear with much more real splendour, as to any advantages from the refinements of civilized life, than an old Scotch laird in the Highlands, sitting in his plaid on a joint-stool, or on a chair of not much better construction, in the corner of his rough, rude, castle-tower." This is a bold assertion, and one that indicates that the writer has no very clear perception of what constitutes the best evidence of the existence of the "refinements of civilized life." The first dull, dark, ill-looking work of mosaic, which Mr. King describes, is a tessellated pavement, which he says "shows great design and masterly execution." The remains of villas discovered in England have for the most part painted walls, even according to Mr. King some proof of refinement, if all other proofs were absent. But the rooms with the painted walls had no fire-places with chimneys, and must have been warmed when needful, "merely by hot air from the adjoining hypocaust." This is a curious example of the mutation of ideas in half a century. The Romans in Britain, according to Mr. King, could have had no comfort or refinement, because they had no open fires, and warmed their rooms with hot air. The science of our own day says that the open fire and chimney are relics of barbarism, and that comfort and refinement demand the hot air. The remains of a hypocaust at Lincoln (Fig. 141) alone indicate something beyond the conveniences possessed by the old Scotch laird sitting on his joint-stool. But, in truth, the bare inspection of the plan of any one of the Roman villas discovered in

189.—Arms and Costume of a Saxon Military Chief.

190.—Arms and Costume of an Anglo-Saxon King and Armour Bearer.

194.—Ringed Mail. Cotton MS. Claud. B. 4

195.—Anglo-Saxon Mantle, Caps, and Weapons.

193.—Costume of a Soldier. From Cotton MS. Tib. C. 6.

191.—Arms and Costume of the Tribes on the Western Shores of the Baltic.

192.—Arms and Costume of Danish Warriors.

196.—St. Michael's Church, St. Albans.

199.—Iona.

 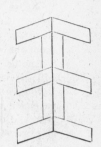

200.—Quoined Work.   201.—Long and Short Work.

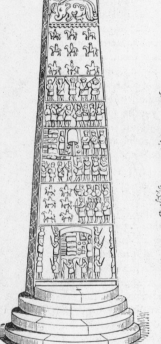

207.—Sueno's Pillar at Forres.

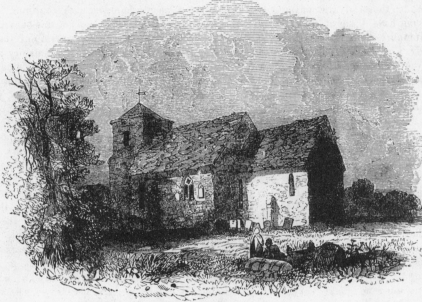

197.—St. Martin's Church, Canterbury.

 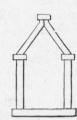 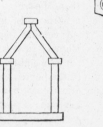 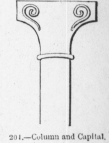

202.—Balustre.   203.—Arch.   204.—Column and Capital.

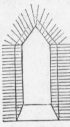 

205.—Window.   206.—Window.

198.—Ruins of the Monastery of Iona, on I-Columb-Kill.

208.—Crosses at Sandbach.

53

England will show that the colonizers brought here the same tasteful arrangements of their private dwellings as distinguished similar remains in the states wholly peopled by Romans. Vitruvius has given us the general plan of a Roman villa (Fig. 176), which we copy, that it may be compared with the plans of Roman villas discovered in England. The most important of these is that at Woodchester, near Stroud, in Gloucestershire, which was discovered by Mr. Lysons in 1795 (Fig. 177). The plan of this remarkable building, which Mr. Lysons has been able distinctly to trace, shows that there was a large open court, or atrium, marked *b*; an inner court, marked *a*; and a smaller court in the wing, marked *c*. Round these were grouped the various apartments and domestic offices, about sixty in number. Mr. King seems to think somewhat meanly of these apartments, as they seldom exceed twenty or twenty-five feet in length, with a proportionate breadth; and because "there is no reason from any remaining traces of any sort or kind to suppose there was ever a staircase in any part, or so much as one single room above the ground-floor."

Another Roman villa, of which we have given the plan (Fig. 179), is described by the same indefatigable antiquary, Mr. Samuel Lysons, who, in consequence of the accidental discovery of a mosaic pavement at Bignor, in Sussex, in 1811, was enabled during that year and the succeeding six years to trace the plan of a building of great extent and magnificence, with rich pavements and painted walls. "Many of the ornaments and general style of the mosaic work bear a striking resemblance to those of the pavements discovered at Pompeii, which could not have been of a later date than the reign of Titus." Sir Humphry Davy in some degree confirms this opinion in a letter to Mr. Lysons: "I have examined the colours found on the walls of the Roman house discovered at Bignor, in Sussex; and I find that they are similar in chemical composition to those employed in the baths of Titus at Rome, and in the houses and public buildings at Pompeii and Herculaneum." We cannot have better evidence that the same arts of design, and the same scientific means of ornament, were employed in Britain as at Pompeii. Accomplished architects have been enabled, from what remains tolerably entire in that buried city, to form a general notion of the internal arrangements of a Roman house. We present such to our readers in the beautiful restorations of Mr. Poynter (Figs. 174, 175, 180, and 181). The villa discovered at Great Witcombe, in Gloucestershire, in 1818 (Fig. 178), exhibits the most complete example of the remains of the Roman baths in this country, several of the walls still existing, from four to five feet above the level of the floors, and most of the doorways being preserved.

The influence of the Roman taste and science upon the domestic architecture of the colonized Britons must no doubt have been considerable. "The use of mortar, plaster, and cement, of the various tools and implements for building, the art of making the flat tiles, and all things connected with masonry and bricklaying, as known and practised by the Romans, must of course in the progress of their works, have been communicated to their new subjects; and it appears that, by the close of the third century, British builders had acquired considerable reputation. The panegyrist Eumenius tells us that when the Emperor Constantius rebuilt the city of Autun, in Gaul, about the end of the third century, he brought the workmen chiefly from Britain, which very much abounded with the best artificers." ('Pictorial History of England,' vol. i.) It would appear, however, that although there can be no doubt that many splendid buildings, such as Giraldus Cambrensis describes as having seen in the twelfth century at Caerleon, were models for the successors of the Romans, no remains of a very high style of art have been discovered in Britain. Mr. Rickman says, "I think it is clear that nothing *very good* of Roman work ever existed in Britain: all the fragments of architecture which have been discovered, whether large or small, whether the tympanum of a temple, as found at Bath, or small altars as found in many places. I believe they were all deficient either in composition or in execution, or in both, and none that I know of have been better, if so good, as the debased work of the Emperor Diocletian in his palace at Spalatro. With these debased examples, we cannot expect that the inhabitants of Britain would (while harassed with continual intestine warfare) improve on the models left by the Romans." ('Archæologia,' vol. xxv.)

It is easy to understand how the Roman architecture of Britain should not have been in the best taste. When the island was permanently settled under the Roman dominion, the arts had greatly declined in Rome itself. In architecture, especially, the introduction of incongruous members, in combination with the general forms derived from the Greeks, produced a corruption which was rapidly advancing in the third century, and which continued to spread till Roman architecture had lost nearly all its original distinctive characters. The models which the Romans left in Britain, to a people harassed with continual invasion and internal dissension, were no doubt chiefly of this debased character. Of the buildings erected for the Pagan worship of the Saxons we have no traces. The re-establishment of Christianity by the conversion of the Saxons was rapidly followed by the building of churches. What was the nature of the material of these churches, whether any of them still exist, whether portions even may yet be found in our ecclesiastical buildings, have been fruitful subjects of antiquarian discussion. There is somewhat of a fashion in such opinions. In the last century, all churches with heavy columns and semicircular arches were called Saxon. Some twenty years ago it was maintained that we had no Saxon buildings at all. The present state of opinion amongst unprejudiced inquirers is, we think, fairly represented in the following candid argument of Mr. Rickman: "On that part of our architectural history which follows the departure of the Romans from Britain, and which precedes the Norman Conquest, there is of course great obscurity; but while in the days of Dr. Stukeley, Horace Walpole, &c., their appears to have been much too easy an admission of Saxon dates on the mere appearance of the semicircular arch, I think there has been of late perhaps too great a leaning the other way; and because we cannot directly prove that certain edifices are Saxon, by documentary evidence, we have been induced, too easily perhaps, to consider that no Saxon buildings did exist, and have not given ourselves the trouble sufficiently to examine our earlier Norman works to see if they were not some of them entitled to be considered as erected before the Conquest." This is the subject which we shall be called upon to illustrate in our next chapter; but in the mean time we refer to some of the details of later Roman art, which we give at page 49 (Figs. 182—188). It is to these forms and arrangements that the architecture of the Anglo-Saxons and Norman is to be traced as to a common source.

The Standard of the White Horse.

CHAPTER III.—THE ANGLO-SAXON PERIOD.

N axe was to be laid to the root of that prosperity which Britain unquestionably enjoyed under the established dominion and protection of the Romans. The military people whom Cæsar led to the conquest of Gaul were, five hundred years afterwards, driven back upon Italy by hordes of fierce invaders, who swarmed wherever plenty spread its attractions for wandering poverty. "The blue-eyed myriads" first came to Britain as allies. The period when they came was one of remarkable prosperity, according to the old ecclesiastical chronicler, whose account of this revolution is the most distinct which we possess. Bede says, that after the "Irish Rovers" had returned home, and "the Picts" were driven to the farthest part of the Island, through a vigorous effort of the unaided Britons, the land "began to abound with such plenty of grain as had never been known in any age before. With plenty, luxury increased; and this was immediately attended with all sorts of crimes." Then followed a plague; and to repel the apprehended incursions of the northern tribes, "they all agreed with their king, Vortigern (Guorteryn), to call over to their aid, from the parts beyond the sea, the Saxon nation." The standard of the White Horse floated on the downs of Kent and Sussex; and the strange people who bore it from the shores of the Baltic fixed it firmly in the land, whose institutions they remodelled, whose name was henceforth changed, whose language was merged in the tongue which they spake. "Then the nation of the Angles, or Saxons, being invited by the aforesaid king, arrived in Britain with three long ships, and had a place assigned them to reside in by the same king, in the eastern part of the island, as it were to fight for their country, but in reality to subdue this."

Britain was henceforth the land of the Angles—Engla-land, Engle-land, Engle-lond. Little more than a century after the settlement in, or conquest of, the country by the three nations of the Jutes, the Saxons, and the Angles, the supreme monarch, or Bretwalda, thus subscribed himself:—"Ego Ethelbertus, Rex Anglorum." The Angles and the Saxons were distinct nations, and they subdued and retained distinct portions of the land. But even the Saxon chiefs of Wessex, when they had extended their dominions into the kingdom of the Angles, called themselves kings of Engla-land. In our own times we are accustomed to use the term Anglo-Saxons, when we speak of the wars, the institutions, the literature, and the arts of the people who for five centuries were the possessors of this our England, and have left the impress of their national character, their language, their laws, and their religion upon the race that still tread the soil which they trod.

The material monuments which are left of these five centuries of struggles for supremacy within, and against invasion from without, of Paganism overthrowing the institutions of Christianized Britain by the sword, and overthrown in its turn by the more lasting power of a dominant church—of wise government, of noble patriotism, vainly contending against a new irruption of predatory sea-kings,—these monuments are few, and of doubtful origin. The Anglo-Saxons have left their most durable traces in the institutions which still mingle with the laws under which we live,—in the literature which has their written language for its best foundation,—in the useful arts which they cultivated, and which have descended to us as our inheritance.

The most enduring monuments are the Manuscripts and the Illuminations produced by the patient labour of their spiritual teachers, which we may yet open in our public libraries, and look upon with as deep an interest as upon the fragments of the more perishable labours of the architect and the sculptor. But of buildings, and even the ornamented fragments of churches and of palaces, this period has left us few remains in comparison with its long duration, and the unquestionable existence of a high civilization during a considerable portion of these five centuries. But it is possible that these remains are not so few as we are taught to think. It has been the fashion to believe that the invading Dane swept away all these monuments of piety and of civil order; that whatever of high antiquity after the Romans here exists, is of Norman origin. We have probably yielded somewhat too readily to this modern belief. For example, Bishop Wilfred, who lived in the seventh century, was a great builder and restorer of churches, and Richard, Prior of Hexham, who lived in the twelfth century, describes *from his own observation* the church which Wilfred built at Hexham. According to this minute description, it was a noble fabric, with deep foundations, with crypts, and oratories, of great height, divided into three several stories or tiers, and supported by polished columns; the capitals of the columns were decorated with figures carved in stone; the body of the church was compassed about with pentices and porticoes. Such a church we should now call Norman. Within the limits of a work like ours it is impossible to discuss such matters of controversy. We here only enter a protest against the belief that all churches now existing with some of the characteristics of the church of Wilfred, must be of the period after the Conquest.

212.—Doorway from the Palace of Westminster.

214.—Capital of a Column in the Crypt of Canterbury Cathedral.

215.—Consecration of a Saxon Church. From Cotton MS.

210.—Edward the Confessor's Chapel, Westminster Abbey,—now used as the Pix Office.

209.—Tower of Earl's Barton Church.

213.—Heads of Windows, Darent Church, Kent.

211.—Windows from the Palace of Westminster.

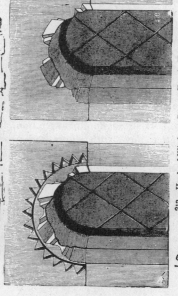

216.—Bosham Church. From the Bayeux Tapestry.

217.—St. Augustine. Royal MS.

225.—Silver Penny of Ceolnoth, Archbishop of Canterbury.

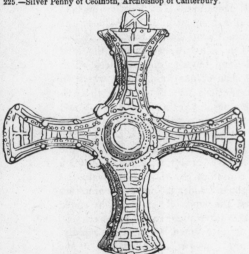

223.—Golden Cross worn by St. Cuthbert, and found on his body at the opening of his Tomb in 1827.

218.—Portrait of St. Dunstan in full Archiepiscopal Costume. Cotton MS.

221.—Bishop and Priest.

219.—Egfrid, King of Northumberland, and an Ecclesiastical Synod offering the Bishopric of Hexham to St. Cuthbert. MS. Life of Bede, A.D. 1200.

224.—St. Dunstan. Royal MS.

222.—Abbot Eunoth and St. Augustine, Archbishop of Canterbury. Harleian MS.

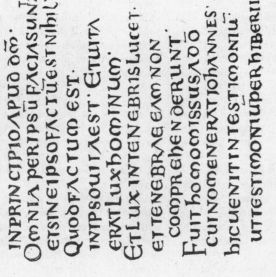

226.—Fac-simile from the Latin Gospels presented by King Athelstane to the Church of Canterbury.

220.—St. Cuthbert. From one of the external Canopies of the Middle Tower of Durham.

No. 8.

When Johnson and Boswell visited Iona, or Icolm-kill, the less imaginative traveller was disappointed:—"I must own that Icolm-kill did not answer my expectations. . . . . There are only some grave-stones flat on the earth, and we could see no inscriptions. How far short was this of marble monuments, like those in West-minster Abbey, which I had imagined here!" So writes the matter-of-fact Boswell. But Johnson, whose mind was filled with the various knowledge that surrounded the barren island with great and holy associations, had thoughts which shaped themselves into sentences often quoted, but too appropriate to the objects of this work not to be quoted once more :—

"We were now treading that illustrious island which was once the luminary of the Caledonian regions, whence savage clans and roving barbarians derived the benefits of knowledge and the blessing of religion. To abstract the mind from all local emotion would be impossible if it were endeavoured, and would be foolish if it were possible. Whatever withdraws us from the power of our senses, whatever makes the past, the distant, or the future, pre-dominate over the present, advances us in the dignity of thinking beings. Far from me, and from my friends, be such frigid philosophy as may conduct us indifferent and unmoved over any ground which has been dignified by wisdom, bravery, or virtue! That man is little to be envied whose patriotism would not gain force upon the plain of *Marathon*, or whose piety would not grow warmer among the ruins of *Iona*."

"The ruins of Iona" are not the ruins of "Saint Columba's cell," of that monastery which the old national Saint of Scotland founded in the midst of wide waters, when he came from the shores of Ireland to conquer a rude and warlike people by the power of the Gospel of peace ; to preach with his followers "such works of charity and piety as they could learn from the prophetical, evange-lical, and apostolical writings ;" and, in addition to this first sacred duty, to be the depositaries of learning and the diffusers of know-ledge. The walls amidst whose shelter Columba lived, training his followers by long years of discipline to the fit discharge of their noble office, have been swept away ; the later erections are crumbling into nothingness (Figs. 198, 199); the burial-place of the Scottish kings is overgrown with rank weeds, and their tombs lie broken and defaced amidst fragments of monumental stones of the less illus-trious dead. Silent and deserted is this "guardian of their bones." The miserable hovels of a few fishermen contain the scanty population of an island which was once trodden by crowds of the noble and the learned. Here the highest in rank once came to bow before the greater eminence of exalted piety and rare knowledge. To be an inmate of the celebrated monastery of Iona was to gain a reputation through the civilized world. This was not the residence of lazy monks, as we are too much accustomed to call all monks, but of men distinguished for the purity and simplicity of their lives, and by the energy and disinterestedness of their labours. Iona sent forth her missionaries into every land from which ignorance and idolatry were to be banished by the workings of Christian love. When the bark that contained a little band of these self-devoted men went forth upon the stormy seas that beat around these western isles, to seek in distant lands the dark seats where Druidism still lingered, or the fiercer worship of Odin lifted its hoarse voice of war and desolation, then the solemn prayer went up from the sacred choir for the heavenly guidance of "those who travel by land or sea." When the body of some great chief was embarked at Corpach, on the mainland, and the waters were dotted with the boats that crowded round the funeral bark, then the chants of the monks were heard far over the sea, like the welcome to some hospitable shore, breathing hope and holy trust. Such are the materials for the "local emo-tion" which is called forth by "the ruins of Iona ;" and such emo-tion, though the actual monuments that are associated with it like these are shapeless fragments, is to be cherished in many a spot of similar sanctity, where, casting aside all minor differences of opinion, we know that the light of truth once shone there amidst surrounding darkness, and that "one bright particular star" there beamed before the dawning.

We have already quoted Bede's interesting narrative of the arrival of Augustine in the Isle of Thanet (p. 34). The same authentic writer subsequently tells us of the lives of Augustine and his fellow-missionaries at Canterbury : "There was in the east side near the city a church dedicated to the honour of St. Martin, formerly built whilst the Romans were still in the island, wherein the queen (Bertha), who, as has been said before, was a Christian, used to pray. In this they at first began to meet, to sing, to pray, to say mass, to preach, and to baptize; till the king being converted to the faith, they had leave granted them more freely to preach, and build or repair churches in all places." On "the east side of

the city" of Canterbury still stands the church of St. Martin. Its windows belong to various periods of Gothic architecture; its external walls are patched after the barbarous fashion of modern repairs; it is deformed within by wooden boxes to separate the rich from the poor, and by ugly monumental vanities, miscalled sculpture; but the old walls are full of Roman bricks, relics, at any rate, of the older fabric where Bertha and Augustine "used to pray" (Fig. 197). Some have maintained that this is the identical Roman church which Bede describes.; and tradition has been pretty constant in the belief that it is as old as the second century. Mr. King has his own theory upon the matter : "Some have supposed it to have been built by Roman Christians, of the Roman soldiery; but if that had been the case, there would surely have been found in it the regular alternate courses of Roman bricks. Instead of this, the chancel is found to be built almost entirely of Roman bricks ; and the other parts with Roman bricks and other materials, irregularly intermixed. There is therefore the utmost reason to think that it was built as some imitation only of Roman structures by the rude Britons, before their workmen became so skilful in Roman architecture as they were afterwards rendered, when regularly employed by the Romans." Whether a British, a Roman, or a Saxon church, here is a church of the highest antiquity in the island, rendered memorable by its associations with the narrative of the old ecclesiastical historian. There is a remarkable font in this church—a stone font with rude carved-work, resembling a great basin, and standing low on the floor. Such a font was adapted to the mode of baptism in the primitive times. In such a church might Augustine and his followers have sung and prayed ; in such a font might Augustine have baptized. Venerated, then, be the spot upon which stands the little church of St. Martin. It is a pleasant spot on a gentle elevation. The lofty towers and pinnacles of the great Cathedral rise up at a little distance ; the County Infirmary and the County Prison stand about it. It was from this little hill, then, that a sound went through the land which, in a few centuries, called up those glorious edifices which attest the piety and the magnificence of our forefathers ; which, in our own days, has raised up institutions for the relief of the sick and the afflicted poor ; but which has not yet banished those dismal abodes which frown upon us in every great city, where society labours, and labours in vain, to correct and eradicate crime by restraint and punishment. Something is still wanting to make the teaching which, more than twelve centuries ago, went forth throughout the land from this church of St. Martin, as effectual as its innate purity and truth ought to render it. The teaching has not even to this day penetrated the land. It is heard at stated seasons in consecrated places ; it is spoken about in our parish schools, whence a scanty knowledge is distributed amongst a rapidly increasing youthful population, in a measure little adapted to the full and effectual banishment of ignorance. Our schools are few ; our prisons are many. The work which Augustine and his fol-lowers did is still to do ; but it is a work which a state that has spent eight hundred millions in war thinks may yet be postponed. The time may come, if that work be postponed too long, when the teachers of Christian knowledge may as vainly strive against the force of the antagonist principle, as the monks of Bangor strove, with prayer and anthem,

> "When the heathen trumpets' clang
> Round beleaguer'd Chester rang."

Whilst we are disputing in what way the people shall be taught, ignorance is laying aside its ordinary garb of cowardice and servility, and is putting on its natural properties of insolence and ferocity. Let us set our hand to the work which is appointed for us, before it be too late to work to a good end, if to do this work at all.

Camden describes a place upon the estuary of the Humber which, although a trivial place in modern days, is dear to every one familiar with our old ecclesiastical history : "In the Roman times, not far from its bank upon the little river Foulness (where Wighton, a small town, but well stocked with husbandmen, now stands), there seems to have formerly stood Delgovitia ; as is probable both from the likeness and the signification of the name. For the British word *Delgwe* (or rather *Ddelw*) signifies the statues or images of the heathen gods ; and in a little village not far off there stood an idol-temple, which was in very great honour even in the Saxon times, and, from the heathen gods in it, was then called God-mund-ingham, and now, in the same sense, Godmanham." This is the place which witnessed the conversion to Christianity of Edwin, King of Northumbria. The whole story of this conversion, as told by Bede, is one of those episodes that we call superstitious, in which history reflects the confiding faith of popular tradition, which does not resign itself to the belief that all worldly events depend solely upon material influences. But one portion of this story has the best elements of high poetry in itself, and has therefore gained little by being versified even by Wordsworth. Edwin held a council of his wise men, to inquire their opinion of the new doctrine which was taught by the missionary Paulinus. In this council one thus addressed him: "The present life of man, O King, seems to me, in comparison of that time which is unknown to us, like to a sparrow swiftly flying through the room, well warmed with the fire made in the midst of it, wherein you sit at supper in the winter, with commanders and ministers, whilst the storms of rain and snow prevail abroad; the sparrow, I say, flying in at one door, and immediately out at another, whilst he is within is not affected with the winter storm; but after a very brief interval of what is to him fair weather and safety, he immediately vanishes out of your sight, returning from one winter to another. So this life of man appears for a moment; but of what went before, or what is to follow, we are utterly ignorant. If, therefore, this new doctrine contains something more certain, it seems justly to deserve to be followed." Never was a familiar image more beautifully applied; never was there a more striking picture of ancient manners—the storm without, the fire in the hall within, the king at supper with his great men around, the open doors through which the sparrow can flit. To this poetical counsellor succeeded the chief priest of the idol-worship, Coifi. He declared for the new faith, and advised that the heathen altars should be destroyed. "Who," exclaimed the king, "shall first desecrate their altars and their temples?" The priest answered, "I; for who can more properly than myself destroy these things that I worshipped through ignorance, for an example to all others, through the wisdom given me by the true God?"

> "Prompt transformation works the novel lore.
> The Council closed, the priest in full career
> Rides forth, an armed man, and hurls a spear
> To desecrate the fane which heretofore
> He served in folly. Woden falls, and Thor
> Is overturned."
>
> WORDSWORTH.

The altars and images which the priest of Northumbria overthrew have left no monuments in the land. They were not built, like the Druidical temples, under the impulses of the great system of faith which, dark as it was, had its foundations in spiritual aspirations. The pagan worship which the Saxons brought to this land was chiefly cultivated under its sensual aspects. The Valhalla, or heaven of the brave, was a heaven of fighting and feasting, of full meals of boar's flesh, and large draughts of mead. Such a future called not for solemn temples, and altars where the lowly and the weak might kneel in the belief that there was a heaven for them, as well as for the mighty in battle. The idols frowned, and the people trembled. But this worship has marked us, even to this hour, with the stamp of its authority. Our Sunday is still the Saxon Sun's-day; our Monday the Moon's-day; our Tuesday Tuisco's-day; our Wednesday Woden's-day; our Thursday Thor's-day; our Friday Friga's-day; our Saturday Seater's-day. This is one of the many examples of the incidental circumstances of institutions surviving the institutions themselves—an example of itself sufficient to show the folly of legislating against established customs and modes of thought. The French republicans, with every aid from popular intoxication, could not establish their calendar for a dozen years. The Pagan Saxons have fixed their names of the week-days upon Christian England for twelve centuries, and probably for as long as England shall be a country.

Some of the material monuments of the ages after the departure of the Romans, and before the Norman conquest, are necessarily obscure in their origin and objects. It was once the custom to refer some of the remains which we now call Druidical to the period when Saxon and Danes were fighting for the possession of the land—trophies of battle and of victory. There are some monuments to which this origin is still assigned; and such an origin has been ascribed to the remarkable stone at Forres, called Sueno's Pillar (Fig. 207). It is a block of granite twenty-five feet in height, and nearly four feet in breadth at its base. It is sculptured in the most singular manner, with representations of men and horses in military array and warlike attitudes; some holding up their shields in exultation, others joining hands in token of fidelity. There is to be seen also the fight and the massacre of the prisoners; and the whole is surmounted by something like an elephant. On the other side of this monument is a large cross, with figures of persons in authority in amicable conference. It has been held that all this represents the expulsion of some Scandinavian

adventurers from Scotland, who had long infested the country about the promontory of Burghead, and refers also to a subsequent peace between Malcolm, King of Scotland, and Sueno, King of Norway. Be this as it may, the cross denotes the monument to belong to the Christian period, though its objects were anything but devotional. Not so the crosses at Sandbach, in Cheshire. These are, no doubt, works of early piety; and they are stated by Mr. Lysons to belong to a period not long subsequent to the introduction of Christianity amongst the Anglo-Saxons (Fig. 208.) If so, we may regard them with no common interest; for the greater monuments of that century, after the arrival of Augustine, when Christianity was spread throughout the land, are, as far as we know and are taught to believe, almost utterly perished. Brixworth Church, in Northamptonshire, which has been so subjected to alteration upon alteration that an engraving would furnish no notion of its peculiar early features, is considered by some to have been erected in the time of the Romans. But this very ancient specimen of ecclesiastical architecture would scarcely be so interesting, even if its date were clearly proved, as the decided remains of some church or monastic buildings of the sixth or seventh centuries—even of some building contemporary with our illustrious Alfred. There may be such; but antiquarianism is a jealous and suspicious questioner, and calls for evidence at every step. We are told by an excellent authority that "an interesting portion of the Saxon church erected by Paulinus, or Albert, [at York] has been recently brought to light beneath the choir of the present cathedral." (Mr. Wellbeloved, in 'Penny Cyclopædia.') This church, founded by Edwin soon after his baptism, was undoubtedly a stone building; and it marks the progress of the arts in this century, that in 669 Bishop Wilfred glazed the windows. The glass for this purpose seems to have been imported from abroad, since the famous Benedict Biscop, Abbot of Wearmouth, is recorded as the first who brought artificers skilled in the art of making glass into this country from France. ('Pictorial History of England,' vol. i.)

Wilfred found the church of York in a ruinous state, on taking possession of the see. He roofed it with lead; he put glass in the place of the ancient lattice-work. Time has brought to light some relics of this church at York, buried beneath the nobler Cathedral of a later age. It is probable that the more ancient churches were as much removed and changed by the spirit of ecclesiastical improvement as by the course of civil strife. One generation repaired, amended, swept away the work of previous generations. We have seen this process in our own times, when marble columns have been covered with plaster, and the decorated window with its gorgeous tracery replaced by a villanous casement. The Norman church-builders did not so improve upon the Saxon; but it is still to be regretted that even their improvements, and those of the builders who again remodelled the Norman work, have left us so little that we can rely upon for a very high antiquity. It would be something to look upon the church at Ripon which Wilfred built of polished stone, and adorned with various columns and porticoes; or upon that at Hexham, which was proclaimed to have no equal on this side the Alps. It would be something to find some fragment of the paintings which Benedict Biscop brought from Rome to adorn his churches at Wearmouth and at Yarrow; but they perished with his library under the ravaging Danes. More than all, we should desire to look upon some fragment of that church which the good and learned Aldhelm built at Malmesbury, and whose consecration he has himself celebrated in Latin verses of considerable spirit. He was a poet, too, in his vernacular tongue; and he applied his poetry and his knowledge of music to higher objects than his own gratification. The great Alfred himself entered into his note-book the following anecdote of the enlightened Abbot, which William of Malmesbury relates:— "Aldhelm had observed with pain that the peasantry were become negligent in their religious duties, and that no sooner was the church service ended than they all hastened to their homes and labours, and could with difficulty be persuaded to attend to the exhortations of the preacher. He watched the occasion, and stationed himself in the character of a minstrel on the bridge over which the people had to pass, and soon collected a crowd of hearers by the beauty of his verse. When he found that he had gained possession of their attention, he gradually introduced among the popular poetry which he was reciting to them, words of a more serious nature, till at length he succeeded in impressing upon their minds a truer feeling of religious devotion." (Wright's 'Biographia Britannica Literaria.') Honoured be the memory of the good Abbot of Malmesbury!

The identical bridge upon which the minstrel stood has long

227.—Saxon Emblems of the Month of January.

229.—Residence of a Saxon Nobleman.

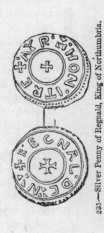

228.—Saxon Emblems of the Month of February.

241.—Silver Penny of Eadgar, King of England.

242.—Silver Penny of Coenvlf, King of Mercia.

236—Saxon Emblems of the Month of March.

239—Convivial party. Harleian MS. No. 603.

238.—Ploughing, Sowing, Mowing, Gleaning, Measuring Corn, and Harvest-Supper.

240.—Chairs. From Harleian MS. No. 603.

243.—Silver Penny of Æthelweard.

244.—Silver Penny of Eadwald, King of Mercia.

237.—Saxon Emblems of the Month of April

61

ago fallen into the narrow stream; the church to which the preacher invited the people by gentle words and sweet sounds has been supplanted by a nobler church, surrounded by the ruins of a gorgeous fabric of monastic splendour. We may not believe, say the antiquaries, that the wonderful porches and the intersecting arches of Malmesbury are of Saxon origin. But, in spite of the antiquaries, they must be associated with the beautiful memory of Aldhelm. His name is not now spoken in that secluded town; but the people there have still their Saxon memories of ancient days. The poor, who have extensive common-rights, say that they owe them all to King Athelstan; the humble children who learn to read in an ancient building called the Hall of St. John, connect their instruction with the memory of some great man of old, who wished that the poor should be taught and the indigent relieved,—for over the ancient porch under which they enter is recorded that a worthy burgher of Malmesbury in 1694 left ten pounds annually to instruct the poor, in addition to a like donation from King Athelstan! We wish that throughout the land there were more such living memorials of the past, even though they were the mere shadows of tradition. It is well for the lowly cottagers of Malmesbury that they are in blissful ignorance that the monument of their Saxon benefactor, in the restored choir of their Abbey Church, belongs to a later period. They look upon that recumbent effigy with reverence—they keep the annual feast of Athelstan with rejoicing. The hero-worship of Malmesbury is that of Athelstan. It has come down from the days of Saxon song, when the victories of the grandson of Alfred were thus celebrated:—

> "Here Athelstan, King,
>   of earth the lord,
>   the giver of the bracelets of the nobles,
>   and his brother also,
>   Edmund the Ætheling,
>   the Elder, a lasting glory
>   won by slaughter in battle
>   with the edges of swords
>   at Brunenburgh.
>   The wall of shields they cleaved,
>   They hewed the nobles' banners."

But Athelstan left the memory of something better than victories. He was a lawgiver; and there are traces in his additions to the Code of Alfred of a public provision for the destitute amongst his subjects. The traditions of Malmesbury have, we doubt not, a solid foundation. He was a scholar, and collected a library for his private use. Some of these books were preserved at Bath up to the period of the Reformation; two of these precious manuscripts are in the Cotton Collection in the British Museum. The Gospels upon which the Saxon Kings are held to have taken their Coronation oath is one of them (see Fac-simile of the 1st Chapter of St. John, Fig. 226). It is not only at Malmesbury that the memory of Athelstan is to be venerated.

We have already alluded to the change of opinion which is beginning to take place with regard to the remains of Saxon architecture existing in this country (p. 54). We do not profess to discuss controverted points, which would be of slight interest to the general reader; and we shall therefore find it the safer course to describe our earliest cathedrals, and other grand ecclesiastical structures, under the Norman period. But it is now pretty generally admitted that many of our humble parish churches may be safely referred to dates before the conquest; and some of the characteristic features of these we shall now proceed to notice. We believe, curious as this question naturally is, and especially interesting as it must be at the present day, when our ecclesiastical antiquities are become objects of such wide-spreading interest, that no systematic attempt to fix the chronology of the earliest church architecture has yet been made. In 1833 Mr. Thomas Rickman thus wrote to the Society of Antiquaries:—" I was much impressed by a conversation I had with an aged and worthy dean, who was speaking on the subject of Saxon edifices, with a full belief that they were numerous. He asked me if I had investigated those churches which existed in places where 'Domesday-Book' states that a church existed in King Edward's days; and I was obliged to confess I had not paid the systematic attention I ought to have done to this point; and I now wish to call the attention of the Society to the propriety of having a list made of such edifices, that they may be carefully examined." We are not aware that the Society has answered the call; but the course suggested by the aged and worthy dean was evidently a most rational course, and it is strange that it had been so long neglected. 'Domesday-Book' records what churches existed in the days of Edward the Confessor;

—does any church exist in the same place now? if so, what is the character of that church? To procure answers is not a difficult labour to set about by a Society; but it is probable that it will be accomplished, if at all, by individual exertion. Mr. Rickman has himself done something considerable towards arriving at the same conclusions that a wider investigation would, we believe, fully establish. In 1834 he addressed to the Society of Antiquaries ' Further Observations on the Ecclesiastical Architecture of France and England,' in which the characteristics of Saxon remains are investigated with professional minuteness, with reference to buildings which the writer considers were erected before the year 1010:—

" As to the masonry, there is a peculiar sort of quoining, which is used without plaster as well as with, consisting of a long stone set at the corner, and a short one lying on it, and bounding one way or both into the wall; when plaster is used, these quoins are raised to allow for the thickness of the plaster. Another peculiarity is the use occasionally of very large and heavy blocks of stone in particular parts of the work, while the rest is mostly of small stones; the use of what is called Roman bricks; and occasionally of an arch with straight sides to the upper part, instead of curves. The want of buttresses may be here noticed as being general in these edifices, an occasional use of portions with mouldings, much like Roman, and the use in windows of a sort of rude balustre. The occasional use of a rude round staircase, west of the tower, for the purpose of access to the upper floors; and at times the use of rude carvings, much more rude than the generality of Norman work, and carvings which are clear imitations of Roman work.

" From what I have seen, I am inclined to believe that there are many more churches which contain remains of this character, but they are very difficult to be certain about, and also likely to be confounded with common quoins, and common dressings in counties where stone is not abundant, but where flint, rag, and rough rubble plastered over, form the great extent of walling.

" In various churches it has happened that a very plain arch between nave and chancel has been left as the only Norman feature, while both nave and chancel have been rebuilt at different times, but each leaving the chancel arch standing. I am disposed to think that some of these plain chancel arches will, on minute examination, turn out to be of this Saxon style."

Mr. Rickman then gives a list of " twenty edifices in thirteen counties, and extending from Whittingham, in Northumberland, north, to Sompting, on the coast of Sussex, south; and from Barton on the Humber, on the coast of Lincolnshire, east, to North Burcombe, on the west." He justly observes, " This number of churches, extending over so large a space of country, and bearing a clear relation of style to each other, forms a class much too important and extensive to be referred to any anomaly or accidental deviation." Since Mr. Rickman's list was published many other churches have been considered to have the same " clear relation of style." We shall therefore notice a few only of the more interesting.

The church of Earl's Barton, in Northamptonshire, is a work of several periods of our Gothic architecture; but the tower is now universally admitted to be of Saxon construction (Fig. 209). It exhibits many of the peculiarities recognised as the characteristics of this architecture. 1st, We have the " long stone set at the corner, and a short one lying on it "—the long and short work, as it is commonly called (Fig. 201). These early churches and towers sometimes exhibit, in later portions, the more regular quoined work in remarkable contrast (Fig. 200). 2nd, The Tower of Earl's Barton presents the " sort of rude balustre, such as might be supposed to be copied by a very rough workman by remembrance of a Roman balustre " (Fig. 202). 3rd, It shows the form of the triangular arch, which, as well as the balustre, are to be seen in Anglo-Saxon manuscripts. 4th, It exhibits, " projecting a few inches from the surface of the wall, and running up vertically, narrow ribs, or square-edged strips of stone, bearing, from their position, a rude similarity to pilasters." (Bloxam's ' Gothic Ecclesiastical Architecture.') The writer of the valuable manual we have quoted adds, " The towers of the churches of Earl's Barton and Barnack, Northamptonshire, and one of the churches of Barton-upon-Humber, Lincolnshire, are so covered with these narrow projecting strips of stonework, that the surface of the wall appears divided into rudely formed panels." 5th, The west doorway of this tower of Earl's Barton, as well as the doorway of Barnack, exhibit something like " a rude imitation of Roman mouldings in the impost and architrave." The larger openings, such as doorways, of these early churches generally present the semicircular arch; but the smaller, such as windows, often exhibit the triangular arch (Figs. 205, 205). The semicircular arch is, however, found in the windows of some churches as well as the straight-lined, as at Sompting, in

Sussex (Fig. 206). In this church the doorway has a column with a rude capital, "having much of a Roman character" (Fig. 204). A doorway remaining of the old palace at Westminster exhibits the triangular arch (Fig. 212). The windows of the same building present the circular arch, with the single zigzag moulding (Fig. 211).

Mr. Rickman has mentioned the plain arch which is sometimes found between the chancel and nave, which he supposes to be Saxon. In some churches arches of the same character divide the nave from the aisles. Such is the case in the ancient church of St. Michael's, St. Alban's, of the interior of which we give an engraving (Fig. 196). The date of this church is now confidently held to be the tenth century, receiving the authority of Matthew Paris, who states that it was erected by the Abbot of St. Alban's in 948.

The church at Bosham, in Sussex, which is associated with the memory of the unfortunate Harold, is represented in the Bayeux tapestry, of which we shall hereafter have fully to speak (Fig. 216). It is now held that the tower of the " church is of that construction as to leave little doubt of its being the same that existed when the church was entered by Harold."

It would be tedious were we to enter into any more minute description of the Anglo-Saxon ecclesiastical remains. The subject, however, is still imperfectly investigated: and the reader will be startled by the opposite opinions that he will encounter if his inquiries conduct him to the more elaborate works which touch upon this theme. It is singular that, admitting some works to be Saxon, the proof which exists in the general resemblance of other works is not held to be satisfactory, without it is corroborated by actual date. Mr. Britton, for example, to whom every student of our national antiquities is under deep obligation, especially for having rescued their delineation from tasteless artists, to present them to our own age with every advantage of accurate drawing and exquisite engraving, thus describes the portion of Edward the Confessor's work at Westminster which is held to be of the later Saxon age; but he admits, with the greatest reluctance, the possibility of the existence of other Saxon works, entire, which earlier antiquaries called Saxon. ('Architectural Antiquities,' vol. v.) The engraving, Fig. 210, illustrates Mr. Britton's description :—

"There are considerable remains of one building yet standing, though now principally confined to vaults and cellaring, which may be justly attributed to the Saxon era, since there can be no doubt that they once formed a part of the monastic edifices of Westminster Abbey, probably the church, which was rebuilt by Edward the Confessor in the latter years of his life. These remains compose the east side of the dark and principal cloisters, and range from the college dormitory on the south to the Chapter-house on the north. The most curious part is the vaulted chamber, opening from the principal cloister, in which the standards for the *trial of the Pix* are kept, under the keys of the Chancellor of the Exchequer and other officers of the Crown. The vaulting is supported by plain groins and semicircular arches, which rest on a massive central column, having an abacus moulding, and a square impost capital, irregularly fluted. In their original state, these remains, which are now subdivided by several cross walls, forming store-cellars, &c., appear to have composed only one apartment, about one hundred and ten feet in length and thirty feet in breadth, the semicircular arches of which were partly sustained by a middle row of eight short and massive columns, with square capitals diversified by a difference in the sculptured ornaments. These ancient vestiges now form the basement story of the College School, and of a part of the Dean and Chapter's Library."

One of the most curious representations of an Anglo-Saxon Church is found in a miniature accompanying a Pontifical in the Public Library at Rouen, which gives the Order for the Dedication and consecration of Churches. (See Fig. 215, where the engraving is accurately stated to be from the Cotton MS.) This miniature, which is in black outline, represents the ceremony of dedication. The bishop, not wearing the mitre, but bearing his pastoral staff, is in the act of knocking at the door of the church with this symbol of his authority. The upper group, behind the bishop, represents priests and monks; the lower group exhibits the laity, who were accustomed to assemble on such occasions with solemn rejoicing. The barrels are supposed to contain the water which was to be blessed and used in the dedication. The form of the church, and the accessories of its architecture, are very curious. The perspective is altogether false, so that we see two sides of the building at the same time; and the proportionate size of the parts is quite disregarded, so that the door reaches almost to the roof. But the form of the towers, the cock on the steeple, the ornamental iron-work of the door, show how few essential changes have been produced in

eight hundred or a thousand years. Some ascribe the date of this manuscript to the eighth century, and others to the close of the tenth century. The figures of the bishop and priest (Fig. 221) are from the same curious relic of Anglo-Saxon art; for all agree that this Pontifical is of English origin. In the 'Archæologia,' vol. xxv., is a very interesting description of this manuscript, in a letter from John Gage, Esq. The writer, in his introductory remarks, gives some particulars of the ancient practice of the dedication of churches :—

"Gregory the Great, in his instructions to St. Augustine, bade him not destroy the Pagan temples, but the idols within them; directing the precinct to be purified with holy water, altars to be raised, and sacred relics deposited ; and because the English were accustomed to indulge in feasts to their gods, the prudent Pontiff ordained the day of dedication, or the day of the nativity of the Saint in whose honour the Church should be dedicated, a festival, when the people might have an opportunity of assembling, as before, in green bowers round their favourite edifice, and enjoy something of former festivity. This was the origin of our country wakes, rush-bearings, and church ales." When Archbishop Wilfred had built his church at Ripon, the dedication was attended by Egfrid, King of Northumbria, with his brother Ælwin, and the great men of his kingdom. The church was dedicated, the altar consecrated, the people came and received communion ; and then the Archbishop enumerated the lands with which the church was endowed. After the ceremony the King feasted the people for three days. The dedication of the church at Winchelcumbe was marked by an event which showed that the Christian morality did not evaporate in ritual observances. Kenulf, King of Mercia, with Bishops and Ealdormen, was present, and he brought with him Eadbert, the captive King of Kent. "At the conclusion of the ceremony, Kenulf led his captive to the altar, and as an act of clemency granted him his freedom." This was a more acceptable offering than his distribution of gold and silver to priests and people. The dedication of the conventual church at Ramsey is described by the Monk of Ramsey, who gives some curious details of the architectural construction of a former church. In 969 a church had been founded by the Ealdorman Aylwin, which is recorded to have been "raised on a solid foundation, driven in by the battering-ram, and to have had two towers above the roof : the lesser was in front, at the west end ; the greater, at the intersection of the four parts of the building, rested on four columns, connected together by arches carried from one to the other. In consequence, however, of a settlement in the centre tower, which threatened ruin to the rest of the building, it became necessary, shortly after the church was finished, to take down the whole and rebuild it." The dedication of this church was accompanied by a solemn recital of its charter of privileges. "Then, placing his right hand on a copy of the Gospels, Aylwin swore to defend the rights and privileges, as well of Ramsey, as of other neighbouring churches which were named."

But the narrative of the circumstances attending the original foundation of this church, as related by Mr. Sharon Turner from the ' History of the Monk of Ramsey,' are singularly instructive as to the impulses which led the great and the humble equally to contribute to the establishment of monastic institutions. They were told that the piety of the men who had renounced the world brought blessings on the country; they were urged to found such institutions, and to labour in their erection. Thus was the Ealdorman, who founded the church of Ramsey, instructed by Bishop Oswald ; and to the spiritual exhortation the powerful man was not indifferent.

"The Ealdorman replied, that he had some hereditary land surrounded with marshes, and remote from human intercourse. It was near a forest of various sorts of trees, which had several open spots of good turf, and others of fine grass for pasture. No buildings had been upon it but some sheds for his herds, who had manured the soil. They went together to view it. They found that the waters made it an island. It was so lonely, and yet had so many conveniences for subsistence and secluded devotion, that the bishop decided it to be an advisable station. Artificers were collected. The neighbourhood joined in the labour. Twelve monks came from another cloister to form the new fraternity. Their cells and a chapel were soon raised. In the next winter they provided the iron and timber, and utensils, that were wanted for a handsome church. In the spring, amid the fenny soil, a firm foundation was laid. *The workmen laboured as much for devotion as for profit.* Some brought the stones; others made the cement ; others applied the wheel machinery that raised the stones on high ; and in a reasonable time the sacred edifice with two towers appeared, on what had been before a desolate waste." Wordsworth has made

245.—Saxon Emblems of the Month of May.

248.—Trombones, or Flutes. From the Cotton MS. Cleopatra.

247.—Dinner Party. Cotton MS.

249.—Drinking from Cows' Horns. Cotton MS.

246.—Saxon Emblems of the Month of June.

254.—Saxon Emblems of the month of July.

260.—Silver Penny of Ceolwulf, King of Mercia

256.—Wheel Plough. (Bayeux Tapestry.)

255.—Threshing and Winnowing Corn.

257.—Harrowing and Sowing. (Bayeux Tapestry.)

261.—Silver Penny of Egbert.

258.—Saxon emblems of the month of August.

262.—Silver Penny of Ethelwulf.

this description the foundation of one of his fine 'Ecclesiastical Sketches:'—

> " By such examples moved to unbought pains,
>   The people work like congregated bees;
>   Eager to build the quiet fortresses
>   Where Piety, as they believe, obtains
>   From Heaven a *general* blessing; timely rains,
>   Or needful sunshine; prosperous enterprise,
>   And peace and equity."

Monarchs vied with the people in what they deemed a work acceptable to heaven. Westminster Abbey was built by Edward the Confessor, by setting aside the tenth of his revenue for this holy purpose. "The devout and pious king has dedicated that place to God, both for its neighbourhood to the famous and wealthy city, and for its pleasant situation among fruitful grounds and green fields, and for the nearness of the principal river of England, which from all parts of the world conveys whatever is necessary to the adjoining city." Camden quotes this from a contemporary historian, and adds, "Be pleased also to take the form and figure of this building out of an old manuscript:—The chief aisle of the church is roofed with lofty arches of square work, the joints answering one another; but on both sides it is enclosed with a double arch of stones firmly cemented and knit together. Moreover, the cross of the church, made to encompass the middle choir of the singers, and by its double supporter on each side to bear up the lofty top of the middle tower, first rises singly with a low and strong arch, then mounts higher with several winding stairs artificially contrived, and last of all with a single wall reaches to the wooden roof, which is well covered with lead."

The illuminated manuscripts of the Anglo-Saxon period (and there are many not inferior in value and interest to the Pontifical which we have recently pointed out) furnish the most authentic materials for a knowledge of the antiquities of our early Church. It is a subject of which we cannot here attempt to give any connected view. Our notices must be essentially fragmentary. As works of art we shall have more fully to describe some of the Illuminations which are found in our public and private libraries. In connection with our church history, it is scarcely necessary for us to do more than point attention to the spirited representation of St. Augustine (Fig. 217); to the same founder of Christianity amongst the Anglo-Saxons (Fig. 222); to the portrait of St. Dunstan (Fig. 218); and the kneeling figure of the same energetic enthusiast (Fig. 224). The group representing St. Cuthbert and King Egfrid (Fig. 219) belongs to the Norman period of art.

The picture history of the manners and customs of a remote period is perhaps more interesting and instructive, is certainly more to be relied on, than any written description. It is difficult for a writer not to present the forms and hues of passing things as they are seen through the glass of his own imagination. But the draftsman, especially in a rude stage of art, is in a great degree a faithful copyist of what he sees before him. The paintings and sculptures of Egypt furnish the best commentary upon many portions of the Scripture record. The coloured walls of the ruined houses of Pompeii exhibit the domestic life of the Roman people with much greater distinctness than the incidental notices of their poets and historians. This is especially the case as regards the illuminations which embellish many Anglo-Saxon manuscripts. Some of these were not intended by the draftsmen of those days to convey any notion of how the various ranks around them were performing the ordinary occupations of life: they were chiefly for the purpose of representing, historically as it were, events and personages with which the people were familiarised by their spiritual instructors. But, knowing nothing of those refinements of art which demand accuracy of costume, and caring nothing for what we call anachronisms, the limners of the Anglo-Saxon chronicles and paraphrases painted the Magi in the habits of their own kings, riding on horses with the equipment of the time (Fig. 283); they put their own harp into the hands of the Royal Psalmist (Fig. 284); and they exhibited their own methods of interment when they delineated the raising of Lazarus (Fig. 289). There are some, but few, Anglo-Saxon pictures of a different character. They are *intended* to represent the industrious occupations, the sports, and the entertainments of their own nation. A series of such pictures is found in a Saxon Calendar, supposed by Mr. Strutt to be written at the commencement of the eleventh century, and which is preserved in the Cotton Library at the British Museum (Tiberius, B. 5). The Calendar is written partly in Latin, and partly in Saxon. The pictures represent the characteristic employments of each Month of the year. The series of engravings of the months, which occupy a

part of this and of the previous sheet of our work, are principally founded, with corrections of the drawing, upon the illustrations of the old Calendar. We probably cannot adopt a more convenient mode of briefly describing the occupations of our Anglo-Saxon ancestors, than by following the order which these pictorial antiquities suggest to us.

JANUARY.

The central portion of the engraving (Fig. 227) represents the ploughman at his labour. Four oxen are employed in the team, and they are guided by a man in front, who bears a long staff. The sower follows immediately behind the ploughman. Fig. 238, which is a literal copy from another manuscript, presents, at once, the operations of ploughing, sowing, mowing, measuring corn into sacks, and the harvest supper. Fig. 256 is a rude representation, from the Bayeux tapestry, of the wheel-plough. Fig. 257, from the same authority, shows us the sower following the harrow—a more accurate representation than that of the sower following the plough. We thus see that the opening of the year was the time in which the ground was broken up, and the seed committed to the bounty of heaven. We cannot with any propriety assume that the seed was literally sown in the coldest month, although it is possible that the winter began earlier than it now does. December was emphatically called Winter-monat, winter-month. The Anglo-Saxon name of January was equally expressive of its fierce and gloomy attributes; its long nights, when men and cattle were sheltering from the snow-storm and the frost, but the hungry wolf was prowling around the homestead. Verstegan says, " The month which we now call January, they called Wolf-monat, to wit, wolf-month, because people are wont always in that month to be in more danger to be devoured of wolves than in any season else of the year; for that, through the extremity of cold and snow, these ravenous beasts could not find of other beasts sufficient to feed upon." We must consider, therefore, that the Saxon emblems for January are rather indicative of the opening of the year than of the first month of the year. There are preserved in the Cotton Library some very curious dialogues composed by Alfric of Canterbury, who lived in the latter part of the tenth century, which were for the instruction of the Anglo-Saxon youth in the Latin language, upon the principle of interlinear translation; and in these the ploughman says, "I labour much. I go out at daybreak, urging the oxen to the field, and I yoke them to the plough. It is not yet so stark winter that I dare keep close at home, for fear of my lord." ('Turner's 'Anglo-Saxons.') We thus see that the ploughing is done after the harvest, before the winter sets in. The ploughman continues, "But the oxen being yoked, and the shear and coulter fastened on, I ought to plough every day one entire field or more. I have a boy to threaten the oxen with a goad [the long staff represented in the engraving], who is now hoarse through cold and bawling. I ought also to fill the bins of the oxen with hay, and water them, and carry out their soil." The daily task of the ploughman indicates an advanced state of husbandry. The land was divided into fields; we know from Saxon grants that they had hedges and ditches. He was as careful, too, to carry upon the land the ordure of the oxen, as if he had studied a modern 'Muck-Manual.' He knew the value of such labour, and set about it probably in a more scientific manner than many of those who till the same land nine hundred years after him. Mr. Sharon Turner has given a brief and sensible account of the Anglo-Saxon husbandry, from which the following is an extract:—

" When the Anglo-Saxons invaded England, they came into a country which had been under the Roman power for about four hundred years, and where agriculture, after its more complete subjection by Agricola, had been so much encouraged, that it had become one of the western granaries of the empire. The Britons, therefore, of the fifth century may be considered to have pursued the best system of husbandry then in use, and their lands to have been extensively cultivated with all those exterior circumstances which mark established proprietorship and improvement: as small farms; inclosed fields; regular divisions into meadow, arable, pasture, and wood; fixed boundaries; planted hedges; artificial dykes and ditches; selected spots for vineyards, gardens, and orchards; connecting roads and paths; scattered villages, and larger towns; with appropriated names for every spot and object that marked the limits of each property, or the course of each way. All these appear in the earliest Saxon charters, and before the combating invaders had time or ability to make them, if they had not found them in the island. Into such a country the Anglo-Saxon adventurers came, and by these facilities to rural civilization soon became an agricultural people. The natives, whom they despised, conquered, and enslaved, became their educators and servants in the new arts, which they had to learn, of grazing and tillage; and the previous cultivation practised by the Romanised Britons will best account for the numerous divisions, and accurate and precise descriptions of land which occur in almost all the Saxon charters. No modern conveyance could more accurately distinguish or describe the boundaries of the premises which it conveyed." ('History of the Anglo-Saxons,' Vol. III., Appendix, No. 2.)

The side emblems of January (Fig. 227) are from manuscripts which incidentally give appropriate pictures of the seasons. The man bearing fuel and the two-headed Janus belong the one to literal and the other to learned art. It is difficult to understand how we retained the names of the week-days from Saxon paganism, and adopted the classical names of the months.

FEBRUARY.

"They called February Sprout-kele, by kele meaning the kele-wort, which we now call the cole-wort, the great pot-wort in time long past that our ancestors used; and the broth made therewith was thereof also called kele. For before we borrowed from the French the name of potage, and the name of herb, the one in our own language was called kele, and the other wort; and as the kele-wort, or potage herb, was the chief winter wort for the sustenance of the husbandman, so was it the first herb that in this month began to yield out wholesome young sprouts, and consequently gave thereunto the name of Sprout-kele." So writes old Verstegan; and, perhaps, if we had weighed earlier what he thus affirms, we might have better understood Shakspere when he sings of the wintry time,

"While greasy Joan doth kele the pot."

The Saxon pictures of February show us the chilly man warming his hands at the blazing fire; and the labourers more healthily employed in the woods and orchards, pruning their fruit-trees and lopping their timber (Fig. 228). Spenser has mingled these emblems in his description of January, in the 'Faëry Queen;' but he carries on the pruning process into February:—

"Then came old January, wrapped well
In many weeds to keep the cold away;
Yet did he quake and quiver like to quell,
And blow his nails to warm them if he may;
For they were numb'd with holding all the day
An hatchet keen, with which he felled wood
And from the trees did lop the needless spray."

MARCH.

The picture in the Saxon Calendar (Fig 236) now gives us distinctly the seed-time. But the tools of the labourers are the spade and the pickaxe. We are looking upon the garden operations of our industrious forefathers. They called this month "Lenet-monat," length-month (from the lengthening of the days); "and this month being by our ancestors so called when they received Christianity, and consequently therewith the ancient Christian custom of fasting, they called this chief season of fasting the fast of Lenet, because of the Lenet-monat, wherein the most parts of the time of this fasting always fell."

The great season of abstinence from flesh, and the regular recurrence through the year of days of fasting, rendered a provision for the supply of fish to the population a matter of deep concern to their ecclesiastical instructors. In the times when the Pagan Saxons were newly converted to Christianity, the missionaries were the great civilizers, and taught the people how to avail themselves of the abundant supply of food which the sea offered to the skilful and the enterprising. Bede tells us that Wilfred so taught the people of Sussex. "The bishop, when he came into the province, and found so great misery of famine, taught them to get their food by fishing. Their sea and rivers abounded in fish, and yet the people had no skill to take them, except only eels. The bishop's men having gathered eel-nets everywhere, cast them into the sea, and by the help of God took three hundred fishes of several sorts, the which being divided into three parts, they gave a hundred to the poor, a hundred to those of whom they had the nets, and kept a hundred for their own use." The Anglo-Saxons had oxen and sheep; but their chief reliance for flesh meat, especially through the winter season, was upon the swine, which, although private property, fed by thousands in the vast woods with which the country abounded. Our word Bacon is "of the beechen-tree, anciently called bucon, and whereas swine's flesh is now called by the name of bacon, it grew only at the first unto such as were fatted with bucon or beech mast." As abundant as the swine were the eels that flourished in their ponds and ditches. The consumption of this species of fish appears

from many incidental circumstances to have been very great. Rents were paid in eels, boundaries of lands were defined by eel-dykes, and the monasteries required a regular supply of eels from their tenants and dependents. We find, however, that the people had a variety of fish, if they could afford to purchase of the industrious labourers in the deep. In the 'Dialogues of Alfric,' which we have already quoted from Mr. Turner, there is the following colloquy with a fisherman: "What gettest thou by thine art?—Big loaves, clothing, and money. How do you take them?—I ascend my ship, and cast my net into the river; I also throw in a hook, a bait, and a rod. Suppose the fishes are unclean?—I throw the unclean out, and take the clean for food. Where do you sell your fish?—In the city. Who buys them?—The citizens; I cannot take so many as I can sell. What fishes do you take?—Eels, haddocks, minnies, and eel-pouts, skate and lampreys, and whatever swims in the river. Why do you not fish in the sea?—Sometimes I do; but rarely, because a great ship is necessary there. What do you take in the sea?—Herrings and salmons, porpoises, sturgeons, oysters and crabs, muscles, winckles, cockles, flounders, plaice, lobsters, and such like. Can you take a Whale?—No, it is dangerous to take a whale; it is safer for me to go to the river with my ship than to go with many ships to hunt whales. Why?—Because it is more pleasant for me to take fish which I can kill with one blow; yet many take whales without danger, and then they get a great price; but I dare not from the fearfulness of my mind." We thus see that three centuries after Wilfred had taught the people of Sussex to obtain something more from the waters than the rank eels in their mud-ponds, the produce of the country's fishery had become an article of regular exchange. The citizens bought of the fisherman as much fish as he could sell; the fisherman obtained big loaves and clothing from the citizens. The enterprise which belongs to the national character did not rest satisfied with the herrings and salmons of the sea. Though the little fisherman crept along his shore, there were others who went with many ships to hunt whales. We cannot have a more decisive indication of the general improvement which had followed in the wake of Christianity, even during a period of constant warfare with predatory invaders.

APRIL.

The illumination of the Saxon Calendar for this month represents three persons elevated on a sort of throne, each with drinking-cups in their hands, and surrounded with attendants upon their festivities (Figs. 237, 267). Strutt, in his description of this drawing, says, "Now, taking leave of the laborious husbandman, we see the nobleman regaling with his friends, and passing this pleasant month in banquetings and music." But he assigns no cause for the appropriateness of this jollity to the particular season. Is not this picture an emblem of the gladness with which the great festival of Easter was held after the self-denials of Lent? April was called by the Anglo-Saxons "by the name of Oster-monat; some think, of a goddess called Goster, whereof I see no great reason, for if it took appellation of such a goddess (a supposed causer of the easterly winds), it seemeth to have been somewhat by some miswritten, and should rightly be Oster and not Goster. The winds indeed, by ancient observation, were found in this month most commonly to blow from the east, and east in the Teutonic is Ost, and Ost-end, which rightly in English is East-end, hath that name for the eastern situation thereof, as to the ships it appeareth which through the narrow seas do come from the west. So as our name of the feast of Easter may be as much to say as the feast of Oster, being yet at this present in Saxony called Ostern, which cometh of Oster-monat, their and our old name of April." Those who are banqueting on the dais in the illumination, have each cups in their hands; the man sitting at their feet is filling a horn from a tankard; the young man on the right is drinking from a horn. There is a clear distinction between the rank of the persons assembled at this festivity; and the difference of the vessels which they are using for their potations might imply that the horns were filled with the old Saxon ale or mead, and the cups with the more luxurious wine. In Alfric's Colloquy a lad is asked what he drank; and he answers, "Ale if I have it, or water if I have not." He is further asked why he does not drink wine, and he replies, "I am not so rich that I can buy me wine, and wine is not the drink of children or the weak-minded, but of the elders and the wise." But if we may reason from analogy, the drinking-horn had a greater importance attached to it than the drinking-cup. Inheritances of land were transferred by the transfer of a horn; estates were held in fee by a horn. The horn of Ulphus (Fig. 292) is a remarkable curiosity still preserved in the Sacristy of the Cathedral at York.

263.—Silver Coin of Athelstan.

268.—Coin of Alfred.

262.—Saxon Emblems of the month of September.

266.—Dance. (Cotton MS.)

265.—Dinner. The Company pledging each other. (Cotton MS.)

267.—An Elevated and richly Ornamented Seat. (Cotton MS.)

271.—Silver Coin of Egbert.

270.—Silver Coin of Ethelwulf.

272.—Silver Coins of Alfred.

264.—Saxon Emblems of the month of October.

279.—Silver Penny of Canute, struck in Dublin.

280.—Silver Coin of Canute.

273.—Saxon Emblems of the month of November.

275.—Feast at a Round Table. (Bayeux Tapestry.)

277.—Saxon Tables. (Harleian MS.)

276.—Wheel-Bed. (Cotton MS.)

278.—Saxon Beds. (Harleian MS.)

281.—Silver Penny of Edward the Confessor.

282.—Silver Coins of Edward the Confessor.

274.—Saxon Emblems of the month of December.

Ulphus was a Danish nobleman of the time of Canute, who, as Camden informs us, " By reason of the difference which was like to rise between his sons about the sharing of his lands and lordships after his death, resolved to make them all alike; and thereupon coming to York with that horn wherewith he was used to drink, filled it with wine, and kneeling devoutly before the altar of God and St. Peter, prince of the apostles, drank the wine, and by that ceremony enfeoffed this church with all his lands and revenues." During the Civil Wars the horn of Ulphus came into the possession of Lord Fairfax, after being sold to a goldsmith; and it was subsequently restored to the church by the Fairfax family in 1675. The Pusey family in Berkshire hold their possessions by a horn given to their ancestors by King Canute (Fig. 290). So Camden informs us; though the inscription upon the horn which records the fact (Fig. 291) is held by Camden's editor, Bishop Gibson, to be of a much more recent date. Nearly all the Saxon representations of convivial meetings—and these are sufficiently numerous to furnish pretty clear evidence of the hospitality of that age—exhibit the guests for the most part drinking from horns (Fig. 249). Whether the wine or mead were drunk from horn or cup, the early custom of pledging appears to have been universal (Fig. 265). According to the old chroniclers, it was the first wine-pledge that delivered over Britain to the power of the Saxons, when the beautiful Rowena sat down in the banqueting-hall by the side of Vortigern, and betrayed him by her wine-cup, and her Waes Heal (Be of health). Robert of Glocester has recorded this first wassail in his rough rhyme, which has been thus paraphrased :

"'Health, my Lord King,' the sweet Rowena said ;
'Health,' cried the Chieftain to the Saxon maid ;
Then gaily rose, and, 'mid the concourse wide,
Kissed her hale lips, and placed her by his side.
At the soft scene such gentle thoughts abound,
That healths and kisses 'mongst the guests went round :
From this the social custom took its rise ;
We still retain and still must keep the prize.'

Selden, who gives the story in his Notes to Drayton, conjectures of the wassail of the English that it was " an unusual ceremony among the Saxons before Hengist, as a note of health-wishing (and so perhaps you might make it wish-heil), which was expressed among other nations in that form of drinking to the health of their mistresses and friends."

MAY.

Spenser has clothed his May with all the attributes of poetry :—
" Then came fair May, the fairest maid on ground,
Deck'd all with dainties of her season's pride,
And throwing flowers out of her lap around :
Upon two Brethren's shoulders she did ride,
The Twins of Leda ; which on either side
Supported her like to their sovereign Queen :
Lord ! how all creatures laugh'd when her they spied,
And leap'd and danc'd as they had ravish'd been,
And Cupid self about her fluttered all in green."

The Saxon name of the month has a pastoral charm about it which is as delightful as the gorgeous imagery of the great poet. " The pleasant month of May they termed by the name of Tri-milki, because in that month they began to milk their kine three times in the day." The illumination of the Calendar carries us into the pleasant fields, where the sheep are nibbling the thymy grass, and the old shepherd, seated upon a bank, is looking upon the lamb which the labourer bears in his arms. The shepherd describes his duty in the Colloquy of Alfric : " In the first part of the morning I drive my sheep to their pasture, and stand over them in heat and in cold with dogs, lest the wolves destroy them. I lead them back to their folds and milk them twice a day, and I move their folds, and make cheese and butter ; and I am faithful to my lord." The garments of the Anglo-Saxons, both male and female, were linen as well as woollen ; but we can easily judge that in a country whose population was surrounded by vast forests and dreary marshes, wool, the warmer material of clothing, would be of the first importance. The fleece which the shepherd brought home in the pleasant summer season was duly spun throughout the winter, by the females of every family, whatever might be their rank. King Edward the Elder commanded that his daughters should be instructed in the use of the distaff. Alfred, in his will, called the female part of his family the spindle side. At this day, true to their ancient usefulness (the form of which, we hope not the substance, has passed away), unmarried ladies are called spinsters. But the Anglo-Saxon ladies attained a high degree of skill in the ornamental work belonging to clothing.

The Norman historians record their excellence with the needle, and their skill in embroidery. Minute descriptions of dress are not amongst the most amusing of reading, although they are highly valuable to the systematic chronicler of manners. It may be sufficient for us to point attention, first to the cloaks, the plain and embroidered tunics, and the shoes of the males (Fig. 285, and incidentally in other Figures). These were the loose and flowing garments of the superior classes, a costume certainly of great beauty. The close tunic of the labourers (Fig. 255) is distinguished by the same fitness for the rank and occupation of the wearers. The practice of bandaging or cross-gartering the hose is indicated in many Anglo-Saxon drawings (Figs. 284, 288). Secondly, the ladies wore a long and ample garment with loose sleeves (the gunna, whence our gown), over a closer-fitting one, which had tight sleeves reaching to the wrist ; over these a mantle was worn by the superior classes, and a sort of hood or veil upon the head (Figs. 286, 287). Those who desire further information upon the subject of the Anglo-Saxon costume may consult Mr. Planché's valuable little work upon ' British Costume,' or the ' Pictorial History of England,' Book II., Chap. VI.

JUNE.

The emblem which we have given for this month (Fig. 246) is assigned to July in the Saxon Calendar; but Mr. Strutt is of opinion that the illuminator transposed the emblems of June and July, as there would be no leisure for felling trees during the harvest time, which is represented in the original as taking place in June and in August. The field operations of August are properly a continuation of those of July, according to Mr. Strutt. But it is not improbable that the hay harvest was meant to be represented by one illumination, and the grain harvest by the other. June was called by a name which describes the pasturing of cattle in the fields not destined for winter fodder. These were the meadows, which were too wet and rank for the purposes of hay. The blythe business of hay-making was upon the uplands. Verstegan says : " Unto June they gave the name of Weyd-monat, because their beasts did then weyd in the meadows, that is to say, go to feed there, and thereof a meadow is also in the Teutonic called a weyd, and of weyd we yet retain our word wade, which we understand of going through watery places, such as meadows are wont to be." The felling of trees in the height of summer, when the sap was up, was certainly not for purposes of timber. It was necessary to provide a large supply of fuel for winter use. In grants of land sufficient wood for burning was constantly permitted to be cut ; and every estate had its appropriate quantity of wood set out for fuel and for building.

JULY.

This was the Heu-monat or Hey-monat, the Hay-month. The July of Spenser bears the scythe and the sickle :—

" Behind his back a scythe, and by his side
Under his belt he bore a sickle circling wide."

These instruments were probably indifferently used in the harvests of the Anglo-Saxons, as they still are in many of our English counties (Figs. 254, 258).

AUGUST.

This was especially the harvest-month. " August they call Arn-monat, more rightly Barn-monat, intending thereby the then filling of their barns with corn." The arable portion of an estate was probably comparatively small. The population of the towns was supplied with corn from the lands in their immediate vicinity. There was no general system of exchange prevailing throughout the country. In the small farms enough corn was grown for domestic use ; and when it failed, as it often did, before the succeeding harvest, the cole-wort and the green pulse were the welcome substitutes. Wheaten bread was not in universal use. The young monks of the Abbey of St. Edmund ate the cheaper barley bread. The baker, in Alfric's Colloquy, answers to the question of " What use is your art ? we can live long without you :"—" You may live through some space without my art, but not long nor so well ; for without my craft every table would seem empty, and without bread all meat would become nauseous. I strengthen the heart of man, and little ones could not do without me." In the representation of a dinner-party (Fig. 247), some food is placed on the table ; but the kneeling servants offer the roasted meat on spits, from which the guests cut slices into their trenchers. We smile at these primitive manners, but they were a refinement upon those of the heroes of Homer, who were their own cooks.

" Patroclus did his dear friend's will; and he that did desire
To cheer the lords (come faint from fight) set on a blazing fire
A great brass pot, and into it a chine of mutton put,
And fat goat's flesh; Automedon held, while he pieces cut
To roast and boil, right cunningly : then of a well-fed swine,
A huge fat shoulder he cuts out, and spits it wondrous fine :
His good friend made a goodly fire ; of which the force once past,
He laid the spit low, near the coals, to make it brown at last :
Then sprinkled it with sacred salt, and took it from the racks :
This roasted and on dresser set, his friend Patroclus takes
Bread in fair baskets ; which set on, Achilles brought the meat,
And to divinest Ithacus took his opposed seat
Upon the bench : then did he will his friend to sacrifice ;
Who cast sweet incense in the fire, to all the Deities.
Thus fell they to their ready food."

CHAPMAN'S TRANSLATION OF THE ILIAD, Book ix.

An illumination amongst the Harleian Manuscripts exhibits to us an interesting part of the economy of a lord's house in the Saxon times. In the foreground are collected some poor people, aged men, women, and children, who are storing in their vessels, or humbly waiting to receive, the provisions which the lord and the lady are distributing at their hall door. It was from this highest of the occupations of the rich and powerful, the succour of the needy, that the early antiquaries derived our titles of Lord and Lady. The modern etymologists deny the correctness of this derivation, and maintain that the names are simply derived from a Saxon verb which means to raise up, to exalt. Horne Tooke, in his 'Diversions of Purley,' maintains this opinion ; and our recent dictionary-makers adopt it. Nevertheless, we shall transcribe old Verstegan's ingenious notion of the origin of the terms, which has something higher and better in it than mere word-splitting : " I find that our ancestors used for Lord the name of Laford, which (as it should seem) for some aspiration in the pronouncing, they wrote Hlaford, and Hlafurd. Afterwards it grew to be written Loverd, and by receiving like abridgement as other of our ancient appellations have done, it is in one syllable become Lord. To deliver therefore the true etymology, the reader shall understand, that albeit we have our name of bread from Breod, as our ancestors were wont to call it, yet used they also, and that most commonly, to call bread by the name of Hlaf, from whence we now only retain the name of the form or fashion wherein bread is usually made, calling it a loaf, whereas loaf, coming of Hlaf or Laf, is rightly also bread itself, and was not of our ancestors taken for the form only, as now we use it. Now was it usual in long foregoing ages, that such as were endued with great wealth and means above others, were chiefly renowned (especially in these northern regions) for their house-keeping and good hospitality ; that is, for being able, and using to feed and sustain many men, and therefore were they particularly honoured with the name and title of Hlaford, which is as much to say, as an afforder of Laf, that is, a bread-giver, intending (as it seemeth) by bread, the sustenance of man, that being the substance of our food the most agreeable to nature, and that which in our daily prayers we especially desire at the hands of God. The name and title of lady was anciently written Hleafdian, or Leafdian, from whence it came to be Lafdy, and lastly Lady. I have showed here last before how Hlaf or Laf was sometime our name of bread, as also the reason why our noble and principal men came to be honoured in the name of Laford, which now is Lord, and even the like in correspondence of reason must appear in this name of Leafdian, the feminine of Laford ; the first syllable whereof being anciently written Hleaf, and not Hlaf, must not therefore alienate it from the like nature and sense, for that only seemeth to have been the feminine sound, and we see that of Leafdian we have not retained Leady, but Lady. Well then both Hlaf and Hleaf, we must here understand to signify one thing, which is oread ; Dian is as much to say as serve ; and so is Leafdian a bread-server. Whereby it appeareth that as the Laford did allow food and sustenance, so the Leafdian did see it served and disposed to the guests. And our ancient and yet continued custom that our ladies and gentlewomen do use to carve and serve their guests at the table, which in other countries is altogether strange and unusual, doth for proof hereof well accord and correspond with this our ancient and honourable feminine appellation."

SEPTEMBER.

The illumination of the Saxon Calendar for this month exhibits the chace of the wild boar in the woods, where he fattened on acorns and beech-masts. The Saxon name of the month was Gerst-monat, or Barley-month ; the month either of the barley harvest or the barley beer making. But the pictorial representation of September shows us the bold hunting with dog and boar-spear. The old British breed of strong hounds, excellent for

hunting and war, which Strabo describes as exported to other countries, was probably not extinct. Even the most populous places were surrounded with thick woods, where the boar, the wolf, and the bear lurked, or came forth to attack the unhappy wayfarer. London was bounded by a great forest. Fitz-Stephen says, writing in the reign of Henry the Second—" On the north side are fields for pasture and open meadows very pleasant, among which the river waters do flow, and the wheels of the mills are turned about with a delightful noise. Very near lieth a large forest, in which are woody groves of wild beasts in the coverts, whereof do lurk bucks and does, wild boars and bulls." All ranks of the Anglo-Saxons delighted in the chace. The young nobles were trained to hunting after their school-days of Latin, as we are told in Asser's ' Life of Alfred.' Harold Harefoot, the king, was so called from his swiftness in the foot-chace. The beating the woods for the boar, as represented in Fig. 231, was a service of danger, and therefore fitted for the training of a warlike people.

OCTOBER.

This was the Wyn-monat, the Wine month of the Anglo-Saxons. Spenser's personification of the month is an image of "Old England :"—

"Then came October full of merry glee ;
For yet his noule was totty of the must,
While he was treading in the wine-fat's sea,
And of the joyous oil, whose gentle gust
Made him so frolic and so full of lust."

The illumination of the Saxon Calendar (Fig. 264) shows us the falconer with his hawk on fist, ready to let her down the wind at the heron or the wild duck. Other illuminations of this early period exhibit the grape-picker and the grape-presser. The wine-press of the time will appear in a subsequent page. Much has been written upon the ancient culture of the vine in England. Bede says, "The island excels for grain and trees, and is fit for feeding of beasts of burden and cattle. It also produces vines in some places." The later chroniclers, who knew the fact, quote Bede without disputing his assertion. Winchester, according to some of the earlier antiquaries, derived its name from Vintonia, the city of the vine ; but this is very questionable. The Bishop of Rochester had a vineyard at Halling ; and one of the bishops, as Lambarde tells us, sent to Edward II. " a present of his drinks, and withal both wine and grapes of his own growth in his vineyard at Halling, which is now a good plain meadow." The same authority says, " History hath mention that there was about that time [the Norman invasion] great store of vines at Santlac [Battle]." He has a parallel instance of the early culture of the vine :—" The like whereof I have read to have been at Windsor, insomuch as tithe of them hath been there yielded in great plenty ; which giveth me to think that wine hath been made long since within the realm, although in our memory it be accounted a great dainty to hear of." Lambarde then particularly describes the tithe of the Windsor vineyard, as " of wine pressed out of grapes that grew in the little park there, to the Abbot of Waltham ; and that accompts have been made of the charges of planting the vines that grew in the said park, as also of making the wines, whereof some parts were spent in the household, and some sold for the king's profit." This is an approach to a wine-manufacture upon a large scale. There can be little doubt that many of the great monasteries in the South of England had their vineyards, and made the wine for the use of their fraternities. They might not carry the manufacture so far as to sell any wine for their profit ; but the vineyard and the wine-press saved them the cost of foreign wines, for their labour was of little account. The religious houses founded in the Anglo-Saxon period had probably, in many cases, their vineyards as well as their orchards. There is an express record of a vineyard at Saint Edmundsbury ; Martin, Abbot of Peterborough, is recorded in the Saxon Chronicle to have planted a vineyard ; William Thorn, the monastic chronicler, writes that in his abbey of Nordhome the vineyard was " ad commodum et magnum honorem "—a profitable and celebrated vineyard. Vineyards are repeatedly mentioned in Domesday-Book. William of Malmesbury thus notices vineyards in his description of the abundance of the County of Gloucester :— " No county in England has so many or so good vineyards as this, either for fertility or sweetness of the grape. The vine has in it no unpleasant tartness or eagerness [sourness, from aigre], and is little inferior to the French in sweetness." Camden, in quoting this passage, adds, " We are not to wonder that so many places in this country from their vines are called vineyards, because they afforded plenty of wine ; and that they yield none now is rather to be imputed to the sloth of the inhabitants than the indisposition of the

283.—Royal Costume, and the Harness and Equipment of Horses. (Cotton MS.)

290.—The Pusey Horn.

291.—Facsimile of the Inscription on the Pusey Horn.

284.—The Harp, accompanied by other Instruments. (Cotton MS.)

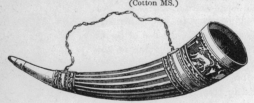

292.—Horn of Ulphus.

288.—Civil Costume of the Anglo-Saxons.

285.—Saxon Cloaks, Plain and Embroidered Tunics, and Shoes. (Cotton MS.)

286.—Costume of a Female, exhibiting the under and upper sleeved Tunic, the Mantle and Hood. (Harleian MS.)

287.—Anglo-Saxon Females. The standing figure is Etheldrytha, a Princess of East Anglia, from the Benedictional of St. Ethelwold.

289.—The Coffin and Grave-clothes. From a Picture of the Raising of Lazarus, in Cotton MS. Nero. C. 4.

72

296.—Entrance of the Mine of Odin, an ancient Lead-Mine in Derbyshire.

298.—Saxon Ships, from an Engraving in Strutt's Chronicle of England, made up from various Saxon Illuminations.

297.—Raising Water from a Well with a loaded Lever. (Cotton MS. Nero, C. 4.)

293.—Wine-Press. (Cotton MS.)

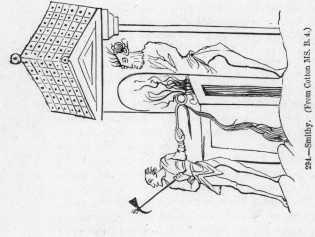

294.—Smithy. (From Cotton MS. B. 4.)

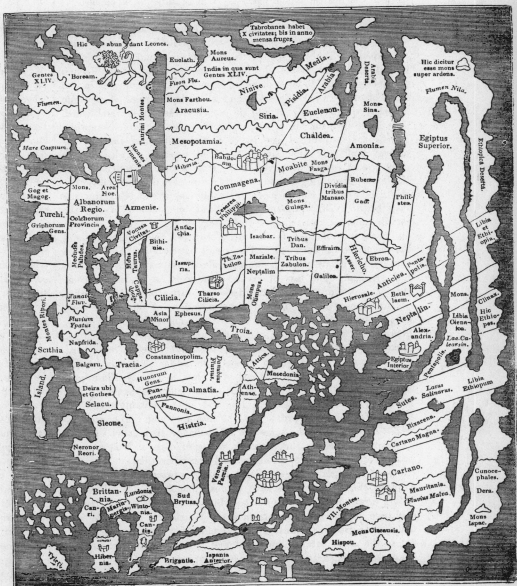

299.—Anglo-Saxon Map of the Tenth Century

295.—Smithy; a Harper in the other compartment. (From Cotton MS.)

climate." This question of the ancient growth of the vine in England was the subject of a regular antiquarian passage-at-arms in 1771, when the Honourable Daines Barrington entered the lists to overthrow all the chroniclers and antiquaries, from William of Malmesbury to Samuel Pegge, and to prove that the English grapes were currants—that the vineyards of Domesday-book and other ancient records were nothing but gardens—that the climate of England would never have permitted the ripening of grapes for wine. The throng of partisans to this battle-field was prodigious. The Antiquarian Society inscribed the paper pellets shot on this occasion as "The Vineyard Controversy."

We have no hesitation in believing that those who put faith in the truth of the ancient records were right;—that vineyards were plentiful in England, and that wine was made from the English grapes. It was not a change in the climate, nor the sloth of the people, that rendered the vineyards less and less profitable in every age, and finally produced their complete extinction. The wine of France was largely imported into England soon after the Norman Conquest. It is distinctly recorded that a passion for French wines was a characteristic of the court and the nobility in the reign of Henry III. The monks continued to cultivate their vines,—as in the sunny vale of Beaulieu, where the abbey, which King John founded, had its famous vineyard; but the great supply of wine, even to the diligent monks, was from the shores of France, where the vine could be cultivated upon the commercial principle. Had the English under the Plantagenets persevered in the home cultivation of the vine for the purpose of wine-making, whilst the claret of a better vine-country, that could be brought in a few hours across the narrow sea, was excluded from our ports, the capital of England would have been fruitlessly wasted in struggles against natural disadvantages, and the people of England would have been for the most part deprived of the use and enjoyment of a superior drink to their native beer. The English vineyards were gradually changed into plain meadows, as Lambarde has said, or into fertile corn-fields. Commercially the vine could not be cultivated in England, whilst the produce of the sunny hills of France was more accessible to London and Winchester than the corn which grew in the nearest inland county. The brethren of a monastery, whose labour was a recreation, might continue to prune their vines and press their grapes, as their Saxon ancestors had done before them; but for the people generally, wine would have been a luxury unattainable, had not the ports of Sandwich and Southampton been freely open to the cheap and excellent wine of the French provinces. This is the course of every great revolution in the mode of supplying the necessities, or even the luxuries, of a people amongst whom the principle of exchange has been established. The home growth for a while supplies the home consumption. A cheaper and better supply is partially obtained through exchange and easy communication—from another parish, another county, another province, and finally from another country. Then the home growth lingers and declines; capital is diverted into other channels, where it can be more profitably employed. Governments then begin to strive against the natural commercial laws, by the establishment of restrictive or prohibitory duties. A struggle goes on, perhaps prolonged for centuries, between the restrictions and the principle of exchange. The result is certain. The law of exchange is a law of progress; the rule of restriction is a rule of retrogression. The law of exchange goes on to render the communications of mankind, even of those who are separated by mighty oceans, as easy as the ancient communications of those who were only separated by a river or a mountain. The rule of restriction, generation after generation, and year after year, narrows its circle, which was first a wide one, and held a confiding people within its fold; but, as it approaches to the end, comes to contain only a class, then a few of the more prejudiced of a class, and lastly, those who openly admit that the rule is for their exclusive benefit. The meadows and the corn-fields of England have profitably succeeded her unprofitable vineyards; and the meadows and the corn-fields will flourish because the same law of exchange that drove out the vineyards will render the home exchange of corn and meat more profitable, generally, to producer and consumer than the foreign exchange. England is essentially a corn-growing and a mutton-growing country; and we have no fear that her fields will have failing crops, or her downs not be white with flocks, if the law of exchange should free itself from every restriction. England was not a wine-growing country, and therefore her vineyards perished before the same natural laws that will give the best, because the most steady, encouragement to her bread-growing and beer-growing capacity.

NOVEMBER.

This was the Wint-monat, the wind-month, of the Anglo-Saxons. Its emblems were the blazing hearth and the swine-killing (Fig. 273). The great slaughter-time was come,—the days of fresh meat were passing away. The beeves, and the sheep, and the hogs, whose store of green feed was now exhausted, were doomed to the salting-tubs. The Martinmas beef,—the beef salted at the feast of St. Martin—is still known in the northern parts of the island; and the proverb which we adopted from Spain "His Martinmas will come, as it does to every hog," speaks of a destiny as inevitable as the fate of the acorn-fed swine at the salting season.

Mr. Strutt, in his explanation of the illumination of the Saxon Calendar, says, "This month returns us again to the labourers, who are here heating and preparing their utensils." He then refers us to another drawing of a blacksmith. The Saxon illumination is very rude. In the centre of the composition there is a blazing fire upon the floor; a group on the right are warming their hands; whilst one man on the left is bearing a bundle of fuel, and another doing something at the fire with a rough pair of tongs. We believe that our artist has translated the illumination correctly, in considering this the fire of the domestic hearth, which the labourers are supplying with fresh billets. But as the subject is interpreted by Mr. Strutt, it refers to the craft of the smith, the most important occupation of early times; and we may therefore not improperly say a few words upon this great handicraftsman, who has transmitted us so many inheritors of his name even in our own day. Verstegan says, "Touching such as have their surnames of occupations, as Smith, Taylor, Turner, and such others, it is not to be doubted but their ancestors have first gotten them by using such trades; and the children of such parents being content to take them upon them, their after-coming posterity could hardly avoid them, and so in time cometh it rightly to be said,—

'From whence came Smith, all be he knight or squire,
　　But from the smith that forgeth at the fire.'"

But the author of an ingenious little book, lately published, on "English Surnames," Mr. Lower, points out that the term was originally applied to all smiters in general. The Anglo-Saxon Smith was the name of any one that struck with a hammer,—a carpenter, as well as a worker in iron. They had specific names for the ironsmith, the goldsmith, the coppersmith; and the numerous race of the Smiths are the representatives of the great body of artificers amongst our Saxon ancestors. The ironsmith is represented labouring at his forge in Fig. 294, and in Fig. 295, where, in another compartment of the drawing, we have the figure of a harper. The monks themselves were smiths; and St. Dunstan, the ablest man of his age, was a worker in iron. The ironsmith could produce any tool by his art, from a ploughshare to a needle. The smith in Alfric's Colloquy says, "Whence the share to the ploughman, or the goad, but for my art? Whence to the fisherman an angle, or to the shoewright an awl, or to the sempstress a needle, but for my art?" No wonder then that the art was honoured and cultivated. The antiquaries have raised a question whether the Anglo-Saxon horses were shod; and they appear to have decided in the negative, because the great districts for the breed of horses were fenny districts, where the horses might travel without shoes (See 'Archæologia,' vol. iii.). The crotchets of the learned are certainly unfathomable. Mr. Pegge, the writer to whom we allude, says, "Here in England one has reason to think they began to shoe soon after the Norman Conquest. William the Conqueror gave to Simon St. Liz, a noble Norman, the town of Northampton, and the whole hundred of Falkley, then valued at forty pound per annum, to provide shoes for his horses." If the shoes were not wanted, by reason of the nature of the soil in Anglo-Saxon times, the invading Normans might have equally dispensed with them, and William might have saved his manor for some better suit and service. Montfaucon tells us, that when the tomb of Childeric, the father of Clovis, who was buried with his horse in the fifth century, was opened in 1653, an iron horse-shoe was found within it. If the horse of Childeric wore iron horse-shoes, we may reasonably conclude that the horses of Alfred and Athelstane, of Edgar and Harold, were equally provided by their native smiths. There is little doubt that the mines of England were well worked in the Saxon times. "Iron-ore was obtained in several counties, and there were furnaces for smelting. The mines of Gloucestershire in particular are alluded to by Giraldus Cambrensis as producing an abundance of this valuable metal; and there is every reason for supposing that these mines were wrought by the Saxons, as indeed they had most probably been by their predecessors the Romans.

The lead-mines of Derbyshire, which had been worked by the Romans, furnished the Anglo-Saxons with a supply of ore (Fig. 296); but the most important use of this metal in the Anglo-Saxon period, that of covering the roofs of churches, was not introduced before the close of the seventh century." ('Pictorial History of England,' Book II. Chap. VI.) It is not impossible that something more than mere manual labour was applied to the operations of lifting ore from the mines, and freeing them from water, the great obstacle to successful working. In the Cotton Manuscripts we have a representation of the Anglo-Saxon mode of raising water from a well with a loaded lever (Fig. 297). At the present day we see precisely the same operation carried on by the market-gardeners of Isleworth and Twickenham. A people that have advanced so far in the mechanical arts as thus to apply the lever as a labour-saving principle, are in the direct course for reaching many of the higher combinations of machinery. The Anglo-Saxons were exporters of manufactured goods in gold and silver; and after nine hundred years we are not much farther advanced in our commercial economy than the merchant in Alfric's Colloquy, who says, "I send my ship with my merchandise (Fig. 298), and sail over the sea-like places, and sell my things, and buy dear things, which are not produced in this land. . . . . Will you sell your things here as you bought them there?—I will not, because what would my labour benefit me? I will sell them here dearer than I bought them there, that I may get some profit to feed me, my wife, and children." The geographical knowledge of the Anglo-Saxons was, no doubt, imperfect enough; but it was sufficient to enable them to carry on commercial operations with distant lands. The Anglo-Saxon map (Fig. 299) is taken from a manuscript of the tenth century, in the Cottonian Library. It was published in the 'Penny Magazine,' No. 340, from which we extract the following remarks upon it:—"The defects of the map are most apparent in the disproportionate size and inaccurate position of places. The island to the left of Ireland is probably meant for one of the Western Islands of Scotland; but it is by far too large, and is very incorrectly placed. The same remark will apply to the islands in the Mediterranean. The form given to the Black Sea appears just such as would be consequent upon loose information derived from mariners. However, in the absence of scientific surveys of any coast, and considering the little intercourse which took place between distant countries, the Anglo-Saxon map represents as accurate an outline as perhaps ought to be expected."

DECEMBER.

The emblem of the Saxon Calendar is that of the threshing season (Fig. 274). The flail has a reverend antiquity amongst us; the round sieve slowly does the work of winnowing; the farmer stands by with his notched stick, to mark how many baskets of the winnowed corn are borne to his granary. Other emblems show us the woodman bearing his fuel homewards, to make his hearth cheerful in the Winter-monat, winter-month; or the jolly yeoman lifting his drinking-horn during the festivities of the Heligh-monat, holy-month, for December was called by both these names. Then was the round table filled with jocund guests (Fig. 275). Then were the harp and the pipe heard in the merry halls; and the dancers were as happy amidst the smoke of their wood-fires, as if their jewels had shone in the clear blaze of a hundred wax-lights (Figs. 248, 266).

The Anglo-Saxon illuminations in the preceding pages, which are fac-similes, or nearly so, of drawings accompanying the original manuscripts in our public libraries, will not have impressed those unfamiliar with the subject with any very high notion of the state of art in this island eight or nine hundred years ago. It must be remembered that these specimens are selected, not as examples of the then state of art, but as materials for the history of manners and of costume. The false perspective, the slovenly delineations of the extremities, and the general distortion of the human figure, will at once be apparent. But there was nevertheless a school of art, if so it may be called, existing in England and Ireland, which has left some very remarkable proofs of excellence, and indeed of originality, in a humble walk of pictorial labour. The illuminated letters of the Anglo-Saxon manuscripts are wholly different from those of any continental school; and they display a gracefulness of ornament, and a power of invention, which may be profitably studied in these our own times when ornamental design in connection with manufactures is escaping from the monotonous barbarism which has so long marked us in such matters as a tasteless and unimaginative people. "The chief features of this species of illumination are

described by Sir F. Madden to be—extreme intricacy of pattern, interlacings of knots in a diagonal or square form, sometimes interwoven with animals, and terminating in heads of serpents or birds. Though we cannot distinctly trace the progress of this art, we may conclude that it continued in a flourishing and improving state in the interval from the eighth to the tenth and eleventh centuries, which were so prolific in Anglo-Saxon works of calligraphy and illumination, that, perhaps, says a competent authority, speaking of this period, our public libraries and the collections abroad contain more specimens executed in this country than any other can produce during the same space of time." ('Pictorial History of England,' Book II. Chap. V.) We give three examples, out of the great variety which exists in this branch of art. The illuminated letter P is of the eighth century (Fig. 301), at which period the illumination of books formed a delightful occupation to the more skilful in the monastic establishments, and was even thought a proper employment by the highest dignitaries of the Church. There is a splendid example known as the 'Durham Book,' which was the work of Eadfrid, Bishop of Lindisfarne, who died in 721. Dunstan himself, at a subsequent period, varied the course of his austerities and his ambition by employing his hand in the illumination of manuscripts. The ornament (Fig. 300) and the letter Q (Fig. 302) are of the tenth century.

But, although the examples are not very numerous, we have proof that the taste thus cultivated in the cloisters of the Anglo-Saxons was occasionally capable of efforts which would not have been unworthy of that period and that country to which we assign the revival of the arts. We are too much accustomed to think that there was no art in Europe, and very little learning, during what we are pleased to call the dark ages. But in the centuries so designated there were, in our own country, divines, historians, poets, whose acquirements might be an object of honourable rivalry to many of those who are accustomed to sneer at their scientific ignorance and their devotional credulity. At the time when Italian art was in the most debased condition, there was a monk in England (and there may have been many more such whose labours have perished) who, in all the higher qualities of design, might have rivalled the great painters who are held, three centuries later, to have been almost the creators of modern art. In the most successful labours of the Anglo-Saxon cloister there was probably little worldly fame; of rivalry there was less. The artist, in the brief intervals of his studies and his devotions, laboured at some work of several years, which was to him a glory and a consolation. He was worthily employed, and happily because his pencil embodied the images which were ever present to his contemplation. He did not labour for wealth amidst struggling competitors. Dante says of the first great Italian artists:—

> "Cimabue thought
> To lord it over painting's field; and now
> The cry is Giotto's, and his name eclips'd.
> Thus hath one Guido from the other snatch'd
> The letter'd prize: and he, perhaps, is born,
> Who shall drive either from their nest. The noise
> Of worldly fame is but a blast of wind,
> That blows from diverse points, and shifts its name,
> Shifting the point it blows from."

There is an Anglo-Saxon collection of drawings in existence, undoubtedly produced in the tenth century, whose excellence is such that the artist might have pretended "to lord it over painting's field" even amongst the Cimabues and Giottos. His name is supposed to have been Godemann; but even that is doubtful. To him, whoever he was, might now be addressed the subsequent lines of Dante:—

> "Shalt thou more
> Live in the mouths of mankind, if thy flesh
> Part shrivell'd from thee, than if thou hadst died
> Before the coral and the pap were left:
> Or ere some thousand years have past?"

But he has vindicated the general claims of his countrymen to take their rank, in times which men falsely call barbarous, amidst those who have worthily elevated the grosser conceptions of mankind into the ideal, showing that art had a wider and a purer sphere than the mere imitation of natural objects. The Benedictional of St. Ethelwold, an illuminated manuscript of the tenth century, in the library of the Duke of Devonshire, is the work to which we allude. It is fully described by Mr. Gage, in the twenty-fourth volume of the 'Archæologia;' and the Antiquarian Society, greatly to their honour, caused to be beautifully engraved in their Transactions thirty plates of the miniatures with which this remarkable

300.—Anglo-Saxon Ornament.
(From MS. of the Tenth Century.)

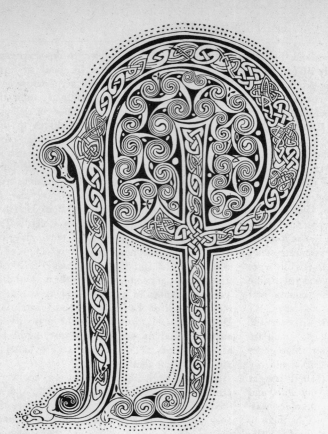

301.—Anglo-Saxon Illuminated Letter. (From MS. of the Eighth Century.)

302.—Anglo-Saxon Illuminated Letter. (From MS. of the Tenth Century.)

303.—From St. Æthelwold's Benedictional. Illumination V.

304.—From St. Æthelwold's Benedictional. Illumination VII.

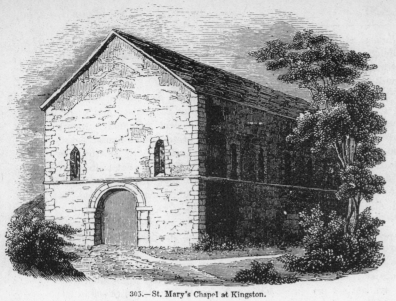

303.—St. Mary's Chapel at Kingston.

306.—Ancient Church, Greensted.

311.—King Edgar. (From Cotton MS.)

308.—Portrait of King Alfred. (Drawn from Coins and Busts.)

312.—Canute and his Queen. (From the Register of Hyde Abbey.)

314.—From Cotton MS.

313.—Seal of Alfric, Earl of Mercia.

310.—Saxon Lantern. (Engraved in Strutt's Chronicle of England.)

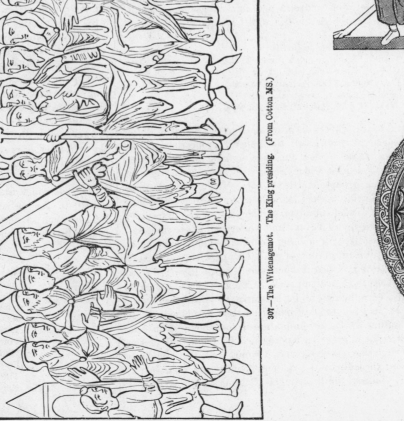

307.—The Witenagemot. The King presiding. (From Cotton MS.)

309.—Alfred's "Jewel."

77

work is adorned. This manuscript was the ancient Benedictional of the See of Winchester; and it is stated at the commencement of the work, that " A prelate whom the Lord had caused to be head of the Church of Winchester, the great Æthelwold, commanded a certain monk subject to him to write the present book; he ordered also to be made in it many arches elegantly decorated and filled up with various ornamental pictures, expressed in divers beautiful colours and gold." At the end of this introduction, or dedication, the writer subscribes his name Godemann. This monk of St. Swithin's subsequently became Abbot of Thorney. Mr. Gage says, " Although it is likely that this superb volume, filled with beautiful miniatures, and ornaments of the richest design, was finished before Godemann had the government of the Abbey of Thorney, we are sure of one thing, that it was executed in this country between the years 963, when Ethelwold received the episcopal mitre, and 984, when he died. . . . That Godemann was the illuminator of the manuscript, as well as the writer of it, I see no reason to doubt. Illumination was part of the art of calligraphy; and generally speaking, the miniature painting and the writing in the early manuscripts are to be presumed the work of the same hand." To furnish a general idea, though certainly an insufficient one, of the remarkable merit of the miniatures of this book, we present copies of the fifth and the seventh plates, as engraved in the ' Archæologia.' Fig. 303 is the second of two miniatures entitled ' Chorus Virginum.' Fig. 304 is the second of four miniatures, each containing a group of three Apostles. It is fortunately unnecessary that we should attempt ourselves any critical remarks on the rare merits of this early work of Anglo-Saxon art; for in the paper in the ' Archæologia ' is inserted a communication from the late Mr. Ottley, whose familiar acquaintance with the works of the early masters, both in painting and engraving, and the general correctness of his judgment, have established for him a high reputation. We extract from his letter a passage which points out not only the beauties, but defects of this work, and of Anglo-Saxon art in general; and further notices the superiority of the best productions of this our early school, both in colour and drawing, to the works of its European contemporaries :—

" In the thirteenth century, as every one knows, the art of painting and sculpture in Italy received new life at the hands of Niccola Pisano, Giunta, Cimabue, and Giotto; from which time they steadily progressed, till the happy era of Giulius the Second and Leo the Tenth. But for some centuries preceding the thirteenth I have sometimes seen reason to conjecture that the arts were in a more flourishing state in various countries distant from Italy than there; to say nothing of Greece, from which, it is probable, the inhabitants of those countries, like the Italians themselves, directly or indirectly, and perhaps at distant periods, originally derived instruction in those matters. That the art of miniature painting, especially, was better known and more successfully practised in France in the thirteenth century, and probably long before, than in Italy, has always appeared to me clear, from the well-known passage in the eleventh canto of Dante's ' Purgatorio,' where the poet thus addresses Oderigi d'Agubbio, a miniature painter, said to have been the friend of Cimabue :—

" Oh dissi lui non se tu Oderisi,
L'onor d'Agubbio, e l'onor di quell' arte
Che alluminar è chiamata a Parisi ?'
('Art thou not Oderigi ? art not thou
Agubbio's glory, glory of that art
Which they of Paris call the limner's skill ?)

" But to return to St. Ethelwold's manuscript. The next thing I would mention is the justness of the general proportions of the figures, especially those larger standing figures of Confessors, female Saints, and Apostles, which occupy the first seven pages of the book. The two groups, entitled Chorus Virginum, are particularly admirable in this respect, as well as for the easy gracefulness of the attitudes of some of them, and the cast of the draperies; so that, had the faces more beauty and variety of expression, and were the hands less like one another in their positions, and better drawn, little would remain to be desired. This deficiency of beauty in the heads, amounting, I fear I must admit, to positive ugliness, appears to have been in a great measure occasioned by the difficulty which the artist encountered in his attempts to finish them with body-colours; as may be seen by comparing these heads with those drawn only in outline in the last miniature in the book; if, indeed, the colouring was not in great part performed by a different person from him who drew the outlines; and, I would add, that the fault is more apparent, throughout the volume, in the large than in the smaller figures. Indeed, the little angels, holding scrolls, or sacred

volumes, especially the two last, have so much gracefulness and animation, are so beautifully draped, and so well adapted in their attitudes to the spaces they occupy, that I hardly know how to praise them sufficiently.

" Wherever the naked parts of the figure are shown, there we have most evidence of the incompetence of the artist; and consequently the figures of the Apostles, whose feet and ankles appear uncovered, are less agreeable than those of the above female Saint. But, as you are aware, this unskilfulness in the art of drawing the naked parts of the human figure is not the fault of the painter, but of the period; and, indeed, it was not until three centuries after the date of this manuscript, that any notable advancement was made in this difficult part of the art.

" The draperies of the figures throughout the volume, with scarce any exception, are well cast; though the smaller folds are often too strongly marked in proportion to the larger ones; which, with the want of any decided masses of light and shadow distinguishing those sides of objects which are turned towards the light from such as are not so, prevents their producing the agreeable effect which they otherwise would do; but this, again, is more the fault of the time than of the artist. The colouring throughout these Illuminations is rich, without being gaudy. It is possible that in the tenth century some of the gay colours, in the use of which the miniature painters of more modern times indulged so freely, were but little known. If I am wrong in this supposition, we must accord to the illuminator of this manuscript the praise of having possessed a more chastened taste than many of his successors."

It would be absurd to pretend that the work attributed to Godemann is an average specimen of Anglo-Saxon art. The illuminations, for example, are very superior to those of the sacred poem known as Cædmon's Metrical Paraphrase of Scripture History, preserved in the Bodleian Library at Oxford. In these the human figure is badly drawn; and there is perhaps more of invention in the initial letters than in the larger compositions. The poem itself is a most remarkable production of the early Anglo-Saxon times. The account which Bede gives of one Cædmon, the supposed author of this poem, is a most curious one :—" There was in this Abbess's Monastery [Abbess Hilda] a certain brother, particularly remarkable for the grace of God, who was wont to make pious and religious verses, so that whatever was interpreted to him out of Holy Writ, he soon after put the same into poetical expressions of much sweetness and compunction, in his own, that is the English, language. By his verses the minds of many were often excited to despise the world, and to aspire to the heavenly life. Others after him attempted in the English nation to compose religious poems, but none could ever compare with him; for he did not learn the art of poetising of men, but through the divine assistance; for which reason he never could compose any trivial or vain poem, but only those that relate to religion suited his religious tongue; for having lived in a secular habit, till well advanced in years, he had never learnt anything of versifying; for which reason being sometimes at entertainments, when it was agreed, for the more mirth, that all present should sing in their turns, when he saw the instrument come towards him, he rose up from table, and returned home. Having done so at a certain time, and going out of the house where the entertainment was, to the stable, the care of horses falling to him that night, and composing himself there to rest at the proper time, a person appeared to him in his sleep, and saluting him by his name, said, Cædmon, sing some song to me. He answered, I cannot sing; for that was the reason why I left the entertainment, and retired to this place, because I could not sing. The other who talked to him replied, However, you shall sing. What shall I sing ? rejoined he. Sing the beginning of creatures, said the other. Hereupon, he presently began to sing verses to the praise of God, which he had never heard."

The ode which Cædmon composed under this inspiration is preserved in Anglo-Saxon, in King Alfred's translation of Bede's Ecclesiastical History : and the following is an English translation from Alfred's version :—

" Now must we praise
The guardian of heaven's kingdom,
The Creator's might,
And his mind's thought;
Glorious Father of men !
As of every wonder he,
Lord Eternal,
Formed the beginning.
He first framed
For the children of earth
The heaven as a roof;
Holy Creator !

> Then mid-earth,
> The Guardian of mankind,
> The eternal Lord,
> Afterwards produced
> The earth for men,
> Lord Almighty!"

The Metrical Paraphrase to which we have alluded is ascribed by some to a second Cædmon; but the best philological antiquaries are not agreed upon this matter. As to its extraordinary merits there is no difference of opinion. Sir Francis Palgrave says, "The obscurity attending the origin of the Cædmonian poems will perhaps increase the interest excited by them. Whoever may have been their author, their remote antiquity is unquestionable. In poetical imagery and feeling, they excel all the other early remains of the North." One of the remarkable circumstances belonging to these poems, whether written by the cow-herd of Whitby, or some later monk, is that we here find a bold prototype of the fallen angels of 'Paradise Lost.' Mr. Conybeare says that the resemblance to Milton is so remarkable in that portion of the poem which relates to the Fall of Man, that "much of this portion might be almost literally translated by a cento of lines from that great poet." The resemblance is certainly most extraordinary, as we may judge from a brief passage or two. Every one is familiar with the noble lines in the first book of 'Paradise Lost'—

> "Him the Almighty Power
> Hurl'd headlong flaming from th' ethereal sky,
> With hideous ruin and combustion, down
> To bottomless perdition, there to dwell
> In adamantine chains and penal fire,
> Who durst defy the Omnipotent to arms.
> Nine times the space which measures day and night
> To mortal men, he with his horrid crew
> Lay vanquish'd, rolling in the fiery gulf,
> Confounded though immortal."

The Anglo-Saxon Paraphrase of Cædmon was printed at Amsterdam in 1655. Can there be a question that Milton had read the passage which Mr. Thorpe thus translated?—

> "Then was the Mighty angry,
> The highest Ruler of heaven
> Hurled him from the lofty seat;
> Hate had he gained at his Lord,
> His favour he had lost,
> Incensed with him was the Good in his mind.
> Therefore he must seek the gulf
> Of hard hell-torment,
> For that he had warr'd with heaven's Ruler.
> He rejected him then from his favour,
> And cast him into hell,
> Into the deep parts,
> When he became a devil:
> The fiend with all his comrades
> Fell then from heaven above,
> Through as long as three nights and days,
> The angels from heaven into hell."

Who can doubt that when the music of that speech of Satan beginning

> "Is this the region, this the soil, the clime
> That we must change for heaven?"

swelled upon Milton's exquisite ear, the first note was struck by the rough harmony of Cædmon?—

> "This narrow place is most unlike
> That other that we ere knew
> High in heaven's kingdom."

It would be quite beside our purpose to attempt any notice, however brief, of the Anglo-Saxon literature in general. Those who are desirous of popular information on this most interesting subject may be abundantly gratified in Mr. Sharon Turner's 'History of the Anglo-Saxons,' in Mr. Conybeare's 'Illustrations of Saxon Poetry,' and especially in Mr. Wright's admirable volume of 'Literary Biography' of 'the Anglo-Saxon period.' The study of the Anglo-Saxon language and literature is reviving in our times; and we have little doubt that the effect will be, in conjunction with that love of our elder poets which is a healthful sign of an improving taste, to infuse something of the simple strength of our ancient tongue into the dilutions and platitudes of the multitudes amongst us "who write with ease." Truly does old Verstegan say, "Our ancient English Saxons' language is to be accounted the Teutonic tongue, and albeit we have in later ages mixed it with many borrowed words, especially out of the Latin and French, yet remaineth the Teutonic unto this day the ground of our speech, for no other offspring hath our language originally had than that." The noble language—"the tongue that Shakspere spake"—which is our inheritance, may be saved

from corruption by the study of its great Anglo-Saxon elements. All the value of its composite character may be preserved, with a due regard to its original structure. So may we best keep our English with all its honourable characteristics, so well described by Camden:—"Whereas our tongue is mixed, it is no disgrace. The Italian is pleasant, but without sinews, as a still fleeting water. The French delicate, but even nice as a woman, scarce daring to open her lips, for fear of marring her countenance. The Spanish majestical, but fulsome, running too much on the o, and terrible like the devil in a play. The Dutch manlike, but withal very harsh, as one ready at every word to pick a quarrel. Now we, in borrowing from them, give the strength of consonants to the Italian; the full sound of words to the French; the variety of terminations to the Spanish; and the mollifying of more vowels to the Dutch; and so like bees, we gather the honey of their good properties, and leave their dregs to themselves. And when thus substantialness combineth with delightfulness, fulness with fineness, seemliness with portliness, and currentness with staidness, how can the language which consisteth of all these, sound other than full of all sweetness?" ('Remains.')

The coins of a country are amongst the most valuable and interesting of its material monuments. The study of coins is not to be considered as the province of the antiquary alone. Coins are among the most certain evidences of history." ('Penny Cyclopædia.') In our engravings we have presented a series of coins, from the earliest Anglo-Saxon period to the time of Edward the Confessor. They begin at page 60, Fig. 232; and continue in every page to page 69, Fig. 282. To enter into a minute description of these coins would be tedious to most readers, and not satisfactory, with our limited space, to the numismatic student. We shall therefore dismiss this branch of Old England's antiquities with a few passing remarks suggested by some of this series.

The little silver coin, Fig. 233, is called a sceatta. This is a literal Anglo-Saxon word which means money; and when, in Anglo-Saxon familiar speech, the entertainer at a tavern is called upon to pay the *shot*, the coin of Victoria does the same office as the *sceat* of the early kings of Kent.

> "As the fund of our pleasure, let each pay his shot,"

says Ben Jonson. The penny is next in antiquity to the sceat. The silver coins of the princes of the Heptarchy are for the most part pennies. There is an extensive series of such coins of the kings of Mercia. The halfpenny and the farthing are the ancient names of the division of the penny; they are both mentioned in the Saxon Gospels. The coins of Offa, king of Mercia (Fig. 234), are remarkable for the beauty of their execution, far exceeding in correctness of drawing and sharpness of impression those of his predecessors or successors. "At the beginning of the ninth century Ecgbeorht or Egbert ascended the throne of the West Saxon kingdom; and in the course of his long reign, brought under his dominion nearly the whole of the Heptarchic states; he is therefore commonly considered as the first sole monarch of England, notwithstanding those states were not completely united in one sovereignty until the reign of Edgar. On his coins, he is usually styled Ecgbeorht Rex, and sometimes the word Saxonum is added in a monogram, within the inner circle of the obverse: some of his coins have a rude representation of his head, and some are without it. From Egbert's time, with very few exceptions, the series of English pennies is complete; indeed, for many hundred years, the penny was the chief coin in circulation." ('Penny Cyclopædia.') The silver pennies of Alfred bear a considerable price; and this circumstance may be attributed in some degree to the desire which individuals in all subsequent ages would feel, to possess some memorial of a man who, for four hundred years after his death, was still cherished in the songs and stories of the Anglo-Saxon population, mixed as they were with Norman blood, as the Shepherd of the people, the Darling of England (Figs. 268, 272). A relic, supposed more strictly to pertain to the memory of Alfred, is now in the Ashmolean Museum at Oxford. It is an ornament of gold which was found in the Isle of Athelney, the scene of Alfred's retreat during the days of his country's oppression. The inscription round the figure, holding flowers, means, "Alfred had me wrought" (Fig. 309). The Saxon lantern, which Strutt has engraved in his 'Chronicle of England' (Fig. 310), is also associated with the memory of Alfred, in that story which Asser, his biographer, tells of him, that he invented a case of horn and wood for his wax candle, by the burning of which he marked the progress of time. The genuineness of Asser's Biography has been recently questioned; but there is little doubt that its facts were

315.—Great Seal of Edward the Confessor.

319.—Harold's Interview with King Edward on his return from Normandy. (Bayeux Tapestry.)

316.—Great Seal of Edward the Confessor.

320.—Harold on his Journey to Bosham. (Bayeux Tapestry.)

318.—Harold taking leave of Edward on his departure for Normandy. (Bayeux Tapestry.)

322.—The Crown offered to Harold by the People. (Bayeux Tapestry.)

321.—Funeral of Edward the Confessor, at Westminster Abbey. (Bayeux Tapestry.)

323.—Coronation of Harold. (Bayeux Tapestry.)

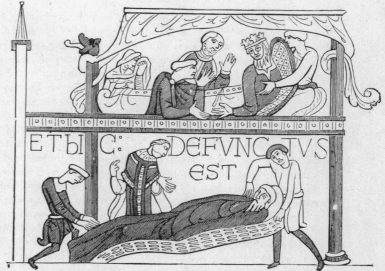

317.—The Sickness and Death of Edward the Confessor. (Bayeux Tapestry.)

329.—Normans carrying Arms and Provisions for the Invading Fleet. (Bayeux Tapestry.)

531.—The Military Habits of the Anglo-Saxons

330.—Battle Scene. (From the Cotton MS. Claud. B. 4.

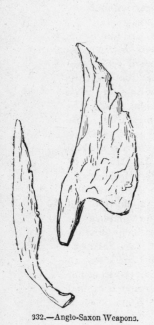

332.—Anglo-Saxon Weapons.

325.—Harold's Appearance at the Court of the Count of Ponthieu. (Bayeux Tapestry.)

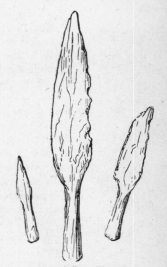

332.—Anglo-Saxon Weapons.

324.—Harold coming to anchor on the Coast of Normandy. Bayeux Tapestry.)

328.—A Ship of the fleet of Duke William transporting Troops for the Invasion of England. (Bayeux Tapestry.)

327.—William giving orders for the Invasion. (Bayeux Tapestry.)

326.—Harold's Oath to William. (Bayeux Tapestry)

No. 11.

81

founded upon an older narrative. The portrait of Alfred (Fig. 308) is copied from that in Spelman's 'Life:' but the materials out of which it is composed are probably not much to be relied upon.

There is a very remarkable object in Berkshire, not a great distance from Wantage, the birth-place of Alfred, which has been considered a memorial of the bravery and patriotism which he displayed even before he came to the throne. In the reign of Ethelred the First, the brother of Alfred, the Danes, who had invaded Berkshire, were routed with great slaughter in a battle known as that of Æscesdun (Ash-tree Hill); and it was contended by Dr. Wise, a learned antiquary of the last century, that the ridge of chalk hills extending from Wantage into Wiltshire was the scene of this battle, and that the White Horse which is cut out on the slope of the chalk is a memorial of this great victory. The White Horse, which gives its name to the hill, and to the fertile valley beneath, is a most singular object. It is a rude figure, three hundred and seventy-four feet in length, formed by removing the turf, and laying bare the chalk, on the north-west face of this hill, just above a lofty and steep declivity, which is visible from the surrounding country. When the afternoon sun shines upon this side of the ridge, the White Horse may be seen from a great distance—as far, it is said, as fifteen miles. Lysons mentions that there was a tradition that lands in the neighbourhood were formerly held by the tenure of cleaning the White Horse, by cutting away the springing turf. An annual festival was once held at this ancient ceremonial labour, called by the people Scouring the Horse. But as the regard for ancient memorials was dying out within the last century, and the peasants of Berkshire were ground down to a worse than serf-like condition of dependence on the poor-rates, the old festival was given up, the White Horse was left to be overgrown and obliterated, and even the memory of Alfred lived no longer amongst his Saxon descendants in these lonely valleys, who had grown up in ignorance and pauperism, because the humanities which had associated their forefathers with their superiors in rank were unwisely severed. The age of festivals, whether of religion or patriotism, is gone. We ought to mention that some antiquaries differ from Dr. Wise, and believe the White Horse to be of earlier origin than the age of Alfred. There can be no question, however, that it is a work of very high antiquity.

The civil government of the Anglo-Saxons, whether under the Heptarchy, or after the kings of Wessex had obtained that ascendency which constituted the united monarchy of all England, is associated with very few existing monuments beyond those of its medallic history. There was an ancient chapel at Kingston existing about half a century ago, in which kings Edrid, Edward the Martyr, and Ethelred are stated to have been crowned. That chapel is now destroyed (Fig. 305). An engraving was made of it whilst the tradition was concurrent with the existence of the old building. Kingston was unquestionably the crowning place of the Saxon kings. There is a remarkable little church existing at Greensted, a village about a mile from Ongar, in Essex. It was described about a century ago in the 'Vetusta Monumenta' of the Society of Antiquaries; and attention has recently been called to it by a correspondent of the 'Penny Magazine.' "In one of the early incursions of the Danes into England (A. D. 870), Edmund, King of East Anglia, was taken prisoner by them, and, refusing to abjure the Christian religion, put to a cruel death. He was a favourite of the people, but especially of the priests; and came naturally, therefore, to be spoken of as a martyr, and his remains to be held in estimation as those of a saint. In the reign of Ethelred the Unready, the Danes, emboldened by the cowardice or feeble policy of the king, who only sought to buy them off from day to day, and made tyrannous by the diminished opposition everywhere offered to them, ravaged the country in all directions, until at length, in the year 1010, 'that dismal period,' as Mr. Sharon Turner calls it, 'their triumph was completed in the surrender of sixteen counties of England and the payment of forty-eight thousand pounds.' In this year the bones of St. Edmund were removed from Ailwin to London, to prevent their falling into the hands of the Danes. They appear to have remained in London about three years, when they were carried back to Bedriceworth (Bury St. Edmund's). A MS. cited by Dugdale in the 'Monasticon,' and entitled 'Registrum Cœnobii S. Edmundi,' informs us that on its return to Bury, 'his body was lodged (hospitabatur) at Aungre, where a wooden chapel remains as a memorial to this day.' It is this same 'wooden chapel' which is supposed to form the nave of Greensted church. The inhabitants of the village have always had a tradition that the corpse of a king rested in it, and the appearance of the building vouches for its great antiquity" (Fig. 306).

The Witenagemot, or the great council of the nation—prelates, ealdormen, and thanes or governors of boroughs, with the crowned king presiding—is represented in one of the Cotton manuscripts in the British Museum (Fig. 307). We have an example of the almost regal dignity of the greater noblemen, in the remarkable seal of Alfric Earl of Mercia, who lived towards the end of the tenth century. The earl not only bears the sword of authority, but wears a diadem (Fig. 313). There are representations of particular monarchs in Anglo-Saxon manuscripts, which are perhaps more valuable as examples of costume than as individual portraits. Such is that of King Edgar (Fig. 311), and of Canute and his queen (Fig. 312).

The seal which we have mentioned (or rather, the brass matrix of the seal) of Alfric, Earl of Mercia, which was found by a labourer in cutting away a bank near Winchester in 1832, is one of several proofs which have set at rest a long-disputed question as to the use of seals among the Anglo-Saxons. The legal antiquaries of the seventeenth century, such as Selden and Coke, speak without any hesitation of charters with seals granted by the Saxon kings. Mr. Astle, a very competent authority, asserted in 1791, that our Saxon ancestors did not use seals of wax appended to their deeds ('Archæologia,' vol. x.). He acknowledged, however, that if such a seal could be found of a date before the time of the Confessor, the argument against their use, derived from the fact that the word Sigillum did not always mean seal, would be set at rest. The opinion of Astle was founded upon that of earlier antiquaries. The late Mr. Douce, in some remarks upon two wax impressions of the seal of the Abbey of Wilton, which he believes to be the original Anglo-Saxon seal, notices these objections: "If Dr. Hickes and the other objectors could have expected successfully to demonstrate that the Saxons used no seals, it was necessary for them to annihilate not only the numerous early seals of the German emperors and French kings, but even the gems and other sigillatory implements of the ancients. It would, indeed, have been a remarkable circumstance, that during a period wherein many of the European monarchs were continuing the immemorial practice of affixing seals to public instruments, the Saxon sovereigns of England, who were not inferior in knowledge and civilization to their contemporaries, and who borrowed many of their customs from Italy and France, should have entirely suspended a practice so well known and established. It is much less extraordinary that a very small number of Saxon seals should be remaining, than that, all circumstances considered, they should not have been frequently used. All that the objectors have been able to prove is, that a great many Saxon instruments were destitute of seals; that some were forged with seals in Norman times; and that the words 'Signum' and 'Sigillum' were often used to express the mere signature of a cross, which nevertheless was the representative of a seal." In 1821, the seal of Ethelwald, Bishop of Dunwich, was found about a hundred yards from the site of the Monastery of Eye. That remarkable seal is now in the British Museum; and Mr. Hudson Gurney, who transmitted an account of it to the Society of Antiquaries, says, "On the whole I conceive there can remain no doubt but that this was the genuine seal of Ethelwald, Bishop of Dunwich, about the middle of the ninth century, and that it sets at rest the question hitherto in dispute touching the use of seals among the Anglo-Saxons."

These few remarks may not improperly introduce to our readers the first of an uninterrupted series of monuments belonging to our monarchical government—the great seals of England. The seal of King Edward the Confessor is represented in Figs. 315 and 316. On one side, according to the description of this seal by Sir Henry Ellis, the king "is represented sitting on a throne bearing on his head a sort of mitre, in his right hand he holds a sceptre finishing in a cross, and in his left a globe. On the other side he is also represented with the same sort of head-dress, sitting. In his right a sceptre finishing with a dove. On his left a sword, the hilt pressed toward his bosom. On each side is the same legend—Sigillum Eadwardi Anglorum Basilei. This seal of King Edward is mentioned several times in the 'Domesday Survey.'" ('Archæologia,' vol. xviii.). The seal of William the Conqueror, which belongs to the next book, is little superior in workmanship to that of the Confessor; and the sitting figures of each have considerable resemblance (Fig. 342). The impression of the seal of the Conqueror is preserved in the Hotel Soubise at Paris, being appended to a charter by which the king granted some land in England to the abbey of St. Denis, in France. This seal establishes the fact that grants of lands immediately after the Conquest were guaranteed by the affixing of a waxen seal; and although this might not be invariably the case, it goes far to throw a doubt upon the authenticity of the old rhyming grant said to be made by

William to the ancient family of the Hoptons, which Stow and other early antiquaries have believed to be authentic. Stow gives it in his 'Annals,' upon "the testimony of an old chronicle in the library at Richmont," omitting three introductory lines, upon the authority of which in the sixteenth century a legal claim was actually set up to the estate of the lords of Hopton :—

> "To the heirs male of the Hopton lawfully begotten :—
> From me and from mine, to thee and to thine,
> While the water runs, and the sun doth shine ;
> For lack of heirs, to the king again.
> I, William, king, the third year of my reign,
> Give to thee, Norman Huntere,
> To me that art both lefe and dear,
> The Hop and Hoptown,
> And all the bounds up and down,
> Under the earth to hell,
> Above the earth to heaven,
> From me and from mine,
> To thee and to thine,
> As good and as fair
> As ever they mine were.
> To witness that this is sooth,
> I bite the white wax with my tooth,
> Before Jugg, Maud, and Margery,
> And my third son Henry,
> For one bow and one broad arrow,
> When I come to hunt upon Yarrow."

We give the above, with some slight corrections, from Blount's 'Ancient Tenures.'

The most extraordinary memorial of that eventful period of transition, which saw the descendants of the old Saxon conquerors of Britain swept from their power and their possessions, and their places usurped by a swarm of adventurers from the shores of Normandy, is a work not of stone or brass, not of writing and illumination more durable than stone or brass, but a roll of needlework, which records the principal events which preceded and accompanied the Conquest, with a minuteness and fidelity which leave no reasonable doubt of its being a contemporary production. This is the celebrated Bayeux Tapestry. When Napoleon contemplated the invasion of England in 1803, he caused this invaluable record to be removed from Bayeux, and to be exhibited in the National Museum at Paris ; and then the French players, always ready to seize upon a popular subject, produced a little drama in which they exhibited Matilda, the wife of the Conqueror, sitting in her lonely tower in Normandy whilst her husband was fighting in England, and thus recording, with the aid of her needlewomen, the mighty acts of her hero, portrayed to the life in this immortal worsted-work. But there is a more affecting theory of the accomplishment of this labour than that told in the French vaudeville. The women of England were celebrated all over Europe for their work in embroidery ; and when the husband of Matilda ascended the throne of England, it is reasonably concluded that the skilful daughters of the land were retained around the person of the queen. They were thus employed to celebrate their own calamities. But there was nothing in this tapestry which told a tale of degradation. There is no delineation of cowardly flight or abject submission. The colours of the threads might have been dimmed with the tears of the workers, but they would not have had the deep pain of believing that their homes were not gallantly defended. In this great invasion and conquest, as an old historian has poetically said, "was tried by the great assise of God's judgment in battle the right of power between the English and Norman nations—a battle the most memorable of all others ; and, howsoever miserably lost, yet most nobly fought on the part of England." There was nothing in this tapestry to encourage another invasion eight centuries later. In one of the compartments of the tapestry were represented men gazing at a meteor or comet, which was held to presage the defeat of the Saxon Harold. A meteor had appeared in the south of France, at the time of the exhibition of the tapestry in 1803 ; and the mountebank Napoleon proclaimed that the circumstances were identical. The tapestry, having served its purpose of popular delusion, was returned to its original obscurity. It had previously been known to Lancelot and Montfaucon, French antiquaries ; and Dr. Ducarel, in 1767, printed a description of it, in which he stated that it was annually hung up round the nave of the church of Bayeux on St. John's day. During the last thirty years this ancient work has been fully described, and its date and origin discussed. Above all, the Society of Antiquaries have rendered a most valuable service to the world, by causing a complete set of coloured fac-simile drawings to be made by an accomplished artist, Mr. Charles Stothard, which have

since been published in the 'Vetusta Monumenta.' The more remarkable scenes of the seventy-two compartments of the tapestry are engraved in our pages : and we may fitly close our account of the antiquities of the Anglo-Saxon period with a brief notice of this most interesting historical record.

In the Hôtel of the Prefecture at Bayeux is now preserved this famous tapestry. In 1814, so little was known of it in the town where it had remained for so many centuries, that Mr. Hudson Gurney was coming away without discovering it, not being aware that it went by the name of the "Toile de St. Jean." It was coiled round a windlass ; and drawing it out at leisure over a table, he found that it consisted of "a very long piece of brownish linen cloth, worked with woollen thread of different colours, which are as bright and distinct, and the letters of the superscriptions as legible, as if of yesterday." The roll is twenty inches broad, and two hundred and fourteen feet in length. Mr. Gurney has some sensible remarks upon the internal evidence of the work being contemporaneous with the Conquest. In the buildings portrayed there is not the trace of a pointed arch ; there is not an indication of armorial bearings, properly so called, which would certainly have been given to the fighting knights had the needlework belonged to a later age ; and the Norman banner is invariably *Argent*, a cross *Or* in a border *Azure*, and not the later invention of the Norman leopards. Mr. Gurney adds, "It may be remarked, that the whole is worked with a strong outline ; that the clearness and relief are given to it by the variety of the colours." The likenesses of individuals are preserved throughout. The Saxons invariably wear moustaches ; and William, from his erect figure and manner, could be recognised were there no superscriptions. Mr. Charles Stothard, who made the drawings of the tapestry which have been engraved by the Society of Antiquaries, communicates some interesting particulars in a letter written in 1819. He adds to Mr. Gurney's account of its character as a work of art, that "there is no attempt at light and shade, or perspective, the want of which is substituted by the use of different-coloured worsteds. We observe this in the off-legs of the horses, which are distinguished alone from the near-legs by being of different-colours. The horses, the hair, and mustachios, as well as the eyes and features of the characters, are depicted with all the various colours of green, blue, red, &c., according to the taste or caprice of the artist. This may be easily accounted for, when we consider how few colours composed their materials."

The first of the seventy-two compartments into which the roll of needlework is divided, is inscribed "Edwardus Rex" (Fig. 318). We omit the inscriptions which occur in each compartment, except in two instances. The crowned king, seated on a chair of state, with a sceptre, is giving audience to two persons in attendance ; and this is held to represent Harold departing for Normandy. The second shows Harold, and his attendants with hounds, on a journey. He bears the hawk on his hand, the distinguishing mark of nobility. The inscription purports that the figures represent Harold, Duke of the English, and his soldiers, journeying to Bosham (Fig. 320). The third is inscribed "Ecclesia," and exhibits a Saxon church, with two bending figures about to enter. This we have given in another place, as an architectural illustration (Fig. 216). The fourth compartment represents Harold embarking ; and the fifth shows him on his voyage. We give the sixth (Fig. 324), which is his coming to anchor previous to disembarking on the coast of Normandy. The seventh and eighth compartments exhibit the seizure of Harold by the Count of Ponthieu. The ninth (Fig. 325) shows Harold remonstrating with Guy, the Count, upon his unjust seizure.

We pass over the compartments from ten to twenty-five, inclusive, which exhibit various circumstances connected with the sojourn of Harold at the court of William. Mr. Stothard has justly observed, "That whoever designed this historical record was intimately acquainted with whatever was passing on the Norman side, is evidently proved by that minute attention to familiar and local circumstances evinced in introducing, solely in the Norman party, characters certainly not essential to the great events connected with the story of the work." The twenty-sixth compartment (Fig. 326) represents Harold swearing fidelity to William, with each hand on a shrine of relics. All the historians appear to be agreed that Harold did take an oath to William to support his claims to the crown of England, whatever might have been the circumstances under which that oath was extorted from him. The twenty-seventh compartment exhibits Harold's return to England ; and the twenty-eighth shows him on his journey after landing. For the convenience of referring to those parts of the tapestry which are connected with King Edward the Confessor, we have grouped them

334.—Orders given for the erection of a fortified Camp at Hastings. (Bayeux Tapestry.)

336.—Duke William addressing his Soldiers at the field of Hastings. (Bayeux Tapestry.)

335.—Cooking and Feasting of the Normans at Hastings. (Bayeux Tapestry.)

337.—Battle of Hastings. (Bayeux Tapestry.)

340.—Group associated with the Conquest.

338.—Battle of Hastings. (Bayeux Tapestry.)

339.—Death of Harold. (Bayeux Tapestry.)

84

342.—Great Seal of William the Conqueror.

341.—William I. and Tonstain bearing the Consecrated Banner at the Battle of Hastings. (Bayeux Tapestry.)

344.—Silver Penny of William I. (From specimen in Brit. Mus.)

343.—Arms of William the Conqueror.

346.—A Norman Castle.

345.—Castle of Lillebonne—General View of Ruins, Church, &c.

348.—The Abbey of St. Etienne (Stephen.) Caen.

347.—Statue of William the Conqueror. Placed against one of the external Pillars of St. Stephen, Caen.

in one page (80), not following their order in the tapestry. The twenty-ninth compartment (Fig. 319) has an inscription purporting that Harold comes to Edward the King. The thirtieth shows the funeral procession of the deceased Edward to Westminster Abbey, a hand out of heaven pointing to that building as a monument of his piety (Fig. 321). The inscription says, "Here the body of Edward the King is borne to the church of St. Peter the Apostle." The thirty-first and thirty-second compartments exhibit the sickness and death of the Confessor (Fig. 317). The thirty-third shows the crown offered to Harold (Fig. 322). The thirty-fourth presents us Harold on the throne, with Stigant the Archbishop (Fig. 323). Then comes the compartment representing the comet already mentioned; and that is followed by one showing William giving orders for the building of ships for the invasion of England (Fig. 327). We have then compartments, in which men are cutting down trees, building ships, dragging along vessels, and bearing arms and armour. The forty-third has an inscription, "Here they draw a car with wine and arms" (Fig. 329). After a compartment with William on horseback, we have the fleet on its voyage. The inscription to this recounts that he passes the sea with a great fleet, and comes to Pevensey. Three other compartments show the disembarkation of horses, the hasty march of cavalry, and the seizure and slaughter of animals for the hungry invaders. The forty-ninth compartment bears the inscription "This is Wadard." Who this personage on horseback, thus honoured, could be, was a great puzzle, till the name was found in Domesday-Book as a holder of land in six English counties, under Odo, Bishop of Bayeux, the Conqueror's half-brother. This is one of the circumstances exhibiting the minute knowledge of the designers of this needlework. The fiftieth and fifty-first compartments present us the cooking and the feasting of the Norman army (Fig. 335). We have then the dining of the chiefs; the Duke about to dine, whilst Odo blesses the food; and the Duke sitting under a canopy. The fifty-fifth shows him holding a banner, and giving orders for the construction of a camp at Hastings (Fig. 334).

Six other compartments show us the burning of a house with firebrands, the march out of Hastings, the advance to the battle, and the anxious questioning by William of his spies and scouts as to the approach of the army of Harold. The sixty-third presents a messenger announcing to Harold that the army of William is near at hand. The sixty-fourth bears the inscription, that Duke William addresses his soldiers that they should prepare themselves boldly and skilfully for the battle. We have then six compartments, each exhibiting some scene of the terrible conflict (Figs. 337, 338). The seventy-first shows the death of Harold (Fig. 339). The tapestry abruptly ends with the figures of flying soldiers.

We have probably been somewhat too minute in the description of this remarkable performance. If any apology be necessary, it may be best offered in the words of Mr. Amyot, in his 'Defence of the Early Antiquity of the Bayeux Tapestry,' which is almost conclusive as to the fact of its being executed under the direction of Matilda, the wife of the Conqueror ('Archæologia,' vol. xix). "If the Bayeux Tapestry be not history of the first class, it is perhaps something better. It exhibits genuine traits, elsewhere sought in vain, of the costume and manners of that age which, of all others, if we except the period of the Reformation, ought to be the most interesting to us; that age which gave us a new race of monarchs, bringing with them new landholders, new laws, and almost a new language. As in the magic pages of Froissart, we here behold our ancestors of each race in most of the occupations of life—in courts and camps—in pastime and in battle—at feasts, and on the bed of sickness. These are characteristics which of themselves would call forth a lively interest; but their value is greatly enhanced by their connection with one of the most important events in history, the main subject of the whole design."

END OF BOOK 1

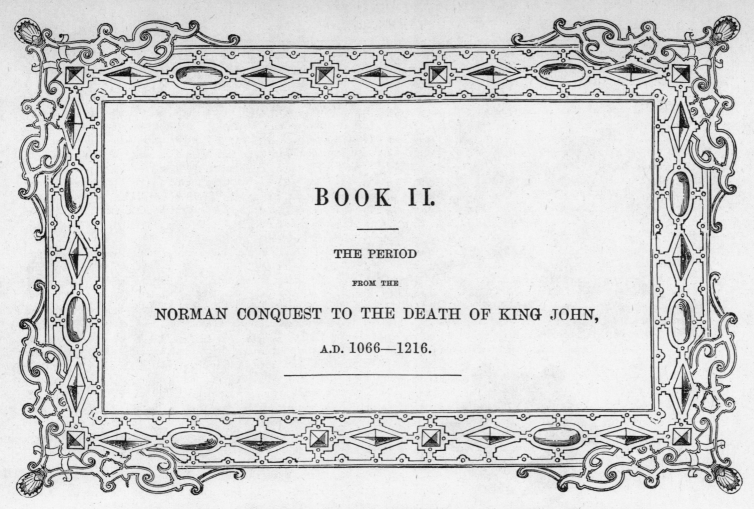

BOOK II.

THE PERIOD

FROM THE

NORMAN CONQUEST TO THE DEATH OF KING JOHN,

A.D. 1066—1216.

CHAPTER I.—REGAL AND BARONIAL ANTIQUITIES.

IN MAGNO NAVIGIO MARE TRANSIVIT, ET VENIT AD PEVENSÆ.

Such is the inscription to the forty-fifth compartment of the Bayeux Tapestry—In a great ship he passes the sea, and comes to Pevensey. The Bay of Pevensey is not now as it was on the 28th of September, A.D. 1066, when this great ship sailed into it, and a bold man, one whose stern will and powerful mind was to change the destiny of England, leaped upon the strand, and, falling upon his face, a great cry went forth that it was an evil omen;—but the omen was turned into a sign of gladness when he exclaimed, with his characteristic oath, "I have taken seisin of this land with both my hands." The shores of the bay are now a dreary marsh, guarded by dungeon-looking towers, which were built to defend us from such another seisin (Fig. 349). The sea once covered this marsh, and the Norman army came a mile or so nearer to the chalk hills, beyond which they knew there was a land of tempting fertility. It must have been somewhat near the old Roman castle that the disembarkation took place, whose incidents are exhibited in the Bayeux Tapestry. Here were the horses removed from the ships: here each horseman mounted his own, and galloped about to look upon a land in which he saw no enemy; here were the oxen and the swine of the Saxon farmer slaughtered by those for whom they were fatted not; here was the cooking, and the dining, and the rude pomp of the confident Duke who knew that his great foe was engaged in a distant conflict. The character of William of Normandy was so remarkable, and indeed was such an element of success in his daring attempt upon the English crown, that what is personally associated with him, even though it be found not in our own island, belongs to the antiquities of England. He was a *stark* man, as the Saxon chronicler describes him from personal knowledge, a man of unbending will and ruthless determination, but of too lofty a character to be needlessly cruel or wantonly destructive. Of his pre-eminent abilities there can be no question. Connected with such a man, then, his purposes and his

success, the remains of his old Palace at Lillebonne (Fig. 345), which may be readily visited by those who traverse the Seine in its steam-boats, is an object of especial interest to an Englishman. For here was the great Council held for the invasion of England, and the attempt was determined against by the people collectively, but the wily chief separately won the assent of their leaders, and the collective voice was raised in vain. More intimately associated with the memory of the Conqueror is the Church of St. Etienne at Caen (Fig. 348), which he founded; and where, deserted by his family and his dependants, the dead body of the sovereign before whom all men had trembled was hurried to the grave, amidst fearful omens and the denunciations of one whom he had persecuted. The mutilated statue of William may be seen on the exterior of the same church (Fig. 347). In England we have one monument, connected in the same distinct manner with his personal character, whilst it is at the same time a memorial of his great triumph and the revolution which was its result—we mean Battle Abbey. When Harold heard—

"That duc Wyllam to Hastynges was ycome,"

he gallantly set forward to meet him—but with an unequal force. He knew the strength of his enemy, but he did not quail before it. The chroniclers say that Harold's spies reported that there were more priests in William's camp than fighting men in that of Harold; and they add that the Saxon knew better than the spies that the supposed priests were good men-at-arms. Mr. Stothard, in his 'Account of the Bayeux Tapestry,' points out, with reference to the figures of the Normans, that "not only are their upper lips shaven, but nearly the whole of their heads, excepting a portion of hair left in front." He adds, "It is a curious circumstance in favour of the great antiquity of the Tapestry, that time has, I believe, handed down to us no other representation of this most singular fashion, and it appears to throw a new light on a fact which has perhaps been misunderstood: the report made by Harold's spies that the Normans were an army of priests is well known. I should conjecture, from what appears in the Tapestry, that their resemblance to priests did not so much arise from the upper lip being shaven, as from the circumstance of the complete tonsure of the back part of the head." Marching out from their entrenched camp at Hastings (Fig. 350), the Normans, all shaven and shorn, encountered the moustached Saxons on the 14th of October. The Tapestry represents the Saxons fighting on foot, with javelin and battle-axe, bearing their shields with the old British characteristic of a boss in

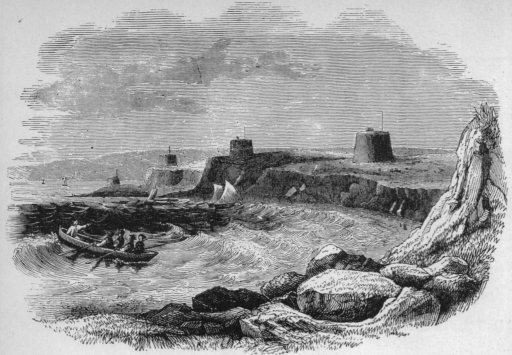

349.—Pevensey Bay, Sussex.

353.—Fire-place, Conisborough Castle.

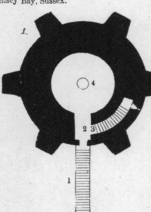

354.—Second Story of Conisborough Castle.

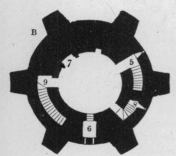

355.—Third Story of Conisborough Castle.

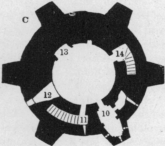

356.—Fourth Story of Conisborough Castle.

352.—William I. granting Lands to his Nephew, the Earl of Brit any. (From the Registrum Honoris de Richmond.)

350.—Hastings, from the Fairlight Downs.

351.—Battle Abbey, as it appeared about 150 years since

357.—Conisborough Castle.

358.—Battle Abbey Gateway.

362.—Walmsgate Barbican, York.

359.—Richmond, Yorkshire.

360.—Richmond Castle from the River Swale.

361.—The Keep of Richmond Castle.

No. 12

the centre. The Normans are on horseback, with their long shields and their pennoned lances. It is not for us to describe the terrible conflict. "The English," says William of Malmesbury, "rendered all they owed to their country." Harold and his two brothers fell at the foot of their standard which they had planted on the little hill of Senlac, and on this spot, whose name was subsequently changed to *Bataille*, was built Battle Abbey (Fig. 351). It was not the pride of the Conqueror alone that raised up this once magnificent monument. The stern man, the hot and passionate man, the man who took what he could get by right and unright, "was mild to good men who loved God." And so he built Battle Abbey.

Robert of Gloucester has thus described, in his quaint verse, the foundation of Battle Abbey :—

"King William bithougt him alsoe of that
    Folke that was forlorne,
And slayn also thorurg him
    In the bataile biforne.
And ther as the bataile was,
    An Abbey he lete rere
Of Seint Martin, for the soules
    That there slayn were.
And the monks wel ynoug
    Feffed without fayle,
That is called in Englonde
    Abbey of Bataile."

Brown Willis tells us that in the fine old parish-church of Battle was formerly hung up a table containing certain verses, of which the following remained :—

"This place of war is Battle called, because in battle here
Quite conquered and overthrown the English nation were.
This slaughter happened to them upon St. Ceelict's day,*
The year whereof. . . . . . this number doth array."

The politic Conqueror did wisely thus to change the associations, if it were possible, which belonged to this fatal spot. He could not obliterate the remembrance of the "day of bitterness," the "day of death," the "day stained with the blood of the brave" (Matthew of Westminster). Even the red soil of Senlac was held, with patriotic superstition, to exude real and fresh blood after a small shower, "as if intended for a testimony that the voice of so much Christian blood here shed does still cry from the earth to the Lord" (Gulielmus Neubrigensis). This Abbey of Bataille is unquestionably a place to be trod with reverent contemplation by every Englishman who has heard of the great event that here took place, and has traced its greater consequences. He is of the mixed blood of the conquerors and the conquered. It has been written of him and his compatriots—

"Pride in their port, defiance in their eye,
I see the lords of human kind pass by."

His national character is founded upon the union of the Saxon determination and the Norman energy. As he treads the red soil of Senlac, if his reformed faith had not taught him otherwise, he would breathe a petition for all the souls, Saxon and Norman, "that there slain were." The Frenchman, whose imagination has been stirred by Thierry's picturesque and philosophical history of the Norman Conquest, will tread this ground with no national prejudices; for the roll of Battle Abbey will show him that those inscribed as the followers of the Conqueror had Saxon as well as Norman names, and that some of the most illustrious of the names have long been the common property of England and of France. But the intelligent curiosity of the visitor to the little town of Battle will be somewhat checked, when he finds that the gates of the Abbey are rigidly closed against him except for a few hours of one day in the week. "The Abbey and grounds can be only seen on Monday," truly says the Hastings Guide. Be it so. There is not much lost by the traveller who comes here on one of the other five days of the week. The sight of this place is a mortifying one. The remains of the fine cloisters have been turned into a dining-room, and, to use the words of the 'Guide-Book,' "Part of the site of the church is now a parterre which in summer exhibits a fine collection of Flora's greatest beauties." This was the very church whose high altar was described by the old writers to have stood on the spot where the body of Harold was found, covered with honourable wounds in the defence of his tattered standard. "Flora's greatest beauties !" "Few persons," adds the 'Guide-Book,' "have the pleasure of admission." We do not envy the few. If they can look upon this desecration of a spot so singularly venerable without a burning blush for some foregone barbarism, they must be made of different stuff from the brave who here fought to the death because they had a country which not only afforded them food and shelter, but the memory of great men and

* St. Calixtus, October the 14th.

heroic deeds, which was to them an inheritance to be prized and defended.

The desecration of Battle Abbey of course began at the general pillage under Henry the Eighth. The Lord Cromwell's Commissioners write to him that they have "cast their book" for the despatch of the monks and household. They think that very small money can be made of the vestry, but they reckon the plunder of the church plate to amount to four hundred marks. Within three months after the surrender of the Abbey it was granted to Sir Anthony Browne ; and he at once set about pulling down the church, the bell-tower, the sacristy, and the chapter-house. The spoiler became Viscount Montacute ; and in this family Battle Abbey continued, till it was sold, in 1719, to Sir Thomas Webster. It has been held, and no doubt truly, that many of the great names that figure on the roll of Battle Abbey were those of very subordinate people in the army of the Conqueror ; and it is possible that the descendants of some of those who roasted for the great Duke the newly-slaughtered sheep on the strand at Pevensey may now look with contempt upon a patent of nobility not older than the days of the Stuarts. But, with all this, it is somewhat remarkable that Battle Abbey, with its aristocratic associations, should have fallen into the hands of a lineal descendant of the master-cook to Queen Elizabeth. Sir Thomas was an enterprising bustling man, who was singularly lucky in South Sea Stock, and had the merit of encouraging the agricultural improvements of Jethro Tull. For the succeeding century of Sir Whistlers and Sir Godfreys, the work of demolition and change has regularly gone forward. The view (Fig. 351) exhibits Battle Abbey as it was about the time that it went out of the Montacute family. Brown Willis, who wrote a little after the same period, thus describes it in his day :—" Though this abbey be demolished, yet the magnificence of it appears by the ruins of the cloisters, &c., and by the largeness of the hall, kitchen, and gate-house, of which the last is entirely preserved. It is a noble pile, and in it are held sessions and other meetings, for this peculiar jurisdiction, which hath still great privileges belonging to it. What the hall was, when in its glory, may be guessed by its dimensions, its length above fifty of my paces; part of it is now used as a hay-barn ; it was leaded, part of the lead yet remains, and the rest is tiled. As to the kitchen, it was so large as to contain five fire-places, and it was arched at top; but the extent of the whole abbey may be better measured by the compass of it, it being computed at no less than a mile about. In this church the Conqueror offered up his sword and royal robe, which he wore on the day of his coronation. The monks kept these till the suppression, and used to show them as great curiosities, and worthy the sight of their best friends, and all persons of distinction that happened to come thither nor were they less careful about preserving a table of the Norman gentry which came into England with the Conqueror."

Horace Walpole has given us a notion of the condition of Battle Abbey, and the taste which presided over it, a century ago. He visited it in 1752, and thus writes to Mr. Bentley : "Battle Abbey stands at the end of the town, exactly as Warwick castle does of Warwick ; but the house of Webster have taken due care that it should not resemble it in anything else. A vast building which they call the old refectory, but which I believe was the original church, is now barn, coach-house, &c. The situation is noble, above the level of abbeys : what does remain of gateways and towers is beautiful, particularly the flat side of a cloister, which is now the front of the mansion-house. A Miss of the family has clothed a fragment of a portico with cockle-shells !"

A general view of Battle Abbey in its present state may be best obtained by passing the old wall, and continuing on the Hastings road for about half a mile. A little valley will then have been crossed ; and from the eminence on the south-east the modern building, with its feeble imitations of antiquity, and its few antiquarian realities, is offered pretty distinctly to the pedestrian's eye. What is perhaps better than such a view, he may, from this spot, survey this remarkable battle-field, and understand its general character. The rights of property cannot shut him out from this satisfaction. The ancient gateway to the abbey, which stands boldly up in the principal street in the town of Battle, is of much more recent architecture than the original abbey. Some hold it to be of the time of Edward the Third ; but the editor of the last edition of 'Dugdale's Monasticon' considers it to be that of Henry the Sixth (Fig. 358).

In the group (Fig. 340) we have given the seal of Battle Abbey, in the lower compartment on the right. The group also contains portraits of the Conqueror and of Harold, views of Pevensey and of Hastings, and a vignette of a Norman and Saxon soldier. The seal of Battle Abbey still remains in the Augmentation Office, attached to the deed of surrender in the time of Henry the Eighth.

The side which our engraving represents exhibits a church, having an ornamented gateway and tower, with four turrets. This, there can be little doubt, represents the church which Sir Anthony Browne destroyed, as churches were destroyed in those days, by stripping the roof of its lead, and converting the timber into building-material or fire-wood.* Time was left to do the rest in part; and as the columns and arches crumbled into ruin, the owners of the property mended their roads with the rich carvings, and turned the altar-tombs into paving-stones—until at last the prettiest of flower-gardens was laid out upon the sacred ground, and the rose and the pansy flourished in the earth which had been first enriched by the blood of the slaughtered Saxons, and grew richer and richer with the bones of buried monks, generation after generation. Truly this is a fitting place for "a fine collection of Flora's greatest beauties." We may be held to speak harshly of such matters; but, as this is the first time we have been called upon so to speak, it may be well that we say a few words as to the course we shall hold it our duty to pursue in all cases where the historical antiquities of our country, and especially where its ecclesiastical antiquities, are swept away upon the principle, just, no doubt, in the main, of doing what we will with our own. The right of private property has no other foundation whatever than the public good. If it could be demonstrated that the public good does not consist with the right of private property, the basis upon which it rests is irrevocably destroyed, and the superstructure falls. But it cannot be so demonstrated. The principle upon which the possessors of Battle Abbey, and a hundred other similar properties in this kingdom, retain their possessions, is a sure one, because it is the same principle that confirms to the humblest in the land the absolute control over the first guinea which he deposits in a Savings-Bank. It would be no greater atrocity, perhaps not so great a one, to reclaim for the Church in the nineteenth century the lands and lordships of the Abbey of Battle, than it was for Henry the Eighth to despoil the Abbey of Battle of those lands and lordships in the sixteenth century. The possessions were wrung from their legal proprietors under the pretext of a voluntary surrender, "with the gibbet at their door." The same process might be repeated under some such pretext of public good. The Church might be again plundered; the possessions of the nobility might be again confiscated; but it would only end in property changing hands. York and Canterbury would have new grantees, and a new Battle Abbey would have a new Sir Anthony Browne. But, looking at all the circumstances under which domains and endowments which are national, at least in their historical memories, have been for the most part originally granted, and are in some instances still possessed, we maintain not only that it is contrary to the spirit of the age, and opposed to the public good, that a continual process of demolition and desecration should go forward, but we hold that, under all just restrictions, the people have a distinct right to cultivate the spirit of nationality, of taste for the beautiful, of reverence for what is old and sacred, by a liberal admission to every fabric which is distinctly associated, in what remains of it, with the history of their country, and the arts and manners of their fore-fathers. It was once contemplated to form an association to prevent the continual destruction of our architectural antiquities. The association has not been formed. But, formed or not, it is no less the duty of those who address the public upon such matters to direct opinion into a right direction; and thus to control those who, in the pride of possession, disregard opinion. It is the continued assertion of this opinion which has at length thrown open the doors of our cathedrals, not so widely as they ought to be opened, but still wide enough to admit those who can pay a little for the sight of noble and inspiriting objects, which ought to be as patent as the blue sky and green trees. It is the assertion of this opinion which has stopped, in some degree, the new white-washing of the fine carved-work of our churches, and the blocking up of their windows and their arches by cumbrous monuments of the pride of the wealthy. But there is yet much to be done. The squire of the parish must have his high pew lowered; and the vicar must learn to dispense with the dignity of his churchwarden's seat blocking up the arch of his chancel. The funds of all cathedrals must in some measure be applied, as they are now in many cases, to the proper restoration of the beauty and grandeur of their tombs and chantries; and not to the destruction of all harmony and proportion, under the guidance of rash ignorance, as formerly at Salisbury. Sacred places which have been made hiding-holes for rubbish, like the Crypt at Canterbury, must be opened to the light. The guardians of our ecclesiastical edifices must, above all, be taught that the house of God was meant to be a house of beauty:

* Horace Walpole was clearly in error in taking the hall, or refectory, for the church.

and that their vile applications of mere utility, their tasteless stalls, their white paint, and their yellow plaster, for the purposes of hiding the glowing colours and the rich imagery of those who knew better than they what belonged to the devotional feeling, will no longer be endured as the badges of a pure and reformed religion; for that religion is not the cold and unimaginative thing which the puritanism of two centuries has endeavoured to degrade it into. We shall do our best not only to direct public attention to the antiquities of our country, and incidentally to the history of our country in a large sense, but we shall take care, as far as in us lies—disclaiming the slightest intention of giving offence to individuals—to contend for a liberal throwing open of those antiquities to the well conducted of the community, whatever be their social position; and to remonstrate against all wanton and ignorant destruction of those remains which wise governments and just individuals ought to have upheld, but which to our shame have in many cases been as recklessly destroyed as if the annals of our country had perished, and we of Old England were a young democracy, rejoicing in our contempt for those feelings which belong as much to the honour and wisdom as to the poetry of civilized life.

———

There is an opinion, which probably may have been too hastily taken up, that previous to the invasion of William of Normandy there were few or no castles or towers of defence in England; and that to this circumstance may be attributed the eventual success which followed his daring inroad. This opinion has had the support of many eminent antiquaries, amongst others of Sir William Dugdale. It is scarcely necessary for us to discuss this point; and therefore, when we come presently to speak of Conisborough Castle, we shall touch very slightly upon the belief of some that it was a Saxon work. That the Conqueror erected castles and impelled his barons to their erection in every part of the kingdom, there can be no doubt. His energy was so great in this mode of defence and protection, that an old Latin chronicler says that he wearied all England with their erection. The general plan of a Norman castle is exhibited in Fig. 346. The keep or dungeon (the tall central building) is numbered 1; the chapel 2; the stable 3; the inner bailey 4; the outer bailey 5; the barbacan 6; the mount for the execution of justice 7; the soldiers' lodgings 8. The following clear and accurate description, by an eminent architect, in the 'Pictorial History of England,' will assist the reader's notion of a Norman castle as conveyed by this ancient plan:—"The Anglo-Norman castle occupied a considerable space of ground, sometimes several acres, and usually consisted of three principal divisions—the outer or lower Ballium (Anglicè, Bailey) or court, the inner or upper court, and the keep. The outer circumference of the whole was defended by a lofty and solid perpendicular wall strengthened at intervals by towers, and surrounded by a ditch or moat. Flights of steps led to the top of this rampart, which was protected by a parapet, embattled and pierced in different directions by loop-holes or chinks, and œillets, through which missiles might be discharged without exposing the men. The ramparts of Rockingham Castle, according to Leland, were embattled on both sides, 'so that if the area were won, the castle-keepers might defend the walls.' The entrance through the outer wall into the lower court was defended by the barbacan, which in some cases was a regular outwork, covering the approach to the bridge across the ditch; but the few barbacans which remain consist only of a gateway in advance of the main gate, with which it was connected by a narrow open passage commanded by the ramparts on both sides. Such a work remained until lately attached to several of the gates of York, and still remains, though of a later date, at Warwick Castle [Fig. 362 exhibits the construction of a barbacan in that of Walmgate Bar, York]. The entrance archway, besides the massive gates, was crossed by the portcullis, which could be instantaneously dropped upon any emergency, and the crown of the arch was pierced with holes, through which melted lead and pitch, and heavy missiles, could be cast upon the assailants below. A second rampart, similar to the first, separated the lower from the upper court, in which were placed the habitable buildings, including the keep, the relative position of which varied with the nature of the site. It was generally elevated upon a high artificial mound, and sometimes enclosed by outworks of its own. The keep bore the same relation to the rest of the castle that the citadel bears to a fortified town. It was the last retreat of the garrison, and contained the apartments of the baron or commandant. In form the Anglo-Norman keeps are varied, and not always regular; but in those of the larger size rectangular plans are the most common, and of the smaller class many are circular. The solidity of their construction is so great, that we find them retaining at least their outward form in the midst of the

N 2

366.—Vignette from the Poem of the Red King.

364.—Great Seal of William Rufus.

365.—Silver Penny of William II. (Brit· Mus.)

370.—Stone in New Forest, marking the site of the Oak-tree against which the Arrow of Sir Walter Tyrrel is said to have glanced.

369.—Yew-tree in Hayes Churchyard.

367.—Hunting Stag. (Royal MS. 2 B. vii.)

368.—Royal Party hunting Rabbits. (Royal MS. 2 B vii.)

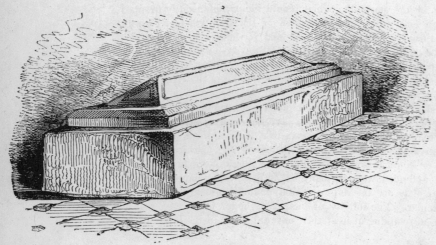

371.—Tomb of Rufus.

372.—Winchester.

374.—Entrance of Rochester Castle.

375.—Rochester Castle: the Keep, with its Entrance Tower.

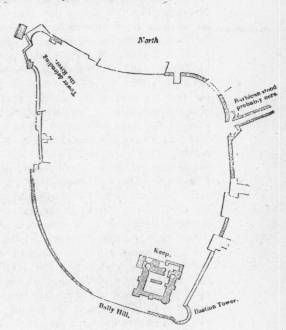

376.—Rochester Castle:—Plan.

373.—Interior of the Remains of the Upper Story of Rochester Castle.

377.—The Tower, from the Thames.

most dilapidated ruin. Time and violence appear to have assaulted them in vain, and even the love of change has respected them through successive generations."

Conisborough Castle, which is pronounced by Mr. King to be of the earliest Saxon times "before the conversion of that people to Christianity," is held by later antiquaries in its extent and arrangement to be a fair representation of the Norman keeps of the smaller class. It is situated in the West Riding of Yorkshire, in the wapentake of Stafforth, and, standing on a steep knowl, commands a splendid view of the winding course of the river Don. It was formerly entered by a drawbridge over a deep fosse. Leland speaks of "the castle standing on a rocket of stone, and ditched. The walls of it have been strong and full of towers." ·By the walls the old topographer means those which surround the keep, which Pennant in his time described as "seemingly circular, and having the remains of four small rounders." The keep, of which a good part is still entire, is a most remarkable building. It was originally four stories high, and is of a circular form, being about twenty-two feet diameter inside. The walls are fifteen feet thick, and they are flanked by six projecting turrets, or square buttresses, running from the top to the bottom, and expanding at the base. The external appearance of the keep does not at first give the impression of its really circular form (Fig. 357). The ground floor or base is described by Pennant as a noisome dungeon of vast depth, at the bottom of which is a draw-well. Fig. 354 exhibits the form of the second story: the steps are numbered 1, the entrance 2, the stairs to the third story 3, the opening to the vaulted story or dungeon below 4. Fig. 355 shows the third story; the stairs from the second floor are numbered 5, the window 6, a closet which shows that our forefathers possessed conveniences which have been thought a modern invention 8, stairs to the fourth story 9; the chimney is numbered 7, and in this and the floor above it is remarkable that the construction of a chimney was not only perfectly well known, but that the form of the opening projecting over the hearth exhibited a degree of elegance which might recommend itself to the tasteless fire-place builders of eight centuries later (Fig. 353). The fourth story is indicated in Fig. 356; a small but well-decorated hexagon room, undoubtedly used as a chapel, formed out of the thickness of the wall and the turret, is numbered 10, the stairs from the third floor 11, the window 12, the chimney 13, the stairs to the platform 14. From this platform there are entrances to six small rooms formed in the six turrets which rise above the parapet. Such were the conveniences of one of the smaller keeps, possessing only a store-room or dungeon, a sort of hall of entrance, two living-rooms, and a chapel, with six pigeon-holes where the retainers slept or cooked their food. Of the larger keeps we shall have particularly to speak when we come to notice the more complete establishment of the feudal system under the immediate successors of the Conqueror. At present we shall content ourselves with a brief description of the Castle of Richmond in Yorkshire, the grant of whose site to its first possessor is distinctly associated with William the Conqueror.

The charter by which the king bestowed the lands of the brave and unfortunate Saxon Earl Edwin upon one of his own followers is thus given by Camden:—" I William, surnamed Bastard, King of England, do give and grant to thee, my nephew, Alan Earl Bretagne, and to thy heirs for ever, all the villages and lands which of late belonged to Earl Edwin, in Yorkshire, with the knight's fees and other liberties and customs, as freely and honourably as the same Edwin held them. Dated from our siege before York." Here then, on this noble hill, nearly encompassed by the river Swale, amidst a landscape of wild beauty, almost of stern grandeur, stands this Castle of Riche-mount, and some of the streets in the little town at its feet have still their Norman names. Alan of Bretagne quickly set to work to defend the broad lands which his kinsman had bestowed upon him, by gathering round him a powerful band safe from attack on this fortressed hill. The castle has been a ruin for three centuries. Even in Leland's time it was a "mere ruin." But yet the great keep, whose walls are ninety-nine feet in height, and eleven in thickness, still defies the wind and the frost, as it once set at nought the battering-ram and the scaling-ladder (Fig. 361). Turrets rise above these walls from the four corners. The keep consisted originally of three stories. The roofs of the two upper stories have now fallen in. There are the ruins of two smaller towers to the south-east and south-west angles of the walls (Fig. 360). The view on the town side is given in Fig. 359.

The grant of lands by the Conqueror to Alan the Breton is represented in a very curious illumination in the register of the Honour of Richmond (Fig. 352). The prolonged resistance made to the power of the Norman invaders in the north brought pillage and slaughter upon the inhabitants of the towns, and confiscation of their lands upon the native chiefs. Villages and manors were given away by scores in every district, to some fortunate follower of the stranger king. It is in Domesday Book, the most extraordinary record of the feudal times, that we can trace the course of the spoliation of the original proprietors of the soil, and the waste and depopulation that had preceded any condition approaching to a tranquil settlement of the country. This book, of which a specimen is given in Fig. 363, is unquestionably the most remarkable monument of the Norman Conquest. No other country possesses so complete a record of the state of society nearly eight centuries ago, as this presents in its registration of the lands of England. By special permission it may be seen in the Chapter-house at Westminster. It was formerly kept in the Exchequer under three different locks and keys. The book familiarly so called really consists of two volumes—one a large folio, the other a quarto, the material of each being vellum. The date of the survey, as indicated in one of these volumes, is 1086. Northumberland, Cumberland, Westmoreland, and Durham were not included as counties in the survey, though parts of Westmoreland and Cumberland are taken. There never was a record which more strikingly exhibited the consequences of invasion and forcible seizure of property. The value of all the estates was to be triply estimated; as that value stood in the time of Edward the Confessor, at the time of its bestowal by the king, and at the formation of the survey. It was found that twenty years after the Conquest the rental of the kingdom was one-fourth less than in the time of thé Confessor; ,and the return was made upon oath. The Saxon chronicler looks upon the Domesday Book as one of the many evidences of the Conqueror's grasping disposition; for he tells us that not a hide or yard of land, not an ox, cow, or hog, was omitted in the census. Later historians have cried up the survey as a monument of the Conqueror's genius for administration. Thierry holds it only to be the result of his special position as chief of the conquering army. This sensible historian has shown, in his notice of Domesday Book, how complete was the spoliation of the Saxon proprietors within twenty years—so complete that the Norman robbers actually record their quarrels with each other for what they call their *inheritance.* Describing the document generally, he says, "The king's name was placed at the head, with a list of his domains and revenues in the county; then followed the names of the chief and inferior proprietors, in the order of their military ranks and their territorial wealth. The Saxons who, by special favour, had been spared in the great spoliation, were found only in the lowest schedule: for the small number of that race who still continued to be free proprietors, or tenants-in-chief of the king, as the conquerors expressed it, were such only for slender domains. They were inscribed at the end of each chapter under the names of thanes of the king, or by some other designation of domestic service in the royal household. The rest of the names of an Anglo-Saxon form, that are scattered here and there through the roll, belong to farmers, holding by a precarious title a few fractions, larger or smaller, of the domains of the Norman earls, barons, knights, serjeants, and bowmen."

The Saxon annalist quaintly writes of the first William, "so much he loved the high deer as if he had been their·father; he made laws that whosoever should slay hart or hind, him man should blind." The depopulation and misery occasioned by the formation of the New Forest have been perhaps somewhat over-stated. A forest undoubtedly existed in this district in the Saxon times. The Conqueror enlarged its circuit and gave it a fresh name. But even William of Jumieges, chaplain to the Conqueror, admits the devastation, in his notice of the deaths of William Rufus and his brother Richard in this Forest:— " There were many who held that the two sons of William the king perished by the judgment of God in these woods, since for the extension of the forest he had destroyed many towns and churches within its circuit." It is this circumstantial statement and popular belief which inspired Mr. William Stewart Rose's spirited little poem of the Red King:—

"Now fast beside the pathway stood
A ruin'd village, shagg'd with wood,
    A melancholy place;
The ruthless Conqueror cast down
(Wo worth the deed) that little town
    To lengthen out his chace.

"Amongst the fragments of the church,
A raven there had found a perch,—
    She flickered with her wing;
She stirr'd not, she, for voice or shout,
She moved not for that revel-rout,
    But croak'd upon the king."

But Mr. Rose does not rest the machinery of his ballad upon tradition alone, or the assertions of prejudiced chroniclers. Adverting to the disbelief of Voltaire in the early history of the New Forest, he points out, in his notes to the poem, what Voltaire did not know, that 'Domesday-Book' establishes the fact that many thousand acres were afforested after the time of Edward the Confessor. The testimony which Mr. Rose himself supplied from his local knowledge is exceedingly curious. "The idea that no vestiges of ancient buildings yet exist in the New Forest, is utterly unfounded, though the fact is certainly little known, and almost confined to the small circle of keepers and ancient inhabitants. In many spots, though no ruins are visible above ground, either the *enceinte* of erections is to be traced, by the elevation of the earth, or fragments of building-materials have been discovered on turning up the surface. The names also of those places would almost, if other evidence were wanting, substantiate the general fact, and even the nature of each individual edifice. . . . . The total rasure of buildings, and the scanty remains of materials under the surface, appear at first a singular circumstance. But it is to be observed, that the mansions, and even the churches of the Anglo-Saxons, were built of the slightest materials, frequently of wood; and that of all countries a forest is the least favourable to the preservation of ruins. As they are the property of the crown, neither the pride nor interest of individuals is concerned in their preservation. . . . . This absence of remains of ruins above the surface need not, therefore, lead us to despair of further discoveries, and these are, perhaps, yet designated by the names of places. May we not consider the termination of *ham* and *ton*, yet annexed to some woodlands, as evidence of the former existence of hamlets and towns?" The historical truth, as it appears to us, may be collected from these interesting notices of Mr. Rose's local researches. The remains of buildings are few, and scattered over a considerable district. The names which still exist afford the best indication that the abodes of men were formerly more numerous. The truth lies between the scepticism of Voltaire as to any depopulation having taken place, and the poetical exaggeration of Pope, in his 'Windsor Forest:'—

> "The fields are ravished from industrious swains,
> From men their cities, and from gods their fanes:
> The levelled towns with weeds lie covered o'er;
> The hollow winds through naked temples roar."

The fact is, that from the very nature of the soil no large population could have been here supported in days of imperfect agriculture. The lower lands are for the most part marshy; the higher ridges are sterile sand. Gilpin has sensibly pointed this out in his book on 'Forest Scenery:'—"How could William have spread such depopulation in a country which, from the nature of it, must have been from the first very thinly inhabited? The ancient Ytene was undoubtedly a woody tract long before the times of William. Voltaire's idea, therefore, of planting a forest is absurd, and is founded on a total ignorance of the country. He took his ideas merely from a French forest, which is artificially planted, and laid out in vistas and alleys. It is probable that William rather opened his chaces by cutting down wood, than that he had occasion to plant more. Besides, though the internal strata of the soil of New Forest are admirably adapted to produce timber, yet the surface of it is in general poor, and could never have admitted, even if the times had allowed, any high degree of cultivation." But, whatever view we take of this historical question, the scenery of the New Forest is indissolubly associated with the memory of the two first Norman hunter-kings. There is probably no place in England which in its general aspect appears for centuries to have undergone so little change. The very people are unchanged. After walking in a summer afternoon for several miles amongst thick glades, guided only by the course of the declining sun,

> "Over hill, over dale,
> Thorough bush, thorough briar,"

we came, in the low ground between Beaulieu and Denny Lodge, upon two peasants gathering a miserable crop of rowan. To our questions as to the proper path, they gave a grin, which expressed as much cunning as idiotcy, and pointed to a course which led us directly to the edge of a bog. They were low of stature, and coarse in feature. The collar of the Saxon slave was not upon their necks, but they were the descendants of the slave, through a long line who had been here toiling in hopeless ignorance for seven centuries. Their mental chains have never been loosened. A mile or two farther we encountered a tall and erect man, in a peculiar costume, half peasant, half huntsman. He had the frank manners

of one of nature's gentlemen, and insisted upon going with us a part of the way which we sought to Lyndhurst. His family, too, had been settled here, time out of mind. He was the descendant of the Norman huntsman, who had been trusted and encouraged, whilst the Saxon churl was feared and oppressed. There is a lesson still to be taught by the condition of the two races in the primitive wilds of the New Forest.

But we are digressing from our proper theme. In these thick coverts we find not many trees, and especially oaks, of that enormous size which indicates the growth of centuries. The forest has been neglected. Trees of every variety, with underwood in proportion, have oppressed each the other's luxuriance. Now and then a vigorous tree has shot up above its neighbours; but the general aspect is that of continuous wood, of very slow and stunted growth, with occasional ranges of low wet land almost wholly devoid of wood. There are many spots, undoubtedly of what we call picturesque beauty; but the primitive solitariness of the place is its great charm. We are speaking, of course, of those parts which must be visited by a pedestrian; for the high roads necessarily lead through the most cultivated lands, passing through a few villages which have nothing of the air of belonging to so wild and primitive a region. Lyndhurst, the prettiest of towns, is the capital of the Forest. Here its courts, with their peculiar jurisdiction, are held in a hall of no great antiquity; but in that hall hangs the stirrup which tradition, from time immemorial, asserts was attached to the saddle from which William Rufus fell, when struck by the glancing arrow of Walter Tyrrell. There is a circumstance even more remarkably associated with tradition, to be found in the little village of Minestead. It is recorded that the man who picked up the body of the Red King was named Purkess; that he was a charcoal-burner; and that he conveyed the body to Winchester in the cart which he employed in his trade. Over the door of a little shop in that village we saw the name of Purkess in 1843—a veritable relic of the old times. Mr. Rose has recorded the fact in prose and verse, of the charcoal-burner's descendants still living in this spot, and still possessing one horse and cart, and no more:—

> " A minestead churl, whose wonted trade
> Was burning charcoal in the glade,
>   Outstretch'd amid the gorse
> The monarch found; and in his wain
> He raised, and to St. Swithin's fane
>   Convey'd the bleeding corse.
>
> And still, so runs our forest creed,
> Flourish the pious woodman's seed
>   Even in the selfsame spot:
> One horse and cart their little store,
> Like their forefather's, neither more
>   Nor less the children's lot.
>
> And still, in merry Lyndhurst hall,
> Red William's stirrup decks the wall;
>   Who lists, the sight may see;
> And a fair stone, in green Malwood,
> Informs the traveller where stood
>   The memorable tree."

The "fair stone," which was erected by Lord Delaware in 1745, is now put into an iron case, of supreme ugliness; and we are informed as follows:—"This stone having been much mutilated, and the inscriptions on each of its three sides defaced, this more durable memorial, with the original inscriptions, was erected in the year 1841, by William Sturges Bourne, Warden." Another century will see whether this boast of durability will be of any account. In the time of Leland, there was a chapel built upon the spot. It would be a wise act of the Crown, to whom this land belongs, to found a school here—a better way of continuing a record than Lord Delaware's stone, or Mr. Sturges Bourne's iron. The history of their country, its constitution, its privileges—the duties and the rights of Englishmen—things which are not taught to the children of our labouring millions—might worthily commence to be taught on the spot where the Norman tyrant fell, leaving successors who one by one came to acknowledge that the people were something not to be despised or neglected. The following is the inscription on the original stone, which is represented at Fig. 370:—

" Here stood the oak-tree on which an arrow, shot by Sir Walter Tyrrell, at a
    stag, glanced, and struck King William II., surnamed Rufus, on the
    breast; of which stroke he instantly died, on the second of August, 1100.
" King William II., surnamed Rufus, being slain, as before related, was laid
    in a cart belonging to one Purkess, and drawn from hence to Winchester,
    and buried in the cathedral church of that city.
" That the spot where an event so memorable had happened might not hereafter be unknown, this stone was set up by John Lord Delaware, who
    had seen the tree growing in this place, anno 1745."

379.—Carlisle Castle.

380.—Carlisle.

381.—St. Mary's Chapel, Hastings, and Ruins of Castle on the Cliff.

382.—Alnwick Castle.

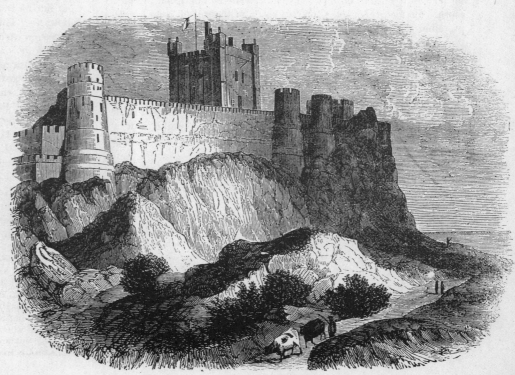

383.—Rock of Bamborough, with the Castle in its present state.

385.—Matilda, Queen of Henry I. From a Statue in the West doorway of Rochester Cathedral.

384.—Great Seal of Henry I.

388.—Mascled Armour.—Seal of Milo Fitz-Walter, Constable of England under Henry I.

387.—Silver Penny of Henry I. From Specimen in Brit. Mus.

390.—Cardiff Castle, as it appeared in 1775.

386.—Monk Bar, York.

389.—Ruins of Reading Abbey, the Burial-place of Henry I., as they appeared in 1721.

In the Cathedral Church of Winchester, which Dr. Milner terms the "ancient mausoleum of royalty" (Fig. 372), is the tomb of William Rufus. "It consists of English grey marble, being of form that is *dos d'âne;* and is raised about two feet above the ground" (Fig. 371). The tomb of the Red King was violated during the parliamentary war in the time of Charles I., and there was found within it "the dust of the king, some pieces of cloth embroidered with gold, a large gold ring, and a small silver chalice." The bones had been enshrined in the time of King Stephen. What remained of these earthy fragments in the sixteenth century had become mixed with the bones of Canute and his queen, and of bishops of good and evil repute. Bishop Fox caused them all to be deposited in one of the mouldering chests which in this Cathedral attract the gaze of the stranger, and carry him, if he be of a contemplative turn, into some such speculations as those of Hamlet, when he traced the noble dust of Alexander till he found it stopping a bunghole.

There are few prospects in England more remarkable, and, in a certain degree, more magnificent, than that which is presented on the approach to Rochester from the road to London. The highest point on the road from Milton is Gadshill, of "men-in-buckram" notoriety. Here the road begins gradually to descend to the valley of the Medway; sometimes, indeed, rising again over little eminences, which in the hop season are more beautifully clothed than are "the vine-covered hills and gay regions of France," but still descending, and sometimes precipitously, to a valley whose depth we cannot see, but which we perceive from the opposite hills has a range of several miles. At a turn of the road we catch a glimpse of the narrow Medway on the south; then to the north we see a broader stream where large dark masses, "our wooden walls," seem to sleep on the sparkling water. At last a town presents itself right before us to the east, with a paltry tower which they tell us is that of the Cathedral. Close by that tower rises up a gigantic square building, whose enormous proportions proclaim that it is no modern architectural toy. This is the great keep of ROCHESTER CASTLE, called Gundulph's Tower (Fig. 375), and there it has stood for eight centuries, defying siege after siege, resisting even what is more difficult to resist than fire or storm, the cupidity of modern possessors. Rochester Castle is, like the hills around it, indestructible by man in the regular course of his operations. It might be blown up, as the chalk hill at Folkestone was recently shaken to its base; but when the ordinary workman has assailed it with his shovel and mattock, his iron breaks upon the flinty concrete; there is nothing more to be got out of it by avarice—so e'en let it endure. And worthy is this old tower to endure. A man may sit alone in the gallery which runs round the tower, and, looking either within the walls or without the walls, have profitable meditations. He need not go back to the days of Julius Cæsar for the origin of this castle, as some have written, nor even to those of Egbert, King of Kent, who "gave certain lands within the walls of Rochester Castle to Eardulf, then Bishop of that see." It is sufficient to believe with old Lambarde, "that Odo (the bastard brother to King William the Conqueror), which was at the first Bishop of Bayeux in Normandy, and then afterward advanced to the office of the Chief Justice of England, and to the honour of the Earldom of Kent, was either the first author or the best benefactor to that which now standeth in sight." Odo rebelled against William II., and was driven from his stronghold and from the realm. The history of the Castle from his time becomes more distinct:—"After this the Castle was much amended by Gundulphus, the Bishop: who (in consideration of a manor given to his see by King William Rufus) bestowed threescore pounds in building that great tower which yet standeth. And from that time this Castle continued (as I judge) in the possession of the Prince, until King Henry the First, by the advice of his barons, granted to William, the Archbishop of Canterbury, and his successors, the custody and office of Constable over the same, with free liberty to build a tower for himself, in any part thereof, at his pleasure. By means of which cost done upon it at that time, the castle at Rochester was much in the eye of such as were the authors of troubles following within the realm, so that from time to time it had a part (almost) in every tragedy." Lambarde, who writes this, tells us truly that in the time of the Conqueror "many castles were raised to keep the people in awe." Such kingly strongholds of oppression were like the "pleasant vices" of common men; they became "instruments to scourge" their makers. Thus, Odo held Rochester Castle against Rufus. The barons successfully maintained it against John. Simon de Montfort carried his victorious arms against its walls, which were defended by the Constable of Henry III. These were some of the tragedies in which Rochester

Castle had a part. But the remains of this building show that its occupiers were not wholly engrossed by feuds and by fighting. The splendid columns, the sculptured arches, of its chief apartments proclaim that it was the abode of rude magnificence; and that high festivals, with luxurious feastings, might be well celebrated within these massive walls (Fig. 373.) This tower, each side of which at the base is seventy feet long, whilst its height is one hundred and twelve feet, has attached to its east angle a smaller tower (probably for domestics), between seventy and eighty feet in height. A partition wall runs up the middle of the larger tower; and the height was divided into four stories. The joists and flooring boards have been torn from the walls, but we see the holes where the timbers were inserted, and spacious fire-places still remain. Every floor was served with water by a well, which was carried up through the central partition. This division of the central tower allowed magnificent dimensions to the rooms, which were forty-six feet in length by twenty-one in breadth. The height of those in the third story is thirty-two feet; and here are those splendid columns, with their ornamented arches, which show us that the builders of these gloomy fortresses had notions of princely magnificence, and a feeling for the beauty of art, which might have done something towards softening the fierceness of their warrior lives, and have taught them to wear their weeds of peace with dignity and grace. Thomas Warton has described, in the true spirit of romantic poetry, such a scene as might often have lighted up the dark walls of Rochester Castle:—

> "Stately the feast, and high the cheer:
> Girt with many an armèd peer,
> And canopied with golden pall,
> Amid Cilgarran's castle hall,
> Sublime in formidable state,
> And warlike splendour, Henry sate,
> Prepar'd to stain the briny flood
> Of Shannon's lakes with rebel blood.
> Illumining the vaulted roof,
> A thousand torches flamed aloof.
> From massy cups with golden gleam,
> Sparkled the red metheglin's stream:
> To grace the gorgeous festival,
> Along the lofty window'd hall
> The storied tapestry was hung;
> With minstrelsy the rafters rung
> Of harps, that with reflected light
> From the proud gallery glitter'd bright."

Fenced round with barbacan and bastion on the land side, and girded with high walls towards the river (Fig. 376), the legal and baronial occupiers of Rochester Castle sat in safety, whether dispensing their rude justice to trembling serfs, or quaffing the red wine amidst their knightly retainers. Even Simon de Montfort, a man of wondrous energy, could make little impression upon these strong walls. But the invention of gunpowder changed the course of human affairs. The monk who compounded sulphur, saltpetre, and charcoal, in their just proportions, made Rochester Castle what it is now. The last repairs which it received were in the reign of Edward VI.; and in that of James I. it was granted by the Crown to Sir Anthony Welldone. His descendant Walker Welldone, Esq., was but an instrument in the hands of mutability to work faster than time. He, good man, "sold the timbers of it to one Gimmit, and the stone stairs, and other squared and wrought stone of the windows and arches, to different masons in London; he would likewise have sold the whole materials of the Castle to a paviour, but on an essay made on the east side, near the postern leading to Bully Hill, the effects of which are seen in a large chasm, the mortar was found so hard, that the expense of separating the stones amounted to more than their value, by which this noble pile escaped a total demolition." (Grose.) The property finally passed into the hands of Mr. Child, the celebrated banker: and it now belongs to the Earl of Jersey, who married the heiress of that house.

The stone bridge at Rochester, over which we still cross the Medway, is a very ancient structure, as old as the time of Edward III. A great captain of that age, Sir Robert Knolles, who, "meaning some way to make himself as well beloved of his countrymen at home as he had been every way dreaded and feared of strangers abroad, by great policy mastered the river of Medway, and of his own charge made over it the goodly work which now standeth." This is Lambarde's account of the matter. But the old Kentish topographer has raked up two ancient documents which show us how great public works were constructed in times when men had first begun to see the necessity of co-operating for public good. The older wooden bridge, which Simon de Montfort fired, and which was wholly destroyed twenty years after by masses of ice floating down the rapid river, was built and maintained at the cost of "divers persons, parcels of lands, and townships, who were of duty bound to bring stuff and bestow both cost and labour in laying it." One of the documents which Lambarde prints is the 'Textus de Ecclesia Roffensi,' which was written in Anglo-Saxon and Latin. It is worth extracting an entry or two, to show how this curious division of labour worked in ancient times. Such a mode of repairing a bridge may provoke a smile; but up to this hour do we retain the same principle of repairing our roads, in the ridiculous statute labour of parishes and individuals. "This is the bridge work at Rochester. Here be named the lands for the which men shall work. First the bishop of the city taketh on that end to work the land pier, and three yards to plank, and three plates to lay, that is from Borstall, and from Cuckstane, and from Frensbury and Stoke. Then the second pier belongeth to Gillingham and to Chetham, and one yard to plank and three plates to lay." And so runs on the record; meting out their work to bishop and archbishop and king, with the aid of lands and townships. These progenitors of ours were not altogether so ignorant of the great principles of political economy as we may have learnt to believe. They knew that common conveniences were to be paid for at the common cost; and that the bridge which brought the men of Rochester and the men of Strood into intimate connexion was for the benefit not of them alone, but of the authorities which represented the State and the Church and the population of the whole district; and therefore the State and the Church and the neighbouring men of Kent, were called upon to maintain the bridge. In these our improved times the burden of public works is sometimes put upon the wrong shoulders.

Gundulphus the bishop, the builder or the restorer, we know not which, of the great keep at Rochester, was the architect of the most remarkable building of the Tower of London. Stow tells us, "I find in a fair register-book of the acts of the Bishops of Rochester, set down by Edmund of Hadenham, that William I., surnamed the Conqueror, builded the Tower of London, to wit, the great white and square tower there, about the year of Christ 1078, appointing Gundulph, then bishop of Rochester, to be principal surveyor and overseer of that work, who was for that time lodged in the house of Edmere, a burgess of London." Speaking of this passage of Stow, the editor of 'London' says, "We see the busy bishop (it was he who built the great keep at Rochester) coming daily from his lodgings at the honest burgess's to erect something stronger and mightier than the fortresses of the Saxons. What he found in ruins, and what he made ruinous, who can tell? There might have been walls and bulwarks thrown down by the ebbing and flowing of the tide. There might have been, dilapidated or entire, some citadel more ancient than the defences of the people the Normans conquered, belonging to the age when the great lords of the world left everywhere some marks upon the earth's surface of their pride and their power. That Gundulph did not create this fortress is tolerably clear. What he built, and what he destroyed, must still, to a certain extent, be a matter of conjecture." And this is precisely the case with the great tower at Rochester. The keep at Rochester and the White Tower at London have a remarkable resemblance in their external appearances (Fig. 377). But we have no absolute certainty that either was the work of the skilful Bishop, who, with that practical mastery of science and art which so honourably distinguished many of the ecclesiastics of his age, was set by his sovereign at both places to some great business of construction or repair. We must be content to leave the matter in the keeping of those who can pronounce authoritatively where records and traditions fail, taking honest Lambarde for our guide, who says, "Seeing that by the injury of the ages between the monuments of the first beginning of this place, and of innumerable such, others be not come to our hands, I had rather in such cases use honest silence than rash speech."

The ruined walls of the Castle of HASTINGS, and the remains of the pretty chapel within those walls, are familiar objects to the visitors of the most beautiful of our watering-places. The situation of this Castle is singularly noble. It was here, according to Eadmer, that almost all the bishops and nobles of England were assembled in the year 1090, to pay personal homage to King William II. before his departure for Normandy. Grose has given a pretty accurate description of this castle, which we abridge with slight alteration. What remains of the castle approaches nearest in shape to two sides of an oblique spherical triangle, having the points rounded off. The base, or south side next the sea, completing the triangle, is formed by a perpendicular craggy cliff about four hundred feet in length, upon which are no vestiges of walls or other fortification. The east side is made by a plain wall measuring nearly three hundred feet, without tower or defence of any kind. The adjoining side, which faces the north-west, is about four hundred feet long. The area included is about an acre and one-fifth. The walls, nowhere entire, are about

eight feet thick. The gateway, now demolished, was on the north side near the northernmost angle. Not far from it, to the west, are the remains of a small tower enclosing a circular flight of stairs; and still farther westward, a sally-port and the ruins of another tower. On the east side, at the distance of about one hundred feet, ran a ditch, one hundred feet in breadth at the top, and sixty feet deep; but both the ditch, and the interval between it and the wall, seem to have gradually narrowed as they approached the gate, under which they terminated. On the north-west side there was another ditch of the same breadth, commencing at the cliff opposite to the westernmost angle, and bearing away almost due north, leaving a level intermediate space, which, opposite to the sally-port, was one hundred and eighty feet in breadth (Fig. 381).

The Castle of CARLISLE was founded by William Rufus. He was the restorer of the city, after it had remained for two centuries in ruins through the Danish ravages. The Red King was a real benefactor to the people at this northern extremity of his kingdom. He first placed here a colony of Flemings, an industrious and skilful race, and then encouraged an immigration of husbandmen from the south, to instruct the poor and ignorant inhabitants in the arts of agriculture. We must not consider that these Norman kings were all tyrants. The historical interest of Carlisle belongs to a later period, and we shall return to it. So does the Castle of ALNWICK (Fig. 382). But we here introduce the noble seat of the Percies, for it was a place of strength soon after the Norman Conquest. In the reign of Rufus it was besieged by Malcolm the Third, of Scotland, who here lost his life, as did his son Prince Edward. Before the Norman Conquest the castle and barony of Alnwick belonged to Gilbert Tyson, who was slain fighting against the invader, by the side of his Saxon King. The Conqueror gave the granddaughter of Gilbert in marriage to Ivo de Vescy, one of his Norman followers; and the Lords de Vescy enjoyed the fair possessions down to the time of Edward I. The Castle of BAMBOROUGH, in Northumberland, carries us back into a remoter antiquity. It was the palace, according to the monkish historians, of the kings of Northumberland, and built by king Ida, who began his reign about 559. Roger Hoveden, who wrote in 1192, describes it, under the name of Bebba, as "a very strong city." Rufus blockaded the castle in 1085, when it was in the possession of Robert de Mowbray, earl of Northumberland. The keep of Bamborough is very similar in its appearance to the keeps of the Tower of London, of Rochester, and of Dover. It is built of remarkably small stones; the walls are eleven feet thick on one side, and nine feet on three sides. This castle, situated upon an almost perpendicular rock, close to the sea, which rises about one hundred and fifty feet above low-water mark, had originally no interior appliances of luxury or even of comfort. Grose says, "Here were no chimneys. The only fire-place in it was a grate in the middle of a large room, supposed to have been the guard-room, where some stones in the middle of the floor are burned red. The floor was all of stone, supported by arches. This room had a window in it, near the top, three feet square, possibly intended to let out the smoke: all the other rooms were lighted only by slits or chinks in the wall, six inches broad, except in the gables of the roof, each of which had a window one foot broad." One of the most remarkable objects in this ancient castle is a draw-well, which was discovered about seventy years ago, upon clearing out the sand and rubbish of a vaulted cellar or dungeon. It is a hundred and forty-five feet deep, and is cut through the solid basaltic rock into the sandstone below. When we look at the history of this castle, from the time when it was assaulted by Penda, the Pagan king of the Mercians, its plunder by the Danes, its siege by Rufus, its assault by the Yorkists in 1463, and so onward through seven centuries of civil strife, it is consoling to reflect upon the uses to which this stronghold is now applied. It was bought with the property attached to it by Nathaniel Lord Crewe, Bishop of Durham, and bequeathed by him to charitable purposes in 1720. The old fortress has now been completely repaired. Its gloomy rooms, through whose loop-holes the sun could scarcely penetrate, have been converted into schools. Boys are here daily taught, and twenty poor girls are lodged, clothed, and educated till fit for service. The towers, whence the warder once looked out in constant watchfulness against an enemy's approach, are now changed into signal-stations, to warn the sailor against that dangerous cluster of rocks called the Fern Islands; and signals are also arranged for announcing when a vessel is in distress to the fishermen of Holy Island. Life-boats are here kept, and shelter is offered for any reasonable period to such as may be shipwrecked on this dreary coast. The estates thus devoted to purposes of charity now yield a magnificent income of more than eight thousand a year. Not only are the poor taught, but the sick

391.—Great Seal of Stephen.

392.—Stephen. Enlarged from a unique Silver Coin in the Collection of Sir Henry Ellis.

394.—Silver Penny of Stephen. From Specimen in Brit. Mus.

397.—Oxford Castle, as it appeared in the Fifteenth Century.

393.—Arms of Stephen.

396.—Tower of Oxford Castle.

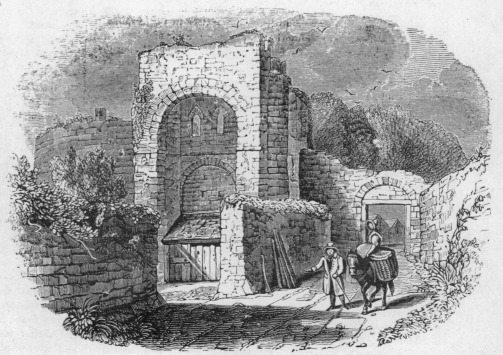

395.—Rougemont Castle.

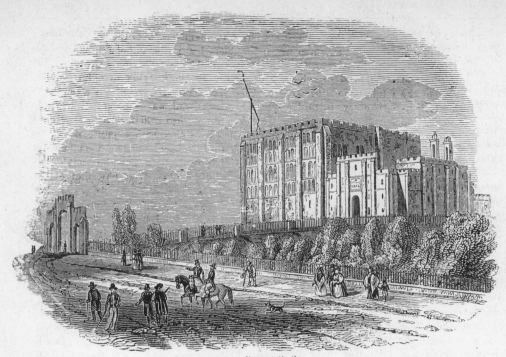

399.—Norwich Castle.

401.—Tegulated Armour.
Seal of Richard, Constable of Chester in the time of Stephen.

398.—South-west View of Norwich Castle.

403.—Standard

404.—Standard.

400.— Winchester.

402—Geoffrey Plantagenet. (Le Bel.) Kerrick's Collect, 6728.

101

are relieved in this hospitable fortress. In the infirmary, to which part of the building is applied, the wants of a thousand persons are annually administered to. Much is still left out of these large funds; and the residue is devoted to the augmentation of small benefices, to the building and enlarging of churches, to the foundation and support of schools, and to exhibitions for young men going to the Universities. When William Rufus besieged this rock of Bamborough, Robert de Mowbray had a steward within the walls, who would have defended it to the death, had not the king brought out the earl his master, who was a prisoner, with a threat that his eyes should be put out unless the castle surrendered. This was a faithful steward. Lord Crewe had an equally faithful steward, after a different fashion, in Dr. Sharpe, Archdeacon of Northumberland, who devised the various means of best applying this noble bequest, and resided on this stormy rock to see that those means were properly administered.

In the fine west doorway of Rochester Cathedral is a statue which is held to represent Matilda, queen of Henry I. (Fig. 385). The marriage of the son of the Norman Conqueror with the niece of Edgar Atheling was a politic measure, which revived the old Saxon feeling in the conquered and oppressed, and made them think that days of equality were in store for them, even under the new race. Matilda the Good was worthy to be a descendant of Alfred. She probably would have been more happy in the cloister to which she had fled for safety during the terrors of the Norman licentiousness, than with her ambitious, daring, profligate, but accomplished husband. Her influence over him did something, no doubt, for ameliorating the condition of her native land. She was a civilizer: she built bridges; she cultivated music. But the promise which Henry had made when he seized the crown, that the old Saxon laws should be restored, was wholly broken as soon as he had fairly grasped the sword of authority. The collection entitled 'The Laws of King Henry I.' is a " compilation of ancient Saxon laws by some private person, and not a publication by authority of the state." The writer of this adds, " The general clamour in England for the Saxon laws of the Confessor, under the three Norman kings, makes it probable that this compilation was made by some private person at the time when the restoration of these laws was called for by, and repeatedly promised to, the nation." ('Ancient Laws and Institutes of England,' published by the Record Commission.) These laws of Edward the Confessor were founded upon older laws, that go back through the times of Canute, and Ethelred, and Edgar, and Athelstan, and Alfred, prescribing many things which are difficult to understand in our present state of society, but upholding a spirit of justice in mercy which later ages have, it is to be feared, not so diligently maintained. The laws of king Ethelred, for example, might furnish a text to be written up in every police court: "And ever, as any one shall be more powerful here in the eyes of the world, or through dignities higher in degree, so shall he the more deeply make 'bôt' (amends, compensation) for sins, and pay for every misdeed the more dearly; because the strong and the weak are not alike, and cannot raise a like burthen." Again here is a noble motto for a judgment-seat: "Let every deed be carefully distinguished, and doom ever be guided justly according to the deed, and be modified according to its degree, before God and before the world; and let mercy be shown for dread of God, and kindness be willingly shown, and those be somewhat protected who need it; because we all need that our Lord oft and frequently grant his mercy to us." This was the spirit of Christianity filling lawgivers with right principles; although some of the institutions of society, such as slavery, were a violation of those principles. For all free men the old Saxon laws were just in their objects, and impartial in their administration. It is easy to understand how they could not exist in connection with the capricious despotism of the first Norman kings, and the turbulence of their grasping retainers. Fortunate was it for the country when a prince arose of such decided character as Henry I.; for he crushed the lesser oppressors, whose evil doings were more constant and universal. It mattered little to the welfare of the country that his unhappy brother Robert was shut up for years in CARDIFF CASTLE, if the king visited his own purveyors with terrible punishments when they ground the people by unjust exactions. In Cardiff Castle (Fig. 390) a dark vaulted room beneath the level of the ground is shown as the place where Robert of Normandy was confined by his brother for twenty-six years. The tradition rests upon no historical foundation whatever, nor, indeed, upon any probability. The gallant but heedless prince, according to William of Malmesbury and other chroniclers, was indeed a prisoner in Cardiff Castle, but surrounded with luxury and magnificence, and provided with minstrels and jesters

to make his life pass away as a gay dream. Matthew Paris tells a curious story, which appears very characteristic of the proud and trifling mind of him whom Beauclerk had jostled out of a throne " It happened on a feast day, that king Henry trying on a scarlet robe, the hood of which being too strait, in essaying to put it on he tore one of the stitches, whereupon he desired one of his attendants to carry it to his brother, whose head was smaller; it always having been his custom whenever he had a new robe to send one cut off from the same cloth to his brother with a polite message. This garment being delivered to Robert, in putting it on he felt the fraction where the stitch had been broken, and through the negligence of the tailor not mended. On asking how that place came torn, he was told that it was done by his brother, and the whole story was related to him: whereupon, falling into a violent passion, he thus exclaimed: ' Alas! alas! I have lived too long! Behold my younger brother, a lazy clerk, who has supplanted me in my kingdom, imprisoned and blinded me! I who have been famous in arms! And, now, not content with these injuries, he insults me as if I were a beggar, sending me his cast-off clothes as for an alms!' From that time he refused to take any nourishment, and, miserably weeping and lamenting, starved himself to death. He was buried in Gloucester Cathedral, where his image, as big as the life, carved in Irish oak and painted, is yet shown." Death levelled these distinctions in the same year. If Robert died of mortification about a cast-off robe, Henry perished more ignobly of a full meal of lampreys. Robert's effigy of heart of oak was carefully repaired by a stranger two centuries ago. The monument of Henry in Reading Abbey, which he founded, perished long since, and scarcely a stone is now left standing of this princely building, to tell the tale of his pious munificence (Fig. 389).

The successor of Henry Beauclerk was also an usurper. The rival pretensions of Stephen of Blois and the Empress Matilda filled the land with bloodshed and terror for nineteen years. From the north to the south, from the Barbacans of York (Fig. 386) to the Palaces of Winchester (Fig. 400), the country was harried by king and baron, by empress and knight. A single burst of patriotism carried the English to fight with one accord at Northallerton, under the car-borne standard of Stephen (Fig. 403). But during the greater part of this period almost every baron's castle had to sustain a siege on one side or the other; and, what was worse, the lands around these strongholds were uniformly wasted by the rapacious garrison, or their plundering assailants. Stephen had given to the nobles the fatal power of fortifying their castles; and it is affirmed that towards the latter end of his reign these "nests of devils and dens of thieves," as Matthew Paris styles them, amounted to the number of eleven hundred and fifteen. A contemporary annalist of the deeds of King Stephen thus describes the miseries of the people during this desolating contest:—" Many abandoned their country; others, forsaking their houses, built wretched huts in churchyards, hoping for protection from the sacredness of the place. Whole families, after sustaining life as long as they could by eating herbs, roots, dogs, and horses, perished at last with hunger; and you might see many pleasant villages without one inhabitant of either sex." There is scarcely a castle of the period that is not associated with some memory of this war of ambition. The Saxon Chronicler says, " In this king's time all was dissension, and evil, and rapine. The great men soon rose against him. They had sworn oaths, but maintained no truth. They built castles which they held out against him." It was thus that Hugh Bigod, who had sworn that Henry had appointed Stephen his successor, was the first to hold out against the king in the CASTLE OF NORWICH, which his ancestor had built. NORWICH was a regular fortress, with a wall and ditch, an outer, a middle, and an inner court, and a keep. The bridge over one of the ditches and the keep still remain. The keep had long since gone through the customary process of being turned into a jail, and the jail being removed it is now gutted and roofless. This keep is a parallelogram, a hundred and ten feet in length by about ninety-three in breadth. The walls are in some places thirteen feet thick, and the tower is seventy feet in height. It was not sufficient for the people in authority in the last century to tear this fine historical monument to pieces, by their fittings up and their pullings down, but they have stuck on their county gaol at one end—a miserable modern thing called Gothic—paltry in its dimensions, and incongruous in its style (Figs. 398, 399). The same process has been resorted to at OXFORD CASTLE. It was built by Robert de Oilies, a Norman who came over with the Conqueror. Not even the romance connected with its history could save Oxford Castle from desecration. It was a little county prison a century ago, and it is a great county prison in our own day. It is something, indeed, to see the strongholds of lawless oppressors becoming monuments of the power of the

Law. We shall speak of more of these presently. But, nevertheless, in a seat of learning, in a place consecrated to ancient recollections, we would gladly have had other associations than chains and gibbets, with the venerable walls from which Matilda escaped through beleaguering hosts in a night of frost and snow, and, crossing the frozen Thames, wandered in darkness for many a mile, till she reached a place of safety. Holinshed tells the story with the simplicity of the elder chroniclers:—"It was a very hard winter that year; the Thames and other rivers thereabouts were frozen, so that both man and horse might safely pass over upon the ice: the fields were also covered with a thick and deep snow. Hereupon, taking occasion, she clad herself and all her company in white apparel, that afar off they might not be discerned from the snow; and so, by negligence of the watch, that kept ward but slenderly, by reason of the exceeding cold weather, she and her partakers secretly in the night issued out of the town, and passing over the Thames, came to Wallingford, where she was received into the castle by those that had the same in keeping to her use: of whom Brian, the son to the Earl of Gloucester, was the chief." The "gaping chinks and aged countenance" of ROUGEMONT CASTLE at Exeter (Fig. 395) are something more in character with the old times than the feeble patchwork of antiquarianism, the parapets and pepper-boxes of our modern castle prisons, pertly bristling up by the sides of these old donjons.

The personal history of Henry II., one of the greatest kings that ever sat upon the English throne, belongs more strikingly to the ecclesiastical than to the civil annals of those times. The story of his wonderful contest with Becket may be best referred to in connection with the scene of Becket's martyrdom. That story was everywhere made familiar to the people by legend and painting (Fig. 411). The romance of Henry's personal history, in connection with Rosamond Clifford, was long associated with the old towers of Woodstock. These are no more; but what they were is shown in Figs. 413, 414.

It is a rare consolation for the lover of his country's monuments, to turn from castles made into prisons, and abbeys into stables, to such a glorious relic of 'Old England' as WARWICK CASTLE. Who can forget the first sight of that beautiful pile, little touched by time, not vulgarized by ignorance? (Fig 417). As he enters the portal through which Gaveston was led to execution, and the king-maker marched in and out to uphold a Yorkist or a Lancastrian pretender to the crown, he feels that he is treading upon ground almost hallowed by its associations (Fig. 415). Cæsar's Tower—that is but a name! Guy's Tower—that belongs to poetry, and is therefore a reality! (Fig. 416). Old Dugdale treated Guy and his legend as a true thing. "Of his particular adventures, lest what I say should be suspected for fabulous, I will only instance that combat betwixt him and the Danish champion, Colebrand, whom some (to magnify our noble Guy the more) report to have been a giant. The story whereof, however it may be thought fictitious by some, forasmuch as there be those that make a question whether there was ever really such a man, or, if so, whether all be not a dream which is reported of him, in regard that the monks have sounded out his praises so hyperbolically; yet those that are more considerate will neither doubt the one nor the other, inasmuch as it hath been so usual with our ancient historians, for the encouragement of after-ages unto bold attempts, to set forth the exploits of worthy men with the highest encomiums imaginable; and therefore, should we for that cause be so conceited as to explode it, all history of those times might as well be vilified." We shall have to return to the fair castle of Warwick: so we leave it, at present, under the influence of Guy and his legends (Fig. 418).

In glancing generally over the subject of the present state of the ancient Castles of England, a striking commentary is afforded to us upon the progress that England has made since they studded the land over with their stately but terrible walls, and gateways, and towers. Look, for instance (to refer only to structures not already mentioned), at FARNHAM CASTLE, in Surrey (Fig. 426), built by Henry of Blois, brother of King Stephen, and forming, no doubt, one of the eleven hundred castles said to have been erected in the reign of that monarch. Eleven hundred castles built in sixteen years! What a scene of violence and strife does not the bare mention of such a fact open to the imagination! It is to that scene Farnham Castle essentially belongs; and if we now gaze upon it, as it is, most strange in all respects appears the contrast between the present and the past associations. The lofty keep stands in a garden forming a picturesque and noble ornamental ruin in the palatial grounds of the Bishops of Winchester, but that is its only value

to the present possessors; it looks down upon the principal street of the place, which probably first grew up into importance under its protection, but it is only now to behold a population exhibiting in a thousand ways their enjoyment of the services of an infinitely more powerful defender—the Law. In numerous other cases our castles have become direct adjuncts to the very power that has thus superseded them. York, Lancaster, and Lincoln Castles are now mere gaols for the confinement, or courts for the trial of prisoners; and that amazing piece of workmanship, which attests to this day the strength of the first of these structures, CLIFFORD'S TOWER (Fig. 423), attributed to the Conqueror, whilst the mount on which it stands is supposed to have been raised by Roman hands, now frowns in unregarded magnificence over the throng of judges, barristers, and witnesses, of debtors and criminals, who pass to and fro through the modern gateway at its feet. Then, again, NEWARK CASTLE (Fig. 425), erected by Bishop Alexander, the well-known castle-building prelate, who seems indeed to have thought he had a mission that way, and who certainly exhibited no lack of zeal in fulfilling it; Newark (i. e., New-Work, hence the name of the town), a rare example for the time of any departure from the principle of considering a castle merely as a stronghold, rather than as a place of residence also; Newark, with its high historical and military reputation, twice unsuccessfully besieged by the Parliamentarians during the Civil War, and only delivered up, not taken, at last in consequence of Charles's own directions when he had given himself up to the Scots—under what circumstances do we behold the ruins of this structure? Why, as if in mockery of that reputation, wooden bowls now roll noiselessly but harmlessly about the close-shaven green, in one part of the castle area, where cannon-balls once came thick and fast, dealing destruction and death on all sides; whilst in another, peaceful men and women now congregate in the "commodious market." Pontefract, or POMFRET CASTLE (Fig. 429), of still higher historical interest, exhibits a change and a moral no less remarkable. The rocky foundation upon which the castle was raised, at an enormous expenditure of time, money, and labour, is now a quarry of filtering-stones, which are, we are told, in great request all over the kingdom; the place, for the maintenance of which the neighbourhood has been so often of yore laid under contribution, now in some measure repays those old exactions from the liquorice-grounds and market-gardens that occupy its site. The liquorice-grounds, we may observe by the way, form quite a distinctive feature of the country immediately surrounding Pontefract, that quietest, and cleanest, and widest-streeted of provincial towns, which, within some fourteen miles of the manufacturing Babel, Leeds, is so little like Leeds, that one might fire a cannon-ball down its main street at noon-day with but very small danger of mischief. We must dwell a little on the history of Pomfret Castle. Royal favour is generally attended with substantial tokens of its existence; but of all English sovereigns who have had at once the will and the power to distinguish their friends in this way, commend us to the Conqueror. The builder of Pomfret Castle was Ilbert de Lacy, who received from William one hundred and fifty manors in the west of Yorkshire, ten in Nottinghamshire, and four in Lincolnshire. Pontefract was among the first, though not it seems previously known by that name, which is said to have been conferred on it by De Lacy from its resemblance to a place in Normandy, where he was born: a pleasant touch of sentiment in connection with one of those formidable mailed barons who struck down at once England's king and liberties on the fatal field of Hastings. The area enclosed by the castle-walls was about seven acres, the walls being defended by the same number of towers. It had of course its deep moat, barbacan, and drawbridge, and its great gateways of entrance. Leland says of the main structure, "Of the Castle of Pontefract, of some called Snorre Castle, it containeth eight round towers, of the which the dungeon cast into six roundelles, three big and three small, is very fair." We should be sorry to wish that the excellent antiquarian had had an opportunity of a closer acquaintance with the "fair" dungeon, but assuredly if he had, he would have chosen a somewhat different epithet, in spite of its external beauty. The dungeons of Pontefract Castle have excited no less fearful interest from their intrinsic character, than from the prisoners who have wept or raved in them to the senseless walls. In the early part of the fourteenth century, Thomas, Earl of Lancaster, uncle of Edward II., married Alice, daughter of Henry de Lacy, and thus became the lord of Pontefract. Among the barons then opposed to the weak and disgraceful government of Edward II. the Earl of Lancaster was conspicuous; but in one of those reverses of fortune which his party experienced, he, with many other nobles and knights, fell into the hands of the royalists, was brought by them to his own Castle of Pontefract, then in their

405.—Great Seal of Henry II.

406.—Henry II. Drawn from the tomb at Fontevraud.

409.—Arms of Henry II.

408.—Silver Penny of Henry II. From a specimen in Brit. Mus.

410.—Planta Genista.

411.—The Martyrdom of Thomas a Becket. From an ancient painting in the Chapel of the Holy Cross, Stratford.

413.—Woodstock.

414.—Woodstock, as it appeared before 1714.

412.—Eleanor, Queen of Henry II. From the Tomb at Fontevraud.

407.—Effigy of Henry II. From the Tomb at Fontevraud.

415.—Entrance to Warwick Castle.

416.—Warwick Castle; Guy's Tower.

417.—Warwick Castle, from the Island.

418.—Ancient Statue of Guy, at Guy's Cliff.

420.—Interior of a Room in Warkworth Castle.

419.—Warkworth Castle.

421.—Ludlow Castle.

No. 14.

105

possession, and there, without even a hearing, beheaded, whilst the other barons were hung. As the owner of the castle and the broad lands sweeping so far away on all sides around it lay helpless in his own dungeons, in the brief interval that elapsed between his capture and horrible death, what thoughts may not, we might almost say must not, have crowded into the brain of the unhappy nobleman! Taught, perhaps, when too late, the wisdom of humanity and love, we may imagine him giving utterance to some such thoughts as those expressed by the poet:—

> "And this place our forefathers made for man!
> This is the process of our love and wisdom
> To each poor brother who offends against us—
> Most innocent, perhaps—and what if guilty?
> Is this the only cure?"

Or as he reflected with unutterable anguish on the beauty of the scene without—that scene on which he had so often gazed with heedless eyes, but that, now that he was to behold it but *once* more, seemed to his imagination bathed in loveliness and romance—could he fail to arrive in some degree at the poet's conclusion?—

> "With other ministrations, thou, O Nature,
> Healest thy wandering and distempered child;
> Thou pourest on him thy soft influences,
> Thy sunny hues, fair forms, and breathing sweets,
> Thy melodies of woods, and winds, and waters,
> Till he relent, and can no more endure
> To be a jarring and a dissonant thing
> Amid this general dance and minstrelsy;
> But, bursting into tears, wins back his way,
> His angry spirit healed and harmonised
> By the benignant touch of love and beauty."

Alas, that the truths here so exquisitely conveyed should be still unregarded! The dungeons of a former day have changed their name, and improved in their superficial characteristics, it is true; but only to fit them for still more extensive application. When "such pure and natural outlets" of a man's nature are

> "shrivelled up
> By ignorance and parching poverty,

and

> His energies roll back upon his heart,
> And stagnate and corrupt, till, changed to poison,
> They break out on him, like a loathsome plague-spot,

we still

> call in our pampered mountebanks;
> And theirs is their best cure! Uncomforted
> And friendless solitude, groaning and tears."

But the dungeons of Pontefract Castle whisper of a still more fearful story than the Earl of Lancaster's. As we walk about among the ruins, and investigate the process of decay, since Gough, the editor of Camden, describes in the last century the remains of the keep as consisting only of the "lower story, with horrible dungeons and winding staircases;" we look with especial interest for the "narrow damp chamber formed in the thickness of the wall, with two small windows next the court," where tradition says the fate of Richard II. was consummated, either by direct violence, as the popular story has it, through the agency of Sir Piers Exton and his band of assassins, some of whom perished in the struggle, or by starvation, as other writers have related the matter. In the short reign of the third Richard, another batch of eminent men underwent the sharp agony of the axe at Pontefract Castle, namely, Woodville, Rivers, Grey, Vaughan, and Hawse. The edifice was finally dismantled and the materials sold, after the civil war, during which it had resisted the parliamentary forces with extraordinary bravery and determination, even subsequent to the death of Charles I.

This said civil war was to our old castles generally, what the Reformation was to our grand and beautiful ecclesiastical remains; with this difference, that the injuries in the one case were necessarily of a much severer character than in the other. Hence we find, in looking back to the history of a large portion of our castles, that they were comparatively in good preservation up to the sixteenth century, and in ruin beyond that time. GOODRICH CASTLE, Herefordshire (Fig. 422), was one of these, the owners of which could boast that the structure dated from a period anterior to the Conquest; and during the civil war it was defended with a courage worthy of its reputation. It is recorded of Goodrich Castle that it held out longer than any other English fortress for the king, with the single exception of Pendennis Castle, in Cornwall. If one could grieve at a matter that necessarily involves so many points for congratulation, we might lament to see how few and comparatively unimportant are the remains of such a castle, interesting to us for its age, and still more by the memory of one at least of its early inhabitants, the brave Talbot of history, and of Shakspere's

Henry the Sixth (First Part). It appears from the records of Goodrich Castle, that when a great man in the middle ages erected a fortress, it was not always the expensive affair we are accustomed to consider it. Goodrich, in the fourteenth century, came into the possession of Elizabeth, daughter of John Lord Comyn, of Badenagh, in Scotland. The notorious Hugh le Despencer and his son, it appears, had taken a particular fancy for portions of this lady's property, and the way they set about the accomplishment of their desires speaks volumes as to the state of society at the period. The lady Elizabeth was suddenly seized, carried into another part of the country, confined for upwards of a year, and finally compelled, from "fear of death," as it is stated in a manuscript cited by Dugdale in his 'Baronage,' to cede to the son her castle of Goodrich, and to the father her manor of Painswick. Certainly, as with these feudal oppressors even-handed justice did often commend the poisoned chalice to their own lips, there is something more than accident in such remarkable conjunctions as the fate of the Earl of Lancaster before mentioned and the character of the dungeons in his castle—in the wrongs done to this lady and the character of the dungeons still traceable among the ruins of her castle. The keep, of Saxon, or very early Norman architecture, originally consisted of three small rooms, one above another; at the bottom was a dungeon, which had *not even a single loop-hole for light or air*, but was connected by a narrow passage with another and smaller dungeon, situated beneath the platform of the entrance-steps of the exterior, which had a very small opening for the admission of air; and thus alone was life preserved even for a time in the inner dungeon. It is a relief to escape from such dreadful recollections of our old castles, to the gay and brilliant scenes that occasionally made them the centres of enjoyment to assembled thousands, when, for instance, the tournament brought from all parts of the country the young and old, rich and poor, the knightly and the would-be knightly, to see lances broken or to break them, to conquer or to be conquered. There were occasions, too, when the exciting and brilliant sports of the tournament were enhanced by peculiar circumstances, calculated in the highest degree to attract, not only the chivalry of Old England, but of Europe, into the lists. One of the most grandly situated of castles is that of PEVERIL of the Peak (Fig. 424), built by a natural son of the Conqueror, whose name it bears. This was some centuries afterwards in the possession of William Peveril, a valiant knight, who had two daughters, one of whom, Mellet, having privily resolved to marry none but a knight who should distinguish himself for his warlike prowess, her father, sympathizing with her feelings, determined to invite the noble youth of England generally to compete for such a prize in a grand tournament. The castle of Whittington, in the county of Salop, was also to reward the victor by way of a fitting dowry for the bride. We may judge of the hosts who would assemble at such an invitation; and even royal blood was among them, in the person of the Scottish King's son. Worthy of the day, no doubt, were the feats performed. Among the combatants, one knight with a silver shield and a peacock for his crest speedily distinguished himself. The best and bravest in vain endeavoured to arrest his successful career. The Scottish prince was overthrown; so was a baron of Burgoyne. Their conqueror was adjudged the prize. Guarine de Meez, a branch of the house of Lorraine, and an ancestor of the lord Fitzwarren, thus wooed and won an English bride, at Peveril's Place in the Peak.

There are two castles that belong to the present period, inasmuch as that their erection chiefly took place in it; we allude to Carisbrook, in the Isle of Wight, and Kenilworth; but as in both cases the most essential points of their subsequent history refer to later periods, we shall confine our present notices to the erection. CARISBROOK (Fig. 427) stands at a short distance from the town of Newport, and near the central point of the isle, of which, from the days of the Saxons and of the isle's independent sovereignty down to a comparatively recent period, it has been the chief defence. The keep, and the great artificial mound on which it stands, are supposed to have been erected so early as the sixth century. Five centuries later, the Norman possessor, Fitz-Osborne, desiring to enlarge his fortress, built additional works, covering together a square space of about an acre and a half, with rounded angles, the whole surrounded by a fosse or ditch. All lands in the isle were then held of the castle, or in other words, of the honour of Carisbrook; and on the condition of serving and defending it at all times from enemies. Of this early building, which still formed only the nucleus of the very extensive and magnificent fortress which ultimately was raised on the spot, the chief remains are the western side of the castle, forming an almost regular parallelogram, with rounded corners; and the keep, on the north, ascended by a flight of seventy-two steps. The lowest story only is preserved. In the centre of the keep there is a well 300 feet deep, telling, by its very formation under such difficult circumstances, the importance of its existence. KENILWORTH (Fig. 430) seems to have derived its name and its earliest castle from the fortress mentioned by Dugdale as standing, even in the Saxon times, upon a place called Hom, or Holme Hill, and which, it is supposed, was built by one of the Saxon kings of Mercia, named Kenulph, and his son Kenelm. Worth, in the Saxon, means mansion or dwelling-place; consequently the formation of the word Kenilworth is tolerably clear. But other writers consider this date as much too modern: to carry back the history of Kenilworth only to a Saxon king is not sufficient; we must go to the Britons at once, and their great sovereign of romance, and perhaps reality—Arthur,

"That here, with royal court, abode did make."

Whatever the beginning of this castle, its end seems certain enough: Dugdale says it was demolished in the wars between King Edmund and Canute the Dane. About a century later, or in the reign of Henry the First, the present castle was commenced by Geoffrey de Clinton, who is stated "to have been of very mean parentage, and merely raised from the dust by the favour of the said King Henry, from whose hands he received large possessions and no small honour, being made both Lord Chamberlain and Treasurer to the said King, and afterwards Justice of England; which great advancements do argue that he was a man of extraordinary parts. It seems he took much delight in this place, in respect of the spacious woods and that large and pleasant lake (through which divers petty streams do pass) lying amongst them; for it was he that first built that great and strong castle here, which was the glory of all these parts, and for many respects may be ranked in the third place at the least with the most stately castles in England." Dugdale ('Baronage') here refers no doubt to the strength, size, and architectural character of the castle; but if its historical importance be considered, or, above all, if we weigh the associations which a single writer of our own age has bound up with its decaying walls, we must assign to it a rank that knows no superior: we must consider the "glory of these parts" might now without exaggeration be more accurately described as the glory of the civilized world.

With a group of border castles—Norham, Warkworth, and Newcastle—we shall conclude for the present our notice of such structures. No mention is made in Domesday-Book of the county of Northumberland, in which these three castles are situated, for the reason probably that the Conqueror could not even pretend to have taken possession of it. And there was then little temptation to induce him to achieve its conquest. Nothing can be conceived more truly anarchic than the state of the country in and around Northumberland at the time. The chief employment of the inhabitants was plundering the Scots on the other side of the Tweed—their chief ambition was to avoid being plundered in return. But the Scots seem generally to have had the best of it; who, not content with taking goods, began to take the owners also, and make domestic slaves of them. It is said that about or soon after the period of the Conquest, there was scarcely a single house in Scotland that was without one or more of these English unfortunates. To check such terrible inroads, castles now began to spring up in every part; to these the inhabitants generally of a district flocked on any alarm of danger; and for centuries such a state of things continued unchanged. A highly interesting picture of domestic border life, and which is at the same time unquestionably trustworthy, has been preserved in the writings of Pope Pius II., who, before his elevation to the pontificate visited various countries in an official capacity—amongst the rest Scotland, to which he was sent as private legate about the middle of the fifteenth century. "The Border Land" naturally attracted his curiosity, and he determined to risk the danger of a personal visit. He thus describes the result. His family name, it may be mentioned, was Æneas Sylvius Piccolomini.

"There is a river (the Tweed) which, spreading itself from a high mountain, parts the two kingdoms. Æneas having crossed this in a boat, and arriving about sunset at a large village, went to the house of a peasant, and there supped with the priest of the place and his host. The table was plentifully spread with large quantities of pulse, poultry, and geese, but neither wine nor bread was to be found there; and all the people of the town, both men and woman, flocked about him as to some new sight; and as we gaze at negroes or Indians, so did they stare at Æneas, asking the priest where he came from, what he came about, and whether he was a Christian. Æneas, understanding the difficulties he must expect on this journey, had taken care to provide himself at a certain monastery with some loaves, and a measure of red wine, at sight of which

they were seized with greater astonishment, having never seen wine or white bread. The supper lasting till the second hour of the night, the priest and host, with all the men and children, made the best of their way off, and left Æneas. They said they were going to a tower a great way off, for fear of the Scots, who when the tide was out would come over the river and plunder; nor could they, with all his entreaties, by any means be prevailed on to take Æneas with them nor any of the women, though many of them were young and handsome; for they think them in no danger from an enemy, not considering violence offered to women as any harm. Æneas therefore remained alone with them, with two servants and a guide, and a hundred women, who made a circle round the fire, and sat the rest of the night without sleeping, dressing hemp and chatting with the interpreter. Night was now far advanced when a great noise was heard by the barking of the dogs and screaming of the geese; all the women made the best of their way off, the guide getting away with the rest, and there was as much confusion as if the enemy was at hand. Æneas thought it more prudent to wait the event in his bed-room (which happened to be a stable), apprehending if he went out he might mistake his way, and be robbed by the first he met. And soon after the women came back with the interpreter, and reported there was no danger: for it was a party of friends, and not of enemies, that were come." (Camden's translation.) Just such a castle of defence for a population, rather than a residence for their lord, we may suppose NORHAM (Fig. 428) to have been built by the Bishops of Durham, about the beginning of the twelfth century; the gloomy ruins which still overhang the Tweed exhibiting no traces of exterior ornament, its walls reduced to a mere shell, its outworks demolished, and a part of the very hill on which it was raised washed away by the river. The keep alone exists in a state to remind us of the original strength and importance of the fortress, when it was so frequently the scene of contest between the people of the two countries. On the accession of Stephen we find David of Scotland besieging and capturing Norham, for Maud, Stephen's rival; a little later the process was repeated by and for the same parties; and then Norham is said to have been demolished. In the reign of John, however, we find it in existence, stronger than ever, and successfully resisting the utmost efforts of the Scots, then in alliance with the revolted English Barons. The next time the defenders were less brave, or less fortunate: in the reign of Edward III. the Scots once more obtained possession of Norham. But we need not follow its history further; so by way of contrast to the scene as represented in our engraving, let us transcribe a glimpse of Norham Castle under more favourable circumstances:—

"Day set on Norham's castle steep,
And Tweed's fair river, broad and deep,
    And Cheviot's mountains lone;
The battled towers, the dragon keep,
The loop-hole grates, where captives weep,
The flanking walls that round it sweep,
    In yellow lustre shone.

"The warriors on the turrets high,
Moving athwart the evening sky,
    Seem'd forms of giant height;
Their armour, as it caught the rays,
Flash'd back again with western blaze
    In lines of dazzling light."
                                        MARMION.

The ruins of WARKWORTH (Figs. 419, 420), in their generally elegant and picturesque outline, present a strong contrast to those of Norham. Residence for the lord as well as protection for his vassals has evidently been studied here. The situation in itself is wonderfully fine. It stands on an eminence above the river Coquet, a little beyond the southern extremity of the town of Warkworth, and commands on all sides views of the greatest beauty and variety. In one direction you have the sea outspread before you, with the Fern Islands scattered over its surface; whilst along the shore-line the eye passes to the Castles of Dunstanborough and Bamborough at the extremity; in another you dwell with pleasure on the richly cultivated valley that extends up to Alnwick Castle; then again in a third, there are the beautiful banks of the Coquet river, dear to salmon-fishers and lovers of native precious stones, many of which are found among its sands; and lastly, in a fourth, you gaze upon an extensive plain inclining seawards, and which is as remarkable for the fertility of its soil, and the amount of its agricultural products, as for the air of peaceful happiness that overspreads the whole—pasture, arable, and woodlands, villages, hamlets, and churches. Such was the site, and the structure was scarcely less magnificent. The outer walls, which are in many parts entire, enclosed a space of about five acres,

423.—Clifford's Tower, and Entrance to York Castle.

425.—Interior of Newark Castle.

422.—Goodrich Castle

421.—Peveril Castle, Derryshire.

429.—Pomfret Castle.

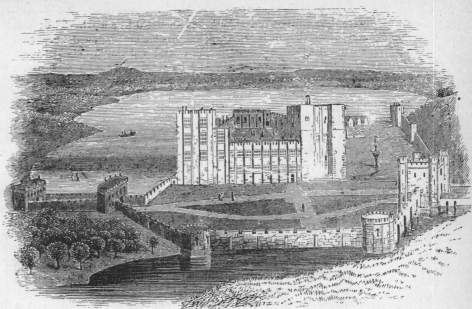

430.—Kenilworth Castle in 1620.—From the Fresco Painting at Newnham Padox.

426.—Ruins of Farnham Castle.

427.—The Keep, Carisbrooke Castle.

428.—Ruins of Norham Castle.

431.—Castle of Newcastle-upon-Tyne.

were about thirty-five feet high, and encircled by a moat. The gateway, of which little is preserved, was a noble building, with numerous apartments for the officers of the castle; and the keep, which was of great size, and octagonal, had its eight apartments with stone vaulted roofs on the ground floor, for the protection, it is said, of cattle brought in from the neighbourhood during any incursion of the Scots; also its great Baronial Hall, nearly forty feet long by twenty-four wide, and twenty high; all of which, though deprived of their roofs, floors, and windows, remain, through the excellence of the masonry, in admirable preservation. Cupidity alone, indeed, has been here at work to destroy. In Leland's time the castle was " well maintained," but in the early part of the seventeenth century the buildings of the outer court, with some others, were stripped of their lead and otherwise dismantled; and in 1672 the noble keep itself was unroofed. Warkworth has for several centuries been in possession of the Percy family. One can hardly mention these names together without also noticing the neighbouring hermitage, which Bishop Percy has made memorable by his poem of the ' Hermit of Warkworth.' This is situated in the perpendicular rocks which form the north bank of the Coquet, about a mile above the town, and consists of " two apartments hewn out of the rock, with a lower and outward apartment of masonry, built up against the side of the rock, which rises about twenty feet high; the principal apartment, or chapel, is about eighteen feet long, seven and a half wide, and seven and a half high, adorned with pilasters, from which spring the groins of the roof: at the east end is an altar with a niche behind it for a crucifix; and near the altar is a cavity containing a cenotaph, with a recumbent female figure having the hands raised in the attitude of prayer. In the inner apartment are another altar and a niche for a couch. From this inner apartment was a door leading to an open gallery or cloister. Steps led up from the hermitage to the hermit's garden at the top of the bank." (Penny Cyclopædia.) Who was the inhabitant of this strange home, and why he inhabited it, are questions that after all we must leave the poets and romance-writers to solve, and they could not be in better hands. It has been supposed that one of the Bertram family, who had murdered his brother, was the tenant of the hermitage, desiring in solitude by unceasing repentance to expiate his crime; but all we know is that the Percy family maintained from some unknown period a chantry priest here.

As the present fortress of NEWCASTLE (Fig. 431) was erected by Robert de Curthose, the eldest of the Conqueror's sons, on his return from an expedition into Scotland, we may judge of the general antiquity of the place by the name then given, the New-Castle. There can be no doubt, indeed, that the spot had been a Roman station, and very little but that in those early days it had been of some importance. After the introduction of Christianity the place became known by the name of Monk Chester, from the number of monastic institutions it contained. On the erection of the fortress, the town took the same name, New-Castle. The tower of this Norman structure remains essentially complete, and forms one of the most striking specimens in existence of the rude but grand-looking and (for the time) almost impregnable Norman stronghold. The first point of attraction to a visitor's eyes on entering Newcastle is that huge gloomy pile; it is also the last on which he turns his lingering glance on his departure. It stands upon a raised platform near the river, majestically isolated in its own "garth" or yard, to which we ascend by a steep flight of steps, spanned near the top by a strong postern with a circular Norman arch, reminding us of the difficulties that formerly attended such ascent when the approval of the inhabitants of the castle had not been previously gained. Crossing the garth to the east side, the one shown in the engraving (Fig. 431), we perceive the extraordinary character of the entrance, which, commencing at the corner on the left hand, and gradually rising, runs through the pile that seems to have been built against the keep rather than forming an integral part of it up to a considerable height, where the real entrance into the keep (originally most richly decorated) is to be found. Through this entrance we pass into one of the most remarkable of halls; it is of immense breadth, length, and height, dimly lighted through the various slit holes, hung here and there with rusty armour, and inhabited by an old pensioner and his family, whose little domestic conveniences when the eye does light upon them (for generally speaking they are lost in the magnitude of the place) have a peculiarly quaint effect. The recesses in various parts formed out of the solid thickness of the wall give us the best idea of its strength; one of these, possibly intended for the minstrels who sung the mighty deeds of the Norman chivalry to men yearning to emulate their fame, is alone of the size of a small and not very small apartment. But let us descend by the winding

staircase to the chapel beneath; recalling as we go a few recollections on the general subject of chapels in castles.

In the plan of an ancient castle (Fig. 346) it will be seen that the chapel forms a component part of the whole; and in turning from the plan to the descriptions of our castles generally, we find in almost every case a similar provision made for the performance of religious duties. It may seem either a melancholy or a consolatory consideration, according to the point of view from which we look, to perceive that in the age to which our present pages refer when the mailed nobles made might right, declared their pleasure and called it law, that then religion, as far as regarded sincere, zealous, and most unquestioning faith, and an indefatigable observance of all its forms and ceremonies, formed also a most conspicuous feature of the same men. To pray for mercy one hour, and be most merciless the next; to glorify the Giver of all good, as the most fitting preparation for the dispensation of all evil; to enshrine their hopes of salvation on the altar of Christ, the divine messenger of love, whilst they pressed forward to the mortal end of all through a continuous life of rapine, violence, and strife;—these were the almost unvarying characteristics of the early Norman lords, the builders of the old castles, where the keep and the chapel yet stand in many places side by side in most significant juxtaposition; the material embodiment of the two principles thus strangely brought together working to the most opposite conclusions, but with the utmost apparent harmony of intention. The great castle-builder provided his walls and his courts, his keep and his dungeons; but a chapel was no less indispensable alike to his station and his actual wants. Beleaguered or free, he must be able at all times to hear the daily mass, or, more grateful still to lordly ears, the pious orison offered up for his own and his family's welfare; he must be able to fly to the chapel for succour when the "thick-coming fancies" of superstition press upon his imagination and appal him by their mysterious influence, or when defeat or danger threatens; there, too, in the hour of triumph must he be found, his own voice mingling with the chant of the priests; at births, baptisms, marriages, and deaths, the sacred doors must ever be at hand; the child fast growing up towards man's estate, who has spent his entire life within the castle walls, looks forward to the chapel as the scene that shall usher him into a world of glory—already he feels the touch of the golden spurs, the sway of the lofty plumes, the thrill of the fair hands that gird on his maiden sword; already with alternating hopes and fears, he anticipates his solitary midnight vigil within the chapel walls. And truly such a night in such a place as this, to which we have descended, below the keep of Newcastle, was calculated to try the tone of the firmest nerves; for though beautiful, exceedingly beautiful it is in all that respects the architectural style to which it belongs, and of which it is a rare example, there are here no lofty pointed windows, with their storied panes, to admit the full broad stream of radiant splendour, or to give the idea of airiness or elegance to the structure. All is massive, great, and impressively solemn (Fig. 432).

The Chapel in the Tower of London (Fig. 433), equally perfect with that of Newcastle, and probably equally ancient, presents in its aspect as remarkable a contrast to that structure as a work erected in the same age, country, and style could have well given us. Here we have aisles divided from the nave by gigantic but noble-looking pillars, being divested of the low stunted character often apparent in Norman ecclesiastical edifices; and their effect is enhanced in no slight degree by the arches in the story above. The chapel is now used as a Record Office. We need only briefly mention the other ecclesiastical building of the Tower, the Chapel of St. Peter, standing in the area that surrounds the White Tower, and which must be of very early date, since we find that in the reign of Henry III. it was existing in a state of great splendour, with stalls for the king and queen, two chancels, a fine cross, beautiful sculpture, paintings, and stained glass. But at whatever period erected, the view (Fig. 434) shows us that material alterations of the original building have probably taken place, though no doubt the pews, the flat roof, and the Tudor monuments are themselves sufficient, in so small a place, to conceal or to injure the naturally antique expression. But there are peculiar associations connected with these walls that make all others tedious in the comparison as a "twice-told tale." In our previous remarks we have glanced at the general uses of the chapels in our old castles; this one of the Tower has been devoted to a more momentous service than any there enumerated; hither, from time to time, have come a strangely assorted company, led by the most terrible of guides, the executioner, through the most awful of paths, a sudden and violent death: in a word, beneath the unsuggestive-looking pavement, which seems to mock one's earnest gaze, and along which one walks with a reverential dread of disturbing the ashes of those who lie below, were buried the innocent Anne Boleyn and her brother, and the guilty Catherine Howard and her associate, Lady Rochford; the venerable Lady Salisbury, and Cromwell, Henry VIII.'s minister; the two Seymours, the Admiral and the Protector of the reign of Edward VI., and the Duke of Norfolk, and the Earl of Essex, of the reign of Elizabeth; Charles II.'s son, the Duke of Monmouth, and the Earls of Balmerino and Kilmarnock, with their ignoble coadjutor, Lord Lovat; above all, here were buried Bishop Fisher, and his illustrious friend More. One would suppose, on looking over such a list of names, that the scaffold, while assuming the mission of Death, was emulous to strike with all Death's impartiality, and sweep away just and unjust, guilty and innocent, with equal imperturbability. It was a short road from the opening to this death-in-life at the Traitor's Gate (Fig. 435), and thence through the gaping jaws of the Bloody Tower (Fig. 436), to the final resting-place of St. Peter's Chapel.

History and ballad, the chronicler and the troubadour, and more effectually than either, the novelist of the North, have made Richard Cœur de Lion one of the favourite heroes of England (Fig. 437). Without the wisdom of his great father, he was the representative of the courage, the fortitude, and the gallantry of the Plantagenets— of the mixed blood of the Saxon and Norman races. We follow the fortunes of the royal crusader over many a battle-field, in which gallantry was always sure of its guerdon from his knightly sword (Fig. 442). We can almost believe in the old metrical romance, which tells us how

> "The awless lion could not wage the fight,
> Nor keep his princely heart from Richard's hand."

(Fig. 444.) The touching friendship of his minstrel, Blondel, tells us that the lion-hearted king had something even nobler in his nature than his indomitable courage and his physical strength. "One day he (Blondel) sat directly before a window of the castle where King Richard was kept prisoner, and began to sing a song in French, which King Richard and Blondel had sometime composed together. When King Richard heard the song, he knew it was Blondel that sung it; and when Blondel paused at half of the song, the King began the other half, and completed it." His was a premature death. But generous as he was, he would have been a dangerous keeper of the rights of England. Of his brother John, the mean and treacherous John, a modern writer finely says: "The strong hands of the two first Plantagenets, Henry II. and Richard Cœur de Lion, his father and brother, were in the dust, and the iron sceptre which they had wielded lay rusting among the heavy armour which an imbecile and coward could not wear" (Pictorial History of England, vol. i.). The heart of Richard, by his own direction, was carried to his faithful city of Rouen for interment, and his body was buried at the feet of his father at Fontevraud: his statue, which was placed upon his tomb in that ancient monastery, is still remaining. It is of painted stone, and this is the principal authority for the portrait of Richard (Fig. 438). Here also is an effigy of his Queen Berengaria (Fig. 440). The faithful city of Rouen did not well keep its faith to the lion-hearted. A splendid tomb was erected over the heart of the king, and it was surrounded by a silver balustrade; but within half a century the faithful city melted the silver. In the year 1733 the chapter of the Cathedral, to effect some alteration in their church, pulled down the monuments of Richard and his brother, and of the great Duke of Bedford, and they laid down three plain slabs instead, in the pavement of the high altar. In 1838 some searches under this pavement were made by the prefect of the department, and amongst the rubbish was found a fine but mutilated statue of Richard (Fig. 439), and a leaden box containing a smaller box, which held all that remained of the lion-heart—something that had "the appearance of a reddish-coloured leaf, dry and bent round at the ends."—"To this complexion we must come at last."

The name of King John has two leading associations—Magna Charta and his murdered nephew. The great dramatic poet of England has so associated the fortunes of Constance and Arthur with the troubles, the fears, and the death-struggles of their faithless kinsman, that we look upon these events through the poetical medium as a natural series of cause and consequence. "The death of Arthur and the events which marked the last days of John were separated in their causes and effect by time only, over which the poet leaps." But the political history of John may be read in the most durable of antiquities—the Records of the kingdom. And the people may read the most remarkable of these records whenever they please to look upon it. Magna Charta, the great charter of England, entire as at the hour in which it was written, is preserved, not

for reference on doubtful questions of right, not to be proclaimed at market-crosses or to be read in churches, as in the time of Edward I., but for the gratification of a just curiosity and an honest national pride. The humblest in the land may look upon that document day by day, in the British Museum, which more than six hundred years ago declared that "no freeman shall be arrested or imprisoned, or dispossessed of his tenement, or outlawed, or exiled, or in any manner proceeded against, unless by the legal judgment of his peers, or by the law of the land." This is the foundation of statute upon statute, and of what is as stringent as statute, the common law, through which for six hundred years we have been struggling to breathe the breath of freedom—and we have not struggled in vain. The Great Charter is in Latin, written in a beautiful hand, of which we give a specimen in Fig. 458.

Runnemede—or Runingmede, as the Charter has it—was, according to Matthew of Westminster, a place where treaties concerning the peace of the kingdom had been often made. The name distinctly signifies a place of council. *Rune-med* is an Anglo-Saxon compound, meaning the Council-Meadow. We can never forget that Council-Meadow, for it entered into our first visions of Liberty:—

> "Fair Runnemede! oft hath my lingering eye
> Paus'd on thy tufted green and cultur'd hill:
> And there my busy soul would drink her fill
> Of lofty dreams, which on thy bosom lie.
> Dear plain! never my feet have pass'd thee by,
> At sprightly morn, high noon, or evening still,
> But thou hast fashion'd all my pliant will
> To soul-ennobling thoughts of liberty.
> Thou dost not need a perishable stone
> Of sculptur'd story;—records over young
> Proclaim the gladdening triumph thou hast known:
> The soil, the passing stream, hath still a tongue;
> And every wind breathes out an eloquent tone,
> That Freedom's self might wake thy fields among."

These are commonplace rhymes—schoolboy verses; but we are not ashamed of having written them. Runnemede was our Marathon. Very beautiful is that narrow slip of meadow on the edge of the Thames, with gentle hills bounding it for a mile or so. It is a valley of fertility. Is this a fitting place to be the cradle of English freedom? Ought we not, to make our associations harmonious, to have something bolder and sterner than this quiet mead, and that still water with its island cottage? (Fig. 455.). Poetry tells us that "rocky ramparts" are

> "The rough abodes of want and liberty."—GRAY.

But the liberty of England was nurtured in her prosperity. The Great Charter, which says, "No freeman, or merchant, or villain shall be unreasonably fined for a small offence—the first shall not be deprived of his tenement, the second of his merchandise, the third of his implements of husbandry"—exhibited a state far more advanced than that of the "want and liberty," of the poet, where the iron race of the mountain cliffs

> "Insult the plenty of the vales below."

Runnemede *is* a fitting place for the cradle of English liberty. Denham, who from his Cooper's Hill looked down upon the Thames, wandering past this mead to become "the world's exchange," somewhat tamely speaks of the plain at his feet:—

> "Here was that Charter seal'd, wherein the crown
> All marks of arbitrary power lays down;
> Tyrant and slave, those names of hate and fear,
> The happier style of king and subject bear;
> Happy when both to the same centre move,
> When kings give liberty, and subjects love."

Our liberty was not so won. It was wrested from kings, and not given by them; and the love we bestow upon those who are the central point of our liberty is the homage of reason to security. That security has made the Thames "the world's exchange;" that security has raised up the great city which lies like a mist below Cooper's Hill; that security has caused the towers of Windsor, which we see from the same hill, to rise up in new splendour, instead of crumbling into ruin like many a stronghold of feudal oppression. Our prosperity is the child of our free institutions; and the child has gone forward strengthening and succouring the parent. Yet the iron men who won this charter of liberties dreamt not of the day when a greater power than their own, the power of the merchants and the villains, would rise up to keep what they had sworn to win upon the altar of St. Edmundsbury (Fig. 463). The Fitz-Walter, and De Roos, and De Clare, and De Percy, and De Mandeville, and De Vescy, and De Mowbray, and De Montacute, and De Beauchamp—these great progenitors of our English nobility—compelled the despot to put his seal to the Charter of Runne-

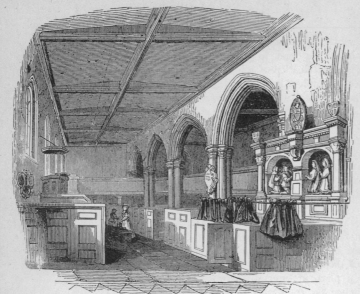

434.—St. Peter's Chapel in the Tower of London.

432.—Chapel in Newcastle Castle.

433.—Interior of the Chapel in the White Tower.

436.—Gateway of the Bloody Tower.

435.—The Traitor's Gate.

437.—Great Seal of Richard I.

438.—Richard I.—From his Tomb at Fontevrault.

440.—Berengaria, Queen of Richard I.
From the Tomb at Fontevrault.

439.—Effigy of Richard I.—From the
Statue found at Rouen.

441.—The Norman Crusader.

442.—Fighting on the Field of Battle.

443.—Avantailes.
a, Helmet of Richard I.
b, Baldwin, Count of Flanders, 1192
c,   „   „   „   1203.

444.—Richard and the Lion.

No. 15.

113

mede (Fig. 459). But another order of men, whom they of the pointed shield and the mascled armour would have despised as slaves, have kept and will keep, God willing, what they won on the 15th of June in the year of grace 1215. The thing has rooted into our English earth like the Ankerwyke Yew on the opposite bank of the Thames, which is still vigorous, though held to be older than the great day of Runnemede (Fig. 457).

Magna Charta is a record. Bishop Nicolson says, "Our stores of public records are justly reckoned to excel in age, beauty, correctness, and authority, whatever the choicest archives abroad can boast of the like sort." Miles, nay, hundreds of miles, of parchment are preserved in our public offices, which incidentally exhibit the progress of the nation in its institutions and its habits, and decide many an historical fact which would otherwise be matter of controversy or of speculation. Nothing can more truly manifest the value of these documents than the fact that the actual place in which this said King John was, on almost every day, from the first year of his reign to the last, has been traced by a diligent examination of the Patent Rolls in the Tower of London. Mr. Hardy has appended to his curious Introduction to these Rolls, published by authority of the Record Commission, the 'Itinerary of King John.' A most restless being does he appear to have been, flying about in cumbrous carriages (Fig. 461) to all parts of England; sailing to Normandy (Fig. 460); now holding his state in his Palace at Westminster, now at Windsor (Fig. 464); and never at ease till he was laid in his tomb at Worcester (Fig. 465). We extract an instructive passage from Mr. Hardy's Introduction:—

"Rapin, Hume, Henry, and those English historians who have followed Matthew Paris, state that, as soon as King John had sealed the Great Charter, he became sullen, dejected, and reserved, and shunning the society of his nobles and courtiers, retired, with a few of his attendants, to the Isle of Wight, as if desirous of hiding his shame and confusion, where he conversed only with fishermen and sailors, diverting himself with walking on the sea-shore with his domestics; that, in his retreat, he formed plans for the recovery of the prerogatives which he had lately relinquished; and meditated, at the same time, the most fatal vengeance against his enemies; that he sent his emissaries abroad to collect an army of mercenaries and Brabaçons, and dispatched messengers to Rome, for the purpose of securing the protection of the papal see; and that, whilst his agents were employed in executing their several commissions, he himself remained in the Isle of Wight, awaiting the arrival of the foreign soldiers.

"That these statements are partially if not wholly unfounded will appear by the attestations to the royal letters during the period in question.

"Previously to the sealing of Magna Charta, namely, from the 1st to the 3rd of June, 1215, the King was at Windsor, from which place he can be traced, by his attestations, to Odiham, and thence to Winchester, where he remained till the 8th. From Winchester he went to Merton; he was again at Odiham on the 9th, whence he returned to Windsor, and continued there till the 15th: on that day he met the barons at Runnemede by appointment, and there sealed the great charter of English liberty. The King then returned to Windsor, and remained there until the 18th of June, from which time until the 23rd he was every day both at Windsor and Runnemede, and did not finally leave Windsor and its vicinity before the 26th of the same month; John then proceeded through Odiham to Winchester, and continued in that city till the end of June. The first four days of July he passed at Marlborough, from which place he went to Devizes, Bradenstoke, and Calne; reached Cirencester on the 7th, and returned to Marlborough on the following day. He afterwards went to Ludgershall, and through Clarendon into Dorsetshire, as far as Corfe Castle, but returned to Clarendon on the 15th of July, from which place he proceeded, through Newbury and Abingdon, to Woodstock, and thence to Oxford, where he arrived on the 17th of that month; and in a letter dated on the 15th of July, between Newbury and Abingdon, the King mentions the impossibility of his reaching Oxford by the 16th, according to his appointment with the barons."

The publications of the Record Commissioners are enriched by the researches of some of our most eminent living antiquarians, who have brought to their task a fund of historical knowledge, and a sagacity in showing the connection between these dust-covered records and the history of our constitution, which have imparted a precision to historical writing unknown to the last age. No man has laboured more assiduously in this field than Sir Francis Palgrave; and he has especially shown that a true antiquary is not a mere scavenger of the baser things of time, but one whose talent and knowledge can discover the use and the connection of ancient things,

which are not really worn out, and which are only held to be worthless by the ignorant and the unimaginative. Sir Francis Palgrave is the Keeper of the Records in the Treasury of the Exchequer, and his publication of the ancient Kalendars and Inventories of that Treasury contains a body of documents of the greatest value, introduced by an account of this great depository of the Crown Records, which is full of interest and instruction. "The custom of depositing records and muniments amongst the treasures of the state is grounded upon such obvious reasons, that it prevailed almost universally amongst ancient nations; nor, indeed, is it entirely discontinued at the present day. The earliest, and in all respects the most remarkable, testimony concerning this practice is found in the Holy Scriptures:—'Now, therefore, if it seem good to the King, let there be search made in the King's Treasure-house, which is there at Babylon, whether it be so, that a decree was made of Cyrus the King to build this house of God at Jerusalem.' 'Then Darius the King made a decree, and search was made in the House of the Rolls, where the treasures were laid up in Babylon.'" The high antiquity of this custom imparts even a new value to our own Treasure Chambers. Those who feel an interest in the subject may consult a brief but valuable article under the head 'Records' in the 'Penny Cyclopædia.' From Sir Francis Palgrave's Introduction to the Ancient Kalendars we extract one or two amusing passages descriptive of some of the figures in p. 121:—

"The plans anciently adopted for the arrangement and preservation of the instruments had many peculiarities. Presses, such as are now employed, do not seem to have been in use. Chests bound with iron;—forcers or coffers, secured in the same manner;—pouches or bags of canvass or leather (Fig. 468); skippets, or small boxes turned on the lathe (Fig. 469);—tills or drawers;—and hanapers or hampers of 'twyggys' (Fig. 470);—are all enumerated as the places of stowage or deposit. To these reference was made, sometimes by letters, sometimes by inscriptions, sometimes by tickets or labels, and sometimes by 'signs;' that is to say, by rude sketches, drawings, or paintings, which had generally some reference to the subject matter of the documents (Fig. 467).

"Thus the *sign* of the instruments relating to Arragon is a lancer on a jennet;—Wales, a Briton in the costume of his country, one foot shod and the other bare;—Ireland, an Irisher, clad in a very singular hood and cape;—Scotland, a Lochaber axe;—Yarmouth, three united herrings;—the rolls of the Justices of the Forest, an oak sapling;—the obligations entered into by the men of Chester, for their due obedience to Edward, Earl of Chester, a gallows, indicating the fate which might be threatened in case of rebellion, or which the officers of the Treasury thought they had already well deserved; —Royal marriages, a hand in hand;—the indentures relating to the subsidy upon woollen cloths, a pair of shears;—instruments relating to the lands of the Earl of Gloucester in Wales, a castle surrounded by a banner charged with the Clare arms;—and the like, of which various examples will be found by inspection of the calendars and memoranda.*

"Two ancient boxes painted with shields of arms, part of the old furniture, are yet in existence, together with several curious chests, coffers, and skippets of various sorts and sizes, all sufficiently curious and uncouth, together with various specimens of the hanapers woven of 'twyggys,' as described in the text.

"One of these hanapers was discovered under rather remarkable circumstances. On the 15th of Feb., in the third year of the reign of Richard II., Thomas Orgrave, clerk, delivers into the Treasury, to be there safely kept, certain muniments relating to the lands and tenements in Berkhampstead, formerly belonging to William, the son and heir of John Hunt, and which the king had purchased of Dyonisia, the widow of William de Sutton, and which are stated to be placed in a certain hanaper or hamper within a chest over the receipt. Upon a recent inspection of a bag of deeds relating to the county of Berks, I found that it contained the hanaper so described, with a

* "The rolls of the Justices of the Forest were marked by the sapling oak (No. 1). Papal bulls, by the triple crown. Four canvass pouches holding rolls and tallies of certain payments made for the church of the church of Westminster were marked by the church (3). The head in a cowl (4) marked an indenture respecting the jewels found in the house of the Fratres Minores in Salop. The scales (5), the assay of the mint in Dublin. The Briton having one foot shod and the other bare, with the lance and sword (6), marked the wooden 'coffin' holding the acquittance of receipts from Llewellin, Prince of Wales. Three herrings (7), the 'forcer' of leather bound with iron, containing documents relating to Yarmouth, &c. The lancer (8), documents relating to Arragon. The united hands (9), the marriage between Henry, Prince of Wales, and Philippa, daughter of Henry IV. The galley (10), the recognizance of merchants of the three galleys of Venice. The hand and book (11), fealty to kings John and Henry. The charter or cyrograph (12), treaties and truces between England and Scotland. The hooded monk (13), advowsons of Irish churches, and the castle with a banner of the Clare arms (14), records relating to the possessions of the Earl of Gloucester in Wales."—(Penny Cyclopædia.)

label exactly conformable to the entry in the memoranda, crumbling and decaying, but tied up, and in a state which evidently showed that it had never been opened since the time of its first deposit in the Treasury; and within the hanaper were all the several deeds, with their seals in the highest state of preservation."

Connected with the subject of the ancient records of the crown may be mentioned the tallies of the Exchequer, which were actually in use from the very earliest times till the year 1834. These primitive records of account have been thus described: "The tallies used in the Exchequer (one is shown in Fig. 471) answered the purpose of receipts as well as simple records of matters of account. They consisted of squared rods of hazel or other wood, upon one side of which was marked, by notches, the sum for which the tally was an acknowledgment; one kind of notch standing for 1000*l*., another for 100*l*., another for 20*l*., and others for 20*s*., 1*s*., &c. On two other sides of the tally, opposite to each other, the amount of the sum, the name of the payer, and the date of the transaction, were written by an officer called the writer of the tallies; and after this was done, the stick was cleft longitudinally in such a manner that each piece retained one of the written sides, and one-half of every notch cut in the tally. One piece was then delivered to the person who had paid in the money, for which it was a receipt or acquittance, while the other was preserved in the Exchequer." The Saxon Reeve-pole, used in the Isle of Portland down to a very recent period by the collector of the king's rents, shows the sum which each person has to pay to the king as lord of the manor (Fig. 473). The Clog Almanac, which was common in Staffordshire in the seventeenth century, was in the same way a record of the future, cut on the sides of a square stick, such as exhibited in Fig. 472.

———

The same combination against the power of the Crown which produced the great charter of our liberties, relieved the people from many regal oppressions by a charter of the forests. We cannot look upon an old forest without thinking of the days when men who had been accustomed to the free range of their green woods were mulcted or maimed for transgressing the ordinances of their new hunter-kings. Our poet Cowper put his imagination in the track of following out the customs of the Norman age in his fragment upon Yardley Oak, which was supposed to have existed before the Normans:—

> "Thou wast a bauble once; a cup and ball,
> Which babes might play with; and the thievish jay,
> Seeking her food, with ease might have purloin'd
> The auburn nut that held thee, swallowing down
> Thy yet close-folded latitude of boughs
> And all thine embryo vastness at a gulp.
> But fate thy growth decreed; autumnal rains
> Beneath thy parent tree mellow'd the soil
> Design'd thy cradle; and a skipping deer,
> With pointed hoof dibbling the glebe, prepared
> The soft receptacle, in which, secure,
> Thy rudiments should sleep the winter through."

But the poet's purpose failed. England is full of such natural antiquities of the earliest period: "Within five and twenty miles of St. Paul's, the Great Western Railway will place us in an hour (having an additional walk of about two miles) in the heart of one of the most secluded districts in England. We know nothing of forest scenery equal to Burnham Beeches (Fig. 476). There are no spots approaching to it in wild grandeur to be found in Windsor Forest; Sherwood, we have been told, has trees as ancient, but few so entirely untouched in modern times. When at the village of Burnham, which is about a mile and a half from the Railway-station at Maidenhead, the beeches may be reached by several roads, each very beautiful in its seclusion. We ascend a hill, and find a sort of table-land forming a rude common with a few scattered houses. Gradually the common grows less open. We see large masses of wood in clumps, and now and then a gigantic tree close by the road. The trunks of these scattered trees are of amazing size. They are for the most part pollards; but not having been lopped for very many years, they have thrown out mighty arms, which give us a notion of some deformed son of Anak, noble as well as fearful in his grotesque proportions. As we advance the wood thickens; and as the road leads us into a deep dell, we are at length completely embosomed in a leafy wilderness. This dell is a most romantic spot: it extends for some quarter of a mile between overhanging banks covered with the graceful forms of the ash and the birch: while the contorted beeches show their fantastic roots and unwieldy trunks upon the edge of the glen, in singular contrast. If we walk up this valley, we may emerge into the plain of beeches, from which

the place derives its name. It is not easy to make scenes such as these interesting in description. The great charm of this spot may be readily conceived, when it is known that its characteristic is an entire absence of human care. The property has been carefully preserved in its ancient state, and the axe of the woodman for many a day has not been heard within its precincts. The sheep wander through the tender grass as if they were the rightful lords of the domain. We asked a solitary old man, who was sitting on a stump, whether there was any account who planted this ancient wood · 'Planted!' he replied, 'it was never planted: those trees are as old as the world!' However sceptical we might be as to the poor man's chronology, we were sure that history or tradition could tell little about their planting." We visited this place in 1841, and this slight notice of it already published may as well be transferred to these pages. But England has a store of popular associations with her old oaks and yews in the vast collection of Robin Hood Ballads.

If there be one district of England over which more than over any other Romance seems to have asserted an unquestionable supremacy—"This is mine henceforth, for ever!"—and over which she has drawn her veil of strange enchantments, making the fairest objects appear fairer through that noble medium, and giving beauty even to deformity itself, it is surely Sherwood Forest. If there be one man of England whose story above the stories of all other men has entered deeply into the popular heart, or stirred powerfully the popular imagination, there can be no doubt but it is the bold yeoman-forester Robin Hood. Who, in youth, ever read unmoved the ballads in which that story is chiefly related, absurd and untrue as undoubtedly many of them are? Who now can behold even a partial reflex of the lives of these joyous inhabitants of the green woods, such, for instance, as 'As You Like It' affords, without a sigh at the contrast presented to our own safer, more peaceable, but altogether unromantic pursuits? It is well, perhaps, that there is now no banished duke "in the Forest of Arden, and so many merry men with him," living there "like the old Robin Hood of England:" for there would be still "young gentlemen" too glad to "flock to him every day, and fleet the time carelessly, as they did in the golden world." But, perhaps, the most decisive proof of the inherent interest of the lives of the Forest outlaws, is not that such interest should simply still exist so many centuries after their death, but that it should exist under the heavy load of mistakes and absurdities that have so long surrounded and weighed it down:— all honour to those whose unerring perceptions and stedfast faith have kept that interest alive! The philosopher has once more condescended to learn from the people whom he should teach. What they would not "willingly let die" under so many circumstances adverse to preservation, he now, in our time, discovers is fit to live, and forthwith satisfactorily proves what millions never doubted, that Robin Hood was worthy of his reputation—that he was no thief, or robber, no matter how these epithets might be qualified in Camden's phrase of the "gentlest of thieves," or Major's of the "most humane and prince of all robbers." Altogether the treatment during late centuries of the story of Sherwood Forest has been at once curious and instructive. The people wisely taking for granted the essentials of that story as handed down to them from generation to generation, and which described Robin Hood as their benefactor in an age when heaven knows benefactors to them were few enough, and which at the same time invested him with all the attributes on which a people delight to dwell, as mirroring, in short, all their own best qualities—hatred of oppression, courage, hospitality, generous love, and deep piety; taking all this, we repeat, for granted, they have not since troubled themselves to ask why they continued to look upon his memory with such affectionate respect. On the other hand, our historians, who were too philosophic (so called) to regard such feelings as in themselves of any particular importance, if they did not even think them decisive against the man who was their object, never condescended to inquire as to his true character, but were content to take their views of him on trust from some such epigrammatic sounding sentences of the older writers as we have already transcribed. And what is the result when they are suddenly startled with inquiry by an eminent foreigner, Thierry, putting forth a strangely favourable opinion of the political importance of Robin Hood?—why, that without referring to a single new or comparatively inaccessible document, a writer in the Westminster Review for March, 1840 (to whom every lover of Robin Hood owes grateful acknowledgments), has shown that there can be no reasonable doubt whatever that it is the patriot, and not the freebooter, whom his countrymen have so long delighted to honour. Of this more presently.

The severity of the old forest laws of England has become a byword, and no wonder, when we know that with the Conqueror a

445.—Great Seal of King John.

446.—Portrait of King John.—From his Tomb at Worcester.

447.—Irish Silver Penny of John.—From a specimen in Brit. Mus.

452.—Great Seal, &c., of King John.

454—Magna Charta and its associations.

53.—Tents.—From a MS. in Brit. Mus.

448.—King John.

449.—Queen Elinor.

450.—William Longespée, Earl of Salisbury.

451.—William Marshall, Earl of Pembroke.

116

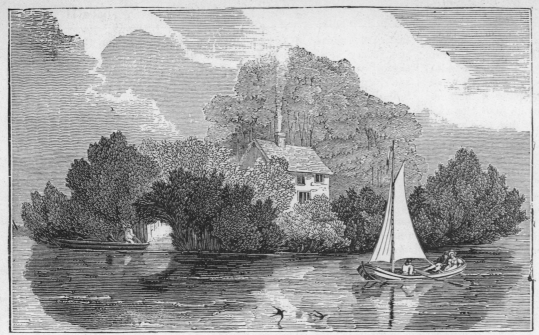

455.—Magna Charta Island.

457.—The Ankerwyke Yew.

459.—Copy of the Seal of King John to the Agreement with the Barons.

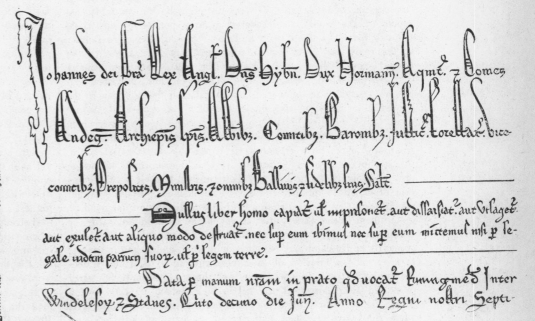

458.—Specimen of Magna Charta, engraved from one of the original Copies in the British Museum. The passages are a portion of the Preamble, the Forty-sixth Clause, and the Attestation.

456.—Runnemede.

sovereign's paternal care for his subjects was understood to apply to red deer, not to Saxon men; and that accordingly, of the two, the lives of the former alone were esteemed of any particular value. But it was not the severity merely that was, after the Conquest, introduced (whether into the spirit or into the letter of the forest laws is immaterial), but also the vast extent of fresh land then afforested, and to which such laws were for the first time applied, that gave rise to so much opposition and hatred between the Norman conquerors and the Saxon forest inhabitants; and that in particular parts of England infused such continuous vigour into the struggle commenced at the invasion, long after that struggle had ceased elsewhere. The Conqueror is said to have possessed in this country no less than sixty-eight forests, and these even were not enough; so the afforesting process went on reign after reign, till the awful shadow of Magna Charta began to pass more and more frequently before royal eyes, producing first a check, and then a retreat: dis-afforesting then began, and the forest laws gradually underwent a mitigating process. But this was the work of the nobility of England, and occupied the said nobility a long time first to determine upon, and then to carry out: the people in the interim could not afford to wait, but took the matter to a certain extent into their own hands; free bands roved the woods, laughing at the king's laws, and killing and eating his deer, and living a life of perfect immunity from punishment, partly through bravery and address, and still more through the impenetrable character of the woods that covered a large portion of the whole country from the Trent to the Tyne. Among the more famous of the early leaders of such men were Adam Bell, Clym of the Clough, and William of Cloudesley (Fig. 479), the heroes of many a northern ballad. But as time passed on, and Normans and Saxons gradually amalgamated, and forgot their feuds of race in the necessity for resisting the oppressions of class, such a life would cease to be honourable; liberty would become licence—resistance to government rebellion. Assuredly the memory of Robin Hood would not have been treasured as it was by our forefathers, if, whilst the country was gradually progressing onwards to peace, order, and justice, he had merely distinguished himself by the exercise of excellent qualities for a very mischievous purpose. What was it, then, that justified such a man in establishing an independent government in the woods, after so much had been done towards the establishment of a more regular authority, and after the people generally of England had patiently submitted, and began in earnest to seek an amelioration of their condition in a legal and peaceable way? It was, in a word, the overthrow of the national party of united Englishmen at the battle of Evesham in 1265, when Simon de Montfort and a host of other leaders of the people fell; when the cause that had experienced so many vicissitudes, and which had assumed so many different aspects at different times, was apparently lost for ever; and when the kingly power, unrestrained by charters—since there were no longer armed bands to enforce them—rioted in the degradation and ruin of all who had been opposed to it. In a parliament called almost immediately after this event which sat at Winchester, and consisted of course entirely of nobles and knights who had been on the victors' side, the estates of *all* who had adhered to the late Earl of Leicester (Montfort) were confiscated at one fell swoop. It is important to mark what then took place. "Such measures," writes Dr. Lingard, whose sympathies are all on the royal side, "were not calculated to restore the public tranquillity. The sufferers, prompted by revenge, or compelled by want, had again recourse to the sword: the mountains, forests, and morasses furnished them with places of retreat; and the flames of predatory warfare were kindled in most parts of the kingdom. To reduce these partial, but successive insurrections, occupied Prince Edward [himself one of the popular party till he found popular restrictions were to be applied to his reign as well as his father's] the better part of two years. He first compelled Simon de Montfort [son of the late earl] and his associates, who had sought an asylum in the Isle of Axholm, to submit to the award which should be given by himself and the King of the Romans. He next led his forces against the men of the Cinque Ports, who had long been distinguished by their attachment to Leicester, and who since his fall had by their *piracies* interrupted the commerce of the narrow seas, and made prizes of all ships belonging to the king's subjects. The capture of Winchelsea, which was carried by storm, taught them to respect the authority of the sovereign, and their power by sea made the prince desirous to recal them to their duty and attach them to the crown. They swore fealty to Henry; and in return obtained a full pardon, and the confirmation of their privileges. From the Cinque Ports Edward proceeded to Hampshire, which, with Berkshire and Surrey, was ravaged by numerous *banditti*,

under the command of Adam Gordon, the most athletic man of the age. They were surprised in a wood near Alton. The prince engaged in single combat with their leader, wounded and unhorsed him; and then, in regard of his valour, granted him his pardon. Still the garrison of Kenilworth [the Montfort family seat] continued to brave the royal power, and even added contumely to their disobedience. To subdue these obstinate *rebels*, it was necessary to summon the chivalry of the kingdom: but the strength of the place defied all the efforts of the assailants; and the obstinacy of Hastings, the governor, refused for six months every offer which was made to him in the name of his sovereign." At length it became necessary to offer something like terms of accommodation; there was danger in such long and successful resistance. So it was declared that estates might be redeemed at certain rates of payment, the highest being applied to the brave Kenilworth garrison, who were to pay seven years' value. They submitted at last. Others still held out, hoping perhaps to see a new national organization, and at all events determined to refuse submission so long as they could. Such were the men who maintained their independence for nearly two years in the Isle of Ely; above all, such were the men who maintained their independence for a lifetime in the forest of Sherwood and the adjacent woodlands. Fordun, the Scottish historian, who travelled in England in the fourteenth century diligently collecting materials for his great work, which forms to this day our only authority for the facts of Scottish history through a considerable period, states, immediately after his notice of the battle of Evesham, and its consequences to all who had been connected, on the losing side, with the general stream of events to which that battle belongs, " *Then from among the dispossessed and the banished arose that most famous cut-throat Robert Hood and Little John.*" If any one rises from the perusal of the mighty events of the reign of Henry the Third with the conviction that Simon de Montfort, to whom in all probability England owes its borough representation, was a rebel instead of a martyr, as the people called him, and that the words so freely used by Dr. Lingard, of pirates, banditti, and rebels, were properly applied to Simon de Montfort's followers, then also they may accept Fordun's opinion that Robin Hood was a cut-throat—*but not else;* they will otherwise, like ourselves, accept his fact only, which is one of the highest importance, and beyond dispute as to its correctness, however strangely neglected even by brother historians. Fordun's work was continued and completed by his pupil, Bower, Abbot of St. Colomb, who under the year 1266, noticing the further progress of the events that followed the battle of Evesham, says, "In this year were obstinate hostilities carried on between the dispossessed barons of England and the royalists, amongst whom Roger Mortimer occupied the Marches of Wales, and John Duguil the Isle of Ely. Robert Hood now lived an outlaw among the woodland copses and thickets." It is hardly necessary after this to add that the one, and, there is but one undoubtedly, ancient ballad relating to Robin Hood, the 'Lytell Geste,' furnishes an additional corroboration of the most satisfactory character; it relates, as its title-page informs us, to "Kynge *Edwarde* and Robyn Hode and Lytell Johan." We may here observe that this ballad, one of the very finest in the language, which for beauty and dramatic power is worthy of Chaucer himself, about whose time it was probably written, had shared Robin Hood's own fate: that is, enjoyed a great deal of undiscriminating and, therefore, worthless popularity. It has simply been looked on as one of the Robin Hood ballads, whilst in fact it stands out as much from all the others by its merits as by its antiquity, and its internal evidence of being written by one who understood that on which he wrote: which is much more than can be said for the ballad-doers of later centuries, when Friar Tuck and Maid Marian first crept into the foresters' company, when the gallant yeoman was created without ceremony Earl of Huntingdon, and his own period put back a century in order that he and the Lion Heart might hob and nob it together. Here, then, we see the origin of Robin Hood's forest career; we see him—the yeoman—doing what the few leaders of the people, the knights and barons whom Evesham had spared, everywhere did also, resisting oppression; the difference being that they fought as soldiers with a better soldier, Prince Edward, and failed; and that he fought as a forester in the woods he had probably been familiar with from boyhood, and succeeded. Without exaggerating his political importance, it is not too much to say that but for Edward's wisdom in conceding substantially, when he became king, what he had shed so much blood to resist while prince, that little handful of freemen in Sherwood forest might have become the nucleus of a new organization, destined once more to shake the isle to its very centre. Edward prevented this result; but, nevertheless, they found their mission. They enabled their leader to become " the representative and the hero of a cause far older and deeper even than that in which

De Montfort had so nobly fallen; we mean the permanent protest of the industrious classes of England against the galling injustice and insulting immorality of that framework of English society, and that fabric of ecclesiastical as well as civil authority, which the iron arm of the Conquest had established. Under a system of general oppression—based avowedly on the right of the strongest—the suffering classes beheld, in a personage like Robert Hood, a sort of particular Providence, which scattered a few grains of equity amid all that monstrous mass of wrong. And when in his defensive conflicts, the well-aimed missile entered the breast of some one of their petty tyrants, though regarded by the ruling powers as an arrow of malignant fate, it was hailed by the wrung and goaded people as a shaft of protecting or avenging Heaven. The service of such a chieftain, too, afforded a sure and tempting refuge for every Anglo-Saxon serf who, strong in heart and in muscle, and stung by intolerable insult, had flown in the face of his Norman owner or his owner's bailiff—for every *villain* who, in defending the decencies of his hearth, might have brained some brutal collector of the poll-tax—for every rustic sportsman who had incurred death or mutilation, the ferocious penalties of the Anglo-Norman forest laws, by ' taking, killing, and eating deer ' " (Westminster Review).

The forest of Sherwood, which formerly extended for thirty miles northward from Nottingham, skirting the great north road on both sides, was anciently divided into Thorney Wood and High Forest; and in one of these alone, the first and smallest, there were comprised nineteen towns and villages, Nottingham included. But this extensive sylvan district formed but a part of Robin Hood's domains. Sherwood was but one of a scarcely interrupted series of forests through which the outlaws roved at pleasure, when change was desired, either for its own sake, or in order to decline the too pressing attentions of the " Sheriff," as they called the royal governor of Nottingham Castle and of the two counties, Notts and Derby, who had supplanted the old elective officer—the people's sheriff. Hence we trace their haunts to this day so far in one direction as " Robin Hood's Chair," Wyn Hill, and his " Stride" (Fig. 486) in Derbyshire; thence to " Robin Hood's Bay," on the coast of Yorkshire, in another, with places between innumerable. But the " woody and famous forest of Barnsdale," in Yorkshire, and Sherwood, appear to have been their principal places of resort; and what would not one give for a glimpse of the scene as it then was, with these its famous actors moving about among it! There is little or nothing remaining in a sufficiently wild state to tell us truly of the ancient royal forest of Sherwood. The clearing process has been carried on extensively during the last century and a half. Prior to that period the forest was full of ancient trees—the road from Mansfield to Nottingham presented one unbroken succession of green woods. The principal parts now existing are the woods of Birkland and Bilhagh, where oaks of the most giant growth and of the most remote antiquity are still to be found: oaks against which Robin Hood himself may have leaned, and which even then may have counted their age by centuries. Such are the oaks in Welbeck Park (Fig. 480). Many of these ancient trees are hollow through nearly the whole of their trunks, but their tops and lateral branches still put forth the tender green foliage regularly as the springs come round. Side by side with the monarch oak we find the delicate silver-coated stems and pendent branches of the lady of the woods; and beautiful is the contrast and the harmony. But everything wears a comparatively cultivated aspect. We miss the prodigal luxuriance of a natural forest, where every stage upward, from the sapling to the mightiest growth, may be traced. We miss the picturesque accidents of nature always to be found in such places—the ash key, for instance, of which Gilpin speaks (Forest Scenery), rooting in a decayed part of some old tree, germinating, sending down its roots, and lifting up its branches till at last it rends its supporter and nourisher to pieces, and appears itself standing in its place, stately and beautiful as that once appeared. Above all we miss the rich and tangled undergrowth; the climbing honeysuckle, the white and black briony, and the clematis; the prickly holly and the golden furze, the heaths, the thistles, and the foxgloves with their purple bells; the bilberries, which for centuries were wont to be an extraordinarily great profit and pleasure to the poor people who gathered them (Thornton); the elders and willows of many a little marshy nook; all which, no doubt, once flourished in profusion wherever they could find room to grow between the thickly set trees, of which Camden says, referring to Sherwood, that their " entangled branches were so twisted together, that they hardly left room for a person to pass.". It need excite little surprise that the outlaws could defend themselves from all inroads upon such a home The same writer adds, that in his time the woods were

much thinner, but still bred an infinite number of deer and stags with lofty antlers. When Robin Hood hunted here, there would be also the roe, the fox, the marten, the hare, the coney, as well as the partridge, the quail, the rail, the pheasant, the woodcock, the mallard, and the heron, to furnish sport or food. Even the wolf himself may have been occasionally found in Sherwood, down to the thirteenth century : in the manor of Mansfield Woodhouse a parcel of land called Wolf huntland was held so late as Henry the Sixth's time by the service of winding a horn to frighten away the wolves in the forest of Sherwood. We must add to this rude and imperfect sketch of the scene made for ever memorable by Robin Hood's presence and achievements, that in another point it would seem to have been expressly marked out by nature for such romantic fame. Caverns are found in extraordinary numbers through the forest. Those near Nottingham are supposed to have given name both to the town and county; the Saxon word Snodengaham being interpreted to mean the Home of Caverns. There are similar excavations in the face of a cliff near the Lene, west of Nottingham Castle. Above all, there is a cave traditionally connected with the great archer himself. This is a curious hollow rock in the side of a hill near Newstead, known as Robin Hood's Stable, but more likely from its aspect to have been his chapel. It contains several passages and doorways cut in the Gothic style, out of the solid rock; and there are peculiar little hollows in the wall, which might have been intended for holy water. Robin Hood's devotion is attested in a thousand ways by tradition, ballad, and sober history. Thus the ' Lytell Geste ' observes :—

> A good maner than had Robyn
> In londe where that he were,
> Every daye or he would dyne,
> Three messes wolde be here.

Fordun's illustration of Robin Hood's piety is an exceedingly interesting anecdote, and one that assuredly would not have found its way into his work unless from his full conviction of its truth. " Once upon a time, in Barnsdale, where he was avoiding the wrath of the King and the rage of the Prince, while engaged in very devoutly hearing mass, as he was wont to do, nor would he interrupt the service for any occasion—one day, I say, while so at mass, it happened that a certain Viscount [the sheriff or governor, no doubt, before mentioned], and other officers of the King, who had often before molested him, were seeking after him in that most retired woodland spot wherein he was thus occupied. Those of his men who first discovered this pursuit, came and entreated him to fly with all speed; but this, from reverence for the consecrated host, which he was then most devoutly adoring, he absolutely refused to do. While the rest of his people were trembling for fear of death, Robert alone, confiding in Him whom he fearlessly worshipped, with the very few whom he had then beside him, encountered his enemies, overcame them with ease, was enriched by their spoils and ransom, and was thus induced to hold ministers of the church and masses in greater veneration than ever, as mindful of the common saying,

> " ' God hears the man that often hears the mass.' "

The life in the forest must indeed have been steeped in joyous excitement. No doubt it had its disadvantages. Winter flaws in such a scene would not be pleasant. Agues might be apt occasionally to make their appearance. One feels something of a shivering sensation as we wonder,

> ————————— When they did hear
> The rain and wind beat dark December, how
> In that their pinching cave they could discourse
> The freezing hours away.

Yet even the rigours of the season might give new zest to the general enjoyment of forest life; we may imagine one of the band singing in some such words as those of Amiens :—

> Under the greenwood tree
> Who loves to lie with me,
> And tune his merry note
> Unto the sweet bird's throat,
> Come hither, come hither, come hither :
> *Here shall he see*
> *No enemy*
> *But winter and rough weather.*

And that very thought would ensure such enemies, when they did come, a genial and manly reception. But reverse the picture, and what a world of sunshine, and green leaves, and flickering lights and shadows break in upon us—excitement in the chace, whether they follow the deer (Figs. 485 and 487), or were themselves followed by the sheriff, through bush and brake, over bog and quagmire—of enjoyment in their shooting and wrestling matches

460.—English Ships, temp. John.

462.—Prison, temp. John.

463.—Altar at St. Edmundsbury.

464.—Room of State, temp. John.

461.—Carriages, temp. John.

465.—Tomb of King John, Worcester.

120

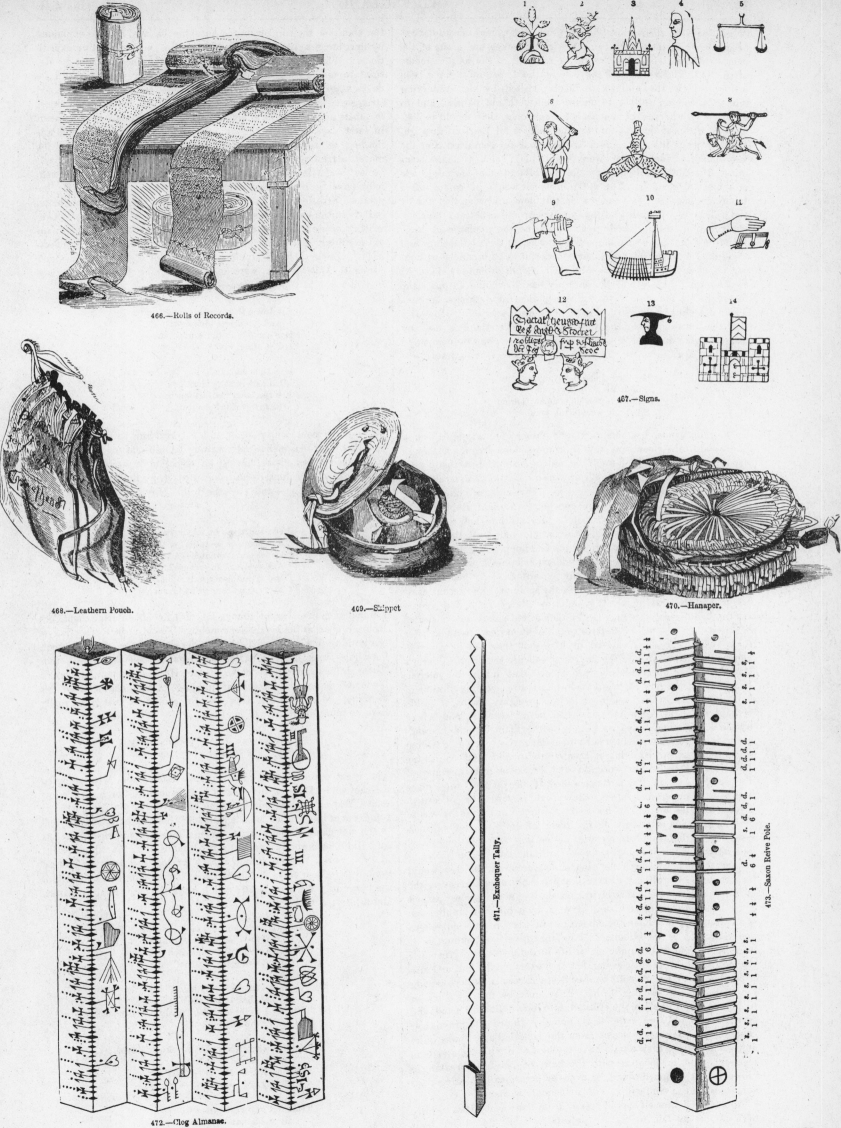

466.—Rolls of Records.

467.—Signs.

468.—Leathern Pouch.

469.—Skippet.

470.—Hanaper.

472.—Clog Almanac.

471.—Exchequer Tally.

473.—Saxon Reive Pole.

(Fig. 484), in their sword-fights (Fig. 483), and sword-dances (Fig. 489); in their visits to all the rustic wakes and feasts of the neighbourhood, where they would be received as the most welcome of guests. The variety of the life in the forest must have been endless. Now the outlaws would be visited by the wandering minstrels, coming thither to amuse them with old ballads, and to gather a rich harvest of materials for new ones, that should be listened to with the deepest interest and delight all England through, not only while the authors recited them, but for centuries after the very names of such authors were forgotten. The legitimate poet-minstrel would be followed by the humbler gleeman, forming one of a band of revellers (Fig. 490), in which would be comprised a taborer, a bagpiper, and dancers or tumblers, and who, tempted by the well-known liberality of the foresters, would penetrate the thick wood to find them. And great would be the applause at their humorous dances and accompanying songs, at their balancings and tumblings; wonderful, almost too wonderful to be produced without the aid of evil spirits, would seem their sleight-of-hand tricks. At another time there would be suddenly heard echoing through the forest glades the sounds of strange bugles from strange hunters. Their rich apparel shows them to be of no ordinary rank. How dare they then intrude upon the forest king? Nay, there is not any danger. Are there not lady-hunters (Fig. 481) among the company? and what says the ballad, the truth of which every one attests?—

> Robyn loved one dere lady,
> For doute of dedely synne;
> Wolde he never do company harme
> That any woman was ynne.

So their husbands, brothers, sons, and fathers hunt freely through Sherwood in their company, safe from the sudden arrow, ay, though even the hated sheriff himself be among them. But there were occasions when the forest would present a much more extraordinary scene than any we have yet referred to. For scores of miles around, what preparations are there not made when the words "Robin Hood's Fair" spread from mouth to mouth, and the time and place of it being held become known! Thither would resort all the yeomen and yeomen's wives of the district, each one hoping to get a "Robin Hood's pennyworth," as the well-understood phrase went, in some courtesy or hood, in handkerchiefs telling their goodness by their weight, in hats, boots or shoes, the spoil of some recent campaign, and bespeaking their general excellence from the known quality of their recent owners. Thither would resort the emissaries of more than one priory and respectable monastery, to look after some richly-illuminated Missal or MS. that they had heard were among the good things of the fair, or to execute the High Cellarer's commission to purchase any rare spices that might be offered. Knightly messengers too would not be wanting, coming thither to look after choice weapons, or trinkets, or weighty chains of gold: perhaps even the very men who had been despoiled, and whose treasures had contributed so largely to the "fair," would be sending to it, to purchase silently back some favourite token at a trifling price, hopeless of regaining it by any other mode. Of course the Jews would flock to Sherwood on such occasions from any and all distances. And as the fair proceeded, if any quarrels took place between the buyers and sellers, a Jew would be sure to be concerned. Even whilst he laughed in his heart at the absurd price he was to give for the rich satin vest, or the piece of cloth of gold of such rare beauty that the forester was measuring with his long bow, generally of his own height, for a yard, and even then skipping two or three inches between each admeasurement, the Jew would be sure to be haggling to lower the price or to be increasing the quantity; till reminded that he was not dealing with the most patient as well as with the most liberal of men, by a different application of the tough yew. Then the adventures of the forest!—indigenous and luxuriant as its bilberries; how they give a seasoning, as it were, to the general conjunction of life in the forest, and prevented the possibility of its ever being felt as "weary, stale, flat, and unprofitable!" Were recruits wanted?—there was a pretty opening for adventure in seeking them. They must be men of mark or likelihood who can alone be enlisted into brave Robin's band, and severe accordingly were the tests applied. In order to prove their courage, for instance, it seems from the later ballads, it was quite indispensable that they should have the best of it with some veteran forester, either in shooting with the bow, or playfully breaking a crown with the quarter-staff, or even by occasionally beating their antagonists when contending with inadequate weapons.

Robin Hood himself should appear from these authorities to have been almost as famous for his defeats, as other heroes for their victories. We suspect that what little portion of truth there is in the tradition thus incorporated into the ballads, may be explained by imagining a little ruse on his part in these recruiting expeditions. When he met with some gallant dare-devil whom he desired to include among his troops, what better method could he devise than to appear to be beaten by him after a downright good struggle? He to beat Robin Hood! It was certainly the most exquisite and irresistible of compliments. The promise of a sergeant in later days to make the gaping rustic commander-in-chief was nothing to it. But suppose we now look at two or three of the more interesting adventures which are recorded in the 'Lytell Geste' as having actually taken place, and which, be it observed, may possibly be as true, bating a little here and there for the poetical luxuriance of the author, as if Fordun had related them: ballads in the early ages were histories. In one part of this poem we find a story of the most interesting character, and told with extraordinary spirit, discrimination of character, and dramatic effect. Whilst Little John, Scathelock (the Scarlet of a later time), and Much the Miller's son, were one day watching in the forest, they beheld a knight riding along:—

> All dreari then was his semblaunte,
> And lytell was his pride;
> Hys one fote in the sterope strode,
> The other waved besyde.
>
> Hys hode hangynge over hys eyen two,
> He rode in symple aray;
> A soryer man than he was one
> Rode never in somers day,

The outlaws courteously accost and surprise him with the information that their master has been waiting for him, fasting three hours; Robin Hood, it appears, having an objection to sit down to dinner till he can satisfy himself he has earned it, by finding strangers to sit down with him—and pay the bill. Having "washed," they dine:—

> Brede and wyne they had ynough,
> And nombles [entrails] of the deer;
> Swannes and fesauntes they had full good,
> And foules of the revere:
> There fayled never so lytell a byrde
> That ever was bred on brere.

After dinner the Knight thanks his host for his entertainment, but Robin hints that thanks are not enough. The Knight replies that he has nothing in his coffers that he can for shame offer—that, in short, his whole stock consists of ten shillings. Upon this Robin bids Little John examine the coffers to see if the statement be true (a favourite mode with Robin of judging of the character of his visitors), and informs the Knight at the same time that if he really have no more, more he will lend him.

> "What tydynge, Johan?"—sayed Robyn:
> "Syr, the Knyght is trewe enough."

The great outlaw is now evidently interested; and, with mingled delicacy and frankness, inquires as to the cause of the Knight's low estate, fearing that it implies some wrong doing on his part. It comes out at last that his son has killed a "Knyght of Lancastshyre" in the tournament, and that, to defend him "in his right," he has sold all his own goods, and pledged his lands unto the Abbot of St. Mary's, York; the day is now nearly arrived, and he is not merely unable to redeem them before too late, but well nigh penniless into the bargain. We need hardly solicit attention to the mingled pathos and beauty of what follows:—

> "What is the somme?" sayd Robyn;
> "Trouthe then tell thou me."
> "Syr," he sayd, "foure hondred pounde,
> The Abbot tolde it to me."
>
> "Now, and thou lese thy londe," sayd Robyn,
> "What shall fall of the?"
> "Hastely I wyll me buske," sayde the Knyght,
> "Over the salt see;
>
> "And se where Cryst was quycke and deed
> On the mount of Calvarè.
> Farewell, frende, and have good day,
> It may noo better be——"
>
> Tears fell out of his eyen two,
> He wolde have gone his waye—
> Farewell, frendes, and have good day;
> I ne have more to pay."

THE CORONATION CHAIR.

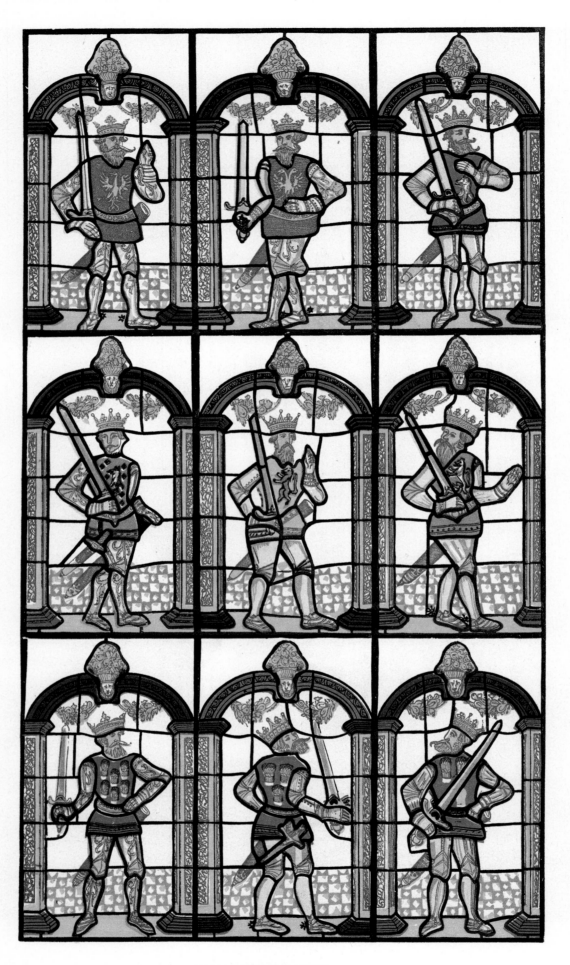

PAINTED WINDOW.

TWO SAXON EARLS OF MERCIA, AND SEVEN NORMAN EARLS OF CHESTER.

ROCHESTER CASTLE.—INTERIOR.

ELIZABETHAN SIDEBOARD, OR COURT CUPBOARD.
IN WARWICK CASTLE.

INTERIOR OF THE TEMPLE CHURCH.

ENTRANCE TO THE CHAPEL OF EDWARD THE CONFESSOR.

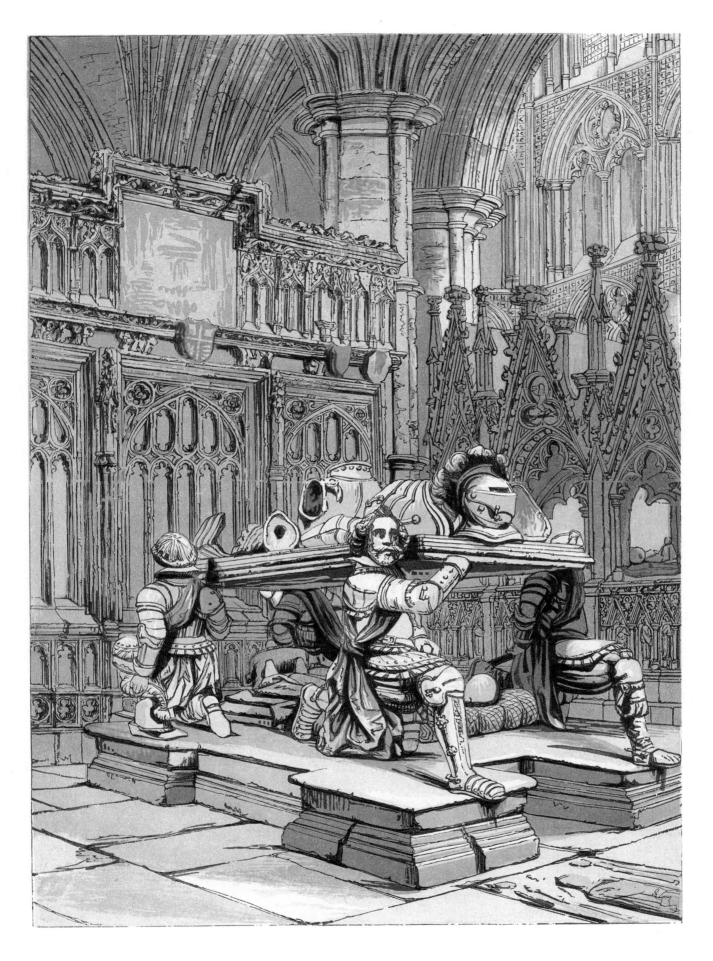

TOMB OF SIR FRANCIS VERE.

IN WESTMINSTER ABBEY.

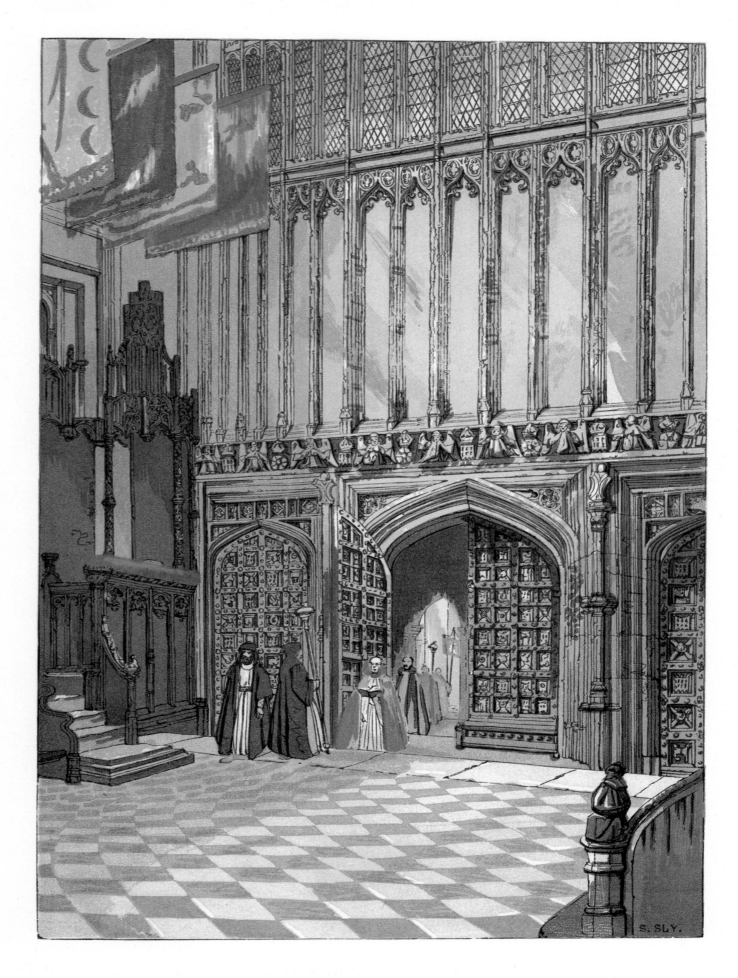

WESTMINSTER ABBEY.——HENRY THE SEVENTH'S CHAPEL.

"Where be thy frendes?" sayde Robyn.
　"Syr, never one wyll me know ;
Whyle I was ryche enow at home,
　Grete bost then wolde they blowe.

"And now they renne away fro me,
　As bestes on a rowe ;
They take no more heed of me
　Then they me never sawe."

For ruthe then wepte Lytell Johan,
　Scathelocke and Much in fere [in company] ;
"Fyll of the best wyne," sayd Robyn,
　"For here is a symple chere."

Before many hours the Knight was pursuing his way with a full
pocket and a full heart to redeem his lands. We must follow him
to York. The day of payment has arrived. The chief officers of
the Abbey are in a state of high excitement, on account of the value
of the estates that will be theirs at nightfall if the Knight comes
not with the redemption money. The Abbot cannot repress his
anticipations :—

"But he come this ylke day,
　Dysheryte shall he be."

The Prior endeavours to befriend the absent Knight, but is answered
impatiently—

"Thou art euer in my berde," sayde the Abbot,
　"By God and Saynt Richarde."

And then bursts in a "fat-headed monk," the High Cellarer, with
the exulting exclamation—

"He is dede or hanged," sayd the monke,
　"By God that bought me dere ;
And we shall have to spende in this place
　Foure hondred pounde by yere."

To make all sure, the Abbot has managed to have the assistance of the High Justicer of England on the occasion by the usual
mode of persuasion, a bribe : and is just beginning to receive his
congratulations when the Knight arrives at the gate. But he
appears in "symple wedes," and the alarm raised by his appearance
soon subsides as he speaks :—

"Do gladly, Syr Abbot," sayd the Knyght ;
　"I am come to holde my day."
The fyrst word the Abbot spoke,—
　"Hast thou brought my pay?"

"Not one peny," sayde the Knyght,
　"By God that maked me."
"Thou art a shrewed dettour," sayd the Abbot ;
　"Syr Justyce, drynke to me."

The Knight tries to move his pity, but in vain ; and after some
further passages between him and the Abbot, conceived and expressed in the finest dramatic spirit, the truth comes out in answer
to a proposition from the Justice that the Abbot shall give two
hundred pounds more to keep the land in peace ; the Knight then
suddenly astounds the whole party by producing the four hundred
pounds.

"Have here thy golde, Syr Abbot," sayd the Knyght,
　"Which that thou lentest me ;
Haddest thou ben curteys at my comynge,
　Rewarde sholdest thou have be."

The Abbot sat styll, and ete no more
　For all his ryall [royal] chere ;
He cast his hede on his sholder,
　And fast began to stare.

"Take [give] me my golde agayne," sayd the Abbot,
　"Syr Justyce, that I toke the."
"Not a peny," sayd the Justyce,
　"By God that dyed on a tree."

A twelvemonth afterwards, and on the very day that the Knight
has fixed for repaying Robin Hood, a magnificent procession of
ecclesiastics and ecclesiastical retainers is passing through the
forest ; and being stopped by the outlaws, who should be at the
head of the whole but our friend the fat-headed monk, the High
Cellarer of St. Mary, York ! Now Robin Hood's security, the only
one that he would take from the Knight, had been that of the
Virgin— what more natural than that he should think the High
Cellarer of the Virgin's own house at York had come to pay him his
four hundred pounds ! It is in vain the holy man denies that he

has come for any such purpose. At last, driven to his shifts, he
ventures a lie when the actual state of his coffers is inquired into.
His return, in official language, is twenty marks. Robin is very
reasonable, and says, if there really be no more, not a penny of it
will be meddled with.

Lytell Johan spred his mantell downe
　As he had done before,
And he tolde out of the monkes male
　Eyght hundreth pounde and more.

No wonder that Robin exclaims—

Monk, what told I thee?
Our Lady is the trewest woman
That ever yet founde I me.

All this is told with a more exquisite humour than our own
partial extracts can do justice to. Anon a second, and to archer
eyes still more attractive pageant, appears. It is the good and
grateful Knight at the head of a hundred men clothed in white and
red, and bearing as a present to the foresters a hundred bows of a
quality to delight even such connoisseurs in the weapon, with a
hundred sheaves of arrows, with heads burnished full bright, every
arrow an ell long, y-dight with peacock plumes, and y-nocked with
silver. The Knight had been detained on his way ; the sun was
down ; the hour of payment had passed when he arrived at the
trysting-tree. His excuse was soon made to the generous outlaw.
He had stayed to help a poor yeoman who was suffering oppression.
The debt was forgiven ; the monks had paid it doubly.

The ballads of Robin Hood which, century after century, followed
the 'Lytell Geste' are, at any rate, evidences of the deep hold
which this story of wild adventure, and of the justice of the strong
hand, long retained upon the popular mind. We have already mentioned how unequal these later productions are to that ancient ballad
which professes to tell the doings of 'Kynge Edwarde and Robin
Hode and Lytell Johan.' Many of these ballads were reprinted by
a scrupulous antiquary, Ritson ; and most of them are to be found
in some collection with which the lovers of early poetry are familiar.
A very neat abridgment of some of the more striking of these
stories was published in 'The Penny Magazine,' in a series of papers
written by the late Mr. Allan Cunningham. To these sources we
may refer our readers. But as the ballad poetry of a country is
amongst the most curious of its records—as the ballads of 'Old
England,' even though they may have been written in the reign of
Elizabeth, or even later, reflect the traditions of the people, and in
many cases are founded upon more ancient compositions that have
perished,—we shall, in each period into which our work is divided,
present one or two ballads entire, without any very exact regard to
the date of their publication, provided they bear upon the events
and manners of the age of which we are treating.

The first ballad which we select for this purpose is from a collection printed in 1607, called 'Strange Histories, or Songes and
Sonets, of Kings, Princes, Dukes, Lordes, Ladyes, Knights, and
Gentlemen ; very pleasant either to be read or songe, and a most
excellent warning for all estates.' Of this curious book there are
only two original copies known to be in existence ; but it has been
recently reprinted by the Percy Society. The principal author of
these poems is held to have been Thomas Deloney, who acquired
great popularity by his books for the people in the end of the sixteenth century, and is spoken of by a contemporary as "the ballad-
ing silk-weaver." The subject of the ballad which we now print
is an interesting event connected with the Norman conquest. We
modernize the orthography, for there is no advantage in retaining
the antique modes of spelling when they have no reference to the
date of a production, or to the peculiarities of its metre. The
'Lytell Geste' could not be thus modernized with the same propriety.

STRANGE HISTORIES.

*The Valiant Courage and Policy of the Kentishmen with Long Tails, whereby
they kept their Ancient Laws and Customs, which William the Conqueror
sought to take from them.*

When as the Duke of Normandy,
　With glistering spear and shield,
Had entered into fair England,
　And foil'd his foes in field,
On Christmas Day in solemn sort,
　Then was he crowned here
By Albert, Archbishop of York,
　With many a noble Peer.

474.—The Forest King.

476.—Burnham Beeches.

477.—Robin Hood, Scarlet, and John.

478.—Robin Hood and the Tanner.—Quarter-staff.

475.—Yew-tree at Fountains Abbey, Ripon, Yorkshire.

481.—Ladies Hunting Deer. (Royal MS. 2 B. vii.)

482.—Cross-bow Shooting at small Birds. (Royal MS. 2 B. vii.)

479.—William of Cloudeslie and his Family in Englewood Forest.

483.—Sword-fight. (Royal MS. 2 C E. 6.)

484.—Wrestling (Royal MS. 2 B. vii.)

Duke's Walking-stick. 480.—Oaks in Welbeck Park. The Seven Sisters.

Which being done, he changed quite
　The custom of this land,
And punish'd such as daily sought
　His statutes to withstand :
And many cities he subdued,
　Fair London with the rest ;
But Kent did still withstand his force,
　Which did his laws detest.

To Dover then he took his way
　The Castle down to fling,
Which Arviragus builded there,
　The noble Briton King.
Which when the brave Archbishop bold
　Of Canterbury knew,
The Abbot of St. Austin's eke,
　With all their gallant crew.

They set themselves in armour bright
　These mischiefs to prevent,
With all the yeomen brave and bold
　That were in fruitful Kent.
At Canterbury they did meet
　Upon a certain day,
With sword and spear, with bill and bow,
　And stopp'd the Conqueror's way.

" Let us not live like bondmen poor
　To Frenchmen in their pride,
But keep our ancient liberty,
　What chance soe'er betide ;
And rather die in bloody field,
　In manlike courage press'd,
Than to endure the servile yoke
　Which we so much detest."

Thus did the Kentish commons cry
　Unto their leaders still,
And so march'd forth in warlike sort,
　And stand on Swanscombe Hill ;
Where in the woods they hid themselves
　Under the shady green,
Thereby to get them vantage good
　Of all their foes unseen.

And for the Conqueror's coming there
　They privily laid wait,
And thereby suddenly appall'd
　His lofty high conceit :
For when they spied his approach,
　In place as they did stand,
Then march'd they to hem him in,
　Each one a bough in hand.

So that unto the Conqueror's sight,
　Amazed as he stood,
They seemed to be a walking grove,
　Or else a moving wood.
The shape of men he could not see,
　The boughs did hide them so ;
And now his heart for fear did quake
　To see a forest go.

Before, behind, and on each side,
　As he did cast his eye,
He spied these woods with sober pace
　Approach to him full nigh.
But when the Kentishmen had thus
　Enclos'd the Conqueror round,
Most suddenly they drew their swords,
　And threw the boughs to ground.

Their banners they displayed in sight,
　Their trumpets sound a charge ;
Their rattling drums strike up alarm,
　Their troops stretch out at large.
The Conqueror with all his train
　Were hereat sore aghast,
And most in peril when he thought
　All peril had been past.

Unto the Kentishmen he sent
　The cause to understand,
For what intent and for what cause
　They took this war in hand ?
To whom they made this short reply :
　" For liberty we fight,
And to enjoy King Edward's laws,
　The which we hold our right."

" Then," said the dreadful Conqueror,
　" You shall have what you will,
Your ancient customs and your law,
　So that you will be still ;
And each thing else that you will crave
　With reason at my hand,
So you will but acknowledge me
　Chief king of fair England."

The Kentishmen agreed hereon,
　And laid their arms aside,
And by this means King Edward's laws
　In Kent doth still abide :
And in no place in England else
　Those customs do remain,
Which they by manly policy
　Did of Duke William gain.

In the possession of Dr. Percy, the accomplished editor of ' Reliques of Ancient English Poetry,' was an ancient ballad entitled ' King John and the Bishop of Canterbury.' The following version of this ballad, in which are some lines found in the more ancient copy, is supposed to have been written or adapted in the time of James I. :—

KING JOHN AND THE ABBOT OF CANTERBURY

An ancient story I'll tell you anon,
Of a notable prince that was called King John ;
And he ruled England with main and with might—
For he did great wrong, and maintained little right

And I'll tell you a story—a story so merry—
Concerning the Abbot of Canterbury :
How for his housekeeping, and high renown,
They rode post for him to fair London town.

An hundred men the King did hear say,
The Abbot kept in his house every day ;
And fifty gold chains, without any doubt,
In velvet coats waited the Abbot about.

How now! Father Abbot, I hear it of thee,
Thou keepest a far better house than me :
And for thy housekeeping, and high renown,
I fear thou work'st treason against my crown.

My Liege, quoth the Abbot, I would it were known,
I never spend nothing but what is my own :
And I trust your Grace will do me no deere,
For spending my own true-gotten gear.

Yes, yes,—quoth he,—Abbot, thy fault it is high,
And now for the same thou needest must die ;
For except thou canst answer me questions three,
Thy head shall be smitten from thy body.

And first,—quo' the King,—when I'm in this stead
With my crown of gold so fair on my head,
Among all my liegemen so noble of birth,
Thou must tell me, to one penny, what I am worth.

Secondly, tell me, without any doubt,
How soon I may ride the whole world about ;
And at the third question thou must not shrink,
But tell me here truly, what I do think.

O, these are hard questions for my shallow wit,
Nor I cannot answer your Grace as yet ;
But if you will give me but three weeks' space
I'll do my endeavour to answer your Grace.

Now three weeks' space to thee I will give,
And that is the longest time thou hast to live ;
For if thou dost not answer my questions three,
Thy lands and thy livings are forfeit to me.

Away rode the Abbot, all sad at that word,
And he rode to Cambridge and Oxenford ;
But never a Doctor there was so wise,
That could, with his learning, an answer devise.

Then home rode the Abbot, of comfort so cold,
And he met his shepherd a-going to fold ;
How now ! my Lord Abbot, you are welcome home
What news do you bring us from good King John ?

Sad news, sad news, shepherd, I must give,—
That I have but three days more to live:
For if I do not answer him questions three,
My head will be smitten from my body.

The first is, to tell him, there in that stead,
With his crown of gold so fair on his head,
Among all his liegemen so noble of birth,
To within one penny of what he is worth.

The second, to tell him, without any doubt,
How soon he may ride this whole world about;
And at the third question I must not shrink,
But tell him there truly what he does think.

Now cheer up, Sir Abbot—did you never hear yet,
That a fool he may learn a wise man wit?
Lend me horse, and serving-men, and your apparel,
And I'll ride to London, to answer your quarrel.

Nay, frown not, if it hath been told unto me,
I am like your Lordship as ever may be;
And if you will but lend me your gown,
There is none shall know us at fair London town.

Now horses and serving-men thou shalt have,
With sumptuous array, most gallant and brave,—
With crosier and mitre, and rochet and cope,—
Fit to appear 'fore our father the Pope.

Now welcome, Sir Abbot, the King he did say,
'Tis well thou'rt come back to keep thy day:
For, and if thou canst answer my questions three
Thy life and thy living both saved shall be.

And first, when thou seest me here in this stead
With my crown of gold so fair on my head,

Among all my liegemen so noble of birth,
Tell me, to one penny, what I am worth.

For thirty pence Our Saviour was sold
Among the false Jews, as I have been told,
And twenty-nine is the worth of thee,
For I think thou art one penny worser than he.

The King he laughed, and swore by St. Bittel,
I did not think I had been worth so little:
Now, secondly, tell me, without any doubt,
How soon I may ride this whole world about.

You must rise with the sun, and ride with the same,
Until the next morning he riseth again,
And then your Grace need not make any doubt
But in twenty-four hours you will ride it about.

The King he laughed, and swore by St. Jone,
I did not think it could be done so soon:
Now from the third question thou must not shrink,
But tell me here truly what I do think.

Yea, that shall I do and make your Grace merry—
You think *I'm the Abbot of Canterbury*;
But I'm his poor shepherd, as plain you may see,
That am come to beg pardon for him and for me.

The King he laughed, and swore by the mass,
I will make thee Lord Abbot this day in his place
Now stay, my liege, be not in such speed,
For alack! I can neither write nor read.

Four nobles a week, then, I will give thee,
For this merry jest thou hast shown unto me;
And tell the old Abbot when thou comest home,
Thou hast brought him a pardon from good King John.

Robin Hood's Well, near Doncaster.

485.—Robin Hood and Little John.

486.—Robin Hood's Stride, or Mock Beggar's Hall, near Burchoven in Youlgrave, Derby.

489.—Sword Dance. (Royal MS. 14 E. iii.)

490.—Country Revel. (Royal MS. 2 B. 7.)

488.—The Parliament Oak in Clipstone Park.

487.—" Will Scarlet, he did kill a buck."

491.—A Carthusian.

492.—A Benedictine.

493.—A Cistercian.

494.—Roger, Bishop of Sarum, 1293.
Salisbury Cathedral.

497.—Costume of an English Mitred Abbot.

498.—Costume of an English Abbess.

495.—Andrew, Abbot of Peterborough, 1199.—Peterborough
Cathedral.

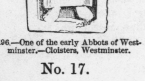

496.—One of the early Abbots of Westminster.—Cloisters, Westminster.

499.—Vision of Henry I.; an ancient drawing, showing the Costume of the Clergy.

500.—Odo, Bishop of Bayeux, pronouncing a
Pastoral Blessing.

No. 17.

CHAPTER II.—ECCLESIASTICAL ANTIQUITIES

HE first century of the Norman rule in England has left behind it more durable monuments of the earnest devotion of the mixed races of the country than any subsequent period of our history. The ecclesiastical distribution of England was scarcely altered from the time of Henry I. to that of Henry VIII. The Conqueror found the archbishoprics of Canterbury and York established, as well as the following bishoprics:—Durham, London, Winchester, Rochester, Chichester, Salisbury, Exeter, Wells, Worcester, Hereford, Coventry, Lincoln, Thetford. Norwich became the see of the bishop of Thetford in 1088. The see of Ely was founded in 1109, and that of Carlisle in 1133. The governing power of the church thus remained for four centuries, till Henry VIII., in 1541, founded the sees of Bristol, Gloucester, Oxford, Peterborough, and Chester, portions of the older dioceses being taken to form the see of each new bishop. The Rev. Joseph Hunter, in his excellent 'Introduction to the Valor Ecclesiasticus of King Henry VIII.,' says, "It is indeed a just subject of wonder that in the first century after the Conquest so many thousand of parish churches should have been erected, as if by simultaneous effort, in every part of the land, while at the same time spacious and magnificent edifices were arising in every diocese to be the seats of the bishops and archbishops, or the scenes of the perpetual services of the inhabitants of the cloister. Saxon piety had done much, perhaps more than we can collect from the pages of Domesday : but it is rather to the Normans than to the Saxons that we are to attribute the great multitude of parish churches existing at so remote an era ; and a truly wise and benevolent exertion of Christian piety the erection of them must be regarded." To describe, with anything like minuteness of detail, any large proportion of these ecclesiastical antiquities, would carry us far beyond the proper object of this work ; but we shall endeavour in this chapter, and in those of subsequent periods, to present to our readers some of the more remarkable of these interesting objects, whether we regard their beauty and magnificence, or the circumstances connected with their foundation and history. Our series of cathedrals will, however, be complete. Mr. Hunter, speaking of the historical uses of the 'Valor Ecclesiasticus' (which has been printed in six large folio volumes, under the direction of the Record Commissioners), says, that in this record " We at once see not only the ancient extent and amount of that provision which was made by the piety of the English nation for the spiritual edification of the people by the erection of churches and chapels for the decent performance of the simple and touching ordinances of the Christian religion, but how large a proportion had been saved from private appropriation of the produce of the soil, and how much had subsequently been given to form a public fund, accessible to all, out of which might be supported an order of cultivated and more enlightened men dispersed through society, and by means of which blessings incalculable might be spread amongst the whole community. If there were spots or extravagancies, yet on the whole it is a pleasing as well as a splendid spectacle, especially if we look with minute observation into any portion of the Record, and compare it with a map which shows the distribution of population in those times over the island, and then observe how religion had pursued man even to his remotest abodes, and was present among the most rugged dwellers in the hills and wilderness of the land, softening and humanizing their hearts. . . . . . But the Record does not stop here. It presents us with a view of those most gorgeous establishments where the service of the Most High was conducted in the magnificent structures which still exist amongst us, with a great array of priests, and all the pomp of which acts of devotion admit ; and of the abbeys and other monasteries, now but ruined edifices, where resided the sons and daughters of an austerer piety, and where the services were scarcely ever suspended."

Who can turn over such a record as this, or dwell upon the minuter descriptions of our country histories, without feeling there was a spirit at work in those ages which is now comparatively cold and lifeless ? Who can lift up his eyes to the pinnacles and towers, or stand beneath the vaulted roof of any one of the noble cathedrals and minsters that were chiefly raised up during this early period— who can rest, even for a brief hour, amidst the solitude of some ruined abbey, as affecting in its decay as it was imposing in its splendour—who even can look upon the ponderous columns, the quaint carvings not without their symbolical meanings, the solidity which proclaims that those who thus built knew that the principle through which they built must endure—who can look upon such things without feeling that there was something higher and purer working in the general mind of the people than that which has produced the hideous painted and whitewashed parallelograms that we have raised up and called churches in these our days? We shall not get better things by the mere copying of the antique models by line and compass. When the spirit which created our early ecclesiastical architecture has once more penetrated into the hearts of the people ; when it shall be held, even upon principles of utility, that man's cravings after the eternal and the infinite are to be as much provided and cared for as his demands for food and raiment ; then the tendencies of society will not be wholly exhibited in the perfection of mechanical contrivance, in rapidity of communication, in never-ceasing excitements to toil without enjoyment. When the double nature of man is understood and cared for, we may again raise up monuments of piety which those who come five hundred years after us will preserve in a better spirit than we have kept up many of those monuments which were left to us by those who did not build solely for their own little day.

In entering upon the large subject of our ecclesiastical antiquities, we have found it almost impossible to attempt any systematic division. Our architecture from the period of the Conquest is generally divided into Anglo-Norman, Early English, Decorative, and Perpendicular. We shall endeavour, as far as we can, to make our chronological arrangement suit these broad distinctions. But as there is scarcely an important building remaining that does not exhibit more than one of these characteristics, and as we cannot return again and again to the same building, we must be content to classify them according to their main characteristics. For example, Canterbury, and Lincoln, and Durham have portions of the earlier styles still remaining in them, and these naturally find a place in the present Book ; but our engravings and descriptions must necessarily include the other styles with which these edifices abound. A little familiarity with the general principles of ecclesiastical architecture will soon enable the reader to mark what belongs to one period and what to another ; and, without going into professional technicalities, we shall incidentally endeavour to assist those who really desire to study the subject. Looking in the same way, not to the date of the foundation, but to the main characteristics of the existing edifice, we shall be enabled to disperse our ecclesiastical materials through some of the subsequent periods into which our little work is divided, not attempting great precision, but something like chronological order. For example, we know that the present Westminster Abbey was not built till the time of Henry the Third, and we therefore postpone our notice of Westminster Abbey, although it was founded by Edward the Confessor, to the period which succeeds the reign of John. Other buildings, such as Salisbury Cathedral, St. George's Chapel at Windsor, and King's College Chapel at Cambridge, being the work of one age, and probably of one architect, do not involve the same chronological difficulties that a cathedral presents which has been raised up by the munificence of bishop after bishop, the choir being the work of one age, the nave of another, the transepts of another, each age endeavouring at some higher perfection. If we are sometimes betrayed into anachronisms, those who have studied this large subject scientifically will, we trust, yield us their excuse.

The noblest ecclesiastical edifices which still remain to us, as well as the ruins which are spread throughout the land, were connected with the establishments of those who lived under the monastic rule. This will be incidentally seen, whether we describe a cathedral, with all its present establishment of bishop, dean, and chapter, or a ruined abbey, whose ivy-covered columns lie broken on the floor, where worshippers have knelt, generation after generation, dreaming not that in a few centuries the bat and the owl would usurp their places. We shall proceed at once to one of the most ancient and splendid of these forsaken places—Glastonbury. We shall not here enter upon any minute description of the engravings numbered 491 to 511, which precede the view of that celebrated abbey. Those engravings represent the costume of the monastic orders of that early period, as well as some specimens of the more ancient fonts and other matters connected with the offices of the church. We shall have to refer to these more particularly as we proceed.

———

GLASTONBURY is one of those few remaining towns in England which seem to preserve, in spite of decay and innovation, a kind of grateful evidence of the people and the institutions from whence their former importance was derived. No one can pass through its streets without having strongly impressed upon his mind the recollections of the famous monastery of Glastonbury, or without seeing how magnificent an establishment must have been planted here, when the very roots, centuries after its destruction, still arrest the attention at every step by their magnitude and apparently almost indestructible character. We have hardly left behind us the marshy flats that surround and nearly insulate the town (whence the old British name of the Glassy Island), and ascended the eminence upon which it stands, before we perceive that almost every other building has been either constructed, in modern times, out of stone, quarried from some architectural ruins, or is in itself a direct remain of the foundation from whence the plunder has been derived; in other words, some dependency of the monastery. The George Inn is not only one of these, but preserves its old character; it was, from the earliest times, a house of accommodation for the pilgrims and others visiting Glastonbury. As we advance we arrive at a quadrangle formed by four of the streets, and from which others pass off; in that quadrangle stand the chief remains of what was once the most magnificent monastic structure perhaps in the three countries. They consist of some fragments of the church, and of two other structures tolerably entire, the kitchen, and the chapel of St. Joseph (Fig. 512). The style of the church belongs to the transition period of the twelfth century, and is of a pure and simple character. The kitchen is a very curious example of domestic architecture, of comparatively recent date; the following story is told of its origin:—Henry VIII. one day said to the abbot, who had offended him, but professedly in reproof of the sensual indulgences which he appeared to believe disgraced the monastery, that he would burn the kitchen; upon which the abbot haughtily replied that he would build such a kitchen that not all the wood in the royal forest should be sufficient to carry the threat into execution; forthwith he built the existing structure. The chapel is a truly remarkable place on many accounts. It presents essentially the same architectural characteristics as the church, but is much more highly enriched. It stands at the west end of the church, with which it communicates by an ante-chapel, the whole measuring in length not less than one hundred and ten feet, by twenty-five feet in breadth. But interesting as the chapel and all the other monastic remains stretching so far around (some sixty acres in all were included within the establishment) must be to every one, it cannot be these alone, or aught that we may infer from them, that gives to Glastonbury its absorbing interest. Strip the locality of every tradition in which real facts have but assumed the harmonious coverings of the imagination, or in which pure fictions have but still made everlasting a fact of their own, that such and such things were believed at some remote time, and are therefore scarcely less worthy of record,—strip Glastonbury of all these, and enough remains behind to render it impossible that it can ever be looked upon without the deepest feelings of gratitude and reverence. Before we look at the soberer facts, suppose we let Tradition lead us at her own "sweet will," whithersoever she pleases. We are, then, moving onwards towards a small eminence, about half a mile to the north-west, noticing on our way the numerous apple-trees scattered about, with their swelling pink buds suggesting the loveliness of the coming bloom; these trees, Tradition tells us, gave to the isle one of its old and most poetical names, Avalon, from the Saxon Avale, an apple. But we

have reached the eminence in question, and are looking about us with keen curiosity, to learn, if we can, from the very aspect of the place, the origin of its curious designation—Weary-all-Hill. Here, Tradition informs us, was the spot where the first bringer of glad tidings to the British heathen, Joseph of Arimathea, sent by Philip the apostle of Gaul on that high mission, rested on his inland way from the seashore where he had landed, and, striking his staff into the ground, determined to found in the vicinity the first British temple for the Christian worship. Hence the name existing to this day of Weary-all-Hill, and hence that peculiar species of thorn, which, springing from St. Joseph's budding staff, tells to a poetical belief the story of its origin, and the period of the year when Joseph arrived, in its winter or very early spring flowers (Fig. 514). The spot itself was no doubt thought too small to rear such a structure upon as was desirable, and therefore the little band of missionaries moved half a mile farther, and there commenced their labours in founding a Christian edifice for the native worshippers, who speedily flocked around them. In that early building St. Joseph himself, continues our authority, Tradition, was buried on his decease; and when, in the lapse of ages, the new faith had become prosperous and magnificent in all its outward appliances, and a new church was erected more in harmony with the tastes, skill, and wants of the age, the site of that primeval building, and the place of Joseph's burial, were still reverentially preserved by the erection over them of a chapel dedicated to the saint's memory. And this is the chapel of St. Joseph, within whose walls we may still wander and commune with our own thoughts, on the importance of the truths which from hence gradually extended their all-pervading influence through the length and breadth of the land. But are these traditions true?— We answer, that in their essence, we have no doubt they are strictly so. Weary-all-Hill may never have been trodden by Joseph of Arimathea's steps; the staff certainly never budded into the goodly hawthorns that so long were the glory of the neighbourhood; but in the subsequent history of Glastonbury, we find ample corroborative evidence to show that there was some especial distinction enjoyed by the monastery, and that that distinction was the fact so poetically enshrined in the popular heart, of its having been the place where the sublime story of the Cross, and its immeasurable consequences, were first taught among us. Thus, in the most ancient charters of the monastery, we find the very significant designation assigned to it—"The fountain and origin of all religion in the realm of Britain:" thus, we find, through the earliest Saxon periods, one continued stream of illustrious persons, showering upon it wealth, privileges, honours, during life; and confiding their bodies to its care after death. What was it that brought the great Apostle of Ireland, after his successful labours, to Glastonbury, a little before the middle of the fifth century; when as yet no monastery existed, and the few religious who performed the service of the church, burrowed, like so many wild beasts, in dens, caves, and wretched huts? What could bring such a man, in all the height of his spiritual success, to such a place? What, but the sympathy that his own exertions in Ireland naturally caused him to feel, in an extraordinary degree, for the place where similar exertions had been previously made in England? Here St. Patrick is said to have spent all the latter years of his life, and to have raised Glastonbury into a regular community. A century later exhibits another retirement to Glastonbury, which also, probably, marks the peculiar attraction that the circumstances we have described had given to it. About the year 530, David Archbishop of Menevia, with seven of his suffragans, came to Glastonbury, and enlarged the buildings by the erection of the chapel of the Holy Virgin, on the altar of which he deposited a sapphire of inestimable value. In 708, all previous exertions to increase the comfort, size, and beauty of the conventual edifice were thrown into the shade by those of Ina, King of Wessex, who rebuilt the whole from the very foundation. At that period, the alleged origin of Glastonbury seems to have been fully believed; it was on the chapel of St. Joseph that the monarch lavished his utmost care and wealth, garnishing it all over with gold and silver, filling it with a profusion of the most costly vessels and ornaments. Still growing in magnificence, scarcely a century and a quarter had elapsed, before new works were commenced, which, when finished, made Glastonbury the "pride of England, and the glory of Christendom." A striking evidence of its pre-eminence is given in the statement that it then furnished superiors to all the religious houses in the kingdom. But when we know who was the abbot of Glastonbury at the period, we may cease to be surprised—it was Dunstan, a man whose connection with it has added even to Glastonbury's reputation. Born almost within its precincts, his mind saturated with all its strange and beautiful legends, he formed a personal attachment to the monas-

501.—Font in Sharnbourn Church Norfolk.

502.—West Side of Bridekirk Font.

503.—East Side of Bridekirk Font.

504.—Font in Berkeley Church.

509.—Marriage of the Father and Mother of Becket. (From the Royal MS. 2 B. vii.)

508.—Baptism of the Mother of Becket. (From the Royal MS. 2 B. vii.)

510.—Burial of a deceased Monk in the Interior of a Convent. (From an ancient drawing in the Harleian MSS.)

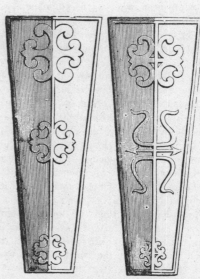

511.—Stone Coffins.—Ixworth Abbey, Suffolk.

505.—Font in Iffley Church.

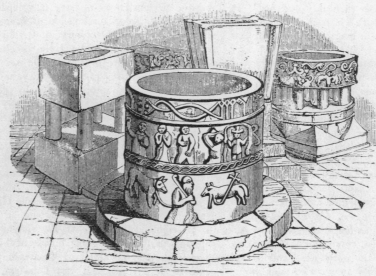

507.—Group of Norman-English Fonts.

506.—Font in Neswick Church.

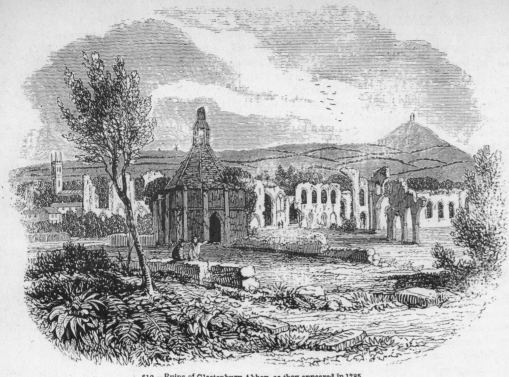

513.—Cup found in the Ruins of Glastonbury Abbey.

512.—Ruins of Glastonbury Abbey, as they appeared in 1785.

514.—The Glastonbury Thorn.

515.—Lewes Priory.

516.—St. Botolph's Priory, Colchester.

133

tery, long before ambition could have led him to connect its advancement with his own; in early life he received the tonsure within its walls; and when, returning for a time, disgusted with the world, or at least that portion of it, Athelstan's court, with which he was best acquainted, he buried himself in privacy, it was in or near the Abbey of Glastonbury that he built himself a cell or hermitage with an oratory, and divided his time between devotion and the manual service of the abbey, in the construction of crosses, vials, censers, and vestments. It is hardly necessary to state that here too he held that meeting with the Evil One which has redounded so greatly to his fame. Those who like to study the hidden meanings that no doubt generally do exist in the most marvellous narrations that have been handed down from a remote time, may find a clue to this one, in the statement of the 'Golden Legend,' printed by Caxton, that the Devil came in the form of a handsome woman. From the period of the abbacy of Dunstan dates the establishment of the Benedictine monks in England, who were brought from Italy by him, and subsequently introduced into his own monastery, in spite of the clamour raised against them, in consequence of their severe discipline, which put to shame the loose and almost licentious habits of the secular clergy. He lost his abbacy, however, for a time, in consequence, and was banished during the reign of Edwy; but returned during that of his successor, Edgar, over whose mind it is well known he obtained the most absolute control. It was probably through this intimacy that Edgar was induced to erect a palace within two miles of Glastonbury, at a most romantic situation still known as Edgarley; and of which structure some interesting vestiges remain,—a pelican and two wolves' heads, attached to a modern house; the last symbol referring to Edgar's tax upon the Welsh people for the extirpation of wolves. The king was buried at Glastonbury, and, we may be sure, in the most sumptuous manner, for the monks owed much to him. What with the privileges conferred by him, and what with those previously possessed, Glastonbury was raised to the highest pitch of monastic splendour. Over that little kingdom, the Isle of Avalon, the abbots were virtual sovereigns; neither king nor bishop might enter without their permission. They governed themselves in the same independent mode: the monks elected their own superior. And, although some reverses were subsequently experienced, as immediately after the Conquest, for instance, the foundation continued down to its very destruction at the Reformation, in such magnificence, that the poor of the whole country round were twice a week relieved at its gates, and when the last abbot, Whytyng, rode forth, he was accustomed to move amidst a train of some sixscore persons. That same abbot died on the scaffold, a victim to the brutal monarch who then disgraced the throne; and a revenue exceeding 3,500l. a-year fell into Henry's rapacious hands.

Such is a mere sketch of the history of the important abbey of Glastonbury; but there is yet one point connected with it, that, in the absence of all other interesting associations, would invest the precincts of Glastonbury with a thousand fascinations. Here King Arthur was buried! Arthur, that hero, whose most romantic history appears so dimly to our eyes through the mists of above thirteen centuries, that we can hardly distinguish the boundaries between the true and false. There can be no doubt, however, of that part of his history which relates to Glastonbury. He died, it is understood, at the battle of Camlan in Cornwall, in 542, and was conveyed by sea to Glastonbury, there buried, and, in process of time, the spot was altogether forgotten and lost. The way in which it was discovered harmonizes with the rest of Arthur's story. When Henry the Second was passing through Wales on his way to Ireland, in 1172, he delighted the Welsh with his politic compliments upon their services in his Irish expeditions. They, full of enthusiasm, wished him all the prosperity that had attended their favourite King Arthur, whose exploits were sung to him as he dined, by one of the native bards. In the song mention was made of the place of Arthur's burial, between two pyramids in the churchyard at Glastonbury. On Henry's return to England, he told the abbot of the monastery what he had heard; and a search was instituted. Of this very interesting event there was fortunately eye-witness one of our chroniclers, Giraldus Cambrensis. Seven feet below the surface of a huge broad stone was found, with a small thin plate of lead in the form of a corpse, and bearing, in rude letters and barbarous style, the Latin inscription: "Hic jacet Sepultus Inclytus Rex Arturius in Insula Avalonia." Nine feet deeper, they found the object of their search, in the trunk of a tree; the remains of Arthur himself were displayed to their eyes, and by his side lay those of his wife Guinever. The bones of the king were of extraordinary size; the shinbone, fastened against the foot of a very tall man, reached three fingers' breadth above his knee. The skull was covered with wounds;

ten distinct fractures were counted; one of great size, apparently the effect of the fatal blow. The queen's body was strangely whole and perfect; the hair neatly platted, and of the colour of burnished gold; but when touched, it fell suddenly to dust, reminding one of the similar scene described in Mrs. Gray's work on 'Etruria,' where the party beheld for a moment, on opening a tomb, one of the ancient kings of that mysterious people, raised and garbed in lifelike and sovereign state, and in which, on the exposure to the fresh air, there was perceptible a kind of misty frost. The next moment all was lost, in the dust of the ground upon which they gazed with so much astonishment. This discovery appears to have excited so deep and permanent an interest, that Edward the First could not be contented without seeing the remains himself: so he came hither with his beloved Queen Eleanor; and the ceremony of exhumation was very solemnly performed. The skulls were then set up in the Treasury, to remain there; the rest of the bodies were returned to their places of deposit, Edward inclosing an inscription recording the circumstances. The stately monument erected over Arthur and Guinever was destroyed at the Reformation, and with it disappeared all traces of the contents.

We conclude with the following spirited lines from Drayton :—

"O three-times famous isle, where is that place that might
Be with thyself compar'd for glory and delight,
Whilst Glastonbury stood? exalted to that pride
Whose monastery seem'd all other to deride :
Oh! who thy ruin sees whom wonder doth not fill
With our great fathers' pomp. devotion, and their skill?
Thou more than mortal power (this judgment rightly weigh'd)
Then present to assist, at that foundation laid,
On whom, for this sad waste, should justice lay the crime?
Is there a power in fate, or doth it yield to time ?
Or was their error such, that thou could'st not protect
Those buildings which thy hand did with their zeal erect?
To whom didst thou commit that monument to keep,
That suffereth with the dead their memory to sleep?
When not great Arthur's tomb nor holy Joseph's grave,
From sacrilege had power their sacred bones to save;
He who that God in man to his sepulchre brought,
Or he which for the faith twelve famous battles fought.
What! did so many kings do honour to that place,
For avarice at last so vilely to deface?
For reverence to that seat which had ascribed been,
Trees yet in winter bloom and bear their summer's green."

Of another monastic establishment of the period in review, St. Botolph's, Colchester, we need not enter into any lengthened notice (Fig. 516). It was founded in the reign of Henry the First, as a Priory of Augustine Canons, by a monk of the name of Ernulph; dissolved, of course, at the Reformation; and the chief buildings reduced to a premature ruin in the civil war, when the great siege of Colchester took place. Parts of the church form the chief remains. The west front has been originally a very magnificent though very early work; the double series of intersecting arches that form the second and third stages of the façade, and extend over the elaborately-rich Norman gateway, are especially interesting; as it is from such examples of the pointed arches thus accidentally obtained by the intersections of round ones that the essential principle of the Gothic has been supposed to have been derived. Some of the lofty circular arches of the walls forming the body of the church also exist in a tolerable state of preservation. The length of the church was one hundred and eight feet, the breadth across the nave and aisles about forty-four. The exceeding hardness of much of the materials used in the construction of this building renders it probable that they had been taken from the wrecks of Roman buildings at Colchester.

The priory of Lewes, in Sussex, of which there are only a few walls remaining (Fig. 515), was founded in 1077, by William, Earl of Warenne, who came into England with the Conqueror. The founder has left a remarkable document in his charter to the abbey, wherein he describes the circumstance which led him to this act of piety. He and his wife were travelling in Burgundy, and finding they could not in safety proceed to Rome, on account of the war which was then carrying on between the Pope and the Emperor, took up their abode in the great monastery of St. Peter at Cluni. The hospitality with which they were treated, the sanctity and charity of the establishment, determined the Earl to offer the new religious house which he founded at Lewes to a select number of the monks of that fraternity. After some difficulties his request was complied with, and the Cluniacs took possession of this branch of their house. The anxiety of the earl liberally to endow this house, and his determination "as God increased his substance to increase hat of the monks," finds a remarkable contrast four hundred and fifty years afterwards. After the dissolution of the religious houses, John Portmari writes to Lord Cromwell of his surprising efforts in *pulling down* the church; and having recounted how he had destroyed this chapel, and plucked down that altar, he adds, " that your Lordship may know with how many men we have done this, we brought from London seventeen persons, three carpenters, two smiths, two plumbers, and one that keepeth the furnace. These are men exercised much better than the men we find here in the country." And yet they left enough " to point a moral."

Tradition and romance have been busily at work respecting the origin and locality of the earliest building dedicated to St. Paul as the chief metropolitan church. It has been supposed to have been founded by the Apostle Paul himself; while there is really some reason to presume that the site, possibly the actual building, had been at first dedicated to the heathen worship of Diana. Ox heads, sacred to that goddess, were discovered in digging on the south side of St. Paul's in 1316; at other times the teeth of boars and other beasts, and a piece of buck's horn, with fragments of vessels, that might have been used in the pagan sacrifices, have been found. The idea itself is of antique date. Flete, the monk of Westminster, referring to the partial return to heathenism in the fifth century, when the Saxons and Angles, as yet unconverted to Christianity, overran the country, observes, " Then were *restored* the whole abominations wherever the Britons were expelled their places. London worships Diana, and the suburbs of Thorney [the site of Westminster] offer incense to Apollo." To leave speculations, and turn to facts. The see of London was in existence as early as the latter part of the second century; though it is not until the sixth that we find any actual reference to a church. But at that period a very interesting incident occurred in the church, which Bede dramatically relates :—When Sebert, the founder of Westminster Abbey, and the joint founder (according to Bede) with Ethelbert, King of Kent, of St. Paul's, died, he " left his three sons, who were yet pagans, heirs of his temporal kingdom. Immediately on their father's decease they began openly to practise idolatry (though whilst he lived they had somewhat refrained), and also gave free licence to their subjects to worship idols. At a certain time these princes, seeing the Bishop [of London, Mellitus] administering the sacrament to the people in the church, after the celebration of mass, and being puffed up with rude and barbarous folly, spake, as the common report is, thus unto him :—' Why dost thou not give us, also, some of that white bread which thou didst give unto our father Saba [Sebert], and which thou dost not yet cease to give to the people in the church?' He answered, ' If ye will be washed in that wholesome font whereat your father was, ye may likewise eat of this blessed bread whereof he was a partaker; but if ye contemn the lavatory of life, ye can in nowise taste the bread of life.' ' We will not,' they rejoined, ' enter into this font of water, for we know we have no need to do so; but we will eat of that bread nevertheless.' And when they had been often and earnestly warned by the bishop that it could not be, and that no man could partake of this most holy oblation without purification, and cleansing by baptism, they at length, in the height of their rage, said to him, ' Well, if thou wilt not comply with us in the small matter that we ask, thou shalt no longer abide in our province and dominions;' and straightway they expelled him, commanding that he and all his company should quit the realm." Thus once more Christianity was banished from London. It was, however, but for a short time. The worship that the great Apostle of the Gentiles preached soon again appeared in the church dedicated to his name; and powerful men vied with each other in raising the edifice to the highest rank of ecclesiastical foundations. Kenred, king of the Mercians, one of these early benefactors, ordained that it should be as free in all things as he himself desired to be in the Day of Judgment. The feeling thus evidenced continued, or rather gained in strength. When the Conqueror came over, some of its possessions were seized by his reckless followers : on the very day of his coronation, however, their master, having previously caused everything to be restored, granted a charter securing its property for ever, and expressing the giver's benedictions upon all who should augment the revenues, and his curses on all who should diminish them. The church of Ethelbert was burnt in the Conqueror's reign, and a new one commenced by Bishop Maurice. That completed, in little more than a century,—when it appeared " so stately and beautiful, that it was worthily numbered among the most famous buildings,"—a great portion of the labours were recommenced in order to give St. Paul's the advantage of the strikingly beautiful Gothic style that had been introduced in the interim, and carried to a high pitch of

perfection. In 1221 a new steeple was finished; and in 1240 a new choir. Not the least noticeable feature of these new works is the mode in which the money was raised—namely, by letters from the bishops addressed to the clergy and others under their jurisdiction, granting indulgences for a certain number of days to all those who, having penance to perform, or being penitent, should assist in the rebuilding of St. Paul's. The subterranean church, St. Faith, was begun in 1256 (Fig. 517). And thus at last was completed the structure that remained down to the great fire of London, when Old St. Paul's was included in the widespread ruin that overtook the metropolis.

And in many respects that Old St. Paul's was an extraordinary and deeply-interesting pile. Its dimensions were truly enormous. The space occupied by the building exceeded three acres and a half. The entire height of the tower and spire was 534 feet (Fig. 522). For nearly 700 feet did nave and choir and presbytery extend in one continuous and most beautiful architectural vista; unbroken save by the low screen dividing the nave from the choir. The breadth and height were commensurate; the former measuring 130 feet, the latter, in the nave, 102 feet. Over all this immense range of wall, floor, and roof, with supporting lines of pillars, sculpture and painting and gilding had lavished their stores; and their effects were still further enhanced by the gorgeously rich and solemn hues that streamed upon them from the stained windows. At every step was passed some beautiful altar with the tall taper burning before it, or some chantry, whence issued the musical voices of the priests, as they offered up prayers for the departed founders, or some magnificent shrine, where all the ordinary arts of adornment had been insufficient to satisfy the desire to reverence properly the memory of its saint, and which therefore sparkled with the precious metals, and still more precious gems—silver and gold, rubies, emeralds, and pearls. Pictures were there too, on every column or spare corner of the walls, with their stories culled from the most deeply-treasured and venerated pages of the Sacred Scriptures; the chief of these was the great picture of St. Paul, which stood beside the high altar in a beautiful " tabernacle" of wood. Then there were the monuments; a little world in themselves of all that was rare and quaint, splendid or beautiful, in monumental sculpture and architecture; and which yet when gazed upon, hardly arrested the careful attention of the beholder to their own attractions, but rather preoccupied his mind at the first sight of them by remembrances of the men to whose memory they had been erected. Here lay two monarchs—Sebba, King of the East Saxons, converted by Erkenwold, Bishop of London, and son of King Offa; and Ethelred the Unready, whose reign might be appropriately designated by a more disgraceful epithet. Here lay also Edward Atheling, or the outlaw, Ethelred's grandson, one of the popular heroes of English romantic history, who lost the kingdom by his father's (Edmund Ironside's) agreement with Canute, to divide the kingdom whilst both lived, and the survivor to inherit the whole, and who was waiting about the Court of Edward the Confessor in the hope of regaining that kingdom, when he died, poisoned, it was suspected, by his rival Harold. Here also lay Saint Erkenwold, the canonized bishop of the see, and in such glorious state as has been accorded to the remains of few even of the mightiest potentates of earth. Among all the marvels of artistical wealth that filled almost to overflowing the interior of Old St. Paul's, the shrine of St. Erkenwold stood pre-eminent. It consisted of a lofty pyramidical structure, in the most exquisitely decorated Pointed style; with an altar-table in front, covered with jewels and articles of gold and silver. Among the former was the famous sapphire stone, given by Richard de Preston, citizen and grocer of London, for the cure of infirmities in the eyes of all those who, thus afflicted, might resort thither. To the mental as well as to the bodily vision this shrine was the grand feature of the cathedral; for the commemoration of the saint's burial was regularly observed with the highest and most magnificent of church ceremonials. Then, in solemn procession, the bishop, arrayed in robes of the most dazzling splendour, accompanied by the dean and other distinguished officers, and followed by the greater part of the parochial clergy of the diocese, passed through the cathedral to the shrine, where solemn masses were sung, and the indulgences granted to all who visited the saint's burial-place, and to those who there offered oblations, recited. Then might have been beheld a touching and beautiful scene; rich and poor pressing forward with their gifts—costly in the one case; a mere mite, like the poor widow's, in the other.

But there were yet mightier spirits among the buried dead of Old St. Paul's. Passing over Sir John Beauchamp, son of the renowned Guy, Earl of Warwick, Henry de Lacy, Earl of Lincoln, one of Edward the First's ablest military officers, and the accomplished Sir Simon Burley, executed during the reign of Richard II., we

517.—St. Faith's.

518.—Paul's Walk.

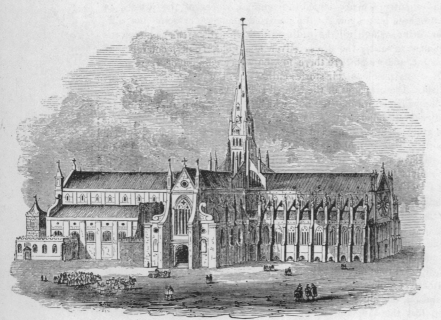

522.—Old St. Paul's, before the Destruction of the Steeple.

520.—Paul's Cross.

521.—East Window, from the Choir, St. Paul's.

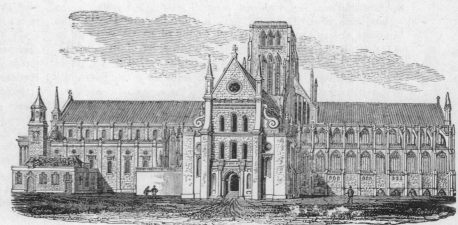

519.—Old St. Paul's Cathedral—South View.

527.—The Western Entrance, Interior, St. Bartholomew's Church.

525.—The Crypt, St. Bartholomew's Church.

529.—Entrance to Bartholomew Close, from Smithfield.

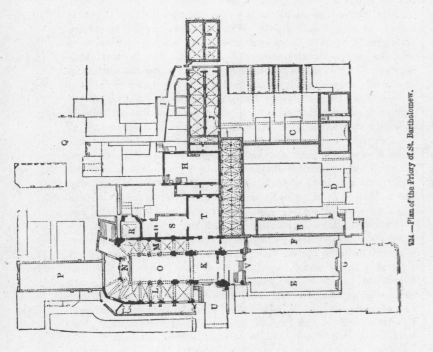

524.—Plan of the Priory of St. Bartholomew.

523.—South Side of St. Bartholomew's Church.

528.—Prior Rahere's Tomb.

530.—Prior Bolton's Rebus.

526.—The Choir, St. Bartholomew's Church.

find that John of Gaunt, "time-honoured Lancaster," was interred in Old St. Paul's beneath a magnificent monument, where athwart the slender octagonal pillars appeared with a very picturesque effect his tilting-spear, and where the mighty duke himself lay in effigy beneath a canopy of the most elaborate fretwork. Beside him reclined Blanche, the duke's first wife, whom Chaucer has made immortal by his grateful verse. In the cathedral was witnessed on one occasion an important scene, with which John of Gaunt was most honourably connected. Wickliffe was cited here to answer before the great prelates of the realm the charge of heresy and innovation. He appeared, but with such a train as seldom falls to the early history of church reform to speak of; it will be sufficient to say, John of Gaunt was at their head. The meeting broke up in confusion. In later times Linacre, the eminent physician, and founder of the College of Physicians, Sir Christopher Hatton, Sir Francis Walsingham, Elizabeth's secretary, and Sir Nicholas, father of Lord Bacon, her keeper of the seals, were all interred in St. Paul's; as were Dean Colet, the founder of St. Paul's School, and the poet Donne, whose effigy yet exists in the present cathedral, disgracefully thrown into a dark corner in the vaults below.

There were many features of Old St. Paul's which, if they did not add to, or even harmonise in our notions with, the religious character of the edifice, certainly added wonderfully to its attractions in the eyes of our more enjoying and less scrupulous forefathers. Thus, did civil war threaten—the martial population of London flocked to the church to witness the presentation of the banner of St. Paul to Robert Fitzwalter, the hereditary Castellan of the city, who came on horseback, and armed, to the great west door, where he was met by the mayor and aldermen, also armed; and, when he had dismounted and saluted them, handed to them the banner, "gules," with the image of St. Paul in gold, saying they gave it to him as their banneror of fee, to bear and govern to the honour and profit of the city. After that, they gave the baron a horse of great value, and twenty pounds in money. Then was a marshal chosen to guide the host of armed citizens, who were presently to be called together en masse by the startling sound of the great bell. Was amusement sought—there were the regular Saturnalias of the Boy-Bishops, and the plays, for which Old St. Paul's enjoyed such repute. The boys of the church seem to have been originally the chief performers, and obtained so much mastery over the art as to perform frequently before the kings of England. Their preparations were expensive, but were evidently more than paid for by the auditors; for in the reign of Richard II. they petitioned that certain ignorant and inexperienced persons might be prohibited from representing the History of the Old Testament to the great prejudice of the clergy of the cathedral. Were great public events passing—had one monarch been pushed from the throne by another or by death—St. Paul's was almost sure to furnish, in one shape or another, palpable evidences of the matter that was in all men's thoughts. Thus when Louis of France came to London in 1216, the English barons present swore fealty to him in St. Paul's; thus, when success now elated the heart of a Henry VI., now of his adversary Edward IV., each came to St. Paul's, to take as it were solemn and public possession of the kingdom; thus, when the body of a Richard II., or of a Philip Sydney, had to be displayed before the eyes of a startled or of a mourning nation, to St. Paul's was it brought—the king to be less honoured in his remains than the humblest of knights, the knight to be more honoured than any but the very best of kings. Were there business to attend to, when all these other sources of interest were unheeded or for the time in abeyance,—then to St. Paul's Walk must the citizens of London have had frequent occasion to go. There were lawyers feed, horses and benefices sold, and set payments made. A strange scene, and a strange company, in consequence, did the cathedral present through the day! "At one time," writes an eye-witness, "in one and the same rank, yea, foot by foot, and elbow by elbow, shall you see walking, the knight, the gull, the gallant, the upstart, the gentleman, the clown, the captain, the appel-squire, the lawyer, the usurer, the citizen, the bankrout, the scholar, the beggar, the doctor, the idiot, the ruffian, the cheater, the puritan, the cut-throat, the high men, the low men, the true man, and the thief; of all trades and professions some; of all countries some. Thus while Devotion kneels at her prayers, doth Profanation walk under her nose" (Dekker's 'Dead Term'). (Fig. 518.)

The undoing of Old St. Paul's forms scarcely a less interesting history than the doing. The Bell Tower was the stake of Henry VIII., when he played at dice with Sir Miles Partridge; the knight won, and the Bell Tower was lost to St Paul's: it soon disappeared. In the reigns of Edward VI. and Elizabeth, the greater part of the sculpture and rich brasses of the interior were destroyed by Puritan hands; whilst the former reign was also marked by the wholesale plunder of the very walls of the outworks of the structure, the chapel and cloisters of Pardon Church Haugh, where the 'Dance of Death' was painted, Shyrington's Chapel, and the Charnel House and Chapel, with their many goodly monuments, in order (such was the base fact) to get the materials, the mere stone and timber, for the new palace in the Strand, Somerset House. Then followed the destruction of the steeple by fire in 1561. Next the civil war, with its injuries. That over, and the State, after the brief interregnum of the Commonwealth, restored to its old ways, came the great fire, and put an end to all that remained of the cathedral, as well as to the many degradations the fine old edifice had experienced. Among these injuries, not the least were the beautifying and restoring processes of Inigo Jones, whose portico might elsewhere have added even to his well-deserved fame, but at St. Paul's only evidenced the mistake the great architect had made, when he fancied he understood the Gothic (Fig. 519).

There are probably few of our readers who, as they have gazed on those architectural wonders of the middle ages, our cathedrals and larger ecclesiastical structures, and thought of the endless difficulties, mechanical and otherwise, surmounted in their construction, but have felt a strong desire to look back to the periods of their erection, and to note all the variety of interesting circumstances that must have marked such events. What, for instance, could be at once more gratifying and instructive than to be able to familiarize ourselves with the motives and characters of the chief founders, with the feelings and thoughts of the people among and for whom the structures in question were reared? If our readers will now follow us into the history of St. Bartholomew Priory, Smithfield, we think we can venture to promise them some such glimpse of those fine old builders at work; and that too founded upon the best of authorities—an inmate of the priory, who wrote so soon after its foundation, that persons were still alive who had witnessed the whole proceedings. We shall borrow occasionally the language as well as the facts of the good monk's history, which has been printed in the 'Monasticon,' and in Malcolm's 'London.' In the reign of Henry the First there was a man named Rahere, sprung and born from low lineage, and who when he attained the flower of youth began to haunt the households of noblemen and the palaces of princes; where, under every elbow of them he spread their cushions, with japes and flatterings delectably anointing their eyes, by this manner to draw to him their friendships. Such was the youthful life of Rahere. But with years came wisdom and repentance. He would go to Rome, and there seek remission of his sins. He did so. At the feet of the shrine of the Apostles Peter and Paul he poured out his lamentations; but, to his inexpressible pain, God, he thought, refused to hear him. He fell sick. And then he shed out as water his heart in the sight of God; the fountains of his nature to the very depths were broken up; he wept bitter tears. At last dawned a new life upon the penitent man. He vowed if God would grant him health to return to his own country, he would make an hospital in recreation of poor men, and minister to their necessities to the best of his power. With returning health to the mind not unnaturally came back health to the body. And now more and more grew upon him the love of the great work he had determined to perform. Visions, as he believed, were vouchsafed to him for his guidance. On a certain night he saw one full of dread and sweetness. He fancied himself to be borne up on high by a certain winged beast, and when from his great elevation he sought to look down, he beheld a horrible pit, deeper than any man might attain to see the bottom of, opening, as it seemed, to receive him. He trembled, and great cries proceeded from his mouth. Then to his comfort there appeared a certain man, having all the majesty of a king, of great beauty, and imperial authority, and his eye fastened upon Rahere. "O man," said he, "what and how much service shouldst thou give to him that in so great a peril hath brought help to thee?" Rahere answered, "Whatever might be of heart and of right, diligently should I give in recompense to my deliverer." Then said the celestial visitant, "I am Bartholomew, the Apostle of Jesus Christ, that come to succour thee in thine anguish, and to open to thee the sweet mysteries of heaven. Know me truly, by the will and commandment of the Holy Trinity and the common favour of the celestial court and council, to have chosen a place in the suburbs of London, at Smithfield, where in my name thou shalt form a church." Rahere with a joyful heart returned to London, where he presently obtained the concurrence of the king to carry out his views. The choice of the place was, according to the monkish historian, who believed but what all believed, no less a matter of special arrangement by Heaven.

King Edward the Confessor had previously had the very spot pointed out to him when he was bodily sleeping, but his heart to God waking; nay more, three men of Greece who had come to London had gone to the place to worship God, and there prophesied wonderful things relating to the future temple that was to be erected on it. In other points, the locality was anything but a favoured one. Truly, says the historian, the place before his cleansing pretended to no hope of goodness. Right unclean it was; and as a marsh dungy and fenny, with water at most times abounding; whilst the only dry portion was occupied by the gallows for the execution of criminals. Work and place determined on, Rahere had now to begin to build; and strange indeed were the modes adopted by him to obtain the gift of the requisite materials, bring together the hosts of unpaid workmen, or to find funds for such additional materials and labour as might be necessary. He made and feigned himself unwise, it is said, and outwardly pretended the cheer of an idiot, and began a little while to hide the secretness of his soul. And the more secretly he wrought the more wisely he did his work. Truly, in playing unwise he drew to him the fellowship of children and servants, assembling himself as one of them; and with their use and help, stones, and other things profitable to the building, lightly he gathered together. Thus did he address himself to one class of persons, those who would look upon his apparent mental peculiarities as a kind of supernatural proof of his enjoying the especial care of the Deity. Another class he influenced by his passionate eloquence in the churches; where he addressed audiences with the most remarkable effect, now stirring them so to gladness that all the people applauded him, now moving them to sorrow by his searching and kindly exposure of their sins, so that nought but singing and weeping were heard on all sides. A third mode of obtaining help was by the direct one of personal solicitation at the houses of the inhabitants of the neighbourhood, in the course of which St. Bartholomew often, it appears, redeemed his promise to Rahere of assistance. Alfun, a coadjutor of Rahere's, the builder of old St. Giles, Cripplegate, went one day to a widow, to see what she could give them for the use of the church and the hospital of St. Bartholomew. She told him she had but seven measures of meal, which was absolutely necessary for the supply of her family. She, however, at last gave one measure. After Alfun had departed with her contribution, she casually looked over the remaining measures, when she thought she counted seven measures still; she counted again, and there were eight; again, there were nine. How long this very profitable system of arithmetic lasted, our good monk does not state. And thus at last was St. Bartholomew's Priory raised, clerks brought together to live in it, a piece of adjoining ground consecrated as a place of sepulchre, privileges showered upon it by the hands of royalty, and the whole stamped, as was thought, with the emphatic approval of Heaven by the miraculous cures that were then wrought in the establishment. Yes, the work was finished, and Rahere made the first prior. No wonder that the people, as we are informed, were greatly astonished both at the work and the founder; or that St. Bartholomew's was esteemed to belong more to the supernatural than the natural. No wonder that as to Rahere it should be asked, in the words of the monkish chronicler, "Whose heart lightly should take or admit such a man *not* product of gentle blood, *not* greatly endowed with literature, or of divine lineage," notwithstanding his nominally low origin? Rahere fulfilled the duties of prior in the beloved house of his own raising, for about twenty years, when the clay house of this world he forsook, and the house everlasting entered.

Of this very building, or rather series of buildings erected by Rahere himself, there remains in a fine state of preservation an important portion, the choir of the conventual church used as the present parish church (Fig. 526). There can be no doubt that we have the original walls, pillars, and arches of the twelfth century; the massive, grand, and simple style of the whole tells truly through the date of their erection. This choir, therefore, forms one of the most interesting and valuable pieces of antique ecclesiastical architecture now existing in England. Among its more remarkable features may be mentioned the continuous aisle that runs round the choir, and opening into it between the flat and circular arch-piers; the elegant horseshoe-like arches of the chancel at the end of the choir; and the grand arches at the opposite extremity, shown in our engraving, on which formerly rose a stately tower corresponding in beauty and grandeur to all the other portions of the pile. The tomb of Rahere is also in the choir, but it is of somewhat later date than the priory. Nothing so exquisitely beautiful in sculpture as that work with its recumbent effigy, and attending monks and angels, its fretted canopies and niches and finials, had yet burst upon old England when Rahere died (Fig. 528). The very perfect state in which it now appears is owing to Prior Bolton, who restored it in the

sixteenth century, as well as other parts of the structure; a labour of which he was evidently very proud, for wherever his handiwork may be traced, there too you need not look long for his handwriting —his signature as it were—a *Bolt* in *tun* (Fig. 530). This prior was an elegant and accomplished man; if even he were not much more. The beautiful oriel window in the second story of the choir which encloses the prior's pew or seat, nearly facing Rahere's monument, as if that the prior might the better look down on the last resting-place of the illustrious founder, was added by Bolton, and has been supposed, for reasons into which we cannot here enter, to be from his own designs. Another part of the ancient structure is to be found in the old vestry-room, which was formerly an oratory, dedicated to the Virgin. Among the burials in the church the most important perhaps was that of Roger Walden, Bishop of London, who rose from a comparatively humble position to the highest offices of the State; he was successively Dean of York, Treasurer of Calais, Royal Secretary and Royal Treasurer, and, lastly, Primate of England, on the occasion of the banishment of Archbishop Arundel by Richard the Second. That ecclesiastic, however, returned with Bolingbroke to his country and office, and Walden became at once a mere private person. Arundel, it is pleasant to relate, behaved nobly to the unfortunate prelate, making him Bishop of London. He died, however, shortly after. Fuller compares him to one so jaw-fallen with over-long fasting that he cannot eat meat when brought unto him. Sir Walter Mildmay, founder of Emanuel College, Cambridge, and Dr. Francis Anthony, the discoverer and user of a medicine drawn from gold (aurum potabile he called it), also lie here buried. There are other monuments not unworthy of notice; though at St. Bartholomew's, as now at most other churches, the major portion refer to those who were, like "Captain John Millett, mariner, 1600,"

Desirous hither to resort
Because this parish was *their* port;

but who have not, like him, told us this in so amusing a manner. Of the other parts of the priory, there remain the entrance gateway (Fig. 529), portions of the cloisters, and of the connected domestic buildings; above all, the refectory, or grand hall, still stands to a great extent entire, though so metamorphosed that its very existence has hardly been known to more than a few. It is now occupied by a tobacco-manufactory and divided into stories; but there can be no doubt that any one who shall attentively examine the place will come to the same conclusion as ourselves, that the whole has formed one grand apartment, extending from the ground to the present roof, and that the latter has been originally of open woodwork. It may help to give some general idea of the magnificent scale of the priory, to state that this hall must have measured forty feet high, thirty broad, and one hundred and twenty in length. Another illustration of the same point is furnished by the plan, which shows the pile in its original state (Fig. 524).* If we look at the part marked O, the present parish church, and the old choir, and see how small a proportion it bears to the entire structure, we have a striking view of the former splendour and present degradation of St. Bartholomew's. The site of the other buildings there marked are now occupied by the most incongruous assemblage of filthy stables and yards, low public-houses, mouldering tenements, with here and there residences of a better character; and in few or none of these can we enter without meeting with corners of immense walls projecting suddenly out, vaulted roofs, boarded-up pillars, and similar evidences of the ruin upon which all these appurtenances of the modern inhabitants have been established. The only other feature that it is necessary to mention is the crypt, which extends below the refectory, and is one of the most remarkable places of the kind even in London, so rich in crypts (Fig. 525). It runs the whole length of the refectory, and is divided by pillars into a central part and two aisles. Popular fancy has not even been satisfied with these suffi-

---

* EXPLANATION OF REFERENCES IN THE PLAN (Fig. 524).

A. The Eastern Cloister, the only one of which there are any remains.
B. The North Cloister, parallel with the Nave.
C. The South Cloister.
D. The West Cloister. The Square thus enclosed by the Cloisters measures about a hundred feet each way.
E. The North Aisle of the Nave.
F. The South Aisle, to which the existing Gateway in front of Smithfield was the original entrance.
G. The Nave, no part of which or of the Aisles now remains.
H. St. Bartholomew's Chapel, destroyed by Fire about 1830.
I. Middlesex Passage, leading from Great to Little Bartholomew Close.
J. The Dining Hall or Refectory of the Priory, with the Crypt beneath.
K. Situation of the Great Tower, which was

supported on four arches, that still remain.
L. The Northern Aisle of the Choir.
M. The Southern Aisle of the Choir.
N. The Eastern Aisle of the Choir.
O. The present Parish Church, forming the Choir of the old Priory Church.
P. The Prior's House, with the Dormitory and Infirmary above.
Q. Site of the Prior's Offices, Stables, Woodyard, &c.
R. The Old Vestry.
S. The Chapter-House, with an entrance Gateway from.
T. The South Transept.
U. The North Transept.
V. The present entrance into the Church.
On the top of the plan is Little Bartholomew Close, on the left Cloth Fair, at the bottom Smithfield, and on the right Great Bartholomew Close.

531.—The Temple Church, from the Entrance.

534.—Porch, Temple Church.

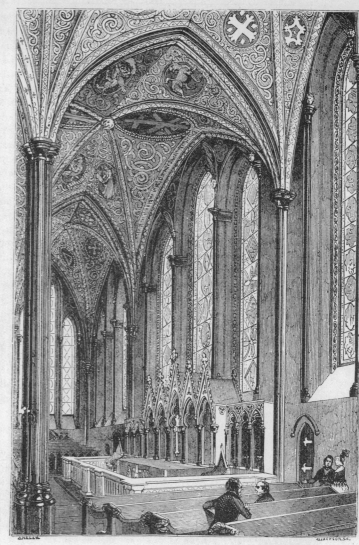

532.—The Western Window, Altar, &c., Temple Church.

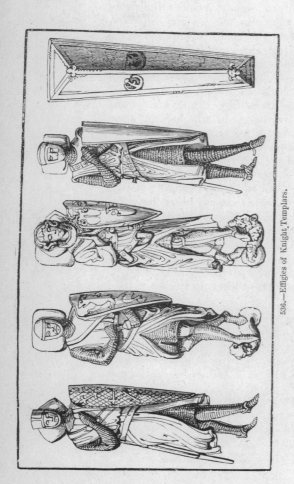

536.—Effigies of Knight Templars.

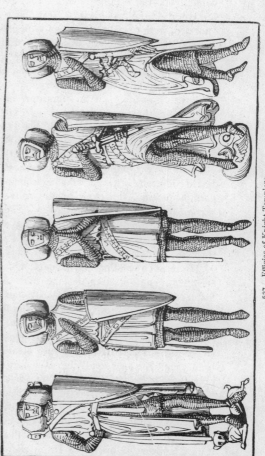

537.—Effigies of Knight Templars.

535.—Interior of the Round, Temple Church.

140

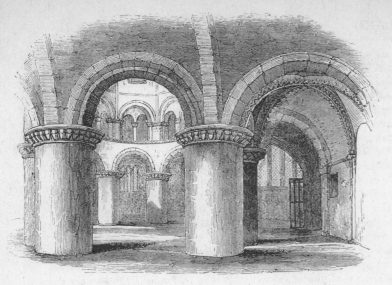

539.—Round Church, Cambridge. Interior.

541.—St. John's Hospital.—From Hollar.

540.—Round Church, Cambridge.

544.—Knight Templar.

543.—Preceptory, Swingfield.

542.—St. John's Gate, Clerkenwell, 1841.

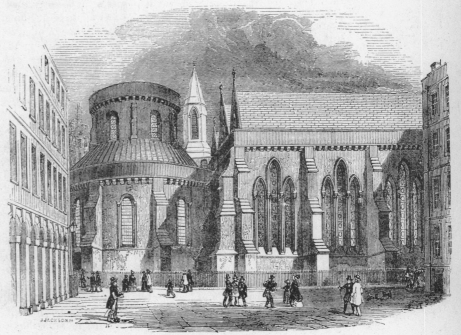

538.—The Temple Church, from the South.

141

ciently noticeable facts as to the subterranean regions of St. Bartholomew's, but has stretched the crypt all the way to Islington, where the prior had his country residence and pleasance or garden of Canonbury; and where the mansion and garden-house of Prior Bolton are still preserved, close by the famous Tower of Canonbury. The tower of course formed a part of the Canonbury estate, which evidently derives its name from the canons of the priory.

Among those extraordinary institutions which from time to time spring up in the world, rise to great prosperity, and in that state exist for centuries together, exercising the most important influence over the affairs of men, and then at last, either through the process of gradual decay or the operations of a more sudden agency, disappear altogether, and leave behind them, as the only traces of their existence, a few mouldering edifices for the antiquary to mourn over or to restore—among such institutions, conspicuous before all others, stand those of the famous Christian warriors, as they loved to designate themselves, the Knights of St. John and of the Temple. And never was there a more deeply-interesting history given to the world than is embodied in the records that tell us of the growth of these Orders, of the picturesque amalgamation at the most opposite qualities of human nature required as the indispensable preliminary of membership, of the active bravery and passive fortitude with which the objects of the Institutions were pursued, of the curiously-intense hatred that existed between the two great Orders, and of their fate, so sudden, terrible, and, in some respects, sublime in the one case, so protracted and comparatively undignified and commonplace in the other. In these pages we can only touch, and that briefly, upon the salient points of such a history. St. John's may be called the oldest of the two Orders, since it dates back to the erection of the Hospital of St. John at Jerusalem, soon after the middle of the eleventh century, when it was founded for the accommodation of Christian pilgrims, in connection with the church of Santa Maria de Latina, built by the Christians of commercial Italy, with the consent of the Mohammedan governors of the Holy Land. But it was then no fighting community: to relieve the hungry, weary, houseless, and sick, of their own faith, whom piety had brought to that far-off land, was their especial vocation. But the kindly offices of the good monks were not limited by the boundaries of creed; the "Infidel" Arab or Turk was also welcome whenever necessity brought him to their doors; a state of things that contrasts powerfully and humiliatingly with the state that was to supersede it.

The influences that transformed the peaceful monks of St. John's into the most turbulent of soldiers did not spring out of common occurrences. The wars of the Crusades broke out, the Saracens were driven from Jerusalem, and Godfrey of Bouillon elected its first Christian sovereign; but the Hospital of St. John remained essentially the same, more prosperous, but not more martial. It should seem, even, that the ambition that alone agitated the members at the time was that of enhancing the legitimate merits of their position, by becoming still more charitable in their charity, still more humble in their humility, still more self-denying in their religious discipline, for in 1120 the Serjiens or Servientes of the hospital formed themselves for such purposes into a separate monastic body under the direct protection of the Church of Rome. But about the same time a little band of knights, nine in number, began to distinguish themselves by their zeal and courage in the performance of a duty self-imposed, but of the most dangerous and important character. They had devoted themselves, life and fortune, to the defence of the high roads leading to Jerusalem, where the Christian pilgrims were continually harassed and injured by the warlike onslaught of the Mussulmen and the predatory attacks of robbers. "Poor fellow-soldiers of Jesus Christ" they called themselves; and poor enough indeed they were, since their chief, Hugh de Payens, was constrained to ride with another knight on the same horse: a memorable incident, which the Order, with noble pride, commemorated in their seal. Such services spoke eloquently to every one. Golden opinions were speedily won. The poor knights soon became rich knights. The little body began speedily to grow into a large one. As a special honour they were lodged, by the church, on the site of the great Hebrew Temple, and the fame of the "Knighthood of the Temple of Solomon" began to spread through Christian Europe. Amid the general excitement of the Holy Wars this junction of the priest and soldier seemed but a most happy embodiment of the prevailing passions, duties, and wants of the age (Fig. 544). Thus, when Hugh de Payens himself set out on a tour with four of the brethren, in order to promulgate more distinctly the objects of the Society, and to seek assistance,

great was the interest and excitement that prevailed wherever they came. They arrived in England in 1128, and were received with the deepest respect by Henry the First and his court. The result of these travels was, that when the four brethren returned to Jerusalem they brought with them in company three hundred of the best and bravest of European chivalry. The new Society was evidently moving the Christian world; what wonder that the monks of St. John felt themselves at last moved too—in the same direction. Within a few years after De Payens' return, and during the spiritual rule of Raymond du Puy, they took up the lance, and rushed forth into the field in rivalry of the brotherhood of the Temple. And between the warlike merit of the two, the knights who had become monks, and the monks who had become knights, it would evidently be impossible to decide; both were the flower of the Christian armies, and the especial dread of the Saracen. The military annals of no country or time exhibit deeds that can surpass, few even that can rival, the prodigies of valour continually performed by these warrior monks. But with wealth, corruption, as usual, flowed in. When one Order (the Templars) possessed nine thousand manors, and the other nineteen thousand, in the fairest provinces of Christendom, it would be too much to expect that humility would long continue to characterize either. The first evidence of the evil spirit that was at work in their hearts was exhibited in their mutual quarrels, which at last grew to such a height that they actually turned their arms against each other; and even on one occasion, in 1259, fought a pitched battle, in which the Knights Hospitallers were the conquerors, and scarcely left a Templar alive to carry to his brethren the intelligence of their discomfiture. This was an odd way to exhibit the beauties of the faith they were shedding so much blood and expending so much treasure to establish among the Saracens, and scarcely calculated to convince the infidel even of the military necessity of acknowledging or giving way to it. The fact is that the decline of the Christian power in the Holy Land may be traced, in a great measure, to these miserable jealousies: it may be doubted whether the two Orders did not, on the whole, retard rather than promote the cause they espoused. But let us now look at their position in this country. The first houses of both were established in London, and nearly about the same time, the Priory of St. John at Clerkenwell in 1100, by Jordan Briset, an English Baron, and his wife; and the Old Temple in Holborn (where Southampton Buildings now exist) founded during the visit of Hugh de Payens, twenty-eight years later. As the Templars, however, increased in numbers and wealth, they purchased the site of the present Temple in Fleet Street, and erected their beautiful church and other corresponding buildings on a scale of great splendour. Both this church and the church of St. John, Clerkenwell, were consecrated by Heraclius, Patriarch of Jerusalem, whom events of no ordinary nature brought to this country; events which threatened to involve something like the entire destruction of the Christians and their cause in the Holy Land, if immediate succour was not granted by some most potent authority. With Heraclius came the Masters of the two Orders; and the hopes of the trio, it appears, were centred on the King of England, who had, on receiving absolution for the murder of Becket, promised not only to maintain two hundred Templars at his own expense, but also to proceed to Palestine himself at the head of a vast army. At first all looked very encouraging. Henry met them at Reading, wept as he listened to their sad narration of the reverses experienced in Palestine, and, in answer to their prayers for support, promised to bring the matter before parliament immediately on its meeting. In that assembly, however, the barons urged upon him that he was bound by his coronation oath to stay at home and fulfil his kingly duties, but offered to raise funds to defray the expense of a levy of troops, expressing at the same time their opinion that English nobles and others might, if they wished, freely depart for Palestine to join the Christian warriors. Henry with apparent reluctance agreed; and "lastly, the king gave answer, and said that he might not leave his land without keeping, nor yet leave it to the prey and robbery of Frenchmen. But he would give largely of his own to such as would take upon them that voyage. With this answer the Patriarch was discontented, and said, 'We seek a man, and not money; well near every Christian region sendeth unto us money, but no land sendeth to us a prince. Therefore we ask a prince that needeth money, and not money that needeth a prince.' But the king laid for him such excuses, that the Patriarch departed from him discontented and comfortless; whereof the king being advertised, intending somewhat to recomfort him with pleasant words, followed him unto the seaside. But the more the king thought to satisfy him with his fair speech, the more the Patriarch was discontented, insomuch that, at the last, he said unto him, 'Hitherto thou hast reigned gloriously, but hereafter thou shalt be forsaken of Him whom thou at this time forsakest. Think on Him, what he hath given to thee, and what thou hast yielded to Him again; how first thou wert false to the King of France, and after slew that holy man, Thomas of Canterbury; and lastly thou forsakest the protection of Christian faith.' The king was moved with these words, and said unto the Patriarch, 'Though all the men of my land were one body and spake with one mouth, they durst not speak to me such words.' 'No wonder,' said the Patriarch, 'for they love thine, and not thee; that is to mean, they love thy goods temporal, and fear thee for loss of promotion; but they love not thy soul.' And when he had so said he offered his head to the king, saying, 'Do by me right as thou didst by that blessed man, Thomas of Canterbury; for I had liever to be slain of thee than of the Saracens, for thou art worse than any Saracen.' But the king kept his patience, and said, 'I may not wend out of my land, for my own sons will arise against me when I am absent.' 'No wonder,' said the Patriarch, 'for of the devil they come, and to the devil they shall go;' and so departed from the king in great ire." (Fabyan.) Two years later, Saladin had put an end to the Christian kingdom at Jerusalem, generously dismissing to their homes his many distinguished prisoners, among whom was Heraclius, and granting to the Christians generally of Europe the possession of the sepulchre of Christ. His liberality experienced no suitable return. A third Crusade was set on foot, the one in which Cœur-de-Lion was engaged, to fail like the previous ones, to be again followed by others, with the same result. In 1291 Acre was besieged by the Sultan of Egypt, and taken after a most terrible conflict, in which the two Orders were nearly exterminated: that event in effect may be said to mark the final defeat of the Crusaders in their long-cherished object of the conquest of the Holy Land.

The Knights of St. John, however, for about two centuries after this, found ample employment of a kind after their own heart; they obtained possession of the island of Rhodes, from whence they kept up continual war,—of a very piratical character, though, be it observed,—against the Turks; but in 1522 Solyman the Fourth, or the Magnificent, after a tremendous siege, in which he is said to have lost upwards of 100,000 men, completely overpowered the defenders, although they fought with a courage that won his respect, and induced him to consent at last that the Grand-master, L'Isle Adam, and his surviving companions, might depart freely whithersoever they chose. He visited his illustrious captive on entering the city, and was heard to remark as he left him, "It is not without pain that I force this Christian, at his time of life, to leave his dwelling." The Emperor Charles the Fifth then bestowed on them the island of Malta, which they fortified with works that render it to this day almost impregnable, but where, after successfully resisting a most formidable attack from the Turkish troops of Solyman, they gradually fell into a mode of life very different from that which had previously characterized them, and which was suddenly brought to a very ignominious conclusion by the appearance of Napoleon, leading his Egyptian expedition, in 1798, and by his landing without opposition, through the mingled treachery and cowardice of the knights; who, however, received their reward: the Order itself was then virtually abolished. It is not unworthy of notice, as evidence of the amazing strength of the place, as well as of the feeling of the French officers at so disgraceful a surrender, that one of them, Caffarelli, said to Napoleon, as they examined the works, "It is well, General, that some one was within to open the gate for us. We should have had some difficulty in entering had the place been altogether empty." A Grand-master and a handful of knights, it seems, do still exist at Ferrara, and possess a scanty remnant of the once magnificent revenue. The Templars experienced a more tragical, but also infinitely more honourable termination of their career, and one that redeemed a thousand faults and vices. Within twenty years after their conduct and misfortunes at the siege of Acre had entitled them to the sympathy of their Christian brethren throughout the world, they were suddenly charged in France with the commission of a multitude of crimes, religious and social; and to convince them that they were guilty, whether they knew it or not, tortures of the most frightful description were unsparingly applied to make them confess. One who did confess, when he was brought before the commissary of police to be examined, at once revoked his confession, saying, "They held me so long before a fierce fire, that the flesh was burnt off my heels; two pieces of bone came away, *which I present to you.*" Such were the execrable cruelties perpetrated on the unhappy Templars in France, where they were also sent to the scaffold in troops, and thus at last the Order was made tractable in that country. In England there was greater decency at least observed. If the torture was applied at all, it was but sparingly, and the confession

obtained was at last reduced to so very innocent an affair, that no man would have been justified in sacrificing life and limb in resistance; so the Templars wisely gave way. All matters thus prepared, the Pope in 1312 formally abolished the Order; and then the world saw the truth of what it had before suspected, namely, that all these atrocious proceedings were but to clear the way for a general scramble for the enormous property of the Order, in which the chief actors were of course the sovereigns of France and England and the Pontiff. They had tried to persuade themselves or their subjects that the rival order of St. John's was to have the possessions in question, and they were nominally confirmed to it: but about a twentieth of the whole was all that the Knights Hospitallers ever obtained.

Of the two churches consecrated by Heraclius in London, that of the Temple alone remains. St. John's was burnt, with all the surrounding buildings of the priory, by the followers of Wat Tyler in the fourteenth century, when the conflagration continued for no less than seven days. The Temple had been previously injured by them on account of its being considered to belong to the obnoxious Hospitallers. We see from Hollar's view of the priory in the seventeenth century (Fig. 541), that previous to the dissolution by Henry the Eighth it had recovered much of its ancient magnificence. But in the reign of Edward the Sixth the " church, for the most part," says Stow, " to wit, the body and side aisles, with the great bell-tower (a most curious piece of workmanship, graven, gilt, and enamelled, to the great beautifying of the city, and passing all other that I have seen), was undermined and blown up with gunpowder; the stone whereof was employed in building of the Lord Protector's house in the Strand." The remains of the choir form at present a portion of the parochial church of Clerkenwell. But there is another relic of the priory, the gateway (Fig. 542), which Johnson " beheld with reverence," and which his successors can hardly look on without a kindred sentiment, were it on his account alone; for here it was that Johnson came to Cave, the publisher of the ' Gentleman's Magazine,' to seek and obtain employment, being at the time poor, friendless, and unknown; nay, so very poor, that he sat behind the screen to eat his dinner, instead of at the printer's table, in order to conceal his shabby coat. The principal part of the gateway now forms the Jerusalem Tavern. The groined roof of the gate has been restored of late years. But we now turn to a remain of the rival metropolitan house of the Templars, which is of a very much more important character.

No one probably ever beheld the exterior of the Temple Church (Fig. 538), for the first time, without finding his curiosity at least excited to know the meaning of its peculiar form, that round—half fortress, half chapter-house like—structure, with such a beautiful oblong Gothic church body attached to it at one side. That the second was added to the first at a later period is sufficiently evident; but we are puzzled by the "Round" as it is called, till we begin to remember who were its founders: the men whose lives were spent in the Holy Land, in a continual alternation of fighting and devotion; whose houses there were one day a place of worship, the next of attack and defence. Such, no doubt, were the origin of the Round churches of England, of which we possess but three others.

The restoration of these fine old works of our forefathers promises to become a marked feature of the present time; and if so, there will be one especial labour of the kind, truly a labour of love to those who have been concerned in it, that will stand out from all the rest, as the grand exemplar of the true spirit that should animate restorers. When the Benchers of the Temple began their noble task, they found nearly all that was left of the original building, walls only excepted, in a state of decay, and everything that was not original, without any exception, worthless. Thus the elaborately-beautiful sculpture of the low Norman doorway, which leads from the quaint porch (Fig. 534) into the interior of the Round, was in a great measure lost; now we see it again in all its pristine splendour. The airy clustered columns of Purbeck marble, which, standing in a wide circle, support with their uplifted, uniting, and arching arms the roof of the Round (Fig. 535), were no longer trustworthy; so they had to be removed entirely, and new ones, at an immense expense, provided; and the ancient quarry at Purbeck, from which so much marble must have been drawn in the middle ages for the erection of our cathedrals, was again opened on the occasion. Everything through the whole church was covered with coating upon coating of whitewash; consequently, all traces were lost of the gilding and colour that had been everywhere expended with a lavish hand, and which now again relieve the walls, in the forms of pious inscriptions in antique letters, which glow in the roofs of the Round and of the Chancel, and which gradually increase into a perfect blaze of splendour towards and around the altar (Fig. 532). The beautiful junction of the two parts of the

547.—The Lady Chapel, St. Mary Overies.

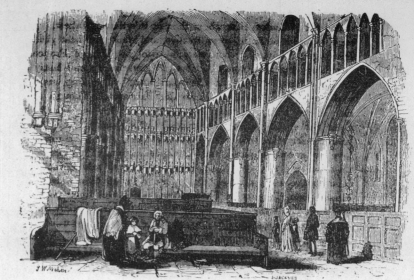

550.—The Choir, St. Mary Overies.

545.— General View of St. Mary Overies, from the South.

548.—Gower's Monument.

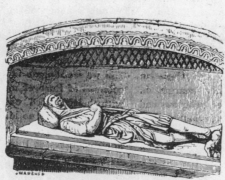

549.—Templar, St. Mary Overies.

546.—Norman Arch, St. Mary Overies.

563.—Finials, Canterbury.

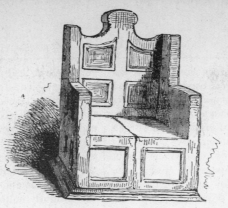

556.—Archiepiscopal Chair, Canterbury.

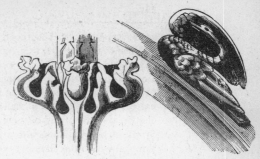

561.—Crockets, Canterbury.

557.—Capital, Crypt, Canterbury.

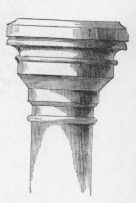

559.—Capital, Crypt, Canterbury.

558.—Base, Crypt, Canterbury.

551.—The Nave of Canterbury Cathedral.

560.—Base, S.E. Transept. Canterbury.

562.—Capital, Canterbury.

561.—Capital, S.E. Transept, Canterbury.

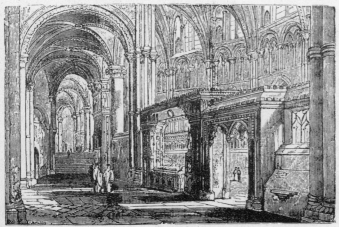

553.—Canterbury.

555.—Font, Canterbury.

554.—Canterbury Cathedral before the Tower was Rebuilt.

entire structure was then concealed by a barbarous screen of the age of Charles the Second, that extended right across between them, and over which was placed the organ; now, once more, the eye ranges along without interruption from the entrance door up to the very altar (Fig. 531), through one of the most beautiful of vistas, and the organ has been removed into a chamber, constructed expressly outside the central window of the chancel, on the north side; the window itself, by slight but judicious alterations, forming a beautiful open screen, through which the chamber communicates with the church. Then, again, the monuments of all kinds but the beautiful, which were formerly let into the very body of the pillars, or placed in other equally incongruous positions, have been removed into the triforium or gallery of the Round; warm, rich-looking tiles have replaced the wooden pavement; gorgeous stained-glass windows again diffuse their magnificent hues upon every object around, and tell in their "panes" the story of Him who died that all might live. In a word, the Temple Church now presents, in most respects, an almost perfect example, on a small scale, of what the grand ecclesiastical structures of the thirteenth century were generally; that is, a consummate and most magical union of all the arts, architecture, painting, sculpture, and music, calculated at once to take man from the world that they might guide him to heaven. With one individual feature of the Temple, we must now conclude our notice of it. On the floor of the Round lie the sculptured effigies of men who belonged to the period of Old England which we have at present under review, and which, as being undoubted originals, are among the most interesting pieces of sculpture we possess (Figs 536, 537). They have lately been restored, with remarkable success, by Mr. Richardson—having become seriously decayed—and now present to us, each in his habit as he lived—Geoffrey de Magneville, that bold and bad baron of the time of Stephen; who, dying excommunicate, was for a time hung upon a tree in the Temple Garden here—the great Protector, Pembroke, who, by his wisdom, assuaged the divisions among his countrymen after the death of John—the Protector's sons, William and Gilbert, the former sheathing his sword; he had fought, and well, but his race was done; the latter drawing it in the service, as he intended, of God in Palestine, when death stopped the journey—and, among others, De Roos, one of the barons to whom the bloodless field of Runnymede has given undying reputation; the exquisitely-beautiful effigy, with the head uncovered, and the curling locks flowing about it, represent that nobleman. These pieces of sculpture were originally, like all the others in the Temple, painted and gilded. We cannot here avoid drawing attention to the head of a seraph, discovered on the wall between the Round and the oblong part of the church during the restoration. The expression is truly seraphic. Traces of colour are even now perceptible; the cheeks and lips have once borne the natural hues of life, the pupil of the eye has been painted blue, the hair gilded. In other heads, also original, the eyes were found to be of glass. How all this reminds one of the customs that prevailed among the Greeks, where some of the most beautiful works the world had ever seen, or would ever see, were thought to be enhanced by means like those we have described.

The very magnificent character of the restoration of the Temple Church, London, has been attended with one undesirable effect—it has drawn away our attention from other labours of a similar and only less important character. Such, for instance, is the restoration of the ROUND CHURCH OF CAMBRIDGE, the oldest of the structures, erected in England in the extraordinary circular form (Figs. 539 and 540). And what gives still higher interest to this building is the fact alleged that it was consecrated in the year 1101, or several years before the institution of the Order of Knight Templars; so that it can hardly be attributed to them. In a paper recently read before the Camden Society, the church is supposed to have been founded by some one interested in the recovery of the Holy Sepulchre at Jerusalem, hence the imitation of the form of that building, and the name; and that the object in view was to make provision for the constant prayers for the success of the Crusaders. We learn from the same pages some other interesting matters. The parish has been traditionally known as the Jewry, which designation, it is supposed, was given to it in consequence of the model of the most sacred of Jewish structures being placed in it. The stained glass votive window, with a saintly figure, which attracts the eyes of visitors to the restored church, it appears, preserves the memory of Bede's legendary residence in the vicinity. Of the restoration of this important structure it is hardly possible to speak too highly. The entire funds, with the exception of some £1,600 still required, have been raised by voluntary subscription, and expended by a little band of ardent and reverential lovers of all that is antique, grand, or beautiful in

our ecclesiastical architecture. The Camden Society especially stands conspicuous in the good work, which has been carried on, we are sorry to learn, through "repeated interruptions and obstructions," and which has—a common case—proved a much more elaborate and costly task than was anticipated. The substantial reparation of the decayed fabric was the object the committee set before themselves; and, much as these words include, it seems that they have found it necessary to add the enlargement of one aisle, the entire erection of another, a new bell-turret, "breaking-up the unsightly uniformity of the rest of the building," the entire fitting of the church with open seats and other necessary furniture in carved oak; and, lastly, the beautiful east window. They have thus involved themselves in debt to the amount before stated, but we do not think they will have relied in vain on the public sympathy and assistance. The stately solemn-looking fabric, so eloquent of those mighty primeval artists, those architectural giants of our early history, who "dreamt not of a perishable home" when they dedicated their skill and cunning to the service of the Almighty, appears again fresh as it were from their very hands. The restoration was completed and the church given up to the parish authorities on the last day of the year 1843, when a statement was made to the world, concerning which great is yet the clamour in local and theological publications. It was discovered that the restorers had erected a *stone* altar, instead of a *wooden* one, and that they had placed a credence—a stone shelf or table—for the display of the elements of the Sacrament. We leave the facts for our readers to weep over, or smile at, as they may see occasion.

Of another of the establishments of the Templars, the PRECEPTORY AT SWINGFIELD, situated about eight miles from Dover, and in which John is said to have resigned his crown to the Pope's Legate, but little now remains, and that is used as a farmhouse, while the foundations may be traced in various parts of the homestead. The eastern part, which was the most ancient (the Preceptory was founded before 1190), exhibits three lancet-shaped windows, above which are the same number of circular ones, and was probably the chapel (Fig. 543).

A few years ago, when the approaches to the new London Bridge were in preparation, an agreement was proposed, and all but concluded, that a space of some sixty feet should be granted for the better display of an old church on the Southwark side, and that a certain chapel belonging to the latter, should be at the same time swept away. The church in question, in short, was to be made as neat and snug as possible, as a fitting preliminary to the new display that it was to be permitted to make. There were persons, however, who by no means approved of the scheme. They said that the Chapel of our Ladye (Fig. 547), which was sought to be destroyed, was one of the most beautiful and antique structures of the kind in England. There were some, even, who held that the fact, that the honoured ashes of good Bishop Andrews lay in it (Bishop Andrews, whose death drew from Milton, no bishop-lover generally, a most passionate elegy), ought to make the place sacred. All this, no doubt, seemed very nonsensical to the framers of the plan in question, who, quietly appealed to the parishioners of St. Saviour's, and obtained the sanction of a large majority to the destruction of the Ladye Chapel. But the persons before mentioned were exceedingly obstinate. They would not be quiet. The Press then took up the matter, and strove might and main to forward the views of these malcontents. At another meeting of the parishioners, the "destructives," to borrow a political phrase, found their majority had dwindled down to three; and, what was infinitely worse, on a poll being demanded, they were left in a minority of between two and three hundred—the beautiful Ladye Chapel and Bishop Andrews' grave were safe. The workmen not long after entered, but it was to restore, not to destroy. Many, no doubt, owe their first personal acquaintance with, if not their first knowledge of the Church of St. MARY OVERIES to the circumstances here narrated, and have been at once surprised and delighted to find so noble and interesting a structure (as beautiful and almost as large as a cathedral) in such a place—the Borough. And when they have been thus led to inquire into the history of the building, their pleasure has been as unexpectedly enhanced. The story of its origin is a tale of romance; poetical associations of no ordinary character attach to its subsequent annals; holy martyrs have passed from the dread tribunal sitting within its walls to the fiery agony of the stake at Smithfield. Stow's account of the origin of St. Mary Overies, derived from Linsted, its last prior, is as follows:—"This church, or some other in place thereof, was of old time, long before the Conquest, a House of Sisters, founded by a maiden named Mary. Unto the which house and sisters she left (as was left her by her parents) the oversight and profits of a cross ferry over the Thames, there kept before that any bridge was builded. This House of Sisters was afterwards, by Swithin, a noble lady, converted into a College of Priests, who, in place of the ferry, builded a bridge of timber." Something like corroborative evidence of the truth of this story was accidentally discovered a few years ago:— "When digging for a family vault in the centre of the choir of the church, near the altar, it was found necessary to cut through a very ancient foundation wall, which never could have formed any part of the present edifice: the edifice exactly corresponds with that of the House of Sisters" described by Stow as near the east part of the present St. Mary Overies, "above the choir," and where he says Mary was buried.

In a wooden box, in the choir, now lies a remarkably fine effigy, of wood, of a Crusader: who he was it is impossible to tell with any certainty, but we venture to think it represents one of the two distinguished persons to whom St. Mary Overies was next largely indebted after the humble ferryman's daughter, and the proud lady, Swithin: those two are, "William Pont de l'Arche and William Dauncy, Knights, Normans," who, in the year 1106, refounded the establishments, on a more magnificent scale, for canons regular (Fig. 546). This Pont de l'Arche was probably the same as the royal treasurer of that name in the beginning of the reign of Rufus. And as carrying still further the records of the connection between St. Mary Overies and the ferry first, and afterwards the bridge, it appears from a passage in Maitland (vol. i. p. 44, ed. 1756), that William Pont de l'Arche, whom we have just seen as the founder of the first, was also connected with the last. If we are right in presuming the Templar to be one of these " Knights, Normans," there can be no doubt too that originally there was also the effigy of the other (Fig. 549): the destructive fires that have from time to time injured the structure explains its absence. There are two curious low-arched niches on the north aisle of the choir; were not these the resting-places of the founders of the priory? We venture to think so, and have placed the Templar in one of them. Aldgod, we may observe, was the first prior of St. Mary Overies. By the fourteenth century, the buildings had become dilapidated; a poet, Gower, restored them; or at least contributed the principal portion of the funds. Gower was married in St. Mary Overies in 1397: and there was at one time a monument to his wife's memory, as well as to his own: the last alone now survives (Fig. 548). This is an exquisitely beautiful work, which has been most admirably restored to all its pristine splendour, and where the quaint rhyming inscriptions in Norman French appear in gay colours, and the effigy of the poet appears radiant in colour and gilding. His head rests on three gilded volumes of his writings; one of them is the 'Confessio Amantis,' his principal and only published work, the origin of which he thus relates:—

In Themse [Thames] when it was flowende,
As I by boat came rowend,
So as Fortune her time set
My liege lord perchance I met;
And so befel as I came nigh
Out of my boat, when he me sigh [saw],
He bad me to come into his barge,
And when I was with him at large
Amonges other things he said,
He hath this charge upon me laid,
And bade me do my business.
That to his high worthiness
Some newe thing I should book.

King Richard the Second's wishes were fulfilled in the 'Confessio Amantis.'

On the pillar seen in our engraving of Gower's monument appears a cardinal's hat, with arms beneath. They refer directly, no doubt, to the beneficence of a very remarkable man, Cardinal Beaufort, Bishop of Winchester, and who in that capacity resided in the adjoining palace, but indirectly to still more interesting matters, in which the busy cardinal had the principal share. Who has not read, and treasured up ever in the memory after, the history of the poet king, James of Scotland, he who, taken a prisoner whilst yet a boy, was kept for many long years in captivity, but educated in the mean time in a truly princely manner; he who, as he has informed us in his own sweet verse, whilst looking out upon the garden which lay before his window, in Windsor Castle, beheld

—————————walking under the tower,
Full secretly new coming her to plain,
The fairest and the freshest younge flower
That ever he saw, methought, before that hour,

and who from that time was no longer heart-whole; he who in all probability was only allowed to free himself from one kind of bondage in order to enter into another, but then that was his marriage with the lady in question, Jane Beaufort, the cardinal's niece;—who

but has been charmed by this romance of reality? It is something then to be able to add, for the honour of St. Mary Overies, that it was within its walls that the ceremony took place. We may add to the foregoing poetical reminiscences, two or three brief, but pregnant sentences, all derived from the same authority, the parish registers. Under the year 1607 we read, " Edmond Shakspere, player, in the church;" and that sums up the known history of one of the great dramatist's brothers. The date 1625 records, " Mr. John Fletcher, a man, in the church;" of whose personal history we know little more. Aubrey thus relates his death: " In the great plague of 1625, a knight of Norfolk or Suffolk invited him into the country: he stayed but to make himself a suit of clothes, and while it was making, fell sick and died; this I heard from the taylor, who is now a very old man and clerk of St. Mary Overy." Lastly comes the most striking entry of all in connection with the year 1640: "Philip Massinger, a stranger." Let us leave the passage, without comment, in all its awful brevity.

The priory was dissolved in 1539, when Linsted, the prior, was pensioned off with 100l. a year. The annual revenue was then valued at 624l. 6s. 6d.

During Wyatt's insurrection in 1554, the insurrectionary troops were posted in Southwark, and the Lieutenant of the Tower bent his ordnance against the foot of the bridge to hinder the passage, and also against the towers of St. Olave's and St. Mary Overies churches. One year afterwards still deadlier weapons were directed against the faith to which St. Mary's belonged, and by its own friends, though in the hope of benefiting it; then was clearly seen the reality of the dangers Wyatt had apprehended, and strove, but unsuccessfully, to avert, in the sittings of a commission in the church, for the trial of those diabolical offenders who dared to have an opinion of their own. Among them first came John Rogers, a prebendary of St. Paul's, who, when questioned by the judge, Bishop Gardiner, asked, " Did you not yourself, for twenty years, pray against the Pope?" " I was forced by cruelty," was the reply. " And will you use the like cruelty to us?" rejoined Rogers. Of course he went to the stake, Bonner refusing him permission to speak to his wife. Bishop Hooper, who was also tried on the same day, was dismissed to the like fate. John Bradford, another of the victims of the St. Mary Overies commission, writing, somewhat about this time, of the death of Hooper, says, " This day, I think, or to-morrow at the uttermost, hearty Hooper, sincere Saunders, and trusty Taylor, end their course, and receive their crown. The next am I, which hourly look for the porter to open me the gate after them, to enter into the desired rest."

The plan of St. Mary Overies is that of a cross, the principal part of which is formed by the Lady Chapel, choir and nave extending from east to west nearly 300 feet; and crossed by the transept near the centre, where rises the majestic tower, 150 feet high. The Anglo-Norman choir (Fig. 550) and transept still remain, and present a fine specimen of the transition state between the comparatively rude and massive structures of the eleventh century, and the more elegant and stately productions of the thirteenth. This portion of the church is now unused; and the pews have consequently been removed. The nave was found a few years ago in so ruinous a state, that it became necessary either to restore it, for which sufficient funds could not be obtained, or build on the site of it a less expensive structure to be used as the parish church, and which should, in some degree at least, harmonize in style with the rest of the pile. The new nave has been rebuilt; but not with such success as to prevent our deep regret for the loss of the old one. Our engraving (Fig. 545) exhibits the church as it was before the rebuilding in question took place. The part nearest the eye shows the old nave. Many objects of interest are to be found in the interior, in addition to those already incidentally mentioned; the screen, for instance, a most elaborate and beautiful piece of sculpture, presumed to have been erected by Bishop Fox, as the pelican, his favourite device, is seen in the cornice. It consists of four stories of niches for statues, divided by spaces, from which project half-length figures of angels. Right up the centre, from the bottom to the top, extend three larger niches, one above another, in the place of the four smaller ones that are found in every other part of the screen; these give harmony, completeness, and grandeur to the whole. Ornament in profusion extends over every part. It will be seen that the screen forms one mass of the richest sculpture; and this, too, is a work of restoration of our own times. The monumental sculpture of St. Mary Overies is particularly curious and interesting, much of it being painted, with the effigies resembling the natural tints of life both in countenance and costume; much of it also referring to interesting personages; and accompanied in some cases by inscriptions which provoke a smile by their quaintness, or

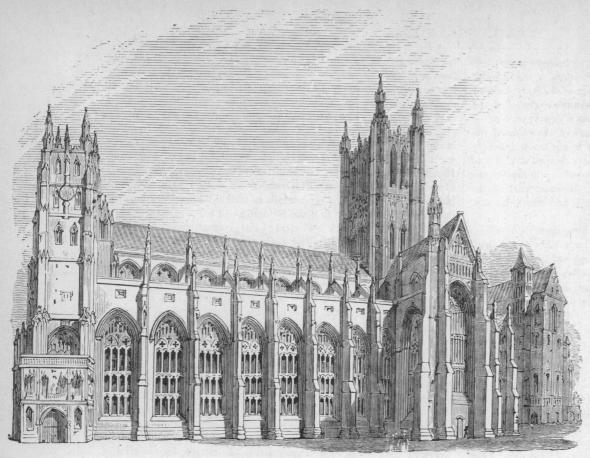

565.—Canterbury Cathedral, South Side.

569.—Staircase in the Conventual Buildings, Canterbury.

568.—Capital and Base, S.E. Transept, Canterbury.

566.—Cathedral Precinct Gateway.

567.—Chapel in Canterbury Cathedral.

572.—Ruins of the Priory of Lindisfarn.

570.—Ruins of the Augustine Monastery at Canterbury.

573.—Abbey Gateway, Bristol. Ancient Window restored.

571.—St. Augustine's Gate, Canterbury.

a sigh by their mournful beauty. Two specimens must suffice to conclude our present notice. On the tomb of a grocer, formerly in the Ladye Chapel, was inscribed,

> Weep not for him, since he is gone before
> To heaven, where grocers there are many more.

On the very large magnificent piece of monumental sculpture which encloses the remains of Richard Humble, alderman of London, his two wives, and his children, we read the following lines, forming part of a poem attributed to Francis Quarles :—

> Like to the damask rose you see,
> Or like the blossom on the tree;
> Or like the dainty flower of May,
> Or like the morning of the day;
> Or like the sun or like the shade,
> Or like the gourd which Jonas had.
>   Even so is the man, whose thread is spun,
>   Drawn out, and cut, and so is done.
> The rose withers, the blossom blasteth,
> The flower fades, the morning hasteth;
> The sun sets, the shadow flies,
> The gourd consumes, and Man he dies.

If Glastonbury may be assumed to have been the spot where the faith of Christ was first expounded to our heathen forefathers, it is certain that it was at Canterbury that it first exhibited all the marks of success, and gave promise of becoming in no very distant period the general religion of the country. There were first heard the teachings of St. Augustine, who may almost be esteemed the real founder of Christianity among us, so great were his achievements in comparison with all that had been done before ;—and there are yet existing two buildings, or parts of buildings, the walls of which may have often echoed with the earnest and lofty eloquence of the illustrious apostle. One of these is St. Martin's Church, already noticed (vol. i. p. 58) : he who would visit the remains of the other, which dispute priority even with St. Martin's itself, must inquire for the crypt or undercroft of Canterbury Cathedral. It is a place that would repay any one for a careful and protracted examination, if the guardians of the sacred edifice had not chosen to shut it up for some twenty years, and to make it a hiding-place for lumber and rubbish. Let the indignation of England call with a loud voice that this crypt shall cease to be desecrated. Nothing more eminently characteristic of the times of its erection perhaps exists in the island. The walls are without ornament, and in that respect contrast strongly with the pillars, upon which the Saxon architect has expended all his fancy. When Ethelbert gave Augustine and his companions leave to settle in the capital of his kingdom, Canterbury, we know, from Bede, that there was a small church existing in the city, which had been previously used for Christian worship, and which must have been then of some age, for Augustine found it necessary to repair and enlarge it. That was the church which, it is supposed, Augustine raised to the rank it has ever since maintained of the first English cathedral, and that is the church of which these rude unornamented walls of the crypt probably yet form an existing memorial. For although it was made little better than a ruin by the Danes in 938, and again, after reparation by Odo, brought to a similar state by the same people in 1011 ; though Canute's extensive restorations were also followed by scarcely less extensive injuries after his decease, and during the early days of the Conquest ; and though, lastly, during the Conqueror's reign, Lanfranc rebuilt the whole almost from the foundation, we still perceive, during all these repairs and restorations, something like evidence of parts of the walls and foundations having been left untouched ; no doubt in consequence of their exceedingly massive and indestructible character. These walls, in short, if we read their history aright, speak to us, in all their simplicity, of a time approaching within a century or two of the life of the Saviour himself, to whom they have been so long dedicated, and of builders whose handiwork can hardly be mistaken for the labour of any other people in whatever part of the world found—the Romans, who are supposed to have built it for the use of their Christian soldiers.

Turning from the plain walls to the curiously-decorated pillars, we evidently pass over several centuries of architectural history. A strange mixture of the simple and the rude with the elaborate and the fantastical do these pillars present, not only in their superficial ornaments, but in their very form ; some are wreathed or twisted, some round, and no two, either of the shafts, or of the capitals, are alike (Figs. 557, 558, and 559). A distinguishing feature of Norman architecture, visible even in its latest and most beautiful stages, namely, breadth and strength, rather than height and stateliness, is here most strikingly developed. The circum-

ference of the shafts is about four feet, and the entire height of plinth, shaft, and capital is only six feet and a half ; from these pillars rise arches of corresponding span, supporting the roof at the altitude of fourteen feet ; the quaint and stunted, yet massive aspect of the place, may from this brief description be readily imagined. To determine the date of the later portions with any precision is impossible ; but there is little question that they belong to a period anterior to the Conquest.

A building thus surrounded by the holiest and most endearing associations was, of course, a continual object of improvement ; scarcely one of its prelates but seems to have done something in the way of rebuilding or enlarging ; a fact strikingly attested by the variety of styles the cathedral now exhibits, even to the least architecturally instructed eyes. Thus while Lanfranc, the Norman, who succeeded Stigand, the Saxon archbishop, in the see, is understood to have left the whole essentially finished, we find Anselm and others of his successors not the less busily at work, pulling down here, and adding there ; and such labours of love were not confined to the archbishops, for it seems that Conrad, a prior of the adjoining monastery, was allowed to participate in them ; who accordingly improved the choir so greatly that the part was for some time afterwards known by his name. But a new and more solemn interest was to invest those walls, than even that derived from their early history. In the second half of the twelfth century, Thomas-à-Becket was the archbishop, and a troubled period did this prelacy become both for the see and England generally. The struggle for supremacy between the royal and the ecclesiastical powers was then at its height : and for a time the former appeared to have triumphed. The beginning of the year 1170 found Becket the resolute assertor of all the rights and privileges of the church, in his seventh year of exile : but unshaken, uncompromising as ever. At last, in July of the same year, the King, Henry the Second, fearing Becket would obtain from the Pope the power of excommunicating the whole kingdom, agreed to a reconciliation, and the two potentates met on the Continent ; the king holding Becket's stirrup as he mounted his horse. The archbishop now prepared for his return. But many warnings of danger reached him. Among others, was one to the effect that Ranulf de Broc, the possessor of a castle within six miles of Canterbury, who had sworn that he would not let the archbishop eat a single loaf of bread in England, was lying in wait, with a body of soldiers, between Canterbury and Dover. The determined spirit of Becket was revealed in his reply. Having remarked that seven years of absence were long enough for both shepherd and flock, he declared he would not stop though he was sure to be cut to pieces as soon as he landed on the opposite coast. But if he had powerful enemies among the nobles and chief ecclesiastics, he had the great body of the people for his friends. As he was about to embark, an English vessel arrived ; and the sailors were asked as to the feelings of the English towards the archbishop ; they replied that he would be received with transports of joy. He landed at Sandwich on the 1st of December, and he was not disappointed in the welcome he had anticipated from his poorer countrymen. But he had already insured his destruction, by an act of extraordinary presumption or courage, for it may be called either ; he had sent before him letters of excommunication, which he had obtained from the Pope, against his old enemies the Archbishop of York, and the Bishops of London and Salisbury. These almost immediately set out for Normandy, to the king, from whom they implored redress. "There is a man," said they, "who sets England on fire ; he marches with troops of horse and armed foot, prowling round the fortresses, and trying to get himself received within them." This was indeed adding fuel to the fire that already burnt in the king's breast : "How !" cried he, in a frenzy, "a fellow that hath eaten my bread,—a beggar that first came to my court on a lame horse, dares to insult his king and the royal family, and tread upon the whole kingdom, and not one of the cowards I nourish at my table—not one will deliver me from this turbulent priest !" These memorable words fell upon ears already inclined perhaps by private hatred to listen to them with delight ; such were Reginald Fitzurse, William Tracy, Hugh de Morville, and Richard Brito, knights, barons, and servants of the king's household ; who, leaving the king to determine in council that he would seize Becket and proceed against him in due form of law for high treason, quietly set out for England to take the matter into their own hands. Whilst Becket was marching about in a strange kind of state, with a host of poor people armed with old targets and rusty lances for his defenders, the conspirators were gradually drawing towards him by different routes. On Christmas-day the archbishop was preaching in the cathedral, with more than his accustomed fervour, his text being "I come to die among you ;" and one cannot but look with a certain amount of admiration and sympathy on the man, notwithstanding the undoubted violence and ambition of the prelate, when we see him performing all the last and most questionable acts of ecclesiastical power, excommunication of personal enemies, with the clearest anticipation of what might be the personal consequences. On that day, he told the congregation that one of the archbishops had been a martyr, and that they would probably soon see another; and forthwith blazed out the indomitable spirit as fiercely and as brilliantly as ever. "Before I depart home, I will avenge some of the wrongs my church has suffered during the last seven years;" and immediately he fulminated sentence of excommunication against Ranulf and Robert de Broc, and Nigellus, rector of Harrow. Three days after, the knights met at the castle of that very Ranulf de Broc; and finally determined upon their plans. The next morning they entered Canterbury with a large body of troops, whom they stationed at different quarters in order to quell any attempt of the inhabitants to defend the doomed man. They then proceeded to the monastery of St. Augustine (Fig. 570) with twelve attendants, and from thence to the palace, where they found the archbishop. It was then about two o'clock. They seated themselves on the floor, in silence, and gazed upon him. There was awful meaning in that glance; a no less awful apprehension of it, in the look with which it was returned. For the murderers to do what they had determined upon, against such a man, and at such a period, was, if possible, more terrible than for the victim to suffer at their hands. At last Reginald Fitzurse spoke: "We come," said he, "that you may absolve the bishops whom you have excommunicated; re-establish the bishops whom you have suspended; and answer for your own offences against the king." Becket, understanding they came from Henry, answered boldly and warmly, yet not without symptoms of a desire to give reasonable satisfaction. He said he could not absolve the archbishop of York, whose heinous case must be reserved for the Pope's judgment, but that he would withdraw the censures from the two other bishops, if they would swear to submit to the papal decision. They then questioned him upon the grand point—supremacy: "Do you hold your archbishopric of the king or the Pope?" "I owe the spiritual rights to God and the Pope, and the temporal rights to the king." After some altercation, in the course of which Becket reminded three of them of the time when they were his liege men, and haughtily said that it was not for such as they to threaten him in his own house, the knights departed, significantly observing they would do more than threaten. Whether the hesitation, here apparent, arose from a desire to try to avoid extremities, or from want of mental courage to perform the terrible act meditated, may be questioned; both influences probably weighed upon their minds. By and by they returned to the palace, and, finding the gates shut, endeavoured to force an entrance. Presently Robert de Broc showed them an easier path through a window. The persons around Becket had been previously urging him to take refuge in the church, thinking his assailants would be deterred from violating a place so doubly sacred—by express privileges, and by its intimate connexion with the growth of Christianity in the country; but he resisted until the voices of the monks, as they sang the vespers in the choir, struck upon his ears, when he said he would go, as duty then called him. Calmly he set forth, his cross-bearer preceding him with the crucifix raised on high, not the slightest trepidation visible in his features or his movements; and when the servants would have closed the doors of the cathedral, he forbade them; the house of God was not to be barricadoed like a castle. He was just entering the choir when Reginald Fitzurse and his companions appeared at the other end of the church, the former waving his sword and crying aloud, "Follow me, loyal servants of the king." The assassins were armed from head to foot. Even then Becket might have escaped, in the gloom of evening, to the intricate underground parts of the cathedral; but he was deaf to all persuasions of the kind, and advanced to meet the knights. All his company then fled, except one, the faithful cross-bearer, Edward Gryme. "Where is the traitor?" was then called out; but as Becket in his unshaken presence of mind was silent to such an appeal, Reginald Fitzurse added, "Where is the archbishop?" "Here am I," was the reply; "an archbishop, but no traitor, ready to suffer in my Saviour's name." Tracy then pulled him by the sleeve, exclaiming, "Come hither; thou art a prisoner!" but Becket perceiving their object, which was to get him without the church, resisted so violently as to make Tracy stagger forward. Even then hesitating and uncertain, hardly knowing what they said, and unable to determine what they would do, they advised Becket to flee in one breath, to accompany them in another. It is probable, indeed, that Becket might have successfully and safely resisted all their

demands, had he condescended to put on for one hour the garb he ought never to have put off—gentleness; but his bearing and language could hardly have been more haughty and contemptuous than now, when he saw himself utterly defenceless and encompassed by deadly enemies. Speaking to Fitzurse, he reminded him he had done him many pleasures, and asked him why he came with armed men into his church. The answer was a demand to absolve the bishops; to which Becket not only gave a decided refusal, but insulted Fitzurse by the use of a foul term that one would hardly have looked for in the vocabulary of an archbishop. "Then die," exclaimed Fitzurse, striking at his head with his weapon; but the devoted cross-bearer interfered; when his arm was nearly cut through, and Becket slightly injured. Still anxious to avoid the consummation of a deed that necessarily appeared so tremendous in their eyes, one of them was heard even then to utter the warning voice, "Fly, or thou diest." The archbishop, however clasped his hands, bowed his head, and, with the blood running down his face exclaimed, "To God, to St. Mary, to the holy patrons of this church, and to St. Denis, I commend my soul, and the church's cause." He was then struck down by a second blow, and the third completed the tragedy. One of the murderers placed his foot on the dead prelate's neck, and cried "Thus perishes a traitor!" The party then retired, and after dwelling for a time at Knaresborough, and finding they were shunned by persons of all classes and conditions, spent their last days in penitence in Jerusalem: when they died, this inscription was written upon their tomb—"Here lies the wretches who murdered St. Thomas of Canterbury." The spot where this bloody act was performed is still pointed out in the northern wing of the western transept, and that part of the cathedral is in consequence emphatically called Martyrdom; the Martyr being the designation by which Becket was immediately and universally spoken of. The excitement caused by the event has had few parallels in English history. For a twelvemonth Divine service was suspended; the unnatural silence reigning throughout the vast pile during that time, making the scene of bloodshed all the more impressive to the eyes of the devout, who began to pour thither from all parts of the world in a constantly-increasing stream. Canterbury then became a kind of second Holy City, where the guilty sought remission of their sins—the diseased health—pilgrims, the blessings that awaited the performance of duly-fulfilled vows. Henry himself, moved by a death so sudden and so dreadful, and so directly following upon his own hasty words, did penance in the most abject manner before Becket's tomb; and two years later gave up all that he had so long struggled for by repealing the famous Constitutions of Clarendon, which had subjected both church and clergy to the civil authority.

It was a noticeable coincidence that only four years after the death of Becket the cathedral was all but destroyed by fire; a calamity that at such a time would hardly appear like a calamity, from the opportunity it afforded of developing in a practical shape the passion that filled the universal heart of England to do something memorable in honour of the illustrious martyr. To say that funds poured in from all parts and in all shapes, gives but little notion of the enthusiasm of the contributors to the restoration of the edifice. The feelings evidenced by foreigners show forcibly what must have been those of our own countrymen. In 1179, says Mr. Batteley, in his additions to Somner's 'Antiquities of Canterbury,' "Louis VII., King of France, landed at Dover, where our king expected his arrival. On the 23rd of August these two kings came to Canterbury, with a great train of nobility of both nations, and were received by the archbishop and his com-provincials, the prior and convent, with great honour and unspeakable joy. The oblations of gold and silver made by the French were incredible. The king [Louis] came in manner and habit of a pilgrim, and was conducted to the tomb of St. Thomas in solemn procession, where he offered his cup of gold, and a royal precious stone, with a yearly rental of one hundred muids [hogsheads] of wine for ever to the convent." The task of rebuilding even a Canterbury Cathedral would be found but comparatively light under such circumstances; so the good work proceeded rapidly towards completion, until the fabric appeared of which the chief parts remain to the present time. It is not, therefore, in its associations merely that the cathedral reminds us at every step we take in it of the turbulent and ambitious, but able and brave priest,—it may really be almost esteemed his monument; for admiration of *his* self-sacrifice, veneration of *his* piety, and yearning to do *him* honour, were the moving powers that raised anew the lofty roof, and extended the long-drawn aisles and nave and choir. The direct testimonies of the people's affection were still more remarkable. Among the earliest additions made after the fire to the former plan was the circular east end,

579.—Early English Capital, Chapter-House
Lincoln.

574.—Lincoln Cathedral.

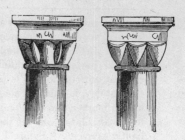

578.—Norman Capitals, Tower, Lincoln.

580.—Early English Turret,
Lincoln.

576—Lincoln Cathedral.

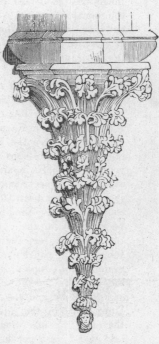

583.—Bracket, Chapter-House, Lincoln.

581.—Gable Cross, Lincoln.

582.—Gable Cross, Lincoln.

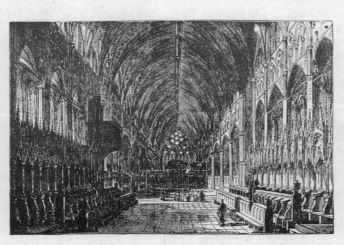

577.—Interior of Lincoln Cathedral.

584.—Bracket, Lincoln.

585.—Boss, Nave, Lincoln.

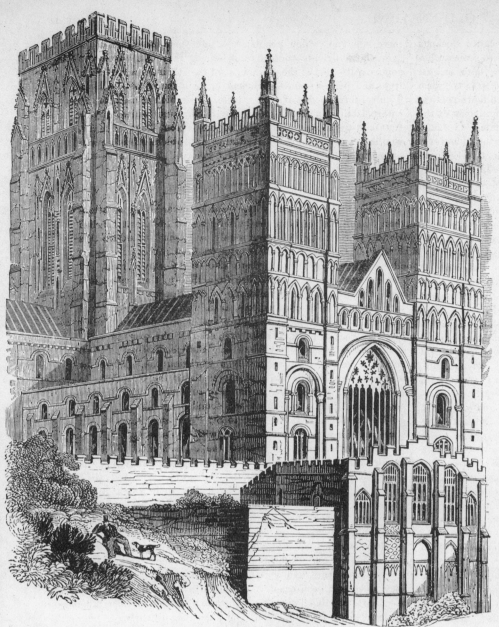

586.—North-west View of Durham Cathedral.

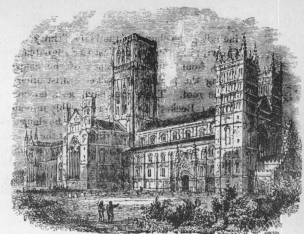

588.—Durham Cathedral.

590.—Stone Chair in the Chapter-House, Durham.

591.—Arcade, Chapter-House, Durham.

587.—Durham.

No. 20.

589.—Durham Cathedral.

including the chapel of the Holy Trinity, and another called Becket's Crown (Fig. 567); the last so designated, according to some authorities, from the circumstance of the chapels having been erected during the prelacy of Becket, whilst others attribute it to the form of the roof. There may have been, however, a much more poetical origin; Becket's Crown was possibly intended to be significant of the crown of martyrdom here won by the slaughtered prelate. It was in that chapel of the Holy Trinity that the shrine, famous the wide world over, was erected, and which speedily became so rich as to be without rival, we should imagine, in Europe. It was "builded," says Stow, "about a man's height, all of stone, then upwards of timber plain, within which was a chest of iron, containing the bones of Thomas Becket, skull and all, with the wound of his death, and the piece cut out of the skull laid in the same wound. The timber-work of this shrine on the outside was covered with plates of gold, damasked with gold wire, which ground of gold was again covered with jewels of gold, as rings, ten or twelve cramped with gold wire into the said ground of gold, many of these rings having stones in them, brooches, images, angels, precious stones, and great pearls." The contents of the shrine were in accordance with the outward display. Erasmus, who obtained a glimpse of the treasures a little before the Reformation, says that under a coffin of wood, inclosing another of gold, which was drawn up by ropes and pulleys, he beheld an amount of riches the value of which he could not estimate. Gold was the meanest thing visible; the whole place glittered with the rarest and most precious gems, which were generally of extraordinary size, and some larger than the egg of a goose. When Henry VIII. seized upon the whole, two great chests were filled, each requiring six or seven men to move it. In strict keeping with the character of the brutal despot was his war with the dead, as well as with the living, when he ordered the remains of Becket to be burned, and the ashes scattered to the winds. The shrine, then, has disappeared, with all its contents, but a more touching memorial than either remains behind—the hollowed pavement—worn away by countless knees of worshippers from every Christian land.

As our ecclesiastical builders seem to have had not the smallest notion of "finality" in their labours—but when a building was even fairly finished, in the ordinary sense of the term, were sure to find some part requiring re-erection in a new style—we find Canterbury for centuries after Becket's death still in progress: the Reformation found the workmen still busy. There is something in all this truly grand, harmonizing with and explaining the mighty ends obtained; reason and feeling alike whisper—Thus alone are Cathedrals built. Yet how deep and pervading the influence of art must have been upon the minds of all who were connected with such structures! Centuries pass, architect after architect dies off, and is succeeded by others, yet still the work grows in beauty, and above all in the loftiest, but under the circumstances apparently the most difficult kind of beauty—expression; each man evidently understands his predecessor so thoroughly, that he can depart from his modes of working—his style, secure still of achieving his principles. Look at Canterbury. How many changes of architectural taste are not there visible; how many different periods of architectural history may not be there traced: yet is the effect anywhere discordant?—Oh, he were indeed presumptuous who should say so! Is it not rather in the highest degree grand and impressive, conveying at once to the mind that sense of sublime repose which belongs only to works of essential unity? We need not subjoin any detailed architectural descriptions. The Cathedral is pleasantly situated in an extensive court, surrounded by gardens, cemetery, the deanery and prebendal houses, and what remains of the archiepiscopal palace, and of other buildings connected with the Cathedral, among which may be mentioned the Staircase (Fig. 569). The Precinct Gate (Fig. 566) forms the principal entrance to this court. As to the Cathedral, the double transepts may be noticed as the most remarkable feature of the plan, which represents, as usual, a cross. The choir is of extraordinary length, nearly two hundred feet, and the great tower is generally esteemed one of the chastest and most beautiful specimens we possess of Pointed architecture. Its height is two hundred and thirty-five feet. The entire length of the building measures five hundred and fourteen feet. One of the two western towers has been recently restored. The Cathedral is exceedingly rich in objects of general interest to the visitor, and may be readily conceived when we consider what a history must be that of Canterbury, how many eminent men have been buried within its walls, what splendid examples of monumental and other sculpture exist there even yet, faint tokens of the wealth art once lavished upon its walls and niches and windows! But among the crowd of interesting objects

there are two which peculiarly attract notice: a sarcophagus of grey marble, richly adorned, and bearing the effigy of a warrior, in copper gilt—that is the monument of the Black Prince, wonderfully fresh and perfect; and an ancient chair in the chapel of the Holy Trinity, formed also of grey marble, in pieces, which is used for the enthronization of the Archbishops of the See, and which, sayeth tradition, was the ancient regal seat of the Saxon kings of Kent, who may have given it to the Cathedral as an emblem of their pious submission to Him who was then first declared unto them—the King of kings (Fig. 567).

———

If St. Augustine's Monastery possessed no other claim to attention than that of having been the burial-place of the great English Apostle of Christianity, it were amply sufficient to induce the visitor to the glorious cathedral to pass on from thence to a space beyond the walls, along the northern side of the Dover road, and there muse over the powers that are from time to time given into the hands of a single man to influence to countless generations the thoughts, feelings, manners, customs, in a word, the spiritual and temporal existence of a great people. Yes, it was here that, after successes that can fall to the lot of few, even of the greatest men, Augustine reposed in 604: he found England essentially a heathen country; he left it, if not essentially a Christian one, still so far advanced to a knowledge of the mighty truths of the Gospel, as to render it all but certain that their final supremacy was a mere question of time. The monastery was founded by him on ground granted by Ethelbert, and dedicated to St. Peter and St. Paul. It was Dunstan who some centuries later, with honourable reverence for Augustine's memory, re-dedicated the establishment to those Apostles and to St. Augustine. Not long after that time Augustine's body was removed into the Cathedral. We fear the pious monks of the monastery must have felt their stock of charity severely tried on the occasion, if we may judge from their known sentiments towards their brethren of Christ Church, who were thus honoured at their expense.

There are some curious passages in what we may call the mutual history of the two establishments. As they both sprang from one source, Augustine, and were of course founded with the same views, they looked on each other, as usual, with feelings that must charm the hearts of those who think it rather creditable than otherwise to be "good haters." Their disputes began early; "neither," says Lambarde, "do I find that ever they agreed after, but were evermore at continual brawling between themselves, either suing before the King or appealing to the Pope, and that for matters of more stomach [pride] than importance; as for example whether the Abbot of St. Augustine's should be consecrated or blessed in his own church or in the other's; whether he ought to ring his bells at service before the other had rung theirs; whether he and his tenants owed suit to the bishop's court and such like." At the dissolution Henry VIII. took a fancy to the monastery, and made it one of his own palaces. Queen Mary subsequently granted it to Cardinal Pole; but on her death it again reverted to the crown; and Elizabeth on one occasion, in 1573, kept her court in it. Subsequently Lord Wotton became the possessor, whose widow entertained Charles II., whilst on his way to take possession of the throne; the note then given to the building may have caused it to be known as Lady Wotton's Palace, which designation is still in use.

We may gather from these facts that the monastery in its days of prosperity must have been an unusually magnificent structure; and, great as have been the injuries since experienced, both in the shape of actual destruction and in the disgraceful treatment of what little was still permitted to exist, no one can look upon the architectural character or extent of the pile, as evidenced in the remains, without being impressed with the same conviction (Fig. 570). The space covered by the different buildings extended to sixteen acres. Of these the gateway (Fig. 571), a superb piece of architecture, is preserved essentially entire.

———

A Monastery at Bristol, dedicated also to St. Augustine, may be here fitly noticed. This was built by Robert Fitzharding, the founder of the present Berkeley family, and a prepositor, or chief magistrate, of the city during the stormy reign of Stephen. The establishment afterwards attained to such a pitch of wealth and splendour, that when Henry VIII. in placing his destructive hands upon the religious houses of England generally, was moved in some way to spare this, he was able to create a bishop's see out of the abbey lands: the abbey church was consequently elevated to the rank it now holds, of a cathedral. As an example of the summary way in which the king's creatures were accustomed to deal with such beautiful and revered structures, it is not unworthy of notice that a part of the church was already demolished, before the arrangement we have mentioned was formally completed. The transept, the eastern part of the nave, and the choir of the original church, are the parts that were saved, and their stately character leaves us grateful for the possession of so much. There is also a tower at the western end of the building, of considerable size and height, and richly decorated. The beautifully arched roof is always looked upon with admiration. The painted windows are also ancient, and therefore interesting. Among the monuments are those to the Eliza of Sterne and to the wife of the poet Mason. But perhaps a still more valuable portion of the Abbey than any we have mentioned is to be found in the gateway (Fig. 573), which has been attributed to an earlier period—the arms of the Confessor are sculptured upon its front,—and which is universally esteemed one of the finest Norman gateways in England.

It is to be observed, in examining the engraving, that the rising of the ground in the course of so many centuries has materially injured the effect of the proportion of the arch to the rest of the edifice; and that the window seen there is not what we now see in the gateway itself, but what we ought to be able to see there; comparatively modern sashes having replaced the antique bay window.

The first view of Lincoln Cathedral obtained by the approaching traveller is something to remember for a lifetime. One of the most beautiful of English structures is certainly at the same time one of the most nobly situated. As we advance towards it from the south, by the London road, we suddenly arrive at the brow of a steep hill, leading down into a fertile valley extending far away to the right and to the left, and through the centre of which the river Witham glides along, whilst immediately opposite rises a corresponding eminence to that on which we stand, at about the distance of a mile or so. In that valley, and stretching up that hill to and over its top, lies outspread before us like a panorama the beautiful city of Lincoln; and crowning the whole stands the glorious Cathedral, its entire length, four hundred and seventy feet, fully displayed, with its two western towers rising at the left extremity, and the grand main tower, truly worthy of its name, lifting itself proudly up from the centre to the height of some two hundred and sixty-seven feet. Such is the first view obtained of Lincoln Cathedral; such the impressions excited by it; and a nearer inspection enhances even the warmest admiration. The architect finds in it the history of his art during two centuries, and those two of more importance (we refer to England only) than all other periods put together, written in styles that make those of words appear tame indeed to his eyes. The sculptor in Lincoln Cathedral looks around him with astonishment at the loftiness of design, as well as consummate beauty of execution, which much of the works that pertain to his own province exhibit. The antiquary finds the blood quickening in his veins as he thinks of the rich storehouse of material that here awaits him, and on which he may exercise, if he pleases, his industry, talents, and zeal for years together; no fear that he will exhaust them. But we are now before the western front, a perfectly unique and stupendous work; simple even to a fault, perhaps, in the general level character of so large a surface, but still sublime in expression, most richly elaborate in ornament, and in the highest degree interesting from the manner in which it tells us, as we look upon it, how it was gradually completed in different eras. There, above all, we perceive in the central portion, including that series of recesses with semicircular arches rising to so many different heights,—the original Norman front of Remigius, the founder of the earliest structure; the pointed window and arch of the central recess alone excepted, which have been substituted for the ancient round ones (Fig. 576). The date of the erection is the reign of the Conqueror, with whom Remigius came over from Normandy. He appears to have been a most enterprising, able, and benevolent man. William of Malmsbury says of him, "that being in person far below the common proportion of men, his mind exerted itself to excel and shine." To show the labourers the spirit that actuated him in rearing the mighty pile, he is said to have carried stones and mortar upon his own shoulders. Of his benevolence it may be sufficient to observe—and the fact is interesting as affording a glimpse of the domestic customs that in some degree ameliorated the frightful misery wrought by the Conquest—he fed daily, during three months of each year, one thousand poor persons; and clothed the blind and

the lame among their number, in addition. Such was the Bishop of Dorchester, who, having removed the see to Lincoln, then one of the most important places in the kingdom, founded the see of Lincoln, and the Cathedral, with the adjoining Bishop's Palace, and other buildings for the residence of the ecclesiastical officers. Unfortunately one pleasure was denied him, that he must have looked forward to with no ordinary emotions; he died the very day before the grand opening of the Minster; to which—warned of his approaching dissolution—he had invited all the most distinguished prelates of the realm to assist in the solemn act of consecration. One of these, the Bishop of Hereford, curiously enough, had excused himself from attending the ceremony, on the ground that he had learnt, by astrology, that the church would not be dedicated in the time of Remigius. Of this early fabric the central portion of the west front is all that now remains; as to the remainder, it has been supposed, by an authority competent to offer an opinion, that it did not materially differ from the present structure in arrangement or size; except that it ended eastwards about sixty feet within the present termination, and that the eastern front formed a semicircular tribune; therefore very unlike the present one, of which it may be said, that if any one desires to see an example of the Gothic, so perfectly beautiful that it is impossible to conceive any more exquisite combination of architectural forms and architectural decorations, let him look upon that eastern front of Lincoln Cathedral.

The building of the Cathedral occupied somewhat more than two centuries; but this did not, as we have partly seen, arise from the circumstance that it was unfinished for so long a time, but that accidents—among them a fire and an earthquake—did great damage to the pile at different periods: another circumstance that no doubt delayed the final completion of the structure was the desire to improve it from time to time as the new and admired Gothic continued to develop fresh beauties and excellencies. Among the bishops to whom, after Remigius, the Cathedral was largely indebted, we may mention Hugh de Grenoble, to whom we owe much of the present fabric, erected by him between 1186 and 1200, no doubt in consequence of the earthquake of 1185. The east or upper transept, with the Chapel attached to it, the Choir, Chapter-house, and east side of the western transept, with parts of the additions to Remigius's west front, are all attributed to Bishop Hugh. Even in this collection of examples of the architecture of but fourteen years, the progression of the art is clearly visible; beautiful as is the Choir, for instance, a pure unmixed specimen of early Gothic, it is far surpassed by the Chapter-house—with its most airy and elegant of interiors—where, in the centre of the lofty octagonal building, rises a stately pillar formed of a group of slender pillars, and which, at a certain height, branch off in all directions, still rising, over the roof. This Bishop, as his name implies, was a native of Grenoble; and so distinguished for his austere piety, that when he died, in 1200, and was brought to Lincoln for interment, the Kings of England and Scotland, who were then holding a conference in the city, went to meet his body at the gates, and bore it on their shoulders to the Cathedral Close, whence it was carried to the Choir by a multitude of the most distinguished personages of the realm, and finally buried at the east end of the Cathedral. Such a man was of course sure to be canonized by the Roman Catholic Church: that ceremony took place in 1220; and sixty-two years later his remains were taken up and deposited in a shrine of pure gold in the Presbytery. The enormous value of this memorial may be conceived from a statement of its dimensions—eight feet by four. The shrine was plundered at the dissolution of the Monasteries, as well as the Cathedral generally. The inventory of jewels, of articles of gold and silver, and of costly vestments taken from Lincoln, fills several folio pages of the great edition of the 'Monasticon.' The Nave, unequalled, it is supposed, in the world for its combined magnitude and beauty of proportion, and the curious Galilee porch, so richly decorated, are among the next additions; the use of the last-named work has thus been explained by Dr. Milner ('Treatise on the Ecclesiastical Architecture of the Middle Ages'):—"There were formerly such porches at the western extremity of all large churches. In these public penitents were stationed, dead bodies were sometimes deposited, previously to their interment, and females were allowed to see the monks of the convent who were their relatives. We may gather from a passage in Gervase, that upon a woman's applying for leave to see a monk, her relation, she was answered in the words of Scripture, 'He goeth before you into Galilee, there you shall see him.' Hence the term Galilee. It is well known that at Durham Cathedral women were not even allowed to attend Divine service except in the Galilee." To a greater man than any we have yet mentioned, Grosteste, we are indebted for the lower portion of the main tower. What powerful kings strove in vain

X 2

594.—Early English Capital, Durham.

592.—Nave of Durham Cathedral.

595.—Capital, Galilee, Durham.

596.—Ornamental Shaft, Door of
North Cloisters, Durham.

597.—Ornamental Shaft, Door of North
Cloisters, Durham.

598.—Norman Moulding,
Durham.

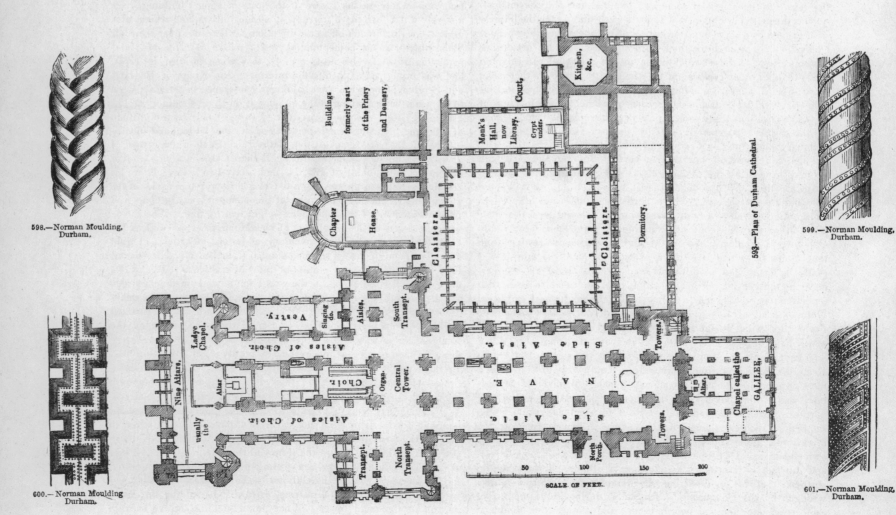

593.—Plan of Durham Cathedral.

599.—Norman Moulding,
Durham.

600.—Norman Moulding
Durham.

601.—Norman Moulding,
Durham.

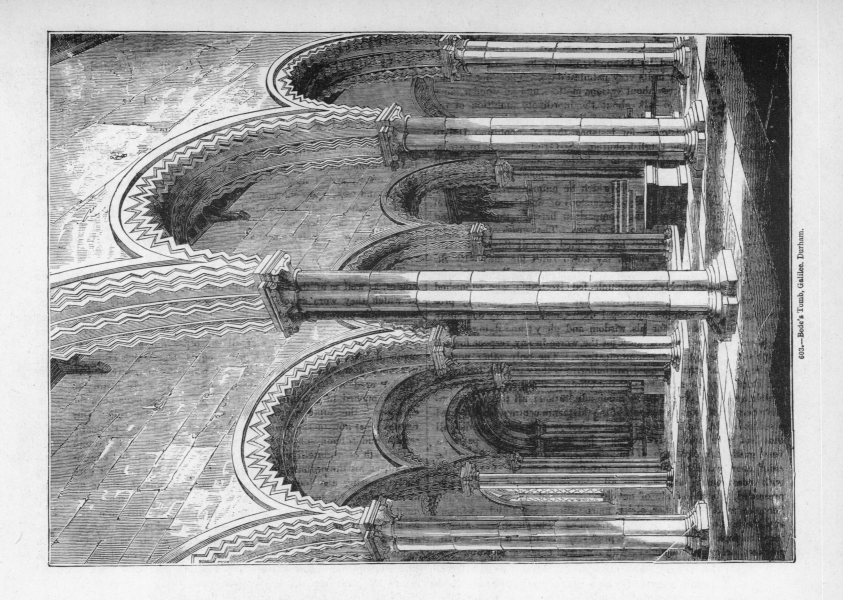

603.—Bede's Tomb, Galilee, Durham.

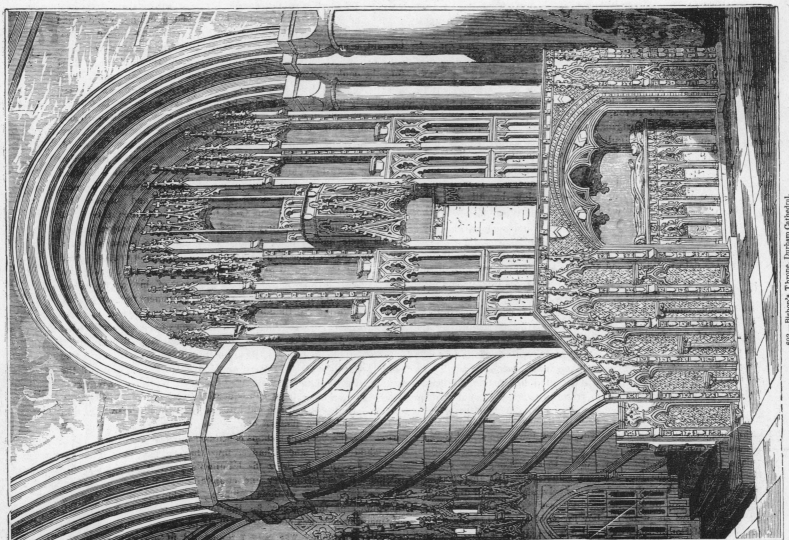

602.—Bishop's Throne, Durham Cathedral.

to do, was accomplished by Bishop Grosteste; he opposed successfully the Papal power in its very palmiest days. The Pope and he, it appears, did not agree about various matters, and no wonder, since he was accustomed to talk about the inordinate ambition of the Pontificate, and to speak disrespectfully of some of its convenient, but not very just, customs—for instance, that of appointing Italian priests to offices in the English church. So Grosteste went to Rome, to see if he could not come to a better understanding with his spiritual superior. His ill success was made apparent on his return, by his publication of a letter, in which he animadverted in no very measured terms upon the gross perversions of the Papal power, and instituted a most unflattering comparison between the living and past possessors of the chair of St. Peter. The wrath of the Pope may be imagined: "What!" he exclaimed, "shall this old dotard, whose sovereign is my vassal, lay down rules for me? By St. Peter, I will make such an example of him as shall astonish the world." He accordingly excommunicated Grosteste; who astonished him, whatever he might have done the world, in return, by proceeding quietly with his episcopal duties, making every one speak of him with reverence for his wisdom and piety; and dying at last, eighteen years afterwards, not a jot the worse in any respect for the Pope's thunders and excommunications. The only other portion of the structure that we need particularize is the east end, including the Presbytery, or space beyond the Choir, and the eastern front, of which we have spoken with so much admiration: all this appears to have been built in the latter half of the thirteenth century; and formed a suitable termination to so grand a work, surpassing, as it did, all that had been previously erected. In these—the earlier parts—a very gradual progression of improvement in the style forms the chief characteristic; but in the Presbytery and east front, while with consummate art we see all the essentials of the former preserved, a striking air of novelty is superadded, and the whole becomes markedly richer, airier, more delicate and stately, without any diminution of grandeur or strength. The buttresses almost cease to look like buttresses, so profusely are they decorated with crockets, creepers, and finials, with clustered columns at the angles, and with brackets and canopies for statues on the faces. The windows now cease to be mere single lights, they are divided into several compartments by mullions; they begin to revel in all the luxuriant variety of geometrical tracery. From the highest to the lowest details, a very "shower of beauty" seems to have suddenly fallen over all; and Time has in most parts dealt so gently with them, that the very freshness of that early period seems to be still preserved.

There are, of course, many matters of interest connected with the erection of the Cathedral, which we have not even referred to, and many others of its general history, or of its individual features, upon which our space either forbids us to comment at all, or but slightly. The Bishop's Porch, at the eastern corner of the southern side of the building, was originally one of the most sumptuous and admirable specimens of mingled architecture and sculpture that even Old England itself could furnish; and, mutilated as the porch now is, more than traces of its superb beauty yet remain. The principal part is the alto-relievo above the doorway, representing the Last Judgment in a style of the loftiest design, that fills one, like the beautiful statue of Eleanor in Westminster Abbey, with astonishment and perplexity: how could such works have been executed in England in the thirteenth or fourteenth century? The various chapels and monumental remains of Lincoln are in themselves a wide field for study and observation; but we can only here remark that among the latter are those of Bishop Remigius, Catherine Swynford, wife of John of Gaunt, and sister of Chaucer's wife, and the remains of a monument, covering the stone coffin of little St. Hugh, a boy alleged to have been crucified by the Jews in derision of the Saviour—a charge absurd enough in all but its consequences: these are painful even to relate. In 1255 one hundred and two Jews were taken from Lincoln to the Tower; and eventually twenty-three were executed in London, and eighteen at Lincoln. The explanation, frightful as is the wickedness it involves, if true, seems to be partially given in the existing record of a commission to Simon de Passeliere and William de Leighton to seize for the king's use, the houses belonging to the Jews who were hanged at Lincoln. Knowing what atrocities were perpetrated, avowedly to make their victims, the Jews, submit to spoliation, there is but little difficulty in believing, however reluctantly, that the spoilers were glad to avail themselves of any conceivable means of directing against that unhappy people the greatest possible amount of popular odium. A painted statue of the boy formerly existed here, bearing marks of crucifixion in the hands and feet, and blood issuing from a wound in the side. The story has been commemorated in the ballad

of 'Sir Hugh, or the Jew's Daughter;' and in the 'Canterbury Tales,' where Chaucer, in the Prioress's Tale, alludes to

> O younge Hugh of Lincoln slain also,
> With cursed Jewess, as it is notable,
> For it n'is but a little while ago: &c.

Great Tom of Lincoln must have a passing word. The old bell, having been accidentally broken in 1827, has been since recast, with the additional metal of the four lady bells that also hung in the great tower; and it now deserves more than its former reputation. Its size and weight are enormous. The height exceeds six feet; the greatest breadth is six feet ten inches and a half; the weight is five tons eight hundredweight. As to tone and volume of sound, the imagination can conceive nothing more grandly, musically solemn.

The records of the foundation of many of our earliest monastic houses, as well as of the faith to the cultivation and dissemination of which they were devoted, exhibit, as we have already partly seen, ample store of miracles on the part of the teachers, responded to by a most unbounded credulity on the part of those who were taught. But all the wonders of all the other religious establishments of England put together, hardly equal those which Durham was once accustomed to boast of, and which were received with implicit credence; for any important event in its early history to have happened in a simply natural manner seems to have been the exception: the supernatural was the mode and the rule. Our readers must not, therefore, be surprised to find that an intrinsically serious and solemn subject has, in the lapse of ages, and through the growth of an intelligent scepticism as to these continual aberrations from all the ordinary laws of nature, become surrounded with many amusing and ludicrous associations. Fortunately the commencement of the history of Durham, which is also the commencement of the history of the introduction of Christianity into that part of the island, has not been impaired by such derogatory influences. Ethelfrith, King of Northumberland, at his death left a widow and seven sons, who were obliged to fly into Scotland, to escape the hands of the usurper Edwin, the boys' uncle. Donald IV. then reigned in Scotland, and being a convert to Christianity, instilled its principles into the minds of the youthful exiles. The eldest son ultimately obtained a portion of his inheritance, after the usurper's death, but relapsed into heathenism, and was murdered by Cadwallon, King of Cumberland, who overran the whole country. It was to do battle with this monarch that Oswald, a second son, then set out from Scotland, and placed himself at the head of the miserable Northumbrians. The utmost force he could collect, however, was so small in comparison with that commanded by Cadwallon, that but for his reliance on the Power so recently made known to him, he must have resigned the contest for his kingdom in despair. Undismayed, he prepared for the bloody fight, and causing a cross to be brought to him in front of the army, he held it with his own hands in an upright posture, while his attendants, animated by his enthusiasm into a similar conviction that they were to be aided by more than mortal influences, heaped up the earth around, and made it fast. Then addressing the men, he said:—"Let us fall down on our knees, and beseech the Almighty, the living and true God, to defend us against this proud and cruel enemy;" and they obeyed him. After devotions, he led on his little band toward the enemy, the whole actuated by a spirit that was irresistible: a complete victory was obtained. Full of gratitude, Oswald sent to Scotland for some holy man, who might assist in the conversion of the inhabitants of his newly-gained dominions; and one was sent whose austere manners proved so little to the taste of the Northumbrians, that Oswald was fain to send him back. He was replaced by Aidan, who seems to have been all that was desired, and who having successfully looked for the most suitable spot, at last fixed on the island of Lindisfarne, where he established a monastery and a bishopric. Of the sanctity of the lives of these primitive Christians of Northumbria we have a kind of testimony in the name subsequently given to the place—Holy Island. But a more direct and interesting evidence is to be found in Bede's charming picture of the lives of the monks during the period that the Scottish bishops continued to fill the office of Abbot. One could almost fancy Chaucer must have had it in view when, at a later period, he drew his inimitable portrait of the "poure parson." "Their frugality and simplicity of life, and parsimony, appeared in the place of their residence, in which there was nothing superfluous or unnecessary for the humblest life. In the church only magnificence was permitted. Their possessions consisted chiefly in cattle, for money was only retained till fit opportunity offered to distribute it to the poor. Places of entertainment and reception were unnecessary, for the religious were visited solely for their doctrines and the holy offices of the church. When the king came thither, he was attended only by five or six persons, and had no other object in view than to partake of the rites of religion, departing immediately after the service: if perchance they took refreshment, it was of the common fare of the monks. The attention of those pastors was confined to spiritual matters only; temporary affairs were deemed derogatory to the holy appointment: and thence proceeded the profound veneration which was paid by all ranks of people to the religious habit. When any ecclesiastic went from the monastery, it was to preach the word of salvation, and he was everywhere received with joy, as a messenger of the Divinity; on the road the passengers bowed the head to receive the holy benediction and sign of the cross, with pious reverence treasuring up the good man's precepts as documents of the most salutary import. The churches were crowded with a decent audience; and when a monk was seen entering a village in his travels, the inhabitants flocked about him, entreating admonition and prayers. On their visitation, donations and riches were not their pursuit, and when any religious society received an augmentation to the revenues of the house, as an offering of Christianity by the donor, they accepted it as an additional store with which they were intrusted for the benefit of the poor." The humble fishermen of Galilee might have recognised kindred spirits in these monks of Lindisfarne.

That most terrible of scourges that was perhaps ever inflicted upon an unfortunate people, a neighbouring nation of pirates, ultimately caused (in connection with another matter, to which we shall refer presently) the removal of the bishopric from Lindisfarne. Again and again the merciless and insatiable Dane burst down upon the island, so Holy to all but him, and destroyed and slaughtered what he could not carry away or make captive; and at last the monks in despair ceased for a time their exertions to make the place retain its original importance. After the Conquest, however, a new Priory was erected, holding the position of a cell only to the former bishopric. The remains of that edifice (shown in Fig. 572) are singularly beautiful in their ruin. Scott has described the whole as forming

A solemn, huge, and dark-red pile,
Placed on the margin of the Isle;

and which, it is to be feared, will be lost to the next generation, notwithstanding the care that is said to have been of late years bestowed on them: the material is a soft red freestone, which wastes rapidly under the action of the elements. About one hundred yards distant from the mainland, with which Lindisfarne itself is connected at low water, and facing the Priory, there stands, on a low detached piece of rock, the foundations of a building upon which most persons look with even deeper interest than on those stately neighbouring ruins. In some parts the walls yet rise a foot or two above the ground: these walls and foundations belonged to a small chapel, dedicated to the saint who was the immediate cause of the removal of the bishopric—St. Cuthbert, himself one of the early prelates. His remains were buried at Lindisfarne. But, having taken up the body about the year 875, and conveyed it away from Lindisfarne to avoid the attacks of the Danes, the Bishop Eandulf and the Abbot Eadred, and all the monastic household, were kept marching to and fro, now alarmed by rumours that the Danes were coming this way, and the monks consequently going that; then again stopped by fresh intelligence, and compelled to diverge into new tracks. No wonder that the good bishop at last felt heartily tired of these incessant and somewhat unseemly manœuvres, and resolved to put an end to them by going over to Ireland. Accordingly the party, which included a great number of the more zealous and attached Christian people, proceeded to the mouth of the Derwent, and took ship; but they had scarcely got out to sea, before a violent storm arose, and drove the vessel back to the spot from whence they had departed. To minds accustomed to look upon all such events as bearing some spiritual meaning, it was considered certain that God thus signified his will that they should not quit England. Food now grew scarce, and the people, driven away by hunger, gradually disappeared, until there were left only the Bishop, the Abbot, and seven other persons to take care of the saintly corpse. In the midst of their distress, one of the number, Hunred, had a vision which greatly comforted the wanderers: they were told through him, by a celestial voice, to repair to the sea, where they would find a book of the Gospels they had lost out of the ship during the storm, and which appears to have been greatly valued, for it was adorned with gold and precious stones. The message then continued, that they would next find a bridle,

hanging on a tree, which was to be placed on a horse that would come to them, and the horse was to be attached to a car that they would also meet with, and thus the body might be carried with greater ease and comfort. Everything happened as foretold; and again the party moved on, following the horse wherever it led. We must not forget to mention, as a very interesting evidence in favour of the truth of all the more natural parts of the story, that at the time of Symeon of Dunelmensis, the ancient historian of the see, from whom this part of our narration is derived, the book was still preserved in the library at Durham, and it is supposed that one of the most valued treasures of the British Museum is this ancient copy of the Gospels. When our travellers had thus spent seven years in incessant motion, Halfdane, the great Danish leader, was seized with a loathsome disorder, which made his presence so unendurable to his fellow-men, that he suddenly went out to sea, with three ships, and there perished. And thus, peace at last blessed the troubled ecclesiastics of Lindisfarne. They went first to the monastery of Cree, where they were "lovingly entertained," and where they stayed for some months. The country at that time was in a terrible state of anarchy; and it is to the credit of the monks that they set to work to reduce the whole into order. It was now the Abbot's turn to have a vision; in which St. Cuthbert appeared to him, and enjoined Eadred to repair to the Danish camp, and there inquire for a youth called Guthred, the son of Hardecnut, who had been sold into slavery; him he was to redeem and proclaim king. It was a bold manœuvre, for if it succeeded, Guthred must be ungrateful indeed not to remember who placed him on the throne. It did succeed; the slave became a monarch; both Danes and Northumbrians, wearied with their perpetual contests and the misery thence produced, acknowledging him at Oswiesdune. And now was seen the ecclesiastical importance of that lucky vision of the Abbot's; the see was formally translated from Lindisfarne to Cunecasestre (Chester-le-Street), and the Bishop Eandulf made the first prelate there; whilst the whole of the land between the Weir and the Tyne was bestowed by Guthred on St. Cuthbert, or, in other words, on the Bishop of Durham, and thus became the foundation of their palatine jurisdiction.

A new alarm, about 995, caused by Sweyn's appearance in England, set the Bishop, and all his clergy and religious, once more on their travels with St. Cuthbert's body. Another miraculous intervention is held to have taken place, and the wandering party were directed to Durham. The spot at that time was strong by nature, but uninhabited, and not easily made habitable—it was so thickly wooded. In the midst was a small plain, which the husbandman had reclaimed; that was the only evidence of civilization the place presented. But there were willing hearts and hands ready to flock thither from all parts, and help these memorable guardians of the most memorable of saints to set up a house and a temple in the wilderness. From the river Coquet to the Tees they came in "multitudes." The trees were grubbed up, and there soon appeared, in the place of the little oratory of wattles first and temporarily put up, dwellings for all the people who had come with the ecclesiastics, and then a church of stone, a more honourable resting-place for the saint than the wattled building, but also intended to be but temporary; for Aldun, the bishop, of course desired to rear a structure worthy of the saint's reputation. There seems little doubt here, also, but that we have followed the details of a true history, the more marvellous portion alone excepted; and a very striking idea they give us of the foundation of one of the most interesting cities of the kingdom. The see was again formally, and for the last time, translated, and hence the Bishopric of Durham. There is a tradition relating to one of the removals of the body thus commemorated by Scott in his 'Marmion:'—

In his stone coffin forth he rides,
A ponderous bark for river tides;
Yet light as gossamer it glides
Downward to Tillmouth cell:

and, strange to say, the tradition may be true. Not only did the coffin exist till within the last few years, perhaps does so still, but was so constructed that statical experiments have proved it to be capable of floating with a weight equal to that of a human body. It was finely shaped, ten feet long, and three and a half in diameter.

The history of the bishops of Durham forms too large a subject even to be glanced at in our pages; so we shall merely give one passage from it, of a noticeable character, and then conclude with a short account of the building around which all these historical recollections, as it were, concentrate themselves—the Cathedral. During the frightful period of the Conquest, which fell with more than its ordinary severity on the northern counties—William, for

603.—Transept, St. Albans.

604.—Waltham Abbey, from the North-West.

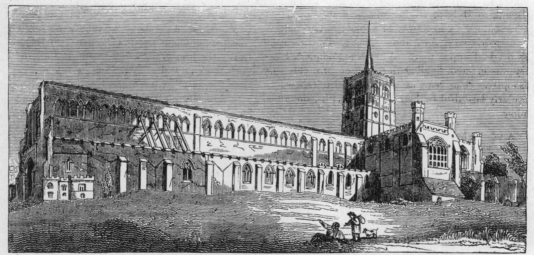

606.—Abbey of St. Albans.

605.—Waltham Abbey.

607.—Nave, St. Albans.

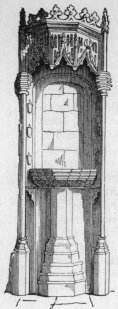

611.—Piscina, Norwich.

613.—Font, Norwich.

615.—Capital, North Transept, Norwich.

617.—Flint Masonry, St. Ethelbert's Gate House, Norwich.

609.—Erpingham Gateway, Norwich.

610.—Norwich.

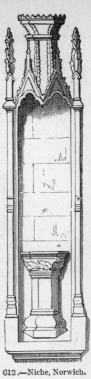

612.—Niche, Norwich.

614.—Pinnacle, Norwich.

616.—Capital, North Transept, Norwich.

618.—Flint Masonry, St. Ethelbert's Gate House, Norwich.

instance, at one time wasted the whole country from York to Durham with fire and sword—the Saxon Bishop Egelwin died a prisoner in the Isle of Ely, of a broken heart, and Walcher, a Norman, was appointed his successor. That ecclesiastic was by no means content to be an ecclesiastic only, no matter what the rank; he purchased the earldom of Northumberland, and thus joined in his own person, for the first time in the see, the spiritual and civil jurisdiction. His success was not at all calculated to encourage imitation. When the people saw the office they had been accustomed to venerate connected with the infliction of legal severities, they began to murmur against the man who had so lowered it, and they did not long confine themselves to murmuring only. On the 14th of May, 1080, Walcher was holding a public assembly at Gateshead in exercise of his obnoxious civil authority; and although large numbers of the people were congregated, there appeared nothing in their appearance and demeanour to excite particular alarm. But suddenly there arose the cry of "Short rede, good rede; slay ye the bishop," which had been the watchword chosen, and at once the people drew arms from beneath their garments and rushed upon the bishop's party, while others set fire to the church. Walcher, seeing escape hopeless, determined to die with dignity, so, veiling his face with his robe, he advanced towards the assailants, one of whom instantly killed him with a lance. Of the succeeding early bishops of the see may be named Ralf Flambard, Hugh de Pudsey, and Anthony Bek, whose life gives one an extraordinary idea of the power occasionally obtained by the more eminent churchmen of the middle ages; he was at once Bishop of Durham, Patriarch of Jerusalem, Governor of the Isle of Man, and, as a military chieftain, able to send his thirty-two banners to the battle of Falkirk. Among the later bishops was Tunstall, of whom, on his return to England, Erasmus touchingly wrote:—"I seem now scarce to live, Tunstall being torn from me; I know not where I shall fly to."

Durham, like Lincoln, enjoys the inestimable architectural advantage of a truly noble site. The city, being nearly surrounded by the river Weir, forms a kind of peninsula, the centre of which rises to a considerable height, with the cathedral at the summit, surrounded at its base by buildings and hanging gardens which descend to the river, and are there continued as it were in the delightful walks of the "Banks," which skirt the water on both sides. The situation of the cathedral and the other ecclesiastical buildings far surpasses any pictures we have ever seen of it—truly beautiful and grand it is! You make your way up to the eminence on which stands the cathedral, through steep and narrow lanes, which bring you into a fine open space, with the cathedral on the south of the square. The palace, or castle (now occupied as the University of Durham), forms another side. You descend to an ancient bridge, and are now under these grand monuments of ancient magnificence. A beautiful walk leads along their base overhanging the river at a considerable height. You cross a noble bridge of modern construction, and find a similar walk on the opposite bank. You have now, following the windings of the river, passed from the west to the south side of the cathedral, and in continuation of it are most picturesque groups of houses rising one above another on the steep bank, embosomed in trees. The winding course of the river brings you now to the east end, and still you have the same grand view of this lordly place. Well might the old bishops feel that theirs was a princely rule, as they gave laws from such a throne.

The cathedral was begun in the reign of Rufus, by Bishop William de Carilepho, and in part or entirely completed by the next bishop, Ralf Flambard. The structure then erected we possess in an all but perfect state. The eastern extremity, where the Nine Altars (see plan, Fig. 593) now stand, was probably in the Norman building semicircular; the nave (Fig. 592) and the choir were open to the timber roof, instead of being vaulted as at present; partial alterations, improvements, and some important additions have also been made; but essentially we have the true Norman building before us, when we gaze upon the noble semicircular arches, and the tall, massive, and in some instances curiously decorated pillars of Durham Cathedral. We may observe by the way that some of these pillars are twenty-three feet in circumference. The Galilee Chapel (Fig. 603), the uses of which are explained in our account of Lincoln Cathedral, was the first addition to the original structure: this was built by Hugh de Pudsey, in the latter half of the twelfth century; and we perceive in it the first of that series of architectural stages, from the Norman to the finished Gothic, which give to Durham, as to some of our other cathedrals, so much artistical value.

The lightness and elegance of the pillars, though in every other respect genuine Norman, strike one at a glance. The great tower, the most important of all the additions, was finished by Richard Hotoun, who became prior in 1290; and who had also the honour of completing the chapel of the Nine Altars. The great western window was the work of Prior John Fossour, about 1350, and the altar-screen, erected at the expense of John, Lord Neville, was finished in 1380 by Prior Berrington. It is painful to have to record that such a building should ever have been allowed to be touched by incompetent and tasteless hands; need we say that they belong to the last century? which, with its predecessor, enjoys an eminence of a peculiar kind—they were, in all that concerns architectural art, the worst periods of English modern history. Durham, at the time to which we refer, underwent a thorough repair, and we suppose, in the ideas of the repairers, *beautifying*—"Heaven save the mark!"—and the result is in many parts too evident. The Galilee was also repaired by Cardinal Langley at the commencement of the fifteenth century, in the exquisitely-florid Gothic of the time. The dimensions of the cathedral are four hundred and eleven feet in length, eighty in breadth, and the main tower two hundred and twelve in height. The interior, as usual, presents many objects of high interest—as the sumptuous bishop's throne (Fig. 602), the stone chair (Fig. 590), and above all, the common tomb of St. Cuthbert and of the Venerable Bede, the author of the valuable Ecclesiastical History to which we are indebted for many of the most interesting facts relating to the establishment of Christianity and Christian houses and temples in England.

[Waltham Abbey and Saint Albans form a page of cuts immediately following Durham. We postpone their description till we have completed our notices of the earlier cathedrals.]

A curious story is told in explanation of the origin of NORWICH CATHEDRAL. During the reign of William Rufus, Herbert de Lozingia, an eminent ecclesiastic, attracted towards himself a degree of unpleasant attention from his spiritual superiors, which ended in his being cited to appear before the Pope at Rome, to answer for simoniacal practices, among which in particular was alleged against him his purchase of the see of Thetford. The punishment was at once characteristic and sensible, and involving what we call poetical justice: he was commanded to build various churches and monasteries at his own expense; and thus Lozingia found enforced upon him a very arduous undertaking for the good of the church, when he had been intending to pursue what he conceived to be more peculiarly his own good. Among the buildings so erected, it seems, were the earliest cathedral of Norwich, and the monastery, both commenced in 1094. Many of our important cities and foundations are accustomed to boast of the public spirit and liberality of their founders or early promoters; the city of Norwich, it will be seen, may date much of its prosperity to qualities of a very opposite kind. Lozingia, however, appears to have been a shrewd—perhaps, after the shame of the exposure, a repentant—man, and to have performed the penance imposed upon him in so creditable a spirit that he was ultimately allowed to transfer the bishopric of which he had been deprived, Thetford, to Norwich, and was there consecrated the first bishop in the cathedral of his own erection. Of this structure it has been supposed by some that we possess no remains, on account of the presumed general destruction of the pile in the extraordinary events that mark the history of Norwich in connection with the year 1272. It appears that from a very early period after the establishment of the monastery, quarrels had broken out between the monks and the citizens, the former asserting their entire independence within their own precincts, the latter maintaining that the charter granted by Henry I. in 1122 gave them right over every part of the city without exception. There was a fair then held at certain times on a piece of ground called Tombland, which lay directly before the gates of the monastery: this spot formed a very bone of contention between the two parties, and at last the bad feelings excited broke out in sudden violence and bloodshed. The monks and their retainers, it matters little which, fell upon the citizens and killed several. The people of Norwich were exasperated in the highest degree. An inquest was held upon the bodies of the dead, a verdict of murder returned against those who had killed them, and a warrant issued for their apprehension. The monks—who seemed to have felt themselves quite safe through the whole proceedings—now thought it necessary to resort to more decided warfare; so having let loose the spiritual artillery at their command, in the shape of a sweeping excommunication of the entire body of citizens, they then took more ordinary weapons into their hands, and amused themselves by picking off a passing citizen, every now and then, by a well-directed shot. If this was their reading of their religious duties, it was only in strict keeping that they should prefer the holiest day for the more important deeds. On the Sunday before St. Lawrence's-day, tired of this desultory warfare, the monastic belligerents sallied forth from their high-walled monastery, with a "great noise, and all that day and night went in a raging manner about the city," killing here and there a merchant or other inhabitant, and plundering here and there a house. They finished by breaking open a tavern kept by one Hugh de Bromholm, where they drank all the wine they could, and left the rest to run waste from the open taps, and then these good and faithful servants returned to their admiring prior. The citizens appear to have remained more patient than one might expect under their provocations, till this last and worst of all. But then the magistrates assembled, word was sent to the king of what had taken place, in order that he might give them redress, and in the mean time a general assemblage of the people was called for the next morning, to arrange measures of defence. They met—an army in numbers, though unfortunately not in discipline. Before the chief persons of influence could instil into their minds the indispensable qualities of order, patience, and firmness, they were borne away by some uncontrollable impulse of anger towards the monastery, where they flung themselves tumultuously against the gates, and endeavoured to force an entrance. The prior resisted for a while the raging storm of assailants, but at last they burnt down the great gates of the close, with the church of St. Albert that stood near, and then swept on, with redoubled energy and determination to fire the chief conventual buildings. The almonry was speedily in flames, then the church doors, then the great tower. Many of the people ascended the neighbouring steeple of St. George's, and from thence, by means of slings, threw fiery missiles into the great belfry, beyond the choir of the cathedral, and thus in a short time the whole building was enveloped in flames. Besides the injury done to the building, the monastery lost all its gold and silver ornaments, its costly vestments, holy vessels, and library of books; for what the fire spared, was carried off by the incendiaries. Most of the monks fled, but the sub-dean, and some of the clerks and laymen, were killed, where they were met with, in the cloisters and in the precincts; others were hurried into the city, to share the same bloody fate; and some were imprisoned. The prior fled to Yarmouth, but it was in order that he might return with fresh strength, and take full vengeance for the sufferings his own disgraceful conduct had brought upon the monastery. He entered Norwich with sword and trumpet in hand—what a picture of the priest militant!—and fell upon the people in their own way, with fire and sword; and having satiated himself, withdrew, to wait, and consider, like the men of Norwich, now that all was over between themselves, what would not both have to answer for to a third party, the government of the country—in other words, the king. Even-handed justice was undoubtedly to be dreaded by both; but that was just the sort of justice that was seldom dispensed when church and laity stood as the disputants on either side of the judgment-seat. Henry's first proceeding was enough to show the citizens what they might expect. He summoned a meeting of the hierarchy, at Eye in Suffolk; and the result was, that an interdict was laid upon the town generally; all persons directly concerned in the riots were excommunicated; thirty-four persons were drawn through the streets by horses, and dashed to pieces; others were hanged, drawn, and quartered, and afterwards burnt; and a woman who was recognised as having set fire to the gates, was burnt alive. And, as on all such occasions in the middle ages, there must be a something forthcoming for the royal treasury, why, twelve of the men of Norwich, no doubt the very richest that could be in any way implicated, were mulcted of their possessions. Such was the punishment of the people; what was the sentence against their opponents and oppressors, who had so recklessly provoked their fury? The prior's conduct was evidently too bad to be altogether looked over, so he was sent to prison for a short time, and whilst there resigned his priory. And that was all. The church did not even suffer in its revenues. Before the interdict was taken off, the citizens were compelled to pay three thousand marks towards the re-edifying of the cathedral, and one hundred pounds in money, for a pix, or cup of gold, weighing ten pounds.

It is strange and lamentable that, after this tragical event, no wise and statesman-like measures were carried into effect to prevent their recurrence for the future; and although the scenes of 1272 were never repeated, the cause of all the jealousy and ill-feeling remained in active operation down to the time of Cardinal Wolsey, when the city formally resigned all jurisdiction within the priory walls; and the priory all power without them. That was just before the Reformation, which settled the matter in its own sum-

mary fashion, by quietly doing away with the monastery altogether. It had been supposed, we repeat, that the church built by Lozinga was entirely destroyed in this fire, and that the present must have been erected in its place. But it is astonishing how any one who had even looked at the cathedral could allow himself for a moment to doubt that the original edifice is still preserved to us. The wood-work, decorations, &c., must certainly have been destroyed, and the structure, generally, seriously injured; but not so seriously as to involve anything like a rebuilding of the whole, for a more characteristically Norman edifice does not exist in the country than the present cathedral of Norwich; and it would be absurd to suppose that such a style would have been adopted at the close of the thirteenth century, when Pointed architecture was giving us some of its most exquisite examples of the perfection to which it had attained. The very plan of Norwich is as unmistakably Norman as the buildings erected on it,—transept without aisles or pillars, choir extending beneath the tower in the centre of the structure, into the very nave itself, circular eastern extremity, forming within a chancel with side aisles running round it, and circular chapels. It is, in a word, the very decided Norman character of Norwich that makes it, notwithstanding its smaller size and comparatively undecorated aspect, its decayed surface, and cramped position, one of the most interesting of our cathedrals. The length of the whole building is four hundred and eleven feet; and the tower, one of the finest specimens of decorated Norman extant, rises with its spire, which is of later date, to the great height of three hundred and thirteen feet. One single ancient statue-tomb of an enriched character, and one such only, is to be found in the church—Bishop Goldwell's, shown in Fig. 620. The plain aspect of the cathedral may, no doubt, be in a great degree attributed to the injuries done in the time of the civil war. Bishop Hall, the satirist, who suffered from both parties, not being apparently partisan enough for either, has given us an interesting account of what took place. In his 'Hard Measure,' he says, "It is tragical to relate the furious sacrilege committed under the authority of Linsey, Tofts the Sheriff, and Greenwood: what clattering of glasses, what beating down of walls, what tearing down of monuments, what pulling down of seats, and wresting out of irons and brass from the windows and graves!—what defacing of arms, what demolishing of curious stone-work that had not any representation in the world, but of the cost of the founder and the skill of the mason! what piping on the destroyed organ-pipes! Vestments, both copes and surplices, together with the leaden cover, which had been newly cut down from over the greenyard pulpit, and the singing-books and service-books were carried to the fire in the public market-place; a lewd wretch walking before the train in his cope, trailing in the dirt with a service-book in his hand, imitating in an impious scorn the tone, and usurping the words of the Liturgy. The ordnance being discharged on the guild-day, the cathedral was filled with musketeers, drinking and tobacconing as freely as if it had turned alehouse."

An interesting appendage of the monastery remains on the south side of the cathedral,—a cloister, also of later date than the original buildings, forming a large quadrangle with a handsome doorway and lavatories. But the most striking feature of the locality is the Erpingham gateway, a truly superb work. Few but will remember the name of the founder as that of the gallant knight of Henry V.'s army, who, while commanding the archers at Agincourt, had the honour of giving the signal for the first momentous forward movement, which he did by throwing his truncheon high into the air, and exclaiming "Now strike!" And they did strike, and with such effect that the French never through the conflict recovered from the blow thus given by the bowmen of England under their gray-headed leader at the very outset. Considering how great a favourite Sir Thomas was with the victor of Agincourt, and the treatment that Lord Cobham received during the same reign for his religious heresy, it is a curious and noticeable circumstance in Sir Thomas's history to find that he too at one time had been dallying with the proscribed Lollard principles, and had exerted himself to promote their diffusion. But Henry Spencer, the "warlike Bishop of Norwich," then ruled over the diocese, who would fain have pursued as short a way with the followers of Wickliffe as he did with those of Wat Tyler. In that most famous of English insurrections, the bishop, unlike many of the more powerful nobles, who shut themselves up in their strong castles, went forth with his retainers to meet the revolters in the field, where he speedily overthrew them; then, having sentenced them in crowds to the scaffold, he laid aside the warrior and judge, and became the ministering priest to his own victims, and exerted himself as busily to save their souls as to destroy their bodies.

621.—From the Prior's Gate Cloisters, Norwich.

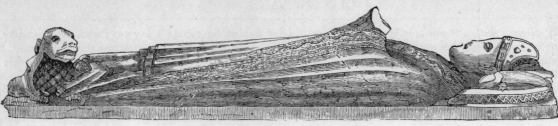

620.—Effigy of Bishop Goldwell, Norwich Cathedral.

622.—From the Prior's Gate Cloisters, Norwich.

623.—Early English Capital, Norwich.

624.—Norman Base, Norwich.

625.—Figure over the Entrance to the Transept, Norwich.

626.—Arcade, North Transept, Norwich.

627.—Finial, Norwich.

619.—Cathedral of Norwich.

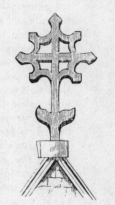

628.—Gable Cross, Norwich.

629.—Norman Arcade, Norwich.

630.—Norman Capital, East End of Gallery, Norwich.

631.—Arcade, Norwich.

164

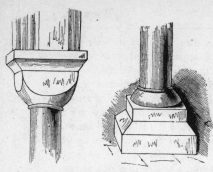

634.—Capital and Base, Worcester.

635.—Tudor Badges, Shrine of Prince Arthur, Worcester.

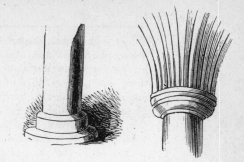

636.—Capital and Base, Chapter House, Worcester.

632.—Worcester, General View.

637.—Effigy of King John, Worcester.

633.—King John's Tomb, Worcester.

638.—Effigy of Lady Harcourt, Worcester.

165

When such a man declared that if he found any Lollards in his diocese, he would make them hop headless, or fry a faggot, to use his own suitable mode of expressing his benignant sentiments, there was no possibility of mistake as to the matter. Lollardism might be safe enough, but it was assuredly a dangerous time and place for the Lollards. Sir Thomas Erpingham seems to have felt this, and to have desisted in time, when he found that not all his popularity deterred the bishop from throwing him into prison: so he agreed, as the price of his release, to erect a gatehouse at the entrance of the precinct, over against the west end of the cathedral, and renounce all heresies for the future. Hence the erection of the gateway shown in our engraving (Fig. 609).

The matter altogether was deemed of such importance, that Henry IV. took steps publicly to reconcile the knight and the bishop, first by declaring in parliament that the proceedings had been good, and that they had originated in great zeal, and then by directing them to shake hands and kiss each other in token of friendship, which they did. The reconciliation, unlike such forced ones generally, turned out real, for Sir Thomas became as willing, as he had already been an unwilling, benefactor to the cathedral; and one of the bequests of his will was a provision of three hundred marks to the prior and convent of Norwich, to found a chantry for a monk to sing daily mass for him and his family before the altar of the holy cross in the cathedral. It has been supposed, from the circumstance that his wife, who died four years after Sir Thomas's imprisonment, made no mention in her will of saints, as was usual, that it was her influence which had led the knight towards Lollardism, rather than any powerful inherent convictions of his own. If so, it ought to be no imputation on his moral courage that he declined making a martyr of himself. One should be very sure what one does think, when stakes and bonfires begin to argue. The interest attached to this gateway, as well as its remarkable beauty, induce us to dwell for a few seconds on its details. Mr. Britton, in his work on Norwich Cathedral, thus speaks of it:—" Amongst the great variety of subjects and designs in the ecclesiastical architecture of England, the Erpingham gateway may be regarded as original and unique; and considering the state of society when it was first raised, and the situation chosen, we are doubly surprised, first at the richness and decoration of the exterior face, and secondly, in beholding it so perfect and unmutilated after a lapse of four centuries. The archivolt mouldings, spandrils, and two demi-octangular buttresses, are covered with a profusion of ornamental sculptures, among which are thirty small statues of men and women, various shields of arms, trees, birds, pedestals, and canopies; most of these are very perfect, and some of the figures are rather elegant. The shields are charged with the arms of Erpingham, Walton, and Clopton, the two latter being the names of two wives of Sir Thomas Erpingham. In the spandrils are shields containing emblems of the Crucifixion, the Trinity, the Passion, &c., while each buttress is crowned with a sitting statue, one said to represent a secular, and the other a regular priest, &c." The first of these priests has a book in his hand, from which he appears to be teaching the youth standing at his side. The regular priest has also his book, but appears to be making no use of it, and turns his eyes idly upon the passengers who may go through the gate. Bloomfield, the historian of the county, thinks this was subtilly designed by Sir Thomas "to signify that the secular clergy not only laboured themselves in the world, but diligently taught the growing youth, to the benefit of the world; when the idle regular, who by his books also pretended to learning, did neither instruct any nor inform himself, by which he covertly lashed those that obliged him to their penance, and praised those that had given him instruction in the way of truth." Sir Thomas himself kneels in effigy in the pediment of the gateway, a remarkable instance to after-times of the power exerted by the clergy of his own day.

In simplicity, we may say plainness of decoration, the exterior of Worcester Cathedral presents a striking contrast to that of Exeter, which we shall presently notice. The outlines of the form are light and beautiful, and the large size gives them grandeur; but those objects achieved, the architects, unlike the architects of our cathedrals generally, seem to have rested content, and to have shunned altogether that elaborate richness of decoration which so generally characterizes these works, and which show so happily the unwearied desires of all concerned to be constantly doing something to render art more worthy of its sublime objects. They were surely the least conceited of men, those old ecclesiastical builders: it is a fine lesson they have bequeathed to the world, and usable in a thousand ways. The noblest temples ever raised by human hands were raised by

them; works that, to all eyes but their own, not only in their own time, but to all time, present and future, appeared and must appear essentially perfect, demanding but one thought and sentiment,—yet compounded of a host of thoughts and sentiments,—admiration, to them, on the contrary, appeared to be but so many centres of study and improvement. Art was long, and life was short, they saw; and they were content, therefore, to labour, each in his allotted space, in the raising of great works for others, and thought nothing of making great names for themselves. It is curious to see at how early a period a kind of antagonist feeling, a desire to check rather than to participate in such enthusiasm, exhibited itself at Worcester. We may premise that the see of Worcester was founded so early as the seventh century, by Ethelred, King of Mercia, and probably a church then existed in the city, on the site of the present building. In 969 the endowments of the cathedral were removed to the church of St. Mary's convent, which then assumed the rank previously attached to St. Peter's, but the latter building, or rather its site, obtained, a few years later, the restoration of its privileges; St. Oswald having, however, first built a new church in the burial-ground. This was burnt by the followers of Hardicanute in 1041, and replaced by an entirely new edifice, erected by Bishop Wulstan. As the workmen were pulling down the remains of the spoiled church, the prelate was noticed weeping. One of his attendants told him he ought rather to rejoice, since he was preparing an edifice of greater splendour and more suitable to the enlarged number of his monks. He replied, "I think far otherwise; we poor wretches destroy the works of our forefathers, only to get praises to ourselves; that happy age of holy men knew not how to build stately churches, but under any roof they offered up themselves living temples unto God, and by their examples incited those under their care to do the same; but we, on the contrary, neglecting the cure of souls, labour to heap up stones." One might fancy that the feeling thus evidenced remained in force at Worcester through all succeeding alterations and reparations, and more particularly those consequent on the extensive damage done in the fires of 1113 and 1202, when both city and cathedral were burnt: and that the plain exterior that we behold to this day at Worcester is in itself but an evidence of it. The works carried on after the fire of 1102 were so important, that the structure was newly consecrated; and it is that building which forms our cathedral. The plan of Worcester is on a very grand scale. It represents a double cross, the extreme length of which is five hundred and fourteen feet, with a noble tower, rising from the intersection of the nave, choir, and western transept, to the height of two hundred feet. This tower is the most embellished of all the exterior portions. The interior is remarkably light and airy. It is rich in both ancient and modern monuments; among the latter, there being several by our modern sculptors, as Roubilliac and the younger Bacon; and among the former, those of Sir John Beauchamp of Holt, beheaded on Tower Hill in the reign of Henry V., and of his lady, both striking examples of early costume; also of Lady Harcourt (Fig. 638), Judge Littleton, Prince Arthur (the son of Henry VII.), and King John. The Prince lies buried in a beautiful chapel of highly ornamented open work, the decorations of which are representative of the union of the white and red roses of York and Lancaster. The tomb of John (Fig. 633), the great object of interest and inquiry with all visitors, stands in the middle of the choir. Before the year 1797 it has been supposed that the remains of the king had been interred in the Lady Chapel, but as an opportunity then offered, during some alteration, of determining the point, an investigation took place of no ordinary interest. The effigy on the top (Fig. 637) was first removed, with the stone slab on which it rested; the interior was thus laid open, where two brick partition walls were discovered, raised no doubt for the more effectual support of the superincumbent mass. After clearing away a quantity of rubbish, and removing one end and a pannel at each side, a stone coffin was found between the brick walls; and when that was opened, the remains of the monarch were visible, much decayed, and with some of the smaller bones no longer seen, but the whole presenting an almost exact counterpart of the effigy on the exterior of the tomb. The only differences were the gloves on the hands, and the covering on the head, which consisted of a crown on the effigy, and of the celebrated monk's cowl on the body, placed there before burial, as a passport through the regions of purgatory. A feeling of the same kind actuated the fierce and bold, but superstitious king, when he desired that his resting-place in his favourite church should be between the bodies of St. Oswald and St. Wulstan, whose effigies, in small, also grace his tomb; the evil spirits, he fancied, would not venture into such company, even to seize him. The hood appeared to have fitted the head exactly, and to have been tied or buckled under the chin by straps, parts of which remained. The body had been wrapped in an embroidered robe, reaching from the neck to the feet, made, it was supposed, of crimson damask, but the cuff, greatly decayed, alone remained. Fragments of the sword and of the scabbard were also found. On the legs there had been some kind of ornamental covering tied round the ancles, and extending over the feet, where the toes were visible through its decayed parts. The exposure of the relics of kingly mortality caused their speedy destruction, the whole mouldering to dust. On ascending the steps of the altar, visitors are shown another object of curiosity—the stone covering the body of William Duke of Hamilton, who fell in the memorable battle of Worcester, in 1651. In the tower is a fine peal of eight bells, each bearing a different inscription. On the last we read:—

> I, sweetly tolling, men do call
> To taste a meat that feeds the soul.

The changes which the names of places have undergone are often strikingly illustrative of the vast extent of time over which the annals of such places extend; Exeter forms a remarkable case in point. In the Caer-Isc of the Britons, signifying the town on the water, we are carried back to the very beginning of all, when the founders in that, as in so many other instances, took as their name for the new place some characteristic circumstance of position. Then in the Isca of the Romans, a Latinized version of the same thing, we are reminded of the dominion of the conquerors of the world. Another change shows us the Roman empire in Great Britain at an end, though the memory of that dominion is preserved in the Saxon Exancestre, that is to say, the Castle on the Ex: from this we pass finally into the great stream of modern history, as we begin to meet with the comparatively modern appellation of Exeter. The ecclesiastical antiquity of the city is no less noticeable; another name ascribed to Exeter—Monketon—seems to show that even in the Saxon times it had become distinguished for the number of these religious ascetics who resided in it. This very remoteness of origin may be the cause why we have been left uncertain of the precise time when the earliest building on the site of the cathedral was begun. All we know on the subject is, that soon after the junction of the sees of Devon and Cornwall, the seat of the united bishopric was removed to Exeter, and Leofric, the bishop, installed with great pomp into the cathedral, in the presence of the Confessor and his queen, both of whom took a prominent share in the ceremony. In 1050, then, the date of this event, there was a cathedral standing in Exeter, but whether recently erected or no is unknown. After the Conquest we find Warlewast, one of the followers of William, busily at work altering and enlarging during the early part of the twelfth century. Happily for him, he did not live to see his labours rendered of no avail by the mischief done to the cathedral during the time Exeter was besieged by Stephen in 1136, and which rendered it necessary for his successor, Chichester, to commence a reparation on the most extensive scale. He seems to have been the very man for the time and the task imposed upon him. A remarkable proof of his zeal, and which was probably exercised in favour of the rebuilding of the cathedral, is given in the statement that he was accustomed to go abroad very frequently in pilgrimage, sometimes to Rome, and sometimes to other places, "and ever would bring with him some one relic or other." (Bishop Godwin.) During the lifetime of Chichester and the three succeeding prelates, the cathedral works were steadily carried on; the last of them, Bishop Marshall, whose sculptured effigy is seen in Fig 647, having the honour of completing the whole before his death in 1206. Whether the large sums of money that had been constantly, and for so long a time, pouring into the Exchequer had begotten something like a love of wealth for other than church purposes in the minds of the chief officers, we shall not venture to decide, but a few years after the religious world was greatly scandalized at some discoveries made at Exeter. Richard Blondly, a recently-deceased bishop, "a man of mild spirit, but very stout against such as in his time did offer any injury to the church," had, it appeared, waxed weaker as he grew older, and allowed his chancellor, registrar, official, and keeper of the seal, with other of the household, to obtain conveyances from him of various estates, advowsons, &c., that then were in his disposition; and for their own private and general benefit. The business was transacted with great secrecy and skill; but the next bishop discovered the whole, and in place of their enjoying the nice little pickings provided, all the great officers of Exeter Cathedral found themselves soon after excommunicated, and doing public penance in their own building openly, upon Palm Sunday, as the indispensable preliminary to their readmission into the Christian body. Before long, however, the masons were again thickly clustering about the cathedral walls and foundations; and bringing the structure to the plan and the state in which a considerable portion of it remains to this day. Peter Quivil was the bishop who thus signalized himself by commencing the great undertaking of bringing the old-fashioned cathedral into better harmony with the architectural knowledge and tastes of the thirteenth century. He may be, indeed, almost called the author of the present cathedral, for what portions of it were untouched by him, and executed afterwards, were built in pursuance of his designs. How extensive these were, may be shown by simply stating that the renovation in the new style, begun by him between 1281 and 1291, and which was ended by Bishop Brentingham, about a century later, extended to every part of the structure, the towers alone excepted. Bishops Stapledon and Grandisson, during this period, particularly distinguished themselves by their architectural labours. Godwin furnishes us with some interesting particulars of the installation of a bishop in the early ages, in his notice of Stapledon's induction to the see. At the east gate he alighted from his horse, and went on foot to the cathedral; black cloth having been previously laid along the streets for him to walk upon. Two gentlemen of "great worship," one on each side, accompanied him, and Sir Hugh Courtney, of the great family of that name, who claimed to be steward of the feast, went before. At Broad-gate he was received by the chapter and choir, all richly apparelled, and singing the Te Deum; and thus they led him to the church. After the service and the usual ceremonies, all parties adjourned to the Bishop's Palace, where a feast, such as the middle ages alone could furnish, was provided. "It is incredible," Godwin remarks, "how many oxen, tuns of ale and wine, are said to have been usually spent at this kind of solemnity." Stapledon's feast would, no doubt, be more than usually magnificent and expensive; for, whatever his faults, something like princely liberality seems to have been one of his characteristic merits.

Exeter College, Oxford, was founded by him, and originally called by his name: Hart Hall, in the same university, also derives its origin from Bishop Stapledon. Unfortunately for him, he was a busy statesman, as well as a zealous prelate. Having held posts of high honour under Edward II., he was found among the adherents of that unhappy prince when, towards the close of the reign, his queen, son, brothers, and cousin marched at the head of an army against him. Edward was in London, and appealed to the citizens, but they gave him so decisive a rebuff, that he fled precipitately, leaving the Bishop of Exeter, Stapledon, as governor. He had scarcely reached the outskirts when the people rose, and, putting aside all opposition, obtained possession of the bishop, and of his brother Sir Richard Stapledon, and executed them both in Cheapside, on the 15th of October, 1326. In the north aisle of the cathedral are two splendid monuments facing each other; they are those of the two brothers. The choir is the principal portion that we owe to Bishop Stapledon. The gorgeous west front, with its almost interminable series, in double tier, of sculptured kings, prophets, apostles, prelates, and distinguished persons, forming one of the richest architectural façades in Europe, is understood to have been raised by Bishop Grandisson, who "sequestering himself from all idle persons," is said to have "kept no more about him than were absolutely necessary, in order to compass the charge of such mighty works; likewise, assembling his own clergy, he persuaded them to bequeath all their goods, &c., to the building of the mother-church of the diocese." After this last circumstance, one need not wonder that he should also be able to prevail "on sundry temporal men to give of their store."

The building, whose gradual formation we have thus traced, now consists of a nave, seventy-six feet wide and one hundred and seventy-five feet long, with corresponding aisles at the sides; two short transepts formed in a peculiar way, namely by two towers, of unmistakeable Norman original, and therefore, to an antiquary, the most interesting parts of the cathedral; a choir of the same breadth as the nave, and one hundred and twenty-eight feet long; to these—the principal feature of the place—must be added, ten chapels, of which the Lady, or St. Mary's Chapel, at the eastern end, is the most important, and the chapter-house. It is hardly necessary to say the interior is in many respects surpassingly noble and beautiful. The delicate and numberless pillars, clustering together into so many solid groups for the support of the nave and choir, always a beautiful illustration of a beautiful thought, the power resulting from union, seem to particularly arrest our attention in Exeter Cathedral. The choir and nave are divided by a screen of the most exquisite character. The chapter-house is, as usual, very

641.—Bracket, Exeter.

643.—Section of Shaft, Exeter.

645.—Bracket, Exeter.

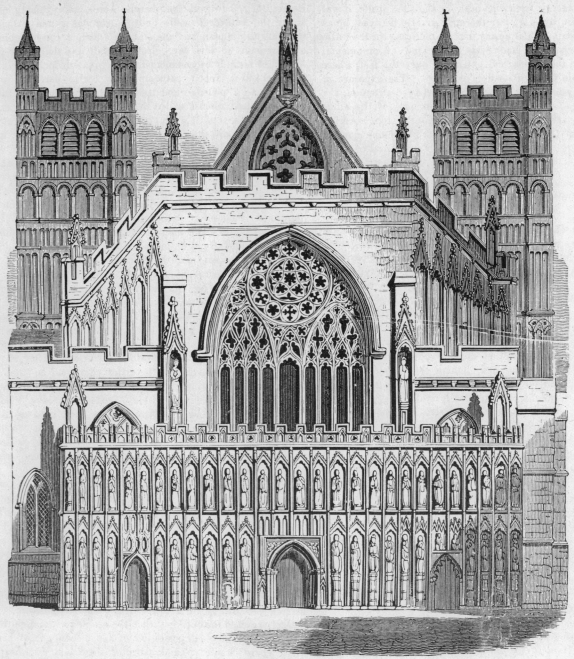

639.—West Front of Exeter Cathedral.

642.—Bracket, Exeter.

644.—Section of Shaft, Exeter.

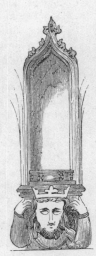

646.—Bracket, Exeter.

647.—Effigy of Bishop Marshall, Exeter.

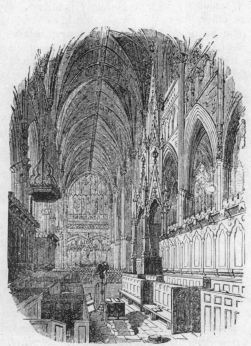

640.—Exeter Cathedral.

648.—Effigy of Bishop Bartholomew, Exeter.

651.—Conventual Seal of Rochester.

654.—Capital of a Crypt Column.

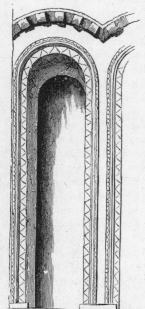

655.—Norman Recess on West Front, Rochester.

657.—Coloured Tile, Rochester.

649.—Principal Entrance and Interior of Rochester Cathedral.

652.—Conventual Seal of Rochester.

653.—Capital of a Crypt Column.

656.—Norman Recess on West Front, Rochester.

658.—Coloured Tile, Rochester.

659.—St. Augustine. From the Door of the Chapter-House, Rochester.

650.—West Front of Rochester Cathedral.

660.—Emblematic Figure of the Mosaic Dispensation. From the Door of the Chapter-House, Rochester.

beautiful; its roof is of oak. The windows of the cathedral generally are very large, and some of them strikingly handsome, with their stained glass. Among the lesser objects of attraction the cathedral presents, may be mentioned the organ, which is probably the largest in Europe, the Haarlem only excepted, and without any exception the finest in tone; the clock in the north tower, which exhibits all the moon's phases, as well as the ordinary time of the day; the great bell, said to weigh twelve thousand five hundred pounds; the episcopal throne, an almost unique example of carved wood-work, forming, as it does, a magnificent pyramid fifty-two feet high, built up of arches, pillars, niches, pannels, crockets, and foliated ornaments; and lastly, the Minstrels'. Gallery, near the middle of the choir, supported by thirteen pillars, with a niche between each two, containing a statue of a musician playing on some instrument. The monastery, we may notice in conclusion, belonged to the Benedictine Order.

Lambarde, the old Kentish topographer, has a curious passage in his 'Perambulation,' on the subject of the comparative insignificance of the diocese of Rochester. "The learned in astronomy," he says, "be of the opinion that if Jupiter, Mercury, or any other planet, approach within certain degrees of the sun, and be burned (as they term it) under his beams, that then it hath in manner no influence at all, but yieldeth wholly to the sun that overshineth it; and some men, beholding the nearness of these two bishoprics, Canterbury and Rochester, and comparing the bright glory, pomp, and primacy of the one, with the contrary altogether in the other, have fancied Rochester so overshadowed and obscured, that they reckon it no see or bishopric of itself, but only a place of a mere suffragan, and chaplain to Canterbury. But he that shall either advisedly weigh the first institution of them both, or but indifferently consider the estate of either, shall easily find that Rochester hath not only a lawful and canonical cathedral see of itself, but that the same was also more honestly won and obtained than even that of Canterbury was." Worthy Master Lambarde's enthusiasm here probably carries him a little too far: however, the history of Rochester shows decidedly enough that its claims to respect and attention are little if at all inferior to the claims of its more potential neighbour, great as those are. Both were founded under the auspices of the same royal convert from paganism to Christianity, Ethelbert; and if Canterbury had an Augustine for its first spiritual superior, Rochester had for its first bishop one of Augustine's companions, Justus. Whilst, therefore, it was natural enough that the former should rise to the very summit of ecclesiastical wealth and power, it was really extraordinary that the latter should as steadily decline till it became what it remains,—the smallest, poorest, and least influential of English sees. The particular causes of this declension appear to have been the wars between the different states of the Heptarchy, then the incursions of the Danes, which left the church in such a state at the time of the Conquest that Divine worship was entirely neglected in it, and the four or five secular canons, who then remained nominally attached to it, found it necessary to eke out their means of subsistence by the alms of the benevolent. The Conqueror, however, still found something to pillage and confer upon his relative, Bishop Odo; and the see seemed about to perish altogether, when Lanfranc, the Archbishop of Canterbury, endeavoured to check the downward progress of Rochester by the appointment of a monk of the Abbey of Bec, for the avowed purpose of achieving a restoration of the old estates and prosperity; and though he died shortly after, his successor was Gundulph, of whom Lambarde says: "He never rested from building and begging, tricking and garnishing, until he had erected his idol building to the wealth, beauty, and estimation of a popish priory." He too was chosen by Lanfranc from the Abbey of Bec; and a tradition recorded by William of Malmesbury gives us an interesting glimpse of the two friends before the conquest of England was dreamt of, and before, therefore, either had any idea of the future power that would be reposed in their hands. The historian says that Lanfranc foretold Gundulph's advancement by a trial of the *Sortes Evangelicæ*, that is to say, opening the book of the Gospels at haphazard, and taking the first text on which the eye rests as the prophetic one. Gundulph, like William of Wykeham, was one of those ecclesiastics who shed a glory upon the middle ages, by their happy union of comprehensive intellects to devise and firm purposes to carry out measures of high importance to the general weal. Whilst he did almost everything for Rochester, recovering, with the assistance of Lanfranc, its former possessions, obtaining the grant of new ones, building a castle, and rebuilding the cathedral, he signalized himself in other quarters by the foundation of a nunnery (at West Malling) and by the erection of

the famous White Tower, the nucleus around which all the assemblages of buildings now known as the Tower of London has gradually grown up. Among his other doings at Rochester, he removed the secular canons, and replaced them by Benedictine monks; and he obtained for the monastery, from Henry I., the privilege of coining. And that was not the only royal favour conferred upon it, and commemorated in the statues of the king and queen in the magnificent doorway of the cathedral. Gundulph who appears to have been confessor to the queen, Matilda, obtained through her means, many gifts and privileges from her husband. The cathedral was in the main completed during the lifetime of Gundulph, who died in March 1107-8, and was buried in his episcopal vestments with great splendour before the altar of the crucifix placed at the entrance of the choir; but the whole does not appear to have been considered finished till 1130, when, on the day of Ascension, a solemn and magnificent dedication of the pile to St. Andrew took place in the presence of King Henry, assisted by all the chief prelates of the country. The cathedral was originally "dedicated to St. Andrew as a token of respect to the monastery of St. Andrew at Rome, from which Augustine and his brethren were sent to convert the Anglo-Saxons; and after the church was rebuilt, Lanfranc did not change the name of its tutelary saint, as he did in his own cathedral, the primate having such confidence in this apostle, that he never transmitted by Gundulph any principal donation without entreating the bishop to chant the Lord's Prayer once for him at the altar of St. Andrew." ['Denne's Memoirs of the Cath. Church of Rochester.'] The festival of St. Andrew was of course kept with great splendour in the monastery; and Gundulph, to enhance the proceedings of the day, made special provision for it, by appointing that there should be reserved out of the estates that he had caused to be settled upon the establishment, what was called a Xenium, from a Greek word signifying a present given in token of hospitality, Gundulph's Xenium seems to have been a very handsome affair, consisting of sixteen hogs, cured for bacon, thirty geese, three hundred fowls, one thousand lampreys, one thousand eggs, four salmon, and sixty bundles of furze, with a large quantity of oats, &c., the whole apparently intended for the entertainment in the bishop's palace of the poor, and strangers generally; for Gundulph expressly says, "If it should happen, contrary to my wishes, that I, or any of my successors, shall be absent from the feast, then, in God's name and my own, I order that the whole Xenium be carried to the hall of St. Andrew, and there, at the discretion of the prior and brethren of the church, be distributed to the strangers and poor, in honour of the festival." The fate of this Xenium forms but one of the many illustrations that the history of our country unhappily furnishes of the fate of the unprotected poor: this provision for a festal day, which must have lightened so many weary spirits by its enjoyments, if it did not even relieve many empty stomachs by its store of food, was ultimately treated as a matter that merely concerned the bishops and the monastery; and hotly enough they disputed it, till the former consented to receive a composition in money in lieu of the provisions in kind: of course we should now look in vain in Rochester for any "open house," ecclesiastical or otherwise, whether on St. Andrew's or on any other day. Of Gundulph's works in the cathedral, the nave forms the principal existing remain, many of the other portions having been seriously injured by the destructive fires that have taken place in Rochester. On the north side of the choir, between the two transepts, there is also a low square tower now in ruins, and known as Gundulph's, the walls of which are six feet thick. It has been doubted, however, whether this was really erected by the architect in question. Parts of the cathedral are recorded as having been built by persons designated simply as monks, rich men, no doubt, who had retired to the cloister of St. Andrew, sick of the vanities and turmoil of active life, and there expended their possessions in the adornment of the house of God. Richard of Eastgate, and Thomas of Mepeham, were the monks who restored and rebuilt the north side of the west transept, after the great fire of 1179; Richard of Waledene the monk, who, about the commencement of the thirteenth century, completed what they had begun by the erection of the south side. How the upper transept and choir came to be re-erected, in the reigns of John and Henry III., forms a curious story, and one strikingly illustrative of the time. In 1201 a rich, benevolent, and pious tradesman, a baker, named William, set out with his servant to perform a pilgrimage to Jerusalem. On the road to Canterbury, a little beyond Rochester, the servant murdered his master, and fled with the property, which had tempted him to the commission of the crime. The corpse was found and taken back to Rochester, where a fate awaited it that the unfortunate William had certainly never anticipated. The monks were probably at the time very anxious to enhance the reputation of their monastery and church in any way they could, and particularly by rebuilding the parts of the latter that had been damaged in the fires, and were therefore quite prepared to appreciate any remarkable circumstance that might happen in connection with their establishment. And such it seems now occurred when the body of William the baker was placed in the cathedral. Miracles—of what nature is not recorded—were wrought at his tomb, the repute of which, spreading far and wide, brought hosts of devotees to Rochester, whose offerings filled the treasury, and gave the monks the necessary funds for the erection of the parts of the cathedral we have mentioned, or, in other words, the whole of the cathedral eastward of the west transept. In 1254 the Pope canonized the murdered traveller, and granted indulgences to all who should visit and make offerings to his shrine,—circumstances that naturally gave a new impetus to the popularity of the tomb and cathedral. The northern part of the east transept, known as St. William's Chapel, preserves to this day the remembrance of these events. The tomb itself has disappeared, though the spot where it stood is marked by a slab in the centre of a square, formed of curiously-figured mosaics. Pilgrims reached the chapel by a small dark aisle, which, after passing between the choir and Gundulph's tower, opens into the former. Midway in the aisle is a flight of steps, worn down to something very like an inclined plane by the innumerable feet that have trodden them. The destruction of the tomb probably took place at the Reformation, when the church generally received considerable damage. During the Civil War the fabric was still more seriously injured by the soldiers of the parliament. These are said to have converted one portion of the cathedral into a carpenter's shop, and another into a tippling-house. From such unpleasant reminiscences it is doubly gratifying to pass to the consideration of the recent doings at Rochester, where the Dean and Chapter have shown that they are fully conscious of the valuable nature of the trust reposed in their hands, and determined to exhibit that consciousness practically. In 1825 a central tower was erected at the intersection of the principal transept, whilst within the last three or four years the interior has undergone a comprehensive repair, including many important restorations of the old details of the structure, such as windows and arches, long filled up, but now once more diffusing a sense of lightness and gracefulness around. The north transept, or St. William's Chapel, has in consequence again become what it originally was, one of the most interesting and beautiful specimens of early English architecture that England anywhere possesses.

The other parts of the cathedral eastward are less decorated, and all those westward, including the nave and west front, are in the main Norman. Of course the perpendicular window in that front (Fig. 650) is the introduction of a much later time. The exceeding richness of the gateway beneath, when the stone was as yet undecayed, and the sculpture exhibited the faithful impress of the artist's hand, is evident at a glance even in the present state. The Chapter House, now in ruins, also exhibits some remarkably fine sculpture, among which may be mentioned the statue of Augustine in the doorway. The dimensions of the cathedral are small when compared with those of cathedrals generally. The entire length is three hundred and six feet, breadth of the nave and side aisles sixty-six feet, breadth of the west front eighty-one feet. There are numerous monuments and chapels; and beneath the choir, and extending its whole length, is a crypt. Among the many eminent bishops of the see may be mentioned Walter de Merton, the founder of the college known by his name at Oxford; the venerable Fisher, the friend and fellow-sufferer of Sir Thomas More, beheaded by the brutal despot Henry VIII.; and the literary trio, Sprat, the poet—Atterbury, the eloquent divine and delightful correspondent of Pope—Pearce, the critic and commentator.

———

The fair of ELY, commencing on the 29th of October, used to exhibit a picturesque kind of memorial of the saint to whom the day had been originally dedicated, and from whom the Isle has derived, in a great measure, its importance; we refer to the ribbons of various colour then offered for sale—no ordinary merchandise, for they had touched the shrine of St. Etheldreda, more popularly known as St. Audrey, and were thence called St. Audrey's ribbons. But this, like so many of our other interesting customs, has shared the fate of the views and sentiments that first gave them birth, and disappeared, and we must now look to the dusty records of our local antiquaries for any tokens of remembrance of the pious lady to whom we owe the foundation of the great religious establishment on the Isle, and therefore remotely of the cathedral itself, which

was connected with it. Yet the history of Etheldreda was one calculated to live in the popular recollection. She was the daughter of Anna, King of East Anglia, who gave her the Isle of Ely as a part of her dowry on her marriage with Tonbert, a nobleman of the same kingdom. After Tonbert's death she married Egfrid, King of Northumberland; but from a very early period all her affections and desires seem to have been placed on a monastic life—we are informed she lived with both husbands in a state of virginity —and so she finally obtained the unwilling consent of the king to her retirement to the cloister, and took the veil at Coldingham. Egfrid, however, who was passionately attached to her, withdrew this permission, and brought her home. Determined to fulfil what she conceived to be her mission, she again left him, secretly, and fled to the Isle of Ely, where she began the erection of the monastery, assisted by her brother, then King of the East Angles. Egfrid, still persevering in his endeavours to compel her to live with him, was (so the monastic writers tell us) warned to desist, by a miracle. As he pursued her with a body of knights, the rock on which she happened at the time to be standing, accompanied by her maidens, was suddenly surrounded by water. After that Etheldreda was allowed to pursue her own way in peace. And then the new monastery was finished, dedicated to the Virgin Mary, and the foundress appointed its first abbess. Bede has given us a striking view of her domestic life in this high office. It appears she never wore any linen, but only woollen garments, ate only once a day, except during sickness, or on occasions of great festivals, and never, except when her ill-health rendered indulgence necessary, returned to bed after matins, which were held in the church at midnight, but made it her custom to continue there at prayers till daybreak. The fame of all this sanctity and discipline gained many and distinguished converts. Persons of the noblest family, matrons of the highest rank, we are told, devoted themselves to religion under her guidance; even some of royal state joined her, resigning all the comforts and luxuries to which they had been accustomed, for the hard fare and severe monotony of a monastic life;—such were Etheldreda's own relatives—Sexburga, her sister, Queen of Kent; Ermenild, Sexburga's daughter; and Wurburga, the daughter of Ermenilda, who succeeded each in turn to the abbacy. Etheldreda died, as she had foretold, of a contagious disorder, and was buried, as she had directed, in a wooden coffin, in the common cemetery of the nuns. The chief events of her life, as here narrated, and others to which we have not thought it necessary to refer, are shown in a series of sculptures which decorate some of the pillars in the cathedral.

In 870 the abbey thus erected was pillaged and destroyed by the Danes, and all its revenues seized for the use of the crown. But King Edgar, in 970, regranted the whole to Ethelwold, Bishop of Winchester, who rebuilt the monastery, and placed a number of monks in it. It was no doubt after this complete restoration that the bishop invited Ethelred, brother of the reigning monarch, Edward the Martyr, to visit Ely, who came with his mother and some of the nobility, and went in solemn procession to the shrine of St. Etheldreda; where the young prince, whose heart seems to have been filled with veneration for the memory of the virgin-wife, promised to become her devoted servant. This was the prince for whom that mother, then present, afterwards murdered her elder born, Edward: Ethelred then ascended the throne, and subsequently evidenced in various ways that he had not forgotten his visit to Ely. As to his mother, Elfrida, the annals of Ely tell of another murder committed by her, only less atrocious than that which has made her memory for ever infamous. Desiring to get rid of Abbot Brithnoth, she is said to have resorted to her usual mode of solving such difficulties—a violent death—and which was thus accomplished. Her servants having heated sharp-pointed irons in the fire, thrust them into the abbot's body beneath the arm-pits; Elfrida considering, probably, that with a little management, as to the display and care of the corpse, she would thus be able to avoid discovery. And, if such was her hope, she was gratified; for the cause of Brithnoth's death appears to have remained unknown till remorse for the murder of her son made Elfrida herself confess this murder too.

The next event in the history of the monastery is connected with one of those struggles against the Normans, that have peculiarly attracted the popular attention. It was in the Isle of Ely that Hereward, "England's darling," as his countrymen affectionately and admiringly called him, held out for a considerable period against all the forces of the Conqueror, causing him a great amount of loss, anxiety, and undissembled rage and mortification; and it was in the famous monastery of the Isle that the patriots appear to have found at first their warmest religious supporters. And although

663.—Athelstane, Ely.

664.—Alwin Ely.

666—Bracket, Ely

661.—Ely Cathedral, North-West.

666—Niche, St. Mary's Chapel. Ely.

667.—Capital, Ely.

668.—Early English Capital, Ely.

660.—Shrine of St. Etheldredra, Ely.

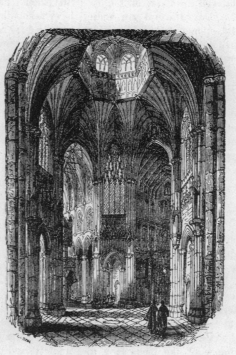

662—Ely Cathedral

670. Vesica Piscis, Ely.

172

673.—Head of Waynflete, Winchester

675.—Font, Winchester.

674.—Effigy of Wykeham, Winchester.

676.—Pinnacle, Bishop Fox's Chantry, Winchester.

677.—Pinnacle, Altar Screen, Winchester.

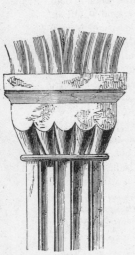

678.—Norman Capital, Winchester.

671.—North-West View of the Cathedral at Winchester.

679.—Norman Capital, Crypt, Winchester.

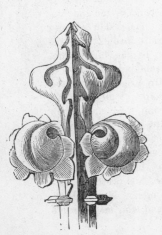

680.—Finial, Winchester.

672.—Winchester.

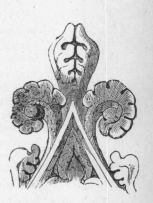

681.—Finial, Lady Chapel, Winchester.

173

there were some recreant few of the monks who, having made a profession of fasting up to a certain point, were so utterly averse to going beyond it, that when provisions grew scarce, they treacherously showed the Normans a way into the Isle, and thus caused Hereward to be at last driven from it; yet the history of William's conduct towards the abbey seems to show that the monks generally had been actuated by nobler principles, and had really given all possible aid to the brave Hereward; on the reduction of the Isle, the furniture and precious jewels of the monastery were seized, and its lands were divided among the Norman chieftains. The firmness of a Norman ecclesiastic alone prevented the ruin that thus seemed to threaten the establishment. Theodwin, having been named abbot by William, refused to enter upon the duties of his abbacy till all the property of the monastery had been restored to it; and so the restoration was made.

A pleasant evidence of the amiable character of the monks of Ely is furnished by an incident that is supposed to have occurred during the time that Theodwin's friend, Godfrey, held the office of Procurator, there having been a temporary vacancy of the abbacy after Theodwin's death. The story also gives a curious illustration of the uses to which our kings were sometimes accustomed to turn the religious establishments of England. Certain knights and gentlemen, who are understood to have belonged for the most part to the best families of the country, and who were officers in the king's army, were sent down by the king to be quartered for a time in the monastery, until he could better provide for them, or until he needed their services. The monks received them well, admitted them to dine with themselves in the common hall or refectory, and at last grew so much attached to them, that when they were called away to go into Normandy, to repress the insurrection of Robert, the king's son, the monks conducted them a portion of the way with solemn procession and singing, and only parted with them at Hadenham, after mutual expressions of deep regret and respect. We need only add to the foregoing historical notices, that Ely was raised into a bishopric by the King Henry I., in 1107, who thus expected to decrease the political importance of the Isle, by dividing the ecclesiastical lands and authority; and that after the dissolution of monasteries, Henry VIII. raised the church to the rank of a cathedral—dedicated to the Undivided Trinity.

A glance at our engraving (Fig. 661) will show that this building is at once noble and remarkable. The elegant lantern-like character of the towers in particular arrests our attention, and we are further surprised to find that the shorter of the two occupies the position generally assigned to the main tower, namely, the centre of the structure, whilst the larger forms a portion of the western front. The interior of the octagon tower presents a no less interesting peculiarity of rich architectural effect. In looking at the date of the different parts of the cathedral, we are naturally curious to know first if there be any remains of Etheldreda's work, and we are answered in the affirmative, and referred to the various antique specimens of masonry now enclosed within, or forming parts of the walls of the neighbouring prebendal houses. Of the cathedral itself, the oldest portion is the transept, which appears to be of the style prevalent in the early part of the twelfth century, and was therefore, in all likelihood, built when the erection of the bishopric gave a new dignity to the church, and demanded, as may have been thought, a more magnificent structure. The transept, therefore, is Norman, with circular arches and heavy pillars; and the nave, which was erected in the same century, does not materially differ from it. Between 1174 and 1189, however, the great western tower was erected by Bishop Rydel, and afforded a noble example of the mighty architectural changes which a single century had brought forth; elegance and beauty were fast growing upon the solid foundation that had been laid for them. Before the close of the same century the Galilee Chapel was built. The presbytery, now used as the choir, was the work of half a century later, when pointed architecture had attained a state of essential perfection: if we contrast the choir of Ely with the choirs of other cathedrals more distinguished for their exquisite architecture, we find that it is mere elaborateness of decoration that makes the difference. And it is no slight merit in the builders of our cathedrals that they knew how to go on elaborating without losing in the process all the more valuable qualities of their productions: it is something to be able to say, after looking at the exquisite purity of the choir of Ely, that the octagon tower is the most beautiful part of the whole building, simply because it is the latest.

The height of this tower is one hundred and seventy feet. The dimensions of the other parts of the cathedral are, the west tower two hundred and seventy feet, transept one hundred and ninety feet, entire length five hundred and thirty-five feet. The monu-

ments present some superb specimens of sculpture—such are the tombs of Bishops Alcott and West,—and some memorials of still higher interest than art can give, though not altogether disconnected with art; we allude more particularly to the tomb of Tiptoft, the ill-fated Earl of Worcester, the patron of Caxton, and a man of such universal accomplishments that, when he was executed at Tower Hill, 1470, it was said, "The axe then did at one blow cut off more learning than was left in the heads of all the surviving nobility."

———

According to certain authorities, more amusing than trustworthy, there was reigning over Britain in the second century, and some twelve and a half centuries after Brute, the descendant of the far-famed Æneas of Troy, ruled in the island, one Lucius, who became a convert to Christianity, and erected a church at Winchester, on the site previously occupied by the chief Pagan temple of the country. Whether the story be true or false, it gives us a striking idea of the antiquity of the cathedral, whose origin is thus carried back to the period where fact and fable mingle inextricably together. The first record of a strictly historical nature, respecting Winchester, seems to be in connection with the seventh century, when the Saxon kings and people of Wessex generally relinquished idolatry; Kinegils, a descendant of that very Cerdic who is said to have destroyed Lucius's structure, setting the example in 635, and began the erection of a new cathedral, of great size and magnificence, which was completed by his successor Kenewalch. The first bishop was St. Birinus, who had been sent over to England by Pope Honorius, and to whom the merit of Kinegils' conversion is attributed.

In this brief statement we may perceive ground to satisfy us that Winchester must have been a place of no ordinary importance, and the direct history of the city tells us that backwards from the reign of Richard the First, through English, Norman, Saxon, and it is supposed even British times, Winchester was really the capital of the island. Of its origin, it were almost idle to speak. "It may possibly have existed," says a writer in the 'Penny Magazine,' "as a village in the woods for a thousand years before the Christian era." The Danes, who, as we have seen, figure so conspicuously and so destructively in the annals of a great proportion of the oldest churches and monasteries of the country, reduced the building once more to a ruin, in 871, to be re-edified, as is supposed, by him whose very name became more terrible to the Danes than their own had been to the afflicted people of England—Alfred. But the earliest portions of the present pile are those which were erected towards the close of the tenth century, by Bishop Ethelwold, who finding the cathedral greatly dilapidated, rebuilt it from the foundation. Some of the most substantial walls and pillars of the existing pile are the presumed remains of St. Ethelwold's labours. With the following century came the Conquest, and a Norman ecclesiastic, Walkelyn, to rule over the see, and introduce his own country's superior knowledge of, and taste for, architecture. His advent was delayed, however, in an unexpected and extraordinary manner. When the Conqueror died, there was but one Saxon bishop to be found in broad England—Wulstan, bishop of Winchester; a man whose only learning was the best of all learning, that which taught him to live a life of spotless purity, humility, and unremitting usefulness. He was required to resign his episcopal staff, by a synod, sitting at Westminster Abbey, on the ground that he was ignorant of the French language. Wulstan rose, on the demand being made, grasped his crozier firmly in his hand and thus spoke: "I am aware, my Lord Archbishop, that I am neither worthy of this dignity, nor equal to its duties; this I knew when the clergy elected, when the prelates compelled, when my master called me to fill it. By the authority of the Holy See he laid this burden upon me, and with this staff he commanded me to receive the rank of a bishop. You now demand of me the pastoral staff, which you did not present, and the office which you did not bestow. Aware of my insufficiency, and obedient to this holy synod, I now resign them; not, however, to you, but to him by whose authority I received them." Advancing then to the tomb of Edward the Confessor, he thus apostrophised the deceased sovereign: "Master, thou knowest how reluctantly I assumed this charge at thy instigation. It was thy command that, more than the wish of the people, the voice of the prelates, and the desire of the nobles, compelled me. Now we have a new king, a new primate, and new enactments. Thee they accuse of error, in having so commanded, and me of presumption, because I obeyed. Formerly, indeed, thou mightest err, because thou wert mortal; but now thou art with God, and canst err no longer. Not to them, therefore who recall what they did not give and who may deceive and be deceived, but to thee who gave them, and art now raised above all error, I resign my staff, and surrender my flock." And so saying, he laid the crozier upon the tomb, and took his place among the monks, as one of their own rank. But lo, a miracle! or what was alleged to be one—the staff became so firmly embedded in the stone, that it could not be removed; an evident token that it was the pleasure of Heaven, that Wulstan should not be deprived of his bishopric: the synod left him therefore in its possession in peace. At his death, Walkelyn, a Norman, was appointed by the king, and it was in his case, as in many others, of prelates appointed by the Conqueror, if they could not satisfy the people of their right, they certainly did convince them of their fitness. Walkelyn built the present tower, part of the present nave and transepts, and altogether made the cathedral so essentially a new work, that it was re-dedicated by him to the Apostles Peter and Paul and the Saint Swithin. Succeeding prelates continued to add and to decorate till Wykeham came, and crowned the whole with the magnificent west front, truly *his* front, as the statue in the pediment seems fittingly to assert, for he was the architect, as well as in a general sense the builder. The character of this distinguished man illustrates so strongly what we conceive must have been the character, in a lesser degree, of many of the prelates to whom we owe our cathedrals, that we should have been glad to have dwelt on it, did our space permit, at more length. As it is, we can only observe, by way of showing the marvellous versatility, as well as lofty excellence in particular pursuits, which men in those early ages often exhibited, unconscious of the practical refutation they were giving to the absurd " philosophy" of later ones, that William of Wykeham, as a man of the world, raised himself, by address and ability, from a very humble position in life, that left him dependent on strangers for his education, to a position which gave him an opportunity of commanding the most lofty; that William of Wykeham, as a priest, was so distinguished in his holy calling, that he was raised by successive steps from the mere clerk to the all-potential bishop; that William of Wykeham, as a statesman, after a similar series of ascending stages, became Lord High Chancellor, and that, too, at a time, the latter part of the reign of Edward the Third and the reign of Richard the Second, when the national affairs were in the most perturbed state; that William of Wykeham, a wholesale restorer and reformer of existing religious foundations, was scarcely less famous as an establisher of new ones in honour, and for the promotion of learning—witness to the last feature those two noble colleges of Winchester and Oxford that were founded by him; that, lastly, William of Wykeham, as an artist, was without rival in his own time, and hardly surpassed in any other. To the man who began his career in this department of his multifarious history, as a clerk of the works to the king, we owe not merely the grand western front of Winchester Cathedral, but such works as England's one palace, among the several so called, Windsor, which assumed, under Wykeham, for the first time, the extent and general arrangement that still prevail through the castle.

Since the bishopric of this noble specimen of *all-sided* humanity, to borrow Goethe's characteristic mode of expression, the chief builder at Winchester has been Bishop Fox, whose statue, under a canopy, terminates in his improvements on the east. But the good work has been continued with admirable spirit and taste in our own days. Not less than forty thousand pounds have been recently expended in restoration, and, what in one instance was still more needed, alteration; we allude to the beautiful choir-screen, that now stands where stood Inigo Jones's elegant, but ridiculously inharmonious, piece of composite handiwork.

Figures of arithmetic sometimes describe better than figures of speech, and we are not sure but that will be the case, as respects the general external aspect of Winchester Cathedral. Whilst the entire length of the structure reaches to five hundred and forty-five feet, the main tower rises only to the height of one hundred and thirty-eight feet: the outspread but stunted expression of the pile may therefore be seen at once. The tower, indeed, rises but twenty-six feet above the roof; the explanation, therefore, is evident—the work remains unfinished. Apart from the west front, however, Winchester is, in many respects, a truly magnificent structure. The view that opens upon the spectator, as he enters by the western door, is one of almost unequalled splendour; he looks through one continuous vista of pillars, arches, and roof, extending to the eastern extremity, where the eye finally rests upon the superb eastern window, that casts its "dim religious light" into the choir. The pillars and arches of the nave are among the most interesting parts of the cathedral: within the clustered columns, that give so light an aspect to those enormous masses of masonry, are hidden

the very Saxon pillars of Ethelwold's structure; within those pointed arches above them, yet remain Ethelwold's semicircular ones; the skilful architect having thus adapted both pillars and arches to the style required, rather than pull them down unnecessarily. The cathedral is rich in monuments: William Rufus lies here, in the choir, in a tomb of plain grey stone. In six mortuary chests, carved in wood, painted and gilt, are buried the remains of Saxon Kings, Kinegils probably among them, and of other distinguished persons, transferred by Bishop Fox from the decayed coffins in which they had been buried. But in an artistical sense, the monumental glory of the cathedral consists in the chantries or oratories of the Bishops Edyngton, Wykeham, Beaufort, Waynflete, and Fox: the last four are among the most superb specimens we possess of these generally beautiful works. One of West's best pictures, the Raising of Lazarus, forms the cathedral altar-piece.

———

The magnificence of Cardinal Wolsey has become a byword, and, as often happens in such cases, has by that very proof of its original fitness almost ceased to be of any practical value; in other words, the term now rises habitually to the mind whenever the subject is before it, in place of, rather than as concentrating and explaining the circumstances and thoughts which originally gave currency to it. But if any one desires to revive the idea of that magnificence in all its primitive freshness of meaning, he need only visit Oxford. Near the southern entrance of the city, with its picturesque series of bridges across the Isis, or Thames, he will find a pile of buildings at first attracting his attention by its general architectural splendour, then by its extraordinary extent, the plan including a cathedral, two great quadrangles, and two courts; lastly by the individual interest attached to almost every separate feature, and more especially the cathedral, the superb west front, the stately hall, and the entrance tower, in which hangs one of the most famous of English bells, Great Tom of Oxford. That pile of building forms Christ Church College and Cathedral, the former being the establishment that Wolsey founded in grateful acknowledgment of the benefits he had derived from the university, and in redemption of the promise which he had consequently made at an early period of his prosperity, to bestow some lasting mark of his esteem upon the place. And splendid as is the edifice, important as are its uses, the one and the other represent but imperfectly the gigantic plan of its founder, which was and is an unprecedented instance of princely beneficence in a country of wealthy men and prodigal benefactors. The best architects of the age were collected together to erect the buildings; and the society for whose accommodation they were to be reared was to consist of one hundred and sixty persons, chiefly engaged in the study of sciences, divinity, canon and civil law, arts, physic, and literature. But the sunshine of royal favour in which the great Cardinal basked became suddenly eclipsed by newer favourites; he fell even more suddenly and signally than he had risen. The crowned despot, however, for once seems to have been moved in a good cause; and either Wolsey's pathetic consignation of his cherished project to the royal care, or the entreaties of the university, caused him to save Christ Church and become its patron. Some years later he translated the see of Oseney, formed by himself out of the monastery of that name, to Oxford, and Christ Church became the cathedral. At the same time the principal estates were granted to the chapter, on condition of their maintaining three public professors of Divinity, Hebrew, and Greek; one hundred students in theology, arts, and philosophy, eight chaplains, and a suitable choir. We have thought it necessary to give this short notice of the origin of the junction of the college with the cathedral, which would otherwise have seemed unaccountable to those ignorant of their history; and, having done that, proceed to notice the structure that more peculiarly belongs to our present section.

Wolsey founded his college upon a site not only time-honoured, but made sacred by its early connection with the growth of Christianity in England, and, to some eyes at least, by one of those pious legends with which church history is so rife; it was on the site of the monastery of St. Frideswida, the church of which yet remained, that he began to build.

We need hardly speak of the antiquity of Oxford itself, since there are learned men who talk of literature having flourished there ever since certain " excellent philosophers with the Trojans coming out of Greece, under the command of Brute, entered and settled in Britain." Whatever truth there may be in this, it seems to be undoubted by any one that it was a place of importance in the British times. But the first event that may be called historical, and that had any great influence over its future fortunes, was one

685.—Pinnacle, Oxford.

682.—Shrine of St. Frideswida, Oxford.

686.—Corbel Shaft, Oxford.

687.—Poppy-head, Oxford.

683.—Christ Church, Oxford.

688.—Poppy head, Oxford.

689.—Boss, Oxford.

684.—Arcade Tower, Oxford.

690.—Norman Capital, Oxford.

691.—Bury St. Edmunds.

692.—Bury St. Edmunds.

693.—Bury St. Edmunds.—1745.

694.—Abbey Gateway, Bury St. Edmunds.

696.—Parliament in Abbey of Bury.

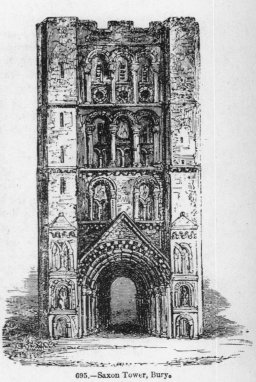

695.—Saxon Tower, Bury.

of which the Cathedral of Christ Church is to this day the palpable embodiment. In 727 Didan, the sub-regulus, or Earl of Oxford, founded a monastery, then dedicated to the Holy Trinity, and in which Didan and his wife were interred. Their daughter, Frideswida, devoted herself to a religious life, and was appointed to the government of her parents' foundation; when an event occurred that incalculably enhanced the popularity of the monastery, and ended in her canonization and the rededication of the monastery to her. Algar, Earl of Leicester, fell in love with her, and allowed his passion so far to exceed all the limits that prudence, as well as religious principle, marked out, as to endeavour to force her, sacred to the service of God as she was by her own choice and the monastic laws, into a marriage. She then concealed herself in a wood at Benson, near Oxford; and the Earl, unable to discover her abode, threatened to fire the city if she was not delivered up to him. "Such tyranny and presumption," observes Leland, "could not escape divine vengeance; he was struck blind! Hence arose such a dread to the Kings of Britain, that none of his successors dared enter Oxford for some time after."

Frideswida died in 740, and was probably buried in a chapel on the south side of the church, for there stood her shrine, until the great fire of Oxford in 1002 (that occurred during the simultaneous massacre of the Danes by Ethelred's order), when it was nearly destroyed, and for a time neglected. But in 1180 the shrine was removed to its present situation, in the dormitory, to the north of the choir; and the worn steps leading to the little oratory, erected at the back of the shrine, show how numerous have been the devotees who have there visited it. In course of time, a new shrine was desired for so popular a saint, which was accordingly erected in 1289, and which remained until the Reformation, when it is said to have been destroyed; but was more probably simply defaced. And even then the relics of the body of St. Frideswida were preserved by some ardent Catholics, and restored subsequently to the church. In the reign of Queen Mary, the remains of the wife of Peter Martyr, the Reformer, were taken up from their resting-place in the Cathedral, and formally condemned to be buried beneath a dunghill: when Elizabeth came to the throne, they were restored with all marked honours; and to prevent any further disturbance in case of a restoration of the older religionists to power, the very singular step was taken of mixing the mouldering relics of the wife of the Protestant reformer with those of the canonized nun and abbess Frideswida. Whether the mingled ashes now lie in the grave of Martyr's wife, or beneath the large altar tomb that is supposed to be St. Frideswida's, and is called by her name, is now unknown. In Fig. 682 this monument is shown; the one to the extreme right, with three stages of decorated architectural work, the lowest being of stone, the other two of wood. Beyond, and next to it, is the very rich monument of Lady Elizabeth Montacute, with her effigy, in the costume of the day, the dress enamelled in gold and colours all over. The third and last monument of the same range is the tomb of Guimond, the first prior; for St. Frideswida's monastery for nuns was subsequently changed into a house of secular canons, and then again into one for regular canons of the order of St. Austin; and thus it remained until Wolsey obtained an order for its dissolution from the Pope, prior to the change he meditated.

There is no reason to suppose that any portions of the pile erected by the parents of Frideswida are preserved in the present Cathedral. At the same time, the architectural character of the oldest portions of the church—early Norman or Saxon—has induced some antiquaries to refer its date to the very beginning of the eleventh century; but the more received opinion is that which attributes the erection to the twelfth century. Much, however, has been added since, as the Chapter House, which, with a highly-enriched Norman doorway, exhibits generally a valuable example of the early English style; the tower of similar architecture (the present spire was added by Wolsey); and the cloisters, which are in the beautiful perpendicular style. Some of the most striking parts of the interior belong to the same period as the cloisters. The roof of the nave is especially deserving of attention, for its curiously-beautiful groining, and for the pendants which stud it over. The size of Christ Church is certainly remarkable, but in the opposite sense to that in which such words are usually applied to such structures: it is, indeed, one of the most *petite* of cathedrals. Its entire length but little exceeds one hundred and fifty feet, and the entire breadth is but fifty-four feet; the transept measures one hundred and two feet, from end to end; the roof is about forty feet high; the steeple, one hundred and forty-six.

Leland, writing of Bury St. Edmunds, some three centuries ago,

observed with unwonted enthusiasm, "The sun hath not shone on a town more delightfully situated;" and we may also add, that the sun doth not now shine on a town, in the whole, more worthy of its natural beauty of position, or of the name which it is said to have borne in the Roman times—the Villa Faustina, or the "happy town." This has partly arisen from the circumstance that a great portion of the place was burnt down in 1806, and has been rebuilt in a handsome manner; but still more must be owing to the feelings and taste of the inhabitants. The river, which, as may be seen in our engravings (Figs. 691, 692), gives so charming an appearance to Bury St. Edmunds from whatever direction viewed, is the Larke; and it contributes no less to the internal than the external aspect, to the comfort than the prosperity of the place. Here we see its waters washing the lower part of the very pretty botanical garden; there bearing along the numerous barges laden with coals and other commodities which they have received about a mile below the town, where the Larke ceases to be navigable to larger vessels. The entrance to that garden is through the "abbey gate," almost the only relic of a monastery which, in architectural extent and magnificence, wealth, privileges, and power, surpassed every other in Great Britain, Glastonbury alone excepted; and the early history of which almost ranks even with that foundation in interest.

In the ninth century the place belonged to Beodric, and was hence called his *worthe* or *cortis*, that is to say, his villa or mansion, and was by that nobleman bequeathed to Edmund, the King and Martyr. How the last-named title was obtained it is our business here briefly to relate, for in the martyrdom of King Edmund we look for the origin of much of the prosperity of Bury, and of the historical interest which now invests its monastic remains. Mingling, as usual, truth and fable, the story runs thus:—Edmund, the brother and predecessor of the great Alfred, succeeding to the throne of East Anglia, was crowned at Bury, on the Christmas-day of 856, being at the time only fifteen years old. In 870 he was taken prisoner by the Danes, and, as he was a Christian as well as an enemy, tortured to death. The Danes first scourged him, then bound him to a tree, and pierced his body all over with arrows; lastly they cut off his head, which they threw into a neighbouring wood. On the departure of these terrible visitors, the subjects of the murdered king sought his remains, that they might inter them with all the honour and reverence due alike to his position and his character. The body was found still attached to the fatal tree; this they buried in a wooden chapel at Hagilsdun, now Hoxne. For a time, all their endeavours to discover the head were ineffectual; but when forty days had elapsed, it was found between the fore-paws of a wolf, which, strange to say, yielded it up quietly, and, stranger still, unmutilated, and then retired into the forest. No wonder that Lydgate the poet, who was a monk of Bury, observes, "An unkouth thyng, and strange ageyn nature." The greatest marvel was yet behind. The head was taken to Hagilsdun, placed against the body in its natural position, when it united so closely with the latter, which was not at all decomposed, that the separation could hardly be traced. The corpse was subsequently removed to Bury, which hence obtained the name of Bury St. Edmunds. Events of this nature were calculated to call forth in the highest degree the pious enthusiasm of the people; and which found, as usual, its development in a magnificent house for religious men, whose lives should be devoted to the honour of the king, martyr, and saint, and of the God in whose service he had so worthily lived and died. Six priests first met, and formed the nucleus. Benefactors of every class, from the highest to the lowest, assisted in the good work; among the earliest of these may be named King Athelstane, and Edmund, son of Edward the Elder. But the time was inauspicious in many respects for rapid or safe progress. The Danes still threatened; and, on one occasion (just before Swein destroyed Bury, in the beginning of the eleventh century), Ailwin, guardian of the body of St. Edmund, conveyed it to London. In the metropolis a new perplexity arose: the Bishop of London, having obtained possession of the treasured remains, by a process that might almost be called a kind of felony, refused to give it up when Ailwin was prepared to return; the guardian, however, was immovably true to his trust, and so, after much altercation, it was again safely deposited in Bury. Peace at last blessed the land, and Ailwin began in earnest the erection of a place that should be esteemed suitable to the memory of him whose mausoleum it was in effect to be. In 1020 he ejected all the secular clergy, and filled their places with Benedictine monks, obtained their exemption from all episcopal authority, and, these preliminaries settled, began the erection of a beautiful church of wood. Two other churches were subsequently raised of the same material. But in 1065 Abbot Baldwyn laid the foundation of a fourth, of stone, and on the most magnificent scale. It was about five hundred feet long: the transept extended two hundred and twelve feet; the western front was two hundred and forty feet broad; no less than twelve chapels were attached in different parts: twelve years were spent in the erection. Of this grand structure there remain but portions of the west front: the chief are, a tower converted into a stable, and three arches, forming originally the entrances into the three aisles of the church, which the utilitarianism of the age has converted, no doubt with considerable self-congratulation at the ingenuity of the idea, into very snug and comfortable dwelling-houses. Notwithstanding all that we know of the influences that have been in operation during the last three centuries to injure or degrade those noble architectural monuments of our forefathers, it strikes one every now and then with a sense of surprise to see how extensive these injuries have been, involving, indeed, in many cases, the almost absolute destruction of piles that, before such influences began to operate, were in the most perfect and apparently indestructible state. When Leland looked upon Bury in the sixteenth century, and said the sun had not shone upon a more delightfully situated town, he added also, nor on "a monastery more illustrious, whether we consider its wealth, its extent, or its incomparable magnificence. You might indeed say that the monastery itself is a town; so many gates are there, so many towers, and a church than which none can be more magnificent; and subservient to which are three others, also splendidly adorned with admirable workmanship, and standing in one and the same churchyard." That was but little more than three centuries ago; yet of all these buildings, which, if even left uncared for to the uninterrupted processes of natural decay, would have exhibited as yet but mere superficial injury, what have we now left? Two of the three smaller churches, a tower and a few arches of the great one, a gateway and part of the walls of the monastery, and another gateway, or tower, which formed the entrance into the churchyard, opposite the western front of the monastic church: and that is, in effect, all. It is, indeed, difficult to believe in the truth of Leland's description, and the description of other writers, who speak in minuter detail of the four grand gates to the abbey, the lofty embattled walls extending so far around, and enclosing, besides the four churches and the necessary monastic buildings of residence, a palace and garden for the abbot, chapter-house, infirmaries, churchyard, and several chapels,—till we begin patiently to explore the traces yet to be found on the spot, and to remember the size and importance of that community which had here for so many centuries its abode. The household of St. Edmundsbury included some eighty monks, sixteen chaplains, and one hundred and eleven servants. The importance of the monastery is shown in its power and privileges. The abbot sat in parliament as a baron of the realm, and in his chapter-house and hall as something more. No sovereign, indeed, could be much more absolute. He appointed the parochial clergy of Bury—all civil and criminal causes arising within the place were tried within his court—the life and death of offenders were in his hand. The monastery coined its own money, and the monarch's into the bargain, when it suited him to obtain its assistance: Edward I. and Edward II. both had mints here. It permitted no divided allegiance in the locality, whether of a spiritual or a temporal nature, and had a very summary mode of setting at rest any question of the kind that might arise. In the thirteenth century, some Franciscan friars came to Bury, and built a handsome monastery; but the monks having by that time, we presume, settled in their own minds that they did not like friars, went and pulled down their building, and drove its tenants forth from the town. Redress appears to have been quite out of the question. Another evidence of the importance of the monastery may be drawn from our knowledge of its wealth. At the dissolution, the commissioners of the king said they had taken from it in gold and silver five thousand marks, a rich cross with emeralds, and also divers stones of great value, but still left behind ample store of plate of silver for the service of the church, abbot, and convent. As to its revenues, a writer in 1727 said, they would have been equal at that time to the enormous sum of two hundred thousand pounds yearly.

We have already noticed the remains of the monastic church. The abbey gate (Fig. 694) was erected in 1327, and is, therefore, above five centuries old, yet notwithstanding its age, and the entire destruction of its roof, remains surprisingly perfect. As a specimen of Gothic architecture it is at once majestic and superb; the height being no less than sixty-two feet, and the fronts, more particularly that on the western or exterior side, being decorated in the most gorgeously splendid style. Among the beautiful decorations of the interior of the gateway is much carved-work, including,

in one part, the arms of the Confessor. But the tower leading into the churchyard (Fig. 695) is, considering its remoter antiquity, as well as its extraordinary magnificence, the most interesting of all the remains of this great religious establishment. It rises to the height of eighty feet, is simple and massive in form, but most elaborately beautiful in decoration—and pure unadulterated Saxon. It is, in a word, one of the finest things of the kind in existence. No records carry us back to the date of its erection. The sculpture upon it is exceedingly curious and valuable as the product of so early a time. Near the base on the western side are two bas-reliefs; in one of which Adam and Eve, entwined by the serpent, typify man in his fallen state; whilst in the other, the Deity is seen sitting in triumph in a circle of cherubim, as representative of man's spiritual restoration. In the interior of the arch are some grotesque figures. The stone of which the edifice is built is remarkable for the number of small shells it contains. Through this gateway we pass to the churchyard, where, as we wander along an avenue of stately and fragrant lime-trees, we perceive, in different parts, the two churches of St. James and St. Mary, and the Shire-hall, erected on the site of the third and destroyed church of St. Margaret; various portions of the abbey ruins; Clopton's Hospital, a modern work of beneficence; and the mausoleum, once the chapel of the charnel, where Lydgate is understood to have resided, and where possibly the greater part of his multifarious writings were composed. His case furnishes a valuable and instructive example of one of the uses of our monasteries—that of nurturing men of learning and literary ability. Lydgate was at once a traveller, a schoolmaster, a philologist, a rhetorician, a geometrician, an astronomer, a theologist, a disputant, a poet; and it is hardly too much to say, that he was all this chiefly because he was also a monk. How many such men may not these institutions have contained, but who did not, like Lydgate, seek for fame beyond the confines of their own monastery! Such encouragement as the Abbot of St. Edmundsbury gave to Lydgate was, in all probability, the rule rather than the exception, in such establishments generally. The pride in the reputation thus reflected upon their house, and the eternal craving for some kind of mental occupation and excitement, which no discipline could entirely eradicate, must have made many a superior encourage such studies, even when he had in himself no particular tendency towards them; but how much more when he had!—and the frequency of the qualification "learning" recorded in accounts of election to monastic government shows that this must have been a matter of common occurrence. We need not then be surprised to see Lydgate allowed to master so many departments of knowledge, or to open a school in the monastery at Bury for teaching some of them, as he did, to the sons of the nobility of his day. Another and equally pleasant instance of the estimation in which he was held is commemorated by a most splendidly illuminated MS. now in the British Museum, forming a life of St. Edmund, and which he presented to Henry VI. when he visited the monastery in 1440: a pension of 7l. 13s. 4d. was the monarch's answering gift; a most princely one, according to the then value of money. Both the smaller churches that we have mentioned as existing are strikingly handsome. St. Mary's has three aisles, divided by two rows of very elegant columns; and the roof of the middle aisle, sixty feet high, is beautifully carved. The roof of the chancel presents an additional feature, carved gilt work on a blue ground, supposed to have been brought from Caen in Normandy. In this church lies Mary Tudor, third daughter of Henry VII., and wife, first, of Louis XII. of France, and afterwards of the Duke of Suffolk: there also, in the middle of the chancel, rests the last Abbot of Bury, John Reeves.

Many events of historical importance are recorded in connection with the monastery. During the wars between Henry II. and his son, the forces of the former marched out of Bury with the sacred standard of St. Edmund, to a spot in the neighbourhood where the enemy was met with, and a battle fought, which ended in favour of the king: to the standard, of course, was attributed the honour of the victory. This incident probably suggested to Richard I the idea of bringing to Bury the rich standard of Isaac, King of Cyprus, which he had taken whilst on his way to Acre and the Holy Land. But the most important of all such events were those connected with the baronial struggle for the great Charter. John arrived from France in October, 1214, full of rage and mortification at the defeat his forces had recently experienced at a place between Lisle and Tournay, and determined to repay himself for his sufferings and losses at the hands of the enemy by increased exactions from his own subjects. FitzPeter, the Justiciary, a man whom John feared, had died during his absence. He laughed

2 A 2

700.—Byland Abbey, Yorkshire.

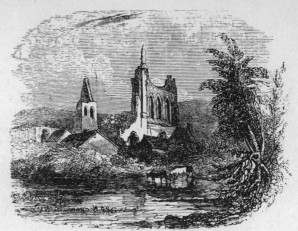

701.—Byland Abbey.

702.—Fountains Abbey.

703.—Walsingham Abbey.

697.—Bermondsey.—Remains of the Eastern Gate-house of the Abbey.

698.—Bermondsey.—Existing Remains of the Conventual Buildings.

699.—Bermondsey.—Remains of the Abbey; from a drawing made immediately before their Demolition.

180

707.—Pershore.

708.—Cross near Pershore.

704.—Priory Church, Hexham. East End.

705.—Tewkesbury.

706.—Tewkesbury.

as the news was imparted to him: "It is well," said he; "in hell he may again shake hands with Hubert our late primate, for surely he will find him there. By God's teeth, now, for the first time, I am King and Lord of England." But the barons were prepared. A league had been already formed with Langton, the Cardinal, and they now agreed to meet: "The time is favourable," they said: "the feast of St. Edmund approaches; amidst the multitudes that resort to his shrine we may assemble without suspicion." On the day in question, the 20th of November, they met, and resolved to demand their rights from the king, in his very court, on the coming Christmas-day. It was a hazardous undertaking, and one from which weak minds might easily be induced to draw back, to which faithless hearts might be as readily instigated to turn traitors; so the solemn sanction of the church was as it were invoked to deter both the one class and the other, if any such there were. The barons advancing in the order of their seniority, one by one, laid their hands on the high altar, and swore that if the king refused the rights they demanded, they would withdraw their fealty, and make war upon him, until he should yield. We need not follow their proceedings further, they are too well known; but the virtual conclusion of the memorable meeting at Bury was the still more memorable one on the plains of Runnymede. Several parliaments have been held in the monastery; the most noticeable is the one that sat in 1447 for the not very estimable or dignified purpose of promoting the object which Margaret, the queen of Henry VI., and her favourite Suffolk, had so much at heart, namely, the destruction of the good Duke Humphrey of Gloucester. Of course that object was for a time concealed, and Gloucester, in consequence, went unsuspiciously to his fate. On the 11th of February, or the very day after the opening of the parliament, he was arrested on a charge of high treason. In less than three weeks from that time he was found dead in his bed; and although no marks of violence were visible when the body was publicly exhibited to the people of Bury St. Edmunds, the impression was universal that he had been murdered. The weak young king, who had consented to all but the last foul proceeding, "thus"—to use, with mere verbal alteration, the words Shakspere has put into the mouth of Gloucester, in the Second Part of Henry VI.—

> ————— King Henry threw away his crutch
> Before his legs were firm to bear his body:
> Thus was the shepherd beaten from his side,
> When wolves were gnarling who should gnaw him first.

But for Gloucester's sudden death, we might have known nothing of the wars of the Roses.

———

So completely has every important vestige of the once famous Abbey of Bermondsey (see Fig. 698) been swept away, that one may pass a hundred times through the streets and lanes that now cover the site, without even a suspicion that any such establishment had ever existed there. A few decaying squalid-looking tenements in the corner of an out-of-the-way court (Fig. 697), a small portion of a gatehouse, with half the rusty hinge still inserted in the stone, scattered masses of wall about the present churchyard, and a few names of streets and squares, as the Long Walk, and the Grange Walk, are the sole relics of the monastery which in its days of splendour was esteemed of so much importance, that great councils of state were frequently held in it. Of the church, which unquestionably was a large and handsome, probably a very magnificent structure, there is not even a trace to be found, unless we may make an exception in favour of a very curious and ancient salver of silver, now used in St. Mary's Church for the collection of alms, and which possibly formed a part of the abbey treasure. The salver presents a view of the gate of a castle or town, with two figures, a knight kneeling before a lady, while she places a helmet on his head. The costume of the knight appears to be of the date of Edward II. This church of St. Mary, we may observe, was built on the site of a smaller one, erected by the monks at a very early period, and, it is supposed, for the use of their tenants and servants. With so little, then, existing at present to stimulate our curiosity as to the past, it will be hardly advisable to dwell at any length upon the subject, though far from an uninteresting one. The founder of Bermondsey was a citizen of London, Aylwin Child, who, in his admiration of the new order of Cluniacs that had just been introduced into England, obtained four monks from one of the foreign monasteries to establish a house of Cluniacs at Bermondsey. The Benedictine rule or discipline was, one would imagine, strict enough for any body of men, however pious; not so thought some of the members of the order themselves; and from

their thoughts and desires gradually arose the order we have referred to. Bermondsey, like the other houses of Cluniacs in England, was considered an alien priory, that is to say, was under subjection to the great Abbey of Cluny in Burgundy, and shared therefore in the fate that befel all such alien houses in the fourteenth century—sequestration. But Richard II. not only restored it to life and activity, but raised it to the rank of an abbey: among his motives for this gracious and important favour, a present of two hundred marks, we presume, ought to be enumerated. At the dissolution Bermondsey was valued at 548*l*. 2*s*. 5½*d*.; and it is remarkable enough that King Henry seems to have really got nothing in this instance by the dissolution; through his unusual liberality, the monks were all pensioned off with sums varying from five pounds six shillings and eightpence to ten pounds yearly, while the abbot's share must have swept away nearly all the rest, amounting, as it did, to 336*l*. 6*s*. 8*d*. King Henry certainly was never more shrewdly managed than by the last Abbot of Bermondsey.

Among the historical recollections of the abbey may be mentioned the residence and death in it of Katherine, who had for her first husband Henry V., and for her second, Owen Tudor, the founder of the Tudor dynasty. Two days before her death, her son by the conqueror of Agincourt, Henry VI., sent to her, in token of his affectionate remembrance, a tablet of gold weighing thirteen ounces, and set with sapphires and pearls. The chief interest, however, that we now feel in the Abbey of Bermondsey arises from the enforced residence of Elizabeth Woodville, whose eventful life finds few parallels in female history. At first the wife of a simple English knight; then, after his death in the wars of the Roses, a wretched widow, pleading at the feet of Edward IV. for the reversal of the attainder that threatened to sweep away the home and estates of herself and children; then the queen of that king, and married by him for the very unpolitical reason that he had fallen passionately in love with her; then again a widow struggling to keep her royal offspring from the murderous grasp of their usurping uncle the Duke of Gloucester,—and who, after their murder in the Tower, became Richard III.; then once more lifted into apparent prosperity by the union of the rival Roses in the persons of her daughter and Henry VII.; and then, lastly, a prisoner at Bermondsey during the very reign of that daughter, and at the instance of that daughter's husband. And there she died, the queen of one king, the mother of the wife of another; and so poor, that in her will, which is touchingly pathetic, we find her leaving her blessing to her child as the only thing it was in her power to bequeath to her. "I have no worldly goods to do the queen's grace, my dearest daughter, a pleasure with, neither to reward any of my children according to my heart and mind." Henry's reason for this harshness appears to have been a belief that she had been instrumental in raising a new Yorkist insurrection in Ireland in 1486, under the leadership of the pretended Earl of Warwick, but really Lambert Simnel, the son of a joiner. He had reason to know she did scheme; for, says Bacon, "in her withdrawing chamber had the fortunate conspiracy for the king against King Richard III. been hatched, which the king knew and remembered perhaps but too well." After the death of his wife, Henry established a yearly anniversary at Bermondsey, when prayers were to be offered for his own prosperity, and for his wife's, his children's, and other relatives' souls; but not a word as to the soul of his wife's mother, the beautiful, intriguing, possibly unprincipled, but certainly most unfortunate, Elizabeth Woodville.

———

Having now noticed in our pages, and at what may be considered sufficient length, some of the more important of the English monasteries, we shall, as a general principle, treat the remainder in groups; passing over most of the subjects in each with a brief, or at least a very partial account, but dwelling, as we may see occasion, on the others. If many highly-important establishments may be thus cursorily dismissed, many also will receive a fair share of attention; whilst, by not attempting what is impracticable in the present instance,—to preserve the individual interest of all, we may hope to convey a more satisfactory impression as to those we select from the multitude. In our first group we include Byland and Fountains Abbey in Yorkshire, Walsingham Priory in Norfolk, Tewkesbury Abbey in Gloucestershire, and Hexham Priory in Northumberland. With such subjects it is indeed difficult to make a choice; but on the whole we may consider Fountains Abbey as the best fitted for lengthened notice.

Among the monastic remains we have had, or may yet have, occasion to notice, there are of course some few that enjoy a marked pre-eminence, either for their history, the beauty of their architectural relics, or the advantages of their local position: they are antiquities that every one feels interested in, that many have personally seen. Fountains Abbey is of this class. Its very name is suggestive of a world of pleasant associations, green ruins with many a legend or story hanging about them, picturesque and attractive as themselves; quiet woods, and delightfully unquiet waters; nooks and corners among rocks or by water-banks, or beneath great overarching trees; a place, in fine, for deep emotion and elevated thought,—where one seems to stand between the Past and the Future, unaffected by all the disturbing influences of the Present; and to look on all things with a sense of newly-aroused powers of apprehension of the truth or falsehood that is in them,—of newly-awakened desire to draw from these chewings of the cud of sweet and bitter fancy the most wholesome nutriment for the every-day business of life, towards which we at last must again, however reluctantly, address ourselves. It is no wonder that Fountains Abbey should have obtained so high or extensive a reputation. All the peculiar advantages above enumerated, as tending to give such relics of "Old England" their fame, are combined in this. It is situated in a beautiful and romantic valley, through which runs the Skell, and in the vicinity of Studley park and pleasure-grounds, the last forming one of the horticultural notabilities of England, a continuous garden of some three hundred acres laid out in the most charming style. For the beauty of the architecture of Fountains Abbey we need only refer to the view (Fig. 702), where the remarkable state of preservation in which the pile generally exists, as well as some indications of the elegance of the prevailing style, will be apparent. On the whole the Abbey ruins form the most perfect specimen that the country possesses of what may perhaps be called the most perfect architectural time,—the age of Henry III. and of Westminster Abbey. All the walls of both church and monastery yet stand, though roofless and with dilapidated windows. The majestic tower, from its unusual position at the north end of the transept, still rises up in serene grandeur. We may walk through the nave and admire the arch of its once glorious eastern window; from thence wander into the "ruined choir" and listen to hymns of praise, albeit the choristers are of a tinier race than of yore. The Chapter House yet tells us of the abbots who sat there in due course of spiritual government, and some of whose tombs now lie beneath our feet, with half-illegible inscriptions; we can still perceive, over the Chapter House, where the library was situated in which the monks read, and the adjoining scriptorium wherein they wrote. It is as long a walk as ever to pace from end to end of the cloisters, and almost as picturesque, with those curious arches overhead formed by the mazy intersections of the groinings of the roof; the kitchen is ready at any moment to glow with "unwonted fires," and renew those old hospitalities of which its two immense fireplaces give one such an expansive idea; the very garden of the monastery still smells sweet and looks fair with quivering leaves and "flowres fresh of hue."

Whilst such the position and such the remains of Fountains Abbey, both at the same time borrow from their past history higher and deeper interest than the picturesque hands of nature or of time could bestow. The monastic *orders* generally, perhaps universally, had their origin in the desire of some one man, or some few men, to check prevailing evils in the lives or views of the people, or of their spiritual teachers, or to carry on still further reformations or improvements already begun. It is easy to imagine that much heart-burning and strife must have frequently resulted from such endeavours; which set brother against brother, divided the once peaceful monastery against itself, which annoyed the idle, or supine, or the licentious, by placing monitors eternally at their elbow. In connection with the records of Fountains Abbey we find a curious and ample account of the growth of such a division: "The fame of the sanctity of the Cistercian monks at Rieval [Rievaulx], the first of that order of Yorkshire, having extended to the Benedictine monastery of St. Mary at York, several of the monks there, finding too great a relaxation in the observance of the rules, were desirous of withdrawing themselves to follow the stricter rules observed by the monks of Rieval. But Galfrid, their abbot, opposed their removal, as being a reflection on his government of the abbey; whereupon, in A.D. 1132, the 33rd of Henry I., Richard, the Prior, went to Thurstan, Archbishop of York, to desire that he would visit the abbey and regulate what was amiss therein, and assist them in their design of withdrawing themselves. The day of visitation being come, the archbishop, attended by many grave and discreet clergy, canons, and other religious men, went to St. Mary's Abbey, whither the abbot had convoked several learned men, and a multitude of monks from different parts of England,

that by their aid he might oppose the archbishop, if requisite, and correct the insolence of those brethren that wanted to leave the abbey. On the 6th of October, A.D. 1132, the archbishop arrived at the monastery, when the abbot, with a multitude of monks, opposed his entrance into the chapter with such a number of persons as attended him; whereupon an uproar ensued: and the archbishop, after interdicting the church and monks, returned; and the prior, sub-prior, and eleven monks withdrew themselves, and were joined by Robert, a monk of Whitby, who went along with them, and were maintained at the archbishop's expense, in his own house, for eleven weeks and five days. . . . The abbot did not cease by messages to persuade the withdrawn monks to return to their monastery, while they at the bishop's house spent most of their time in fasting and prayer. However, two of them were prevailed on to quit the rest, and go back; and yet one of the two repenting, soon returned to those who were for a more strict way of life." It is to these monks of St. Mary's that Fountains Abbey owes its origin; they were its founders, and very interesting were the circumstances of the foundation, as related by the same writer, Burton ['Monast. Eboracen.']. "At Christmas, the archbishop, being at Ripon, assigned to the monks some land in the patrimony of St. Peter, about three miles west of that place, for the erecting of a monastery. The spot of ground had never been inhabited, unless by wild beasts, being overgrown with wood and brambles, lying between two steep hills and rocks, covered with wood on all sides, more proper for a retreat of wild beasts than the human species. . . . Richard, the Prior of St. Mary's at York, was chosen abbot by the monks, being the first of this monastery of Fountains, with whom they withdrew into this uncouth desert, without any house to shelter them in that winter season, or provisions to subsist on; but entirely depending on Divine Providence. There stood a large elm in the midst of the vale, on which they put some thatch or straw, and under that they lay, eat, and prayed, the bishop for a time supplying them with bread, and the rivulet (the Skell) with drink. Part of the day some spent in making wattles to erect a little oratory, whilst others cleared some ground to make a little garden." A clump of yew-trees, it appears, however, offered a better shelter, and to these they removed, and there remained during the erection of the monastery. Some of these trees, we believe, still remain, and are of such extraordinary size and so close together, as to corroborate the statement of the uses to which they were put above seven centuries ago. The monks adopted the Cistercian rule, and placed themselves in direct communication with the famous founder of it, St. Bernard, who sent them a monk from his own monastery of Clairvaux, to instruct them alike in spiritual and temporal affairs. Some cottages were now built, and ten other persons joined them. Terrible, and all but intolerable, as were the difficulties these men endured, their enthusiasm seems to have never slackened for a moment; they were even liberal in their severest destitution. At a time when they were obliged to feed on the leaves of trees, and herbs boiled with a little salt, a stranger came and begged for a morsel of bread; two loaves and a half were all that the community possessed; and one was given to the applicant, the abbot saying, "God would provide for them." Almost immediately after, two men came from the neighbouring castle of Knaresborough with a present of a cartload of fine bread from Eustace Fitz-John, its lord. Left, however, entirely to the assistance of the Archbishop of York, they were, at the end of two years, about to retire to the Continent, on the invitation of St. Bernard, when prosperity at last dawned upon them; Hugh, Dean of York, falling sick, caused himself to be taken to Fountains, and settled all his immense wealth upon the community. From that time the monks steadily progressed until their establishment became one of the most distinguished in the kingdom. Its territorial wealth seems almost incredible. From the foot of Pinnigant to the boundaries of St. Wilfred, a distance exceeding thirty miles, extended without interruption its broad lands. There is a circumstance in the later history of the abbey, which, taken in connection with those already narrated as to its earlier, forms a striking commentary on the causes of the rise and fall of all such institutions. William Thirske, the last but one of all the long line of abbots, was expelled for stealing from his own abbey, and afterwards hanged at Tyburn!

Byland Abbey (Fig. 701) needs but few words. It was founded in 1177 by Roger de Mowbray, the nobleman whose estates were sequestrated by Henry I. for disloyalty, and then given to another nobleman, also of Norman extraction, who took the Mowbray name, and founded the great family of the Mowbrays, Dukes of Norfolk and Earls of Nottingham. The exquisite form of the lancet windows yet remaining in a part of the ruins, shows that Byland has

709.—Tynemouth.

710.—Tynemouth Cliff.

711.—Easby Abbey.

184

714.—Devil's Bridge, South Wales. Built 1187.

715.—Well of St. Keyne, Cornwall.

716.—Warkworth Hermitage.

been a beautiful and stately pile. The memory of our "Lady of WALSINGHAM" demands longer pause before the beautiful ruins of the priory at that place. It is difficult to account for the reputation obtained by this monastery. In 1061, a lady, the widow of Richoldis de Favarches, erected a small chapel in honour of the Virgin Mary, in imitation of the Sancta Casa at Nazareth; and to this chapel, the lady's son added a Priory for Augustine canons, and built a church. In these facts there does not appear to be anything at all unusual or remarkable; not the less, however, did the shrine of our Lady, erected in the chapel, become the most popular place of resort, without exception, that Old England contained. Even Thomas à Becket's shrine at Canterbury seems to have been hardly so much visited. Foreigners came hither from all parts of the world, guided, as they fancied, by the light of the milky way, which the monks of Walsingham persuaded the people—so Erasmus says—was a miraculous indication of the way to their monastery. Many kings and queens were among the pilgrims: above all, let us not forget to mention, for the sake of the strange contrast the incident presents to the subsequent acts of the same man, Henry the Eighth came hither in the second year of his reign, and walked barefoot from the village of Basham. Not many years after, the image of our Lady was burnt at Chelsea, to the horror of the Roman Catholic world; and who should direct the act, but that same quondam worshipper and royal pilgrim to Walsingham, King Henry. Prior to the dissolution of the monastery, Erasmus visited it. The chapel, he says, then rebuilding, was distinct from the church, and contained a smaller chapel of wood, with a little narrow door on each side, where strangers were admitted to perform their devotions, and deposit their offerings; that it was lighted up with wax torches, and that the glitter of gold, silver, and jewels would lead you to suppose it to be the seat of the gods. A Saxon arch, forming part of the original chapel, still exists; and there also remain extensive portions of the church and monastery, among which may be especially mentioned, on account of its exceeding beauty, the lofty arch, sixty feet high, which formed the east end of the church, and two wells called the Wishing wells, from which whoever drank of the waters obtained, under certain restrictions, whatever they might wish for: at least so many a devotee was told and believed. Most of the convent ruins are now included in the beautiful pleasure grounds of a modern residence known as Walsingham Abbey. (Fig. 703.)

TEWKESBURY Church, as it is called, but which for size, plan, and magnificence may rank among our cathedrals, was, before the dissolution of monasteries, the church of the Abbey of Tewkesbury, originally founded in the Saxon times by two brothers, Dodo and Odo, who both died in 725. During the reign of the Confessor, an incident occurred which led to the temporary ruin of the foundation, and which is too remarkable to be passed without notice. Bithric, Earl of Gloucester, was sent into Normandy, on an embassy, and whilst there, Matilda, daughter of Baldwin, Earl of Flanders, fell so passionately in love with him, as to forget the delicacy of her sex and make her feelings known to him who had called them forth. Whether the earl disliked the Norman lady, or was already in love with an English one, we know not, but he at all events so discouraged the advances made that the love, as is not unfrequent in such cases, changed to hate, and left but one desire in Matilda's heart, that of vengeance. The earl no doubt laughed at threats from such a quarter, and returned to England, where most probably the circumstance was altogether forgotten. But by-and-by, news came that Matilda had married Duke William of Normandy. Time passed again, and rumours of invasion at the hands of this Duke William filled all England; and truly the duke came at last, and England was conquered. Then too came the time that Matilda had never, it seems, ceased to look forward to. She personally solicited the conqueror to place Bithric at her disposal, and having obtained possession of his person, threw him into prison at Winchester, and there he died. Many of his estates were at the same time seized by Matilda, among them the town and abbey of Tewkesbury. By William Rufus, however, the church and monastery were re-granted to Robert Fitz Hamon, who rebuilt the whole about 1102. "It cannot be easily reported," says William of Malmesbury, "how highly he exalted this monastery, wherein the beauty of the buildings ravished the eyes, and the charity of the monks allured the hearts of such folk as used to come thither." Among the interesting features of the interior of this Church may be particularized the monuments of the nobles and others slain in the fatal battle of Tewkesbury. (Figs. 705, 706.)

HEXHAM Church (Fig. 704) was also the church of a famous monastery, and, like Tewkesbury, owes its preservation, in much of its ancient magnificence, to the fact of its being used after the Reformation, as a place of worship for the town and parish. The plan is cathedral-like, including nave, choir, and transepts, though the nave, having been burnt by the Scots in the time of Edward the First, has never been rebuilt. The architecture generally is of the twelfth century, but there are both later and earlier portions; some of the last indeed being supposed to be remains of a structure that formed one of the marvels of Saxon England, the church erected by Wilfrid, Archbishop of York, in the latter part of the seventh century. It has been thus glowingly described by one who assisted to restore it from the ruin into which it had fallen. Wilfred "began the edifice by making crypts, and subterraneous oratories, and winding passages through all parts of its foundations. The pillars that supported the walls were finely polished, square, and of various other shapes, and the three galleries were of immense height and length. These, and the capitals of their columns, and the bow of the sanctuary, he decorated with histories and images, carved in relief on the stone, and with pictures coloured with great taste. The body of the church was surrounded with wings and porticos, to which winding staircases were contrived with the most astonishing art. These staircases also led to long walking galleries, and various winding passages so contrived, that a very great multitude of people might be within them, unperceived by any person on the ground-floor of the church. Oratories, too, as sacred as they were beautiful, were made in all parts of it, and in which were altars of the Virgin, of St. Michael, St. John the Baptist, and all the Apostles, Confessors, and Virgins. Certain towers and blockhouses remain unto this day specimens of the inimitable excellence of the architecture of this structure. The relics, the religious persons, the ministers, the great library, the vestments, and utensils of the church, were too numerous and magnificent for the poverty of our language to describe. The atrium of the cathedral was girt with a stone wall of great thickness and strength, and a stone aqueduct conveyed a stream of water through the town to all the offices. The magnitude of this place is apparent from the extent of its ruins. It excelled, in the excellence of its architecture, all the buildings in England; and, in truth, there was nothing like it, at that time, to be found on this side the Alps." [Richard, Prior of Hexham.] It can hardly be supposed there were English architects to design, or English workmen to execute such a building, in the seventh century: both classes were brought from Rome.

In dealing with a second group, we may commence with the venerable and picturesque ruins of the monastery of EASBY, which are near the village of that name, about a mile and a half from Richmond, and on the rocky and well-wooded banks of the Swale. Rould, Constable of Richmond Castle, was the founder, about the year 1152. Its inhabitants were members of the then recently introduced order of Premonstratensian Canons, who lived according to the rule of St. Austin. Their dress was entirely white—a white cassock, with a white rochet over it, a long white cloak, and a white cap; and a picturesque addition to one of the most picturesque of houses and scenes, these white canons must have formed. Our cut (Fig. 711) shows the more important of the existing remains, which are well described in Dr. Whitaker's 'Yorkshire:'—

"By the landscape painter and the man of taste the ruins of this house, combined with the scene around them, have never been contemplated without delight. But admiration and rapture are very unobserving qualities; and it has never hitherto been attended to, that this house, though its several parts are elaborate and ornamental, has been planned with a neglect of symmetry and proportion which might have become an architect of Laputa. Of the refectory, a noble room nearly one hundred feet long, with a groined apartment below, every angle is either greater or less than a right angle. Of the cloister-court, contrary to every other example, there have been only two entire sides, each of which has an obtuse angle. From these again the entire outline of the church reels to the west, and though the chapter-house is a rectangle, the vestry is a trapezium.* Once more: of the terminations of the north and south aisles eastward, one has extended several yards beyond the other; the choir also is elongated, out of all proportion. The abbot's lodgings, instead of occupying their usual situation, to the southeast of the choir, and of being connected with the east end of the cloister-court, are here most injudiciously placed to the north of the church, and therefore deprived, by the great elevation of the latter, of warmth and sunshine. The abbot's private entrance into the church was by a doorway, yet remaining, into the north aisle of the nave. To compensate, however, for the darkness of his lodg-

* Trapezium, a figure where the four sides are neither equal nor parallel

ings, he had a pleasant garden, open to the morning sun, with a beautiful solarium,* highly adorned with Gothic groinings at the north-east angle.

"But to atone for all these deformities in architecture, many of the decorations of this house are extremely elegant. Among these the first place is due to the great window of the refectory, of which the beauties are better described by the pencil than the pen. This, with the groined vault beneath, appears to be of the reign of Henry III. North-west from this are several fine apartments, contemporary, as appears, with the foundation; but the whole line of wall, having been placed on the shelving bank of the Swale, has long been gradually detaching itself from the adjoining parts, and threatens in no long period to destroy one of the best features of the place. On the best side of the imperfect cloister-court is a circular doorway, which displays the fantastic taste of Norman enrichments in perfection. A cluster of round columns, with variously adorned capitals, is surmounted by a double moulded arch, embossed with cats' heads hanging out their tongues, which are curled at the extremities. Above all is an elegant moulding of foliage. Not far beneath is a large picturesque tree (perhaps truly) distinguished by the name of the Abbot's elm. The abbey gateway, still in perfect repair, is the latest part of the whole fabric, and probably about the era of Edward III."

On a bold bluff rock, looking out upon the German Ocean, stand the ruins of the PRIORY OF TYNEMOUTH. We pass into the consecrated ground, which is still used as a burial-place, through a barrack, the buildings of which have been partly erected out of the materials of the Priory. When we are within the Priory inclosure we see artillery pointing seaward and landward,—sentinels pacing their constant walk, and in the midst the old grey ruin, looking almost reproachfully upon these odd associations. There is one living within constant view of this ruin—a writer who has won an enduring reputation—to whom the solitude of a sick-room has brought as many soothing and holy aspirations as to the most pure and spiritual of the recluses, who, century after century, looked out from this rock upon a raging sea, and thought of a world where all was peace. The scene which is now presented by the view from Tynemouth is thus described by the writer to whom we allude, in 'Life in the Sick-room.' What a contrast to the scene upon which the old monks were wont to look! (Fig. 710.)

"Between my window and the sea is a green down, as green as any field in Ireland, and on the nearer half of this down hay-making goes forward in its season. It slopes down to a hollow, where the Prior of old preserved his fish, there being sluices formerly at either end, the one opening upon the river, and the other upon the little haven below the Priory, whose ruins still crown the rock. From the Prior's fish-pond, the green down slopes upwards to a ridge; and on the slope are cows grazing all summer, and half way into the winter. Over the ridge, I survey the harbour and all its traffic, the view extending from the lighthouses far to the right, to a horizon of sea to the left. Beyond the harbour lies another county, with, first, its sandy beach, where there are frequent wrecks—too interesting to an invalid—and a fine stretch of rocky shore to the left; and above the rocks, a spreading heath, where I watch troops of boys flying their kites; lovers and friends taking their breezy walk on Sundays; the sportsman with his gun and dog; and the washerwomen converging from the farm-houses on Saturday evenings, to carry their loads in company, to the village on the yet farther height. I see them, now talking in a cluster, as they walk each with her white burden on her head, and now in file, as they pass through the narrow lane; and finally they part off on the village green, each to some neighbouring house of the gentry. Behind the village and the heath stretches the railroad; and I watch the train triumphantly careering along the level road, and puffing forth its steam above hedges and groups of trees, and then labouring and panting up the ascent, till it is lost between two heights, which at last bound my view. But on these heights are more objects; a windmill, now in motion and now at rest; a limekiln, in a picturesque rocky field; an ancient church tower, barely visible in the morning, but conspicuous when the setting sun shines upon it; a colliery with its lofty wagon-way, and the self-moving wagons running hither and thither, as if in pure wilfulness."

The original choice of the situation for the Priory appears to have been dictated by that benevolence which was characteristic of

---

* Solarium, as the name implies, signifies a place exposed to the sun, and was applied originally to places on the tops of houses where the Romans used to take air and exercise. In the present instance it means simply a garden or summer-house.

---

the early religious foundations. Tynemouth Priory was a beacon to the sailor, and when he looked upon its towers he thought of the Virgin and Saint Oswin, who were to shield him from the dangers of the great waters. That the situation, at the mouth of a river, and on an elevated site, early recommended the place as suitable both for military defence and religious purposes, is evident from the fact that Robert de Mowbray, about the year 1090, fled hither, and defended himself within its walls against William Rufus (against whom he had conspired); but, after a time, finding that he could hold out no longer, he sought "sanctuary" at the altar of the church, from which, however, he was taken by force, and, after suffering a tedious imprisonment, was put to death. The monastery at one time enjoyed considerable wealth. It possessed twenty-seven manors in Northumberland, with their royalties, besides other valuable lands and tenements. At the dissolution, in 1539, there was a prior, with fifteen prebendaries and three novices. The annual revenues of the priory were then estimated (separate from the Abbey of St. Alban's, on which it depended) at 397l. 10s. 5d. by Dugdale, and at 511l. 4s. 1d. by Speed. The prior, on the surrender of the monastery, received a pension of 80l. per annum. The site and most of the lands were granted in the 5th of Edward VI. to John Dudley, Earl of Northumberland; but by his attainder in the next year it reverted to the Crown, in which it remained till the 10th of Elizabeth. During the reign of Elizabeth the place was occupied as a fortress. Camden says, "It is now called Tinemouth Castle, and glories in a stately and strong castle."

The following description of the remains is from a small work published at North Shields in 1806. There is very slight alteration at the present time, for the ruins are now carefully preserved.

"The approach to the priory is from the west, by a gateway tower of a square form, having a circular exploratory turret on each corner; from this gateway, on each hand, a strong double wall has been extended to the rocks on the sea-shore, which from their great height have been esteemed in former times inaccessible. The gate, with its walls, was fortified by a deep outward ditch, over which there was a drawbridge, defended by moles on each side. The tower comprehends an outward and interior gateway, the outward gateway having two gates at the distance of about six feet from each other, the inner of which is defended by a portcullis, and an open gallery; the interior gateway is, in like manner, strengthened by a double gate. The space between the gateways, being a square of about six paces, is open above to allow those on the top of the tower and battlements to annoy assailants who had gained the first gate.

"On passing the gateway, the scene is strikingly noble and venerable; the whole enclosed area may contain about six acres; the walls seem as well calculated for defence as the gateway tower; the view is crowded with august ruins; many fine arches of the priory are standing. The most beautiful part of these remains is the eastern limb of the church, of elegant workmanship. The ruins are so disunited, that it would be very difficult to determine to what particular office each belongs. The ruins which present themselves in front, on entering the gateway, appear to be the remains of the cloister, access to which was afforded by a gateway of circular arches, comprehending several members inclining inwards, and arising from pilasters. After passing this gate, in the area many modern tombs appear, the ground being still used for sepulture. The west gate entering into the abbey is still entire, of the same architecture as that leading to the cloister. The ground, from the cloister to the south wall, is almost covered with foundations, which, it is presumed, are the remains of the Priory. Two walls of the church are standing: the end wall to the east contains three long windows; the centre window, the loftiest, is near twenty feet high, richly ornamented with mouldings. Beneath the centre window at the east end is a doorway of excellent workmanship, conducting to a small but elegant apartment, which is supposed to have contained the shrine and tomb of St. Oswin." (Fig. 709.)

PERSHORE, a name derived, it is said, from the great number of pear-trees in the vicinity, is delightfully situated on the northern bank of the Avon. The origin of the town is probably to be dated from the foundation of the abbey here in the seventh century, by Oswald, one of the nephews of Ethelbert, King of Mercia. The patrons of the establishment seem to have had some difficulty in making up their minds as to what particular religious community should be permanently settled in it, for at one time we find secular clerks at Pershore, then monks, then seculars (females) again, and lastly, from 984, Benedictine monks. Legend has been busy concerning the early history of Pershore. One Duke Delfere usurped the possessions, and in consequence—so it was

718.—Crypt: St. Peter's, Oxford.

720.—Castleacre Priory, Norfolk.

717.—Dryburgh Abbey.

719.—The Abbey of Rievaulx.

721.—Aspatria.

712.—Christchurch, Hampshire.

722.—Doorway of Barfreston Church, Kent.

723.—Barfreston.

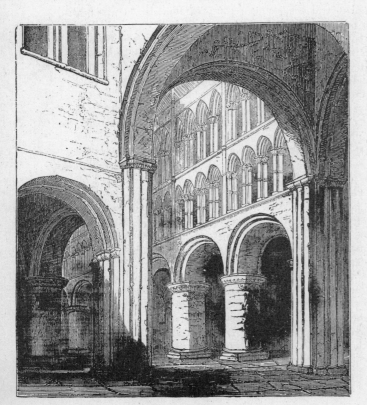

713.—St. John's, Chester.

724.—Iffley.

189

generally believed—died eaten up by vermin. Oddo, another Mercian duke, to whom the estates had passed, was so moved by Delfere's miserable fate, that he not only restored the lands, but made a vow of celibacy, in order that no son of his should ever be guilty of the sacrilege of endeavouring to obtain repossession. There remain of the abbey some vestiges of the monastic buildings, a part of the entrance gateway, and considerable portions of the church, as in the tower, the southern part of the transept, and a chapel, all included in the existing church of the Holy Cross. (Fig. 707.) Near the gateway we have mentioned, stood the small chapel of St. Edburga, to whom the abbey was dedicated. This lady was a daughter of Edward the Elder, and distinguished herself even in her childhood by her scholastic and pious tastes. Her father one day placed before her a New Testament and several other books on one side, and some fine clothes and rich jewels on the other, and desired her to choose. The princess at once took the books. The king, thinking, no doubt, he was bound to obey what he esteemed such decisive tokens of her proper position in life, immediately placed her in a nunnery at Winchester, where she died, and where her bones were preserved for ages after, as invaluable relics.

No one need be surprised at the magnificence of the ancient priory of CHRIST CHURCH, Hampshire (Fig. 712), as that magnificence is attested to the present day by the church, when the circumstances related of the erection are considered. The first establishment of the house is lost in the darkness of antiquity, but in the twelfth century we find Ralph Flambard, that turbulent and oppressive, but able and zealous prelate, busily engaged rebuilding the whole, and obtaining the necessary funds by seizing the revenues of the canons, allowing each of them merely a sufficiency for his subsistence. We may imagine the confusion, the dismay, the uproar, though, unfortunately, no Sydney Smith was then among the oppressed to record their feelings and sentiments as on a somewhat similar occasion in our own time. The Dean, Godric, resisted the bishop with all possible energy, but was, in consequence, degraded from his office, and obliged to seek refuge on the Continent ; and though he was ultimately allowed to return, it was only in a spirit of due obedience to his superior. Flambard, having removed all opposition, levelled the old buildings to the ground, and raised the new ones, of which considerable portions exist to this day : these are to be found in the nave, the south-western aisle, and the northern transept. But let it not be supposed that Flambard obtained all the honours of this mighty work. According to a legend told by the monkish writers, he had supernatural assistance. Whenever the workmen were engaged in their labours, there was observed one workman of whom no one could tell from whence he came, or what he was, except that he exhibited a most extraordinary indefatigability in the business of raising the monastery, and an equally extraordinary liberality in declining to be paid anything for what he had done ; at the times of refreshment, and of settlement of wages, he was ever absent. And so the work progressed, until near completion. One day a large beam was raised to a particular place, and found, unfortunately, to be too short. The interrupted and embarrassed workmen were unable to remedy the defect, and retired to their dwellings for the day. The next morning, when they returned to the church, there was the beam in its right position, longer even than was required. The strange workman immediately occurred to every one's thoughts ; and the general conclusion was, that the Saviour himself had been the supernatural assistant. The dedication of the pile to Christ was in later ages attributed to this circumstance, and hence comes the name of Christ Church. Nay, if there are any persons very anxious about the legend, we believe they may yet find some who will show them in the church what they hold to be the very miraculous beam itself. It is probable that Christ Church was originally founded in the earliest days of Christianity in England, on the site of a heathen temple, the usual mode in which the shrewd missionaries of Rome at once attested the triumph of the new over the old religion, and reconciled the people to the change, by adopting their habitual places of worship. In the course of the last century there was discovered, in the Priory foundations, a cavity about two feet square, that had been covered with a stone cemented into the adjoining pavement, and which contained a large quantity of bones of birds,—herons, bitterns, cocks and hens. Warner, a local antiquarian writer, observes that, among the Romans, "many different species of birds were held in high veneration, and carefully preserved for the purposes of sacrifice and augural divination. Adopting the numerous absurdities of Egyptian and Grecian worship, their tolerating conquerors had affixed a sacredness to the cock, the hawk, the heron, the chicken, and other

birds ; the bones of which, after their decease, were not unfrequently deposited within the walls of the temple of the deity to whom they were considered as peculiarly appropriated." Portions of the Priory yet remain, and a visitor to the neighbourhood occasionally hears of the Convent Garden, now a meadow, of Paradise, the appropriately-named place of recreation for the scholars of Christ Church school, and forming also a relic of the Priory,—of vestiges of fish-ponds and stews. But the church is the only important part of the Priory now existing, which, apart from its architectural characteristics, exhibits many interesting features. Including St. Mary's Chapel at the eastern end, and the Tower at the western, the Church extends to the distance of three hundred and eleven feet. The parts of the building which may be separately distinguished are the Norman remains already noticed, the Porch or principal entrance, and the Tower, with the Great Window nearly thirty feet high. On the under sides of the benches of the stalls, are a series of satirical and grotesque carvings, representing, there can be little doubt, the monkish opinions of the friars. In one is seen a fox with a cock for his clerk, preaching to a set of geese, who are greedily imbibing the doctrines he puts forth. In a second the people are typified by a zany, who, while his back is turned upon his dish of porridge, is saved the trouble of eating it by a rat. A third exhibits a baboon with a cowl on his head, reposing on a pillow, and exhibiting a swollen paunch. From what we know of the origin of the friars, who sprung up to reform the state of idleness and sensuality into which the monks and clergy generally had fallen, one would think the last of these pieces of carved satire must have told much more strongly against its authors than its objects. Another very curious carving is the Altar-piece, which Warner supposes to be coeval with Bishop Flambard. If so, it is one of the most extraordinary things of the kind existing in England. The carving represents the genealogy of Christ, by a tree springing from the loins of Jesse. On each side is a niche, one containing a statue of David, the other Solomon. Above these sit the Virgin with the child Jesus, and Joseph, and surrounded by the Magi. Projecting heads of an ox, and an ass, remind us of the manger, and of the flight to Egypt. Still higher are shepherds with their sheep, the former looking up toward a group of angels, over whom, at the apex of the carving, God extends his protecting arms. Exclusive of all these figures, which are mostly mutilated, there are niches which contained nine others, and there are a host of small figures of saints, thirty-two in number, also in niches, and each bearing his particular emblem or distinguishing mark. The chief individual memories of Christ Church are connected with the noble family of the Montacutes, Earls of Salisbury. By them was the noble Tower at the west end erected in the fifteenth century ; by them were the two small Chantries in the North Transept raised ; by them was the beautiful, but mutilated Chapel—to the north of the altar—left to excite the admiration of visitors to the Church by its beauty, to stir at the same time their deepest sympathies and warmest indignation, as it reminded them of the noble and most unhappy lady whose fate that mutilation may be said to commemorate. The chapel was erected by Margaret, Countess of Salisbury, for her own resting-place, when in due course of nature she should have need of it. But the venerable mother of the eloquent Cardinal Pole, the man who had refused to minister to the depraved appetites of Henry, and subsequently held him up to the scorn and abhorrence of the European world, was not likely to die a peaceful death in England during that monarch's lifetime. In 1538 the chief relatives of the Cardinal, namely Lord Montacute and Sir Geoffrey Pole, his brothers and the Countess, his mother, were suddenly arrested with the Marquis of Exeter and others, on a vague charge of aiding the Cardinal, as the King's enemy ; and Geoffrey, the youngest, having pleaded guilty and made a confession involving the remainder, on a promise that he should be pardoned for so doing, the two noblemen were beheaded on Tower Hill. A month afterwards, on the ground of some alleged discoveries made through the wreck of a French vessel on our shores, fresh arrests took place ; and parliament was instructed to pass bills of attainder against the living mourners of the recent victims of the scaffold,—namely, the Countess of Salisbury, her grandson the child of Lord Montacute, and the widow of the Marquis of Exeter, and with them were associated two knights. The Countess was then seventy years of age, but behaved not the less with so much firmness and presence of mind on her examination before the Earl of Southampton and the Bishop of Ely, that these personages wrote to their employer, Cromwell, saying she was more like a strong and constant man than a woman, and that she denied everything laid to her charge ; and that it seemed to them either that her sons had not made her " privy or participate of the bottom and pit of their stomach, or that she must be the most arrant traitress that ever lived." Some of the Countess's servants were examined, and, no doubt, tampered with; still no sufficient material for a criminal trial was to be obtained. What next? Dismissal to their homes, no doubt, under almost any other English monarch: not so under the rule of the cruel Henry; so a bill for their attainder, without the form of a trial, was obtained from the parliament, which should be considered scarcely less infamous than the King to allow itself, as it did, to be the constant agent of his personal malignity. The two knights were executed; the Marchioness of Exeter was pardoned some months later, and what became of the boy does not appear: but as to the Countess, two years after the high nobility and commons of England had authorized the murders sought at their hands, and when men's minds thought the affair had reached its bloody conclusion at last, the people of England were horrified, those at least whom the never-ceasing wholesale state executions had not entirely brutalized, to hear that the aged Countess had been dragged to the scaffold after all, on the ground of some new provocation given by her son, Cardinal Pole, and that one of the most frightful scenes in English history had taken place on the occasion of the poor lady's death. When told to lay her head on the block, she answered, " No! my head never committed treason; if you will have it, you must take it as you can." The executioner strove to detain her, but she ran swiftly round the scaffold, tossing her head from side to side, while the monsters struck her with their axes, until at last, with her grey hair all dabbled in blood, she was held forcibly to the block, and an end put to her misery. There is, as we have already partly intimated, an appendant to this awful picture to be found in the history of Christ Church. It might have been supposed that even Henry would be glad to let such events pass as soon as possible into oblivion; but his satellites knew him better; so when the commissioners were at work at the time of the Reformation, they took care to tell him, in relation to their visit to Christ Church— " In the church we found a chapel and monument made of Caen stone, prepared by the late mother of Reginald Pole for her burial, which *we have caused to be defaced*, and all the arms and badges clearly to be delete [erased]."

On one side of the tower, at the west end of ST. JOHN'S CHURCH, CHESTER, may be seen the figures of a man and a hind; in that rude pictorial representation we have a record of the origin of the foundation of St. John's, between eleven and twelve centuries ago; when King Ethelred was admonished in a vision that he should erect the sacred pile on a spot where he would see a milk-white hind. When entire, this building was worthy of its kingly founder, having been at once large and magnificent. But one limb after another of the edifice has disappeared, until now there remains little more than the nave of a building that once had its transepts, and choir, and chapels, on the true cathedral scale. And that nave, with its mighty pillars and arches, seems sadly shorn of its dignity by the alterations and fittings up, including wooden galleries, that have taken place to render the church suitable to our modern notions of the accommodation required for a congregation. (Fig. 713.) There are two interesting traditions connected with St. John's. When, according to the monkish writers, Edgar took that famous water excursion of his in a barge on the Dee, rowed by eight kings, it was to the church of St. John that he, taking his station at the helm, personally directed their course, and then returned to his palace. If this story be but of doubtful authenticity, we fear our other will be still less entitled to credence. Giraldus Cambrensis, in reference to the brave but unfortunate Harold, slain at Hastings, says that he " had many wounds and lost his left eye with the stroke of an arrow, and was overcome, and escaped to the county of Chester, and lived there holily, as men troweth, an anchorite's life in Saint James's cell, fast by St. John's Church, and made a good end, as it was known by his last confession." The believers in the existence of Harold at Chester, long after he was supposed to have been killed at Hastings, have been accustomed to show, by way of supporting their views, a small antique-looking building overhanging a high cliff on the south of the churchyard, and known as the Anchorage. Two bodies, deposited in coffin-shaped cavities, have been found in the rock close by—no doubt the bodies of those who have tenanted the Anchorage. But if we would follow the remains to their undoubted resting-place, we must visit WALTHAM ABBEY.

WALTHAM ABBEY, or Holy Cross, is situated on the eastern bank of the river Lea, at the distance of twelve miles and a half from London; the latter name is derived from a holy cross, asserted to have been brought hither by miraculous means during the reign of Canute. Tovi, standard-bearer to Canute, founded here a religious house for two priests, to whose charge the sacred relic was

committed. After the death of Athelstan, the son and successor of Tovi, the estate, it appears, reverted to the crown. The lordship was then given by the monarch (Edward the Confessor) to Harold, on condition that he should build a college, and furnish it with all necessaries, relics, dresses, and ornaments, in memory of Edward and his spouse Editha. Harold in consequence rebuilt the church, increased the number of priests to twelve, one of whom was the governor, under the title of dean, gave it ample endowments, and, so far as the time permitted, made it an excellent school of learning. No less than seventeen manors were granted on this occasion by Harold, and confirmed to the establishment by the charter granted by Edward. Previous to the fatal battle of Hastings, Harold here offered up his vows; and he afterwards was brought here for interment with his two brothers, by their unhappy mother Githa, who with great difficulty obtained Harold's remains from the Conqueror. The canons on Harold's favourite foundation also experienced William's resentment. It is said that he despoiled them of all their moveable wealth; their lands, however, he left nearly entire. Waltham continued a college until 1177, when it was dissolved on the alleged account of the debauchery of the members, by Henry II., and an abbey for regular canons founded in its stead, whose number, according to Farmer, in his 'History of Waltham Abbey,' amounted to twenty-four. The Conqueror's charter was confirmed, as were also various subsequent additional grants, and two new manors were granted.

In 1191 Waltham was made a mitred abbey. Richard I. gave to the abbey the whole manor of Waltham, with great woods, and park called Harold's park, and other lands, as well as the market of Waltham. Henry III. frequently resided here, and, as a mark of his favour, granted the Abbey a fair, to be held annually for seven days. During this reign the church was again solemnly dedicated in the presence of the king and many of the principal nobles. The body of Edward I. was brought here in 1307, with great pomp, where it remained for no less than fifteen weeks, during which time six religious men were chosen weekly from the neighbouring monasteries to attend it night and day. The abbey was surrendered to Henry VIII. at the dissolution, on the 23rd of March, in the thirty-first year of his reign, by Robert Fuller, the last abbot, who had previously made a vain effort to avert the impending ruin by presenting the king with the magnificent seat of Copt Hall. The net annual income at this period was 900*l*. 4*s*. 3*d*.

The only remains of the monastery are, a portion of the conventual church, which now forms the parish church, an entrance gateway and bridge across an arm of the Lea, some vaulted arches forming a kind of dark passage of two divisions, and some broken walls. The church must have been a magnificent specimen of Norman architecture, if it were only from its great size. An idea of the extent may be conveyed by stating that the site of Harold's tomb, which stood either in the east end of the choir or in a chapel beyond, is no less than one hundred and twenty feet distant from the termination of the present edifice. The original church consisted of nave, transept, choir, and chapels. There was also a large tower rising from the intersection of the transept, containing " five great tunable bells." Part of this tower having fallen, the remainder was undermined and blown up, the choir, tower, transept, and east chapel at once demolished. The nave and some adjacent chapels alone remained: the nave, as before stated, with its side aisles, forms the body of the present church. (Figs. 604, 605.) This is about ninety feet in length, and in breadth, including the side aisles, forty-eight feet; it is in the Norman style, with round massive piers dividing the nave from the aisles, semicircular arch, and zigzag enrichments. One of these piers on each side is decorated with spiral and another with very bold and rude zigzag indentations, which, it is supposed, were formerly filled up with brass or other metal. Above the first range of arches, supported on the piers we have mentioned, are two other tiers of arches: those of the second tier corresponding in width with those of the first, but being lower in height; the arches of the third tier are three to each arch of the lower tiers, with a window pierced in the middle one. The roof is modern and plain. At the west end of the church is a heavy square embattled tower, eighty-six feet high, bearing date 1558. From the south side of the church projects the Lady-chapel, now used as a vestry and school-room, under which is a fine arched crypt, " the fairest," says Fuller, who was the incumbent from 1648 to 1658, " I ever saw." Another little chapel, at the south-east end, is now a repository for rubbish. These chapels have some beautiful portions in the decorated English style. The windows in the south aisle have been but little altered. There is a fine wooden screen, bearing the arms of Philip and Mary, and a font, which appears to be very ancient. Near the screen there was

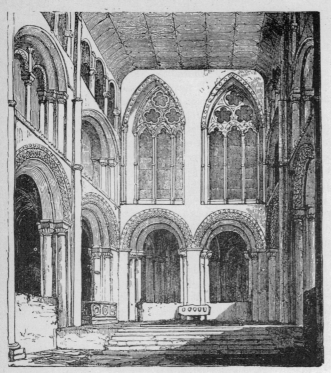

725.—Romsey Abbey.

726.—The Abbey Church, Romsey, Hampshire.

730.—Norman Window.—Castor Church, Northamptonshire.

727.—Doorway, Romsey Abbey, Hants.

731.—Norman Window.—St. Cross.

728.—St. Cross, near Winchester.

729. St. Cross

734.—Stewkley Church, Buckingham...re.

732.—Interior of Holyrood Chapel.

735.—St. Peter's, Northampton.

733. Oxford Cathedral.

736.—Sanctuary, Westminster.—From a sketch by ·Dr. Stukeley, before its destruction in 1775

formerly a painting on glass of Harold; this was destroyed by the Puritans during the reign of Charles I. Farmer observes that the church "is observed by all artists, and the most curious, to stand the exactest east and west of any other in Great Britain." The abbey refectory is reported to have stood eastward of the church, and the stables on the spot now known as the Abbey Farm. The gateway we have mentioned is in a much later style of architecture than the church. Two stone coffins have been found at different periods, each of which was at first thought to be Harold's, but there appears to have been no proof of the correctness of the supposition

Near the abbey mills is a wide space of ground called the Bramblings, but formerly known by the name of Rome-land; owing, it is supposed, to the rents having been appropriated to the see of Rome. On this spot Henry VIII. had a small pleasure-house, which he occasionally occupied in his visits to Waltham. One of these visits led to an important event—the introduction of Cranmer to Henry, and his consequent elevation to influence and authority.

If history were altogether silent on the subject of Verulam, and we knew nothing of the slaughter of its countless thousands of Roman inhabitants by the Britons under Boadicea, and of other scarcely less important events, that show the place to have been one of the most ancient and distinguished of British and Roman towns, a walk through the neighbourhood of its more modern representative, St. Albans, even at the present day, would tell us our footsteps were among the memorials of a mighty people, that we looked upon the site of what must have once been a great and magnificent place. There is no mistaking the character of these huge fragments of wall, or of these gigantic embankments, not unaptly denominated the Verulam Hills, or of the extent of the place both walls and embankments formerly enclosed. Nay, even the very Abbey Church of St. Albans, stamped as it is with an expression of the extremest antiquity in its general style of architecture, tells of something infinitely more ancient, in the heterogeneous materials of which it is built,—tiles, bricks, flints, the débris of Roman Verulam. But if we avail ourselves of the assistance of history, our wonder and admiration are indefinitely enhanced. Before London as yet was, Verulam existed, not only as an important city, but as the seat of a line of princes, the Cassii. After their overthrow, and the complete establishment of the dominion of the masters of the world, Verulam was one of the few places that rejoiced in the honour and advantages attending the elevation to the rank of a municipium or free city. Its wealth, as well as its large population, at the time of the British outburst under Boadicea, is evident from the allusion to it made by Tacitus, who seems to intimate that its riches formed an additional inducement with the Britons to attack it, and from the number of persons—seventy thousand—who are said to have fallen in Verulam, London, and some other less important places. It may be easily supposed that St. Albans must be a rich mine for the antiquary to delve in, though its choicest treasures have probably been already gathered. "Were I to relate," says Camden, "what common report affirms of the many Roman coins, statues of gold and silver, vessels, marble pillars, cornices, and wonderful monuments of ancient art dug up here, I should scarcely be believed." One of the most important discoveries was made some nine centuries ago, during the time of Abbot Eadmer, who having employed men to ransack the ruins, they "tore up the foundations of a great place in the midst of the ancient city; and while they were wondering at the remains of such large buildings, they found in the hollow repository of one wall, as in a small press, among some lesser books and rolls, an unknown volume of one book, which was not mutilated by its long continuance there; and of which neither the letters nor the dialect, from their antiquity, were known to any person who could then be found; but the inscriptions and titles in it shone resplendent in letters of gold. The boards of oak, the strings of silk, in great measure retained their original strength and beauty. When inquiry had been industriously made very far and wide concerning the notices in this book, at last they found one priest, aged and decrepit, a man of great erudition, Unwon by name, who, knowing the dialect and letters of different languages, read the writing of the before-mentioned book, distinctly and openly. In the same manner he read without hesitation, and he explained without difficulty, notices in other books that were found in the same room and within the same press; for the letters were such as used to be written when Verulam was inhabited, and the dialect was that of the ancient Britons then used by them. There were some things in the other books, written in Latin, but these

were not curious; and in the first book, the greater one, of which I have made mention before, he found written 'The History of Saint Alban, the proto-martyr of the English,' which the church at this very day recites and reads; to which that excellent scholar Bede lends his testimony, differing in nothing from it. That book in which the 'History of St. Alban' was contained, was deposited with the greatest regard in the treasury of the abbey; and exactly as the aforesaid presbyter read the book written in the ancient dialect of England or Britain, with which he was well acquainted, Abbot Eadmer caused it to be faithfully and carefully set down by some of the wiser brethren of the convent, and then more fully taught in the public preachings. But when the history was thus made known, as I have said, to several, by being written in Latin, what is wonderful to tell, the primitive and original work fell away in round pieces, and was soon reduced irrecoverably to dust." (Whitaker's 'Ancient Cathedral of Cornwall.') As may be supposed, the name, St. Albans, is derived from the saint, whose history was thus strangely discovered. Alban, or Albanus, was a Roman citizen of Verulam, who, during the dreadful persecution instituted by Dioclesian against the Christians, gave shelter to one of their ministers or priests, named Amphilabus, who had fled to Verulam from Wales. His retreat was unfortunately discovered, and the judge of the city sent soldiers to arrest him; when Albanus, who had received some private intimation of their approach, sent away his guest in safety, and then putting on his habit, presented himself to the soldiers as the man of whom they were in search. By them he was conveyed to the judge; where, throwing off his cloak, and revealing himself, he proceeded to defend the act of heroism he had performed, by one still more heroic,—a bold and unequivocal declaration of his belief in the doctrines of the Cross. Great was the excitement and indignation. At first he was scourged with the utmost severity, in the hope of inducing him to recant; but seeing all efforts ineffectual, he was taken the same day to a neighbouring hill, and there beheaded. Two miracles are related as having occurred at his death. The bridge over the river was so narrow that the multitudes who crowded to see the execution were unable to pass, until Albanus prayed that the waters might be divided and afford a safe passage. This was done; and the executioner, in consequence, refused to perform his office, and was himself condemned to death on account of his scruples. The other miracle has been thus recorded by a poetical writer of the time of James I., in an inscription which was placed below a painted window in the abbey, representing the martyrdom:—

> "This image of our frailty, painted glass,
> Shows where the life and death of Alban was.
> A Knight beheads the martyr, but so soon,
> His eyes dropt out to see what he had done;
> And leaving their own head, seem'd with a tear
> To wail the other head laid mangled there:
> Because, before, his eyes no tears would shed,
> His eyes themselves like tears fall from his head.
> Oh, bloody fact, that whilst St. Alban dies,
> The murderer himself weeps out his eyes."

After the execution, the people of St. Albans had the story of Albanus's disgrace, as they esteemed it, engraved upon marble and inserted in the city walls. Even then, however, no doubt St. Albans was secretly divided against itself; and men were heard still whispering to each other in solitary corners in something like the words of the scientific martyr of a later time—"It moves;" for both Bede and Gildas state that but a very few years later a church was founded, in honour of Alban, on the very spot where he had suffered. And then, too, the public record of his disgrace disappeared from the walls, to give place to the triumphant memorials of the new religion. And in high veneration did the place, afterwards known as St. Albans, remain from that time forward, though it was not till the eighth century that it enjoyed the honours, usually accorded to all such sacred spots, of having a house of religious persons established on it. Offa, the great Mercian king, being then in much trouble of mind as to various incidents of his career, and more particularly as to the murder of Ethelbert, sovereign of the East Angles, determined to set all right by founding a monastery. Then came the question as to the whereabout. After a while, being at Bath, as Matthew Paris, the historian of the abbey, tells us, in the rest and silence of night, he seemed to be accosted by an angel, who instructed him to raise from the earth the ashes of the body of the first British martyr, Alban, and place them in a suitably-ornamented shrine. To Humbert, Archbishop of Lichfield, and Unwona, Bishop of Leicester, his special counsellors, did Offa communicate the particulars of this vision; when the whole three set out to search for the relics. As they approached Verulam, the king saw a light, as of a torch shining over the town, and, as a harbinger of success, gladly was it welcomed. "When the king, the clergy, and the people," continues the historian, "were assembled, they entered on the search with prayer, fasting, and alms, and struck the earth everywhere with intent to hit the spot of burial; but the search had not been continued long when a light from heaven was vouchsafed to assist the discovery, and a ray of fire stood over the place, like the star that conducted the Magi to find the Holy Jesus at Bethlehem. The ground was opened, and, in the presence of Offa, the body of Alban was found." It was then taken in solemn procession to the church before mentioned, which had been erected on the very spot where Alban had been beheaded, and there deposited in a shrine enriched with plates of gold and silver. Offa himself placed a circle of gold, inscribed with Alban's name and title, round the skull. And then was commenced the erection of the monastery around the church; a matter deemed of such vast importance, that Offa made a preliminary visit to Rome to procure the requisite powers and privileges, obtained at no less a cost than the making perpetual the payment of Peter-pence by the English nation (a custom that did last for several centuries), but which previously had been granted by Ina merely for the maintenance of a Saxon college at Rome. On his return to England, a great assembly was held at Verulam, of the nobles and prelates, when it was resolved that the monastery should not only be on a large scale, sufficient, indeed, for the accommodation of one hundred monks, but so amply endowed as to be able to exercise the rites of hospitality to the many travellers who passed through the neighbourhood along the Watling Street in their journeys between London and the North; a gratifying trait of the feelings, as well as an interesting glimpse of the manners of Saxon England. The monks were all carefully selected from the houses most distinguished for the regularity of discipline. The first stone was, of course, laid by Offa, who laboured at the undertaking with a zeal and perseverance that were, considering his position and the many duties it imposed, really extraordinary; and although the buildings were mostly erected in the course of the first four or five years, death found him still busily engaged in his labour of love and piety, rather than of remorse, in which it first originated. A touching story is told concerning his burial. From some unexplained cause, Willegod, the first abbot, seems to have thought it his duty to refuse permission to inter the remains of Offa in the monastery; two months after Offa's death, Willegod himself died, partly through the grief he is said to have felt on account of that refusal. In the history of the subsequent abbots of St. Albans we might find ample materials for an interesting volume; we can, therefore, only attempt to select here and there a passage. During the lifetime of the eleventh abbot, Ælfric, some alarm was felt lest, in the ravages of the Danes, the remains of St. Alban might fall into their unrespecting hands; and in consequence the monks came to a determination which does great credit to their shrewdness, and which led to an incident strikingly illustrative, in various points, of the monkish character. A wooden chest was brought, into which were put the saint's relics, and the costly shrine, into which, we presume, they had been placed by Offa; to these were added some of the most valuable effects of the monastery. The chest, with its precious contents, was then let into a secret cavity in the wall of the church, and securely closed up. A few of the monks only were admitted into the abbot's confidence. This completed one part of the arrangement. Another and very rich-looking chest was now obtained, and the bones of a common monk placed therein with great show of respect. This, with some of the ornaments of the church, and an old ragged cloak, which it was insinuated was the very cloak that Amphilabus had worn, and in which Alban went disguised before the judge, were sent to the monks of Ely to take care of, who received them with undissembled joy. After the alarm had subsided, Ælfric demands his chest and other deposits; but the monks are determined to take such care of them, as never again to let them leave their own walls. Ælfric implores—but they care not; Ælfric threatens, and at last they are somewhat frightened; a schism takes place in the monastery, some insisting upon the return of the martyr's remains, some insisting upon their detention; at last, however, there is a sudden unanimity; they will return the chest, but first open the bottom very subtilly, and replace the relics by others. No sooner, however, does Ælfric examine the chest on its return, than he sees the imposition, and forgetting his own deception in his indignation at the deception of his brethren of Ely, exposes the whole affair, to the sorrow of many a pious spirit, the mirth of many a merry one, and the never-ending annoyance and mortification of the poor monks of the Isle.

If the monastic character, but too often, it is to be feared, was justly chargeable with these little deceptions, it had many excellent qualities by way of counterpoise. The records of the abbey of St. Albans exhibit various instances of noble devotion to the public good. Thus the predecessor of Ælfric, Leofric, son of the Earl of Kent, and afterwards Archbishop of Canterbury, during the prevalence of a grievous famine, first expended for the relief of the people the treasures that had been set apart for the erection of a new church, and then sold the very materials, the slabs of stones, the columns, and the timber that had been dug up for the same purpose from the inexhaustible quarry of the ruins of Verulam. To these also he added the gold and silver vessels that belonged to the church and to his own table. His wise liberality caused much dissension among the monks, but he had his reward in his own inward satisfaction, and in the gratitude of his fellow-men generally, some of whom, the most exalted in rank, warmly supported him. Another abbot, the successor of Ælfric, Leofstan, confessor to the Confessor, cut down the thick groves and woods that covered the Watling Street, and which had become the haunts of wolves, wild boars, stags, and wild bulls (these were among the inhabitants of Old England), as well as of a still more terrible class of ravagers, the human robbers and outlaws who made plunder their trade. And yet a third abbot must be mentioned, Frederic, descended from Saxon royal blood, and with the true current still pouring through his veins. It was his misfortune to be Abbot of St. Albans at the period of the Conquest. William, after the battle of Hastings, had gradually made way to London; but finding his entrance resisted, roamed about the country for some time, doing all the mischief he could, thereby intimating, we presume, to the people, the advantage of quickly coming to a better understanding with such a reckless and potent enemy. On his return towards London, his road lay through St. Albans. As he approached that place, the passage was found to be stopped by masses of great trees that had been felled and drawn across the road. The Abbot of St. Albans was sent for to explain these demonstrations, who, in answer to the king's questions, frankly and fearlessly said, "I have done the duty appertaining to my birth and calling; and if others of my rank and profession had performed the like, as they well could and ought, it had not been in thy power to penetrate into the land so far." Not long after, the same Frederic was at the head of a confederacy, determined, if possible, to compel William to reign like a Saxon prince, that is, according to the ancient laws and customs, or to place England's darling, Edgar Atheling, in his room. William submitted for a time, and, in a great council at Berkhampstead, swore, upon all the relics of the church of St. Albans, that he would keep the laws in question, the oath being administered by Abbot Frederic. In the end, however, the Conqueror grew too strong to be coerced into any measures, however nationally excellent or desirable, and he does not seem to have cared much about oath-breaking, unless indeed it was when he had exacted the oath—the unhappy Harold, for instance, found that no light matter—and so William became more oppressive than ever. St. Albans, as might have been anticipated, suffered especially from his vengeance; he seized all its lands that lay between Barnet and London-stone, and was with difficulty prevented from utterly ruining the monastery. As it was, the blow was enough for Frederic, who died of grief in the monastery of Ely, whither he had been compelled to fly.

We have before had occasion to notice the many able and zealous men whom William introduced into our bishoprics, and abbatial offices, in the place of the Saxon dignitaries, whom he displaced or killed off: St. Albans forms no exception to this general rule. Paul, said by some to be the king's own son, was made abbot, who signalized his rule by a rebuilding of the entire abbey, church included, from the enormous masses of materials that had been previously collected from the Roman city. The "young monks" of the abbey possessed a less gratifying recollection of him. To these "young monks," says Matthew Paris, "who, according to their custom, lived upon pasties of fresh meat, he prevented all inordinate eating," by first stinting them in quantity, and then in substituting kar-pie, or herring-pie, made of "herrings and sheets of cakes." One would have supposed there was no need of stinting the use of that dish. The new church was consecrated by the succeeding abbot, Albany, 1115, when a goodly company were present, including Henry I. and Queen Maud, with a crowd of prelates and nobles, all of whom were for eleven days entertained by the abbey at its own cost. The spiritual connection of St. Cuthbert with the abbey began in this abbot's time, who is said to have enjoyed "a wonderful cure of a withered arm" through the saint's intercession. From the period of the erection of the new church, the abbey gradually began to recover its lost prosperity,

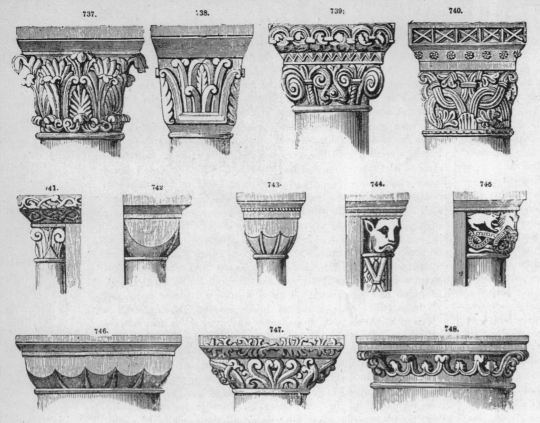

Norman Capitals

737. Jumieges.   738. Sanson-sur-Rille.   739. St. Peter's, Northampton.   740. Steetly, Derbyshire.   741 and 747 St. John's, Chester

742, 743 and 746. Rochester Cathedral.   745. Canterbury.   746. St. Georges de Bocherville.   748. Oxford.

779.—Specimen of Lombardic Architecture.

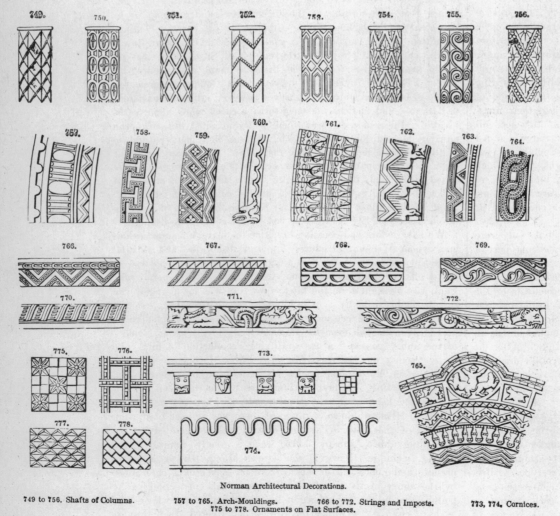

Norman Architectural Decorations.

749 to 756. Shafts of Columns.   757 to 765. Arch-Mouldings.   766 to 772. Strings and Imposts.   773, 774. Cornices.

775 to 778. Ornaments on Flat Surfaces.

780.—Specimens of Lombardic Architecture.

781.—Norman Intersecting Arches, Lincoln.

782.—The Husbandmen. Vision of Henry II.

783.—Costume of the Time of John.

784.—Horse beating a Tabor.

785.—Fishing with a Seine Net.

786.—Horse beating a Tabor.

787.—Bob-Apple.

790.—Costume of Norman-English Ladies in 12th Century.

788.—Horse Baiting.

789.—Water Tournament.

791.—Bird-catching by Clap-net.

792.—Ancient Quintain; now standing at Offham, Kent.

793.—Playing Bears.

794.—Bowling.

197

and to rise to even greater splendour. Abbot Gorham's rule marks perhaps the most important era of this progress. He procured exemption for the abbey from all ecclesiastical jurisdiction other than that of the Pope, a favour obtained through the personal recollections of the latter—Adrian, the Englishman, who then filled the chair of St. Peter, and who had been born at Abbot's Langley. To this was added a grant of precedence; "as St. Alban was distinctly known to be the first martyr of the English nation, so the abbot of his monastery should at all times, among other abbots of the English nation, in degree of dignity be reputed first and principal." Many disputes and heartburnings arose through these privileges: the Bishops of Lincoln were discontented to be deprived of their usual jurisdiction; the abbots of Westminster, of what they seem to have considered their proper seat, the one of highest honour and dignity in parliament. In the second point the Abbots of St. Albans were ultimately defeated through the supineness of one of their number, who was content to be foremost in learning; but in the first they were perfectly successful, the Bishops of London giving up all opposition, after a very marked interference by royalty, during the abbacy of Gaurine. The king happened at the time to be a visitor to the abbey, and thus addressed the astonished prelate: "By the eyes of God, I was present at the agreement. What is it, my lord of Lincoln, that you would attempt? Do you think these things were done in secret? I, myself, and the most chosen men of the realm, were present; and what was then done is ratified by writings the most incontestable, and confirmed by the testimony of the nobles. The determination stands good; and whoever sets himself to combat this abbot and monastery, combats me. What seek you?—to touch the pupil of mine eye?" "By no means, your majesty," we can fancy the astounded prelate replying in a troubled and tremulous voice, and retiring back into perpetual silence on the subject thenceforth.

Literature and the arts appear to have ever found a welcome reception at St. Albans. The most eloquent of the monastic historians, Matthew of Paris, was a monk here, as was also Roger de Wendover, from whom the former transcribed a portion of his history; and William Rishanger, who continued the narration from the point where Matthew ceased. Then again, we read of several scribes and copyists being constantly employed in the monastery in the twelfth century, by Abbot Symond, and of a house having been built expressly for copyists in the fourteenth century. But the most interesting event of a literary nature, connected with the abbey, was the introduction of printing, almost immediately after its first introduction into England by Caxton. The earliest book known to be issued by the great English printer, from an English office, is dated 1474; the first book printed at St. Albans is of the date 1480, in which year no less than three publications appeared. The most remarkable of the St. Albans productions was the curious 'Gentleman's Recreation,' printed here in 1486, and which consists of three treatises, having for their subjects hawking, hunting and fishing, and coat armour; and the principal author or compiler of which was a lady of rank and the head of a religious house, the nunnery of Sopwell, a subordinate establishment to the abbey. It was an interesting fact that two abbeys, those of Westminster and St. Albans, should have been the first English printing-offices; that the new art, one of the first consequences of which was the Reformation and the dissolution of monasteries, should have had monks for its earliest patrons. The arts have fared no less worthily than literature at the hands of the abbots of St. Albans, from the earliest times. Paul, the first Norman abbot, adorned the space behind the high altar of the church with "stately painting." The shrine, made in 1129, by Abbot Gorham, for the relics of St. Alban, had for its artificer Anketill, who had been Mint-master to the King of Denmark, and who, during the construction of the superb work intrusted to him, appears to have grown so much attached to the abbey, that he would not afterwards leave it, but took the cowl and became a member. When the great repair and improvements of the church took place during the rule of Abbot Trumpington, in the thirteenth century, and when, among other beautiful works, St. Cuthbert's Screen was raised, we find, extraordinary as the fact seems and worthy of all admiration, that the chief architects and sculptors were the abbey's own members, namely, its Treasurer, Richard of Thydenhanger; its Keeper of the Seal, Matthew of Cambridge; its Sacrist, Walter de Colchester: as to the last of whom, Matthew Paris says he was at once excellent in painting, sculpture, and carving. Looking at these and the many similar instances already pointed out, and which are probably but so many indications of the multitude of facts of the same kind that have been left unrecorded, it seems hardly possible to overrate the beneficial influence which these religious

establishments of Old England must have had upon the national mind, humanizing, harmonizing, and ennobling it in a thousand ways, apart from any religious merits, and in spite of their many and notorious religious abuses.

All that is necessary to give a reader who has not seen St. Albans a faint glimpse of what it is (and those who have seen it do not need our aid), may be briefly told. With a preliminary reference, therefore, to the engraving (Fig. 606), we may state that its amazing size, the great variety of architectural styles, comprising, we verily believe, every one ever known in England from the days of the Saxons down to the fifteenth century, including the entire rise, prosperity, and fall of the Gothic, and the strange medley of the materials used in the construction, these are the characteristics that first strike every beholder. The building is in the form of a cross, extending from east to west about six hundred feet, and from north to south, along the transepts, more than two hundred feet. A square tower of three stages of stories, with a spire, rises at the intersection. In the interior, the famous screen of St. Cuthbert divides the choir from the nave (Fig. 607); whilst the altar or Wallingford's screen is placed, as its name implies, over the altar, separating the choir from the presbytery: this is one of the most beautiful pieces of stone-work in the country, of the age of Edward IV. Although finished in the time of Abbot Wallingford, it was planned and commenced by Abbot Whethamsted, as his arms upon the screen yet show. Whethamsted was one of the worthies of St. Albans, a most liberal, able, and indefatigable man. During his rule the wars of the Roses were at the height, and we need only mention the names of the two great battles of St. Albans, in one of which Henry VI. was defeated and made prisoner, and in the other was successful, in order to intimate that the Abbot of St. Albans must have had a troubled time of it. This monument is one of the most remarkable in the church; where also, among many other monuments, may be particularly mentioned those of Abbot Ramryge, and of Humphrey, Duke of Gloucester, whose fate we have already alluded to in our pages. St. Alban himself lies in the presbytery, where a stone in the middle of the pavement bears the inscription: "S. Albanus Verolamensis, Anglorum Proto-Martyr, xvii Junii, ccxcvii:" a date that does not exactly agree with the period referred to by the story, 'The Emperor Dioclesian's persecution of the Christians,' which took place in 303.

On the 3rd of February, 1832, a part of the wall of the upper battlement on the south-west side of the abbey fell upon the roof below, in two masses, at an interval of five minutes between the fall of each fragment. The concussion was so great that the inhabitants of the neighbouring houses described it as resembling the loudest thunder; and the detached masses of the wall came down with such force that a large portion of the roof, consisting of lead and heavy timber, was driven into the aisle below. Besides the damage thus occasioned, the abbey generally has been a good deal out of repair for several years. The nave has been restored; but there is still a great deal to be done, which cannot be attempted by local subscription. This is a national work; and a grant from Parliament might be far better employed on such a superb structure —having no revenues of its own—than on many a trumpery edifice —a Buckingham Palace, for example, or a National Gallery—of our own day.

———

Though no monastery at any period, the church and hospital of St. Cross present to this day so much the semblance of a monastery, in the general style of its buildings, and their juxtaposition with the noble church, and in the dress of the members, whom on our visits we see wandering about in the precincts, each in his black cloak, and with a large silver cross on his breast, that with a little exercise of the imagination one may easily fancy the old Catholic times revived, and half anticipate, as we pace silently and thoughtfully along towards the sacred edifice, that we shall hear the masses sung for the souls of some great departed—Henry de Blois, perhaps, King Stephen's brother, who first founded the establishment, or Cardinal Beaufort, who refounded it, and with much greater magnificence. But the place is, in truth, a monument simply of the charity of our forefathers, and we need not look in any part of England for one more worthy of them. The hospital was originally founded for thirteen poor men: these were to reside within its walls, and receive a daily allowance of three and a quarter pounds of bread, a gallon and a half of beer, besides mortrel, an ancient and no doubt very good kind of egg-flip, and besides a quantity of wastel bread, or dainty cakes. Then there was fish in Lent for dinner, flesh at other times, and an excellent supper always provided. But the building here on our left as we enter the first quadrangle, and called Hundred Men's Hall, reminds us that we have not mentioned the whole provision made by the warlike but charitable bishop for the poor. One hundred of the most indigent inhabitants of Winchester were provided with a dinner in that hall every day, and as their respective allowances were more than even the sharpest-set appetites required, they were permitted to take the remainder home with them; it was, in short, a dinner for their families as well as themselves. To both these classes were added the religious and other officials, who comprised a master, steward, four chaplains, thirteen clerks, and seven choristers, all educated in the hospital. This, to our notions, should seem pretty well for one charitable establishment; but Bishop Blois' successor thought he could do better, and so added another hundred poor men to the daily dinner in the halls. Lastly, having sunk through corruptions,—its revenues having been plundered and wasted,—Cardinal Beaufort thought it only dealing in a liberal spirit with the hospital, after William of Wykeham had enforced restitution of the old estates, to do something to raise them still higher in amount than they had ever been, and make the most hospitable of institutions still more hospitable. So thirty-five members were at once added to the thirteen for whom a permanent home and maintenance had been provided; and two priests and three nuns to the religious body, the last to wait upon the sick in the infirmary. And to what has all this dwindled? Here are stately buildings; walks, grass-plots, and flower-borders, all in the trimmest order; lodges for the brethren, each having his three rooms, and some hundred a year to spend in them, in the most comfortable manner, for he may follow a trade or profession in the College, may have his wife and family with him there if he pleases; but how many brethren are there of the forty-eight that were here maintained? Why, some eleven or twelve. Beaufort wished his charity to be called the "Alms House of Noble Poverty;" and it has generally been supposed he meant thereby to aid reduced gentlemen in their lowest estate; the modern and practical reading has been, that the Noble Poverty intended to be benefited was that particular state of pecuniary difficulty which is only evidenced in a non-capability of maintaining faithful old servants at its own expense, and which, therefore, kindly hands them over to the care and expense of the hospital. Let it not also be overlooked that any one who knocks at the porter's gate before the day is "too far spent," may receive a horn of ale and a slice of bread; few, except pleasure-seeking tourists, do come for such a purpose, but we must own, now that the extensive process of feeding two hundred poor men of Winchester daily has been quietly got rid of, it is as well not to mind these bread and ale casualties, which form the only existing vestige of the custom, particularly as they are generally well paid for in gratuities. Of course, in these remarks we refer to no particular persons or time; there is no saying when or how the change was consummated; it has been in process for centuries; but it does stir one's indignation to see the property of the poor, wherever we look, thus silently filched from them. It is but a simple matter of arithmetic to estimate what must have been the value *now* of endowments that four centuries ago supported entirely forty-eight families, and partially two hundred more. The church, we may add, yet remains in many respects as Blois himself left it. It is of the cathedral form, with a huge massive Norman tower at the intersection of the transept by the nave and chancel or choir. (Figs. 728, 729, 731.) The very antiquity, of course, gives interest to the structure; but it possesses features of a higher kind in its architectural characters, which have been deemed of such importance, that Dr. Milner thought the Gothic was actually discovered from the accidental effect produced by some peculiar intersections of circular arches in the chapel or church of St. Cross.

Romsey Church, the chief remain of Romsey Abbey, is generally supposed to have been built by the kings Edward the Elder and Edgar; but the regularity of the plan, no less than the finished character of the workmanship of the building, have induced high authorities, Mr. Britton for instance, to attribute the erection to the latter part of the eleventh or beginning of the twelfth century—the very periods that the records of the abbey have made so full of interest, in connection with its internal affairs. Royally founded—Romsey seems also, through a succession of abbesses, to have been long royally governed. But it is not that circumstance simply that has invested the fine old church and the neighbouring ruins with an attraction even more potent than that of their architecture. We have more than once had occasion to mention the good queen Maud or Matilda, the wife of Henry I.; it was from Romsey Abbey the king took her to become his bride, and under very important circumstances. She had been educated here from her childhood, under the care of the Abbess Christina, her relative, and

cousin to the Confessor, who had evidently cherished in Maud a lofty spirit, well becoming the daughter of the King of Scotland, and a descendant on the mother's side of the great Alfred. As she grew up, many suitors appeared, among them Alan, Earl of Richmond, who died before he could obtain an answer from the king, Rufus; and William de Garenne, Earl of Surrey, who does appear to have obtained an answer and a refusal. When Rufus died, and Henry came to the throne, a new, and what most women would have thought a dazzling, prospect opened upon Maud; the young king himself appeared as her suitor. But the recollections of the bloody field of Hastings, on which had been destroyed the nationality of her country, pressed stronger upon her mind than the personal advantage which might accrue to herself from marrying the son of the Conqueror; so she desired to be permitted to decline the match. But the country and the people she so loved were even more interested than Maud in the success of the proposal. She was told she might restore the ancient honour of England, and be a pledge of reconciliation and friendship between the two races; whilst otherwise their enmity would be everlasting. Maud could not resist that argument, and at last reluctantly consented. But now a new difficulty arose. Many among the Normans, who were not at all desirous of seeing an end put to the state of things that had given them so much power, asserted that Maud was positively a nun; that she had been seen wearing the veil, which made her for ever the spouse of Christ. Maud's explanation is one of those very interesting passages of ancient history which give us a true and most melancholy picture of the state of the people during the first few years after the Conquest. Having denied that she had ever taken the veil, she said, "I must confess that I have sometimes appeared veiled, but listen to the cause: in my first youth, when I was living under her care, my aunt, to save me, as she said, from the lust of the Normans, who attacked all females, was accustomed to throw a piece of black stuff over my head, and when I refused to cover myself with it she treated me very roughly. In her presence I wore that covering, but as soon as she was out of sight I threw it on the ground, and trampled it under my feet in childish anger." The chief ecclesiastics of England in solemn council determined, in effect, that this explanation was sufficient, by declaring Maud free. The marriage accordingly took place, and threw a momentary gleam of sunshine over the hearts of the miserable Saxon people. The history of another abbess suggests less gratifying materials for reflection. It is an old story,—that of human passions stifled, and therefore burning but with greater intensity, within the walls of the cloister, whither the unhappy man or woman has retired, in the hope of obtaining a peace denied them in the world—that peace which passeth all understanding. But old though this story be, it is ever full of instruction, ever sure of sympathy, when we are permitted to throw the veil aside, and see the true being who is hidden beneath. Such cases are necessarily rare, indeed almost confined to those most awful of events in the histories of our monasteries, when, bursting through all the restraints it had voluntarily imposed upon itself, but which force subsequently maintained, the heart of the unhappy recluse has demanded, at any hazard, its restoration to the general heart of humanity, to share again in all the cares and distresses and exacting demands of the world, but also in all the pleasurable enjoyments which are for ever welling up at our feet, even at the most unexpected times, and in the most unanticipated places, when we pursue with steady purpose the path that duty has marked out for us. If it be true that without occasional solitude the best of us may pass through life in ignorance of that which, of all other things, it most concerns us to know—ourselves, it is no less true, that without a participation in all the healthful activities of life, we shall most probably learn nothing either of ourselves or of others: in a word, we may vegetate, but can hardly be said to live. In the records of Romsey we have a glimpse of one of those terrible struggles between human affections and mental aspirations—between the continual beatings of the heart against its cage for liberty, and the chill repressive bonds of custom, aided by the fearful whisperings of the conscience, "This thing that thou desirest, it were wickedness to do." The termination of the struggle, however, was less tragical than such terminations have too often been, probably from the fact that the culprit was at once an abbess and a princess. Mary was the youngest and, at the time of her entering the abbey, only surviving daughter of King Stephen; a circumstance that, taken in connection with her subsequent history, renders it probable there was some extraordinary reason for her assuming the veil. From a simple nun, she was raised to the rank of abbess, on the first vacancy perhaps, but it soon became evident that her affections did not that way tend; the religious world of

795.—Ship-building.

796.—Coiner at Work. From the Capital of a pillar at St. Georges de Bocherville, Normandy.

797.—Corn Sacks and Store-basket.

798.—Chairs. Ancient Chessmen. (Brit. Mus.)

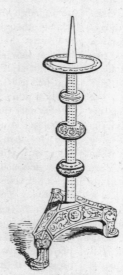

799.—Candlestick.

800.—Ancient Chessmen. (Brit. Mus.)

801.—Reaping and Gleaning.

802.—Corn Hand-mill.

803.—Cradle.

804.—Sarcophagus. Said to be Archbishop Theobald's, Canterbury.

805.—Ornamental Letter of the 12th Century.

806.—Threshing.

200

807.—London Bridge, Southwark side

808.—London Bridge, 1209

809.—Building a House.

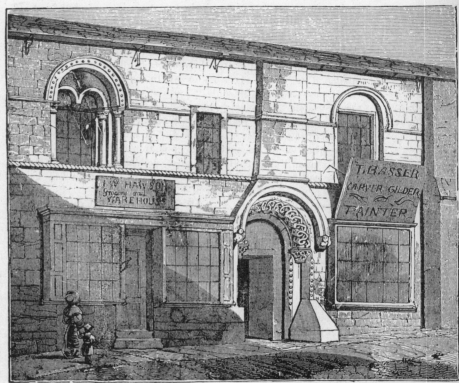

812—Jew's House at Lincoln.

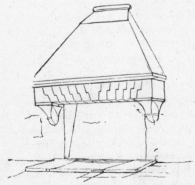

810—Fireplace, Boothby Pagnel, Manor-House

811.—Elevation of a Norman House (Bayeaux Tapestry.)

813.—Fire-bell Gate (and Curfew), Barking, Essex

No. 26.

201

England was suddenly surprised and horrified to hear that the abbess of Romsey had been secretly conveyed to Flanders, and there married to Matthew, son of the earl of that country. To compel her return to the monastery under such circumstances, much less to punish the offender for leaving it, was out of the question; but if the lovers could not be prevented from living together, as they continued to do for no less than ten years, they could be harassed by the incessant interferences and alarmed by the extreme denunciations of the spiritual powers; and these at last seem to have made their union unendurable. So after the long period mentioned, during which two children had been born, the unfortunate abbess was fain to seek a reconciliation with the Church, by consenting to a divorce, and then returning to her monastery. God help her! There needs no record to tell us that she must have had a weary time of it for the remainder of her life. The church is pleasantly as well as commandingly situated, with the green and quiet-looking churchyard of Romsey on this side (Fig. 726), and a pretty little garden on that; here a paved court, once the court of the abbey—there the Sessions Hall, on the site of the monastic buildings, in which the abbess and her nuns and the father confessors once resided. The oldest and most interesting parts of the structure are the chancel, transepts, and eastern part of the nave, which are all of the richest as well as purest Norman style (Figs. 725, 727); the other or western portion was Gothic. In the interior are some memorials of the lady abbesses, and an inscription, charming for its simplicity, "Here lies Sir William Petty;" referring, it is hardly necessary to say, to the well-known and estimable ancestor of the Marquis of Lansdowne. From the top of the towers a delightful view is obtained of the surrounding country; though, until of late years, visitors who ascended to the spot were generally drawn thither to examine Nature on a more limited scale, or, in other words, to admire an apple-tree that had grown upon a small quantity of mould, and there flourished, and put forth its flowers and fruit, regularly as the seasons came, for two or more centuries, and only died at last of sheer old age.

Among the churches of Oxford valuable for their antiquity, the most remarkable is St. Peter's in the East, one of the many relics about which the learned disagree as to their Saxon or Norman origin. It is not certainly known when or by whom it was founded, but it is generally attributed to St. Grimbald, who intended his remains to lie in the crypt (Fig. 718); but the good saint, being nettled by some disputes between him and his scholars, indignantly removed his monumental preparations to Winchester. The crypt designed for that honour remains the most remarkable part of St. Peter's. It has a vaulted roof, and low massive pillars in four ranges, and looks altogether like a subterranean cathedral on a small scale. In the churchyard lies the antiquary Hearne. Aspatria is a long straggling village in Allerdale, below Derwent. The church is dedicated to St. Kentigern, and of rich Norman style. (Fig. 721.) A gigantic skeleton was found in a chest in the neighbourhood; on its left side lay a broadsword, five feet in length; on the right a dirk, a foot and a half in length, the handle studded with silver. Other discoveries have been also made. Barfreston Church is a highly-prized remain of architectural antiquity, seated in a remote and barren part of Kent, on open downs. (Fig. 723.) At the Domesday Survey it formed a part of the vast estates of the Bishop of Bayeux. Subsequently it was attached to the castle at Dover. Its dimensions are unusually narrow, suited to the scanty population of the district. The most interesting part of the structure is the south or principal portal, which, in every point of view, is elaborate and sumptuous, with some extraordinary allegorical sculpture. (Fig. 727.)

Castle Acre Priory, in Norfolk, another invaluable relic of the Early Normans, forms a direct contrast to Barfreston in magnitude, grandeur, and wealth. It was founded in or before 1085, by the first Earl Warren and Surrey, whose favourite residence, of all the one hundred and forty lordships that he received from his father-in-law the Conqueror, was at the castle here. The French monks of Cluni were first introduced into England by this Earl, at the time when foreign priests were overrunning the land, until "neither governor, bishop, nor abbot remained therein of the English nation." At first, Castle Acre Priory was a mere cell to the Cluniac Abbey of Lewes in Sussex, and the rapidity of its growth to an establishment of the first class is rather a remarkable instance of the liberal piety of the stern warriors of old-time. The first, second, and third Earls Warren,—then their successors of the Plantagenet blood, the Earls of Warren and Surrey—and lastly, the Fitzalans, Earls of Arundel and Surrey, successively extended the

endowments, until in 1283 we find the prior in possession of "four hundred and sixty acres of arable land, twenty of pasture, ten of meadow, five water-mills, and fishing liberty 'in pure alms,' besides other lands held by thirty-six tenants, a court baron, two folds, two free boars, and two bulls," while subordinate to Castle Acre were four cells, an hospital, and a priory. A lofty stone wall enclosed this stately establishment, which occupied twenty-nine acres. The arrangement of the interior can be distinctly ascertained; and this is a peculiarity that lends much interest to Castle Acre, of which we shall avail ourselves to give some definite notion of the place in its palmy days, as an illustration of the sort of life led in the larger monasteries of the middle ages, and the accommodations they provided. There were four principal divisions:—the Church, the Cloister, the Prior's Lodge, and the detached offices. A great part of the beautiful west front of the church remains, picturesquely broken. (Fig. 720.) Each side the great entrance was a tower: there was also a central tower, of which the only remain is a tall irregular mass of rocky flint masonry. The pious brethren celebrated two solemn masses daily in the church. A small chapel was attached to each transept, for the use perhaps of the lordly patrons. The Almonry and Sacristy adjoined the north transept, walled from it, and three points seem to have been especially consulted —convenient nearness to the church, remoteness from the more private parts of the monastery, and easy access to the public entrance. The Almonry was for the entertainment of poor mendicants, against whom its doors were never closed. The Cloister was a square of above one hundred feet, separated by a wall from the cemetery. Fancy can readily conjure up the silent, solemn figures of the black monks pacing these dim arched walks with breviary in hand, meditating, or muttering their Latin prayers; or gliding one by one into the Chapter House that stood east of the Cloister— some, perhaps, with the not very agreeable expectation of reproof, or even severe punishment, for some point of discipline neglected, or serious fault committed—and there entering each into his separate cell; and as we can trace eighteen cells on either side, we perceive thirty-six to be the number of inhabitants of the house. The prior and sub-prior occupied distinct stalls at the upper end. Here, as we have intimated, public confession of faults was made and correction administered; for the Cluniac (which was the principal) branch of the Benedictines was exceedingly strict in all discipline. Here the prior consulted with the brethren on the affairs of the abbey, and here the young monks studied singing, being not only required to sing in the choir, but also to chant psalms during their work. Between the refectory and kitchen was a yard or garden for the admission of servants and lay brethren, and which formed *their* place of correction. The meals in the refectory were restricted to one daily, except at certain periods, when two were allowed, and nothing could be eaten on any pretext after evening service. The strictest silence was preserved, signs being substituted for speech. The staple food was bread and wine, and the remnants were immediately distributed to the poor in the almonry. The meal ended, the monks retired into the locutory or parlour, where conversation was allowed. In the dormitory every monk had his bed and his chest in a separate cell, opening into a common passage running through the centre. The scriptorium, for writing, copying, and illuminating manuscripts, and the library, adjoined the parlour; and in the same portion of the establishment were the hall and chambers for the novices, generally mere boys, sent hither for education.

It was to the foreign religious orders introduced into England that we owe whatever intellectual improvement was imported at the Conquest, and none were more useful in that respect than the order of monks domiciled at Castle Acre. They were highly esteemed as learned and holy instructors. The pupils were kept apart from the monks, except in the refectory and parlour. The prior's lodge is now a farm: a ladder long ago displaced a flight of stone steps leading up to the prior's door, by which he was enabled to receive guests of quality, or visitors on business, independent of the Convent. A stone basin for holy water under an arch we believe still remains outside the door, where those performed their ablutions who sought his venerable presence. Two richly-storied windows lighted the fathers' dining-room, which still retains the name, one an oriel of nine panels, on the glass of which was painted the arms of the priory, of the Earls Warren and Arundel, of Mowbray, Duke of Norfolk, and of England and France. The prior's chapel adjoined, and the officiating priest and servants entered it by means of a narrow passage behind the prior's bedroom, in order to avoid passing through his private apartments. He was always a foreigner, appointed by the houses of Cluni in France, so long as they exercised jurisdiction over the English houses of their order, and drew from them heavy tribute. In another of the prior's rooms was the broken portraiture, on the glass of the window, of one of the Earls of Arundel, in armour, with a broadsword, and on his surcoat his arms and the remnant of a legend, " My trust ys."— The porter's lodge is a very good specimen of the flint masonry of Henry VII., and it is a curious circumstance that all the arches, buttresses, and window-frames are of a very hard red brick, burned in the several shapes required. The detached offices consisted of an infirmary for the sick, gatehouse, stables for the monastery and for strangers, malthouse, brewhouse, millhouse, &c. There was also a little detached chapel, placed with kind and prudent thoughtfulness where two highways meet, in order to incite the passing traveller to pray, and at the same time to intercept the casual offerings which might otherwise have been carried to some altar in the parish church farther on.

At the Reformation, Thomas Malling, prior of Castle Acre, and ten of his monks, surrendered the whole to his highness Henry VIII., on account of " certain causes, them their souls and consciences especially moving." The ruins have suffered as much from wanton and mercenary injuries, as from time and storms : almost every house and cottage in the village contiguous contains some undisguised evidence of the plunder of the priory. Still, the ruins are unusually ample and various. Wherever buildings have stood, walls or foundations remain, and prominences of the grass-grown soil mark the proportions and dimensions.

A finer situation for a monastic retreat could hardly be conceived, than that in which RIEVAULX ABBEY has been placed. (Fig. 719.) Probably, as a father's sorrow for his only child—a son, killed by a fall from his horse—was the occasion of the foundation of this abbey, so the choice of a site was influenced by the same feeling, which prompted Sir Walter L'Espee, the founder, to seek relief in the gentle influences of this beautiful scenery, where, in 1131, he allotted a " solitary place in Blakemore " to some Cistercian monks, sent by St. Bernard, abbot of Carival, a most devout man, into England. This " solitary place " was surrounded by steep hills covered with majestic woods. The angles of three valleys were near, with each a rivulet running through them, that passing by where the abbey was built, and being called Rie, the vale of this religious house was called Rieval, and the house the Abbey of Rieval or Rievaulx. William, one of the monks sent by St. Bernard, a man " of great virtue and excellent memory," began the building of the abbey, which was endowed by Sir Walter L'Espee, who, since the loss of his son, caring no longer for wealth, devoted the greater part of his possessions to advance that blessed religion in which he found all his solace. The ruins themselves are noble, and prove the abbey to have been of great extent; but it is the fascinating scenery and the touching circumstances of its foundation that lend the greatest charm to Rievaulx Abbey.

There is little to be said of ST. PETER'S OF NORTHAMPTON ; it is peculiarly one of those beautiful and antique architectural works that must be seen to be appreciated. Anything more curious in most of its details seldom offers. (Fig. 735.) Its situation near the castle leads to the supposition that it owed its rise to one of the first Norman lords of Northampton, probably within fifty years after the Conquest. It was the privilege of this church, that a person " accused of any crime, and intending to clear himself by canonical purgation, should do it here, and in no other place of the town, having first performed his vigils and prayers in the said church the evening before."

STEWKLEY CHURCH is another of the fine old churches the era of whose erection is unknown. (Fig. 734.) Dr. Stukely mentions it as " the oldest and most entire he ever saw, undoubtedly before the Conquest, in the plain ancient manner," &c. But the enthusiastic doctor was never at a loss for a bold decision, whatever he might be as to proofs on which to found it. The shape is a parallelogram, ninety feet by twenty-four. Half the length is allotted to the nave, and one-fourth to the chancel, which is vaulted with stone. In the remaining space, two round arches support a square tower, whose upper part is surrounded with thirty-two small intersecting circular arches attached to the wall. The windows are small ; the mouldings are decorated with zigzag sculpture. It stands in the large village of Stewkley, in Buckinghamshire. It is not unworthy of notice that IFFLEY CHURCH, on the banks of the river Isis, about a mile and a half from Oxford, bears a marked resemblance to the church just mentioned, and belonged to or enjoyed the protection of the same monastery as that with which Stewkley was connected, —the Priory of Kenilworth. It will be a sufficient testimony of its antiquity to say it is known to have been in existence before 1189. (Fig. 724.) The old tower has a commanding aspect, and the sculpture on the western doorway, rude though it be, possesses greater

charms for many an antiquary than works of infinitely greater beauty, in its allegorical character and in its astronomic insignia.

If the old abbey ruins of DRYBURGH, and the many interesting spots in the neighbourhood for miles around, were places especially dear to Scott, how much more must they now be to us, since he has invested them with all the sweet, and lofty, and solemn recollections connected with his own life, and death, and burial among them ! Not a pile of old grey wall, not a crag, or wimpling burn, but has its own peculiar association with the great poet. In one part we behold

> —— those crags, that mountain tower,
> Which charm'd *his* fancy's wakening hour,

where, in the poet's childhood,

> —— was poetic impulse given
> By the green hill and clear blue heaven,

and where he sat whilst the old shepherd knitted stockings, and discoursed most eloquent music, to Scott's ears, of tales and ballads of the border, which lay all about them, so that the shepherd could point out the very scenes of which he spake ; " and thus," as Washington Irving observes, " before Scott could walk, he was made familiar with the scenes of his future stories ; they were all seen as through a magic medium, and took that tinge of romance which they ever after retained in his imagination. From the height of Sandy Knowe he may be said to have had the first look out upon the promised land of his future glory." Then in another part, not far distant, we have Abbotsford itself, that romance in stone and lime ; whilst about midway between these scenes of his earliest and latest days lies Dryburgh, secluded among trees, with the broken gables rising upwards from among and above them. (Fig. 717.) And it is impossible to overlook the singularly appropriate and harmonious conclusion to the poet's life, which his burial here suggests. The ripple of the favourite river that soothed his dying ear murmurs by his grave ; the " misty magnificence " of his own native and beloved skies hangs eternally over him ; its bleak winds whistle and howl through the picturesque Gothic ruins which form his last earthly dwelling-place ; sounds that he ever delighted to revel in, objects that of all others he looked on with the most unfading interest and reverence. Years before his death, he had looked forward to Dryburgh as his place of burial, though the idea was not always suggested to him in a very agreeable manner. Dryburgh, originally a house of Premonstratensian canons, founded in the reign of David I., came in 1786, by purchase, into the hands of the Earl of Buchan, who was proud of the sepulchral relics it contained of Scott's ancestors, and accustomed to boast of the honour he should one day have of adding the minstrel himself to the number—an allusion not at all relished by the object of it. And if ever there was a nation of mourners, it was when that day at last came. " The court-yard and all the precincts of Abbotsford," says Mr. Lockhart, Scott's son-in law and biographer, " were crowded with uncovered spectators as the procession was arranged ; and as it advanced through Dornick and Melrose, and the adjacent villages, the whole population appeared at their doors in like manner, almost all in black. The train of carriages extended, I understand, over more than a mile ; the yeomanry followed in great numbers on horseback, and it was late in the day ere we reached Dryburgh. Some accident, it was observed, had caused the hearse to halt for several minutes on the summit of the hill at Bemerside, exactly where a prospect of remarkable richness opens, and where Sir Walter had always been accustomed to rein up his horse. The day was dark and lowering, and the wind high. The wide enclosure at the Abbey of Dryburgh was thronged with old and young ; and when the coffin was taken from the hearse, and again laid on the shoulders of the afflicted serving-men, one deep sob burst from a thousand lips. Mr. Archdeacon Williams read the Burial Service of the Church of England ; and thus, about half-past five o'clock in the evening of Wednesday, the 26th September, 1832, the remains of Sir Walter Scott were laid by the side of his wife in the sepulchre of his ancestors, ' In sure and certain hope of the resurrection to eternal life, through our Lord Jesus Christ, who shall change our vile body that it may be like unto his glorious body, according to the mighty working whereby he is able to subdue all things to himself.' "

By a not unnatural transition we pass from Dryburgh, so connected with Scott's personal and poetical history, to HOLYROOD and the Canongate in Edinburgh, which he has rendered scarcely less interesting memorials of himself, by making the neighbourhood

814.—Henry III.—From his Tomb in Westminster Abbey.

815.—Great Seal of Henry III.

818.—Ruins of Kenilworth in the 17th Century.

819.—Bridge at Evesham.

816.—Penny of Henry III.

817.—Penny of Edward I.

820.—Edward I.—From a Statue in the Choir of York Minster.

821.—Edward I.

822. - View of Kenilworth Castle from the Gate-House

823.—Great Hall, Kenilworth.

the locality of some of the most stirring and admirable scenes of his prose fictions. "This is the path to Heaven," saith the motto attached to the armorial bearings of the Canongate: alas! too many have found that if it was so, it was in anything but the sense originally intended by the words: it is to be hoped they did find Heaven, but it was Death that, lurking in the palace, opened the door. We have not here, however, to deal with the palace of Holyrood, but the ancient abbey of the same name, founded by David I., and under circumstances truly miraculous, if we may believe Hector Boece, whose account we here abridge and modernize. David, who was crowned king of Scotland at Scone, in 1124, came to visit the Castle of Edinburgh three or four years after. At this time there was about the castle a great forest full of harts and hinds. "Now was the Rood-day coming, called the Exaltation of the Cross, and, because the same was a high solemn day, the king passed to his contemplation. After the masses were done with vast solemnity and reverence, appeared before him many young and insolent barons of Scotland, right desirous to have some pleasure and solace by chace of hounds in the said forest. At this time was with the king a man of singular and devout life, named Alkwine, canon of the order of St. Augustine, who was long time confessor afore to King David in England, the time that he was Earl of Huntingdon and Northumberland." Alkwine used many arguments to dissuade the king from going to the hunt. "Nevertheless, his dissuasion little availed, for the king was finally so provoked, by inopportune solicitation of his barons, that he passed, notwithstanding the solemnity of the day, to his hounds." As the king was coming through the vale that lay to the east from the castle, subsequently named the Canongate, the stag passed through the wood with such din of bugles and horses, and braying of dogs, that "all the beasts were raised from their dens. Now was the king coming to the foot of the crag, and all his nobles severed, here and there, from him, at their game and solace, when suddenly appeared to his sight the fairest hart that ever was seen before with living creature." There seems to have been something awful and mysterious about the appearance and movements of this hart, which frightened King David's horse past control, and it ran away over mire and moss, followed by the strange hart, "so fast that he threw both the king and his horse to the ground. Then the king cast back his hands between the horns of this hart, to have saved him from the stroke thereof," when a miraculous Holy Cross slid into the king's hands, and remained, while the hart fled away with great violence. This occurred "in the same place where now springs the Rood Well." The hunters, affrighted by the accident, gathered about the king from all parts of the wood, to comfort him, and fell on their knees, devoutly adoring the holy cross, which was not a common, but a heavenly piece of workmanship, "for there is no man can show of what matter it is of, metal or tree." Soon after the king returned to his castle, and, in the night following, he was admonished, by a vision in his sleep, to build an abbey of canons regular in the same place where he had been saved by the cross. Alkwine, his confessor, by no means "suspended his good mind," and the king sent his trusty servants to France and Flanders, who "brought right crafty masons to build this abbey," dedicated "in the honour of this holy cross." The cross remained for more than two centuries in the monastery; but when David II., son of Robert Bruce, set out on his expedition against the English, he took the cross with him; and when he was taken prisoner at the battle of Neville's Cross, the cross shared the monarch's fate. It subsequently became an appendage of Durham Cathedral. The abbey to which the cross had belonged received still more direct injury at the hands of the English in later times. When the earl of Hertford (afterwards Protector Somerset) was in Scotland in 1544, he gratified his fanaticism by the ruin of the stately abbey, leaving nothing of all its numerous and beautiful buildings but the body of the church, which became the parish church. This was subsequently made the Chapel Royal: and royally and elegantly it appears to have been fitted up, with its organ, and its stalls for the Knights of the Thistle; but the Presbyterians, scandalized not only at the organ, but at the mass that was performed in the chapel during the reign of the second James, once more destroyed it, at the Revolution. During the excitement the very graves were stripped of their contents; among the rest Darnley's remains were exposed and his skull purloined. His thighbones were of such gigantic size as to confirm the truth of the statements as to his stature, seven feet.

Of the monument in the belfry of Richard, Lord Belhaven, who died in 1639, Burnet relates the following anecdote in his 'History of his own Time:'—Charles I., in the third year of his reign, sent the Earl of Nithsdale into Scotland with a power to take the surrender of all church lands, and to assure those who readily surrendered that the king would take it kindly and use them well, but that he would proceed with all rigour against those who would not submit their rights to his disposal. "Upon his coming down," continues Burnet, "those who were most concerned in such grants met at Edinburgh, and agreed that when they were called together, if no other argument did prevail to make the Earl of Nithsdale resist, they would fall upon him and all his party in the old Scottish manner and knock them on the head. Primrose told me one of these lords, Belhaven, of the house of Douglas, who was blind, bid them set him by one of the party, and he would make sure of one. So he was set next to the Earl of Dumfries: he was all the while holding him fast; and when the other asked him what he meant by that, he said, ever since the blindness was come on him he was in such fear of falling, that he could not help holding fast to those who were next to him. He had all the while a poignard in his other hand, with which he had certainly stabbed Dumfries if any disorder had happened." Of the once magnificent abbey there now only remains the exquisitely-beautiful architectural relic shown in Fig. 732; those clustered columns and arches, and windows and walls, are now the only memorial of that wealthy and potential community, whom King David made the owners of so many priories, and churches, and lands, the enjoyers of privileges of market and borough, the lords of courts of regality, the dispensers of those curious modes of determining guilt or innocence—trial by duel, or by the fire and water ordeal. These ruins alone survive to remind us of the greater ruin of which they form the symbol.

One of the most important events recorded in our annals in connection with the privilege of Sanctuary, furnishes us incidentally with a very striking view of the nature of that privilege, and of the classes of the people who chiefly used or abused it; we refer to the residence of the queen of Edward IV., and her younger son, the Duke of York, in the Sanctuary of Westminster, of which the building shown in page 193 (Fig. 736) formed at once the church below and the place of residence for the sanctuary people above. This remained till 1775, and was then, with great labour and difficulty, on account of the strength of the walls, demolished. Edward died in 1483, and shortly after the queen received intelligence, a little before midnight, in the palace at Westminster, that her eldest son, now Edward V., was in the hands of his uncle Gloucester, and that although he was treated with all seeming reverence, his and her nearest relations and friends had been arrested and sent no man knew whither. In great alarm, the queen suddenly removed to the place where, in a time of former difficulty, when her husband was a fugitive on the seas, she had obtained shelter, and where her eldest son had been born—the neighbouring Sanctuary. The Lord Chancellor (the Archbishop of York) received, by a secret messenger the same night, similar information from Lord Hastings, with the assurance that "all should be well." "Be it as well as it will," observed the startled Chancellor, "it will never be as well as it hath been;" and therewith he called his armed retainers about him, and then taking the Great Seal, hurried with kindly promptitude to the queen. It was a woful picture —that which he beheld on reaching Westminster, the unhappy mother sitting alow on the rushes, all desolate, and dismayed, whilst around her crowds of servants were hurrying into the Sanctuary with chests and packages trussed on their backs, that they had brought from the palace, and in their haste breaking down the wall in one part to make a nearer way. Lord Hastings' message fell even more coldly on the queen's ear than on the archbishop's. "Ah! woe worth him," said she, "he is one of them that laboureth to destroy me and my blood." Having delivered the seal, with a warm protestation of his own fidelity, the archbishop departed to his home; but the first glance of the river at daybreak seems to have cooled his generous enthusiasm. As he looked from his chamber window he beheld the Thames full of the Duke of Gloucester's servants, watching that no man should go to sanctuary, nor any leave it unexamined. He began to think he had been somewhat rash, and so sent for the Seal back. He had done enough, however, to make him a marked man. At the next meeting of the Privy Council, he was sharply reproved, and the Seal taken from him and given to the Bishop of Lincoln. And now arose the question, what was to be done concerning the queen, and her younger son, the Duke. Gloucester, of course, saw from the first that to attain the crown both the princes must be destroyed; one was in his hands, but the other in the most impregnable of strongholds, the Sanctuary. When the council met to debate this matter, Gloucester opened the proceedings in a tone of injured innocence, complaining of the queen's malice against the counsellors of her son, in thus exposing them to the obloquy of the people who would think they were not to be trusted with the guardianship of the king's brother. Then he referred to the lonely position of the king, who, naturally unsatisfied with the company of ancient persons, needed the familiar conversation of those of his own age: and then came the pertinent question,—with whom rather, than his own brother? The speaker continued by observing "that sometimes without little things greater cannot stand;" and in the end advised that a man of credit with all parties should be sent to the queen to remonstrate with her, and if that failed, then to take the child by force, when he should be so well cherished, that all the world should vindicate them and reproach her. The archbishop of York undertook the office of mediator, but spoke strongly and solemnly against the proposed breach of sanctuary, which, he said, had been so long kept, and which had been more than five hundred years before hallowed, at night, by St. Peter in his own person, and accompanied in spirit by great multitudes of angels; and as a proof, the archbishop referred to the Apostle's cope then preserved in the abbey. "And never," observed the archbishop, was there " so undevout a king as durst violate that sacred place, or so holy a bishop as durst presume to consecrate it. God forbid that any man should, for anything earthly, enterprise to break the immunity of that sacred Sanctuary, that hath been the safeguard of many a good man's life, and I trust, with God's grace, we shall not need it. But for what need soever, I would not we should do it. . . . There shall be of my endeavour no lack, if the mother's heart and womanish fear be not the let." The Duke of Buckingham's speech was fiery and bold, to suit Gloucester. Catching up the prelate's words, he exclaimed, "Womanish fear! nay—womanish frowardness! for I dare well take it upon my soul, she well knoweth there is no need of any fear for her son or for herself. For, as for her, there is no man that will be at war with a woman. Would God some of the men of her kin were women too; and then should all be soon in rest. Howbeit there is none of her kin the less loved for that they be of her kin, but for their own evil deserving. And nevertheless, if we love neither her nor her kin, yet there was no cause to think that we should hate the king's noble brother, to whose grace we ourselves be of kin; whose honour, if she as much desired as our dishonour, and as much regard took to his wealth as to her own will, she would be as loth to suffer him from the king as any of us be. For if she have wit (we would God she had as good will as she hath shrewd wit), she reckoneth herself no wiser than she thinketh some that be here, of whose faithful mind she nothing doubteth, but verily believeth and knoweth that she would be as sorry of his harm as herself, and yet would have him from her if she bide there." After some further remarks, the duke favoured the council with his views on the subject of sanctuaries generally, and the passage is one of high interest and value in an historical sense. "And yet will I break no sanctuary; therefore, verily, since the privileges of that place and other like have been of long continued, I am not he that will go about to break them; and in good faith, if they were now to begin, I would not be he that should be about to make them. Yet will I not say nay, but that it is a deed of pity, that such men as the sea or their evil debtors have brought in poverty, should have some place of liberty to keep their bodies out of the danger of their cruel creditors; and also if the crown happen (as it hath done) to come in question, while either part taketh other as traitors, I like well there be some place of refuge for both. But as for thieves, of which these places be full, and which never fall from the craft after they once fall thereunto, it is a pity the Sanctuary should screen them, and much more man-quellers, whom God bade to take from the altar and kill them, if their murder were wilful; and where it is otherwise, there need we not the sanctuaries that God appointed in the old law. For if either necessity, his own defence, or misfortune draweth him to that deed, a pardon serveth, which either the law granteth of course, or the king of pity may. Then look we now how few Sanctuary men there be whom any favourable necessity compel to go thither; and then see, on the other side, what a sort there be commonly therein of them whom wilful unthriftiness have brought to nought. What rabble of thieves, murderers, and malicious heinous traitors, and that in two places especially; the one the elbow of the city [that of Westminster] and the other [St. Martin's-le-Grand] in the very bowels. I dare well avow it, weigh the good that they do with the hurt that cometh of them, and ye shall find it much better to lack both than to have both; and this I say, although they were not abused as they now be, and so long have been, that I fear me ever they will be, while men be afraid to set their hands to amend them; as though God and St. Peter were the patrons of ungracious living. Now unthrifts riot and run in debt upon the boldness of these places; yea, and rich men run thither with poor men's goods, there

they build, there they spend, and bid their creditors go whistle. Men's wives run thither with their husbands' plate, and say they dare not abide with their husbands for beating. Thieves bring thither their stolen goods, and live thereon riotously; there they devise new robberies, and nightly they steal out, they rob and rive, kill, and come in again, as though those places gave them not only a safeguard for the harm they have done, but a licence also to do more." A remarkable conversation here ensued, in which it was agreed on all sides that the goods of a Sanctuary man should be delivered up for the benefit of creditors, as well as stolen goods to the owner; and that Sanctuary should only preserve to the debtor his personal liberty in order to get his living; a striking practical anticipation of the wise and benevolent measure at this very moment before Parliament. Circuitously as the wily speaker advanced towards his mark, he was all the while advancing. having thus prepared the minds of his listeners to listen to reasonable limitations of the privileges of sanctuary, he observed in the concluding part, "If nobody may be taken out of Sanctuary that saith he will bide there, then if a child will take Sanctuary because he feareth to go to school, his master must let it alone; and as simple as the sample is, yet is there less reason in our case than in that; for therein, though it be a childish fear, yet is there at the leastwise some fear, and herein is there none at all. And verily I have often heard of Sanctuary men, but I never heard erst of Sanctuary children." The effect of the speech was tolerably decisive; the Lord Cardinal went to see if he could obtain the child by fair means, though there seems to be no doubt but that, if he failed, the council generally were satisfied of the propriety of taking him by foul ones. The result is but too well known—the child was given up to his uncle, to perish with his brother in the Tower.

The warriors and feudal chiefs of the olden times have left stirring names behind them; we trace their exploits with breathless interest in many a chronicle and many a legend; their memories are a spell; but what has become of the names and the memories of the less noisy workers through the middle ages, the builders of our glorious Gothic cathedrals, the collectors of our libraries, the good Samaritans of the poor, the disseminators of morality and devotion, the healers of the sick, and the benefactors of the common people in a hundred common ways, that are so unobtrusive, they are apt to escape us altogether? Where, for instance, is the record of the monk who first conceived the bold design of throwing a bridge over the deep chasm of the mountain torrent Mynach? If the utility of a design be the best test of its excellence, and the difficulties that must be overcome the most signal evidences of the architect's skill, few men have been better entitled to remembrance; but history, busy with the doings of the illustrious great —which, Heaven knows, have been but too often little enough— had no time to waste on such matters or on such men. And we fear tradition can hardly be received as a satisfactory authority in the present case, since it assigns the enemy of souls as the author of the bridge. (Fig. 714.) The year 1187 has been supposed to be the date of the work, but all is conjecture; the only thing we can with tolerable safety state is, that we must look for its munificent and able builders in the Cistercian Abbey which has left its ruins in the neighbourhood. As a general rule, it should seem that in these early times bridges and roads for the general convenience were works about which few troubled themselves; the people had not been used to such luxuries, for one thing, and then the works involved much labour and little present fame, so they would have been left undone, but that, as usual, the monks, the civilizers, stepped in and did them themselves. The chasm in question was impassable until the bridge was built, which remained, for nearly six hundred years, the only means of communication between the opposite sides. About the middle of the last century there were discovered some symptoms of weakness and decay, when the county (Cardigan) built another bridge over it, leaving the original structure an honourable memorial of the skill and practical benevolence of Old England, and a picturesque addition to this most delightful picturesque of scenes. An interesting description of the falls, and of the romantic scenery around, appeared in the ' Penny Magazine' for 1834, to which we may refer our readers. The ruins of the Cistercian Abbey are still to be seen near Hafod, a place of high reputation for its beauty, and where Johnes, the translator of Froissart, so long resided. Two difficult paths lead down from each end of the bridge to the rocky sides of the chasm, but the direct descent is lower down, nearly under the comfortable inn called the Hafod Arms. From the back windows of this house we look upon the great falls of the Rhydal, situated at the head

224.—Queen Eleanor.—From her Tomb in Westminster Abbey.

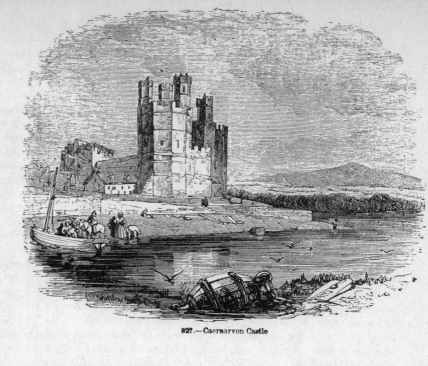

227.—Caernarvon Castle

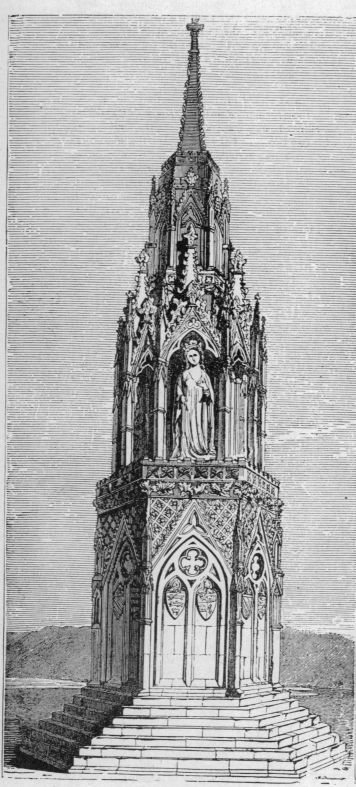

825.—Waltham Cross

228.—Great Seal of Edward I.

829.—Conway Castle.

830.—Beaumaris Castle.

831.—Pembroke Castle.

832.—Harlech Castle.

of a rocky glen ; and we hear, but cannot see, the four falls of the Mynach.

———

A poet,* we regret to say no longer living to enjoy the honours of a reputation as universal as it was well earned, tells, in humorous verse, the story that has made the well of St. Keyne (Fig. 715) popular for many an age among all classes of the people, and which still invests its waters with a certain air of romance, finely harmonizing with their picturesque appearance and position in a little green nook some two miles and a half south of Liskeard.

> A well there is in the west countrie,
>   And a clearer one never was seen ;
> There is not a wife in the west countrie
>   But has heard of the well of St. Keyne.
>
> An oak and an elm tree stand beside,
>   And behind does an ash tree grow,
> And a willow from the bank above
>   Droops to the water below.
>
> A traveller came to the well of St. Keyne,
>   And pleasant it was to his eye,
> For from cockcrow he had been travelling,
>   And there was not a cloud in the sky.
>
> He drank of the waters so cool and clear,
>   For thirsty and hot was he,
> And he sat him down on the grassy bank
>   Under the willow tree.
>
> There came a man from the neighbouring town
>   At the well to fill his pail,
> By the wellside he rested it down
>   And bade the stranger hail.
>
> "Now art thou a bachelor, Stranger?" quoth he,
>   "Or if thou hast a wife,
> The happiest draught thou hast drank this day
>   That ever thou didst in thy life.
>
> "Or has your good woman, if one you have,
>   In Cornwall ever been?
> For, and if she had, I'll venture my life
>   She has drank of the well of St. Keyne."

———

* Robert Southey.

> "I left a good woman who never was here,"
>   The stranger he made reply ;
> "But that my draught should be better for that,
>   I pray thee answer me why?"
>
> "St. Keyne," quoth the countryman, "many a time
>   Drank of this crystal well ;
> And before the angel summon'd her
>   She laid on its waters a spell.
>
> "If the husband of this gifted well
>   Shall drink before his wife,
> A happy man henceforth is he,
>   For he shall be master for life.
>
> "But if the wife should drink of it first,
>   Alas for the husband then—"
> The traveller stoop'd to the well of St. Keyne
>   And drank of its waters again.
>
> "You drank of the waters, I warrant, betimes,"
>   He to the countryman said ;
> But the countryman smiled as the stranger spoke,
>   And sheepishly shook his head.
>
> "I hastened as soon as the wedding was o'er,
>   And left my good wife in the porch ;
> But, faith! she had been wiser than I,
>   For she took a bottle to church."

The pious lady who gave these miraculous virtues to the well, and consequently her name, St. Keyne, appears to have been a virgin of the royal British blood ; her father was Braganus, Prince of Brecknockshire. About the year 490 she came to Mount St. Michael, Cornwall, on a pilgrimage, and there remained so long that her nephew, Cadoc, went to fetch her. The people, however, had grown no less attached to her than she to them, and refused her permission to depart, until, as the poet informs us, an angel summoned her, and of course all parties were bound to obey the mandate. The well of St. Keyne was then endowed with its marvellous properties, in memory of her, and perhaps by way of suggesting a piece of excellent domestic philosophy,—namely, that in the married state to live happily together there must be an acknowledged supremacy ; but whether that attaches to the man or woman, as superior wit and mental characteristics may determine, St. Keyne does not seem to have thought very material, and we are very much disposed to be of the same opinion.

CHAPTER III.—POPULAR ANTIQUITIES.

 HE domestic features of the Anglo-Norman Period cannot be better commenced, perhaps, than by a glance at the most important, our shipping, which then first began to emerge from obscurity. The Saxon had nearly lost the naval arts which King Alfred had taken such pains to advance. The preparations for the Norman Invasion, that employed workmen of all classes in building (Fig. 795) and equipping ships, lasted, we are told, "from early spring all through the summer months;" and when completed, the Normans, Flemings, Frenchmen, and Britaignes, who composed William's host, were conveyed to the English shores in about three thousand vessels, of which six or seven hundred were of considerable size, and the rest small craft or boats. We have an interesting description of the duke's own bark, which led the van, and "sailed faster than all the rest." It had been presented for the occasion by his wife Matilda, an instance of her affectionate zeal in a cause thought just and holy by great numbers, and sanctified by the Pope, whose consecrated banner floated from the vessel's top, with a cross upon it, as a rallying-point for all the religious as well as martial enthusiasm of his forces. Matilda's bark shone conspicuous by day for its splendid decorations, and in the darkness of the night for the brilliant light that burned at the mast-head. It was painted with the three lions of Normandy, its vanes were gilded, its sails of different bright colours, its figure-head—a child sculptured with a drawn bow, the arrow ready to fly against the hostile land. The duke's first care, after disembarking his troops, was to erect defences for the protection of his ships. But this armament was, as it were, got up for the occasion, and must have, in a great measure, disappeared with it,—the merchants no doubt requiring and obtaining the return of their vessels to the more legitimate demands of commerce. William did not live to possess a navy of his own, though he often felt the want of it, and took especial pains to obtain one. Among the wisest of his regulations for the defence of the kingdom, that he had mastered by his resistless energy, was the establishment of the Cinque Ports. Other towns on the coast were also bound to supply ships, and, on emergency, he and his successors scrupled not to seize the whole in the merchant service. The son of the Conqueror showed glimpses of the spirit that should animate a sovereign desiring naval success. On the occasion of news suddenly reaching him of an outbreak in Normandy, he hurried from the chace in the New Forest, and, deaf to the cautious remonstrances of his nobles, galloped to the nearest port, and embarked in the first vessel he found, although it was blowing a gale of wind, and the sailors entreated him to have patience till the storm should abate. "Weigh anchor, hoist sail, and begone!" cried Rufus, with all his great father's scorn of danger: "did you ever hear of a king that was drowned?" The sailors made no answer, put to sea, and landed their royal passenger at Barfleur on the following day. Most of the old historians are of opinion, that the drowning of the nephew of Rufus, Prince William, was a judgment for the presumption of the uncle. Barfleur, where Rufus had landed, was the ill-omened place of Prince William's embarkation, with his French bride, his sister and brother, and a host of gay young nobles. The melancholy shipwreck is well known; but we recur to it for a brief mention of the ill-fated ship and its captain, as characteristic of the manners and sea-life of the period. When all was ready for a short and pleasant expedition to England, which was to include the king, with his numerous retinue, Thomas FitzStephen, a mariner of some repute, presented himself to the king, and, tendering a golden mark, said, "Stephen, son of Evrard, my father, served yours all his life by sea, and he it was who steered the ship in which your father sailed for the conquest of England. Sire king, I beg you to grant me the same office in fief: I have a vessel called the *Blanche-Nef*, well equipped, and manned with fifty skilful mariners." The king could not accept FitzStephen's offer for himself, as he had selected his own vessel, but gave his permission that the "White Ship" and its gallant captain should take charge of the prince and his retinue, amounting, with the crew, to about three hundred persons. The captain had a sailor's pride in the speed of his craft and the qualities of his crew, and though hours passed away before he left the shore, he promised to overtake every ship that had sailed before him. There was feasting and dancing and drinking on deck at the prince's expense, and the men "drank out their wits and reason" before the White Ship started from her moorings, which was not till night. But what cared those joyous young hearts beating with love, and happiness, and pride, with the bright moonlight above them, the wind fair and gentle, and FitzStephen, proud of his charge, at the helm, while every sail was set, and the sturdy mariners plied the oar with the utmost vigour, cheered on by the boyish princes and their companions? The rest is well known. The fate of the fine-spirited captain is worthy of the deepest pity. Swimming among the dying and the dead, he approached two drowning sufferers, and anxiously said—"The king's son, where is he?" "He is gone," was the reply; "neither he, nor his brother, nor his sister, nor any of his company, has appeared above water." "Woe to me!" cried FitzStephen, and then plunged to the bottom. The honour of his art, so deeply concerned in the high trust that had been reposed in him, was more to him in that appalling moment than his own life. The loss of a depraved and heartless prince like William, who gave the worst possible promise for a future king, was of much less real consequence than that of a mariner like FitzStephen.

Henry II. paid great attention to maritime affairs. When he embarked for the conquest of Ireland, he had four hundred vessels with him; some that would be considered even *now* of large size, and one of the "chiefest and newest" capable of carrying four hundred persons. Some time before his death he began expressly to build vessels for the voyage to Palestine; and when his son, Richard I., succeeded, he found these preparations so far advanced, that he was soon able to launch or equip fifty galleys of three tiers of oars, and many other armed galleys, inferior in size to them, but superior to those generally in use. He had also selected transports from the shipping of all his ports; "and there is not much danger in assuming," observes Southey, "that, in size and strength of ships, this was the most formidable naval armament that had as yet appeared in modern Europe." Indeed, an English *royal* navy had begun at last decidedly to grow. Cœur-de-Lion drew up a singular scale of punishments for keeping order among his crews and forces: a murderer was to be lashed to the dead body of his victim, and thrown overboard; or if in port or on shore, buried alive with it. For lesser injuries the offender was to lose his hand, or if there was no bloodshed, suffer so many times ducking over head and ears. Bad language was fined; theft punished by tarring and feathering, of which species of punishment this is the earliest instance on record. When we next read of this custom in connection with the outposts of civilization in the United States it will be only just to remember where it originated. A severer punishment for theft, perhaps when the crime was of an aggravated kind, was to leave the offender on the first land the ship reached, and abandon him to his fate. Richard's fleet sailed from Dartmouth, and being all constructed both to row and to sail, they must have made a gallant show, glittering in every part with the Crusaders' arms, and covered with an endless variety of banners painted on silk. The general form of the galley, of course, must have varied a little through a period of a hundred and forty years. At first it seems to have been long, low, and slender, with two tiers of oars, and a spar or beam of wood, fortified with iron, projecting from the head, for piercing the sides of the enemy. The poop and prows are seen to be very high in Richard's fleet. He had some galleys, shorter and lighter than the rest, for throwing Greek fire, then a favourite mode of destruction both on land and sea. No English or, we may add, European fleet, had ever accomplished so

2 E 2

833.—Ruins of Roslin Castle.

834.—Conway Castle.

835.—Ruins of Roslin Castle and Chapel.

836.—Ruins of Kildrummie Castle.

837.—Dunfermline Abbey, Fife; the Burial-place of Bruce.

838.—Rock of Dumbarton.

839 —Gate betwixt the upper and lower parts of Dumbarton Castle.

840 —Edinburgh Castle.

841.—Prudhoe Castle, Northumberland.

long and difficult a navigation as that attempted by Richard. But the mariners had good faith in St. Nicholas, the guardian of distressed seamen, and it has been said that the beatified Becket also had received special directions to watch over these crusading barks. The first dawning of a stupendous power like that of the present British navy must inspire deep interest, therefore we have particularly dwelt on such glimpses of its progress as the period affords. In the reign of John we find his forces embarked in five hundred vessels, opposed to a French fleet of three times their number, at Damme, then the port of Bruges. This was a memorable encounter, as not only did the French then put forth their first great fleet, but the engagement was the first of all those sanguinary encounters which have since taken place between the two nations. And a melancholy beginning it was for the French. Their navy was annihilated. This victory transported the English with joy, and, of course, was proportionably felt with bitterness by their neighbours. Indeed, the enmity between the two nations scarcely slumbered or slept afterwards. It is said that John, in consequence, had the presumption to claim for England the sovereignty of the seas, and to declare that all who would not strike to the British flag were lawful spoil;—a pretty feature in the man who made the kingdom, as far as he could, a mere fief of Rome.

Next in importance to the shipping come the building arts of the Normans. Many of their extraordinary castles have been already described in this work; they sprang up all over the kingdom to defend the Norman lords in their new territories. The religious edifices which they produced in unexampled profusion, taste, and splendour, lie also beyond our present purpose. But to their house and street architecture, embellishment, and decoration, we must devote a short space. The Norman style of building was a sudden expansion and gradual refinement of the Saxon, and a branch of the Romanesque. Its chief recognisable points are the round-headed arch, generally with ornaments of a plain but decided character; windows narrow and few, simple vaulting, massive arch-piers, few battlements and niches, and no pinnacles. It was, in the main, a stern and unelaborated style, for the evident reason that it had to be adapted to a society living in a state of civil warfare. But it was admirably adapted to this end: its perfect fitness to repel every engine of war then known is evident at a glance; and their construction was so perfect and massive, that they could only be destroyed by extreme violence or many centuries of neglect. It has been observed as rather singular, that among all the imitations, often paltry enough, of modern architects, they should have so seldom attempted the Norman, which contains much that, if duly weighed by some bold inventive genius, might open new paths. Contracted space was an unpleasant feature in Norman residences. Such were the smaller class of country-houses, those numerous dwellings, for instance, built in form of towers—peel-houses, as they were called in the border country between England and Scotland. Sometimes several hundred persons would be kennelled, rather than lodged, in one of these dark and narrow dens. The principal room solely accommodated the lord, who, after banqueting with an uncivilised crowd of martial retainers, and spending the evening listening to the lay of the minstrel, viewing the dancers and jugglers, and laughing at the buffooneries that were practised for his amusement, repaired to his rug bed in the same place, spread on straw on the floor, or on a bench. If a lady shared the rule of the tower, she had also one apartment, for all purposes; and as for the inferior members of the family, including servants and retainers, often a very great number, they spread themselves every night over the lower rooms on a quantity of straw. Such was Anglo-Norman life, with one extensive class. As skilful architects, the Norman builders of course adapted their buildings to the positions they occupied. The peel-houses lay much exposed, hence everything was sacrificed to security, and the light of day could scarcely penetrate the thick and solid walls, through the narrow slits that served for windows. But the dwellings of the nobility and wealthy classes that were more sheltered—as for instance under the protection of some larger fortress, or congregated in a town—were rather lighter less contracted, and more decorated. Specimens of this sort remain in good preservation at Lincoln, which might be designated a Norman city, for it is full of Norman remains, and was at the Norman period a most wealthy, strong, and magnificent place. That remarkable building the Jew's House (Fig. 812) presents a good example of enriched street-architecture of the period. The prevalent custom was to build domestic residences with timber, many remains of which, in immense beams intersecting each other, and of great durability, were within these few years visible in many places in the same ancient city. But the Jew's House, and a few others elsewhere, are of stone. There is another Norman house

in Lincoln deserving especial mention, a mansion, vulgarly designated John of Gaunt's Stables, but it should rather be called his Palace, of which there seems little doubt it formed an important feature. In our day the very numerous rooms in this valuable relic have been turned into repositories for soot, but we can trace the whole arrangement of the interior. Fronting the street we have a round archway that immediately arrests attention, a very fine one of that period. The upper story is gone which contained the chief apartments; the lower is only lighted with loopholes, as usual. We pass under the archway, and, in its sullen shade, dungeon-like portals appear on each side. But the archway admits us to a quadrangle, or square court, round the sides of which are hidden, as it were, the stables, a sort of long, low, vaulted, and pillared hall, and the various offices—all of a gloomy, confined character—that belonged to such an establishment. It has been thought that the idea embodied in such specimens of Norman domestic architecture might be adapted and improved in some of our palaces—that of concealing all the miscellaneous rooms around enclosed court-yards, and placing the principal apartments connectedly on one grand story over the ground-floor; and thus the custom originally prompted by danger, might now be modified to promote that simple dignity and harmonious splendour which are so sadly deficient in many of our public buildings. Another feature of Norman residences was the moveable staircase on the outside of the Norman house (Fig. 811), whose utility, in case of a hostile attack, is obvious. The upper apartments generally had no communication with the lower. Of the Palatial style of the period, William Rufus's Hall at Westminster survives—a splendid monument—and will be noticed more particularly hereafter. The great halls generally were divided into three aisles of two rows of pillars. Previous to the Conquest, the Normans were distinguished by a taste for magnificent buildings, and however the necessities of defence restrained that taste, it broke forth at every possible opportunity. One antique sketch of this time (Fig. 809) shows the whole process of the erection of the important edifices that arose during the more tranquil part of the Anglo-Norman Period. There is the lordly principal, stating probably the dimensions, and giving the architect his own views of the outline and character of the building, while the latter listens, and explains his work, and artificers of different grades are busy at the various executive processes. The number of builders and artificers employed was greater than at any former period, and their skill was much superior. Invention was naturally stimulated under such circumstances. William of Sens, employed as an architect by Lanfranc, Archbishop of Canterbury, constructed a machine for loading and unloading vessels, and for conveying weights by land. One of the most important works of the period, London Bridge (Fig. 808), first constructed of timber, and afterwards of stone, the production of an ecclesiastical architect, will be treated of at length in another place. The gateway to the buildings placed on the bridge (Fig. 807) exhibited a hideous spectacle of blackened and ghastly human heads bristling on spear points; a scene expressive of the worst spirit of war, and strangely at variance with the harmonizing influence of industry and the arts which the Normans cultivated. London at this period possessed neither grandeur nor conveniences, taken on the whole; the common people lived in very poor dwellings, intersected by narrow miry lanes, the whole enclosed by walls. The manor-house of the period presented in many respects a great contrast to one of the present day. Although chimneys, when introduced, resembled the modern (Fig. 810), the coarse habits which existed side by side with magnificent taste and talent, induced the preference of a hearth in the midst of the hall, whence the smoke of wood and turf (for coals were seldom used) ascended to blacken the roof. Fashion partially banished the tapestry from the best rooms, and painted wainscoting was preferred. Ornamental carved furniture (such as the chairs, Fig. 798) enriched the stern and sombre interior of this feudal home. The fabrication of armour gave a lively impulse to the metallic arts, for which the lord had workshops on his estate, and many beautiful articles were produced for church and household display. Candlesticks (Fig. 799) were furnished with a spike at top on which the candle was stuck, sockets being of later contrivance. The coins of this period are of great rarity. Royal mints continued in the chief towns and on the principal estates; and in the reign of Stephen every castle was said to have its mint. There was but one coin, the silver penny (at least no other has come down to us), and the penny was broken into halves and quarters, to form halfpence and farthings. In Fig. 796 we see an Anglo-Norman coiner at work. The dress and implements of many of the rural labourers employed on the different manors, often on the lands held by the monks, who were the greatest improvers of agriculture and gardening, may be understood by a reference to our engravings, which are copied from manuscripts of that time. We have there the ordinary labourers of the soil (Fig. 782), reapers and gleaners (Fig. 801), thrashers (Fig. 806), millers (Fig. 797, 802); and besides these, there were shepherds, neatherds, goatherds, cowherds, swineherds, and keepers of bees. The fisheries (Fig. 785) were productive. In Kent, Sussex, Norfolk, and Suffolk were herring fisheries. Sandwich yielded annually forty thousand herrings to the monks of Christ Church, Canterbury; and in Cheshire and Devonshire there were salmon fisheries. In Cheshire, one fishery paid one thousand salmon annually as rent. The rent of marsh or fen land was generally paid in eels.

Our great woollen manufacture is to be dated from this period. The art of weaving cloth we owe to the Flemings. In 1197 laws were laid down regulating the fabrication and sale of cloth. Linen was also manufactured. The guilds, or incorporated trades, date their origin from this period. The weavers, fullers, and bakers, were the earliest; other trades followed: but the next period is the chief one when these important and peaceful associations were formed. Thus far, their object seemed mutual succour, but it was extended afterwards. Ladies of rank employed themselves in embroidering tunics and veils and girdles for themselves, robes and banners for their knightly husbands and sons, gorgeous vestments for their favourite clergy, storied tapestry for their chosen church. The native English at the Conquest were said to be a rude and illiterate people, but William and his successors loved and favoured learning, which had its chief source with the Arabs that had conquered Spain. This was the golden age of Universities. But attainment rested with the clergy. The common people we do not wonder to find untaught, for that has been generally their fate everywhere, but the nobility were scarcely better. There were two great classes, equally proud and eminent, dividing between them the mastery of the rest. These were the men of the sword and the men of the pen—in other words, the soldiers and the monks. Scholastic logic stood first in the rank of studies, and lorded it over all other. Abstruse learning was indeed followed with such intense zeal as to be fatal to polite literature. Poetry was cast out contemptuously to glee-singers and troubadours; and though rather more respect was paid to music, it was only such as was suited to the choir. The most elegant art practised in the monasteries was the emblazoning of initial letters (Fig. 805) in manuscript books. The scribe usually left blanks for these letters, which were afterwards filled up by artists, who exercised a rich invention in the pattern, and executed them with the aid of gold and silver. As the twelfth century advanced, these manuscript books were often made of prodigious size. The sports of the Norman lords were chiefly hunting and hawking; the English were forbade to use dogs or hawks, and had to resort to gins, snares, and nets (Fig. 791), when they durst follow these sports at all. It was some time before the

Conqueror or his successors permitted the tournament, which might have been dangerous before the two nations became amalgamated; but the noble students of chivalry practised military sports, of which the principal was the quintain, in which the young man tilted with his lance at a shield or Saracen elevated on a pole or spear, past which he rode at full career.

This exercise was imitated by the young men who were not blessed with noble birth; a sand-bag being in that case substituted for a shield or a Saracen, and a quarter-staff for a lance (Fig. 792). To this were added the water-quintain and the water-tournament (Fig. 789), rendered more exciting by the chance of immersion in the river in case of a failing blow. Such pastimes strengthened the muscles and the nerves, and inured a warlike race to take delight in overcoming difficulty, encountering peril, and enduring pain. But if these promoted the courage and agility required in war, others, even for children's enjoyment, stimulated a horrid love of cruelty and bloodshed. Excellent schoolmasters they must have been, whose pupils were in the regular habit of bringing a fighting-cock on the Tuesday of Shrovetide to school, which was turned into a pit for their amusement. And a suitable preparative this was for such manly sports as that of horse-baiting (Fig. 788). There might be less inhumanity, perhaps (though the process of teaching was barbarous enough, no doubt), in the curious feats animals were taught to perform, as that of bear-playing (Fig. 793), and horses beating a war point on a tabor (Figs. 784, 786). But, happily, we have traces that the Norman-English delighted sometimes in sports more innocent: we can fancy them sitting absorbed in the intellectual game of chess (Figs. 798, 800), or enjoying the fresh air, the green grass, the summer sun on the bowling-green (Fig. 794), or bursting with obstreperous laughter by the rustic fireside at the game of bob-apple (Fig. 787). The general time of retiring to rest was at sunset in summer, and eight or nine in winter, when the *couvre feu*, cover fire, or curfew-bell, was rung. The Conqueror, though he did not (as supposed) originate this custom, no doubt employed it as a means of repressing the spirit of the English. In some remote places the curfew still "tolls the knell of parting day," and from towers to which, like that of Barking (Fig. 813), it has lent its name. The dead among the common people were buried without coffins. The Conqueror was thus laid in a shallow grave lined with masonry. When stone coffins were used by the wealthy classes, they were let into the ground no lower than their depth. Gradually they came to be placed entirely above the ground, and then the sides were sculptured. The tomb in the engraving is of this kind (Fig. 804). The costume of the Normans of both sexes was chiefly Oriental, borrowed from the Crusades of this period (Figs. 783, 791). The most remarkable exception was the singular knotted sleeve of the ladies, as shown in Fig. 791.

END OF BOOK II.

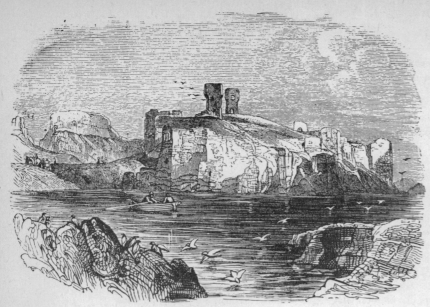

842 — Ruins of the Castle of Dunbar

843. — Stirling Castle.

844. — Lancaster.

845 — Field of the Battle of Chevy Chase (Bird.)

846 — Stirling.

847.—Dunluce Castle.

848.—North Gate, Athlone, Leinster.

849.—View of Stirling Castle.

850.—View of Tantallon Castle, with the Bass Rock in the distance.

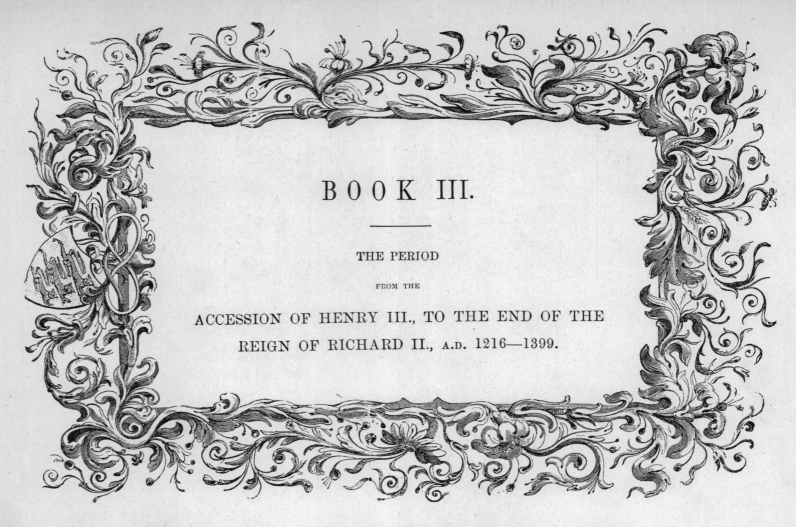

BOOK III.

THE PERIOD

FROM THE

ACCESSION OF HENRY III., TO THE END OF THE

REIGN OF RICHARD II., A.D. 1216—1399.

CHAPTER I.—REGAL AND BARONIAL ANTIQUITIES.

HE circumstances attending the coronation of Henry III. (Figs. 814, 815) in his boyhood might have taught him in his mature years a very different mode of rule from that he adopted, and which led to events almost without parallel for importance in our history: the establishment of something like an equal system of justice, and the rise of the Commons of England, are but two of the great events of the period of which we are now about to treat; both, strange but cheering to say, brought about by the endeavours of Henry III. and his ministers to govern unjustly and arbitrarily, but both, alas! purchased at the sacrifice of much of the best and purest blood of the nation, in all ranks of society. When John died, his son Henry was but in his tenth year. And what a state of confusion surrounded the helpless boy!—Louis the French Dauphin in the land with an army of French troops, and supported by the chief English barons, who had invited him over as their last refuge against John's tyranny. But a great and good man was then living—Pembroke, soon afterwards declared the Protector; who, collecting together at Gloucester the different branches of the royal family, as well as a host of the principal men of both political parties, suddenly appeared among them, and placing the young Henry, with all due honour and ceremony, before the assembled prelates and nobles, said, "Albeit the father of this prince, whom here you see before you, for his evil demeanours hath worthily undergone our persecution, yet this young child, as he is in years tender, so is he pure and innocent from those of his father's doings," and so called upon them to appoint him their king and governor, and drive the French from the land. The assembly received the speech with cordial greeting, and the coronation ceremony was immediately hurried on. The crown had been lost in the Wash, so a plain circlet of gold was used. Pembroke was appointed the royal guardian, and the governor of the kingdom. That appointment saved Henry his throne, and the people of England their nationality. Pembroke, who fully appreciated the motives of the disappointed barons, caused the Magna Charta to be revised and confirmed, with the view of satisfying them, and his character testified to all men that the act was done in good

faith. The result was soon perceptible in the breaking up of the moral strength of the dangerous and unnatural confederacy. Then came the battle, or "Fair," of Lincoln, in 1217, in which the French and English allies were completely overthrown; and when Pembroke, hurrying from the ancient city with its bloody streets the same evening to Stow, was able to assure the trembling boy-king for the first time that he was really lord of England. Pembroke dealt firmly but generously with the allies, and before long Louis had returned to La belle France, and the barons of England were once more united in support of their own monarch. Englishmen could again look on one another without rage or humiliation, again feel what the poet has so nobly expressed:—

> This England never did, nor never shall,
> Lie at the proud foot of a conqueror,
> But when it first did help to wound itself.
> Now these her princes are come home again,
> Come the three corners of the world in arms
> And we shall shock them: Nought shall make us rue,
> If England to itself do rest but true.

Here was matter for reflection for the longest life; a storehouse of facts from whence King Henry might have drawn without difficulty the practical philosophy of restraining his many expensive, and despotic, and nationally-degrading inclinations. Unfortunately, he, like so many of his royal brethren, had learnt nothing by misfortune. That his father failed and suffered in his contest with the people, seemed only a reason why the son should risk similar results. The period of Henry's marriage with Eleanor, daughter of the Count of Provence, seems to mark with tolerable accuracy the period of the commencement of the struggle between him and his subjects. His minister, the Poictevin Bishop, Des Roches, had given him a double course of practical instruction as to how he should rule, although the people and the barons so little appreciated their share in the example, that they compelled Henry, in 1234, to dismiss him, with a whole host of his countrymen, not only from power, but from the island. Henry comforted himself on his marriage by taking Gascons and Provençals into his favour, since they would not let him have Poictevins; and upon them he lavished all possible wealth and honours. The barons remonstrated, and the king, wanting money, promised to behave better. When he next asked for funds, he was told of broken promises, and an oath was exacted. That broken too, the barons became more and more annoying and disrespectful; charged Henry with extravagance, and at last said in the most unmistakable English, they would trust him no longer, and therefore, if he wanted them to give him money, he must allow them to add to the gift a few public officers of their choice, such as the Chief Justiciary, Chancellor, and so on. The king thought he would much rather stretch his prerogative a little over those especially subject to it, in matters of fine, benevolence, and purveyance; rob the Jews, and beg from everybody else; and admirably he did all these things. Even this hardly sufficed, so in 1248 he again met his barons in parliament, to see what they would do for him, but soon left them in disgust; they would provide nothing but lectures upon his past conduct, and advice as to his future; except, indeed, on their own conditions. Some new manœuvres were then tried, which really do great honour to Henry's ingenuity, whatever they may prove as to his baseness and cupidity. The Holy Land had long been a fruitful theme, so a new expedition was talked of, and money obtained from the pious. Then the king began to "invite himself sometimes to this man, and sometimes to that, but nowhere contenting himself with his diet and hospitage, unless both he, his queen, and son Edward, yea, and chief favourites in court, were presented with great and costly gifts, which they took not as of courtesy, but as of due." (Speed.) Of course under such circumstances Henry could retrench his own household, which he did with a free hand. There was no harm, too, in selling the crown plate and jewels, when fresh ones were so attainable. "But who will buy them?" said he to his advisers. "The citizens of London," was the matter-of-course reply. Indeed, appears to have thought the king to himself I must look after these wealthy Londoners; and he did so in good earnest. Among his other freaks, he established a new fair at Westminster, to last for fifteen days during the whole of which time he shut up all the citizens' shops: we need not add that he made a very profitable fair of it for himself. That there were men in England who neither could nor would endure such government was to be expected; but one's admiration is especially warmed to find there were English women who could tell the king plain truths in plain words. The young widowed Countess of Arundel having failed to obtain what she alleged to be hers in equity, thus addressed him before his court: "O, my lord king, why do you turn away from justice? We cannot now obtain that which is right in your court. You are placed as a mean between God and us, but you neither govern us nor yourself, neither dread you to vex the church diversely, as is not only felt in present, but hath been heretofore. Moreover, you doubt not manifoldly to afflict the nobles of the kingdom." Henry listened with a scornful and angry look, and then cried out in a loud voice, "O, my lady countess, what? have the lords of England, because you have tongue at will, made a charter, and hired you to be their orator and advocate?" But the lady had as much wit and presence of mind as courage, and answered, "Not so, my lord; for they have made to me no charter. But that charter which your father made, and yourself confirmed, swearing to keep the same inviolably and constantly, and often extorting money upon the promise that the liberties therein contained should be faithfully observed, you have not kept, but, without regard to conscience or honour, broken. Therefore are you found to be a manifest violator of your faith and oath. For where are the liberties of England, so often fairly engrossed in writing? so often granted? so often bought? I, therefore, though a woman, and all the natural loyal people of the land, appeal against you to the tribunal of the fearful judge," &c. The king was overawed, but of course remained unchanged; and the lady, as Matthew Paris tells us, lost her charges, hopes, and travail. When women thus speak, men must begin to act. A confederacy was soon formed, and the barons "determined to come strong to Oxford at Saint Barnabas-day." According to their agreement they appeared in an imposing body before the king, "exquisitely armed and appointed, that so the king and his aliens should be enforced, if they would not willingly assent." Of course their demand was the old demand—the Charter; but there was a new and very important addendum, that the country should be ruled, according to its provisions, by twenty-four men, to be then and there chosen by the assembly. There was no help for it. William de Valence, indeed, blustered and refused to give up any castle which had been given to him, when he was quietly told the barons would certainly have either his castle or his head. The Poictevins then present, seeing things look so serious, made no more scruple about what they should do, but decamped as fast as they could from Oxford, nor rested till the Channel was between them and the Britons. The leader of the confederated barons was the king's brother-in-law, Simon de Montfort, a Frenchman by the father's side, but in every other respect one of the truest of Englishmen. Before events had

shown Henry the lofty and commanding spirit that his oppressions had raised, he had a kind of prescience of the fact, which is somewhat remarkable. Being one day, in the month of June, in his barge on the Thames, there came on so heavy a storm of rain, thunder, and lightning, that Henry impatiently caused himself to be set down at the nearest mansion, which happened to be Durham House, where the Earl of Leicester then was. De Montfort came forth to meet him, and seeing the king's alarm, observed, "Sir, why are you afraid? the tempest is now past." Henry, looking at the speaker with a troubled and lowering aspect, replied, "I fear thunder and lightning above measure; but, by the head of God, I do more fear thee than all the thunder and lightning of the world." The quiet dignity of the earl's reply was admirable:—"My liege, it is injurious and incredible that you should stand in fear of me, who have always been loyal both to you and your realm, whereas you ought to fear your enemies, such as destroy the realm and abuse you with bad counsels." The war, towards which all things had been long tending, at last broke out. In 1264 there met at Lewes two great armies, the one headed by the king, and his son Prince Edward, who had till recently supported the barons, the other by De Montfort, whose soldiers were directed to wear white crosses on their breasts and backs, to show they fought for justice. The result was a complete triumph for the popular party; the king was taken prisoner in the battle, and the prince yielded himself also to captivity the day after, as a hostage of peace. De Montfort's power was now supreme over England, and though there appears not the smallest proof that he ill-used it, some among his brother nobles grew jealous, especially the Earl of Gloucester. By his contrivance Prince Edward escaped; whose address and energy speedily raised once more a powerful royalist army. Seldom has a general been placed in a more difficult position. His own father was in De Montfort's hands — the feelings of the more enlightened of the people, those resident in the chief towns, were in favour of the "traitors" (a designation easily applied when no other as serviceable can be)—above all, the bravest of England's chivalry were the men who had to be overthrown. Through all Edward's subsequent career, so brilliant in a military sense, there is no event that does more credit to his skill than the strategy by which he succeeded in placing himself between two bodies of the enemy, preventing them from joining each other, or simultaneously attacking him; and then confronting the chief adversary thus shorn of a considerable portion of his strength. There appeared, it seems,

In that black night before this sad and dismal day
Two apparitions strange, as dread heaven would bewray
The horrors to ensue : Oh most amazing sight !
Two armies in the air discerned were to fight,
Which came so near to earth, that in the morn they found
The prints of horses' feet remaining on the ground ;
Which came but as a show, the time to entertain,
Till the angry armies joined to act the bloody scene.

Such, according to the Warwickshire poet Drayton, and the old chroniclers, were the dire portents by which the great battle of Evesham was preceded. The scene of this sanguinary encounter has been thus described in 'William Shakspere, a Biography,' from personal observation :—

"About two miles and a half from Evesham is an elevated point near the village of Twyford, where the Alcester Road is crossed by another track. The Avon is not more than a mile distant on either hand, for, flowing from Offenham to Evesham (Fig. 819), a distance of about three miles, it encircles that town, returning in nearly a parallel direction, about the same distance, to Charlbury. The great road, therefore, passing Alcester to Evesham, continues, after it passes Twyford, through a narrow tongue of land bounded by the Avon, having considerable variety of elevation. Immediately below Twyford is a hollow now called Battlewell, crossing which the road ascends to the elevated platform of Greenhill." It has been remarked by a careful observer that the Battlewell could not have been *in* the scene of action, though so near it. It is now a mere puddle at the bottom of an orchard. The declivity there was on the right wing of Prince Edward's army, and the troops may have used the well for filling their canteens previous to the action, but no part of the fight could have actually occurred on that spot, unless we suppose that Edward's van and centre had both given way, and they had fallen back on their reserve. But we have nothing to bear this out. Edward, early in the day on the 4th of August, 1265, appeared on the heights above Evesham; and it seems most probable that he was never driven from that vantage-ground so far as the hollow of Battlewell. And now, having seen the place of this great strife of armies, we will glance at these armies themselves

851.—Edward II. From the Tomb at Gloucester.

852.—Great Seal of Edward II

853.—Berkeley Castle

854.—Blacklow Hill, near Guy's Cliff

855.—Queen Philippa. From the Tomb in Westminster Abbey.

856.—Effigy of Edward II. Gloucester Cathedral.

857.—Edward III. From the Tomb in Westminster Abbey.

858.—Windsor Castle.

859.—Windsor Castle, temp. Edward III.

860.—Tournament. Knights entering the Lists.

861.—Great Seal of Edward III

862.—Great of Edward III.

864.—Half-Groat of Edward III.

863.—Penny of Edward III.

865.—Edward III. and the Countess of Salisbury

221

on the morning of the eventful day. The young soldier at the head of the royalists, recently escaped from the custody of the veteran whom he is now to oppose, was the prince, burning to revenge his defeat and captivity, and to release his father the king. The great object of his manœuvres was to prevent a junction of the forces under Simon de Montfort and his eldest son. In order to effect this it was necessary to keep the old earl on the right bank of the Severn, with which view he destroyed all the bridges and boats on the river, and secured the fords. But the earl himself was not to be out-manœuvred by his clever young adversary—he managed to cross, and encamped at first near Worcester, hoping hourly that his son would join him. But Simon the younger, though he does not appear to have been deficient in patriotism or courage, was no match for genius in war like Edward. He was surprised near Kenilworth by night, lost his horses and his treasure, and most of his knights, and was compelled to take refuge, almost naked, in the castle there, which was the principal residence of the De Montfort family. This, though as yet he knew it not, was a death-blow to the earl, who, still hoping and expecting with impatience to meet his son, marched on to Evesham. There he waited, but waited in vain. The day before the fatal 4th, no shadow of the truth clouding the confidence he felt in his son, he had solemn masses performed in the Abbey Church, and expressed himself well assured that his son would join him presently, and that Heaven would uphold his cause against a perjured prince. "The next morning he sent his barber Nicholas to the top of the abbey tower to look for the succour that was coming over the hills from Kenilworth. The barber came down with eager gladness, for he saw, a few miles off, the banner of young Simon de Montfort in advance of a mighty host. And again the earl sent the barber to the top of the abbey tower, when the man hastily descended in fear and horror, for the banner of young De Montfort was nowhere to be seen, but, coming nearer and nearer, were seen the standards of Prince Edward, and of Mortimer, and of Gloucester." ('William Shakspere.')

The devotion of the leaders of the popular party to the cause they had espoused, and to each other, now received a noble and touching proof. "While escape was still possible, a generous rivalry led each leader to persuade others to adopt that mode of safety which he rejected for himself. Hugh le Despenser and Ralph Basset, when urged to fly, refused to survive De Montfort, and the great leader himself, when his son Henry affectionately offered to bear the brunt of the battle alone, while his father should preserve his life by flight, steadily answered, 'Far from me be the thought of such a course, my dear son! I have grown old in war, and my life hastens to an end; the noble parentage of my blood has been always notoriously eminent in this one point, never to fly or wish to fly from battle. Nay, my son, do you rather retire from the fearful contest, lest you perish in the flower of your youth; you are now about to succeed (so may God grant) to me, and our illustrious race, in the glories of war.'" ('The Barons' War,' by W. H. Blaauw, Esq., M.A., 1844.)

The danger attending the junction of such powerful personages, the grief and disappointment at the evident discomfiture of his son —fifteen of whose standards were presently raised in exulting mockery in front of the Royalist forces on the Evesham heights, and apprehension for that son's fate, must have altogether sorely tried the earl, who had the further bitterness of reflecting that Gloucester and his powerful father had been with him at the head of the barons, and had deserted him merely out of jealousy of his superior popularity. His greatest friend and counsellor was now armed to crush him. Under all these painful feelings, and seeing not only on the heights before him, but also on either side and in his rear, the heads of columns gradually blocking up every road, he exclaimed at once in despair and admiration, "They have learned from me the art of war." And then, instantly comprehending all that must follow, he is said to have exclaimed, according to one writer, "God have our souls all, our days are all done;" and according to another writer, "Our souls God have, for our bodies be theirs." But, as we have seen, had retreat been allowed him, he was not the man to avail himself of it. Having marshalled his men in the best manner, he spent a short time in prayer, and took the sacrament, as was his wont, before going into battle. Having failed in an attempt to force the road to Kenilworth, he marched out of Evesham at noon to meet the prince on the summit of the hill, having in the midst of his troops the old King Henry, his prisoner, encased in armour which concealed his features, and mounted on a war-horse. As the battle grew more and more desperate, the earl made his last stand in a solid circle on the summit of the hill, and several times repulsed the charges of his foes, whose numbers, as compared with his own, were overwhelming. Gradually the royalists closed around him, attacking at all points. There was but little room, so the slaughter was confined to a small space, and it is fearful to picture to one's self the slow but sure progress of the work of death during that long summer afternoon and evening. Every man, valiant as a lion, resolved neither to give nor take quarter. In one of the charges the imbecile Henry was dismounted and in danger of being slain; but he cried out, "Hold your hand! I am Harry of Winchester," which reaching the ears of the prince, he fought his way to his rescue, and succeeded in carrying him out of the mêlée. At length the barons' forces, wearied by the nature of the ground, which compelled them to be the assailants, and worn out by the determined resistance of the royalists, wavered in their attacks. At the going down of the sun, which they were never more to see setting in that western sky, Leicester himself with his son Henry, and a handful of friends and retainers, were struggling on foot against a host of foes, who were animated by the exhilarating consciousness that the victory was theirs. And now the scene began to close; the earl's horse was killed under him, but De Montfort rose unhurt from the fall, and fought bravely on foot. Hope, however, there was none. It is said, that feeling for the brave youth who fought by his side, his son Henry, and for the few bravest and best of his friends that were left of all his followers, he stooped his great heart to ask the royalists if they gave quarter. "We have no quarter for traitors," was the merciless answer, on which the doomed veteran again exclaimed, "God have mercy upon our souls, our bodies must perish!" and rushed amid his foes with resolute despair. But Mr. Blaauw describes him as answering to those who summoned him to surrender, "Never will I surrender to dogs and perjurers, but to God alone." At last he saw his gallant son Henry fall, his noble adherents were then cut to pieces, and, finally, the veteran chief himself dropped, his sword still in his hand. The prophecy was verified which had been uttered twelve years before by the dying lips of the far-seeing Bishop of Lincoln, Robert Grosteste, whose views of the national abuses were as strong as De Montfort's, and who was one of the most popular reforming spirits of that age, though at his death matters were not so desperate as they grew afterwards. "Oh, my dear son!" cried the venerable old man, laying his hands on the head of De Montfort's son Henry, "you and your father will die on one day, and by the same kind of death, but in the cause of truth and justice." This contemporaneous testimony to the worth of the cause which De Montfort upheld to the last gasp is worth something, for all writers concur in praising Grosteste's clear and vigorous discernment and high rectitude. He was the last man to apply the words truth and justice to treasonable or selfish cabals.

The remnant of the defeated army was pursued to Offenham, a mile and a half from Evesham, where the slaughter was very great, the bridge having been, probably, cut away by the Prince's troops to prevent their retreat. The reservoir now called Battlewell is supposed to have been so choked with dead bodies, as to have remained long useless to the neighbouring peasantry, but this seems questionable. The bloody contest lasted from two in the afternoon till nine at night. No prisoners were taken: of one hundred and eighty barons and knights of De Montfort's party, there was not one knowingly left alive; although some ten or twelve of the knights, who were afterwards found to breathe when the dead were examined, were permitted to live if they could. A more savage, inhuman carnage never disgraced England; or one that inflicted more widely-diffused and permanent sentiments of distress and horror. These sentiments have found undying record in a ballad written at the time in the Anglo-Norman French, which has been thus translated by Mr. George Ellis:—

In song my grief shall find relief;
  Sad is my verse and rude;
I sing in tears our gentle peers
  Who fell for England's good.
Our peace they sought, for us they fought,
  For us they dared to die;
And where they sleep, a mangled heap,
  Their wounds for vengeance cry.
On Evesham's plain is Montfort slain,
  Well skill'd he was to guide;
Where streams his gore shall all deplore:
  Fair England's flower and pride.

Ere Tuesday's sun its course had run
  Our noblest chiefs had bled:
While rush'd to fight each gallant knight,
  Their dastard vassals fled;

Still undismay'd, with trenchant blade
They hew'd their desperate way:
Not strength or skill to Edward's will,
But numbers give the day.
　　　　　On Evesham's plain, &c.

Yet by the blow that laid thee low,
Brave Earl, one palm is given;
Not less at thine than Becket's shrine
Shall rise our vows to Heaven!
Our church and laws, your common cause:
'Twas his the church to save;
Our rights restored, thou, generous lord,
Shalt triumph in thy grave.
　　　　　On Evesham's plain, &c.

Despenser true, the good Sir Hugh,
Our justice and our friend,
Borne down with wrong, amidst the throng
Has met his wretched end.
Sir Henry's fate need I relate,
Or Leicester's gallant son,
Or many a score of barons more,
By Gloucester's hate undone?
　　　　　On Evesham's plain, &c.

Each righteous lord, who brav'd the sword,
And for our safety died,
With conscience pure shall aye endure
The martyr'd saint beside.
That martyr'd saint was never faint
To ease the poor man's care:
With gracious will he shall fulfil
Our just and earnest prayer.
　　　　　On Evesham's plain, &c.

On Montfort's breast a haircloth vest
His pious soul proclaim'd:
With ruffian hand the ruthless band
That sacred emblem stain'd:
And to assuage their impious rage
His lifeless corse defaced,
Whose powerful arm long saved from harm
The realm his virtues graced.
　　　　　On Evesham's plain, &c.

Now all draw near, companions dear,
To Jesus let us pray
That Montfort's heir his grace may share,
And learn to Heaven the way.
No priest I name: none, none I blame,
Nor aught of ill surmise:
Yet for the love of Christ above
I pray, be churchmen wise.
　　　　　On Evesham's plain, &c.

No good, I ween, of late is seen
By earl or baron done;
Nor knight or squire to fame aspire,
Or dare disgrace to shun.
Faith, truth, are fled, and in their stead
Do vice and meanness rule;
E'en on the throne may soon be shown
A flatterer or a fool.
　　　　　On Evesham's plain, &c.

Brave martyr'd chief! no more our grief
For thee or thine shall flow;
Among the blest in Heaven ye rest
From all your toils below.
But for the few, the gallant crew,
Who here in bonds remain,*
Christ condescend their woes to end,
And break the tyrant's chain.
　　　　　On Evesham's plain, &c.

It was a striking evidence of the indestrucibility of the principles for which De Montfort had fought and perished, that even in the hour of full success the king did not dare to revoke the Great Charter; and when he and a parliament held at Winchester passed severe sentences against the family and adherents of De Montfort, he provoked a new resistance, which occupied Prince Edward two years to put down. Kenilworth Castle especially (Figs. 818, 822, 823) resisted all efforts of the besiegers; and at last it became necessary to offer reasonable terms. The "Dictum de Kenilworth" was consequently enacted, and gradually all parties submitted. And thus ended the last armed struggle in England for Magna Charta; which, extra-

* The few knights above mentioned who were found still alive among the bodies of the slain.

ordinary as it may seem, became now for the first time an instrument of the highest practical value; in other words, the people, while appearing to lose everything by the overthrow of Evesham, in reality gained all they had so long struggled for; and their benefactor was the very man who had been their ruthless scourge, King (before Prince) Edward. Henry died on the 15th of November, 1272, and was buried in the beautiful Abbey of Westminster, a portion of which he had recently erected; and as Edward was then in the Holy Land, the Earl of Gloucester and other barons present put their bare hands upon the corpse, and swore fealty to the absent prince. In 1274 Edward returned to England and was crowned. (Figs. 821, 828.) And now, recalling for a moment the recollection of the power of the insurgents even after the battle of Evesham, and the comparatively favourable terms they were able to obtain, we shall understand the impelling motives to that course of legislation and government which Edward thought proper to pursue. We shall see that he had taken home to himself the lesson that had been thrown away upon his father; and was inclined to hazard no more experiments in favour of bad government. The corrupt administration of justice had been perhaps of all others the evil the people most suffered from under the Norman dynasty, and had most desired to get rid of by the Charter. Here is one evidence that their object was at last achieved:—In 1290 Edward caused some of the chief officers of justice to be dismissed from their offices, and fined, after a complete and disgraceful exposure in parliament: the chief justice himself, Sir Thomas Weyland, was among them. All the other officers who were innocent or less guilty were at the same time compelled to swear that from thenceforth they would take no pension, fee, or gift of any man, except only a breakfast or the like present. This was indeed fulfilling Magna Charta. It was this for which in a great measure the barons had appeared in irresistible combination at Runnymede, had conquered at Lewes, had been slaughtered at Evesham. The old trick of state policy, but which unfortunately is, in a practical sense, as new and common as ever, was once more successfully practised,—if reformation could no longer be delayed, the reformers might be, and were, got rid of: and thus did the government satisfy its pride—it no longer at least appeared to be coerced—whilst it could at the same time claim with some show of propriety the people's gratitude for the good it vouchsafed to them. Edward proceeded with the good work he began; though not always without a little gentle pressure being exercised upon him. Thus in 1298, finding dissatisfaction growing, and that among the dissatisfied were such men as Humphry de Bohun, Earl of Hereford and Essex, and Roger Bigod, Earl of Norfolk and Marshal of England, he, among other concessions, again agreed to confirm the Great Charter, and the Charter of Forests, and also that there should be no subsidy nor taxation levied upon the people without the consent of the prelates, peers, and people. And how were the people, it may be asked, to give their consent? The answer to that question involves the most important event that ever occurred in English history,—the rise of the system of borough representation, for which there is every reason to suppose we are indebted to the great man whom most historians have noticed but to misunderstand and calumniate, Simon de Montfort. It was between the two battles of Lewes and Evesham that that nobleman, in calling a parliament, issued the earliest known writs requiring each sheriff of a county to return, together with two knights of the shire, two citizens for each city, and two burgesses for each borough within its limits. In this matter, too, what does King Edward, in his 23rd year, but permanently confirm his antagonist's far-seeing and comprehensive act, so that when he consented that no taxation should be levied without the consent of the people, he used no specious words, there were the people sitting in parliament to give or refuse funds. As an evidence of the gigantic character of this innovation, we may notice the number of members respectively sent to the House during Edward's reign—seventy-six shire representatives, and two hundred and forty-six city and town representatives. Two other illustrations of Edward's conduct as a legislator in carrying out the principles for the maintenance of which he had slaughtered the advocates (we ought not ever to forget that), will not be out of place. In 1305 he sent out an extraordinary commission all over the country to inquire concerning malefactors, of whatever rank, and to administer severe punishments on the spot. There was no longer any trifling with corruption: the king was terribly in earnest. If to all that we have said we now add Sir Matthew Hale's remark by way of summing up, we shall at once do justice to Edward and to those who impelled him into the career, which, when in, he so nobly pursued. Sir Matthew says that more was done in the first thirteen years of his

866.

867.—The Siege of Calais.

868.—Machines used for the Defence of Stone Walls against the action of Battering Rams.

869.—Attack on the Walls of a besieged Town. The cut shows two forms of the Battering Ram in use for making breaches in the fortifications.

870.—Machines used for boring holes in fortified walls, to make openings for the action of the Battering Ram.

871 —Joan of Eltham. From his Tomb in Westminster Abbey.

872.—Genoese Archer, winding up or bending his Cross-bow.

874. —Ancient Gate of Coventry, 1842.

875.—St. George at Dijon.

873.—The Battle of Cressy.

876.—Battle of Poictiers.

No. 29.

reign to settle and establish the distributive justice of the kingdom, than in all the next four centuries. Let us pass to another, less important, but even more interesting, phase of Edward's life—let us look at him in his domestic relations. It is recorded of him that when he received (in Calabria) intelligence of his father's death, and at a period not long after the loss of an infant son, he was so moved that some surprise was expressed that he should grieve more for the loss of his old father than for his own offspring. "The loss of my child," observed Edward, "is a loss which I may hope to repair; but the death of a father is a loss irreparable." The sentiment was at once touching and beautiful, and reveals the same spirit that afterwards bequeathed so sweet a recollection to the world in his conduct as a husband.

If it be true, as one of our poets remarks, that (we quote from memory)

" It is the heart which glorifies this life,"

then was there a glory shining about that of the king of Castile's daughter, Edward's wife Eleanor (Fig. 824), who with lips, as an old writer quaintly observes, "anointed with the virtue of lovely affection," drew the poison from the wound which her husband had received at Acre, in Palestine, from Azazim, a Saracen, of the murderous sect of Assassini : hence our word "assassin." Eleanor gained an immortal memory by this extraordinary example of conjugal affection; but that she did it not for fame, but love, is touchingly evident in the feelings of grief, admiration, and gratitude with which Edward cherished her memory after her death in 1291. She was married to him at Bures in Spain, crowned with him the day of his coronation, lived his wife, "in lovely participation of all his troubles and long voyages" thirty-six years, and died either at Grantham, or at Hardeby, near Grantham in Lincolnshire, as Edward was on his way to Scotland, when he first began to insinuate himself into the affairs of that kingdom. But Edward's passion for ruling and oppressing the Scots succumbed now to a holier feeling. His journey was stopped, he gave all his thoughts to his faithful and devoted partner's remains, which were embalmed, and the internal parts laid in Lincoln Cathedral, the body itself being conveyed to Westminster. A long and melancholy journey the mourning king made with it to the chapel of King Edward the Confessor; and the nation, to whom Eleanor had been a "loving mother," sincerely sympathized in his grief. The mournful procession rested in its progress at Lincoln, Stamford, Dunstable, St. Albans, and Charing, then a village, and some other places, about fifteen in all, at every one of which, when the beloved and noble-hearted woman had passed from mortal view, Edward, to perpetuate the memory of her virtues and his love, erected a beautiful Gothic building in the form denominated a cross. (A view of the Charing Cross is given in Fig. 826.) Of all these, three only now remain; namely, at Geddington, Northampton, and Waltham—of which the last and most beautiful would probably by this time have been also lost, but for the good taste and liberality of the neighbouring gentry and others, who caused it to be restored. Its graceful form and elegant style may be best understood from the engraving (Fig. 825.) No one can look upon it without lamenting the loss of so many of its fellows, not only for their beauty, but for the sake of the events they so beautifully record. If, however, pinnacles and battlements and fretwork fail, there is no danger that the heroic self-sacrifice, the holy love and sorrow, which these crosses commemorate, will ever be forgotten. Would we could linger upon such recollections of the great Edward! for when we leave them, it is to look upon the darker side of the monarch's character, as shown in his Welsh and Scottish wars.

Edward had not so completely established his military fame in the Crusades as to be content to settle down to peace. It was not enough that in Palestine and Italy and France he had lifted the national honour of England—as honour was then understood—from the depths to which it had sunk under his father's rule; it was not enough that all the talk among the delighted people was of Edward and his adventures;—he had a great scheme at heart, in comparison with which all he had yet done were trifles. He saw that before England could mount very high in the scale of nations, the whole of the island of Britain must be essentially one undivided power, instead of three. Leaving foreign conquest, therefore, to his successors, he fixed his powerful will on the accomplishment of this unity. The princes of Wales and Scotland were bound by some indefinable species of feudal vassalage to the English crown, and this he took for the foundation of his advances. A world of misery ensued to the brave people fighting for their independence; we cannot have too much sympathy for them;—nor, on the other hand, too high an appreciation of the essential idea which lay beneath all

Edward's barbarities, if we consider the value of that unity now, when England, Scotland, and Wales are so happily and indissolubly bound together by the only fitting ties, common sympathies and common interests.

It is recorded that one day as Henry II. rode through some part of Wales, attended by a splendid retinue of his English chivalry, he looked with a contemptuous eye on the Welsh gentlemen riding on their rough ponies, and on the poorer sort who were clad in sheep's or goats' skins. A mountaineer approached the great king, and said, with a noble pride, "Thou seest this poor people—but, such as they are, thou shalt never subdue them ;—that is reserved alone for God in his wrath." The mountaineers were, therefore, not likely to yield their mountain fastnesses an easy conquest. For some time a fearful struggle had been going on against certain great barons of England, who had erected regular chains of fortresses in South Wales; but at the critical moment when the fate of the whole country was at stake, the native princes and clans fell at variance amongst themselves. Rees ap-Meredith, Prince of South Wales, and David, brother of the ruler of the northern principality, Llewellyn, joined Edward with their vassals to fight against Llewellyn. Edward had been long intriguing with Llewellyn's subjects, corrupting the chiefs by bribes and promises, and encouraging the prince's enemies; and then, on pretence of Llewellyn's not obeying a summons, as a great vassal of the English crown, to his coronation and parliament at Westminster, though he denied him a safe-conduct thither, had seized as a prisoner Elinor de Montfort, daughter of the great earl who fell at Evesham, the contracted bride of Llewellyn, as she was on her voyage from France to Wales, with Emeric, her young brother. The fiery Welsh prince bitterly complained of these insults done to him in a time of peace, and retaliated by falling on the English on his borders, and demanded hostages, and the liberation of Elinor de Montfort before he would go to court. But Edward did not want him there now. He had procured from his parliament and the Pope sentences of forfeiture and excommunication against the prince, and at midsummer he crossed the Dee with a fine army, took the Castles of Flint and Rhuddlan, drove the prince to the mountains, and there girded him in by land and sea, so that no supplies could reach him. Llewellyn defied cold and hunger and distress for several months, but at last was reduced to accept the hard conditions offered him at Rhuddlan Castle;—that he should pay a fine of fifty thousand pounds, cede his principality as far as the river Conway, and do homage, deliver hostages, and pay annual tribute for the isle of Anglesey, which poor remnant of his possessions was to revert to the English crown if Llewellyn died without male issue. The fine being practically impossible in so poor a country, Edward afterwards remitted it, and Llewellyn was appeased for a time by receiving the hand of his bride in the presence of Edward and Queen Eleanor, and Alexander of Scotland. No heirs arose from this alliance, which circumstance working upon the mind of David, Llewellyn's brother, who had married an English earl's daughter, and some children rising around him, he cursed his own folly, which, besides bringing ruin on his country, had deprived them and himself of the succession of the principality. The bards and peers prophesied that the ancient race should recover their supremacy, and that the Prince of Wales should be crowned king in London. Alas! this prophecy was to be differently realized from what they expected. On the night of Palm Sunday, March 22, 1282, David surprised and took the strong castle of Hawardine, belonging to Roger Clifford—"a right worthy and famous knight," according to the English; "a cruel tyrant," according to the Welsh—and the lord, who was caught in his bed, was wounded and carried off prisoner. A general insurrection extended itself from the Snowdon heights throughout the whole of Wales, but the chief seat was the mountainous tract called Snowdon (the Saxon translation of the Welsh *Creigie 'r Eira*, the Crags of the Eagles), which included all the highlands of Caernarvonshire and Merionethshire, as far east as the river Conway. Never did people make a more gallant stand for independence than the natives of these "crags;" and it would have been impossible to dislodge them, had not their scientific enemy cut down their woods, and opened roads in previously inaccessible places by means of his "thousand" pioneers; and after driving them into the very remotest and wildest fastnesses among the rocks, employed Basques from the Pyrenees, whose method of fighting, and whose general habits and manners, differed little from those of the Welsh people, to hunt them down like bloodhounds. One after another, their entrenched positions were forced, but never without the greatest difficulty and loss. David, whose unnatural treason had been a great cause of the ruin of the country, now joined Llewellyn, evidently with the strongest purpose to redeem his honour; and a fierce but most unequal struggle ensued, in which Edward was twice defeated, and on the last of these occasions obliged to fly for protection to one of his castles. The other mischance thus occurred. It appears that Llewellyn having no ships to oppose to Edward's fleet, the English easily enclosed the coast, and were enabled to take the island of Anglesey. On St. Leonard's day, while Edward was at Aberconway with some Gascon lords and Basques, his soldiers laid down a bridge of boats across the Menai Strait (where the Suspension Bridge now is), and in their impatience to encounter the Welsh on the mainland, crossed before it was finished, and waded through the water when the tide was out. They landed, and busied themselves in reconnoitring some entrenchments of the Welsh, until the tide rolled in, and made deep water between them and the unfinished bridge of boats. The armed Welsh people, who had been watching them stealthily, then rushed down upon them, and drove them into the sea, where, loaded with armour, many sank, and, between the waves and the sword, there perished thirteen knights, seventeen squires, and several hundred foot-soldiers. But what signified a few reverses to Edward? Reinforcements continually crossed the Dee, or came up from the coast, and as a crushing blow, he caused an army to march on the rear of the Welsh through South Wales. False friends, it seems most likely, advised Prince Llewellyn to leave the war in his own principality to the command of his brother David, and advance to meet the new invaders. At Bualth, in the valley of the Wye, the forces of the prince appear to have been suddenly and treacherously withdrawn from him, so that he was left with only a few followers, just as the savage Earl of Mortimer appeared with a body of English on the other side the river, and surprised him before he had time to put on his armour. The prince fell, murdered, as it has been said, rather than slain in battle. His head was sent to the Tower of London, where it was exhibited crowned with willow, in mockery of the Bardic prophecy. And then came a repetition of the policy that we have already commented upon; the Welsh prince got rid of—why, Edward could not do too much for the Welsh people. So he proceeded to institute a series of wise regulations to render them submissive, civilized, and contented, whilst he flattered their well-known pride by adroitly leading them to indulge the delusive hope that his infant son, born among them in Caernarvon Castle (Fig 827), should have the separate government of their country. He strongly fortified the castle just named, as well as Conway Castle (Figs. 829 and 834) and many others,—Beaumaris Castle (Fig. 830) was built later in the reign;—and, to finish his conquest, divided the lands at the foot of Snowdon among his great barons, who gave them to others in fief, when the territory soon became studded over with towers and strongholds for defence, and many a savage feud occurred afterwards between these petty feudal tyrants and the natives. The last of the old princely line, David, held out resolutely six months longer, and then perished, like his brother, by treachery. He and his wife and children were carried in chains to the Castle of Rhuddlan, and condemned, by a parliament at Shrewsbury, first, to be dragged by a horse to the place of execution, because he was a traitor to the king, who had made him a knight; secondly, there to be hanged, because he had murdered several knights in Hawardine Castle; thirdly, to have his hands burned, because he had done the deed on Palm Sunday; fourthly, to be quartered, and have his limbs hung up in different places, because he had conspired the king's death—an atrocious sentence, but fulfilled to the letter. Some years later, the patriots of the border fairly drove the English over the marches; and it cost Edward months of personal hardships and dangers, during a severe winter among the Crags of the Eagles, before his policy and arms united could bring their last champion, Madoc, to surrender. The sacred summits of Snowdon were again invaded, the country wasted with fire and sword, the principal Welsh chiefs consigned to dungeons for life, and the bards, who had contributed so greatly to keep alive the patriotic flame in the people's hearts, massacred—so at least tradition and poetry relate. How finely Gray pictures one of these inspired seers pouring out his vengeful predictions of misery to Edward's line, must be fresh in every one's recollection; yet the passage will bear repetition :—

> Ruin seize thee, ruthless king!
>   Confusion on thy banners wait!
> Though fann'd by Conquest's crimson wing,
>   They mock the air with idle state.
> Helm, nor hauberk's twisted mail,
> Nor e'en thy virtues, Tyrant, shall avail,
> To save thy secret soul from nightly fears,
> From Cambria's curse, from Cambria's tears.

> Such were the sounds that o'er the crested pride
>   Of the first Edward scattered wild dismay,
> As down the steep of Snowdon's shaggy side
>   He wound with toilsome march his long array.

> *   *   *   *

> On a rock whose haughty brow
>   Frowns o'er old Conway's foaming flood,
> Robed in the sable garb of woe,
>   With haggard eyes, the poet stood
> (Loose his beard and hoary hair
> Streamed, like a meteor, to the troubled air),
> And with a master's hand and prophet's fire
> Struck the deep sorrows of his lyre.

The one half of his great design accomplished, Edward, after four years' rest from war, addressed himself, with equally stern, farseeing, and unprincipled policy, to the other. He took his ground, as with Prince Llewellyn, on the homage question. During his father's reign (in the year 1251) this point was mooted, when the young king of Scots, Alexander III., did homage to Henry for his English possessions, and homage was demanded of him also for the kingdom of Scotland. Alexander's reply was singularly intelligent, spirited, and firm for a boy of eleven years of age :—"He had been invited to York to marry the Princess of England, not to treat of affairs of state; and he could not take a step so important without the knowledge and approbation of his parliament." This noble boy two years before had sat at Scone on the "sacred stone of destiny," which stood before the cross at the eastern end of the church; and while there, after the bishop of St. Andrews had knighted and crowned him, a grey-headed Highland bard, stepping forth from the crowd, addressed to him a long genealogical recitation in the Gaelic tongue, beginning, "Hail, Alexander, King of Albion, son of Alexander, son of William, son of David," &c., and thus carried up the royal pedigree through all its generations to the legendary *Gothelus, who married Scota, the daughter of Pharaoh*, and who was therefore the contemporary of Moses. Alexander honoured his lengthy lineage. The daughter of Pharaoh might have been proud of her descendant; for his was the rare praise of making his subjects happy, at least so far as kings can make men so. He was universally beloved; and under his pious and judicious rule, the Scots enjoyed twenty years of quiet, within and without; wealth, arts, and social life progressed; and the designs of Edward on the Scottish independence had no room to expand. But in 1286, as Alexander was riding on a dark night between Kinghorn and Burnt Island, on the northern shore of the Frith of Forth, his horse, on which he had galloped forward from his attendants, stumbled with him over a high cliff, at a place now known as King's Wood End, and he was killed on the spot. This fatal event extinguished for a long period the prosperity of Scotland. Three promising children of Alexander had died before him. One had left a daughter, Margaret, who was now scarce four years old, under the charge of her father Eric, King of Norway. Margaret had been distinctly appointed by her grandfather, in 1284, to succeed him on the throne of Scotland failing other issue; but this settlement was new, and distasteful to warlike men, who would scarcely submit to a manly sovereign, much less to a feeble girl; but the difficulty and danger of the question, who was to succeed, if she did not, as well as respect to the niece of Alexander, might have kept the majority of the chiefs on her side, had she not fallen sick and died, as she was on her passage to England, where she was to have stayed until good order was re-established in Scotland. Edward and the estates of Scotland were both desirous to have married her to Edward's eldest son, which would have united the sceptres of England and Scotland pacifically and effectually, and so accomplished Edward's design without any of the miseries that followed the early death of the "maid of Norway." A fierce controversy commenced who should succeed to the throne, thus left vacant by the extinction of the line of William the Lion; which, though it had included ten related households, had been entirely swept away in a single century. The descendants of the brother of William the Lion, David, Earl of Huntingdon, were now the nearest heirs—John Baliol and Robert Bruce. In hopes, it seems, that Edward would act as a just umpire for the conflicting estates of Scotland in this weighty business, they met him at Norham, on the English side the Tweed, in May, 1291; when those who had not been previously prepared for the divulging of Edward's mind, were stricken aghast to find that, preparatory to proceeding with the conference, he must be recognised as Lord Paramount of Scotland, and fealty must be sworn to him. There was a dead silence—broken by one voice venturing to say that while the throne was vacant, no answer could be given. "By holy Edward! whose crown I wear," the king sternly exclaimed, "I

2 G 2

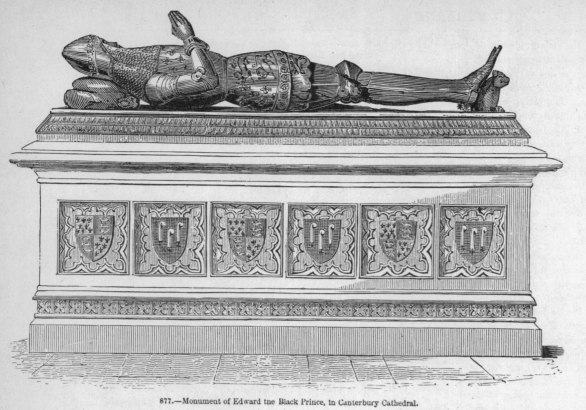

877.—Monument of Edward the Black Prince, in Canterbury Cathedral.

878.—Ordeal Combat or Duel. (Royal MS. 14 E. iii.)

879—Knights Combating. (Royal MS. 14 E. iii)

881.—St. Mary's Hall, Coventry; Court Front.

880.—Knights Jousting. (Royal MS. 14 E. iii.)

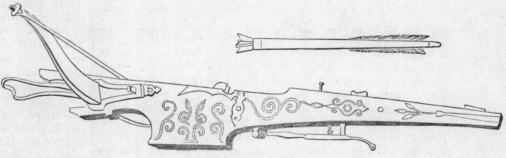

882.—Cross-bow and Quarrel.

883.—Ships of the time of Richard II. (Harl. MS. 1319.)

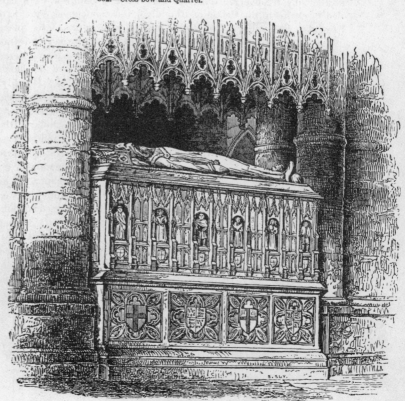

884.—Tomb of Edward III.

885.—Edmund of Langley.

886.—Richard II. (Portrait in the Jerusalem Chamber.)

887.—John of Gaunt.

888.—Great Seal of Richard II.

889.—Portrait of Richard II. (Illumination in Metrical History.)

890.—Half-Groat of Richard II

891.—Groat of Richard I

892.—Penny of Richard II.

893.—Banishment of Bolingbroke and Norfolk by Richard II.

894.—Richard II. and Gower.

will vindicate my just rights, or perish in the attempt." The chiefs craved time, and obtained it with difficulty. The king provided for opposition by issuing writs to his northern military tenants to assemble at Norham the day after that of the second conference, with "horses, arms, and all their powers." And there was no mincing the matter in any respect; Edward's chancellor, speaking in his name, clearly stated that he meant not to relinquish his right of property in the kingdom of Scotland hereafter. Robert Bruce, Lord of Annandale (grandfather of the great Bruce), the proper heir of Scotland, was the first at the next meeting, at Holywell Hough, opposite Norham, to surrender Scotland's independence. Being peremptorily asked whether he acknowledged Edward as Lord Paramount of Scotland, and was willing to ask and receive judgment from him in that character, Bruce definitely, expressly, publicly, and openly declared his assent. Seven other competitors for the crown, at that time, and an eighth, with John Baliol, the next day, followed this odious and unpopular example. The rival princes having thus for selfish ends at once disgraced and ruined their country, a great deal of hypocritical pretence of deliberation by Edward on their claims took place, with the aid of a large body of commissioners, forty being chosen by Bruce, forty by Baliol, and twenty-four by the king, who, however, reserved the privilege of adding *as many more as he pleased*. The commission sat at Norham and Berwick, during many months, which the king employed in procuring a solemn surrender of the kingdom of Scotland by the regents into his own hands, and of all the castles of Scotland by their holders in trust; and it is surprising to note the confidence with which his word seems to have been taken that he would make full restitution in two months from the date of his award in the cause of the succession. One Scotsman alone acted, says Lord Hailes, " with integrity and spirit on this trial of national integrity and spirit,"—Gilbert de Umfraville, Earl of Angus, who refused to deliver the castles of Dundee and Forfar, without an obligation to indemnify him from Edward and all the competitors. The next degradation was the swearing of fealty, performed voluntarily by Bruce and his son, by Baliol, and many chiefs, but by only one churchman, it is said. To make all ranks sign the rolls of homage as his vassals, from bishops and earls, down even to the burgesses, Edward made a progress through Scotland, and sent out his officers to receive the oaths, and whosoever refused were torn from their homes and imprisoned. The oppressor at length resumed his seat as umpire for the Scottish crown in the great hall of the Castle at Berwick, where at one meeting he declared "that Bruce should take nothing in the competition with Baliol," and at another, "that John Baliol should have seisin of the kingdom of Scotland," *but* that this judgment "should not impair his (Edward's) claim to the *property* of Scotland." Baliol was crowned at Scone, and a very tractable vassal he proved in all respects; he suffered with exemplary patience all Edward's rough usage, such as compelling him to appear in the English courts to answer as a defendant all sorts of causes, brought by his own subjects, until the indignities were pushed a little too far even for *him*, and on being compelled to appear as usual in an English parliament in 1293, to answer an appeal concerning lands in Fife, instead of making his defence in due form, he said, "I am King of Scotland. To the complaint of the appellant, or to aught else respecting my kingdom, I dare not make answer without the advice of my people." " What means this?" cried the tyrant. "You are *my* liege man; you have done homage to *me*; you are here in consequence of *my* summons." Baliol, remaining steady to what he had said, was adjudged guilty of contempt of court and open disobedience. The appellant had damages granted him, and the three principal towns and castles of Scotland, with their royal jurisdiction, were said to be forfeited to Edward. Baliol and Scotland had by this time a tolerable experience of what vassalage to Edward meant; so, in hope of relief, they turned to France, who was then at war with Edward, and were soon doomed to feel in consequence the vengeance of their English master. In the siege of the town of Berwick, he himself, mounted on his horse Bayard, was the first who leaped over the dike. The carnage that followed is one among the many ineffaceable blots on the memory of this great but unrelenting man; infancy, womanhood, old age, all were butchered that came within reach of the victors' swords. Thirty Flemings, posted in a building called the Red House, which the resident merchants of their nation held by the tenure of defending it at all times against the English, stood out gallantly, and refused to surrender; the building was then fired, and every man perished in the flames. Baliol, soon after this frightful scene, sent to Edward a bold ecclesiastic, the Abbot of Aberbrothock (or Arbroath) to deliver this solemn renunciation of his allegiance and fealty. "What a piece of madness of the foolish

traitor!" exclaimed Edward : "since he will not come to us, we will go to him."

The castle of Dunbar (Fig. 842) had been given up to the Scots by the Countess of March, whose husband was at the time serving Edward, and a fresh contest for it took place between the English, under Earl Warenne, and Baliol's army, in which ten thousand Scots perished. In about two months, Roxburgh, Dumbarton, Jedburgh, Edinburgh, Stirling, and all the other important fortresses, were in Edward's hands, and the conquest was complete. Baliol again crouched at Edward's feet, and, in the churchyard of Strathkathro, in Angus, stood, it is said, with a white rod in his hand, to detail his offences against his liege lord, committed through false counsel and his own simplicity, and concluding by resigning his kingdom and people to the English king. After this disgraceful exhibition, Edward exercised his usual wisdom, in settling the government of the conquered country on prudent, moderate, and popular principles. But the Scots could not be reconciled to a foreign yoke. Wallace arose, the second son of the Knight of Ellerslie, endowed with strength, stature, courage, decision, military genius, the talent for command, a stirring though rude eloquence, an enthusiastic patriotism, and a fierce and unextinguishable hatred of the English dominion. He first appeared as a kind of petty chief lurking in woods and wilds, with a small band of outlaws, infesting the English quarters. Sir William Douglas, who had commanded the castle of Berwick during the siege, was the first person of note who joined this outlaw chief, with his vassals, attracted by the reputation of his successful exploits. By a bold and brilliant attack they took Scone, and overran the neighbouring country. Other chiefs crowded to their banners, among them—most welcome of all—the young Bruce, grandson of Baliol's competitor, and eventually the restorer of the Scottish monarchy.

But when the greatest effort was to be made by the associated warriors, against Surrey, Percy, and Clifford, and their immense army, it was discovered that Wallace was a plebeian! It was impossible—quite impossible—that the proud blood of Scotland could submit to the guidance of a plebeian. So the hero was deserted by all but one noble-hearted as well as noble-blooded man, Sir Andrew Moray of Bothwell. The followers of the nobles, however, having none of their masters' objections, rallied in great numbers round Wallace, who soon found that the people generally of his native country were ready to devote their lives to the cause under his direction. And so they marched and countermarched—increasing in numbers at every step—and taking castle after castle, until they appeared forty thousand strong, in addition to some one hundred and eighty horse, before Stirling itself (Figs. 843, 846, 849), that almost impregnable stronghold, the possession of which both English and Scotch alike considered indispensable to success. It must have been in the main a rude and tumultuous host, though courage, enthusiasm, and numbers made ample amends for what was lacked in discipline. To oppose the Scotch appeared an English army of fifty thousand infantry and a thousand horse. Negotiation was spoken of to Wallace: "Return," he said, to those who came to him, " and tell your masters that we come not here to treat, but to assert our rights, and to set Scotland free. Let them advance; they will find us prepared."

The prudent commander of the English saw that to accept this defiance would involve his men in certain destruction; for while he had been marching on Stirling, Wallace, leaving the siege of the castle of Dundee to the citizens, had hurried his whole force to the banks of the Forth, and partially concealed them in the best position behind the neighbouring high grounds, before the English came up. Surrey remained a night without making any movement, but gave way at last to the forward zeal of his men, and the angry remonstrances of Cressingham, the Treasurer, who protested "against the waste of the king's money, in keeping up an army, if it was not to fight." This Cressingham had been Governor of Scotland for Edward, and made himself peculiarly odious to the Scottish people by imitating, on a limited scale, the oppressions of his royal master. Not many hours after, his blood was mingling with the waters of the Forth, and so intense was the hatred his cruelties had excited, that his skin was preserved by the Scots in small pieces, "not as relics, but for spite," and Wallace himself is said to have had a sword-belt made of it—such were the unchristian feelings of revenge cherished even by the best men of that age. The morning of the 11th of September, 1297, dawned on a fearful scene at the Bridge of the Forth, a narrow wooden structure, that Surrey's host could not have crossed in many hours, had they been totally unmolested; how great then was the folly of the experiment with a powerful and skilful foe on the other side! Half the rash and eager English had hardly reached the Stirling bank—they had not had time to form—when down rushed the Scots from the heights, possessed themselves of the extremity of the bridge, and fell on that portion of the divided army which was thus placed in their power. Thrown into confusion, the English perished by thousands, as they advanced upon the Scottish swords, or were forced backward into the river, which presented a sickening sight, crimsoned with gore, and choked with human bodies. Only one of all that had crossed escaped, Sir Marmaduke Twenge, who spurred his horse back through the force that guarded the bridge, and cut his way to the opposite side. Surrey, seeing this man acquit himself so boldly, charged him with delightful naïveté, to occupy Stirling Castle with what troops he might be able to collect of the fragments of the army, since the whole had not been able conveniently to manage it, and then mounted his horse and never stopped till he reached Berwick. The loss of the Scots at Stirling Bridge is mentioned as trifling—it was great to Wallace, for the only man of note that fell was his most faithful friend, Sir Andrew Moray. This, the most important of a rapid and continuous series of triumphs, at once restored Wallace to the favour and countenance of the Scottish nobility, and the king of England, while engaged in Flanders, received the astounding tidings that this new man of the people—this leader of a little band of outlaws, this plebeian without family, influence, or wealth, supported by merit alone, had wrenched from the English every fortress in Scotland, from one end of the kingdom to the other. Edinburgh Castle (Fig. 840) was one of the first that surrendered. A letter has been recently discovered written to the authorities of Lübeck and Hamburg by Wallace at this period, informing them that their merchants should now have free access to all parts of the kingdom of Scotland, seeing that the said kingdom, by the favour of God, had been recovered by war from the power of the English. There was something almost superhuman in this sudden clearance, for though Edward's absence might have rendered it rather more easy, the spirit of Edward was largely infused into the English warriors who supported his conquest, and they had their own peculiar interests in the conquered country to nerve them, independent of national and military feelings of glory. Wallace's friend, the young Sir Andrew Moray, son of the veteran who fell at Stirling, we now find sharing with him the chief command of the Scottish army, in an invasion of England. They stayed in Cumberland some time, and wasted the country as far south as the walls of Newcastle. A famine in Scotland, most probably attributable to the devastation made by the English, seems to have chiefly impelled Wallace to push his triumphs thus far. He was now at the very pinnacle of power. At the Forest Kirk, in Selkirkshire, he received the supreme rule of the kingdom, under the title of "Guardian of Scotland;" and this with the consent and approbation of the nobility. Though thus himself virtually king, Wallace acted in the name of John Baliol, "King John," who lived as unlike a king as could be desired, by any party, at his own demesne of Bailleul in Normandy, whither he had been allowed to go on the king of England's releasing him from confinement at the intercession of the Pope. His holiness was less successful in the letters he granted the Scots to Edward, to induce him to desist in his endeavours against Scottish independence. Edward swore a terrible oath "that he would not desist," and to the Scots' threats he replied, with a disdainful smile, "Have you done homage to me (as to the chief lord of the kingdom of Scotland), and now suppose that I can be terrified with swelling lies, as if, like one that had no power to compel, I would let the right which I have over you to slip out of my hands? Let me hear no more of this: for if I do, I swear by the Lord I will consume all Scotland from sea to sea." The Scots replied as boldly, "They would shed their blood for defence of justice and their country's liberty." Arms again could alone decide the question. Edward caused his military tenants to assemble at York, on the Feast of Pentecost, and he led them in person to Roxburgh, and along the eastern coast of Scotland. His march lay through a country made desolate and deserted as he approached; his army found no provisions to subsist on, no spoil to animate their spirits, no enemy to wreak their vengeance upon for his inhospitality; and of their own ships, with the supplies, which had been sent forward to the Frith of Forth, they could hear no news. Hunger and disappointment were not the only difficulties Edward had to encounter. At Templeliston, between Linlithgow and Edinburgh, where he stopped to wait for his fleet, he was told that thousands of his soldiers, Welshmen, rankling under the remembrance of their own country's wrongs, were on the point of going over to the Scots, with whom, we are sure, they must have sympathised deeply. "I care not," said Edward loftily; "let my enemies go to my enemies: I trust that in one day I shall chastise

them all." The famished army were about to retreat to Edinburgh, when the Earls Dunbar and Angus came privately at daybreak to the quarters of the soldier-bishop of Durham, with information that a Scottish army was near in the wood of Falkirk. When Edward heard of it, he cried in a rapture, "Thanks be to God, who hitherto hath delivered me from every danger: they shall not need to follow me; I will forthwith go and meet them." The army that night was lying in the fields; the king himself on the ground, his horse standing beside him. A terrible shout from the Scottish army is said to have startled the animal, as his royal master was putting his foot in the stirrup; it threw him to the earth, and, striking with the hinder heels, broke two of his ribs. In the confusion occasioned by the accident, a cry arose that the king was killed or seriously wounded, and the calamity was attributed to treachery. But Edward speedily restored confidence, by mounting the same horse which had injured him, and, regardless of the pain he suffered, marshalling his host, and giving orders to march on the foe. They passed Linlithgow, and then the advanced-guard of the enemy was seen on the ridge of a hill in front. Soon after the whole Scottish army was descried, forming, on a stony field, at the side of a small eminence in the neighbourhood of Falkirk. To explain the execrable desertion which Wallace experienced in the disastrous battle that ensued—the whole of his horse galloping away during the heat of the action, without striking a blow—we must refer to the envy and aristocratic pride of the Scottish nobility, who, Fordun relates, were in the habit of saying, "We will not have this man to rule over us." The archers and lancers on foot were only moved from the position in which Wallace planted them by repeated charges of Edward's cavalry, and through their being left unsupported; but the treachery or cowardice of the horsemen was fatal, they were borne down, and fifteen thousand perished; the rest fled with Wallace to Stirling. The English shortly came after him, but found him gone, and the town burned. After this defeat, Wallace gave up all such authority as the Commonwealth of Scotland had formerly granted unto him for the preservation of their freedoms; and the great rivals, Bruce and Comyn, and the Bishop of St. Andrews, shared the supreme rule. It is painful to trace the hero's subsequent career. Ingratitude drove him back to the wild life from which his resplendent talents and virtues had raised him. He was again a wandering guerilla-sort of chief, harassing the English on their marches, and in their camps and castles. Meanwhile it fared ill with his distracted country. The battle of Roslin (the Castle of Roslin is shown in our engravings, Figs. 833 and 835), won by Comyn and Bruce and the combined nobility, was speedily followed by the reappearance of Edward, who swept through Scotland almost unobstructed, marking every step by devastation and blood. One after another the places of strength quietly opened their gates to him. Brechin Castle is a memorable exception. Its commander, Sir John Maule, whilst the English were battering the walls, stood in defiance on the ramparts, coolly and contemptuously wiping off with a towel the dust and rubbish that fell on him. He was struck by a missile. As he was expiring, his men inquired if they might *now* surrender the castle, but he reproached them for cowards. The castle was given up the next day. Oaths of fealty were once more taken to Edward, who, at the close of this new conquest, wintered at Dunfermline. All that now remained in arms for Scotland, except the friends of Wallace, gathered at Stirling, under Comyn; but Edward and his cavalry routed these without difficulty, except such as took refuge in the castle. The spirit of the nobility of Scotland now completely yielded. Edward granted a general capitulation for all who had been in arms for Scotland, by which Comyn and many chiefs of rank, stigmatized as traitors, were suffered to live at freedom and retain their estates, subject only to fines at the king's pleasure. It was the glorious distinction of William Wallace that his name stood entirely alone as excluded from the capitulation, though he was told that he might, if he pleased, "render himself up to the will and mercy of Edward." What that will and mercy was, he had too soon to experience. At a parliament held at St. Andrews, he and Fraser, and the garrison of Stirling, being summoned, and not appearing, they were outlawed. Fraser eventually surrendered, but Wallace and the garrison held out. The rhyming chronicler Longtoft informs us (though the fact is perhaps to be doubted) that Wallace was hidden in the forest of Dunfermline, whence he sent some of his friends to Edward with a proposal to yield himself if his life and heritage were assured to him by a sealed writing of the king's. But Edward, "full grim," cursing Wallace and all his traitorous supporters, made the most decisive of replies by setting a price of three hundred marks upon his head. Wallace is then said to have "in mores and mareis with robberie him fedis."

895.—Westminster Hall, with the ancient surrounding Buildings restored.

896.—Parliament assembled for the Deposition of Richard II.

897.—The Savoy.

898.—Meeting of Richard II. and Bolingbroke.

899.—Pontefract Castle temp. Charles II.

900.—Richard II. and Bolingbroke arrived at London.

232

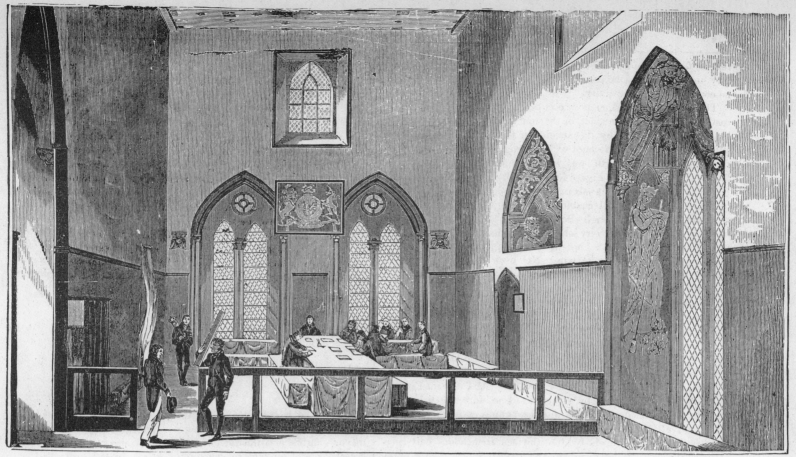

901.—The Painted Chamber.

902.—Minstrels' Pillar, Beverley.

903.—Principal Entrance to Westminster Hall.

904.—Knights Jousting. (Royal MS. 14 E. iii.)

905.—Funeral of Richard II. (Illumination in Froissart.)

that is, fed himself by robbery in moors and marshes, by which we may understand, that he continued to prey on the English whenever he could find an opportunity.

The garrison of Stirling now occupied Edward's attention. The castle was one, and the chief, of the four principal fortresses of the kingdom of Scotland (by the articles of the Union these four are still kept up), and, on account of its strength and its commanding the passage of the Forth, was highly important to both parties. Our views of the castle (Figs. 843, 846, 849) as seen from different parts, towering above the steep and precipitous slopes of the hill on which it is built, will enable the reader who is a stranger to this stronghold of the early Scottish kings and Scottish independence to comprehend the very serious difficulties to which Edward I. in his old age addressed himself, with the fire and daring of a youth who had his spurs to win. Not even the circumstance of his being struck by the stones and javelins from the castle, not even the arrow that lodged in his armour, could deter him from conspicuously exposing himself, as he directed in person every contrivance for battering down the walls and sending winged death among the brave defenders.

Sir John Oliphant, the commander, being required to surrender, requested time to go to France to the exiled Sir John Soulis, from whom he had his trust: "Am I to wait for *his* orders?" cried the old king. "Defend the castle, if you will." And defended it was, to the very last extremity, by a garrison of no more than a hundred and forty soldiers, during three months, against a mighty English force, and all Edward's military tactics. For the first month, so little impression was made by the thirteen tremendous battering-engines, the best in the kingdom, and the darts, armed with brass, cast from the springals, that the business must have grown tedious, for we find Edward writing to his sheriffs of London, Lincoln, and York, to buy up all the bows, quarrels, and other engines of war that were to be found in their districts, and to the Constable of the Tower to send a supply from the stores at his command. In our engravings (Fig. 882) the form of the cross-bow and quarrel may be seen, and in Figs. 868 to 870 is illustrated the whole process of battering the walls as carried on in the period under review. Slow, but sure, after that the work of destruction went on, till the strong fortress lay in ruins. Imagination shrinks to conceive the horrors experienced during these two last months by the stubborn garrison, and the thirteen noble ladies who shared the sufferings and dangers of their husbands, fathers, and brothers. And what a moment must that have been when the cry went forth amongst them, that the food which they had been anxiously eking out day after day was gone! Little wonder that, weak and worn as the strongest must have been, by the time Edward's troops had them at their mercy, that the twenty-five noble gentlemen who were among the garrison, had not spirit left to reject the only chance of life, but suffered themselves to be led forth in mournful procession to the feet of the conqueror, who was never either more magnanimous or more cruel than his stern purposes required. Excepting two ecclesiastics, all were stripped to their shirts and under garments, and all knelt with trembling and tears, acknowledging their guilt, and casting themselves on his mercy. Edward did not consider it quite necessary to destroy those who could be compelled to this degrading submission; they were permitted to breathe,—but in dungeons. A harsher doom was reserved for the unconquerable Wallace—the last hope of despairing Scotland. Among the prisoners there appears to have been one Ralph de Haliburton, who, tempted, it is said, by Edward's offers of liberty and reward, undertook to manage, in some way that is not clear to us, to betray the hero to the English. And he accomplished his undertaking: Wallace was conveyed as a prisoner to Dumbarton Castle, then held by "the false Menteith."

The gigantic rock of Dumbarton (Fig. 838), at the junction of the rivers Leven and Clyde, retains unchanged the gloomy grandeur that darkened around the hero as he was led up the guarded steep (Fig. 839), and the memory of his imprisonment by the English throws around it a romantic and imperishable interest, that receives some addition from the fact of his two-handed sword being reverently preserved within the walls of the fortress. The name of Menteith has since that age been coupled with many a malediction, as that of a false Scot, by whom Wallace was betrayed. But it appears Menteith was only false to Wallace in so far as he was false to Scotland. Dumbarton he held for Edward, and his unpopularity arose from his disgraceful task of receiving and confining the great champion of his nation, and sending him to England to suffer all that the malice and fears of his foes could suggest. Wallace was led in triumph through London, "all men and women wondering upon him." With what feelings could

these curious wonderers have gazed on that tall, majestic form, which had borne the brunt of so many battles, which we are sure had known no pampering in the forests, moors, and marshes, and which was glorious with a martyr's devotion to as holy a cause as ever soldier fought for? Were there no tears shed among the women of those eager crowds when they thought of his murdered wife, of his father and his brother, and his dearest friends, slain in the same cause for which he had now to pour out his own blood? Did no thinking minds there find the conclusion flash upon them that their king had taken a wrong path to reach his great designs? Perhaps lurking in the multitude was some true Scot, who, as his heart melted with grief, secretly cursed the proud factions who had been the cause of Wallace's overthrow: nay, we can imagine some repentant noble with bitter regrets exclaiming in the depths of his soul as the hero disappeared, strongly guarded, into the house of William Delect in Fenchurch Street, there to lodge until his trial the next day in Westminster Hall—

> We are selfish men;
> Oh! raise us up, return to us again;
> And give us manners, virtue, freedom, power.
> Thy soul was like a star, and dwelt apart;
> Thou hadst a voice whose sound was like the sea:
> Pure as the naked heavens—majestic, free.
>
> WORDSWORTH.

Next day he is exhibited on horseback, passing from Fenchurch Street to Westminster: John Seagrave, and Geoffrey, knights, the mayor, sheriffs, and aldermen of London, and many others, both on horseback and on foot, accompanying him. In the great hall at Westminster he is placed on the south bench, and submits to the paltry mockery of a crown of laurel, because it had been commonly reported that he had said he ought to wear a crown in that hall. Yet never were laurels worn with truer glory. Never does prisoner appear to have behaved to his unscrupulous judges with a more quiet, serene dignity. When Sir Peter Malorie, the king's justice, impeached him of treason, he replied, "He was never traitor to the king of England; but for other things whereof he was accused, he confessed them." And certainly Wallace never had acknowledged fealty to the English king, therefore could be no traitor to him. This fact is his great distinction above all the other Scottish patriots. His neck had *never* submitted to the degrading yoke. He was as true to the Scottish independence as if it had never been assailed. And as Edward must have despaired of ever bending such a man to his rule, and was never sure while Wallace lived that he would have any rule left to be submitted to, the patriot's death, to his eyes, was inevitable. Accordingly, on the 23rd of August, 1305, the hero of Scotland was executed in the same manner as the last Prince of Wales, being dragged at the tails of horses to the common place of execution, the Elms in West Smithfield, hanged on a high gallows, and, while he yet breathed, his bowels were taken out and burnt before his face. The head was then cut off, and set up on a pole on London Bridge, his right arm was sent for exhibition to Newcastle, his left to Berwick, the right foot and limb to Perth, the left to Aberdeen. The English king thus concluded an infamous act in the most infamous manner. Obeying the dictates of state policy (that phrase so fruitful in all ages of national crime and misery), Edward was determined to have Scotland at any cost: then how else, but by such exhibitions, was he to deter others from imitating Wallace's example? But the "politician" that, as Hamlet says, "would circumvent God," lives often to find he has only circumvented himself: so was it now with our great king. Only six months after Wallace's death appeared Bruce in arms, and asserting his own right to the throne. Edward had everything to undertake anew for the subjugation of Scotland. That Bruce should be the leader of the new movement was a fact that personally enhanced to Edward the irritating sense of his formidable claims. He had forgiven his coquetting, as it were, with his struggling countrymen, and permitted him, at his father's death, to take unmolested possession of all the family estates; he even held him in such favour, probably from the remembrances of his friendship with Bruce's father, who had fought by his side in the Holy Land, that he was accustomed to receive his opinions on Scottish matters with marked respect. Edward evidently concluded that Bruce had finally renounced all views on the throne of his native country; and great, no doubt, was the shock when he was undeceived. Intelligence suddenly reached him that Bruce and the influential Bishop of St. Andrews had bound themselves to support each other against all persons whatsoever, and neither to undertake any business of importance without the other. A third party was made acquainted with that significant treaty—Comyn, who, through Baliol, might be considered to have a claim to the throne. To him Bruce said, "Support my title to the crown, and I will give you all my lands; or bestow on me your lands, and I will support your claim." Comyn resigned his own title; an agreement was written and sealed, and oaths of faithfulness and secrecy were pledged to each other. Comyn, regretting probably his decision, violated his oath to Bruce, and divulged what had passed to Edward. The king one evening, thrown off his guard by having drunk more wine than usual, told some lords who were with him of Bruce's treasonable schemes, and his own resolution to take vengeance on the offender. The Earl of Gloucester, Bruce's relation, desirous to save him without compromising himself, despatched to him a pair of spurs and a piece of money. Bruce, who was in London, set out immediately for Scotland, having, it is said, his horse's shoes reversed, that he might not be traced in the snow. He went straight to his castle of Lochmaben; and on the way the treachery of Comyn was made more clear to him by some letters that he intercepted, which a messenger was bearing from Comyn to Edward, urging Bruce's imprisonment or death. The bearer of these Bruce slew on the spot, and then sought Comyn at Dumfries. Their meeting took place in the convent of the Minorites, a place whose selection was dictated, apparently, by the conscious fears of Comyn. After a violent scene, in which Bruce reproached Comyn for his detestable breach of faith, Bruce stabbed his rival with his dagger, as they stood together by the high altar. Leaving the sanctuary in haste, he called "to horse," and his attendants, Alexander Lindsay and Roger Kirkpatrick, observing him pale and extremely agitated, inquired what had happened. "I doubt I have slain Comyn," said he. "You doubt?" exclaimed Kirkpatrick; "I'se mak sicker" (I'll make sure); and he darted into the church and finished the murder, killing Sir Robert Comyn also, who, hearing the scuffle, ran in to the defence of his nephew. The judges, sitting in a hall of the castle, hearing a confused alarm, barricaded the doors. But the followers whom Bruce had suddenly collected threatening to force an entrance by fire, they surrendered. Bruce had but few with him at first, and these mostly young; but the news of the revolt spread like wildfire, and his force increased, so that many of the English officers fled before him: but it does not seem that he was able to collect any considerable army for some time. On the 27th of March, 1306, Bruce was twice crowned at Scone, sitting under a banner wrought with the arms of Baliol, which the Bishop of Glasgow had kept concealed in his treasury. The regal coronet was first set on the young king's head by the Bishop of St. Andrews; but the Countess of Buchan, whose brother, Duncan, Earl of Fife, inherited an ancient privilege of crowning the Scottish kings, while he was absent from his domain *assisting the English*, hurried, "with all his great horse," to Scone, and with her own hands exercised her family right, by placing the symbolic circlet a second time on the brow of Robert Bruce. This anecdote will serve to illustrate the enthusiasm which was excited throughout Scotland for Bruce, who had at last stepped into his proper place, though he had not reached it by quite as straight a path as we, looking coolly upon that past time of difficulty and temptation, might desire.

Edward, now in his last sickness, prepared, nevertheless, to go out against Bruce in person, though aware that his death was near. At the knighting of his son, the Prince of Wales, he gave a magnificent feast, when two swans, covered with nets of gold, being set on the table by the minstrels, the aged monarch rose, and solemnly vowed to God and to the swans that he would take vengeance for Comyn's murder, and punish the Scottish rebels; then turning to his son, and addressing the splendid assembly, which included a great number of noble youths who had been knighted by the prince, he conjured them after his death not to inter his body until his successor should have performed this vow. The new-made knights, with the prince at their head, departed next morning for the borders, the infirm king following slowly in a litter. For some time Bruce's reign promised to be but a short and unhappy one. He passed from misfortune to misfortune; he lost nearly all his followers; his brothers were one after the other sent to the gallows; his wife, and other female relatives, made prisoners and taken into England; Nigel, the most accomplished and beloved of his five brothers, had been taken while gallantly, but unsuccessfully, defending Bruce's queen and daughter in his Castle of Kildrummie (Fig. 836). He began to be even pursued by bloodhounds, as though he were a mere wild beast. His adventures during this period read like a passage in a romance. At last his never-failing courage and address met their reward. Friends and adherents again flocked to his banner; he reduced various districts to his authority, and at last routed the English

guardian of the kingdom, Pembroke, in a pitched battle. King Edward from his sick bed had directed all the recent operations that had thus unsuccessfully ended at last: there was nothing for him, but he must go on himself, dying as he was. So he went into the cathedral of Carlisle and offered up his litter, and then mounting his horse, the well-known voice was once more heard directing the march onwards to the border. The effort was too much for him. At Burgh on the Sands he was compelled to stop for the night, and there, the next morning, he died, immovable in purpose as ever; expending his last breath, according to Froissart, in making his son swear that he would boil his body in a cauldron, bury the flesh, and keep the bones to be carried at the head of an army against the Scots every time they should rebel.

It was little anticipated by the nation that the new king would so soon disobey the command of his dying father, by recalling Gaveston, who, for "abusing the tender years of the prince with wicked vanities," had been banished on two different occasions, especially as he thus incurred that father's solemn curse. But so it was; and to make matters worse, some of the most eminent men in the realm were persecuted because they had had the courage and public spirit to treat the prince's favourite as he deserved. Walter de Langton, Treasurer of England, was imprisoned, and had his goods confiscated, because, in the late king's days, he had dared to reprove the prince and complain of Piers Gaveston. The very different conduct of a later monarch, Henry V., towards the judge who had committed him, whilst Prince Henry, to prison, forms a striking contrast. This Gaveston, for some service rendered by his father, had been brought up with the young Edward, and thus was the friendship established between them, that led to such disastrous consequences to both, and to so much disgrace to the nation at large. Gaveston "had," says an old historian, "a sharp wit in a comely shape, and briefly was such an one as we used to call *very fine*." (Speed.) He possessed also great courage and skill in arms, as he had proved in the Scottish war, and in the tournaments, where he had overthrown the most distinguished of our baronial chivalry. On the other hand, he was luxurious to the last degree, proud as regards himself, insolent to others, and oppressive and capricious to those in any way subjected to his control. He was fond of nicknames. Thomas, Prince of Lancaster, the king's cousin, was "a great hog," and a "stage-player;" the Earl of Pembroke was "Joseph the Jew;" Guy, Earl of Warwick, the "black dog of Ardenne." These were dangerous men to jest with in this fashion; even if there had been nothing in the favourite's public conduct to lay hold of. But while they thus saw themselves treated with contempt, they also saw all the great enterprises neglected, upon which they, as devoted followers of Edward I., had set their hearts, more especially the Scotch wars. They saw the king's court given up to sensuality and riot. They knew also that the riches of the kingdom were being converted to Gaveston's private use; that Edward, besides conferring on him the Earldom of Cornwall, a dignity hitherto reserved for princes of the blood, and marrying him to his sister's daughter, gave him the funds collected for the Scottish war, and for the Crusades, as well as his ancestors' jewels and treasures, even to the crown worn by his father, which the barons not unnaturally looked upon as a symbol of the result that Edward possibly dreamed of, the declaration of Piers Gaveston as his successor.

The young queen added her voice to the general complaint. Through Gaveston, the king had been drawn on to injure her in the highest respects. Her appeal to her father, the French king, was followed by the Gascon knight's third banishment, in June, 1309, which, however, was merely to Ireland, and as governor. But he would not take warning; in October he returned, in defiance of a known decree, "that if at any time afterwards he were taken in England, he should suffer death." An angel from heaven could not have been more welcomed by Edward, who evidently would rather lose crown, kingdom, queen and all, than Piers Gaveston. The lords, with the "great hog," Thomas Earl of Lancaster, at their head, looking upon the return with very different eyes, met, and agreed to send respectfully to Edward, to desire that Gaveston should be delivered into their hands, or driven out of England. The king vacillated, knowing peace must be kept with the lords, yet unwilling to sacrifice his own foolish or worse than foolish desires. At last, losing patience, the lords took arms. Gaveston endeavoured to defend himself in Scarborough Castle (of which the crumbling ruins now only remain, Fig. 919), while the king went to York to seek an army for his relief. But before any force could be collected for such a purpose, Piers Gaveston, on the 19th of May, 1312, capitulated to the Earls Pembroke and Percy

906.—Ruins of St. Stephen's Chapel.

907.—Restoration of St. Stephen's Chapel.

908.—Chepstow Castle

909.—Leaning Tower of Caerphilly

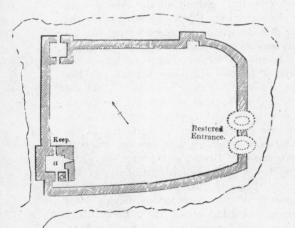

914.—Plan of Castleton Castle.

911.—Gateway to Cowling Castle.

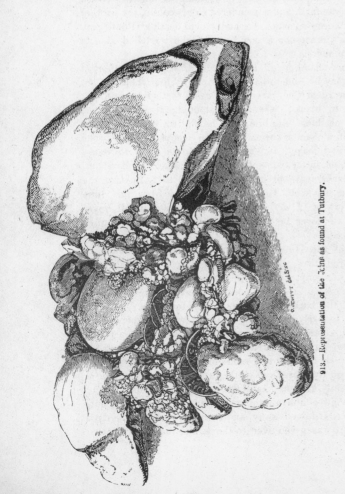

913.—Representation of the Kilns as found at Tutbury.

912.—Interior of Tutbury Castle-Yard.

237

who pledged their faith, it is said, that he should be kept unharmed in the castle of Wallingford. At Dedington, a village between Oxford and Warwick, the Earl of Pembroke, who escorted him, left him for a night under the pretext of visiting the Countess of Pembroke, who was in the neighbourhood. Gaveston seems to have remained full of confidence, as usual, until he was roused from his sleep by the startling order to "dress speedily." He obeyed, descended to the courtyard, and found himself in the presence of the "black dog of Ardenne." He must have repented then his wretched wit, for he knew the stern Warwick had sworn a terrible vow that he would make the minion feel "the black dog's teeth." A deeper darkness than that of the night must then have overshadowed the wretched Gaveston. No help was at hand. Amid the triumphant shouts of the large armed force that attended Warwick, he was set on a mule, and hurried thirty miles through the night to Warwick Castle (Figs. 415, 416, 417, and 917), where his entrance was announced by a crash of martial music. He stood trembling and dismayed before the dais, whereon sate in terrible array his self-constituted judges, the chief barons. During their hurried consultation, a proposal was made, or a hint offered, that no blood should be shed : but a voice rung through the hall—"You have caught the fox; if you let him go, you will have to hunt him again." Let Gaveston's deserts be what they might, the faith pledged at the capitulation at Scarborough ought to have been adhered to; but it was otherwise determined by the barons. He had been taken once more on English ground, and he must die. As Gaveston had been insolent in his prosperity, so now he lost all manly spirit under the fear of death. The "old hog" was now a "gentle lord," and the unhappy man kneeled and prayed to him and the rest for mercy—but found none. There is a little knoll about two miles from the castle, on the edge of the road that leads from Warwick to Coventry, and on it yet exists a stone bearing the following ancient inscription : "P. Gaveston, Earl of Cornwall, beheaded here, 1312." Within the present century, the cross shown in Fig. 851 has been erected by the possessor of the adjoining mansion, Guy's Cliff. The news of this event threw the king into an agony of tears, and he resolutely refused to declare Gaveston a traitor. While he lamented, and pined for revenge, the national councils were distracted, the national spirit and power declined. He now determined to renew the war in Scotland, which he had dropped almost immediately after his father's death. But the posture of affairs demanded the skill and indomitable energy of the first Edward; and as these qualities were as notoriously absent in his son, it was not difficult to foresee what must be the conclusion. Bruce had by this time so completely established his authority as king in Scotland, as to be able to make an inroad into the dominions of the English monarch, in order to take vengeance for the sufferings that the English governors had inflicted upon his country. Edward would have concluded a truce—as a preliminary, possibly, to peace; but Bruce, confident in his strength, declined. War then was inevitable. The final struggle took place at Bannockburn, for the defence of the castle of Stirling, the last of the castles held by the English, and where Edward concentrated all his forces for its defence. His defeat was as signal as it was in every way humiliating. His army, which greatly outnumbered that of the enemy, was cut to pieces; the slain, at the lowest computation, comprised one hundred and fifty-four lords and knights, seven hundred gentlemen, and ten thousand common soldiers : whilst the Scotch reckoned the entire loss at no less than fifty thousand persons. The king himself was pursued for sixty miles. By this battle Bruce achieved the final independence of the Scottish nation, and the permanent settlement of his own family on the throne, which he had so well and hardly earned. He lived to see peace concluded between the two nations, by the recognition of that independence in an English parliament, and died in 1329, after some two years of pious solitude, in a castle at Cardross, on the northern shore of the Frith of Clyde, and was buried in the magnificent abbey church of Dunfermline, founded by King Malcolm Canmore, and, after the celebrated Iona, the common burial-place of the kings of Scotland. About twenty-six years ago the skeleton of the royal warrior was disinterred, and found to measure above six feet : a cast was at the same time taken of the skull; a pleasant bonne-bouche for our phrenologists. The highly-picturesque ruins of the abbey are shown in Fig. 837.

Under these distressing circumstances, what was poor King Edward to do? where to find consolation? He found out at last what he would do—he would have another favourite. It is true that the kingdom was already miserable enough, without the addition of new feuds about new court minions. A striking evidence of the disorganized state of England at the time is brought

to our recollection by the view of Leeds Castle (Fig. 927), where the queen, whilst travelling in Kent, was actually denied shelter, and part of her escort killed. But it was the fate of the king to sink deeper into disgrace at every fresh step taken in his career; so he had his favourite, peculiarly inauspicious as the times were. Unhappy king! he was to pay dearly for these indulgences. The young Despenser, a dependent of the Earl of Lancaster, was the object of royal favour. Upon him Edward bestowed in marriage another daughter of his sister the Countess of Gloucester, and large possessions. Again the barons appeared in arms, and the favourite, with his father, was banished. Then they were recalled by Edward and for a time the barons were foiled at their own weapons The Earl of Lancaster fell into the hands of the royal party, and was beheaded, as we have already had occasion to notice, in the Castle at Pomfret. Many others of the leaders on the same side also perished; and altogether the triumph of the Despensers seemed complete. But now arose a new element of danger to Edward, in the person of his own queen, who, being sent by him to France to endeavour to treat with her brother, Charles IV., concerning the British territories in France, which he was fast taking possession of, instead of fulfilling her mission, at once gave vent to the feelings of disgust and hatred which her husband's conduct had excited in her mind, and plunged into the very midst of the party of English malcontents that she found at the French court, driven from their own country by the enmity of the favourite. By a trick she and her chief confederate, Mortimer, got possession of the person of the young Prince Edward, afterwards Edward III., who was then affianced to Philippa (Fig. 855), daughter of the Earl of Hainault, on condition that that nobleman should aid the confederation with troops and money. Thus prepared, she threw off the mask, and set sail for England with a force of three thousand men. On her disembarkation at Orwell, in Suffolk, all the chief men in the kingdom joined her, including even Edward's own brother, the Earl of Kent. The king thus saw at once combined against him his wife, his son, his brother, his cousins, and all the might of England. Round the banner of Edward of Caernarvon there rallied not one man. He had to fly out of London with none but the two Despensers, the Chancellor, and a few of their servants. It did not help his cause a jot offering a thousand pounds for Mortimer's head. Edward ceased now to be spoken of seriously as a king. The elder Despenser, whose capital offence was grasping at the honours and estates of others, first fell, his own garrison rising in mutiny against him in the castle of Bristol, and giving him up to his enemies, who exhausted a truly fiendish barbarity in the execution of this old man of ninety years. The favourite next suffered from the vengeance of the confederates, having been given up by the country-people, and he too was sent to the gallows; though not before the helpless and hopeless monarch, who had been now tossing on the tempestuous seas, now hiding among the Welsh mountains, had come forth and surrendered to his cousin, the brother of the Earl of Lancaster, whom he had put to death at Pontefract. Not a sword was drawn nor a bow bent for the wretched king in any part of his dominions.

In the presence-chamber of Kenilworth Castle, soon after, a deputation, that may be said to have been sent by the whole nation, stood before Edward of Caernarvon, who came forth from an inner room, "gowned in black;" when, understanding their errand, it "struck such a chillness into him, that he fell to the earth, lying stretched forth in a deadly swoon." When recovered, "he broke forth into sighs and tears," and was addressed in these words :— "I, William Trussel, in the name of all men of the land of England, and of all the parliament—procurator, resign to thee, Edward, the homage that was made to thee, sometime, and from this time forward now following *I defy thee*, and prive thee of all royal power; and I shall never be attendant to thee, as for king, after this time." (Speed.)

The Steward of the Household then broke his white wand of office, and declared that all persons were freed from Edward's service. This ceremony, usually performed at a king's death, completed the process of dethronement. We should be glad to be spared mention of the barbarous doings which followed. Edward it seems, was too tenderly treated by Lancaster; so a keeper was found, Maltravers, a man whose natural ferocity had been sharpened by the cruel wrongs he had suffered at the hands of Edward and his favourites. The poor prisoner was made to travel about by night a good deal, and to go from castle to castle, in order that his residence might not be certainly known. Lord Berkeley, of Berkeley Castle, was the last who gave him anything like humane treatment, but, falling sick, he was detained away, and then Edward, on one dark night in September, was given over to the tender mercies of "two hell-hounds, that were capable of more villanous despite than becomes either knights or the lewdest varlets in the world," Thomas Gurney and William Ogle. What passed within the walls of Berkeley Castle (Fig. 853) may be but too truly guessed from the horrible screams and shrieks of anguish that were heard without, even so far as the town, " So that many, being awakened therewith from their sleep, as they themselves confessed, prayed heartily to God to receive his soul, for they understood by those cries what the matter meant." The body was publicly exposed with a pretence of innocence, as showing no outward marks of violence; but the horribly distorted countenance confirmed to the eye what the shrieks had told to the ear,—Edward II. had been murdered; some, at least, of his enemies by this very act showing themselves worse even than the monarch they had destroyed. Altogether it would be hardly possible to find any other period of our history so full of individual wickedness, and national misery and degradation, or one so un-relieved by any of the gentler or nobler influences. The personal appearance of the weak and wretched man, to whom these sad con-clusions must be mainly attributed, is shown in the engravings (Figs. 851, 856), and on his great seal (Fig. 852).

Though the reign of Edward III. (see the portrait and insignia, Figs. 857 and 861), one of the most brilliant in English history, nominally commenced from the period of the death of his miserable father, it was not till the young monarch had delivered himself from the bondage of his father's murderers, who were no other than his mother and her favourite, Mortimer, that he was able to show himself as he was, and to make England what he thought England ought to be. In his eighteenth year Edward became a father, his queen Philippa then giving him a memorable son, the Black Prince of future history; and Edward thought it high time to take into his own hands the power which Mortimer exercised over the destinies of the country. But that nobleman was known to be as unscrupulous in maintaining as he had been from the first in possessing himself of power: the Earl of Kent, Edward's uncle, had already been sent to the gallows, on one of the most extra-ordinary charges perhaps ever recorded in our criminal annals, that he had designed to raise a dead man to the throne, his murdered brother Edward II., whom he had been led to think was still alive. Caution was then of high importance, or Edward III. might have shared the fate of his two distinguished relatives. Parliament about the time met at Nottingham, and Edward, his mother, and Mortimer, were all lodged in the castle. Edward's chief confidant in the enterprise meditated was Lord Montacute, who was seen one morning by one of Mortimer's people riding away into the country after a secret conference with Edward. The favourite took the alarm, and that very day charged the young king in council with confederating against him and the queen-mother. Edward denied the charge, but Mortimer was incredulous. Nottingham Castle was no place to be suddenly taken by assault, however skilfully or powerfully made; and Isabella, to prevent treachery, was accustomed to have the keys brought nightly to her bedside. So Mortimer appears to have felt safe. But that very night, Lord Montacute returned in the darkness with a strong party, the governor of the castle having privily agreed to open to them a secret subterranean passage which led into the castle, from a spot covered with brushwood and rubbish, on the outside of the base of the castle hill. These cavities in the earth, we may observe in passing, form a distinctive feature of Nottingham and the neighbourhood, and are supposed to have given name to the city and the shire—Snotenga-ham, the Saxon word, meaning, " the home of caverns." The engraving (Fig. 922) shows some of these caves, which are supposed to communicate with the castle. At midnight the party entered the cavern: at the foot of the main tower they were joined by Edward, and they all passed noiselessly on to a hall adjoining the queen-mother's chamber. Here they paused, hearing voices,—they were those of the Bishop of Lincoln and others sitting with Mortimer in council, to prevent probably the very tragedy now about to be consummated. Suddenly the door was burst open, and two knights killed who sought to defend it. Isabella in an instant was among the armed crowd, imploring her " sweet son " to spare the " gentle Mortimer;" and he was spared for the moment, but taken out of the castle in safe custody. The next day Edward publicly proclaimed himself virtual as well as nominal king, and soon after Mortimer was hung at the "Elms," and the guilty queen-mother shut up for life in her manor-house at Risings, where, however, Edward paid her her regular and respectful visits. And now Edward was free to begin the course that he had so long yearned for

There are few of our readers who will need to be told that the four-

teenth century was the golden age of chivalry in Europe; the period when all the conflicting qualities conjoined in that one word were carried to their extremest stages of development; or that Edward and his son the Black Prince were among the most perfect individual examples of what, according to the loftiest practical standard, the true knight should be, namely, pious but intolerant, romantic in love and licentious, brave and cruel in war, the gentlest of the gentle in peace; selfish and unprincipled in the pursuit of his own interests, yet occasionally capable of the most graceful and generous devotion to the feelings of those whom he had most deeply injured: and, lastly, ever a hero in the fulfilment of the especial duties enjoined by the knightly creed,—as in the redressing of wrongs, when he was not the wronger; the interposing his own body in battle to guard his liege lord from danger, when he did not happen to be fighting against him; the spreading the knowledge of the doctrines of peace by war, even though it were to make them detestable in the eyes of the learners, as they saw what they wrongly, but naturally, conceived to be their legitimate fruits in the conduct of the expounders. Whilst such the time, it was certainly an extraordinary coincidence that it should have such an historian as Froissart (Fig. 866), in whose pages the events that so thickly crowd them borrow a new lustre, and obtain a new interest, one, indeed, possibly more permanent than any of their own. It may be questioned whether there would now have been any popular recollection of a large portion of the doings of chivalry in the fourteenth century for their own sake; but Froissart recorded them, and there was no longer any question upon the matter. One could half wish, indeed, that the native deformity of warfare had not been veiled in such seductive colours. In the ensuing notice of the reign of Edward, we shall no longer follow the narrative form that we have thought advisable in connection with his more immediate predecessors, but select from different portions of his career a few of the leading incidents, as illustrative of the peculiarly chivalrous character of this sovereign and his age; and in so doing we shall, of course, generally follow the delightful records of the historian just named. And first we will look to Edward's life for an example of the chivalric love of the period, and which forms the subject of our engraving (Fig. 865).

During the early part of their reigns, the kings of Scotland and England were constantly at war; and on one occasion the former, David, laid siege to the castle of Wark, belonging to the Earl of Salisbury, then a prisoner in Paris, but which was so bravely defended by his countess, that David could make no impression on it. At last, understanding that some of the garrison had succeeded in getting out and passing his army in safety, and were then on their way to seek succour from King Edward, who was at York, he raised the siege, after another unsuccessful assault, and departed. He had scarcely gone, when Edward appeared before the castle, he and his men sore travelled in consequence of the haste they had made, and no less " sore displeased " that the enemy had not waited to fight them. The rest we must give in Froissart's own inimitable style:—" And as soon as the king was unarmed, he took ten or twelve knights with him, and went to the castle to salute the Countess of Salisbury, and to see the manner of the assaults of the Scots, and the defences that were made against them. As soon as the lady knew of the king's coming, she set open the gates, and came out so richly beseen, that every man marvelled of her beauty, and the gracious words and countenance she made. When she came to the king, she kneeled down to the earth, thanking him of his succours, and so led him into the castle to make him cheer and honour, as she that could right do it. Every man regarded her marvellously; the king himself could not withhold his regarding of her, for he thought that he never saw before so noble nor so fair a lady: he was stricken therewith to the heart with a sparkle of fine love that endured long after; he thought no lady in the world so worthy to be beloved as she. Thus they entered into the castle hand in hand; the lady led him first into the hall, and after into the chamber nobly apparelled. The king regarded so the lady that she was abashed. At last he went to a window to rest him, and so fell in a great study. The lady went about to make cheer to the lords and knights that were there, and commanded to dress the hall for dinner. When she had all desired and commanded, then she came to the king with a merry cheer, who was in a great study, and she said, ' Dear sir, who do ye study so for? Your grace not displeased, it appertaineth not to you so to do; rather ye should make good cheer and be joyful, seeing ye have chased away your enemies, who durst not abide you: let other men study for the remnant.' Then the king said, ' Ah, dear lady, know for truth that since I entered into the castle there is a study come to my mind, so that I cannot cheer, but muse; nor

910.—Strand Gate, Winchelsea.

916.—Hertford Castle

917.—Guy's Tower, Warwick Castle.

915.—Southampton Gate; North Front.

918.—Tunbridge Castle.

920.—Ruins of Scarborough Castle.

922.—West Gate and Holy Cross Church, Canterbury.

919.—Corfe Castle, Dorsetshire.

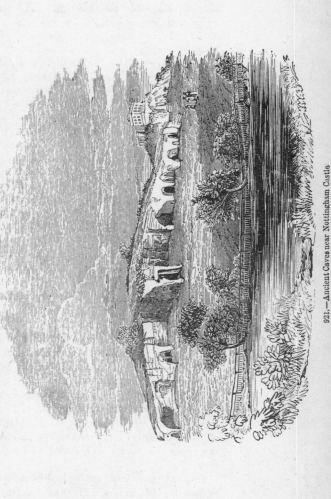

921.—Ancient Caves near Nottingham Castle.

I cannot tell what shall fall thereof: put it out of my heart I cannot!' 'Ah, sir!' quoth the lady, 'ye ought always to make good cheer, to comfort therewith your people. God hath aided you so in your business, and hath given you so great graces, that ye be the most doubted [feared] and honoured prince in all Christendom; and if the king of Scots have done you any despite or damage, ye may well amend it when it shall please you, as ye have done diverse times or [ere] this. Sir, leave your musing, and come into the hall, if it please you; your dinner is all ready.' 'Ah, fair lady,' quoth the king, 'other things lieth at my heart, that ye know not of: but surely the sweet behaving, the perfect wisdom, the good grace, nobleness, and excellent beauty that I see in you, hath so surprised my heart, that I cannot but love you, and without your love I am but dead.' Then the lady said, 'Ah! right noble prince, for God's sake mock nor tempt me not. I cannot believe that it is true that ye say, nor that so noble a prince as ye be would think to dishonour me and my lord my husband, who is so valiant a knight, and hath done your grace so good service, and as yet lieth in prison for your quarrel. Certainly, Sir, ye should in this case have but a small praise, and nothing the better thereby. I had never as yet such a thought in my heart, nor, I trust in God, never shall have, for no man living: if I had any such intention, your grace ought not only to blame me, but also to punish my body, yea, and by true justice to be dismembered.' Herewith the lady departed from the king, and went into the hall to haste the dinner. Then she returned again to the king, and brought some of his knights with her, and said, 'Sir, if it please you to come into the hall, your knights abideth for you to wash; ye have been too long fasting.' Then the king went into the hall and washed, and sat down among his lords, and the lady also. The king ate but little; he sat still musing, and as he durst he cast his eyes upon the lady. Of his sadness his knights had marvel, for he was not accustomed so to be; some thought it was because the Scots were escaped from him. All that day the king tarried there, and wist not what to do: sometimes he imagined that honour and truth defended him to let his heart in such a case dishonour such a lady, and so true a knight as her husband was, who had always well and truly served him: on the other part, love so constrained him, that the power thereof surmounted honour and truth. Thus the king debated in himself all that day and all that night; in the morning he arose and dislodged all his host, and drew after the Scots to chase them out of his realm. Then he took leave of the lady, saying, 'My dear lady, to God I commend you till I return again, requiring you to advise you otherwise than you have said to me.' 'Noble prince,' quoth the lady, 'God, the father glorious, be your conduct, and put you out of all villain thoughts. Sir, I am, and ever shall be, ready to do you pure service, to your honour and to mine.' Therewith the king departed all abashed." It speaks much for Edward's disposition that a few days after he made the release of the Earl of Salisbury the subject of an express item in a treaty with the French king, and was shortly " at London, making cheer to the Earl of Salisbury, who was now come out of prison." But Edward had not quite resolved to forget the enchantress. He gave a splendid feast in the city of London, to bring her once more within the sphere of his influence. She came, sore against her will, for she thought well enough wherefore it was; but she durst not discover the matter to her husband; she thought she would deal so as to bring the king from his opinion. . . . . All ladies and damsels were freshly beseen, according to their degrees, except Alice, Countess of Salisbury, for she went as simply as she might, to the intent that the king should not set his regard on her, for she was fully determined to do no manner of thing that should turn to her dishonour nor to her husband's. We cannot think she would have looked less lovely in Edward's eyes for the simplicity of her attire; but let us hope the high feelings that prompted its adoption gave a better tone to his own. It was this same model of conjugal fidelity of whom the well-known anecdote of the Garter is told, that gave rise to the illustrious order of Knights Companions, to which monarchs are in our own time proud to belong. " Evil be to him that evil thinks," said the king, to rebuke the smiles of his courtiers, when the fair countess accidentally dropped her garter. We can well appreciate his feelings, in determining to make that trivial incident the foundation of a lasting memorial of his admiration for a creature as far above most of her sex for the grace and purity of her soul, as for the exquisite beauty of her form.

Edward possessed an excitable temperament, which is some excuse for his errors. He was imaginative, and we can hardly ourselves escape being misled a little by the golden mist of romance in which most of his actions were enveloped. We have seen him in love; let us now watch him at his sports at his great castle of Windsor. We see him there fired with the idea of rendering England the centre of the world of honourable arms, himself the foremost man of that world, and carrying on a fantastic rivalry of knightly pageants with Philip of Valois, king of France. The proud Order just referred to (which some literal-minded sages profess to doubt he founded) was placed under the patronage of a name which only the wildest enthusiasm could have made holy. St. George of Cappadocia, primate of Egypt in the fourth century, had been put to death by the pagans of Alexandria: ample was the provocation given; but, nevertheless, he had suffered from the detestable pagans, and that was enough, with a little legendary colouring, to make a martyr of him. Our early Crusaders had read of him in their calendars and martyrologies, and they found him installed among the Eastern Christians under the winning appellation of St. George the Victorious—a characteristic which the sculptor of St. George at Dijon (Fig. 875) had evidently in view. These circumstances, and their gratitude for the assistance they imagined the beatified St. George had rendered them at the siege of Antioch, led to their adopting him as patron of soldiers. His saintship under Edward III. rose to a higher place, as patron of chivalry, and tutelar saint of England. A chapel in his honour was built or enlarged by Edward at Windsor, and although the present edifice is of later date, we cannot anywhere have a livelier idea of the impressive and imaginative splendours of knighthood than in this exquisite fabric, where the banners and escutcheons of the Knights Companions glitter above their carved stalls, within which we trace the armorial bearings of each knight of the Order from the time we are treating of. Another of Edward's fanciful acts was to build a round chamber at Windsor, two hundred feet in diameter, and call it the Round Table, for the accommodation of a brotherhood of knights, established during a splendid tournament, in the eighteenth year of his reign. For the original idea of this we must look to the popular romance of chivalry, in which King Arthur and the Knights of his Round Table shone conspicuous. Their pageants, Froissart tells us, were held at Windsor in the sixth century; and the public mind, grown as fanciful as that of the king, no doubt, enjoyed amazingly the actual revival of King Arthur's institution before their eyes, with all possible splendour, on the very spot tradition associated with its original glories. But Philip of Valois would have a Round Table too, and even the imposing assemblies of the Knights of the Garter were in danger of being thrown into the shade by the attractive pageants of his brother king on the other side the Channel. It was about 1350 that Edward began the erection of the great castellated works which were to form the vast regal castle. In 1356 Edward made one of his chaplains, William of Wykeham, chief architect, on a salary of a shilling a day. Imagination had left political wisdom so far in the rear, that the pattern of " true manhood, courteousness, and gentleness," saw no error in impressing artificers to make his castle, whether they liked his wages or not, and took no hint from their frequently stealing away to other employments that offered better; nor could he find any better remedy than a prison for the deserters, and penalties for those who employed them. The castle was finished about 1374, and was in extent and general arrangement the same as we now see it. (Fig 859.) But so much had notions of interior convenience changed by the last century, that a separate building had to be made for the royal family of George III. The noble pile underwent so much tasteless disguising, that at length there was " neither character nor grandeur to recommend it to the eye;" so an inventive writer signing Mela Britannicus, when a restoration of the old chivalric castle was under discussion in 1824, proposed to erase the whole pile, make one level of the site, and erect in its centre " *a compact Grecian edifice of moderate extent.*" This advice was declined by parliament, who granted three hundred thousand pounds to reinstate the castle, " as far as it consistently could be, in what was, or what might be supposed to have been, its original character." This object has not been very rigidly carried out, but the appearance of antiquity on the whole is obtained; and with all its faults, this castle is the only royal residence of any grandeur that we can boast. Here, then, at stately Windsor (Figs. 858, 859), the most dazzling spectacles of chivalry took place; here were not the " feasts of reason," but of fancy, that glow through our young dreams in such delightful hues. We listen with beating hearts to the king's heralds, clad in wondrous blazonry, proclaiming far and wide the coming tourney,—we follow with curious interest the successive arrivals of knights of heroic name from all parts of Christendom, who have Edward's letters of safe-conduct to pass and repass the realm,—we gaze with marvellous awe on their armies of retainers, their gleaming banners and lances, and shining mail; and amongst that part of the dazzling congregation within the lists in Windsor Park, who

"Assume the port
Of stately valour,"

our kindling eyes watch for the towering white ostrich plumes that distinguish our royal Edward, and that youthful prince of finest promise in the coal-black armour by his side. Well, the grand passage of arms (Fig. 860) is over. There may have been blood shed; but the true knight slays and dies with equal coolness, for, like Othello, nought does he in hate, but all in honour. Alas! poor imagination; such are its weak delusions. Hark! the minstrels' merry music summons to the banquet, where imagination is still the presiding deity. What a scene of gorgeous enjoyment! We have seen something like its form revived in modern days,—but the spirit cannot be revived; *that* has altogether evaporated, like the breath of its perfumes. The spirit of chivalry is dead. The impressive magnificence of the hall, the mixture of the warlike, the superb, and the picturesque in costume, the joy-inspiring wines of France and Spain, and Syria and Greece, the lays of Froissart, that lent to the scenes the charms of poetry and song (the poet is often forgotten in the historian), these and such-like circumstances were mere accessories to the peculiar enjoyments that arose out of the honours paid to the warriors for renown and ladies' love—the throbbing hopes of the young aspirants of chivalry, and the thrilling interest of the ladies in the perilous encounters, whose recollection and anticipation gave the chief zest to these happy hours of secure festivity.

From the chivalric preliminaries of and preparations for war, turn we now to war itself. We shall not, of course, enter into the oft-told story of the English claims upon the French throne, the armed assertion of which led to the memorable siege of Calais, and the battles of Cressy and Poictiers in the present reign. It will be sufficient to state, that war exemplifies most strikingly the inconsistencies of chivalry before alluded to. Whilst begun in injustice, and most ruthlessly carried on, seldom at the same time has a war exhibited so many touching and graceful examples of individual nobility of mind and kindliness of heart upon the part of its originators. The battle of Cressy occurred during the retreat of the English towards Ponthieu, followed by the French King Philip, at the head of an immense army, who were flushed with the hope of an easy conquest, and only alarmed lest their prey should escape. They were destined to learn better what the English were. When Edward had found a place to his mind, he quickly prepared for the fight that he saw must take place. The night before Saturday, the 6th of August, 1346, Edward, says Froissart, "made a supper to all his chief lords of his host, and made them good cheer. And when they were all departed to take their rest, then the king entered into his oratory, and kneeled down before the altar, praying God devoutly that if he fought the next day, that he might achieve a journey to his honour. Then about midnight he laid him down to rest, and in the morning he rose betimes and heard mass, and the prince, his son, with him, and the most part of the company, were confessed and houseled. And after the mass said, he commanded every man to be armed, and to draw to the field, to the same place before appointed. Then the king caused a park to be made by the wood side, behind his host, and there was set all carts and carriages, and within the park were all their horses, for every man was afoot; and into this park there was but one entry." We need hardly say the prince here mentioned was him whose deeds made the very colour of his armour among men a kind of symbol of all that was heroically brave and chivalrous; that it was the Black Prince, who in the battle of Cressy was to give the promise of the future conqueror of Poictiers. Edward arranged the English in three battalions, and then leaping "on a hobby with a white rod in his hand, one of his martials on the one hand, and the other on the other hand, he rode from rank to rank, desiring every man to take heed that day to his right and honour: he spoke it so sweetly, and with so good countenance and merry cheer, that all such as were discomfited took courage in the seeing and hearing of him. And when he had thus visited all his battles [battalions] it was then nine of the day: then he caused every man to eat and drink a little, and so they did at their leisure; and afterwards they ordered again their battles. Then every man lay down on the earth, and by him his salet and bow, to be the more fresher when their enemies should come." They were thus found by the French, who came on with cries of 'Down with them,' 'Let us slay them;' but as the English objected in their own peculiar way to both processes, the battle quickly commenced. The Genoese cross-bow men (see our engraving, Fig 872) were first ordered to advance, which they did unwillingly as being

utterly fatigued with their march. However, they went with great cries, which the Englishmen taking no notice of, they shot fiercely with their cross-bows. Then the English archers stepped forth one pass [pace], and let fly their arrows so wholly, and so thick, that it seemed snow." The Genoese were presently discomfited by the storm, and thrown into confusion: "Slay the rascals," then called out the sage king of the French, and the French men-at-arms ran in and killed a great number of them, while of course the Englishmen "shot wherever they saw the thickest press." The slaughter under such circumstances was terrible. As the fight thickened, the blind king of Bohemia called upon his people to lead him forward so that he might strike one stroke with his sword. They did so, and "to the intent that they might not lose him in the press, they tied all the reins of their bridles each to other, and set the king before to accomplish his desire, and so they went on their enemies." The whole party were found after the battle still united, but—in death. The king's crest appears to have been an eagle's pinion, from which the man by whose hands he fell plucked three feathers: the very mention of the words, "the Prince of Wales's feathers" will tell us who he was, and remind us of the mode in which the event of the blind hero's death has been made memorable. But this was not the only incident of the day in which the Black Prince's courage had been recorded. His "battalion at one period was very hard pressed; and they with the prince sent a messenger to the king, who sat on a little windmill hill;" then the knight said to the king, "'Sir, the Earl of Warwick, and the Earl of Oxford, Sir Reynold Cobham, and others, such as be about the prince, your son, are fiercely fought withal, and are sore handled, wherefore they desire you, that you and your battle will come and aid them: for if the Frenchmen increase, as they doubt they will, your son and they shall have much ado.' Then the king said, 'Is my son dead, or hurt, or on the earth felled?' 'No, Sir,' quoth the knight, 'but he is hardly matched, wherefore he hath need of your aid.' 'Well,' said the king, 'return to him and to them that sent you hither, and say to them, that they send no more to me for an adventure that falleth, as long as my son is alive; and also say to them that they suffer him this day to win his spurs, for, if God be pleased, I will this journey be his, and the honour thereof, and to them that be about him.'" No wonder these words "greatly encouraged the prince and his party, and made them only repine that they had sent to him at all. The battle was at last won, and the French when they were able to estimate the amount of their loss, found the appalling result to be—the death of the king of Bohemia, the Duke of Lorraine, the Earl of Alençon, the Count of Flanders, and eight other counts, two archbishops, seven lesser nobles, twelve hundred knights, and about thirty thousand of the soldiery. The miserable French monarch, Philip, was one of the latest to quit the field. As to the feelings of the prince and his father on meeting when all was over (see Mr. Harvey's design, Fig. 873), life could have hardly promised to have in store for either any other pleasure so exquisite as was then felt on that bloody but glorious field of Cressy; by the father, to have such a son—by the son, to have exhibited himself before such a father.

The siege of Calais was begun only five days later; and if the English anticipated an easy success, they were soon to find their error. Our military annals furnish few cases of more determined and noble resistance than that maintained for so many months by the burghers of Calais under the command of John de Vienne, a commander worthy of the commanded: it would be impossible to award him higher praise. Famine attacked them even more fiercely than Edward, and still they resisted; and it was only when, after almost incredible fortitude, they saw their last hope dashed to the ground, at the very moment they anticipated relief,—it was only when Philip came towards Calais, and then, not liking the aspect of the English defence, turned and went back again, that they allowed themselves to think of submission. But Philip's cruel desertion was a deathblow. They sent to Edward; who, however, would listen to no terms but unconditional submission. The noble Sir Walter Manny, however, spoke for them; and, at last, mercy was promised to all but six of the chief burgesses, who were to come to him bareheaded, barefooted, with ropes about their necks, and the keys of the town and castle in their hands. Let those who would see what is true—as compared with what is but, after all, factitious—glory, look at the conduct of the burghers of Calais, and contrast it with the conduct of the best of the European chivalry. The people of Calais were summoned by the market-bell into the market-place, and there the conditions of mercy were made known. "Then all the people began to weep, and make much sorrow, that there was not so hard a heart, if they had seen them, but that would have had great pity of them: the captain [John de Vienne] himself wept piteously. At last a most rich burgess of all the town,

923.—Baynard's Castle.

924.—Ruins of the Savoy Palace, 1711.

925.—Bodiam Castle, Sussex.

926.—Arundel Castle.

927.—Leeds Castle.

928.—Betchworth Castle.

929.—North West View of Salisbury Cathedral.

930.—Salisbury Choir.

933.—Early English Foliage Bracket.

934.—Gable Crosses.

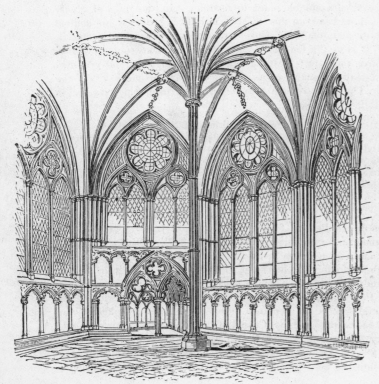

931.—Chapter House, Salisbury.

932.—Salisbury.

245

called Eustace de Saint Pierre, rose up and said openly, 'Sirs, great and small, great mischief it should be, to suffer to die such people as be in this town, either by famine or otherwise, when there is a means to save them. I think he or they should have great merit of our Lord God, that might keep them from such mischief. As for my part, I have so good trust in our Lord God, that if I die in the quarrel to save the residue, that God would pardon me; wherefore, to save them I will be the first to put my life in jeopardy.' When he had thus said, every man worshipped him, and divers kneeled down at his feet, with sore weeping, and sore sighs. Then another honest burgess rose and said, 'I will keep company with my gossip Eustace;' he was called Jehan d'Aire. Then rose up Jacques de Wisant, who was rich in goods and heritage; he said also that he would hold company with his two cousins likewise; so did Peter of Wisant, his brother: and then rose two others; they said they would do the same. Then they went and apparelled them as the king desired. Then the captain went with them to the gate; there was great lamentation made of men, women, and children at their departing. Then the gate was opened, and he issued out with the six burgesses, and closed the gate again; so they were between the gate and the barriers." Then they were handed to Sir Walter Manny, with an earnest injunction on the part of John de Vienne, that he would interfere to save them; an injunction, however, that Sir Walter needed not. When they were presented to the king, "they kneeled down and held up their hands, and said, 'Gentle king, behold here we six, who were burgesses of Calais, and great merchants; we have brought the keys of the town and of the castle, and we submit ourselves clearly unto your will and pleasure, to save the residue of the people of Calais, who have suffered great pain. Sir, we beseech your grace to have mercy and pity on us, through your high nobles.' Then all the earls and barons and others that were there wept for pity. The king looked *felly* on them, for greatly he hated the people of Calais, for the great damage and displeasures they had done him on the sea before. Then he commanded their heads to be stricken off. Then every man required the king for mercy, but he would hear no man in that behalf. Then Sir Walter of Manny said, 'Ah, noble king, for God's sake refrain your courage; ye have the name of sovereign noblesse; therefore, now do not a thing that should blemish your renown, nor to give cause to some to speak of you villanously; every man will say it is a great cruelty to put to death such honest persons, who by their own wills put themselves into your grace to save their company.' Then the king wryed away from him, and commanded to send for the hangman, and said, 'They of Calais had caused many of my men to be slain, wherefore these shall die in likewise.' Then the queen, being great with child, kneeled down (see Fig. 867), and sore weeping, said, 'Ah, gentle Sir, sith I passed the sea in great peril, I have desired nothing of you; therefore now I humbly require you, in the honour of the Son of the Virgin Mary, and for the love of me, that ye will take mercy of these six burgesses.' The king beheld the queen, and stood still in a study a space, and then said, 'Ah, dame, I would ye had been as now in some other place; ye make such request to me that I cannot deny you, wherefore I give them to you, to do your pleasure with them.' Then the queen caused them to be brought into her chamber, and made the halters to be taken from their necks, and caused them to be new clothed, and gave them their dinner at their leisure, and then she gave each of them six nobles, and made them to be brought out of the host in safeguard, and set at their liberty." Froissart, unhappily, was deceived as to their being freed. Edward, if he could not make up his mind altogether to resist the entreaties of his friends not to do a deed which would have made him infamous for ever, was at the last ungracious enough to keep them prisoners: in the records of the Tower of London we read of the entrance of John de Vienne and the six burgesses.

The battle of Poictiers (Fig. 876) was fought and won by the Black Prince alone, and under circumstances of disproportion in the number of troops engaged on each side, quite as remarkable as those of Cressy, while the results were still more signal. Among the prisoners after the conflict was the French King John, son of Philip of Valois. His capture is one of the most interesting as well as most important incidents of the battle. Undeterred by their frightful losses at Cressy, so directly brought on by their mismanagement and conceit, the French directed their vast army at Poictiers with the same want of skill and prudence, and in consequence soon found the battle going as terribly against them. And as, when the mischief was done, Philip of Valois had distinguished himself by his personal courage in the former battle, so did his son now imitate his example in this, fighting on foot, battle-axe in hand; as though doing the duty of a man-at-arms could retrieve the consequences of the

neglect of duty as a commander. By his side was a boy of sixteen, who, whilst his elder brethren fled, exhibited a heroism as remarkable, considering his age, as anything in the history of the great English prince, whom the boy of sixteen stood in arms with his countrymen to oppose. Keeping his eyes constantly on his father, and neglecting all thoughts of himself, he cried out, as he saw any blow about to be struck at the king, "Father, guard yourself on the right; guard yourself on the left," &c. John was twice wounded, and once beaten to the ground, but he rose again, replying with fresh blows to every fresh requisition to surrender. A young French knight attached to the English army at last forced his way towards him "by strength of his body and arms;" in the hope of moving him: "Sir, yield you," he said as he drew near. "The king beheld the knight, and said, 'To whom shall I yield me? Where is my cousin the Prince of Wales? If I might see him, I would speak to him.' Denis answered and said, 'Sir, he is not here; but yield you to me, and I shall bring you to him.' 'Who be you?' quoth the king. 'Sir, I am Denis of Morbecque, a knight of Artois; but I serve the king of England, because I am banished the realm of France, and I have forfeited all I had there.' Then the king gave him his right gauntlet, saying, 'I yield me to you.'" It was with great difficulty, however, and not till especial assistance had been rendered, that John was brought in safety to the English quarters, the whole of the knights and others around struggling each to make him his particular conquest. The conduct of the Prince of Wales that night at supper towards his captive guest, and which was but the commencement of an unbroken series of kindly and graceful attentions, is well known. John was brought to England, and received with chivalrous courtesy by King Edward; then, after the lapse of two or three years, allowed to return to France, to see if the French people would consent to Edward's terms, which were, that on full and entire sovereignty being yielded to him over Guienne, Poictiers, and Ponthieu, he would renounce all other claims to France. The terms, however, being declined by John's subjects, he most honourably returned to his captivity, and died in the palace which had been assigned as his residence, the Savoy (Figs. 897, 924), the chief metropolitan residence of Edward's fourth son, the famous John of Gaunt. And what was the end of these brilliant displays of skill and courage? of all this outpouring of human blood? of all the cities, and towns, and villages of beautiful France burnt and wasted and pillaged? Why, that at the close of Edward's reign matters remained just as they were at the commencement: we were as far off as ever from the attainment of our object.

The Black Prince in the later period of his life appears to have been necessitated through illness to become something more of the citizen than must have altogether suited his taste. Coventry (Figs. 874 and 881) became his favourite place of residence; a circumstance the visitor will find recorded in the remarkable St. Mary's Hall, that richest and in every way completest of specimens of English architecture in the fifteenth century. Its foundation was connected with the growth of the guilds of Coventry, which, first established in the reign of Edward III., rapidly rose into prosperity, and required a suitable place to meet in. In the reign of Henry VI. nothing less than this St. Mary's Hall (Fig. 881) would content the taste and wealth of Coventry, and an honourable memorial, truly, it is of the founders. A tapestry in it, constructed in 1450, measures thirty feet by ten, contains eighty figures, and is a fine specimen of the artistical as well as of the mechanical skill of the time. The verses referring to the Black Prince, which we find in the Hall, tell us that

Edward, the flower of chivalry, whilom the Black Prince hight,
Who prisoner took the French King John, in claim of Grandame's right;
And slew the King of Beame in field,—whereby the ostrich pen
He won and wore on crest here first; which posie bore *Ich Dien*.
Amid these martial feats of arms, wherein he had no peer,
His bounty eke to shew, this seat he chose, and loved full dear;
The former state he got confirmed, and freedom did increase,
A president of knighthood rare, as well for war as peace.

The prince died in 1376, in his forty-sixth year. The beautiful monument in Canterbury Cathedral (Fig. 877) marks his last resting place. Just twelve months after, his father followed him; too late, unfortunately for his fame, for he turned driveller in his old age, and died without a single friend by his side; the very lady, Alice Perrers, whom he had so favoured, deserting him when there was nothing more to be gained by his smiles or lost by his frowns. He of course rests in the "Chapel of the King," the Choir of Westminster Abbey, and beneath the monument shown in our engraving (Fig. 884). An admirable summary of the domestic character of this reign has been given by Sir James Mackintosh:—"During 2 reign of fifty years, Edward III. issued writs of summons, which are extant to this day, to assemble seventy parliaments, or great councils. He thus engaged the pride and passions of the parliament and the people so deeply in support of his projects of aggrandisement, that they became his zealous and enthusiastic followers. His ambition was caught by the nation, and men of the humblest station became proud of his brilliant victories. To form and keep up this state of public temper was the mainspring of his domestic administration, and satisfactorily explains the internal tranquillity of England during the forty years of his effective reign. It was the natural consequence of so long and watchful a pursuit of popularity, that most grievances were redressed as soon as felt, that parliamentary authority was yearly strengthened by exercise, and that the minds of the turbulent barons were exclusively turned towards a share of their sovereign's glory. Quiet at home was partly the fruit of fame abroad." The great national assemblies were not fixed at Westminster before the latter part of this reign. We have a lively picture of their previous roving habits in the 'Westminster Review:'—"The constitution of King, Lords, and Commons was accustomed to scamper, as fast as the state of the roads would admit, all over the kingdom, from Berwick-upon-Tweed to the Land's End. Within one year it would hold its parliamentary sitting at Carlisle and Westminster, in the following year at Exeter and Norwich, or at Lincoln and Worcester. . . . . Not only were the early parliaments holden in different towns, but they frequently moved from place to place daily during the session." Our imperious senators and their insolent retainers often scattered the opposite of blessings among the common people, whom they honoured with the charge of entertaining them, and the country generally had cause to be gratified with the settlement at Westminster. The supreme judicial courts had been fixed here some time, and so have remained to this day. One of the good things secured in Magna Charta was an article to the effect that the court for finally deciding actions between man and man, the court of Common Pleas, should be settled in one place, instead of following the king's court hither and thither, by which many of the poorer orders were cut off from redress, because they could not afford time nor money for journeys. The courts of Exchequer and Chancery, and of King's Bench, so called from the monarch sitting on a bench raised above the seats of the judges, as well as the courts just mentioned, still sit in the venerable hall of the old palace of Westminster, as they have done more than five hundred years, though the palace itself was deserted by the court for Whitehall in the time of Henry VIII., in consequence of a fire that nearly consumed the ancient pile. Westminster Hall as it now stands (Figs. 895, 903) was rebuilt in the reign we are about to enter upon, in 1389. We cannot discover at what period the Hall was deserted by the peers for the "Old House of Lords," which adjoined the Painted Chamber on the south. The House of Lords recently destroyed was formed in 1800 out of the old Court of Requests, which had formed, it is believed the banqueting-hall of the old palace before Rufus built the grand hall used for parliaments. The Painted Chamber (Fig. 901) was used by Edward III. for holding a parliament in 1364. Why this apartment was so named was not ascertained until the beginning of this century, when the old tapestry being removed, paintings were disclosed containing a multitude of large figures, and representing battles. In the manuscript itinerary of Simon Simeon and Hugo the Illuminator, dated 1322, we find a remarkable mention of these ancient relics :—"To the same monastery (Westminster Abbey) is almost immediately joined that most famous palace of the king, in which is the well-known chamber on whose walls all the history of the wars of the whole Bible are exquisitely painted, with most complete and perfect inscriptions in French, to the great admiration of the beholders, and with the greatest regal magnificence."

A noticeable feature of Edward's reign was the separation of the Commons from the Lords in 1377, on the ground that they could not have a president of their own while the two assemblies sat together. Their meetings were not characterised by refinement, whatever honesty of purpose they may have had to boast. "Debates were carried on more by the eloquence of the *fist* than the tongue," and private broils seemed to occupy them quite as much as the duty to which the early Commons professed to confine themselves, that of studying the welfare, complaining of the grievances, and supplying the defects of the places they came to represent.

The want of éclat and glitter about them was, however, one cause why they were so disrespectfully regarded by the higher powers, for scenes quite as much at variance with the calmness of deliberative wisdom were frequently occurring among the Lords, as well as among the Commons. We have an amusing anecdote of the abbot of Westminster and the Commons, while the latter sat in the chapter-house of the abbey, their first distinct place of meeting. On one occasion the Commons, forgetting the solemn purposes of their assembling, became so riotous, and created so great a turmoil, that the abbot waxed indignant at the profanation, and collecting a sufficiently strong party, turned the whole legislative wisdom out of his house, and swore lustily that the place "should not again be defiled with a like rabble." Nevertheless, the Commons continued in the chapter-house until the time of Edward VI., when St. Stephen's chapel was adapted for their use. The engraving of this chapel restored (Fig. 907) is designed to illustrate its supposed appearance prior to Edward VI. It was then an unique and superb little fabric, rebuilt by Edward III., about the time when he commenced the castle of Windsor. The adaptations to the Commons' use, made from time to time, completely hid its beauties. At the beginning of this century, the admission of the new Irish members rendered enlargement necessary ; when, on the removal of the wainscoting, it was discovered that the old walls and roof had been entirely covered with painting, gilding, and rich ornamental work, in the very best style of the arts in the fourteenth century. As to the architecture, we need only refer to the engraving of the restoration already mentioned, and the engraving of the appearance of the chapel after the fire of the houses (Fig. 906), when, as was observed at the time, it was really wonderful to see the sharpness and beautiful finish of the mouldings, the crockets, the embossed ornaments, and other running workmanship in stone, notwithstanding the violence which the chapel had suffered from ancient destroyers and modern improvers, and notwithstanding that it had come out of the fiery furnace of so fierce a conflagration.

The reign of Richard of Bourdeaux, son of the Black Prince, begins in sunshine and splendour :—

> Fair laughs the morn, and soft the zephyr blows,
>   While, proudly rising o'er the azure realm,
> In gallant trim the gilded vessel goes,
>   Youth on the prow, and pleasure at the helm ;
> Regardless of the sweeping whirlwind's spray,
> That, hush'd in grim repose, expects his evening prey."
>
> GRAY.

The portrait in royal robes (Fig. 886) brings before the mind the enthusiastic rejoicings that welcome the beautiful boy as he is brought from the Tower to be crowned at Westminster. There are around him a devoted multitude of nobles, knights, and esquires, that dazzle his eye with their costly adornments. The streets they pass through on their gorgeously-caparisoned coursers are hung with floating draperies, the windows are full of gazers. The air resounds with rapturous shouts, "God bless the royal boy! Long live King Richard!" In Cheapside golden angels bend to him from the towers of mimic castles, presenting crowns; and at other places he is met by beautiful virgins of his own age and stature, robed in white, who blow leaves and flowers of gold in his face, and, as he approaches nearer, they fill gold cups from the conduits flowing with wine, and hand to him. High and low delight to honour him for his father's sake. His plastic imagination is of course most highly wrought upon by the magnificent pageants, and by the unbounded adulation that he witnesses on all sides. They bewilder his reason, and make him fancy himself a god, long before he has learned to be a man.

Do we find nothing in the picture given us by Froissart of his prime (Fig. 889) that looks like a consequence of the injudicious treatment he received in boyhood ? "There was none so great in England that dared speak against anything that the king did. He had a council suitable to his fancies, who exhorted him to do what he *list*: he kept in his wages ten thousand archers, who watched over him day and night." Do we wonder to find that he is buried in selfish luxury; that he only regards the misery of his people to add to it; or that he resorts to craft, injustice, and cruelty to protect his "precious crown" from those of his peers whom he calls his foes, because they have dared to whisper caution to the foolish dreamer ?

There is one pleasant side, certainly, to this part of his life. Like his illustrious grandfather, Richard was a poetically-minded man, and loved and promoted the arts. The engraving (Fig. 894) gives us a glimpse of him as a literary patron, while it interests us also as a glimpse of the manners of the times. The king's luxurious barge and the lowly boat of the poet Gower have met on the busy Thames. The king invites the poet into the barge, and there, calmly sailing, converses at large with him, while the fresh breeze plays in the silk-embroidered awning. This was the occasion when

935.—Capital.

937.—Canopy.

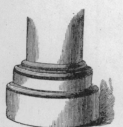

939.—Base.

936.—Capital.

938.—Bracket.

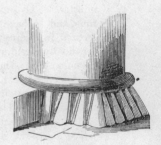

940.—Base.

950.—West Front of York Minster

941.—Boss.

947.—Decorate Foliage.

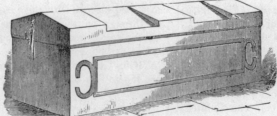

949.—Coped Tomb.

948.—Decorated Foliage.

942.—Boss.

944—Boss.

946.—Finial.

945.—Finial.

951.—York, from the Ancient Ramparts.

955.—Capital, Chapter-House.

959.—Archbishop Savage.

960.—Archbishop Gray.

951.—Pendant, Chapter-House.

956.—Sculpture over West Door.

962.—Sculpture over West Door.

952.—Interior of the Choir of York Minster

963.—Bracket.

957.—Bracket.

958.—Capital, Crypt.

964.—Capital, Crypt.

953.—York. General View.

954.—Choir. York.

No. 32.

249

Gower received command to pen a new book, which proved to be the 'Confessio Amantis.'

We are loth to turn from gentle scenes like this; scenes for which Richard was as peculiarly fitted as he was altogether unfit for the stern duties of the governor of a kingdom convulsed by storms of no ordinary kind. The important event shown in Fig. 893 occurred on the 16th of September, 1398. King Richard is there seen banishing Mowbray, Duke of Norfolk, Earl Marshal of England, and his own cousin, Henry of Derby, afterwards called Bolingbroke. Henry was the only son of the eldest of the two princes that survived Edward III.'s seven sons: these two were John of Gaunt (Fig. 887), Duke of Lancaster, and Edmund of Langley (Fig. 885), Duke of York. It appears that, shortly before, Bolingbroke, riding between Swindon and London, was overtaken by Mowbray, who said to him, "We are about to be ruined." "For what?" asked Bolingbroke. "For the affair of Radcot Bridge," answered Mowbray. "How can that be, after his pardon and declaration in Parliament?" "He will annul that pardon," said Mowbray: "and our fate will be like that of others before us." And then he spoke of Richard's well-known duplicity and faithlessness, positively asserting that the king and his minions were at that very time planning to destroy other peers as well as themselves. "If such be the case, we can never trust them," observed Hereford. "So it is," said Mowbray; "and though they may not be able to do it now, they will contrive to destroy us in our houses ten years hence." This conversation reached the king, and Bolingbroke declared it true in open parliament. Norfolk, having surrendered on proclamation, denied the story flatly, and accepted Hereford's gage of defiance. A court of chivalry was held, lists were set up at Coventry for a trial by combat, in accordance with the custom of the times (Figs. 878, 879). "Now I shall have peace from henceforward," said Richard to himself; but could he have looked into the future, how different would have been his exclamation! The combatants were ready, their lances in rest, their beavers closed, the trumpet had sounded, Bolingbroke had started six or seven paces forward, when the heralds cried, "Ho! Ho! the king has thrown his warder down." Their spears are taken from them, and two long hours of suspense conclude with an unequal and arbitrary sentence. Norfolk dies in his exile broken-hearted, but Bolingbroke has a younger and more buoyant spirit, and he is sustained by the ardent sympathies of hosts of friends, who feel his wrong their own. His humble and courteous manners—

"Off goes his bonnet to an oyster-wench,"

says the poet—have won for him the love of all classes, and the proofs he has given of a cool, sagacious intellect and high energies lead them to look on him as the star of their hopes, which will one day shine brightly forth, although a cloud is now upon it.

Passing over ten months, the engraving of ships of the time of Richard II. (Fig. 883) brings us, with a trifling exercise of imagination, to an event little dreamed of by the deluded Richard—the return of Henry, now in his own person Duke of Lancaster, his father having died during his exile. He has stolen from France with a few friends and servants, taking advantage of Richard's absence from his kingdom to quell some tumults in the south of Ireland. He hovers about the coast at first, as if doubtful of a welcome; but his wrongs are fresh in the minds of his countrymen, especially that most inhuman one, Richard's seizure of his inheritance on his father's death, in one fell swoop,—gold, lands, and honours, even to the household furniture. Thousands of swords are ready to leap from their scabbards to compel the tyrant to make him restitution. With their aid he will have his dukedom, and dwell again in his native air, or find a speedy grave. With this resolution Henry lands in Ravenspur in Yorkshire, on the 4th of July, 1399, unfurls the standard of revolt, and finds, in a wonderful short space of time, that he may not only be duke but—king.

Can a few months have so completely changed the relative positions of the injurer and the injured, as we find in the first meeting of Richard and Bolingbroke, at Flint Castle (Fig. 898)? Alas, poor king! Bolingbroke has scattered all his splendour and power like a dream. The chief castles and towns, including London itself, have flung wide their gates to the banished man. All—all is Bolingbroke's. And around the fortress to which he has been entrapped by Northumberland are countless thousands of armed men, and these, too, are Bolingbroke's. In gentle words must the proud monarch speak to his "Fair cousin of Lancaster;" a welcome most foreign to his heart must he offer, standing before him with uncovered head. Henry is sincere enough in his part of the greeting, and every word stings like a serpent. "My lord, I am come somewhat before my time, but I will tell you the reason.

Your people complain that you have ruled them harshly for twenty-two years, but; if it please God, *I will help you to rule them better*." What could Richard say to this unsolicited offer of assistance? "Fair cousin, if it pleaseth you it pleaseth me." The interview involves feelings too intense to be sustained long. No more is said between them; but, with a loud and stern voice, Bolingbroke commands the king's horses to be brought forth. The next of the three pictures we have copied (Figs. 896, 898, 900) from the interesting and remarkably beautiful series of illuminations in a metrical history of Richard's expedition to Ireland, and of the events immediately ensuing, written by a "Frenchman of mark" in his suite, shows us Richard's humiliating entry into London in the train of his cousin, serving as a sort of foil to set off his greatness. Passing by the immaterial circumstance that the illumination represents the personages on foot, apparently because about to enter the tower (Fig. 900), Shakspere's matchless description of the sad spectacle will be a better explanation than any words of ours :—

> "The duke, great Bolingbroke,
> Mounted upon a hot and fiery steed,
> Which his aspiring rider seemed to know;
> With slow, but stately pace, kept on his course,
> While all tongues cried—God save thee, Bolingbroke!
> You would have thought the very windows spake,
> So many greedy looks of young and old
> Through casements darted their devouring eyes
> Upon his visage; and that all the walls
> With painted imag'ry, had said at once—
> Jesu preserve thee! welcome, Bolingbroke!
> Whilst he, from one side to the other turning,
> Bare-headed, lower than his proud steed's neck,
> Bespake them thus : I thank you, countrymen ;—
> And thus still doing, thus he passed along.
>
> *   *   *   *   *
>
> As in a theatre, the eyes of men,
> After a well-grac'd actor leaves the stage,
> Are idly bent on him that enters next,
> Thinking his prattle to be tedious :
> Even so, or with much more contempt, men's eyes
> Did scowl on Richard : no man cried, God save him ;
> No joyful tongue gave him his welcome home ;
> But dust was thrown upon his sacred head,
> Which with such gentle sorrow he shook off—
> His face still combating with tears and smiles,
> The badges of his grief and patience—
> That had not God, for some strong purpose, steeled
> The hearts of men, they must perforce have melted,
> And barbarism itself have pitied him. "

Of course no time was lost in formally deposing the helpless king, an event that forms the subject of the next engraving (Fig. 896), where we see the nobles met for that purpose in the very hall of Westminster that Richard had rebuilt, and which remains to this day a magnificent memorial of his artistical tastes. Near the vacant throne sits Bolingbroke, while the resignation of Richard,—extorted by the fear of death, but *said* to have been made with a merry countenance,—is read and accepted by the parliament; then, shouts of joy from the concourse of people without, make sweet music in the duke's ears. He rises, amid a hush of expectation; and there has been nothing in his surprising conquest to prevent us from giving him credit, for feelings at this solemn moment more elevated and pure than those of mere selfish ambition. He deliberately approaches the throne, stops close to it, solemnly crosses himself, and makes his claim in these words:—"In the name of God the Father, Son, and Holy Ghost, I, Henry of Lancaster, challenge this realm of England, because I am descended by right line of blood from the good lord King Henry III., and through that right, that God of his grace hath sent me, with help of my kin, and of my friends, to recover it; the which realm was in point to be undone, for default of government, and undoing of the good laws." The claim being responded to most joyfully and heartily, he kneels in prayer on the steps of the throne, and then mounts them, and takes his seat. Henry IV. is King of England.

For the last scene of all, that ends this strange eventful history, we turn to Pontefract Castle (Fig. 899), whither Richard, on the recommendation of the House of Peers, has been privately conveyed; and it is not without a shudder we quote Gray's fine lines, indicating the fate that, it is but too probable, here closed the career of the royal captive, within five months of his deposition :—

> "Fill high the sparkling bowl,
>   The rich repast prepare,
> Reft of a crown, he yet may share the feast;
>   Close by the regal chair,
>   Fell thirst and famine scowl
> A baleful smile upon their baffled guest."

We can hardly believe that Henry would sanction so detestable

STRATFORD CHURCH.

INTERIOR, SEEN FROM THE DOOR.

CHANTRY CHAPEL.
ADJOINING THE BEAUCHAMP CHAPEL, WARWICK.

METHLEY HALL

OLD ENGLAND

A PICTORIAL MUSEUM

OF NATIONAL ANTIQUITIES

VOL. I.

1847

CHAUCER.

A FAC-SIMILE OF AN ILLUMINATION IN THE BRITISH MUSEUM.

SCREEN AT THE WEST FRONT, EXETER CATHEDRAL.

CHOIR OF ELY CATHEDRAL.

DRYBURCH ABBEY.

a cruelty, for it appears that he was not without personal regard for his royal relative, and had refused to take his life when the Commons petitioned him to do so. The Percies, before the battle of Shrewsbury, distinctly charged Henry with having caused Richard to perish from hunger, thirst, and cold, after fifteen days and nights of sufferings unheard of among Christians; but their grounds for that dreadful charge do not appear, and the variety of rumours as to the mode of Richard's death, and the very fact of his having died at all being doubted by many people for a number of years, make the imputation against Henry a very doubtful one. In the beginning of March, 1400, Richard's body—or what was asserted to be such—was brought out of Pontefract Castle (Fig. 899), in funeral procession, and conveyed to London, to the new king, who paid to it all possible respect, and interred it with great state in Westminster Abbey.

———

There are many highly picturesque castellated remains of this period scattered over England, which we have been unable to introduce in our sketches of regal history; we shall therefore briefly review them in connection with the baronial.

In the reign of Henry III., Prince Edward, fighting for his father against the barons, took Tunbridge Castle (Fig. 918) from Gilbert Rufus, Earl of Clare, Gloster, and Hertford. The first of this family who comes under our notice is the founder of Tunbridge Castle and town, Richard FitzGilbert, a follower of the Conqueror. Tunbridge was long a place of consequence, and its walls have echoed to the clangour of many a martial and many a festive scene, under the Badlesmeres and Cobhams, as well as the more legitimate owners. Chepstow Castle (Fig. 908), on the beautiful Wye, rose into existence at the same time, and descended from the same family to the possession of the Plantagenets, Herberts, and Somersets. And a noble ruin Chepstow forms, and finely harmonizes with one of the finest of scenes; nestling in foliage above the romantic cliff whose shadow slumbers on the stream. The Fitzwalters, a branch of the same family, possessed Old Baynard's Castle, London, founded by Baynard, one of the Conqueror's bold adherents, on the Thames, conspicuous among the martial residences of Old London until its destruction by fire in 1428. The Fitzwalters claimed to be Chatellans and chief standard-bearers of London. In 1214, Robert Fitzwalter held a conspicuous post of honour as general of "the army of God and the Holy Church;" by which the great charter, on which our national liberties were founded, was extorted from John. His daughter, "the fair maid of Essex," had attracted the notice of the licentious king, whose base passions led to his demolition of her father's castle, one of the causes which induced the citizens of London to think it time to arm for the protection of their households, as well as for national liberty. Gilbert Strongbow, son of Gilbert de Clare, was made Earl of Pembroke by King Stephen. Pembroke Castle (Fig. 838) was given to the family of De Valence by Henry III. We find Aymer de Valence, Earl of Pembroke, one of Edward I.'s most efficient generals against the Scottish king, Robert Bruce. The situation of the fortress is the extremity of a rocky promontory; its style, Norman mixed with early Gothic. The Norman family of Umfranville received from William the Conqueror the ancient Northumbrian castle of Prudhoe, deriving its appellation from the *proud* eminence it occupied, and keeping guard over a dangerous border district inhabited by a fierce and unsettled people. Many of the Umfranvilles seem to have distinguished themselves in opposing the incursions of the Scotch. Odonel in 1174 gallantly defended Prudhoe against the Scottish King William. He had the character of an oppressive lord to his poorer neighbours. Gilbert, who died in 1245, is called by Matthew Paris "a famous baron, the flower and keeper of the northern parts." But they were not always on the side of England. Three Umfranvilles were Earls of Angus. It was one of them who so honourably distinguished himself as a Scotchman by his integrity and spirit when Scotland succumbed the first time to the encroachments of the English on its independence. The last Umfranville of any note was Vice-Admiral of England in 1410; Robin Mend-Market he was facetiously styled, after bringing from a Scotch war large spoils of cloth and corn: he died at Bonjie in Anjou. The Tailboys, and then the Percies, have since succeeded to the possession of Prudhoe. Having alluded to the wars in Scotland and the border, we may next refer to the great Scottish family of Douglas, whose history blends itself with that of the majestic relic of Tantallon Castle, East Lothian (engraved in Fig. 850), until all traces of both are lost in the uncertain haze of the far past. The surges of the German Ocean beat in vain against that rock which stands out among them as if proud of its burden, though it is but a ruin; and the stormy blasts are weary with trying to overthrow

that range of solid wall, which has defied alike wars and the elements through unnumbered centuries, and still lifts its shattered front and mournful-looking tower to tell of the Douglas and his deeds. The might of the family was bound up in that of the castle, and its overthrow, according to the old Scottish proverb, was [read] as impossible a thing as "To ding down Tantallon and make a bridge to the Bass" (a celebrated rock, two miles distant from Tantallon, out at sea). Among the many famous Douglases, one was the firm supporter of Bruce in his worst adversities, and the commander of the centre of the Scottish van at Bannockburn; who died fighting with the Saracens as he was bearing the heart of his royal master to the Holy Land. He is called "the good Sir James;" but that his goodness was after the fashion of other heroes of that age, and did not exclude ferocity and cruelty, we have a notable instance in the tradition of the Douglas border, still current in the vicinity of Douglas Castle, and mentioned by Scott in 'Castle Dangerous.' After recovering his castle from the English, Douglas mercilessly slew all his prisoners, and burned them on a heap of malt, corn, and wine-casks, and all else that he could find in the castle that he was not able to carry away. The rivalry of this great border family with the Percies, also Borderers, led to the remarkable contest called, in song, the Battle of Chevy Chase, fought on the 15th of August, 1388 (Fig. 845). Percy vowed he would take his pleasure in the border woods three days, and slay the Douglas deer. Earl Douglas heard of the rash vaunt: "Tell him," said he, "he will find *one* day more than enough." Percy's aim was the armed encounter thus promised. We see him at Chevy Chase with his greyhounds and fifteen hundred chosen archers. After taking his sport at the Douglas's expense, gazing on a hundred dead fallow-deer and harts, tasting wine and venison cooked under the greenwood tree, and saying the Douglas had not kept his word, when

> Lo, yonder doth Earl Douglas come,
> His men in armour bright,
> Full twenty hundred Scottish spears
> All marching in our sight,
>
> All men of pleasant Tiviot-dale,
> Fast by the river Tweed.
> "O cease your sport," Earl Percy said,
> "And take your bows with speed."

Soon after this

> The battle closed on every side,
> No slackness there was found,
> And many a gallant gentleman
> Lay gasping on the ground.

The mail-clad leaders combated hand to hand, until the blood dropped from them like rain. "Yield thee, Percy," cried Douglas, "I shall freely pay thy ransom, and thy advancement shall be high with our Scottish king."

> 'No, Douglas," quoth Earl Percy then,
> "Thy proffer I do scorn;
> I would not yield to any Scot
> That ever yet was born."

Almost immediately he dropped, struck to the heart by an arrow. "Fight on, my merry men," cried he with his dying breath. Percy took his hand: "Earl Douglas, I would give all my lands to save thee." These were *his* last words. He was slain; and with these true essences of chivalry, fell the flower of Border Knighthood, Scotch and English, and squires and grooms, as ardent to fight and as fearless to die as their renowned masters. There does not seem to have been a spark of hate or malice in a fight one of the most desperate and sanguinary ever recorded; it was only to decide which name—Percy or Douglas—should blaze the brightest in the rolls of chivalry, and to add another jewel to one or other of the glittering wreaths of martial victories that bound the brows of the rival nations. The result pleased the pride and touched the best feelings of both houses—both nations; and all the more, because, though the Scots had the best at the last, the struggle was in fact pretty equally balanced, for they had the superiority of numbers. The same intense and wide-spread love of war displayed at Chevy Chase animated other neighbours of England beside the Scotch, and prompted all to be forward, like Percy, at aggression, in order to stimulate to arms. Hence the fortifications whose remains meet our view in every old English town, and more especially those exposed to attacks from the sea, such as the Strand Gate, Winchelsea (Fig 914), for which town Edward I. designed great things, as one of the Cinque Ports; but the sea proved stronger than the monarch, and as old Winchelsea had quietly submitted to be submerged, so Edward's Winchelsea yielded gradually to sand and water, amidst which it has long resigned all flattering dreams of importance, and dwindled to little better

2 K 2

966.—Capital.

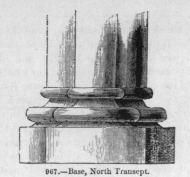

967.—Base, North Transept.

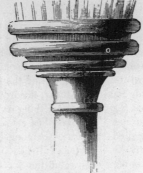

968.—Capital, Chapter-House.

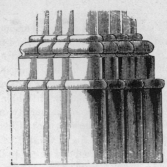

969.—Base, Chapter-House.

970.—Bracket.

971.—Dripstone Termination.

974.—From the Door, Chapter-House.

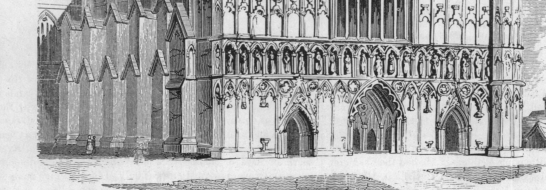

965.—Lichfield Cathedral. General View.

972.—Western Doorway.

975.—Western Doorway

973.—Dripstone Termination.

976.—Dripstone Termination.

977.—Bracket, Chapter-House.

978.—Finial

979.—Capital.

980.—Crotchet

981.—Bracket, Chapter-House.

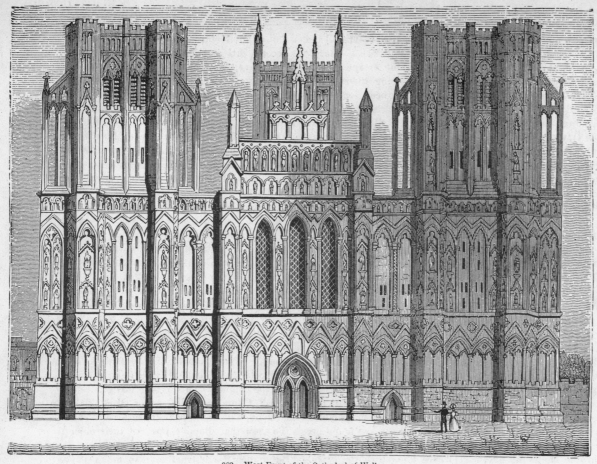

982.—West Front of the Cathedral of Wells

983.—Interior of Wells Cathedral.

985.—Capital, Wells.

986.—Boss.

987.—Bracket.

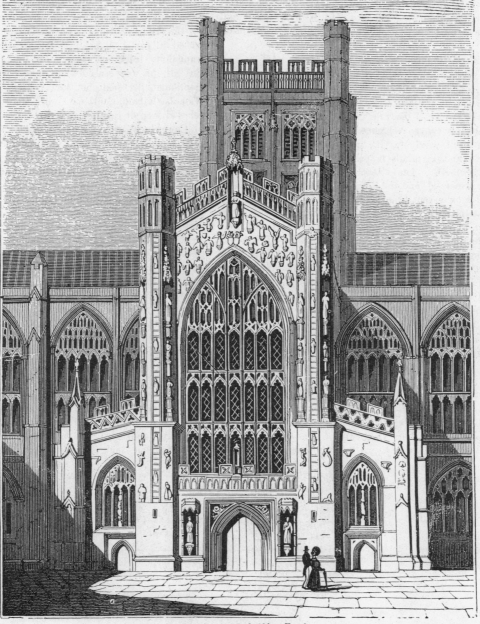

984.—West Front of Bath Abbey-Church.

988.—Capital, Wells.

989.—Boss.

990.—Bracket.

than a village, though the villagers now and then may be excused for dwelling on those days when two or four hundred ships, according to some doubtful records, rode at ease in the harbour. The invasions of the French caused Southampton to be fortified under Edward III. and Richard II. The two valiant lions on the large and fine gate (Fig. 918) anciently adorned a bridge which crossed a ditch before the gate, but ditch and gate are among the things that were. Athlone (Fig. 848), a town on what was almost the only high road from Dublin to the wild retreats of the Connaught province, from which independence was not finally wrested before 1590, was in consequence carefully fortified to interrupt fugitives, and serve as a guard over that dangerous district. Dunluce Castle (Fig. 847) is one of many ruins along the extensive coast of Antrim, in the province of Ulster, whose histories are almost wholly wrapped in oblivion. A powerful chief, under the Earl of Ulster, seems to have held it about the time of Edward Bruce's ambitious attempts at sovereignty in Ireland, when he was actually made king of Ulster. The Despensers, ruined by the fatal fondness of their weak king Edward II., possessed Caerphilly Castle, a place of very remote antiquity, whose ruins, situate in a deep valley, are among the most extensive and grand that Britain can boast. The Leaning Tower (Fig. 909) is but a fragment, held together entirely by the strength of the cement, being eleven and a half feet out of the perpendicular;—a singular appearance, explained by the tradition that the tower was blown up when the Despensers were besieged by the barons. The Welsh proverb, "It is gone to Caerphilly," signifying a direction something the reverse of good, does not speak much for the character of the lords of this place in the old days. To the family of our first religious martyr among the English nobility, Lord Cobham, Cowling Castle, in Kent, is to be ascribed. The bold and handsome gateway (where the groove of the portcullis is still distinct), and the ivy-clad tower, seen in Fig. 911, add picturesqueness to the tranquil farm, with its orchard and garden, that now occupy the demesne ; they are nearly all that are left standing of John de Cobham's massive square edifice, raised in the reign of Richard II., with its moat and flanking towers, and on a part of which the following inscription was set up :—

> Knoweth that beth, and shall be
> That I am mad in help of the contre,
> For knowing of which thyng
> This is chartre and wytnessing.

Arundel Castle (Fig. 926) has for many centuries enjoyed a privilege given to no other residence in the kingdom, that of conveying the title of Earl to its possessor without creation. From the Albinis and Fitzalans it passed by marriage to the Howards under Elizabeth. Some venerable walls of the ancient castle have been preserved, and the keep is converted to a singular use : it is a cage for owls, sent from North America to the possessor of the modern magnificent residence. Two Fitzalans perished by the axe ; Edmund, at Hereford, for arming against Edward II. and the Despensers; and Richard Fitzalan, in King Richard II.'s actual presence, according to Froissart, for conspiring against him here, with many others of the high nobility. The people of England mourned for this last earl as a martyr, for he was one of the few nobles who stood out for *their* liberties. Arundel's death was one of the last and most odious of Richard's multiplied tyrannies. It is said the shade of the injured earl, covered with blood, and reproaching him for his injustice, often "revisited the glimpses of the moon" in Richard's dreams. Not many months after, the earl's brother, Thomas, Archbishop of Canterbury, banished in the same cause, set the crown of Richard on Bolingbroke's head. Of course the Arundels found favour with the new king. We find the earl's second son, John Fitzalan, had leave from him to embattle his manor-house at Betchworth (Fig. 928) : the present old mansion stands on the castle site. The Lancasters finish our sketch of the barons of the fourteenth century. A few fragments on a breezy

eminence are all that is left of their once regal Castle of Tutbury (Fig. 912). Here the second earl and his men made his memorable escape over the river Dove, while Edward II.'s troops were forcing their entrance at the gates. A vast sum of money, that he had been long amassing for the civil war, was secured in a chest intrusted to Leicester, and lost amid the hurry of that dismal night. Not till 1831 was the treasure discovered. The reader will find an account of this interesting event in No. 166 of the 'Penny Magazine.' Fig. 913 represents the singular manner in which the coins were found imbedded in the hardened soil, to which they almost seemed to have grown. The famous John of Gaunt held the earldom of Derby, of which Castleton Castle (Fig. 910), built by Peveril of the Peak, a natural son of the Conqueror, formed a part. This place has been already spoken of in a previous part of our work. Gaunt possessed also the Honor of Hertford, and at Hertford Castle (Fig 916) he and the rest of the chivalric family of Edward III. paid many generous attentions to the French King John, their guest and prisoner. The London palace of Gaunt, the Savoy (Figs. 897, 924), was John's assigned residence. Here, we are told, every effort was made to make him forget that he was a captive, but this was impossible ; when he was entreated to lay aside his melancholy, and derive consolation from cheerful thoughts, John smiled mournfully, and answered in the words of the sweet Psalmist of Israel, "How shall we sing in a strange land?" The dukedom of Lancaster, as held by Gaunt, was a sort of petty kingdom, of which the town of Lancaster (Fig. 844) was the capital. This prince was extremely unpopular with the English Commons, who, under Wat Tyler, burned his palace of the Savoy, and would have taken his life could they have found him. To show that plunder was not their object, they proclaimed death to all who should take or secrete anything found in the palace. But among the destruction of so much plate, gold, and jewels, it was hardly wonderful one man's integrity should fail him. The theft of a silver cup did not pass unobserved, and the stern rebels, to vindicate the purity of their motives, flung the culprit with the cup into the flames, or, as some chroniclers say, into the Thames, saying, "We be zealous of truth and justice, and not thieves or robbers." In the last century the Savoy (Fig. 924) served in part "as lodgings for private people, for barracks. and a scandalous infectious prison for the soldiery and for transports." But all this has ceased some time. In the great insurrection just mentioned, perished, on Tower Hill, Simon de Sudbury, son of Nicholas Tibald, gentleman, of Sudbury, in Suffolk. He was eighteen years Bishop of London, and, on being elevated to the Archbishopric of Canterbury, rebuilt the walls and west gate (Fig. 921). In Stow's Annals we have an appalling account of his death :—" Being compassed about with many thousands, and seeing swords about his head drawn in excessive number, threatening to him death, he said unto them thus : 'What is it, dear brethren, you purpose to do? What is mine offence committed against you, for which ye will kill me ? You were best to take heed, that if I be killed, who am your pastor, there come not on you the indignation of the just Revenger, or at the least, for such a fact, all England be put under interdiction.' He could unneath pronounce these words before they cried out with a horrible noise, that they neither feared the interdiction nor the Pope to be above them. The Archbishop, seeing death at hand, spake with comfortable words, as he was an eloquent man, and wise beyond all wise men of the realm ; lastly, after forgiveness granted to the executioner that should behead him, he kneeling down offered his neck to him that should strike it off; being stricken in the neck, but not deadly, he, putting his hand to his neck, said thus : 'Aha! it is the hand of God.' He had not removed his hand from the place where the pain was, but that being suddenly stricken, his finger ends being cut off, and part of the arteries, he fell down ; but yet he died not, till, being mangled with eight strokes in the neck and in the head, he fulfilled a most worthy martyrdom." His body lay unburied till the next afternoon, and then his head was set up on London Bridge.

CHAPTER II.—ECCLESIASTICAL ANTIQUITIES.

UR cathedrals will now again demand attention; and in resuming the series of the preceding period, we shall commence with that of SALISBURY, the records of which are unusually full and particular. The bishopric of Salisbury was created by the union of the sees of Wilton and Sherbourne, which was done by order of Lanfranc, Archbishop of Canterbury, in 1075. The seat of the bishop was fixed at Old Sarum (of which we have already spoken, p. 6), and there a cathedral was built. Old Sarum, however, was a fortified town, and the priests and the soldiers soon began to quarrel, and though for a while by the authority of their superiors kept in check, during the troublous times of Richard I. their enmity broke out into open contest. In the 'Chronicles' of Holinshed we have a piquant account of the matter. "In the time of the civil wars," he tells us, "the soldiers of the castle and canons of Old Sarum fell at odds, insomuch that after often brawls they fell at last to sad blows. It happened, therefore, in a Rogation week, that the clergy going in a solemn procession, a controversy fell between them about certain walks and limits, which the one side claimed and the other denied. Such also was the hot entertainment on each part, that at last the castellans, espying their time, got between the clergy and the town, and so coiled them as they returned homeward, that they feared any more to gang about their bounds for the year." This occurred while Herbert Poore (or Pauper) was bishop; and he, anxious to avoid a recurrence of such uncomely doings, and being, notwithstanding his name, a wealthy man, petitioned the king to be permitted to remove his see to a more convenient place. To this Richard readily assented; but the removal did not take place, the bishop prudently recalculating the expenses attending such a step, and determining, on second thoughts, that they were beyond his ability to bear.

Herbert died in 1217, and was succeeded by his brother Richard Poore, a man of lofty purpose and resolute character. His first care was to carry out the object his brother had failed to accomplish. Determined not to submit to military control, and to remove the scandal of the continued strife between the canons and castellans, he took such measures as soon caused all difficulties to melt as snow. He applied first to Gualo, the Legate of the Pope, then in England, and having obtained letters from him in support of his application, he despatched special messengers to Rome to obtain the sanction of the Pontiff to the removal of the cathedral and its officers. His holiness, Pope Honorius, having first made due inquiries into the propriety of such removal, acceded to it, and issued his Bull accordingly.

So far all was well, but all was not done yet. Our bishop had resolved on raising no common structure, and no ordinary sum was needed for the purpose. His first step was to call a chapter, and having explained his intentions, he induced each canon and vicar—himself setting the example—to bind himself to appropriate one-fourth of his income, for seven years successively, towards defraying the expenses of the new structure. A contract or obligation was accordingly drawn up in regular form—for the bishop evidently knew his men—and signed and sealed by each in due order on "the day of Saints Processus and Martinianus," 1218. The next thing to be done was to fix on an eligible site; and here the bishop was, it is said, miraculously aided. He had long pondered where it should be, when, as he lay on his bed one night thinking of the matter, the Virgin appeared to him in a vision and told him to build it in Merry-field. Where this field was, however, he was not told, and none of his canons knew. But it happened that as he passed by some soldiers who were trying their bows, he overheard one of them wager that he could shoot his bolt into Merry-field. "And where may that be?" said our delighted prelate. Of course he was speedily informed, and in Merry-field he fixed his mark;

erecting immediately a temporary wooden chapel there. He now set about collecting money in all quarters, with a tact and success that could hardly be surpassed in our own day. He sent preachers and deputations everywhere, to collect from the religious part of the community, as we do now; and though he had not fancy-fairs or bazaars in which to sell pretty toys, he issued what found then more ready purchasers—pardons and indulgences for all who should contribute to the good work. And he found plenteous help. The king, Henry III., as we shall see, granted a charter, the nobles sent rich gifts, and the poor gave of their poverty—many of them giving also their labour freely.

All being thus ready, Richard proceeded to commence his cathedral. He has left us a record of every step of his progress; having commanded his Dean, William de Wanda, to draw up a chronicle thereof. The ceremony of laying the foundation was a gorgeous one. The young king, and all the principal nobility and clergy of the realm, were invited, and everything that could add dignity or splendour to the solemnity was provided. Henry, indeed, was absent, being engaged negotiating a treaty with the Welsh at Shrewsbury; but there was a large assemblage of lords and prelates, and a huge multitude of people collected in Merrifield on the day of St. Vitalis the Martyr (April 28), 1220, to witness and aid in commencing a structure that they hoped should be not unworthy of Him whose presence filleth the earth. The bishop, first having performed divine service in the wooden building he had raised,—reverently put off his shoes, and, accompanied by all the clergy chanting the Litany, proceeded in procession to the place of foundation. He then consecrated the ground, solemnly dedicating it for ever to the service of the Holiest. He next turned to the people, and addressed them in a suitable sermon. Then taking in his hands the necessary instruments, he proceeded to lay the first stone for Pope Honorius, the second for the Archbishop of Canterbury, and the third for himself; William Longspee, Earl of Salisbury, who was present, then laid the fourth stone, and his wife, Elai de Vitri, Countess of Salisbury, laid the fifth. Certain noblemen added each a stone after her; and then the several officers of the cathedral did the same. The people shouting and weeping for joy, and all "contributing thereto their alms with a ready mind, according to the ability which God had given them." We have followed the account given by De Wanda, but there is a difference in that of Bishop Godwin, according to which Pandulph, the Pope's Legate, laid the five stones; the first for the Pope, the second for the king, the third for the Earl of Salisbury, the fourth for the countess, and the fifth for the bishop.

The bishop and his canons appear to have left Old Sarum soon after the foundation of the new cathedral was laid; and the people of the old town left with them. Indeed, there was little to bind them to the old place, for the wealthier sort had suffered like inconveniences and oppression from the military with the canons, and the poorer, says Harrison, feared to lose their "bellie-cheere (for they were woont to have banketing at everie station, a thing commonly practised by the religious of old, wherewith to link in the commons unto them, whom any man may lead whether he will by the bellie; or, as Latimer said, with beefe, bread, and beere"). Richard, careful to provide for the people, or for the importance of his office, procured from the king a charter creating New Sarum a cathedral city, with all the privileges and immunities for the citizens that they possessed in the old city, and that belonged to other cathedral towns. Holinshed has thus recorded this removal in his 'Chronicle,' A. D. 1221, vol. ii. p. 202, ed. 1587:—

"This year the priests or canons that inhabited within the king's castle of Old Salisbury removed with the bishop's see unto New Salisbury, which by the king was made a city. The bishop Richard procured this removing through the king's help, who was very willing thereunto, as it seemed by his charters largely granted in that behalf."

One who had proceeded thus far so vigorously in his work was not likely to stop short now everything was advancing so favour

992.—Shrine of Ethelbert, King of the East Saxons, formerly on the High Altar of Hereford Cathedral.

993.—Parapet, Peterborough.

994.—Arch of the Cloisters, Peterborough.

995.—Recesses. Peterborough

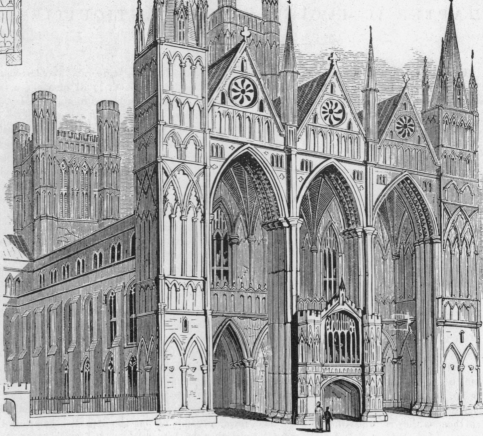

991.—Peterborough Cathedral.

996.—Parapet, Peterborough.

997.—Inscription on Ethelbert's Shrine.

998.—Ancient West Window of Hereford Cathedral.
999. Modern ditto.

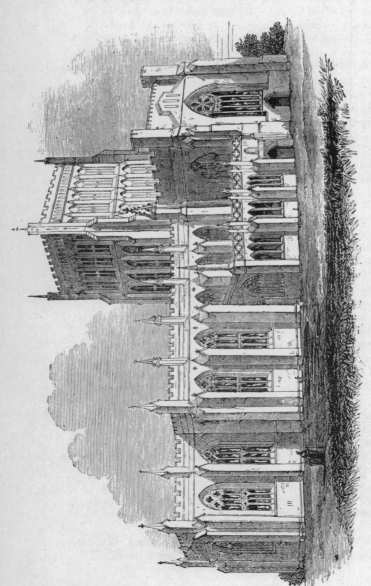

1000.—Bristol Cathedral.

1001.—Gloucester Cathedral.

1002.—Hereford Cathedral.

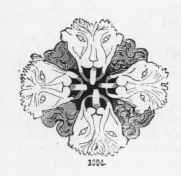

1004.

1005.

1004, 1005.—Rosettes on the Tomb of Bishop de la Wich.

1003.—Chichester Cathedral.

1006.—Chichester. Carving on the Floor of the Presbytery. The inscription is, "Ici gist le couer Maud de."

1009.—Ornamental Gable, Carlisle.

1007.—Carlisle Cathedral.

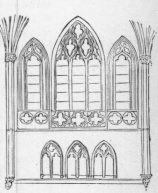

1008.—Part of Nave, Carlisle.

ably. We find him, accordingly, issuing decrees which made those canons who failed to contribute as they had agreed, liable to have their corn seized from their prebendal acres, and sold for the amount due. He set in motion also every contrivance his active mind could devise to hasten on the works, and so successfully, that in about five years the church was deemed sufficiently forward for the performance of divine service. His dean, De Wanda, he now joyfully directed to cite all the canons to be present on Michaelmas Day, 1225, when the cathedral would be solemnly opened. The noble heart of Richard Poore doubtless glowed with devout thankfulness, and perhaps something of honest pride, when he struck the first stone of the building; but how much more intensely must it now have beaten as he saw the pile, in all its beauty and completeness of proportions, stand thus far finished! We may be sure that it was with lofty feelings he gazed on this

Glorious work of fine intelligence,

and remembered that it was *his* work.

The solemnity at the opening of the cathedral was not less splendid than that at its foundation. The service commenced on the vigil of Michaelmas by the bishop, in the presence of the Archbishops of Canterbury and of Dublin, consecrating three altars in the Cathedral: one, situated in the east, to the Trinity and All Saints, for the continual performance of mass to the Blessed Virgin, who had showed him so great favours; another, in the north, to St. Peter; and the third, in the south, to St. Stephen, the proto-martyr, and the rest of the martyrs. On the following day, Otto, the Pope's Nuncio, the archbishops already named, many bishops, a large array of the nobility and magnates of the land, and a great multitude of people being assembled, Richard preached to them a sermon, and then advancing into the church, whither as many as could followed, he there solemnly celebrated divine service. On the Thursday following, the youthful monarch, attended by the famous Hubert de Burgh, his grand justiciary, went to the cathedral. The mass of the glorious Virgin was there heard by the king, who then offered at the altar ten marks of silver and one piece of silk; and granted to the church the privilege of a yearly fair of eight days' continuance. The justiciary then made a vow that he would give a golden Text (or Bible for the use of the altar) with precious stones, and the relics of divers saints, in honour of the B.V.M., and for the service of her church. Again, we are told, on the day of the Holy Innocents the sovereign and his justiciary visited Salisbury Cathedral and heard mass there. On this occasion "the king offered one gold ring with a precious stone, called a ruby, one piece of silk, and one gold cup, the weight of ten gold marks. When the mass was concluded, he told the dean that he would have the stone which he had offered, and the gold of the ring, applied to adorn the Text which the justiciary had given; but as to the cup he gave no particular directions. The justiciary caused the Text which he had before given to be brought, and offered it with great devotion on the altar. They then all repaired to the bishop's house, where they were honourably entertained." To complete all, we learn that "in the year 1226, on the Feast of Trinity, which was then on the 18th of the calends of July, the bodies of three bishops were translated from the castle of Sarum to the new fabric, viz., the body of the blessed Osmund, the body of Bishop Roger, and the body of Bishop Joceline."

We have dwelt at some length on the proceedings connected with the foundation and opening of Salisbury Cathedral, because it is not often that we can so minutely follow them in contemporary narrative as in this instance, and because it is interesting to be able to trace a series of ceremonies no doubt much like those on similar occasions of which we have no authentic accounts. Our sketch is, however, but a slight and hasty one, compared with the elaborate picture from which we have drawn it. Our notice of the further progress of the building to its completion may be much more brief. Although thus opened for divine service, the building was not finished: Richard was in 1229 translated to the wealthier see of Durham, and the works which he had carried forward so zealously appear to have proceeded much more slowly under his successor, for at his death in 1246 the church was still unfinished. It was, however, continued by the next bishop, William de York, and completed by Giles de Bridport in 1258. On the 28th of September in that year it was accordingly "fully dedicated," in the presence of Boniface, Archbishop of Canterbury, and a large assemblage of prelates, peers, and people. Thus, then, the church was completed in thirty-eight years, at an expense of 40,000 marks, or 26,666l. 13s. 4d. sterling. But although the church was completed at that time, the upper part of the tower and the spire, with part of the chapter-house, were not erected till a somewhat later period.

They were supposed to have been added by De Wyville, Bishop of Salisbury, to whom there is in existence a grant by Edward III. of "all the stone walls of the former cathedral church of Old Sarum, and the houses which lately belonged to the bishop and canons of the said church, within our castle of Old Sarum, to have and to hold, as our gift for the improvement of the church of New Sarum, and the close thereunto belonging."

The cathedral, whose erection we have thus somewhat closely followed, stands pre-eminent among English ecclesiastical edifices for the symmetry of its proportions, the harmonious adjustment of its various parts, the elaborate richness of its members, and the grandeur of the whole. (Fig. 932.) A building of more chaste splendour, or more nearly approaching perfection, is scarcely within reach of the imagination. Fortunately, too, it is situated in an open space where the full effect of its stately dimensions may be readily seen. The north-west view (Fig. 929) exhibits it to great advantage; but to be fully appreciated it must be seen under every combination of light and shadow, and from every point of view. When illuminated by the splendour of a summer moon its appearance is remarkably solemn. The broad masses of shadow, the strange streaming light that flickers over the Gothic tracery, the lofty spire assuming then a loftier and more unearthly aspect, and the deep quiet around, impress the mind with a feeling almost of awe. Then would the tones of the midnight mass be felt as only accordant with the grave sentiments that have been aroused. But at whatever time it be seen, the visitor will be ready to exclaim with the poet—

They dreamt not of a perishable home
Who thus could build.

Lest it should be thought that we too highly praise our cathedral, we will quote the opinion of one concerning it who seldom errs in warmth of expression, and whose judgment will be readily acknowledged. Rickman says, "This edifice has the advantage of being built in one style, the Early English, and from an uniform and well-arranged plan. . . . . On the whole this cathedral presents an object for study hardly equalled by any in the kingdom; the purity of its style, and the various modes of adapting that style to the purposes required, deserve the most attentive consideration." But we must give a somewhat more particular account of the building. It consists "internally of a nave, with two lateral aisles; a large transept, with an eastern aisle branching off from the tower; a smaller transept with an aisle east of the former; a choir with lateral aisles; a space east of the choir, and a Lady-chapel at the east end. On the north side of the church is a large porch, with a room over it; and rising from the intersection of the transept with the nave is a lofty tower and spire. South of the church is a square cloister, with a library over half of the eastern side; a chapter-house; a consistory court; and an octangular apartment called the muniment-room." The preceding extract is from Britton's 'History of Salisbury Cathedral,' from which work we also take the following principal dimensions. Extreme *length* 474 feet; interior 450 feet. *Widths.* West front externally, 112 feet, and 217 more to the southern extremity of the cloister wall; great transept externally, 230 feet; interior of nave 34 feet, and with aisles 78 feet; great transept, N. to S. 206 feet; width of ditto with aisle, 57: small transept N. to S. 145 feet; width 44 feet: width of choir and aisles, 78 feet; of Lady-chapel, 37 feet. The *heights* of the vaulting of the nave, choir, and transepts, 81 feet; of the aisles and Lady-chapel, 40; externally, parapet 87 feet; point of roof 115 feet; parapet of tower 207 feet; and summit of spire 404 feet. The cloister forms a square of 181 feet within the walls, and is 18 feet wide between the side walls and windows; the height of the vaulting is 18 feet. The chapter-house is 58 feet in diameter, internally, and 52 feet high to the vaulting.

We have spoken of the general effect of the edifice: in looking at its parts we may remark, that while the west front has been objected to as having an air of stiffness—of which, however, we took no account when before it—the eastern end has been uniformly admired for its lightness and grace, and for the elegance of its arrangement. The whole of the exterior is singularly beautiful. The windows—of which there is a popular saying that they are as many as there are days in the year—are handsome specimens of the Early English or Pointed style; and the north porch is rich and picturesque. But the most striking feature is the spire. The architect is said to have been desirous to carry his spire higher than any other in England; and he did so. It is much taller than any in this country, though not so high as those of Strasburgh and Mechlin. It rises from a tower constructed, at least the two upper stories, as we have said, at a more recent period than the body of the church. He must have been a daring man who determined on such a work! but he was a wise one too: he knew that it was not enough to dare greatly. He set about his work in the same spirit as he had conceived it. He laid down 387 feet of new foundation, strengthened the tower internally and externally by flying buttresses, and, as Price informs us, added to it 116 additional supports, exclusive of bands of iron. But with all his care it was seen, soon after the capstone was laid, that a slight settlement had taken place on the west side; this, however, has never increased. From the same authority we learn that its declination is as follows:—At the top of the parapet of the tower, the wall declines 9 inches to the S. and 3¾ to the W., whilst at the capstone of the spire the declension is 24½ in. to the S. and 16¼ to the W. Britton does not think the spire beautiful; but we take leave to differ from him. The chapter-house (Fig. 931) is an interesting building. Internally it is very beautiful and highly enriched; there are some finely-carved capitals and some sculpture above the arches; over the capitals is a series of seven curious bracket-heads, one of them appearing to be a representation of the Trinity; beneath the arches there were formerly circular paintings; it is lighted by eight windows of remarkably beautiful form, and once filled with stained glass; the floor is formed of glazed tiles, and no doubt the whole was originally highly embellished. A plinth and stone seat is carried round the interior wall, and this is elevated at one end of the room a step higher than elsewhere, and divided into seven compartments, which were originally intended for the bishop and his dignitaries: whilst the other niches, of which there are thirty, were intended for the canons; and one seat on each side the door was for the chancellor and treasurer. The cloister occupies a square area on the south side of the nave, and extends from the transept to the west end. It is separated from the church by an open space called the Plumbery, and consists of a continued arcade, with a wall on one side and a series of openings on the other. The interior of the cathedral is less ornate than that of some others; it is marked by simplicity and harmony of proportions, and is light and elegant in appearance. The effect is much injured by the organ, which, with its ungainly screen (a modern excrescence), effectually breaks the vista of lofty arches. The choir (Fig. 930) is grand and imposing. The nave, which is lofty and narrow, has ten arches on each side, supported by clustered columns; over these are two other series, the upper division, called the clerestory, having a succession of glazed windows of three lights each. The Lady-chapel is a beautiful room with a vaulted ceiling supported by slender pillars of Purbeck marble. In the north transept is a curious lavatory. There are a great many fine monuments, especially those of Bishops Bridport and Metford, and the elaborate chantry-chapel to Bishop Audley: there are other ancient monuments interesting for their costumes; with many modern ones by Rysbrach, Bacon, Flaxman, and Chantrey, with one to Sir Colt Hoare, Historian of Wiltshire, by Joseph—which, though not remarkable in any other respect, is said to be an admirable likeness. But there is one monument of quite a unique character—to a chorister, or boy-bishop. (Fig. 1026.) It was discovered in the prelacy of Bishop Duppa, under the seats near the pulpit, and is now placed in the nave. The Rev. J. Gregorie, a prebend of Salisbury at the time, wrote a dissertation on the subject of boy-bishops, from which it appears that it was the custom of the choristers to elect on the day of St. Nicholas one of their number to be bishop; and he was not only clothed in episcopal robes and put on a mitre, and carried a crozier, but performed all the functions of a bishop, from the day of his election, the 6th of December, till the 28th, being Innocents' day. The details he gives are very curious, but we have not space for them here; we merely add that this is supposed to be a monument raised to one who died during the possession of his brief authority. The organ-screen, as we mentioned, is modern; it was erected by Mr. Wyatt: the organ is the gift of George III. There are several stained windows, some modern; one is from a design by Sir Joshua Reynolds, another from one by Mortimer.

We have very little to add to the history of the cathedral. The Commonwealth soldiers were quartered in it, and, as in most other of our ecclesiastical edifices, committed great devastation. Seth Ward, who had expended twenty-five thousand pounds on the reparation of Exeter Cathedral, on his translation to the see of Salisbury immediately set about repairing its cathedral and palace at his own expense, and employed Sir Christopher Wren to survey the edifice. More recently it has been repaired under the direction of Mr. Wyatt, some of whose alterations are in very questionable taste. Among the eminent men who have held the bishopric we may name Cardinal Campeggio, the papal Legate, so well known for his connection with the trial of Catherine of Arragon. When Wolsey was disgraced, Campeggio was dispossessed of his see by the angry

monarch; Jewell, the Reformer; Duppa, the friend of Charles I.; Gilbert Burnet, whose amusing 'History of his Own Times' affords so much curious information respecting an important period in the history of our country; Hoadly, and Sherlock.

The origin of the see of York belongs to the earliest successful introduction of Christianity into our island. Among the forty companions of Augustine was one

of shoulders curved and stature tall,
Black hair, and vivid eye, and meagre cheek,
His prominent feature like an eagle's beak;
A man whose aspect doth at once appal
And strike with reverence

This monk, whom our ecclesiastical poet, closely following the prose of his venerable predecessor, thus describes in sonorous verse, was named Paulinus. As soon as his great leader had gained firm footing among the men of Kent, having succeeded in converting the king and his court, with a large number of the people, Paulinus, being full of zeal for the propagation of the faith, resolved to attempt the conversion of Edwin, the Saxon king of Northumbria, and *Bretwalda*, or leader of the Britons, who held his court at Eboracum, the York of these recent times. The fervour of Paulinus soon wrought on the heart of that monarch; but though he yielded a mental assent, he resolved to call a meeting of his councillors to deliberately consider the matter, before he openly declared himself a convert. The proceedings of the Council, which terminated in a resolution to adopt the Christian religion, are fully related by Bede, whose account of the breaking-up of the Council is worth quoting—the translation is Wordsworth's:—" Who, exclaimed the king, when the Council was ended, shall first desecrate the altars and the temples? I, answered the chief Priest, for who more fit than myself, through the wisdom which the true God hath given me, to destroy, for the good example of others, what in foolishness I worshipped? Immediately, casting away vain superstition, he besought the king to grant him, what the laws did not allow to a priest, arms and a courser; which mounting, and furnished with a sword and a lance, he proceeded to destroy the idols. The crowd seeing this, thought him mad—he, however, halted not; but, approaching, he profaned the temple, casting against it the lance which he had held in his hand, and, exulting in acknowledgment of the worship of the true God, he ordered his companions to pull down the temple with all its enclosures." Edwin was baptized, with his two sons, Coiffa the priest, and the chief of his nobles, in a little wooden oratory that had been hastily constructed. But soon the monarch, anxious to erect a building more suitable to His worship whom he now served, and stimulated, as some say, by the persuasions of Paulinus, laid the foundation of a noble church of stone, enclosing in it the wooden oratory in which he had been baptized—on the site of this building stands the present magnificent York Minster. Paulinus, after a while, received from Rome the title of Archbishop of York, and with it the pallium, that vestment which, after being consecrated by the sovereign pontiff, and applied to the tomb of St. Peter, is sent only to metropolitan bishops: Augustine had before received it as Archbishop of Canterbury. Edwin was slain before the edifice he had commenced was brought to a conclusion; it was finished by his successor Oswald. Those were troublous times, and Paulinus was compelled to fly into Kent, where he died. York was now left for thirty years without a bishop —Christianity was repressed, and the church fell into ruins. St. Wilfred, towards the close of the seventh century, restored it, but it was finally destroyed by fire in the year 741. About thirty years afterwards a new church, and, as is plain from contemporary memorials, a far more splendid one, was begun and completed by the Archbishop Albert. This edifice met with a similar fate to the one it had replaced, being destroyed in a conflagration that consumed a great part of the city, in the early part of the reign of William the Conqueror. A small portion of the crypt of this Saxon church, comprising also, as is thought, a part of the structure raised by Edwin, has been recently discovered beneath the choir of the present Minster, in the course of the excavations rendered necessary by the fire in 1829. Archbishop Thomas, who was appointed to the see in 1070, rebuilt the church from its foundation; but—with a singular infelicity of fortune—it was again destroyed by fire in the year 1137. It now lay for some time in ashes, although that Archbishop Thurston *intended* to rebuild it is clear from an Indulgence (always the prime instrument in such matters) issued by Joceline, Bishop of Salisbury, which states that " Whereas the Metropolitan Church of York was consumed by a new fire and almost subverted, destroyed, and miserably spoyled of its ornaments," he released all such as bountifully contributed towards its re-edification from forty

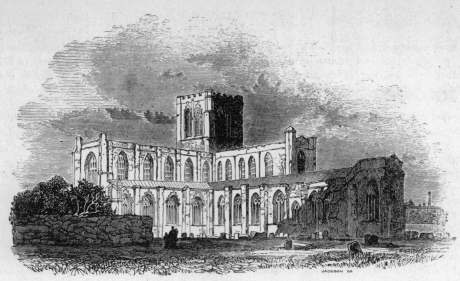

1011.—Chester.

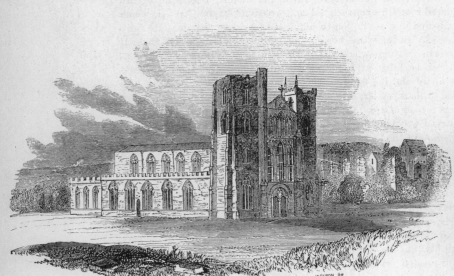

1013.—Llandaff.

1012.—St. Asaph's.

1014.—St. David's.

1010.—Bangor.

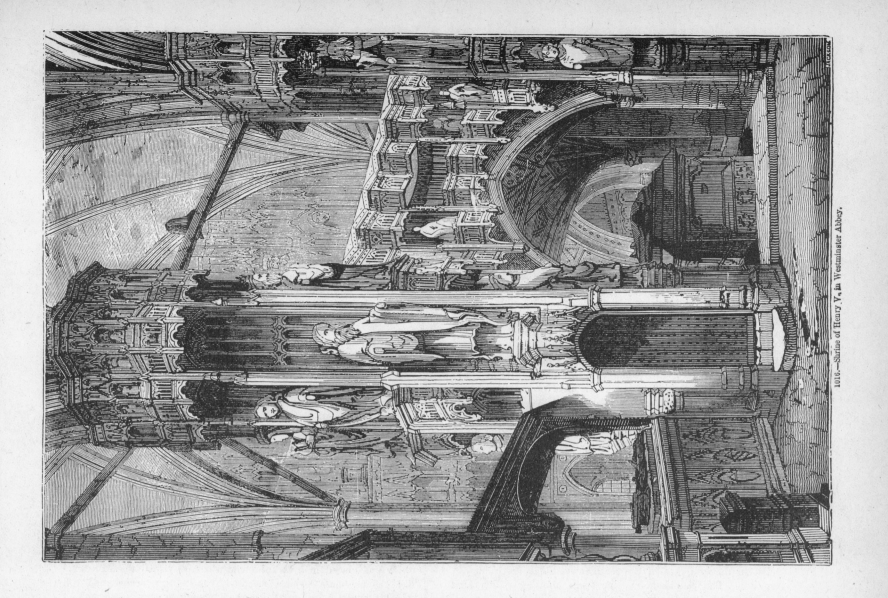

1016.—Shrine of Henry V., in Westminster Abbey.

1015.—Westminster Abbey. North Aisle, looking West.

261

days of penance enjoined. But it was reserved for Archbishop Roger, the sturdy opponent of Thomas-à-Becket, to effect its restoration. Soon after Walter Grey succeeded to the archbishopric, he commenced the present south transept, about the year 1200 or 1225. This is the oldest part of the existing edifice; from this time we are able to trace its gradual progress. The north transept is also believed to have been commenced by Walter Grey, but it was completed in the year 1260, by John le Romaine, treasurer of the church. His son, John le Romaine, who had been appointed Archbishop of York, laid the foundation of the nave in 1291, but he did not live to complete it. Archbishop Melton carried on the work with vigour, issuing indulgences to all who would aid, and, what required more self-denial, subscribing seven hundred pounds of his own money for the purpose. Other assistance was not lacking. The Lords Vavasour and Percy of Bolton contributed, the one stone from his quarries, and the other wood from his grounds; money was sent by some, and others gave their labour. It was not, however, till the year 1360 that the nave was finished by Archbishop Thoresby. This prelate was one of the most munificent contributors towards the erection of York Minster. Besides completing the nave, he removed the choir which Archbishop Roger had built, and laid the first stone of the present choir on the 29th of July, 1361, though it was many years before it was finished. Archbishop Thoresby contributed of his own money one thousand two hundred and sixty-seven pounds—a very large sum in those days—besides the materials of his mansion at Shireburn, towards building the choir. He was largely assisted by Pope Innocent VI., who "granted indulgences of two years and two quarters" to all who assisted in its erection. Urban V. also granted an indulgence of one year (1366), and Urban VI. gave to the Dean and Chapter the revenues of the Church of Misterton for ten years for the same purpose. The central tower was probably erected by John Skirraw, a prebendary of York, about the time of the completion of the choir: the towers at the west end of the cathedral were erected by John de Bermingham, about the year 1402; his name, with the figure of a bear, was to be seen cut in bold relief in the west face of the south tower till its destruction in the last fire. The chapter-house, the finest building of its kind in existence, is believed to have been commenced near the close of the thirteenth century, and finished about fifty years afterwards.

The building whose gradual rise we have thus traced, although wanting, of course, the uniformity of one constructed from a well-arranged plan, is a magnificent, almost a sublime structure. Even its irregularity is rather seen in the details than in the whole; its form being nearly regular, though its parts are somewhat discordant in style. It is not fortunate in its situation, which is low and confined, yet its mass and the grand scale on which every part is constructed, render it an imposing object from whatever point it is viewed. It is perhaps best seen as a whole from the Ramparts (Fig. 951), although with the disadvantage of looking down upon it—always the worst way of looking at an architectural object. The west front (Fig. 950) is very grand: the immensity of the structure here appears very striking.* The several parts, too, are singularly beautiful. The window is pronounced by an excellent judge to be "an unrivalled specimen of the leafy tracery that marks the style of the middle of the fourteenth century." The lofty towers arising from the western aisles are uniform and very graceful; they are terminated by pinnacles and supported by buttresses, in every part highly enriched. Almost the whole of this front is adorned with a profusion of sculpture and tracery. Over the door is the figure of Archbishop Melton, with, on one side, a statue of Lord Percy (mentioned above) holding a piece of un-hewn wood in his hand, and on the other a corresponding statue of Lord Vavasour holding in his hand a rough block of stone, to typify their benefactions to the church. The door is the only part that will perhaps bear an objection at this end, and it certainly appears too small as compared with the largeness of the other parts. The south transept is a noble piece of workmanship. Attached to it is a fine porch, over the entrance of which there used to be a clock of the time of Henry VII., with wooden figures to strike the hours, similar to those that formerly stood at St. Dunstan's Church in Fleet Street, but they were removed with the clock some years back. The central tower is a very noticeable feature, and is very fine, but appears hardly high enough compared with those at the western end, being only one hundred and ninety-eight feet high, while they are two hundred and one feet to the top of the pinnacles: it has been supposed that it was intended to be crowned by a lofty spire. The interior of the edifice from the vastness of its

* The entire length of the church externally is five hundred and nineteen feet, the width of the west front above one hundred feet.

dimensions, and the internal length, is four hundred and eighty-three feet: the simplicity of its lines and the subdued splendour of the whole produces a powerful impression on the mind, lessened somewhat, it may be, by the recent appearance of so large a part of it—the roof of the nave and choir having been unfortunately destroyed by the fires that occurred within our own memory. The cathedral consists internally of a nave, choir, and Lady-chapel, each with its two aisles; north and south transepts, with two aisles, and a lantern in the centre; and a chapter-room, with a vestibule on the north side. The choir is shown in Figs. 952 and 954. The transepts at the north and south extremities are very dissimilar to each other. The elevation of that on the north side presents five tall and very beautiful windows, commonly known as "the five sisters;" above these are five other lancet windows of varied heights. The south transept is neither so regular nor so finished as the other, though rather richer in the details. The nave is remarkably beautiful, and the aisles are unequalled for grandeur in this kingdom; they are as lofty as those at Westminster, but not so narrow. The east window has an effect of surprising splendour as it is seen from the interior. Drake in his 'Eboracum,' says, "It may justly be called the wonder of the world both for masonry and glazing. It is very nearly the breadth and height of the middle choir." By the scale affixed to his engraving of it, it is about seventy-eight feet high and thirty feet wide. It is divided into compartments, each containing the representation of an historical event; in all about two hundred subjects are represented. "It was begun to be glazed at the expense of the Dean and Chapter, anno 1405, who then contracted with John Thornton of Coventry, glazier, to execute it. He was to receive for his own work four shillings a week, and to finish the whole in three years. The indenture further witnesses that he should have one hundred shillings sterling every of the three years, and if he did his work truly and perfectly he was to receive ten pounds more for his care therein." ('Ebor.,' 517.) There is a singular elaborate and very interesting screen that must just be noticed. It contains statues of the Kings of England from William I. to Henry V., and also that of James I., which was placed in a vacant niche when he visited the Minster. The chapter-house—which, as the Yorkists are accustomed to boast, is among houses what the rose is among flowers*—is a noble room of an octagonal form, its angular diameter being sixty feet, and height of the central base from the floor sixty-two feet. The roof is unsupported by any pillar. "Seven arched windows fill as many of its sides; the other is solid, with tracery on the walls to answer the pattern on the windows. The whole circumference, below the windows, except at the entrance, is occupied by fifty-four canopied stalls of stone, for the canons who composed the chapter. The canopies of these stalls afford early specimens of that beautiful tabernacle-work, as we are accustomed to call it, which soon afterwards was more elaborately ornamented. The columns of the stalls are of Petworth marble; the lines of their canopies are not very complex, but the sculpture is executed with great skill and spirit." (Britton's *York Cathedral*.) The roof, which is simple and elegant, is of wood, and was not long since adorned with paintings and gilding. Over the door is a row of thirteen niches, formerly, it is thought, filled with statues of the Saviour and his Apostles.

The monuments are numerous, but not so fine as in some other cathedrals, while there is at least an equal number of absurd ones. Drake observed this more than a century back. "For instance, in our own church," he says, "who can bear to read a long dull encomium on a child of six years old, where the author, some trencher scholar to the family no doubt, shamefully dresses it up in the garb and gravity of threescore? Or refrain from laughter if you can, when you are told by an old doating doctor of divinity, that his wife, who he says died of her twenty-fourth child, stood death like a soldier, and looked as lovely in her coffin as a young blooming virgin!" Some of the ancient monuments are, however, very beautiful. The most important is that of Archbishop Walter Grey, who built the south transept in which it is placed. It is a splendid relic of the thirteenth century. It consists of two tiers of trefoil arches, supported by eight slender columns, with capitals of luxuriant foliage, sustaining a canopy divided into eight niches, with angular pediments and elaborate finials. On a flat tomb under the canopy is an effigy of the archbishop in his pontifical robes. There is also a fine monument of Archbishop Bowet, of the early part of the reign of Henry VI.; and others to Archbishops Rotherham, Savage, &c. A very beautiful recumbent statue of the youthful Prince William de Hatfield, the second son of Edward III., should not be overlooked. It is engraved in C. Stothard's 'Monu-

* Ut rosa flos florum,
Sic est domus ista domorum.

mental Effigies,' as are also some others that are curious for their costumes. Many of the old monuments were defaced by the soldiers of Cromwell; and of those that were left, some were much broken and others entirely destroyed in the late fires. Among the remarkable things contained in the cathedral—for, like Westminster, York can boast of its antiquities and its "curiosities"—is an ancient chair, in which it is said several Saxon kings were crowned; it is now used by the archbishops at ordinations and other solemnities. There is also a large ivory horn, which is mentioned by Camden, who has the following citation from "an ancient author," respecting the donation of which it serves as a token:—" Ulphus, the son of Toraldus, governed in the western part of Deira, and by reason of a difference like to happen betwixt his eldest son and his youngest, about his lordships when he was dead, he presently took the course to make them equal. Without delay he went to York, and taking the horn wherein he was wont to drink, he filled it with wine, and kneeling upon his knees before the altar, he bestowed upon God and the blessed St. Peter all his lands." By this horn the chapter holds estates of great value a little east of York, which are still "de Terra Ulphi." Another "curiosity" is a wooden head found in the tomb of Archbishop Rotherham when a new pavement was laid down. This prelate died of the plague, and it is supposed "that he was immediately and unceremoniously interred, and that an image was afterwards solemnly buried in the church in the insignia of the deceased prelate." Before the Reformation the cathedral possessed several indubitable relics, two or three of which we may name as a sample of the ware then most valued. There were some bones of St. Peter; two thorns from the crown of our Saviour; a tooth of St. Apollonia; part of the brains of St. Stephen; and not least perhaps were the relics of three Archbishops of York, namely, some hair of St. William, a cloth stained with the blood of Scroop, and an arm of St. Wilfrid, enclosed in an urn of silver. In our notice of Salisbury Cathedral we have spoken of boy-bishops; among the jewels formerly existing here, of which Dugdale gives a list, was " a small mitre set with stones for the bishop of the boys, or, as he was anciently called, the barne bishop, also a pastoral staff and ring for the same."

There are few prelates of celebrity who have held the see besides those we have already named. The St. William above mentioned was a nephew of King Stephen, and was in high repute during his life for his holiness; after his death many miracles were said to be worked by his remains, and about one hundred and fifty years afterwards he was canonized by Pope Nicholas: on this occasion his bones were taken up and reinterred with great solemnity in the nave, in presence of King Edward I., his queen, eleven bishops, and a large number of other important personages. A splendid shrine was erected over his remains, but it was destroyed at the Reformation. When the new pavement was laid down, his tomb was opened: this occurred in May, 1732, and Drake, the historian of York, was present. At a depth of about a yard a stone coffin was discovered, and inside it a leaden box, in which were the bones of the saint in tolerable preservation: he appeared to have been about five feet six inches in height—which is perhaps worth noticing, as it is not often there is an opportunity of taking the height of a real saint. The bones were carefully replaced. Another archbishop—by no means a saint—was Geoffrey, son of Henry II. by Fair Rosamond. He had held the see of Lincoln previously to that of York, but was compelled to give it up by the Pope, as he performed none of its duties, choosing rather to accompany his father in his wars against the Scots. He was the favourite son of Henry, whose last request was that Richard would appoint him to the Archbishopric of York. This Richard did, but made him pay exorbitantly for the office. The rest of his life was spent in quarrels, first with William de Longchamps, the Chancellor, then with John and the Pope, and to the end of his life with his own canons; he remained a bishop militant to the last. Shakspere's " Scroop, Archbishop of York," will be remembered for the part he took against Henry IV., and for his tragical fate. Cardinal Wolsey also held the see, but he never visited his diocese.

The earlier churches, as we have seen, were successively destroyed by fire; the present Minster has twice narrowly escaped a similar fate. The first time was on the 2nd of February, 1829. It was the work of a maniac, Jonathan Martin, who had concealed himself in the Minster the preceding day, Sunday, after prayers. His own account of his proceedings displays no little of that shrewdness so often observed in such persons. He hid himself, he said, in the belfry till the clock struck half-past one, singing hymns; he then got down into the body of the church; when he "got to the great door of the prayer-place," he said, " I found it locked. I then fastened the cord on one side (he had cut one of the bell-ropes

to assist him), and got to the top of the door, and let myself down in the inside. The first thing I did was that of getting all the books that I could, and cushions that were necessary, piled them up in two heaps, and set one pile on fire at the archbishop's throne, and the other at the right-hand side of the organ; but before I set it on fire, I scrambled up the pulpit side, and cut off the gold lace all round the pulpit, with my razor, and after that I cut off all the silk velvet I could get. When half-past two o'clock struck, I lighted my fires; that at the archbishop's throne burnt very fast, but the other burnt very slowly. I stayed half an hour in the place watching it. At three o'clock I started out on my journey." He was soon apprehended and tried, but acquitted on the ground of insanity. He was of course sent to a lunatic asylum, where he died, in October, 1838. Some fanatic notions seem to have been floating in his bewildered brain; his own statement of his reason for committing the act is as follows:—" I set fire to the Minster in consequence of two remarkable dreams. I dreamt that one stood by me, with a bow and a sheaf of arrows, and he shot one through the Minster door. I said I wanted to try to shoot, and he presented me the bow. I took an arrow from the sheaf and shot, but the arrow hit the flags and I lost it. I also dreamt that a large thick cloud came down over the Minster, and extended to my lodgings; from these things I thought that I was to set fire to the Minster." By this fire the whole of the roof of the choir, two hundred and twenty-two feet long, was destroyed, with the woodwork on each side; and the walls above the arches of the choir were so much damaged that it was found necessary to rebuild them; the organ was burnt, and the altar-screen so much injured as to render a new one necessary; the communion plate, too, was melted. No time was lost in repairing the parts injured; the restorations were scarcely completed when another fire occurred, hardly less destructive in its results. A workman, who had been employed to repair the clock, with most culpable negligence left his candle burning when he quitted his work. This was on the evening of May 20, 1840, and by nine o'clock the south tower, in which he had been employed, was discovered to be in flames. By twelve o'clock the south tower was destroyed, and the whole of the roof of the nave had fallen in. The progress of the flames was checked by the great tower, but the amount of damage sustained was very great—in an antiquarian view irreparable. Mr. Smirke, who had so successfully restored the choir, has since been employed in reconstructing the south tower and the nave. The works are now almost completed, and it is said with entire success. When we saw them some time back, they certainly appeared to us to be performed with great judgment; but it was difficult to decide as to the general effect from the place being so occupied by the scaffolding.

———

We cannot better commence our notice of LICHFIELD CATHEDRAL than with a short story. Penda was King of Mercia, the most extensive and powerful of the kingdoms of the Saxon heptarchy. The princes whose dominions lay contiguous to his had been induced to cast aside their pagan idols, and assume the name of Christians. Penda was continually engaged in war with them, and obtained, some writers believe undeservedly, the character of a sanguinary persecutor. The Middle Angles, or English, who inhabited Leicestershire, were at the time governed by his eldest son, Peda, to whom the authority had been delegated. In 653 this young prince arrives on a visit at the court of Oswy, a converted King of Northumbria. Oswy has a daughter, Alchfleda, for whom the pagan prince conceives a passion. Oswy consents to the marriage, on condition that the young idolater is baptized into the Christian faith. Love prevails, and Peda returns to his own province with his bride, and four priests, who are to teach his people the new religion. Troubles rapidly thicken around him. His wife proves unworthy of his attachment, his father and his father-in-law are involved in a cruel war, whilst he cannot consistently take part with either, for though he may suspect Oswy of having decoyed him into the recognition of Christianity, from secret motives of selfish ambition, yet he cannot help his father without aiding paganism, and violating his baptismal vows; nor, on the other hand, can his wishes to see Mercia a converted kingdom induce him to draw the sword for his father's inveterate enemy, who is seeking to enhance his own dominions by Penda's ruin. After two years' warfare the ambitious Northumbrian attains his object. Penda is defeated in battle, and slain, and Oswy adds King of Mercia to his other titles. Nor is this all; from 642 to 670 he is also Bretwalda, that is, Emperor of the whole Heptarchy. He seems to have been one of the most ferocious, vigorous, and ambitious spirits of his day. His unhappy son-in-law, Peda, was permitted for twelve months to share his triumphs (he ruled over the

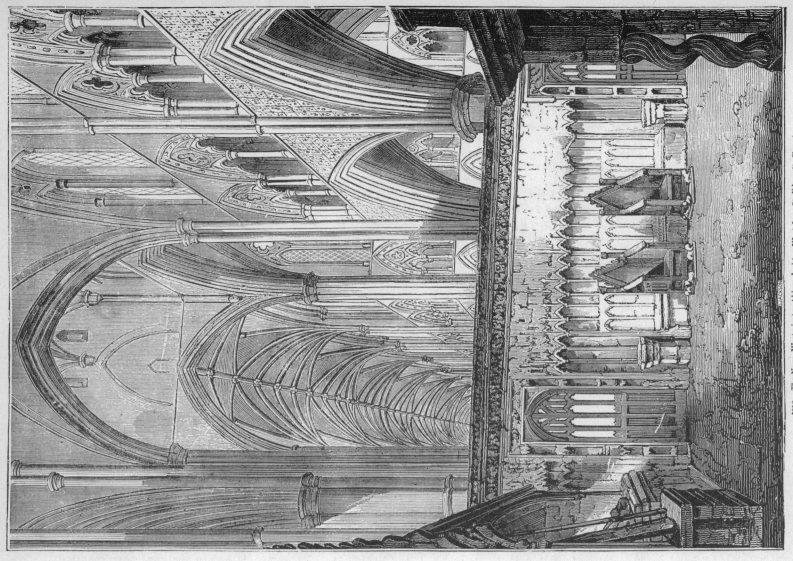

1018.—The Nave, Westminster Abbey, looking West from St. Edward's Chapel.

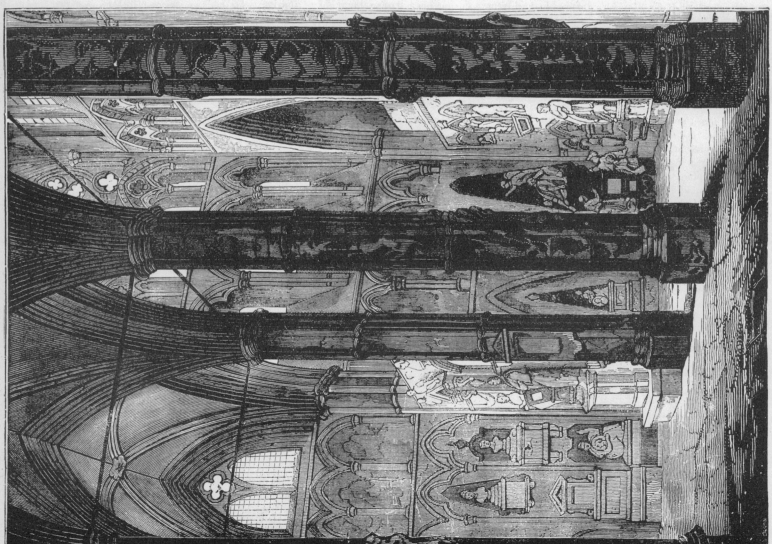

1017.—Poets' Corner, Westminster Abbey.

264

1019.—Front of the Northern Transept, Westminster Abbey.

1020.—Funeral of Henry V.

1021.—Choir of Westminster Abbey.

1022.—Westminster Abbey and Hall in the Seventeenth Century.

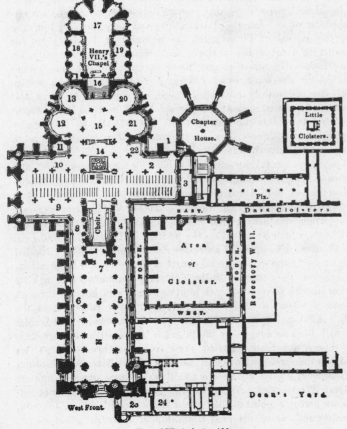

1023.—Plan of Westminster Abbey.

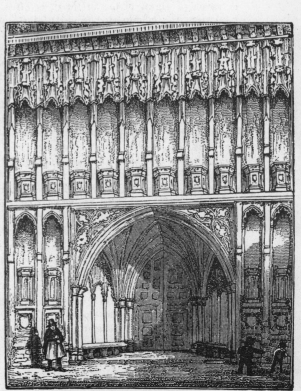

1024.—Westminster Abbey, Western Entrance.

Mercians south of the Trent, the chief part of his father's dominion), but was then basely murdered, and according to general belief, by his treacherous wife, at the instigation of her father. Oswy had now removed his enemy and the heir of his enemy, and was at the summit of his desires; but he was as incapable of moderation in the use of power as in attaining it, and was ultimately driven from Mercia by an insurrection, to give place to Wulfhere, a younger brother of Peda, but who was, like his father Penda, a determined pagan. This Oswy and his converted son-in-law Peda were the first founders of Lichfield church and monastery; and one of the four priests that we have mentioned as having been brought out of Northumbria by Peda to his own dominions was Diuma, the first bishop of the great see of Mercia, which included nearly half of England. The conversion of King Wulfhere was accomplished, we are told, by a most unique miracle, and the narration, as given by the monks of Peterborough, introduces us to a very illustrious personage in Catholic history,—St. Chad, the first bishop who established the see at Lichfield, and whose relics were worshipped here upwards of a thousand years after. At one time, probably when the pagan Wulfhere was persecuting the Christians of his kingdom, Ceadda, or Chad, or Chadd, for his name is spelled in various ways, lived as a hermit in a cell by the side of a spring, where his only nourishment was the milk of a doe. The two sons of Wulfhere, accidentally discovering his retreat, were induced by the eloquent instructions of the recluse not only to keep secret his place of abode, but to change their own faith. Wulfhere, having some reason to suspect what had occurred, watched his sons to the cell, whither they were in the habit of resorting to engage in devotional exercises with their teacher. In his fury, Wulfhere slew them in the sight of the venerable man, who fled in terror, to seek for himself another hiding-place. But Wulfhere was more a violent than a hard-hearted man. Remorse and grief led him to the feet of the hermit, of whom he sought forgiveness and consolation, and begged that he would intercede with heaven for him. Ceadda seized the favourable occasion to turn the yielding heart of the king to the faith he had persecuted; and as a proof of the power of that faith, which it would have been wonderful indeed if mortal man could have resisted, *hung Wulfhere's cloak on a sunbeam.* With or without the miracle, Wulfhere became one of the most ardent of converts, and the legend is valuable as giving an insight into the sufferings of the early English Christians, and the manner in which (apart from mysteries of the cloak-and-sunbeam sort, which were no doubt often gratuitously added afterwards) the faith of Jesus gradually superseded the Saxon idolatries. It may be mentioned, in passing, that the corruptions defiling that holy faith were fewer at that time than they became afterwards. The Anglo-Saxon bishops were less magnificent personages than those of subsequent ages. Their sees were fixed in retired villages, and they loved seclusion and simplicity, and spent a great part of their lives in prayer and meditation and Christian communion, approximating indeed near to the Apostolical standard. Thus, Ceadda, in the house he built for himself, near the monastery, in the humble village of Lichfield, was wont to read and pray with a few, that is, seven or eight, of the brethren, as often as he had any spare time from the labours and ministry of the word. That he was a pure and zealous minister of God there is not a doubt; and it is a pity that with the truth of his history so much adulteration should be blended: though one feels not unwilling to be credulous, when we read of the pleasant songs of angels with which his transit from this painful life to a happy immortality was announced and solemnized.

In the history of the see, the first event of moment is the splitting of the Mercian diocese into five separate bishoprics by Theodore of Canterbury, by whom Ceadda had been made bishop; a clear indication this how the new faith had prospered in Mercia under Ceadda and his three predecessors since Diuma. The next event, about 786, is the elevation of Lichfield into an archbishopric, comprehending the kingdoms of Mercia and the East Angles: this was done by Pope Adrian, at the suit of Offa, a warlike king of Mercia, who, having conquered the kingdom of which Canterbury formed a part, and having a personal hatred to the archbishop, did not choose his prelates should be in subjection in any way to the humbled province, or to a man whom he regarded as his enemy. But the honour lasted only during the life of him who had obtained it " fraudulently and surreptitiously," as the Synod of 803 declared when deciding to resume the pall, and compel Lichfield to return to her ancient duty to the metropolitical see of Canterbury. Under the Norman regime the see of Lichfield was removed to Chester, thence subsequently to Coventry, and thence back again to Lichfield, but in connection with Coventry. The see of Lichfield and Coventry is the present designation.

The primitive church of Lichfield was rebuilt by Heeda, in 700, who brought St. Chad's bones to a shrine he had prepared, and dedicated the edifice to him. In the twelfth century Roger de Clinton " built it new" to the honour of St. Mary and St. Chad, and his church was the foundation of the present cathedral, which on the whole is of the style of the thirteenth and fourteenth centuries: Bishop Heyworth, in the fifteenth, is stated by Fuller to have completed it. If not one of our very noblest cathedrals, Lichfield is able to boast a harmony and elegance, and especially a picturesqueness, highly original and attractive. In length it is four hundred and ten feet, in width one hundred and fifty-three. The engraving will convey a better idea than any description of the three remarkable and elaborately wrought spires, the chief of which is two hundred and eighty feet high. (Fig. 965.) The west front abounds in "exquisite imagerie," now sadly mutilated by time and war. Walter Langton's Lady-Chapel, which enclosed St. Chad's miraculous shrine, is very beautiful, with its high and rich windows filled with stained glass brought from the nunnery of Herckenrode in Liege. We are permitted to have a free view of every part of the exterior of this cathedral by the fine open space around it, which is elevated above the rest of the city, and is entirely under the cathedral jurisdiction.

During the civil wars this close sustained no less than three sieges, alternately from Puritans and Cavaliers, in the course of which it is said that two thousand cannon-shot and fifteen hundred hand-grenades were discharged at the cathedral. In the first siege Lord Brook was shot by a gentleman of the Dyott family, who was on a battlement of one of the cathedral towers, and saw his lordship directing a battery on the east gate of the close, while partially sheltered under the porch of a small house. Lord Brook had vowed the destruction of this " hateful temple of episcopacy," and prayed for some especial token of God's favour during his enterprise. He had the token, said the royalists, but not as he had anticipated. As the event occurred on St. Chad's day, of course the saint had the credit of interposing for Lord Brook's punishment. The memory of these sanguinary times seems now little to accord with the aspect of the cathedral close, with its tranquil lawn-like verdure—its fine old trees—its quiet mansions—and its sheet of water, one of Lichfield's three ancient pools. Near the close was formerly a willow tree, the delight of Johnson's " early and waning life," and even still more so of Miss Seward's; it was the ornament of Stowe Valley, the subject of every writer, the gratification of every naturalist, and the admiration of every traveller. Dr. Johnson never visited this city but he proceeded to his favourite willow, a description of which was drawn up at his desire, by Dr. Jones, for the 'Gentleman's Magazine' for 1731. This willow, after having often been shattered by the high winds, was finally uprooted in the night of April 28th, 1829. ('Family Topographer,' vol. iv. p. 262.)

In the wars just mentioned the cathedral was so much injured as to be almost deemed beyond repair; but what cannot be accomplished by zeal? On the Restoration, and only the very morning after the arrival of Dr. Hacket, the bishop, that dignitary set his servants to remove the rubbish, and helped vigorously with his own hands. He made extraordinary exertions to get money contributed for the work, besides being profuse with his own means, until the melancholy ruin once more was restored to form and beauty; but not exactly as we now see it, for in 1788 it was found necessary to obtain the services of Mr. Wyatt, to institute a thorough repair, involving some important alterations, the expense being met by subscriptions.

The almost total absence of ancient tombs, monuments, and brasses is deeply to be regretted: we owe this, as well as the destruction of the cathedral records, to the two periods so fatal to our great ecclesiastical houses. Henry VIII. swept away among other treasures of the church and see, every shrine, except St. Chad's, which he spared on the petition of Bishop Rowland Lee. The Puritans accomplished a greater destruction, when they stabled their horses in the nave, placed courts of guard in the cross aisles, and relieved their sterner duties (as party statements tell us) by tearing up the pavements, and hunting a cat with hounds through the sacred edifice to delight themselves with the echoes from the roof. Among the modern mementoes of the dead, there is one that will long be sought by the pilgrims of art with feelings only less reverential than actuated their religious predecessors: we allude to the far-famed piece of statuary of the Sleeping Children, by Chantrey, placed above the tomb of the two grand-daughters of Dean Woodhouse. When we can turn from this to lesser objects, we perceive a bust of the " great cham " of literature, Johnson, which reminds us of his long friendship with Garrick, that began at Lichfield, where David was one of the three pupils of Johnson's school, and from whence both started off together to try their fortunes in London, and both to be most successful. Miss Seward's monument, with Scott's inscription, provokes a smile even *here* by the recollection of the vain lady and her works, and the ludicrous dilemma in which an unhappy passing expression of admiration placed him. Here too is a monument of Lady Mary Wortley Montagu, the firm-minded experimentalist of vaccination.

Pacing meditatively the "long-drawn aisles," the sweet and solemn chimes of the bells recall an anecdote of the enthusiastic churchman Hacket, the first of whose peal of six was hung when he was near death. He went from his chamber into the next room, where he could better catch the sound, seemed exceedingly gratified, and blessed God who had favoured him with life to hear it, at the same time observing it would be his passing-bell—and so it was, for he went back to his chamber and left it no more until he was borne to the grave. Among the curiosities of the library is a remarkable book with strange drawings, said to be a thousand years old, in Saxon characters, entitled the Gospels of St. Chad; also a Koran taken from the Moors; and a folio illuminating Chaucer.

It has been a cherished tradition in Lichfield, that the place was originally chosen for the bishop's seat in order to keep in honoured remembrance the martyrdom of a thousand Christians under Dioclesian and Maximilian, and a spot called Christian Field is pointed out as the scene of the slaughter. Dr. Johnson's opinion, and which he took care to put into his Dictionary, that Lichfield means "a field of the dead," is relied on in confirmation of the story. But the antiquarian doctors differ among themselves—so who shall decide? Dr. Stukely derived the name from the marshes about; Mr. Britton, curiously enough, believes, after all, that it means *Pleasant Field.* This interpretation at all events harmonizes most with modern Lichfield, that stands in a verdant valley (nearly in the centre of England), with gentle hills on every side.

There appears to have been at BATH a body of religious men from the very earliest ages of Christianity, who had their house near the springs, which according to tradition were first discovered by Bladud, son of Lud Hudibras, who, being infected with the leprosy, was banished from the palace, and found an asylum with a swineherd, who employed him to watch his pigs. "Then," however, in the words of a humorous "Zomerzetshire" poet, who has somewhat richly treated a rich subject,

> Bladud did the pigs invect, who grunting ran away,
> And vound whot waters presently, which made 'em vresh and gay.
> Bladud was not so grote a vool, but zeeing what pig did doe,
> He beath'd, and wash'd, and rins'd, and beath d, from noddle down to toe.
> Bladud was now (Grammercy, pig!) a delicate vine boy,

and returned to his friends, and ultimately succeeded to the throne of Lud Hudibras, when he erected a city around the springs, to commemorate the circumstance of his own recovery, and blazon their fame abroad to aid in the recovery of others. And so Bath became, says tradition—not very trustworthy, we fear in this instance—the capital of the British monarchs. Bath was, in truth, a Roman city, chosen, like many other of their cities, solely on account of its hot springs.

This house of religious devotees appears to have undergone many changes of constitution, to have experienced many vicissitudes of fortune. Among its earliest benefactors were Osric, a Saxon king, Offa, king of Mercia, Athelstan, and Edgar. During the insurrection of Odo, Bishop of Bayeux, in the reign of Rufus, the town and monastery were burnt and ruined. The circumstances of its restoration are not a little remarkable. A monk of Tours, one John de Villula, who, like many of his brethren, practised medicine, settled at Bath, and, says the historian Warner, though nothing more than an empiric, found means to accumulate a large fortune by his practice, which included the imposing upon the ignorance and credulity of the invalids who flocked to the healing waters of the city. Nothing less would content John de Villula's ambition than the purchase of Bath, which he managed by a payment to Rufus of five hundred marks, and its restoration to prosperity and splendour by the re-erection of its chief edifices, including the church and monastery. And all this he accomplished. Still unsatisfied, he next sought to remove to Bath the see of Wells, and again he was successful, through the professional process of anointing the king's hands, as Matthew Paris slily observes, with "white ointment." The conclusion to the whole was, that Henry I. very fittingly and justly marked his sense of Villula's public spirit by confirming all the existing privileges of Bath, and conferring new; and that, in 1106, Villula, then *Bishop of Bath,* gave the whole, with a more than princely generosity, to the monastery, reserving to himself and successors the right of appointing the

prior, who was thenceforth to rule in the place of the abbot of former times. And now, looking at John de Villula's earlier life by the light of his later, may we not conclude that the modern historian has probably been a little too hasty in his judgment, when he brands such a man as an empiric and an impostor?

Bath Cathedral (Fig. 984) has one architectural feature which distinguishes it in an interesting manner from all other English buildings of the same class: it was the latest of the whole in the period of its erection, having been begun in the reign of Henry VII. and finished in the reign of the second James. Oliver King was the bishop to whom the commencement of this good work was owing; and the circumstances that made him determine to undertake such a mighty task in those degenerate days are not unworthy of narration. "Lying at Bath, and musing or meditating one night late, after his devotions and prayers for the prosperity of Henry VII. and his children (who were all in most part living), to which king he was principal secretary, and by him preferred to his bishopric—he saw, or supposed he saw, a vision of the Holy Trinity, with angels ascending and descending by a ladder, near to the foot of which there was a fair olive-tree, supporting a crown, and a voice that said, 'Let an Olive establish the crown, and let a King restore the church.' Of this 'dream or vision' he took exceeding great comfort, and told it divers of his friends, applying it to the king, his master, in part, and some part to himself. To his master, because the olive being the emblem or hieroglyphic of peace and plenty, seemed to him to allude to King Henry VII., who was worthily counted the wisest and most peaceable king in all Europe of that age. To himself (for the wisest will flatter themselves sometimes), because he was not only a chief counsellor to his king, and had been his ambassador to conclude the most honourable peace with Charles VIII., ... but also, because he carried both the Olive and the King in his own name, and therefore thought he was specially designed for this church work, to the advancement of which he had an extraordinary inclination. Thus though (as St. Thomas of Aquina well noteth) all dreams, be they never so sensible, will be found to halt in some part of their coherence, and so perhaps may this; yet most certain it is, he was so transported with his dream, for the time, that he presently set in hand with the church (the ruins whereof I rue to behold even in writing these lines), and at the west end thereof he caused a representation to be graved of this his vision of the Trinity, the angels, and the ladder; and on the north side the olive and crown, with certain French words which I could not read, but in English is the verse taken out of the book of Judges, chap. ix.:

> "Trees, going to choose their king,
> Said—Be to us the Olive King, &c." *

The "French verses" here mentioned were most probably merely a later translation of the English one which is understood to have been inscribed on the part in question; and the window to which Harrington refers in the words "at the west end," is at the present time one of the glories of the cathedral, representing, by means of many figures, the dream we have described, and which led to the re-erection of the pile. The author from whom we have quoted the foregoing passage was the well-known poet, and the godson and favourite of Elizabeth; and to him we are indirectly indebted for the completion of the cathedral. Being left unfinished by Bishop King, and the Reformation coming to arrest all such architectural labours, the edifice fell into a very dilapidated state, although in the reign of Elizabeth certain benefactors stepped forward and did something. But in Harrington's time, according to his own words above transcribed, the church remained in ruins, and he then determined, if he could, to be instrumental in its restoration. And an opportunity soon occurred. Whilst Bishop Montague was at Bath, on his primary visitation, and walking in the grove, he was suddenly caught in a shower, which induced him, on the invitation of Sir John, to seek shelter in the church. The knight took him into the north aisle, then entirely roofless, which made the bishop remark that this situation did not shelter him from the rain. "Doth it not, my lord?" said the knight: "then let me sue your bounty towards covering our poor church; for if it keep not us safe from the waters above, how shall it ever save others from the fire beneath?" The appeal was successful; Bishop Montague set to work, and all but completed the cathedral.

And the edifice, when finished, though not large (the extreme length is two hundred and ten feet, extreme breadth one hundred and twenty-six), looked noble, with its superb central tower, and formed altogether a very pure and beautiful example of the latest period of Pointed architecture; but it has been reserved for the present time to show practically how little such work was appreciated, by

* Harrington's 'Nugæ Antiquæ.'

1025.—Howden Church.

1026.—Tomb of the Boy-Bishop, Salisbury.

1028.—Franciscan, or Grey Friar.

1027.—Ruins of Netley Abbey.

1029.—Dominican, or Black Friar.

1030.—View of Tintern Abbey.

1033.—Winchester College

1034.—New Abbey, Kirkcudbrightshire. (From an Original Sketch.)

1035.—Lich-Gate at Beckenham.

1032.—Leicester Abbey.

1031.—Tintern Abbey.

making in it the most extensive and most injurious alterations. The remarkable square east window was supported by square towers; these the clever improvers of the nireteenth century have changed into octagonal pinnacles. The—but it is idle to particularise—for in short the whole character of the cathedral has been wantonly destroyed,—it *was* called, from its general lightness and elegance, the lantern of England; we may keep the title—but if so, let it be as we hang lights against dangerous places in our streets, to *warn* rather than to attract. We may add that the interior is crowded with monuments of all shapes, sizes, and materials, a heterogeneous assemblage, which may excuse the somewhat irreverent tone of the lines—

> These walls, adorned with monument and bust,
> Show how Bath waters serve to lay the dust.

The first religious oratory in Britain is said by monastic writers to have been built of "wreathed twigs" at Glastonbury, by Joseph of Arimathea and eleven other disciples of St. Philip; and that hence arose the conversion to Christianity of the native Britons of the district in which Wells and Glastonbury are situated. If the legend be true, the doctrines thus taught were soon effaced, for when the West Saxons possessed the country, the Italian missionary Birinus, observing how deeply all were sunk in idolatry, paused in his progress, as he was journeying to parts beyond the dominion of the English, where he had intended to sow the seed of the Holy Faith, and addressed himself to the difficult task of enlightening the hearts of the pagans he saw around him, wisely concluding that the need of knowledge could nowhere be greater. It was a work of time to uproot the deeply-seated pagan superstitions; and the West Saxons had so far relapsed into their old infirmities, as greatly to incense Pope Formosus, who issued a thundering missive; fulminating eternal damnation against their king, Edward the Elder (the son and successor of Alfred), and all his subjects, if they should invalidate this decree, namely, that among other changes, in consequence of the West Saxons having been left seven years without a pastor, three new bishoprics should be forthwith instituted among them. One of these three was WELLS. Doubts have been cast on the genuineness of the Pope's missive; but, at all events, the see was certainly formed about this period—the beginning of the tenth century. It seems generally believed that the first church was built at Wells two centuries earlier, in 704, by King Ina, and that it was a religious seminary, dedicated to St. Andrew, because placed near a medicinal and miraculous spring reverenced as St. Andrew's well, and sometimes called the Bottomless Well; and this account is based both on tradition and probability, although there is no evidence in contemporary documents to stamp certainty upon it. The connection of a common and honoured origin was not forgotten by the houses of Glastonbury and Wells. A distinguished monk or abbot of Glastonbury was often elected to be bishop of Wells; and in the reign of Richard I. the abbey of Glastonbury was annexed to this see, in exchange for Bath. The means by which this was accomplished are most remarkable. Savaric, bishop of Wells, had earnestly coveted the abbey, on account, it would seem, of its great wealth; and being a kinsman of the Emperor of Germany, he employed his secret influence with that monarch to seize Cœur-de-Lion on his return from the Holy Land, in order to make one of the conditions of the king's release his surrendering the abbey of Glastonbury to Savaric. For the proof of this story we have a record of Henry III., mentioned by Stow; and Cœur-de-Lion afterwards declared "that the abbey had been extorted from him by force and terror." Savaric, however, kept his prize, and removed his see thither.

The undaunted founder of the present cathedral (Figs. 982, 983) was Joceline de Welles, who "built it new from the very foundation," in the year 1239. "No one," says the Canon of Wells, in 'Anglia Sacra,' "had ever been like this man, and we have never seen a successor equal to him." The body of the church, from the west end to the middle of the choir, is visibly of or about the time of this prelate. The style is pointed, but bears strongly upon it the impress of the Norman architecture out of which it had just arisen, being much more ponderous and sombre than the Eastern parts of the fabric, built in later times. The quadrangular main tower, resting on four broad arches, is particularly massive, even to a fault.

Mr. Britton observes, that in passing through the choir toward the eastern end, lightness and richness and elegance grow on us until we arrive at the part about the altar, which is exceedingly florid and beautiful. Even this, however, is far surpassed by the exquisite Lady-Chapel—that perfect gem of ecclesiastical architecture, which, placed amid so much that is glorious beside, seems to us like a sweet fanciful episode to a noble poem. As the Lady-

Chapel is the most superb, so is the west front the grandest portion of the edifice. The mere account of the sculpture upon it is truly astonishing, comprising an assemblage of one hundred and fifty statues of life size, and above three hundred smaller ones. The niches are beautifully decorated, and the canopies rest on slight and elegant pillars of finely-polished marble. The quadrangle of the cloisters measure on each side from one hundred and fifty to one hundred and sixty feet. The two western towers, erected toward the end of the fourteenth century, and the chapter-house, a handsome octangular building fifty-two feet in diameter, sustained on one central pillar, are, among the other portions of the edifice, peculiarly deserving notice. The dimensions of the pile are as follows:—371 feet in length from east to west; 135 feet the transept or extreme breadth; 160 feet the height of the main tower; and 126 feet the height of the west tower. The whole cathedral, both within and without, forms one of the grandest of our national architectural effects. A more majestic object can hardly be conceived than it presents as seen from all the great roads leading to the ancient city, to which it imparts an aspect of great dignity. Nature, too, has favoured the spot. The Mendip Hills on the north, in form like an amphitheatre, and the rich and green meadows on the south, present lofty and beautiful combinations, finely harmonizing with the stately work of human intelligence before them. We may here observe that several of the bishops of Wells of the middle ages were wont to pursue the unclerical sports of hunting and hawking,—nay, we are told that Ralph de Salopia (the builder of that lofty and embattled wall, with its broad moat, that gives such a fortress-like character to the episcopal palace of Wells, and also the founder of the Vicar's Close) actually destroyed by hunting *all the wild beasts* of Mendip forest; and Reginald Fitz-Joceline, a bishop of most rare geniality of temperament, was not only passionately fond of the field-sports of his time, but took pains that his successors might enjoy them also, for he obtained from Richard I. liberty for the bishops of Wells to keep dogs for hunting throughout all Somersetshire. But if it could not be said of Joceline that cure of souls was his chief aim, neither could it be said that he was oppressive or ambitious, inasmuch as he relieved the city burgesses from feudal offices of a servile nature, and when offered the dignity of archbishop, replied with tears, that "so far was he from having any ambitious desire of that place, that it was a great grief unto him to be chosen, and that he would be very glad if they would take some other in his room: howbeit (quoth he), if they will needs stand to their election, though with grief and heart's sorrow, I must and will accept of the same." There was often a little affectation of humility in such cases, and probably those who were so bent on forcing Fitz-Joceline to the archiepiscopal throne, had little doubt that his reluctance would soon wear away: it did not, however; for though he submitted, he was taken suddenly ill, put on a monk's cowl, and so died. This sporting taste in the episcopals of Wells seems to be commemorated in the monument of Salopia in the cathedral, which presents two dogs, collared, at the feet of the bishop's effigy. The other sepulchral memorials of Wells are chiefly of antique date.

PETERBOROUGH CATHEDRAL (Fig. 991) is another of the ecclesiastical foundations which we owe to Peda or Peada, the son of the pagan monarch Penda, converted, through the instrumentality of human love, to divine worship. He it was who founded the Benedictine Abbey of Medeshamstead, which in course of time became one of the most magnificent in England, and of which, under the name of Peterborough, we possess a noble remain in the church. In our account of Penda and his son, in the notice of Lichfield Cathedral, we have spoken of the conversion of the brother of the latter Wulfhere; the records of Medeshamstead furnish us an interesting glimpse of the subsequent conduct of this prince. That valuable but in general brief record of ancient events, the Saxon Chronicle, for once in its notices is tolerably diffuse. It states that "In Wulfhere's time Medhamstead waxed very rich. He loved it much, for the sake of his brother Peda, and for the love of his wed-brother Oswy, and for the love of Saxulf the abbot. He said, therefore, that he would dignify and honour it by the counsel of his brothers, Ethelred and Merwall; and by the counsel of his sisters, Kyneburga and Kyneswitha; and by the counsel of the archbishop, who was called Deus-dedit; and by the counsel of all his peers, learned and lewd [unlearned], that in his kingdom were. And so he did. Then sent the king after the abbot, that he should immediately come to him. And he so did. Then said the king to the abbot, 'Beloved Saxulf, I have sent after thee for the good of my soul, and I will plainly tell thee for why: my brother Peda and my beloved friend Oswy began a Minster, for the love of Christ and

St. Peter. But my brother, as Christ willed, is departed from this life; I will, therefore, entreat thee, beloved friend, that they earnestly proceed on their work; and I will find thee, thereto, gold and silver, land and possessions, and all that thereto behoveth! Then went the abbot home and began to work. So he sped as Christ permitted him: so that in a few years that Minster was ready." The Chronicle goes on to describe the interesting circumstances attending the opening and dedication, when the charter of its estates and privileges was granted in the presence of all the chief nobility of the kingdom. It may serve as an example of the spirit of these Saxon princes, and show how impossible they thought it was to render too much to God in return for all he had given them, to state that the lands then conferred extended nearly twenty miles east and west, and that in the erection of the buildings the foundation-stones were of such dimensions that eight yoke of oxen could with difficulty draw one of them.

The known wealth of the abbey of course made it a mark for the assaults of the Danes, during the period they harassed England with their piratical attacks. About 870 they came hither, after the destruction of the neighbouring monastery of Croyland, and, on finding the gates closed against them, besieged the abbey. For some time the monks appear to have successfully resisted, notwithstanding that the walls were battered by some species of warlike engine. Talba, the brother of the Danish leader Hubba, was slain by a stone from the walls, and that casualty led to the destruction of the entire body of inmates. An entrance was forced by the vindictive Hubba, who then slew—it is said with his own hand, but this can hardly be true—every one of the monks, eighty-four in number, including the Superior. Whatever was valuable, and that could be removed, was then taken away, and the monastery burnt: for fifteen days the fire continued.

From the state of desolation into which this horrible event plunged the establishment, Edgar raised it about 970, who, not content with a mere restoration, appears to have made it even more splendid and wealthy than before. The "golden burgh" or golden city was the name fittingly applied to it by some; but Peter-burgh from the name of the patron saint, gradually superseded both that and the earlier designations.

The same kind of sweeping destruction, followed by the same kind of persevering and Christian liberality in restoration, has twice since the Danish attack been experienced by Peterborough; namely, during the insurrection under Hereward le Wake, in the wars against the Conqueror, and during an accidental fire in the year 1116. But the result was, that, down even to the very dissolution of monasteries, Peterborough was one of the most magnificent and powerful of English abbeys. Some rude old rhymes descriptive of the characteristics of several monasteries of the neighbourhood, seem to imply that it was not a little puffed up by its distinctions. They run thus:—

> Ramsay, the rich of gold and fee;
> Thorney, the flower of many fair tree;
> Croyland, the courteous of their meat and their drink;
> Spalding, the gluttons, as all men do think;
> *Peterborough the proud;*
> Sautrey by the way—that old abbey—
> Gave more alms in one day than all they.

The cathedral was begun immediately after the fire of 1116, by Abbot John de Sais, a Norman, and finished, in all its greater parts at least, before the close of the century. The style, therefore, is Anglo-Norman, and remarkable for its solidity of construction and aspect. The more noticeable architectural features may be briefly summed in—the low central tower which forms a lantern, the double transepts with a tower at the extremity of the north-western only, the semicircular eastern end, the lofty and richly-decorated portico, in three compartments, that forms the western front, the *wooden* roofs of the nave, transepts, and choir, and the very beautiful fittings and decorations of that choir, entirely completed in the style of Edward III. The dimensions of the cathedral are—length 476 feet, breadth at the great transept 203 feet, length of the western front 156 feet, height of central tower 184 feet. The devastations of the civil war have left but few specimens of monumental sculpture. Two burials of no ordinary interest have taken place here—Mary Queen of Scots, whose body was afterwards removed by her son King James to Westminster Abbey, and Catherine of Arragon, the noble and suffering wife of that ignoblest and most brutal of husbands, Henry VIII. However, if a credit it be that he did not altogether disregard her dying injunctions, let him have the benefit of it. Heaven knows, they were simple and easy enough. "When I am dead," she says, according to the words of her most faithful chronicler, the great poet,

> Let me be us'd with honour; strew me over
> With maiden flowers, that all the world may know
> I was a chaste wife to my grave: embalm me,
> Then lay me forth: although unqueen'd, yet like
> A queen, and daughter to a king, inter me.

Poor and yet rich Catherine, thou hast been "used with honour!" The flowers wet with tears, have been, and will continue to be, in spirit at least, dropped over thee, in lands the very name of which thou never heardest of, and to ages more distant than any of us may venture to compute.

———

To Lichfield and Peterborough we have now to add GLOUCESTER, in enumerating the services of the family of Penda in the cause of the new faith they had embraced under such peculiar and interesting circumstances. Wulfhere, who had assisted to finish at Peterborough what his brother Peda had begun, appears to have thought it necessary to mark in a more independent manner his sympathy with his brother's views, his gratitude to the class of men who were so active in extending the knowledge of Christianity, and, above all, his piety towards the God who had been so newly declared unto him: hence the establishment at Gloucester. Of course there are no remains of a building so early as the seventh century: whether time would have permitted any parts of Wulfhere's structure to descend to us we know not, for fire, that agent of destruction which sooner or later, either through design or by accident, invariably attacks all such mighty memorials of the past, has been busy at Gloucester. The most ancient portions of the cathedral are the crypt, the chapels that surround the choir, and the lower part of the nave—all erected, it is supposed, by Bishop Aldred in the latter half of the eleventh century, and all forming a portion of his "New Minster." This was burnt with the monastery about 1087, and it is supposed by the same fire that destroyed a great portion of the city; the incendiaries were the adherents of that Robert, the son of the Conqueror, who now lies in the cathedral, with his effigy "carved to the life in heart of oak." Here too is laid, beneath a very remarkable *bracket* monument, Abbot Serle, who after the fire rebuilt the edifice, with the exception of the parts above named. To this excellent abbot William of Malmesbury pays the high compliment of adducing him as an example that England was not then destitute of virtue; and another writer, a monk of the same monastery, shows that Serle had even achieved the difficult task of becoming a prophet in his own immediate sphere. Godfrey, the prior, says—

> The Church's bulwark fell when Serlo died,
> Virtue's sharp sword, and Justice's fond pride:
> Speaker of truth, no vain discourse he lov'd,
> And pleas'd the very princes he reprov'd.
> A hasty judgment, or disordered state
> Of life or morals, were his utter hate.
> The third of March was the auspicious day
> When Serlo wing'd through death to life his way.

He died in 1104. Whether any portion of his edifice remains appears doubtful: so many circumstances, of injury and reparation and improvement are recorded, that it is most probable that the cathedral has been entirely rebuilt since his time, with the exception of those older portions which existed before him; for we find distinct notices of the raising of the south aisle and transept between 1310 and 1330; of the commencement of the choir soon after this period; of the erection of the cloisters between 1351 and 1390; and of the chapel of Our Lady toward the close of the fifteenth century; and lastly, of the noble tower, with its four beautiful and delicate pinnacles, which was completed in the beginning of the sixteenth. (Fig. 1001.) One of the abbots who was concerned in these rebuildings, Abbot Thokey, deserves especial mention, not so much for what he did in that way himself, as for what he was the means of enabling his successors to do. About 1319 Edward II. paid the abbey a visit, and was received with great honour. As he sat in the hall, he noticed on the walls the portraits of his kingly predecessors, and jocosely asked if his own were among them. The abbot, desiring apparently to pay some great compliment, answered, that he hoped to have him in some more honourable place. The words were unmeaning enough then, but proved to be prophetic ones. Edward was murdered at Berkeley Castle, and three several monasteries refused to receive the corpse, dreading the anger of the ruling powers. Abbot Thokey, however, stepped forward, brought it in honourable procession to his monastery, and there interred it near the great altar. That event gave the monastery an incalculable increase of wealth, popularity, and influence; for the young Edward speedily overthrew his father's murderers, and then—why then, every one was glad, were it but for the son's sake, to come and pay

1036.—Malmesbury Abbey.

1038.—Porch of Malmesbury Abbey.

1037.—Arch in Transept of Malmesbury Abbey.

1037*.—Arms of Malmesbury.

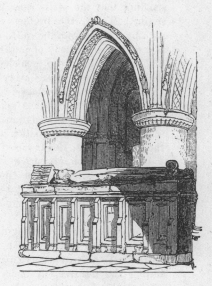

1039.—Tomb in Malmesbury Abbey.

1040.—Kirkstall Abbey.

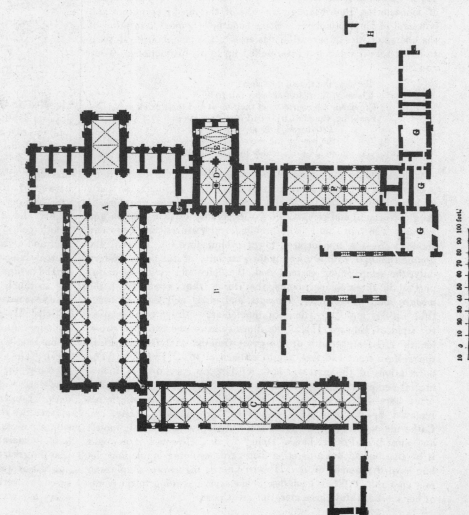

1041.—Plan of Kirkstall Abbey.

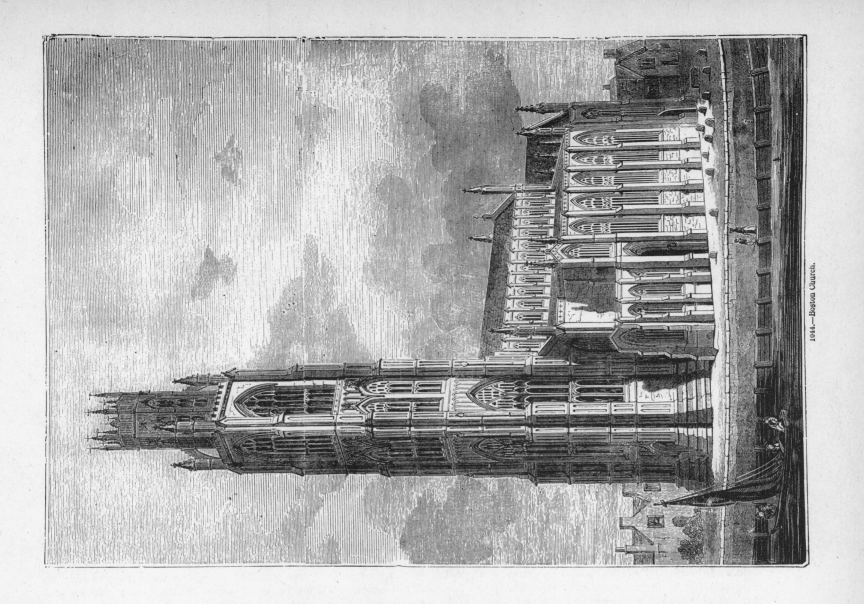

1044.—Boston Church.

1043.—Redcliffe Church, Bristol.

No. 35.

their respects to the dead father's shrine. Offerings flowed in a continually glittering stream. The monks at one time were obliged—painful obligation!—to sell some hundred pieces of silk interwoven with gold, their treasury became so very crowded. That Edward and his family should pay special attention to the shrine was only to be expected. We find the former, at a certain period, when he was in danger of shipwreck, vowing a golden ship if he escaped; and he performed the vow, but subsequently redeemed the ship for one hundred pounds. Among the family offerings may be mentioned a heart and urn of gold, by Queen Philippa, and a gold cross, given by the Black Prince.

During the abbacy of Horton—a name never mentioned by ancient monk of Gloucester without a blessing, for he provided that the anniversary of his death should be celebrated by a mass, the priests wearing vestments of blue velvet, interwoven with little moons and stars—probably of silver, and by a distribution of wine, wassail, and pittance, or money;—during this abbacy Richard II. held a parliament at Gloucester, and kept his own court in the monastery, where, it appears, the laws of arms were regulated in the refectory, the House of Lords sat in the common hall, and the Commons in the chapter-house. The abbey was so crowded, as to look more like a fair than a house of religion, and the green plat in the cloisters was so trampled down by the wrestlers and ball-players, that not a vestige of green grass was to be seen. Does not this little passage in the history of Gloucester monastery give us curious glimpses of the public business and private sports of an English king in the fourteenth century, when the court regulating the laws of arms seems to have been a kind of third estate, and when the court precincts formed an arena for the display of gymnastic sports? How the pious and sedate monks must have been puzzled at the whole affair! how whimsically out of place they must have felt themselves, wandering about amidst such gay and reckless and turbulent throngs!

We need not add much to the particulars of the cathedral incidentally given in the previous pages. The choir is the portion which more especially attracts admiration; a writer in the 'Transactions of the Society of Antiquaries' observes of it, that "the great elevation of the vault, the richness of the design, the elaborate tracery which covers the walls, and the vast expanse of the eastern window, render it an almost unrivalled specimen of the florid style of architecture." The whispering-gallery has been mentioned by Lord Bacon. We allude to it for the sake of the verse inscribed on the wall:—

Doubt not but God, who sits on high,
Thy secret prayers can hear,
When a dead wall thus cunningly
Conveys soft whispers to the ear.

In its extreme length the cathedral measures 423 feet, the nave 171, the choir 140, the Lady-Chapel 92; the north and south transepts each 66 feet; the height of the tower is 225 feet. The alabaster tomb of Edward II. is the most interesting among the monuments. Here, too, is a statue to that truly good and great man who, while the civilized world was ringing with his fame, and waiting to shower wealth and honours upon him if he would but come to receive them, stayed quietly in his native village, content with the fulfilment of his ordinary duties, and happy in the knowledge that they left him ample leisure to promote by unceasing labour the discovery that has immortalized the name of—Edward Jenner.

The history of HEREFORD CATHEDRAL introduces to us a love-story of a very different character and termination to that related in our notice of Lichfield, though, like that, tending powerfully to promote the progress of Christianity, in times when such progress must have seemed, to all but its enthusiastic promoters and guides, a very uncertain and hazardous business. Offa, king of Mercia, had a daughter, beloved by Ethelbert, king of the East Angles, who in consequence sought her hand. Offa, receiving his advances in a friendly spirit, invited him to his palace at Sutton, some three miles from Hereford, and on his arrival treated him with great kindness, and professed, perhaps sincerely, his desire for an alliance. Offa's queen, however—a person of the most unscrupulous and ambitious character—thinking the occasion a fitting one for enabling her husband to add Ethelbert's dominions to his own, induced Offa to forget alike what was due to Ethelbert as a king, a man, and as her guest, and to give consent to the horrible crime proposed—Ethelbert's murder. The unfortunate king was speedily beheaded; or, as some writers state, precipitated into a hollow space beneath her bed-chamber, and there stifled by the queen's agents. And now miracles occurred, if we are to believe the monkish annalists. "On the night of his burial, a column of light, brighter than the sun,

arose towards heaven;" and three nights after, the figure of the wounded king appeared to Brithfrid, a nobleman, and commanded him to carry the body to a place called *Stratus Waye*, and to inter it near the monastery there. Brithfrid, with the aid of another column of light, proceeded on his journey, bearing the head and body in a carriage. On the way, the head accidentally fell, but was found by a blind man, who picked it up and restored it to the driver, receiving as a reward his sight. On their arrival at the place now known as Hereford, they interred the body. Asser, Alfred's biographer, says, that so numerous and considerable were the miracles then and there performed, that Offa sent two bishops to Hereford to inquire into the matter; they beheld the cure of a Welsh nobleman afflicted with palsy; and at once believed. Offa, on receiving their report, did the same, and conferred a tenth of all his possessions on the saint, that is to say, on the church where he was buried. He also built a magnificent tomb over Ethelbert's remains. Nor was that all: he actually set out on a pilgrimage to Rome, by way of penance, and whilst there, consented to subject his kingdom to the payment of Peter's pence;—which, by the way, was making his subjects, who were innocent, do penance too. To these circumstances we owe the origin of Hereford Cathedral; for although there was a church on the site before the period of the occurrences in question, it was through them only that the religious establishment obtained fame, wealth, and ecclesiastical rank. One of the first results, apart from Offa's munificence, was that Milfrid, governor of the province under King Egbert, built a new church, a stone structure, which, having become decayed by the beginning of the eleventh century, was rebuilt by Bishop Athelstan. That building, again destroyed by the Welsh in an incursion about 1055, it was reserved for one of the admirable Norman prelates whom (to his honour be it said) the Conqueror appointed, Robert de Lozing, or Lozinga, to raise the proud fabric once more from ruins. To his labours, then, we owe the commencement of the existing cathedral (Fig. 1002). Of this ecclesiastic's death an interesting and not at all improbable story is told; for although an able priest, mathematician, and architect, he is known to have been so superstitious as to decline attending the dedication of the cathedral of Lincoln, when invited by Remigius, on the ground that he had consulted the stars and found them unpropitious. It appears that during the illness of Wulstan, bishop of Worcester, Lozing, being then at court, beheld the form of his friend in a dream, who said to him, "If you wish to see me before I die, hasten to Worcester." Hurrying to the king, Lozing obtained leave to depart, and travelling night and day, he reached Cricklade, where, overcome by fatigue, he slept. His friend there again appeared, saying, "Thou hast done what fervent love could dictate, but art too late. I am now dead; and thou wilt not long survive me: but lest thou shouldst consider this only a fantastic dream, know that after my body has been committed to the earth a gift shall be given to thee, which thou shalt recognise as having belonged to me." Lozing proceeded to Worcester on the following morning, where, truly enough, the good old bishop, the last of the Saxon ecclesiastics, lay dead. Lozing performed the obsequies, and was preparing to depart, when the priest said to him, "Receive as a testimony of our departed lord's love his lambskin cap which he wore." No wonder the words caused Lozing's "blood to run cold;" or that the coincidence wrought out its own greatest marvel in Lozing's death. Wulstan died in January; Lozing, in June of the same year, 1094.

At Hereford, as at Bath, the restorers have been at work in the true spirit of the restorations *of the last century*; that is, to add and to take away, to beautify and make comfortable, and to make neat, without the smallest reference to the original design of the edifice, or indeed to any design whatever. That a distinguished name, Wyatt's, is connected with such unworthy proceedings in relation to a building that all architects should look on with reverence and wonder, makes the matter only the more painful. Our space will not permit us to pause over any descriptive details: we can therefore only observe, the cathedral stands near the banks of the beautiful Wye; that the chief external characteristic of its appearance is the broad, low, but highly enriched square tower; that the original west front is lost, having been destroyed by the fall of its tower, and that we have one by Mr. Wyatt in its place as contemptible as that was noble; and, lastly, that the interior presents many architectural objects of high interest, in addition to some very old and very highly decorated monuments. In its extreme length the cathedral measures 325 feet; the extent of the great transept is 100 feet; the height of the body of the church 91 feet. There were two exceedingly beautiful appendages of Hereford Cathedral, the chapter-house and a genuine Saxon chapel; for the destruction of both, the dignitaries of the cathedral during the last century must enjoy all the merit or disgrace. For ourselves we should say it was a merit, if the alternative was, as is most probable, that the building should be pulled down, or what they would call *restored*.

In the aisles of CARLISLE CATHEDRAL (Fig. 1007) there is a very remarkable series of ancient legendary paintings from the histories of St. Anthony, St. Cuthbert, and St. Augustine, or St. Austin, the founder of the order of Austin Canons. Over each subject is a distich, in uncouth rhyme. The series relating to St. Austin commences with a picture beneath which we read an explanation of its subject—

> Her [here] fader and modʳ of Sanct Austyne
> Fyrst put him her to learn doctrine ;

and then proceeds to show us, with extraordinary minuteness and correctness, all the different phases of the saint's career, from the time that his parents thus early bent his mind to study, up to the period of his burial at Pavia. At one period, we see he has become a distinguished scholar, but proud in his tastes and immoral in his conduct, and a defender of the early heresies, until the sermons of St. Ambrose and the tears of his mother Monica bring him back to the purity and truth of the Gospel—not, it appears from these rhymes, without miraculous interposition :—

> Her wepyng and walying, as he lay,
> Sodonly a voice thus herd he say,
> "Tolle lege, Tolle lege."

Bishop Tanner remarks of Carlisle, " This is the only episcopal chapter in England of the order of St. Austin ;" and, we may add, that while Carlisle Cathedral was of this order, all the rest of the English religious houses connected with our cathedral churches were Benedictines. As this, then, was the peculiarly distinctive feature of the establishment, it was a happy thought that of placing on the walls a complete pictorial narrative of the life, fame, and teachings of the founder of the Austin rule. In respect to St. Cuthbert, bishop of Lindisfarn, Egfrid, king of Northumberland, gave the town of Carlisle, walled and rebuilt, to him ; and in 686 the saint " was carried by the townspeople," says Bede, " to see their walls." Carlisle continued an appendage of the see of Lindisfarn until 1133, when Henry I. made it a separate see, and also founded the priory and built the cathedral. A religious institution had previously been founded at Carlisle by St. Cuthbert, or about his time (the seventh century), which Walter, a priest and follower of the Conqueror, had attempted to revive. As some parts of the present fabric are as old as the Saxon times, Henry I. must have remodified and enlarged an older structure. The nave and south aisles were built by William Rufus, and the choir—the finest part of the church—between 1363 and 1397, when indulgences and remissions of penance were granted to such of the laity as contributed money, materials, or labour to the holy work. The priory, to which the cathedral was attached, " wanted not for relics of saints, for Waldeive, the son of Cospatrick, Earl of Dunbar, brought from Jerusalem and Constantinople a bone of St. Paul and another of St. John the Baptist, two stones of Christ's sepulchre, and part of the Holy Cross, which he gave to the priory, together with a mansion near St. Cuthbert's church where at that time stood an ancient building called Arthur's Chamber, taken to be part of the mansion house of King Arthur, the son of Uther Pendragon, of memorable note for his worthiness in the time of ancient kings." (Denton's MSS.) In the civil wars of the Commonwealth, Carlisle Cathedral was sadly curtailed of its fair proportions ; what was left of the nave is now converted into a separate parish church, the cathedral service being performed in the choir. The chapter-house and cloisters disappeared in these wars, and the ancient refectory has been used for the modern chapter-house. Dr. Paley was Archdeacon of Carlisle, and has a monument here. There are some ancient sepulchral remains ; but it seems scarcely to be known for whom any of them were originally intended. A small chapel of St. Catherine's, adjoining the transept in the south aisle, was separately founded and endowed by John de Capella, a citizen of Carlisle, previous to 1366, at which time an attempt was made to deprive it of some of its revenues ; but Bishop Appleby interrupted this process in a peculiarly decisive way, ordering public notice to be given that he should excommunicate the parties by *bell, book, and candle,* unless restitution were made before the expiration of ten days : no doubt the threat was successful, for it was an awful one in that day. In a chamber of the deanery is a curious painted ceiling, and on the sides of the cross-beams several couplets, and this inscription :—

> Symon Senus, Prior, sette yis roofe and scallope here,
> To the intent wytbin thys place they shall have prayers every daye in the year.
> Lofe God and thy prynce, and you neydis not dreid thy enimys.

As the cathedral appears at present, it seems to be of various styles, and the material of which it is composed, a coarse reddish freestone, is unfavourable to architectural beauty ; but nevertheless, at a distance it is still imposing, an effect greatly to be attributed to the elevation of the city on an eminence of a lozenge shape formed by the swelling banks of three rivers, the Eden, Caldew, and Peteril, and to the flat plain that extends all around this picturesque capital of one of the most picturesque of counties, until it terminates in mountain, cloud, and mist. " Bonny Carlisle," as it is called in old Border Song, was once a strong border town ; and the ancient garrison-fortress still seems to stand as a guard near the cathedral, conspicuous at the distance of many miles. It used also to be sung,

> The sun shines fair on Carlisle wa' ;

but though the sun still shines fair as ever on Carlisle, very little of those celebrated walls or their bulwarks now meet its rays, and, happily, there is no longer any necessity for them.

There is little in the architecture of CHICHESTER CATHEDRAL (Fig. 1003), and not much in its history, that will need a lengthened notice. The original cathedral was founded and the building completed towards the close of the eleventh century. In the year 1114 it was greatly injured by fire, and, though soon restored, it was entirely destroyed by a second fire in the year 1186. Bishop Seffrid, who had been appointed to the see about this time, immediately commenced the renovation of the cathedral. According to some of the historians, he built the church from its foundations ; while others say that he " engrafted upon the remaining walls a new work, adapting it to the style and architectural ornaments peculiar to the age in which he lived." Be that as it may, it is agreed that his building is the nucleus of the existing cathedral : it consisted of the " present nave with its single aisles, the centre arcade with its low tower and transept, and of the choir." It was consecrated by Seffrid on the 13th of September, 1199 ; but he had not quite completed it at his death in the year 1214. There is little remarkable about it, except that it presents one of the earliest specimens of a stone groined roof : the cathedral having been twice burnt already owing chiefly to its wooden roof, Seffred resolved in his church to prevent, if he could, a similar disaster. Great additions and alterations were made to Seffrid's structure during the three next centuries, and its architecture consequently shows the marks of many periods. The lateral towers belong, at least up to the second tier, to the original church ; that facing the south exhibits four elegant examples of early Norman arches ; the arches in the third tier are of the tall lancet shape. The central tower was begun by Bishop Neville in the year 1222 ; the spire was raised about the year 1337—it is nearly three hundred feet high, and bears a considerable resemblance to that of Salisbury Cathedral, though much less graceful. (Fig. 1003.) In the interior of the cathedral may be seen some of the earliest applications of the Sussex, or Petworth marble, so much used in our ecclesiastical edifices of the " Early English " period. We cannot say much for the appearance of Chichester Cathedral ; it is indisputably the least handsome of our cathedrals. The outside is unadorned ; and there is nothing in the general form to redeem the inelegance of the details. During the great Revolution it suffered much from the Commonwealth soldiers ; and part of its present uncomely appearance may be laid to the charge of their fanaticism and the want of taste displayed in the subsequent restorations. The northern tower, for instance, was so much injured in the siege of 1642, that it fell a few years afterwards, and the present unsightly tower was substituted for it in the year 1791. The ugly western window too is modern, Cromwell's soldiers having entirely destroyed the old one. Nor is the cathedral fortunate in its site, which is low, and it is surrounded by houses. The entire length of the cathedral is four hundred and seven feet ; of the transepts, one hundred and fifty feet ; the nave and aisles are seventy-eight feet wide. The interior is plain. At a short distance from the north-west angle of the cathedral stands a campanile, or bell-tower, one hundred and twenty feet high. It has four detached turrets at its summit, exactly similar to those at the base of the spire, whence it is thought that it was built at the same time, to receive the bells from the old tower.

The only noticeable circumstance in the history of Chichester Cathedral is its treatment by the parliamentary soldiers, to which we have just alluded. When the city was taken by Waller, in 1642, some of the troops were quartered in the church, and the devastation they committed was terrible. They threw down the organ and destroyed the screen, stripped the tombs of their brasses and defaced the sculpture, broke down the pulpits, pews, and taber

1045.—Stone Church.

1046.—South Door of Stone Church.

1047.—Stone Church: Nave and Chancel

1048.—Hadley Church Tower and Beacon.

1049.—Lutterworth Church. Wickliffe's Rectory.

1050.—Chilton Church.

1052.— St. Nicholas-Church, Newcastle-upon-Tyne.

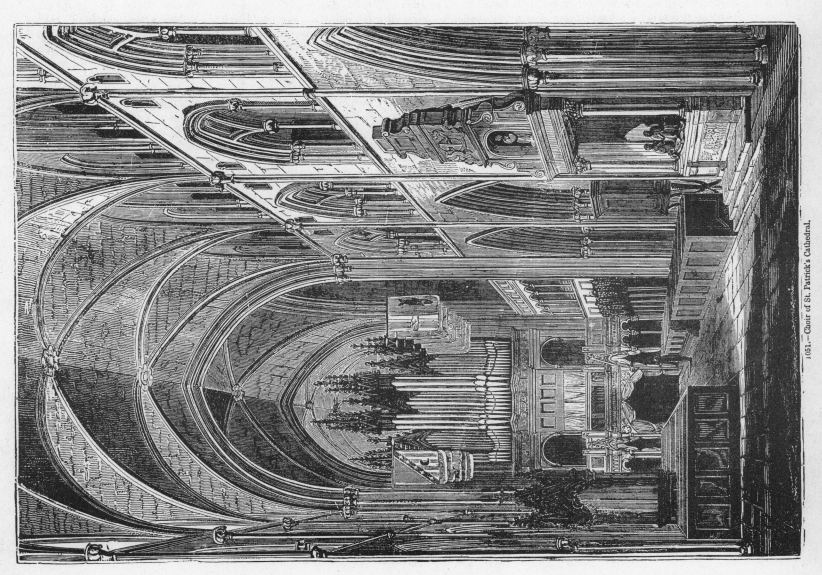

1051.— Choir of St. Patrick's Cathedral.

nacle-work, and tore into fragments the Bibles and service-books, scattering their leaves over the church; in addition to which they defaced the carvings both of the interior and exterior of the church, and broke the stained windows. Yet a few years afterwards another party was sent, under the command of Sir Arthur Haslerig, to finish the work of destruction, which it was alleged had been left incomplete; and they did finish it. As we have said, the restorations subsequently made were without the least regard to propriety; but in 1829 the interior was restored to much of its original character. When we were at Chichester a few years back, there was some talk of bringing the exterior to something more of consistency, but we believe nothing has been done yet to that end.

On the walls of the south transept are some remains of two singular pictures painted about the year 1519, for Bishop Sherburne, by Theodore Bernardi, an artist he had invited from Italy for the purpose. They were designed to represent two "principal epochs" in the history of the cathedral of Chichester—the foundation of the see of Selsey by Caedwalla, and the establishment of his own four prebends—rather unequal epochs, it should seem. These pictures were defaced after the siege, and repaired without much skill after the Restoration: there is little artistic merit in them; whatever value they may possess is antiquarian. There is another by the same hand, which contains a series of portraits of the Bishops of Chichester, and of the kings of England from the Conqueror to Henry VII. These have been since brought down to George III. When the interior was repaired some years back, four stone coffins, supposed to be those of bishops, were discovered, in one of which was the skeleton, it is thought, of Stigand (1070), with episcopal robes and insignia, and a large and curious thumb-ring, an agate set in gold. One was the black marble coffin of Bishop Ralph, having his name engraved on it—being one of the oldest with a name existing in England. There are some interesting monuments in the cathedral. Among others the splendid chantry of St. Richard; the tomb of William Chillingworth, the learned and able defender of Protestantism; Flaxman's monument to the poet Collins, &c. The Lady-Chapel is appropriated to the monuments of the family of the Duke of Richmond: a large vault was constructed under it in the year 1750. Over the entrance to this vault is a stone with the inscription "Domus Ultima," on which Dr. Clarke, one of the Residentiaries, wrote an epigram that has been classed among the first in our language. It has so much point that, though often printed, we may quote it as a little relief to our dull details :- —

> Did he who thus inscribed this wall
> Not read, or not believe, Saint Paul,
> Who says there is, where'er it stands,
> *Another house,* not built with hands;
> Or may we gather from these words,
> That house is not a—House of Lords?

Early in the times of the Saxons, there was a religious house dedicated to St. Peter and St. Paul at CHESTER, which was then an important fortified place on the English frontier next Wales, and had rendered itself remarkable as one of the very last of the strong positions wrenched from the native British. In 875 the event occurred to which Chester chiefly owed its celebrity in later times. We have made frequent mention of Wulfhere, in connection with the kingdom and diocese of Mercia, and the five sees taken out of it, one of which was Chester. That remarkable convert from Paganism had, it seems, a daughter, scarcely less remarkable than himself, who became a nun or abbess of Chester (William of Malmesbury), and after her death her relics were placed in an honoured sepulchre at Heanburgh, where they remained for two centuries; until fear of the Danes led to their being removed to Chester for safety. A new community of secular canons, in honour of this sainted lady and St. Oswald, was now formed at this place, under King Athelstan, and grew rapidly into notice; but at the Norman Conquest it was deprived of much of its lands, and the great Norman Earl of Chester, Hugh Lupus, swept it aside altogether, to make room for a Benedictine colony from Bec, in Normandy. "The earl," says Pennant, "possibly did not care to trust his salvation to the prayers of the *Saxon* religious," at a time when sickness and a troubled conscience made him feel that there was particular need of effectual intercession for him with the offended majesty of Heaven. He richly endowed the new Benedictine brotherhood, and his countess Ermentruda and his numerous tenants followed his example; so that the abbey was inundated with the good things of this life in all shapes—lands, manses, chapels, churches, woods, plains, and tithes, together with privileges of fishing with one vessel and ten nets, and all the profits

of the profitable feast of St. Werburgh. Before the great abbey gate, at this feast, were ranged the booths for the merchants, who brought wares of all kinds from various lands, and disposed them beneath coverings of reeds, which the monks were especially chartered to gather from Stanlaw Marsh. Here, too, was erected the moveable theatre for the performance of the Chester Mysteries, attributed by some writers to the inventive brain of a monk of this abbey, Randle or Ralph Highden, and by Mr. Markland to one of the earlier brethren, or to several of them unitedly. Two or three of the manuscripts of these Chester interludes have come down to us; there are twenty-four mysteries in each, and their subjects are the most striking incidents of the Scriptures, both old and new. There was a strange privilege (and one on which many reflections might be offered, were they not irrelevant to our present purpose) afforded to malefactors coming to the great fair—they were not to be arrested, however heinous their crimes might be, unless they committed some *new* offence. The concourse of loose people which such a regulation insured we might have fancied rather detrimental than otherwise to the interests of Chester. There was an occasion however, when it proved of signal service, if not to the town, to its earl, Randle the Third, who being surrounded in the castle of Rhudland by a Welsh army, and in imminent danger, despatched a messenger to Robert de Lacy, his general or constable, for assistance. Lacy was attending the fair, when immediately he and his son-in-law, Ralph Dutton, collected a numerous body of minstrels, musicians, and various idle persons, and led them to the relief of his lord. The Welsh, descrying from a distance the approach of this extraordinary army, and of course unaware of the materials of which it was composed (for Lacy had done the best he could to place them in battle array), broke up the siege, and the earl was saved. The grateful lord bestowed some remarkable privileges on Lacy for his prompt and very original services—he had " full power over all the instruments of the earl's preservation." Every anniversary of the event was also to be distinguished by a gathering of the county musicians and minstrels, who "were to play before him and his heirs for ever, in a procession to the church of St. John; and, after divine service, to the place where he kept his court. The minstrels were then to be examined concerning their lives and conversation, and whether any of them played without annual licence from their lord, or whether they had heard any words among their fellows tending to his dishonour." (Pennant.) The annual procession of the Chester minstrels was not discontinued before the middle of the last century. The privileges enjoyed by Lacy and his heirs descended to the Dutton family, whose steward presided over the courts for the examination of the minstrels, from whom they claimed at the feast four bottles of wine, a lance, and a fee of fourpence-halfpenny. The jurisdiction of the Duttons over the minstrels has been recognised by parliaments, as late as George II., and clauses "saving their rights" have found their way into modern Vagrant Acts.

We have other curious glimpses afforded us of the manners and pastimes of the Benedictines of St. Werburgh. The hospitality or the abbey appears to have been of the most splendid character; its dependants resembled those of the great barons in number and importance. A curious document shows us that at a period when the number of the actual monks was by no means considerable (supposed about twenty-eight), the abbey cook was allied to families of importance; that his office was honorary—a feudal tenure by which he held several manors; and that he had kitchen perquisites worth a regular recovery in the Portmote Court. Among the remains of the abbey may be mentioned the great abbey-gate, and the cloisters which form a quadrangle one hundred and ten feet square, in the style of the fifteenth century. The south walk is gone, but on that side six semicircular arches on short pillars indicate the places of sepulchre of the Norman abbots. We need hardly say that the refectory, or dining-hall of the abbot and his brethren, was a noble apartment: where good living was so highly appreciated there was not likely to be a want of ample and handsome accommodation: the style is of the thirteenth century. The Bishopric of Chester dates from the reign of Henry VIII., who founded within the site of the Abbey of Werburgh a new episcopal see and a cathedral church, which foundation Elizabeth confirmed, and added to its endowments, in order "that the Holy Gospel of Christ may be preached constantly and purely, that the youth of the kingdom may be instructed there in good learning, that hospitality may be exercised by the dean and prebends aforesaid, and the poor be there continually relieved." The cathedral thus instituted is an irregular, spacious, heavy building, of the red stone of the county, and chiefly of the times of Henries VI., VII., and VIII. (Fig. 1011.) The space occupied by the conventual buildings is very great, and we scarcely need any other evidence of the grandeur of the ancient establishment. The sculptured stone-case of the city of Chester's tutelar saint, Wer-burgh, is used as the bishop's throne. The chapter-house of the cathedral is interesting, not only for the great beauty of the archi-tecture, but on account of the burial in it of Hugh Lupus, by his nephew, the builder of the chapter-house, Randle the First. In 1724, the remains of the great earl were there discovered in a stone coffin, on which was sculptured a wolf's head, in allusion to the name. There was originally, it seems, a rhyming inscription annexed, commencing—

> Although my corpse it lies in grave,
> And that my flesh consumed be,
> My picture here now that you have,
> An earl sometime of this city,
> Hugh Lupe by name, &c.

The sword of Hugh, we may observe, is preserved in the British Museum

———

"On the first establishment of Christianity in Britain," says the Rev. J. Evans ('Beauties of England and Wales'), "the particular assemblies of people for the purpose of divine worship were desig-nated by the appellation côr, a circle, society, or class. These côr-an afterwards received the name of their respective evangelical instructors, as côr-Bybi, côr-Illtud, côr-Deiniol, &c. When any one of these was invested with paramount authority over certain others, it assumed the distinctive name of Ban-côr, or the supreme society." Hence the present BANGOR. The cathedral (Fig. 1010) stands in a narrow fertile vale, at the base of a steep rock; the city, founded by Maelgyn Gwynedd, a sovereign of North Wales, as early as the sixth century (Cressy), forms but one narrow crooked street, of a mile in length, with openings to the water-side. This Maelgyn had rendered himself notorious by his guilty life, and, anxious to make his peace with God and his offended people, he left his throne and government, and became a penitent recluse in the monastery that had a few years before (in 525) been founded by Deiniol or Daniel, son of the Abbot of Bangor Iscoed, as a cell to his father's house; but which afterwards became so much more famous than its parent, as to be distinguished from it by the appellation vawr, or great. But the first novelty of this change over, Maelgyn soon grew disgusted with a life so opposed to all his previous habits, and once more went back to his old excesses, and persevered in them to the last. To appease, probably, his own conscience, silence his murmuring subjects, and at the same time soothe Deiniol, he caused him, as the founder of the monastery, to be made a bishop; the con-vent church, then a cathedral, to be flatteringly dedicated to him; and bequeathed some few lands with certain franchises to the chapter. Such was the origin of the diocese of Bangor, its constitution, and revenues (never very great). In 1118 Archbishop Baldwin and Giraldus de Barri, the preachers of the Crusades, came to Bangor, through a serpentine ravine that fatigued them excessively; the archbishop sat down on an oak torn up by the violence of the winds, and began to be very amiable and pleasant with the Crusaders who accompanied him, when the sweet notes of a bird in a wood adjoin-ing led to a discussion as to what bird it was. "The nightingale was never heard in this country," it was observed; the archbishop, significantly smiling, replied, "The nightingale followed wise coun-sel, and never came into Wales; but we unwise counsel, who have penetrated and gone through it." After being rested and refreshed in Bangor by Guy Ruffyus, the bishop, Archbishop Baldwin cele-brated mass in the cathedral, and, "more importunate than per-suasive," compelled him to take the cross, amid the general lamenta-tion of his people, who seemed broken-hearted at the prospect of his departure from them. (Hoare's 'Giraldus.') In the cathedral, built in 1102 (the previous one was destroyed at the Conquest), that characteristic scene occurred, in which King John, irritated by opposition to his rapacity, displayed his violent and tyrannic disposition by seizing the Welsh bishop as he was officiating at the altar. A handsome ransom procured the bishop's release, for money was John's prime object, especially as the discovery had been forced on him, in the course of several visits to Wales, that it was far easier in his rage to vow the extermination of the whole Welsh race, than to fulfil that vow when it was made. In the revolt of Owen Glendwr, 1402, Bangor Cathedral was once more reduced to a wreck, and so remained during nearly a century. The old choir was then rebuilt by Bishop Dean, and the tower and nave by his successor, Bishop Skeffington, in 1532. The next bishop, Bulkeley, alienated much of the church property, and, says Godwin, "having sacrilegiously sold away five bells out of the steeple of his cathedral, and going to see them shipped off, he was on his return homewards struck with blindness, insomuch that he never saw afterwards."

This can hardly be true, or the bishop must have possessed extra-ordinary faculties, for there are many writings of his in existence, dated during the years of his supposed deprivation of sight. The present excellent condition of the cathedral is attributable to Dr. Warren, its liberal improver at the beginning of the present century. Several ancient Welsh princes, besides many bishops and ecclesiastics, have been buried here. The most interesting sepulchral relic is a tomb of Prince Owen Gryffydd, in an arched recess.

At the same time that Maelgyn Gwynedd, as we have just seen, governed North Wales, his uncle Cadwallon seems to have been in possession of that little province of the princedom which now forms the county of Flint; and to him fled from persecution Kentigern, or, as the Scottish historians call him, St. Mungo, Bishop of Glasgow, and was received with generous hospitality. Cadwallon assigned him a pleasant spot on the banks of the turbulent stream Elwy, which a little below falls into the river Clywd, where he built, about 560, the church called Llan Elwy, and founded a monastery for religious instruction and devotion. Kentigern allowed his monks (at one time said to have been nearly a thousand in number) no indolent careless life, for his regulations provided that one-half should labour whilst the rest prayed, and that the twofold duty should be reciprocally performed. Recalled to his own see in his native country, he left this flourishing institution to the care of Asa, or Asaph, a pious scholar. Whether Kentigern had been a bishop here we know not; but Asaph is certainly styled in ancient writings episcopus Asaphensis. And thus was founded the see-cathedral of ST. ASAPH. The cathedral, an unpretending struc-ture, situated on the summit of a small hill (Fig. 1012), has a square embattled tower in the centre, ninety-three feet in height, whence a delightful prospect is obtained of the rich and extensive Vale of Clwyd. The nave and transept contain some fine parts of decorated English style, and the window at the east end of the choir is especially ob-servable for its painting, copied from a picture of Albano; but as to the choir itself, rebuilt under Bishop Shipley, that is of no style or character whatever: we are told that the Perpendicular has been aimed at; this may be, but the architect has shot strangely wide of his mark. The monuments are neither numerous nor very impor-tant; the principal one is that of Bishop David Owen, who died 1512. St. Asaph being a frontier town, it followed, as a necessary conse-quence, that its cathedral would be in frequent peril during the fierce wars that so often broke out between the high-spirited Cam-brians and their encroaching and powerful neighbours. To these wars we trace the loss of the church records, and the destruction by the English, in 1282, of the first stone cathedral, that had super-seded St. Kentigern's timber structure. The present building may be dated from 1284; for though it was afterwards burnt by Owen Glendwr in 1402, its walls were left standing, and these—after eighty years of desolation and neglect—were incorporated with the gradually-renewed cathedral of St. Asaph. The sees of Bangor and St. Asaph were united a few years ago.

———

We have before had occasion to speak, in terms not very com-plimentary, of those who have been concerned in the restorations of some of our great ecclesiastical edifices; persons who, whatever their intentions or abilities, have injured the buildings it was their especial duty to guard from injury; who have degraded art, and made the country itself contemptible by showing it as unable to appreciate the value of those heirlooms which form no inconsider-able portion of its truest wealth. But none of the cases to which we refer are to be compared for a moment with that of LLANDAFF (Fig. 1013), where the ecclesiastical and architectural Vandals of the last century, finding the old western front out of repair, actually erected a new one across the nave nearer the centre of the pile, leaving the original arcade to decay; and what, think you, gentle reader, was the character of the said new front? Why, Grecian! After that we can hardly be surprised at anything—not even at the erection of a Grecian portico around the altar, which was also done at Llandaff. That, however, has been removed; how long, may we ask, will it be before the other piece of barbarism will share the same fate? The condemned west front is just what might be expected from the proceedings we have mentioned,—one of the most interesting and valuable portions of the cathedral, with nu-merous delicately-executed lancet windows, of different sizes, and a fine tower at the northern angle. The other tower was thrown down by a great storm in 1703. The entire length of the church is three hundred feet, the breadth eighty. The Lady-Chapel and the chapter-house, both in the decorated English style, are among the more interesting appendages of the edifice. The episcopal palace, close by, a ruin, was destroyed, it is said, by Owen Glendwr.

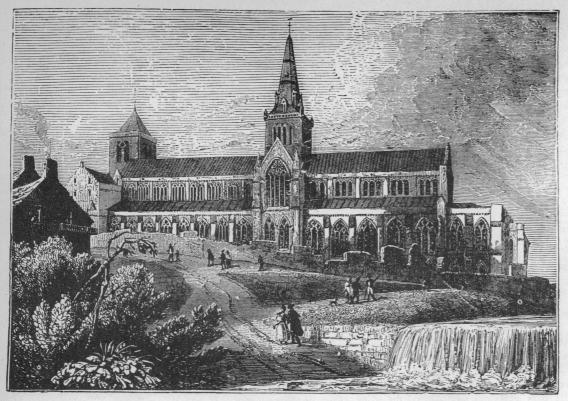

1053.—Glasgow Cathedral.

1054.—Kelso.

1055.—St. Magnus, Kirkwall.

1056.—Jedburgh.

1057.—South-east View of Melrose Abbey.

1058.—Melrose Abbey.

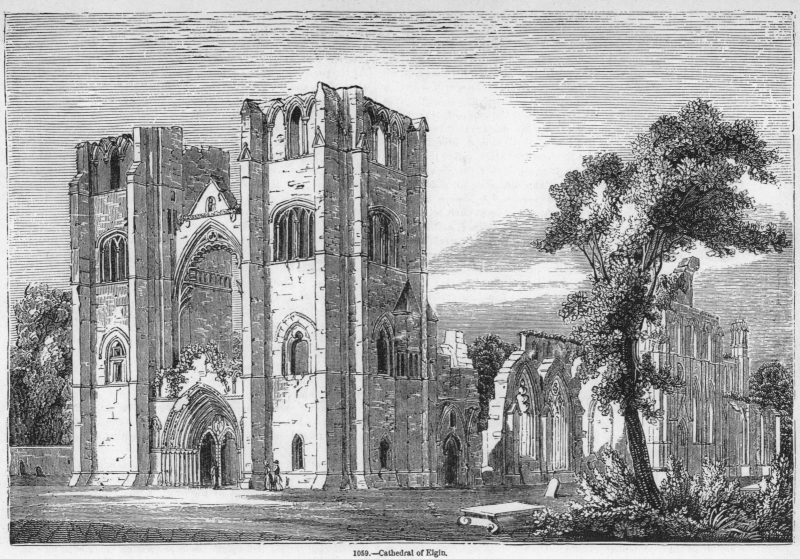

1059.—Cathedral of Elgin.

1060.—Cathedral of Kildare.

The cathedral of St. David (Fig. 1014), we hardly need say, derives its name from the tutelary saint of Wales and Welshmen; but that is the least part of its connection with the holy man, as we shall see by a brief notice of his life. He was the son of a Prince of Cardigan (whose name we need not transcribe, considering that it requires some seven words—and those Welsh ones—to do so), and was born about the middle of the fifth century. After a long period of study, first of general knowledge and literature, and secondly of divinity, he settled in a secluded place called the Valley of Roses, established a religious house, and brought around him a considerable number of scholars. The discipline he caused to be observed was unusually strict and severe. All were bound to labour with their own hands for the common welfare, all gifts or possessions offered by unjust men were to be refused, and a hatred of wealth was to be cherished. "They never conversed together by talking but when necessity required, but each performed the labour enjoined him, joining thereto prayer or holy meditations on divine things; and having finished their country work, they returned to their monastery, where they spent the remainder of the day till the evening in reading or writing. In the evening, at the sounding of a bell, they all left their work, and immediately repaired to the church, where they remained till the stars appeared, and then went all together to their refection, eating sparingly and not to satiety. Their food was bread with roots or herbs seasoned with salt, and their thirst they quenched with a mixture of water and milk. Supper being ended, they continued about three hours in watching, prayers, and genuflections. As long as they were in the church it was not permitted to any to slumber, or sneeze, &c. After this they went to rest, and at cockcrowing they rose, and continued at prayer till day appeared. All their inward sensations and thoughts they discovered to their superior, and from him they demanded permission in all things. . . . . Their clothing was skins of beasts." ('Acta Sanctorum Martyrum.') Rapidly did the place, and still more so its founder, rise into repute. When the Pelagian heresy, as it was called, reappeared in Wales, a synod was called, about 519, to endeavour to check its progress. Moved by repeated entreaties, David at last consented to repair thither and personally engage in the undertaking; and, says Giraldus, "When all the fathers assembled enjoined St. David to preach, he commanded a child which attended him, and had lately been restored to life by him, to spread a napkin under his feet; and, standing upon it, he began to expound the Gospel and the law to the auditory. All the while that his oration continued, a snow-white dove, descending from heaven, sat upon his shoulders; and, moreover, the earth on which he stood raised itself under him till it became a hill, from whence his voice, like a trumpet, was clearly heard and understood by all, both near and far off." If any doubt the truth of these somewhat marvellous statements let them go to the spot, and there to this day they will assuredly find a little hill, and a church (Llanddewi-Brefi) built upon it in commemoration of the event above mentioned. To return, however, to St. David: it appears the assembly were so delighted with his eloquence and zeal in opposing the obnoxious doctrines, that they unanimously called upon him to accept the arch-bishopric of Caerleon, one of the three archiepiscopal seats (York and London being the others) into which England was then divided. David accepted the honours and duties, but on the condition of removing the see to Menevia, the establishment he had founded in the Valley of Roses. The period of these interesting events was the reign of that most interesting of sovereigns—King Arthur. Five-and-twenty archbishops in succession filled the archiepiscopal seat, and then the last of the number withdrew with all his clergy to Brittany, and after the lapse of some time the see became subject to Canterbury. Such was the origin and history of the present bishopric of St. David's.

The cathedral stands near the seashore, amidst the wreck of various religious edifices, and in a city which itself is but a wreck of what it was, when pilgrims thronged from all parts of Britain to pay their respects to St. David's shrine, which is still preserved in the cathedral, and exhibits four recesses for the receipt of offerings. Pope Calixtus ordained that two pilgrimages to this place should be reckoned as equivalent to one to Rome. Among the monarchs who are known to have come hither may be mentioned the Conqueror, Henry II., and Edward I. and Eleanor. Giraldus relates a pleasant anecdote in connection with the visit of the second Henry. Across the river Alan, which runs through the cathedral precincts, there was in very ancient times a beautiful marble bridge consisting of a single slab, measuring ten feet in length, by six in breadth and one in depth. "Henry II., on his return from Ireland, is said to have passed over this stone before he entered the church. Proceeding towards the shrine of Saint David, habited like a pilgrim

and leaning on a staff, he met at the White Gate a procession of the canons, coming forth to receive him with due honour and reverence. As the procession moved along, a Welsh woman threw herself at the king's feet, and made a complaint against the bishop of the place, which was explained to the king by an interpreter; the woman, immediate attention not being paid to her petition, with violent gesticulations, and a loud and impertinent voice, exclaimed repeatedly, "Vindicate us this day, Lechlavan! Revenge us and the nation in this man!" alluding to a vulgar fiction and proverb of Merlin, that a king of England and conqueror of Ireland should be wounded in that country by a man with a red hand, and die upon Lechlavan on his return through Menevia. The king, who had heard the prophecy, approaching the stone, stopped for a short time at the foot of it, and, looking earnestly at it, boldly passed over; then turning round and looking towards the stone, thus indignantly inveighed against the prophet: "Who will hereafter give credit to the lying Merlin?" One of the bystanders then called out in a loud voice, "Thou art not that king by whom Ireland is to be conquered, or of whom Merlin prophesied!"

The cathedral, which was erected by Peter, the forty-ninth bishop, is partly in the Norman, partly in the Pointed style, three hundred and seven feet long, with a lofty square tower at the west end, and a lofty choir. The bishop's throne is of exquisite workmanship, and the rood-loft-screen and roof are greatly admired. Giraldus Cambrensis, from whose writings we have borrowed the preceding anecdotes, lies buried here, obtaining in death that position among the bishops of the see which he failed to obtain in his lifetime; but to which his virtues and the twice-recorded suffrages of the Chapter of St. David's so well entitled him.

It is not unamusing or uninstructive to mark how, in the record of our great ecclesiastical establishments, as we ascend step by step towards the contemplation of the greatest, the importance of the alleged miracles that shed such a halo round the foundation, as well as the position of the alleged founder, grow in a like proportion, till nothing less than the presence and exertions of St. Paul himself will suffice to explain the first erection in London of the famous church that bears his name; whilst, to do honour to the ceremony of the consecration of its great rival at Westminster, a St. Peter must not only be directly concerned, but the apostle must be brought down from heaven, centuries after his death, to share in the very pleasant business of self-dedication. When Sebert, king of the East Saxons, overthrew, in the beginning of the seventh century, the temple of Apollo, which, according to Flete, a monk of Westminster, had previously occupied that "terrible place," so overrun with thorns as to have obtained the name of Thorney Island, he built on the site a Christian temple, and thus, if other ancient authorities speak truly, restored the worship which that most perplexing of monarchs, King Lucius, first established there, on his conversion to Christianity, about the year 184. Mellitus, Bishop of London, encouraged Sebert in the good work, which was at last fully completed, and about to be opened with great splendour by the bishop. St. Peter, however, anticipated him. One evening, as a fisherman was busy in his vocation on the banks of the Thames, just opposite to Thorney Island, a figure suddenly appeared to him, and requested to be taken across the river. On reaching the other side, the fisherman was desired to wait awhile; and the figure presently disappeared into the new church. All this seemed very strange to the fisherman, but as he gazed on the church it suddenly became lighted up with a most unearthly-looking blaze of light, and then choral hymns were heard as from innumerable hosts of angels. The trembling fisherman knew then it must be St. Peter he had rowed across the river, and that the new church was then being dedicated by a heavenly priesthood. St. Peter himself soon reappeared, confirmed what the fisherman had supposed, and bade him go at daybreak to Mellitus to inform him of what had passed, observing, at the same time, that the bishop would find, in corroboration of the statement, marks of consecration on the walls of the edifice. The apostle concluded by bidding the fisherman cast his nets into the river, and take one of the fish he should catch to Mellitus; the fisherman did so, and a truly miraculous draught of the finest salmon (which was undoubtedly a Thames fish in those days) rewarded his services, and assured him of the truth of all these marvellous occurrences when the apostle had vanished. Mellitus, on hearing the fisherman's tale, hurried to the church, and there truly enough he found marks of extinguished tapers and of the chrism; so, instead of rededicating the pile, he contented himself with the celebration of mass. Now it is a remarkable feature of this story, that one of the rights of the abbey of Westminster, that of claiming a tenth of all the fish caught in the Thames within certain limits, which existed for many centuries, was avowedly asserted and admitted on the ground that St. Peter told the fisherman that neither he nor his brethren should ever want fish so long as they gave a tenth to the church he had just dedicated.

Sebert's church had many benefactors in the course of the next three centuries; but up to the time of the Confessor, the building and revenues were on a scale far from commensurate with the spiritual rank to which it had been elevated by St. Peter. The monastery also, it may be observed, had suffered greatly from the Danes. Whilst King Edward, however, was in exile during the Danish invasion, he vowed a pilgrimage to Rome, if God should please to restore him to his throne. He was restored, and Edward prepared to fulfil his vow; but his nobles persuaded him to send an embassy instead, and the Pope granted absolution of the vow on condition that the sums of money that were to have been spent in the journey, should be bestowed on some religious house dedicated to St. Peter. Just at the very critical time, it happened that a monk of St. Peter's at Westminster, a man of great sanctity and simplicity of manners, it is said, had a dream, which showed that the apostle himself condescended to point out the establishment that should be the fortunate recipient of the king's treasures. Wulsine, the monk in question, was asleep one day, when St. Peter appeared to him, and thus spake: "There is a place of mine in the west part of London, which I chose, and love, and which I formerly consecrated with my own hands, honoured with my presence, and made illustrious by my miracles. The name of the place is Thorney; which having, for the sins of the people, been given to the power of the barbarians, from rich is become poor, from stately, low, and from honourable is made despicable. This let the king, by my command, restore and make a dwelling of monks, stately build, and amply endow: it shall be no less than the house of God, and the gates of Heaven." Edward implicitly believed the dream to be a special interposition to decide all his doubts, and at once set to work in such a spirit that a new pile soon appeared, which was, indeed, for the times, stately built, and as amply endowed as a tenth part of all the king's property, and an extensive set of relics of the most inestimable character, could make it. It was a sad grief to Edward that he could not witness its consecration; the day, the Feast of the Innocents, was appointed, the chief nobility and clergy throughout England were summoned, all was ready, when he fell ill, and his queen, Editha, was obliged to preside in his absence: however, he had lived to see the whole completed; to learn the particulars even of the last concluding ceremony, and that was much: he died almost immediately after, and was of course buried in the edifice he had erected. Of the Confessor's building there are still some very interesting remnants preserved, as the Pix Office, and the parts adjoining against the east cloister and the south transept, all evidencing the simple grandeur of the original structure, which, says Matthew Paris, was built *novo compositionis genere*,—an evidence, it seems to us, that the Norman style of architecture was then new in England. Admired, and deservedly, as that style was at the period in question, men could have little supposed that in less than two centuries after, another king, Henry III., should find it necessary to pull down the greater part of the Confessor's building, in order to raise it anew, more in harmony with the architectural tastes of his day; still less could they have supposed that such presumption—as it must have seemed to them—would be excused by the fact, that the rebuilding would really be an improvement on their own noble church. That it was so, we need only walk into the existing Westminster Abbey, to satisfy us, for the present edifice is, in a great degree, the pile so rebuilt by Henry. He it was who erected the chapel of the Confessor, which forms the rounded end of the choir, or the apsis of the building, the four chapels in the ambulatory, that extend around the choir, a considerable portion of the choir itself, a small portion of the nave, the transepts, and probably the chapter-house. We may complete the necessarily brief notice that our space compels us to give of the erection of the abbey, by observing that the nave thus begun was carried further in the reign of Edward I., and gradually finished, with the other portions of the edifice, in the course of the thirteenth and fourteenth centuries, and that the grand close to the whole works took place in the reign of Henry VII. by the erection of the chapel, not unhappily named the world's wonder. The great central tower and the western towers, however, were still unbuilt, and so to this time the former remains; the latter have been added by the architect of St. Paul's, in a style that makes us regret he did not confine himself to St. Paul's and works of a kindred character; most assuredly he was profoundly ignorant of the character and merits of the productions to which he presumptuously applied the epithet of "Gothic crinkle-crankle."

In walking round the exterior of the Abbey, the parts that more especially attract the eye are the wonderfully rich and elaborate chapel of Henry VII., forming the rounded eastern extremity of the pile—the north transept, formerly called, on account of its extreme beauty, Solomon's Porch (Fig. 1019)—the western or chief front, with the towers which Wren raised to the present proportions—and the doorway shown in our engraving (Fig. 1024) beneath, which, when the niches were filled with their proper statues, must have formed a glorious specimen of the sculpture of the middle ages. Scarcely less interesting than these great features of the exterior of the abbey itself are its numerous adjuncts. It was to the Jerusalem Chamber, which rests against the northern corner of the base of the west front, that Henry IV., on falling ill in the Abbey, desired to be carried, saying,

> It hath been prophesied to me many years,
> I should not die but in Jerusalem,
> Which vainly I supposed the Holy Land;
> But bear me to that church and there I'll lie,—
> In that Jerusalem shall Harry die.

Then, again, there are close by the various domestic buildings still remaining of the old monastery, as the cloisters and the college dining-hall, the last a most perfect specimen of an old refectory, and still used for its original purpose, though the monks are changed into the boys of the Grammar-School of Westminster, who were connected with the cathedral foundation by Henry VIII. after the dissolution of the monastery. In the cloisters stood formerly a little chapel dedicated to St. Katherine, which was used for the meeting of synods. Hollinshed has recorded some rather *amusing* circumstances respecting one of these assemblies, held in 1176, before the Pope's legate:—"When the legate was set, and the archbishop on his right hand, as primate of the realm, the Archbishop of York coming in, and disdaining to sit on the left, where he might seem to give pre-eminence unto the Archbishop of Canterbury (unmannerly enough, indeed), swash'd him down, meaning to thrust himself in betwixt the legate and the Archbishop of Canterbury. And where, belike the said Archbishop of Canterbury was loth to remove, he sat himself in his lap; but he scarcely touched the archbishop's skirt, when the bishop and other chaplains, with their servants, stept to him, pulled him away, and threw him to the ground; and beginning to lay on him with bats and fists, the Archbishop of Canterbury, yielding good for evil, sought to save him from their hands. . . . . . . The Archbishop of York, with his rent rochet, got up, and away he went to the king, with a great complaint against the Archbishop of Canterbury; but when, upon examination of the matter, the truth was known, he was well laughed at for his labours, and that was all the remedy he got. As he departed so be-buffeted forth of the Convocation-house towards the king, they cried upon him, 'Go, traitor, thou that diddest betray that holy man Thomas (à-Becket); go, get thee hence, thy hands yet stink of blood!'" But of all these architectural offsets the chapter-house is that which demands our warmest admiration. Nothing can be imagined more exquisitely beautiful than must have been the entrance in the east cloister, or than the building to which that entrance leads—nay, we might almost say, than they still are, in spite of decay, mutilation, and the most disgraceful neglect on the part of the dignitaries of the abbey. Here exist many important traces of painting on the walls, and the floor has still large portions of the original pavement, most beautifully tessellated. The chapter-house is now used for a Record-office, and is therefore a closed place to the public; the same may be said of the adjoining Pix-office, which, as before stated, forms the chief remains of the Confessor's pile.

Whatever the beauty or intrinsic value of the architecture of Westminster Abbey—and it is impossible to estimate either too highly—there are few who can yield to that architecture the attention it deserves; for the very first glimpse of the building conjures up a host of associations of a more absorbing and stimulating character. This is the church, we say to ourselves, in which so many kings have been crowned, or buried; in which so many of England's greatest men sleep their last sleep, statesmen and warriors, poets, philosophers and philanthropists, actors, artists, musicians—the illustrious by their genius or virtues—and with no inconsiderable sprinkling of the illustrious merely by rank or courtesy. It would be difficult to find a parallel in any age or country to the wealth stored up in the vaults of this one building—this truly national mausoleum—this fine old Abbey of Westminster. Through century after century England has poured into it a large proportion of those whose memory the world would not willingly let die, till every part of the pile, nave, choir, transepts, and ambulatory, have been filled to

1061.—Upper Chapel of St. Thomas, London Bridge.

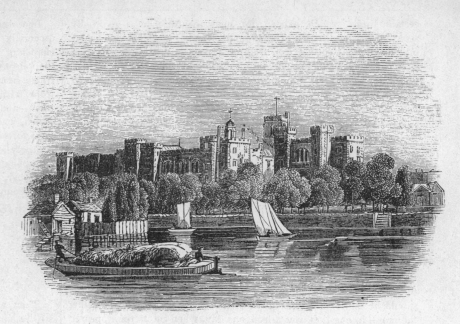

1064.—Lambeth Palace, before the recent alterations.

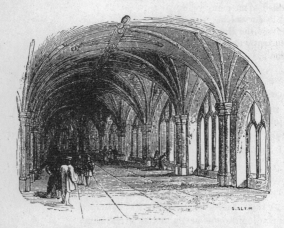

1062.—Lower Chapel, or Crypt, of St. Thomas.

1066.—Archbishop reading a Papal Bull (Harl. MS. 1319.)

1065.—Doorway in Lollards' Tower.

1067.—Specimen from a Copy of Wycliffe's Bible in the British Museum. (Royal MS. I. C. viii.)

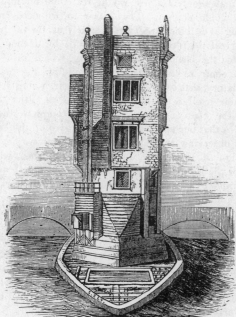

1063.—The Chapel of St Thomas converted into a House and Warehouse.

1068.—Tomb of Archbishop Grey, York Cathedral.

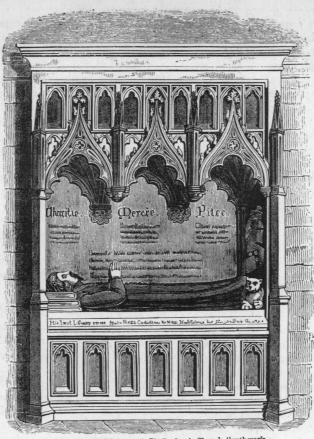

1069.—Gower's Monument, St. Saviour's Church, Southwark.

1070.—Tomb of William of Windsor and Blanch de la Toar, Westminster Abbey.

1071.—Early English. Capitals, York Cathedral.

1072.—Decorated English Capitals, York Cathedral.

1073.—Tomb of Aymer de Valence, Westminster Abbey.

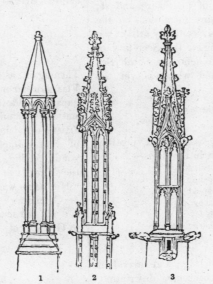

1075.—Pinnacles: 1, Early English, from Wells Cathedral; 2, Decorated English, from St. Mary's, Oxford; 3, Decorated English, from York Cathedral.

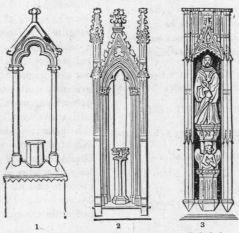

1076.—Niches: 1, Early English, from Salisbury Cathedral, 2 and 3, Decorated English, from York Cathedral.

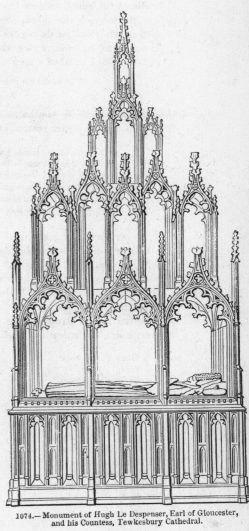

1074.—Monument of Hugh Le Despenser, Earl of Gloucester, and his Countess, Tewkesbury Cathedral.

overflowing, and the stream has found vent only in the cloisters surrounding. Let us begin in them our hasty observations. There lie in strange juxtaposition with some of the earliest abbots of the monastery, a host of actors and actresses, as Barry, Betterton, Foote, Mrs. Bracegirdle, Mrs. Cibber, and Mr. Yates—several musicians, among whom we may mention Lawes, Milton's friend, and the composer of the original music to 'Comus,' Sir John Hawkins, the musical historian, and Benjamin Cooke, with the appropriate musical score of the Canon by twofold-augmentation engraven on his monument. The great engraver, Vertue, also lies in the cloister.

We will now enter, in fancy at least, by the great western door; the only mode, let us observe, in which the authorities permit the public to use that approach; in ignorance, probably, that the builders, when erecting that grand entrance, saw no grander purpose to which it could be put than to allow a people to draw nearer to their God, and so planned all things in accordance for due architectural effect; or, if not in ignorance, is it, then, that the authorities shut up their chief doors, simply because money-taking—a very pleasant, but not peculiarly Christian or even reputable-looking process, under the circumstances—would look too bad at that part of the church, and so the affair is smuggled up into a *corner?* Well, we enter, in fancy at all events, by the western door, and at once the full and vast magnificence of the nave—one of the most elegant, and, without exception, the highest in England—is before us, extending far away its glorious columnar ranks and airy sweeps of arches. As we wander along towards the choir, and then turn, the gorgeous western window breaks upon us with its Jewish patriarchs wrapped, as it were, in all the coloured glories of one of the most glorious of sunsets. What beds of purple and amber! what streams of golden light! But we have no time to pause, with this endless array of monuments, busts, and statues before us. A few preliminary words as to the route we propose to take, and we must hurry along as fast—ay, almost as fast as one of the abbey guides himself could wish, even though he were reckoning up at the time how many more sets of visitors might be driven through the abbey before closing-time. If the reader will look at the plan of the abbey (Fig. 1023),* he will be able readily to follow us as we advance along the right side, or southern aisle of the nave, then back again, and along the left side, towards the north transept: from thence into the ambulatory, as far as Henry VII.'s Chapel, and then round by the other half of the ambulatory, to the south transept, or Poets' Corner, on the other side of the choir; and so, lastly, into the choir itself. Among the many memorials on the walls of the south aisle of the nave that more peculiarly attract the eye or interest the mind, are those to Craggs, the Secretary of State, who was so deeply concerned in the nefarious South Sea Scheme as to sink under the exposure, and who was yet the satirist's *beau idéal* of a man

> Who broke no promise, *served no private end;*
>
> POPE.

and Mrs. Oldfield, the actress, whose vanity was lashed, possibly with not much better reason, by the same poet in the lines—

> Odious! in woollen! 't would a saint provoke
> (Were the last words that poor Narcissa spoke):
> No, let a charming chintz and Brussels lace
> Wrap my cold limbs and shade my lifeless face:
> One would not, sure, be frightful when one's dead!
> And—Betty—give this cheek a little red.

Then we have Congreve, in his full-bottomed wig; and several of a military character, including one of the most *outré* description, Admiral Tyrrell's; and one that has drawn tears down many a fair cheek, as it suggested the melancholy particulars of its owner's fate—unfortunate, brave, noble André, whose very chivalric generosity of disposition seems to have led him into a position that he must have abhorred in the abstract more than most other men, and so brought upon him a spy's death. Well, we can sympathize with him, with-

out questioning the justice or the expediency, in a military sense, of Washington's severity towards him, which was exercised under circumstances of no ordinary nature: it was not simply that André had put off the British uniform for secret objects, but to arrange the particulars of an act of the most diabolical treachery towards the American cause, then meditated by the unsuccessful but ever-infamous Arnold. This monument has suffered frequent mutilation; and Charles Lamb, with malicious sportiveness, made the circumstance an instrument of attack on his friend Southey's change of political opinion. Designating the injury as the wanton mischief of some schoolboy, fired, perhaps, with some notion of transatlantic freedom, he observed to Southey, "The mischief was done about the time that *you* were a scholar there. Do you know anything about the unfortunate relic?" Remembering Roubiliac's monument to Newton at Cambridge, it is but an act of charity to pass Kent's quietly by, which stands on one side of the entrance into the choir. Of the memorials along the northern aisle of the nave, we may first mention that of the sublime coxcomb Kneller, who was, says Pope, in the inscription,

> By Heaven, and not a master, taught;
> Whose art was Nature, and whose pictures thought.

Major Rennell, Tierney, Spencer Perceval, so strangely assassinated by Bellingham, with Freind, Woodward, and Mead, the memorable trio of physicians, are among the names that are read upon the walls, as we pass on towards the part where the projecting choir narrows the space. Here the "spoils of time" become rich indeed in one particular class of eminent men, who in this abbey excite even more than usual interest, on account of their living as well as their dead connection with it; we find here one of the finest of the great ecclesiastical English musicians, Dr. Croft, who was organist of the abbey; Blow, another admirable musician; Dr. Burney, the historian of music; Samuel Arnold, also organist to the abbey; and, lastly, Henry Purcell, who might almost be called the Shakspere of the art, on account of the height and variety of his powers, and of whom some one—Dryden, it is supposed—has finely said in the inscription, he has "gone to that blessed place where only his harmony can be exceeded."

The north transept is the wealthiest part of the abbey for memorials of a miscellaneous kind, but especially statesmen. Here lie, within a short distance of each other, Chatham, Pitt, Fox, Castlereagh, Canning, Wilberforce, and Grattan,—all their party contests over—

> A few feet
> Of sullen earth divide each winding-sheet.
> How peaceful and how powerful is the grave,
> That hushes all!

Then again, as specimens of art, there are, among numerous others, Flaxman's monument of Judge Mansfield, one of the noblest, perhaps *the* noblest of the specimens of modern sculpture; Chantrey's statue of Canning; Westmacott's memorial of Fox, and the same artist's exquisite group of a mother and child. Lastly, as examples of what epitaphs may become when dictated by true sentiment or poetic feeling, let us commend to all readers the inscription on the Newcastle monument, in which the Duchess says of herself, "Her name was Margaret Lucas, youngest sister to the Lord Lucas of Colchester; a noble family, for all the brothers were valiant, and all the sisters virtuous;"—and this, placed upon a plain tablet to Grace Scot, 1645:—

> He that will give my Grace but what is hers,
> Must say her death hath not
> Made only her dear Scot,
> But virtue, worth, and sweetness widowers.

In a part of the transept, now divided from it by a wall of monuments, is that most picturesque of monumental works, Sir Francis Vere's, where the knight lies in effigy on the bottom, whilst four knights at the corner, all full length, but kneeling figures, support a table or canopy above, on which rest the warrior's arms, his helmet, breastplate, and other accoutrements. Roubiliac was seen one day gazing upon one of these figures, with his arms folded, and evidently quite absorbed in its contemplation. "Hush!" said he to one who approached, pointing at the same time to the figure: "He will speak soon." We need not go far to inquire into the value of this praise; Roubiliac's own and most distinguished work, the Nightingale monument, is close by, almost exceeding the legitimate bounds of art by the powerful fidelity of its representation. The king of terrors is seen suddenly arising from the depths below, and about to cast his fatal dart at the victim, a female; who is supported by her husband with one hand, whilst with the other he endeavours in frantic agony, to avert the threatened blow.

Scarcely less attractive are the funeral memorials in the ambulatory, though we cannot even mention the names of most of them. Here, or in the chapels that we find on our left, are the colossal statues of Telford and Watt, the last most absurdly placed in the *petite* and exceedingly beautiful chapel of St. Paul,—how it got there is a mystery to us; General Wolfe's monument; various works of the character of Lord Hunsdon's, that is to say, stately and magnificent, but most intolerably cumbrous and heavy; and lastly, tombs of some of the early abbots of Westminster, and of a bishop, Ruthall, who died, it is supposed, from mortification at an unlucky mistake he made:—having drawn up a book on state affairs, he sent it, as he thought, to the king; but, unfortunately, the book really sent turned out to be an inventory of his treasure; —an awkward accident to have occurred at any period of English history; what then must it have been when the king so favoured was—Henry VIII.? We might here, too, stop to mention the beautiful tomb of the standard-bearer of Henry V. at Agincourt; but the monument of that sovereign himself is before us, and draws us onward by its superior attractions.

The engraving of the shrine of Henry V. (Fig. 1016) shows us the headless effigy of the hero-king on his tomb, shadowed by an arch deep and solemn, through which the spectator, as he stands with his back toward the choir, may obtain his first view of the dim porch and radiant chapel of Henry VII. This chantry is "adorned with upwards of fifty statues: on the north face is the coronation of Henry V., with his nobles attending, represented in lines of figures on each side; on the south face of the arch the central object is the king on horseback, armed cap-à-pie, riding at full speed, attended by the companions of his expedition. The sculpture is bold and characteristic; the equestrian group is furious and warlike; the standing figures have a natural sentiment in their actions, and simple grandeur in their draperies, such as we admire in the paintings of Raphael and Masaccio" (Flaxman). In the very flower of his youth, in the flush of victory, enjoying such fortune and happiness as kings are rarely blessed with, Henry V. died. His had been a brief reign, but he had had his

One crowded hour of glorious life,

and had left a name to be remembered by his countrymen with unfading admiration and delight. He was a second Black Prince to them, the model of all chivalric virtue. They placed him by that hero's side in their gallery of great ideals; and he gained by the contrast. He was a man, says the historian Walsingham, "sparing of words, resolute in deeds, provident in council, prudent in judgment, modest in countenance, magnanimous in action, constant in undertaking, a great almsgiver, devout to Godward, a renowned soldier, fortunate in field, whence he never returned without victory." He died in France in 1422, and was carried to Paris, to the church of Notre Dame, where high funeral obsequies were performed, in the presence of a concourse of lords of England, France, Normandy, and Picardy. Thence he was borne to Rouen, to remain there until all was prepared for a progress to England worthy of his rank and deeds. Paris and Rouen, it is said, offered large sums of gold to have his remains interred among them; but England would almost as soon have sold her independence. There was but one place of sepulchre for Harry the Fifth, St. Peter's Abbey. And if the mourners could not gaze on his actual form, they at least saw him with the eyes of fancy, in the effigy that Speed tells us was artificially moulded and "painted according to life; upon whose head an imperial diadem of gold and precious stones was set, the body clothed with a purple robe furred with ermine; in his right hand it held a sceptre royal, and in the left a ball of gold: in which manner it was carried in a chariot of state, covered with red velvet, embroidered with gold, and over it a rich canopy, borne by men of great place."

The king of Scotland, and many princes, lords, and knights of England and France, went with the procession out of Rouen: "the chariot all the way compassed about with men, all in white gowns bearing burning torches in their hands; next unto whom followed his household servants, all in black; and after them the princes, lords, and estates, in vestures of mourning adorned; then two miles distant from the corpse, followed the still-lamenting queen, attended with princely mourners, her tender and pierced heart more inly mourning than her outward-sad weeds could in any sort express. . . . . And thus, by sea and land, the dead king was brought unto London, where through the streets the chariot was drawn with four horses, whose caparisons were richly embroidered, and embossed with the royal arms, the first with England's arms alone, the second with the arms of France and England in a field quartered, the third bore the arms of France alone, and the fourth three crowns, or, in a field azure, the ancient arms of King Arthur —now well-beseeming him who had victoriously united three kingdoms (France, England, and Ireland) in one."

The clergy chanted the service for the dead as the bier was borne with slow steps to St. Paul's, where the parliament of the nation were assembled to witness the celebration of the grand obsequies. The procession then moved to Westminster Abbey (Fig. 1020), and the body, after its long pilgrimage, rested at last. This superb chantry rose to grace the spot: and thrice a day mass was sung in it for the repose of the hero's soul. And if now we could conjure up the living presence of the valiant Henry, we have but to gaze on that shield and war-saddle fastened on the columns, and on that battered casque which he wore at Agincourt, and which is now set up on the wooden bar, conspicuous between the entrance towers: compared with these relics, sculpture, tomb, and effigy are, to our feelings, as regards him, but cold abstractions. The mutilations of the effigy happened at the suppression of the abbey by Henry VIII., when that monarch, who was generally so very fond of taking off heads because he did not like them, took off this, from an opposite principle—he loved it, like Othello, "not wisely, but too well"—it was of solid silver. The body and tomb he also stripped of their silver and gilded ornaments. Queen Katharine of Valois, who had first placed that costly effigy on her husband's tomb (Speed), and who most probably erected the whole chantry, suffered a worse because a more directly personal desecration after her death. "She was buried in Our Lady's Chapel," says Speed, "within Saint Peter's Church, at Westminster; whose corpse was taken up in the reign of King Henry VII., her grandchild, when he laid the foundation of that admirable structure (the chapel of Henry VII.), and her coffin placed by King Henry in her husband's tomb, hath ever since so remained, and never reburied: where it standeth, the cover being loose, and to be seen and handled of any that will." It was reported that the body was left thus strangely exposed by Katharine's own appointment, "in regard of her disobedience to King Henry, for being delivered of her son at the place he forbade."

Pepys says of one of his visits to the abbey: "Here we did see, by particular favour, the body of Queen Katharine of Valois, and I had the upper part of her body in my hands, and I did kiss her mouth, reflecting upon it that I did kiss a queen, and that this was my birthday, thirty-six years old that I did kiss a queen." In 1776 the remains were at last restored to the seclusion of the grave in St. Nicholas' Chapel. That Henry, her grandson by a second marriage, in building his "world's wonder," should not have had grace enough to treat with ordinary decency the corpse of his ancestress, is, we presume, only to be accounted for by the fact that he was in such continued anxiety about his own soul, that neither the souls nor bodies of any one else, however nearly related to him, could receive much attention. For the welfare of that soul he erected this sumptuous edifice, into which we now enter, and in which, to use Washington Irving's words, stone seems, by the "cunning labours of the chisel, to have been robbed of its weight and density, suspended aloft as if by magic, and the fretted roof achieved with the wonderful minuteness and airy security of a cobweb." For the good of his soul, Henry did cause to be carefully erected, in his own lifetime, the most sumptuous of monuments for his soul's mortal tenement; a monument which lends new grace and splendour to the surpassing loveliness of the chapel in which it stands. Lastly, it was for the especial good of his soul, that he directed three masses to be performed daily before his tomb *while the world should last*. It is but justice to state, that another of the great artistical treasures of the chapel, the tomb of Margaret, Countess of Richmond, executed by the same masterly sculptor, Torregiano, shows that Henry did, upon some occasion or other, find time to cast one pious and filial thought towards the memory of his mother and her soul. This mother seems to have had in her composition all the warlike aspirations that her son, however personally brave, lacked, or was too politic to give scope to. Camden says of her, that she was accustomed to remark that, "on the condition that the princes of Christendom would combine themselves and march against the common enemy, the Turk, she would most willingly attend them, and be their laundress in the camp." Such enthusiasm was thrown away upon her royal son; had there been opportunity for outwitting the Mohammedans, he might have been induced to try his skill, but fighting them was quite another matter. Among the many other interesting monuments in the chapel, we may especially particularize those two superb ones, which cover respectively the remains of Mary Queen of Scots, and her cousin and persecutor Elizabeth; the monument of the young princes murdered in the Tower, Kings James and Charles II., Monk, Duke of Albemarle, King William and Queen Mary, George II.

1077.—Piscina, Gloucester Cathedral.

1078.—Piscina, Great Gidding, Northamptonshire.

1079.—Piscina, Romsey, Hampshire.

1080—Piscina, Hexham, Northumberland.

1081.—Piscina, Hexham, Northumberland.

1082.—Piscina, Burford, Oxfordshire.

1086.—Early Brass (inlaid in stone)

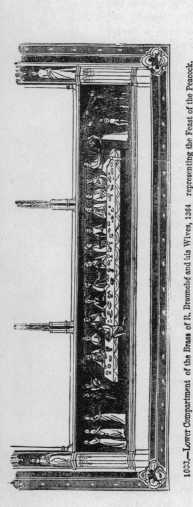

1033.—Lower Compartment of the Brass of R. Braunché and his Wives, 1364 representing the Feast of the Peacock.

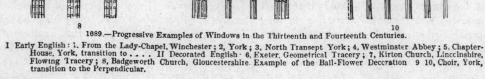

1087.—Brass of Bishop Compton.

1089.—Progressive Examples of Windows in the Thirteenth and Fourteenth Centuries.

I Early English : 1. From the Lady-Chapel, Winchester ; 2, York ; 3, North Transept York ; 4, Westminster Abbey ; 5. Chapter-House. York, transition to . . . . II Decorated English : 6, Exeter, Geometrical Tracery ; 7, Kirton Church, Lincolnshire, Flowing Tracery ; 8, Badgeworth Church, Gloucestershire. Example of the Ball-Flower Decoration 9 10, Choir, York, transition to the Perpendicular.

1083.—Piscina, Salisbury, Cathedral.

1084.—Piscina, Bapchild, Kent.

1085.—Piscina in Norman Arch, Bapchild, Kent.

090.—Froissart and Sir Espaing de Lyon.

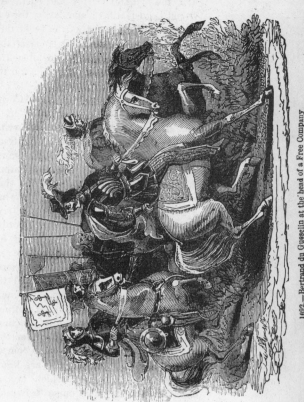

1092.—Bertrand du Guesclin at the head of a Free Company.

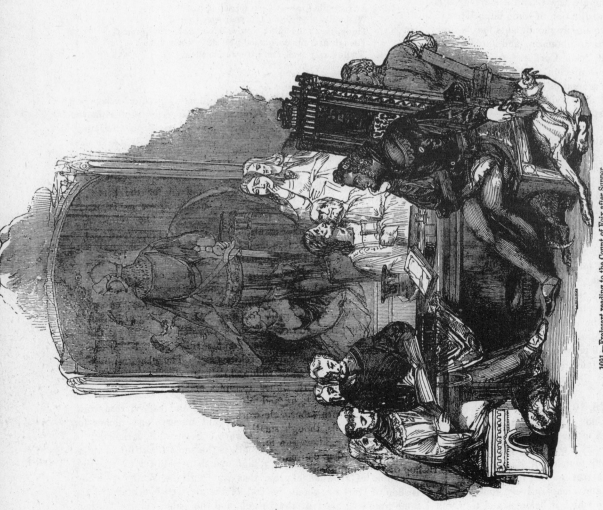

1091—Froissart reading to the Count of Foix after Supper.

2093.—Long-bow Archers   (From an original Drawing.)

and the "butcher" of Culloden, Addison, and his patron and friend Lord Halifax; and, lastly, the exquisitely-beautiful recumbent statue by Westmacott, of the Duke de Montpensier. We must not quit the chapel without a glance at the banners of the Knights of the Bath, that, hung on high along the chapel walls, remind us of the superb ceremony of installation that takes place in this chapel on the creation of a new knight.

We pass on now towards Poets' Corner (Fig. 1017), casting a mere passing glance into the chapels that lie by our side on the left. One of the most poetical of prose writers has given us his impressions of this, the more peculiarly attractive part of the whole abbey, and we cannot do better than transcribe the passage, for such writers enhance, by the personal sentiments they excite in connection with themselves and their visits, the sentiments they may have occasion to express with regard to what they felt and saw. "The monuments," observes Washington Irving, "are generally simple, for the lives of literary men afford no striking themes for the sculptor. Shakspere and Addison have statues erected to their memories; but the greater part have busts, medallions, and sometimes mere inscriptions. Notwithstanding the simplicity of these memorials, I have always observed that the visitors to the abbey remain longest about them. A kinder and fonder feeling takes place of that cold curiosity or vague admiration with which they gaze on the splendid monuments of the great and the heroic. They linger about these, as about the tombs of friends and companions; for indeed there is something of companionship between the author and the reader. Other men are known to posterity only through the medium of history, which is continually growing faint and obscure; but the intercourse between the author and his fellowmen is ever new, active, and immediate: he has lived for them more than for himself; he has sacrificed surrounding enjoyments, and shut himself out from the delights of social life, that he might the more immediately commune with distant minds and distant ages. Well may the world cherish his renown; for it has been purchased, not by deeds of violence and blood, but by the diligent dispensation of pleasure. Well may posterity be grateful to his memory; for he has left it an inheritance, not of empty names and sounding actions, but whole treasures of wisdom, bright gems of thought, and golden veins of language."

It is hardly necessary to enumerate the separate stars of this poetical Milky-way; but there is a distinction of some importance to be observed: some of our poets have simply monuments here—such are Shakspere, Milton, Butler, Gray, Thomson. and Goldsmith; whilst others were really interred in Poets' Corner. As we wander about this little spot—surely the most precious any age or country can boast of—we have beneath or around us the ashes of Chaucer (fit name to commence the custom of burying poets in the abbey, worthy leader of the illustrious host that were to follow), Spenser, prince of poets, Beaumont, Drayton, Cowley, Dryden, Rowe, Prior, Gay, Denham, Macpherson, the author or discoverer of Ossian, Samuel Johnson, Richard Brinsley Sheridan, and the poet who has just put off his mortality to put on immortality, Thomas Campbell. The words "O rare Ben Jonson!" inscribed on the wall near the door, remind us that Ben Jonson, though not buried in the corner, lies in the abbey, in the north aisle of the nave; and a curious story is told as to the grave. The Dean of Westminster rallied the poet one day about his burial in the abbey vaults. "I am too poor for that," said Jonson; "and no one will lay out funeral charges upon me. No, sir, six feet long by two wide is too much for me: two feet by two will do for what I want." "You shall have it," replied the Dean; and so the conversation ended. On the poet's death, continues the story, a demand was made for the space promised, and a hole made in it eight feet deep, and the coffin deposited therein *upright*. Many other eminent men enjoy the honourable companionship of the poets,—such are the musician Handel, the actors Garrick and Henderson, the men of learning Casaubon and Camden, the divine South, the architect Chambers, &c.

And now, in the choir (Figs. 1018, 1021), do we reach what may be called the holiest spot of the pile, not only in a religious, but in an artistical sense. Here, in the chapel of the kings, at the back of the choir, from which it is divided only by a screen, rests the monarch who may be considered the original founder of the pile, Edward the Confessor, beneath a monument that speaks, if ever stone did speak, of the primeval simplicity and comparatively rude magnificence of the Anglo-Saxon times, to which it belongs, and to which it at first sight carries back our thoughts. And what a circle of dead monarchs surround him!—Henry III., Edward I., Edward III., Richard II., and Henry V.; with Queens Eleanor (a monument so beautiful, that it may be questioned whether, in the whole

world of art, there is aught else that can surpass it), Philippa, and Anne of Bohemia, the spouse of the unfortunate Richard. Then against the screen are the two coronation-chairs, one of them with the stone of destiny beneath, whose real history (see Fig. 1018 of our work) goes back so far, and through such marvellous details, that a little faith may carry us even to end in the fabulous; and we may believe that it *was* the very stone that Jacob laid his head upon during the night of his memorable dream. And what a history is suggested by these chairs of the ceremonies that have taken place in this abbey from the days of Harold, the successor of the Confessor, down to our own times, on the accession of every new sovereign! What thoughts are not forced upon the mind as we turn from these types of the glory attending the rise of the kingly sun to those that speak of its setting;—sometimes still more gloriously —sometimes, alas! as in poor Richard's case, in tempest and deepest gloom. "It would be hardly possible," we have had occasion to observe elsewhere, "to present a more impressive lesson on the mutability of earthly glory than is afforded by the contrast between the two grand ceremonials which connect the history of our sovereigns for so many centuries with that of Westminster Abbey. The few steps upward to the throne, and the few downward into the grave; the airy sweep of the beautiful pointed arches, tier above tier, and the low and narrow vault; the spirit-stirring splendours of one pageant, and the sombre and dread magnificence of the other; the new-born hopes, which, binding king and people for the time in a common sympathy, make the past appear as nothing, the future all —and, alas! the melancholy comment provoked when all is over, as to the necessity for the repetition of the process:—these are but the regular and almost unchanging phenomena of the momentous ebbing and flowing of regal life which meet us in the memories of the abbey. It were a curious question to inquire whether those who have been the chief actors in such different ceremonials, have ever, during the one, thought of the other; whether, among all the monarchs who have passed along in their gorgeous robes, and beneath the silken canopy which the proudest nobles have been most proud to bear, there has been one to whom the secret monitor has whispered, in the words of a writer (Dart) better known as the historian than as the poet of the cathedral,—

> While thus in state on buried kings you tread,
> And swelling robes sweep spreading o'er the dead;
> While, like a god, you cast your eyes around,
> Think, then, oh! think, you walk on treacherous ground;
> Though firm the chequered pavement seems to be,
> 'Twill surely open, and give way to thee.

Never, probably, has there been a time of greater misery or humiliation for England than during the sovereignty of Ethelred the Unready, when the kingdom was about to pass from the family of the glorious Alfred to the Northern Pirates, by whom it had been so long harassed. Ethelred inherited no spark of the genius of his ancestor; and that dreaded consummation he made no decisive effort to avert, except by bribing the adventurers of the "Raven's" standard with his subjects' gold. To get this, he instituted the regular tax of the Dane-Geld, or Gold for the Danes, which he levied with such cruel rigour that he grew as odious to his people as even the terrible Northmen. The religious houses, having settled endowments, were a ready prey; and the monastery of Peterborough is recorded as one of those which, having failed to pay its Dane-geld, suffered loss of land and estate. Thus it was that the manor and collegiate establishment of St. Peter at HOWDEN (or Hovedon) passed from the Peterborough monks to the crown. We know scarcely anything of its after history, except that it was dissolved by Edward VI., and that, excepting a portion which is now the parish church, all was left to decay. And yet the place has been a considerable one, for the ruins (Fig. 1025) are extensive and of beautiful Gothic architecture. The chapter-house is one continuous specimen of rich and delicate ornament in stone. Here are thirty seats with ribbed canopies and carved rose-work, seven windows full of light and elegant tracery, and niches for statues garnished with tabernacle-work. Some antiquarians go so far as to say that this, though small, is the most beautiful chapter-house in England. There is a high and shapely tower overtopping the ruins of Howden church, that was built by Walter Skirlaw, Bishop of Durham, about the end of the fourteenth century, at the same time with part of the church, and the palace of the Durham bishops, also a ruin. The Book of Durham, quoted by Camden, gives Howden tower an origin similar to the tower of Babel, on the plain of Shinar—that is to say, it was to save the people of this district in the event of the rivers Ouse and Derwent flooding the land. The population must have been very scanty, judging by the accommodation provided for them in the interior of this tower. With all deference to Camden, however, the story is not deserving of credit.

To the desecrators of the fine old relics of England we commend the story told of a builder of Southampton, in connection with NETLEY ABBEY (Fig. 1027). Soon after the beginning of the last century, Mr. Walter Taylor purchased this abbey, intending to pull the whole fabric to pieces, and with the materials erect a town-house at Newport, and dwelling-houses at other places. After the contract had been made, some of Mr. Taylor's friends appear to have been conversing with him on the unworthiness of it, and uttered the forcible remark, that "*they* would never be concerned in the demolition of holy and consecrated places." Mr. Taylor then began to feel less satisfied with his undertaking; and his family have since related that he related to the father of Dr. Isaac Watts a dream that he had, in which, whilst taking down the abbey, the keystone of the arch over the east window fell from its place, and killed him. Dreams were held in more respect a century ago than they are at present; but Mr. Watts's advice went no further than recommending that the builder should not *personally* be concerned in the destruction of the abbey. His advice, such as it was, was not followed. Mr. Taylor superintended the operations of his workmen at their melancholy task; and, singularly enough, while he was removing some boards within the *east* window, to admit air, a stone fell upon his head and fractured his skull. The injury was not at first deemed mortal; but the decree had gone forth—the spoiler of the holy edifice was doomed—he died under the operation of extracting a splinter. It might certainly be said that the accident of the surgeon's instrument slipping aside and piercing the brain was the immediate cause of death, and not the *stone;* but we can think only of the moral bearing of the incident, nor will a little superstition on this point be amiss, if it induce certain people to lay more reverent hands on time-honoured remains like Netley Abbey. In fact, the feelings of awe and fear produced by this occurrence *have* been useful in preserving what we now see from more attempts of the same sort: and we rejoice at it. The wise law-giver of Israel has said, "Cursed is he that removeth the ancient landmarks;" and here is a landmark not only ancient, but also otherwise sacred. "*Materials,*" indeed! When will it be remembered that the value of such fragments is not in stones, or brick, or mortar—hardly even in the artistical fashioning of them—but in their associations! An enlightened German tourist thus speaks of Netley:—"One principal cause of the beauty of English ruins is the dampness of the climate, which covers them so immediately with a mantle of verdure. At Netley Abbey the court-yards, chapels, halls, and chambers, are all filled with trees, the edges of the walls covered with plants, and the ivy has hung its rich garlands round every elegant column and window-frame. In the centre of the largest space within the ruins, some speculator has established a table where the traveller may obtain ginger-bread and ginger-beer, soda-water and biscuits, and the vender of these dainties has set up his tent in the cell of one of the monks. The trees and bushes seem here as if they were representing the scenes in Ovid's Metamorphoses. A thorn, covered with its red berries, seems to be looking out of one of the windows at the Southampton Water, as once the young daughters of the Earl of Hereford, or some among the 103 descendants of the Marquis of Winchester, may have done. Instead of porters and tall lacqueys, two tall trees keep watch at the gate; and, instead of horses, we find in the stables fine specimens of the stately ash. For the aged crones who may once have tenanted its chimney corners, we find there knotted and gnarled trunks; and the church is filled with plants and shrubs, which seem like a metamorphosed congregation of devout worshippers. Beyond the abbey the ground rises a little, and thence I had the view of the sea through its arched windows." (Köhl's 'England,' 1844.)

It is said that Netley Abbey tower, of which we see the fragments of a spiral staircase, was once a mark for seamen. Our forefathers designated the scene amid which the ruins are situated, Letley, or, Pleasant Place, the most beautiful features of which are the fine bay called Southampton Water, the gentle slopes of rich green verdure, and the woods that screen the abbey from the busy world. Grandly the wintry blast sounds in these woods, as it sweeps through crypt and chapter-house and refectory, and seems to raise in the chapel (whose rich roof lies broken on the ground, and whose interior is exposed to the gaze of all the host of heaven) echoes of long-departed strains of prayer and praise. The monks of Letley came from the neighbouring Cistercian monastery of Beaulieu, and their abbey was founded about 1239. It was dissolved in the first

year of Edward VI., and passed to the possession of the eminent Sir William Paulet, who retained his office of High Treasurer of England, through the perilous changes of the reigns of Henry VIII., Mary, and Elizabeth, owing his safety to his partaking more of the nature of the willow than the oak. The Earls of Hereford next held Netley Abbey, and inhabited part of it, until it grew too dilapidated. But without calling up remote particulars of history, we have here abundant materials for interest and suggestive thought.

> Fallen pile! I ask not what has been thy fate;—
>   But when the weak winds, wafted from the main,
>   Through each lone arch, like spirits that complain,
> Come hollow to my ear, I meditate
> On this world's passing pageant, and the lot
>   Of those who once might proudly, in their prime,
>   Have stood with giant port; till, by time
> Or injury, their ancient boast forgot,
> They might have sunk, like thee; though thus forlorn
>   They lift their heads with venerable hairs
> Besprent, majestic yet, and as in scorn
>   Of mortal vanities and short-lived cares;
> E'en so doth thou, lifting thy forehead grey,
> Smile at the tempest, and time's sweeping sway.
>
>   BOWLES.

Of the large world of monachism, just previous to the rise of the mendicant orders, we might truly exclaim, in the words of Hamlet,—

> Fye on't! O fye! 't is an unweeded garden,
> That grows to seed; things rank and gross in nature
> Possess it merely.

A few illustrations of its overseers and guides, the leading clergy, about the twelfth and thirteenth centuries, will be proof enough of the general degeneracy. They (the monks and clergy together) held nearly half the lands of England, yet were still unsatisfied. At one time, in the twelfth century, we hear it said of a great prelate, Roger, Bishop of Sarum, or Salisbury, that "was there anything adjacent to his possessions which he desired, he would obtain it either by treaty or purchase, and if that failed, by force." At another time, we see an archbishop of Canterbury, Boniface, in the thirteenth century, sweeping down among his pastoral flocks to strip them of all he can by mean and tyrannic devices, putting the revenues at his control into his own private purse, and quartering himself and his retainers wherever he can find entertainment; and all the while fully prepared with bell, book, and candle for whoever may be disposed to question the holiness of his proceedings. How the riches of these spiritual leaders were spent we are at no loss to comprehend; for it is said of one bishop that he " wasted his wealth on hawks and hounds;" of others, that they were courtiers, politicians, men of pleasure, men of the world, who thought far more of a fine dinner than a fine sermon, of a good cook than a good preacher, of a purse of gold than all the souls that were to be saved in their dioceses. All were men of magnificence, or at least with very rare exceptions. It was said of that consummate churchman, Becket, "that he wished to be greater than the saints, and better than St. Paul:" and many others assumed, like him, the port of super-human beings moving about in this sublunary world, to which they only appeared to have deigned to belong. And the spiritual power and influences they possessed were backed, whenever necessary, by force of a more temporal nature, such as bands of armed retainers and strongly-fortified castles. As for the rules of the respective orders, they had ceased to be regarded both by great and small clergy. A simple Archbishop of Rouen once gave it as his opinion that certain bishops ought to live as their orders enjoined, humbly and quietly, without meddling with military affairs, or building castles or places of war: he found few to agree with him. Of the spirit of these Christian pastors we have a striking instance in the little incident that gave rise to this novel doctrine. At Oxford, when a court was held there, the numerous and disorderly retainers of the Bishops of Lincoln, Ely, and Sarum—the last the same Roger before mentioned—happening to quarrel with the Earl of Brittany's retainers, drew their swords, and killed a knight in the fray. The sovereign was not sorry for that "disgraceful blood-shedding," because he was able to imprison these three holy fathers, and make them ransom themselves with some of their *fortresses* and treasures. At the Conquest, and often afterwards, the high clergy were mounted on war-steeds, clad in full panoply, and directed the siege or headed the attack; not forgetting afterwards to draw their lots with the rest for their share of the booty. In every civil commotion they were prominent, turning their palaces into fortresses, calling up their knightly vassals, and performing with them (to say the truth) as splendid achievements in war as the more legi-

1091.—The Black Prince presenting his Banner to Sir John Chandos.

1095.—Death of "The Squire."

1096.—Tournament. (From Pluvenal's 'Art of Horsemanship.')

1097.—Mounting of a Cannon. (From Froissart.)

1098.—A, Ancient Cannon raised from the Godwin Sands, and supposed, from a coat of arms which it bears, to have been made about the year 1370. B, Chamber for loading. C, Spanish Cannon of the same date. D, Chamber for Loading. E, F, Earliest forms of English Cannon, from Examples in the Tower of London.

1099.—Portrait of Bertrand du Guesclin.

1100.—Bertrand du Guesclin fully armed.

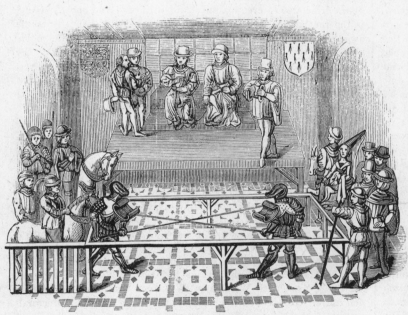

1102.—Tilting-match between Nich. Clifford and J. Boucmell. (From Froissart.)

1101—Accepting the Challenge.

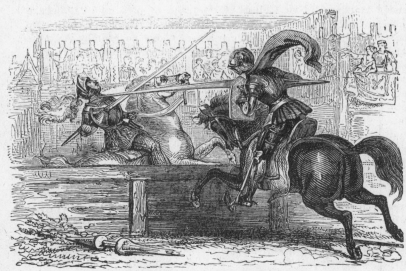

1103.—Young Bertrand du Guesclin at the Tournament.

1104.—A Herald reading his Despatches.

293

timate martialists. A few lights, and but a few, shone through the murky atmosphere; for human goodness cannot be wholly quenched. The famous Grosteste was one of the purest and noblest of bishops, who lived through the most miserable times of church profligacy under King John and Henry III., and whose successless struggles for the cleansing of the Augean stables furnish us with a most dismal picture of the state of our English monasteries, and of the utter impossibility of reforming them so long as there lived a priest at Rome ready to listen to every appeal to him that came strengthened by a bribe, and sufficiently powerful to shelter all the vices of Christendom. The good Fulk Basset, Bishop of London, and others, might also be mentioned, but these only made the darkness of the times more visible, until suddenly, in the beginning of the thirteenth century, day seemed to brighten around, and was joyfully hailed by the friends of mankind, in the institution of religious orders adopting the habits of life and teaching once practised by the Saviour and his Apostles.

At Assisi, in Umbria, in 1182, was born Francis, son of Peter de Bernardino, a wealthy merchant: he was at first christened John by his mother Pica, but his father, returning after an absence, changed that name to the one which was afterwards destined to become illustrious. Francis early acquired French, intending to adopt his father's profession; but, about 1206, the whole current of his mind underwent a singular change; a fit of sickness opened to him new worlds of thought—at once and for ever he abandoned the dissolute life he had been some time leading, and gave himself to prayer, to poverty, and to solitude. The good folks of Assisi deemed him mad; but his father was more disposed to blame his will than his infirmity, and, in the hope of coercing him to return to common duties, shut him up in a prison. This proving ineffectual, another plan was tried for reclaiming Francis, by taking him before the Bishop of Assisi, and requiring him to renounce his right in the paternal property. Francis was prepared and willing to make even this sacrifice for his principles. He surrendered *all*, even to the last article of his clothing, and from that time a coarse habit of grey cloth, tied with a common cord round his waist, and reaching to his ankles, superseded the handsome habiliments of the rich merchant's son. His feet were bare, only protected from the earth by rude sandals, and his head was shaded by a grey cowl. Such, with the addition of an occasional cloak, was the garb uniformly adopted by his followers, the Grey Friars (Fig. 1028). In 1210 and 1215, the rule of St. Francis was approved by the Pope and the Council of Lateran. In 1211 he had his first church near Assisi; and no later than 1219, when Francis was but thirty-seven, he enjoyed the title of "Seraphic Father," and held a chapter of some five thousand friars. He was no longer thought *mad*. His death took place at Assisi, in 1226, and he was canonized four years after. In a great measure, men are created by their times. Powerful and new minds were just then loudly called for, and they sprang up at the call. There was a contemporary of St. Francis, born in another land, and with whom it does not appear he had any communication, yet they seem to have been inspired with perceptions, zeal, and talents nearly identical, were canonized within five years of each other, and were the founders of orders so nearly alike, that the chief difference we can discover was, that the habits of the followers of Dominic de Guzman were black, with a white rochet (Fig 1029), and those of Francis grey. The Dominicans first entered England. Thirteen Spanish friars and a superior came, with high testimonials and recommendations from the Pope and other leading men of the holy see; they came on foot, being forbidden to mount on horseback by the humility of their rule; they came teaching the poor and ignorant, who had almost ceased to hear the voice of a preacher, and they came with so little of the cumbersome formality of ecclesiastical worship, that their portable pulpits and altars were set up in the streets and highways. Great was the sensation these zealous strangers excited. They asked no revenues or lands, they sought no glorification of themselves; they only desired permission to teach and pray, and to subsist on the alms of the pious. These poor preaching-friars became ere long the ornament and support of our greatest university at Oxford, where they grew eminent for all the learning of the time. Their second house was the noted Black Friars at London, near the present Blackfriars Bridge. The Franciscans very soon followed the Dominicans, and were generously entertained by the latter. Their first English house was at Canterbury; their second, the Grey Friars of London, where part of the buildings of the magnificent monastery that rose on the site still remains in the famous Blue-Coat School of Christ Church. In the course of time this church, built and endowed by royalty and nobility, came to be a place of sepulchre for four queens and nearly seven hundred persons of quality; whilst the Black Friars' Church in

the same metropolis was equally gorgeous and equally fashionable, it being generally believed that to be interred there, in the habit of that order, preserved the dead from the Great Enemy. No wonder other men endeavoured to imitate St. Francis and St. Dominic in founding mendicant orders, or in bringing previous orders near to their standard. A very modest fraternity arrived in 1244; they only asked from the opulent a house to live in, and exemption "from being *reproached by any one*;" meekly promising excommunication to those who failed to comply with the latter demand. Two London citizens accommodated these Crossed or Crutched Friars, who were distinguished by carrying an iron cross in their hands (changed to silver afterwards); and by wearing a cross of cloth on their garments, at first of grey, then red, and lastly blue. Gerard, prior of St. Mary de Morillo, at Bologna, in 1169, first instituted this order of friars, whose houses were dedicated to the holy cross. The Carmelites, or White Friars, "originated from the hermits of Mount Carmel, who inhabited the mountain which Elias and Eliseas, Elija and Elisha, inhabited" (Pennant). Another order was "for such married people as were desirous of repentance," as a sign of which they wore sackcloth. They were taken under the special protection of Queen Eleanor, wife of Edward I., under the designation of Friars Penitents, or Friars of the Sac. There were also Trinitarians, or Maturines, Austin Friars, Bethlemites, Friars of St. Anthony of Vienna, Friars de Pica, Bonhommes, or good men, introduced in 1283, by the Earl of Cornwall, and many others. Prosperity proved soon fatal to the moral elevation of all these different friars, or *freres* (brethren), precisely as it had done to the monkish orders and their clergy before. "The barefooted friar" came to be ludicrously associated with a pampered, indolent, sensual life; and the proverb, "It is not the cowl that makes the friar," expresses how wofully they too (like their predecessors the monks) had degenerated from their early professions. New men were *again* demanded to create a new state of things: and one was found in the memorable rectory of Lutterworth (Fig. 1049). Wickliffe arose, the morning star of the Reformation, and began the noble movement that was to make glorious his name by unsealing the Book of Books, and enabling the people to gather for themselves, without the interposition of monk, friar, or priest, the saving truths of the Gospel, in a popular version of the Scriptures. Our engraving (Fig. 1067) is a specimen of Wickliffe's translation.

To our notice of the friars of the thirteenth century, we name two bishops worthy of better times. Others might have been mentioned had space permitted. The century following had its lights also. Monastic and clerical morality in England had little improved, when a poor boy was placed in the "great Grammar School of Winchester" by a generous lord of the manor of Wykeham. The boy did not turn out one of those prodigies of musty lore of which the monastic ages were so fond; but he had rare talents for architecture, and that was an equally sure passport to preferment in the middle ages. A mightier patron than the Lord of Wykeham—Edward III.—fostered the genius and rewarded the exertions of the rising man, until William of Wykeham was presented with a rich mitre. He proved a great builder in other than architectural respects. His diocese of Winchester underwent at his hands a thorough purification and renovation; but his crowning work, and which he lived to see complete and flourishing, was the bestowment of his wealth for the good of posterity in provision for a liberal and exalted education for those who had not the means to pay for it—and the erection for this purpose of two extensive buildings, New College, Oxford, and its preparatory College of Winchester. The latter opened with its full establishment in 1393, on the site of the old grammar-school, chosen no doubt by Wykeham from grateful remembrance of the kindness and instruction which he had received there. The Winchester foundation has withstood successfully the innovations of time, that has changed all things about it. We have still the seventy poor Wykehamite Scholars of Winchester, forming with the two masters the holy number of seventy-two, that of the early disciples; the warden and ten fellows (who have appointments for life) still stand for the eleven apostles, and the sixteen choristers still represent the four great and twelve lesser prophets. We have even still the Gothic style, and the antique arrangement of the various erections in and about the college, similar to those of Eton and Oxford Schools. The approach through two courts, beneath an ancient tower and gateway (Fig. 1033), wears the secluded and venerable air of a learned retreat of monastic days. The beautiful chapel and hall speak worthily of the architect-bishop's genius. In the cloisters (one hundred and thirty-two feet square) is John Fromond's Chantrey, built in 1430; it was deprived of its chaplain at the Reformation, and converted into a library by Dr. Pinke in 1629. In one of the schoolrooms we find some ancient admonitory symbols, offering the scholar three alternatives, a bishop's cap and staff, with a motto in Latin, signifying that he may stay and learn; an inkstand and a sword, with a motto meaning, that if he does not choose to learn, he may leave; and finally a rod, that needs not the motto attached, so unmistakably does it imply that if he will neither learn nor leave, he must submit to something more disagreeable. A noble schoolroom was built by the "Wykehamites" in 1687, at a cost of 2592*l.* Over the entrance is the bronze statue of William of Wykeham, that was modelled, cast, and presented to the college by the father of Colley Cibber. One of the curiosities of the college is a figure illustrative of a good servant according to the ideas of our ancestors: it is compounded of a man, a stag, an ass, and a hog, severally representing, we presume, the intellect of mind, the swiftness of foot, the gentleness of temper, and the accommodating character of appetite, that ought to be at the master's service. One would like to see a corresponding figure, showing what the master thought *he* ought to be, to be worthy of such an attendant. We must conclude this sketch by a touching extract, after premising that there are upwards of a hundred boys not on the foundation lodged in a spacious quadrangular building contiguous to the college, many of them belonging to wealthy or distinguished families. "At the close of the school year, the scholars break up, after having solemnly sung, in the presence of the assembled clergy and gentry of the neighbourhood, the hymn of 'Dulce Domum,' known throughout England, and said to have been composed by a poor Wykehamist, condemned as a punishment to remain at school during the holidays. The story goes that after composing this song and the melody to it, he continued singing it incessantly, till languishing more and more, in vain longing for his home, he fell sick and died. The æsthetic value of the composition is of course not great, but it is so expressive of the feelings which animate millions of hearts, that it has spread from Winchester to Eton, Harrow, Westminster, and all public schools, and is everywhere sung with enthusiasm. The mail coaches used formerly at Christmas and other holiday times to be filled with boys, singing this favourite ditty, and holding in their hands little banners, on which 'Dulce Domum' was inscribed in great letters." (Köhl's 'England,' 1844.)

Canons have been often mentioned in connection with cathedral and collegiate establishments. They lived a modified monastic life under the control of the bishop, by whom they were often sent out into the rural districts to teach the ignorant population, and perform among them the rites of religion. For a long time they thus sufficed, during the primitive ages of the Anglo-Christian religion, instead of a parochial clergy. They were also students and interpreters of the great canon laws, those emanations of the legislative wisdom of the successors of St. Peter, to which all Europe rendered obedience. It was by these canons' assistance, as a sort of privy council, the bishop exercised his extensive powers. Such, before 1105, were the canons, a class still attached to our episcopal establishments, generally under the denomination of prebendaries, though the ancient ideas of their duties are quite extinct. After 1105 they were called Seculars, to distinguish them from the Regulars, who lived more like monks, but not so strictly, although they kept close in their monasteries, instead of going forth to teach. The regular canons' first home in England was at Colchester. Tanner mentions above one hundred and seventy-five houses of canons and canonesses in England and Wales. Of these houses the great lords, as in other orders of monachism, were the chief founders. Among them, Robert Bossu, Earl of Leicester, in 1143, established LEICESTER ABBEY (Fig. 1032), for one of the reformed canon orders, of St. Mary's Pré; that originated in the diocese of Laon in Picardy, where the Virgin herself had, it was asserted, pointed out a place to be its head. Leicester Abbey became rich and fashionable, and the place of rest and refreshment for monarchs and other great personages (Richard II. and his queen and courtiers among the rest), as they passed to and from the North. It is now a mere heap of ruins (Fig. 1032), destitute of form or dignity, and deriving its chief interest from its having been the scene of the death of one of the most remarkable personages of the detestable reign of Henry VIII.—Cardinal Wolsey. The common reproach that human nature loves to trample on fallen greatness was not borne out in the instance of Wolsey's precipitate descent from high fortune. He found himself indeed deserted by the minions of the court, but the common people, to whom he had been disguised by prosperity, found out in his adversity that he was possessed of amiable and estimable qualities, and would have risked even their lives to rescue him from his tormentors, and take him to the sea-coast, where he might escape to another

land. But no! Wolsey indeed looked to another land for safety, but that was beyond this world. He had been twenty years the dearest friend of Henry, and he could not survive this bitter reverse:

> Blow, blow, thou winter's wind,
> Thou art not so unkind
>   As man's ingratitude.

The suffering prisoner had reached Sheffield Park when he was attacked by a mortal sickness. A fortnight's illness left him in the last extreme of feebleness, so that he could scarcely sit upon his mule. It was growing evident to those who had charge of him, that there would be no dungeon but the grave for Wolsey: that the Tower would not number him among its list of victims, that the axe would thirst in vain for his blood. He was passing out of the reach of earthly potentates. In the full consciousness of this, when, late on the third evening, he and his keepers reached Leicester Abbey, and the abbot and monks came out with burning torches at the gates to receive him, with the honour rather due to his former than his present condition, he said to the abbot, "Father, I am come to lay my bones among you." The weeping brethren carried him from his mule to a bed, where swoon followed swoon. His memorable last words were then uttered to the lieutenant. "Master Kingston, I pray you have me commended most humbly to his majesty, and beseech him, on my behalf, to call to his gracious remembrance all matters that have passed between us from the beginning, especially respecting Queen Catherine and himself, and then shall his conscience know whether I have offended him or not. He is a prince of most royal courage, and hath a princely heart—for, *rather than miss or want any part of his will, he will endanger one half of his kingdom.* And I do assure you, I have often kneeled before him in his privy chamber, sometimes for three hours together, to persuade him from his appetite, and could not prevail. And, Master Kingston, this I will say—*had I but served God as diligently as I have served the king, he would not have given me over in my grey hairs.* Howbeit this is my just reward for my pains and diligence, not regarding my service to God, but only my duty to my prince." Never did deathbed speech contain a more profound or pathetic moral. He died soon after. It was at midnight that the heartbroken Cardinal was interred by the brethren of Leicester Abbey, in the chapel of Our Lady in the church, with no solemnity except such as was essential to the awful duty, and arose out of heartfelt reverence and sorrow.

Before the Conquest, the only order of monks known in England was the Benedictine, instituted early in the sixth century, and first generally established by St. Dunstan in the tenth. One of the principal of their houses was at MALMESBURY, the buildings of which occupied forty-five acres of ground. It was the second establishment for extent and importance in the west of England. The founder was a Scotchman of the seventh century, Maidulph, or Maydulph, first known at Malmesbury as a teacher. When he had collected a few pupils who were willing to forsake the world for a monastery, he began to build one. Neither master nor pupils could have been in possession of much worldly wealth; for though we may presume they had the alms of the pious to help them, yet for some time they could scarcely manage to live. But this did not last long. Their humble house was in a few years transformed into all the magnificent complication of a great abbatial structure, endowed by Saxon bishops, and Saxon kings, Ina, Athelstan, Edgar, Edward the Confessor, and others. The first founder lived to be a rich abbot. He was associated with Aldhelm, a monk still of note as a Saxon writer. To honour Aldhelm's memory after his decease, King Athelstan chose him for his patron saint, and bequeathed his own body to be buried in the abbey. The altar tomb in our engraving (Fig. 1039) has been called King Athelstan's, but the situation does not correspond with the spot mentioned by William of Malmesbury as the place of his burial, which was under the high altar. The style also is later than the age of Athelstan. The tomb has been examined, but contained no vestiges of interment. Whom the royal-robed effigy is intended to represent we shall probably never discover, but we know that other Saxon kings have been interred in this abbey beside Athelstan. The Norman era, fatal to many Saxon monasteries, advanced this; the Norman kings being pleased to shed over Malmesbury the genial sunshine of their favour. About the end of the eleventh century was born the valuable old English historian whom we have just quoted, William, called "of Malmesbury," because he was an inmate of this abbey. He was placed here in his boyhood, became librarian and precentor (Leland), and ultimately refused the mitre. The number of works

1105.—Guildhall, Chichester.

1107.—The School of Pythagoras, Cambridge

1108. A Tower which formerly stood on the Bridge at Oxford.

1106.—Watergate Street, with the external View of the "Rows" at Chester.

1109.—Croyland Bridge.

1113.—Interior of a Chester "Row."

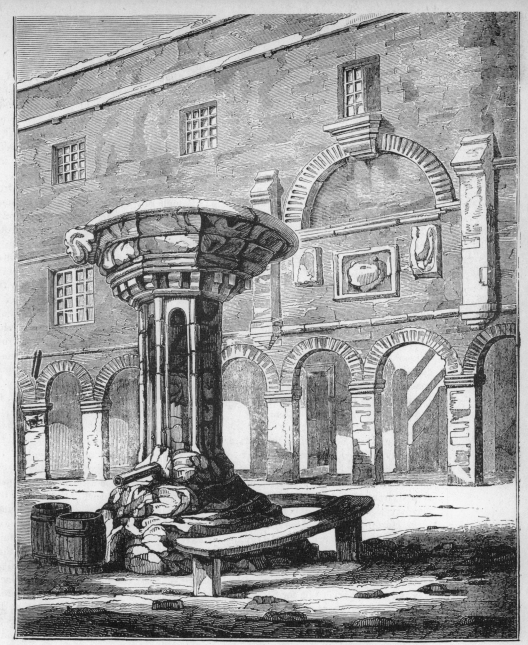

1110.—"Pant" in front of the Freemen's Hospital, Newcastle-upon-Tyne.

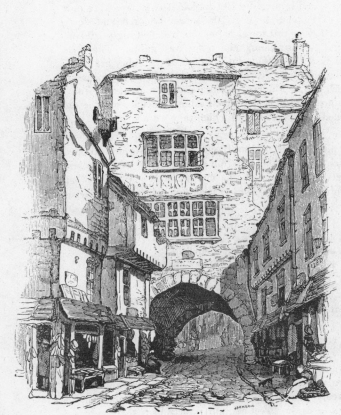

1111.—Black Gate, Newcastle.

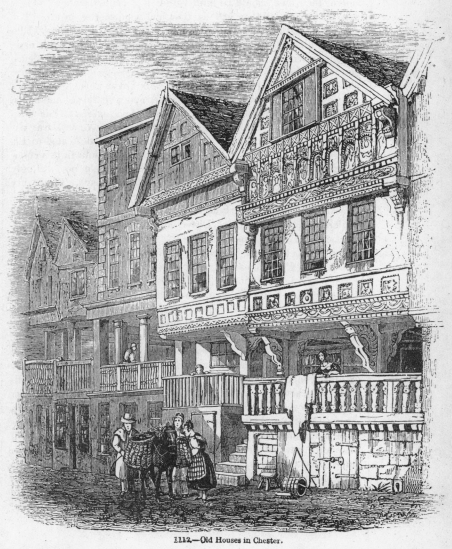

1112.—Old Houses in Chester.

that he produced speaks much for the life of the Malmesbury recluses, as we may fairly presume he was not the only one of them who spent his time in quiet trains of thought, or in the exercise of the pen. Life in the monastic communities was no doubt eminently favourable to mental pursuits, when there was any taste or desire for such occupations, and we find this evidenced not only in literary and architectural, but in various other productions. Thus we find one monk, Oliver of Malmesbury, who lived in the abbey about the same time as William, making a daring and novel experiment in mechanical art, like that of Johnson's flying philosopher in 'Rasselas.' One day he presented himself on the top of a lofty tower, in the centre of a pair of wings that he had contrived for sailing through the air. Great was the admiration and wonder of the beholders, when Oliver boldly sprang forth into that element which had hitherto eluded man's skill. But Oliver's pinions unfortunately proved no more trustworthy than those that betrayed their author in the Happy Valley. He flew a furlong space (it is said), and then dropped, fracturing his limbs. Fig. 1036 gives us an exterior view of all that remains of this proud establishment—a few fragments of the abbey church, "that right magnificent thing" (Leland). The time of its erection is referred generally to that of Roger, Bishop of Sarum, in the twelfth century. The character of the whole is massive, large, and curiously decorated. The grand southern porch (Fig. 1038) is the finest part. The arch of the transept (Fig. 1037) is also well worthy of attention.

Though the Benedictines were, as a body, averse to new forms of religion, they became the source of many. One reformer of this primary body was an abbot of Cîteaux in the bishopric of Châlons, in Burgundy, where he had founded a house, to be more retired from the world than the Benedictines generally deemed necessary. The third abbot of Cîteaux was an Englishman, Stephen Harding, canonised as St. Etienne, who may be esteemed the real founder of the order les Cîteaux, or Cistercian, that began in his time first to make a name in the world. Until the period of the French Revolution, the abbots of Cîteaux were superiors-general of the whole order. A marked feature of the Cistercians was and is their reverence for St. Bernard, the founder, it is said, of sixty houses. He was abbot of Clairvaux, or Clareval, in the diocese of Langres. The Cistercians are also designated Bernardines. The sudden rise of this great order was truly remarkable. Within fifteen years five hundred abbeys sprang to light, in solitary and uncultivated places, it being a rule of the body that no house, even one of their own, should be built within a certain distance. Their own historians say they had six thousand monasteries in all. The English Cistercians came from Aumone Abbey in Normandy, 1128. Walter Giffard, Bishop of Winchester, established in his new-founded abbey at Waverley. The abbots of this place had precedence in the chapters, and over all the order in England. At the suppression, by Henry VIII., there were thirty-six Great Bernardine houses in this country, besides many smaller, and twenty-six nunneries. The monks wore white habits at their religious exercises, but when they went abroad the white gown over the white cassock was exchanged for a black gown. All their houses were dedicated to the Virgin. Those that remain of the ancient foundations in this country are mostly ruins, but such ruins as one would not willingly exchange for most modern and complete establishments. The beauty and solitariness of their situations of course greatly enhance the effect of the relics of their beautiful and lofty architecture. In slightly noticing some of the chief Cistercian houses in England, such as Kirkstall, Tintern, and Melrose, the thoughts not unnaturally revert to the house of White Monks, located in Charnwood Forest, where some Cistercians of our own day are busily occupied in completing a Cistercian abbey on the largest scale, with a Gothic church that may almost rival those of the middle ages.

Henry de Lacy, in the reign of Stephen, being in a bad state of health, made a vow that if he should recover he would build an abbey in honour of the blessed Virgin and the Cistercian order. He *did* recover, and at once set about fulfilling his vow. It seems that he held the town and appurtenances of Bernoldswic, or Bernoldswie, in fee of Hugh Bigod, Earl of Norfolk, himself a munificent benefactor to holy church. This property was made over by Lacy to Abbot Alexander, "Prior of Fountains," and called St. Mary's Mount. Alexander brought twelve monks and ten converts from Fountains, and became abbot of Lacy's new monastery. But it was ill provided against the rigours of the wintry season, and war added to the distress of the monks. After enduring much from hunger and cold, during six months, the abbot in very despair began to look about for some better place, where the abbey would be more likely to flourish, and the inmates have more chance of

comfort. He found this place in a beautiful and well-wooded dale through which the river Aire flowed clear and full. Here he selected the site of a new abbey, close on the river margin. There was plenty of stone in the neighbourhood for building, and abundance of fuel, which, with water, formed three great indispensables for the undertaking. But what seems to have chiefly determined Abbot Alexander in his choice, was the finding already settled here a few anchorites. Lacy now obtained a grant of the land necessary for the abbey from William of Poictou or Poiteven, to whom and his heirs the monks of Kirkstall paid five marks annually. The church, built entirely at Lacy's expense, the two dormitories for monks and lay-brothers, the refectory, cloister, chapter-house, and other offices, were all built during the good Alexander's long abbacy. Lacy supplied the brethren with money and provisions, and other patrons soon followed, who must have been very liberal, if we may judge from the large possessions Kirkstall ultimately acquired.

The plan of the abbey (Fig. 1041) exhibits an arrangement common to all such edifices. The beauty of the present ruins (Fig. 1040) is enhanced by the grand masses of ivy that in some parts clothe it from the ground to the topmost fragment. The style involves the changes from Early Norman to Pointed. In fine weather, especially on Sundays, the neat little village of Kirkstall, placed at a most convenient distance for the pleasure-seekers of busy Leeds, is quite thronged by manufacturing artisans and others, who wander about the celebrated abbey, and on the banks of the Aire, devoid, for the most part, of sympathy with its original purposes, but fully alive to the two interesting facts—all they know of it—that it is beautiful and old. Some, as they peep into the remains of cells and cloisters, long to know more of those who formerly tenanted them; or, as they attempt to climb the dim and perilous steps to the remains of weird-looking galleries, fancy the moonbeam glancing through the deep shadows to be the form of a white monk, or, gazing with still deeper awe, not to say fear, into the inscrutable vaults, shudder as they recall to mind all the terrible stories of which they have ever read in history or in fiction of monks entombed alive, for striving to burst the stern cold barriers which they had placed between themselves and the world of human nature. In another respect KIRKSTALL ABBEY is unfortunate in its nearness to the great depôt of woollens; there was not room enough, it seems, in that big town for tall chimneys, and rows of formal factory windows, and great unsightly masses of stone and mortar, but they must encroach on a domain sacred to the poetry of the past, and so rob Kirkstall, in our opinion, of half its charms.

The Black Canons were introduced into Scotland about the same time as in England. One of their houses was at JEDBURGH, the inmates of which came from Beauvais in France, early in the twelfth century. It suffered greatly in the visitations of the English, was pillaged and burned by Surrey, in 1253, at the storming of Jedburgh, and injured by Hertford in 1545. We have now only the ruins of the church (Fig. 1056), two hundred and thirty feet in length. The central tower is one hundred feet high. There are two beautiful Norman doors, and a fine west gable. The style is Norman and Early English. Foundations of the abbey are traceable to a considerable distance. The burial-ground is very spacious. Jedburgh parish was in old days celebrated for its castles, fortified dwellings, and magnificent ecclesiastical establishments; and for the picturesque woodland scenery amid which they were situated.

One of the pious works of the Bigod, Earl of Norfolk, alluded to in our notice of Kirkstall, was the abbey church of TINTERN, whose ruins adorn that part of the margin of the Wye between Monmouth and Chepstow, which has been so celebrated by tourists and poets.

> How oft,
> In darkness, and amid the many shapes
> Of joyless daylight, when the fretful stir
> Unprofitable, and the fever of the world,
> Have hung upon the beatings of my heart,
> How oft, in spirit, have I turned to thee,
> O sylvan Wye! Thou wanderer through the woods:
> How often has my spirit turned to thee!

The poem containing these lines, composed a few miles above Tintern Abbey, on revisiting the banks of the Wye, July 13, 1798, must be known to most of our readers. Familiar almost as household words are some of the thoughts it contains—thoughts which, whilst we trace the outward and visible objects described in the poem, interpret to us, in sweet and mournful music, their spiritual purposes. Nor is this all. They lead us to admire and rejoice in the sympathy that unites pure and lofty minds of all ages and creeds, whether Catholic fathers, such as those who selected the romantic and pastoral vale of Tintern, and then invested the spot with a higher interest by the erection of their beautiful monastery —or Protestant bards like Wordsworth, who have drawn inspiration from it, and added yet another charm to Tintern by their writings. Wordsworth and the early monks seem to have felt with equal intensity, that—

> Nature never did betray
> The heart that loved her : 'tis her privilege,
> Through all the years of this our life, to lead
> From joy to joy : for she can so inform
> The mind that is within us, so impress
> With quietness and beauty, and so feed
> With lofty thoughts, that neither evil tongues,
> Harsh judgments, nor the sneers of selfish men,
> Nor greetings where no kindness is, nor all
> The dreary intercourse of daily life,
> Shall e'er prevail against us, or disturb
> Our cheerful faith, that all which we behold
> Is full of blessings.

We have a singular distant view of the ruin from a spot at a little distance on the other side the river, presenting fine illusory effects. It seems to stand in the front of an interminable forest. The grand east window, set in shrubs and ivy, is changed into a majestic portal, through which we gaze on a vista whose limits baffle us, so indefinitely are they prolonged by the foliage twined about columns, and dropping from arches, and clustering beyond the opposite extremity of the ruin, the arch of the western window. The best near view of the shell of the Abbey Church is given in Fig. 1031. The total loss of the tower is unfortunate, as in consequence there is felt a deficiency of elevation to harmonize the exterior. It happens too that the most prominent parts left standing are gables of common, formal, and obtrusive outline. The roof of the church, like the tower, has long ago fallen. Other parts of the building are in tolerable preservation, and amply justify the praise bestowed upon it by Mr. Rickman, that, "in beauty of composition and delicacy of execution, it yields to few edifices in the kingdom." Tintern is chiefly noted for the fine perspective of the interior (Fig. 1030). No jarring point meets us there. All is antique and regular, airy and grand. The smooth and verdant turf contrasts well in colour with the grey walls, and by preserving the original level of the ground, preserves also the original proportions of the building. It seems likely that the choir of the church was first built, as in 1268, William of Worcester informs us, the abbot and monks entered it and celebrated mass at the high altar. The style was Early English, passing gradually into Decorated, as the edifice advanced to completion. The abbey was founded a short time previous to the church (in 1131), by Walter de Clare, grandson to Walter Fitzosbert, Earl of Eu. Some remains of the abbot's lodge and fratry are close to the water's edge, and droop their ivy clusters over it. The monks' cells are partly incorporated into miserably poor tenements, the abodes of indigent people, whose unseemly rags and importunate solicitations for alms by no means enchance the natural associations of the place. One cannot but remember that their forefathers were in all probability very differently cared for. Well, time has swept away worse things than the spirit of Catholic love and reverence for the poor ; which is ill exchanged for the cold, selfish policy that prevails too much in our own age.

Some of the general features of the great abbeys of the Cistercian order, that we have noticed in England, we find repeated in the Scottish houses MELROSE and NEW ABBEY. The former, the mother Cistercian church of Scotland, was founded in 1136, by that "sore saint for the Crown," as James VI. styled his ancestor, the royal David I., when he found how his revenues were impoverished by that saint's pious doings. The monks came from Rivaulx Abbey in Yorkshire ; they were wealthy and numerous (nearly a hundred), and have left no good character behind them. The old border ballad thus slily alludes to their luxury and rapacity—

> O the monks of Melrose made gude kale
> On Friday, when they fasted :
> They wanted neither beef nor ale
> As long as their neighbours' lasted.

As usual, the remains are those of the church (Fig. 1057). The length of the nave and choir together is two hundred and fifty-eight feet, that of the transept one hundred and thirty feet. In this fabric, in Mr. Hutchison's opinion, are the finest lessons in, and the greatest variety of Gothic ornaments that the island affords.

Francis Drake, writing in 1742, also observes, "Mailross, I shall take it upon me to say, has been the most exquisite structure of the kind in either kingdom." Lastly comes the poet, also pointing out, as the great architectural attractions of Melrose its intricate and exquisite stone carving :

> Nor herb nor floweret glistened there
> But was carved in the cloister arches as fair.

And he settled the business. The beauties of Melrose became a point of fashionable faith. By day and night, the great and the small crowded about it, in consequence of the descriptions in the famous "Lay." Some who had never heard of Melrose before, never forgot it after ; some cared nothing about it *then*, and only followed in the popular wake to be able to say they had seen it ; but all pressed to look for the shadow of the blood-red cross that marked where the wizard lay ; and all, even the most prosaic people, talked poetry about Melrose by moonlight (Fig. 1058), and repeated the famous lines, and even made Johnny Bower, the "decent-looking little old man in a blue coat and red waistcoat," get up a kind of artificial illumination, when the moon was in eclipse.

> If thou wouldst view fair Melrose aright,
> Go, visit it by the pale moonlight ;
> For the gay beams of lightsome day
> Gild but to flout the ruins grey.
> When the broken arches are black in night,
> And each shafted oriel glimmers white ;
> When the cold light's uncertain shower
> Streams on the ruin's central tower ;
> When buttress and buttress, alternately,
> Seem framed of ebon and ivory ;
> When silver edges the imagery,
> And the scrolls that teach thee to live and die ;
> When distant Tweed is heard to rave,
> And the owlet to hoot o'er the dead man's grave ;
> Then go—but go alone the while,
> Then view St. David's ruined pile ;
> And, home returning, soothly swear
> Was never scene so sad and fair.

A point of high interest not generally known, though Scott himself mentions it, is connected with this abbey. We have elsewhere said that the royal Bruce bequeathed his heart to the care of his tried friend and companion in arms, Sir James Douglas, to be conveyed to the Holy City in Palestine. After "the good Sir James" had fallen, fighting with the Moors in Spain, the glorious relic found its way back to its native clime, and was enshrined in "Old Melrose." There are some interesting sepulchral remnants. "I can never forget," says Mrs. John Ballantyne (in a number of 'Chambers's Edinburgh Journal,' of September, 1844), "the awe-striking solemnity with which he (Scott) pronounced an elegiac stanza inscribed on a tombstone in Melrose Abbey :

> "Earth walketh on the earth,
> Glistering like gold ;
> Earth goeth to the earth
> Sooner than it wold.
> Earth buildeth on the earth
> Palaces and towers ;
> Earth sayeth to the earth,
> All shall be ours."

Among the other curiosities of New Abbey, in Kirkcudbright Stewartry, Scotland, is a small curious gate leading into the abbey, and an escutcheon, supposed to bear the Abbey arms, with an inscription over it in old English, "Choose time of need." In those arms is a heart, in allusion to a touching circumstance relating to the foundation of the abbey by the mother of John Balliol, that unpatriotic or incapable king, who brought disgrace on Scotland, such as only a Wallace and a Bruce could wipe away. She was a coheiress of Alan, the last of the ancient lords of Galloway, and the wife of John Balliol, lord of Barnard Castle. He died in 1269, and his heart was preserved by the beloved woman who mourned for him. She enclosed it in a beautiful ivory box, highly ornamented, and bound with enamelled silver, and then caused it to be set in the wall near the high altar of the New Abbey. From that relic and memorial of true affection, the abbey was called afterwards, Dolce Cor, or the abbey of Sweet-heart. Henry, the first abbot, died on a journey to Cîteaux ; Eric, the second, was among the free barons who swore fealty to Edward I. on his undertaking the arbitration between the claims of Balliol and Bruce and other competitors for the crown of Scotland. Gilbert Brown the last abbot, was an active Catholic controversialist, "a busy trafficker for Rome and Spain," and sat in Parliament when

1118.—The Talbot, 1841.

1114.—Portrait of Chaucer.

1115.—The Tabard.

"In Southwark at the Tabard as I lay,
Ready to wenden or my pilgrimage
To Canterbury with devout courage,
At night was come into that hostelry
Well nine and twenty in a company
Of sundry folk by adventure yfal
In fellowship, and pilgrims were they all,
That toward Canterbury wolden ride."
Canterbury Tales

1117.—The Tabard. (From a Drawing about 1780.)

1116.—The Tabard. (From Urry's edition of Chaucer, 1720.)

1119.—The Knight and the Squire.

1120.—The Sergeant-at-Law and the Doctor of Medicine.

1121.—Cardinal's Hat. (Royal MS. 16 G. vi.)

1122.—Male Costume time of Edward II. (Royal MS. F.M. Sloane MS 346.)

1123.—The Monk and the Friar.

1124.—The Parson and the Clerk of Oxenford.

the Confession of Faith was adopted, 1560. The commissioners of the Assembly particularly noticed him in their list of grievances, and so Abbot Brown had to forsake his abbey, and betake himself to concealment. He eluded his enemies until 1605, and then the people attempted his rescue. Happily, the edge of persecution had been dulled before he was cast into prison, and after lying in Blackness and Edinburgh castles long enough to be convinced that all was over for his church in Scotland, he was allowed to retire into France, where he died, at Paris, in 1612.

New Abbey stands in a small valley or "bottom," by the river Nith. A large portion of the English coast is included in the varied and extended prospect seen from the abbey, and from the tower Loch-Kindar is visible, with its little island and ancient ruin. The parish of New Abbey (formerly Kirkander) extends to the Solway Frith, and consists of low and high ground, the latter broken into rocks, hills, mosses, and muirs. On one of the heights near the abbey, some fragments, called the Abbot's Tower, mark what was once the private residence of the abbots of Sweet-heart. The abbey ruin is begirt with a space of twenty acres, designated "the Precinct," that used to be enclosed with a wall of most substantial fabric, of which little is left, but that little exhibiting stones of a ton weight each, even near the top. Beside the ruins of the church, of light decorated Gothic (Fig. 1034), there is a part of the Chapter-house standing. A parish kirk in 1731 was formed out of the ruins of the other buildings. There are very antique tombstones in the burial-ground. One bears a cross and a large and broad sword—an anomalous union, unless the ingenious artist meant to shadow forth the two opposite principles which rule this world. Lord Kames published an account of a very singular ash-tree which formerly grew from some seed dropped on one of the abbey walls, and which was supplied with nourishment from a runner that descended to the earth.

Among the less distinguished classes of monachism that also sprang out of the original Benedictine, may be mentioned that to which KELSO ABBEY, in the town of Kelso, Roxburghshire, belonged. It acknowledges the same founder as Melrose, St. David. Kelso was repeatedly burned or otherwise injured during the English invasions. The ruins (Fig. 1054) are of mingled styles, the Norman predominating. At a certain period they were injured by incongruous additions for the use of a church congregation; but, to the credit of all concerned, these blemishes have been removed, and we see the building now in all its own unadulterated and venerable grandeur.

Considering that Ireland is a Catholic country, we feel some surprise and disappointment to meet with so few Gothic remains in it of magnitude or importance. The chief structure of this kind, though not the most antique, is St. PATRICK'S CATHEDRAL, in Dublin, situate at the foot of the declivity, on the ridge of which stands the Castle and another Cathedral of older foundation. St. Patrick's is an imposing pile: the most beautiful part is the choir (Fig. 1051), to which the handsome roof, the monuments, the stalls and banners of the Knights of St. Patrick (their installation takes place here), and other accessories, give a very striking if not altogether harmonious effect. The Cathedral was first erected by Archbishop Comyn, about the end of the twelfth century. Being consumed by fire in 1362, through the negligence of " John the Sexton," Minot, a successor of Comyn in the primacy, began two years after to build it up again. How much he thought of his work we may see in the device on his seals, where he appears holding the steeple in his hands. As we walk round the interior to view the memorials of the dead who have found a place in St. Patrick's, two especially rivet our attention, that of Swift, who was Dean of St. Patrick's, and that of his ill-starred and most amiable wife, poor Stella. When we read in his inscription of his resting "where bitter indignation can tear his heart no more," we are led to moralize on the source of that bitter indignation, which was not, as he wished us to believe, the vices and follies of mankind, so much as the failure of his ambitious aspirations; and we cannot wonder how a heart that was undeniably fraught with strong and generous feeling could be so lamentably deficient in magnanimity. When we look to Stella's tablet, we half anticipate some expression of her bitter indignation against the eccentric being who caused her so much suffering, and it seems very likely broke her heart: but woman's wrongs are seldom paraded before the world, like those of the loftier sex; in Stella's case they are not, however, and never can be, forgotten.

As St. Patrick's Cathedral is the chief specimen of Gothic architecture in Ireland, so is GLASGOW CATHEDRAL (Fig. 1053) the most perfect relic of the kind in Scotland, or anywhere else, in the opinion of some of its frequenters and admirers. It is one of the four remarkable points of Glasgow, namely, the Cathedral, the Green, a great public esplanade, the Trongate, a noble specimen of a street, and the graceful river Clyde, said by a Glasgow poet to be—

Glory of that and all the world beside.

Mr. Robert Chambers tells us that on these four " the native of Glasgow principally grounds his ideas regarding the consequence of the city," and that he would defend them from any species of violation, as though they were his personal instead of public property. And this has been proved as well as said. When the zeal of the Puritans was working so much mischief in ecclesiastical edifices, an order went forth bearing the signatures of A. Argyle, James Stewart, and Ruthven, to " tak down the hail images " of Glasgow Cathedral, " cast down the altaris, and purge the kirk of all kind of monuments of idolatrye," and so make a general bonfire of all the most precious objects of antiquity. The pious Destructives thus let loose, it seemed likely that even the reservations in the order, that neither the " dasks, windocks, nor durris " should be in " ony ways hurt or broken, either glassin wark, or iron wark," would have been neglected, and thus the whole fabric destroyed, but for a sagacious provost's recommendation that before the old church were destroyed a new one ought to be built. After this there was a second attack by a body of workmen sent with beat of drum, but the sturdy craftsmen and burgesses rallied to the rescue, headed by their deacons, and fully prepared to bring the matter to a life and death issue. It did not, however, reach that extremity. On their threatening that the first man who dared to pull down one stone, should not live to pull down another, it was deemed best to treat with the defenders pacifically, and, in short, they saved the grand old Cathedral. This has been described by a master hand :—" Ah, it's a brave kirk, none o' yere whigmaleeries and curliewurlies and opensteek hems about it,—a' solid weel-jointed mason wark, that will stand as lang as the warld, keep hands and gunpowther aff it." Andrew Fairservice is perfectly right in his character of the pile ; it does indeed seem to defy all the ordinary processes of decay, and besides is pervaded by so awful an expression, that it may almost be entitled to the epithet sublime. This expression—made up of gloom and majesty—is not lessened by the ancient and irregular cemetery, crowded every inch with mementos of death, and bordered on one side with the broken battlemented wall, shown in the engraving, and on the other with a wild and sombre ravine, whose opposite bank exhibits the modern pillar and statue of John Knox, looking, says Mr. Chambers, like the " spirit of the reformer come back to inveigh, with outstretched arm, against the Cathedral, and, if possible, complete the work which he left unfinished at his death." The scene might be in a desert, so completely is the Cathedral isolated from the populous and flourishing city around.

The spirit of restoration has not left Glasgow unvisited ; and Köhl makes a striking reflection in connection with the recent repair of St. Kentigern's Cathedral. " It possesses," he observes, " the finest crypt in Great Britain. I regret I could not obtain a sight of it, on account of the repairs that were in progress, adding another to the hundreds and hundreds of public churches of Europe under repair and restoration in the year 1842. Ten years more, and Gothic Europe will stand around us as it stood in the fourteenth and fifteenth centuries." This crypt was used, from the time of the Reformation down to the beginning of the present century, as a church, called the Barony Kirk ; and the extraordinary aspect of the place will at once recur to every one's mind when it is remembered that it was the place where Rob Roy so mysteriously appointed the assignation with Frank Osbaldiston. And here, we may add, St. Kentigern was buried.

The Reformation in Scotland, which had so nearly caused the destruction of Glasgow Cathedral, spared one other building of the same kind, and only one—the Cathedral of ST. MAGNUS, at the seaport town of KIRKWALL (Fig. 1055), the capital of the Orkney Islands, and this pile too has become familiar to us through the writings of the great novelist, who has made the neighbourhood the scene of his romance of 'The Pirate,' and with happy propriety ; for the spot chosen may be said to have been dedicated from the very earliest period to the service of those who adopted on the largest scale the principle—

That they should take, who have the power,
And they should keep, who can.

The Orkneys formed the general rendezvous of the Danish pirates, and the Cathedral itself was founded by a Danish monarch, Olave. Rollo, Earl of Orkney, was the conqueror of Normandy, and the ancestor of the conqueror of England. It will be seen from the engraving that St. Magnus' is in excellent condition; it is still the parish church.

REDCLIFF CHURCH, Bristol (Fig. 1043), is still more closely identified with one of the great names of our national literature, Chatterton, a name so suggestive of melancholy considerations as to make us, to a certain degree, unfit for the contemplation of its more cheering and glorious ones, and which should chiefly occupy our attention. But, alas! we cannot do justice to the poetry, from the all-absorbing character of our recollections of the poet. Over every line and verse rests the awful shadow of the boy-suicide. It was on the steps of the porch of this church of Redcliff that Chatterton, as yet a child of eight or ten years of age, was accustomed to rehearse the first heirs of his invention to his playmates. It was in one of the towers in Redcliff Church that the parchments were found which first probably suggested to Chatterton the idea of issuing his poems in the garb of antiquity, such as he could easily borrow from those black-letter writings. It was in the aisles of Redcliff Church that he was generally found wandering about, or else seated by one of its tombs, that of Canynge, when missed for any extraordinary length of time by his mother and sister, engaged, no doubt, in developing more and more satisfactorily to himself his mighty scheme. Lastly, it was toward that same Redcliff Church that, even when absent, all his thoughts were directed; he could not stroll through the neighbouring meadows but he was most likely on some sudden impulse to turn, throw himself on the green sward, and there, fixing his eyes upon the venerable structure, remain lost, as one of his companions has described him, in a species of ecstasy. Poor Chatterton! it is difficult to say which was the unhappiest case: thine, involving a deception in which thou sawest no immorality, but which led to ruin; or the world's, which being deceived, saw, like Horace Walpole, no differences in deception—"All of the house of Forgery are relations"—and so treated the poet (and one of the proudest, because one of the poorest and most sensitive, of poets that ever trod the earth), who had deceived it *into* the possession of a body of the most glorious and original poetry, just as if he had juggled it out of the possession of a bundle of those "promissory notes" which Walpole so brutally, we might almost say infamously, dares to insinuate the poet's literary skill might have led him to fabricate. Walpole has been charged with Chatterton's death; that is cruel: heaven knows there rests enough on his memory in connexion with Chatterton without that imputation. "Oh ye," exclaimed Coleridge, reflecting on some of these things, "who honour the name of *man*, rejoice that this Walpole is called a *lord!*" The pile thus memorably connected with our poetical history is undoubtedly the finest parish church in England; and, indeed, possesses all the lofty beauty of a Cathedral. The erection was begun in the thirteenth century. One of the chief benefactors was Chatterton's Canynge, an eminent merchant of the reign of Edward the Fourth.

Among the more important churches erected in the period of which we treat, that of NEWCASTLE-UPON-TYNE holds an honourable place (Fig. 1052). It crowns a bold eminence, and forms from every point of view the chief ornament of the town. The founder was St. Osmond, Bishop of Salisbury; the time, the reign of William Rufus. Henry I. gave the church to the canons of Carlisle. It was burned in 1216, and rebuilt, as supposed, about 1359. The most remarkable feature is the steeple, two hundred and one feet high, erected in the reign of Henry VI., which is of the most elegant character, in the form of an imperial crown: the tall pinnacle is hollow, the stones only four inches broad: indeed, of such airy construction is the whole tower, that it has been observed, a man could carry with ease under his arm the largest stone contained in it. During a siege in 1644, a Scottish general threatened to destroy this steeple, unless the keys of the town were delivered to him. The people of Newcastle were sadly distressed between such alternatives, until their mayor ordered that some Scotch prisoners, who had been taken in the struggle for the mastery of the town, should be sent to the top of the steeple: "And then," said he, "our enemies shall either preserve it, or be buried in its ruins." There was no more talk of annihilating the steeple.

The tower of BOSTON CHURCH, Lincolnshire (Fig. 1044), if less graceful in its outlines, is still very beautiful, and of far greater height than St. Nicholas, rising as it does to three hundred feet. The top forms an elegant lantern, from which formerly issued the guiding or saving light for the mariners in the Boston and Lynn Deeps during the hours of darkness. The somewhat excessive height of the tower is owing to this particular use of it. The model from which this fine piece of architecture was taken was the tower of the

great church at Antwerp. No wealthy lord or prelate built the church at Boston; it originated in the pious feelings of its people. In 1309 the first stone was laid, and Margery Tilney put five pounds on it, two other persons the same, "and these were the largest sums given at that time." There is not a church in England without cross-aisles to be compared with Boston's for magnitude; it is at the same time well proportioned, and of capital masonry. The town was the ancient Icanhoe of Bede, where St. Botolph, a famous abbot of the seventh century, had a monastery.

A beacon-tower, of ruder fashion than that of old St. Botolph's, and used generally for less peaceful purposes, is to be seen at HADLEY CHURCH, Middlesex (Fig. 1048). "Before the reign of Edward III., beacons were but stacks of wood set up on high places, which were fired when the coming of enemies was descried; but in his reign pitch-boxes, as now they be, were, instead of those stacks, set up; and this properly is a beacon." (Lord Croke.) The pitch-box, or fire-pot, is still remaining at Hadley; and a picturesque object it is, reminding us of the warlike days when watches were regularly stationed at such places, and horsemen, called hobbelars, according to Camden, waited by, "to give notice in daytime of an enemy's approach, when the fire would not be seen." A perilous task these watches and hobbelars must have had of it, for of course it would be an object with the enemy to seize the beacons to prevent alarm spreading. Many a deadly fray that has left no record may have occurred on this tranquil and rural spot.

But worse even than such encounters, as bringing into play a thousand times worse passions, are those private feuds that often spring up where nature seems most peculiarly to invite to peace and love. One of these has given a bad reputation to the rural parish of CHILTON, Bucks. In the reign of Charles II., at the Aylesbury Assizes, Larimore, an Anabaptist preacher of Chilton, by the advice of Sir John Croke, grandson of the celebrated judge, and lord of Chilton manor, carried a bill of indictment against the incumbent of Chilton Church, Robert Hawkins, charging him with burglary on the house of Larimore, and with feloniously taking away, "by force and arms," two gold rings, one white holland apron, two pieces of gold, and nineteen shillings in silver. The judge was the good Lord Hale, whose presence lends great interest to the extraordinary trial that followed (see Knight's 'English Causes Célèbres'), and which at that day was one of life and death. It opened with a challenge of two jurymen by the parson, because he had been informed "they were no friends to the Church of England," whose cause he evidently considered bound up with his own. The Anabaptist made his case so clear and strong, in spite of the close questioning of the judge, and the cross-fire of the acute and undaunted parson, that before three witnesses had been heard, Lord Hale observed, "Here is enough sworn, if believed, to hang twenty men." "I doubt not to clear myself, notwithstanding their evidence, if I may but be heard," stoutly rejoined the parson. "You *shall* be heard," said Lord Hale. Still, with all the ready logic and tact of the parson, the case grew darker and darker; his life seemed not worth a straw. But at this most critical point the scale began to turn—malice on account of a lawsuit began to appear among the prosecutor's motives. An honest fellow sent to witness that the parson stole a pair of boots of him, took the judge and court by surprise; showing that from the time of the parson pressing for tithes, the lord of the manor and his son, the Anabaptist, and several farmers and yeomen of Chilton, sought by persuasion and threats to make him swear falsely against the parson. Other exposures as striking followed: and, in short, by the time Hawkins began his sermon-like defence, regularly divided, and formal in its inductions, few could have had a doubt of his having been the victim of one of the most atrocious conspiracies that ever disgraced humanity, and which thus originated;—"I was," says Hawkins, "entertained by Mr. John Croke, of the parish of Chilton, in the county of Bucks, Baronet, to attend as chaplain in his house, and also to serve the cure of the said parish, for which he did, under his hand and seal, promise to pay me fifty pounds per annum, he being impropriator of the said parish, and to pay it by quarterly payments. When I had faithfully performed my duty in both these capacities above two years, and in all that time had received no money from him, but upon some occasions had lent him several sums out of my pocket, at last I was somewhat urgent with him for money; and then he told me plainly, that I did not know him as yet, for he had cheated all persons he had ever dealt with, and I must not expect to speed better than they had done. I told him I hoped for better things from him; but he replied, that he never intended to pay me any money, and that therefore I might take my course." Hawkins did take his course—up to London; where he found the baronet had been outlawed on account of debt, his manor

1125.—The Prioress and the Wife of Bath.

1126.—The Franklin and the Merchant.

1127.—Female Costume, time of Richard II.
(Royal MS. 16 G. 7., and Harleian MS 4379.)

1128.—Ladies' Head-dresses   (Royal MS. 15 D. ii.)

1129.—Female Costume, time of Edward III.
(Royal MS. 19 D. ii)

1130.—Miller, Manciple, and Reeve.

1131.—The Ploughman and Shipman.

1135.—Ladies' Costume, time of Edward I. (Sloane MS. 3983.)

1136.—Head-dresses, time of Edward II. (Royal MS. 14 E. iii)

1132.—Carpenter, Haberdasher, Weaver Dyer, and Tapestry maker.

1137.—Female Dress, time of Edward II. (Sloane MS. 346.)

1138.—Male Costume, time of Edward III. (Royal 19 D. ii., and Strutt.)

1139.—Male Costume time of Richard II. (Royal MS. 20 B. vi., and Harleian MS. 1319.)

1133.—The Host and the Cook.

1131.—Sumpnour and Pardoner.

of Chilton extended into the king's hands, and a lease of the rectory granted to the creditors who had pursued him. This lease they re-granted to Hawkins, to pay him for his spiritual services, who then went back to Sir John Croke, offering to deliver it up if he would pay what was due. The baronet, however, set him at defiance, per-suaded his tenants to do the same, and so lawsuits began against Larimore and others, who in return joined with the baronet in the nefarious scheme thus happily exposed. The last witness examined was a King's Bench officer, who had had Sir John in charge, and who, when asked what he had to say, said he dared not speak on ac-count of the threats that had been used. When he did speak, under the judge's protection, he said he had overheard a private conversa-tion between Sir John and the Anabaptist, in the course of which the following conversation took place:—Larimore remarked, " The parson is too hard for us still." Sir John replied, " If thou wilt but act, I will hatch enough to hang Hawkins." " But how shall we bring this to pass?" asked Larimore. " Canst thou not convey some gold or silver into Hawkins' house, and have a warrant ready to search; and then our work is done?" The worthy baronet, after some further instructions concluded—" Charge him with flat felony—and force him before me, and no other justice—and I'll send him to gaol without bail, and we'll hang him at the next assizes." Judge Hale seems to have been perfectly appalled with these revelations. " Come, come, Larimore, thou art a very villain: nay, I think thou art a devil," said he. Presently he added, addressing the justices—" Gentlemen, where is this Sir John Croke?" They said he was gone. " Is Sir John Croke gone? Gentlemen, I must not forget to acquaint you (for I had thought Sir John Croke had been here still), that this Sir John Croke sent me this morning two sugarloaves for a present, praying me to excuse his absence yesterday." Of course the judge had sent them back. With the loaves came also a letter, which the judge produced from his breast. The result was the entire acquittal of Hawkins, who obtained compensation from his enemies, and that Sir John Croke was deprived of his commission of the peace. He afterwards sold his ancestral manor of Chilton, and died in poverty and disgrace. His only son, Sir Dodsworth Croke, also concerned in the plot, reached old age, and died in great destitution. He was the last of a family that had come in at the Conquest under the name of Blount, and which is traceable to still more remote periods in a great Italian race. Some of their mailed effigies are still in the old parish church of Chilton. (Fig. 1050.)

The trial of the Chilton parson furnishes an example of the romantic incidents often to be found linked with our rural parish churches and the country gentry. We have not much of this to boast in the next village church which our artist has engraved for us (Fig. 1045). Yet STONE CHURCH associates itself with several important Kentish families, and more especially with those who have successively been the owners, through some five centuries, of Stone Castle. In the last reign but one (Edward III.) of the period whose remains we have at present under review, Sir John de North-wood held the castle, and about that time, or the previous reign, when the second form of the Gothic, the Decorated, was displacing the Early English, this church was built in the place of an earlier one, founded probably in Saxon times. In 995 we find Stone given by King Ethelred to the church and see of Rochester, and the bishops often resided here afterwards. To that see the manor of Stone still belongs. In Stone Church we have a good deal of the trefoil, quatrefoil, rose, and other ornaments of the decorated Gothic. Fig. 1047 exhibits another beautiful feature, tall and slender columns linked by light and elegant arches, dividing the nave from its two aisles. The chancel is seen through a single arch of the same graceful form. Traceried arches on each side show the circular figure which is so common in the Early English style. A more flowing tracery prevails in the windows, especially the large east one. Round the chancel runs a low range of trefoil, headed arches, in relief, springing from slight pillars of grey marble. The door-head in Fig. 1046 presents a cluster of rich mouldings one within the other. The tower is extremely curious for its scientific construction. Not to mar the lightness of the nave and aisles, it is open beneath on three sides, which rest on arches. At the same time, to give it stability, the fourth side is solid from the foundation of the church, supported by two graduated buttresses of considerable strength and projection, and by two light and elegant flying buttresses that shoot directly athwart the north and south aisles. Such tact and precision are evinced in the design and execution of the tower, that it has been from the first, is, and is likely to remain, immovable and solid as any piece of Gothic work-manship in the land. The chapel adjoining the chancel was built

by a lord of Stone Castle of the reign of Henry VII. Sir John Willshyre, Knt., comptroller of the town and marches of Calais. He and his lady were interred under a rich altar-tomb, with an arched recess behind, where, in addition to niches and other orna-mental work, there is a cornice of grapes and vine-leaves, and the arms of Sir John and Dame Margaret.

In Gough's 'Sepulchral Monuments' is engraved a remarkable brass in Stone Church. Such memorials, we may take this occasion to observe, were but in very partial use before the middle of the present period; after that they rapidly became general among all ranks, were often extremely elaborate in point of ornament, and of elegant design. The brass in the chancel of Stone Church is inlaid in a slab in the pavement, about six feet in length. The figure represents a priest in his canonical vestments standing in the centre of a cross composed of eight trefoil arches, and adorned with vine-leaves. The stem of the cross rises from four steps, and on it is a Latin inscription. Another inscription is on a scroll over the priest's head; and a third round the face of the arches. The whole is about to be completely restored. We are happy to see this very beautiful and appropriate architectural decoration coming again into use. Among the other services of the Cambridge Camden Society, this especially demands grateful mention.

Quitting for the present the fertile and pleasing subject of village antiquities, we can only give a passing glance to one feature that is occasionally presented to our notice, the ancient canopy over the rustic churchyard gate, beneath whose cover the dead brought for interment used to be set down to rest awhile. Such is the one at Beckenham (Fig. 1035), in the same county with Stone; they were called *lich*-gates, *lich* signifying a " corpse."

The county town of Elgin was one of the most noted Scottish towns of Saxon and Norman times for its monks and friars, and ecclesiastical establishments, to say nothing of its royal fort. It was in the diocese of Moray; and Bishop Andrew Moray, or *of* Moray, early in the thirteenth century received instructions from Pope Honorius to build a new cathedral for that diocese, in consequence of requests that had been made to his Holiness. The situation pointed out was at Spynie, a mile and a half northward from the present ruin. This did not please Bishop Andrew, for, as he care-fully represented to the Pope, all the provisions for that part of the country were to be had at Elgin; and if the establishment were at Spynie, the canons would be put to inconvenience to fetch their provisions from the former place. Pope Honorius felt the full force of the objection, and Elgin was the place fixed upon, and there, in 1224, the first stone was laid of a building to be called, " in all time coming," the cathedral church of the diocese of Moray. That edifice did not long exist; a bishop of the next century, Alexander Barr, had lands in Badenoch, which were seized by the freebooting and ferocious lord " the Wolf of Badenoch," whose rank as a prince (he was a son of Alexander II. of Scotland) rendered it difficult for the bishop to obtain redress. The spiritual sword was resorted to: the lord of Badenoch was excommunicated; a punishment that only served to stimulate him to phrensy, and set him, in the summer of 1390, burning and wasting all before him. The town of Forres, situated twelve miles from Elgin, including its manse and church, was first laid in ruins, and then Elgin itself, its cathedral, the church of Maison Dieu, and eighteen houses of canons and chaplains. After this sweeping revenge, in which the Wolf of Badenoch seemed to have fully expended his rage and animosity against the bishop, he cooled down, began to see that all he could do was, after all, as nothing compared with the terrors of the Church, and so he submitted himself to a public declaration of penitence, and humbly received absolution at the hands of Walter Trail, bishop of St. Andrews, in Blackfriars Church at Perth. The Bishop of Moray immediately began rebuilding ELGIN CA-THEDRAL (Fig. 1059), which was finished in about twenty years, and resembled Lichfield Cathedral, excepting that it was far more extensive and elaborate; indeed few finer structures, for symmetry, loftiness, or sculpture, adorned the palmiest days of Catholic Scotland. The cause of its decay was the stripping off the lead which covered it, in 1568, by the Regent Morton, in order to raise money for the payment of his troops. The judgment of God, it was said, lighted on the ship in which the lead of Elgin and Aberdeen Cathedrals was to be conveyed to Holland. Scarce had it left the coast of Scotland, when vessel, cargo, and crew went to the bottom of the sea. Elgin Cathedral had originally five towers; the main one fell on Easter Sunday, 1711, with a mighty crash. A few minutes before, a crowd of persons had been standing close by, and it seemed almost miraculous that no one was hurt. The two largest remain-ing towers command a delightful prospect. The churchyard is very large, and peculiarly suggestive of historical memories on account of the Scottish kings and chieftains who lie buried in it. The college attached to the cathedral had walls extending nine hundred yards, in which were four gates. The houses and gardens of the bishop and twenty-two canons stood within the area. The gateway left in part of the wall had formerly an iron gate, portcullis, and watchman's lodge.

At KILDARE, in Ireland, still remain the relics of a small building in which, previous to the thirteenth century, the holy fire of St. Brigid used to be kept burning. It was suppressed at that period by Henry de Loundres, Archbishop of Dublin, a man who seemed to rise above many of the superstitions of his age. After his death it was revived, and only ceased at the Reformation. One of the popular saint's disciples, Conlæth, under St. Brigid's directions, founded, in the beginning of the sixth century, the ancient cathedral of Kildare (Fig. 1060), of which the choir only is now in use, the nave and transepts having been completely ruined in the civil wars of the seventeenth century. The successor to St. Conlæth in the bishop's throne was Aodh Dubh, who had been previously an abbot and a monk, and king of Leinster. The history of this ancient see is almost a blank from the days of the kingly recluse to 1272, when Simon of Kilkenny died, and a dispute concerning the succession left the see vacant seven years. Pope Nicholas III. put an end to the quarrel by nominating Nicholas Cusack. William Miagh succeeded in 1540; who seems to have done individually what the nation did collectively—halt between two opinions, but verging nearer to Protestantism than Catholicism. The next bishop, Thomas Lancaster, consecrated by Browne, Archbishop of Dublin, in July, 1550, was altogether Protestant. But the Reformed Church has not profited much in any way by the acquisition of Kildare. The second Protestant bishop, Alexander Craik, shamefully and absurdly alienated the diocese lands and manors to one Sarsfield, taking in return nothing but tithes of scarcely any worth. The poverty of the see in consequence, the absence of any suitable residence for the bishop, and the very great disproportion between the number of Catholics and Protestants, there being on a fair average eight of the former to one of the latter, naturally led the way to the enactment of William IV., that at the next vacancy Kildare should be united to the see of Dublin, and that the deanery of Christ Church, and the Preceptory of Tully, which Kildare had held since 1681, on account of its impoverished condition, should vest in the Ecclesiastical Commissioners. We may observe, in conclusion, that if the establishment of Kildare has for some time taught little that is in accordance with the religious faith of the inhabitants, it must at least be entitled to some credit among them for its educational exertions, ranking eighth among the thirty-two dioceses of Ireland in that respect.

Not all the admirable works of benevolence, piety, and art which the people of England during the present period owed to Catholicism, could sustain its wondrous hierarchy in the proud position it occupied at the close of the last. Step by step through every reign we can trace its retrograde progress. The statute *circumspecte agatis* of 13 Edward I. established a firm settlement of the limits of the hitherto oppressive ecclesiastical courts—the statute of Westminster the First made ecclesiastics guilty of crimes amenable to temporal judges, and gave the crown the control of their property—the first Statute of Mortmain restrained that grand source of the Church's acquisition of wealth, the making over of lands to it by the laity—another statute of the same vigorous and fearless monarch cut away all the host of benevolences and tributes by which Rome had impoverished this country; and though Edward II. cared little whether his subjects were in subjection to Rome or not, his parliament carried forward the perilous work. One of the principal charges made against Edward at his deposition was, that he had given allowance to the bulls of the see of Rome (Fig. 1066). Edward III. was fashioned more after his grandsire's mould; he at first tried calm expostulations, to which his Holiness replied menacingly and contemptuously, informing him that the emperor of Germany and the king of France had lately submitted to the Holy See. Edward then took another tone, and apprised the pontiff, that if both the emperor and the French king should take his part, he (King Edward) was ready to give battle to them all, in defence of the liberties of his crown. And he followed this characteristic speech by equally characteristic acts. Citations of the king or any of his subjects to the court of Rome were immediately declared unlawful, and several penalties attached to them, for all over whom our crown had any power; no English priest was permitted to accept a benefice by any foreign provision; no one

was to aid papal interference with English presentations; and the crowning assumption of Rome since the reign of King John, that England was her vassal and bound to pay her annual rent, was put an end to at last, by the declaration made solemnly by parliament, that John's disgraceful surrender of his kingdom was null and void. Finally, under the last reign (Richard II.), there was added to all the other edicts for the assertion and security of our temporal rights against the encroachments of the Romish power, the famous Statute of Premunire. Thus far Rome had contested every inch of ground, but had been fairly defeated, because England was at unity with herself, and determined on shaking off the yoke. But now, a new kind of opposition arose, still further to injure the Roman Catholic church. The temporal power only hitherto had been attacked, men now stepped forth to attack its spiritual conduct and principles; these were Wickliffe and Wickliffe's disciples. And the country was soon deeply agitated by the news that Wickliffe had been cited before the Bishop of London, and delegates sent from the Pope "expressly to inquire into the matter." What was intended by this inquiry seemed to be well understood, and the people, to whom martyrdom for religious opinions was yet new, rallied for the protection of Wickliffe. Princes and nobles also took the alarm. The delegates must have seen at once there was nothing to be done at St. Paul's, when the offender arrived attended by two such friends as John of Gaunt and Percy, Lord Marshal. In order to be more private, another council was held at Lambeth Palace (Fig. 1064). The council took place, but they were disappointed in regard to the privacy. The proceeding was too awful in its character and probable consequences for the sagacious and free-spirited citizens of London and others of the commons to permit it to reach a conclusion without their voices being heard. They forced themselves into the archbishop's chapel, where the council sate, "to speak," says Walsingham drily, "on Dr. Wickliffe's behalf." The delegates were startled by these determined and self-appointed advocates. And if a doubt remained in their minds concerning what course they should take, that doubt was fully dispelled by the arrival of Sir Lewis Clifford from the queen-mother, peremptorily forbidding them to proceed to any definitive sentence. Then, "as the reed of a wind shaken, their speech became as soft as oil, to the public loss of their own dignity, and the damage of the whole Church. They were struck with such a dread, that you would think them to be as a man that heareth not, and in whose mouth are no reproofs." (Walsingham.) And so the council broke up in most admired disorder, Wickliffe for form sake being commanded to put forth no more such propositions in his sermons, or in the schools, as those he had presented in writing to the council. The baffled delegates and the leading English clergy at the same time must have been fully aware that the obnoxious propositions (especially the leading one, that the Bible is the only infallible rule of faith) had already spread far and near,—perhaps had instinctively guessed that the result would be the loosening of the very roots of Catholicism in England. To the alarm thus engendered we may no doubt attribute the immediate preparations that were made to check the movement, and which failing, were only pursued with the greater eagerness and intensity, until what was intended for a wholesome spiritual correction became savage ferocity, and ended in the sacrificial horrors of the fifteenth and sixteenth centuries. Archbishop Chicheley's Lollards' Tower was attached to Lambeth Palace very soon after Wickliffe's sudden death. We need not inquire the purpose of its uppermost room, planked all over, ceiling, walls, and floor—the eight rings riveted in the wall inform us but too plainly; we need not ask why those doors and their frameworks are so massy and strong; and we can even dimly surmise the mysterious purposes of the Post Room, with its stout central pillar, that forms the lower story, and from which we ascend to the Lollards' dungeon by the same stairs which so many of the noble army of English martyrs have ascended before us: the door (Fig. 1065) stands open which proved to numbers the confines of life and death. In the next period we shall have to speak of the deeds of some of the heroic men for whom all these things were made ready.

"I well remember," says Pennant, "the street on London Bridge [removed gradually during the last century], noisome, darksome, and dangerous to passengers from the multitude of carriages; frequent arches of strong timber crossed the street from the tops of the houses, to keep them together, and from falling into the river. Nothing but use could preserve the repose of the inmates, who soon grew deaf to the noise of falling waters, the clamours of watermen, or the frequent shrieks of drowning wretches." How potent this "use" was we have an instance in Nichols's 'Literary Anecdotes.' Mr. Baldwin, a haberdasher, who

1140.—Library Chair, Reading Table, and Reading Desk
(Royal MS. 15 D. iii.)

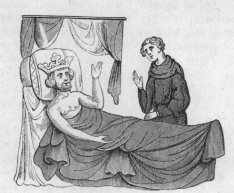

1141.—Bed. (Royal MS. 14 E. iii.)

1142.—Bed. (Royal MS. 15 D. iii.)

1143.—Mummers. (Bodleian MS.)

1144.—Quarter-staff. (From the old Ballad of Robin Hood
and the Tanner.)

1145.—Playing at Draughts. (Harleian MS. 4431.)

1146.—Chair. (Royal MS. 14 E. iii.)

1147.—Hand-Organ or Dulcimer, and Violin.
(Royal MS. 14 E. iii.)

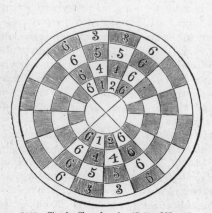

1148.—Circular Chess-board. (Cotton MS. and
Strutt.)

The Figures show the places of the Pieces:—1, The
King—2, The Queen, or Fevee—3, The Castle,
Rook, or Rock—4, The Knight—5, The Bishop
or Alfin—6, The Pawns.

1149.—Hand-Bells. (Royal MS. 15 D. iii.)

1152—Great Seal of Henry IV.

1153.—Henry IV. (From the Tomb at Canterbury.)

1154.—Signature of Henry IV., consisting of the initials H. R. (for Henricus Rex)
(From Cotton MS. Vesp. F. xiv.)

1150.—The Coronation of Henry IV.

1155.— Queen Joan of Navarre, second Wife of Henry IV. (From the Tomb at Canterbury.)

1151.—Coronation of Henry IV. (Harleian MS. No. 4679.)

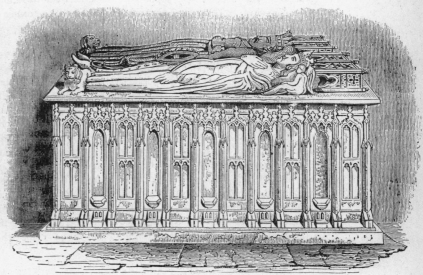

1156.—Tomb of Henry IV. and his Queen, at Canterbury Cathedral.

was born in a house that had been built over the ancient chapel of St. Thomas-à-Becket on the bridge, and lived in it all his life, being ordered, at the age of seventy-one, to go to the country for a change of air, could not sleep " for want of the roaring lullaby that he had been always used to hear." The same Baldwin, or Yaldwin, discovered the remains of the tomb of Peter of Colechurch, the original architect of London Bridge, who died in 1205, three or four years before his great work was fully completed. The tomb was found under a staircase which Mr. Baldwin was repairing. It is singular no curiosity should have been felt to search for the body. Peter, curate of St. Mary, Colechurch, is one of the few of the great ecclesiastical architects of the middle ages of whom any record, however brief, has been preserved. He built a London Bridge of wood, before that celebrated one of stone which rendered him famous, and both were preceded by others which were successively swept away by battle, flood, or fire. There used to be a popular saying that Peter of Colechurch's London Bridge was built upon woolpacks, because its cost was defrayed by a tax upon wool. That bridge came to be the scene of many of the most stirring events of English history, some of which we shall have hereafter to refer to. In the insurrection of 1381, Sir William Walworth, Mayor of London, anticipating the arrival of Wat Tyler, and his commons of Kent, fortified the bridge, raised the drawbridge (which formed one of the arches), and fastened a great chain of iron across. "Then the commons of Surrey, who were risen with others, cried to the wardens of the bridge to let it down and give them entry, whereby they might pass, or else they would destroy them all : whereby they were constrained by fear to let it down and give them entry, at which time the religious [of the chapel] present were earnest in procession and prayer." The insurgents were not deterred, it seems, by the terrible spectacle of decapitated heads stuck on poles over the Traitor's-gateway Tower, which formed another of the singular characteristics of the ancient bridge. Over that Traitor's Gate the noble features of William Wallace long blackened in the wind, accompanied by others perhaps as little deserving such a situation. The shocking exhibition was kept up as late as the Restoration. We do not read that the peace of the realm suffered in consequence of its cessation. It might be that some spectacles, only less shocking, of our own day, might be discontinued with as little harm.

We have thus slightly noticed some of the most interesting of the features of Old London Bridge, for the sake of the chapel on the tenth or centre arch, Peter of Colechurch's burial-place, and which was built with and perished at the same time as the bridge. Our engravings (Figs. 1061, 1062) represent the ancient appearance of its interior, and the changed form of its exterior in the last century. The lower chapel, or crypt, was twenty feet high, with vaulted roof and clustered columns, in beautiful Early English style. The ranges of windows in both the upper and lower chapels looked out over the river. The crypt was last used as a paper-warehouse, and although at high-water mark the floor was always from ten to twelve feet under the surface, yet such was the excellence of the materials and the masonry, that not the least damp or leak ever happened, and the paper was kept as safe and dry as it would have been in a garret." (Smith's 'Ancient Topography of London,' 1701.) A fish-pond, grated over, had been made in the sterling of the long pier on which the chapel stood. When the tide was over the sterling, the fish were carried in at the bars, and at ebb they were left in the pool. Persons used to go down through the chapel to fish in this pond. The last transformation the chapel underwent, some time before its final destruction, was the shrouding the upper part under brickwork and boarding, whilst a crane for taking in goods from the river for the paper-warehouse assisted to render the lower chapel of St. Thomas-à-Becket as unlike itself in former times as anything could well be.

Architectural details and changes, even of an order so interesting to the imagination as the Gothic, will better please unprofessional readers, and be more clearly understood by them, in our pictorial representations than in any written descriptions. We will not bewilder them, therefore, in technical phrases, or presumptuously attempt in these pages to impart a knowledge which can only be the fruit of careful study of the science. A few hints only will be requisite as explanatory of the engravings to convey a general understanding of the progress of art in the thirteenth and fourteenth centuries. And first it will be necessary to bear in mind that the historical periods into which this work is divided are *not* the periods of its architecture. For instance, in the century we have now to treat of, we have the close of the First Pointed style, the Early English, or Lancet, extending through the reign of Edward I.; the whole of

the Second Pointed style, or Decorated, which lasted through the reigns of Edward II. and III.; and the beginning of the Perpendicular, that thoroughly English style, commencing with Richard II. And of all these reigns that of Edward III. produced works in the highest state of perfection—works which, the more they are investigated, inspire delight, wonder, and reverence, so bold and lofty are the principles of their composition found to be, so rich the fancy lavished on them, and so surpassing the skill with which those principles and that fancy have been embodied in the inert material. We proceed now to show the more obvious transitions of the art from the First Pointed Style to the beautiful Decorated, leaving the Perpendicular to the next period, to which it properly belongs. In the first place, the pointed arch, itself, which had been too narrow, too sharp at the point, and ungracefully turned (with exceptions, of course), became now of the most exquisite outlines and proportion; then the upper part of the arch in windows grew generally more superb. If the reader will take the trouble to observe the gradual elaboration of the ten examples of window arches given in Fig. 1089, it may easily be comprehended how the length of the clustered column came to be better proportioned to the rise of the arch, and more beautifully modelled; how the bow of the arch slowly expanded into perfect ease and grace, and how it came to be filled up with exquisite flowing tracery, and edged and finished with an endless variety of ornaments. If from the windows we turn to the four specimens of tombs (Figs. 1068, 1069, 1073, 1074), and recall to mind the example we gave of the simple sarcophagus, with scarcely any ornament and no canopy, that prevailed towards the close of the last period, no difficulty will be felt in comprehending how much had since been done in this great branch of Old English art. The different forms of tombs succeeded each other in something like the following order :—coffin-shaped stones, prismatic and plain at top ; the same, prismatic and carved at top, with crosses plain or otherwise ; altar-tombs, sometimes with, sometimes without effigy or effigies ; and then the same with the tester or arch over it, with vine or oaken foliage. Archbishop Grey's tomb (Fig. 1068) shows the next advance; he died in 1225. The altar-tomb or table is lower than it afterwards became ; the figure of the archbishop is in pontificals, stretched upon it. The canopy is composed of arches, pinnacles, and other Gothic ornaments, rather heavy on the whole. The tombs of Aymer de Valence, 1324 (Fig. 1073), and of Hugh le Despenser, 1359 (Fig. 1074), display the canopy over the altar-tomb in its full perfection. Both evince extraordinary splendour and originality of imagination. We are never weary of admiring in the one (that of Valence) the free span of the main arch, the bold and singular variations of the subordinate arches, the gorgeous gable, the spear-like pinnacles that taper upwards from airy buttresses, the mixture of heraldic devices and sculpture (especially the graceful little group mourning at the head of the earl), and the high finish of every part. In the other canopy we have an assemblage of open arches in four tiers, and scarce know which to praise the most, the novelty of the design, the lightness of the effect, the flowing curves, the exquisite proportioning of each to each, or the fairy-like adorning. The poet Gower's monument (Fig. 1069) was built in 1408, after the decorated Gothic had passed into the third style, called the Perpendicular. We have already described it in connection with the beautiful church that contains it, St. Mary Overies. This class of tombs is chiefly to be found in cathedrals, in small chapels, with the accompaniments of piscinas, niches, altar monuments, &c. Finally, many tombs of this period were, as has been previously observed, inlaid with brass (Figs. 1087, 1089), having inscriptions in cameo or intaglio. Gough, in his ' Sepulchral Monuments,' mentions one in the choir of St. Margaret's church at Lynn, " So highly finished and so exquisitely embellished, that one knows not what censure to pass on those tasteless topographers who content themselves with a hasty transcript of its epitaph. . . . . . This admirable brass, the execution of some Cellini of the fourteenth century, is a monument of a burgess of one of our most commercial and opulent boroughs. The inscription, in Gothic letters round the verge, sets forth that Robert Braunche and his two wives Letitia and Margaret are buried under it, and that he died October 15, 1364." Beside the usual decorations, there is represented, under three principal figures, a feast (Fig. 1088), that " for the splendour of the table and company, the band of music and attendants, might pass for some grand anniversary celebrated in the wealthy town, perhaps the feast of St. Margaret, their patroness, or the fair-day granted them by King John, or perhaps the Mayor's feast, when Mr. Braunche held that office, 1349 or 1359. He may be seated at the upper end or right hand of the plate, and the aldermen and their wives in a row below him.

In confirmation of this last conjecture one might even fancy one sees, among other decorations of the table, the silver cup which King John had presented to the town at his last visit, 1216, above a century before. Among the delicacies of this splendid table one sees the *peacock*, that *noble bird*, the *food of lovers* and the *meat of lords* (such are the epithets bestowed on it by romance writers). Few dishes were in higher fashion in the thirteenth century, and there was scarcely any royal or noble feast without it. They stuffed it with spices and sweet herbs, and covered the head with a cloth, which was kept constantly wetted to preserve the crown. They roasted it and served it up whole, covered after dressing with the skin and feathers, the comb entire, and the tail spread. Some persons covered it with leaf gold, instead of its skin, and put a piece of cotton dipped in spirits into its beak, to which they set fire as they put it on the table. The honour of serving it up was reserved for the ladies most distinguished for birth, rank, or beauty, one of whom, followed by others and attended by music, brought it up in the gold or silver dish, and set it before the master of the house, or the guest most distinguished for his courtesy or valour; or, after a tournament, before the victorious knight, who was to display his skill in carving the favourite fowl, and take an oath of valour and enterprise on its head. The romance of 'Lancelot,' adopting the manners of the age in which it was written, represents King Arthur doing this office to the satisfaction of five hundred guests. A picture by Stevens, engraved by L'Empereur, represents a peacock-feast. M. d'Aussy had seen an old piece of tapestry of the thirteenth century representing the same subject, which he could not afterwards recover to engrave in his curious history of the 'Private Life of the French.' It may flatter the vanity of an English historian to find this desideratum here supplied.

We have mentioned pinnacles, piscinas, and niches. All these, as well as the capitals of the pillars (Figs. 1071, 1072), partook of the same spirit of progress as we have seen manifested in windows and tombs. The first of our three specimens of pinnacles (Fig. 1075) shows the period when they were rare and plain : the second and third, when they shot up at the sides of almost every arch, and on the top of every buttress, and when, enlarged in size and added to the square tower, they became lofty and beautiful spires that seemed to point to heaven, and so formed a singularly appropriate and striking ornament, which gave the last finish to the Christian Church of the middle ages. The Latin word piscina is used to indicate a stone basin for the holy water ; it was a cavity in a niche, generally near an altar, for the use of the priest previous to the celebration of mass, &c. It was furnished with a pipe to carry off waste water. (Figs. 1077, &c.) The plain niches of the thirteenth century became gorgeous tabernacles in the fourteenth (Fig. 1076), and were filled with statuary, executed often with consummate art.

1158.—King with his Privy Council. (Harleian MS. No. 4379.)

1157.—English Ships of War of the Fifteenth Century. (Harleian MS. 4374 and 4379.)

1159.—A Parliament of the time of Henry V. (Harleian MS. No. 2278.)

1163.—Henry of Monmouth.

1165.—Sir W. Gascoigne.

1160.—Ancient Gateway of Queen's College, Oxford.

1162.—Portrait of Owen Glendower. (From his Great Seal, engraved in the Archæologia.)

1164.—Richard II. knighting Henry of Monmouth.

1161.—Earl of Westmoreland.

1166.—Southampton.

1167.—The English Fleet.

1169.—Street in Harfleur.

1168.—Entry of Henry V into London.

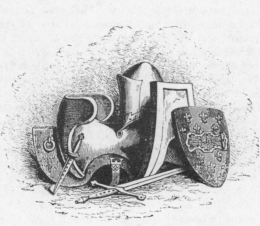

1170.—Helmet, Shield, and Saddle of Henry V.

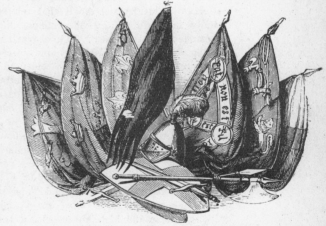

1171.—Banners used in the Battle of Agincourt.

1172.—Archbishop Chicheley.

1173.—Henry V. being armed by his Esquires.

1174.—Montacute, Earl of Salisbury.

1175.—Sir Thomas Erpingham.

No. 40.

CHAPTER III.—POPULAR ANTIQUITIES.

N directing our attention to the Manners and Customs of the period under review, Chivalry again first demands notice: for although a system built up as it were for war, it was not, like our military system, a mere blank as regards domestic life in time of peace. The warrior of the middle ages was still a warrior, though for a time he had left the battle-field for the family hall; with the difference, that whereas in the one case he fought, in the other he was always to a certain degree preparing for fighting. If he read, his book was tolerably certain to be some romance of chivalry; if he interfered in the education of his children, it was almost literally to teach the young idea how to shoot; his sports were mostly but so many military exercises; to him if peace had its victories as well as war, it was only in the tilting-match (Figs. 1102), or in the tournament, with all its "pomp and circumstance" (Figs. 1096, 1103), that he found them. All this was at once necessary to, and a consequence of, the system. Success in battle then depended in a very great degree on the personal and individual skill, courage, and prowess of the knights and other men of rank among the combatants, and to develop these qualities therefore was the primary object of the whole social system of feudalism: on the other hand, the opportunities afforded for display and for obtaining reputation were a continual incentive to men to admire and carry out most vigorously the system they submitted to. All this was to be changed, though gradually, by the appearance of the terrible engines of war—cannon, which are said to have been used at the battle of Cressy, and of which one of the earliest forms is shown in our engraving (Fig. 1097).

We have already had occasion to speak of Froissart as the historian of Chivalry and of all that relates to it, and have incidentally furnished various illustrations, chiefly from his pages, of its manners and customs. The engraving of Froissart and Sir Espaing de Lyon (Fig. 1090) reminds us of the indefatigable zeal and industry which the historian added to his other accomplishments for the labour of love he had undertaken. We behold him there on his way to the court of Gaston de Foix, or, as he was called for his manly beauty and love of hunting, Gaston Phœbus, one of the last of a now extinct class in Europe, the sovereign nobles, who enjoyed every kingly privilege and power but the name. Froissart thus relates his motives in commencing this journey:— "Considering in myself how there was no great deeds by arms likely toward in the parts of Picardy or Flanders, and seeing that peace were made between the Duke and them of Ghent, and it greatly annoyed me to be idle; for I knew well that after my death this noble and high history should have his course, wherein divers noble men should have great pleasure and delight: and as yet, I thank God, I have understanding and remembrance of all things past, and my wit quick and sharp enough to conceive all things showed unto me touching my principal matter; and my body is yet able to endure and suffer pain; all things considered, I thought I would not let [cease] to pursue my said first purpose; and to the intent to know the truth of deeds done in far countries, I found occasion to go to the high and mighty prince, Gaston, Earl of Foix and Béarn. For I well knew that if I might have that grace to come into his house, and to be there at my leisure, I could not be so well informed of my purpose in none other place of the world. For thither resorted all manner of knights and strange squires for the great nobleness of the said earl." On his way he fell into company with Sir Espaing de Lyon, a knight attached to the Earl of Foix, and a very pleasant and valuable meeting it was for Froissart, for he received from Sir Espaing a world of information, not only as to the character of the great man he was going to visit, but as to history (often most eventful) of the places through which lay their route. One little specimen of their conversation must

suffice. As they passed a ruined castle, the knight observes, "The Count of Foix on a night sent his brother, Peter de Béarn, with two hundred spears, and with them four hundred villains [the knight of course speaks in a social, not in a moral sense] of the county, charged with fagots, much wood, and torches; and they brought it to the bastide, and then set fire thereon, and so burnt the bastide, and all them that was therein, without mercy; and since it was never made again." Froissart was received by Gaston de Foix in a most kindly and liberal spirit, excited evidently by the simple consideration that the guest was a man of letters. As a kind of literary bonne-bouche the prudent historian had brought with him a book of songs, ballads, rondeaux, and virelays, the product of the Duke of Bohemia's leisure hours, and collected by himself as the duke's protégé, and this book De Foix was especially glad to see. "Every night after supper," says Froissart, "I read therein to him; and while I read there was none durst speak any word, because he would I should be well understood; whereat he took great solace" (Fig. 1091).

One of the most minute and in every way complete descriptions of a great noble of the middle ages, is Froissart's account of the appearance, character, and habits of Gaston de Foix: it is too long for us to transcribe here; we will only observe, therefore, that the limitation with which all Froissart's statements must be received as to the virtues of the heroes of chivalry, are nowhere more indispensable than here. One can hardly believe that the man whom he characterizes as in everything so perfect that he could not be praised too much, who loved that which ought to be loved, and hated that which ought to be hated, is the same man of whose cruelty to his son, a mere boy, he elsewhere relates so piteous a narration.

The interesting incident that forms the subject of another of our engravings (Fig. 1094) we borrow from the same writer's account of the campaign of the Black Prince in Spain, who went thither to assist Pedro, or Peter the Cruel, to regain the throne he had lost by his misdeeds, and which was occupied by his half-brother Enrique or Henry. The latter, at the head of a large army, advanced to meet the combined army of the English and their allies, and on the evening of the 2nd of April, 1366, the combatants confronted each other before Najara, which is situated a few miles from the banks of the Ebro. The battle did not commence till the following morning, when the armies advanced towards each other just as the "sun was rising up," and a great beauty, Froissart says, it was to behold the battalions and the armour shining against the sun. It was when all was prepared, that the event we have referred to occurred. Sir John Chandos, whose name as a knight and a commander is only a little less famous than his sovereign's, and his sovereign's son's, the Black Prince, "brought his banner rolled up together to the prince, and said, 'Sir, behold here is my banner; I require you to display it abroad, and give me leave this day to raise it; for, Sir, I thank God and you, I have land and heritage sufficient to maintain it withal.'" No knight, we may observe, could raise his banner unless he had a train of not less than fifty men-at-arms, with their usual complement of archers and followers. "The Spanish King and the Black Prince then took the banner between their hands, and spread it abroad, the which was of silver, a sharp pyle gules, and delivered it to him, and said, 'Sir John, behold here your banner; God send you joy and honour thereof.' Then Sir John Chandos bare his banner to his own company, and said, 'Sirs, behold here my banner, and yours; keep it as your own;' and they took it, and were right joyful thereof, and said that by the pleasure of God and St. George they would keep and defend it to the best of their powers; and so the banner abode in the hands of a good English squire, called William Allestry, who bare it that day, and acquitted himself right nobly." The battle ended, as usual, in favour of the English, though Pedro did not permanently profit by it, for he died at last by the hands of his brother, in a kind of unpremeditated duel to which mutual hatred had led them on meeting, and Henry afterwards reigned the unquestioned king of Castile.

A very remarkable person was taken in the battle of Najara, De Guesclin, one of the most popular and renowned of French warriors, who commanded that day a body of French soldiers, and who, previously, at the head of thirty thousand men, chiefly consisting of those military freebooters called the Free Companies (see Fig. 1092), had been the principal instrument of Henry's accession to the throne of Castile. As Nature had not fitted him for success in one of the objects of a knight's ambition, love, he devoted himself with the greater earnestness to the other, war: as he used himself to say, "I am very ugly, and shall never please the ladies; but I shall make myself dreaded by the enemies of my king." At the early age of seventeen he distinguished himself in the tournament (Fig. 1103); then, entering on a military career, rapidly rose to fame and rank. After the battle of Poictiers, it was to him that France was indebted for the successful maintenance of the struggle against the English power; though he was himself on one occasion so unfortunate as to fall into their hands. When peace was concluded, he was liberated, and immediately performed a service scarcely less valuable than any for which his country was indebted to him, that of ridding it of the vast number of disbanded soldiers, native and foreign, who, under a variety of leaders, roamed about, exercising all kinds of oppression. These, at the French king's request, Du Guesclin undertook to remove. So calling them about him, he commenced with a magnificent gratuity of two hundred thousand golden florins, promising them as much more on the road, if they would follow him. They did so with the utmost enthusiasm, and after a visit to the Pope at Avignon, to make him take off the excommunication he had laid on the "Companies," and to tax him to the amount of one hundred thousand francs—by way of reminder, we presume, that he was not to do so again—they were conducted by their commander, not against the Saracens, as had been intended, but against Pedro of Castile. The result we have seen, so far as regards those for and against whom he fought. As to himself, the circumstance of his release from his captivity furnishes another and scarcely less striking illustration than any we have given of the graceful generosity of chivalry in its better moods. Du Guesclin remaining a long time at Bordeaux, the continental head-quarters of the Black Prince, a friend of his hit upon the ingenious scheme of suggesting to the captor that it was believed by some persons that he only kept Du Guesclin a prisoner because he was afraid of restoring him to liberty. That was enough; the prince sent for the French warrior, and said he only asked one hundred francs for his ransom, or even less, if that was too much. Du Guesclin immediately offered one hundred thousand golden florins, but the prince said it was too much; seventy thousand was then offered, as being the lowest sum the prisoner would allow to be given, and thus it was settled. On his release Du Guesclin rejoined his friend Henry, and helped to restore him to the Castilian throne. To the engravings already mentioned in connection with his history, we append two (Figs. 1099, 1100) that may afford a glimpse of his appearance.

The last illustration of the spirit of chivalry that we shall at present give, and which forms the subject of the engraving (Fig. 1102), refers to the period immediately after the peace concluded in 1379 between De Montfort, Duke of Brittany, and the French, when the English, who had been in alliance with the former, under the command of the Duke of Buckingham, set out to make the best of their way home, having received a "safe-conduct" from the Constable of France. Among them were a party of knights, who one day rested in the town, near the castle of Josselyn, where the Constable then was. Whilst there, certain Frenchmen of the castle, knights and squires, courteously came to see them, "as men of war oftentime will do" with each other, says Froissart, and "especially Englishmen and Frenchmen." Among the attendants of the knights of the two nations that met, were two who had been previously acquainted, one an English squire called Nicholas Clifford, the other the French Earl of March's squire "and one that he loved entirely," called John Boucmell. When they had "beheld each other" and communed together awhile, the following conversation ensued. "Nicholas," observed the Frenchman, "divers times we have wished and desired to do deeds of arms together, and now we have found each other in place and time where we may accomplish it. Now we be here before the Constable of France, and other lords that be here present, therefore, I require you, let us have now three courses afoot with a spear each of us against other." The Englishman answered, "John, ye know right well we be here going on our way, by the safe-conduct of my lord, your Constable; therefore that ye require cannot be done, for I am not the chief of this safe-conduct, for I am but under these other knights that be here; for though I would here abide, they would not do so." Again the French squire urged the acceptance of the challenge (Fig. 1101). "Nicholas, excuse you not by this means; let your company depart if they list, for I promise you by covenant, the arms once done be-

tween you and me, I shall bring you into the vale of Cherbourg without damage or peril; make ye no doubt thereof." But the English squire had no armour with him, neither he nor his company; a custom possibly with knights when thus travelling under safe-conduct. John Boucmell would not be answered with this objection; he had harness of different sorts at his command, they should be brought before Clifford, and after he had made his choice from them, Boucmell would make his. We can well understand and appreciate the feelings of our gallant countryman at being compelled by a sense of propriety, as he evidently felt he was, still to decline so generous an antagonist. However, he promised him he would take advice, and added, that at all events, as soon as they came into each other's neighbourhood, which they expected would shortly be the case, that he would come to him, and deliver the challenge he so despised. "Nay, nay," was the reply, "seek no respite. I have offered, and yet do offer you so many things so honourable, that in no wise ye can depart, saving your honour, without doing deeds of arms with me, sith I require you of it." And so they parted, the Englishman probably not choosing to be compelled even by such remarks into a line of conduct he had determined to avoid, but evidently stung with them, and "sorer displeased than he was before." But this conversation reached the ears of the French Constable, who at once saw how to obviate all difficulties, and determined that the trial of skill should take place. So when the English knights waited upon him to make arrangements for their departure, he told them pleasantly that he arrested them all as his guests, and that on the morrow after mass they should see deeds of arms done between the two squires. The remainder we must tell in Froissart's own inimitable style. "Then these two squires, John and Nicholas, advised them well of the battle that they must furnish the next day; and so in the next morning they both heard one mass and were confessed, and leaped on their horses, and all the lords of France on the one part, and the Englishmen on the other part, and so came all together to a fair plain place without the castle of Josselyn, and there tarried. John Boucmell had made ready two harnesses, fair and good, according as he promised to the English squire, and then he said to him, 'Nicholas, choose which ye will have;' but he would in no wise choose, and gave the first choice to the French squire, and so he took the one and armed him therewith, and Nicholas did help to arm him, and so did he in like wise again; and when they were both two armed, they took good spears all of one length, and so each of them took his place and came a fair pace afoot each against other; and when they should approach, they crouched down their spears, and at the first stroke Nicholas Clifford strake John Boucmell on the breast, and the stroke did slide up to the gorget of mail, and the spear-head did enter into his throat, and did cut asunder the jugular vein, and the spear broke, and the truncheon stuck still in the squire's neck, who was with that stroke wounded to death: the English squire passed forth, and went and sate down in his chair. When the lords saw that stroke, and saw how the truncheon stuck still, they came to him and took off his bascinet, and drew out the truncheon; and soon as it was done he turned about without any word speaking, and so fell down dead suddenly, so that the English squire could not come to him time enough, *for he had certain words to have stanched him* that would have holpen: but when he saw that he was dead, he was sore displeased because of that adventure, seeing how he should slay so valiant a man of arms. He that then had seen the Earl of March would have had pity to see what sorrow he made for his squire, for he loved him entirely. The Constable recomforted him, and said, 'In such deeds of arms let no man look for nothing else; though this evil fortune be fallen on our squire, the English is not to blame, for he cannot amend it!' Then the Constable said to the Englishmen, 'Sirs, let us go and dine; it is time:' and so the Constable, against their goodwill, had them with him into the castle to dinner, for he would not break his promise for the death of his squire. The Earl of March wept piteously for his squire, and Nicholas Clifford went to his lodging and would not dine in the castle, what for sorrow, and for doubt of the French squire's friends. But the Constable sent so for him, that it behoved him to go to the castle; and when he was come, the Constable said, 'Certainly Nicholas, I believe verily, and see well how ye be sorry for the death of John Boucmell; but I excuse you, for ye cannot amend it: for as God help me, if I had been in the same case as ye were in, ye have done nothing but I would have done the same, or more if I might; for better it is a man to grieve his enemy, than his enemy should grieve him: such be the adventures of arms;' so they sate down at the table and dined at their leisure." This touching incident forms the subject of two of our engravings (Figs. 1102, 1095)

1176.—Portrait of Henry V.

1177.—Katherine.

1179.—Noble of Henry V.

1180.—Half-Noble of Henry V.

1178.—Great Seal of Henry V.

1181.—Quarter-Noble of Henry V

1182—Groat of Henry V.

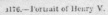

1185.—Signature of Henry V.

1184.—Penny of Henry V.

1183—Half Groat of Henry V.

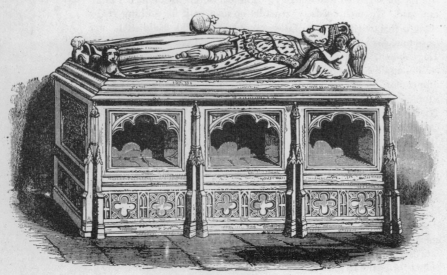

1187.—Tomb of Henry V. in Westminster Abbey.

1186.—Henry V. and his Court.

1183.—Henry VI. in his Youth.

1193.—Great Seal of Henry VI.

1196.—Penny of Henry VI.

1195.—Half-Groat of Henry VI.

1194.—Groat of Henry VI.

1192.—Henry VI.—A.D. 1450.

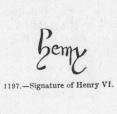

1197.—Signature of Henry VI.

1189.—Portrait of Henry VI.

1190.—Henry VI. and Court. John Talbot receiving a Sword.

1191.—Marriage of Henry VI. and Margaret of Anjou.

The establishment of regular colleges for the residence of students in separate communities, commenced about the middle of the thirteenth century, and thus considerably changed as well as improved the two great Universities of Oxford and Cambridge. It may not be uninteresting to glance at university life previous to that time. It presents many curious features. In the first place, the number of students is quite startling; they were counted by tens of thousands. The old Oxford historian, Anthony-a-Wood, tells us that many of them were mere "varlets who pretended to be scholars," who "lived under no discipline, neither had any tutors, but only for fashion sake would sometimes thrust themselves into the schools at ordinary lectures; and when they went to perform any mischiefs, then would they be accounted scholars, that so they might *free themselves from the jurisdiction of the burghers*." A pretty lawless state of society those unfortunate burghers must have lived in: all sorts of violent crimes were perpetrated, and the townspeople who generally suffered from them, had no redress but such as they could enforce by a hasty resort to arms, or obtained from the tardy and ineffectual interference of the king or high clergy. How these disorderly crowds of *students* were all boarded and lodged it is almost impossible to tell. The school of Pythagoras at Cambridge (Fig. 1107), a Norman house or hostel, is said to have been used for the residence of scholars there. It seems pretty evident that they fared as they could, each according to his means among the surrounding villages or townsfolk. We have a few glimpses of the university teachers. Hebrew was taught at Oxford by Jews, long resident there; Greek was a recent study taught by a monk from Athens, called Nicholas the Greek. It is pleasant to find among these professors of learning, at a time when the clergy were scrambling for wealth and power and pomp, some who stood apart in dignified simplicity and humility, asserting practically in their lives the beauty and glory of knowledge, and making it to them its own exceeding great reward. Thus we read, in 1362, the rector and masters of the faculty of arts petitioned for a postponement of the hearing of a cause in which they were parties, because "we have difficulty in finding the money to pay the procurators and advocates, whom it is necessary for us to employ, *we whose profession it is to possess no wealth*." The vow of the Franciscan friars enjoined poverty, manual labour, and study; and though only a few years had elapsed since they first entered Oxford, the university had become thoroughly imbued with their principles, and its leading men were either Franciscans or the patrons of Franciscans. The most eminent of the former class was Roger Bacon, who had been persuaded to join them by Robert Grosteste, their most distinguished and, indeed, their first patron at Oxford. These two scholars were contemporaries, and in all respects kindred minds; their training, their studies, their conflicts, their whole career, were almost identical in their leading points, and furnish us with a striking illustration of the state of learning at that period, and the difficulties and dangers that beset those who dared to start from the beaten track. We see Bacon, in the first instance, as the younger brother and disciple of Grosteste: both had been placed at Oxford early in life, both had finished their studies (so far as study depended upon school) at the first university in Europe, that of Paris, then resorted to by all who aspired to the honoured name of scholar. Both had returned to Oxford with laurels on their brows, there to drink inspiring draughts of pure faith and morality from the new orders of friars, and to receive from them quickening impulses of mental advancement. And both *did* advance: both were distinguished mathematicians; students of languages; and diligent collectors of such books as were then to be had: in twenty years Bacon spent two thousand livres (French) in books and instruments, no doubt through the liberality of the opulent friends of the learned mendicants. Both also searched into the operations of nature, real and imagined; and whilst Grosteste strenuously opposed the moral and spiritual depravities of the church, Bacon, undistracted by the arduous and stormy duties into which his friend had plunged when he became a bishop, ascended the heights of philosophical discovery, and produced his 'Opus Majus.' There are thoughts scattered like gems through that work, which will bear the closest comparison with the wisdom of his illustrious namesake of a later time (who curiously enough, exhibits a striking mental resemblance to him), whilst at the same time a beautiful ease and simplicity pervade the whole composition; indeed nothing finer of the kind was produced for several ages. The mechanical discoveries indicated in his writings, especially the telescope and gunpowder, are very remarkable, as showing how thought may anticipate all things; for, be it carefully observed, the most valuable of Bacon's discoveries were, it is quite manifest, of *imagination and reflection solely*, without actual experiment. ('Penny Cyclopædia —Bacon.) The common ideas of "Friar Bacon" have always represented him as a magician, who made a brazen head that could answer questions concerning futurity. Grosteste divides the credit of this wondrous invention with Bacon; but the truth is that the charge of magic originated with the monks, by whom Bacon and Grosteste (and all the friars) were heartily detested. Anthony-a-Wood wittily shows us how little their researches could be understood. "The clergy," says he, "knew no property of the circle, except that of keeping out the devil; and thought the parts of a triangle would wound religion." The court of Rome was equally the foe of the spirit of free investigation which these early reformers were spreading. Both were successively in their old age cited to Rome; the one to answer for his actions, the other for his writing. Grosteste was excommunicated, and after his death narrowly escaped having his bones flung out of Lincoln Cathedral; Roger Bacon suffered ten years' rigorous confinement at Rome, and was only released at the intercession of some powerful nobles. But he was worn out by captivity and grief, and died in 1292, a few months after he had returned to Oxford, where he was buried in the Franciscan church. There was formerly a tower on the bridge at Oxford (Fig. 1108), which was traditionally said to have been Bacon's study; perhaps, then, it was to that tower the bigots hastened on Bacon's death to search for his papers, and immediately placed under lock and key all they could find; which in process of time were consumed by insects. But enough has been left to show us that their author stands in the very foremost rank of Old England's scientific and philosophical minds.

To obtain, in the present day, the best idea of the aspect of an English city in the middle ages, we must go to CHESTER, which preserves its original aspect, with such remarkable completeness that even the surrounding wall is still to be found there; though that work of defence, so common in former times, is attributed by tradition to Cymbeline—that is to say, to a period a century before the birth of Christ. Having been altered at different periods, and much reduced in height, as no longer needed for their original object, these walls, some two miles round, now serve the much pleasanter purpose of a promenade for the inhabitants. And, as Kohl observes, a very "curious promenade it is; sometimes up hill and sometimes down; at one point closely wedged in between houses, while at another the narrow path passes under some ancient watchtower; here it runs under a gateway, and there we must descend a flight of steps, because the wall has been cleared away to make room for a street; now we pass behind the venerable cathedral, and now in front of the spacious old castle, which has been converted into a military barrack. The antiquity of Chester will be tolerably evident from these remarks, and its importance in past times is equally worthy of notice. Kohl says, it may be considered as the "mother of Liverpool, for at a time when nothing was yet known of Liverpool commerce on the Mersey, the fame of Chester and her trade on the Dee was widely spread in Germany, Spain, and France." Liverpool, however, has proved but an ungrateful child, for, taking advantage of the injury done to the navigation of the Dee by accumulations of sand, it has gone on flourishing at the parent's expense, until it has grown into all its present magnitude and power, and left Chester in all its present comparative insignificance.

The interior of Chester is even still more extraordinary than the exterior, on account of a feature that appears to be peculiar to the place, and which has sadly puzzled all our antiquarians to account for or explain the origin of. We allude to the long covered public passages called Rows (Figs. 1106, 1113), that extend through the first floor of the houses parallel with the streets. The best description we have seen of these Rows is that by the pleasant writer before mentioned; although, as he observes, "the thing is not very easy to describe. Let the reader imagine the front wall of the first floor of each house to have been taken away, leaving that part of the house completely open towards the street, the upper part being supported by pillars of beams. Let him then imagine the side walls also to have been pierced through, to allow a continuous passage along the first floors of all houses. How the people of Chester came, in this way, to spoil their best floors in so many of their houses, is a matter that was never made perfectly clear to me. We have also a number of towns in Germany, particularly in Silesia and the Austrian dominions, where covered passages, for the accommodation of the public, have been made to run through or round private houses; but then these passages or galleries are always on the ground floor, and on a level with the street." The two great intersecting streets are to a considerable extent constructed on this plan, and as those, as well as the other streets of

Chester exhibit in the simplicity of their plan very clear evidence of their builders—the Romans, who made Chester the station of their twentieth legion, it is not improbable that Pennant may be correct in considering that the peculiar mode of construction exhibited in the Rows may have existed from the Roman period. Other antiquarians are satisfied that the Rows were intended for defence, and therefore attribute their design and erection to the ages when the city was exposed to continual attacks by the Welsh and the Scots; in order that, if the citizens failed to keep their enemies outside the walls, yet that they might still be able to prevent them from taking possession of the place. It is certainly much in favour of this theory that the Rows were in later times found of great importance for military purposes; it is asserted, that in the civil wars, the possession of the Rows decided the possession of Chester, whether for the Royalists or the Parliamentarians.

"It must not be imagined," continues Kohl, "that these Rows form a very regular or uniform gallery. On the contrary, it varies according to the size or circumstances of each house through which it passes. Sometimes, when passing through a small house, the ceiling is so low that one finds it necessary to doff the hat, while in others one passes through a space as lofty as a saloon. In one house the Row lies lower than in the preceding, and one has in consequence to go down a step or two, and, perhaps, a house or two further, one or two steps have to be mounted again. In one house a handsome new-fashioned iron railing fronts the street; in another, only a mean wooden paling. In some stately houses, the supporting columns are strong and adorned with handsome antique ornaments; in others, the wooden piles appear time-worn, and one hurries past them apprehensive that the whole concern must topple down before long. The ground-floors over which the Rows pass are inhabited by a humble class of tradesmen, but it is at the back of the Rows themselves that the principal shops are to be found. This may give an idea of how lively and varied a scene is generally to be witnessed here. Indeed, the Rows are often full of people, either making their little purchases in the shops, or mounting to their boarded floors, to avoid the disagreeable pavement of the streets. Perhaps these Rows may be connected with another singularity pointed out to me at Chester. The streets do not, as in other towns, run along the surface of the ground, but have been cut into it, and that moreover into a solid rock. The Rows are in reality on a level with the surface of the ground, and the carriages rolling along below them are passing through a kind of artificial ravine. The back wall of the ground-floor is everywhere formed by the solid rock, and the court-yard of the houses, their kitchens, and back buildings lie generally ten or twelve feet higher than the street." A place so rich in these broad features of antiquity could hardly be destitute of many of its minor and more ordinary details. A more richly picturesque example of domestic street architecture, than is shown in our engraving (Fig. 1112) of some of the old houses of Chester, it would be hardly possible to find or to desire.

Among the places which one often hears of, but few ever see, may be reckoned CROWLAND or CROYLAND in Lincolnshire, famous for its abbey. It lies in the very heart of the fens; and the traveller whom business or accident takes there for the first time, say from Spalding or Market Deeping, will not speedily forget either the way by which he reaches it, or the place when reached. For miles the road extends through a dead flat, where endless drains, occasional large sheets of water, pollard willows, and, if he be fortunate, a flight of wild ducks, are the only objects that meet his gaze. Not a habitation or a human being anywhere appears. The road itself, at times necessarily raised to a considerable height, causes him many a twinge of fear as to the consequences of his horse starting at any sudden occurrence, and dropping the vehicle over the undefended edge; and if another vehicle meets him in such places he must have confidence indeed in the animal, if he does not get out, and, carefully holding him by the head, draw him within a very few inches of the edge, and there keep him standing while the other equipage passes. But the town is reached, and the superb ruins of the monastery at once attract the eye, and suggest all kinds of pleasant anticipations as to the place itself. Curiously are we disappointed. Never surely before were there so many dull and spiritless-looking houses congregated together; the drains that run through some of the streets seem to have shed over everything their own stagnant qualities. Not a good-looking public building of any sort relieves the tedium of brick and mortar—nay, we question whether there is such a thing as a public building in the place: we certainly remember none, though some years have passed since we were there. A handsome-looking or superior mansion is almost equally scarce: strange as the fact at first may appear, we were informed that there was not a

single person resident in Crowland that could be supposed even to aspire to the rank of a country gentleman. We think we do recollect a few trees, but are not at all sure about flowers. In a word, a place more completely out of the world, as it were, one cannot well imagine. And yet after all Crowland is an interesting place. It is interesting, if it be only to see how completely time has swept away every incidental vestige of the magnificence of the abbey, which had few rivals in the country; and the very existence of which one would now be inclined to doubt, did not the existing ruins still stand there to be its witnesses. It is interesting also for another structure—the one exception to the universal blank of the town—the bridge, which is at once the oldest and most extraordinary structure of the kind in England. It is triangular, having three roadways meeting at the top in a common centre, which is high in proportion to the other dimensions of the edifice This curious form, and its steepness, rendering it useless except for pedestrians, though horses *might* cross it—whilst at the same time neither need it—have induced antiquarians to suppose the whole to be simply a material embodiment of the idea of the Trinity. It seems to us that whilst the builders did intend to shadow forth one of the grand mysteries of their religion, they intended its immediate use to be that of a proper bridge for foot passengers over the two drains that there met and mingled their waters beneath, and which drains were probably too wide to be crossed without its assistance; though horsemen might ford them. The drains have long disappeared, and hence the wonder with which a visitor looks upon the strange and apparently unnecessary bridge. The period of its erection is said to have been 860; but the style implies a much later date, bringing it down to the era upon which we now write. The statue seen in our engraving (which exhibits the bridge as it appeared in the last century) is now so much mutilated, that hardly a feature is discernible. We can see, however, it represents a king; and may therefore be a statue of Ethelbald, who founded the monastery about the beginning of the eighth century (Fig. 1109).

The castle of NEWCASTLE-UPON-TYNE, that extensive and majestic relic of the war times of Old England, has already engaged our attention (see page 110): we have also alluded to the ancient importance of the town; we have now to glance at the fragments which time has left us of the walls, to which both the town and castle were mainly accustomed to trust for security. The great Norman fortresses had generally two walls: the outer one of Newcastle enclosed three acres of ground; the inner joined it at two places, and formed a second enclosure, within which, thus doubly intrenched, stood the main buildings of the fortress. The outer wall had a main entrance and two posterns; the inner wall had the same. Of all these entrances and walls nothing now remains but the Black Gate (Fig. 1111), which was the great gateway of the outer wall, built in the time of Henry III. at a cost of about five hundred and fourteen pounds old money. As we now see it, it is apt to convey a gloomy impression of Norman character and times: in passing under the low and narrow arch, louring and characteristic is the effect of the great depth, thirty-six feet, and suggestive of thoughts of the awful dungeons of the mighty barons and the deeds of cruelty too often perpetrated in them; and we thank God that it is given to us to live in other times. Two lofty circular towers formerly added to the strength and majesty of this gateway, and one of them is still very perfect towards its base, but the rest of the structure is mixed up with confused masses of extraneous building. The town of Newcastle, independent of the castle, had been walled from a very early period: in proof of which a strong barrier of earth remains behind the priory of Black Friars. But by the time of Edward I. these walls had become quite inadequate to the defence of the inhabitants; the Scots entered and ravaged the town at will, and at one of their visits, in addition to making the customary use of fire and sword, carried off a rich citizen to Scotland. The captive, being ransomed after a short confinement, formed a resolution to prevent such unpleasant accidents for the future. So he employed his wealth in rebuilding the fortifications; and in that great undertaking was assisted by the rest of the inhabitants of Newcastle, and encouraged by the king. The result was a rampart twelve feet high and eight feet thick, strongly resembling, it is said, the walls of Avignon. They extended two thousand seven hundred and forty yards, with a fosse or ditch running along the foot outside sixty-six feet broad, and named the King's Dykes. There were *seven* gates in them, and *seventeen* round towers, "between every one of which were, for the most part, two watch-towers, made square, with the effigies of men cut out in stone upon the tops of them, as though they were watching." (Bourne.) These great works were not completed until the reign

1198.—Duke of Bedford.

1199.—Talbot, Earl of Shrewsbury.

1200.—Old Monument of Joan of Arc. Rouen.

1201.—Rouen.

1203.—Effigy upon the Tomb of John Talbot.

1202.—Talbot, the great Earl of Shrewsbury, presenting a Book of Romances to Henry VI.
(Royal MS. 15 E. 6.)

1204.—Lydgate presenting his Poem of 'The Pilgrim' to the Earl of Warwick and Salisbury. (Harleian MS. No. 4826.)

1206.—Queen Margaret.

1205.—Westminster Hall.—Treaty between Henry VI. and Richard, Duke of York.

1207.—Richard, Duke of York.

1208.—Richard Nevil, Earl of Warwick.

1210.—Battle of Barnet. (From an Illumination in a MS. at Ghent.)

1209.—Cardinal Beaufort.

1211.—Field of Battle near Barnet.

1213.—Humphrey, Duke of Gloster.

1212.—Fields near St. Albans.

of Edward III. The town was then divided into twenty-four wards, according to the number of gates and round towers upon them. All the free burgesses of each ward buckled on their harness as soldiers for its defence whenever there was a cry of danger; and regularly, in the reign of Henry IV., did a hundred of those burgesses pace the bulwarks nightly. In the opinion of Leland, "the strength and magnificence of the wauling of this town far passeth all the waulles of the cities of England, and most of the towns of Europa." The relics of these noble ramparts are fast becoming obliterated, like many of the minor curiosities of this fine old town, among which may be mentioned the public conduits of peculiar construction, "having each a small square reservoir before them for retaining the water for the the use of horses, or common domestic purposes." (Brand.) Pond was anciently pronounced pand, according to Dr. Thomas Shaw, and Skinner derives the word from the Anglo-Saxon *pyndan*, to enclose or shut up. On the Scottish and English borders, *pand* seems to have been converted into *pant*, meaning a little reservoir or pond. In a deed of 1450 a public conduit in the market-place of Durham, similar to the pants of Newcastle, is described in Latin and Anglo-Norman as "the fountain head, vulgarly called the 'Pant' head." The pant of which we have given an engraving (Fig. 1110) stands in front of the Freemen's Hospital, or the Hospital of the Holy Jesus. The charity was founded in 1683, by the mayor and burgesses, for the relief of freemen and freemen's widows, or sons and daughters of freemen, being unmarried. The buildings erected for this purpose stood on a piece of ground called the Manors, and the institution was incorporated under the title of "The Master, Brethren, and Sisters of the Hospital of the Holy Jesus." The hospital was thus described by Bourne, upwards of a century ago, in his account of Newcastle :—"You ascend to it by stairs from the High-street, and then enter into a pleasant field, on the north side of which is the said hospital. It is three stories high, and the under story is adorned with piazzas, which are about sixty yards in length, and make a very agreeable walk. About the middle of the piazzas is the entrance into the second and third stories, and over against this entrance is a fountain (very much beautified) for the use of the hospital." Some of the many pants in Newcastle are beautiful, others merely curious. The want of water that Newcastle has, to a certain extent, experienced for ages, evidently led to the erection of the pants. In the last century, the common council, in order to obviate the deficiency, accepted the liberal offer of a neighbouring gentleman to supply the town with water from his property, on their preparing aqueducts. Other provision has since been made.

Whilst Froissart was busily engaged collecting materials for his great history, and journeying from land to land in order to increase their amount, or obtain additional verifications of their correctness, an Englishman was no less actively employed in the study of the manners and customs, and modes of thought, of his own countrymen, of all ranks and classes of society, and embodying the result of his experience in poems that were to be at least as permanent as his contemporary's prose, and infinitely more valuable. Froissart recorded but one feature of his age, the most conspicuous undoubtedly, but one so little calculated for durability, that the record has become in the lapse of ages chiefly interesting and valuable for its own sake. Chaucer also described the men of the fourteenth century; but in doing so, went so much deeper beneath the surface, that he at the same time described human nature under a thousand varying aspects; the consequence is, we turn with ever-fresh instruction to his pages. Froissart's *beau idéals*—the gentle warriors who set and kept Europe in a blaze—are happily extinct; but the characters of the 'Canterbury Tales' yet seem to live, breathe, and move among us, so thoroughly individual are they, so thoroughly men and women, having all our own peculiarities, humours, follies, virtues, and vices. Through all literature we may look in vain for any parallel to the amazing amount and variety of descriptive powers of the highest class, lavished in the small space occupied by the prologue to the great poem we have named; and yet that prologue hardly bears a smaller proportion in quantity to the rest of the 'Canterbury Tales,' than do the powers exhibited in it to those which the poet's complete works reveal. In a word, of the few supreme master spirits that stand out above all other of the illustrious of the earth, Chaucer is one. The design of the poem itself is one of almost unequalled skill and magnificence. Taking that exceedingly picturesque feature of Old England, the pilgrimages, and availing himself of the opportunity such occasions offered for the mingling of different ranks (we need hardly say that such unnatural and pernicious extreme social divisions as mark our time were unknown in Chaucer's), he brought together as the dramatis

personæ of his "Comedy not intended for the Stage," a most complete and picturesque set of examples of all the different classes of society. These he causes to meet, himself among the number, at the Tabard, now the Talbot, in Southwark, a place especially favoured by pilgrims departing from London, and which still preserves much of its antique character. There are reasons even for believing that the very gallery, along which Chaucer himself may have walked as a pilgrim, among pilgrims, and the room where they may have dined, still exist. (See 'London :—The Tabard,' Vol. i. No. IV.) Our engravings (Figs. 1116, 1117, 1118) show the progress of the changes that have from time to time modernised other portions of the original Tabard. In the engraving of the supper (Fig. 1115), the artist has aimed to restore the pilgrims' room of the Tabard, and to exhibit the pilgrims as Chaucer has described them at supper. The meal scarcely over, the Host, evidently excited with some unusual thought, rises. Chaucer says of him—

> A seemly man our hoste was with all
> For to have been a marshall in a hall ;
> A large man he was, with eyen steep,
> A fairer burgess is there none in Cheap.
> Bold of his speech, and wise and well ytaught,
> And of manhood him lacked righte nought.
> Eke therto was he right a merry man ;

evidence of which is afforded by his address to the company. Having told them how welcome they were to his "herberwe," or inn, he adds :—

> Fain would I do you mirth, an I wist how.
> And of a mirth I am right now bethought
> To do you ease, and it shall cost you nought.
> Ye go to Canterbury ; God you speed.
> The blissful martyr [Becket] quite [requite] you your meed,
> And well I wot as ye go by the way,
> Ye shapen you to talken and to play ;
> For truely comfort ne mirth is none
> To riden by the way dumb as the stone ;
> And therefore would I maken you disport,
> As I said erst, and do you some comfort.
> And if you liketh all by one assent
> Now for to standen at my judgement,
> And for to worken as I shall you say
> To-morrow, when ye riden by the way :
> Now by my father's soule that is dead,
> But ye be merry, smiteth [smite] off my head :
> Hold up your hands withouten more speech.

The pilgrims thought it not worth while to "make it wise," so agreed to his proposal, and bade him give what verdict he pleased. And now the Host explains the idea that he has been brooding over all the supper-time :—

> This is the point, to speak it plat and plain ;
> That each of you, to shorten with your way
> In this viage [journey] shall tellen tales tway ;
> To Canterbury ward, I mean it so,
> And homeward he shall tellen other two
> Of aventures that whilom have befall
> And which of you that beareth him best of all,
> That is to say, that telleth in this case
> Tales of best sentence and most solace,
> Shall have a supper at your aller cost
> Here in this place, sitting by this post,
> When that ye come again from Canterbury.

Such is the proposal of the Host, but fortunately that is not all he has to say, or we should have wanted through the ensuing pilgrimage the life and soul of the party, and the poet would have wanted the most important of the links by which to connect the stories that form the staple of the poem. So the liberal-hearted and joyous Harry Bailly tells them that he will himself ride with them at his own cost, and be their guide. The pilgrims not only received this offer in the spirit in which it is made, but asked him to undertake the office of governor on the pilgrimage, and the judge of the tales that are to be told, observing, in short, that they will be ruled by him in "high and low." Lots are now drawn to see who shall tell the first tale, and the Knight is the man. The pilgrims soon after retire to bed, and the following morning they depart on their way to Thomas á-Becket's shrine. Having thus briefly sketched the plan of the poem, we will now pause to look a little more in detail at the characters of the pilgrims. We may, however, add to this notice of the Host, a few words on a character who accompanies the party as a man of business rather than a pilgrim (Fig. 1133)—

> To boil the chickens, and the marrow bones,
> And poudre marchant tart and galingale—

delicacies (we mean, the marchant tart and galingale) of which the said pilgrims had a better understanding than we confess we have. There is no difficulty in respect to his other accomplishments—

> Well could he know a draught of London ale;
> He coulde roast, and seethe, and broil and fry
> Baken mortrewés, and well bake a pie;
> For blanc-manger that made he with the best.

The mortrewes consisted of meat—generally pork—brayed in a mortar (une mortreuse), and mixed with milk, eggs, spices, &c.: and we fancy we should be inclined to relish the composition from such able hands, always providing that the saffron were omitted with which it used to be "coloured very deep." But the *blanc-mange* we should decidedly object to, personally, if made according to an ancient recipe in 'A Proper New Book of Cookery,' 1575:— "Take a capon, and cut out the braune of him *alive*," &c. Among all our modern improvements, let us be thankful for increased humanity in the treatment of the helpless creatures that have to die —not always that we may live—but too generally that we may abound in luxuries. Even our improvements in this respect have by no means reached their limits. The cry of pain stills ascends to the Maker and Father of All from his humble creatures; and to an extent that few would believe who do not enter deeply into the mysteries of the gastronomic art. It is strange that man, who shares so much of their nature, should continue so long insensible to the tortures he inflicts. In vain still are we told,—

> Never to blend our pleasure and our pride
> With sorrow of the meanest thing that feels.

We see by the mention of London ale, that our metropolitan breweries have enjoyed their high reputation for a long period. Perhaps the earliest allusion to an English cook's shop is contained in some lines in another part of the 'Canterbury Tales,' where the Host banters the Cook for selling in *his* shop the fly-blown stubble goose, and for his re-dressing of his provisions—the Jack of Dover—probably a kind of pasty,

> That hath been twiés hot and twiés cold.

One might have expected that a poet manifesting such wonderful discernment as Chaucer would have brought into view the absurdities of knight-errantry, but we suppose the high and beautiful qualities of the chivalric character had too much won on his imagination; and so he gave us his picture of the sedate, wise, and veteran warrior,

> That from the timé that he first began
> To riden out, he lovéd chivalry,
> Truth and honour, freedom and courtesy:

who was in all respects

> A very perfect gentle knight.

Chaucer speaks of his worthiness in "his lorde's war," a passage which may not unaptly be illustrated by a few remarks on the military system of the Middle Ages. Every knight, except the sovereign, whatever his degree, was military vassal to some superior lord, bound to arm at his call, and attend him forty days in the field. This tenure by knights' service was performed as an equivalent for so much property in land, sufficient to maintain and equip him without ordinary labour. Such property was called a knight's fee. The heads of the nation settled the maximum value of knights' fees, the object being to create as many as possible, in order to have an ample supply of knights for war. When the king wanted their aid, he issued his writs to his tenants-in-chief, each possessing large property in land, and rated respectively at so many knights' fees. On the appointed day, and at the appointed spot, came these tenants-in-chief, with their standards unfurled, as rallying points for their respective hosts. On receiving their sovereign lord's writs, *they* had issued their own summonses to the knights, for whose appearance they were responsible. Their tenants in fee, again, had called together *their* tenants, holders of half or quarter knights' fees, and bound to render only half or quarter the ordinary term of military service. A beautiful and gallant sight it must have been, to behold such an army of knights as were often raised by our Edwards, and Henries, and Richards, all mounted and equipped to the very best of their ability in the mixed stern and gorgeous panoply of the order, and attended by squires only a little less proudly apparelled than their masters.

We have seen how much cause English sovereigns often had to wish that any other system existed rather than that which made the barons so powerful for the control of royal despotism, and left them only less ready to war against than for their liege master. But there was yet a third resource for the restlessness of chivalry. When there was no enterprise stirring in England, they could go abroad, and revive a sort of little Holy war, now that the Crusades

had ceased, by entering into the service of princes who had embraced Christianity, or who supported without embracing it (for such cases there were), and who, either to defend or increase their territories, still waged war against the infidels. Thus, for example, did Bolingbroke in his youth, and Edward III.'s youngest son, Thomas of Gloucester; and thus did the knight, who may have been Chaucer's model, so closely does the history of his adventures in different parts of the world, as described on his tomb, and copied in Leland's 'Itinerary,' agree with the adventures of Chaucer's hero. We refer to "the noble and valiant knight, Mathew de Gourney," who died in 1406, aged ninety-six years. It appears he "was at the battle of Benamaryn, and afterwards at the siege of Algezir against the Saracens, and also at the battles of L'Escluse, of Cressy, of Deyngenesse, of Peyteres [Poictiers], of Nazare, of Ossey, and at several other battles and sieges in which he gained great praise and honour." Chaucer's knight has been at three victories won by Pierre de Lusignan, king of Cyprus: that of Satalie, the ancient Attalia, in 1352; that of Alexandria, in 1365; and that of Loyas, a town in Armenia, in 1367: he has served with the knights of the Teutonic order in Prussia: he has journeyed for adventures in Lithuania, and Russia, and Africa; he assisted in 1344 to take from the Moorish king of Granada that very city of Algezir or Algeçiras, mentioned in the above epitaph; and he has been with the lord of Palathie in Anatolia, against a Turkish infidel: in short, he has been altogether in fifteen mortal battles, besides thrice slaying his foe in the lists. The knight's appearance is that of one who has outlived the chivalric love of personal display. His gipon, or short cassock, is but of fustian, and "all besmottered," or soiled, with his habergeon, or coat-of-mail, whilst the horse he rides on, though good, is not gay (Fig. 1119).

The Squire may be considered as representing the Knight in his youth; and in connection with him we must again refer to the training of the order. The boy from infancy was taught to reverence and emulate knighthood; he played with chivalric toys, his dawning imagination was impressed with chivalric splendours, and at seven years old he was first taken from the society of the ladies of the household, and allowed to take the degree of page to a knight, and commence that companionship and those exercises which were at once to stimulate his mind to love and yearn for war, and render his body agile and robust, and in other respects thoroughly fitted for it. The precocious warrior became a no less precocious lover. The boy was expected to devote himself to some young maiden, and to study to deserve her favour next to that of Heaven. At fourteen he enters his second novitiate and becomes a squire. The first arms he is to wear are laid on the church altar and are blessed with all solemnity by the priest, who girds them on in the presence of his near relations and friends, whilst the young heart of the future hero swells proudly with the foretaste of fame. Glowing hope and ambition fill up the next seven years, during which he goes on practising all martial exercises with constantly-increasing severity, not, however, forgetting to master at the same time all polite accomplishments. Occasional excursions with his knightly tutor give the finishing touch to the novitiate's character. And thus at last we have such a result as the poet has embodied in the following exquisite description:—

> With him [the Knight] their was a young Squiér,
> A lover and a lusty bachelor,
> With lockés curl'd as they were laid in press;
> Of twenty year of age he was, I guess.
> Of his statúre he was of even length;
> And wonderly deliver [active, agile] and great of strength.
> And he had been some time in chevachie [a chivalric expedition]
> In Flanders, in Artois, and in Picardy;
> And borne him well, as of little space [considering his little experience],
> In hope to standen in his lady's grace.
> Embroidered was he [his garments] as it were a mead
> All full of freshé flowrés, white and red.
> Singing he was, or floyting [fluting] all the day;
> He was, as fresh as is the month of May.
> Short was his gown, with sleevés long and wide,
> Well coulde he sit on horse, and faire ride.
> He coulde songés make, and well indite,
> Joust, and eke dance, and well pourtray, and write.
> So hot he lovéd, that by nightertale [night-time]
> He slept no more than doth the nightingale.
> Courteous he was, lowly and serviceable,
> And carved before his father at the table—

as was the custom at the time.

The final ceremony of knighting, at the age of twenty-one, was highly solemn, and designed to give the aspirant a profound impression of the dignity and responsibility of the profession of arms. Hence the rigorous fast, the night vigil in the church—the

1214.—Edward, Prince of Wales.

1215.—Chertsey.

1217.—Edward IV

1218.—Queen Elizabeth Woodville.

2216.—Tomb of Henry VI., formerly at Windsor.

1219.—Signature of Edward IV., R. E. (for Rex Edwardus).

1221.—Groat of Edward IV.

1222.—Half-Groat of Edward IV.

1223.—Penny of Edward IV.

1220.—Great Seal of Edward IV.

1224.—Angel of Edward IV.

1225.—Half-Angel of Edward IV.

324

1226.—Edward IV.

1227.—Edward IV. and his Court. (Royal MS. 15 Edward IV.)

1228.—Earl Rivers presenting Caxton to Edward IV. (MS. Lambeth Palace Lib.)

1229.—Signature of Edward V.

12.1.—Signature of Richard III.

1232.—Great Seal of Richard III.

1233.—Groat of Richard III.

1234.—Penny of Richard III.

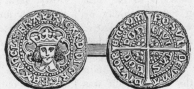

1235.—Half-Groat of Richard III.

1230.—Richard III.

1236.—Anne, Queen of Richard III.

325

strict confession, sacrament, and solemn mass—the sponsorship required for the aspirant's good conduct—the instruction in his duties from priest and lord—and the inspiring attentions he received after the magical *accolade*, when the fairest and the best thronged about him to buckle on his new and splendid armour, and to bring near the charger on which the belted knight was to shine forth as a newly-risen sun upon the multitudes waiting without. Such circumstances could hardly fail to make the character that was desired. Few were the recreants that, according to its own standard, disgraced the rolls of English knighthood.

From the men of war, turn we now to the men of law and physic (Fig. 1120). The

> Sergeant of the Law, wary and wise,

was chosen from the most opulent and learned of the profession. The investiture with the robes and coif was attended with much pomp and ceremony. Generally several sergeants were created at one time, and held their seven days' feast in one of the chief London palaces. A new sergeant was obliged to be rather more generous than, we dare say, he always liked. He was required to spend not less than four hundred marks—a great sum in those days—for the dinner, for rings distributed among officers and other notable men in the king's courts, and for suits of cloth to his household and all persons who were fortunate enough to be of his acquaintance at the time. The Sergeant, we are told, had often been at "the Parvise." The Parvis of London has been supposed to have been situate in Old Palace Yard, before Westminster Hall, or, with more likelihood, at St. Paul's. Dugdale mentions "the Pervyse of Paul's." It was a sort of law school, where "not only young lawyers repaired to learn, but old sergeants to teach and show their cunning."—(Waterhouse.) Chaucer's Sergeant is not a man to hide his light under a bushel. Not only

> Discreet he was, and of great reverence,

but

> He seeméd such, his wordés were so wise.
> Nowhere so busy a man as he there n' as ;
> And yet he seemed busier than he was.

The sergeant often acted as judge at assizes, and was apparently a personage of greater importance in some respects than his modern namesake. A peculiar source of profit, attached to that as well as to other important legal offices, were the "robes," which Chaucer mentions in connection with "fees," and which seem to have been almost as important. Summer and winter these were regularly supplied out of the king's wardrobe, and most probably upon all great public occasions. Money was then scarce in England, and all possible payments were made "in kind."

In connection with the title of Doctor of Physic we may observe that there are examples of degrees taken in the medical science nearly as early as the Conquest; for instance, the Bachelor of Physic at Oxford. Passing over the poet's hint that the doctor, having enriched himself in a pestilence, has "kepté what he won," and the witty two-edged sarcasm at physic and his professors, in the shape of a defence of the latter—

> For gold in physic is a cordiál,
> Therefore he loved gold in speciál,—

let us inquire into a subject of more general interest, as showing us the state of the profession in the fourteenth century—what were the doctor's professional qualifications? His study, it appears, was but little in the Bible, that is one negative fact; the positive information, if less amusing, is somewhat more direct and explicit. Chaucer gives us a catalogue of the books which the doctor *did* study. Esculapius, Hippocrates, Galen, and Dioscorides are there, with Rufus, a physician of Ephesus during the time of Trajan ; and we may observe, in reference to these, that all our medical knowledge rests on Greek foundations. Then follow the later commentators and improvers upon those originals : Haly, John Serapion, and Avicen, Arabians of the eleventh century ; Rhasis, an Asiatic physician who lived at Cordova in Spain in the century previous ; Averroes, professor in the university of Morocco, who taught in the Moorish schools of Africa and Spain ; Damascene, who wrote on various sciences before the Arabians or Saracens brought medicine into Europe ; and Constantinus Afer, a monk of Cassino in Italy, a *Saracen* (one of the few converts to the faith of the Crusaders), who formed the Salernitan School, chiefly by translating Arabian and Grecian medical writings into Latin. Lastly, we find in the doctor's library the writings of the chief medical contemporaries of Chaucer: Bernard, a professor of medicine at Montpelier, the author of many treatises ; and John Gatisden, a fellow of Merton College, where the poet himself was educated, and who was author of the 'Rosa Anglica,' a popular

medical work. Gatisden was the first *English* court physician. Several of the above list of authors were writers on astronomy, as it was then called, though by this was chiefly meant divination by the stars, a science in the East still deemed essential to the healing art, whence our old English professors of Physic and Astrology derived both. Astronomy, says Roger Bacon, is the *better* part of medicine. Our doctor was well grounded in this indispensable knowledge of the heavenly bodies; by his magic natural he was able to tell immediately the proper hours for his operations, and determine when a propitious star would be in the ascendant; his genius also extended to the cause of every malady, be it cold or hot, or moist or dry (into these divisions were diseases of all kinds then classified, under the Arabic system of Physics) ; he knew also where it was engendered, and of what humours ; and with this perfect understanding, he was able to give the sick man his remedy presently, having ready at hand his apothecaries (or druggist, as we now call the class referred to) to send him lectuaries and drugs. One could have hoped that death would have been completely vanquished by such "a very perfect practisour." It is true the bard adds an insinuation that rather modifies our respect both for him and his apothecaries—

> For each of them made other for to win :
> Their friendship was not newé to begin.

Unfortunately for the dignity of the medical profession and the health of the people, their too close friendship promises to last. Drugs ignorantly or heedlessly administered still make patients for the doctors ; and doctors find ample employment, in return, for drugs.

What we have said elsewhere of the pride and profligacy which had crept into the monastic system receives complete confirmation in Chaucer's descriptions of the Monk and Friar (Fig. 1123). The Monk, though only the superior of a cell—that is, a subordinate monastery—has all the pride and luxury of an abbot. His sleeves purfled with the finest fur (then a most expensive ornament), his hood fastened with a curious gold pin, a love-knot in the greater end (though jewellery was forbidden in monastic rules), his supple boots, his horse of great estate, are hints not to be mistaken. Epicureanism is legibly written on his bald head and face, shining like glass, or as though they had been anoint ; and we can almost anticipate the finishing touch to the whole—

> He was a lord full fat, and in good point.

His golden bridle-bells, jingling in a whistling wind as clear and loud as his chapel bell, also gives us a lively idea of the conspicuous state with which he rides abroad. Some instances have been given in this work of hunting prelates : we are not, therefore, surprised to find many a dainty horse in our monk's stable, or that he had greyhounds swift as birds of flight, or that he was a hard rider, and spared no cost in the prosecution of his favourite sports. To be sure, the rule of St. Maur and St. Benedict, that he professed, forbade all these things, but it was too old and narrow for him ; his philosophy was to let old things pass out of sight, and to follow the new. From this " fair prelate " turn we to the companion portrait of the Friar—how lamentably changed since Francis of Assisi and St. Dominic, scarcely two hundred years before, revived the original apostolic purity, simplicity, and *poverty* of the Holy Catholic Church. The Friar so far resembles the Monk that he wears no threadbare cope, like a poor scholar, but a semicope of double worsted, round as a bell out of the press, and looks like a master or a pope. But his enjoyments are of a more popular and social character. He is wanton and merry. No brother of all the orders four (Dominican, Franciscan, Carmelite, and Augustine) can make himself so agreeable, or has such fair language—

> Somewhat he lispéd for his wantonness
> To make his English sweet upon his tongue.

As a capital boon companion, he is much beloved, and familiar with all the franklins of his country district—a jovial class of old English gentlemen, who keep open house and a plentiful table. He carries knives and pins in his tippet to give " fairé wives :" he is as strong as a Champion. He knows well the taverns in every town, and every " gay tapstére." Among his popular delights are harping and singing, that make his eyes twinkle like stars in a frosty night : and certainly, says Chaucer, he had a merry note. So much for the Friar in his worldly relations, and his spiritual ones exhibited a marvellous resemblance. He heard confession with great sweetness of manner, and his absolution was pleasant. He had a large charity for human infirmities. He knew the human heart to be a stubborn thing ; therefore, instead of prayers and tears, as outward signs of penitence, the amiable confessor was willing to compound with them for *silver* instead. The Friar boasts a humility peculiar to himself: he pays a certain rent for an exclusive right of begging in "his haunt," and in that haunt he exhibits himself the best beggar of his fraternity. There is one allusion to a beautiful old custom, full of the spirit of Christianity, in the sketch of this character—the love-days for the reconcilement of differences; but this, like all the other pious customs of the primitive times, had been corrupted, and turned into a roystering occasion, better suited to draw out our Friar's genial qualities than to promote any abstract goodness.

In striking contrast to the luxurious and unprincipled Monk and Friar, we are presented with a pair of portraits (Fig. 1124), drawn with an utter absence of pretension or ornament, yet more perfect and grand, intellectually, religiously, and morally, than any it was ever our good fortune to meet with. This is the description of the first :—

A good man was there of religión
That was a pouré parson of a town,
But rich he was of holy thought and work,
He was also a learned man, a clerk
That Christés gospel truély would preach.
His parishens devoutly would he teach
Benign he was, and wonder diligen
And in adversity full patiént.

. . . .

Full loth were him to cursen for his tithes ;
But rather would he given out of doubt
Unto his pouré parishens about
Of his off'ring, and eke of his substánce.
He could in little thing have suffisance.
Wide was his parish, and houses far asunder,
But he ne left not for no rain nor thunder,
In sickness and in mischief [misfortune] to visit
The farthest in his parish, much and lite [rich and poor],
Upon his feet, and in his hand a staff.

. . . .

Out of the Gospel he the wordés caught,
And this figúre he added yet thereto :—
That if gold rusté, what should iron do?

. . . .

And though he holy were, and virtuous,
He was to sinful men not dispitous [not wanting in pity],
Nor of his speeché dangerous, nor digne [disdainful],
But in his teaching díscreet and benign.
To showén folk to heaven with fairéness,
By good ensample was his business.
But it were ony person obstinate,
What so he were of high or low estate,
Him would he snibben sharply for the nonés [occasion].
A better priest I trow that no where none is ;
He waited after no pomp ne reverence,
Ne maked him no spiced conscience,
But Christés love, and his Apostles twelve
He taught, but first he followed it himself.

With all our enlightenment we have not advanced beyond this surpassing conception of a Christian pastor, which is so free from bigotry that almost any class of the sincere followers of Jesus might adopt it for their own. If there be any character worthy to stand beside this pouré parson, it is Chaucer himself must furnish it in the Clerk of Oxenford. There is the same touching simplicity and sublime elevation of character exhibited ; the same wonderful penetration into the essentials of human position and duties. We shall wait long before we see a more admirable summary of the true student than is conveyed in the last line—

Gladly would he learn, and gladly teach.

Three ladies are amongst the pilgrims—a nun, a prioress, and a Wife of Bath (Fig. 1125). The Nun is a kind of duenna, and servant of the Prioress. The description of the latter is a delicate morceau of the richest comedy, levelled at the fine-ladyism of convent life, and at the same time a picture of feminine nature for all time, in which beauty and meekness mingle so closely, one hardly knows which predominates.

Ladies taking the veil in our own day discard their baptismal name for another of pious or fanciful association, by which they are henceforth to be known. To this custom the fashionable Prioress may have been indebted for hers—of fascinating sound— Madame Eglantine. She was no doubt a very finished specimen of refinement, as we may see in her smile so coy and "full simple," in her pretty and innocentest of oaths, " by Saint Eloy"—in her singing the service divine so sweetly " entuned in her nose,"—in her elaborately precise behaviour at meals,—and in her superfine French, spoken

After the School of Stratford atte Bow,

where candidates for the cloister received the polish of which we

are giving an example. That school taught, it seems, a French of its own, for French of Paris was as unknown to the Prioress as to some of the boarding-school ladies of our own time, who pride themselves on the polite language. Then, too, mark the exquisite sensibility of her nature—

She was so charitable and so piteóus,
She wouldé weep if that she saw a mouse
Caught in a trap, if it were dead or bled.
Of smallé houndés had she, that she fed
With roasted flesh, and milk, and wasted bread [cakes of the finest flour],
But soré wept she, if one of them were dead,
Or if men smote it with a yerdé [rod] smart,
And all was conscience and tender heart.

The other lady, who is seen in the same engraving with this exquisite gentlewoman, has a face " bold and fair, and red of hue." She is a dame of the burgess' class, habited in a hat as broad as is a buckler or a targe, a fote-mantle, or riding-skirt, girdled round the hips, and fine scarlet red hose. Her masculine disposition is indicated by the sharp spurs on her feet, and her gay temper not only by her gay dress, but also by her ready laugh and carp (repartee). She has been a most unwearied pilgrim to holy places. No less than three times has she been at Jerusalem, and " passed many a strange stream :" she has been also to Rome, to Boulogne, to Cologne, and other places. It needs but little consideration to perceive how such rovings, often without any, or very inadequate protection, were likely to injure the growth of true womanly qualities ; their too frequent results we see more than hinted at in the history of this Wife of Bath, who

Couldé much of wand'ring by the way.

The town just named was famous for cloth-making, and the " Wife," it appears, so far excelled in the art as even to surpass " the famous manufactures of Ipres and of Ghent." Thus she had made herself comparatively wealthy, and was able to gratify her passion for dress, wearing coverchiefs on her head on a Sunday of the finest texture, and so heavy that they might have weighed a pound. Perhaps her very immoralities induced her to lavish money on church ceremonies to appease her conscience. This was an easy and agreeable way to heaven. In her eagerness to be the first at the " off'ring," and in her being so wroth as to be out of all charity if any wife in all the parish went before her, we have a humorous hint how female vanity helped to fill the church coffers under the semblance of piety. She had had five husbands at the church door —the marriage service, for the most part, being then performed in the entrance porch, instead of at the altar.

In Chaucer's Franklin (Fig. 1126) we have the old English gentleman in all his glory, the rich landed proprietor settled upon his own estate, looking after his own and his tenants' interest, and settling, nominally at least, half the public business of his neighbourhood. He is one with whom charity may begin at home ; but, if so, only becomes therefore the more sensible of the enjoyment that it may be the means of diffusing when sent abroad. So though his beard be white as the daisy, and his complexion of the true sanguineous hue, though he be

Epicurus owen son,
That held opinion that plain delight
Was verily felicity parfite—

though his house is so nobly supplied with provisions that the poet humorously observes it snowed there with meat and drink, who can help loving and admiring him? We know he would like all his fellow-creatures to look as rosy and enjoy the same philosophy as himself, and therefore keeps something very like open house for the country round. Mr. Warton observes, " that his impatience if his sauces were not sufficiently poignant, and every article of his dinner in due form and readiness, is touched with the hand of Pope or Boileau." This Mr. Todd calls a happy observation, and it is meant certainly for high praise ; but we apprehend a time is not very distant when Pope and Boileau will be honoured by its being said (if with truth it can be) that they touch satire with the hand of Chaucer.

The mercantile spirit of gain, absorbing everything into its own self, our bard hits off in a single line in his description of the Merchant. He was,

Sounding alwáy th' increáse of his winning.

Much of the Merchant's anxieties were for the well-keeping or guarding of those great highways of his trade, the seas and rivers. At the Exchanges, well could he " sheldes," sell, that is, French crown-pieces with a shield on one side. The worldly prudence of the

1238.—Richard III.

1237.—Portrait of Richard III.—The arms from a design by J. R. Planché, Esq. At top—Bosworth Field; at the bottom—Ludlow Castle and Richard's Lodging-House at Leicester.

1239.—Richard III.

1240.—Duke of Norfolk.

1241.—John Howard, first Duke of Norfolk.

1242.—The Bloody Tower.

1243.—Anne, Queen of Richard III.

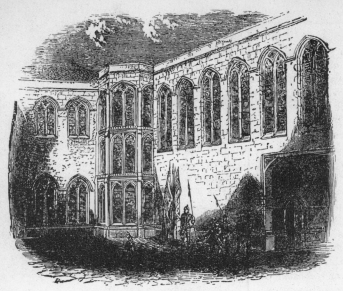

1245.—Crosby House.

1244.—Tamworth Castle.

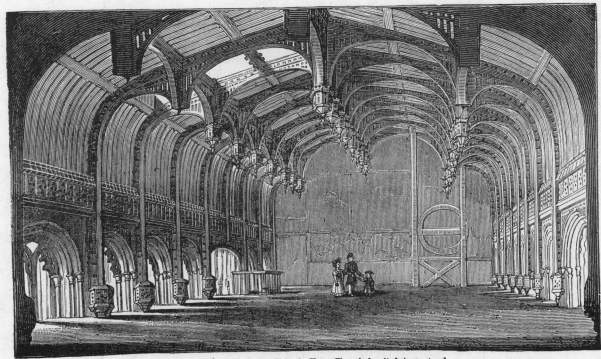

1246.—Interior of Crosby Hall, the Upper Floor, before its being restored.

1248.—Lord Stanley.

1247.—Leicester.

1249.—Thomas Howard, Earl of Surrey.

329

No. 42.

merchant also well expresses the class. His bargains and agreements were made with great care, and no man could tell how his affairs stood in regard to debts, so closely and secretly he governed them. In personal matters, we fancy he would surprise his commercial descendants, could he suddenly step in among them. His beard was forked, the style of his dress *motley*. He sat high on his horse, perhaps on a high saddle, and wore a Flanders beaver hat, and boots tight and neat. We might illustrate the character of the merchant by actual personages of the time, but space forbids; so we pass on to the

Miller, Manciple, and Reve (Fig. 1130). The Miller is the very personification of low mirth and churlish humours; a stout carle, full big of brawn and bones: a famous wrestler, and a goliardeis, so called from Golias, a man of wit at the end of the twelfth century, the founder of a jovial sect, which, if the miller may be taken as a specimen, was not singularly full of moral or Christian graces. It is intimated there was a good deal of dishonesty in the miller-trade, in regard to the corn intrusted to be ground; the character before us, it is said, could well steal corn, beside cheating his customers in their reckonings in some peculiar way. "And yet," exclaims Chaucer, "he hath a thumb of gold, pardie;" alluding to the use of the thumb in testing the qualities of the meal as it came from the spout; on which the old proverb was founded, "Every honest miller has a thumb of gold." Mr. Todd thinks the passage may mean, that, notwithstanding his thefts, he was an honest miller —as honest as his brethren. This uncultivated fellow is prone to jangling and scandalous speech; but, happily for those who are to share his society, he has a bagpipe with him, and can well "blow and soun" upon it (this being an English rustic accomplishment), and so he led the pilgrims out of town. Certainly a curious instrument to announce the approach of a religious cavalcade, and played by a no less unseemly performer; for the miller's face was pale with drinking, and from the same cause he sat uneasily on his horse; to say nothing of other traits of his outward man—the mouth wide as a furnace, the sow's-ear bristles on his nose, the beard red as a fox and broad as a spade, &c.

The Reve, though not a whit more prepossessing, is a very different man for all that. He is particularly slender, with close-shaved beard, and hair docked like a priest's. His choleric nature tells sad things for the poor hinds and their bailiffs under his control as steward of a manor. Every sleight of cunning he knew perfectly; and "they were adread of him as of *the death*;" to which doom, by the way, many of them were liable without judge or jury, at the lord's behest, which would often mean in practice at the steward's. The reve's bargains, it appears, were often made for his own advantage more than for his lord's, and hence he was richly furnished with secret stores; nevertheless, he could please his lord subtilely, and bend him to his own purposes,

And have a thank, and get a côte and hood.

By covenant or agreement he had to give reckoning for the whole estate since his lord was twenty years of age, and that under close auditorship; so, after all, anxieties and cares may have made him the irritable and unpleasing man he is, and be the cause of that unsocial temper which is manifested in his riding over the "hinderest of the rout."

Placed in juxtaposition with this steward of a landed estate, is a steward of a temple—the manciple, as the officers were called who served the different inns of court, colleges, and other public institutions. The word was derived from the Latin *manceps*, and signified, more particularly, a superintendent of a bakehouse, and from thence a baker generally. The office, which chiefly related to provisions, yet exists; as, for instance, at the London Charter-House. This gentle manciple is exceedingly wise in the purchase of provisions; on which Chaucer exclaims, "Now is not that of God a full fair grace," that a wit wholly uncultivated should surpass, and, we presume, take advantage of the wisdom of a heap of learned men!

In the Ploughman (Fig. 1131) we have a direct and delightful testimony to the worth of the obscure; and more especially of the poor tillers of the soil, those of whom laws and lawmakers had hardly begun to take any cognizance, except to keep them in bondage, in spite of all the efforts they were making to rise above it. Chaucer did much for this degraded class when he showed prejudice and injustice how the best Christian virtues often graced their lot —in their peaceful and charitable lives, in their contentedness to labour not alone for self, but for every pouré wight that needed help, "for Christe's sake." And more sweet and effectual we are sure did such brotherly help prove, than the ostentatious and humiliating charities of the rich and proud. Willingly also out of

his small substance—the fruits of his husbandry and his cattle—did the ploughman pay tithes; he was therefore a rural tenant, and, as such, one of a class of which we could say much did space permit. Most of the rural tenantry were in a state of villanage—and hence unable to remove from the place of their settlement to any other spot on the wide earth, were their desire ever so strong; for they formed essentially a part of the estate of the feudal lord, as much as any tree that grew thereon. There is nothing in the description of the ploughman to inform us whether he was a rural tenant in villanage, or *free*. His being on pilgrimage is quite consistent with the former condition, for, to the honour of the Catholic system, its rites and ceremonies were for poor as well as rich, bond as well as free, and the feudal lords under its influence permitted their bondmen often to quit their contracted sphere for the great world in a journey of pilgrimage, for which they furnished them with letters patent that signified the time when they were to return. It is delightful to think what a blessed relief from a monotonous round of servile toil and constant confinement to one scene must have been afforded by such a custom. When, therefore, we are disposed to smile at pilgrimages, let us think of the poor, who owed so much to them. Another beautiful feature of the system must not be overlooked. The poor pilgrim would meet with gratuitious entertainment at the different monasteries and hospitals where such travellers were received, and be assisted in intermediate stages by their fellow-pilgrims of larger means. The ploughman rides on a mare—horses were not used, or rarely, in husbandry; when one horse was kept, therefore, as in the present case, it was simply for riding.

The true British sailor of Chaucer's time exhibited nearly the same strong traits as our own brave tars. The Shipman in the engraving is clad in a gown of falding (coarse cloth) to the knee, and in the Prologue he rides on a common hack, called a rouncie, as well "as he couthe," considering he is little accustomed to such a situation. "For aught I know," says the poet, "he was of Dartemouth;" that place being as famous then for ships and shipmen as now Portsmouth is. He took his share of the perils of war, and rather a large one, and carried his dagger or short sword hanging by a lace about his neck and under his arm. All the trade-vessels were liable to be called at any hour to fight the king's enemies; and there was, we are afraid, a spice of the piratical spirit in them— they thought no harm sometimes to fight as knights fought on land, for the glory and love of the thing, and also for the spoil. If our shipman fought and had the higher hand, why then, wherever he was he sent his ships and prisoners home to their respective lands— first, however, we presume, helping himself with perfect freedom to all that was valuable among the contents of the prizes. The shipman had no nicety of conscience, as we see demonstrated in his conduct at Bordeaux, where he drew full many a draught of wine while the chapman slept. But liberal indulgence is to be made for a sailor's aberrations, and Chaucer's shipman was in the main "a good felaw, hardy and wise." In his stout "barge," the Magdalen, he had sailed far and near.

With many a tempest had his beard been shake.

As for his craft, he knew the tides, the streams, the strands, from Hull to Carthage, the heavens from "Jotland to the Cape Finisterre," and every creek in "Bretagne and Spain;" a knowledge that says much indeed for the naval enterprise of England, even so early as the fourteenth century.

We have next five London citizens (Fig. 1132)—very flattering representatives of the wealth and consequence of our great metropolis at that comparatively early period. Each is attired in a "fresh and new" and handsome livery of "a solemn and great fraternity;" their knives adorned with silver, instead of the ordinary brass. Each looked well worthy to sit on a guildhall dais (raised platform), and to be made an alderman—a dignity their good wives would have not the smallest objection to. For is it not

Full fair to be ycleped Madame,
And for to go to vigils [festival eves] all before [taking precedence,]
And have a mantle royally ybore?

The five trade companies represented by these burgesses were the haberdashers, carpenters, weavers, dyers, and tapisers, or makers of tapestry, then a highly-important trade.

The ecclesiastical abuses of his day are the poet's next mark; and vividly are they shown up to utter scorn and abhorrence, through the medium of the Sumpnour and Pardoner (Fig. 1134). The Summoner was so called from delivering the summonses of the archdeacons to persons discovered to have deviated from the straight path in morals or manners, in witchcraft, defamation, church reves, testaments, contracts, lack of sacraments, usury, simony, and loose life; for such is the list of cases under the summoner's control given in the Frere's Tale. The worthy officer employed spies to inform him what offenders it "*availed*" to punish, or to draw into evil, in order that they might become open to punishment. Full privily it seems the Sumpnour could pull a finch, or, as we should say, pluck a pigeon, by which we understand that he was in the habit of deceiving and plundering the unsuspecting. On the other hand, to give him his due, he was never backward to sell his silence; he would countenance the worst deviation from rectitude for a quart of wine; and if he found liberal treatment, would teach the offender to have no care of the archdeacon's curse, and in all friendliness argue with him that money could clear all. "Purse is the archdeacon's hell," said he; until the dupe discovered a worse probably in a *significavit*, or writ of excommunication; when his case really did reach the archdeacon. The Sumpnour's attainments, person, and tastes correspond with his vocation. We see him crowned with a gay garland, large enough to set up over an alehouse sign: he has made him a buckler of *a cake*; he has a fire-red *cherubinnes* face, with whelkes white, and knobbes sitten on his cheeks—

> Well loved he garlic, onion, and leeks,
> And for to drink strong wine as red as blood;
> Then would he speak, and cry as he were wood [mad].
> And when that he well drunken had the wine,
> Then would he speaken no word but Latíne.
> A fewé termés could he, two or three,
> That he had learned out of some decree.
> No wonder is—he heard it all the day,
> And eke ye knowen well, how that a jay
> Can crepen "Wat!" as well as can the pope.
> But whoso would in other thing him grope,
> Then had he spent all his philosophy.
> Aye, questio quid juris, would he cry.

Quid juris? often occurs in Ralph de Hengham, a law-writer and Chief Justice of King's Bench in the reign of Edward I.—who, after having stated a case, makes use of these words, and then proceeds to answer the question as to what is the law?

The people of this country have long ceased to suffer from the vexatious inquisitions and impositions of Summoners or Archdeacons; they have also ceased to be credulous of relics, such as used to be exhibited by the Sumpnour's amiable friend and compeer the Pardoner; and it could not have been otherwise, after exposures like those which Chaucer gave; for the truth must have been at once and deeply felt, and the conclusion, to common sense, irresistible. The searcher after transgressions, and the vendor of Holy Church's pardons for them, sing together, as they ride; the Pardoner taking the lead, in "Come hither, love, to me!" and the Sumpnour joining in the burden in a voice louder than a trumpet. The Pardoner affects fashion,

> Him thought he rode all of the newé get,

but does not exactly see himself as others see him. His hair in parted locks, yellow as wax, overspreads his shoulders. His hood is trussed up in his wallet, and a small cap, with an ornament on the front, leaves those dishevelled locks all bare to the free admiration of his fellow-pilgrims, and as many others as choose to gaze. His glaring eyes resemble those of a hare. But what of his craft?—his wallet lies on his lap,

> Bretful of Pardon come from Rome all hot.

From Berwick unto Ware there is not another such a Pardoner; so rich is he in potent relics, including a covering of a pillow for Our Lady's veil, a morsel of St. Peter's sail when he walked on the sea, a glass containing "pigges bones," &c., with which, when he found "a poure parson dwelling up on lond," he would make more money in one day than the parson got in two months; and so, says the poet, more broadly than he wont, "he made the parson and the people his apes." The cheat is amusingly candid with the pilgrims, and describes the processes of his trade. On entering a church, he preaches commandingly to the people, informs them he is sent from the pope, and shows his bulls, and "our liegé lordé's seal," on his patent, that no man be so bold as to disturb him in Christ's holy work. Then his precious relics are displayed, and he fairly tells the pilgrims,

> By this gaud have I wonnen, year by year,
> A hundred marks since I was Pardoner.

If any have opposed his or his brethren's practices, the unlucky offender cannot escape being defamed falsely in the course of the Pardoner's preaching; for, though the "noble Ecclesiast" does not tell the proper name, men well know whom he means, by signs and other circumstances: and thus he spits out his venom under the colour of holiness. Such was one of the modes taken to suppress the truth in Chaucer's day, and the shameless frauds practised on the people were thus often acquiesced in through fear. Chaucer, having made the Pardoner boldly confess his own love of lucre, adds,

> *Therefore* my theme is yet, and ever was,
> Radix malorum est cupiditas.
> [The love of money is the root of all evil.]

The principal changes of Costume during the five reigns of the period now drawing to a close will be found so amply exhibited in our engravings as to require little verbal comment. Four of the six examples of ladies' head-dresses in the reign of Henry III. (Fig. 1128) exhibit the hair enclosed in a caul of gold, silver, or silk network: the veil added on one of the heads was called a peplum; and a round hat or cap was also sometimes worn. A beautiful style for the fair and young was the chaplet without the caul, encircling the braided hair with goldsmith's work, or a wreath of nature's jewels—natural flowers. The grey hairs of age, or the sad brows of widowhood, were shadowed with the wimple, or head-kerchief. To this was added, in the time of Edward I. (Fig. 1135), the gorget, a cloth wrapped once, twice, or thrice round the throat, so as utterly to conceal it, and then fastened with a great quantity of pins on either side the face, higher than the ears. "Par Dieu!" exclaims Jean de Meun, the continuator of Lorris's 'Roman de la Rose,' "I have often thought in my heart, when I have seen a lady so closely tied up, that her neckcloth was nailed to her chin, or that she had the pins hooked into her flesh." These head and throat cloths are now peculiar to the habits of nuns, but the cloistered votaresses of old seem to have followed, perhaps often *led*, the fashions of their time. Extravagance in dress was the exception, not the rule, under Edward I., when sterner business engrossed men's minds, and the king himself despised ornament; "it was absurd," he said, "to suppose he could be more estimable in fine than in simple clothing." The head-dresses of Edward II. (Fig. 1136) consisted of a picturesque chaperon or hood, worn by both sexes, and twisted or folded into fanciful shapes. The ladies' costume of this reign (Fig. 1137) gives us the *apron*, called by Chaucer a barme or lap-cloth. The fashions took an entire change in the very lengthened reign of Edward III. The long streamers or tippets in the two engravings of male and female costume form (Figs. 1129, 1138), in our opinion, a more conspicuous than elegant ornament; but in the effigies of William of Windsor and Blanche de la Tour (Fig. 1070), daughter of Edward III.,—examples of the dresses generally worn by the nobility on peaceful occasions—we meet with better taste, particularly in the habit of the princess, in the graceful folds of the lower robe, in the picturesque jacket, bordered with fur (or other costly ornamental materials), and in the mantle flowing down the back, gathering in a voluminous train at the feet, and held on the shoulders by a band of jewels across the full breadth of the chest, thus leaving the arms free, and the whole front of the dress fully displayed. The very prevalent *cote hardie*, worn by William of Windsor, was formed of the richest materials, buttoned closely down the front, and fitted the figure perfectly. In length it descended a very little below the hips, round which was worn a broad and gorgeous girdle. These were the "gay cotes graceless," said, by the Scots, to make England "thriftless." Could the wearers of them now mingle in the sombre-looking crowds of our streets, how they would wonder at the change of tastes which had banished from male attire all their rich variety of material and colour, all their shining embroidery and jewelled arms! and they would think us grown a very dull and spiritless people. Nor less would the subjects of Richard II. marvel to see men living and moving about England without elaborated edges to their garments, of leaves or other forms, without letters or mottoes on them in shining silver, silk, or gold, without party-coloured hose, or excessively short jackets, and even—most wonderful of all—without that fashion of fashions, the long-ypiked shoes, fastened up with silver chains. So we, could we some century or two hence walk these streets, might wonder to find perhaps that the very fashions we now write of as obsolete trifles of the past, were again occupying the fancy and the industry of no small proportion of the nation—such an insubstantial, vacillating, and comparatively uninventive thing is this same *Fashion*.

Of the domestic furniture of the thirteenth and fourteenth centuries the beds of the nobility (Figs. 1141, 1142) were most lavishly adorned. The simple form was that of a railed box or crib;

1251.—Storming a Fort. (Harleian MS. 4379.)

1250.—Archers. (From various MSS. of the 14th Century.)

1252.—Siege of a Town.

1253.—Breaching-Tower; Archers behind their Pavison, Cannon, Crossbow-men, &c.

1254.—Tournament. (Harleian MS. 4379.)

1255.—Tournament. The Melée. Thirty on each side. (Harleian MS. 4379.)

1254.—From an Illumination, Harl. MS. 2278. Temp. Henry VI

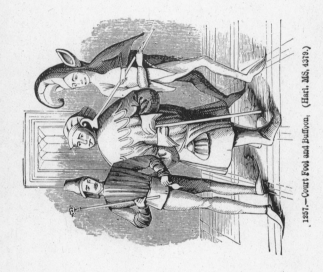

1257.—Court Fool and Buffoon. (Harl. MS. 4379.)

1256.—Court Mummers. (Harleian MS. 4379.)

1260.—Windsor Castle. Great Quadrangle.

1259.—Windsor Castle, North Front and Terrace.

the "brasses," or rails of costly material: the draperies at the head magnificent in substance and in armorial blazonry. In the wills of our old nobility, one bed is mentioned "powdered with blue eagles," one of red velvet, with ostrich feathers of silver, and heads of leopards of gold; others of black velvet, black satin, blue, red, and white silk, &c. Cloth of gold and silver coverlets, and rich *fur of ermines*, are also specified; and sheets of fair white silk, and pillows from the East. The earliest mention of carpets in this country is in the romance of 'King Arthur,' where they are described of silk, "poynted and embroidered with images of gold." The square-backed chair (Fig. 1146) was frequent in the mansions of the thirteenth century. In the fourteenth, they, and other articles combining household utility and elegance, were modified by the pointed architecture, and partook of the beautiful variety of its forms: thus, in the engraving of library furniture (Fig. 1140), we see in the reading-table a miniature spire or pinnacle, with little pointed arches.

We cannot greatly compliment our forefathers on the sport called mummings (Fig. 1143), in which men masqueraded as brutes; but it seems they were determined to have mirth, however they procured it. *We*, perhaps, err on the other hand, and may be too fastidious to be happy. Quarter-staff (Fig. 1144) was the glory of the stout old English peasant or yeoman, in which, as far as we can learn, he was without a competitor in any foreign nation. Draughts (Fig 1145) and chess were amusements of the higher ranks. The circular board (Fig. 1148) is peculiar: the chessmen differed somewhat in form and name from ordinary chessmen. Dulcimer and violin players (Fig. 1147) were among the regular musical performers mentioned in the roll of Edward III.'s household. Hand-bells (Fig. 1149) were also played upon.

But one fact more remains to complete our notices of the 13th and 14th centuries—an extraordinary and all but unaccountable fact, that, previous to the year 1400, when we enter on a new period, not a single specimen of musical invention can be traced—not a dancing tune, or minstrel accompaniment, or church air—though never was a people apparently more keenly alive to the charm of music in connection with the services of the church, with poetry, and with dancing. We should say, therefore, that there *was* plenty of genuine national music, but that it was either unwritten, or that all the MSS. of the art have been lost.

The incidental illustration of costume, furniture, &c., contained in our series of the Chaucer portraits, will not, of course, escape the reader's attention in connection with this department of our subject.

END OF BOOK III.

BOOK IV.

CHAPTER I.—REGAL AND BARONIAL ANTIQUITIES.

THE interest attending the lives of English monarchs generally commences with the act of coronation (Figs. 1150, 1151). In the case of Henry IV. it may be rather said to have ended there. No doubt, that of the three insurrections that disturbed his reign, there was one destined to be long remembered; but the household names connected with that event are those of the great leader, Owen Glendower (Fig. 1162) himself, of his coadjutor, Hotspur, and their youthful conqueror, Henry of Monmouth, not of Henry of Bolingbroke, however deeply the latter was concerned in the issue. Yet was this, as far as King Henry IV. was personally concerned, the most important event of his reign. The future poet-king of Scotland, then a boy, was taken on the seas, and kept in a long captivity: some trifling movements were made in connection with the still-asserted claim of sovereignty over France, and laws were passed declaring that relapsed Lollards, or Lollards who refused to abjure their faith, should be burned; and that was in effect the sum of Henry IV.'s reign. A dreary contrast to the brilliant anticipations caused by his early career: it seemed as though all the genius and energies with which nature had blessed him had been lavished upon the one grand act of his life—the obtaining the English throne—and which, when obtained, he could thus make little or no worthy use of. It appears, indeed, tolerably evident, that remorse preyed upon his mind for his conduct towards Richard, as well it might, if, as has been supposed, he had any hand in, or previous cognizance of, the murder. From being one of the most popular of kings, he became one of the most universally disliked. His friends changed to enemies. His own son became in his lifetime the cynosure of all eyes and hearts: the mightiest man in England was one of the most desolate; Henry could not but perceive that his subjects were weary of him, and looked forward with eager hopes to the day that should see their darling Harry of Monmouth on the throne. To crown all, he suffered from bodily ailments and mental superstitions, and both enhanced in a thousand ways all his other anxieties. He fancied that Heaven would not permit his descendants to enjoy the crown, and at last meditated a pilgrimage to the Holy Land, in order to soothe his conscience, and probably believing too that he should be thus fulfilling the divine behests, as conveyed to him through the prophecy, which had said he should die in Jerusalem. One day whilst he was praying before the shrine of the confessor in Westminster Abbey, he was seized with an apoplectic fit. The attendants carried him to the abbot's apartments, and there laid him down in the chamber which still exists, apparently unaltered against the corner of the western front. He inquired the name of the place;—"the *Jerusalem* Chamber," was the answer. Here Henry IV. died. He was buried at Canterbury, where a sumptuous table-monument (Fig. 1156) bears the effigies of himself and his second wife, Joan of Navarre. Portraits of both, with the great seal, will be found among our illustrations (Figs. 1153, 1155).

Popular as Henry of Monmouth, the prince, had been, sage men shook their heads as they thought of the consequences when he should become king. They remembered that

> His addiction was to courses vain;
> His companies unletter'd, rude, and shallow;
> The hours filled up with riots, banquets, sports;

whilst, on the other hand, they had

> Never noted him in any study,
> Any retirement, any sequestration
> From open haunts and popularity.

Yet had they chosen to look for the soul of good beneath all these things evil, they would have seen it was a most promising and noble soul—one that might accomplish all that other enthusiastic minds only dreamed of, when the right time and circumstances came. We allude not so much to his courage, that shone out so suddenly and so brilliantly in his defeat of the best warrior of his own country and times, in the great northern insurrection, but rather to those romantic incidents which no doubt mainly made him so popular with the people, who in this, as in a thousand other cases, showed their practical wisdom. One of these is supposed to have been afterwards commemorated on the silver coins of Henry V. (Figs. 1181, 1182). The time referred to is the latter part of Henry of Bolingbroke's reign, when, being "somewhat crazy, and keeping his chamber," he received news daily of his son's loose excesses, and heard constructions placed upon them, that at last alarmed him for the safety of himself and crown. When the knowledge of these dreadful suspicions reached the Prince, he

1261,—The Tower in the 15th Century

1265.—The Jewel House.

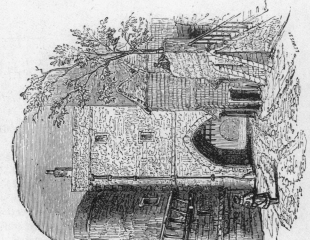

204.—The Bloody Tower— North Side.

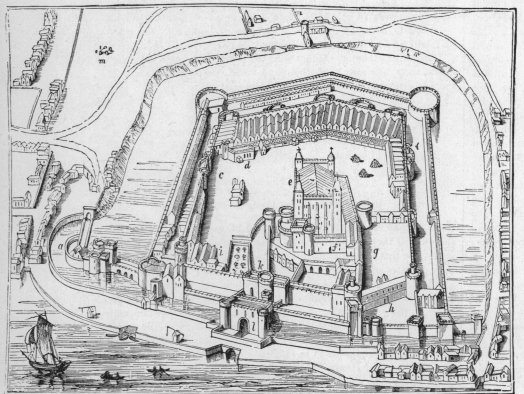

1262.—The Tower of London.

From a Print published by the Royal Antiquarian Society, and engraved from the Survey made in 1597, by W. Haiward and J. Gascoigne, by order of Sir J. Peyton, Governor of the Tower.—*a*, Lion's Tower ; *b*, Bell Tower ; *c*, Beauchamp Tower ; *d*, The Chapel ; *e*, Keep, called also Cæsar's, or the White Tower ; *f*, Jewel House ; *g*, Queen's Lodgings ; *h*, Queen's Gallery and Garden ; *i*, Lieutenant's Lodgings ; *k*, Bloody Tower ; *l*, St. Thomas's Tower (now Traitor's Gate ; *m*, Place Execution on Tower Hill.

1263.—The Tower. Temp. Henry VI.

1267.—Great Hall of Eltham Palace.

1266.—Hall of Eltham Palace.

1268.—Coventry.

1269.—Sandal Castle.

1270.—Great Court of Warwick Castle.

1271.—Pomfret Castle.

strengthened himself with his chief friends, and well-wishers, and with such a troop repaired to his father's court, as a greater in those days had not been seen. (Otterborne.) The manner of his approach is described by an eyewitness, the Earl of Ormond of Ireland. He attired himself in the garb of his college (Queen's, at Oxford, Fig. 1160), " a gown of blue satin, full of oylet holes, and at every hole a needle hanging by a silken thread ;" which, in fanciful explanation of the name of the founder of the college, Eglesfield, was to represent *aiguille*, a needle, and *fil*, thread. We may add, as showing the thoughts upon the mind of the prince, in thus arraying himself, that it had been from a very early period a custom for the bursar of the college to give to each student on New Year's Day the implements just mentioned, with the words, " Take this, and be thrifty." Going, then, to Westminster, with these tokens about him of his faith in, and gratitude for, the peaceful and honourable instruction that had been afforded him in the academic lore of the university, he commanded his followers to wait by the fire in the hall, and then passed on with one of the household to the presence of his father. " The king," continues Earl Ormond, " weak then with sickness, and supposing the worst, commanded himself to be borne into a with-drawing chamber, some of his lords attending upon him, before whose feet Prince Henry fell, and with all reverent observances, spoke to him as followeth :—Most gracious sovereign and renowned father, the suspicion of disloyalty, and divulged reports of my dangerous intendment towards your royal person and crown, hath enforced at this time, and in this manner, to present myself and life at your Majesty's dispose. Some faults and mis-spent time (with blushes I may speak it) my youth hath committed ; yet these made much more by such fleering pickthanks that blow them stronger into your unwilling and distasteful ear. The name of sovereign ties allegiance to all ; but of a father, to a further feeling of nature's obedience, so that my sins were double if such suggestions possessed my heart : for the law of God ordaineth that he which doth presump-tuously against the ruler of his people shall not live, and the child that smiteth his father shall die the death. So far, therefore, am I from any disloyal attempt against the person of you, my father and the Lord's anointed, that if I knew any of whom you stood in the least danger or fear, my hand, according to duty, should be the first to free your suspicion. Yea, I will most gladly suffer death to ease your perplexed heart ; and to that end I have this day prepared myself both by confession of my offences past, and receiving the blessed Sacrament. Wherefore I humbly beseech your grace to free your suspicion from all fear conceived against me with this dagger, the stab whereof I will willingly receive here at your Majesty's hand, and so doing, in the presence of these lords, and before God at the day of judgment, I clearly forgive my death. But the king, melting into tears, cast down the naked dagger (which the prince delivered him), and raising his prostrate son, embraced and kissed him, confessing his ears to have been over-credulous that way, and promising never to open them again against him. But the prince, unsatisfied, instantly desired that at least his accusers might be produced, and, if convicted, to receive punishment, though not to the full of their demerits ; to which request the king replied that, as the offence was capital, it should be examined by the peers, and therefore willed him to rest contented until the next parliament. Thus by his great wisdom he satisfied his father from further suspicion, and recovered his love, that nearly was lost."

The other incident we have alluded to originated in the arraign-ment of one of Prince Henry's servants, before the bar of the King's Bench, for felony. Receiving intelligence that he was to be sentenced to death, the prince posted thither, and found him strongly fettered, and about to be conveyed away for execution ; he immediately commanded his fetters to be struck off, and the felon set free. A command so sudden and peremptory, perfectly astonished and awed the court. In the midst of the panic the chief justice, Sir William Gascoigne (Fig. 1165), stood up, and showed the prince that his seat was the king's ; that laws were the sinews of the commonwealth ; that the prince himself was sworn to do justice, and must yield an account for all that he did ; that he honoured the prince as the eldest son of the sovereign ; but to set free the prisoner he could not, having so apparently endangered his life to the law : and therefore he (the chief justice) desired the prince, if he held the prisoner in such esteem, to save him by pardon from the king, and not to infringe the law, which he told him plainly, *he should not do*. The prince, more enraged by denial, began to resort to violence to enforce his will ; but the chief justice firmly forbade him, commanding him upon his alle-giance to cease from such riot, and to keep the king's peace ; but he was interrupted by Prince Henry, who in a fury stepped up to the bench, and gave Sir William Gascoigne a blow on the face.

The imperturbable judge was not daunted by the outrage, but sat still in his place, and with a bold countenance said, " Sir, I pray you remember yourself ; this seat of judgment, which here I possess, is not mine, but your father's, to whom and to his laws you owe double obedience. If his highness be thus contemned, and his laws violated by you, that should show yourself obedient to both, who will obey you when you are a sovereign, or minister execution to the laws that you shall make ? Wherefore, for this attempt, in your father's name, I commit you prisoner unto the King's Bench, there to remain until his Majesty's pleasure be further known." The storm-fit of the young man was as brief as violent ; he stood mute by the judge, greatly abashed ; and fixing his eyes on his reverend face, laid down his weapons, made an humble obeisance and departed to prison ! When the king heard of this extraordinary scene, he greatly rejoiced that he had a son capable on reflection of such obedience to the laws, and a judge so upright to administer them without either favour or fear. Yet he thought fit to mark his sense of his son's offence by removing him from the presidency of his privy council, and placing his second brother in his stead—a punishment that was deeply felt, but which by no means diminished his general popularity. The sparkles of a better hope were indeed beautifully visible in these ever-memorable and touching incidents ; and no sooner had the breath left his father's body, according to Shakspere, than they merged in the full effulgence of as dazzling a reign as English heart or ambition had learned to desire. Then,

> Consideration like an angel came
> And whipped the offending Adam out of him ;
> Never came reformation in a flood
> With such a heady current, scouring faults ;
> Nor never hydra-headed wilfulness
> So soon did lose his seat, and at all once,
> As in this king.

We are often tempted to ask ourselves, as we pause on the early records of his reign, can this be the same " mad compound of majesty" that played the masquer at Gadshill, and in the Boar's Head Tavern, at Eastcheap, to draw out the humorous vices of the " fat rogue" Falstaff ? Now, his " unlettered, rude, and shallow " companions must not approach him within ten miles, or alter their manners—a most necessary decree, albeit harsh of sound. His " riots, banquets, and sports" are forsaken all ; and instead," every day after dinner, for the space of an hour, his custom was to lean on a cushion set by his cupboard, and there himself received petitions of the oppressed, which with great equity he did redress." His conduct towards the remains of Richard II. was of the same lofty character. They were exhumed by his command, and buried in Westminster Abbey, beside the murdered king's beloved wife Anne of Bohemia. In the funeral procession Henry himself walked as chief mourner. There was in all this evidenced a peculiarly graceful and generous disposition ; and the circumstances are perhaps enhanced, as well as in some degree explained, by our knowledge that Henry of Monmouth had been knighted by the unfortunate Richard only a little time before his ruin by Henry's own father's hands. The young king's magna-nimity towards his enemies deserves also especial admiration. The son of Hotspur was restored to the family estates. Mortimer, the rightful king by descent, was set free from his long captivity, though his name afterwards, as before, was used by those whom no excellence could induce to lay aside their machinations. But as regards Mortimer himself, what danger accrued ? Did Henry live to rue the nobleness of his act of mercy ? We have an answer in the fact, that Mortimer accompanied Henry to France, fought for him, bled for him (he was wounded at Harfleur), and was by his kind master sent home in all care and confidence, to get well again. Thus did the new sovereign win golden opinions from all sorts of people, and found, as true wisdom teaches us we may find, that in so doing it was not at all necessary to dim their lustre to his own conscience, even on the severest self-examination.

The French war, criminal as *we* must now consider it in the abstract to have been, was recommenced by him under much more excusable circumstances than usual. With a sense of a kind of right, there was mingled a just feeling of indignation at the treatment that his honourable overtures for peace received. In the first year of his reign, application was made to Charles VI., king of France, for an alliance with his daughter, the Lady Katherine. The ambassadors, says one French writer, were told " the king had no leisure to think on that business ;" or, according to another authority, Franciscus Rosienius, " The king, scornfully smiling, answered, that France was neither destitute of dukes nor he at leisure to think about the proposition." It was also commanded, that the Duke of Burgundy and all other princes of the blood should make no alliance of marriage with England. The English peers, highly exasperated, met immediately (Fig. 1159); and then was made the famous oration of Archbishop Chichely (Fig. 1172) for a war with France for the conquest of the country; in which he repeated the old arguments with new force, and brought to bear upon the subject an amount of knowledge that might well help to blind Henry to the true character of the policy that the head of the Church—the *Christian* Church of England—advised: namely, war; and one of the worst of wars—a war of acquisition. The archbishop's speech, indeed, may furnish a most valuable lesson to those persons, still too numerous, who think every kind of proceeding, as well as of faith, may be justified by isolated extracts of Scripture, read too in the most literal manner: instead of basing both, as they ought, on a careful consideration of its general tenor and spirit. War was determined on by the assembled council unanimously: and a summons was sent forthwith to France to surrender Normandy, Aquitaine, Guienne, and Anjou. It could not have been made at a worse time for France, which was then reduced to a state of anarchy by her lawless aristocracy, who had been at war with one another, and had oppressed the French people of that fair land during twenty years. The profligate dauphin, who had the upper hand in the state, was at once so foolish and so vulgarly impudent as to send a ton of tennis-balls to King Henry as "bullets most fit for his tender hands, who had spent his youth more among rackets" than in matters of state. Henry quietly answered, that he would repay the dauphin's present with balls of more force, against whose stroke the gates of Paris should not prove rackets sufficiently strong to make them rebound. Immediately he prepared to keep his word, aided with all the wealth, enthusiasm, skill, and courage of England. In what state, we may ask, was France meanwhile? One illustration will suffice by way of answer. "What," cried the poor people of France, when they heard of the mighty preparations for depriving their land of its independence—"what can the English do to us more than we suffer from our own princes?" And when the burghers and others did offer to defend France, they were refused with haughty insolence—none but *gentlemen* were worthy of that honour. For this the said *gentlemen* had to suffer a sore penance. A sincere and manly policy was also wanting in all French negotiations at that time, or respectable terms might have been made. Failing these, the English Parliament met to vote supplies for the war—Henry's uncle, Beaufort (Fig. 1209), opening the proceedings with a speech turning upon the text, "Whilst we have time let us work the good work." On the following April fifteen prelates and twenty-eight peers met in council at Westminster (Fig. 1158), and heard with enthusiasm Henry's announcement of his firm purpose to head in person the war on France, and leave his brother, the Duke of Bedford (Fig. 1198), regent during his absence.

> Now all the youth of England are on fire,
> And silken dalliance in the wardrobe lies.
> Now thrive the armourers, and honour's thought
> Reigns solely in the breast of every man.
> They sell the pasture now to buy the horse,
> Following the mirror of all Christian kings
> With winged heels.

The French began now to feel something of Henry's own earnestness, with a difference however. At the last moment attempts at negotiation were made by a French ambassador, a spirited ecclesiastic, who told Henry he would be either made captive, driven into the sea, or slain. "We shall see," said Henry, and dismissed him with rich presents and marks of honour. At Southampton (Fig. 1166), where rode his mighty fleet of vessels (Figs. 1157, 1167), he was delayed by the conspiracy of some lords who, professing to adopt Mortimer's cause, but receiving, it is supposed, French gold, and acting upon French instructions, had determined upon the almost inconceivable wickedness of killing the youthful and admirable sovereign. Fortunately the plot was discovered, and the plotters sent to the scaffold. The twelve or fourteen hundred vessels at last set sail, bearing an army of six thousand five hundred horse and twenty-four thousand foot. The landing, near Harfleur, occupied three days, and they might have been opposed with effect, but all was perfectly quiet. The siege of Harfleur occupied thirty-six days; then the victorious Henry passed through the streets (Fig. 1169), not proudly as a conqueror, but barefooted to the church of Saint Martin, "where with great devotion he gave most humble thanks unto God for this his first achieved enterprise." The dauphin, declining Henry's challenge to personal combat, prepared to assemble the whole strength and chivalry of France at Rouen. Sickness now attacked the English; shipful after shipful of diseased men were sent home, until a mere remnant was left, and the chiefs began to urge the king to re-embark at once. "No," said Henry, "we must first see, by God's help, a little more of this good land of France, which is all our own. Our mind is made up to endure every peril rather than they shall be able to reproach us with being afraid of them. We will go, an if it please God, without harm or danger; but if they disturb our journey, why then we must fight them, and victory and glory will be ours." So, with at the utmost but nine thousand men, he prepared to pass through Normandy, Picardy, and Artois, to Calais; an attempt so daring as almost to reach the point of imprudence; but then Henry knew that his men, as well as himself, were prepared to perish rather than return without glory to their countrymen, who remained so full of expectation. So *Forward!* was the word. French armies, fresh and vigorous, were gathering from all directions under the mightiest chiefs of the realm on the line of his route; but still the cry was, Forward! Attacks multiplied, famine pressed, sickness weakened, and fatigue lay heavy on the strongest. Still they went on—those gallant hearts—until they saw before them the river Somme, where every bridge had been broken down, every fort fortified, and where multitudinous columns of horse and foot covered the opposite bank. Yet that river must be crossed. A chaplain of the army says, "I and many others looked bitterly up to heaven, and implored the divine mercy." Much time was lost in trying to force a passage, and had the French fallen on their rear we should not have had to record the battle of Agincourt. Get over, however, ultimately they did, baggage and all. The French constable fell back disconcerted on the Calais road: the English followed, and, as it seemed, to certain death. When all the war strength of France had assembled, they sent notice to Henry they should give him battle. He replied, calmly and firmly, that "he meant to march to Calais,—not to seek them,—but left the issue to God;" and then regularly and steadily he pursued his dismal route, men dropping about him continually. The French made their stand at the village of Agincourt: Henry did the same in another village close by. Night intervened, and the moon shone over combatants thus picturesquely contrasted: "The French, gallant, fresh, and, through vain hope of honour, already mounted above men of mean rank: the English, weak, weary, and sore starved, made no such show, and yet their courage was no less than the other. The one spending the night before battle in feasts, triumphs, and other-like sports, distributing their captives, dividing their spoils, and decreeing none to be saved but the king and his nobles, all others must die or be incurably maimed: the other, trimming their arrows, sharpening their spears, buckling their armours, and refreshing their bodies for the next day; and, beside other observances, by the light of the great fires made in the French camp the English discerned what was therein done, and took the advantage of their order and ground." Those "other observances" of the English included also solemn preparation for death, and exhilarating *martial music*. Next morning "the beauty and honourable horror of both the armies no heart can judge of, unless the eye had seen it: the banners, ensigns, and pennons (Fig. 1171), streaming in the air, the glistering of armours, the variety of colours, the motion of plumes, the forests of lances, and the thickets of shorter weapons, made so great and goodly a show." The armies thus ranged, awhile stood still and faced each other. Then King Henry, in bright armour (Fig. 1173), distinguished by a rich coronet on his helmet, mounted on a horse of "fierce courage," with the royal standard borne before him, with cheerful countenance and words full of resolution, rode through his ranks. "We have not come," said he, "into our kingdom of France like mortal enemies, *we have not burnt towns and villages*, we have not outraged women and maidens, like our adversaries at Soissons;" where, in addition to these atrocities, two hundred brave English prisoners had been hung like dogs. The allusion had an almost electric effect. Still there was cause enough to make the most brave warrior doubtful of the issue. Walter Hungerford [Shakspere says the Earl of Westmoreland (Fig. 1161)] wished that some of the many men then living in idleness in England could be present there. "No," exclaimed Henry, "the fewer there are, the more honour; and if we lose, the less will be the loss to our country. But we will *not* lose; fight as you were wont to do, and before night the pride of our numberless enemies shall be humbled to the dust." And so it was. The wonderful success of the English in this battle has been attributed chiefly to the perfect unity of spirit among them; and the disgraceful failure of the French to their divisions. "The Constable," says M. de Barante, an eminent writer, "was, by right of his office, the commander-in-chief of the French army, but there were with him so many princes who had wills of their own, that it was not easy for him to obtain obedience." The consequence was, that the very numbers which gave the French all their mighty strength proved unwieldy and confused in action; whilst Henry, with his mere handful of men, laid his plans with such consummate art, and

1272.—West-Gate. Canterbury

1273.—Present state of Borthwick Castle.

1274.—Moveable Tower of Archers, Cannon, &c. (Royal MS.

1275.—Tomb of Sir John Crosby

1276.—St. George's Chapel, Windsor.

1278.—Eton College.

1277.—St. George's Chapel, Windsor, South Front.

prompted their execution with such calm unwavering confidence, that his little army proved perfectly irresistible. Next to Henry's genius, it was the bravery and skill of the fine old English bowmen that won Agincourt. As the bow was a vulgar weapon, they had no competitors on the other side, where all stood on their gentility; so, undismayed by the far-stretching and innumerable ranks of heavily-mailed and splendidly-adorned horsemen, they threw aside their leathern jackets, and waited like eager hounds in the leash for the king's order to begin the attack. Near noon Henry gave the welcome words—"Banners, advance!" and in the enthusiasm of the moment the leader of the archers, Sir Thomas Erpingham (Fig. 1175), *threw his truncheon into the air*, and cried aloud, "Now strike!" The archers ran forward to within bow-shot of the French, planted their stakes, and did great havoc by the rapidity and impetuosity of their flights of arrows. Some confusion was produced by a charge from the great leading division of the foe; but the archers rallied, and leaving their stakes, and slinging their bows behind them, grasped their billhooks and hatchets, and with bare and brawny arms sprang among the knightly melée, making the welkin ring again with the war-shout of England. Many a famous gentleman of France sank before them, including the Constable himself, and speedily the French dead became so numerous as to form a kind of wall, on the top of which our men leaped to continue the fight. The encounter of the *chivalry* of England and France nevertheless took place with fearful odds against the former. The beautiful nature of Henry here again shone out: he was seen planted by, or, according to Speed, bestriding the fallen body of his brother Clarence and beating off the assailants. The stroke of a battle-axe brought the hero himself to his knees, and after that the coronet on his casque was cut through by a similar blow; but he who made it was instantly slain, as he was in the act of calling out to Henry "I surrender myself to you, I am the Duke of Alençon." The battle was closed in effect with his fall. And certainly never, under a Hannibal or a Napoleon, was there one more wonderful, whether we regard the mighty energies lavished on it—the discrepancy of numbers—the genius of the conqueror—or the death-roll of noble names, numbering, it is thought, eight thousand gentlemen of France, seven of whom were personal relatives of the French king, and a hundred and twenty knights-in-chief, or banner-knights. Like the Black Prince, Henry brought back to England with him an illustrious captive the Duke of Orleans, who had been pulled out from under a heap of slain. As to John of France, so to this royal duke was the most marked courtesy paid. Once when Henry was trying to console him, the king is recorded to have given this striking testimony to the misery of France:—"If God has given me the grace to win this victory, I acknowledge that it is through no merits of mine own. I believe that God has willed that the French should be punished; and if what I have heard be true, no wonder at it; for they tell me that never were seen such a disorder, such a licence of wickedness, such debauchery, such bad vices, as now reign in France. It is pitiful and horrible to hear it all, and certes, the wrath of the Lord must have been awaked."

At Dover the English rushed into the sea to meet their victorious king, on his return, and actually bore him on their shoulders to the shore. We call ourselves the *sober* English—our forefathers had plenty of fire in their veins, as was very clear not only in that reception, but through all the subsequent proceedings. As Henry rode toward London, never was such enthusiasm—such rapture—such boundless and passionate love beheld as everywhere welcomed him. And they admired him the more for his modesty, in not allowing his broken casque and bruised arms (Fig. 1170) to be carried before him (Fig. 1168). The victory of Agincourt opened the way to Henry's alliance with Catherine (Fig. 1177), princess of France, to his being adopted heir and regent of France, and virtually to his exercising over it the power of a king. And to give the climax to the greatness of Henry V., and to show the true origin, after all, of the people's love for him, we may observe, on the one hand, that the "poor people of France" grew happier under his rule than they had been for many a day, and honoured his death only with less intensity than Henry's own subjects, who, on the other, there is every reason to believe, never had occasion to make *one complaint of his government* (Fig. 1186). Worth a thousand such brilliant victories as Agincourt is that one homely-sounding fact. His death and burial have already been described in our account of Westminster Abbey, it will only be necessary therefore to refer to the page in question (Fig. 287), and to our additional engraving (Fig. 1187) representing the tomb in the abbey, with the effigy of Henry, to which we have restored the head. The personal appearance of Henry is represented at very different periods of his life in our engravings of the boy (Fig. 1163) and the warrior (Fig. 1176): see also the great seal (Fig. 1178).

When Henry V. died, his son, named after himself, was but nine months old: the unsettled character thus given to the reign at its commencement, followed it to its premature and terrible close. It would have been impossible to have found a better regent than was chosen to exercise rule during the king's minority: the very name of Humphrey the Good (Fig. 1213) was a tower of strength; and notwithstanding the weakness that almost invariably characterizes regencies, all seems to have gone well in England, until the boy for whom so much had been done to smooth the way to actual as well as nominal power, grew to a man, and showed his utter unfitness for his position. Henry, it has been said, would have made an excellent monk: no wonder, therefore, that he did make a very bad king. His intentions were admirable; but served only as a foil to show off his utter want of power to perceive what he should intend, and the absence of all firmness in carrying resolve into execution. Two great events mark his reign: the loss of all, or nearly all, that his father had gained in France; and the wars of the Roses, which deprived him of all that his birthright had given him in England: for the first he was in no way personally answerable; the second may be considered to have entirely originated in his own infirmity of character.

Whilst Duke Humphrey became Protector at home, another and elder brother, the Duke of Bedford (Fig. 1198), equally or even more highly gifted, assumed the administration of affairs abroad—that is to say in France. We are not about to detail step by step the decline of our power in that country, which proceeded steadily, if slowly, in spite of occasional victories, and in spite of the most consummate prudence and energy. It is true, there was a time when the duke thought he could recover the lost ground; and so, in 1428, he prepared to make a great effort for the extension of the English sovereignty beyond the Loire. The posture of affairs was encouraging in many points, but especially in these—that France, like England, had a very young monarch, and was divided against itself, through the jealousies and hatred of the two great houses of Orleans and Burgundy; the latter of whom was now in alliance with the English. The city of Orleans was besieged by the Earl of Salisbury (Fig. 1174); and Charles saw no hope of saving even that last bulwark of his kingdom. Then it was that a new and extraordinary personage appeared upon the scene, whose doings could be only accounted for in her own age by the supposition that they were connected with sorcery—and who in ours, and in all succeeding ages is, and will be, a subject for the deepest sympathy and warmest admiration, not only on account of her melancholy fate, but also for her lofty and beautiful character. The mists that so long obscured the life of Joan of Arc—and which, among many other manifestations of its effects, caused Voltaire to injure permanently his own reputation by misunderstanding and ridiculing hers—have passed away; and poets and philosophers in all countries have rivalled each other in the fervency and grandeur of their tributes to her genius and virtue. Schiller in Germany, and Southey in England—two names that at once occur among others—are for ever bound up with the memory of the heroic French peasant's daughter. Joan was born in 1410 or 1411, in the little hamlet of Domremy, near the Meuse, on the borders of Champagne; and there it was that she imbibed her rustic superstitions and her fervent public spirit; for even in that remote district village rose against village—Burgundians against Armagnacs (the Orleans party). And what was it but those superstitions and that public spirit acting upon a generous and enthusiastic temperament, that made the girl of thirteen a marvel unto her fellow-villagers, and ultimately caused the woman to excite the wonder of a world? Among the superstitions was one to the effect that France would be yet saved by a virgin; it was not long before Joan conceived the idea that it was she who was to realize the faith. Then strange visions were hers; she saw a great light, from amidst which a voice proceeded, bidding her be devout and good, and promising her the protection of Heaven. Rising with the demands made upon her, Joan prepared herself for the great work, and, as a commencement, vowed eternal chastity. Again and again came the voices, until Joan found them her constant companions and advisers. At last they bade her take the grand step, and act—they prompted her to quit her parents and home, take arms, and drive the foe before her until the young king should be able to be crowned in the national place of coronation, Rheims. Joan may have smiled to herself in her calmer moments as she recapitulated such a programme of proceedings; but the smile would be succeeded by a still calmer expression of confidence, as with eyes mirroring, as it were, the shadows of the future that passed before her mind, she gazed deeply into her own nature, and saw that she was equal to the position. But she was a maiden, she was young, she was friendless—and still she hesitated. The incursions of a band of Burgundians into her native village, and the destruction of her beloved church, decided her. The voices then became even still more practical. They not only bade her commence her mission, but directed her as to the best mode—she was to go to De Baudricourt, the governor of Vaucouleurs. Joan did so, and was treated with contempt. But there were others who believed, in spite of De Baudricourt's scepticism. The whole history of human kind shows how mighty is the power of self-conviction, when we would influence others. No scheme, however absurd and pernicious, but has obtained disciples through its influence: nothing greatly good will ever be achieved in its absence. Among the converts whom Joan of Arc's faith in herself had induced to arrive at a similar conclusion, were two gentlemen, named John of Metz and Bertram of Poulegny: these ultimately obtained permission of the governor of Vaucouleurs to conduct her to the dauphin; so it was evident that even he was moved at last, though the paramount motive with him in sending her may have been his desire to do anything that might have a tendency to raise the French from their desperate condition, and enable them to raise the siege of Orleans. Joan's powers were put to a severe trial on her first appearance at court: she was required to recognise Charles as he stood amongst his nobles, undistinguished in any way from them. She did so. Even that was not enough. It was agreed she had a mission—but was it from heaven, or from the Evil One? A body of ecclesiastics proceeded to determine that point. Her chastity, of which the most unquestionable evidence was obtained, proved, according to the notions of the day, that Joan of Arc was indeed commissioned by God to deliver France from her enemies; even though she declined to perform miracles, answering ever to such requests—"Bring me to Orleans, and you shall see. The siege shall be raised, and the dauphin crowned king at Rheims." Joan was now raised to the rank of a military commander; she arrayed herself in suitable armour, and sent for a sword from Fierbois, where she said one would be found buried within the church. The sword was dug up at the spot indicated; Joan, it is to be observed, had spent some time at Fierbois previously. It was not long before Orleans was relieved by the entrance of a body of French with Joan at their head, though not by the path that she would have chosen if the French leaders would have permitted her—right over the English fortifications. Their spirits, however, raised by this first successful step, the French speedily consented to follow Joan, or La Pucelle, as she was called, to attack the English strongholds. They were forced one after another. The English behaved as of yore, but it was of no avail against men who fought with a more than mortal bravery, such confidence had been instilled into their hearts by their young and beautiful and religiously-inspired leader. Joan herself shared in one of the fiercest assaults, and was wounded by an arrow in the shoulder just as she was about to ascend a scaling-ladder. She was taken aside, and for a moment the woman overcame her—she wept: but the sight of her standard in danger renewed all her heroism—she forgot her wound, leaped up, ran back, and presently the irresistible French drove all before them. The siege was then raised; and in one week Orleans was altogether free from its terrible enemy. It is not necessary to enumerate the remaining steps of her wonderful career; suffice it us to say, that in spite of the presence of the bravest of the English warriors, our countrymen were everywhere beaten; until, at the battle of Patey, even John Talbot himself, the famous Earl of Shrewsbury (Fig. 1199), was not only defeated, but taken prisoner. Within three months after the first appearance of Joan on the scene, Rheims opened its gates without attempting to strike a blow in defence; and Charles was crowned, where the virgin had prophesied he should be. With that act her work may be said to have been essentially accomplished. She had roused and animated the national feeling and courage, and there was no longer any danger of permanent defeat; a consideration that must have been full of consolation to her under the frightful circumstances attending the close of her career. In May, 1430, she was taken prisoner by the Burgundian party, who ultimately handed her over to the English. And then commenced the proceedings which were to make for ever infamous all those directly concerned in them. Under pretence of trial, this maiden, not yet arrived to the age of womanhood, was for month after month harassed by unceasing examinations and interrogations, in order to draw from her the acknowledgement of the influences which had actuated her, and which might then form the groundwork for the charge of sorcery which it was desired to bring against her. Of course the reverend and learned inquisitors were successful; one by one they drew forth the statement of the visions, and the belief in them that Joan's highly-wrought enthusiasm had given rise to. More than all, they obtained from her a declaration that she declined to submit to the

ordinances of the church, whenever her voices told her to resist; which was in effect but saying that she would follow the guidance of that inward light which had been given to her, and by which alone she, and all of us, can safely walk, seeing that it is the power which must test all things before we can worthily accept anything—church ordinances not excluded. But ignorance is ever intolerant of what it does not understand; and Joan's judges, having had no experience of the influences that determined her to lofty and sublime action, could only attribute the whole to some evil spirit, for which again poor Joan was to become bodily responsible. She was declared guilty of heresy and schism, and threatened with the stake if she did not acknowledge her visions to be false, forswear male habits and arms for the future, and own how deeply she had erred. These are the tricks that men play with human nature, before high heaven, and which are indeed sufficient to make angels weep, or a Mephistopheles laugh. Joan indignantly resisted. The scaffold was prepared at Rouen (Fig. 1201); the victim brought forth. The bishop of Beauvais read the sentence; and while he was reading, the pious men who would have moved heaven and earth to induce her in effect to destroy her soul—by saving it in their way—were very solicitous about the dangers to her body. Joan was moved. The frightful aspect of the scene was too much for her. She uttered some words of contrition; a form of confession was instantly produced, and to that the miserable, wretched creature—not daring to pause to think of what she did—signed with a cross, the only signature she could make. She was led back to prison under a sentence of perpetual imprisonment. Well, was this not enough for the most bigoted of all earthly men, for the most hard of heart of all Joan's unnatural *French* enemies? No; the inconceivably cruel and base men in whose hands she was, placed her male attire in her dungeon, hoping, we presume, either thoroughly to break down every particle of the heroine's lofty and undaunted nature, by showing her to herself as too timid to give vent in any way to the feeling that was certain to rise in her heart at the sight of these tokens of her glorious career; or to entrap her, should she be induced by any revulsion of sentiment to put them on once more. Joan did put them on; and with them all her original faith, courage, and fortitude. She heard her voices reproaching her with her pusillanimity; she determined to be true to them and herself. She told her persecutors, "What I resolved, I resolved against truth: let me suffer my sentence at once, rather than endure what I suffer in prison." Her fate was then sealed irrevocably. Again the scaffold and the faggots were prepared; again the vast sea of upturned and unpitying faces met the eye of the friendless maiden in the market-place of Rouen; again she wept, but not again was there to be the smallest symptom that Mercy had any place in the world. She was burnt, and her ashes afterwards thrown into the Seine. The old monument (Fig. 1200) marks at once the scene of the transaction, and the opinion of Joan's later countrymen upon it. There have been some not very profitable discussions as to *where* the infamy of this execution chiefly lies; whether with the English, who sanctioned and, as it were, superintended the murder (the great Cardinal Beaufort (Fig. 1209) was present, but was so overcome as to be obliged to retire before the close), or with the French of Joan's own party, who made not the smallest effort to rescue her, although she had done everything for them,—or, lastly, with the French of the opposite party, who first took her captive, and then were in effect her real executioners: it seems to us that, the different circumstances of each party considered, they may on the whole divide the merit of the deed pretty equally between them. This tragedy, consummated in 1431, for a time checked the retrograde progress of the English authority in France; the more especially that the spell having been removed, which chilled all the fire of our troops, such men as the Duke of Bedford and the Earl of Shrewsbury recovered the supremacy naturally belonging to their great skill and indomitable energy; but in 1435 the duke died, and eighteen years later the earl was defeated and killed in battle. And with brave John Talbot, the man whom sovereigns and people had alike delighted to honour (see the portraits and other engravings illustrative of his career, Figs. 1190, 1199, 1202, 1203), we lost also every inch of ground we had possessed in France, Calais only excepted. Such was the issue of one of the great questions of the reign of Henry VI. We now address ourselves to the other, involving that period so peculiarly interesting to all Englishmen, the Wars of the Roses.

The origin of the poetical designation given to these wars is supposed to have been an incident that took place in the Temple Gardens on the Thames, when were present the chief of the younger branch of the Lancastrian or kingly family, the Duke of Somerset, and the chief of the Plantagenets, the Duke of York. These two are quarrelling; and Plantagenet, impatient at perceiving that the

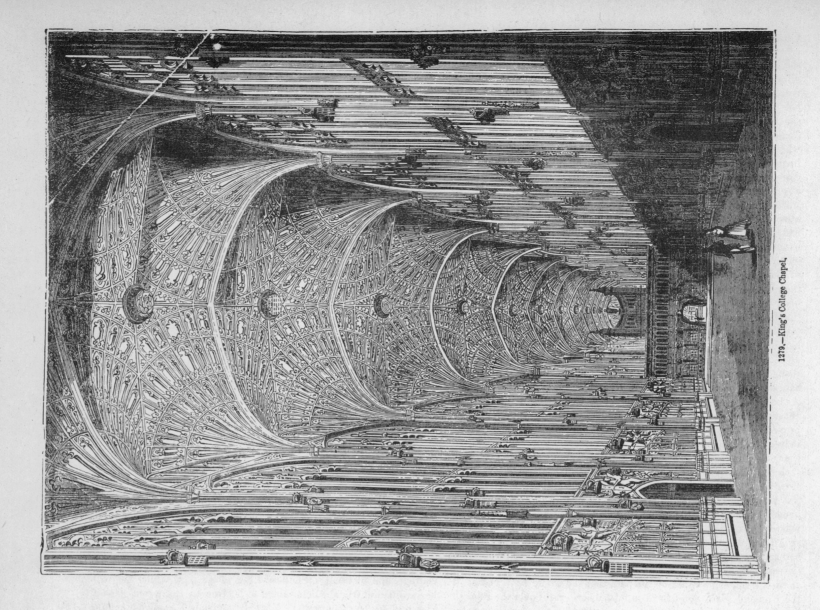

1279.—King's College Chapel,

1280.—King's College Chapel.

1281.—Doorway, King's College Chapel, Cambridge.

1282.—Dutch Church, Austin Friars.

1283.—Crypt, Guildhall.

1284.—Porch of St. Alphage.

1285.—Interior of St. Helen's.

1286.—Tower of St. Michael's, Cornhill.

1287.—Cloisters, Charter-House.

1289.—St. Michael le Quern.

1288.—Inner Gateway, Charter-House.

nobles around seem unwilling to give an opinion as to which of the disputants is right, and probably attributing their unwillingness to their deference to Somerset's position as the great man of authority and influence on the kingly side, exclaims—

> " Since you are tongue-tied, and so loth to speak,
> In dumb significants proclaim your thoughts :
> Let him that is a true-born gentleman,
> And stands upon the honour of his birth,
> If he suppose that I have pleaded truth,
> From off this brier pluck a *white rose* with me."

Somerset accepts the challenge, and immediately adds :—

> " Let him that is no coward, nor a flatterer,
> But dare maintain the party of the truth,
> Pluck a *red rose* from off this thorn with me."

The nobles pluck their red and white roses, in mute expression of their opinions of the previous argument; and possibly at the same time half intimating their anticipation of the coming mightier one, for which also they thus take sides. Suffolk plucks the red rose; he is with Somerset—Warwick the white; he is with Plantagenet. Add to the former the other powerful members of Somerset's family—the Beauforts, and especially the great cardinal; add to the latter, the Earl of Salisbury, Warwick's father, and we see with tolerable accuracy the two great baronial divisions formed during the struggles for political power that each party so ardently desired, as involving under such a sovereign as Henry VI. all the real powers of sovereignty.

Before, however, these parties became so formed, and so confronted each other, most, if not all of the members of both, had found ample employment in getting rid of a man whose nature was of too lofty a kind to descend to the intrigues they so much delighted in, and who saw too plainly the evils of faction to allow them even to pursue their own way unmolested. This was the Duke of Gloucester, the king's uncle and presumptive heir,— the *good* Duke Humphrey, as the people admiringly and affectionately designated him. He had been placed at the head of the Council of Regency, immediately after the death of Henry V.; but there was also in that Council Henry Beaufort, Bishop of Winchester, a man of the most unbounded ambition, and who never ceased his endeavours to supplant the duke, until, failing every other means, he succeeded at last by having the young king, a boy of eight years old, crowned, and Gloucester's office of Protector abolished. If any evidence were needed that it was Beaufort's unprincipled ambition that was the real cause of all the contentions that kept England for so many years in trouble, and which had more than once nearly broken out into civil war, it is furnished by this act—on the face of it a dishonest one. If Gloucester were an unfit Protector, why another might have been appointed; but to pretend that the eight-year old king did not want a Protector at all, was, under the circumstances, perhaps a stroke of subtle policy, but not one calculated to win our admiration for its ecclesiastical author. Beaufort thus succeeded, and Gloucester descended to the position of a mere peer of the realm. But even then he so exposed the misdoings of the new governors, as to bring upon the cardinal the necessity of asking and obtaining from parliament an immunity for all *crimes* committed up to a certain period. The hatred of the Beauforts towards "good Duke Humphrey," under such circumstances, may be imagined; and as he had attacked, to the great satisfaction of the nation at large, the custom of choosing statesmen from the church, the whole body of churchmen shared the cardinal's feelings, and sought to compass his ruin. Other influences were in operation to aid them in that object. In 1445 Henry had married (Fig. 1191) the beautiful but unprincipled and masculine-minded daughter of the King of Sicily (Fig. 1206), who speedily showed to the English people her contempt alike for her husband and their notions of morality, by lavishing every mark of favour that it was in her power to bestow on the minister who had negotiated the marriage, the Earl of Suffolk. These two now sought to concentrate in themselves all the power of the realm, and, as the people believed, for the worst purposes. One man, again, stood in *their* way—" the good duke;" who was also the man, as Margaret, no doubt, took care to remember, who had opposed Henry's marriage with her when first proposed. For the events that follow, it is now impossible to say to which party, that of the queen and her favourite, or that of the Beauforts, we should attribute them. Suffice it that Gloucester's utter ruin *was* determined upon and accomplished, and must therefore have had its agents. If his inveterate enemies who obtained the credit of such deeds were innocent, they have certainly been very unfortunate.

Gloucester's wife was first attacked. Being a great patron of learning, the duke supported constantly in his house certain doctors and clerks, among whom was one Roger Bolingbroke, an adept in all the astrological mysteries of the day. The duchess, thinking somewhat too curiously of her husband's prospects, is supposed to have been desirous to know the time of the king's death, and to have held, therefore, consultations with the clerk as to the means of discovery. The simple credulity of the duchess is evident, for it was proved she had sought for love-philters to secure the constancy of her husband; but it was not proved that she had sought to hasten as well as to know the period of Henry's death as charged against her; and which it was stated she strove to accomplish by keeping by her a wax figure endowed with such magical sympathy, that in proportion as it wasted away, when melted before a fire, so would the flesh and substance of King Henry wither and dissolve. She was found guilty, however, and sentenced to perpetual confinement, besides doing public penance at three different places in London. The duke, whatever his emotions, stifled them, and instead of breaking out into violence, as may have been hoped, appeared patient and resigned. A short time after, a parliament was summoned at Bury St. Edmund's; the duke went without suspicion, was arrested for high treason, and in a few days later found dead in his bed : murdered there can hardly be a doubt. Our great poet makes both Suffolk and the cardinal participators in the crime. Beaufort, strangely enough, survived the duke but six weeks. His dying thoughts, as described by Shakspere, present the most awful picture of a criminal and despairing mind that the whole range of literature can afford,—

> Died he not in his bed? Where should he die?
> Can I make men live, whe'r they will or no?
> O! torture me no more, I will confess—
> Alive again? then show me where is !
> I'll give a thousand pounds to look upon him.—
> He hath no eyes, the dust hath blinded them.—
> Comb down his hair; look, look, it stands upright
> Like lime-twigs set to catch my winged soul !—
> Give me some drink; and bid the apothecary
> Bring the strong poison that I bought of him.

The amiable monarch, who bends over him, anxious for his soul's welfare, solemnly adjures him,—

> Lord Cardinal, if thou think'st on heaven's bliss,
> Hold up thy hand, make signal of thy hope.—
> He dies, and makes no sign.

Now, if the poet were right in attributing the murder of good Duke Humphrey, in part to this old man of eighty years, as the concluding act of a life full of turmoil, and ambition, and worldly acquisition,—and we have seen how much ground there is to presume Shakspere *was* right in so doing,—who, in that case, shall say that penetrating beneath the surface, and discarding the mere conventionalities of the bed of death, the dramatist has not given us the essential *truth* after all, even though it be known that the cardinal bade all present pray for him, and that when he could no longer enjoy his enormous wealth in person, he still made it subservient to his fame, by directing that a considerable portion of it should be expended in works of charity?

Suffolk was now supreme in power, and the formidable insurrections under Jack Cade may be taken as evidence of the character of his government, which became at last unbearable to other classes of the people of England than those which had followed Cade. The Commons impeached the favoured minister, and were evidently determined upon his conviction and death. The queen was no less determined to save him; and the weak Henry having been induced to throw himself into the breach, Suffolk was banished for five years— to the discontent of both parties. The people endeavoured to seize him, and execute justice in their own summary fashion; but he escaped, and embarked for the Continent. As the two small vessels that carried him and his retinue were between Dover and Calais, they were brought-to by a great ship-of-war, the Nicholas, from whence presently came orders for the duke to come on board. As Suffolk stepped upon the deck, he was received by the significant salutation, "Welcome, traitor !" For two days, however, his fate remained uncertain, the captain of the Nicholas, in the mean time, constantly communicating with the shore; but on the third day a boat came alongside, with block, axe, and executioner all prepared; and Suffolk was speedily sent to his great account. And thus, one by one, were the men swept away from the scene, upon which a more important actor than any of them had been long, but secretly waiting for a favourable opportunity to enter and play his part. This was the Plantagenet of the Temple Gardens, the man in whose person centred the real right to the throne, as the lineal descendant from the *third* son of Edward III.; except,—and the exception of course, in ordinary circumstances, ought to be a decisive one,—possession, and the long-continued sanction of the nation through three reigns, were to be considered as making permanent the seizure of the throne by Bolingbroke, who was descended from the *fourth* son of the king before named. But it must be confessed the circumstances of Henry's reign were not ordinary ones. That king was not only weak at the best of times, but unable, at certain periods, even to appear to exercise kingly authority. And although there was no hope of supplanting the good duke, had he lived to succeed his nephew, that difficulty was removed by his assassination. And, in short, Richard Plantagenet (Fig. 1207), to speak of him by the name that Shakspere has made familiar, determined to aim, at least, at the attainment of the 'golden round;' continuing, however, to act with his usual prudence and secrecy, and confine his exertions for a time to the task of winning the Parliament of England to his cause, by his great deference to their authority, in all the offices entrusted to him, and more especially in the protectorship of the realm, rendered necessary during the king's fits of aberration. He took up arms, it is true—and more than once—but that was with the full sympathy of the nation at large, and in order to check the continual machinations of the court party, of whom Queen Margaret was still the ruling spirit, and Somerset—a Beaufort in ambition as well as in blood—the professed leader. And here, as in all the private events that we have spoken of, circumstances worked most favourably for Plantagenet; as enabling him to draw together all the armed force that he could, and yet in so doing to appear but as a supporter of the people generally, against a most unpopular minister. The aspect of affairs, therefore, when the wars of the Roses really began, was this:—two great baronial parties in the state struggling for political power, and for each other's destruction, and one of the two at the same time concealing beneath its ostensible claims, others of an infinitely more important and dangerous kind. And it is only by keeping in view the complex character of the wars at their commencement, and the insincerity almost necessarily imposed upon the combatants by their position and views, that we can understand how Englishmen became engaged in such deadly hostilities with so little apparent principle to fight for on either side—how such battles as that of St. Albans (Fig. 1212) came to be fought, for no other evident reason but to decide whether Plantagenet or Somerset should be chief minister. In that bloody field the royalists lost their leader, Somerset, with other nobles; and the king himself, a warrior only in his appearance (Fig. 1192), fell into the hands of the Duke of York, as prisoner. Still the latter contented himself with a kind of modest reversion to his former state of protector, with, however, this important change in the terms of his appointment, that he held it during the parliament's, and not the king's pleasure. And that was all the use he made of the battle of St. Albans. He had not even the gratification of obtaining what he had most probably all along hoped and wrought for, a formal parliamentary declaration that he should be the successor to the throne. And soon after, all hopes of this nature were destroyed by the birth of a prince. The duke, however, does not appear to have esteemed the event by any means of the decisive character that might have been anticipated. As the nation generally looked upon the child as the son of Suffolk, and not of King Henry, the Duke of York found it easy to do the same; and so abated, it should seem, no jot of heart or hope that he would yet be king of England. If so, it was clear that there must be some more powerful acting mind than the duke's at work, and that mind he found in his great coadjutor Warwick, one of the most eminent—perhaps, on the whole, the most eminent—of English nobles. (Fig. 1208.) This eminence was partly owing to position: the Nevil family, to which the earl belonged, was, it is supposed, at that time the most extensively-connected family ever known in England; and the earl himself was immensely rich; but his eminence was still more directly based on his personal qualities: on his unbounded hospitality; his frank and affable bearing; on his eloquence and general talents; on his military skill: so that with all classes of men he was necessarily popular. The people seem to have almost adored him. And it must be acknowledged, he had found a happy mode of preparing them to appreciate all his excellences. "When he came to London," says Stow, "he held such a house, that six oxen were eaten at a breakfast, and every tavern was full of his meat; for who that had any acquaintance in that house he should have had as much sodden and roast as he might carry upon a long dagger." In fine, he kept open house wherever he resided; and it has been estimated that not less than *thirty thousand* persons were fed daily at his different mansions during the period of his prosperity. Such was the man who bound up his fortunes with Plantagenet, and really did for him all that was done.

He it was who chiefly won the battle of St. Albans, and thus marked himself out for the especial attacks of the queen and her party. Thus when Henry, once more interposing with kind thoughts and desires, patched up a formal reconciliation between Margaret and Plantagenet, and induced them to walk together most lovingly hand in hand with him to St. Paul's, it was Warwick who first experienced the hollowness of the reconciliation, in an attempt to assassinate him in the streets of London, in consequence of which he suddenly left the metropolis. It was he, again, who, after the parliament that met at Coventry in 1459 had attainted him, with Plantagenet, and all their chief friends, shortly returned to express his opinions of the attainder, at the head of thirty thousand men. It was he who then gave Plantagenet the courage and determination to throw aside the mask, at last, and declare his purpose; and most characteristic was the duke's method of doing so. He returned from Ireland, entered London with an armed retinue, and made the best of his way to the House of Lords. Awful was the state of excitement and expectation as to what he was about to say—what do. He went straight to the throne, and laid his hand upon the gold cloth that covered it; he was evidently about to announce himself as king—but his old vacillation checked him even then: he paused, looked around, and then stood still, in the position he had taken. What a picture of his mind did not that position present? The Archbishop of Canterbury asked him if he would not visit the king in the adjoining palace. The duke replied that Henry ought rather to wait upon him—that he was subject to no man in that realm—but, under God, was entitled to all respect and *sovereignty*. Still there was no explicit and formal claim made. But in a week *that* too followed; and after much discussion—conducted, however, under the very awkward circumstance that Warwick's great army was at hand—the House of Lords suggested that Henry should retain the crown during his life, and that Richard, Duke of York, should succeed him. (Fig. 1205.) The Yorkists agreed; but the Lancastrians flew to arms, headed by Margaret herself, now not unnaturally anxious to maintain her son's rights to the throne. And thus at last, the objects of all parties became open, their movements real, and the wars of the Roses began in earnest. And these wars may nearly all be comprised in the history of the illustrious noble of whom we have spoken. The battle of Northampton was won by Warwick, and the king taken prisoner for a second time. That success was followed by a reverse, at the battle of Wakefield, in which Plantagenet, with all his long-cherished hopes, disappeared from the busy and bloody scene, that had been got up more especially for his advantage; he was defeated by Queen Margaret, and slain. Warwick's father, the Earl of Salisbury, was also taken prisoner, and beheaded by the savage female conqueror. But the death of the Duke of York caused no pause in the terrible action that was going on; it rather, indeed, infused new vigour into it, by the introduction of the duke's son, a brave and able warrior, who at first took his father's title of Duke of York, but soon after that of Edward IV., King of England.

These wars of the Roses, we may observe by the way, tried all parties' fortitude pretty severely. The cast of a die was hardly a more uncertain thing than the issue of a battle. The victor had hardly either time or inclination to congratulate himself on the conquest of to-day, for it was not at all improbable that he would be beaten to-morrow. The vanquished, again, suffered not only the ordinary humiliations of defeated men, but had always superadded the anguish arising from the tremendous losses invariably inflicted upon their friends and kindred on all such occasions. But both parties went on till they got used, we suppose, to all kinds of horrors, and until the only possible end to their mutual intensity of hatred, was utter exhaustion.

To the loss of his father, as a consequence of Plantagenet's defeat at Wakefield, Warwick soon after added the disgrace of his own defeat at St. Albans, Margaret again being the successful opponent; but this was before the junction of Warwick and the new Duke of York. After that junction, all opposition for the time was beaten aside, and the combined forces entered London, and Edward was formally declared king. Instead of Westminster Abbey, however, Towton was destined to be the scene of Edward's virtual coronation. There it was that he was to be his own champion, not in vain words, but by deeds such as the winning of a battle; there was he anointed—by the sweat that ran down his brows, as he reposed from his labours after that well-fought and successful field. Edward IV. was then indeed King of England; and to the miserable but still persevering and resolute Margaret herself there could have appeared little ground for hope, except through the severance of Edward and Warwick; and that event, little as it could have been anticipated, did occur, in connection

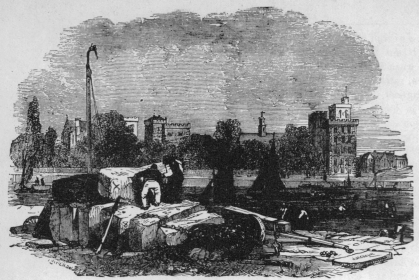

1290.—Lambeth Palace, from the River.

1292.—The Chapel.

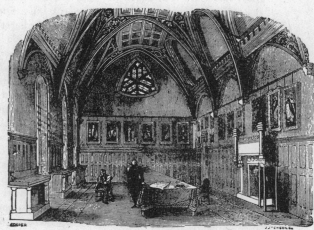

1293.—The Guard-Room.

1291.—Gateway.

1294.—Lollards' Prison.

1295.—Great Hall.

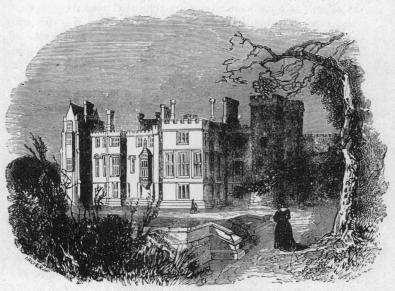

1296.—Lambeth Palace. Garden View.

1297.—Holy Well at Northampton. Dedicated to St. Thomas-à-Becket.

1298.—Font in Coventry.

1300.*—Chapel of Ely House.

1239.—Coventry Pageant.

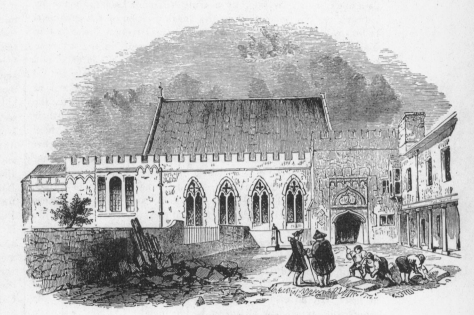

1300.—Ely Palace, 1772.

1301.—Beauchamp Chapel, Warwick.

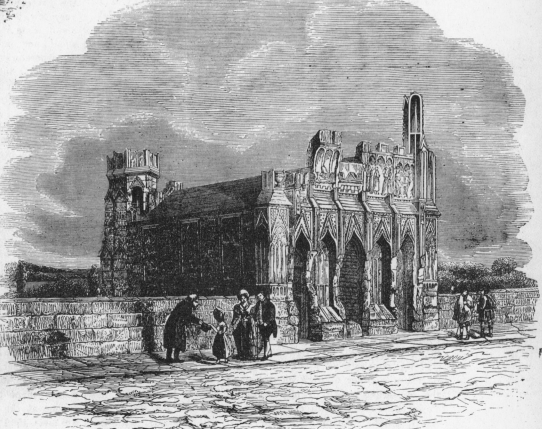

1302.—Edward the Fourth's Chapel on Wakefield Bridge.

549

with one of the many romantic stories of which these wars of the Roses are full.

King Edward went one day to visit the Duchess of Bedford, who had married a second husband, Sir Richard Woodville, and was then living at her manor of Grafton, near Stony Stratford. The duchess's daughter Elizabeth was present, the young and beautiful widow of a Lancastrian knight who had been killed at the second battle of St. Albans and lost his estates by forfeiture. Availing herself of the opportunity, Elizabeth, kneeling at the feet of Edward, implored him, for the sake of her helpless and innocent children, to reverse the attainder. The beautiful supplicant gained at once her estates and the king's heart, who married her secretly on an appropriate May morning, in the year 1464. After considerable delay and preparation, Edward caused the nobility and chief estates of the kingdom to meet him at Reading Abbey, where Edward's brother, the Duke of Clarence, and Warwick, overcoming their great indignation at the marriage, took the fair queen (Fig. 1218) by the hand, and introduced her to the assembly. Edward rewarded them by shortly after making the queen's friends his bosom counsellers and the recipients of his bounty, to the exclusion of the Nevils, who had previously enjoyed both, and who had so well deserved them. The growing division was increased by the marriage of Edward's brother, Clarence, to one of Warwick's daughters, and, it is said, by a truly villanous attempt made by Edward on the honour of another near relation of the great earl in his own house. At all events a new insurrection broke out in Yorkshire in 1468, followed almost immediately, to the astonishment of Europe, by the capture of the king by Clarence and Warwick. Reconciliations and ruptures now again succeeded in the most perplexingly rapid and unexplained succession; and at the next pause it was Clarence and Warwick who were at the bottom of the wheel, or, in other words, who were flying for their lives to the Continent. There they met Margaret. The next marvel for the gossips of England to dilate upon, was the news that the apparently irreconcilable enemies, who had each upon his or her head the blood of the other's nearest and dearest kindred, had made a solemn compact of alliance (secured by the marriage of Prince Edward to Warwick's second daughter), and that they were preparing to invade England. Sudden and almost as causeless, to all appearance, as the changes of a dream, were those that now followed. England was invaded—Henry VI. was again proclaimed king—Margaret, Warwick, and Clarence march to London— Edward, in his turn, now becomes the continental fugitive—the Nevils are reinstated in all their offices. Well, shall we not rest at last? By no means. Edward IV., of course, has to act all the same manœuvres over again, so he too invades England, with the assistance of his brother-in-law the Duke of Burgundy—his brother Clarence joins him—Warwick advances to meet the invaders— and at Barnet, on the 14th of April, 1471, the opposing forces encounter each other. The result of that battle (Figs. 1210, 1211) is the defeat of the Lancastrians, the death of their leader Warwick, and peace for England, produced, as we have before intimated, by the utter exhaustion of the principal element of the wars, the ambitious and turbulent nobles, who were nearly all destroyed in them. It is true that, only a few days after, the indefatigable Margaret was again at the head of an army; but the struggle was but momentary, and may be rather called a slaughter than a battle, though of the most decisive character. Margaret and her son (Figs. 1206, 1214) were both taken. "What brought you to England?" said King Edward to the prince. "My father's crown and mine own inheritance," was the bold reply. He immediately received a blow on the mouth with the king's gauntleted hand; and that brutal act was the signal for his murder, which was performed by Clarence and Gloucester, afterwards Richard III., who thus fittingly makes his first important appearance as a public man. One thing only remained to do. Edward returned to London on the 21st of May, and on that very evening, or the following morning, the poor captive in the Tower, who had undergone more alternations of fortune during the few previous years than we have space to mention, was found lifeless. He was buried at Chertsey monastery (Fig. 1215), though subsequently his remains were removed, and it is said to Windsor, where a tomb (Fig. 1216) was erected to his memory. Popular rumour seems to have had ample reason for attributing Henry's murder to Richard of Gloucester, to whose subsequent career we now pass on, seeing that the remainder of Edward's reign presents, as regards himself, no features either of high interest or intrinsic importance, unless the mysterious death or murder of his brother Clarence in the Tower be considered an exception. Edward died on the 9th of April, 1483. Portraits of him (Figs. 1217, 1226), with his autograph and great seal (Figs. 1219, 1220), and his coins (Figs 1221 to 1325), and a view of his Court (Figs. 1227, 1228), will be found among our engravings.

———

At the time of his father's decease, the Prince of Wales was with his maternal uncle, the Earl of Rivers, at Ludlow Castle; and the Duke of York, his brother, in the care of his mother, Queen Elizabeth Woodville, at London. Poor boys! They wept, no doubt, when the mournful tidings reached them; but with far more reason might they have mourned for themselves could they have seen into the heart of the powerful uncle who claimed the charge of them under the title of *Protector*. That uncle, Richard of Gloucester, had many advantages to recommend him to a nation who set great price on strong manly qualities in their rulers: he was an accomplished warrior, and through all the vicissitudes of the previous reign had been Edward's companion in arms, and his sagacious and energetic adviser. And if there were men in England able enough to foresee danger from the high position to which a character of such force was raised by Edward's death, and who might try to prevent any injury to those who interposed between the duke and his right of succession to the throne; there was, probably, on the other hand, a great proportion of the nation who wished that he *were* king, in their apprehensions of the troubles of a royal minority, and in their admiration of Richard's talents. Thoroughly aware of all he had to hope and all he had to fear, and with a mind fixed, it would seem, on assuming the sceptre that he professed to hold for his nephew, Gloucester marched instantly from the Scottish border, where he was commanding an army against the Scots, and on reaching York on his way to London summoned the gentlemen of the north to swear allegiance to Edward V.: he was himself the first to take the oath. Arrived at London, he seemed to be very earnest about the preparations for the young king's coronation, whilst in reality he was clearing the way for his own. His chief adviser was the Duke of Buckingham, his cousin, and their subtle deliberations were carried on daily at a mansion in Bishopsgate Street, built by Sir John Crosby, an Alderman of London, who was knighted by Edward IV. after his landing at Ravenspur in 1471. The mansion (Fig. 1245), known as Crosby Place, is one of the most interesting antiquities of our metropolis. Here, and most probably in the Hall (Fig. 1246), sat Gloucester and his friend in deliberation; and "To turn the eyes and minds of men from perceiving their drifts," says Sir Thomas More, they sent for lords from all parts of the realm to the coronation. "But the Protector and the duke, after that they had set the Lord Cardinal, the Archbishop of York, the Lord Chancellor, the Bishop of Ely, the Lord Stanley, and the Lord Hastings, then lord chamberlain, with many other noblemen, to commune and devise about the coronation in one place (the Tower), in part were they in another place [Crosby Place] contriving the contrary, and to make the Protector king. To which council, albeit there were admitted very few, and they very secret, yet began there, here and there about, some manner of muttering among the people, as though all should not long be well, though they neither wist what they feared nor wherefore: were it that before such great things men's hearts, of a secret instinct of nature, misgive them, as the sea without wind swelleth of itself some time before a tempest; or were it that some one haply somewhat perceiving, filled many men with suspicion though he showed few men what he knew? Howbeit, somewhat the dealing itself made men to muse on the matter, though the council were close; for, by little and little, all folk withdrew from the Tower and drew to Crosby Place in Bishopsgate Street, where the Protector kept his household. The Protector had the resort, the king in a manner desolate; while some for their business made suit to them who had the doing, some were by their friends secretly warned that it might haply turn them to no good to be too much attendant about the king without the Protector's appointment; who removed also divers of the prince's old servants from him, and set new about him. Thus many things coming together, partly by chance, partly of purpose, caused at length, not common people only, who wave with the wind, but wise men also, and some lords eke, to mark the matter and muse thereon; so far forth that the Lord Stanley, who was afterwards Earl of Derby, wisely mistrusted it, and said, with the Lord Hastings, that he much misliked these two several councils, 'for while we,' quoth he, ' talk of one matter in the one place, little wot we whereof they talk in the other place.' "

Yet neither of these lords seem to have had any idea, when they rode to the meeting of the two councils the next day, in what a fearful shape the mystery was to be unfolded to them. Let us glance at the scene. They enter the council-chamber—the lords are met—the Protector in a particularly agreeable mood. He leaves them awhile, and returns with an aspect so entirely changed, as to strike all present with astonishment and fear. He bares one of his arms, that had been shrunken from his infancy, and exhibits it as a proof of the sorceries of traitors that are seeking to destroy him and Buckingham, and all the old nobility. Ferociously he glares on those he is about to destroy. Suddenly the room fills with armed men, and Stanley narrowly escapes a deathblow by lowering his head below the council-board. Every one knows the fate of the amiable and courtly Hastings, the incorruptible friend of Edward IV. and of his heirs. With scarce breathing-time between a doom utterly unexpected and its execution, he was barbarously beheaded on a log of wood that happened to be lying on the green within the Tower. This was the first of the state murders which rendered that green, and the fearful spot where it is said *the grass will not grow*, so memorable. Indeed the whole fortress, instead of a portion of it, might from that time have justly borne the name attached to the gateway leading into the area—the Bloody Tower. (Figs. 1242 and 1264.) Only two days after a similar scene was enacted before Pontefract Castle, where died three of the queen's near relations. By such acts, and by making free use of the dungeon, Gloucester swept aside or awed into passiveness many whom he could not tempt to support him by active measures. Throughout all these and other events originating in his ambition, a remarkable acquaintance with human character is displayed by Richard, and a singular power of operating upon it for the furtherance of his own selfish ends. Nowhere is this more apparent than in his choosing to divulge his intentions through oratorical appeals to the people, made *for* instead of *by* him, by the principal orators of the day—Dr. Shaw, the preacher at Paul's Cross, and the Duke of Buckingham, who from the hustings of Guildhall declaimed to the citizens, as Dr. Shaw had done on the previous Sunday, on the bastardy of Edward IV. and his children, and his luxurious vices, in contrast with the noble duke of Gloucester. A cry was attempted to be raised of "Long live King Richard!" but it was a feeble cry, and short-lived, and Buckingham could only draw from the respectable part of his audience a promise to *think of it*. This was disconcerting; nevertheless, as if the acclamations had been unanimous, Buckingham expressed a very earnest gratitude; and, proceeding to collect as many influential persons as he could, led them to Baynard's Castle, the residence of the Duchess of York, mother of Edward IV., Clarence, and Gloucester. The arch dissimulator appeared surprised at the embassy who there craved audience of him, and with great humility listened to a long address offering him the crown and royal dignity in the name of the three estates of the realm. After much modest reluctance, Richard of course felt it to be his duty to obey the voice of *the people*, so next day he was declared King of England and France in Westminster Hall. He began his reign by popular acts of justice and clemency, and might perhaps have kept his usurped greatness, and after all not have proved one of the worst of kings, but for the murder of the children that he had in his charge. Buckingham had fallen from him, and was heading a great rising of the people throughout Kent, Essex, Sussex, Berkshire, Hampshire, Wiltshire, and Devonshire; and, to check this perilous movement, Richard imagined it necessary to destroy the young princes on whose behalf it was made; and this step, by the horror it excited, and the enemies it multiplied around him, proved his ruin. A man in his particular confidence, one John Greene, was secretly sent to Sir Robert Brakenbury, constable of the Tower, with a letter, and sufficient credentials, directing Sir Robert "in any wise" to put the children under his charge to death. Brakenbury had probably been induced to take an oath of secrecy, for he received the terrible command "kneeling before our Lady." He had either too much fear or too much conscience to obey (though his refusal must have been nearly as dangerous), for Greene returned to report the failure of his embassy, "whereat King Richard took such displeasure and thought, that the same night he said to a secret page of his, 'Oh! whom shall a man trust? They that I have brought up myself—they that I thought would have mostly served me—even those fail, and at my commandment will do nothing for me.' 'Sir,' quoth the page, 'there lieth one in the pallet-chamber without that I dare well say, to do your Grace pleasure the thing were right hard that he would refuse.'— Meaning by this Sir James Tyrrel." To this Sir James, Richard according to the narrative of Sir Thomas More, opened his thoughts regarding the princes, and Sir James "devised that they should be murdered in their beds, and no blood shed: to the execution whereof he appointed Miles Forest, one of the four that before kept them, a fellow fleshbred in murder beforetime; and to him he joined one John Dighton, his own horsekeeper, a big, broad, square, and strong knave." The merciless deed is thus described:—"Then, all the others being removed from them, this Miles Forest and John Dighton, about midnight, came into the chamber, and suddenly wrapped them up amongst the clothes, keeping down by force the feather-bed and pillows hard upon their mouths, that within a while they smothered and stifled them, and, their breaths failing, they gave up to God their innocent souls into the joys of heaven, leaving to their tormentors their bodies dead in bed; after which the wretches laid them out upon the bed, and fetched Tyrrel to see them; and when he was satisfied of their death he caused the murderers to bury them at the stair-foot, meetly deep in the ground, under a great heap of stones." In 1674 the bones of the royal victims were discovered beneath a circular flight of stairs winding up to the chapel of the White Tower; and thence they were removed, by order of Charles II., to Henry VII.'s Chapel at Westminster. Richard had now to learn that he had for once failed egregiously in his policy, for instead of resting quiet under the sway of so inhuman a tyrant, because he had the power to strike terror into their hearts, the English at once sent to Bretagne, to invite to their throne a young man of the Beaufort branch of the great House of Lancaster, who from five years old, as he himself afterwards told the French historian, Comines, had been either in prison or under strict surveillance. The boy was in the hands of the Yorkists in Ragland Castle when Jasper Tudor, Earl of Pembroke, his uncle, who was attainted at Edward IV.'s accession, stole secretly from France, and, at imminent personal hazard, carried off young Henry to Pembroke Castle, and thence to sea, when they were driven by stress of weather into the port of Bretagne. Duke Francis the Second detained both in honourable captivity, until the Earl of Richmond was chosen by the chiefs of the English nobility to cope with Richard III. for the throne. The experiment was hazardous, considering Richmond was wholly inexperienced in war. After the death of Edward IV.'s sons, his eldest daughter, Elizabeth, was the rightful sovereign of England, and the offer made to Richmond was conditional on his marriage with her—he therefore took a solemn and public oath to complete that alliance when he should have conquered Richard. Henry's personal claims were very defective. The Beauforts were illegitimate descendants of John of Gaunt and Catherine Swynford; and it is not clear that the patent of legitimacy subsequently entered on the rolls of Parliament, after the marriage of Gaunt and Catherine, admitted them to the right of regal succession; but even granting that it did, there were in existence nearer offshoots of the Lancastrian tree, though, being aliens in all respects but this, the nation paid small regard to them. The only other Lancastrian beside Henry who was at all formidable was the Duke of Buckingham; the mother of each was a Beaufort. It does not seem to be known with any accuracy what first induced Buckingham to fall from Richard; but it is clear family interest would weigh with him in supporting Henry, to whom he stood next in a right line of succession. He might naturally dream that royalty for himself might be attainable. But Buckingham was not moulded for great enterprises; his party broke asunder without a blow, and he fell into Richard's hands and was beheaded instantly. All the hopes of the nation were then concentrated on Richmond; whose name, Henry Tudor, suggested a train of associations connected with his descent that, though not amounting to a claim, operated a good deal in his favour. As grandson of Sir Owen Tudor and the widow of the lamented Henry V., he was a descendant of the Welsh sovereigns and the royal house of France. The prophecy of Henry VI. would also be remembered. One day, as he was washing his hands at a great feast, happening to cast his eye on Henry, then a boy, he said, "This is the lad that shall possess quietly that we now strive for." (Bacon.) The prophecy might have been in Edward IV.'s mind when he so repeatedly importuned Duke Francis of Bretagne to render up the young earl. To the duke's stedfast refusals, dictated it would seem by generous solicitude for the safety of his guest or prisoner (since he could hardly have anticipated at that time a restoration of the Lancastrian dynasty), Richmond owed most likely his escape from the practices that had summarily shortened the lives of Duke Humphrey and Henry VI. After the first abortive attempts of his friends in England, during which he reached the Devon coast but did not land, Richmond was driven from his former shelter in Bretagne by the power of King Richard, and resorted to France, where, after an interval of nearly two years, he prepared for his second descent with a small army of foreign adventurers and English exiles, placing his reliance entirely on the aid he should receive after landing.

In this reliance, and in the generally bold character of the attempt, he insured for himself success. Those whom King Richard had planted to defend the coasts suffered the invaders to land

1303.—Guy's Cliff in the 17th Century.

1304.—Chapel at Guy's Cliff.

1308.—Stratford Church: West End.

1305.—Church of Aston Cantlow.

1309.—Ancient Font, formerly in Stratford Church.

1306.—The Parish Churches, Evesham.

1307.—Stratford Church.

1310.—Front of Henry V.'s Chantry Westminster.

1311.—Luton Church.

1312.—Inlaid Brass Monument of Eleanor Bohun, wife to Thomas of Woodstock, Duke of Gloucester.—Died 1399.

1313.—Font in East Dereham Church, Norfolk.

1314.—Northleach Church, Norfolk.

1315.—Weston Church.

1316.—Leatherhead Church.

without obstruction at Milford Haven, and to march on unopposed as far as Tamworth Castle (Fig. 1244). Let us see how Richard had employed the time. After the first failure of Henry he passed various acts that show him to have been fully equal to the comprehension and advancement of the economical welfare of the country; therefore making it still more to be regretted that he should not have known better what were his true interests than to pollute himself with blood and murder, when he was in possession of so much more effectual means for working out his objects. His restless fears were as furies goading him to destruction. To prevent the alliance of Richmond and Elizabeth, he would have married that princess to his own only son, Edward; and when the untimely death of the latter stopped that scheme, Richard had the insanity and wickedness to propose to her himself; and she, his own niece, the sister of the poor boys he had murdered, is said to have been not merely willing but eager to accept the offer—and this whilst Richard's queen, Anne (Figs. 1236 and 1243), yet lived, though presently after she died, as suspected, of poison. Surely Elizabeth of York must have dissembled through fear of her uncle. Ratcliff and Catesby, two of Richard's most trusted advisers, have the merit of dissuading him from this infamous scheme, by assuring him it would rouse the indignation of the people from one end of the kingdom to the other. Then Richard publicly disclaimed all intentions of the kind, though the grossness of the falsehood could only serve to sink him lower in public estimation. Another of Richard's cruelties was the beheading of Collingbourne, a gentleman whose only crime was his being the author of a popular rhyme—

The cat, the rat, and Lovel our dog,
Rule all England under a hog:

alluding to Ratcliff, Catesby, Lord Lovel, and Richard, whose crest was a wild boar. But the tyrant's career was soon to draw to a close. His power and influence rapidly declined. He was without money, and durst not ask supplies. Forced loans destroyed the little remnant of his popularity in London. Hourly he heard of his nobles passing over to Richmond. Many that remained excused themselves on various pretences from arming in his defence. Under these wretchedly disheartening circumstances, the genius of the last-crowned Plantagenet shook off every encumbrance, and displayed itself in a promptitude, ability, and decision worthy of any of his great progenitors. He sent forth a proclamation, drawn up with infinite skill, according to which Henry Tudor could have no claim to the crown of England but by conquest,—had bought the aid of the ancient enemies of France by the surrender in perpetuity of all those rights in France that the English had won so hardly, and by promises of gifts of all that was valuable in England; and he was coming with bands of robbers, murderers, and attainted rebels. Therefore Richard called on "all true and good Englishmen" to arm against these invaders, promising himself, like a diligent and courageous prince, to spare no labour or peril in their behalf. By such energetic measures, under every disadvantage, Richard was able to march toward Leicester with a large force; but, according to the Oriental metaphor, having sown the wind, he was now to reap the whirlwind. Deserters went over in crowds to his enemy, and Richard saw around him very few in whom he could place any faith. The two armies left the towns of Tamworth and Leicester (Fig. 1247) at the same time precisely; they then encamped during the night before the battle, Richmond at Atherston, and Richard near Bosworth, and took up their final positions on Redmore plain on the morning of the 22nd of August, 1485. The desertions, still increasing, filled Richard with the worst forebodings. These haunted him when he lay down to rest before arming for the fight, and in his sleep he fancied himself pulled and hauled about by terrible devils, so that in the morning he looked "piteously," and had not that alacrity, and mirth of mind and of countenance, that he was accustomed to have before he came toward the battle. (Hall.) Nevertheless his soldiers beheld him on the following morning riding on horseback through their ranks, bravely apparelled, with the crown on his head, and marshalling all into due order. When Richard saw the earl's force had passed a morass that lay between the armies, he "commanded with all haste to set upon them; then the trumpets blew, and the soldiers shouted, and the king's archers courageously let fly their arrows. The earl's bowmen stood not still, but paid them home again. The

terrible spot once passed, the armies joined and came to hard strokes, where neither sword nor bill was spared; at which encounter the Lord Stanley [who headed one of the three divisions of Richard's army] joined with the earl, having three thousand men with him." The junction at this moment had been sagaciously planned. The movement, extending as it did throughout Richard's army, was completely bewildering; all was confusion and uncertainty. "Some," says Fabyan, "stood hovering afar off till they saw to which side victory should fall." Of the nobility with Richard, only two were perfectly faithful to him to the last—John Howard and his son, whom Richard had created first Duke of Norfolk (Figs. 1240, 1241) and Earl of Surrey (Fig. 1249). Our readers will remember the scroll found by Norfolk in his tent in the Shaksperian scene—

Jockey of Norfolk be not too bold,
For Dickon thy master is bought and sold.

Norfolk made a most gallant attack on the earl's van, which might have carried victory with it, had the other great leaders supported him. Sir Richard Ratcliffe, Sir Robert Brackenbury, and a few other knights, also fought and died nobly for their master. The fierce struggle had lasted near two hours, and Richard's doom seemed certain, when single-handed he nearly retrieved all misfortunes. He was told that the Earl of Richmond with a small number of men-at-arms was not far off, separated it would appear from the rest of the army; and as Richard marched nearer, he recognised him "by certain demonstrations and tokens which he had learned of others." On a sudden he spurred "out of side of the range of his battle, leaving the avant-gardes fighting, and like a hungry lion ran with spear in rest towards him." His attack was made with resistless might. Richmond's standard-bearer was instantly slain and the standard thrown down. Sir John Cheney, a man of great force and strength, met him hand to hand, but was overthrown, and others who tried to stop his way to Richmond shared the same fate. Before the troops of Richmond perceived his imminent danger, the earl and the king were met, and the earl, though he received the shock most bravely, was at last giving way before the deadly thrusts of Richard, and beginning to despair alike of life and throne, which at that moment rested indeed upon the hazard of the die, when Sir William Stanley, who, like his father, had the command of three thousand of Richard's men, suddenly destroyed the last hope of Richard, by turning upon him: then, and not till then, fell Richard III., "manfully fighting in the midst of his enemies." The Stanleys unquestionably caused his defeat and death, and it was Lord Stanley (Fig. 1248) who, on the spot now called Crown Hill, picked up his battered and bloodstained crown, and placed it on Richmond's head. We should have been glad to see more of the old chivalric generosity actuating the victor's treatment of his rival's dead body, which was stripped, flung over a horse, exposed ignominiously for three days, and buried without respect in the church of Greyfriars in Leicester. We have given four portraits (Figs. 1230, 1237, 1238, 1239), besides those on the coins and great seal (Figs. 1232 to 1235), of this remarkable man. Excepting one, they contradict the vulgar notions of his person. He may have had some slight deformities, and his stature was low, but his features were rather handsome, and his aspect polished. The best notion of the historical Richard III. is to be gained from the portrait that we have surrounded by localities of Bosworth Field (Fig. 1237). It was originally published by the Royal Antiquarian Society. This shows him young—he was, indeed, scarce thirty when he seized the crown, and only in his thirty-third year when he died. The positions of the encampments and armies on Bosworth Field may be yet distinctly traced; though the ancient barren wild, without a hedge or tree, gleams and glows beneath the summer sun with the products of cultivation. The well of which it is said Richard drank during the heat of the combat, was drained and closed when Dr. Parr visited it in 1812, and wrote his Latin inscription for a monument. There have been dug up at various times, shields, crossbows, arrow-heads, halberds, armour, spears, skeletons, &c. In taking leave of Bosworth, we must observe, that the contest was not on that extensive scale which we might have anticipated, considering its eventful character, involving as it did the death of Richard, and the introduction to the throne of England of the Tudor race of sovereigns.

CHAPTER II.—ECCLESIASTICAL ANTIQUITIES.

ALL that is fair must fade, or at least for a time appear to do so, is a rule as applicable to architectural styles as to every thing else; and so, having traced the rise of the beautiful Gothic, through its simplest up to its sublimest developments, we have now, on entering upon a third period, to speak of its decline, of which a too rank prosperity seems to have been the predisposing cause. It is as if the great artists of the day had grown so habituated to their labours, that when they found they could rise no higher, why, they were even content to descend lower, so long as they were still going on; a wise determination, if they had but changed the direction of their labours, and endeavoured to raise some other style to the level of the Gothic, instead of lowering the Gothic itself, while pursuing their experiments. As it was, they set to work to "gild refined gold," and with no better success than might have been anticipated. A style of which decoration is the peculiarly distinctive characteristic sprung up, and was intermingled with a style which had ever been the theme of wonder and admiration on account of the stern beauty and consummate grandeur of its outlines: the two could not harmonize on terms of equality; every principle of art forbade it; and the result was the predominance of the first, and the consequent gradual degradation and ruin of the Order to which both belonged. But even in that ruin, the Gothic, like a dying flower, scattered abroad the seeds of a vigorous progeny, which, under the name of the Tudor Domestic architecture, forms to this day the most valuable of all styles for general purposes, which combines at once all the qualities that can be derived for the largest or the smallest public or private building (ecclesiastical edifices of course excepted), which, in a word, will give us the sumptuous magnificence of the Houses of Parliament, or the picturesque comfort of the suburban or roadside cottage, with its bay window and gabled roof. It is no doubt from the very want of a direct or highly-elevated purpose in the minds of the promoters of this third stage of the Gothic, that the names given to their style have been so various, and all so comparatively inadequate or inapplicable. Of these, perhaps the best known, but the least architecturally expressive, is the Tudor, given no doubt on account of the period when the style was so much in vogue,—the reign of Henry VII., the first of the Tudor family who occupied the throne of England. The Depressed Arch order is good, inasmuch as it shows at once the very feature in which it chiefly differed from the previous Pointed Arch style; but very bad in this—that the arch became a less and less conspicuous feature, and consequently did not, for long at least, stand in the same relation to the style that the Pointed Arch did to the Gothic. We come next to the name by which the style is generally spoken of in scientific works, the Perpendicular, which is derived from the mullions, or slender strips of stone that divide the windows longitudinally, and the panellings that so largely decorate all otherwise vacant spaces of wall. But on such grounds, as has been well observed, Horizontal Architecture would be quite as fit, if not indeed a more fitting designation. If the reader will turn for a moment to the three engravings at the top of page 356, he will see in the first—a window from St. Mary's, Oxford (Fig. 1317)—something like a Perpendicular effect; but in the second—a door from the ruined Bishop's palace, Lincoln (Fig. 1318)—the broad square label over the door gives a decidedly Horizontal expression to the whole; while lastly, in the third, showing the window in the nave of Winchester Cathedral (Fig. 1319), the transoms (or stone strips that cross the mullions, and with them form the inner framework of a window) are so numerous that the window becomes cut up into panels, to which the names Perpendicular and Horizontal become equally applicable, and equally unmeaning. But there are other points that make the second the more appropriate of the two as applied to the style; such for instance as the depression of the arch already alluded to, which conveys the idea of an approximation to the horizontal, in the arch of Eton College (Fig. 1278), and also the string-courses marking the different stories of an edifice, which when bold and prominent, as in the building just mentioned, aid materially to increase the horizontal and to decrease the perpendicular effect. Lastly, it is to be observed, that none of these names convey the slightest idea of all the other features of the style—the increased expansion of the windows, and the frequently embattled character of their transoms, nor of the gorgeous tracery of the fan-roofs, and their vast pendants suspended in mid air, as if to mock, in very wantonness of artistical skill, the fears and precautions of ordinary architects; neither do they suggest ought of the wondrous luxuriance of heraldic emblazonry that enriched the buildings of the style, and formed in themselves one of their most peculiar features. Looking at all these circumstances, perhaps we shall agree that the only name we have not yet mentioned, the Florid, is on the whole the best.

To judge of the effect of the combination of all these qualities, one must pay a visit to Henry VII.'s Chapel at Westminster, King's College, Cambridge, or St. George's Chapel, Windsor, three perfect and unadulterated examples of Florid architecture. Writers date the decline of the Pointed architecture from the introduction of this style, and abstractedly we have in a preceding sentence agreed with them. The purity of the Gothic was spoiled no doubt; but when we look upon the superb works just named, one can hardly help echoing the remark of a friend of ours to his lady, who remonstrated that some choice dish would be spoiled by his method of dressing it:—"I like it spoiled," was the quiet reply. Assuredly one must have very little taste, or a great deal of it, who does not like the spoiled Gothic.

In all the characteristics of the style that we have enumerated, King's College, Cambridge, begun in the reign of Henry VI. and finished in that of Henry VII., stands pre-eminent. Decoration runs riot there, and the sense aches again at the beauty and splendour and variety that everywhere meet the gaze. Floor alone excepted, the whole is, to begin with, one mass of panelling in all the forms of panelling. One thinks nothing can exceed the elaborate splendour of the entrance-doorway (Fig. 1281) until the painted windows meet the gaze; yet both these again presently appear to be surpassed by the roof, composed entirely of arches of the most airy and most indestructible construction, and covered with exquisite fan-like tracery, beside which all previous decoration seems so insignificant, that we feel to want a new word to express worthily the character of that which makes the chapel of King's College glow as it were with a *lighter* kind of light. And yet we are told of what *was* intended, of the grandeur and magnificence that *were* to have been exhibited, had not the wars of the Roses interrupted the good King Henry in his projects! Some interesting records have been preserved as to the mode of proceeding in those days, from which it appears that when a king wanted some grand chef-d'œuvre of the arts, he had only to send out his commands to that land of romance in the days of Henry VI., as well as in the days of Shakspeare and Ben Jonson—Southwark, and the matter was in effect settled. At the time fixed there were the windows, or doors, or roofs required; or, in fine, a St. George's, a King's College, or a Henry VII.'s Chapel. In these records we find, for instance, contracts for the windows of King's College, and for the "orient colours and imagery" with which they were to be adorned, drawn up in the same matter-of-fact manner that one would now employ if a number of mere modern sashes were concerned; *and yet the "orient colours and imagery" came.*

Leaving our readers now to trace out for themselves, by the aid of these preliminary remarks and our numerous engravings of the period in question, the many modes in which the Perpendicular style then developed itself, we proceed to notice the more important and interesting of the buildings represented in those engravings, occasionally, perhaps, in connection with their archi-

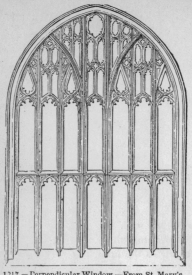

1317.—Perpendicular Window.—From St. Mary's Church, Oxford.

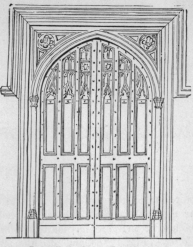

1318.—Perpendicular Door.—From the Bishop's Palace, Lincoln.

1320.—Specimen of Old Paintings in St. Stephen's Chapel.

1319.—Nave of Winchester Cathedral.

1321.—Effigy of Beatrice, Countess of Arundel. In Arundel Church.

1322.—Effigy of Lady de Thorpe. In Ashwelthorpe Church, Norfolk.

1323.—Effigy of Sir Thomas Peyton, Isleham Church, Cambridgeshire.

1325.—Robert Chamberlain, Esquire to Henry V. (Cotton MS. Nero, D 7.)

1326.—Effigy of Richard Beauchamp, Earl of Warwick. From his Monument in the Lady-Chapel, St. Mary's Church, Warwick.

1327.—Effigy of Michael de la Pole, Earl of Suffolk. Haversham Church, Notts.

1324.—Effigy of Lady Peyton. Isleham Church, Cambridgeshire.

1328.—Effigy of Sir Robert Grushill. Haversham Church, Notts.

1329.—The Duke of Bedford and St. George.—From the Bedford Missal.

1330.—Richard Beauchamp, Earl of Warwick, as a Pilgrim, worshipping at the Holy Sepulchre, Jerusalem. From a MS. of Rouse's History of the Earls of Warwick, in the Cottonian Library (Engraved in Strutt's Regal and Ecclesiastical Costume).

1331.—Transcriber at Work.

1332.—Convocation of Clergy. (From the Harl. MS. 4379.)

1333.—Friar Preaching from a Moveable Pulpit.—(Royal MS. 14 E. iii.

1334.—Passage of the Host. Cripples worshipping.—(Cotton MS. Nero, D. i.)

tectural characteristics, but generally in the more popular view—of their uses and history. We may begin with St. George's Chapel and Eton; the last founded by the same monarch, and at the same time, as King's College, Cambridge, and indeed connected with it as a preparatory school. A poet thus introduces us to Eton and Windsor:—

> Ye distant spires, ye antique towers,
>   That crown the wat'ry glade,
> Where grateful Science still adores
>   Her Henry's holy shade!
> And ye, that from the stately brow
> Of Windsor's heights, the expanse below
> Of grove, of lawn, of mead survey,
>   Whose turf, whose shade, whose flowers among
>   Wanders the hoary Thames along
> His silver winding way!

Standing on the finest part of the noble terrace (Fig. 1259) on "Windsor's heights," the matchless prospect described by Gray, in his celebrated ode 'On a distant Prospect of Eton College,' is before us in all its beauty and glory, glittering under a bright October sun, and a crisp keen atmosphere, that brings out all the attractions of the "silver winding" Thames, and throws into most picturesque prominence the antique towers of Eton, a most interesting and ornamental feature of the view.

Let us be thankful that the exclusive spirit which debars the people from so many of the fairest scenes as our fair island has not shut up this noble terrace, from which, as from a vantage-ground, we now resume our notices of the chivalric history of Windsor (see p. 242), whose knightly sovereigns seem still to rule the place from their urns. Windsor appears still pervaded by their spirit—still to echo back the sound of their footsteps—still to be glorified by their pomps. Our thoughts are here carried back, age after age, through Tudor and Plantagenet dynasties, through the various scenes they have enacted here (too many even for the briefest enumeration), to that earliest period, when, from the first battlements, rude and stern, of the fortress and hunting-seat of William the Conqueror and William Rufus, fair dames looked forth over the thick woods and tangled vales to see the Norman chivalry—

> With cry of hounds, and merry blasts between,
> . . . . chase the fearful hart of force.
> EARL OF SURREY.

That period was the first principal epoch in the history of Windsor Castle. Of the second we have spoken in Edward the Third's chivalric career. But we must say a few words more on his buildings, and the purposes to which he applied them. First, as to the distribution. Most people know that Windsor Castle extends around two principal areas, divided by the "proud keep," and called the Upper and Lower Wards; the upper being of grand extent. Thus did Edward III. arrange his home. St. George's Hall, used for the high festivals of the Knights of the Garter, is on the north side of the great quadrangle, or Upper Ward (Fig. 1260), and looks so antique and chivalric that one might almost fancy we have but to step in to behold the Round Table itself, with Edward and all his knights in their glory around it. The hall forms an oblong room of vast length, and terminates a continuous line of state apartments, to which the public are admitted. Most truly does this grand quadrangle deserve the epithet by which it is distinguished; "grand" it is unquestionably, in its combination of large space, with regularity of form in the ranges of buildings, and general dignity of style. Invention in Gothic architecture had so far ceased by the time of Charles II., that the monarch could find no better substitute for Edward III.'s buildings in this quadrangle than the style of Louis XIV.! But the bad taste of that change has been remedied, and hence the present fine quadrangle. Fine as it is, however, its chief interest to an imaginative mind must consist in its suggestions of the old days, when Edward's thick embattled walls, and narrow towers, and crooked steps, and loopholed apologies for windows, letting in a few rays of light in confined and rude apartments, were here watched by mailed warriors, and pierced ever and anon by some shrill trumpet-blast, indicating a new arrival to share the boundless hospitality of Windsor, and try a passage of arms with its renowned knights. Those were indeed the palmy days of Windsor: with all its modern improvements and heightened refinements, we must not look to see their like again,—no—not even under our present youthful and pageant-loving sovereign.

The interval of twenty-one years between the "jousts, tournaments, dances, carols, and great and beautiful repasts" in honour of Edward's bridal with Philippa of Hainault, in 1328, and the first grand installation of the order that promises to be an immortal memorial of the king's unfortunate passion for the lovely and noble-hearted Countess of Salisbury—marks the rise of Windsor to the

zenith of its glory, when its fame went abroad over the earth. It was a great day, that anniversary of St. George in 1349, when twenty-five of England's best and bravest knights, banded together by the order of the Garter, and headed by a king in all respects their fitting leader and glorious exemplar, walked in solemn procession, amid a concourse from all the nations that then partook of the chivalric fire, and laid their honours and their arms at the feet of the Most High, in the College or Free Chapel of St. George (Figs. 1276, 1277), that had been founded expressly for the new Order, and for the maintenance of poor knightly brethren, who might there offer up prayers for the weal of the souls of the knights-companions. In this, as in a thousand other instances, we see how deeply the precept "He that giveth to the poor lendeth to the Lord" had entered into the hearts and minds of our ancestors, and consequently into all their institutions; and thus it is that these institutions, notwithstanding the mighty revolutions of society, still constantly arrest the eye in some shape or other, to reproach our colder faith and charity. Gorgeous and protracted was that first festival of St. George; full of knightly skill and daring the martial encounters. The knights-companions, bound to assist and defend each other by the oath of the "golden badge of unity" (Speed) and of martial honour, boldly met all comers, and challenged the best of the heroes of all lands. The chief ladies, who presided at the festival, with Queen Philippa at their head, were splendidly attired, in the habit of the order, wearing the garter around the left arm, and were called *Dames de la Fraternité de St. George.* The sehonours were conferred from time to time upon a certain number of distinguished ladies until a century after, when they began to fall into disuse. Charles I. and his queen would have revived them, had not the civil wars prevented.

The habit of the knights-companions was for a long time chiefly distinguished by its colour (blue), and by embroidered garters, over the mantle, tunic, and hood, all three then prevalent parts of royal and noble costume. The knights' tunics were lined with miniver, the sovereign's with ermine, fur being then a most costly and fashionable ornament. Henry VIII. added the collar and the greater and lesser medallion of George killing the dragon. The blue riband was Charles II.'s addition. The habit, when worn in full, with all the insignias, has a most magnificent appearance. The variety of rich and resplendent objects, each having its own associations, feasts at once the eye and the imagination. There are the blue velvet mantle, with its dignified sweep, the mode of crimson velvet, the heron and ostrich plumed cap, the gold medallion, the blazing star, the gold-lettered garter, to all which may be added the accessaries that rank and wealth have it in their power to display; as, for example, the diamonds worn by the Marquis of Westminster at a recent installation, on his sword and badge alone, worth the price of a small kingdom, or, richer still, her present Majesty's jewels, that seem to have been showered by some eastern fairy over her habit of the Order, among which the most beautiful and striking feature is, perhaps, the ruby cross in the centre of the dazzling star of St. George.

The second sovereign of the Order of the Garter was Richard II., in whose reign the knights of England sought elsewhere for fame, though there was plenty of revelling at Windsor, and on a scale of the most extraordinary magnificence. There is a very singular fact in connexion with this king and St. George's Chapel, that might raise many conjectures. The chapel was falling to ruin, and no less a person than Geoffrey Chaucer was made "clerk of the works" for its repair, with a salary of two shillings a day. He did not, however, long occupy the post. We wonder if *impressing* "carpenters, stone-cutters, and other workmen" quite met with the bard's approbation. The absurdity and injustice of such a system is so apparent now, that one hardly likes to find an illustrious name like the poet's connected with it, though in truth the subject of the right of the poor to dispose of their labour was in Chaucer's time little understood even by their best friends. We perhaps err on the other side, and, by not taking sufficient care to see that our people are all thoroughly employed, do too often in effect, under the semblance of affording freedom to industry, in reality secure to it only its own misery and degradation.

After the great poet and his ill-starred master had been gathered to the grave, Henry of Bolingbroke, having spent his chivalric energies in foreign wars "for the faith," and his ambition in compassing the crown, shut up his state captives here, where one—the lineal heir of the throne—pined thirteen years, until the accession of a more magnanimous and fearless king, who set wide his rival's prison doors, and became his true friend and companion in arms. When this "mirror of all Christian kings" (Henry V.) with his "grace and myght of chivalry" went forth to France—to die—

he left his young queen, Katherine of France, at Windsor, and there was born "Henry of Windsor," the sixth of that name, who had, perhaps, less of chivalric ardour in his composition than any king that ever sat on the English throne, which was the secret of his melancholy fate; for none but a very able or a very chivalric king could possibly then have governed the bold and ambitious English. His relics found their way from the Tower to St. George's Chapel, where they were worshipped, if not as a hero's, yet as a saint's, and miracles were long believed to take place at his tomb (Fig. 1216).

A new epoch in the chivalric history of Windsor would have opened with the reign of Edward IV., if that monarch, so cruel and brave in war, so gay and affable in peace, could have accomplished what he wished. During the few happy years that relieved his tempestuous career, he laboured hard to restore the declining genius of chivalry; but well as he was fitted for the task, it was too difficult even for *him*, though assisted by the general desire of the nation, and by the stimulus given by the first printed books—the chivalric romances—of the Caxton press. Firearms were also fast dissipating the prestige attached to knightly skill; commerce and literature were opening new and boundless fields for the energies that had been wasted hitherto on war. A more enlightened religious faith was introducing new refinements and enhancing the value of life; and, in short, chivalry was already as a lamp of the night, whose beams grew wan and useless in the radiance of the opening day of knowledge. Finding that neither authoritative edicts, brilliant example, nor liberal encouragement could bring back the old ardour, Edward IV. was fain to solace himself with the shows instead of the substance of chivalry; and even in them was no less strikingly exhibited the growing spirit of the time. The tournaments, for instance, of the fifteenth century (Figs. 1254, 1255), provided with such care for the protection of the combatants, that the chief object of the sport, the development of martial bravery, was lost; and the fire of emulation burned so low in the breasts of the chief knights of the time, that they were content to have the number of blows that should be struck, reduced to as mechanical a precision as any of the commonest arrangements of the tilt-yard. The shock of the war-horses, that had formed one of the leading perils of the encounter, was prevented by a double barrier of partitions dividing the hostile parties, and stretching across the area of the lists; whilst the thrust of the lance and the sword was also rendered harmless enough by the points being blunted. (Sir Walter Scott.)

We are not surprised to find Edward, under such hopeless circumstances, turning to other courtly delights. One day the Lord Mayor of London, and the aldermen and their wives, received his summons to attend him at Windsor,—not to present addresses, or to perform any other state formality—no—but simply to "hunt in his company, and he himself to be merry with them." (Stow.) One can hardly help smiling to think of grave and solid burgesses, unused to courtly amusements or courtly society, riding might and main in Windsor's glades after the jovial king and his favourites and parasites; and when the sport was done (a trying sport to them, very likely), banqueting in the gay silk tents that Edward set up in his summer hunting for the ladies, "wherein," says Comines, "he treated them after a magnificent manner," his humour and person being, in the words of the same excellent judge, "as well suited to gallantry as those of any prince I ever saw in my life, for he was indisputably the most beautiful man of his time." Whilst at Windsor these worthy city guests of Edward IV. would probably do something more for their monarch's amusement than simply hunt; they could not "ride in the mumming," as their forefathers had done at the Christmas festival of Henry IV., and for which the said civic mummers "had great thanks?" What would our present city dignitaries say to amusing our court in this way; capering grotesquely before the highest personages of the realm in visors and suits of buckram, representing wild men and women, birds, beasts, and angels? (Fig. 1256.)

But there was other sport at Windsor. There was one personage who, we imagine, must have been particularly dreaded by the mayor and aldermen at Windsor, for many would be the quips and cranks he would have at their expense as he stood at the king's elbow, ready to receive their largesses, and those of the rest of the company, for his biting wit. But then, mayor and aldermen would know full well, there was no restraining the court fool (Fig. 1257), and if they winced a little, why, so did others: and, after all, without the relish of the mirth he created, pageants and sports would have been but indifferent enjoyments. When spirits grew dull, who like him could brighten them? The jingle of the bells attached to his motley yellow-fringed garments, the flourish of his bauble—a staff

with a blown bladder or zany head at the top of it, the shake of his ass's ears, and his various *practical* jokes, made even the grave gay, and prepared men of all moods to abandon themselves to the humours of the time. The court fool is thus painted, not over favourably, in 'Lodge's Wit's Miserie,' 1599:—" In person comely in apparel courtly, but in behaviour a very ape, and no man: his employment, it is asserted, was to coin bitter jests, and to sing profligate songs and ballads; give him a little wine in his head, he is continually fleering and making of mouths: he laughs intemperately at every little occasion, and dances about the house, leaps over tables, outstrips men's heads, trips up his companion's heels, burns sack with a candle," and performs a great many other madcap and mischievous feats, in the course of which his morals, it is more than hinted, "lose all quality of fastidiousness." Such was the darker and coarser side of the picture; but under much of the fool's folly and caustic insolence would be often conveyed useful truths, that durst only be uttered by all-licensed lips, and the utterance of which was indeed virtually a part of the court fool's office, which required of course anything but a fool to fill it successfully, and was sometimes rewarded by kinder feelings in the royal master than their respective positions might seem to warrant. There were affection and regret in the exclamation of the distracted Lear—"And my poor fool is hanged!" Bouffon in French and Buffoon in English have been occasionally used as synonymous with court fool. The word is derived from *buffa*, a corrupted Latin word of the middle ages, meaning "a slap on the cheek:" Buffe and Buffet in the old French, and Bofetada in Spanish, were of the same sense. At present the Italian Buffone means a ludicrous fellow, but not always a contemptible one; and this seems to have been the idea of the court buffoon or fool of the fifteenth century, who was a regular officer of the royal household from the Conquest to Charles II.

Lest too much of the sweets of life should cloy, the appetite was sharpened now and then by a war-movement, intended for Scotland or France, the latter got up manifestly as a pleasant stimulus, on the old pretensions. In 1475, Garter king-at-arms was sent by Edward as herald to make a suitable demand. What followed is so rich in traits of character, that we must find room for it in passing. Louis XI., "the Fox," whom two of the greatest romance writers of England and France have, each in his own peculiar way, made familiar to the world as a character supereminent for craft and cruelty, was seated with the lords of the French court when Garter with due form delivered to him a letter from Edward IV. of England. The sight of it must have created a painful commotion in the mind of Louis, for though he despised his brother king's effeminate luxuries, he knew and feared the warlike propensities to which Edward was no less prone. The crown must have seemed just then to shake upon his head. He took care to read the letter first *to himself* as he sat, and found his worst fears verified. He was requested, in very elegant and polite terms, to render up the sovereignty of France as the inheritance of King Edward, and it was suggested that, in the event of a refusal, there might be more French wars. For either alternative Louis had no relish whatever, but lest some of his court might, he withdrew into another room, and sent quietly for the herald, to whom he professed the most wonderful respect and affection for his master, who he knew had been set on to this step by others, and he showed Garter how desirable for both England and France would be a peaceful accommodation, using various arguments, the best of which, to the herald's mind, would be the three hundred crowns that Louis's own royal hands put into his pouch, with a promise of a thousand more when the good peace should be completed. The least that Garter could do in return was to give so very generous and so very amiable a king the best advice he could think of, and then go back to make a mediatory report of his embassy. So much for Garter. The French nobles had now to be dealt with. There were, says Comines, the historian, and a sharer in the scenes he describes, "many persons waiting outside during the king's private discourse with the herald, all of them impatient to hear what the king would say and to see how his majesty looked when he came forth. When he had done, he called me," continues Comines, "and charged me to entertain the herald till he ordered him some other company, that might keep him from talking privately with anybody. He commanded me likewise to give him a piece of crimson velvet of thirty ells; which I did. After which, the king addressed himself to the rest of the company, gave them an account of his letters of defiance, and calling seven or eight of them apart, he ordered the letters to be read aloud, showing without the least sign of fear in the world; *and indeed he was much revived by what he had got out of the herald.*" Louis was not, however, to get rid of his adversary so

1335.—Male Costume in the time of Henry IV

1336.—Male Costume in the time of Henry V.

1337.—Female Costume in the time of Henry V   (Royal MS. D 3.)

1338.—Male Costume in the time of Henry VI.

1339.—Servant, to prevent treachery, tasting the Wine before serving it at Table.
(Royal MS. 14 E 3.)

1340.—Female Costume in the time of Edward IV.   (Cotton MS.
Nero, D 9, and Royal MS. 15 E. 2.)

1341.—Law Habits of the fifteenth century.   (Collected from various contemporary MSS. Engraved in Strutt's
'Angel-Cyunan.'

1342.—Saying Grace   (Royal MS. 14 E 3.)

1343.—Female Costume in the time of Edward IV.   (Cotton MS.
Nero D 9, and Royal MSS. 15 E 2 and 15 E 4.)

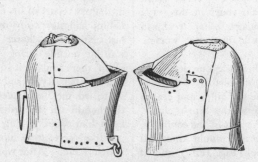

1345.—Tilting Helmets in the time of Henry V.—In
Cobham Church, Kent.

1344.—Female Costume in the time of Henry VI.

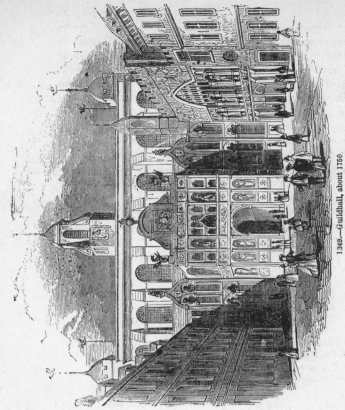

1349.—Guildhall, about 1750.

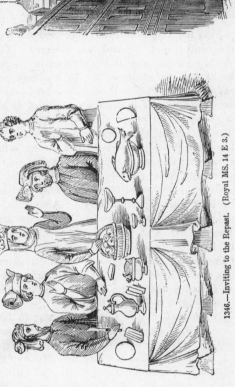

1346.—Inviting to the Repast. (Royal MS. 14 E 3.)

1348.—Restoration of the ancient Thoroughfare from Westminster to London.

1347.—Dining-room and Kitchen. (Harleian MS. 4375.)

1350.—The Hall. Guildhall.

No. 46.

easily as he hoped. Edward landed in France in 1475 with a choice army. Louis's fears were intense, but he knew how to disguise them. One thing was clear to him, there must be no more Agincourts, no more pitched battles. The only antidote of the English, a Pope had said, was the Scotch. Louis had found out another. They were a straightforward, unsuspicious people, these English, and Louis resolved to dupe them. It is most amusing to read in the narrative of Comines, how the simplicity of our warriors, king and all, was operated upon by Louis, who, exulting in his superior guile, despised them for the quality that was in reality one of their greatest ornaments. He won their hearts by the same kind of false professions and profuse liberality that had been so successful with the Garter herald; they were his dear and honoured guests; nothing was too good, too troublesome, or too costly, that he could provide for their accommodation or enjoyment. At his very first meeting with Edward on the bridge of Picquigny, near Amiens, when the kings saluted each other from the opposite sides of a strongly-grated barrier, Louis at once found the way to Edward's good graces by telling him jocosely he should be glad to see him at Paris, where he should have for his confessor the Cardinal of Bourbon, who would grant him pleasant absolution for any little peccadilloes he might commit there in the way of love and gallantry. A treaty was soon concluded; but to Louis's vexation, Edward accepted the invitation given. "Certes," observed Louis to Comines, in his characteristic way, "our brother of England is a very fine man, and a warm admirer of the ladies; he might chance to find some dame at Paris so much to his taste, as *to tempt him to return*; his predecessors have been too often in Paris and Normandy already, and I have no great affection for his company on this side the Channel, though ready to hold him as friend and brother on the other side of the water." Edward however did *not* go to Paris, but returned to England, fairly bowed, as it were, out of the country which he had entered with such lofty determinations to make his own.

But it is time that we should speak of the most memorable of all the incidents of Edward's life at Windsor, his rearing of the exquisitely superb St. George's Chapel, the general effect of which on the imagination, and especially in the choir (Figs. 1276, 1277), has been already alluded to, though to convey an adequate impression of it, to one who is a stranger to the place, would be next to impossible. King's College Chapel, and Henry the Seventh's Chapel, unrivalled for gorgeousness, must yield to St. George's in diversity, chasteness, and elegance. Though called a chapel, it is more like a small cathedral; indeed, by the word chapel our forefathers generally meant a small church, in which sense it was here applied, St. George's Chapel being the church to the royal College of Windsor, composed of canons, poor knights, and various officers and attendants. The first founder of both the college and collegiate chapel was Henry I. Of the chapel, rebuilt by Henry III., there remain to this day evident traces in the range of closed arches on the south side of the Dean's cloisters, and some others behind the altar. We readily perceive other styles also after that date, and previous to the florid Gothic of Edward IV.; but these interminglings of the productions of various periods by no means mar the perfection of the whole as a work of consummate art. The merit of the new design belongs probably to Richard Beauchamp, Bishop of Salisbury, and first chancellor of the Garter, whose religious profession did not prevent him from having a most intense devotion to chivalry, which led him, "out of mere love towards the order" of the Garter, "daily to attend the advancement and progress of this goodly structure." Beauchamp commenced the work about 1476, and died before it was completed. The gifted knightly architect, Sir Reginald Bray, then followed up the high task, and brought to it equal genius and taste. He too died while the fabric was in progress, and after that we find, in 1507, that the groined ceiling of the choir was intrusted to two freemasons, John Hylmer and William Vertue, who agreed to construct it for seven hundred pounds by the Christmas of 1508. The rich stalls of the knights companions, and other decorations of the choir, were chiefly added by Henry VIII., at whose death all the solid masonry, roof, side chapels, and embellishments were nearly if not quite finished. Thus piece by piece were the richest productions of the middle ages composed, till the whole attained to full development, and the glorious composition, as it has been beautifully said of King's College Chapel, seemed as if "knit together by the fingers of angels." One is never tired of wondering at the exhaustless invention of the architects of these royal chapels. The roof of St. George's presents a distinct novelty, of the boldest and most luxuriant fancy. Between the fan-work runs a central space, filled up with diversified pannelling, enriched with pendants. To effect this, it was necessary to widen the nave more than usual,

though the aisles are left of the ordinary proportion; and, observes Dalloway, "they have all the magic perspective of the cloisters at Gloucester," and are "even improved by loftiness." The magnificent west window, as at King's College Chapel and Henry the Seventh's, fills up the whole width of the nave: the stained glass was collected here from other windows of the chapel, in 1774, and the whole has been recently perfected. The side chapels, or chantries, commemorative of illustrious personages of the fifteenth and sixteenth centuries, are highly beautiful, and in perfect keeping with the rest of the fabric. One of the most unique of tombs is found in the chapel, being the iron or steel work by Quintin Matsys placed over the remains of Edward IV., who was buried here with great pomp, near the tomb of Henry VI., the guilt of whose death he probably shared with the Duke of Gloster, who had the general infamy of it. Pope, struck by the circumstance of the rival kings of York and Lancaster thus neighbouring each other in the peaceful shadows of the grave, writes—

> Let softest strains ill-fated Henry mourn,
> And palms eternal flourish round his urn;
> Here, o'er the martyr king, the marble weeps,
> And, fast beside him, once-fear'd Edward sleeps,
> Whom not the extended Albion could contain,
> From old Bolerium to the German main.
> The grave unites, where e'en the great find rest,
> And blended lie the oppressor and the oppress'd.

Some workmen repairing the chapel in 1789, perceived an aperture in the side of the vault where Edward was interred. This being enlarged, and the interior laid open in the presence of the surveyor and two of the canons, the skeleton of the monarch was found enclosed in leaden and wooden coffins, the latter measuring six feet three inches in length. The head was reclined to the north side; there was no appearance of cere-cloth or wrapper, rings, or other insignia. The bottom of the coffin was covered with a glutinous muddy liquor, about three inches deep, of a strong saline taste. It is somewhat singular that the coffin of his queen in the same tomb should have been found entirely empty. She died in confinement in Bermondsey Abbey, about three years after her consort, and is supposed to have been secretly interred. Among other celebrated personages interred in St. George's Chapel, we may briefly enumerate Henry VIII. and Jane Seymour, Charles I., the Crookback's victim Hastings, both the gifted ecclesiastical and knightly architects of the chapel, many of the noble Beauforts; and in Wolsey's tomb-house, first built by Henry VII., to which a subterranean passage leads from the foot of the altar, various members of the present royal family, down to King William IV.

One should not simply see St. George's Chapel, but stay to hear Divine service performed in it, if we would feel in all their power the influences of the place. It has been observed in the paper 'Windsor, as it Was' ('Penny Magazine'), "I account it one of the greatest blessings of my life, and a circumstance which gave a tone to my imagination, which I would not resign for many earthly gifts, that I lived in a place where the cathedral service was duly and beautifully performed. Many a frosty winter evening have I sat in the cold choir of St. George's Chapel, with no congregation but two or three gaping strangers, and an ancient female or so in the stalls, lifted up to heaven by the peals of the sweetest of organs, or entranced by the Divine melody of the *Nunc Dimittis*, or of some solemn anthem of Handel or Boyce, breathed most exquisitely from the lips of Vaughan. If the object of devotion be to make us feel, and to carry away the soul from all low and earthly thoughts, assuredly the grand chaunts of our cathedral service are not without their use. I admire—none can admire more—the abstract idea of an assembly of reasoning beings offering up to the Author of all good their thanksgivings and their petitions in a pure and intelligible form of words; but the question will always intrude, does the heart go along with this lip service? and is the mind sufficiently excited by this reasonable worship to forget its accustomed associations with the business, and vanities, and passions of the world? The cathedral service does affect the imagination, and through that channel reaches the heart. In no place of worship can the cathedral service harmonise better than with St. George's Chapel. It does not impress the mind by its vastness, or grandeur of proportions, as York —or by its remote antiquity, as parts of Ely; but by its perfect and symmetrical beauty. The exquisite form of the roof—elegant yet perfectly simple, as every rib of each column which supports it spreads out upon the ceiling into the most gorgeous fan—the painted windows—the rich carving of the stalls of the choir—the waving banners—and, in accordance with the whole character of the place, its complete preservation and scrupulous neatness—all these, and many more characteristics which I cannot describe, render it a gem of the architecture of the fifteenth century."

The close proximity of Eton and Windsor is a fact familiar to most persons, however personally unacquainted with the neighbourhood. The two places, indeed, are essentially one, though lying in different counties, and on opposite sides of the Thames. There was a time, also, it appears, when the lords of Windsor and of England thought that the college of Eton really should be as united by the laws of its establishment, as by the circumstances of the locality to Windsor. Edward IV. petitioned Pope Pius II. to remove the foundation and unite it to Windsor, on the ground of the heavy expenditure required to finish the establishment begun by Henry VI. at Eton; and then, curiously enough, when his wishes had been formally carried into effect, he again petitioned the Pope (Paul II.) to undo what had been done, urging that he had been deceived. But for the comparatively peaceable character of the establishment then meditated, namely, a provost, ten priests, four clerks, six choristers, and twenty-five poor men, with the leaven only of twenty-five riotous scholars, one might have supposed that Edward had felt some misgiving in his mind, in the interval, as to the inroad the new institution might make upon his own comfort at Windsor if brought too close.

The bronze statue of Henry VI. that meets our gaze in the quadrangle, as we approach the academic buildings, shows us, as all works so situated should, the founder of the pile; though the monarch's labours were, as we have incidentally seen, interrupted, and by a cause that every one readily divines—the wars of the Roses, and his own constantly-increasing misfortunes, which terminated only in a bloody and secret death. This statue is not the only one of the unfortunate Henry at Eton, there is another by Bacon in the chapel; a part of the structure that stands out, externally, from the generally plain character of the rest of the pile, not only in materials, being of stone, while the buildings generally are of brick, but also by its pretensions and beauty, the college exhibiting little of either of those qualities elsewhere. The aspect of the whole has been likened to the aspect of the well-known St. James's Palace, London. Lupton's Tower, in the centre of the façade shown in our engraving (Fig. 1278), was the last portion erected of the ancient structure, and was only finished in the early part of the reign of Henry VIII.

The assemblage in the chapel at prayer of such a number of the "flower of English aristocratic youth," as Köhl justly designates them, must be indeed a stirring sight, and one, at the same time, calculated to beget high and solemn speculations, "particularly when it is recollected that the past annals of Eton prove that whoever at any time sees six hundred scholars assembled, sees among them a great number whose names and lives will hereafter become interesting to the whole world. How many famous lawyers and authors, how many distinguished statesmen, ecclesiastics, generals, and admirals have received their education at Eton, and knelt on their knees in this chapel, morning and evening? how many future famed and influential heroes, statesmen, actors, and legislators knelt there at that moment among the rest?" The writer of this passage speaks of something as appearing strange and unbecoming to him, a German, namely, the order of the congregation, "commoners" above "poor scholars," and "noblemen" above commoners. There is no such distinction whatever at Eton, either in chapel or school. Rank, except the rank of scholastic merit, is entirely unknown.

Of the three chief schools of England, Eton, Winchester, and Westminster, the first is the most important in numbers, wealth, and popularity. Of the two objects that the founder had at heart, the educating youth and providing for old age, the first alone has been observed, and the second apparently sacrificed to it; no "poor and infirm old men" now form any part of the foundation. At the head of Eton we find a provost, a vice-provost, and six fellows. These together constitute, as it were, the senate that rules the little world of Eton. The executive government may be said to be carried on by the head-master, with a numerous corps of under-masters and assistants. Lastly, as to the body for whom all this machinery exists; it is divided into two classes, the one consisting of the seventy scholars, who form a part of the foundation, and who wear the black college gown; and the other, formed of the 'Oppidans," or scholars who are simply sent to Eton to receive their education, and who, having no other connection with it, are boarded in the different houses established for that purpose in the town of Eton. The college is of course anything but a cheap school. Even for the king's scholar, that is, one of the seventy all of whom should be poor boys, the incidental charges are perfectly incompatible with the means of very poor parents.

For those parents who, without being wealthy, have still sufficient means to secure for their sons a king's scholarship at Eton, the college offers great advantages. Even the fagging system, brutal as it has been, and brutal to some extent it must remain whenever the powers given by it rest in the hands of a boy-tyrant (ever the worst of tyrants), yet even that system gives to the king's scholar a means of asserting his independence and dignity, which might otherwise be seriously compromised by the thoughtless or selfish recklessness of the purse-proud young merchant or haughty young lordling. Then, too, there are the continually-recurring vacancies for the king's scholars at King's College, Cambridge, according to the arrangement of the royal founder of both, where they are at once provided for, and after three years succeed to fellowships. An ancient festival called Montem takes place every three years. It has been supposed that it sprung from another custom, one of the most popular in the middle ages, known by the name of the boy-bishop. "What merry work," says Bishop Hall, in his 'Triumphs of Pleasure' (written in the seventeenth century), "it was here in the days of our holy fathers (and I know not whether in some places it may not be so still), that upon St. Nicholas, St. Katherine, St. Clement, and Holy Innocents' day, children were wont to be arrayed in chimers, rochets, surplices, to counterfeit bishops and priests, and to be led with songs and dances from house to house, blessing the people, who stood grinning in the way to expect that ridiculous benediction! Yea, that boys in that holy sport were wont to sing masses, and to climb into the pulpit to preach (no doubt learnedly and edifyingly) to the simple auditory : and that was so really done, that in the cathedral church of Salisbury (unless it be defaced) there is a perfect monument of one of these boy-bishops (who died in the time of his young pontificality), accoutred in his episcopal robes, still to be seen." This very interesting monument (Fig. 1206, p. 268) will be found among our engravings. The boy-bishop of Salisbury, here referred to, is actually said to have had the disposal of any prebends that might fall vacant during his brief term of authority. The custom was abolished by Henry VIII.; and then it was, in all probability, that the scholars of Eton, setting their wits to work how to obey the statute and yet keep their holiday, hit upon the Montem. We know that there was a boy-bishop of Eton in papal times;—we know that a boy dressed in a clerical habit formed at one time a part of the existing ceremony, and read prayers, evidently representing the abolished bishop; and, lastly, we know that the present Montem did, up to the middle of the last century, take place on the very day originally set apart for the pranks of the mitred youthful ecclesiastic.

Among the Norman visitors to King Edward the Confessor's court, who first gave England a foretaste of what they were afterwards to suffer from that imperious and warlike people, was Eustace, Earl of Boulogne, who, on his return, engaged in a disgraceful affray at Dover, arising out of the insolence of his armed followers as he marched them through the town : eighteen perished for their presumption, and the bold Norman earl fled for his life before the English whom he had insulted. He was, however, protected by the king, and became the husband of Goda, the Confessor's sister, a match that could not be very pleasing to the English nation. Earl Eustace bestowed the manor of St. Mary, called also Lanchei, and Lamhea, now Lambeth, the property of Goda his wife, on the bishops of Rochester, who by certain exchanges in the twelfth century transferred it to the archbishops of Canterbury.

The removal of the chief residence of the archbishops from Canterbury to London was a consequence of some of those factions which in the twelfth and thirteenth centuries so disturbed the Catholic constitution, and at the same time revealed how much evil there was latent in its system. The primates of Canterbury were at enmity with the monks thereof: on the side of the primates was the sovereign of England; on the side of the monks was the pontiff of Rome. Archbishop Baldwin tried to set up a rival house for canons regular at Hackington near Canterbury, but the monks, backed by the Pope, soon put a stop to that plan. Archbishop Hubert next resolved to carry out what Baldwin had failed in, only at another place, the manor of St. Mary at London. Richard I. approved Hubert's scheme, and the important fabric was set about with due energy. In a sad state of agitation, the Canterbury monks, terrified lest the glorious and gainful relics of St. Thomas-à-Becket should be taken from them, to lend a lustre and bring

1351.—Great Chatfield Manor-House, Wilts.

1352.—House at Grantham, Lincolnshire.

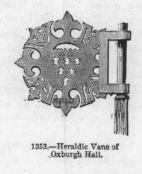

1353.—Heraldic Vane of Oxburgh Hall.

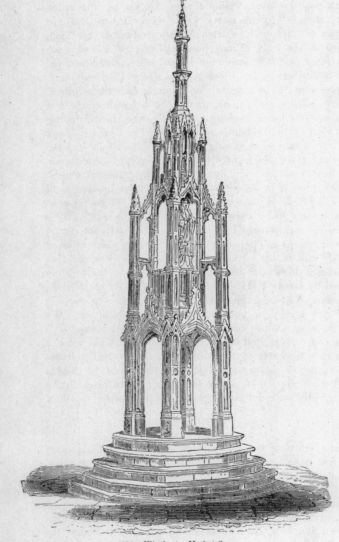

1354.—Winchester Market-Cross.

1355.—The Almonry, Westminster, where Caxton's Printing-office was.

1356.—House of the Fifteenth Century, at Leicester. In which it is said Richard III. slept the night before the Battle of Bosworth.

1357.—Chimney-piece at Tattershall Castle.

1358.—Vault under Gerard's Hall.

1359.—St. Mary's Hall: Street Front.

1360.—St. Mary's Hall: Interior

1361.—Street in London: Cheapside

1332.—Street in London.

1363.—Street in London.

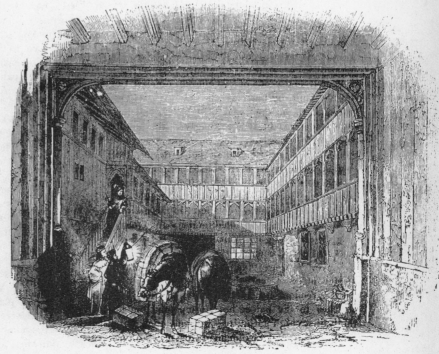

1364.—An Inn Yard.

substantial offerings to the rising establishment at London, again implored the help of the supreme head of the church. It was not denied. Bull rapidly followed bull, high-toned and threatening, commanding Hubert to desist, and the king to cease to support him. These tremendous missives in a short time bowed the iron wills of Archbishop Hubert and of Cœur-de-Lion, who found it easier to cope with savage beasts and Saracens than with the Pope. But Hubert was not compelled to return to reside at Canterbury, and thus that city lost an honour which it never afterwards regained.

For some years the primates seem to have been but humbly lodged in the manor-house of St. Mary's parish; until another of the fiery discords of the age, still more remarkable than the preceding, was the occasion of an edifice being erected worthier of its exalted inhabitants. Archbishop Boniface was one of the foreign prelates whom the king in the thirteenth century had favoured the country with, a person without the least fitness for a spiritual vocation, though installed at the very summit of the English church. Not content with the princely revenues he received, Boniface was in the habit of making what he styled his *visitations*, that is, travelling in great pomp, and with a vast retinue, from monastery to monastery, parish to parish, at the expense of those whom he visited, who suffered cruelly under his shameless exactions. One of these visitations brought him to the priory of St. Bartholomew in Smithfield, "where, being received with procession in the most solemn wise, he said that he passed not upon the honour, but came to *visit* them." The canons, who might well shrink at the word from *his* mouth, knowing what was meant by it, answered that they, "having a learned bishop, ought not, in contempt of him, to be visited by any other; which answer so much offended the archbishop, that he forthwith fell on the sub-prior, and smote him on the face, saying, 'Indeed, indeed! Doth it become you English traitors so to answer me?' Thus raging, with oaths not to be recited, he rent in pieces the rich cope of the sub-prior, and trod it under his feet, and thrust him against a pillar in the chancel with such violence that he had almost killed him. But the canons seeing their sub-prior almost slain, came and plucked off the archbishop with such force that they overthrew him backwards, whereby they might see he was *armed* and prepared to fight. The archbishop's men, seeing their master down, being all strangers, and their master's countrymen, born at Provence, fell upon the canons, beat them, tore them, and trod them under foot. At length the canons, getting away as well as they could, ran, bloody and miry, rent and torn, to the Bishop of London to complain: who bade them go to the king at Westminster and tell him thereof. Whereupon four of them went thither; the rest were not able, they were so sore hurt. But when they came to Westminster the king would neither hear nor see them, so they returned without redress. In the mean season the whole city was in an uproar, and ready to have rung the common bell, and to have hewed the archbishop into small pieces; who was secretly crept to Lambeth, where they sought him, and, not knowing him by sight, said to themselves, 'Where is that ruffian —that cruel smiter? He is no winner of souls, but an exacter of money, whom neither God nor any lawful or free election did bring to this promotion: but the king did unlawfully intrude him, being unlearned, a stranger born, and having a wife,'" &c. (Stow.) Instead of receiving redress, those who had been so grossly injured were presently excommunicated by the archbishop. The Pope then stepped in to adjust the affair, and with a shrewd eye to the splendour and profit of the church, ordered Boniface to do penance for his fault, by building for the see of Canterbury a rich palace at Lambeth, in the room of the then existing manor-house. And the palace was built accordingly. Six hundred years of mighty changes for England and the church have rolled away since that atoning act, and we cannot help wishing that with the palace the custom had survived in which it originated. How would the land be studded over with noble edifices, if every distinguished offender of the Boniface kind had been so put to his purgation!

There are few antique edifices in the metropolis more reverenced and cherished by the inhabitants than Lambeth Palace. It is not hidden out of sight, as many are. Its conspicuous position on the banks of the Thames (Fig. 1290), where all who pass up or down the river between Westminster and Blackfriars, or across it at the former place, must behold the edifice literally embosomed in green woods, renders it widely familiar. But the strong interest that attaches to the palace has more potent foundations than this. We think of its high antiquity; we remember that it has been the place of judgment and confinement for many of our earliest martyrs to Protestant principles; visions of splendour float before the mind, as we recall the visits so often made to the palace by our kings and queens, especially Mary and Elizabeth. Mary completely furnished the palace at her own expense for Cardinal Pole, whom she frequently visited: and Elizabeth during her long reign honoured successive archbishops in the same way, especially Parker and Whitgift, staying sometimes two or three days together, and being magnificently feasted. The barges of these high visitors still to the wandering fancy seem to move to and fro in the sunlit river in all their glitter and pomp, and between banks fairer than the Thames now possesseth. In such day-dreams, of course good Queen Bess figures conspicuously in her ruff and hooped petticoat: we see her landing at Lambeth Palace, and handed forth by the courtly archbishop, who however, we suspect, would gladly lose the honour of the visit, if at the same time he could avoid hearing his gracious mistress's somewhat free-spoken words. It is not pleasant, for instance, after one's lady has been expending all her energies in the entertainment of a queen, to hear the guest at departure express her thanks in the fashion of Elizabeth to Archbishop Parker's lady: "Madam I may not call you, and Mistress (a word used then in a disreputable sense) I am ashamed to call you, so I know not what to call you, but yet I do thank you;"—and all because her self-sufficient Majesty does not like the clergy to be married!

Supposing the reader to be a stranger to the existing palace, we will take leave to usher him into its precincts, and conduct him through it, reviving by the way a few—it can be but a few—of the memories that attach to particular parts. The entrance gate of the outer palace-court first impresses us by its extraordinary height and size. The most beautiful part of it is the groined roof under the deep arch. This we see at once is a relic of the rich Gothic of the fifteenth century. The whole gate was rebuilt about 1490 by Cardinal Morton, in the place of the "Great Gate" that we find mentioned in the steward's accounts of the palace in the reign of Edward II. That would be a sort of castle-gate, better suited, according to our modern notions, to the home of a warrior than a prelate. But prelates' houses were, in effect, castles; often regularly fortified, and in times of civil commotion defended against sieges and attacks, like any of the regular fortresses. At that great old gate, in the reign of Edward I., the daily fragments of the house were distributed, and every Friday and Sunday a loaf of bread was given to every beggar that came, sufficient for a day's sustenance. On high festival days one hundred and fifty pence (old money) were given to one hundred and fifty poor people, besides all which good Archbishop Winchelsey sent provisions, money, and apparel to the aged, the sick, and the unfortunate who were either ashamed or unable to beg. The venerable Protestant Archbishop Parker, the translator of the Bible, already mentioned, was as eminent as any of his Catholic predecessors for his liberality to the destitute and the stranger; and if the reader turn to our engraving of the gateway (Fig. 1291), he will perceive by the groups of poor persons gathering at the gate, that the old custom has not grown entirely obsolete. But the gate has gloomier memories. A low door under the arch leads to a mysterious-looking room, with ponderous stone walls, having three strong iron rings in them, and a name—*Grafton*—inscribed, said to be that of one who perished here. This was a reserve-prison for Lollards when the tower that bears their name was full. We enter now the outer palace-court. A picturesque ivy-covered wall on the left divides us from the beautiful and well-known Bishop's Walk by the Thames. On the right is the Great Hall and Manuscript-room, the latter a fireproof modern erection, containing many precious literary curiosities of the middle ages. Before us is the Water Tower, built of brick, and the Lollards' Tower, of stone, whose sad and fearful history provokes without satisfying the curiosity. Of those who have been immured or perished in it we have few records beyond their handwriting on the walls of the Lollards' prison in the upper part of the tower (Fig. 1294) The carved stonework of the exterior of the windows is mouldered with age; the statue of Thomas-à-Becket is gone from its lofty and beautiful niche; but so long as a stone of that worn tower remains, it will be gazed on with intense and reverent emotions for the sake of the heroic men who laid with incalculable pains and cemented with their blood the foundations of our inestimable religious freedom. Glory to them for ever! and as for their persecutors and murderers, sure we are, that those most worthy of the name of martyrs would breathe for them the prayer of Christ, "Father, forgive them, for they know not what they do." Neither ought *we* to judge them harshly.

On entering the great hall (Fig. 1295), its noble dimensions first take us by surprise, then the lofty and richly-painted window opposite excites our admiration. In it are collected beautiful relics from other windows of the old palace, including the portrait of Archbishop Chicheley, builder of the Lollards' tower and rebuilder of the old hall, first built most likely by Boniface. Chicheley's hall would of course be of the architecture of his time, the beginning of the fifteenth century, and Gothic being then in its perfection, his work would doubtless be a considerable advance on Boniface's. But it was not destined to last. Scot and Hardyng, two of Charles the First's judges, having Lambeth Palace granted them by the Commonwealth, pulled down the hall, and sold the materials. Archbishop Juxon after the Restoration rebuilt it on the ancient model, at a cost of ten thousand five hundred pounds. The distinguishing feature of the hall is its roof, of timber, most richly carved, with a series of broad semicircular arches. The old uses of the hall were dining and feasting; it is a place for feasting still to antiquaries and scholars; for whom few greater enjoyments could be devised than to turn them loose among the books of the very valuable library that now occupies all the available space of the hall. This library was formed by Archbishop Bancroft, who died in 1610; and after experiencing strange vicissitudes and wanderings, it seems now safe and settled at last.

The great quadrangle, or inner court, has a beautiful and dignified effect, with its lofty trees here and there overhanging the walls; its ornamental cross, supporting lamps, on a little green in the centre; its ranges of buildings, where we see in regular succession a buttressed side of the great hall, with an elegant modern porch, the guard-room, with a curious and beautiful gable window, and the splendid new palace of the primates of Canterbury. The old buildings thus superseded about twelve years ago, were famous for a fig-tree, the last of those which had been planted by Cardinal Pole. They were of the Marseilles kind, and bore what those who liked green figs esteemed delicious fruit. There are yet some shoots of this tree growing between the buttresses of the hall.

No part of the palace has a more quaint and beautiful expression than the guard-room (Fig. 1293); mention of which occurs in the steward's accounts of the time of Henry VI. The guard-room of Boniface's palace had then been rebuilt. The designation of the guard-room, and the arms kept here from the period of the middle ages, speak forcibly to the mind of the military character of their archiepiscopal owners, and of their deficient comprehension of the doctrines of the Gospel that they presumed to teach. Around the walls of the guard-room extends an unbroken chronological line of portraits of archbishops, from Warham to Sutton, with a few of earlier date. The earliest is that of Arundel, the brother of that Earl Arundel previously mentioned as beheaded by Richard II. While one brother thus perished, the other joined Bolingbroke in his banishment, and, returning to England with him, shared his triumphs. It was this Arundel by whom Bolingbroke was crowned. But he, the tonsure of whose hair, as Fuller observes, was alone the cause of "the keeping of his head," had not been improved in tenderness of heart by adversity: he sent the first English martyr to the stake—William Sawtre, priest of St. Osyth's, London—who was condemned in accordance with the provision of the famous law passed against relapsed heretics, in the second year of the reign of Henry of Bolingbroke. The ceremonial of degradation preliminary to Sawtre's execution was calculated by its formality and impressiveness to produce a strong effect on the minds of all who witnessed it. In his priestly garments, holding in his hands the chalice of the host, and its paten or lid, Sawtre was brought into St. Paul's Cathedral, before Arundel and six bishops. The sentence of degradation fell in solemn tones from the archbishop's lips, while he took from the poor priest the chalice and paten, and his casule, or scarlet robe. Sawtre then ceased to be a priest. The New Testament was put in his hands, and taken away, and the stole or tippet removed from his neck; and Sawtre was then no longer deacon. His alb or surplice, and the maniple on his left wrist, were next taken off; and Sawtre's sub-deaconship had departed from him. A candlestick, taper, and small pitcher given up; and his office of acolyte was gone. With his book of exorcisms he surrendered the power of exorcist; with his book of daily lessons, his task of reader; with his sexton's surplice and church-door key, a sexton's authority; and by way of finish, his priest's cap was taken from his head, the tonsure obliterated, and the cap of a layman put on instead. Thus stripped of all dignity, except such as he derived from his intrepid constancy to the truths he advocated,—with a recommendation to mercy that only adds to our disgust and horror,—the victim was formally delivered over by Arundel to the high constable and marshal of England. Sawtre was burned in Smithfield, in 1401, amid a vast multitude of people, whose feelings at a sight so new and dreadful i: is hardly possible to analyze, but who surely never could have allowed such a revolting act to be perpetrated, if they had seen, however dimly, in anticipation the awful character and extent of the passions that, once let loose, were to rage through the length and breadth of England, destroying its best and bravest sons, putting strife between the dearest friends and relations, turning the domestic hearth into a pandemonium, with bigotry set up on high as the only household god.

Whilst Arundel thus endeavoured to keep down the new opinions, he strove more and more to encourage and enforce the practice of the old. Fresh saints and fresh holydays were added to the calendar; religious processions (see the Passage of the Host, Fig. 1334) became more frequent and magnificent; altars and images of all kinds were crowded more thickly into the churches; priests partook of the spirit of their chief leader, and grew more zealous; friars preached in their moveable pulpits about the streets (Fig. 1333): the holy wells at Northampton (Fig. 1297), and other places, the shrines of Becket, and our Lady of Walsingham, were each the resort of countless pilgrims. Rome, nay Jerusalem itself (Fig. 1330) was haunted by titled and wealthy and pious wanderers from Old England. But not the less did the heresy still lift its low but clear and thrilling voice, not the less were there to be found believers in it, ready to endure martyrdom for its sake. One of the most remarkable of the next chosen two or three victims was a man, whose death, we regret to say, reflects disgrace on a reign, otherwise free from all that can personally lessen our love and esteem for the ruler, that of Henry V. When he came to the throne, he found the Lollards following the guidance of one of his own early friends and associates, Sir John Oldcastle, or as he was often called in right of his wife, Lord Cobham. At first Henry would not let Arundel work his pleasure upon such a heretic, but would talk with him himself. The young king could do much; but there was one thing he could not do—roll back in Cobham's heart and mind the stream of thought by which he had been borne on to the haven where he had anchored at last. It is a fearful evidence of the bigotry that exists in us all, to find such a man as Harry the Fifth making up for the want of the legitimate success of reason by the illegitimate assistance of threats of the stake and the flames. Cobham thought it time then to withdraw to his manor and castle of Cowling, in Kent, but was obliged speedily to surrender to an armed force, and submit himself a prisoner to those who came to guide him to the Tower of London. At his examination by a synod of prelates and abbots, he debated every point raised with the utmost ardour and self-confidence, and so was sentenced to the martyr's doom. But Henry granted a respite of fifty days, and during that time Cobham escaped. It was a critical moment. Something decisive must be done. He determined to raise the Lollards in arms, and so endeavour at once to secure the prosperity of the cause. He failed, miserably failed; first, in the attempt to seize Henry at Eltham Palace, and secondly, in his idea of seizing London, where, instead of the twenty-five thousand men that he hoped to have met in St. Giles's Fields, scarcely a hundred assembled, aware, probably, that the king had discovered their intentions, and was prepared. Cobham for a time escaped, but at a later period, when his hopes for the progress of Lollardism induced him, it is said, to invite the Scots, he was taken prisoner, after a gallant struggle, arraigned before the House of Lords, and finally condemned to be hanged as a traitor and burnt as a heretic. A frightful sentence, but executed in all its horrors. He was hung up by the armpits, and actually roasted alive, in the same place where his followers had previously suffered.

Quitting the guard-room by a passage leading through some private apartments down to the vestry, we pause a minute to admire the valuable antique chest kept in the vestry, supposed of Chinese work, exceedingly rich and elaborate, and then enter the chapel (Fig. 1292). Here the walls and windows appear in the main as old as the palace built by meek Archbishop Boniface. When Laud first came to Lambeth, the stained windows were "shameful to look on, all diversely patched, like a poor beggar's coat." It was charged against Laud afterwards, "that he did repair these windows by their like in the mass-book." But Laud replied, that he and his secretary had made out the story as well as they could by what was left unbroken. / That "story" was man's history from the creation to the day of judgment—the types in the Old Testament being painted on the side windows, the antitype and verity in the New on the middle windows. Laud also set up the beautiful oaken screen and other decorations, now disguised by paint. In this chapel Miles Coverdale assisted to consecrate Archbishop Parker, who was afterwards buried at Lambeth. An inscription for his monument was shown to the subject of it while he lived. He replied, he could not assume the description of such a character to himself, but he would so make use of it as to attain, as far as possible, the good qualities and virtues it specified. It is a pity that the writers of laudatory epitaphs generally do not in the same way anticipate death, and thus give the object of their praise a chance at all events, of conforming

1365.—Old House at Warwick.

1367.—Furniture of a Bed-room of the time of Henry VI. (Harleian MS. 2278.)

1366.—Old Timber Houses at Coventry.

1368.—Ancient Kitchen at Stanton Harcourt.

1369.—A Bed-room in the time of Edward IV. From Rouse's Hist. of Rich. Beauchamp, Earl of Warwick. (Cotton MS. Julius, E 4.)

1370.—Criminals conducted to Prison. (Harleian MS. No. 4374.)

1371.—Criminals conducted to Death. (Harleian MS. No. 4374.)

1372.—Caxton.—With Paper-marks.

1375.—Shooting at Butts. (Royal MS, 19, c. viii.)

1373.—Woodcut of a Knight. (From Caxton's 'Game of the Chess.')

1376.—St. Alban's. Hawking Party.

1374.—Couvre-fen.

1377.—Whitsun Morris-Dance.

his life to the epitaph, since they will not make the epitaph conform to the life. These good qualities and virtues did not prevent the Archbishop's remains from being most unworthily treated. He had been no good friend to the Puritans, and when Scot and Har-dyng, as we have said, had the palace granted them, Colonel Scot, desirous of turning the chapel into a hall or dancing-room, demo-lished Parker's monument. Not satisfied with that, Hardyng ex-humed the corpse of the Archbishop, sold the leaden covering, and buried the venerable relics *in a dunghill*. There it remained until the Restoration, when Sir William Dugdale, hearing accidentally of that dastardly outrage, repaired immediately to Archbishop San-croft, who obtained an order from the House of Lords for re-inter-ment of the desecrated relics in Lambeth chapel. On a stone we read the result. The body of Matthew Parker, archbishop, here rests *at last*. His monument is also restored, and is in that part of the chapel divided from the rest by the screen. The painted windows were destroyed in the civil wars.

Again we stand in the green and handsome quadrangle, and turn to inspect the irregular and embattled front of the new palace, which, if not in entire accordance with the old remains (or they would have exhibited a compound of styles), do honour to the taste and skill of Mr. Blore, the architect. The entrance-hall is espe-cially admirable; the staircase has an elaborately worked balustrade: at the top, a screen of three arches opens to the corridor, which, on the right, conducts to the principal apartments of the new palace, and on the left, to those of the old. One front of the palace looks on the gardens (Fig. 1296), which are charmingly laid out, and have altogether an air that makes us, on entering, ask ourselves in sur-prise—Can this be indeed London?

A terrible year for England was the year 1348. There were solemn masses and prayers in the churches, fastings and humiliations in the monasteries, processions of public penitents scourging themselves in the streets, funeral bells tolling by night and by day. Fear and horror sat on every countenance. The cry of lamentation was heard from almost every house: the Destroyer had gone forth—there was a mighty pestilence in the land. This had begun in the heart of China, traversed the deserts of Cobi, the wilds of Tartary, the Levant, Egypt, Greece, Italy, Germany, and France, and entered this country by the western coast. On its route, it had desolated or depopulated whole regions. We may imagine with what terror our countrymen must have anticipated its presence among them; alas! the reality far exceeded even their fears. Amidst the chilly winds and rains and mists of November, it entered London. The poor people having thus to endure the winter's cold at the same time that they were exposed to this ghastly and awful visitant, and living generally pent up in great numbers in dirty, narrow, ill-ventilated streets, so favourable to the progress of disease, it is impossible even to estimate the amount of their actual sufferings; but the amount of their dead is knowledge suf-ficient. The churchyards of London were soon filled, and more room was demanded. The devout feeling so prevalent, made people unwilling to bury even the infectious bodies of the deceased in any but consecrated ground and in the neighbourhood of a house of prayer. The dead were not therefore, as in later instances, huddled into the earth in any fashion, to get them out of the way of the living, but fields were bought or bestowed by the wealthy and pious, to make new churchyards of. One of these fields was called "No Man's Land," though had it belonged to no one, Ralph Strat-ford, Bishop of London, could not have purchased it for the purpose just stated. "No Man's Land" was walled round, consecrated, and a church built on it. The situation was between the north wall of the present CHARTER-HOUSE in Wilderness Row and Sutton-Street. "It remained," says Stow (writing more than two centuries ago), "till our time by the name of Pardon Churchyard, and served for burying such as desperately ended their lives, or were executed for fe-lonies; who were fetched thither, usually in a close cart, bayled over, and covered with black, having a plain white cross thwarting, and at the fore-end a St. John's cross without, and within a bell ringing by shaking of the cart, whereby the same might be heard when it passed; and this was called the Friary Cart, which belonged to St. John's, and had the privilege of sanctuary." No Man's Land, in its turn, became filled, and in an appallingly short space of time. So a noble knight next gave thirteen acres adjoining Pardon Churchyard, which were called the Spittle Croft, and afterwards the "New Church Haw." This new piece of ground was conse-crated by the same Bishop of London who gave and hallowed the other; and a chapel was built, in which masses were offered up for the sufferers. This chapel stood about the centre of the present Charter-House Square. There was employment enough for the priests who prayed in it, for within the year, fifty thousand persons, cut off by the pestilence, were interred in that one burial-ground. The same noble knight, after the plague had passed away, in a spirit probably of devout thankfulness that it had so passed, devoted the spot permanently to the support of a body of religious, twenty-four in number, of the strictest of all monkish orders, the Carthusians. That knight we can readily believe to have been "noble," were there nought else known of him; but his name was Sir Walter Manny, one of the bravest and most skilful of English warriors (though not English-born), and the man who, with Queen Philippa, divides in some degree with the more important actors the admiration raised in our minds by the ever-memorable events of the siege of Calais, an event that has been for several centuries, and no doubt will for ever remain, best known by its connection with the simple but much-meaning words—the Citizens of Calais. That story has been already narrated in these pages, so we will here speak of another incident in the life of Manny. Edward on one occasion sent him to the continent with a body of troops to relieve the Countess de Montfort, who, while her husband was a prisoner in the power of Philip, King of France, was besieged by Montfort's enemy, Charles de Blois, who sought to seize his duchy of Brittany. The countess, however, in her castle of Hennebon, made a gallant and protracted defence, under such extreme privations as induced the stoutest warriors about her to prepare for surrender; well on that occasion was Froissart's description of her borne out—she dis-played the "courage of a man and the heart of a lion" until the joyful moment when the English ships were descried bringing assistance. We can well imagine with what enthusiastic and grate-ful feelings the countess must have welcomed Sir Walter Manny and his troops. They were handsomely entertained; but the next day the knight had to begin the serious business that he came for: the siege had to be raised; the enemy driven from their camp. He was making inquiries of the countess concerning the state of the town and of the enemy's army, when, looking out of a window, and seeing a large machine placed very near, probably one of the moveable towers of the day (see our engravings, Figs. 1253, 1274), under cover of which operations were carried on by the enemy against the castle walls, to the great annoyance of the defenders, Sir Walter, with a few other bold knights, resolved to destroy it. Accordingly, "They went to arm themselves, and then sallied quietly out of one of the gates, taking with them three hundred archers (Fig. 1250), who shot so well, that those who guarded the machine fled, and the men-at-arms, who followed the archers, falling upon them, slew the greater part, and broke down and cut in pieces the large machine. They then dashed in among the tents and huts, set fire to them, and killed and wounded many of their enemies before the army was in motion. After this they made a handsome retreat. When the enemy were mounted and armed, they galloped after them like madmen. Sir Walter Manny, seeing this, exclaimed, 'May I never be embraced by my mistress and dear friend if I enter castle or fortress before I have unhorsed one of those gallopers. He then turned round, and pointed his spear towards the enemy, as did the two brothers of Land-Halle, le Haze-de-Brabant, Sir Yves de Tresiquidi, Sir Galeran de Landreman, and many others, and spitted the first coursers. Many legs were made to kick the air. Some of their own party were also unhorsed. The conflict became very furious, for reinforcements were perpetually coming from the camp, and the English were obliged to retreat towards the castle, which they did in good order until they came to the castle-ditch; there the knights made a stand until all their men were safely returned. . . . . The Countess of Montfort came down from the castle to meet them, and with a most cheerful countenance kissed Sir Walter de Manny and all his companions, one after the other, like a noble and valiant dame." (Froissart.) Under such a commander the castle precincts soon became too hot to hold the French: the siege was raised.

The establishment founded by this very "perfect gentle knight," and in which he was buried (Fig. 1372) with solemn pomp, amidst the regrets of the whole English nation, was called the Chartreux House, from Chartreux, a place in France, where, about 1080, the order originated; hence the corrupted English name of the Charter-House. The rule prohibited the eating of flesh, and of fish, unless it were given to them; and beside these prohibitions, one day in each week was set apart for fasting on bread, water, and salt. The monks slept upon cork, with a single blanket to cover them; they rose at midnight to sing their matins, and none were permitted to go beyond the bounds of their monastery, except the prior and proctor, and they only on indispensable business. Their habit was white, with a black cloak.

During about a century and a half, the history of Sir Walter Manny's monastery presents no particular event to engage our attention, the best proof of the contented and quiet lives passed within its walls; but at the period when the religious houses were dissolved, the monks of this place rise suddenly into prominence, and become ever memorable for their honest and high principles, tried by the extremest inflictions of cruelty and oppression, which they had to endure at the hands of one who has had few superiors in the art of testing how far human fortitude can go in what it esteems to be a good cause. And that very fact is, indeed, the one, and the only one source of consolation that is presented to us in tracing the more sanguinary proceedings of Henry VIII.

In our notices of Lambeth Palace, we had occasion to allude to the sufferings of the early Protestants in England under the Catholic heads of the church in the fifteenth century; in the melancholy fate of the Charter-House monks in the sixteenth we have to exhibit a counter-picture, in which the conscientious Catholics are made to undergo equal wrongs under Protestant ascendancy. The evil was the same on both sides, each in turn making his own convictions the tribunal by which to judge and punish those of the other. This has been an error of ages, and still exists, we fear, among nearly all classes of thinkers and believers. The most vital point of the old religion was deemed by its professors in the Chartreux Monastery to be Papal Supremacy. They refused, therefore, to take the oaths that set up the king in the pope's place. The prior and the proctor, named Houghton and Middlemore, were in consequence sent to the Tower, and tortured into a temporary submission. But they were not then permitted to return to the monastery. Three governors were appointed in their stead; "most wise, learned, and discreet men" they were styled; and such they proved themselves in all that could tend to promote their royal master's designs on the monastic revenues, in corrupting the minds of such of the monks as were open to corruption, and in procuring the destruction of the remainder. They assembled the whole community, which had also submitted, and informed them that all heresies and treasons were pardoned up to that day, but that death would follow the commission of new offences. Then they demanded the keys of the convent from the prior, and took the regulation of the receipts and expenditure into their own hands, accounting for both only to the king thenceforward. And thus commenced a system of persecution, almost without parallel even in the worst ages of religious bigotry. Before, however, the monks were called upon to exert all the strength alike of body and mind that they possessed, their superior, the prior, renouncing the safety that his first partial submission had promised, showed them the path they should pursue, and proved himself worthy to be their superior by the way in which he himself trod it. He, with four others, all Carthusians, and two of them, like himself, heads of houses, perished at Tyburn, and their bodies being quartered, one of Houghton's quarters was set over his own gate. Such was the position of affairs when the triad of governors began their subtle practices upon the monks generally of the monastery. Ffyloll, the most influential, it would seem, of the three governors, wrote from time to time to Cromwell, the equally unscrupulous and time-serving minister of Henry VIII.; and his letters afford us much insight into the proceedings of these worthies. It appears they altered and broke up the arrangements of the establishment by gentle degrees. The large charities and hospitalities of the monastery were thus attacked. Ffyloll "learns" that the proctor used to account for an expenditure, chiefly for hospitality, charity, and buildings, of 1051*l.* a year, the regular receipts being 642*l.* 4*s.*, and the deficiency made up by the benevolence of the city of London. And the monks, "not regarding this dearth, neither the increase of their superfluous number, neither yet the decay of the said benevolence and charity [nor, we may add, the ruin that was fast coming on them], would have and hath that same fare continued that then was used, and would have plenty of bread and ale and fish given to strangers in the buttery and at the buttery-door, and as large distributions of bread and ale to all their servants and to vagabonds [travellers] at the gate as was then used." These bounties, Ffyloll, under favour of his worship, Cromwell, deems necessary to have diminished; and diminished, of course, they are, as a step merely to their entire suppression. But Ffyloll had not yet done interfering with the buttery. "I think, under correction of your mastership, that it were very necessary to remove the eleven lay-brothers from the buttery, and set eleven temporal persons in that room, and likewise in the kitchen, for in those eleven offices lie *waste of the house.*" One of Ffyloll's petty persecutions was the endeavour to compel the lay-brothers and steward to dine on flesh in the refectory; irritated, it would seem, by their carrying messages to and from the confined monks. How the privacy of the brethren's

cells was invaded, and their lightest actions subjected to the worst constructions, we may easily perceive in the following extract:— "It is no great marvel though many of these monks have heretofore offended God and the king by their foul errors, for I have found in the prior and proctor's cells three or four sundry printed books, from beyond the sea, of as foul errors and heresies as may be, and not one or two books be new printed alone, but hundreds of them; wherefore, by your mastership's favour, it seemeth to be more necessary that these cells be better searched, for I can perceive few of them but they have great pleasure in reading of such erroneous doctrines, and little or none in reading of the New Testament, or in other good book." In a postscript to another communication, Ffyloll sends Cromwell a list of all the monks, with a significant G and B placed before each name. Better endeavours than those of coercion were not wanting to persuade them to bend to the king's authority, by friends who pitied their sufferings and trembled for their final fate.

Archbishop Cranmer sent for two of the monks, Rochester and Rawlins, to try what his kind persuasions could effect. One was gained, whom the Archbishop kept with him, and induced to lay aside his religious habit, and to depart from the abstemious rules of his order; but Rochester was sent back to his monastery, and to his fate. The confessor-general of the monks of Sion, who had himself conformed to the king's supremacy, also tried the power of friendly importunities. He had "found by the word and will of God, both in the Old and New Testament, great truths for our prince, and for the Bishop of Rome nothing at all." Therefore, he beseeches them, "die not for the cause; save yourselves and your house; live long, and live well, to the honour of God; wealthy by your prayers, and edifying by your life to the people. Subject yourselves to your noble prince; get his gracious favour by your duty doing to his grace." A noted friar was brought to preach to them, but they refused to hear him, after they found that he sought to draw them from the faith they esteemed most holy. Books, entitled 'The Defence of Peace,' were distributed among them by one William Marshall, but though, on consideration of their new prior's consent, they were induced to receive these books, twenty-three out of twenty-four were almost immediately returned unread, and the twenty-fourth, after being kept four or five days by John Rochester, was *buried* by him—an act which, says Ffyloll, "is good matter to lay to them." By the accumulation of such "good matter," these unhappy men were ere long brought to their fearful end. From first to last, only six were drawn aside from their resolution, the rest were executed, like their prior, or perished no less miserably in prison, under the influence of filth, neglect, cruelty, and despair, until, in the words of a Mr. Bedle, whose loyalty to his sovereign seems to have been accompanied by something very like blasphemy to his Maker, they were all despatched by "the hand of God." Henry, alone at last in his glory, sat down to count the proceeds, namely, some six hundred and twenty-two pounds a-year from the revenues of the Charter-House, being twenty less than the proctor used to account for, which twenty the king graciously vouchsafed as a retiring pension to the new prior, Trafford, who had been appointed after the murder of the old, to give perhaps an air of legality to the surrender. Subsequently, the monastery buildings and site, whilst passing from one proprietor to another, under favour of the king, put on a new aspect, and became a noble mansion. In the reign of Elizabeth, Thomas Howard, Duke of Norfolk, made it his chief residence, and built most of the existing edifice (Figs. 1287, 1288). His son sold the whole to the founder of the Charter-House, Thomas Sutton, of whom we may have to speak in a future page.

From the ecclesiastical buildings represented in our engravings, as belonging either partially or wholly to the Perpendicular period of architecture, we may now first select for brief notice a group of country churches. That of Stratford-upon-Avon (Figs. 1307, 1308), perhaps of all others the dearest to Englishmen, on account of the ashes it holds,—consists generally of Early English, with additions in the late Perpendicular style: of which the chancel especially forms a very fine specimen. And here Shakspere was buried, needing not the remarkable invocation contained in the lines on his grave-stone, to secure the sacredness of his repose. There was here also at one time the font (Fig. 1309), in which, no doubt, he was baptized. But after having been long disused, the relic was found in the old charnel-house, from whence it was turned out as a piece of decayed and worthless stone into the churchyard. But even utilitarianism itself is not always sufficiently utilitarian; the parish clerk, when he looked on the despised old font, saw that it was worth something still—it would make an excellent pump-trough—and so

1378.—Bowling-Ball (From a MS. in the Douce Collection.)

1379.—Tumbling. (From Sloane MS. 264.)

1380.—Two-wheeled Plough. (From Harleian MS. No. 4374.)

1381.—Trap-Ball.

1382.—River-Fishing. (From Harleian MS No. 4374.)

1383.—Drummers. (Engraved by Strutt, from the Liber Regalis, Westminster Abbey.)

1384.—Golf, or Bandy-ball. (From a MS. in the Douce Collection.)

1385.—The Dance in the 'Garden of Pleasure:' from the 'Roman de la Rose.'—(Harl. MS. 4425.)

1386.—Hoodman Blind. (Bodleian MS.)

1387.—Leaping through a Hoop. (Ancient MS. engraved in Strutt's Sports.)

1388.—Club-ball. (From a MS. in Bodleian Collection, and Royal MS. 14 B 6.)

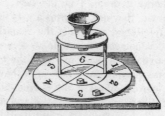

1389.—Ancient Dice-Box.

1390.—Shuttle-Cock. (From a MS. in the Douce Collection.)

372

pump-trough it became. In time, however, the relic attracted attention, was bought, and thenceforward carefully preserved. It now decks the garden of a gentleman at Stratford, and few gardens in England can boast of a greater treasure. Yet one cannot but ask—Is that its proper place? When shall we learn in England, the truth that one might have supposed was too evident to remain long unlearnt or unpractised, that the reverential care of all that is directly concerned with a great man's life and history, is the best of all monuments to his memory? What piece of sculpture, though it be by a Chantrey or a Westmacott, and reared in the most magnificent of national mausoleums, even in Westminster Abbey itself, ever excited a tithe of the interest that is felt on looking on the humblest relics of a man of genius in the spot where he was born, where he lived, or where he died? The first may teach us to think of him, the second will assuredly make us both think and feel *with* him. The font in question, we may add, though mutilated, has been evidently beautiful, and worthy of a time that abounded in exquisite pieces of sculpture, devoted to the same or similar purposes: let the reader look, for instance, at the font of East Dereham church, Norfolk (Fig. 1313), and the piscina (Fig. 1298, p. 349, where it has been accidentally miscalled a font).

From Stratford Church and font, we turn not unnaturally to the church of Aston Cantlow (Fig. 1305), in the heart of the woodland district, some five or six miles in a north-west direction, where the poet's father and mother were married; and to Weston (Fig. 1315), also in the neighbourhood of Stratford, where no doubt the wandering bard has often paused to admire the picturesque building, perhaps to "stand by and mark" while some funereal procession passed into it, and his imagination busied itself with the feelings stirred to the very depths of the mourners' hearts; or, pleasanter occupation, to gaze with earnest and admiring eye upon some village bride led in all her virgin loveliness to the altar by the youth of her choice, to whom with quivering lips, but unfaltering heart, she resigns the care of her future life and welfare. Evesham churches (Fig. 1306), we are happy to say, exhibit a kind of parallel feeling in connection with fine structures to that we so anxiously desire to see infused into the hearts of the people in connection with their illustrious men. That beautiful church of St. Lawrence,—formerly connected with the neighbouring Abbey, from the top of which Simon de Montfort's messenger hastily descending, announced the appalling news of the approach of the army that was to crush the patriots—that church in which to this hour exists the exquisitely decorated tomb of Clement Lichfield, the last abbot, and the munificent builder of the sumptuous gateway that still arrests the eye of every visitor to Evesham,—even that edifice, so interesting alike for its intrinsic and extrinsic features, was allowed to moulder away year after year till the whole was in a state of ruin. But the reviving love of middle age architecture has embraced the church of St. Lawrence in its active ministrations, and the pile is in consequence restored. Of the other three churches included in our group, Luton in Bedfordshire (Fig. 1311), Northleach in Gloucestershire (Fig. 1314), and Leatherhead in Surrey (Fig. 1316), we need only particularise the first, and that not so much for the sake of its noble architecture, which may be best appreciated in our engraving, but in order that we may say a few words upon an adjunct of Luton church, the adjoining chapel, erected by John, Lord Wenlock, prior to the year 1461. The following lines, from a manuscript in Harleian Miscellany, British Museum, appear to have been formerly inscribed in the chapel over his remains :—

> "Jesu Christ, most of might,
> Have mercy on John le Wenlock, knight,
> And of his wife Elizabeth,
> Who out of this world is passed by death;
> Who founded this chapel here.
> Help them with your hearty prayer,
> That they may come to that place
> Where ever is joy and solace."

This John Wenlock was knighted by Henry VI., made Constable of Bamburg Castle, and chamberlain to the Queen. Having gained great wealth, he lent the king a sum of money exceeding a thousand pounds, for which he received an assignment of certain moneys granted by the parliament. For this service he received the order of the Garter. He was dreadfully wounded at St. Albans. In 1459 he went over to the Duke of York, and was attainted by the Lancastrian parliament. He fought well at Towton, was created a baron, employed in several embassies, and advanced to the distinguished and important office of Lieutenant of Calais. He changed sides again, and raised forces for Warwick and Margaret of Anjou. He commanded the middle ward of the army at Tewkesbury. At the first brunt his old vacillations returned; he was standing with his troops in the market-place when he should have supported the commander-in-chief, the Earl of Somerset who, returning to ascertain the cause of being left without aid in his fierce charge upon the enemy, rode up to Wenlock, and with one blow of his battle-axe cleft his head.

For a second group of churches we take four metropolitan edifices. Two of these are dedicated to the same saint, namely, St. Michael le Quern (Fig. 1289), so called from the *corn*-market in the immediate neighbourhood, and St. Michael's Cornhill (1286), to which Wren, after the fire, first put an Italian body to the existing Gothic tower, and then, fifty years later, on pulling down the tower, added a Gothic tower to the existing Italian body, as though his tastes and the requirements of the structure were constantly playing at cross purposes. The other two are the church of St. Alphage, of which, however, the porch (Fig. 1284) is the only existing remain possessing any pretensions to antiquity, which belonged to the old Elsing priory; and Ely Place (Fig. 1300), the once famous metropolitan seat of the bishops of Ely, of which the engraving (Fig. 1300*) shows the last, but fortunately a most important relic, namely, the chapel. Many a pleasant passage in the history of the palace might we here dilate upon: gladly should we dwell upon the life of the saint Etheldreda, to whom the chapel of Ely Place, as well as the parent foundation, the Cathedral of Ely, was dedicated—that daughter of one of our West-Anglian monarchs, who, having devoted herself in heart to heaven, and being compelled by circumstances into marriage at two different periods of her life, still persevered "with both husbands to live in a state of virginity." Then—how John of Gaunt, that great progenitor of kings, not only English, but Spanish, died at Ely Place, whilst residing here after the destruction of the Savoy by the followers of Wat Tyler; how the Serjeants' feasts used to be held in the great hall of Ely Place, with a magnificence that almost outstrips belief; how Sir Christopher Hatton, who danced into Ellzabeth's good graces and—the Chancellorship, lived here; and how Bacon and Coke came to Ely Place at the same time as suitors to the daughter of Lady Hatton, who by marriage inherited the Chancellor's name and property: how all these and a host of other pleasant and suggestive incidents took place, we should indeed be glad to pause awhile and narrate; but the remembrance of the encroachments we have already made upon our space forbids. There are, however, two other matters that we must notice, the Shaksperian incident of the strawberries, and the characteristic letter that a bishop of Ely caused the virgin queen to write. When Gloucester was meditating the murder of Hastings, and had called the council in the Tower as already described, Hollinshed (from Sir T. More) observes :—"These lords so sitting together, communing of this matter, the Protector came in amongst them, first about nine of the clock, saluting them courteously, and excusing himself that he had been from them so long, saying merrily that he had been a sleeper that day. After a little talking with them, he said unto the Bishop of Ely, 'My lord, you have very good strawberries at your garden in Holborn; I require you let us have a mess of them.' 'Gladly, my lord,' quoth he, 'would God I had some better thing as ready to your pleasure as that!'" and therewith he sent his servant for a mess of strawberries; who, when he returned, must have found Hastings dead in the area of the Tower—his master under arrest—confusion, distrust, and horror on every countenance. It may be naturally asked, how Ely Place came to pass from the possession of its episcopal owners. The answer forms another proof of the great favour Sir Christopher Hatton enjoyed at the hands of his mistress; and how evanescent, after all, that favour was. It was Sir Christopher who, having taken a liking to the palace, urged his mistress to obtain it for him, first on a temporary, but afterwards on a permanent tenure. She did so with some difficulty, and then ultimately kept it herself, when the Chancellor fell into the queen's debt, and through her exacting demands broke his heart. Another bishop had in the interval succeeded to the see, and was not at all inclined to fulfil the enforced bargain which his predecessor had made: then it was that Elizabeth wrote the following letter, a model for absolute sovereigns who would like to gratify their wishes without any troublesome expenditure of time in expressing them :—

"Proud Prelate,—

"You know what you was before I made you what you are now: if you do not immediately comply with my request, by G—d I will unfrock you.

"ELIZABETH."

The bishopric, however, in the end lost Ely Place, though it obtained in the last century a fee-farm rent of a hundred a year in compensation.

The only ecclesiastical buildings now remaining to be noticed are those which we have specially reserved as being in some important respects relics of those events that have made the period so memorable, namely, the Wars of the Roses. In one of those quiet little neighbourhoods which the pedestrian occasionally lights upon, to his great surprise, in the very heart of busy, bustling, restless London, stands the Dutch church, as it is called; which, in spite of its name and its Dutch congregation, is essentially an English structure, and one of no ordinary magnificence. That church, large and noble as it is (Fig. 1282), was nothing more than the nave of the church of the Austin Friars, once resident here. The spire, that "beautifullest and rarest spectacle" in London, has long disappeared; so have the monuments that once lined its walls with work after work in apparently interminable range, each as you walked along in front seeming to grow more and more rich in architectural beauty, more and more interesting from their associations with the great and influential of the land. Here lay, for instance, Edmond the half-brother of Richard II., Humphrey Bohun, the munificent founder of the pile in 1253, and Richard, the great Earl of Arundel, beheaded by Richard II. Here too, to pass on to its later history, was "poor Edward Bohun," Duke of Buckingham, interred after his execution; and all these names, if the most conspicuous, form but a very small proportion of the important personages whose ashes were disturbed and left to be scattered by the winds of heaven, when the possessor of the estate, in the beginning of the seventeenth century, pulled down the steeple and choir, and sold the monuments for one hundred pounds: that worthy was the "most noble" Marquis of Winchester. But there were a class of nobles who lie buried in the church of the Austin Friars, that we have not yet mentioned,—the victims of that most fratricidal, we might almost call it suicidal, War of the Roses. Vere, Earl of Oxford, beheaded 1463, was the first and most unhappy of these men; for the others did, at all events, fall sword in hand on the field of battle. These were the lords who perished at the battle of Barnet in 1471, and who were all buried together in the body of the church.

A short walk eastward from the Dutch church, and we find ourselves in another, and scarcely less interesting building for its general associations, and for its connection with the wars in question. This is the church of St. Helen's in Bishopsgate (Fig. 1285), formerly the remains of a priory of Benedictine nuns, whose long row of carved seats against the wall yet exist in the structure. As the burial-place of Sir Thomas Gresham St. Helen's is most popularly known. That truly illustrious merchant lies in the corner shown in our engraving; his arms are emblazoned in the window above. But the monument that more especially attracts us at the present time is that of Sir John Crosby and his lady, with their effigies, a truly beautiful piece of sculpture. (Fig. 1275.) Sir John, the founder of Crosby Hall, was an alderman of London, and the holder of various other important offices—a fact that no doubt made his accession to the friends of Edward IV. a matter of importance: by Edward he was knighted during the adventurous march from Ravenspur to London.

A mission given to Sir John the following year marks most decisively the confidence reposed in him by the Yorkists. He was sent with other eminent persons to the Duke of Burgundy to arrange various matters, amongst the rest, most probably, the treaty of alliance which, as we have already seen, Edward sought to make prior to his invasion of France. From Burgundy the party proceeded to the court of the Duke of Brittany, to conclude a similar treaty, and where also, observes Stow, they hoped to have gotten the two Earls of Pembroke and Richmond. So that Edward was already conscious of the exact quarter from whence danger was to be apprehended, though he could have little foreseen what course Richmond's endeavour would take, namely, the overthrow of the murderer of his—Edward's—own children. The ambassadors wrought so subtilly that they at last persuaded the two nobles to return to England, and they were actually about to embark at St. Malo, when the minister of the Duke of Brittany, foreseeing probably the destruction that assuredly would have fallen upon them, caused a delay, and Richmond at last took the alarm and disappeared.

But whilst the church of the Austin Friars and the church of St. Helen's thus in some particular features carry us back into the sanguinary times of the two rival houses, there is one building, that in spot, purpose, and founder is entirely devoted to them, forming at once a memorial of its greatest actors, and its most deeply tragical incidents. Many will anticipate the words—the chapel on Wakefield Bridge. (Fig. 1302.) The building that had previously occupied the site was, it appears, a wayside chapel. We cannot better describe this class of structures, once so numerous in and so important to Old England, than

in the words of the authors of an account of Wakefield Chapel, just published, by John Chessell and Charles Buckler:—"Wayside chapels were the only ancient places of public worship with which burial-grounds were not locally connected. They had no walled enclosures, and could never have been more alone than many are now on the highways to Walsingham. Those near Hillborough have been planted on the bleak brows of elevated ground near the roadside, and are without particular architectural distinction, being little oblong buildings of square breadth throughout, as plain in design as in their figure. The walls are roofless and broken, the cracks and chasms serving to channel away the water from the moss-grown summit. The interior, which could once afford rest to the weary and a pittance to the distressed, is now too desolate to be sought as a shelter by cattle. No marvel then that travellers in later days have neglected to turn a few paces out of the way to visit these ancient relics. They would find them not altogether uninteresting, but overgrown with briers, and half filled up with heaps of old rubbish. No kind of sepulchral memorial has been discovered within or on the outside of any of these edifices, often as death must have overtaken the pilgrim on his way. Chances of this kind were not provided for by a consecrated space for burial, as the custom of entombing the dead around the sanctuary in which the living assembled for worship was never extended to wayside chapels, neither was the administration of baptism nor the celebration of matrimony included in the duties prescribed to them, as was sometimes the case in privileged instances in assistant chapels belonging to districts at a distance from the mother church." The simple but sufficient and admirable object aimed at by the founders of these buildings, appears to have been to cheer the heart of the fainting pilgrim, or traveller, or mendicant, by affording him a temporary rest and refreshment for soul and body, and comfortable assurance of better entertainment further on. And as along the roads that religious pilgrims traversed they were the most needed, why, there were they the most frequent.

Let us now see how it was that the wayside chapel on Wakefield Bridge, founded, it is supposed, in the reign of Edward II., became alienated from its original purpose, and transformed into the superb little structure that now, in spite of decay and neglect, meets the eye. The first battle that followed the attempt of the House of Lords to compromise the respective demands of Henry VI. and Richard Plantagenet, Duke of York, was that of Wakefield, which took place between the town and the neighbouring castle of Sandal (Fig. 1269), the property of Plantagenet, who himself commanded the Yorkist army, with the aid of the Earl of Salisbury, whilst the Lancastrians were led by the Duke of Somerset, the Earls of Northumberland and Devon, the Lords Clifford, Dacres, and Nevil; and who were as superior in numbers of troops as of noble leaders. As the fight began, "the Duke of York with his people descended down in good order and array, and was suffered to pass forward toward the main battle; but when he was in the plain ground, between his castle and the town of Wakefield, he was environed on every side, like a fish in a net, or a deer in a buckstall; so that he, manfully fighting, was within half an hour slain and dead, and his whole army discomfited;" and with him perished nearly three thousand men, including some of the duke's most trusty friends, and many "young gentlemen and heirs of great parentage in the south part, whose lineages revenged their deaths" within a short period after. Chief of these was the innocent Duke of Rutland, the fourth son of the Duke of York, scarce of the age of twelve years, whose murder by the ruthless Clifford, one of the chief supporters of Margaret of Anjou, is touchingly narrated by the same authority—Hall: "Whilst this battle was in fighting, a priest called Sir Robert Aspall, chaplain and schoolmaster to the young Earl of Rutland, ... a fair gentleman, and a maidenlike person, perceiving that flight was more safeguard than tarrying, both for him and his master, secretly conveyed the Earl out of the field, by [past] the Lord Clifford's band, toward the town; but ere he could enter into a house he was by the said Lord Clifford espied, followed, and taken, and by reason of his apparel demanded what he was. The young gentleman, dismayed, had not a word to speak; but kneeled on his knees imploring mercy, and desiring grace, both with holding up his hands, and making dolorous countenance, for his speech was gone for fear. 'Save him,' said his chaplain, 'for he is a prince's son, and peradventure may do you good hereafter.' With that word, the Lord Clifford marked [recognised] him, and said, 'By God's blood, thy father slew mine, and so will I do thee and all thy kin; and with that word stuck the Earl to the heart with his dagger, and bade his chaplain bear the Earl's mother and brother word what he had done and said." Certainly a more barbarous act than this never disgraced the chivalry of England. It filled all right-feeling men with disgust and abhorrence, and even by many of his own party the deed was condemned, and the doer of it stigmatised, in the words of Hall, "a tyrant, and no gentleman." Hollinshed describes the death of the Duke of York as not occurring in the heat of the fight, but after it was over, under circumstances fully as barbarous as those attending his son's death. "Some write that the duke was taken alive, and in derision caused to stand upon a mole-hill, on whose head they put a garland instead of a crown, which they had fashioned and made of segges [sedges], or bullrushes, and having so crowned him with that garland, they kneeled down afore him, as the Jews did to Christ, in scorn, saying to him, "Hail, king without rule! hail, king without heritage! hail, duke and prince without people or possessions!' And at length, having thus scorned him with these and divers other the like despiteful words, they stroke off his head," which they presented to the queen, Margaret, whose whole conduct shows with what pleasure she must have looked upon the bloody ruin of her chief and, as she then thought, most dangerous enemy. The head was by her order fixed on the gates of York, and a paper crown placed upon it in mockery. It was not long, however, before all these brutal proceedings were avenged by others scarcely, if at all, less brutal; and then Edward, in pious and filial sorrow, erected near the place where his father had been slain, and on the very bridge where his brother had been so foully murdered, the chapel that to this day attracts the eye of the traveller by the Manchester and Leeds Railway, on the southern side of the Wakefield station. This, too, we may add, is one of the structures that, long neglected, is now again attracting attention, and about to be restored by the Yorkshire Architectural Society. All honour to the gentleman who, we understand, originated the movement in its favour—the Vicar of Wakefield.

In examining works of extraordinary architectural beauty or grandeur, one feels something of the same desire to know all about the men who produced them, and the circumstances under which they were produced, that we feel in every little bit of gossip relating to the history of a great poem, or painting, or piece of music; with the difference, however, that it too often happens that the only records we have of the first come through bills of .expenses, or such similar media, and thereby lose in passing nearly all the real interest they possessed; while when we do know anything of the second, our knowledge must, from the less public and mechanical character of the superficial operations, be more or less attractive. But not even such documents can absolutely destroy the charm that invests the subject of the origin of a great edifice; and Beauchamp Chapel, Warwick, forms a strong case in point. Of this structure, attached to the church of St. Mary, Warwick, we need hardly repeat the oft-told tale of its exquisite beauty of proportion and decorative detail (see Fig. 1301). A more useful labour will be to give some idea, by means of the valuable papers printed in Britton's 'Architectural Antiquities,' of the mode in which the executors of Richard Beauchamp, Earl of Warwick, who died in 1439, went to work to erect the chapel that he had in his lifetime devised, and the altar-tomb to his memory, which now stands in the centre of the chapel. These accounts do not apply to the raising of the walls, but to their adornment when finished. First, there are the windows to be supplied with stained glass, which is settled by the following agreement with John Prudde, of Westminster, glazier, who, on the 23rd of June, in 25 Hen. VI., "Covenanteth, &c., to glaze all the windows in the New Chapel in Warwick with glass beyond the seas, and with no glass of England; and that in the finest wise, with the best, cleanest, and strongest glass of beyond the sea, that may be had in England, and of the finest colours of blue, yellow, red, purpure, sanguine, and violet, and of all other colours that shall be most necessary, and best to make rich and embellish the matters, images, and stories that shall be delivered and appointed by the said executors, by patterns in paper; afterwards to be newly traced and pictured by another painter in rich colours at the charges of the said glazier: all which proportions the said John Prudde must make perfectly, to fine, glaze, anneal it, and finely and strongly set it in lead and souder, as well as any glass is in England. Of white glass, green glass, black glass, he shall put in as little as shall be needful for the showing and setting forth of the matters, images, and stories. And the said glazier shall take charge of the same glass, wrought, and to be brought to Warwick and set up there, in the windows of the said chapel, the executors paying to the said glazier for every foot of glass, 2s., and so for the whole, 91l. 1s. 10d." To the evidence of liberality that spared no cost in the attainment of the object sought, given in this curious document, we may observe, that after the windows were finished, alterations were made, enhancing their generally sumptuous charac-

ter, especially by the addition of pictures, including the marriage of the Earl of Warwick, and these also were "set forth in glass and most fine and curious colours." Next to the agreement with the glazier comes that with the carpenter for desks, poppies, seats, sills, planks, an organ-loft, &c. The walls have now to be painted, so the. executors are off again to the metropolis, where they secure the services of John Brentwood, citizen and stainer of London, who, on the 12th of Feb., 28 Hen. VI., "doth covenant to paint fine and curiously to make at Warwick, on the west wall of the new chapel there, the doom of our Lord God Jesus, and all manner of devices and imagery thereto belonging, of fair and sightly proportion, as the place shall serve for, with the finest colours and fine gold; and the said Brentwood shall find all manner of stuff thereto at his charge, the said executors paying therefore 13l. 6s. 8d." But the painter of the walls must not also be the painter of the sculpture, so for them Kristian Coleburne is engaged, a painter dwelling in London, who, on the 13th of June, 32 Hen. VI., "Covenanteth, &c., to paint in most fine, fairest, and curious wise, four images of stone ordained for the new chapel in Warwick, whereof two principal images, the one of Our Lady, the other of St. Gabriel the angel, and two less images, one of St. Ann, and another of St. George: these four to be painted with the finest oil colours, in the richest, finest, and freshest clothings, that may be made of fine gold, azure, of fine purpure, of fine white and other finest colours necessary, garnished, bordered, and powdered in the finest and curiousest wise, all the cost and workmanship of painting to be at the charge of the said Kristian, the executors paying for the same 12l." The marbler follows the painters, who undertakes the erection of the tomb, and the adjoining part of the chapel pavement; then another marbler, with a founder and a coppersmith, who together agree to provide the metal ornaments, the latten-plates, for the tomb, consisting of one large plate, and two narrow ones to go round the tomb, with hearse, shields of arms, inscriptions, &c., which are to be gilded with the finest gold, and the whole executed at a cost of 125l. of the money of the fifteenth century. But the tomb is not yet prepared for the effigy that is to crown the whole; some fourteen images of lords and ladies, called weepers, of a certain size, and some eighteen angels, are needed. William Austin, the "founder" of the previous agreement, undertakes this labour, alone; covenanting "to cast, work, and perfectly to make, of the finest latten to be gilded, that may be found, viz.: images embossed of lords and ladies in divers vestures, called weepers, to stand in housings made about the tomb, those images to be made in breadth, length, and thickness, &c. to fourteen patterns made of timber. Also he shall make eighteen less images of angels to stand in other housings, as shall be appointed by patterns, whereof nine after one side, and nine after another Also he must make an hearse to stand on the tomb, above and about the principal image that shall lie in the tomb, according to a pattern; the stuff and workmanship to the repairing to be at the charge of the said Will Austin. And the executors shall pay for every image that shall lie on the tomb, of the weepers so made in latten, 13s. 4d., and for every image of angels so made 5s.; and for every pound of latten that shall be in the hearse 10d., and shall pay and bear the costs of the said Austin for setting the said images and hearse." And now, at last, the tomb is complete, with the single but important exception of the effigy of the deceased earl, the founder of the beautiful work around. William Austin's services are here a third time in requisition, who—doth covenant "to cast and make an image of a man armed of fine latten, garnished with certain ornaments, viz.: with sword and dagger, with a garter, with a helm and crest under his head, and at his feet a bear muzzled, and a griffon, perfectly made of the finest latten, according to patterns." Our modern sculptors may like to know what was the cost of such a statue—engraved in p. 356, Fig. 1326—it was just 40l. of the money of the time. But who made all the *patterns* that are so constantly referred to in all the agreements? We wish we could answer the question, but unfortunately we are there left in the dark. Among the executors was one called Will. Berkswell, priest, who was dean of the collegiate church; Mr. Britton thinks he was also the architect of the chapel. If so, the inexhaustible variety of these "patterns" was probably owing in a great measure to him.

The Richard Beauchamp to whom we are indebted for this liberal and artistical expenditure, was a man of no ordinary importance in his day. In the reign of Henry IV. he did good service against Glendower and the Percies; in the reign of Henry V. he was one of the glorious few at Azincourt—

> Harry the King, Bedford, and Exeter,
> *Warwick*, and Talbot, Salisbury and Gloucester:

and lastly, in the reign of Henry VI., the youthful king was confided chiefly to his tutelage. He died in the castle at Rouen, leaving behind him a name of the highest honour,—the *Good* Earl. One of the most interesting incidents of his life was his pilgrimage to the Holy Land (Fig. 1330), where he was magnificently entertained by the Soldan's lieutenant, on the ground that "he was descended from the famous Sir Guy of Warwick; whose story they had in books of their own language."—*Dugdale.*

Among the many wild and picturesque legends told by Old English Chroniclers of the early heroes of England, there is none more popular than that just referred to, which has made the name of Guy as famous to this day as those of King Arthur and St. George the Victorious. The story in question can be traced back to the twelfth century, and whatever of truth there may be in the events to which it relates, belongs probably to a period not much earlier, though usually assigned to the tenth century, and the reign of Athelstan. The tradition runs to the effect that in the year 926 the Danish and Norwegian powers, who then kept the country in continual terror, invaded England and advanced as far as Winchester. Athelstan saw the crown about to depart from him, and his only hope lay in being able to find a champion who might cope successfully with a champion of the Danes in a single combat that was to decide the fate of Athelstan and of England. There were stout and skilful warriors among the Saxons, but none, it would seem, who durst engage with the Dane, a man of gigantic size and prowess, a sort of Goliath among the Philistines: his name was Colbrand, and he was an African or a Saracen; hence probably the interest felt in Guy among the Saracens, of which Dugdale gives us so pleasant an evidence. Amidst the fear and distress which this dark and terrible giant excited among our Saxon forefathers, Athelstan was favoured by a vision, directing him to the man whose valour was to save his country in her dire extremity. "Like a palmer poore" appeared this hero, chosen by heaven itself, for the momentous ordeal: he had just landed at Portsmouth from the Holy Land. Athelstan engaged him, acting on his faith in the vision, and knowing nothing of the palmer's history and fitness. The hour of trial and peril arrives. If the giant conquers, England her king will be enslaved to the "Lord Danes." It is a fearful venture. All outward advantages are on Colbrand's side. Does he not seem to shake the solid earth with his tread, as, in the sight of a multitude of English and of Danes, he advances toward his victim? Does he not swell with disdain and defiance to even more than his ordinary vastness of dimensions? And Athelstan, when he hears the foreboding murmurs of his people, and the scornful threats of the insolent foe, regrets he not his trust in the vision? Is he not sick to the soul with agonizing suspense as the combat begins, and the sword-strokes rattle on the casques and shields? He averts his gaze, and adds his prayer to the many that are ascending around him. Suddenly,

the sun breaks out from behind the cloud that had enveloped their fortunes. Colbrand falls! The "palmer poore" is victor. The welkin rings with shouts of joy from the English host. Overpowering is the grateful enthusiasm of the liberated people. But, shrinking from the general gaze, desiring no earthly glory, the pilgrim-hero retires from the scene. To the king alone, and on a promise of secrecy, he reveals himself as Guy, the renowned Earl of Warwick. Therewith he passes from Athelstan's presence to strict retirement, in the neighbourhood of his castle of Warwick. There, with his own hands, as the peasants about Guy's cliff now tell us, he hewed out a cave, in which he lived and died. His remains were interred by his beautiful countess, Felicia, who most probably applauded the superstitious delusion which had consigned her to solitude and sorrow, and worshipped her husband's memory in consequence as that of a glorious saint. Guy's cliff (Fig. 1303) is situate a mile and a half from Warwick, by the river Avon, that here winds through beautiful meads and rocks and woods, the centre of one of the most lovely and romantic of scenes. The cave is not the only local memorial of the ancient hero; armour is preserved in the castle that, according to tradition, he once wore; a rude statue of him, eight feet high, was carved from the solid rock by Richard Beauchamp, the same Earl of Warwick who founded the chapel on the cliff (Fig. 1304), and the contiguous buildings, as well as the more superb Beauchamp chapel. The right hand of the statue held a drawn sword, the left arm supported a shield; the sword-arm and the sword, and the left hand are now wanting: a leg was also deficient, but "a new one was bestowed a few years back by a female statuary of rank and deserved celebrity, while on a visit to the castle" ['Beauties of England and Wales']. The Hon. Mrs. Damer, we presume, is the lady here referred to. The legend of Guy was doubtless the attraction that drew a greater hero than Guy to visit the hermitage, Henry V., who was about to found a chantry on the cliff for two priests, but his illness and early death prevented it. In his father's reign, and in the reign of Edward III., there was a hermit resident at Guy's cliff; other recluses have most probably dwelt there, whose lives have passed in holy quiet without a record. But there is one hermit of this "house of pleasure" and "place meet for the Muses" (Leland), of whom we *have* a record—John Rous, the antiquary, son of Geffrey Rous of Warwick. He was a chantry priest at Guy's cliff, and officiated daily in its chapel. Having acquired considerable learning at Oxford, he surrounded himself here with his books, and employed most of his time in writing chronicles of his country and a history of Warwickshire and its famous earls, without manifesting the smallest desire to win the notice or applause of the world, but sufficiently rewarded by the gratification afforded him by his studies: he died in 1491.

CHAPTER III.—POPULAR ANTIQUITIES

T is with curious feelings and thoughts that we contemplate such a view of the metropolis of the Middle Ages as is furnished in our engraving of the approach towards the City from Westminster (Fig. 1348). A kind of doubtful wonder seizes us when, looking for the localities that have become celebrated over half the globe, we have to recognize them under such very different aspects, in so very different a scene. One can hardly believe that the pastoral landscape in the foreground, stretching away on the left into the country around Hampstead and Highgate, and scattered over with isolated mansions, farms, and homesteads, whilst on the right it extends down literally to the river's *strand*, broken, however, at intervals by the embattled mansions and "pleasances" of the nobility, should be really the same place along which the throng of men, women, and children, coaches, omnibuses, cabs, now passes from "morn to dewy eve," and long after, without apparent cessation or rest. One may look in vain to trace in the Convent Garden of the view any resemblance to the present Covent Garden, though the flowers bloom there as of yore, only in a thousand times greater luxuriance and beauty and variety. How one of the pious monks would have stared at the sight of gorgeous cacti suddenly put among his little collection! How he would have luxuriated over a pine-apple!

The first of the mansions along the old route towards St. Paul's was Durham Place; on a line with it, farther on, were Essex House and York House, names chronicled in historic and poetic pages. The old church of St. Mary, Strand, appears at the bend of the road, on its left side. Looking towards the river, we see the silver current flowing on to the foot of the many-arched Old London Bridge, loaded with houses, gates, and chapel; the airy pinnacles of St. Mary Overies appear on its right, the Tower of London on its left, and nearer the front of the picture Old St. Paul's, whose elevated position, and queenly height and dignity, attest the cathedral of the great metropolis, only, instead of the grand Grecian dome that lords it over modern London, a most beautiful, bold, and elegant Gothic spire is there seen to pierce the sky. Glancing from the general view, to that of one of the streets of London (Figs. 1362, 1363), we are enabled to judge of the extent, arrangement, and character of the houses generally, of the ancient metropolis. Art was not then merely art for the great. The merchant and the small trader had their homesteads built substantially and picturesquely; and when, on the occasion of a public pageant, the windows were adorned with rich tapestry and the streets festooned with garlands of flowers, it would be hardly possible to desire a more agreeable picture, even without the royal personage and his splendid train for whom the show might be got up; as, for instance, when the boy-king, Henry VI., returned from his coronation at Paris. Cheapside (Fig. 1361) was the principal place for the exhibition of the more important features of these old pageants; where the towers full of singing angels and allegorical characters were set up, where the conduits flowed with wine, and around which another garden of Eden seemed spontaneously to grow.

Let us turn aside for a few moments to look at Guildhall, presenting a very altered aspect from the Guildhall of the last century (Fig. 1349), and both as unlike as they could be made to the first building erected here in the year 1411, when a "little college" was changed into the great Guildhall; funds having been obtained by large gifts from the different companies, and by a mode that reminds us of, and no doubt was borrowed from, the custom of raising money for the great ecclesiastical foundations; it seems "offences of men were pardoned for sums of money towards this work;" at the same time "extraordinary fees were raised, fines, amerciaments," which continued more or less for the space of ten years. Among the particular

benefactors were the executors of Richard Whittington, who gave thirty-five pounds towards paving the hall with Purbeck marble. That hall (Fig. 1350), notwithstanding the disgraceful treatment it has undergone as respects externals, and which makes one of the most noble and stately of buildings look to a stranger approaching it as one of the most supremely ugly that it was ever his fortune to behold —that hall still remains, and within needs only the superficial restoration of the old architectural style in the upper story, and a new roof, and the being relieved of those two pretty monstrosities, Gog and Magog, that give one the idea that the mayor, aldermen, and common council of the metropolis of the British empire must be a parcel of overgrown children playing at government, rather than dealing with their duties in that lofty abstract spirit which they require,—there want but these alterations and renewals to make the interior of the Guildhall a very noble specimen of the architecture of the fifteenth century. The crypt (Fig. 1383) below the hall is scarcely less interesting. It seems to have been a custom at the period in question to build these strange-looking places, too low and dark to have been intended for any very public or important proceedings, too beautiful to be mere vaults beneath the halls of great mansions. There is the same at Crosby Place; the same at Gerard's Hall (Fig. 1358).

It would be superfluous to say that the historical recollections of Guildhall are of no ordinary weight and interest. Here it was that Garnet the Jesuit, that extraordinary man, was tried for his connection with the Gunpowder Plot, and, after a most skilful and elaborate defence, condemned. Here was Throckmorton placed on his trial for treason as a friend of Sir Thomas Wyatt, and for once, by his consummate skill, by his mingled boldness and tact, obtained what was little less than a miracle, a verdict of not guilty from a packed jury, the members of which were well-nigh ruined for their honesty. Here was the brave Anne Askew doomed to the last fiery trial of the strength of her religious principles; and here did Richard, Duke of Gloucester, through his mouthpiece Buckingham, first seek in public the suffrages of the citizens of London to make him king, and very amusing were the proceedings, or would be, if there were not such tragical "issues" behind. Buckingham commenced by an allusion that found a powerful echo in the hearts of his hearers: he spoke of the tyrannies and extortions of Edward IV., who had taxed the pockets and patience of the Londoners pretty severely; thence he led them to the consideration of his amours, which some present had probably especial reason to remember in their desolate and ruined homes, and so, by easy stages, the grand point was attained, of preparing the auditory to listen to the assertion that Edward himself was only an illegitimate son of Richard Plantagenet the late Duke of York, *therefore* as the Lords and Commons had sworn never to submit to a bastard, what was to be done but to acknowledge Gloucester as king? and that, Buckingham energetically called upon them to do. He paused—there was dead silence. No wonder that even Buckingham himself was for the moment "marvellously abashed." Recovering his presence of mind, he said privately to the mayor and others, who had been gained over, "What meaneth this, that the people be so still?" "Sir," was the reply, "perchance they perceive [understand] you not well." Of course, Buckingham could amend that, and therewith, somewhat louder, rehearsed the same matter again, in other order and in other words, so well and ornately, and nevertheless so evidently and plain, with voice, gesture, and countenance so comely and so convenient, that every man much marvelled that heard him; and thought that they never heard in their lives so evil a tale so well told. But were it for wonder or fear, or that each looked that other should speak first, not one word was there answered of all the people that stood before; but all were as still as the midnight, not so much rouning [speaking privately] among them, by which they might seem once to commune what was best to do. When the mayor saw this, he, with other partners of the council, drew about the duke, and said that the people had not been accustomed there to be spoken to but by the recorder, which is the mouth of the city, and haply to him they will answer. With that the recorder, called Thomas Fitzwilliam, a sad (serious) man and an honest, which was but newly come to the office, and never had spoken to the people before, and loth was with that matter to begin, notwithstanding, thereunto commanded by the mayor, made rehearsal to the commons of that which the duke had twice purposed himself; but the recorder so tempered his tale that he showed everything as the duke's words were, and no part of his own; but all this no change made in the people, which alway after one stood as they had been amazed." One cannot but admire the fortitude of Buckingham in persevering under such very discouraging, and personally humiliating circumstances, but he came to do certain work, and do it he would and did. So, changing his style, he began to stand somewhat upon his dignity, without abating, however, in the particular affection he had conceived for the citizens. So, again coming forward, " ' Dear friends,' said he, ' we come to move you to that thing which, peradventure, we so greatly needed not, but that the lords of this realm and commons of other parts might have sufficed, saying, such love we bear you, and so much set by you, that we would not gladly do without you that thing in which to be partners is your weal and honour, which as to us seemeth, you see not or weigh not, wherefore we require you to give us an answer, one or other, whether ye be minded, as all the nobles of the realm be, to have this noble prince, now protector, to be your king?' And at these words the people began to whisper among themselves secretly, that the voice was neither loud nor base, but like a swarm of bees, till at the last, at the nether end of the hall, a bushment of the duke's servants, and one Nashfield, and others belonging to the protector, with some prentices and lads that thrusted into the hall amongst the press, began suddenly, at men's backs to cry out as loud as they could, ' King Richard! King Richard!' and then threw up their caps in token of joy, and they that stood before cast back their heads *marvelling thereat, but nothing they said.* And when the duke and the mayor saw this manner, they wisely turned it to their purpose, and said it was a goodly cry and a joyful to hear *every man with one voice,* and no man saying nay." Of course, there was no resisting such an expression of opinion, and Buckingham departed to persuade the reluctant Gloucester to take upon him the sovereignty of England. How the latter must have enjoyed the narration of his friend's exploits! if, indeed, for either enjoyment could exist, under such hazardous and unprincipled movements.

As to the Tower, seen with such propriety looming in the background of our view, we may begin by observing that some important reparations were made in it during the reigns of Edward IV. and Richard III., connected probably with the rapidly-increasing uses that it was put to, especially as the grand state-prison of England. We have an evidence of what Edward IV. was thinking about, in the attempt of his officers to set up their own scaffold and gallows on Tower Hill; but the city resisted, and the sheriffs successfully maintained their right of superintending the business of extinguishing human life, with all its then usual revolting and cruel accompaniments.

Our plan and engravings furnish a tolerably comprehensive view of the Tower in what may be called its complete state. We see in the first (Fig. 1262), the shape of the site, and the arrangement and names of the different buildings; whilst in the last, we see the exterior of the Tower in the time of Henry VI. (Fig. 1263); then the interior (Fig. 1261), shown us in a more useful than artistical way, with the French prisoner of Agincourt, the Duke of Orleans, busy writing, surrounded by his guards; and lastly comes, in addition to the engravings already given of parts of the Tower, the view of the old Jewel House (Fig. 1265), and the north side of the Bloody Tower, or gateway (Fig. 1264), which was so termed, " for the bloodshed, as they say, of those infant princes of Edward IV., whom Richard III., of cursed memory (I shudder to mention it), savagely killed *two together, at one time.*" So says W. Hubbocke, the orator who welcomed James I. when he visited the Tower, in 1604, and who gives us a new impression of the transaction, evidently hardly knowing which was worse, the murder or its climax, the killed " two together, at one time."

What, thinks the reader, is the Duke of Orleans doing at such an evidently important time? Some treaty, is it, he is about to sign, that shall restore him to his country, and give peace hereafter between England and France? No; the duke is writing simply— poetry! and the guards looking on with such interest and attention are watching the process of gestation. Talk of knowledge under difficulties! if this is not the pursuit of poetry under difficulties, no matter how unnecessary or self-created we know not what is. We

can imagine when an approving hem! broke forth from the satisfied poet, how the long-silent guards must take advantage of the pause, and give way to their hems! too; then if some lame line will not get into easier paces, some thought will not leave the palpable obscure where it is first born, and the poet looks round unwittingly upon the faces of the sympathising men-at-arms, how he may be answered by some satirical rascal's cough here, and a sudden droop or turn of the head there, lest royalty should see its anxieties doubled like Wordsworth's swan and shadow. Then, as a poet when he has pleased himself, must read his production aloud, to hear how it sounds, what a pleasant little knot of critics are at hand, not only to form opinions, but to express them too—when they get safely away to the buttery-hatch among their companions.

That the Tower of London was formerly a royal palace as well as a royal fortress and prison, we are forcibly reminded by a sight of the regalia still kept here. The small tower in which they were exhibited until the recent fire stands at the north-east angle of the great area. The first mention of these jewels occurs in the reign of Henry III., who, returning from France, commanded the Bishop of Carlisle to replace them in the Tower, as they were before. The same king pledged them to certain merchants of Paris: being redeemed, they were again pledged to the merchants of Flanders by Edward III., and a third time to the merchants of London by Richard II., when they were placed in the charge of the Bishop of London and the Earl of Arundel. Henry VI. also pledged to his wealthy uncle, Cardinal Beaufort, as security for seven thousand marks, an immense quantity of such valuables, which were all to be forfeited if the borrowed moneys were not repaid by the feast of Easter, 1440. Being returned in safety to the Tower, the crown jewels were permitted to rest until the accession of the great spoiler, Henry VIII., who ordered his minister Cromwell to go to the jewel-house and take therefrom as much plate as he thought could possibly be spared, and coin it immediately into money. Even after this characteristic reduction, the royal treasure remained of great value and variety, as appears by an inventory made by order of James I.

The regalia at present in the Tower includes five crowns: St. Edward's (made at Charles II.'s coronation, to replace the one which the Confessor is supposed to have worn), the crown of State, the queen's circlet of gold, the queen's crown, and the queen's rich crown. Of these the first and fourth are proper coronation crowns. Three of the most precious of jewels are on the state crown—a ruby, a pearl, and an emerald, seven inches round. Here also are the other coronation jewels: the orb, emblem of universal authority, borrowed from the Roman emperors; the ampula, or eagle of gold, containing the anointing oil; the curtana, or sword of mercy, borne between the two swords of justice, spiritual and temporal; St. Edward's staff, which is a sceptre of gold, four feet seven inches and a half long, with a small foot of steel, and a mound and cross at top; four other sceptres of gold and precious stones (one of these discovered in 1814, behind some old wainscoting in the jewel-house); the queen's ivory rod, a short sceptre of ivory and gold, made for the queen of James II., &c., &c.

The office of " master and treasurer of the jewel-house " was one of great honour and profit in the old days. The regalia was first exhibited to the public in the reign of Charles II., when the direct emoluments were reduced, and the " show " permitted by way of compensation. In the same reign an incident occurred that would in all probability have put a stop to the custom almost as soon as it was begun, but for the circumstance just narrated. Among the notorious men of that day, one of the most notorious was a Colonel Blood, a native of Ireland, who under the Commonwealth had occupied a very respectable position in society, having received a grant of land for his services as a lieutenant in the field, been in the commission of the peace, and married a gentleman's daughter of Lancashire. The Irish act of settlement blighted his fortunes, and threw him on the world a restless, discontented, desperate man. He headed an Irish insurrection for surprising Dublin Castle, and seizing the person of the lord lieutenant, the Duke of Ormond. Failing in this, he made himself still more notorious, by a most extraordinary and daring attempt to seize and hang at Tyburn the same duke on the night of the 6th of November, 1676, in revenge for Ormond's having dealt that doom on some of the colonel's friends in the insurrection. The duke was actually tied on horseback to a confederate of Blood's, when timely aid saved him. This brief summary of Blood's career may prepare the reader to understand the character of the man, who was concerned in one of the most extraordinary attempts that the annals of felony can furnish. During the reign of Charles II. the keeper of the regalia was one Talbot Edwards, an old and confidential servant of Sir Gilbert Talbot, master of the Jewel-house. Edwards, with his wife and daughter, dwelt in the domestic apart-

SHRINE OF HENRY THE FIFTH.

THE CHOIR—WESTMINSTER ABBEY.

WOLSEY'S HALL, HAMPTON COURT.

TOMB OF MARY, QUEEN OF SCOTS.—WESTMINSTER ABBEY.

HOUSE OF JOHN KNOX, EDINBURGH.

TOMB OF QUEEN ELIZABETH ——WESTMINSTER ABBEY.

PAINTED SCREEN. SAINT GEORGE'S CHAPEL.

ST. GEORGE'S HALL, WINDSOR.

ments adjoining the place where the treasure was kept. One day there came a respectable-looking parson and his wife, to whom Edwards was exhibiting the jewels, when the lady was suddenly taken ill. To call his wife to render assistance was naturally the keeper's first thought, and to invite the sufferer to a private room as naturally occurred to Mrs. Edwards. The lady recovered; but the civility and kindness of the worthy old couple and their daughter, and the gratitude of the strangers, led to a continuance of their intimacy, and to a proposal from the parson of a marriage between his nephew and the keeper's daughter. All this was arranged before the lover's appearance on the scene; and of course the old people and their daughter were worked up into a state of high expectation by the time when the first meeting of the pre-affianced pair was to take place. The nephew came at the appointed time, attended by his uncle and two other friends. Leaving their horses at St. Catherine's gate, they walked through the Tower to the jewel-house, at the door of which, one of the gentlemen—(all of whom it afterwards appeared were furnished with daggers, pocket-pistols, and rapier-blades in their canes)—made some slight pretence for remaining while the others entered. The parson wished his friends to be shown the regalia, as Mrs. and Miss Edwards did not immediately appear, and, accordingly, the unsuspecting keeper entered the jewel-room with them. Hardly was the door closed, when a cloak was thrown over him, and a gag forced into his mouth: he was then informed of the true character of his visitors, and their real object, which the reader will have already foreseen. The pretended parson was Colonel Blood, the nephew and friends his associates, with whose assistance he was determined to possess himself of the regalia of England, an object so bold, and so certain it would seem to ordinary eyes of failure, that none but men who fancied there was a kind of glory in acts of outrageous wickedness, if requiring great courage, would have set their lives upon the hazard of such a cast. Edwards, faithful to his trust, resisted them manfully, and the poor old man was beaten and stabbed before he could be quieted; his life, probably, was only saved by the singularly opportune arrival of his son from Flanders. The confederate who watched at the door below had attempted to stop the young man, and inquired with whom he would speak. Edwards, probably wishing to give his family an agreeable surprise, and supposing perhaps that the person was stationed there on duty connected with the Tower, answered he belonged to the house, and ran up stairs. What a meeting for father and son after a long separation! At the moment when the robbers were interrupted, Blood had slipped the crown under his cloak, one of his associates had secreted the orb, the other was filing the sceptre into two parts. At the stranger's appearance there was an instantaneous flight, to stop which the wounded keeper relieved from his gag, shouted "Treason and murder!" his daughter, waiting near, heard and repeated the cry, as she rushed into the open air. The warders of the tower seemed panic-stricken. The first whom the fugitives encountered, on trying to stop them, received a pistol-shot; the second did not so far provoke them, and they passed the drawbridge. As they ran along the Tower wharf, they joined in the shouts of "Stop the rogues!" thus bewildering the pursuers. They would probably have got clear off but for the courage of a brother-in-law of young Edwards, a Captain Beckman, who followed and stopped them. Blood fired at him, but, missing his aim, was secured. The crown was still beneath his cloak, and he struggled hard to keep it. His witty exclamation, when he saw that all was over, "It was a gallant attempt, however unsuccessful; it was for a crown," affords good evidence how far he was from repentance or fear. Strange to say, he had, after all, little cause to be afraid. At a time when the most trivial felonies were so frequently punished with death, one is amazed that so audacious a criminal should be spared; but how much more, to find him in a short time actually elevated to the dignity of a *favourite* at court, so that it became the mode for suitors to make application to the king through Colonel Blood; whilst the petty reward to the keeper and his son, of three hundred pounds, was delayed so long that the orders for the money were previously disposed of at half the nominal value. Little as we know Charles II. was inclined to estimate mere probity and loyalty in comparison with wit, humour, and a bold spirit, and much as he might sympathize with a "fine, gay, bold-faced villain," it seems wonderful that his majesty could not have contented himself with benefiting the accomplished colonel in a private way, instead of letting all the world perceive how little he regarded the laws he proposed to rule by. But conceit, like charity, covers a multitude of sins. Charles was not proof against that compliment paid to his august person by the colonel in the circumstance, as related by himself, that he had been once deterred from taking the king's life

from among the reeds by the Thames side above Battersea, as he had *undertaken to do*, by a sudden and irresistible "awe of majesty." The public opinion of Colonel Blood's elevation is apparent, in an epigram by one of the witty and profligate lords of Charles' court, the noted Rochester:—

> Blood, that wears treason in his face,
> Villain complete in parson's gown,
> How much he is at court in grace
> For stealing Ormond and the crown!
> Since loyalty does no man good,
> Let's steal the king, and outdo Blood.

From the London of the fifteenth century, suppose we now direct our attention to the COVENTRY of the same period, as one of the most important and interesting of English provincial towns. It was at that period that the magnificent St. Mary's Hall was erected (see page 246), of which we subjoin additional engravings of a street view (Fig. 1359), and a view of the interior (Fig. 1360). Of course no essential difference need be looked for between the general style and appearance of the houses of the wealthy and other inhabitants of Coventry (Fig. 1367) and those of houses belonging to the same classes in London. Coventry, too, was, like London and all our principal cities of the middle ages, fortified: its appearance from a distance may be seen in the view of Coventry (Fig. 1268), which represents Edward IV. in arms, and encamped against his formidable enemy, the Earl of Warwick, who is lodged with his forces in the town. The time is a little before the terrible and decisive battle of Barnet. In that representation of Coventry is suggested what the known history of Coventry confirms—its importance in a military point of view. We refer not to its brick or stone walls and entrenchments, but to the spirit, wealth, and liberality of the inhabitants. In the year 1448, Coventry alone fitted out 600 armed men for service. The attention paid to it by the chief rulers of the nation evidences in a striking manner its rank among the towns of Old England. It was, as has been previously stated, the favourite residence of the Black Prince. In Coventry have sat two of those parliaments which have achieved as it were an individual reputation for their doings: the first being that of 1404, composed entirely of laymen; the other that of 1459, which, for the numbers of attainders it issued against the Yorkist party, received the appellation of *Parliamentum Diabolicum*. A better known, as well as still more important incident in the history of Coventry, was the meeting there in the time of Richard II., when Bolingbroke and Norfolk were to decide their quarrel, by personal combat, after the fashion of the chivalric code. We have on more than one occasion alluded to this custom, and have given various engravings illustrative of the proceedings; we have also described, from Froissart, an actual deed of arms, that, though ending unhappily, was intended to have been only a friendly encounter; we may now add, from Holinshed, an account of the preparation for a more deadly encounter, and where mightier combatants were concerned. At the time appointed, "the Duke of Aumerle, that day, being high constable of England, and the Duke of Surrey, marshal, placed themselves between them, well-armed and appointed; and when they saw their time, they first entered into the lists with a great company of men, apparelled in silk sendall, embroidered with silver, both richly and curiously; every man having a tipped staff to keep the field in order. About the hour of prime came to the barriers of the lists the Duke of Hereford, mounted on a white courser, barded with green and blue velvet, embroidered sumptuously with swans and antelopes of goldsmiths' work, armed at all points. The constable and marshal came to the barriers, demanding of him what he was; he answered, 'I am Henry of Lancaster, Duke of Hereford, which am come hither to do mine endeavour against Thomas Mowbray, Duke of Norfolk, as a traitor untrue to God, the king, his realm, and me.' Then, incontinently, he sware upon the holy evangelists, that his quarrel was true and just, and upon that point he required to enter the lists. Then he put by his sword, which before he held naked in his hand, and putting down his vizor, made a cross on his horse, and with spear in hand entered into the lists, and descended from his horse, and set him down in a chair of green velvet, at the one end of the lists, and there reposed himself, abiding the coming of his adversary.

"Soon after him entered into the field with great triumph, King Richard, accompanied with all the peers of the realm, and in his company was the Earl of St. Paul, which was come out of France in post to see this challenge performed. The king had there above ten thousand men in armour, lest some fray or tumult might rise amongst his nobles, by quarrelling or partaking. When the king was set in his seat, which was richly hanged and adorned, a king-at-arms made open proclamation, prohibiting all men in the name of the king, and of the high-constable and marshal, to enterprise or attempt to approach or touch any part of the lists upon pain of death, except such as were appointed to order or marshal the field. The proclamation ended, another herald cried, 'Behold here Henry of Lancaster Duke of Hereford appellant, which is entered into the lists royal to do his devoir against Thomas Mowbray, Duke of Norfolk, defendant, upon pain to be found false and recreant.' The Duke of Norfolk hovered on horseback at the entrance of the lists, his horse being barded with crimson velvet, embroidered richly with lions of silver and mulberry trees; and when he had made his oath before the constable and marshal that his quarrel was just and true, he entered the field manfully, saying aloud, 'God aid him that hath the right;' and then he departed from his horse, and sate him down in his chair, which was of crimson velvet curtained about with white and red damask. The lord marshal viewed their spears to see that they were of equal length, and delivered the one spear himself to the Duke of Hereford, and sent the other unto the Duke of Norfolk by a knight. Then the herald proclaimed that the traverses and chairs of the champions should be removed, commanding them on the king's behalf to mount on horseback, and address themselves to the battle and combat. The Duke of Hereford was quickly horsed, and closed his beaver, and cast his spear into the rest, and when the trumpet sounded set forward courageously towards his enemy six or seven paces. The Duke of Norfolk was not fully set forward, when the king cast down his warder, and the heralds cried, 'Ho, ho!' Then the king caused their spears to be taken from them, and commanded them to repair again to their chairs, where they remained two long hours, while the king and his council deliberately consulted what order was best to be had in so weighty a cause."

The banishment, return, and change of dynasty that followed this —for Richard—most unfortunate interference, we have already narrated. But there is something for which Coventry has been, nay is, even more famous than for any or all of these events, stirring as is the interest and high as is the argument concerned in them; need we say we allude to its pageants? It is something to see one of these even in the present day, when the vital spirit that was of old infused into them has to a great degree departed. And a stranger who sees that pageant for the first time, is at no loss to understand its origin, and must be of somewhat unexcitable materials if it does not revive in his mind, however faintly, the romance with which he heard, in his boyish days, the very story that now comes before his eyes in so palpable a shape. Amidst the general accessories of processions—here, however, richer and more picturesque than usual —amidst the exhilarating music, the waving ribands and feathers, the motley assemblage of woolcombers and men in armour, Bishop Blaize, Jason, and puffy aldermen, city companies, and St. George of England, all superbly habited, amidst all these comes a lady riding on a beautiful grey horse, her long hair flowing over her beautiful limbs, enveloped in flesh-coloured muslin—the representative of that Lady Godiva who—but the story is too good to be told in the end of a sentence, and though well known, never, to our mind, tires by repetition. Best of all, even that class of antiquaries who so much delight in destroying for other people the enjoyments they cannot appreciate themselves, even those laborious mischief-makers have been unable with all their researches to do more with the story of Godiva than—in essentials at least—confirm it. One undeniable evidence is as good as a thousand; such a one is furnished by the inscription that formerly existed in a window at Coventry, set up so far back as the reign of the second Richard. Thus it ran:—

"I, Luriche, for the love of thee
Doe make Coventre tol-free."

Thus Luriche, or Leofric III. was one of the aldermen or earls of Coventry, in the time of Canute, and obtained a bad reputation for his oppressive conduct, more especially in matters relating to taxation and finance. In vain did the citizens remonstrate and entreat for relief. The great business of commerce, then beginning, was too little understood by any of the rulers of the people to induce them to show any particular favour to the men or the towns whose prosperity depended upon it, while in too many cases their only feelings and desires seem to have been to act like the boy with his eggs in the fable, and, by seizing all that could be laid hold of at once, stop all future growth and supply. Such a man this Leofric seems to have been; and the rising town of Coventry might possibly have been effectually checked and have gone to ruin, leaving not even its name to future times, but for the interposition of his Countess, a very beautiful, pious, and modest woman, who, unable to endure the sight and knowledge of the people's distress, added her prayer to theirs, and constantly importuned her husband to remove the cause, and would not be silenced. Irritated at what

he looked upon as a mere unreflecting desire to be charitable at the expense of his heavy revenues, Leofric appears to have thought he would at once put a stop to all further intercessions, by naming some impossible condition as the price of his consent; so in a moody humour one day told her, that when she would ride on horseback, naked, through the town of Coventry, he would grant the remission of tolls desired. "But," returned the Countess quickly, "will you give me leave so to do?" He could not of course but be consistant with his humour, so said "Yes." And before he had really dreamt, perhaps, of the possibility of his wife taking him at his word, the compact was at once settled by her. As the news flew abroad, Coventry must indeed have been in a strange state of excitement and expectation; but was it true? A public announcement soon decided that question; it was ordered that all persons on pain of death should keep within doors, and away from their windows, the shutters being at the same time universally closed. At the appointed time, the Countess came forth, beautiful and innocent as the poet has painted our first mother in her first days of innocence; and the physical beauty was but a type of the mental beauty that had determined upon such a deed: and both must have been alike strange and abashed, and shrinking as it were within themselves, at the sudden revelation of themselves they were called upon to make. One man, a tailor, disobeyed the proclamation; and may we not consider our knowledge that their was such a one as a kind of evidence that there were few, or no more, and that the general feelings and thoughts of the inhabitants were worthy of the occasion, namely, thankful, lofty, almost reverential, and utterly incapable of receiving the service their benefactress did them, in any other spirit than that in which it was offered? And thus, with her long hair drooping over, and almost concealing her form, her head bowed, and a strange but glorious confusion of womanly fears and fancies for herself, womanly tenderness and resolve for her poor clients floating through her brain, can we imagine Godiva, pursuing her way, till the eventful ride was over, and her lord, forgetting all those unworthy motives that must have actuated him in allowing her to do what she had done, and borne away by a new sense of the truly noble and beautiful being that it was his happiness to call wife, would receive her with open arms at his gates, and give her not only what she had asked for the people at Coventry, but what must have been still dearer, personally to herself, his own fervent admiration and respect. However this may have been, it is certain that Coventry was relieved, and that Coventry, to this day, neither forgets, nor intends to forget, what it owes to the Lady Godiva.

This is no doubt the essentially popular event in the history of Coventry; but considered simply as a pageant on the one hand, or as regards its connection with the dramatic literature of England on the other, there yet remains to be noticed the most important of the exhibitions that have made the city so famous; we allude to the performances of the mysteries that from a very early period have taken place in Coventry, and which were there carried to a higher pitch of splendour than in any other part of England, unless the Chester plays may be considered an exception. The place of performance was the street or churchyard, the stage a moveable platform (Fig. 1299), the actors and managers the trading companies or guilds, and the subjects the most solemn of the Bible themes. To the histrionics of the fifteenth century there appeared no difficulty whatever in getting up a play that should represent the Creation, or Fall of Man, the Nativity, or Crucifixion of Christ; nay, even the last solemn day of Judgment, were quite within their means—at least so they thought. Nothing of course was too expensive for such representations; and in the items that have been preserved of the cost of particular plays, there are some amusing evidences of the knowledge of the importance of the property-man and machinist, and of the want of knowledge of the boundaries that divide piety from what looks like blasphemy, but which is so only in look, for we know it was all done in innocence and perfect simplicity. Here are some items from Sharp's 'Dissertation' on these pageants:—"Payd for 2 pound of hayre for the Divill's head, 3s.; mending his hose, 8d.; black canvas for shirts for the damned, 4s.; red buckram for the wings of angels (represented by naked children), 7s.; paid for a cote for God, and a payre of gloves, 3s." The auditory were not unworthy of such magnificent preparation and subjects. The King and royal family, the nobles and chief ecclesiastical dignitaries of England, were usually present, with a host of strangers from different parts of the kingdom. The crafts went previously through the streets in solemn procession. The times of performance were chiefly the Christmas and Whitsun Holidays. The pageants were rightly so named, for the dialogue was generally rude, with very little or no plot, and the whole formed a succession of scenes, rather than a connected story. We may here glance at the pageant of the Birth of Christ and offering of the Magi, and which included also the Flight into Egypt and Murder of the Innocents. This, according to the principle of division of different parts of a general series among different companies, was prepared by and at the expense of the company of Shearmen and Tailors. The piece opens amidst the sound of harp and trumpet, and Israel appears prophesying the blessing that awaits mankind. The poet does not trouble his head about niceties, so presently several centuries are passed over, and Gabriel comes to announce to Mary her share in the great transactions that are about to take place. This is followed by a conversation between Mary and Joseph, and then preparations are made for the first appearance on the scene of the wonderful stranger. This is done with fine poetic feeling. It is night, and the scene represents a field where shepherds are scattered about, who are cold, and heavy in spirit, when a star shines, and the song of *Gloria in excelsis Deo* is heard. Immediately follow three songs, sung in parts, treble, tenor, and bass (the music, a simple kind of melody, is preserved); the singers being the shepherds, and certain women who represent the mothers of the country sorrowing over Herod's cruel edict.

> "O sisters two, how may we do
>   For to preserve this day
> These poor younglings, for whom we do sing,
>   By, by, lully, lullay.
>
> "Herod the king in his raging,
>   Charged he hath this day
> The men of might, in his own sight,
>   All young children to slay.
>
> "That woe is me, poor child, for thee,
>   And ever mourn and say
> For thy parting, neither say nor sing
>   By, by, lully, lullay."

The star now guides the shepherds to the "crib of poor repast," where the child Jesus lies, and the shepherds present their offerings, one his pipe, another his hat, a third his mittens. The action now moves on with more rapidity. Prophets come declaring where he would not be born, namely, in halls, castles, or towers, in order to enhance the humility of the chosen place; Herod's messenger follows; then the three kings, who seek to persuade Herod to recal his cruel decree, but in vain, and so at last the slaughter takes place, the infant Jesus being previously carried off into Egypt. With two specimens of the author's powers respectively in pathos and fury, we conclude our notice of the Shearmen and Tailors' pageant. Whilst one mother thus entreats for mercy—

> "Sir Knightes, of your courtesy,
>   This day shame not your chivalry,
>   But on my childe have pity';"

another threatens all and sundry in these words—

> "Sit he never so high in saddle
>   But I shall make his brains addle,
>   And here with my pot-ladle
>   With him will I fight."

"There is abundant evidence," observes the author of an admirable article on the English Drama in the 'Penny Cyclopædia,' "that the Romish ecclesiastics, in their first introduction of this kind of representations, especially that part of them relating to the birth, passion, and resurrection of Christ, had the perfectly serious intention of strengthening the faith of the multitude in the fundamental doctrines of their church; and it seems the less extraordinary that they should have resorted to this expedient, when we reflect that, before the invention of printing, books had no existence for the people at large. But it is no less certain that the repetition of these exhibitions rapidly worked upon the popular mind an effect which, it is likely, the priestly dramatists themselves had not contemplated in the first instance: it developed the universally latent passion in the breast of social man for spectacle in general, and for dramatic spectacle especially, for its own sake. Here again was the strongest encouragement of all for the clergy to persevere in their dramatic efforts. Finding the lively pleasure which the people took in this mode of receiving religious instruction, they were tempted to add, according to their barbarous ability, embellishment after embellishment to the simple copies which they had originally presented of the most remarkable passages of Scripture story, until the profane exhibition itself, the miracle *play*, and not the sacred subject of it, became the sole object of interest to the people who composed the audience at these representations, as, also, it certainly became the primary object of the greater part of the ecclesiastics who took part in getting them up." And, starting from this point, it is easy to perceive how, step by step, the growing power went on, until became what it now is, the richest division of the richest of national literatures.

In the beginning of the present chapter we alluded to the manifold uses to which the florid Gothic style of architecture became applicable during the present period: this is one of its distinctive features as compared not only with all previous forms of the Gothic, but as compared with most other styles of architecture by whatever name known. In carrying this style, which had been hitherto an exclusively ecclesiastical one, into buildings intended for domestic purposes, the alterations and adaptations were not at first very considerable. The parts were on a smaller scale, and exhibited some specialties of composition; but their details and ornaments, even the doors and windows, were essentially the same. But gradually new members sprang up, the chimney, for instance, and gave at once a domestic expression to the whole. Bays and oriels also became highly beautiful and picturesque parts of the new style. Then the timber roof began to rival the ecclesiastical stone ones; and, although originated, like them, in an earlier period, were carried in the present one to the highest pitch of mechanical skill and artistical effect. The arch of timber in a simple form is frequently found in buildings of the thirteenth and fourteenth centuries. In Westminster Hall, completed in 1399, we find one of the earliest examples of a novel method of constructing and ornamenting the open roof; and which in its turn led the way to the more elaborate roofs of Eltham Palace, Crosby Place, &c.

In the castellated structures of the period we find the new domestic style blended with what may be called the old domestic style of those barons who were always attacking or being attacked, and whose houses therefore exhibited more of wall and battlement, tower and turret, than any of the lighter features that speak of social comforts, splendour, or refinement. And thus, according to the peaceable or the turbulent characters of their possessors, did the mansions that were built in the fifteenth century partake more or less of the Domestic or the Military aspect. Generally speaking, the difference within half a century was very great. What, for instance, can be more striking than on turning from the view of the Westgate, Canterbury (Fig. 1272), with its solid towers, and machicolated gateway, breathing as plainly as stone and mortar and iron can, defiance and war, to the contrast presented in the elegant range of building that forms a part of the great court of Warwick Castle (Fig. 1270)? Yet but a small interval of time occurred between the erection of these structures. Warwick Castle generally is, we may notice in passing, what the first sight of it suggests, the growth of long centuries, and no product of any one founder or architect, any more than of one style. We need not dwell on the individual architectural characteristics of some of the other buildings of the period, represented in our engravings; such for instance as the Manor-house of Great Chatfield in Wiltshire (Fig. 1351), an Inn-yard (Fig. 1364), or the houses in Warwick (Fig. 1365), Grantham (Fig. 1352), and Leicester (Fig. 1350), where Richard III. slept the night before the battle of Bosworth; whilst of the merely decorative features of domestic architecture, the chimney-piece at Tattershall Castle (Fig. 1357), and the heraldic vane of Oxburgh Hall (Fig. 1353), it will be sufficient to observe that they show very happily that love of heraldic display which forms a characteristic of the style and time. The Crosses, that so picturesquely adorned our old English towns, are not unworthily represented in the Market-cross at Winchester (Fig. 1354).

How necessary it was, even so late as the fifteenth century, to make every mansion of a certain rank capable of military resistance, is shown in a very remarkable manner, in that collection of letters known as the Paston Letters, recently edited from an earlier edition, by Mr. A. Ramsay, and which consists generally of the correspondence of the Pastons and their connections between the years 1440 and 1505. It appears that in 1459, the celebrated warrior Sir John Fastolf died, and left by will to the respectable family of the Pastons his relations, in Norfolk, "the estate of Caister." The Duke of Norfolk laid claim to the same estate, which he asserted Sir John had already given to him in his lifetime. Out of these opposite claims litigation arose, and the Letters furnish some curious examples of the manner in which it was carried on. After seven years spent in preliminaries, one of which was a bargain for the purchase of the estate from one of Fastolf's executors, in order to put his right on the most solid ground possible, the duke proceeds to *besiege* the manor-house, a course of action that no one seems to have thought for a moment inconsistent with the most formal respect for law; indeed, the age was one of legal formality, and the Pastons and the Norfolks were the very concentration of its spirit. While the duke prepared for his attack on the Caister manor-house,

Sir John Paston, knight, a distinguished soldier, who had succeeded his father as chief of the family, sent help for the defence from London, where he was living. On his brother John devolved the perilous task of resisting the duke's men at Caister. The soldiers sent by the knight are described by him in his letter to his brother as "four well assured and true men to do all manner of thing that they be desired to do in safeguard or strengthening of the said place;" and he says, "they be proved men, and cunning in the war and in feats of arms; and they can well shoot both guns and crossbows, and amend and string them, and devise bulwarks, or any things that should be a strength to the place; and they will, as need is, keep watch and ward: they be sad (serious) and well-advised men, saving one of them which is bald, and called William Penny, which is as good a man as goeth on the earth, saving a little, he will, as I understand, be a little copshotten (high-crested), but yet he is no brawler, but full of courtesy," &c. Kindly regarding their comforts, he points out that a couple of beds must be provided for them, and further explains that he prefers sending such men from a distance, to relying upon the neighbouring people, who might be timid on account of the losses they may bring upon themselves, and so discourage the "remanent," that is to say, we presume, the great body of the knight's own servants and retainers, whom, no doubt, these skilled men of war were brought down from the metropolis to guide and instruct. The siege now goes on week after week, the law taking not the slightest notice. On the 12th of September we learn from another letter, written by the mother of Sir John, that the garrison are getting pressed.

"I greet you well," she writes, "letting you weet that your brother and his fellowship stand in great jeopardy at Caister, and lack victuals; and Daubeney and Berney (two friends who had joined him in the defence) be dead, and divers other greatly hurt; and they fail gunpowder and arrows, and the place is sore broken with guns of the other party, so that, unless they have hasty help, they be like to lose both their lives and the place, to the greatest rebuke to you that ever came to any gentleman, for every man in this country marvelleth greatly that ye suffer them to be so long in so great jeopardy without help or other remedy." Fresh strength too is to be given to the besiegers: the duke, she says, has sent for all his tenants to come to Caister on the following Thursday, when "there is there like to be the greatest multitude of people that came there yet; and they purpose then to make a great assault; for they have sent for guns to Lynn and other places, by the sea's side, that with their great multitude of guns, with other shot and ordinance, there shall no man dare appear in the place; therefore, as ye will have my blessing I charge you and require you that you see your brother be holpen in haste." The anxious mother, however, living at a distance, finds from Sir John's answer that matters are not so bad as she anticipates. The grand difficulty is the want of money, and it is really surprising, as well as touching, to hear this man of rank and property say, "I have but ten shillings, and wot not where to have more; and moreover, I have been ten times in like case or worse within this ten weeks." Under such circumstances, and contending against a nobleman, it is not difficult to foresee the result; the garrison were obliged to surrender, and then—what does the brave defender, John Paston, but prepare to engage in the service of the very duke who had overthrown him; a fact partly perhaps to be attributed to the duke's behaviour when he had achieved his wishes, and partly to the feeling of the time, which allowed men to engage in these affairs without any particular animosity towards each other. Eventually the Pastons got back their property, the duke having died, and the duchess having been from the first friendly to them.

A few words by way of appendage to this part of our subject may here be devoted to the subject of our engravings, representing the storming of a fort (Fig. 1251), the siege of a town (Fig. 1252), and the chief machines used on such occasions, namely, the breaching and the moveable towers (Figs. 1253 and 1274). Cannon we see were now in constant use. The art of attacking fortified places was greatly advanced by the English during the period under review, as the French found to their cost when Henry V. was among them. Every town that he attacked he took: a fact that forms a striking contrast to the state of things but a few years before, when, for instance, Edward III. was kept for a whole twelvemonth before Calais, wasting his resources and losing his temper. Henry's engineers, it appears, drew their lines of contravallation and circumvallation, approached by entrenchments, ran their secret mine through the bowels of the earth, battered the walls with rams as well as artillery, showered darts, stones, and bullets over the ramparts and their defenders. As a specimen of one of the fortresses built in the fifteenth century, consisting essentially of a mere tower, or keep, mounted with extensive fortifications, therefore

evidently intended for defence, and not for accommodation, we may refer to Borthwick Castle, in Scotland (Fig. 1273), erected about 1430, an edifice well known as having been frequently visited by Mary, Queen of Scots, an honour which it owed to its proximity to the castle of Crichton, the property of Bothwell. Sir Walter Scott tells a good story of the nobleman to whom Borthwick then belonged. In consequence of a process betwixt Master George Hay de Minzeans and the Lord Borthwick (in 1547), letters of excommunication had passed against the latter, on account of the contumacy of certain witnesses. William Langlands, an apparitor or macer of the see of St. Andrews, presented these letters to the curate of the church of Borthwick, requiring him to publish the same at the service of high mass. It seems that the inhabitants of the castle were at this time engaged in the favourite sport of enacting the Abbot of Unreason, a species of *high jinks*, in which a mimic prelate was elected, who, like the Lord of Misrule in England, turned all sort of lawful authority, and particularly the church ritual, into ridicule. This frolicksome person with his retinue, notwithstanding the apparitor's character, entered the church, seized upon the primate's officer without hesitation, and dragging him to the mill-dam on the south side of the castle, compelled him to leap into the water. Not contented with this partial immersion, the Abbot of Unreason pronounced that Mr. William Langlands was not yet sufficiently bathed, and therefore caused his assistants to lay him on his back in the stream, and duck him in the most satisfactory and perfect manner. The unfortunate apparitor was then conducted back to the church, where, for his refreshment after his bath, the letters of excommunication were torn to pieces, and steeped in a bowl of wine, the mock abbot probably being of opinion that a tough parchment was but dry eating. Langlands was compelled to eat the letters and swallow the wine, with the comfortable assurance that if any more such letters should arrive, during the continuance of this office, they should "a' gang the same gait."

Anthony Bec, the famous military Bishop of Durham, in the thirteenth century, was guardian of the legal heir of the manor of ELTHAM,—William de Vesci,—grandson of the powerful baron, John de Vesci. As covetous as he was warlike, Bec possessed himself of the manor, depriving the heir of his right. A large and splendid mansion was built by the bishop, in place, it would seem, of an earlier manor-house. Ultimately the property reverted to its original possessor, John of Eltham. Edward II.'s sovereign son was born here in 1315. Parliaments met several times at Eltham in the reign of Edward III., who, with his heroic sons, here celebrated great feasts and festivals, for the solace of John the captive king of France. Edward IV. almost entirely rebuilt the palace, of which the hall was the noblest part. In that hall, he celebrated the Christmas of 1483, as Christmases of old were wont to be celebrated, with bountiful hospitality for high and low, and abundance of mirth and sport. The palace was much enlarged by Henry VII. His barons dined with him daily in the hall. In its finished state at that time, the structure was extensive and magnificent. Four quadrangles were enclosed within a lofty wall and deep wide moat. The principal entrance consisted of a bridge and gateway in the north wall. Another gate with a bridge opened in the south wall. The hall, chapel, and state apartments were the principal interior features. A garden and three parks surrounded the palace, stocked with deer, and adorned by noble trees. Such was the fine old palace of Eltham previous to the rise of the new palace at Greenwich, which stole away all its lustre, and caused it to be deserted, if we except an occasional visit from royalty down to the period of James I. Its decline was hastened by the commonwealth. The parks were broken into, the deer dispersed and killed by soldiers and others. The greater part of the buildings were completely destroyed. Charles II. after his restoration was too intent on his pleasures to think about recovering or preserving any part of the melancholy wreck. The old palace was turned into a quarry, and stones were carried away for any and every purpose; indeed the whole would have gone, most likely, but for the hall being converted into a barn, a circumstance to which we owe the preservation of one of the most beautiful architectural specimens of the reign of Edward IV., whose symbol, the expanded rose, is visible in different parts of it. Mr. Buckler observes, "The interior is magnificent. The taste and talent of ages are concentrated in its design; and it is scarcely possible to imagine proportions more just and noble, a plan more perfect, ornaments more appropriate and beautiful; in a word, a whole more harmonious than this regal banqueting-room." The forms of the windows are admirable; but the timber roof (Fig. 1267) is the great attraction of this valuable remain. "The main beams of the roof

are full seventeen inches square, and twenty-eight feet long, perfectly straight and sound throughout, and are the produce of trees
of the most stately growth. A forest must have yielded the choicest
timber for the supply of this building; and it is evident that the
material has been wrought with incredible labour and admirable
skill." Of late years this rich and noble roof has been restored
by Mr. Smirke, at the expense of the government. The area of
the palace is still surrounded by a high stone wall and a broad deep
moat, now converted into a garden, over which are two bridges.
At Eltham, as at a hundred other great and ancient places, there
has long existed a tradition that subterranean passages existed; and
true enough such passages have been found. We learn from a little
pamphlet published a few years ago, that under the ground floor
of one of the apartments of the palace, a trap-door opens into a
room under ground, ten feet in length, which conducts the passenger to the series of passages, with decoys, stairs, and shafts, some of
which are vertical, and others on an inclined plane, which were
once used for admitting air, and for hurling down missiles and
pitchballs upon enemies, according to the mode of defence in those
ancient times; and it is worthy of notice that, at points where weapons from above could assail the enemy with the greatest effect,
there these shafts verge and concentrate. About five hundred feet
of passage have been entered and passed through in a direction west,
towards Middle Park, and under the moat for two hundred feet.
The arch is broken into the field leading from Eltham to Motting-
ham, but still the brick-work of the arch can be traced farther.
Proceeding in the same direction, the remains of two iron gates, completely carbonized, were found in that part of the passage under the
moat; and large stalactites, formed of super-carbonate of lime,
hung down from the roof of the arch, which sufficiently indicate the
lapse of time since these passages were entered.

Glancing at the interior of the mansions of the fifteenth century,
something or other of novelty to our eyes every where presents
itself. The antique bed-rooms (Figs. 1366, 1369), the couvre-
feu (Fig. 1374), which gave name to the custom that the Normans
made so odious, the kitchens (Fig. 1347), all speak of habits differing materially from our own; and still more do some at least of
the arrangements for the feast (Figs. 1339, 1342, 1346), and
especially that of the servant on his knees tasting the wines to satisfy
the guests there was no death in the cup. A very interesting view
of the enconomy of the house of the chief personage in the realm, has
been just made public (by means of the Athenæum, Nov. 16), in
the Travels of Leo von Rozmital, the brother of George, King of
Bohemia, who, with a retinue including the narrator, Tetzel, visited
England during the reign of Edward IV. Tetzel, after having
confirmed the truth of the usual remark as to Edward's own handsome person, adds, that he " has the finest set of courtiers that a
man may find in Christendom. After some days he invited my
Lord Leo and all his noble companions, and gave them a very
costly feast, and also he gave to each of them the medal of his
order, to every knight a golden one, and to every one who was not
a knight a silver one; and he himself hung them upon their necks.
Another day the king called us to court. In the morning the
queen (Elizabeth Woodville) went from child-bed to church with
a splendid procession of many priests, bearing relics, and many
scholars, all singing, and carrying burning candles. Besides there
was a great company of women and maidens from the country and
from London, who were bidden to attend. There were also a great
number of trumpeters, pipers, and other players, with forty-two of
the king's singing men, who sang very sweetly. Also, there were
four and twenty heralds and pursuivants, and sixty lords and knights.
Then came the queen, led by two dukes, and with a canopy borne
over her head. Behind her followed her mother and above sixty
ladies and maidens. Having heard the service sung, and kneeled
down in the church, she returned with the same procession to her
palace. Here all who had taken a part in the procession were
invited to a feast, and all sat down, the men and the women, the
clergy and the laity, each in his rank, filling four large rooms.
Also, the king invited my lord and all his noble attendants to the
table where he usually dined with his courtiers. And one of the
king's greatest lords must sit at the king's table upon the king's
stool, in the place of the king; and my lord sat at the same table,
only two steps below him. Then all the honours which were due to
the king had to be paid to the lord who sat in his place, and
also to my lord; and it is incredible what ceremonies we observed
there. While we were eating, the king was making presents to all
the trumpeters, pipers, players, and heralds; to the last alone he
gave four hundred nobles, and every one, when he received his
pay, came to the tables and told aloud what the king had given
him. When my lord had done eating, he was conducted into

a costly ornamented room, where the queen was to dine, and
there he was seated in a corner that he might see all the expensive provisions. The queen sat down on a golden stool
alone at her her table, and her mother and the king's sister stood far
below her. And when the queen spoke to her mother or to the
king's sister, they kneeled down every time before her, and remained
kneeling until the queen drank water. And all her ladies and
maids, and those who waited upon her, even great lords, had to
kneel while she was eating, which continued three hours (!) After
dinner there was dancing, but the queen remained sitting upon her
stool, and her mother kneeled before her. The king's sister danced
with two dukes, and the beautiful dances and reverences performed
before the queen—the like I have never seen, nor such beautiful
maidens. Among them were eight duchesses, and above thirty
countesses and others, all daughters of great people. After the
dance the king's singing men came in and sang. When the king
heard mass sung in his private chapel my lord was admitted: then
the king had his relics shown to us, and many sacred things in
London. Among them we saw a stone from the Mount of Olives,
upon which there is the footprint of Jesus Christ, our Lady's girdle,
and many other relics." This is altogether about the most extraordinary picture of the life of royalty in England ever presented;
and one can with difficulty believe that it really refers to a time not
quite four centuries removed from our own.

A peculiar and very significant evidence of the value placed upon
books in days when authors were few, and copies of their writings
could only be obtained by the labours of the transcriber (Fig. 1331),
is furnished to us by the very numerous cases recorded of the
presentation of books to persons of high rank, amidst circumstances
of great ceremonial. In some cases that presentation seems to have
taken place from the single desire of the poet or writer to obtain
patronage; or show, in a graceful manner, the appreciation of services
already enjoyed. Thus Lydgate presents his poem of the 'Pilgrim'
to Thomas Montacute, Earl of Salisbury (Fig. 1204). In other
cases, the object appears to have been to make some offering
of unusual value and magnificence; and what could be more valuable or magnificent in the eyes of a man like Henry VI., than the
Missal presented to him on his coronation by his uncle the Duke of
Bedford, one of the most beautiful and elaborate specimens of the
art of illumination ever produced before or since? The manuscript
contains fifty-nine drawings of the most highly-finished character,
nearly the size of the page (eleven inches by seven and a half),
and above a thousand tiny miniatures, in addition to the border of
foliage, and other rich and exquisite decorations. In one of these
(Fig. 1329) we have the only portrait known of the duke, at whose
cost it was executed. Then again, other nobles who desired to gratify their monarch by such gifts, happily combined with the gratification of that feeling their desire to call his attention to subjects in
which they felt a peculiar interest: some such feeling it was, we
may conclude, that led the Earl of Shrewsbury to present to the
same king a book of romances (Fig. 1202); and how the circumstance seems to explain, and, in our estimation, to enhance the exploits
of brave John Talbot! But a mighty change came over the spirit
of literature, small as were its earliest manifestations. The famous
mercer, William Caxton (Fig. 1372), came back to England with
those few, and simple, and rude implements which had cost him so
much wealth, labour, time, and anxiety to obtain; and then, from the
precincts of Westminster Abbey, speedily issued the art of printing.
And certainly it is an extraordinary fact, that the power that was
to destroy the supremacy of the Roman Catholic Church, with
all those rank abuses which a gentler mode of treatment might
have failed to remove, should have issued as it were from its
own bosom; and one calculated to enhance our estimation of that
church; for, of all the services rendered by it to humanity—
and who can doubt but that these were many and momentous?—
none can be compared with that which we owe to it, in connection
with the most magical of all arts and instruments—printing and the
press. It almost seems, as though she had been conscious that the
manifold corruptions that had gathered around her, crippling her
energies, and bending her once erect forehead towards the earth,
had removed all chance of future usefulness, and that, therefore,
she had used all her remaining strength to summon up a new
and infinitely more potent spirit to take her place, and continue
with increase of success proportioned to the increase of means, the
good work that the church had in its days of purity begun and
carried on, all things considered, so well and wisely for many a
century, which, in some respects at least, would have been " dark
ages" indeed, but for her exertions. It is certain, at all events,
whatever the notions and thoughts of the men who did welcome the

new thing, that inattention to its possible effects formed no part of them. Among the enemies of printing, there was a bishop who said plainly, "If we do not destroy that remarkable invention, it will destroy us." Caxton—a name ever to be revered by all who have faith in and a yearning for the progress of mankind, which he, in connection with the establishment of such a literature as that of England, has done more perhaps to promote than any other man, working with similar material agencies—Caxton came to England about 1473 or 1474, and—ominous locality!—was located, it has been supposed, in the scriptorium of the abbey, the place where its transcribers were wont to be employed; at all events it is certain that he began to print in some building either forming a part of the actual abbey, or directly connected with it; and that the Abbot Milling, and probably Milling's successor, Esteney, patronised him. Caxton's residence appears to have been a house in the Almonry (Fig. 1355). Caxton's publications were of a very miscellaneous character, such as treatises on heraldry, hawking, and chess (Fig. 1373); romances of religion and literature; translations of classical works; chronicles, &c.; all, no doubt, carrying out, as far as circumstances would permit, his desire, which was to make the books capable of "instructing the ignorant in wisdom and virtue." But Caxton, too, must be presented at court, and make his offering—a most memorable one—the first English printed book ever presented to an English monarch. On our engraving (Fig. 1228), copied from the illumination of a beautiful manuscript at Lambeth Palace, we see two persons engaged in the ceremony of presentation. Caxton's fellow-labourer (for he worked as a contributor to the Caxton press) and patron is the Lord Rivers, the most accomplished of all the men who fell as the victims of the sanguinary wars of the Roses. He was beheaded, with Lord Grey, Sir Thomas Vaughan, and Sir R. Hawse, at Pomfret, by order of Richard III., immediately after the death of Edward IV., and in order, evidently, to get them out of the way of his projected usurpation. "O Pomfret! Pomfret!" is the passionate address of Lord Rivers, as he, with his companions, goes to execution (Fig. 1271)—

> ———"O thou bloody prison—
> Fatal and ominous to noble peers!
> Within the guilty closure of thy walls
> Richard the Second here was hacked to death;
> And for more slander to thy dismal seat
> We give to thee our guiltless blood to drink."
> *Shakspere*. Richard III.

The War of the Roses, it has been observed, was essentially a barons' war, and thus the people were but little interested either way in the conclusion. It is a well-known fact that the former were, for once, the chief sufferers, and that the latter were generally spared by both parties; but not the less is it certain that the peaceful pursuits of industry must have been fearfully arrested (Fig. 1380); that the ploughshare was too often turned into a sword, and that a state of general disorder must have ensued, calculated to impoverish and demoralise all within its influence, and especially the poorest and most ignorant peasantry. The string of miserable malefactors going to prison (Fig. 1370), and the dreadful processions issuing from it towards the scaffolds (Fig. 1371), that so often met the startled gaze, thrusting their hideous outlines athwart the blue and serene-looking sky, were symptoms of a worse mischief done to the national heart and intellect by these unnatural wars, than the disappearance even of that long line of nobles who were their more prominent and more lamented victims.

But they are ended at last, and affairs gradually fall into the old channel. Commerce revives; the tradesman looks busy and contented. Literature and art continue their respective missions. The ministrations of the church assume somewhat of their former influence, now that the practical anomaly of an atmosphere of war is removed from the houses of peace and of God. The towns again exhibit their magnificent religious plays; the villages once more resound with the clamour of the popular sports; the mummers and the tumblers (Fig. 1379) arouse not only the mirth of the rustics but—what the wars had checked—their liberality; the drums (Fig. 1383) are beaten by hands that seem to know the influence of better living than the poor performer has been lately in the habit of experiencing; the green sward that had been trampled by unaccustomed feet is re-levelled for the bowls (Fig. 1378); the ball again flies across the green from the hand, the trap (Fig. 1381), or the club (Fig. 1388); and if the boys leap through their hoops (Fig. 1387), as before—to them war itself has been but a new subject for sport—their parents look on with a fresh feeling of satisfaction; if shuttlecock (Fig. 1390) and hoodman-blind (Fig. 1386) have not ceased to be played, there is now assuredly more of the players' hearts in the sports. The bow, however, is neglected—a significant fact—the people have had enough of war, and so their own favourite weapon is laid aside. The government of Edward IV.—a thing of force—grows alarmed at the idea of any decrease of the materials of force, and so the popular sports are condemned, and the instruments used in them are to be destroyed—dice (Fig. 1389) among the rest; and shooting-butts (Fig. 1375) are to be erected in every township. But the edict fails; the use of the bow still declines; and the government, as it ceases to find the materials for its armies always ready among its subjects generally, leans more and more towards a chosen portion of them—the growing hired and standing army of England.

The systematic slaughter of the most distinguished warriors engaged in the wars of the Roses, must have given a fresh impulse to the desire already strongly and universally felt of making armour more and more impregnable, and complete from head to foot. An evidence of the importance previously attached to this subject is furnished by the fact that when Bolingbroke was preparing for the ordeal trial at Coventry, he sent to Galeazzo, Duke of Milan, for a choice suit of armour. The duke placed all his stock before the messenger, and when he had chosen what he liked, sent with him four of the best armourers out of Milan to attend to the fitting of it to Bolingbroke's person. About 1400 plate armour began to supersede the old chain mail, and—that accomplished—grew in a few years more and more rich and fantastic. In our engravings are exhibited various stages of the progress of plated armour, beginning with the suits worn by Henry V.'s squire, of which the plumed bascinet of war is a striking feature (Fig. 1325), and by the Earl of Suffolk (Fig. 1327); and then onwards through the suits of Sir Robert Grushill (Fig. 1328), Richard Beauchamp, Earl of Warwick (Fig. 1326), and Sir Thomas Peyton (Fig. 1322). The helmets shown in Fig. 1245 are tilting helmets only, and were not worn in war. Looking at the richness and splendour of some of these examples of the armour of the fifteenth century, we can better appreciate the incident related by Froissart in connection with Raymond, the nephew of Pope Clement, whose beautiful armour was the cause of his destruction: he was taken prisoner, and put to death by his reckless captors, for the sake of the dazzling shell in which he had enveloped himself. With a few words on costume we conclude. This was in some respects an age of fashionable monstrosities. Let the reader who would enjoy a quiet laugh at the expense of our ancestors, look for instance at the head-dresses of the ladies, square (Fig. 1337), horned (Fig. 1344), steepled (Fig. 1324), and winged (Fig. 1343), and then contrast them with the exquisitely graceful figure and dress exhibited in the brass monument of Eleanor Bohun (Fig. 1312) in Westminster Abbey, which is a proof after all how solid are the foundations of good sense and fine taste: what the sculptor of that effigy admired, and had a circle around him prepared to admire also, we look upon with exactly the same sentiment. It is Fashion again, that whimsical fantastic being, who must be answerable for all these head-dress vagaries, as well as for the equally numerous and equally absurd characteristics of portions of the male costume (Figs. 1335, 1336, 1338, 1340), one of which, the long sleeves, thus fell under the quaint satire of the poet Occleve:—

> What is a lord without his men?
> I put case, that his foes him assail
> Suddenly in the street, what help shall he
> Whose sleeves encumbrous so side trail
> Do to his lord,—he may not him avail;
> In such a case he is but a woman;
> He may not stand him in stead of a man;
> His arms two have right enough to do,
> And somewhat more, his sleeves up to hold.

END OF VOLUME 1

INDEX

TO THE

ENGRAVINGS OF VOLUME I.

3 D

OLD ENGLAND:

A PICTORIAL MUSEUM

OF

REGAL, ECCLESIASTICAL, MUNICIPAL, BARONIAL,

AND POPULAR ANTIQUITIES.

EDITED

By CHARLES KNIGHT.

IN TWO VOLUMES.—VOL. II.

CONTENTS OF VOLUME II.

ILLUMINATED ENGRAVINGS OF OLD ENGLAND.

VOLUME II.

<hr>

. Some of these Engravings are described at the pages to which they are respectively assigned in the following list. Others are not so described, although they are placed with reference to the general subject to which they belong. Where such description is not found in the text, we here subjoin a more particular notice of the Engraving.

THE passage to Wolsey's Hall is by a flight of stone steps, above which is a richly-groined ceiling, with the carving still quite sharp, though three hundred years have passed away since it was executed. The entrance to the hall is at the west end, beneath the minstrels' gallery, which, projecting under the west window, casts a comparative gloom over the approach, and, when the hall is first seen, produces an effect of light and splendour almost startling. The hall is one hundred and six feet long, forty feet wide, and sixty feet high. The roof is supported by a carved timber framework, which stretches across the wide and lofty room in a series of magnificent arches, each central arch springing from two pendents, suspended from the points of two arches which spring on each side from brackets between the windows. Carved timber, resembling the framework of Gothic windows with their tracery, fills up the space between the arches and the ceiling. The carving is exceedingly rich, and the whole is painted and finished off in burnished gold. The hall is lighted by six Gothic windows high above the floor on each side, a great window at the west end, another at the east end, seen over the top of the screen which separates the hall from the withdrawing room, and a beautiful oriel window on the south side, which, reaching almost from the floor to the roof, pours its abundant light on the dais, or raised portion of the pavement at the upper end appropriated to the most distinguished persons. The canopy of the oriel window, consisting of pendents of carved stone, is of singular beauty. The east and west windows and the oriel are decorated with stained glass executed by Mr. Willement. The walls on each side of the hall are hung with arras tapestry, consisting of eight pictures, each of which represents one of the principal events of the life of the patriarch Abraham. The whole series includes ten pieces; the other two are in the public dining-room at Hampton Court Palace. The tapestry belonged to Henry VIII., and has descended to the present times as a portion of the royal wardrobes. It is not known by whom the designs were made, but they have been ascribed, with some degree of probability, to Bernard von Orlay, of Brussels, who went to Rome when he was young, and became a pupil of Raphael. He afterwards returned to Brussels, and is known to have made other designs for tapestry. The tapestry beneath the minstrels' gallery is of still earlier workmanship. There are various other appropriate decorations in Wolsey's Hall, which for brilliancy and gorgeousness of effect are probably unrivalled in Europe or in the world.

THE monument of Mary, Queen of Scots, is in the south aisle of Henry VII.'s Chapel, Westminster Abbey. It consists of a table-tomb, on which is a recumbent marble effigy of Mary, well sculptured, by Stone, and apparently an excellent likeness. The tomb is enclosed by marble pillars, which support a lofty ornamented entablature, forming a vaulted canopy over the effigy. The material of which the whole is constructed is white and black marble, and the architecture in the Classic style, which had gradually been coming into fashion, and which had then almost entirely superseded the Gothic.

Mary's monument is a structure resembling that of Queen Elizabeth, which is in the north aisle of Henry VII.'s Chapel; both were erected by Mary's son, James I.: Stone was the sculptor of both, and though we cannot admire the style of architectural decoration, it must be admitted that both are sumptuous and stately monuments. The table-tomb, with a recumbent effigy on the top and kneeling effigies round the sides, immediately in front in our engraving, is that of Lady Margaret Douglas, afterwards Countess of Lennox, who was the mother of Lord Darnley, Mary's husband, and grandmother of James I. She was the great-granddaughter of Edward IV., granddaughter of Henry VII., sister of James V. of Scotland, and nearly related to many other royal personages.

THE architectural embellishments of tombs in England, in every successive period, have had a close connection and correspondence with the prevailing forms of architecture in edifices. In the reign of James I., by whose direction the monument of Queen Elizabeth was erected in Westminster Abbey, Gothic architecture had been entirely superseded by the Grecian, Roman, and Italian, the forms of which, we venture to say, were less beautiful, certainly less appropriate to the embellishment of English tombs. The monument of Queen Elizabeth is constructed of white and black marble, and consists of a table-tomb enclosed by two sets of six columns with Corinthian capitals, each set supporting an entablature from the interior of which springs a semicircular arch, forming a vaulted roof, which is surmounted by an attic, ornamented with the royal arms and other decorations. The recumbent effigy of the queen is of white marble: the features seem to be exceedingly well represented by the sculptor, Nicholas Stone. The tomb stands in the north aisle of Henry VII.'s Chapel, above the remains not only of Elizabeth, who died in 1602, but those also of her sister, Queen Mary, who died in 1558 Mary has no effigy.

5. PAINTED SCREEN IN ST. GEORGE'S CHAPEL, WINDSOR. . . . .

ON the south side of the south aisle of the choir of St. George's Chapel, Windsor, adjoining the south transept, is a small chantry chapel, formerly called Oliver King's Chapel, but now the Aldworth Chapel, in consequence of the several members of the Aldworth family, paternal ancestors of Lord Braybrooke, having been buried in it. Oliver King, who built the chapel, was Bishop of Bath and Wells, and appears to have been buried in Bath Cathedral, pursuant to his will. He was registrar of the order of the Garter, and secretary to the four royal personages whose likenesses he caused to be painted on the oak panel of which our coloured wood-engraving is a representation. The panel is opposite to the chantry chapel, on the north side of the south aisle of the choir. The figures represent Henry VI., his son Prince Edward, who was murdered after the battle of Tewkesbury, Edward IV., and Henry VII. Each person is painted as standing on a pedestal, on the front of which are his armorial bearings, supporters, and devices. The inscription beneath the figure is in Latin, and solicits our reader to pray for the soul of Oliver King, professor of law, &c., and chief secretary to the above princes; and beneath the panel is a marble tablet inscribed to the memory of the Duke and Duchess of Gloucester.

The remains of Edward IV. are deposited at the east end of the north aisle of the choir. Over a large stone slab, on which is inscribed "King Edward IIII., and his queen Elizabeth Widdville," is an open screen of iron gilt in the form of a pair of gates between two towers, the whole curiously and beautifully wrought in Gothic tabernacle-work. The body of Henry VI. was first buried in the abbey of Chertsey, in Surrey, but was afterwards removed to St. George's Chapel, and deposited in the south aisle of the choir.

6. ST. GEORGE'S HALL, WINDSOR. . . . . "

THE magnficent banqueting-room in Windsor Castle, called St. George's Hall, is two hundred feet long, thirty-four feet wide, and thirty-two feet high. The length of the original hall has been much increased, by throwing into it a second apartment, formerly used as a chapel, and divided from the hall by a gallery. Verrio, employed by Charles II., painted the walls and ceiling, on which he represented English kings and statesmen, partly in Roman costume celebrating a Roman triumph, partly as allegorical and mythological characters; and when he had completed his absurd work, with no less absurdity and still greater presumption inscribed over the tribune at the top of the hall :—" Antonius Verrio, Neapolitanus, non ignobili stripe natus, ad honorem Dei, augustissimi Regis Caroli Secundi, et Sancti Georgii, molem hanc felicissima manu decoravit " (Antonio Verrio, born of a race not ignoble, to the honour of God, the most august king Charles II., and St. George, decorated this structure with a most felicitous hand). St. George's Hall, however, has since been entirely purified from these productions of false taste and vanity. It is lighted by a range of tall pointed-arch windows in the south wall, while corresponding Gothic recesses in the north wall contain portraits of the sovereigns of England from James I. to the present time; the walls are wrought in Gothic panels of dark-coloured oak; the ceiling is adorned with the armorial bearings of all the Knights of the Garter, from the institution of the Order to the present time; and heraldic insignia, borne in shields, of some of the more early Knights, are placed on the walls between the windows and the recesses. St. George's Hall, as it appears at present, not only from its vast length, but for the simplicity, propriety, and richness of its decorations, ranks as one of the most splendid apartments in Europe.

7. HALL IN OCKWELLS MANOR-HOUSE . . . .

THE old manor-house of Ockwells is situated about one mile westward from Bray, in Berkshire. It is one of those mansions built chiefly of timber framework, of which many yet remain in England, some of them almost as large as palaces and little less magnificent, picturesque without, with their bay windows and ornamental gables, and rich in timber-roofs, oak panelling, and carved furniture, within. Sixty or seventy years ago a large part of Ockwells manor-house was burnt down. Of the part which remains, now converted into a farm-house, the gables are striking and richly carved. The panelling of the hall and the fine oriel window divided by mullions into six lights yet remain, but the timber roof has been covered up and formed into a flat ceiling. The upper windows are still filled with the original painted glass. The mansion was built by John Norreys, lord of the manor of Ockholt in the parish of Bray, who in 1465 left a considerable sum by will for the completion of the building. The paintings in the windows consist of coats of arms of the Norreys family, and of those of Henry VI., Margaret of Anjou, the abbot of Westminster, Beaufort duke of Somerset, Edmund last earl of March, Henry duke of Warwick, De la Pole duke of Suffolk, and other noble and distinguished persons.

8. WHITEHALL CHAPEL . . . . "

THE interior of the Banqueting House, Whitehall, has been used as a place of worship, under the name of Whitehall Chapel, ever since the reign of George I. The Banqueting House, which was begun by Inigo Jones in 1619, and completed in about two years, was almost the only part of Whitehall Palace which escaped destruction by the fire which occurred in 1698. The loftiness of the exterior, the boldly projecting cornices and window-mouldings, the half-columns, pilasters, and wreaths of fruit and foliage, altogether produce an effect in the highest degree rich and picturesque, and render it one of the most beautiful of the public buildings of London. The interior (the gallery built for the use of the Household Troops having been removed a few years ago) now appears worthy of the exterior—the room, of vast size and noble proportions, being seen in all its original magnificence. A handsome gallery runs along the two sides; the organ-gallery and organ are over the door. The great attraction of Whitehall Chapel is the ceiling, painted in oil by Rubens, in 1630, for Charles I. It is divided into nine compartments; the largest, of an oval form, in the centre, representing the apotheosis of James I., and two others, of a square form, exhibiting James I. as protector of peace, and as seated on his throne, appointing Charles I. as his successor. In the side compartments are genii, who are loading carriages with corn and fruits: the carriages are drawn by lions and other animals. All the figures are of colossal dimensions. Like most large paintings on ceilings, they are somewhat heavy in effect and oppressive to examine; but the colouring is very brilliant, harmonious, and rich.

14. KING'S COLLEGE CHAPEL, CAMBRIDGE . . . . "

THE Chapel of King's College, Cambridge, is one of the finest specimens in the kingdom of the later or perpendicular English architecture. The exterior is noble, but the interior presents a combination of magnificence and beauty almost without a parallel. The foundation-stone was laid in September, 1447, in the reign of Henry VI., but the building was not completed till July, 1515, in the reign of Henry VIII. The agreement for the painted windows was not made till 1526, and the screen and part of the stalls were not erected till 1534. The name of the architect was Cloos, or Close, whose son Nicholas Cloos became a Fellow of King's College in 1443, and Bishop of Lichfield in 1452. The entire length of the Chapel inside is 291 feet, the breadth 45½ feet, and the height 78 feet. The roof is a vast canopy of stone wrought into the most exquisitely delicate tracery, the key-stones forming large and beautiful pendents in the centre, from which the ribs of the arches, with their accompanying tracery, radiate in all directions. The chapel is lighted from the sides by twenty-four Gothic windows, each of which is nearly fifty feet high, and is filled with the most brilliant painted glass, representing Scripture subjects, the designs of which are so excellent that they have been ascribed to Julio Romano, who was living at the time when they were executed. The great east window is also filled with painted glass; the great west window alone is plain. The glass of the whole of these beautiful windows is now (1845) undergoing a complete cleaning and burnishing, each window being taken out in succession for the purpose. The altar-piece is a beautiful painting of the Taking down from the Cross, purchased as the production of Ricciarelli (Daniele di Volterra), but which has been ascribed to Raphael. A screen of curiously-carved Gothic tabernacle-work, surmounted by the organ and organ-loft, about the middle of the chapel, separates the ante-chapel from the choir. The carved stonework of the ante-chapel is exquisitely rich, but the pannelling of the stalls and the tabernacle-work of the choir are not in equally good taste, and do not harmonize well with the style of the rest of the chapel.

15. CHAPEL OF ST. JOHN'S COLLEGE, CAMBRIDGE . . . .

Between pages 268 and 269

THE chapel is one of the original structures of St. John's College, the foundation-charter of which is dated April 9, 1511; it forms a part of the east court, or first court, which was completed in 1516, and which then constituted the college. The entire length of the chapel is 120 feet, the breadth 27 feet; and it is divided into a chapel and ante-chapel by the organ-gallery, in which an excellent new organ has been set up. The chapel only is shown in our coloured wood-engraving. A new roof has been recently constructed, the timber framework of which is plain, but appropriate and handsome. The stalls are of Gothic tabernacle-work elaborately carved; a new brass eagle-desk is greatly admired; and indeed the fitting up of the chapel is altogether in the best taste. The east window is of elegant design, and the painted glass with which it is filled produces great richness of effect. The altar-piece, painted by Sir Robert Ker Porter, represents John the Baptist preaching in the wilderness; the commanding figure of the preacher and the deep attention of the hearers are very impressively exhibited. In the ante-chapel are some ancient tombs: that of Archdeacon Ashton, an early benefactor, is much mutilated: he is represented in his robes, with a skeleton beneath him; and the tomb exhibits also the quaint emblem of his name—an ash upon a tun. Choral service is performed on the evenings of Saturday and Sunday, and on the mornings of those Sundays when the sacrament is administered.

1391.—Henry VII. (From the Tomb in his Chapel at Westminster.)

1394.—Henry VII.

1392.—Henry VII. (Cotton, Caligula, B. 6.)

1395.—Great Seal of Henry VII.

1393.—Elizabeth, Queen of Henry VII. (From the Tomb in his Chapel at Westminster.)

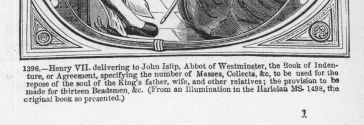

1396.—Henry VII. delivering to John Islip, Abbot of Westminster, the Book of Indenture, or Agreement, specifying the number of Masses, Collects, &c, to be used for the repose of the soul of the King's father, wife, and other relatives; the provision to be made for thirteen Beadsmen, &c. (From an Illumination in the Harleian MS. 1498, the original book so presented.)

OLD ENGLAND.

BOOK V.

THE PERIOD

FROM THE

ACCESSION OF HENRY VII. TO THE END OF THE REIGN OF ELIZABETH.

A.D. 1485—1603.

CHAPTER I.—ANTIQUITIES OF THE CROWN AND THE STATE.

 MEMORABLE period of English history is the one to which we have now arrived, for it " was that of the birth of modern policy, and that in which the foundations were laid of the still-enduring system of the European states. Nothing that was then established has been greatly shaken since: all the changes that have since taken place have been little more than the growth and development of the arrangements that were then made, and the principles that were then called into action. This reign, therefore, may be considered as the beginning of the modern history of England." (' Penny Cyclopædia.') If, therefore, that " policy " and that " system " have failed in some respects to secure what we now begin to perceive is the true end of government—the happiness of the governed, we have only to look back at the originator of both—Henry VII.—to be thankful that matters are not worse; for assuredly few men ever lived, who combined in themselves at once so much external and internal power, arising from their position and their intellect, with so little desire for the improvement or exaltation of the people, or even for their well-being in the state in which he found them, as the founder of the Tudor dynasty. Look but at his objects as we find them developed in the actions of his reign! They were first, and naturally enough, to secure himself upon the throne, which successive insurrections endangered: secondly, to erect his sovereignty into as absolute a despotism as all existing laws and customs which he respected in the letter would admit of, by all kinds of violation of their spirit: thirdly, by extracting from his subjects the last sixpence that could be wrung from them by oppressive though still legal exactions, and there ended his objects—no, we forget, there was one more. Henry, having achieved all these, set lastly to work to save his very precious soul, not by undoing all that was evil, or selfish, or unjust in his previous life, as though conscious that they were the things that put it in peril, but by provision for the due lodgment of his soul's mortal tenement in a sumptuous resting-place (Fig. 1396), and by the establishment of masses, to be said or sung daily for ever. Having succeeded in circumventing all men with whom he had had to deal in his lifetime, one could almost fancy he had practically arrived at the idea that he could circumvent God when he was about to die, and so reach heaven by his own way. And now that he has been dead for above three centuries, and that the masses have been discontinued in consequence of his own son's religious policy, for nearly as long, Henry still seems as it were to be guarding against all surprise from the powers of evil,—to be lying defended by entrenchment within entrenchment. First, there are the walls of that sacred edifice, Westminster Abbey, to be passed; then the most sacred part of that sacred edifice, the altar, interposes, beyond which Henry lies buried in his chapel; and even when that chapel is reached, there is the tomb itself (Fig. 1397), surrounded by high brazen walls, and guarded at every corner and side by saints and angels. With Henry rests his wife, Elizabeth of York, daughter of Elizabeth Woodville; and though their perishable parts have been long reduced to dust and bones, they are most worthily represented in their habits as they lived in the admirable effigies above (Figs. 1391, 1393), which with the monument forms a work of the most sumptuous and masterly character. The sculptor was Torregiano.

It would be impossible to give any sufficient idea of the power and subtlety of the mind of this extraordinary man, for, like himself, it was seldom visible, whether in life or death, but from behind a screen. Looking at his own idea of government as simply that of self-aggrandizement, it was complete, equal to all things. When Richard had to be struck down, no man of pure action could have done the thing better—more straightforwardly—more energetically: he knew well, that was no time for bribing, flattering, menacing, persuading; the adventurer for a throne that is preoccupied must strike suddenly would he strike successfully, and while men's minds are fermenting with the ideas his claim has instilled: when that subsides—routine—the every-day business and placidity of life, above all the prestige of actual sovereignty, become immoveable forces standing in his path. Bosworth was won heroically, at the imminent hazard of the adventurer's life; but once a king, never again do we find Henry repeating the same line of conduct under what he esteemed essentially different circumstances. He is always where he is wanted, knowing, guiding everything; but not where he is not wanted, in the van of the battle, risking in his person his crown and dynasty. It is a strange fact, and one calculated powerfully to show the influence of the times in which men live in moulding even the most powerful characters, that the three princes who stand out above all others as the actual impersonations of state-cunning, lived at the same time; they were Ferdinand of Spain, Louis XI. (whom Scott has made so familiar to us in his ' Quentin Durward'), and Henry VII.

With these prefatory remarks we now proceed to notice that event in Henry's reign which was the most personally important to him; which engaged his attention for several years, and must have cost him much secret anxiety and mortification; which, in a word, left him uncertain that his sovereignty might not, as during the wars of the Roses, be changed to banishment or death, within the next year, month, or week. We allude to the insurrections or invasions that had for their object the placing Perkin Warbeck on the throne, as the real son of Edward,—he who was supposed to have been murdered with his elder brother by Gloucester in the Tower, —and which followed a very similar outbreak, founded upon the claims of the nephew of Edward, the Earl of Warwick, who had been and was confined in the great state-prison at the time that a baker's son, Lambert Simnel, undertook to personate him, and so far succeeded as to induce many to support him. His pretensions, however, were put an end to by the battle of Stoke in 1487.

In the year 1494, Lord Bacon tells us in his admirable 'History of Henry VII.,' "the news came blazing and thundering over into England that the Duke of York was sure alive," the youngest of the two sons of Edward IV., supposed to have been murdered by Richard III. in the Bloody Tower. The story ran, that the eldest of the boys, Edward V., had indeed died as was reported, but that the other had been spared by the murderers, and secretly conveyed over sea; that the party who had him in charge suddenly forsook him, and that he had long wandered in divers countries before he came to the true knowledge of his royal birth, and the wrongs he had sustained. A number of the gentry and nobility of England, who considered they had great reason to be discontented with the character and government of Henry, sent over to Flanders, where Perkin was, Sir Robert Clifford, knight, "as one that had seen and known the true Richard," to inform himself and them "whether he was indeed as he seemed." Sir Robert, after seeing and conversing with the young man, asserted most positively "that this was indeed Richard Plantagenet, the true Duke of York, and that he well knew him for such." On this report, an extensive conspiracy was formed to recover the English crown for its supposed heir. But that task was not easy with a man of such consummate craft and experience as Henry VII. He undeceives his good people. He tells them who the Duke of York really is, for he too has sent out emissaries to inquire. The aspirant's name is Peterkin or Perkin Warbeck. He is a merchant's son, and a converted Jew. He was born in the Flemish city of Tournay; lived much with English merchants in Flanders; and had been recently travelling about Europe as servant to Lady Brompton, wife of an English exile. In case this version of the story fail to set all to rest, the coasts are strongly guarded, to impede the landing of enemies, or the escape of fugitives. Men's minds are greatly puzzled with these contradictory statements, and what puzzles them still more is the princely state in which the hero of this mysterious romance has been living for two years past, in Ireland, in France, and in Flanders. The king has hardly enjoyed his throne during that time, what with fears about the stranger, and anxious labours to overthrow his plans. Henry has watched his slightest movements, openly or by spies. Let us glance over the events of those two years.

It was in the beginning of May, 1492, that the so-called Duke of York first made, as it were, his public appearance, landing in the Cove of Cork from Lisbon. The place was well chosen, for Ireland had been attached with all the vehemence of her ardent nature to the house of York, since the father of Edward IV. had governed it. The citizens of Cork and their mayor warmly declared for the grandson of the well-remembered and honoured duke. The name of Richard of York rang through the greater part of Ireland. Many Irish nobles were ready to draw the sword for him; and, says the historian Speed, "he so enchanted that rude people with the charms of false hopes and mists of seemings, as he was sure of partakers in great plenty." Charles VIII. of France, hearing, and probably believing, that the Duke of York lived, gave him a royal invitation, received him in a royal manner, and caused him to be royally treated by the whole French court. "Duke Richard" had a French guard of honour to attend his person, and a princely maintenance. But such rapid ascents in the scale of fortune are not unfrequently attended by as rapid falls. Charles of France, though but twenty-three years old, and of a romantic mind and dissipated character, had not neglected the lesson his father, Louis XI., taught him so carefully in his childhood:—"The prince who could not dissemble was utterly unfit to reign over a civilized people." (Varillas.) Charles could dissemble, and was almost equal already to that brightest specimen of king-craft then on the earth—Henry VII.—with whom he, like nearly every other sovereign in Europe, was at enmity. Charles threatened to let the adventurer loose in England, backed by a French army; a threat to which he was chiefly indebted for the peace of Estaples, the conclusion of which terminated Perkin's expectations for the time in France. When Henry asked, however, the surrender to him of his enemy, Charles answered, that it would be inconsistent with his honour, as we know it was his policy. Another treaty might be wanted some day. There was plenty of hope for Perkin, notwithstanding this disappointment. Sir George Nevil, and Sir John Taylor, and about a hundred English exiles, had bound themselves to him in Paris, and his

fame in France must have induced many others to join his standard. And now whither should Richard of York go for protection and help, but to Margaret of York, his aunt, widow of Charles the Rash, Duke of Burgundy, who lived in sovereign state on the lands left her by her husband for her dower in the Netherlands?

After a studied and imposing scrutiny of his claims, she embraced him as her dear nephew, the living image of her loving brother Edward IV., exhibiting excessive joy for his miraculous preservation, and hailing him by the title by which he was known among his followers from that hour—The White Rose of England. The Flemish nobility paid him suitable honours, and he was appointed a guard of thirty halberdiers. Such is a hasty summary of the fortunes of this extraordinary personage, before the news came, as Bacon says, blazing and thundering, that he was in truth the Duke of York, lineal king of England.

And now, "the king, looking circumspectly to his matters, purposed to pacify the storms and blasts that he perceived to be growing, rather by policy and counsel than by dubious war."— (Bacon.) His dark unsocial character broke forth into momentary light and splendour. Twenty-three Knights of the Bath were created, and a gorgeous entertainment given on the occasion. On Hallow-mass, or All-Saints day, to please the people of London, Henry and his queen walked in a grand procession, wearing their crowns, and "Our Lord Harry" (the infant Henry VIII.) was shown to the admiring gaze in the arms of Lord Shrewsbury. "Our Lord Harry" is made useful in other ways; it is attempted by his means to restore his father's lost popularity. The people hope in him, who hope no more from the king. So the prince, at four years old, is made Lieutenant of Ireland, with a deputy; and this, and some other popular acts, turn the variable hearts of the Irish from the man whom they had so enthusiastically supported. The White Rose bloomed no more in Erin.

The conspiracy in England was put down by baser—we had almost said by murderous—measures: Henry set to work without favour or remorse. The false Clifford and an associate, seduced by the king's money and promises, betrayed the whole party, who relied on Clifford as their chief. The proceedings were conducted with extraordinary secrecy and prudence. The impending ruin was only felt in the fall. Many persons of note were arrested, on one day (1494), and brought to London before Henry. The startling news drove many others to sanctuary. Then the axe began its deadly work, and Henry contrived it so, that of those to whom his gracious clemency was extended, *few lived long after.*" There was one sharer in this tragedy, whose death left a peculiarly deep and ineffaceable stain on Henry's career. It was well known that to Lord Stanley, his mother's husband, he chiefly owed his crown—that to Sir William Stanley he owed his life, when Richard III. charged him so furiously at Bosworth. Yet no gratitude for these, or other important services, could prevent him from sending Sir William Stanley to the block. Stanley had nobly disdained to deny or excuse his fault, when, by the most elaborate and hypocritical contrivances, Henry had caused him to be accused by the treacherous Clifford. It was on his *own confession* the Lord Chamberlain suffered. But what was his crime after all? The worst accounts stated, he had sent Perkin money, and undertaken to establish him in England, others that he had merely said, "if he were sure Perkin was the son of Edward IV., he would never bear arms against him." We have another clue to this odious state-murder—Stanley happened unfortunately to be "the richest subject for value in the kingdom." The party of the White Rose were now, as Bacon graphically describes, "like sand without lime, ill bound together, especially as many as were English, who were at a gaze, looking strange upon one another, not knowing who was faithful to their side, but thinking that the king, what with his baits, and what with his nets, would draw them all unto him that were anything worth." To add to the adventurer's difficulties, the Flemings, suffering from an interdiction of commerce between England and Flanders, by which Henry tried to compel Philip of Burgundy to use his authority for expelling the White Rose from the dominions of his grandmother, the Duchess Dowager, began to murmur, and threaten the cause of their distress, who, thus harassed on every side, rashly resolved to risk all on one bold cast, and invade England. But Henry had prepared for such desperate attempts. A few hundred foreigners and English exiles landed near Deal, in 1495, and tried to raise the country for the invader, who waited the result at sea, with sails bent. A remnant only of these daring adherents were driven back to the sea-shore, after a sharp fight, and returned with their leader, under press of sail, to Flanders. One hundred and sixty-nine prisoners taken in the struggle were driven to London, tied together like a great team of cattle, and every man put to a miserable death.

1398.—Henry VII.'s Trial of Weights and Measures.   From Harl. Coll.

1400.—Sovereign of Henry VII.

1401.—Rose-Rial of Henry VII.

1402.—Groat of Henry VII.

1399.—Perkin Warbeck's Groat.

A silver coin supposed to have been struck by the Duchess of Burgundy for distribution among Warbeck's followers. (Drawn from the original in the British Museum.)

1403.—Half-Groat of Henry VII.

1397.—The Great Brass Screen enclosing the Altar Tomb of Henry VII. and his Queen in his Chapel at Westminster.

1404.—Penny of Henry VII.

1406.—Henry VIII. (From a Picture by Holbein in Trinity College, Cambridge.)

1405.—Henry VIII.

1407.—Henry VIII (Cotton MS. Vespasian, F. 13.)

1408.—Great Seal of Henry VIII.

1409.—Henry VIII

1410.—Henry VIII.

5

and gibbeted for "sea-marks or lighthouses to teach Perkin's people to avoid the coast, because the king thought that to punish a few for example was gentleman pay, but for rascal people, they were to be cut off, every man, especially in the beginning of an enterprise." Those who had fought for Henry at Deal were paid in rich *promises*, and in promises only. Soon after, Henry achieved the banishment of the White Rose from Flanders, by means of a "great treaty of commerce," binding Philip to prevent the duchess from assisting or harbouring the king's rebels. That done, surely Henry might repose himself. Nevertheless, he continued, to observe all his (the adventurer's) ways "with as much curiosity as was possible."

For some time a cloud no bigger than a man's hand had been hovering in the direction of Scotland, where Henry's spies would no doubt inform him that James IV. was in correspondence with the Duchess of Burgundy and her protégé. James's character was to be feared. He was very young, ardent, thoughtless, just the man to enter heart and soul into the Pretender's scheme, especially under the stimulus of indignation at the partial exposure of certain dark and treacherous plots in which Henry had engaged with some of James's most favoured subjects, to seize their master's person and place him in Henry's power. James welcomed the fugitive at his court, whither he came with his foreign adherents, Speed says a "well-appointed company," strongly recommended by the King of France and the Duchess of Burgundy. Some of James's advisers, when they heard the highly plausible account of himself set forth by the White Rose, tried to convince the king to "repute all but for a mere dream, and illusion;" the majority, however, thought far differently, and "the king was finally deceived by error, as most of others, though most prudent princes, had been before." (Andreas.) Once more then Perkin Warbeck flourished as a prince. Tournaments and great festivals were held in his honour; he was exhibited to the admiring and applauding Scottish people in a royal progress; he was addressed by James constantly as "cousin;" he received in marriage the beautiful Lady Catherine Gordon, nearly related to the House of Stuart; and a war on his behalf was commenced with the assistance of France and Burgundy. James summoned all his lieges to meet him in arms at Lauder, and when all was ready crossed the border with the White Rose, under the title of Richard IV., preceded by a declaration of war, and a proclamation by Richard, calculated to produce a striking effect. This was a crisis indeed for Henry; but he came through it with his characteristic success. To be sure, his bribed myrmidons at the Scottish court had failed in seizing Perkin at night in his tent, as they had devised, and open negotiations had been equally nugatory; but Lord Bothwell and the Earl of Buchan, and other base-hearted traitors to James among the Scottish nobility, were reporting to him every movement of the war, so that he could anticipate all, provide for all. Success for the enterprise was almost impossible amid such intrigues and treachery, aided, too, as they were by the jealousies and divisions that rent in pieces the invading army—the French quarrelling with the Flemings and Germans, and the Scots with all the foreigners alike; and by the national prejudices of the English against Warbeck's supporters, men whom they considered their natural enemies, and whose excesses on their march in Northumberland added to the bitterness of their opposition. Perkin is reported to have said, that he would rather lose the throne than gain it by the sufferings of Englishmen; but James taunted him with being over-tender to the nation which would acknowledge him neither as their king nor as their fellow-subject. All these causes, combined with the scarcity of provisions, lead to a retreat over the border without a single battle being fought, and so was the adventurer's cause lost in Scotland. How little the royal supporters of the White Rose had calculated on such a termination of the enterprise, we have evidence in the silver coin struck by the Duchess of Burgundy for distribution among his followers (Fig. 1339), and the treaty by which Richard agreed on attaining the throne to deliver to James the castle and town of Berwick, to pay fifty thousand marks in five years, and advance him a certain sum of money.

Trouble and danger pressed hard now on the adventurer. In 1497, he had to bid adieu to Scotland, for James had grown hopeless and weary of his cause, and consented to become the son-in-law of Henry. But again the subtle king failed to have his enemy surrendered to his tender mercies. With every mark of generous regret, James dismissed his friend, with an escort of horse to the seaside at Ayr, where a ship had been privately got ready, commanded by Robert Barton. The most delicate attentions had been paid to the comfort of the wanderer and his devoted wife, who left all to follow him. A few attached friends shared their miserable journey. An extract from a letter of King Henry to Sir Gilbert Talbot, in 'Ellis's Letters,' will show the sort of difficulties that lay

before them, and what was the next step in their career. "Whereas Perkin Warbeck and his wife were lately set full poorly to the sea by the King of Scots, he after landed within our land of Ireland in the wild Irisherie, where he had been taken by our cousins, the Earls of Kildare and Desmond, if he and his said wife had not secretly stolen away." Thus, Ireland having failed him a second time, Cornwall was the next and last place of refuge of the wanderers. They had been invited thither by the Cornishmen, who had promised faithfully to serve him. They were "a stout, big, and hardy race of men" chiefly poor and rude, but full of courage and manliness. Scarcely three months before, two thousand of them had fallen like heroes at Blackheath, in an insurrection to resist Henry's shameful extortions of money, on the ground of paying troops to oppose Warbeck. The blacksmith-orator of Bodmin, whose harangues stimulated that rebellion, went to the scaffold after the battle of Blackheath, cheering himself, "that yet he hoped thereby, that his name and memory should be everlasting." No common motives could have actuated that rude blacksmith; and he has obtained the renown he desired. "King Richard IV." landed at Whitsand Bay, and marched to the blacksmith's native place, where he raised an enthusiastic army, who despised death in his cause. They advanced into Devonshire, where the people joined them cautiously. The siege of Exeter was a bold, desperate, but unsuccessful attempt, in which massive gates and walls, in an admirable state of defence, were sought to be forced without artillery or engines. The strong hand and the stout heart could do much, but not accomplish impossibilities. After repeated assaults, the Cornish retired, and their Devon allies crept home, and returned to their allegiance to the wise and fortunate King Henry. What was now to be done? The adventurer saw small hope of aid in any quarter—had nowhere to lay his head in safety. Perhaps, had he followed his own judgment, he would have returned to St. Michael's Mount, where he had left his fair and unhappy wife for present security, and have bade adieu to England and all his aspiring hopes. But the unconquerable spirit of the Cornishmen urged him onwards. They told him they would die for him to a man. So on they went. The country people on their line of march wished them success, but held aloof from the dreadful hazard. At Taunton they were met by a numerous and imposing royal army, with Henry himself in the rear. There was not a shadow of hope for him in the encounter. Through the gloom of the evening, he beheld on his own side a mere handful, comparatively, of men, brave and true certainly, but scarcely clothed, and utterly unfurnished for such a war. Their sacrifice appeared inevitable. After every preparation had been made by their leader for battle, and he had ridden through the ranks with a cheerful countenance, he, in the night-time, appalled and smitten with despair, mounted a swift horse, and fled—and so sealed his ruin. In the morning, the Cornishmen, paralysed at the discovery of his desertion, surrendered. The ringleaders only were put to death. The rest were dismissed, but, poor fellows, naked and starving.

So ended the war-movements of the White Rose.

Henry immediately sent a troop of horse St. Michael's Mount, to seize the Lady Catherine, anticipating the possibility of the birth of an heir to his rival's pretensions, "in which case the business might not have ended in Perkin's person." But it proved otherwise. When brought before Henry as a captive, she blushed and wept bitterly; and well she might weep, believing, as she did, that her husband had been most deeply wronged, and dreading even worse misfortunes than those they had suffered. Already Henry's troops were surrounding the sanctuary of Beaulieu, where Perkin had taken refuge. Thither the king sent his well-instructed agents to persuade the young man to accept his pardon, which one without help or hope of course could not reject. We may judge the intense curiosity with which the king then for the first time beheld *from behind a screen* this spectre of his fears, which had haunted him seven years,—probably, in secret, longer. Henry entered London with his captive, riding in procession, but took good care the feelings of the Londoners were not unnecessarily excited by seeing the handsome hero of so many wonderful adventures treated ignominiously. He could not of course prevent the crowds who pressed to gaze, from being generally touched with respect and pity. Some six or seven months were spent by the White Rose in an honourable sort of captivity at court, until Henry had drawn from him all that was to be drawn by means of a secret commission, of which nobody heard any results calculated at all to explain the mysterious parts of the story. At last, all were to be satisfied who had ever doubted. The adventurer escaped;—*how*—probably Henry and his myrmidons knew better than their unfortunate victim, who was soon re-delivered up by the prior of the sanctuary of Sheen, on another promise of pardon

Possibly it had been hoped to have obtained possession of the fugitive without such a promise. At all events, it seems new schemes were thought necessary. The young man was compelled, probably through the influence of fear, of which he seems to have been highly susceptible, to submit to the unutterable degradation of sitting in the stocks before the door of Westminster Hall, and in Cheapside, and there reading what was stated to be a confession of his birth, connections, and the origin of his pretensions, though its contradictions and reservations were so numerous that the whole seems to have been generally disbelieved, then and since. The confession thus explained the origin of his pretensions. Having been "dressed in some clothes of silk," when he first landed at Cork, the people *took it into their heads* that he must be the son of the Duke of Clarence, the Earl of Warwick, kept a prisoner in the Tower from his childhood, or a bastard son of Richard III., or, lastly, which it was finally determined he should be, the Duke of York. By the enemies of King Henry, he was made *against his will*, to learn English, and they taught him what he should do and say. This degrading confession evidently softened Warbeck's share in the business as much as was consistent with the object. That object attained—or Henry fancied so—nothing remained but to take the life of the prisoner, for which Henry's brains were again tasked for a skilful scheme, and very skilful, it was. That troublesome Plantagenet in the Tower, the son of the Duke of Clarence, whose claims Henry could *not* throw suspicion on, might he not be cut off with Warbeck? The two cousins—if Warbeck was the son of Edward IV.—were *permitted to be together*. Warbeck won the entire friendship of the earl. Mutual misfortunes would promote mutual attachment, and talk of escaping could hardly be avoided under such circumstances. Suddenly they were accused of a plot, which it was said was discovered just in time to prevent its taking effect, and to save the governor of the Tower from being murdered, in order to get at the keys of the Tower. They were separately tried, Warwick on the *ground that he sought to make Perkin king*, by a set of judges, whose only notion of justice seemed to be the king's pleasure. Perkin perished at Tyburn in 1499; his confession was read again on the scaffold, and he declared it true; but even this, it was believed by many, might have been extorted by some peculiar threats of torture, or promises of pardon at the last moment. Warwick was beheaded on Tower Hill, and his fate added one more to the many examples that history presents of the atrocities of state *policy*.

Walpole, in his 'Historic Doubts,' maintains that Perkin Warbeck was a true prince, and even Bacon, who treated him as an impostor, says, the matter remained *almost* a mystery to his day; Henry's "showing things by pieces and dark-lights had so muffled the story." We leave the difficult question with an extract from the powerful and affecting (supposing it to be true) proclamation of Perkin, when he, "so distressed a prince," put himself into the Scottish king's hands. It was there stated, that Henry, as his extreme and mortal enemy, so soon as he had knowledge of his being alive, imagined and wrought all the subtle ways and means he could to devise his final destruction. That the said mortal enemy had not only falsely surmised him to be a feigned person, giving him nicknames, and so abusing the world, but that also, to defer and put him from entering into England, he had, offered large sums of money to corrupt the princes with whom he had been retained, and made importunate labour to certain servants about his, the said Richard's person, to murder or poison him, and others to forsake and leave his righteous quarrel, and to depart from his service, as Sir Robert Clifford and others. And thus, that every man of reason might well understand, that the said Henry needed not to have moved the aforesaid cost and importunate labour if he had been such a feigned person.

In appearance, Perkin Warbeck was eminently handsome, and in that and other traits strongly resembled Edward IV., his presumed father. His general manners were as eminently princely. Bacon observes that "with long, and continual counterfeiting, he was turned by habit almost into the thing he seemed to be," but it would seem from his immediate popularity, that when Perkin *first began* to counterfeit, he was just as princely. Old historians say that he had a "fine natural wit," and Bacon expresses a high admiration of the skill with which for so long a time he played his part. To us it seems, that his skill is less evident than his opportunities, and his conviction of his own rights. He was too tender of heart, and too alive to fear, for his mighty task. His strength failed under it. Preferring to lose the crown, rather than gain it by the sufferings of Englishmen, was not the language of an unprincipled impostor, especially under the circumstances of its utterance: for the fine spirit of humanity which prompted that remarkable expression, most likely

ruined him with the foreign adventurers, who thought to have pillaged the country at will through which they marched. Amiability seems to have been Perkin Warbeck's principal characteristic. He was enthusiastically admired and loved by thousands in all the countries where he received support. One of his earliest adherents, the mayor of Cork, died with him. James of Scotland turned into money for Warbeck not only the royal plate, but the very gold chain which he was accustomed to wear. Had the White Rose not had faithful servants constantly about him, was it likely he would have escaped assassination? The fact of his wanderings being shared, when hardly a glimmering of hope shone on his perilous path, by such a woman as Lady Catherine Gordon, who, says Bacon, "in all fortunes entirely loved" him, and that of the heir of the Duke of Clarence preferring Warbeck's claims to his own, are conclusive as to the powerful love and faith which the wanderer inspired.

The widowed Lady Catherine lived long in the court of Queen Elizabeth of York, admired for her beauty and respected for her virtues. She was popularly called "The White Rose," in memory of her ill-fated husband. She was at last re-married to Sir Matthew Cradoc, of North Wales, ancestor of the Earls of Pembroke, and was buried with him in the old church of Swansea, where still remains their tomb and epitaph.

We conclude our notice of Henry VII. with an anecdote that may show him in a somewhat less tragical, but equally characteristic aspect. "There remaineth to this day a report, that the king was on a time entertained by the Earl of Oxford (that was his principal servant both for war and peace) nobly and sumptuously, at his Castle at Henningham. And, at the king's going away, the earl's servants stood, in a seemly manner, in their livery-coats, with cognizances, ranged on both sides, and made the king a lane. The king called the earl unto him and said, 'My lord, I have heard much of your hospitality, but I see that it is greater than the speech. These handsome gentlemen and yeomen which I see on both sides of me are sure your menial servants.' The earl smiled, and said, 'It may please your grace, that were not for mine ease. They are most of them my retainers, that are come to do me service at such a time as this, and chiefly to see your grace.' The king started a little, and said, 'By my faith, my lord, I thank you for my good cheer, but I may not endure to have my laws broken in my sight; my attorney must speak with you.' And it is part of the report that the earl compounded for no less than fifteen thousand marks." (Bacon.) The earl's parade was a violation of the statute against "Liveries"—that is against great men having retainers wearing livery-coats and badges.

———

There is after all, something touching and beautiful in the constancy of the people's faith that the new sovereign will be better than the old one, no matter how bad that old one has been, no matter how fervent the love and admiration he too had once excited and so cruelly disappointed. And in that faith, however unreasoning, there is a deep wisdom, which those who can *only* pity the people's delusions, or smile at the absurdity of their expectations, would do well to study, for assuredly *their* error is infinitely greater. Whilst they seeing so deeply into the machinery of existing society, and reasoning simply from what they see there, measure the future by it; the people, on the contrary, who are less familiar with the artificialities of life, are, at all times of national excitement, only the more open to a perception of its essentials; hopeful words hover upon unaccustomed lips; there is a kind of projection of the universal heart and mind onwards into the future: the people are, in a word, obeying as by instinct what will some day be taught them as the chief duty of existence by their intellects, the law of progression or improvement; and are therefore in the main wiser and happier than those who sneer at their truthfulness, or than those who, as governors, abuse instead of justifying it, by assuming their own proper position as leaders in the great onward march. Thus it ought to be, thus yet we may hope it will be. Never perhaps has this faith been more severely tested than by the reign of Henry VIII., for the popularity in which he began his reign was no less striking than the detestation in which it closed. When his father died he was in his eighteenth year, of handsome person, frank manners, and cheerful disposition, running a little into excess, perhaps, as evident in his love of pleasure; but even that was hardly esteemed as a fault in the man who succeeded the morose, unsocial, unloving, and unloved Henry VII. The reign, too, began well in more than one respect: the young king married the woman whom the people would certainly have selected for him had the choice been in their hands, Catherine of Arragon (Fig. 1412), the young widow of Henry's brother, Arthur, who had died soon after their marriage. Another event, immediately following this, was

1411.—Henry VIII. granting the Charter to the Barber-Surgeons.

1412.—Queen Catherine. (From a Miniature by Holbein.)

1414.—Palace at Bridewell.

1416.—Trial of Catherine.

1415.—Henry VIII. Maying at Shooter's Hill.

1413.—Henry VIII. and his Council. (From Hall's Chronicle, 1548.)

1417.—The Embarkation of Henry VIII. at Dover, May 31, 1520. (From the large Print published by the Royal Society of Antiquaries, engraved after the Original Picture preserved in Hampton Court.)

1418.—The Field of the Cloth of Gold. (From the large Print published by the Royal Society of Antiquaries, engraved after the Original Picture preserved in Hampton Court.)

1419.—Henry VIII. at the Field of the Cloth of Gold.

1420.—Eltham Palace.

calculated still more to popularize the new king and government; this was the arrest and prosecution of the two favourite finance ministers of Henry, Empson and Dudley. Both were lawyers; and to serve Henry's purpose and their own, had "turned law and justice into wormwood and rapine." Never, at any other period, had the people of this country endured such infamous exactions under the authority of a royal government. Packs of spies and other myrmidons were kept in every part of the kingdom to assist these ministers to make fines and forfeitures for offences, many of which were of their own invention. "A rabble" was kept for juries, until juries were found to be better dispensed with altogether, as well as arrests by indictment: in the place of both, the officers seized by "precept," and their masters, for the purpose of extorting money, tried by commission in their own houses. Though the guilt of these men was equal, their characters differed. Dudley, who was of a good family, was remarkable for eloquence of speech, "one that could put hateful business into good language." His associate was of lower extraction, the son of a sieve-maker, "who triumphed always upon the deed done, putting off all other respects whatsoever." To save the character of the late king, their master and employer, and some others of the existing government, and to escape the disagreeable duty of restitution to the victims of the state robbers, they were condemned as traitors to Henry VIII. for a pretended conspiracy, and, after a year of misery in the Tower, executed, in accordance with numerous petitions, on Tower Hill, in 1510. Their spies and informers suffered fearfully in the storm of universal indignation and abhorrence. Many were pilloried, or exposed on wretched horses, riding the reverse way; and some were actually torn in pieces by enraged mobs.

In his sports, pageants, and general habits of life, there was a magnificence not unmingled with a sense of the poetical and the picturesque, which still further endeared the young Henry to the people of England. We can well understand with what pleasure the tales must have been told and listened to of Henry's coming into London in the habit of a yeoman of the guard, to behold the festivities of Midsummer-eve, or of his excursions into the country on May-day morning. One of the most picturesque of chroniclers, Hall, thus describes an incident of this kind, which stands in strange and refreshing contrast to the scenes of the later years of the same king's reign:—

"The king and the queen, accompanied with many lords and ladies, rode to the high ground of Shooter's Hill (Fig. 1415) to take the open air, and as they passed by the way they espied a company of tall yeomen, clothed in green, with green hoods, and bows and arrows, to the number of two hundred. Then one of them, which called himself Robin Hood, came to the king, desiring him to see his men shoot, and the king was content. Then he whistled, and all the two hundred archers shot and loosed at once; and then he whistled again, and they likewise shot again; their arrows whistled by craft of the head, so that the noise was strange and great, and much pleased the king, the queen, and all the company. All these archers were of the king's guard, and had thus apparelled themselves to make solace to the king. Then Robin Hood desired the king and queen to come into the green wood, and to see how the outlaws live. The king demanded of the queen and her ladies if they durst adventure to go into the wood with so many outlaws. Then the queen said, if it pleased him, she was content. Then the horns blew till they came to the wood under Shooter's Hill, and there was an harbour made with boughs, with a hall, and a great chamber, and an inner chamber, very well made, and covered with flowers and sweet herbs, which the king much praised. Then said Robin Hood, Sir, outlaws' breakfast is venison, and therefore you must be content with such fare as we use. Then the king departed, and his company, and Robin Hood and his men them conducted; and as they were returning there met with them two ladies in a rich chariot, drawn with five horses, and every horse had his name on his head, and on every horse sat a lady with her name written. On the first courser, called Camde, sat Humiditie, or Humide; on the second courser, called Mameon, rode Lady Vert; on the third, called Pheaton, sate Lady Vegetave; on the fourth, called Rimphom, sate Lady Pleasance; on the fifth, called Lamfran, sate Sweet Odour, and in the chair sat the Lady May, accompanied with Lady Flora, richly apparelled; and they saluted the king with divers goodly songs, and so brought him to Greenwich." (Hall.)

The young king was not unmindful of another source of popularity,—the glory, as it was esteemed, of warfare; he joined the Holy League, formed by the Pope, the Emperor, and the King of Spain, against France; and after one unsuccessful expedition, determined to go over to the Continent in person, and emulate the deeds of his ancestry. But there was then lying in the Tower one Edmund de la Pole, Earl of Suffolk, who in the reign of Henry VII. had fallen under the monarch's suspicions, fled, but ultimately been beguiled back into England and—the Tower; where, however, he was kept alive in consequence of a promise that Henry had given the King of Castile, in whose dominions Suffolk had found refuge. But even on his deathbed his pious care for his soul did not prevent him from leaving directions that this unfortunate nobleman should be put to death. Suffolk's time was now come, Henry's son and successor understood perfectly what was the real nature of the earl's guilt; it was this, his mother was a Plantagenet —the sister of Edward V., and his brother, Richard de la Pole, had entered into the service of Louis, at the same time assuming the ominous appellation of the "White Rose." It appears the council of government thought the people so strongly inclined to the house of York, that they represented to the king, that if he should die without issue, they would probably take Edmund de la Pole out of the Tower, and make him king, instead of confirming the sovereignty to Henry's sister Margaret. What was to be done then? Simply, said these hoary-headed, grave, unimpassioned men, cut off the earl's head: and it was done—without trial, or pretence of any kind of legal proceedings. Alas! the people had been used to these occasional evidences of the nature of state policy; so with a natural shudder or two, the bloody act was passed over, and forgotten; and away went Henry to the war, amidst the acclamations and songs of the people—

> The rose will into France spring,
> Almighty God him hither bring,
> And save this flower which is our king;
> This rose, this rose, this royal rose!

The result, however, hardly equalled the expectation; the chief battle fought was that of Guinegaste, in 1513, when Henry, with the assistance of the Emperor Maximilian, defeated the French; but the behaviour of the beaten army was such as to prevent the conquerors from reaping any great amount of glory. Early in the battle a panic seized the French horse, which became utterly irresistible when the mounted English archers and some German horse poured down upon them like a storm, almost as terrible for its cries of "St. George! St. George!" as for its arrowy sleet; in vain did their officers, comprising some of the bravest chivalry of France, strive to arrest, to shame them; they struck spurs into their horses and fled, leaving their leaders who did not feel inclined to participate in their unseemly haste, prisoners in the English hands. The very flower of all chivalry, the illustrious Bayard, was among these captives. Henry, in receiving them, could not help complimenting them upon the great speed their men had put into their horses, and the Frenchmen joining in the laugh, owned it had been nothing but a battle of Spurs. By that name has the engagement (Fig. 1433) been subsequently known.

Henry had evidently very little call to the fighting vocation, so the year after a treaty was concluded with Louis, by which the latter agreed to marry Henry's sister Mary. We may here add, that the French king died only three months after his marriage, when his queen married the man to whom her heart had been long secretly devoted, Charles Brandon, the king's favourite, who had been raised by Henry to the rank of Viscount Lisle, and after the murder of de la Pole, to the Dukedom of Suffolk (Fig. 1434). From that marriage sprang Lady Jane Grey's claim to the throne; she was the grand-daughter of Suffolk and Henry's sister.

But if Henry's own operations were not of a nature to rival, much less to eclipse, those of the victors of Crecy or Azincourt, there was nearer home an event taking place, under the guidance of one of his lieutenants, that was calculated to reflect the highest military splendour upon his reign.

Whilst Henry was on the Continent, there came to him, from Scotland, Lyon king of arms, bringing defiance and declaration of war from James IV., Henry's own brother-in-law (through the marriage of which we have already spoken in our notice of Perkin Warbeck). Henry quietly replied that the Earl of Surrey, who was in the marches, would know how to deal with the herald's master, and so dismissed him. The confidence in the earl was to be nobly justified. The Scottish king entered England with one of the most formidable armies that had ever invaded our country; and after some preliminary manœuvres in the besieging and taking of sundry border castles, including those of Norham and Wark, he advanced to meet the English under the Earl of Surrey, who had sent forward a challenge to fight him on the following Friday, if he dared to wait so long on English ground. James paused at Flodden Hill, an offshoot from the Cheviot, which was strongly and naturally defended by the deep river Till, a tributary of the Tweed.

running along in front, and by the steepness of its own sides. It is rather amusing to find Surrey complaining of James's good generalship in fixing himself in such an admirable position : he had " put himself into a ground more like a fortress or a camp, than any indifferent ground for battle to be tried." James, not the less, stood still. Surrey now thought it advisable to see what generalship would do for him. So turning aside, he marched towards the rear of Flodden Hill, as if intending to occupy an eminence that lay beyond, between James and Scotland. The Scotch were evidently very indignant at the movement, whatever was meant by it, so determined to interfere, and, in short, were already out-generalled from their position. Setting fire to their huts, they descended under cover of the smoke, and in dead silence—

> Nor martial shout nor minstrel tone
> Announced their march : their tread alone,
> At times the warning trumpet blown,
> At times a stifled hum,
> Told England, from his mountain throne
> King James did rushing come.
>   *Marmion.*

England, however, was quite prepared ; whilst, on the contrary, there were two among the most eminent of the council of the Scotch who doubted the prudence of the attack :—Lord Lindsay of the Byres, a rough old soldier, pointed out the great inequality of the stakes to be played for and hazarded by the two countries. Scotland might lose its king, and the best of all its chivalry : England could but lose an army and its officers, and had plenty more to put forth in their room. The answer to Lindsay was a threat to hang him at his own gate. The Earl of Angus, the terrible " Bell-the-cat " of a former day, but who was now very old, was told in reply to a similar appeal, that if he were afraid, he might go home. The veteran warrior burst into tears, and turning to go away, said, " My age renders my body of no use in battle, and my counsel is despised ; but I leave my two sons and the vassals of Douglas in the field : may old Angus's foreboding prove unfounded !" James remained unshaken, and his followers, generally, were quite determined to conquer or die for him. The armies were remarkably equal in number, containing about thirty thousand men each. The battle began on the 9th of September, and continued with varying fortunes for some time. The English ordnance at first did great execution among the Scotch, but these, making only the more haste to join close battle, the Earl of Huntly and Lord Home broke down with their forces from the left wing upon a part of the right wing of their adversaries, with irresistible impetuosity, and swept away all opposition. Whilst, however, many of their soldiers dispersed in search of plunder, the English retaliated by a similarly fierce and, after a long struggle, similarly successful charge. And so the battle went on. Charge rapidly followed charge from each side, and constantly absorbed fresh portions of the respective armies, till nearly the whole were engaged ; the leaders, however, still keeping aloof ; till at last Surrey found himself also compelled to advance, when James, who had been waiting for that movement, started forward to meet him, and so from end to end there was one vast continuous line of battle. And a more tremendous conflict has seldom excited or afflicted humanity than now ensued. And, had no particular errors been committed on one side or the other, it is impossible to say how the battle of Flodden Field might have terminated. But the selfish though brave Earl of Home, thinking his men had done and suffered enough in the outset, when desired by his colleague, the Earl of Huntly, to advance once more, replied that they had done their part, and the rest must do as well. Then, again, the Highlanders, who were on the right, being terribly galled by the English arrows, as they descended a hill, broke from all restraint and discipline, threw away their shields, and rushed upon their enemies with their broadswords and battle-axes. Confounded for a moment, the English still stood firm, and kept cool—closed every rank and square the moment it was broken, and at last, feeling as it were their way to success with these new antagonists, they began to turn back the tremendous crowd, and then themselves to advance, when the Highlanders, being unable to re-form, were cut to pieces. The battle now thickened round James's own post, as it grew evident to both sides that both he and his army were in the extremest jeopardy. And noble was the fortitude now exhibited alike by king and people—

> The English shafts in volleys hailed,
> In headlong charge their horse assailed ;
> Front, flank, and rear, the squadrons sweep,
> To break the Scottish circle deep,
> That fought around their king.

> But yet, though thick the shafts as snow,
> Though charging knights like whirlwinds go,
> Though bill-men ply the ghastly blow,
> Unbroken was the ring ;
> The stubborn spear-men still made good
> Their dark impenetrable wood,
> Each stepping where his comrade stood
> The instant that he fell.
> No thought was there of dastard flight !
> Linked in the serried phalanx tight,
> Groom fought like noble, squire like knight,
> As fearlessly and well,
> Till utter darkness closed her wing
> O'er their thin host and wounded king.
> Then skilful Surrey's sage commands
> Led back from strife his shattered bands ;
> And from the strife they drew,
> As mountain-waves from wasted lands
> Sweep back to ocean blue.
> Then did their loss his foeman know ;
> Their king, their lords, their mightiest, low ;
> They melted from the field, as snow,
> When streams are swollen and south winds blow,
> Dissolves in silent dew.
> Tweed's echoes heard the ceaseless plash,
> While many a broken band
> Disordered through her currents dash—
> To gain the Scottish land ;
> To town and tower, to down and dale,
> To tell red Flodden's dismal tale,
> And raise the universal wail.
> Tradition, legend, tune, and song,
> Shall many an age that wail prolong ;
> Still from the sire the son shall hear
> Of the stern strife, and carnage drear,
> Of Flodden's fatal field,
> Where shivered was fair Scotland's spear,
> And broken was her shield !

The body of James was found among a heap of dead, and recognised by several who knew him well. Surrey caused it to be carried to the monastery of Sheen, near Richmond, where it was interred. Many in Scotland refused to believe that James had been killed, but asserted that he had been seen alive after the battle, and that he had gone on a pilgrimage to the Holy Land. They particularly objected to the English story, on the ground of the non-production of the iron belt that James constantly wore round his body, in penance for his youthful rebellion and the death of his father. But James may have laid it aside when preparing to participate personally in the fight of Flodden : at all events, if the English did not produce the iron belt, they did show James's sword and dagger (Fig. 1435), as well as a turquois ring that had belonged to him, all of which are still carefully preserved in Heralds' College, London. The number of the dead on both sides in this terrible battle was very great ; that of the Scotch amounted to eight or nine thousand, among whom were included, beside the king and his natural son, the Archbishop of St. Andrew's, twelve earls, fifteen lords and chiefs of clans, a bishop, two abbots, a dean, and a countless host of the principal gentry of the country. " Scarce a Scottish family of eminence," says Sir Walter Scott, " but had an ancestor killed at Flodden ; and there is no province in Scotland, even at this day, where the battle is mentioned without a sensation of terror and sorrow." A greater sudden calamity perhaps never fell upon a nation than this defeat.

Another of the efforts of the time to raise England in the scale of nations, by the increase of her power for attack or defence, deserves especial mention from its bearing on the subsequent history of the country. Up to the reign of Henry VII. our navy consisted merely of vessels furnished at short notices by the Cinque Ports, or which were borrowed with or without leave from the merchant service generally. But that politic sovereign saw the importance of a navy of higher warlike capacities, and so commenced the royal navy of England by the erection of the " Great Harry." His son Henry VIII. continued what his father had begun : his direct motive, however, for so doing being to emulate Francis I., who had built the " Caracon," a vessel of one thousand tons burden, and carrying one hundred guns ; so our king must have his " Henri Grace-à-Dieu " (Fig. 1432) of equal burden, but carrying twenty-two guns more. We should strangely err if we were to liken this vessel to one of our one hundred and twenty gun ships. " Henri Grace-à-Dieu " was built more for show than use ; with the exception of thirteen, her guns were of the smallest calibre. She steered badly, rolled incessantly, and so, after making a great deal of noise in the European world, was disarmed and left to decay. The French vessel was burnt by accident at Havre. The impulse given to the movement for the creation of a royal navy was not,

1423.—Hever Castle. (From an original Sketch.)

1422.—Queen Anne Boleyn. (From a Painting by Holbein.)

1425.—Group of Christening Gifts.

1421.—Brass of Sir Thomas Bullen.

1424.—Palace at Greenwich. Returning from the Christening.

1426.—Middle Quadrangle of the Palace at Hampton Court.

1430.—Queen Anne of Cleves. (From a Painting by Holbein.)

1427.—Queen Jane Seymour. (From a Drawing by Holbein.)

1428.—Henry VIII. delivering the Bible to Cranmer and Cromwell. (Being a portion of the Engraved Title-page of Cranmer's, or The Great Bible.)

1429.—Trial of Lambert before Henry VIII. in Westminster Hall. (From a Drawing in the King's Library and some old Prints.)

however, allowed to subside into inaction; fresh ships were built; the dockyards of Deptford, Woolwich, and Portsmouth were formed; the Admiralty and Navy Boards were organized. By the end of the reign of Elizabeth the royal navy numbered forty-two ships. James I. surpassed all his predecessors in one respect; he built the largest of all ships up to his own time, called the Prince. Another distinguished ship was that erected in the following reign, the "Sovereign of the Seas" (Fig. 1431), which was one hundred and twenty-eight feet long and forty-eight feet broad, and carried one hundred and six guns.

Turning from these records of military and naval proceedings, let us follow the victor of Flodden Field into the council-chamber (Fig. 1413), that we may obtain some insight into the civil government of Henry, and make acquaintance with some of the more eminent men there seated in debate, and who, a few years later, were to be the chief actors in one of the most extraordinary series of events that English annals record. During the earlier years of the reign, Surrey, as Lord Treasurer, and Fox, Bishop of Winchester, had struggled for supremacy as the adviser of royalty; but the latter, finding he was losing ground, hoped, it seems, by placing one in his interests in the office of king's almoner, to strengthen his own power, and counteract that of Surrey. The man chosen was Wolsey, dean of Lincoln, then in the prime of life, recommended by courtly and fascinating manners, and only wanting opportunity to achieve that public greatness to which his ardent ambition aspired. Let us take a brief glance at his previous career. Thomas Wolsey was born at Ipswich, in Suffolk, 1471. His father, Robert Wolsey, is said to have been a butcher, and certainly was an obscure person, but possessed of sufficient means to afford his son an early preparatory education, and then to send him to the university of Oxford. His talents must have been precociously developed, for he graduated at fifteen, and thus gained the honourable name of the Boy Bachelor. For some years after that, his progress was sure, though slow: he became fellow of his college, received ordination, and taught the grammar-school adjoining Magdalen College. Three sons of the Marquis of Dorset were among his pupils, and it was from the marquis that, at the age of twenty-nine, he received his first clerical appointment to the living of Lymington, in Somersetshire. His character at Lymington was not quite in harmony with his holy vocation. It is said that he was once drunk at a neighbouring fair, and that Sir Amias Poulet confined him in the stocks for this irregularity. Whether this was the true cause or not, Wolsey certainly suffered that degradation, and in after days revenged himself for it on Sir Amias Poulet. But, notwithstanding, the priest of Lymington seems to have been on the whole a gifted, sagacious, and attractive person. One of the valuable friends he gained was Sir John Nafont, a Somersetshire gentleman, who held the office of treasurer of Calais. Being sick and old, Sir John made Wolsey his deputy, and rendered him more substantial service by introducing him to Henry VII. Wolsey became king's chaplain. The first decided proof he gave of his high abilities and usefulness for a king's service, was his rapid comprehension of the imperfectly-expressed instructions of Henry VII. in reference to negotiations for a marriage, and the rapidity of his movements in making the requisite journey to Flanders, when rapidity was of great importance to the king: Wolsey had actually returned before his master knew that he was gone; so that had Henry VII. lived much longer, Wolsey would probably have ascended in his favour as he ascended in the favour of Henry's son and successor, though not to so high a point; for, whilst Wolsey had little beyond the knowledge of state-craft (deemed indispensable in those days, and, unhappily, not altogether renounced in ours) in common with the one, all his tastes and habits strikingly harmonized with the tastes and habits of the other. And Wolsey was not a man to hide his light under a bushel, to allow such a gracious master as Henry to remain ignorant of the existence of such a useful servant as the dean of York, who, it appears, thus summed up the relative duties of king and minister:—"The king should hawk and hunt, and, as much as him list, use nonest recreations. If so be he should at any time desire suddenly to become an old man by intermeddling in old men's cares, he should not want those (meaning himself) that would in the evening, *in one or two words*, relate the effect of a *whole day's consultation*." Yes, Wolsey was the very man the pleasure-loving king needed; to pass "like another Mercury," in the words of an old writer, "between this our Jove and the senate of the lesser gods." Henry was as little disposed to the business of the state "as a wild ox to be yoked to the plough," and Wolsey gave up his capacious intellect and energetic powers entirely to its performance, and went on through a series of years, gradually absorbing all power to himself, until he was more completely at

the head of all the interests of the kingdom of every kind than was its sovereign.

Within the first year of Henry's reign, the favourite rose from plain Almoner to *Lord* Almoner, and received gifts of valuable lands and houses in St. Bride's parish, Fleet Street, that had been forfeited by Empson. Every year for the next seven years added to his preferments and to his wealth. In 1510 he was rector of Torrington; in 1511, canon of Windsor, and Registrar of the Order of the Garter; in 1512, prebendary of York; in 1513, dean of York and bishop of Tournay in Flanders; in 1514, bishop of Lincoln and archbishop of York; in 1515, cardinal and chancellor of England; and in 1516, Legate-à-latere, an extraordinary dignity received from the pope, which gave the last finish to his greatness, by making him nearly as mighty as a pope over the clergy of England.

His wealth, from all these sources, was truly prodigious; and it was augmented from the dioceses of Bath, Worcester, and Hereford, which he held for foreign prelates, allowing them fixed stipends far below the annual proceeds collected. Then he held in commendam the rich abbey of St. Albans, and had stipends from the kings of France and Spain, and the doge of Venice. All which revenues formed collectely an income more vast than has ever been enjoyed by any subject of England before or since. At one time it fully equalled the crown revenue. The residences of the great cardinal were of course numerous—attached to his several preferments. The principal one was York Place (Fig. 1439), afterwards called Whitehall, an extensive palace, that had been for centuries a seat of the prelates of York, and which was furnished with every luxury by Wolsey. But he desired to build himself a more original and magnificent abode, that should outvie every palace in the kingdom. So the manor-house of Hampton Court was removed, and near it the palace of Hampton Court soon grew into stately height and breadth. It was on a design of such largeness, utility, and magnificence, as none but a Wolsey could have ventured to conceive or execute. The highly-ornamented buildings, all of brick, were to be disposed in *five* courts. The interior arrangements comprehended no less than two hundred and eighty beds for visitors of rank.

Of the edifice thus built by Wolsey, and which was enlarged by Henry VIII. afterwards, there remain the chapel, the great hall, and various chambers and domestic offices (Fig. 1426). The remainder of the pile is of later date, and chiefly of William III.'s erection. The household of the cardinal was truly royal. From five to eight hundred persons were engaged in his service, including fifteen knights and forty squires. He numbered many persons of rank among these, as, for instance, the Earl of Derby and Lord Henry Percy: but such persons seem generally to have been the "beggared descendants of proud barons." His steward was always a dean or a priest; his treasurer, a knight; his comptroller, an esquire; and his master-cook wore daily "damask, satin, or velvet, with a chain of gold about his neck." His gentleman-usher was Cavendish, his biographer. The cardinal held a levee every morning early, after a short mass, at which he appeared clad all in red. When he went forth, it was in great state (Fig. 1443). As a priest, he rode on a mule, but that touch of professional humility was contradicted with the greatest care in the trappings of the animal, in his own attire, and by the number and appearance of his retinue. The saddle and saddle-cloth were of costly crimson velvet, the stirrups of silver gilt. His fine portly figure was exhibited in silk and satin robes of the richest possible texture, and the finest scarlet or crimson dye. Sables of great price covered his shoulders; gloves of red silk his hands; and his very shoes were of silver gilt, *inlaid with pearls and diamonds*. He was immediately preceded by two priests, tall, and as handsome men as could be found, to carry two ponderous silver crosses; before the priests went two gentlemen, each bearing a silver staff; before these, a person of rank bore his cardinal's hat (Fig. 1436); and foremost of all rode a pursuivant-at-arms, with a massive mace of silver gilt. Other officers, with spearmen, &c., swelled his train, riding on fine coursers, highly trained and richly caparisoned. Before such displays, those of the proudest churchman of the former days, Thomas-à-Becket, sink to insignificance. But if we would see Wolsey in the full orb and blaze of his magnificence, we must view him in the far-famed Field of the Cloth of Gold (Figs. 1418, 1419); for his was the presiding mind of that costly and gorgeous affair.

There were at the time three powerful, spirited, and popular princes in Europe, of varying degrees of ability—the Archduke Charles, Francis, and our Henry. What a notion does it not give us of the cardinal's power, to find him in effect the mainspring of the movements of all! It was after having experienced the peculiar inconvenience of having offended Wolsey, and after having by secret means, that may be readily guessed at, effected a reconciliation with him, that Francis entered into a treaty of alliance with Henry, which was presently followed by a proposal for a meeting between them, and an appointment for the purpose. It was postponed in consequence of the death of the Emperor Maximilian, when all the three kings we have named became rivals for his crown, which falling to Charles, by far the greatest of the three, gave occasion for the noble saying of Francis, that "in ambition, as in love, a discarded suitor ought never to cherish resentment." That affair over, and the three kings to appearance on amicable terms, the summer of 1520 was fixed for the gay and splendid journey to France. The English court had removed from Greenwich to Canterbury, then in all its ecclesiastical pride and splendour; and the court was on the eve of embarkation, when the Emperor Charles most unexpectedly anchored at Hythe, having arrived on the pretext of visiting Queen Catherine, his aunt, but in reality to win over his "most dear friend" the Cardinal not to injure his interests in the negotiations that were about to ensue between Francis and Henry. Wolsey went out of Canterbury with a train of gentlemen and nobles, and in his barge met the emperor on the water. They landed together under a canopy of gold and embroidery, beneath the symbol of the black eagle of Germany. The conference of the Emperor and the Cardinal cost the former some magnificent presents, a promise of his influence to make Wolsey pope, and an appearance of reverence for and submission to Wolsey's judgment, not usual with crowned arguers. The result of that conference was esteemed by the Emperor worth its price; of such potency was Wolsey's influence in all the state business of the time. Charles's errand was done; but he stayed four days, to make a show of conferring with the king, who spent the greater part of one night conversing with him in Dover Castle; to visit his aunt, the Queen at Canterbury, outside of which Wolsey again met him, Charles riding by Henry's side,—the Cardinal at the head of a grand procession of the clergy; and, lastly, to make his offerings at the shrine of Thomas-à-Becket, that shrine of which it is said gold was the meanest thing about it, situated in a cathedral of which we are told that every part "was enlightened with the lustre of most precious stones,"and " abounded with more than royal treasures." The day of the Emperor's departure was that of the embarkation at Dover of Henry and his whole court (Fig. 1417), who on the 4th of June, 1530, arrived at the lordship royal of Guisnes, the place selected for the joyous meeting. The arrangements for the accommodation of so many illustrious persons, the etiquette that should be observed, the disposal of time, and the conduct of the festivities, had not been adjusted without long and anxious deliberations. Wolsey was the life and soul of the whole business; to him everything was confided by both monarchs, Francis thereby intending to pay the Cardinal a delicate kind of compliment, that must, however, have fallen but flatly in comparison with that secret promise of the popedom, of Francis's rival the Emperor. The two sovereigns could not have done better. Wolsey lavished so much poetic fancy on the pageant, that he might have been nothing but a romantic dreamer of fairy-land all his life, instead of one who wielded the destinies of nations. Let us approach the temporary lodging provided for the English court. On the green plain (Fig. 1418) stands a fountain, gilded with find gold; there is a statue of the jolly god, Bacchus, carousing: of the wine, which flows freely by conduits, white, red, and claret, all people are invited to drink. Read those golden letters over his head—" Faicte bonne chere quy voudra." Near Bacchus, we have another device: Cupid, on a gold-wreathed column, supported on four lions. The arrow is in the bow, the string is drawn ready " to strike the young people to love." Bacchus and Cupid ornament the entrance to a kind of fairy palace, an extraordinary production for such a temporary purpose. Eleven hundred workmen, chiefly cunning artificers from Flanders or Holland, have been employed on it; part of the framework was made in England. It is " set on stages, by great cunning and sumptuous work." It encloses square courts and divers fountains, being in form a vast quadrangle, each side of which is one hundred and twenty-eight feet long. In one particular we have a characteristic specimen of Henry's invention; a wild man, with bow and arrows, conspicuous in front of the palace, with a Latin motto underneath, " He whom I support prevails." Imagery abounds in every part. Round about the great tower, in the windows, and on the battlements, appear men of war ready to cast great stones, and figures of ancient princes, " Hercules, Alexander, and the like." The exterior covering of the palace is sail-cloth painted like squared stone; the interior is hung with the richest arras. The numerous apartments include state-rooms and a chapel,

which form the most resplendent parts of the whole; their very walls gleaming with jewelled embroidery; their altar and tables loaded with plate. The pavilion provided for Francis, and the lesser tents by its side (whose ropes were of blue silk twisted with gold of Cyprus), appear to have been even more remarkable for imaginative design. The exterior of the pavilion presented to the eye a vast dome covered all over with cloth of gold, stretched out by ropes and tackle, and sustained by a mighty mass. The interior hollow of this dome *imitated the firmament* by means of azure velvet, and "craft of colours," and stars in gold-foil. The destruction of these gay tents was premature; they were laid " all in the dirt " by a tempestuous wind, and the French monarch was therefore obliged to lodge in an old castle near the town of Ardres, during the fortnight the gaieties lasted. The first two days the Cardinal riveted all eyes upon himself, while arranging a treaty with Francis, as Henry's high ambassador. He

> The articles of the combination drew
> As himself pleased, and they were ratified
> As he cried, Thus let be.

He was highly entertained by Francis; and the French " made books, showing the triumphant doings of the Cardinal's royalty; as, of the number of his gentlemen, knights, and lords, all in crimson velvet, with marvellous number of chains of gold, the multitude of horses, mules, coursers, and carriages that went before him with sumpters and coffers—his great silver crosses and pillars—his embroidered cushions—and his host of servants, as yeomen and grooms all clad in scarlet."

After the treaty came the meeting of the two kings, in the valley of Andren; thus described by Hall, who was present at it: " Then the king of England showed himself some little forward in beauty and personage (Fig. 419), the most goodliest prince that ever reigned over the realm of England: his grace was apparelled in a garment of cloth-of-silver damask, ribbed with cloth of gold, so thick as might be; the garment was large, and plaited very thick . . . of such shape and making that it was marvellous to behold. . . . Then up blew the trumpets, sackbuts, clarions, and all other minstrels on both sides, and the kings descended down toward the bottom of the valley of Andren, in sight of both the nations, and on horseback met and embraced. 'My dear brother and cousin' said the French king, 'thus far to my pain have I travelled to see you personally. I think verily that you esteem me as I am, and that I am not unworthy to be your aid. The *realms and seigniories in my possession demonstrate the extent of my power.*' Henry replied, ' Neither your realms nor other the places of your power are a matter of my regard, but the steadfastness and loyal keeping of promises comprised in charters between you and me. I never saw prince with my eyes that might of my heart be more beloved; and for your love have I passed the seas into the farthest frontier of my kingdoms to see you." Then " the two kings alighted, and after embraced with benign and courteous manner each to other, with sweet and goodly words of greeting." After a banquet in a gorgeous tent, " and spice and wine given to the Frenchman, ipocras was chief drink of plenty to all that would drink." The next scene of excitement was the camp, an enclosure nine hundred feet long and three hundred broad, surrounded by broad moats, and, partially, by the galleries and scaffolds for the two queens and the court ladies. In the midst of this enclosure was an artificial mount, on which a hawthorn-tree for England, and a raspberry-tree for France, seemed to grow with interlaced stems and branches. The shield of Henry, bearing the arms of England within the garter, was hung on one tree; the shield of Francis on the other, bearing the arms of France within a collar of the order of St. Michael. To that mount the two kings rode side by side, attended by noble gentlemen, and armed to defend the field against all comers, as brothers-in-arms, according to a proclamation that had been sounded abroad in all the chief cities of Europe for months before. Their tents, richly adorned, stood at the entrance to the camp, and two cellars close at hand were stored with wine, as free to all men as water. The ladies who sat as spectators were most brilliantly attired, especially the Queen Catherine, whose very foot-cloth was powdered with pearls. The splendid equipments of the nobles were such, that many Frenchmen are said to have carried their estates on their backs, and many, both French and English, were ruined by the expense they incurred. Six days were spent in tilting with lances, two in tourneys with the broadsword on horseback, and two in fighting on foot at the barriers. The feats of the warriors were registered in a book; but these would not seem to have been very formidable, since the kings, who fought five battles each day, invariably came off victorious! The English sport of wrestling engaged an humbler sort of combatants. Henry, however,

1434.—Duke of Suffolk.

1431—Sovereign of the Seas.

433.—Battle of the Spurs. (From the ancient Picture in the possession of the Royal Society of Antiquaries.

1435.—Sword and Dagger of James IV., and Two Knights' Banners, used at the Battle of Flodden Field.

1432.—Henri Grace à-Dieu. (From a Picture in Greenwich Hospital.)

16

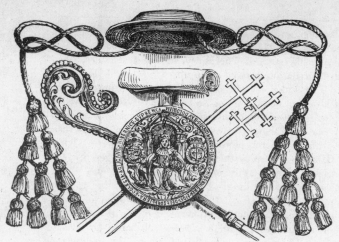

1436.—Cardinal's Hat, &c.

1437.—Cardinal Wolsey.

1438.—Chancellor's Costume.

1439.—York Place.

1440.—Duke of Buckingham

1641.—Westminster Hall; Buckingham embarking for the Tower

1442.—Street near Westminster Abbey; Coronation of Anne Boleyn.

himself challenged his brother of France to try a fall with him, and caught hold of his collar. Francis, being very agile, threw his grace. Henry then rose and demanded revenge, but the gentlemen standing by wisely interposed. A pleasing anecdote is told of Francis; who, perceiving that the English were partially labouring under distrust of the French, which marred their free enjoyment of the sports and festivities, early one morning left his castle, unknown to his court, taking with him only a page and two gentlemen. Thus comparatively unprotected, he entered Henry's tent, and said sportively to Henry, who was in bed, that he was now his (Henry's) prisoner. Henry, thanking him, arose, and threw a splendid collar over his neck. Francis gave in return a rich bracelet, and, with the most graceful familiarity, proceeded to perform the duty of a valet, assisting his grace of England to dress, warming his shirt, spreading out his hose, and trussing his points. Then Francis, remounting his horse, rode back to Ardres; near which he met some of his court, and his faithful and plain-speaking friend, Fleuranges, who addressed him bluntly, "Sir, I am right glad to see you back again, but let me tell you, my master, that you were a fool to do the thing you have done; and ill luck betide those who advised you to it!" "And that was nobody," said Francis, gaily; "the thought was all my own, and could have come from no other head." After that proof of sincerity from Francis, the best feeling seemed to prevail on all sides; and the golden time closed with a rapid succession of banquets and balls, and maskings and mummings, in which the kings and the ladies performed their parts. "But pleasures must have their intermission—and kings, if not by their greatness, are by their affairs severed." Thus Francis returned towards Paris; and Henry, after visiting the Emperor of Germany, to London; which he and his court reached "all safe in body, but empty in purse." When all the excitement of the show had passed away, the painful consideration of its expense caused many complaints. Among the dissatisfied was one whose character and fate form a tragical and interesting episode of the reign of Henry; or, what was for many years the same thing, of the period of Wolsey's power.

Edward Stafford, Duke of Buckingham (Fig. 1440), one day held the basin to the king for him to wash his hands; when his majesty had done, Cardinal Wolsey dipped his hands immediately in the same water, which the duke, "disdaining to debase himself to the service of a priest," managed to shed in his shoes. The Cardinal, understanding the import of the action, for indeed this was not the only evidence Buckingham had given of a desire to lower his arrogance, made a threat, well remembered afterwards, that he would sit on the duke's skirts. The king, also, secretly hated Stafford. "Being yet a child," says the Bishop of Hereford, "I have heard ancient men say, that by his bravery of apparel and sumptuous feasts, he exasperated the king; with whom, in these things, he seemed to contend." Like his father, Henry VIII. could partake of his nobles' generous hospitality while he sought the most convenient way to ruin them. Stafford, entertaining the king at his splendid seat at Penshurst, little dreamed that his wealth and popularity, and the large number of his retainers, there made visible to the royal eyes, were regarded as so many capital offences. His frank, sincere, hearty nature would nave disdained to surmise that he could be an object of jealousy and suspicion, where the greatest affection was pretended, and where every disposition was apparent to advance him to the highest offices of the state: (Stafford was the last Lord High Constable of England.) His danger, as a son of that Duke of Buckingham (Richard III.'s friend and victim), whose personal claims to the crown as a Beaufort had stood next to those of Henry of Richmond, seems scarcely to have caused Stafford an anxious thought: otherwise policy would have taught him to beware of rendering himself conspicuous; much less of presuming to cast a reflection on the king's absolute wisdom in the matter of the expense created for his nobles, to the ruin of many of them, by the Field of the Cloth of Gold. He took no warning from the summons to the Star Chamber of Sir William Bulmer, who had left the king's service to enter into his, and where for that change of service, he was compelled to beg pardon on his knees as for a "serious crime." That was a very significant sign of the coming storm: but though it irritated the duke, he was far from comprehending its portentous character as regarded himself. Immediately before or after his own seizure, secret arrests took place of his chancellor, confessor, steward, and a friar Hopkins, a prophet with whom the duke had been in communication, after the fashion of those credulous times, during about eight years. The friar had first won the duke's faith by his successful prophecies that Henry would return safe from the French war, and that if the King of Scots crossed the borders he would surely die. The prospects of the duke and his family had, of course, engaged friar Hopkins's

particular attention, and it seems he had hinted that the duke's son would succeed Henry VIII. on the throne.

Stafford was at his estate of Thornbury, in Gloucestershire, when an unexpected invitation arrived from the king to the Court at Greenwich. The duke set out on this his last journey without the remotest idea that he was going to his death. Having reached Windsor, he lodged there one night; and his fears were first excited by observing that three knights, who had followed him on the road to Windsor, with a "secret power of men-at-arms" were "lying close by." His eyes were farther opened to his danger, by the marked disrespect of a creature of the court, one Thomas Ward, gentleman-harbinger to the king. Suspense, fear, and indignation spoiled his appetite for breakfast in the morning, for we are told "his meat would not down." Mounting his horse, he rode with his treacherous guard as far as Westminster, where he took barge for Greenwich, which it was not intended he should reach. In passing the "bridge" (a jetty or quay) at York House, Stafford landed with four or five servants, and desired to speak with "my Lord Cardinal." Wolsey declined to see him on the plea of indisposition. "Well," said the unfortunate duke, "yet will I drink of my lord's wine as I pass." One of the cardinal's gentlemen then conducted him with much reverence into the cellar, where the duke drank; but seeing that "no cheer to him was made," he changed colour and departed. A little farther down the river, his barge was hailed and boarded by Sir Henry Marney, captain of the body-guard, who was attended by a company of yeomen of the guard. Sir Henry arrested him as a traitor, in the king's name; took him on shore, and conducted him through Thames-street to the Tower, amidst universal astonishment and regret, for no man was more beloved. The secret processes that were then in constant use in the Tower for torturing the body, and by this means, and also by threats and bribery, breaking down the mind, were, it is more than probable, applied to the duke's servants freely, until they were ready to say whatever was required of them. On the 13th of May, Stafford was brought before a body of peers, chosen by the king and the Duke of Norfolk, as High Steward; and charged with tempting friar Hopkins to make traitorous prophecies, by means of messages and personal conferences;—tampering with the king's servants and yeomen of the guard by means of presents and promises;—with saying, when reprimanded for retaining Sir William Bulmer, that if his arrest had been ordered, he would have plunged his dagger into the king's heart;—and with declaring his determination after Henry's death, to cut off the heads of the lord cardinal and some others and seize the government. To these charges Buckingham at first contented himself with replying, that, were all proved, as there had been no overt act, there could be no treason. But he was informed by the chief justice that he was mistaken: merely imagining the death of the king constituted sufficient treason; and words sufficient evidence. Stafford then made a complete defence; repelling charge by charge, denying every particular of guilt, and demanding to be confronted with his accusers; they were brought, and the sight of them must have given the duke the keenest anguish: they were Hopkins, De la Court, his confessor, Perk, his chancellor, and Sir Charles Knevitt, his own cousin, and formerly his steward; who all performed the parts assigned to them; and thus, in the words of the Shaksperian scene of Buckingham's condemnation (described in a conversation between two gentlemen in a street near Westminster-hall), "Both," says the duke, alluding to his own and his father's fate,

> Fell by our servants, by those men we loved most.

The Duke of Norfolk (Fig. 1449) (formerly Earl of Surrey), the victor of Flodden Field, pronounced sentence; and,

> Albeit unused to the melting mood,
> Dropped tears as fast as the Arabian trees
> Their medicinal gums.

"My Lord of Norfolk," said Stafford, when he had finished, "you have said to me as a traitor should be said unto; but I was never none. Still, my lords, I nothing malign you for that you have done unto me: may the eternal God forgive you my death as I do. *I shall never sue to the king for life*: howbeit, he is a gracious prince, and more grace may come from him than I desire. I desire you, my lords, and all my fellows, to pray for me."

On leaving Westminster-Hall, the axe was borne before the duke with the edge toward him. At the water-side his own barge was ready (Fig. 1441) to convey him to the Tower. Sir Thomas Lovel respectfully requested him to take his customary seat on the cushions and carpet; but he declined, saying, bitterly, "When I came to Westminster I was Duke of Buckingham, but now I am nothing but Edward Stafford, the poorest wretch alive." Three days intervened between his trial and appearance on the scaffold on Tower-hill. He persisted to the last in his refusal to implore the king's mercy ; and died amid the groans and lamentations of the people, whose feelings at the event are expressed in the exclamations of one of the gentlemen in the play—

> O, this is full of pity! Sir, it calls,
> I fear, too many curses on their heads
> That were the authors

And thus passed on the course of public business in England during the first eighteen years of the reign of Henry VIII.; and if the period were not a very glorious one for the sovereign, it was at all events sufficiently pleasant to him ; and, on the whole, appears to have been, at the same time, a peaceable and prosperous one for the people. Up to the year 1527 not a cloud was perceptible upon the horizon that might suggest even to the keenest sighted of observers the coming tempest: the chief elements of which, the king's own passions, were as yet comparatively unknown in their true character and tendencies, having been untried by temptation and difficulty, and therefore kept within decorous bounds. But before the close of that year, the temptation and the difficulty came ; —the passions were let loose—to prey, not only upon their owner, or upon all that he himself had most loved and favoured, but upon the country that was placed beneath his charge. England has had many a fiery ordeal to go through, many a blow to recover from, that has steeped her to " the very lips " in misery and degradation, but it may be doubted whether she ever suffered so much as during the last few years of the reign of Henry VIII.: when government became a thing of the executioner and the shambles, and religion a stalking-horse for the most shameless licentiousness ; when to be known as a good man was the sure step to ruin ; and when, in a word, there was no way open to those who had the misfortune to be born to, or who had achieved distinction, but that of participating in all the tyrant's cruelties and baseness, or of swelling themselves the number of his victims. It is true that out of the monstrous mass of evil one good arose—the Reformation ; although every sincere Protestant must feel in his heart a kind of regret that it did not happen at any other period of English history ; for one more calculated to stain a great and glorious principle it would be impossible to find.

About the time we have mentioned a young lady returned from France, who had gone thither some years before in the retinue of Henry's sister, Mary. She was the daughter of Sir Thomas Boleyn or Bullen, and Lady Elizabeth Howard ; and no doubt possessed, in a very eminent degree, those personal attractions, and that fascination of manner, which were calculated to arrest the attention of the king, who appears to have become immediately and deeply enamoured of her. One noticeable proof of the earnestness of his passion is the sensitiveness of perception it called forth in him—lover-like. Among the lady's admirers *he* is said to have been the first to discover her favourite, namely, the Lord Percy, son of the Earl of Northumberland. Wolsey, in whose family the young nobleman had been brought up, soon removed this difficulty. Percy was sent into the country, and forced into another marriage, and Anne was consoled by finding that she had only exchanged a noble for a kingly lover.

It would be gratifying to be able to think that Henry's religious scruples on the subject of his previous marriage with Katherine —his eldest brother's widow—were of an earlier date than the existence of this passion ; but unhappily his statements to that effect are not to be trusted in opposition to his deeds, which show that, during the whole process of the divorce, he was constantly communicating with her who was to take Katherine's place, when that tedious but momentous event should be consummated. Anne Bullen behaved throughout the whole affair with the utmost prudence. She had determined to be the king's wife, not his mistress : and from that determination ensued events, the importance of which, in relation to the destinies of the country, it is hardly possible to overrate. Hever Castle (Fig. 1423), Kent, was the family residence of the Bullens ; and there Anne Bullen chiefly resided during the period in question ; and there, according to tradition, the bugle-horn was often heard sounding from the top of a neighbouring hill—Henry's announcement to his lady-love of his approach. A regular correspondence by letter was also kept up ; and some of the king's epistles are still preserved in the library of the Vatican.

The first step taken for the attainment of a divorce was an application to the Court of Rome in 1527, the very year when Anne

Bullen is supposed to have returned from the Continent. For two years did the legal proceedings then drag their slow length along, and in that very delay, and the consequent presumed coolness of the head of the Romish Church, it is probable we must look for one of the causes of Henry's appearance before the world in a character of all others the most unsuitable to him, that of a religious reformer ; and to make the whole business more ludicrous, a reformer in the path of the man—Luther—whom he had some years before stepped forth to attack in a Latin treatise on the Seven Sacraments, and with such success—so at least the Pope said—that the title of Defender of the Faith was bestowed on Henry VIII., in token of the Papal approbation. The simple clue to this marvellous change, and the still more marvellous conduct that followed, is to be found in the fact, that the actual queen was a sincere and ardent Catholic, whilst her rival was understood to be disposed towards the new views ; in consequence, there was a gradual concentration around the one of the friends of the Protestant cause, met by a similar congregation round the other, of the supporters of the old religion.

The day so long anxiously looked for came at last, the 21st of June, 1529, and the king (then residing in the ancient palace of Bridewell, Fig. 1414), the queen, and the principal courtiers, assembled within the hall of the Black Friars, for the trial of the legality of the royal marriage (Fig. 1415) ;—Wolsey and Campeggio, the Papal Legate, sitting as judges ; Henry on their right hand, Katherine, with four friendly bishops, on their left. The king's name was called, and he answered, Here! The queen's was similarly uttered, but found no response. The citation was repeated, when the unhappy lady, rising in great agitation, crossed herself devoutly, as if soliciting the protection of Heaven, and then throwing herself at Henry's feet, appealed to him in the most moving language. " Sir, I you beseech, for all the love that hath been between us, and for the love of God, let me have justice and right ; take of me some pity and compassion, for I am a poor woman and a stranger, born out of your dominions. I have here no assured friend, much less impartial counsel, and I flee to you as to the head of justice within this realm. Alas, Sir! wherein have I offended you, or on what occasion given you displeasure . . . . that you should put me from you? I take God and all the world to witness that I have been to you a true, humble, and obedient wife ; ever conformable to your will and pleasure. Never have I said or done aught contrary thereto, being always well pleased and contented with all things wherein you had delight or dalliance, whether it were in little or much ; neither did I ever grudge in word or countenance, or show a visage or spark of discontent." She reminded him that for *twenty years* she had been his true wife ; that their parents, who determined the union, were amongst the wisest of princes ; that she cannot but be wrongly dealt with, since she has only such advice as he assigns to her ; and in fine, she entreats, " in the way of charity, and for the love of God, to spare her the extreme power of the court, until she may advise with her friends in Spain ; and if he will not extend to her so much impartial favour, why, let his will be fulfilled : she commends her cause to God." And therewith, to the astonishment of every one, Katherine, with a low obeisance to the king, walks hastily out of the hall.

The business, however, proceeded ; but in a few days it became evident that neither of the cardinal judges had much love for the vocation, and one of them, Campeggio, adjourned the court. The disappointment was so keen, that Henry's brother-in-law, the Duke of Suffolk, struck the table passionately with his fist, exclaiming— " Never did cardinal bring good to England." Wolsey stung by the brutal insult to his brother commissioner, as well as himself, forgetting everything for the moment but his natural and generous feelings, answered Suffolk with great dignity and force. These few words probably sealed Wolsey's ruin. Anne Bullen and her friends already suspected him of lukewarmness in their cause ; Suffolk joined with them heart and soul ; and it was not long before the results were made evident to the nation at large. Henry set out on a progress ; and men wondered to hear that the all-powerful minister was left behind. Wolsey rode after the court, was received by the king with his old familiarity, at Grafton, in Northamptonshire, and again, it appeared, the cardinal was safe ; but on the following morning he was ordered to London, and never more saw his master. Some time after, on proceeding to the Court of Chancery, he found he was to be subject to the law, instead of, as of old, engaged in administering it ; bills being filed against him by the attorney-general, for having exercised the function of Papal legate : that he had done so with the approbation of Henry and the Parliament, mattered nothing to either, when the former wanted to destroy him. Wolsey perceived his danger, and strove to save himself by sub-

1443.—Wolsey and his Suite.

1446.—Leicester Abbey.

1444.—Henry and Anne sending Dr. Butts with token of favour to the sick Cardinal.

1445.—Wolsey surrendering the Great Seal.

1448.—Wolsey's Tower, Esher.

1447.—Ruins of Leicester Abbey.

1449.—Thomas Howard, Duke of Norfolk.

1450.—Gardiner.

1451.—Henry Howard, Earl of Surrey.

1452.—Sir T. More.

1453.—Family of Sir T. More. (From Holbein.)

1454.—Queen Katherine Howard. (From a Painting by Vander Werff.)

1455.—Cranmer.

1456.—Queen Katherine Parr. (From a Painting by Holbein.)

21

mission. On condition of retaining his ecclesiastical rank and preferment, he gave up all his personal estates, valued at half a million of crowns; that was something, but Henry wanted more. So the Dukes of Suffolk and Norfolk came to him at York Place, and told him the king was coming to live there, and that he must confine himself to his house at Esher (Fig. 1448). Any thing more? Yes, he must surrender the great seal (Fig. 1445). "My lords," said Wolsey, with spirit, "the great seal of England was delivered to me by the hands of my sovereign; I hold it by his majesty's letters patent, which along with it have conferred on me the office of chancellor, to be enjoyed during my life; and I may not deliver it at the single word of any lord, unless you can show me your commission." The commission was speedily obtained, and Wolsey almost as speedily sank under his misfortunes.

One gleam of hope burst upon him. Henry, hearing that a slow fever was upon him, and that he was dying, relented for a moment, and sent his favourite physician, Butts, to him (Fig. 1444), with kind words and gifts, which wonderfully restored Wolsey. But it was no more than a gleam, and the cardinal's prospects were immediately after as gloomy as ever. He was left at Esher, for a time, in such a state that he could hardly command the necessaries of life. And when he removed from Esher (Fig. 1448), and travelled towards York, and began to regain by his manners much of the popularity he had lost, he was suddenly stricken to the heart by an arrest for treason. On his way to London, as a prisoner, he died, as has been already described [Vol. i. p. 295], at Leicester Abbey (Figs. 1446, 1447).

Cranmer (Fig. 1445) now rose into power, and upon the same question that had caused Wolsey's fall, but by taking the opposite side. As the last evidently was inclined to move only so far as Rome would sanction his every step, the first began with the bold advice to consider the marriage by reference to the Bible—the English divines—the English universities—in short, to any thing, or any body rather than the Pope. That was the very thing for Henry. Cranmer was sent for, and employed at first in endeavouring to persuade the Pope of the propriety of the divorce, and, when that failed, set to work to carry out his own views. In 1531 an English convention declared Henry the One Protector of the Church (thus virtually destroying the Papal supremacy), and his marriage with Katherine contrary to the law of God. In 1533 Cranmer was made Archbishop of Canterbury, and, in the same year, Anne Bullen obtained the object of her long-cherished desire—the throne, by a private marriage with the king, afterwards publicly confirmed at Lambeth by Cranmer. Her coronation (Fig. 1442) took place on the 1st of June, 1533.

Thus Anne Bullen was at last Queen of England, and Katherine deposed. At first all things smiled upon the beautiful and light-hearted woman who now presided over the domestic arrangements of the court. A daughter—Elizabeth—was born; and loud and long were the congratulations, magnificent the feastings and processions of the christening (Fig. 1425). But ere three years had passed, the poisoned chalice that Anne had been instrumental in offering to the late queen, was commended to her own lips, under circumstances a thousand times more terrible. Katherine died in the beginning of 1536, and within six months after, Queen Anne Bullen, who in the pride of her heart had said, on hearing of Katherine's death, "she was now indeed a queen," discovered that, as she had supplanted her royal mistress, so was she about to be supplanted by one of *her* maids of honour. It is said that the premature birth of a son was brought on by discovering some unseemly familiarity between Henry and Lady Jane Seymour; and the death of that son in consequence completed her ruin.

There was a grand tilting-match in Greenwich Park, on May-day, 1536, and Henry and Queen Anne were present. Suddenly the king rose, and departed to London, with six attendants only. The principal challengers in the sport were Viscount Rochford, the queen's brother, and Henry Norris, one of the grooms of the stole, who, it soon afterwards appeared, were marked out for destruction with the queen. Anne waited at Greenwich in fearful suspense till the next day, when she was met on the water, by her uncle Norfolk, Audley the Chancellor, and Cromwell, and arrested for adultery. She fell on her knees, exclaiming wildly—"O Lord, help me! as I am guiltless of that whereof I am charged." The Tower received her—that gloomy entrance to the realms of death: and she was confined in the chamber where she had slept the night before her coronation. Here again, falling on her knees, she cried, "Jesus have mercy on me!" and wept and laughed convulsively—"Wherefore am I here, Mr. Kingston?"—she then asked of the lieutenant of the Tower. "When saw you the king? where is my sweet brother?" and hardly waiting for a reply, broke into

the pathetic exclamation—"Oh, my mother, thou wilt die of sorrow!" Fully aware of her terrible position, she afterwards exclaimed—and her words were soon verified—"I shall die without justice!" Kingston, the servile tool of Henry, had the impudence to reply, "There was justice for the meanest subject in England;" at which Anne laughed loudly, half, probably, in delirium, half in mockery, of the justice that the lieutenant talked of. She knew, none better, what justice Katherine had received; and that knowledge told her every thing as to the treatment she would experience herself. The usual crafty and treacherous means were taken to entrap her into saying something that could criminate her; but, in extenuation of such levities with the courtiers, as it is said she acknowledged (if they were not in great part the invention of her foes), it must be remembered that she had been used to French manners. There is a tone of innocence that appeals strongly to the heart in the well-known letter Anne wrote from her "doleful prison" to Henry:—"Try me, good king," she supplicates, "but let me have a lawful trial, and let not my sworn enemies sit as my accusers and judges; yea, let me receive an open trial; for my truth shall fear no open shames. . . . . But if you have already determined of me, and that not only my death, but an infamous slander, must bring you the enjoyment of your desired happiness, then I desire of God that he will pardon your great sin . . . . and that he will not call you to a strict account of your unprincely and cruel usage of me, at his general judgment-seat. . . . . My last and only request shall be, that myself may only bear the burden of your grace's displeasure, and that it may not touch the innocent souls of those poor gentlemen, who, as I understand, are likewise in strait imprisonment for my sake. If ever I have found favour in your sight—if ever the name of Anne Bullen hath been pleasing in your ears—then let me obtain this request." We scarcely need say, Henry paid no regard to the letter. Anne's judges were chosen by him; and they proved worthy his choice: the brave peers of England, with Norfolk at their head, did not blench from their horrid task. Norfolk had wept when he sentenced Buckingham, but he had sat on other murderous tribunals since then, and grown used to the "bloody business:" we hear of no tears when he doomed his young and beautiful niece to infamy and a scaffold.

As all records of the trial were carefully destroyed soon after—a significant fact—we shall not attempt to enter into any of its revolting and utterly untrustworthy details, which were only gained by bribery or torture. We are told by an old writer, who is supported by all Protestant authors of the time, that "having an excellent quick wit, and being a ready speaker, she did so answer to all objections that, had the peers given in their verdict according to the expectation of the assembly, she had been acquitted." The day after Anne's condemnation, the lieutenant of the Tower wrote to Cromwell:—"This day at dinner the queen said that she should go to Antwerp, and is in hope of life;" but that hope was of short duration, and interrupted by fits of anguish and despair, and delirious levity.

The third day after her trial she sent for the lieutenant of the Tower, early in the morning, to speak in Cranmer's presence of her innocence. After that she sent for him a second time, and said—"Mr. Kingston, I hear say I shall not die before noon, and I am very sorry there for; for I thought to be dead by this time, and past my pain." Kingston replied—"That it should be no pain, it was so subtle." "I heard say the executioner was very good, and I have a little neck," said Anne, putting her hands about it, and laughing heartily. On Cranmer devolved the melancholy task of preparing the half-insane victim for death. It is pitiable to see this eminent man, through fear of his own destruction, participating in deeds so abhorrent to common sense and humanity. When the tyrant's influence could make such men his instruments, can we wonder that a feminine spirit, whose only strength was its sensibility, should be darkened and perverted by it even in its last agony? In her address to the nobility and city companies, admitted to witness her execution, she says—"*A gentler or more merciful prince was there never;*" and "to me he was ever a good, gentle and sovereign lord." After this sad mockery she submitted to her fate, repeating, "Christ have mercy on my soul! Lord Jesus receive my soul!" until, with one skilful stroke of the axe, the executioner of Calais severed that fair small neck, and Anne Bullen was no more. And how did this gentle, merciful prince, await the news of her death? In solitude was he? or in tears? Neither. But, certainly, he was anxious and impatient, because he was waiting to begin a jovial hunt in Epping Forest. At last he heard the signal-gun. Up then started he. "Ah! it is done! the business is done! Uncouple the dogs, and let us follow the sport." He returned in the evening, gay; and next morning married Jane Seymour (Fig. 1427). She had not time to grow out of his liking, for she died within little more than a twelvemonth, after giving birth to a son, subsequently Edward VI. Anne of Cleves (Fig. 1454) succeeded Jane Seymour; and not suiting her royal husband, was put away with her head safe on her neck in six months after her marriage. That union, however, mainly caused the ruin of the minister, Cromwell, who had planned it—so he went to the block instead. Next came the Lady Katherine Howard (Fig. 1454), with whom Henry remained content for two years, and then he beheaded her, on the charge of adultery. Lastly, in the following year, he married Katherine Parr (Fig. 1456), widow of Lord Latimer, who, after one very narrow escape, survived him.

We return now to the extraordinary series of events connected with the religious history of the reign, which, beginning with the single desire to put away a wife that he was tired of, ended in Henry's all but putting away the religion that had been for so many centuries established in this country. The refusal of the papal government to sanction Katherine's divorce, and its promulgation of the annulment of that divorce, when the English churchmen, with Cranmer at their head, did so divorce her, completed the schism between the English and the Roman governments; and measure after measure was framed by Henry and his parliament, under the guidance of Cromwell (who had been Wolsey's secretary), to destroy every vestige of the old connexion. One of these was the oath of supremacy, which declared the King the head of the Church. Another was the dissolution of the monasteries, chiefly carried into effect by Cromwell. A third was the virtual introduction of Protestantism by the dissemination of the Scriptures in the popular version. (Fig. 1428.) And every one of these measures had its own peculiar series of victims.

The two new statutes, which made it high treason for an Englishman to deny that the king was in all respects a fit and proper person to preside over the whole spiritual Church of England, or that his marriage with his good queen's maid of honour was perfectly lawful and right, though they filled dungeons and scaffolds, and made the year 1535 hideous with a series of murders of the eminent and the excellent—yet brought forth some good out of their manifold evils: for, by applying the touchstone to the moral truth of such men as Fisher and More, who embraced death rather than consent to either statute, they have been the means of enriching our annals with the histories of martyrs for truth's sake, who will command admiration as long as those annals exist.

The classical Erasmus thus describes the happy household of the author of the Utopia, from which the master-spirit was removed without the shadow of a crime, to endure a lingering confinement of thirteen months in the Tower of London:—" With him (Sir Thomas) you might imagine yourself in the academy of Plato. But I should do injustice to his house by comparing it to the academy of Plato, where numbers and geometrical figures, and sometimes moral virtues, were the subjects of discussion: it would be more just to call it a school and an exercise of the Christian religion. All its inhabitants, male and female, applied their leisure to liberal studies and profitable reading, although piety was their first care. No wrangling, no angry word, was heard in it; no one was idle; every one did his duty with alacrity, and not without a temperate cheerfulness." Holbein, in his way, has made this happy family scarcely less familiar to us than Erasmus in his (see our Engraving, Fig. 1453). More (Fig. 1452) had a fellow-sufferer in the Tower—the excellent Fisher, Bishop of Rochester—who also refused to bend his conscience to the King's will, in respect to the statutes. Deeply affecting is it to read More's own statements (made in reply to interrogatories put to him after Fisher's death) of the "divers scrolls and letters" that passed between them, by means of a poor man, called George, the lieutenant's servant, "whereof the most part contained nothing else but comfort, and words from either to other, and declaration of the state that they were in, in their bodies, and giving of thanks for such meat or drink that the one had sent to the other." It would seem that the bishop more often received than sent the "comfort" and the "meat and drink;" for his heartless keepers left him deficient even of the merest necessaries, although he was near fourscore years old, and in sickness and pain. The chancellor was treated with equal severity, and denied at last even the books and writing materials with which he had relieved his solitude. But the filial heroism of his married daughter, Margaret Roper, aided by others of his family and friends, mitigated in some considerable respects the hardships imposed on him, and, probably, enabled him to lighten also those of his fellow-prisoner. In June, 1535, that fellow-prisoner was tried and condemned as a traitor, for saying the king could not be the head of the Church. If Henry's destructive appetite might have brooked a short pause, he had been saved the

odium of thus rudely thrusting into the grave an old man, who was already verging upon it by the process of natural decay; and who had been the friend of his father, and of his grandmother, the Countess of Richmond, by whose dying breath he had been recommended as a good and wise counsellor for her inexperienced grandson. But Henry was dead to all grateful remembrance: the most sacred obligations were of no weight with him, while possessed with the fierce thirst of blood. His savageness rises almost to sublimity when he exclaims, on hearing that Pope Paul III. had sent the imprisoned bishop a cardinal's hat—"Ha! Paul may send him the hat—I will take care that he have never a head to wear it on." Very soon, indeed, that head, with its reverend white hairs, was seen set up over London Bridge, and, with exquisite brutality, the face turned towards the Kentish Hills, where his best years had been spent, whilst the mutilated body of this ancient friend of the king's family —this accomplished restorer of ancient learning, whose excellence as a Christian priest was almost without a spot—was exposed naked to the vulgar gaze, and then buried in Barking churchyard, coffinless and shroudless. More was yet left in the Tower dungeons, none of whose terrors could make him to himself untrue. His sharpest trial was doubtless the entreaties of his afflicted family, and especially of his beloved daughter, Margaret, who wrote to him letters of vehement tenderness to induce him to save himself by bending to the king's will; but he only replied by exhorting her to patience, and desiring her to pray for him. His last letter to her was written with a piece of charcoal, and he had no paper but a few scraps left in his way by some unknown hand. How gloriously the firm and cheerful mind of the Christian philospher triumphed over all this anguish and privation, is shown in a letter that he sent forth from his prison, to open, if possible, the hearts and minds of his foes towards him. In it he says—"I pray for his highness, and all his, and all the realm. *I do nothing harm; I say no harm; I think none harm; and wish everybody good: and if this be not enough to keep a man alive, in good faith I long not to live.* I am dying already; and, since I came here, have been divers times in the case that I thought to die within one hour. And, I thank our Lord, I was never sorry for it, but rather sorry when I saw the pang past; and, therefore, my poor body is at the king's pleasure. Would to God my death might do him good!" His trial came. Dressed in a coarse woollen gown, instead of the usual Chancellor's robes (Fig. 1438)— looking the mere wreck of his former self—with hair grown white, and frame bowed and weakened by long confinement, so that he was obliged to support himself on a staff, and with countenance pale and wasted, he stood in that Hall of Westminster where he had formerly presided as judge. The contrast between his accustomed and present state, and his altered aspect, strongly stirred the sympathies of the audience. His intellect, it was soon perceived, had lost nothing of its high powers. Though his eye was hollow, it sparkled still with vivacity; the music of his eloquence was still such as to be dreaded by his predetermined judges, and his moral intrepity was unshaken by all that he had suffered, and all he had to dread. Pardon was offered on condition of his doing the king's will. More declined it. The tedious verbiage of the indictments did not confuse him; but, when they had been read, he exposed the false pretences on which they were based. Neither by word nor deed had he done anything against the king's marriage with Anne Bullen; he had, indeed, disapproved of it, but he had never expressed this disapprobation except to the king, who had commanded him on his allegiance to give his real opinion. All he had done in regard to the king's supremacy over the church, was to be silent thereon, and silence was not treason. So argued More, who, having been judge and chancellor, thought he knew the law; but the judges had a different reading of it; they affirmed that silence *was* treason, and sentenced him accordingly. More then a second time addressed the court, after being twice rudely prevented. Casting aside all reservations, all fears, all hopes, he burst out with the electrifying words, that what he had hitherto concealed he would now openly declare—the oath of supremacy was utterly unlawful! He regretted to differ from the noble lords whom he saw on the bench, but his conscience would not permit him to do otherwise. He had no animosity against them; and he hoped that; even as St. Paul was present and consented to the death of Stephen, and yet was afterwards a companion saint in heaven, so they and he should all meet together hereafter. "And so," he concluded, "may God preserve you all, and especially my lord the king, and send him good counsel." His son had been present at the trial; and, as More left the bar, rushed through the hall, fell on his knees, and begged his blessing. A still more affecting interruption took place as More was walking through the streets of London back to the Tower, the axe borne before him, and officers and halberdiers surrounding him. The dismal procession had reached

1457.—Old Trinity House. (From a Print in Pennant's Collection.)

1458.—Bramber Castle.

1459.—Naworth Castle.

1460.—Sandown Castle, near Deal.—One of Henry VIII.'s Fortresses.

1461.—George (Gold) Noble of Henry VIII.

1462.—Gold Crown of Henry VIII.

1463.—Gold Half-Crown of Henry VIII.

1464.—Shilling of Henry VIII.

1465.—Wolsey's Groat.

1466.—Wolsey's Half-Groat.

1467.—Penny of Henry VIII.

24

1468.—Edward VI. (From a Painting by Holbein.)

1469.—Great Seal of Edward VI.

1470.—Edward VI. and his Council. (From a Woodcut on the Title to the Acts of Parliament, 1551.)

1473.—Old Somerset House.

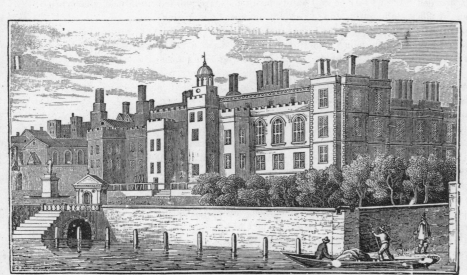

1474.—Old Somerset House

1471.—Statue of Edward VI.

1472.—Edward VI. (Cotton MS. Vespasian, F. 3.)

1475.—Edward VI.

the Tower wharf, when Margaret Rope pressed through the armed throng, and hung, sobbing, on his neck. Her father tried to console her. He blessed her, and the last agonizing farewell was said, and he was once more moving on, when again she burst through the guard, again clasped his neck and wept. More, too, then wept, repeating his blessing and pious consolation. The unutterable pathos of the scene melted guards and people: the former could with difficulty nerve themselves to divide the father and daughter. But divided they were. More had then done with this life, and with a cheerful spirit prepared to enter on the next. The witty sayings recorded of him in his last hours, we have seen somewhere found fault with, as unbecoming an occasion so awful. To More there was no awfulness about it. He was full of the happiest anticipations of the great change; and was too truthful to affect a formality and gloom foreign to his natural character. When he heard that the king had mercifully commuted the hanging, drawing, and quartering, into simple decapitation—"God preserve all my friends from such royal favours!" exclaimed he. The framework of the scaffold being weak, some fears were expressed lest it might break down. "Mr. lieutenant," said Sir Thomas, "see me safe up; and for my coming down, let me shift for myself." When the executioner asked pardon, More said to him, "Friend, thou wilt render me to-day the greatest service in the power of man; but my neck is very short; take heed, therefore, that thou strike not awry, for the sake of the credit of thy profession." Not being permitted to address the spectators, he simply declared that he died a faithful subject and a true Catholic: then after prayer, quietly laid his head on the block, saying, with a smile, as he bade the headsman hold his hand until he removed his beard— "My beard has never committed any treason." Thus he died. And what said the English nation—that nation ever famous for its hatred of tyranny in all its forms—to these detestable murders? One would expect that nobles and commoners would have risen as one man to remove Henry from the throne that he was no more fitted to enjoy than a mere wild animal, whose furious passions he emulated. But no: England permitted the monster to go on perpetrating many more such murders. Such was the effect of extreme dread. Echoes, however, of suppressed murmurs, could not be entirely shut out from palace walls; and these added to the restlessness and disquiet that ever haunted the tyrant. From abroad, there came to him still louder and more potential voices of rebuke—from Rome, from Germany, from France. No desire of amicable alliance with him could prevent Charles and Francis from speaking out. The former sent for Sir Thomas Elliott, the English ambassador, and said to him, "My lord ambassador, we understand that your master has put to death his faithful servant and grave and wise counsellor, Sir Thomas More." Elliott replied that he had heard nothing of it. "Well," said Charles, "it is but too true; and this will we say, that if we had been master of such a servant, of whose abilities ourself have had these many years no small experience, we would rather have lost the best city in our dominions than so worthy a counsellor."

The English ambassador at the French court also heard of the matter in severe terms; and Francis told him that his master should banish, not take the lives of, such offenders. And no doubt he would have been glad to have given More a welcome in his own dominions. Henry, greatly incensed, replied they had suffered by due course of law: that they were worthy of a ten times more terrible death; and if they had a thousand lives, all were forfeited. Thus, through foreign countries, Henry must have half anticipated the opinions of posterity on his crimes. What he thought and felt upon the matter, we may learn with tolerable certainty from his anxiety to prevent those opinions from spreading in England; as was shown by his interdicting all communication with foreigners. Erasmus, in a letter to a friend, in the August of this year, says, that "the English were living in such a state of terror that they could not write to foreigners or receive letters from them."

If the victims of another of the great events of the reign—the dissolution of monasteries, begun in 1535 by the energetic Cromwell, and all but completed by 1540—comprised no names so illustrious as that of the author of the 'Utopia,' they were fearfully numerous; and the measure involved a lamentable amount of social disorganization. We speak not simply of the effects of the dissolution on the monasteries concerned, but also of the effects on the people of England at large, which, though less outwardly apparent, were scarcely less potent. Hosts of poor men and women had been accustomed to look up to the monks as their natural friends and protectors, and to congregate around the religious houses from which they obtained supplies of food, and which were also their hospitals, infirmaries, and dispensaries. When the monks were dispersed, and the monasteries broken up, a terrible amount of suffering must have been the inevitable consequence; for not only were

the poor thus suddenly deprived of their accustomed resources, but their numbers were greatly swelled by the addition to their ranks of those who had formerly been their benefactors. And if we cannot on the whole regret that monastic institutions were abolished, we can still acknowledge the existence, and lament the fate of the many excellent men that they fostered. It is worthy of note, that amongst this order alone do we find any considerable number of men who had at once the principle and the courage to oppose the brutal tyrant who occupied the throne. We shall not here add to the horrors that the reign has already forced upon our attention, any notice of the sufferings and heroism of the monks during the dissolution of their houses, for we could not give a more striking example than the fate and conduct of the brethren of the Charter House (described in the previous volume, page 371). We confine ourselves therefore here to an equally characteristic, though less tragical evidence, that the monks and friars still possessed something of the old spirit of self-devotion.

When Henry had married and crowned Anne Bullen in defiance of the church of Rome, and when men, though anticipating—and generally in great alarm—further and more decided exhibitions of opposition to the papal ascendancy, were still too much awed to speak out their opinions of that marriage, and the disgraceful treatment that Katherine had received, there was one "simple man" of the order of Observants, Friar Peto by name, who dared to beard the lion in his very den, namely, the palace chapel at Greenwich, where he preached before the king. He chose for his theme 1 Kings, c. 22, the latter part of the story of Ahab, reading, "Even where the dogs licked the blood of Naboth, even there shall the dogs lick *thy* blood also, O king." Then he proceeded to speak of the lying prophets which abused the king; and continued—"I am Micheas (Micaiah) whom thou wilt hate, because I must tell thee truly that this marriage is unlawful; and I know I shall eat the bread of affliction and drink the water of sorrow: yet, because our Lord hath put it into my mouth, I must speak of it." Henry bore this quietly. Next Sunday Dr. Curwen preached in the same place, and gave Peto many ill names, saying that no subject should speak so audaciously to princes; and after much more that was calculated to please the king, broke out with, "I speak to thee, Peto, which makest thyself Micheas, that thou mayest speak evil of kings; but now thou art not to be found, being fled for fear and shame, as being unable to answer my arguments." It was true, Peto was not present, but a brother friar of the same house, called Elstow, was; who, standing up in the rood-loft, with all Peto's boldness, exclaimed, "Good Sir, you know well that Father Peto, as he was commanded, is gone to a provincial council holden at Canterbury, and not fled for fear of you, for to-morrow he will return again. In the mean time I am here, as another Micheas, and will lay down my life to prove all those things true which he hath taught out of the Holy Scriptures; and to this combat I challenge thee before God and all equal judges: even unto thee, Curwen, I say it, which art one of the four hundred prophets into whom the spirit of lying is entered, and seekest by adultery to establish succession, betraying the king unto endless perdition, more for thine own vain-glory and hope of promotion than for the discharge of thy clogged conscience, and the king's salvation." Henry's own voice of thunder bade the daring speaker hold his peace. Next day both the friars were brought before the council, and severely rebuked. The Earl of Essex told them that they deserved to be put into a sack and thrown into the Thames. Elstow smilingly replied, "Threaten these things to rich and dainty folk which are clothed in purple, and fare deliciously, and have their chiefest hope in this world! for *we* heed them not, but are joyful that for the discharge of our duties we are driven hence; and, thanks to God, we know the way to heaven to be as ready by water as by land, and therefore care not which way we go." Dr. Curwen was made a bishop; the friars—it is rather remarkable—were permitted to live in the banishment which they shared with all of their order.

The victims of the third great movement of the reign, the introduction of Protestantism,—or what in course of time ended in Protestantism,—it might have been supposed would have been few in number: since it was the king and his ministers who were constantly accelerating that movement in their own way. But no: Henry was as impartial as he was fantastic in his cruelty; and so, Protestants and Catholics were seen on the same hurdle going to execution: the one for denying or opposing the king's supremacy, as the head of the Catholic Church, and the other for denying or opposing what happened to be the king's doctrinal views for the moment;—both therefore on religious grounds. Well might the foreigner exclaim, who beheld the spectacle which appalled and might have instructed both parties, "Good God! how do people make a shift to live here, when papists are hanged, and anti-papists are burnt!" As to the Protestants, it is clear that their persecution went on with the greatest severity just when the measures of government were most directly calculated to promote the final establishment of their views. Thus the year 1538 witnessed the setting up in the churches generally throughout the kingdom, of copies of the newly-translated Bible, and the tuition of the people, in English, of the Lord's Prayer, the Creed, and Commandments; the same year also witnessed the memorable trial of Lambert, a schoolmaster, previously a priest, for his disbelief of the Real Presence. Henry presided in person at the trial in Westminster Hall (Fig. 1429), robed in white silk; and *Cranmer* was also engaged in it. Cranmer, who but shortly after, in fact as soon as he safely could, publicly avowed the same opinions as Lambert, was now put in peril; for the Bishop of Chichester, in opening the business, made a remarkable statement, which furnishes decisive evidence of Henry's utter want of devotion to any other system of religion than that which his own superstition, cupidity, wilfulness, and reckless passions, had built up, and his determination that while he reigned, his subjects' religion should be compounded of similar or equally worthless materials. The bishop said that Lambert had appealed to the king, who, in consequence, was inclined to credit a report that many credulous people were persuaded that he had embraced the tenets recently put forth in Germany. It was true, continued the bishop, that the king had shaken off the intolerable yoke of Rome, had expelled the monks from their monasteries, who were no better than drones in the bee-hive, had abolished the idolatrous worship of images, and had committed to his subjects the reading of God's word; but as for other things, he had determined there should be no change whatever in his reign, and this his purpose he now intended publicly to manifest. This was the commencement of Lambert's trial, who must have seen at once there could be no hope of justice under such circumstances. When the bishop had done, Henry rose, and said, "Ho! good fellow, what is thy name?" Lambert, kneeling, replied, "his real name was Nicholson, but that of many he was called Lambert." "Ha!" was the rejoinder, "hast thou two names? I would not trust a man with two names, were he my own brother." This was worse, still worse for the unhappy prisoner. The king, again speaking, next inquired, "Fellow, what sayest thou touching the Sacrament of the Altar? Wilt thou agree to the doctrine of the church, or wilt thou deny that the Eucharist is the real body of Christ?" and therewith the pious king uncovered his head. Presently, a whole army of theologians were let loose upon the prisoner, including Cranmer, Gardiner, Tunstall, and we know not how many other bishops; and though the odds were sufficient to confuse and overpower Lambert, and to prevent him from doing justice to his cause, they did not shake *him*. Five hours the disputation continued; and considering that Henry was one of the disputants, that fact was enough to seal the fate of the still unconvinced heretic. As it grew dark, and torches were brought into the fine old hall, the king, growing tired, turned to Lambert once more, and said, "What sayest thou now, fellow, after these solid reasons of such learned men? Art thou satisfied? Wilt thou live or die?" "I commit myself," said the prisoner, "into the hands of your majesty." "Then," said Henry, in words of unmistakeable meaning, "commit thyself into the hands of God." Upon which the prisoner exclaimed with admirable gentleness of speech, and consistency of purpose, "My soul, indeed, I do commend unto God, but my body I yield unto your Grace's clemency." Of course the reader is prepared for Henry's conclusion: "Then must thou die; for I will not be the patron of heretics." And Lambert was burnt in Smithfield immediately after, and under circumstances of suffering more than usually atrocious. Such was the treatment of Protestants even whilst the government under the management of Cromwell and Cranmer was fast verging toward Protestantism; though, be it observed, the year following Lambert's execution these two statesmen received a severe check, through the rising influence of Gardiner (Fig. 1450), who succeeded in passing the bloody statute against heretics (that is to say, against Protestants), and in 1540 caused Cromwell himself to be sent to the block.

In his latter years, Henry, growing impatient of inaction, and not having, perhaps, sufficient opportunity in England to slake that unquenchable thirst of blood which possessed him, went to war with France, and re-asserted the old claim of sovereignty over Scotland. The savage brutality of his instructions to the Earl of Hertford, when the latter invaded Scotland, in 1544, almost surpasses belief. We question whether the worst band of pirates ever arranged beforehand such a scheme of wholesale murder and misery, as we find carefully set down in those instructions:—
"Sack Holyrood house, and as many towns and villages about

Edinburgh as ye conveniently can; sack Leith, and burn and subvert it, and all the rest, *putting man, woman, and child to fire and sword*, without exception, when any resistance shall be made against you; and, this done, pass over to the Fife land, and extend like extremities and destructions in all towns and villages whereunto ye may reach conveniently, not forgetting, amongst all the rest, so to spoil and turn upside-down the cardinal's town of St. Andrew's, *as the upper stone may be the nether*, and not one stick stand by another, *sparing no creature alive within the same*, especially such as either in friendship or blood be allied to the cardinal [Beatoun];" and so "*this journey shall succeed most to his majesty's honour*." To *his* majesty's honour perhaps it might. Whatever this king could desire he always found nobles and ministers to execute. Hertford obeyed literally his instructions. One example may suffice. The tower of Broom House was burnt by him, and in it a noble lady with her whole family. But neither such instructions, nor Henry's schemes for taking off by secret assassination those whom he could not destroy by open warfare, nor bribing every man of rank or influence who would take a bribe to ruin his country, sufficed to enable Henry to obtain possession of Scotland; and the consciousness of his failure evidently harassed the last few months of his life. Burning more heretics, and beheading more nobles, who did not sympathise with his career, helped, however, to divert his thoughts and energies in some degree from the Scots. Katherine had a wonderfully narrow escape of going to Smithfield; and although by her address she saved herself, one of the ladies who had introduced heretic books into the court, the young, beautiful, and heroic Anne Askew, suffered instead. The king's illness was now daily increasing: and certainly a more truly wretched creature did not exist in the wide world than was this monarch of England, who could command all men and things to obey him, except the laws of Nature; these were now taking fearful vengeance for his violation of them. He had grown so fat and unwieldy that he could only be removed from room to room by the aid of machinery. An old ulcer in the leg kept him in fearful pain, and made the very air about him offensive to all who approached. And the state of the body was but a faithful revelation of the state of the mind: his irritability had increased to that degree, that the slightest word that offended put him in a state of frenzy. He suspected every one. Anything like a cheerful or agreeable sensation appears to have been unknown to him. Yet, consistent to the last, even when he began to feel "the inevitable necessity of death," he could not cease from shedding blood. The Howards were marked. The Earl of Hertford, his brother, and their friends, between whom and the Howard family a bitter rivalry had long subsisted, urged on their destruction. Had the elder Norfolk only been singled out, there had been something like retribution in the proceedings, for he had assisted many to a like doom, having scrupled at nothing that the despot desired him to do, whether it were to betray, torture, or destroy: but Norfolk's son—the flower of the English nobility—the gallant, accomplished, poetical Surrey (Fig. 1451)—what had he done, or what could he be supposed to have done, that he was to be prematurely cut off from a life that was opening to him such delightful vistas? Why he had, *long before*, quartered the royal arms with his own, in accordance with the decision of the heralds, and which it is all but certain he had a right to do: and therefore he had a design upon the throne. It is said the king really suspected him of a design against the princess, afterwards queen, Mary. Not a shadow of proof of treasonable designs was furnished; but the jury obeyed their masters—he was found guilty, sentenced, and suffered under the axe. His father would have experienced the same fate, but that, by the strangest good fortune, Henry died on the very night that was intended to have been Norfolk's last; and so he was respited, though left in confinement till the accession of Queen Mary, who, regarding him as a victim of the Protestant party, gave him his liberty, when old age and sorrow must have almost taken away the relish of it.

That the king's death was in but too complete accordance with his life, we may see in the facts just stated, that blood—still blood—engaged his thoughts. It is true he did not know he was dying; no one had dared to tell him so, even when the physicians wished that he should be warned. Sir Anthony Denny at last undertook the dangerous task, and performed it manfully; and, as often happens in such cases, found that his courage and straightforwardness had carried him safely through. Henry sent for Cranmer, who came just in time to exhort the dying monarch to hope for God's mercy through Christ, and to receive in answer a last grasp from his hand. A few moments later, and Henry was dead.

It is wonderful that England did not lose its wits for joy when the relief that it must have so long panted for came at last, and

1476.—Lady Jane Grey.
(From an original Picture in the collection of the Earl of Stamford and Warrington.)

1477.—Foot Soldier, 1508.

1478.—Foot Soldier, 1540

1479.—Gold Sovereign of Edward VI.

1480.—Crown of Edward VI·

1481.—Shilling of Edward VI.

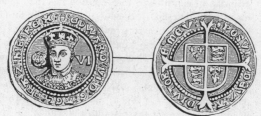

1482.—Sixpence of Edward VI.

1483.—Groat of Edward VI.

1484.—Penny of Edward VI.

1485.—Queen Mary. (From a Painting by Holbein.)

1486.—Great Seal of Queen Mary.

Marye

1487.—Mary. (Cotton MS. Vespasian, F. 13.)

1488.—Philip of England and Spain. (From a Painting by Titian.)

1489.—King Philip. (Husband of Queen Mary.)

1490.—Gold Rial of Queen Mary.

1491.—Gold Sovereign of Queen Mary.

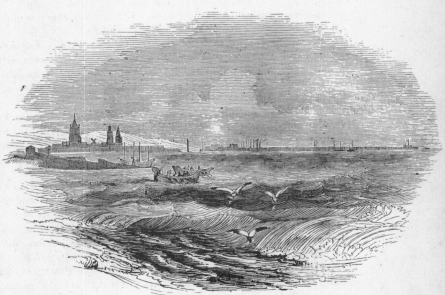

1492.—Calais from the Sea. (From an Old Print.)

men could once more move about in freedom, and speak out what they thought in safety. A young monarch ascended the throne, and, according to all accounts, a most excellent monarch he would prove. The people were familiar with many a story of his piety, and learning, and beneficence. Kings' ministers had been astonished at him almost from his birth. When he was not *eleven months old*, the Chancellor Audley wrote a letter to Cromwell especially to thank the king for the licence he had enjoyed of visiting his lord prince's grace, the youthful Edward. In that letter Audley hardly knew how to express sufficiently his admiration of the youthful wonder he had beheld. "I assure your lordship," he writes, " I never saw so goodly a child of his age, so merry, so pleasant, so good and loving countenance, and so earnest an eye, as it were a sage judgment towards every person that repaireth to his grace; and, as it seemeth to me, thanks be to our Lord, his grace increaseth well in the air that he is in. And albeit a little his grace's flesh decayeth, yet he shooteth out in length, and waxeth firm and stiff, and can stedfastly stand, and would advance himself to move and go if they would suffer him; but, as to me seemeth, they do yet best, considering his grace is yet tender, that he should not strain himself, as his own courage would serve him, till he come above a year of age. . . . *I cannot comprehend nor describe the goodly towardly qualities that is in my lord prince's grace*," &c. If he were such a being at eleven months, what might he not become at the age of eleven years, was the very natural idea, no doubt, of many of his loving subjects. And there was one who, writing when he had reached the age just mentioned, and about a year or so after his accession, thought that the warmest anticipations were borne out by the result. "If ye knew," he says, "the towardness of that young prince (Figs. 1468, 1471, 1475), your hearts would melt to hear him named, and your stomach abhor the malice of them that would him ill; the beautifulest creature that liveth under the sun; the wittiest, the most amiable, and the gentlest thing of all the world," &c.

The mainsprings of government under Henry VIII. had been the unbridled passions of the sovereign; during the reign of Edward, the ambitious intrigues of the nobles for power were become the supreme influences of the state. The Earl of Hertford, who executed Henry's gentle behests in Scotland, and who subsequently in the same country outstripped even all these former doings, when he had no such orders to excuse him,—Hertford was declared Protector, and made Duke of Somerset, and for a time maintained his supremacy. The Earl of Southampton endeavoured to oppose his influence; but was speedily frightened out of office as well as out of all interference, by a threat of prosecution for high treason on the ground of some informality he had committed.

The Protestant religion then became in effect the established faith of the country; Somerset having the powerful aid of Cranmer, who, "being now delivered from that too awful subjection that he had been held under by King Henry, resolved to go on more vigorously in purging out abuses." Bishops Gardiner and Bonner made a firm stand; so they were arrested, and sent to the Fleet Prison. The Protestantising of the State went on for some time without check. Divine service was performed in English in the royal chapel; images were removed from the churches throughout the kingdom, the cup was allowed to the laity, nomination of bishops conferred on the king, all ecclesiastical processes were to run in his name, the Bloody Statute was repealed, the use of the Prayer Book established, the laws prohibiting priests from marrying repealed, and, among other doings, an act was passed in which we fancy the young Edward's hand may be traced. We read in the preamble of the act for abolishing the ancient laws against eating flesh on certain days, and reconfirming the custom, "the king's majesty, considering that due and godly abstinence is a mean to virtue, and to subdue men's bodies to their soul and spirit, and considering also specially that fishers, and men using the trade of living by fishing in the sea, may thereby the rather be set to work, and that by eating of fish much flesh may be saved and increased," &c. Marks of very juvenile legislation here we should say. The king had been in the council (Fig. 1470) when that measure was determined upon.

Once more an insurrection broke out; the religious changes forming probably the most influential of the grievances complained of; and it was not until much blood had been shed that the revolters were dispersed, when, as usual, the gallows began its work.

While discontent and rebellion were thus pervading the land, the ministers were busier than ever in their intrigues. Before that insurrection, Somerset had found a rival in his own brother, Admiral Lord Seymour, who strove to supplant him in the Protectorship; but Somerset had caused him to be cut down with as little remorse as he would have destroyed a noxious weed that lay in his way; and

of course on the old pretence, high treason; after that event it was Somerset himself who was similarly smitten by another noble, the Earl of Warwick, son of the infamous Dudley, who with Empson obtained such bad eminence in Henry VII.'s reign. It is presumed that Warwick had been only making a tool of the one brother previously to get rid of the other, so that there might remain but one for *him* to get rid of. He now accomplished his ends. Somerset had become very unpopular on various grounds, but most of all perhaps for his rapacity and religious indecency in connection with the foundation of that noble pile in the strand, which (rebuilt in the last century by Sir William Chambers) still bears his name. When Somerset, it appears, commenced operations in the Strand, he wanted more room, so he unscrupulously demolished an inn of chancery, called Strand Inn, or Chester's Inn, and the episcopal houses of the bishops of Lichfield, Worcester, and Llandaff, and the church and churchyard of St. Mary-le-Strand. This done, he had still to obtain materials for the work. Timber and rubble were then in use for common houses, bricks not being generally employed, whilst stone was confined to the nobility, and brought from over sea. Stone, then, was the material chosen for Somerset's palace; but to wait for its arrival by the ordinary means was too tedious for him, so he found it nearer at hand, by making so many quarries of the charnel-house of old St. Paul's, and the chapel over it, and a large cloister on the north of St. Paul's, called Pardon Churchyard. Numerous and valuable monuments were in that cloister, which also contained the curious paintings called the Dance of Machabray, or the Dance of Death. All were swept away without remorse, till only a bare plot of ground was left where the cloister had stood. The steeple and part of the church of the priory of St. John of Jerusalem were also transformed into parts of Somerset House. Strype observes, *in excuse*, "yet this notice of former superstitions was gained by this barbarity, that among a great number of rotten carcasses were found caskets full of pardons safely folded and lapped together in the bottom of their graves; which Dr. Haddon himself had observed when they digged dead men out of their graves, and carried away their bones," &c. Such shocking violations of public feeling and private rights excited universal detestation and horror. By many also the very time chosen for his undertaking was looked on as a proof of his unpatriotic selfishness. It was said, "that when the king was engaged in such wars, and when London was much disordered by the plague, that had been in it for some months, he was *then* bringing architects from Italy, and designing such a palace as had not been seen in England." The building was begun in March, 1546. The site occupied an area of six hundred feet from east to west, by five hundred north and south. The principal architect is believed to have been John of Padua, an Italian. It was the first building (Figs. 1473, 1474) of Italian architecture executed in this country. Within less than three years after its commencement, its owner went to the block: it is most probable, therefore, that he never inhabited it. Edward's notice in his private journal of his uncle's death, does not say much for his feeling; under the date, Friday, 22nd of January, he writes, "The Duke of Somerset had his head cut off on Tower Hill, between eight and nine in the morning." Another story shows him in a more honourable light. When Joan Boecher was condemned as a heretic, and delivered over to the secular power for execution in Smithfield, Edward shrank with horror from the warrant which he was asked to sign. An eminent ecclesiastic— we regret to say—Cranmer, endeavoured to reason him out of his scruples; but the simple, unsophisticated boy, was not to be convinced, and although, with tears in his eyes, he yielded at last, he told Cranmer solemnly, that if the act were wrong, he, Cranmer, would have to answer for it to God, since it was done in submission to his authority. Cranmer is supposed to have been moved by this warning, and to have striven to save Joan by long-continued persuasion; but no one could have known better than Cranmer the inutility of such persuasion: poor Joan was immoveable, and so she went to the stake.

Traits like this, aided by the exhibition of a wise and active benevolence, in the founding of such great and valuable establishments as Christ Church, London, certainly gave promise of one worthy of the name and duties of a king, when riper years should add intellectual vigour to his other qualifications. But in 1552 he was seized with the small-pox, and though he recovered, the disease left him so debilitated, that he sank gradually, and died on the 6th of July in the following year, being then fifteen years and eight months old.

During Edward's illness the intriguers set to work with tenfold activity and unscrupulousness. Among the noblemen of the court was the Duke of Northumberland, who thought the opportunity a favourable one for excluding the Catholic Mary from the succession, and placing himself virtually though not actually on the throne. How he hoped to accomplish this we shall presently see.

In illustration of the relative value of love and fear in promoting virtue and learning, the amiable and enlightened Roger Ascham, who, in matters of education, possessed a discernment far beyond his age, relates an interview that he had with the youthful Lady Jane Grey, daughter of the Duke and Duchess of Suffolk, and granddaughter of Charles Brandon, and Mary, the sister of Henry VIII. "Before I went into Germany," says Roger Ascham, "I came to Broadgate, in Leicestershire, to take my leave of that noble lady Jane Grey, to whom I was exceeding much beholden. Her parents, the duke and the duchess, with all the household, gentlemen and gentlewomen, were hunting in the park. I found her in her chamber reading Phædon Platonis in Greek, and that with as much delight as some gentlemen would read a merry tale in Bocace (Boccaccio). After salutation and duty done, with some other talk, I asked her, why she would lose such pastime in the park? Smiling, she answered me, 'I wis all their sport in the park is but a shadow to that pleasure that I find in Plato. Alas! good folk, they never felt what true pleasure meant.' 'And how came you, madam,' quoth I, 'to this deep knowledge of pleasure? and what did chiefly allure you unto it, seeing not many women, but very few men have attained thereunto?' 'I will tell you,' quoth she, 'and tell you a truth, which, perchance, ye will marvel at. One of the greatest benefits that ever God gave me is, that he sent me so sharp and severe parents, and so gentle a schoolmaster. For, when I am in presence either of father or mother, whether I speak, keep silence, sit, stand, or go, eat, drink, be merry, or sad, be sewing, playing, dancing, or doing anything else, I must do it, as it were, in such weight, measure, and number, even so perfectly as God made the world, or else I am so sharply taunted, so cruelly threatened, yea, presently, sometimes with pinches, nips, and bobs, and other ways, which I will not name for the honour I bear them, so without measure disordered, that I think myself in hell, till time come that I must go to Mr. Elmer; who teacheth me so gently, so pleasantly, with such fair allurements to learning, that I think all the time nothing whiles I am with him. And when I am called from him, I fall on weeping, because, whatever I do else but learning, is full of grief, trouble, fear, and whole misliking unto me. And thus my book hath been so much my pleasure, and bringeth daily to me more pleasure and more, that in respect of it, all other pleasures, in very deed, be but trifles and troubles unto me!'"

Lady Jane Grey (Fig. 1476) spoke and wrote, correctly and fluently, the Greek, Latin, Italian, and French languages, and understood Hebrew, Chaldee, and Arabic! Astonishing acquisitions certainly for one who was as yet a mere child in age—though wiser than many at fourscore. Her love of retirement arose from no personal defects, as sometimes happens, for she was calculated to shine in any society by her grace and beauty, which, combined with sweetness of temper and skill in the usual female accomplishments, rendered her in every respect a delightful companion. But her parents only prized her extraordinary excellence to advance their ambitious projects by it; and the consequence was, that to the other hardships and injuries that she had suffered through them, she had to add the sacrifice of her life. With the assistance of the powerful Duke of Northumberland, they resolved to make her a queen, without reference to her inclinations, and contrary to all right and reason, since she could only reign by the forcible exclusion of the three nearer heirs—Mary, Elizabeth, and Mary of Scotland—and for that injustice had no excuse in the will of the English people. As a preliminary step the hapless young lady was led to the bridal altar, to give her hand to the son of the Duke of Northumberland, Lord Guilford Dudley, to whom she was fondly attached, although it is very plain that the match was formed with little reference to what would promote her peace, but as a measure of selfish policy. The mind of Edward VI. was therefore, in his dying hours, perverted to the unjust act of settling the crown upon Lady Jane, which was done at the suggestion of the Duke of Northumberland, who chiefly influenced the king; the fallacy of that act being, the presumed stability which the accession of Lady Jane would give to the Protestant interest. What she herself would think of it appears to have been correctly anticipated, for not until four days after the king's death was she informed of the dignity that was to be forced on her. Then who can harshly blame her, if, so young, the tenderness of the bride and the reverence of the daughter overcame the reluctance that she expressed? who can wonder that she had not firmness to resist the vehement arguments and entreaties of her husband, and of those to whom she had been trained from infancy to render the

most implicit obedience? Lady Jane, thus urged, assumed the fatal diadem—perhaps the last woman on earth to whom, under almost any circumstances, it could have been desirable. Her guiltless usurpation was brief enough. Within ten days of her proclamation and exhibition as queen, and her taking up her residence in that character in the Tower of London, the rightful heiress, Mary, was in full possession of all of which it had been attempted to deprive her, and Queen Jane and her young consort had to come down from their thrones, and to bid an eternal farewell to all earthly glory. The Tower Palace became almost instantaneously the Tower Prison. In the Beauchamp Tower (Fig. 1532) the letters A N E, inscribed on the wall, was attributed to the hand of Lord Guilford.

Northumberland perished at once on the block, but Lady Jane and her husband had probably been spared, but for Wyatt's ill-managed insurrection, which broke out on the news of the queen's intended marriage with the cruel bigot of Spain, King Philip, and was supported by *Lady Jane Grey's father*, the Duke of Suffolk. The insurrection failed, and not only involved all those in ruin who had directly promoted it, but those in the Tower, who assuredly desired nothing so much as a peaceable unambitious life. Within a week after Wyatt's discomfiture, it was determined that Lady Jane and her husband should both die, and on the same day. Fecknam, a Catholic Dean of St. Paul's, was sent to endeavour to change her faith, but all his learned arguments failed with one who was more than his equal in controversy. Lady Jane preserved her fortitude admirably through the closing scenes of her life; and, that it might not be shaken, refused a farewell meeting with Lord Guilford on the morning of the fatal day. It would foment their grief, she said, rather than be a comfort in death, and they should shortly meet in a better place, and more happy estate. But she had a severer trial to endure than this would have been. From the window of "Master Partridge's house," where she was lodged, she beheld Lord Guilford going to execution, and exchanged with him her last parting signal. He passed on—to Tower Hill—was brought back in a cart to be buried in the Tower Chapel, and she looked upon his headless trunk! That such an exhibition was not spared to such a wife, shows the brutal insensibility of those in authority who regulated the proceedings. "O Guilford, Guilford!" exclaimed the unhappy lady rising even in her agony to the highest sublimity of Christian heroism, "the antepast is not so bitter that thou hast tasted, and which I shall soon taste, as to make my flesh tremble: it is nothing compared to the feast of which we shall partake this day in heaven." She immediately went forth to her own scaffold, which for privacy was on the Tower Green, "in countenance nothing cast down, neither her eyes anything moistened with tears, although her gentlewomen, Elizabeth Tilney and Mistress Helen, wonderfully wept." Holding a book in her hand, she prayed till she came to the scaffold. There in her modest address to the bystanders, she stated that she had justly deserved punishment for suffering herself to be made the instrument, though unwillingly, of the ambition of others, and that she hoped her fate might serve as a memorable example in aftertimes. The executioner beginning to unrobe her, she desired him to let her alone, and turned to her attendants, who performed that melancholy office. He then requested her to stand on the straw, which she did, saying, "I pray you despatch me quickly." As she knelt, she inquired, "Will you take it off before I lay me down?" "No, madam," was the reply. Then she tied her handkerchief about her eyes, and, *feeling for the block, she said, "Where is it? Where is it?"* One of the standers-by guided her thereunto, and she laid her head down, and stretched forth her body, and said, "Lord, into thy hands I commend my spirit;" and so died—at seventeen years old!

It was an unfortunate contrast for Mary that presented itself to every one's eye, between the queen thus deposed from her short-lived sovereignty, and the queen who took her place; so immeasurably was Lady Jane Grey the superior of Mary in all but her acquirements.

We may compare with the portraits of Mary by Holbein (Fig. 1485), and on her seal (Fig. 1486), and coins, &c. (Figs. 1490 to 1496), the account given by the Venetian ambassador Michele, who described her as a woman of low stature, thin, and delicate; her face more than middling pretty: but then he adds, that her eye was so piercing as to induce fear as well as reverence in those she looked upon; her voice thick and loud, like a man's; and her general aspect and appearance that of one sickly and ill. She too, in her childhood, had been the theme of as much admiration among the courtiers as we have seen her brother was. Though still comparatively young (thirty-seven years), her constitution had been infirm from childhood, and dreadfully shattered by the troubles she had passed

1493.—Shilling of Mary.

1494.—Sixpence of Mary.

1495.—Groat of Mary.

1496.—Penny of Mary.

1497.—Great Seal of Queen Elizabeth.

1499.—Elizabeth.

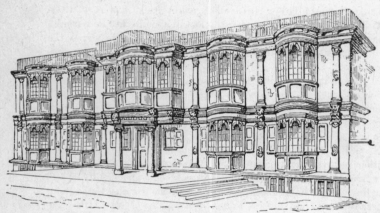

1498.—Old Palace at Greenwich.

1500.—Elizabeth.

1501.—Queen Elizabeth. (From a Painting by Zucchero.)

1502—Gold Rial of Queen Elizabeth.　　　1503.—Gold Angel of Queen Elizabeth.　　　1504.—Crown of Queen Elizabeth.

1505.—Shilling of Queen Elizabeth.

1506.—Sixpence of Queen Elizabeth

1507.—Groat of Queen Elizabeth.

1508.—Penny of Queen Elizabeth.

1509.—Elizabeth.　(Harleian MS. 285.)

Think your Country your home', the inhabitants your neighbours, all freinds your children, and your children your own Sowl; endeuouring to surpass all these' in liberality and good nature'.

1510.—Facsimile from Elizabeth's Translation of a Dialogue in Xenophon between Hiero and Simonides.

1511.—St. James's.

1512.—Richmond.

1513.—Nonsuch House　(From Speed's 'Theatre of Great Britain.')

through; such as the deposition of her mother Katherine; the declaration of her own illegitimacy (subsequently reversed by her father); and the progress of the new views, which had consequently caused her much anxiety, not only in the abstract, but personally and practically. She had, like every one else (except here and there a chancellor and a bishop, a monk or a friar), succumbed during her father's reign of terror, but had pertinaciously refused to succumb any longer. On the 18th of March, 1550, King Edward wrote in his journal:—"The lady Mary, my sister, came to me at Westminster, where, after salutations, she was called with my council into a chamber; where was declared how long I had suffered her mass, in hope of her reconciliation; and how now being no hope, which I perceived by her letters, except I saw some short amendment, I could not bear it. She answered, that her soul was God's, and her faith she would not change, nor dissemble her opinion with contrary doings. It was said I constrained not her faith, but wished her not as a king to rule, but as a subject to obey; and that her example might breed too much inconvenience."

Mary's name, indeed, had then become the "tower of strength," of the Catholics; and everything was hoped from her, if, as seemed probable, she should be called to the throne. She did not disappoint their expectations, at least as far as her will and wishes were concerned. And it was a most critical time. The new religion had undoubtedly made much progress; but England at large was only as yet thinking about, rather than actually embracing it; and kindness and liberality on the part of the ministers of the old faith, and of the Government, would assuredly, in multitudes of cases, have revived the affections that had been chilled, and have repressed the wandering impulse even in its birth. A very different course, however, was adopted; and Protestantism became the avowed or secret belief of a large proportion of the nation, before Mary's death stopped the almost unbroken series of fires that blazed away in Smithfield. So certainly is it one of the laws of our being (given, like all other laws, for our advancement and true happiness) that whatever prevents truth by preventing the free belief in—and expression of— what appears to be true, recoils invariably on those who have used the unlawful weapons. As men at one time were constantly burning each other for their opinions; so at another, when they have outgrown that lamentable error, they still cling to an error of a kindred nature, and similarly punishable; namely, that the looking at facts through individual opinions is a just means of measuring the character of men and events. Protestants have no doubt too often exaggerated Mary's bigotry and cruelty, and have kept back those better traits which modify her otherwise unamiable character. Unhappily, after every allowance, enough remains to startle and horrify us. The Catholic historian Dr. Lingard, admits that after expunging from the lists of martyrs promulgated by the Protestants the "names of all who were condemned as felons or traitors, or who died peaceably in their beds, or who survived the publication of their martyrdom, *or who would for their heterodoxy have been sent to the stake by the reformed prelates themselves*, had they been in possession of the power," &c., it will still be found " that in the space of four years about two hundred persons perished in the flames for religious opinions." And what illustrious men were there not included among these victims—Hooper, Ferrar, Latimer, Ridley, and Cranmer!—The last, as we have already seen, far from innocent himself as regards others of the crime committed upon him. Mary's political advisers were Gardiner, Cardinal Pole, and Bonner; but the last was the chief instigator of the religious persecutions.

The military results of the reign may be likened to the religious in this,—that while they were signalised by an event—the loss of Calais—which deeply affected the people of England, from the queen downward, the loss was really a permanent gain. It was impossible that Calais could ever have been looked upon by the French as a proper appanage of England; our possession of it, therefore, would have remained a constant source of jealousy and incitement to warfare. It was in consequence of her marriage with Philip of Spain (Figs. 1488, 1489), that Mary was induced to join the latter country in a war upon France; and that junction gave the French, under the Duke of Guise, the opportunity of besieging and taking the place (Fig. 1492) in question in 1558. Calais was thus reannexed to the French dominions. Our queen, it is said, never recovered the blow. She died in the same year; and on her deathbed observed to her attendants, "that, if her breast should be opened after her decease, ' Calais' would be found written upon her heart." The palace of St. James (Fig. 1511) was the place of her decease.

We cannot better conclude our notice of a reign so short, and yet so full of horrors, than with a glimpse of Mary's better nature.

In her will, to which no attention was paid, she speaks thus touchingly of her mother, the excellent Katherine:—"And further I will that the body of the virtuous lady and my most dear and well-beloved mother, of happy memory, Queen Katherine, which now lieth buried at Peterborough, shall, within as short time as conveniently may after my burial, be removed, brought, and laid near the place of my sepulchre, in which place I will my executors to cause to be made honourable tombs or monuments for a decent memory of us."

———

Once more did the hearts of the people expand with hope and joy as a new sovereign, Elizabeth (Fig. 1500, 1501), was proclaimed in the streets of London; where the tables were spread for " plentiful eating, drinking, and making merry;" and where the bells by day, and the bonfires by night, kept up a perpetual round of manifestations of the royal popularity. It was, we think, a favourable evidence of the soundness of heart of the English people, and their desire to have no more favour or disfavour shown to either religious party, that the junction of Catholics and Protestants in the Queen's Council, immediately after her accession, did not apparently in the slightest degree affect the general congratulations that were showered upon her. Her coronation went off most brilliantly. Never were the prophecies in Latin and English, in prose and verse, better listened to from the prophets who stood here and there along the route; never did pageants seem to be more worthily presented or received; never were words that fell from royal lips more rapturously caught up, to be treasured ever after:—and some of those words were worth all the respect they enjoyed. " Be ye well assured," said Elizabeth, at one part, " that I shall stand your good queen." At another part she noticed an ancient citizen, who wept and turned his back,—" I warrant you it is for gladness," was Elizabeth's happy comment. Her behaviour generally was as enchanting as her speech. " How many nosegays did her grace receive at poor women's hands!—how oftentimes staid she her chariot when she saw any simple body offer to speak to her grace! A branch of rosemary given her grace, with a supplication, by a poor woman about Fleet Bridge, was seen in her chariot till her grace came to Westminster, not without the marvellous wondering of such as knew the presenter, and noted the queen's most gracious receiving and keeping the same." (Holinshed.)

Much anxiety was naturally felt by all devout and earnest men as to what course Elizabeth would take upon religious matters; and they were not left long in the doubt engendered by the *juste milieu* character of her earlier proceedings. Nor would she be moved till it suited her from the doubtful kind of position she had taken up. Bacon records that " on the morrow of her coronation (it being the custom to release prisoners at the inauguration of a prince) " she " went to the chapel; and, in the great chamber, one of her courtiers, who was well known to her, either out of his own motion, or by the instigation of a wiser man, presented her with a petition, and, before a great number of courtiers, besought her, with a loud voice, that now this good time, there might be four or five more principal prisoners released : these were the four evangelists and the apostle St. Paul, who had been long shut up in an unknown tongue, as it were, in prison; so as they could not converse with the common people. The queen answered very gravely, that it was best first to inquire of themselves whether they would be released or not :" an answer that her grandfather, Henry VII., might have envied her the power of making under such delicate circumstances. But the reading of the Liturgy in English had been already authorised, and other measures followed that showed the country had obtained a Protestant queen. In effect, the affairs of the church reverted to their state under Edward VI., with an immense increase of the accompanying influences that were calculated to prevent any second relapse. Gradually Elizabeth was drawn by political considerations into a more and more decided support of the new, and opposition of the old faith, till on the one hand we find her recognised throughout Europe as the head of the Protestants; and on the other, till we perceive such severe measures adopted against the Catholics as the banishment on pain of death of Jesuit and popish priests. Many were subsequently executed under this cruel law.

Of a reign so long, so important, and so exceedingly brilliant, it is here of course impossible to do more than present some of the features which are at once the most salient and the most illustrative of the characters of the sovereign and the time. Thus the queen's love-passages and continual dallyings with the question of marriage may be incidentally noticed in connection with her favourite Leicester; her continental wars find appropriate mention in the account of Sir Philip Sidney (a fairer example of the best spirit of chivalry than it was ever the fortune even of a Froissart to behold or to paint) ; the chief source of that discontent among Elizabeth's subjects which sought to break out into insurrection is revealed in the sad narrative of Mary Queen of Scots ; the heroic spirit of the "fair virgin throned by the west" nowhere shines so clearly as through the records of the defeat of the Armada ; and, lastly, the fate of the Earl of Essex, and the consequent sufferings of his mistress, "point the moral" to the "tale" of her personal history.

We may fitly precede these matters with a few notices of a miscellaneous kind relating to Elizabeth, but all of which bear more or less upon the character of the sovereign who was to exercise so important an influence, and for so long a time, over the destinies of England, nay, we might say without exaggeration, of Europe.

We have enumerated her lovers after she became queen of England ; but the list would not be complete without the addition of those who had previously exhibited their attachment to her (or to their own interests, in a profession of attachment to her). Putting aside, then, those advances made for her hand when she was two years old by Francis of France for his son the Duke of Angoulême, and the alliance proposed for her when she was in her thirteenth year, with Philip of Spain—her first suitor, when she had arrived a little nearer the years of womanhood, was the Protector's unfortunate brother, the Admiral, Lord Seymour. One of the crimes charged against him was that he had plotted to force the Princess Elizabeth to marry him ; and the scandal of the day talked of familiarities that had passed between them, and of the affection that she bore to the Admiral. The next and more public claimant for her hand was the eldest son of Christian III. of Denmark, but she refused him ; and King Edward, her brother, seems to have been quite content with the refusal of his "sweet sister Temperance," as he was accustomed to call her. Edward was, indeed, much attached to Elizabeth, and fond of seeing her at his court, assigning her at such times Somerset House (Fig 1520) as a place of residence.

Then in Mary's reign came Erick XIV. of Sweden, and was also refused ; Elizabeth gaining a sister (after all the anger and jealousy caused by her presumed participation in Wyatt's insurrection) whilst she lost a lover, by saying she would never marry without Mary's consent. And making every allowance for the ambition that actuated many of those proposals, before and after the accession to the throne, there can be no question that Elizabeth's person and mind were calculated to stir the imagination and warm the heart of the young, romantic, and unselfish, quite as much as the crown —that she was soon to, or did, wear—dazzled the eyes and stimulated the schemes of older and more worldly men. Camden's description of her may stand as a parallel portrait by the side of Ascham's description of Lady Jane Grey :—"She was of admirable beauty, and well deserving a crown ; of modest gravity, excellent wit, royal soul, happy memory, and indefatigably given to the study of learning ; insomuch, as before she was seventeen years of age she understood well the Latin, French, and Italian languages, and had an indifferent knowledge of the Greek. Neither did she neglect music, so far as it became a princess, being able to sing sweetly, and play handsomely on the lute. With Roger Ascham, who was her tutor, she read over Melancthon's Common Places, all Tully, a great part of the Histories of Titus Livius, certain select orations of Isocrates (whereof two she turned into Latin), Sophocles' tragedies, and the New Testament in Greek, by which means she both framed her tongue to a pure and elegant way of speaking," &c. A facsimile of a passage from one of Elizabeth's translations into English will be found among our engravings (Fig. 1510).

The third and last of the Princess's lovers whose names have been recorded was Edward Courtenay, whose connection with Elizabeth involved some very peculiar features. There is reason to suppose that both the sisters were enamoured of him ; for it is said that Mary, who released him from the Tower and made him Earl of Devon, intended to marry him, until she learned his preference for Elizabeth. He became involved with the latter in Wyatt's insurrection, one of the objects of which was to bring about their marriage, in order to secure a Protestant reigning family. Mary's state motives and jealousies thus enhanced by the keenest personal feelings, Elizabeth and her lover were placed in imminent danger. Elizabeth was arrested, brought to London, and after some delay committed to the Tower. It was the morning of Palm Sunday ; and every one was ordered to "keep the church, and carry the palms." In attempting to "shoot" the bridge (old London bridge) she narrowly escaped destruction. The barge stopped at Traitors' Gate (Fig. 435), but Elizabeth refused to land. She was then told by one of the lords that she would have no choice, and therewith he offered her his cloak to defend her from the rain ; but putting it aside with

a "good dash," she stepped out, and placing one foot on the stairs, exclaimed, "Here landeth as true a subject as ever landed at these stairs ; and before thee, O God, I speak it, having none other friend but thee alone." She was ultimately released from the Tower, though still confined for a time at different places, among the rest at the beautiful palace built by her grandfather at Sheen or Richmond (Figs. 1512, 1517). Courtenay was allowed to take a trip to the Continent, where he died in dissipation, brought on, it is said, through his disappointments. Elizabeth used in after time to say of this period, that she had fully expected death ; that she knew that her sister had thirsted for her blood.

It is an odd combination, that of a great coquette with a great sovereign ; yet it is as certain that Elizabeth was the one as the other. Her lovers or suitors were so numerous that it is hopeless to attempt to mention them all. But among the earlier ones after her accession, were Philip of Spain ; Charles, Archduke of Austria ; James Hamilton, Earl of Arran, the head of the Scottish Protestants ; Erick XIV., King of Sweden ; and Adolphus, Duke of Holstein— all foreigners : at home there were Sir William Pickering ; Henry, Earl of Arundel ; and Robert Dudley, afterwards the Earl of Leicester (Figs. 1542, 1544), who appeared to be the chief favourite. And on reading the highly interesting account of Elizabeth's manners and conversation given by Melville, the ambassador in England of Mary Queen of Scots, we see that Leicester was not altogether mistaken in his notions of the probability that he might be able to ally himself to the royalty of England. Elizabeth, says Melville, expressed great desire to see Queen Mary ; and as that could not easily be managed, appeared to take great delight in a picture of her sister of Scotland.

"She took me," he continues, "to her own bedchamber, and opened a little cabinet, wherein were divers little pictures wrapped within paper, and their names written with her own hands upon the papers. Upon the first that she took up was written 'My lord's picture.' I held the candle, and pressed to see that picture so named ; she appeared loth to let me see it, yet my importunity prevailed for a sight thereof, and I found it to be the Earl of Leicester's picture. I desired that I might have it to carry home to my queen, which she refused, alleging that she had but that one picture of his. I said, Your Majesty hath here the original, for I perceived him at the farthest part of the chamber speaking with Secretary Cecil. Then she took out the queen's picture and kissed it, and I adventured to kiss her hand for the great love evinced therein to my mistress. She showed me also a fair ruby, as great as a tennis-ball : I desired that she would send either it or my Lord of Leicester's picture as a token to my queen. She said, that if the queen would follow her counsel, she would, in process of time, get all that she had ; that in the meantime she was resolved, in a token, to send her with me a fair diamond." Growing late, she appointed eight the next morning as the time when Melville should again see her, and when she was accustomed to walk in the garden. On meeting again, they spake of the customs of foreign countries ; the buskins of the women were not forgot, and he was asked what country's weed or dress he thought most becoming gentlewomen.

"The queen said she had clothes of every sort, which every day thereafter, so long as I was there, she changed. One day she had the English weed, another the French, and another the Italian, and so forth. She asked me which of them became her best? I answered, in my judgment the Italian dress ; which answer I found pleased her well, for she delighted to show her golden-coloured hair, wearing a caul and bonnet, as they do in Italy. Her hair, rather reddish than yellow, curled, in appearance, naturally. She desired to know of me what colour of hair was reputed best, and which of them two was fairest? I answered, the fairness of them both was not their worst faults. But she was earnest with me to declare which of them I judged fairest. I said she was the fairest queen in England, and mine in Scotland. Yet she appeared earnest. I answered they were both the fairest ladies in their countries ; that her majesty was whiter, but my queen was very lovely. She inquired which of them was of highest stature? I said my queen. Then, saith she, she is too high ; for I myself am neither too high nor too low. Then she asked what exercises she used? I answered, that when I received my dispatch the queen was lately come from the Highland hunting ; that when her more serious affairs permitted, she was taken up with reading of histories ; that sometimes she recreated herself in playing upon the lute and virginals. She asked if she played well. I said reasonably, for a queen. That same day, after dinner, my lord of Hunsdon (Fig 1514) drew me to a quiet gallery, that I might hear some music

1514.—Lord Hunsdon.

1515.—Queen Elizabeth surrounded by her Court. (From a Print by Vertue.)

1516.—State Carriage of Queen Elizabeth. (From Hoefnagel's Print of Nonsuch Palace.)

1517.—Richmond Palace. (From an old Drawing engraved in the Second Volume

1518.—Ancient View of St. James's and Westminster.

1520.—Somerset House.

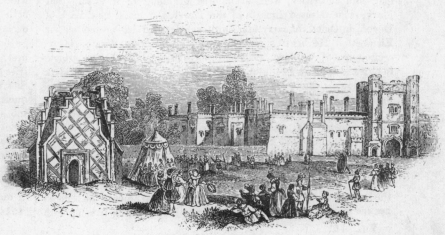

1519.—St. James's Palace. (From a Print by Hollar.)

1523.—The Spanish Armada.

1524.—The Spanish Armada attacked by the English Fleet. (From the Ancient Tapestry in the House of Lords, destroyed in the late Fire at the Houses of Parliament.)

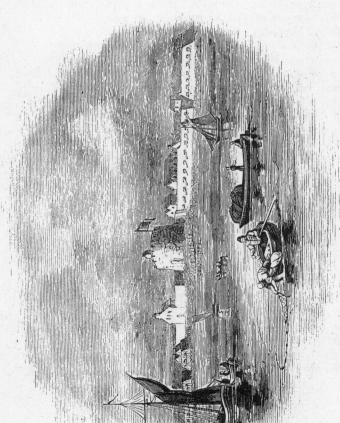

1521.—Tilbury Fort. (From a Picture by Laymaker, engraved by Kip, about 1680.)

1522.—Tilbury Fort.

but he said he durst not avow it, where I might hear the queen play upon the virginals. After I had hearkened awhile I took by the tapestry that hung before the door of the chamber, and seeing her back was towards the door, I ventured within the chamber and stood a pretty space, hearing her play excellently well; but she left off immediately so soon as she turned about and saw me; she appeared to be surprised to see me, and came forward, seeming to strike me with her hand, alleging that she used not to play before men, but when she was solitary, to shun melancholy. She asked me how I came there. I answered, as I was walking with my lord of Hunsdon, as we passed by the chamber door I heard such melody as ravished me, whereby I was drawn in ere I knew how, excusing my fault of homeliness as being brought up in the court of France, where such freedom was allowed, declaring myself willing to endure what kind of punishment her majesty should be pleased to inflict upon me for so great an offence. Then she sat down low upon a cushion, and I upon my knees by her, but with her own hand she gave me a cushion to lay under my knee, which at first I refused, but she compelled me to take it. She then called for my Lady Strafford out of the next chamber, for the queen was alone. She inquired whether my queen or she played best. In that I found myself obliged to give her the praise. She said my French was very good, and asked if I could speak Italian, which she spoke reasonably well. I told her majesty I had no time to learn the language, not having been above two months in Italy. Then she spake to me in Dutch (*German*), which was not good; and would know what kind of books I most delighted in: whether theology, history, or love-matters. I said I liked well of all the sorts. Here I took occasion to press earnestly my dispatch. She said I was sooner weary of her company than she was of mine. I told her majesty that though I had no reason of being weary, I knew my mistress's affairs called me home. Yet I was stayed two days longer that I might see her dance, as I was afterwards informed; which being over, she inquired of me whether she or my queen danced best? I answered, the queen danced not so high or disposedly as she did. Then, again, she wished that she might see the queen at some convenient place of meeting. I offered to convey her secretly to Scotland by post, clothed like a page, that, under this disguise she might see the queen, as James V. had gone in disguise with his own ambassador to see the Duke of Vendome's sister, who should have been his wife; telling her that her chamber might be kept in her absence as though she were sick; that none need be privy thereto except Lady Strafford and one of the grooms of her chamber. She appeared to like that kind of language; only answered it with a sigh, saying, "Alas, if I might do it thus!" Leicester was appointed to convey the ambassador from Hampton Court to London, and on the way did not scruple to ask what Melville's mistress, the Queen of Scotland, thought of him for a husband—a proposal that had originated with Elizabeth, apparently for the pleasure of seeing Leicester refuse it on her account. Melville answered as he had been commanded by Mary, very coldly, and Leicester then disclaimed all pretence of aiming to marry so great a queen.

Assuredly, however, Leicester's thoughts were constantly at work to enable him to compass a marriage with a still greater queen, though year after year passed away, and still he seemed no nearer to the goal. Perhaps his hopes were never higher, or his chances generally greater, than at the time of Elizabeth's memorable visit to him in the mansion that had been her own gift.

How vividly Scott has revived the old glories of Kenilworth no English reader can need to be informed; but it may not perhaps be so generally known, that the influence exercised by the magic pen of the novelist has done something more than this: it has preserved the existing ruins themselves, by a spell almost as effectual as though some enchanter of fabulous story had waved his wand over every crumbling tower and gateway, and averted at once all the ordinary processes of spoliation and decay. It was indeed a memorable hour for Kenilworth, when, some six-and-twenty years ago, that a "man of middle age, with a lofty forehead and a keen grey eye, slightly lame, but withal active, entered its gatehouse (Figs. 1540, 1541), and having looked upon the only bit of carving left to tell something of interior magnificence (Fig. 1545), passed into those ruins, and *stood there silent for some two hours.* Then was the ruined place henceforward to be sanctified. The progress of desolation was to be arrested. The torch of genius again lighted up 'every room so spacious,' and they were for ever after to be associated with the recollections of their ancient splendour. There were to be visions of sorrow and suffering there too, "woman's weakness—man's treachery" (William Shakspere: a Biography). Of Amy Robsart, the victim

of that "treachery," and whose unhappy form we see moving about in those "visions of sorrow," it will be sufficient to say, that whilst Scott has, with perfect propriety and adherence to the probable truth, connected Amy's sufferings with the aims of her husband upon the hand of Elizabeth, and chosen the period of the queen's visit to Kenilworth for his display of both, it is here necessary to premise, that the unfortunate lady really died at Cumnor many years before the visit; and, it is most likely, in the way described by the novelist. It may also be stated that notwithstanding one wife was thus, according to the general belief of the time, murdered by her husband, to get her out of his path toward the throne, Leicester is actually supposed to have married a second, the widow of Lord Sheffield, and to have attempted to poison her, for the same reason that had prompted the previous murder: but she escaped; and hoping, perhaps, to avoid all further danger, gave way to Leicester's threats, and married Sir Edward Stafford. The earl, however dearly he had paid for it, certainly succeeded in obtaining and keeping Elizabeth's favour, which was most convincingly shown by and during the visit to Kenilworth, of which we now proceed to speak.

On Saturday the 9th of July, 1575, about eight in the evening, Elizabeth arrived within "a flight shoot" of the first gate of the castle, where, upon the leads and battlements, stood "six trumpeters, hugely advanced, much exceeding the common stature of men in this age, who had likewise huge and monstrous trumpets counterfeited, wherein they seemed to sound."—It was but seeming —the real trumpeters were hidden behind the giants. Before they sounded, Sibylla, "comely clad in a pall of white silk, pronounced a proper poesy in English rhyme and metre."

> The rage of war fast bound in chains
> Shall never stir nor move;
> But peace shall govern all your days,
> Increasing subjects' love.

Elizabeth made her entrance through the gate of the tilt-yard, not the great gateway. Advancing to Mortimer's Tower, which led into the base-court, she was met by a mighty porter, "tall of person, big of limb, and stern of countenance," who demanded the cause of the disturbance, but, seeing the lion aspect of the queen, dropped on his knees in the tenderest and humblest of moods. Then was heard the welcome of the "harmonious blasters," the trumpeters. The next greeting she received was from a more interesting sort of personage—an enchanted Lady of the Lake—who, "upon a moveable island, bright blazing with torches," in the fine pool that enhanced so greatly the beauty of Kenilworth, floated to land, and met her majesty with a "well-penned metre," describing a very extraordinary history. She said she had been concealed within the lake since the days of King Arthur, on account of the incessant war and confusion; but that now she delivered lake and dominion into the hands of the queen. Elizabeth, with that ready wit that characterised her, said she had thought the lake her own, but would confer with the lady on the subject at some more convenient time. The queen then moved on through a very fairy land for loveliness, amidst bursts of the most joyous music. More welcome still!—the queen had to listen to certain Latin verses; and then "did follow so great a peal of guns, and such lightning by firework," that "the noise and flame were heard and seen twenty miles off." The first day Elizabeth spent at Kenilworth, being Sunday, was partially one of rest, with music and *dancing* in the evening. In the afternoon of Monday the queen rode to hunt the hart. Returning by torchlight, she is met by a salvage man, coming forth out of the woods, "with an oaken plant, plucked up by the roots, in his hand, himself foregrown *all in moss and ivy;* who for personage, gesture, and utterance beside, countenanced the matter to very good liking." This savage, in his moss and ivy, has an attendant, "Echo," and repeats verses, which were "devised, penned, and pronounced by Master Gascoigne; and that (as I have heard credibly reported) *upon a very great sudden.*" So we are told by one of the two chief authorities who has described these festivities, no less a person than Master Gascoigne himself (Fig. 1543)—meaning, no doubt, to heighten our surprise at the extraordinary merit of his invention. Nor are such lines as these to be despised. We have read worse—and better:—

> The winds resound your worth,
> The rocks record your name,
> These hills, these dales, these woods, these waves,
> These fields pronounce your fame.

In his enthusiastic acting, Master Gascoigne had an accident that might have proved serious. When the savage had learned at last that he was in the presence of the greatest of queens and goddesses, he, thunderstruck, and "for the more submission," observes Laneham,

Gascoigne's rival recorder, "broke his tree asunder, and cast the top from him," when "it had almost light upon her highness' horse's head; whereat he startled, and the gentleman much dismayed."

Tuesday was spent in music and dancing, and Wednesday in the chace. On Thursday Elizabeth enjoyed the sport of bear-beating, then in high favour with the polite circles. The bears had been brought especially from London; and the masters of her majesty's games had the chamberlain's warrant to travel peaceably with them, and to press all ban-dogs that should be needful. They were brought into the inner court, for the especial diversion of the queen and her ladies. The imposing spectacle is described with much unction by Master Laneham, whom we have quoted above as a narrator of the proceedings at Kenilworth. "It was a sport very pleasant of those beasts; to see the bear, with his pink eyes, leering after his enemies' approach, the nimbleness and wait of the dog to take his advantage, and the force and experience of the bear again to avoid the assault: If he was bitten in one place how he would pinch in another to get free; that if he was taken once, then what shift, with biting, with clawing, with roaring, tossing, and tumbling, he would work to wind himself from them; and when he was loose, to shake his ears twice or thrice, with the blood and the slaver about his visnomy, was a matter of a *goodly relief*." The bear-baiting took place in the day-time, and at night there was a "very strange and sundry kinds of fireworks," which, by the way, were then so new as to excite great wonder and delight. Friday and Saturday were too damp and gloomy for out-door recreation; but on the ensuing Sunday, "after divine service in the parish church," and "a fruitfull sermon" there in the forenoon, a "Merry Marriage" was performed. The procession was set in order in the tilt-yard, to make it show in the castle before the great court, where the queen beheld it from a window. There were "sixteen wights, riding-men, and well beseen;" the bridegroom, "in his father's tawny worsted jacket," a straw hat, with a capital crown steeple-wise on his head; a pair of harvest-gloves on his hands, as a sign of good husbandry; a pen and inkhorn at his back, for he would be known to be bookish; lame of a leg, that in his youth was broken at foot-ball; well beloved of his mother, who lent him a muffler for a napkin, that was tied to his girdle for [fear of] losing it. It was no small sport to mark this minion in his full appointment; that, through good tuition, became as formal in his action, as had he been a bridegroom indeed." The morris-dancers followed, with Maid Marian, and the fool; bride-maids "as bright as a breast of bacon," of thirty years old apiece; a freckled-faced red-headed lubber, with the bride-cup; the "worshipful bride, thirty-five years old, of colour brown bay, not very beautiful indeed, but ugly, foul, and ill-favoured;" and lastly, many other damsels "for bridesmaids, that for favour, attire, for fashion, and cleanliness, were as meet for such a bride as a tureen ladle for a porridge pot." This ridicule of a rustic ceremonial, endeared to the country people, did no great honour to the good taste of Leicester as a country lord, and could have been anything but gratifying to many who witnessed it. "By my troth," says Laneham, however, "it was a lively pastime; I believe it would have moved a man to a right merry mood, though it had been told him that his wife was dying." Gascoigne had prepared an elaborate masque in two acts, of Diana and her Nymphs. "This show," says the poet, "was devised and penned by Master Gascoigne, and being prepared and ready (every actor in his garment) two or three days together, yet never came to execution. The cause whereof I cannot attribute to any other thing than to lack of opportunity and seasonable weather." The piece concluded in these words :—

A world of wealth at will
You henceforth shall enjoy
In wedded state, and therewithal
Hold up from great annoy
The staff of your estate ;
O Queen, O worthy Queen,
Yet never wight felt perfect bliss
But such as wedded been.

The Coventry men, "my lord's neighbours there," who next were determined to attract the notice of her Majesty, and who had petitioned her to be permitted to perform their "old storial show" of the Saxons and the Danes, now commenced operations, and their spectacle formed the most permanently interesting feature of the whole proceedings. This play, as originally performed by the men of Coventry—"expressed in actions and rhymes after their manner" —was a complicated historical event; in short "a regular model of a complete drama" (Percy). We have no clear account of the spectacle, but there were Danish and Saxon lance-knights on horse-

back, who had furious encounters with spear and shield, sword and target; there were footmen fighting in rank and squadron, and "twice the Danes had the better, but at the last conflict beaten down, overcome, and many led captive for triumph by our English-women." The chief points of the action snowed how the English arose to free themselves from "outrage and insupportable insolency," and "how valiantly our Englishwomen, for love of their country, behaved themselves." On another day, the magnificent masque of the Lady of the Lake was represented: one incident of which must conclude our notices of the pleasant pastimes of Kenilworth. When the spell by which the Lady of the Lake had been enthralled was broken, Henry Goldingham, one of the favoured wags of the court, was to have appeared as Arion riding on a Dolphin, in order to regale her majesty with a song. When the time came for him to commence, he found his voice so husky from the effects of the water that he found he could not get on ; so he threw off his vizor—swore he was no Arion, but only honest Harry Goldingham ! "which blunt discovery pleased the queen better than if it had gone through in the right way." But after all the profusion of show there was one spectacle that Leicester could *not* exhibit, and the absence of which renders unsatisfactory all the rest : it was that of a contented' grateful, happy tenantry. Leicester had none such—he had been an oppressor ; and his character in other respects was probably better understood at home than it was at court.

Yet, neither secret crimes nor public magnificence won Elizabeth ; and, tired of the pursuit, Leicester married a third wife, the Countess of Essex, after, it is supposed, a second murder, that of the Earl of Essex, her husband. On Leicester's death, Kenilworth was left in the possession of his brother, the Earl of Warwick, and the inheritance only bequeathed to his son, Sir Robert Dudley, whom during his life he had basely disowned. Sir Robert lost even the reversion of the property so grudgingly dealt out to him, through the rapacity of King James, assisted by Leicester's widow. The generous Prince Henry, on whom Kenilworth was bestowed, negociated with Sir Robert Dudley for the purchase, but only a fifth of the purchase-money was ever paid, and on Prince Henry's death, Charles took possession of Kenilworth as his heir. Cromwell next divided the castle and lands among his captains and counsellors, and the whole from that time went to ruin. "The ground plot of Kenilworth Castle," as it was in 1640, enables us to trace all the leading divisions of the fabric —with the pleasance and the pool or lake, the performances on which formed decidedly one of the chief attractions of Elizabeth's visit. That fine natural lake is now almost dried up; and the tilt-yard where Elizabeth made her grand entry, and the base court where she graciously conversed with the enchanted lady, and the inner court where the bears were baited, are strewn with the ruins of Leicester's proud castle. The whole scene, indeed, presents a saddening contrast to that we raise up to the mind's eye when we think of the Mortimer's Tower where the gigantic porter met the queen, and the buildings where she was entertained and lodged, "all of the hard quarry stone ; every room so spacious, so well belighted, and so high-roofed within ; so seemly to sight by due proportion without ; in daytime on every side so glittering by glass—at nights, by continual brightness of candle, fire, and torchlight, transparent through the lightsome windows, as it were the Egyptian Pharos relucent unto all the Alexandrian coast." No longer can royalty hear in the presence-chamber, or in the privy-chamber, the sweet incense of adulation and homage; they and the hall (Fig. 1541), and every other part of that sumptuous edifice, are now entirely broken into ruins ; but still such ruins as, by their extensiveness and beauty and romantic associations, leave eye, heart, and fancy content to desire nothing more than there lies before him. (Figs. 430, 818, 822, 823.)

Let us, without inquiring "too curiously" into his motives, end our notices of Leicester with the pleasantest of the associations connected with his name—the Hospital for infirm men founded by him at Warwick, and which now affords a very handsome provision for a master and twenty brethren. The picturesque character of the buildings is shown in Mr. Harvey's drawing (Fig. 1546).

———

A more striking proof of appreciation of the merits of a subject, by a sovereign whose judgment was of any value, was never probably vouchsafed, than the peremptory command of Queen Elizabeth that Sir Philip Sidney (Figs. 1547, 1548) should not embark with Sir Francis Drake in his second expedition against the Spaniards in the West Indies, "lest she should lose the jewel of her dominions." The man thus singled out by the discerning Elizabeth as one whom in an especial manner, she delighted to honour, received about the same time a token no less remarkable of the admiration he had

1525—Arms from the Tower Armoury.

1526—Camp at Tilbury.

From our base in-va-ders, From wick-ed men's de-vice,

O God! a-rise and aid us, And crush our e-ne-mies!

Sink deep their po-tent na-vies! Their strength-en'd spi-rit break!

O God! a-rise and help us, For Je-sus Christ his sake.

1527.—Song of Thanksgiving.

1528.—Procession to St. Paul's.

40

1530.—Howard.

1529.—Gresham. (From a Painting by Sir Ant. More.) Drake. (From a Painting at Nutwell Church.) Cavendish and Frobisher. (Anonymous Pictures engraved by Van der Gucht.) Hawkins. (Old Anonymous Print.)

1531.—Raleigh.

1532.—Interior of the Beauchamp Tower.

1533.—Sir Walter Raleigh in the Tower.

1534.—Hayes Farm, Devonshire, Birthplace of Sir Walter Raleigh.

inspired in other countries: the crown of Poland was offered to him, and—which may be taken as a proof, probably, that Sidney was superior even to the common weakness of great men, ambition—was, according to Fuller, declined; though other accounts make it appear probable that Elizabeth opposed his accepting it. It is a delightful relief, in wading through the crime, misery, and pettinesses of personal ambition, that form so large a portion of past history, to light upon an episode so fresh and beautiful as that of the life and death of this admirable character, whose name is as a magic talisman to call up the recollection of all kinds of noble and graceful deeds. As Sir Philip was the jewel of Elizabeth's dominions, so is the Sidney family the jewel of the English aristocracy. Of Algernon Sidney, Wordsworth's "later Sidney," the eminent martyr-patriot, identified with one of the grandest epochs of the national progress, we must speak hereafter. A characteristic feature of the mind of Sir Philip Sidney was that chaste and imaginative sentiment, which assisted so materially to refine and purify the taste and morals of his times, and was poured out in his various works, especially in his Arcadia; "the perusal of which," says the Retrospective Review, "excites a calm and pensive pleasure, at once full, tranquil, and exquisite." But the work on which his reputation as an author is chiefly based is the noble 'Defence of Poesie,' a work that not only exhausts the subject, but displays it also in the best possible manner. Cowper happily styles him "warbler of poetic prose." The Arcadia was composed in retirement at Wilton, the seat of the Countess of Pembroke, the

Sidney's sister, Pembroke's mother—

of Jonson's well-known epitaph. In that beautiful spot Sidney sought to recover his composure of mind, disturbed by a quarrel with the Earl of Oxford, in which he seems to have exhibited some impetuosity of temper—the only defect ascribed to him. As the Arcadia was written in a great measure for his sister's enjoyment, he affectionately called it the Countess of Pembroke's Arcadia. The charming scenery around the family mansion of the Sidneys at Penshurst (Fig. 1552), in Kent, where Sir Philip was born, has a visible harmony with the best productions of the mind that was reared in it. It has been described in a spirit and with a power worthy of its own fame and beauty by Ben Jonson; so we must transcribe some at least of his nervous and fine lines. Jonson's allusion to the tree called "Sidney's Oak" (Fig. 1553) will not be the less relished when it is known that it still exists, an object of frequent pilgrimage with the lovers of poetry and romance.

> Thou art not, Penshurst, built to envious show
> Of touch, or marble; nor canst boast a row
> Of polished pillars, or a roof of gold;
> Thou hast no lanthorn whereof tales are told,
> Or stair, or courts; but stand'st an ancient pile,
> And these grudged at, art reverenced the while.
> Thou joy'st in better marks; of soil, of air,
> Of wood, of water; therein thou art fair;
> Thou hast thy walks for health as well as sport;
> Thy Mount to which the Dryads do resort,
> Where Pan and Bacchus their high feasts have made
> Beneath the broad beech and the chestnut shade.
> That taller tree, which of a *nut was set*
> *At his great birth, where all the Muses met;*
> There in the writhed bark are cut the names
> Of many a sylvan taken with his flames,
> And thence the ruddy Satyrs oft provoke
> The lighter Fauns to reach thy Ladies' Oak.

Approaching the mansion, or "castle," as it is called (Fig. 1551), through an interesting village churchyard—the latter, with its church (Fig. 1549), divided from the mansion by a noble row of trees—the tranquil and rustic beauty of the scene enhanced by many a time-hallowed association, well prepares us for the touching memorials of the hero of the "lyre and sword," that are to meet our gaze within those picturesque walls and towers. Penshurst has long been under process of restoration, and still the work goes on. The two principal fronts are very long: one presents a façade of Tudor windows, battlements, turrets, and towers; whilst the other, amid great variety of details, shows us large triple-arched windows, the lofty gable of the Banqueting Hall (of the time of Edward III.), in which Ben Jonson had often sat an honoured guest, and wings with towers, decorated windows, and sloping roofs. As we cross the threshold we feel a touch of "hero worship" steal over us; for here, if anywhere, we are made to comprehend that

Great men have been among us:

and we remember Jonson's explanation of the pre-eminence of the Sidneys:—

> They are and have been taught religion; thence
> Their gentler spirits have sucked innocence;
> Each morn, and even, they are taught to pray
> With the whole household.

There is a portrait of Sir Philip at Penshurst peculiarly expressive of the depth and tenderness of his feelings in the family relations, and so affords fresh traits of his altogether charming nature. This is a double portrait of himself and his younger brother Robert, their arms linked together, and the faces full of love, mingled in the one case with something of the protector, and in the other with an expression of full confidence in the protection.

In a letter to Robert, his brother Philip is set up as a model for his guidance: a model which he is to imitate in all "his virtues, exercises, studies, and actions." The writer of that letter was, in truth, one of Sir Philip's warmest admirers; for he adds, "he is a rare ornament of his age, the very formula that all well-disposed young gentlemen of the court do form also their manners and life by." . . . . Again—"He hath the most virtue that I ever found in any man." The writer of that letter was Philip's father, Sir Henry Sidney. A proud and happy man to be able to write such a letter of his own son! It is but justice to observe that this very appreciation is the best evidence of Sir Henry's merits; and may induce us to attribute no slight portion of the character of Philip to the father and friend who had watched over and guided its development.

Yet this all-accomplished, all-perfect, Sir Philip failed where failure might least have been anticipated—in love. The portrait of the "Stella" of his poems, the "Philoclea" of his Arcadia, whom he describes with a pencil dipped in the fairest colours, also meets our view at Penshurst. Lady Penelope Devereux, which was her real name, was the object of Sidney's ardent love; but she formed another marriage, and he seems to have wisely sought consolation by imitating her example. He wedded Frances, daughter of Sir Francis Walsingham. Stella afterwards added to the notoriety she had attained through Sidney's passion for her—but under far different circumstances—by her unhappy connection with Mountjoy, Earl of Devonshire. Mrs. Jameson has given us an interesting account of her in the 'Romance of Biography.'

Sir Philip evidently only wanted opportunities and exigencies calculated to arouse the heroism of a patriot, to have been as eminent in that particular as Algernon Sidney afterwards became. Sir Philip's bold letters, entitled the 'Remonstrance,' issued when the queen seemed about to form a marriage with the Duke of Anjou (another lover), was an interference with the will of his sovereign that might have cost him his head, had not that sovereign known better than some of her predecessors how to value truth in her courtiers. His 'Discourse in defence of the Earl of Leicester,' his uncle, in answer to an attack by Parsons, the Jesuit, in a tract called 'Leicester's Commonwealth,' does less credit to his judgment than to his earnestness and sincerity of purpose; for to all appearance, Leicester as ill merited the support of such a nephew, as he did the favour of his queen. Indeed, Sir Philip seems to have begun to discover his uncle's imperfections when associated with him in the command of troops in Holland, in the fatal expedition that cost him his life. Whilst there he frequently expressed his disapproval of Leicester's conduct as general. Sir Philip's sword lies on one of the tables at Penshurst, and is shown to visitors. Its form is singular. The handle is about sixteen inches long; the cross-piece is a ragged staff, with bears at the extremities; and on each side of the blade, a little way above the handle, is a kind of short spike. One gazes at the deadly relic with a thrill and a shudder: it speaks eloquently of the field of strife where the young "English Petrarch," as Sir Walter Raleigh calls him, received his death-wound.

When the war between the people of the Netherlands and Spain was raging, and Elizabeth took part with the former, she appointed Sidney governor of Flushing. After the exhibition of conspicuous and successful bravery, Sidney and his troops accidentally met a force of about three thousand marching to relieve Zutphen, a town of Guelderland. An engagement ensued, almost under the walls of the town. Sidney's horse was shot under him, and, while making a third charge, he received a musket-bullet in the left thigh, a little above the knee. He was carried out of the battle-field, "in which sad progress, passing along by the rest of the army, where his uncle the general was, and being thirsty with excess of bleeding, he called for some drink, which was presently brought him; but as he was putting the bottle to his mouth he saw a poor soldier carried along, who had eaten his last at the same feast, ghastly casting up his eyes at the bottle; which Sir Philip perceiving, took it from his head before he drank, and delivered it to the poor man with these words: 'Thy necessity is yet greater than mine.'" (Lord Brooke.)

After many days of severe suffering, he died at Arnheim, on the 7th October, 1586, experiencing all the consolation that the tender attentions of Lady Sidney and his faithful secretary, William Temple, could bestow. The body was conveyed to England, lay many days in state, and was interred in Old St. Paul's Cathedral (Fig. 1550), attended by seven deputies, one for each of the Seven United Provinces, and by a great number of peers, his friends, and others. There was a general mourning for him observed throughout the land—*the first of the kind* known in England. The Universities published three volumes of elegies on his death. Spenser composed one, under the title of Astrophel. The summary of his character is thus given in the Retrospective Review: "Sir Philip Sidney was a gentleman finished and complete, in whom mildness was associated with courage, erudition mollified by refinement, and courtliness dignified by truth. He is a specimen of what the English character was capable of producing when foreign admixtures had not destroyed its simplicity, or politeness debased its honour. Of such a stamp was Sir Philip Sidney, and as such every Englishman has reason to be proud of him." "He trod," says the author of the 'Effigies Poeticæ,' "from his cradle to his grave amid incense and flowers, and died in a dream of glory." On the whole, it is evident, that in his own time there never was a man more a favourite in public or in private life, in the court or the camp, as an author or as a hero; nor will the statement require any extensive modification if we refer to times other than his own—or, in a word, to posterity. If his merits were very nicely balanced in comparison with those of many men who have lived and died in partial neglect, it might be found there had been some of the illusions of romance in this excessive admiration; but there would still be sufficient ground for pronouncing, with the writer in the Review just named, Sir Philip Sidney one of the very noblest men of Old England.

There were troubles gnawing at the heart of Elizabeth all the while she appeared to be enjoying the highest happiness that the world could bestow; those troubles were fear and jealousy of her cousin, Mary of Scotland (Fig. 1557), whose pretensions to the throne of England alarmed the sovereign, as much as her personal beauty excited the envy of the woman. And, it must be allowed, Elizabeth had cause to fear her beauteous rival in regard to the safety of the crown she wore; for, since the death of the late Queen of England, when claims were put forth on the behalf of Mary Queen of Scots, whose grandmother was the eldest daughter of Henry VII., those claims had continued to be urged with great pertinacity by her ambitious uncles, the princes of Lorraine; the youthful Mary, as Dauphiness of France, and the Dauphin, her husband, on every occasion of their appearing in public, had been ostentatiously greeted as king and queen of England; the English arms were engraved on their plate, embroidered on their banners, and painted on their furniture; and Mary's own favourite device was, at the time, the two crowns of France and Scotland, with the motto *Aliamque moratur*, meaning that of England. Nor had this been all; when Mary left France, after the Dauphin's death, and subsequently, when riper years might have begun to render her less at the mercy of her interested advisers, she refused to abandon the claims that had been set up for her, and which were supported, according to the notions of every Catholic in England, by the canonical laws of the Romish church. Anne Bullen's marriage, in their estimation had been unlawful, and had been pronounced null and void by a sentence of the Church; whilst, at the same time, the attainder of Elizabeth's blood had not been reversed even by her own parliament—Elizabeth having been too sagacious to risk the re-opening of the question. Such were the relative grounds of the rivalship for the sovereignty of this nation between the two queens—depending solely on the question of Elizabeth's legitimacy—which, set aside, would leave Mary undoubted heiress of the succession. Religious feeling, it will be seen, was at the root of the whole matter. The mother of Elizabeth had been a Protestant; Elizabeth now stood at the head and front of universal Protestantism; and the Scottish Reformers, a most determined body, linked themselves with her interest, and the interests of her Reformed people, and were the bitterest enemies of their own Queen. On the other hand, Mary's Catholic adherents called for the stake and the fire to destroy their adversaries: just as if they had endured nothing that ought to have taught them the inutility of such arguments; just as if they were incapable of seeing that the dread of their cruel intolerance was hourly weakening their hold on the popular affections, and involving the mistress whom they loved in their own certain and rapidly advancing ruin. It was asserted by James Stuart (Mary's half-brother, and prior of St. Andrew's) that *his* sole motive for acting as a leader of the Scottish party who

distrusted and warred against her, was the extirpation of the old superstition, for the honour of God, and the good of Scotland; and there can be little doubt that it was the ruling motive also of others of that party, with their great leader, John Knox.

At the coming over of the widowed Mary from France, where she had dwelt since her fifth year, where she had shared in the polite education of the French king's own daughters, in one of the first convents of the kingdom, and been the idol of the whole French court and people, it is said that, as the coast of the happy land of her youth faded from her view, she continued to exclaim, "Farewell, France! farewell, dear France! I shall never see thee more!" and her first view of Scotland only increased the poignancy of these touching regrets; so little pains had been taken to "cover over the nakedness and poverty of the land." Tears sprang into her eyes when, fresh from the elegant and luxurious court of Paris, she saw the wretched ponies, with bare wooden saddles, or dirty and ragged trappings, which had been provided to carry her and her ladies from the water-side to Holyrood. And then the palace itself: how different from the palaces in which she had lived in France! It was dismal and small, consisting only of what is now the north wing. (Fig. 1559.) The state-room and the bed-chamber which were used by her yet remain with the old furniture; and much of the needle-work there is said to have been the work of her own hands. Then the melody with which they greeted her—her poor rude Scottish subjects—"Two or three hundred violinists, *apparently amateur performers*, held a concert all night below her windows, and prevented her getting an hour's sleep after the fatigues of the sea. Mary, though suffering under the effects of this dire serenade, received the compliments of these 'honest men of the town of Edinburgh' as it was intended, and even ventured to hint a wish that the concert might be repeated." (Sir Walter Scott.) Such graceful good humour had not been deserved, for with something worse than the bad taste that had dictated the "dire serenade," she had been ushered into Edinburgh by pageants so contrived as to cast derision on the faith to which it was known she was strongly attached. All this was but a foretaste of the bitterness to come. She had been promised that she should exercise her own religion in her own establishment; but John Knox sternly declared that to import one mass into the kingdom of Scotland would be more fatal than to bring over a foreign army of ten thousand men. Thus the poor queen, who had lived hitherto in one long happy dream, had now to be awakened, as it were, by a peal of thunder, to see a long train of miseries and troubles coming on in the distance, and threatening to overwhelm her.

The first Sabbath in Holyrood had nearly been stained by the blood of her priest at the very altar foot, where in the palace chapel he attempted to celebrate mass. "Shall that idol, the mass, again have place? It shall not!" exclaimed the excited Reformers; and the young Master of Lindsay called out in the court-yard of the palace, that the idolatrous priest should die the death according to God's law. Even James Stuart, who stood with his drawn sword at the chapel door to prevent this shocking outrage, had to pretend that he did so only to prevent any Scot from entering to witness the abominable ceremony within. Poor Mary must have felt as if she had suddenly lighted among a nation of savages—and truly these proceedings were savage; notwithstanding the latent "soul of good" that existed in them. The second Sunday brought out Knox against her in a thundering sermon on idolatry. Then he tried to convert her, and "knocked at her heart" until she was bathed in tears before his fierce rebukes. What was to follow, if she were *not* converted, was shadowed forth so as to be sufficiently understood by the hearers, in Knox's daily prayer—"That God would turn her heart, now obstinate against God and his truth; and if his holy will were otherwise, that he would strengthen the hearts and hands of the chosen, and the elect, stoutly to withstand the rage of tyrants."

At present all the tyranny was on the petitioner's side. Mary understood something of toleration, though she *was* a Catholic, and rebuked her stern teacher on account of "his severe dealing with all men that disagreed with him in opinions," and "willed him to use more *meekness* in his sermons." A removal to Stirling did not abate her troubles; and again tears were wrung from her by the vehemence of the Reforming preachers and their followers, who threatened with death all who should dare to partake in the idolatry of the mass. Overborne by all this violence, she followed her half-brother's advice, banished the monks and friars, and by other concessions obtained leave to remain a Catholic herself—provided she kept all the ceremonials of Catholicism out of the public view. These restrictions appeared just, no doubt, to the nation, then in the midst of its grand struggle for spiritual freedom; but they reflect no credit on the cause. Never, it has been

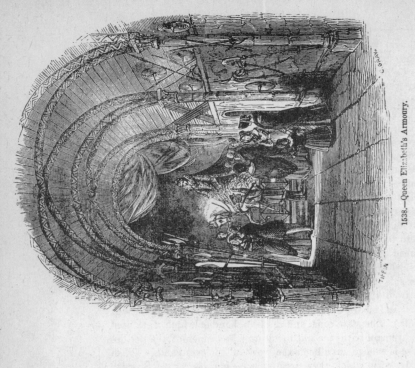

1538.—Queen Elizabeth's Armoury.

1537.—Drake.

1539.—Remains of Upnor Castle, temp. Eliz.

1535.—Elizabeth Castle, Jersey.

1536.—View of Mount Orgueil Castle: Women Gathering Sea-weed.

1540.—Kenilworth Gate.

1541.—Entrance to the Hall, Kenilworth.

1543.—Gascoigne.

1542.—Earl of Leicester.

1544.—Leicester.

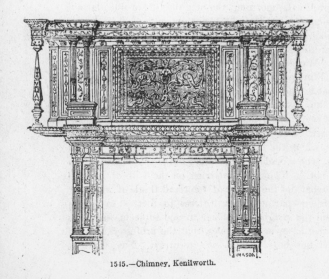

1545.—Chimney, Kenilworth.

1546.—Leicester's Hospital, Warwick.

remarked, was crowned head so braved and insulted by bishop or pope, even in the darkest periods of the darkest ages, as this delicately-framed and sensitively-minded woman and queen of nineteen years old by John Knox. To give another example or two:—During her absence from Holyrood, some of the populace of Edinburgh broke into her chapel, defiled the altar, and committed all kinds of indecent outrages. Mary, indignant, had two—*only*—of these rioters indicted; when Knox wrote circular letters to " the faithful," men of the strong hand and iron heart, charging them to come up to Edinburgh and *protect their persecuted brethren* What was meant the faithful well knew, and so did Mary and her privy council, before whom Knox was summoned. He appeared with defiance on his lips—with language utterly unsuited to the presence in which he stood;—yet he went forth again freely acquitted. What hope after that could Mary have had of living at peace in Scotland? Knox was in the habit of usually designating Mary " the Jezebel " in his sermons in the pulpit, and this before any impropriety whatever had appeared in her conduct, beyond that of being a Catholic, and fond of hunting and hawking, music and dancing, which, indeed, were all crimes in the opinions of the puritanical disciplinarians of the new faith. Knox was unsoftened when " with winning sweetness " Mary promised him ready access to her whenever he should desire it, and entreated him, if he found her conduct blameable, to reprehend her in private, rather than vilify her in the kirk before the people. He replied, it was her duty to go to the kirk to hear him,—not his duty to wait upon her. At another time he told her that he would submit to her even as Paul submitted to Nero; and he did not scruple to regale her ears with proofs from Scripture of the holiness of regicide, and of the slaughter of Catholic priests. These are but specimens of Mary's sufferings in the days of her innocence, to which we will add another. " It is now called in question," writes Randolph to Cecil, " whether the queen, *being an idolatress*, may be obeyed in all civil and political actions. I think marvel of the wisdom of God, that gave this unruly, stout, and cumbersome people no more substance or power than they have, for then they would run wild." Some time after, the same writer says, in reporting the progress of Mary's unhappiness in Scotland, " So long as the queen is in heart divided from her subjects through the diversity of religion, there is neither that quietness of mind, nor peace in conscience, that is most to be desired in true service to their sovereign; nor can I yet see how her fate will long continue, seeing the self-same seeds remain, that were the occasion of the former mischief."

Four years after her return from France, Mary again married; her second husband being her cousin, Henry Stuart, Lord Darnley, heir of the noble house of Lennox. The rites observed were those of the Romish church; and Mary neither consulted her parliament in forming the union, or in investing the object of her love with the sovereign dignity and title. But, though Knox and others murmured, the people generally appear to have become so much attached to Mary as to think little of the irregularity. And now for a brief period Mary seems to have tasted once more something like happiness. But it was indeed brief. Chatelard, a French poet, had come over with Mary, and obtained her favour by his poetical effusions. But, forgetting her position as a queen and a wife, he exhibited his personal attachment to Mary in a manner that was most audacious and unbecoming: the government interfered, and the poet was barbarously executed. His conduct in his last hours—repeating verses from Ronsard instead of his prayers, and his dying speech, " Farewell to the most beautiful and most cruel queen that ever lived "—showed, to say the least of it, a state of mind requiring gentler discipline than the axe. Chatelard was succeeded in Mary's favour by David Rizzio, who was at first her musician, but subsequently her French secretary; and in that position became so obnoxious to Mary's husband, Darnley, and to the Scottish Reformers, that a plot for his destruction was concocted. From the former Rizzio might have expected different treatment, seeing that he had been Darnley's confidant in his courtship of Mary, and had aided him by every means in his power; from the latter he could have no hope of mercy, if he were once in their power, for he had committed the horrible crime in their eyes of corresponding in his official capacity with the Pope of Rome. No proof of any guilt on Rizzio's part seems to have been sought or required: it was enough that he was hated (by Darnley, because Rizzio—among other obnoxious features of his conduct—had remonstrated with him on his treatment of the queen), and being hated, he was suspected; assassination was determined upon, and also that it should take place before Mary's eyes at a time, too, when she was expected shortly to become a mother. Of the character and conduct of Darnley, *the husband*, that little trait alone furnishes an unanswerable evidence. A bond was signed by the conspirators, by which Darnley took the whole under his special protection: that was on the 1st or the 5th of March. On the 9th of the same month Mary was sitting at supper in Holyrood house, engaged in quiet conversation with the Countess of Argyle and the governor of Holyrood, whilst Rizzio, as was his custom, sat also at supper at a side-table, when the door suddenly opened, and the king stalked in, placed himself at the back of the queen, and glared in terrible significance on the doomed secretary. Lord Ruthven followed: he had risen from the bed of sickness to share in the bloody deed, and now appeared in complete armour, looking pale and ghastly. The other conspirators followed, also armed. Ruthven, in sepulchral accents, bade Rizzio come forth, for the place he sat in did not become him. Mary started up, and inquired of Darnley if he knew anything of this foul proceeding, and on receiving his denial of any such knowledge, commanded Ruthven, on pain of treason, to quit her presence. In the mean time Rizzio had run round to her on whom alone all his chances of life rested, and seizing Mary's garments, cried aloud for protection and justice. Instantly the table was overturned by Ruthven and the others, Darnley seized Mary's arm, and Rizzio was torn away. The first to strike was George Douglas, who, pulling out the king's own dagger, aimed so violent a blow upon the unfortunate Italian, that the blade was buried up to the hilt in his body and so left. What a scene!—the groans of the dying victim as he was dragged away into an ante-chamber, and there despatched by no less than *fifty-six* blows!—the shrieks of the female attendants!—the unutterable anguish of Mary, to see such a deed done on such a man, and by her own husband and his associates!—the ruffian Andrew Ker standing with his cocked pistol before her, and, lastly, Morton, the Chancellor of Scotland, guarding the door, to prevent any assistance being rendered to Mary from without!

In reference to Chatelard and Rizzio, there appears to be no evidence that the queen's conduct was liable to any more serious charge than that of indiscretion; but in the next important event of her life, the connection with the Earl of Bothwell, her name was to suffer in the eyes of others than her enemies. Three or four years before the murder of Rizzio, this Bothwell had been an outlaw, having, in addition to his other offences, spoken words of the queen that irritated her so grievously that she swore he should never have favour at her hand. He watched his time and opportunity, however, and obtained the favour so unreservedly that when, after the murder just mentioned, Mary persuaded Darnley to fly with her from Edinburgh, it was to the castle of Dunbar they fled, where Bothwell, as the custodian, received them. Another presumed evidence of the queen's partiality was given in 1566, when Bothwell was despatched as Lieutenant of the Marches, to Leddesdale, then in a state of revolt. Whilst there, he was " deadly wounded by John Elliott, *alias* John of the Park, whose head was sent into Edinburgh thereafter." Mary rode from Jedburgh, forty rugged miles, to see Bothwell, and returned the same day, so harassed in mind, and wearied in body, that a fever seized her, and her life was despaired of. After this it seems Bothwell pressed Mary to agree to a divorce; but she declined, on account of her son, (afterwards James I. of England). Bothwell soon found a way out of the difficulty that threatened to overthrow his project; and a characteristic way it was, of this bold, bad man. In January, 1567, when the king and queen were at Edinburgh, Bothwell was heard to say " it was the queen's mind that the king should be taken away." On the 9th of the following month, when the latter was lying ill of the small-pox in the Kirk of Field, Mary spent the evening with him. At twelve she left him for a masque, kissing him as she took her leave, and putting one of her rings on his finger. About two in the morning, the neighbourhood was alarmed by a loud explosion, which brought every one out of doors to see what had happened: they found the king's lodgings blown up, and the dead body of the king lying under a tree at a short distance from the ruins. We *may* hope that Mary knew nothing of this murder; but it is impossible to doubt that Bothwell was the chief murderer, and that he did it to gain possession of her hand.

Little more than two months after Darnley's death, Mary was one day on a journey to see her son, when she was met near Linlithgow by Bothwell and a great party, who carried her to the Castle of Dunbar, where the former was heard to boast, he " would marry the queen, who would or who would not; yea, whether she would herself or not." They were married on the 15th of May at Holyrood. And what did the people of Scotland think of all this? Mary's flight with her partner from fortress to fortress to escape the consequences of the indignation of her armed subjects, furnishes the answer. It must be owned, however, that the professed motives of the leaders will not bear a moment's scrutiny. Nay, there is reason to believe, they were the very men who had indirectly aided in the perpetration of the murder that they now called upon heaven and earth to punish.

Three weeks after the marriage of Bothwell and Mary, Morton, Maitland, and others of her worst enemies, rose in arms ostensibly to punish Bothwell, to free the queen from his control, and secure the person of her son; in other words, to protect Mary and the prince against Bothwell. But secretly it was determined to dethrone the queen, and crown her son. They attempted to seize her and Bothwell in Borthwick Castle, near Edinburgh; when she was reduced to disguise herself in male attire in order to escape, and, mounted on a common saddle, to ride after her husband to the castle of Dunbar. The confederates then assumed the supreme power, and issued proclamations calling on all the queen's people to join their standard under pain of being deemed murderers of the late king; and they printed detailed statements of the crimes of Bothwell. In the main then this was a confederacy of the nobles; and the evil motives that lurked beneath their fair pretences seem to have been tolerably understood by the more rational and disinterested middle orders. Instead of joining them, some sent to Mary troops to enable her to oppose them. Two thousand fighting men from the Lothians and the Merse instantly answered the queen's appeal for aid, and gathered at Dunbar. Mary, with a spirit and decision that would have done credit to her lion-hearted cousin of England, —but unfortunately with less cautious sagacity—left her safe retreat, without waiting for those reinforcements of her army (which would probably have enabled her to recover all she had lost of queenly power), and marched towards Edinburgh. Halting at Gladsmuir, she caused a proclamation to be read to her followers, in which she declared that her late marriage with Bothwell had been contracted and solemnized *with the consent and at the persuasion* of the chiefs of those now in insurrection against her, as their own handwritings testified; and affirming, that though they affected to fear for the safety of her son (who was at the very time in their own possession), yet they only aimed at overthrowing her and her posterity, in order that they themselves might enjoy the supreme power. She had been forced to take arms, she said, for her own defence, and would reward the valour of her faithful followers with the confiscated lands of the traitors. After spending the night at Seton, she the next morning (Sunday) advanced to Carberry Hill, where the Lords met her: the Earl of Morton commanding one division of troops, the Earl of Athole another.

Mary sent her French ambassador, the aged Le Croc, to prevent, if possible, a battle, by assuring the insurgents that she was desirous to avoid bloodshed, and willing to grant an amnesty for all that had passed. The Earl of Morton answered that they had not taken arms against the queen, but against the murderer of the king, and that if she would deliver up Bothwell, or put him from her company, they would return to obedience; otherwise, "they would make a day of it." To this the Earl of Glencairn added, they were not come to that field to ask pardon, but rather to *give* it. Bothwell also sent to the lords, offering to prove his innocence by single combat. There were two acceptances of that challenge, which Bothwell objected to, as they were from men of inferior rank. Then he singled out the Earl of Morton, a man who may be considered his equal in guilt. The combat was to be on foot, with two-handed swords; however, it did not take place. Lord Lindsay volunteered to take the place of Morton, laid aside his armour for the purpose, and falling on his knees in the presence of the whole army, prayed that God might in his mercy protect the innocent, and punish the murderer of the king. But Mary would not consent to this meeting. The accounts of her surrender at Carberry Hill (Fig. 1558) differ: according to some, Bothwell demanded a promise of fidelity from Mary, and then riding swiftly away to Dunbar Castle, left her to be dealt with as the ruthless hearts of her foes might dictate. According to others, Morton and some of the nobles secretly urged him to flight, lest, being taken, he might impeach them of their share in Darnley's murder. Others again state, that the queen sent to desire that Kirkaldy of Grange, who enjoyed the high praise of being Scotland's best soldier, and who seems to have been one of the most honourable, might wait upon her to settle terms of accommodation. The laird of Grange was sent accordingly, with full powers; and he proposed that Bothwell should pass off the field until the cause was tried, and that Queen Mary should return to the counsels of her nobles, who bound themselves thenceforward to honour, serve, and obey her majesty. Mary acquiescing, Kirkaldy took Bothwell by the hand and desired him to depart, which he did. Then the laird took the queen's bridle-rein, and led her down the hill, where Morton, meeting her, ratified the assurances that had been given by Kirkaldy, saying, she should be more honoured and

obeyed than any of her progenitors had ever been. But their object once attained, the treatment she received at the hands of her lords became as strongly marked as ever with coarse cruelty and bad faith. The armed ranks closed around her with fearful gestures and reproaches; her ears were assailed by cries from the low rabble and common soldiery (who readily imitated the temper of those above them) that she ought to be burned as a papist—a prostitute —and a murderess. Amid this horrid clamour she began to move toward Edinburgh, where she arrived at seven in the evening, in tears, and covered with the dust of the roads. There she was made to pass on horseback—a public spectacle of disgrace—through the principal streets, some of the mob carrying a white banner before her, on which was rudely painted the figure of her husband Darnley, lying strangled under a tree, and a figure of Prince James, his son, kneeling beside it with a label issuing from his mouth, bearing these words, "Judge, and avenge my cause, O Lord." To this terrible day succeeded a no less terrible night: the yells of the populace continuing to resound about the provost's house in which she was lodged, until daylight brought back again to her sight the hideous banner—the first object that presented itself.

Bothwell fled to Dunbar, and thence departed in a vessel for the Orkney Islands, but being pursued directed his course towards the Danish shores, and was taken prisoner by the Danes. An account has been printed by the Bannatyne Club of "The examination of Bothwell when he was taken by a Danish man-of-war on his flight from Scotland, and brought to Bergen in Norway," 28th September, 1567. The examiners of Bothwell state, "that when Chrestene Olborrig arrived here, in Bergen, with his royal majesty's man-of-war called the Biornenn (the Bear), he brought with him two armed Scottish pinks (ships of a small size) which he found in his royal majesty's seas and waters." These small ships had been met armed and manned, "yet having no document, letter of marque, passport, or ship's papers, such as respectable sailors usually have, and ought to have and produce." Among those on board—Scottish people —there was "one dressed in old, torn, and patched boatswain's clothes, who sometime thereafter stated himself to be the supreme governor of all Scotland," and assumed a high tone. This was Bothwell. It was a notorious pirate vessel in which he was taken. He pretended to have nothing on board that he cared for preserving; but on search being made, a box was found filled with letters and papers, some printed, some written, among which were the Scottish proclamations declaring the crimes with which he was charged, and offering a reward for his apprehension. There was a letter in the box written to him by Queen Mary, in her own hand; but unfortunately the contents are only noticed in a very general way in this curious document. It seems nearly certain that Bothwell continued a prisoner of the Danish government till madness led the way to his death in 1576, in the castle of Malmoe or Malmary, in the province of Schoenen, now a part of Sweden, then belonging to Denmark. The authenticity of his "dying testament," in which he is said to have solemnly declared upon oath that he himself murdered Darnley by the counsels of Murray, Morton, and others, rests in partial doubt.

Let us now turn to the miserable queen, whose very life was in danger from the wild rage of the Reformers. Sir Nicholas Throgmorton, a special envoy from Elizabeth, writing to his court, says, he could get no access to Queen Mary, and it would be nearly impossible to induce the lords to send Prince James into England— a plan which Elizabeth and Cecil much desired. He adds, " I found them (John Knox and Craig) very austere in this conference. What I shall do hereafter I know not. They are furnished with many arguments, some parts of Scripture, some of history, some grounded (as they say) upon the laws of this realm, some upon practices used in this realm, and some upon the conditions and oaths made by their princes at their coronation. The lords still speak reverently and mildly about Mary, yet I find by intelligence that the queen is in very great peril of her life, by reason that the people assembled at this convention *do mind vehemently the destruction of her.*"

This convention was the Assembly of the Kirk, with George Buchanan at their head, then in close league with the lords of the Secret Council. From Edinburgh Mary was removed to Lochleven (Fig. 1560), a castle situated on an islet in the loch, or lake, which bears that name, in Kinross-shire, and commanded by the ferocious Lord Lindsay of the Byres, and Ruthven, Rizzio's chief murderer. When such men were her keepers, we may easily judge what were her sufferings. The very sight of Ruthven must have been almost a present death, reviving memories so fearful. The possessor of Lochleven was Sir William Douglas, presumptive heir to the dark Morton. To the honour of Kirkaldy of Grange, he gave no assent

1547.—Sir Philip Sidney. (From a Painting by Sir Anthony More.)

1548.—Sir Philip Sidney.

1549.—Penshurst Church.

1550.—Funeral of Sidney.

1551.—Penshurst Castle.

1552.—Penshurst. General View.

1553.—Sidney's Tree.

1554.—North Front of Burghley House.

1555.—Robert Cecil.

1556.—Gateway at Cowdry.

1557.—Queen Mary of Scotland. (From a Painting by Zucchero.)

1558.—The Surrender of Mary Queen of Scots, at Carberry Hill.
(From the old Picture engraved by Vertue, and published by the Royal Society of Antiquaries.)

to these proceedings; but, much incensed, charged the lords with breaking their word, and having made him, an honourable soldier, the means of deceiving the queen with lies. But they answered that Mary, having since her confinement written affectionately to Bothwell, and promised still to share his fortunes, had forfeited the benefits of the treaty. It seems very doubtful whether such a letter had been written, especially when we find that Bothwell's quitting the kingdom did not procure her liberation, but that it was then declared she should be dethroned, not on his account, but for general misgovernment (as if she had in reality ever been able to govern the kingdom at all!), and yield the crown to her son, and her half-brother, the Regent Murray. And under such keepers as Lindsay and Ruthven, no wonder the signature of abdication was at last wrung from her. Mary became a subject of her own infant son, who was crowned at Stirling in 1567. But Mary was as much a queen in her own estimation after her deposition as before—her spirit rose above her unparalleled misfortunes, and she received comfort from the knowledge that she had devoted friends, who would not rest until they had accomplished her escape. She was enabled to communicate with them secretly, and to concert measures. There were ambushes placed round the lake, and fleet horses provided. One morning, the queen's laundress, coming early as usual, Mary, disguised in her dress, went out of the castle, and entered a boat to cross the lake. One of the rowers said, merrily,—"Let us see what manner of dame this is," and attempted to pull down the muffler that covered her face; Mary put up her hands to prevent the action, when they were perceived to be very fair and white, and their suspicions were aroused. Mary, self-possessed and courageous, then speaking to them as a queen, charged them, for their lives, to row her over to the shore; but they took her back to her prison, promising, however, to keep her attempt secret from her keepers, which promise they seem to have violated. George Douglas was lingering at a little village, "hard at the loch side," with Semple and Breton, two of Mary's faithful servants, to receive her, had she landed. The fact that she had so nearly accomplished her desire, no doubt stimulated rather than depressed the mind of the Queen, and it was not long before she repeated her attempt. There was then a "poor simple lad" in the castle, "Little Douglas," a relative of the owner of the castle, and whose proceedings no one dreamed of looking after on account of his simplicity. By Mary's directions he was induced to steal the keys from the keeper's chamber, in the middle of the night, and presently the Queen was once more outside the castle-gates, which were carefully locked upon the keeper by the prisoner, and the keys thrown into the loch. Then Mary hurried into a small boat with a single female attendant, and was quickly rowed across by the stout-hearted "Little Douglas" to the opposite side, where she was received with transports of joy by some of her adherents, and borne swiftly away.

Once more at large, her friends assembled, and Mary found herself in a very short space of time at the head of a considerable army. The Regent Murray, her half-brother, advanced to oppose her, and the armies met at Langside between Glasgow and Dumbarton, and attacked each other with desperate fury. Mary remained on a neighbouring hill watching the progress of the fight, which for a while appeared to be favourable to her; but at last Morton, with a detachment, sweeping suddenly round an eminence, charged her troops in flank, broke and routed them. The battle was lost. Once more the unhappy Queen was a fugitive. For nearly sixty miles, almost without pause or rest, did she continue the headlong flight, and then stopped at Dundrennan Abbey to consider what farther chances there remained for her almost desperate cause. Should she yield herself to the mercy of her subjects? who would in all probability be merciless; or take refuge in France? whither, unhappily, there appeared to be no means of going; or, lastly, throw herself in full confidence on the kindness and generosity of Elizabeth? who, notwithstanding some equivocal-looking acts, had used many kindly words in connection with her fair "sister" and cousin. Mary determined upon the last course. It was a fatal one, though its results were not at first to be made apparent; nor is it easy to see that Mary on the whole could have acted with a greater probability of saving herself. Elizabeth refused to see Mary; but offered to mediate between her and her Scottish subjects. Elizabeth, it is to be remembered, desired in secret the crown of Scotland as much or more than Mary had ever appeared in public to desiderate the crown of England. Mary declined the offer, refusing to be regarded in any other light than as Queen of Scotland. From that time her fate appears to have been determined—an endless captivity. She was immediately cut off from all communication with her subjects, excepting such as it was

thought proper to allow; and was moved about from place to place the better to ensure her safety. The hapless victim again and again implored Elizabeth to deal generously—justly with her. "I came," said she, "of mine own accord—let me depart again with yours; and if God permit my cause to succeed, I shall be bound to you for it." And in the latter part of the same letter she writes in these touching terms:—"Good sister, be of another mind, when the heart and all shall be yours, and at your commandment. I thought to satisfy you wholly, if I might have seen you. Alas! do not as the serpent that stoppeth his hearing, for I am no enchanter, but your sister and natural cousin," &c.

Our space will not admit of any details of the perplexed and tedious proceedings connected with the commission that sat at York to determine, as it were, between the three parties—Elizabeth, Mary, and the Regent of Scotland, whether Mary were or were not innocent. It is evident that Elizabeth was predetermined that the Regent Murray should prove his own sister Mary guilty; but the proofs, it seems, were too slight, too unworthy even of credence for her and her minister, and so in the end she admitted that Murray had not proved his charges. Neither on the other hand, had Mary, it was alleged, proved aught against the honour and loyalty of Murray, so he was left quietly in his government, and Mary still kept carefully in her captivity. The pretence now was, that Mary was a lawful prisoner, and might not depart till she had satisfied Elizabeth for the wrong done in claiming the crown of England. It was the old fable of the Wolf and the Lamb acted yet once more.

One of the greatest lessons of history is—that which we believe a careful study of all history affords—the constant retribution that the crimes of state-policy bring back upon their authors. Few have experienced this more severely than Elizabeth. The sovereign who would not have had one real enemy among her subjects but for this imprisonment, made hosts of enemies by it, and embittered her own life little less than she embittered the poor prisoner's. Scheme after scheme was formed for the relief of Mary among the Catholics of England, and it is highly probable that the views of the disaffected may have reached, as was supposed, to the dethronement of their own sovereign. Before we notice the most interesting and painful of these schemes, Babington's, we may notice a previous one that had for its object the marriage of the Queen of Scots to the Duke of Norfolk. Elizabeth more than once, it is said, spoke to Norfolk in such a way that he could hardly be sure whether she was seeking to discover his supposed secret views, or desirous to promote them. But he answered cautiously that the project had not originated with him, nor did it meet his wishes. Elizabeth then observed, "But though you now mislike of it, yet you may percase be induced to like of it for the benefit of the realm, and for mine own security." The Duke, knowing something of his royal mistress's meaning and disposition, answered, "that no reason could move him to like of her that had been a competitor to the crown; and if her majestey would move him thereto, he would rather be committed to the Tower, for he meant never to marry with such a person where he could not be sure of his pillow." But there were noble tempters at work to destroy Norfolk. Leicester and others impelled him to address Mary privately, and when he did so all his letters were conveyed to the Queen. Then Leicester turning ill, confessed with sighs and tears the plot, and was fondly pardoned. Of course Norfolk could not under such circumstances be treated with great severity, so he received a reprimand, and promised to drop the project. He went into the country. After a time he was invited to court by Elizabeth; on the way to London he was arrested, and sent to the Tower, the pretence being that fresh discoveries had been made of his treasonable machinations. Whilst there the impending storm burst out in an insurrection of the Catholics headed by the Earls of Northumberland and Westmoreland. It was, as usual in such cases, a failure, and brought ruin on all concerned in it: and among the rest on the ducal captive in the Tower, the plotting lover of the Queen of the Scots—the Duke of Norfolk, who was tried and beheaded.

But if the schemes of Norfolk and his coadjutors, and the growing alarm as to the intentions of the Catholics that pervaded England, rendered Mary's position exceedingly dangerous, it was reserved for some still more arduous and enthusiastic friends to be the immediate instruments of her utter ruin. Among the Catholic youth of England, whom the tale of Mary's misfortunes had moved most deeply, was one Anthony Babington, a young man of family and fortune. With him several others joined—men of his own stamp, intellectual, high-spirited, and enthusiastic; the last men to have become conspirators, under any ordinary circumstances, but whose sympathies for Mary had been wrought to so high a pitch that they were prepared to hazard every danger in order to accomplish her deliverance. But a traitor was among them who regularly informed Walsingham of their proceedings. They were notwithstanding allowed to go on: as that statesman, with the cold-blooded policy common to the time (and we wish we could add to his time only), desired to implicate Mary in their plot. So for *months* together he and his tool, Pooley, continued to draw the unfortunate gentlemen more and more closely into their toils, till the preparations were complete, and then instantaneously the whole party were pounced upon, one only escaping. Seldom has a court of justice witnessed a trial that excited more admiration or pity for the subjects of it than the trial of Babington and his associates; seldom has the scaffold visited its bloody punishment upon men who seemed less deserving of it, when all the extenuating features of their scheme were remembered. One of them, Tichborn, declared on the scaffold that friendship alone induced him to conceal Babington's designs. Another, Jones, had said previously that he could not destroy his dear friend, Thomas Salisbury, by divulging the plot when it became known to him. A third, Bellamy, shared the terrible fate of the whole, simply because they had met at his house. And now, at last, the most illustrious of all the victims was to be struck—Mary, whose death there can be little doubt had been long and anxiously desired. Her trial was prepared by Burghley, Walsingham, and others of the Council of the Queen, who then at the eleventh hour hesitated. Leicester, divining the thoughts of Elizabeth—the difficulty of obtaining a sentence that should seem to the world as just as it was intended to be fatal, proposed his mode—poison. Walsingham objected—it was contrary to God's law; but Leicester sent him a preacher to convince him he was mistaken. These kind, gentle, good men now talked of shortening Mary's life by severer treatment, and as a healthy and beautiful woman had already been changed into a cripple—why, there was no doubt the thing could be done. The trial, however, was determined upon; and a body of titled and other judges named. And how were they to bring Mary—a sovereign of another country—before such a tribunal? By an act passed after Babington's conspiracy, declaring that the person for whom such attempts should be made should be incapable of the crown of England, and prosecuted to death, if he or she should be judged guilty by twenty-four or more of the Privy Council and House of Lords. An act, therefore, passed *after* the commission of the alleged crime it was to punish! and treating as a subject of England one on whom the government of England had not the smallest claim, except as on a prisoner of war!

Though Mary, after enduring the rigours of nineteen years' confinement, had become in body but a wreck of her former self, her heart and mind remained as beautiful as ever, if indeed they had not grown more beautiful, as they certainly had become more lofty, by the sobering and purifying processes of long affliction. About the period that it was decided she should be subjected to trial, her wanderings from place to place (just as the fears or objects of the government prompted) ceased, by her removal to Fotheringhay (Fig. 1561), where her mortal pilgrimage was to end. The precautions taken for her safe custody were of the most marked character. There was a standing order that she should be shot if she attempted to escape, or if others attempted to rescue her. When she was taken to Fotheringhay it was by a circuitous route, and under the pretext of giving her a change of air to recruit her shattered health. One of the regulations of Fotheringhay was hardly calculated to advance that object. It was ordered that if "any noise or disturbance in Mary's lodgings, or in the place where she was," took place, she was to be killed outright. This (possibly hoped-for) event did not happen. Another incident shows the character of the precautions taken in Mary's lodgings for the restoration of health. One night Mary had a narrow escape from being consumed by fire, in consequence of the wretched chimney of her dungeon becoming ignited. Elizabeth now began to perceive that there was no avoiding the process she had put off so long, contrary to the advice of her ministers, one of whom—Walsingham—lamented that she "was not prepared to do things in season, and work her own security as she ought." Elizabeth *was* now prepared. Thirty-six commissioners came to Fotheringhay, bringing a letter from her to Mary, charging her with being accessory to Babington's conspiracy, and informing her that they were to try her for that and other treasons. Mary was not so crushed by anguish and despair but that she could receive even this dreadful message with spirit and dignity. Composedly and firmly she replied, stating her sufferings and wrongs, and refusing to acknowledge the commissioners, adding, "My notes and papers are taken from me, and no one dares appear to be my advocate."

She was again asked, the next day, if she persisted in her refusal: and replied, she did, most firmly. "But this I had quite forgotten. The Queen says, I am subject to the laws of England, and to be tried and judged by them, because I am under the protection of them; but to this I answer, that I came into the kingdom an independent sovereign, to implore the Queen's assistance, not to subject myself to her authority. Nor is my spirit so broken by past misfortunes, or so intimidated by present dangers, as to stoop to anything unbecoming a crowned head, or that will disgrace the ancestors from whom I am descended, or the son to whom I leave my throne. If I must be tried, princes alone can try me: they are my peers: and the Queen of England's subjects, however noble, are of a rank inferior to mine. Ever since my arrival in this kingdom I have been confined as a prisoner. Its laws never afforded me protection: let them not be perverted now, to take away my life." In answer to that noble denial of the right of her judges to try her, "men learned in the civil and canon laws" strove to *persuade* her to compliance, whilst Burghley and the Chancellor Bromley *threatened*. Mary then grew heated—she would die a thousand deaths rather than submit to such dishonour—she was heart-whole still, and would not derogate from the honour of her ancestors the Kings of Scotland, by owning herself a subject to the crown of England—she would rather perish utterly than answer as the Queen's subject and a criminal. Burghley interrupted her, "We will nevertheless proceed against you to-morrow, as absent and contumax." "Look to your consciences!" was Mary's indignant and impetuous reply. Then Vice-Chamberlain Hatton threw out a speech that—at the critical moment—turned the poor Queen's resolution, and induced her—after all she had said—to yield to the will of her enemies. "If you are innocent, you have nothing to fear; but by seeking to avoid a trial, you stain your reputation with an everlasting blot." For her name's sake—which was dear to Mary, though slander had said so oft and loudly she was indifferent to it—for her name's sake—to clear that—if it were possible—if such a thing as justice were in reality attainable—she at last, with certain reservations, consented, and took her seat in the presence-chamber of Fotheringhay Castle, at the upper end, near a vacant chair of state, representing her hard-hearted cousin—on the 14th of October, 1586. The commissioners were ranged before her on either side the hall, on benches. She had no assistant in that trying hour—no papers—no witnesses—yet, with her wonderful self-possession and address, she, says Dr. Lingard, "for two whole days kept at bay the hunters of her life."

The especial subjects of the trial were Mary's alleged endeavour to induce foreign powers to invade England, which there can be little doubt she had done, and which she had a perfect right—putting the question of prudence aside—to do; and the support it was alleged she had given to attempts at assassination of Elizabeth, which she denied repeatedly and in the most energetic manner:—she would never, she said, make shipwreck of her soul by engaging in such a bloody crime; and we see no reason to disbelieve her. She was found guilty, of course, and the commissioners departed from Fotheringhay.

In the following month parliament implored Elizabeth to put Mary to death. Elizabeth in her reply said that even now, although she had been convicted of treason, if she thought Mary would repent, and her emissaries not pursue their designs—or that if they were two milk-maids with pails upon their arms, and it was merely a question which involved her own life without endangering the religion and welfare of her people, she would most willingly pardon all her offences. But whilst Elizabeth thus conveyed to the world the idea of her own unwillingness to proceed in the business, the speech contained passages that rendered it inevitable that she should be called on to forego that unwillingness. In fact it is sufficiently evident, that to do the crime determined upon with as great an air of innocence as possible, was the real aim of all Elizabeth's speeches and acts during the few terrible weeks that elapsed between Mary's sentence and execution.

Even the last hours of the victim were embittered by unnecessary miseries. A sincere Catholic—she was insulted by the officious labours of two Protestant ecclesiastics; and a few days after they left her, the inconceivably paltry and brutal annoyance was inflicted upon her of tearing down from her apartment the insignia of royalty. Mary now wrote her last letter to Elizabeth, in which, disclaiming all malice and resentment, and thanking God that she was come to the end of her troublesome pilgrimage, she proceeded to ask certain favours. "Fearing as I do the secret tyranny of some persons, I beg you not to permit the sentence to be executed upon me without your knowledge; not from fear of the torment which I am very ready to suffer, but on account of the reports

1560.—Lochleven Castle; the hills overlooking the Loch are the Lomonds.

1561.—Fotheringay, as it appeared in 1718. (From a Print in Bridge's 'Northamptonshire.')

1559.—Holyrood House, the ancient Royal Palace of Edinburgh. (From an Original Drawing made in 1828.) Only a portion of the left or north wing of the present building existed in the time of Mary.

1562.—Tomb of Mary Queen of Scots, in the south aisle of Henry VII.'s Chapel, Westminster Abbey.

1564.—The Misfortunes of Arthur

1565.—The Merry Wives of Windsor played before the Queen

1566.—Harefield.

1563.—Play acted before Elizabeth.

1567.—Tilt-yard, Westminster.

which, in the absence of witnesses above suspicion, might be spread respecting my death, as I know has been done in the case of others of different condition. To avoid which I desire that my servants shall be spectators and witnesses of my death, in the faith of my Saviour and in obedience to his church." She also desired permission for her servants to leave England in peace, and quietly enjoy the small legacies she had bequeathed to them, and that her own body might be conveyed for burial to France. Such were the favours that Mary besought of her cousin in her last letter, and in the name of Christ, and by their near relationship—the memory of their common ancestor Henry VII., and by Elizabeth's own royal dignity.

The French king made an ineffectual effort to arrest execution through the mouth of an ambassador. There was another sovereign from whom a demonstration of a very different kind might have been expected—Mary's son, James, now king of Scotland, and heir to the throne of England. But he too contented himself with sending ambassadors, one of them so thoroughly in Elizabeth's interest that he promoted the business he came to stop. The other, Melville, the recorder of the interesting conversation before transcribed, was honest, earnest, and able, but utterly unable by himself to avert the impending blow. He told Elizabeth the chief nobility of Scotland would give themselves as hostages to secure her against any plot on Mary's account aimed at the English throne; and his answer was Elizabeth's scornful comment addressed to Leicester and others that stood around. But why was the Scottish queen so dangerous? inquired the envoys. "Because she is a papist, and they say she shall succeed to my throne," was Elizabeth's reply. To that it was rejoined that Mary would divest herself of her right in favour of her son James. Then Elizabeth shrieked out, "She hath no such right. She is declared incapable of succeeding." It was further urged that James was a Protestant; when, if Elizabeth's religious professions had been honest, it is clear that such a renunciation by Mary in favour of a king of such belief must have been sufficient to have satisfied her. Her reply, however, must have convinced all parties that she wanted no satisfaction but that of the scaffold. "Is that your meaning?" she screamed out. "Then should I put myself in worse case than before. By God's passion, this were to cut mine own throat. He shall never come into that place or be party with me!" Melville subsequently besought her in the most earnest manner to delay the execution: "No, not for an hour,"—and Elizabeth left them. James withdrew his ambassadors, and for a moment there was probably some alarm as to his intention; but when it was found that all his exertions to save a doomed mother were expended in an order to the clergy of Scotland to pray for her, it was justly concluded that happen what might to Mary, there was no danger to be apprehended to England from over the border.

Before we turn to the last scene of all at Fotheringhay, we must say a few words upon one of the darkest incidents of the reign, the project for Mary's private assassination. It is but too clear, that Elizabeth wished to have the unhappy prisoner made away with secretly, in order, no doubt, that she might deny all participation in her death afterwards. When Davison, Elizabeth's secretary, had laid the warrant for execution before her, and it had been signed, and he was about to leave the apartment, she complained of Sir Amyas Paulet and others, who, she said significantly, might have rendered the signing of the warrant unnecessary. Growing bolder, she then expressed a wish that he (Davison) or Walsingham should write to Sir Amyas and Sir Drew Drury, in order to sound them. Davison answered her it would be lost labour, but promised that such a letter should be written. In the course of the day Walsingham wrote the letter; in which the two secretaries told the two jailers that they found her majesty noted in them a lack of care and zeal, in that they had not in so long a time found some way to shorten the queen's life; and also a lack of care for their own particular safeties, or rather for the preservation of religion and of the public good. With other allusions calculated to stir up their religious bigotries, and to convince them of the justice of putting to death one guilty of matters "so clearly and manifestly proved," the writers of this atrocious document proceed to remark that their queen "taketh it most unkindly towards her, that men professing that love towards her that you do, should, in any kind of sort, for lack of the discharge of your duties, cast the burden upon her; knowing as you do, her indisposition to shed blood, especially of one of that sex and quality, and so near to her in blood as the said queen is." Paulet's answer was soon received. Although a bigot, he was too honest probably to do what was required of him—too sagacious not to perceive that if he did it, his gracious mistress might the very next hour give him up to justice as Mary's murderer,

and so have the benefit of the murder without its odium, at *his* expense. Therefore, deploring deeply that he had lived to see such an unhappy day, when he was required to do an act that God and the law forbade, he said his goods and his life were at her Majesty's disposal, but God forbid that he should make so foul a shipwreck of his conscience, or leave so great a blot on his posterity, as to shed blood without law and warrant. When Elizabeth heard this, she had the audacity still to urge Davison to proceed with the "bloody business," telling him she knew one Wingfield, who, with others, would have done it. Had Elizabeth tried him already in similar affairs? But Davison, who had been disinclined from the first to have anything to do with such a foul murder, now urged strongly its injustice and dishonour. Elizabeth was thus perforce obliged to take the responsibility upon herself of Mary's death.

On the 7th of February, 1587, Mary received the announcement that Shrewsbury, the Earl Marshal, had arrived, attended by three other earls, Kent, Cumberland, and Derby, and by Beale, the clerk of the Council, and by certain ministers of the Gospel. She rose from her bed, dressed, and sat down by a small table; her servants, male and female, being ranged on each side of her. Then the earls entered, and Beale read the death-warrant. A long, melancholy, and agitating conversation ensued, commenced by Mary, who, crossing herself devoutly, said, "that she was ready for death—that it was most welcome to her: though she had hardly thought that, after keeping her twenty years in a prison, her sister Elizabeth would so dispose of her." A book lay beside her, on which she laid her hand, solemnly protesting that, as for the attempted assassination of Elizabeth, she had never imagined it, never sought it, never consented to it. "That is a popish Bible, and therefore your oath is of no value," brutally exclaimed the Earl of Kent. "It is a Catholic Testament," replied the queen, "and therefore, my lord, as I believe that to be the true version, my oath is the more to be relied on." This just reply led to a long discourse from the Earl of Kent, in the coarsest taste, in which he advised her to lay aside her "superstitious follies and idle trumperies of popery," and accept the services of the Protestant Dean of Peterborough. Mary declined, and asked for her own chaplain and confessor; but the consolation of his attendance was denied her. After further talk, Mary, alluding to James of Scotland, asked whether it were possible that her only son could have forgotten his mother. Then came the thrilling inquiry—when she was to suffer. "To-morrow morning at eight," replied the Earl of Shrewsbury, and he was greatly agitated. As the earls rose to depart, Mary inquired if Naue, her late secretary, were dead or alive. She was told alive, in prison. "I protest, before God," exclaimed Mary, putting her hand again on the Catholic Testament, "that Naue has brought me to the scaffold to save his own life. But the truth will be known hereafter." Mournful must have been the scene when Mary was again left alone with her faithful attendants; but presently she bade them dry their tears, and hasten supper, "for that she had a deal of business on her hands." She asked one who waited on her during the meal, whether the force of truth was not great, since, notwithstanding the pretence of her conspiring against the queen's life, the Earl of Kent had just told her that she must die for the security of *their religion!* Then alluding to his clumsy attempt to move her faith, she smiled and said he was an unfit doctor to undertake conversion. After supper her servants were called to the table, and *she drank to them all;* they pledging her in return upon their knees, weeping, and imploring forgiveness for any past offences. Mary forgave them, and then *asking forgiveness of them,* gave them Christian advice as to their future conduct in life. Having distributed among them the few things she had, she retired to her chamber, and wrote her last will on two sheets of paper, and then three letters, one to the King of France, one to her cousin the Duke of Guise, and a third to her confessor. Praying and reading alternately filled up the hours till four o'clock, when she slept till break of day. Then rising, she re-assembled her attendants, read her will to them, distributed all her clothes, except what she had on, bade them farewell, and retired to kneel before an altar in her oratory until the last summons came. About eight, the sheriff of the county entering the oratory, she arose, took down the crucifix, and came forth with an air of pleasantness and majesty, attired in a black satin gown, with a veil of lawn descending to her feet. A chaplet hung at her girdle; the ivory crucifix was in her right hand. The lords and her keepers waited in an ante-chamber, and the procession was formed to the Castle-hall. Among those assembled was Sir Robert Melville, who had been denied access to her for the last three weeks, and who now fell upon his knees, lamenting with a passion of tears his hard fate, to have to bear such sorrowful news into Scotland. Mary, who in her proudest and brightest days had ever been ready to listen to his counsel, and to rely on his fidelity, must have been deeply affected, but preserving her fortitude, said to him, "Good Melville, cease to lament, but rather rejoice, for thou shalt now see a final period to Mary Stuart's troubles. The world, my servant, is all but vanity, and subject to more sorrow than an ocean of tears can wash away." Giving a farewell message to her son, King James, she burst into tears, and continued, "I die true to my religion, to Scotland and to France. God forgive them that have thirsted for my blood 'as the hart longeth for the water-brooks !'." Melville still weeping, Mary, kissing him, said, "Once more farewell, good Melville, pray for thy mistress and queen." She then besought the lords to treat her servants with kindness, and permit them to stand by her at her death. The coarse and inhuman Earl of Kent objected; they would be troublesome to her majesty, and unpleasing to the company—they would put some superstitious trumpery in practice—and perhaps there *would be a dipping their handkerchiefs in her Grace's blood.* "My lords," said Mary, "I will give you my word they shall deserve no blame, nor do such things as you mention; but, poor souls, it would do them good to see the last of their mistress; and I hope your mistress, as a maiden queen, would not deny me, in regard of womanhood, to have some of my women about me at my death. Surely you might grant a greater favour than this, though I were a woman of less rank than the Queen of Scots." The lords remaining silent, "Am I not cousin to your queen?" she exclaimed with some vehemence, "descended from the royal blood of Henry VII., a married Queen of France, and anointed Queen of Scotland?" After much consultation, she was permitted to have with her two of her maids, named Kennedy and Curle, her apothecary and surgeon, and her house-steward, Melville. The scaffold, in the great hall, was raised about three feet from the ground, surrounded with rails, and covered all over with black cloth, as were also a stool for the queen to rest upon, a cushion for her when she knelt, and the block. Without change of countenance Mary ascended the scaffold, and seated herself. The Earl of Kent stood on her right hand, the Earl of Shrewsbury on her left. The headsman from the Tower, in a suit of black velvet, stood, with his assistant, immediately in front of her. She looked cheerful and easy during the reading of the warrant, and, after the loud "God save Queen Elizabeth!" which broke from certain of those who were admitted to see her die, she reminded them that she was a sovereign princess, not subject to the laws and punishments of England, but brought to suffer by injustice and violence. She declared again, she had not sought Elizabeth's death, and added, that, from her heart, she forgave all her enemies. One would think there had been an end of petty torments by this time— but no—the dean sent by Elizabeth began to harass her by a discourse on her life, opinions, and prospects. "Mr. Dean," said Mary, "trouble not yourself, I am fixed in the ancient religion, and by God's grace, I will shed my blood for it;" but he would go on, and even told her, if she did not discard her cherished faith, she must inevitably be dammed to all eternity. "Good Mr. Dean," said Mary, "trouble not yourself about this matter. I was born in this religion, I have lived in this religion, and I will die in this religion;" and to mark her displeasure turned aside from him; but the dean, turning round the scaffold, again faced her, and thundered out his sermon. The Earl of Shrewsbury then ordered him to cease preaching, and begin prayer. Whilst he did so in English, Mary prayed alone in Latin, repeating fervently the penitential Psalms; but when he had done she also prayed in English for the Church, her son, and Queen Elizabeth. Then, kissing the crucifix, she cried, "As thy arms, O Jesu, were stretched upon the cross, so receive me, O God, into the arms of mercy." "Madam," said the Earl of Kent, "you had better put such popish trumpery out of your hand, and carry Christ in your heart." Mary answered, "I can hardly bear this emblem in my hand, without at the same time bearing him in my heart." Even that was not the last insult. Her women were not quite quick enough in disrobing her, and the executioners rudly pulled off a part of her attire. Mary observed to the earls, she was not used to be undressed by such attendants, or before so much company. Her servants now gave a loose to their emotions, but she put her finger to her lips, kissed them again, and bade them pray for her. Then the maid Kennedy took a handkerchief edged with gold, in which the Eucharist had formerly been enclosed, and fastened it over her eyes. The executioners led her to the block, and the queen, kneeling on the cushion before it, said, with a clear, unquailing voice, "Into thy hands, O Lord, I commend my spirit!" Unfortunate to the last, it took three strokes to cut the neck asunder. Thus perished the beautiful Mary Queen of Scots, in her forty-fifth year.

We may end this sad and humiliating narrative, by observing,

that in spite of the continual failure of her endeavours before the execution, to ensure a scapegoat who should bear the odium of Mary's death, Elizabeth was not the less determined to have a victim afterwards, who might at least seem to have been the most guilty party. Of course the very man who had kept her from the perpetration of the murder she had really wished, was the very man to suffer now for the execution that she had to profess she had not wished—nor intended to have taken place. So poor Davison, instead of being let off like Burghley and the others, with a show of royal displeasure, was utterly ruined by a fine of 10,000l., and his committal to the Tower for the whole of the remainder of the reign.

Among the events that make memorable the reign of Elizabeth, none were regarded with a more lively gratification by sovereign and by people than the voyages of discovery and conquest made by the bold English sea-captains, some of whom sprang from the humblest classes. The source of that gratification was partly national, because the Spaniards arrogated to themselves not only the dominion of the whole New World, called then the Indies, but the sole right to navigate the vast Indian sea; and the prospects of crushing that arrogant assumption, of leaving Englishmen free to range the world of waters, and to open ports of trade, and colonies that might enlarge the boundaries of English dominion, as yet but narrow, were too tempting to allow of much nicety as to the strict honour and honesty of the means. But there was another source of interest in those voyages—the adventurers went out poor to return rich; they seemed to find in those far regions gold and treasure without limit. Not that they enriched themselves in the mode they had first anticipated. When Frobisher (Fig. 1529) returned from that famous expedition, of which the appellation "Frobisher's Strait," leading to Hudson's Bay, still so constantly reminds us, in the accounts of modern attempts to discover a north-west passage, he brought with him a piece of black stone, very heavy. A portion of the stone, being thrown upon the fire some time afterwards, by the wife of one of the mariners who had been with Frobrisher, and then taken out again and quenched in vinegar, glittered like gold, and upon being subsequently fused, was found to contain some of the precious ore. It was not long after that discovery before a second expedition was fitted out, expressly for the collection of the black stone. Plenty of it was obtained; and shortly a third expedition departed from our shores, which had the two-fold object in view of discovering a north-west passage and bringing home some of the black stone. But the passage was not discovered; nor do we find that either the government or the adventurers grew rich with the gold.

But the gold was still to be obtained; and Drake (Figs. 1529, 1537) showed the way. Born of poor parents in Devonshire, he had been placed as apprentice with the master of a little coasting bark, and in that condition, "pain, with patience, in his youth, knit the joints of his soul, and made them more solid and compact" [Fuller].

One Sunday, in August 1573, when the townsfolk of Plymouth were at church, news was brought that Francis Drake, already known as the Devonshire hero, was returned from voyaging on the Spanish Main. Forgetting all the proprieties of the day, the place, and the occasion, forth rushed the worshippers out of the church, until "there remained few or no people with the preacher." Running to the harbour, where the rovers were anchored, great was the welcoming and the joy. No end to the eager inquiries concerning the marvels that Drake and his men had seen and performed! Surely there must have been a charmed life in those three frail barks in which the adventurers had encountered such great dangers, and by means of which they had been enabled to cross the Isthmus of Darien, where Drake directed his longing gaze towards the waters of the great Pacific (an ocean as yet closed to English enterprise), and uttered that passionate prayer to God, that he might have "life and leave once to sail an English ship in those seas." And that prayer was realized, in Drake's next memorable voyage, when (if we except John Oxenham, who had served as a sailor and cook under Drake, and who merely floated a pinnace on the South Sea, and was taken and executed as a pirate by the Spaniards) he was the very first English captain to whom appertained that honour.

> The fair breeze blew, the white foam flew,
>   The furrow followed free;
> *They* were the first that ever burst
>   Into that silent sea.—COLERIDGE.

It was in these voyages that the men of the sixteenth century discovered how gold was to be obtained from the Spanish territories and seas of the New World. The first voyage had been signalized

1568.—Essex House.

1569.—House of M. Beaumont, the French Ambassador.

1571.—Essex.

1572.—Exterior of Beauchamp Tower, from the Parade.

1573.—Arundel House.

1574.—Essex House.   (From Holliar's 'View of London,' 1647.)

1579.—Westminster Abbey and Hall.

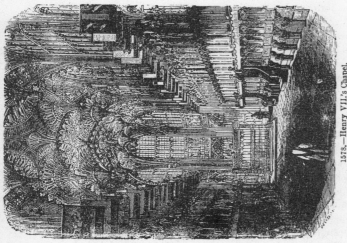

1578.—Henry VII.'s Chapel.

1575.—Funeral of Queen Elizabeth.

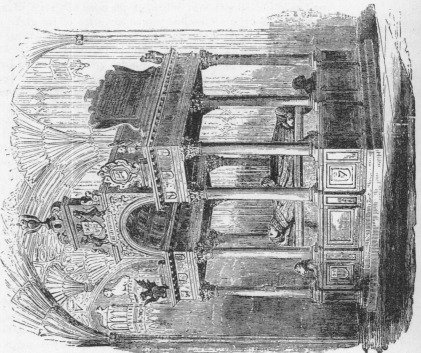

1576.—Tomb of Queen Elizabeth, in the north aisle of Henry VII.'s Chapel, Westminster Abbey

1577.—Interior of Henry VII.'s Chapel.

by many a desperate encounter, by the boarding of many a goodly Spanish ship, and even by the storming of a Spanish town—Nombre de Dios. And the fruits were visible to the eyes of Drake's wondering and admiring countrymen, in the solid silver and gold, and in the variety of other rich things with which every inch of spare room in their barks was crammed: demonstrations of success that admitted no question. No wonder that Drake next time was able to go out with five instead of three small vessels, and a company of one hundred and sixty-four "gentlemen" adventurers, and choice seamen, the former including some young men of noble blood, who accompanied the expedition to "learn the art of navigation," after Drake's own peculiar fashion. Having obtained the secret sanction of Elizabeth, who was then at peace with Spain, these resolute pupils of the "hero," and their companions, proceeded to attack and plunder the Spanish possessions and the Spanish ships. Their first lessons were afforded on the coasts of South America, often with complete success. Especially memorable, in this memorable voyage, was Drake's landing at Port Julian, on the coast of Patagonia, near the Strait named after the first circumnavigator of the globe half a century before Drake (who was the second), the Portuguese Fernando de Magalhaens. It was here that striking incident occurred—the discovery of a gibbet—which greatly comforted Drake and his men, as a proof that Christian people had been there before them—the severest, though most unintentional, satire ever uttered. Drake at the same place proceeded to show that he could improve on this Christian example, by putting to death, under circumstances that give the act the aspect of a foul murder, a gentleman of high birth and education, "Master Doughtie." After many extraordinary adventures and discoveries, the rovers obtained an immense booty by plundering the Spanish towns on the coast of Chili and Peru. Among many other vessels they took, was a royal galleon called the "Cacafuego," richly laden with plate. The whole voyage round the globe occupied two years and nearly ten months. At last, after spending many months on the almost unknown southwestern coast of America—after sailing right across the Indian Ocean from Java, and doubling the Cape of Good Hope—Drake once more reappeared in Plymouth harbour, on the 26th of September, 1579. The queen, Camden informs us, "received him graciously, and laid up the treasure he brought by way of sequestration, that it might be forthcoming if the Spaniards should demand it. His ship she caused to be drawn up in a little creek near Deptford, upon the Thames, as a monument of his so lucky sailing round the world, where the carcase thereof is yet to be seen. And having, as it were, consecrated it as a memorial with great ceremony, she was banqueted in it, and conferred on Drake the honour of knighthood. At this time, a bridge of planks by which they came aboard the ship, sank under the crowd of people, and fell down with an hundred men upon it, who, notwithstanding, had none of them any harm. So that that ship may seem to have been built under a lucky planet." It was called the "Pelican;" and after having been long honourably preserved at Deptford, has gone to decay since Camden's time, and been broken up, but one of the planks is still in existence, converted into a chair, now in the possession of the University of Oxford.

Queen Elizabeth paid a considerable sum out of the treasure brought home by the great navigator to certain merchants who sent to her court to demand satisfaction for having been "unjustly robbed." The rest of the booty rewarded the privateers. If most of the English, with their queen, gloried in the advantages that unquestionably resulted from these naval exploits, there were some few at least who had regard to the rights that had been violated; for, according to Camden, nothing troubled Drake more than the refusal of some of the chief men at court to accept the gold which he offered them, because it was "gotten by piracy." The names of those chief men would have been worth preserving. On the other hand, it does not seem to have been piracy that the Spaniards complained of most. They of course saw, and with most excited passions, that their exclusive naval dominion was about to be wrested from them. Mendoza, the Spanish ambassador, complained with arrogant violence of Drake's having so much as dared to sail in the Indian Sea. Elizabeth's spirited reply is the first instance of the absolute assertion of England's right of navigating the ocean in all its parts, a right none has since that time been able to take from us. She told Mendoza plainly that a title to the ocean could not belong to any people, or private persons, "forasmuch as neither nature, nor public use and custom, permitteth any possession thereof." This was indeed one of the occasions when Elizabeth's clearness of intellect and determined will achieved advantages of priceless value to the empire.

Another of these adventurers "by flood," and whose career may

be said to have run in parallel lines to the career of Drake and of Frobisher, was Thomas Cavendish (Fig. 1529), whose primary motive for his expedition was the common one of Elizabeth's days, that of repairing in the Spanish Main the fortunes wasted in the English court. He, too, circumnavigated the globe, and in a shorter space of time than had ever before been known: namely, in two years, one month, and a few days. He was but twenty-two when, fired by the hope of emulating Drake, he undertook the command and chief pecuniary risk of the undertaking, selling or mortgaging for the purpose all that remained of the estates he had inherited from his father on coming of age the year before, and which he had already seriously diminished to accompany Sir Richard Grenville to Virginia and the West Indies. Geographical discoveries of considerable value marked this, as well as most other of these half-patriotic, half-buccaneering voyages. Cavendish was the first to point out to the English the local advantages of the island which was subsequently to be immortalized as the prison and the deathplace of Napoleon. In a letter written by Cavendish on his return, to Lord Hunsdon, Elizabeth's chamberlain and favourite, he thus enumerates his exploits—"I burnt and sunk nineteen sail of ships, small and great; and all the villages and towns that ever I landed at I burned and spoiled." Cavendish had now made himself rich, and Elizabeth made him a knight. And so he returned to his former way of life, until fresh expeditions became necessary. A second was formed, but not by Cavendish alone, or even under his exclusive command, to which circumstances we may attribute its failure and his death at twenty-nine years old, worn out by vexation, as he was on his way back to England. It seemed as though the youthful veteran were unable to endure the meeting with his countrymen, under circumstances so different from what they anticipated.

And what did the King of Spain think, say, or do, when he thus saw his power made contemptible throughout the world; his fair towns burnt and pillaged, his ships of treasure continually intercepted? Religious considerations must have sufficiently embittered his mind against England, had there been nothing more. But when he found England assisting his revolting subjects in the Netherlands to throw off at once his rule and their old faith, and when he further beheld the same country harassing beyond endurance his faithful, peaceable American subjects, it is easy to perceive that his mind must have been excited to the highest pitch of indignation and excitement. Nay, it is but just to acknowledge, that the way in which he prepared to meet these evils at their very source, by attacking and conquering England, exhibited a courage of purpose and comprehensiveness of view highly calculated to excite the admiration of the people against whom they were to be directed.

It was in or about 1586 that the first rumour appears to have reached England of the intention of Philip of Spain to invade England with a vast force. But it was not till after the execution of the Queen of Scotland in 1587, that anything decisive appears to have been known. Philip, feeling no doubt a great deal of just horror at her death, and possibly professing even more than he did feel, immediately denounced Elizabeth as a murderer, and hurried on his preparations for the invasion without any attempts at concealment. Elizabeth strove to pacify him, but in vain; so Drake was sent to destroy all the Spanish ships he could find in the Spanish harbours, and to prevent, or at least to delay, the preparations of the invading fleet. With thirty sail he swept into the Cadiz roads, burned, took, or sank, thirty ships (some of the largest size), and secured a considerable quantity of spoil for the benefit of the merchant-adventurers with him: then turning back along the coast, between Cadiz Bay and Cape St. Vincent, disposed in a similar manner of nearly one hundred vessels, and demolished four castles. Drake called this "singeing the King of Spain's beard." Sailing to the Tagus, he then challenged the Marquis Santa Cruz, who was the appointed general of the Spanish Armada, and captured before his eyes, the "St. Philip," a great ship loaded with the richest merchandise. De Cruz, the best sailor of Spain, forbidden by the orders he had received from the court of Madrid to accept Drake's challenge, though his was the superior force, took it so much to heart, that it is said he fell sick in consequence, and soon after died. These brilliant performances of Drake proved of sufficient consequence to delay the sailing of the Armada more than a year.

Incessant and portentous were the rumours still flying to and fro as to the vast character of the Armada; the preparations for which only went on the more vigorously in consequence of the check received from Drake. The Pope renewed a bull of excommunication that had previously been fulminated against Elizabeth, and endeavoured to aid by temporal supplies the efforts of his spiritual artillery. Philip on his part levied troops wherever it was possible to levy them, hired ships from the Genoese and Venetian republics, took possession of all that belonged to his Neapolitan and Sicilian subjects, hurried on the building of new ones in Spain and Portugal, formed a vast fleet of flat-bottomed boats in Flanders, and constituted an army of 34,000 men under the command of the Duke of Parma, who were to embark in them and be carried over to the doomed English coast. And some, no doubt, in England were alarmed at the magnitude of the danger that threatened : some no doubt looked to see the fulfilment of that prophecy of which Stow speaks, namely, that the year 1588 "should be most fatal and ominous unto all estates," adding, that it was plainly discovered "that England was the main subject of that time's operation." But such timid and apprehensive spirits were few and utterly uninfluential. The native courage never shone out more brilliantly than at the period in question. From high to low, from the palace, the parliament-house, the church, the theatre—everywhere—was heard the cheering enthusiastic voice of scornful defiance. Never were the brief but significant words, Let them come ! heard from a greater variety of speakers of all ages and temperaments. And if, as is supposed in ' William Shakspere, a Biography,' it was during this eventful period of expectation that ' King John ' was produced, how the theatre must have rung again and again to hear such passages as the following recited ; how from mouth to mouth, through the wide theatre of England, every man, whilst he prepared to become, if need be, an actor in the mighty tragedy that was to be played before the world, must have exulted as he repeated the poet's sentiments :—

> This England never did, nor never shall,
> Lie at the proud foot of a conqueror,
> But when it first did help to wound itself.
> Now these her princes are come home again,
> Come the three corners of the world in arms,
> And we shall shock them : nought shall make us rue,
> If England to itself do rest but true.

In November Elizabeth summoned a great council, in which she included the bravest and ablest of her military and naval officers. Among these Raleigh (Fig. 1531) occupied a conspicuous position—a man whose genius, and turbulence, and misfortunes, have made him one of the most interesting characters of our history. He, like Drake, was born in Devonshire (Fig. 1537). Whilst yet very young, he had, as a soldier, given promise of the courage and ability he afterwards exhibited. His fitness to shine as a courtier was clearly proved in the incident which Sir Walter Scott has helped to familiarise to us, though with a slight inaccuracy of fact, Raleigh at the time having been in actual attendance on the queen, instead of owing to the occurrence his first introduction to her notice. The essential truth, however, is the same in the fact and in the fiction—for Raleigh certainly owed to it much of his influence with the great queen. Elizabeth, while taking a walk, came to a miry part of the road, and hesitated to proceed, which the young courtier perceiving, he plucked off his rich plush cloak, and spread it before her feet. Elizabeth was of course delighted with so delicate an act of flattery, and the more so when she perceived it came from a particularly handsome young man ; so Raleigh's cloak, as it has been observed, procured for him many a *good suit*. Elizabeth, after knighting Raleigh in 1584, bestowed her royal favours on him with a lavish hand ; until perceiving that his demands kept more than even pace with her liberality, she attempted to check his forwardness with the sharp question, "When, Sir Walter, will you cease to be a beggar ?" But Sir Walter—his mistress's equal in readiness of wit and worldly tact—replied, "When your gracious majesty ceases to be a benefactor." Raleigh, as we have said, was one of the great council of war called to deliberate on the posture and management of affairs, and the queen was soon to find that her favourite was prepared to justify her favours by better claims than mere courtship. He took a leading part in the deliberations, and to him more than to any other we appear to owe the gallant and momentous determination to meet the invaders at sea, and not wait for their landing. And now in earnest England began its preparations. The very best men were selected to fight the national battles. **Lord** Howard of Effingham (Fig. 1530)—a *Catholic*—as popular as he was brave and wise, was made High-Admiral, Drake was made Vice-Admiral, Frobisher and Hawkins (Fig. 1529) were commissioned as chief officers. Raleigh, as a soldier, had command of the land-forces appointed for the defence of the part of the coast where the danger appeared the most imminent—Cornwall. But we may here observe in anticipation, that Raleigh was not one to stand idle on land when he found the Spaniards, according to his own advice, were to be struggled with on the water ; and so, when the Armada had passed up the Channel, he hastened, with all the

ardour of his chivalric spirit, to join the British fleet, and to distinguish himself among the most eminent of the men who commanded it.

A gratifying evidence of the universal patriotism of England was afforded by the conduct of the Catholic party, who, forgetting, or not choosing to remember, that the avowed object of the Armada was the promotion of its own peculiar religious views, and who, generously forgiving the government the harsh treatment it had received and still continued to receive, pressed forward with the greatest enthusiasm to fill the ranks of the defenders of the country. But they were Catholics, they were told, and, notwithstanding the rank, and wealth, and devotion of many of their number, could not be admitted to places of honour and trust : well, then, they would serve as common soldiers or common sailors, they replied—and, to their eternal honour be it said, they did so. There was one act of Elizabeth's, however, in the highest degree calculated to encourage such generous feeling : she placed, as we have said, a Catholic at the very head of the British fleet : not, of course, because he was a Catholic, but in consequence of his great qualifications, which Elizabeth could not afford to lose the benefit of at such a time. But this sagacity in the choice of her chief officers of state was one of Elizabeth's most striking and important characteristics, and one that never deserted her. It is true that she was unjust to herself and to her country, in the desire to oblige or promote such a favourite as Leicester ; but his case forms the solitary exception, and it may be doubted whether, in any real emergence, she would have suffered even him to have misled her. Thus if we look at the arrangements we have described, we perceive that when the Armada is expected, it is Raleigh who is sent to the foremost post of danger on the land, and Lord Howard and Drake with their companions who are commissioned to bear the brunt of battle at sea ; but Leicester, notwithstanding the apparent dignity of his position as Lieutenant-General to the Queen, and commander of the chief army prepared to oppose the Spaniards, is really kept almost by her side as she moves about between London and Tilbury, surrounded by a knot of other and better men to guide the councils of war, under the influence of her own powerful and masculine mind.

Few localities of England, memorable for their associations with great national events, are so calculated to excite our national pride or our feelings of loyalty, as that which, opposite Gravesend, on the northern bank of the Thames, meets our view, as we sail to or from London on the river, whose navigation Tilbury Fort commands. This fort (Figs. 1521, 1522), originally built as a mere block-house by Henry VIII., was first fortified by Elizabeth, who formed there the famous camp (Fig. 1526), traces of which remain in the neighbourhood. Here were the head-quarters of all the armies collected from all parts of the land and all orders of the people. "It was a pleasant sight," says Stow, "to behold the soldiers as they marched towards Tilbury, their cheerful countenances, courageous words and gestures, dancing and leaping wheresoever they came ; and in their camp their most felicity was hope of fight with the enemy : where ofttimes divers rumours rose of their foe's approach, and that present battles would be given them ; then they were joyful at such news, as if lusty giants were to run a race." And the commander, woman though she were, was worthy of such soldiers. Tilbury and Elizabeth are names associated everlastingly with one of the grandest of national recollections. In connection with Tilbury, Elizabeth is remembered —not as the merciless oppressor of Mary Queen of Scots—nor as the vain coquette with whom no flattery could be too gross—but as a sovereign who, in the extremest hour of her country's peril, stepped forward prepared to share with the humblest of her subjects the immediate, as well as the remote perils, toils, and anxieties that actual war brings upon the actors in it. Putting on her armour and mounting her war-horse, with the truncheon of command in her hand, she thus addressed her "loving people" at Tilbury : —"We have been persuaded by some that are careful of our safety, to take heed how we commit ourselves to armed multitudes, for fear of treachery ; but I assure you, I do not desire to live to distrust my faithful and loving people. Let tyrants fear ! I have always so behaved myself, that, under God, I have placed my chiefest strength and safeguard in the loyal hearts and good-will of my subjects : and, therefore, I am come amongst you at this time, not as for my recreations and sport, but being resolved in the midst and heat of the battle to live or die amongst you all—to lay down for my God, for my kingdom, and for my people, my honour and my blood even in the dust. I know that I have but the body of a weak and feeble woman, but I have the heart of a king, and of a king of England too ; and think foul scorn that Parma or

1580.—Cranmer, on the morning of his Execution, making the Confession of his Protestantism, after Dr. Cole's Sermon in St. Mary's Church, Oxford, at the moment when the Friars and other Papists present were about to pluck him down from the "Stage set over against the Pulpit, of a mean height from the ground," on which the Archbishop was placed, "in a bare and ragged gown, and ill-favouredly clothed, with an old square cap exposed to the contempt of all men." (From Fox's 'Acts and Monuments.')

1582.—Chained Bible.

1583.—Stone at Hadleigh to commemorate the Martyrdom of Dr. Taylor.

1581.—Cuthbert Simpson on the Rack. (Being a portion of the Cut representing his sufferings in Fox's 'Acts and Monuments.')

1584.—James Baynham doing Penance.

1585.—Martyrdom of Anne Askew and others.

1586.—Burning of Person, Testwood, and Filmer, before Windsor Castle. (From Fox's 'Acts and Monuments.')

60

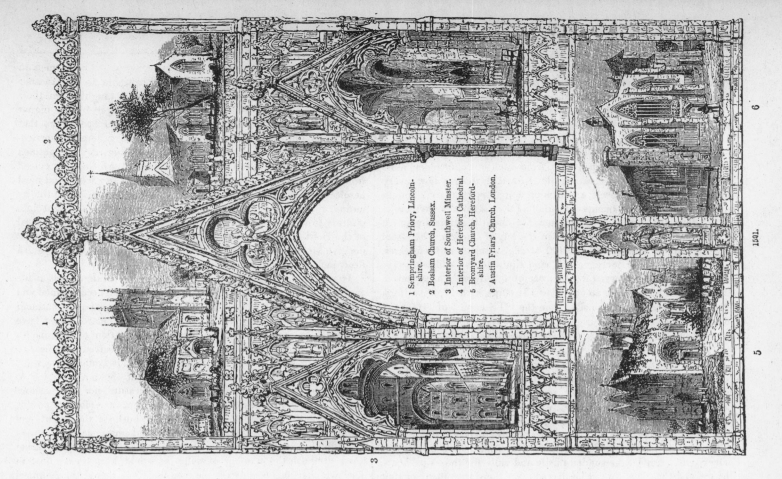

1 Sempringham Priory, Lincolnshire.
2 Bosham Church, Sussex.
3 Interior of Southwell Minster.
4 Interior of Hereford Cathedral.
5 Bromyard Church, Herefordshire.
6 Austin Friars' Church, London.

1591.

1590.—Old St. Paul's School. Founded 1509.
As it appeared before the Great Fire.

1589.—Latimer

1588.—King's School, Canterbury. Founded 1432.
(From an old Print.)

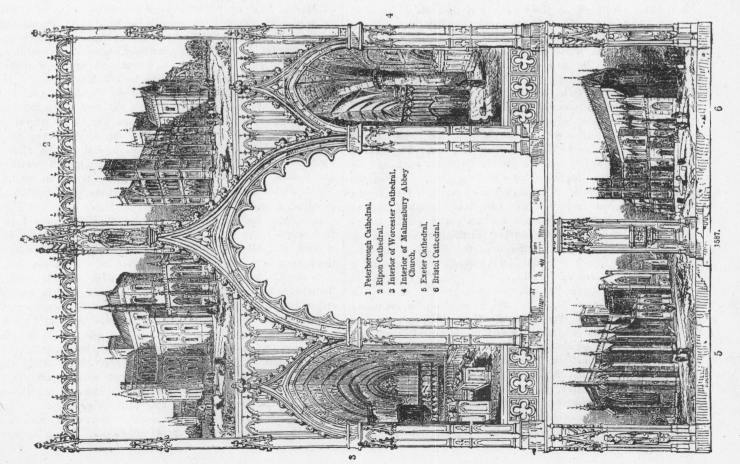

1 Peterborough Cathedral.
2 Ripon Cathedral.
3 Interior of Worcester Cathedral.
4 Interior of Malmesbury Abbey
  Church.
5 Exeter Cathedral.
6 Bristol Cathedral.

1587.

61

Spain or any prince of Europe, should dare to invade the borders of my realms! To which, rather than any dishonour shall grow by me, I myself will take up arms—I myself will be your general—the judge and rewarder of every one of your virtues in the field. I know already by your forwardness, that you have deserved rewards and crowns, and we do assure you on the word of a prince, they shall be duly paid you." We may readily understand how such speeches, at such a time, from such a commander, must have excited the enthusiasm of the armed listeners; how every man must have felt himself a citizen of a country that would surely prove to be what its opponents denominated their Armada—invincible. Altogether, the men of England under arms at the time amounted to 130,000, exclusive of the levies of the city of London, which sent forth a body of picked men, 10,000 strong, an army in themselves, of the first order for courage, skill, and equipments; and who were honoured as they deserved, by the care of the queen's own person. The English naval force amounted to 181 ships, with 17,472 sailors. The ships varied greatly in size, from the " Triumph " of 1100 tons, down to those—by far the largest number—whose tonnage severally was below 200. The entire tonnage was 31,985.

It is well known that the victors of Waterloo received their first summons to the battle in a ball-room. We have a parallel to this fact (we will not call it surprise, since high authorities differ upon that point), in a similar one which occurred to the Vice-admiral Drake and his officers, who were playing bowls on the Plymouth Hoe, when one Fleming, a Scottish privateer, brought the intelligence that he had seen the Spanish fleet off the Lizard. The cool self-possession of Drake at that exciting moment was never surpassed. Amidst the sudden bustle and calls for the ships' boats, he insisted the game should be played out; there was plenty of time both to win the game and beat the Spaniards!

The wind was blowing hard against them when the two Admirals sailed out of Plymouth harbour to meet the Armada. They were in uncertainty as to its destination, which therefore it was their first business to discover, by watching its motions. This opportunity was afforded them on the following Saturday, the 20th of July, when the spectacle—at once grand and terrible—displayed itself of the Invincible Armada approaching majestically the devoted British shores. It appeared a close crescent—*seven miles broad* (Fig. 1524)—and was in great part composed of what seemed more like floating castles than ordinary vessels. One would fancy that the boldest among the bold, in the comparatively insignificant-looking knot of ships that have come out to meet this mighty host, must have quailed at such an extraordinary and portentous sight. But the very magnitude of the Spanish vessels was a good augury to the experienced English mariners—and at once the plan seems to have been formed that made them victorious throughout all the conflicts that followed, spite of every disadvantage. This plan was—avoiding close fighting and boarding wherever it was possible and trusting very much to the capibility of their ships for rapid motion in the hands of the skilful men who guided them. It was soon found, too, that the Spanish guns being mounted so high often fired over them, whilst the English were able to make every shot do its work. The Armada, under the guidance of the duke de Medina, made no attempt to land, as had been anticipated, at Plymouth, and where Raleigh was waiting most ardently its coming; but continued its course through the Channel, in pursuance of the order that had been given to make for the coast of Flanders, and there form a junction with the Duke of Parma, whose troops were to be carried away for the invasion of England. The contest commenced with a slight brush, to use the favourite technical term between some of the English ships and those in the rear of the Spanish train, in which, unfortunately for the reputation of the Armada, one great invincible was completely crippled, and so rendered useless to its owners; and another not only subjected to the same fate, but involving the further mortification of becoming very useful to the destroyers, for the English took it, and found in the prize 55,000 ducats, all which Drake distributed, with a truly princely generosity, among the sailors.

Howard and Sir Walter Raleigh, with as large a fleet as they had been able to collect, on the 23rd of July encountered the whole Armada (Fig. 1522) off Portland. Sir Henry Wotton compared the battle that ensued, and which lasted nearly the whole of that day, to a morrice-dance upon the waters!—by which he meant to describe the active and airy movements of the English ships, dancing, as it were, about the castle-like galeasses of the Spanish, tacking hither and thither, pouring in their fire on all sides, and sheering off out of range before the Spaniards had time to reload, then returning to give another broadside, and as rapidly darting off again. But some of the British ships had very nearly been caught

during and in consequence of these manœuvres. The seamen in their ardour forgot that wind was as indispensable as enthusiasm; but when the sudden cessation of the former taught them their error, they redeemed themselves from their danger by the higher manifestation of the latter. Among the separate encounters that took place during and immediately after the general "morrice-dance," the most remarkable was that of five English merchantmen led by Frobisher's great ship, the " Triumph," which being cut off from the rest of their fleet, were in close action *two hours*, and most heroically sustained themselves in that terrible position until, by means of sweepers and tow-boats, a squadron was brought into position to their rescue, in obedience to a signal from the Ark Royal of the Lord Admiral. The same squadron had just achieved a most decisive victory of its own—having cut off a division of the Spanish fleet, and crippled every ship in it.

It is painful to think, that all the admirable arrangements made for the defence of the kingdom should have been accompanied and their success endangered by a mistimed desire to save the national funds. It is a startling fact that, after all, the Spaniards might have succeeded in landing through the mere operation of Elizabeth's parsimony; for just before they came, she received intelligence that a storm had so injured the Armada that it could not sail for a year, and in consequence ordered some of the largest ships to be laid up, and the crews discharged; a measure not only perilous in itself as regards the amount subtracted from the defensive power, but calculated to throw over the whole business the doubt and hesitation which are so fatal in great national emergencies. Howard of Effingham flatly refused to obey the order, replying that rather than diminish the number of ships he would keep them afloat at his own charge. Such were the men who then served the country! But the queen, far from being warned by this incident against the danger she incurred by the miserable desire to save her purse, left the fleet unprovided with a sufficiency of gunpowder! Thus the very day after Frobisher's gallant defence of the merchantmen, the English found they had no means of continuing the engagement till supplies reached them. A day was lost in consequence. When the fleets again met on the morning of the 25th, the English had scarcely recommenced the fight in good earnest, and began to warm with their success, when they found once more all the gunpowder gone!

On the 27th the Spaniards anchored before Calais, and messengers were sent overland to the Duke of Parma, urging him to send fly-boats to enable Medina to cope with the English ships—those morrice-dancers—whose guns and balls were so eternally bounding about his ears, and knocking his ships to pieces without waiting for a polite return. But the English allies—the Dutch—took care of the duke of Parma's fly-boats, so that he could render no aid until he was first aided by the breaking up of the blockade that paralysed his exertions by keeping him shut out from the sea. Then the Duke of Medina made up his mind to continue his route to Dunkirk, as originally arranged, and rescue his brother of Parma before venturing to England, but he found the impertinent English were not inclined to let him. The Spanish admiral however arrived in sight of Dunkirk, when the wind fell to a dead calm, and for a whole day he was kept stationary hemmed in by 140 English sail, " fit for fight, good sailors, nimble and tight for tacking about." The close array of the Armada, and the excellent disposition made by its commander—the ships of largest size being ranged next the enemy, and the lesser anchored between them and the shore—induced Lord Howard to refrain from attack, until a plan was devised for breaking their order, so that they might be dealt with in divisions. In the dead of night this plan was put in operation. Favoured by darkness, the tide, and a rising gale, two English captains, named Young and Prouse, conducted eight small ships close to the Spanish line, and there left them hastening back in their boats. The ships had been filled with pitch, sulphur, rosin, wildfire, and other combustibles, and the Spaniards now beheld them wrapt in flames, driving down before the wind on the different divisions of their fleet! In the expectation of their explosion the alarm was fearful. The whole Armada was in confusion immediately. "The fire of Antwerp! the fire of Antwerp!" cried some, remembering certain terrible fire-ships that had been used against them by the Dutch in the Scheldt. Some cut their cables, others weighed their anchors, and let their ships run before the wind, without knowing what course to take. Many of the ships, in their hurry to escape, ran against one another, and were so injured as to be of no further use. The explosion of the fire-ships terminated the danger, but not the mischiefs produced by it; the Spaniards were scattered all about, some far out unprotected in the wide sea, some among the shoals of Flanders. Few heard the signal gun from the Duke of Medina's ship recalling all to their former position, and the dawning morning exhibited them in all their disorder to their exulting adversaries, who forthwith proceeded to deal in a still more effectual manner with the squadrons thus dispersed and broken. One great ship after another was taken, sunk, or burnt. Among the incidents of this period that more especially remind us of the frightful character of war, may be mentioned the fate of a large Biscayan galleon. This ship, one of the largest and most important of the whole Armada, was subjected to a most terrible fire. An officer on board at last proposed to surrender, but was immediately killed by another for having made a proposal esteemed so dishonourable. He, too, in his turn, was killed by the brother of the first, and while these events were going on, the ship sunk under the English fire. The story here told was narrated by the few survivors who were picked up out of the sea by the English sailors. The courage, indeed, of the Spaniards, was fully equal to that of our own men, but they were less skilful, and fought in vessels utterly unsuited for the contest in which they were engaged. And so the long-cherished vision of the conquest of the hated country of England melted into thin air. The Spaniards, it is true, called out for revenge; but their leader perceived the utter futility of all further attempts, and determined to make the best of his way home. The proudest of nations must submit to one of the most humiliating of defeats. Those chalky cliffs, " with all that they inherit,"—

> This royal throne of kings, this scepter'd isle,
> This earth of majesty, this seat of Mars,
> This other Eden, demi-paradise ;
> This fortress, built by Nature for herself,
> Against infestion and the hand of war,
> This happy breed of men, this little world ;
> This precious stone set in the silver sea,
> Which serves in it the office of a wall,
> Or as a moat defensive to a house,
> Against the envy of less happier lands ;
> This blessed plot, this earth, this realm, this England—

was not to be penetrated—this year at least—by landing the Invincibles. Alas! what would not the Spaniards give to have the opportunity of rechristening the Armada with some more modest title!

The Armada retreats, steering round by Scotland, to avoid the narrow seas. " There was never anything pleased me better," writes Drake to Walsingham, " than the seeing the enemy flying with a southerly wind to the northward. We have the Spaniards before us, and mind, with the grace of God, to wrestle a fall with them. God grant that we have a good eye to the Duke of Parma; for, with the grace of God, if we live, I doubt it not but, ere it be long, so to handle the matter with the Duke of Sidonia, as he shall wish himself at Saint Mary's Port, among his lime-trees."

And what prevented Drake from enjoying himself in his own way? *Want of gunpowder again !* When they came to examine their provisions they found a general scarcity both of powder and shot ; and so they too were fain to return home, leaving the Spaniards unmolested. " Another opportunity was lost, not much inferior to the other, by not sending part of our fleet to the west of Ireland, where the Spaniards of necessity were to pass, after so many dangers and disasters as they had endured. If we had been so happy as to have followed their course, as it was both thought and discoursed of, we had been absolutely victorious over this great and formidable navy, for they were brought to that necessity that they would willingly have yielded, as divers of them confessed that were shipwrecked in Ireland" (Sir William Monson).

A part of the English fleet did, however, follow the Spaniards all along the English and Scottish coast, as far as the Frith of Forth; but this was a lame and impotent conclusion, deeply disappointing to the nation, and keenly lamented by may of its rulers. A letter written on the 8th of August from Tilbury Fort by Secretary Walsingham to the Chancellor, makes this comment, exonerating at the same time the general of the fleet from the blame :—" I am sorry the Lord-Admiral was forced to leave the prosecution of the enemy through the want he sustains ; our half-doings doth breed dishonour, and leaveth the disease uncured."

But the elements fought against the unfortunate Spaniards when the English had ceased to do so. As they rounded the Orkneys a fierce tempest swept over them, dashing some of the ships to pieces on the coasts on each side, sinking others with every soul on board, and driving no less than thirty upon a place near the Giant's Causeway, Ireland, still known as Port-na-Spagna. The miserable inmates of these vessels were either butchered by the Irish in cold

blood, or were for the most part drowned, on again committing themselves in their shattered vessels to the deep. Other vessels were driven back into the English Channel, and taken.

After about three months' absence, the Armada arrived at the Bay of Santander. But how changed from what it was when it set out ! It moved in a narrower space than seven miles now ; for only sixty of the fleet of one hundred and thirty sail were left. And the giant ships spoke most eloquently in their aspect of the treatment they had received. The spectre-like appearance of the once hardy and robust sailors told better than words of the sufferings they had undergone. Instead of taking England for King Philip, both ships and men had been unable to obtain even a reasonable amount of credit and safety for themselves.

As to the Duke of Parma, condemned all the while to inaction, Drake no doubt correctly anticipated his feelings in his letter to Walsingham, in which he says, " I take [him] to be as a bear robbed of her whelps : and no doubt but, being so great a soldier as he is, that he will presently, if he may, undertake some great matter, for his credit will stand now thereupon."

The defeat of the Armada was of course felt to be a great national deliverance, and celebrated with deep and universal joy. Passing over the great fires at Southwark, the demonstrations of victory displayed at London Bridge, and the first general but irregular exhibition of religious thankfulness, bursting out also into song and music that are still preserved (Fig. 1527), the 19th and 24th of November were especially set apart, the first as a holyday to be observed by all people throughout the realm, the latter as a day on which the queen would make her own public acknowledgments. Her love for her country and her people, her pride in their fame, her sleepless anxiety for their prosperity, can never be denied, whatever else may be said in disparagement of her ; and we cannot but think, that it was not merely joy for the security of her crown that glowed in that mighty heart when, after issuing from Whitehall Palace, and riding in her chariot through the crowded streets (Fig. 1528) and her train of heroes and statesmen, Queen Elizabeth knelt down at the west door of St. Paul's, and openly and audibly praised God " who had thus delivered the land from the rage of the enemy." Nor was this the only evidence of feelings too powerful to be restrained within formal limits, with which Elizabeth surprised the noble assembly on that occasion. After a sermon " wherein none other argument was handled, but only of praises and glory to be rendered unto God," she broke forth again with a full heart, exhorting all the people to thankfulness, " with most princely and Christian speeches." When we read of such scenes, it is not difficult to understand how Elizabeth won the name of " Good Queen Bess," or why her name is still traced as it were in golden characters in the history of the English people.

———

The personal life and habits of sovereigns of vigorous intellects, generous tastes, and who are actuated by desires to raise their country in the scale of nations as the truest mode of raising themselves, are ever matters of high importance ; in Elizabeth's case they were pre-eminently so. Unless, indeed, we except the love-passages of her history, she had no *private* life ; for in all she said and did, she was still carrying out the views—generally enlightened and comprehensive, sometimes the reverse—that had been determined upon in the council or in her own mind. And even these love passages of the woman were on the whole efficiently controlled by the prudence of the sovereign.

Among the most wonderful phenomena of Elizabeth's time, the sudden rise and almost as sudden prosperity of the drama will ever stand foremost ; it would not be too much to say that the queen should share a portion of the merit of that movement. To her state policy was doubtless in some degree owing the general freshness and invigoration of the national heart and mind that so characterised the time, and rendered dramatists and audience alike worthy of each other ; to her private encouragement, the theatre was still more directly indebted for the stamp of approbation that was at once discriminating and royal, and therefore productive of the most beneficial influence on the fortunes of the stage. Some memorable instances are on record of performances that have taken place before her. In the beginning of 1558 certain gentlemen of Gray's Inn presented before the Queen at Greenwich, the 'Misfortunes of Arthur, Uther Pendragon's son' (Fig. 1564); among these certain gentlemen was Francis Bacon, then Reader of Gray's Inn. About the same period, it is supposed a play involving, as regarded the dramatist, issues of an infinitely more important kind, was presented

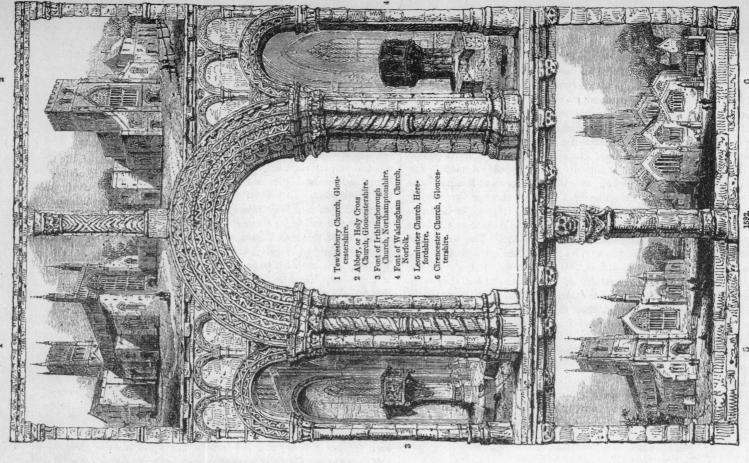

1 Tewkesbury Church, Gloucestershire.
2 Abbey, or Holy Cross
Church, Gloucestershire.
3 Font of Irthlingborough
Church, Northamptonshire.
4 Font of Walsingham Church,
Norfolk.
5 Leominster Church, Herefordshire.
6 Cirencester Church, Gloucestershire.

1592.

1591.—Merchant Tailors' School ; the present Building.
(Engraved from an original Sketch.)

1593.—Westminster School. (From an old Print)

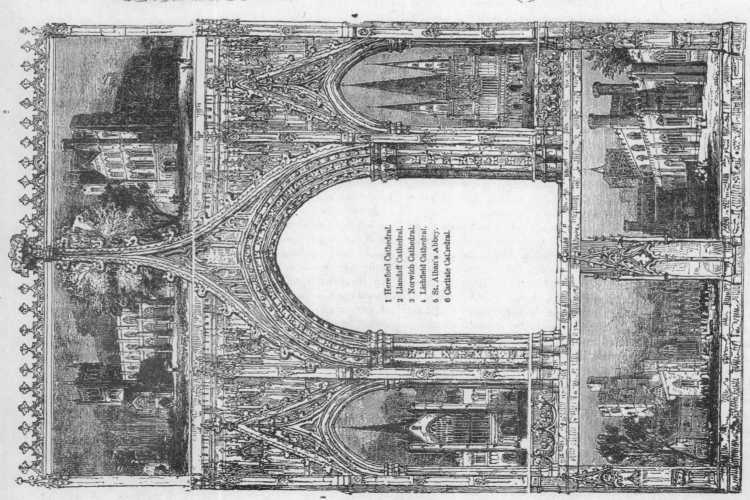

1 Hereford Cathedral.
2 Llandaff Cathedral.
3 Norwich Cathedral.
4 Lichfield Cathedral.
5 St. Alban's Abbey.
6 Carlisle Cathedral.

1595

1596.—Magdalen Bridge and the Tower of Magdalen College. (From an original Drawing by W. A. Delamotte.)

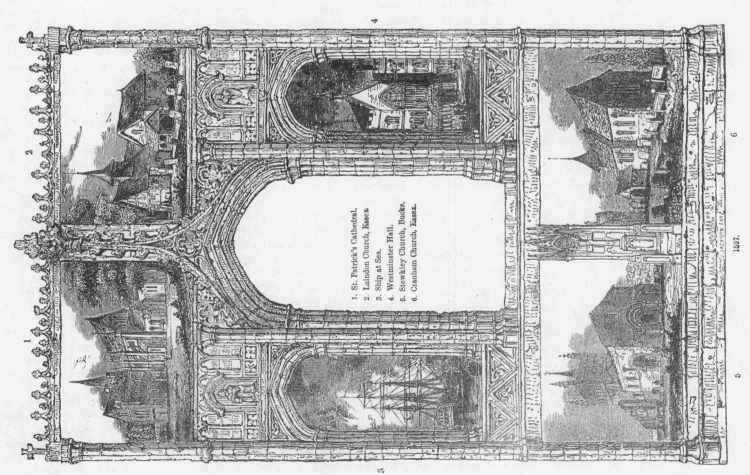

1. St. Patrick's Cathedral.
2. Laindon Church, Essex.
3. Ship at Sea.
4. Westminster Hall.
5. Stewkley Church, Bucks.
6. Cranham Church, Essex.

1597.

before Elizabeth (probably the Love's Labour Lost, Fig. 1563), by William Shakspere. The fact at all events is certain that early plays of Shakspere were performed at an early period of his dramatic life before the queen; it is no other than Ben Jonson who records the poetic

Flights upon the banks of Thames,
That so did take Eliza;

and it is hardly possible to overrate the effect that such encouragement must have had upon the career of the young dramatist. And the favour thus early accorded evidently continued to the close of Elizabeth's reign. One of the pleasantest of traditions says that the Merry Wives of Windsor was written at her command and by her direction, and that she was so eager to see it acted, that she commanded it to be finished in fourteen days; and was afterwards very well pleased at the representation (Fig. 1565). Others add that the idea of the comedy was suggested to Elizabeth by her admiration of the character of Falstaff in Henry IV., and that she desired to see him in love. The date of that representation was in all probability 1593, in which year it is known there was a visit made to Windsor, such as that referred to by Dr. Caius:—"Dere be a Garman duke come to de court has cosened all de host of Branford and Reading." Nay the very name of the Duke was preserved sufficiently for all who knew the story to enjoy it, without committing the royal audience to the impropriety of laughing so very barefacedly at the recent guest—the Count of Mümpel*gart*, or, as the dramatist had it in his early copies, *Gar*momble.

In her progresses Elizabeth had, it is clear, one steadily-formed object in view—that of reducing the wealth, and thereby the political power of her noble and wealthy subjects. She had learnt alike the policy and the mode of carrying it out from her grandfather, that incarnation of subtle statecraft, Henry VII.—but then how she bettered the instruction! He could not have ventured to have made in a life-time the number of visits she made in a single year. He was hated in so doing; she made her guests, as Otway says, " in love and pleased with ruin :" which in some instances it wellnigh brought on them. To attempt to describe all Elizabeth's movements, even in one single progress, would be quite out of the question here. Take a single year, 1561. Starting from Westminster, she went to the Mint, coined some pieces of money, and gave them away, and from thence passed to the Charter House. From the Charter House, four days after, she went to the Savoy to sup with Mr. Secretary Cecil, afterwards Lord Burghley. At last she was fairly off into Essex, and visited Lord Rich at Wanstead, the Earl of Oxford at Havering, Sir John Grey at Purgo House in the same parish, Sir Thomas Davy at Loughton Hall, Sir William Petre at Ingatestone, and so to the mansion, built by her father, of New Hall or Beaulieu, near Chelmsford. Then came the turn of the corporations. Colchester, Harwich, and Ipswich each had the honour to entertain her Majesty. Next a fresh round of private visits, in which we know not how many Tollemaches, Waldegraves, and Morleys were honoured by the opportunity of showing their loyalty by their hospitality and profuse expenditure. As a crowning *bonne-bouche*, she stayed at Hertford above a fortnight, a pretty treat for the inhabitants, who had to bear the royal costs. At last she returned to her own house at Enfield, and from thence a little later towards her palace of St. James (Figs. 1511, 1519), the hedges and ditches between Islington and Charing Cross being cut down or filled up, to allow free way for the thousands of people who flocked out to meet and welcome her home. Among the places visited on other progresses, may be enumerated Sandown Castle (Fig. 1460), Cowdry, in Sussex (Fig. 1556), and Harefield (Fig. 1566), the mansion of the Lord Keeper Egerton, a place doubly endeared to the lovers of poetry; there Shakspere's Othello was played by his own company; there Milton fixed the scene of his Arcades.

A remarkable print engraved by Vertue (Fig. 1515) from an old picture he found in 1647 at Lord Digby's seat at Coleshill, shows us the kind of state in which the Virgin-Queen moved in these progresses. In that print, " the Queen," to use the words of the antiquary-engraver's own description, " is seated in a canopy-chair of state, carried by six gentlemen; several Knights of the Garter, with their collars of that most noble order, walking before the Queen, and many favourite ladies following in the train. The yeomen of the guard follow, and the band of gentlemen-pensioners line the way. Amongst the Knights of the Garter, Dudley, Earl of Leicester, is nearest to the Queen. Henry, Lord Hunsdon (see also Fig. 1514), carries the Sword of State before her Majesty. As these knights walk two and two, the next is William Cecil, Lord Burghley, Lord High-Treasurer, with his white staff in his hand. Next before him is Charles Howard, admiral, afterwards Lord Nottingham. The other three

Knights of the Garter (Lords Clinton, Russel, and Sussex), as those before mentioned, each of them having a ribbon about his neck, with a small gem or intaglio appendant to it; thereon a profile of her Majesty's countenance, which additional ornament, it is conjectured, was designed to represent these noblemen to be the Queen's favourites. The place where this procession appears to be is within the enclosure of the court-yard of Hunsdon House; the back part is the prospect in this picture; they are passing round, as it were, by the aqueduct, to come to the front entrance. This house was entirely built by King Henry VIII., and afterwards the front only new rebuilt by Lord Hunsdon, as it still remains, both ways being encircled with water, and two arched bridges to pass over to the house. As the back front is the prospect to this picture, so at a distance, on a hill, appears a small old castle, perhaps Stortford Castle, by which the river Stort passes, and joins the river Lea at Stansted, where, near the bridge, are boats or skiffs purposely represented, &c. I have some reasons to think that amongst the ladies that follow the Queen, the foremost in white may be the Lady Hunsdon; on her right hand Lord Hunsdon's sister, Lady Katherine, who was wife to Admiral Howard; and next behind, in a dark grave habit, Lady Mary Bolen, mother of Lord Hunsdon : all the ladies are richly adorned with jewels to grace the solemnity of this procession. And as this noble lord was captain of the band of gentlemen-pensioners, he might order or appoint their attendance (as they appear) to line the way with their partisans in their hands." To this part of the pageant, we must not forget to add another that accompanied some of the progresses, although it was doubtless judiciously kept in the back ground—we refer to the " Smutty regiment who attended the progresses, and rode in the carts with the pots and kettles, which, with every other article of furniture, were then moved from palace to palace," and to whom in consequence " the people in derision gave the name of *black* guards, a term since become sufficiently familiar, and never probably explained " [Gifford]. Such exhibitions would be presented whenever the Queen moved about between Greenwich and Westminster (Fig. 1516), St. James's, and Nonsuch, and Somerset House (Figs. 1473, 1474, 1520), and Enfield, and Richmond (Figs. 1512, 1517, and Hampton Court, the different homes of royalty : for not even the mistress of all these palaces could, or at least did, command furniture enough for half of them. Among these palaces Nonsuch, if only for its peculiarities, demands a few words of notice. If we were to be content to take without inquiry the panegyrics that writers have given of it, we should say it was worthy of its name, that in the world there were *none such* beside. " One might imagine," it has been said, " everything that architecture can perform to have been employed " on it. If we look, however, to the engraving (Fig. 1513), we shall see that the fantastic expression of the whole was its true distinction. " The palace itself," says one who saw it in its palmy days, " is so encompassed with parks full of deer, delicious gardens, groves ornamented with trellice-work, cabinets of verdure, and walks so embowered by trees, that it seems to be a place pitched upon by Pleasure herself to dwell in along with Health." The gardens were decorated with many columns and pyramids of marble, and fountains of the most ingenious but artificial character, all showing like the palace the magnificence and the bad taste of the founder.

In concluding these episodical notices of the private life of Elizabeth, let us look at her at home; and through the medium of one who had the ability to describe in no ordinary manner the remarkable scene that was opened to him—Paul Hentzner—a German, who came to England in 1598, in the suite of a young German nobleman. His work is in Latin, but has been translated by Horace Walpole. Hentzner thus describes her march, as it may be called, from the domestic apartment to the chapel of the palace at Greenwich :—

" First went gentlemen, barons, earls, knights of the garter, all richly dressed, and bare-headed; next came the Chancellor, bearing the seals in a red silk purse, between two; one of which carried the royal sceptre, the other the sword of state, in a red scabbard, studded with golden fleurs-de-lis, the point upwards; next came the queen, in the sixty-fifth year of her age, we are told, *very majestic*; her face oblong, fair but wrinkled; her eyes small, yet black and pleasant; her nose a little hooked, her lips narrow, and her teeth black (a defect the English seem subject to, from their too great use of sugar); she had in her ears two pearls, with very rich drops; she wore false hair, and that red; upon her head she had a small crown, reported to be made of some of the gold of the celebrated Lunebourg table; her bosom was uncovered, as all the English ladies have it till they marry; and she had on a necklace, of exceeding fine jewels; her hands were small, her fingers long, and her stature neither tall nor low; her air was stately, her manner of speaking mild and obliging. That day she was dressed in white silk, bordered with pearls of the size of beans, and over it a mantle of black silk, shot with silver threads; her train was very long, the end of it borne by a marchioness; instead of a chain she had an oblong collar of gold and jewels. As she went along in all this state and magnificence, she spoke very graciously, first to one, then to another, whether foreign ministers, or those who attended for different reasons, in English, French, and Italian; for besides being well skilled in Greek, Latin, and the languages I have mentioned, she is mistress of Spanish, Scotch, and Dutch; *whoever speaks to her, it is kneeling:* now and then she raises some with her hand. While we were there, W. Slawata, a Bohemian baron, had letters to present to her; and she, after pulling off her glove, gave him her right hand to kiss, sparkling with rings and jewels—a mark of particular favour; *wherever she turned her face, as she was going along, everybody fell down on their knees.* The ladies of the court followed next to her, very handsome and well shaped, and for the most part dressed in white. She was guarded on each side by the gentlemen-pensioners, fifty in number, with gilt battle-axes. In the ante-chapel next the hall where we were, petitions were presented to her, and she received them most graciously, which occasioned the acclamation of 'Long live Queen Elizabeth!' She answered it with, 'I thank you, my good people.' In the chapel was excellent music; as soon as it and the service was over, which scarce exceeded half an hour, the queen returned in the same state and order, and prepared to go to dinner." In the meantime Hentzner had cared more to see the preparations for the dinner than to partake in the service of the chapel, so while Elizabeth was still at prayers, he saw her table thus set out:—"A gentleman entered the room bearing a rod, and along with him another who had a table-cloth, which, after they had both kneeled three times with the utmost veneration, he spread upon the table, and, after kneeling again, they both retired. Then came two others, one with the rod again, the other with a salt-cellar, a plate, and bread; when they had kneeled as the others had done, and placed what was brought upon the table, they too retired with the same ceremonies performed by the first. At last came an unmarried lady (we were told she was a countess) and along with her a married one, bearing a tasting-knife; the former was dressed in white silk, who, when she had prostrated herself three times in the most graceful manner, approached the table, and rubbed the plates with bread and salt, with as much awe as if the queen had been present; when they had waited there a little while, the yeomen of the guards entered, bare-headed, clothed in scarlet, with a golden rose upon their backs, bringing in at each turn a course of twenty-four dishes, served in plate, most of it gilt; these dishes were received by a gentleman in the same order they were brought, and placed upon the table, while the lady-taster gave to each of the guard a mouthful to eat of the particular dish he had brought, for fear of any poison. During the time that this guard, which consists of the tallest and stoutest men that can be found in all England, being carefully selected for this service, were bringing dinner, twelve trumpets and two kettle-drums made the hall ring for half an hour together. At the end of all this ceremonial a number of unmarried ladies appeared, who, with particular solemnity, lifted the meat off the table, and conveyed it into the queen's inner and most private chamber, where, after she had chosen for herself, the rest goes to the ladies of the court."

In the year of Hentzner's visit a gloom was thrown over the brilliant circle that surrounded the queen in her every movement, by the death of its most distinguished member—William Cecil, Lord Burghley. Let us pause awhile over the recollections suggested by the event. Let us follow him into his splendid seclusion at the place from whence he derived his title.

The era of palaces, as the sixteenth century has been felicitously called, numbered among its proudest productions Burleigh, or Burghley House, Northamptonshire, still a splendid example of Elizabethan or Tudor-Gothic architecture. Most of the grand palatial edifices of this kind were reared by the high officers of state or nobility; and Burghley owes its grandeur, if not its origin, to William Cecil. "My house of Burghley," writes Cecil in 1585, "is of my mother's inheritance;" and speaking of the stately structure he was erecting in the place of the former, he adds, "I have set my walls on the old foundation, . . . and yet one side remaineth as my father left it me." Several dates about the present Burghley House point out the Lord Treasurer's buildings. Near one of the entrances within the central court is the inscription— 'W. Dom. De Burghley, 1577." Beneath a turret is the date 1585, when extensive additions were made; and the present grand entrance appears to have been built in 1587. While the work was going on, or, as Cecil facetiously expressed it, while his great house

at Burghley was sweeping, he retired to Wothorp, about two miles distant, "out of the dust." The dates given above show the mansion principally to have been the work of Cecil's age, when he found time to exchange the cares of the nation for the delightful task of forming this splendid retreat. The relaxation of such a mind must still have greatness in it. The planning, decorating, and enjoying, his residence at Burghley, were among Cecil's relaxations. And well the habits of the state veteran in his retired leisure harmonised with all the better parts of his public career. Accustomed to say that a man false to his God could not be expected to be true to any other, Cecil was, in his own private life, faithful both to God and man in the essential requirements of his position His piety is said to have been sincere and elevated; yet no one could be less of an ascetic in his family or social connexions. Though abstemious in his own diet, he kept and delighted in a liberal table; and if it was not his wont to set it "in a roar" with the warmth and genuineness of his humour, or the brilliant coruscations of his wit, he was yet facetious and merry enough to produce an equally desirable effect—unalloyed cheerful enjoyment. He had, too, that art which should be esteemed the highest evidence of good breeding, the art of making all who sat at his table share in the general enjoyment, by drawing forth from all those qualities in which they severally shone. Fuller says of him, "He had a pretty wit-rack in himself to make the dumb to speak, and to draw speech out of the most silent and sullen guest at his table, to snow his disposition in any point he should propound." The hospitality of Burghley House to its wealthy neighbours was not more marked than its charity to the poorer: both were luxuries as well as duties to its princely owner. Among his other high delights, was the "pure" and "substantial world" of books, and the garden—scarcely an inferior world to those who care to study it. The self-control and equanimity of temper which had distinguished Cecil in the great trials of his public life, were equally exercised in those pettier vexations that often overcome the wisest when withdrawn from the influence of the public eye. And even when growing infirmities and the loss of his dearest companion for forty-five years, the estimable Mildred, his wife, rendered him occasionally irritable and capricious, it was truly affecting to behold how the venerable old man strove immediately by all the means in his power to make atonement. That was an enviable reflection to which he gave utterance when he said, "I entertain malice against no individual whatever, and I thank God that I never retired to rest out of charity with any man."

The time at length arrives—

> When, like a thrice-told tale,
> Long rifled life of sweets can yield no more,—(YOUNG)

and Cecil was prepared to

> Toss fortune back her tinsel and her plume,
> And drop this mask of flesh behind the scene.

He is on his death-bed. Children—friends—domestics—admiring, reverencing, loving, lamenting,—gather about him; the world grows darker and darker—the future brighter and brighter; and, at last—in perfect peace—Cecil expires. The voice of England's greatest statesman is heard no more. Burghley's chief glory was his integrity; he was almost the first thoroughly *honest* minister who had kept the coffer of the state without helping himself clandestinely to some of its contents, and to whom no touch or stain of financial extortion attached, as was indubitably proved, when Elizabeth sifted his affairs so rigorously after his decease. As for his abilities to guide the nation, their best evidence was Elizabeth's deference to his judgment, and even her occasional unwilling submission to it, at those periods when she had been betrayed into a deviation from the high path which she had marked out for herself. His impartiality in dispensing patronage was equally remarkable with his fine discrimination of character: whence it seemed as if he were resolved to render England "distinguished above all nations for the integrity of her judges, the piety of her divines, and the sagacity of her ambassadors." To these high merits we may add another, that though to him we chiefly owe the firm and final settlement of our Reformed Church, he was so far from being a bigot, that his habit of encouraging free discussion has been especially noticed. And, notwithstanding Cecil's participation in some of the besetting sins of the age, as political ingratitude, political intrigue, and political bending of right and justice to might and expediency, his life was on the whole a most noble one, and the termination as noble. With the elevating impressions that it leaves on our mind fresh upon us, we approach his mansion, which is still in great part as he built it, though various additions and alterations have added

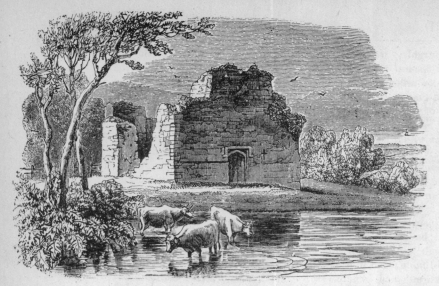

1598.—Court-a-Street Chapel, in the Parish of Aldington, Kent; where the Holy Maid of Kent uttered her prophecies in presence of the image of the Virgin, through which she pretended to receive her Inspirations. (From an original Drawing.)

1599.—The Boundary Elm, Stratford

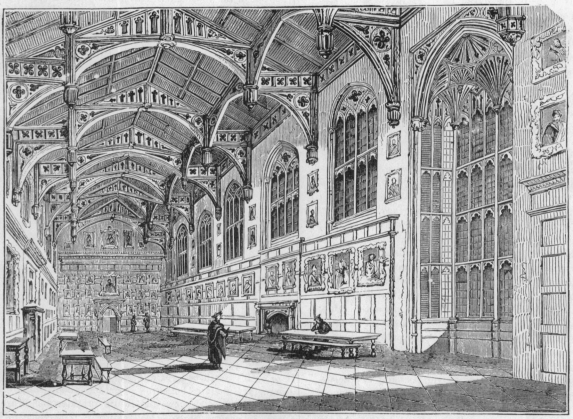

1601.—Interior of Christ Church Hall. (From an original Drawing by W. A. Delamotte.)

1602.—Christ Church, Oxford, in the Sixteenth Century.

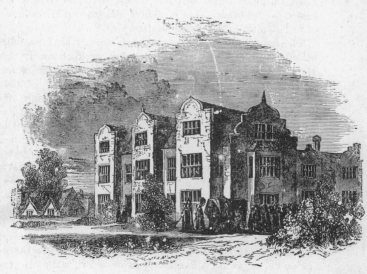

1600.—Nunnery at Salford.

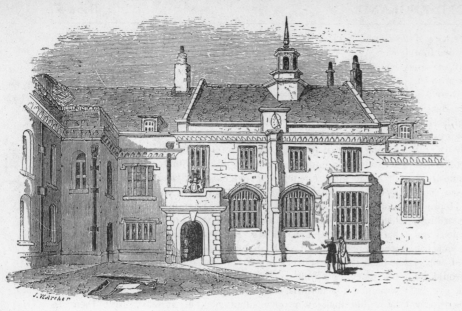

1606.—The Great Hall, Charter-House.

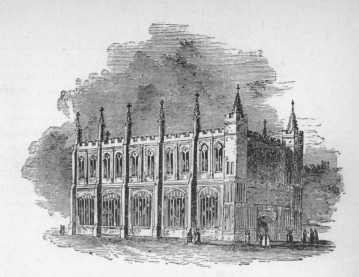

1605.—Divinity Schools, Oxford, in the Sixteenth Century.

1304.—Interior of the Bodleian Library.

1607.—Inner Court of Stratford Grammar-school.

1603.—Balliol College, Oxford, in the Sixteenth Century

1604.—Ancient View of Cambridge.

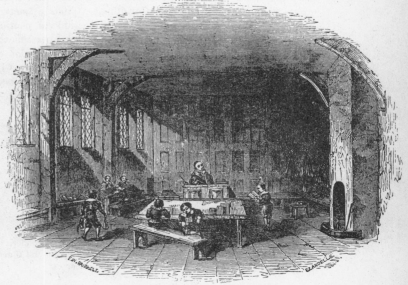

1608.—Interior of Stratford Grammar-school.

69

greatly to its size, so that one of the most striking characteristics of Burghley House is its vast extent. On entering the park we first find ourselves in a winding road between an avenue of lofty trees. Then the park opens, presenting from time to time, as we proceed, lesser avenues of trees, or green alleys, as we may call them; at the end of one of which, filling up its entire breadth, appears Burghley House, with its towers and cupolas, and picturesque pillar-like chimneys, and its tall chapel spire. Truly magnificent in expression is the north front (Fig. 1554), and indeed the character of the whole pile can be given in no better word than that of magnificence. Even if we dislike the general style or taste of the composition, there can be no question of its possessing the quality we have named in a very eminent degree. The plan of Burghley House is a square, with a court in the centre. The windows are very striking, on account of their breadth. Thus, the great hall, spacious and lofty as it is, contains but two windows, and the ball-room has but one, a bow-window. The vast and varied collection of works of art, for which Burghley is especially remarkable, it would be quite impossible here to particularise. They enchant the eye, or inform the mind, in every part. Of the carving, we can only mention the oaken roof of the great hall, a work of the richest beauty:—of the pictures, those of the eminent persons of Lord Cecil's time, and especially the portrait of Essex, and Marcus Gerard's "Queen Elizabeth at an advanced age," which exhibits her usual excess of ornament in dress, and features expressive of a proud and somewhat chilling character. Her visit to Burghley is commemorated by the preservation of the bed in which she lay, with its ancient hangings of green and gold brocade. The scenery which Elizabeth and her Lord Treasurer would gaze on from Burghley's broad windows is the same also—in essentials—as that we gaze on, a paradise of wood, and stream, and lawn, extending in particular directions into prospects of unusual extent and beauty.

William Cecil was succeeded by his son Robert (Fig. 1555), not only in the barony of Burghley, but also in the still higher dignity of prime minister, in which he displayed abilities not unworthy of his predecessor.

We now approach the close of the reign, and the period of those incidents which, in causing the disgraceful death of a brave, accomplished, and estimable man, shortened the life of the sovereign who sentenced him; and showed, by that melancholy evidence, that Elizabeth's heart was for once deeply touched. Strange as it must seem to us, considering Elizabeth's age, and the number of her past favourites, there is no resisting the conclusion, that of all the romantic personal connections in which she delighted to engage, her last favourite was also the most real favourite, the one for whom she had (and perhaps for him only) a genuine affection; and him she sent to the scaffold. The reader anticipates the name—Essex (Fig. 1571), familiar to us still in connection not only with the abstract history of the events in question, but with the locality where the imprudent Earl lived at the time he so deeply committed himself.

In passing through Devereux Court in the Strand, a little beyond Temple Bar, the observer, pausing to look up at the front of the once famous Grecian Coffee-house, sees a small bust, and will probably feel, like us, touched when he learns that it is a semblance of the great Earl who once lorded it over the neighbourhood, and finally quitted it under such tragical circumstances. Passing on, he will find himself in Essex Street, at the bottom of which a pair of tall and massive stone pillars with Corinthian capitals attract his eye; these pillars are the sole remains of the magnificent mansion (Fig. 1568), left by will to Essex by his guilty mother's second husband, Leicester, to whom he owed his favourable introduction at court. Within its walls, both under the name of Essex House, and Leicester House, the poet of the 'Fairy Queen' was a frequent guest. Thus writes he of both owners, whilst the last (Lord Essex) was its master:—

> Next whereunto there stands a stately place,
> Where oft I gayned giftes and goodly grace
> Of that great lord, which therein wont to dwell,
> Whose want too well now feels my friendless case:
> But oh! here fits not well
> Olde woes, but joyes, to tell
> Against the bridale daye, which is not long:
> Sweet Themmes! runne softly till I end my song.
>
> Yet therein now doth lodge a noble peer,
> Great England's glory, and the world's wide wonder,
> Whose dreadful name late through all Spaine did thunder,
> And Hercules' two pillars standing near

> Did make to quake and fear:
> Faire branch of honour, flower of chevalrie!
> That fillest England with thy triumph's fame,
> Joy have thou of thy noble victorie.

Spenser was a dependent on Leicester, and most probably on Essex, by whom he was interred in Westminster Abbey.

Essex had more than once offended the Queen before he gave the last and unpardonable offence in 1600. Only two years before, having differed from Elizabeth in respect to some Irish appointment, Essex was so imprudent and ungallant as to turn his back upon her with the most unequivocal evidences of anger and scorn. The Queen, naturally stung by the insult, gave him a box upon the ear, and bade him go to the devil. The Earl immediately clapped his hand upon his sword, and when the Lord-Admiral stepped in between him and Elizabeth, he swore that he neither could nor would put up with such an affront—that he would not have taken it from the hands of Henry VIII. himself. He then rushed out of the place, and went to his country-house at Wanstead; there he remained for months, deaf to all the entreaties of his friends that he would make a proper submission, or at least leave them to conclude a reconciliation. Camden and others date Essex's ruin from this period; but we think wrongly, unless it be simply meant that the recollection of this affair would enhance the Queen's exasperation when another and more important incident left his life legally in her hands, and so led to his death. But assuredly there is enough evidence that, as far as the Queen's affection as well as favours were concerned, Essex, when he did re-appear at court, resumed his former position.

Unhappily for Essex, he was appointed to the government of Ireland, part of which was then in a state of rebellion. He might have dealt successfully with the difficulties of his task, had he received all proper aid from the minister at home. But Robert Cecil and Raleigh were his enemies, and made the most of every failure. The instruments also by which he was to work were not left to his own selection; having named his friend the Earl of Southampton general of the horse, the appointment was revoked, to the great humiliation and injury of Essex. Under such circumstances, it is unfair to measure Essex's conduct by its results, which were most unsatisfactory. The Earl indeed seems to have been possessed by the constant reflection that the enemies he had to contend with were not the wild and rebellious Irish, but the smooth-tongued English courtiers. So one day he arrived most unexpectedly at the gates of the Queen's palace, and being admitted, ran hastily up to the royal bedchamber, where Elizabeth had just risen, and met him with her hair about her face. She received him in a manner that fulfilled his most sanguine hopes. He had from Ireland conveyed to his mistress his poetical wishes, most poetically expressed, that he might live "in some unharmed desart most obscure,"

> From all society, from love and hate
> Of worldly folk; then should he sleep secure.
> Then wake again, and yield God every praise,
> Content with hips and hawes, and bramble-berry;
> In contemplation parting out his days,
> And change of holy thoughts to make him merry
> Who, when he dies, his tomb may be a bush,
> Where harmless robin dwells with gentle thrush.

And now that he had returned from his unthankful Irish government, he found Elizabeth so far sympathising with his tastes and the difficulties he had had to contend with, that when he left her he was heard to thank God that though he had suffered much trouble from storms abroad, he found a sweet calm at home. That very evening he was ordered to consider himself a prisoner in his room. Eight lingering and wretched months passed; and then Essex wrote to the Queen. But there was no answer for three long months more, when he was released, but ordered to keep away from the court. Essex had a valuable patent for the monopoly of sweet wines; it was about to expire—he asked for its renewal; it was denied:—"In order to manage an ungovernable beast, it is necessary to stint his provender," was Elizabeth's harsh comment upon the request. That treatment only made the "ungovernable beast" still more furious and desperate. He began to listen to the suggestions of his secretary, one Cuffe, a man "smothered under the habit of a scholar, and slubbered over with a certain rude and clownish fashion that had the semblance of integrity;" who advised him to remove his enemies—Sir Robert Cecil, Raleigh, and others—from the Queen's court and council by force. Essex hesitated, and was lost. Extensive preparations were made; too extensive to be kept secret from the men against whom they were directed. But although warned by an anonymous note to be careful of his safety, and informed that the palace-guard had been doubled, Essex—instead of obeying the summons he had received to attend before the Privy Council—sent out messengers in all directions during the following night to call his friends together, as his life was threatened by Raleigh and Lord Cobham, excusing himself to her Majesty's Council, then assembled at Salisbury Court, on the pretence of sickness. Next morning (Sunday, February 8, 1601) there were joined with him the Earls of Rutland and Southampton, the Lords Sandys and Mounteagle, "with a troop of gallant gentlemen their followers," about 300 altogether. Among them were Danvers, Blount, Catesby, Owen Salisbury, and many other familiar names of that time. Zeal for the Earl—alas! without judgment—burned in every breast. They saw him injured, degraded, and almost driven into a state of frenzy by a faction whose intrigues were marked with the sorest ingratitude and malicious cunning. It was, indeed, but too true what Elizabeth herself once said, alluding to her intriguing courtiers—" In those (former) days force and arms did prevail, but now the wit of the fox is everywhere on foot, so as hardly a faithful or virtuous man may be found." The wit of the fox had been turned against Essex, who possessed it not, nor desired to possess it, nor to feign it,—amongst others by Robert Cecil, who had laid many a snare for the fiery young favourite, and by Walter Raleigh. Against such men Essex was not formed by nature or by principle to contend. What could the gusty and unequal counsels of passion do for him, but convert misfortune into total ruin? With his armed force—that fatal Sunday morning—Essex was about to set forth to force his way to the Queen, and to avail himself of the collection of citizens expected to be at Paul's Cross during sermon-time, when he hoped to induce them to take arms for him. Before the Earl had left the house, there arrived the Lord Keeper of the Great Seal, the Chief-Justice Popham, Sir William Knollys, who was Essex's uncle, and the Earl of Worcester, all four men highly esteemed by Essex, and sent by the Queen apparently to try what soothing remonstrances could effect. They were admitted by a wicket gate, most of their attendants, however, being excluded.

In the court,—full of Essex's armed partisans,—the Lord Keeper put off his hat and said, that he and those with him were sent to understand the meaning of this assembly, "and to let them know, that if they had any particular cause of grief against any person whatsoever, they should have hearing and justice." "There is a plot laid against my life," answered Essex vehemently; "letters have been forged in my name—men have been hired to murder me in my bed—mine enemies cannot be satisfied unless they suck my blood." The Chief Justice assured him the queen would see him righted if he explained the matter, and the Lord Keeper seconding these promises, desired him to declare his grief, if not openly, yet in private, and he doubted not but to procure him full satisfaction. A tumultuous movement interrupted the conference, and voices cried aloud to Essex, "They abuse you, my Lord—they betray you—you are losing time." The Lord Keeper immediately covered his head, and, turning towards the multitude, with a louder voice said, "I do command you all, upon your allegiance, to lay down your weapons and to depart." His words were overpowered by impetuous shouts. "Kill them! kill them! keep them for hostages! Away with the Great Seal!" Essex was not the man to stain himself with the murder of those who were but performing a duty, and in the most temperate and proper manner. He led them to his "book chamber," where they hoped to prevail with him in private conference, but he would not hear them, and bidding them have patience half an hour, he left them, bolting the door, and planting there a guard of musketeers. Instantly drawing his sword, he rushed out of the house, followed by most of the gentlemen in arms. His first disappointment was the finding the city streets empty, and no preaching at Paul's Cross, for the politic Elizabeth and her advisers had sent timely orders to the mayor and aldermen. Those who did see Essex and his followers as they ran tumultuously through the streets, and who heard the earl shout, "For the queen, my mistress! For the queen! For the queen! A plot is laid for my life!" re-echoed by the other gentlemen, instead of joining the earl as they were entreated to do, contented themselves with crying, "God bless your honour!" or else gazed in blank astonishment, either not knowing or mistaking the cause of the excitement. Citizens—artificers—prentices—none joined him —not a man! and the ill-fated earl, after passing through Ludgate and Cheapside, not knowing what to do, entered the house of a "supposed friend" (Smith), then one of the sheriffs, who, "seeing the multitude, avoided himself out at a back door, when presently in divers parts of the city Essex was proclaimed a traitor, to the no less grief of the citizens, than fear of his followers." One of the

latter, a most esteemed and trusted servant of the earl, to provide for his own safety, hurried to Essex House, to Sir John Davis, who had charge of the four counsellors, and pretending to be sent by the earl, caused all four to be released. Many other of his friends now deserted Essex, who about two in the afternoon, leaving the house of the Sheriff, came to Gracechurch Street, and there attempted to make a stand; but though the mayor and others were at the upper end of the street, "no one citizen or servant showed him any sign of assistance" (Speed). He retired again towards St. Paul's, meaning to pass Ludgate by the way that he came, but his progress was interrupted by barricades of empty carts, and several companies of pikemen and other troops called out by the Bishop of London. The earl was twice shot through the hat, and forced back. Sir Christopher Blount, his stepfather, after being severely wounded in the head was taken prisoner. Young Tracy was slain, and several others injured. Retreating into Friday Street, Essex grew faint, and desired drink of some of the citizens, which they gave him. At Queenhithe he took boat, and "with a mind distracted he rowed up the river, and landed at the water-gate of his own house, which he presently fortified," with the full purpose of dying in his own defence—still, however, cherishing a hope that the citizens would join him. That hope was soon dissipated. Essex House was stormed by the Lord Admiral, yet not a man came to his relief. The Countess of Essex, the Lady Rich, and their gentlewomen, were permitted to depart, and then the garden was forced, so that the soldiers reached the very walls of the house. At that moment, when Essex's defeat and ruin appeared certain, an affecting incident occurred. Captain Owen Salisbury stood openly at a window bareheaded, seeking to obtain a soldier's rather than a rebel's death. A musket bullet from some person in the street struck him in the side of the head;—"Oh, that thou hadst been so much my friend as to have shot but a little lower!" he exclaimed. As it was, however, the wound answered its purpose; he died the next morning. Essex was by that time in the hands of his foes; at ten o'clock at night he had yielded, desiring only that he might be civilly used, and that he might have an honourable trial. He was first taken to Lambeth House, where for an hour or two he remained with the Lord Archbishop ("his ever most loving, but then most mournful friend"); from thence he was with some other lords conveyed to the Tower.

Essex was tried and condemned; the terrible nature of the proceedings being immeasurably enhanced to the unhappy prisoner by the consideration that one of his dearest friends, Southampton, stood by his side sharing in his danger, and that another, whom Essex had held scarcely less dear, and to whom he had rendered services for which a life-long gratitude might have been expected, stood foremost among the accusers who thirsted for his blood—that was the "greatest—meanest of mankind"—Bacon. Essex and Southampton were both condemned. The nobility of Essex's nature was never more apparent than then; being asked why judgment of death should not be passed upon him, his answer was principally an earnest appeal for his friend Southampton's life, being indifferent to his own. To the advice of the Lord Steward that he should implore the Queen's mercy by acknowledging and confessing all his offences, he replied patiently but with dignity, that he could not ask for mercy in that way; he begged her Majesty's forgiveness in all humility; he would rather die than live in misery; he had cleared his accounts, had forgiven all the world, and was ready and willing to be out of it.

He was executed on Ash-Wednesday, the 25th of February, at about eight in the morning, in an inner court of the Tower, most probably on the spot where a quadrangular space of ground is still marked by the different colour of the stones, in the front of the Beauchamp Tower (Fig. 1572): the spot on which so much noble blood has been poured forth, in sacrifice to the evil spirits of Ambition, Tyranny, and State-selfishness. At the time this able warrior, tolerant statesman, and accomplished man thus perished, let it not be forgotten that he was but comparatively young—not having reached his thirty-fourth year.

Let us now pass over some two years. The people who had so loved and admired Essex, and so regretted and almost resented his fate, that when his harsh mistress and executioner went abroad, the altered greeting of her subjects was too marked to be overlooked and mistaken—even these have well-nigh forgotten him in the variety and incessant sequence of new events and new actors. But there is one who remembers him—Elizabeth herself. Sickness has begun to seize her. But there is a deeper malady than physician can cure at work in her breast. She will take no medicine. The heat that parches her mouth and her stomach so violently, that she is often in danger of being stifled by it, is but weak to that consuming fire that is preying upon her heart. So deep a melan

1610.—Charlcote Church.

1609.—Boldre Church, Hampshire.

1611.—Bishopton Chapel.

1612.—Houghton Regis Church, Bedfordshire.

1613.—Meadows near Welford.

1614.—Old Church of Hampton Lucy.

1615.—Clifford Church.

1616.—Bromley Church, Kent.

1617.—Lynton Parsonage, Devonshire.

1618.—Stoke Church, Buckinghamshire.

1619.—Seathwaite Chapel, Lancashire.

1620.—Chelsea Church, from the River.

choly stamped upon her face and behaviour, that even the most ordinary observers take notice of it. Fatigue is wearing down her once powerful frame, but she will take no rest—such as her bed can give her. Her attendants grow alarmed. It is whispered that she is dying. Her ministers and others see it is necessary that some violence even shall be used, when they behold her lying on the floor in a state of such regal desolation as perhaps no poet or painter ever imagined—propped by cushions, her finger in her mouth, her eyes open, and fixed ever on the ground. By violence, in fact, she is drawn to bed at last, on the 21st of March, 1603—in time to die there, three days after.

And what was the meaning of this extraordinary prostration of heart and intellect? Some say it was excited by her reflections touching the succession; why it would be impossible to say, since James was a Protestant, and though a son to Mary, had done as much as he well could, without violating all appearances of decency, to divest himself in his dealings with Elizabeth of every feeling and duty that attached to his relationship. Others said it was because her council had constrained her to grant a pardon to the Earl of Tyrone for his Irish insurrection; a cause as evidently inadequate as the other to the effect produced. There remained but one solution of the difficulty—that it was grief and remorse for the fate of the Earl of Essex; a solution that was readily caught up and acquiesced in by the public, and with the greater avidity, on account of the romantic narration of circumstances connected with Elizabeth and Essex that accompanied it, and explained the mystery that hung over the execution of such a man by one who was understood to have had so much love for him. We entreat our reader's particular attention to this narration, for a reason that we shall presently explain. The writer is Dr. Birch, who collected the particulars and published them in his 'Negotiations,' and whose account has been reprinted in the 'Memoirs of the Peers of England during the Reign of James,' from which we here transcribe.

"The following curious story was frequently told by Lady Elizabeth Spelman, great-grand-daughter of Sir Robert Carey, brother of Lady Nottingham, and afterwards Earl of Monmouth, whose curious memoirs of himself were published a few years ago by Lord Corke:—When Catherine Countess of Nottingham was dying (as she did, according to his lordship's own account, about a fortnight before Queen Elizabeth), she sent to her Majesty to desire that she might see her, in order to reveal something to her Majesty without the discovery of which she could not die in peace. Upon the Queen's coming, Lady Nottingham told her that while the Earl of Essex lay under sentence of death, he was desirous of asking her Majesty's mercy in the manner prescribed by herself during the height of his favour; the Queen having given him a ring, which, being sent to her as a token of his distress, might entitle him to her protection. But the Earl, jealous of those about him, and not caring to trust any of them with it, as he was looking out of his window one morning, saw a boy with whose appearance he was pleased; and, engaging him by money and promises, directed him to carry the ring, which he took from his finger and threw down, to Lady Scroope, a sister of the Countess of Nottingham, and a friend of his Lordship, who attended upon the Queen; and to beg of her that she would present it to her Majesty. The boy, by mistake, carried it to Lady Nottingham, who showed it to her husband, the admiral, an enemy of Lord Essex, in order to take his advice. The admiral forbade her to carry it, or return any answer to the message; but insisted upon her keeping the ring. The Countess of Nottingham, having made this discovery, begged the Queen's forgiveness; but her Majesty answered, '*God may forgive you, but I never can*,' and left the room with great emotion. Her mind was so struck with the story, that she never went into bed nor took any sustenance from that instant; for Camden is of opinion that her chief reason for suffering the Earl to be executed was his supposed obstinacy in not applying to her for mercy. . . . . . In confirmation of the time of the Countess's death," continues the compiler, "it now appears from the parish-register of Chelsea, extracted by Mr. Lyson ('Environs of London,' ii. 120), that she died at Arundel House (Fig. 1574), London, February 25th, and was buried the 28th, 1603. Her funeral was kept at Chelsea, March 21, and queen Elizabeth died three days afterwards!"

Now we have a story to tell too. When in 1564 Mary Queen of Scots married Darnley, she sent to her fair cousin of England a diamond-ring in the form of a heart, in token of the event and her own affection. The ring was accompanied by some Latin verses by the chief Scottish scholar and poet of his time—Buchanan, and which have been thus rendered into English :—

> This gem behold, the emblem of my heart
> From which my cousin's image ne'er shall part;
> Clear in its lustre, spotless, does it shine,
> 'Tis clear and spotless, as this heart of mine.
> What though the stone a greater hardness wears,
> Superior firmness still the figure bears.

According to information which has been communicated to us with an implicit faith on the part of our informants, that was the ring presented by Elizabeth to Essex, as being the most precious it was in her power to give him; that was the ring given by poor Essex to the boy to be carried back to its giver in token he asked his life in a manner that would have made Elizabeth but too happy to grant it, and which being kept back by the Countess of Nottingham, induced Elizabeth to allow him to "perish" in what she esteemed "his pride;" that was the ring which, returning into Elizabeth's hand, when the Countess of Nottingham on her death-bed made her fearful revelations, subsequently passed into the hands of Elizabeth's successor, and the original giver's son, James.

We have spoken at some length of the voyages of discovery begun with such remarkable energy and success in Elizabeth's reign: the movement continued through succeeding reigns, and one of its consequences was the establishment of several of our West Indian colonies by Sir Thomas Warner, who had been James's lieutenant of the Tower, and who at his return received the memorable ring from James as a peculiar mark of the value that was placed upon his services: and the ring has remained from that time to this in the possession of Sir Thomas Warner's family, who placed it upon their shield of arms, with the motto, "I hold from the King," and there it still forms a conspicious feature.* We hardly need add that the ring is kept in the strictest custody, as the most precious of all the family heir-looms. It consists simply of a plain circle, of a size to fit the thumb, and of a heart, formed of a rose diamond, which is fastened upon and across it at one part of the circle.

The particulars of the closing scene are highly interesting, and in the main so characteristic of Elizabeth as to bear evidence of their truth; though their authenticity has been questioned on the ground that those who surrounded her may have thought proper to make her speak as it best suited their objects that she should speak. On the 22nd she was asked by Secretary Cecil (who was accompanied by the Lord Admiral and the Lord-Keeper) to name her successor. Starting, Elizabeth said, "I told you my seat has been the seat of kings; I will have no *rascal* to succeed me." One could almost imagine that her thought was, that the ministers would raise an Englishman—perhaps one of themselves—to the kingly dignity; for what followed appears to show that she could not have meant to refer to James as the "rascal." Cecil asked her what she meant by the words—no rascal? She answered, a king should succeed her; and who could that be but her cousin of Scotland? Was that her absolute will? they inquired; but she would bear no more questioning. Some time after, and while she lay speechless on her bed, Cecil again besought her to give them a sign if she would have the king of Scots to succeed her. Elizabeth then raised herself suddenly up, and clasping her hands together, held them over her head in evident signification of a crown. She died early the next morning, seemingly in a stupor, and free from pain; having reigned forty-four years, and being then sixty-nine years of age.

* In returning our warmest thanks to the lady who has furnished us with the means of tracing the history of this most interesting of gems, and who has the best possible means of knowing the accuracy of the facts upon which that history rests, we believe we may add, that the absence from England of the head of the family, who holds a high official appointment in one of the West Indian colonies, alone prevents us from giving a representation of the ring among the engravings of the present period. The ring is, as we have stated, looked upon, and justly, as a precious heir-loom; it is deposited in one of the most respectable of London banking-houses, and only permitted to be seen by the direct permission of the head of the family. We have reason to hope we shall be able to include it in the engravings of the next period.

CHAPTER II.—ECCLESIASTICAL ANTIQUITIES.

HE general history of the progress of the mighty religious changes that mark the present period, has been glanced at in connexion with the proceedings of the monarch whose personal conduct and state policy mainly originated those changes, and in connexion with the favour or disfavour shown to them by his successors, down to the final establishment of the new faith during the reign of Elizabeth. And our previous notices of the subject have been necessarily confined, for the most part, to such generals. But if we consider that every step in that eventful progress was won by the most sublime heroism on the part of individual men and women, many of them humble in position, and unknown even now by name, many of them among the most learned and eminent of the land,—if we consider the variety of circumstances evidenced by the fact, that the contest lay not only between people of the same county, city, town, village, or hamlet, but even in thousands of cases between the inhabitants of the same house; where parents were divided against their children, or the wife against her husband,—if we consider these circumstances, we may readily understand why the complete history of the English Reformation unites all the interest of a deeply interesting and most tragical romance, with the record of facts more truly momentous perhaps in their ultimate operation on the national mind and prospects, than any that have happened in England since the Romish missionaries first preached in it the doctrines of Christianity. Some of the passages of that romance we now proceed to give.

Various signs and portents gave warning of the coming Reformation even so early as the reign of Henry VII., while yet the Romish clergy stood firm on their proud eminence, controlling or performing nearly all the business of the nation. The favourite doctrines and traditions of the church began to be brought in question, its ancient customs to fall gradually into disuse. In particular, the holy images and shrines of the kingdom found fewer and fewer visitants and offerings; for new opinions concerning their true character began to find utterance among the common people. Thus, one John Blomstone was accused of saying, "there was as much virtue in an herb as in the image of the Virgin Mary, and that it was foolishness to go on pilgrimage to the image of Our Lady of Doncaster, Walsingham, or of the Tower of the city of Coventry; for a man might as well worship the blessed Virgin by the fireside in the kitchen as in the foresaid places, and as well when he seeth his mother or sister as in visiting the images, because they be no more but dead stocks and stones."

Richard Higham of Coventry, again, was charged with saying, that if "Our Lady of Tower was put into the fire, it would make a good fire,"—by no means so innoxious a truism as might at first sight appear, being tantamount to recommending that the said "Our Lady of Tower" should be burned, and so he was understood, no doubt. John Falkes, of the same place, was still more plainspoken. "Her head shall be hoar or [ere] I offer to her that is but a block: if it could speak to me, I would give it an halfpenny-worth of ale."

It was in vain attempted to stop the movement by severe laws, carried out to the severest extremes, even to the fire and the stake. The torrent rolled on—the more fiercely for the impediments cast in its way. Every single victim gave rise to a host of others. One of the modes of torment is thus described:—"Their necks were tied fast to a post or stay with towels, and their hands holden that they might not stir, and so the iron being hot was put to their cheeks, and thus bare they the prints and marks of the Lord Jesus about them." More refined cruelty was practised on the feelings and affections, as in the case of William Tylsworth, in Amersham. who was burnt in 1506: the flames that consumed him were lighted by his only daughter: whom the wretches who managed the execution

compelled to perform that horrid office. The deeply affecting story of Laurence Ghest also, "burned in Salisbury for the matter of the Sacrament," is another example: "He was of a comely and tall personage, and otherwise, as appeareth, not unfriended, for the which the bishop and the close (the canons) were the more loth to burn him, but kept him in prison the space of two years. This Laurence had a wife and seven children, wherefore, they thinking to expugn and persuade his mind by stirring of his fatherly affection toward his children, when the time came which they appointed for his burning, as he was at the stake, they brought before him his wife and his foresaid seven children. At the sight whereof, although nature is commonly wont to work in other, yet in him, religion overcoming nature, made his constancy to remain immoveable; in such sort, as when his wife began to exhort and desire him to favour himself, he again desired her to be content, and not to be a block to his way, for he was in a good course, running toward the mark of his salvation; and so, fire being put to him, he finished his life, renouncing not only wife and children, but also himself, to follow Christ. As he was in burning, one of the bishop's men threw a firebrand at his face; whereat the brother of Laurence, standing by, ran at him with his dagger, and would have slain him had he not been otherwise staid" (Fox). All these cases belong to the reign of Henry VII.

In the reign of Henry VIII. a powerful impulse was given to the movement by the tales that now came more frequently than before to the popular ear, in illustration of the dissolute lives of the monks in their monasteries, which was in fact acknowledged by the Papal bulls. The great abbey of St. Alban's had become especially infamous for its profligacy. Almost every kind of vice is ascribed to its inhabitants, in the letter still extant of the Catholic Archbishop Morton to the Abbot, commanding reform. This was a fact calculated most powerfully to influence the minds of the people against the religion to which the monks belonged; for it is always to be remembered, that the theory of their life was to fulfil the desire for a very high state of human purity and holiness, which is common more or less to all men of thoughtful, enthusiastic natures, and which they alone professed to be able to fulfil. But when imposture was found very frequently accompanying profligacy, when it was seen that the ministers of a religion were often practising upon the credulity of its votaries, it became a still easier matter to connect the individual with the faith, and to look on both with the same disgust. When the Dominicans and the Franciscans were at enmity with each other, and the latter betrayed the scandalous impositions of the former, it was no wonder the people went further than the tale-bearers would have had them, and believed the worst of both parties. Here is but one of many cases on record: at Boxley, in Kent, there was a crucifix of great size, known as the Rood of Grace, and which was held in especial veneration; as well it might be, considering the extraordinary character of the image of Christ that was upon it. This image, when worshippers knelt before it and presented their offerings, would roll its eyes, bend its brows, move its lips, shake its head, hands, and feet, whilst it graciously inclined its body in acknowledgment; or whilst, if displeased, it exhibited its displeasure in an equally intelligible manner. But among the crowds of devotees who flocked to Boxley, there was one Nicholas Partridge, who, when he bent before the Rood of Grace, occupied himself much more curiously than devoutly in trying to penetrate into the mystery of the image. He seems to have been so interested by the result as to have determined to pursue his inquiries further, and watching his opportunity, lighted at last upon an inner world of springs and wheels that looked very much like the work of some exceedingly skilful but unprincipled human agents. What an exhibition was that to be exposed to the people of England, and their monarch Henry VIII.! who, to see and enjoy it with his own eyes, had the Rood brought to court, where it was made to nod, wink, bow, and perform all its other amusing evolutions, amid the laughter of the unthinking, and the sorrow and disgust of the truly pious, of each and all denominations! That exposure was not made until the latter part of the

1621.—Bristol.

1622.—Evesham.

1623.—Stratford Church Avenue.

1624.—Bengeworth Church, seen through the Arch of the Bell-Tower at Evesham

1625.—The Bell-Tower, Evesham.

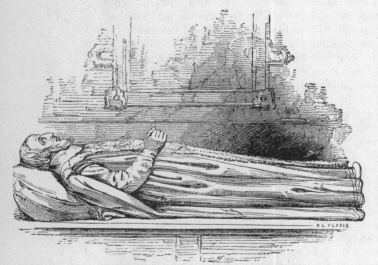

1626.—Monument of John Combe, in Stratford Church

1627.—Monument of Sir Thomas Lucy, the younger, in Stratford Church.

1628.—The Clopton Monument in Stratford Church.

1629.—East Window of St. Margaret's Church, Westminster.

1632.—General Costume in the time of Henry VII. Selected from L'Imagination de la Vraye Noblesse, Royal MS. 19 C. viii.; and Roman de la Rose, Harl. MS. 4225.

1631.

1630.

1634.—Suit of Fluted cap-a-pie Armour. Temp. Henry VII.

1633.—Suit of very Long-breasted Armour.

1636.—Suit of Demi-Lancer's Armour. Temp. Henry VII.

1653.—Suit of Black Armour of a Knight of St. George. Temp. Henry VII.

reign; but similar exposures of the same kind, though of a less exciting degree, marked also the earlier.

Particular incidents had in some cases the effect of appearing to reform the belief of particular and important portions of the commonwealth. Thus was it with the people of the city of London, who, however prepared previously to change, do not seem to have actually changed until the death of the citizen Hunne, in 1514; then they performed the operation almost *en masse*. Hunne had dared to sue a Romish parson for bringing him, the king's subject, before a foreign power,—the pope's legate, then sitting in the Spiritual Court. The church, in revenge, shut him up as a heretic in the Lollards' Tower of St. Paul's, where he was privily murdered, and subsequently the body burned in Smithfield. The excitement was terrible; and the metropolis was in effect reformed by that affair.

Of the individual cases of martyrdom that occurred during the reign of Henry VIII., two are especially interesting, those of James Baynham and Anne Askew. The execution of Person, Testwood, and Filmer before Windsor Castle (Fig. 1586) in 1544 need only be thus referred to in passing. James Baynham was brought before Sir Thomas More, the Chancellor, at his house in Chelsea, in 1531, on the ground of heresy; and was detained there in a kind of free custody for a time. But when More, according to the account of Fox, saw he could not prevail in perverting him to his sect, he "cast him in prison in his [More's] house, and whipped him at the tree in his garden, called the Tree of Troth, and after sent him to the Tower to be racked; and so he was, Sir Thomas More being present himself, till in a manner he had lamed him, because he would not accuse the gentleman of the Temple of his acquaintance, nor would not show where his books were; and because his wife denied them to be at his house, she was sent to the Fleet, and their goods confiscated." We trust Fox's well-known credulity has here a little misled him: that the illustrious Chancellor was not altogether free from the besetting sin of the age's intolerance is probable, but he could hardly have been the author of the excessive inhumanity here ascribed to him. Baynham, in the end, consented to abjure his heresies, and do penance. On one Sunday in February, 1532, the good people of London were regaled with the sight of a procession in which Baynham appeared conspicuous, making the best of his way to Paul's Cross. There the penitent stood on high, with a lighted taper in one hand and a bundle of fagots in the other (Fig. 1584), and listened to a sermon befitting the occasion. Baynham was then permitted to return to his home uninjured—he had escaped—and loud and long, no doubt, were the congratulations of his Catholic friends. One month only, however, elapsed before Baynham once more called his friends together, and spoke of the deep anguish he felt at his conduct. The following Sunday he was in St. Austin's Church, and there, to the astonishment of the congregation, he stood before them in his pew, "declaring openly with weeping tears, that he had denied God, and prayed all the people to forgive him, and to beware of his weakness, and not to do as he did." His fate was now sealed irrevocably. But it was desirable to obtain a second recantation, and these were the gentle methods employed. "A fortnight he lay," continues Fox, "in the bishop's coal-house in the stocks, with irons upon his legs; then he was carried to the Lord Chancellor's, and there chained to a post two nights; then he was carried to Fulham, where he was cruelly handled by the space of a sevennight; then to the Tower, where he lay a fortnight, scourged with whips to make him revoke his opinions: from thence he was carried to Barking, then to Chelsea, and there condemned, and so to Newgate to be burned."

Anne Kyme, or Askew, was a young married lady of good family. Her father was Sir William Askew, of Kelsey, in Lincolnshire; her husband, Kyme, a neighbour, with whom she had been forced into a marriage whilst very young, and probably from mercenary motives, as Kyme was wealthy. Anne was beautiful, high-spirited, and intellectual: and presents another example of the learned ladies of whom that age was so rife. Anne's learning led to serious results. She had studied the Scriptures profoundly, and, drawing her conclusions upon religious matters from them, became a convert to the Reformed faith. What her intellect taught her to believe, her tongue dared to avow, though the Bloody Statutes were then in full force, sending martyr after martyr to the rack and to the stake, and she could have had no reason to expect exemption from the fiery ordeal. Her first and her bitterest adversary was her own husband, who drove her—the mother of his two children—from his doors. Anne went to London to sue for a separation. There the sufferer for conscience' sake met with friends among the ladies resident at court. Queen Catherine Parr herself most probably

favoured Anne, and became, as we have before pointed out, almost if not quite a convert to the views which Anne fearlessly taught and disseminated, both verbally, and by distributing books and tracts of the Reformers. Catherine's stolen readings of some of these prohibited productions, and her strong tendency to believe in them, led to that doctrinal dispute with Henry, which was so near proving fatal to her. "A good hearing this," exclaimed the savage controversialist king, "when women become such clerks; and a thing much to my comfort, to come in my old age to be taught by my wife." But Catherine soon saw her error and her danger, and, when he uttered the words, "Kate, I know you, you are become a doctor," she made him believe that her opposition had been solely designed to beguile him of the sense of his bodily pain. "Ah!" cried he, "is it so, sweetheart? Then we are friends again." And so when the Chancellor Wriothesly, who had orders to arrest Catherine, came with forty men of the guard, Henry received him with various choice epithets—as knave! arrant knave! fool! beast!—and Wriothesly was glad to make the best of his way out of the royal presence. That was a scene Wriothesly was not likely soon to forget; the remembrance of it may have given him additional energy in that other and most revolting one, when he *applied his own hand to the rack* on which lay Anne Askew in torture, hoping to extort from her something that might enable the *fool* and *beast* yet to bring on his royal mistress, or some of those about her person, the doom she had so narrowly escaped. But Anne could not be brought by any anguish to say that which might compromise them. At her examination in the Tower, when she was asked how she had gained comfort and food in prison if she had no powerful friends—a question that, as well as the reply, opens a dreadful view of her prison-sufferings—she replied, "*My maid bemoaned my wretched condition to the apprentices in the streets*, and some of them sent me money, but I never knew their names. Her examiners were certain that many ladies had sent her money, and so it is clear they had, at the greatest possible risk. Pressed hard on this point, Anne said, "My maid once told me that a man in a blue coat had given her ten shillings for me, saying that they came from Lady Hertford; and at another time, that a man in a violet coat had given her eight shillings for me, saying that they came from Lady Denny; but whether these accounts are true, I have no certain knowledge: I can speak only as to the young woman's report." Some of the council were supposed to have rendered her secret support, but she denied this. She went to Smithfield as heroically as she had gone to the dungeon and the rack. No one was prosecuted on her testimony, but it is very possible that her influence and example assisted to bring others to the fiery furnace of martyrdom: indeed we find a gentleman of the royal household died with her—and for the same particular crime, disbelieving the real presence. They were chained to separate stakes, and at two others stood a Shropshire clergyman and a poor London tailor—also victims to the Bloody Statutes. A pulpit was reared opposite, in which preached the apostate Shaxton, formerly Bishop of Salisbury, who, after forfeiting his bishopric rather than sanction the passing of the Six Articles—after enduring long poverty and captivity—had given way at last under the fear of death, and now exhibited the pitiable spectacle of a weak, false denier of his conscience, who, to obtain a miserable livelihood from court, spent his learning and abilities in endeavouring to pervert others. His example was not a very inviting one, and Anne Askew had already refused to follow it, when he came to the Tower from the commission to persuade her to renew more effectually a submission with which, when she was first arrested, she had obtained a temporary freedom on bail. Anne had gathered courage from suffering since then, and sharply reproved him for his falsehood, telling him it had been better for him if he had never been born. His declamation and appeals were just as unsuccessful now. She and her heroic companions rejected the renewed offers of pardon on recantation made at the conclusion of his discourse, and thus with wonderful courage died (Fig. 1585).

It is of course to the reign of Mary that the "noble army of martyrs" chiefly belongs; and as we read of their heroism and their sufferings, it is difficult to say which of two opposite and contradictory feelings predominates—an earnest and reverential admiration that makes us proud to think we are men, since humanity can raise itself to such heights of self-sacrifice, or a sense of the deepest humiliation and abasement to be one of a class of beings that can inflict such revolting tortures upon its own kind, on account of speculative differences of belief. All the horrors we have hitherto had occasion to describe in connexion with the reign of Henry were revived, though, it must be owned, from more honest motives, in the reign of Mary, which happily was almost as brief as it was "bloody;" commencing in February, 1555, with Rogers at Smithfield, Bishop Hooper at Gloucester, and Dr. Taylor at Hadleigh, where a well-known stone (Fig. 1583) still marks the place, and ending in 1558, after the immolation at the altar of bigotry of nearly three hundred persons. Speed thus classifies them. Five bishops, twenty-one divines, eight gentlemen, eighty-four artificers, a hundred husbandmen, servants, and labourers, twenty-six wives, twenty widows, nine unmarried women, two boys, and *two infants*—of whom, he says, one was whipped to death by Bonner, and the other, coming first into life whilst the anguished mother was surrounded by the flames, was made (wilfully) to share its parent's doom. But these facts only bring before us a part, and hardly the most considerable part, of the sufferings of our martyrs. Many of them were subjected to the most horrible barbarities before execution; hosts of others endured the mere preliminary inflictions, who escaped the final agony by submission, or through other causes. Strype, with Coverdale for his authority, says some were "thrown into dungeons, noisome holes, dark, loathsome, and stinking corners; other some lying in fetters and chains, and loaded with so many irons that they could scarcely stir. Some tied in the stocks with their heels upwards; some having their legs in the stocks, and their necks chained to the wall with gorgets of iron. Some with hands and legs in the stocks at once. Sometimes both hands in and both legs out; sometimes the right hand with the left leg, or the left hand with the right leg, fastened in the stocks with manacles and fetters, having neither stool nor stone to sit on, to ease their woeful bodies. Some standing in Skevington's gyves, which were most painful engines of iron [compressing the limbs together], with their bodies doubled; some whipped and scourged, beaten with rods, and buffeted with fists; some having their hands burned with a candle to try their patience, or force them to relent; some hunger-pined, and some miserably famished and starved." The known treatment of Cuthbert Simpson furnishes an apt commentary upon this passage. We learn from one of his letters written to his friends to describe his treatment in the Tower, that he was first set in a rack of iron (the gyves before mentioned), in order to induce him to tell the names of the members of a body of religious reformers, of whom he was the deacon; then, on another day, that he had his two fore-fingers bound together, and an arrow drawn between them so rapidly that the blood burst out, and the arrow brake; and lastly, that he was twice put on the rack, the engine properly so called, and in which position he is represented in our engraving (Fig. 1511).

But the names that have most deeply entered into the hearts of Englishmen in connexion with the mighty business of the Reformation, are those of Ridley, Latimer, and Cranmer, the three most illustrious of Mary's victims. Ridley was a powerful preacher, and an able denouncer of what he deemed popish superstitions. He first attacked the images and holy water, then transubstantiation, then other doctrines; and he became the assistant of Cranmer in framing the celebrated forty-one Articles. The enlightened charitable institutions founded by Edward VI. owed, it is well known, their origin to a sermon of Ridley's. The bells that rung for Queen Mary's accession, rang Ridley's knell. He was at once flung into prison, and there remained until brought forth to debate on the doctrines that he denied, if that could be called a debate which took place amid a perfect Babel of uproar, hissing, and hooting. Ridley was a practised and courageous controversialist; but he was at last fain to exclaim, amid the overpowering clamour, "I have but one tongue, I cannot answer at once to you all." In the opinions of his friends, however, he acquitted himself with triumphant ability. Next day, good old Latimer—he was then upwards of eighty—was brought to be baited in the same arena—St. Mary's church, Oxford, so weak and faint after his imprisonment, that he could hardly stand. "Ha! good masters," said he, "I pray ye be good to an old man. You may be once as old as I am: you may come to this age and this debility." And how was his prayer responded to? He had presently to exclaim, that in his time and day he had spoken before great kings more than once, for two or three hours together, without interruption; "but now," says he, "if I may speak the truth by your leaves, I cannot be suffered to declare my mind before you, no, not by the space of a quarter of an hour without snatches, revilings, checks, rebukes, taunts, such as I have not felt the like in such an audience all my life long." How this famous controversy ended under such circumstances we need not say. When next Ridley, Latimer, and Cranmer were brought before the public eye in St. Mary's church, they were asked if they would now turn or not; but they bade them read on (their condemnation) in the name of God, for they were *not* so minded. Eighteen months after, in the ditch on the north side of Oxford, now a part of the town itself, and marked by the beautiful sculptured Martyrs' Memorial that

has recently been erected, the stakes and fagots were reared fo the execution of Ridley and Latimer. Ridley—firm and strong of mind and frame—came to the spot with a lively step, but turned back to meet his feebler brother-martyr, and, kissing him on the cheek, encouraged him: "Be of good heart, brother; for God will either assuage the fury of the flames, or strengthen us to bear it." There was the usual sermon, with the text, "Though I give my body to be burned, and *have not charity*, it profiteth me nothing." Many fearful and fantastic cases are on record of the misuse of Scripture texts; but we hardly know one more extraordinary than this. Men burning their fellow-men for their opinions, with a preliminary lecture on charity! Certainly, Dr. Smith's sermon was to very little profit, for the martyrs showed no disposition to change. Ridley, ever prompt, immediately prepared for the last ordeal—taking off his own clothes, and giving them away to the bystanders, with whatever trifling articles he had about him, such as a new groat, some nutmegs, bits of ginger, and a dial. Latimer had to be stripped by others. The two stood up by the fagots, and the chains were bound round them. During this operation a change seemed to pass over the venerable Latimer (Fig. 1589). The spirit had before been willing enough, though the flesh was weak: but now, with his shroud about him, he seemed no longer decrepit, withered, bowed—but erect, and "as comely a father as one might behold;" and gave utterance to that ever-memorable prophecy— "*Be of good comfort, Master Ridley, and play the man; we shall this day light such a candle, by God's grace, in England, as, I trust, shall never be put out.*" And did they not? Gunpowder was fastened to each. Latimer was quickly put out of pain with its assistance, but it was long before the fire penetrated through the mass of fuel to the gunpowder that hung about Ridley's neck: so that it did not explode until his extremities were consumed. He bore his tortures with unquailing courage. Burnet considers him to have been the ablest man—for piety, learning, and solid judgment— of all that adorned the Reformation.

Five months later, perished Cranmer, after a continual series of endeavours to shake his constancy, which, alas! were for a time but too successful. His enemies, with a truly Satanic malignity, induced him to wreck his conscience in the hope of saving his life, and then would not spare that life. How unutterable must have been the anguish of Cranmer's mind at the hour of the discovery of the position in which his weakness had placed him! And, once humiliated, his enemies prepared to bow him utterly to the earth— to steep him to the very lips in moral degradation. We may imagine what a susceptible and essentially upright spirit, as Cranmer's was, must have suffered when—on the very eve of appearing before a God of truth, and of leaving a last example to the world—he was reduced to utter that equivocation, if no worse, to Dr. Cole, Provost of Eton, whom Mary sent to him—that he remained firm in the *Catholic* faith, as he had recently professed it; and when he consented to transcribe and deliver a recantation that had been prepared for him to speak when he came to the place of death. But Cranmer could not die thus a traitor to himself. Relieved, in some degree, from the terrible presence of fear by the certainty of his doom, his higher nature began to assert itself. His enemies— little anticipating the scene that was to ensue—required his recantation to be read in public, before his execution; so they took him to St. Mary's church, and set him on a stage or platform, raised a moderate height from the ground, and placed in front of the pulpit in which Dr. Cole was to preach the last sermon Cranmer was to hear. The archbishop's dress was a bare and ragged gown, and an old square cap, "in which he was exposed to the contempt of all men." But there were heroic thoughts at work that were to glorify for ever that base garb, and to redeem, most grandly, all past errors and vacillations. After Dr. Cole's exhortation, Cranmer spake, and these were some of his words: "Now," said he, "I come to the great thing that troubleth my conscience more than any other thing that I ever said or did in my life; and that is, the setting abroad of writings contrary to the truth which I thought in my heart, and writ for fear of death, and to save my life, if it might be; and that is, all such bills which I have written or signed with mine own hand since my degradation, wherein I have written many things untrue. And forasmuch as my hand offended in writing contrary to my heart, therefore my hand shall be first punished. For if I may come to the fire, it shall be first burned. And as for the pope, I refuse him, as Christ's enemy, and Antichrist, with all his false doctrine." He was not allowed to conclude, but he had said enough —quite enough to excite the bitterest hate of his enemies, and to ensure for ever the reverence of all other men. He was pulled down (Fig. 1580) from the platform by the "friars and other papists" present, and with all haste brought to the ditch over against Balliol

1638.—Suit of Armour with Lamboys, presented by the Emperor Maximilian to Henry VIII.

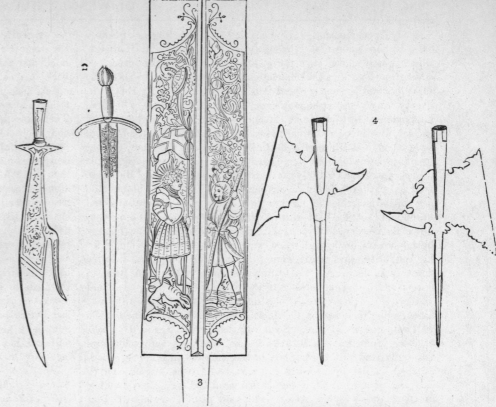

1636.—1, Glaive-blade of the time of Henry VII.; 2, Sword engraved by Albert Durer before 1528; 3, Military Costume engraved on the annexed Sword; 4, Halbert-heads of the time of Henry VII.

1641.—Suit of Puffed and Engraved Armour, 1510.

1637.—Tilting Helmet of the time of Henry VII.

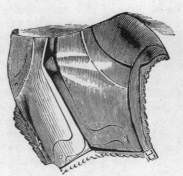

1642.—Breastplates of the time of Henry VIII.

1639.—General Costume in the time of Henry VIII. (Selected from Holbein's 'Dance of Death.')

1640.—Military Costume in the time of Henry VIII. (Selected from Cotton MS. Augustus iii.)

1613.—General Costume of the time of Edward VI.
(Selected from the Ancient Picture of his Coronation Procession from the Tower to Westminster.)

1644.—Costume.—French, 1574 (Montfaucon). German, 1577 (Weigel). Burgundian, 1577 (Weigel).

1645.—Suit of Ribbed and Engraved Armour. (From Meyrick and Skelton's Ancient Arms and Armour.)

1646.—Ladies' Head-Dresses of the Sixteenth Century. . From Mr. Ady Repton's Tapestry.

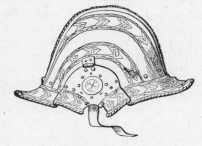

1647.—Coursing-Hat.

1648.—Costume.—Venetian, 1590 (Titian). Spanish, 1577 (Weigel). French, 1581 (Boissard).

1649.—Men's Caps, Hats, and Bonnets of the Sixteenth Century. (From Mr. Ady Repton's Tapestry.)

College, where Ridley and Latimer had before suffered. Here they stripped him to the shirt, took off his shoes, bound him to the stake, and lighted the fire. Cranmer stood perfectly self-possessed—resolved: no weak murmur escaped him. When he saw the eager flames rising, he neither shrunk from the pain nor the death they were to inflict, but thrusting his right hand into them, was heard repeatedly exclaiming, "This unworthy hand! This unworthy hand!" and continued to the last to hold it out. "When the fire raged more fiercely," says Godwin, "his body abided as immoveable as the stake whereto he was fastened, and lifting up his eyes toward heaven, he exclaimed, Lord Jesus, receive my spirit!" And so he died; a more truly brave man than others, who, not having the same quick and subtle imagination to disturb them in their purposes, obtained the reputation which really belonged to those who, like Cranmer, seeing and feeling in all their intensity the horrors that had to be encountered, did so at the last encounter and conquer them.

Turning from the effects of the religious changes of the sixteenth century upon the national mind, and on the individual persons who most actively promoted them, whether as victims or persecutors, we are reminded, by the groups of cathedrals and other ancient churches (in pages 61 and 64), of the effect of those changes upon the buildings devoted to God, upon the services performed in them, and, above all, upon their officiating priests.

The effect of these changes on our ecclesiastical structures can only be described in one word—as most lamentable. The noblest series of edifices, as a whole, that the world possesses, were, prior to the Reformation, enhanced by a no less noble series of adornments of the highest character, from the hands of painters and sculptors, and artistical decorators, whose very existence in such number, and of such excellence, in this country, centuries ago, seems but as the dream of some enthusiastic antiquary; so complete has been the gulf that the Reformation, and other and later influences, have put between our England and their England—between us and them. It is impossible to overrate the injury done to art by our reforming forefathers: we can only hope that the good done to religion was an ample counterbalance. But, it was said, all these artistical decorations are *superstitious*: that was the idea that worked so much destruction among our sculptured angels, holy saints, and courageous martyrs; it was that which pulled down our exquisitely-carved rood-lofts and our richly-painted windows (St. Margaret's Westminster, Fig. 1629, one of the latest of the class, may show there was some excuse for the long-prevailing notion of the lost art); it was that which tore up our decorated brasses, that had made the very floors radiant with the grace and fancy of the artist, and the sweet and holy piety expressed in the life-breathing effigy of the departed spirit, as it still clasped the hands in prayer, still looked up towards the sky, year after year, and century after century, as though absorbed into so high a state of spiritual being, that it cared not to break the spell that bound it. Perhaps no class of works (with the exception of the pictures, which, being easily moveable, were entirely swept away) suffered more than the brasses. The windows were elevated, and so were a large proportion of the sculptures, and modes and seasons were therefore requisite for their extensive injury; but every zealot who entered the sacred edifice could set to work with a chisel and a hammer to strip away a beautiful brass from the floor, or mutilate it, when it was not convenient to finish the business: consequently the art of monumental brasses has also become, until of late years, a "lost," one—the relics having been too few, too unimportant, or too much hidden from the general eye, to have kept the art in recollection for any practical purposes. Both these lost arts, however, we hope yet to see entirely found again: assuredly we have, within the last few years, made a good beginning. We may add that the value of our ancient brass memorials, as examples of costume, is now not only generally acknowledged, but turned to excellent account. Our two engravings (Figs. 1630, 1631) furnish interesting data of this kind.

The idea of the idolatrous nature of the images, relics, and shrines of the churches of the middle ages, had fast possession of great numbers of the English people, by the time the minister Cromwell, in 1537, commenced his war against them. There were plenty of willing hands to light the consuming fires for the famous shrines then brought to London—comprising, among others, those of our Lady of Walsingham, Ipswich, and Islington—that had been enriched with the offerings of many generations of worshippers. The most sumptuous of the works destroyed at this crisis was Thomas-à-Becket's shrine at Canterbury. And, once begun, the proceedings were vigorously carried on. In the following year, Cromwell thus issued his commands to the clergy:—"Such feigned images as ye

know in any of your cures to be so abused with pilgrimages, or offerings of anything made thereunto, ye shall, for avoiding of that most detestable offence of idolatry, forthwith take down, and without delay; and shall suffer from henceforth no candles, tapers, or images of wax to be set afore any image or picture, but only the light that commonly goeth across the church by the rood-loft, the light before the sacrament of the altar, and the light above the sepulchre, which, for the adorning of the church and divine service, ye shall suffer to remain."

There was a pause in the latter years of Henry VIII.'s life (for he was then a Catholic, and a more intolerant one than any of his predecessors); and on the accession of his Protestant heir, Edward, Cranmer and the Protector appeared dubious about reviving it. The constantly-increasing portion of the people who had embraced Protestantism waited for some time patient, though in a state of great suspense; but growing weary of the delay, they again renewed their labours. We give one or two examples, curiously illustrative of the very equivocal posture of affairs at the time.

The curate and churchwardens of St. Martin's, in Ironmonger Lane, London, took down the crucifix, and the images and pictures of the saints, and painted the walls instead with texts of Scripture. They were cited before the council on the complaint of Bonner; and having asked pardon, the council, "in respect of their submission, and of some other reasons which did mitigate their offence," did not imprison them, but ordered them to provide a crucifix, or at least some painting of it till one were ready, and to beware of such rashness for the future."

On May-day following, the people of Portsmouth pulled down the images and crucifixes from the walls of various churches in that town. In one of the latter, the image (or statue) of St John the Evangelist, that stood in a chancel by the high altar, was taken away, and a table of alabaster broken. An eye was also bored out, and the side pierced, of an image of Christ crucified.

Gardiner complained loudly, but Ridley led a still louder outcry on the side of the popular feeling, by a Lent sermon against images and holy water, which rang from one end of the kingdom to the other. The excitement was at its height, when an order (in Febuary, 1548) for the removal of *all* images restored tranquillity among the Protestants. And as Edward, or Edward's ministers, like Henry VIII., had no objection to make public reforms aid their private interests, the seizure was ordered, for the king's use, of all the plate, jewels, vestments, and general furniture of the sacred edifices, that could be spared—which meant, in effect, the barbarous dismantling of them to relieve temporary difficulties of the treasury, or enrich the royal wardrobe. "Among other things that came into the king's possession, by virtue of this commission, was good store of linen, good and bad, as surplices, altar-cloths, towels, napkins," &c. (Strype.) The amount of treasure gained by these unscrupulous proceedings was almost incredible. The great cathedrals of course furnished the richest booty. Bishop Ridley petitioned that the "haberdashery" of the churches, found in his diocese of London, might be given up to him for the benefit of the Christ Church Hospital, and this was conceded; but the churches were everywhere left in a state almost of primitive plainness.

The religious services in the English churches were not changed suddenly, but by slow and intermitting movements. The first—of momentous character—was the introduction of the Scriptures in the common language. The *first* printed English translation of any part of the Scriptures was Tyndal's New Testament, published in an octavo volume, at Antwerp, in 1526, and circulated secretly but largely throughout England—to the great discomfort of Wolsey and the Roman Catholic dignitaries generally. Burnet tells a pleasant story respecting this book:—"Tunstall, then Bishop of London, being a man of invincible moderation, would do nobody hurt, yet endeavoured as he could to get their books into his hands; so, being at Antwerp in the year 1529, as he returned from his embassy at the treaty of Cambray, he sent for one Packington, an English merchant there, and desired him to see how many New Testaments, of Tyndal's translation, he might have for money Packington, who was a secret favourer of Tyndal, told him what the bishop proposed. Tyndal was very glad of it; for, being convinced of some faults in his work, he was designing a new and more correct edition; but he was poor, and the former impression not being sold off, he could not go about it: so he gave Packington all the copies that lay in his hands, for which the bishop paid the price, and brought them over and burnt them publicly in Cheapside. This had such an hateful appearance in it, being generally called a burning of the word of God, that people from thence concluded there must be a visible contrariety between that book and the doctrines of those who so handled it, by which both their prejudice against the clergy and their desire of reading the New Testament was increased. So that, next year, when the second edition was finished, many more were brought over; and Constantine (one of Tyndal's associates) being taken in England, the Lord Chancellor, in a private examination, promised him that no hurt should be done him if he would reveal who encouraged and supported them at Antwerp; which he accepted of, and told that the greatest encouragement they had was from the Bishop of London, who had bought up half the impression. This made all that heard it laugh heartily, though judicious persons discerned the great temper of that learned bishop in it."

The first printed translation of the entire Bible in English was that of Miles Coverdale, also issued from a continental press, in 1535. An interesting incident marks the reception of this book at court. Various opinions having been expressed about the work, Henry VIII., says Burnet, "ordered divers bishops to peruse it. After they had had it long in their hands, he asked their judgment of it: they said there were many faults in it. But he asked, upon that, if there were any heresies in it? they said they found none. Then, said the king, in God's name, let it go abroad among my people." Coverdale himself related this anecdote to the audience at St. Paul's Cross. Pending the preparation of the new translation (Cranmer's) that had been ordered, Cromwell directed that Coverdale's should be obtained for every parish, and chained to a pillar or desk of the church for all to read at their pleasure (Fig. 1582).

An innovation of the same period was the Book of Homilies, designed to be read to the people by such as were not licensed to preach; consisting mostly of plain and practical paraphrases of Scripture, with serious exhortations and short explanations of difficult passages, "that show the compiler of them was a man both of good judgment and learning" (Burnet). A more important Book of Homilies (Cranmer's, or prepared under his direction in 1547) was provided for such priests as could not preach, who were ordered by Edward VI., in a preface, to read them every Sunday. This is the Book of Homilies mentioned in our Prayer-Book—with a third, of 1562—as containing "a godly and wholesome doctrine." Some of our forefathers had a different notion of it. "It is strange," says Strype, "to consider how anything, be it never so beneficial and innocent, oftentimes gives offence. For a great many, both of the laity as well as the clergy, could not digest these homilies; and therefore, sometimes, when they were read in the church, if the parishioners liked them not, there would be such talking and babbling in the church that nothing could be heard." The bad reading of the priest was often one cause of this. "He would so hawk it, and chop it," says Latimer, "that it were as good for them [the parishioners] to be without it, for any word that could be understood." The reader, indeed, often understood it as little as the listeners; sometimes, like them, did not want to understand it.

From the period of these Homilies we may date the existing practice among clergymen of the Establishment of reading their sermons. Before, pulpit discourses had been extemporaneous when delivered at all. The permission of the cup to the laity in the Sacrament of the Lord's Supper—the surrender of the doctrine of the necessity of auricular confession to a priest, and the substitution, by those who pleased, of confession to God—the addition to high mass, matins, and to even-song, of readings in English from the New Testament—were additional changes with which the reign of Edward was ushered in. But the mass itself was soon doomed to give way, and the mass-book to be superseded by the book of Common Prayer, as at present received and celebrated. Probably few of our readers are aware that this was compiled out of the different forms of the Mass-Book used in different parts of the kingdom—as that of York, used in the north; that of the Church of Sarum, used in the south; and those of Lincoln, Hereford, and Bangor, used in their respective dioceses. The chief novelties were the rendering of the whole into English, and the introduction of the Litany. At first the Litany contained a petition for deliverance from the Bishop of Rome, but this was struck out in the reign of Elizabeth. The book was printed, and ordered to be used by all ministers in the celebration of divine service.

The services of the churches were thus completely Protestantised, when Mary ascended the sovereign seat of the empire, and threw all back into its old state, as in the last year of the reign of Henry VIII.

But again a Protestant sovereign ruled England, and the overjoyed nation beheld the reformed worship re-established, and the word of God disseminated among all ranks in an intelligible form. Cranmer's great Bible was twice reprinted—namely, in 1562 and

1566—but, being found incorrect, the sacred text underwent a careful revision, under the superintendence of Archbishop Parker, who divided it in portions, and distributed them amongst many able divines—Grindal, Bentham, Sandys, Horn, Cox, Goodman, and others. The whole, when completed and bound together, formed a splendid folio volume, interspersed with maps and cuts, and was called Parker's, or the Bishops' Bible. This was the authorised translation until the reign of James I., when our present version was produced. But the Bishops' Bible was not altogether acceptable to certain classes of the Protestant community, who preferred, instead, a *new* translation by Miles Coverdale, and other learned men then residing on the Continent. Among these classes were the Puritans, the disciples of Nonconformity; which, says Fuller, "in the days of King Edward was conceived; which afterwards, in the reign of Queen Mary (but beyond sea at Frankfort), was born; which in the reign of Elizabeth was nursed and reared; which, under King James, grew up a young youth, or tall stripling; but towards the end of King Charles's reign, shot up to the full strength and stature of a man, able not only to cope with, but conquer the hierarchy, its adversary:" and, the writer might have added, to pull down dynasties; and, in the end, while the form of government reverted to the old position, to change permanently its entire spirit. All classes of men are accustomed to speak of the glorious Revolution of 1688, but assuredly that revolution was only a phase of the one that had preceded it—happily, the final phase; then the great movement that had caused the expenditure of so much blood settled down into quiet: renouncing its extremer views, but obtaining ample security for the adoption of those which it deemed most necessary to the grand object, good government. And all this mighty series of events, the fame of which has spread to the remotest corner of the earth, are but so many developments of the one apparently slight influence that we before alluded to—the change wrought by the religious policy of our government during the sixteenth century upon the officiating priests of the churches. At first the effect must have been more ludicrous than tragical or seemly; seeing, as men did, nearly the whole body of clergy shifting now in a body towards Catholicism, on one side, when Henry VIII. commanded; then back again at the behests of Edward's ministers towards Protestantism, on the other; then again to extreme Catholicism when Mary ascended the throne, and yet once more reverting to the new faith at the bidding of Elizabeth. There were exceptions, of course. The Catholic bishops refused the oath of supremacy at the commencement of the last-named reign, and others were consequently appointed to their sees; but we find it especially noted that the great body of the parochial clergy performed, as usual, the now familiar movement, and changed most peaceably. But the very magnitude and comprehensiveness of this humiliation was calculated to draw the attention of earnest minds, and so prepare the way for the removal of the scandal.

Whilst the entire framework of the ancient religion had been subjected, bit by bit, to the most searching examination, and men had drawn from the labour a conviction that manifold abuses existed in it, and that some sweeping processes of purification were necessary, it was not to be supposed they would agree as to the exact amount of change required. Some desired to stop at this point, and some at that, a little further on; but none had found the mode by which alone these differences can be reconciled—equal intellectual freedom for all to move just as they pleased. The commencement was little more than a question of vestments, but gradually embraced the whole subject of the church liturgy, ceremonies, and discipline. The Puritans, as the name expresses, were those who desired an especially *pure* system of worship—one far advanced beyond the views of those in authority, reformers though they were. An honourable name is his who was the first (or among the first) to divide the body of religionists amongst themselves, that had so recently divided from the disciples of the older worship; that name is Hooper's. After long wandering in exile, and chiefly in Switzerland, then the stronghold of the more extreme religious reformers, he returned, with many others, during the reign of Edward. Being nominated to the bishopric of Gloucester, he refused the oath of supremacy in the terms in which it was couched, and would not assume the prescribed habit for consecration. He listened, unconvinced, to the persuasions of his Puritan friends, Bucer and Peter Martyr, as well as Cranmer and Ridley, and was accordingly sent to the Fleet, for contumacy, in 1551, and there lay until he consented to a compromise. He was to wear the vestments on high occasions, but to be excused on common ones. This was looked on by many as a paltering with the truth, and "lost him much of his popularity" (Burnet). It was his fate afterwards, however (as we have already seen), to assert his principles, not only in defiance

1650.—Lord Willoughby. (In this cut is shown the half-armour of a general officer, the costume and accoutrements of a pikeman, an archer, and a musketeer, of the Elizabethan period.)

1651.—Sir Horace Vere.

1652.—"And an old porter to relieve the poor at his gate."

1653.—"With an old hall hung about with pikes, swords and bows.
* * * * * *
With a good old fashion, when Christmas was come,
To call in all his old neighbours with bagpipe and drum."

84

1656.—" With a new-fangled lady, that is dainty, nice, and spare,
Who never knew what belonged to good housekeeping and care."

1653.—" And never knew what belonged to coachmen, footmen, or pages.
* * *
Who buys gaudy-coloured fans to play with wanton air,
And seven or eight different dressings of other women's hair."

1655.—" With an old falconer, huntsman, and a kennel of hounds,
That never hawked or hunted but in his own grounds.
* * *
And a new smooth shovel-board whereon no victuals ne'er stood."

658.—" A new French Cook, to devise fine kickshaws and toys."

1654.—" I like a flourishing young gallant, newly come to his land,
Who keeps a brace of painted madams at his command."

1657.—"With an old buttery hatch worn quite off the hooks,
And an old kitchen that maintained half a dozen old cooks."

of the terror of imprisonment, but of the flames of martyrdom, in which he perished heroically in 1555.

But it was not until the reign of Elizabeth that, as Fuller observes, Puritanism was "nursed and reared," and then by the curious process of endeavouring to destroy it. The great influx of exiles from Switzerland—nearly the whole of whom were in effect Puritans—gave a mighty impulse to the growing distaste for all that had been preserved by the Reformers of the creed that had been reformed. Objections were urged against the spiritual claims of bishops—their sole right of ordination and discipline—their temporal dignities—the titles and offices of the various cathedral officials—the jurisdiction of the spiritual courts—the promiscuous admittance to the communion-table—to many things in the Liturgy —to passages in the marriage and burial offices—to the prohibition of the clergyman from using his own prayers in public service— to godfathers and godmothers—to confirmation—to apocryphal books read in the church—to Lent and holidays—to cathedral worship, chantings, and organs—to pluralities and non-residency— to church patronage in the hands of the crown, bishops, and lay patrons, instead of election by the people: and, in fact, there appears to be no end to the list of the things objected to in the Establishment. The Puritans might have almost said in a word, "We object to everything." But the Establishment could not be more offensive to them than were their views as to what it should be to Elizabeth, who loved pomp and magnificence, for their own sakes, and who at first desired to keep as much of both as possible in the church for the sake of her Catholic subjects; desiring then to lessen rather than increase the difference between them and their Protestant countrymen. It would have been well for the country, and for her reputation and fame, had she never lost this desire. It was determined to put down Puritanism with a strong hand. A committee of divines was constituted to examine and alter, if necessary, the Liturgy of Edward: Archbishop Parker was at their head—"a parker, indeed, careful to keep the fences, and shut the gate of discipline, against all such night-stealers as would invade the same" (Fuller). Some alterations were made:—for the worse, in the opinion of the Puritans, as showing a still more decided leaning to popery. And then the famous Act of Uniformity was passed (in 1558), which, while it empowered the Queen and the commissioners to ordain further ceremonies and rites, forbade, under severe penalties, the performance of divine worship in any other manner than that prescribed by the Prayer-Book. The immediate effect of this Act was startling. In all parts of the kingdom the clergymen, refusing to obey, quitted their churches. And, says the historian Neal, "It was impossible, with all the assistance they could get from both universities, to fill up the parochial vacancies with men of learning and character. Many churches were disfurnished for a considerable time; and not a few mechanics, altogether . . . .unlearned. . . .were preferred to dignities and livings; who, being disregarded by the people, brought great discredit on the Reformation; while others, of the first rank for learning, piety, and usefulness in their functions, were laid by in silence. There was little or no preaching all over the country." The Bishop of Bangor had but two preachers in his diocese. In some country towns and villages there was not so much as a homily read for many months together. Baptisms and burials were with difficulty provided for.

Many of those who still continued to officiate, did so, it is said on the ground that they feared the nation, thus left without spiritual guidance, might relapse into popery; but it appears also that for some years the new Act was not violently enforced. Where men stayed in their churches, and enjoyed the sympathy of their congregations, they were allowed for a time to continue their own mode of worship, as though their violation of the Act were unknown; but that was only a temporary toleration, no doubt for political purposes. So, in 1564, the Queen's attention was called to the matter, and a paper presented to her showing how the Puritans deviated from her Act; and a very striking picture has been preserved in that paper of the religious customs of the Puritans in their churches, which modes, for variety, might be named Legion. "Some perform divine service and prayers in the chancel, others in the body of the church; some in a seat made in the church, some in a pulpit, with their faces to the people; some keep precisely to the order of the book, some intermix Psalms in metre; some say with a surplice, and others without one. The table stands in the body of the church in some places; in others it stands in the chancel; in some places the table stands altar-wise, distant from the wall a yard; in others in the middle of the chancel, north and south; in some places the table is joined, in others it stands upon tressels; in some the table has a carpet, in others none. Some administer

the communion with surplice and cap, some with surplice alone, others with none; some with chalice, others with a communion cup, others with a common cup; some with unleavened bread, and some with leavened. Some receive kneeling, others standing, others sitting; some baptize in a font, some in a basin; some sign with the sign of the cross, others sign not; some minister in surplice, others without; some with a square cap, some with a round cap, some with a button cap, some with a hat; some in scholars' clothes, some in others." It was high time for the ministers of persecution to be let loose, thought Elizabeth; and with her characteristic energy did she cause the poor Nonconformist or Puritan preachers to be persecuted accordingly. All were ejected who would not conform rigidly to the established rites, habits, and ceremonies, as laid down in the Rubric. Great numbers of ministers, any deservedly in high esteem, were thus left destitute. "They travelled up and down the countries, from church to church, preaching where they could get leave, as if they were apostles; and so they were with regard to their poverty, for silver and gold they had none." (Bishop Jewel.) When the Nonconformists could not obtain the churches to preach in, or when the weather was too cold or the persecution too hot for them to hold forth in the streets, fields, and woods, they sought the privacy of the houses and other buildings of their disciples, and these were our earlier "conventicles:"—the parents of that numerous progeny which, under the name of chapels or meeting-houses, now extend over the entire country, and in which the worshippers of God may meet without dreading, as of old, that before the service closes, their beloved pastor, perhaps even themselves, may be borne away to prison, there haply to perish from neglect or ill treatment: such was the treatment their forefathers experienced from Elizabeth. Nor was the communication stopped in one direction allowed to be opened in another. There was no "free press" for the persecuted religionists. If they dared to vindicate their opinions that way, a Star Chamber matter was made of it. The printer and publisher forfeited all the copies, were imprisoned three months, and could never print afterwards. The sellers, binders, and stitchers were also fined 20s. for every book; and no places or persons were safe from search, on suspicion of secreting books or pamphlets against the Queen's ordinances.

The trodden-down Puritans now began to turn upon the foot that crushed them. Instead of retracing their steps back to the churches they had forsaken, "it was," says Neal, "debated among them whether they should use as much of the Common Prayer and service of the Church as was not offensive, or resolve at once, since they were cut off from the Church of England, to set up the purest and best form of worship, most consonant to the Holy Scriptures, and to the practice of the foreign reformers. The latter of these was concluded upon: and accordingly they [in 1566] laid aside the English Liturgy, and made use of the Geneva Service-book." So far, however, was the Church from discovering the madness of the course that was thus estranging the hearts of a large portion of the community, and raising up a power that was ultimately to shatter it to pieces, its leaders were impatient because more rigorous measures were not taken, and caused, from time to time, the persecution that was dying away to be freshly renewed; and they had their excuse—there were always hosts of victims found. The Act, passed in 1571, for enforcing the Articles, threw a hundred clergymen out of their livings. Still Puritanism advanced with giant strides, thriving wonderfully upon the unpromising food provided for it. In 1583 Dr. Whitgift became archbishop, and thought he would have a wrestle with this portentous monster. So within a few weeks after his installation, many hundreds more of the clergy were ejected, and left without a home wherein to lay their heads, because they would not subscribe to a new set of articles issued by him. Then going to the Queen and the minister, he obtained a new commission, with powers of inquisition and punishment more extensive than had ever before been granted. Whitgift himself drew up the articles of examination for the clergy who might be brought before the commission, and submitted them to Cecil, among others, for approval. His (the minister's) reply speaks volumes:—"I have read over your twenty-four articles,. . . . and I find them so curiously penned, that I think the Inquisition of Spain used not so many questions to comprehend and to trap their priests." But the archbishop had put his hand to the work, and was determined to go resolutely on with it. So in 1592, the Act, rightly stigmatised as "atrocious," was passed, which subjected every one to imprisonment who did not, at least once in every month, go to the legal church; and, after imprisonment, if they did not conform, to banishment, from which if they returned they were to be put to *death*.

It has been frequently observed that Elizabeth executed no one on account of religious opinions, but the observation is a mere juggle. To call heresy treason, or any other equally bad name, and then to punish the "treason" with a traitor's fate, wonderfully resembles religious martyrdom at all events; and such martyrdom was undoubtedly inflicted. But lest there should be any possible chance of doubting her readiness to inflict the last extremities of executive power on sufferers for conscience' sake, Elizabeth actually burnt two German Anabaptists who were guilty of the unspeakable crime of coming to England to tell Englishmen they believed Christ took not flesh from the body of the Virgin, that infants should be re-baptized, that no Christian man should be a magistrate, and that it is not lawful to take oaths. Connected with this affair we may here say a few words on a very eminent Puritan—John Fox, the martyrologist—"the first man I have seen depicted with a broad-brimmed hat and band," says the Rev. Mr. Tyson, in Nichols' 'Literary Anecdotes.' Fox was one who refused to subscribe to the articles of religion as finally settled, and this prevented him from rising in the Church above the prebend in Canterbury Cathedral, given him by Cecil. He had been an early sufferer for his opinions in exile in Germany, and returned, with the rest of the English exiles, on Elizabeth's accession. Elizabeth always respected him, and used, it is said, to style him "father." The veracity and honesty of his statements in his celebrated narrative of the sufferings of Protestants is unimpeached; though they may not be free from slight mistakes. No man of his time was held in higher regard for moral excellence. From recording the cruelties of the Catholics, Fox had learned in some degree the lesson of toleration, then almost unknown, and he laboured to instil it into others, including his sovereign. When Elizabeth was about to burn these two Anabaptists for errors of doctrine, as by law established, he wrote to her a Latin letter, beseeching for their lives. In this he ventures to say, "To roast alive the bodies of poor wretches that offend rather through blindness of judgment than perverseness of will, in fire and flames raging with pitch and brimstone, is a hard-hearted thing, and more agreeable to the practice of the Romanists than to the custom of the gospellers." To save their lives at any price, he suggests all the variety of punishments that just fall short of it, and concludes, "This one thing I most earnestly beg, that the piles and flames in Smithfield, so long ago extinguished by your happy government, may not now be again revived.' Elizabeth, however, had said, "Thus it shall be," and thus it was. The poor Anabaptists died—the only sacrifices of the kind that stained her reign, though many others were hanged for no greater crimes.

As we shall have occasion to enter still more largely into the progress of Puritanism in the next period, we shall conclude our present notice of it by an evidence of the extent to which its principles had spread during the reign of Elizabeth, as evidenced by its parliamentary power. When the House of Commons met in November, 1584, immediately after these proceedings of the archbishop had thrown the country into a greater ferment than ever, they began to pass bills for restraining the power of the Church. One had actually passed, when the Queen sent down her lord treasurer to tell them how highly she was offended by their daring to encroach on her supremacy, and attempting what she had already forbidden; and the Speaker was commanded to see that no bills of ecclesiastical reformation were exhibited, or if exhibited, not to read them; and the House succumbed. How the first Charles would have liked to have been able to settle matters in this quiet off-hand way!

———

Among the engravings not yet noticed of the chapter upon which we are at present engaged, there are several illustrative of our public schools and colleges (pages 61, 64, 65, 68, 69), which will be most conveniently referred to in connection with many others of a similar character belonging to the next period, where the subject of education will be treated of as a whole, in a chapter expressly devoted to it; and which chapter will then take the place of the usual ecclesiastical chapter. It can be hardly necessary to mention that we have now reached a point when Gothic architecture underwent something like a total eclipse. The religious history of the time, at which we have glanced in previous pages, is sufficient to account fully for this phenomenon. The style had been, from its very beginning, essentially a thing of the older form of Christian faith—had grown with its growth, and strengthened with its strength—and therefore naturally declined when it declined, precisely because it was so intimately connected with it. Men stopped not to consider what were its inherent and abstract qualities, in order to see whether they were equally applicable to a reformed as to an unre-formed system of worship—it was sufficient that in them they had,

according to their views, seen "idols" worshipped—had heard mass performed, and witnessed all the other rites and ceremonies which now became so loathsome to their eyes. Happily the Gothic *had* abstract qualities in it, too valuable and robust, to be utterly ruined by any accidental circumstances. In the nineteenth century we see it on all sides reviving, and reproaching us, as it were, in the mute eloquence of its beautiful forms, for the neglect with which we have so long treated it.

In thus dismissing the ancient Gothic structures of Old England, we may observe that there will be found among our engravings, in addition to the long and magnificent series of buildings previously represented, engravings of many others; some chosen on account of their intrinsic importance, others as being the latest of the kind that were erected. Few of these require special notice. The ruins of Sempringham Priory, Lincolnshire (Fig. 1591), are chiefly interesting as reminding us that the village was the birth-place of the Englishman who founded a monastic order—Sir Gilbert de Sempringham—and who *was* a prophet in his own country, for here at his native place was the first Gilbertine house established. The Holy Cross or Abbey Church of Shrewsbury (Fig. 1592, here, in error, called Gloucestershire) forms the chief remains of a Benedictine house whose abbot sat in parliament, and wore those magical emblems of power, the sandals, mitre, and gloves. The house was especially famous for its connexion with the Welsh female martyr and saint, St. Winifrede, whose relics were brought to the abbey in the reign of Stephen, and became one of the chief causes of its subsequent wealth and prosperity. Alas! the proud abbots little dreamt that the day would come when their stately buildings should be sold to a "tailor of the town," and be pulled down by him for the sake of the value of the materials.

The present aspect of the interior of Holy Cross impresses one with the idea of a majestic simplicity. Among the interesting tokens of past splendour that have been preserved is a richly decorated stone pulpit. There is a curious passage in the history of the church, and one which is very apposite to the subject that has recently engaged our attention—namely, the stripping of the ecclesiastical edifices of all their adornments by the reformers. In the last century the impulse given in the two preceding centuries seems to have been fairly worn out at Shrewsbury, among the parishioners at least, though not in the mind of their spiritual guide. There was, prior to 1728, a picture of the Crucifixion in the church. The vicar of the day, desiring a revival, we presume, of the old feelings, and not considering that every one of the exciting motives of the early reformers had ceased to exist, began a new crusade against art by removing the picture. The parishioners remonstrated; and lampoons on both sides were circulated. The two here following present probably a family likeness to many of the lighter documents that were scattered about during the period of the growth of Puritanism. Thus ran the attacks upon the vicar, hinting apparently at a worse motive than mistaken zeal:—

> The parson's the man,
> Let him say what he can,
> Will, for gain, leave his God in the lurch;
> Could Iscariot do more,
> Had it been in his power,
> Than to turn his Lord out of the church?

To this it was replied—

> The Lord I adore
> Is mighty in power,
> The One only living and true;
> But that lord of yours,
> Which was turned out of doors,
> Had just as much knowledge as you.

> But since you bemoan
> This god of your own,
> Cheer up, my disconsolate brother:
> Though it seems very odd,
> Yet if this be your god,
> Mr. Burley * can make you another.

The South-Well, whose name is associated with one of the most interesting and venerable of our minster-churches (Fig. 1591), is a spring that rises about half a mile southward of the town of Southwell in Nottinghamshire, and is known as the "Lord's Well;" forming another of those very numerous holy wells of the middle ages, which enjoyed such peculiar reverence that pilgrimages were made to them, and oratories often built over or near the spot, to receive the prayers and the offerings made by their worshippers. Southwell Minster would no doubt draw many of the faithful to its

* A painter of Shrewsbury.

1660.—Chichester Market Cross.

1661.—Southwark in the Sixteenth Century.

1662.—Remains of the Gate-House of Wolsey's College, Ipswich.

1663.—Market-Cross at Malmesbury.

1664.—Coventry Cross.

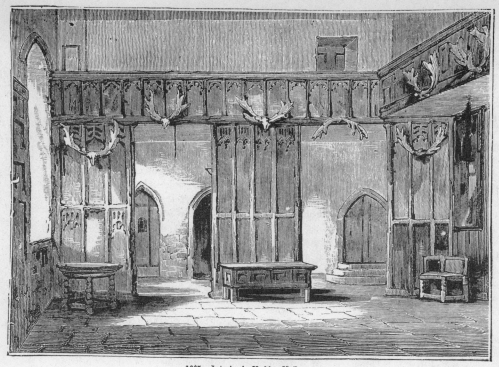

1665.—Interior in Haddon Hall.

1667.—Wollaton, Northamptonshire.

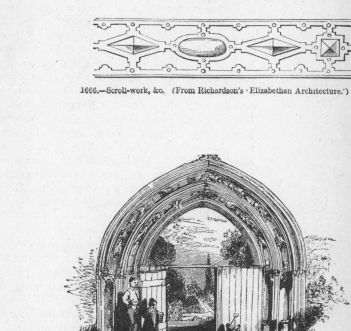

1666.—Scroll-work, &c. (From Richardson's 'Elizabethan Architecture.')

1668.—Ancient Gateway, Evesham.

1669.—House formerly standing at the corner of Chancery Lane, in Fleet Street. Temp. Edward VI. (From Smith's 'Topography of London.')

1670.—Hardwick Hall, Derbyshire.

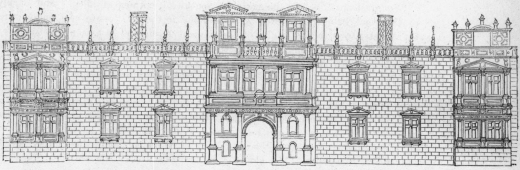

1671.—Somerset House. (From the Original Collection of Drawings, by John Thorpe, in the Library of Sir John Soane's Museum.)

time-honoured altars by the fame not only of this, but also of the other wells within its precincts : these were, the Holy Well, on the right of the cloister—the Lady's Well, filled up in consequence of a clergyman being drowned in it one dark night—and St. Catherine's Well, still famed for rheumatic cures. The situation of Southwell is of a romantic woodland character. The town and Minster are surrounded with trees, and beautiful wood-crowned hills rise around, with the river Greet—famous for its trout—winding at their base. The founder of the Minster was no less a personage than Paulinus, the missionary sent by Pope Gregory to convert the idolatrous West Saxons, and who became Archbishop of York. With no ordinary sentiments one approaches a building like this, the oldest in England, with the single exception of St. Augustine's of Canterbury : venerable in its appearance, and rich in the accumulated associations of twelve centuries. And then the architecture—comprising all the different styles of Gothic art that have prevailed in England at different periods up to the fifteenth century ;—what a field for study is there—Saxon pillars and arches, Norman doors and windows, Decorated-English screens and chapter-houses ! The entrance to the last is especially beautiful, revelling in foliage most exquisitely sculptured. There are three towers, which, with the nave and transepts, are all of fine bold Norman character, the central tower being very massive, the other two richly ornamented. The screen forms a kind of small cloister, in three divisions, ornamented with the most delicate and lavish fancy, and exhibiting extraordinary geometrical skill. The whole of this valuable remnant of antiquity is, we are happy to say, in excellent preservation, public subscriptions having enabled the guardians of the Minster to institute thorough repairs ; which were but just in time, however—for the whole pile had long been decaying.

Before the Reformation there had been a long and brilliant period for Southwell ; during which, a succession of monarchs, and nobles, and prelates, vied with each other in adding to its wealth and splendour, while the popes fenced it round with their decrees. All this ceased, never to be revived, under the religious policy introduced by the Tudor dynasty. First, Henry VIII. expelled its priests and dissolved its charities. But there were earnest friends of the ancient establishment at court, as well as in the county of Nottingham, and Cranmer in particular obtained the favour of a declaration that Southwell should remain the mother-church of the county—which it still is. Then, in the following reign, the chapter was dissolved. To Edward VI., however, succeeded Mary, who restored the ancient establishment ;—to last, as it proved, but for a short time in the Catholic form, for next came Elizabeth's new code of laws drawn up for a reformed chapter. After which, Southwell enjoyed an interval of repose, and still held a dignified position, as the only church in England, except Ripon (Fig. 1587, of late years made the cathedral of the new bishopric of Ripon), that was both collegiate and parochial. The desecrations of the edifice in the civil wars were just of the same kind as we have had to speak of in other great churches—arising of course from the facilities they offered for the temporary lodgment of troops, and the value of the lead and other materials in great emergencies. Some of the iron rings by which Cromwell's soldiers fastened their horses to the walls of Southwell Minster were remaining as late as 1793.

The tombs here which have survived all these ravages include two that we look upon with peculiar interest : one is a most ancient relic, placed under a circular arch, in shape exactly like a coffin ; the other a large alabaster tomb and effigy of Archbishop Sandys, one of the numerous Reformed divines who fled to Germany on the accession of Queen Mary, and returned on Elizabeth's to play a conspicuous part in most of the great operations of her reign. Sandys was one of the commission by which Mary Queen of Scots was tried and condemned. He was engaged in a more honourable way as one of the translators of Parker's or the Bishops' Bible, but latterly obtained an inevitable notoriety as a persecutor of the Puritans, whose principles he had formerly professed.

We must not conclude this notice of Southwell, without alluding to the remarkable discoveries of bodies, one in the south aisle of the Minster, one in the vaults of the ancient Archbishop's palace in the Minster-yard : the former almost furnishes a parallel to the wizard of Scott's 'Lay ;' it lies in the grave in cloth of silver tissue, with leather boots on, a wand by the side, and on the breast something like a silver cup with an acorn or bunch of leaves on its top. How long it had so lain there was no clue to discover, except that the skull was sufficiently thin and transparent to show that its owner must have lived at a very distant period. The teeth however were all sound, and so was even the stitching of the boots, though the leather tore like paper. The skeleton in the palace vault was also

entire—*standing upright*, booted and spurred, with military weapons at its feet. A strange spectacle ! An axe was left in the cleft skull, having evidently given the death-wound. There had been previously a tradition that when Charles I. was in Southwell, and had his head-quarters in the palace, a deserter or spy had been thrust by some of his soldiers into a vault or well, and there slain. Does not the fact of the finding (in 1740) of the skeleton just named offer a terrible testimony of the truth of the tradition !

The high embattled tower of Bromley Church (Fig. 1616), with its turret at one corner, is visible over the quiet scenery of the Ravensbourne river, long before we approach near to the church itself. The entrance is an advanced covered porch, so common to our country churches. It is a Sabbath afternoon, and before we enter that porch, the touching quietude and sweet solemnity of the scene around tempt us to linger and meditate awhile at our ease in the grave-yard where

> The rude forefathers of the hamlet sleep

in their mossy graves, chequered by sunlight and shade of green trees.

There is a stone here on the outside of the church, with an inscription from Dr. Hawkesworth, the author of ' The Adventurer,' and ' Almoran and Hamet,' and the translator of ' Telemachus.' It is a memorial of a blacksmith's wife, Elizabeth Monk, who being childless, " an infant to whom and to whose father and mother she had been nurse (such is the uncertainty of temporal prospects) became dependent upon strangers for the necessaries of life ; to him she afforded the protection of a mother. Her parental charity was returned with filial affection, and she was supported in the feebleness of age by him whom she had cherished in the helplessness of infancy." This touching example of humble generosity and grateful remembrance is more salutary to the mind that will receive it, than many deeds of sounding note. We have few records of the virtues of the poor and lowly, and the rarity makes this peculiarly acceptable. In Bromley Church the writer of the inscription himself lies. A Latin memorial reminds us of the sorrows of a still greater man, Dr. Johnson, who here interred his beloved wife, three days after he had finally discontinued his ' Rambler,' in consequence of grief and sad foreboding.

Truly good men are unhappily too rare to be ever passed by in silence by those who earnestly desire to honour goodness as the quality that, above all others, really ennobles humanity. And such a man was William Gilpin, whose memory is for ever connected with the church of Boldre, in Hampshire (Fig. 1609), in which, in the spirit of Chaucer's poor parson—

> Christes lore, and his Apostles twelve,
> He taught, but first he followed it himselve.

And if, unlike the poor parson, William Gilpin in the early part of his career, desired wealth, and worked strenuously in his vocation as a schoolmaster till he had obtained it, we have, in the still flourishing schools of Boldre that he founded, delightful evidence of the unselfish and noble objects he had in view. He achieved those objects, and then he rested as he had said he would rest, content. Having obtained the sum of ten thousand pounds, he returned to Boldre and there commenced a life of active usefulness that has been only too much overshadowed by the growth of his literary reputation. But indeed it is not too much to say that Gilpin is one of the most delightful writers in the language. No one can have read his Lives of the religious Reformers—men doubly interesting to him, inasmuch as he not only reverenced them, but his own ancestors were among the number—without feeling the inexpressible charm of his simply style ; whilst of his work on Forest Scenery it may be said, that he is one of the very few writers who impress us with the idea of his being equal to the subject. The grandeur and magnificence of external nature, the endless changes of its beautiful and deeply interesting phenomena, were familiar to his heart and mind, were evidently worshipped by him in the spirit of one who looks through Nature up to Nature's God, and were described by him, with the subtlest skill, in that style of mingled power and simplicity which is so characteristic of the great original whom he most deeply studied. But William Gilpin was not only a good schoolmaster, one of the best of pastors, and an original and charming writer ; he drew also with such feeling and power, that when his very numerous sketches were sold, after his decease, they realised a sum far exceeding their previously estimated value : the proceeds were assigned, as he had directed, to the school. He lived, as one desires to see all such men live, to a good old age—eighty ; and was, buried in the parish from which for many, many years he had hardly been absent a single day. His widow also lies in Boldre churchyard, expressing, in the inscription above, her hope " to be raised in God's good time, when it will be a new joy to see several of their good neighbours who now lie scattered in those sacred precincts around them." In the precincts of Boldre there was formerly a very remarkable natural curiosity, which Gilpin carefully examined and described; and, as a passing (though by no means peculiarly favourable) example of his picturesque style of composition even in level passages, we extract his account of it. " A cottager who lived near the centre of the village heard frequently a strange noise behind his house, like that of a person in extreme agony. Soon after, it caught the attention of his wife, who was then confined to her bed. She was a timorous woman, and being greatly alarmed, her husband endeavoured to persuade her that the noise she heard was only the bellowing of the stags in the forest. By degrees, however, the neighbours on all sides heard it; and the circumstance began to be much talked of. It was by this time plainly discovered that the groaning noise proceeded from an elm which grew at the bottom of the garden. It was a young, vigorous tree, and to all appearance perfectly sound. In a few weeks the fame of the groaning tree was spread far and wide; and people from all parts flocked to hear it. Among others it attracted the curiosity of the late Prince and Princess of Wales, who resided at that time, for the advantage of a sea-bath, at Pilewell, within a quarter of a mile of the groaning tree. Though the country people assigned many superstitious causes for this strange phenomenon, the naturalist could assign no physical one that was in any degree satisfactory. Some thought it was owing to the twisting and friction of the roots; others thought that it proceeded from water which had collected in the body of the tree, or perhaps from pent air: but no cause that was alleged appeared equal to the effect. In the mean time the tree did not always groan—sometimes disappointing its visitants—yet no cause could be assigned for its temporary cessations, either from seasons or weather. If any difference was observed, it was thought to groan least when the weather was wet, and most when it was clear and frosty; but the sound at all times seemed to come from the roots. Thus the groaning tree continued an object of astonishment, during the space of eighteeen or twenty months, to all the country around; and, for the information of distant parts, a pamphlet was drawn up, containing a particular account of all the circumstances relating to it. At length, the owner of it, a gentleman of the name of Forbes, making too rash an attempt to discover the cause, bored a hole in its trunk. After this it never groaned. It was then rooted up, with a further view to make a discovery: but still nothing appeared which led to any investigation of the cause. It was universally, however, believed that there was no trick in the affair; but that some natural cause really existed, though never understood." Who can say how much of the Grecian and other mythologies may not have originated in such accidental phenomena occurring among a highly-imaginative people? Assuredly, in the earlier periods of the world's history, the groaning tree of Baddesley would have been deemed a clear case of some imprisoned mortal or god.

The character of this good pastor reminds us of another, who in his little vill ge world obtained some reputation for his zeal, though his fame has hardly extended beyond his own precinct. Among our cuts will be found a representation of one of the smallest, quaintest, and most picturesque of parsonage-houses—Lynton (Fig. 1617), situated in the parish of that name, high up among the rocks of the north of Devonshire, which extend in a magnificent range from Exmoor to Morte Bay. The parsonage was built in 1560, and continued to be used till the commencement of the eighteenth century, when the incumbent, a man of some property, erected a larger house. That in so doing his heart was not puffed up with any unseemly pride is tolerably evident from his custom of riding about the lanes of the neighbourhood of the "Valley of Stones," on a Sunday, before service, to collect his flock together. Since his death the little parsonage has been again used; but a later vicar having built a still handsomer residence than the house we have mentioned (which has been pulled down), we see the new standing " in striking contrast with the old parsonage-house beside it, which is now called Ivy Cottage, and with its stone staircase and diminutive windows has an air of great antiquity inside; outside, geraniums in full blossom have been seen flourishing beneath its shade in the month of December." (' Penny Mag.,' 1844.)

For a third example of the parochial clergyman, let us pass to another and distant part of England, still more distinguished for its mountainous and sublime scenery: let us drop in fancy, as it were, on the bank of the Duddon, the river that for some twenty-five

miles divides Cumberland and Lancashire; and which Wordsworth has, both in his prose and in his poetry, immortalized. Here in the secluded hamlet of Seathwaite, lived, as the curate of its chapel (Fig. 1619), " Wonderful Robert Walker;" and the circumstances of his life show there was some foundation for the title popularly accorded to him. Having been a "sickly youth," he was bred as a scholar, then became a schoolmaster, and finally curate of his own native place, Seathwaite, with the magnificent income of *five* pounds a-year, which was gradually increased to about fifty pounds: a cottage also was provided. He married, and his wife brought him some forty pounds. And these were all of what may be called the regular sources of income he possessed. Yet this man, with a family of twelve children, eight of whom grew up and were respectably educated, was munificent in his hospitality, charitable to the poor, and died, sixty years afterwards, worth two thousand pounds. Was he not indeed " Wonderful" Robert Walker? Of course there was no magic or mystery in the business, but a great deal of patient industry and inventive intellect. He spun all the wool, and his family made all the clothes that were required; and he educated the parishioners' children while he spun. Then he aided his neighbours in the business of sheepshearing, haymaking, and other agricultural operations, where sudden accessions of labour are occasionally required, and of course they repaid him with interest, on the acre or two of ground that he had, and which he personally tilled. He was the scrivener of the neighbourhood, and his brewer: it may be noticed, that, when any one drank the ale in his house, he charged twopence a quart more for it than if taken to the usual place, an adjacent field—an exquisite little touch, as it seems to us, of the pastor-dignity that he wisely thought proper to observe amidst the many avocations that were, according to general notions, of a not very pastor-like nature. But to us the Swiss-like simplicity and homeliness of all this is delightful. And surely men like Robert Walker are, above all others the men to understand truly the hearts and minds of their flocks, to sympathise with them; and in such understanding and such sympathy lies the grand secret of success with our fellow-men in all ages and climes. How the little chapel harmonises with the character of its former curate, may be seen at a glance in our engraving (Fig. 1619). It is a low oblong building, with an unpretending porch and belfry, the bell-rope hanging in primeval simplicity on the outside. Walker lies in the churchyard, with an inscription to his memory. In leaving Seathwaite we cannot resist the pleasure of transcribing from Wordsworth a charming passage descriptive of the scenery around, approaching from Coniston, over Walna-scar, and descending into a little circular valley, through which flows the Duddon. He says, " This recess, towards the close of September, when the after-grass of the meadows is still of a fresh green, with the leaves of many of the trees faded, but perhaps none fallen, is truly enchanting. At a point elevated enough to show the various objects in the valley, and not so high as to diminish their importance, the stranger will instinctively halt. On the foreground, a little below the most favourable station, a rude foot-bridge is thrown over the bed of the noisy brook foaming by the wayside. Russet and craggy hills of bold and varied outline, surround the level valley, which is besprinkled with grey rocks plumed with birch-trees. A few homesteads are interspersed, in some places peeping out from among the rocks like hermitages, whose site has been chosen for the benefit of sunshine as well as shelter; in other instances, the dwelling-house, barn, and byre, compose together a cruciform structure, which, with its embowering trees, and the ivy clothing part of the walls and roof like a fleece, call to mind the remains of an ancient abbey. Time, in most cases, and nature everywhere, have given a sanctity to the humble works of man that are scattered over this peaceful retirement. Hence a harmony of tone and colour, a consummation and perfection of beauty, which would have been marred had aim or purpose interfered with the course of convenience, utility, or necessity. This unvitiated region stands in no need of the veil of twilight to soften or disguise its features. As it glistens in the morning sunshine it would fill the spectator's heart with gladsomeness. Looking from our chosen station, he would feel an impatience to rove among its pathways— to be greeted by the milkmaid—to wander from house to house, exchanging ' good morrows' as he passed the open doors; but at evening, when the sun is set, and a pearly light gleams from the western quarter of the sky, with an answering light from the smooth surface of the meadows—when the trees are dusky, but each kind still distinguishable—when the cool air has condensed the blue smoke rising from the chimneys—when the dark, mossy stones seem to sleep in the bed of the foaming brook—*then* he would be unwilling to move forward, not less from a reluctance to relinquish

1672.—Hulme Hall, Lancashire.—Front View.

1673.—Ornamental Brick Chimneys.—1. East Barsham Manor-House.   2. Hampton Court.   3. Eton College.

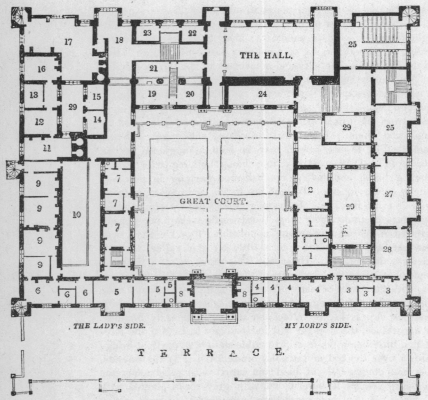

1674.—Plan of Buckhurst House, Sussex.

1675.—North Side of the Priory Cloisters, Christ's Hospital.

1676.—The Duke's House, Bradford. (From Richardson's 'Elizabethan Architecture.')

1677.—Staircase at Claverton, Somersetshire.
(From Richardson's 'Elizabethan Architecture.')

1678.—House in the High Street, Stratford.

1679.—John Shakspere's House in Henley Street. (From an old Print.)

1681.—Chimney Corner of the Kitchen in Henley Street.

1682.—Old Houses, Evesham.

1680.—House in Henley Street.

1683.—House in Charlcote Village.

1685.—Interior of Old English Cottage.

1684.—Shottery Cottage.

what he beholds, than from an apprehension of disturbing by his approach the quietness beneath him."

Reserving Stoke Church, and the several buildings, monuments, &c., connected with the career of William Shakspere, for mention elsewhere, we close our ecclesiastical notices with a few words on Chelsea Church (Fig. 1620); not on account of its beauty, for it is very much the reverse, but on account of the deep interest that attaches to the man whose supposed mausoleum it is—Sir Thomas More. We say supposed, for there is good reason to doubt the statements of Weever and Anthony Wood, that his daughter Margaret buried the body here soon after the executioner had performed his bloody office on it. She is known to have removed the body of Bishop Fisher, More's friend and fellow-sufferer, from the place where it was deposited, to St. Peter's church in the Tower, in order that it might be near her father's; and it is hardly probable that she would have been able subsequently to remove the latter to Chelsea. The imprisonment she was subjected to, for obtaining by purchase the head of her beloved parent, speaks decisively as to this point. Poor Margaret!—she had, after all, the consolation of reflecting that, however much she had suffered in consequence of her filial desire to possess the melancholy relic, she was allowed at last to keep it in peace, and to cause it to be buried with her in the church of St. Dunstan, Canterbury.

But if More's body does not lie at Chelsea Church, which is of course still very doubtful, it is certain that he intended to lie there, and erected for himself the beautiful tomb, still remaining, in which he was to be interred. It is a powerful testimony to the excellence of a life, when the owner, long before its probable close, can sit down to labours of this kind, not in a spirit of restless vanity to anticipate other men's praise, or in jealous alarm of their neglect, or worse than neglect, but in the honest desire to consider what he has been, and what, so far as time may permit, he ought yet to become. Such was More's spirit in penning the inscription, in Latin prose and verse, on his own monument. "Good reader," says he, in conclusion, "I beseech thee that thy pious prayers may attend me while living, and follow me when dead; that I may not have done this in vain; nor trembling may dread the approach of death, but willingly, for Christ's sake, undergo it; and that death to me may not be altogether death, but a door to everlasting life." There is one very remarkable and important passage in the inscription. More describes himself as not disliked by the good for a strict performance of his high duties, and as "dreaded only by thieves, murderers, and *heretics*." The friend who restored the inscription in the last century left out the word "heretics," and has been praised as "judicious" for so doing. The kindness and propriety of feeling are undeniable, but we doubt the judiciousness. History shows that More was to some degree a persecutor: there is no denying the fact—it was More's only blemish. But does not this inscription show, beyond question, another important fact—that More did only what he thought a sacred duty, and not to please any set of men, or in compromise of any principle, for purposes of temporary expediency? He erred, but it was the error of the age; and the "judicious" friend of More is, to our minds, he who shows how the error originated. Rightly looked at, there is nothing even in the dreadful persecutions of Baynham (before described) to make us love or reverence the *man* More one jot less than we are impelled to do by the knowledge of his, in every other respect, beautiful and noble career.

Sir Thomas More had a foreshadowing of his fate when his name was included in a bill for "Misprision" or concealment of treason—the treason being the prophecies of Elizabeth Barton, the Holy Maid of Kent. Cranmer, Latimer, and Cromwell, had the task of investigating these prophecies. The result we may briefly state. The Holy Maid had been a sufferer from excessively severe fits, of an epileptic character, which her ignorant neighbours attributed to supernatural influence, and her delirious ravings were accordingly treasured up as prophecies. The chief place with which these prophecies were connected was the chapel of Court-a-Street, in Kent (Fig. 1598). The king grew curious about this supernaturally gifted person, and showed her prophecies, as printed and circulated by her friends, to Sir Thomas More, who was so far from lending himself to the deceit or delusion, that he said he saw nothing in them worthy notice. "A right simple woman might speak it of her own wit well enough." After that, Henry had a private interview with the prophetess, who told him that, if he accomplished the divorce he was seeking, he would die an infamous death within seven months. When an illustrious character like More was to be smitten for a merely passive and respectful opposition to that measure, we cannot wonder that the poor creature who had the daring to utter such prophecies was instantly marked out for death. The Star Chamber sentenced her to appear in public at Paul's Cross on a Sunday, and declare herself an impostor, which she submitted to, probably in the hope of saving her life; but if so, she was soon disappointed: royal justice was yet unappeased; and this intrinsically worthless affair employed the High Court of Parliament. The bill of indictment included a number of persons who were supposed to have aided and abetted, or at least concealed, the "treasons" of which she was accused. One of these was More, as we have before stated; and there was another, afterwards More's fellow-prisoner and fellow-martyr, the venerable Fisher, Bishop of Rochester. It was thus Henry first attempted to frighten these eminent persons into an approval of the divorce and the suppression of the monasteries. More's name he afterwards withdrew, but Fisher had to compound with the Crown for his "misprision." Parliament was still sitting, when by its doom *seven* victims were drawn to Tyburn—the nun, and six of her friends.

There are many other objects of curiosity or interest in and around Chelsea church. There is an elaborate piece of sculpture here by Bernini, so well known for the bust of Charles I. The monument of Dr. Chamberlayne reminds us of a tragi-comical story not unworthy of mention. He was the author of a popular work on the state of England in 1668, and of various writings on religious and political subjects, but of nothing calculated to raise the admiration of his fellow-countrymen to any very high pitch. He had, however, it seems, works that were to astonish them, but not then—no, posterity only was worthy of the books he would bequeath to the world. So we read on his monument, first, and in order to challenge our respectful attention, that Dr. Chamberlayne was an "English gentleman, a Christian, and doctor of laws, descended from the ancient Norman family of the Earls of Tanquerville." And then comes the important announcement:—"He was so studious of good to all men, and especially to posterity, that he ordered some of his books, covered with wax, to be buried with him, which," says the writer, with delightful modesty, "may be of use in times to come." We are then told by the friend who erected the monument as a testimony both of respect and grief, and who is the author of the inscription, that it is not to be "rashly violated." Now, this was a very pretty mystery to perplex living men, who naturally desired to participate in the concealed intellectual treasures of the tomb; but a century having elapsed, it was thought posterity might claim its own, and so in 1791 there was a project for opening the place of deposit, and seizing these Sibylline leaves. But, alas! their labours had been anticipated by Time, who had so injured the tomb, that nooks and crannies were opened for the admission of air: when the interior was examined-not a trace of the mystic volumes remained behind. What may we not have lost!

In the churchyard of Chelsea rest two men, each, in his path, admirable: Sir Hans Sloane, and Philip Miller, the author of the 'Gardener's Dictionary'—a work that puts to shame all subsequent attempts of the same kind, so full is it of enlightened views, so rich in the facts of experience, and so plainly but popularly written. Here too rest Shadwell, the poet-laureate; Mossop, the actor; Dr. Kenrick; and Sir John Fielding, whose honourable name, suggesting as it does recollections of his half-brother the great novelist, must not make us forget his own reputation as a most able and active magistrate.

CHAPTER III.—POPULAR ANTIQUITIES.

MONG the comprehensive series of illustrations of the costumes of Old England during the reigns of Henry VII. and VIII., Edward, Mary, and Elizabeth, contained in pages 77, 80, 81, 84, we may select a few as suggesting special points of information or interest. In the right-hand figure of the engraving of general costume of the reign of Henry VII. (Fig. 1632), we perceive something of that blending of the male and the female attire which characterised the fashionable dresses of the day, and which made Strutt complain that it was frequently impossible to discover to which sex the wearer belonged. Even the names of portions of the habit exhibit, to our eyes, the same kind of confusion. The author of the 'Boke of Kervynge,' quoted by Strutt, says to one of the officers of royalty, "Warm your sovereign his *petticoat*, his doublet, and his *stomacher*, and then put on his hose, and then his shoes or slippers, then straiten up his hose mannerly, and tie them up, then lace his doublet hole by hole," and so on. The first use of the word petticoat, in its present restricted sense, is said to be that contained in the following passage from the history of the famous clothier, Jack of Newbury, who lived in the reign of Henry VIII. His wife's maidens, who are employed in spinning, are described as arrayed

In *petticoats* of stamel red,
And milk-white kerchers on their head,
Their smock-sleeves like to winter's snow,
That on the western mountains flow,
And each sleeve with a silken band
Was fairly tied at the hand.

The elegant style of slashing (see also the same cut) now began to make its appearance. Camden, in his 'Remains,' tells a pleasant story of a shoemaker of Norwich, named John Drakes, who, in the time of Henry VIII., coming to a tailor's, and finding some fine French tawney cloth lying there, which had been sent to be made into a gown for Sir Philip Calthrop, took a fancy to the colour, and ordered the tailor to buy as much of the same stuff for him, and make him a gown of it, precisely of the same fashion as the knight's, whatever that might be. Sir Philip, arriving some time afterwards to be measured, saw the additional cloth, and inquired who it belonged to. "To John Drakes," replied the tailor, "who will have it made in the self-same fashion as yours is made of." "Well," said the knight, "in good time be it : I will have mine as full of cuts as thy shears can make it." And both garments were finished according to the order. The shoemaker, on receiving his gown slashed almost to shreds, began to swear at the tailor, but received for answer, "I have done nothing but what you bade me ; for as Sir Philip Calthrop's gown is, even so have I made yours." "By my latchet!" growled the shoemaker, "I will never wear a gentleman's fashion again." ('History of British Costume.')

The female costume of Henry VII.'s reign has been smartly touched off by the poet-laureate of the day, Skelton, who, in his humorous description of a well-known hostess, gives us this picture of the dress of females of the middle class :—

In her furr'd flocket,
And grey russet rocket,
Her duke of Lincoln green ;
It had been hers I ween
More than forty year,
And so it doth appear,
And the green bare threads
Look like sea-weeds
Withered like hay,
The wool worn away

And yet I dare say,
She thinks herself gay
Upon a holyday,
When she doth array,
And girdeth in her gates,
Stitched and pranked with plates,
Her kirtle Bristow red,
With cloths upon her head,
They weigh a ton of lead.
She hobbles as she goes,
With her blanket hose,
Her shoon smeared with tallow.

It will be remembered that Chaucer speaks of the coverchiefs on the head of the wife of Bath, observing,—

I durste swear they weigheden a pound ;

and that he alludes to her "shoes full moist ;" so it appears that these customs at least had not changed from his to Skelton's time, except that the kerchiefs had grown more and more heavy, until, with a little exaggeration it must be owned, the satirist says

They weigh a ton of lead.

In the reign of Edward the flat cap made its appearance (Fig. 1650), and gradually descending from grade to grade, becomes at last eternally popular, if not eternally worn, upon the heads of the bold 'prentices of London. The general dress of the citizens at that time is preserved for us to our own day in the garb of the blue coat boy of Christ's Hospital. Stockings of silk first made their appearance in England about the same time. Their novelty and value are shown very strikingly in the fact that Sir Thomas Gresham made a formal present of a pair to the youthful Edward. Elizabeth's reign witnessed the existence of the first pair of English manufacture, as it did also the manufacture of worsted stockings. Stow informs us that William Rider, apprentice to Thomas Burdet, at the foot of London Bridge, saw a pair of knit worsted stockings at an Italian merchant's that had been brought from Mantua. He immediately borrowed them, made a similar pair, and presented them to the Earl of Pembroke. That was the first pair of worsted stockings knit in England. The next step was the invention of the stocking-frame, connected with which is a somewhat tragical story. The inventor was William Lee, a gentleman and scholar. Tradition attributes the origin of his invention to a pique he had taken against a towns-woman with whom he was in love, and who it seems, neglected his passion. She got her livelihood by knitting stockings, and, with the ungenerous object of depreciating her employment, he constructed this frame, first working at it himself, then teaching his brother and other relations. He practised his new invention some time at Calverton, a village about five miles from Nottingham ; and either he or his brother is said to have worked for Queen Elizabeth. The other stocking-manufacturers used every art to bring his invention into disrepute : and it seems they effected their purpose for that time, as he removed from Calverton, and settled at Rouen in Normandy, where he met with great patronage ; but the murder of Henry IV. of France, and the internal troubles subsequent to that event, frustrated his success, and he died at Paris of a broken heart. Stow says that Lee not only manufactured stockings in his frame, but "waistcoats, and divers other things." ('History of British Costume.')

Among all the fashionable absurdities of the female dress in Elizabeth's time, the ruff and wings truly stand out the most conspicuous. The best examples of these novel enormities are to be found in the well-known portraits of the queen herself (see page 32). No ordinary skill or preparation was sufficient to produce these edifices of muslin—these fortifications of lace. Up to the second year of the reign holland had been used, and, when Elizabeth must have lawn and cambric, no one could starch or stiffen them. It was a case for extraordinary exertions, and extraordinary exertions were made ; some Dutch women were sent for, who

1690.—The Old Blue Boar, Holborn.

1689.—Remains of Stoke Manor House.

1687.—Ancient Manor-House, Vauxhall.

1691.—Marylebone House.

1686.—Garden of New Place.

1688.—Carter's Hall Passage, with the Old Townhall, Oxford.

1692.—Charlcote House, from the Garden.

1693.—Charlcote House, from the Avenue.

1694.—A Peep at Charlcote.

1695.—Charlcote House, from the Avon.

1696.—The College, Stratford.

1697.—Ancient Hall in Stratford College

1698.—Leeds Castle, Kent.

sufficed for a time, and until the advent of a greater artist in clear-starching, Mistress Dingham Vander Plasse, a Fleming, who in 1564 came to London, and rose immediately into high reputation, both as a professor of the art and a teacher. Her lessons were of course expensive; four or five pounds (of the money of the sixteenth century) a scholar, and twenty shillings in addition for instruction as to the making of the starch. Stubbs, who, in his 'Anatomy of Abuses,' attacks every change that does not please his very decided puritanical and unimaginative tastes, speaks with amusing severity of "this liquid matter which they call starch," wherein it appears "the devil hath learnt them to wash and dive their ruffs." The starch it seems was made not only of different grain, as wheat flour, bran, of roots and other things, but also of different colours, white, red, blue, and purple. But starch alone was not sufficient; there was also a "certain device made of wires, crested for the purpose, and whipped all over either with gold, thread, silver, or silk," in ringlets, called an "under-propper." Upon these were erected the "stately arches of pride"—the starched ruff row upon row, till we come finally to the "master-devil ruff," rich beyond mea-sure in gold, silver, or silk lace, and which sparkled all over with suns, moons, stars, and other devices.

The male fashionables had their pre-eminent absurdity too—the wide breeches, of which Strutt quotes from the Harleian MSS. the following ludicrous memorandum:—"That over the seats in the Parliament-house there were certain holes, some two inches square, in the walls, in which were placed posts to uphold a scaffold round about the house within, for them to sit upon who used the wearing of great breeches stuffed with hair like woolsacks, which fashion being left the eighth year of Elizabeth, the scaffolds were taken down and never since put up!"

Armour, in the reigns of the present period (see pages 77, 80, 81, and 84), is chiefly distinguished by the constant increase of splen-dour in its most important features. It became ribbed, and fluted, and otherwise adorned. Skill, fancy, and reckless expenditure, are fairly exhausted upon it. Among the valuable series of examples in the Armoury of the Tower we find the suits attributed or that really belonged to Henry VII. (Fig. 1394), Henry VIII. (Figs. 1409 and 1638), Edward VI. (Fig. 1475), and Sir Horace Vere (Fig. 1651). Of all these, Henry the Eighth's is by far the richest; showing that was in his time the art of the armourer reached its climax. Alterations were subsequently made, one of which, the practice of russetting, certainly added to the superb effect of the armour, but on the whole nothing more truly magnificent, beautiful, and costly, has been seen in England than the suit that startles every visitor to the Armoury into enthusiasm, when he reaches the central recess of the room, and sees an effigy of bluff King Hal arrayed in it. This was presented to Henry by the Emperor Maximilian. The entire suits for both horse and rider are washed over with silver, and enriched with exquisite engrav-ings of legends, devices, mottos and arms, or in some parts of still more important subjects, as on the breastplate, where there is a figure of St. George. On one of the joints is inscribed the German word glück, meaning good luck, and referring, it is sup-posed, to the marriage of Henry with Catherine of Arragon. Two incidental evidences of the claim of the suit to the high rank we have assigned to it are not unworthy of mention: it was so admired by the giver, as to have been either copied for or from a similar suit for himself, which is now preserved in the little Belve-dere palace, Vienna, and so prized by the receiver, that he caused himself to be represented in one exactly corresponding with it in form and style, for his great seal (Fig. 1408). The russet armour, of which Edward the Sixth's suit presents an example, was produced by oxidising the surface of the metal, and then smoothing it. The russet, when inlaid with gold, as in Edward's suit, has an exceedingly rich appearance. It had also the advantage of being kept bright and clean with greater ease than the plain polished steel.

The principal heroes of Queen Elizabeth's Tilt (now Palace) Yard (Fig. 1567), we are told by Pennant, were Sir Henry Lee of Ditchley, Master of the Armoury, and George Earl of Cumberland. Sir Henry constituted himself the queen's knight or champion in the martial sports, and made a vow to present himself armed at the Tilt Yard on the 27th of November in every year. Thus commenced the annual exercises of arms in this reign, for which Sir Henry formed a society of twenty-five of the most distinguished gentlemen of the court. In the thirty-third year of Elizabeth's reign the then aged knight resigned his office of president, and his proud title of the Queen's Champion, in favour of the Earl of Cumberland. The ceremony of resignation was in the most imaginative and exalted spirit of chivalry in its palmiest days. Edward III. and his knights

could not have resigned themselves more completely to its exciting illusions, than did Elizabeth, the veteran lord of the martial sports, and his gallant companions, on this occasion. Early on a morning unusually cheerful and sunny for the month of November, the citizens of London thronged to occupy the galleries erected for spectators in the Westminster Tilt Yard, where seats were ready to be had, if paid for in gold pieces. The best seats were let at very high prices, or set apart for the city and court dignitaries. There were several tiers of seats of varying degrees of honour, stretching entirely round the Tilt Yard. The appearance of these crowded galleries was exceedingly gay and splendid:—covered with coloured cloths fringed with gold; the feathers in the caps of the gentlemen everywhere in graceful and joyous motion with the play of the breeze: and their festival dresses, of all sorts of silk and satin materials, shining with gems and with gold and silver embroidery. The ladies, of course, were equally brilliant; and every here and there the partizans of the soldiery caught the bright rays of the sun. On this animating assemblage looked down the ancient Hall and Abbey; the shadowy form of the latter relieved by the glorious light that flamed in its Gothic windows. And the air breathed by the crowd was not of pent-up streets, but of fresh fields, and pastures, and gardens. Hark! there are bursts of martial music, and all eyes turn to the queen, who takes her place amidst the rapturous homage of her most "loving people." She sits opposite the entrance to the Hall, in the "Queen's Gallery," under a rich canopy, and around her are gathered her most favoured courtiers and her beautiful maids of honour. The tilting begins. The combatants are habited in armour, richly engraved, and gilded, with grotesque and imaginative devices. Loudly the people applaud the well-run course; but the passion for war in earnest breaks out now and then in something very like murmurs because the sport is found to leave all the knights scathless. "Why, after all, this is but child's play, compared with the jousts of the knights of old!" some burley citizen or bold apprentice is heard to remark: and in the general feeling of that lamentable falling-off, chivalry is dis-cerned to be dying away, and these brilliant shows are but transient revivals that usher in the final close of all.

The jousts being over, the queen's aged knight, who has now done his devoirs in her service for the last time, presents himself at the foot of the stairs leading to the queen's gallery. Just then, one of those cunning surprises takes place, without which no fête of that age would have been considered complete. The earth, as it were, suddenly opening, there appeared an extraordinary and most beau-tiful little chapel or temple of white taffeta set upon pillars of porphyry, arched "like unto a church," with many lamps burning in it, and the roof fretted with rich Gothic work and gilding. An altar appeared within, covered with cloth of gold, and lighted by two large wax candles in rich candlesticks. On this were laid "certain princely presents," Sir Harry Lee's parting memorials to the queen. Strains of enchanting sweetness issued from the temple as the aged knight drew near the throne, and Mr. Hales, "her Majesty's servant, a singer," of admirable voice and skill, accom-panied the instruments with these touching verses, supposed to be addressed by Sir Henry to the queen:—

> My golden locks time hath to silver turn'd,
> (Oh, time! too swift, and swiftness never ceasing,)
> My youth 'gainst age, and age at youth hath spurn'd;
> But spurn'd in vain—youth waneth by increasing—
> Beauty, strength, and youth, flowers fading been,
> Duty, faith, and love, are roots, and evergreen.
>
> My helmet now shall make an hive for bees,
> And lovers' songs shall turn to holy psalms;
> A man-at-arms must now sit on his knees,
> And feed on prayers that are old age's alms.
> And so from court to cottage I depart,
> My saint is sure of mine unspotted heart
>
> And when I sadly sit in homely cell,
> I'll teach my swains this carol for a song;
> Blest be the hearts that think my sovereign well,
> Cursed be the souls that think to do her wrong
> Goddess, vouchsafe this aged man his right,
> To be your beadsman now, that was your knight.

The knight then laid his goodly gifts at her Majesty's feet, and repeated the burden of the song, declaring that, although his youth and strength had decayed, his duty, faith, and love remained perfect as ever; and his hands, instead of wielding the lance, should now be held up in prayer for her Majesty's welfare; and he trusted she would allow him to be her beadsman, now that he had ceased to incur knightly perils in her service. Elizabeth, in reply, paid him some well-merited compliments on his gallantry, and desired him still to attend the annual jousts to direct the knights. The new champion was then presented and accepted. Sir Henry's esquires presented their master's armour at the foot of the throne, and, after he had himself put on a side-coat of "black velvet, pointed under the arms, and covered his head (in lieu of a helmet), with a buttoned cap of the country fashion," he assisted to invest the Earl with his own armour, and to mount him on his horse, amid thundering artillery, martial music, and cheers and huzzas from nobles and people.

Sir Henry Lee died in 1611, at eighty years of age. Scott has caught with delightful effect the leading traits of this amiable character, his enthusiastic loyalty, courage, and honourable feeling. And few who delight in that masterly delineation in Woodstock, will care much for the chronological inaccuracy of placing him in the reign of Charles II. instead of that of Elizabeth.

In the Percy Reliques there is a song belonging to the early part of the seventeenth century, which shows very picturesquely the domestic life of the reign of Elizabeth, while lamenting the changes that had taken place in the interval between the two periods. The song, in somewhat altered words, has recently become a second time highly popular. The version we are about to give, and which is made the subject of a series of engravings in pages 84, 85, was printed by Percy from a black-letter copy in the Pepys Collection. Thus it runs :—

> An old song made by an aged old pate,
> Of an old worshipful gentleman, who had a great estate,
> That kept a brave old house at a bountiful rate,
> And an old porter to relieve the poor at his gate (Fig. 1652) ;
>   Like an old courtier of the queen's,
>   And the queen's old courtier.
>
> With an old lady, whose anger one word assuages,
> This (who) every quarter paid their old servants their wages,
> And never knew what belonged to coachmen, footmen, nor pages (Fig.
> But kept twenty old fellows with blue coats and badges;   [1659)
>   Like an old courtier, &c.
>
> With an old study filled full of learned old books ;
> With an old reverend chaplain, you might know him by his looks ;
> With an old buttery-hatch worn quite off the hooks,
> And an old kitchen, that maintained half a dozen old cooks (Fig. 1567) ;
>   Like an old courtier, &c.
>
> With an old hall hung about with pikes, guns, and bows,
> With old swords and bucklers, that had borne many shrewd blows,
> And an old frieze coat to cover his worship's trunk hose,
> And a cup of old sherry to comfort his copper nose ;
>   Like an old courtier, &c.
>
> With a good old fashion, when Christmas was come,
> To call in all his old neighbours with bagpipe and drum (Fig. 1653),
> With good cheer enough to furnish every old room,
> And old liquor able to make a cat speak and man dumb ;
>   Like an old courtier, &c.
>
> With an old falconer, huntsman, and a kennel of hounds,
> That never hawked nor hunted except in his own grounds (Fig. 1655) ;
> Who, like a wise man, kept himself within his own bounds,
> And when he died he gave every child a thousand good pounds;
>   Like an old courtier, &c.
>
> But to his eldest son his house and land he assigned,
> Charging him in his will to keep the old bountiful mind,
> To be good to his old tenants, and to his neighbours be kind ;
> But in the ensuing ditty you shall hear how he was inclined ;
>   Like a young courtier of the king's,
>   And the king's young courtier.
>
> Like a flourishing young gallant, newly come to his land,
> Who keeps a brace of painted madams at his command (Fig. 1654),
> And takes up a thousand poudns upon his father's land,
> And gets drunk in a tavern till he can neither go nor stand;
>   Like a young courtier, &c.
>
> With a new-fangled lady, that is dainty, nice, and spare,
> Who never knew what belonged to good housekeeping or care (Fig. 1656) ;
> Who buys gaudy-coloured fans to play with wanton air,
> And seven or eight different dressings of other women's hair ;
>   Like a young courtier, &c.
>
> With a new-fashioned hall, built where the old one stood,
> Hung round with new pictures that do the poor no good,
> With a fine marble chimney, wherein burns neither coals nor wood,
> And a new smooth shovel-board whereon no victuals ne'er stood ;
>   Like a young courtier, &c.
>
> With a new study stuff'd full of pamphlets and plays,
> And a new chaplain that swears faster than he prays,
> With a new buttery-hatch that opens once in four or five days,
> And a new French cook to devise fine kickshaws and toys (Fig. 1658) ;
>   Like a young courtier, &c.
>
> With new titles of honour, bought with his father's old gold,
> For which sundry of his ancestors' old manors are sold ;
> And this is the course most of our new gallants hold,
> Which makes that good housekeeping is now grown so cold,
>   Among the young courtiers of the king,
>   Or the king's young courtiers.

The cities of England generally, and especially that of London, pursued steadily their onward career through the whole of the earlier reigns of the period. But a still more rapid impetus was given in the prosperous era of Elizabeth. And their royal mistress was one of the first to congratulate her citizens on their commercial successes in her own pleasant ways; she either visited them, and so helped them to spend the fruits of their industry, or she condescended to borrow whatever she thought they had to lend, on her own terms. Thus, hearing how the good people of Bristol were thriving, she naturally desired to witness with her own queenly eyes the city of which such pleasant rumours were always flying about. She might think too she had done something personally to promote their prosperity. In 1558, immediately on her accession, she had granted them a charter confirmatory of their old privileges ; and three years later exempted them finally from the charge of keeping the Marches of Wales. It was in 1574 that Elizabeth set out on her visit, calling on her way at Berkeley Castle, where the Lady Berkeley, sister of the Duke of Norfolk beheaded by Elizabeth for his presumed connection with the Queen of Scots, petitioned on her knees her Majesty's favour, in connection with some lawsuit then pending. " No, no, my Lady Berkeley," was the harsh reply, " we know you will never love us for [on account of] the death of your brother." This has been called a knowledge of human nature ; to us it seems a knowledge only of the most worldly part of human nature. A generous act generously performed might have changed the whole current of the unhappy petitioner's thoughts. But such was state-wisdom under the Tudor dynasty. Magnificently, of course, did the corporation of Bristol receive their gracious virgin queen. The mayor's house was set apart for her accommodation ; and thither she was led by the whole of the incorporated companies, with their gay banners flying, and the cheerful music ringing through the air. A pageant as usual formed a part of the reception proceedings, and the artist-poet was Thomas Churchyard. The main feature was Fame's address, who thus speaks of herself and the royal visitor :—

> Nor fleet of foot, nor swift of wing, nor scarce the thought in breast,
> Nor yet the arrow out of bow, nor wind that seld' doth rest,
> Compares with me, quick world's report, that some calls Flying Fame,
> A burst of praise, a blast of pomp, or blazes of good name.
> The only land that kings do seek, a joy to catch estate ;
> A welcome friend that all men love, and none alive doth hate,
> Salutes the Queen of rare renown, whose goodly gifts divine
> Through earth and air, with glory great, shall pass this trump of mine.
> And knowing of thy coming here, my duty bade me go
> Before, unto this present place, the news thereof to show.
> No sooner was pronounced the name, but babes in street 'gan leap ;
> The youth, the age, the rich, the poor, came running all on heap ;
> And clapping hands, cried mainly out, " O blessed be the hour!
> Our Queen is coming to the town with princely train and power !"

The still more elaborate pageant of a succeeding day deserves especial notice for its bearing on the commercial views of the time. In them Dissension strove to set Wars and Peace by the ears, urging upon the latter the " vanity " of prowling about for pelf; and that if they

> Abide at home till cannons roar,
> The plaster comes too late to salve the sore,

and exciting the former, by telling them,

> Peace calls you rogues, and Swashing Dicks, that stand upon your braves,
> A swarm of wasps, a flock of wolves, a nest of thieves and knaves,
> That live by spoil and murthers vile, and triumph still in blood.

No wonder Wars grew indignant to hear that they are thus vilified, and so the poet with proper discrimination makes them the first to advance to do battle at the instigations of Dissension. A tremendous attack takes place, and the fort of Feeble Policy is soon won. The main fort of Peace still holds valiantly out ; but at last is so reduced to extremities, that a gentleman actually swims " over the water in sore danger, clothes and all," to obtain aid from the queen, who is thus perforce made one of the component parts of the pageant. Wars now begin to use persuasion ; but the good soldiers of Peace shake their heads, wisely observing—

> Our trade doth stand in civil life, and *there our glory lies*,
> And not in strife, the ruin of states, a storm that all destroys,
> A heavy bondage to each heart that freedom's fruit enjoys—

an admirable evidence of the good sense of the Bristolians ; and very emphatically did the queen express her approbation of the sentiment of the pageant: at the conclusion she sent the soldiers two hundred crown-pieces. Here again Elizabeth was worthy of herself, her country, and her time. It is impossible to overrate the effect that such marked approbation of the growing desire for

1699.—Clopton Bridge, Stratford.

1703.—Statue of Sir Thomas Gresham

1700.—Foot-bridge above the Mill, Stratford.

1701.—Bidford Grange.

1702.—Sir Thomas Gresham's Exchange, London.   (From a Print in the Guildhall Library.)

1705.—London, from Blackfriars, in the Sixteenth Century.

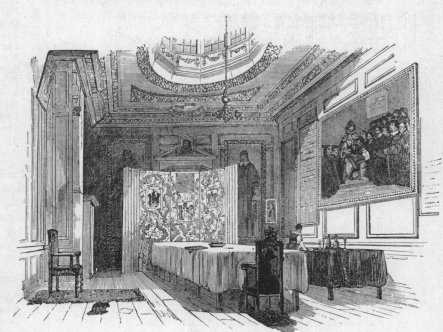

1706.—Court-Room, Barber-Surgeons' Hall.

1704.—Portrait of Sir Thomas Gresham

1707.—Mill at Arundel.

1708.—The Mill, Welford.

1709.—Interior of Merchant Tailors' Hall, Threadneedle Street

1710.—Mercers' Hall, Cheapside.

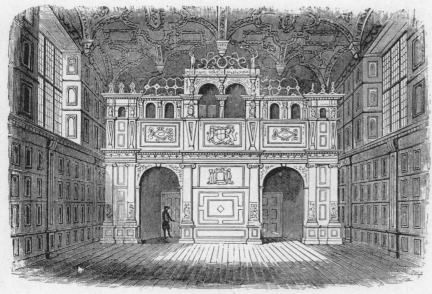

1711.—Leathersellers' Hall, London. (From an Old View engraved in Malcolm's 'History of London.')

1712.—Smithfield

1713.—Wharf of the German Merchants of the Steel-yard in Thames Street (From Hollar's print in 1641.)

1714.—Public Washing-grounds, 1582. (Harleian MS. 3469.)

peace and peaceable pursuits must have had upon the trading and commercial interests of the kingdom.

But we must turn to London, and its Exchange (Fig. 1702), and the munificent founder of that Exchange, Gresham (Figs. 1703, 1704), for the most striking evidences of Elizabeth's consciousness of the best mode to make her native land truly great among the nations of the earth. During the reign of Edward VI. the Duke of Northumberland had been Gresham's chief patron and supporter in the arduous task then begun by that great financial reformer; and when the duke fell, in consequence of his attempt to place Lady Jane Grey on the throne, Gresham feared his fortunes had sunk too. But at the very first council held by Elizabeth at Hatfield, where she was residing at the time of her accession, she received the merchant-prince most graciously: and even told him—conscious of the difficulties he had to contend with—she would keep one ear shut from his enemies, in order that it might be ever open to him: on that same occasion it was that Gresham tendered his memorable advice, first, that all the debased coin of the realm should be turned into fine, of a specific weight; secondly, that the Steelyard merchants should not be allowed the restoration of their "usurped" privilege; thirdly, to grant as few licences as possible; fourthly, to incur little or no debt beyond the seas; lastly, to keep her credit with her own merchants at home as they were the men who would stand by her in her necessities. Much, indee , does England owe of its present power and wealth, to the advice that day given by Gresham; for the whole of it, with the exception of the licences, was acted upon: his remarks became, subsequently, so many axioms in our financial system.

It is not, however, to be supposed that Elizabeth, who was so very fond of deciding matters by the summary process of saying it was her will, and therefore the thing was to be done out of hand, would immediately understand or appreciate all the subtleties of Gresham's commercial wisdom. So, even while she proceeded to carry out his views, she also allowed herself many little liberties that seem ludicrous enough now, but which sadly hampered Gresham in his movements. It was, for instance, a difficult matter for him to establish his sovereign's credit as a borrower at home, when she was already too well known there. Let us give an example or two.

One day the lord mayor comes to the ironmongers with her commands, that they prepare immediately the sum of 60*l.*, to be lent to her for "one whole year;" and this, says he to them, is to be taken "of the stock of your hall, and, if you have not so much in store, then you must borrow the same at interest, at the only costs and losses of your hall;" and of this they were to fail at their "peril!" But this is not the whole or the best part of the story. Having overfilled her coffers with the citizens' money, by such and similar means, she returned some of it; but how?—why, by loans varying from 50*l.* to 200*l.*, on security of gold and silver plate, or other equally satisfactory deposits; for which loans of money, to its proper owners, her Majesty charged *only* seven per cent. Poor citizens!—obliged to borrow back upon security, at seven per cent., the money they had lent for nothing, and without any security! The ludicrous injustice of the whole business can only be paralleled by the story told of the late Dey of Algiers, who is said to have been very fond of playing with his courtiers at whist for large stakes, but with one little peculiarity in the mode of playing the game: he always insisted upon his right to name the trump card, after looking at his own hand.

In other respects the citizens had cause to look with suspicion upon Elizabeth whenever she had aught to say to them concerning money. At one time she introduced lotteries, and desired her loving friends, the Companies, to avail themselves of the brilliant advantages they offered. The idea had been taken from the continental governments, but it does not seem that the speculators in her majesty's lotteries were as much fascinated as she was with them. There is a sly satiric couplet in the books of the Merchant Tailors of the time, which tells with quiet significance what their views were:—

> One bird in the hand is worth two in the wood;
> If we get the great lot it will do us good.

With regard to Gresham's other proposed reforms:—the debased coinage was restored under his own superintendence—an act in itself sufficient to immortalize him; and the Steelyard merchants did not recover their monopoly. We may here observe that the Esterlings, or Germans, had settled in England so early as the reign of Ethelred, and had been our earliest instructors in the art of commerce. Numerous privileges had been bestowed upon them, and for several centuries their monopoly was, like many other

monopolies, highly beneficial; but, by the reign of Edward VI. it was thought, and no doubt rightly, that the foreign commerce of England had grown too vast a thing to be any longer the exclusive property of any particular body of men, so their privileges were abolished: and Elizabeth, by Gresham's advice, confirmed that abolition. Their guildhall was on the banks of the Thames (Fig. 1713), not far from London Bridge, and contained two of Holbein's fine pictures—the Triumph of Riches and Poverty. There remains but to notice the matter of the granting of licences, and in them Elizabeth did not follow the judicious advice tendered her;—it was found *too* pleasant to have the opportunity of personally rewarding some favourite public servant, as a Leicester or a Raleigh—*too* convenient to have the opportunity of punishing one who had offended by declining to renew a grant, or even perhaps by withdrawing it, without waiting for the period of renewal. Elizabeth's treatment of Essex, in the matter of the licence for sweet wines, will not be forgotten by our readers. So this fruitful source of abuse was preserved, to be in later times the means of adding fresh fuel to the flames, when sovereign and people began to look with jealous and angry eyes upon each other. The licence system was worse than the lotteries, for it was a direct and positive infringement on the chief powers and rights of the Companies, for the most selfish purposes, and without the least regard to consequences. It was attempted with the leathersellers. Edward Darcy, a hanger-on of the court of Elizabeth, held from her a patent to search and seal all the leather through England: and he found it, Strype tells us, "a very gainful business to him." No doubt he did, but the leathersellers did not find it equally so to them; and the whole body assumed a posture of determination to procure a revocation of the patent. The wardens of the Company were threatened—were imprisoned—but stood out manfully against the unjust innovation, until they had conquered it; though the snake was only scotched, not killed. Patents soon multiplied rapidly, until a list was read one day in the House of Parliament that included currants, salt, iron, powder, cards, calf-skins, felts, leather, ox-shin bones, train-oil, and a host of other produce. Well might a member ask, "Is not bread among the number?" and reply, after the astonished response, "Bread!" "Yes, I assure you, if affairs go on at this rate, we shall have bread reduced to a monopoly before the next parliament." The system itself was bad enough—transferring important commercial powers from communities, respected and partially responsible, to single individuals; but it was made worse by the original patents becoming matters of sale. They were disposed of to the highest bidders, who, regardless of aught but their own private advantage, raised commodities to what prices they pleased, and so put "invincible restraints upon all commerce, industry, and emulation in the arts."

If, in passing through Lombard Street, the stranger pauses a moment before the banking-house of Stone, Martin, and Co., he may please himself by reflecting that he looks upon the site where stood Gresham's shop, with the grasshopper as a sign above, and that all about was the scene of the only Exchange known to the merchants of London during the early part of the reign of Elizabeth. If he then passes round to Cornhill, and looks upon the magnificent building recently erected there, he may further amuse himself by the reflections which that palpable evidence of the growth of the power of which Gresham may be said to have all but laid the foundation is calculated to call forth; and the building itself, as a building, is, we need scarcely say, but the representative of the one erected by Gresham. It did not accord with his notions of the dignity of English merchants to be obliged to meet in a narrow street, to be there "constrained either to endure all extremes of weather, viz. heat and cold, snow and rain, or else to shelter themselves in shops" (Stow); so he determined, in the liberality and princeliness of his disposition, to build a home for them. All he asked of his fellow-merchants was a site. With the assistance of Flemish materials, Flemish workmen, and a Flemish architect, who worked after a Flemish model (the Bourse of Antwerp), the edifice was raised, with shops round it as at present (Fig. 1702); and although for a time the circumstance that those shops were unlet caused Gresham some anxiety, Elizabeth soon settled the matter for him by the éclat given to the building by her visit in 1570, when she named it the Royal Exchange. Heywood, in a play on the subject, makes Gresham at the banquet (given by him to Elizabeth on the same day) produce a pearl of immense value, crush it to powder, and then drink it off in a cup of wine:

> Here fifteen hundred pound at one clap goes!
> Instead of sugar, Gresham drinks the pearl
> Unto his queen and mistress · pledge it, lords.

And if the passage has no other value, it shows the notion that prevailed generally of Gresham's wealth and liberality. The building thus raised by him was burnt down in the great fire. We conclude our notice of it with a glowing description of its contents from the pen of one who wrote upon the effects of the dire calamity just mentioned, in a vein of no ordinary eloquence :—" How full of riches was that Royal Exchange!—Rich men in the midst of it, rich goods above and beneath! These men walked upon the top of a wealthy mine, considering what Eastern treasures, costly spices and such-like things, were laid up in the bowels (I mean the cellars) of that place. As for the upper part of it, was it not the great storehouse whence the nobility and gentry of England were furnished with most of those costly things wherewith they did adorn either their closets or themselves? Here, if anywhere, might a man have seen the glory of the world in a moment! . . . . . . What artificial thing could entertain the senses, the fantasies of men, that was not there to be had? Such was the delight that many gallants took in that magazine of all curious varieties that they could almost have dwelt there (going from shop to shop like bee from flower to flower), if they had but had a fountain of money that could not be drawn dry. I doubt not but a Mahomedan, who never expects other than sensual delights, would gladly have availed himself of that place and the treasures of it for his heaven, and have thought there was none like it." (Rev. Sam. Rolle.)

Among the few halls of the civic Companies that escaped the fire, there are two especially worthy of note—the hall of the Leather-sellers (Fig. 1711), a sumptuous specimen of internal domestic architecture of the age of Elizabeth; and the hall of the Barber-Surgeons (Fig. 1706), reminding us of the time when the pursuits of pharmacy and hair-cutting, surgery and the trimming of a beard, were considered to have some sort of practical connection with each other. The hall itself is one of the most charming little places, notwithstanding its antiquity, that London can boast of; nor need we be surprised at that, when we know Inigo Jones was concerned in its erection, and that it possesses the famous picture by Holbein (Figs. 1411) of the granting of the charter to the Company by Henry VIII. Holbein owed his favour at court to Sir Thomas More, in whom he found a most liberal patron, and in whose house at Chelsea he resided three years. More once invited Henry VIII. to his house, and had Holbein's best pictures displayed to advantage in the gallery. Henry, as Sir Thomas had expected, admired the pictures, and was then introduced to the painter, who was forthwith taken into the royal service, assigned a pension, and an apartment in White-hall, where the king was forming a collection of pictures. Nor was this all; the pictures Holbein painted for the king were paid for separately. The blood-stained tyrant thus, as in many other instances, evinced his possession of one redeeming quality—an appreciation of the fine arts. He had already sought, by munificent offers, to draw within his dominions the divine Raffaelle and Titian, but failed; and he was now only the more delighted to do all that a king might do, to honour the genius of Hans Holbein. One of the painter's tasks was a design for the magnificent gate-house which Henry built before his palace, opposite the entrance into the tilt-yard. There is a story told of Holbein and the king, in which Henry shows to more advantage than perhaps anywhere else. Holbein was occupied at his easel when a nobleman of high rank, who forcibly intruded upon him, so roused his ire that he actually had the temerity to thrust his lordship down stairs. Reflection immediately succeeding impulse, he sought the king, and informed him of what had happened. Presently came the nobleman with his complaint; which, but for Holbein's promptness, would have been nearly certain to have cost the painter his patron, perhaps his life. Henry defended the painter, and charged his accuser not to contrive or adopt any mode of revenge, on pain of his high displeasure, "You have not now to deal with Holbein," Henry sternly remarked, "but with me. Remember that of seven peasants I can make as many lords, but I cannot make one Holbein."

Merchant Tailors' Hall (Fig. 1709) is modern, the old one having been swept away, with nearly all the other buildings of the same kind, in the fire: we may not therefore look upon the actual edifice in which so many of our older monarchs and nobles have been feasted up to the time of Henry VII., who sat down "openly there in a gown of crimson velvet of the fashion " of a member. But the present building has its recollections too, nor do we know that they will yield in interest to those of its predecessor. It was in that hall that James I. was greeted with " great and pleasant variety of music of voices and instruments, and ingenious speeches;" and where to do him pleasure, such men as Ben Jonson assisted in the preparation of the poetical parts of the entertainment, and Dr. Bull

in the musical—the latter giving us, in perpetual remembrance of the occasion, the air of " God save the King." Mercers' Hall (Fig. 1710), of which Gresham was a member, is also modern. It stands upon a most interesting site. Here was the house of Gilbert Becket, a yeoman who whilst following his lord to the Holy Land during the Crusades, was taken prisoner by a Saracen emir, and confined in a dungeon. The emir had a daughter who saw and pitied the captive. Pity in this instance proved akin to love, and under the influence of these tender feelings she contrived to set him free. Gilbert returned to England, leaving his benefactress behind, pining in sorrow for his loss, which at last grew so insupportable that she determined to seek him through the world. She went to the nearest port, and embarked on the sea, the words " London" and "Gilbert" being all the directions she had to guide her. The first sufficed to convey her to the English capital; but when there she could only wander from street to street, repeating, with touching pathos, the other—" Gilbert !"—" Gilbert !" How the fond and single-hearted girl succeeded in finding Gilbert, the story sayeth not, but she did find him, and was rewarded for all her troubles—obtained the fruition of all her hopes. The yeoman welcomed her with tears of joy, had her immediately baptized (Fig 508), and was then united to her in marriage (Fig. 509): the son of the fair pagan and the yeoman was the far-famed Thomas-à-Becket.

In connection with these leading Companies, it will not be out of place here to state that the shopkeepers of London generally exposed their wares open to the street until about the reign of Queen Anne. The shops themselves were small and dark, in consequence of the overhanging upper stories. In some parts of London a few of these ancient depôts of metropolitan trade may still be traced. The old-clothes-shop of the present day will give a good notion of the sort of shop called a " frippery," as it existed in the time of the Plantagenets and Tudors; only the word " frippery" is hardly perhaps to be taken in the modern sense, but as applying to general clothing, often of a sufficiently substantial kind. Our engraving (Fig. 1718), of a print dated 1587, shows the shop entirely open at the front, a clothier at work, and garments hung upon lines for sale.

———

"Heaven be praised," says Malcolm, one of the historians of London, "that Old London was burnt!" and if his very unantiquarian enthusiasm in the cause of improved domestic arrangements ran away with his humanity and judgment, the remark still shows no less justly than forcibly the character of the streets and houses of the old city that were destroyed, and which were of course pretty much what they had been for centuries before. Holinshed admits that during the reign of Elizabeth, London had a very mean appearance in comparison with most foreign cities. The foreigners who came over with Philip of Spain, during the reign of Mary, described the houses as built with "sticks and dirt." But in the general movement of the nation in Elizabeth's time, architectural art was not left behind. On all sides highly picturesque and beautiful edifices were seen to rise. We need only refer in passing to Marylebone House (Fig. 1691)—the ancient Manor House, Vauxhall (Fig. 1687)—the house formerly standing at the corner of Chancery Lane (Fig. 1669)—the old Blue Boar, Holborn (Fig. 1690)—and Somerset House (Fig. 1671, that has been previously described): all, with the Exchange, belonging to the present period. As examples of the picturesque effect of a street in the olden time when seen under the most favourable aspect, we may call attention to the views of Southwark (Fig. 1661) and of Bucklersbury (Fig. 1715;) whils, ftor a more comprehensive view of London, as a whole, we turn to another engraving (Fig. 1705), where the point of sight is from the old Black Friars. With the inn we have named is connected one of those remarkable incidents which, in themselves apparently trifling, determine the fate of empires. When Charles I. was in the hands of the Scots, he endeavoured to take advantage of the then very peculiar aspect of affairs to make terms, secretly, with the different parties who stood disunited among themselves, but all banded against him. Among the rest he entered into secret negotiations with Cromwell; and had he been sincere, he might in all probability have saved his throne and life. It appears that one day, in the year 1649, when Lord Broghill was riding between Cromwell and Ireton, Cromwell said to him, that if the late king had followed his own mind, and had had trusty servants, he would have fooled them all; and that at one time they really intended to close with Charles. Broghill asked a question or two, to which Cromwell freely replied, saying, " The reason why we would once have closed with the king was this: we found that the Scots and the Presbyterians began to be more powerful than we;

1715.—"Bucklersbury in simple time."

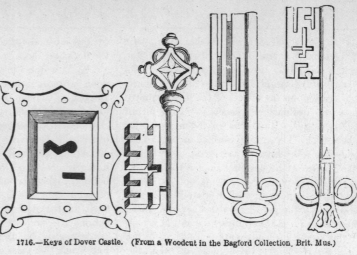

1716.—Keys of Dover Castle. (From a Woodcut in the Bagford Collection, Brit. Mus.)

1717.—Water-carrier

1718.—A Frippery.

1719.—Watchmen. (From Dekker.)

1722.—The Watch, with "cressets" and "beacons." (Grouped from Hollar.)

1720.—Miners' Standard Dish, Wirksworth, Derbyshire.

1721.—Conduit in West Cheap

1723.—"Lanthorn and a whole candle light! Hang out your lights! Hear!"

1724.—The Marching Watch.

1727.—Middle Temple Hall.

1728.—Lincoln's Inn Gateway.

1725.—Sir Edward Coke.

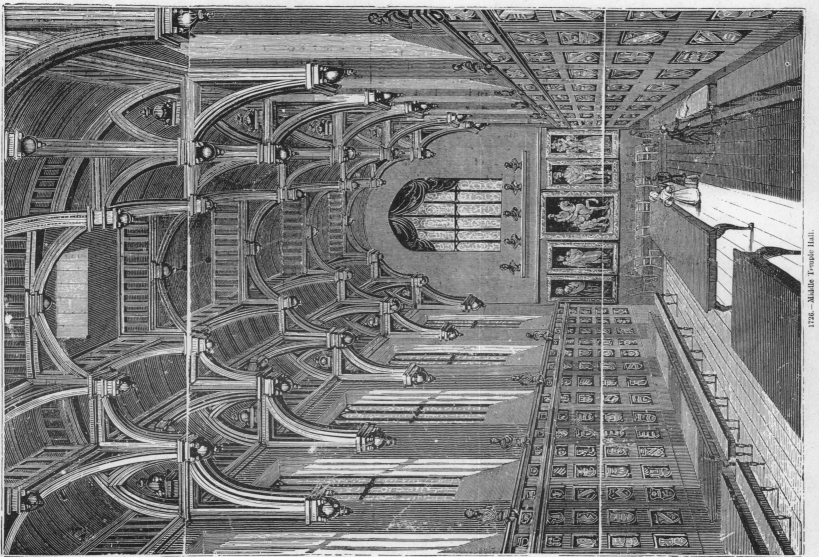

1726.—Middle Temple Hall.

No. 62.—Vol. II.

and if they had made up matters with the king, we should have been left in the lurch; therefore we thought it best to prevent them, by offering first to come in upon any reasonable conditions." Cromwell went on to say, that while he and his party were occupied with these thoughts, they received information from one of their spies, who was of the king's bedchamber, that their doom was decreed by Charles, as they might see, if they could only intercept a letter from the king to the queen, which letter was sealed up in the skirt of a saddle, and the bearer would be that night at the Blue Boar Inn, in Holborn, where he was to take horse for Dover. Accordingly, Cromwell, and Ireton, his son-in-law, disguised as troopers, with one trusty fellow with them, went to the Blue Boar, called for cans of beer, and continued drinking till the man with the saddle came in, when they seized the saddle, ripped up the skirts, and there found the letter. In it the king informed the queen that he was now courted by both factions—the Scotch Presbyterians and the army—and which bid fairest for him should have him; but he thought he should close with the Scots sooner than the other. In further confirmation of the duplicity of Charles, as brought to light by intercepted letters, we have Richardson's statement, to whom, and to Pope and Lord Marchmont, Lord Bolingbroke said, that Lord Oxford had often told him that he (Lord Oxford) had seen, and had had in his hands, an original letter that King Charles I. wrote to the queen, in answer to one of hers that had been intercepted, and then forwarded to him, wherein she had reproached him for having made those villains too great concessions. These concessions were chiefly, that Cromwell was to be Lieutenant of Ireland for life; that an army should be there kept, which should know no head but the lieutenant; and that he should have a Garter. In the reply of Charles to the queen, he said, she should leave *him* to manage, who was better informed of all circumstances than she could be; but she might be entirely easy as to whatever concessions he should make them; for that he should know in due time how to deal with the rogues, who, instead of a silken Garter, *should be fitted with a hempen cord.* This letter Lord Oxford said he had offered five hundred pounds for. It was this letter which was seized at the Blue Boar. Cromwell, as soon as he had read it, took horse and went to Windsor. It had determined Charles Stuart's fate.

West Smithfield has, from very early times, been celebrated for three especial uses—as a place of execution, of martial and festive show, and as a horse and cattle market. It was the chief scene of Protestant martyrdom; previous to which, its fires were occasionally lighted for the immolation of some unfortunate individual supposed to have been guilty of sorcery. Here the celebrated "Witch of Eye" was burned in the reign of Henry VI. Most of the Plantagenet kings held tournaments at Smithfield : and none were more gorgeous or striking than the seven days' feast held by Edward III., in honour of Alice Perrers, his worthless paramour, designated on this occasion "The Lady of the Sun." As early as 1174, when Fitz-Stephen wrote, Smithfield was celebrated as a horse-fair. He says, "Without one of the gates, in a certain plain field, on every Friday, unless it be a solemn festival, there was a great market for horses, whither earls, barons, knights, and citizens repair, to see and to purchase." Our cut (Fig. 1712) of Smithfield in the Elizabethan period, shows it then retained its celebrity for the sale of horses; and who knows not that the same characteristic still remains ?

The number of buildings erected in the course of the early part of Elizabeth's reign alarmed the government, and a proclamation was issued, forbidding the erection of any but houses of the highest class, within three miles of the city. Mandates of this nature are apt to excite a smile, seeing how small the London was that was to be thenceforth prevented from enlarging its boundaries, and seeing into how vast a thing the city has really swelled. But whilst we smile we may ask ourselves the question,—Since, in the nineteenth century, we are beginning to perceive that the let alone system of government is not by any means the perfection of government—and since, in reference to the very question before us, we are ourselves beginning to take very decided steps to check the evils found to result from leaving private cupidity or ignorance to build as they please—ought we not to inquire, whether our ancestors might not have had an inkling of the same truth that we now perceive, but without viewing, so clearly as we do, the true modes of carrying it into practical effect? In short, was it not that they interferred in a wrong way, rather than that they interferred at all, that made their legislation a nullity, and left it, though hardly with justice, a laughing-stock for those who only see their failure, and

do not care to inquire into its causes, or the true motives of those who failed?

The chief extension of London during the present period appears to have been westward, along the north bank of the Thames, where many of the nobility, as we have already seen, erected "fair and stately mansions," of which Northumberland House is now the last existing representative.

In 1532 an Act was passed for improving and paving the city. The streets of London are therein described as "very foul and full of pits and sloughs, very perilous and noyous, as well for all the king's subjects on horseback as on foot, with carriages." To add to the "perilous" character here spoken of, the streets were narrow and crooked, rendered gloomy by day by the projecting upper stories and confined space, and perfect pits of darkness by night, relieved only by casual lights in the houses, or by the passing torches or cresset lights that attended the progress of passengers of consequence. Then the accommodations *in* the houses were often as bad as the accommodations of the streets without. Picturesque effect in construction was constantly obtained at the sacrifice of health and safety. Thatched roofs, and plaster and timber materials, were favourable to fire, as the denseness of the buildings, and the pent-up rooms, into which the air could hardly penetrate, and where gloom and dirt prevailed, were favourable to disease ; and we see the consequences of such arrangements in the continually-recurring conflagrations that formed one of the popular objections to a residence in London—and in the fearful "plague," now happily known no more in the metropolis that was formerly seldom free from its ravages. The change that has taken place in respect to both these destructive calamities is calculated to encourage many of the best hopes of philanthropists as to the removal of the evils that still exist ; fever, for instance, itself a "plague" of the most fearful character ; but being more regular and less obtrusive in its opera tions, though scarcely less fatal *on the whole,* does not excite half the attention that a plague ever commanded.

As, in tracing Gresham's metropolitan labours, we are naturally pleased to see that even thus early the fruits of commerce were made subservient to still higher tastes and enjoyments than the mere promotion of fresh commerce, so, in glancing over the chief provincial towns of England, we see that there too liberality and art were found in connection with the pursuits of the workshop, the counter, and the desk. Would we could perceive the corporations of the present day beautifying their towns, and promoting the tastes of their citizens, by the erection of such structures as the halls and market-crosses of the fifteenth and sixteenth centuries! And for what objects were they erected? Why, in some cases, these beautiful little temples, as they almost deserve to be called, sprang up in the midst of our towns merely for the shelter and accommodation of "poor market-folks, to stand dry when rain cometh" (Leland). And in them were admirably combined utility, benevolence, and ornament. Cobbett, speaking of Malmesbury in his 'Rural Rides,' says, "There is a market-cross in this town, the sight of which is worth a journey of hundreds of miles to see." (Fig. 1663.) It is an octagon, of stone, with flying buttresses. There is appended to it a decorated turret, also octagonal, with a niche on each side, filled with figures in basso-relievo. "The men of the town made this piece of work," says Leland, writing in the reign of Henry VIII., "*in hominum memoriâ*"—that is to say, within the memory of man. Cobbett is scarcely less enthusiastic about the situation of the town, than the particular piece of architecture contained in it, that so struck his fancy. He says, "This town, though it has nothing particularly engaging in itself, stands upon one of the prettiest spots that can be imagined. Besides the river Avon, which I went down, in the south-east part of the country, here is another river Avon, which runs down to Bath, and two branches or sources of which meet here. There is a pretty ridge of ground, the base of which is a mile, or a mile and a half, wide. On each side of this ridge, a branch of the river runs down, through a flat of very fine meadows. The town and the beautiful remains of the famous old abbey stand on the rounded spot which terminates this ridge; and just below, nearly close to the town, the two branches of the river meet, and then they begin to be called the Avon. The land round about is excellent, and of a great variety of forms. The trees are lofty and fine : so that, what with the water, the meadows, the fine cattle and sheep—and, as I hear, the absence of hard-pinching poverty— this is a very pleasant place."

Chichester Market Cross is still more beautiful than that of Malmesbury ; indeed, Mr. Britton considers it to be "the most enriched and beautiful example of this class of buildings in England ;" and if the reader will turn to our engraving (Fig. 1660), he will, we think, give every credit to this judgment, for certainly it is difficult to imagine anything of the kind *more* rich or more beautiful. The form is an octagon. There is a large central column, from which numerous bold ribs spring upward to the vaulted roof. The walls are panelled, and have a parapet, pinnacles, and flying buttresses, and the whole is sustained on eight pier buttresses. The cross was erected by Bishop Story near the close of the 15th century. There are shields attached to the buttresses, on which his arms are impaled with those of his sovereign.

Many of our old English towns, we have had occasion elsewhere to remark, had their origin in religious establishments, founded by the early teachers of Christianity. Evesham, in Worcestershire, is one example of this religious creation, for which we are indebted to St. Egwin, bishop of the Wicci, in the time of the Anglo-Saxons. An ancient legendary life of St. Egwin has a curious story relative to the foundation of St. Egwin's church. In the territory of the Wicci was a place called Hetheholme—wild—solitary—utterly destitute of cultivation—overgrown with brambles, and wrapped continually in the vapours exhaled from the marshy soil. St. Egwin obtained a gift of this unpromising place from Ethelred, King of the Mercians. A number of swine were kept by Egwin in the forest, for his own use and for that of his religious associates. One of the four swineherds appointed to look after those " pigs of the servants of God " going once too far into the woods, lost a pig which had hid itself in the thickets. While he was looking after it, he met three glorious virgins, all shining brightly as the sun, holding in their hands a beautiful book, and dancing. The swineherd turned pale with fear and amazement, and hastened home to his master, who, delighted at the vision, went to the wood, and beheld the fair celestials whilst he was in the act of offering up his prayers. Our readers will readily anticipate that the interview was commemorated by the erection of the church. The name of Evesham or Eovesham was derived from the swineherd's name, Eoves. The inmates of the abbey attached to the church of St. Egwin did not always confine themselves rigidly to rules of self-mortification. An abbot who succeeded in 1213 was very unpopular for keeping the brethren many days on dry bread, and giving them bad small beer, instead of " the jolly good ale and old," which in old song our monks are said to have so well loved. The feast of the Holy Trinity was a very blithe time in Evesham Abbey and town. Then every monk had his capon and his quart of wine—the prior, his two capons and half-flagon of wine—the abbot, his three capons and whole flagon. When a death took place, the deceased did not lose his general allowance for a whole year afterwards, for though it could no longer comfort his body, it was considered that it might benefit his soul, by bestowing it on some poor person. And the thought, we are sure, carried a blessing with it, though not perhaps exactly in the way supposed.

The chief relics of the Abbey are the Abbot's Tower, and a gateway that formerly led to the Chapter House; the latter now opening upon a pleasant scene,—the cultivated land let out in allotments to the poor and industrious people of the town, and the former showing to us in the distance the church of Bengeworth (Figs. 1625, 1624). The Abbot's Tower, begun in 1533 by Abbot Clement Lichfield, is exceedingly beautiful, with arches most gracefully turned and richly wrought, the summit finished with eight pinnacles springing from an open embattled parapet. Its height is 110 feet, and this is all that remains of the once sumptuous house which had its sixteen altars, its one hundred and sixty four gilded pillars, its chapter-house, cloisters, refectory, dormitory, buttery, treasury, almonry, granary, and storehouse, in addition to domestic buildings suitable for the accommodation of a family of some eighty-nine monks, with almost as many servants to wait upon them.

The town (Fig. 1622) stands on the pleasant banks of the ever-memorable river Avon. It has two principal streets, wide, and clean, and cheerful ; and some very picturesque-looking antique houses (Fig. 1682). The vale of Evesham boasts a rich, luxuriant soil ; and the extensive gardens near the town, which supply Evesham and other neighbouring towns and villages with fruit and vegetables, greatly enhance the beauty of the place. The corporation long possessed the power of trying and executing for all capital offences, except high treason. Even as late as 1740, a woman was burned in the town for petty treason.

The Guildhall of Chichester (engraved in page 296 of our first volume) affords a striking commentary upon the changes that the country has experienced. It was at first part of a castle built in the feudal days by Hugh de Montgomery, who was created Earl of Chichester and Arundel by the Conqueror. Next the castle

became a convent ; the fourth Earl of Arundel having given it to the Grey Friars in 1233. Lastly, at the dissolution, Henry VIII. granted the whole to the mayor and corporation, who kept the chapel of the Grey Friars for their Guildhall, and let the remainder on lease. Two other buildings may be briefly dismissed : the old Town Hall of Oxford (Fig. 1688), burnt down at Christmas, 1824, and the exquisitely beautiful Cross of Coventry (Fig. 1664), which reminds us that the inhabitants of Coventry in the last century had not even the taste to admire what their forefathers had the liberality and taste to build, and so caused one of the finest pieces of architecture in the kingdom to be pulled down.

A group of country mansions and manor-houses, some of them suggesting recollections of no ordinary nature, may here engage our attention. Gray the poet opens his humorous descriptive poem, ' The Long Story,' with these spirited verses :—

> In Britain's isle, no matter where,
>   An ancient pile of building stands ;
> The Huntingdons and Hattons there
>   Employed the power of fairy hands—
>
> To raise the ceiling's fretted height,
>   Each panel in achievements clothing,
> Rich windows that exclude the light,
>   And passages that lead to nothing.
>
> Full oft within the spacious walls,
>   When he had fifty winters o'er him,
> My grave Lord-Keeper led the brawls ;
>   The seals and maces danced before him.
>
> His bushy beard, and shoe-strings green,
>   His high-crowned hat and satin doublet,
> Moved the stout heart of England's queen,
>   Though Pope and Spaniard could not trouble it.

The grave Lord-Keeper here alluded to was Lord Chancellor Hatton, who resided in the fine old manor-house of Stoke Pogis, Buckinghamshire (Fig. 1689), where he was succeeded by Lord Chief Justice Coke, who entertained Queen Elizabeth in 1601 ; on which occasion he presented her with jewels upwards of a thousand pounds in value. The ancient pile that Gray describes was in great part taken down in 1789. What remains is of a delightfully picturesque character, and is seen rising from amidst groups of the most charming masses of green and bright foliage. There is still left the wide old kitchen, and a fire-place broad enough for the roasting of an ox, with heraldic sculpture about it. The manor and manor-house were sold by the Cobhams in the last century to William Penn, the son, we presume, of the eminent quaker. Lady Cobham inhabited it when Gray lived at his mother's cottage, about half a mile distant. The verses we have quoted arose from a visit which two ladies residing at the Manor-house paid him at the cottage. Gray's admirable mother now lies in Stoke churchyard, with his aunt, who had lived with her, and shared the toils by which she was enabled to give her son a learned education. Gray placed over his aunt a plain flat stone with an unpretending epitaph ; and writing to his mother in her affliction, he says, " However you may deplore your own loss, yet think that she is at last easy and happy." He himself now sleeps as easily and happily, and in the same churchyard, and by his mother's side, according to his particular desire. It is a solemn and secluded place, shadowed with funereal-looking trees, as yew, cypress, and dark pine.

> Hark how the sacred calm that breathes around
>   Bids every fierce tumultuous passion cease ;
> In still small accents whispering from the ground
>   A grateful earnest of eternal peace.

It is said, and with very much probability, that this was the scene of the ' Elegy written in a Country Churchyard.' The ' ivy mantled tower,' where

> The moping owl does to the moon complain
> Of such as, wandering near her secret bower,
> Molest her ancient, solitary reign,

aptly applies to the tower of Stoke Church, a most venerable structure. The entrance is a massive wooden porch. The late Mr. John Penn, of Stoke Park, a descendant of the Penns of Pennsylvania, erected a monument to Gray, near the churchyard, in a garden. Lines from the ' Elegy ' and from the ' Ode on a distant Prospect of Eton College ' are inscribed on its four sides.

Hulme Hall, Lancashire (Fig. 1672), may be looked on as a fair specimen of the very numerous timber-houses that form so conspicuous a class in the domestic architecture of Elizabeth's time. And most picturesque buildings they were, with their gable

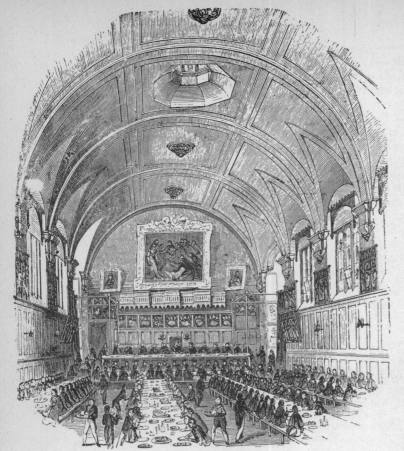

1729.—Lincoln's 'nn Hall.

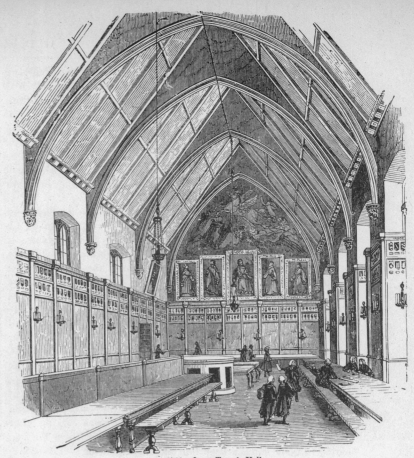

1730.—Inner Temple Hall.

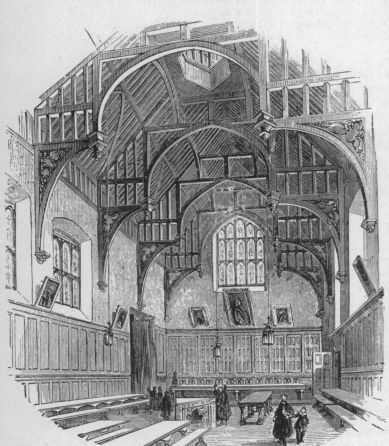

1731.—Gray's Inn Hall.

1733.—The Whirligig.

1732.—Clock at Hampton Court.

1734.— Man and Woman in Stocks.

"A stockes to staye sure and safely detayne
Lazy, lewd leuterers that lawes do offend." (Harman's 'Caveat,' &c.

1735.—The Brank.

1736.- Genings and Blunt.

HALL AT OCKWELLS, BERKSHIRE.

WHITEHALL CHAPEL.

MONUMENT OF LORD BACON

IN ST. MICHAEL'S CHURCH, NEAR ST. ALBANS.

STATUE OF CHARLES I. AT CHARING CROSS.

ST. PAUL'S CATHEDRAL—LOOKING WEST.

ST. STEPHEN'S, WALBROOK.

MILTON'S MONUMENT IN ST. GILES'S CHURCH, CRIPPLEGATE.

KING'S COLLEGE CHAPEL. CAMBRIDGE.

1737

1738.—Spenser.

1741.—Drayton.

1740.—Samuel Daniel

1739.—Spenser.

1742.—Jonson

1743.—John Taylor.

1744.—George Chapman.

109

roofs, and numerous projections, their carvings and their pinnacles. Hulme Hall no longer exists. It was pulled down a short time since. Our engraving was taken just before its demolition. The place belonged to the family of Prestwick from the middle of the fifteenth to about the middle of the seventeenth century. A curious mystery may be said still to attach to the spot. The dowager Lady Prestwick, during the Civil War, encouraged her son, who belonged to the Royal party—but apparently had been wavering in his allegiance on account of pecuniary difficulties—to remain firm to the Royalist cause, saying she had treasure to supply him with. It was supposed she referred to some hidden stores about Hulme. But when she was dying she was speechless, and so, if she had a secret of the nature supposed, it was buried with her. Nothing remarkable has since been discovered at Hulme.

The bountiful and "home-keeping" country gentlemen of good estate in Elizabeth's time may be fitly represented by the "King of the Peak," as Sir George Vernon—the last male heir of the Vernon family in Derbyshire who inherited the manor of Haddon—was named by his country neighbours. He died in the seventh year of Queen Elizabeth's reign. His mansion, Haddon Hall, now the seat of the Duke of Rutland, was disposed around two irregular courts, and consisted of various suites of apartments, which were all completed nearly as we now behold them, in the reign of Henry VIII. The hospitable feasts of the King of the Peak would be held in the Hall (Fig. 1665), where there is a raised floor at the upper end, and two side galleries supported on pillars. The amount of good cheer that was in requisition for the table may be readily imagined, when we look at the magnitude of the culinary furniture in the kitchen—the two vast fire places—the irons for sustaining a surprising number of spits—and the enormous chopping-blocks.

The hospitality of Haddon Hall has been frequently revived in the ancient spirit since Sir George Vernon died. The first Duke of Rutland kept seven score servants here, and his twelve days' feasts at Christmas will be long remembered. Two hundred couple have danced in the Long gallery within the present century. That gallery occupies the whole south side of the second court, and is floored with oak planks, said to have been cut out of a single tree which once grew in the garden. It is wainscoted also with curiously carved oak. But Haddon, like many other magnificent abodes, appears, on close examination, evidently built when *comfort* was not a peculiarity of art in household construction. The doors are very rudely contrived, except when picturesque effect is the object; few fit at all close, and their fastenings are nothing better than wooden bolts, clumsy bars, or iron hasps. To conceal these defects, and exclude draughts of air, tapestry was put up, which had to be lifted in order to pass in or out; and when it was necessary to hold back these hangings, there were great iron hooks fixed for the purpose. All the principal rooms, except the gallery, were hung with loose arras, and their doors were concealed behind.

The universal rage for building in the sixteenth century (felt by no one more than Henry VIII., who built, improved, or completed no less than ten palaces) caused a rapid development of the new style then in process of formation—the Tudor-Gothic. This style was in effect (as has been shown more fully in the previous period) the latest form of the ecclesiastical Gothic, but modified by the necessities and proprieties of a domestic residence. Thus, more light was required for a room than for the interior of a chapel or a church; so the fronts of houses became one vast expanse of glass. "You shall have sometimes fair houses so full of glass, that one cannot tell where to come to be out of the sun or cold." (Bacon.) Chimneys of all shapes and sizes, and some of them exceedingly ornamental (Fig. 1673), sprang up. But in Elizabeth's time a new element came into operation. Italian art was introduced. Henry VIII., in a spirit of rivalry with Francis of France, had sought to bring foreign artists to England; and though Raffaelle and Titian declined the invitation, other eminent men from different parts did come; among them Holbein, the universal artist. Many of the chief buildings erected after the middle of the sixteenth century show the influence of the Italian architects.

Somerset House (Fig. 1671), already noticed, was built by John of Padua, and became, as the first Italian edifice erected in England, an example for others to follow. But the English architects did not servilely copy them or any other works. They preserved some of their own Tudor-Gothic tastes; they admired, and therefore added, something from the Italian; they also admired, and therefore also borrowed from Holbein and the German and Flemish schools, and the result was, unquestionably, magnificence.

As presenting, generally, a notion of the plan of Elizabethan mansions of the first rank, Buckhurst House, Sussex (Fig. 1674), may be usefully studied. This was built about 1560 by the author

of the glorious poetical Induction to the Mirror for Magistrates Lord Buckhurst, afterwards Lord Treasurer and Earl of Dorset. We regret to say, not only for the sake of the building, but for the associations connected with its author, that Buckhurst has long since disappeared. But magnificent as were these great mansions in their size, arrangement, and general aspect, there was little even in them that would harmonize with our notions of what the interiors should be to correspond with such exteriors.

Walpole justly observes, with regard to the mansions of the sixteenth century, "Space and vastness seem to have made their whole ideas of grandeur; the palaces of the memorable Countess of Shrewsbury are exactly in this style. The apartments are lofty and enormous, and they knew not how to furnish them. Pictures, had they had good ones, would have been lost in chambers of such height: tapestry, their chief moveable, was not commonly perfect enough to be real magnificence. Fretted ceilings, graceful mouldings of windows, and painted glass, the ornaments of the preceding age, were fallen into disuse. Immense lights, composed of bad glass, in diamond panes, cast an air of poverty over their most costly apartments."

Hardwick, in Derbyshire, between Chesterfield and Mansfield, the property of the Duke of Devonshire, is one of the "palaces of the memorable Countess of Shrewsbury" here referred to. A strange story is told in explanation of this lady's building propensities. A tradition, recorded by Walpole, says the Countess was told by a fortune-teller that she should not die whilst she continued building; so she went on, erecting mansion after mansion, until her proceedings were arrested one winter by a hard frost, which rendered the workmen unable to continue their labours, and then she died. Two or three portraits of the Countess, or as she is more popularly called, Bess of Hardwick, are to be found here. The gallery (Fig. 1670) is of the amazing extent of 195 feet, and contains some interesting pictures; among them one of Mary Queen of Scots, whose residence as a prisoner in the mansion has given to it a still higher interest than is attached to the well-known Countess its founder. Mary spent a considerable portion of her long nineteen years of imprisonment at Hardwick, during which time she occupied some of her dreary hours by embroidering the black velvet chair-covers that are still preserved in the mansion. Indeed, one of the most delightful features of the place is its perfectly Elizabethan character. Everything remains unaltered from the days of the two queens—the oppressor and the oppressed. Mrs. Radcliffe's description of the place, as she saw it in the close of the last century, remains, we believe, true to the letter at present. "The second floor," she writes, "is that which gives its chief interest to the edifice, as nearly all the apartments were allotted to Mary (some of them for state-purposes); and the furniture is known, by other proofs than its appearance, to remain as she left it. The chief room, or that of audience, is of uncommon loftiness; and strikes by its grandeur, before the veneration and tenderness arise, which its antiquities and the plainly-told tale of the sufferings they witnessed excite. The walls, which are covered to a considerable height with tapestry, are painted above with historical groups. The chairs are of black velvet, which is nearly concealed by a raised needle-work of gold, silver, and colours, that mingle with surprising richness, and remain in fresh preservation. The upper end of the room is distinguished by a lofty canopy of the same materials, and by steps which support two chairs. In front of the canopy is a carpeted table, below which the room breaks into a spacious recess, where a few articles of furniture are deposited, used by Mary: the curtains are of gold tissue, but in so tattered a condition that its original texture can hardly be perceived; this, and the chairs which accompany it, are supposed to be much earlier than Mary's time. A short passage leads from the state-apartment to her own chamber, a small room, overlooked from the passage by a window, which enabled her attendants to know that she was contriving no means of escape through the others into the court. The bed and chairs of this room are of black velvet embroidered by herself; the toilet of gold tissue; all more decayed than worn, and probably used only towards the conclusion of her imprisonment here, when she was removed from some better apartment in which the ancient bed, now in the state-room, had been placed."

"Sir Francis Willoughby," says Walpole, "at great expense, in a foolish display of his wealth, built a magnificent and most elegant house, with a fine prospect." The house here referred to is Woollaton Hall, Nottinghamshire (Fig. 1667), erected from the design of John Thorpe, one of the most eminent architects of his day. The interior is rich in works of art. Our space will only allow us to mention a single picture—a portrait of Sir Hugh Willoughby, who fell a victim to that ardent love of adventure which so characterised the period. He fitted out three ships at the private expense of a society of merchants, who supported him in the enterprise; and set out, beguiled by that ignis fatuus, or rather, as we might say, by those *northern lights*, which still tempt men to subject themselves to the most terrible extremes of cold, and privation, and danger, in the hope of discovering a north-east passage. Having proceeded so far as Spitzbergen, the Edward Bonaventure, commanded by Captain Richard Chancellor, was separated from the other vessels by a gale; and soon after, Sir Hugh discovered land. He was unable to set foot upon it; but the place is supposed to have been either the coast of Nova Zembla, or the island of Kolgen. Sailing thence westward they came to the mouth of the river Arzina, in Russian Lapland. "This haven," says a journal of the expedition, printed by Hakluyt, and which subsequently found its way to England after the writer had perished, "runneth into the main about two leagues, and is in breadth half a league, wherein are very many seal-fishes and other great fishes: and upon the main we saw bears, great deer, foxes, with divers strange beasts; as ellans and such others, which were to us unknown, and also wonderful. There remaining in this haven the space of a sevennight, seeing the year far spent, and also very evil weather, as frost, snow, and hail, as though it had been the depth of winter, we thought it best to winter there. Wherefore we sent out three men south-south-west to search if they could find people, who went three days' journey, but could find none. After that we sent other three westward four days' journey, which also returned without finding any people. Then sent we three men south-east three days' journey, who in like sort returned without finding of people or any similitude of habitation."

Thus far we follow their proceedings to the month of October. Next, we learn from a will of Gabriel Willoughby, a kinsman of Sir Hugh, which also found its way to England (it is supposed through the Russians), that some at least of the party were alive in January, 1554; lastly, we discover from Anthony Jenkinson's account of a voyage to Russia in 1558, that the whole company had perished. Chancellor's ship, which had lost sight of the others, escaped for a time, but on its return towards England was wrecked, and all but a few seamen drowned. So that of the whole expedition, only a few of the crew of this one ship returned in safety. Whether it was through a want of fuel alone, or whether it was from being attacked, as has been supposed, with the scurvy, at the same time that they were suffering from other privations, that Sir Hugh and his men perished, we have no means of discovering. From the period of their entering the mouth of the Arzina—that 'harbour of death"—and sending out their exploring parties, all is wrapped in impenetrable obscurity. The poet of the 'Seasons,' in his Winter, gives the most probable, as well as the most poetically tragical explanation, making due allowances of course for the artistical treatment of the subject that was necessary to his purpose.

> Miserable they!
> Who, here entangled in the gathering ice,
> Take their last look of the descending sun;
> While, full of death, and fierce with tenfold frost,
> The long, long night, incumbent o'er their heads,
> Falls horrible. Such was the Briton's fate,
> As with first prow (what have not Britons dar'd?)
> He for the passage sought, attempted since
> So much in vain, and seeming to be shut
> By jealous Nature with eternal bars.
> In these fell regions, in Arzina caught,
> And to the stony deep his idle ship
> Immediate seal'd, he with his hapless crew,
> Each full exerted at his several task,
> Froze into statues; to the cordage glued
> The sailor, and the pilot to the helm.

Of old castles, as well as old churches, we take our leave in the present period. Their uses had passed away. Many of those built in imitation, to a certain extent, of the ancient castellated style, were but superficial imitations, calculated to please the still lingering military tastes of the owners, but utterly unsuited for the real wear and tear of military defence. Indeed, Elizabeth, as well as her father, would no doubt like to have seen the man who would have ventured to have erected a real stronghold in her time. Power enough was reserved for the aristocracy, but it was to be henceforth the power of station and wealth only, whether exercised in public or in private life. So, although castles were erected, and strong ones too, no subjects were the builders. There were to be defences provided, not to facilitate internal warfare, but as a protection from foreign aggression. Henry VIII. caused a chain of fortresses to be raised for the protection of the northern and

eastern coasts—as Sandown (Fig. 1460), and others. To Elizabeth we owe the commencement of the castle named after herself at Jersey (Fig. 1535), in which Clarendon resided for two years, and wrote a large portion of his 'History of the Rebellion.' Mount Orgueil (Fig. 1536), also in Jersey, commandingly situated on a rocky headland that projects forward into the sea, is famous as the prison of Prynne, and the residence of Charles II. during a part of his exile. Upnor Castle (Fig. 1539), on the Medway, a little below Chatham—now completely in ruins—is distinguished as being one of the last, if not the very last, of those places of defence that were built on the old principles of fortification. Upnor is also distinguished by the fact that it fulfilled, on one important occasion, all that could ever have been hoped from it. The Dutch, under De Ruyter, in 1667, appeared suddenly at the mouth of the Thames, and Van Ghent, the vice-admiral, was despatched with seventeen lighter ships and eight fire-ships, to sail up the Medway. The port of Sheerness was taken, the stores destroyed, and again the Dutch moved on. Monk, Duke of Albemarle, made every disposition that the suddenness of the attack permitted. He sunk several vessels in the channel of the river, and drew a chain across; behind which he placed three large men-of-war, that had been recently taken from the Dutch. Van Ghent, however, swept on, favoured by wind and tide, broke the chain, and forced his way between the three ships, and then, leaving them in one tremendous blaze of fire, again advanced, with six men-of-war and five fire-ships, until he reached Upnor Castle. The gross neglects of this time of corruption prevented the valour of the English sailors being of use to their country. Upnor could only make a feeble resistance; and it was more from good luck than skill or courage in the defenders of their country that Van Ghent soon retreated. On his way back he burnt three ships, one of them commanded by Captain Douglas, who, in the general confusion arising from the unexpectedness of the attack, had received no orders to retire. So there he stayed, conscious that his destruction was inevitable. "It shall never be said that a Douglas quitted his post without orders," were the last words uttered by him. Soon after, ship, captain, and crew all perished.

We cannot better take leave of the general subject of castles, than with a few words upon a fortress that formed a most perfect example of the class in all its genuine strength, and sternness, and inconvenience for residence, and which, to the regret of those who like to have something better than mere descriptions of antiquity to rely upon, has been recently much damaged by fire. Naworth (Fig. 1459) stood on the edge of a ravine, had walls of enormous thickness, and was altogether in the style of a castle of the fourteenth century; when all such works were built with the expectation that occasions might arise to test their strength, and with more than expectation—the certainty—where castles like Naworth were concerned. To the strength of wall, and narrowness of window, that marked the exterior of such places, must be added, in order to combine their chief characteristics, the dungeons within for prisoners, and the fire-places of the hall, which were really of almost incredible dimensions. That of Naworth was seventeen feet broad. Scott has made the dungeons of the castle familiar to us. William of Deloraine, in the 'Lay of the Last Minstrel,' says—

> And when I lay in dungeon dark
> Of Naworth Castle long months three,
> Till ransomed for a thousand mark,
> Dark Musgrave! it was long of thee.

The chief associations of Naworth are those connected with "Belted Will." The nobleman thus popularly designated was the son of Thomas, fourth Duke of Norfolk, executed by Elizabeth, grandson of the poet Surrey, executed or murdered by Henry VIII., and brother of the Lady Berkeley that we have so recently mentioned as the unsuccessful petitioner to Elizabeth when the queen was on her way to Bristol. William Howard would have fared but ill had his fortunes entirely depended upon Elizabeth, who took and kept possession of his father's estates. But, in his fifteenth year, he was married to his father's ward, Lady Elizabeth Dacre, who brought him Naworth, and other large possessions, and thus in essentials restored him to the position of which he had been deprived. This marriage—so convenient—and between parties who were afterwards accustomed to say they could not at the time of their union "make above twenty-five years both together,"—could hardly have been expected to turn out also a happy one; but it did, and eminently so. Their prospects, it is true, were for a time clouded by an unjust claim to the estates; and, when that was legally overthrown, by Elizabeth's still more disgracefully unjust conduct in keeping them out of the rights solemnly awarded

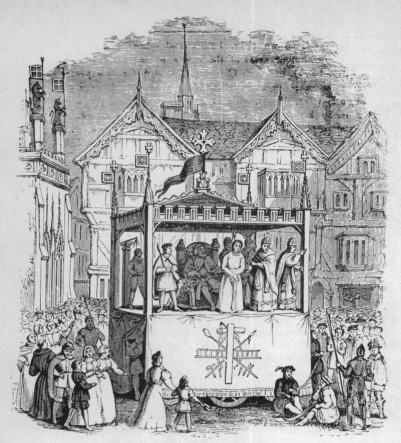

1745.—Performance of a Dramatic Mystery at Coventry.

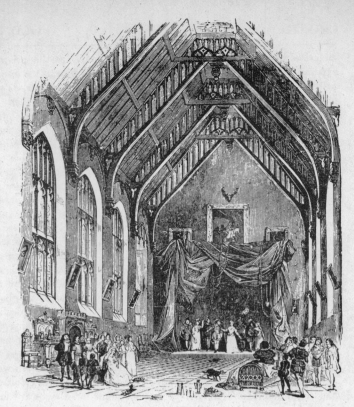

1746.—Itinerant Players

1747.—The Falcon Tavern

1748.—The Globe Theatre, Bankside

1749.—The Paris Garden Theatre, Southwark.

1750.—Hall of the Middle Temple.

1751. — Portraits of Shakspere.

1753.—The Bailiff's Play.

1754.—The Globe Theatre.

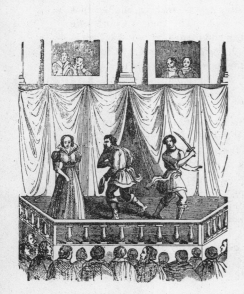

1752.—View of the old Stage and Balcony.

1756ª.—Court Fool

1755.—Richard Burbage.

to them by the law. And she robbed them in the end of 10,000*l.* before she would consent to grant them their own. That was in the year 1601. Soon after she died; and then the fortunes of the Howards brightened. The son of Mary did not forget what the Duke of Norfolk and his children had suffered for Mary's sake. The elder brother's son, Thomas Howard (the collector of the famous marbles), was restored to all that had been lost, excepting only the ducal title; and William Howard was appointed to a post of honour in his own native county—the wardenship of the marches. It was in this position that his energetic—probably severe—measures obtained for him so dreaded a name that the Scottish mothers are said to have been accustomed to frighten their children with it. It is but right to observe that the constant incursions of the borderers from one country into the other had become just that kind of abominable nuisance, that every honest and sensible man in either country must have ardently desired to see put down. The causes in which border warfare had originated—hostility between England and Scotland—had passed away; and the whole business, and the actors in it, had become nothing better than so much robbery by so many banditti. So it was a conclusive day's work that caused any moss-troopers to be seized by the officers of Belted Will. The fact that they were moss-troopers was all that had to be proved, and they were then immediately sent off to Carlisle—the place where, as Fuller says, "the officer always does his work by daylight;" or, if that were inconvenient, why there was a grove of tall oaks in the vicinity of the castle, and there, after the fashion of Le Petit André in 'Quentin Durward,' their moss-trooping was brought to a close. A somewhat awful story is told, in connection with this judicial expedition, which we must hope is not strictly true, though it sounds likely enough. Belted Will was a scholar, and devotedly fond of his books. One day, when he was intently engaged with some favourite author, a trooper hastily came to him to report that a man of uncertain character from the Scottish border had been captured, and desired to know what they should do with him. Lord William, angry at the interruption, exclaimed, "Hang him, in the devil's name!" Soon after, however, he proposed to inquire into the case, when he found that the unfortunate captive had been hung out of hand, in literal obedience to the orders he had given. We naturally feel curious as to the choice of books by such a student. It appears that Homer's Iliad, Shakspere's Plays, and Purchas's Pilgrim, with the works of Camden, Speed, and Raleigh, were among the contents of Belted Will's library. One book had the autograph of the venerable Bishop of Rochester, Fisher; given by him, probably, to a member of the Howard family. The contents of the castle at the time of its destruction were very varied, and—in an historical and antiquarian sense—valuable. The most attractive of all the curiosities was the belt, from which the Lord of the Marches derived his popular cognomen. Scott thus describes his appearance:—

> Costly his garb, his Flemish ruff
> Fell o'er his doublet shaped of buff,
> With satin slashed and lined;
> Tawny his boot, and gold his spur:
> His cloak was all of Poland fur;
> His hose with silver twined;
> His Bilboa blade, by marchmen felt,
> Hung in a broad and studded belt;
> Hence in rude phrase, the borderers still
> Called noble Howard, Belted Will.

The belt in question was of foreign manufacture, studded over with pieces of metal, so as to form a rhyming German distich, that expressed the admonitory truth to the wearer—powerful as he might be, there was One still more powerful.

Some witty, but, we believe, unknown writer, has said in reference to the cognizance of the Inner Temple—a winged horse, and of the Middle Temple—a lamb:—

> As by the Templars' haunts you go,
> The Horse and Lamb displayed,
> In emblematic figures, show
> The merits of their trade.
>
> That clients may infer from thence
> How just is their profession;
> The lamb sets forth their innocence,
> The horse their expedition!
>
> O, happy Britons, happy isle!
> Let foreign nations say;
> Where you get justice without guile,
> And law without delay!

Another writer, professing to reply to this, has, with equal wit, enforced the same lesson, in a different manner:—

> Deluded men! their holds forego,
> Nor trust such cunning elves;
> These artful emblems tend to show
> Their clients, not themselves.
>
> 'T is all a trick, these all are shams
> By which they mean to cheat you;
> But have a care, for you're the lambs,
> And they the wolves that eat you.
>
> Nor let the thoughts of no delay
> To these their courts misguide you;
> 'T is you 're the showy horse—and they
> The jockeys that will ride you!

Among the "haunts" here referred to, the part called the Temple Garden is at once the most interesting and the best known. "It is, indeed, the most elegant spot in the metropolis," observes Charles Lamb,—a partial judge; but that very partiality, which made it *his* favourite "haunt," adds a new charm to the Temple Gardens, to all the admirers of "Elia." Yet in many respects the place is worthy of the lively attachment which he all his life expressed for it. The neighbourhood, even in its least attractive portions, is classic ground. On the one hand is Whitefriars, the "Alsatia" of our older writers, and in which are laid some of the most thrilling scenes of the 'Fortunes of Nigel.' On the other hand are the localities rendered memorable by the misfortunes of the Earl of Essex. The "Silent Highway" glides on before. Thousands of busy chirping sparrows flutter about the old trees by the river side, reminding one of the rookery introduced in Queen Anne's time by Sir Edward Northey, of which colonization Mr. Leigh Hunt remarks,—"It was a pleasant thought; supposing that the colonists had no objection. The rook is a grave, legal bird, both in his coat and habits: living in communities, yet to himself, and strongly addicted to discussions of *meum* and *tuum*." As one walks here, varied and curious are the pictures that arise to the imagination of the long line of generations that have delighted to wander in the precincts of the Temple. Here have been exhibited all costumes, from the imposing robes and armour of the Knights Templars, and the rich vesture of the lordly priest, down to the cocked-hat and ruffles, satin small-clothes, and silk stockings of the lawyers of the reign of George the Third; who at times, casting professional gravities aside, would here laugh and discourse with all the gaiety of heart of school-boys released from their tasks. Shakspere, above all, has immortalized the Temple Garden by making it the scene of the origin of the factions of York and Lancaster—the place where the red and white roses were first plucked and worn as badges of the great houses that during so many years kept England in a flame.

Stow, writing in the reign of Elizabeth, describes the Inns of Court and Chancery at that time as "a whole university of students, practisers, or pleaders, and judges of the laws of this realm, not living on common stipends, as in the other universities it is for the most part done, but of their own private maintenance, as being altogether fed either by their places or practice, or otherwise by their proper revenues, or exhibition of parent and friends: for the younger sort are either gentlemen, or sons of gentlemen, or of other most wealthy persons. Of these houses there may be at this day fourteen in all, whereof nine do stand within the liberties of this city, and five in the suburbs thereof." These fourteen were the four Inns of Court—Inner Temple, Middle Temple, Lincoln's Inn, and Gray's Inn,—all still existing and flourishing, and ten Inns of Chancery, of which eight now remain. The Inns of Court were frequented by the sons of the nobility and gentry, at a cost of something like twenty marks per annum; while the Inns of Chancery were more especially occupied by the sons of merchants and others, whose means would not admit of the large expenditure we have named. The first were called *apprenticii nobiliores*, the latter simply *apprenticii*, or apprentices.

In the Inns of Court, as at present constituted, there are three bodies: the students; the barristers—the last of course chosen, in due course of time and study, from the first; and the benchers, or governing body, a kind of permanent committee selected from the barristers, and generally from those only who have become Queen's counsel. These benchers, or "ancients," as they were formerly called, are armed with almost unlimited power for the governance of their respective inns. We will now take a brief glance at each of these establishments.

In the reign of Elizabeth the gentlemen of the Inner Temple were celebrated for their gallantry, accomplishments, and sumptuous hospitality. Many of the Privy Council of the Queen sat at 'he splendid feast of 1561, celebrated in the Inner Temple Hall, and Elizabeth herself, on the 18th of January after, witnessed what is probably the oldest English tragedy, 'Ferrex and Porrex,' performed before her at Whitehall by the "gentyll men of the Temple." These gentyll men seem to have been as famous for dance and song as for their histrionic powers. At their numerous revels, the order of merriment seemed to be this: after dinner the play was enacted; then one or more of the barristers sang carols or songs; and lastly, the judges and benchers led the dance round the sea-coal fire in the centre of the hall, escorted by the Master of the Revels (annually elected at Hallowe'en), and the rest of the company followed their example with hearty good will. As to the festival fare: at Christmas-day breakfasts, there was brawn, mustard and malmsey; and at dinner the boar's head was presented, amidst the joyous sounding of minstrelsy. At the feast given to Palaphilos, Prince of Sophie, or, in common prose, Dudley, Earl of Leicester, Gerard Leigh tells us, there was such abundance of "tender meats, sweet fruits, and dainty delicates, that it seemed a wonder a world to observe the provision; and at every course the trumpeters blew the courageous blast of deadly war; with noise of drum and fife, with the sweet harmony of violins, sackbuts, recorders, and cornets, with other instruments of music, as it seemed Apollo's harp had tuned their stroke."

The masques and plays of the Templars were often the productions of men of genius; sometimes fellows of the Society, sometimes regular dramatists. Decker, in his 'Satire' against Ben Jonson, says, "You shall swear not to bombast out a new play with the old ining of jests stolen from the Temple Revels."

Pennant refers us to the 'Origines Juridiciales' for the relation of other of the enjoyments of the Templars in those days, such as the humours of the three courtiers of the Lord of Misrule, and the hunting the cat and the fox round the hall, with ten couples of hounds. Of the doings of this Lord of Misrule, of whom we hear so much in connection with old English amusements, and especially among the generally grave lawyers, we have a glowing account from the Puritan Stubbs; who in this, as in various other passages, not only interests us in the things he condemns so abusively, but evidently enjoys them himself more than he would like to acknowledge. "First," says he, "all the wild heads of the parish conventing together, choose them a grand captain (of mischief), whom they ennoble with the title of my Lord of Misrule; and him they crown with great solemnity, and adopt for their king. This king anointed, chooseth for him twenty, forty, threescore, or a hundred lusty-guts like to himself, to wait upon his lordly majesty, and to guard his noble person. Then, every one of these his men he investeth with his liveries of green, yellow, or some other wanton colour. And as though that were not gaudy enough, they bedeck themselves with scarfs, ribbons, and laces, hanged all over with gold rings, precious stones, and other jewels; this done they tie about either leg twenty or forty bells, with rich handkerchiefs in their hands, and sometimes laid across over their shoulders and necks, borrowed for the most part of their pretty Mopsies and loving Bessies. . . . . Thus, all things set in order, then have they their hobby-horses, dragons, and other antics, together with their pipers, and thundering drummers, to strike up the devil's dance withal; then march these heathen company towards the church and church-yard, their pipers piping, their drummers thundering, their stumps dancing, their bells jingling, their handkerchiefs swinging about their heads like madmen, their hobby-horses and other monsters skirmishing among the throng; and in this sort they go to the church (though the minister be at prayer or preaching) dancing, and swinging their handkerchiefs over their heads in the church, like devils incarnate, with such a confused noise that no man can hear his own voice. Then the foolish people, they look, they stare, they laugh, they fleer, and mount upon forms and pews, to see these goodly pageants solemnised in this sort. Then, after this, about the church they go again and again, and so forth into the churchyard, where they have commonly their summer halls, their bowers, arbours, and banqueting-houses set up, wherein they feast, banquet, and dance all that day, and, peradventure, all that night too. And thus these terrestrial furies spend the Sabbath-day in the country."

The ancient hall of the Inner Temple is no more. The one built on its site (Fig. 1730), though not a very large, is a fine room; and as viewed when illuminated, with the judges and leading lawyers of England seated at one of their grand dinners on the "state," or dais, and the rising men, the students, and ordinary practitioners of the law, at the long tables stretching down to the carved screen—it forms a striking picture. The members of the Inner Temple dine in the hall daily during Term-time. Among

the other contents of the hall is a full-length portrait of a great man, Coke (Fig. 1725), whose memory, if it be connected with some painful associations, suggests much more calculated to arouse our reverence and enthusiasm.

The common law of England, which, according to Lord Bacon, "had been like a ship without ballast," owes much of its present form to Sir Edward Coke. His father was a bencher of Lincoln's Inn. Coke was first a member of Clifford's Inn, a dependent of the Inner Temple, which latter he entered in 1572. He was subsequently reader at Lyon's Inn, where, says Lloyd, in his 'State Worthies,' "his learned lecture so spread forth his fame, that crowds of clients sued to him for his counsel." Whilst reader of the Inner Temple, the plague drove him thence to his Suffolk mansion at Huntingfield, when he was escorted as far as Romford by no less than nine benchers, and forty other of his fellow members of the Inner Temple. If we except his bigoted severity on some state trials, and his truly savage prosecution of Raleigh, we may safely assert, that, as a judge of long standing, we have never had one more generally admirable—and, without any exception, never one more learned, more indefatigable or energetic, more independent or uncompromising, when the powers above him would have turned him and his high office to their own selfish and despotic purposes. His standard of what became "an honest and just judge" was exceedingly lofty, and he scrupled not to offend any one, even the sovereign himself, to act up to it. As late as his seventy-ninth year, in the reign of Charles I., Coke was found in the English Parliament, boldly asserting and defending the constitutional rights of the people of England, and he was the foremost man concerned in framing the Petition of Right in 1628. One of his last public acts may stand almost as a parallel to Lord Chatham's celebrated appearance in the House of Parliament, when near his death, to pour out his passionate eloquence on a great national cause that strongly engaged his heart. Rushworth describes the aged Coke as "overcome with passion" at the prospect of the coming troubles, and as "forced to sit down when he began to speak, through the abundance of tears." But when the time-worn patriot did speak—to denounce the Duke of Buckingham as the cause of all the evil—who among the excited auditory would ever forget that spirited outburst of sorrowful indignation? His death took place in 1663, whilst he was in the act of repeating, "Thy kingdom come, Thy will be done."

The Middle Temple Hall, of course, would also have its "revels" and its plays; and they would partake of the same spirit and character as those in which their brethren of the other Temple delighted. But there is an incident of its histrionic history, the very recollection of which has, centuries later, become a matter of deep interest, from its connexion with one of whom we know so little, that the commonest, and abstractedly most unimportant facts of his life, assume in our eyes an inexpressible charm. One of the Middle Temple students, John Manningham, kept a diary, or table-book, from Christmas 1601[2], to April 1603[4]; in which he notes, on Feb. 2, 1601—"At our feast we had a play called 'Twelfth Night, or What You Will,'" a brief record, of whose value, John Manningham, when he wrote it, would seem to have had little notion; or that those few simple words would cause his own otherwise obscure name to be written and spoken of in far distant times, and lend a permanent attraction to the hall where that record is preserved. The 'Twelfth Night,' it is supposed, was played by lawyers on that feast day, for the first time after its creation. Most likely the bard himself was present, and many a kindred spirit of the bright galaxy by which that golden age of English poetry was adorned. But other times came. Fancy, and feeling, and joyousness of heart, became profaned, polluted, in the reign of Charles II.; and we do not wonder to find the virtuous Evelyn, who had been elected one of the comptrollers of the Middle Temple revellers, retiring from the noisy scene, resigning his staff of office, and hastening away to spend the Christmas with his brother in the purer and soberer country scenes of his beloved Wotton. In 1668 he was tempted, it seems, to go to see the revels at the Middle Temple, but they pleased him no better than before. He speaks of them as "an old, but riotous custom," and as having "relation neither to virtue nor policy." Between such fantastic extravaganzas as the ancient revels, and the abstruse studies and grave pursuits of law, there appears to modern eyes a singular discrepancy. But the matter is simple and natural enough. The same human heart throbs beneath all bosoms, and precisely in proportion to the restraints placed upon its impulses in one direction, will be its efforts to escape from the thraldom in another. And it is one of the most melancholy of errors to endeavour to prevent this natural and most beneficial tendency. And as to the opinions of others, why it is fools only

1758.—Monument at Stratford.

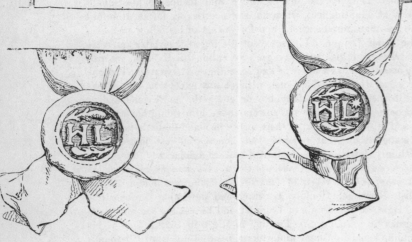

1756.—Autographs of Shakspere

1759.—Bust at Stratford.

1760.—Ben Jonson

1757.—Chancel of Stratford Church

1761.—The Fortune Theatre, Golden Lane, Barbican.

116

1762.—Edward Alleyn.

1763. John Lowin.

1764.—Thomas Greene.

1765.—Thomas Sackville.

1766.—Beaumont.

1767.—John Fletcher.

1768.—Nathaniel Field.

1769.—Philip Massinger.

770.—Thomas Dekker.

who are imposed upon by that "mysterious carriage of the body" which is put on to "hide the defects of the mind."

The Middle Temple Hall (Figs. 1726, 1727) was completed in 1572, after ten years had been spent in its erection. It is the largest and most sumptuous of the halls of the inns of court. The arms of a great number of eminent lawyers who have received their legal education in the society are emblazoned on the windows. There is also much rich carving; but the principal feature of the place is the famous painting, by Vandyke, of Charles I. on horseback. The Hall abuts on the garden, where stands what was, until very recently, the only fountain in London—an object made familiar in our own day, through the pages of 'Martin Chuzzlewit,' to countless thousands who never saw, and are never likely to see the spot in question.

The well-known gateway of Lincoln's Inn (Fig. 1728) was built in the early part of the sixteenth century. The cost of its erection was nearly all defrayed by a member of Lincoln's Inn, Sir Thomas Lovell, who was a knight of the Garter, and the founder of Holywell Nunnery. The only memorials of him left are placed over the gateway. The Inn itself, next in importance to the Inner and Middle Temple, long maintained with these a rivalry of sports, as well as of professional honour. The Temple Master of the Revels was a Lord of Misrule; here, at Lincoln's Inn, he was "the King of the Cocknies" (Pennant), or, the King of Christmas-day. The dramatic nature of these sports presents some curious points. Assumed characters seem to have been so numerous as to require limitation in the unceremonious edicts of the Benchers; and "Jack Straw" and "all his adherents" they banished utterly, on pain of a forfeit of five pounds to every fellow offending by such personation. Pepys tells us that Charles II. visited Lincoln's Inn to see the Christmas revels of 1661, "there being, according to an old custom, a prince and all his nobles, and other matters of sport and charge." During the great contest of principles between the Puritans and the Royalists, there were many of the fellows of the learned societies of the law to whom the revels were distasteful, partly on account of their licentious disorderliness, partly through the gloomy prejudices of the "new learning" against all amusements. The celebrated Prynne was a member of Lincoln's Inn, and the lawyers of the different inns combined in a masque of more than ordinary magnificence to "confute" his famous book, the 'Histrio-Mastix,' for which he was tried. Lord Cottington remarked in the court, that "If Mr. Prynne should be demanded what he would have, he liked nothing; no state or sex; music dancing, &c., unlawful even in kings: no kind of recreation, no kind of entertainment,—no, not so much as hawking: all are damned." There was pertinent truth in this. And there was searching wit, as well as truth, in the Earl of Dorset's remark in his speech—"My Lords, when God had made all his works, he looked upon them, and saw that they were good; this gentleman [Prynne], the devil having put spectacles on his nose, says that all is bad." And so, to remove those spectacles, and make Prynne see clearer, his enlightened, witty, eloquent judges proceeded to cover him with abuse, to fine him 10,000l., to eject him from the bar, expose him in the pillory, doom him to everlasting bondage in prison with no book but the Prayer Book, which his principles disavowed, and with neither pen, ink, nor paper; and to brand and mutilate him in a manner truly frightful. Yet, when Sir Simon d'Ewes visited him shortly after in the Fleet, he found the sufferer calm and firm, and even cheerful, the "rare effects of an upright heart and a good conscience." It might have been some manifestation of the spirit of Puritanism in Lincoln's Inn, which led to that remarkable order in the seventh year of James I., by which the under barristers were actually "put out of Commons, for example sake," for their not dancing on the previous feast of Candlemas, "when the judges were present;" and they were threatened, if the like fault were repeated, they should be fined, or "disbarred." Neither in size nor appearance is Lincoln's Inn Hall (Fig. 1729) equal to either of the Temple Halls; but it is, nevertheless, a handsome room. It was commenced in 1506. At the end is a painting by Hogarth, Paul preaching before Felix, which all Hogarth's admirers must regret he ever attempted. Many a brilliant name has its emblazoned escutcheon here: among the lawyers—Perceval, Canning, Brougham, Lyndhurst; and among the clergymen who have been preachers to the honourable society—Heber, Warburton, and Tillotson—names ever to be revered. But that which most of all strikes our attention in the Hall is the noble statue of Erskine, and while we look upon it, that affecting description of his, of his entrance upon his professional career, touchingly arouses our sympathies for the early struggles of genius. He was surrounded with pecuniary difficulties. when he rose to speak in public for the first

time. Overcome with confusion, he was about to sit down again. "At that time," he used to relate, "I fancied I could feel *my little children tugging at my gown*, so I made an effort—went on—and succeeded."

Gray's Inn Hall (Fig. 1731) is superior to that of Lincoln's Inn or the Inner Temple, and little inferior to the Middle Temple Hall. Its chief architectural attractions are its timber roof, carved wainscot, and emblazoned windows. It was completed in 1560. Some of the revels of the "practisers" of Gray's Inn seem to have drawn upon them evil report, especially on the "ferial" days. An order of the reign of Henry VIII., forbidding the fellows to depart out of the Hall during revels, until they are ended, under penalty of 12d., seems to indicate pretty plainly the nature of some of their laxities—the students would be masquerading in the streets, as well as in the Hall. Indeed, we need little more information as to the sort of life they generally led, than the following memorandum in Pepys's 'Diary,' and the anecdote related by the great Cecil's old historian of his Gray's Inn days. Pepys says—"Great talk of how the barristers and students of Gray's Inn rose in rebellion against the benchers the other day, who outlawed them, and a great deal to do; but now they are at peace again." The gambling propensities of the members are strikingly illustrated in the anecdote of Cecil:—"A mad companion having enticed him to play, in a short time he lost all his money, *bedding, and books* to his companion, having never used play before. And being afterwards among his other company, he told them how such a one had misled him, saying he would presently have a device to be even with him. And with a long trouke he made a hole in the wall, near his playfellow's bed-head, and, in a fearful voice, spake through the trouke: 'O mortal man, repent! Repent of thy horrible time consumed in play, cozenage, and lewdness, or else thou art damned, and canst not be saved.' Which, being spoken at midnight, when he was all alone, so amazed him, as drove him into a sweat for fear. Most penitent and heavy, the next day, in presence of the youths, he told with trembling what a fearful voice spake to him at midnight, vowing never to play again; and calling for Mr. Cecil, asked him forgiveness on his knees, and restored him all his money, bedding, and books. So two gamesters were both reclaimed with this merry device, and never played more. Many other the like merry jests I have heard him tell, too long to be here noted."

The plays of the lawyers were sometimes aimed at popular abuses. Thus, in 1527, John Roos, a student of Gray's Inn, and afterwards sergeant-at-law, gave deep offence to Wolsey by writing a comedy, that was acted here, reflecting on clerical arrogance and pomp; Roos was degraded and imprisoned for that offence. In the works of Beaumont and Fetcher there is a 'Masque of the Gentlemen of Gray's Inn.'

In old times, Gray's Inn, like the other Inns of Court, was famous for its Mootings, occasions when the barristers and students met to debate *moot* points of law in the form of imaginary cases, certain parties undertaking the plantiff's case, and others the defendant's. In modern times debating societies have taken the place of the Mootings. Curran, a member of Gray's Inn, has given us an entertaining description of his *début* at one of these societies:—Upon the first occasion of our assembling, I attended, my foolish heart throbbing with the anticipated honour of being styled 'the learned member that opened the debate,' or 'the very eloquent gentleman who has just sat down.' All day the coming scene had been flitting before my fancy, and cajoling it: my ear already caught the glorious melody of 'Hear him! hear him!' Already I was practising how to steal a cunning sidelong glance at the tear of generous approbation bubbling in the eyes of my little auditory; never suspecting, alas! that a modern eye may have so little affinity with moisture, that the finest gunpowder may be dried upon it. I stood up—my mind was stored with about a folio volume of matter; but I wanted a preface, and for want of a preface the volume was never published. I stood up, trembling through every fibre; but, remembering that in this I was but imitating Tully, I took courage, and actually proceeded almost as far as 'Mr. Chairman,' when, to my astonishment and terror, I perceived that every eye was riveted upon me. There were only six or seven present, and the little room could not have contained as many more; yet was it, to my panic-struck imagination, as if I were the central object in nature, and assembled millions were gazing upon me in breathless expectation. I became dismayed and dumb; my friends cried 'Hear him!'—but there was nothing to hear. My lips, indeed, went through the pantomime of articulation; but I was like the unfortunate fiddler at the fair, who, upon coming to strike up the solo that was to ravish every ear, discovered that an enemy had maliciously soaped his bow; or rather, like poor Punch, as I once saw him, grimacing a soliloquy, of which his prompter had most indiscreetly neglected to administer the words." For some short time after the unfortunate aspirant was greeted with the appellations of "Orator Mum," or "Stuttering Jack Curran,"—but they were soon exchanged for others expressive of universal and ardent admiration of the most eminent orator that Ireland had yet produced. From the time of Demosthenes to the present, such has been the experience, in a more or less degree, of most of our men of genius.

As late as the middle of the last century, a number of petty punishments were in operation in this country that have been since entirely swept away. Of these some were highly ludicrous—some barbarously cruel. Drunkards were paraded through the town, wearing a tub instead of a cloak, a hole being cut out at the bottom for the head to pass through, and two small holes in the sides, through which the hands were drawn. This was called "the Drunkard's Cloak" (Fig. 1810). Scolds had their heads enclosed in a sugarloaf-shaped cap, made of iron hooping, with a cross at the top, and a flat piece of iron projecting inwards, that was laid upon the tongue; a string was attached behind, and by that the scold was led through the streets. The Brank (Fig. 1735), as this invention was named, seems to have been in common use, with minor modifications of form. Trifling offences were sometimes punished by the Whirligig (Fig. 1733), a round wooden cage turning on a pivot; the culprit being enclosed, and whirled round with such velocity that extreme sickness ensued—and thus it proved in reality a punishment highly distressing and dangerous, and therefore shamefully unsuited to the correction of slight aberrations. The Stocks are still, we believe, occasionally used, though the sooner they too become obsolete the better. They were founded on the same principle as the Drunkard's Cloak and the Brank—that of humiliating exposure; and women, as we perceive by our engraving (Fig. 1734), were equally liable with men, Harman's 'Caveat' mentions—

> A stockes to staye sure, and safely detayne
> Lazy leud leuterers that lawès do offend.

In this same 'Caveat, or Warning for Common Cursetors, vulgarly called Vagabonds,' whose author, a poor gentleman, had drawn it up "for the utility and-profit of his native country"—we have a great deal of curious information of the wandering orders of the sixteenth century. Among these were the Rufflers, or sturdy beggars; the Upright Men, who were chiefly vagabond chiefs; the Priggers of Prances, or horse-stealers; the Abraham Men, pretended lunatics (hence the vulgar phrase of shamming Abraham); and the Counterfeit Cranks, who affected sickness. The same author gives an amusing, yet, properly considered, melancholy account of one of these latter worthies, whose portrait, besides that of an Upright Man, named Nicholas Blunt, trim and comfortable-looking (Fig. 1736), is given as an illustration to his 'Caveat.' The poor afflicted Counterfeit Crank, Nicholas Genings, while the 'Caveat' was going through the press, appeared under the author's lodgings at the White-Friars, where he hoped for gain from two or three great ladies. The author watched the proceedings of this man, penetrated his imposture, questioned him, and almost reduced him to confession; but at that critical point the Crank, not exactly liking his position, started off. He was taken, after a long and difficult pursuit, in the house of "an honest Kent yeoman," many miles from town. To make sure of him, he was stripped naked, and merely wrapped in an old cloak. But they must be cunning who could hold him even under such circumstances. He was presently running naked over the fields, and completely baffled his enemies among the metropolitan wilds of vagabondism. After two months, in a new disguise, Nicholas Genings re-appeared one New Year's Day in White-Friars. The author of the 'Caveat' again discovered him, and again he fled; but this time Genings was less happy in his exertions—being taken at Fleet Bridge, and lodged in Bridewell. He was pilloried at Cheapside, "went in the mill while his ugly picture was a-drawing, and then was whipt at a cart's tail through London," the said picture borne before him in procession. Then followed another period of confinement in Bridewell, and, after this purgatory, the miserable rogue was dismissed, on condition that "he would prove an honest man, and labour truly to get his living." Much likelihood of this result—for one so publicly marked and degraded! With all deference to our ancestors' wisdom, the means were hardly adapted to that end.

Few words are recalled with deeper interest than those which speak so emphatically of the state of feeling among our ancestors,—than the two forming the almost magical phrase—*Merry England*; —and few, at the same time, excite a more painful sense of regret, incessantly reminding us, as they do, how little is left to us of the old things, or how little we have substituted of new calculated to keep alive the same genial and wholesome habit of enjoyment. It is a truly noble endeavour, that of making ourselves a great nation: but we violate the very first law of our nature, in not keeping ourselves, in the mean time, a happy nation. The clouds, however, we may hope, are in some degree passing away. And the very references to these past times, which are becoming more and more frequent, are the best auguries of the influences they are destined to exert on future ones. We could not, if we would—nor is it at all desirable, if we had the power—revive the exact modes in which the cheerful temperaments of our forefathers developed themselves; but there was nevertheless, much in those modes that should be restored to us. The poetry of an old English May-day, the overflowing hospitality of an old English Christmas, or the picturesque splendour of the old English trade festivals,—why should we not adapt these to our own peculiarities of thought and opinion?—why should we not make these, among other of the "red-letter days" of the Calendar, as typical as ever of the glow and sunshine of genuine national happiness?

The times of Elizabeth are those which more especially have obtained the appellation to which we have referred: let us, then, take a rapid glance at the most important of the occasions on which merry England delighted to exhibit itself. And what can we begin with but May-day? The delicate green of the young leaves is everywhere refreshing the eye with its beauty, and gladdening the heart with its promise of the more luxuriant, sunny, shade-chequered world of embowering foliage to come. Already begin the old games of the battle of Summer and Winter. The youth are divided into two troops, "the one in winter livery, the other in the gay habit of the spring." Of course the victory is to the Spring, and is celebrated with triumphant carrying of green branches and May flowers, and singing aloud songs of joy, of which the burthen is to the effect—"We have brought the summer home." May-day Eve comes. At midnight the people assemble, divide into companies, and go to the woods, groves, and hills, and there spend the first hours of the dawn; now bathing their faces with the dew of the grass—a sovereign recipe for rendering them beautiful—now collecting branches of trees, chiefly of the birch; laden with which they return, singing loud, as Chaucer says, "against the sunne sheen." "But the chiefest jewel they bring from thence is the May-pole, which they bring home (Fig. 1782) with great veneration; as thus:—they have twenty or forty yoke of oxen, every ox having a sweet nosegay of flowers tied to the tip of his horns; and these oxen draw home the May-pole; . . . which they covered all over with flowers and herbs; bound round with strings, from the top to the bottom; and sometimes it was painted with variable colours, having two or three hundred men, women, and children following it with great devotion. And, thus equipped, it was reared, with handkerchiefs and flags streaming on the top; they straw the ground round about it; they bind green boughs about it; they set up summer halls, bowers, and arbours hard by it; and then fall they to banqueting and feasting, to leaping and dancing about it." Is not this a charming description of a most charming incident?—yet is the writer—Stubbs—Puritan Stubbs. It is true he says something about a "stinking idol" and a "heathen" custom; there his Puritanism exhibits itself, and perhaps the more sourly on account of a kind of instinctive consciousness of the seductiveness of the subject, and of his own treatment of it. Could we desire a more satisfactory evidence how deeply the poetical nature of a May-day had sunk into the people's hearts, than these curious practical contradictions on the part of its Puritan denouncer? If Stubbs was not a lover, however unwillingly or unconsciously, of the beautiful custom his intellect teaches him to condemn, we will never again trust to the animating spirit of an author. With what unction does he not enter into the details of the proceedings! The *sweet* nosegays tied on the tips of the horns was surely a superfluous adjective for him and his object; and those summer halls and bowers he speaks of, have a sound that reveals plainly enough how the Puritan's spirit revels in them, whatever may be the unlikeliness of seeing him bodily there. Well—

> The May-pole is up,
>   Now give me the cup,
> I'll drink to the garlands around it,
>   But first unto those
>   Whose hands did compose
> The glory of flowers that crown'd it.
>
> *A Pleasant Grove of New Fancies,* 1657.

1771.—Richard Pynson, died 1530.

1772.—John Day, died 1584.

1777.—The Wake.

1773.—Wynkyn de Worde, flourished 1493—1533.

1774.—Robert Copland, died 1548.

1775.—Thomas Berthelet, died 1555.

1776.—Robert Wyer, flourished 1527—1542.

1771 to 1776.—Marks of the early English Printers.

1778.—The Fair.

1779.—Bringing in the Yule Log on Christmas Eve.

1780—Bringing in the Boar's Head at Christmas

126

1781.—Plough Monday: Dance of Bessie and the Clown.

1782.—Bringing in the Maypole on May Morning

1783.—May Day.

1784.—Milkmaids' Dance, with pile of Plate, on May Day.

1785.—Playing at Bucklers.—Maids dancing for Garlands.

1786.—May-pole before St. Andrew Undershaft.

Let us suppose the scene to be London; where the most famous of the May-poles was the one of St. Andrew, on Cornhill, called "Undershaft," on account of the great height of the shaft or pole, which soared above the steeple (Fig. 1786). On that spot, now so covered with houses, the masquers and mummers then played their pranks, the music filled the air with its sweet and joy-inspiring sounds, and the vicinity everywhere presented the aspect so delightfully described by Herrick in the line—

Each field grew a street, *each street a park:*

so luxuriantly was every dwelling enclosed in the green riflings of the neighbouring woods. There, too, year by year, was exhibited the loveliest and most poetical of all the May-day scenes; and which has been thus described by a delightful but little known poet,—

I have seen the Lady of the May
Set in an arbour (on a holy-day)
Built by the May-pole, where the jocund swains
Dance with the maidens to the bagpipe's strains,
When envious night commands them to be gone,
Call for the merry youngsters, one by one
And, for their well performance, soon disposes
To this a garland interwoven with roses;
To that, a carved hook or well-wrought scrip
Gracing another with her cherry lip;
To one, her garter; to another then,
A handkerchief cast o'er and o'er again:
And none returneth empty that hath spent
His pains to fill their rural merriment.

Browne's Pastorals, 1625.

Next the Lord of the May leads the wilder revels of the night;—carried too often to excess: till morris-dancers and crowd are dispersed by the rising of another day, upon faces, whose wan appearance tell plainly that the springs of enjoyment are, for the present, exhausted.

Among the adjuncts of May-day one of the pleasantest sights was that presented by the Milkmaid's Dance. Many a fair, fresh, cleanly-looking group, in the prettiest and gayest of country costumes, with bright scarfs and ribbons, and garlands, came dancing (Fig. 1784) before their customers' doors, with one of their number in the centre, supporting a brilliant pyramid of May flowers, and polished silver cups, tankards, and salvers, borrowed for the occasion.

It seems that even now there are nooks and corners of England where May-day still preserves a kind of supremacy and honour. In many of the villages of Surrey, we are told that, "During the last few days of April, the village children go about the meadows, and, collecting all the cowslips they can find, form them into garlands, chaplets, &c., and on May morning they assemble, and, uniting in bands, carry their garlands, arranged commonly on two hoops crossed vertically, and fixed on poles, about the neighbourhood; and very pretty they look. They have nosegays of other flowers also, but cowslips (or paigles, as they call them) are the chief; and with these their bonnets and caps are also trimmed. We have seen some of these little processions that looked as charming as those troops of Italian children carrying flowers which Mr. Uwins paints so delightfully."—(Thorne's 'Rambles by Rivers.')

From spring, in all its youthful prime, let us turn, if only for the sake of the contrast, to winter; and mark, while our ancestors did all they could to enhance and to enjoy the "spirit of life in everything," that so characterises the one season, how they ameliorated the rigour of the other, and made it, if "frosty," also "kindly." And here again bursts out the enthusiasm of the poet, who made it his pride and his pleasure to

Sing of May-poles, hock-carts, wassails, wakes,

and the thousand other things that made life in his day so much more full of nurture for the poet's existence than in our own. And what, after all, is the poet's spirit but the very flower and essence of the spirit of the nation to which he belongs? Whatever is good for him will assuredly, in a lesser or greater degree, be good for us all. Herrick thus bursts out in his 'Christmas Ceremonies:'—

Come, bring, with a noise [of music],
My merry, merry boys,
The Christmas log to the firing;
While my good dame, she
Bids ye all be free,
And drink to your hearts desiring.

With the last year's brand
Light the new block, and,
For good success in his spending,

On your psaltries play,
That sweet luck may
Come while the log is a-teending,
Drink now the strong beer,
Cut the white loaf here,
The while the meat is a-shredding,
For the rare mince-pie,
And the plums stand by,
To fill the paste that's a-kneading.

The more sober prose writers of the period confirm the truth of the picture of Christmas domestic life here given. No old custom sounds more cheering to the heart of the comfort-loving English than the burning of the Yule-log on Christmas-eve, that used to be attended with such ceremony and blithesomeness. First, there was the bringing the ponderous mass into the hall (Fig. 1779) with procession of retainers and servants, with lights flaring in all directions, with uproarious shouts and glee, that moved the very souls of the highest and meanest present, with beating of drum, and blowing of trump, and breathing of flutes. Then there was the critical lodgement upon the hearth, happily capacious enough for the mightiest log, and whose chimney gaped wide to receive and welcome the flood of flame and sparks that full soon set at nought all radiance but their own. A goodly sight; and in itself enough to inspire the whole community that gambolled, and danced, and ate, and drank, and masqueraded in its glorious presence. The use of the Yule-block is supposed to have originated in partly the same notion as the fires in the open air of Midsummer (to which we shall presently refer), with the difference only of being made within doors. Christmas-day comes, and fresh enjoyments come with it.

From the ancient tract 'Round about our Coal-Fire,' we are able to follow pretty accurately the forms of the more substantial parts of the great entertainment in the mansions of many of the country gentry. With the first faint dawn of the wintry day, the tenants and neighbours of the worthy landholder entered his hall. Woe betide the cook-maid, if, early as it is, she has not got the hackin, or great sausage, boiled; in that case two young men take her by the arms, and run her round the market-place for her laziness. However, she was generally prepared, and so were all those whose duty it was to give the tenants and neighbours their first Christmas cheer. The strong beer was broached, and the black-jacks went plentifully about, with toast, sugar, nutmeg, and good Cheshire cheese. From the daybreak so hospitably begun, to the final close of the Christmas holidays, the great table was kept constantly covered. "The sirloins of beef, the minced-pies, the plum-porridge, the capons, turkeys, geese, and plum-puddings, were all brought upon the board: every one ate heartily, and was welcome, which gave rise to the proverb, 'Merry in the hall when beards wag all.'"

The far-famed boar's-head was anciently the first dish on Christmas-day, wherever it was conveniently to be had. It was carried up to the principal table (Fig. 1780) with great ceremony, whilst a carol was sung. In a set of Christmas carols, printed by Wynkyn de Worde, we have the following jovial strains:—

A CAROL, BRINGING IN THE BOAR'S HEAD.

Caput Apri defero,
Reddens laudes Domino.

The Boar's Head in hand bring I,
With garlands gay and rosemary;
I pray you all sing merrily,
Qui estis in convivio.

The Boar's Head, I understand,
Is the chief service in this land;
Look wherever it be fande,
Servite cum cantico.

Be glad, lords, both more and lasse,
For this hath ordained our steward
To cheer you all this Christmasse,
The Boar's head with mustard.

But there is yet a third festival that must be described; one of so imposing a character that it drew an English monarch privately into London to witness and enjoy, as an ordinary spectator, all its spirit-stirring pageantry. "On Midsummer-eve, at night, King Henry came privily into West Cheap of London, being clothed in one of the coats of his guard." (Stow, 1510.) This was when Henry, as Cavendish says, was "a young, lusty, and courageous prince, entering into the flower of pleasant youth;" and when his amusements were of a healthy, tasteful, imaginative kind,—"shooting, singing, dancing, wrestling, casting of the bar, playing on the recorders, flute, virginals, and in setting of songs and making of ballads." (Hall.) On such occasions, the atmosphere appeared to be "all in flame," owing to the light of the numerous bonfires; and

The wakeful shepherd by his flock in field,
With wonder at that time far off beheld
The wanton shine of thy triumphant fires
Playing upon the tops of thy tall spires.
　　　　　　　Richard Niccols, 'London Artillery.'

The fires and lights that formed so prominent a feature of the festival of St. John the Baptist, are supposed by the late Dr. Milner, the Roman Catholic bishop, to have been suggested by that well-known and beautiful metaphor, "He was a bright and shining light" (John v. 35); and by John's "bearing witness to the light" (John i. 7) The ancient homily on the subject says, "In worship of Saint John the people waked at home, and made three manner of fires,"—a bone-fire, a wood-fire, and Saint John's fire. The first fire was to drive away dragons and disease; "the second fire was made of wood, for that will burn light, and will be seen far; for it is the chief of fire to be seen far, and betokening that Saint John was a lantern of light to the people." The blaze would be seen afar off, "especially in the night, in token of St. John's having been seen from far in the spirit by Jeremiah. The third fire, of bones, betokeneth John's martyrdom, for his bones were burnt," by the Emperor Julian, according to the homilist; who had the body disinterred for the purpose, and "cast the ashes in the wind." Other authorities have suggested different origins for the custom, as the Druid fires, and the Pagan worship of sun and fire: the sun at the feast of St. John attaining the highest place in the zodiac.

On this as on other festivals London seemed to be turned into one continuous wood or garden; but, it appears, that some particular plants enjoyed especial favour on Midsummer-eve. No wonder, when we consider that many of them were to be the book of fate to many a pair of lovers. The poet of the time says, the

Young men round about with maids do dance in every street,
With garlands wrought of motherwort, or else with vervain sweet,
And many other flowers fair, with violets in their hands,
Where as they all do fondly think, that whosoever stands,
And through the flowers beholds the flame, his eyes shall feel no pain.

The orpine appears to have been also a highly treasured plant, commonly under the name of Midsummer-men. "The people of the country delight much to set it in pots and shells on Midsummer-even, or upon timber, slates, or trenchers daubed with clay, and so to set or hang it up in their houses." Lovers had another mode of divination in connection with it. Two plants were stuck up, and if they bent towards each other, the persons whom they represented would be united in marriage; if the contrary way, the lovers' hopes would be blighted. Branches of green birch, and lilies, were also in great request for Midsummer-eve decorations.

Another feature of the time was indeed delightful, for the warm unselfishness of spirit in which it must have originated, and in connection with which alone it could have continued to exist. The

Tables set were plentifully spread,
And at each door neighbour with neighbour fed;
Where modest mirth, attendant at the feast
With plenty, gave content to every guest;
Where true good-will crowned cups with fruitful wine,
And neighbours in true love did fast combine;
Where the Law's pick-purse, strife 'twixt friend and friend,
By reconcilement happily took end.—*Niccols.*

But the grandest part of the festival was the Marching Watch (Fig. 1724). These comprised about two thousand men, some mounted, some on foot; some called "demilances," riding on great horses; some gunners, with harquebuses and wheel-locks; some archers in white coats, bearing bent bows and sheafs of arrows; some pikemen in bright corslets; others billmen, with aprons of mail. The Cresset train (a pitchy rope, in an iron frame, raised high on a shaft) (Fig. 1722) amounted also to nearly two thousand men, each cresset having one to bear it, and one to serve it. The Constables of the Watch made an imposing part of the pageant, each with his glittering armour and gold chain, his henchman following him, his minstrel before him, his cresset bearer by his side. In the rear of all these passed the City Waits, then came the morris-dancers, Robin Hood, Friar Tuck, Maid Marian, and the rest. The Mayor with his train, his sword-bearer, henchmen, footmen, and giants, came after the morris-dancers: and then came the sheriffs. The windows facing the streets were opened wide, and

Kings, great peers, and many a noble dame,
Whose bright, pearl-glittering robes did mock the flame
Of the night's burning lights, did sit to see
How every senator in his degree,
Adorned with shining gold and purple weeds,
And stately mounted on rich trapped steeds,

Their guard attending, through the streets did ride,
Before their foot bands, graced with glittering pride
Of rich gilt arms, whose glory did present
A sunshine to the eye, as if it meant,
Among the cresset lights shot up on high,
To chase dark night for ever from the sky.—*Niccols.*

The Setting of the Watch of Midsummer-eve, seems to have meant the stationing of these armed and mailed ranks, singly or in groups, about the streets of the city, to guard it during this night alone. In the 31st of Henry VIII. the king abolished the Marching Watch, and the cost of the great pageant was to be devoted to a substantial standing watch, for the safety of the city. So, instead of harnessed constables, London had the watchman with halberd and lanthorn (Fig. 1723) calling to the sleeping inmates of the houses to hang out their lights, as they were ordered to do on dark winter evenings. From Queen Mary's reign to the Commonwealth this watchman added a bell to his halberd and lanthorn (Fig. 1719). Dekker seems to have had considerable objections to these disturbers of the public peace: a bellman, he says, is "the child of darkness; a common night walker; a man that had no man to wait upon him, but only a dog; one that was a disordered person, and at midnight would beat at men's doors, bidding them (in mere mockery) to look to their candles, when they themselves were in their dead sleeps."

According to Milton's 'Penseroso,' the bell had rather a contrary effect from what might seem intended:

The bellman's *drowsy* charm,
To bless the doors from nightly harm.

And so, step by step, do we get down from the picturesque men of the old Midsummer-eve, to the comfortable looking and useful, but not at all picturesque, policemen of our day.

As the close of the festival draws nigh, the youths who

Thus till night they danced have, they through the fire amain
With striving minds do run, and all their herbs they cast therein,
And then with words devout and prayers they solemnly begin,
Desiring God that all their ills may there consumed be;
Whereby they think through all that year from agues to be free.
　　　　　　　The Popish Kingdom.

And so ends Midsummer-eve.

Such then were May-day, Christmas, and Midsummer; such, with modifications suited to their origin and seasons of observance, were Easter and Whitsuntide. But our ancestors would have looked upon the year as dull indeed if these were all the holidays it brought them in its revolving course, not only must every period have its own particular festival, but also every apostle and saint, every trade and calling, we might almost say every city, town, or village. Wakes, and fairs, and feasts—Plough Monday, Shrove Tuesday, Holy Thursday, Good Friday,—but indeed there is no end to the list of holidays observed with more or less of enthusiasm by the English in the olden time. But numerous as these were, not only had their mirth-loving spirits stomachs for them all, but even the regular undistinguished working days of each week must be made to yield time for the cultivation of enjoyment. Here is a picture of London streets a few centuries ago:—

In the days of Fitz-Stephen the city youths were wont to use their bucklers like fighting men; and the city maidens were often in the fine evenings "dancing and tripping till moonlight" in the open air. These customs continued to the time of Stow, who says, "the youths of this city also have used on holidays, after evening prayer, at their masters' doors, to exercise their wasters and bucklers; and the maidens, one of them playing on a timbrel, in sight of their masters and dames, to dance for garlands hanged athwart the streets" (Fig. 1785); and he adds, "which open pastimes in my youth, being now suppressed, worser practices within doors are to be feared." Truly, we think they are.

It will not be necessary for us to go into any lengthened details of the numerous holidays above named; but there are particular features of some of them not unworthy of notice. There is, for instance, the grotesque dance of Bessy and the Clown, and their followers (Fig. 1781), on Plough Monday; the primary object of which, like most others of the revels of the poor, was to collect money. And whoever refused to aid in furnishing the means of convivial enjoyment for the poor ploughmen, was pretty sure of a tangible evidence of resentment in the soil of his threshold being ploughed up, when practicable, by the plough that the dancers dragged up. Bessy was a ploughman dressed as an old woman; the Clown figured in a fox's skin, or that of some other animal, with the tail hanging down his back. The ploughmen who drew the plough were generally "gallant young men," in white shirts, uncovered by coat or waistcoat, but decorated with a great number

1787.—Hunting.

1788.—Hawking.

1789.—Grand Falconer.

1790.—Shooting

1791.—Archery.

1792.—Cross-bowman

1793.—Fishing.

1794.—Otter-hunting.

1795.—Hurling.

1796.—Bear-baiting in the Seventeenth Century.

1797.—Carved Hunting-Horn of the Sixteenth Century, belonging to Earl Ferrers.

1798.—Christmas.

1799.—Barley-break.

125

of ribbons folded into roses. As many as twenty young men would be in the yoke of one plough.

Shrove Tuesday, again, had its own especial source of amusement, and a very discreditable one it was. "He also would to the threshing of the cock" (Fig. 1807), says a manuscript life of the fourth Lord Berkeley, preserved at Berkeley Castle, a proof that this ancient barbarity, the chief distinguishing feature of Shrove Tuesday, was by no means confined to the plebeian vulgar. "In our wars with France, in former ages," says the 'Gentleman's Magazine' for 1737, "our ingenious forefathers invented this emblematical way of expressing their derision of, and resentment towards that nation [the Latin name for a cock, 'Gallus,' also signified a Frenchman]; and poor Monsieur at the stake was pelted by men and boys in a very rough and hostile manner." Sir Charles Sedley's epigram implies another origin: in it he says—

> Mayst thou be punish'd for *St. Peter's* crime,
> And on Shrove Tuesday perish in thy prime

But there is yet a third account by an old German author, Cranenstein:—"When the Danes were masters of England, and lorded it over the nations of the island, the inhabitants of a certain great city, grown weary of their slavery, had formed a secret conspiracy to murder their masters in one bloody night, and twelve men had undertaken to enter the town-house by a stratagem, and seizing the arms, surprise the guard which kept it; and at which time their fellows, upon a signal given, were to come out of their houses and murder all opposers: but when they were putting it in execution, the unusual crowing and fluttering of the cocks about the place they attempted to enter at, discovered their design; upon which the Danes became so enraged that they doubled their cruelty, and used them with more severity then ever. Soon after they were freed from the Danish yoke, and to revenge themselves on the cocks, for the misfortune they involved them in, instituted this custom of knocking them on the head on Shrove Tuesday, the day on which it happened. This sport, though at first only practised in one city, in process of time became a national divertisement, and has continued ever since the Danes first lost this island." As late as 1759, the 'London Daily Advertiser' records the exertions of the justices of the city and liberty of Westminster to suppress the Shrove Tuesday sport, the result being, that "*few cocks* were seen to be thrown at, so that it is to be hoped this barbarous custom will be left off." The hope is happily realised. But we must not forget that the Puritans were the first to oppose (on principle) all such inhumanities. Cock-fighting was hardly less prevalent. The flag that used to float over the theatre to tell that one of Shakspere's dramas was in the act of performance, was often opposed by the counter-attraction of another flag, placed over some building near to indicate the combat of a main of cocks.

Another custom, over whose extinction we also have reason to rejoice, was the brutish exhibition of bear-baiting (Fig. 1796). For this our forefathers do not appear to have been willing to wait the recurrence of any particular season or holiday: they must have it at all times of the year. How much Elizabeth partook of the then national ferocity, as well as of the national courage and talent, is strikingly exemplified in her well-known partiality for this amusement: witness the Kenilworth entertainments. Fashion is not nice when monarchs lead the way. This detestable sport grew in high favour with the nobility and gentry. Bear-gardens abounded in London; and, to heighten the luxury, it was served in various modes. Sometimes the bear was hoodwinked, and thus surrounded with a circle of men, who roused it into frenzy by lashing it with whips.

The ceremonies on Palm Sunday (Fig. 1811) have been so completely described by a versifier of the time, that we cannot do better than quote his account:—

> Here comes that worthy day wherein our Saviour Christ is thought
> To come unto Jerusalem, on ass's shoulders brought;
> When as again these Papists fond their foolish pageants have,
> With pomp and great solemnity, and countenance wondrous grave
> A wooden ass they have, and image great that on him rides.
> But underneath the ass's feet a table broad there slides,
> Being borne on wheels, which ready drest, and all things meet there for,
> The ass is brought abroad and set before the church's door;
> The people all do come, and boughs of trees and palms they bear,
> Which things against the tempest great the parson conjures there,
> And straightway down before the ass upon his face he lies,
> Whom there another priest doth strike with rod of largest size:
> He rising up, two lubbers great upon their faces fall,
> In strange attire, and loathsomely, with filthy tune they bawl:
> Who, when again they risen are, with stretching out their hand,
> They point unto the wooden knight, and singing as they stand,

> Declare that that is he that came into the world to save
> And to redeem such as in him their hope assured have;
> And even the same that long agone, while in the street he rode
> The people met, and olive boughs so thick before him strewed.
> This being sung, the people cast the branches as they pass,
> Some part upon the image, and some part upon the ass;
> Before whose feet a wondrous heap of boughs and branches lie;
> This done into the church he straight is drawn full solemnly:
> The shaven priests before them march, the people follow fast,
> Still striving who shall gather first the boughs that down are cast;
> For falsely they believe that these have force and virtue great,
> Against the rage of winter storms, and thunder's flashing heat.
> In some places wealthy citizens, and men of sober cheer.
> For no small sum do hire this ass with them about to bear;
> And mannerly they use the same, not suffering any by
> To touch this ass, nor to presume unto his presence nigh.
>   When as the priests and people all have ended this their sport,
> The boys do after dinner come, and to the church resort;
> The sexton pleased with price, and looking well no harm be done:
> They take the ass, and through the streets and crooked lanes they run,
> Whereas they common verses sing, according to the guise,
> The people giving money, bread, and eggs of largest size.
> Of this their gains they are compelled the master half to give,
> Least he alone without his portion of the ass should live.
>   *Naogeorgus, translated by Barnabe Googe.*

Truly here were holidays and amusements enough to make any country "merry," but they were by no means all. The whole classes of field and of military sports, in which men from the highest down almost to the lowest ranks of society participated, yet remain to be noticed. Exhilarating to all hearts was the sound of the hunter's horn, heard

> From the side of some hoar hill
> Through the high wood echoing shrill.

Or even of its poetical echoes in song:—

> The hunt is up, the hunt is up (Fig. 1787),
> Sing merrily we, the hunt is up;
> The birds they sing,
> The deer they fling;
>   Hey nony, nony,—no;
> The hounds they cry,
> The hunters they fly;
>   Hey trolilo, trolilo.
> The hunt is up.—*Douce.*

This, again, was a sport greatly enjoyed by Elizabeth, as we learn from an interesting anecdote. Once visiting Berkeley Castle while the Earl was absent, she found on the estate a noble collection of deer; and, consulting only her own royal will, instigated by the Earl of Leicester, forthwith proceeded to hunt them down with such hearty energy, that, in one day, there fell no less than twenty-seven prime stags. The Earl of Berkeley, on his return, was greeted with the tidings of the reckless slaughter of the valuable animals he had preserved with so much care. Highly exasperated, he at once broke up his enclosures, and dissolved his hunting establishment, resolved, at least, that her Majesty should take no more such liberties with his property. Soon after, he was warned by a friend at court that the Queen was indignant against him for what he had done, and that the Earl of Leicester had an eye to the Berkeley estates, and their owner's head. This recalled him to a more prudent course, and saved him.

There was one sport exclusively confined to the noble and wealthy orders of society—hawking—which chiefly flourished and declined during the present period. To a people who found habitually much more of pleasure than of pain or annoyance in the overcoming of difficulties, and who retained much of what our phrenologists would call the destructive principle, no sport could be more attractive than this, especially when it comprised the additional gratification of a splendid spectacle. The meeting of gallants and ladies (Fig. 1788) afforded an admirable opportunity for the exhibition of fine dress. The galloping over hill and dale in the invigorating breeze, and amid country scenery, was highly exhilarating and delightful; and the many daring and dexterous feats which had to be accomplished, in order to follow the course of the hawk and its prey during the aërial chase and combat, gave full exercise to courage and energy. The sport required no less resolution when followed on foot: with the aid of a hawking-pole desperate leaps were taken over hedge and ditch. In making one of these leaps Henry VIII. nearly perished; his hawking-pole broke, he fell short in the mud, and his dread Majesty had to be indebted to the ready help of a footman to save him from being smothered. But these are trifles to your true sportsman. He was *not* smothered—that's enough; so on he goes with greater zest than ever from the excitement of the check. Oh,

'T is royal sport! Then, for an evening flight,
A tiercel gentle, which I call, my masters,
As he were sent a messenger to the moon
In such a place flies, as he seems to say,
See me, or see me not! The partridge sprung,
He makes his stoop; but wanting breath, is forced
To cancelier; then with such speed, as if
He carried lighting in his wings, he strikes
The tumbling bird, who even in death appears
Proud to be made his quarry.—MASSINGER.

But the nobility began to find one serious inconvenience attending the sport—it was very expensive. Good falcons sold excessively high, and a large establishment had to be kept up for their care and training. The Grand Falconer in his full dress, with the falcon on his wrist (Fig. 1789), was a most poetical-looking personage; and his assistants, bearing the perches for the hooded birds, slung from their shoulders, no less so. But poetry too often must yield to convenience. The fowling-piece in its use required no such costly apparatus, and there was a novelty besides in the sort of skill it demanded: so from this time the sport that had existed since the days of Alfred—a favourite with most of the gentle-born and chivalric spirits of England—fell into disuse.

In hurling (Fig. 1795)—a game chiefly enjoyed by the middle and lower classses—it was when parish matched with parish that there came the "tug of *sport*." Then the ball was driven "over hills, dales, hedges, ditches,—yea, and thorough bushes, briars, mires, plashes, and rivers."

Otter-hunting, now exceedingly rare, was formerly an animated sport among watermen, the dwellers near the rivers, and sportsmen—such as Izaak Walton and his friends. Izaak most animatedly describes the search—"Look! down at the bottom of the hill there, in that meadow, chequered with water-lilies and lady-smocks; there you may see what work they make; look! look! you may see all busy; men and dogs; dogs and men; all busy." Every place of possible concealment in the banks was examined—and at last the otter was found. Then barked the dogs, and shouted the men! Boatmen pursue the unlucky animal on the water. Horsemen dash into the shallower parts (Fig. 1794). The otter swims and dives to escape them, but the dogs are thoroughly trained, and all her arts are fruitless. She perishes in their grasp in the water, or is run up a bank and despatched by the huntsmen's spears.

One of the most amusing of the military sports was that which was in great favour in London during Easter holidays, the water-quintain (Fig. 1808), already described in a former period. We may here add, that it appears to have been most popular about the reign of Henry II.; but Stow describes it as in existence so late as the reign of Henry VIII.: "I have seen also in the summer season, upon the river of Thames, some rowed in wherries with staves in their hands, flat at the fore-end, running one against another; and, for the most part, one or both of them were overthrown and well ducked."

Archery, till the beginning of this period, remained the popular military sport, forming, as it still did, a most efficient, and therefore most popular, instrument of actual warfare.

The memorable victory of Flodden Field speaks trumpet-tongued of the might of the English bow as late as the reign of Henry VIII. But the days were now at hand when its fame was to exist but in bygone records, when as a national weapon it was to cease entirely from the land. This change took place about the close of the reign of Elizabeth, previous to which the cross-bow (Fig. 1792), so long prohibited by statutes and penalties, had for some time almost superseded the use of the regular bow, except occasionally in the chase, or when the other was used for exercise and amusement. And even that use soon ceased. Stow, in 1598, exclaims, "What should I speak of the ancient daily exercises in the long-bow by citizens of the city, now almost clearly left off and forsaken? I overpass it. For, by the means of closing in of common grounds, our archers, for want of room to shoot abroad, creep into bowling-alleys, and ordinary dicing-houses, near home." Only four years before this was written, in 1594, there existed in Finsbury Fields alone, no less than one hundred and sixty-four archers' targets, set up on pillars, crowned with some fanciful device. The Finsbury archers gradually degenerated in skill, and were often satirized. Thus D'Avenant :—

Now lean attorney, that his cheese
Ne'er pared nor verses took for fees,
And aged proctor, that controls
The feats of Puck in court of Paul's,
Do each with solemn oath agree
To meet in fields of Finsbury ;
With loins in canvass bow-case tied
Where arrows stick, with mickle pride ;

With boots pinned up, and bow in hand,
All day most fiercely here they stand,
Like ghost of Adam Bell and Clymme :
Sol sets for fear they'll shoot at him.

At Mile End the gorgeous archery festival took place annually, which was known as Prince Arthur's Show (Fig. 1805); the "prince" being formally recognised, under that title by Henry VIII., who, going once to see the performances, was so pleased, that he even confirmed by charter, the "famous Order of Knights of Prince Arthur's Round Table or Society." The prince was rivalled in a friendly way by another potentate of similar pretensions and standing—the Duke of Shoreditch, whose train, at the annual festival in 1583, contained three thousand archers skilled to ply "the grey goose wing." There were on that occasion no less than nine hundred and forty-two chains of gold worn by the company. A wedge of gold was presented to that "duke" by a "marquis," whose page flung to the populace glistening spangles from a box. The creation of the first Duke of Shoreditch happened thus: his real name was Barlow, and he was a member of the king's body-guard. In an archery match at Windsor, when all the competitors had shot except Barlow, Henry cried to him, "Win them, and thou shalt be duke over all archers." Barlow surpassed the best of the previous shots ; and the king, asking him where he resided, and being told Shoreditch, immediately named him Duke of Shoreditch.

Riding at the ring (Fig. 1809) superseded the joust, as being the most graceful, and the safest also, of chivalric exercises. The skill consisted in careering gracefully at a small ring suspended nearly on a level with the rider's eyebrow, sending the point of the lance through the circle, and (the fastening readily yielding) bearing it off as a trophy. This favourite courtly amusement was reduced to a regular science by the end of the period. We may here transcribe Ascham's views of what in the sixteenth century were the accomplishments required for the complete English gentleman. They are "to ride comely, to run fair at the tilt or ring. to play at all weapons, to shoot fair in bow, or surely in gun ; to vault lustily, to run, to leap, to wrestle, to swim, to dance comely, to sing, and play of instruments cunningly ; to hawk, to hunt, to play at tennis, and all pastimes generally which be joined with labour, used in open place, and in the daylight, containing either some fit exercise for war, or some pleasant pastime for peace ;" and these "be not only comely and decent, but also very necessary for a courtly gentleman to use." And with this we conclude our notices of the materials that went to the building up of the fabric of England's mirth and enjoyment, in the days when she was called the "Merry," believing, as we do, that whatever forms may be chosen, the spirit of that mirth and enjoyment *must* be revived. "In England," says M. Léon Faucher ('Manchester in 1844'), "the bow is perpetually on the stretch ; and hence the sole danger which can menace such a nation."

We have seen in preceding pages some evidences of the eventful and magnificent character of the Elizabethan era. A monarch executed on the scaffold, an Armada defeated, a new religion permanently established, are but the foremost among the mighty crowd of incidents that make the political history of the time so full of interest. And the domestic phenomena of the country present a corresponding grandeur of development. Never in the history of the world, before or since, did great men spring up so numerously ; and deeply gratifying it is to add, not in the majority of cases for mere temporary purposes. The very circumstances that made so many of them less individually important in a worldly point of view while they lived, was but one of the necessary conditions of the splendour of the immortality that awaited them when the patronising "lord" would be forgotten, or only remembered in connection with his "humble servants"—the poor players, when even the powerful intellect of royalty, and the deep sagacious lore of the statesman, would be remembered and admired chiefly as important influences that had been ; whilst the men who amused their leisure hours would be daily and hourly moving and guiding the world. Oh, never should the great poet or artist forget, even in his hours of deepest gloom, the wonderful compensations that are in store for his every pang of disappointment or humiliation! And on the other hand, never should the world forget to test the character of its worship of all the powers that be, by occasional retrospections, which may serve to show it how little it has understood the powers that were to be. It is not admiration, still less is it worldly state and splendour, that our intellectual monarchs demand ; it is the apprehension of the Beautiful and the reverence for the Good, that they themselves feel beyond all other men,

1800.—Tric-trac. (From a Painting by Teniers.)

1801.—A Knotted Garden.

1802.—Bowling-green.

1803.—Bank's Horse.

1804.—The Wedding.

1805.—Arthur's Show.

1806.—Water Quintain.

1807.—Cock-throwing. Shrove Tuesday.

1808.—Quarter-staff.

1809.—Tilting at the Ring.

1810.—The Drunkard's Cloak.

1811.—Palm Sunday. Procession of the Wooden Ass.

1812.—Quintain. (From Pluvenal.)

1813.—Tilting. (From Pluvenal.)

that should in some modified form be extended towards them : it is in such a spirit they study Nature, and the Creator of Nature, and become worthy of their "calling ;" it is in such spirit we should study them, with the certainty of raising ourselves in the scale of intellectual and moral being as our reward for so doing.

It is no new but always a pertinent remark, that when above all such men as those who make illustrious the latter part of the sixteenth century, *one* is seen to rise, towering far above his fellows, we have at once the best general illustration of the stupendous intellectual altitude of William Shakspere. Looking then upon his presence in the sixteenth century as the most distinguishing characteristic of it, let us, by the aid of the very complete series of engravings given in our work, follow his steps with as much accuracy as the known facts or received traditions permit ; leaving untouched the merely probable in the speculation, as out of place in these pages. Of course we begin at Stratford-upon-Avon ; then, that is to say about the middle of the sixteenth century, one of the pleasantest of old English towns ; composed as it was in a great measure of timber houses, often picturesquely beautiful (see an example still remaining in the High Street : Fig. 1678), and situated generally each in its little garden. Stratford derived its name from the *street* or road upon which it stood ; and the *ford* across the Avon, which had, before the days of bridges, to be crossed by the primitive mode of wading through it on foot, or by the assistance of a trusty horse. A wooden bridge at last marked the advancing progress of civilization, and then, in due course of time, a stone one (Fig. 1699) ; still known by the name of its liberal founder—Clopton, an alderman of London.

At Stratford, on the 23rd of April, the poet was born ; and tradition says in the room of the house in Henley Street (Figs. 1679, 1680, 1681), which is known to have then belonged to his father, an alderman of Stratford. In the early part of the present century a butcher held the premises, who put up the following inscription : —

WILLIAM SHAKSPEARE WAS BORN IN THIS HOUSE.

N.B.—A HORSE AND TAXED CART TO LET.

This unseemly juxtaposition of facts no longer exists. We now read simply—

THE IMMORTAL SHAKSPEARE WAS BORN IN THIS HOUSE.

There ought not to be, but there is, much to create painful sensations in the contemplation of this building. As we trace its history, and reflect upon its present position, we are compelled to ask ourselves if the poet, the idol, as he has almost been esteemed, of his countrymen, has, after all, met with any of those attentions which can alone show the unselfish character of our enthusiasm. There is little merit in going to see 'Othello' performed, or in sitting down to read 'As You Like It.' Nor do hosts of commentators make better evidence of the reality of a nation's love and respect. Nine-tenths of them have been but too anxious for their individual glorification to be able to spare any corner of their own hearts for genuine enthusiasm ; how then should they excite such feeling in the heart of their readers ? But, let us ask, what have we done to show, in a quiet, earnest way, the truth and depth of our reverence for his memory ? What national holiday, or feast, commemorates his birthday—brightest as it is in the calendar ? What national monument have we to show ? What measures have we taken for the security even of the very house that pilgrims have come from the most distant parts of the world to visit, or of the other relics of his presence in his birthplace ? Answer the recorded facts of the last half-century.—There was at the garden of New Place, the poet's own residence, a noble mulberry-tree, planted, says an old tradition, by his own hand. Generation after generation of the most distinguished men of their time had sat under its shade, enhancing, if aught could enhance, the value of its associations. That tree was coolly cut down, in 1756, by the clergyman who then had possession of New Place, in order that he might save himself the trouble of showing it to visitors. And when the very just indignation of the people of Stratford was exhibited towards the author of this outrage, he pulled down the house itself, in which Shakspere had lived and died. We mention this at present merely for the sake of illustrating the question—what may not be the fate of the house in which the poet was born ? *That* yet exists ; but it is to our minds saddening and humiliating to have it to say—there is not the smallest security that it may not be pulled down to-morrow. Already strange tricks have been played there. We have seen within the last twenty-five years, an alleged descendant of Shakspere—one of the Harts—a poor old woman, ejected from the house, where she had been accustomed to obtain a lucrative and

very fitting livelihood (in the absence of a better provision being made for her) ; and we have seen that same person, when so ejected, covering the entire walls of the room with whitewash where the poet was born, in order to obliterate the names with which the whole surface was scribbled over—forming, unquestionably, the richest and most interesting series of autographs that ever were collected into one place. The poor creature had a natural feeling of the injustice done to her, direct and indirect, but not enlightenment enough to consider the true character of the mode in which she exhibited her resentment. The whitewash has been partially removed : but, we repeat, the house itself may be pulled down to-morrow, for aught the nation has done to avert such destruction. It may seem a bold, even a wild, speculation, but we really must ask, would it be impossible for this empire, on which the sun never sets, to purchase that little tenement in Henley Street, Stratford-upon-Avon ?

Shakspere's father has naturally been the subject of a great deal of industrious inquiry—since his position, character, and attainments must have so materially influenced the early history of the poet. Aubrey's account of both is delicious for its absurdity. "The poet's father," he says, "was a butcher, and I have been told heretofore by some of the neighbours, that when he was a boy he exercised his father's trade ; but when he killed a calf he would do it in a high style, and make a speech. There was at that time *another* butcher's son in this town that was held not at all inferior to him for a natural wit, his acquaintance and coetanian, but died young"—of course, what was the use of their both living ? It was altogether, we think, a very graceful act of this other embryo Shakspere to go quietly out of the way. And, by-the-by, what a capital verification is here afforded of a popular theory ; that Nature, when she wants great men, will bring them forth. In the sixteenth century she wanted a Shakspere so badly, that she made two, lest one might be unkindly nipped in the bud. Making them both butchers too ! Can there be a doubt as to her determination ? Rowe says Shakspere's family were of "good figure and fashion there, and are mentioned as gentlemen. His father, who was a considerable dealer in wool, had so large a family, ten children in all, that though he was his eldest son, he could give him no better education than his own employment." A passage from Harrison's 'Description of England' (as has been shown in 'William Shakspere : a Biography') appears to explain these and other apparently contradictory statements. He complains that men of "great port and countenance are so far from suffering their farmers to have any gain at all, that they themselves become graziers, BUTCHERS, tanners, SHEEPMASTERS, woodmen, and *denique quid non*, thereby to enrich themselves, and bring all the wealth of the country into their own hands, leaving the commonalty weak, or as an idol with broken or feeble arms, which may in time of peace have a plausible show, but, when necessity shall enforce, have a heavy and bitter sequel."

It is certain, at all events, that when John Shakspere, the father, wooed Mary Arden in the neighbouring village of Wilmecote, and was married to her (probably) in the church of Aston Cantlow (Fig. 1305), he was a man of substance ; and that five years later he gloried in a coat-of-arms, granted by Heralds' College, on account of services rendered by his great-grandfather to Henry VII., possibly on the field of Bosworth.

Let us now glance at the neighbourhood of Stratford—those scenes where the boy-poet spent so many and the most important years of his life. Much of what he afterwards poured forth for the delight and instruction of mankind, had there been first hived up in his ever-busy brain. There is nothing grand in the scenery of the neighbourhood—nothing remarkable for lofty beauty ; but independent of all associations, the scenery possesses the charms of an undulating and richly-wooded surface, in the very highest state of cultivation, and exhibits much even of the picturesque and romantic on the banks of the river that glides through it ; for we must not read too literally D'Avenant's poetical statements, that in consequence of the departure of the poet from the scene

The piteous river wept itself away
Long since, alas !

The Avon is indeed the holy of holies, as it were, to that great natural temple in which the poet chiefly performed his own worship of Nature as her high-priest.

Far from the sun and summer gale,
In thy green lap was Nature's darling laid ;
What time, where lucid Avon strayed,
To him the mighty mother did unveil
Her awful face : the dauntless child
Stretched forth his little arms, and smiled

"This pencil take," she said, "whose colours clear
Richly paint the vernal year;
Thine, too, these golden keys, immortal boy!
This can unlock the gates of joy;
Of horror that, and thrilling fears,
Or hope the sacred source of sympathetic tears."—GRAY.

In all probability the poet has himself described his own beloved river in the exquisite and well-known passage in the 'Two Gentlemen of Verona:'—

The current, that with gentle murmur glides,
Thou know'st, being stopped, impatiently doth rage;
But, when his fair course is not hindered,
He makes sweet music with the enamelled stones,
Giving a gentle kiss to every sedge
He overtaketh in his pilgrimage;
And so by many winding nooks he strays.

How much of interest, as well as of beauty, the Avon, from Kenilworth to Evesham, comprises, is strikingly shown by the mere enumeration of the places comprised within that range:—Guy's Cliff, famous in legendary romance; the proud and magnificent Warwick Castle; the precipitous scenery of Fulbrooke and Hampton Wood; the romantic Hatton Rock, with the confined current rushing swiftly at its base; the pleasingly picturesque scenery of Stratford; the bold and striking marl-cliffs of Bidford; the luxuriant irregularity of Charlecote, and many a sweet tranquil spot, whose loveliness is as yet unknown to fame. Then, again, if the reader be an artist, we commend him heartily to the Avon below Charlecote (Fig. 1694). If he have the true feeling of his art, there is a place to enjoy it. There is a study of models, not *from* but *in* Nature—of beauteous forms, and lights, and shadows, and expression, that might inspire another Gainsborough—or an English Claude Lorraine. The fisherman, or the pilgrim to the localities of Shakspere—whose boat glides noiselessly under the overhanging boughs, may furnish points of unity amid the rich variety of wooded banks, cultivated slopes, flat grassy meadows, long ranges of willow or alder trees, islands of sedge, and lowly homesteads, about which the very peace of Heaven seems to brood. To this part of the Avon may aptly apply the description in the following lines:—

Thy pastures wild,
The willows that o'erhang thy twilight edge,
Their boughs entangling with the embattled sedge;
Thy brink with watery foliage quaintly fringed,
Thy surface with reflected verdure tinged.
Thomas Warton's Monody, written near Stratford.

"Eight villages," it has been noticed, "in the neighbourhood of Stratford, have been characterised in well-known lines by some old resident, who had the talent of rhyme. It is remarkable how familiar all the country people are to this day with the lines, and how invariably they ascribe them to Shakspere:—

Piping Pebworth, dancing Marston,
Haunted Hillborough, hungry Grafton.
Dudging* Exhall, Papist Wicksford,
Beggarly Broom, and drunken Bidford."
William Shakspere: a Biography.

With the last-mentioned place tradition has connected the poet's movements still more closely. About a mile from Bidford (Figs. 1701, 1793) there was, until within the last twenty years or so, a crab-tree (Fig. 1791) long known as Shakspere's crab-tree. The story runs to the effect, that the young poet was one of a party who accepted a challenge for a drinking-bout from certain topers at Bidford, and was in the course of the contest so overcome, that when he set out on his way homeward he was unable to proceed any farther than the crab-tree, and there accordingly he laid him down, and was sheltered by its branches from the night dews. It is a silly story, first told by a silly old twaddler, Samuel Ireland, and may fairly be given over to the goodies.

No other portion of the biography of such a man as Shakspere can have half the interest that attaches to the period of his youth; that all-important period, between boyhood and manhood, when the mighty business of culture is going on, and, when, in the poet's earliest works, the *flower* of the poet's mind becomes apparent, and tells us what the *fruit*, under favourable circumstances, shall be. Unhappily all this portion of Shakspere's career is wrapped in an obscurity that is even denser than the cloud that hangs over his life generally. We do know many things with tolerable certainty that relate to his family, marriage, fortune, and the general tenor of his subsequent career; but here we have nothing but traditions to guide us, most of them probably containing some truth, and most of them, no doubt, disguised by a great deal of fiction. We must,

* Sulky, in dudgeon.

however, make the best of them. And we shall find that, on the whole, they show that the boy-poet led in all probability the very life outwardly that was best fitted for him—a desultory, roving, changeable life, that gave ample scope to the free growth of the wonderful inner life, of which not even himself, much less others, could have had any adequate conception. Rowe, as we have seen, states that the poet's father "had so large a family, ten children in all, that, though he was his eldest son, he could give him no better education than his own employment." He adds, "He had bred him, it is true, for some time at a free-school, where it is probable he acquired what Latin he was master of: but the narrowness of his circumstances, and the want of his assistance at home, forced his father to withdraw him from thence, and unhappily prevented his further proficiency in that language." The free-school here mentioned would no doubt be the grammar-school of Stratford (Figs. 1603, 1608).—But, if another tradition be true, there was a school in which the poet was a teacher, instead of a scholar. "Though, as Ben Jonson says of him, that he had but little Latin and less Greek, he understood Latin pretty well, for he had been in his younger years a schoolmaster in the country" (Aubrey). But we have not yet exhausted the list of pursuits in which he is said to have been engaged; to the butcher, glover, wool-dealer, and school-master, must be added that of an attorney's clerk, and a gardener or florist; both these last avocations being attributed to him by particular persons, on the ground of his minute knowledge of their technicalities, as well as of their spirit. Lastly, these traditions conduct us to the very threshold of the edifice of his fame—the theatre. "This William," adds Aubrey, was "naturally inclined to poetry and acting;" and "began early to make essays at dramatic poetry, which at that time was very low." Here we at last rest on something like a trustworthy foundation. At the time Aubrey especially refers to, when the poet was about eighteen, there can, we think, be no doubt that he was inly communing with himself on the gigantic and sublime task that lay before him, the creation of a new drama, and from the humblest of materials,—the pageants (Fig. 1299) and the mysteries (Fig. 1745) he was no doubt accustomed to see repeatedly at Coventry, and the rude plays which the itinerant companies performed in some large barn, town, or gentleman's hall (Fig. 1746).

But it is ever a fearful and perilous thing for youth to leave its home to launch forth upon the wide world; and especially with one in whom the domestic affections and ties were so strong as they must have been in William Shakspere. As yet, therefore, he lingered at Stratford; and about the same time entered into an engagement that must have appeared to ordinary eyes likely to keep him for ever there, by compelling him to adopt one or other of the ordinary modes of obtaining a livelihood. Let no visitor to Stratford fail to visit also Shottery, the "prettiest of hamlets," and the place where the poet wooed and won his bride. Here were doubtless poured forth in all the intensity of reality the overflowings of a spirit, whose mere reflex, or second self, sufficed to the production of a 'Romeo and Juliet.'

We have described a May-day, with its central picture of the May-Queen in her arbour;—but let us imagine Shottery to be the scene (Fig. 1783), Anne Hathaway to be the Lady of the May, and William Shakspere among the dancers; and what a combination is there not presented to our gaze! Yet it is likely enough that Shottery has more than once witnessed that combination: for she was eminently beautiful, and he one who could not be otherwise than a chief actor in all such sports.

Shakspere's marriage-bond, discovered a few years since, describes his wife as "Anne Hathway, of Stratford, in the diocese of Worcester, maiden." The Hathaways had been settled forty years at Shottery. In an action against Richard Hathaway, 1576, John Shakspere, the father of the poet, appears in a precept as his bond man. Lady Barnard the grand-daughter of Shakspere, makes bequests in her will to the children of Thomas Hathaway "her kinsman." To these facts, tradition adds, and has done so for many years, that at the cottage represented in our engraving (Fig. 1684) Anne Hathaway lived. It is a rustic, homely relic of Old English picturesqueness—with thatched roof, and time-worn timber beams with tall trees about it, and pleasant pastures. Within is preserved a very ancient carved bedstead, that has been handed down from descendant to descendant, time out of mind. Other relics were purchased from the cottage by David Garrick at the Stratford Jubilee. A chair—called Shakspere's courting-chair—was taken off by Mr. Samuel Ireland; and thus, to gratify particular individuals, has this interesting place been stripped of its most precious memorials.

Let us now past to Charlecote. The beautiful stream glides past the mansion. It is not greatly changed from what it was in the days of Elizabeth. The picturesque outlines—the smooth emerald lawns—irregular banks—and abundant foliage of trees—some of which, for aught we can tell, may be old enough to have once attracted the gaze of the great bard himself—these, and the graceful deer, so admirably suited by Nature to tenant such a scene—make up a whole, of which the eye scarcely ever wearies, whilst the memory of the traditions that connect Shakspere with Charlecote, adds an inexpressible charm (Figs. 1692, 1693, 1695).

"An extravagance that he was guilty of forced him both out of his county, and that way of living which he had taken up; and though it seemed at first to be a blemish upon his good manners, and a misfortune to him, yet it afterwards happily proved the occasion of exerting one of the greatest geniuses that ever was known in dramatic poetry. He had, by a misfortune common enough to young fellows, fallen into ill company, and, amongst them, some that made a frequent practice of deer-stealing, engaged him more than once in robbing a park that belonged to Sir Thomas Lucy, of Charlecote, near Stratford. For this he was prosecuted by that gentleman, as he thought, somewhat too severely; and in order to revenge that ill usage, he made a ballad upon him. And though this, probably the first essay of his poetry, be lost, yet it is said to have been so very bitter, that it redoubled the prosecution against him to that degree, that he was obliged to leave his business and family in Warwickshire for some time, and shelter himself in London." (Rowe's Life of Shakespeare.)

Rowe, it will be observed, states the ballad, is "*lost*." Half a century after he wrote this, Oldys, the antiquarian, says, "There was a very aged gentleman living in the neighbourhood of Stratford (where he died fifty years since), who had not only heard from several old people in that town of Shakspeare's transgression, but could remember the first stanza of that bitter ballad, which, repeating to one of his acquaintance, he preserved it in writing; and here it is, neither better nor worse, but faithfully transcribed from the copy which his relation very courteously communicated to me." The stanza, first published by Capell, seventy years after Rowe wrote, corresponded word for word with that of Oldys. It is as follows:—

> A Parliament member, a justice of peace,
> At home a poor scare-crow, at London an asse;
> If Lowsie is Lucy, as some volke miscalle it,
> Then Lucy is Lowsie, whatever befall it.
>   He thinks himself great,
>   Yet an ass in his state,
> We allow by his ears but with asses to mate.
> If Lucy is Lowsie, as some volke miscall it,
> Sing Lowsie Lucy, whatever befall it.

The entire ballad, says Malone, was afterwards "found in a chest of drawers that formerly belonged to Mrs. Dorothy Tyler, of Shottery, near Stratford, who died in 1778, at the age of eighty." The additional stanzas are these:—

> He's a haughty, proud, insolent knighte of the shire,
> At home nobodye loves, yet there's many hym feare.
> If Lucy, &c.
>
> To the sessions he went, and dyd sorely complain,
> His park had been robed, and his deer they were slain.
> This Lucy, &c.
>
> He said 't was a ryot, his men had been beat,
> His venison was stole, and clandestinely eat.
> So Lucy, &c.
>
> So haughty was he when the fact was confess'd
> He said 't was a crime that could not be redress'd.
> So Lucy, &c.
>
> Though luces a dozen he paints in his coat,
> His name it shall Lowsie for Lucy be wrote;
> For Lucy, &c.
>
> If a juvenile frolick he cannot forgive,
> We 'll sing Lowsie Lucy as long as we live;
> And Lucy the Lowsie a libel may call it:
> We 'll sing Lowsie Lucy, whatever befall it.

Mr. Thomas Jones, who dwelt at Tarbick, a village in Worcestershire, a few miles from Stratford-upon-Avon, and died in 1703, aged upwards of ninety, remembered to have heard from several old people at Stratford, the story of Shakspere's robbing Sir Thomas Lucy's park, and their account of it agreed with Mr. Rowe's; and they added, the ballad was stuck upon the park gate, which exasperated the knight to apply to a lawyer at Warwick to proceed against him. Mr. Malone is of opinion that the ballad is an entire forgery; the same belief is expressed in 'William Shakspere,' with the difference, that the first stanza is an old, the rest a modern forgery. Mr. De Quincey urges that the first was a "production of Charles the Second's reign, and was applied to a Sir

Thomas Lucy, not very far removed, if at all, from the age of him who first picked up the precious filth: the phrase 'parliament member' we believe to be quite unknown in the colloquial use of Queen Elizabeth." To this it has been added, "Sir Thomas Lucy, who was on terms of intimacy with the respectable inhabitants of Stratford, acting as arbitrator in their disputes, was not very likely to have punished the son of an alderman of that town with any extraordinary severity, even if his deer had been taken away. To kill a buck was then an offence not quite so formidable as the shooting of a partridge in our own times." ('William Shakspeare.')*

There is one particular series of incidents in the history of Stratford, that, could we trace their exact consequences, would be found, we think, to have had the most momentous influence on the character and fortunes of the poet. We have already alluded to the pageants and mysteries, and the performances of the itinerant players; all of which, there cannot be a question, a youth of Shakspere's tastes, situated in such a locality (Coventry is but a few miles from Stratford), must have been familiar with. But there were representations that can be connected with still greater certainty with the poet's experience, the Bailiff's Plays (Fig. 1753) at Stratford. The books of the corporation show payments made by them for dramatic performances, on many different occasions: some referring to the time when the William Shakspere of fifteen or sixteen years of age might have sat to witness them; and some referring to the year when the father of that same William Shakspere was himself the bailiff, or patron of the players. Those who know the seductions of the histrionic art to the young of all classes, however well or ill qualified to succeed in it, will see how greatly these circumstances were calculated to set on fire the spirit of a highly-imaginative youth; how calculated to turn all his as yet untried and undetermined energies into the direction they suggested; how in short they may have originated, fostered, and matured the histrionic and dramatic aspirations of William Shakspere; for let it never be forgotten, that he *was an actor* as well as a poet: and that whilst we have no evidence that can for an instant be relied on to show that at any time of his life he had ceased to honour the actor's calling, we have unanswerable testimony to his sense of its lofty value, in the well-known passages of Hamlet, where the true mission of the Stage is pointed out, in words that will last as long as the art itself. He must be bold, indeed, who will say that *that* is not a noble mission. Perhaps the actor does not fulfil it:—then make him. Displace the unworthy; and let better men step into their places. Of all vulgar errors, one of the most absurd, mischievous, and we might almost say cruel, is that which constantly seeks to depreciate the character and position of a body of men, and then turn round upon them and complain that they are not—what you would not let them be.

But who were those players at Stratford? Why, in one word the *best* in the kingdom; another important circumstance in the history of the poet. Between 1569, when his father was bailiff or chief magistrate, to 1580, we find that no less than seven distinct companies were engaged in the performance of the Bailiff's Plays. These were, the Queen's Players; her favourite the Earl of Leicester's; the Earl of Worcester's, the Earl of Warwick's, Lord Strange's, the Countess of Essex's, and the Earl of Derby's. It may be necessary here to state, that in Shakspere's time all such companies found it both advisable and necessary, for the purposes of existence and protection, to place themselves under the wing of great personages, and were then known accordingly by the names of their respective patrons. Hence do we preserve at this day at our principal theatres the title of Queen's Servants.

We have referred to the presence of the Queen's Players at Stratford; this was in the year 1587: only two years later we find Shakspere a salaried member of that very company, performing, of course, with them in the metropolis, and already so far advanced upwards that he was also become a shareholder in the concern. How in so short a space so much was achieved, is a question of no ordinary moment. He appears to have been at Stratford so late as 1585, as under that date the register records the births of two of his children; yet within four years, that is to say by 1589, we find him occupying the position described. What were the steps that enabled him to begin public life so favourably as these circumstances imply he did, and to advance so rapidly when he had entered upon it? The tradition related by Pope, and recorded by Johnson, saith:—

"Coaches being yet uncommon, and hired coaches not at all in use, those who were too proud, too tender, or too idle to walk, went on horseback to any distant business or diversion. Many came on horseback to the play; and when Shakspeare fled to London from

* We may here correct an error connected with Sir Thomas Lucy's monument (Fig. 1627). It is not, as there stated at Stratford, but at Charlecote.

the terror of a criminal prosecution, his first expedient was to wait at the door of the playhouse, and hold the horses of those that had no servants, that they might be ready again after the performance. In this office he became so conspicuous for his care and readiness, that in a short time every man as he alighted called for Will Shakspeare, and scarcely any other waiter was trusted with a horse while Will Shakspeare could be had. This was the first dawn of better fortune. Shakspeare, finding more horses put into his hand than he could hold, hired boys to wait under his inspection, who, when Will Shakspeare was summoned, were immediately to present themselves, —'I am Shakspeare's boy, Sir.' In time, Shakspeare found higher employment; but as long as the practice of riding to the playhouse continued, the waiters that held the horses retained the appellation of Shakspeare's boys."

In 'William Shakspere' it is conjectured that the Blackfriars Theatre might have had Shakspere's boys to hold horses, though not Shakspere himself, in order to accommodate the visitors to his theatre, perhaps to draw some additional pecuniary profit to himself, and to afford a guarantee by his name for the security of the horses —when horse-stealing was one of the commonest of occurrences. It is at all events, we think, clear, that this horse-story affords no explanation of Shakspere's position among the Queen's players at the age of twenty-five. But let us now see whether the real facts are not after all, tolerably clear. First, there can be no doubt that by that time the poet must have produced some of his plays; and if he had done so, we need seek no other explanation of his early success. Nashe alludes to 'Hamlet' in the very year in question, 1589, and if there be a remote possibility that he did not refer to Shakspere's earliest version of that tragedy, but to some older production, there can be none whatever, we think, that the passage in Spenser's 'Thalia,' written in 1591, refers to the illustrious poet. From the tenor of that passage it will be perceived, indeed, that he had not only found time to grow famous, but to suffer one of those temporary obscurations that the greatest men in all pursuits have been liable to.

> Where be the sweet delights of learning's treasure,
>   That wont with comic sock to beautify
> The painted theatres, and fill with pleasure
>   The listeners' eyes and ears with melody:
> In which I late was wont to reign as queen,
> And mask in mirth with graces well beseen?
>
> O! all is gone; and all that goodly glee,
>   Which wont to be the glory of gay wits,
> Is laid a-bed, and no-where now to see;
>   And in her room unseemly Sorrow sits,
> With hollow brows and grissly countenance,
> Marring my joyous gentle dalliance.
>
> And him beside sits ugly Barbarism,
>   And brutish Ignorance, ycrept of late
> Out of dread darkness of the deep abysm,
>   Where being bred, he light and heaven does hate:
> They in the minds of men now tyrannize,
> And the fair scene with rudeness foul disguise.
>
> All places they with folly have possessed,
>   And with vain toys the vulgar entertain:
> But we have banished, with all the rest
>   That whilom wont to wait upon my train,
> Fine Counterfesance, and unhurtful Sport,
> Delight, and Laughter, decked in seemly sort.
>
> All these, and all that else the comic stage,
>   With season'd wit, and goodly pleasure graced,
> By which man's life in his likest image,
>   Was limned forth, are wholly now defaced;
> And those sweet wits, which wont the like to frame,
> Are now despis'd, and made a laughing game.
>
> And he, the man whom Nature self had made
>   To mock herself, and Truth to imitate,
> With kindly counter, under mimic shade,
>   Our pleasant Willy, ah! is dead of late:
> With whom all joy and jolly merriment
> Is also deaded, and in dolour drent.
>
> Instead thereof, scoffing Scurrility,
>   And scornful Folly, with Contempt, is crept,
> Rolling in rhymes of shameless ribaldry,
>   Without regard, or due decorum kept;
> Each idle wit at will presumes to make,
> And doth the Learned's task upon him take.
>
> But that same gentle spirit, from whose pen
>   Large streams of honey and sweet nectar flow,
> Scorning the boldness of such base-born men
>   Which dare their follies forth so rashly throw,
> Doth rather choose to sit in idle cell
> Than so himself to mockery to sell.

Thus, to our mind, is one of the most valuable documents we possess for the Shaksperian biography. From this, then, we learn that there had been genuine comedy in existence; but the false— the abusive—the shameless—the worthless, had driven it forth: a madness of licentiousness had possessed the stage under Robert Greene and his wild companions, and "pleasant Willy," true to his own godlike nature and mission, retired. There were at that time in existence, in all probability, the 'Two Gentlemen of Verona,' 'Love's Labour's Lost,' 'The Taming of the Shrew,' the 'Midsummer Night's Dream,' and others which he afterwards revised. We *know* that ten years after there were in existence nine of his comedies, besides eight histories, or historical plays, and three tragedies; all of which must have been written in nine years!— according to the common and absurd theory that represents Shakspere *beginning* to write in 1591.

It is not difficult, then, to see in these circumstances, though, as it were, darkly and afar off, how the poet began public life; but we can even put our finger upon what were, in all probability, the very agencies that first connected the unknown William Shakspere with the flourishing Servants of her Majesty. Among these were Thomas Greene, John Hemynge, and Richard Burbage. Thomas Greene was a comic actor, who obtained such celebrity that one play, not written by him, was emphatically called his— *Greene's Tu Quoque* (see his portrait, Fig. 1764). He, too, was a poet. Speaking of himself he observes, in a passage the authenticity of which has been questioned, but hardly, we think, on sufficient grounds,—

> I prattled poetry in my nurse's arms,
> And, born where late our Swan of Avon sung,
> In Avon's streams we both of us have lav'd,
> *And both came out together.*

At a much later period (1614) Greene notes, in his memorandum book, "My cousin Shakspere coming yesterday to town, I went to see him how he did." But Hemynge—also an honoured name, for it is that of one of the two literary executors of the poet, to whom we are indebted for the first complete edition of his plays—Hemynge is also said to have been the poet's fellow-countryman, and even to be of the very same hamlet of Shottery, from whence Shakspere took his bride. Lastly, and this perhaps is the most important of the whole, there is reason to believe that Richard Burbage (Fig. 1755), the son of the head or manager of the company of the Queen's players, was an intimate friend of the young poet before the name of either had been trumpeted forth through the world of England as the rivals, respectively, in dramatic literature and the histrionic art, of the greatest men of antiquity. It was said of Burbage and Shakspere, "they are both of one country, and indeed almost of one town." These words occur in a letter from Lord Southampton, introducing Burbage and Shakespere to the protection of the Lord Chancellor Ellesmere, when threatened in some way by the Lord Mayor and aldermen of London (Mr. Collier's 'New Facts regarding the Life of Shakespere,' 1835). In 'William Shakspere' it is imagined that Burbage and Shakespere first went to London together. However that may have been, it is highly probable that they began life together, under the guidance of Burbage's father, and it is certain that they long continued it together. Burbage himself became manager of the London Blackfriars theatre, in connexion with Hemynge, and continued the intimate friend of the poet to the latest hour of Shakspere's life. They were, it is supposed, nearly of the same age, and their course ran parallel—the one the greatest actor, the other the greatest poet of the English stage. Richard Burbage was one of the three professional friends mentioned in Shakspere's will; and it is to be remembered that the actor's reputation was chiefly founded on the writings of the poet, his friend: a circumstance *he* never forgot. Two of his daughters were named Juliet, and hence it is supposed that Romeo was originally performed by Burbage. In Richard III. he was greatly admired. Bishop Corbet tells us, in his 'Iter Boreale,' that his host at Leicester

> When he would have said King Richard died,
> And called "a horse, a horse," he Burbage cried

Some of the other characters in which he most excelled are mentioned in the anonymous elegy that, after lying long in MS., was first published in the 'Gentleman's Magazine' for 1825, a copy of which, quoted by Mr. Payne Collier in 'Annals of the Stage,' contains the following lines:—

> He's gone, and with him what a world are dead,
> Which he revived to be revived so!
> No more young Hamlet, old Hieronymo,
> King Lear, the cruel Moor, and more beside,
> That lived in him, have now for ever died.

The elegy thus concludes :—

> And thou, dear earth, that must enshrine the dust,
> By heaven now committed to thy trust,
> Keep it as precious as the richest mine
> That lies entombed in the rich womb of thine ;
> That after times may know that much-loved mould
> Fro others' dust, and cherish it as gold.
> On it be laid some soft but lasting stone,
> With this short epitaph endorsed thereon,
> That every one may read, and reading weep :
> " 'Tis England's Roscius, Burbadg, that I keep."

Phillpot's additions to Camden's 'Remains' dismiss the gifted actor more briefly—" Exit Burbage."

With three such friends, then, as Greene, Hemynge, and Burbage, all supposed to have been intimate with Shakspere in their youth, all so qualified to appreciate his dawning powers, and to give immediate opportunity for bringing them to the test, we can attribute but little weight to the effects of the deer-stealing incident, if ever so true ; and we must smile at the absurdity of the idea that William Shakspere's first introduction to the London theatre was in the position of a mere holder of horses at its doors. Rowe's narrative, on the other hand, is, in all probability, true when it states he was first received into the company in a very mean (by which is meant a very humble) rank ; for it implies nothing more than this :—A young poet of twenty-one, strongly spoken of by a friend in the company, desires to be admitted. He has probably been driven somewhat hastily and prematurely to adopt the vocation of an actor as an indispensable condition of his obtaining a livelihood, whilst his writings as an author are gradually brought forward, and under such circumstances can neither expect himself, nor desire others to expect for him, anything *but* a humble certainty for the present ; accompanied, however, by ample and most important opportunities for the future. When these opportunities arrive, no one knows better than he the value of the

> tide in the affairs of men,
> Which, taken at the flood, leads on to fortune ;

and never was man better prepared for a venture. He is eminently successful. Such, it seems to us, was in truth the transit of William Shakspere, from utter obscurity into the full blaze of a reputation that, with only very slight periods of eclipse, has ever since that time grown brighter and brighter, until its radiance now spreads over and illumines no inconsiderable portion of this vast globe with its many and widely-differing peoples, each possessing its own literary galaxies, but which even to themselves appear pale in the comparison.

Let us now glance at the different theatres with which the poet became connected. The *début* both as actor and poet was made probably at the Blackfriars ; which stood on the spot now known as Playhouse Yard, and situated upon that mean thoroughfare of bye but busy lanes that lead, by a shorter rout than the principal one, from the middle of Ludgate Hill to Blackfriars Bridge. The place is miserably dull and dingy-looking, and one can hardly fancy it could ever have been the scene of such brilliant intellectual displays. The Blackfriars was one of the private theatres, which differed from the public ones in these particulars :—they were entirely roofed over, instead of having, as in ordinary cases, the stage only covered ; there was a regular pit, instead of a mere inclosure ; the performance took place in them by candle-light, in which feature they alone anticipated the modern custom ; and lastly, in them, as devoted to the amusement of the higher classes of spectators, a seat on the stage could be obtained as a matter of right ; though this last custom prevailed also in a lesser degree at all the theatres. The stools on the stage were hired at sixpence each. Two companies performed at the Blackfriars, the one that Shakspere belonged to, and the other consisting of children, who were denominated the children of the Chapel. It was by these youthful players that Ben Jonson's ' Case is Altered ' and his ' Cynthia's Revels ' were performed. It is to them, doubtless, that the passage in ' Hamlet ' applies : " There is, Sir, an aiery of children, little eyases, that cry out on the top of question, and are most tyrannically clapped for 't ; these are now the fashion ; and so berattle the common stages (so they call them), that many, wearing rapiers, are afraid of goose quills, and dare scarce come thither."

In the preliminary chorus to ' Henry the Fifth ' we find the poet located in another theatre :—

> Pardon, gentles all,
> The flat unraised spirit, that hath dared
> On this unworthy scaffold to bring forth
> So great an object ; Can this Cockpit hold

> The vasty fields of France ? or can we cram
> Within this *wooden O*, the very casques
> That did affright the air at Agincourt ?

In the words the " Cockpit " and the " Wooden O," the Globe Theatre (Fig. 1748) is described, which was erected about 1593, in consequence, probably, of the increasing prosperity of Shakspere's company. This, notwithstanding the poet's purposed depreciation of the building, from an artistical desire to elevate the imaginations of the auditory to the height of the argument that was about to engage their attention, was, as the audience of course knew well enough, the largest and finest theatre that had been yet built in the metropolis. And within its walls took place, it is to be presumed, the first performance of all those works which belong, or are supposed to belong, to the full maturity of the poet's genius, as ' Lear,' ' Macbeth,' ' The Tempest,' the Roman plays, and ' Henry the Eighth.' A serious accident marked the introduction of the last-named piece. In a letter from Sir Henry Wotton to his nephew (June, 1603), he writes—" I will entertain you at present with what hath happened this week at the Bankside. The king's players had a new play, called ' All is True,' representing some principal pieces of the reign of Henry VIII., which was set forth with many extraordinary circumstances of pomp and majesty, even to the matting of the stage ; the knights of the order, with their Georges and Garters ; the guards with their embroidered coats, and the like ; sufficient, in truth, within a while, to make greatness very familiar, if not ridiculous. Now King Henry, making a mask at the Cardinal Wolsey's house, and certain cannons being shot off at his entry, some of the paper or other stuff wherewith one of them was stopped did light on the thatch, where, being thought at first but an idle smoke, and their eyes more attentive to the show, it kindled inwardly, and ran round like a train, consuming, within less than an hour, the whole house to the very grounds. This was the fatal period of that virtuous fabric, wherein yet nothing did perish but wood and straw and a few forsaken cloaks ; only one man had his breeches set on fire, that perhaps had broiled him, if he had not, by the benefit of a provident wit, put it out with bottle ale." In the original stage directions to Shakspere's ' Henry the Eighth,' Act i. Scene 4, we read " drums and trumpets, chambers discharged," which, with the mask at Cardinal Wolsey's house, attests the play that Sir Henry Wotton speaks of as ' All is True ' to have been really that of ' Henry the Eighth.' ' All is True ' may have been the first title, and this idea is strengthened by the prologue, which earnestly impresses the *truth* of the story. That it was also called ' Henry the Eighth ' we know by a letter to Sir Thomas Puckering, from Thomas Lorkin, descriptive of the event told by Sir Henry Wotton, the destruction of the Globe. It is there expressly called ' Henry the Eighth.' The accident seems to have been turned to profitable account, by the improvement of the building, in its re-erection the following year.

> Where before it had a thatched hide,
> Now to a stately theatre is turned.—*Taylor, the Water-Poet.*

In the passage we have quoted from Sir Henry Wotton, the extraordinary pomp and majesty " *even* to the matting of the stage " —his curious comment on the Georges and Garters and embroidered coats—the clumsy management of the cannons— and the *thatched* theatre—shows how comparatively unfamiliar were those who first witnessed the representation of the most wonderful series of plays the world has seen, with those costly and laboured contrivances to which in our day the soul of the art has been sacrificed. Poetry, wit, passion, humour, wisdom, could be relished by our ancestors without them. Burbage and Thomas Greene could move all hearts to tears or laughter without them ; and though there can be no objection to add all kinds of appliances that the skill of the painter, the decorator, the carpenter, and the mechanist can devise, if properly subordinated in an artistic spirit, there is every objection to our having these things given us in the place of the other ; as too many managers have done of late years. One illustration of the stage economy of our ancestors is delightful for its almost infantine simplicity. In Greene's ' Pinner of Wakefield ' two parties are quarrelling :—" Come, Sir," says one ; " will you come to the town's end, now ?" " Ay, Sir, come," replies his adversary. And in the next line, having, we may suppose, made as distant a movement as the narrow stage admitted of, he continues, with amusing faith in the imaginative power of the audience,— " Now, we are at the town's end, what shall we say now ?" As to the scenes—in Shakspere's early days they would seem to have been often dispensed with altogether. Sir Philip Sidney ridicules " Thebes written in great letters on an old door." An important part of the old stage was the balcony (Fig. 1752), with windows facing the audience. Here sat the first Juliet; here the court beheld the play in 'Hamlet;' and here, when the balcony was not wanted for the piece, the gallants or dramatic authors that hovered about the stage would sit to view the performance.

Among the other theatres of London which obtained considerable popularity may be noticed the Paris Garden (Fig. 1749), which was used for bear-baitings as well as for the performance of plays, and the Fortune (Fig. 1761), built by Alleyn the actor (Fig. 1762), and founder of Dulwich College, whose history proves how completely he made it worthy, in a pecuniary sense, of its name.

From this brief glance at the state of the drama in the metropolis during Shakspere's time, we return to the poet's history. Whatever the cause of the eclipse that we have referred to as obscuring his reputation, it was but for a moment; and about, or at least immediately after, the accession of James to the throne, we find him in his right position, as the "observed of all observers." The first theatrical performance before James in England was by Shakspere's company, purposely sent for to Wilton by the king, whilst the public theatres were closed, from fear of increasing the plague by "concourse and assembly of people." Malone says, "King James bestowed especial honour upon Shakespere." His authority seems to have been chiefly the Advertisement to Lintot's edition of Shakspere's poems. "That most learned Prince and great patron of learning, King James the First, was pleased with his own hand to write an amicable letter to Mr. Shakespeare: which letter, though now lost, remained long in the hands of Sir William Davenant, as a credible person now living can testify." The story is partially corroborated by the known fact, that the poet's plays formed the staple amusement of the court.

Let us now follow him into his retirement (about 1604) at the place so associated with all his early hopes and struggles, and joys and sorrows—Stratford—the place that was evidently, from first to last, tenderly endeared to him. Here, or in its neighbourhood, he, and his wife, and his children were born; and here had one of the last died. Here too he had closed the eyes of a beloved father and mother; where else should his children perform the like office for him? So he purchased, as early as 1597, a house in Stratford; the best one, it is said, in the town. Sir Hugh Clopton had been its builder in the reign of Henry VII., and in his will it was described as the "great house." It was also, as Dugdale informs us, a "fair house, built of brick and timber." It was called New Place, and here no doubt the poet had his knotted garden (Fig. 1801), and luxuriated in that most useful as well as delightful of all recreations to the student—horticulture. "His garden was a spacious one. The Avon washed its banks; and within its enclosures it had its sunny terraces and green lawns, its pleached alleys and honeysuckle bowers (Fig. 1616). If the poet walked forth, a few steps brought him into the country. Near the pretty hamlet of Shottery lay his own grounds of Bishopton, then part of the great common field of Stratford. Not far from the ancient chapel of Bishopton, of which Dugdale has preserved a representation (Fig. 1611), and the walls of which still remain, would he watch the operation of seed-time and harvest. If he passed the church and the mill, he was in the pleasant meadows that skirted the Avon in the pathway to Ludington. If he desired to cross the river, he might now do so without going round by the great bridge: for in 1599, soon after he bought New Place, the pretty foot-bridge (Fig. 1700) was erected, which still bears that date." ('William Shakspere.') Tradition will have it, that the estate was purchased by means of the assistance of Shakspere's chief patron and friend, Lord Southampton, the nobleman who was so deeply concerned in Essex's revolt. "To him 'Venus and Adonis,' or a sketch of it, the first poetic work given by Shakspere to the world, most likely before he left Stratford, was dedicated. In the letter before mentioned, written by the earl to the Chancellor Ellesmere, he thus, after speaking of Burbage, continues, "The other is a man no whit less deserving favour, and my especial friend, till of late an actor of good account in the company; now a sharer in the same and writer of some of our best English plays, which as your lordship knoweth, were most singularly liked of Queen Elizabeth, when the company was called upon to perform before her Majesty at court at Christmas and Shrovetide. His most gracious Majesty King James also, since his coming to the crown, hath extended his royal favour to the company in divers ways and at sundry times. This other hath to name William Shakespeare; and they are both of one county, and indeed almost of one town: both are right famous in their qualities, though it longeth not to your lordship's gravity and wisdom to resort unto the places where they are wont to delight the public ear. Their trust and suit now is, not to be molested in their way of life, whereby they maintain themselves and their wives and families (being both married and of good reputation), as well as the widows and orphans of some of their dead fellows." Another paper was found with the letter, referring to negotiations for the purchase and sale of the Blackfriars, and containing the following:—

" Item. W. Shakespeare asketh for the wardrobe
and properties of the same playhouse, £500, and
for his four shares, the same as his fellows Burbidge
and Fletcher, viz. £933 s6 d8   £1433 s6 d8 "

From all this we see, first, that whilst it is highly probable the Earl of Southampton would have assisted the poet in the way presumed by the tradition, it is still more probable that the poet did without that assistance, having such ample resources of his own. The letter tells us that he had retired from the stage; but we know that he still continued to do, what was in every way of infinitely more importance—write for it. A Diary found two or three years ago, in the library of the London Medical Society, has some facts of considerable interest respecting the poet's later years. The writer was the Rev. John Ward, vicar of Stratford, the date from 1648 (thirty-two years after the poet's death) to 1679. Referring to Shakspere, he says "he frequented the plays all his younger time, but in his elder days lived at Stratford, and supplied the stage with *two plays every year*: and for it had an allowance so large, that he spent at the rate of 1000l. a year, as I have heard."

There is a notion yet lingering in too many corners of this civilized world, that poets require to be half starved in order to be induced to sing. Those who have chiefly given it credence are little aware how in so doing they expose themselves. We may doubt as to the applicability of their ideas to the poets, but we cannot doubt of the character of the mind in which such ideas originate. In short, they tell us, though quite unconsciously, that they have no faith in goodness and greatness; and that is all they can tell us. But how did the poet use the latter years of a life thus placed beyond all fear of poverty? Why, the very first work of his full leisure was that one, which was unquestionably the sublimest of all his productions— 'Lear.' His latest works were 'Coriolanus,' 'Julius Cæsar,' and 'Antony and Cleopatra,' the commencement, it is supposed, of a new and grand series of dramas, suddenly cut short by what we must consider his premature death, at the age of fifty-three. This event must have been as unexpected as it was premature, for only a month before he describes himself in his will as being in "perfect health and memory (God be praised!)" The Diary before mentioned has these few but weighty words—"Shakspere, Drayton (Fig. 1741), and Ben Jonson had a merry meeting; and it seems, drank too hard, for Shakspere died of a fever there contracted." This was on the 23rd of April; the birth-day was also the day of death. He left a wife and two children. His real estates were bequeathed to his eldest daughter. It was the object of Shakspere by this will to perpetuate *a family estate*. In doing so, did he neglect the duty and affection which he owed to his wife? He did not. His estates, with the exception of a copyhold tenement, expressly mentioned in his will, were *freehold*. His wife was entitled to *dower*. She was provided for amply, by the *clear and undeniable* operation of the English law"—(Life of Shakspere,—Penny Cyclopædia).

It was a sad day in Stratford—that 25th of April—which was chosen for the poet's burial. We know not who were present, but cannot doubt but that Stratford had seen few such occasions. As the mourners passed through the beautiful church avenue, their own grief must have been controlled by the overpowering and most sublime reflections forced upon them, that they were then representing the sadness and desolation of a world. Onward to the church moves the procession; and as the final service proceeds, thoughts of the scope and character and permanency of his writings will intrude, and suggest that, after all, such a death is but a kind of mockery—a submission to the letter of the terrible law of the great King of Terrors, but a triumph over its spirit. There should be another word than death for the cessation of the mere bodily life of a great poet.

Beneath the well-known bust (Figs. 1758, 1759) in, the scarcely less known-chancel (Fig. 1767), we read the verses commencing—

Stay passenger, why goest thou by so fast.

Near the monument, on the floor, is a flat stone, bearing the lines—

Good Frend for Jesus sake, forbeare
To digg t—e Dust EncloAsed He.re
Bless be t—e man ᵗ⁄ᵧ spares t—es stones,
And curst be he ᵗ⁄ᵧ moves my Bones.

It is probable that this stone did not originally belong to the poet's monumental relics ; but presuming that it did, we think we can furnish a proof, that we do not remember to have seen yet given, that they were not Shakspere's, leaving their un-Shaksperian character in style, thought, and feeling quite out of the question. *The very same verses have been used elsewhere*, and therefore there can be little doubt they formed a part of the regular stock in trade of the sexton in the seventeenth century. We have ourselves, within the last few months, either seen them on an ancient monumental stone, or transcribed from some such stone, in the pages of a topographical work ; we forget which : but we are certain as to the fact, and that they were applied to some obscure person.*

Near Shakspere's monument is that (by the same sculptor) of John Combe (Fig. 1626) ; a name made familiar to us by Aubrey's story. "One time," he says, the poet was at a tavern at Stratford when "an old rich usurer was to be buried. He makes there this extemporary epitaph :—

> Ten in the hundred the devil allows,
> But Coombes will have twelve, he swears and vows :
> If any one asks who lies in this tomb,
> 'Hoh !' quoth the devil, ''tis my John o' Coombe.' "

If such an epitaph were written at all by the poet, we may depend upon it that it was at a very different time than Aubrey speaks of— probably in the presence of its subject, and as much for his mirth as that of any one else. The Clopton monument (Fig. 1628) is also in Stratford Church.

We conclude by referring the reader to the portraits (Fig. 1751) and autographs of Shakspere. Of the last it is neccessary to state, in explanation of the alteration of the mode of spelling the poet's name here adopted, that it has been shown in the 'Pictorial Shakspere' that all the six authentic autographs (Fig. 1756) spell the name as it is there spelled.

It is of course quite out of the question that we should here attempt to notice individually Shakspere's rivals in the dramatic art, who were almost as wonderful for their number as for their respective excellences. The imagination indeed recoils from the attempt to weigh and estimate the amount of intellectual wealth that was then devoted to the service of the stage. Put Shakspere aside—forget him, if that be possible—and we should only be a little less filled with wonder and admiration at the powers of such men as would still remain—Marlow, Ben Jonson (Figs. 1742, 1760), Beaumont and Fletcher (Figs. 1766, 1767), and Massinger (Fig. 1769) ; or, could they be also put aside, and their very existence ignored, still a fresh host of men, each a giant, would step forth to challenge our respect and admiration :—A Dekker (Fig. 1770), a Chapman (Fig. 1744), a Ford, a Webster, a Field (Fig. 1768), and others of almost equal mental calibre.

If this spontaneous and mighty combination of minds to found our English drama is calculated to impress us with a deep sense of its grandeur and incalculable importance, there is another combination of the same men that suggests visions of an atmostphere, almost too brilliant and delightful for this working-day world. What would not one give to have listened, for but one hour, to the conversations at the Falcon Tavern (Fig. 1747) by the Bankside, when its usual circle of guests was complete ! Here took place the "wit-combats," of which Fuller speaks, between Shakspere and Ben Jonson : "which two I behold like a Spanish great galleon, and an English man-of-war : Master Jonson (like the former) was built far higher in learning ; solid, but slow, in his performances. Shakespeare, like the English man-of-war, lesser in bulk, but lighter in sailing, could turn with all tides, tack about, and take advantage of all winds by the quickness of his wit and invention." We have a slight example of the genial spirit of their mirth, in the ' Merry Passages and Jests ' compiled by Sir Nicholas Lestrange :—

"Shakespeare was godfather to one of Ben Jonson's children ; and after the christening, being in a deep study, Jonson came to cheer him up, and asked him why he was so melancholy. ' No, faith, Ben (says he), not I, but I have been considering a great while, what should be the fittest gift for me to bestow upon my godchild ; and I have resolved at last.' ' I prythee, what ?' says he. 'I' faith, Ben, I'll e'en give him a dozen good Latin [or latten, an inferior metal] spoons, and thou shalt translate them.' " In answer to this pleasant bit of satire on Ben's excess of learning, ould come no doubt a tremendous broadside against Shakspere's

want of it ; for to have " little Latin and less Greek," would be no learning at all in the poet-scholar's eyes. Another of these places of convivial meeting was the Mermaid ; and one of the actors has himself recorded the character of the performance in lines that show at the same time how well he must have played his own part. Beaumont (Fig. 1766), then scarcely sixteen, writing to Jonson, says—

> Methinks the little wit I had is lost,
> Since I saw you ; for wit is like a rest
> Held up at tennis, which men do the best
> With the best gamester. What things have we seen
> Done at the Mermaid ! heard words that have been
> So nimble, and so full of subtile flame,
> As if that every one from whence they came
> Had meant to put his whole wit in a jest,
> And have resolved to live a fool the rest
> Of this dull life ; then when there had been thrown
> Wit able enough to justify the town
> For three days past,—wit that might warrant be
> For the whole city to talk foolishly,
> Till that were cancelled ; and when that was gone,
> We left an air behind us, which alone
> Was able to make the two next companies
> Right witty ;—though but downright fools, mere wise.

It is to be remembered that there were others equally qualified to share in and to promote these wit-combats besides the dramatic writers, and whose claims were most readily admitted. The chief actors of course found a place. Men like Burbage and Lowin (Figs. 1755, 1763) were an honour even to such a time. Then there were the poets, some or other of whom were no doubt constantly to be found among the illustrious assemblage. Surrey (Fig. 1737), of whom we have before spoken, was of an earlier date : so was Ascham (Fig. 1737), nor perhaps would it have comported with his grave but still genial character, or his position at the right hand of monarchs, to have visited the Mermaid or the Falcon, had he been alive ; but there were Spenser (Figs. 1738, 1739), and Drayton (Fig. 1741), and Daniel (Fig. 1740), and the Water-Poet (Fig. 1743) ; above all, there was Herrick, one of the most delightful whenever he does not think proper to make himself one of the most disgusting of poets. He too has recorded, in his own way, in an epistle to Jonson, his impressions of these extraordinary meetings :—

> Ah, Ben !
> Say how, or when,
> Shall we thy guests,
> Meet at those lyric feasts,
> Made at the Sun,
> The Dog, the Triple Tun ?
> Where we such clusters had,
> As made us nobly wild, not mad ;
> And yet each verse of thine
> Outdid the meat, outdid the frolic wine.
> My Ben !
> Or come agen
> Or send to us
> Thy wit's great overplus ;
> But teach us yet
> Wisely to husband it,
> Lest we that talent spend ;
> And having once brought to an end
> That precious stock, the store
> Of such a wit the world should have no more.—*Herrick.*

The Printers may fitly find place in immediate proximity to the men whose writings their art did so much to preserve for the delight and instruction of posterity. Wynkyn de Worde was the friend, associate, and successor of Caxton. No less than four hundred and eight books are ascribed to his press. Robert Coplande was an assistant of de Worde's and himself dabbled in poetry. Pynson, also (as supposed), an assistant of Caxton, became the first King's Printer. Berthelet, Wyer, and Day were all men eminent in their vocation. The last named, John Day, was the chief printer of the Reformation. It was from his press that Fox's ' Book of Martyrs' issued ; or, as the fact has been paraphrased—

> He set a Fox to write how martyrs run
> By death to life. Fox ventured pains and health
> To give them light ; Day spent in print his wealth.

The marks of all these men will be found among our engravings (Figs. 1771—1776). Day's mark is poetically expressive of the day-spring of the Reformation : a sun rising over a landscape, and a sleeper being awakened with the exclamation, " Arise, it is day !"

1814.—Edinburgh in the Seventeenth Century.

1815.—Holyrood House.

1816.—James the Sixth of Scotland and First of England.

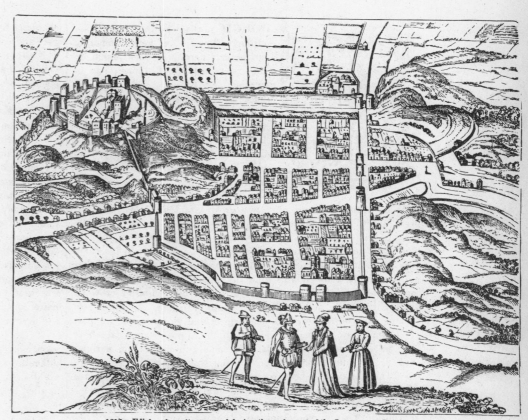

1817.—Edinburgh, as it appeared during the early part of the Seventeenth Century.
(From a Print of the Period.)

1818.—Western Front of Holyrood Palace.

1819.—Anne of Denmark, Queen of James I.
(From a Painting by Cornelius.)

BOOK VI.

THE PERIOD

FROM THE

ACCESSION OF JAMES I. TO THE END OF THE STUART DYNASTY.

A.D. 1603—1688

CHAPTER I.—ANTIQUITIES OF THE CROWN AND STATE.

 HOUGH not in himself, when familiarly known, a very romantic character, there had been much in the past history of James VI. of Scotland, to invest him with the hues of romance in the eyes of those over whom he was to reign with the title of James I. of England. He was the son of Mary Queen of Scots, and Darnley, and was born in the castle of Edinburgh, in 1566; and the circumstance that he should be called, in right of Mary, to reign over two great kingdoms, when she had been sent to the scaffold for only, at the most, desiring to do so, was calculated to strike forcibly upon the popular imagination. The same may be said of the kind of life he had led in his early years—so full of portentous events—and mysteries! The father murdered only a few months after his birth: the mother made prisoner, and compelled to abdicate in his favour: himself crowned at Stirling when he was but little more than a year old:—to become the constant subject of intrigue and violence on the part of the ambitious nobles, who desired to obtain possession of the boy-king in order to carry on the government in his name, perhaps even to put him altogether out of the way, after the fashion in which his father had been spared any further trouble in the cares of the world. Bothwell, we may be sure, had he succeeded in his attempts to induce the honest and estimable Earl of Mar to resign his youthful charge, would not have been very scrupulous, not even for Mary's sake, in ridding himself of such a formidable obstacle to the crown. But the Earl was inflexible, and kept James safe at Stirling through one regency after another. His education, in the mean time, was chiefly conducted by George Buchanan (Fig. 1737) and three other eminent Scottish scholars, under the general superintendence of the Earl of Mar's brother, Alexander Erskine.

As the boy grew in years his position became modified by that growth; not only inasmuch as those who desired to use him for their own purposes could now profess that he was able, in some degree, to administer the affairs of the nation, but also, that the youthful monarch no doubt really began to have his own wants and wishes in state matters. Unhappily there was then about him no one who was both honest enough and powerful enough to tell him of his incapacity, and compel him to leave the business of the government in the hands of capable and properly appointed ministers. Some such effect was aimed at, in all probability, as well as the preliminary removal of a tyrannical and unprincipled minister (Morton), by a body of the Scottish nobles, when, in 1578, they assembled in solemn council, and requested James to take the government into his own hands; but that attempt failed from the Papistical tendency of some of the members of the government that succeeded Morton's: so the unpopular minister regained his power, increased, by the failure of his adversaries, a hundredfold. James, too, was now placed in his hands; and, for a time, everything smiled upon the Earl of Morton. But youthful royalty is seldom lacking in zeal to use prematurely the powers that it knows are to be eventually confided to it; James's personal

character began to exhibit itself. And a fearful succession of dangers and calamities was the consequence.

First, the twelve-year-old monarch must have his favourites. One of the earliest was Esmé Stuart, of the Scottish and royally connected house of Lennox, but born in France, where he was known as the Lord D'Aubigny. James made him also Lord Aberbrothick, Earl of Lennox, Duke of Lennox, Governor of Dumbarton Castle, Captain of the Royal Guard, First Lord of Bedchamber, and Lord High Chamberlain. Another favourite was Captain James Stuart, son of Lord Ochiltree. He, it appears, was made of sterner stuff than Esmé Stuart, and wanted something more substantial than honours or even wealth. It was well known that Morton, the chief minister, had been concerned in the murder of Darnley, but it was little anticipated that any man was to be found to charge him with the crime even in the very council chamber. But this Captain Stuart, acting on a preconcerted scheme with James, did; and before Morton could recover from his surprise at the attack, he was a prisoner. Trial quickly followed upon arrest, and execution upon trial. The guilty Morton was sent to his last account, and the two Stuarts succeeded to his power. The boy-king and his favourites, then, for a time, revelled in the exercise of a perfectly uncontrolled despotism.

If the people of Scotland had been inclined to bear patiently such a state of things, the nobility were not; in fact it would be difficult to tell what state would have been agreeable to men who all desired to be masters. What Chaucer applies to love, they applied to government—

Each man for himself, there is none other:

and a pretty state of confusion their turmoils and struggles produced! Something now was to be done, and it was not long before the old policy was determined upon. In Scotland everybody's panacea for improvement in the affairs of government was—Catch the king. So the Earls of Mar, Glencairn, and Gowrie, with many others of the nobility, took counsel together, and the result was, James was caught in the castle of Ruthven, where he had been invited by the Earl of Gowrie, a son of the Ruthven who murdered Rizzio. This enterprise is known in Scottish history as the Raid of Ruthven. As to the favourites, the one—Esmé Stuart, Duke of Lennox—was banished, and soon after died in France; the other—James Stuart, created by James, Earl of Arran—was imprisoned. Queen Elizabeth, we may observe, was very busily engaged at this time in supporting the views and movements of the conspirators who also received the sanction of a Convention of the National Estates. Behold the boy-king once more in effect a prisoner—his aspiring wings clipped—and the nation for a while at peace, and enjoying apparently a nearer approach than they had long known to good government. Truly a wretched state of things to James and his personal friends! How shall they alter it?

He is at Falkland, one of the three summer palaces of royalty; Linlithgow (Fig. 1822) and Perth being the others. If he could but escape to the castle of St. Andrews (the ruins of which—Fig. 1824—attest to a later time their original strength), he might defend himself until his name—the "king's name"—should build him up a "tower" of greater "strength" in the shape of a powerful army of his subjects. He made the attempt—it was successful: the infamous Arran was recalled; the Earl of Gowrie, notwithstanding a distinct promise of pardon, was sent to the block; and all the other sharers in the Raid of Ruthven were declared guilty of high treason. James at the age of seventeen, was again in possession of an unbridled sovereignty, a circumstance of which his favourite Arran enjoyed substantially the benefit. The King's character was becoming more and more developed, but in directions that could excite no feeling of alarm in the breast of the most ambitious minister—provided only he remained the favourite. Two illustrations of his character here offer. James became a pensioner of Elizabeth; and to please her wrote a letter to his unhappy and imprisoned mother in such unfeeling terms, that she, in her anguish, threatened to leave the load of a parent's curse upon his head.

Unfortunately for James's minister, the sole contingency on which depended the loss of power happened—another favourite arose. This was the Master of Gray, quite as well qualified as himself, by an utter want of honesty of purpose, or true dignity of feeling or behaviour, to fill the coveted post. Arran acted with shrewdness, —he appeared to honour, even while he got rid of, the unpleasant intruder, by giving him the appointment of ambassador to England. But there, the shrewd English politicians gained over the ambassador to their own views, among which was the destruction of Arran, who was not even esteemed valuable enough to play the part of an English tool. While, therefore, the Master of Gray returned to bask in the sunshine of his gracious young sovereign's favour, a body of ten thousand men, headed by the lords concerned in the Raid of Ruthven, entered Scotland in 1585, and advanced to Stirling, where James and Arran were lying. There was no help for it; the one must fly—the other make the best terms he could. All this was peculiarly unpleasant to James—his will thwarted, his favourite gone; but then he remembered he had another favourite, and he was consoled; he began to think of the grandeur of the prospect that dawned upon him from England, and he was content. True, his mother was beheaded on the scaffold, soon after, by his very kind friend and ally, Elizabeth; and that affair naturally excited a little uneasiness, and demanded a little bluster; but Elizabeth was considerate enough to make allowance for both—and then all was right. Excellent woman!—she neither stopped the pension nor prevented his accession to the throne. But no doubt he thought to himself—What dangers had he not escaped from! Like Parolles he had much reason to be thankful that he was not "great of heart." The worst was, that his favourite had acted with too keen an insight into his ultimate wishes, had been too zealous and indiscreet in his labours; for he allowed it to become known that he had actually forwarded the execution he was sent to stay; so it was indispensable that he should be dismissed and disgraced.

James is thirty-three, and he must have a bride, since no very eligible personage offers to fill up the vacancy left by the Stuarts, and Arran, and the Master of Gray, in the king's heart. His chosen queen was the second daughter of Frederick II., King of Denmark; who set out for Scotland, but the elements drove her back to Upslo in Norway, and there James joined her. Queen Anne (Fig. 1819) is described in very different colours by her friends and by her enemies; the one holding her up as a restless intriguer, not only in politics, but in gallantry; the other as a person deserving of high respect. One of the many strange incidents that mark the history of James, and by which his years might almost be counted, arose out of her bridal voyage. It was said that various persons—witches—had raised the storm by which the Queen's life had been endangered on the seas: these were taken up, examined, and *tortured*, when they stated that Francis Stuart, Earl of Bothwell, a grandson of King James V., had employed their art for the raising the storms in question. Stuart was accordingly committed to prison, a circumstance that seems to have raised in him a spirit of revenge, fostered, perhaps, by another spirit that required no raising—the spirit of ambition. Once more the king was to be caught—even in his chief palace of Holyrood (Figs. 1815, 1818). On the night of the 27th of December, in 1561, the daring Earl made a forcible entrance by the aid of his retainers, and after setting fire to several apartments, nearly reached the King's chamber, before any alarm was given; then, however, he was compelled to retreat. His pretence was that of expelling the Chancellor, Maitland, from the King's council, but his real object was shortly made apparent by another failure to seize James at Falkland, and lastly, by his success in that object, on the 24th of July, 1593, when he appeared suddenly at Falkland from England, broke into the palace, and made James his prisoner. He then demanded a pardon, and the dismission of Maitland; both of course were granted, and Bothwell remained minister paramount for his period of "brief authority."

With one other incident of James's Scottish history we conclude

these preliminary notices:—Shortly before James came to England a singular and still mysterious tragedy took place in Scotland, which rendered the names of Falkland and Perth (Fig. 1826;—or St. Johnstoun, as Perth was commonly called) memorable all over the three kingdoms. There was a published account sent abroad from the hand of James himself, headed, "A discourse of the unnatural and vile conspiracy attempted by John, Earl of Gowrie and his brother, against his Majesty's person, at St. Johnstoun, upon Tuesday the fifth of August, 1600, printed at London by Valentine Sims." James was staying at Falkland at the period when the narrative commences; "and being daily at the buck-hunting (as his use is in that season), upon the fifth day of August, being Tuesday, he rode out (Fig. 1823), to the park, between six and seven of the clock in the morning, the weather being wonderful pleasant and seasonable. But before his Majesty could leap on horseback, his Highness being now come down by the equerry, all the huntsmen, with the hounds attending his Majesty on the green, and the court making to their horses, as his Highness' self was, Master Alexander Ruthven, second brother to the Earl of Gowrie, being then lighted in the town of Falkland, hasted him fast down to overtake his Majesty before his on-leaping, as he did." The Master of Ruthven and his brother were both highly popular young noblemen, sons of the Earl of Gowrie, who was beheaded for the Raid of Ruthven, and grandsons of the Ruthven who assisted in the murder of Rizzio. Alexander, "bowing his head unto his Majesty's knee (although he was never wont to make so low a courtesy), drawing his Majesty apart, he begins to discourse unto him, with a very dejected countenance, his eyes ever fixed upon the earth." A countryman, he said, had been found near Perth the evening before, who had "a wide pot, all full of coined gold, in great pieces," hidden under his cloak. The man was lodged in Gowrie Castle, and the King was earnestly requested to come and examine him there. A pot of gold was certainly a very likely bait for a king so sorely in need of gold as James was. However, he refused to go, and rode away after the hounds: but he could not forget that tempting pot of gold, and so musing and wondering he called Ruthven back, and said he would go with him to Perth after the chase, which lasted from about seven of the clock in the morning until eleven and more, being one of the greatest and sorest chases that ever his Majesty was at." The buck slain, James, Ruthven, and a few attendants rode to Perth (Fig. 1826), Ruthven hastening first to warn the Earl of his coming. James's fears seem to have been excited on the road, by the "raised and uncouth staring and continued pensiveness" of the Master of Ruthven, whom he imagined to be somewhat beside himself. Those fears increased when the Earl met him from the castle with four-score of servants and friends, who were mostly armed, whilst James's servants were few and unarmed. The Earl had only had a few minutes to prepare for his coming, and having been in the midst of his dinner, had ridden out in haste with such a train as could be collected on the instant.

On reaching Gowrie Castle, James was annoyed by having to wait a full hour for his dinner, and when it did come, it was very indifferently furnished forth; the "sorry cheer" being excused on the plea of the suddenness of the King's coming. His Majesty being sat down to his dinner—such as it was—he observed that the Earl stood very pensive, and with a dejected countenance, at the end of the table, often whispering over his shoulder "one while to one of his servants, and another while to another; and ofttimes went out and in." The King was, after dinner, conducted by Master Alexander Ruthven to a distant part of the Castle, to see the man with the treasure. He was led "up a turnpike (winding stairs) and through two or three chambers, Master Alexander ever locking behind him every door as he passed." Presently they entered a little study, called the "gallery chalmer," where there indeed stood a man, but certainly no prisoner, for he had a dagger at his girdle. Master Alexander locked "the study door behind him; and at that instant, changing his countenance, putting his hat on his head, and drawing the dagger from that other man's girdle, held the point of it to the King's breast, avowing, now that the King behoved to be in his will, and used as he list; swearing many bloody oaths, that if the king cried one word, or opened a window to look out, that dagger should presently go to his heart; affirming that he was sure that now the king's conscience was burthened for murdering his father." James reasoned with him on the enormity of the offence, and promised, "if he would spare his life, and suffer him to go out again, he would never reveal to any living flesh what was betwixt them at the time." Moved, the young man then put off his hat, and promised that his life should be safe. He went out to bring in the Earl his brother, leaving the king in the

1821.—Canongate Gaol, Edinburgh.

1823.—Falkland.

1820.—Heriot's Hospital, from the Castle Hill, Edinburgh.

1822.—Linlithgow.

1824.—Castle of St. Andrew's.

1825.—James I. (From a Painting by Vandyke.)

1826.—Perth, and its Vicinity.

1827.—Great Seal of James I.

1828.—James I.

1829.—Glamis Castle.

577

charge of the man (the Earl's steward), who had stood "trembling and quaking, like one condemned." He declared himself ignorant of ...is master's purpose, and said that he had been locked in the closet just before the King came, without his leave being asked. Alexander Ruthven returned, told James that he must die, and proceeded to bind his hands with a garter. Breaking from his gripe, James seized the hand which Ruthven already had laid upon his sword, and the two at the same moment of time clasped each other's throats, Ruthven having two or three of his fingers in the king's mouth, to prevent him from crying out. In this terrible position, James is said to have exclaimed to his assassin:—"Albeit ye bereave me of my life, ye will nought be King of Scotland, for I have both sons and daughters." He managed to drag Ruthven to the window, where his piercing cry, "I am murdered," reached some of his servants, whom the Earl had attempted to mislead, by saying to them the King had departed by a back way. Sir John Ramsey was the first to save his master, and hence became his especial favourite. Finding a private entrance of the "Blak Turnpike," or secret stairs, with the door standing open, he hurried up, stabbed the Master of Ruthven with his dagger, and thrust him out at the door, just as Sir Thomas Erskine and Sir Hugh Herries were also coming up to the king's rescue, who finally despatched him on the stairs. After these, came up the Earl of Gowrie, who was instantly "stricken dead with a stroke through the heart, which Sir John Ramsey gave him." The alarm had been caught by others, and the Duke of Lennox, the Earl of Mar, and their company, were forcing the doors with hammers. The Earl of Gowrie was Provost of Perth, and his mysterious death occasioned a great outcry in the town. The people of Perth uttered "most irreverent and undutiful speeches against his Majesty," and gathering about the place, cried out "Bloody butchers! traitors! murderers! Ye shall all die! Give us forth our provost! Woe worth ye greencoats! woe worth this day for ever! Traitors and thieves! that have slain the Earl of Gowrie." So far was the popular feeling from sympathising with James, that they believed him "a doer, and not a sufferer." (Galloway's discourse before the king.) The clergy (remembering the Presbyterian tendencies of the Ruthvens) refused to read James's 'discourse' from their pulpits, and one Mr. Robert Bruce, a distinguished minister, when urged to bend, said that though he *respected* his Majesty's account of the affair, he would not answer for *believing* it. He was deprived and banished. Under these circumstances, that man was most loyal who blackened most the character of the Earl of Gowrie. At the judicial investigation, Master William Reid deposed to certain magical characters found in his lord's pocket after his death; that he always kept the characters about him; and that in *his* opinion it was for no good. One James Weimis of Bogy had had conversations with the Earl on mysterious subjects: the Earl had spoken of serpents made to stand still at the sound of one Hebrew word; of an Italian necromancer with whom he had had dealings; of a man who had been hanged after his prediction of the event. Weimis had counselled the Earl to beware with whom he did communicate such speeches, who answered that he would communicate them to none except great scholars. The truth was, the Earl and his brother were men of rare cultivation of mind, literary and scientific; they had added all the various knowledge that could be obtained by travel to such accomplishments as Scotland then afforded. The excellence and refinement of their characters would perhaps have continued to outweigh the king's account in the estimation of most, had not other evidence accidentally corroborated much if not all of his story, nine years after it was published. Various motives have been ascribed to the brothers by various writers, but chiefly personal ambition. The attempt has partly been traced to the contrivance of Elizabeth, with whose ambassador, Sir Henry Neville, the Earl of Gowrie had contracted an intimate friendship in Paris, and from whom he had received marks of especial favour. On this supposition, the real object would have been once more to catch in order to coerce James, and thus be able to control his government—the very object effected by the Raid of Ruthven sixteen years before, which had also been instigated by Elizabeth. The conduct of James at that time was not likely to have been forgotten by the sons of the earl, who had been put to death for his share in the "Raid," after James had formerly pardoned him. It has been supposed that some of the incidents of this Gowrie conspiracy were made use of by Shakspere in his 'Macbeth.' Glamis Castle (Fig. 1825), the traditionary scene of the murder of Duncan, is in the neighbourhood of Perth. But this tragedy, and the reflections and suspicions created by it, were gradually forgotten, as a new and extraordinary state of things opened upon the two neighbouring countries, in the approaching union by the "golden link" of James's crown.

One of the most peculiar positions in which England has ever been placed with regard to the regal succession, was when, on the death of Elizabeth, a foreign king succeeded to the throne, and who was not foreign only, but the head of a people between whom and the English people there had been constant and bitter hostility for many centuries. And that the event in question was as important and beneficial as it was peculiar, is shown most forcibly, when we turn our eyes from the present relations of Scotland and England, to look on the similar relations of Ireland with this country. Had we not obtained Scotland in just the way we did, though at the cost of letting Scotland appear to obtain us, we should probably have seen there the same melancholy results that Ireland exhibits. Ought we not as a nation to draw from these facts their most transparent moral, that in politics there *is* a something infinitely worse than a "blunder"—namely, a disregard for the rights of other nations; and that the crime brings with it its own punishments of disappointment, suffering, and humiliation, to all parties. We have not had the miserable gratification of being able to say we conquered Scotland, and therefore, in truth, in the best of senses, we have conquered her; that is, wherever our own religion, morals, literature, art, science, or knowledge of government have been superior, that superiority has taken possession of the minds of the people, and produced its natural consequences. On the other hand, we have conquered Ireland, in order to show our extreme moral weakness; we have neither been able to impart to her our own civilization, or knowledge, or prosperity, or point out to her a way to work out such social requisites for herself. Is it not then high time that all such conquests should be treated as suicidal; as conferring ruin on the one hand—deep mortification and disgrace, too often the preliminaries of ruin, on the other?

It cannot either be said that it was owing to the great enlightenment of the monarch whose destinies called him to preside over the two nations, under circumstances seemingly so critical. We have already seen enough of James's character to be satisfied on that point. All the subtler and deeper influences that unite or divide nations were left for the most part to take their own course as far as King James was concerned. One thing only was expected from him, that he should not hand over his new kingdom as a prey to the courtiers and greedy expectants of all kinds of the old one; but James understood no such niceties: and England was not spoiled at the beginning of his rule by the indulgent fulfilment even of that humble expectation. On the contrary, the prodigality with which he distributed the honours and riches that flowed into his hands among his Scottish favourites or companions and followers, completely disgusted the people of this country at the very outset. But the course of affairs had determined that James could be their king without dishonour, and the English government that he ought to, and should be—so they acquiesced.

James at this eventful period was in his thirty-seventh year. Let us pause for one moment to glance at the person of the monarch who was to hold such a conspicuous position in the eyes of the European world. He was by no means a handsome man. On the contrary, his appearance (Figs. 1816, 1825) is described as having been as unprepossessing and as undignified as can be well conceived. His legs were too weak to carry his body, his tongue was too large for his mouth, he was goggle-eyed—with eye-balls ever rolling, yet vacant,—he was slovenly and dirty in his dress, ungainly in his carriage, and displayed the pusillanimity of his nature by all sorts of contrivances against assassination, one of which was the wearing his doublet so thickly wadded as to be dagger-proof. We may complete the picture by the addition of the traits which Bacon's account of his impressions of James the first time he saw him furnishes:—"Your lordship shall find a prince the furthest from vain glory that may be, and rather like a prince of the ancient form than of the later time: his speech is swift and cursory, and in the full dialect of his nation, and in speech of business short, in speech of discourse large. He affecteth popularity by gracing them that are popular, and not by any fashion of his own; he is thought somewhat general in his favours; and his virtue of access is rather because he is much abroad, and in press, than that he giveth easy audience; he hasteneth to a mixture of both kingdoms and nations, faster, perhaps, than policy will well bear. I told your lordship once before my opinion, that methought his Majesty rather asked counsel of the time past than of the time to come."

The hollowness of mere worldly ties could scarce find a better illustration than the eagerness with which several of Elizabeth's eager courtiers hastened to Edinburgh to her no less eager heir to communicate the "glad tidings" of her decease. One John Ferrour afterwards claimed to have been prime messenger but that honour seems rather to have belonged to one of Elizabeth's own relatives, Sir Robert Carey, son of Lord Hunsdon, who was on the watch in Richmond Palace the night of the Queen's death, when his sister, Lady Scrope, stole from the deathbed of the Queen to tell him that all was over. Before Cecil and the other lords of the Council had time to collect their thoughts, Sir Robert had taken flight. A journey to the sister kingdom was not then quite so easy as at present, and, with all his speed, Sir Robert did not enter Edinburgh until the night of the 26th of March—Elizabeth having expired at three o'clock of the morning of the 24th. Until the official report arrived, James amused himself with guarding the precious secret. The official report took four days more to reach Edinburgh. It was sent by the Council, among whom the son of the great Cecil had sat as chief. James had been proclaimed, and generally accepted by the English nation. What a relief for the longing heart of the poor Scottish king! Doubts and fears, an undistinguishable throng, must have been harassing his spirits, lest after all, the golden dream might turn out an illusion. He must have recollected that no less than thirteen or fourteen claims to the succession had been talked of before now; and he would have often shivered at the name of Arabella Stuart (descended, like him, from the eldest daughter of Henry VII.); and often have trembled at the thought of the descendants of the favourite sister of Henry VII.—Mary, wife of Charles Brandon, Duke of Suffolk—to whom Henry's will had bequeathed his crown, in case of his own children—Edward, Mary, and Elizabeth—leaving no heirs. Happily for James some doubts hung over this will; and Sir Robert Cecil—zealous servant!—had secured the dangerous Arabella,—whilst all the other diverse claims seemed to be forgotten, or set aside as by common consent. In case of tumult, too, Sir Robert Cecil had given the country a sample of the prompt determination with which any opposition to the new Sovereign would be put down, by arresting eight hundred persons in two nights, and sending them to serve on board the Dutch fleet—under the convenient appellation of "vagabonds;" and thus, all dangers past, James the Sixth of Scotland was in addition James the First of England.

Not happening to have the strongest head in the world—the absolute assurance of his good fortune almost turned it. Farewell now to all the thousand ills which he had endured whilst wearing the barren name of King in Scotland, without being allowed to do as he liked in his government, without money to spend, often without even personal freedom. He was going now to a far different state of things. He could now do exactly as he chose. He would be absolute King. He would have an endless store of wealth. In fact, there hardly seemed a limit to what he would have, or what he would do. If the blessing of this change seemed almost too great for belief, there was tangible evidence before him in the money sent by Cecil for his journey to London, and without which he would have had to stay where he was.

But, though the English Council were awaiting his august presence in the most agreeable of humours, they found themselves rather in an awkward dilemma when James sent to ask for the Crown jewels of England for his Queen! They felt themselves obliged to delay complying with this request. Well, no matter, James could go, if his wife remained behind; and so he prepared to take leave of Edinburgh, and think only thenceforward of London.

Few men could have left such a place, and their birth-place, without some feeling of regret, but James was excusable even if no such feeling had place in his mind. It had been connected, in his mind, with too many horrors: the murder of Rizzio before his mother's eyes, and the repeated attempts on his own person, had probably left him little relish for the natural beauties of the city. The Edinburgh, too, of the beginning of the seventeenth century was a very different thing from the Edinburgh of the middle of the nineteenth. It was anything but a "city of palaces" when James was familiar with it.

Our engravings of Edinburgh (Figs. 1814, 1815, 1817, 1821)—which exhibit the city in the time of James—will suggest to such of our readers as are acquainted with Auld Reekie the principal alterations that have been made in the appearance of the city since that time. We see in them, also, a building that reminds us of one of the host of persons who prepared to accompany James, and were scarcely less anxious than himself for a sight of the promised land. We refer to George Heriot, the "Jingling Geordie" of Scott's 'Fortunes of Nigel,' and the King's goldsmith, whose previous and subsequent career we may here dismiss in a few words. He was descended from a family of some consequence, the Heriots of Trabrown, in East Lothian. George Heriot followed his father's trade, and had flourished so well in it, that, in a space of ten years, his accounts against James's queen for jewels, &c. had amounted

to nearly forty thousand pounds. Like most of his order at that time, Heriot was a banker as well as a goldsmith, and ministered to the necessities of the needy great, receiving plate and gems for security. From these united sources his wealth grew, until, in 1624, when he died, he left—after providing for all who had any just claim on him—between twenty-three and twenty-four thousand pounds in trust with the Edinburgh magistrates, for building an "Hospital and Seminary for Orphans," in imitation of Christ's Hospital in London: and thus arose one of the noblest establishments in Great Britain. The building (Fig. 1820) forms a conspicuous feature in the chief views of Edinburgh.

On the 6th of April James set out for Berwick, where he made his first halt, wrote to thank the Council for their money—told them he meant to enter York in state progress in "solemn manner," and desired them to send thither "all such things as they in their wisdom thought meet," hinting that their coming to meet him would be agreeable, though he did not press this, "the journey being so long;" and he desired them to consider whether it would be more honour for the deceased Queen to have the funeral finished before he came, or to wait and have him present at it. This was an indirect mode of telling the Council that he wished all that melancholy business done with as soon as possible; so Queen Elizabeth was speedily consigned to her tomb in Westminster, in the presence of fifteen hundred voluntary mourners clad in deep black. One could hardly wish the great Queen to have been better attended. In Henry VII.'s Chapel now lie her remains, in strange juxtaposition with those of her "sister" of Scotland; the monuments of the two—so like in their appearance (Figs. 1562, 1575) —looking for all the world just as though they had been indeed sisters in love during life, and now in death were not to be divided. To return to Elizabeth's successor at Berwick: in the exuberance of his delight, he actually mustered courage to fire off a great piece of ordnance in his own honour. From Berwick, after having written to ask for all that he could think of that would embellish his regality—coaches, horses, litters, jewels, stuffs, and a Lord Chamberlain, "which was very needful,"—he travelled on by exceedingly slow stages (banqueting wherever he could with the English nobility or gentry) to Newcastle, which he reached *seven* days after quitting Berwick. At Newcastle a bright idea occurred: he would have coins of his own. It had been the custom in England for "his progenitors" to have "some new monies made in their own name against the day of their own coronation." So he wrote to have new coins of gold and silver prepared. Settling his arms, quarterings, and mottoes, furnished him with some more pleasant employment. In two days after leaving Newcastle, he reached the house of Sir William Ingleby at Topcliff, when he sent off *another* letter to the Council, chagrined at their not coming and bringing him the crown jewels. Then he went on to York, at the rate of about fifteen miles a day. No child, luxuriating over some unaccustomed delicacy, ever spun out its enjoyment with greater ingenuity and zest than James in this progress. At Topcliff he was gratified by a secret conference with Secretary Cecil. Three days of banqueting and parade were spent at York, where he knighted no less than thirty-one persons—a prerogative of his dignity that he greatly delighted in, having already knighted fourteen before he came to York, and conferring the same honour on eighteen more at Worksop, in Nottinghamshire, and eight when he came to Newark Castle. At the latter place the intoxicated King—for so we may style him with strict propriety—not content with making one of his prerogatives ludicrous, exhibited another— the most awful that can be placed in the hands of a mere mortal— in a light that must directly have opened the eyes of many to the unfitness of the new sovereign for his position.

Stow says, "In this town, and in the court, was taken a cutpurse doing the deed, and being a base pilfering thief, yet was all gentlemanlike in the outside: this fellow had good store of coin found about him, and, upon examination, confessed that he had, from Berwick to that place, played the cutpurse in the court. The king, hearing of this gallant,"—ordered him—to be examined or tried?—No; but to be hanged up forthwith; and hung he was! James's opinion of his own omnipotence he expressed in words as well as in deed: "Do I make the judges?" he is said to have joyously exclaimed to some of his English counsellors. "Do I make the bishops? Then, God's wounds! I make what likes me law and gospel." On the road between Newark and Belvoir Castle the sapient King knighted four persons, and *forty-five* at Belvoir. Another amusement had been added by this time, equally characteristic—hunting along the road; but as James, with all his prerogatives, and his courtiers' care in bolstering him up, could not manage to ride even tolerably, he got a fall, though, observes

1830.—Hatfield House.

1831.—Coronation of James I.

1832.—St. James's Palace, and City of Westminster. (Temp. James I.) Viewed from the Village of Charing. (From an ancient Picture engraved in Nichols's Progresses.

1833.—Banqueting House, Whitehall; and Gate-House, supposed to have been designed by Hans Holbein.

1834.—Banqueting-House, Whitehall.

1835.—Print of Garnet's Straw.

Bates.   R. Winter.   C. Wright.   J. Wright.   Percy.   Fawkes.   Catesby.   T. Winter.
1836.—The Gunpowder Conspirators.   (From a Print published immediately after the discovery.)

1837.— Garnet's Straw

my lord out of the loue i beare to some of youer frendz
i haue a caer of youer preseruacion therfor i would
aduyse yowe as yowe tender youer lyf to deuys some
excuse to shift of youer attendance at this parleament
for god and man hathe concurred to punishe the wickednes
of this tyme and thinke not slightlye of this aduertisment
but retere youre self into youre contri wheare yowe
maye expect the event in safti for thowghe theare be no
apparance of anni stir yet i saye they shall receue a terrible
blowe this parleament and yet they shall not seie who
hurts them this councel is not to be contemned becauss
it maye do yowe good and can do yowe no harme for the
dangere is passed as soon as yowe haue burnt the letter
and i hope god will giue yowe the grace to mak good
use of it to whose holy proteccion i comend yowe

1838.—Fac-simile of the Letter to Lord Monteagle.

Guido Fawkes

Guido

1840.—The Autographs of Guido Fawkes
before and after torture.

To the right honorable
the lord mounteagle

1839.—Superscription of the Letter.

1841.—House of the Conspirators at Lambeth   (From an old Print.)

1842.—Vault beneath the Old House of Lords   (From an Original Drawing.)

Cecil—surely with covert satire—in relating the accident, "It is no more than may befall any other great and extreme rider as he is, at least once every month." Behold his Highness then at last at Theobalds Park, Cecil's sumptuous seat, where four days were spent in receiving the homage of all the Lords of the Council, kneeling, (a gratification sufficient surely to deserve the making of twenty-eight more knights,) in the remodelling of a new Cabinet by Cecil, and in the enjoyment by James of luxuries and elegancies to which he had lived a stranger until this progress, and which had filled him with astonishment at every English gentleman's house that he visited. After a journey of five weeks, James at last came in sight of London: and how did he take possession of his new capital—the nucleus of all the greatness of the kingdom he was called to reign over? Truly—thus: after being met at Stamford Hill by the lord mayor and aldermen in scarlet robes—"From Stamford Hill to London was made a train with a tame deer, that the hounds could not take faster than his Majesty proceeded." After this ludicrous first presentation of himself to the metropolitans, he stopped at the Charter House at six in the evening, and there made another bevy of new knights.

James was crowned on the 25th of July; and a Dutch print of the time, copied in our engraving (Fig. 1831), shows us, as clearly as if we were present, all the different stages of the ceremony. In more antique times it would have been considered that the occasion was accompanied by evil omens. The weather was unusually dull and rainy; and the plague raged so violently that the people were forbidden to go to Westminster (Fig. 1832) to see the shows and pageants. Nor was it long before events took place that might ha satisfied the believers in such evil portents that they had not be mistaken.

When Cecil so managed matters that James, on his way to London, spent four days at Theobalds (Fig. 1843), he rightly considered he had succeeded in avoiding all opposition to his own private views—that in a word, he had completely outmanœuvred his rivals and enemies; especially Raleigh and Lords Grey and Cobham:—and so they found. The two lords were left without a chance of promotion; and Raleigh was deprived of whatever posts he held, the government of the island of Jersey alone excepted. At the same time great dissatisfaction was felt by the Catholic and the Puritan bodies on account of James's faithless violation of the promise he had given of toleration. And now began various plots and projects, which were, it seems, ultimately reduced into two—the "Bye" and the "Main." As to the object of the "Bye,"—first and foremost it appears the poor king was once more to be caught; for the English conspirators seem to have taken a fancy to that custom of their Scottish brethren in revolt. He was then—just as in Scotland—to be compelled to change his ministers, grant toleration, and a free pardon to all the plotters. Much more than this was charged against the persons concerned; but, in cases of failure, that is so commonly done, that we need take little notice of such allegations. The "Main" was undoubtedly a very grave affair, having for its aim the elevation of Arabella Stuart to the English throne. Here Cobham was the chief actor; although it was suspected a more able and dangerous person, Raleigh, was behind the scenes. And as it is chiefly for his sake that we refer to these plots, we shall simply premise that they were discovered—it is supposed through the common medium, a treacherous confidante—and that Grey, Cobham and many others were tried, found guilty, and sentenced to death. Raleigh was tried separately; and few historical trials have excited a deeper or more permanent interest.

He was charged with conspiring to kill the king—to raise a rebellion, in order to change religion and subvert the government—and for these purposes to incite the king's enemies (especially the Spaniards) to invade the realm. Certain overt acts were then alleged, showing, if true, that Raleigh and his confederates of the "Main" intended to put Arabella Stuart in the place of James. The trial began at eight in the morning, and lasted till eleven at night. Raleigh at the time laboured under great disadvantages; he had irrevocably offended the sovereign, whatever the issue of the present trial; and, on the other hand, he knew the people felt no sympathy with him. He had been at once proud and rapacious. But the genius and better nature of the man so shone out on this eventful day, that the feelings of his countrymen generally seem to have been completely changed as they heard how virulently he was attacked, and how gallantly he defended himself. The chief evidence produced against him was a confession by Cobham, which charged Raleigh with being the first mover of the plot.

Coke—(would it were possible to forget altogether his share in the proceedings of the day, for they have dimmed eternally an illustrious name!)—Coke began in a manner that showed the spirit of the prosecution, by referring to the horrible intentions of the "Bye." "I pray you, gentlemen of the jury," interposed Raleigh, "remember I am not charged with the 'Bye,' which was the treason of the priests." Coke replied—"You are not, but it will be seen that all these treasons, though they consisted of several parts, closed in together, like Samson's foxes, which were joined in their tails, though their heads were separated." Presently Coke grew heated, and not satisfied with the charges in question, must add others calculated to inflame the minds of the jury. Raleigh, he said, was "a damnable atheist," the "most vile and execrable of traitors." "You speak indiscreetly, barbarously, and uncivilly," returned the prisoner. But Cooke continued—"I want words to express thy viperous treasons." "True, for you have spoken the same thing half a dozen times over already," was the witty reply of the self-possessed Raleigh.

If, in this fierce conflict of debate, where life depended (on the one side) upon a successful parry to every thrust, Sir Walter interested all present, and in fact obtained an advantage over his prosecutors by making them lose their temper, he rose to a still higher point, whenever he could, without interruption, address himself directly to the business of defence. "I was not so bare of sense," he observed in one part, "but I saw that if ever this state was strong and able to defend itself, it was now. The kingdom of Scotland united, whence we were wont to fear all our troubles; Ireland quieted, where our forces were wont to be divided; Denmark assured, whom before we were wont to have in jealousy; the Low Countries, our nearest neighbours, at peace with us; and instead of a Lady [Elizabeth] whom *Time had surprised*, we had now an active king, a lawful successor to the crown, who was able to attend to his own business. I am not such a madman as to make myself in this time a Robin Hood, a Wat Tyler, or a Jack Cade." The poetical elegance and delicacy of the thought expressed in the three words we have Italicised, was perhaps never surpassed; and they become the more beautiful when we reflect that there was no courtier-like need for such delicacy in referring to Elizabeth's age, since she was no longer living to show either pleasure or displeasure at the allusion.

In answer to some compliment to Cobham, who, according to Coke, had been drawn into evil by Raleigh, the latter said Cobham was "a poor, silly, base, dishonourable soul." And certainly the evidence that followed was conclusive as to the truth of the statement. The prisoner produced a letter written by Cobham in the Tower since his arrest for the plot, completely exonerating Raleigh before "God and his angels." Coke, in answer, produced another letter, written by Cobham only the day before, repeating the charges he had first made. Raleigh, in explanation, said, that Cobham's wife had urged him to save himself by accusing his friend; and immediately demanded that his accuser should be brought before him. It makes one shudder to think of the treatment experienced at that time by all men whom a government chose to call traitors:—the demand was made in vain. Again it was urged. "My lord," said Raleigh earnestly, "let Cobham be sent for; I know he is in this very house! I beseech you, let him be confronted with me! Let him be here openly charged upon his soul—upon his allegiance to the king, and if he will then maintain his accusation to my face, I will confess myself guilty." Still in vain was the demand made. The crown lawyers would not notice it, but endeavoured to bear him down by a torrent of words. But there they failed. "I will have the last word for the king," exclaimed Coke. "Nay, I will have the last word for my life," was the reply. "Go to!—I will lay thee upon thy back for the confidentest traitor that ever came to the bar." This was too much for some present who could interfere. Cecil reproved Coke, and said he was harsh and impatient. Hereupon the great attorney-general sat down. Raleigh was found guilty, and sentenced to death, with all the usual barbarities. The intelligence was immediately taken to James, and the feelings of the messengers show very strikingly how Raleigh had that day won "golden opinions" from nearly all present. "The two first that brought the news to the king were Roger Ashton and a Scotchman; whereof one affirmed, that never any one spoke so well in times past nor would do in the world to come; and the other said that, whereas when he saw him first, he was so led with the common hatred that he would have gone a hundred miles to have seen him hanged, he would ere he parted have gone a thousand to have saved his life. In one word, never was a man so hated, and so popular in so short a time." (Sir Dudley Carleton).

Monday was fixed for Raleigh's death. A window in his prison opened on the castle-green of Winchester, through which he may have beheld some of his fellow-sufferers pass by on their way to the scaffold, perhaps even have dimly discerned the "bloody handling" to which they were subjected; and have endeavoured to familiarise himself, by that terrible example, with the horrors of his own impending execution. Two priests went first, who died boldly, notwithstanding the fiendish barbarities inflicted upon them. George Brooke, a gentleman, followed. He was dressed in a black satin suit, a richly-worked nightcap, and black damask gown : for the possession of this last article the sheriff and the headsman could not help quarrelling, even upon the scaffold. Markham and the Lords Grey and Cobham were also to die the same day. But, as their time arrived, the condemned men, and the spectators who came to watch their dying pangs, found a series of the most extraordinary and fantastic surprises prepared for them ; such as could have issued from no brain but that of King James.

Markham, after taking his last farewell of his friends on the scaffold, was respited for two hours, on pretence that he was badly prepared for Heaven. Lord Grey, after going to the scaffold like a bridegroom, supported on each side by two of his best friends, and attended by a troop of young noblemen, and after having made his last supplication to God, and whilst waiting the death-signal, was taken away—because King James would have Lord Cobham go before him. Lord Cobham—who it was afterwards conjectured was deeper in the mystery than most people—came up to die with a show of bravery most unexpected by those who knew the character of his mind. But he, like Grey and Markham, was respited, and they were brought back to confront him. No wonder they looked strangely and wildly upon each other, " like men beheaded and met again in the other world ;" for Grey and Markham, if not Cobham also, believed the others dead. The scene was most dramatically got up.

" Now all the actors being together on the stage (as use is at the end of a play), the sheriff made a short speech unto them, by way of interrogatory, of the heinousness of their offences, the justness of their trials, their lawful condemnation, and due execution there to be performed ; to all which they assented : then, said the sheriff, see the mercy of your Prince, who of himself hath sent hither the countermand, and given you your lives. There was then no need to beg a *plaudite* of the audience, for it was given with such hues and cries that it went from the castle into the town, and there began afresh." All this was very prettily contrived for effect—but the three lives would have been lost if James's messenger had only arrived an hour later, or if James had not bethought him that the respite had gone off without his signature, and just sent for it back in time.

The reprieve of these men involved of course the reprieve of Raleigh. But James was not sagacious enough to do more, and endeavour to attach to his interests the men he had spared from the scaffold, by a frank pardon, and restoration to their position and estates. Raleigh, the poet—warrior—discoverer—statesman, so fitted by nature and education to become one of the foremost men of his time, had a really useful public career been opened to him, was left to pine away in long captivity in the Tower, a place that it might reasonably have been supposed would have proved but a more lingering agency of death to one distinguished for the activity of his character and the vivaciousness of his disposition. But adversity does indeed, like the fire, only purify and make more rich the true metal. Whatever doubt or difference of opinion may exist concerning the other portions of Raleigh's career, there can be none as to the elevation and beauty of his life during his thirteen years of bondage in the great State Prison. He seems, in the truest spirit of wisdom, to have looked about him on all sides in order that he might gather together what remained to him of consolation and enjoyment ; as for the rest, why he obtained all that he desired from the depths of his own hitherto unstudied nature, where he found a thousand springs of solace and delight, that in the turmoil of the world he had left uncared for. Never before could the affection of his wife have appeared so precious to him as now that she shared his hours of loneliness and bondage. It was in connection with her that he had first known what it was to be a prisoner (Fig. 1533) within these gloomy walls. He had secretly carried on an intrigue with her—while she was as yet but Elizabeth Throckmorton, a maid of honour to the Queen ; but when it was discovered that she ought to have been Lady Raleigh—for that offence the virgin Queen threw Raleigh into the Tower. Yet he married the object of his love, and was after a time set at liberty. In the Tower one of their two children was born. There, also, Raleigh became an ardent student.

Mrs. Hutchinson, in the fragment of autobiography attached to her Life of her husband, Colonel Hutchinson, says, " Sir Walter Raleigh and Mr. Ruthin, being prisoners in the Tower, and addicting themselves to chemistry, she (my mother) suffered them to make their rare experiments at her cost, partly to comfort and

divert the poor prisoners, and partly to gain the knowledge of their experiments, and the medicines to help such poor people as were not able to seek physicians." Raleigh was, like most scientific men of his day, an alchemist, and a believer in the philosopher's stone. Nay, he was satisfied he had discovered a remedy for disease, and when the Queen was ill she agreed to try the illustrious prisoner's medicine, and received, or fancied she received benefit from it. That circumstance alone must have led Raleigh's friends, if not himself, to hope for a pardon ; but though Prince Henry, the King's eldest son, joined his mother in petitions for grace, James was inexorable. But to study merely for his own improvement was not the extent of Raleigh's prison aspirations. He considered he possessed high literary powers, as the author of the answer to Marlowe's " Come live with me and be my love " well might. The verses, thus commenced, have been attributed to Shakspere, and are worthy of him ; and the answer in question, beginning with the words

If all the world and love were young,

are worthy of *them*. The subject that Raleigh was bold enough to undertake was a ' History of the World,' one of the most gigantic schemes ever seriously proposed and attempted to be carried out by one man. Its immediate purpose was to instruct the young Prince we have named, who had won the heart of Raleigh, as well as of his countrymen generally, by the precocious nobility of his disposition, his talents, and accomplishments, and perhaps in no slight degree also by his utter dissimilarity to the character of his father. More personal reflections would also have their effect on Raleigh —the Prince had said that none but his father would keep such a bird in such a cage. The first part alone of the work was accomplished ; which, commencing with the creation, ended about a century and a half before the Christian era. Why he there ceased is explained in the following passage, which shows us at the same time the lofty character of portions of the book that was prematurely brought to a close :—

" O, eloquent, just, and mighty Death ! whom none could advise, thou hast persuaded ; what none hath dared, thou hast done ; and whom all the world hath flattered, thou only hast cast out of the world and despised ; thou hast drawn together all the far-stretched greatness, all the pride, cruelty, and ambition of man, and covered it all over with these two narrow words—*Hic jacet* !

" Lastly, whereas this book, by the title it hath, calleth itself the ' First Part of the General History of the World,' implying a second and third volume, which I also intended, and have hewn out ; besides many other discouragements persuading my silence, it hath pleased God to take that glorious prince (Henry) out of the world to whom they were directed."

Prince Henry, who whilst a mere child gave every sign of future greatness, died on the 6th of November, 1612, before he was nineteen. Our engraving (Fig. 1844) of him, and the young Lord Harrington (to whom his dignified father afterwards gave a grant for the coining of base farthings in brass, instead of the 30,000*l.* that he claimed for attending the King's daughter to 'the Rhine at her nuptials), well expresses the spirited and martial character of which he gave so many striking indications. Once, as he was tossing his pike, the French ambassador asked him if he had any message for the King of France. " Tell him what I am now doing," was the significant reply, in the spirit of a young Harry the Fifth. His early appreciation of superior minds was shown in his enthusiasm for such men as Raleigh. He was devout also, and became the hope and pride of the Puritans, who had this rhyme commonly in their mouths—

Henry the Eighth pulled down the abbeys and cells,
But Henry the Ninth shall pull down bishops and bells.

Like his mother, Prince Henry availed himself of the medical skill of Raleigh. One of the last cordials that he took, a few hours before he died, was sent from Raleigh's prison.

During a part of his thirteen years of confinement, Raleigh did not suffer from any pecuniary troubles, his estate having been assigned in time to trustees for the benefit of his family. But James having taken a fancy for a new minion, young Robert Carr, nothing would do but he must confer on him that fair estate of Sherborne, in Dorsetshire, which Raleigh had taken such pride and pleasure in, and with such lavish cost had adorned with orchards, gardens, and groves, " of much variety and great delight." This unprincipled alienation James was enabled, with Chief Justice Popham's assistance, to accomplish, by taking advantage of the omission of some slight technicality in the deed. Raleigh, however, determined to appeal directly to Carr. " For yourself, sir," said he, " seeing your fair day is now in the dawn, and mine drawn to the

1843.—Hall at Theobalds, the favourite Residence of James. (From an Original Picture at Hinton St. George.)

1844.—Prince Henry and Lord Harrington. (From an old Picture at Earl Guildford's, Wroxton.)

1845.—Procession of James I. on the Thames.

1846.—York House.

1847.—Cobham Hall.

1848.—Earl and Countess of Somerset. (From a print of the period.)

148

1849.—Palace Yard. (From Hollar.)

1850.—Holland House.

1851.—Wolsey's Hall, Hampton Court.

1852.—James I. (From a letter to his son Charles, while on his Spanish love-making expedition, beginning, "My dear babie." (Harleian MSS. No. 6987.)

1853.

1854.—Procession of James I. to St. Paul's, accompanied by the Prince of Wales and many of the Nobility, on Sunday, March 26, 1620.

149

evening, your own virtues and the king's grace assuring you of many favours and of much honour, I beseech you not to begin your first building upon the ruins of the innocent; and that their sorrows with mine may not attend your first plantation." He continues, "I therefore trust, sir, that you will not be the first who shall kill us outright, cut down the tree with the fruit, and undergo the curse of them that enter the fields of the fatherless; which, if it please you to know the truth, is far less in value than in fame." The favourite had not nobleness of heart enough to forego the prize from considerations merely of abstract justice or generosity; he took no heed of the letter. Lady Raleigh then threw herself, with her children, at the King's feet, and implored him to spare the remnant of their fortunes. But James was unmoved. "I maun ha' the land—I maun ha' it for Carr," was his characteristic exclamation; and the beautiful, noble-hearted woman, was turned away with her children, despoiled of all. But yet a heavier misfortune awaited her, and one that assumed the cruellest of shapes in which evil can assail us—promise of good: her husband's death on the scaffold was to be brought about as a consequence of her husband's liberation from his long imprisonment in the Tower. Raleigh had before found life when he had expected death; he was now to find death when his heart and mind were all newly awakened to the pleasures and prospects of life. In one of his bold voyages he had visited Guiana, in South America, the fabled El Dorado, or Land of Gold, of the Spaniards, which, though discovered by them, was left unconquered, and without any European settlement. Raleigh, if he did not find whole cities of gold and silver and precious metals, yet did find some signs of a gold-mine near the banks of the Orinoco. His enterprising spirit, and his desire for the liberty so long denied, induced him to propose to Secretary Winwood an expedition to secure and work that golden mine, which he was confident would yield exhaustless treasure. He undertook, with the aid of his friends, to fit out the ships and provide for all expenses, asking only his liberty, and an ample commission. Winwood recommended James to accept the offer. James, then almost destitute of money, caught at it eagerly; but he was soon chilled, on reflecting that Spain claimed by papal bull all these regions. No matter that the claim was of a disputable nature—James was too cowardly to like meddling with it, when war might be the consequence. He thought with Hudibras,

> Alas! what perils do environ
> The man that meddles with cold iron.

But James could not forget El Dorado—nor Raleigh, whom he now began to talk of as a brave and skilful man. The release from prison was gained by some noble friends of Raleigh, through the favourite that succeeded Carr—Villiers, whose uncles, Sir William St. John and Sir Edward Villiers, received 1500l., and then Raleigh came forth from the Tower.

This extraordinary man seems to have recovered immediately some of his old haughty asperity, likening himself to Mordecai, and the fallen Somerset (Robert Carr), whom he had left in the Tower, to Haman; which coming to James's ears, revived the prejudice against him in the royal mind, through which he had suffered so long and grievously. This prejudice, and fear of the Spaniards, still kept James undecided about the expedition, on which Raleigh had now staked his every earthly hope. But at last he plucked up courage to consent, and Raleigh was permitted to prepare for the expedition. In the mean time "the old sentence still lies dormant against him, which he could never get off by pardon, notwithstanding that he mainly laboured in it before he went; but his Majesty could never be brought to it; for he said he would keep that as a curb to hold him within the bounds of his commission and of good behaviour." (Howell's *Letters*.) Raleigh induced many gentlemen of quality to venture their properties and persons upon the design; a debt of 8000l. was paid to him; Lady Raleigh sold her estate of Mitcham for 2500l.; and at last, on the 28th of March, 1617, the energetic adventurer set sail with fourteen vessels, having pledged his word to the King and the Spanish ambassador that he would not sail for any Spanish possession, but only for that country over which England could claim a right by priority of discovery and consent of the natives; and that there should be no hostile collision between him and the Spaniards, except in self-defence. Had that pledge been more carefully observed, all might have gone well.

At the very outset the ships were driven by a storm into the Cove of Cork, where they lay nearly four months. After that they had a long and arduous voyage before the land of Guiana was reached. Forty-two men had beeen ill and died, on board the admiral's ship alone; others were disabled. Raleigh, himself, had been at at the point of death, and was obliged, it is said, to remain at the island of Trinidad, being incapable of walking; whilst he sent another, with his gallant son, in command of five ships up the river, to "the star that directed them thither"—the mine of gold. Yet in good hope he wrote to his wife from Guiana: "To tell you that I might here be King of the Indians were a vanity. But my name hath still lived among them here. They feed me with fresh meat, and all that the country yields. All offer to obey me."

No braver leaders than Captain Keymis and young Raleigh could have been chosen: Keymis was devoted to Raleigh, and had suffered much for his sake. He knew the mighty hazard of the present enterprise; but he was deficient in prudence to guide it. Perhaps Raleigh himself—with that moral defectiveness that remains a serious blemish on the brightness of his fame—was paying slight regard to his promise to James not to enter into collision with the Spaniards. It seems probable that he had fixed nimself at the island of Trinidad to prevent them from following Captain Keymis. The latter was ordered, if he found the mine "rich and royal," to plant himself beside it, of course at any hazard; if not, to bring away a basket or two of gold-ore to pacify the King. Keymis found a Spanish settlement—St. Thomas—and landed between it and the mine. It was a perilous juxtaposition, that of the Spaniards and these determined eager men. The Spaniards surprised Keymis in the night, and put many of his people to death; and the next day the town of St. Thomas was assaulted by the English. A desperate fight took place, and among the slain on one side was a near relation of the Spanish ambassador in England, Gondomar, who was watching Raleigh's enterprise with great suspicion; and on the other, the brave young son of Raleigh, who was cut down at the head of his own company of pikemen. His fall maddened the English party, and they seemed to have stopped at no atrocity. They drove the Spaniards away, set the town on fire, and then searched for treasure; but, luckless at all points, they found no more than two ingots of gold and two empty refining-pots.

More disasters followed, and Keymis returned to the island of Trinidad to meet the bitter upbraidings of his chief, who told him he must leave it to himself to answer for his conduct to the King and State. Keymis then shut himself in his cabin, and committed suicide. To complete the confusion, the crews mutinied; and Raleigh was left with only five ships and a few desperate adventurers, who urged him to enrich himself and them by following the example of the Drake and Cavendish school of heroes. Raleigh was strongly tempted; and though he refused at first, and sailed with "brains broken" (his own expression) to Newfoundland to get his ships refitted, he was soon obliged, by a fresh mutiny, to promise to intercept certain treasure-galleons. They were *not* intercepted, however, and Raleigh—poor in all senses—returned to Plymouth to be once more a state prisoner.

His men foretold that if he returned his ruin was certain: but he persisted; for the Earls of Pembroke (Fig. 1862) and Arundel were bound for his return, and he must discharge those friends from their engagement. So were his motives explained by his younger son, Carew, many years after his father's death. And how was that death compassed? Raleigh, it is true, had brought no gold, and he had offended most grievously the Spaniards; but James could not send him to the scaffold on either ground; and the Spanish ambassador would be satisfied with nothing less than his destruction. In brief, they must revive the *old sentence!*—and this was actually done, and Raleigh's death-warrant signed, with an interval of thirteen years and upwards between it and the condemnation. A more flagrantly unjust act was never committed. Not even this treatment broke down Raleigh's fortitude. He had prepared himself to be "equal to either fortune;" and since the worst had come upon him, he would even accept it patiently. He spent the last night at the Gatehouse, Westminster. There he took his leave of his wife. She had one consolation to speak of even at that time—his body had been granted to her. "It is well, Bess," said he, "that thou mayest dispose of that dead, thou hadst not always the disposing of when alive." How calm, how wonderfully calm he was during this terrible night, we may gather from the fact that he could moralize, in his finest vein, on the nature of the life he was about so suddenly to leave!

The following verses are understood to have been written on a fly-leaf of his Bible the night before the execution:—

> Even such is Time, that takes on trust
> Our youth, our joys, our all we have,
> And pays us but with age and dust:
> Who, in the dark and silent grave,
> When we have wandered all our ways,
> Shuts up the story of our days.

The scaffold was erected in Old Palace Yard, Westminister (Fig.

1849), on the morning of the 29th of October, 1618. The spectators —a vast number—included many of the chief men of the day. Sir Walter, who had been with difficulty brought to the scaffold through the press, having cheerfully saluted the assembly, and being about to make his farewell speech, observed, that as he wished to be heard by the three noblemen whom he perceived seated at a window—Arundel, Northampton, and Doncaster, he would strain his voice. "Nay," replied Lord Arundel, " we will rather come down to the scaffold ;" which immediately he and several other lords did, whom Raleigh saluted one by one with as composed an air as if he were receiving them in his own private dwelling, in happiness and security. We can give but a meagre outline of his speech. He replied to all the charges against him—except those relating to his conduct against the Spaniards, which he passed over in utter silence. No so that heaviest charge against him with the public, if not with the King— his part in the death of Essex, for which there is little doubt he had at times suffered much remorse. He tried to palliate his conduct— " It doth make my heart to bleed to hear that such an imputation should be laid upon me ; for it is said that I was a prosecutor of the death of the Earl of Essex, and that I stood in a window over against him when he suffered in the Tower, and puffed out tobacco in disdain of him. I take God to witness that I *had no hand in his blood*, and was none of those that procured his death. I shed tears for him when he died ; and as I hope to look God in the face hereafter, my Lord of Essex did not see my face when he suffered ; for I was afar off, in the Armoury, where I saw him, but he saw not me." Unhappily there is a letter of Raleigh's still in preservation, urging Sir Robert Cecil by the most strenuous arguments to press Essex " down "—not to " relent" toward him, and to have no fear of con- sequences. It is *possible*, however, and we would fain hope it was so, that his ingratitude to Essex was simply that of having, as he said in his last speech, belonged, to a " contrary faction ;" and there- fore helped to " pluck him down," without intending to have Essex put to death. " My soul," said Raleigh, " hath many times since been grieved that I was not nearer to him when he died ; because, as I understood afterwards, he asked for me at his death, to have been reconciled unto me." The sheriff would have delayed his execution a short space, offering, as the morning was sharp, to take him from the scaffold to warm himself by a fire. " No, good Mr. Sheriff, let us dispatch," answered Raleigh, with admirable firmness ; " for within this quarter of an hour mine ague will come upon me, and, if I be not dead before then, mine enemies will say that I quake for fear." After a most admirable prayer, he ro c up, clasped his hands, and said, " Now I am going to God." He calmly took leave of the assembled gentlemen ; and, in bidding farewell to the Earl of Arundel, entreated him to desire the King that no scan- dalous writing to defame him might be published after his death. Then he turned to the block, poised the axe, felt its edge, and, smiling said—" This is a sharp medicine, but it will cure all diseases." He kneeled down, and adjusted his neck to the block ; and, rising, told the executioner he would himself give the signal by raising his hand, and then, said he, " Fear not, but strike home !" He then again laid himself down, but was requested to alter the position of his head. " So the heart be right, it is no matter which way the head lies," remarked he. He gave the signal ; and finding that the executioner hesitated, he exclaimed, with the most surprising for- titude—" What dost thou fear ? Strike, man !" Two blows dis- missed the intrepid and gifted Raleigh to his final rest. He was then in the sixty-seventh year of his age.

We append to these notices of Raleigh a few words upon his ungenerous enemy, Carr.

In Scotland, James had once a beautiful boy as page, Robert Carr or Kerr, of the border family of Fernyherst. Carr had been early taught to expect that his personal charms, with gay dress and accomplished manners, would make his fortune at court. To gain the manners, he was sent to the usual finishing-school, France ; and, on his return, ere yet of age, an accident threw the for- tune in his way. At a grand tilting-match at Westminster, Carr, as esquire to Lord Dingwall, had to present his lord's shield to the King, when his horse threw him, and his leg was broken. The King became his chief nurse and doctor, and shortly, his school- master too, giving him a Latin lesson every day. Carr being knighted and made a gentleman of the bedchamber, James went about the court hanging on his neck or his arm, pinching his cheek, smoothing his ruffled garments, or gloating on his face. He was loaded with presents from court suitors. The favourite he had supplanted, Sir Philip Herbert, Earl of Montgomery (Fig. 1864), brother of William Herbert, Earl of Pembroke, was one of his bosom friends. " But, above all, was Sir Thomas Overbury, his Pythias " (Weldon)—a man of abilities superior to Carr, and who

would have been moderate, if the swarm of court flatterers would have let him. Carr soon rose to be Viscount Rochester, member of the Privy Council, Knight of the Garter, Lord Chamberlain, and, in effect, Prime Minister, whilst the favourite's favourite performed the duties of State Secretary. Among the ladies of the court, by whom Rochester was greatly admired, was one supremely beautiful, witty, and fascinating, married to the son of Queen Elizabeth's victim, Essex. At the period of that marriage Lady Frances Howard was but thirteen, her husband fourteen. They were kept apart four years—an interval that proved fatal to Essex's influence with his bride. Whilst he was on the Continent, the lovely girl was attracting admirers in the profligate court of James. Her chief counsellor was Mrs. Turner, almost as beautiful and fascinating as herself, who had been her early companion, as a dependent in her father's house, and was now a physician's widow, gay and dissolute. The Countess conceived a passion for Rochester, and Mrs. Turner assisted her to gain his love, by means of puppets, pictures, enchanted papers, and magic spells, furnished by a conjuror at Lambeth. Whether Rochester was influenced by these arts, or by the " magic natural " of her beauty and wit, Overbury was soon employed in pen- ning to her ardent love-letters, and contriving stolen interviews. The Countess next resolved, at the expense of her own eternal infamy, to get a divorce from her husband, on a disgraceful pretext, in order to wed with Rochester. Here Overbury to save his friend from such dishonour, spake boldly to him of the " baseness of the woman." Rochester told his mistress this, and she vowed Overbury's destruction. She offered 1000*l*. to Sir John Wood to kill him in a duel. Her friends tried to get him sent on a mission to Russia : he declined it ; and then Rochester, enslaved by the charms of the Countess, denounced his friend to the King as insolent, disobedient, and intolerable, both to himself and the sovereign. Overbury was sent to the Tower ; its lieutenant was removed, and a dependent of the Countess and Rochester put in his place. During several months three kinds of poison, procured by Mrs. Turner, were administered to Overbury in small doses in medicines, soups, and other food. He died—it was said of an infectious disease—and was hastily buried in a pit within the Tower. The next day the Countess gained a sentence of divorce : and then the delighted monarch of all England and Scotland celebrated her second shameful marriage with royal pomp, creating Rochester Earl of Somerset for the occasion. Whether Somerset knew much or little of the murder, he was a changed man after his friend's death. James, not liking that change, had the murder sifted. The actual perpetrators, including the fair Mrs. Turner, were hung at Tyburn : the actual authors were more leniently dealt with. Both were imprisoned : and, as we have seen, the Earl was in the Tower when Raleigh left it in triumph to conduct his ill-fated expedition. After a few years' confinement they retired into the country—the dream of passion over—to reproach and hate each other ! Somerset was allowed by James 4000*l*. a-year : and it seems *certain* that the motives of all this unwonted liberality to a fallen favourite was, however startling it may sound, some *dreadful secret*, by which Somerset, if driven to desperation, might have irretrievably ruined his sovereign in the eyes of the world. The portraits of the Earl, and the " beautiful devil " the Countess, will be found among our engravings (Fig. 1848).

If the reader will turn to the engraving of a group of men in another page (Fig. 1836), he will look upon the chief actors in one of the most extraordinary plots ever devised by suffering and desperate men to relieve themselves o an intolerable load of political oppression and wrong—no matter at what cost—whether of life, honour, or even of the cause itself for which they struggled. Popular notions of history are too often but of a doubtful character, to say the best of them : here they cease indeed to be doubtful, because they are so clearly wrong. That a great, nay, a stupendous crime, was meditated, is beyond question, and so far our Fifth of November observances do not mislead the young and ignorant. But how is it that equal care has not been taken to show that those against whom the crime was directed were in a great measure the real authors of it, and ought therefore to share in the odium that attaches to the whole transaction ? If such observances—tending, as the one in question does, to perpetuate divisions and jealousies, and heart burnings between man and man—must be maintained, let us at least take care that some spirit of equal justice shall be contained in them. The Gunpowder conspirators paid a fearful penalty for their unaccomplished treason : there is no need, nor is it very honourable to blacken their motives and life in addition. Let us look at them as they were—not as they have been painted by prejudice, and bigotry and fear ; and then alone shall we be able to obtain from the fearful tragedy of life in which they were the actors its important

1855.—Sir Hugh Middleton. (From a Portrait by Cornelius Jansen.)

1856.—William Alexander, Earl of Stirling.

1857.—Lord Bacon and his Localities. (The portrait from the engraving by Marshall, 1641, prefixed to Bacon's 'Life of Henry VII.' Beneath the portrait his arms, taken from Marshall's portrait; the Chancellor's Mace, Autograph of King James, and other insignia of office, from original authorities. At the top, to the left, York House, from a drawing by Hollar, engraved in Wilkinson's 'Londini Illustrata;' to the right, Old Gray's Inn, from a Print in Pennant Collection, Brit. Mus. At the left side Gorhambury, from a drawing of the remains of the original mansion by Neale, 1810, engraved in 'Beauties of England and Wales;' and Highgate, with the Old Church, from a Print by Chatelaine, 1740. At the bottom, St. Michael's Church, St. Alban's, from a drawing in George III.'s Collection, Brit. Mus.)

1858.—Chadwell Springs.

1859.—Bacon.

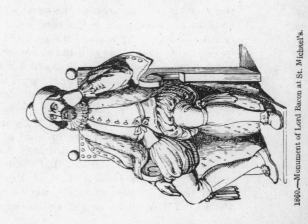

1860.—Monument of Lord Bacon at St. Michael's.

152

1861.—William Drummond.

1863.—Drummond—(From a Portrait by Cornelius Jansen).   Hawthornden—(From an Original Drawing).

1862.—William Herbert, Earl of Pembroke

1864.—Philip Herbert, Earl of Montgomery.

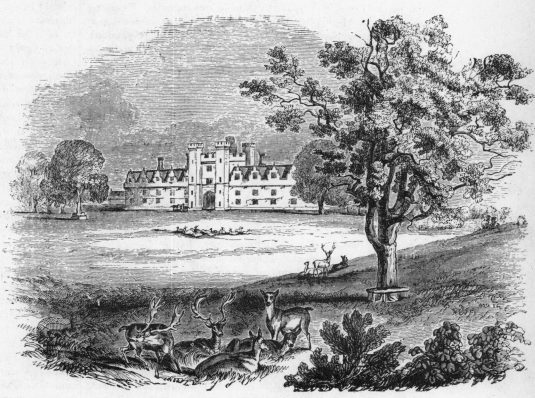

1865.—Knowle House and Park, Kent.

and ever useful moral. A brief glance at the names and histories of the men contained in that remarkable group will show us how little their characters agree with the common notion of them—that they were but so many blood-thirsty ruffians. The principal figure, with his hand on his sword, a chain over his shoulder, and who wears a dress of gentlemanly fashion, was the chief contriver and sustainer of the plot—*not* the famous Guy, but Catesby, a gentleman of family and fortune. The ruling passion of his being is seen not only in this attempt, but in his previous support of the rash Essex on the ground that the Earl had promised liberty of conscience. When that hope failed, he had striven by intrigues at the principal Catholic courts of Europe, those of France and Spain, to secure the same great end; but failing utterly, disappointment rankled in his breast, and influenced him to adopt at last the bloody and unscrupulous project of blowing up King, Lords, and Commons at one blow. By the side of Catesby are the two men who first embraced his scheme: Guy Fawkes, who is on the left; and Thomas Winter, who is on the right of the spectator. To Winter, Catesby first opened his plan. He was a gentleman of Worcestershire, but had spent much of his time abroad as a soldier of fortune in the Low Countries, and, what was of great importance to Catesby, had long acted at the court of Spain as a secret agent of the English Catholics. At first he recoiled in disgust and horror from the proposal; and though subsequently he was swayed by the master-mind to his purposes, he agreed only on the condition that one more effort should be made to induce the King of Spain to mediate between James and his Catholic subjects. The effort was made—failed—and left Winter as "bloody, bold, and resolute" as Catesby could have desired. Fawkes, the vulgar melodramatic monster of the popular creed, was also a soldier of fortune, and had obtained in that vocation both respect and credit. His mind appears to have been chiefly remarkable for a quiet determination of purpose that was so irrespective of all personal consequences as to approach very nigh to heroism; indeed, had his judgment but have guided him into an equally dangerous and unsuccessful, but *good* course of action, he would have deserved emphatically the title of a hero. It may be added that the birth, manners, and appearance of Guy Fawkes were those of a gentleman. He was induced to join the plot through the instrumentality of his old friend and associate, Thomas Winter. The figures whose heads alone are visible in the centre of the picture represent the two next who joined: their names are John Wright, esteemed one of the best swordsmen of his time; and Thomas Percy, a distant relation of the great house whose family name he bore, and who was the steward to the head of the house, the Earl of Northumberland. Percy was one of the most violent of the whole set. When James was about to become King of England, Percy had been sent by the English Catholics to Scotland to ascertain how he was disposed to deal with them. James, then in a mood to promise anything likely to help him to his wishes, gave his word that he would tolerate the Mass, albeit "in a corner." Percy and those who sent him were completely deceived, and Percy in consequence thirsted for vengeance. Despising the caution of his confederates, it was he who, at a meeting at Catesby's lodgings, before the Gunpowder Scheme was propounded, opened the terrible subject of debate by the fiery exclamation—"Well, gentlemen, shall we always talk, and never do?"

Before opening the particulars of his scheme to the four earliest coadjutors, Catesby demanded from all a solemn oath of secrecy. A few days after they met at a lonely house in the fields, beyond St. Clement's Inn, and there the oath was accepted by each, on his knees. Thus it ran:—"You shall swear by the blessed Trinity and by the sacrament you now propose to receive, never to disclose, directly or indirectly, by a word or circumstance, the matter that shall be proposed to you to keep secret, nor desist from the execution thereof until the rest shall give you leave." Catesby then told them his plan of blowing up the Houses of Lords and Commons by gunpowder on the first day that the King should be present in the parliament. They all then went up stairs to another apartment, where they found a Jesuit missionary, Father Gerard, who administered the sacrament. There is reason to doubt whether the objects which were thus solemnized were made known to Gerard.

The three remaining personages of the engraving joined the conspiracy later. The one holding the paper in his hand, with the words "The Oath" inscribed on it, is Robert Winter, a brother of Thomas; next to him, on the one side, is Christopher Wright, a brother of John Wright, and on the other is Bates, Catesby's servant, who was suspected by Catesby to have discovered some inkling of what was going on, and who was therefore at once taken into the confidence of the party, in the hope of binding him to them. And he justified his master's confidence in him—such as it was. These are all the conspirators who figure in the engraving; but

there were others who were drawn into the same dreadful business as it progressed; namely, Robert Keyes (or Kay), a poor Catholic gentleman, who undertook the care of the house at Lambeth (Fig. 1841), where the combustibles were guardedly collected in small quantities at a time; John Grant, a Catholic gentleman of Warwickshire, who had been plunged into profound melancholy by the treatment he had received on account of his religious views; and three other gentlemen, admitted on account of their pecuniary ability to furnish the supplies of horses, ammunition, &c., that were to be provided to aid the insurrection that was to burst out immediately the grand blow was struck:—these were Ambrose Rookwood, long a bosom friend of Catesby, whose chief motive for joining the conspiracy was a romantic determination to share *his* dangers and aims; Sir Everard Digby, also a dear friend of the arch-conspirator, a young man of great wealth, and of an enthusiastic disposition, who yielded only after a severe struggle with his feelings, and love for his wife and two children; and lastly, Francis Tresham, son and heir of Sir Thomas Tresham—a gentleman who, in his own pathetic words, had suffered "full twenty years of restless adversity and deep disgrace, only for testimony of his conscience." Had the conspirators but stopped before admitting this—the last man who was admitted —the scheme would in all probability have succeeded, and have been followed by consequences too momentous even for us to venture to give them shape or name. But Tresham was related to Catesby, he was able to furnish the immense sum of two thousand pounds to the common stock, and so his character—that of a fickle, mean-spirited, untrustworthy man—was overlooked; he was admitted, and England in consequence (according to all probability) saved from the infamy that some of her misguided sons strove to attach to her.

And what a lesson for bigotry does not this Gunpowder Conspiracy form, in whatever way it be read. None but bigots of the worst description, though for a time placed in the position of sufferers, could have devised such a scheme of relief; none but bigots revelling in the plenitude of power could have inflicted wrongs capable of driving their fellow-men to such wild extremities. And what have either gained by their conduct? What could either have gained by it, had the issue been different? Is there a single Catholic living who thinks the plans of Catesby and his companions have, or could have, promoted his faith—devoted as they were to its service? Is there a single Protestant who can gratify himself by the reflection that the purity and strength of his own individual belief, or its prosperity generally with his fellow-men, can be traced to any of those numerous repressive laws against Popery, that have been passed from the days of James I. to our own. Look where we will, through all history, the result is the same; force may keep down the belief you would encourage, but can never promote it; whilst the endeavour often transforms men into fiends, the world into a hell. Were this the popular as it is the real moral of the Gunpowder Treason, it would be well that the Fifth of November custom should be most sedulously and religiously guarded from falling into disuse.

It is an inquiry that rises almost instinctively to the lips, as we weigh again and again the awful character of the deed they meditated—did the conspirators exhibit no irresolution of purpose—no symptoms of their desire to avoid these bloody conclusions? Alas! If they *could* once form and commence the project, the state of things was such as effectually to prevent any hesitation in going on with it. Look but for one moment at the influences at work upon their minds during that interregnum of their labours, when, Percy having purchased a house adjoining the parliamentary buildings, they were waiting impatiently to commence operations, but were delayed by its being taken possession of for a short time for the transaction of some public business. At the previous Lancashire assizes, six seminary priests and Jesuits were tried, condemned, and *executed* for simply remaining within the realm. As though that horrible evidence of the treatment that Catholic priests were in future to expect in England were not sufficient, their whole flocks were told they could be swept at once into the meshes of a similar law, if they heard mass from a Jesuit or seminary priest.

What the Catholics of England thought of all this, we may best judge by asking ourselves what we—Protestants—should feel if we saw our spiritual advisers executed on the scaffold because they persisted in attending to their duties, and if we were further made aware that we should be guilty of felony for only listening to them and receiving their ministrations. But there were men among the Catholics who had little sympathy with the movements of Catesby and Guy Fawkes—men who allowed their indignation to take a proper channel. We may imagine the interest with which the conspirators, during the pause of which we have spoken, would watch the effect of an appeal to the justice and good feeling of the government. There may have been in more than one breast the thought—If that appeal be successful, we must retrace our steps.

It was Mr. Pound, a Catholic gentleman of Cheshire, who caused the appeal to be made in the form of a petition to James, complaining of the persecution to which his co-religionists were subjected, and more especially of the recent proceedings. The answer was a summons to the Star Chamber! followed by imprisonment in that place of torture, second only to the Tower, the Fleet Prison; the pillory twice, where he was to have been nailed by the ears, but that a majority of one or two thought—perhaps because the criminal was so *very* aged—he should be spared his ears; and, lastly, a fine of one thousand pounds. This is in truth no romance, though it looks like it; the event took place in England, and not where we might be supposed to look for such scenes—in some far-off barbarous land. It was scarcely necessary after that to tell the conspirators that more priests were being hunted down—that fines were multiplying daily against those who held any connection with them—or that the sword of the law was about to receive a keener edge in *next parliament;* they had already in their determination disposed of that parliament: it might meet, but should never separate; it should fall at once into a common ruin with the walls and roofs that gave it shelter. No sooner was the house in Westminster at liberty, than Catesby, and the four gentlemen he had first drawn into his scheme, re-entered it one dark night of December. They kept close, afraid of attracting notice by going abroad, and had prepared a quantity of provisions such as would keep—hard eggs, dried meats, and pasties. The wall to be pierced was found of tremendous thickness (three yards, and of stone)—too much, indeed, for the few gentlemanly though resolute hands that laboured at it. The number of conspirators—five—was therefore augmented by the introduction of Keyes and C. Wright. "All which seven," said Fawkes subsequently, "were gentlemen of name and blood; and not any were employed in or about this action (no, not so much as in digging and in mining) that was not a gentleman. And while the others wrought I stood as sentinel to descry any man that came near; and when any man came near to the place, upon warning given by me they ceased until they had a notice from me to proceed; and we seven lay in the house, and had shot and powder, and we all resolved to die in that place before we yielded or were taken." A prorogation of parliament, now announced, caused them to cease for a time their labours, and disperse; it being agreed that they should neither meet nor associate in public, nor correspond by letter on any point whatever connected with the plot. By the time they recommenced working they were ten in number. "Their ears were acutely sensible to the least sound—their hearts susceptible of supernatural dread. They heard, or fancied they heard, the tolling of a bell deep in the earth under the Parliament House, and the noise was stopped by aspersions of holy water" (*Pictorial England*). One morning they experienced a greater alarm: there was a sudden rushing sound heard over their heads. They thought they were discovered: but Fawkes, ever the first where danger was most imminent, went to reconnoitre, and found that the sound proceeded from a coal-cellar occupied by one Bright, who was now selling off his stock preparatory to his removal. As the experienced eye of Fawkes ranged over the place, he saw at once its superior fitness for their purpose, as compared with the place they were then excavating. The cellar or vault (Fig. 1842) was situated immediately beneath the House of Lords, and could they obtain possession of it they might bring their severe task to an immediate termination. So the vault was hired, and the combustibles speedily placed in it. Many barrels of gunpowder were conveyed from Lambeth by night, the iron crowbars and other tools used by the confederates were thrown among them, in order to widen the trench, and then the whole was carefully concealed by faggots. Lumber also was scattered about to give the place as natural an aspect as possible for the locality and purpose to which it was ostensibly devoted. By May, 1605, all was completed.

The preparations for the insurrection then engaged attention. Fawkes went to Flanders, to endeavour to secure foreign co-operation before the blow was struck; and Sir Edward Baynham to Rome, to be ready, when all was over, to explain to the Pope that the conspirators' object was the establishment of Catholicity. The other chief confederates spent the spare interval of time in collecting horses, arms and powder—the material, in short, for equipping suddenly a Catholic army. As the day of meeting of the parliament approached, it was finally arranged that the mine should be fired by a slow match, by Fawkes, who would then have a quarter of an hour to escape. On the same day Sir Everard Digby was to have ready a large body of Catholic gentry at his seat in Warwickshire,

assembled on the pretence of hunting, to form the nucleus of the insurrection. Lastly, as they wanted one of the King's sons to become, under their auspices, the future king, Percy was also on the same day to seize the Prince Henry, and bear him off; or if he accompanied his father to the house and was destroyed, then the Duke of York, afterwards Charles I., was to be taken instead.

And now arose a momentous question. Most of the confederates had dear friends or relations in parliament—were these to perish? The agitation of this question almost shook the resolution of the conspirators. Tresham had two Catholic brothers-in-law in the Upper House, Stourton and Mounteagle; Percy was nearly related to the Earl of Northumberland; Keyes' heart bled for Lord Mordaunt, his benefactor, who had given food and shelter to his destitute wife and children; and there was one, the young Earl of Arundel, whose safety all were anxious to secure. Catesby tried to argue down these weaknesses. Most of the Catholics, he was of opinion, would be absent, since they could not hope to prevent the passing of new penal laws against their religion. "But with all that," added the remorseless and determined chief, "rather than the project should not take effect, if they were as dear unto me as mine own son, they also must be blown up." This was unpalatable enough to several of the conspirators; but the danger of giving any specific warning to so many persons was evident; and it was agreed, though reluctantly, that no express notice was to be given, but that all should be at liberty to use such persuasion upon general grounds as they thought likely to be most successful. But there was one who remained unsatisfied by this arrangement. Catesby, Thomas Winter, and Fawkes were together at White Webbs, three days after the first agitation of the business, when Tresham unexpectedly appeared, and required, in passionate terms, that Mounteagle should be warned. They refused, and high words ensued. Seeing they were determined, he desired the plot to be deferred, as he could not yet furnish the money he had promised. Tresham then went away; and, there can scarcely be a doubt, opened to the nobleman in question the tremendous secret, and advised with him how it might best appear to come from some other quarter. So ten days before the opening of parliament, Mounteagle suddenly appeared at his mansion at Hoxton, where he seldom visited, ordered a supper to be prepared, and, as he was sitting at it, about seven in the evening, his page presented him a letter, that he said he had just received from a tall man, whose features he could not distinguish in the dark. Mounteagle opened it, and, seeing it had neither date nor signature, tossed it to a gentleman in his service, desiring him to read it aloud. The letter, of which we give a facsimile (Fig. 1838), does not, it will be seen, point out the exact nature of the danger that threatened the "parliament;" though the words "a terrible blow," and "they shall not see who hurts them," go as near to the truth as its author dared venture in order to keep up the character assumed—that of a man who desired to save Mounteagle, but also to conceal and help to carry out the project that endangered him.

Mounteagle directly rode off to Whitehall, and, the King being absent—he was hunting at Royston—showed it to Cecil and several other ministers. Cecil and Suffolk were the real interpreters of the mysterious epistle, though they chose to flatter the King by ascribing the discovery—that it was meant to blow them up with gunpowder—to the "divine spirit" by which he was inspired when they laid it before him on his return; "thereby miraculously discovering this hidden treason." By Cecil's advice the "devilish practice" was not to be interrupted till the last moment—the conspirators were to be allowed "to go on to the end of their day." They, too, had their warning, if they would have taken it. And this matter should not be overlooked in judging of Tresham's conduct; for in all probability due warning to them formed a part of his plan. Mounteagle's gentleman communicated to Thomas Winter the delivery of the letter to Cecil. Winter apprised Catesby, who at once pronounced that Tresham had betrayed them. His having absented himself several days made this all the more probable. He, however, promptly attended the summons of Catesby and Winter; and it says much for his courage that he dared to hold so perilous an interview. Fixing their searching eyes on his countenance, they accused him of the letter, and were prepared, if he exhibited fear or confusion, to stab him to the heart on the spot. He was firm and steady in his denial; and they were silenced and disarmed—if not perfectly convinced. And Tresham may have hoped that all danger was thus averted both from the victims of the plot and the agents. How could he suppose the last would go on under such circumstances? But he knew them not. Having succeeded in throwing aside all the ordinary feelings of humanity, they had become but so many incarnations of one idea, and could no more put that idea aside than they could bid their busy brains to cease to work or

1866.—Thirty-shilling Piece.

1868.—Fifteen-shilling Piece.

1867.—Sovereign

1869.—Half-Sovereign.

1866 to 1869.—Gold Coins of James I.

1870.—James I. lying in State.   (The hearse and decorations designed by Inigo Jones.)

1871.—Crown

1872.—Shilling.

1875.—Penny

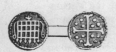

1876.—Halfpenny

1873.—Sixpence

1874.—Twopence

1877.—Charles I. (Painted by Vandyke as a model for the Bust sculptured by Bernini.)

1878—Queen Henrietta Maria. (From a Painting by Vandyke.)

1879.—Great Seal of Charles.

1880—House at Portsmouth in which the Duke of Buckingham was assassinated.

188 —Charles I. (Harl. MS. No. 6988.)

1882.—Charles I and Armour-bearer (Vandyke.)

1883.—Charles I.

157

their hearts to stop their life-supporting pulsations: it had become everything to them. So even now that they knew the secret was all but made public—they would go on; merely first satisfying themselves that the cellar had not been searched, by sending Fawkes, as yet ignorant of the letter, to examine it. He found all as he had left it; and then Catesby and Winter excused themselves for having placed him in such danger without a warning; but he coolly replied, he would have gone just as readily if he had known all; and he undertook to return to the cellar once every day till the 5th of November—and he kept his word with astonishing nerve through the doubtful and anxious time that followed. On Sunday the 3rd of November, Lord Mounteagle's gentleman informed the conspirators of the importance attached to the letter by King James. One cannot but pity and sympathize with the sufferings of Tresham, from whom, no doubt, this second warning also came. He saw all the men to whom he had so solemnly pledged his honour that he would preserve their secret and promote their object, going almost wilfully to the scaffold, in consequence of his faithlessness to them. Seeing both these warnings fail, the very same evening that the second had been given he appeared, during an interview with Thomas Winter, in great agitation and distress, and he said, too, *that to his certain knowledge they were all lost men, unless they saved themselves by immediate flight.* That very night, as usual, Fawkes went to keep watch in the cellar! There was time and opportunity for all to have been saved, but the precious interval was desperately thrown away. Even Tresham, whom the other conspirators suspected of being in communication with their adversaries, neither sought flight nor concealment. The fiery Percy insisted on their keeping their ground to see the result of Monday, the last day before the terrible event, on the afternoon of which John Wright and Catesby were to ride off to join Sir Everard Digby at Dunchurch.

That Monday did bring with it an event that would have spoken trumpet-tongued to any men less determined—less infatuated than these Gunpowder conspirators. In the afternoon of the 4th the Lord Chamberlain Suffolk and Lord Mounteagle went to the old House of Lords. They stayed some time in the Parliament Chamber, and then descended to the vaults and cellars, pretending that some of the King's stuffs were missing. Opening the door of the conspirators' vault, they saw, standing in a corner, "a very tall and desperate fellow." The Chamberlain carelessly asked him who he was. He replied, he was a servant to Mr. Percy, and stated that he was looking after his master's coals. "Your master has laid in a good stock of fuel," said Suffolk; and he and Mounteagle left the place without saying more. What next? Why, Fawkes hurried off to tell Percy, and then returned to the cellar! His reasoning to himself was, no doubt, simply this—He had undertaken to guard the cellar, and at the appointed time to fire the train; it was their duty to withdraw him if it was indispensably necessary that he should be withdrawn. They did not do so; and, for aught he knew, they had still a hope of success; so he stayed. Had such gallant self-sacrifice but been exhibited in a noble cause, there would have been no bounds to the world's admiration And—strange obliquities of human nature!—he thought his conduct had that indispensable quality; the "light that led astray" was indeed to his eyes a "light from heaven."

All this while, what, let us ask, did the government really know? More, we think, than was professed from a mere perusal of the letter. Mounteagle, like Tresham, may have stipulated for secrecy as regarded any information given by him; and it is only on such an hypothesis that we can understand why the examination just mentioned should be left to so late a period. If the ministers knew all, they could afford to let the conspirators play on their game as long as possible, and they would desire to pursue that policy in order to entrap and obtain evidence against them, without using their secret sources of knowledge. But if they knew no more than the letter told them, they might have mistaken the mode of destruction intended—which might, after all, burst out upon them from some unexpected quarter —and, at all events, the delay at such a critical time might give the conspirators time to escape. We have no doubt, therefore, that Mounteagle, while holding open ample opportunities for their escape, did really furnish the government with information as to the essentials of the plot.

Midnight came, and Fawkes thought, as all seemed quiet, he would look forth. He stepped out from the cellar, and in an instant found himself pinioned, and in the presence of a company of armed men, under the command of Sir Thomas Knevet, a magistrate of Westminster. He was searched, and matches and touchwood found upon him. Going into the cellar, a dark lantern was found behind the door. The party went on, removed the faggots, and the whole business in all its horrors stood revealed to them but too plainly, in

the sight of the six-and-thirty barrels of gunpowder that were ranged along the wall. They questioned Fawkes, who was as frank as he had been courageous. He at once avowed his purpose to Sir Thomas, adding "that if he had happened to be within the house when he took him, he would not have failed to have blown him up, house and all:"—a pleasant assurance for the listeners!

Fawkes was taken to Whitehall, and into the royal bedchamber, where he was confronted with the King and Council, who did not half like his appearance, bound though he was, for his looks darted scorn and defiance, and his voice was bold, his answers keen and cutting as a two-edged sword. To the questions put to him he answered, his name was John Johnson, he was servant to Mr. Percy. He was sorry he had not succeeded in his purpose. The King asked how he could have the heart to destroy his children and so many innocent souls that must have suffered. "*Dangerous diseases require desperate remedies,*" replied Fawkes, and that, no doubt, was the substance of the delusive arguments by which the infatuated men had supported themselves throughout. One of the Scottish courtiers inquiring why so many barrels of gunpowder had been collected, Fawkes replied, "One of my objects was to blow Scotchmen back into Scotland." He was pressed to name his accomplices, but answered with quiet contempt, "he could not make up his mind to accuse any." In subsequent examinations he was tried by temptations, as well as threats, to betray his accomplices, but remained unalterably firm in his refusal. His intellectual self-possession also continued as striking as ever. When told it was useless to deny their names, as their flight had discovered them—" If that be so," was his apt reply, " it would be superfluous for me to declare them, seeing by that circumstance they have named themselves." He readily confessed all his own guilt—said he was ready to die— but rather wished ten thousand deaths than to accuse his friends. Whilst in that frame of mind, on the 8th of November, he signed his deposition with a bold and steady hand. What passed during the next two days is shrouded in darkness; but we can more than guess at the nature of its fearful mysteries. The "gentler tortures" were to be first used unto him, " *et sic per gradus, ad ima tenditur ;** and so God speed you in your *good work.*" Such were the instructions issued by James to the keepers of Fawkes. How the mandate was obeyed may be best understood from an examination of the signature on the 10th instant, of the same man who had signed so boldly on the 8th. The contrast (Fig. 1840) suggests horrors too appalling for the imagination to dwell upon. And as there is a limit to the extremest powers of endurance, Fawkes's tormentors appear to have succeeded in discovering it, and so making him confess to a certain degree what had passed. But it appears that even then he did nothing really calculated to injure any one, as the other conspirators by their conduct declared themselves openly to the world, when they learnt that Fawkes was taken.

Percy and Christopher Wright rode off (Catesby and John Wright having already gone) to the gathering at Dunchurch; Rookwood and Keyes, being little known in London, waited to see what turn affairs might take. In the morning, going abroad they saw horror and amazement on every countenance, and then they knew that all was over. Keyes fled at once. Rookwood—the last to linger—waited till noon, to gain more intelligence, then mounted and in little more than six hours rode a distance of eighty miles. His route lay at first over Highgate Hill and Finchley Common, and he was crossing the latter when he overtook Keyes, and they rode side by side as far as Turvey in Bedfordshire, where Keyes parted from him. Rookwood dashed on to Brickhill, and there overtook Catesby and John Wright. The three soon after overtook Percy and Christopher Wright, and all five swept along over hill and down as fast as some of the fleetest horses in England could bear them. Two or three of the party even threw their cloaks into the hedge to ride the lighter. Escape was easy at one of the sea-ports. But they still hoped. The second part of their plan might succeed, though the first had failed. The entire Catholic party might yet be induced to aid them.

In the mean time, Sir Everard Digby, having assembled his party at Dunchurch on the 5th of November, rode off to Ashby Ledgers, to hear what was the result of the plot. That evening, the five fugitives from London, covered with sweat and half dead with fatigue, appeared before the house of Lady Catesby, and burst into an apartment where a party of expectant Catholics (including Winter and Digby) were sitting down to supper. When Rookwood and the rest had told their tidings, a rapid consultation was held, and bold and vigorous measures at once decided on. The note of war was to be sounded through the land, the Catholics resident on

---

* And thus by degrees we may proceed to extremities.

the route to Wales were to be summoned instantly to join them. But, at starting, *all* Sir Everard's guests at Dunchurch forsook the cause, on hearing what the plot had been, and especially that it had failed. They stole away privily in the night, leaving none to aid, except a few servants and retainers. The conspirators were, however, no longer able to retrace their steps, and some of them would not if they could. They still resolved to raise the country, or lay down their own lives, of which they had grown sufficiently weary.

Riding through Warwick, they carried off some cavalry horses from a stable, leaving their own tired ones in their place. At Grant's house of Norbrook they were joined by a few servants. On the third night after leaving London they reached Holbeach, on the borders of Staffordshire, and rested at a house belonging to one Stephen Littleton. Every rational hope was by this time cut off.—" Not *one* man," as Sir Everard Digby afterwards observed, " came to take our part, though we had expected so many :" and in despair he forsook his companions, with the professed intention of hastening some expected succours. Scarcely had he left, before some gunpowder placed before the fire to dry exploded, and seriously injured three or four of the conspirators, among whom was Catesby. No wonder they began at last to lose their self-possession and confidence. Rookwood and others, " perceiving God to be against them, prayed before the picture of Our Lady, and confessed that the act was so bloody, as they desired God to forgive them." Presently the house was surrounded by the whole *posse comitatus* of the county, with Sir Richard Walsh, the sheriff, at their head. But though these men now began to tremble from the fear of God, they defied man even in this their last extremity. They were called upon to surrender, but the call was an idle one. Fire was set to the house by one body of the assailants, whilst an attack was made upon the gates by another. The doomed men—doomed in their own determination as well as by their conduct—presented themselves fearlessly, sword in hand, to the assailants. One of them, Thomas Winter, was disabled by a shot in the arm. With a nobility of feeling on the part of the criminal, that can be acknowledged without lessening our horror of the crime, Catesby cried out to his helpless friend, " Stand by me, Tom, and we will die together." And as he said, so it was. Whilst—standing back to back—Catesby defended both, two bullets, shot from the same musket, severally gave them their death-wounds. Catesby was just able to crawl into the house on his hands and knees, seize the image of the Virgin that stood in the vestibule, clasp it fervently, and that was all. The two brothers, John and Christopher Wright, and Percy experienced the same merciful end; though Percy lingered until the next day. All the other conspirators were taken into custody either here or elsewhere, and the executioner finished what the provincial sheriff had begun. We need not excite the loathing of our readers by a description of the sort of execution that the Christian governors of England in the seventeenth century enforced : suffice it to say, that no words the language affords can be too strong to express its brutality. Yet, consistent to the last, the miserable men bore their tortures with exemplary patience and fortitude. The place of execution was the west end of St. Paul's churchyard. The fate of Tresham is remarkable. Before the day of trial he died in the Tower, not without exciting suspicions among the people of England who were of his own creed that he had been foully dealt with.

Comprehensive as was this destruction of the men who had themselves aimed to destroy on such a gigantic scale, the affair—and the excitement caused by it—was not yet at an end. It was supposed that the Jesuits, who had been only recently introduced into England, were privy to the plot. Henry Garnet was then the Superior of the Order ; a post for which he was eminently qualified, not only in the opinion of his friends, but of his enemies ; though there might be some difference in the minds of the two as to the character and value of the particular qualifications required. The great lawyer Coke, when Garnet was tried, eulogized his fine natural gifts, and said he was " by birth a gentleman, by education a scholar, by art learned, and a good linguist." For several years he had followed various occupations in the neighbourhood of London in order to disguise the real one. He had been concerned in the treasonable intrigues with the king of Spain just before Elizabeth's death, and was suspected of other seditions, but had purchased a general pardon at James's accession. He continued, however, to associate with disaffected Catholics, including many of the nobility. The regard in which he was held by them was carried to the extremest enthusiasm. Lady Anne Vaux, for instance, after her father's death, followed his fortunes with romantic devotion. Such a person representing such an Order, capable of the most profound craft, and actuated by a restless spirit of intrigue and ardent fanaticism, was certainly to be feared by such a government as that which was oppressing the

Catholics. It is very difficult to fathom the real extent of the Jesuits' connection with the plot, but there is no doubt that many of the Order in England and on the Continent were aware of it. As to Garnet himself, it is certain that very shortly before the plot was discovered he was with a company of persons, most actively engaged in it, on a pilgrimage to St. Winifred's Well, in Flintshire ; and at the very time when Fawkes was preparing to fire the deadly train under the Parliament House, Garnet was in the neighbourhood of the general rendezvous of the conspirators at Coughton. A proclamation of attainder against Garnet, Greenway, Gerard, Oldcorne, and three other Jesuits having been issued, Greenway and Gerard fled to the Continent. What had become of Oldcorne and Garnet no one could or would tell.

About that time Humphrey Littleton, being condemned to death at Worcester for only harbouring two of the conspirators, told the sheriff of Worcester, in order to save his life, that some of the priests mentioned in the royal proclamation were at Hendlip Hall, near Worcester. Sir Henry Bromley with a sufficient force was sent to make search. He first surrounded the mansion ; but as Mr. Abingdon, the owner (a brother-in-law of Lord Mounteagle), was absent, there was of course little or no resistance, and he took possession and commenced a rigorous scrutiny. Mr. Abingdon soon returned, and, regarding the lives of his friends (Oldcorne was his domestic priest) more than his own, or than truth, denied solemnly that any such persons were hidden there, and offered to die at his own gate if any such should be found in his house—or the shire. Sir Henry, however, pursued his scrutiny, for the intricacy of the building kept his suspicions alive. It was full of the most extraordinary hiding-places. No less than eleven secret " conveyances " came to light ; " all of them having books, masoning stuff, and popish trumpery in them, except two that had apparently been discovered before, and so were distrusted." A manuscript now in the British Museum details the singular discoveries made in the course of the protracted search, which was unattended by any decided result until the fourth day, " when, from behind the wainscot in the galleries " came out of their own accord two persons, who proved to be Garnet's confidential servant Owen, and Chambers. It was directly believed that their superiors were hidden in some other part of the building, and four days more were spent in minute examination of the edifice. But after all, the Jesuits might have remained secure, had they not been driven forth, like Owen and Chambers (who had had but one apple between them for several days), by want of food. They came out of a *chimney*—from a secret entrance curiously covered over with brickwork, and made fast to planks of wood, and coloured black like the other parts of the chimney. The place of concealment within seems to have been supplied with light and air from a funnel that appeared externally as a chimney. Such nourishment as caudles, broths, and warm drinks had been attempted to be conveyed to the Jesuits through a quill or reed passed through a hole into the chimney of a gentle woman's chamber. This curious old mansion seems to have been built in great part for the express purpose of concealing distressed Catholics. It was pulled down in the present century. A view of it will be found among the illustrations of the Popular Antiquities.

It was a striking evidence of the respect felt for Garnet even by his enemies, that they did not put him upon the rack. But whatever unusual mercy they exhibited towards him, was more than compensated for by their infamous treatment of his unfortunate companions. We need but give one example.

Nicholas Owen, Garnet's confidential servant, whose fidelity to his master formed his only crime, refused to give evidence against him. The ruthless barbarity of the State engines was employed to force him. He was suspended by his thumbs from a beam, and endured the torture without flinching in his constancy ; but being told to expect the rack on the following day, he in the interval complained of illness ; and before he was to be again tormented, as he sat down to dinner, on a chair that his keeper had the humanity to bring him, he besought the man to make his broth hotter on a fire in an adjoining room. The keeper complying found him, when he came back with the broth, lying on the floor with straw pulled over him, his countenance pale and ghastly. The poor fellow, to avoid the coming agony, and keep unsullied his fidelity, had actually rent open his body with a blunt dinner knife, and so he died. Such were the scenes hidden from the public eye by the blood-stained walls of the " Towers of Julius." Truly they should be called (not " London's " but) England's " lasting shame."

Since force would not succeed, there was another tried and much-esteemed agency—fraud, to experiment with : the keepers of the Tower were equally adepts at both. Garnet's keeper pretended

1884.—Old Star Chamber, Westminster; pulled down after the late Fire of the Parliament.

1885.—Cheapside, with the Procession of Mary de Medicis on her Visit to Charles I. and his Queen. (From La Serres' "Entree Royale de la Regne Mère du Roy." 1638.)

1886.—St. Giles and the Old Tron Church, Edinburgh, in the time of Charles I. (From an old Print.)

1887.—Cecil, Earl of Salisbury—after Zucchero.   Prynne—old Picture of the Prynne Family   Ireton—Anonymous Print.
Pym—Print by Vander Gucht.   Wentworth, Earl of Strafford—Vandyke.

1888.—Medal struck in honour of the Earl of Essex, bearing on one side a Portrait of the Earl, and on the other the two Houses of Parliament; the King presiding in the Lords, and the Speaker in the Commons.   Engraved from the Parliamentary series executed by Simon, the celebrated Medallist of the period.

1889.—Design of Inigo Jones for Whitehall.   The front towards the Park.

1890.—The Front towards Charing Cross.

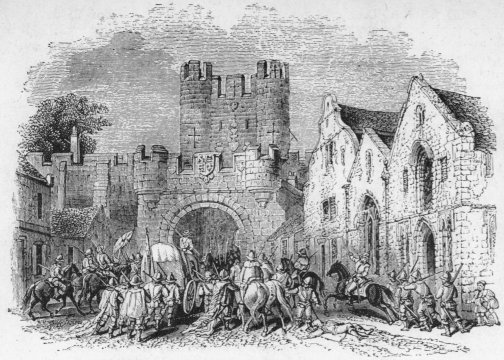

1891.—York Micklebar Gate, with the arrival of a Royalist Baggage-train.

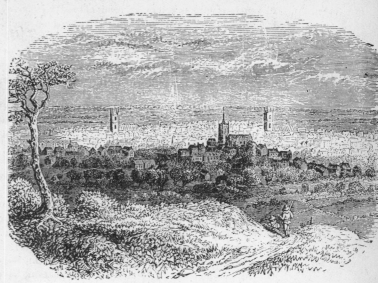

1893.—Reading, from Caversham Hill. (From an Old Print.)

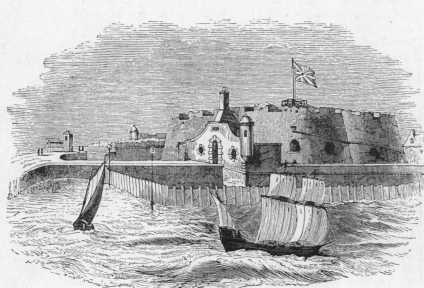

1892.—Castle of Hull, temp. Charles I. (From an old Plan of the Town.)

1894.—Dublin, temp Charles I.

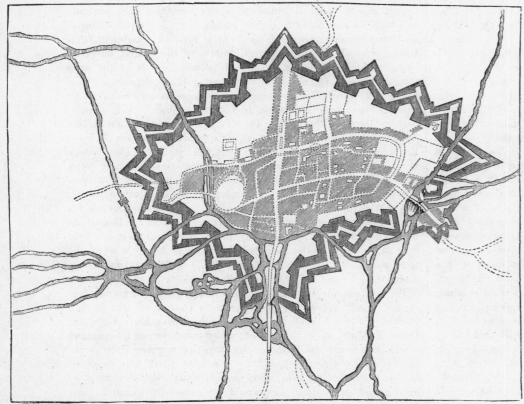

1895.—Plan of Oxford, with the Lines raised for its Defence by Charles I. (From an Old Print by Anthony Wood.)

1896.—Oxford. (From a Drawing by Hollar)

to venerate him as a martyr, and offered to convey letters to his friends. He conveyed them in reality to the council. The Jesuits, however, were not to be caught in so commonplace a trap as this. Then Oldcorne was put in an adjoining cell, and the keeper showed a concealed door through which they could converse, but recommended extreme caution. This time the Jesuits were snared. They spoke of how they should arrange their defence. Garnet said he must needs confess that he had been at White-Webbs in Enfield Chase with the conspirators, but he would maintain he had not been there since Bartholomew-tide: adding, "And in truth I am well persuaded that I shall wind myself out of this matter." Other things Garnet said connecting him with the conspirators—little conscious that all the while Cecil's secretary and a magistrate were taking notes of every unguarded word. It was chiefly on the oaths of these "spials set on purpose" that Oldcorne and Garnet were put to death. They boldly denied the "spials,'" testimony, till the rack extorted confession from Oldcorne, who was executed with a brother priest, Strange, and several other persons. Garnet's statements in the Tower are reported contradictorily by the Catholics and the authorities concerned. When shown Oldcorne's examination, he said, his friend might accuse himself falsely, but he would not do so. Then, say the Catholics, he was led to the rack, and made sundry admissions to escape torture: the authorities say, these admissions were made by him freely, when he saw it was useless to persist in denial. The admissions, however gained, sound like the truth, though not perhaps all the truth. When Fawkes went to Flanders, Garnet had recommended him to Baldwin the Jesuit. Catesby at one time asked him in general terms if a design meant to promote the Catholic faith were lawful, in which it would be necessary to *destroy a few Catholic friends* together with a *great many heretical enemies.* Garnet answered—"In case the object were clearly good, and could be effected by no other means, it might be lawful among many nocents to destroy some innocents." After this it is not easy to have much sympathy with the "martyred" Jesuit—one is more inclined to pity the men who were deceived by such guides. Garnet also admitted that he had long been accessary to the plot, which had been disclosed to him by Greenway, who had learned it under the sacred seal of confession from Catesby and Thomas Winter: but, added Garnet, he had done his best to dissuade the conspirators from their design. Garnet's trial took place in Guildhall. James was present in one corner—the Lady Arabella Stuart in another. Coke spoke forcibly for hours. Garnet could evidently have done the same, but was not permitted. So rude, indeed, were the interruptions that James declared the Jesuit had not had fair play. He "carried himself very gravely and temperately," and the audience were charmed in spite of themselves. His defence essentially was this:—The laws of the church did not permit him to reveal any secret obtained in the confessional; but that what he could do he had done—namely, strove to prevent the execution of the plot. From that defence, and beyond the admissions already specified, he could not be moved. But they were enough in the opinion of the jury—or rather in the opinion of the government, for political juries in those days had no opinions: Garnet was found guilty, condemned, and (after some delay in the vain hope of further avowal) executed.

Surely at last this dreadful business will begin to disappear from the public gaze, and leave the angry feelings aroused by it to fall back into their more usual and placid state? Far from it. From the Jesuit's ashes sprung up a new wonder—a professed miracle. The first who announced it to the world was one Wilkinson, a tailor, who said that, as he stood near the place of Garnet's execution, there was cast towards him—"*how*, he knew not"—an ear of straw that had been put in a basket with the martyr's head and quarters. This sacred straw he afterwards delivered to a Mrs. N., a matron of singular Catholic piety, who enclosed it in a bottle, which being rather shorter than the straw, it became slightly bent. A few days afterwards, showing the bottle to a certain noble person, that person, looking attentively, said—"I can see nothing in it but a man's face!" Mrs. N. and Wilkinson, in astonishment, themselves then examined the ear of straw again and again, and distinctly perceived a human countenance. The fame of the miracle rapidly spread both in England and on the Continent. The face improved with keeping. It expanded and grew sublime. A crown of sunlike rays encircled it. A cross appeared on the forehead. An anchor came out of the ears at the sides. (Figs. 1835, 1837.) We seldom find the privy councils of that period acting so sensibly as in respect to this notorious imposition—for such they *proved* it to be—and then left all parties concerned in it to suffer the only suitable punishment—universal contempt. In concluding these notices of the Gunpowder Conspiracy we have, alas!

yet to mention its worst feature—the effect upon those who were to have gained so much by it. We have already shown that one of the predisposing causes of the plot was the rumour that the penal sword was to receive a yet keener edge in the ensuing parliament: but the feelings and thoughts of those who had so desired to whet it were now a thousand times more bitter and relentless and oppressive than ever. Truly the sword was sharpened. Laws inflicting every conceivable kind of injury and humiliation on the Catholics were passed by immense majorities; and the only wonder is that they did not at at last do what so many of their most enthusiastic spirits desired—break out into open war, and at once die, or relieve themselves from the worse than Egyptian bondage in which they were placed. But the truth was, they were weighed down—lowered in their own estimation (though they, as a body, were perfectly guiltless)—by the gigantic wickedness of the Gunpowder Plot, and became in consequence an unresisting prey.

In the house lately occupied by Messrs. Roake and Varty in the Strand, is preserved a part of an old ceiling, that probably others like ourselves have gone on a pilgrimage to see—as the last remnant of the interior of a mansion famous on many accounts, but especially for its connection with one of the greatest of Englishmen, Francis Bacon. It was in York House (Fig. 1846) that Sir Nicholas Bacon, Elizabeth's Lord Keeper, was residing at the time of the birth of his son; and it was there, in all probability, the latter spent those years of early boyhood which exhibited such striking traits of what the manhood was to be. As the future philosopher was made evident in incidents like that of the boy leaving his playmates to inquire into the cause of an echo in St. James's Street, so was the future courtier as remarkably revealed when, in answer to Elizabeth's question as to his age, the reply was—"I am just two years younger than your majesty's happy reign." Even the courtier's reward was foreshadowed by the same incident; the queen, in expressing her pleasure at Francis's address and wit, called him her "young Lord Keeper." In these pages we can only glance at the steps by which the rise of such a man, in his twofold character, was accomplished. We may refer at the commencement, once for all, to the engraving (Fig. 1857), which exhibits Bacon's portrait, and the different localities with which the great epochs or events of his life and career are connected. Of York House we have already spoken. Beside it is shown Old Gray's Inn (Fig. 1857), where, after spending some years at the University of Cambridge, and experiencing the overthrow of his brilliant prospects in consequence of his father's sudden death, Bacon entered as a student; determined, no doubt, to work his way upward to the eminence he desired, through all opposing obstacles, since he could no longer hope to reach it by the more facile path that his birth and position had promised to open to him. It is surprising how Bacon's example could ever have been cited by those who would inculcate the doctrine that lofty poetical and philosophical genius is incapable of that drudgery which the pursuits of life too frequently demand; still more extraordinary is it that Bacon's own biographers should fall into the same misconceptions. It is an undoubted fact, that while his mind was teeming with projects of the loftiest character in connection with literature and philosophy, he was at the same time so earnest a student of the law that in his twenty-second year he was called to the bar—obtained almost immediately a considerable practice—was made a bencher in his twenty-fourth year—counsel extraordinary to the queen in his twenty-eighth—Lent double reader to his Inn in his thirtieth year, in which position he gave to the world a work on a difficult subject, the 'Statute of Uses,' which is still of authority. These advancements, rapid as they were, exhibit all the characteristics of an elevation depending not upon favour, but upon true merit, exhibited in the legitimate way. It was only natural that after such a connection Bacon should feel a warm and unfading attachment to Gray's Inn; and the feeling has been as warmly and permanently reciprocated. The memory of his last visit is carefully cherished there. The house in which he lived was burned down in 1676, but No. 1 of Gray's Inn Square stands upon its site. The walls of the chambers on the north side of the staircase are covered with the wainscot rescued from the fire. In the garden a very few years ago were some trees that he had planted. The books of the Society abound with his autographs. Bacon had not, as we have seen, relied much on his friends and connections to aid him in the earlier stages of progress; but as the nephew of Lord Burleigh, and the cousin of the Cecils, he could hardly avoid hoping that when he had thus entitled himself to honour and promotion, both would be cheerfully granted. But although he was humble, if not servile, in his attention to them, they disappointed him in his every hope; having, perhaps, no sympathy with his intellectual character, and certainly looking on him with jealousy on account of his friendship for Essex. How the real ignorance of the "practical man"—just when he is most pluming himself upon his penetration, and upon his knowing so much—appears, from the representation of the Cecils to the queen that Bacon was a *speculative*—therefore a dangerous individual in the realities of business! Bacon had his errors, and worse, in the management of business, as we shall subsequently see; but it was from no incapacity to transact worldly business in a worldly manner: in truth he became only too worldly. In justice to the Cecils, it must be stated, they did appear to do something for their able kinsman: they procured him the reversion of a post worth 1600*l.* a-year when it fell to him—just twenty years later. Bacon observed upon the gift—it "mended his prospect, but did not fill his barn."

Turning from the Cecils in hopelessness, Bacon joined himself still more closely than before to the fortunes of Essex, and asked of him the office of Attorney-General. Essex tried his utmost; but the Cecils were too influential: and the generous earl, deeply mortified, wrote thus to Bacon—"You fare ill because you have chosen me for your mean and dependence. You have spent your time and thoughts in my matters. I die, if I do not somewhat toward your fortune. You shall not deny to receive a piece of land, which I will bestow upon you." Bacon accepted an estate at Twickenham worth 2000*l.* But he knew the world, and advised his benefactor not to turn all his estates thus into obligations, like the Duke of Guise, in France, for he would find many bad debtors. We fear few men ever found worse than did Essex in Bacon himself. The latter deserted him at his utmost need—appeared as counsel against him—employed his talents in magnifying his crimes—and after the earl's execution, to please the queen, wrote 'A Declaration of the Practices and Treasons attempted and committed by Robert Earl of Essex,' printed by authority. There is certainly one excuse to be urged for this conduct: Bacon probably throughout fulfilled the odious task intrusted to him *less* harshly and vindictively than any one else would have done: it appears that the first draught of the Declaration just mentioned was reckoned by the queen and her advisers much too mild; and the former observed, "I see old love is not easily forgotten."

It was not until the accession of James that Bacon found he was at last about to achieve the high fortunes he desired, and for which he worked so hard—publicly by honourable means—privately by those flatteries, and intrigues, and solicitations, of which the less said the better for those who do not love to dwell upon the dark side of so illustrious a character. He was first knighted—then made a King's Counsel—next Solicitor-General—and still he climbed the ladder: he obtained in succession the appointments of a joint Judge-ship of the Knight Marshal's Court—Attorney-General—member of the privy council—and, at last, of the office of Lord Keeper: the dream of early ambition, fostered perhaps by Elizabeth's royal lips, was realized. There still remained, however, an Alp beyond all these Alps—the Lord High Chancellorship; and that too was obtained on the 4th of January, 1618. Here, as in all the other cases we have mentioned, the man was worthy of the office: but did not, unhappily, obtain it because he was worthy. The ready pliancy with which he could previously promise James to make the post subservient to the sovereign's will and pleasure, had doubtless much more to do with his success. James even, it should seem, was a little uneasy lest he should carry his sycophancy to unnecessary lengths; for in his advice to Bacon at the time he placed the seals in his hand, he told him not "to extend the royal prerogative too far." This, for James, is rich indeed. Let us now pause a moment to glance at Bacon's position at the commencement of the most eventful year of his life—a year, indeed, so eventful, all things considered, perhaps hardly any other man's life affords. He had now obtained the highest honour the State could give. His literary reputation was established, and steadily advancing, though his great work was yet to appear. Once more he was in the home of his father, and residing there in the enjoyment of higher rank and magnificence than that father had known. It was also, as we have seen, his birthplace; it was a scene in every way calculated to hold one of those solemn birthday-festivals from which as from a height men generally are accustomed to look back on the past, to gaze forward into the future. And few such birthdays have been seen as that of Bacon at York House (Fig. 1846), when he celebrated his sixtieth year, amid a splendid galaxy of genius and talent, and rank, and wealth, and power. Ben Jonson was one of the guests—and a delighted one, as he had taken care to record in some of his verses.

All things, he says, seemed to smile about the old house—"the fire, the wine, the men,"—and Bacon seemed to him the most enviable of mankind. He was

> England's High Chancellor, the destined heir,
> In his soft cradle, to his father's chair,
> Whose even thread, the Fates spin round and full,
> Out of their choicest and their whitest wool.

And now, having achieved all those personal objects on which he had so long set his heart; having dazzled the eyes of his contemporaries with the splendour of his abilities, his success, and the magnificence of his tastes and modes of life, which made York House remind many of York Place and its owner (Wolsey), he next addressed himself to a task that was to make him appear even still more illustrious in the eyes of posterity. The same year that beheld his elevation to the Chancellorship, and the holding of the feast on his sixtieth birthday, the 22nd of January, beheld also the publication of his immortal work, the 'Novum Organum.' What a lesson to those who would achieve reputation is afforded by the growth of that production! It was, in strict truth, the labour of a lifetime. Even "whilst he was commorant at the university, about sixteen years of age (as his Lordship hath been pleased to impart to myself), he first fell into the dislike of the philosophy of Aristotle; not for the worthlessness of the author, to whom he would ever ascribe all high attributes, but for the unfruitfulness of the way, being a philosophy (as his Lordship used to say) only strong for disputations and contentions, but barren of the production of works for the life of man. In which mind he continued to his dying day." (Dr. Rawley, Bacon's chaplain and biographer.)

The rejection of the old system was, very naturally, accompanied by a desire for a new one, which, step by step, year by year, Bacon proceeded to build, undiverted by the pressure of his weighty business, unseduced by the reputation that his other writings from time to time brought him. One illustration of the man of genius, in his glorious workshop, we must give:—Twelve separate times was the 'Organum' copied, in consequence of the constant revision it underwent! When the book was published, it realized what the ardent young author had, some forty years before, said to himself it should be; and therefore then called it—"The greatest birth of time."

Bacon, if he was not the author of the Inductive Philosophy, was the first to unfold it; to show its infinite importance, and to induce the great body of scientific inquirers to place themselves under its guidance. (Professor Playfair.) He turned the attention of philosophers from speculations and "contentions" upon remote questions, and fixed it upon those productive of works for the benefit of "the life of man." He first showed philosophy its proper objects, the promotion of human happiness and the alleviation of human suffering. The key to this philosophy is contained in the famous aphorism that commences the 'Novum Organum:'—"Man, who is the servant and interpreter of nature, can act and understand no further than he has, either in operation or in contemplation, observed of the method and order of nature." In the same work Bacon observes, "Men have sought to make a world from their own conceptions, and to draw from their own minds all the materials which they employed; but if, instead of doing so, they had consulted experience and observation, they would have had facts, and not opinions, to reason about; and might have ultimately arrived at the knowledge of the laws which govern the material world." Truths these, that may be justly called divine, as calculated to teach us the all-important knowledge that nature, which is but the visible manifestation of the Deity, is, and must eventually appear, harmonious in its working; and that the discords of human life are the result of ignorance of its laws. In the few sentences we have quoted, Bacon has given us a solid foundation for the erection of that greatly improved and infinitely happier state of being, that men in all ages have dreamed of.

With the publication of the 'Organum' Bacon's life should have ended. How different then had been our views of him! less true, unquestionably—perhaps less useful, but a thousand times more satisfactory and gratifying. About the time to which we refer, rumours flew abroad impeaching the integrity of the Lord Chancellor. Soon after, the rumours were strengthened by the fact that a Committee of the Lower House (which, for the first time, was beginning to undertake the correction of popular abuses with a high hand) began to inquire into the proceedings of the law courts, and ended by recommending proceedings against the Lord Chancellor: "a man endued with all parts, both of nature and art, as that I will say no more of him, being not able to say enough." So spake Sir Robert Philips, who reported for the Committee to the Lords. There were laid to Bacon's charge by the Commons no

1897.—Prince Rupert's House, Barbican, as it appeared before its recent demolition.

1898.—Manor-house of Hampden, and Church where John Hampden lies interred.

1899.—Puritans destroying the Cross in Cheapside. (From a Contemporary Print in the Pennant Collection, Brit. Mus.)

1900.—Newbury: Donnington Castle in the Distance. (From an Old Print.)

1901.—Sermon at St. Paul's Cross on Good Friday. (From a Drawing in the Pepysian Library. This Cross was erected about 1450, and remodelled in 1595.)

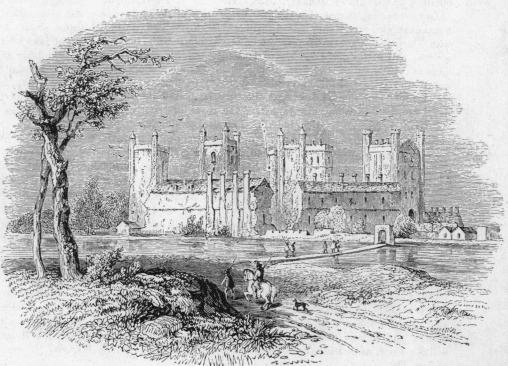

1902.—Basing House after the Siege.

164

Sr. beinge comanded by you to this service, I thinke my selfe bound to ac= quaint you with the good hand of God towards you and vs, Wee marched yesterday after the Kinge whoe went before vs from Daventre to Haverbrowe, and quartered about six miles from him, this day wee marched towards him, Hee drew out to meete vs, both Armies engaged, wee, after 3 howers fight, very doubtful att last routed his Armie, killed and tooke about 5000. very many officers

I wish this action may begett thankfullness, and humilitye in all that are conerned in itt, Hee that ventures his life for the libertye of his cuntrie, I wish Hee trust God for the libertye of his conscience, and you for the libertye Hee fights for, In this Hee rests whoe is

your most humble servant

Oliver Cromwell

Juno. 14.th 1645.
Haverbrowe.

1904.—Anderson's Place, Newcastle. The House in which Charles was delivered to the Parliamentry Troops. (From an Original Drawing made before its demolition in 1836.)

1905.—Obelisk on Naseby Field. Erected to commemorate the Battle. (From an unpublished Lithograph.)

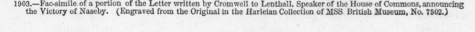

1903.—Fac-simile of a portion of the Letter written by Cromwell to Lenthall, Speaker of the House of Commons, announcing the Victory of Naseby. (Engraved from the Original in the Harleian Collection of MSS. British Museum, No. 7502.)

1906.—Uxbridge. Showing, to the right, the House (called the Treaty House) in which the Commissioners held their Sittings.

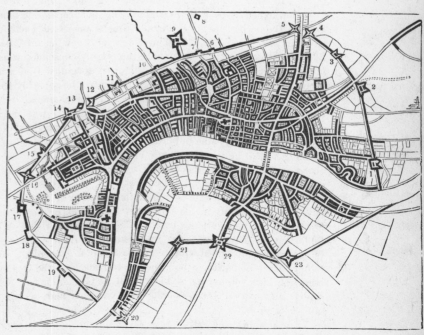

1907. Plan of City and Suburbs of London, as it appeared fortified in 1643.

less than twenty-two distinct acts of bribery and corruption. The prosecution was encouraged by the king and Buckingham, as the latter wanted the seals for his minion, Bishop Williams.

Here is one of the cases:—

A gentleman named Aubrey, who had been almost ruined by expenses and delays in the course of a suit in Chancery, was advised by some of the hangers-on of the Chancellor to make him a present. The unfortunate suitor had not the means, but obtained a hundred pounds with great difficulty from a usurer; and Bacon received the sum thus gained, some of his dependents assuring the gentleman that all would go well. He relied on these promises, which proved deceptive. "A killing decree" plunged him in despair, and he exposed the whole transaction. This example may suffice; but there were worse cases even than this one. Bacon could not deny them. And so "this poor gentleman, mounted above pity, fell down below it; his tongue that was the glory of his time for eloquence (that tuned so many sweet harangues), was like a forsaken harp hung upon the willows, whilst the waters of affliction overflowed the banks. And now his highflying orations are humbled to supplications, and thus he throws himself and cause at the feet of his judges before he was condemned." (Sir Arthur Wilson.) He said, he understood some justification had been expected from him, but the only justification he should make should be out of Job: "I have not hid my sin, as did Adam, nor concealed my faults in my bosom." Extenuating circumstances he left to their "noble thought," and submitted himself wholly to their "piety and grace." This to them as judges; but addressing them as peers and prelates, he also told them a story out of Livy, to show that the questioning of men in eminent places hath the same effect as their punishment: adding, "My humble desire is, that his majesty would take the seals into his hands, which is a great downfall, and may serve, I hope, in itself, for an expiation of my faults." A distinct confession to all the charges specially brought against him was required, and Bacon did not refuse it. He felt he had fallen so low already that he could hardly fall lower. A deputation waited on him, to know whether this second complete acknowledgment was his voluntary act. He replied with tears, "It is my act—my hand—my heart. Oh, my lords, spare a broken reed." His prayer was so far granted, that he was excused from publicly appearing in court to hear the judgment passed on him,—a fine of forty thousand pounds, imprisonment in the Tower during the king's pleasure, incapability in future of any office of state or seat in parliament, and banishment from within twelve miles of the court. The king's object being to degrade him from his position, the other parts of his sentence were eventually remitted. And thus Bacon bade farewell to the court, where it had been fortunate for his fame if he had never come.

And what was the secret impulse to the commission of all this guilt, so likely from the first to bring with it all this degradation and ruin of one who should have been in all things, as he was in much, one of the noblest of God's creatures?—The weakness, too common with men of genius and taste, an unbounded love of magnificence, that cannot stoop to square its wants with its means. In the cases to which we refer, and we confine our observations solely to these, it matters little what the amount of attainable wealth is, it will still be found insufficient. Double the income to day, the expenditure will be trebled or quadrupled to-morrow. During the latter years of Bacon's life he possessed, even in his adversity, an income of 2500l. a-year; yet when he died he was 22,000l. in debt. He was himself thoroughly conscious, when too late, of his error. One day, while the charges against him were in process of examination, as he entered his house, the superbly-habited menials rose to receive him. "Sit down, my masters," was the bitter remark, "your rise has been my fall." It was the same year (1618) that witnessed the elevation to the Chancellorship—the prosperous birthday—the publication of the work, hardly overrated in being called the greatest birth of time—that also witnessed the charges of corruption, the humiliation, the fall, and the punishment.

It is pleasant to be able to reflect that a world of goodness must have existed after all in Bacon's heart and mind, or he would not have kept so many friends by his side at such a crisis. We are told, that as Prince Charles was returning from hunting, "he espied a coach, attended with a goodly troop of horsemen;" and on inquiry learned that these horsemen were friends of the Chancellor, escorting him voluntarily to his retreat at Gorhambury. Charles smiled, and said, "Well, do what we can, this man scorns to go out like a snuff."

After a short and fitful fever of ambitious hopes to regain his position by constant prayer and flatteries, directed to the prince just

named, among others, Bacon trusting that as "his father the king had been his *creator*, so he his son, would be his *redeemer*," he settled down into peace at last, in the quiet and lovely solitudes of Gorhambury, near St. Albans (Fig. 1857), where his father had built a splendid mansion. Scientific pursuits, and the society of his friends, became thenceforth everything to him. Hobbes, then a young man, was among his friends and ardent admirers. Bacon, it is said, "was wont to have him walk with him in his delicate groves, when he did meditate; and when a notion darted into his lordship's mind, Mr. Hobbes was presently to write it down, and his lordship was wont to say that he did it better than any one else about him: for that many times when he read their notes, he scarce understood what they writ, because they understood it not clearly themselves." (Aubrey's 'Lives of Eminent Persons.') The manner of his death had a kind of poetical fitness and beauty about it. Travelling, says Aubrey, in his carriage, when snow lay on the ground, Lord Bacon began to consider whether flesh might not be preserved by snow as well as by salt. He determined to make the experiment, and, alighting at a cottage near Highgate (Fig. 1857), bought a hen, and stuffed it with snow. This so chilled him, that he could not return home, and went to the Earl of Arundel's house at Highgate. The earl was absent, and the domestics in charge of the place, while intending to show Lord Bacon every respect, unfortunately put him into a damp bed, which decided his fate. He died in a few days, having previously written a letter to the Earl of Arundel, in which he compared himself to the elder Pliny, "who lost his life by trying an experiment about the burning of Mount Vesuvius." Bacon adds, that his own fatal experiment "succeeded excellently well." In his will he wrote, "For my burial, I desire it may be in St Michael's Church, St. Albans; there was my mother buried, and it is the parish church of my mansion-house of Gorhambury, and it is the only Christian church within the walls of old Verulam." This church is drawn at the foot of the localities in the engraving (Fig. 1857). In the same document also occur these impressive words—"For my name and memory, I leave it to men's charitable speeches, to foreign nations, and the next ages." Bacon's faithful friend and secretary, Sir Thomas Meautys, erected a monument to his memory (Fig. 1860), and was himself buried at his feet.

Two or three other eminent men of James's reign may be here noticed; and among them the author of what has been styled "one of the most extensive works of the kind which the history of the civilised world can anywhere furnish. I question," continues the writer of this passage, "if the celebrated aqueducts in ancient Rome equalled in magnitude, most assuredly not in extent, the beneficial effects of this undertaking." The work thus spoken of is the formation of the New River by Sir Hugh Middleton, the subject of Jansen's noble picture (Fig. 1855). Here again is enforced the truth of which we have spoken in our notices of Bacon, that the bearing up against, in order ultimately to triumph over, difficulties and disappointment, is one of the conditions of the accomplishment of any great undertaking, and in itself forms to our mind a greater and more truly glorious thing than the special object achieved can possibly be. He began in 1608. He had to bring his river from the springs of Chadwell (Fig. 1858) and of Amwell, in Hertfordshire, by a circuitous way that extended an ordinary route of nineteen miles to thirty-eight; he had to deal with every variety of soil, "now oozy and muddy, and now rocky and hard," and with all kinds of surfaces, so that whilst one while he had to make his trench descend thirty or forty feet, in other places "it required a sprightful art again to mount it over a valley in a trough between a couple of hills, and the trough all the while borne up by wooden arches, some of them fixed in the ground very deep, and rising in height above twenty-three feet." He had to make innumerable drains, sewers, and bridges; he had to do all this when mechanical and engineering science were far below their present state; he had at the same time to soothe jealous and influential persons along his route, who could be soothed, or oppose them by every means in his power, when nothing but sturdy opposition would do; he had to complete all by a given (short) time; lastly, and worst of all, he had, in addition to his other difficulties, to contend against a lack of funds; and that cause stopped him when nothing else could, and when he had thrown his own splendid fortune, without a sigh as to its fate, into the undertaking, and had induced friends to do the same. The city, to its disgrace be it said, refused to help him; and then King James did; not, be it observed, from any absurdly Quixotic desire to aid in a work that should be a glory to his reign, but because he was admitted to a share of all the profits that were in the end to be realised. Middleton was not mistaken in that view, although unhappily for him, the prosperity of the New

River Company dated from a period many years later than he had anticipated. It was only in the nineteenth year after completion (1613) that any dividend was declared; that dividend amounted to just 11l. 19s. 1d. per share. A share has since that time sold for 14,000l. Still there is reason to hope that Sir Hugh (he was knighted by James—one of the few examples of the king's wisely conferring that honour) lived to see and to share in for a brief time the success of the great work of his life.

The death of Prince Henry was the means of raising to notice one of the most genuine poets of Scotland, and the first and best of that country who composed in pure and classic English, namely, William Drummond of Hawthornden (Figs. 1861, 1863), who wrote an elegy on that prince, which Milton afterwards partly imitated in 'Lycidas,' and which no less an authority than Ben Jonson pronounced "all good." Five years later, the same eminent dramatist honoured Drummond by going to Scotland on foot to visit him, and staying at Hawthornden three weeks. The scene of that memorable visit is as poetical as heart could desire. It still remains little changed. The house is very ancient, and exhibits all the picturesque variety of mullioned windows, clustered chimneys, and gable roof. It is planted on the edge of a tremendous cliff of limestone, from which another cliff is divided only by the river that flows between. Both are richly covered with woods. On the face of one of the precipices is a ledge leading to a hollow cavern, containing an old table and a seat. Here Drummond composed the 'Cypress Grove,' after a dangerous fit of illness. The rock contains other nooks still more singular. There are four small rooms, excavated, according to tradition, before the time of Wallace and Bruce, who found shelter in them during their distresses. Two are dark, and one is lighted by a hole in the wall, which appears externally as though a stone had merely fallen out by accident. It is a long and toilsome descent to the river, but the view there obtained richly repays the trouble. Its passage is romantically obstructed by fallen rocks, more or less hid in the stream, which chafes and bubbles and brawls, as if endued with a living spirit. The purple heath is everywhere conspicuous among the foliage of trees, bushes, and wild plants, that clothe every recess of the lofty and overhanging rocks. Such is and was Hawthornden, where Drummond was born, wrote, lived the greater part of his lifetime, and died in 1649. His fine sensibility seems to have been at once his bliss, his inspiration, and his bane. Love and Sorrow formed the wings of his Muse. His betrothed died on the eve of their wedding-day, and the melancholy induced in consequence was poured out in song :—

> Do not disdain, dear ghost, this sacrifice,
> And though I raise not pillars to thy praise,
> My offerings take, let this for me suffice,
> My heart a living pyramid I'll raise;
> And whilst kings' tombs with laurels flourish green,
> Thine shall with myrtle and these flowers be seen.

Later in life his feelings were strongly engaged in the cause of Charles I., and he exerted his literary talents in his favour. The execution of Charles, after Drummond had been compelled to supply his quota of men to serve against him, plunged the poet again into a melancholy, and shortened his days. The moral of the history of this too tender and unworldly spirit Drummond has himself given :—

> Love, which is here a care
> That wit and will doth mar;
> Uncertain truce, and a most certain war;
> A shrill, tempestuous wind,
> Which doth disturb the mind,
> And, like wild waves, all our designs commove;
> Among those powers above
> Which see their Maker's face,
> It a contentment is, a quiet peace,
> A pleasure void of grief, a constant rest,
> Eternal joy, which nothing can molest.

Inigo Jones's first patron was William Earl of Pembroke (Fig. 1862), who, charmed with his talent for drawing, sent him abroad to study. On the Continent, Jones found himself in a new world; he became a follower of Palladio, and sought to ascertain the elements of ancient art, and to apply them with taste to modern wants and usages. The old orders of architecture were as yet utterly unknown to his countrymen, so were the Italian modifications of them, except as mere ornaments. He resolved to introduce Italian art on the principles of Palladio into England—by which he created here a new epoch. Twice Jones visited Italy, pursuing

his studies there, conversing with its great men, and exploring its ruins. In the interval between these visits he was at the court of Christian IV. of Denmark, or inventing those famous masques with Ben Jonson for the amusement of the court of James, which have shed the charms of poetry and imagination over what was in many respects one of the most unpoetical and unimaginative of courts. Subsequently the dramatist and the architect quarrelled, and "Surly Ben" was severe upon him in the satirical characters of In-and-In Medley and Lantern Leatherhead. Jones's chief offence seems to have been his having prospered in the world, and the satire wounded most the hand that penned it.

The fame of Inigo Jones has been rendered immortal by his designs for the erection of a new royal palace (Figs. 1889, 1890), that would have been the grandest in existence had it been finished according to the plans that have been bequeathed to us, bating some errors which have crept in most likely from the hands of those who have issued the designs since their author's death. Three years after James's accession he had removed the " old, rotten, slight-builded Banqueting House " erected by Elizabeth at Whitehall, and in its stead built another " very strong and stately, being every way larger than the first : there were also many fair lodgings new builded and increased." In 1619 this " fair Banqueting House " was consumed by fire, and then Inigo Jones was employed to design the new palace in question. Its proposed dimensions were startling : the exterior buildings were to have measured 874 feet on the east and west sides, 1152 feet on the north and south, and there were to have been seven courts within. The Banqueting House (Figs. 1915, 1916) was the only part the artist was allowed to finish ; but he could not have left us a better evidence of what he meant the whole to become. The following note is published by Pennant from Walpole, as showing the trifling pay which was given to Jones whilst engaged in superintending the erection of the Banqueting House :—" To Inigo Jones, surveyor of the works done about the king's houses, 8s. 4d. per diem, and 46l. per ann. for house-rent, a clerk, and other incidental expenses." Even on such a scale James could not support the expense ; and James's successor lived in too troubled times to undertake so vast a work.

In drawing to a close our notices of the reign of James, we may make a few observations upon the personal character of that monarch. The many different aspects under which we have had occasion to look at him, bring out in strong relief the chief traits of his character. Such are his constitutional timidity—his unmanly love of favourites—his utter want of feeling, not only for them when he was tired of them, but for his nearest and dearest relatives, witness his conduct to his mother—his busy, meddling, prying propensities—his abilities, which are generally acknowledged—his want of prudence and dignity, that made even his best friends secretly ashamed of him—his taste alike for true magnificence, as shown in the delightful masques of Whitehall, and for empty show, as is made evident in the numerous pageants and processions by water (Fig. 1845) and land (Fig. 1854), in which we find him so often engaged —his appreciation of eminent men, such as Shakspere, Bacon, Ben Jonson, Jones, shared, however, it must be owned, by men of the calibre of the king's "philosophical poet," William Alexander, Earl of Stirling (Fig. 1856)—his insincerity, of which the Catholics had especially painful evidence—and, lastly, his despotic words, principles, and acts, which, falling like seed upon the hearts and minds of the people of England, gave birth, like the teeth of Cadmus, to a most portentous progeny of armed men, mutually bent on each other's destruction, in the time of James's son and successor. To complete the picture of this sovereign's character, however, we must add a few words upon the last feature of it—his love of despotism ; and upon some traits not yet noticed, relating to his personal and mental tastes. When Christian IV., King of Denmark, paid a visit to England in 1606, a feast was given to James and him at Theobalds (Fig. 1843), by Cecil. Two facts may suffice to show the spirit of these domestic enjoyments under the eye of the British Solomon : both monarchs got so drunk, that James had to be carried to his bed by his courtiers ; whilst Christian, on the way to his room, missed his proper route, and found the way into the apartments of the Countess of Nottingham, whom he insulted in the grossest manner. The effects of such examples were truly lamentable. An eyewitness of this very entertainment says— " Men who had been shy of good liquors before, now wallowed in beastly delights ; the ladies abandoned their sobriety, and were seen to roll about in intoxication," (Harrington.) As to the traits of the king's mental tastes that we have not yet mentioned, it would be unpardonable to forget James the author, in James the anything else. And such an author ! the variety of whose writings are as

1908.—Newark Castle. (From an original Drawing.)

1909.—Remains of Colchester Castle (From an original Drawing.)

1910.—Carisbrook Castle, in its present state. (From an original Drawing.)

1911.—Carisbrook Castle; showing the window from which Charles I. attempted to escape.

1912.—Trial of Charles I. (From a Print in Nalson's Report of the Trial, 1684.) A, the King. B, the Lord President Bradshaw. C, John Lisle; D, William Say: Bradshaw's assistants. E, Andrew Broughton; F, John Phelps; Clerks of the Court. G, Oliver Cromwell; H, Henry Marten; the Arms of the Commonwealth over them. I, Coke; K, Dorislaus; L, Aske: Counsellors for the Commonwealth. The description of the plate ends with these words:—"The pageant of this mock tribunal is thus represented to your view by an eye and ear witness of what he heard and saw there."

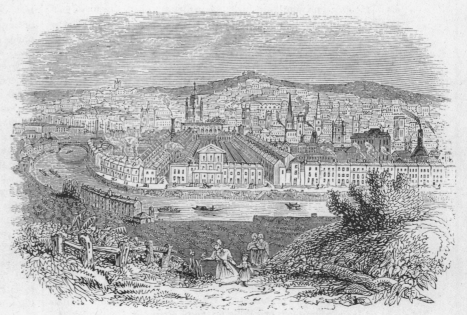

1913.—Bristol in the Seventeenth Century.

1914.—"The George." *a*, upper side; *b*, under side; *c*, upper side, raised, showing a portrait of Henrietta Maria.
(From the original Print by Hollar.)

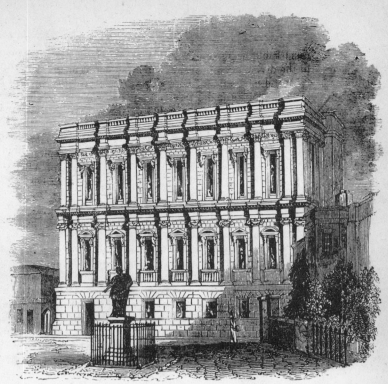

1916.—Banqueting-room; from the Inner Court.

1917.—Twenty-shilling Piece.

1918.—Ten-shilling Piece.

1919.—Angel.

1917 to 1919.—Gold Coins of Charles I.

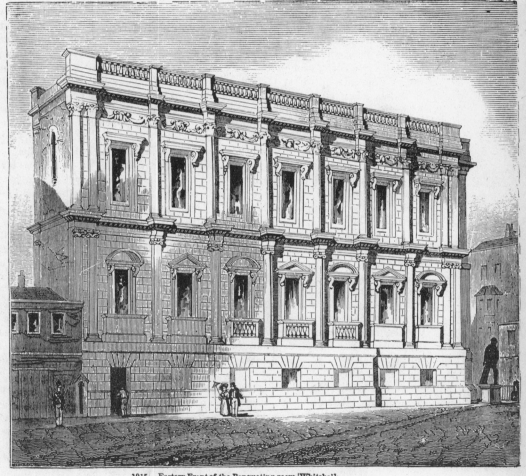

1915.—Eastern Front of the Banqueting-room, Whitehall.

1920.—Oxford Crown.　　　　1921.—York Half-Crown.　　　　1922.—Shilling.

remarkable as their extent. Was he not at one time "a prentice in the divine art of poesy?" Did he not at another time have such "fruitful meditations" on a part of the Revelation of St. John, that he could not keep the results from the world? Was not his name one of the literary strongholds of the believers in witchcraft, and of those who opposed the introduction of tobacco? Was he not, in fine, the historian and expounder of his own life, and government, and views, in his publications on the Gowrie Conspiracy, the 'Laws of Free Monarchies,' the 'Apology for the Oath of Allegiance,' the 'Remonstrance for the Right of Kings,' and the 'Discourse of the Manner of the discovery of the Powder Treason'? It would be superfluous, after this, to speak of James's learning, or the displays of it that he so delighted in. And here let us notice what we may not have another favourable opportunity for so doing—the greatest act, all things considered, of his government—the translation of the Bible, which was begun and completed under his auspices, and really suggested, to his credit be it said, by himself. Early in his reign a conference of divines of different opinions had been held at Hampton Court (Fig. 1851), in which much was said of the imperfection of the then existing translations. " I wish," observed James, "some special plans were taken for a uniform translation, which should be done by the best learned in both universities, then reviewed by the bishops, presented to the privy council, and, lastly, ratified by royal authority, to be read in the whole church, and no other." The suggestion thus made was caught up, and carried out in the spirit and manner proposed. Forty-seven of the best biblical scholars undertook the great labour of love, who presently divided themselves into six classes, each undertaking a portion of the Scriptures. The system then pursued was admirably calculated to develop individual ability and check individual biases or errors. Each member of a class translated the whole of the portion set apart to his class; then the class met, and revised as a body their separate versions. One general version was next agreed upon by the class, which was subsequently revised by each of the other classes. Two of the classes sat at Cambridge, two at Oxford, and two at Westminster. It should be observed, however, that the translators were not left as perfectly free as they should have been, in order to produce a perfectly accurate and faithful translation. They were directed to make as few deviations as possible from the Bishops' Bible, then the one in common use, and they were to keep in the old ecclesiastical words—such as church: both circumstances that theological disputants of more zeal than learning should bear in mind when they battle upon the narrow ground of single sentences, phrases, or even as is often the case, upon single words. Three years were spent in the undertaking—namely, from 1607 to 1611. Among the few men engaged who have obtained any great celebrity for their other writings or lives, was included the admirable Bishop Andrews, whom we have mentioned in an earlier part of the work as buried in St. Mary Overies. The Bible thus completed was printed by Robert Barker in 1611.

The further illustration that we wished to give of James's character cannot be better conveyed than in a passage from one of his speeches, delivered at Whitehall to the members of both Houses of Parliament. We must premise that they had declined to vote sufficient funds to support James's extravagant expenditure; and when Cecil attempted to supply the deficiency by imposing duties on various kinds of merchandise on the authority of mere orders in council, they became at once clamorous in their complaints of the illegality, and resolute in their determination to put a stop to it. And now for the speech: "Kings are justly called gods," said James; ' for that they exercise a manner or resemblance of divine power upon earth; for if you will consider the attributes of God, you shall see how they agree in the person of a king. God hath power to create or destroy, to make or unmake, at his pleasure; to give life, or send death; to judge all, and to be judged nor accountable to none; to raise low things, and to make high things low, at his pleasure; and to God both soul and body are due. And the like power have kings: they make and unmake their subjects; they have power of raising and casting down, of life and death: judges over all their subjects, and in all causes, and yet accountable to God only. They have power to exalt low things, and abase high things, and make of their subjects like men of chess—a pawn to take a bishop or a knight, and to cry up or down any of their subjects as they do their money. And to the king is due both the affection of the soul and the service of the body of his subjects." All that might be very true: but the Commons decidedly objected to the earthly divinity's taxing currants and broadcloth.

There was one, however, who listened to all these assertions of the right divine of kings with a deep conviction of their truth; and whilst perhaps impatient at their broad and straightforward avowal,

was secretly determined, when his time should come, to proceed with greater subtlety and determination in the same path, and doubting not but his efforts would be attended with greater success. That was Prince Charles, the heir-apparent to the throne. And at last the time—too often, we fear, anxiously looked for by princes in Charles's position—did come; his father died at Theobalds on the 8th of April (new style), 1625; and before the breath was well out of his body, his successor heard (no doubt with a kindling of the blood that no grief could overpower) the Knight Marshal proclaiming Charles I., King of England, Scotland, France, and Ireland. Charles's life seems to have been prolific of omens: perhaps the most striking of them all was the blunder made by this Knight Marshal, Sir Edward Zouch, who, according to the letter-writer, Howell, called Charles the rightful and dubitable heir; but he was set right by Mr. Secretary Conway, and then said *indubitable.*"

At first the usual promise, though in fainter tones, was given by rumour, of the future excellence of the King. His father's funeral was magnificently conducted (see our engraving of the Lying in State, Fig. 1870); and many saw in that circumstance a devoted son's pious care. Then, too, the court buffoons and jesters were dismissed; and the courtiers, awed by the example of their head, put on an air of decorum, which was refreshing to the eye, if too superficial to excite any deeper sentiment. The zealous piety of the young monarch was loudly spoken of; and one supposed evidence of it received with peculiar gratification by many—he was to drive away all recusant Papists. Lastly, he was to pay the debts of his father, mother, and brother, even at the cost of disparking some of his parks and chaces. There was one awkward fact to counterbalance all this supposition: he *might* perform these good things but in the mean time he *had* taken to the councils of the sovereign the profligate friend of the prince—Buckingham; the "Steenie" who had accompanied "Baby Charles" in his romantic expedition to Spain some years before, in order that he might see and converse with his proposed bride, and prevent the delays of the diplomatists. That match was hardly broken off, before a treaty with France was negociated for the hand of Henrietta Maria, sister of Louis of France. Only three days after Charles's accession, he ratified the conditions of the treaty, and sent Buckingham to bring the Queen home to her future subjects. Charles met her at Dover Castle. " The King took her up in his arms, kissed her, and talking with her, cast down his eyes towards her feet (she seeming higher, than report was, reaching to his shoulders), which she soon perceiving discovered, and showed him her shoes, saying to this effect 'Sir, I stand upon mine own feet: I have no help by art. Thus high I am; and am neither higher nor lower!' She is nimble and quick, black-eyed, brownhaired, and, in a word, a brave lady." (Fig. 1878.) The *couleur de rose* that beautifies all new governors in the eyes of the governed gave Henrietta Maria so many charms, that they even made her—a bigoted Catholic, with some twenty-nine priests and other religionists of her persuasion in her train—appear as half ready to embrace Protestantism. All these misconceptions were but too soon to be removed. Charles, it was found, had all his father's political and religious views, with talents and means peculiarly his own to promote them; whilst, as if to throw fresh elements of discord into affairs already but too full of them, his Queen, so far from becoming a convert to the episcopal notions of her husband, or the growing puritanical ones of a large portion of the people, exhibited her attachment to the creed of her fathers in modes more ostentatious than was necessary, or could be warranted by any abstract desire to maintain the rights of conscience. Whitehall swarmed with Catholic priests, and Catholic friars ran in and out the Queen's private chamber with a licence that was somewhat unseemly, to say the least of it. Here was cause enough to make Charles odious in the eyes of Protestant England, had there been nothing else to excite divisions between them.

The whole religious policy of our government was based upon the principle that it alone professed the truth, and that other religionists, basing their faith upon falsehood, were to be dealt with in the severest repressive spirit. And yet the head of that government, who was bound to enforce laws against the Catholics which would have appeared cruel beyond measure even to those who originated and approved of them, if they had not been satisfied they were just and necessary on the ground above stated, this King, the chief of a Protestant League, had married a Catholic! Either, then, men thought he had no faith in the principle upon which these repressive laws were based, and every penal punishment inflicted through their operation was frightfully unjust, and Charles at the same time a hypocrite to profess to believe in them; or he had knowingly committed a great outrage upon his conscience, and the consciences of the people of England, for mere purposes of state expediency; and at the same time given a heavy blow to the very existence of such laws for the future :—the Queen a Catholic, how could Charles carry on the persecution of Catholics? Had the people then known all, they would have been indeed exasperated. Charles had actually sworn to the French King not to enforce these penal laws. But here—and thus early—came into play one of Charles's chief characteristics, one upon which he much valued himself, and which, in the end, led him in all probability to the scaffold—his skill in management; in other words, his insincerity and double dealing. So when, as if to test him, his first parliament conjured him to put these laws in execution,—instead of stating what he had pledged himself to, he returned a gracious answer, which was necessarily, therefore, a deceitful one. Such was the state of feeling when Charles was crowned, amid ceremonies as remarkable for the punctual performance of all due splendour and solemnities as for the absence of everything like popular enthusiasm. Let us now glance at two or three incidents that may serve to show the practical effect of Charles's conduct and views upon the conduct and views of his subjects.

It is the opening of the second session of parliament, and Charles in person addresses the members in a short speech, remarking that he is no orator, but desires to be known by his actions. Herewith he refers them to the Lord Keeper, Sir Thomas Coventry. Sir Thomas, duly warmed by the consideration that he is the King's mouth-piece, expatiates upon the condescending goodness of the King, in actually admitting, nay inviting, his subjects to conference and counsel with him. The Commons listen, and immediately after proceed to divide into sections and standing committees, in order to canvass grievances, and bring the King's favourite, the detested and incompetent Buckingham, to punishment. Sixteen capital abuses are presently charged against him, including monopolies, prodigality, and malversation; and, above all, the illegal levying of the duties of tonnage and poundage, without the consent of parliament. Some recent degradations of the English flag, by unsuccessful expeditions on sea and land, are also laid at the door of the "great delinquent." Charles sees an impending petition for impeachment, and anticipates it by a message. "I must let you know, that I will not allow any of my servants to be questioned among you, much less such as are of eminent place, and near unto me," &c. Again the answers are startling—the stoppage of the question of supplies, and more vigorous progress with the accusation against Buckingham; and again Charles sends to the House. He is growing heated and impatient. Words of fearful and dangerous import are spoken to the Commons by the Lord Keeper, conveying threats that disobedience will be followed by dissolution. Two members are also required to be punished for their insolent discourses in the House. To prevent the possibility of mistake, Charles himself once more addresses the Commons, bidding them remember that parliaments are altogether in his power for their calling, sitting, or dissolution; and repeating the threat of how he will use that power, if they do not please him. What answer now? The Commons retire to deliberate; they lock the door of the House to keep out all intruders, and place the key in their Speaker's hands. The business grows too serious to be continued, for the present at least; so the King draws back, in order again to advance by another mode,—conciliation; but the Commons remain firm, and Buckingham is impeached. Immediately after the failure of this attempt to prevent the Commons from fulfilling one of the most important of their duties, the King subjected himself to a similar defeat in a quarrel with the Lords, caused by his arresting one of their members on some paltry pretence. The Lords asked for him once, twice, and then stopped all business until their request was granted. Charles was obliged to give him back to the House out of the Tower. Yet scarcely had he recovered from the first sting of that humiliation before he arrested two members of the Lower House, Elliot and Digges, with no other effect than again to be compelled to give them up, by the Commons also refusing to proceed with any business till satisfaction were given. The impeachment of Buckingham proceeded. The charges were made, even the defence was begun, when a message, still more decidedly menacing, was sent down demanding a subsidy without delay or condition. The Commons immediately proceeded to prepare their answer; and that preparation was an answer to Charles. He dissolved the Parliament—his second in two years—and before it had passed a single act.

And now the country learned what were the "other resolutions" Charles had threatened to take. He and his favourite devoted all their skill and energy to the business of raising supplies for the one wanted money, and was apparently not unwilling to test the extent of his power in raising it; and the other naturally grew more and more devoted to his master, as he saw that he was his

sole defence from the attacks of the people's representatives. So duties were levied upon imports and exports; exactions connected with the religious dissentients from the Established Church were rigorously enforced; voluntary loans were sought, and London was especially honoured by a demand for 120,000l. All these not sufficing, forced loans on a gigantic scale were adopted, on the pretence of assisting the Protestant cause in the Low Countries. Every person was to contribute according to his rating in the late subsidy, and to be paid out of the *next*;—a hopeful prospect; yet those who refused were imprisoned, if rich; marched off to serve in the army or navy, if poor. Among the former was John Hampden. These were but unhappy subjects for Charles to have to talk over with his third Parliament, when he would think proper to summon it; and matters were made worse by the failure of another of Buckingham's foreign expeditions, that for the relief of Rochelle; yet he still proceeded to add fresh subjects of grievance, even to the very last moment. The writs for a third Parliament were issued in January, 1628, and it was to meet on the 17th of March: in that short interval the King managed to do three things, all most damaging to his cause. He sent out commissioners to collect more money, and to inform the people that the meeting of Parliament would depend upon their success; but was obliged to recall them on account of the general excitement. He then imposed some new mercantile duties on his own authority, which the very judges were obliged to declare illegal; and so there too, he was compelled to retrace his steps. Lastly he entertained the plan of bringing over some thousands of foreign mercenaries, which, reaching the ears of the people, roused them to such a pitch of excitement, that they determined to send to the House men more decidedly democratic than before. So that in effect Charles had, as compared with the state of things during the previous session, prepared more and weightier causes of quarrel for the consideration of a much more hostile and determined Parliament. It was that Parliament which the Lord Keeper thus addressed : "If this" (the grant of supplies) "be deferred, necessity and the sword may make way for others. Remember his Majesty's admonition; I say, remember it." It was that Parliament also which, with such men as Sir Thomas Wentworth and Pym (Fig. 1887), Coke, Elliot, and Selden, at its head, wrung from Charles a document that may be ranked, in practical importance, with our old Magna Charta—we refer to the famous PETITION OF RIGHT. Its essentials may be thus described: commencing with a reference to the statute of Edward I., which declared that no tollage nor aid could be levied without the consent of Parliament; and with a similar reference to the Act of the 25th year of Edward III., which declared that thenceforward no person should be compelled to make any loans to the King; and to other laws of the realm, making provision against benevolences; they proceeded to complain of the recent violations of all those unquestioned laws, and of the imprisonment and injuries inflicted upon those who had refused to submit. Invoking Magna Charta, they then continued to show that by that charter it had been enacted that no freeman should suffer in person or property, except by the lawful judgment of his peers; and yet divers persons had been of late imprisoned without any cause shown, and when they had been brought before the justices by writ of habeas corpus, had been detained by Charles's special command and returned to prison, still without any charge being made against them. Lastly, omitting some minor matters, they complained of the establishment of martial law among the troops destined for the continental wars, which they probably had a fear might be only a preparatory step to the declaration of martial law over the people at large, and which they alleged, already had been the instrument of much injustice. They ended by praying that all these practices should cease. And after some ineffectual attempts to evade giving his decided sanction, Charles found himself compelled to assent. And thus one of the greatest and most bloodless victories was achieved for the people of England. The Commons immediately gave the King five subsidies, and for a moment all looked well. It was but for a moment. A warm remonstrance from the Commons to the King, on the subject of Buckingham's conduct, again offended him. But a still more important question arose. It appears that he had secretly determined to keep the power of levying the tonnage and poundage duties, which had not been expressly mentioned, but by implication, founded on their character and the recorded opinions of Parliament, which were virtually included in the Petition of Right. If but one single tax were left free from the control of the people's representatives, not only was the principle violated, but who could tell but that an able and determined sovereign, like Charles, might ultimately manage to make that tax, like Aaron's rod, capacious enough to swallow up all the others? So while the Commons prepared to pass the bill

1923.—Sixpence.

1924.—Fourpence.

1923 to 1926.—Silver Coins of Charles I.

1925.—Penny.

1926.—Halfpenny.

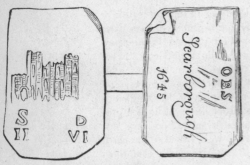

1927.—Scarborough Half-Crown.

1928.—Newark Shilling.

1929.—Beeston-Castle Shilling.

1930.—Colchester Shilling.

1927 to 1930.—Siege Pieces of Charles.

1931.—Arms of Commonwealth.

1932.—Great Seal of the Commonwealth.

1933.—Twenty-shilling Piece.

1934.—Ten-shilling Piece.

1933 and 1934.—Gold Coins of the Commonwealth.

1935.—Crown.

1936.—Shilling.

1941.—Pewter Farthing of Commonwealth.

1937.—Sixpence.

1938.—Twopence.

1939.—Penny.

1940.—Halfpenny.

1935 to 1940.—Silver Coins of the Commonwealth

1942.—Copper Farthing of the Commonwealth.

172

1943.—Silver Crown.

1944.—Silver Shilling.

1945.—Silver Sixpence. 1946.—Copper Farthing

1943 to 1946.—Coins of Oliver Cromwell.

1947.—City of Worcester. (From an old Print.)

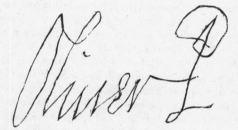

1948.—Oliver—Protector.
(From a Patent dated 5th July, 1655. Harl. MSS. No 7592.)

1949.—The Protector Oliver Cromwell. (From a Painting by Vandyke.)
Picture in the British Museum.

1850.—Oliver Cromwell's Wife. (From an Anonymous Print of the Period
in which she is styled "Protectress and a Drudge.")

1951.—At top—View of Worcester. (From an old Print.) The battle was fought on the foreground meadows. In the centre, the flight of Charles before the Parliamentary Soldiers; designed from various contemporary portraits of Charles II., Harrison, Lilburne, Bradshaw, and others. At the bottom, the old wooden house, in the Corn-market, Worcester, in which Charles lodged.

authorizing the levy of those duties for a year, they also prepared a remonstrance against the King's previous conduct in levying them without their consent. That remonstrance Charles did not choose to receive; he suddenly prorogued the House. And the mighty questions at issue were again left in a state calculated to stir and inflame men's minds to a height so dangerous, that we can only understand the King's conduct by supposing that he had seen from · the first their true meaning and antagonism, and was determined to try to decide them at any cost in his own way.

Buckingham, however, was no longer to aid him in this task. A new expedition, that was to reverse all former defeats, was set on foot to relieve the Protestants of Rochelle, and Buckingham departed to take the command. He rested at Portsmouth on his way; and there, as he was leaving his lodging (Fig. 1880), surrounded by a crowd of French refugees and others, he was stopped for a moment in the hall by one of his officers: at that instant a knife was plunged into his heart. The unhappy man had just strength to draw it forth, stagger, and fall, with the word "villain!" on his lips—and that was all. A mightier power than the Commons —Death—had at once impeached and punished him. No one saw the blow given, nor knew the hand from which it had come. The Frenchmen were suspected, and, in the bustle and horror, and indignation of the time, were in great danger. Presently many of Buckingham's officers and others came rushing into the house, crying—"Where is the villain? Where is the butcher?" A man then walked calmly forth from the kitchen of the house, where he had been standing unnoticed, and said, "I am the man!—here I am!" It was with great difficulty that he was saved for further inquiry, from those who would have cut him down upon the spot. He had anticipated that fate, and prepared accordingly a written explanation, which was found fastened inside his hat. It contained these words:—"That man is cowardly and base, and deserveth not the name of a gentleman and soldier, that is not willing to sacrifice his life for the honour of his God, his King, and his country. Let no man commend me for the doing of it, but rather discommend themselves as the cause of it; for if God had not taken our hearts for our sins, he had not gone so long unpunished.—John Felton." The assassin proved to be a gentleman by birth, and a soldier by vocation. His chief motive appears to have been a conviction that Buckingham was so shielded by the royal favour that the punishment he (Felton), in common with the people at large, believed he deserved, would never be inflicted; therefore he took it into his own hands. As the news flew abroad, it is worthy of note in what a different spirit it was received by those who were very fast becoming two parties—the king and the people. The last greeted Felton with blessings as he passed along the road on his way to the Tower. Charles was at church, "when Sir John Hippesley came into the room with a troubled countenance, and without any pause in respect of the exercise they were performing, went directly to the King and whispered in his ear what had fallen out. His Majesty continued unmoved, and without the least change in his countenance, till prayers were ended, when he suddenly departed to his chamber, and threw himself upon his bed, lamenting with much passion, and with abundance of tears, the loss he had of an excellent servant; and the horrid manner in which he had been deprived of him; and he continued in this melancholic discomposure of mind many days." (Lord Clarendon.) It appears that Charles's self-control on the first receipt of the fatal news, deceived many of those worthy persons who look at all things upon the surface; they even said the accident was not very ungrateful to him, as ridding him of so unpopular a minister. It was a great mistake, and did the King gross injustice. Whatever we may think of Charles the king, there are but few points of view in which Charles the man does not appear estimable; a deep, warm, generous nature seems to have been ever exhibited by him to those he loved.

Some it appears, acting upon this mistake, hoped to thrive by the detraction of Buckingham; and they got their reward. It has been noticed by Lord Clarendon that from that time forward Charles "admitted very few into any degree of trust who had ever discovered themselves to be enemies to the Duke, or against whom he had manifested a notable prejudice." He paid the Duke's debts, buried him in Westminster Abbey, and took his wife and children under his protection. Felton was of course executed. One of the great causes of the Civil War, the difference between the King and the people as to who should possesss the right to tax, which meant, in other words, who should possess the right to govern, and whether Englishmen should or should not enjoy political liberty, being now, we trust, made sufficiently clear, we pass to another, which involved the equally if not more momentous question of religious liberty.

There must have been much of deeply rooted honest conviction as well as much that was brave and heroic about Charles, to have enabled him to devise and endeavour to carry out his gigantic scheme of sovereignty, involving, as it did, the guidance of men's spiritual as well as temporal interests, in opposition to the views and principles of a great majority of their number. One who had had less faith in "the divinity that doth hedge in a king," would not have ventured so much in the endeavour to establish that faith as the practical rule for all the great business of the state; one who had had less courage would at all events have been content to deal with such mighty difficulties piecemeal. But Charles, true— ever true—to that absorbing passion and belief of his life, and thinking, perhaps rightly, that he could not deal as he wished with one alone, without in the mean time compromising in some degree his presumed right to deal with the other, determined to stand or fall by the idea of a sovereignty that should be in power and irresponsibility on all questions—"one entire and perfect chrysolite." His memorable coadjutor and adviser in the religious warfare he undertook was Laud, a man of whom it was said at the university, that he was "at least very Popishly inclined," and who had already given earnest of his fitness for Charles's purposes by his journey to Scotland with King James, for the purpose of modelling the Scottish Church after the fashion they had devised both for it and the Church of England. On the death of Buckingham, Laud became the King's chief minister. A notice of two among the various remarkable religious movements made by him in that capacity may form a fitting parallel to the notices already given of the political movements of the reign.

Whilst Charles was doing his best to put down democracy, Laud with equal zeal, and with as little discretion, set to work to put down Puritanism. Let us see how. Alexander Leighton, the father of the celebrated Bishop, a man lacking temper, but learned and able, published an 'Appeal to Parliament, or Sion's Plea against Prelacy." The book, directed against the Queen and the Bishops, was "disrespectful, fanatic, and in some respects brutal;" but instead of leaving him to the operation of the ordinary law, if his offence was so bad as properly to come within the verge of law, he was called to the Star Chamber at Westminster (Fig. 1884), a place that now began to rise into a bad eminence, and there examined. He pleaded honestly and with proper submissiveness, that he had offended through zeal, and not through any personal malice. The sentence was degradation from the ministry, public whipping in the Palace Yard, the pillory for two hours, an ear to be cut off, a nostril slit, and a brand inflicted on one cheek of S. S., meaning Sower of Sedition. In what a state the hearts and minds of the men must have been who could thus exhaust their ingenuity to heap torture upon torture—injury upon injury—we leave our readers to judge. That was Laud's way of teaching men how to love his church. But will it, can it be believed, that after all these barbarities were executed, and before the wounds were healed, this unhappy man was again dragged forth to punishment; again whipped—pilloried—his other ear cut off—his other nostril slit, his other cheek branded?—Or that when all was over, that the victim was sent back to perpetual imprisonment? Need we wonder at any institution or any men being swept away at last by a people like the English, when such was the state of things—such the powers that were sought to be consolidated among them? As we have before had occasion to allude to Prynne (Fig. 1887), who soon joined Leighton as a fellow-sufferer, we shall for the present say no more of him, but shift the scene of our inquiries to Scotland.

On Sunday, the 23rd of July, 1637, dense crowds of people were collected round the church of St. Giles, in the Tron-Gate, Edinburgh (Fig. 1886). A bold experiment was to be tried; the imposition of a new Liturgy upon the Scottish churches generally, and St. Giles's was the first place where the new service was to be performed. The archbishops, the bishops, the lords of session, and the civic magistrates, were all present by command. The dean opened the service-book and began to read, but his voice was overpowered by the cries and exclamations of indignation and abhorrence that arose. The Bishop of Edinburgh, the appointed preacher for the day, stepped into the pulpit, and spoke earnestly to the congregation of the holiness of the place. The storm now burst out with greater fury, and from clamour the people proceeded to violence: a woman threw a stool with such force that it would probably have killed the bishop upon the spot, but that it was arrested in its course. Sticks were now produced, and stones and dirt were seen flying thickly about. Some cried "Down with the priests of Baal!" others "A pape! a pape!" and "Anti-Christ!" And still more menacing voices were distinguished, urging the people to "Thrapple him!" "Stone him!" The Archbishop of

St. Andrews and other eminent persons interfered with no better success: they were repelled by curses. At last the provost and the bailies cleared the church of some of the more violent, and then again was the service attempted, and with great difficulty carried through. But on leaving the church the Bishop of Edinburgh was thrown down by the multitude, and nearly trodden to death. Riot upon riot followed, and still the new Liturgy was forced down the Scottish people's throats, until the end was, the formation of the great National Covenant, whereby the subscribers undertook to maintain their old form of worship—the Presbyterian—at every hazard. Such was the success of the new League, that before the end of April (1638), " he was scarce accounted one of the reformed religion that had not subscribed to this Covenant, and the church and state were divided into two names, of Covenanters and Non-Covenanters: the Non-Covenanters consisting first of papists, whose number was thought small in Scotland, scarce exceeding six hundred; secondly, some statesmen in office and favour at the time; thirdly, some who, though they were of the reformed religion, were greatly affected to the ceremonial of England, and Book of Common Prayer." (May.) These last three, and comparatively unimportant classes, Charles and Laud made friends of—the first, comprising all the rest of the nation, they changed into determined enemies. There wanted but union between them and the Puritans and patriots of England, to combine the greater portion of Charles's English and Scottish subjects in resolute opposition to his darling measures, and circumstances were powerfully tending to create that union. The Scotch were the first to appeal to arms, and single-handed, against him; but as if they could not have enough of difficulty to contend with, Charles and Laud lost no time in England in driving matters to such an extremity, as that the best men among its patriots saw no other resource than to imitate and aid their northern brethren.

We have already noticed one of the religious victims of the Star Chamber: we may now mention one of the political also. In 1638, about the very time that the Scotch were in a state of insurrection, John Lilburne (Fig. 1952) and John Warton were summoned to the Star Chamber, for unlawfully printing and publishing libellous and seditious books: and, which was supposed to enhance the crime, the having printed such books in direct opposition to a recent decree by Laud, that placed the press under a licensership: another step in the eventful career that was to conduct both minister and sovereign to a little-dreamt-of conclusion. When desired to take an oath to answer the interrogations of the court, both prisoners refused; Lilburne observing that no free-born Englishman ought to take it, not being bound by the laws of his country to criminate himself. It was this speech that caused Lilburne to be subsequently known as " Free-born John." Persisting in their refusal, the Lords of the Star Chamber ultimately committed them to a confinement in the Fleet until they should conform, fined them 500l. each, and directed that they should procure sureties for their good behaviour before enlargement. This would have been severe enough in all conscience for an offence of which there is no evidence that it was really an offence at all; but it would have lacked consistency with the punishment passed on the religious " seditionists " before mentioned. So the court took care to preserve its consistency by torturing one of the two new prisoners; of course the one whose bold and enthusiastic language was so especially objectionable to the authorities of the Star Chamber. There was no need to repeat the exact punishment of Leighton or Prynne: Lilburne could be very well punished by directing that he should be whipped from the prison to the pillory, and thence back to the prison. It was a punishment shrewdly calculated to break down by its degrading associations the spirit of the victim, and keep others like him from following his example. It did not prove successful, however. The pillory was fixed as far as possible from the prison—namely, at Westminster, between the Palace-yard and the Star Chamber; and through all that distance, we are told, Lilburne was " smartly whipped." Yet whilst he was thus whipt at the cart, and stood in the pillory, he uttered many bold speeches against tyranny and bishops, &c.; and when his head was in the hole of the pillory, he scattered sundry copies of pamphlets (said to be seditious), and tossed them amongst the people, taking them out of his pockets; whereupon the court of Star Chamber, then sitting, being informed, immediately ordered Lilburne to be gagged during the residue of the time he was to stand in the pillory, which was done accordingly; and when he could not speak, he stamped with his feet, thereby intimating to the beholders he would still speak were his mouth at liberty." On his return to the Fleet he was placed as directed, with irons on his hands and legs, in the ward " where the basest and meanest sort of prisoners " were " used to be put." A fire, however, broke out in the prison, and thinking

Lilburne, in his desperation had caused it, there was a cry raised by the citizens who lived in the adjoining narrow streets, of " Release Lilburne, or we shall all be burnt." In consequence, " Free-born John " was removed by the warder to a place where he could at least get a little air.

There were now no parliaments in England. Charles had met his latest in 1629; and from that period up to 1640 no successor was summoned. The king, therefore, was governing by the mere exercise of his own will; or as he termed it, by his prerogative. Taxation, as well as everything else, of course depended upon his pleasure. The subjugation of the constitution was for the time complete. But such a state of things could not last for ever. All courage was not confined to the Houses of Parliament. At length the long-stifled flame burst out in connection with the resistance of a man whose name all parties have since spoken of with respect, and whom most have delighted to honour—Hampden. One of the taxes levied by Charles was denominated ship-money. This, in 1636, Hampden refused to pay; and other freeholders of his parish – Great Kimble, in Buckinghamshire—followed his example. The crown lawyers were ordered to proceed. The cause was tried in Michaelmas Term, 1637. The whole of the judges were present on the bench. Hampden's advocates chiefly relied upon Magna Charta, and the famous statutes of the first and third Edwards before mentioned; and above all upon the Petition of Right, which Hampden had helped to secure for the country. In answer, the court advocates did not hesitate to take their stand on the presumption that the monarchy of England was an *absolute monarchy*—that the power of the King was, above all law, and statutes, and parliamentary devices. " This power," it was urged, " is not in any way derived from the people, but reserved unto the King, where positive laws first began," &c. So spoke Charles's attorney-general Bankes. And if men's eyes were not clearly open before as to Charles's purposes, there was at all events, no possibility of mistaking them now. Here was at once presented by this trial the theory and the practice of despotic government. But the judges, reversing the wholesome customs of our day, went beyond, instead of seeking to moderate, the statements of the advocate. Justice Berkeley, referring to the position assumed by one of Hampden's counsel, Holborne—the sovereign could take nothing from the people without the consent of the representatives—said : " Mr. Holborne is utterly mistaken therein. The law knows no such king-yoking policy. The law is itself an old and trusty servant of the King's; it is his instrument or means which he uses to govern his people by." Still it was a portentous business; and the judges hesitated and talked, and talked and hesitated, through three terms; and at last one judge, Croke, boldly spoke out—The thing was illegal. He had from the first had misgivings; but had silenced them, from a dread of the consequences—ruin to himself and family. It is delightful to reflect upon the influence that brought him back to the path of duty. It was his wife's, who, whilst fully aware of his danger, strengthened him to encounter it. " She was," says Whitelock, " a very good and pious woman; and told her husband upon this occasion, that she hoped he would do nothing against his conscience for fear of any danger or prejudice to him or his family; and that she would be contented to suffer want or any misery with him rather than be an occasion for him to do or say anything against his judgment and conscience." The example was infectious. Justice Hutton took up his post beside Justice Croke. Judgment was finally entered against Hampden in June, 1638; but whatever moral effect might have been produced by a unanimous decision of the judges was utterly lost as it was. The money became more difficult to collect than ever.

Wentworth, subsequently Earl of Strafford (Fig. 1887), who now shared with Laud the chief business of the government under Charles, seems to have been so great an admirer of the whipping discipline, that he would have even had Hampden whipped ! " Mr. Hampden," he writes to Laud, " is a great *brother* [Puritan], and the very genius of that nation of people leads them always to oppose, both civilly and ecclesiastically, all that authority ever ordains for them. But in good faith, were they rightly served, they should be whipped home into their right wits; and much beholden they should be to any that would thoroughly take pains with them in that sort." There is tolerable proof that Strafford seriously meant what he said in this passage—perhaps had actually advised it; for he again writes :—" In truth I still wish Mr. Hampden, and others to his likeness, were well whipped into their right senses. And if the rod be so used that it smart not, I am the more sorry." The poet Burns has finely observed upon the effect that would be produced could we see ourselves as others see us: we may vary and somewhat differently apply the thought in observing—Oh ! that our statesmen could but

1952.—Col. John Lilburne.

1953.—Cromwell dissolving the Long Parliament. (From a Painting by Benjamin West.)

1954.—Cromwell's House.

1955.—Ruins of Dunbar Castle. (From an original Drawing.)

1956.—Cromwell's Great Seal for Scotland.
The reverse exhibits the Cross of Scotland surmounted by Cromwell's Paternal Arms. (From Simon's Medals.)

1957.—Boscobel House.

1958.—Richard Cromwell. (From a Miniature by Cooper.)

1959.—Dorothy, wife of Richard Cromwell.

A PERFECT DIVRNALL OF THE PASSAGES In Parliament:

1960.—Head of a Newspaper of the Seventeenth Century.

1961.—Arms of Oliver Cromwell

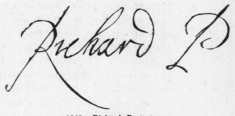

1962.—Richard, Protector
(From a Patent in Lansdowne Collection. No 1236.)

1963.—Great Seal of Richard Cromwell. Obverse.

1961.—Great Seal of Richard Cromwell. Reverse.

see themselves as posterity will see them! However, they did not whip Hampden, nor did they do what most likely he was prepared for—send him to the Tower to join his dear friend Eliot, who, for his patriotic conduct, was dying by inches from sickness in hopeless imprisonment.

At last Charles, having exhausted all the modes of raising money that even his notions of prerogative could suggest, determined to try once more a parliament. This was in 1640: eleven years after the dissolution of the previous parliament. What he could have hoped from this proceeding it is difficult to conceive. Every grievance that the men of 1629 had complained of, existed for the contemplation of the men of 1640, but in an infinitely more aggravated shape; and surrounded by hosts of other grievances that made even the former almost insignificant in the comparison—as for instance, the gigantic grievance of Charles's having governed altogether for so long a period without parliaments. As we remember this, and the treatment received by all who had opposed the arbitrary proceedings of the government, whether in political or religious matters, we may understand the general state of feeling that prevailed in the new House of Commons. In three weeks it shared the fate of its predecessors. But already Charles was beginning to experience the more serious consequences of his policy. The Scotch, who had taken up arms against him some time before, actually entered England in the same year; and in his straits a fifth parliament was called—his last—the ever-memorable Long Parliament. Its first act was to conclude the union, of which we have before spoken, with the Scottish insurgents; and at once it was in the possession of a power before which the King's sank, for a time, helpless. Charles was formally stripped of all his objectionable prerogatives, by a series of enactments; and as to his chief advisers, Laud was sent to the Tower, which he was only to be released from in order to mount the scaffold four years later; whilst Strafford was at once attainted, found guilty, and executed. The day of retribution had indeed come at last. The most conspicuous of the men who promoted the proceedings against both Strafford and Laud was Pym (Fig. 1887), one of the greatest of the many great men this eventful time produced.

But though bent for a while by the first violence of the storm, nothing could be farther from Charles's thoughts than a real resignation to the will of the country. He began gradually to prepare for the terrible conclusion that had been so long foreseen by men of all parties, even by those who dreaded to express it in words—a Civil War. It matters little on which precise question the war broke out at last; had not the Militia Bill—which reposed the military power of England in the hands of the Parliament—been in dispute, something else would. The real issues remained as of old for decision—should there be a constitutional or a despotic government in England?—and as the Parliament could not yield without undoing all they had done, and incurring eternal infamy, and as Charles would not, there was nothing left but the sword wherewith to determine the mighty controversy. And both parties prepared to use that weapon as effectually as possible. Charles issued his commissions of array, inviting or enjoining all men to bring him money, arms, and harness, for which he pledged as security his forests and parks, and agreed to pay interest at the rate of eight per cent.; whilst, on the other hand, the Parliament commanded all persons to put in execution the ordinances it had previously made respecting the militia. Each party was obeyed by its respective adherents, and England presented almost suddenly the aspect of a universal camp. Everywhere were exhibited the musters or marching of troops, the carrying to and fro of military stores, the hurrying of noblemen, gentlemen, citizens, and yeomen, to join the king at York, where he first took up his position, or to swell the numbers of the military array for the Parliament, at the headquarters of the county to which they respectively belonged. In looking generally at the supporters of the two belligerents, it appears that the more prosperous, civilized, and commercial portions of the community stood for the Parliament; and those which possessed less of these characteristics, for the King. Thus, whilst in the county of Derby the Parliament had hardly a single adherent of note, London was enthusiastic in its favour, collected an army from among its own citizens, and opened a kind of public treasury for the receipt of gifts, to which "not only the wealthiest citizens and gentlemen who were near dwellers, brought in their large bags and goblets, but the poorer sort, like that widow in the Gospel, presented their mites also; insomuch, that it was a common jeer of men disaffected to the cause, to call this the thimble and bodkin army." The time was to come when the bravest and skilfullest troops of Charles were to find the thimble and bodkin had changed somehow into weapons that *they* vainly contended against.

One of the first movements of the Royalists, before the war had actually broken out, was an attempt to obtain possession of the strong fort of Hull (Fig. 1892), a place of great strength and importance. But the governor, Sir John Hotham, though hesitating as to which power he should obey, found that his own son and his officers were decided Parliamentarians, and jealous and watchful of himself. So Charles was defeated in obtaining quiet possession of the place, and, being without ammunition, was unable to force it. As he was retreating in bad spirits, he was revived by the news that Portsmouth had declared for him, with Colonel Goring, a deserter from the Parliament, at its head. At that time the first virtual declaration of war, though still not assuming war's formal shape, may be said to have been made by Charles, by a proclamation requiring all men who could bear arms to repair to him at Nottingham by the 25th of August. And there, at the time named, "the *Standard* was erected about six of the clock in the evening of a very stormy and tempestuous day. The King himself, with a small train, rode to the top of the castle hill; Varney, the Knight-Marshal, who was standard-bearer, carrying the standard, which was then erected in that place with little other ceremony than the sound of drums and trumpets. Melancholy men observed many ill presages about that time. There was not one regiment of foot yet brought thither, so that the trained bands which the sheriff had drawn together were all the strength the King had for his person and the guard of the standard. There appeared no conflux of men in obedience to the proclamation. The arms and ammunition were not yet come from York (see our engraving, Fig. 1891), and a general sadness covered the whole town. The standard was blown down the same night it had been sent up, by a very strong and unruly wind, and could not be fixed again in a day or two, till the tempest was allayed. This was the melancholy state of the King's affairs when the standard was set up." (Lord Clarendon.)

The chief Royalist commander next to Charles was his nephew Prince Rupert, a brave and able, but exceedingly rash officer, who did Charles more harm than good, by bringing the feelings and practices of the mere soldier of fortune into a contest where men were fighting for the most part from a consciousness of its overwhelming necessity, and were inclined to do nothing in hate, but all in honour, and who were least of all prepared to become plunderers or banditti. On account of his unscrupulous conduct in these matters, Prince Rupert became known as Prince Robber among the English people. The supreme command of the Parliamentary troops was conferred on the Earl of Essex, whom we have in an earlier page mentioned as the son of Elizabeth's favourite and victim, and as the youthful husband of the equally youthful lady who was afterwards known as the profligate Countess of Somerset. It was on Sunday, the 23rd of October, 1642, that the combatants first met fairly in the field of battle at the base of Edgehill, in Warwickshire. The Royalists occupied the hill. Charles was there in person, arrayed in complete armour (Figs. 1882, 1883), and acted as his own commander-in-chief. The brave veteran soldier, the Earl of Lindsay, was called the chief general beneath the King; but disgusted, with Prince Rupert's insolence, he regarded himself only as the possessor of the nominal dignity, and therefore placed himself, pike in hand, at the head of his own regiment. The Royalists were the most numerous, the Parliamentarians the strongest in ordnance. For some hours the combatants gazed on each other, as if reviewing the past and the future, recalling the recollections of the one, and meditating on the awful possibilities of the other; and as if such considerations, though it must not shake long-fixed resolves, still made each unwilling to incur the reproach of firing the first battle gun. At last the Parliamentarians, who were compelled to take the initiative, on account of the position of their antagonists, fired their artillery twice, and, it is said, towards that part where the King was reported to be. The Royalists returned the fire, then descended the hill, and, surrounding the King's standard, advanced. The Parliamentarians rushed forward to charge them, and the shock of encounter so long looked for—yet so much dreaded—was experienced at last. The Royalists repulsed their assailants, and Prince Rupert then dashed forward with his cavalry, from the right wing, upon the Parliamentary troops opposite, commanded by Sir James Ramsay; broke and dispersed it, and followed the fugitives right out of the field, as far as a neighbouring village, where his troops—admirable soldiers! —began to plunder. In the mean time, the right wing of the Parliamentarians, under Sir William Balfour, made a charge upon the Royalists that was equally successful; and then, avoiding Rupert's childish eagerness, fell back upon the main body ready again for active operations. Essex now sent forward two regiments of foot to attack the Royalist foot that surrounded the standard of Charles—a severe struggle took place, neither could advance, and neither would retreat, until Balfour again charged in the Royalist rear, and with such effect that Charles presently saw his main body—the defenders of his standard—routed, and hurrying precipitately down the hill, and the standard itself captured. Here too fell his best officer, the Earl of Lindsay, who, mortally wounded, was taken prisoner with his son, and Colonel Vavasour. Sir Edward Varney was also killed; he was a gentleman who was understood to have been engaged on that side not for any good opinion of the cause, but "on the point of honour." The battle, however, was not won; for the Royalists rallied on the top of the hill, of which they continued to keep firm possession. Just then Prince Rupert returned, flushed with conquest and booty—to find that the Royalist army had been well-nigh ruined through his absurd conduct, and to experience a tremendous attack from the forces which he had probably thought were by this time scattered to the winds, before he could replace his soldiers in their old position. In this indecisive way ended the first battle of the Civil War, and at a cost of no less than four thousand lives. The spot where so much precious blood was poured forth was known as the "Vale of the Red Horse!" No wonder that there were men, such as the able and eloquent Sir Benjamin Rudyerd, who still earnestly hoped for, and strove to effect an accommodation; and they were so far successful as to obtain a suspension of hostilities on the part of the Parliamentarians. And how did Charles use the opportunity?— Why, he attempted to surprise London: conduct that can only be characterized as exhibiting very bad faith, to speak of it in the mildest terms. The attempt was only defeated through the heroic courage of a small body of troops posted at Brentford, under Colonel Hollis, who, notwithstanding the immense disparity of numbers, kept their ground until the gallant regiment of Lord Brooke, and the still more famous one known as the Green Coats of Hampden (enrolled by himself from among his own tenantry and friends, and trained by himself), came up, when the three regiments, supporting each other, completely stopped the way. The excitement in the metropolis was very great: "All that night the city of London poured out men towards Brentford." The Parliament, in its indignation at the trick that had been played them, voted that they would never again enter into any accommodation with Charles; but, excusable as the resolution was, they were too wise in the end to keep it, but remained up to all but the last moment prepared still to treat. But it must never be forgotten that it was these tricks, that were so often occurring, and the general insincerity of Charles's behaviour, that induced men finally to adopt the conclusion that no terms could be safely made with him.

Passing over a multitude of incidents, such as the siege of Reading (Fig. 1893) by Essex, which was taken in ten days—the general skirmishing war in the north, where Fairfax, as yet a young man, was fast rising into reputation as a Parliamentary officer—we must pause to notice an event connected with one of the many Royalist excursions from Oxford (Fig 1896), where the King had established his head-quarters.

The event in question was one of the saddest of the Civil War, being no less than the death of the brave and patriotic Hampden; and at a time, too, when many persons, dissatisfied with the slow progress making under Essex, were hoping to see Hampden raised to the chief command. On the night of the 17th of June, he was posted at Watlington, where an alarm reached him that Rupert was in the neighbourhood. He immediately despatched a message to Essex, advising him to send troops instantly to stop the passage of the bridge of Chiselhampton, the route that the Royalists must take in order to recross the Cherwell on their way back to Oxford: and then he immediately hurried forward to seek the Prince, and engage him. The combatants met among the standing corn of Chalgrove Field, and a fierce and bloody struggle took place, in which Hampden, whilst in the act of charging the enemy, received two carabine balls in the shoulder, which broke the bone, and lodged in the arm. Bending his head in agony over the horse's neck, he left the field, and turned to go to his father-in-law's house, which was in the neighbourhood, but the way was blocked by Rupert's troopers; so he determined to go to Thame. And there he died, after six days of intense suffering; which did not, however, prevent him from writing letter after letter to urge the Parliament to exhibit a more resolute and active spirit; and to the commander-in-chief to beg him to correct the errors to which he (Hampden) had fallen a victim—and, by concentrating his army for the support of the metropolis, set at defiance Rupert's flying excursions. He was buried in the parish church of Hampden (Fig. 1898), his Green Coats following him bare-headed, their arms reversed, their ensigns and drums muffled, and singing the while the Ninetieth Psalm. The grief, and indeed alarm, of the Parliamentarians, at the loss of such

a man was most signal. And this blow was followed by another equally calculated to depress their spirits—the defeat of their army in the north by the Royalist Earl of Newcastle. But a man of whom as yet little notice had been taken by the nation generally, an officer in the Parliament's army, now began to emerge from the comparative obscurity of his position.

Sir Philip Warwick, a Royalist, speaking of the House of Commons at the commencement of the Long Parliament, says—"I came one morning into the House well clad, and perceived a gentleman speaking (whom I knew not) very ordinarily apparelled; for it was a plain cloth suit, which seemed to have been made by an ill country tailor; his linen was plain, and not very clean; and I remember a speck or two of blood upon his little band, which was not much larger than his collar; his hat was without a hat-band; his stature was of a good size; his sword stuck close to his side; his countenance swollen and reddish; his voice sharp and untunable; and his eloquence full of fervour." Such was Oliver Cromwell, before confidence in his powers, derived from the test of experience, and the influence of the lofty position he attained, had conferred upon him that majesty of demeanour which characterised him in his later days, and which is so strongly impressed upon his portraits (Figs. 1949, 1953). Cromwell now came upon the scene, and quickly the aspect of affairs changed. The mere military men of the day must have been strangely bewildered by his successes. He had had no previous experience in warfare; had not made it his study; had no particular taste for it: then, too, he was a man of a mature age, forty-three, and could no longer be supposed to possess that plastic quality of mind which readily adapts itself to an entirely new state of things. But, however inexplicable, the facts were not to be denied, that it was he who trained his own regiment into such a state of military perfection that the bravest and most skilful Royalist troops where unable to compete with it; that it was he who checked the victorious arms of the Earl of Newcastle; scattered to the winds the levies that were coming to the Earl's assistance; gained the victory near Grantham; and saved the Parliamentarian general, Lord Willoughby, from destruction at Gainsborough; and all in the course of his first and brief campaign. At that point he was arrested by superior numbers, and compelled to retreat, and for a time we hear little more of Oliver Cromwell.

Tracing the merest outlines of the succeeding events, we may state that the war now rapidly spread all over the country; the Queen raised the spirit of the loyalists of the west of England by her presence among them; the Earl of Newcastle was, as we have shown, promoting Charles's cause with marked success in the north; whilst the King himself, taking up his head-quarters at Oxford, and rendering his position there as strong as a complete circle of fortifications could make it (Fig. 1895), encouraged his friends, and kept at bay his enemies, through all the midland districts. Among the many other advantages that attached to Charles's residence at Oxford, was one that no doubt he hoped much from, namely, that while keeping the metropolis in check, he might by some sudden movement obtain possession of it. One not very creditable attempt of the kind we have noticed. To prevent all danger of another, the Londoners, who seem to have gone heart and soul with the Parliament, set to work to erect defences: May, the Parliamentary historian, says, "The example of gentlemen of the best quality, knights and ladies, going out with drums beating, and spades and mattocks in their hands, to assist in the work, put life into the drooping people." So that, in a space of time that seems hardly credible, twelve miles of entrenchment were finished, encircling the entire capital, and studded at intervals throughout with bulwarks, hornworks, redoubts, and batteries.* We cannot resist the pleasure of noticing a defence of another kind, made by the poet Milton, then resident in London. His fortification was the following noble sonnet written

WHEN THE ASSAULT WAS INTENDED TO THE CITY.

Captain, or Colonel, or Knight in arms,
Whose chance on these defenceless doors may seize,

* We subjoin a list of these in explanation of the plan (Fig. 1907) :—1. Gravel Lane, a bulwark; 2. Whitechapel Road, a hornwork; 3. Near Brick Lane, a redoubt; 4. Hackney Road, Shoreditch, a redoubt; 5. Kingsland Road, Shoreditch, a redoubt; 6. Mount Mill, a battery and breastwork; 7. St. John Street, a battery and breastwork; 8. Islington Pound, a small redoubt; 9. New River, Upper Pond, a large fort with bulwarks; 10. The hill east of Blackmary's hole, a battery and breastwork; 11. Southampton House, now the British Museum, two batteries and a breastwork; 12. Near St. Giles's Pond, a redoubt; 13. Tyburn Road, a small fort; 14. Oxford Road, now Oxford Street, by Wardour Street, a large fort; 15. Oliver's Mount, a small bulwark; 16. Hyde Park Corner, a large fort; 17. Constitution Hill, a small redoubt and battery; 18. Chelsea Turnpike, a court of guard; 19. Tothill Fields, a battery and breastwork; 20. Vauxhall, a quadrant fort; 21. St. George's Fields, a fort; 22. Blackman Street, a large fort; 23. Kent Street, a redoubt.

1965.—Charles II and the English Ambassadors, at the Hague, arranging the terms of his Restoration. (From a Print by Vliet.)

1966.—Charles I. (From a picture by Sir Godfrey Kneller.)

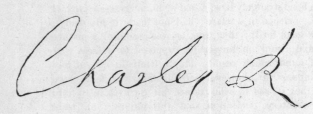

1967.—Charles II. (From the original in Harleian Library.)

1968.—Landing of Charles II. at Dover. (From a painting by West.)

1969.—Market-Cross of Edinburgh: Execution of Argyle. (From a Drawing of the time.)

1970.—Great Seal of Charles II.

1971.—Catherine of Braganza. (From an original Painting Pepysian Library.)

180

1972.—Pest-House Tothill Fields. (From Hollar.)

1976.—Old Horse Guards, St. James's Park. (From a Painting by Canaletti.)

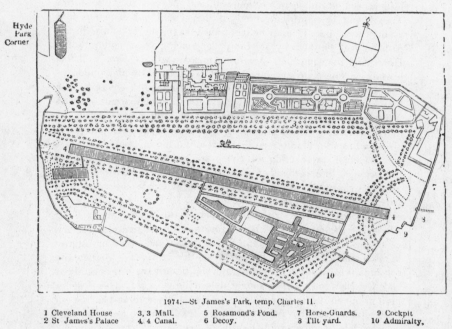

1974.—St James's Park, temp. Charles II.

1 Cleveland House   3, 3 Mall.   5 Rosamond's Pond.   7 Horse-Guards.   9 Cockpit
2 St James's Palace   4, 4 Canal.   6 Decoy.   8 Tilt yard.   10 Admiralty.

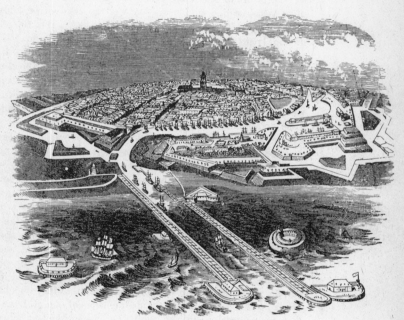

1973.—Dunkirk, temp. Charles II.

1975.—Medal in Commemoration of the Restoration.

1977.—London before the Great Fire. (From the Print by Hollar.)

1978.—Medal exhibiting a First-rate Ship of War struck to commemorate the appointment of James, Duke of York, Lord High Admiral.

If deed of honour did thee ever please,
Guard them, and him within protect from harms.
He can requite thee, for he knows the charms
That call fame on such gentle acts as these.
And he can spread thy name o'er land and seas,
Whatever clime the sun's bright circle warms.
Lift not thy spear against the Muses' bower :
T'.e great Emathian conqueror did spare
The house of Pindarus, when temple and tower
Went to the ground : and the repeated air
Of sad Electra's poet had the power
To save the Athenian walls from ruin bare.

Happily no opportunity was afforded of testing the efficiency of the poet's defences. Charles saw it was useless to make any attempts upon London.

The battle fought at Newbury (Fig. 1900), near which is Donnington Castle, the supposed residence of the poet Chaucer, was a serious blow to the Royalists ; fifteen hundred of them fell, with an unusual number of officers of rank, among whom was the universally-lamented Lord Falkland, the King's secretary of state. A still weightier calamity for Charles was the complete union of the Scotch Covenanters and English Parliamentarians that took place in 1643, when the National Covenant of the Scots merged into the "Solemn League and Covenant" of the two kingdoms. And one of the modes adopted by Charles to meet this most formidable combination—that of bringing over Catholic troops from Ireland to aid him—was calculated to do him more harm than good in a country where the chief mass of his supporters, as well as the entire body of his opponents, had a great horror of "Papists." But the main body of the Irish recruits had scarcely been six weeks in the country before Fairfax fell upon them, killed two hundred, and made prisoners of fifteen hundred ; and thus summarily settled the question of Irish interference. But Charles had to suffer the additional mortification of hearing that many of his own English troops in the north had refused to fight for him, on hearing of the Irish arrangements ; and that one Royalist, Sir Edward Deering, had in his disgust even returned to the Parliament he had before deserted, and thrown himself upon their mercy, rather than fight for Charles under circumstances so revolting to his conscience. These were indeed the things that from first to last were continually depriving Charles of the moral strength that his cause would otherwise have possessed. He left himself and all those who fought for him, no one principle, high and unadulterated, by the light of which they could with a clear conscience and a zealous spirit move onward at his call, excepting that of the right divine of sovereignty —a principle too weak alone to bear the structure he would have reared upon it No one ever had more ardent or devoted followers ; but he asked too much when he required that they should run all risks of life and fortune for the maintenance of one abstract principle that was so precious to him, whilst he hesitated not to violate in all possible ways other principles that ought to have been even dearer to himself, and which were dearer to them. The most determined Royalist still put his "Fear God" *before* his "Honour the King ;" and must have found his faith in the second law somewhat deteriorated, when he saw that king equivocating, to say the least of it, with his conscience as to the first.

Pass we now over the death of Pym in 1643—the calling of a Parliament at Oxford in 1644—Royalist of course, so that two Parliaments sat at the same time in England—the ineffectual attempt at negotiation made by the King and his "mongrel parliament," as he more humorously than prudently called the Oxford one, and come at once to the events that bring Cromwell again before our eyes, as the real influencer of the destinies of the nation.

The Civil War was, as we have seen, a religious as well as a political struggle ; the Royalists generally adhering to the Episcopal form of government, whilst the Commonwealth men were as generally Puritans. But the Puritans were also divided into two parties, the Independents and Presbyterians, who looked on each other with only less dislike than they felt towards their common enemy. And here too a kind of affinity between religious and political views discovered itself ; making the Presbyterians, who leaned towards the support of monarchical and aristocratic institutions, also yearn to establish *their* church on the base made by the ruin of all others, and abhor toleration as one of the worst of crimes ; whilst the Independents, holding more decidedly democratic notions as to civil government, desired toleration for all Christian bodies in the ecclesiastical policy of the country. Cromwell, Selden, St. John, Vane, Whitelock, were all Independents, whilst their Scotch allies were almost to a man Presbyterians ; and so were the chief officers of the Parliamentary army, as the Earls of Essex and Manchester. Here were ample elements of discord,

and for a time the cause of the Parliament suffered in various ways from them ; but chiefly in the spirit of indecision that these differences appear to have inspired in the minds of the military commanders. Suspicions grew rife that both Essex and Manchester were shunning rather than seeking a decisive success against the King, lest they should at the same time give too great a power to that party among their own supporters, of whom they were in dread. Nor were there wanting facts to support these views. A large army having been placed under the command of Manchester, with Cromwell as his lieutenant-general, the battle of Marston Moor was fought on the 2nd of July, and the Royalists completely routed. The important garrison of York surrendered immediately after, and, in fact, the entire command of the north of England may be said to have suddenly changed hands. The second battle of Newbury followed ; and, though the issue was indecisive, the Parliamentarians were left in possession of the field ; yet, twelve days after, Charles was allowed to return to the scene of action, and take away the artillery he had left in Donnington Castle, before the very eyes of the enemy. The Commons, in their indignation, ordered an inquiry, when Cromwell at once charged his superior officer with acting as though he thought "the King too low and the Parliament too high." From that moment the Presbyterian leaders sought to destroy Cromwell, and he to overthrow them. They began by inquiring secretly if they could not denounce him as an "incendiary ;" and he continued even more boldly in the path he had entered, by solemnly denouncing their policy to the House and the country. According to some writers, Cromwell was a confused rambling speaker ; it will be difficult to find much of either quality in the following weighty sentences :—"It is now time to speak, or for ever to hold the tongue : the important occasion being no less than to save a nation out of a bleeding, nay, almost dying condition, which the long continuance of the war hath already brought it into ; so that, without a more speedy, vigorous, and effectual prosecution of the war, casting off all lingering proceedings, like soldiers of fortune beyond sea, to spin out a war, we shall make the kingdom weary of us, and hate the name of a parliament. For what do the enemy say ? Nay, what do many say that were friends at the beginning of the Parliament ? Even this—that the members of both Houses have got great places and commands, and the sword into their hands ; and, what by interest in Parliament, and what by power in the army, will perpetually continue themselves in grandeur, and not permit the war speedily to end, lest their own power should determine with it. This I speak here to our own faces is but what others do utter abroad behind our backs. I am far from reflecting on any ; I know the worth of those commanders, members of both Houses, who are yet in power ; but, if I may speak my conscience without reflection upon any, I do conceive, if the army be not put into another method, and the war more vigorously prosecuted, the people can bear the war no longer, and will enforce you to a dishonourable peace. But this I would recommend to your prudence, not to insist upon any complaint or oversight of any commander-in-chief upon any occasion whatsoever ; for as I must acknowledge *myself* guilty of oversights, so I know they can rarely be avoided in military affairs : therefore, waiving a strict inquiry into the causes of these things, let us apply ourselves to the remedy which is most necessary ; and I hope we have such true English hearts and zealous affections towards the general weal of our mother country, as no member of either House will scruple to deny themselves and their own private interests for the public good, nor account it to be a dishonour done to them, whatever the Parliament shall resolve upon in this weighty matter." It was soon made evident to what this bold and remarkable address pointed ; some one moved that all members of Parliament, whether of the House of Lords or of Commons, should be excluded from all command and offices ; Vane seconded the motion, and, before the House rose, it was carried : and by this stroke of subtle policy the Presbyterian leaders were not only put aside, but could hardly, without injury to their reputation, even appear to complain. It was and is impossible to deny that if the House was determined to prosecute the war vigorously, the way to do it was to employ officers whose sole interest would be to carry out to the best of their ability the desires of the House. Under these circumstances passed the famous "Self-denying Ordinance," by which of course Cromwell among the other military members was excluded. But it is supposed, and it is highly probable, that the profound sagacity of the men who appear to have originated this movement—Cromwell, Vane, and St. John—saw that the aristocratic Presbyterians once put aside, some opportunity would be sure to occur for the reintroduction of Cromwell : and so it happened. After another ineffectual attempt at negotiation by a body of commissioners who met at Uxbridge (Fig. 1906), the war was renewed vigorously; some slight reverse happened, and immediately the Commons sent Cromwell to the scene of action. He performed the duty committed to him with his usual skill, courage, and success. But other dangers threatened, the Royalists were concentrating their forces; some great effort was about to be made; so now Fairfax sent to the Commons to request that they would again dispense with the Ordinance in Cromwell's case, and nominate him second in command —a post that had been left vacant on the remodelling of the army— for (it is supposed) the very man who now received a commission of three months' date to fill it. And whether he had planned and guided all these things from the first, or whether in truth his reappointment had been quite unexpected by him when the Self-denying Ordinance was passed, the time was at all events come when he had the opportunity of testing personally the value of the counsel he had then given. The speedy, vigorous, and effectual prosecution of the war, was now to a great extent in his own hands. It must have been an anxious question with the Parliament, seeing how determined he was to speedily settle the business, to know how the settlement should come, whether in ruin or triumph. The battle of Naseby (Northamptonshire) was his answer. Of two armies that when they met were about equal in numbers, the result was, ere they parted, that one had lost in slain between six and seven hundred men, and five thousand prisoners, besides twelve brass field-pieces, two mortars, eight thousand stand of arms, forty barrels of powder, its entire bag and baggage, and, among other matters, above a hundred standards; whilst the loss of the other army was confined to about a hundred men. It is sufficient to say that Cromwell was at Naseby, to tell on which side the mighty loss, and the gain, respectively lay. The battle, fought on the 16th of June, 1645, sealed the fate of Charles so far as it depended upon military issues. We may imagine the state of feeling in the House of Commons, when the letter, of which we give a fac-simile (Fig. 1903), was read aloud within its walls. The obelisk, shown in our engraving (Fig. 1905), was raised at Naseby in grateful commemoration.

But there was a more formidable enemy of Charles than the army of the Parliament—his own determined insincerity; and the capture of a handful of letters at Naseby, expressive of his true sentiments on various matters then in dispute, rendered his cause a thousand times more hopeless, than even that decisive battle. What a scene was that in a public hall in London, where these letters were read aloud in the presence of a great body of the most distinguished citizens and members of Parliament, and it became known to the world that the man who had solemnly declared "I will never abrogate the laws against the Papists," had already in secret pledged himself to abrogate them; that the man who had said with a show of generous indignation, "I abhor to think of bringing foreign soldiers into the kingdom," had been encouraging his Queen to strain every nerve to induce foreign princes to send him troops; that, lastly, the man who had but a short time before consented during negociation to give the Parliament its title of Parliament, was all the while doing it with the mental reservation that calling them so was not so acknowledging them; a distinction difficult to understand in one sense, but quite clear in another, namely, that Charles was prepared to keep no faith whatever with those whom he so often appeared to be ready to negociate with.

Successes in Scotland achieved by the Marquis of Montrose, who like a meteor darted to and fro, and certainly brought in his train the calamities that our superstitious forefathers were wont to attribute to the movement of the erratic denizens of the air, for a time deluded Charles with hopes of success; but at last Montrose was caught in one of his Parthian-like movements, and his wings effectually clipped by the Covenanters. And now the King began to feel personally, with a constantly-increasing severity, the dangers and miseries of his position. The chief officers quarrelled more violently than ever, and even the best of them lost their energy. The old Marquis of Newcastle had left the country after the battle of Marston Moor, in disgust probably at the conduct of Charles's nephew, Prince Rupert. That prince himself gave mortal offence to Charles by the surrender of one of the most important places then remaining in the possession of the Royalists, Bristol (Fig. 1913), and after a siege of some four days only, although he had assured Charles he would keep it for four months. And now that the utter failure of the Scottish Royalists plunged them all in despair, fresh broils drove the unhappy King almost to frenzy, and ended in the withdrawal of the Prince, with many other officers, and a body of horse, with the intention of quitting the country. Charles was then at Newark, with the armies of the Parliament rapidly closing around him.

He was now driven from place to place with hardly a moment's rest; and not even his rank, or the number and quality of his supporters, sufficed to preserve him from those physical sufferings and privations which must have appeared to him, when contrasted with his past grandeur, like some hideous dream. The coins of Charles (pp. 169, 172), at this period, speak most eloquently of the tenor of his career. We have them of different mints—as, the Oxford crown, the York half-crown, and so on (Figs. 1920, 1921); deteriorating so greatly in value, as his affairs grew worse, that at last, the siege pieces, as they were denominated, can hardly be called coins at all. One sort consisted of mere bits of silver plate, with a castle rudely stamped upon them, supposed to be that of Scarborough (Fig. 1927). A mode adapted by the Queen of raising supplies does honour to her ingenuity. Miss Strickland, in the recently published volume of her work on the 'Queens of England,' says:—"At this period, Henrietta had recourse to the painful expedient of soliciting personal loans for the service of her royal husband, not only from the female nobility of England, but from private families, whom she had reason to believe well affected to the cause of loyalty. To such as supplied her with these aids, she was accustomed to testify her gratitude by the gift of a ring, or some other trinket from her own cabinet; but when the increasing exigencies of the king's affairs compelled her to sell or pawn in Holland the whole of her plate and most of her jewels for his use, she adopted an ingenious device, by which she was enabled at a small expense to continue her gifts to her friends, and in a form that rendered these more precious to the recipient parties, because they had immediate reference to herself. Whilst in Holland she had a great many rings, lockets, and bracelet clasps made, with her cipher, the letters H. M. R., Henrietta Maria Regina, in very delicate filigree of gold, curiously entwined in a monogram, laid on a ground of crimson velvet covered with thick crystal, and like a table diamond, and set in gold. These were called 'the Queen's Pledges,' and presented by her to any person who had lent her money, or rendered her any particular service, with an understanding that, if presented to her Majesty at any future time when fortune smiled on the Royal cause, it would command either repayment of the money advanced, or some favour from the Queen that would amount to an ample equivalent. Many of these interesting testimonials are in existence; and in families where the tradition has been forgotten, have been regarded as amulets which were to secure good fortune to the wearer. One of these Royal pledges, a small bracelet clasp, has been an heir-loom in the family of the author of this life of Henrietta; and there is a ring, with the same device, in possession of Philip Darrel, Esq., of Coles Hill, in Kent, which was presented to his immediate ancestor by that Queen." But it was all in vain. The King had embarked in an enterprise that was from the first dangerous, and now proved to be impracticable: and he was too proud, or too rigidly fixed to his principle of government, to make a sudden and handsome retreat, throw himself at once into the arms of the people, and be thenceforward what they wished—the king of a free and happy nation. That would have saved him even yet; but Charles was actually mad enough to incur all the danger, without entitling himself to any of the grace or advantages of the act: he gave himself up in 1646 (Fig. 1904) to his Scotch rather than his English subjects, and they presently handed him over to the latter.

Charles was now, then, at last a prisoner in the hands of the Parliament. Yet still he hoped. One delusion after another, founded upon that unsurest of all foundations—intrigue, had crumbled away; yet still he put faith in this one—the excitation of dissension between the two parties who had together conquered him. But though they engaged in what might be almost called a deadly struggle for the mastery, the contest was in effect but brief: the Independents triumphed, and Cromwell obtained the entire control of the army, in spite of the Presbyterian majority in the Parliament. From that moment Cromwell was evidently entitled to rule the destinies of England. And having by a sudden movement succeeded in removing Charles from the custody of the Parliamentary Commissioners to his own, he might feel that the path was open for him to the attainment of the highest point that even his ambition might suggest. In estimating the character of that wonderful man, and endeavouring to judge whether he was like most other of the Commonwealth men, pursuing what he believed the best interests of the country, or selfishly caring only for what he thought to be his own, it is most important to observe his conduct at this period, when Charles was in his hand, the army his devoted instrument, and a large portion, perhaps the great majority of his countrymen, his warm admirers. To allow Charles to regain his power, no matter how restricted, was to set at rest for ever any unlawful and

1979.—London during the Great Fire, from the Bankside, Southwark.

1980.—The Royal Exchange, previous to the Fire in 1838.

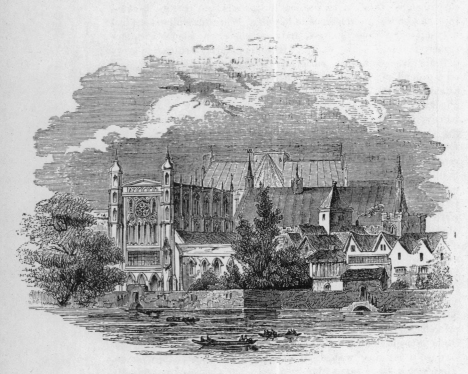

1981.—Houses of Parliament, from the River: temp. Charles II.

1982.—The Monument.

1983.—Burning of Newgate. Old St. Paul's in the background.

1984.—The Savoy Palace, in 1661. (From Visscher's 'London.')

1985.—Dutch Fleet in the Medway: Burning of Sheerness. (From a Drawing of the time of Charles II.)

1986.—Clarendon House: Arrival of the King in state.

1987.—Clarendon House.

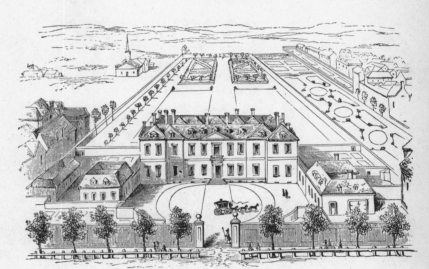

1988.—Burlington House.

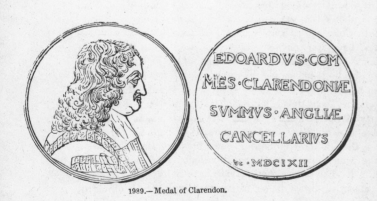

1989.—Medal of Clarendon.

1990.—Medal struck to commemorate the Popish Plot. (From the Original in the Brit. Mus.)

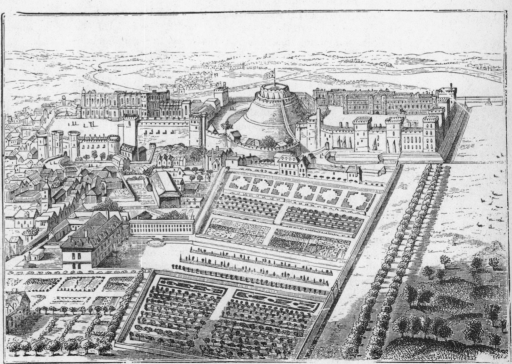

1991.—Palace of Windsor. (From Kip's Delices de la Grande Bretague.)

unprincipled aspirations, by whomsoever held : whilst to crush him, now that he could be crushed, was to open a thousand opportunities for their realization. What was Cromwell's course ? The remarkable incident described in an earlier part of our work in connection with the Blue Boar Inn, in Holborn, furnishes the answer. Cromwell did treat with Charles, until he found that he was dealing with one who would not only break whatever pledges he made the moment he was again in power, but would make a jest of putting the halter round his (Cromwell's) neck, as the practical mode of fulfilling a promise of the Garter. Up to this time there had still been a chance of Charles's restoration to power; this last act of faithlessness sealed his fate irretrievably.

All this while, the King himself appears to have remained insensible to his fatal vice; and bewailed his misfortunes with an earnestness, pathos, and poetical power, that strangely remind us of, and hardly lose by the contrast with the lamentations of the second Richard, in Shakspere's play. Whilst in confinement in Carisbrook Castle, in the Isle of Wight (Fig. 1910), and where he made an ineffectual attempt to escape (see our engraving, Fig. 1911), he wrote the verses from which the following are selected :—

> Nature and law, by thy divine decree
> The only sort of righteous royalty,
> With this dim diadem invested me.
>
> The fiercest furies, that do daily tread
> Upon my grief, my grey discrowned head,
> Are those that owe my bounty for their bread.
>
> The Church of England doth all faction foster,
> The pulpit is usurped by each impostor ;
> *Extempore* excludes the *Pater Noster.*
>
> The Presbyter and Independent seed
> Springs with broad blades : to make religion bleed
> Herod and Pontius Pilate are agreed.
>
> The corner-stone's misplaced by every paviour :
> With such a bloody method and behaviour
> Their ancestors did crucify our Saviour.
>
> With my own power my majesty they wound,
> In the king's name the king himself's uncrowned :
> So doth the dust destroy the diamond.

The ability displayed in these lines will no doubt surprise many, who may not have been aware that Charles was in truth a man of fine literary genius. He was also an excellent critic, distinguished alike for the depth and the universality of his views of art ; and we use the word in its general, not in its more limited sense. The Rev. Mr. Gilpin justly observes that " the amusements of his court were a model of elegance to all Europe, and his cabinets were the receptacles only of what was exquisite in painting and sculpture ; none but men of the first merit found encouragement from him, and those abundantly ; Jones was his architect, and Vandyke his painter." The same writer adds, " Charles was a scholar, a man of taste, a gentleman, and a Christian ; he was everything but a king. The art of reigning was the only art of which he was ignorant."

The trial (Fig. 1912) was commenced on the 20th of January, 1648 : Westminster Hall was the scene, the judges a body of Commissioners, numbering one hundred and thirty-five, and including the chief officers of the army, as Fairfax, Cromwell, Ireton, Waller, Skippon, Harrison, and others, three noblemen, most of the members of Parliament (now consisting entirely of independents, in consequence of the " purge " administered by Colonel Pride at the door of the House of Commons), four aldermen of the city, three serjeants-at-law, twenty-two knights and baronets, with some citizens of London and country gentlemen. Bradshaw was President, who thus addressed Charles at the commencement of the proceedings :—" Charles Stuart, King of England : the Commons of England, being deeply sensible of the calamities that have been brought upon this nation, which are fixed upon you as the principal author of them, have resolved to make inquisition for blood ; and, according to that debt and duty they owe to justice, to God, the kingdom, and themselves, they have resolved to bring you to trial and judgment, and for that purpose have constituted this high court of justice, before which you are brought." Coke, the solicitor-general, then rose, but was interrupted by the King, who, tapping him on the shoulder with his cane, cried, " Hold ! Hold !" As he did so, the head of the cane dropped on the ground, and Charles, as he subsequently said to the Bishop of London, was greatly shocked at the incident. Coke then, in few words, stated the substance of the charge, which he handed over in writing to the clerk to be read at length. As the officer began, Charles once more exclaimed, " Hold !" but presently he sat down, " looking sometimes at the high court, sometimes up to the galleries ; and having

risen again, turned about to behold the guards and spectators, sat down again, looking very sternly, and with a countenance not at all moved, till these words—namely, " Charles Stuart to be a tyrant, a traitor," &c., were read ; " at which he laughed, as he sat, in the face of the court." The essential charge was, of course, that he was the author of the Civil War, and of its deplorable consequences to the country. His answer to the charge being demanded, Charles rose, and though he had a natural impediment in his speech, that at ordinary times inconvenienced him, his voice was now as steady and free as his deportment was majestic and fearless. He demanded to know by what authority he had been brought there. " I was not long ago," he said, " in the Isle of Wight . . . . I treated there with a number of honourable lords and gentlemen, and treated honestly and uprightly. I cannot say but they did very nobly with me. We were upon a conclusion of the treaty. Now, I would know by what authority, I mean lawful,—for there are many unlawful authorities in the world, thieves and robbers by the highways,—but I would know by what authority I was brought from thence, and carried from place to place. Remember I am your lawful King. Let me know by what lawful authority I am seated here,—resolve me that, and you shall hear more of me." The President said he was there by the authority of the people of England, whose elected King he was. Charles replied that England was never an elective kingdom, but an hereditary kingdom for near these thousand years. He added, " I stand more for the liberty of my people than any here that come to be my pretended judges." " Sir," said Bradshaw, " how well you have managed your trust is known. If you acknowledge not the authority of the Court, they must proceed." Charles, pointing to Colonel Cobbet, said he had been forcibly brought hither by him. He did not come there as submitting to the Court ; and added, " I see no House of Lords here, that may constitute a Parliament ; and the King, too, must be in and part of a Parliament." To which Bradshaw replied, " If it does not satisfy you, *we* are satisfied with our authority, which we have from God and the people. The Court expects you to answer ; their purpose is to adjourn to Monday next." The guard was then directed to take the King away, who, as he left the court, pointed to the sword of justice, and said, " I do not fear that."

The interval was spent by the judges in the most solemn manner, with prayer, preaching, and with a fast ; and on the Monday the business proceeded. Charles still questioned the legality of the Court, and said that a king could not be tried by any jurisdiction upon earth—that he resisted not only for himself, but for the sake of the liberties of the people of England. He was proceeding, when Bradshaw interrupted him : he could not be suffered any longer to dispute the authority of the Court. Charles persisted, and was again stopped by the President, and this was repeated so many times, that at last Bradshaw directed the serjeant-at-arms to remove the prisoner from the bar. " Well, Sir," then exclaimed Charles, " remember that the King is not suffered to give in his reasons for the liberty and freedom of all his subjects." " How great a friend you have been," rejoined Bradshaw, " to the laws and liberties of the people, let all England and the world judge." Another adjournment now took place, followed by a private meeting of the judges, at which it was determined that if he was still contumacious, no further time should be granted. At the third sitting in Westminster Hall, Coke craved speedy judgment, and Bradshaw addressing Charles, bade him answer whether he were guilty or not of these treasons. Charles asked if he might speak freely. He was told after pleading he should be heard at large, and Bradshaw invited him to make the best defence he could against the charge. " For the charge," exclaimed the King, " I value it not a rush ; it is the liberty of the people of England that I stand for ; I cannot acknowledge a new Court that I never heard of before." He proceeded, and, though interrupted, for some time continued to do so between the interruptions, until the President called out, " Clerk, do your duty." The officer then formally asked him for a positive and final answer ; but still no satisfactory reply being obtained, Bradshaw said, " Sir, this is the third time that you have publicly disowned this Court and put an affront upon it. How far you have preserved the liberties of the people your actions have shown. Truly, Sir, men's intentions ought to be known by their actions ; you have written your meaning in bloody characters throughout this kingdom. But, Sir, you understand the pleasure of the Court. Clerk, record the default. And, gentlemen, you that took charge of the prisoner, take him back again. " Sir," said Charles, " I will yet say one word to you. If it were my own particular, I would not say any more to interrupt you." " Sir," rejoined Bradshaw, " you have heard the pleasure of the Court, and you are, notwithstanding you will not understand it, to find that you are before a Court of justice." With these ominous words the Court adjourned for the third time.

The fourth and fifth days of trial went on in the King's absence: the judges having determined they would for their own satisfaction hear witnesses. The sixth day was expended in consideration of the sentence. On the seventh day Charles was again conducted to the Hall, amid cries of "Justice! Justice! Execution! Execution!" As he entered with his hat on as usual, he saw the President was robed in scarlet, and the commissioners in "their best habits." There was also a solemnity of aspect about the Court that no one in Charles's position could mistake—he was to die. The moment he reached the bar he desired to be heard, and when told the Court must be heard first, he urged with still greater earnestness his prayer, saying that hasty judgment was not soon recalled. Bradshaw assured him he should be heard before judgment was given, and remarked upon his previous refusal to answer to the charge brought against him in the name of the people of England. Suddenly a female voice cried out, "No, not half the people!" but it was silenced, and the President, at the close of his speech, signified that the Court were prepared to hear him. "I must tell you," began the King, "that this many a day all things have been taken away from me, but that I call more dear to me than my life, which is my conscience and honour; and if I had a respect to my life, more than to the peace of the kingdom and the liberty of the subject, certainly I should have made a particular defence; for by that, at leastwise, I might have delayed an ugly sentence, which I perceive will pass upon me." . . . . He then expressed a desire to be heard in the Painted Chamber before the Lords and Commons, adding, "I am sure what I have to say is well worth the hearing." He was told in answer, that this was but further declining of the jurisdiction of the Court, which was founded on the supreme authority of the Commons of England, and his prayer for a hearing in the Painted Chamber was at once refused. It has been supposed that Charles referred to a proposal for abdicating in favour of his son; but his whole conduct through the trial shows that his object was to evade if possible the jurisdiction of the Court, and gain time, in the hope that something or other might occur to save at once his life, throne, and principles of government. Even the natural disinclination of men to be engaged in such a weighty business he might think was a circumstance in his favour, and might generate a favourable feeling for him if only time were obtained. And an incident that occurred at the moment of the refusal of his request, supports the view that delay was his best policy, always provided that he was not prepared to throw himself frankly upon the Court, and, whilst asserting the conscientiousness of his motives, renounce them, without the smallest reservation, for the future. That was the only chance, even if the time were not too late for any course to save him; but he would not—perhaps was satisfied that he ought not to submit; and he was in the hands of men who by this time understood thoroughly his character and modes of action, and were determined to leave no opportunity open for his evading the awful judgment that they were prepared to pass.

The incident to which we refer was the conduct of one of the Commissioners, John Downes, a citizen of London, who in his excitement kept on saying to those around him, "Have we hearts of stone? Are we men?" He now rose, and addressing the Court, said, "My lord, I am not satisfied to give my consent to this sentence. I have reasons to offer against it. I desire the Court may adjourn to hear me." In some confusion the Court did adjourn, and left Charles in a fearful state of suspense. They returned in about half an hour, unanimous in their purpose. "Serjeant-at-arms, send for your prisoner," exclaimed the sonorous voice of Judge Bradshaw; and the King, who had been spending the interval in deep conference with Bishop Juxon, returned to his seat at the bar. "Sir," then said Bradshaw, "you were pleased to make a motion for the propounding of somewhat to the Lords and Commons for the peace of the kingdom. Sir, you did in effect receive an answer before the Court adjourned; truly, Sir, their withdrawing and adjournment was *pro forma tantum* [for form only], for it did not seem to them that there was any difficulty in the thing; they have considered of what you moved, and have considered of their own authority. Sir, the return I have to you from the Court is this—that they have been too much delayed by you already." The King, at the conclusion of the President's speech, having said that he did not deny the power they had, again implored a hearing in the Painted Chamber. But still, it is to be observed, not a glimpse of any really tangible proposition to be made when he got there, did he afford. After again refusing in the name of the whole Court, Bradshaw addressed himself to the weighty business of delivering judgment, and the reasons for the awful sentence it involved. He

told Charles that the law was his superior, and that he ought to have ruled according to law—that as the law was superior to him, so were the people of England superior to the law, as its author and parent. He reminded the King that there were things called parliaments—that anciently they were kept twice in the year, that subsequently they had been appointed to be held once in the year; whereas, what the intermission of parliaments had been in his (the king's) time, was very well known; and what during those intermissions he had arbitrarily introduced among the people, was also too well known and felt. Referring then to the sitting of the still existing Parliament, the Long Parliament, he continued, "What your designs, and plots, and endeavours, all along have been, for the crushing and confounding of this Parliament, hath been very notorious to the whole kingdom. And truly, Sir, in *that* you did strike at all; for the great bulwark of the liberties of the people is the Parliament of England. Could you but have confounded that, you had at one blow cut off the neck of England; but God hath pleased to confound your design, to break your forces, to bring your person into custody, that you might be responsible to justice."

Precedents were then cited: and among the many incidents that, it was alleged, could be found in the histories of both Scotland and England, the particular cases were referred to of Charles's own grandmother, Mary Queen of Scots, set aside in favour of her son James (Charles's father), and of Edward II. and Richard II.; and truly, said the President, whoever should look into the stories of those kings should not find the articles charged against them come near in height and capitalness of their crimes to those charged against Charles I.

He next proceeded to assert, that a contract exists between sovereign and people—that the bond is reciprocal; the sovereign is as much bound by his coronation oath as the subject is bound in his allegiance, and that if this bond be once broken, farewell sovereignty! He then continued in these words,—"Sir, that which we are now upon, by the command of the highest court, is to try and judge you for your great offences. The charge hath called you tyrant, traitor, murderer." A startling "Hah!" from Charles here burst forth. "Sir," continued Bradshaw, "it had been well if any of these terms might justly have been spared." He concluded by protesting that through these proceedings all the judges had God before their eyes, and by recommending Charles to take the example of the repentance of King David as one proper for him to imitate. Charles in a hurried tone said, "I would desire only one word, before you give sentence—only one word." Bradshaw said the time was past. Again Charles pressed, but was reminded by Bradshaw that he had not owned their jurisdiction, that he merely looked upon them as a sort of people met together, that they all knew what language they had received from his party—remarkable words, and signifying, we think, how deeply Charles had injured himself by resisting the Court, if there were any well-founded hopes of accommodation in his mind, founded upon the concessions he was prepared to make. Of course, if he had no such hopes—was prepared with no such concessions—he could not have adopted any course more politic than the one we have described. Unfortunately for him, his policy was understood and resisted. Disclaiming all knowledge of the language referred to, Charles again begged to be heard, but Bradshaw sternly told him they had given him too much liberty already; that he ought to repent of his wickedness, and submit to his sentence. Then, in louder tones, he said, "What sentence the law affirms to a traitor, a tyrant, a murderer, and a public enemy to the country, that sentence you now are to hear. Make silence! Clerk, read the sentence." The clerk did so. The concluding words ran thus:—"For all which treasons and crimes this Court doth adjudge, that he, the said Charles Stuart, as a tyrant, traitor, murderer, and public enemy to the good people of this nation, shall be put to death, by severing his head from his body." Charles, with a look upward to Heaven, said, "Will you hear me a word, Sir?" "Sir," was the reply, "you are not to be heard after sentence." In great agitation, the King rejoined, "No, Sir?" "No by your favour," said Bradshaw, and continuing, "Guards, withdraw your prisoner." Still struggling to be heard, the unhappy King exclaimed, "I may speak after the sentence, by your favour, Sir. I may speak after the sentence, ever. By your favour—" He was stopped by the "Hold!" of the President. Again Charles stammered forth, "The sentence, Sir, I say, Sir, I do—," but was again stopped by the "Hold!" of the immoveable Bradshaw. "I am not suffered to speak: expect what justice other people will have," muttered Charles, and therewith he turned away, and left the Hall with his guards. Thus ended this momentous trial; and whatever may be thought of the

1992—Bothwell Bridge,—where the Scotch Covenanters were defeated, 22nd June, 1679.) (From an original Drawing.)

1993.— Bass Rock,— with the Prison of the Covenanters.

1994 — Medals struck to commemorate the Murder of Sir E. Godfrey   (From the Originals in the Brit. Mus.)

1995—The Rye-House.

1996.— Belvoir Castle temp Charles II

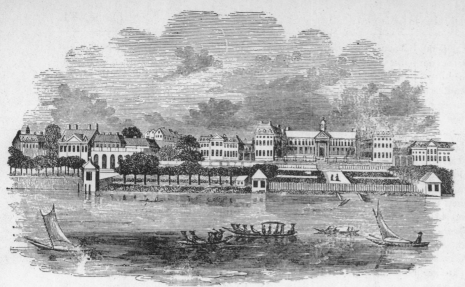

1997.—Chelsea Hospital, as it appeared in 1715.

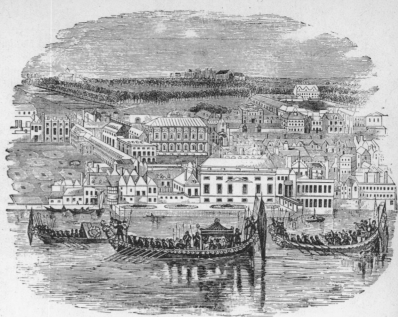

1998.—Whitehall and adjoining Buildings, with a Royal Aquatic Procession.

2004.—James II. (From a Picture by G. Kneller.)

1999.—Whitehall as it appeared before the Fire of 1691.

2000.—Guinea. Charles II.

2001.—Crown. Charles II.

2002.—Shilling. Charles II.

2003.—Halfpenny. Charles II.

2006.—Great Seal of James II.

2005.—James II. (From an Original in Harleian Library.)

abstract justice or injustice involved in it, considerations that depend of course upon the political views of the thinker, there can be no question of the moral grandeur of the scene, and the mighty character of the chief actors in it. From beginning to end, we perceive through the whole an order, a solemnity, and a right intensity of purpose, that could only spring from conscientious and deeply seated (even if mistaken) views of the overwhelming necessity of the deed. The respect paid to Charles throughout is unmistakeable. There was no pettiness about his adversaries. It cannot indeed be denied that the Commonwealth men were justified in their proud vaunt, that they had acted neither meanly nor timidly; that what they had done was not done in a corner, but openly in the eyes of all England, and of the world. We may here add, that tradition points out Cromwell's house in Clerkenwell (Fig. 1954), as the place where the death-warrant was signed.

The memory of King Charles "the Martyr" has been more endeared to the popular mind by his tender and indulgent parental character, than by any nice appreciation of the merits of the cause in which he suffered. The affecting scene of his last parting from his young children, when they came from Sion House to St. James's Palace to bid him farewell, shortly before his execution, has been a favourite subject for pictorial representation, and there are few who can contemplate it unmoved. Charles, taking the princess up in his arms, kissed her, and gave her two seals with diamonds, praying for the blessing of God upon her, and the rest of his children, "and," adds Whitelock, with pathetic simplicity, "*there was a great weeping.*" The King's last night on earth was spent tranquilly. He slept more than four hours, his attendant, Herbert, resting on a pallet by the royal bed. The room was dimly lighted from a great cake of wax set in a silver basin. Before daybreak Charles aroused his attendant, saying, "He had a great work to do that day," and proceeded to attire himself with unusual care, observing, "Death is not terrible to me; and, bless God, I am prepared." Bishop Juxon being called in, Charles spent an hour with him in prayer, and received the Sacrament. He then said, according to Sir Philip Warwick, "Now let the *rogues* come; I have heartily forgiven them, and am prepared for all I am to undergo." About ten o'clock there was a gentle tap at the door; Charles commanded Herbert to open it, which he was almost too agitated to do. Colonel Hacker—paler than the King—announced that they were ready. The way from St. James's to Whitehall was through the open Park, and past the Horse-Guards (Fig. 1976). The Park was filled with companies of soldiers; drums were beating, colours flying. Charles walked rapidly and erect between Colonel Tomlinson and Bishop Juxon, followed by some of his own gentlemen and servants bareheaded, and by a guard of halberdiers. A solemn and respectful silence pervaded the multitude, save when, here and there, some full heart vented its emotion in a prayer or blessing. The royalist writer Warwick—and he only—states, that one of the commanders, to disturb the King, asked him, Whether he were not consenting to his own father's death? to which the King answered, "Friend, if I had no other sin, —I speak it with reverence to God's majesty—I assure thee, I would never ask him pardon."

The scaffold not being quite ready, the King was led through the long gallery of the Banqueting House to his own Council Chamber, where dishes of meat were prepared for him; but he declined them, having resolved to touch nothing after the consecrated elements. Lest, however, he might be seized with faintness on the scaffold, which his "murderers" might misinterpret, he was induced by Bishop Juxon to accept a glass of claret and a piece of bread about twelve at noon. Soon after, the King came out of the Banqueting House (Figs. 1915, 1916) on the scaffold (through, it is supposed, one of the windows, made into a door for the occasion), "with the same unconcernedness and motion that he usually had when he entered it on a masque night," according to the testimony of an eye-witness located in the neighbouring Wallingford House. Again were heard raised for him the loud and frequent prayers of both men and women; nor did the soldiers rebuke them for these expressions of sympathy, "but by their silence and dejected faces seemed afflicted rather than insulting." To as many as could hear him, Charles addressed a long speech, in which he said he felt it his duty as an honest man, a good king, and a good Christian, to declare his innocence. He called God to witness that he never did begin a war upon the Parliament—they began it with him by claiming the militia. He said that God would clear him; that being in charity with all, he would not lay this guilt upon the two Houses; he hoped they were free from it. He then continued by observing that "ill instruments between him and the two Houses had been the chief cause of all this bloodshed. . . . Yet for all this, God forbid

I should be so ill a Christian as not to say that God's judgments are just upon me. . . . An unjust sentence (alluding to the death of Strafford) that I suffered to take effect is punished now by an unjust sentence upon me." He forgave all the world, the causers of his death in particular: "who they are God knows; I do not desire to know; I pray God forgive them." He emphatically appealed to the people on behalf of his son and successor, and then made that ever-memorable remark—which contained in brief the whole question at issue between him and his opposers—"that the people ought never to have a share in the government—that being a thing nothing pertaining to them!" It is certainly difficult after this to understand what Charles meant by calling himself the "martyr of *the people;*" for in these words he clearly showed himself an unmistakeable martyr to the principle of regal despotism. He concluded with a prayer, in which all who heard him no doubt joined fervently—that the people might take those courses that were best for the good of the kingdom and their own salvation. His speech, done, he said to Colonel Hacker—"Take care that they do not put me to pain:" and to one of the masked headsmen—"I shall say but very short prayers, and then thrust out my hands for the signal." Putting on his cap, he said—"Does my hair trouble you?" and when it was all put up under his cap, he said to the bishop—"I have a good cause, and a gracious God on my side."

"You have now," said Juxon, "but one stage more; the stage is turbulent and troublesome, but it is a short one; it will soon carry you a very great way—it will carry you from earth to heaven."

"I go from a corruptible to an incorruptible crown, where no disturbance can be," were the last words of Charles; and the Bishop responded—"You are exchanged from a temporal to an eternal crown—a good exchange."

The last action of the King, before stooping to the block, was to take off his cloak, and give his ornament of the George (Fig. 1914) to Juxon, with the mysterious word—"Remember." A single blow from one of the two masked figures sufficed: the other then held up the bleeding head, with the words—"This is the head of a traitor."

———

The all-absorbing character of the questions at issue in the Civil War has prevented us from pausing to note any but the most prominent of the multitude of incidents that marked its course, full of interest as many of the others are. The writer of romance may here find an ample storehouse of materials, in the effects upon domestic life of this great splitting up of the country into two hostile parties. It often happened that the son was on the one side, and the father on the other—that brothers and friends, long parted, met again on the field of battle, to fight with all their strength and energy against each other's cause, if they did not even allow their own bloody weapons to cross—that the lover rushed into the field to preserve his principles and lose his mistress—or, when she, though belonging to a hostile family, still sympathised with him, to shun with anxious care the carrying home to herself the horrors of war by personal attack on her kindred. A question suggests itself to all Englishmen as they look upon this exciting and dreadful time: How did the national character bear the demoralizing wear and tear that warfare ever involves, and especially such warfare? Happily the question can be most satisfactorily answered. Neither rapine nor cruelty, nor that dishonour which is worse than death—none, in short, of those horrors which add a deeper dye even to war itself, characterized this stupendous contest. Writers on both sides have charged this man and that with sanctioning such excesses; but if we omit only those minor occasions in which obscure individuals occasionally took advantage of the public disorder to gratify their own evil passions, as such persons always do, and will—we shall find that, on the whole, the Civil War stands out, when looked at from that point of view, as pre-eminently a contest of principle, and not needlessly embittered by wanton injuries and malice. Clarendon, indeed, speaking of the battle of Naseby, says the victors "left no manner of cruelty unexercised that day, and in the pursuit killed above one hundred women, whereof some were the wives of officers of quality." But what says the author of the 'Pictorial England' to this statement? Why, that "here the Royalist drew from the stores of his imagination and hatred, for neither in this battle and rout, nor in any other in England, were such atrocities committed."

A class of incidents connected with the Civil War, of the highest interest, are the sieges that were constantly taking place of the chief towns, castles, and fortified places, down even to the humblest gentleman's manor-house, which often stood out most bravely long after prudence would have dictated submission. We will here briefly mention two of the sieges that most strongly excited the feelings of the people of England.   The city of Colchester had not long before surrendered to the Royalists, and been garrisoned by a strong force under the command of Sir Charles Lucas and Lord Goring, when Fairfax arrived in 1648, with a determination te restore it to the Parliament.   His purposes were very summary—he would storm and take the place at once (Fig. 1909).   But after a severe struggle for several hours, he found he must alter his plans, and trust to the more tedious but also more safe course of blockade.   Week after week passed, and the Royalists remained firm.   Their provisions began to fail : still they yielded not.   The flesh of horses and dogs became a precious food, and still no sign of surrender.   But in truth there was a particular reason for this.   The garrison stood in a dangerous position ; they were fighting without a warrant.   England generally having submitted, the King at last had given up the contest, and ordered all his chief officers to yield the places then held for him.   This contest, therefore, was a wanton expenditure of blood.   But the leader had also a motive for engaging in such resistance.   Lord Goring knew that, if taken, death was his most probable doom.   At the beginning of the war, he had, as we have seen, most treacherously deserted the Parliament, while in command at Portsmouth, and given up that place to the King.   But if the Royalists could endure under such circumstances within, of course their opponents could continue to press them more and more severely from without.   So after eleven terrible weeks, the garrison was compelled to surrender at discretion, or at least with only the guarantee of the lives of the soldiers and inferior officers.   Goring was reserved to be dealt with by the Parliament, as was the Lord Capel, who was with him at Colchester.   The two next chief officers, Sir George Lisle and Sir Charles Lucas, were conducted to the exterior of the castle walls and shot; a terrible punishment—but it would be wrong to say an unjust or an unnecessary one.   The moment the *war* ceased, the very value attached by the conquerors to the blood of the people would dictate extreme measures with those who, hopelessly and wantonly, caused it to flow, by mere isolated and unauthorised efforts.

The defence of Basing House has given a kind of immortality to its brave owner, the Marquis of Winchester.   It was first invested in 1643, by the Parliamentary troops ; and though they did not succeed in forcing it, they continued from time to time for two whole years their harassing attacks.   On one of the occasions when it was besieged, the bravest and most successful of the Parliamentary generals before the more prominent appearance of Cromwell and Fairfax on the scene, Sir William Waller—or as the soldiers and people used to call him, William the Conqueror—attempted to carry Basing House by assault three distinct times within nine days.   But he was repelled each time, with severe loss.   To a later summons of surrender the Marquis replied, that " if the King had no more ground in England than Basing House, he would maintain it to the uttermost."   He was, however, narrowly pressed at this time, for his provisions became exhausted, and he was at last compelled to signify to Charles that he must surrender in the course of ten days if no assistance was rendered.   The assistance came, and the Parliamentarians were as far off as ever from the possession of the coveted place.   Their reputation now became concerned.   It was a bad example for their cause—that of a Royalist mansion holding out in spite of all their efforts.   It must be taken—Cromwell himself must be despatched thither.

We may judge that the mansion was at once strong and formidable, when we glance at the character of the walls as they appeared even in a state of ruin (see our engraving, Fig. 1902) ; and when we know that it was defended by ten pieces of ordnance and from three to five hundred soldiers.   But the Marquis had now to deal with the master spirit, and with the usual result.   It was not long before the Speaker of the House of Commons received the following letter from Cromwell :—" Sir,—I thank God I can give you a good account of Basing.   After our batteries placed, we settled the several posts for the storm : Colonel Dalbeere was to be on the north side of the house next the Grange ; Colonel Pickering on his left hand ; and Sir Hardresse Waller's and Colonel Montague's regiments next him.   We stormed this morning after six of the clock : the signal for falling on was the firing from our cannon, which being done, our men fell on with great resolution and cheerfulness.   We took the two houses without any considerable loss to ourselves.   Colonel Pickering stormed the new house, passed through and got the gate of the old house, whereupon they summoned a parley, which our men would not hear.   In the meantime Colonel Montague's and Sir Hardresse Waller's regiments assaulted the strongest work, where the enemy kept his court of guard, which, with great resolution, they recovered, beating the enemy from a whole culverin (a piece of ordnance so named), and from that work ; which, having

done, they drew their ladders after them, got over another work, and the house wall, before they could enter.   In this, Sir Hardresse Waller, performing his duty with honour and diligence, was shot in the arm, but not dangerously.   We have had little loss ; many of the enemies our men put to the sword, and some officers of quality ; most of the rest we have prisoners, amongst which are the Marquis and Sir Robert Peake, with divers other officers, whom I have ordered to be sent up to you.   We have taken about ten pieces of ordnance, much ammunition, and our soldiers a good encouragement,"—in other words, booty—consisting of money, jewels, provisions, furniture, to the estimated value of 300,000*l.*

The monarchy had ceased to exist : England was now a Republic.   The House of Lords was abolished as " useless and dangerous ;" though Harry Marten, the well-known wit, proposed with biting sarcasm an amendment, that the word. " dangerous " should be omitted from the act of abolition.   The king's statues were taken down from the Exchange and other places.   An elaborate declaration was written and published in the English, Latin, French, and Dutch languages, in explanation and in justification of the king's execution and the change of the form of the government.   Six of the old judges who agreed to act were reappointed, the estimable Whitelock received the Great Seal (Fig. 1932), whilst St. John, who, it is said, " almost as much as any single man had helped to make this memorable revolution," became chief justice.   A permanent executive Council of State was formed of forty members, comprising seven noblemen, with Whitelock, St. John, Fairfax, Cromwell, the brave and popular Skippon, Sir Harry Vane, Harry Marten, Bradshaw, and Ludlow.   Bradshaw was the president of this council, *John Milton* the secretary.

Altogether, a council so distinguished for the ability of its members has never before or since sat in England.   The promise given by the constitution of this body that the administration of affairs would be conducted with extraordinary vigour, was no less markedly afforded in other directions.   Thus, while the army remained under the command of those who had made it invincible, the navy was removed from the care of the Earl of Warwick, and placed under the control of the three best officers of the day, of whom the chief was Blake.   At the Admiralty again sat Vane, as the guiding spirit.   In the church, the men of the Commonwealth did as little as possible, but what they did was well done.   Retaining the Presbyterian form of worship, they infused into it a spirit previously unknown to Presbyterianism—toleration.

The first great business of the Commonwealth was the repression of the attempt made simultaneously in Ireland and Scotland to raise the eldest son of the late king to the supreme government, under the title of Charles the Second.   The Irish, after a short but most murderous campaign, were completely overpowered by Cromwell, who returned to England, and was met several miles before he reached London, by the " Lord-General Fairfax, accompanied by many members of Parliament and officers of the army, with multitudes that came out of curiosity to see him of whom Fame had made such a loud report."   The Scotch movement was a more portentous affair.   The same religious views that had influenced the Scotch to resist and to help so powerfully to destroy Charles I., because he wanted to force his religion on them, now prompted them to endeavour by force of arms to force their religion on their former coadjutors—the English.   And as they thought their views would be forwarded by inducing Prince Charles to act with them, they hesitated not to bribe him by the engagement to support his claim to the throne of Great Britain, if he would subscribe to their Covenant, and consent to various restrictions which in effect made the sovereignty they promised little better than a name.   But then, thought Charles, the conquest of England!—if he could by their means achieve that !   He was soon decided, and, in imitation of his father's fatal error, consented to lay aside conscience for the sake of what he thought policy.   The Commonwealth men, with a wise and prudent desire to avoid hostilities, publicly declared that they had no design to impose upon the Scottish people anything opposed to their inclination—that they might choose their own government, provided only they left the English nation to exercise a similar right, and live under the establishment *they* had chosen.   But the Scotch, unable to brook the triumph of the party of the Independents in this country, called Charles to join them on the conditions we have stated, raised troops, proclaimed their new king, and denounced the English Parliament as regicides and traitors.   Well, then, thought the Commonwealth men, if they will fight us, we will not trouble them to cross the border, but seek them in their own country.

Fairfax having declined the command of the invading army, (he

2007.—Maria Beatrix, of Modena,
Queen of James II. (From a Picture by Sir P. Lely

2010.—Back View of Lady Place, Hurley.

2008.—Crown. James II.

20 2—Medal Struck in honour of the Petitioning Bishops.
(From a Specimen in the British Museum.)

2009—Halfpenny James II.

20 1 —Vaults of Lady Place.

2013.—James II.

2017.—Convocation or Chapter House, St. Paul's, in 1704.

2014.—Archbishop Leighton.—From an anonymous Print.   Bishop Hall.—From the Picture in the Gallery of Emanuel College Cambridge.   Bishop Burnet.—From a Picture by Sir Godfrey Kneller.   Bunyan.—From a Print engraved by Sharp after an anonymous Picture.   Barrow.—From a Picture by Isaac Whood, in Trinity College, Cambridge.   Dr John Owen.—From a Print by Vertue.

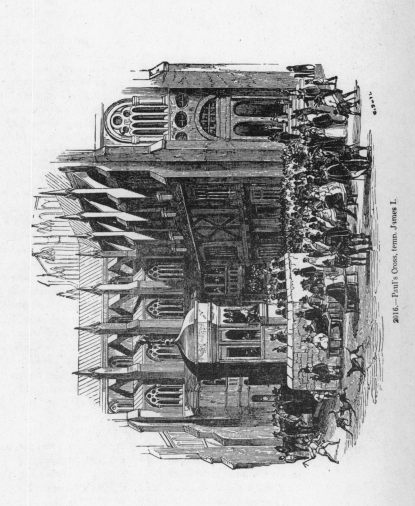

2016.—Paul's Cross, temp. James I.

2015.—Archbishop Abbot.—From an Original Picture in Lambeth Palace.   Bishop Taylor.—From an Original Picture in All Saints College, Oxford   Fox.—From an anonymous Print.   Archbishop Laud.—From a Picture by Vandyke.   Archbishop Usher.—From a Picture by Sir Peter Lely.

was a Presbyterian, be it remembered, in his religious views, though participating generally in the movements—because sympathising with the politics of the Independents), Cromwell was named Captain-General of all the forces. This was on the 26th of June; within three days later he was on his way to the Borders to teach the Scots what that law meant to which they had appealed. But they were more wary than might have been anticipated from the readiness with which they had rushed into the contest. They took care to keep out of the dreaded Englishman's way, hoping to harass his soldiers by continual skirmishing, and by keeping them through the winter in an unsuitable climate. They had every reason to be delighted with the result of their policy, as they saw it being developed daily in the growing weakness of the English army, in the scarcity of provisions, that affected them most seriously, and, at last, in a march that looked very like a retreat, towards Dunbar, where supplies might be obtained from the English shipping. And it was a retreat. The English having reached Dunbar, shipped their sick and their heavy luggage, and prepared themselves to return into England. But the Scotch thought that now the time was come for them to fight. The numbers of the respective forces were very satisfactory to them, 12,000 men on the one side, 27,000 on the other—their own. The Scotch, indeed, as they continued to gather more and more thickly upon the hills adjacent to Dunbar, appeared "like a thick cloud, menacing such a shower to the English as would wash them out of their country, if not out of the world." Cromwell was in the low grounds or fields, hoping, rather than expecting, that they would descend to attack him. But when the Scottish preachers showed their armed flocks from Scripture that the victory must be certain, they began to descend; and as Cromwell saw what they were doing, he burst out with the triumphant, and as it proved, in one sense at least, prophetic cry, "The Lord hath delivered them into our hands!" It was not till the next morning, however, that any opportunity offered of attack, when Cromwell attempted to force one of the passes that commanded the enemy's position. A terrific struggle ensued, and, as had often before happened, it was not until Cromwell led up his own regiment of Ironsides that the defenders of the pass were dispersed. A body of horse now swept down upon the English, and at the same moment the newly-risen sun burst through the morning mist, and revealed the two armies distinctly to each other. Then it was that there was heard far and near, the spirit-stirring voice of him whose tones no one could mistake—"Now let God arise, and his enemies shall be scattered!" Four thousand dead and ten thousand captive Scotchmen, told in awful language of the might they had so recklessly provoked.

It has been said of King Charles II., that he never said a foolish thing and never did a wise one; but there was one act of his life in which the latter part of the observation receives a decided contradiction. Whilst one place after another surrendered to Cromwell in consequence of the battle of Dunbar, and whilst the remains of the Scottish army showed by their movements how deeply they had taken to heart their indiscretion in attacking Cromwell under any circumstances, Charles suddenly dashed across the Border, and swept along with the utmost possible speed towards London. Cromwell had never dreamt of his doing this; and certainly we shall never again find Charles exhibiting any proofs that such wise and sudden and eventful decisions were characteristic of him. The great soldier was out-manœuvred. But quick as lightning he hurried after him, cut to pieces instantaneously a body of Royalists headed by the Earl of Derby that attempted to arrest his progress, and presently formed a junction with the troops despatched from London on the first news of the attempt, and thus reinforced, sat down before Charles at Worcester, assured master of the game: even in numbers his army was superior to that of the Royalists. So the Severn was crossed on the 30th of September, and the attack made with irresistible power. Charles was presently flying for his life (Fig. 1951), and it was only with the greatest difficulty, and after a variety of hairbreadth escapes, that he reached France. Cromwell was welcomed back by the Parliament with fresh honours, and a pension of 4000l. a-year was added to that of 2000l. a-year they had before settled on him. We must not forget to add, that these movements in Ireland and Scotland ended in the annexation of both countries to the dominions of the Commonwealth: the map of the united British Islands thenceforward graced its great seal (Fig. 1932).

The Dutch were the next to experiment with the temper and strength of the young but most vigorous power; and they had no doubt the more confidence in so doing from reflecting that Cromwell was not a sailor, and that their chief strength lay on the seas. But our navy had its Cromwell too, as they found to their cost. The first engagement between Blake and the Dutch admiral Van

Tromp occurred on the 19th of May, 1652, when the latter was compelled to sheer off with the loss of two ships. This defeat was followed by a victory, which so elated the Dutch, that forgetting they had obtained the victory simply through the greater number of ships engaged on their side, Van Tromp had the exquisite vanity to put a broom at his mast-head, signifying that he meant to sweep the English seas clear of the ships of the Commonwealth. The English with extraordinary rapidity again prepared for the contest; and Blake found himself in the beginning of 1653 master of eighty men-of-war, and having Monk and Dean among his officers. Blake and Van Tromp met on the 18th of February, Van Tromp's force amounting to seventy-six men-of-war and thirty merchantmen, most of which were armed. The first day's proceedings ended in the loss of six Dutch ships; whilst not a single English ship was either destroyed or taken, to partially balance the account. The struggle, interrupted by the night, recommenced with the morning; and the second day the Dutch summed up their losses as one man-of-war taken by boarding and many merchantmen captured. They were now in full retreat. The third day was Sunday, when Blake again brought his antagonist to action, until a breeze that sprung up in the afternoon enabled Van Tromp to shelter himself against the Calais Sands. The entire damage the English had received during the three days, amounted to but one ship of war, and a somewhat heavy list of killed and wounded; on the other hand, the Dutch found that eleven ships of war, thirty merchant-vessels, and two thousand five hundred men had been taken or destroyed. Such was the issue of the contest between the Commonwealth's navy and the navy of the power that was previously esteemed the most formidable of all maritime nations.

But whilst thus victorious everywhere abroad, there were unhappily discords arising at home. The Parliament had now existed so long, that it became unwilling to set any limit to its period of power. It seems, indeed, to have grown jealous of the army, and of the intentions of the army's great leader—feelings that were fully reciprocated by them. "If there were personal ambition and the intoxication of power on both sides, there were certainly on both sides —as well on that of Cromwell as on that of the Vanes, the Martens, and the other Commonwealth men, high and noble and patriotic motives. Each in fact wished for power for the establishing or working out a system which each deemed the best for the peace, the happiness, and the glory of the nation; and in justice to Oliver Cromwell it must be avowed that his scheme of social policy was in itself one of the purest which had as yet entered into the mind of any statesman, and one that adapted itself more readily to the character and habits of the community than the more finely-drawn theories of the republicans. This wonderful man had certainly a long and doubtful struggle, not merely with his former friends, but now republican opponents, but also with his own heart and conscience; and he was quiet, or at least abstained from any very open act, until the Parliament betrayed an intention of coalescing with the Presbyterians, who in their hearts hated both Cromwell and the Parliament alike." ('Pictorial England,' vol. iii. p. 408.) Then it was, that, after a long preliminary conversation, he asked Whitelock (and the choice of such a man says much for the conscientiousness of the questioner), "What if a man take upon him to be king?" The answer was unfavourable. And though, in an affair of such magnitude, the idea of sovereignty was no more to be lightly thrown aside than lightly taken up, Cromwell not only did not make himself king, when it is certain he could have done so, but he declined the honour almost against his own opinions, when a large majority of a Parliament that had been called by him formally requested him to take the magic title.

But how had the Long Parliament been at last induced to dissolve? Cromwell, his chief officers, and some members of the Parliament, were earnestly engaged one day at his lodgings in White-hall, considering what was best to be done in respect to the government of the country and the dissolution of the Parliament, when Colonel Ingoldsby arrived in great haste to say that the House was passing with all possible speed a bill that had been brought in for the dissolution, and which contained clauses that would have insured the admission of a number of Presbyterians in the next Parliament, men determined to overturn the existing government. Cromwell, in a high state of excitement, sent for a party of soldiers, whilst the members present ran back to the house. Presently Cromwell, attended by Lambert and other officers, and a file of musketeers, arrived at the doors, and, leaving the soldiers outside, he entered, and took his seat. He sat and listened in silence, until the Speaker was about to put the motion, when rising, he said to Harrison, whom he had beckoned to his side, "Now is the time— I must do it." Harrison advised consideration, and Cromwell sat down for about a minute, then rose, and taking off his hat, addressed the House. The state of his mind was soon made apparent by his language. He called the members deniers of justice, oppressors, and said that they were planning to bring in the Presbyterians, who would lose no time in destroying the cause they had deserted. He was told by Sir Harry Vane his language was unparliamentary. "I know it," was the reply; and instantly Cromwell started forward from his seat into the body of the house, and there walked up and down, his hat on his head, pointing to different members, and heaping reproaches upon them. Thus, with his finger raised against Sir Harry Vane, he said, "One person might have prevented all this, but he is a juggler, and hath not so much as common honesty." Here the indignant exclamations of Vane, Wentworth, and Marten interrupted him; but their voices were borne down by the louder and sterner tones of Cromwell, as he shouted forth, "I'll put an end to your prating; you are no Parliament; I'll put an end to your sitting. Get ye gone! Give way to honester men." Then stamping with his foot, the house was instantly filled with armed men. Pointing to the Speaker, he said to Harrison, "Fetch him down!" and seeing the Speaker hesitated to obey Harrison's demand, he again cried, "Take him down!" and the Speaker submitted. Algernon Sydney, then a young man, and one of the purest and most enthusiastic of the republicans, was sitting close by: "Put *him* out," was the next command. Sydney refused to go; until, at the reiteration of the order, Harrison and Worsley, another officer, put their hands upon him, when he moved towards the door. The Mace now attracted Cromwell's attention: "Take away that bauble!" he said. How highly he had strung up his nerves to the task he had undertaken, we see in the treatment received by those who ventured to urge a word of remonstrance. To Alderman Allen, who said that if he would send out the soldiers all might yet be repaired, he retorted with a charge of embezzlement in the office of treasurer of the army. Challoner was a drunkard, Sir Peter Wentworth an adulterer, and Henry Marten a—something little better. When Vane cried out as he passed Cromwell, "This is not honest; yea, it is against morality and common honesty;" the comment was, "Sir Harry Vane, Sir Harry Vane! the Lord deliver me from Sir Harry Vane!" But, observes Whitelock (himself understood to have been a participator in the shower of abuse that had been falling so plentifully), "Among all the Parliament, of whom many wore swords, and would sometimes brag high, not one man offered to draw his sword against Cromwell, or to make the least resistance against him, but all of them tamely departed the house." With the keys in his pocket, Cromwell returned to Whitehall, and told the Council of Officers, still sitting there, what he had done; observing, "When I went to the house, I did not think to have done this; but perceiving the Spirit of God strong upon me, I could no longer consult flesh and blood." The Council of State were dissolved the same day, by the same means—force—Bradshaw, its president, yielding to what could not be resisted, but speaking as sternly and uncompromisingly to Cromwell as he had ever done to Charles on the Trial in Westminster Hall. The great events of the day are not unworthily commemorated in West's well-known picture (Fig. 1953).

The evident necessity of giving unity and steadiness to the policy of the government, soon dictated the measure which placed Cromwell at the very summit of earthly power. He was declared Lord Protector in 1653, and under that title enjoyed an amount of power that no kingly authority could exceed, and which was used for the exaltation of the national character among the nations of the world, with an energy, a dignity, and a success, that few kings have ever been able to rival. "Perhaps no government was ever more respected abroad," says Sir Walter Scott. At home his difficulties were too great to be utterly surmounted, even by *his* lofty genius. Under the influence of Charles's attempt to change the government from a comparatively free one to a despotism, and under the influence of the events which that attempt brought on in natural and possibly inevitable sequence, society had to a great extent resolved itself into a chaos of conflicting elements. Episcopacy stood against Puritanism, royalty against republicanism, or even free monarchy, Independency against Presbyterianism, and all these against Catholicism. Each again stood in opposition to its nearest neighbour and apparent friend. This man wanted to go thus far, and that man to go not half the distance; and in the inevitable movements of the time each considered the other had deserted him, and was a traitor to the principles on which they had mutually based their cause at the commencement. The consequences were—not so much any outward exhibition of a desire to overthrow the existing government (though this was not wanting, and had to be kept down by a strong hand), as the difficulty, if not

the impossibility, of governing constitutionally. It is impossible, for instance, to doubt the desire of Cromwell to restore to the Parliament all its ordinary privileges, for again and again he made the attempt; but he found that in each case they were more anxious to undo what was settled in government, than to apply themselves earnestly to the task of aiding that government to restore to England peace, order, and prosperity. All his efforts therefore failed to do more than preserve a tolerably quiescent state of things during his life; and, wanting his hand afterwards, the whole then fell into disorder; and an able soldier, but not at all remarkable man, either for his talents or elevation of mind, or his political honesty, stepped in, put aside, almost without an effort, the Protector's son, Richard Cromwell (Fig. 1958), and handed over the throne of England, without a single real security, to the son of the man who had been dethroned and executed for despotism. To seek a settlement of the affairs of the nation by inviting back the lineal heir to the throne, may have been the truest policy; but surely there can be no doubt as to the baseness of the man who had himself fought for freedom, against the father, sacrificing everything to the son, when the amplest means were in his hand to have secured all that the principles of his own previous life had taught him were indispensable to good government. It is true that Charles solemnly and publicly promised indemnity for the past, and liberty of conscience for the future; but the worthlessness of a mere promise recent events had but too clearly shown. But Monk knew what he was doing, when he contented himself with this, and with giving some good advice to his future king as to the management of the people of England; and the Duke of Albemarle of a later day, one of the most favoured and most honoured of the servants of royalty, saw no doubt sufficient reasons to be thankful that he had, as George Monk, exercised such a delicate discrimination as to his own interest and his gracious master's views. The Commissioners of the new and Presbyterian Parliament who met Charles at the Hague (Fig. 1965) were equally complaisant, and the mockery soon over.

We may here say a few words upon a most important influence that had been called into existence during the Civil War—the Newspaper. The first known publication of the kind includes the period from Nov. 3, 1640, to Nov. 3, 1641; and so rapidly did the newspapers then increase in number, that it has been calculated above a hundred had appeared before the death of Charles, and eighty more between that event and the Restoration. These were at first published weekly, then twice, and even at last thrice a week. Our engraving (Fig. 1690) shows the heading of a newspaper of the time. But the disseminators of news were more than rivalled by the disseminators of opinions. *Thirty thousand* pamphlets are said to have been written during the Civil War and Commonwealth.

———

Cromwell died on the 3rd of September, 1658, the anniversary of his battles of Dunbar and Worcester, praying with his last breath that God would not forsake the people; "but love and bless them, and give them rest, and bring them to a consistency." In May, 1660, Charles II. landed at Dover (Fig. 1968); and very soon began, in his way, the work of bringing England to "consistency." Instead of seeking to allay all heartburnings and jealousies by endeavouring to sink the melancholy past in oblivion, the worst passions ever aroused by the war were but tame in comparison with those which were now allowed free range over the lives and fortunes of the men of the Commonwealth. Even the dead could not be permitted to rest in peace. The remains of Cromwell, Ireton, and Bradshaw were exhumed from their resting-place in Westminster Abbey, for the infliction of the ineffably mean revenge of hanging them upon a gibbet at Tyburn. If aught worse could be done than this, it was done in the similar exhumation of the remains of the *mother* and *daughter* of Cromwell (women, it is said, who had been "models of female domestic virtue"), with the remains of Pym, Blake, and others. The living opponents of Charles offered, of course, much more satisfactory objects of vengeance. They *could* be made to feel all that hatred and cruelty had it in their power to inflict upon them. So one after another the eminent men of the Commonwealth were sent for trial, and from thence to the gallows, until the public mind began to sicken at the bloody doings of the executioner, and, worst of all, until it became known that even the infernal cruelties in which he was commanded to luxuriate were found utterly powerless in breaking down the fortitude of the victims; who, even in their extreme agonies, gloried in the Cause for which they suffered. Harrison, as he was on his way to the place of execution at Charing Cross, was asked by a brutal bystander—"Where is your good Cause now?" "Here it is," said Harrison, clapping his hand to his heart; "and I am going to seal it with my blood." Carew's last words were that if the business were to be done over again, he would do it, and that

2021.—North-east View of St. Paul's Cathedral.

2022.—North-west View of St. Paul's Cathedral.

2020.—Sir Christopher Wren.

2019. Sir Christopher Wren's first Design for St. Paul's.

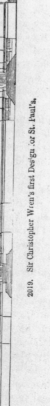

2018.—Inigo Jones's Portico, St. Paul's.

2023.—Festoon from St. Paul's.

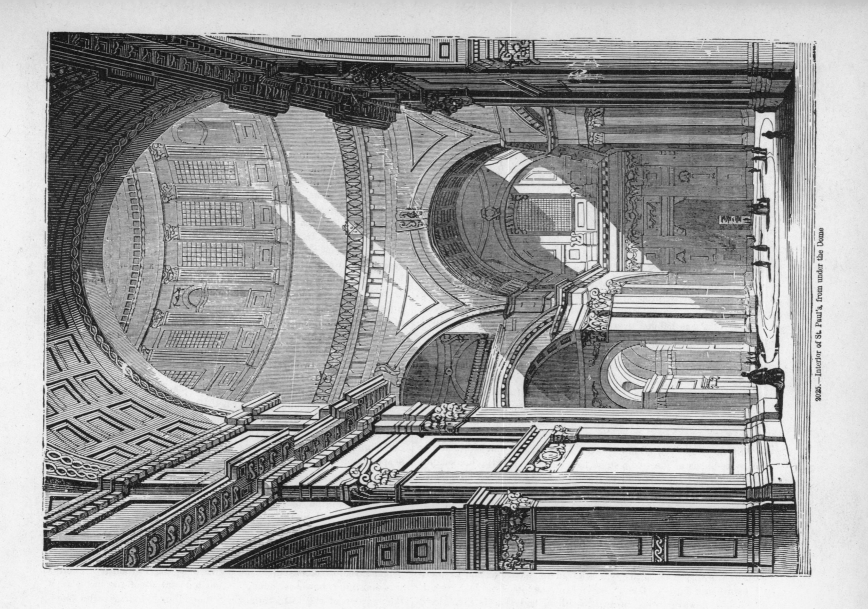

2025.—Interior of St. Paul's, from under the Dome

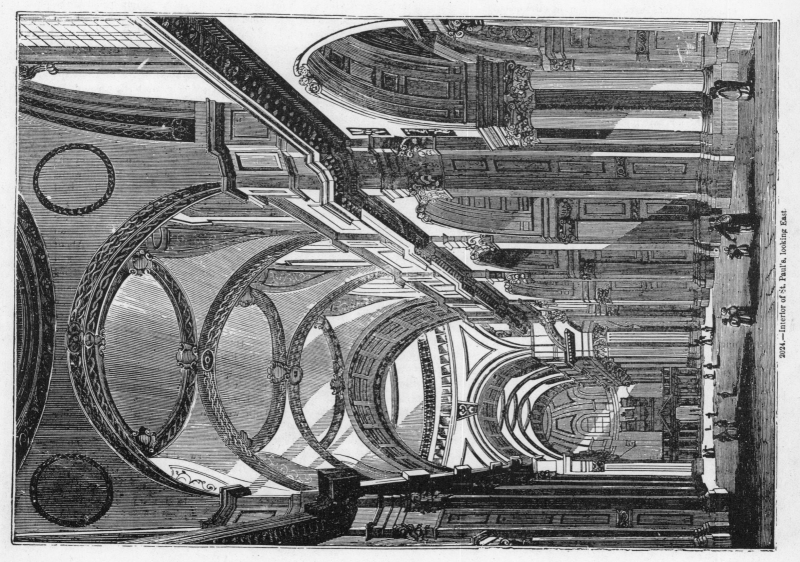

2024.—Interior of St. Paul's, looking East.

the blessed Cause would not be lost. Coke, the solicitor-general of the king's trial, after referring to his endeavours for a reform of the laws, and for cheap and expeditious justice, said, he too was far from repenting of his conduct. Hugh Peters, who was brought on the scaffold before his own execution, in order that he might see all the indescribable barbarities of quartering, &c., carried on upon Coke, was asked by the executioner, who came to him rubbing his bloody hands, how he liked that work. The answer was a bidding to do his worst; and when the old preacher ascended the scaffold, he said to the sheriff, " Sir, you have butchered one of the servants of God before my eyes, and have forced me to see, in order to terrify and discourage me, but God has permitted it for my support and encouragement;" and, incredible as it seems, he died with a serene smile upon his face. Colonel Scot would have addressed the people, but was not permitted: " Surely," said he, " it must be a very bad cause which cannot suffer the words of dying men." No wonder Charles was advised not to proceed further. And for a time there was a pause. But Sir Harry Vane was too eminent a mark to be overlooked. He was handed over to the executioner; though prudence dictated that his death should be by the axe alone. Special directions, however, were given that he should be effectually silenced if he attempted to address the spectators. No doubt he would repeat there, what he had said in taking leave of his wife and children, " I die in the certain faith and foresight that this Cause shall have its resurrection in my death." He did endeavour to speak, but the drummers and trumpeters silenced him, and though the sense of shame produced a temporary lull, during which he spoke of his life and of the wars, the trumpets were immediately sounded, and the very note-books of those who stood near demanded by the lieutenant: " He treats of rebellion, and you write it," said he. Six note-books were accordingly given up at his command. In the end, Vane found that it was useless to struggle for the free delivery of his thoughts, so he submitted his head to the block. There was another man in imminent danger at this time, whose death the world through all time would have mourned; happily England was spared that calamity and shame. Milton, after having been actually committed to the care of the serjeant-at-arms, was allowed to depart on the payment of exorbitant fees—a favour, it is said, he owed to D'Avenant. His books, however, were burnt. Scotland had also its executions, of which the chief was the Earl of Argyll, who was beheaded close by the Market-Cross of Edinburgh (Fig. 1969). In glancing at the character of these executions, and the circumstances under which they took place, one is almost led to suppose that Charles thought the foundations of his government, as the builders of the terrible Tower of London thought of that structure, could only be properly laid in blood. But they were content with beasts'—he required human blood. Thus, at all events, it was, that he sought to reduce the jarring and disunited elements of society into a state of " consistency." Our readers may ask, where was the promised indemnity for the past?—Where indeed !

But when all these frightful preliminaries of the reign of the new king were over, the grand questions remained to be solved as to what the character of his rule would be, as to how much happier and better he would make the nation. Contrasts were inevitable, in the nature of things, between the two governments approximating so nearly to each other in point of time, but standing in such deadly opposition, owing to the circumstances under which one of them had been developed. It is evident, indeed, that the contrast was carefully cherished by Charles and his favourites. Thus—to begin with his personal habits, and the aspect of the court during his rule: A dignified simplicity of behaviour, a genial sense of enjoyment, an earnest and lofty observance of all moral and religious duties, had characterised Whitehall (Figs. 1949, 1950) whilst under the control of Cromwell and his wife, and his son's wife (Fig. 1959), and other estimable relatives. How matters changed under Charles's influence let Evelyn tell (speaking of Whitehall, but his remarks of course apply to Windsor (Fig. 1991), or wherever else the court happened to be): he states, " I can never forget the inexpressible luxury and profaneness, gaming, and all dissoluteness, and, as it were, total forgetfulness of God, (it being Sunday evening,) which this day se'nnight I was witness of, the king sitting and toying with his concubines—Portsmouth, Cleveland, Mazarine," &c. This was but a *week* before Charles's death, but the end was in accordance with the beginning. When his bride, Catherine of Braganza (Fig. 1971), was brought over, one of the first persons introduced to her by her husband was Lady Castlemaine; and, says Clarendon, " Whether her majesty in the instant, knew who she was, or upon recollection found it afterwards, she no sooner sat in her chair but her colour changed, and tears gushed out of her eyes, and her nose bled, and she fainted." And when Charles saw her thus moved, merely because he had introduced his mistress to her notice, he felt, we are told, " wonderful indignation."

In the policy of the reign, also, the government, it might be supposed, had gone upon the principle of contrast with that of the previous administration. As Cromwell had won Dunkirk, so Charles sold it (Fig. 1973). As Cromwell had made foreign states follow as it were in his wake through the difficult and stormy sea of European politics, Charles not only determined to repay the obligation by a reversal of the English position, but to bind himself by the receipt of a pension from one country (France), to do all that could be reasonably expected of him in that position. Cromwell, when he did involve the nation in a war, was sure to carry it through successfully, and, in the usual sense of the word, gloriously: Charles was as sure to make the incapacity of his government only the more evident when he did fight, than when he let it alone. To how low a pitch the reputation of England must have sunk when the Dutch sought us in our rivers, and burnt our shipping and our ports, Sheerness (Fig. 1985) included, before the very eyes of the people of England, we leave our readers to judge. Much of the responsibility of the disgrace—and as regards the French pension, infamy—attaches to Clarendon, the Royalist historian, Charles's chancellor; it was he who advised the sale of Dunkirk—he who taught Charles the advantage of pecuniary dependence on a foreign power. He had his reward in two senses. The king's liberality enabled him to build Clarendon House (Figs. 1986, 1987), one of the most magnificent mansions of the time; and, on the other hand, the indignation of the people broke out, not only in sarcasms, such as christening Clarendon House, " Dunkirk House," but in such deeper sentiments as ultimately found vent in a parliamentary impeachment, and in the Chancellor's being driven from power and from the country.

And as with the foreign, so with the home affairs. The internal peace, which had formed the chief motive of many Englishmen for desiring Charles's recall, never came. In 1678 there was the excitement caused by the pretended Popish plot of the notorious Titus Oates, who professed to have discovered all kinds of wonderful atrocities about to be perpetrated by the Catholics. There was one thing, however, unhappily but too real about the business; the murder of the magistrate, Sir Edmondbury Godfrey, who had first received Oates's deposition, and other confidential communications from one Coleman, an agent and factotum of the Duke of York, the king's brother, who was said to be implicated in the plot. Sir Edmondbury was discovered, with his neck broken, upon Primrose Hill, near London. Neither the real murderers—nor the cause of the murder—were ever discovered. The sensation produced by these mysterious events is shown by the different medals (Fig. 1994) that were struck in commemoration of the event by the Protestants. That excitement had scarcely subsided, when it was succeeded by the signs of a new contest between King and Parliament. Whether Charles thought the people had, by the very act of his recall, shown their approval of his father's conduct, or whether he thought the time favourable for a renewal of his father's policy, even in opposition to their views, Charles began to dissolve parliament after parliament, one of them within a week of its sitting. Next we find the Covenanters of Scotland, driven to frenzy by the intolerable injustice of Charles's minister, the Duke of Lauderdale, breaking out in open insurrection; and, after the defeat at Bothwell Brig (Fig. 1992), being hunted and cut down like wild beasts, or thrown into horrible dungeons, in places where—as at the Bass Rock (Fig. 1993)—every species of cruelty could be inflicted upon them without hindrance, and almost unknown to the world. About the same time, we find also, that in England men of high rank and social position, and of the most unblemished honour, lovers of peace and order, but also haters of evil government, were beginning to band secretly together in order to repeat, if necessary, the terrible lesson that had been so lately but apparently fruitlessly given. We have no space to enter into the particulars of the Rye House Plot, so named from the place (Fig. 1995) where it was said an attempt was to have been made on the life of Charles, or into the views of the chief actors connected with it; it will be sufficient to say, that the government of the second Charles found that it could not exist in safety whilst men like Lord William Russell and Algernon Sydney were alive. So both went to the scaffold on convictions for high treason. We need hardly remind our readers that it was on the trial of Lord William Russell that the affecting and noble scene occurred of his wife stepping forward to act as his secretary; and that it is Algernon Sydney who is mentioned in Wordsworth's well-known lines:—

Great men have been among us—hands that penned
And tongues that uttered wisdom; better none;

The later *Sydney*, Marvell, Harrington,
    Young Vane, and others who called Milton friend.

Sydney's last words were remarkable. He did not offer to speak on the scaffold, and when asked to do so, he replied that he had made his peace with God, and had nothing to say to man. But he delivered a paper to the sheriff, the concluding words of which show that the principles for which the Commonwealth had striven, though modified by circumstances, were still actively at work. Sydney in his paper, thus addresses the Almighty: "Grant that I may die glorifying thee for all thy mercies, and that at the last thou hast permitted me to be singled out as a witness of thy truth, and, even by the confession of my very opposers, for that old Cause in which I was from my youth engaged, and for which thou hast often and wonderfully declared Thyself." And that "old Cause" was yet to know some taste of success. The "glorious Revolution" of 1688 was but the establishment of many of the most essential of their principles.

We must not, in concluding our notice of Charles, forget those whom he so ungratefully took care not to remember—his own and his father's friends in adversity, as his treatment of them shows so powerfully his character, nor would it be proper to pass without an allusion, at least, to his expenditure in all kinds of debauchery of the funds voted by Parliament for a monument to his father. And, as if to put the seal to the contempt into which his memory was to fall, there seems good reason to suppose, that while at his death he preserved all the appearance of dying in the Protestant faith, he was secretly communicating with a Catholic confessor, brought to him by his brother.

Amidst all the other sufferings and trials of the English people during the seventeenth century, they had to contend with frequent visitations of the plague. In the year 1665 alone, there were destroyed by it in London a hundred thousand persons, and those whom it spared must, for the most part, have been left in a state that rendered life of little value. Our engraving of the Pest House, Westminster (Fig. 1972), reminds us of one of the many numerous houses of that kind that were dispersed about London. The fearful year just named was, however, to witness, as far as we can discern, the last of its deadly triumphs. And it was to be stopped by an agency that but too fearfully harmonised with its own terrors. It was by the great fire of London that the great plagues of London were to be destroyed.

A little after midnight of Saturday, the 2nd of September, 1666, Farryner, the king's baker, in Pudding Lane, according to his own positive statement, went through every room of his house, and carefully raked up the only fire in it, in a room paved with bricks. Soon after, on the morning of the 3rd, his house was on fire, and the flames spread in so extraordinary a manner, that above three hundred houses were burned down by the beginning of the next forenoon. The fire was blown into greater fierceness by a strong east wind, and its career rendered more easy and irresistible by the unusual drought that had prevailed during the past month, that had of itself half burnt up the timber houses with which the narrow streets were crowded. In the first hurry and excitement of the alarm, the terrible enemy met no opposition; the citizens were distracted and bewildered—the Lord Mayor at his wits' end. When Charles sent to command him to spare no houses, but pull down before the fire every way, he was found by Pepys wandering helplessly in Cannon Street, and replied, "Lord, what can I do? I am spent; people will not obey me. I have been pulling down houses, but the fire overtakes us faster than we can do it." So the venerable and picturesque city submitted to its fate. From the Bankside, Southwark (Fig. 1979), Pepys and Evelyn, on the evening of Monday, the first day of the fire, wandered about to gaze on the wondrous spectacle, which at one time appeared as one vast and entire arch of "a most horrid, malicious, bloody flame."

"I saw," writes Evelyn, "the whole south part of the city burning, from Cheapside to the Thames, and all along Cornhill (for it likewise kindled back against the wind, as well as forward), Tower Street, Fenchurch Street, Gracious (Gracechurch) Street, and so along to Baynard's Castle, and was taking hold of St. Paul's Church, to which the scaffolds contributed exceedingly. The conflagration was so universal, and the people so astonished, that, from the beginning, I know not by what despondency or fate, they hardly stirred to quench it; so that there was nothing heard or seen but crying out and lamentation, running about like distracted creatures, without at all attempting to save even their goods; such a strange consternation there was upon them, so as it burned, both in breadth and length, the churches, public halls, Exchange, hospitals, monuments, and ornaments, leaping after a prodigious manner from house to house, and street to street, at great distances from one to the other; for the heat, with a long set of fair and warm weather, had even ignited the air, and prepared the materials to conceive the fire, which devoured, after an incredible manner, houses, furniture, and everything. Here we saw the Thames covered with goods floating, all the barges and boats laden with what some had time and courage to save; as on the other, the carts, &c., carrying out to the fields, which for many miles were strewed with moveables of all sorts, and tents erecting to shelter both people and what goods they could get away. Oh, the miserable and calamitous spectacle! such as haply the world had not seen the like since the foundation of it, nor to be outdone till the universal conflagration of it. All the sky was of a fiery aspect, like the top of a burning oven, and the light seen for above forty miles round about for many nights. God grant mine eyes may never see the like! who now saw above ten thousand houses all in one flame: the noise and crackling and thunder of the impetuous flames, the shrieking of women and children, the hurry of people, the fall of towers, houses, and churches, was like a hideous storm, and the air all about so hot and inflamed that at last one was not able to approach it; so that they were forced to stand still and let the flames burn on, which they did for near two miles in length and one in breadth."

The clouds of smoke from this tremendous conflagration extended near fifty miles in length, and travellers riding at noonday might be "some six miles together in the shadow thereof, though there were no other cloud besides to be seen in the sky."—(Vincent.) Among the incidents that naturally attracted peculiar attention were the burning of some of the public buildings, which included works of the finest Gothic architecture. Their destruction, in more than one case, formed spectacles equally singular, glorious, and fearful. The Guildhall, for instance, being formed of solid oak, stood in the midst of the vast fiery furnace like "a bright shining coal, as if it had been a palace of gold, or a great building of burnished brass." All Monday night, and until about Tuesday at noon, the fire was unchecked, was irresistible; but gradually it retreated as the use of gunpowder for the expeditious blowing up of the houses on its route, created gaps too wide for it to pass over. Had this plan been resorted to earlier, as "some stout seamen proposed," the city might have been saved, but "some tenacious and avaricious men, aldermen, &c., would not permit" it, "because their houses must have been of the first."—(Evelyn.) Five days after the breaking out of the fire, Evelyn thus describes the great city, as it lay a blackened, gigantic, and most awful ruin:—

"I went this morning on foot from Whitehall as far as London Bridge, through the late Fleet Street, Ludgate Hill, by St. Paul's, Cheapside, Exchange, Bishopsgate, Aldersgate, and out to Moorfields, thence through Cornhill, &c., with extraordinary difficulty, clambering over heaps of yet smoking rubbish, and frequently mistaking where I was; the ground under my feet so hot that it even burnt the soles of my shoes. . . . At my return I was infinitely concerned to find that goodly church, St. Paul's, now a sad ruin, and that beautiful portico (Fig. 2018), for structure comparable to any in Europe, as not long before repaired by the late king—now rent in pieces, flakes of vast stone split asunder, and nothing remaining entire, but the inscription on the architrave, showing by whom it was built, which had not one letter of it defaced. It was astonishing to see what immense stones the heat had in a manner calcined, so that all the ornaments, columns, friezes, capitals, and projectures of massy Portland stone flew off, even to the very roof, where a sheet of lead covering a great space (no less than six acres by measure) was totally melted: the ruins of the vaulted roof falling, broke into St. Faith's, which being filled with the magazines of books belonging to the stationers, and carried thither for safety, they were all consumed, burning for a week following. . . . There lay in ashes that most venerable church, one of the most ancient pieces of early piety in the Christian world, besides near one hundred more; the lead, iron-work, bells, plate, &c., melted; the exquisitely wrought Mercers' Chapel, the sumptuous Exchange, the august fabric of Christ Church, all the rest of the Companies' Halls, splendid buildings, arches, entries, all in dust; the fountains dried up and ruined, whilst the very water remained boiling; . . . subterranean cellars, wells, and dungeons, formerly warehouses, still burning in stench and dark clouds of smoke, so that in five or six miles traversing about I did not see one load of timber unconsumed, nor many stones but what were calcined white as snow. The people who now walked about the ruins appeared like men in some dismal desert, or rather in some great city wasted by a cruel enemy; to which was added the stench that came from some poor creatures' bodies, beds, and other combustible goods. Sir Thomas Gresham's statue, though fallen from its niche in the Royal Exchange, remained entire when

2026.—Tomb of Sir Christopher Wren.

2028.—Interior of St. Stephen's, Walbrook.

2027.—St. Paul's Choir.

2029.—A Parallel of some of the principal Towers and Steeples built by Sir Christopher Wren.

St. Dunstan in the East.   2, St. Magnus.   3, St. Benet, Gracechurch-street.   4, St. Edmund the King. Lombard-street.   5, St. Margaret Pattens.   6, Allhallows the Great.
7, St. Mary Abchurch.   8, St. Michael, Cornhill.   9, St. Lawrence, Jewry.   10, St. Benet Fink.   11, St. Bartholmew.   12, St. Michael, Queenhithe.   13, St. Michael Royal.
14, St. Antholin, Watling-street.   15, St. Stephen, Walbrook.   16, St. Swithin, Cannon-street.   17, St. Mary-le-Bow.   18, Christ Church, Newgate-street.   19, St. Nicholas,
Cole Abbey.   20, St. Mildred, Bread-street.   21, St. Augustin, Watling-street.   22, St. Mary Somerset.   23, St. Martin, Ludgate.   24, St. Andrew by the Wardrobe.
25 St. Bride, Fleet-street.
The scale is expressed by St. Paul's in the background.

2030.—St. James's Westminster.

2031.—Lich Gate, Pulborough.

2032.—Sir Dudley Carleton's Monument, Westminster Abbey.

2033.—Sutton's Monument, at the Charter House.

2034.—Bow Church and Cheapside.

all those of the Kings since the Conquest were broken to pieces; also the standard in Cornhill and Queen Elizabeth's effigies, with some arms on Ludgate, continued with but little detriment, whilst the vast iron chains of the city streets, hinges, bars, and gates of prisons [Newgate was among the edifices destroyed; see our engraving, Fig. 1983], were many of them melted and reduced to cinders by the vehement heat. Nor was I yet able to pass through any of the narrower streets, but kept the widest; the ground and air, smoke, and fiery vapour continued so intense that my hair was almost singed, and my feet unsufferably surbated [battered, bruised, sore]. The by-lanes and narrower streets were quite filled up with rubbish; nor could any one have possibly known where he was, but by the ruins of some church or hall that had some remarkable tower or pinnacle remaining. I then went towards Islington and Highgate, where one might have seen two hundred thousand people of all ranks and degrees dispersed and lying along by their heaps of what they could save from the fire, deploring their loss and, though ready to perish for hunger and destitution, yet not asking one penny for relief, which to me appeared a stranger sight than any I had yet beheld. His Majesty and Council, indeed, took all imaginable care for their relief by proclamation for the country to come in and refresh them with provisions.

The amount of destruction is thus summed up in the inscription that remains to this day, on the north side of the Monument, erected in commemoration of the event:—" Eighty-nine churches, the City gates, Guildhall, many public structures, hospitals, schools, libraries, a vast number of stately edifices, thirteen thousand two hundred dwelling-houses, four hundred streets; of twenty-six wards it utterly destroyed fifteen, and left eight others shattered and half burnt. The ruins of the city were four hundred and thirty-six acres from the Tower by the Thames side to the Temple Church, and from the north-east gate along the City Wall to Holborn Bridge. To the estates and fortunes of the citizens it was merciless, but to their lives very favourable (only eight being lost), that it might in all things resemble the last conflagration of the world."—(Translation of the Latin inscription by Maitland.) The loss was estimated at nearly eleven million pounds sterling!

It is melancholy to reflect how little value has been generally placed by those who have had the care of princes in their youth, upon the influences that were most likely to affect the personal happiness and welfare of their pupils in after life. The accident of position has been alone thought worthy of attention, whilst the substantial interests of the human heart and brain that were to heave and throb beneath the ermined robe and the golden crown have been strangely neglected. The minds called to such mighty responsibilities have a natural tendency to swell into something unreal and fantastic, and require solid mental and moral qualities to keep that tendency within reasonable limits. But this very tendency has been studiously encouraged in the education of our princes; and yet we wonder that but once in a thousand years an Alfred comes. These remarks have been suggested and are forcibly illustrated by the training of James II. (Figs. 2004, 2013). Whilst a boy, Lord Byron had been made his governor—a man said to have been well qualified for the trust; but before James had reached his fourteenth year, he was taught by those around him to consider it a lessening of his dignity to be governed; and before long we find, as the natural results of this and similar treatment, a " firm resolution " existing in the young prince's mind " never to acknowledge he had committed an error." May we not see prefigured in these words James's whole character and reign and fate?

James ascended the throne without any opposition on his brother's death, and the court immediately assumed an outward show of decorum that belied the real private life of its master. He had been only less famous for his mistresses, for instance, than his brother. One of the most noted of his favourites was Lady Denham, who died at Burlington House (Fig. 1988) under very suspicious circumstances. In his first speech to the Privy Council, James told them he had been reported to be a man desirous of arbitrary power, but that that was not the only story that had been made of him. And then, as a comment upon his words—and it explained them but too clearly—his first deed was to proclaim the continuance of certain duties, that expired with his brother's reign, and which, constitutionally, the Parliament alone could re-establish. Another of his deeds was to secure the continuance of the French pension enjoyed by his brother. It is true, he determined to call a Parliament, but, as he said to his intimates, " Hereafter it will be much more easy for me to put off the assembling of Parliament, or to maintain myself by other means which may appear more convenient

to me." Such, then was the effect of the Restoration, that, only twenty-five years afterwards, the Parliament and King were again anticipating being in opposition to each other, notwithstanding the overthrow of the parties from whom the parliament of Charles I. had been chiefly formed. A more striking evidence it would be impossible to desire, that the contest from the first had been, and continued to be, a real contest between the nation at large, that desired a free—and the king, who desired a despotic government.

But James, like his father, could not be content with one object to struggle for, however vast that may be; nay, it should almost seem that he thought his father had not even gone far enough in his attempt; he had only tried to reduce the Church as well as the State into a despotism, and had been content to leave it still a Protestant Church. James must have nothing less than a Catholic establishment by the side of a civil despotism. At first matters looked very promising for him. He so managed the election or his first Parliament, that he declared, with some exultation, there were not forty of them that he would not himself have chosen: it must indeed have been a nice Parliament. And although insurrections broke out both in Scotland and in England, the leaders, Argyll and Monmouth, were quickly overthrown, taken, and sent to the scaffold. But when the Parliament had been prorogued, and re-assembled, and when James had coolly informed them that in the interim he had appointed many Catholic officers, and dispensed with the legal test of conformity to the Establishment, even his own charming House of Commons began to murmur, " though as 't were afar off." This little manifestation of opinion was at once silenced by a violent message from James. The only member who ventured to remonstrate, and to express a hope that they were all Englishmen, and not to be frightened by a few hard words, was summarily marched off to the Tower.

The task of abolishing Protestantism in England, was therefore to be carried on with unflinching vigour. On the 27th of April, 1688, James brought on the crisis by commanding a declaration of indulgence to be read by the clergy in all the churches. Then met together at Lambeth, in solemn deliberation, the Seven Bishops, who under that designation subsequently became so famous; they were—the Archbishop Sancroft, and Bishops Lloyd of St. Asaph, Ken of Bath and Wells, Turner of Ely, Lake of Chichester, White of Peterborough, and Trelawny of Bristol (Fig. 2012). The result was the preparation of a petition, stating their aversion to the act demanded of them, for many reasons, but especially because Parliament had often declared such a power as that exercised by James was illegal. This was presented to the King, who by way of answer, sent the whole seven to the Tower.

The excitement of the people may be imagined, especially of those who were eye-witnesses of the conveyance of the bishops by water from Whitehall (Figs. 1998, 1999), to the Tower, and thence, at a later day, to Westminster Hall, to be tried. The greater part, indeed, of the immense concourse of spectators on both occasions actually knelt and prayed aloud for them as they passed. They were found " Not Guilty " of the false, fictitious, malicious, pernicious, and seditious libel charged against them. Here was a severe check. But James would not understand it. Two of the judges were dismissed, and the whole body of the English clergy (two hundred only excepted) ordered to be prosecuted for disobedience to the King's command. What was to be done?—the condition of affairs thus desperate, another Civil War apparently about to burst in all its horrors upon the country? Eminent men met in secret council at Lady Place, Hurley (Fig. 2010), where, it is said, certain important documents connected with the determination that was come to, were signed in a recess of the vaults (Fig. 2011): the determination was, that the Prince of Orange should be called in to aid the English people. He had married James's daughter, and was therefore acceptable to many of the Royalists, but had of course no claim to the throne, therefore was more likely to study the interest of those who might elevate him to that dignity. Above all, he had been unflinchingly true to his own republic, notwithstanding many temptations, and had thus given earnest that he would be equally true in whatever new relations he might form. He was, consequently, on the whole, the very man required to establish a compromise between the long-conflicting parties and principles of English politics. William landed at Torbay on the 4th of November, 1688, and James presently found himself without a friend or a soldier or a subject by his side, to remind him he had been King of England. So having previously sent his wife, Maria Beatrix (Fig. 2007), and the young prince his son, over to France, he followed them, and was for a time withdrawn from the eyes of his former subjects; who were, however, to find that they had not yet done with him

CHAPTER II.--ECCLESIASTICAL ANTIQUITIES.

E need not again enter into the vast subject of the religious history of England during the seventeenth century, seeing that during that time it became inextricably mixed up with the political history, and has therefore already engaged our attention. We propose therefore to devote a short chapter to brief notices of some of the more remarkable divines who lived during the period, but of whom we have hitherto had no opportunity to speak; and to a few words upon the re-erection of the metropolitan churches, destroyed by the fire.

Both Fuller and Clarendon have expressed a belief, that had the system of severity to the Nonconformists pursued by Archbishops Whitgift and Bancroft, in the reign of Elizabeth, not been interrupted by the different views of Abbot (Fig. 2615)—(who was made Archbishop of Canterbury in 1610, by James I.)—Calvinism and dissent would have been extirpated from England, and hence the political and religious convulsions of the next reign would have been prevented; or, in other words, we presume the nation would have been less prepared to resist Charles's despotic views. But Abbot did interrupt the excessive fierceness of persecution, and would probably have done so, even if he had foreseen the consequences that are said to have ensued. When in 1627 Dr. Manwaring was brought to the bar of the House of Lords for having asserted in a sermon that "The King is not bound to observe the laws of the realm concerning the subjects' rights and liberties, but that his royal will and command in imposing loans and taxes, without common consent in parliament, doth oblige the subjects' conscience upon pain of eternal damnation," Abbot, in the fulfilment of the duty committed to him of reprimanding the offender, expressed very energetically his abhorrence of so audacious a doctrine. A discourse of a similar description having been delivered by a Dr. Sibthorp in Abbot's own diocese, the Archbishop refused to license it; upon which Laud actually had the boldness to obtain the suspension of Abbot—his own ecclesiastical superior. What a view does this not give us of the sort of advisers and prompters that were about Charles I.! When Abbot died, his enemy Laud succeeded him.

Bishop Hall (Fig. 2014), who claims, and justly, the authorship of the earliest satires in the language, was also one of Laud's marked men. He was too earnest in attending to his own and his flock's spiritual welfare to be able to spare time to follow Laud in his ecclesiastical campaigns, so the term of opprobrium usually applied to moderate Episcopalians was cast upon him—Puritanism. At last, in his indignation, he determined to meet the charge direct. He says, "Under how dark a cloud I was hereupon, I was so sensible, that I plainly told the Lord Archbishop of Canterbury [Laud], that rather than I would be obnoxious to those slanderous tongues of his misinformers, I would cast up my rochet. I knew I went right ways, and would not endure to live under undeserved suspicions." The revenues of his bishopric were of course sequestrated, with the other sees, by the Parliament, and during his latter days Hall suffered so much from poverty and harsh treatment, that they wrung from him a book of complaint, called 'Hard Measure.'

Who has not, in childhood or in youth, read the 'Pilgrim's Progress?' Who has not felt deeply interested in after years in tracing the remarkable history of the author (Fig. 2014)—first a tinker, then a soldier in the army of the Parliament, than a Baptist minister, lastly a prisoner for twelve years and upwards? He supported himself in prison by making tags and laces; and it was then that the 'Pilgrim's Progress' was undertaken. Bunyan's confinement was one of the results of the ecclesiastical policy of Charles II.'s government; and, strange to say, his release was the result of the policy of a still more bigoted king, James II. But then James's motive in proclaiming toleration, and causing the discharge of such

men as Bunyan was, in order that he might reach circuitously what could not be reached directly—toleration for the Catholics, as a preliminary to their supreme power.

Among those men who have been conspicuous for what may be termed the complete goodness and loftiness of their mind and character, Isaac Barrow (Fig. 2014) must hold a conspicuous place. Although a staunch Royalist, he received the most gratifying testimonials of merit from the University of Oxford, at a time when the parliamentary influence was all powerful, and when men's deserts were less thought of than their politics. And the hopes excited by the student were realized by the mature man. Barrow became highly distinguished as a mathematician; he obtained a rank among the first of English divines. We may here relate an amusing anecdote of him in the pulpit:—Being invited to preach for Dr. Wilkins (afterwards Bishop of Chester, &c.) in a parish church in London, his appearance (which was that of an apprentice) drove the whole of the congregation away, except a few persons, among whom was Mr. Baxter, the Non-Conformist, who declared afterwards that he could have sat all day to hear him, much to the confusion of the congregation, who had complained to the rector of his substitute. An apprentice, when he came down from the pulpit, said to him, "Sir, be not dismayed, for I assure you it was a good sermon." On being asked what he thought of this person, he said, "I take him to be a very civil person, and if I could meet with him, I'd present him with a bottle of wine." His moral character was at least on a par with his intellectual. We must not, as with the lives of most eminent churchmen, reckon the successes of his life by the preferments he received, but by those he declined from conscientious and high-principled motives. He resigned the post of Gresham professor of Geometry, because he considered it incompatible with that of the Lucasian professorship, to which he had been subsequently appointed; he refused a valuable living that was offered on condition of teaching a pupil, because he considered the offer as simoniacal; but the most remarkable of all these sacrifices was the resignation of the Lucasian professorship before mentioned; for the very unworldly reason that there was a young man of high promise whose interests and objects he thought the office would advance. Barrow was not deceived as to the promise. That young man was Isaac Newton. Many stories, some of them very entertaining, are told of his courage: here is one story that illustrates not only that quality, but something better:—Being on a visit at a house with a garden attached, he rose early in the morning, and was wandering about, when a large dog, usually kept chained by day, but let loose at night for the protection of the house, attacked him. Barrow seized the animal by the throat, threw him, and lay upon him, and whilst he kept him down, considered what he should do with him in that exigency. To kill him, was naturally his first thoughts; but he soon perceived that there would be injustice in the deed, for the dog only did his duty, and he himself was in fault for rambling out before it was light. Happily he was at last released from his dangerous position, by making his cries heard by the inmates of the house. And this is told of him, who was in his youth of so quarrelsome a disposition, and altogether so ill-conditioned a boy, that his father is reputed to have said, that if God should take any of his children, he hoped it would be Isaac.

Let us now glance at a scene in Whitehall during the Protectorate, that may make us acquainted with two other of the eminent men of the day. Cromwell was there, expecting as his visitor George Fox (Fig. 2015), the founder of a new sect—the Quakers. With Cromwell was his intimate friend, Dr. John Owen (Fig. 2014), a man of learning, amiability, and of exemplary character. The commencement of the intimacy between the two was marked by circumstances honourable to both. Cromwell having heard him preach, was so pleased, that when he went to Ireland he took Owen with him, in order that he might superintend the college of Dublin, then a very onerous task. The appointment with Fox had been made the previous day; when, as Cromwell was riding in his coach in the park, Fox rode to the side of the vehicle, in order to remonstrate with the

2035.—Henry Prince of Wales. (From Drayton's Polyolbion.)

2036.—Anne of Denmark, Queen of James I. (From Strutt.)

2037.—English Lady of Quality. (Hollar's Ornatus Muliebris, 1640.)

2038.—Gentlewoman. (Hollar's Ornatus Muliebris, 1640.)

2039.—Merchant's Wife of London. (Hollar's Ornatus Muliebris, 1640.)

2040.—Citizen's Wife of London. (Hollar's Ornatus Muliebris, 1640.)

2041.—Lady Mayoress of London. (Hollar's Theatrum Mulierum.)

2042.—Countrywoman with Mufflers. (Speed's Map of England.)

2043.—Musketeer 1603. (From a Specimen at Goodrich Court, engraved in Skelton's Armour.)

2044.—Cavalier, 1620. (From a Specimen at Goodrich Court; engraved in Skelton's Armour.)

2045.—Infantry Armour, 1625. (From a Specimen at Goodrich Court; engraved in Skelton's Armour.)

2046.—Pikeman, 1635 (From a Specimen at Goodrich Court.)

2047.—Soldier of Trained Band, 1638.

2048.—Cuirassier, 1645. (From a Specimen at Goodrich Court.)

2049.—Oliverian, or Puritan. (Jeffrey's Dresses.

2050.—Helmets, 1645. (From Specimens at Goodrich Court.)

2051.—Dragoon, 1645. (From a Specimen at Goodrich Court.)

Protector against the severities that had been exercised upon the "Friends." At parting, Cromwell, as Fox says, had invited him to his house the next day. He tells us also that before he went, one of Cromwell's "maids, whose name was Mary Sanders, came to me at my lodging, and told me her *master* came to her, and said he would tell her some good news. When she asked him what it was, he told her George Fox had come to town. She replied, that was good news indeed, (for she had received truth,)" parenthetically remarks the self-complacent dispenser of that truth; "but she said she could hardly believe him, till he told her how I met him, and rode from Hyde Park to St. James's gate with him." The invitation was of course accepted, and Fox, and the friend who accompanied him, began to speak of the "inward light" they possessed, but which Cromwell said was a natural light. "But we," continues Fox, "showed him to the contrary;" adding, "the power of the Lord God arose in me, and I was moved in it to bid him lay down his crown at the feet of Jesus. Several times I spoke to him to the same effect. Now I was standing by the table, and he came and sat upon the table's side by me, and said he would be as high as I was; and so continued speaking against the light of Christ Jesus; and went away in a light manner."

Among the great writers in divinity, Jeremy Taylor (Fig. 2015) holds the highest place, not merely relative to this, but to any period. He has been called "the Spenser of our prose writers;" and it has been said that "his prose is sometimes almost as musical as Spenser's verse." He, too, suffered from the troubles of the time, whilst the Parliament was in the ascendant, and during the period of the Commonwealth; but the Restoration brought with it some compensations. An Irish bishopric was conferred upon him; also a seat in the Irish privy council. But it seems that, as the husband of a natural daughter of Charles I., as an ardent loyalist, and, above all, as a man of the most brilliant abilities, his friends seem to have thought him entitled to preferment nearer home. The reason alleged for his not receiving that mark of the royal favour is, at all events, creditable to Bishop Taylor's honesty and unflinching love of truth. "Charles," suggests Bishop Heber, "may not have been unwilling to remove to a distance a person whose piety might have led him to reprove many parts of his conduct, and who would have a plausible pretence for speaking more freely than the rest of the dignified clergy."

If only as one of Milton's polemical antagonists, Archbishop Usher (Fig. 2015), would deserve attention, but his own virtues and learning need no adventitious circumstances to entitle his memory to respect and honour. The estimation in which he was held by his antagonists speaks trumpet-tongued as to his character. Thus, although during the eventful period of the troubles of the reign of Charles I. he wrote against the lawfulness of taking up arms against the king; when arms had been taken up and the Royal cause defeated, and himself plunged in the general ruin that awaited men of his own public position and political and religious views, it was no other than Cromwell himself who pensioned and caused to be treated with the utmost respect the fallen archbishop; and when he died in 1656, it was Cromwell again, who caused him to be buried in Westminster Abbey. It is not without reason that some of those who have called Cromwell a usurper have added—that it must be confessed he was a truly magnanimous one.

If the period of the Civil War was one to test men's souls, we may say they stood the test admirably, and developed an amount of courage, ability, and virtue, that must have been utterly unanticipated, and which might have lain dormant in a quieter period of the world's history. It is surprising, as we glance over the names of the men who are now engaging our attention, to perceive how the excellence of one life seems to animate all, notwithstanding the modifications wrought by individual tempers or circumstances, placing them frequently at the very opposite points of the political compass. There would be no end, indeed, to our task, were we to endeavour to mention all the men of the period whose names are deservedly held dear by every class of Christians. With two more, therefore, we close the list. Our first shall be Leighton (Fig. 2014), Archbishop of Glasgow—a man whom not all the exciting and disturbing influence of parties could induce to step aside, either to the right or to the left of the path that he believed to be the right one. It was a custom with the dignitaries of the Scottish Church, a little before the Civil War, to ask the clergy in their assemblies, "Whether they preached to the times?" meaning in effect, did they take advantage of their position to inculcate in their sermons the views of those in authority. When the question was put to Leighton, he replied, with inimitable delicacy of sarcasm upon the conduct of his fellows, and with a lofty feeling of what should be his and their conduct—"When all my brethren preach to the times, suffer me to preach about eternity." The other

personage to whom we alluded is Bishop Burnet (Fig. 2014), the well-known author of the 'History of the Reformation,' and of the 'History of his Own Time,' works neither distinguished for soundness of judgment nor impartiality, but highly informing, and written by one whose life in every way testifies that he was a good man. In the corrupt court of Charles II. Burnet was tested, and found to be incorruptible. In 1682 overtures were made to him to the effect, that if he would join the Court party and come over to the King's interests, he should have the bishopric of Chichester. He not only refused, but about the same time wrote to Charles his celebrated letter, commenting upon and reproving in severe language his public conduct and his private vices. Charles read the letter twice over, and then threw it into the fire. Not many months after, news was brought to Charles that Burnet had attended Lord William Russell to the scaffold; and immediately certain offices he held were taken from him. The most important part of Burnet's public life was the share he took in the Revolution of 1688. The Prince of Orange had not a more zealous and efficient friend through all that business than Burnet, who accompanied the Prince to England as his chaplain, and when the one became King William III., the other was speedily known as the Bishop of Salisbury.

Burnet's reputation has received some damage from the wits. When the 'History of his Own Time' was published, Swift wrote 'Short Remarks' upon it; and no doubt the worthy bishop would have been as well pleased if they had been still shorter. Arbuthnot made a parody upon it. But the most pungent and most successful of all the attacks was that of Pope, whose 'Memoirs of P. P., Clerk of the Parish,' present a too severe but most irresistibly amusing burlesque of Burnet's garrulity and conceit. These systematic attacks may have been partially owing to the bishop's known contempt for the profession of literature. It was he who spoke of "one Prior," and was punished by a stinging epigram, in which he was referred to as "one Burnet." It was he also, who, in one of his pamphlets, had called Dryden a monster of profligacy, for which Dryden gave him a niche in the 'Hind and Panther.'

After the fire, the great work of restoration was confided to Wren: and it progressed so rapidly, that ten thousand houses arose in four years, and it was not long before the re-erection of the public buildings, and more especially the churches, were also begun. The eighty-five churches destroyed within the City walls were replaced by fifty-one of Wren's erection, beside his new church of St. James, Westminster (Fig. 2030), and two that he rescued from the general ruin, St. Andrew's, Holborn, and St. Clement Danes. These churches are chiefly remarkable for their beautiful towers and steeples. We have given a parallel of some of the principal of them in our engraving (Fig. 2029), where they have for their background the mighty shadow of the architect's crowning work, the imperial dome of St. Paul's. One of the most popularly known and appreciated of all Wren's churches is Bow Church, Cheapside (Fig. 2034), in style an adaptation from his favourite classical authority, the Temple of Peace, at Rome. Of St. Stephen's, Walbrook (Fig. 2028), it has been said—"Had the materials and volume been so durable and extensive as those of St. Paul's Cathedral, Sir Christopher Wren had consummated a much more efficient monument to his well-earned fame than that fabric affords."—(Britton and Pugin's 'Illustrations of the Public Buildings of London.') But in referring to what Wren did not do, both here and elsewhere, we must bear in mind how difficult a matter he often found it to command the necessary funds even for what he did. It is only where he was permitted freely to develop his plans, and where he could think that he was not wasting his strength in enriching parts which few could behold, through the contraction of the streets or thoroughfares, that we can rightly estimate the architect's powers; and, in the fullest meaning of the words, *no* such opportunity was ever afforded him, not even in St. Paul's. Is not the grandeur of the whole of that building unquestionable? but how much grander would it have been had his first design (Fig. 2019), or even his later ones, been fully carried out!

At the commencement of the work, Sir Christopher Wren writes in the 'Parentalia'—"An incident was taken notice of by some people as a memorable omen: when the surveyor in person had set out upon the place the dimensions of the great dome, and fixed upon the centre, a common labourer was ordered to bring a flat stone from the heaps of rubbish (such as should first come to hand), to be laid for a mark and direction to the masons: the stone, which was immediately brought and laid down for that purpose, happened to be a piece of a gravestone, with nothing remaining of the inscription but this single word, in large capitals, '*Resurgam*' (I shall rise again)." The favourable omen was fully realised; and the second rising of St.

Paul's can scarcely be deemed inferior to the first, notwithstanding the advantage which the Gothic style generally has over the Italian-Roman style of Wren, both in its superior beauty and its fitness for the purpose in question. The dome alone of modern St. Paul's is enough to enable the building to stand up in rivalry against the mighty reputation of its predecessor. The interior of the Cathedral is of course fine, but does not correspond in grandeur of design with the exterior. The most favourable points of sight are from the western doorway, looking east (Fig. 2024), and from immediately beneath the dome (Fig. 2025). But the first impression, even in this last-mentioned spot, is somewhat disappointing to a careful observer, who comes with the impression of the exterior fresh upon his mind. The dome to such a one seems to have shrunk in space—to have descended in height most strangely. On inquiry he learns that the exterior dome is—if the word must be used—a sham; and covers two others, of which the lowermost only forms the real internal arch of the Cathedral.

If the artistical decorations of St. Paul's be taken as an evidence of the state of art in England at the time, which we believe they may with justice, we shall be compelled to entertain but a very low opinion of the latter. With but one exception, Gibbons' work in the choir, none of the original decorations are worth mentioning, apparently because, with the exception of Gibbons, none of the eminent sculptors of the day were employed. If, for instance, we desire to see any of the chief productions of the most fashionable English sculptors of the seventeenth century, Nicholas Stone, we must go to the Charter House to gaze upon his Sutton monument (Fig. 2023), or to Westminster Abbey, where we shall find his memorial of Sir Dudley Carleton (Fig. 2032). The carved wood-work of the choir (Fig. 2027), to which we have referred, is truly beautiful. Gibbons was dwelling in an obscure cottage at Deptford, carving the Stoning of St. Stephen, after Tintoretto, when Evelyn first drew him into notice. "The King saw the carving at Sir R. Browne's chambers, and was astonished at the curiosity of it, but was called away, and sent it to the Queen's chamber. There a French peddling woman, who used to bring baubles out of France for the ladies, begun to find fault with several things in it, which she understood no more than an ass or a monkey. So, in a kind of indignation, I caused it to be taken back, and sent down to the cottage again."

But the generous appreciation of Evelyn was soon followed by the appreciation of the King, and Court, and nation.

Wren himself is among the many eminent persons who rest under the mighty dome. He lies in the crypt (Fig. 2026); and over the entrance into the choir are these words in Latin:—"If you would behold his monument, look around."

One famous appendage of the old Cathedral had fallen before the Great Fire, and did *not* rise again. One of the last sermons preached from Paul's Cross (Figs. 1901, 2016), on the 30th of May, 1630, was attended by Charles I., who came in state to St. Paul's, and first heard the service in the Cathedral, and after that took a seat prepared for him in the open air before the door, to hear the sermon. The abolition of bishops, deans, and chapters took place in 1642, and was followed, in 1645, by the destruction of St. Paul's "Cross in the churchyard, which had been for many ages the most noted and solemn place in the nation for the gravest divines and greatest scholars to preach at;" and at the same time were destroyed all the rest of the crosses about London and Westminster, by further order of the said Parliament; among these may be enumerated the Cross of Cheapside (Fig. 1899). Another of the dependencies of old St. Paul's exists at this day—as repaired by Wren—the Convocation or Chapter House (Fig. 2017), in appearance a tall, substantial, dingy-looking mansion, in which the Convocation or parliament of the clergy sit, at the meeting of a new parliament of the kingdom, in order, it would seem, to prorogue themselves immediately. In the reign of William III., an energetic endeavour was made to turn the nominal into a real ecclesiastical parliament; but the ungracious age would not permit it; so the members of the Convocation meet, dream of, and occasionally perhaps sigh over the past glories of the Church, and then go away to repeat the process next time, and from thenceforward *ad infinitum*.

The Savoy (Fig. 1984) had been another famous meeting-place for Divines. Here the Independents drew up their Declaration of Faith in 1658; and here, three years later, a body of Episcopal met a body of the Presbyterian clergymen, and endeavoured to arrange the Book of Common Prayer to their mutual satisfaction. The attempt, however, failed. Baxter was one of the controversialists upon this occasion.

2052—Costume of the Nobility and Gentry, temp. Charles II.
(Selected from Ogilby's Coronation of Charles II., 1662, and Prints by Silvester, 1664.)

2053—Costume of the Commonalty, temp Charles II.
(Selected from Prints by Hollar and Silvester, 1664.)

2055.—"Fair Lemons and Oranges!"

2054—Costume of the Nobility and Gentry temp. James II.
(Selected from Sandford's Coronation of James II., 1687.)

2056—"Pots to mend!"

2057.—"Old Shoes for some Brooms."

2058.—"Four for Sixpence, Mackerel!"

2059.—Hackney Coachman, 1680.

2060.—Mountebank

2061.—"Oh Raree Show!"

2063.—Sir Hudibras addressing the Mob.

2065.—The Flight of the Bear.

2062.—Hudibras and Ralph.

2064.—The Bear at the Stake.

CHAPTER III.—POPULAR ANTIQUITIES.

HE changes during the century comprised between the commencement of the reign of James I. and the abdication of James II., are perhaps more remarkable than in any similar space of time which the history of English costume can furnish. Dress may be said during that period to have had both its age of gold and its age of lead. Nothing could be finer than the dresses Vandyke loved to paint: nothing more unnatural or absurd than the costume Kneller was often compelled to draw—we hope without loving it. The ancient beaux and belles of the latter part of the seventeenth century, in peruke and commode—with snuff-box and fan, taking their evening walk in the Mall, could comment to children and grandchildren on a hundred varieties of the popular aspect since they were young—since Queen Anne of Denmark (Fig. 2036) and her ladies went abroad in the enormous wheel fardingale, standing collar, and buckram bust of the Elizabethan style, and the gentlemen of the royal household and court in the ungainly stuffed and plaited garments that originated in the cowardly fears of her husband, King James I. We may glance at a few of the most conspicuous of these changes, and begin with those of the hair and its appendages. In the reign of Queen Anne of Denmark, the hair of the ladies was still frizzled, and crisped, and tortured into wreaths and borders, and " underpropped with forkes, wires," &c. (Stubbs), as in the time of Elizabeth, her predecessor. For some time after, the hat, often steeple-crowned, with a round or broad flapping brim, continued to shade the tresses of the middle classes generally (Figs. 2039 to 2042). The French hood was long a favourite wear with the puritanical gentlewoman. Then there was the " cap-kercher, and such like," of which Stubbs speaks. A fashionable lady would

wear a flowing coronet to-day,
The symbol of her beauty's sad decay;
To-morrow she a waving plume will try,
The emblem of all female levity:
Now in her hat, then in her hair is drest;
Now, of all fashions she thinks change the best.
Dramatic Pastoral, 1631.

Many a fair aspiring citizen also laid herself open to the censure of Luke, in the ' City Madam :'—

The reverend hood cast off, your *borrowed* hair
Powdered and curled, was, by your dresser's art,
Formed like a coronet, hanged with diamonds
And richest orient pearls.—MASSINGER.

But for once in the seventeenth century there was to be a time when the loveliest ornament bestowed by Nature on the human form was to be set free from unnatural constraint, as far as fashion was concerned. The glossy ringlets of the young gentlewoman of 1640 (Fig. 2038) drooped to the neck in all their native luxuriance, negligently confined by a simple rose, jewel, or bandeau of pearls. This is the style that has been transmitted to us in the bewitching portraits of the beauties of the Court of Charles II.; but its reign was too genuinely beautiful not to be brief, so it was succeeded by one of the most extraordinary contrasts conceivable, the tower, or commode, a regularly built-up pile of hair and ornaments. As to the decoration of the gentlemen's heads, it seems that after frizzing up the hair from the forehead, as in the portrait of Prince Henry (Fig. 2035), and suffering it to share in the freedom and luxuriance of that of the other sex, in the reign of Charles I., they next thought they would supersede it altogether; and, following the example of the ladies before mentioned *borrow* their hair. The French, from whom we have derived so many agreeable fashions, as if to counterbalance the obligations incurred, gave us also that odious invention of the flatterers of the " Grand Monarque," the peruke or periwig—made in imitation of his long waving curls

when he was a little boy. Charles II., most tasteless and fantastic in all his innovations, adopted the fashion, and very soon not a gentleman's head or shoulders was complete without the French wig. That was not the worst; the picturesque Spanish Sombrero did not suit the new contrivance; so it was flung aside for the sugar-loaf hat set round about with feathers or ribbons—we leave our reader to judge of the ludicrous effect in the general costumes of this reign (Fig. 2052). Archbishop Tillotson is the first English prelate represented in a wig, but the appendage was in his case small and natural-looking. "I can remember," he observes, in one of his sermons, " since the wearing the hair below the ears was looked upon as a sin of the first magnitude; and when ministers generally, whatever their text was, did either find or make occasion to reprove the great sin of long hair, and if they saw any one in the congregation guilty in that kind, they would point him out particularly, and let fly at him with great zeal." The age of full-bottomed wigs, however, had arrived, and the barbers were to fulfil their august mission. It became dangerous to one's intellectual reputation to resist. Farquhar, in his comedy of ' Love and a Bottle ' (1698), observes, that a full wig was as " infallible a token of wit as the laurel."

The fardingale of the sixteenth and beginning of the seventeenth centuries—most of our readers are aware—was the originator of the hooped petticoat of the eighteenth. An amusing story is told of this exquisite monstrosity in Bulwer's ' Pedigree of the English Gallant.' When Lady Wych, wife of the ambassador from James I. to the grand Seignior, appeared with her waiting-women in fardingales in the presence of the Sultaness, the latter was amazed at the extraordinary size of their hips, and seriously inquired if that shape was peculiar to the natural formation of the English women, and Lady Wych was obliged to explain the whole mystery of the dress, before she could convince the Sultaness that they were not in reality so deformed as they appeared to be. And when they had so convinced her, we fear the Sultaness would hardly congratulate them on the new views they had opened to her as to the objects of dress. But there was something liked even better than the fardingale; namely, the exercise of a capricious fancy that knew no limits of taste or sense: so of the lady of the time it is said, in illustration of the passion for extreme and continual changes,—

Now calls she for a boisterous fardingall;
Then to her hips she'll have her garments fall.

As with the hair, so with the dress: there was a time during this century (the period of the war) when ladies of fashion were contented to imitate nature. And if the rich flowing train be esteemed an innovation upon what may be called a natural style of costume, it was a very pardonable one. After the Restoration, this continued the style of the Court for some considerable time; but the century went out, and its successor came in, with so many flounces and furbelows, that the wearers seemed all " in curl,"—" like one of those animals," as Addison says, " which in the country we call a Friezland hen." In some respects the gentlemen offered a still broader mark for the satirist. The huge trunks of James I. were changed into " the long sawsedge hose, and breeches pinned up like pudding-bags," of which Ben Jonson speaks in his ' Tale of a Tub,'—a fashion that at once signifies its Dutch origin. The straight and loose nether garments of the Vandyke costume met the ruffles of the boot tops, and were richly fringed or pointed. After these came Charles II.'s " petticoat breeches;" which Randal Holmes, 1659, thus describes: " The lining, being lower than the breeches, is tied above the knees: the breeches are ornamented with ribands up to the pocket, and half their breadth upon the thigh; the waistband is set about with ribands, and the shirt hanging out *over them*." These choice inventions again subsided under James II., and, as though to restrain all future unseemliness of bulk, were tied beneath the knee. The Puritan (Fig. 2049) or Oliverian, in every article of his dress contrasted with the Cavalier (Fig. 2044), as by his contempt of the caprices of fashion, by his choice of coarser and darker stuffs, and by his rejection of ornament; but in the doublet especially this contrast was remarkable. That of the Puritan was homely, sombre, and plain; that of the Cavalier of silk, satin, or velvet, of the richest colours, with loose full sleeves, slashed in front; or, for military service, it was the buff coat, as much adorned as the nature of the dress could possibly admit of: the collar of this superb doublet was of the costliest point lace; a sword-belt of the most magnificent kind crossed over one shoulder; whilst a rich scarf encircled the waist, and was tied in a large bow at the side.

Charles II. curtailed the doublet of its fair proportions, made it excessively short, and opened it in front to display a rich shirt, bulging out, without any waistcoat: then it must have holland sleeves, of extravagant size and fantastical contrivance, as in our engraving (Fig. 2052), where one figure appears so absurdly disguised with these sleeves, and with the periwig,—projecting shoe-ties, and other singularities, as to appear almost unreal. In a short time, however, all this was sobered down—but not until Charles II. with all his fopperies and vices had passed for ever from the scene. The sleeves of the ladies' dresses, and the drapery and ornaments of the bust, continued in admirable taste throughout the greater part of the century. The free use of the Vandyke lace had often a fine effect, as may be seen in our engravings of the Lady of Quality (Fig. 2037), and the rich Merchant's Wife (Fig 2039).

Massinger in 'The City Madam' (1659), speaks of the ladies' slippers, or

> Rich pantables, in ostentation shown,
> And roses worth a family;

while Taylor the Water-Poet, tells us a gallant would

> Wear a farm in shoe-strings edged with gold,
> And spangled garters worth a copyhold.

The courtier's wide boots, so finely in keeping with the rest of his chivalric and magnificent dress, appears to have almost banished the shoes thus richly adorned, which, however, regained their popularity under Charles II., when they were ornamented with large projecting bows of ribbon. In the next reign (James II.) succeeded the sober substantial shoe, with very high instep.

We cannot stay to dwell on all the other changes that characterized the dresses of the period: as in the

> — gaudy cloak three mansions' price almost:

or in the vests, coats, and waistcoats: nor shall we attempt to use any other language than the poet's in enumerating the host of articles of wear and ornament that filled the wardrobes or occupied the dressing-tables of the votaries of fashion; the

> Chains, coronets, pendants, bracelets, and ear-rings;
> Pins, girdles, spangles, embroideries, and rings;
> Shadows, rebatoes, ribands, ruffs, cuffs, falls,
> Scarfs, feathers, fans, masks, muffs, laces, cauls,
> Thin taffanies, cobweb-lawn, and fardingals,
> Sweet falls, veils, wimples, glasses, crisping-pins,
> Pots of ointment, combs, with poking-sticks and bodkins,
> Coifs, gorgets, fringes, rolls, fillets, and hair-laces.
> *Dramatic Pastoral.*

The great starched ruff had been rendered unfashionable by the fair Mrs. Turner's making her exit in one at Tyburn. But for some time the matronly part of the community favoured them, and they often appeared in the full dress of the great civic dames, as in our engraving of a Lady Mayoress (Fig. 2041). The fan, exhibited in the cut just referred to, and in that of the Lady of Quality, was a most elegant and picturesque ornament for a lady's hand: it was composed of ostrich or other rare and costly feathers. The carved fan, its successor, however beautiful in itself, is not for a moment to be compared with it. In a licentious age we shall generally find that masks are prevalent—of course, therefore, they were in that of Charles II. The muffler, an article of dress at least as ancient as the time of the prophet Isaiah (iii. 19), and in all probability very much older, had not yet ceased to defend the elderly or the delicate English female from the perilous winter cold of our bleak climate. Among the country people (Fig. 2042), however, they would be more prevalent than in towns. Lastly, let us observe, that if from parts we turn to costume as a whole, there is one figure among our engravings—that of the Merchant's Wife of London (Fig. 2039)—which may be taken as a model of gracefulness and unaffected elegance—in short, of true taste.

Armour, on the decline at the close of the last period, continued to be used through the Civil Wars, though it did not exactly justify James I.'s characteristic praise—that it not only saved the life of the wearer, but hindered him from doing hurt to anybody else. Many a life was lost, clad in complete steel or nearly so, and many a life was taken by the heavily-armed cavalry soldier. Helmets

(Fig. 2050) or head-pieces were invariably worn in the field. Those of the Cavalier (Fig. 2044) and Cuirassier (Fig. 2048) were in general crowned with plumes. The Dragoon (Fig. 2051), whose order was first raised in France in 1600, by the Marshal de Brisac, wore in our armies a stout buff coat with deep skirts. Infantry armour (Fig. 2045) consisted of back and breast pieces, worn over a buff coat, and with throat pieces and skull-cap, the cheeks being also defended. One of our military cuts represents a soldier of the Trained Bands, 1638 (Fig. 2047); a name which may remind some of our readers of Cowper's famous hero—

> A train-band Captain eke was he
> Of famous London Town.

The trained bands were the ridicule of the Cavaliers, as being composed of apprentices, artisans, and shopkeepers of London: they were called the "thimble and bodkin army," on account of their being supported in their resolute stand against Charles I. by all sorts of contributions from poor and rich in and around London. But they proved the chief means by which the first important victory was gained over Charles, in a battle in which even Clarendon says they "behaved themselves to wonder."

When the pikemen and musketeers of these civic militia first became actual soldiers, their costume was not altogether that of the regular military Pikemen (Fig. 2046) and Musketeer (Fig. 2034), but they "marched to the field in high-crowned hats, collared bands, great loose coats, long tucks under them, and calves'-leather boots;" and in this dress "they used to sing a psalm, fall on, and beat all opposition to the devil."—(Shadwell's comedy of 'The Volunteers.')

———

Alexander Gell, a bachelor of divinity, was sentenced to lose his ears and to be degraded from the ministry, for saying of Charles I. "that he was fitter to stand in a Cheapside shop, with an apron before him, and say 'What lack ye?' than to govern a kingdom." Scott, in his 'Fortunes of Nigel,' has for ever popularized the custom here referred to, of the shopkeepers of Cheapside, and other principal thoroughfares of London, standing at the doors of shops, resembling booths or stalls, and emulating one another's sweet voices in the constant cry, "What lack ye? What d'ye lack?" Among the cries of London, then, may safely be included the occupations of its tradesmen generally; who kept up, as it were, a daily fair, all through the metropolis. Much of the trade of London was carried on by itinerants, then a more respectable and thriving class than at present; these, too, had their cries; and their vociferations more than rivalled those of the shopkeepers. Among the noisiest of them were the venders of oranges, fish, and brooms. The orange-woman's cry, though shrill, was often musical—

> Fair lemons and oranges (Fig. 2055),
> Oranges and citrons!

"Four for sixpence, mackerel!" (Fig. 2058) was the cry of a fish-wife, such as we still hear every day. "Old shoes for some brooms!" (Fig. 2057) indicated a state of things when street-barter was much more extensively practised than at present, though the custom has by no means disappeared. If we do not so often as of old hear the cry of "Pots to mend!" (Fig. 2056), and if the tinker has ceased to be the popular personage he once was, the fraternity has not yet wholly gone out; his utility has preserved him. The absence of utility, or we may rather say, positive mischievousness, has caused the disappearance of other street-trading classes; and among them, of the Medical Mountebank (Fig. 2060), who, during three centuries or more, travelled with his wonderful appliances for the cure of all diseases. At markets and fairs, and other crowded places, would he exhibit his pills and phials, and endeavour to sell them to the people by means of humorous or bombastic speeches. From such jocosities the famous mountebank of 1547, Dr. *Andrew* Borde, was called "Merry Andrew"—a name still applied to all of the mountebank genus. The popular character of the mountebank seems to have undergone very little change from the days of Dr. Borde to those when the 'Spectator' immortalized the Hammersmith *Artist*, and his irresistible jest of giving five shillings to every native of Hammersmith, for the exceeding love he bore to the place; and who fulfilled his generous purpose by giving them a quantity of physic for sixpence, that he assured them was constantly sold for five shillings and sixpence. Truly the mountebank belonged to an amusing though most impudent and unprincipled class. How he was accustomed to make even roguery itself an instrument for the dissemination of philosophy, the well-known tale "Conceit can kill, conceit can cure," informs us. Indeed, we may say of him as Henry V. said of Falstaff, we could well have spared a better man

2068.—Hudibras subdued by Trulla.

2069.—The Knight and Squire conveyed to the Stocks.

2066.—The Bear Rescued.

2067.—Combat of Hudibras with Orsin and Cerdon.

212

2072.—Procession of the Skimmington.

2071.—The Knight and Squire released from the Stocks.

2070.—The Lady visiting the Knight in the Stocks

2073.—Escape of Hudibras and Ralpho.

From the same curious collection of originals whence our cut of the mountebank is taken, we present to the reader's view an old English Raree-showman (Fig. 2061), whose name, Caulfield tells us, was Old Harry. The contents of his raree-show were various and wonderful, especially to the eyes of the rising generation. There were—

> The fleas that run at tilt
> Upon a table;

a tame hedgehog, a wonderful snake, and other such specimens of the marvellous.

About the reign of James I. the drivers of both private and public vehicles had no other accommodation than a bar, or driver's chair, placed very low behind the horses: in the following reign (Charles I.) they ride more after postilion fashion; after the Restoration they appeared with whip and spurs (Fig. 2059); and towards the end of the century mount to a "coachman's box." This *box*, covered with a *hammer*-cloth, was often in reality a box; and within it, or in a leather pouch attached to it, were tools for mending broken wheels or shivered panels, in the event of accidents occurring in the street or road, which were by no means uncommon; in consequence, first, of the defective construction of the vehicles—(D'Avenant says they were "uneasily hung, and so narrow that I took them for sedans on wheels") (Figs. 2131, 2132); in the second place, from the clumsy driving of carmen in the crowded thoroughfares; and in the third place, and principally, from the nature of the streets themselves, full of all the worst perils a coachman could have to encounter. What a picture is that Gay has left us, in reference to the beginning of the eighteenth century, when, if there was any difference, we may presume there must have been some improvement upon the state of the streets that prevailed during a little earlier period!—

> Where a dim gleam the paly lantern throws
> O'er the mid pavement, heapy rubbish grows,
> Or arched vaults their gaping jaws extend,
> Or the dark caves to common-shores descend;
> Oft by the winds extinct the signal lies,
> Or smother'd in the glimmering socket dies
> Ere Night has half rolled round her ebon throne;
> In the wide gulf the shatter'd coach o'erthrown
> Sinks with the snorting steeds; the reins are broke,
> And from the crackling axle flies the spoke.

The sedan (Figs. 2129, 2130), which is still occasionally to be seen emerging from the oblivion into which we thought it had passed for ever, was in full vogue during the present period.

If the wittiest writer in the English—perhaps, indeed, in any—language had but been also an unprejudiced observer of the men and things he described, 'Hudibras' would to this hour have stood unrivalled since the days of Chaucer, as a glowing, life-like view of the state of English society, and as a piece of most wholesome satire of all that was absurd, or vicious, or criminal in it. Unhappily Butler's partiality is as notorious as his wit; and it is indispensable that we get rid of the faintest notion of any real likeness between the "Presbyterians" and "Independents" of his verse, and the men who overthrew Charles and Laud, before we can properly estimate and enjoy the amazing amount of literary wealth that has been expended upon the work in question. True courage and dignity, for instance, are among the last qualities the writer of 'Hudibras' would appear to be willing to ascribe to the "rebels," yet if *he* forgets that they overthrew his strong and gallant party, with a king at their head, *we* cannot; neither is it easy to find aught calculated to arouse contempt (whatever deeper emotions may be called into existence) when we read of the conduct of the Puritans in their prosperity during the trial of Charles, or in their adversity, when they sealed with their blood, at the Restoration, the cause they thought so just and holy. But perhaps the most striking of all evidences of Butler's unfitness to judge of those to whom he was politically opposed, is his mention of a contemporary writer, Withers, one of the truest poets that ever adorned a country, but who being a Puritan *must* also be a fool—in 'Hudibras.' Butler, appealing to the Muse, says—

> Thou that with ale, or viler liquors,
> Didst inspire Withers, Prynne, and Vickers,
> And force them, though it was in spite
> Of Nature, and their stars, to write:—&c.

The fact appears to be that Butler did not draw the materials for his great satire from any one party or sect alone, but that he did endeavour to fasten the odium and ridicule excited by his exposure solely upon those particular bodies to whom he had been politically opposed. The consequences are just what Butler ought to have expected,—we reject his cherished and extravagant bigotries, and admire him less, to say the least of it, for having imposed upon us such a task. But when all is done, we find ourselves in possession of a work that must ever be looked upon with interest, and admiration, and wonder, for the broad and unctuous humour, the brilliant and sparkling wit, and the depth and universality of satirical observation that overflows in every page. There are few better evidences of literary greatness than may be found in the frequency with which an author's phrases and sentences, or peculiar thoughts, are perceived to be mingling in the common business and conversations of life. Now we are all constantly quoting Butler, from the statesman—who, when he propounds a new measure, reminds us that

> Doubtless the pleasure is as great
> Of being cheated, as to cheat—

down to the cynical humourist of the fireside, who tells his good dame

> There are no bargains driven
> Nor marriages clapp'd up in heaven,
> And that's the reason, as some guess,
> There is no heaven in marriages.

The poet informs us at the commencement, that

> When civil dudgeon first grew high,
> And men fell out they knew not why;
> When hard words, jealousies, and fears
> Set folks together by the ears;

in other words, when the Civil Wars began, then did Hudibras, or, as Butler calls him, Sir Knight,

> abandon dwelling,
> And out he rode a-colonelling.

A long description of the Knight's intellectual qualities now ensues, from which we learn that

> although he had much wit,
> He was very shy of using it;

and that he was extremely learned, extremely critical—he could

> divide
> A hair 'twixt south and south-west side,—

extremely eloquent, and poetical in his eloquence—

> he could not ope
> His mouth, but out there flew a trope,—

and, lastly, very religious, though belonging to a party who

> prove their doctrines orthodox
> By apostolic blows and knocks,

and whose

> chief devotion lies
> In odd perverse antipathies;
> In falling out with that or this,
> And finding somewhat still amiss;
> More peevish, cross, and splenetic,
> Than dog distract, or monkey sick;
> That with more care keep holy-day
> The wrong, than others the right way;
> Compound for sins they are inclined to,
> By damning those they have no mind to.

The wit of these lines, subtle and anatomizing as it is, is even less remarkable than the vivid truth of character conveyed in them. Who does not know many a Hudibras, now actively bustling about the world, engaged in schemes at once Quixotic, fanatical, and what is, or looks terribly like, hypocrisy? Of the Knight's outer man we must let the poet speak at length:—

> His tawny beard was th' equal grace
> Both of his wisdom and his face;
> In cut and dye so like a tile,
> A sudden view it would beguile:
> The upper part whereof was whey;
> The nether, orange mixed with grey.
> This hairy meteor did denounce
> The fall of sceptres and of crowns.

In form the Knight was somewhat heavy behind; but then—

> To poise this equally, he bore
> A paunch of the same bulk before;
> Which still he had a special care
> To keep well crammed with thrifty fare;
> As white-pot, butter-milk, and curds
> Such as a country-house affords;
> With other victual, which anon
> We further shall dilate upon,
> When of his hose we come to treat,
> The cupboard where he kept his meat.

His doublet was of sturdy buff,
And though not sword, yet cudgel-proof;
Whereby 'twas fitter for his use,
Who fear'd no blows, but such as bruise.
His breeches were of rugged woollen,
And had been at the siege of Bullen;
To old King Harry so well known,
Some writers held they were his own.
Through they were lined with many a piece
Of ammunition bread and cheese,
And fat black-puddings, proper food
For warriors that delight in blood.

The poet remarks that the statement that the old knights-errant did not eat, is false; and instances King Arthur, who, he says, was accustomed to carry, in a huge pair of round trunk hose, enough meat for himself and all his knights. But to continue the description of Hudibras:—

His puissant sword unto his side,
Near his undaunted heart, was tied;
With basket-hilt that would hold broth,
And serve for fight and dinner both.
In it he melted lead for bullets,
To shoot at foes, and sometimes pullets,
To whom he bore so fell a grutch,
He ne'er gave quarter t' any such.
The trenchant blade, Toledo trusty,
For want of fighting was grown rusty,
And ate into itself for lack
Of somebody to hew and hack.
The peaceful scabbard where it dwelt,
The rancour of its edge had felt;
For of the lower end two handful
It had devoured, 'twas so manful;
And so much scorn'd to lurk in case,
As if it durst not show its face.
In many desperate attempts,
Of warrants, exigents, contempts,
It had appear'd with courage bolder
Than Serjeant Bum invading shoulder.
Oft had it ta'en possession,
And pris'ners too, or made them run.
This sword a dagger had, his page,
That was but little for his age;
And therefore waited on him so,
As dwarfs upon knights-errant do.
It was a serviceable dudgeon,
Either for fighting or for drudging.
When it had stabb'd, or broke a head,
It would scrape trenchers, or chip bread;
Toast cheese or bacon; tho' it were
To bait a mouse-trap, 'twould not care;
'T would make clean shoes; and in the earth
Set leeks and onions, and so forth
It had been 'prentice to a brewer,
Where this and more it did endure;
But left the trade, as many more
Have lately done, on the same score—

an allusion to Cromwell, that was no doubt mightily enjoyed by all the Royalists. He, however, does not appear to have been himself engaged in the brewing business, as is here intimated, although his parents were.

The Knight, as we see in the first (Fig. 2062) of the series of engravings by Mr. Harvey, contained in pages 209 to 220, has a companion not unworthy of himself. This is his Squire,

whose name was Ralph,
That in th' adventure went his half:
Though writers, for more stately tone
Do call him Ralpho, 'tis all one:
And when we can, with metre safe,
We'll call him so; if not, plain Ralph:
(For rhyme the rudder is of verses,
With which, like ships, they steer their courses).
An equal stock of wit and valour
He had laid in; by birth a tailor.
The mighty Tyrian queen, that gain'd
With subtle shreds a tract of land,
Did leave it with a castle fair
To his great ancestor, her heir;
From him descended cross-legged knights,
Fam'd for their faith and warlike fights
Against the bloody cannibal,
Whom they destroy'd both great and small.
This sturdy Squire, he had, as well
As the bold Trojan knights, seen hell;
Not with a counterfeited pass
Of golden boughs, but true gold-lace.
His knowledge was not far behind
The Knight's, but of another kind,
And he another way came by 't:
Some call it Gifts, and some New Light:

A lib'ral art that costs no pains
Of study, industry, or brains.
His wit was sent him for a token,
But in the carriage crack'd and broken;
Like commendation nine-pence, crook'd,
With—To and from my love—it look'd.

This ninepence was a common coin prior to the year 1696, when all the money that was not milled was called in, and this particular one kept in thenceforth. The custom of bending a coin till it became "crooked," and usable as a lover's token, survived, however, almost down to our own time, as the prolific numbers of deformed pieces, everywhere seen in circulation but a few years ago, sufficiently show.

Ralph, it appears, was one of those who referred every question to the light that had been vouchsafed to him—the New Light, as it was commonly called, of which Butler says,

'T is a dark lantern of the spirit,
Which none see by but those that bear it:
A light that falls down from on high,
For spiritual trades to cozen by.

Of course, under such circumstances, Ralph considered himself infallible. The poet tells us he was a deep occult philosopher, who understood Jacob Behmen, and was familiar with the Rosicrucian lore; who could explain the discourses of birds, and the origin of matter; and who, without the aid of astrology, could foretell all mighty things that were to happen, as great diseases, battles, and inundations. Such, then, were the pair who set forth to seek adventures.

There is a town in the western parts of England, whither

people did repair
On days of market, or of fair,
And to crack'd fiddle and hoarse tabor
In merriment did drudge and labour.

In this last line, so characteristic of our rural population at the present time, we see that the mirth of which we hear so much in connection with old England, was still anything but a spontaneous, impulsive, habitual joyousness of character. What Butler said in the seventeenth century is precisely what foreigners say of us in the nineteenth—that we do drudge and labour even in our recreations.

But something more than the ordinary attractions of a market or fair have now

rak'd together village rabble;
'T was an old way of recreating,
Which learned butchers call Bear-baiting:
A bold advent'rous exercise,
With ancient heroes in high prize;
For authors do affirm it came
From Isthmean or Nemean game:
Others derive it from the Bear
That's fixed in northern hemisphere,
And round about the pole doth make
A circle, like a bear at stake,
That at the chain's end wheels about,
And overturns the rabble rout;
For, after solemn proclamation
In the bear's name (as is the fashion,
According to the law of arms,
To keep men from inglorious harms,)
That none presume to come so near
As forty foot of stake of bear.

The poet here describes exactly the preliminaries of the famous bull-runnings of Tutbury in Staffordshire, where the "solemn proclamation" was made in these words—"That all manner of persons give way to the bull, none being to come near him by forty foot, any way to hinder the minstrels, but to attend to his or their own safety, every one at his peril." (Plot's 'Staffordshire.') Towards the scene of this bear-baiting, which we learn from a subsequent passage was at Brentford, the Knight

his course did steer,
To keep the peace 'twixt dog and bear—

as he believed he was bound to do. And on his way he explained to the Squire his views, and why he thought it best to save the expense of Christian blood, and try by mediation to compose the quarrel without blows. As he justly observes—

Are not *our* liberties, our lives,
The laws, religion, and our wives,
Enough at once to lie at stake
For Cov'nant and the Cause's sake,
But in that quarrel, dogs and bears,
As well as we, must venture theirs?

Ralph agrees that it is an unchristian sport, unlawful alike in name and substance,—that, as to the name,

2074.—Hudibras and Sidrophel.

JACKSON SC.

2075.—Combat of Hudibras and Sidrophel.

2076.—Hudibras and the Goblins.

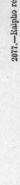

2077.—Ralpho rescuing the Knight.

2080.—The Assembly alarmed.

2081.—The Assembly dispersing.

2079.—'Poor Presbyter.'—Field preaching.

—'A mongrel kind of church dragoon.'

the word Bear-baiting
Is carnal, and of man's creating ;

and as to the thing itself,—

A vile assembly 'tis, that can
No more be proved by Scripture than
Provincial, classic, national ;
Mere human creature cobwebs all.

Ralpho is here, under colour of agreeing with the Knight on the bear-baiting question, slily enforcing his views of the similar un-lawfulness of Hudibras's favourite religious bodies ; the Knight being a Presbyterian, whilst Ralph is an Independent, if not even " something more "—an Anabaptist. So

Quoth Hudibras, I smell a rat ;
Ralpho, thou dost prevaricate ;

and one of the numerous arguments between the two that are found in the poem, is begun, but for the time interrupted by the Knight's reflection, that neither the time nor place was suitable. The field is not far off where they must give the world a proof of deeds, and not words, and the Godly must not be deceived. At the same time he remarks in a strain not unworthy of the real men and real events that Butler covertly alludes to, but it must be owned a little incon-sistent in their earnestness and truth with the particular individual and incident in question, that success is a

mark no mortal wit,
Or surest hand, can always hit ,
For whatsoe'er we perpetrate,
We do but row, we're steer'd by Fate,
Which in success oft disinherits,
For spurious causes, noblest merits.
Great actions are not always true sons
Of great and mighty resolutions ;
Nor do the bold'st attempts bring forth
Events still equal to their worth,
But sometimes fail, and in their stead
Fortune and cowardice succeed.

In the concluding part of this speech we find the poet clearly iden-tifying Hudibras with one who is understood to have been his patron :—

'Tis sung, there is a valiant Mameluke
In foreign land ycleped [Sir Samuel Luke*],
To whom we have been oft compared
For person, parts, address, and beard.

The name we have enclosed in brackets is that of the gentleman, a Puritan, and one of Cromwell's officers, in whose service Butler spent some time, and it is evidently the name with which Butler intended the hiatus to be filled.

Let us now pass to the place where the bear, chained to his stake (Fig. 2064), is waiting the attacks of the dogs, and the assemblage of people is constantly increasing around. The doughty warrior having approached with due care so as to make himself acquainted with their numbers and order, and having charged his pistols, and drawn with great difficulty his rusty sword from the scabbard, has advanced directly before them, and is now, as the artist shows him (Fig. 2063), addressing the people, and their leaders—Crowdero, the fiddler ; Orsin, the bearward ; Talgol, the butcher, " mortal foe to cows ;" Magnano, the tinker, who in magic was as

deeply read
As he that made the brazen head ;

Trulla, his female—but not very feminine companion ; Cerdon, the cobbler, of whom it is said,

preaching was his chiefest talent.
Or argument, in which being valiant,
He used to lay about and stickle
Like ram or bull, at conventicle ;

and lastly, Colon, a bold man of war, but cruel and remorseless.

The description of the combat would suffer from any analysis, besides being out of place here, in which we only notice the poem as an illustration of manners. The engravings which we give will furnish the best notion of the costume of the time, and of the com-bat itself (Figs. 2066, 2067, 2068, 2069, 2070, 2071).

The procession of the Skimmington (Fig. 2072) forms the subject of one of our illustrations. This was a pageant formerly common enough in England, but which has now fallen into such general disuse, that only faint traces of the custom are to be found. Here is But-ler's description of the Skimmington :—

---

* Or, should it not be,—Sir Sammy Luke ?

First, he that led the cavalcate
Wore a sow-gelder's flageolet,
On which he blew as strong a levet,
As well-feed lawyer on his brev'ate ;
When over one another's heads
They charge (three ranks at once) like Sweeds.
Next pans, and kettles of all keys,
From trebles down to double bass ;
And after them, upon a nag,
That might pass for a forehand stag,
A cornet rode, and on his staff
A smock display'd did proudly wave.
Then bagpipes of the loudest drones,
With snuffling broken-winded tones,
Whose blasts of air, in pockets shut,
Sound filthier than from the gut,
And make a viler noise than swine
In windy weather when they whine.
Next one upon a pair of panniers,
Full fraught with that which for good manners
Shall here be nameless, mix'd with grains,
Which he dispens'd among the swains,
And busily upon the crowd
At random round about bestow'd.
Then, mounted on a horned horse,
One bore a gauntlet and gilt spurs,
Ty'd to the pummel of a long sword
He held revers'd, the point turn'd downward.
Next after, on raw-bon'd steed,
The conqu'ror's Standard-bearer rid,
And bore aloft before the champion
A petticoat display'd, and rampant ;
Near whom the Amazon triumphant
Bestrid her beast, and on the rump on't,
Sat face to tail, and bum to bum,
The warrior whilom overcome ;
Arm'd with a spindle and a distaff,
Which as he rode she made him twist off :
And when he loiter'd, o'er her shoulder
Chastis'd the reformado soldier.
Before the dame, and round about,
March'd whifflers, and staffiers on foot,
With lackeys, grooms, valets, and pages,
In fit and proper equipages ;
Of whom, some torches bore, some links,
Before the proud virago-minx,
That was both Madam and a Don,
Like Nero's Sporus, or Pope Joan ;
And at fit periods the whole rout
Set up their throats with clam'rous shout.

Hudibras's ire is greatly excited by the spectacle ; he says it is heathenish, and points out a variety of circumstances illustrative of a pagan origin ; and although Ralph takes a more common-place and sensible view of the custom, the knight determines to interfere, and therefore advances and addresses the crowd, urging the dis-honour it does to women, and the services they had rendered to the Cause. Our engraving of the Escape of Hudibras and Ralph may show (Fig. 2073) the ill success of the Knight's eloquence.

The poet next opens to us quite a new chapter in literary his-tory, having for its object the exposure of one of the most extra-ordinary classes of deceivers the world has ever seen, men who often no doubt deceived themselves, but who were ever deceiving others, and yet were still trusted in, and allowed to exercise a most potent influence over the conduct not only of men, but of nations. We refer to the astrologers ; and more particularly to the profes-sional ones. Butler has the great merit of having been the very first eminent writer who attacked the irrational faith in astrology, and who showed the stuff of which the art and its paid expounders were made. Of course we must make allowances for a little exag-geration : the man, Lilly (Fig. 2158), for instance, was probably a much less contemptible personage than Butler makes his other self, Sidrophel ; but the professional astrologer class unquestionably afforded ample materials for the masterly exposures of Hudibras.

The most eminent of the names intimately connected with astro-logy, in modern times at least, is that of John Dee (Fig. 2155), a man of remarkable ability and learning, who at the age of twenty made a tour on the Continent for the purpose—unusual with per-sons of his age—of holding scientific converse with the most emi-nent European scholars. In 1543 he was made a fellow of Trinity College, Cambridge, just then founded by Henry VIII. ; but, five years later, we find him entering into a kind of voluntary exile, by a second Continental expedition, caused by the suspicions he had excited at home of his dealings in the Black Art, in which term, however, all kinds of legitimate studies that the vulgar could not understand were included. Dee, for instance, was an able astro-nomer and a skilful mechanician ; and these attainments alone, had he not been an astrologer also, would have sufficed to have made him one in the eyes of the world of England in the sixteenth century. While on the Continent he wrote those prefaces and lectures on Euclid referred to by Butler in the character of Sidrophel, who, he says, had

> road Dee's prefaces, before
> The Dev'l and Euclid, o'er and o'er.

Dee returned to England during the reign of Edward VI., and was presented at Court, and received a pension, which he subsequently resigned for a country rectory. But in the reign of Mary the old suspicions revived in a still more concentrated and dangerous shape: he was accused of practising against the queen's life by enchantment; but the charge ultimately fell to the ground. In this matter Dee appears as a friend of the princess, afterwards Queen Elizabeth, who on her accession caused him to be consulted as to the choice of a propitious day for her coronation; and subsequently, as supposed, employed him on more than one occasion, as a secret messenger abroad. The rumours of his dealing with the devil all this time, grew more and more into belief with the populace, who at last assembled round his house at Mortlake in Surrey, and destroyed his collection of books, instruments, &c., and would probably have killed him and his whole family but for their escape.

It is in connection, however, with another personage, Edward Kelly (Fig. 2156), that the lovers of the miraculous have become most familiar with the name of Doctor Dee. Kelly entered his service as an assistant in 1581, and then, according to the ordinary accounts, were commenced the "conversations with spirits." The two magicians, it seems, had a black mirror, formed, some say, of a stone, others, of a piece of polished cannel coal; and in this they could at pleasure induce the angels Gabriel and Raphael to appear at their invocation. Thus we read in Hudibras,

> Kelly did all his feats upon
> The devil's looking-glass—a stone.

It is also said that they transformed base metals into gold in the castle of a Bohemian nobleman, where in consequence they lived in great affluence; but there seems much reason to believe that from first to last Elizabeth was accustomed to employ Dee as a " secret intelligencer " on the Continent, and that therefore Dee did not care to contradict the marvels told of him, since they turned away the public attention, both at home and abroad, from the nature of his real avocations; the appointment of Dee to the Wardenship of the College of Manchester in 1595, supports this view; as it appears to be a reward suitable to such a man for long political services. Many of the particulars of Dee's life are obtained from the autobiographical memoirs of the next astrologer we shall mention, William Lilly, the Sidrophel to whom Butler will presently introduce us in his version of the character.

Lilly's entrance into the world was in the humble capacity of servant to a mantua-maker; but it was not long before he exchanged this post for that of a kind of clerkship to the Master of the Salters' Company, who, being an illiterate man, required some one to keep his accounts. When he died, Lilly married the widow, who was wealthy; and after her death, Lilly by a second marriage still further improved his fortunes. And then, under the superintendence of a clergyman who had been expelled the church for fraudulent practices, he began the study of astrology, and speedily made himself such an adept in it, that his fame extended far and wide; and men of all parties, during the troublous times of the war, sought his advice and the benefit of his lore. Thus we find him at one time high in the favour of King Charles I., who even asked his opinion as to the propriety of agreeing with the Parliamentary propositions; whilst at another, he is under engagements with the Parliament, to furnish them with " perfect knowledge of the chiefest concerns of France ;" and on yet a third occasion, sitting as one of the members of the close commission of the Parliament who are debating the subject of the death of the monarch just named. But Lilly's popularity with the million chiefly originated in his almanac, which he began to publish in 1644, under the title of ' Merlinus Anglicus, Junior.' This obtained an amazing circulation, and was followed by a host of similar productions, of whose authors, John Gadbury (Fig. 2157) was one of the most notorious in his own day, whilst Francis Moore (Fig. 2154) even yet remains famous in ours. There is one incident of Lilly's career which illustrates very forcibly the state of public opinion at the time: a rumour prevailed about the year 1634, that vast treasures were hidden beneath the cloisters of Westminster Abbey, and at last Lilly was called in to decide the question by the use of Mosaical or miners' rods. The permission of the dean had to be sought, and it was granted; but only on the condition that he should have a share in the proceeds. Lilly, in the darkness of

night, attended by thirty gentlemen, each carrying a hazel rod, stalked in solemn array into the cloisters, where graves were opened, coffins removed, and the rods incessantly applied, but without effect; when suddenly a great storm burst out, and the imaginations of the explorers, already sufficiently excited by the place, the time, and the mysterious nature of the influence they were endeavouring to put into operation, became utterly uncontrollable, and the whole party scampered away in a frenzy of alarm, as fast as their legs could carry them. It is to be hoped the dean had a " share " of this, the only result of the unseemly disturbance of the ashes of the dead, that he had sanctioned in the hope or profit. Turn we now to Butler's astrologer, Sidrophel (Figs. 2074, 2075), who

> had been long t'wards mathematics,
> Optics, philosophy, and statics,
> Magic, horoscopy, astrology;
> And was old dog at physiology:
> But, as a dog that turns the spit,
> Bestirs himself, and plies his feet
> To climb the wheel, but all in vain,
> His own weight brings him down again;
> And still he's in the selfsame place
> Where at his setting out he was:
> So in the circle of the arts,
> Did he advance his nat'ral parts;
> Till falling back still for retreat,
> He fell to juggle, cant, and cheat,
> For as those fowls that live in water
> Are never wet, he did but smatter;
> Whate'er he labour'd to appear,
> His understanding still was clear.
> Yet none a deeper knowledge boasted,
> Since old Hodge Bacon and Bob Grosted.
> Th' intelligible world he knew,
> And all men dream on't to be true;
> That in this world there 's not a wart
> That has not there a counterpart;
> Nor can there on the face of ground
> An individual beard be found,
> That has not in that foreign nation
> A fellow of the selfsame fashion;
> So cut, so colour'd, and so curl'd,
> As those are in th' inferior world.
> He 'ad read Dee's prefaces, before
> The Dev'l and Euclid, o'er and o'er;
> And all th' intrigues 'twixt him and Kelly,
> Lascus and the Emperor, would tell ye;
> But with the moon was more familiar
> Than e'er was almanac well-willer;
> Her secrets understood so clear,
> That some believed he had been there,
> Knew when she was in fittest mood
> For cutting corns, or letting blood;
> When for anointing scabs or itches.

Butler then amuses himself at the expense of the newly-established Royal Society. Sidrophel's power and skill were as great as his knowledge was extensive:

> He made a planetary gin
> Which rats would run their own heads in,
> And come on purpose to be taken,
> Without the expense of cheese or bacon;

He could

> Fire a mine in China here
> With sympathetic gunpowder;

and do a thousand other marvellous things, far surpassing any that were understood by the philosophers who assembled in Gresham College. It is no injury to say of a body that, even in its commencement, exhibited a most honourable enthusiasm for learning, with a great deal of talent, to enable them to develop that enthusiasm wisely, that it did enter into some absurd speculations, and thus afforded a fair mark for Butler's satire. What, for instance, does the reader think of a grave body of men, commissioning one of the most eminent of their members, Boyle, to examine if it were true that a fish suspended by a thread would turn towards the wind? Or what would he think, could he see them all congregating earnestly around their table in order to judge with their own eyes whether or no a spider could get out of a circle formed by a powdered unicorn's horn?

We pass over the incidents of Hudibras and the Goblins (Fig. 2076), and the rescue of the Knight (Fig. 2077), and merely glance in passing to one or two matters, including, however, a pair of portraits, in which Butler has personified the two parties who were opposed to the Royalists. The first is the poor Presbyter, who, in consequence of the triumph of the Independent party is—

2083.—Hudibras writing the Letter

2085.—Butler's House, Pershore.

2082.—Hudibras consulting the Lawyer

2084.—The Lady receiving the Letter from Ralpho.

220

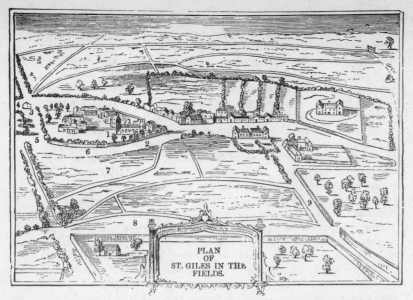

2087.—Westminster, about 1666.

2086.—1. The first St. Giles's Church. 2. Remains of the Walls anciently enclosing the Hospital precincts. 3. Site of the Gallows, and afterwards of the Pound. 4. Way to Uxbridge, now Oxford Street. 5. Elde Strate, since called Hog Lane. 6. Le Lane, now Monmouth Street. 7. Site of the Seven Dials, formerly called Cock and Pye Fields. 8. Elm Close, since called Long Acre. 9. Drury Lane.

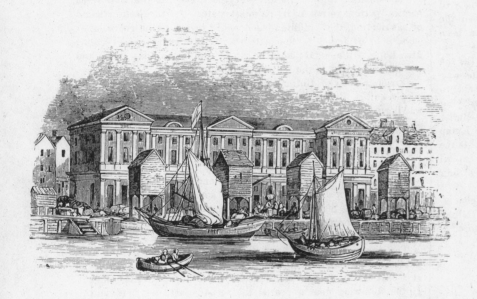

2088.—The Custom House, London, as it appeared before the Great Fire. (From a Print by Hollar.)

2089.—Barbican. (Designed from old Maps and Elevations, temp. James and Charles I.)

2090.—London Bridge, about 1616.

2091.—Palace-Yard Stairs, 1641

221

now reduc'd,
Secluded and cashier'd, and chous'd!
Turn'd out and excommunicate
From all affairs of church and state;
Reformed t' a reformado saint,
And glad to turn itinerant,

and preach to his brethren in belief wherever he can, even in the open fields, or by the mountain side, as represented in our engraving (Fig. 2078); where, however, the "Poor Presbyter" appears more as inspired by the lofty, devout, poetical feeling that was really characteristic of his class, than as actuated by the sentiments which the satiric poet attributes to him. The other portrait (Fig. 2079) is of the early friends but later enemies of the Presbyterians—

The Independents (whose first station
Was in the rear of reformation,
A mongrel kind of church-dragoons,
That serv'd for horse and foot at once,
And in the saddle of one steed
The Saracen and Christian rid:
Were free of ev'ry sp'ritual order,
To preach, and fight, and pray, and murder):

a picture that, if it does not accurately represent the men of the particular time referred to, does something better, namely, represents a class who belong to all past and present times—the men with whom the Church is ever "militant"—the Lord apparently remembered but as "a man of war."

Towards the termination of the canto, Butler describes a body of the Independents sitting in council, just about the time when the Presbyterian members of the House of Commons, who had been driven away, were restored to it, and were thus enabled to overpower the Independent majority of the Rump Parliament (as the remains of the Long Parliament were called), and prepare the way for the restoration of the kingly power. A messenger, said to have been Sir Martyn Noell, suddenly arrives with the terrifying intelligence of the state of public feeling (Fig. 2080). Butler makes this messenger dilate at length upon the fitness of the Rump as an emblem of government, until a near and loud shout puts the whole assembly into a frenzy of alarm, and gives the poet a capital opportunity, and which he makes the most of, for describing their escape (Fig. 2081).

Hudibras's next movement in his love-suit is admirably characteristic of the business-like character of his passion. On Ralph's advice he determines to win the lady by force of law, since force of deception may not, more particularly as Ralph put it—

Your case is clear; you have her word,
And me to witness the accord.

So he goes to a lawyer—a chosen one, and worthy of the business in hand—with his case (Fig. 2082). The dryness of ordinary legal transactions is a byword; their wit and irresistible humour, however, are the only features that strike us in 'Hudibras.' The lawyer assures Hudibras he has as good and just a cause of battery as heart can desire; and advises him, while the conjuror is proceeded against, to try privately all he can do with the lady —to

spare for no trepans
To draw her neck into the bans;
Ply her with love-letters and billets,
And bait 'em well, for quirks and quillets,
With trains t' inveigle and surprise
Her heedless answers and replies.

The Knight relishes the advice much; so he leaves the lawyer; and, presently, behold him seated at his table in the seclusion of his study (Fig. 2083), inditing the

mouse-trap lines,

with his subtlest skill, and which, when finished, Ralph conveys and delivers to the lady (Fig. 2084). She answers it in an epistle as long as his own: and there the poem abruptly terminates, being, in short, unfinished: a circumstance that can only be explained by noticing the manner of its composition; which we may do in a brief sketch of the life of the poet.

And that life is curiously out of harmony with what we should expect from one who, in his writings, plunged so deeply into the grand disputes of the time. We not only do *not* find him in the armed ranks of the Royalists, but we *do* find him enjoying the friendship of one of the most eminent of the Parliamentary men, Selden, and living in the house of another, Sir Samuel Luke, one of Cromwell's officers. Prior to this, all we know of Butler may be summed up in a few words: born the son of a small farmer, and educated in the Free-school at Worcester, he was unable to complete his education in the ordinary way, at the university, and therefore engaged himself as clerk to Mr. Jeffreys, a magistrate of his native county, with whom he spent all his leisure hours in self-education —studying at once history, poetry, music, and painting. His views were materially forwarded by an introduction to the Countess of Kent, who admitted him to the use of her valuable library. It was at this time he was on intimate terms with Selden. Subsequently he entered into the service of Sir Samuel Luke, whom he has endeavoured to hold up to everlasting ridicule in 'Hudibras.' It is not until after the Restoration that we find him connected personally with the Royalists, as holding the position of secretary to Richard, Earl of Carbury, Lord President of the Principality of Wales, who, when the Court of Marches was revived, made Butler steward of Ludlow Castle—a highly honourable post. He now married, his wife being a lady of fortune; but the whole of her property was lost by its being invested in bad securities. Tradition has affirmed that Butler died in absolute poverty; but there is good reason to believe that tradition, for once, errs widely. It would be disgraceful, and should seem impossible, for the poet to be reduced to such a state of distress as has been supposed, when he could number among his friends, intimates, and patrons the nobleman above named—the second George Villiers, Duke of Buckingham, and the Earl of Dorset. But we know, from too many instances, that "Put not your trust in *patrons*" ought to have been taken as the soundest rule of life for every poet, even at the time when poetical patronage was in its palmiest state. A more solid ground of satisfaction, that tradition has erred in regard to the poet's latter days, is to be found in the statement of his friend and executor, Mr. Longueville, who declares that he died in no one's debt, and was never exposed to the indigence supposed.

Our engraving of Butler's house (Fig. 2085), or, as the country people call it, Butler's Cot, exhibits the building in which the poet was born. It is a very humble-looking place, situated in the village of Strensham, near Pershore. It appears from Mr. Thorne's 'Rambles by Rivers—the Avon,' that a tradition yet floats about the neighbourhood, that the bear-baiting scenes of Hudibras were derived from Butler's own personal history; that it was he who was first put in the stocks—then released, and the "Knight" of the village put in his room; and that, in consequence, the poet was obliged to leave Strensham in a somewhat hasty manner. Possibly here, as elsewhere, it is the poem that has given birth to the tradition, and not the tradition that originated the poem.

The three cantos that form the first part of 'Hudibras' were published in 1663, and became immediately so popular, that even at Court its sparkling epigrammatic verses began to pass current. In the following year appeared the second part: but between this and the third, no less than fourteen years elapsed; and before the conclusion could be prepared, the poet died, in his sixty-eighth year. He was buried in the churchyard of St. Paul's, Covent Garden. In designing 'Hudibras,' there is no doubt Butler had in view the immortal Spanish romance, 'Don Quixote;' but nothing can well be more unlike than the two works. Don Quixote never ceases to interest you, or to make you sympathise with him amidst all his extravagance; the Knight, under no circumstances, does either the one or the other. The Don is as consistent as the English Knight is altogether inconsistent. So again of the poems. The one is full of poetry, and of all sorts of shady nooks and corners where the imagination loves to rest: the other is, on the whole, sadly destitute of poetry, and presents such a continuous world of glitter, that anything like repose is quite out of the question. Cervantes still observes the modesty of nature; Butler ever forgets it: Cervantes binds individual and universal character indissolubly together—each true, and each enhancing the other; Butler, in his utter untruth to the individual, does much to impair the fidelity of his universal portraits. But here the natural buoyancy of genius saves him, and makes his production one that, with all its faults, is still destined for immortality.

In giving a few notices of the London of the seventeenth century, we may begin with a part now undergoing greater changes than ever—St. Giles, or, as it was called in its days of long grass and buttercups, and stiles dividing meadow from meadow, St. Giles-in-the-Fields (Fig. 2086). This, in the time of James I., formed a separate hamlet adjoining Westminster; but it was speedily to lose its rural character, and become a part of the rapacious ever-growing monster city, by the erection of a range of continuous houses between the two. There was one feature of St. Giles that made it but too well known throughout England. At a certain public-house criminals about to be hung used to stop on their way to Tyburn.

and receive their last draught of ale from "St. Giles's Bowl." Passing on from St. Giles towards Westminster, we are reminded, by the names of the streets in the neighbourhood of Covent Garden, of the periods when they were erected. Thus, we have James Street, from James I.; Charles Street, from Charles I.; Henrietta Street from Charles's queen; all of which were laid out by Inigo Jones. Of a later date are Catherine Street, named in honour of Catherine of Braganza, Charles II.'s wife; and Duke Street and York Street, in similar honour of Charles's brother, the Duke of York, subsequently James II. Going still farther in the same direction, and gazing upon the magnificence of Pall Mall, St. James's Square, and other streets of the vicinity, we are struck by Anderson's observation (made about the middle of the last century):— "I have met with several old persons in my younger days who remembered when there was but one single house (a cake-house) between the Mews-gate at Charing-Cross and St. James's Palace gate."

It has been observed by an old writer, Howel, that the union of the two crowns of England and Scotland in 1603, conduced not a little to unite the two cities of London and Westminster (Fig. 2087); "for," says he, "the Scots, greatly multiplying here, nestled themselves about the Court; so that the Strand, from the mud walls and thatched cottages, acquired that perfection of building it now possesses:" and thus went on the process which made London, according to the quaint fancy of the writer just named, like a Jesuit's hat, the brims of which were larger than the block; and that induced the Spanish Ambassador, Gondomar, to say to his Royal Mistress after his return from London, and whilst describing the place to her,—" Madam, I believe there will be no city left shortly, for all will run out of the gates to the suburbs."

During this incessant, but very natural, overflow of places too full, into places as yet comparatively empty, many buildings, or vestiges of buildings, of great interest, were of course every now and then swept away, leaving little more than a name to remind us of what has been, and often unfortunately not even that. Names indeed, in matters of antiquity, will undoubtedly carry us a long way. Thus, for instance, mention to the poetical antiquary the name of Old Palace-yard Stairs (Fig. 2091), and his thoughts are at once carried back to the days when the monarchs of England swept along in all the gorgeous magnificence that characterized their own costumes, and the costumes of the nobles, gentlemen, and hosts of retainers that accompanied their every step, as they quitted the old Palace of Westminster, and descended the "stairs" to their barge, which, like Cleopatra's, burned on the water, and which, when it moved, was followed by others only less brilliant and costly; the whole appearing upon the breast of the river like some gigantic lustrous and many-coloured serpent, winding with sinuous course along the "silent highway," and, as though it were an Egyptian god, greeted by the acclamations of the multitudinous people along the banks, and by the continual outbursts of exulting minstrelsy. Many relics of the past, however, that we would wish to preserve in constant recollection, have not been thus fortunate; they have left no name behind, and therefore would, but for the labours of the topographer, be utterly lost. We do not know why there should not be memorials of great buildings, as well as of great men, that have passed away; since the second excites much the same kind of interest as the first; we do not care for the stones and bricks and mortar, but for what events have taken place in them —what processes humanity has therein passed through, calculated to purify or to exalt, or to give to the world examples of what it should shun or emulate. Great buildings, then, are but great men one step removed. And we should, accordingly, much like to see in Palace Yard, immediately opposite the entrance into the Hall, a stone bearing some such inscription as this: "Here stood the clock-tower, referred to in the following passage from the historian of London:—A certain poor man, in an action of debt, being fined the sum of thirteen shillings and fourpence, Randolphus Ingham, Chief Justice of the King's Bench, commiserating his case, caused the court-roll to be erased, and the fine reduced to six shillings and eightpence; which being soon afterwards discovered, Ingham was amerced in a pecuniary mulct of eight hundred marks. which was employed in erecting the said bell-tower on the north side of the said enclosure, opposite Westminster Hall gate; in which tower was placed a bell and a clock, which, striking hourly, was to remind the judges in the Hall of the fate of their brother, in order to prevent all dirty work for the future. However, this fact seems to have been forgotten by Cailyn, Chief Justice of the King's Bench, in the reign of Queen Elizabeth, by his attempting the razure of a court-roll; but Southcote, his brother judge, instead of assenting

to this, plainly told him that he had no inclination to build a clock-house."

The pedestrian of the seventeenth century proceeded from Westminster to London by means of a road in which it required all his care and skill to avoid sinking up to the knees every now and then in mud. Did we not know how used were the people of that time to such a state of the public ways, we should suppose the owners of the splendid palaces that extended in an almost continuous range along the Strand, would be subject to many a hearty anathema for suffering, and obliging others to suffer from, so grievous a nuisance. And, if we imagine ourselves for a moment standing at the period in question with our back against Temple Bar, and looking towards Westminster, we shall have before us the view shown in our engraving (Fig. 2095), and be aware that the dirty streets were only an accompaniment of a still greater, because more dangerous, nuisance—narrow streets. The view represents the old Butcher Row (granted by Edward I. to the country butchers, who were not permitted to enter the city), and which was truly of "Row" like dimensions. Yet such was the entrance into the city whose reputation had spread to the farthest corners of the world. Opposite neighbours could almost shake hands out of their several windows, and certainly could with ease carry on a conversation upon all that was passing below. Gay has well described the locality:—

> Where the fair columns of St. Clement stand,
> Whose straitened bounds encroach upon the Strand;
> Where the low penthouse bows the walker's head,
> And the rough pavement wounds the yielding tread;
> Where not a post protects the narrow space,
> And, strung in twines, combs dangle in thy face;
> Summon at once thy courage, rouse thy care.
> Stand firm, look back, be resolute, beware,
> Forth issuing from steep lanes, the collier's steeds
> Drag the black load; another cart succeeds;
> Team follows team, crowds heap'd on crowds appear,
> And wait impatient till the road grow clear.

The substitution of the great buildings on the north side of St. Clement's for those standing there in the seventeenth century, was the patriotic work of an alderman of London. The poet in these and the following lines shows that by the beginning of the seventeenth century the palatial edifices of the Strand were fast disappearing, and the whole neighbourhood assuming the characteristics of the nineteenth century:—

> Behold that narrow street, which steep descends,
> Whose building to the slimy shore extends;
> Here Arundel's famed structure rear'd its frame;
> The street alone retains the empty name.
> Where Titian's glowing paint the canvas warm'd,
> And Raphael's fair design with judgment charm'd,
> Now hangs the Bellman's song, and pasted here
> The coloured prints of Overton appear.
> Where statues breath'd, the works of Phidias' hands,
> A wooden pump or lonely watch-house stands;
> There Essex' stately pile adorn'd the shore;
> There Cecil's, Bedford's, Villiers',—now no more.

But if Villiers's house—Buckingham Palace—be gone, there is a remarkable relic of it left—the Water-gate (Fig. 2096), one of Inigo Jones's most admired works.

Directing a passing thought towards Bangor Court, Shoe Lane (Fig. 2097), where stood until the present century the Elizabethan building which had once formed the palace of the Bishops of Bangor, we may direct our course to Drury Lane. In the time of James I., we are told, Drury Lane was a "deep, foul, and dangerous" road between the village of St. Giles and the Strand, though here too were to be found some of the mansions of the nobility. At the corner of Drury Lane and Wych Street stood Drury House, built by Sir William Drury, a commander in the Irish wars, in the reign of Queen Elizabeth, who perished in a duel with Sir John Burroughs, that arose out of a foolish dispute about precedency. At Drury House the zealous but unwise friends of the Earl of Essex, in the same reign, resolved on the counsels that destroyed him. In Drury House lived also Sir Robert Drewry, the patron of the poet Donne (Fig. 2167), and who, after the death of an earlier patron, assigned him and his wife an apartment in his own house, rent free, and " was also a cherisher of his studies, and such a friend as sympathised with him and his, in all their joys and sorrows." It was at this period of Donne's life that the incident occurred which forms so interesting a portion of his biography. Sir Robert, being about to depart on an embassy to France, requested the poet's company; but he, at the solicitation of his wife, then near her confinement, and who said her divining soul boded her some ill in his absence, begged to be excused. Sir Robert still pressed the

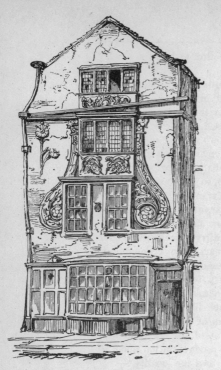

2092.—House formerly standing in Little Moorfields.

2093.—Craven House, Drury Lane.

2094.—House formerly standing in Long Lane, Smithfield.

2095.—Butcher Row, Temple Bar.

2096.—Water-gate, Buckingham or York House.

2097.—Bangor House, Shoe Lane.

2098.—Lighthouse erected at Plymouth, 1665. (From a Print by Kip.)

2099.—The Broad Stone, East Retford, Nottinghamshire,—on which Money, previously immersed in Vinegar was placed in exchange for Goods during the Great Plague. (From an Original Drawing.)

The prospect of
BERMINGHAM
from Ravenhurst (neere London road)
on the South east part of the towne 1640

2100.—View of ancient Birmingham.

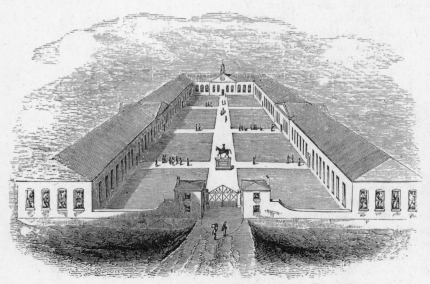

2101.—The great Cloth-market, Leeds, established by Edward III., as it appeared about 1640. (From a Print in the King's Library, Brit. Mus.)

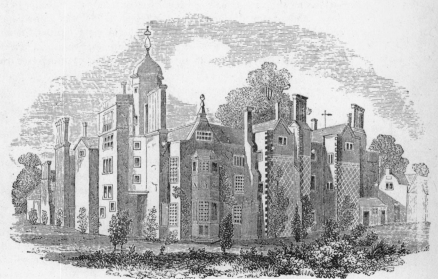

2102.—Hendlip House, near Worcester, pulled down since 1800

matter earnestly, and Donne again sought his wife's consent and obtained it. Some of the poet's first verses commemorate the parting. Speaking in them of his own and his wife's soul, he says,

> If they be two, they are two so
> As stiff twin compasses are two
> Thy soul, the fix'd foot, makes no show:
> To move ; but doth if the other do.
> And though it in the centre sit,
> Yet, when the other far doth roam,
> *It leans, and hearkens after it,*
> And grows erect when that comes home.

Let us observe by the way, that one hardly knows which to wonder at most, the exquisite poetical beauty of the feeling of these lines, or the excessively unpoetical character of the material agencies by means of which that feeling is developed. But such was the characteristic of Donne, and others like him, who seem to have had no notion of the pursuit of poetry except under difficulties. Whilst in Paris the incident occurred to which we have referred. Charming old Izaak Walton, Donne's biographer,—would every good man could have such a biographer !—shall describe it in his own words. We have merely to premise that Donne was left a short time after dinner one day, in the dining-room alone. "Sir Robert returned within half an hour, and as he left, so he found, Mr. Donne alone; but in such an ecstasy, and so altered as to his looks, as amazed Sir Robert to behold him; insomuch that he earnestly desired Mr. Donne to declare what had befallen him in the short time of his absence. To which Mr. Donne was not able to make a present answer; but, after a long and perplexed pause did at last say, 'I have seen a dreadful vision since I saw you; I have seen my dear wife pass twice by me through this room, with her hair hanging about her shoulders, and a dead child in her arms; this I have seen since I saw you.' To which Sir Robert replied, 'Sure, Sir, you have slept since I saw you, and this is the result of some melancholy dream, which I desire you to forget, for you are now awake.' To which Mr. Donne's reply was, 'I cannot be surer that I now live, than that I have not slept since I saw you; and am as sure that, at her second appearing, she stopped, and looked me in the face, and vanished." A servant was immediately sent off to England to satisfy Donne, who returned on the twelfth day with the intelligence that Mrs. Donne had been delivered of a dead child, after a long and dangerous labour, on the same day, and about the same hour, of the supposed appearance of the apparition.

There is preserved a statue of Donne, the remarkable aspect of which suggests correctly a remarkable origin. Towards the close of his devout and most holy life, he was persuaded by a friend, Dr. Fox, to have a monument made. So Donne sent for a carver to make him an urn. "Then, without delay, a choice painter was got to be in readiness to draw his picture, which was taken as followeth :—Several charcoal fires being first made in his large study, he brought with him into that place his winding-sheet in his hand, and having put off all his clothes, had this sheet put on him, and so tied with knots at his head and feet, and his hands so placed as dead bodies are usually fitted to be shrouded and put into their coffin or grave. Upon this urn he thus stood, with his eyes shut, and with so much of the sheet turned aside as might show his lean, pale, and death-like face, which was purposely turned towards the east, from whence he expected the second coming of his and our Saviour Jesus Christ." He was then drawn, and from the drawing, which he was accustomed continually to contemplate, in order to prepare himself for death, the statue (Fig. 2168) was subsequently moulded. The frame of mind in which the poet quitted life may be best seen in the verses he composed on his death-bed, entitled 'Hymn to God, my God in my sickness.' One of the verses runs thus :—

> Since I am coming to that holy room,
> Where, with the Choir of Saints, for evermore
> I shall be made thy music ; as I come
> I tune my instrument here at the door,
> And what I must do then, think here before.

And where does the reader suppose this deeply-interesting statue is to be found ? It ought to be in some honoured place in St. Paul's ; not that we should expect that deans and chapters would care much about the mere *poet* Donne, illustrious though his memory be ; but then he was also Dean of St. Paul's. And the statue, though endangered and slightly injured in the Great Fire, was saved. Where then can it be ? asks the reader, who has visited St. Paul's, but seen nothing of the Donne memorial. We will tell him. If we descend into the vaults beneath, he will find, huddled up together in a very dark corner, a few broken pieces of sculpture; as though cast aside till it was convenient for them to be removed

with other rubbish ; and there is Donne's monument. We wonder that the same spirit that suggests such close attention to the twopences above, has not suggested some attention to this most interesting piece of sculpture below. To use the language but too well understood at St Paul's—*It might draw.*

In the seventeenth century Drury House was rebuilt by the well-known and universally-admired Earl of Craven, and thenceforward called Craven House (Fig. 2093).

Among the many men of heroic mould who graced the seventeenth century, this nobleman is one who claims a peculiarly honourable mention, not so much for his enthusiastic courage, gallantry, and loyalty—though in these qualities few have exceeded him—as for his energetic and self-devoted philanthropy, during those terrible calamities of his time, the plagues and fires of London. We have already given an engraving of the Pest-house in the fields at Westminster (Fig. 1972). This was a lazaretto built by Lord Craven, for the reception of the victims of the terrible plague that preceded the Great Fire. But the Earl was not satisfied with building a pest-house, and then going to shelter his nobility in some safe retreat in the country, as most others of his class did, who had residences in the doomed city ; but, on the contrary, he remained to the last in the very midst of the pestilence, to preserve order and mitigate the horrors of the disease. And this he did " with the same coolness as he fought the battles of his beloved mistress, Elizabeth, titular Queen of Bohemia, or mounted the tremendous breach of Creutznach." The importance and value of such an example must have been very great, not only on that trying occasion, but on others when Earl Craven exerted himself for the public safety ; for there were few or no public regulations calculated for such emergencies, and the affrighted populace looked altogether for guidance and support to those above them in rank. It came at last to be said of the Earl, in reference to fire in the metropolis, that his very horse smelt it out. The white horse on which Lord Craven appeared mounted in the painting on the wall at the foot of Craven Buildings, was most probably the same sagacious quadruped who was thus popularly known and appreciated in the lifetime of its rider. With Craven House is associated the memory of the Queen of Bohemia, daughter of James I., mentioned above. Here the Earl, her devoted lover and champion, brought her to reside in her fallen estate, when she was wholly dependent on him. It is supposed they were privately married. She died a few months after the removal. Subsequent to that event, at the period of the " Glorious Revolution," Earl Craven held for James II. the important post of chief of the guard at St. James's Palace, when the soldiers of the Prince of Orange arrived to displace him and his party. The Earl resolutely refused to depart, and nothing could shake that resolution but an order from James himself. Then with " sullen dignity " he gave the command to his men, and they marched away. Disappointed in love and loyalty, his " bruised arms hung up for monuments "—and sad ones they must often have been to his eye—Lord Craven survived long enough to witness the extinction of the Plague (a blessing well obtained at the cost of the Great Fire) and the chances much lessened of the recurrence of similar calamities in the metropolis, by its being rebuilt of less combustible materials. Two of the latest specimens of the old English timber houses which contributed so much to the former fires, will be found among our engravings (Figs. 2092, 2094), one of them elaborately carved. The Earl died in 1697.

Craven House, we may add, was taken down by the late Mr. Astley, who purchased the site for the construction of " the Olympic Pavilion," in which he exhibited his equestrian performances. We have at present in its stead the Olympic Theatre.

Old London Bridge (Fig. 2090) has been already described ; and it will be sufficient to say of Barbican (Fig. 2089) (so called from the watch-tower, that stood here in connection with the original fortifications of London), that it formed, during the seventeenth century, one of the spots favoured by the nobility as places of residence. Here, for instance, was the house (Fig. 1897) of Prince Rupert, or, as the people would have it, Prince Robber ; the nephew and favoured officer of Charles I. Having had occasion, in a previous chapter, to say much with regard to the evil parts of the life and character of Charles's son and successor, the " Merry Monarch," it is but just, as well as agreeable, to add here a notice of one act of his reign that may serve, in a slight degree, as a counterpoise :—he founded Chelsea Hospital (Fig. 1997). The site had been occupied by a college instituted by James I., but it never prospered, and during the Civil Wars was broken up. The architect of the Hospital was Wren, and the foundation-stone was laid by Charles II. himself, in the presence of the chief nobli:

and gentry of the kingdom. The building was completed in 1690, after eight years' labour, and at an expense of 150,000*l.* There are probably few persons unacquainted with the tradition that ascribes the honour of the original suggestion of this noble work of charity to Nell Gwyn, the orange-girl, and the best of all the king's numerous mistresses. Without attempting here to enter into any description of this establishment, we may adduce, as passing illustrations of its gigantic character, that it boards, lodges, clothes, and finds pocket-money, or pay, for some five hundred or more military invalids, or in-pensioners; and that it provides pay alone for some eighty-five thousand out-pensioners, distributed throughout the country, each in his respective home.

One of the first things that arrests the attention of the inquirer into the state of trade and commerce in England during the present period, is the extraordinary advance that took place immediately after the Restoration. It might have been expected that the Civil War would have thrown the country back so far, that a century or two would have been required to enable it to regain its former position. That it was not so, was partly owing to the wise measures of Cromwell, who called together what in effect was our first Board of Trade, to consult how the traffic and navigation of the Republic might be best promoted and regulated, and partly owing to the impetus that all business experienced when the civil commotions ended, or appeared to have ended, with the Restoration. Thus, to compare a period some years before the war broke out, with one some years after it, and when all its more visible consequences had passed away, we find that the entire value of the exports and imports of the country amounted in 1613 to 4,628,586*l.*; whilst in 1669 they amounted to 6,259,413*l.* But we derive from Sir Josiah Child (Fig. 2176), an eminent London merchant, who published in 1668 'New Discourses of Trade'—evidences more easily appreciable than any figures can furnish of the growing prosperity of England. First, he says, "We give generally now one-third more money with apprentices than we did twenty years before. Secondly, notwithstanding the decay of some and the loss of other trades, yet, in the gross, we ship off now one-third more of our manufactures, and of our tin and lead, than we did twenty years ago. Thirdly, newbuilt houses in London yield twice the rent which they did before the conflagration in the year 1666; and houses immediately before that fire generally yielded one-fourth more rent than they did twenty years ago. Fourthly, the speedy and costly rebuilding, after that great fire in London, is a convincing, and to a stranger an amazing, argument of the plenty and late increase of money in England. Fifthly, we have now more than double the number of merchants and shipping that we had twenty years ago. Sixthly, the course of our trade, from the increase of our money, is strangely altered within these twenty years, most payments from merchants and shopkeepers being now made with ready money; whereas formerly the course of our general trade ran at three, six, nine, and eighteen months' time."

Sir William Petty, again, in his 'Political Arithmetic,' published in 1676, tells us the Royal Navy had doubled or quadrupled its numbers within forty years; that the number and splendour of coaches, equipages, and household furniture had greatly advanced; whilst the postage of letters had increased from *one* to *twenty.* We shall merely add to these satisfactory evidences a calculation by Dr. Davenant (Fig. 2176), who estimates that the whole land of England was only worth 72,000,000*l.* in the beginning of the seventeenth century, and at the Revolution of 1688, 252,000,000*l.*! Agriculture therefore, as well as Commerce, was again flourishing. The implements of husbandry, and of the sister art, horticulture (Figs. 2133 to 2148), were again taken up by the hands that had only laid them down to become soldiers, and with renewed zest and energy, on account of the novelty of the employments. No longer did England exhibit—as during the war—the aspect of a land

> full of weeds; her fairest flowers chok'd;
> Her fruit-trees all unprun'd; her hedges ruined;
> Her knowts disorder'd; and her wholesome herbs
> Swarming with caterpillars.

England, in a word, was again prosperous, and upon the whole, we may judge, the people were happy.

For the source of much of this prosperity we must look to the new commercial connections that had been formed during the century. America had been colonised, first, by a host of adventurers, and then by the Pilgrim Fathers, flying from religious persecution at home—the West India trade had grown into importance—the East India Company had been formed, and had succeeded in establishing the foundation of an entirely new and mighty empire. The introduction of tea had of course no particular effect upon the trade of the

period, but was to be followed by consequences of the highest moment, and which are only at the present day beginning to develop themselves in our new relations with the Chinese. The poet Waller wrote some lines on the birthday of Queen Catherine, entitled 'Of Tea, commended by her majesty,' in which he says—

> The best of queens and best of herbs we owe
> To that bold nation which the way did show
> To the fair region where the sun doth rise,
> Whose rich productions we so justly prize.
> The Muse's friend, Tea, does our Fancy aid;
> Repress those vapours which the head invades;
> And keeps that palace of the soul serene,
> Fit on her birthday to salute the queen.

The "bold nation" is the Dutch, whose East India Company imported the first tea into Europe. Its price in England was for some time enormous. In 1664 the East India Company itself could only procure two pounds and two ounces, when they wanted to make a present to Charles II., and they paid for it at the rate of forty shillings a pound. In all this increase of wealth and comfort, London of course took the lion's share; the days had long passed away when as a port it ranked but a little higher in reputation than the ports of Boston, Lynn, and Southampton; and it began to be a general subject of complaint out of London, how it monopolised "traffic by sea and retailing by land, and exercise of manual arts also." The Custom-house of London, the building shown in our engraving (Fig. 2088), was burnt down in the Great Fire. In other towns of England, however, indications present themselves, showing that they share in this prosperity, each in its own particular way: Plymouth erects its lighthouse (Fig. 2098) to guide the constantly-increasing concourse of ships that pass to and from its harbour; and Leeds builds its immense Cloth-Hall, the forerunner of those edifices which at the present day strike the visitor with surprise by their extent and simple plainness—features that suggest forcibly the gigantic amount and the primitive modes of the business done within them.

Just before the time for commencing business (eleven o'clock, if we remember rightly), one may see a crowd of respectable business-like men standing about in front of the gates of the Coloured-Cloth Hall (Fig. 2101). Suddenly a bell rings, the gates open, and the merchants—for such they are—hurry in; and a curious and noticeable scene presents itself in the interior of the buildings that extend round the immense area or quadrangle of the Hall. The space is divided into six rows or streets, each row having two ranges of stands, and the size of each stand being just twenty-two inches. These are the manufacturers' shops, and their respective names are inscribed in front. But the amount of business done on those little counters would astonish a stranger as much as the speed with which it is transacted. They offer few facilities for huxtering—these great Cloth-Halls. Just one clear hour is allowed for buying and selling; then a bell rings, and before another quarter of an hour has elapsed, all business must be brought to a conclusion, or the servants of the Hall will help to conclude it in their own way, by levying fines on the offenders. No sooner have the merchants left the Coloured-Cloth Hall than they hasten to the White-Cloth Hall, situated in another part of the town, where everything proceeds as before. The cloth exhibited for sale at these times is undressed, the merchants themselves undertaking the labour of finishing it for the markets. The period under review was a severe one for Leeds. It suffered much from the Civil War, but still more from the plague, which at one time reduced it to such a state that the very grass grew in its streets. But after these calamities had been passed through, Leeds entered as it were upon a new career; it obtained a charter from Charles II. to protect its merchants, cloth-workers, and other inhabitants, from the frauds that various dishonest persons were practising in the preparation of woollen cloths, and from that time steadily improved in prosperity, till it became one of the most important of English manufacturing towns.

In the year 585, Cridda, a Saxon military adventurer, by whom the Saxon kingdom of Mercia was founded, gave Birmingham to one of his lieutenants, named Ulwine, the original of the present common surname Allen. At the Conquest, the Saxon Ulwines, or Allens, were still in possession, but they had then to make way for the Norman barons FitzAusculph, to whom they became subordinate by feudal tenure—still, however, residing on the estate. The FitzAusculphs, or lords of Birmingham, inherited in peaceful and regular succession until 1537, when a melancholy story is told, in Dugdale's 'Antiquities of Warwickshire,' of the last Lord de Birmingham. The ambitious and rapacious Duke of Northumberland (the same who endeavoured to set Lady Jane Grey on the

2103.—Herstmonceaux Castle, Sussex.

2105.—East Basham, Norfolk.

2104.—Newmarket Racecourse temp. Charles I.

2106.—Inn at Charmouth.

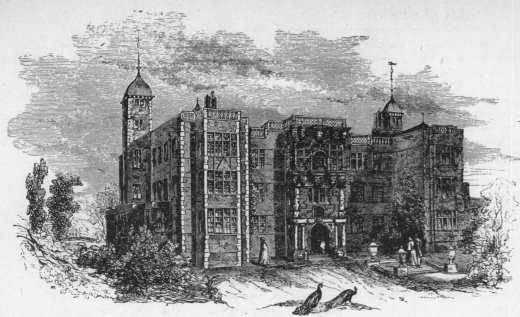

2107.— Charlton House, Kent.

2112.—Farm-house built of the materials of Queenborough Castle

2108.— Hill Hall, Essex.

2109.— Windmill at Chesterton, Warwickshire.

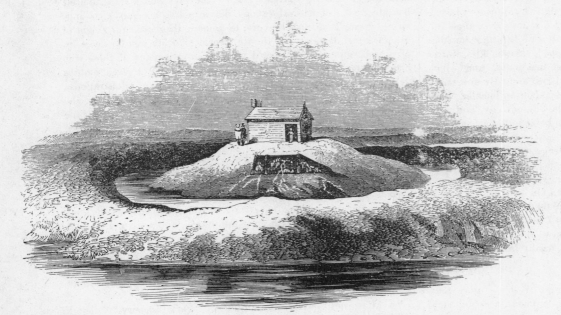

2110.—Site of Queen Philippa's Castle Queenborough, Kent.

2111.—Queenborough Castle. (From an Outline on the Font of Queenborough Church.)

throne, and perished for that unjustifiable attempt), desired to possess the manor of Birmingham, and sounded its possessor, Edward de Birmingham, respecting the disposal of it. Edward de Birmingham, however, did not choose to part with his ancient family inheritance, and rejected the duke's proposals. To dispossess him of it, a stratagem was then resorted to of so extraordinary a nature as to read like a fiction: some villains were hired to commit a highway robbery on one of their own confederates, at the moment of time when Edward de Birmingham should be passing. This having been effected, it was sworn that he was present as an accessary, and Edward de Birmingham was accordingly dragged from his ancestral home, from honour and affluence, to receive the doom of a highway robber. There was but one way left for him to escape a felon's miserable death—the duke would use his influence with the king—if the manor of Birmingham were made over to him. Made over it was, and then the plundered Lord de Birmingham retired into a melancholy obscurity, with 40l. a-year for the subsistence of himself and his wife. Even after the execution of the duke by Queen Mary, there was no restitution made; and the estate passed by favour of the queen to the Marrow family, by whom it was sold at the beginning of the last century. The residence of the ancient Lords of Birmingham was a moated and castellated manor-house, the site of which is now converted into a cattle-market; it was situate at the southern extremity of the town, below St. Martin's Church. In 1538, Leland thus describes Birmingham:—"The beauty of Birmingham, a good market-town in the extreme parts of Warwickshire, is one street going up along, almost from the left side of the brook up a meane hill, by the length of a quarter of a mile. I saw but one parish church in the town. There be many smiths in the town, that used to make knives and all manner of cutting-tools, and many lorimers, that make bitts, and a great many naylors, so that a great part of the town is maintained by smiths who have their iron and sea-coal out of Staffordshire." A hundred years after this description was written, Birmingham remained apparently (Fig. 2100) much the same. The date of our view is 1640, about which time Birmingham was rendering itself memorable by its advocacy of the popular cause against Charles I The unjust tax he imposed under the name of Ship-Money, which the patriot Hampden so nobly resisted, was also vigorously resisted by the men of Birmingham. But it is for its connexion with the useful arts and manufactures that Birmingham is, and ever has been from unknown antiquity, most famous. We see from Leland, that in the sixteenth century Birmingham was in repute for its cutlery. Before the war the forges of Birmingham were set actively at work for the supply of the Parliamentary troops with swords and other military arms. To these sources of profit, after the Restoration, were added the manufacture of many new, ingenious, and costly, metal articles, for which a demand had been created by the progress of the national refinement, and by the luxurious tastes of Charles the Second's court. The Revolution of 1688 gave a new impetus to Birmingham. At one of his levees, William III. was expressing regret that he was obliged to import his arms from Holland at much expense and with great difficulty, when Sir Richard Newdigate, a member for Warwickshire, recommended his Birmingham constituents as being fully competent, if duly patronised, to supply them. Sir Richard was immediately dispatched to Birmingham with an extensive order; and the opportunity thus afforded was so improved, that no English sovereign or minister of state has since had to complain of any necessity for importing these implements. Among the principal manufactures of Birmingham since the seventeenth century may be mentioned shoe-buckles, introduced into England by the monarch just mentioned, and which employed five thousand Birmingham artisans annually for many years; and buttons, that, unlike the great trade in buckles, have continued with unabated popularity to the present day, and now comprise about sixty separate branches of handicraft—as many as six hundred millions of shanks being made here every year. But the period of the discovery of the steam-engine forms perhaps the most important epoch in the history of the modern town, when there opened for her population a new and vast field of enterprise, in which it has reaped wealth and renown, in connection with a hundred different forms of industry; as in the making of buttons, guns, cast-iron and plated ware, and toys (though Birmingham is no longer what Burke called it, the "toy-shop of Europe"); in japanning, glass-blowing, and though last, hardly least—the manufacture of steel pens.

We have already spoken, in general terms, of the plagues that desolated England; but there is in the circumstances of such calamities so much to bring out into powerful relief the more latent qualities of human nature, that we shall not deny ourselves the pleasure of here pausing awhile to tell one of the many stories with which the country was rife a century or two ago, but which now, through the cessation of the actual visits of the plague itself, and the consequent diminution of the interest felt regarding its previous visitations, are only to be heard of in books. If the reader will look upon the representation of the stone at East Retford in Nottinghamshire (Fig. 2099), and consider what must have been the state of things when man could only thus approach man for the purpose of exchanging the commonest necessaries of life, he will have some idea of what was passing in various parts of England whenever the plague was among our forefathers. And with such a stone is our story connected.

During the plague of 1666, a box of cloth was sent from London, to a tailor at Eyam in Derbyshire, who no sooner opened it than he fell ill, and presently died; and, with but one exception, his whole family shared the same fate. From the tailor's house the contagion spread with almost incredible rapidity to house after house in the village, selecting in every case victims, if it did not sweep away the entire household. Recovery of those attacked was hopeless. The sick were in effect dead; and if anything could add to the horror of such a scene, it was the desire necessarily felt in most cases that death, when impending, should be expedited, in order to keep down as much as possible the terrible virulence of the disease. The churchyard being speedily filled, graves were dug on the neighbouring hill sides and in the adjoining fields, and there with frightful haste the festering bodies were thrown.

The minister of Eyam at that time was a Mr. Mompesson, a young man of twenty-eight, married, with two children. His wife, at the outset, besought her husband earnestly to save them all by flight; but he was no holiday pastor—nothing would induce him to leave his miserable flock. But she must not remain, nor their children. The devoted wife agreed to send away the children, but would never abandon him. So they remained together. And now, wherever danger was most imminent, there was the noble-minded pastor sure to be found, for there were those who most needed his consolation. But Mompesson was as enlightened and energetic to avert evil, as he was brave and heroic in enduring it. He persuaded the whole body of his parishioners to determine to stay within a certain line marked out by him and the Duke of Devonshire, who remained at Chatsworth to assist him, so that all communication with the surrounding country should be stopped: within that line provisions and other necessaries were to be obtained by means of stones placed at certain parts of the boundary, upon which the dealers were to place what they brought, then go away and return again—to find the money deposited in a trough of clean spring water. Some of these troughs are still to be found at Eyam.

Mr. Mompesson did not even allow the church service to cease, thinking no doubt that it was more than ever necessary at such a time; but as a meeting in the church would be dangerous and imprudent, he caused his congregation to assemble in a little dell, called Cucklett Dale, situated a short distance from the town. This dell and its tenants formed an extraordinary and impressive scene. On one side were craggy rocks; upon the other, high overarching trees; and between, at the bottom, low down, ran brawling along a little stream. Here the preacher, placing himself beneath a kind of natural canopy, discoursed to his audience—in a spirit elevated, we may be sure, to a more than ordinary height of grandeur and devotion—of the transitoriness of life, and the necessity of a preparation for the world to come, which many of those who listened were shortly and prematurely to enter. For seven months did this noble-hearted pair continue their active ministrations; and by her forethought was he in all probability saved, for she persuaded him to have an excision in his legs, to carry off the complaint in case of infection; that provision, it is said, was tested, and succeeded; but as to herself, she died whilst in the very enjoyment of her husband's escape.

The stricken-hearted man had, however, the satisfaction in the end of seeing his measures to prevent the diffusion of the plague beyond Eyam completely successful; and when it ceased there, and men had time to look back, and consider the conduct of their benefactor, they did so with most full hearts, and with a universal feeling of gratitude that repaid Mompesson, as much as aught earthly could repay him, for all he had suffered. Nor were other acknowledgments wanting. He rose to the rank of prebendary, and had even the deanery of Lincoln offered to him, but this he declined in favour of his friend Dr. Fuller.

"I know not," writes the author of 'Park Scenery,' "that I ever felt more seriously and solemnly impressed than on my visit to this place. The dreadful power of that disease which, while it prevailed in London, appalled the whole empire, and in the following year unpeopled the village of Eyam, is here strikingly exemplified. Six headstones and one tabular monumental stone yet remain to tell the tale of the total extinction of a whole family, with the exception of one boy, in the short space of eight days. The inscription, though much worn, may still be distinctly traced. The respective dates are—

Elizabeth Hancock, died August 3, 1666.			
John Hancock, sen.	,,	4	,,
John Hancock, jun.	,,	7	,,
Oner Hancock	,,	7	,,
William Hancock	,,	7	,,
Alice Hancock	,,	9	,,
Anne Hancock	,,	10	,,

The very name of Philippa of Hainault, Queen of Edward III., lends interest to any place with which it has been connected, no matter how slightly; but as an evidence of the honour in which she was held by her husband, the fact that Queenborough, in the Isle of Sheppey, was thus designated at Edward's express command, after a few days' residence in the Castle with Philippa, is of importance, and invests the place with associations that make a visit to it more attractive than any existing remains are sufficient to explain. A moat, with an elevation of soil in the centre (Fig. 2110), and a well two hundred feet deep, that still furnishes an inexhaustible supply of excellent water, are all that mark the site of the castle in which the royal pair lodged, and which had been then but just finished by the most eminent architect of his day, William of Wykeham. Some of the materials of the castle undoubtedly exist, but only in the shape of a farm-house (Fig. 2112), that has been built from them. A curious view of the castle has been preserved in an equally curious manner: on the front of Queenborough Church there is an outline representation of it: this has been copied in our engraving (Fig. 2111). The pile was destroyed during the Commonwealth, because "the whole was much out of repair, and no ways defensive of the Commonwealth or the island on which it stood, being built in the *time of bows and arrows;* and that as no platform for the planting of cannon could be erected on it, and it having no command of the sea, although near unto it, it was not fit to be kept, but demolished;" and so—demolished it was.

Herstmonceaux Castle (Fig. 2103), Sussex, is distinguished as being one of the finest existing examples of that period in the history of architecture, when fortified mansions began to lose something of their former dreary dungeon-like aspect, while still preserving much of their original strength. The days had gone by for subjects to maintain a regular siege, and therefore no attempt was made to render the castle of the fifteenth century fit for such rough work; but feuds between neighbouring barons, or even sudden and temporary attacks arising from political causes, rendered it necessary still to keep the moat and the drawbridges, the portcullised gateway and machicolated cornice, the strong towers and loop-holed turrets, in all their former integrity. At Herstmonceaux there was also provision made, by means of furnaces in the turrets, for pouring down upon besiegers melted lead or pitch. The builder was Sir Roger de Fiennes, treasurer to Henry VI., and who had accompanied the conqueror of Azincourt in his French expeditions. Among the many stories of baronial life preserved in connection with the old mansions of England, there is one of a very tragical nature relating to Herstmonceaux. In the reign of Henry VIII. Lord Dacre was the possessor of the estate. One night he went with other young men into a neighbouring park, in order to shoot some deer; but being encountered by the keepers, an affray ensued, and one of the latter was killed. Lord Dacre and three other gentlemen were tried and condemned. It is said that some of Henry's unprincipled courtiers, who wanted the large estates of the unfortunate young man—he was but in his twenty-fourth year—got about him, and persuaded him to plead guilty, and that thus he was destroyed. On the day of execution "he was led on foot, between the two sheriffs of London, from the Tower, through the city to Tyburn, where he was strangled as common murderers are." No wonder there was much "noise and lamentation" made at this unhappy end of a "right towardly gentleman, and such a one as many had conceived great hope of better proof." (Holinshed.)

Herstmonceaux at a later period passed into the possession of the Bishop of Chichester; and while his son resided there Horace Walpole visited the place, and wrote a pleasant account of what he saw. In one passage he observes, "They showed us a dismal chamber, which they call Drummer's Hall, and suppose that Mr.

Addison's comedy is descended from it." The castle was dismantled in the latter part of the last century. What now remains —a mere shell of the former Herstmonceaux—is carefully preserved.

It is a curious and instructive contrast to compare with Herstmonceaux—a true castle, but in which the domestic mansion was beginning to show itself—with East Basham Hall in Norfolk (Fig. 2105), which forms a true and most beautiful mansion, but in which the traces of old castellated architecture are everywhere conspicuous. It appears from the dates of the erection of the two piles, that it took nearly a century to complete the transformation. And truly significant, in its stately elegance, is Basham Hall, of the more peaceable days that must have dawned for England before any one would have erected a pile so utterly defenceless against warlike attacks. It is supposed to have been completed in 1540. This is also a ruin. Hill Hall, Essex (Fig. 2108), begun just after Basham was completed, carried still further, and, indeed, completes the change that had been so long in progress. Nothing whatever in its front reminds you of the feudal days of Old England. It is commodious, handsome, but common-place, in comparison at least with the Tudor style, which the architect seems to have so determinedly renounced. The founder of Hill Hall was Sir Thomas Smith, principal Secretary to the youthful Edward VI.

Charlton House, Kent (Fig. 2107), the seat of Sir T. M. Wilson, is a fine specimen of yet another style of building to any of those just mentioned, and which came into use in the early part of the seventeenth century. In form the mansion is an oblong square, with projections at the end of each front, turreted, and the whole surrounded at the summit by an open balustrade. Among the curiosities of the interior is a chimney-piece, with a slab of black marble finely polished, in which Lord Downe is said to have seen a robbery committed on Blackheath, or, according to Dr. Plot, at Shooter's Hill. The story adds, that he sent out his servants, and they apprehended the thieves. The chief apartments are the saloon and the gallery; the former is exceedingly rich in ornament: on one side of the chimney-piece is a figure of Vulcan, in alabaster; on the other, one of Venus. The gallery is upwards of seventy-six feet in length, with stained windows. It contains a valuable collection of insects, minerals, fossils, and other natural relics, collected by Lady Wilson. The park and pleasure-grounds are extensive, and include some delightful scenery.

The architecture of Hendlip House (Fig. 2102) may be carefully compared with that of some of the buildings above-named. It belongs to the same century as Basham Hall, but possesses distinct characteristics of its own. The interesting incidents connected with the discovery of the Jesuits at Hendlip have been narrated in a previous page (159). The Windmill at Chesterton, Warwickshire (Fig. 2109), is said to be by Inigo Jones.

The sumptuous furniture exhibited in our two pages of engravings (232, 233) is, of itself, sufficient to prove the truth of the statements before noticed, as to the advances made during the present period in wealth and luxury. One could not desire to see a more beautiful bedroom, for instance, than that (Fig. 2114) in which James I. was accustomed to sleep during his visit to Knole in Kent, and which is, to our minds, only the more attractive for a kind of grave stateliness that pervades the whole. The mothers of the present day may, perhaps, feel interested in knowing what kind of article a cradle was about three centuries ago: their curiosity may be gratified, if they will look at our drawing (Fig. 2113), where no doubt they have as handsome a specimen before them as the time could produce: the cradle being that which was used for the infant James of Scotland, afterwards King of the united countries. The articles generally represented in the pages in question explain themselves at once through the eye; it will be sufficient therefore for us to notice any peculiar features of furniture and household adornments. The former was occasionally turned to other than what may be called its legitimate purposes. Sir W. Penn had a chair, known as King Harry's chair, in which, whenever a stranger sat down, he found himself suddenly in the grasp of two powerful but inanimate arms, and exposed, for as long as the bystanders pleased, to their jests and merriment. Embroidery was the staple ornament for bed-curtains and hangings; but early in the seventeenth century hangings of paper and of leather came also into use. A still nobler species of ornament for walls consisted of the paintings that now began to cover them, and which were often by the finest masters—Rubens and Teniers, Vandyke and Rembrandt; mixed with which were to be seen many a glorious specimen of Holbein and Jansen, and not unfrequently of the illustrious early painters of Italy. And that the owners were proud of them was sufficiently evidenced

2114.—James I.'s Bedroom at Knole, Kent. (The Chairs are of a later date.)

2113.—James I.'s Cradle. (From a Print in Nichols' Progresses.)

2115, 2116.—Furniture of the Sixteenth Century. (Selected from Specimens and Prints of the Period.)

2117, 2118.—Furniture of the Sixteenth Century. (Selected from Specimens and Prints of the Period.)

2119.—Furniture of the Sixteenth Century. (Selected from Specimens and Prints of the Period.)

2120.—Furniture of the Sixteenth Century. (Selected from Specimens and Prints of the Period.)

2121.—Sideboard, with Plate, &c. (From Specimens in Private Collections.)

2122.—Library Furniture. (The Chair from one presented by Charles II. to Sir C. Ashmole, preserved in the Ashmolean Museum, Oxford; the Table and Bookcase from Sir P. Lely's Portrait of Killigrew; and the rest from Specimens in Private Collections.)

2123.—State Bed, Dressing-glass, &c. (From Specimens at Penshurst and in Private Collections.)

2124.—Sitting-room Furniture. (From Specimens in Private Collections.)

2125.—Sofas, Stools, and Cabinets. (From Specimens in Private Collections, and Pictures by Sir P. Lely.)

by the price that such works commanded, and by the care with which they were ever treated. No frame could be too costly to enshrine these productions in a manner that the owners thought worthy of them.

Turkey and Persian carpets were in use, but not on the floor, except occasionally in regal apartments. Our forefathers still trod upon rushes or mats, and kept their valuable carpets upon the *tables*, where their beauty would be more readily seen and preserved. The famous Gobelin tapestry appeared in England towards the close of the century, or not long after the establishment of the manufactory at Gobelin. But the tapestry previously in use in England must have been very beautiful, if Spenser's description of it, in the time of Elizabeth, may be taken as strictly true :—

> ——round about, the walls yclothed were
> With goodly arras of great majesty,
> Woven with gold and silk so close and near,
> That the rich metal lurked privily,
> As faining to be hid from envious eye :

and the very same feature is referred to in a description of tapestry belonging to the Anglo-Saxon period. We read in the poem of Beowulf, that in the great wine-chamber

> There alone variegated with gold
> The web on the walls.

Both James I. and Charles II. endeavoured to revive the art of *weaving* tapestry, that had been introduced into the country during the reign of Henry VIII. A memorable incident occurred in connection with these attempts : five, if not more, of the Cartoons of Raphael were worked in tapestry at Mortlake ; and, what is still more important, the Cartoons we now possess—and which are perhaps the most valuable of all existing works of art—were, it is supposed, bought by Charles I. expressly for the purpose of their reproduction in tapestry. In order to support decorations of this kind, frames appear to have been erected at little distances from the wall, and upon these the tapestry was suspended ; hence the opportunities (so freely made use of by the old dramatists) for persons to conceal themselves, in order to listen to what might be passing in the apartment. The hanging of the tapestry was the business of the grooms of the chamber, who in royal progresses went forward previously, in order to get all prepared. From an anecdote that has been related of Henry IV. of France, it appears that the designers of tapestry were accustomed to compliment or please their patrons and employers by introducing into the work such political allusions or representations as were most likely to be acceptable. Henry, in order to pay especial honour to a papal legate when visiting St. Germain-en-Laye, sent orders that the finest tapestry should be hung up. This order was obeyed, and a suit chosen, that was decorated with emblems ridiculing the Pope and the Roman Court. Henry's wise minister, Sully, was however at hand, and he soon discovered, and changed the suit, which had turned up at so very awkward a time.

It is now agreed on all hands that an abundant supply of wholesome water in our dwellings is the first essential for the enjoyment of health and domestic comfort ; yet, but two centuries ago, our ancestors in this metropolis were obliged to fetch all they needed from the nearest conduit or the river, or to purchase for their use of the water-carriers, who in the time of James I. went about the streets bearing large cans upon their shoulders. This state of things exists to the present day in Paris—the centre of European elegance and refinement. The first of the conduits of London was built near Bow Church, in Cheapside, in the reign of Henry III. ; and one of the latest appears to have been erected at Leadenhall in 1655, and which formed, at the same time a fountain and a graceful architectural street ornament (Fig. 2127). There were others scattered about London, of which they formed a characteristic and most picturesque feature. That unknown Hogarth of the seventeenth century, the author of the original print, of which a woodcut copy now remains in the British Museum, headed " Tittle-Tattle, or the several Branches of Gossiping " (Fig. 2126), has made his own peculiar comment on this custom of his time. The women of the seventeenth century, it appears, were fond of meeting and gossiping at the conduits, and were ready even to enter into most unfeminine contests for their right of precedence there. This may serve to give us a glimpse of many little partialities entertained towards these convenient places of public resort, and that served to prolong their existence. These ancient gossipings at the conduits may be paralleled by a lively scene that now and then in a severe winter frost occurs amongst ourselves. Whoever has seen a " Plug in a Frost " (Fig. 2128), and the groups gathered about it, when their

own pipes and cisterns at home are so frozen that the water cannot flow, may have a lively idea of the meetings at the conduits of old London.

In 1582 the want that had begun to be felt of water in the houses was attempted to be supplied by one Peter Morris, an enterprising Dutchman, who made " a most artificial forcier " for the purpose, which the lord mayor and aldermen went to view ; when Morris, to prove the power of his machine, threw water from it over St. Magnus Church. The city granted him a lease for the use of the Thames water, and one of the arches of London Bridge (Fig. 1616), for five hundred years. Two years later he obtained the use of another arch for a similar period. Peter Morris's waterworks long formed one of the great sights of London ; but as their supply to the inhabitants reached only " so far as Gracechurch Street," we cannot form a very high opinion of them, excepting as they gave the first impetus to the endeavours made from time to time afterwards to supply the important deficiency. In 1594 waterworks of a similar kind were erected near Broken Wharf, which supplied the houses in West Cheap and around St. Paul's as far as Fleet Street. Queen Elizabeth, alive to all the great interests of the people she governed, did not overlook this matter : she issued a grant for cutting and conveying a river from any part of Middlesex or Hertfordshire to the city of London, but died before any man had come forward to execute that great work of utility. It was not until the next reign that Hugh Middleton, " citizen and goldsmith," commenced and completed (as we have already seen in a former page), the herculean labour.

Horse-racing is in itself a sport recommended by many attractions to all who delight in the exhibition of the powers of this beautiful and generous-spirited creature : and deeply is it to be regretted that a sport so suited to the national taste should be degraded and made mischievous by the gambling and profligacy that accompany it. We have here, however, only to do with the sport, independent of its dangerous concomitants. Newmarket, as the metropolis of the sporting world, has obtained a European reputation. The course, which extends four miles in length, is considered to be the finest in existence. The fame of Newmarket began soon after the destruction of the Spanish Armada. Some horses, which had escaped from the wrecked vessels, are said to have been exhibited here, and to have astonished those who beheld their extraordinary swiftness. In a very short space of time, racing had grown fashionable, and James I. and his Court became so enamoured of the sport, that a house was erected at Newmarket for their accommodation. At the time of the Civil War this house sustained considerable injury ; and Charles II., on ascending the throne, and becoming chief patron of the turf, ordered it to be rebuilt. Part of it is still standing, with the extensive stables adjoining that were formerly used for the royal stud. The racing establishment of Newmarket is chiefly valuable for the training of horses, which is here conducted with such skill and success on the training-ground on the southern side of the town of Newmarket, that great numbers are exported, and very many sold at such advanced prices as none could merit but animals of the most consummate excellence. The thorough-bred English horse, such as he is produced at Newmarket, stands indeed almost without a rival. Our engraving (Fig. 2104) represents the course in the time of Charles I.

One of the most interesting passages of the history of the Great War is Charles the Second's escape after the battle of Worcester, and which we may here narrate in connection with two buildings represented among our engravings, namely, Boscobel House (Fig. 1957) and the Inn at Charmouth, both places that Charles had but too much reason to remember to the latest day of his life, as reminding him of the most eventful periods of his altogether eventful flight. For some hours after the battle he kept with a large body of horse, under the command of General Leslie, but having little faith in their safe retreat into Scotland, he determined to leave them, and trust to his own individual efforts. He departed therefore at night with two servants, and at daybreak the following morning he dismissed them also, having however first made them cut off his hair. Completely wearied, he now lay down on the ground in the borders of Boscobel Wood, Staffordshire, and, notwithstanding his dangers, slept soundly. On waking, another fugitive from the battle-field, Captain Careless, who had been enjoying the shelter of an oak-tree, joined him, and persuaded him to ascend to the same secure place. While they were in the tree, they saw many persons pass, and heard them talking loudly how they would use the King if they caught him. It is in remembrance of this incident that " oak-apple day " is still observed in Devonshire and other parts of England. On the 29th of May, Charles's birth-day, and the date of his restoration, many a rustic may be seen in the streets of Exeter with his little sprig of oak-leaves stuck in his hat, and the "apples" superbly gilded. Such at least was the custom in our boyish days.

As night approached, the half-famished pair descended, and went to the cottage of a poor man, who gave Charles the shelter of a barn full of hay, where he immediately fell asleep, notwithstanding his hunger, while Careless went on to explore the country farther. The King now obtained his first meal since the parting with his servants—it was of bread and buttermilk—homely fare, but as he himself, in effect, said, the most delicious he had ever tasted. On the third night a man came from the Captain, to guide Charles to another cottage, twelve miles distant. A deeper disguise was now adopted. The alteration wrought by cutting off his hair, and by staining the face brown with walnut-tree leaves, was completed by Charles's inducing his poor host to change dresses with him, even to the very shirt. No looking-glass, we should say, was at hand, to give Charles an idea of the full effect of his toilet at this time, but as he glanced over his exterior habiliments, he must have been amused, amidst all his anxieties, by reflecting upon the strange appearance he presented. In a contemporary tract the garb of the future King of England is thus described:—"He had on a white steeple-crowned hat, without any other lining besides grease, both sides of the brim so doubled up with handling, that they looked like two waterspouts; a leather doublet, full of holes, and almost black with grease about the sleeves, collar, and waist; an old green woodriff [woodman's] coat, threadbare and patched in most places, with a pair of breeches of the same cloth, and in the same con-dition, the slops hanging down to the middle of the leg; hose and shoes of different parishes; the hose mere grey stirrups, much darned and clouted, especially about the knees, under which he had a pair of flannel stockings of his own, the tops of them cut off; his shoes had been cobbled, being pieced both on the soles and seams, and the upper leathers so cut and slashed, to fit them to his feet, that they were quite unfit to befriend him either from the water or dirt." Even thus disguised, Charles would not run any unnecessary risk, so he and his guide crossed fields, climbed over hedges, and jumped over ditches, in order to avoid the high roads. But the shoes he had put on began to pinch intolerably, and he threw them away, and walked without. Growing more and more weary, and footsore, the unhappy wanderer at last stopped, and threw himself upon the ground in utter despair, declaring that he would rather hazard being taken than proceed under so much misery. Again and again he did this, still however plucking up fresh courage, and thus at last the cottage was reached, where he once more took up his quarters in a barn.

Having succeeded in arriving at the house of a magistrate in Staffordshire, where he could stay for a time in tolerable safety, Charles enjoyed a temporary rest, and recovered from his unusual fatigue. But there was a reward offered for him by the Parliament, and his position was considered so dangerous, that he *must* be got out of the country as speedily as possible. So a romantic scheme was devised and put into execution. He was transformed into "William," nephew of the magistrate, Mr. Lane, and placed on horseback, with the magistrate's daughter, Miss Lane, behind him as a " cousin,"·to go on a visit to Bristol, for the sake of his health, which was very bad, so bad indeed (with the " ague") that poor "William" was obliged to retire alone to his chamber in every house they stopped at on their route. The house of a relation of Mr. Lane at Bristol was thus reached in safety, and there the King spent some days before venturing another movement towards the sea-side. At last, however, Charles again set out, accompanied by Lord Wil-mot (subsequently the notorious Earl of Rochester), and reached the inn at Charmouth (Fig. 2106), near Lyme, in Dorsetshire, where the sagacity of a smith had wellnigh sealed Charles's fate. A horse, having been taken to be shod, or, as others say, having been accidentally examined, the man remarked the horse must have tra-velled far, as he said his shoes had been made in four different coun-ties. An alarm was raised, and the inn searched, but Charles had just escaped. Through county after county the fugitive moved about for some time, until his fears and miseries were ended by his embarkation at Brighton in a vessel, which speedily landed him at Fecamp, in Normandy.

Of the Edinburgh of the seventeenth century (Fig. 1886), Taylor, the Water-Poet, has given us a description from personal observa-tion, in his 'Penniless Pilgrimage.' Many of our readers are possibly aware that Taylor, during the reign of James, "travelled," to use his own words, " on foot from London to Edinburgh in Scot-

land, not carrying any money to or fro, neither begging, borrowing, or asking meat, drink, or lodging "—an agreeable proof of the hos-pitality that then pervaded Old England. A man of no higher standing in life or in literature than the Water-Poet would find it difficult now to accomplish Taylor's task. He however got through it in gallant style. On entering Edinburgh he was, it appears, penniless and worn out with fatigue, but the good folks of the northern capital soon restored him to strength and spirits. " I found," he says, " entertainment beyond my expectation or merit; and there is fish, flesh, bread, and fruit, in such variety, that I think I may offenceless call it superfluity." Having visited the castle, which he describes as "both defensive against any opposition and magnifick for lodging and receipt," he thus continues his description of Edinburgh :—"I descended lower to the city, wherein I ob-·served the fairest and goodliest street that ever mine eyes beheld, for I did never see or hear of a street of that length, which is half an English mile from the Castle to a fair port [gateway] which they call the Nether Bow, and from that port the street which they call Kenny Gate is one quarter of a mile more, down to the King's Palace, called Holyrood House, the buildings on each side of the way being all of squared stone, five, six, and seven stories high, and many bye-lanes and closes on each side of the way, wherein are gentlemen's houses, much fairer than the buildings in the High Street, ..or in the High Street the merchants and trades-men do dwell, but the gentlemen's mansions and goodliest houses are obscurely founded in the aforesaid lanes: the walls are eight or ten feet thick, exceeding strong; not built for a day, a week, a month, or a year; but from antiquity to posterity, for many ages." His notice of Leith, the port of Edinburgh, seems remarkable to us now, not only as exhibiting England in the position of a corn-exporting country, but as exporting it to the Continent. He says he had been credibly informed that in the course of one year 320,000 bushels of corn had been sent to Spain, France, and other countries; so that, says he, it " makes me wonder that a kingdom so populous as it is, should nevertheless sell so much bread-corn beyond the seas, and yet to have more than sufficient for themselves."

Certainly the love of field and other out-of-door sports, felt by James I., forms as strong a proof as need be desired of their attract-iveness, for they made him—a coward—positively brave enough to venture upon all the dangers arising from infuriated and desperate wild animals in the hunt—the breaking of poles, and a variety of other mishaps common to hawking-parties (Fig. 2150), or getting some particularly unpleasant blow from an unlucky ball at tennis. Yet these were all especially favourite games with James I.; so much so, indeed, that they interfered very materially with the national business. Whenever the ministers wanted to consult him upon any matter of sudden and particular importance, they were fortunate, in-deed, if they had not to seek him at Newmarket among the horses, or at Royston, among the dogs, engaged in the hunt. Mr. Edward Lascelles, in a letter to the Earl of Shrewsbury, tells an agreeable story of a stroke of practical satire that was played off on the King. " There was one of the King's special hounds, called Jowler, missing one day. The King was much displeased that he was wanted; not-withstanding, went a hunting. The next day, when they were on the field, Jowler came in amongst the rest of the hounds: the King was told of him, and was very glad; and, looking on him, spied a paper about his neck, and in the paper was written—' Good Mr. Jowler, we pray you to speak to the King (for he hears you every day, and so doth he not us), that it will please his majesty to go back to Lon-don, for else the country will be undone; all our provision is spent already, and we are not able to entertain him any longer.' " The affair was "taken for a jest," as it should have been, but also for *no more*. We are told, as the conclusion, that the King "intends to lie there yet a fortnight." At this very time religious and state affairs of the highest importance were engaging the attention of every thoughtful man in England; it was the period when the nation was just about to be shaken to its very centre by the Gunpowder Plot.

The most favourable circumstances for learning what a great hunt really was in the seventeenth century, were those connected with the gatherings that annually took place in the Scottish Highlands; and at such a gathering the Water-Poet was present in the course of his penniless expedition. The hunts on such occasions lasted for several weeks, the season being the early part of the autumn. Then "many of the nobility," says Taylor, " do come into those Highland countries to hunt, where they do conform themselves to the habit of the Highlandmen, who for the most part speak nothing but Irish; and in former time were those people which were called the Red-Shanks. Their habit is shoes with but one sole apiece: stockings (which they call short hose) made of a warm stuff of

2126.—Water-carriers.

2127.—Conduit at Leadenhall, erected 1665

2128.—Plug in a Frost.

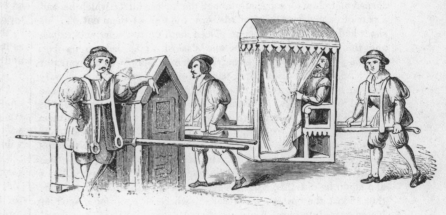

2129.—Sedan Chairs   (From Prints and Paintings of the Period.)

2130.—Sedan 1638

2131.—Coaches of the time of Charles II. (Selected from Prints.)

2132.—Hackney Coaches. (Selected from Braun's 'Civitates Orbis Terrarum,' 1584, and various Prints and Paintings of the Period.)

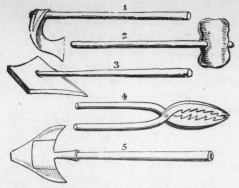

2133-2137 Husbandry Implements. (From Gervase Markham's 'Farewell to Husbandry,' 1620.)

1. Hack for breaking Clods after Ploughing. 2. Clotting Beetle for breaking Clods for Harrowing. 3. Clotted Beetle for Wet Clods. 4. Weeding Nippers. 5. Paring Shovel, for Clearing Ground and destroying Weeds.

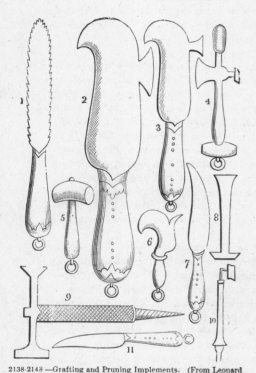

2138-2148—Grafting and Pruning Implements. (From Leonard Mascall's 'Countryman's New Art of Planting,' 4to. Lond. 1592.)

1. Saw. 2. Great Knife, with Chesill-head. 3. Pruning-knife. 4. Chesill with a Wimble-bit. 5. Mallet. 6. Vine Knife. 7. Slicing Knife 8 Grafting Chesill. 9. Hammer, with a File and Piercer. 10. Scraper, to 'cleanse your Mosse-trees'' 11. Grafting Knife Each Instrument was fastened by a ring or button to the girdle of the labourer.

2151.—Tennis Court. (From Commenius's 'Orbis Sensualim Pictus,' 1658.)

2149.—The Tinkhell.

Through heather, mose, 'mongst frogs, and bogs, and fogs,
'Mongst craggy cliffes, and thunder-battered hills,
Hares, hinds, bucks, roes, are chas'd by men and dogs.
Taylor's *Sonnet*

2150.—James I., and attendants, Hawking. (From a 'Jewell for Gentry,' 1614.)

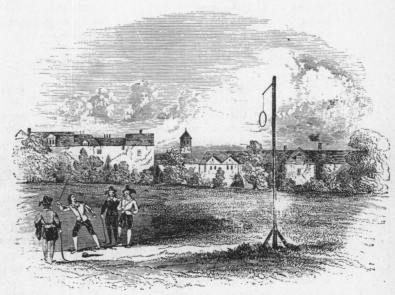

215 Pall-mall in St. James's Park. (From a Picture of the Period, engraved in Carter's 'Westminster.')

237

divers colours, which they call tartan; as for breeches, many of them, nor their forefathers, never wore any, but a jerkin of the same stuff that their hose is of, their garters being bands or wreaths of hay or straw, with a plaid about their shoulders, which is a mantle of divers colours, much finer and lighter stuff than their hose, with blue flat caps on their heads, a handkerchief knit with two knots about their neck; and thus are they attired. Now their weapons are long bows and forked arrows, swords and targets, harquebusses, muskets, dirks, and Lochaber axes. With these arms I found many of them armed for the hunting. As for attire, any man of what degree soever that comes amongst them, must not disdain to wear it; for if they do, they will disdain to hunt, or willingly to bring in their dogs; but if men be kind unto them, and be in their habit, then are they conquered with kindness, and the sport will be plentiful. This was the reason that I found so many noblemen and gentlemen in those shapes." And a very good reason too; though there was another that an artist might have urged, the delightfully picturesque as well as appropriate effect of such costumes among the mountains and upon the heather. Taylor, having been made a Highlander for the occasion, accompanied the establishment of the Lord Erskine; for of course no one in his senses ventured without due provision for his daily wants, into a part of the country where not a house, corn-field, or habitation of any nature could be seen for "twelve days" together; but in their room, "deer, wild horses, wolves, and such like." And in a very luxurious manner did the Lord Erskine keep his establishment; "the kitchen being always on the side of a bank, many kettles and pots boiling, and many spits turning and winding, with great variety of cheer, as venison baked, sodden, roast, and stewed beef, mutton, goats, kid, hares, fresh salmon, pigeons, hens, capons, chickens, partridge, moorcoots, heathcocks, caperkellies, and termagants (ptarmigan), good ale, sack, white, and claret, tent (or allegant) with most potent aqua-vitæ." The real purveyors of all these goodly stores were the "falconers, fowlers, fishers," who whilst enjoying their respective sports, under more than usually stimulating and encouraging circumstances, fed the camp abundantly. At last the hunt begins. "Five or six hundred men do rise early in the morning, and they do disperse themselves divers ways; and seven, eight, or ten miles compass, they do bring or chase in the deer in many herds (two, three, or four hundred in a herd) to such a place as the noblemen shall appoint them; then, when the day is come, the lords and gentlemen of their companies do ride or go to the said places, sometimes wading up to the middle through bourns and rivers: and then they being come to the place, do lie down on the ground till those foresaid scouts, which are called the Tinkhell, do bring down the deer. But as the proverb says of a bad cook, so these Tinkhell men do lick their own fingers; for besides their bow and arrows, which they carry with them, one can hear now and then a harquebus or a musket go off, which they do seldom discharge in vain. Then after we had stayed there three hours or thereabouts, we might perceive the deer appear on the hills round about us (their heads making a show like a wood), which being followed close by the Tinkhell, are chased down into the valley where we lay; then all the valley on each side being waylaid with a hundred couple of strong Irish greyhounds, they are let loose as occasion serves upon the herd of deer, that with dogs, guns, arrows, dirks, and daggers, in the space of two hours, fourscore fat deer were slain (Fig. 2149), which after are disposed of, some one way and some another, twenty and thirty miles, and more than enough left for us to make merry withal at our rendezvous." Taylor, whilst full of the impressions excited by this hunt, produced two sonnets: the lines beneath our engraving, commencing

Through heather, mosse, 'mongst frogs, and bogs, and fogs,

are taken from one of them.

Charles I. had unhappily little time for sports, but Charles II. was, like his grandfather, a perfect devotee to them. His personal habits, indeed, were in many respects of a very manly nature. Prince George of Denmark complained once to him he was growing fat. "Walk with me, and hunt with my brother [the Duke of York]," was the reply, "and you will not long be distressed with growing fat." The morose-minded bigot—the Duke here named—was as fond of out-of-doors sports as all the rest of his family. Charles's remark gives us a glimpse of his hunting enthusiasm, and we learn from Pepys, that the first time he ever saw the game of pall-mall (Fig. 2115) was when the Duke was playing it in the Park. The new game speedily became fashionable. The present Pall-Mall, London, not only derives its name from this sport, but points out the locality where the gossip watched the Duke's play. The Mall, it appears

from Pepys, had to be very carefully made and kept, to fit it for the sport. He says, the keeper told him as he was sweeping it; that the earth was mixed, and covered over all with powdered cockle-shells, that made it "bind," as gardeners say of their gravel. In dry weather the surface, however, would turn to dust, and deaden the spring of the ball. Nor was pall-mall the only novelty in which Pepys saw the sport-loving Duke engaged. Another time he followed him into the Park, "where, though the ice was broken, he *would* go slide upon his skaits, which I did not like; but he slides very well." This is one of the earliest notices we possess of the now favourite English sport of skating; Evelyn refers to it as being after the "manner of the Hollanders;" so that it is most probable the Cavaliers had learnt the art during their exile, and brought it back with them to England at the Restoration. Tennis (Fig. 2151) was so eagerly pursued by Charles II., that having once caused himself to be weighed before and after playing the game, he found that he had lost weight in the interval to the amount of four pounds and a half. We perceive from the engraving of the Billiards of the seventeenth century (Fig. 2153), that the game was altogether different from what it is now. There were two instead of three balls, and a pair of little arches near the centre of the table, instead of the six "pockets" that are at present to be found attached on its outer edges, namely, one at each of the four corners, and one on each side, at the middle.

———

The love of the country for its own sake, and for the sake of the many pure and tranquil enjoyments that it never fails to yield to all who look for them, had glowed no doubt in many an English heart, and given a sweetness to many an English life, before Izaak Walton sallied forth from his little linendrapery shop (seven feet and a half long, by five wide), in the Royal Burse, in Cornhill, or from the half-shop that he afterwards occupied in Fleet Street, whose corresponding portion was tenanted by a hosier, and, laying aside business, "went a fishing with honest Nat and R. Roe;" but, at least, Izaak was the first of that pleasing class of modern writers, the end and aim of whose productions is to allure others to the same love and study of nature, and to the enjoyments connected with it.

'The Complete Angler, or Contemplative Man's Recreation, appeared in 1653; and its reception shows that the public taste—as yet uncorrupted by the example of Charles II. and his Court—could appreciate, and relish with hearty zest, a book breathing of all the freshness of unsophisticated rural life, and of the quiet pastoral scenes amidst which it had been designed and the materials for it collected, and which was also enriched by the fruits of long experience and a most unworldly wisdom. Izaak lived to see his book re-issued four times, so popular did it shortly become. And popular it has ever since remained, and so must remain while poetry, truth, and simplicity are dear to us. Is the reader familiar with good old Izaak's "Recreations?" If so, then, in fancy, he must often have risen with the early dawn to ramble with him in his character of Piscator, and with his scholar Venator, down the banks of the Lea, Walton's beloved river; he must often have breakfasted with them under the sycamore boughs in the open air, the water rippling and murmuring at their feet, and the eastern rays yet shining gloriously upon it. When caught in the "smoking" summer shower, he has sat with them under the honeysuckle hedge, fascinated by the sweet voices of the fair milkmaid and her mother, singing "that smooth song which was made by Kit Marlowe:"

Come live with me and be my love,
And we will all the pleasures prove
That vallies, groves, and hills, and fields,
Woods or steepy mountains yields.

And we will sit upon the rocks,
Seeing the shepherds feed their flocks,
By shallow rivers, to whose falls
Melodious birds sing madrigals.

And I will make thee beds of roses,
And a thousand fragrant posies,
A cap of flowers and a kirtle
Embroidered all with leaves of myrtle:

A gown made of the finest wool,
Which from our pretty lambs we pull;
Fair-lined slippers for the cold,
With buckles of the purest gold:

A belt of straw and ivy buds,
With coral clasps and amber studs;
And if these pleasures may thee move,
Come live with me and be my love

The shepherd swains shall dance and sing,
　For thy delight each May-morning;
If these delights thy mind may move,
　Then live with me and be my love.

And how full of wisdom, even to overflowing, the eloquent old man is: "Let me tell you," he says to his scholar, "there be many that have forty times our estates, that would give the greatest part of it to be healthful and cheerful like us, who, with the expense of a little money, have eat, and drank, and laughed, and angled, and sung, and slept securely; and rose next day, and cast away care, and sung, and laughed, and angled again, which are blessings rich men cannot purchase with all their money. Let me tell you, scholar, I have a rich neighbour that is always so busy that he has no leisure to laugh; the whole business of his life is to get money, and more money, that he may still get more and more money; he is still drudging on . . . . he considers not that it is not in the power of riches to make a man happy." So, "Let us not repine," he adds, "if we see another abound with riches, when, as God knows, the cares that are the keys that keep those riches, hang often so heavily at the rich man's girdle, that they clog him with weary days and restless nights."

We are sorry there is a shady side to Izaak's wisdom. "The scholar" of our day will often smile at the preference given to angling above all other pursuits as a means of attaining the happy and holy frame of mind which Izaak so delightfully commends; but that smile must often be changed into a frown, and he may be half inclined to turn away in disgust, when he reads one of Walton's barbarous directions for impaling live-bait for the angle, and will for the moment almost sympathise with Byron's wish that the

　　　———quaint, old, cruel coxcomb, in *his* gullet
　　　Should have a hook, and a small trout to pull it.

But we must recollect that Walton himself is perfectly unconscious of saying anything that can expose him to censure when he advises that the frog impaled on the hook shall be used as tenderly "as though you loved him," in order "that he may live the longer!" Both in innocence as well as in every other excellent quality, angling, according to Izaak, is pre-eminent. With combined wit and enthusiasm, he somewhere writes, "We may say of angling, as Dr. Boteler said of strawberries, 'Doubtless God could have made a better berry, but doubtless God never did,' and so (if I might be judge) God did never make a more calm, quiet, innocent recreation than angling."

After the day's sport, Piscator takes his scholar to a house where he himself has often before found rest and refreshment; it is called Bleak Hall, and is situated about a mile from Edmonton, by the Lea side. Bleak Hall (Fig. 2163) is not a mansion, as its name would seem to imply; but simply "an honest alehouse, where might be found a cleanly room, lavender in the windows, and twenty ballads stuck about the wall; with a hostess both cleanly, and handsome, and civil." Piscator values the fish he has caught too highly to have them spoiled in the cooking. So they are dressed in accordance with his own views, and the pair sit down to supper, and what with good liquor, tale-telling, song-singing, and other recreations, they spend a delightful evening, before they retire to the bed which is so "white," and smells so sweet of the "lavender."

The building now known as Bleak Hall was formerly a kitchen, with a room over it (ascended by a staircase outside), called the "fisherman's locker," from its having been used as a place of deposit for their tackle. If it be not the identical hall of Walton, as has been supposed, it must have been a similar "alehouse" for fishermen on the Lea river; but if we cannot satisfy ourselves thoroughly of the identity of this interesting relic of the "contemplative man," no such doubt exists in respect to another, of equally interesting associations, the veritable "Fishing House" (Fig. 2162) on the banks of the Dove, built by Walton's true disciple and adopted son, Charles Cotton the poet, who resided in the neighbourhood. The situation of this little building was exactly such as might be anticipated—isolated, in a fine smooth stream, with a bowling-green close by, and meadows and mountains around. Well might the visitor exclaim in the words of Viator, "Now, I think this a marvellous pretty place!" when he looks "from the brink of the hill upon the river," and the "vale it winds through like a snake."

Izaak, in a marginal note to Cotton's account of this place, says, "Some part of the fishing-house has been described, but the pleasantness of the river, mountains, and meadows about it cannot, unless Sir Philip Sidney or Mr. Cotton's father were again alive to do it." This allusion to Cotton's father appears to be but one of the many tokens of affection that existed between Walton and Cotton—an affection as beautiful in its way as anything about them. This is still further shown by the initial letters of their respective names that Cotton had placed upon the fishing-house, "twisted in cypher;" and by the fact, that as in life they loved each other, so in death they were undivided; their reputation being indissolubly connected in the 'Complete Angler,' by the addition of Cotton's second part, which is not unworthy of its position. A few years ago the fishing-house was in a ruinous state, the roof decayed, the inscription illegible, the table broken, and moss and weeds overrunning the whole, whilst a broken window afforded the only entrance. Yet even thus it gave a touching interest to the romantic river. Since then, however, a spirit that we rejoice to perceive breaking from its lethargy, that of veneration for the ancient landmarks, has cleared away the intrusive vegetation, removed the fallen fragments, and restored the whole to its primitive state. In legible characters may now again be read, as of old, "Piscatoribus Sacrum;" and there, too, is the "twisted cipher" over the door, and the date of the erection, 1674. The interior also has its stone floor and dozen comfortable arm-chairs, "marble table and all, in the middle." In short, we recognise with delight the complete restoration of Cotton's own fishing-house. It is sheltered, we should add, by a few yew and other trees. Altogether it would be difficult to imagine a place that more predisposes one to trains of high and solemn thought; and Cotton himself has done justice to it. To read 'The Retirement' here, is like listening to one's own feelings and sentiments, expressed with more than one's own power:—

　Farewell, thou busy world, and may
　　We never meet again;
　Here I can eat, and sleep, and pray,
　And do more good in one short day
　Than he who his whole age outwears
Upon the most conspicuous theatres,
Where nought but vanity and vice appears.

　Good God! how sweet are all things here!
　How beautiful the fields appear!
　　How cleanly do we feed and lie!
　Lord! what good hours do we keep!
　How quietly we sleep!
　　What peace, what unanimity!
　How innocent from the lewd fashion
Is all our business, all our recreation!

　Oh, how happy's here our leisure!
　Oh, how innocent our pleasure!
　Oh, ye valleys! oh, ye mountains!
　Oh, ye groves, and crystal fountains!
　How I love, at liberty,
　By turns to come and visit ye!

　Dear Solitude, the soul's best friend,
That man acquainted with himself dost make,
　And all his Maker's wonders to intend,
　　With thee I here converse at will,
　　And would be glad to do so still,
For it is thou alone that keeps the soul awake: &c.

Near the fishing-house stood Beresford Hall, Cotton's residence, where Walton, in his old age, found the ease and retirement so congenial with the favourite pursuits of his past life. His wife, "a woman of remarkable prudence and of the primitive piety," was the daughter of Thomas Ken of Furnival's Inn, and sister of Dr. Ken, Bishop of Bath and Wells. This union connected him intimately with the Royalist party; and Charles II. distinguished him by the perilous honour of conveying the "lesser George" to London, after the defeat at Worcester. But Walton was no reckless partisan. Ashmole says of him, that he was "well known, and as well beloved of *all* good men." He lived forty years after his retirement from business in 1643, spending most of his time in the houses of distinguished persons, whose friendship he had won by his goodness and his writings, or with whom his matrimonial alliance had connected him. Walton wrote several works besides his principal one, 'The Complete Angler,' and all were distinguished for charming simplicity, affecting moral sentiment, and impressive wisdom. His coadjutor, Cotton, furnishes a sadder history; his is the oft-told tale of opportunities wasted, and life declining into poverty as well as old age. His accomplishments, wit, and amiable disposition might have rendered him both happy and eminent, had he possessed more prudence or more wealth; but wanting both of those prime requisites of success in the world, he fell into difficulties and died insolvent, leaving behind him just such productions as serve to heighten our regret for the loss of what he might have done.

2153.—Billiards. (From 'School of Recreation,' 1710.)

2154.—Francis Moore, 1657. (From an anonymous Print published at that date.)

2155.—Dee

2156.—Kelly.

2157.—John Gadbury 1658

2158.—Lilly.

240

2159.—Group of Portraits

CAMDEN. SHAKSPEARE. H. JONES. RALEIGH. BACON.

2160.—Raleigh's House, Pied Bull, Islington.

2161.—Hooker.

2162—Cotton's Fishing house.

2163.—Bleak Hall.

2164.—Selden

2165—Gallery of the Arundel Marbles.

The groups of portraits of eminent men (Figs. 2159, 2174) that appear among our engravings, may be viewed as representing something more than the mere fanciful linking together of so many contemporaries; they may suggest—not infelicitously—the peculiar ties of sympathy, intercourse, and friendship, that, directly or indirectly, bound the whole together. Of the great men of the latter part of the sixteenth and early part of the seventeenth centuries, all those who were living at any one time—poets, dramatists, philosophers, historians, men of art or science—appear to have been personally familiar with each other. Defective as our knowledge of this matter must be in relation to a period in which Shakspere could live, and leave behind him so little materials for a history of his individual life and character, we can yet trace the links of this intellectual chain with tolerable precision and certainty. Thus, for instance, to begin with the one who stood highest in worldly position—the prose-poet and philosopher, the Lord Chancellor Bacon. He was the intimate friend of Essex: and Essex was the patron and friend of both Shakspere and Spenser. Could we restore the past, and have the chambers of Essex House in the Strand suddenly laid open to us, on some favourable occasion, we should see—there can be little or no doubt—three of the greatest of England's sons, the authors of the 'Novum Organon,' 'Hamlet, and the 'Fairy Queen,' in high commune together. Then, we know that Bacon and Jonson were personally intimate: on the Chancellor's sixtieth and memorable birthday, the poet was an honoured guest. As to Jonson himself he was everybody's friend, except at such times as he had taken it into his head to become, for a brief while, almost everybody's enemy. He was the friend of Shakspere; and delightful is it to recollect the particular incident in which their friendship is said to have originated, although the story is held to be somewhat apocryphal. "It began," says Rowe, "with a remarkable piece of humanity and good nature. Mr. Jonson, who was not at that time altogether unknown to the world, had offered one of his plays to the players, in order to have it acted; and the persons in whose hands it was put, after having turned it carelessly and superciliously over, were just upon returning it to him with an ill-natured answer, that it would be of no service to their company, when Shakspere luckily cast his eye upon it, and found something so well in it as to engage him first to read it through, and afterwards to recommend Mr. Jonson and his writings to the public." Inigo Jones was of course intimately connected with Jonson. The Masques of Whitehall have given a "Beaumont and Fletcher" kind of indivisibility to their names. Jonson, however, it must be confessed, was not an amiable man; so, when Jones offended him, tremendous was the storm poured down upon the artist's devoted head. Camden was Jonson's tutor, and we should say that seldom has scholar owed more to a master than in this case. But the poet's obligations to the learned and estimable antiquary did not end with the tuition of Westminster School. We learn from Wood that when Jonson early in his career was in great distress, and compelled to work as a common bricklayer in the erection of Lincoln's Inn, some gentlemen who saw him took compassion on him, and drew attention to his case. He was then sent, it is said, by his former master, Camden, who had probably lost sight of him for a while, to Raleigh, who made him tutor to his son, and sent him with the latter to the Continent. And thus began Jonson's connection with Raleigh, which ultimately extended even to their literary productions. Jonson wrote for the 'History of the World' an account of the Punic War; and though Raleigh neither acknowledges this nor many similar pieces of assistance that he is said to have received, it is Jonson who may give us the full explanation, though in few words. He said Raleigh "esteemed more fame than conscience." Here is indeed the key to Raleigh's whole character. Nor did divisions of countries keep asunder our great men. Jonson walked on foot to Hawthornden to see Drummond. Jonson, again, was a friend of Selden, "the great philologist, antiquary, herald, linguist, statesman, and what not." (Wood.) Jonson called him "monarch of letters," and lent him books out of his valuable library, that Selden could nowhere else find. And through Selden the men of the earlier part of the seventeenth century are connected with those of a little later time. He appears to have known all familiarly. We find him contributing notes to Drayton for his 'Poly-Olbion,' sharing in all the proceedings that led to the Civil War; and whilst for the most part acting on the side of the Parliamentarians, and agreeing with much of the views of such men as Milton, was on friendly terms generally with the Royalists: it is Clarendon who writes the most glowing of eulogiums upon his character;—we have seen in a previous page that Butler was one of his associates. A curious fact in relation to Milton and Selden may be here mentioned. Cromwell first desired Selden to write an answer to the 'Eikon Basilike'—and it was

after his refusal that Milton undertook and accomplished the task.

With Milton we might commence a similar series of literary connections. Marvel and Harrington were among his most intimate friends; and the latter established a club, known as the Rota, at the Turk's Head in Palace Yard, where, at one time or another, were no doubt to be seen every literary man of any eminence at the time, whose political position or views did not keep him away. We do not know whether Dryden was ever among the audience, but we do know that he was very proud of what little personal communication did take place betwixt him and the author of the 'Paradise Lost.' One of the oddest of these communications was that relating to the work just mentioned. Aubrey says Dryden went to the illustrious poet "to have leave to put his 'Paradise Lost' into a drama in eclogue. Mr. Milton received him civilly, and told him he would give him leave to tag his verses." Dryden was one of the earliest members of the Royal Society, and therefore in continual personal communication with such men as Waller, Denham, and Cowley, Boyle, Hooke, and Barrow, and others of equal learning and ability.

To these notices many similar ones might be added—such as that Hobbes made it his pride to act as amanuensis to Bacon—that it was Raleigh who introduced Spenser to Elizabeth, and who founded the Mermaid Club in Friday Street, the resort of all the most eminent intellects of the day, and so on. But enough has probably been said to give some idea of the close personal intimacy that existed among the eminent men of the periods in question; and which, in itself, shows how much more genial, to say the least of it, was the heart of society then than now, when the literary, artistical, and scientific writers have so little connection with each other, when each is divided into so many "cliques," and when among all our "re-unions" nothing like the pre-eminently intellectual unions of the Mermaid, the Falcon, or the Devil's Tavern, are in any quarter to be found. We have our great societarian meetings plentiful enough, but they live and move and have their being in the public eye, and possess, therefore, little or nothing of the characteristic of the older assemblages that we refer to. *Their* greatest charm was the *abandon* that prevailed among them—a circumstance as favourable to the development of many intellectual qualities, as to the enjoyment of them.

In selecting from the men we have recently named some few for especial comment, we must not forget one or two others whom we have not had occasion to mention. There is poor old Stow:—had he no recognised place among the eminent men of his day? Was he shut out from the mighty circle of mind that then surrounded England as it were with a halo of light? By no means. The Earl of Leicester, Spenser's patron, patronised him; though, as the patronage went no further than hearty thanks and commendations for a book written at the earl's request, we will not place much stress upon it. Archbishop Parker gave him more effectual encouragement in his antiquarian labours. Bacon and Camden knew him so well—in the best sense of knowledge—that they quoted facts from him on the bare strength of his statement that they *were* facts. Ben Jonson and he took their walks together, as we learn from an anecdote that has been preserved by Drummond of Hawthornden, in the record of his remarkable conversations with the illustrious Ben. He says Jonson told him that as he and Stow were walking together, they met two lame beggars; Stow asked them, "What they would have to take him to their Order?" A superstitious mind would of course connect this incident by more than ordinary relations with the remarkable circumstances that accompanied the close of Stow's life.

He was the son of a tailor, and himself bred to the business. But the customs of the past soon drew away his attention from the costumes of the present, and he became an ardent chronicler and antiquarian. About 1560, when he was thirty-five years of age, he set out on a pedestrian journey through England, for the purpose of examining the historical manuscripts that were then lying scattered about in great profusion in the libraries of cathedrals and other public buildings. At the same time he collected, so far as his scanty means would permit, all sorts of old books and manuscripts—just then a plentiful commodity, owing to the dissolution of the monasteries by Henry VIII. The loss inflicted upon literature by that act can hardly, indeed, be estimated. Bishop Bale ('Declaration') has given us a melancholy view of the state of things that prevailed in consequence:—"A number of them which purchased these superstitious mansions" (the monasteries and other religious houses), "reserved of those library books some to serve their jakes, some to scour their candlesticks, and some to rub their boots; and some they sold to the grocers and soap-sellers, and some they sent over sea to book-binders, not in small numbers, but at times whole ships full. Yea, the universities are not all clear in this detestable fact; but cursed is the belly which seeketh to be fed with so ungodly gains, and so deeply shameth his native country. I know a merchant-man (which shall at this time be nameless), that bought the contents of two noble libraries for forty shillings price: a shame it is to be spoken. This stuff hath he occupied instead of grey paper, by the space of more than these ten years, and yet hath he store enough for as many years to come." A priceless service, then, Stow must have rendered to the history of his country, by wandering about to collect the most precious of those scattered leaves. Necessity—a cruel one he must have felt it—interrupted these labours of love, and drove him back to the shop; until Dr. Parker, archbishop of Canterbury, to his honour be it remembered, assisted him with the means to resume his important vocation. The book suggested by the Earl of Leicester, a 'Summary of English Chronicles,' appeared in 1566. Above thirty years later, or in 1598, he put forth the work by which he is to this hour popularly known—his 'Survey of London;' a work that has formed, and must ever form, the basis of all accounts of the great British metropolis. Eight years he spent on this survey; a long time under any circumstances, but fearfully so to Stow, who was labouring under poverty and sickness, and extreme old age through the whole of it. The worst privation was the interruption of his labours by the ailments that attacked him. "He was afflicted near his end very much with pain in the feet; which perhaps was the gout. In the year 1602 or 1603, he was fain to keep his bed four or five months with it; where he observed how his affliction lay in that part that fomerly he had made so much use of, in walking many a mile to search after antiquities and ancient books and manuscripts. He was now within a year or two of a good old age, that is, fourscore years." (Strype.) In the very absoluteness of his needs the poor old man determined to apply for relief to the country for which he had done so much; and in what manner, thinks the gentle reader, was he compelled to do this? The answer is, the gracious and formal consent that was granted by the English Solomon, that the historian might go a-begging through certain districts of the country! To this effect, a paper was regularly drawn up, signed and sealed by James I., and addressed to "all and singular, archbishops, bishops, deans, and their officials; parsons, vicars, curates, and to all spiritual persons; and also to all justices of peace, mayors, sheriffs, bailiffs, constables, churchwardens, and headboroughs; and to all officers of cities, boroughs, and towns corporate; and to all other our efficient ministers, and subjects whatsoever, as well within liberties as without, to whom these presents shall come." The reasons for the issue of the grant are thus stated in the preamble: Stow, as a citizen of London, had "for the good of the commonwealth and posterity to come, employed all his industry and labour to commit to the history of chronicles all such things worthy of remembrance as from time to time happened within this whole realm, for the space of five and-forty years, until Christmas last past (as by divers large and brief chronicles of his writing may appear), besides his great pains and charge in making his book called his 'Survey of London,' wherein he spent eight years in searching out of ancient records concerning antiquities both for London and Southwark." Accordingly, in answer to his humble suit, and in recompense of his labours and travail, and towards his relief now in his old age, power, licence, and authority are granted to Stow or his deputy, to ask and gather the alms and charitable benevolence of his majesty's loving subjects in thirty-six counties. These included the whole of England; Cornwall, Northumberland, Westmoreland, and Cumberland alone excepted. The paper then concludes, "We will and command you, and every of you, that at such time and times as the said John Stow or his deputy, the bearer hereof, shall come and repair to any of your churches or other places, to ask and receive the gratuities and charitable benevolence of our said subjects, quietly to permit and suffer them so to do without any manner your let and contradiction; and you the said parsons, vicars, and curates, for the better stirring up of a charitable devotion, deliberately to publish and declare the tenor of these our letters patent unto our said subjects; exhorting and persuading them to extend their liberal contributions in so good and charitable a deed." Strype has given us the means of forming some slight notion of Stow's success. The parish of St. Mary Woolnoth, London, contributed seven shillings and sixpence. Stow died in 1605, and was buried in the church of St. Andrew Undershaft, where a monument (Fig. 2166) was erected to his memory by his wife, which still remains.* Maitland tells a disgraceful story of the removal of his bones in 1732, to make way for those of some richer person. Opposite this church it is said

* A *coloured* engraving of this monument will form the frontispiece to Vol. II.

Stow lived, and used to witness year by year the scenes that he so picturesquely describes as taking place there on the 1st of May, when the Maypole was taken down from the hooks where it hung below the eaves of the neighbouring houses, and after it had been decorated with long and gaily-coloured streamers, was set up before the church; while quickly around its base, the summer-houses, bowers, and arbours were erected of green boughs, the Lord and Lady of the May selected, their braveries of dress put on—and the dances, the music, the shouts, the feastings—the mirth—the enjoyment—raised by rapid steps to their highest pitch. At one time, all this was put down by authority, in consequence of an attack made upon the foreigners resident in London, on one May-day—long known subsequently as the Evil May-day. But it should seem that already puritanism was directing its efforts against the national holidays. About the time that people began to talk of the restoration of the pole of St. Andrew of Undershaft to its legitimate uses, a clergyman preached against it at Paul's Cross. ' I heard his sermon," says Stow, "and I saw the effect that followed. For in the afternoon of that present Sunday, the neighbours and tenants . . . over whose doors the shaft had lain, after they had dined to make themselves strong, gathered more help, and with great labour raising the shaft from the hooks whereon it had rested two-and-thirty years, they sawed it in pieces, every man taking for his share so much as had lain over his door and stall. . . . . Thus was this 'idol,' as he, *poor man*, termed it, mangled, and burnt."

Stow appears to have been peculiarly thrown in the way of observing this worthy clergyman's behaviour. In the following anecdote we hear more of "Sir Stephen," as he was called, and obtain a fearful glimpse of the time, to say nothing of a bit of information as to Stow's own local position that comes in at the end. In the third year of Edward VI. a great insurrection broke out in Norfolk, Suffolk, Essex, and other parts, and "Strict orders being taken," says Stow, "for the *suppression of rumours*, divers persons were apprehended, and executed by martial law, amongst the which the bailiff of Rumford in Essex was one, a man very well beloved. He was early in the morning of Mary Magdalen's day (then kept holiday) brought by the sheriffs of London and the knight-marshall to the well [or pump] in Aldgate, there to be executed upon a gibbet set up that morning; where, being on the ladder, he had words to this effect:—' Good people, I am come hither to die, but know not for what offence, except for words spoken by me yesternight to Sir Stephen, curate and preacher of this parish, which were these:—He asked me, "What news in the country?" I answered, "Heavy news." "Why?" quoth he. "It is said," quoth I, "that many men be up in Essex; but, thanks be to God, all is in good quiet about us." And this was all, as God be my judge.' Upon these words of the prisoner, Sir Stephen, to avoid reproach of the people, left the city, and was never heard of since amongst them to my knowledge. I heard the words of the prisoner, for he was executed upon the pavement of my door, where I then kept house." One hardly knows whether to wonder most at the execrable character of this murder, or at its ineffable stupidity. Acts like these, it must be acknowledged, form an ugly reverse to the picture of merry England. We learn from another of Stow's half-public, half-private stories, that property was as recklessly played with as life by the great men of his day. The Drapers' Hall in Throgmorton Street stands on the site of a magnificent palace erected by Sir Thomas Cromwell, afterwards Earl of Essex, the favourite minister of King Henry VIII. "This house," says Stow, "being finished," and Cromwell "having some reasonable plot of ground left for a garden," but not so much as he desired, "caused the pales of the gardens adjoining to the north part thereof, on a sudden to be taken down, twenty-two foot to be measured forth right into the north of every man's ground, a line to be there drawn, a trench to be cast, a foundation laid and a high wall to be builded. My father had a garden there, and there was a house standing close to his south pale; this house they loosed from the ground, and bare upon rollers into my father's garden twenty-two foot ere my father heard thereof; no warning was given him, nor other answer when he spake to the surveyors of that work, but that their master, Sir Thomas, commanded them so to do. No man durst go to argue the matter, but each man lost his land; and my father paid his whole rent, which was 6s. 8d. the year, for that half which was left." Stow adds quietly, but severely, "This much of mine own knowledge have I thought good to note, that the sudden rising of some men causeth them to forget themselves." Not the least interesting part of this story is the fact that a house could be moved in the sixteenth century with as much ease and success apparently as in the nineteenth, and with a great deal less noise and wonder.

2166.—Stow's Monument, in the Church of St. Andrew Undershaft.

2169.—Inigo Jones.

2170.—Harvey. (From a Portrait by Cornelius Jansen.)

2168—Statue of Donne.

171.—Milton at the age of Nineteen.

2167.—Donne.

2172.—Portrait of Milton.

2173.—Milton and his Localities.—1, The Portrait, from an etching by Cipriani, after a picture formerly in the possession of Jacob Johnson.—2, Ludlow Castle, from a view drawn in 1750.—3. Chalfont, from a woodcut in a series of views of Poets' residences.—4. Christ's College, Cambridge, from a print in Ackermann's Cambridge.—5, St. Giles's, Cripplegate, with part of the London Wall, from a view in Wilkinson's 'Londiniana.'

2175 —Chancel of St. Giles, Cripplegate.

2176
Sir Dudley North.   (From a Print by Vertue.)
Dr. Davenant.   (From an anonymous Print.)
Sir Josiah Child   (From an anonymous Print.)

2178.—Essex's Ring.

2177.—Sculpture on Thynne's Monument in Westminster Abbey

2174.—Milton, from a Miniature by Faithorne.—Ray, from a Picture in the British Museum.—Temple, from a Picture by Sir Peter Lely.—Dryden, from a Picture by Hudson, in Trinity College, Cambridge.—Hobbes, from a Picture by Dobson, in rooms of Royal Society.—Boyle, from a Picture in the Collection of the late Lord Dover

2179.—Alderley Church

What Charles I. did for painting in England, when he formed at Whitehall the first collection of pictures deserving the name of national, was done with equal zeal and ability, and more extensive opportunities, by the Earl of Arundel for sculpture, when he brought together at his mansion in the Strand, the matchless collection of antique marbles that have ever since been known by his name. But to a certain extent even the credit of Charles's collection should belong to the Earl, as it was he who recommended and by his own example stimulated the King to the task. The mode in which the Earl set to work to accomplish the object he had determined to attain, is peculiarly worthy of notice. The exclusive services of two of the most accomplished men of the day, Evelyn and Mr. (afterwards Sir William) Petty, were secured by the Earl, and the former despatched to Rome, while the latter undertook a journey of no ordinary hazard to the Greek Islands and the Morea. Petty's expedition was full of interest. Having ransacked the islands of Paros and Delos with indefatigable zeal and a proportionate success, he took his way towards Smyrna, was shipwrecked opposite Samos, and escaped with his life only. In one hour all the fruits of his past labour were swept away. But instead of despairing, and doing nothing, there was only the more reason, he thought, for going on. And he was rewarded. At Smyrna he obtained many most valuable marbles—among them the Parian Chronicle, so called from its having been made (as supposed) in the Isle of Paros, nearly two hundred and fifty years before the birth of Christ. It consists of a block of marble, and contained in its perfect state an account of the principal events in Grecian history for more than thirteen hundred years. If aught more be needed to show what a truly precious fragment of antiquity this is, we may extract one or two—from among the numberless—passages of the highest interest and historical value.—" Since Xerxes formed a bridge of boats on the Hellespont, and dug through Athos, and the battle was fought at Thermo[py]lae, and the sea-fight by the Greeks at Salamis against the Persians, in which the Greeks were victorious, 217 years: Calliades being Archon at Athens." Again: " Since Euripides, being 43 years of age, first gained the victory in tragedy 17[9] years, Diphi[los] being Archon at Athens. But Socrates and A[naxa]goras lived in the time of Euripides." The letters and figures in the brackets were supplied by Selden and others, in the place of those which had been effaced in the original.

When at length the Earl had collected together the results of the labours of his enthusiastic coadjutors and of his enormous expenditure, he found himself in possession of some thirty-seven statues, one hundred and twenty-eight busts, and two hundred and fifty marbles with inscriptions, in addition to various sarcophagi, altars, and a great number of fragments, and in addition also to a collection of gems of inestimable value. With these Arundel House was speedily adorned as never before was adorned any mansion in England. The inferior and mutilated statues were placed in the garden, and the statues and busts formed the gallery. Would the reader like to be able to take a single glance into that gallery as it then was? Our engraving (Fig. 2165) will enable him to do so.

As magnificent a spirit certainly reigned in the breast of this Earl of Arundel as in the breasts of any of the men who have been most famous for that quality. He honoured living artists as much as dead ones; and while he ransacked the world to discover any works that might yet exist of the one, he did all that lay in his power to promote the production of works that he thought ought to exist from the hand of the other. He patronised Inigo Jones and Vandyke; he brought over from Holland Wenceslaus Hollar, the engraver; he employed Nicholas Stone, Le Sœur, and Fanelli, the sculptors; while other able men he maintained altogether. No wonder that Clarendon should be able to say, " His expenses were without any measure, and always exceeded his revenue."

What remains of this noble collection, after the terrible inroads made upon it by the Parliament during the Civil War, by the Earl's own descendants in putting it up for sale, by repairing artists who ruined whatever they undertook to restore, by bequests, and so on —are now deposited at Oxford; part of them having been bequeathed to the University by the son of the founder of the collection, and the remainder by the Countess Dowager of Pomfret.

From Broad Street to Cripplegate is but a short way, according to ordinary modes of reckoning; yet, if we remember that Milton was born in the first, and died in the last, and that his whole and mighty life lies, in a sense, between them, the distance will appear strangely lengthened to the dullest imagination. We propose, as briefly as possible, to follow the local steps of the poet's life, pausing awhile

where he paused, and recall the recollections that he has bequeathed to every spot where he found for a time an abiding place or home. He was born, as we have said, in Broad Street, in the parish of Allhallows. His father was a scrivener; and the sign that was fixed over the door spoke of more than business to those who understood it—the Spread Eagle there represented formed the armorial bearing of the family. Poets, of all persons, are, by the very laws of their temperament, peculiarly subject to parental influences, and must benefit or suffer to an all-important degree by their wisdom or folly—care or neglect—love or want of love. Milton had, in a word, one of the best of fathers, and was therefore one of the happiest of sons. And again and again the poet has taken opportunity to express in his own manner his affectionate and grateful sense of what he owed to him, and of his father's own skill and accomplishments. In a passage of his Latin poem *Ad Patrem*, translated by Cowper, he says,

> Thou never badest me tread
> The beaten path, and broad, that leads right on
> To opulence, nor didst condemn thy son
> To the insipid clamours of the bar,
> The laws voluminous, and ill observ'd.

In another passage he says to his father—

> Thyself
> Art skilful to associate verse with airs
> Harmonious, and to give the human voice
> A thousand modulations, heir by right
> Indisputable of Arion's fame.
> Now say, what wonder is it if a son
> Of thine delight in verse; if, so conjoin'd
> In close affinity, we sympathize
> In social arts and kindred studies sweet?

Under such a parent progress in whatever was undertaken would be rapid, and it was especially so with the youthful Milton. Whilst his education proceeded with such rapidity—first at St. Paul's School, and then at Cambridge—that he became one of the most accomplished of scholars before the years of manhood were reached, he at the same time cultivated the divine art with so much assiduity and success, that his scholastic attainments sink into comparative insignificance as the young poet rises before us, giving promise of the very highest future excellence. Milton was but fifteen when he went to Cambridge, and entered Christ's College (Fig. 2173). A mulberry-tree planted by his own hand flourishes in the college-garden to this hour. One of the most romantic incidents of the poet's life occurred here, if it occurred at all. It is well known that the poet was eminently handsome. Our portraits of him at different periods (in pages 244, 245) afford ample proofs of this, especially the one that exhibits him in the bloom of youth (Fig. 2171), when he was about nineteen years of age. A still more forcible testimony to his personal beauty is the appellation given to him by his fellow-collegians—they said he was the " Lady of the College," and Milton by no means relished the compliment " Wandering one day, during the summer, far beyond the precincts of the University, into the country, he became so heated and fatigued, that reclining himself at the foot of a tree to rest, he shortly fell asleep. Before he awoke, two ladies, who were foreigners, passed by in a carriage. Agreeably astonished at the loveliness of his appearance, they alighted, and having admired him as they thought unperceived, for some time, the youngest, who was very handsome, drew a pencil from her pocket, and having written some lines upon a piece of paper, put it with a trembling hand into his own. Immediately afterwards they proceeded on their journey. Some of his acquaintance, who were in search of him, had observed this silent adventure, but at too great a distance to discover that the highly-favoured party in it was our illustrious bard. Approaching nearer, they saw their friend, to whom, being awakened, they mentioned what had happened. Milton opened the paper, and with surprise read these verses (in Italian) from Guarini:—' Ye eyes! Ye human stars! Ye authors of my liveliest pangs! If thus when shut ye wound me, what must have proved the consequence had ye been open?" The story here told was first made public in a newspaper of the last century; which added also, that, " Eager from this moment to find out the fair incognito, Milton travelled, but in vain, through every part of Italy;" but this can be only a poetical flourish of the narrator, for it was later in life that he left his own country to travel on the Continent.

Notwithstanding Johnson's humiliating statement, who " is ashamed to relate what he fears is true, that Milton was one of the last students in either University that suffered the public indignity of corporal correction," it is certain that he had great reason to be satisfied with his College residence. His abilities commanded admiration, and as to the treatment he generally received, we have the best of testimonies—his own—that he met with more than " ordinary favour and respect," and " above any of his equals " at the hands of the fellows of the College. But he did not like Cambridge, or the country around it, and he did like home. In his Latin elegy, addressed to Charles Deodati, and which was probably written when he was about nineteen, he thus delightfully speaks of his affection for—and his content to stay at—home, rather than return to the University :—

> I, well content, where Thames with influent tide
> My native city laves, meantime reside ;
> Nor zeal nor duty now my steps impel
> To reedy Cam, and my forbidden cell ;
> Nor aught of pleasure in those fields have I
> That to the musing bard all shade deny.
> 'T is time that I a pedant's threats disdain,
> And fly from wrongs my soul will ne'er sustain.
> If peaceful days in letter'd leisure spent
> Beneath my father's roof be banishment,
> Then call me banish'd ; I will ne'er refuse
> A name expressive of the lot I choose.

Who was the " pedant" mentioned in the above lines ? and what were the " wrongs " the poet complains of ? It must be owned there is here some support given to Johnson's statement. Yet supposing it to be true, neither the offence given, nor the person by whose order the punishment may have been inflicted—not even the punishment itself, which was one that *had* been common enough—was therefore *necessarily* of a character to degrade Milton in the eyes of his associates, or, for any length of time, in his own. Punishments are sometimes inflicted in universities, as well as elsewhere, that have the effect of enhancing the general respect for and sympathy with the sufferer. Milton's high-principled unbending character may have easily led him into collision with some one of the men in authority ; on the question, for instance, of the politics of the day, that were fast assuming a most portentous aspect under the guidance of the new monarch, Charles I.

Milton leaves Cambridge, and his father soon after leaves London for a country residence ; a delightful change in every way, and one that has left memorable proofs of its influence upon the poet. At Horton, in Buckinghamshire, where the family took up their new residence, the exquisite pair of poems, ' L'Allegro ' and ' Il Penseroso,' with ' Lycidas ' and ' Comus,' were all, it is supposed, written. And every one of these poems breathes, as it were, a fresh and pure country air. Here, too, the ' Arcades ' was composed and performed at Harefield House, the seat of the Countess Dowager of Derby, the actors being that lady's children. To Harefield and its beautiful owner the following lines are supposed to have been applied :—

> Towers and battlements it sees
> Bosom'd high in tufted trees,
> Where, perhaps, some beauty lies
> The cynosure of neighbouring eyes.

The engravings of Harefield, given in an earlier page of our work, happily illustrates the first couplet of this passage. The circumstances in which ' Comus ' originated are peculiarly interesting. Warton writes—" I have been informed from a manuscript of Oldys, that Lord Bridgewater, being appointed Lord President of Wales, entered upon his official residence at Ludlow Castle with great solemnity. On this occasion he was attended by a large concourse of the neighbouring nobility and gentry. Among the rest came his children, in particular Lord Brackley, Mr. Thomas Egerton, and Lady Alice,

> to attend their father's state,
> And new-entrusted sceptre.

They had been on a visit at a house of their relations, the Egerton family, in Herefordshire ; and in passing through Heywood Forest were benighted, and the Lady Alice was even lost for a short time." Such is one record of this accident—' Comus ' is another. Milton prepared it to be performed at Ludlow Castle (Fig. 2173), as a Michaelmas festivity, and the actors in the real were also the actors of the dramatic story.

Milton's Italian journey (undertaken after his mother's death in 1637) was full of incidents calculated to impress deeply a poetical mind. It will be sufficient to mention his personal interviews with Galileo, Grotius, and the patron of Tasso, Manso. But to our minds, a still more important feature of this expedition is the proof it affords of Milton's patriotism. Whilst other men were in many instances hastening to leave England on account of the political troubles that just then assumed a much more alarming aspect than they had ever done before since the commencement of the struggle, Milton on the contrary, hastened home

And now he is once more in London ; the city of his affections and his pride. In the epistle to Deodati he had thus addressed London :—

> Oh city, founded by Dardanian hands,
> Whose towering front the circling realms commands !
> Too blest abode ! no loveliness we see
> In all the earth, but it abounds in thee.

And although in the interim he had been better able to judge of the truth of the admiration expressed in these lines than he could be when he wrote them, it does not appear that he had learned to love or admire his native place one jot the less. We find him from henceforth constantly residing there, when not called or driven away by the temptations of love or the threatened dangers of the plague. In 1643 he married. His wife was the daughter of a gentleman at Forest Hill, Oxfordshire, a Royalist—a circumstance that augured ill for Milton's future happiness. And it was not long before she parted herself from him, by declining to return from her father's when she had gone home on a visit. Milton's twofold comments upon this act were most characteristic. He published various treatises in justification of his right to repudiate her under such circumstances ; and then he began to pay his addresses to a young lady of great beauty. About that time the poet called one day at the house of a relation in St. Martin's-le-Grand, and there suddenly appeared before him his wife, who cast herself upon her knees, and begged him earnestly to forgive her. No one can help connecting this scene with the famous one in ' Paradise Lost,' where Eve prays Adam's forgiveness of the sin into which she has led him ; and the result in both cases was the same. Of Milton, like Adam, it may be said—

> Soon his heart relented
> Towards her, his life so late, and sole delight,
> Now at his feet submissive in distress.

He forgave her ; and if he thought at all of the possibility that the distress into which her friends had by this time fallen was partly the cause of her return, he only showed it by his magnanimity in assisting that family—politically opposed though they were—by every means in his power, even to the taking the whole, father, mother, brothers, and sisters into his own house.

Let us here pause a moment to see what the poet had been doing since his return from Italy, and what he was preparing to do. Education, that mightiest of subjects—that basis of all national schemes of social, moral, or political reformation—at first engaged his mind. He adopted a new system of tuition, and applied it to the education of his nephews, John and Edward Phillips. Other pupils were subsequently added. We cannot here enter into Milton's system ; suffice it to say, that its paramount object appears to have been to form good citizens ; its chief principle, in details, the stimulating thought rather than memory into action. He began his public career about the same time by the publication of various treatises and tracts, one among which, ' The Reason of Church Government,' contains the passage that gives us beyond question the most deeply interesting glimpse that was ever afforded to the world of the motives of a great poet in preparing himself for the accomplishment of the mightier tasks that he has set before him. Speaking of his visit to Italy, where he perceived that some poetical trifles he had in his memory—composed whilst he was under twenty—were received with written encomiums, which the Italian is not forward to bestow on men this side the Alps, " I began," he continues, " thus far to assent, both to them and divers of my friends here at home ; and not less to an inward prompting, which now grew daily upon me, that by labour and intent study (which I take to be my portion in life), joined to the strong propensity of nature, I might perhaps leave something so written to after times, as they should not willingly let it die. These thoughts at once possessed me ; and these others—that if I were certain to write as men buy leases, for three lives and downward, there ought no regard to be sooner had than to God's glory, by the honour and instruction of my country. For which cause, and not only for that I knew it would be hard to arrive at the second rank among the Latins, I applied myself to that resolution which Ariosto followed against the persuasions of Bembo, to fix all the industry and art I could unite to the advancing of my native tongue ; not to make verbal curiosities the end—that were a toilsome vanity—but to be an interpreter and relater of the best and safest things among mine own citizens throughout this island in the mother dialect. That what the greatest and choicest wits of Athens, Rome, or modern Italy, and those Hebrews of old did for their country, I in my proportion, with this over and above, of being a Christian, might do for mine ; not caring to be once named abroad, though perhaps I could attain to that, but content with these British islands as my world, whose fortune hath hitherto

2482.—Great Seal of William and Mary.

2183.—Medals of William and Mary.

2184.—Embarkation of the Prince of Orange at Helvoetsluys.

2181.—Queen Mary   (From a Painting by Sir Godfrey Kneller.)

2180.—William III.   (From a Painting by Sir Godfrey Kneller.)

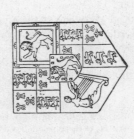

2186.—Arms of William I.

2185.—Landing of William III. at Torbay.   (From a Print after Stothard.)

2187.—Regalia.

2188.—Earl of Albemarle, temp. William III. (From Kneller.)

2189.—Kinsale. (From an Old Drawing.)

2191.—Battle of the Boyne. (From West's Picture.)

2192.—Medal struck to commemorate the Battle of the Boyne. The King crossing the River at the head of his Troops.

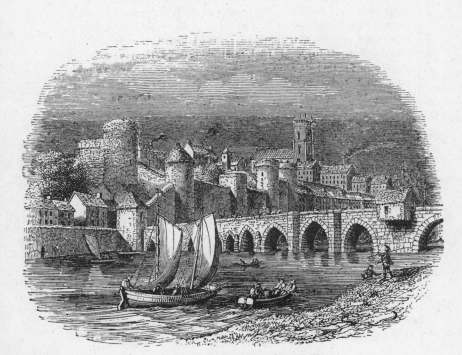

2190.—Limerick showing a portion of the Old Walls

2193.—Medal struck to commemorate the siege of Londonderry. Obverse: Advance of the English Fleet to relieve Londonderry; in front, Bust of King William, crowned by Valour and Abundance. Reverse. Poverty and Slavery holding a broken Crown of Laurel over the head of Louis XIV.

been, that if the Athenians, as some say, made their small deeds great and renowned by their eloquent writers, England hath had her noble achievements made small by the unskilful handling of monks and mechanics." He then proceeds to speak of what his mind in "the spacious circuits of her musing" hath contemplated; as the epic, with its modes of treatment, and its subjects;—the dramatic—and so on. The Scripture, he remarks, affords fine subjects; and he specifies, in the most magnificent prose sentences that ever flowed from mortal pen, the Apocalypse of St. John, as "the majestic image of a high and stately tragedy, shutting up and intermingling her solemn scenes and acts with a sevenfold chorus of hallelujahs and harping symphonies." 'Paradise Lost,' we see, is as yet in the dim distance, but *approaching*. In the mean time clear to nis mind as the goodness of God himself, who gives the poet his peculiar gifts, are the objects of the poetical mission. His abilities "are of power, beside the office of a pulpit, to inbreed and cherish in a great people the seeds of virtue and public civility; to allay the perturbations of the mind, and set the affections in right tune; to celebrate, in glorious and lofty hymns, the theme and equipage of God's almightiness, and what he suffers to be wrought with high providence in his church; to sing victorious agonies of martyrs and saints, the deeds and triumphs of just and pious nations, doing valiantly through faith against the enemies of Christ; to deplore the general relapses of kingdoms and states from justice, and God's true worship. Lastly, whatsoever in religion is holy and sublime, in virtue amiable or grave, whatsoever hath passion or admiration in all the changes of that which is called fortune from without, or the wily subtleties and reflexes of man's thoughts from within: all these things, with a solid and treatable smoothness, to point out and describe." It required a Milton to shape such a task; and how he, in the end, accomplished it, all men know. But that end was not as yet. He had to contend with his own friends by publishing treatises in favour of the Liberty of the Press, that were ever after to be so many text-books on the subject for posterity; he had to renew from time to time his attacks against his opponents, for supporting what he conceived to be royal and ecclesiastical tyranny. Nor did his labours cease even when the king was overthrown and beheaded. The men of the Commonwealth required that the world should know the motives that had actuated them in their tremendous career; who so fit as Milton to give the world the requisite knowledge? The tract on the 'Tenure of Kings and Magistrates, proving that it is lawful to call to account a Tyrant or wicked King,' &c., therefore appeared.

Cromwell was not the man to leave a Milton unemployed in the public service, if he could be induced to enter into it. The poet became the Foreign Secretary of the State at one of the most eventful periods in all English history. He takes up his residence at Whitehall. Thenceforth for some time the will of the most potent uncrowned king that ever ruled Britain was expressed in language that is probably also without parallel, for its nervous strength and classic elegance. It must be remembered that the whole of the communications between England and foreign states during the Protectorate were made in Latin. It is said that the poet kept up here a kind of semi-royal state; holding a weekly table for the entertainment of foreign ministers and persons of learning. It is most likely that Aubrey's remarks applied to this period. He says of Milton, "He was mightily importuned to go into France and Italy; foreigners came much to see him, and much admired him, and offered to him great preferment to come over to them; and the only inducement of several foreigners that came over into England was chiefly to see [Oliver Cromwell, the] Protector, and Mr. J. Milton; and would see the house and chamber where he was born. He was much more admired abroad than at home." Suddenly a terrible calamity fell upon the poet. What it was he tells us in one of his noble sonnets.

Addressing his friend Cyriack Skinner, he writes—

> Cyriack, *this three years' day*, these eyes, though clear,
> To outward view of blemish or of spot,
> Bereft of light, their seeing have forgot;
> Nor to their idle orbs dark night appear
> Of sun, or moon, or star, throughout the year,
> Of man or woman. Yet I argue not
> Against Heaven's hand or will, nor bate a jot
> Of heart or hope; but still bear up and steer
> Right onward. What supports me, doth thou ask?
> The conscience, friend, to have *lost them*, *overplied*,
> In Liberty's defence, my noble task,
> Of which all Europe rings from side to side.
> This thought might lead me through the vain world's mask
> Content, though blind, had I no better guide.

Milton left Whitehall in 1652, and finally quitted the post of

Secretary in 1655, the period of the composition of the above sonnet; but it does not seem to have been noticed that the poem explains *why* he left Whitehall: it was that day three years before the day of its composition that he lost his sight; the inference therefore is irresistible, that as he became suddenly blind in 1652, and left Whitehall in 1652, that he left at the time of his deprivation, on account of its incapacitating him for his duties. It might be desired that he should continue to hold nominally, perhaps in part really, his post until it was seen whether the blindness would pass away or be confirmed. In 1655, when he wrote the sonnet, it was but too evidently confirmed; and so the poet resigned the office. A pension of 150*l*. was assigned to him by Cromwell.

On leaving Whitehall, Milton removed to a house in Petty France (now Queen-Square Place), Westminster; the very same that Jeremy Bentham lived in for so many years, and at his death left to his friend and executor Dr. Bowring. A friend of ours, who had occasion when a boy to see Bentham in his garden, remembers the enthusiasm with which the philosopher spoke of the poet's walking in the same place. Milton's blindness was but the first of a series of blows calculated to test his fortitude to the uttermost. In the house just named he lost his wife, married again three years later (a most happy union it should seem), and within a single twelve-month lost her too, by the same cause—childbirth. His twenty-third sonnet forms her best memorial—

> Methought I saw my late espoused saint
> 　Brought to me, like Alcestis, from the grave,
> 　Whom Jove's great son to her glad husband gave,
> 　Rescued by force from death, though pale and faint.
> Mine, as when wash'd from spot of childbed taint,
> 　Purification in the old law did save,
> 　And such as yet once more I trust to have
> 　Full sight of her in heaven without restraint,
> Came, vested all in white, pure as her mind;
> 　Her face was veiled, yet to my fancied sight
> 　Love, sweetness, goodness in her person shin'd
> So clear, as in no face with more delight.
> 　But oh, as to embrace me she inclin'd,
> 　I wak'd, she flew, and day brought back my night.

Next came the Restoration, when the poet was proscribed. And certainly a more zealous, as well as more able opponent, the Royalists had not. Up to the last moment Milton attempted to stem the reflux of public feeling towards monarchy. These were bold sentences to write when their author might so soon be called upon to answer for them :—" What I have spoken is the language of that—which is not called amiss—the good old cause. If it seems strange to any, it will not seem more strange, I hope, than convincing, to backsliders; thus much I should perhaps have said, though I were sure I should have spoken only to trees and stones, and had none to cry to but with the prophet, 'O, earth, earth, earth!' to tell the very soil itself what her perverse inhabitants are deaf to. Nay, though what I have spoken should happen (which Thou suffer not, who didst create mankind free, nor Thou next, who didst redeem us from being servants of men!) to be the last words of our expiring liberty." And they were the last words for many a long year.

Milton was proscribed; and when he found concealment in a friend's house in Bartholomew Close, a proclamation was issued for his apprehension, and for the similar apprehension of another Commonwealth-man, Goodwin, in these terms: "The said John Milton and John Goodwin, are so fled, or so obscure themselves, that no endeavours used for their apprehension can take effect, whereby they may be brought to legal trial, and deservedly receive condign punishment for their treason and offences;" that is to say, we presume, hanging, drawing, and quartering, after the style of the bloody handling of Harrison and his fellow-sufferers at Charing Cross. But the poet escaped the first "pelting of the pitiless storm" (it is said a mock funeral was performed to mislead the authorities); and subsequently, when the government had grown a little less thirsty of human blood, he was allowed to escape under the Act of Indemnity. He is stated to have owed this good fortune to Davenant, to whom some years before Milton had rendered a similar service. If he was not committed to the hangman, however, some of his books were: a bad answer to their contents, to say the least of it.

Peace at last: and time and opportunity for the realization of the dreams of enthusiastic youth, and which had only grown dearer and assumed a more practical shape to the mind of the mature man. So whilst other men of his age (fifty-two), and who had passed through a tithe of his troubles, would have been content to let the world glide along as it would, for the few years of life that remained to them, Milton sat down to a task far mightier than any that had ever before engaged even him. And what a privilege was that enjoyed by Milton's friends, of looking, after a while, upon the results of his labours—of reading for the first time, from the author's own manuscripts, as yet virgin to the world—'Paradise Lost.' Such a privilege was enjoyed by Elwood the quaker, who had acted occasionally as his secretary. When the Plague broke out in London in 1665, Elwood took a house for Milton at Chalfont, in Buckinghamshire. Here Elwood came one day to see him, and after some "common discourses," he says, "had passed between us, he called for a manuscript of his, which being brought, he delivered it to me, bidding me take it home with me, and read it at my leisure, and when I had so done, return it to him, with my judgment thereupon. When I came home, and set myself to read it, I found that it was that excellent poem which he entitled 'Paradise Lost.'" It was in this same "pretty box" (Fig. 2173), as Elwood called it, at Chalfont, that 'Paradise Regained' was written.

Milton's last London residence was in Bunhill Fields: it was there that Dryden, and no doubt a host of other eminent men, from time to time visited him. Not unfrequently he was found sitting before the door, enjoying the sunshine, wrapped in a coarse grey coat—blind, but not the less seeing a thousand times more truly, and vividly, and usefully, than those around him who laboured under no similar deprivation. The serene wisdom that characterizes him whenever he is not engaged in actual disputation—a large exception, it must be owned—is in nothing more evident than in his habits. It would be difficult to imagine a more beautiful domestic life than Milton's. His biographer, Todd, says, "Of wine, or any strong liquors, he drank little. In his diet he was rarely influenced by delicacy of choice; illustrating his own admirable rule—

> The rule of "not too much," by temperance taught,
> In what thou eat'st and drink'st; seeking from thence
> Our nourishment, not gluttonous delight.

He once delighted in walking and active exercise, and appears to have amused himself in botanical pursuits; but after he was confined by age and blindness, he had a machine to swing in for the preservation of his health. In summer he rested in bed from nine to four; in winter to five. If at these hours he was not disposed to rise, he had a servant by his bedside to read to him. When he first rose he heard a chapter in the Hebrew Bible, and commonly studied till twelve; then used some exercise for an hour; then dined; afterwards played on the organ or bass-viol, and either sung himself or made his wife sing, who he said had a good voice but no ear. It is related that when educating his nephews, he had made them songsters, and sing from the time they were with him. No poet, it may be observed, has more frequently or more powerfully commended the charms of music than Milton. He wished, perhaps, to rival, and he has successfully rivalled, the sweetest descriptions of a favourite bard, whom the melting voice appears to have often enchanted—the tender Petrarch. After his regular indulgence in musical relaxation, he studied till six; then entertained his visitors till eight; then enjoyed a light supper; and after a pipe of tobacco and a glass of water, retired to bed."

And death itself came as sweetly and gently as sleep must have done, after days so spent. The friends in the room did not know the actual moment of his departure. He was buried, where his father had been buried before him, in the church of St. Giles, Cripplegate (Fig. 2175): and if the visitor there can for a moment put aside the all-absorbing consciousness of the intellectual grandeur that seems to issue forth as it were from that little six feet of earth, and thence radiate into the furthermost corners of the earth—if he can forget this, and recall in a more staid spirit the various associations of the place, he cannot but be struck with some surprise at the peculiarly happy conjunctions that the history of the church exhibits. Here Milton's friend and patron, the all-powerful Protector, was married to Elizabeth Bourchier; here do we find in the parish register, one entry after another relating to the Brackleys, and Egertons, and Bridgewaters, just as though the parish authorities, in their admiration of the poet and their pride in his memory, had thought it would be but a graceful act of attention to collect here the facts relating to the births, marriages, and deaths, of the noble family who had originated and first performed 'Comus.' At the same time we think it very likely that if the authorities were asked their opinion of the matter, they would, in their modesty, disclaim the compliment, and say it was because the Earl of Bridgewater had a metropolitan residence in the neighbourhood.

If there had been no other fact to distinguish the England of the seventeenth century than the discovery of the circulation of the blood, it would have stood out, through all time, as one of the most eventful eras in the history of scientific progress. As usual, the

very extent and originality of the discovery unfitted men's minds for receiving it, and the discoverer was added to the list already, alas! but too long, of those who have been martyrs for Truth's sake. We often hear various kinds of causes alleged for the persecution of Galileo: it was bigoted individuals—it was the Inquisition—it was the Catholics—and so on; but in sober truth Persecution is of no particular class or religion, profession, or condition; the practical rule has hitherto been in all countries—proscribe what you do not understand—punish those who dare to think themselves so very much more enlightened than we are; and thus Harvey in England, by offending the prejudices of men of education and intellect—his professional brethren—fares no better than Galileo in Italy, when he cannot square his astronomical system with the religious notions of the Pope! The portrait in the apartments of the College of Physicians is in itself a revelation of human suffering and fortitude such as it seldom falls to the lot of painter to bequeath to the world. That portrait is by Cornelius Jansen; and our copy of it (Fig. 2170) may give some slight notion how worthy it is of his reputation, and of the painful, yet in many respects noble, recollections that it is calculated to recall.

But Harvey's, though the greatest, is not the only name of his own time that is illustrious in the annals of science. It was then that Ray (Fig. 2174) may be said to have laid the foundations of the science of botany. In 1682 he published his new method of classifying plants, which, after it had undergone some improvements by his own hand, at a later period formed the basis of the system which has since obtained such wide acceptation in connection with the name of Jussieu. The characteristic of this system is, that it arranges all plants according to natural affinities, so far, of course, as our skill and knowledge can guide us to these affinities. But Ray experienced in a lesser degree the same kind of treatment as Harvey; the system was too great an innovation. Curious and most instructive is the result. Ray's discoveries were allowed to sink into oblivion, or something very like it; Linnæus arose, and with wonderful skill and industry, constructed an entirely artificial system, which, as it did not establish any remarkably new and original *principles*, was received with universal favour: all our botanical books, those of very recent date alone excepted, have been founded upon this method: and the result is, that the best European botanists agree that the whole is one splendid error—our botanical books are worthless, and the despised Ray's system, carried of course farther, and made more perfect than by him, but still his system, is recognised as the only true one. To many of our readers these remarks may appear strange: we transcribe, therefore, for their satisfaction, a sentence or two from the pages of a periodical publication of high character, and edited by one of the most eminent botanists of the present time. In answer to a correspondent of the 'Gardener's Chronicle,' Dr. Lindley writes, "The Linnæan system of botany is not worth learning, and we cannot do you the disservice of recommending you a book on the subject." And again, "the Linnæan botany *teaches nothing but names*, and these with less certainty and advantage than the natural system. It had its use in former days, but is now abandoned by all botanists." It is a clear case, we fear. There is no help for it: we must burn our Linnæan-system books: or, better still, keep them to remind us and our children, that when fresh alleged improvements are put forward, we shall act wisely not to reject them because of their originality, but remember Linnæus and Ray.

Robert Boyle's name (Fig. 2174) must be added to those of Harvey and Ray, though in his own time his contemporaries would have thought the connection of three such personages ridiculous, so high stood Boyle's reputation, so low the reputation of his two contemporaries. Posterity, if it has not exactly reversed that position, has at least a little lowered Boyle and very much elevated Harvey and Ray. After all allowances, it appears to be unanimously agreed that Boyle was a great experimental philosopher, and one who, if he did not enrich science with any pre-eminent discoveries, did much to promote that state of knowledge and feeling in which both new discoveries will be made and old ones turned to increased advantage. In Boyle's life there are many incidents of a highly-interesting nature, as showing into what unscientific paths men of science then wandered. Boyle was a famous chemist; and his researches in chemistry caused him to indulge in the belief that he would discover, nay, that he almost had discovered—the art of transmutation of metals. Isaac Newton even was alarmed. In a letter written by him in 1676, he thus expresses himself: "But yet because the way by which mercury may be so impregnated has been thought fit to be concealed by others that have known it, and may, therefore, possibly be an inlet to something more noble, *not to be communicated without immense damage to the world*, if there should be any

2194.—Glencoe.

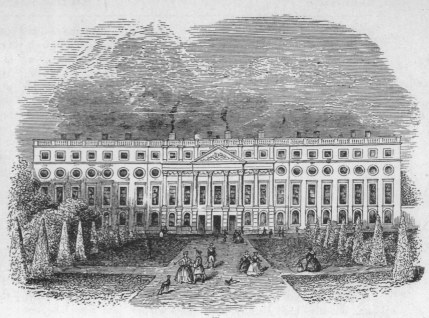

2195.—Hampton Court Palace. (From a Print of the time.)

2196.—Medal struck to commemorate the able Conduct of the Queen, after the Defeat of the English and Dutch Fleets in the Channel, in June 1690. Obverse. Bust of the Queen. Reverse · The Tower on the one side, and the Dutch ships careening on the other; in front, the Queen extending a Trident in her right hand.

2199.—Great Seal of William III.

2200.—Crown of William and Mary.

2201.—Shilling of William and Mary

2197.—Londonderry. (From an Old Print.)

2198.—Autograph of King William

2202.—Shilling of William III.

2203.—Halfpenny of William III

2204.—Queen Anne. (From a Portrait by Sir Godfrey Kneller.)

2206.—Arms of Anne.

2205.—Prince George of Denmark. (From a Portrait by Sir Godfrey Kneller.

2207.—Great Seal of Anne (before the Union with Scotland)

2208.—Medal struck to commemorate the Victory of Oudenarde.

2209.—Medal struck to commemorate the Battle of Blenheim. On the Obverse are Portraits of Prince Eugene and the Duke of Marlborough. On the Reverse, the Battle of Blenheim, showing the rout of the French army and the Surrender of Marshal Tallard.

2210.—Medal struck to commemorate the Surrender of Lille.

verity in Hermetic writers; therefore I question not but that the great wisdom of the noble author [Boyle] will sway him to high silence, till he shall be resolved of what consequence the thing may be." Boyle had faith too in spirits. Lastly, he had faith in what we now call Mesmerism: for it seems clear that the performances of Mr. Greatraks in the seventeenth century were identical with those of the disciples of Mesmer in our own time. And it is certainly very remarkable that the cures alleged to be performed by the gentleman we have named should have been attested by such men as Boyle, Cudworth, Andrew Marvell, Wilkins, Patrick, and Flamsteed; the last of whom went over to Ireland purposely to be touched, and said he was "eye-witness of several of his cures." Marvell signed two certificates in one day, of cures effected by Greatraks; one, of a tumour in the breast, as large as a pullet's egg, by twice stroking; and the other of a general soreness and pains in the body, which were "run out" by the same means. Greatraks is described as a man of "graceful personage and presence." He used neither "charms nor unlawful words;" but attributed his power to a "ferment implanted in his body." He took no money for his services, and appears altogether to have been a man of estimable character, and of disposition and habits little suited to the notoriety he obtained.

If Boyle and his fellow-labourers in the walks of science erred by giving too ready a belief to the marvellous, it may be doubted whether this error is not more rational, as well as less dangerous, than the one of an opposite kind, which induces men to disbelieve everything they cannot make palpable to the outward senses, or which they do not find in harmony with their preconceived notions of the economy of Nature. The moment science ceases to inquire or to speculate, it stops. It was not by mathematical demonstrations that Newton really discovered the law of gravitation; they only followed whither the imagination had gone before, and proved that the sublime height from whence as from a tower the imagination had seen the end of all, was no "baseless fabric" of a vision. That the man of science can speculate on the truth of the greatest marvels—absurdities as we generally call them,—and yet confer on science benefits that its matter-of-fact followers never dream of till they are realized, does not admit of question: the discoverer just named was, as we have seen, a believer in the transmutation of metals.

But there were beliefs of a past time, that one cannot be too grateful to see are beliefs no longer. Such was the faith in witches, which induced the high-minded and virtuous Sir Matthew Hale to condemn two poor women to death for an impossible crime. This took place at the assizes at Bury St. Edmund's, in the year 1655. In the course of the trial Hale avowed his belief in witchcraft; and this may have helped to influence the jury in finding them guilty. Both were executed. This incident formed the only blemish in the otherwise pure and unsullied character of one of the best of English judges. The church of Alderley (Fig. 2179), in Gloucestershire, contains, as is most fitting, his remains; for in that village Hale was born.

BOOK VII.

THE PERIOD

FROM

THE REVOLUTION TO THE END OF THE REIGN OF GEORGE II.

A.D. 1688—1760.

CHAPTER I.—ANTIQUITIES OF THE CROWN AND THE STATE.

ILLIAM III.'s expedition to England may be termed the art of invasion made easy. It is true he had to make extensive preparations, collect a large army of soldiers (14,000), and provide a magnificent fleet to bear them from shore to shore in safety. It is true also that a hurricane somewhat discomposed him when he had embarked at Helvoetsluys (Fig. 2184), and set out on his voyage; for it compelled him to put back to Helvoet, and gave an opportunity to the well-wishers of King James to spread the report that the expedition was deferred. But again starting, with the flag waving to and fro from his own ship, declaring by its motto his purposes to the world—" I will maintain the Protestant religion and the liberties of England,"—William now passed the straits of Dover unmolested by any English fleet, and landed in perfect comfort at Torbay, where many of the invaded came forward full of enthusiasm to greet him (Fig. 2185). This invasion might almost be said to be too easy—and to have somewhat spoiled him for any difficulties that might occur. Having marched to Exeter, and not finding there the full cordiality of feeling he had anticipated, he had half a mind to go back, and punish those who he thought had not been sufficiently zealous in preparing for him a proper reception, after inviting him over, by publishing their names, and then leaving them to James's tender mercies. But the military and legal butcheries of Kirk and Jeffreys, that had followed the Monmouth insurrection, and spread the deepest misery and horror through Devonshire, Somerset, and adjoining counties, might well have excused the people of Devon from being lukewarm in any new schemes relating to the throne. But William advanced, entered London, waited in dignified silence, while the Houses of Lords and Commons deliberated what they should do under such extraordinary circumstances, declined—without giving time for its being formally proposed—the Regency that James's adherents desired in order to preserve intact their master's right to the throne; declined also the proposition (founded upon a similar desire) of reigning in right merely of his wife, Mary, James's daughter, and accepted, when at last it was fairly offered to him in conjunction with his wife (Figs. 2180, 2181), the throne of the British realms.

But if the tenor of all these preliminary proceedings were of a very unusual character, matters were soon to fall into the ordinary train; ease of obtaining the throne to give place to arduous efforts for maintaining it; negotiations and punctilios to broad swords and cannon balls. The royal bigot who had fled from England was " scotched, not killed;" the powerful Louis XIV. of France took up his cause, not so much perhaps for the sake of legitimacy, as in order to injure his most dangerous enemy—William of Nassau; who had now added to the power he already possessed, through his wisdom, courage, and devotion to the cause of Protestantism, all the influence that the sovereignty of England must naturally bestow.

The defender of the Protestants of the Continent now became a greater safeguard than ever to his friends, a source of infinitely greater apprehension to his enemies. Roman Catholic Ireland was, of course, to be the battle-field. There James hastened with a powerful army. As he left the French court, Louis, embracing him, said, " The best wish I can give you is, that I may never see you again." Near Bantry Bay, James's French fleet met what he thought ought to be his own English fleet, and the latter were beaten off. When the French ambassador extraordinary, who accompanied James, exulted over this defeat of the English sailors, James sadly replied, " It is the first time." He landed at Kinsale (Fig. 2189). The siege of Londonderry (Fig. 2197) was one of the earliest events of importance that occurred. This was heroically defended by the townspeople, who were chiefly Protestants. Having no faith in William's governor, Colonel Lundy, they deposed him, and put in his place Walker the Presbyterian minister, and Major Baker. The gallant minister had already raised a regiment at his own expense to oppose James, and endeavoured ineffectually to prevent the advance of the besiegers of Londonderry. The siege commenced about the middle of April, 1689, and the inhabitants were speedily reduced to a terrible state by the want of provisions. But every day supplies were expected from William by sea, and the two governors did all they could to inspire the people with courage and fortitude. Baker died in June, and then the sole command devolved on the minister, who proved to be one of the very best of soldiers. He was always to be seen where he was most wanted, now tightening the indispensable bonds of discipline, now preaching in the cathedral, now heading a rallying party from the gates. And at last the siege was raised; Major-General Kirk having succeeded in passing with three ships over a boom that James had erected in the river. A medal (Fig. 2193) was struck to commemorate this important success.

With so overwhelming a proportion of the people of Ireland in his favour, James was not however to be put down by ordinary fighting;—William determined to go over to Ireland in person; and the two kings were speedily confronting each other on the same soil; though not at so short a distance as to enable them to decide the contest by a bold encounter. There was much skirmishing, and a great deal of delay, before an opportunity of this kind was fairly offered to both parties. But at last it began to be noticed that the hostile armies drew near and nearer to each other, until on the 29th of June, when James crossed the river Boyne, and took up his position on its right bank, William was so near at hand, that on the 30th he too reached the river at the same point, and prepared for battle. The armies were very large: William's consisting of 36,000 English, French, Dutch, and Danes; James's of 27,000 French and Irish, independent of a body of troops who held Drogheda for him, on his right, so as to command the road to Dublin. The commanders included brave and eminent men on both sides. William had with him Duke Schomberg, and his son Count Schomberg, Generals Ginkel, Douglas, and Kirk; whilst for James fought the Dukes of Tyrconnell and Berwick, Generals Hamilton and Sarsfield, the Count Lauzun, and other able French

2213.—Blenheim House, Woodstock, from the Park.

2214.—Wood's Irish Halfpennies.

2215.—Medal struck to commemorate the Battle of Ramilles. On the one side, the Battle is represented at the moment of victory; on the other is an emblematic representation of the Union of England and Holland. Behind the Figure of England, on a Pillar inscribed with the three first letters of his name, stands a Bust of Marlborough, and opposite to it another of D'Ouwerkerke

2211.—Charles Montague, Earl of Halifax,—from a Picture by Sir Godfrey Kneller. Lord Chancellor Somers,—from a Picture by Sir Godfrey Kneller. Henry St. John, Viscount Bolingbroke.—from an anonymous Etching. Robert Walpole, Earl of Orford.—from a Painting by Pond. Robert Harley, Earl of Oxford.—from an anonymous Print. Sidney, Earl of Godolphin,—from a Painting by Sir Godfrey Kneller

2212.—Blenheim House, Woodstock

2218.—Royal Hospital, Greenwich.

2219.—North Front of Chelsea Hospital.

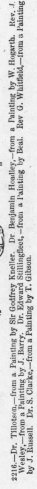

2216.—Dr. Tillotson.—from a Painting by Sir Godfrey Kneller. Dr. Benjamin Hoadley.—from a Painting by W. Hogarth. Rev. J. Wesley.—from a Painting by J. Barry. Dr. Edward Stillingfleet.—from a Painting by Beal. Rev G. Whitfield.—from a Painting by J. Russell. Dr. S. Clarke.—from a Painting by T. Gibson.

2217.—Great Seal of Queen Anne (after the Union of England and Scotland).

officers. But then there was William, a host in himself; whilst as far as James's military abilities or courage were concerned, his troops would have been as well if not better without him than with him. An accident, however, had nearly wrought an overwhelming counterbalance in James's favour. As William, on the night of his arrival on the Boyne, rode up and down with his staff to examine the enemies' position, and judge how he might best attack them, two field-pieces were brought to bear upon his party, and fired with such precision, that a man and two horses were killed by the first shot, very near to William's side. A second shot followed, which grazed the bank of the river, then bounded along, *en ricochet*, as military men say, until it passed right across the King's shoulder, and tore away some little flesh. Lord Coningsby, riding up immediately, clapped his handkerchief to the wound; but William said he needed it not—that the ball should have come nearer to do him harm, and then after the wound was dressed proceeded with his employment, continuing on horseback nearly the whole of the day. But James's soldiers, seeing the confusion produced among the party fired on, jumped at once to the conclusion that William was killed, and sent off expresses to that effect to Dublin, to Paris, and to the other chief capitals of Europe. It may not be without interest here to state, that the handkerchief is to this hour carefully preserved in a cabinet at Cassiobury, the seat of the Earl of Essex, and by the side of the cabinet is Cooper's picture representing the incident we have described.

Towards night, William called his officers together, not exactly to ask their opinion, but rather to tell them what he had determined: he would pass the river on the morrow. Immediately all possible preparations were made. The men were to wear in their hats green boughs or sprigs, to distinguish them from the French and Irish, who wore pieces of white paper as cockades. At midnight, William rode amidst the light of torches through every part of the camp. When day broke, in all the splendour of one of the finest of summer mornings, the troops were roused, and by the time the sun was up, the leading divisions were on the march. Ten thousand horse and foot presently moved towards the fords below Slane, and five thousand of James's army advanced to dispute their passage. The contest was sharp, but short and decisive. James's officer, Sir Neale O'Neill, fell dead at the head of his regiment at the first charge; and his opponent, General Douglas, was soon firmly posted on the opposite bank. And now there opened a still more portentous attack from the centre of William's position. Admidst a general movement of Enniskillen infantry, regiments of French Huguenots, and of large bodies of cavalry, a dense mass of Dutch blue guards were in particular seen to advance, their drums beating a march, till they reached the water's edge, when they dashed eight or ten abreast into the river, and crossed towards the centre of James's army, which was partly covered by ditches and breastworks, and partly hidden by intervening heights. A tremendous fire was opened upon the guards as they reached the middle of the river, but they moved on, reached the opposite bank, and dislodged their enemies. The Huguenots and Enniskilleners crossed a little lower down, whilst the cavalry made way between them and the Dutch guards. But the attacks upon them were so fierce that the Huguenots were broken and lost their commander, and some of the horse driven back. Schomberg here started forward, passed the river, placed himself at the head of the Huguenots, and, pointing to the French Catholics in James's army, cried out, in words that must have had a most stirring effect upon those to whom they were addressed, "Come, gentlemen, see your persecutors!" but even as he spoke a ball passed through his neck, and the old veteran was presently dead. "The people here say that the German troops had offered violence to an Irish country girl, for which her lover swore he would take revenge; but being unable to discover the actual miscreant, he selected their general, and slew him." [Kohl.] Schomberg's loss was followed by another that was very much felt after the battle, if not at that time. Walker, the heroic defender of Londonderry, was here killed. It was high time for William to charge in person; which he did with the Enniskillen regiment, who now rallied, and redeemed themselves from the disgrace of their momentary retreat. William, with his sword drawn, though hardly able to carry it through the pain and stiffness of his wound the day before (Fig. 2191), directed them and the Dutch guards right against the centre of James's army, where, however, no James now was;—that prudent monarch was already thinking of the road to Dublin, and endeavouring to place himself in a convenient nearness to it. But his troops fought better for their master than he did for himself; and though they were driven back by the overwhelming impetus of William's attack, they rallied, and even repulsed their enemies for a time so vigorously, that the King was in great personal danger. But from all quarters the charges grew more and more frequent and severe; again and again the Irish and French were compelled to retreat, till, in a word, it was evident the battle was lost, when there was a rapid dispersion of the mighty force, that promised in the morning to restore James to his three kingdoms. The French alone retreated in good order. James's precautions for escape were perfectly successful; he went off under the protection of General Sarsfield's regiment of cavalry, and swept along as fast as fear could carry him to Dublin. Meanly enough, he endeavoured to throw the blame of the defeat on the brave Irish. As he reached the Castle of Dublin, and Lady Tyrconnell advanced to meet him, he said to her, "Your countrymen, the Irish, madam, can run very quick;" the stinging answer was, "Your majesty excels them in this as in everything else, for you have won the race." This was unpleasant; but James was not to be deterred by it from continuing his flight at so rapid a pace that he rode to Waterford by the next night, a distance of more than a hundred miles. Here he had shipping ready, and he at once embarked for France. As he ascended the side, the wind blew off his hat; General O'Farrell, to prevent his catching cold, put his own hat on the King's head, who seems to have been touched by the single act of kindness so far as to try to say something noticeable on the occasion. So he observed, "That if, through the fault of the Irish, he had lost a crown, he had gained a hat from them in its place." But the wit was on a par with the truth of the observation. An obelisk of grand proportions commemorates the battle, and marks the spot where William received the wound of which we have spoken. The medal, shown in our engraving (Fig. 2192), was cast in similar remembrance of the event, and of the personal bravery of the conqueror. "My friend," writes Kohl, "who had grown up in the neighbourhood, informed me, that at the present moment all the details of the battle live in the memories of the people who dwell around, and are handed down from generation to generation; and not these particulars alone, but all the high relationships and entire genealogies of the distinguished persons who were engaged in it. The Irish traditions still possess the peculiar precise character of the traditions of nations who have no books, and whose memory is therefore the stronger. In them everything is described with the greatest accuracy—the localities, the physiognomies, the speeches—just as if the people had seen everything themselves."

But the Irish were not cast down. They had lost a great battle, it was true; but had they not also got rid of James for a time from among them? Their opinions of the man for whom they were still willing to risk everything (because they thought that the interests of religion were bound up in his success) are forcibly shown in their remark, that if the English would only change kings with them, they would be glad to fight over again the battle of the Boyne. With great spirit did they make the best of their unhopeful position: and at Limerick (Fig. 2190), even the all-conquering William was brought to a stand-still. He battered—he made breaches—he assaulted, but was driven back, and nearly killed by a cannon ball. Then he formed more batteries, opened more breaches, guarded his troops by trenches, and again tried an assault with just so much success as to make more annoying the subsequent failure; he carried the covered way and effected a lodgment, but was then forced back again with heavy loss. And there for a time William was fain to let the siege rest, as far as he was personally concerned, for his presence was required in England. In the following year, Limerick capitulated, and in so doing put an end to the war in Ireland.

Through the transactions that have here been slightly noticed, as well as through all the others connected with his management of the public affairs of the nation over which he had been called to govern, William's conduct was of a character calculated generally to engage our respect, and never to call forth sentiments of an opposite nature. But we must now speak of a matter which has stamped lasting disgrace on his memory, and on the memories of every one who was connected with it, either as advisers or as the chief executive instruments: we refer to the slaughters among the wild and sublime rocks of Glencoe. After Ireland had ceased to trouble the new King, Scotland took up the ball, and harassed him incessantly with skirmishings, and plots, and all the outward manifestations of a wide-spread dissatisfaction with his dynasty. His most openly avowed enemies were the Highlanders. Lord Breadalbane thought that a good opportunity offered of turning their hostility, and directing it in favour of King William by a general pardon, a sum of money for division among them, and pensions to their chiefs, the sole but important condition being that four thousand clansmen should be held ready to resist any French invasion. The scheme was liked in high quarters, and a proclamation issued that all the rebels who took the oaths to the new government before the 1st of January, 1692, should be pardoned.

But the Duke of Hamilton had other schemes of his own to oppose to Lord Breadalbane's, and the Highland Chiefs had no faith in the pecuniary honesty of the parties who would have to pay them the money. So they sought to play a double game; they wrote to James to solicit his acquiescence in their submission, which they engaged to throw off when necessary for his interests; and they also endeavoured to instil doubt into William's mind as to the fidelity of his supporters and ministers. Lord Breadalbane and the Scottish Secretary of State then, it should seem, determined to keep no measures with the chiefs, but make them submit, or destroy them like so many wild beasts. It was proposed by Breadalbane, and agreed to by their master, King William, that such of the Highlanders as still held out in opposition to his government should have that sort of execution practised upon them which was known in Scotland as " letters of fire and sword." This was bad enough, under the circumstances, as it is clear that the clans were prepared to submit if treated with clemency and frankness as well as firmness; but even this determination becomes a trifle in conjunction with what was done. The moment the clans saw clearly their danger they submitted, and hurried in to take the oaths. There was one exception—Macdonald of Glencoe, the hereditary enemy of Lord Breadalbane; he paused awhile, unable perhaps to stomach submission to *his* orders, perhaps even fearing he would be in some way treacherously dealt with. But on the last day of the year, and of the term of pardon offered, he wisely made up his mind to yield, and so went to Fort William to take the oaths. The officer in command refused to administer them, on the ground that he was not a civil magistrate. The old chief had then no resource but to go on through rough roads and bad weather to Inverary, which he was unable to reach until two or three days had elapsed. Still, the sheriff, not anticipating the diabolical purposes of some of Macdonald's enemies, after some hesitation, administered the oaths, and the chieftain returned to his home. It has been supposed that William was deceived as to the circumstances when a warrant for execution was obtained from him. But supposing that he did not know that Macdonald had in effect submitted within the period named, it is inconceivable that his ministers should have ventured to practise so far upon him as not even to let him know that he *had* submitted—though in a formal sense —too late. So that, putting the king's conduct in the best light, if we acknowledge, for the moment, that he did not violate his pledge, he did condemn a whole band of men, about seventy in number, to murder—there can be no other word for it—because one man, their chief, whom they were bound to obey, had done the right act, but in a trifling degree, at the wrong time. But how much worse was the conduct—how much deeper the infamy, that attaches to his ministers, Secretary Dalrymple and Lord Breadalbane! They knew the chief had in effect submitted within the allotted time. And what are the excuses offered for them or their master? It is said that the Secretary thought " mercy would be thrown away upon them, because they had been in the irreclaimable habit of making incursions into the low countries for plunder, and because he had himself obtained a pardon for them from King William, when, one of the clan having discovered his accomplices in a crime, the rest had tied him to a tree, and every man of the tribe had stabbed him with a dirk, Glencoe, the chieftain, giving the first blow." [Memoirs of Dalrymple.] But it has been justly observed " all this was Highland law and Highland usage ;" and if the authorities thought the clans should be exterminated therefore, they should have said so, instead of offering a pardon. But supposing the Macdonalds guilty of these crimes, how did the administrators of law and justice in a Christian country proceed to teach the erring men? Why, by the committal of the two crimes that in all ages and countries have been thought the most detestable—murder and the blackest treachery.

In the secluded valley of Glencoe all was peace and satisfaction. The submission of the chief had hushed reasonable fears. Their late enemy William was no longer their enemy; and they might hope from his magnanimity that he would become their friend. It was with pleasure therefore that they beheld one day a body of soldiers, commanded by Captain Campbell of Glenlyon, a relative by marriage of their chief, enter their valley and take up their quarters among them. They were brother-highlanders, too:— how could they make them sufficiently welcome? Day by day passed on; the strangers ate and drank and made merry among their hospitable entertainers; entered—as men in such close companionship must—into all the little joys and sorrows, and hopes and expectations of the domestic life which they for the time spared; made perhaps their individual friendships among the children; and then—one night, when the glen was covered with

darkness, and the Macdonalds one and all were asleep, rose and *butchered them.* The chief and thirty-eight of his clansmen were rapidly despatched; and the rest would have experienced the same fate, but for a touch of foolish remorse that came over one of the murderers. He exclaimed—somewhat loudly and passionately perhaps—to a brother soldier that he liked not the work—that he had not the courage to kill them so. That speech was heard by one of those who yet slept—a son of Macdonald—and so a portion of the clan escaped. William, alarmed no doubt at the horror that the deed excited throughout Europe, sent down a commission of inquiry, which ended exactly as might have been anticipated, supposing William to have really sanctioned all that had passed, and to have possessed throughout a tolerably correct view of the case— *but not else.* The Secretary alone was punished—by dismissal : and his punishment was a mere screen for his master's reputation ; accordingly he was soon re-employed. Campbell's 'Pilgrim of Glencoe,' and Mr. Sergeant Talfourd's recent work on the same subject, testify, among other productions, how deep and permanent has been the impression made by these atrocities.

Glancing for a moment at the private life of William, it does not seem to suggest to us any very amiable or gratifying reminiscences. He was cold, haughty, and formal, and however great in war and politics, was little or nothing out of them. His tastes were at once bad and imitative. Thus when he built at Hampton Court the great and eastern fronts that we still find there, he thought nothing of the beautiful style of the other parts of the building that Wolsey had erected ; he thought only of imitating the *Grand Monarque.* And although, again, he had Wren for his architect, he could not even leave him to do his best. Walpole tells us that Wren submitted another design for the alterations of the Palace, which was " in a better taste," and " which Queen Mary wished to have executed, but was over-ruled." William, however, was delighted with the result, of which our engraving (Fig. 2195) shows one aspect ; he said, as we are told in the 'Parentalia,' that the new apartments, for good proportions, style, and convenience jointly, were not paralleled by any palace in Europe ;" so that the *Grand Monarque* was beaten after all. Of the Queen's taste, on the other hand, Wren speaks in the highest terms. She " pleased herself from time to time in examining and surveying the drawings, contrivances, and the whole progress of the present building, and in giving thereon her own judgment, which was exquisite." Let us here observe that Mary had much of her husband's talent for business ; as she proved on some trying occasions when he was absent, and all the duties of a King devolved upon her. The medal we have engraved (Fig. 2195) records one of these periods ; another was when James thought he was all but restored to the British throne. He had then a great French fleet ready ; he had reason to believe that the commander of the English fleet was favourable to his interests; that Marlborough, already the people's soldier of promise, would lead his armies; and lastly, that the Princess Anne, his second daughter, who was in England, would bring over to his cause the great body of English churchmen. But the Queen, with vigorous hand, soon put down the real danger—the plottings at home; Marlborough was made sure of in the Tower for a few days; and the English sailors as speedily, when they met the French, settled the foreign threatenings. The famous battle of La Hogue was fought in James's own presence, who, as he saw his countrymen and former subjects destroying the French ships and all his hopes by their invincible bravery, exclaimed with truly national feeling, " See, my brave English sailors !" The Princess Anne, who resided, by the way, at Hampton Court, was in danger at this crisis. She had really expected her father's success, though not at all desiring it (the Parliament had declared her the successor to the throne, if William and Mary died without issue) ; and, in consequence of her expectation, somewhat committed herself. But the Government contented itself with watching her ; and but a few years passed before she became the mistress of that Government. Mary died in 1695, and William in 1702, when Anne became immediately Queen of England, being then in her thirty-eighth year.

That peculiar reversal of the ordinary position of wifehood which occurs when a Queen in her own right marries, and thus holds as a subject bound in obedience to her the husband she has sworn to obey, a position exhibited in our own country at present, was first presented to England by Anne and her husband Prince George of Denmark, to whom she was married long before her accession to the throne. The Tudor Queen Mary's case, it will be remembered, was very different. The English Parliament authorised her husband, Philip of Spain, to bear the title of king during his wife's life. But Prince George had not, nor has her present Majesty's

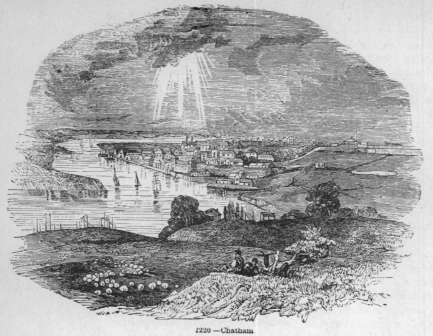

2220—Chatham

2221.—Parliament House and Square Edinburgh

2222.—Medal struck in London on the occasion of Sacheverell's Trial.—The Doctor's Portrait was accompanied by different
Reverses to suit the opinions of purchasers. In one case the Reverse would be a Mitre, emblematic of the Church of
England and in the oth r a head of the Pope as the Representative of the Roman Catholic Church The Inscriptions,
which are continuous would then, in either case read—'H Sach D D is firm to thee.'

2224.—Crown

2225.—Shilling.

2226 —Halfpenny.

2224 to 2226.—Coins of Queen Anne.

2227 —Autograph of Queen Anne.

2223.—The Regalia of Scotland.—a, b, Sceptres; c, Sword of State; d, Scabbard of ditto

228.—George I. (From a Portrait by Sir Peter Lely.)

2230

2229.—Sophia of Zell, Wife of George I. (From the Strawberry-Hill Drawing.)

2231 to 2236.—Queen Anne's Farthings Complete Set.—The first of the series, on the lower line, is the one so highly valued by Collectors.

2237.—James Francis, the Old Pretender. (From a Picture by A. S. Belle.)

2238.—Great Seal of George I.

husband any regal power or name whatever. The cause of the difference that prevails between the position of the wife of a King in his own right, who is crowned and recognized as Queen, and the position of the husband of a Queen in her own right, who remains only a private subject, is no doubt the greater jealousy felt by the State of interference in the one case than in the other. The ordinary law of marriage, that the husband's intellect and will should predominate in all questions relating to the weighty business of life, remains uninterfered with in the first instance; but were that same law to be fully acted on in the second, the effect would be practically a setting aside of the very principle of hereditary government; thus in the eighteenth century it would not have been the personage chosen by the Parliament, Anne, who would have ruled England, but George of Denmark—a gentleman that the Parliament certainly never would have chosen under any circumstances implying full freedom of choice. Quietly therefore, but decidedly, does the State express its opinion as to the behaviour it desiderates in a Prince Consort, by the difference we have pointed out. Of course we do not mean by these remarks to imply that there is no difference between Queen Regnants and Queen Consorts, or, in other words, between a Queen in her own and a Queen in her husband's right. There must be naturally a very great and self-evident difference here, as in all other cases of derived, as compared with original power.

Whilst upon a subject so intimately connected with the outward shows and pomps of sovereignty, let us pause to add a few words upon the Regalia, exhibited in another page (Fig. 2187). The Regalia, properly so called, are represented grouped on the left side of the engraving. The two crowns are the crown of state and the imperial crown. The imperial crown is also called St. Edward's crown, as having been made for the coronation of Charles II., to supply the place of the old crown (which bore the name of Edward the Confessor) destroyed, along with the other ancient regalia, by order of Parliament. The imperial crown "is the crown royal," which is set upon the King's head; the crown of state is for the accommodation of the King, to be worn in procession. The crown of state, represented above, was made for the coronation of George IV., the old one having been broken up. A new crown of state has been made for the present Queen, which contains all the jewels of the former crown, with many additional ones. Four swords are used at a coronation. The sword of state, represented above as sheathed in its ornamental scabbard, and the three swords of mercy and of justice. The sword of mercy is the curtana, or the pointless sword; the sword of spiritual justice is obtusely pointed; but the point of the sword of justice of the temporality is acute. St. Edward's staff is represented above as crossing the imperial crown; it is a large golden rod, with a mound and cross at the top, and is carried before the King in the procession to the coronation. The sceptre and the virge, or rod, are represented crossed in the foreground of the engraving. The sceptre, surmounted by a mound and cross, is placed in the King's right hand, and the virge, or rod, surmounted by a cross and dove, is placed in the left hand. The globe, or orb, surmounted by a cross, is supposed to have been used originally as a type or emblem of sovereignty. The other portion of the regalia are the spurs, of fine gold, curiously wrought, the ring, and the armil, or armilla, which is used in the ceremony of investiture. That portion of a regalia which is used when a Queen Consort is crowned consists of a crown of state, a circlet of gold, an orb similar to the King's sceptres, and a ring. They are grouped on the right side of the wood-cut, the sword of state crossing them.

The Scottish regalia (Fig. 2223) comprise a crown, whose circle or rim was made for Robert Bruce, a sceptre that belonged to James V., a sword presented by Pope Julius II. to James IV., and various other articles of interest as well as value. The well-known Scottish crystals, called "Cairngorms," are used extensively in the adornment of these insignia: which "have had," Kohl observes, "a more singular fate than any other in Europe, excepting perhaps the crown of Hungary. They entirely disappeared for more than a hundred years, and no one knew where they had been placed. In the year 1707, the period of the [legislative] union of Scotland with England, through the patriotism of some Scottish gentlemen, they were packed in a chest and concealed in the wall of an upper chamber of the castle, where they are now exhibited. This precaution was adopted, I believe, in the apprehension that the English might carry them off to London. Their place of concealment was afterwards completely lost sight of, until they were discovered again, for the first time, in 1818, and after the breaking down of the wall exposed to daylight—or at least to waxlight; for the small low room in which they lie, within a grating of iron, is lighted by spermaceti candles, being quite inaccessible to the light of the sun."

If we look at the reign of Anne, in order to discover the most truly important of the events that signalize it, we shall, perhaps, select one that is seldom heard of now-a-days, although its consequences affect us hourly, and, it will be acknowledged, in all respects beneficially : we allude to the amalgamation of the legislatures of England and Scotland into one, an act which made the "Union" for the first time a real and permanently concluded event. This was not accomplished without a great deal of excitement in Scotland. More than once it was feared that the last sittings of the Scottish legislature in the Parliament House (Fig. 2221) would be accompained by bloodshed. The Great Seals of Anne before (Fig. 2207) and after (Fig. 2217) this Union are given in another page. But if we look at the same reign with the eyes of those who lived at the time, it is warfare abroad and intrigue at home, the last in its way as gigantic as the first, that alone seem to occupy all thoughts and energies, from the sovereign downwards to her humblest subjects. It was then that some of England's mightiest victories both by sea and land were obtained; it was then that the fates of governments depended upon the good-will of chamberwomen, and a statesman's fitness for his office had to be decided by his skill in commanding the familiar back-stairs' entry to the palace; it was then that party warfare rose to its highest pitch, and left the names Whigs and Tories so perfectly wrought as it were into the very intellectual being of the nation, that from that day nearly down to our own it has not known how to debate the simplest or the most abstruse question of politics until it was first decided by which of the two appellations it should be called.

We need not, like Lord Byron, ask for a hero for this age, who shall represent it in its essentials,—the man of his day, in the eyes of his contemporaries, still holds and must ever hold the same position. John, Duke of Marlborough, might have said with greater truth than the French king—"The State!—it is me!" Let us, for a brief time, imagine ourselves on a visit to that particular spot in England where the recollections of this period and of its chief moving spirit seem to be the most freshly and fittingly remembered. We will premise merely one or two points—very necessary to be known, but which we shall certainly hear nothing of at the place we propose to visit, respecting the Duke's conduct in the early part of his career. Whilst as yet but Colonel Churchill, and enjoying only in anticipation the success that the great French warrior Turenne had predicted for "his handsome Englishman," he married, and was thus rescued from a very dissipated career. The lady was Sarah Jennings, who, as his wife, became subsequently scarcely less famous than himself. She had, like her husband, been placed in early youth in the household of the Duke of York, afterwards James II., and there acquired the powerful influence over James's second daughter, Anne, which, when the latter became queen, was productive of such momentous consequences. This lady was beautiful, and possessed a truly masculine vigour of intellect, added, unfortunately, to a very imperious temper. Both Churchill and his wife, it will be seen, were therefore intimately connected with the interests of James. And the duke's conduct after their marriage was of a nature to deepen whatever of grateful recollections they felt for him before. Both still remained in his service: confidential missions were from time to time intrusted to the Colonel; he was raised to a Scotch barony, and on James's accession further promoted to an English peerage by the title of Baron Churchill. James now placed the most unbounded confidence in him. When William of Nassau was known to be coming over to England, Churchill took the command of a large body of troops to oppose his advance—left James full of hope from his known skill and courage, and presumed devotion; and the end was—that Churchill went over as coolly as possible to the invader. It was thus he obtained his elevation to the earldom of Marlborough, bestowed by William when he became king. It was barely possible, still, that he had acted from a desire to secure the interests of the nation, and in opposition to all his own personal views and predilections. But not content with one act of treachery, John Churchill liked the game he had played so well that he tried it over and over again upon the very same parties. Now that William was king, he corresponded and intrigued with his former benefactor, James; in short, it is but too evident that Churchill, through all these transactions, thought only of advancing his own selfish interests, no matter at what cost. William knew him thoroughly; and so while he encouraged him to be honest to him by frequent employments, he warned and in some degree prevented him from an opposite course by intervals of imprisonment, or by cashiering him. Yet so strong was the influence of his abilities upon the mind of the king in his dying hour, that he recommended Marlborough to his successor as the fittest person to "lead her armies and direct her councils." And he did both.

About eight miles from Oxford, and close by the town of Woodstock, we find ourselves in the vicinity of an extensive park, through which, at favourable openings, we look upon an edifice surprising for its magnificence and apparent extent, even in this country so thickly studded over with palace-like mansions. But this is in truth a palace, and of the first order. And here is an inscription, referring no doubt to its history, on the stately Corinthian arch or gateway before us. It is in Latin; but for the benefit of the unlearned there is a translation on the park side of the gate. As we read it, we perceive that all around us is but an evidence of what a generous nation can bestow on those who have greatly served it. This is Blenheim Palace, built for the most part with the money granted by a grateful parliament and queen. And the architect was a man of true genius, notwithstanding Pope's satirical epitaph—

Lie heavy on him earth; for he
Laid many a heavy load on thee.

This is Sir John Vanbrugh's greatest work, and it is worthy of him who, in a different walk, produced the 'Provoked Wife' and the 'Confederacy,' and was one of the very first of English comic dramatists. Mr. D'Israeli has devoted a chapter of his 'Curiosities of Literature' to the subject of the "secret history of the building of Blenheim," which shows the great difficulties the artist had to contend with in consequence of the irregularity of the supplies of money, and the conduct of the duchess, who, after the duke's death, had the superintendence of the erection. In the end, the "wicked woman of Marlborough," as Vanbrugh calls her, discharged him from his post, and refused to pay him what was due of his salary. But the work was at last completed in accordance with the architect's original designs—therefore, whatever merits attach to the palace must unquestionably he ascribed to him.

But what is this we read in the concluding part of the inscription? —"The services of this great man to his country, the *Pillar* will tell you, which the Duchess has erected for a lasting monument of his glory, and her affection to him." An excellent idea! Would that every one who has enjoyed the public bounty could feel an equal pride in recording publicly the reasons thereof! As we approach nearer to the castle, pausing every instant to admire the exquisite union of nature and art exhibited in the grounds, and the constantly changing character of the aspects in which the palace presents itself—now so picturesquely beautiful, now so solemnly grand, we arrive at a large sheet of water, winding through a deep valley, and crossed by a bridge of stone of such large dimensions that the centre arch has a span of one hundred feet. This bridge unites the hills on each side. Ah, there is the pillar! a fluted Corinthian one —standing on an eminence in the centre of a lawn—and the Roman figure on the top represents, of course, in accordance with the taste of the eighteenth century, the British hero. And here, on the pillar, there is indeed a full account of the duke's services inscribed. It will take one some half hour or more to read it. It is said, however, to have been written by Bolingbroke;—author and subject, therefore, alike command attention and inspire interest. We can only deal with it by snatches. It commences with a brief but comprehensive and clear view of the causes of the war in which William and Anne were engaged. "Philip, a grandson of the house of France, united to the interest, directed by the policy, supported by the arms of that crown, was placed on the throne of Spain. King William III. beheld this formidable union of two great and once rival monarchies. At the end of a life spent in defending the liberties of Europe, he saw them in their greatest danger. He provided for their security in the most effectual manner. He took the Duke of Marlborough into his service.

"Ambassador Extraordinary and Plenipotentiary
To the States-General of the United Provinces."

The Duke contracted several alliances before the death of King William. He confirmed and improved these: he contracted others after the accession of Queen Anne; and re-united the confederacy, which had been dissolved at the end of a former war, in a stricter and firmer league.

"Captain General, and Commander in chief
Of the Forces of Great Britain."

"The Duke led to the field the armies of the allies. He took with surprising rapidity Venlo, Ruremonde, Stevenswaert, Liege. He extended and secured the frontiers of the Dutch. The enemies whom he found insulting at the gates of Nimeghen were driven to seek for shelter behind their lines. He forced Bonne, Huy, Limbourg, in another campaign. He opened the communication of the Rhine, as well as of the Maes. He added all the country between these rivers to his former conquests.

"The arms of France, favoured by the defection of the Elector of Bavaria, had penetrated into the heart of the empire. This mighty body lay exposed to immediate ruin. In that memorable crisis the Duke of Marlborough led his troops, with unexampled celerity, secrecy, and order, from the ocean to the Danube. He saw, he attacked; nor stopped but to conquer the enemy. He forced the Bavarians, sustained by the French, in their strong entrenchments at Schellenberg. He passed the Danube. A second royal army, composed of the best troops of France, was sent to reinforce the first. That of the Confederates was divided. With one part of it the siege of Ingolstadt was carried on: with the other the Duke gave battle to the united strength of France and Bavaria. On the 2nd of August, 1704, he gained a more glorious victory than the histories of any age can boast. The heaps of slain were dreadful proofs of his valour: a marshal of France, whole legions of French, his prisoners, proclaimed his mercy. Bavaria was subdued, Ratisbon, Augsburg, Ulm, Meminghen, all the usurpations of the enemy were restored. From the Danube the Duke turned his victorious arms towards the Rhine and the Moselle; Landau, Treves, Traerback were taken. In the course of one campaign the very nature of the war was changed. The invaders of other states were reduced to defend their own!" The reader has here as vivid a description as could well be given him, in the shape of a summary, of the doings of the Duke of Marlborough during one campaign. And he has only to imagine all this, repeated over and over again, with fresh names—we know not how many times, for we have hardly quoted a fourth of the inscription—to arrive at a very fair notion of the extraordinary character of the Duke's abilities and successes; which fully equal those of the greatest military commanders the world has ever seen. He must have kept the Parliament, and the press, and the medallist tolerably busy at home, with the mere duties of passing thanks for them, and recording, and diffusing the knowledge of them among the people, and in making artistical memorials of them to be bequeathed to later times. Among our engravings will be found four medals illustrative of as many important successes achieved by the Duke. One relates to the battle of Ramilies (Fig. 2215); another to the siege and taking of Oudenarde (Fig. 2208); the third to the siege of Lisle (Fig. 2216). "A numerous garrison," continues the inscription, "and a marshal of France, defended the place. Prince Eugene of Savoy commanded, the Duke of Marlborough covered and sustained the siege. The rivers were seized, and the communication with Holland interrupted. The Duke opened new communications, with great labour and greater art. Through countries overrun by the enemy, the necessary convoys arrived in safety. One alone was attacked. The troops which attacked it were beaten. The defence of Lisle was animated by assurances of relief. The French assembled all their force: they marched towards the town. The Duke of Marlborough offered them battle without suspending the siege. They abandoned the enterprise. They came to save the town: they were spectators of its fall." The fourth medal refers to the greatest of all the Duke's victories, and the one that led to the gift of Blenheim—of course the battle of that name—and the "more glorious victory than the histories of any age can boast," of the passage of the inscription already transcribed.

It was after a series of the most intricate and skilful manœuvres that, at the dawn of the day before that of the battle, Marlborough and Prince Eugene (whom the medallists happily represented as the Castor and Pollux of modern military life, see our engraving, Fig. 2209) found themselves with their respective armies once more in close union, on the banks of the Danube, and prepared to resist the attacks, that appeared to be imminent, of the immense Gallo-Bavarian army, commanded by Marshal Tallard, General Marsin, and the Elector of Bavaria, whose "defection," as the inscription has told us, had enabled the French to penetrate to their present position. Whilst Marlborough and the Prince were surveying the ground, they ascended a church tower, and distinctly perceived the quarter-masters of the enemy marking out a camp between Blenheim and Lutzingen, in the place of the one he then occupied. It was at once determined to give battle whilst the removal was going on. But the enemy was stronger both in numbers and position—urged some of the officers. "I know the danger," said the Duke in reply, "but a battle is absolutely necessary, and I rely on the bravery and discipline of the troops, which will make amends for our disadvantages." During the night the French and Bavarians

2240.—Medal Struck to commemorate the Battle of Dumblane.

2239.—Perth. (From an old Print.)

2242.—Crown.

2243.—Shilling.

2244.—Halfpenny.

2242 to 2244.—Coins of George I.

George R

2241.—Autograph of George I.

2245.—George II. (From a Portrait by Sir Godfrey Kneller.)

2246.—Autograph of George .I.

2247.—Queen Caroline (From a Painting by Vanderbank.)

2218.—Medal struck to commemorate the Capture of Porto Bello by Admiral Vernon. (From an Original in the British Museum.)

2249.—Medal struck to commemorate the Battle of Dettingen. (From an Original in the British Museum.)

2250.—Great Seal of George II. (No perfect impression is known to exist.)

2251.—Charles Edward Stuart, the Young Pretender. (From a French Print.)

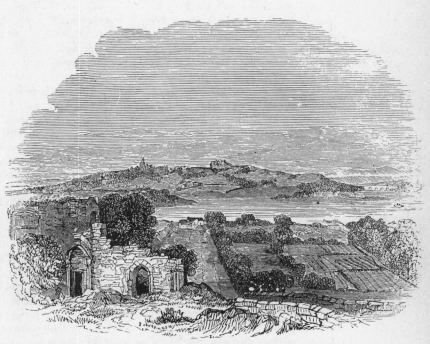

2252.—The Forth, from Cambuskenneth Abbey; Stirling in the distance. (From an Old Print.)

began to move to their new camp, and at two in the morning of Sunday—the day of battle—the duke and the prince prepared to follow them, over very difficult ground, and hardly certain, even to that time, as to what precise spot they would have to occupy. The prince led the right wing, the duke the left. The ground was intersected with ditches and little streams. Most circumspectly was the advance made. Every inch of ground within reach was examined—every hill, and wood, and large water-course in front were rigidly scrutinized. And at one point the two generals rode forward to obtain a still more accurate view of their opponents' position. By seven o'clock they had approached so near that the outposts and picquets of the French and Bavarian army drew back rapidly from all points, and the columns of their main body obeyed the warning and formed in order of battle. Their number amounted to about 56,000 men : they were opposed to about 52,000.

The Elector and General Marsin commanded the left, at Lutzingen. Tallard held the right—the post of honour—or that of the greatest danger, by the side of the little village of Blenheim. The village itself was occupied by three brigades, who were strengthened by every possible means—palisades, gates, barricades—by blocking up every little open space with felled trees, empty carts, or even boards, every foot of defence at the same time having its concealed defender,—by fortifying the church tower and a little old castle close by with musketeers,—by a whole battalion of artillery distributed over every convenient spot; and lastly, by an advanced barricade, formed of waggons, between the village and the Danube, behind which a brigade of dismounted dragoons were posted. The artillery was under the command of General Clerambault, whose orders were to maintain the village to the last extremity—a tremendous position indeed to assail, and one that might have cast a little apprehension into the hearts of the bravest soldiers. But, of course, it is precisely where the enemy is strongest that in ordinary cases he must be sought ; so was it here. While Eugene moved forward and attacked the Elector and Marsin, Marlborough, after a short cannonade, in which he had been very nearly struck by a ball, led on the left, to attempt the more fearful part of the undertaking, by Blenheim. To increase his difficulties, a little river, the Nebel, had to be crossed. Lord Cutts was sent forward to the village, while Marlborough advanced along the banks of the Nebel, under a heavy storm of grape-shot, in order to be ready to interpose between the two great divisions of the French army, which he saw were very inefficiently connected. Lord Cutts, disregarding the grape-shot, threw fascines into the river, got across, and marched right towards the terrific position we have described. All was silence until he was within some thirty paces of the defences, when such a volley burst forth that no inconsiderable portion of the whole number of the English were at once swept down. On they went, however ; General Rowe, who was at the head of the leading brigade, actually striking his sword into the palisade before he gave the word to fire. But even then, what could be done by men everywhere exposed, against others equally brave, who were everywhere sheltered ? The chief officer fell : one-third of the soldiers of that leading brigade were lying prostrate. However bitter their feelings, they must retreat : in so doing they were attacked by a body of gens d'armes. The Hessians, however, came up to their support, and drove back the French horse ; and Lord Cutts speedily brought up in their place a large body of our own cavalry, notwithstanding the great difficulty found in crossing the swamps. Other brigades now arrived, and the fight waxed fiercer, and over a larger space. It has been noticed that the national animosities between the French and English were remarkably conspicuous at this period. The officers of the two countries crossed their swords between the palisades, and the English soldiers, too impatient to load their pieces, thrust with their bayonet points through the defences, or struck over them with the butt-ends, at their opponents. Still it was all useless. The one body remained sheltered and the other exposed ; and their losses and successes were in accordance with their respective positions. Lord Cutts was beaten back to a rising ground.

Marlborough all this time watched those two great and partially sundered divisions, of which we have spoken, with the eyes of some magnificent bird of prey, preparing to pounce upon a quarry that is hardly less powerful than itself, and may prove much more so if aim and opportunity be not exact. At last he darted forward, his infantry crossing the river by means of little bridges, his cavalry by planks and fascines ; formed on the opposite bank of the Nebel, threw back, as by a mere impatient wave of his arm, the charges of the French and Bavarian cavalry, and then paused one instant in calm but grim expectation of the arrival of the artillery under the Prince of Holstein-Beck, who found such great difficulty in passing

the Nebel, on account of the desperate charges of an Irish brigade in the pay of the French King, that Marlborough was obliged to gallop to his aid, drive back the French, and help the prince over. Another inexplicable movement or two was made by the man on whom all eyes were now directed in intense expectation, and behold, he and Prince Eugene, in short the whole confederated army, were joined, and ready to burst in with irresistible force between the doomed divisions of the French and Bavarian army. Tallard must have now seen, too late, his ruinous error, in making the separation in question. At five in the afternoon, with the cavalry formed in two lines, and the infantry in their rear, Marlborough, amidst a terrific fire of musketry and cannon, moved forward, and ascended a steep hill, where the French horse had gathered together, with a part of Tallard's infantry. The skill and bravery of these troops shook him for an instant—he paused, and was even driven back ; but as he receded, the fiery storm poured faster and faster from his own side upon the enemy, until at last it overpowered them ; then there was a fresh charge from Marlborough, and the cavalry were broken, and the infantry were presently all dead men or prisoners. In vain Tallard sent to demand from the Elector a reinforcement, or an attack by way of diversion on the rear of those who were so destroying him. Prince Eugene gave the Elector full and very unsatisfactory employment for every man he had. Nor was there time to draw from Blenheim the troops now wasted there. Tallard found himself suddenly borne down by the whole force of Marlborough's horse ; and about as suddenly his troops were flying in every direction, seeking vainly for safety in the waters of the Danube, or in the marshes of Hochstadt ; in some cases whole battalions laying down their arms at once, and crying for mercy. After this Tallard might think it mattered little that among the countless prisoners *he* was one. The troops who held the almost impregnable position of Blenheim, after a sharp struggle, surrendered. The loss of the French and Bavarians on that fatal day is said to have exceeded thirty-five thousand men, including those who were slain, drowned, or taken prisoners.

Passing over all the other deeds recorded by the inscription, we find the result thus stated :—" The French acknowledged their conqueror, and sued for peace." The famous Treaty of Utrecht was concluded in 1713.

The parliamentary vote for the magnificent building before which we now stand in admiration was 500,000*l.*, but much more than that sum was ultimately expended. We shall not attempt to lead our reader through, in order to make him familiar with the contents of, all the great apartments of Blenheim—from Corinthian portico to hall, hall to bay-window room, thence to the duke's study, east drawing-room, grand cabinet, little drawing-room, saloon, state drawing-room, state bed-chamber, and so on, according to the usual round of visitation, but say in brief, that all are in the most sumptuous possible style ; and that among the more conspicuous features of the treasures of Blenheim are the magnificent library, and some of the finest paintings of Rubens, which were presented by the States of Holland to the great duke. A statue of Anne, in white marble, by Rysbrack, adorns the library, and is noticeable not only for its own excellence, but for the reminiscences aroused by it, which are not altogether of the character that one would anticipate from merely reading the record on the pillar, of the duke's services to his mistress, and the rewards he received, of his dukedom, and this most superb of palatial mansions. At first, so enthusiastic, nay romantic, was the friendship felt by Anne for Marlborough's wife, and through her in a lesser degree for him, that the queen could not be content to correspond under all the formalities of rank, but, as Mrs. Morley, must write to her dear Duchess under the name of Mrs. Freeman. But the queen was a Tory, the duchess a Whig ; and as gradually the former yielded to her prepossessions, and the latter somewhat imperiously opposed them, and made her mistress throw herself into the arms of the people she most disliked—the love of youth passed away, and was succeeded by a still more cordial hatred. And then the duke, whose services were before the world, was to be degraded on account of these private feelings and views. He endeavoured, not in a very manly and dignified manner, to avert the storm, but failed, and withdrew to the Continent until the death of Anne, and the accession of George I. (Fig. 2228), who restored him to office and favour, and thus enabled him to pass the last few years of his life in somewhat like the sunshine he had deserved.

The career of the Duke of Marlborough is so essentially the same thing as the reign, in a political sense, of Anne, that we need not add to the foregoing view of both, anything more than a few words upon the group of portraits of Anne's chief ministers, Whig and Tory. The former were the Lord Chancellor Somers, Walpole, Earl of Orford, and the Earl of Halifax : the latter, Harley, Earl of Oxford, and St. John, Viscount Bolingbroke, the subtlest and in some respects loftiest spirit of the whole. Godolphin, like Marlborough himself, had at first a leaning towards the Tories, but gradually he turned towards the other party, and before he died had the reputation of being a very good Whig. It was during his administration that Marlborough's brilliant victories were obtained, and the legislative union of England and Scotland consummated; yet such was the power and baseness of faction at the time, that he was suddenly dismissed by a letter, of which the bearer was a livery servant! This dismissal he owed to the prince of intriguers and back-stair statesmen, Harley, who was aided by the influential services of the bed-chamber woman, Mrs. Masham. Mr. Hallam, looking at the results of the interference of this lady on the one side, and her enemy, the Duchess of Marlborough, on the other, observes, " It seems rather a humiliating proof of the sway which the feeblest prince enjoys even in a limited monarchy, that the fortunes of Europe should have been changed by nothing more noble than the insolence of one waiting woman and the cunning of another. It is true that this was effected by throwing the weight of the crown into the scale of a powerful *faction*; yet the House of Bourbon would probably not have reigned beyond the Pyrenees, but for Sarah and Abigail at Queen Anne's toilette."

The terms Whig and Tory demand a few words of explanation. They rose into use about 1670. It appears the friends of the Duke of York (James II.) were at first called Yorkists, which " served," says Roger North, " for mere distinction, but did not scandalise or reflect enough. Then they came to *Tantivy*, which implied *riding post* to Rome." Next it was observed " that the Duke favoured Irishmen; all his friends, or those accounted such, by appearing against the exclusion [of the Duke of York from the throne], were straight become *Irish*, and so *wild Irish*, thence *Bog-trotters*, and in the *copia* of the factious language the word *Tory* was entertained, which signified the most despicable savages among the wild Irish, and being a vocal clever-sounding word, readily pronounced, it kept hold, and took possession of the foul mouths of the faction; and everywhere, as those men passed, we could observe them breathe little else but Tory, together with oaths and damnation." So much for the origin of one of the great party nicknames; now as to the other. Of course the " Tories " were not to be so called without repaying their opponents in their own coin. How was that to be done? " Birmingham Protestants " was thought of, as reminding us of the false groats counterfeited at that place, and other epithets and designations; but at last, in allusion apparently to the objecting, fault-finding characteristic of the opposition mind, they hit upon the name *Whig*—a Scotch word signifying corrupt, sour whey. At first, then, Tory was applied to the favourers of James, and Whig to the favourers of William III.; from whence the words soon became fixed designations for those who supported arbitrary and despotic—as contrasted with " constitutional "—principles in Church and State. As an illustration of the vehemence with which these principles struggled for the mastery during Anne's reign, though happily in more peaceable arenas than the battle-fields of the commonwealth, we may mention the case of Dr. Sacheverell, who turned the pulpit into a forum for the expression of the extremest Tory views, and excited the whole nation into a state of the highest ferment. He was impeached and convicted, but punished so mildly that he was considered as really acquitted. He then took a journey through England, which proved a perfect triumph, so prevalent yet among the people were the views he had advocated. Medals were cast in his honour, the most amusing feature of which was their adaptability to the different religious views of purchasers. Those who thought the Doctor was promoting the Romish Church, bought one with a picture of the Pope on the reverse, whilst those who attributed to him a firm devotion to the English Church, bought one with a mitre, as symbolic of that establishment. The Doctor's portrait was on the obverse, with the words, " I am firm to thee." You turned the medal, and according as you saw the Pope or the mitre, you saw to which he meant he was firm. (Fig. 2222.)

Passing for an instant from these disputes about the best forms and principles of government, let us mention one practical event of the reign of Anne, upon the value and importance of which all good men were agreed—the opening of Greenwich Hospital. At first erected as a royal palace, and used as such by Charles II., it was owing, it is said, to the benevolent thoughtfulness of Queen Mary that her husband, William, was induced to agree to the foundation of a hospital for disabled seamen, and to consent to Wren's proposal that " Greenwich House " should be assigned for the purpose. It was then in an unfinished state. Wren undertook to complete and greatly enlarge it—to put it, in short, into the state in which we find it at present (Fig. 2218). The hospital was opened in 1705.

VOL. II.

Before we touch upon the events that occupied so large a portion of the thoughts of King, Government, and People, during the reigns of the two first Georges—the attempts made by the son and grandson of James to re-obtain possession of the throne for their family—we may narrate, in connection with a very unromantic personage, one of the most romantic of historical passages. In 1682, George, son of the Elector of Hanover, married Sophia Dorothea of Zell (Fig. 2229), a young, beautiful, and highly accomplished woman, and therefore, as the result showed, peculiarly unsuited to his tastes. The Princess had the misfortune to offend one of her husband's father's mistresses, and thence probably all her subsequent misfortunes may be dated. While her husband was absent with the army, there came to the electoral court Philip, Count of Königsmark, a brother of the man who had obtained in London, a few years before, a kind of infamous reputation by his assassination of Mr. Thynne in Pall Mall in the open day, an incident commemorated on the monument of the unfortunate gentleman in Westminster Abbey (Fig. 2177). The Count, as a member of an ancient and distinguished family, was received by the Elector with respect, and, it is said, with more than respect, on account of his handsome person, by Sophia Dorothea of Zell; but there does not appear to be any evidence that her indiscretion proceeded farther than mere coquetry and flirtation with the Count; and, in looking at what followed, it is only just to observe that even if she were faithless to her husband, he had been already notoriously untrue to her. Incited by the secret representations of the lady before referred to as the enemy of the young Princess, the Elector immediately commanded the Count to leave his dominions. Before he did so, he obtained, some say without the Princess's previous knowledge, a private interview with her, to kiss hands on taking his departure. On leaving her bedchamber, where he had been introduced by the ladies in waiting, he disappeared, and from that day Count Königsmark was never again seen alive, and his fate was left buried in the profoundest mystery. The Princess was placed under arrest; and soon after her husband, it was stated, obtained a sentence of divorce from the Consistory. Horace Walpole observes, " Of the circumstances that ensued on Königsmark's disappearance I am ignorant; nor am I acquainted with the laws of Germany relative to divorce and separation; nor do I know or suppose that despotism and pride allow the law to insist on much formality when a sovereign has a reason or a mind to get rid of his wife." The detention of the Princess Sophia, thenceforward known as the Duchess of Halle, in the solitary castle of Ahlen, on the river Aller, for the whole remainder of her life, thirty-two dreadful years, seems to make it doubtful that any real divorce had taken place; and when George ascended the English throne, in right of his grandmother, Sophia, Electress of Hanover (the nearest *Protestant* member of the old royal family of England, to whom the English parliament had confirmed the throne, should Anne die without issue), the people of this country, instead of seeing the court presided over by one who would have given lustre to it by her beauty, accomplishments, and abilities, had the degrading spectacle before their eyes, of a monarch whose tastes were, if possible, lower even than his morals. Horace Walpole thus describes his two favourites, the Duchess of Kendal and the Duchess of Darlington:—The last he saw at his mother's in his infancy, and " whom I remember," he says, " by being terrified at her enormous figure." She had " two fierce black eyes, large and rolling, beneath two lofty arched eyebrows, two acres of cheeks overspread with crimson, an ocean of neck that overflowed and was not distinguished from the lower part of her body," &c. The other he saw when he had obtained permission to gratify his boyish passion to see the King. " The night but one before he began his last journey, my mother carried me, at ten at night, to the apartment of the Countess of Walsingham, on the ground floor towards the garden at St. James's, which opened into that of her aunt, the Duchess of Kendal. Notice being given that the King was come down to supper, Lady Walsingham took me alone into the Duchess's ante-room, where we found alone the King and her. I knelt down and kissed his hand. He said a few words to me, and my conductress led me back to my mother. The person of the King is as perfect in my memory as if I saw him but yesterday. It was that of an elderly man, rather pale, and exactly like his picture and coins (Figs. 2238, 2242-2244); not tall, of an aspect (Fig. 2228) rather good than august, with a dark tie-wig, a plain coat, waistcoat, and breeches of snuff-coloured cloth, with stockings of the same colour, and a blue riband over all. So entirely was he my object that I do not believe I once looked at the Duchess: but as I could not avoid seeing her on entering the room, I remember that just beyond his Majesty stood a very tall, lean, ill-favoured old lady," &c. No wonder that " the mob of London were highly diverted at the importation of so uncommon a

2253.—Preston Tower (Near which the Battle was fought.

2254.—Seaton House.

2255.—View of the City of Carlisle.

2256.—Birthplace of Colonel Gardiner.

2257.—Carlisle Castle.

2258.—The House in which the Pretender lodged at Derby.

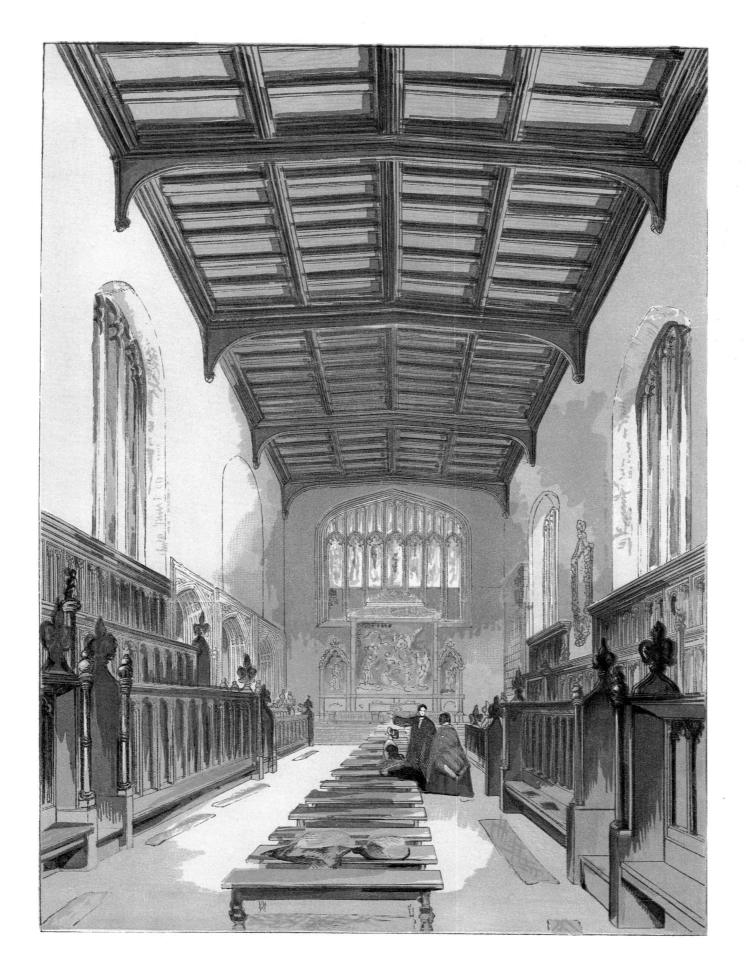

ST. JOHN'S COLLEGE CHAPEL, CAMBRIDGE.

THE BODLEIAN LIBRARY. OXFORD.

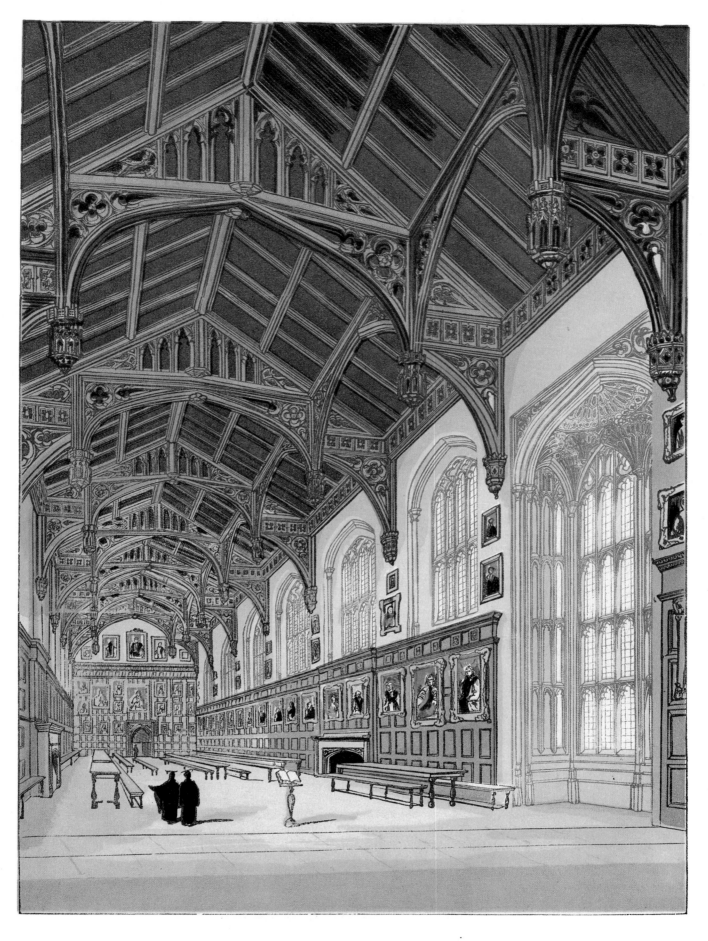

CHRIST CHURCH HALL OXFORD.

OLD PALACE AT GREENWICH.

SMEATON'S EDDYSTONE LIGHTHOUSE.

THE SHAKSPERE JUBILEE AT STRATFORD-UPON-AVON.

STATUE OF SIR ISAAC NEWTON AT CAMBRIDGE.

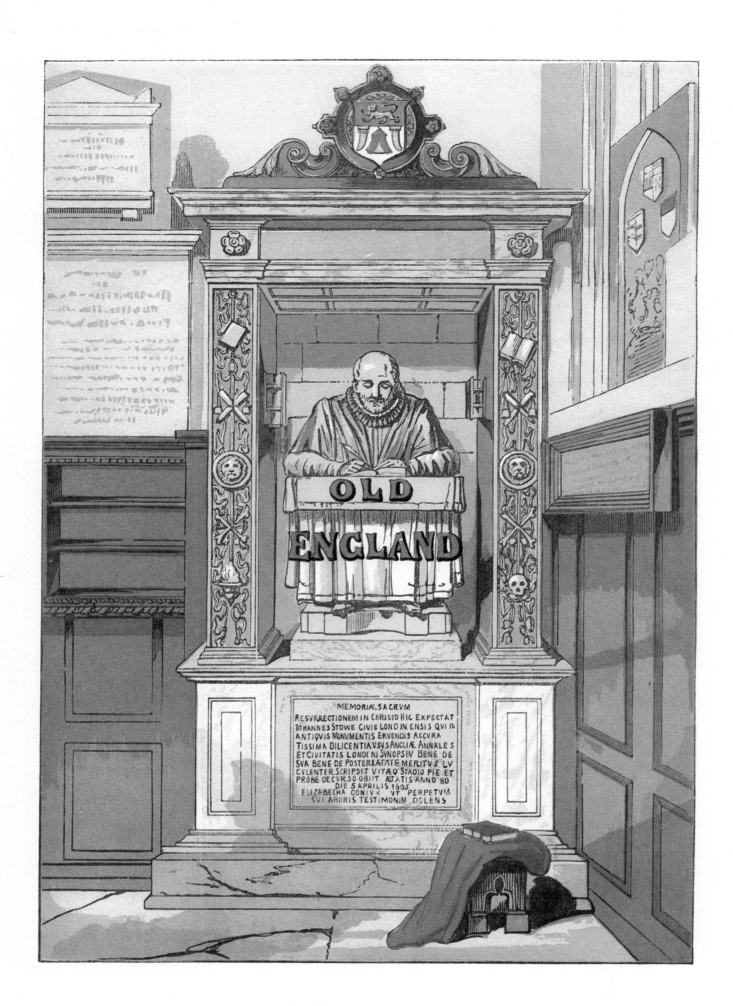

OLD

ENGLAND

MEMORIÆ SACRVM
RESVRRECTIONEM IN CHRISTO HIC EXPECTAT
IOHANNES STOWE CIVIS LONDINENSIS QVI IN
ANTIQVIS MONVMENTIS ERVENDIS ACCVRA
TISSIMA DILICENTIA VSVS ANGLIÆ ANNALES
ET CIVITATIS LONDINI SYNOPSIN BENE DE
SVA BENE DE POSTERAATATE MERITVS LV
CVLENTER SCRIPSIT VITÆQ STADIO PIE ET
PROBE DECVRSO OBIIT ÆTATIS ANNO 80
DIE 5 APRILIS 1605
ELIZABETHA CONIVX VT PERPETVM
SVI AMORIS TESTIMONIM DOLENS

2259.—Falkirk.

2260.—Culloden, or Drummossie Moor.

2261.—The Young Pretender in Highland Costume. (From a Portrait in the possession of Mr G. A. Williams, Cheltenham.)

2262.—Lord Lovat. (From a Drawing made by Hogarth the morning before his lordship's execution.

2263.—Flora Macdonald. (From a Painting by Ramsay.)

2264.—Medal struck to commemorate the Battle of Minden.

seraglio." The son of the King, Prince, afterwards King George II., had, it appears, perfect confidence in his mother's innocence, and once made a bold but unsuccessful attempt to see his mother by riding through the river, and endeavouring to gain admittance, but the gaoler, Baron Bulow, sternly refused his request. It has even been asserted that his father, as though himself half inclined towards the same belief, once made some proposals for reconciliation, when he received this answer from his injured wife:—"If what I am accused of be true, I am unworthy of his bed; and if the accusation is false *he is unworthy of me:* I will not accept his offer." When her death, so long protracted, drew nigh at last, she wrote, if we are to believe the account given by Lockhart of Carnwarth, to the King a letter containing a "protestation of her innocence, a reproach for his hard usage and unjust treatment, and concluded with a summons or citation to her husband to appear, within the year and the day, at the divine tribunal, and there to answer for the long and many injuries she had received from him. As this letter could not, with safety to the bearer, be delivered in England or Hanover, it was given to him in his coach on the road [in the 'last journey' that Walpole speaks of]. He opened it immediately, supposing it came from Hanover. He was so struck with these unexpected contents, and his fatal citation, that his convulsions and apoplexy came fast on him. After being blooded, his mouth turned awry; and they then proposed to drive off to a nearer place than Osnaburgh, but he signed twice or thrice with his hand to go on, and that was the only mark of sense he showed." Lockhart says he obtained this relation from a person of "superior rank and great esteem," and that he had before heard it imperfectly from a "lady of quality." When the new King, George II. (Fig. 2245), took his first journey to Hanover after the death of his father, he caused some alterations to be made in the electoral palace, when at last the body of Königsmark was discovered under the floor of the Princess Sophia's dressing-room, so that he had been buried, in all probability, beneath the very spot where he had been murdered.

Among the rumours that from time to time were disseminated through England during the reign of Anne, were some that showed, if true, she was strongly inclined to restore the regular line of her family's succession. Thus it was whispered that her brother, the son of James II., had once clandestinely made his way into England, and had actually visited her at the palace, in order to concert with her measures to defeat the Hanoverian succession. It seems certain that she had a strong desire, and that so also had Bolingbroke and others of her ministers, to secure the throne to her brother; and most natural, on her part, was the wish. She could not but sympathise with his misfortunes, and with the disappointment that he experienced in seeing himself finally excluded by the English parliament from the throne. Her dying words were said to have been an expression of pity for him. The "Pretender," all things considered, had certainly powerful excuses for his pretensions, and for his determination to press them even at the point of the sword.

It was on the 6th of September, 1715, that his standard was set up by the Earl of Mar, at Braemar in Scotland. Before long, the rebels, as they were called, were established at Perth (Fig. 2239), twelve thousand strong, in cavalry and infantry. After some hesitation, and many ineffectual movements, they marched into England, but with so little success, notwithstanding the many advantages they possessed, that on one and the same day (the 13th of November) nearly fifteen hundred Jacobites surrendered themselves prisoners at Preston, and their army, under the Earl of Mar, was defeated at the battle of Dumblane (Fig. 2240); and on that day also the news arrived of the treachery of Lord Lovat (Fig. 2262), who had yielded the pass of Inverness. It was not long before London witnessed a sad spectacle. A long train of prisoners entered the metropolis, each pinioned with cords upon the back of a horse, which was led by a foot soldier, the drums of the accompanying troops beating a triumphal march. This, though the first, was by no means to be the last of the sad evidences that met the eyes of the Londoners, of devotion to the Pretender's cause, notwithstanding the ruin and misery that from time to time overwhelmed his partisans.

In spite of this ill success, the Pretender came over personally to Scotland, was proclaimed, assumed royal state, formed his court, and granted honours: knights and peers sprung up under his creative hand, to enjoy, however, but for a short time their new dignities. But even while all this gallant show of assured success was made to the world, James and his council were discovering that the expedition was a failure, and beginning to exert all their energies to run away from instead of to fight their enemies. A satirist might have said that in this they showed more skill and alacrity than in any

other portion of the expedition. They raised new batteries, destroyed place after place to prevent the English from obtaining supplies or shelter, and in one way or another raised such a bustle that every one thought some grand attack must be contemplated; but when the Earl of Argyll, on the part of King George I., pressed forward, the Jacobites retreated to Dundee, and then, more suspicious still, were ordered by their commanders to march to Montrose, where certain French ships of war lay at anchor. Suddenly the troops refused to move. The idea had crossed their minds that they were going to be sacrificed—that they were helping to secure James's escape, and then would be themselves left to the kindly consideration of Argyll's dragoons and troopers. How very unjust, nay, how unkind, after all the labours of the sovereign and his council! The Earl of Mar must have blushed to have found himself under the necessity of assuring them that the King was going to place himself at their head, and make a bold stand at Aberdeen. If he did not, his countenance must have been of brass; for while, to deceive the troops, the Pretender's horses and body-guard were all drawn up before his door, that he might, as had been promised, lead them, that careful personage was slipping out at the back door, walking as quickly as he could to the Earl's lodgings, and from thence proceeding to the sea-shore, where a boat conveyed him and the Earl to a French ship. Seventeen other persons of consequence were got off in safety at the same time. So ended this expedition. Let us here avail ourselves of a very striking description of the chief actor in it, written by one of his own partisans. It will show us in a great measure, the cause of that want of enthusiasm that pervaded all the business operations of an army who were individually inclined to be full of enthusiasm for him and his cause. "His person very tall and thin, seeming to be inclined to be lean rather than to fill up as he grows in years. His countenance (Fig. 2236) pale, yet he seems to be sanguine in his constitution, and has something of a vivacity in his eye that perhaps would have been more visible if he had not been under dejected circumstances, and surrounded with discouragements which, it must be acknowledged, were sufficient to alter the complexion even of his soul as well as of his body. His speech was grave, and not very clearly expressing his thoughts, nor over-much to the purpose; but his words were very few, and his behaviour seemed always composed. What he was in his diversions we know not. Here was no room for such things: it was no time for mirth; neither can I say I ever saw him smile. . . . . We found ourselves not at all animated by his presence; and if he was so disappointed in us, we were tenfold more so in him. We saw nothing in him that looked like spirit. He never appeared with cheerfulness and vigour to animate us; our men began to despise him; some asked if he could speak. His countenance looked extremely heavy. He cared not to come abroad amongst our soldiers, or to see us handle our arms, or do our exercise. Some said the circumstances he found us in dejected him; I am sure the figure he made dejected us." How could such a man conquer? It is only wonderful that he should have made the attempt amidst so many dangers.

And what was the fate of the unhappy prisoners who had been led so ignominiously into the metropolis? A thousand of them having petitioned to be transported to the North American colonies, had their prayer granted, but many others, less fortunate, were executed. Among the prisoners, the most important were the Earls of Wintoun, Kenmure, Derwentwater, Carnwarth, and Nithsdale, and the Lords Widdrington and Nairn; all of whom had been taken at Preston. On the 19th of January they were brought to the bar of the House of Lords, where they knelt, and with one exception (Lord Wintoun), confessed their guilt, and begged for mercy. Sentence of death was pronounced, and preparations made for the execution. Shocking as their sentence must seem if it be remembered that in every part of the nation, not excluding the houses of legislature, there were men who agreed in the views of the condemned men, and thought they had only done their duty, yet King George I. was as obdurate as though they had been the vilest possible of miscreants. Watching their opportunity, the ladies of Nithsdale and Nairn suddenly stepped forth from behind a curtain as the king passed through an apartment in St. James's, and throwing themselves at his feet, pleaded for their husbands' lives. He could listen, but would not be moved. Lord Nairn, however, was saved by the interposition of one of the ministers, Lord Stanhope, who had been his school-fellow. For the other lords every possible effort was made. As bribes had been taken before in similar circumstances, sixty thousand pounds were offered for the life of Lord Derwentwater, but in vain. In vain also the heart-rending grief of the young Countess of Derwentwater, assisted though she was by the Duchesses of Cleveland and Bolton. These three ladies were all introduced at one time to the royal bed-chamber, but with no better success than the other ladies had obtained in their personal application. Yet there were men in the houses of parliament who, rising above the cruel selfishness and short-sighted policy of these proposed executions, raised their voices for mercy toward their opponents. Steele—honour to his memory for it—was one of those men. In the Lords there was actually a motion carried for an address to the king for a reprieve; but the mover, a minister and a Tory, was immediately turned out of the Cabinet. It was finally decided that two of the lords who were less deeply implicated, Carnwarth and Widdrington, should be pardoned, but the rest were ordered for execution. On the following morning, to the astonishment of the people of London, who had heard that three were positively to be executed, two only appeared on the scaffold at Tower Hill, the English Lord Derwentwater, and the Scottish Lord Kenmure. Both died bravely, and regretting their plea of guilty, as they had done but their duty to their true sovereign, as they considered him, James III. But where was the third victim, the Earl of Nithsdale? Why, one cannot avoid feeling a sense of pleasure in saying it, he had escaped, and was hidden in impenetrable secrecy, from the vengeance of his enemies. He had been saved by the noble devotion of his wife: how, she herself has told us, through the medium of a letter addressed to her sister, Lady Lucy Herbert, Abbess of the Augustine nuns at Bruges. Immediately after the House of Lords had expressed itself so favourably toward the question of the reprieve of the condemned lords, she says, she thought she could draw some advantage from it in favour of my design, "so hastened to the Tower, where, affecting an air of joy and satisfaction, I told all the guards I passed by, that I came to bring joyful tidings to the prisoners. I desired them to lay aside their fears, for the petition had passed the house in their favour. I then gave them some money to drink to the lords and his majesty, though it was but trifling; for I thought that if I were too liberal on the occasion they might suspect my designs, and that giving something would give them good humour and services for the next day, which was the eve of the execution." Her next business was to find assistants. Mrs. Mills, her landlady, and a lady, Mrs. Morgan, to whom she had been introduced by a friend, agreed to help her in her hazardous and difficult task of getting her husband out of the Tower, and if they succeeded, then the friend—Mrs. Evans—was to receive him. The fearful character of the circumstances inspired the Countess with more than ordinary skill, courage, and presence of mind She says, "When we were all in the coach *I never ceased talking, that they might have no leisure* to reflect. Their surprise and astonishment on my first opening my design to them, had made them consent without ever thinking of the consequences." On their arrival at the Tower Mrs. Morgan was first introduced, as the Countess was only allowed to take in one person at a time; and that lady had concealed about her person the clothes that Mrs. Mills was to put on when she had given those she wore to the earl. When the clothes were safely deposited in the cell, the Countess took Mrs. Morgan back to the staircase, begging her aloud to send the maid to dress her, and saying she was afraid she would be too late with her last petition, unless her maid came immediately. "I despatched her safe, and went partly down stairs to meet Mrs. Mills, who had the precaution to hold her handkerchief to her face, as was very natural for a woman to do when she was going to bid her last farewell to a friend on the eve of his execution. I had indeed desired her to do it, that my lord might go out in the same manner. Her eyebrows were rather inclined to be sandy, and my lord's were dark and very thick; however, I had prepared some paint of the colour of her's to disguise his with. I also bought an artificial head-dress of the same coloured hair as her's, and I painted his face with white, and his cheeks with rouge, to hide his long beard, which he had not had time to shave. All this provision I had before left in the Tower. The poor guards, whom my slight liberality the day before had endeared me to, let me go quietly with my company, and were not so strictly on the watch as they usually had been; and the more so, as they were persuaded, from what I had told them the day before, that the prisoners would obtain their pardon. I made Mrs. Mills take off her own hood, and put on that which I had brought for her. I then took her by the hand, and led her out of my lord's chamber, and in passing through the next room, in which there were several people, with all the concern imaginable I said, 'My dear Mrs. Catherine, go in all haste and fetch me my waiting-maid; she certainly cannot reflect how late it is; she forgets that I am to present a petition to-night, and if I let slip this opportunity I am undone, for to-morrow will be too late. Hasten her as much as possible, for I shall be on thorns till she comes.' Everybody in the room, who were chiefly the guards'

wives and daughters, seemed to compassionate me exceedingly; and the sentinel officiously opened the door. When I had seen her out, I returned back to my lord, and finished dressing him. I had taken care Mrs. Mills did not go out crying as she came in, that my lord might the better pass for the lady who came in crying and affected: and the more so because he had the same dress she wore. When I had almost finished dressing my lord in all my petticoats, I perceived that it was growing dark, and was afraid that the light of the candles might betray us; so I resolved to set off. I went out leading him by the hand, and he held his handkerchief to his eyes. I spoke to him in the piteous and most afflicted tone of voice, bewailing bitterly the negligence of Evans, who had vexed me by her delay. Then said I, 'My dear Mrs. Betty, for the love of God, run quickly, and bring her with you. You know my lodging, and if you ever made despatch in your life, do it at present, I am almost distracted with the disappointment.' The guards opened the doors, and I went down stairs with him, still conjuring him to make all possible despatch.

"As soon as he had cleared the door, I made him walk before me, for fear the sentinels should take notice of his walk; but I still continued to press him to make all the despatch he possibly could. At the bottom of the stairs I met my dear Evans, into whose hands I confided him. I had before engaged Mr. Mills to be in readiness before the Tower to conduct him to some place of safety, in case we succeeded. He looked upon the affair as so very improbable to succeed, that his astonishment when he saw us threw him into such consternation that he was almost out of himself; which Evans perceiving, with the greatest presence of mind, without telling him anything, lest he should mistrust them, conducted him to some of her own friends, on whom she could rely, and so secured him, without which we should have been undone. When she had conducted him and left him with them, she returned to find Mr. Mills, who by this time had recovered himself of his astonishment. They went home together, and having found a place of security they conducted him to it.

"In the meanwhile, as I had pretended to have sent the young lady on a message, I was obliged to return up stairs, and go back to my lord's room in some feigned anxiety of being too late, so that everybody seemed sincerely to sympathise with my distress. When I was in the room, I talked to him as if he had been really present, and answered my own questions in my lord's voice as nearly as I could imitate it; I walked up and down, as if we were conversing together, till I thought they had time enough thoroughly to clear themselves of the guards. I then thought proper to make off also. I opened the door, and stood half in it, that those in the outward chamber might hear what I said; but held it so close that they could not look in. I bade my lord a formal farewell for the night, and added that something more than usual must have happened to make Evans negligent on this important occasion, who had always been so punctual in the smallest trifle; that I saw no other remedy than to go in person; that if the Tower were still open when I finished my business, I would return that night; but that he might be assured I would be with him as early in the morning as I could gain admittance into the Tower; and I flattered myself I should bring favourable news. Then, before I shut the door, I pulled through the string of the latch, so that it could only be opened on the inside. I then shut it with some degree of force, that I might be sure of its being well shut. I said to the servant as I passed by, who was ignorant of the whole transaction, that he need not carry in candles to his master till my lord sent for them, as he desired to finish some prayers first. I went down stairs, and called a coach," and so, in short, she escaped, as well as her husband. After some days' concealment in an obscure house, the Venetian ambassador unwittingly enabled them to leave London, by sending down his coach to Dover to meet his brother. Through the assistance of one of his servants, the earl, having been dressed in livery, was conveyed to that place among the ambassador's retinue. At Dover he embarked for Calais, and reached the French coast in safety in so short a time, that the captain, who knew nothing of his passengers, remarked, that if they had been flying for their lives the wind could not have served them better. The Earl of Wintoun also escaped from the Tower, but as there does not seem to have been any desire to act upon the sentence passed against him after his trial, the escape itself may have been connived at, to rid the government of difficulty.

We shall not here follow any further the fortunes of the Old Pretender, but take up the account of the movements made on the part of his family, when his son Charles Edward came forward as the leader, in the years 1744-1745. After the destruction by the

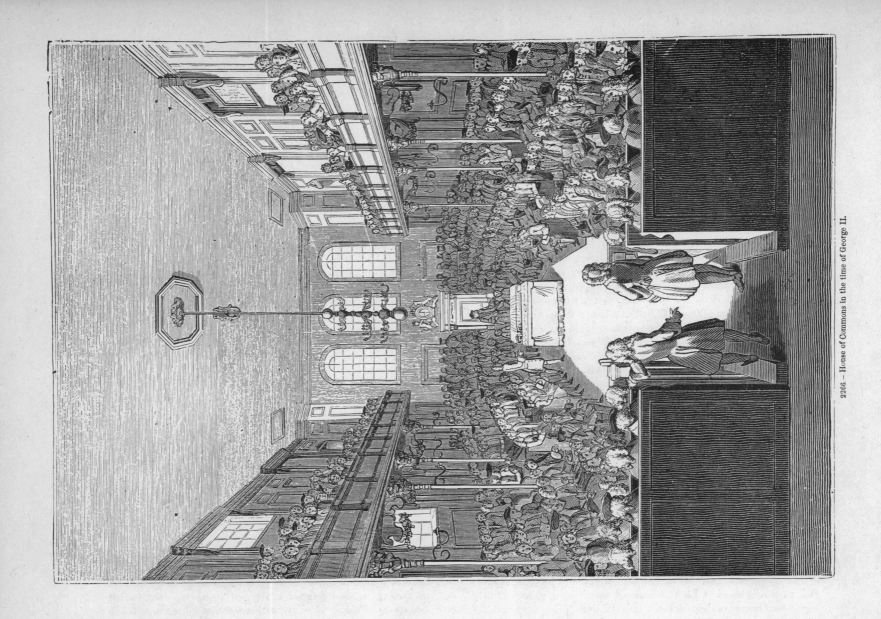

2266 — House of Commons in the time of George II.

2265 — House o Lords in the time of George II.

2267.—Medal struck to commemorate Hawke's Victory in Quiberon Bay
(From an Original in the British Museum.)

2268.—Crown.

2272.—Taylor Institute, Oxford, erected 1844.

2269—Shilling.

2270.—Halfpenny.

2268 to 2270.—Coins of George II

2271. Oxford, from the Abingdon Road.

conjoined effects of a violent storm and the attack of the British navy, of a magnificent fleet, bearing an army of 15,000 men, he crossed the Channel with only two ships; and one of these was so much damaged in an encounter that took place with one of King George's cruisers, that it was obliged to put back into Brest. But the prince went on in the other, saying he would either die or be crowned: the Old Pretender, it is to be observed, had resigned his claims to his son.

The King of England, George II., was at the time absent at Hanover; Scotland was guarded by few troops; the Highlanders generally were thirsting for revenge for their former defeats, and for an opportunity to displace a government that they detested:—not without reason, as Glencoe reminds us. Although the English government at first treated the affair with ridicule, the progress of the Young Pretender soon changed their sentiments. Accordingly, George hurried back from Hanover, and a proclamation was issued, offering a reward of 30,000l. to any one who should secure the person of the Pretender's eldest son; an act that the latter met in a similar spirit by proclaiming a reward of 30,000l. for the apprehension of the Elector of Hanover. The Forth (Fig. 2252) was passed by means of a ford, and Colonel Gardiner's dragoons, instead of fulfilling their promise of cutting the rebels to pieces if they made an attempt to cross, turned tails, and trotted away. The city of Edinburgh was given up to Charles without a struggle, and for a brief time, as he moved to and fro in the regal halls of Holyrood House, he might persuade himself he had re-won his inheritance. Home, the poet, saw him there. He says of him, that his figure and presence (Figs. 2251, 2261) "were not ill-suited to his lofty pretensions. He was in the prime of youth, tall and handsome, and of a fair complexion." The armies met near Prestonpans, in Haddingtonshire, the English setting up a great shout, to which the Highlanders replied. The former were commanded by Cope, who occupied a position in which Prestonpans lay on his right, and Seaton House (Figs. 2253, 2254) and the sea on his left. Charles's army was lodged among the declivities near the little town of Tranent. Between the combatants extended a morass, crossed by hedges and dry stone dykes, with here and there willow-trees scattered about. During the night that ensued, while both armies lay in profound silence and apparent sleep, a Jacobite gentleman of the name of Anderson offered to guide the prince to a spot where the morass might be crossed unseen by the enemy. He was led by the officer to Charles, who was stretched asleep upon the ground, with a sheaf of peas for his pillow. It was determined to trust to the knowledge and fidelity of this gentleman. At daybreak, while the ground was covered by fogs and mists, the Highlanders moved forwards, in almost unearthly quiet, three abreast. As they drew near to the spot in question, they disturbed some mounted dragoons in picquet, who called out, Who goes there?—then, hardly pausing for an answer, rode off to give the alarm. Still more rapidly, then, the Highlanders moved forwards, crossed the morass, which in some places took them in up to the middle, and formed in perfect order on the other side. The ground that now intervened between the armies consisted of an extensive corn-field. "Harvest," says Home, "was just got in, and the ground was covered with a thick stubble, which rustled under the feet of the Highlanders as they ran on, speaking and muttering in a manner that expressed and heightened their fierceness and rage." A battery of cannon, that fired upon them as they advanced, was speedily taken possession of. Colonel Gardiner with his regiment in vain endeavoured to stem the torrent; and then, when the infantry saw the ill success of their artillery and horse, they appear to have wavered; and as the Highlanders, claymore in hand, rushed upon them, were presently broken, and driven to seek safety in flight, where flight was possible, or otherwise in surrender. Sir John Cope himself was among the fugitives, and it is said that he fled in headlong speed to Berwick, where Lord Mark Ker welcomed him with the observation that he "believed he was the first general in Europe that had brought the first tidings of his own defeat."

After a pause of some weeks in Scotland, the young Pretender determined to march upon England. His friends urged him to reconsider this determination; but after three several discussions in council, he said to them, "I see, gentlemen, that you are determined to stay in Scotland and defend your country; but I am also resolved to try my fate in England, even if I should go alone." He went, but of course, not alone; and his success was for some time tolerably satisfactory to his adherents. Carlisle (Fig. 2257) was besieged, and surrendered to the Duke of Perth. And then Charles boldly resolved to march direct for London. At Manchester he was joined by two or three hundred men under the command of Colonel Townley. There, too, as well as at Preston, the bells rang out a cheering welcome. Still there were no symp-toms of a general rising in his favour. His wellwishers seemed deterred, by the frightful danger they would incur, from aiding him, until he had given decided earnest of his permanent success. It was clear that the issue was fast approaching. Three several armies, moving in as many different directions, were preparing to stop the way to the metropolis, and drive back the bold invader. On the 4th of December the entire rebel army was encamped at Derby (the house in which the Pretender lodged (Fig. 2258) is, we believe, still standing at the bottom of Full Street), and their antagonists were not far off. The Duke of Cumberland, the English king's son, was at the head of an army who held possession of Lichfield, Coventry, and Stafford. And now the courage and determination of the rebels began to melt away. First they thought they would endeavour to avoid the Duke, and still push on towards London; then that they would retreat. The Young Pretender, though much dissatisfied at this course, was induced to adopt it on the advice of the brave and able Lord George Murray, who desired to form a junction with another army that was advancing from Scotland to their aid. So they returned to Scotland, and the junction was completed. The rebels then numbered nine thousand men. Stirling was attacked, but the castle held out, although the town was occupied. And now once more the forces of King George and of his rival confronted each other at Falkirk (Fig. 2259), and the former were completely routed. Thus two royal armies had been beaten in the field. The matter began indeed to look serious. King George trembled for his crown. But his cause was in potent hands—those of his son, the Duke of Cumberland, who was now also in Scotland, following with a kind of dogged determination and confidence, that looked ominous, the steps of the rebel force. And so again they avoided him, by suddenly raising the siege of Stirling, and retreating towards Inverness. Here a bold attempt was made upon the person of the chief causer of the war. Lord Loudon, who was at Inverness, hearing that the Prince had only five or six hundred men with him, set out one evening in the dark to surprise him. Charles lodged that night at the seat of the laird of Mackintosh. Lady Mackintosh in some way or other (it is supposed by means of letters from her mother) heard of this attempt, and prepared to resist it. Saying not a word to the Prince, she ordered five or six men well armed, and who were under the guidance of a smith, to watch the road from Inverness. As the troops of Lord Loudon came stealthily and rapidly along, the little band fired upon them, and began to call upon all the Macdonalds and Camerons who were lying concealed—as the royalists, at least, believed—in order to surprise them whilst they sought to surprise the Pretender. They thought themselves, in short, out-manœuvred—and they were so, but only because they so thought. They hurried back instantly, and the lady's stratagem was completely successful. Yet, ever behind them moved on that dreaded Duke, his portentous shadow "thrown before," dimming the sunshine of every success. Inverness was taken, but to what end?—the Duke, they heard, was marching there too. So they left it, and went on towards Nairn. And there they would stop—and confront him. But when, following them there, the royalists entered Nairn at one end, they found the rebels quitting at the other.

However, on the 15th of April, 1746, the whole rebel army was drawn out in order of battle upon Drummossie Moor (Fig. 2260), about a mile and a half from Culloden House. And while the men were refreshing themselves for the combat that they now knew was imminent, Charles and his council determined upon a night attack. The Duke's army lay then at Nairn. At eight o'clock in the evening the Highlanders set forth, but were so hindered on their way by the darkness, that at two in the morning they were still three miles from Nairn. A drum was now heard. The Duke of Cumberland had obtained intelligence of their approach, and was prepared. Weary, and out of spirits, the rebels returned to Culloden, and lay down to sleep. It was but for a short time. Once more the Duke pursued—at eight o'clock his forces were actually in sight—by one, they were upon the Highlanders, opening a cannonade. The Duke's previous experience of their particular objection to meet him had led him to the conclusion that they would not now fight. But he was to be undeceived in that matter. When his ordnance began to play upon them with the most murderous effect, "they came," says one of the English officers, "running forward in their furious wild way on our right, where his Royal Highness had placed himself to receive them, imagining the greatest push would be there. They came down three several times within a hundred yards of our men, firing their pistols and brandishing their swords; but our soldiers appeared as if they took little notice of their bravadoes." A similar feeling induced the clan MacIntosh to start forth from the centre of the rebel army, and endeavour to bring the contest to as summary.a conclusion as possible. What followed has been so vividly described in Chambers's 'History of the Rebellion,' that we avail ourselves of the passage :—" A Lowland gentleman, who was in the line, and who survived till a late period, used always, in relating the events of Culloden, to comment with a feeling of something like awe upon the terrific and more than natural expression of rage which glowed in every face and gleamed in every eye as he surveyed the extended line at this moment. Notwithstanding that the three files of the front line of English poured forth their incessant fire of musketry—notwithstanding that the cannon, now loaded with grape-shot, swept the field as with a hail-storm—notwithstanding the flank fire of Wolfe's regiment, onward, onward, went the headlong Highlanders, flinging themselves into, rather than rushing upon the lines of the enemy, which indeed they did not see for smoke, until involved among their weapons. It was a moment of dreadful agonizing suspense, but only a moment, for the whirlwind does not sweep the forest with greater rapidity than the Highlanders cleared the line. They swept through and over that frail barrier almost as easily and instantaneously as the bounding cavalcade brushes through the morning labours of the gossamer which stretch across its path ; not, however, with the same unconsciousness of the events. Almost every man in their front rank, chief and gentleman, fell before the deadly weapons they had braved ; and although the enemy gave way, it was not till every bayonet was bent and bloody with the strife. When the first line had been completely swept aside, the assailants continued their impetuous advance till they came near the second, when being almost annihilated by a profuse and well-directed fire, the shattered remains of what had been but an hour before a numerous and confident force, at last submitted to destiny, by giving way and flying. Still a few rushed on, resolved rather to die than to forfeit their well-acquired and dearly-estimated honour. They rushed on, but not a man ever came in contact with the enemy. The last survivor perished as he reached the points of the bayonets."

It appears that there was a particular reason why the Highlanders suffered so greatly in the beginning of this attack, notwithstanding their success in breaking the line. A new mode of managing the bayonet was adopted. Previously the bayonet-man attacked the adversary who stood direct before him, but now he was trained to single out the one who stood opposite to his next neighbour on the right hand. The consequence was, that his body was in a manner defended on the left by the target of the Highlander in front, whilst he found the right of the Highlander, whom he thus obliquely attacked, quite exposed to his thrust. "This manner," it is said, "made an essential difference; staggered the enemy, who were not prepared to alter their way of fighting, and destroyed them in a manner rather to be conceived than told. This sanguinary commencement of the battle proved also in effect its conclusion. It is true that other clans partially imitated the example of the Mac Intosh clan, but soon stopped short, and fled : and all else that day were but flight and pursuit, the cries of the dying, and the exulting shouts of the victors—the suffering and horror, carnage and butchery. Prince Charles advanced with the intention to endeavour to rally the Highlanders, but Sir Thomas Sheridan not only strenuously opposed this desire, but led the Prince's horse by the bridle away from the field. On the other hand, a less favourable view has been given of his conduct. It is said that this hesitation occurred at a time when hesitation was disgraceful as well as ruinous. Some of the Highland regiments yet kept their ground, when Lord Elcho rode up to Prince Charles, and earnestly exhorted him to make one final attempt to rally his troops, and, at least, to die like one worthy of a crown. But Charles hesitated, and Lord Elcho, seeing that then indeed all was lost, turned away with execrations, swearing he would never again see his face. Nor did he. The loss of the Highlanders on that day amounted altogether to nearly two thousand five hundred men, two-thirds of whom had been put to death *after* the battle. It was the savage cruelty of this pursuit, and the still worse proceedings that followed, that caused the Duke to receive a name that even in his own day made his " glory " but a mockery, and which promises to stick to his memory as long as that memory itself shall exist. " The King," says Horace Walpole, " is much inclined to some mercy, but the Duke, who has not so much of Cæsar after a victory as in gaining it, is for the utmost severity. It was lately proposed in the city to present him with the freedom of some company ; one of the aldermen said aloud, then let it be the *Butchers*'." A word, however, as to the British " Cæsar " during " the victory." The noble and witty letter-writer appears to have forgot that Cæsar did not gain his reputation by fighting and winning battles in which his forces, as compared with the enemy's, numbered two to one ; yet that was but the proportion of the royalist and the rebel forces at

Cullod n. Among the host of popular ballads that sprung into existence, in record of the chief incidents of this rebellion, and of the feelings excited during its progress, there are few more pathetic than the one containing the lines—

> Drummossie Muir, Drummossie day,
> A waefu' day it was to me!
> For there I lost my father dear,
> My father dear, and brethren three.

And thus unsuccessfully ended the last of the organized schemes for the restoration of the expelled Stuart line. The solemn decision of the people of England upon their unworthiness for the position to which they had been called was confirmed now and for ever. And, like a hunted deer, the miserable Prince Charles found himself flying hither and thither, with hardly a moment's rest for body or mind, harassed and tortured by fatigues and misery that one might say were beyond endurance, but that they were endured by this young representative of a long line of kings. It is at this period in truth, that the most painfully-interesting part of his career commences. It is his sufferings and his romantic adventures, and the sacrifices that were made for him by his adherents, during the few months that elapsed between the battle of Culloden and his escape from the country, that have made the subject so full of attraction, and which have rendered his name a fond recollection, even to this hour, in the districts where he found shelter.

The Prince's first movement after the battle was a flight to the castle of the man who had deceived alike him and the English government—a man so old that he had long had, as it were, one step in the grave, and yet who knew no better mode of spending the last few years, days, or hours that might elapse before the other must follow, than plotting, and juggling, and breaking faith with every one who trusted him. To the castle of the old, wily, and powerful Fraser of Lovat (Fig. 2262), Charles Stuart now for the first and last time took his way. Sir Walter Scott thus describes the meeting, on the authority of an eye-witness :—" A lady, who, when a girl, was residing in Lord Lovat's family, described to us the unexpected appearance of Prince Charles and his flying attendants at Castle Dounie. The wild desolate vale, on which she was gazing with indolent composure, was at once so suddenly filled with horsemen riding furiously towards the castle, that, impressed with the belief that they were fairies, who, according to Highland tradition, are visible to men only from one twinkle of the eyelid to another, she strove to refrain from the vibration, which she believed would occasion the strange and magnificent apparition to become invisible. To Lord Lovat it brought a certainty more dreadful than the presence of fairies or than even of demons. The towers on which he had depended had fallen to crush him, and he only met the Chevalier to exchange mutual condolences." Lovat and the other chieftains agreed to keep their clans together, and abide if necessary a mountain warfare until they might exact honourable or merciful conditions. And had the Prince seconded their efforts, no doubt they would have succeeded. The English government had too much reason to be alarmed at any show of resistance, not to be willing to agree to reasonable conditions for getting rid of it, if they could not of themselves, and by force at once put it down. But the prince most probably thought to himself, that whilst *they* might gain or save everything personally important to them as life, property, or rank, by such a course, he could only still further endanger his own life by staying ; and he possibly even thought that there might be such a thing as the servants making favourable terms by the sacrifice of the master. Lord Lovat's character was enough to generate such suspicions. So he determined to trust only to himself, and get away in secret as fast as possible to France. For a time he concealed himself in the islands of North and South Uist, dwelling in the huts of the fishermen or wherever he could find shelter, and supported by the bounty of the islanders. But the hunters were upon his track. General Campbell searched the islands of Barra and of South Uist : and Long Island, where also Charles hid himself, was surrounded by ships of war. Strange to say, at one period, while he was tossing about in the rough waters surrounding these islands, he saw and might have reached with ease two French frigates, which would at once have borne him off in safety ; but they were mistaken for English vessels, and so helped only to increase the unfortunate fugitive's alarms. How he managed to escape the hot pursuit that was made for him through the islands is wonderful. Ever moving about as the hunters moved, it is only to be accounted for by the circumstance that nearly all the residents must have been in the secret, and have proved themselves worthy of the confidence reposed. Still the reward was 30,000*l.* !—the position terrible. It was idle to suppose that the capture could be much longer prevented if the Prince stayed within so limited and so strongly guarded a space. Yet how could he move

2273. Radcliffe's Library.

2274.—Christ Church, Oxford.

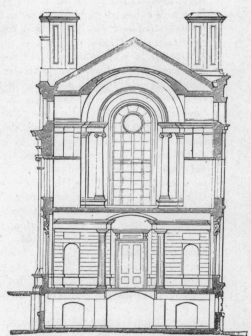

2275.—Section of King's College Library, Cambridge.

2277.—Gate of Botanical Garden at Oxford.

2276.—Queen's College, Oxford, in the Sixteenth Century.

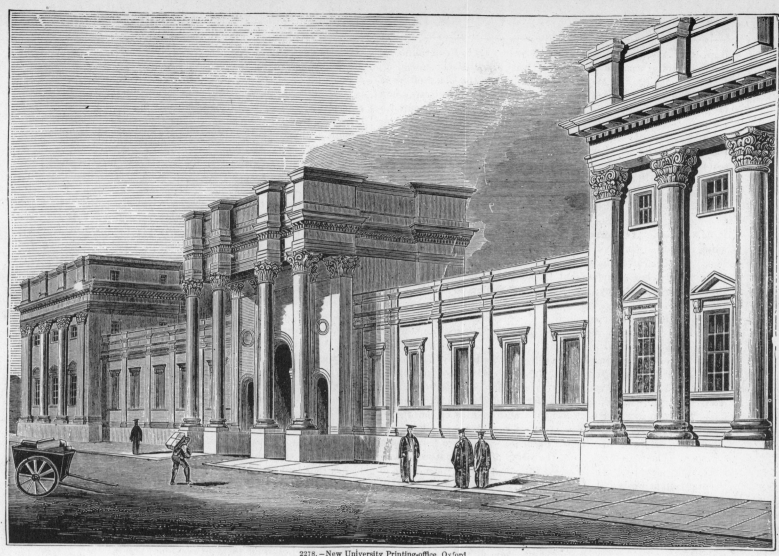

2278.—New University Printing-office, Oxford.

2279.—Caius Gate of Honour, Cambridge

2280.—The Pepysian Library. Magdalen College, Cambridge.

from it? A woman gave him the answer, who had determined to risk everything to save him. This was Flora Macdonald (Fig. 2263), the daughter of Macdonald of Melton, in the island of South Uist. She was introduced to Charles, and undertook to convey him to Skye, habited in female apparel, as her maid. She procured a passport accordingly for herself and Betty Burke—not a soul being allowed to leave the island without this authority. One circumstance was favourable to her views; her stepfather, Hugh Macdonald, who secretly sympathised with the misfortunes of the Young Pretender, was one among the commanders who pursued him. It was he who granted this passport. Another danger—that of scandal—the gallant-minded maiden put aside without a thought or a fear, after the first moments of hesitation and scruple. Her own man-servant was to be with her. As a striking feature of the actors, and the highly-wrought state of feeling that prevailed among them, it may be mentioned that Charles's only follower, O'Neil, offered to marry her in order to allay her scruples; but she declined the offer, while fully appreciating the delicacy, and chivalry of feeling in which it had originated.

At length, with the assistance of Lady Clanronald, Flora completed her preparations, and the two ladies, with the servant of the latter, Mackechan, went to seek him. He was found in a wretched hut by the sea-side, roasting a sheep's liver for his dinner; and when he saw tears starting from the eyes of those who beheld his occupation, he remarked gaily, and with true wisdom, that it might be well for other royal personages to go through the ordeal that he was enduring. The next morning witnessed the transformation of the Prince into Betty Burke. But the party were not able to embark till night, as wherry after wherry with armed soldiers were seen to pass the spot. Their destination was the island of Skye. And what a memorable night was that in which they then trusted themselves to the waters that washed the Hebrides! Except the Prince himself, all were in wretched spirits, worn out by fatigue, privation, and fear. The night was rainy. But Flora, notwithstanding, fell asleep, while Charles, who had begun to sing to cheer them, now continued singing in the hope of prolonging her slumbers. When the sail had to be re-adjusted, he guarded her with his hands during the operation. She found him thus employed, with his hand stretched over her, when she awoke: what a subject for a picture! At daybreak they knew not where they were, being out of sight of land. But at last they perceived looming through the distance the great headland of Skye, and made all haste to land at a point called Waternish. To their horror they suddenly found themselves almost in the very middle of their enemies—there was a party of militia on the shore, a boat at the water-side. Happily the tide was out, the beach long and rough, and the boat had no oars. The militia shouted to them to land, an invitation that was of course declined; and then they were fired upon. The Prince bade the boatmen not "mind the villains;" and when they remarked that their apprehensions were only for him, said, "Oh, no fear of me!" Eventually he stretched himself at the bottom of the boat, but it was only because Flora refused to do so until he himself did the same. No one was hit; and they were soon out of danger from the soldiers' fire.

Flora had intended to lodge her charge in the house of Sir Alexander Macdonald, who was himself at that very time in attendance on the Duke of Cumberland, and therefore from home; but whose wife, Lady Margaret, was a Jacobite in heart, and prepared, as far as her presence and wishes were concerned, to aid the Prince's escape. But several of the King's soldiers were at that very time in her house, and Flora had the courage and presence of mind to meet the commanding officer, Lieutenant Macleod, in Lady Margaret's drawing-room, and answer all his questions, as to where she had come from, where she was going, and so forth. Lady Margaret was naturally alarmed to hear of the arrival of the Prince at such a time; but it was speedily arranged that he should be conducted to the house of a gentleman named Kingsburgh, who was also present, and a sound Jacobite; while Flora, to make all safe, waited behind for a time, keeping the officer in conversation. Kingsburgh, it should seem, went reluctantly to meet the fugitive, who accosting him told him that "his life was now in his, Kingsburgh's, hands to dispose of; that he was in the utmost distress, having had no meat or sleep for two days and two nights—sitting on a rock, beat upon by the rains, and when they ceased ate up by flies; he conjured him to show compassion but for one night, and he should be gone. This moving speech, and the visible distress prevailed, for he was meagre, ill-coloured, and overrun with the scab."

Among the party who accompanied Flora when she rode off after Charles and Kingsburgh, were two servants, who knew nothing of

the weighty business that was being transacted, and whom Flora desired to get rid of before again entering into personal communication with the Prince. One of these servants, as they passed the two pedestrians on the road, was struck by Betty's unfeminine movements, and said to Flora, "See, what long strides the jade takes! I dare say she's an Irishwoman, or else a man in woman's clothes." Flora said, no doubt she was an Irishwoman, and so stopped that very alarming conversation. When these servants, with their mistress (who was in the secret), had departed, and Flora had joined the pair, they were troubled to find the people quitting church, and coming along the road, as they advanced. For Betty was still the observed of all observers. And as everybody knew Kingsburgh, why they could talk with and question him freely. We may judge of his annoyance and difficulty. But at last he got rid of them by a happy thought. "Oh, sirs," said he, "cannot you let alone talking of your worldly affairs on the Sabbath, and have patience till another day?"

As Lady Kingsburgh (so the laird's wife was called) that night after supper discoursed over with Flora all the moving adventures that she had experienced, she asked what she had done with the boatmen who brought them to Skye. Flora said she had sent them back to South Uist. It was immediately pointed out to her that they might fall into the English officer's hands, and divulge the all-important news of his movements. Flora in consequence determined to change the female garb that very night. It was a wise determination;—and offered the only chance of redeeming the oversight that had been made. Within a week after Charles had landed at Skye, he was followed by Captain Ferguson, who was in possession of every particular as to his disguise and companions; the boatmen having been seized and compelled to speak. With keen sagacity he now followed his footsteps. He learned that Flora had been at Lady Margaret's, but no tall female servant. He learned that she had also been at Kingsburgh, and that there the tall female had been seen among Flora's attendants. Kingsburgh professed to have taken no notice of these attendants. But Captain Ferguson discovered that she, or he, had been placed in the best bed, so Kingsburgh was marched off to a prison, and which he did not leave for a twelvemonth. Flora herself was soon also in custody. And still growing nearer and nearer to the fugitive, Captain Ferguson and his associates were shortly able to hem him completely in, within a very limited circle of posts—ignorant of his precise position, but feeling sure, for the first time, that he was within their grasp. He had then too reached the mainland. These military posts were so close to each other, that Charles had to creep up the channel of a brook in order to avoid two of them. He was accompanied now by Macdonald of Glenaladale, and after fresh difficulties and adventures, succeeded in reaching with him the hill of Corado, situated between Kintail and Glenmoriston. Here, in a wretched cave, suited to their and his fallen and desperate fortunes, Charles found a few of his most faithful followers, who knew him notwithstanding his strange aspect and appearance, and fell on their knees before him.

The poet Home thus describes Charles's dress at this time:—"He had a coat of coarse dark-coloured cloth, and a wretched yellow wig, with a bonnet on his head. His brogues were tied with thongs so worn that they would hardly keep on his feet. His shirt was saffron, and he had not another." Here Charles stayed between five and six weeks, supported by the same means as his companions, who "lifted" whatever they wanted from wherever they could obtain it. He then moved along over the tops of the mountains, in a stormy night, to another hut, and from thence to a "Cage" that one of his devoted followers, Clunie, had fitted up for the shelter of himself and a wounded friend and fellow-chieftain, Lochiel. The maker of the Cage was also its describer, and it must have been, as he says, "a great curiosity." It appears it was situated on the face of a very rough, high, and rocky mountain, called Letternilichk, still a part of Benalder, full of great stones and crevices, and some scattered wood interspersed. "The habitation called the Cage, in the face of that mountain, was within a small thick bush of wood. There were first some rows of trees laid down, in order to level a floor for the habitation; and, as the place was steep, this raised the lower side to an equal height with the other; and these trees, in the way of joints and planks, were levelled with earth and gravel. There were between the trees growing naturally on their own roots, some stakes fixed in the earth, which with the trees were interwove with ropes made of heath and birch twigs, up to the top of the Cage, it being of a round, or rather oval shape; and the whole thatched and covered with fog [moss]. This whole fabric hung, as it were, by a large tree, which reclined from the one end, all along the roof, to the other, and which gave it the name of the Cage. And by chance there happened to be two stones at a small distance from one another in the side next the precipice, resembling the pillars of a chimney, where the fire was placed. The smoke had its vent out here all along the face of the rock, which was so much of the same colour that one could discover no difference in the clearest day. The cage was no larger than to contain six or seven persons; four of whom were frequently employed playing at cards, one idle looking on, one baking, and another firing bread and cooking." Ample provisions were laid in before the Prince arrived. "There was plenty of mutton, an anker of whiskey containing twenty Scotch pints, some good beef sausages made the year before, with plenty of butter and cheese, besides a large well-cured bacon ham." Upon the entry of Charles into the Cage, he "took a hearty dram, which he sometimes called for thereafter to drink the health of his friends. When some minced collops were dressed with butter in a large saucepan which Lochiel and Clunie carried always about with them, being the only fire-vessel they had, his Royal Highness ate heartily, and said, with a very cheerful countenance, 'Now, gentlemen, I live like a prince.'" However, he was now near his long and terrible journey's end. He left the Cage on hearing that two French frigates were waiting for him, and, travelling only by night, reached Lochnanuagh, and re-embarked for France at the very spot where he had landed from that country in order to achieve the conquest of Great Britain.

And what became of poor Flora? As might have been expected, she was the theme of universal admiration. It is even said that the King's own son, Frederick, Prince of Wales, and father of George III., did not hesitate to express his sympathy with the popular views of her conduct. His consort having condemned Flora, the Prince replied, "Let me not hear you speak thus again, Madam. If you had been in the same circumstances, I hope in God you would have acted as she did." As Flora was on her way towards Leith, she found on board the same vessel, and also in captivity, Captain O'Neil, who had before offered to marry her, and who had first advised her to embark in the enterprise that had ended so successfully as regards the Prince. She went up to him, and slapping his cheek gently and playfully, said, "To that black face do I owe all my misfortunes." Never, perhaps, did monarch hold a more popular levee than Flora Macdonald, when, having anchored at Leith, the public wished to come on board to see her. The clergyman of Leith was among the visitors, and has left us a record of his impressions of her conduct and appearance. He says, "Although she was easy and cheerful, yet she had a certain mixture of gravity in all her behaviour, which became her situation exceedingly well, and set her off to great advantage. She is of a low stature, of a fair complexion, and well enough shaped. One would not discern by her conversation that she had spent all her former days in the Highlands; for she talks English (or rather Scots) easily, and not at all through the Earse tone. She has a sweet voice, and sings well; and no lady, Edinburgh bred, can acquit herself better at the tea-table than what she did when in Leith-roads." She was subsequently taken to London, and confined for a short time in the house of a private family; but when the Act of Indemnity passed, July, 1747, she was set at large. She subsequently married the son of Kingsburgh, her partner in loyalty and danger, and, after a long and adventurous life, died at Skye in 1790.

Lamentable was the fate of hosts of other adherents of the young Pretender. The executioner went to work with frightful assiduity and remorselessness. Among the most pitied of the victims were the Lords Kilmarnock and Balmerino: among the least pitied was the old Lord Lovat, caught like a rat in a trap, where his cunning might no longer avail him. Even the Tower, he thought and said, would not have been able to hold him, if he had been a little younger man. And when it was replied that much younger men had been kept there, he replied, "Yes, but they were inexperienced; they had not broken so many jails as I have. On his trial he laughed and jested, even whilst the sentence was being pronounced. The day before execution Hogarth took his portrait (Fig. 2262). The old man was in the best possible spirits. He said he would die as a Christian, and as a Highland chief should do—*not in his bed*. On the scaffold he sat down and talked with great composure to the people, quoting Horace in the course of his remarks. Walpole, who said he "had been *living* at old Lovat's trial," was of course not absent from the execution. He thus describes the behaviour of Lovat:—"He died extremely well, without passion, affectation, buffoonery, or timidity; his behaviour being natural and intrepid." He had said that he would be hanged, for that if beheaded he should be struck upon the shoulders; but

the executioner was skilful, and performed his horrible office so expertly that the one blow sufficed.

Of all those who fell at the battle of Prestonpans the most regretted was Colonel Gardiner, a man as much esteemed by his superiors for his military skill and courage, as by a large body of those persons who have generally little sympathy with the class to which he belonged, for his character and conduct as a man. His life, indeed, formed a kind of new era in what may be called the English soldier's domestic history. Before Colonel Gardiner's time the state of morality among military men was very low indeed; and as to religion—it consisted in a hurried prayer now and then, when danger threatened, but had no practical effect in exalting the feelings, or principles, or business of daily life. Gardiner did not differ from his brethren up to a certain period of his career. He was dissolute and reckless; nor did what he afterwards esteemed his first warning—a remarkable wound in his neck, received at the battle of Ramilies—work any change in his conduct. But in July, 1719, when he had retired to his chamber for the night, he took up for an hour's diversion, a book in which his profession was spiritualized. Suddenly "he thought he saw an unusual blaze of light fall on the book while he was reading, which he at first imagined might happen by some accident in the candle. But lifting up his eyes, he apprehended to his extreme amazement, that there was before him, as it were suspended in the air, a visible representation of the Lord Jesus Christ upon the cross, surrounded on all sides with a glory; and was impressed as if a voice, or something equivalent to a voice, had come to him to this effect (for he was not confident as to the very words), 'Oh, sinner! did I suffer this for thee, and are these the returns?'" The Colonel's excellent biographer, Dr. Doddridge, remarks on the possibility of his having fallen asleep and dreamt this vision; whilst it has been supposed by other writers that the mind had been in a peculiarly susceptible and imaginative state; to which also a fall that the Colonel had experienced a little time before might have contributed, by slightly injuring the brain. Colonel Gardiner, however, was perfectly satisfied that he had experienced a "a supernatural soliciting," and he obeyed the call. Thenceforward he became a man of the most exemplary piety.

As illustrating at once the effect of this conversion, which made a great noise throughout the country, and the state of the military profession at the time, we may here give an interesting anecdote. The Colonel had invited the commanding officer of the troops, then at Edinburgh, to dine with him at his house at Bankton. Knowing —too well—the habits of the guests he had to entertain, and at the same time determined not to compromise his own sense of what was right, he addressed them, when they were all assembled, with an air of mingled respect and firmness, saying that he had the honour to be a justice of the peace in that county—and therefore sworn to put the laws in execution, and among the rest those against swearing. He entreated them, accordingly, to be on their guard, and hoped that if any oath or curse did escape them, they would consider his animadversions as a necessary part of the duties of his office, and as implying no want of deference to them. The commanding officer received this address in the proper spirit; and said he would himself pay the penalty if he offended. He even undertook the office of watching for violators of the law during the Colonel's temporary absences from the room, and was, no doubt, not a little amused by the opportunity he found of fining one of the persons present on such an occasion.

That the Colonel's religious views did not prevent him from being an excellent soldier was strikingly proved at the battle, in which, as we have seen, he lost his life. His behaviour, indeed, stands out in marked contrast to the behaviour of the English officers generally, and especially of their commander, who has been immortalized in no pleasant fashion by the author of the well-known ballad—

Hey, Johnny Cope, are ye wauking yet?

The Colonel, it appears, was wounded in the very beginning of the combat, by a bullet in the left breast, which made him give a sudden spring in the saddle. His servant wished him to retreat, but he said it was only a flesh wound, and fought on. Presently he received a second shot, which lodged in the right thigh. When his regiment fled, Gardiner, with characteristic courage and presence of mind, seeing a party of foot fighting near him, without any officer to guide them, close by the park wall of his own happy home, he said, "These brave fellows will be cut to pieces for want of a commander;" and riding up to them, exclaimed, "Fire on, my lads, and fear nothing!" At that moment, a Highlander armed with a scythe fastened to a long pole, struck at him, and his sword was seen to fall from his hand. He was then dragged from his

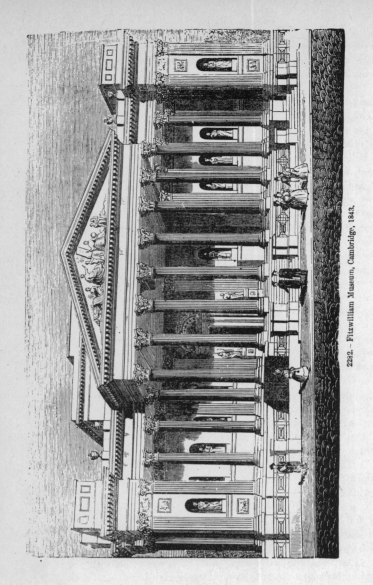

2282.—Fitzwilliam Museum, Cambridge, 1843.

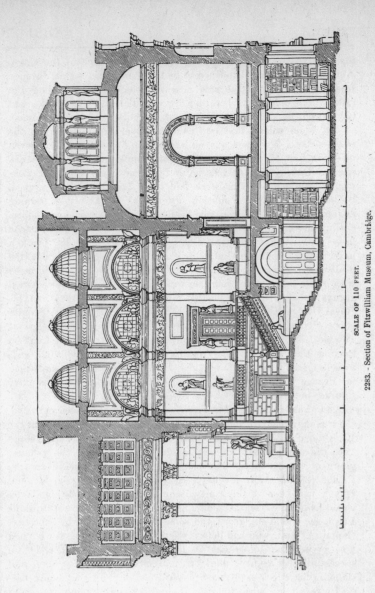

SCALE OF 110 FEET.

2283.—Section of Fitzwilliam Museum, Cambridge.

2281.—Bridge connecting the Colleges of St. John's, Cambridge.

2284.—Library of Trinity College Cambridge

2285.—St. Olave's School, Southwark (as rebuilt).

2286.—Lady Owen's School (as rebuilt)

2288.—Costume of William III.

2287.—Bedford School (as rebuilt).

2290.—Costume of Queen Mary. (From two Prints of the time.)

2289.—William III (From a Print dated 1694.)

2291.—Gentlemen of the reigns of Queen Anne George I and II (From Jeffrey's Collection, published in 1757) a, 1700-15; b, 1735; c, 1745; d, 1755

horse, and had scarcely touched the ground before another High-lander struck him on the back of his head. The dying man's last act was to wave his hat as a signal to a faithful servant that he should fly. The man did so, but returned disguised two hours after the engagement, and found the Colonel still breathing; but he died the same morning in the house of the minister at Tranent.

Our engraving (Fig. 2256) exhibits the house in which he was born, which is situated in a sequestered spot between Blackness Castle and Borrowstoness, in Linlithgowshire, and commands a delightful view of the Frith of Forth.

We shall not, of course, plunge into the almost unfathomable sea of European politics during the reigns of the first and second Georges; but content ourselves with the mention of two or three of the particular incidents that have obtained so wide a reputation as to be still popularly remembered, when the circumstances and motives in which they originated are forgotten, or at least have ceased to command any general interest. Thus few now-a-days care to know about the war with Spain in 1739; but there are few who do not still warm with enthusiasm as they read of the skill and courage with which Admiral Vernon reduced Portobello (Fig. 2248), in the Isthmus of Darien, in the course of that war. The battle of Dettingen (Fig. 2249), fought in 1743, by our own king in person, and with great bravery, is a pertinent matter still to us. And lastly, though no doubt it was a great source of satisfaction to Englishmen in the eighteenth century that the French had been driven back to the Rhine, we in the nineteenth should listen to the statement of the facts with lack-lustre eyes, but that we hear of the mode in which the feat was accomplished, namely, by the great battle of Minden (Fig. 2264), fought in 1759, when English gallantry was, if possible, more than usually conspicuous.

There is, however, another class of foreign operations that affect us very differently. The events we have named, and a host of others like them, have left no permanent record behind them that can satisfactorily explain their utility. They look like so many tremendous evidences of a belief on the part of the most civilised nations of the earth, that it is a part of the economy of Nature that they should fight with one another, and therefore that they have sought for causes for warfare, rather than merely fought when the causes of themselves came. It seems, therefore, an approach to common sense to become selfish under such circumstances, and fight for territories, instead of "balance of power," or "glory;" and so obtain results that posterity shall at least see and understand. The reign of George II. was to be for ever remembered in connection with such efforts and successes. Wolfe won Canada at the cost of his own life, by winning the battle of Quebec; Clive in effect won the East Indies by overpowering the native combatants, and driving out the French from almost every one of their possessions in that most real of *El Dorados*. Of the ministers who, during the two reigns in question, guided the public affairs, two only need be mentioned. One is Sir Robert Walpole, a man of greater ability even than contemporaries give him credit for, able as he was acknowledged to be, and all-powerful as he evidently was, but whose name has also become synonymous with all the arts of political corruption. The other is that of a younger man, who began to rise as Walpole began to fall, and who, when rebuked by the brother of Walpole for his presumption, is reported by Johnson to have said, "The atrocious crime of being a young man, which the honourable gentleman has with such spirit and decency charged upon me, I shall neither attempt to palliate nor deny, but content myself with wishing that I may be one of those whose follies may cease with their youth, and not of that number who are ignorant in spite of experience." The acclamations of a crowded House of Commons (Fig. 2266) no doubt carried home to the quarter at which they were levelled the severe but polished sarcasms of this remarkable speech, for the speaker was then rapidly becoming popular. It was the elder Pitt who thus spiritedly defended himself. His character and influence, however, belong not to 'Old England.' It is in connection with the reign of George III., and with events of which the excitement and party feeling have hardly yet entirely subsided, that his name became illustrious.

CHAPTER II.—POPULAR ANTIQUITIES.

HE last of the colleges that can be properly said to belong to 'Old England'—we refer to Worcester College, Oxford—was founded in the year 1714; we may, therefore, in connection with the present period, glance at the general subject of Education, as viewed in association with the two principal English universities, and with some of the more important of the public schools that yet exist in our great towns.

If in one of those magic freaks of which eastern tales are so full, a person who had never seen Oxford or Cambridge, nor paid much attention to aught he might have read about them, were set down just outside one of these cities, say, for instance, Oxford, and on the Abingdon road (Fig. 2271), and were conducted from thence into its streets and among its population, he would be apt to think he had been transported to some foreign country; so unlike in various respects would seem the aspect of the place as compared with the aspect of other English towns. The ladies, it is true, dress there much as elsewhere; but the gentlemen—some in black togas and black square caps—others with their robes displaying rich red silk linings, and wearing lace and embroidery, and yet others who move resplendently about beneath quantities of gold lace and gold thread—what are these who wear the most picturesque of dresses with so picturesque and gallant an air?

Turning from these, who form so large a part of the entire population of the place, the place itself presents new cause for wonder and admiration. Never surely before were so many magnificent edifices congregated in so limited a space. Private buildings and public ones have here reversed their usual numerical proportion. Here, if anywhere, may one speak with propriety of a city of palaces. And then the gardens—those paradises of peaceful delight—which seem as though each must join at some corner or other the one nearest to it, and so the whole extend all over Oxford. Truly, it is a thing worth remembering, the first sight of the students and the streets of this famous University.

We will imagine ourselves for the moment in the position of one who walks through the city with an intelligent Freshman, explaining as he goes whatever object arrests the eye, or that suggests itself as matter of inquiry to the thoughts of the new comer, who is, of course, as usual, full of the novelty of the place and his own future in connection with it. The first things that surprise him are the bridges. Whether he comes from the south, east, or west, the entrance into the town is still by bridges. With something like poetical emotion he looks down from the western one, should his route lie that way, for it spans the waters of the classical Isis—the stock figure for prize poems innumerable. Or should he come from the south, he pauses at Folly Bridge to look at the spot where was Friar Bacon's study, and haply wonders whether Nature is here dealing—by this odd conjunction of names—in one of those little bits of practical satire of which she often seems to be fond. Or if, lastly, he come with the great stream that pours in eastwards, chiefly from London, the street view that there presents itself may fix him spell-bound with admiration. It has been said that this High-street is one of the finest in Europe; and without having gone all over Europe to obtain materials for the comparison, one can feel tolerably sure it must be so. But what, he asks, is this building here by the bridge, that we have just passed? What a curious old pile it is, and what a beautiful pinnacled tower!

That is Magdalene College (Fig. 2280), founded by William of Wayneflete, and the tower is said to have been designed by Wolsey; but the story appears to rest on no better foundation than the fact that Wolsey was a bursar of the college at the time. And he is but one of the many eminent men who have issued forth from its walls into the active business of the world, including Bishop Wilkins, the poet Daniel, Sir Harry Vane, Sir Julius Cæsar, Lord Clarendon, Sir Matthew Hale, and others. A noticeable feature of Magdalene College is the custom, that it is bound to observe by statute, of playing the entertainer whenever Royalty visits Oxford.

And that modern and magnificent pile of building in the Grecian style, with the queenly statue in front?

That is Queen's College, founded by the confessor of good Queen Philippa, and was so called probably in order to commemorate his admiration and affection for that admirable woman. Not only she herself, but other queens since that time, have delighted to honour the establishment; so that it peculiarly deserves the name it bears. Queen Charlotte owes the especial respect paid to her in the erection of the statue over the gateway to a gift of 1000*l.* towards the building of the quadrangle. The victor of Agincourt was here educated, and there was in a room over the gateway a very ancient portrait of him in glass. The engraving (Fig. 2276) represents the ancient College, over whose gateway Henry V. is said to have lodged when a student. Barnard Gilpin and the poet Collins were also members of Queen's. But now turn your eyes to the opposite side of the street, to the long and grand-looking front of University College, with its double gateways, and towers, and statues; that is the parent establishment of the whole university; and if tradition and some writers are to be believed, had no less a personage for its founder than the great Saxon king Alfred, who is understood to have resided at one period in Oxford with his three sons. The story has at least this much evidence to be put forth in its favour; we know Oxford to have been become reputed as a place of study so far back as the time of the Confessor. And it is not an uninteresting occupation to contrast the state of the university in its earlier stages with its present sumptuous magnificence. The university began humbly, with mere schools for the instruction of youth attached to religious houses, or supported by the masters and other inhabitants of Oxford. There were schools for grammar, sophistry, arts, medicine, law, divinity, &c. When many of the scholars resided together in the secular schools or houses of study, these establishments became known as halls or hostels, and governors were appointed to superintend the discipline and instruction. No regular plan, however, can be traced until the foundation or revival of University College by Walter de Merton in 1247; but his statutes were gradually adopted, with alterations, by other succeeding colleges. These facts, on the whole, give us a kind of glimpse of the mode of formation of the present university. And comparatively rude and simple as the arrangements no doubt then were, as compared with the elaborate system that now prevails, there is one startling fact in connection with this foundation or revival of Merton College; there were then at Oxford no less than fifteen thousand scholars! It is a common remark to say that these and the thirty thousand students of the reign of Henry III. are mere exaggerations: but apparently the assertion is made on no better foundation than the fact that no such state of things prevails now.

And what is that hybrid-looking building a little farther on, where ancient and modern architecture seem to have tried to amalgamate, but have only very indifferently succeeded?

That is All Souls'; or to give it its proper statute designation, "The College of the Souls of all faithful people deceased, of Oxford;" seeming to convey the idea of a sort of spiritual cemetery. Perhaps some malicious tongues would say it is so in its business of education; but the names of the men who have been educated there—Linacre, the first great English physician, Leland, Jeremy Taylor, Wren, the poet Young, Blackstone, Heber—form a triumphant answer to the calumny. It appears that the idea so quaintly expressed was chiefly intended to apply to the praying for the good estate of Henry VI. and the Archbishop Chicheley, who was the founder, and also for the souls of Henry V. the Duke of Clarence,

2292.—Costume of the Nobility and Gentry, temp. William and Mary. (From Prints by Romain de Hooge, 1689, and Costumes by Myer, 1691.)

2293.—Costume of the Commonalty, temp. William and Mary. (From Prints by Romain de Hooge, 1689 and Mauron's Cries of London.)

2294.—General Costume, temp. Anne. (From Prints dated 1706—1709, and figures in Jeffrey's Collection.)

2295.—General Costume, temp. George I. (Selected from early works of Hogarth.)

2296.—General Costume, temp. George II. (From Prints of the Trial and Execution of the Rebel Lords, 1746.)

2297.—Military Costume, temp. George II. (Selected from Hogarth's March to Finchley.)

2298.—Ladies of the reign of George II. (From Jeffrey's Collection.
a, 1735 ; b, 1745 ; c, 1755.

2299.—Fashionable Costumes, 1765.

2300.—A Minuet.

2301.—Scene in the Fair Penitent.

2303.—House of Commons in the time of Sir R. Walpole.

2302.—Garrick as Macbeth.

2304.—Alamode, 1735. Mall in St. James's Park.

2305.—Alamode, 1745. Mall in St. James's Park.

and of all those dukes, earls, barons, knights, and esquires, and other English subjects, who had fallen in the war with France. A pious thought. The hecatombs of human victims that had been sacrificed to that brilliantly conducted but unjust war might well seem to need some expiation. We must examine the interior at another opportunity; suffice it therefore at present to tell you there is a statue, by Bacon, of Blackstone, among the works of art of the College, and that one of the finest libraries in England is to he found at All Souls'. We refer alike to the place and its extent. The one measures one hundred and ninety feet in length, by thirty-two feet and a half in breadth, swelling out in the centre to above fifty feet, whilst the height, forty feet, is sufficient to allow of a gallery that extends round three sides of the room. And the whole sprung from the munificence of a single individual, Colonel Codrington, governor of the Leeward Caribbee islands. As to the books, it may be briefly said that they form one of the finest collections that even Oxford, so rich in literary wealth, can boast of, and is constantly increasing. It was something to lay the first stone of such a building; and for once, literary and learned men exhibited a proper respect for their own order, by choosing one of themselves for the honour. Could they have a better man than the author of the 'Night Thoughts'? Let us pause here a moment at this noble opening—called after a well-known name, and who has been a truly princely benefactor of Oxford—Radcliffe Square. The buildings on its eastern side are, as you see, part of All Souls', and the remainder belonged to the now extinct foundation of Hertford College. On the opposite or western side, that range of buildings of antique cast, and with the beautiful Gothic entrance gateway, belongs to the College of Brazen Nose.

Brazen Nose!

Yes, an odd name, and arising from an odd combination of circumstances, some of which are among the most interesting features of the history of the university. From the earliest period the members of the university and the townspeople were engaged in continual broils, breaking out sometimes into such violence that bloodshed ensued. The townspeople, however, appear to have had the best of it, and so again and again their antagonists withdrew from the place, and left Oxford without a university. At one time Northampton was the place of their retreat; at another, Stamford in Lincolnshire. At this last-named place we have often paused to gaze upon the remains of a Norman gateway belonging to one of the colleges thus established. On the door there was of old an iron ring fixed in a nose of brass, to serve the purpose of a knocker, and the college became known through that feature as Brazen Nose. On the return to Oxford, which took place after a little time, the members of the college took the name with them, and left it attached to one of the two halls that were removed when the present establishment was founded on their site. And that foundation reminds us of the very important period to which it belongs. It is a curious, but perhaps, when thoroughly examined, very natural circumstance, that the fourteenth century, which marks the revival of modern learning, should be distinguished by very high individual genius—Chaucer's works, for instance, were then produced—and also the sixteenth, when English literature had, as far as we can yet judge, reached its culminating point; but that the century between should be remarkable for the absence of any literary productions of a permanently high intrinsic value. And yet that is the century in which so gigantic a movement was made in the establishment of houses of learning. Here at Oxford, for instance, was Brazen Nose founded in 1511; Corpus Christi, in 1517; Cardinal, by Cardinal Wolsey, in 1525 (and which on his fall fell too); Henry VIII.'s, in 1532 (an intended continuation of Wolsey's, but dissolved in 1545, when was erected in its stead) Christ Church, also by Henry; Trinity, in 1554; St. John's, in 1557; and Jesus, in 1571. And at Cambridge a parallel state of feeling and activity prevailed. It has been observed that "this indeed was the natural and proper direction for the *first* impulse to take that was given by the revival of letters: the actual generation upon which the new light broke was not that in which it was to be expected it should do much more than to awaken the taste for true learning, or at most the ambition of excellence: the power of accomplishment could only come in the next era. The men of the latter part of the fifteenth century, therefore, were most fitly and most usefully employed in making provision for the preservation and transmission to other times of the long-lost wisdom and eloquence that had been found again in their day—in building cisterns and conduits for the precious waters that, after having been hidden for a thousand years, had burst their fonts, and were once more flowing over the earth." ('Pictorial England,' vol. ii. p. 813.) Now, though this is in the main no doubt as true as it is eloquent, it appears to us to require some mo-

dification. Dante, Petrarch, and Boccaccio in Italy, and Chaucer in England, were the real revivers of modern learning and literature, by the impulse that their genius and learning and literary tendencies gave to the study of the ancients; and they all belong to the fourteenth, not to the fifteenth century. The "first" impulse, therefore, in England was really one to stimulate production, as in the works of Chaucer and Gower; for it is clear that they were influenced, and deeply, by the Italian movement. But the sudden energy aroused in individual minds would no doubt subside with them, and then the general mass of society would remain to be affected in the mode above described. But stay, here we are opposite what is called the University Church, because the members of the university commonly attend here; sometimes to please themselves, sometimes because they happen to have been pressed into the service, as, with their thoughts and their feet running in some contrary direction, the proctor happened to meet them. And an amusing thing it is, though not exactly in accordance with the sentiments that the sight of such a place should call forth, to see that official on some particularly successful occasion entering with his reluctant train. "Of course, all the pressed men walk out of the church the moment they are in it. There is no one to prevent them, as the authorities sit in a different part. One of the proctors, once meeting a gownsman walking away from the church just as he himself was going there, stopped and indignantly asked him, 'Is this the way to St. Mary's sir?' 'No, sir, that is the way,' said the youth, pointing out the spire to the offended dignitary." You smile, but beware; jokes with proctors are very well when perfectly successful, but uncommonly awkward in every other case.

And what is that splendid circular many-sided building, with its Corinthian columns and dome, in the centre of the square? (Fig. 2273.)

The Radcliffe Library, rich beyond measure, as it should be, in books of medicine and natural history, and forming altogether one of the most magnificent individual bequests ever known in the country. Radcliffe's biography gives us some indication of the circumstances that may have influenced him. He was first a student here, though a very strange student. He had so few books that Dr. Bathurst, the President of Trinity, once on a visit to him in his rooms, asked him where was his library? "There, sir," said Radcliffe, pointing to some glass vials, a herbal, and a skeleton, "there, sir, is Radcliffe's library." And it would be well if every student could make such good use of his books. He became a fellow, took the degree of Doctor of Medicine, and went out, as it was called, a Grand Compounder, with all the usual splendid ceremonies, including a general procession of the members of the college, who went with him, who was bareheaded, to the Convocation House. In the mean time he had obtained a very high reputation for professional skill; in short, he was emphatically a prophet in his own country, and—what does not often follow—able to maintain or even to advance his reputation when he went elsewhere. In London he speedily became known, and courted; his caustic wit aiding in no slight degree the fame of his cures. He once said to Dr. Mead, "I love you, and now I will tell you a sure secret to make your fortune; *use all mankind ill.*" Happily there is not the smallest need to accept his philosophy for anything more than a superficial view of the nature of men, for we know he did a very great deal in the way of using them well: in hosts of cases he alleviated or cured the diseases that afflicted or threatened to bring to a premature close the lives of his fellow-men, and which were often perfectly intractable in all other hands, and thus added, in no slight degree, to the comfort and enjoyment of his fellow-creatures. Radcliffe was, in short, the Abernethy of his day. His London residence was in Bow-Street, Covent Garden, and next to him resided the painter Kneller, a juxtaposition that with two such men was sure to lead to some passages of arms between them. And so, when they quarrelled about the door into the garden that the painter threatened to close up, he was told he might do aught but paint it; to which his retort, at once witty and kindly, was, that he could take anything from the doctor but physic. Radcliffe is another instance to be added to the many that before existed, of men who were misers to themselves or their contemporaries in order to benefit posterity. He has owned that he was "avaricious, even to spunging, whenever he any way could save, at a tavern reckoning, a sixpence or a shilling among the rest of the company, under pretence of hating (as he ever did) to change a guinea, because (said he) it slips away so fast. He could never be brought to pay bills without much following and importunity, nor then, if there appeared any chance of wearying them out." (Richardson). His death furnishes a very different moral to his life than he could have ever anticipated. It was brought on, it is said, by the public indignation and excitement at his refusing to attend Queen Anne when she was dying. Such was the man who left 40,000l. to build a library at Oxford, and other large funds to provide for repairs, the librarian, and the purchase of books. And various other bequests were also left, in one way or another, to the university, of such value that, in addition to the constant and handsome support of two travelling fellowships in connection with University College, his executors have been able to build entirely the Infirmary and the Observatory of Oxford (the last at an expense of 30,000l.), and to render great assistance to other charitable and important establishments.

But Oxford possesses a yet more important library than this—a library that has obtained an European reputation for the amazing extent and value of its contents; and which is, properly speaking, the public library of the university. There it is—forming a part of that great quadrangle, which ranges along the northern side of the square. The original founder was the good Duke Humphrey, who gave the library a superb collection of manuscript books, one only of which—out of it is said six hundred—now remains. The existing specimen is a folio MS. of Valerius Maximus, most elegantly decorated. Sir Thomas Bodley, a favoured public servant of Elizabeth, set to work about the close of the sixteenth century to restore to Oxford a library. He gave his own collection, worth 10,000l., to begin with. Such examples are apt to be infectious from their very impressiveness and magnificence. He found it so. Never was there such a sudden inroad of books into a building before or since. Every corner, however remote, began to fill; at last there was not an inch of space remaining—and still the stream poured on. So a new library, the present one, was erected; and subsequently the university added the three other sides of the quadrangle, forming the schools, &c. To give an adequate idea of the contents in any short space were impossible. It is not one, but a dozen libraries collected together. A poetical mind would probably be most interested in the choice collection of the earliest editions of Shakspere here preserved. The German, Kohl, was chiefly interested with the topographical portion. "Every shire has here its own department, and I was astonished at the minute accuracy with which the petty history and geography of every village, hamlet, and parish in England was here detailed. In some cases the history of every family of any importance was given." It is unpleasant to be told by the same writer that "Access to the library is granted very sparingly, and even the students have to pay an annual sum for the use of it." Our view represents its interior (Fig. 1602).

The Divinity Schools (Fig. 1605), the very ancient piece of architecture that you see there, connected with the Bodleian Library and the more modern schools, was also founded by Humphrey of Gloucester. In that same pile, too, we shall find all that remains in a collective form of the famous Arundelian marbles (Fig. 2165).

And what is that handsome building, with the portico, in the open square beyond?

The Clarendon Printing-office, erected from Vanbrugh's designs; a very satisfactory and tangible evidence of the value of a copyright. That edifice was built with the profits of the famous 'History of the Rebellion,' Clarendon's son having given the copyright to the university. One may here muse over the extraordinary changes that a few years may produce in the views and condition of men; when we see the University of Oxford at one period sending forth, with the stamp of its authority and sanction, a work steeped in bitterness towards those who had fought in the senate or in the field against Royalty, and then, when we see at another, and but a little earlier one, Cromwell in the position of Chancellor—the same post that the Duke of Wellington now holds; Kohl may well observe, "These are the two most remarkable Chancellors of Oxford I ever heard of." The University Printing-office is a distinct building, situated at the back of the Observatory, and forms one of the "lions" of Oxford (Fig. 2278). Think of a "press-room" two hundred feet long and twenty-eight wide! But the office enjoys privileges that sufficiently account for the vast business preparations that here meet the eye. There are but three printers in England entitled to issue the Bible without notes or comments: they are the King's printer in London, and the printers of Oxford and Cambridge Universities.

We need not stop to describe the theatre further than to say that here the principal public meetings of the university are held, and that it was one of the works by means of which Wren stepped upwards to the highest pinnacle of architectural reputation. The Ashmolean Museum, that you see there adjacent to the theatre, was also from Wren's designs; and the establishment itself is interesting as being the first public collection of the kind that existed in England. But Elias Ashmole was the very man to collect all sorts of curiosities in natural history or the arts. He had a faith in them beyond the faith of those who now collect such things. He was, in a word, an alchemist, and had every expectation of finding the philosopher's stone—and who should say in which stone, or odd piece of metal, or other "curiosity," he might find it! He even studied Hebrew in order to a better understanding of the old Hermetic writers. But he gave up the pursuit at last, and settled down into a very active and able antiquarian. He aided Dugdale; he was intimate with the Tradescants of Lambeth. These last were men after his own heart. They believed in griffins; and rocs that can truss elephants; and why not? did not the historian Sindbad see the birds? And yet, while we smile at these credulities, we forget how often they are in truth no credulities at all, but the mere readiness of the believer to own that there may be more mysteries in heaven and earth than are dreamt of in men's philosophy. The man of science of the present day, who would have rejected with scorn the Tradescants' relics of the griffin and the roc,—would, no doubt, have done the same with the marvellous relic of the dodo, long placed in the same category, but now universally acknowledged to be a part of a creature that has existed, though it may now be extinct. And it is often thus: he who has the most faith in the possibilities of Nature is in the long run the more likely to be right than those who, undertaking the mission of interpreters, limit her in every direction by the range of their own senses. Nevertheless, we own we should like to inquire at the museum what has become of the griffin and the roc—or their representative fragments. They should be still preserved as parts of the Museum of the Tradescants, which they bequeathed to Ashmole, and which he gave to the university, with his own additions. Should either of the two great Archæological Societies hold their meetings at Oxford, we hope that they will not overlook either the roc or the griffin.

We must now quit the chief streets for a time. Oxford does not display all her wealth there, though it must be acknowledged she does pretty well.—Near the museum, but more hidden among the retired parts of the city, we find Lincoln, Exeter, and Jesus Colleges; whilst in another direction, beyond the Clarendon Printing-office already mentioned, is Wadham College. The first of these is almost a holy place in the eyes of a great body of the people of England, thousands of whom, too, never saw or cared about universities or colleges, or aught that belongs to them. It was in Lincoln College that John Wesley prepared himself for the gigantic task that he had determined upon; it was there, in effect, that he laid the foundations of Methodism. His brother Charles was, at the time to which we refer, a member of Christchurch, and belonged to a little band of religious students whose pursuits and views may be gathered from the epithets so plentifully showered upon them. These were the holy club—the godly club—bible moths—bible bigots—sacramentarians—Methodists. And certainly their habits of life were calculated not only to attract attention, but ridicule in the eyes of the great mass of their fellow-students. Not content with the divinity that in one shape or other they were obliged to familiarise themselves with, they must, of their own accord, devote their Sunday evenings to that express study. And when they got laughed at for so doing, they only replied, if they replied at all, by giving up secular business on all other nights, and so devoting the entire week to religious exercises and reading. Twice in each week they communicated; hence the name fastened upon them of Sacramentarians. They had also their weekly fast-day. They were, in a word, constantly engaged in devout exercises, prayer, meditation, and self-examination. So much for their discipline among themselves, which gave promise of something like a restoration of the old severities of monachism in its purest days. One member, it is said, shortened his life by them. Beyond the walls of the college the Methodists exhibited themselves as the visitors to the sick, or the poor, or the imprisoned. Such were the men that John Wesley joined about the year 1729. And if aught more need be added to show what a remarkable association this must have been, it will be found in the fact that Hervey, the author of the Meditations in a Churchyard, and Whitfield were among them. How Whitfield was of very respectably-descended but poor parents—got there is worth narrating. Not long before, he had been assisting his mother (a widow) in the business of her tavern, and, as he himself states, with a kind of exultation in his abasement.—"At length I put on my blue apron and my snuffers, washed mops, cleaned rooms, and in one word became a professed and common drawer for nigh a year and a half." Subsequently his mother became still less able to aid his views as to a university education, which he ardently desired, and for which he was prepared, having been an excellent scholar at the grammar-school of Gloucester. But after a time

2306.—Lamplighter.

2307.—Linkboy

2308.—Watchmen

2309.—Footman with Flambeau.

2310.—Cobbler's Stall, 1760

2311.—London Shoeblack, 1750

2312.—Sir Roger de Coverley and the 'Spectator.'

2313.—Sir Roger de Coverley and the Picture Gallery.

2314.—Sir Roger de Coverley leaving Church.

2315.—Sir Roger de Coverley as Sheriff.

2316.—Sir Roger de Coverley and the Hare.

" a young student," he continues, " who was once my school-fellow, and then a servitor of Pembroke College, Oxford, came to pay my mother a visit. Among other conversation he told her how he had discharged all college expenses that quarter, and saved a penny. Upon that my mother immediately cried out, ' That will do for my son !' Then turning to me, she said, ' Will you go to Oxford, George ?' I replied, ' With all my heart !' Whereupon, having the same friends that this young student had, my mother without delay waited on them. They promised their interest to get me a servitor's place in the same college ;" and were successful. Whitfield, a year after, joined the little circle of which he had heard so much. Gradually, however, the numbers declined. The physical hardships were probably too much for them, or doubts began to exist as to their necessity ; so the seven-and-twenty dropped down to five. And for a time even Wesley himself disappeared from the scene : he went to America with a party of Moravians—and on Whitfield alone was left all the burden and heat of the day. But he had enthusiasm enough to triumph over all difficulties. Methodism began to number its disciples by hundreds and thousands. And then Whitfield set out for America at the very time that Wesley was departing for England. And by a noticeable coincidence the two ships passed each other which bore respectively the two friends, neither of whom were conscious that they were thus changing places. As yet Wesley, according to his subsequent statements, had not obtained those true views of Christianity that were to be productive of such amazing energy and self-devotion. One night, however, he happened to go, unwillingly, to a society in Aldersgate-street, and heard some one read Luther's ' Preface to the Epistle to the Romans,' and he was " converted." The time, we were told, was a quarter before nine in the evening, the day Wednesday the 29th of May, the year 1738.

It was not until Whitfield's return from America that any very important movements were made. One of the first steps then taken was preaching in the open air, Whitfield, with characteristic ardour, leading the way. The effect was magical. Crowds followed them everywhere, though all were not convinced, and though many sought, by violent means, to hinder others from being convinced. The first act that looked like dissent from the Established Church, by those who had been bred in her communion, was Wesley's sanction of lay preaching. He consented, with some hesitation, that a person of the name of Bowers, who had never entered into holy orders, should preach in Islington church-yard. Presently the two founders quarrelled and divided ; and though they subsequently were reconciled, their respective followers remained permanently distinct from each other. But, divided or in union, the movement they had originated went on with giant strides. Wesley hardly rested two days in the same place, nay, in the rural districts hardly two hours. He preached, rode on—preached again, and again rode on—and so continued till he had ridden from forty to sixty miles, and addressed four or five different congregations between day-break and night-fall. No weather stopped him : no other care or pleasure distracted his attention. When he married, he made it an express stipulation that he should not be expected to preach one sermon nor travel one mile the less. Whitfield's career was essentially the same, varied only in its details. He not only made it his general rule to traverse England and Scotland through, yearly ; but he thought no more of a voyage every now and then to America than we do now that steamboats waft us over in twelve or fourteen days. He was in some respects more popular than Wesley ; for men of the highest intellect delighted in his fervid eloquence even when they had no sympathy with his doctrinal views. The man who could bring a Chesterfield and a Bolingbroke, a Hume and a Franklin, to hear him preach, needs no other vouchers of his intellectual power : and to this power was added worthy instruments for its exercise. Whitfield's voice could be heard, it is said, to the distance of half a mile, and was as flexible and expressive as it was strong ; " capable of taking every various tone of emotion, and whether poured forth in thunder or in softer music, making its way to the heart with irresistible force and effect. Then he gesticulated, he stamped, he wept with a tempestuous abandonment, to which the most successful efforts of the counterfeit passions of the stage seemed tame and poor." (Life of Whitfield, in ' Penny Cyclopædia.') And so these good and great men—for they were both—went on rejoicingly, making themselves the awakeners, civilizers, and spiritual guardians and advisers of the poor, at a time when no other body of religionists took any particular trouble upon the matter. This is the glory of Methodism, and one that no change of position, no adversity, can deprive it of.

Exeter College reminds us of one of those tragical incidents that throw so deep a gloom over many of the earlier portions of English history. It was founded by Walter de Stapledon, Bishop of Exeter, in 1314. That prelate was left by Edward II. governor of the city of London at the time that he fled from it with his unworthy favourites the Despensers, in order to avoid the threatened attacks of the nobles who were then advancing towards the metropolis, having all the sympathy and support that Edward's own wife, son, brothers, and cousin, could give them. No sooner had he disappeared than the London populace rose, and murdered the royal officer—the Bishop of Exeter : an act of " bloody sacrilege," as Speed phrases it. Two of the scholarships of this college were founded by William Gifford, who rose from being a poor shoemaker's apprentice to the editorship of the potent ' Quarterly Review,' a publication that he did much to establish as well as to conduct. These scholarships show that he had no desire to forget the lowliness of his origin. They are intended solely for natives of his own county, Devonshire, and with a preference for the inhabitants of his own town, Ashburton. This kind of local partiality forms a characteristic of the colleges generally ; some of them being indeed expressly founded for the assistance of particular parts of the country. It was thus with Jesus College, established by a patriotic Welshman, in the reign of Elizabeth, for the special benefit of his countrymen. Wadham College exhibits a similar preference for the good people of Somersetshire and Essex. We must approach close to this. Over yonder gateway you will find a great room : you must at your leisure visit it. In that room was established the most illustrious of all English societies, ancient or modern. You will not, I am sure, be unwilling to hear something of the circumstances.

One of the most eloquent writers of the present day has wittily illustrated the peaceful and studious character of the mind of a man who was a most distinguished ornament of this University, Sir Thomas Browne. He says, " he had no sympathy with the great business of men." In that awful year when Charles I. went in person to seize the five members of the Commons' House, when the streets resounded with shouts of ' Privilege of Parliament !' and the King's coach was assailed by the prophetic cry, ' To your tents, O Israel !'—in that year, in fact, when the Civil War first broke out, and when most men of literary power were drawn by the excitement of the crisis into patriotic controversy on either side— appeared the calm and meditative reveries of the ' Religio Medici.' The war raged on. It was a struggle between all the elements of government. England was torn by convulsions and red with blood. But Browne was tranquilly preparing his ' Pseudodoxia Epidemica ;' as if errors about basilisks and griffins were the fatal epidemic of the time ; and it was published in due order in that year, when the cause which the author advocated, as far as he could advocate anything political, lay at its last gasp. The King dies on the scaffold. The Protectorate succeeds. Men are again fighting on paper the solemn cause already decided in the field. Drawn from visions more sublime—forsaking studies more intricate and vast than those of the poetical sage of Norwich—diverging from a career bounded by the most splendid goal—foremost in the ranks shines the flaming sword of Milton. Sir Thomas Browne is lost in the quincunx of the ancient gardens ; and the year 1658 beheld the death of Oliver Cromwell and the publication of the ' Hydriotophia.'

But it would be a mistake to suppose that it was only Browne who was thus playing the imaginative recluse at a time when all the world of England was in arms. It is really to our minds a very striking as well as interesting circumstance, to perceive that the Royal Society itself may be said to have been originated at exactly the same time, and of course exactly under the same circumstances. It was just three years before the execution of Charles that several lovers of knowledge and science agreed to meet together and form themselves into a club, where the distracting subjects of politics and religion should be excluded, so that Cavalier and Parliamentarian, Episcopalian and Puritan, might meet in harmony on the same common ground, of desire to enlarge the boundaries of learning—and, what is an inevitable consequence, at the same time enlarge their own minds. A German, Mr. Haak, had the honour of originating the idea ; which was speedily adopted by Dr. Wilkins, afterwards Bishop of Chester ; Waller, the famous mathematical scholar ; Goddard and Ent, well-known physicians ; with others of kindred views, including Foster, the professor of astronomy of Gresham College. They met where they found it most convenient—sometimes at the houses of members, sometimes in Gresham College. Boyle called them the " Invisible " Society. Wilkins, Waller, and Goddard went to Oxford in 1651, having obtained appointments there, and speedily drew around them thers who could help them to carry on at Oxford a similar society. Doctors Seth Ward, Bathurst, Petty, and an eminent physician of the name of Willis, with Rooke, whose name is too well known to need illustration, joined them. At first they met at Petty's lodgings, in the house of an apothecary, who gave them access to his drugs for the purposes of examination. A little later Boyle, who had joined them, accommodated them occasionally in his apartments, he being then settled at Oxford. But the chief place of meeting seems to have been in this great room over the gateway of Wadham College, where they were the guests of Dr. Wilkins. In 1659, the chief members of the society found themselves again in London, united to the former association, and with one man of no ordinary mark or likelihood, among many others, joined to their numbers, Christopher Wren. Two years after the Restoration, Charles II. granted them a charter of incorporation, and the Royal Society was firmly established in the land. There must have been something like pride and exultation felt by the earliest members, when they fixed for the first time to a document that stately-looking token of their independence, the society's seal. And beyond all praise were the motives of those scientific men of the seventeenth century. Would that every new institution of a parallel nature would adopt at starting an equally clear and noble declaration of principles! It was agreed by the society's resolutions—"That records should be made of all the works of nature and art of which any account could be obtained; so that the present age and posterity might be able to mark the errors which have been strengthened by long prescription, to restore truths which have been long neglected, and to extend the uses of those already known; thus making the way easier to those which were yet unknown. It was also resolved to admit men of different religions, professions, and nations, in order that the knowledge of nature might be freed from the prejudices of sect, and from a bias in favour of any particular branch of learning, and that all mankind might as much as possible be engaged in the pursuit of philosophy, which it was proposed to reform, not by laws and ceremonies, but by practice and example. It was further resolved that the society should not be a school where some might teach and others be taught, but rather a sort of laboratory where all persons might operate independently of one another." (Article, " Royal Society," in the ' Penny Cyclopædia.') To carry out their magnificent schemes the members divided into committees; and these divisions alone, if we knew nothing more of the views of the founders of the society, would be sufficient to prove that we have gone back rather than advance since that time in the two grand essentials of all such associations—that is, enthusiasm to inquire, and wisdom to know how and as to what it were best to begin to inquire. There were nine committees; and passing over the more obvious subjects dealt with, we may particularize the committee on histories of trade—the committee for collecting all the previously observed phenomena of nature, all made and recorded experiments—and the committee for improving the English tongue—especially for philosophical purposes. Such universality of scope attracted to their place of meeting, Gresham College, nearly all the men of eminence of the time. Dryden was there—so was Waller, and Cowley, and Denham—so was Sir Kenelm Digby—so were Ashmole, and Aubrey, and Barrow. Would the reader like to be able to take a peep at this remarkable body of men in their very *sanctum sanctorum?* A Frenchman, Sorbiere, the historiographer of Louis XIII., affords us the opportunity. Having noticed that the beadle went before the President with a mace—the very one, by the way, that was the subject of Cromwell's command in the House of Commons, "Take away that bauble!"—he continues: " The room where the society meets is large and wainscotted; there is a large table before the chimney, with seven or eight chairs covered with green cloth about it, and two rows of wooden and matted benches to lean on, the first being higher than the other, in the form of an amphitheatre. The president and council are elective; they receive no precedency in the society, but the president sits at the middle of the table in an arm-chair, with his back to the chimney. The secretary sits at the end of the table on his left hand; and they have each of them pen, ink, and paper before them. I saw nobody sit in the chairs; I think they are reserved for persons of great quality, or those who have occasion to draw near the president. All the other members take their places as they think fit, and without ceremony; and if any one comes in after the society is fixed, nobody stirs, but he takes a place presently where he can find it, so that no interruption may be given to him that speaks. The president has a little wooden mace in his hand, with which he strikes the table when he would command silence; they address their discourse to him bareheaded till he makes a sign for them to put on their hats; and there is a relation given in a few words of what is thought proper to be said concerning the experiments proposed by the secretary. There

is nobody here eager to speak, that makes a long harangue, or [is] intent upon saying all he knows; he is never interrupted that speaks; and difference of opinion causes no manner of excitement, nor as much as a disobliging way of speech; there is nothing seemed to me to be more civil, respectful, and better managed than this meeting; and if there are any private discourses held between any, while a member is speaking, they only whisper, and the least sign from the president causes a sudden stop, though they have not told their mind out. I took special notice of this conduct in a body consisting of so many persons and of such different nations."

The first practical business recorded, appears to have been the appointment of Wren to conduct certain experiments on the vibrations of pendulums, and of Lord Brouncker (the president after the incorporation), to prepare instructions for others to conduct experiments on the Peak of Teneriffe, relating to temperature, moisture, and so on. We shall only add to these notices of the society a few words relating to one of its members, who joined in 1672. In that year there was among the members elected Isaac Newton; and between one and two years later, we read in the book an order of the council to excuse Isaac Newton from the customary payment of a shilling weekly. If, as it appears probable from the circumstance, his means were straitened, his appointment to the wardenship of the Mint in 1695 completely relieved him. In 1703 he was elected president of the society, and so remained until his death. His experiments on light and colours were among the earliest papers that gave a permanent lustre to the published ' Transactions of the Society.' But the most mutually honourable circumstance of this connection was the publication of the ' Principia ' by the Society at its own expense, and at a time too when it was somewhat in difficulties as regards money matters. Newton sat for the last time as president on the 28th of February, 1727—and the 20th of March he was dead. "I know not," he had said a little time before, " what I may appear to the world; but to myself I seem to have been only like a boy playing on the sea-shore, and diverting myself in now and then finding a smoother pebble or a prettier shell than ordinary, whilst the great ocean of truth lay undiscovered before me." What a lesson of humility for the world at large, to think that a Newton could thus speak!

Hark, what a noble-sounding bell!

That is Great Tom of Oxford that you have so often heard of. Is it not fine? And very fond of hearing himself Great Tom is. Every evening, for instance, not content with summoning together all the fellows (" students" they are here called) of the college—Christ's (Fig. 2274)—from their wandering in the town and elsewhere, he must give each of them his own particular warning. So not till he has pealed out his 101 strokes, that being the number of the " students," will he cease. Christchurch, you have no doubt heard, is the richest, most magnificent, and most celebrated of all the collegiate establishments of Oxford. It is the especial resort of the sons of the richest gentry and higher aristocracy of England. Kohl reminds us that Sir Robert Peel was educated here. It has been honoured by hosts of men who have belonged to a different aristocracy,—men who are seldom acknowledged to be illustrious during their lives, but whom none deny to be so for ever afterwards. Sydney, Ben Jonson, and Otway, Locke, Penn, and Canning, were all members of Christ's. The founder was Wolsey; and everything one sees here harmonises with the associations suggested by his name, although his scheme was but in part accomplished. A view of Christ Church in the sixteenth century is elsewhere engraved (Fig. 1602). The front of the pile is three hundred and eighty-two feet long. The hall measures one hundred and fifteen feet by forty, and is fifty feet high. And as if these dimensions were not in themselves enough to distinguish it from most other famous English halls, the roof is of elaborately carved oak, and among the contents are an extensive collection of pictures. Even the kitchen of Christ Church is on such a scale as to be alone worth a visit. " It is said to be the largest kitchen in England, much larger than that of Windsor Castle, or even that of the Reform Club. It is of course very splendid, and complete in all its arrangements." (Kohl.) It is delightful to see how thoroughly and unselfishly in earnest Wolsey was for the completion of his foundation according to the gigantic original design. When power, royal favour, and with them nearly all else that were dear to Wolsey's heart were departing, or rather we might say had departed—he pleaded more strenuously for the completion of Christ Church than for anything else. The brutal king was influenced; but being as shabby as he was brutal, determined, while he listened to the entreaties of his former dear friend and servant, and to the entreaties of the university, to re-found the establishment so as to deprive Wolsey of all the merit of the deed. But that was impossible. He

2318.—Sir Roger d. Coverley and the Beggar.

2317.—Sir Roger de Coverley and the Gipsies.

2320.—Sir Roger de Coverley at the Playhouse.

2319.—Sir Roger de Coverley at Westminster Abbey

has only after all deprived Wolsey of the name. It should have been the Cardinal's—it is Christ's. But who forgets that it is in effect his? The noble cathedral of Christ Church, which forms the chapel to the college, has been mentioned elsewhere (vol. i. p. 175).

But let us here pause to take another street view of Oxford. We are now in St. Giles's Street, which crosses Oxford from the north to the centre of the town. What length and breadth—and then what a magnificent avenue is formed by the row of elms on each side,—what fine terminations to the vista—St. Giles at one end, St. Mary Magdalen at the other, two thousand feet distant! But see, another college, St. John's, noted for its beautiful little gardens; and yet others, as we move on, still keep pressing forward, as it were, upon our attention. There is New College, which Khol designates as "one of the handsomest in Oxford. Its gardens are splendid, commanding wide and beautiful prospects of the surrounding country. How luxurious must be study and meditation among the ivy-clad ruins and rich verdant groves of these antique gardens!" Next we have Balliol, of which we give an engraving (Fig. 1603) of its appearance in the sixteenth century, founded by the father of him who made the name so famous, John Balliol, King of Scotland; Trinity, Corpus Christi, Oriel, Merton, Pembroke, and Worcester. And there are five halls which differ from the colleges in this— they are not endowed with estates, but are simply so many places for the residence and education of students, under proper superintendence. In addition to all these are various other buildings, worthy of more attention than we can now pay to them. Let us however take a glance, if but one, at the stately façade of the Taylor Institute (Fig. 2272); and also at the entrance gateway (Fig. 2277) of the Botanical Gardens, which were designed by Inigo Jones.

A great British university is a centre of which the radiations extend all over the kingdom in the shape of such schools as Eton, Harrow, Westminster (Fig. 1593), St. Paul's (Fig. 1590), Christ's or the Blue Coat School, Charter-House (Fig. 1606), Merchant Tailors' (Fig. 1594), King's school at Canterbury (Fig. 1588), and hundreds of others, known for the most part as grammar-schools, of which St. Olave's, Southwark (Fig. 2285), the Bedford school (Fig. 2287), and Lady Owen's, in Goswell-street, London (Fig. 2286), may be taken as examples. Generally in these a university education forms the termination of the scholastic vista, no matter how few or how many the number of those who endeavour to reach it. It is in consequence an almost self-evident fact that the quality and mode of the education given in the schools will be materially influenced by the quality and modes of the education in favour at the universities.

Of course Cambridge is in many essential respects similar to Oxford. We confess for our own part we were almost as much disappointed at the first sight of Cambridge as we were beyond measure charmed and gratified by the first sight of the sister university. But this impression certainly wears away, in part, as you become more thoroughly acquainted with Cambridge. Much has been done, especially along the banks of the Cam, to improve upon the ancient appearance of the place (Fig. 1604), since Milton wrote—

Next Camus, reverend sire, came footing slow;
His mantle hairy, and his bonnet sedge—

and since he spoke of the absence of trees to make a shade. There are now some truly magnificent avenues of limes and chestnuts. Dyer, in his 'History of Cambridge,' contrasts Oxford and Cambridge with not more partiality towards the latter than might have been reasonably anticipated from a Cambridge man. He says, "It may be admitted that the public walks of our sister university have some superior charms over those we are now describing; the walks are generally more winding, without so many formal straight lines and acute angles; the trees have greater variety of foliage (and consequently you have bolder lights and shades), and there is more of underwood and shrubbery amidst their fine oaks, beech, birch, and elms. But still our walks have their peculiar beauties adapted to the place; and the walk planted with limes from Clare Hall forms a vista lengthened and of admirable effect. You might say, perhaps, that Oxford has not anything of the kind equal to this. Taking into consideration the beauty and grandeur of the several buildings to be seen from Clare Hall or King's College, Oxford must yield to Cambridge; nor must you say this is not Grasmere nor Keswick; there is no scene of the kind throughout all England that can be compared with these. The aspect, too, is the best that could be, both for the walks and effect on the adjoining buildings.'

The oldest of the colleges is Peter's House, or St. Peter's, which was endowed in 1257; the youngest, Downing College, established within the last quarter of a century. The most magnificent, if only on account of its chapel (see vol. i. p. 355), is King's College: the largest, Trinity; and which claims by right the honour of entertaining Royalty whenever it visits Cambridge. Queen Elizabeth was a visitor, and found her scholar-subjects so cordial in their reception, that she stayed five days; during which time, to allay jealousies, as well as to gratify her own curiosity, she visited every one of the houses. Queen Anne's visit here had a consequence of a memorable kind. Whilst she held her court at Trinity Lodge, she knighted Isaac Newton. Poor Trinity—for she then was poor—was obliged to borrow 500l. to defray the expenses of its hospitality on that occasion. But the most magnificent of all the feasts to Royalty that Trinity has given, is said to have been the banquet for George II. in 1728. A perfect shower of degrees then fell, to do honour to the time, upon the students of the university. No less than fifty-eight persons were made Doctors of Divinity. The library of Trinity, an edifice said to be unrivalled for magnificence and convenience (Fig. 2284), was built by means of a subscription of its members, under the auspices of Barrow.

It may give some idea of the grand scale in which everything is established at Trinity, to state that it possesses, besides its sixty fellowships, its sixty-nine scholarships, and its numerous exhibitions or pensions for the assistance of poor students, no less than sixty-five rectories, vicarages, and perpetual curacies,—that is to say, they are all in its gift. The actual number of its members generally approaches towards two thousand. One of the finest of all sights, or sounds, may be enjoyed in the chapel of this college, or of King's, on Sundays and on certain holidays, when the full cathedral service is chanted, and the students attend in white surplices. "The effect of this on a Sunday evening, when there are between three or four hundred thus assembled in the long narrow aisles of Trinity, is very striking—with the tones of one of the finest organs, struck by one of the finest players in England, pealing upon the ear."

With some omissions, the same observances take place in the chapel of St. John's. The "Johnians are always known by the name of pigs; they put up a new organ the other day, which was immediately christened Baconi Novum Organum." But the Johnians have of late years put up something more than this—an entirely new and superb pile, which is now picturesquely connected, by a bridge (Fig. 2281), with the older one. But perhaps the most picturesque thing in Cambridge is the Caius Gate of honour, belonging to Gonville and Caius College, the founder of which, Dr. Caius, an eminent physician, built three gates, one of which was named and inscribed the Gate of Humility; the second, the Gate of Virtue; the third, the Gate of Honour (Fig. 2279). Pembroke College originated in a very affecting circumstance. It takes its name from the Countess of Pembroke, whose husband, during the reign of Edward, was accidentally killed at a tournament held in honour of their wedding-day. The countess, plunged in melancholy, retired from the world and made acts of charity her only solace. The foundation of Pembroke College was one of these acts. The chief peculiarity of Corpus Christi, or Bene't's (Benedict's) College, is its foundation by the brethren of two ancient guilds, who desired not so much to promote learning generally, as to train up young men who should be well fitted to make prayers, and perform masses for the souls of departed members of the said guilds. Cromwell was a student of Sussex College; and it is supposed by some that he gave an evidence of his attachment to the university by saving the painted windows of King's College chapel, when threatened by the Puritans. But there is also another motive that might be attributed to him for such an interference, and which people often forget in estimating his character. He who saved the Cartoons—and whose great delight was in listening to sacred music—might be safely esteemed a lover of the arts for their own sake. His illustrious secretary, Milton, was a sizar of Christ's College. We shall only mention one more establishment, Jesus College—of which Gilbert Wakefield tells a humorous story in connection with a Dr. Boldero, a master, who is buried in the chapel. This gentleman had been treated with severity during the Protectorate for attachment to the royal cause, in which the Bishop of Ely had been an equal sufferer. On a vacancy of the mastership, Boldero, without any pretensions to the appointment, plucked up his spirits, and presented his petition for the place to the bishop. "Who are you?" said the bishop; "I know nothing of you; I never heard of you before!" "My lord, I have suffered long and severely for my attachment to our royal master, as well as your lordship. I believe your lordship and I have been in all the gaols in England." "What does the fellow mean? Man! I never was confined in any prison but the Tower." "And, my lord," replied Boldero, "I have been in all the rest myself." The bishop made Boldero master.

Some of the numerous public buildings of the University challenge our admiration. Perhaps the most recent is also the finest—the Fitzwilliam Museum (Figs. 2282, 2283). As an instance of individual munificence, this may parallel Dr. Radcliffe's bequests at Oxford. Viscount Fitzwilliam at his death in 1816, bequeathed to the University, in addition to his books and pictures, and other collections, *a hundred thousand pounds* in the South Sea Annuities, of which the interest alone was used in the erection and permanent endowment of the Museum. The Pepysian Library (Fig. 2280) was the gift of the well-known gossip to his own college, Magdalen, He has given us the particulars, in his own inimitable way, of two visits he paid to Cambridge, one when he was led up to the Senate House to vote, the other later in life, when he amused himself by coming, as it were, incognito to the college. As to the last, he says, "I took my boy and two brothers, and walked to Magdalen College; and then into the butteries as a stranger, and there drunk of their beer, which pleased me as the best I ever drunk; and hear by the buttery-man, who was son to Goody Mulliner, over against the college, that we used to buy stewed prunes of, concerning the college and persons in it; and find very few that were of my time." Pepys was in his way a very able public servant, and no doubt, in private life, a kindly and good man. James II. must have felt a more than ordinary attachment to him to do what he did. The news of the landing of the Prince of Orange was brought to him as he sat to Kneller for his portrait, which was to be given to Pepys; but, instead of hurrying away, he bade the artist finish the picture, that his friend might not be disappointed. This is about the most graceful incident that we remember of James's history. An exceedingly valuable portion of the Pepysian library is the collection of English ballads, in five great folio volumes. The work that contributed so materially to revolutionize and to improve our poetical tastes in the last century, Percy's 'Reliques of Ancient Poetry,' was chiefly formed from the contents of these volumes.

Giving a kind of new reading of Milton's "Better to reign in hell than serve in heaven," the beaux and belles of the eighteenth century thought it better to be original even in the extremest absurdities of costume than to imitate the most graceful of the habits of their forefathers. You can hardly think of an eminent man of the time but up rises a figure with the imposing periwig shaking its curls before you, waistcoat descending almost to the knees, and the whole ending with breeches, stockings, and high-lows—for, notwithstanding the silver buckles, and some little peculiarities of their own, those shoes in which the gentlemen of the time stalked about were but modern high-lows; and indeed the whole style of the adornments of the nether man are precisely those which, in humbler materials and colours, find favour among our coal-heavers. Is it that they are the very conservatives of dress?—that they have preserved the garb of their grandfathers, whilst all the world around them has been seduced by the successive attractions of pantaloons and trousers?

And can it be that it was but from a century to a century and a half ago that men from the monarch William III. (Fig. 2289) downwards, wore a dress of this kind (see the different views of costume in pages 284, 285); that the slow, graceful, and stately minuet (Fig. 2300) filled the place that quadrilles and polkas now occupy; that footmen were forbidden to carry swords or offensive weapons; that ladies wore patches on their faces explanatory of their politics; that gentlemen made it a point to look like modern beadles (see the front figure in Alamode 1735, Fig. 2304), and to carry great oaken staves as tall as themselves, with the ugliest possible faces carved upon them; that persons of both sexes walked about with their heads in a state somewhat resembling the lawyer's after leaving the flour-bag, in one of our popular farces? Could these and a hundred other fantastic peculiarities, of which we have now not a trace left, have belonged to a time so little removed from our own, that many an aged man now living may have heard his father describe nearly the whole from his own youthful experience?

Can it, again, be London, of which it was written at the same period,—

> Prepare for death if here at night you roam,
> And sign your will before you sup from home.
> Some fiery fop, with new commission vain,
> Who sleeps on brambles till he kills his man,—
> Some frolic drunkard, reeling from a feast,
> Provokes a broil and stabs you for a jest.

> Yet even these heroes, mischievously gay,
> Lords of the streets and terror of the way,
> Flush'd as they are with folly, youth, and wine,
> Their prudent insults to the poor confine:
> Afar they mark the flambeau's bright approach,
> And shun the shining train and gilded coach.

A pretty picture of the streets of the metropolis of the British empire. Where and who were the guardians? Alas, poor fellows, notwithstanding their tremendous weapons, they had enough to do to take care of themselves, whenever it was most desirable that they should be protecting others. But we need only take one glance at them to understand the matter. We present a group (Fig. 2308). Do they not remind us of forms that have not long since vanished from our own eyes?—Look they not like so many spectral watchmen revisiting the glimpses of the moon, and haunting the places from which they were banished by the new police?

Ay, now we begin to track the England and the London of the eighteenth into the England and London of the nineteenth century. Often in our boyhood, as we passed through some of the older squares of the metropolis, have we wondered to ourselves what could be the meaning of those straight trumpets—for so we thought them—affixed on each side of the doors. Were they placed there, as at old castles in old times, for visitors to blow upon and rouse the inhabitants? We live to learn; our trumpets were extinguishers—flambeau extinguishers (Fig. 2309). When the "gilded coach" had set down the party from the theatre, or the masquerade, or the rout, the "flambeau" was thrust into the extinguisher; and the neighbourhood relapsed into its usual darkness.

As to lamplighters (Fig. 2306), and link-boys (Fig. 2307), and street shoe-cleaners (Fig. 2311), we have them all yet—unless the last has very recently disappeared. Many will remember the man who stood at the edge of a court in Fleet Street, a few years ago. Was he in truth the last of all his race? The cobbler's stall (Fig. 2310) is still to be found in many a corner:—

> No jutty, frieze,
> Nor buttress, nor coign of vantage, but this bird
> Hath made his pendant bed.

We fear it is a bad sign of the morals of the fraternity that—

> Where they most do breed and haunt, we have observ'd
> The air is

anything but "delicate" with the fumes of the public-house, to which they have attached their nests.

But let us now turn to the pages of those who, in a time so fruitful of materials, began their rambles of observation, and gave us as the result, the series of well-known papers entitled the 'Spectator.' Let us glance over the pages of Steele and Addison; men who were as minute as they were comprehensive, as profound and eloquent as they were shrewd and witty; as kindly and just towards individuals, as they were severe and uncompromising towards the vice and folly that prevailed among them. One of the earliest papers that refer to the manners and customs of the period (and such only shall we notice), shows us that masques and masquerades were then in the height of their popularity, and yet that they were not then much more distinguished for innocence, or for the skilful personation of the characters assumed, than at present, when some worthy manager endeavours to revive those good old money-making scenes. Truly "we have had now and then rakes in the habit of Roman senators, and grave politicians in the dress of rakes." And still "the misfortune of the thing is, that people dress themselves in what they have a mind to be, and not what they are fit for." We have had our judges "that danced a minuet, with a Quaker for his partner, while half a dozen harlequins stood by as spectators;" a Turk drinking off his "two bottles of wine," and a Jew eating his "half a ham of bacon." We have before had occasion to observe how fashion seems eternally to reproduce itself—making the dress of to-day the mere revival of the dress of some former day, sufficiently long past to be forgotten. The 'Spectator' on one occasion speaks of a little muff, of silver garters buckling below the knee, and of fringed gloves; two out of the three, the little muff, and the fringed gloves—or what we take to be the same—gloves edged at the wrist with lace, may again be seen constantly in our streets. And though we have not now the multitudes of signs that formerly kept up an eternal creak over the head of the pedestrian, there is yet no lack "of blue boars, black swans, and red lions, not to mention flying pigs, and hogs in armour, with many other creatures more extraordinary than any in the deserts of Africk."

The fair sex, as was but proper, enjoyed the chief attention of

2322.—Death of Sir Roger de Coverley announced to the Club.

2325.—The Palace Gate, St. James's.

2324.—Sedan Chair.

2321.—Sir Roger de Coverley at the Temple Stairs.

2323.—State Coaches.

2326.—Sofa, Chairs, Cabinet. &c., temp. William III. and Anne. (Selected from Specimens at Penshurst and in Private Collections.)

2327.—Sitting-room Furniture, temp. William III. (Selected from Specimens at Knowle and in Private Collections.)

2328.—Cabinet, Chairs &c., temp. William III. and Anne. (From Specimens in Private Collection.)

2329.—Bed, Cabinet, Chairs, &c., temp. George I and II (From Specimens in Private Collections and in Prints of the Period.)

2330.—Sitting-room Furniture, temp. George I. and II. (From Specimens in Private Collections, and in Prints of the Period.)

2331.—House built by Inigo Jones, in Great Queen Street.

the 'Spectator,' in these questions of dress and habits of life; an attention, however, that the ladies would no doubt have gladly spared. Let us for a moment imagine what would be the sentiments and words of a fine lady of the time, as number after number of the provoking publication was placed on the table. There, exclaims she, as one of them is perused, we have got rid of our old head-dresses, and are busy considering how best to replace it with something equally striking and new, and now everybody is to laugh at us, by being told—" There is not so variable a thing in nature as a lady's head-dress. Within my own memory I have known it rise and fall above thirty degrees. About ten years ago it shot up to a very great height, insomuch that the female part of our species were much taller than the men (Fig. 2290.) The women were of such enormous stature, that we appeared as grasshoppers before them. At present the whole sex is in a manner diminished and shrunk into a race of beauties that seems almost another species. I remember several ladies who were once very near seven feet high, that at present want some inches of five. How they came to be thus curtailed I cannot learn. Whether the whole sex be at present under any penance which we know nothing of; or whether they have cast their head-dresses in order to surprise us with something of that kind which shall be entirely new; or whether some of the tallest of the sex, being too cunning for the rest, have contrived this method to make themselves sizeable, is still a secret; though I find most are of opinion, they are at present like trees new lopped and pruned, that will certainly sprout up and flourish with greater heads than before." Next, our fans, it appears, do not quite please him, and so he must expose all the little trickeries that have been sacred from time immemorial. The ladies must be represented as having an academy for the instruction of the right mode of managing their weapon. An impertinent correspondent is even allowed to say he has undertaken the duty of drilling them in the most approved style of military science. " The ladies," says he, " who carry fans under me, are drawn up twice a-day, in my great hall, where they are instructed in the use of their arms, and exercised by the following words of command: handle your fans—unfurl your fans—discharge your fans—ground your fans—recover your fans—flutter your fans." And as though the inuendo was not plain enough, Mr. Spectator must go into particulars, showing that the whole business is rank flirting, and coquetry, and affectation. And though we know as well as he does, perhaps after all better, that " there is an infinite variety of motions to be made use of in the flutter of a fan," and that there is " the angry flutter, the modest flutter, the timorous flutter, the confused flutter, the merry flutter, and the amorous flutter," what business has he or his readers with it? But, indeed, he stops at nothing. Another of his pretended correspondents, supposed to be writing to him during his absence, tells him, in order that he should tell the world, their hooped " petticoats, which began to heave and swell before you left us, are now blown up into a most enormous concave, and rise every day more and more:" (and so, it appears, from our engravings, Alamode 1735, Fig. 2304, and Alamode 1745, Fig. 2305, remained for a long time). He follows us in our walks, where, if a lady happens to be dressed something rakishly, he describes at length the extra-ordinary young *gentleman* he had seen; he watches us to the theatre, and retails all the little conversations that we carry on during the play; he penetrates to our library, and becomes very sarcastic on the mingling of our books, and the dear old china; and very witty on the sorts of books that he finds there, in company : ' Locke on the Understanding,' with a paper of patches in it, and a Spelling Book; a book of novels, and the Academy of Compli-ment—all the classic authors in wood, and Clelia, which opened of itself in the place that describes the two lovers in a bower—' Taylor's Holy Living and Dying,' and ' La Ferte's Instruc-tions' for country-dances. But worst of all—the—what shall I call him? this most impudent of Spectators—finds his way into our bedrooms—exposes all the little delicate mysteries of the toilet—says coarsely of our slight tintings, we " paint." Nay, that there are some of us " so exquisitely skilful in this way, that give them but a tolerable pair of eyes to set up with, and they will make bosom, lips, cheeks, and eyebrows by their own indus-try." In a word he calls us Picts! And then, too, to complain of our male valets-de-chambre, and to print, as though it was some-thing so very extraordinary, that he had himself " seen one of these male Abigails tripping about the room with a looking-glass in his hand, and curling his lady's hair a whole morning together. I know who he means well enough. Above all—that charming fashion that we brought over from France, of receiving company in bed when we are not very well, or have got the vapours. I am told he denounces that. Let us see, where is the paper?—" The

lady, though willing to appear undrest, had put on her best looks, and painted herself for our reception. Her hair appeared in a very nice disorder, as the night-gown which was thrown upon her shoulder was ruffled with great care." Hem—well—and what's this?—" As the coquettes who introduced this custom grew old, they left it off by degrees; well knowing that a woman of three-score may kick and tumble her heart out, without making any impression." There's a malicious thought for you!

These were strokes that must and did tell indirectly, if not directly. The fine lady would carry it off with a high hand for a time, but not the less did she find, now in this quarter, now in that, and at last in her own mind, an opinion growing up that disconcerted her in spite of all her thoughtlessness and waywardness. The genial love and wisdom that pervaded the Spectator's lucu-brations were ever winning their way into and healing the wound that the searching exposure made. Men and women discovered (almost for the first time) that it was not very difficult even to laugh at themselves, when it was an Addison and a Steele who made others laugh at them. Take this little picture, for instance, from the same paper that we have just been referring to, descriptive of ladies receiving visitors in bed. " It is a very odd sight that beautiful creature makes when she is talking politics with her tresses flowing about her shoulders, and examining that face in the glass which does such execution upon all the rude standers-by. How prettily does she divide her discourse between her women and her visitants! What sprightly transitions does she make from an opera or a sermon to an ivory comb or a pincushion! How have we been pleased to see her interrupted in an account of her travels by a message to her footman, and holding her tongue in the midst of a moral reflection by applying the tip of it to a patch!" Now the very intellectual power required for all this piquant sort of coquetry involved the power to perceive its absurdity when pointed out in so exquisite a manner. Would that all satirists at least would give their days and nights to Addison, in order to learn how they may really exercise their tremendous power with the greatest amount of benefit to their fellows.

It appears that this custom of ladies receiving visitors in their bed-rooms was used, like every other available influence, for party political purposes. The second daughter of the Duke of Marlbo-rough for instance, commonly known as the Little Whig, had, like her mother, the impetuous and haughty Duchess Sarah, a very beautiful head of hair. So when it was desired to secure the votes of certain gentlemen of the Tory party—young and romantic men perhaps, who could not be corrupted by mere bribes, the policy was for the Little Whig to receive them at her toilet, and converse with them whilst her fair tresses were let out and sported with on pretence of dressing them; until the visitor was caught in their magic snares, and paid the price of his vote to get away again. Many a politician no doubt had sighed, as he repeated, with the poet—

And beauty draws us with a single hair.

But now for a portrait of another kind. It is that of the country gentleman of the sixteenth century, as Steele and Addison painted him, partly perhaps *from* the life as it existed, partly *to* the life that it was desired to make exist. And how refreshing it is to turn from the contemplation of a society that could present so many fantastic aspects as those we have noticed, to the delightful sim-plicity of mind and goodness of heart that characterise a Sir Roger de Coverley. We are told he is a gentleman of Worcestershire, of ancient descent. " His great-grandfather was inventor of that famous country-dance which is called after him. All who know that shire are very well acquainted with the parts and merits of Sir Roger. He is a gentleman that is very singular in his behaviour, but his singularities proceed from his good sense, and are contradictions to the manner of the world only as he thinks the world is in the wrong. However, this his view creates him no enemies, for he does nothing with sourness or obstinacy; and his being unconfined to modes and forms makes him but the readier and more capable to please and oblige all who know him. When he is in town he lives in Soho-square," then the most genteel part of London. It appears Sir Roger keeps a bachelor " by reason he was crossed in love by a perverse beautiful widow of the next county to him. Before this disappointment Sir Roger was what you call a fine gentleman, had often supped with my lord Rochester and Sir George Etherege, fought a duel upon his first coming to town, and kicked Bully Dawson in a public coffee-house for calling him a youngster." This Bully Dawson was a man worth kicking. He was a debauchee in his habits, a swaggerer in his behaviour and discourse, a sharper in principle and practice; so that whenever opportunity offered for punishment, there would no doubt be a long arrear of offences to be settled. Sir Roger's ill success with the widow made him "serious for a year and a-half, and though, his temper being naturally jovial, he at last got over it, he grew careless of himself, and never dressed afterwards. He is now in his fifty-sixth year, cheerful, gay, and hearty; keeps a good home botn in town and country; a great lover of mankind; but there is such a mirthful cast in his behaviour that he is rather beloved than esteemed. His tenants grow rich, his servants look satisfied, all the young women profess to love him, and the young men are glad of his company. When he comes into a house he calls the servants by their names, and talks all the way upstairs to a visit. I must not omit that Sir Roger is a justice of the quorum; that he fills the chair at quarter-sessions with great ability, and threemonths ago gained universal applause by explaining a passage in the Game Act." Such is Sir Roger de Coverley.

The Spectator being invited by him to spend a month in the country, goes to the baronet's seat, where they stroll about together (Fig. 2312), the good knight only showing him to the country gentlemen of the county from a distance, and begging them in the Spectator's own hearing not to let him see them, for that he hates to be stared at. And there fresh traits of Sir Roger's character are constantly made apparent to him. He so seldom changes his servants "that you would take his valet-de-chambre for his brother his butler is grey-headed, his groom is one of the gravest men that I have ever seen, and his coachman has the look of a privy counsellor." He has a chaplain in his house, who has lived with him thirty years, chosen by the baronet for his good sense rather than his learning—Sir Roger did not want to be insulted with Greek and Latin at his own table—for his clear voice, amiable temper, and his skill at backgammon. His choice has been a wise one. Not a lawsuit has there been in the parish since the chaplain came. If the parishioners quarrel, they appeal to him; and if that fails—as in a few rare cases only—then they appeal to Sir Roger himself.

Sir Roger, like most other gentlemen of his birth and position, has his picture-gallery, and filled much in the usual way with portraits of his ancestors (Fig. 2313). The history of all these is described to the Spectator; from him who wore the vast jutting coat and small bonnet of Henry VII.'s time, a costume preserved in the yeomen of the guard of the nineteenth as well as the eighteenth century, down to the one whom Sir Roger took to be the honour of the house—a man as punctual in all his dealings as a tradesman, and as generous as a gentleman; and who would have thought "himself as much undone by breaking his word, as if it were to be followed by bankruptcy," and who was, finally, a brave man; he had narrowly escaped being killed in the civil wars, "for," said he, "he was sent out of the field upon a private message the day before the battle of Worcester." So private, no doubt, that one may feel satisfied that no temptations would induce this "brave" ancestor of Sir Roger to expose its nature.

We must now follow this beau ideal of the good old English gentleman to church. The interior is adorned with texts in various parts, chosen by the baronet, and wherever we look some token of his munificence meets the eye. Even the hassocks and prayer-books are his gift—a subtle stroke of his policy to induce the congregation to kneel and join in the responses. He has also had them taught by an itinerant singing-master how to sing properly the tunes of the psalms. "As Sir Roger is landlord to the whole congregation, he keeps them in very good order, and will suffer nobody to sleep in it besides himself; for if by chance he has been surprised into a short nap at sermon, upon recovering out of it he stands up and looks about him, and if he sees anybody else nodding, either wakes them himself, or sends his servant to them." When the sermon is over, "nobody presumes to stir till Sir Roger is gone out of the church. The knight walks down from his seat in the chancel between a double row of his tenants (Fig. 2314), that stand bowing to him on each side: and every now and then inquires how such a one's wife, or mother, or son, or father do, whom he does not see at church; which is understood as a secret reprimand to the person that is absent."

Sir Roger has served as a sheriff, and rode in procession at the head of a whole county, with music before him, a feather in his hat, and his horse well bitted (Fig. 2315). Of course, he is a keen sportsman. "He has in his youthful days taken forty covies of partridges in a season: and tired many a salmon with a line consisting of but a single hair." He is a distinguished foxhunter, "having destroyed more of those vermin in one year than it was thought the whole county could have produced." And indeed the knight had swelled the native-bred animals by sending for great numbers out of adjoining counties, and turning them loose by night, in order that he might catch them again the next day. All his dogs are so well

matched, that the voices make a complete concert. He sent back one hound that was presented to him because he was a bass, whereas he wanted a counter-tenor. The Spectator is witness to a hare-hunt, in which the knight's goodness of heart makes him save the poor animal just at the last moment, by taking her up in his arms (Fig. 2316), and delivering her to a servant, to be let loose in an orchard where he has others of these prisoners of war.

Sir Roger and the Spectator on one occasion light upon a troop of gipsies; and it may be considered as an evidence (so far as a period of a century and a quarter is concerned) of the unchangeable character that has been ascribed to this remarkable people, to find Addison describing them exactly as we should describe them now, unless it be that we might speak of them as a trifle more honest, or at least more under the wholesome fear of the law than he does. At first, says the Spectator, "my friend was in some doubt whether he should not exert the justice of the peace upon such a band of lawless vagrants; but not having his clerk with him, who is a necessary counsellor on these occasions, and fearing that his poultry might fare the worse for it, he let the thought drop," as many a modern country magistrate no doubt has done many a time for exactly the same reason. So Sir Roger contents himself with giving the Spectator "a particular account of the mischiefs they do in the country, in stealing people's goods, and spoiling their servants If a stray piece of linen hangs upon a hedge, says Sir Roger, they are sure to have it: if the hog loses his way in the field, it is ten to one but he becomes their prey; our geese cannot live in peace for them; if a man prosecutes them with severity, his hen-roost is sure to pay for it. They generally straggle into these parts about this time of the year, and set the heads of our servant-maids so agog for husbands, that we do not expect to have any business done as it should be while they are in the country. I have an honest dairy-maid who crosses their hands with a piece of silver every summer, and never fails being promised the handsomest young fellow in the parish for her pains. Your friend the butler has been fool enough to be seduced by them; and though he is sure to lose a knife, a fork, or a spoon, every time his fortune is told him, generally shuts himself up in the pantry with an old gipsy for above half an hour once in a twelvemonth. Sweethearts are the things they live upon, which they bestow very plentifully upon all those that apply themselves to them. You see now and then some handsome young jades among them; the sluts have very often white teeth and black eyes." Sir Roger and the Spectator cannot, of course, do less then have their fortunes told (Fig. 2317), and in both cases the operation is performed very satisfactorily. The hints about the widow are particularly relished by Sir Roger. But he subsequently finds he has paid well for his gratification. The gipsies have picked his pockets.

Charity and hospitality are conspicuous traits of Sir Roger's character. Of course he must not forget he is a magistrate. The Spectator overhears him chiding a beggar for not finding work, but he sees him in the end slip a sixpence into his hand (Fig. 2318). As to his hospitality, the good old customs are kept up at his mansion in their fullest integrity. "I have often thought," says Sir Roger, "it happens very well that Christmas should fall out in the middle of winter. It is the most dead, uncomfortable time of the year, when the poor people would suffer very much from their poverty and cold, if they had not good cheer, warm fires, and Christmas gambols to support them. I love to rejoice their poor hearts at this season, and to see the whole village merry in my great hall. I allow a double quantity of malt to my small beer, and set it a-running for twelve days to every one that calls for it. I have always a piece of cold beef and a mince-pie on the table, and am wonderfully pleased to see my tenants pass away a whole evening in playing their innocent tricks, and smutting one another." Happy landlords! happy tenantry! ye are no fiction. Few were the manor-houses in England a century or two ago, that did not present such scenes at all such times.

And we may here observe, that we wish to illustrate the manners, customs, and men of the age, and not the 'Spectator,' or that most perfect of its gems, the individual character of Sir Roger; except, indeed, so far as the two aims are indissolubly bound together; we dwell, therefore, only on those points which may best promote the object we have in view. Sir Roger, like his country prototype whom Addison probably had in view, is proud of his historical knowledge, though derived simply from 'Baker's Chronicle.' He comes to London, and accompanies the Spectator on a visit to Westminster Abbey, where he is quite puzzled at the story of the maid of honour who killed herself by a prick of a needle, and at last observes, "I wonder that Sir Richard Baker has said nothing of her." But when he gets to the Sword of Edward III. (Fig. 2319),

2333.—Guy's Cliff, Warwickshire.

2332. Wilton House.

2336.—The Royal Observatory, Greenwich.

2335.—Old Watering-house, Knightsbridge, as it appeared in 1841.

2334.—Mansion in Moor Park.

2339.—South Front of Castle Howard, Yorkshire. (Vanburgh.)

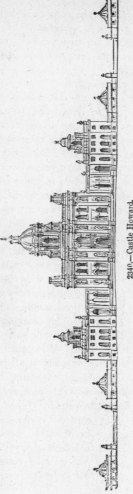

2340.—Castle Howard.

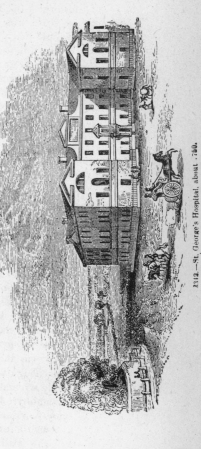

2342.—St. George's Hospital, about 1760.

2337.—Blenheim.

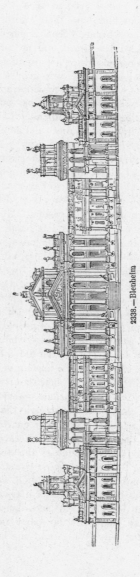

2338.—Blenheim.

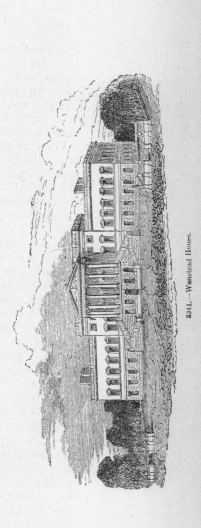

2341.—Wanstead House.

Sir Richard Baker and he are at once at home, and so the whole history of the Black Prince is narrated. Sir Roger is a Tory, as we learn from his remark on being shown the headless Henry V., and told that the silver head had been stolen years before—" Some Whigs, I'll warrant you."

The pair go to the playhouse, Sir Roger not having been there for twenty years before. On the last occasion he had seen the 'Committee,' having been previously satisfied it was a good Church of England comedy ; now he proposes to see 'The Distressed Mother,' a tragedy recently brought out. An interesting illustration of the state of the streets as regards their insecurity, and of the tendency of the country visitor to believe them even worse than they were, here occurs. The knight inquires if there be no danger from the Mohocks, and states that he had thought he had fallen into their hands the previous evening, when two or three lusty black men had followed him half way up Fleet Street. But if, as is most probable, these lusty black men were Mohocks only in the worthy knight's imagination, the class was real, and terrible, and villanous enough. It was headed by a president, whom they called the Emperor of the Mohocks. Their objects, it appears, may be summed up as comprising every kind of detestable outrage they could think of, on the persons of those who fell into their hands, during the night, in the streets of London. To prepare for their sport, they drank themselves into a kind of frenzy, when they sallied out sword in hand, and woe to those they met with. Watchmen were especial objects of their vengeance ; but they were not at all particular as to the sort of persons they attacked, always excepting those who were numerous enough to hold out a reasonable prospect of defence. The unmanly wretches did not spare women. Some Mohocks were known as tumblers, because they turned the females whom they caught topsy-turvy on their heads. Another class were very fond of throwing a woman into a barrel, and then setting it rolling down a steep part, as Snow Hill. Sometimes the persons caught were "tipped the lion," that is to say, had their noses violently flattened, and their eyes gouged out with the fingers. The dancing-masters were those Mohocks who chiefly luxuriated in making their victims cut capers by continually pricking them with their swords. But the most favoured of all these diversions was the one in which it was thought something like wit and humour were mingled with the other enjoyments. A body of Mohocks would give chase to some person before them, raising a regular view-halloo, and shouting "A sweat! a sweat!" When they had overtaken their trembling prey, they formed in a circle about him, with their swords drawn, the points upwards. The sport now began. Some one behind pricked him in the legs or elsewhere, with a sword, and he turned round to avert the attack ; then some one else drew his attention by the same mode in a different direction ; and so he was kept wheeling round and round, until cruelty had exhausted its appetite, and he was dismissed, as being sufficiently sweated. The Mohocks borrowed their name from a well-known tribe of Red Indians. These are the gentry that Sir Roger desires to guard against, and amusing is the account of his precautions. A friend, Captain Sentry, is to accompany them. When they all met at Sir Roger's house, the captain " bid Sir Roger fear nothing, for that he had put on the same sword which he made use of at the battle of Steenkirk. Sir Roger's servants, and among them the butler, had, I found, provided themselves with good oaken flails, to attend their master upon this occasion. When we had placed him in his coach, with myself at his left hand, the captain before him, and his butler at the head of his footmen in the rear, we conveyed him in safety to the playhouse, where, after having marched up the entry in good order, the captain and I went in with him, and seated him betwixt us in the pit. As soon as the house was full and the candles lighted, my old friend stood up, and looked about him with that pleasure which a mind seasoned with humanity naturally feels in itself at the sight of a multitude of people who seemed pleased with one another, and partake of the same common entertainment. I could not but fancy to myself, as the old man stood up in the middle of the pit (Fig. 2320), that he made a very proper centre to a tragic audience." Sir Roger now plays the critic, and in a delightfully amusing manner, but as his various observations do not bear upon the manners and customs of the stage at the time, we may here throw in a few remarks derived from other quarters.

Sir Roger, we see, had previously taken care to go to a good Church of England comedy ; a touch of the Spectator's satire, we presume, of the custom then prevalent on the stage, of introducing party religious and political allusions. Of course this custom would leave men generally to choose their plays as they now choose their newspapers, that is to say, in accordance with their own predilections. We may judge how far party feeling was carried, when we learn that the lady Whigs and the lady Tories sat on opposite sides of the house. But Addison's own history, or rather the history of one of his books, shows this feature of the time in a peculiarly interesting manner. No inconsiderable portion of the success that marked the production of 'Cato' in 1712 was caused by the circumstance that each of the two opposite parties claimed its sentiments as being in accordance with and supporting their own. The chief part was performed by Barton Booth, one of the most eminent of English actors. During the performance a purse of fifty guineas was collected in the boxes by the Tories, and presented to him as a "slight acknowledgment of his honest opposition to a perpetual dictator, and in dying so bravely in the cause of liberty." So that even the actor was perforce enlisted into the cause of party. If such was the favour shown to 'Cato' by the Tories, its popularity with the Whigs was necessarily still greater, as the author was one of themselves, without, however, the fanaticism and absurdity that too many of them generally exhibited. The state of things here described was attended by an important consequence to the interest of the stage. Annoyed by the unceasing storm of attacks that the petty dramatists of the day kept up on him and his administration, Sir Robert Walpole brought in a bill, in 1737, prohibiting the representation thenceforward of any play until the sanction of the Lord Chamberlain had been obtained. And so dramatists to this hour, no matter what their character, genius, or position, must submit their productions to the perusal of a government official, on account of the demerits of their predecessors in the reign of George II.

The stage appointments had now risen to a high pitch of splendour. Nothing could be more superb or costly, but also nothing more absurd, than the costumes then worn by the greatest actors, even by Betterton and Garrick. The Roman Cato, the Trojan Hector, the Danish Hamlet, the Scottish Macbeth, and in short all the chief heroes of tragedy, were played in the same garb —the dress of a gentleman of the day. The same with the ladies. Cleopatra was the very pink of perfection, in her hooped petticoats, stomacher, and powdered commode, and with the richly ornamented fan in her hand (Figs. 2301, 2302). Not the least striking part of the business is this, that although in the 'Spectator' we find many of the absurdities of the opera pointed out with the keen perception that we should anticipate from the accomplished writers, the similar absurdities of the English stage quite escape attention. Addison's own Cato exhibited himself in a "long wig, flowered gown, and lackered chair."

Sir Roger's next important movement in the business of sight-seeing is his visit to Vauxhall, then called Spring Garden. It was the usual mode to go thither by water. A charming trait of Sir Roger's character occurs at the outset. "We were no sooner come to the Temple Stairs but we were surrounded with a crowd of watermen, offering us their respective services. Sir Roger, after having looked about him attentively spied one with a wooden leg (Fig. 2321), and immediately gave orders to get his boat ready. As we were walking towards it, "You must know," says Sir Roger, "I never make use of anybody to row me that has not lost either a leg or an arm. I would rather bate him a few strokes of his oar, than not employ an honest man that has been wounded in the queen's service. If I was a lord or a bishop, and kept a barge, I would not put a fellow in my livery that had not a wooden leg." Our readers will mark the illustration here given of old London life. It appears there were still noblemen and bishops who "kept a barge" for moving up and down the Thames.

On the way to Vauxhall the knight turns two or three times to survey the great city, and his observations remind us of an event of the time that materially changed the appearance of London. He "bid me observe how thick the city was set with churches, and that there was scarce a single steeple on this side Temple Bar. 'A most heathenish sight!' says Sir Roger. 'There is no religion at this end of the town. The fifty new churches will very much mend the prospect ; but church work is slow, church work is slow.'" Well might the good knight say so ; a considerable portion of those fifty churches never came into existence. The Act for their erection was passed in 1710, and one of the objects to be attained by them was the "redressing the inconvenience and growing mischiefs which result from the increase of *Dissenters* and Popery." Among the churches that *were* erected we may mention that fane where, says the poet Savage,

God delights to dwell, and man to praise ;

namely, St. Martin's-in-the-Fields, built by Gibbs (Fig. 2367); and the Church of St. Mary Woolnoth, erected by Hawksmoor (Fig 2366.)

At length the party reach Vauxhall, so called from Faux Hall the manor-house that originally belonged, it is supposed, to one of King John's soldiers of fortune, a well-known Norman, named Faulk de Brent. Addison's description of the place is very short, but very much to the purpose. The chief period of visiting it was probably the spring (hence the name), for he says, the garden is "excellently pleasant at this time of the year (May). When I considered the fragrance of the walks and bowers, with the choirs of birds that sung upon the trees, and the loose tribes of people that walked under their shades, I could not but look upon the place as a kind of Mahometan paradise." The lovers of Burton ale may be interested in knowing that this was the beverage that Sir Roger and the Spectator partook of, with a slice of hung-beef, a century and a quarter ago at Vauxhall. The gardens, we may add, had not yet risen to the zenith of their reputation. About twelve years after the date of Addison's paper on the subject of this visit, Mr. Jonathan Tyers, a friend of Hogarth's, opened them in a style of novel magnificence, and then Vauxhall in a very short time assumed the character that it has ever since borne, and became the great attraction of the day. The boxes were painted by Hayman with copies from Hogarth's pictures. One peculiarly magnificent work of art graced the gardens, Roubiliac's statue of Handel. This was the first important evidence of his genius that the sculptor exhibited to the English public, and it immediately brought him into repute. It was cut in the dwelling-house at the Gardens, where Handel sat; and the resemblance was so forcible, that a person who had never seen Handel, discovered him one night as he walked in the Gardens, merely by the knowledge that the statue had given him of the musician's face. In a work of such excellence in higher qualities, this is indeed a merit also worth mentioning. Some poet paid Roubiliac the following compliment:—

> That Orpheus moved a grove, or rock, or stream
> By music's power, will not a fiction seem;
> For here as great a miracle is shown—
> A Handel breathing, though transform'd to stone.

But Sir Roger's career now draws to a close. As the club to which the Spectator, Sir Roger, and several of the other characters that are from time to time introduced, belong, is sitting one evening, news is brought of the good knight's death (Fig. 2322); which, according to a Whig justice of the peace, Sir Roger's enemy and antagonist, had been caused by catching a cold at the county sessions, as he was very warmly promoting an address of his own penning, and in which he succeeded to his wishes. But Sir Roger's butler gives a very different version; who ascribes his visit to the sessions to a determination to see justice done to a poor widow woman and her fatherless children, that had been wronged by a neighbouring gentleman. And it seems he died as he had lived, thinking still how he could best promote the interest and comforts of all around, and especially of those who, he considered, had been in a sense committed to his charge, namely, the poor of his estate, and the servants of his household. From high to low there is therefore in the will a kind word, and gift for all. The butler thus continues his letter to the Spectator, in a passage that we extract as containing a charming picture of the customs that once prevailed in England when death came to the Manor-house:—"He has bequeathed the fine white gelding that he used to ride a-hunting upon to his chaplain, because he thought he would be kind to him; and has left you all his books. He has moreover bequeathed to the chaplain a very pretty tenement with good lands about it. It being a very cold day when he made his will, he left for mourning to every man in the parish a great frieze coat, and to every woman a black riding-hood. It was a most moving sight to see him take leave of his poor servants, commending us all for our fidelity, whilst we were not able to speak a word for weeping. As we most of us are grown grey-headed in our dear master's service, he has left us pensions and legacies, which we may live very comfortably upon the remaining part of our days. He has bequeathed a great deal more in charity, which is not yet come to my knowledge; and it is peremptorily said in the parish, that he has left money to build a steeple to the church; for he was heard to say some time ago, that if he lived two years longer, Coverley Church should have a steeple to it. The chaplain tells everybody that he made a very good end, and never speaks of him without tears. He was buried according to his own directions, among the family of the Coverleys, on the left hand of his father, Sir Arthur. The coffin was carried by six of his tenants, and the pall held by six of the quorum. The whole parish followed the corpse with heavy hearts, and in their mourning suits; the men in frieze, and the women in riding-hoods."

Vauxhall had a formidable rival in Ranelagh, which possessed attractions peculiarly its own, and views of both will be given

hereafter. The water, for instance, formed a pretty feature of the gardens, whilst the rotunda was a building of extraordinary pretensions, size, and magnificence.

Here public breakfasts were held and here concerts and other musical performances were given. The musical reputation of Ranelagh is sufficiently established by the fact that Dr. Arne was engaged o add choral and instrumental accompaniments to the glees and catches that were sung there. Here also masquerades were held, and in a style of dress that exposed the sharers in them to a still severer satire than Addison or Steele had found necessary. A writer in the 'Connoisseur,' one of the many publications that afterwards sprung up in consequence of the success of the 'Spectator' and the 'Tatler,' announces a remarkable species of entertainment that he understands is to take place at Ranelagh, namely, a naked masquerade, when the weather gets hot enough. "One set of ladies, I am told, intend to personate water-nymphs bathing in the canal; three sisters, celebrated for their charms, design to appear together as the three Graces; and a certain lady of quality, who most resembles the goddess of beauty, is now practising, from a model of the noted statue of Venus de' Medici, the most striking attitudes for that character. As to the gentlemen, they may most of them represent very suitably the half-brutal forms of Satyrs, Pans, Fauns, and Centaurs." That this satire had a solid foundation, we learn from many corroborating circumstances. It is after a masquerade here that the ruin of one of Fielding's female characters—in 'Amelia'—is accomplished. But, after all the chief attraction of Ranelagh seems to have been very much the same that draws people to such places now, the desire to see and be seen. Bloomfield pleasantly ridicules the empty character of the amusements there in some of his verses. He says,

> To Ranelagh once in my life
>   By good-natur'd force I was driven,
>   he nations had ceas'd their long strife,
>   And Peace beam'd her radiance from Heaven.
> What wonders were here to be found
>   That a clown might enjoy or disdain?—
> First, we traced the gay circle all round,
>   Ay—and then we went round it again.

Another verse gives us some touches of costume, and shows that it was not only in masquerades the ladies wore their dresses so very scanty:—

> A thousand feet rustled on mats—
>   A carpet that once had been green;
> Men bow'd with their outlandish hats
>   With corners so fearfully keen.
> Fair maids, who at home in their haste
>   Had left all clothing else but a train,
> Swept the floor clean as slowly they paced,
>   Then—walk'd round and swept it again: &c.

Ranelagh existed until the beginning of the present century. The rotunda was pulled down in or about 1805—and Ranelagh was no more. Its beautiful gardens, adjoining those of Chelsea College, are now covered with houses.

We have given in an earlier page (Fig. 2216) a group of portraits of the most eminent divines of the period at present under review; two of these, Wesley and Whitfield, have been already noticed in our account of Oxford—we may here say a few words upon the others. William III. used to observe of the man he had raised to the deanery of St. Paul's immediately after his own elevation to the throne, and on whom he subsequently conferred the archbishopric of Canterbury,—William used to say of Tillotson, that there was no honester man, and that he himself had never had a better friend. Excellent and in every way unobjectionable as was this appointment, it excited a great deal of envy and discussion at the time; partly because Tillotson leaned neither to the Catholics nor to the Calvinists, and still less to the body of those who, in their practice at least, were men of no religion; but partly, also, because it was remembered that he had been bred a Puritan, had acted as tutor in the family of Cromwell's Attorney-General, Prideaux, and, lastly, had married Cromwell's niece. The archbishop did not long enjoy the exalted position to which he had attained; he died within four years of his appointment, and was buried in the church of the parish (St. Lawrence in the Jewry) where he had laid the foundations of a better reputation than any archbishopric could establish for him, by the delivery of his well-known sermons. Stillingfleet rose at the same time, and by the assistance of the same royal hands, to the high dignity of a bishopric; and, to say nothing of his able and zealous controversial writings in the cause of Protestantism, he had by one particular

2344.—The Mansion of Strathfieldsaye, the Seat of the Duke of Wellington, from the River Loddon.

2347.—Courts of Law. Westminster Hall, about 1750.

2346.—Islington, 1780.

2343.—Chatsworth.

2345.—Westminster Bridge.

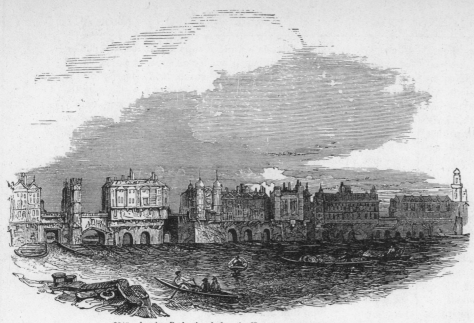

2348.—London Bridge just before the Houses were pulled down in 1760

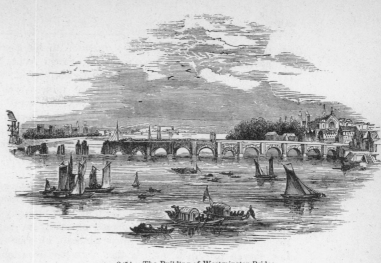

2351.—The Building of Westminster Bridge

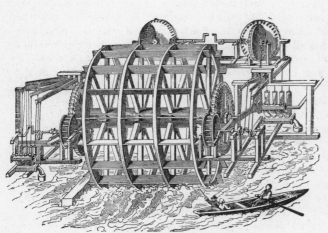

2349—Water-works at Old London Bridge

2350—Hogarth's View of Old Houses on London Bridge

2357.—The Old College, Warwick Lane, as it appeared in 1841.

2354.—The Mansion-House 1771.

act done something to challenge attention to his merits, should an opportunity offer for rewarding them: when James II. revived the Court of Ecclesiastical Commission, Stillingfleet declined to become a member. One of the host of persons who combated his views, or whose views he combated, was the great philosopher Locke. Among the bishop's writings we may mention the work on the antiquities of the British church, from which we learn that he inclined to a belief in the truth of a deeply interesting tradition connected with the establishment of Christianity in England, namely, that the Apostle Paul visited Britain.

As Bishop Stillingfleet distinguished himself as one of the opponents of Unitarianism, so on the contrary Bishop Hoadley was, if not exactly a supporter of that sect, at least strongly inclined to favour opinions which were supposed especially to belong to it. Bishop Hoadley was also the great advocate of what were called Low-church principles, and in that character a curious and very complimentary incident occurred to him. He published a work on the 'Measure of Obedience to the Civil Magistrate,' which Bishop Atterbury, a man in all respects opposed to him in opinions, denounced. Hoadley then defended himself, and with such spirit that the House of Commons presented an address to Queen Anne representing the signal service he had done in the cause of civil and religious liberty. Another of his publications, a sermon on the text "My kingdom is not of this world," roused a much more formidable contention; the Bangorian controversy (so called because Hoadley was then Bishop of Bangor) was originated by it. Dr. Hoadley, the physician, and author of one of our standard comedies—'The Suspicious Husband,' was the son of the bishop.

Samuel Clarke was a name that in its owner's day could not have been pronounced in any mixed company of intelligent men without rousing at once warm friends and equally warm enemies. Never hardly was a life more fruitful in controversy. He was continually publishing works on philosophy or religion; and almost every one raised up its own particular set of opponents. In his sermons on the 'Being and Attributes of God,' he attacked Spinosa; but in such a manner that it was doubted by many whether he had not rather thrown back than advanced his object. Pope refers to Clarke when he writes—

And reason downward till we doubt of God.

His lectures on the 'Evidences of Natural and Revealed Religion' laid him open to the lash of another writer, as capable as Pope himself of making the satire permanent. Every reader of 'Tom Jones' must remember Square, and his "fitness of things." Fielding borrowed the phrase from Dr. Clarke, who said morality consisted in the immutable differences, relations, and eternal fitness of things. Baptism, the Trinity, Free Will, Primitive Doxologies, were among the other subjects which he discussed with all sorts of opponents, and with all the ardour of his busy and powerful mind. We are told that when he took his degree of Doctor of Divinity, in consequence of his appointment to be chaplain to Queen Anne, such a logical conflict ensued between him and the professor, James, as never was heard before in the schools of Cambridge; and we can well believe it. Newton, we may observe, was Clarke's intimate friend. The latter did much to introduce the writings of the great philosopher into notice. He published a Latin translation of the 'Treatise on Optics;' and Newton in a princely spirit gave him in return 500l. for his five children. He died in 1729.*

Among the few public exhibitions of royal pageantry that are still to be occasionally seen in London, there is one—a levee at St. James's Palace, that never fails to attract a curious multitude of spectators. Yet even the most regular of the levee-hunters among these would find it difficult, we think, to recognise the same essential scene, under the very different aspect that it bears, if we look back upon a levee-day at St. James's in the eighteenth century (Fig. 2325). Everything seems changed: the carriages (Fig. 2323) are very unlike our carriages—a large portion of the distinguished visitors come in sedans, the chairmen of which (Fig. 2324) seemed to be dressed as sumptuously as though they intended to take their burdens into the very presence of royalty; the place itself is so narrow, that it is wonderful how the guests can all arrive in any reasonable time at their destination: everything, we repeat, seems changed except the old palace itself, and the hearts and minds of the human actors in the show,—those who are going in—the privileged and gratified few, and those who must stay without—the curious and scarcely less gratified many.

The sedan chair was in the eighteenth century a favourite mode

* We have to express our thanks to a correspondent for pointing out an error in the notice of Walker, the hero of Londonderry. He was not a Presbyterian, as there stated, but the Episcopalian rector of Donoughmore.

of conveyance, not merely, as we might suppose, for delicate ladies, or scarcely less delicate gentlemen, but for general purposes. And they were very cheap, considering the nature and severity of the service afforded; a shilling an hour, or a guinea a week, were the common prices for the sedan and its two bearers, who were mostly Irishmen, and proverbial for their firm thick-set build, and immense calves to their legs. It is curious to note that the sedan obtained its popularity in spite of the objections that were raised when they were first introduced; but which objections have overthrown them at last. It was not pleasant to our forefathers, this idea of making men beasts of burden; though they soon got over the sentiment, and began to enjoy the sin—if sin it were, leaving it to a later generation to grow virtuous and renounce the luxurious vehicle. The introducer of the sedan was Prince Charles, afterwards King Charles I., who on his return from his romantic but not very creditable love-expedition into Spain with "Steenie" (Buckingham) brought back with him three sedan chairs. Two of these were given to the favourite, and he immediately used them; and in consequence "the clamour and noise of it was so extravagant, that the people would rail on him in the streets."

If one were to judge of the taste of the eighteenth century simply by its furniture (Fig. 2326, 2327, 2328, 2329, 2330), we should say it was at once refined, elegant, and original; nay, we have only to glance in the windows of some one or other of the commercial palaces of Regent or Oxford Street, to perceive that if there be any thing in them more than ordinarily attractive, it is almost certain to be some revival or imitation of the styles so fashionable in this country during the last century, in connection with the names of Louis Quatorze and Louis Quinze of France. And these names remind us that the English taste for such furniture was not original; but had come from the same quarter from whence our countrymen had before obtained no inconsiderable portion of the architectural, artistical, poetical, and dramatic tastes that still prevailed among them.

It was during the same period that the best English houses became for the first time what we should call completely furnished. We have altered and improved, and in some cases have perhaps altered without improving upon, the furniture of the eighteenth century, but we have added little of decided novelty and importance to it. The little nick-knackeries of the present day have only replaced an equally various and indescribable tribe belonging to an earlier one. Old China was the all-absorbing passion of the female subjects of Anne, as Berlin wool is of those of her present Majesty; and for our parts, we dare not venture a word of opinion as to the respective merits of the taste in these matters of the two eras.

There was one novelty, however, of the eighteenth century of a permanently valuable character; mahogany then began to be used in England. Dr. Gibbons, a physician of London, brought over the first block, towards the close of the previous century; this block was manufactured into articles of ornament, and excited universal admiration. Painted and gilded woods speedily lost all their attractions, and the new comer carried all before it, until it became almost the only material used in cabinet-making.

In architecture the present period certainly could claim some originality: for it produced, though it did not apparently justly appreciate, Vanbrugh, whose great work of Blenheim we have already noticed. And it is not an uninteresting task to compare some of the views of this building (see the additional engravings,—Figs. 2337, 2338) with views of Castle Howard, the architect's first important achievement, and with other buildings of his time, the product of various contemporary artists.

Who can look without admiration upon the superb front of Castle Howard (Fig. 2339, 2340)? Who can avoid being instantly impressed with the idea that this is indeed, whatever its faults, true architectural grandeur? And the more you look, the more the stately and picturesque, yet withal solemn beauty of the pile grows upon you. The play of light and shade—the constantly-changing outline, the climbing as it were of its more salient points one above another, till the loftiest, in the shape of the tower, surmounts and tranquilly looks down upon everything else, are all features of the exterior of Castle Howard, that strike alike the most unarchitectural and the most professional of spectators. Vanbrugh had here full scope for the display of his genius. He had neither littleness of space nor littleness of patrons to deal with. The front of Castle Howard extends to no less than six hundred feet, or two hundred yards! The contents of the interior are worthy of such an exterior To give a mere catalogue of the pictures would occupy no incon siderable space in our pages. Ask for what master you please, and you can be shown specimens of his finest days. But as even in such collections, there is generally one work that stands out beyond all others, partly by its surpassing excellence, partly by the natural tendency of the mind to collect, as it were, all its strength for admiration and remembrance and enjoyment, upon one picture, rather than lose the whole in the vague dreamy kind of wonder that such a multiplicity of artistical wealth is apt to generate,—so at Castle Howard there is a favourite—a focal centre to attract and concentrate the dispersing rays of admiration. This is the Three Maries with the dead body of Christ, by Annibal Carracci. The money value of such works is but a poor evidence of their intrinsic value; yet it is an evidence. For this picture, then, it is said the Court of Spain offered as many louis d'ors as would cover it, or in a simpler mode of calculation, something like 8000l. Nay, it is even added, that this offer has been outstripped in our own country.

In articles of virtù Castle Howard is of course rich to repletion; for the time of its erection and furnishing was the time, above all others, when such things were sought with avidity, and purchased at incredible prices. But the most precious article of this class that Castle Howard possesses was a gift; and the giver was a man who could enhance the value of the thing given, by the mere fact that it was a gift from him. We refer to the small cylindrical altar, about four and a half feet high, that stands in the Museum, and of which the verses inscribed on its top record the history:

Pass not this ancient altar with disdain,
'Twas once in Delphi's sacred temple rear'd,
From this the Pythian poured her mystic strain,
While Greece its fate in anxious silence heard.

What chief, what hero of the Achaian race
Might not to this have clung with holy awe?
Have clung in pious reverence round its base,
And from the voice inspired received the law?

A British chief, as famed in arms as those,
Has borne this relic o'er the Italian waves
In war still friend to science, this bestows,
And *Nelson* gives it to the land he saves.

It is but an act of justice to the founder of this noble edifice, and the patron of Fanbrugh, to state, that at a certain portion of the park the visitor will find an open place formed by the meeting of four avenues of great trees, and in the centre of that place stands an obelisk a hundred feet high, which informs us that "Charles, the third Earl of Carlisle, of the family of the Howards, erected a castle where the old castle of Hinderskelf stood, and called it Castle Howard. He likewise made the plantations in this park, and all the outworks, monuments, and other plantations belonging to this seat. He began these works in the year 1712, and set up this inscription An. Dom. 1731."

Wilton House (Fig. 2332) looks tame and common-place in the comparison with Castle Howard, though great men have been at work upon it: the original designer was Hans Holbein; and when his pile was injured by fire, the restorer was Inigo Jones. But since the time of the latter artist, Mr. Wyatt has been also very busy at Wilton, and according to the opinion of Sir Richard Hoare, not with the most satisfactory results. In short, as the building now is, it belongs to neither of the great men we have named, nor can it be said altogether to be a product of their successor. A specimen of Holbein's architecture, however, does still exist—a porch and gateway at one end of the gardens. This is of strikingly beautiful proportions,—contains two series or stages of pillars, one above the other, and has recesses with busts.

But in its contents Wilton may vie with Castle Howard, or any other of those great mansions which make our English noblemen appear like so many inferior sovereigns on their own domains, whilst in its associations Wilton surpasses nearly all of them. Its hall, for instance, contains nearly two hundred pieces of ancient sculpture, many of them literally of incalculable value—and there are paintings of the first order by Rubens, Holbein, Vandyke, &c., and a host of other masters. It was at Wilton, again, that Massinger was born (he was the son of a retainer of the Pembroke family). It was at Wilton that Philip Sydney wrote the 'Arcadia,' and probably made love to Lady Penelope Devereux, the Philoclea of that romance, Sidney's sister being then the Countess of Pembroke—and lastly, it was upon this lady that Jonson wrote his well-known epitaph—

Underneath this marble hearse
Lies the subject of all verse—
Sidney's sister, Pembroke's* mother!
Death, ere thou hast killed another,

* The next earl.

Wise and fair and good as she,
Time shall throw a dart at thee.

Moor Park (Fig. 2334) was originally built by the unfortunate Duke of Monmouth: subsequently it belonged to a gentleman, Mr. Styles, who, having obtained a splendid fortune by the South Sea scheme, was wise enough to keep it—by withdrawing in time; and by him the brick building was cased over with stone as we now see it, and the noble portico added. Subsequent alterations have, however, given the building somewhat of an all-portico character. The wings added by the fortunate speculator were taken away by an unfortunate one, who subsequently possessed the mansion. This gentleman threw up a good place—a directorship at the East India Board, in the hope of obtaining a still better at the Board of Control under Fox's famous India Bill; but when disappointments clipped the pinions of his soaring hopes, he cut off the wings of his mansion at Moor Park too, and sold the materials, as though to show his consciousness of how he had been misled, and his determination that the lesson should not be again repeated.

It is curious how the all-portico character of the exterior finds a correspondence of expression in the all-saloon character of the interior. This saloon—or entrance-hall—is very large, and according to the ideas of the last century, very magnificent, with its gilt-railed gallery, its marble door-cases opening in all directions, above as well as below, and each surmounted by great pieces of sculpture, its endless series of white stucco compositions on the walls, and its mass of painting and gilding on the ceiling. Here too there is a series of immense and very showy pictures, three in number, illustrative of Ovid's story of the Metamorphosis of Io. But as to any *architectural* beauty, or elegance, or picturesqueness—as to any general expression of architectural grandeur or architectural character of any sort—the less said the better, in connection with the hall of Moor Park. Yet such as it is, it is the whole: there is no other part of the interior in which there has been any attempt made to raise domestic convenience into Art. Step out of the chief hall into the smaller one behind (probably the original hall of the Duke's mansion), and you are disagreeably impressed by the contrast. This saloon is dark and gloomy, without being at all solemn and impressive; and when you are told that those are the pictures that you see there on the walls and ceiling, for which Sir James Thornhill recovered 3500l. in a court of law, you can hardly help wishing that the jury had sat on the spot to determine the case with the gaudy subjects of the demand before them. They would assuredly have revenged upon Sir James the headache his works would have given them after an hour or two of their company.

The next step is still worse—as it conducts us to the staircase, which is absolutely mean. There are pictures here too on the walls, but there is no spot of ground large enough to stand upon to look at them in comfort. This was the way they worked in the last century; Mr. Styles, the South Sea speculator before mentioned, spent 150,000l. in the improvement of Moor Park, yet left this staircase.

The apartments contain many objects of interest, and one of them, the drawing-room, is truly superb and beautiful. The grounds of Moor Park were highly celebrated whilst the taste lasted from which their peculiar attractions had sprung. They formed, in the opinion of Sir William Temple, the "perfectest figure of a garden" he ever saw. As a peculiarly favourable example therefore of the style of gardening produced in the seventeenth, and forming the beau ideal of the eighteenth century, we may here transcribe Sir William's account of Moor Park. Having observed that it was "made by the Countess of Bedford, esteemed amongst the greatest wits of her time, and celebrated by Dr. Donne [the poet], and with very great care, excellent contrivances, and much cost," he proceeds to his description of the results:—"It lies on the side of a hill upon which the house now stands, but not very steep. The length of the house, where the best rooms and of most use and pleasure are, lies upon the breadth of the garden; the great parlour opens into the middle of a terrace gravel-walk that lies even with it, and which may be, as I remember, three hundred paces long, and broad in proportion; the border set with standard laurels, and at large distances, which have the beauty of orange trees out of flower and fruit. By this walk are three descents, by many stone steps in the middle and at each end, into a very large parterre. This is divided into quarters by gravel walks, and adorned with two fountains and eight statues in the several quarters. At the end of the terrace-walk are two summer-houses, and the sides of the parterre are ranged with two large cloisters open to the garden upon arches of stone, and ending with two other summer-houses even with the cloisters, which are paved with stone, and designed for walks of shade, there being none other in the whole parterre. Over these

2355.—Cornhill, the Exchange, and Lombard Street. (From an Old Print.)

2358.—Fleet Ditch, 1749.

2361.—The Treasury, from St. James's Park, 1775

2356.—Old East India House, 1726

2360.—The South-Sea House.

2362.—The Admiralty, as it appeared before Adam's Screen was built.

2363.—Surgeons' Theatre, &c., Old Bailey.

2367.—St. Martin's Church.

2364.—Pall-Mall, about 1740.

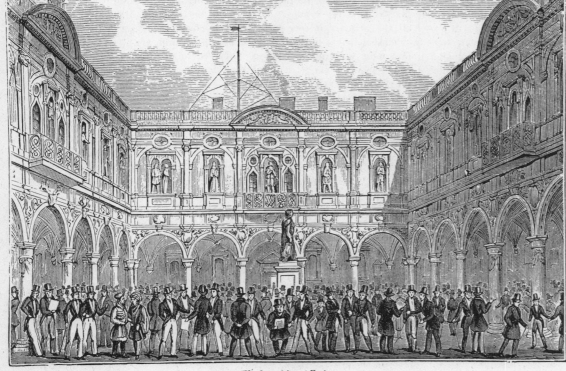

2365.—The Second Royal Exchange.

2366.—St. Mary Woolnoth, Lombard Street.

two cloisters are two terraces covered with lead, and fenced with balusters; and the passage into these airy walks is out of the two summer-houses at the end of the first terrace-walk. The cloister facing the south is covered with vines, and would have been proper for an orange-house, and the other for myrtles and other more common greens, and had, I doubt not, been used for that purpose, if this piece of gardening had been then in as much vogue as it is now. From the middle of this parterre is a descent by many steps, flying on each side of a grotto that lies between them covered with lead, and flat, into the lower garden, which is all fruit-trees ranged about the several quarters of a wilderness, which is very shady; the walks here are green, the grotto embellished with figures of shell-work, fountains, and water-works. If the hill had not ended with the lower garden, and the wall was not bounded by the common way that goes through the park, they might have added a third quarter of all greens; but this want is supplied by a garden on the other side of the house, which is all of that sort, very wild, shady, and adorned with rough rock-work and fountains. This was Moor Park when I was acquainted with it, and the sweetest place, I think, that I have seen in my life, either before or since at home or abroad." Reading this, how could Lord Anson, the great navigator, when he purchased Moor Park, let loose Mr. Capability Brown among the greens, and the shady places, and the fountains? Or how could Mr. Brown himself talk of the *capabilities* of a place that was already the very acme of perfection, and persuade his employer to let him pull the whole to pieces, as he did, and reconstruct it? Yet it must be owned, as one sees what he made of the ground, and what his successors, under the direction of the present proprietor, the Marquis of Westminster, have made of them, there does not seem to be felt the smallest regret for the destruction of this " sweetest " of all gardens.

And it is after reading of such a place we should go to see the grandest and most beautiful of all English gardens in our own time —that of Chatsworth. There, too, we shall find fountains, though the child's toys of the one become indeed sports for men in the other. Think of a fountain that sends up a column of water nearly *three hundred feet* high—in other words, to the height of the top of St. Paul's! Think of *such* a fountain shaking its loosening silver in the sun! This is indeed the " Emperor " of fountains; and, like other emperors, requires large supplies: say, for instance, an acre of water of a foot in depth hourly. Another fountain at Chatsworth is as fairy-like and enchanting as the Emperor is grand and royal in its character; this sends up various jets, that rise and fall in such a peculiar manner that you can scarcely repress the almost involuntary exclamation when you first see it—Why, the water is dancing! And so it is;—inspired by the artistical skill of its designer. Chatsworth, too, has its rocks. And what rocks! One can hardly expect to be believed in stating the dimensions and weights of the pieces of which it is composed. There are single masses weighing upwards of three hundred and seventy tons! But mark too to what purposes all these magnificent materials are turned. The mistake is not made here of treating them as an end in garden scenery—they are only the means of producing some grand effect not indigenous to the place, but which shall still be made to appear as indigenous. So in one part of the grounds of Chatsworth the rocks form an exact imitation in all their savage grandeur of the Strid at Bolton Abbey in Yorkshire, the original design being (which is probably by this time completed) to have a mountain torrent, some three hundred feet long, with banks thirteen or fourteen feet high. Contrast this with the " shell-rock work " of Sir William Temple's sweet gardens. But in short it is useless to pursue the parallel, which we only instituted for the purpose of showing how much purer and loftier the taste of the present day is in such matters than it was but a hundred or two years ago, when Nature everywhere bore the stamp of extreme artificiality, whereas now our best landscape gardeners seek rather to give to the highest efforts of their art something of the impress of Nature.

The fountains and rock-work of Chatsworth, vast as they are, appear to be only on the proper scale to accord with everything about them. One of the most magnificent conservatories in existence is at Chatsworth, and almost overpowering are the sentiments of wonder and admiration that it excites as you pass along the stateliest of terraces, Solomon's Walk, and through the rock garden to the upper terrace, and catch from thence the first view of the " Mountain of Glass." And beyond all comparison as this is in size with the various other erections that are found in the different parts of the ground, as the Orangery, the Musa House, the Greenhouse, the Orchidaceous House, Camellia House, and so on—yet would some of these, if placed singly in almost any other grounds be considered remarkable for their dimensions and general excel-

lence of adaptation to the purposes for which they were erected. Then Chatsworth has not only its flower gardens of different kinds and styles, but its Arboretum; and the Duke of Devonshire, we believe, has even his own collector, whose business it is to explore the most distant parts of the world for new floral treasures wherewith to enrich the Palace of the Peak. In brief, all the arrangements of the gardens are on the very largest and most magnificent scale, and such as, we believe, taken for all in all, are without parallel in any part of the world. It is not often the Sovereign of England can look upon a place where the finest of her own gardens look almost insignificant in the comparison, and where there has been such an outlay that even she might hesitate to venture to incur an equal expenditure; yet when Her Majesty visited Chatsworth just two years ago, some such thoughts must have been suggested by the sight of the surpassing grandeur that met her eyes.

On the whole the " palace " itself is not unworthy of the scene around it; and that is high praise. It was planned by William Talman, Comptroller of the Works to William III., but it was reserved for the present Duke to finish what Talman began, and in finishing to enlarge and improve at the same time. And though this sort of process is one that generally ends in the production of works that have no harmony of idea apparent through all their members, it is not so at Chatsworth, as our engraving will sufficiently show. It will be there seen (Fig. 2343) that the mansion has a very stately, simple, and expressive aspect. Its interior is, as a matter of course, as sumptuous as the taste and skill, aided by unlimitable pecuniary means, can make it. Some of Gibbons's very choicest wood-carvings are here. And here, too, are a class of works that were famous, and are still notorious, if only on account of the positions they occupy,—the very large and very bad pictures that Pope so justly commented on. It should seem indeed that the satirist had Chatsworth itself in his eye, for it is in its *chapel* that Verrio's master-piece is to be found. Pope writes:—

> And now the *chapel's* silver bells you hear,
> That summon you to all the pride of prayer;
> Light quirks of music, broken and uneven,
> Make the soul dance upon a jig to heaven.
> On painted ceilings you devoutly stare,
> Where sprawl the saints of Verrio and Laguerre.

Now one of the works in the chapel by Verrio is a painting of the Ascension that covers the ceiling, and Laguerre was with Verrio at Chatsworth, acting as his assistant.

Chatsworth has had some noticeable guests—guests, we mean, of a comparatively permanent character. Mary Queen of Scots was a prisoner here. Hobbes, the philosopher of Malmesbury, had his chief home at Chatsworth. Lastly, when Tallard was brought to England as a prisoner by Marlborough after the battle of Blenheim, he resided for a short time with the Duke of Devonshire. With the politeness and felicity of thought and diction that have been considered so characteristic of his countrymen, the marshal, when he took leave of Chatsworth, said to the Duke, " When I return to France, and reckon up the days of my captivity in England, I shall leave out all that I have spent at Chatsworth."

Strathfieldsaye (Fig. 2344), like Blenheim, is a memorial of the English nation's gratitude to one of her very greatest warriors for *his* greatest victory. And, as in the case of Marlborough, all the honours it was in the State's power to bestow had been exhausted before the battle of Blenheim was won, and it was therefore most powerless just when it desired to be most powerful in expressing its sense of the mighty services rendered',—so was it with the Duke of Wellington before the battle of Waterloo; in each case, therefore, all that could be done was to confer a magnificent estate upon the conqueror, accompanied by such universal and enthusiastic expression of thankfulness as made the gift a thousand times more precious.

Two hundred thousand pounds were accordingly granted after the battle of Waterloo; and this sum was added to various other sums that had been previously granted, making in all seven hundred thousand pounds. Truly it is something to serve England! The estate purchased is held from the crown by the tenure of the presentation of a tri-coloured flag on the 18th of June—a pleasant mode of making even the acknowledgment of lordship only another opportunity for recording the merits of the vassal, and of reminding the descendants of both, of the price paid for the estate—Waterloo.

Strathfieldsaye is situated in the north of Hampshire, near the place so dear to antiquarians, and so interesting to others also—the Roman Silchester. The Park is small, but pleasant, of an undulating surface, well-wooded and watered. The name appears to be derived from Strath—a stretch of level ground with elevated sides:

field—a word requiring no explanation; and Say—from a family of that name, who originally possessed the manor. Before it came to the Duke's possession, the two Chathams, father and son, both possessed the estate, and resided here. Guy's Cliff, Warwickshire (Fig. 2333), has been already noticed (vol i. p. 376). Wanstead House (Fig. 2341) may be referred to as a favourable specimen of the style of Colin Campbell, one of the architects who shared with Kent the patronage of Lord Burlington. Street architecture in the period exhibits no improvement upon the individual specimens that have been preserved of an earlier date, as, for instance, the house built by Inigo Jones in Great Queen Street (Fig. 2331). This forms an interesting specimen of street domestic architecture of the higher class; while the old watering-house at Knightsbridge (Fig. 2335), with its rest for the porter's load in front, may be contrasted with the palatial character of Jones' mansion as a specimen of the residences of the middling classes of London about the same—down to a much later—time.

It is a common question with those who are apt to look upon themselves as really practical men, whenever new discoveries or new efforts for discovery are made in scientific matters, to ask—what good? The history of the foundation of Greenwich Observatory furnishes a very striking illustration of—as well as a very happy answer to—the common fallacy involved in such questions; which assume that no steps are to be taken in the path of knowledge, unless we are assured as to the exact amount and nature of our rewards for so doing. Before the latter part of the seventeenth century, there was no national Observatory. Men had been from the earliest times aware in a vague way of the advantages of some astronomical lore to those who in Chapman's words ploughed "Neptune's salt wilderness," yet still no efforts were made to establish a place for the express advancement of the science by means of careful and continuous observations. And why? Simply, we presume, because our statesmen and others saw no especial practical object to be attained, and would not move without. In the sixteenth and seventeenth centuries, the business of navigation began to assume a much more imposing aspect than it had ever done before, and the art of navigation became in consequence of the most signal importance. Yet still nothing was done until it began to be remarked that if the motion of the Moon among the Stars could be exactly pointed out before a ship left England, the crew would at any part of their voyage have the means of discovering their longitude, by observing what position the moon then occupied among the stars; and thus determining the exact London time. A plan founded upon this principle was proposed to Charles II. by a Frenchman, named St. Pierre, but it was then found there were no exact lunar tables in existence, and that the scheme was impracticable simply on such grounds. No doubt there ought to have been such tables; and had astronomers received the attention and assistance they had a right to ask, no doubt they would have been ready when they were wanted. Of course practical men of all kinds now knew the defect, and set to work to remedy it. Charles II. caused the Observatory at Greenwich to be erected (Fig. 2336), and Flamsteed was appointed Astronomer Royal. But the impulse died before it had accomplished anything like a complete working agency for the attainment of its desires—so the Observatory was left without instruments, and the whole project might have fallen to the ground, but for Flamsteed's public spirit, who made what instruments he could, and expended his own money in purchasing the remainder. The accuracy that has been since attained in our lunar and all other astronomical tables by the labours of Flamsteed and his successors, and the value of these tables to navigation, are now matters thoroughly and universally understood. But this is not the only or the most important proof of the truth of the position we have assumed, that Greenwich Observatory affords. That establishment, as we have seen, however long wanted, could not be obtained, till practical evidence was given of its necessity; and in that necessity, and in the delay that men found inevitable, because they had made no previous preparation, they might have discovered the folly of dictating to Science the terms upon which she shall live and move. But, we repeat, the fallacy of the "what good?" kind of questioning, receives a happy and most complete answer in the records of the Greenwich foundation. "The first edition of Newton's 'Principia' had appeared shortly before Flamsteed had supplied himself with his best instruments; and at Newton's request many of Flamsteed's observations on the Moon, deduced as was then practicable, were communicated to him to aid in perfecting the theory deduced from the principle of universal gravitation. The time at which these observations were made was in fact a most critical one; when the accurate observations

were needed for the support of the most extensive philosophical theory that man had invented." (Penny Cyclopædia.) And they were ready. But where would they have been, if the founders of the Observatory had received no other assurance than a vague one of the advantages that *must* result to science from its erection, and so on? And this, though the mightiest, is far from being the only assistance that scientific men have derived from the erection of the Observatory, independent of the direct purposes for which it was called into existence.

The every-day business of the Observatory cannot be better described than in the words of the writer from whom we borrowed the previous passage:—"It is not devoted to the gazing at planets or nebulæ, or to the watching the appearances of the spots in the sun, or the mountains in the moon, with which the dilettante astronomer is so much charmed; it is not to the measures of the relative positions and distances of double stars, or the registering the present state of the nebulous bodies which appear liable to change—measures and registers of great importance, but which possess a charm sufficient to persuade private observers to undertake the observations, and which do not demand extreme nicety of adjustment of the instruments, nor require much calculation afterwards. But it is to the regular observation of the sun, moon, planets, and stars (selected according to a previously arranged system) when they pass the meridian, at whatever hour of the day or night that may happen, and in no other position; observations which require the most vigilant care in regard to the state of the instruments, and which imply such a mass of calculations afterwards, that the observation itself is in comparison a mere trifle. From these are deduced the positions of the various objects, with an accuracy that can be obtained in no other way: and they can then be used as bases to which observations by amateur astronomers, with different instruments, can be referred." Nothing need be added to this passage in explanation of the duties of the Astronomer Royal and his assistants, nor as to their relative position with respect to the many persons who, spread through the country, use their leisure and pecuniary means in an honourable and delightful manner, by the promotion of astronomical science.

We have referred to the great value of the Observatory to the class of men for whom it was especially erected; but we must not forget that it is now becoming still more valuable to them, by making itself apparently less so. It has been found that clocks or watches of great excellence will enable the mariner to determine the exact London (or Greenwich) time without any further aid. The Royal Observatory, therefore, is doing its best to give him such instruments, by receiving on trial chronometers of every kind of construction, to see which is the most accurate. As many as sixty of these have been undergoing the severe ordeal of the Observatory at once. That was during the period when prizes were given for the best; a system no longer in existence. But by such trials, which are still continued, the chronometer has been raised to an extraordinary pitch of excellence.

We may conclude these notices with a somewhat amusing and certainly very striking evidence of the practical disfavour that was shown by society at large to those who studied science for its own sake, and for the consequences that flow from it,—but, be it observed, only to such men; as though Science did not choose to make her revelations to any but her loving and confiding disciples. When Flamsteed sent those observations on the moon to Newton, that were so full of importance to the latter, he mentioned the circumstance to Dr. Wallis, in a letter that was published. This aggrieved the great philosopher, who wrote to Flamsteed, "I do not love to be printed on every occasion; much less to be dunned and teased by foreigners about mathematical things; *or to be thought by our own people to be trifling away my time about them*, when I should be about the King's business." If the people here referred to could have been made aware that we should now think about the "King's business," in contrast with what we should now think about the "trifles," they would have been strangely perplexed and astonished; if indeed they did not summarily settle the business by a deep sigh over the coming degeneracy of human nature. It may have been in this slight circumstance that the ill-feeling originated, which was afterwards so unpleasantly apparent, between Flamsteed and Newton in their well-known quarrel. But it is always an ungracious and seldom a useful task to dwell on the weaknesses of great men; so untold by us shall be all the hard names they called each other, and the severe retorts that followed in rapid succession, from side to side.

There are probably few persons who have not noticed with surprise the apathy—as they cannot but call it—of persons resident in

2368. Hall of Doctors' Common

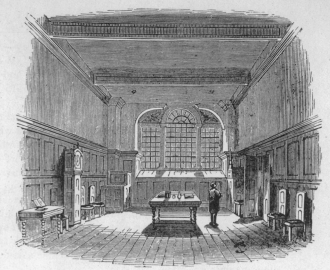

2369.—Vestry-room, formerly Court of Arches, St. Mary-le-Bow.

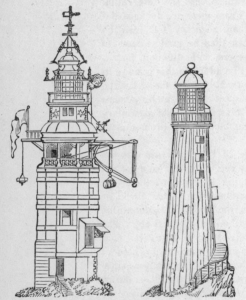

2370.—A, Winstanley's, and B Rudyerd's Lighthouses.

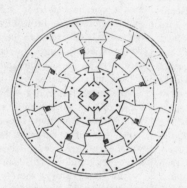

2371.—Horizontal Section of the lower and solid part of the Eddystone Lighthouse; showing the mode in which the courses of stone are dovetailed together.

2372.—Eddystone Lighthouse in a Storm.

2374.—North Foreland Lighthouse, 1834.

2373.—East side of the Eddystone Lighthouse.

2277.—St. Alban's Head, Dorsetshire.

2278.—The Thames at Wallingford.

2275.—Sheerness Dockyard, and First-rate Man-of-War lying off the Pier

2276.—Lynn, as it appeared at the commencement of the Eighteenth Century

remarkable scenes or places to the objects that have brought them, and are constantly bringing others as pilgrims, to gaze on the wonders they have so long heard of—and so long yearned to see. Take London for instance. How delightful it is to watch the pleasure that young intelligent spirits feel and exhibit on their first entrance into that mightiest of human lives. To persons familiar with all the things that excite astonishment and admiration in the minds of visitors, there are no " lions " half so attractive as those who come to look at the "lions." It is too often forgotten by persons who are surprised to see us calm amidst the sights and wonders that make them enthusiastic, that the impulse of novelty that moved them is lacking with us; and when novelty dies away, there survives only the love and admiration that has been called forth by truly worthy objects. Such sentiments, under ordinary circumstances, delight not in display, but are the most true when most serene and unobtrusive.

How many are there in London who, for aught they talk about Westminster Abbey or St. Paul's, might never have entered their doors, and yet in whose hearts rests for ever a deep sense of their solemn and impressive beauty and grandeur, mingling with and elevating their thoughts in many an hour of solitary communion, or even influencing them unconsciously into a sympathy with higher things, when business and the cares of the world are most actively pressing upon them !

Yet since the mere reflection in another's feelings of what we have ourselves once felt, is so agreeable to us, one cannot but sometimes wish we knew less of the things about us, in order that we might begin again to know more, or at least seem for the moment to do so, in the momentary activity of thought and enjoyment thus produced. And what is Antiquarianism, in a popular sense, but a kind of possible substitute for this impossible desire? What is it that gives Antiquarianism its greatest charm, when it is permitted by its nurses to have any charms, but that it enables us, when wearied of the sights of the present, to run back and enjoy the sights of the past? And as Time is ever bringing fresh changes, so is he therefore ever heaping up fresh materials for this kind of recreation. The great features of London, for example, may remain on the whole much the same now that they were a century or so ago ; yet on looking back to the metropolis at the earlier period, we find differences sufficiently extensive and numerous to interest us. Many of these differences we have already taken opportunities to point out ; and others may be here thrown together into a collective form. We will suppose ourselves to be following the steps of a visitor to the metropolis during the last century, after he has been the formal round regularly pointed out to him and to his class, and when he is beginning a more independent career—starting hither and thither just as the whim of the moment or his book-knowledge of metropolitan localities may suggest. Westminster Bridge was then building. Of course he went to see it, if it were only because he had heard the scheme so much laughed at, and seen how manfully its supporters had fought their way through parliament. Crowds were congregated around the workmen, and many of them had an expression in their countenances that showed there would be mischief, did not the " I would," wait upon the " I dare not." Some talked of the ferries that it would destroy, and the distress it would bring upon the watermen and their fellows. Others prophesied the destruction of the very navigation of the Thames, and of hosts of lives of the men who were engaged on the river. One orator hoped the bridge itself would be the first to experience the terrible resentment of Father Thames : and another significantly added—amid a general expression of sympathy and approval— " Wait till you see it built." It was evident, after all, that the thing was looked on as impossible. Presently the visitors heard exclamations—" There he is—that's the Swiss "—and Labelye, the architect, was seen bustling about, now encouraging the artisans by his cheerful countenance and assured tones, that ill agreed, however, with his doubting and aching heart—and now explaining with great deference. except when for the moment he forgot himself in his earnestness, to the pompous-looking " Commissioner " by his side, how he would remedy that difficulty that had been experienced. how he would obviate this objection that had just been put forward. His doubt, however, is not as to his powers, but as to the means that will be afforded to him to evidence his powers. He works in the constant dread of being stopped in his labours by the incredulity and illiberality that prevail with regard to them, even in quarters where he might have least expected to find such obstacles. But he goes on—and triumphs. The bridge was completed (Fig. 2345). And our visitor might have seen one near the bridge, who, we might say, judged correctly of the success that would attend Labelye's efforts, or he would otherwise have hardly thought it

advisable to bind up with it a work of his own. The Venetian artist Canaletto was there, making a drawing of the scene (Fig. 2351), that will live even when in the progress of engineering skill and public taste, the bridge of Labelye shall be replaced by an improved structure.

The visitor then pursued his way to the Fleet Ditch, which Pope had immortalized to him and all readers, and was presently quite satisfied as to the justice of the character given to the

King of dykes! than whom no sluice of mud
With deeper sable blots the silver flood—

of the Thames, into which the sluice opened (Fig. 2358), at the spot where Blackfriars Bridge has been since erected. And the visitor would smile as he remembered the invitation which the goddess of the poem—(the 'Dunciad')—gives to her favoured heroes—

Here strip, my children; here at once leap in,
And prove who best can dash through thick and thin.

Ascending the hill, the visitor began to look for the College of Physicians. He had no need to ask the way. He knew—Garth had told him long before in his ' Dispensary '—that it stood

Not far from that most celebrated place
Where angry justice shows her awful face ;
Where little villains must submit to fate,
That great ones may enjoy the world in state ;

or, in more prosaic language, Newgate. He also knew by what signs and tokens he might recognise the building when he was within sight of it. He knew that it had

A dome, majestic to the sight,
And sumptuous arches bear its awful height ;
A golden globe, placed high with artful skill,
Seems to the distant sight a gilded pill.

And thus aided he soon finds the College of Physicians ; the old college, as we now call it, but which then stood too high in reputation for any one to anticipate the time when it should become necessary to have a new one. And those who may now go through the professionally deserted place, and see in what really excellent preservation the whole yet is, even to the admirable wood carvings, will learn that the necessity for change has been of that kind merely which sprung from the desire to be in a more agreeable atmosphere than that of the butchers, and to possess a more splendid building, according to the present tastes, than even a Wren could give the wealthy and dignified licentiates and fellows of medicine. And certainly it is a strong contrast—that of the College of Physicians at the corner of Pall Mall, and that of the College of Physicians in Warwick-lane (Fig. 2357). If after visiting these we go to the house in Knight Rider-street, where the college was first founded, we have a very fair visible representation in the three buildings of the history of the rise of the professors of the healing art in this country during the last three centuries and a quarter. That house in Knight Rider-street was the residence of the most eminent of our early physicians, Linacre ; and he it was who founded the college, and allowed the members the use of his own house for their meetings during his lifetime, and subsequently gave it to them in perpetuity. As curious illustrations of the state of the profession, and of a portion of the professors, we may here mention that there was a time when the College of Physicians made astrology one of the subjects in which it examined ; and a time, still nearer to our own, when surgeons were impressed in shoals like so many seamen : warrants of impressment are still to be found among the records of the Barber-Surgeons' Company. But indeed it was only a century ago that the legislature recognised any particular difference between the excision of a man's leg and of his beard, by incorporating the surgeons into a separate college. These met first in Monkwell Street, and then built themselves a handsome pile in the Old Bailey, next to Newgate, in order, we suppose, that their theatre (Fig. 2363) might be adjacent to the horrid instrument that then alone, legally speaking, supplied them with subjects for dissection. We have somewhere met with a strange story of this building, said to have been told by John Hunter, in one of his lectures. When the operators were about to dissect the body of a criminal who had only been recently cut down, they discovered to their astonishment and horror that he was alive. They might have wished to spare the unhappy wretch from a double punishment, and yet have felt that their duty was imperative not to conceal the circumstance. They sent to the sheriffs, who took the man back to Newgate, from whence he was allowed by the King to depart for a foreign country.

As visits to London were not quite so common in the last century as now, when a person did come he had generally a variety of commissions to execute for friends in addition to his own business.

Our visitor has promised to inquire concerning a will at Doctors' Commons, so he bends his way thither, surprised to find what an unambitious-looking place it is—this great national will depository of which he had heard so much; this place of purgatory for the unhappy wedded, from whence the unfaithful depart to the Tartarus of public infamy, and their released partners to the Elysium—if they so please, and so estimate the state—of a new marriage. And the visitor here is deeply interested in all the departments of the great business of Doctors' Commons. In the Will-office he amuses himself by watching the emotions that are exhibited in the countenance of some of the will-explorers as they discover that they have been remembered, as they could wish, by the "excellent deceased," or only after the fashion that Peter Pindar attributed to royalty—"remembered to be forgot," by the "miserable ingrate." In the hall of Doctors' Commons (Fig. 2368) he is chiefly struck by the mode in which the business is managed of the different courts that sit here, namely, the Court of Arches, the supreme ecclesiastical court of the province of Canterbury; the Prerogative Court, for the determination of all will causes; the Consistory Court of the Bishop of London; and—an odd connection—the Court of Admiralty. The counsel in any particular case, after a long series of preliminary movements, come into Court, each armed with a formidable batch of papers that include the examinations of all witnesses, taken, however, under the responsibility of the examiners as to their correctness, and then the two advocates begin the war upon each other, and in the end the judge settles the business, without ever seeing a witness or any of the parties concerned. Many, like the visitor, have perhaps wondered how the powers of Doctors' Commons originated. The answer is, that they are but the remains of the once formidable system of ecclesiastical government that pervaded every department of the State, and when ecclesiastics thought the care of the temporal wealth of the community quite a much their business as the care of its spiritual aspirations. It sounds hardly credible at the present day, when we are told that testamentary causes came under the ecclesiastical jurisdiction of Doctors' Commons, "at a period when the bishops and other clergy claimed the property of intestates, to be applied to pious uses, without even being required to pay their debts. In the course of time this claim had been considerably limited, and the clergy were obliged to pay the debts of the intestate out of his property before any of it could be applied to pious uses. Subsequent restrictions had, however, required that the property of the intestate *should be given to his widow and children*; and afterwards it was enacted, that where such relations did not exist, the property should go to the next of kin, and failing these, should go to the crown." Does not this read as a fiction? Is it conceivable that there could ever have been a time when the clergy could systematically and avowedly take from the widow and children the property of the deceased husband and father? Yet the statement to this effect was made in the House of Commons; the speaker was Dr. Nicholls, an authority on such a point alike beyond suspicion of an unfavourable bias or a want of sufficient knowledge.

Our visitor of the last century next proceeded towards the centre of all English as well as of all metropolitan commerce, and which, curiously enough, has been so from the days of the Romans downwards—we refer of course to the spot upon which stand the Merchants' Exchange, the Mansion-House of Mayoralty, and the Bank, whose names have scarcely less weight in the most distant part of the world than in the neighbourhood of their own Threadneedle and Lombard Streets. The scene that met his eyes at the junction of Cornhill and Lombard Street (Fig. 2355) was very different from that we at present see. The Exchange was partly shut up among houses, instead of presenting the magnificent façade to the opening of Cheapside that now makes every one who approaches in that direction pause in admiration as he draws near to it. The Mansion House was then building, the governing officer of the city having never before had any residence especially set apart for him. It is noticeable how often we trace this kind of neglect of the outward shows of power when the power itself is most active and unquestioned; and then as that begins to decay, how much more magnificent and prosperous it begins outwardly to look. The Lord Mayor of London is no doubt in our own era a really important and most laboriously-worked dignitary; but there is also no doubt that in individual power he is but a shadow of what he was in past times, when he maintained a position equalling baronial rank, and when the government of the civic community not only meant what it does not now mean—the government of London—but was a government almost approaching to the despotic, though extended over willing and anything but enslaved subjects; when, lastly, the

first citizen was also the first merchant, first patriot, first soldier of the community, and qualified, therefore, alike to administer the extensive and somewhat intricate business of the municipality which included supervision over every trade, and over every person engaged in it; to regulate all the relations of London with foreign countries; to stand as a bulwark between grasping sovereigns and his fellows; to fight even, should fighting become necessary, either against or for that sovereign, and at the head of citizen troops, that were probably then among the very best of English soldiers.

The visitor now heard the chimes of the Exchange playing one of their favourite and popular tunes, and he hastened thither:—paused for a moment to gaze on the statue of Gresham at its entrance, and then stepped quickly in, to the scene that Addison had already made tolerably familiar to him, but with that kind of "familiarity" which breeds respect and interest, rather than "contempt."—Gresham's, or the first Exchange, we have already described [Vol. I. p. 102]. The Exchange our visitor looked upon (Fig. 2365) was the second, and built by Wren after the fire had destroyed Gresham's; and this, we need scarcely say, is the one that was recently destroyed by the same agency, and replaced by the present pile. It was therefore the second Exchange that the illustrious essayist referred to, when he said, "There is no place in the town which I so much love to frequent as the Royal Exchange;" and as the picture he describes was the same that our visitor looked upon, we cannot do better than transcribe his description:—"It gives me," he continues, "a secret satisfaction, and in some measure gratifies my vanity, as I am an Englishman, to see so rich an assembly of countrymen and foreigners consulting together upon the private business of mankind, and making this metropolis a kind of emporium for the whole earth. I must confess I look upon high Change to be a great council in which all considerable nations have their representatives. Factors in the trading world are what ambassadors are in the politic world: they negotiate affairs, conclude treaties, and maintain a good correspondence between those wealthy societies of men that are divided from one another by seas and oceans, or live on the different extremities of a continent. I have often been pleased to hear disputes adjusted between an inhabitant of Japan and an alderman of London; or to see a subject of the Great Mogul entering into a league with one of the Czar of Muscovy. I am infinitely delighted in mixing with these several ministers of commerce, as they are distinguished by their different walks and different languages. Sometimes I am jostled among a body of Armenians; sometimes I am lost in a crowd of Jews; and sometimes make one in a group of Dutchmen. I am a Dane, Swede, or Frenchman at different times; or rather, fancy myself like the old philosopher, who upon being asked what countryman he was, replied that he was a citizen of the world. This grand scene of business gives me an infinite variety of solid and substantial entertainment. As I am a great lover of mankind, my heart naturally overflows with pleasure at the sight of a prosperous and happy multitude, insomuch that at many public solemnities I cannot forbear expressing my joy with tears that have stolen down my cheeks. For this reason I am wonderfully delighted to see such a body of men thriving in their own private fortunes, and at the same time promoting the public stock." Presently the essayist illustrates the genial character of the commercial spirit in a very happy series of illustrations, borrowed from the history of English horticulture. He says, "If we consider our own country in its natural prospect, without any of the benefits and advantages of commerce, what a barren and uncomfortable spot of earth falls to our share! Natural historians tell us that no fruit grows originally among us besides hips and haws, acorns and pig-nuts, with other delicacies of the like nature; that our climate, of itself, and without the assistance of art, can make no further advance towards a plum than a sloe, and carries an apple to no greater perfection than a crab; that our melons, our peaches, our figs, our apricots, and cherries, are strangers among us, imported in different ages and naturalized in our English gardens; and that they would degenerate and fall away into the trash of our own country if they were wholly neglected by the planters and left to the mercy of the sun and soil. Nor has traffic more enriched our vegetable world than it has improved the whole face of Nature among us. Our ships are laden with the harvest of every climate; our tables are stored with spices, and oils, and wines; our rooms are filled with pyramids of China, and adorned with the workmanship of Japan; our morning draught comes to us from the remotest corners of the earth; we repair our bodies by the drugs of America, and repose ourselves under Indian canopies. My friend, Sir Andrew, calls the vineyards of France our gardens; the Spice Islands our hot-beds; the Persians our silk-weavers; and

2379—Canterbury

2381.—Lincoln

2380.—Portland, from Sandsfoot Castle. (Henry VIII.)

2382.—Lincoln

2385.—Plymouth.

2386.—Reading, from Caversham Hill. From an Old Print.

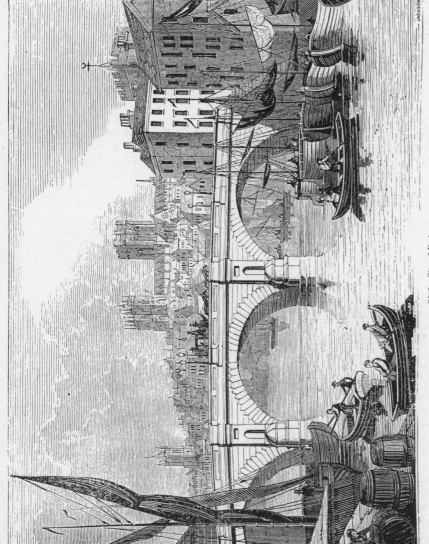

2383.—City of York.

2384.—St. Andrew's, as it appeared about 1740.

the Chinese our potters. Nature, indeed, furnishes us with the bare necessaries of life, but traffic gives us a great variety of what is useful, and at the same time supplies us with everything that is convenient and ornamental. Nor is it the least part of this our happiness, that whilst we enjoy the remotest products of the north and south, we are free from those extremities of weather which gave them birth; that our eyes are refreshed with the green fields of Britain at the same time that our palates are feasted with fruits that rise between the tropics. For these reasons there are not more useful members in a commonwealth than merchants. They knit mankind together in a mutual intercourse of good offices, distribute the gifts of nature, find work for the poor, and wealth to the rich, and magnificence to the great. Our English merchant converts the tin of his own country into gold, and exchanges his wool for rubies. The Mahometans are clothed in our British manufacture, and the inhabitants of the Frozen Zone warmed with the fleeces of our sheep." One of the most striking features of the late Exchange—Addison's Exchange, as we may call it—was the range of statues, by Cibber chiefly, that decorated the quadrangle. These suggest to the essayist the concluding passage of a paper, which is even more than ordinarily full of the wisdom and quiet eloquence that characterise the 'Spectator.' "When," he says, "I have been upon the Change, I have often fancied one of our old kings standing in person where he is represented in effigy, and looking down upon the wealthy concourse of people with which that place is every day filled. In this case how would he be surprised to hear all the languages of Europe spoken in this little spot of his former dominion, and to see so many private men, who in his time would have been the vassals of some powerful baron, negotiating like princes, for greater sums of money than were formerly to be met with in the royal treasury. Trade, without enlarging the British territories, has given us a kind of additional empire. It has multiplied the number of the rich, made our landed estates infinitely more valuable than they were formerly, and added to them an accession of other estates as valuable as the land themselves."

Such were the merchants on 'Change. Our visitor was desirous of seeing them off 'Change, and so, being himself a mercantile man, obtained an introduction, which enabled him to follow them to their warehouses or counting-houses facing the streets, and thence into the hidden retreats behind, where suddenly the visitor found himself stepping out of some dark and narrow court, into apartments most richly and picturesquely furnished. He soon found, too, that many of the very greatest merchants did not attend the Exchange at all, but were only to be met with at one or other of the famous coffee-houses—Robins's, Jonathan's, and Garraway's, in Change Alley. The last of these—Garraway's—seemed to suggest to him thoughts of a not very cheering character. He remembered Swift's lines—

Subscribers here by thousands float
And jostle one another down,
Each paddling in his leafy boat,
And here they fish for gold and drown.

Now buried in the depths below,
Now mounted up to Heaven again,
They reel and stagger to and fro
At their wits' end, like drunken men.

Meantime, secure on *Garraway* cliffs,
A savage race, by shipwrecks fed,
Lie waiting for the foundered skiffs,
And strip the bodies of the dead.

Probably also the visitor remembered how his youthful patrimony had been squandered away among this " savage race," the brokers of Change Alley, during the madness of the South Sea scheme. After a glance at the interior of the coffee-house (which, be it observed, yet remains and flourishes), he went on toward the building that had obtained so evil a reputation, the South Sea House in Threadneedle Street (Fig. 2360), which the essays of Elia have since invested with a new interest, and which was already putting on much of the aspect that Lamb so charmingly describes. The bubble had long before burst, and " the magnificent portals ever gaping wide " began to disclose to the view " a grave court, with cloisters and pillars, with few or no traces of goers-in or comers-out—a desolation something like Balclutha's " in 'Ossian.' And the visitor, as he stood in grave and thoughtful mood before it, might then have said, " This was once a house of trade, a centre of busy interests. The throng of merchants was here, the quick pulse of gain, and here some forms of business are still kept up, though the soul be long since fled." The folly of the deluded in this South Sea scheme, the stupendous knavery of the deluders, and the all-pervading mischief and misery which affected England in consequence, are but too well known

and should form an everlasting lesson to us, of the dangers that attend the attempt to make short cuts to wealth.

And as the visitor threaded his way up Cornhill, and went on pondering upon the history of the gigantic bubble, it seemed like a sudden light thrown upon the subject, when the old East India House (Fig. 2356) met his eye. Here was a token of what commerce can do when it pursues its old course, of making sure of one step before it takes another, instead of rearing—as at the South Sea House—magnificent-looking fabrics upon nothing. How soon the adventurers of the one were up to the highest pinnacle of apparent prosperity! How many years were spent by the adventurers of the other before they had even obtained an honourable position on the great East Indian continent! But yet a little longer the adventurers go on—and the first class are ruined, and not a word or look of sympathy attends their fall; while the second have become the virtual sovereigns of a region that really was what the South Sea Islands, on an infinitely smaller scale, were only thought to be.

Of course our visitor did not forget the water-works on London Bridge; nor, as he approached the venerable old pile, could he avoid being struck with its exceedingly picturesque character, a feature in a great measure owing to the battlemented gateways, and to the masses of old houses that had clustered together upon it so thickly, that they even overhung, and seemed ready to fall into, the water. Hogarth, in a part of his sixth plate of Marriage-à-la-Mode (Fig. 2350), and Pennant in his work on London, enable us to revive the scene that then met the visitor's eyes. Pennant says, " I well remember the street on London Bridge, narrow, darksome, and dangerous to passengers, from the multitude of carriages; frequent arches of strong timber crossed the street from the tops of the houses, to keep them together, and from falling into the river." Through this narrow way the visitor moved along, casting a glance as he went at—but not daring to stop to examine—the shops of the pin and needle makers, which notwithstanding their position, were so attractive, that the economical ladies from the West End would come thither to make their purchases. At last he looks down upon the famous water-works, which then occupied no less than five arches of the bridge, and had become, by successive additions and improvements, a unique and truly ingenious and powerful piece of mechanism (Fig. 2349). By this was the city chiefly supplied for a long period of time. The founder was Peter Morris, who erected the first work in 1582; they were removed by Act of Parliament in 1822.

The visitor now took boat, and returned up the Thames towards Westminster, desiring to see the Supreme Courts of Law in Westminster Hall (Fig. 2347), those landmarks of the past which still tell us in their names—Court of King's Bench, Court of Exchequer, and so on—of the time when justice was looked upon but as an emanation from royalty, government but as an instrument for filling the king's coffers; and which still remain, notwithstanding all other changes on the same spot where they first became fixed, after ceasing their ambulatory progresses through the country. A curious and unseemly custom we are apt to think this itinerating system. Yet it is possible that we have not taken the right view of it. It may have been, after all, a partial fulfilment of the very demand that has sprung up in our own day—that for, to speak figuratively, justice at every man's own door. When the monarch moved about and the court followed in his train, who can say but that it was the practice fixed by opinion (for there has been always some kind of atmosphere of opinion, even for the most despotic) that the monarch should in ordinary cases regulate these movements by some consideration of the legal necessities of his subjects? Whilst in the neighbourhood, our visitor strolled on towards St. James's Park, to see some of the other public offices, among which the business of government in modern times is distributed. First there was the Treasury (Fig. 2361), originally the Cock-Pit of Harry the Eighth's palace of Whitehall; then the Horse-Guards; then the Admiralty, as it appeared before Adam's screen was built (Fig. 2362); but there was no telegraph in those days, sticking its tall beam of timber up towards the sky, and making the passers-by wonder how long it will be before it again begins to work—or if it be working, what can be the nature of the information it conveys. So our visitor, thinking of all sorts of naval heroes, past, present, and future, who had looked or would look towards that building as their Polar star, he wandered on into Pall Mall (Fig. 2364), and was presently lost in the contemplation of the variety of persons—dresses, equipages, shops, houses, &c.—that there met his eye, and in the hosts of literary recollections, satirical and others, which the very name of Pall Mall aroused. Here it was that the shoemakers were accustomed to exhibit those delicate slippers which provoked the ire of Isaac Bickerstaff, and especially that pair " with green lace and blue heels." Here was situated the coffee-house which the same censor satirized by giving notice " to all the ingenious gentlemen in and about the cities of London and Westminster, who have a mind to be instructed in the noble sciences of music, poetry, and politics, that they repair to the Smyrna coffee-house in Pall Mall, between the hours of eight and ten at night, where they may be instructed gratis, with elaborate essays by word of mouth, on all or any of the above-mentioned arts. The disciples are to prepare their bodies with three dishes of Bohea, and purge their brains with two pinches of snuff."

But what would the frequenters of Pall Mall at the present day think of a smock-race taking place there? So late as 1733 this choice amusement drew crowds to Pall Mall. And what shop is this before which the visitor has stopped? It is Dodsley's—once a poet-footman, now an enterprising bookseller; a man who obtained in this last position the respect of all who knew him, and whose shop was the resort of the ablest and most distinguished men in London, either as writers engaged by him, or as idlers for the hour seeking to enjoy a pleasant lounge. Dodsley may be said to have been to a certain extent the patron of both Johnson and Burke, for he gave literary employment to both, when they most needed it, and thus aided materially their subsequent advancement. Wistfully does the visitor look at all who go in and out. He knows not but there may be among them the men we have named, or others of equal eminence. Nay, Dodsley is even the publisher of Pope;—but then he would know *him* well enough.

There is a class of works occasionally attempted, of such vast, and to most men's eyes insurmountable, difficulty, that when accomplished even the works themselves become less impressive than the qualities of mind that could alone achieve such successful results: their moral overshadows their physical grandeur. Such a work has been the Thames Tunnel in the present century; such a work was the Eddystone lighthouse in the last century. The rocks to which the word Eddystone has been applied (from the eddies, no doubt, the stones cause in the surrounding water) are situated in the English Channel, about fourteen miles from Plymouth. At high water they are covered, and at no time do they project very much above the surface of the sea. As might have been expected, therefore, from such rocks in such a position, many terrible accidents occurred through the ignorance of the unfortunate mariners, who frequently saw them not until they struck upon them, and went down in the very sight of the port that they felt, as it were, they had already reached. Who could build a lighthouse upon these destructive rocks? Again and again the question was agitated: and at last a Mr. Winstanley undertook the bold task. He was a kind of amateur engineer, and possessed of independent property. He had, therefore, ample leisure for making the attempt, and he possessed the tastes that would make his severest labours—labours of love. He began in 1696, and finished it in about four years. He was, no doubt, proud of his work, deeply gratified with the everlasting fame that he thought awaited him. It is said that he frequently declared that his only wish was that he might be in it during the greatest storm that ever blew under the face of the heavens. Such was the strength of the lighthouse in his opinion. He was to be terribly undeceived. If the rocks and waves were to have a master—he was not the man; and tragically poetical was the punishment for his attempt. One night during the progress of some repairs he was in the lighthouse with his workmen. A tempest of the kind he had so desired came—the next morning all was gone—engineer, workmen, lighthouse—not a vestige appeared to be left to assure the spectators that they did not dream it was there the tall building had been erected, until it was discovered that there was just one piece of iron chain that Nature herself, as if in sport and mockery of man's ambition and failure, had driven so deep into a chasm, that nothing could move it.

It was not likely that any further attempt would be made until fresh calamities should again stimulate fresh hope and enterprise to prevent their recurrence for the future. Some hapless vessel perished, with nearly the whole of the crew; and then again there were calls for the lighthouse. Parliament authorized the erection, and presently a second amateur was found bold enough to undertake the Herculean task. This was John Rudyerd, a silkmercer on Ludgate Hill. Wishing to profit by experience, he determined, as Winstanley had built the lighthouse partly of stone, he would construct his entirely of wood; Winstanley's had been angular, his should be round (see the engraving of both, Fig. 2370). He began in 1706, completed it in 1709; and this at least promised to be perfectly successful. Year after year passed on—storms beat—the waves rose wildly around and dashed over the slender structure, but it still

remained unshaken. Even the severe tempest of September 26th, 1744, left it unscathed. But at last the evil day came, when the powers of the air and water, having vainly gathered together and concentrated their utmost force in the endeavour to strike down the building of Rudyerd, as they had struck down the building of his predecessor, called to their aid another element—fire. About two in the morning of the 2nd of December, 1755, one of the three men, Henry Hall, who had the management of the pile, went up to snuff the candles in the lantern, which he perceived to be full of smoke, and when he opened the door flame burst forth. A spark, it is supposed, had in some way or other ignited the woodwork. The man, who was in his ninety-fourth year, but full of physical and mental activity, immediately shouted to his companions, who were in bed asleep, to come to his assistance, and in the mean time threw water up as well as he could upon the fire, which was burning four yards above him. There was but a tubful of water; and when his companions were at last roused, and came to his aid, they could only keep running up and down a distance of seventy feet, with as much water as they could carry. The lead of the roof now began to melt, and came down in a torrent upon the brave old man, who then, and not till then, descended with the others from room to room as the fire crept down after them, until they were at last compelled to seek the shelter of a hole on one side of the rock. There they remained until almost stupefied, and, until, probably, they had given up all hopes of escape; when they were released by boats from the shore. Some fishermen had seen the lighthouse on fire, and immediately given the alarm. The most extraordinary and painful part of this incident was the fate of the old man. He said he had swallowed some of the molten lead; and the only effect of his statement was to make people believe the fire had injured his wits rather than his stomach. Still he persisted in his view that the doctors could do him no good, unless they took the lead from him. On the twelfth day he died—was opened—and there, truly enough, was a piece of lead, weighing nearly half a pound.

And still *the* lighthouse had to be built. There must be no more timber structures. Yet who was to construct one of stone, capable of resisting the immense action of the elements about the Eddystone rocks? The Royal Society was applied to; and the President answered the application by a recommendation of Mr. Smeaton. And he accepted the undertaking; though now the opinion as to the impracticability of the work had become more general than ever.

He began on the 5th of August, 1756, and the foundations were cut before the expiration of the season. That was the engineer's opening campaign. On the 12th of June, 1757, the first stone was laid, and others rapidly followed, until by August, 1759, the entire stonework of the building was completed. Of the ingenuity that was brought to bear upon the performance of this part of the process, the view of an horizontal section, showing the dovetailing of the stones together (Fig. 2371), forms a very striking memorial. Of the patience with which the work had to be pursued, no better illustration can be desired than the statement of the fact that during the whole period of erection, extending to a little more than three years, there had been but four hundred and twenty-one days on which it was possible for the men to be on the rock; and of these days only so small a portion could be used, that the whole time really spent upon the erection of the lighthouse did not amount to sixteen weeks. Of his care for others during such dangerous operations, we need only say, in the words of Smeaton himself, that the whole was accomplished " without the loss of life or limb to any one concerned in it;" of his own courage and participation in the perils of the work we had wellnigh had too conclusive an evidence given; he was nearly lost upon one occasion when he was returning in a sloop with some of the labourers to the shore.

This lighthouse has had its trials too; but the waves and winds of Eddystone have found their master. The greatest storms have burst upon it without effect. In 1762 there was one of so furious a character, that a certain person who had been in the habit of predicting the destruction of the building, said if it stood *that* it would stand anything until the day of judgment. In the morning there was the lighthouse safe as ever—not even a pane of glass broken in the lantern. No wonder there were people who now went a little to the opposite extreme. The men of Plymouth began to talk of the inhabitants of the lighthouse being rather more secure under their building, exposed to all the violence of winds and water, than they were themselves in their houses, endangered by the former only. Our engravings (Figs. 2372, 2373) show the form of the lighthouse, and many readers will recognise in it the architect's model. It was Nature who taught him how to resist herself—she bade him mark how the oak withstood the mightiest warfare that the elements

2389.—Exeter. (From an Original Print.)

2390.—Thomas Lombe's Silk Mill, Derby.

2387.—Gloucester. (From an Old Print.)

2388.—Ranelagh Gardens, Rotunda, &c., 1751.

2391.—Bartholomew Fair, 1721. Lee and Harper's Booth
(From a Painted Fan of that date.)

2392.—Faux, the Conjuror.

2393.—Dancing-dolls. Hogarth's Southwark Fair.)

2394.—Posture-master.

2395.—Dancing-dolls.—Italian.

2396.—Vauxhall in 1751.

2397.—Rosamond's Pond, 1752.

could wage against it—she bade him study the form she had given to that tree as the best calculated for its defence: he did so, and went and copied it for his Eddystone Lighthouse.

Glancing from the Eddystone and other lighthouses (see an engraving of North Foreland lighthouse, Fig. 2374) that protect the way to the different ports of England, we may let our attention rest for a few moments upon the ports themselves. The important events of the history of Plymouth (Fig. 2385), such as its being again and again attacked by the French, its sufferings at different periods from the plague, and the two sieges it experienced during the Civil War, when the Royalists endeavoured in vain to force their way into it, all belong to an earlier time. So also does one of the great works that have made its name famous—Drake's noble achievement of bringing water from Dartmoor, by a channel twenty-four miles long, for the supply of Plymouth. But the reign of William III. witnessed the establishment of the dockyard, esteemed one of the finest in the world, and the consequent foundation of the great town of Plymouth Dock, as it was formerly, or Devonport, as it is now called. This dockyard forms one of the most interesting of all sights, on account of the gigantic scale and the perfect system of management, even in the minute details, of all the arrangements for the building, repairing, rigging, and so on, of great ships for the navy. Thus the blacksmiths' shop is a building two hundred and ten feet square, contains forty-eight forges, and consumes annually one thousand three hundred chaldrons of coal, and in front of it, piled upon the wharf, are hundreds of anchors, some of them weighing five tons. The rigging-house is four hundred and eighty feet long, three stories high, and forms one side of a quadrangle, the area of which is composed entirely of stone and iron, and called the *combustible* storehouse, though incombustible would be the more appropriate name, since it is the contents of the house alone that are inflammable, and for that reason are placed here. Then there are rope-houses one thousand two hundred feet long, where cables are manufactured of one hundred fathoms, measuring twenty-five inches round, and weighing singly above one hundred and sixteen hundredweight; also a boiling-house, mast-house, mast-pond, &c.; and everything else in and about Plymouth connected with the public service is on the same grand scale. The harbour of Hamoaze is so big that all the great men-of-war of all the states of the world could probably be comfortably accommodated in it at the same time. And this is but one of the harbours of Plymouth. Another, called the Catwater, an estuary of the river Plym, will hold a thousand vessels of ordinary size. The fortifications, partly old, partly of the last, and partly of the present century, are, as a matter of course, as strong as English engineering science can possibly make them. Lastly, there is the Breakwater, composed of vast stones thrown together till they formed an immense rampart—or dyke—nearly a mile long, which was commenced in 1812. All these great works, combined with the natural position of Plymouth as a chief place for the collection of the navies of this country, whether for the purposes of defence or offence, have raised Plymouth and the adjoining places to a high pitch of prosperity. No one can walk through their streets without perceiving what a great number of handsome houses have been erected of late years, or without admiring the liberal spirit apparent in their numerous public buildings, their churches, their splendid hotel and adjacent theatre—built by the corporation, their baths and hospital, their libraries, Athenæum, Plymouth and Mechanics Literary and Scientific Institutions; the iron bridge, a most beautiful structure, the floating steam-bridge, the railroad to Dartmoor, and so on.

Chatham (Fig. 2220) owes a considerable part of its present importance to the measures taken in the last century to strengthen the defences of the place. De Ruyter had proved their miserable inefficiency in 1667. Having taken Sheerness (Fig. 2375), he sent a part of his fleet to Chatham, and caused several ships to be burnt or sunk there, and one to be carried away. Something, it is true, was done immediately afterwards to remedy this dangerous state of affairs, but not enough. In the reign of Anne two Acts of Parliament were passed for the extension of the dockyards, arsenals, &c. But as all remembrance of the original cause of alarm died away, the matter sunk into comparative neglect till the threats of invasion by the French caused from time to time a series of active but intermitting labours to be carried on. When our continental brethren were very menacing, then, and then only, were the workmen at Chatham very busy. And so gradually the place became surrounded by almost impregnable defences. The dockyard here, too, as at Plymouth, is on a very large scale, and Chatham enjoys an especial reputation for the excellence of its machinery in all the public departments. Two or three other features of Chatham

deserve notice, namely, the school for engineers, established in 1812; the Naval Hospital, that originated in a suggestion made by William IV, when he was Duke of Clarence and the Lord High Admiral; and the establishment, consisting of four ships, for convicts, who are employed in the dockyard and arsenal. The entire list of the royal or national dockyards of England comprise Deptford, Woolwich, Chatham, Sheerness, Portsmouth, Plymouth, and Pembroke.

Beyond their general aspect in the present period, which our engravings may best show, there is little demanding attention in the views of Lynn (Fig. 2376) in Norfolk, the capital, as it might be called, of the fenny districts of England, or in those of St. Alban's Head, Dorsetshire (Fig. 2377), Portland, from Sandsfoot Castle (Fig. 2380), so famous for its quarries, and the Thames at Wallingford (Fig. 2378). And as we have already had various occasions to speak of all those cities whose glory is their cathedrals and other remains of high antiquity, we may pass over the views of Canterbury, Lincoln, York, Gloucester, and Exeter, contained in pages 316, 317, and 320, with only a momentary pause to note any especial changes that may have taken place in either of them during the eighteenth century. Canterbury, for instance, then obtained the charming walk that now so much interests every visitor to the venerable place. It was in 1790 that an alderman of the city, Mr. James Simmonds, converted a large artificial mound standing close to the old wall, and in a field called the Donjon field, into a mall for the inhabitants, by cutting serpentine paths all round it, so as to make an easy ascent to the summit. A terrace also was formed within the wall 600 yards long, and connected with the walks of the mound, and additional walks were made in the field before mentioned. The principal of these has a double row of limes on each side. The inhabitants, to their credit be it mentioned, gave the finishing touch to the work, by erecting a pillar on the top of the mound in commemoration of the patriotic founder. In York the assembly-room was erected in the same period, and is considered one of the finest buildings of the kind in England. It was erected after a design by Palladio, and by an amateur architect, the Earl of Burlington. Lastly, Exeter owes to the same period its charter, which George III. granted in 1770, and its stone bridge over the Ex, which cost 20,000l.

St. Andrew's, in Scotland, was formerly an important place, with its opulent merchants, its fair lasting for several weeks, to which hundreds of vessels resorted from all parts of the commercial world, its wide and bustling streets, its cathedral, its university. What it had become by the last century is shown in our engraving (Fig. 2384), or may be briefly summed up in the words of Dr. Johnson, who visited it in 1773. " One of its streets is now lost : and in those that remain there is the silence and solitude of inactive indigence and gloomy depopulation." Since then, however, there has been a great revival, and St. Andrew's may yet recover all its former prosperity. Its university, the most ancient in Scotland, has an income of 3000l. a year; and Mr. Bell, the founder of the Madras system of education, has given 45,000l. for the establishment of a Madras College. These establishments alone are amply sufficient, under ordinary good management on the part of those who have influence in the affairs of the town, to secure its prosperity. The antiquities of St. Andrew's are exceedingly interesting. In the parish church is a monument to Archbishop Sharpe, showing in rude sculpture his murder. The university buildings are, in parts, of handsome appearance. The cathedral is a ruin, but there are portions still standing, which may serve to show the architecture of the pile. Then there are relics of three monasteries. A fragment of the arched roof of one of them exhibits a beautiful specimen of the pointed style. The ruins of a castle, a cave, and various other features, help to swell the long list of matters that the antiquary finds so full of material for his enjoyment and study at St. Andrew's. But the most precious to him of all these relics of the past is the chapel founded, it is said, by St. Rule, or St. Regulus, and which, according to the most careful observers, must be at least a thousand years old. But as this chapel is connected with the foundation of the town, we must here briefly tell the story of the saint in question. He was, it appears, the abbot of a monastery of Patras, in Achaia, in the fourth century. At a certain time he was warned in a dream to depart without delay to an island called Albion, situated, he was told, at the very extremity of the western world. The saint was obedient and zealous. He collected together seventeen monks and three nuns, and with these, and some of the relics of St. Andrew, to guard the party from danger, set out to reach the strange and distant place to which he had been directed. While, probably, he was wondering how near he was to the spot, or by what token he would be satisfied of its correctness, he was wrecked in a bay; the shores of which were covered with wood and infested with huge and fierce wild boars. Nothing was saved but the lives of the party and the sacred relics of St. Andrew. So there could be no doubt that it was here, in this unpromising-looking place, that the saint's lot was ordained to be cast. He speedily set to work among the natives, and converted their governor, the King of the Picts, who erected a chapel in honour of the pious man. Of course St. Andrew's bay was the bay in question—the chapel the chapel of St. Regulus. Hence, too, the origin of the name of the town.

———

Commerce, like war, has its chivalry, and like that, is indebted for no inconsiderable part of its possessions to those who may be called its most distinguished knights. Let us give one striking example. There were in London at the beginning of the last century three brothers of the name of Lombe, carrying on the business of silk-throwsters. They had been previously manufacturers at Norwich. These gentlemen were deeply impressed with the disadvantage England laboured under through its being compelled to receive all its silk thread from Italy, where machinery of a very superior kind had been applied to the manufacture, with such success, that the English manufacturers were totally unable to compete with the Italian. How could the nature of this machinery be discovered? Would it be possible to send any one to Italy who might succeed in fathoming the secret? But then the hazard of so doing! We are informed in a document subsequently issued by one of the brothers, that the Italians, "by the most severe laws, preserved the mystery among themselves for a great number of years, to their inestimable advantage. As, for instance, the punishment prescribed by one of their laws for those who discover or attempt to discover anything relating to this art is *death*, with the forfeiture of all their goods, and to be afterwards painted on the outside of the prison walls, hanging to the gallows by one foot, with an inscription denoting the name and crime of the person; there to be continued for a mark of perpetual infamy." Not the less, however, was one of the brothers Lombe determined to risk this frightful punishment; and the only point of consideration was, how the attempt might be best and most safely made. The firm had an establishment at Leghorn for the purchase of raw silk sold by the Italian peasantry at the markets and fairs; and of course there were scattered about among the Italian ports and chief towns many other English mercantile houses. Now it was a custom among the English merchants engaged in this trade, to send their sons and apprentices to the houses of their agents or correspondents in Italy, in order to obtain a complete knowledge on the spot of the transactions between the two countries with which they were to be afterwards so intimately connected. The idea of the brothers was to take advantage of this custom, and send the youngest of the three to attempt the discovery of the Italian processes of silk-throwing. But the circumstance that it was necessary to send a very young man, made the danger greater—the chances of success less. But there are young men whose youth consists only in their age; such a man was John Lombe. He set out for Leghorn in 1715. One of his first movements was to go as a visitor to see the silk-works; for they were occasionally shown under very rigid limitations, such as that they could be seen only when in motion—the multiplicity and rapidity of the machinery making it impossible then to comprehend them—and the spectator was also hurried very rapidly through the place. At first young Lombe thought he could have accomplished his object in this way, by going again and again, under different disguises. One time he was a lady—another a priest. He was as generous too with his money as he could be without exciting suspicion. But it was all in vain. He could make nothing of the hurried glimpses he thus obtained; and every effort to see the machinery put in motion, or at rest, failed. He now tried another course. He began to associate with the clergy; and being a well-educated man and of liberal tastes, he succeeded in ingratiating himself with the priest who acted as confessor to the proprietor of the works. And however revolting it is to our notions of patriotism to see a man who should be of more than ordinary moral elevation playing the traitor both to his country and to his friends, there can be no doubt of the fact that this priest's assistance was obtained by Lombe. Neither do we think there can be any doubt of the means by which that assistance was won. Hardly any bribe could be too great, that enabled the young adventurer to succeed in his object. A plan was now devised and put in execution, for Lombe's admission into the works. He disguised himself as a poor youth out of employ, and went to the directors with a recommendation from the priest, praising his honesty and diligence, and remarking he had been inured to greater hardships than might be supposed from his appearance. Lombe was engaged as a boy to attend a

spinning-engine called a filatoe. He had now evidence afforded of the sufficiency of his disguise, or rather perhaps of the fulness of the confidence the directors placed in the priest who had sent him; he was accommodated with a sleeping-place in the mill. In a word, his success was as it were at once secured. But even then he had an arduous and most hazardous task to perform. After he had done his thorough day's work—the secret work of the night had to begin; and if discovered in that employment!—the young man must have felt many a cold shudder pass over him as he contemplated such a possibility. Even the few appliances he required were an additional source of danger; their discovery would have opened the eyes of the directors to what was going on. It appears there was a hole under the stairs where he slept, and there he hid his dark lantern, tinder-box, candles, and mathematical instruments. And now the work went rapidly on. Drawing after drawing was made from different parts of the machinery, and handed over to the priest, who called occasionally to inquire how the poor boy got on that he had recommended. The priest handed the drawings over to the agents of the Messrs. Lombe, who transmitted them to England piecemeal in bales of silk. And thus at last every portion of the machinery from beginning to end was accurately drawn, and the all-important secret—a secret no longer.

It would have been suspicious to have left the works until a ship was ready to place the suspected out of reach; so Lombe stayed in the mill. And this, as well as all the other circumstances we have narrated, may show how shrewd a head was placed upon these young shoulders. But the ship came, Lombe immediately went on board, and was off. And instantly—so quick did the suspicion he had anticipated arise—instantly was there an Italian brig despatched in pursuit. And the English merchant would have been more than one of the knights of commercial chivalry—he would have been a martyr to the cause—had not the English vessel been the better sailer.

It is said the priest was tortured; but a much more probable version of his fate is that suggested in the 'Gentleman's Magazine,' where it is observed that after Mr. John Lombe's return to England an Italian priest was much in his company. Of course no one in his senses would have done what the priest did, and have stayed to see what his countrymen thought of him.

And after all it does not seem certain that John Lombe was not one of the martyrs of trade. He died at the age of twenty-nine, and there is a tragical story told of his death, which is likely enough to be true. It is said the Italians, when they heard of the whole affair, sent over a female to England, commissioned to poison him. Lombe had brought with him from Italy two natives of that country, who were accustomed to the manufacture for which he had risked so much. The woman obtained the ear of one of these, and succeeded through his means in administering a deadly poison.

Sir Thomas Lombe, the head of the house, having thus obtained the long-desiderated secret, built his famous silk-mill at Derby (Fig. 2390). And though since that time many others have been erected in the neighbourhood, which as a matter of course surpass it in every respect, yet there is none of them that can give a stranger a tithe of the pleasure that he feels on witnessing the first mill of the kind established in England, and under such extraordinary circumstances.

———

Our streets now-a-days are growing very dull in contrast with what they were one, two, or three centuries ago. There are more elegant shops now, more articles calculated to tempt the curiosity or the pocket, within their windows; but where are the picturesque signs, the animated cries of the tradesmen at the doors—the witty or humorous gibes bandied between apprentice and apprentice, making the old street resound again as with so many intellectual crackers? where are the fops who dare now to court public admiration, like the fops of a former day, by the most fantastic extravagance? where are the shouts of "Clubs! Clubs!" by day—or the " A Sweat! A Sweat!" of the Mohocks by night? where, above all, are the smock-races of Pall Mall, the foot-ball contentions of the Strand, and a variety of other popular sports—where the tight-rope stages—the puppet-shows that enabled the genius of a Powell to blaze out so gloriously before the world—where are the dancing-bears, where the medical mountebanks? Alas! Punch alone seems to support successfully his claim to a vested interest in our public thoroughfares: Punch alone seems to be truly immortal. But let us at least trace with emotions befitting the occasion the more leading features of the rise and fall of the history of street sports and recreations during the last and previous century.

And how is it we have no learned horses now? What has become of the art of equine education, that the subjects of Elizabeth

2398.—Folly House, Blackwall. (From an Old Print.)

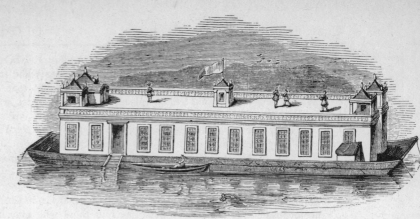

2399.—Floating Coffee-house on the Thames.

2400.—Foot-ball in the Strand.

2401.—Stratford Jubilee.

2402.—White Conduit House, 1749; the Conduit in front.

2403.—Game of Shinty.

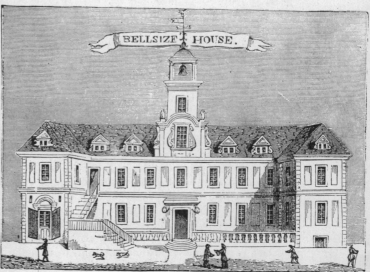

2404.—Bellsize House.

2405.—A Fleet Marriage Party. (From a Print of the time.)

2406.—Examination of the Warden of the Fleet. (From Hogarth's Picture.)

2407.—Jonathan Wild.

2408.—Gang of Prisoners being conveyed to Trial. (From an original Drawing.)

2409.—Sir John Fielding.

2410.—Portrait of Hogarth, painted by himself.

alone could witness such exhibitions as that of Bankes's horse (Fig. 1803, page 326)? Let no one be placing this illustrious animal on a level with the learned pig, or any other of the brute literati. Raleigh himself did not disdain to notice the horse in his 'History of the World.' And of course it was an event, the advent of such a creature. Raleigh's words are in connection with the master : " If Bankes had lived in olden times, he would have shamed all the enchanters in the world : for whosoever was most famous among them could never master or instruct any beast as he did " his famous horse Morocco, for so was he called. Then again a bishop—even a sedate bishop—(Hall)—condescends to speak in his satires of

Strange Morreco's dumb arithmetic.

And yet a greater than either has also helped to immortalise him. When we read in 'Love's Labour Lost,' that " The dancing horse will tell you," it is to Bankes's horse that Armado is referred for information. And what was it the horse did to excite such admiration? Sir Kenelm Digby tells us, he " would restore a glove to the due owner after the master had whispered the man's name in his ear ; and would tell the just number of pence in any piece of silver coin newly showed him by his master." But these were among his ordinary feats. One of his extraordinary ones seems to have been the telling the Sieur de Melleray, in Paris, not only the number of francs in a crown, but in so doing making regular commercial allowance for the depreciation of the coin at that exact time. In short, such were the horse's performances, that in France he and his master had a narrow escape from being taken up and burnt as wizards. Bishop Morton speaks of the story as told to him by Bankes himself, " from his own experience in France among the Capuchins, by whom he was brought into suspicion of magic, because of the strange feats which his horse Morocco played (as I take it) at Orleans, where he, to redeem his credit, promised to manifest to the world that his horse was nothing less [or, as we might say, anything rather] than a devil. To this end he commanded his horse to seek out one in the press of the people who had a crucifix in his hat : which done, he bade him kneel down unto it ; and not this only, but also to rise up again and to kiss it." ' And now, gentlemen,' quoth he, ' I think my horse hath acquitted both me and himself ;' and so his adversaries rested satisfied : conceiving (as it might seem) that the devil hath no power to come near the cross." And yet, unhappily, there does seem reason to fear that superstition found at a later time the victims that escaped her now. Jonson says—

Among these Tiberts [cats] who do you think there was ?
Old Bankes the juggler, our Pythagoras'
Grave tutor and the learned horse ; both which
Being, beyond sea, burned for one witch,
Their spirits transmigrated to a cat.

Whether these lines are to be taken as recording a truth or no, it is impossible to say. The fate of the pair rests in obscurity. And this public recreation may be taken as an example of a class that especially delighted our ancestors (another bishop, Burnet, speaks of his seeing an elephant play at ball), and who, consequently, rewarded their prompters so liberally as to encourage them to develop their skill to the utmost ; for of course it is hardly necessary to say, that in all such cases the real wonder is the ingenuity and patience of the human teacher, rather than the capacity of the brute performer ; though even that is worthy of more attention than it has received. The ordinary theories of instinct seem to us quite inadequate to explain the multiplied and varying and individual manifestations of animal sagacity that have been recorded. The Raree-showman, given in an earlier page (Fig. 206), stood between this class and the class of those who had no other share in the wonders they exhibited than the business and profits of exhibition. He had such natural monstrosities as Jonson speaks of in the 'Alchemist,'—a strange calf with five legs—a huge lobster with six claws—tame hedgehogs and wonderful snakes ; but he had also

The fleas that run attilt
Upon a table—

and which must have acquired no ordinary amount of tuition before they mastered the accomplishment. This part of the raree-showman's exhibition has been revived in our own days with eclat, under the title of the " Industrious Fleas."

We *have* seen the Dancing-dolls (Fig. 2395), but that is all we can say ; for rarer and rarer becomes their presence in our streets. And they are under the guidance of Italians. The Englishmen have given them up. (Fig. 2393.) Was it thought society was growing too old for them? If so, perhaps *Young*

England may give us back the dancing-dolls among the other revivals it promises us.

Posturising was a favourite exhibition ; and the art had its great man, about the period of the Revolution, in Joseph Clark (Fig. 2394). No motion, however unnatural or preposterous, was impossible to him. He could be a cripple, a hunchback, a big man, a little man—and, in short, set at nought all the laws of anatomy in so complete a manner, that he deceived one of the most celebrated surgeons of the day, who dismissed him as an incurable cripple. Scientific men were so interested in Joseph Clark, that a record of the case found its way into the ' Philosophical Transactions.' It is there stated that " Clark had such an absolute command of all his muscles and joints, that he could disjoint almost his whole body."

Street fairs, too, are passing away ; and if only those who are anxious for their overthrow will take care not to be misunderstood, and show, by the institution of other and better-managed holidays, that they are not at all desirous to lessen the amount of the people's enjoyment, already much too small, no one need regret the circumstance. Streets are no places for them. Contrast an old Bartholomew fair-day with the fair in Hyde Park at the time of the Queen's coronation! Why, the two seem as though they ought not to be classed under the same appellation. A child—nay, the most nervous and delicate invalid—might have gone in perfect safety, and with much enjoyment, if only to see how others enjoyed themselves, through the countless thousands of the one ; whilst in the other, any man of intelligence who might once pass through it, would hardly know which most to wonder at—the danger and difficulty of getting at the recreations offered, or the pitiful and degrading character of those recreations when reached. Nearly all that was really full of interest in the fairs of a former day has disappeared, or has dwindled into exhibitions calculated to beget disgust rather than interest at their barefaced—unintellectual—and in every way vagabond character. This degradation is, however, of long date. If in some respects the Bartholomew Fair of the last century was better, there were many also in which it was worse ; and without entering into particulars, it will be sufficient to point to the proclamation issued by the lord mayor in 1702, for the suppression of the " great profaneness, vice, and debauchery too frequently practised there." Our engravings of Lee and Harper's booth (Fig. 2391), and of Vaux the conjuror's (Fig. 2392), are copied from painted fans of the time. The conjuror of late years seems to have lost his popularity at fairs—partly, perhaps, because the more practised *artistes* have withdrawn from them. In their systems each must be the only sun.

The foot-ball playing in the Strand (Fig. 2400), to which we incidentally referred, is spoken of by various authors. Stubbs refers to it as a " bloody and murthering practice, rather than a fellowly sport or pastime," and those who have seen the game played in the present century, as we have seen it in the fields around Exeter, must acknowledge that it is painful work for the shins, and that the players do not trouble themselves about the consequences of their kicks, when they grow thoroughly excited in the sport. There was a work published some years ago by a French author, M. Souvestre, on Brittany, in which there occurs a most glowing description of the same game (there called the *soule*), as played in that province. We extract a passage that forms a complete illustration of the strong terms used by the Puritan recorder in connection with the English game :—" The ball or *soule* is at first carried on only by the weakest players : the strong keep aloof. They look on with crossed arms, throwing out to the combatants encouragement or hisses, but they take no part in the mêlée, save by from time to time leaning with the strength of their hands upon some knot of players, so as to drive them ten paces off, to roll in the dust over and over the others. But, little by little, these preludes excite them, and whip their blood up. The *soule*, taken and retaken, is already far from the place where it was launched. The outskirts of the township are near : all feel the time is come to interfere. The most impatient lets himself go : the first blow is given ; and then a cry is raised : all join the fight, and push and strike : nothing more is heard but complaints, curses, threats—the rude and dull sound of fists punishing flesh. Blood soon flows, and at its sight a sort of frenzied intoxication possesses the *souleurs*. The spirit of a herd of wild deer seems to awaken in the hearts of the men. . . They are mingled confusedly—they press on each other ; they writhe one above the other : in an instant the players form only one single body, above which may be seen arms rising and falling incessantly, like the hammers of a paper-mill. At a great distance, faces—pale or bronzed—show themselves—disappear—then rise again, bloody, *marbled* with blows. In proportion as this strange mass struggles and heaves, it is seen to melt and to diminish, because the weaker get struck down, and the contest continues over their bodies; generally the last two combatants on the two sides meet face to face, half dead with fatigue and pain. It is then that he who has yet some strength escapes with the *soule*. Feebly pursued by his exhausted rival, he soon reaches the neighbouring *commune*, and thus obtains the prize so fiercely disputed." (Translation in 'Westminster Review,' Aug. 1838.)

D'Avenant's Frenchman [Entertainment at Rutland House] thus pleasantly satirizes the English custom of choosing such unfavourable localities for the game. " I would now make a safe retreat, but that methinks I am stopped by one of your heroic games, called football; which I conceive (under your favour) not very conveniently civil in the streets; especially in such irregular and narrow roads as Crooked Lane. Yet it argues your courage, much like your military pastime of throwing at cocks. But your mettle would be more magnified (since you have long allowed these two valiant exercises in the streets) to draw your archers from Finsbury, and during high markets let them shoot at butts in Cheapside." Still the game went on. In the early part of the last century, Gay, in his 'Trivia, or the Art of Walking the Streets,' says—

> The 'prentice quits his shop to join the crew;
> Increasing crowds the flying game pursue.

In shinty (Fig. 2403), which is so favourite a sport in the Highlands of Scotland, the ball is struck by a stick, and the object with each party is to drive it beyond certain opposed boundaries. This game is essentially the same as that formerly known as hurling in England. Golf was also once popular in this country. Nay, the very best golf-player upon record is said to be no other than King James II.; surely the last man one would expect to see engaging, much less excelling, in this or any other genial sport. Yet, as we have before had occasion to observe, he was an excellent player at Mall, one of the first skaters in point of time in this country, whilst as to his golf-playing, Kohl says he had but one rival, an Edinburgh shoemaker of the name of Paterson. When the traveller just named was in Scotland he met with a most enthusiastic golfer, who explained the sport and all its adjuncts to him in the most amusing manner. We learn from this that the leather of the ball must be first of all soaked in boiling water, and the interior stuffed with feathers by means of an ingenious little machine. Then it must be painted several coats thick with white-lead to distinguish it from the green and other colours of the field, and to give it the requisite hardness. The head or knob of the club or kolbe must have the right bend, and be neither too heavy nor too light—must be at once strong and elastic, and be filled with lead, and strengthened by a plate of iron on the side that strikes the ball. The wood of the handle must be very carefully chosen, and where the hand grasps it, bound with silk, in order to ensure a better hold. But to do all this requires skill and experience; or, as the describer observed to Kohl—" Gracious powers! to make the thing properly is the immense difficulty!"

The parks of London were, of course, in the last century as in the present, the most frequented of all the public walks: and we find continual reference to them in the writings of the day. Swift, we find, was regularly walking in St. James's Park, except when the Mohocks were more than usually threatening. In one passage, under the date of January, 1711, he writes, " Delicate walking weather, and the canal and Rosamond's Pond full of the rabble, sliding, and with skaits, if you know what that is." The Rosamond's Pond, here referred to (Fig. 2397) as a favourite resort of skaiters, was also but too well known through its tragical associations. Beneath the print in the Pennant Collection, we read, " The south-west corner of St. James's Park was enriched with this romantic scene. The irregularity of the trees, the rise of the ground, and the venerable Abbey, afforded great entertainment to the contemplative eye. This spot was often the receptacle of many unhappy persons, who in the stillness of an evening plunged themselves into eternity."

We have not hitherto noticed one appendage of the dress of the day, the bag-wig, which has such an irresistibly ludicrous effect in the works of the satirical painters and caricaturists of the last century. So we may here give an amusing story from a publication of the period, illustrative of the very general use of this article of costume. We read in the volume of the 'Annual Register' for 1761—" June 24. Last Sunday some young gentlemen belonging to a merchant's counting-house, who were a little disgusted at the too frequent use of the bag-wig made by apprentices [and others, down] to the meanest mechanics, took the following method to burlesque that

elegant piece of French furniture. Having a porter just come out of the country, they dressed him in a bag-wig, laced ruffles, and Frenchified him up in the new mode, telling him that if he intended to make his fortune in town, he must dress himself like a gentleman on Sunday, go into the Mall in St. James's Park, and mix with people of the first rank. They went with him to the scene of action, and drove him in among his betters, where he behaved as he was directed, in a manner the most likely to render him conspicuous. All the company saw by the turning of his toes that the dancing-master had not done his duty; and by the swing of his arms, and his continually looking at his laced ruffles and silk stockings, they had reason to suppose it was the first time he had appeared in such a dress. The company gathered round him, which he at first took for applause, and held up his head a little higher than ordinary; but at last some gentlemen joining in conversation with him, by his dialect detected him, and laughed him out of company. Several, however, seemed dissatisfied at the scoffs he received from a parcel of 'prentice boys monkeyfied in the same manner, who appeared like so many little curs round a mastiff, and snapped as he went along, without being sensible at the same time of their own weakness."

The most noted public places of entertainment during the eighteenth century (after Ranelagh and Vauxhall, already noticed) appear to have been Bellsize House, in the Hampstead Road (Fig. 2404), the Floating Coffee-House on the Thames (Fig. 2399), the Folly House, Blackwall (Fig. 2398), and the White Conduit House (Fig. 2402). We need only describe the first. Bellsize consisted of an ancient and stately manor-house, with a large park and handsome gardens, and commanding, as those who may now be familiar with the spot well know, a charming prospect. In 1720 the opening advertisement explained to the public the nature of the entertainment proposed to be given there, " the park, wilderness, and gardens " in the meantime having been " wonderfully improved, and filled with variety of birds which compose a most melodious and delightsome harmony. Every morning at *seven o'clock* the music begins to play, and continues the whole day through; and any person inclined to walk and divert themselves in the morning, may as cheaply breakfast there, on tea or coffee, as in their own chambers." Coaches were to ply between Hampstead and Bellsize to fetch visitors at sixpence each; and lastly, there is an announcement, which, however calculated to encourage hesitating visitors then to come to the place, would have a very different effect now. Imagine the proprietors of Vauxhall, for instance, putting at the bottom of their bills—" For the security of the guests there are twelve stout fellows completely armed, to patrol betwixt London and Vauxhall, to prevent the insults of highwaymen and footpads which may infest the roads." Yet such, with the mere alteration of the word Vauxhall for Bellsize, was the conclusion of the first advertisement issued from this place of entertainment.

There was something fresh, pleasant, and poetical about the idea of these early morning recreations; and, whether on that account or other less innocent causes, Bellsize became so fashionable that on one occasion the Prince and Princess of Wales dined there. But rapidly the place degenerated. The twelve armed men swelled up to thirty—the breakfasts, and huntings, and fishings became less attractive than the deep play and the illicit love intrigues that were carried on under cover of the dance or the concert, or the quiet walk in the extensive and secluded grounds.

There was one class of the community—parents—who must have had a great horror and dread of Bellsize, and all such places, on account of the fatal facility that existed for every sharper or adventurer, whether male or female, to inveigle some young, wealthy, and credulous partner into a Fleet marriage. What that was is worth showing. No feature of London in the last century was more noticeable, few more important for evil. A person could not then pass frequently along Fleet Street or Ludgate Hill without having such occasional interrogatories put to him as—" Would you like to be married, sir?" If he looked in a window in the same neighbourhood it was most probable he saw a card, or a large board, with the announcement, " Weddings performed here!" Even the newspapers spread far and wide the tempting invitation in the shape of advertisements, one of which is here transcribed verbatim :— " Marriages, with a licence, certificate, and a crown stamp, at a guinea, at the new chapel, next door to the china-shop near Fleet Bridge, London, by a regular-bred clergyman, and not by a Fleet parson, as is insinuated in the public papers; and that the town may be freed [from] mistakes, no clergyman, being a prisoner in the Rules of the Fleet, dare marry; and to obviate all doubts, this chapel is not in the verge of the Fleet, but kept by a gentleman who was lately chaplain on board one of His Majesty's men-of-war,

2414.—The Politician.

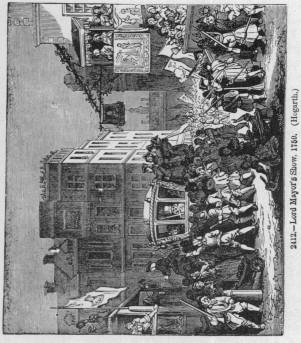

2412.—Lord Mayor's Show, 1750. (Hogarth.)

2411.—Boy. (From Hogarth's 'Noon.')

2413.—Temple Bar. (Hogarth.)

2421.—From Hogarth's 'Progress of Cruelty.'

2415—2420.—Swift, from a Picture in the Bodleian Library.—Locke, from a Picture by Sir Godfrey Kneller.—Hogarth, from a Picture by himself.—Newton, from a Picture by Vanderbank.—Addison, from an anonymous Picture.—Pope, from a Picture by Hudson.

2422.—Seal of the Royal Society.

2423.—Woolsthorpe Manor-house, Sir Isaac Newton's birthplace.

2424.—Sir Isaac Newton's House.

2425.—Prynne.

2426.—Davenant.

2427.—Observatory at Greenwich.

and likewise has gloriously distinguished himself in defence of his king and country, and is above committing those little mean actions that some men impose on people, being determined to have everything conducted with the utmost decency and regularity, such as shall all be supported in law and equity." But the most amusing feature of the place was to see the contention that was aroused if a carriage appeared with a couple bound for the Fleet. Up they rushed, clustering, struggling on each side of the window—one shouting, "Madam, you want a parson? I am the clerk and registrar of the Fleet!" Another, "Madam, come with me; that fellow will carry you to a little peddling alehouse!" And yet a third, "Go with me; he will carry you to a brandy-shop!" So one is speedily chosen, if only to get rid of the rest, and the pair descend, with the bridesmaid following quick after, as soon as she has released her immense hoop from the temporary restrictions it has experienced. The clergyman—a pretty fellow, we may be sure —advances to meet them, all smiles: he expects to be well paid from the appearance of the pair. Such is the nature of the scene presented in an interesting print of the time, copied in our engraving (Fig. 2405). And how is the ceremony performed within? Let us step in and see. As the party ascend the prison stairs and pass along the gallery, they receive various invitations to stop—a coal-heaver is especially pressing: "This," says he, "is the famous Lord Mayor's chapel; you will get married cheaper here than in any other part of the Fleet." The chaplain who has got the job looks daggers at him, but receives a horse-laugh in reply. And, by-the-by, the pair are fortunate,—their worthy conductor is sober to-day. They enter his rooms. There is a hint about brandy and wine, which the excellent priest deals in as well as wedlock; and both are called for. And the ceremony now proceeds, and is performed on the whole decently enough. It is the last bit of professional dignity or pride left in the functionary's heart—the going solemnly through the service: he is even indignant when jokes are played upon him, and tries hard to obtain credit for his rigid sense of the proprieties. All that sort of thing of course ceases with the conclusion of the ceremony; and woe betide the bridegroom if he has not made up his mind to pay handsomely, even according to the Fleet standard, otherwise he will not soon forget the Fleet parson's lesson in Billingsgate.

This is but a literal description of what was taking place daily and hourly in the Fleet prison or precincts. And most calamitous frequently must have been the results of the unions thus formed. There is an entry in one of the registers full of significance:— "William —— and Sarah ——: he dressed in a gold waistcoat, like an officer; she a beautiful young lady with two fine diamond rings, and a black high-crown hat, and very well dressed—at Boyce's. N.B.—There was four or five young Irish fellows, seemed to me, *after* the marriage was over [we beg the reader to mark the rascal's cunning], to have deluded the young woman." False names, half names, or even no names at all, would do with these most liberal gentry; and if all that was not sufficient, they would get up a "sham" certificate of marriage without any marriage taking place. A marriage of to-day could be dated back for a twelvemonth or two; if bride or bridegroom could not conveniently come, there was one ready to act proxy; women who were in debt might come here, be married to a husband regularly attached to the place for the purpose, and as soon as married part to meet no more—he quite content for a handsome gratuity to be liable to all her debts; she able to laugh at her old creditors, and take in new ones. Lastly, if money was short, you might go "upon tick," as the 'Register' has it; but then, we presume, the security was unexceptionable.

A roaring trade was thus obtained. As far as mere income was concerned, it was almost as good for a clergyman to be put into the Fleet for debt, and become popular there, as to achieve some of the highest dignities of the church. Wyatt was one of these popular Fleet parsons; he received, as we learn from his own memorandum book, 57l. 12s. 9d. (money of the last century, be it observed) for a single month's marriages. William Dare's average complement was some one hundred and fifty or two hundred couple a month: he had a curate to assist him. The most notorious of them all was Keith, "who had constructed a very bishopric for revenue in May Fair, by performing that charitable function for a trifling sum which the poor successors of the apostles are seldom humble enough to perform out of duty."—(Walpole.) But the glory of the Fleet marriage system was to depart from it at the inexorable fiat of King, Lords, and Commons. A new Marriage Bill was brought forward in 1753, making the publication of banns indispensable, and was passed, though in the face probably of the most determined opposition that a successful bill ever met with. Most ludicrous were the reasons alleged against it. A naval captain remarked

that he had once given forty of his crew leave to go on shore, and the whole returned married: of course, therefore, he was aghast at the idea of a bill that would stop all such proceedings for the future. The last marriages in the Fleet were fixed to take place on the 24th of March, and the utmost use was made of the time afforded. In one day Keith married one hundred and seventy-three pairs; and in the last—the terrible 24th—we have records of above three hundred marriages having taken place, and even that number may not have included the whole.

These Fleet marriages speak trumpet-tongued of the state of the Fleet prison; of course they were only possible through the connivance of the authorities. Yet it should seem that the marriages only took the place of still more detestable abuses: when cruelty and cupidity were stopped in one way, the cupidity, at all events, found vent in another. It was but a few years before the Fleet marriage system was in the very height of prosperity that a memorable inquiry was carried on, which has been ever since referred to as one of the earliest and most important of the series of movements made by philanthropists for the amelioration of prison discipline. There had been for half a century a sort of general consciousness in the minds of the people that all was not as it should be at the Fleet. Prisoners had petitioned—inquiries had been made, followed by some slight attempts to redress the evils that were most apparent. But it was not till 1727 that anything really important was done. A parliamentary commission of working and determined men then began to inquire into the state of the Fleet, and some pretty discoveries they made. From beginning to end the whole management of the prison, first under Mr. Huggins, and then under Mr. Bambridge—such were the wardens' names— was one gigantic system of extortion from all who had anything to be extorted—and of cruelty to those who had not. A prisoner of ordinary respectability, for instance, was not carried direct to the prison but to one of Bambridge's sponging-houses, where the hourly expenses might almost be counted in guineas. Yet to get away from this place, and into the prison, was not to be thought of without a fee proportionate to the advantages relinquished. So the fee was paid, and the prisoner inducted into the Fleet, where a new series of demands awaited him. In short, the expenses in the case of a gentleman who had four detainers lodged against him were estimated at 45l. 1s. 0d., for nothing more than the right of quiet residence and the liberty of the rules in the place where his creditors had sent him. But even that sum, after a time, was thought insufficient, and fresh payments required. Some would resist them, who had never resisted before, as seeing the hopelessness of satisfying such harpies. The gentleman just referred to, an architect, did so. And what were the consequences? He was arrested whilst enjoying what he had purchased—the right of moving about in the precincts— thrown into the sponging-house as before, and had actually to repeat the former processes, of paying to get away from it, and then paying to get again into the prison. It is most probable that the unhappy gentleman's means were utterly exhausted, and he was unable to do what was required. But the small-pox was raging in the sponging-house, and the new prisoner had never had that disease. In frantic language and alarm he begged to be removed, and the tipstaffs were men for once, and seconded the petition; but the governor, no doubt with scorn of their soft hearts, rejected the prayer. Mr. Castles died, leaving a widow and a numerous family in the deepest pecuniary and mental distress. An enormous income was levied by this system. But Bambridge was ambitious and inventive; he wanted and obtained more. Prisoners occasionally found their way into the Fleet—rich smugglers, for instance—who could afford to pay well for being themselves smuggled out of it. That method Bambridge made so good use of, that we find he actually broke the prison wall down, in a certain part, repeatedly, in order to allow one Boyce to pass through it. Another person— a prisoner—was sent to France to buy wines; pay for them with bills drawn on a tipstaff of the prison, which were duly accepted and honoured till a sufficient amount of credit had been obtained, when the tipstaff suddenly refused to accept any more; the drawer returned to prison, and both sat down with the governor to count and divide the profits. And then, in their despair, we suppose, of discovering any new modes of realising, their insatiable hands began to tamper with the prisoners' poor-box! After that trait it were idle to add anything.

From all these practices the very poor prisoners were necessarily free. But the practices could not be maintained without victims to show the consequences of any resistance to them; the poor were therefore, in a word, all victims. And there can be no doubt that even *murders* were perpetrated; for although on a subsequent protecution of Bambridge and others, by the crown, a verdict of Not Guilty was recorded, it was evident to all men that it was in a legal sense only that the evidences of guilt were insufficient. Among these helpless victims of the gaol there was a Portuguese who had been confined for months in a filthy dungeon, manacled and shackled, and whose sufferings had been so severe, and bred in him such a terror of the inflictors, that when in the course of his examination he heard something that appeared to imply that Bambridge would return again to the Fleet as Warden, he fainted, and the blood streamed from his mouth and nose. It was in spontaneous manifestations like this, quite as much as in the sight of the infernal instruments of tyranny, or the explanation of the mode of using them, that the Committee, and through them the public, arrived at a correct notion of the atrocious system of the prison government. Hogarth and Thomson have each helped to make memorable these incidents: the first, in his view of the examination scene, where Bambridge stands—no one can mistake him—on the left hand (Fig. 2406), and the second, in his lines in the ' Seasons '—

And, here, can I forget the generous hand,
Who, touched with human woe, redressive searched
Into the horrors of the gloomy gaol,
Unpitied, and unheard, where misery moans,
Where sickness pines, where thirst and hunger burn,
And poor misfortune feels the lash of vice,
While in the land of liberty, the land
Whose every street and public meeting glow
With open freedom, little tyrants raged :
Snatched the lean morsel from the starving mouth:
Tore from cold wintry limbs the tattered weed ;
E'en robb'd them of the last of comforts, sleep :
The free-born Briton to the dungeon chain'd,
Or, as the lust of cruelty prevailed,
At pleasure mark'd him with inglorious stripes,
And crushed out lives, by secret barbarous ways,
That for their country would have toiled or bled.
O great design ! if executed well,
With patient care, and wisdom-tempered zeal.
Ye sons of mercy ! yet resume the search,
Drag forth the legal monsters into light,
Wrench from their hand oppression's iron rod,
And bid the cruel feel the pain they give :
Much still untouched remains ; in this rank age
Much is the patriot's weeding hand required.

If any readers have been surprised by the Bellsize announcement before spoken of, showing the audacity of highwaymen and footpads but a century ago in the suburbs of London, what will they think to hear that they actually formed a design to waylay and rob the queen in the very streets of London in the year 1728, as she returned, without state, from a supper in the city, to St. James's? And most probably they would have accomplished their purpose but that, after all, the villains were but of a mongrel kind, and could not confine themselves to their ambitious purpose ; so when the queen's carriage did pass, they were busily engaged upon the person and possessions of an alderman of London, Sir Gilbert Heathcote, who was then going home from the House of Commons. This impudent attempt naturally excited an unsual degree of attention and activity, and the consequence was, that for a brief time there was so vigorous a system of repression adopted, that, says Maitland, " the streets were soon cleared of those wicked and detestable rogues, many of whom being apprehended, they were justly condemned and executed for their many enormous crimes." Our engraving (Fig. 2408) shows a batch of such men going to prison. Unhappy wretches ! There can be no doubt of the necessity of keeping down such a class, but much might be said upon the " justice " of sending them to the gallows. Look at the history of most of them, as we may see it illustrated in the following passage from the ' Annual Register' for 1765 :—" March 25. At an examination of four boys detected at picking pockets, before the Lord Mayor, one of them, admitted as evidence, gave the following account: a man who kept a public-house near Fleet Market had a club of boys whom he instructed in picking pockets and other iniquitous practices. He began by teaching them to pick a handkerchief out of his own pocket, and next his watch, by which means the evidence at last became so great an adept, that he got the publican's watch four times in one evening, when the master swore his scholar was as perfect as one of twenty years' practice. The pilfering out of shops was the next art. In this, his instructions to his pupils were, that at such chandlers' or other shops as had latches, one boy should knock for admittance for some trifle, whilst another was lying on his belly close to the latch, who, when the first boy came out, the latch remained on jar, and the owner being withdrawn, was to crawl in on all fours, and take the tills or anything else he could meet with, and to retire in the same manner.

Breaking into shops by night was the third article ; which was to be effected thus : as brick walls under shop-windows are generally very thin, two of them were to lie under a shop-window as destitute beggars, asleep, in appearance, to passers by ; but when alone, were with pickers to pick the mortar out of the bricks, and so on till they had opened a hole big enough to go in, when one was to lie as if asleep, before the breach, till the other had accomplished his purpose."

Thus did the idle and ignorant boys grow up into expert pickpockets and burglars as men ; and if still further back we pursue their history, we should see them as infants in such scenes as are only brought together, not exaggerated, in Hogarth's ' Gin Lane,' or, in a word, in such scenes as St. Giles's revealed a few months ago, and as a hundred other places reveal at present, to the inquiring eyes in the very neighbourhood of all that is most wealthy, and enlightened, and magnificent in the metropolis of the British empire. While they exist, crime must exist. And surely no one will suppose that St. Giles's is gone, because its place can be no longer found. The inhabitants are dispersed—but whither? No provision has been made—the " improvements " concern not them ;—even the very dispersion, as in the case of infectious diseases, may only cause every seperate batch to establish a new St. Giles's, if the philanthropist does not set to work in earnest to better their mental, moral, and physical condition.

This too, was the period of a peculiar state of things in the history of crime—happily well nigh extinct now—the robbing, or causing others to rob, for the sake of restoring the property to the owners on receiving large gratuities. In other works, this was the time when Jonathan Wild flourished. (Fig. 2407.) Fielding has not only dignified this personage by the name of the Great, but made him the nominal subject for one of the most masterly satires in the language. Wild's professed position before the world was that of a represser rather than an encourager of thieves ; he was—emphatically—the Thief Taker. And he did take thieves, and a great many of them, but only when they did not belong to his set of jackals, or when, if they did so belong, they turned troublesome, rebellious, or unprofitable. And then Jonathan Wild served both himself and the public at the same time, by giving them up to justice. We may present two examples of his mode of doing business. The first illustrates his fearless, cool way of taking possession of his former friends when he wanted them to serve him by submitting to trial and its consequences. Wild, be it observed, is the narrator of his own doings. A man, nicknamed the Grinder, was thus wanted by the Great Jonathan. So a warrant for his apprehension on account of a robbery committed by him and two others was obtained, and Jonathan hastened to execute it. " I went to a house he frequented in Crown Court, St. Giles's. Tom Eaves [who was possibly in Wild's secret confidence] happening to see me before I got in, he thrust the door too, and stood against it. I swore, if they would not open it I'd fire through, and clear the way directly. Upon this I was let in ; and searching the house, I found the Grinder under the bed, and so secured him and Eaves." Some dialogue now ensued, and Eaves observed that he could make himself an evidence. " Can you so ?" then replied Wild : " Very well ! So," he continues, " I took care of my two chaps ; and next day I went in quest of the other two, Picket and Avery, whom I knew to be old snatch-pockets, and it was not long before I met 'em in the street. ' So,' says I, ' where are you two gentlemen a-going ?' They said they had heard the Grinder was taken, and they were going to inquire how he came off. ' Came off !' says I : ' he is not come on yet ; but you shall go and see—I'll carry you to him.' ' No,' they said ; they were satisfied with what I had told them. ' But,' says I, ' he'll take it ill if you don't go ! and why should you be against it ?' ' Because,' says Picket, ' as we have sometimes been in his company and drank with him, may be he may swear some robbery upon us.' ' May be so too,' says I, ' and for that very reason I must take you with me.' " And somehow or other, the poor wretches were obliged to go.

Blueskin, one of Wild's associates, has obtained scarcely less notoriety than Wild himself. He, at last, fell under the mighty fiat ; was taken, tried, and sentenced to the gallows. Wild was to be a witness against him ; and his conduct under these circumstances shows us how worthy he was to be the original of Fielding's history—how truly, in his way, he was Great. A day or two before the trial, Jonathan went to see Blueskin in the Bail-dock. Another prisoner and victim, Simon Jacobs, was present. It is necessary to premise, that 40l. was then paid to those who were the means of bringing felons to the gallows—blood-money, as the payment has been popularly called. To this Jacobs Wild first addressed himself. " I believe you will not bring 40l. this time. I wish Joe " (meaning Blueskin) " was in your case ; but I'll do my

2428.—Dryden.

2429.—Bishop Berkeley.

2430.—Rowe.

2431.—Dryden.

2432.—Sydenham. (From a Portrait by M. Beale.)

2433.—Sir John Vanbrugh.

2434.—Pope.

2435.—Dennis.

2436.—Entrance to Pope's Grotto.

2437.—Pope's Tree, at Binfield, Berks.

2438.—Warburton.

2439.—Johnson.

2440.—Goldsmith's House, Green Arbour Court.

2441.—Boswell.

2442.—Old Academy in St. Martin's Lane.

2143.—Sir Joshua Reynolds.

2444.—Garrick.

2445.—Captain Coram. (From Hogarth's Picture.)

2446.—Zoffany's Picture of the Royal Academicians, 1773.

2147.—Horace Walpole, after Muntz

333

endeavour to bring you off as a single felon," that is to say, as one liable only to transportation, or the lesser punishments. "Then turning to me," continues Blueskin, for it is his narrative we are following, "he said, 'I believe you must die. I'll send you a good book or two, and provide you a coffin; and you shall not be anatomized.'" There is nothing in Fielding to surpass this. Can any one wonder that the maddened convict, drawing a clasped penknife, rushed upon his destroyer, and awoke him, at least for a moment, from his sublime indifference—his deep peace—on the subject of all other men's sufferings and feelings, by cutting his throat. That was not, however, a death in harmony with the peculiar greatness of Wild's life. A more elevated agency was to be concerned. He was trapped at last in the meshes of an act passed almost for his especial benefit. This act made it felony, and punishable by death, to take money for recovering stolen goods, without bringing the offender to justice. Jonathan was tried on the 24th of May, 1725, and though—failing every other resource—he handed a paper to the jury setting forth his claims as a public benefactor, and presenting in full the names of thirty-five robbers, twenty-two house-breakers, and ten returned convicts he had brought to the gallows, it was all useless; they were determined to hang him, and he was hanged. And seldom has the world been freed from a more intolerable social curse. The mention of Fielding's name in connection with this subject, reminds us of the very able, though blind magistrate, his brother, Sir John Fielding (Fig. 2409), who presided at Bow Street till his death in 1780.

The Stratford Jubilee in 1769 originated with Garrick, and though we may smile at some of the modes in which the founder and his coadjutors carried out their views, the affair has at least this merit; it gave an unusual opportunity for the exhibition of the national enthusiasm in all that is connected with the name and honour of William Shakspere. Persons of all ranks, social and intellectual, were drawn together at Stratford on the occasion, and in vast numbers. An octagonal theatre that would contain a thousand persons was erected close to the river; and as one of its chief ornaments Garrick caused a bust of the bard to be placed in it; —the one that he subsequently gave to the Corporation, and which is now in the Town Hall. The ceremonies or performances, or whatever they might be called, began on the 6th of September, and lasted three days. There was a public breakfast in the Town Hall; an oratorio—'Judith'—in the church; a dinner—of course— which was eaten in the amphitheatre; a ball; recitations by Garrick of a poetical Ode, and a prose oration, in honour of Shakspere; fireworks; a horse-race; and above all, a kind of walking masque (Fig. 2401), representative of the different characters of the plays. A triennial Shaksperian festival is still observed in the town.

Contemporary with Garrick was the illustrious painter of English life and manners, William Hogarth. There has never lived an artist who performed so thoroughly and so well the business to which he devoted his life and talents. He possessed in the highest degree those qualities which specially endowed him for the work, namely, a faculty of observation which, while it comprehended everything, never missed the minutest details, or failed to fasten upon the most striking and suggestive—a facile mastery of the arts, both of the painter and engraver, which leaves nothing to be desired on the score of fidelity, of breadth, or of expression—and a keen sense of humour, which was restrained from wandering into extravagance or caricature, by his profound reverence for nature and truth. To these qualities should be added his unparalleled industry and perseverance, which alone could have enabled him to paint and to engrave with his own hand, a prodigious number of works, excellent as masterpieces of art and teeming with the profoundest moral significance. A brief glance at the life of such a man will not be uninteresting or uninstructive.

William Hogarth was born in London in the year 1698. He began to draw faces and figures as soon as he could hold a pencil; he scrawled them on his slate and copy-books at school, and when paper was wanting, or a whitewashed wall did not happen to be within reach, would jot them down on his thumb-nail. His natural guardians, ignorant of the mighty genius thus instinctively striving for development, endeavoured by discouragements to cure him of the habit of "making faces," but finding that impossible, at length apprenticed him to an engraver of arms, and left him to take his course. His first employment was the engraving of lions' heads, griffins, hands and daggers, and such like rubbish of heraldry, together with bill-heads for shopkeepers. But he soon grew more ambitious, and began to execute small plates and frontispieces for the booksellers. These were succeeded by his illustrations of

Butler's Hudibras, a remarkable series full of grotesque humour, and manifesting considerable power in drawing, which brought him into note, and laid the foundation of his early fame. In the meantime he had been practising arduously as a painter, and there is reason to believe had almost from the very first essays mastered the mystery of colour. His first exhibited picture was a representation of Wanstead Assembly, "a conversation piece," in which the portraits were all taken from life.

Like most men of large capacity, Hogarth was nothing wanting in confidence or self-esteem. At thirty he began to think of settling in life, and paid his court to the daughter of Sir James Thornhill, the greatest English painter of the day. Sir James at first repudiated the idea of any connection with the homely and self-asserting engraver, and cavalierly denied his consent to the match. The future Shakspere of art was not to be rebuffed: the lady and he had made up their minds—and the unwilling parent must be won over to the agreement. Hogarth set to work anew, and, inspired by his passion, produced a series of drawings which he intended should vindicate his claim to the honour of the alliance he sought. He sent them to Thornhill, and at the same time renewed his application for the daughter's hand. Sir James, astonished, saw himself excelled in his own art by the pertinacious suitor, and was generous enough to withdraw his opposition. Hogarth married the daughter of the great man in 1730.

It was shortly after his marriage, that Hogarth decorated the gardens of Vauxhall with some admirable sketches, for which he received no other payment than a free ticket of admission. But in 1733 he gave to the world his well-known pictures of "The Harlot's Progress," a work which stamped his reputation among the best judges. These were followed in rapid succession by those moral histories and satires of vice and folly with which we are all so familiar, the "Rake's Progress," "Marriage-a-la-Mode, the Election Prints, "Industry and Idleness," &c., &c.; all of which towered far above the critical faculty of his day.

Upon the conclusion of the war by the treaty of Aix-la-Chapelle, Hogarth went to France, and while sketching the old gate of the town of Calais, was taken up for a spy, hauled before the authorities, and put into confinement; from which, however, he was speedily released. His first care on returning home was to commemorate the event in that famous print "The Roast Beef of Old England," which he has made the vehicle of satire for affairs other than French.

Hogarth prospered in his day, but it was rather as a tradesman than an artist. He painted portraits, but being too honest to flatter, gained but little in that department of art. He painted historical pictures, but herein he mistook his vocation, and won more reproach than reputation. His income, which was never large, was derived mainly from the sale of his engravings; but his wants were few, his wife practised the virtues of economy, and thus he was enabled to lead an independent life.

In the year 1753, Hogarth published his "Analysis of Beauty,' a characteristic work, which illustrates rather coarsely his independence of character, but which contains a great deal of valuable artistic truth mingled with errors and crotchets. In it he ridicules the stupidity of the connoisseurs who ran mad after the old masters and neglected living merit; he reduces the rules of colouring, as it was practised in his day, to the simplest elements; and he claims for himself the discovery of the waving line, as the line of beauty. In the preparation of this work he had the assistance of Dr. Hoadly, his own want of education, which is often betrayed by the mis-spelling of the inscriptions appended to his prints, incapacitating him for such a task.

In 1757 he became sergeant-painter to King George II., and it was probably this promotion that induced him to set up his carriage. He appears, however, never to have become habituated to the use of such a luxury—for riding out in it one day to visit the Lord Mayor of London; and having protracted his stay till a heavy shower came on, he was bowed out by a different door from that by which he entered, and hastening off on foot through the rain, arrived at home wet through to the skin. When, at his dripping apparition, his wife asked him where he had left the carriage— "Oh," said he, unconcernedly, "I forgot that I had such a thing;" a case of absence of mind charmingly illustrative of the man.

The temper of Hogarth was not of the mildest. He was roused to wrath by provocations which ought not to have stirred his bile, and was not easily pacified. This disposition led him into frequent quarrels, and induced him to employ that time and those talents in caricaturing his adversaries, which would have been much better applied in the legitimate pursuit of his art. The last years of his life were embittered by rancorous quarrels with Wilkes and Churchill. The satire of the latter, especially, galled him exceedingly, and to say the truth, was of a most butcherly and unprincipled kind. According to some of his biographers the quarrel with Churchill shortened his days, and sent him prematurely to his grave. He died in 1764, and was interred in the churchyard of Chiswick, where he had resided for some years. His friend Garrick wrote the following epitaph, which is inscribed on his tomb :—

> Farewell, great painter of mankind !
> Who reached the noblest point of art;
> Whose pictured morals charm the mind,
> And, through the eye, correct the heart.
>
> If Genius fire thee, reader, stay :
> If Nature touch thee, drop a tear :
> If neither move thee, turn away,
> For Hogarth's honoured dust lies here.

It is not necessary at this time of day to insist upon the merits of Hogarth's performances either with the pencil or the graver. In the use of the latter implement he has been excelled by his successors, and is left far behind by the talent of the present day ; but as a painter it may be safely averred that he has had no rival up to the present hour. The Marriage-a-la-Mode, now in the National Gallery, and the Election Pictures, now in Sir John Soane's Museum in Lincoln's Inn Fields, attest his superiority to all succeeding British artists who have attempted the same walk of art. Both these works are superior in drawing, and inventive originality, and the last named especially is superior in boldness and facility of handling, to those of any painter since his time. During Hogarth's life there wanted but one thing to the fulness of his fame, and that was, an appreciation on the part of the public of his real genius. They looked upon him as a maker and seller of prints: had their eyes been open they would have seen in him the Michael Angelo of every-day life, and something more—a silent preacher of great and enduring truths. Had he lived a century later, the present generation would have seen him reverenced and honoured—knighted by his sovereign, and enriched beyond the reach of desire by the price of his labours. As it was, he sold his paintings for less than one-twentieth of the sums they would now realize at a public auction ; and trusted for the reward of his industry to the sale of his prints. But no man need regret that he lived when he did : the work he wrought in his day was one eminently needful to be done ; in a non-reading age, he preached pictorial sermons to all, which all could see and understand ; and by holding the social vices of our forefathers up to general reprobation, he contributed more than any other moralist to social reform. Were this his sole claim to remembrance, we should be bound to venerate his name ; but he did more than this—he raised the character of English art, and taught foreign nations to respect in him a worthy rival of their noblest artists.

The specimens of Hogarth's works engraved in the present volume will be found numbered consecutively from 2410 to 2414 inclusive. They are too well known to require any explanation here. We need only remark that the picture of Temple Bar has a historical value, as illustrative of a phase of street life in London on the 5th of November, which our modern sense of order and decorum has done away with for ever.

Two of the greatest names in the history of England, or indeed of the world's philosophy, belong to the present period ; they are Newton and Locke (Figs. 2426, 2419.) And it is a matter calculated to excite solemn and most instructive reflection, that the same period of time should witness such great advances made alike in the discovery of the laws of the material and of the intellectual universe.

The boyhood of Isaac Newton was chiefly remarkable for exhibitions of mechanical ingenuity ; a wind-mill and a water-clock were among the early productions of his little workshop, but in other matters—especially in the regular departments of education—he was more than usually backward ; and therefore held no honourable rank among his schoolfellows of the Grantham Grammar School. But one day the boy who was above him gave him a severe kick in the stomach, which caused great pain. From what follows it should seem that it was this boy's superiority in the class that enabled him to perpetrate these brutalities with impunity ; for Isaac Newton at once determined to get above him, and laboured incessantly until he had done so. And—the impulse given—he went on, and rapidly became the first boy in the school.

It was intended by his mother, after the death of her second husband, in 1656, that Isaac should assist in the farm at Woolsthorpe, where he was born, and he was accordingly taken from school and sent on market-days to Grantham, in the company of an aged domestic, to purchase provisions and other necessaries for the family, or to sell the farm produce. At Grantham, however, he was generally found in the garret of an apothecary, where he had previously lodged, and where there were a few old books to rummage over, that afforded more interest and profit, in his view, than the market could. Neither could he be depended upon to come home directly : wherever there happened to be a piece of machinery, such as a water-wheel, on or near the high road, there was Isaac sure to loiter. His wise as well as kind mother now resolved not to thwart such powerful tendencies, so she sent him back to school : and subsequently a relative enabled him to go to the university. Little in apparent amount is known of the kind of life he led there, but that little is all-important ; and makes up in a great degree for deficiencies. One of his uncles found him one day under a hedge, wholly absorbed in the solution of a mathematical problem. Thus is his whole university life concentrated in a few words.

We shall not attempt to follow the various steps he made in raising himself into the position he was thenceforward to occupy, probably to the end of all time—that is, as the author of the first of all human productions that have the explanation of the material phenomena of the universe for their subject. We shall merely glance at those personal incidents which are ever so deeply interesting in connection with our great men. Foremost of these is the event that has made a little cottage in a little hamlet of Lincolnshire (Fig. 2423),—already a precious spot, since it was there Newton was born,—still more the object of almost sacred regard upon the parts of all those, a constantly-increasing number, who can fully understand and appreciate the vast and sublime character of the discovery to which the event led, and who see no reason to be ashamed of their faith in a tradition as likely to be true as it is popular. It was at Woolsthorpe, sayeth this tradition, whither Newton had retired in 1665-6, that one day as he sat in the garden, or orchard, his attention was peculiarly attracted by the fall of an apple. *Why* did it fall? That sort of question he had often asked himself before, and had endeavoured by elaborate and most persevering study to answer; but at this particular time,—and such times perhaps occur to all great men in connection with their crowning achievement—he was more than usually inspired with the considerations excited by this simple incident, and he set to work with increased energy and determination, to endeavour to satisfy himself. The end was, as is well known, the discovery of the law that regulates the order of sun, moon, earth, and planets, and the apparently eternal repetition of the same or similar series throughout the visible and invisible regions of space, as well as of the fall of that apple in the orchard of Woolsthorpe, namely, the law of gravitation. An interesting anecdote is told in relation to the final process of this discovery. When he endeavoured at Woolsthorpe to verify by demonstration his hypothesis, he found the figures fail him ; the issue of his calculations showed—to his mind—he had erred. But, in fact, the error was in some of the materials that he had been obliged to use, for want of better ; those connected with the length of the earth's radius. However, he threw aside the whole subject, and only resumed it when he had heard accidentally of a fresh measurement that had been made by Picard. He took a note of the result of that measurement, and again retraced the whole ground, and as he drew nearer and nearer to the conclusion, and saw the extreme probability that he was right—and weighed the mighty importance of the truth that would be established if he were, he grew so excited that he was unable to go on personally with the calculations : so a friend finished them for him ; the supposed was indeed the true law: it was no longer an hypothesis—it was a matter of demonstration.

The apple-tree that used to be pointed out to visitors, as the one from which the particular fruit in question fell, no longer exists, having been thrown down by the wind. A drawing of it was preserved, and another tree grafted on the stock. Our engraving represents, with literal fidelity, the exterior of the place. It lies at the bottom of a little slope. Within we are shown the room where Newton was born. A marble tablet has been placed over the chimney-piece, with the inscription—" Sir Isaac Newton, son of Isaac Newton, lord of the manor of Woolsthorpe, was born in this room on the 25th of December, 1642." Beneath are inscribed Pope's magnificent lines :—

> Nature and Nature's laws lay hid in night;
> God said " Let Newton be,"—and there was light.

Some of the anecdotes told of the philosopher are amusing enough, but they possess a higher interest than belongs to mere amusement; the causes of his absence of mind, for instance, are constantly impressing themselves upon us, even when we smile at the ludicrous character of its effect. Dr. Stukeley once went to see him. He was shown into a room, and there left. Time passed on, and as the antiquarian was hungry, and probably also aware how hopeless it was get his friend the philosopher away from his eal-

2448.—Horace Walpole.

2449.— View from the Garden of Strawberry Hill.

2450.—The Gallery, Strawberry Hill.

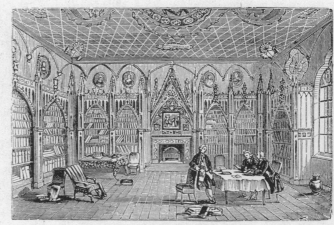

2451.—The Library, Strawberry Hill.

5452.—Tonson.

2453.—Dunton.

2454.—Guy.

2455.—Cave.

2456.—Dampier, from an anonymous Print.— Anson, from a Medal by Pingo.

336

culations in any reasonable time, if he happened to be much absorbed, he quietly began his dinner upon a fowl that had been prepared for Newton, and speedily demolished it. At last Newton came down, prepared for dinner; but seeing the fowl gone, was evidently much surprised; and excused himself to Dr. Stukeley by saying,—" You see, Doctor, how very abstract we philosophers are; I really imagined I had not yet dined !" We may contrast this dilatoriness and inattention to domestic matters with the rapidity and readiness of his intellect in what were to him the true business and enjoyment of life. When Bernouilli had proposed a problem, for the solution of which six months were given, and Leibnitz had requested an extension of the time, Newton did the business in about as many hours. Again, when Leibnitz himself prepared a problem that he intended should puzzle all the European philosophers, Newton solved it within half a day after it came to hand. Another anecdote of Newton is tolerably well known; not so the most serious consequences that followed the incident in question. There is in existence a manuscript diary, kept by a student of Cambridge, Mr. Pryme, commencing with the year 1685: in this document it is written under the date of the 3rd of February, 1692, that the writer had that day heard of the destruction of Newton's MSS. on the theory of colours, "established upon thousands of experiments which he had been twenty years of making, and which had cost him many hundreds of pounds." By connecting what follows in the diary with the popular story that was in circulation before the diary was known anything of, and which, in essentials, mutually confirm each other, we find that the circumstances were of the following nature :—Whilst Newton had gone to the morning chapel, he left in his study a favourite dog; who, by some means or other, overturned a lighted taper, which set fire to the precious papers, and consumed them. On Newton's return, he discovered the calamity. " Oh, Diamond, Diamond !" he exclaimed to the unconscious animal, " little do you know the mischief you have done me !" The diary says, he was so affected at his loss, that " every one thought he would have run mad ;" and there is but too much evidence to show that the event did for a time unsettle Newton's intellects.

We may add a few particulars to the information conveyed by our portrait (Fig. 2416). In person Newton was short, and somewhat corpulent; his hair was of a silvery grey, his eye bright and penetrating; his disposition was of a reserved nature; his conversation had nothing in it of brilliancy. He owed the honour of knighthood to Queen Anne. He lived in a house in St. Martin's Street, Leicester Square (Fig. 2424), for many years, and built himself an observatory. Thence he removed to Kensington, where he died.

Of his connection with the Royal Society we have already spoken in a previous page. The seal of this society will be found among our engravings (Fig. 2422).

It is curious that two of the most powerful thinkers that have yet arisen among men, should have had remarkably weak bodies in infancy. It was said of Newton that he could have been put into a quart pot when a baby. As for Locke, he was destined for the profession of medicine, but was of so infirm a constitution that he was unable to practise. His well-known portrait (Fig. 2419) conveys much of the expression of illness and suffering. Locke's private life became, for a considerable period, of a not very quiet or satisfactory kind, through an accidental circumstance, the formation of an acquaintance with Lord Ashley, afterwards Earl of Shaftesbury (Dryden's Achitophel), in whose house he went to reside. This connection brought him into intercourse with all the more eminent men of the day, and caused him occasionally to be employed by government. But it also involved him to a certain extent in the misfortunes of his patron, after the failure of the Duke of Monmouth's expedition. Locke was one of eighty-three persons whom the English Envoy demanded to be given up by the States-General. The Revolution, among its other blessings, restored to England John Locke: a situation worth 200l. a year was also conferred upon him by the government. And from that time his life flowed on as smoothly as it could be well desired. The Essay on the Human Understanding was published in 1690. The success of this work was immense. Locke was already widely known as the earnest advocate of civil and religious liberty. His reputation as a true patriot and sound philosopher was still further enhanced by the publication of his second letter on Toleration, and his treatises on Government. In these he placed, in direct opposition to the idea maintained by some advocates of the fallen Stuart dynasty—that Adam was the first governor by God's own ordinance, and that kings were Adam's representatives—his own very different views, namely, that the legitimacy of a government depends solely and ultimately on the popular sanction; or, in other words, on the consent of men, making use of their reason to unite together into

societies. Locke was as a man all that his greatest admirers could hope that he should be, in order to harmonise with his writings. A lover of liberty, he was content to take his share of the sufferings it involved, and to grant to others all that he desired for himself. A teacher of toleration, he did not, as too many have done, and do, preserve their consistency only so long as there is no very strong temptation to depart from it. Nothing induced—nothing, we believe, could have induced him to consent to the persecution of any man for the expression of a conscientious belief. One trait of his mind conveys too valuable a lesson for us all, to be overlooked in these pages. He was once asked how it was he had contrived to accumulate such extensive and deep stores of knowledge. His reply was to the effect that he attributed what little he knew to the not having been ashamed to ask for information; and to the rule he had laid down, of conversing with all descriptions of men on those topics chiefly that formed their own peculiar professions or pursuits.

Hogarth, in addition to all his other claims to our attention, adds that of being one of the virtual, though not the nominal, founders of the Royal Academy; and though it was the last thing upon which he would have been anxious to have been complimented. He was the chief of the persons who were connected with the Academy—a mere private assemblage of artists for drawing from the living figure, &c.—from which the Society of Incorporated Artists sprang; and from which society again, at a later period, branched out the Royal Academy. But when the members of the old Academy—who met at Hogarth's own house in St. Martin's Lane—endeavoured to obtain royal favour, and an act of incorporation, he not only refused to join them, but even expressed publicly his opinion that the only motive was that a few bustling characters, who had access to people of rank, thought they could thus get a superiority over their brethren, be appointed to places, and have salaries, as in France, for telling a lad when an arm or a leg is too long or too short. The artists succeeded in their aim, and were incorporated in 1765. The permanence of any such institution, however, would have been a very questionable matter, but for an influence that accidentally sprang up, and gave it the stability that prosperity in pecuniary matters gives to everything, as society is now constituted. When the Foundling Hospital was completed, there was a desire expressed for paintings on the walls. But the charity could not pay artists, so some of the eminent men of the day offered to work for it gratuitously. Hogarth was the most conspicuous and active of these benefactors. He painted the founder, Captain Coram, and he also painted the Adoption of Moses by Pharaoh's Daughter; of which a critic has observed— " There is not perhaps in Holy Writ another story so exactly suitable to the avowed purpose of the foundation." His March to Finchley became also the property of the institution, in the mode before pointed out. Other painters entered into this noble rivalry of beneficence and artistic skill. Reynolds painted the portrait of the Earl of Dartmouth; Ramsay that of Dr. Mead; Wilson and Gainsborough filled certain small compartments with exquisite bits of landscape; Hayman and others contributed still more ambitious pictures; and, lastly, Rysbrack placed over the mantelpiece of the room now used as the Committee-room, the beautiful piece of sculpture that attracts the eye of every lover of the arts who may visit the Hospital. Such an assemblage of works was of course exceedingly attractive; and thus painters for the first time in England began to perceive what might be done by public and collective exhibitions. The experiment was partially tried at the great rooms of the Adelphi, in connection with a system of premiums given by the Society, then recently established, for the Encouragement of Arts, Manufactures, and Commerce. There was no charge made for admission: the price of the catalogue— sixpence—furnished the only profit. The number of visitors was so considerable, that a place at Spring Gardens (by Charing Cross) was engaged next year, the price of the catalogue raised to a shilling, and none allowed to enter who could not, either by himself or by his party, show a catalogue. Samuel Johnson noticed this exhibition; and his remarks are not very flattering to his discernment. Having observed that the " exhibition has filled the heads of the artists and the lovers of art," he adds, " Surely life, if it be not long, is tedious, since we are forced to call in the assistance of so many *trifles* to rid us of our time. We may contrast this with Reynolds's reply to Dr. Tucker, Dean of Gloucester, who happened to say in his presence—" A pin-maker is a more useful and valuable member of society than Raphael." " That," said Reynolds, with not more severity than the case demanded, " is an observation of a very narrow mind—a mind that is confined to the mere object of commerce— that sees with a microscopic eye but a part of the great machine of the economy of life, and thinks that small part which he sees to be the whole. Commerce is the means, not the end of happiness or pleasure; the end is a rational enjoyment by means of arts and sciences:" and so on. After Johnson's comment, it is somewhat surprising to find him obliging the artists by writing the advertisement to the third exhibition. Reynolds had probably been the means of inducing him to reconsider the matter upon which he had so hastily and unwisely expressed himself. The Exhibition was now decidedly successful; and the artists quarrelled about the disposal of the money: some cried out for statues—some for a mansion—some for a gallery of paintings—and some thought it best to keep the money, and make the most of it. A split in consequence took place. The more valuable members of the Society withdrew; among them were Reynolds and West; and through West, who had but recently obtained the personal patronage of George III., the seceders exerted themselves to obtain an independent charter of incorporation. The news of their success fell like a thunderbolt upon the others. The manner was, if possible, worse than the matter of the communication. Kirby, the painter, was just then elected to the Presidency of the Incorporated Artists. One day he went to the King, was admitted to the royal presence, where he found West, who was busily engaged upon his picture of Regulus. The President looked upon painter and painting, and, of course, commended both; then, turning to the King, he said, "Your Majesty never mentioned anything of this work to me. Who made the frame? It is not made by one of your Majesty's workmen; it ought to have been made by the royal carver and gilder." "Kirby," said the monarch, "whenever you are able to paint me such a picture as this, your friend shall make the frame." The President then turned to the young American. "I hope, Mr. West, you intend to exhibit this picture." West replied, "It is painted for the palace; and its exhibition must depend upon his Majesty's pleasure." "Assuredly," interposed George III., "I shall be very happy to let the work be shown to the public." "Then, Mr. West, you will send it to my exhibition?" inquired the President. "No," replied the King, "it must go to my exhibition—that of the *Royal Academy*." And this, according to the narrator of the story, Mr. Allan Cunningham, was the first public intimation made of the foundation of the present institution.

The earliest home of the Royal Academy was in St. Martin's Lane (Fig. 2442). Thither went Reynolds and West to meet and join the new body. As they entered, every man rose, and saluted the former with the single word—President! This admirable choice says much for the artists who made it. Reynolds, like most other great men, was, when he first appeared, a heretic in the eyes of his brethren. Hudson was his master; and this gentleman went to see his former pupil when he had returned from prosecuting his studies in Rome. Some pictures were lying about—a boy in a turban especially caught Hudson's attention. "Reynolds," exclaimed he, with an oath, "you don't paint so well as when you left England!" An eminent portrait painter of the name of Ellis also went to see him. "Ah, Reynolds," said he, "this will never answer; why you don't paint in the least like Sir Godfrey [Kneller]." Hereupon Reynolds explained that he acted upon his own views of art, and stated them at length; but at the conclusion Ellis strutted off with the words, "Shakspere in poetry, and Kneller in painting; d——e." The honour so peculiarly honourably conferred showed, however, that it required but a little time to enable his brother artists generally to appreciate as it deserved the new style of painting. And the glory that Reynolds conferred upon them, their institution, and, above all, upon their art, has surpassed all they could have anticipated. The Discourses on Art, a work which time and increased study and knowledge only makes appear more valuable, were delivered orally to the members of the Academy. The style of these writings, apart from their matter, is so clear and noble, that many persons to this hour believe they were in part written by Burke; but as far as we have ever been able to learn, for no other earthly reason than that they are so excellent. Men are always loth to believe that such pre-eminence can be obtained in such different walks as those of the actual painter and the literary and philosophical art-critic.

Aided by a curious and very able picture of the assemblage of all the members of the Academy in their hall, on a drawing night, let us take a peep at them, and tell who and what are the men composing the Royal Academy, some few years after its establishment. The picture in question (Fig. 2446) was painted by Zoffany, who appears in it, in his own proper person, on the left of the picture, seated, and with his palette in his hand. This gentleman went at one time to Florence, at the invitation of the Grand Duke, and was there accosted by the Emperor of Germany, who

was then on a visit to the Duke. Pleased with his works, the Emperor inquired his name. Zoffany told him. "What countryman are you?" "An Englishman," was the reply. "Why your name is German." "True," said Zoffany, "I was born in Germany —that was accidental; I call my country that where I have been protected." We shall not therefore ourselves call him a foreigner, although he came to England from a foreign country whilst a young man, and, under the patronage of the Earl of Barrymore, rose in a very short time to high reputation. His theatrical works are among his best and most widely-known productions. The picture of the Academy, however, is, in its class and scope, first rate.

Behind Zoffany, in a standing posture, is West, who at a later time became the President of the Academy—the culminating point of a career that from birth seemed to have been shaped out as a remarkable one, if we take into consideration the very peculiar circumstance of his position. His birth was premature, in consequence of the excitement of a field-preaching scene, to which his mother had gone; his only teachers were the Red Indians, who instructed him in some little matters relating to the properties of colours; above all, his parents were Quakers, the last body of people from among whom we generally look for any example of individual excellence in the imaginative arts. But, as in the case of Newton so lately noticed, and in hosts of other cases, Nature has taught parents, through their love, the wisdom that they would never have learnt through the operations of their intellect—that is, to let their children follow the course to which they have exhibited a powerful and unequivocal bias. Never, perhaps, has this kind of wisdom been more broadly asserted in opposition to what the utterers had previously thought wisdom, than in the case of one of the Quaker friends of the West family, when a meeting had taken place to debate what should be done with the young innovator, who persisted in practising what the very doctrines of the society forbade. The speaker of the following sentences was John Williamson:— "You have all heard, that by something amounting to inspiration, the youth hath been induced to study the art of painting. It is true that our tenets refuse to own the utility of that art to mankind; but it seemeth to me that we have considered the matter too nicely. God has bestowed on this youth a genius for art—shall we question his wisdom? Can we believe that He gives such rare gifts but for a wise and good purpose? I see the Divine Hand in this. We shall do well to sanction the art and encourage this youth." The audience, thus addressed, responded unanimously to the speaker's views. Young West was called in, and there, standing in the presence of the whole society, received perhaps the noblest exhortation on the true uses and mission of art that has ever been delivered. "Painting has been hitherto employed to embellish life, to preserve voluptuous images, and add to the sensual gratifications of man. For this we classed it among vain and merely ornamental things, and excluded it from amongst us. But this is not the principle, but the misemployment of painting. In wise and in pure hands it rises in the scale of moral excellence, and displays a loftiness of sentiment and a devout dignity worthy of the contemplation of Christians. I think genius is given by God for some high purpose. What the purpose is let us not inquire—it will be manifest in his own good time and way. He hath in this remote wilderness endowed with the rich gifts of a superior spirit this youth, who has now our consent to cultivate his talents for art. May it be demonstrated in his life and works that the gifts of God have not been bestowed in vain; nor the motives of the beneficent inspiration, which induces us to suspend the operation of our tenets, prove barren of religious or moral effect!" It is only simple justice to West to say that such precious seeds fell upon no unworthy soil; his picture of Death upon the Pale Horse, and the Death of General Wolfe, are works of which our nation may be proud: and the whole of his other productions exhibit that lofty moral purpose, which the illustrious though comparatively obscure John Williamson had impressed upon him, as the true end of all the labours of genius. As marking an era in art, let us also here relate, in West's own language, an anecdote in connection with one of the paintings just named—the Death of Wolfe. "When it was understood that I intended to paint the characters as they had actually appeared on the scene, the Archbishop of York called on Reynolds, and asked his opinion: they both came to my house to dissuade me from running so great a risk. Reynolds began a very ingenious and eloquent dissertation on the state of the public taste in this country, and the danger which every innovation incurred of contempt and ridicule, and concluded by urging me earnestly to adopt the costume of antiquity, as more becoming the greatness of my subject than the modern garb of European warriors. I answered that the event to be commemorated happened in the year 1758, in a region of the world unknown to the Greeks and Romans, and at a period when no warriors who wore such costume existed. The subject I have to represent is a great battle fought and won; and the same truth which gives law to the historian should rule the painter. If instead of the facts of the action, I introduce fiction, how shall I be understood by posterity? The classic dress is certainly picturesque, but by using it I shall lose in sentiment what I gain in external grace. I want to mark the place, the time, and the people; and to do this I must abide by truth. They went away then, and returned again when I had the painting finished. Reynolds seated himself before the picture, examined it with deep and minute attention for half an hour; then rising, said to Drummond, 'West has conquered—he has treated his subject as it ought to be treated: I retract my objections. I foresee that this picture will not only become one of the most popular, but will occasion a revolution in art.'"

Peter Pindar's attacks on West are familiar to everybody. It cannot be denied that they were frequently well deserved, nor that they were frequently called forth for the not very sufficient reason that the painter enjoyed too exclusively the royal patronage. Peter, in one poem, represents George III. as a girl placing West as a daisy in a garden,

Thinking the flower the finest in the nation,

and who visits it, and waters it—

Then staring round, all wild for praises panting,
Tells all the world it was *its own* sweet planting;
And boasts away, too happy elf!
How that it found the daisy *all itself*.

The next seated and prominent figure (going regularly round from the left of the picture) is Hayman, the friend and coadjutor of Hogarth: it was he who painted the Vauxhall pictures after Hogarth's designs. Next, of course, our reader will recognise the President, if it be only from Goldsmith's well-known lines:—

When they talk'd of their Raphaels, Correggios, and stuff,
He shifted his *trumpet*, and only took snuff.

Behind Reynolds, on his right, half sitting on the corner of the table, is Sir William Chambers, the author of the well-known and valuable work on architecture, and the builder of the present Somerset House. On the other side of Reynolds is Dr. William Hunter, professor of anatomy, and brother to John Hunter. The two figures (one wearing spectacles), who are examining the position of the man who is officiating as the model, are Yeo and Zuccarelli, an Italian artist, who began a very successful career in England by painting scenes for the Opera; and elevated behind them is seen the portly figure of Richard, or, as he was more commonly called, Dick Wilson. This juxtaposition of Zuccarelli and Wilson reminds us of a scene a few years later, when the two were also in company, but when one at least, and to a certain extent the other, had the world all before them where to choose, but with no recognised pretensions that might support them in their choice. Wilson began by painting portraits; and whilst a student at Rome, for some time made them his chief consideration. One morning, while he was waiting for the coming of his friend Zuccarelli, he took up a pencil to beguile the time, and sketched the landscape that lay before him, as seen through the open window. When Zuccarelli came, he looked at this sketch, was surprised, and asked him if he had ever studied landscape. "No," said Wilson. "Then I advise you to try, for you are sure of great success," was the unhesitating remark of Zuccarelli. The French painter, Vernet, confirmed Zuccarelli's opinion. Wilson took heart, and began. How he ended, let those who have seen his Niobe, and other pictures of that class, either in the original or even in prints, say for themselves. It is, we believe, an unanimous decision that "Dick Wilson" is our greatest, because our loftiest, landscape painter. But if such men as Zuccarelli could see this, it took the world a long time to see it too—so long, indeed, that poor Wilson could not wait, but died before his reputation became completely established. Here is one illustration of the treatment that this artist received from his countrymen. *After* the Niobe had appeared, his only standing resource were the pawnbrokers, and we may readily judge what sort of prices those gentry paid him: and even that failed. He went one day to sell a new picture; but the pawnbroker, taking him up stairs, showed him a pile of paintings, and said to him in a kindly manner, "Why, look ye, Dick, you know I wish to oblige, but see! There are all the pictures I have paid you for these three years." And so at last Wilson, the painter of Niobe—a work now of almost inestimable pecuniary value—had to live by making sketches for half a crown a-piece; and when a lady once ordered two pictures of him, he was actually without the means of obtaining the requisite canvas and

other materials. Happily one gleam of sunshine descended to cheer his last hours: at the death of a relative he became possessed of a little property in Wales, and there he died.

It must be acknowledged that Wilson's habits and manners had almost as much to do with his distress as the apathy of his professing admirers, or the ignorance of the rulers of the fashionable world of taste: he was consequently held in no personal respect. A brother painter, however, ought to have known better than to presume upon this to insult him, as Zoffany did in the original sketch of his picture of the Academy, by putting a pot of beer at Wilson's elbow. Wilson heard of the circumstance, went immediately and bought a cudgel, and expressed his determination to thrash his brother Academician for his impudence. Zoffany immediately removed the offensive feature, and the matter went no farther. Between Dr. Hunter and Wilson is Bartolozzi, the eminent engraver, who first distinguished himself in England by his design for tickets for select operatic performances. In this comparatively humble walk he so roused the jealousy of the English engraver, Strange, that he ventured to say Bartolozzi could do nothing else. Bartolozzi answered the illiberal and oracular judgment by his engraving of Clytie after Annibale Caracci, and of the Virgin and Child after Carlo Dolce. From that time Strange stood alone in his opinion, even if he himself was not now convinced of his error, as to Bartolozzi's merits. His taste was as exquisite as it was versatile. He was as successful in rendering the sublimity of the great Michael Angelo as the excessive refinement and delicacy of Cipriani, his early friend and countryman, and who, like him, settled in England. Cipriani stands in the picture behind West.

The painter who is giving to the model the handle that is suspended from the ceiling for the support of his arm, is Moser, one of the most active of the members during the formation of the Royal Academy. Over his head, to the right, are suspended the portraits of two lady Academicians: one of them represents Angelica Kauffmann. "And now," as Peter Pindar says,

for Mister Nathan Hone,

the tall gentleman who stands immediately beneath and between these portraits, and whom the bard thus addresses:—

In portraits thou'rt as much alone
As in his landscapes stands th' unrivall'd Claude.

The slight difference between the two being—that one is alone in excellence, the other in the opposite quality. What this gentleman lacked in ability he thought to make up by a liberal use of the interest that personalities are but too apt to excite. The little artists of the day had got hold of a very amusing notion explanatory of the superior success of Reynolds, namely, that he pilfered wholesale from them; that nothing of theirs was safe near him—figures, groups, attitudes were all the same to him—he seized whatever he could catch. So "Mister Nathan Hone" painted a picture in which an enchanter appeared surrounded by various works of art and prints; and beneath these were slight but sufficient indications of those works by Sir Joshua, which were supposed in some respects to resemble and to have been borrowed from them. Considering Mister Nathan Hone intended to exhibit his picture in the Royal Academy exhibition, this was tolerably bold; but it was not enough for him: so, in reference to some flirtation that said to have passed between Sir Joshua and Mrs. Kauffmann, there was a representation of that lady introduced. Of course the Academicians, as soon as they beheld the picture, returned it at once to its author, who then vainly endeavoured to shuffle out of the business, by declaring he had not intended any such allusions. On the extreme right of the picture, appears Richard Cosway, the best miniature painter of his day. This gentleman, like the late Mr. Varley, seems to have thought himself qualified to speak of matters beyond the ordinary ken of human vision. At one of the Annual Royal Academy dinners, he told a brother member that he had that morning been visited by Mr. Pitt, who had died some four years before. "Well, and pray what did he say to you?" "Why," answered Cosway, "on entering the room he expressed himself prodigiously hurt that during his residence on the earth he had not encouraged my talents." Lastly, over Cosway's shoulder appears Nollekens, the sculptor, a man capable of the meanest and the most generous deeds—at once rude and illiterate—and yet a graceful and refined artist. His conduct to Chantrey should never be forgotten, and may be fitly contrasted with Strange's conduct to Bartolozzi before mentioned. Chantrey, then a young and utterly unknown sculptor, sent to one of the exhibitions a bust of Horne Tooke; it was placed, as is but too often the case, not in accordance with his merit, but the artist's position. Nollekens happened to see it.

He stopped—turned it round—took it up—and at last said, "Here's a fine—a very fine work; let the man who made it be known—remove one of *my* busts, and put this in its place, for well it deserves it." Such conduct outweighs a thousand faults; and Nollekens' faults were after all chiefly such as affected himself rather than others.

We have now mentioned the names of four out of the six painters who may be chiefly looked upon as the founders of the British school of painting—namely, Hogarth, Reynolds, West, and Wilson; the other two being Gainsborough and Barry. Each of these men has produced works that in their respective kinds have probably never been surpassed; each of them has been to a certain extent an originator. Gainsborough and Barry joined the Academy after Zoffany had painted his picture. We must, however, supply the omission by a few words on each of them.

Gainsborough was the son of a poor man residing at Sudbury in Suffolk, and enjoyed but little scholastic education. That a real education, however, did begin at a very early career, is sufficiently certain, when we know that he had painted several landscapes before he was twelve years old. In fact his boyhood was almost entirely spent in wandering about among the rich woods and along the pastoral streams of his native county, and in sketching whatever object struck his fancy. Subsequently he became a pupil of Hayman, whom we have mentioned as one of the personages of Zoffany's picture, but he did not remain long in that position. He was ambitious to achieve independence, so he painted portraits on his own account at the age of nineteen, and soon after married. He went first to Ipswich, then to Bath, but in 1774 he returned to London, and from that time went steadily on towards the highest possible reputation, and what were its natural accompaniments—pecuniary emolument and social distinction. Reynolds was one of his earliest admirers. When Gainsborough offered his Girl and Pigs for sale at the price of sixty guineas, Reynolds took it and paid a hundred. Gainsborough, too, admired Reynolds more than any other living man, more indeed than he cared to acknowledge; for the President in some way offended him. But when he was dying, he sent expressly for Sir Joshua, who came of course, full of emotion; and heard his last words—"We are all going to Heaven, and Vandyke is of the company."

Gainsborough was an amateur musician; and it is well known what a passion amateurs have for their pet enjoyment, and which in men of fine intellect becomes only the more conspicuous, because of the vigour that they must throw into everything that interests them. Gainsborough's passion was most enthusiastic—most amusing. It was not simply that an exquisite piece of melody would bathe his soul in bliss or move him to tears, or that the grander combinations of the musician would make his mind swell with admiration and sympathy, as when Handel, for instance, let loose the storm of sounds, but rode upon them as their master; his love for the art reflected itself on every person and everything connected with it. Not only were musicians the finest fellows under the sun, but their very instruments seemed to his eyes worthy of an almost awful respect and love. Smith, who wrote the life of Nollekens, found Gainsborough one day listening to the playing of a first-rate performer on the violin—a Colonel Hamilton. His cheeks were wet—he stood speechless in admiration. The colonel stopped. "Go on," exclaimed the excited painter, "and I will give you the picture of the Boy and the Stile which you so often wished to purchase of me." The colonel did so, and as his reward took away the long-coveted prize. So much for the art itself; as to his veneration for the instruments of the art, his friend Jackson tells the following capital story:—"He happened on a time to see a theorbo in a picture of Vandyke's, and concluded, because perhaps it was finely painted, that the theorbo must be a fine instrument. He recollected to have heard of a German professor, and ascending to his garret, found him dining on roasted apples, and smoking his pipe, with his theorbo beside him. 'I am come to buy your lute: name your price, and here's your money.' 'I cannot sell my lute.' 'No, not for a guinea or two; but you must sell it, I tell you.' 'My lute is worth much money: it is worth ten guineas.' 'Ay! that it is—see, here's the money.' So saying, he took up the instrument, laid down the price, went half way down the stairs and returned. 'I have done but half my errand. What is your lute worth if I have not your book?' 'What book, Master Gainsborough?' 'Why, the book of airs you have composed for the lute.' 'Ah! sir, I can never part with my book!' 'Pooh; you can make another at any time:—this is the book I mean; there's ten guineas for it—so, once more good day.' He went down a few steps, and returned again. 'What use is your book to me if I don't understand it? And your lute: you may take it again if you won't teach me to play on

it. Come home with me and give me the first lesson.' 'I will come to-morrow.' 'You must come now.' 'I must dress myself.' 'For what? you are the best figure I have seen to-day!' 'I must shave, sir.' 'I honour your beard!' 'I must, however, put on my wig.' 'D—n your wig! Your cap and beard become you. Do you think if Vandyke were to paint you, he'd let you be shaved?'" The professor acccordingly went.

It is not often permitted even to the wisest and most influential of patrons to be able to raise from poverty and obscurity two such men as the poet Crabbe and the painter Barry; yet this was Burke's proud and honourable distinction. He was present at an exhibition of art in Dublin, where there was a picture that attracted universal attention. The subject may be thus described :—St. Patrick having converted the barbarian king of Cashel, he demanded immediate baptism. The saint, hastening to obey the glad message, struck his iron-pointed crozier into the ground, and in so doing overlooked the circumstance that he had driven it through the king's foot. With a fine adherence to the literal as well as to a high spiritual truth (for all history shows that pain, if not actually lessened by some process that we are ignorant of, *seems* lessened when the imagination is highly excited), the painter had represented the king as bearing the torture without the slightest manifestation of his suffering, while the ceremony proceeded. Every person inquired, "Who was the painter?" No one knew. But presently there emerged from the crowd a poorly-clad young man, who, with his lips quivering with the emotion of success, declared that it was his work. The sages present would not believe it. Who ever heard of genius in poverty? And poor Barry, for he it was, hurried away. But, as we have said, Burke was present. He followed the young artist, made his acquaintance, and sent him to Rome; and Burke had ample reason to congratulate himself on his judgment. Barry's first picture (Venus rising from the Sea) did not excite much notice; but that was but a comparative trifle to the fact that it deserved all the attention that could possibly be paid to it; and when, after some years, he painted the great pictures at the Adelphi, the world was but too glad to express its admiration and wonder. These are now acknowledged to be among the grandest, perhaps the very grandest, productions of the English school.

Unhappily Barry was of an irritable, captious temper. Elected a member of the Royal Academy, he did nothing but quarrel with the members, from the President (West) downwards, until they ejected him. Even his friend and benefactor, Burke, became for a time estranged by Barry's attacks upon men whom Burke held in the highest honour, and for whom he felt the deepest personal affection—as, for instance, Reynolds. Yet beneath all these ebullitions of his ungovernable temper, that made his tone in his literary controversies so offensive, the essentials of what he had to say were for the most part at once true, important, and noble. He wanted to have a more lofty ideal set up by the professors of art generally than was then the case. His own maxim reveals the man—as he really was when stripped of all superficial characteristics—*No cross, no crown*; and he himself had both in those pictures in the Adelphi. When he began them he was worth just sixteen shillings; yet, single-handed, he launched himself upon the mighty undertaking, with no other prospect of obtaining a livelihood the whole time (they occupied him six years) than by working at night at any kind of miscellaneous employment that might offer; and notwithstanding the most rigid economy, this resource occasionally failed; and then what Barry suffered, the imagination is unwilling to think of. He never borrowed a sixpence; and when, after long labouring at the works, the intentional benefactor was obliged so far to stoop as to ask for assistance from the Society, they refused him. He received, however, at subsequent periods, two donations of fifty guineas each; and that was all, until the works were finished, when the exhibition produced him nearly a thousand pounds. Excellent Jonas Hanway was one of the earliest visitors: he had hardly taken a peep round before he ran back, and insisted upon paying a guinea for admission, instead of the shilling he had paid.

———

We were among the thousands of persons who, two or three years ago, flocked to Twickenham, to see the place that had obtained so wide a celebrity under the name of "Strawberry Hill." And curiously disappointed we felt at the first glance of the building (Fig. 2449); there was something to our eyes positively ludicrous in the contrast between the reality and the associations that its "Gothic" reputation naturally excited. The old English architects—the men who made the Gothic what it was in the days of its highest prosperity—were men of some invention; but certainly they never imagined such a specimen of the Gothic as this architectural labour of love by Horace Walpole (Figs. 2447, 2448). A "plaything-house" he found it; and he was very pleasant and witty

2457.—James Watt.

2458.—The Ocean Steamer.

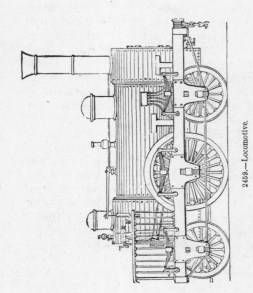

2459.—Locomotive.

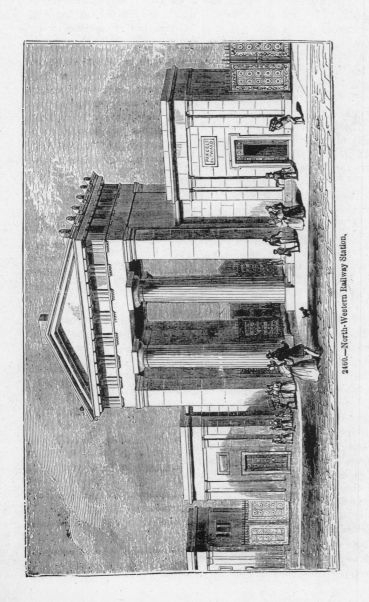

2460.—North-Western Railway Station.

2461.—Primrose Hill Tunnel.

in his description of the place in that state; but we think he might have been at least equally amusing on the state in which he left it—a plaything-house to the last. Writing, on June 8, 1747, to his dear friend Conway (Walpole's friendship for this gentleman is the one trait of unalloyed unselfishness in his character), he says—"You perceive by my date [Twickenham] that I am got into a new camp, and have left my tub at Windsor; it is a little plaything-house that I got out of Mrs. Chevenix's shop, and is the prettiest bauble you ever saw. It is set in enamelled meadows, with filigree hedges—

> A small Euphrates through the piece is roll'd,
> And little fishes wave their wings in gold.

Two delightful roads that you would call dusty supply me continually with coaches and chaises; barges as solemn as Barons of the Exchequer move under my window. Richmond Hill and Ham walks bound my prospects; but, thank God, the Thames is between me and the Duchess of Queensberry; dowagers as plenty as flounders inhabit all around, and Pope's ghost is just now skimming under my window by a most poetical moonlight. The Chevenixes had tricked the cottage up for themselves. Up two pair of stairs is what they call Mr. Chevenix's library, furnished with three maps, one shelf, a bust of Sir Isaac Newton, and a lunar telescope without any glasses."

And up "two pair of stairs" the Earl of Orford's showy library (Fig. 2451) was also to be found when Strawberry Hill, with all its precious contents, was lately laid open to the public gaze; nay, the very staircase—whitewashed, and too narrow for more than one person to ascend or descend at the same time—remained, we presume, in its original state. Everywhere the same incongruities were visible. The place teemed—overflowed with treasures of art and vertu—but they were packed away in such places, and in such a style, as to give the whole the appearance of a superior kind of shop for the sale of such things, rather than the aspect of a building that should in all respects reflect the elegant tastes, and show how well used had been the wealth and the leisure of its aristocratic owner. Strawberry Hill, for instance, must have its chapel in one part of the grounds, and knowing that there was a shrine by Cavalini in it, one's imagination is naturally a little excited by the anticipated splendour of the place: when you get there you find the shrine true and beautiful enough, but it is so large that the chapel looks merely like a box built over it, and profusely ornamented with Gothic adornments.

But the contents of Strawberry Hill were indeed well worth going to see—so rich were they, so varied, and so apparently inexhaustible. They covered every spare inch of wall, they filled every cupboard, or shelf, or niche, they loaded every table. And it was a noticeable and pleasant occupation to mark where the stream of spectators seemed most to pause in curiosity and admiration. Sir Joshua Reynolds's large picture of the three daughters of the second Earl of Waldegrave attracted especial attention; and well does that beautiful picture deserve it. The ladies were ever enraptured with the china room. And those who looked at their catalogue would see some characteristic evidences of the mind of the accomplished and able gossip who had collected them. He thus notices two "Saxon tankards, one with Chinese figures, the other with European. These tankards are extremely remarkable. Sir Robert Walpole drank ale; the Duchess of Kendal, mistress of King George I., gave him the former. A dozen or more of years afterwards the Countess of Yarmouth, mistress of King George II., without having seen the other, gave him the second, and they match exactly in form and size." On the chief staircase the exceedingly beautiful armour of the gallant French monarch, Francis the First, won universal admiration; it was of steel, gilt, and covered with engravings in bas-relief of his exploits. The couvre-feu, or curfew, was sure to stop the onward movement of the fashionable crowds. So, too, did the antique silver clock, which had been originally a present from Henry VIII. to Anne Bullen. But the gem of the collection, if we may trust to the opinions of the visitors, as shown in their eager desire to press into the front of the circle of admirers, was the silver bell by Benvenuto Cellini, which was entirely covered with the most delicate and beautiful workmanship. For ourselves, we remember nothing that pleased us more than a bas-relief of Eleonora, the mistress of Tasso, revealing, however, little or nothing of the personal beauty for which, as well as for her intellect, the poet has immortalized her. The most elegant part of the mansion was the gallery (Fig. 2450).

But these, and all the apparently inexhaustible stores of Strawberry Hill—upon which the proud and gratified owner found it necessary to expend above a hundred quarto pages of description—are scattered to the four corners of the earth. And as we think of this utter breaking up and dispersion, the words recur to the mind from his letter to Conway, 1761 :—

"I am writing, I am building—both works that will outlast the memory of battles and heroes! Truly, I believe, the one will as much as t'other. My buildings are paper, like my writings, and both will be blown away in ten years after I am dead: if they had not the substantial use of amusing me while I live, they would be worth little indeed."

This prophecy has proved true enough as regards the one department of his exertions; as to the other, some at least of his writings are destined no doubt to be much more permanent. As a letter writer his reputation never stood higher than at the present moment.

It was at Strawberry Hill that Walpole set up his printing-press in 1757, by means of which he printed most of his own works, and some others. And with this press, the adding to and arranging his pictures, books, and curiosities—continual letter writing—and occasional attempts at more ambitious composition, as in his 'Castle of Otranto' and 'The Mysterious Mother,' Walpole whiled his life away very pleasantly, and kept himself from being too closely mixed up with the public men and public business of the day. He had evidently no political ambition, or with his position—as the son of one of the most powerful ministers who ever ruled England—and with his unquestioned talents, he might have commanded the very highest posts and dignities. But Walpole's character was full of contradictions. A more thorough aristocrat in feeling and manners never lived; yet did he patronize republican principles, and when he was elevated to the peerage through the death of a nephew, he did not even care to take his seat in the Upper House, and he used the title as seldom as possible. Then again, though a distinguished member of another republic, that of letters, and having in every way the habits of literary men, he never mingled among them, seldom spoke of them but with contempt—his own especial favourites, such as Gray, of course, excepted. Here is a specimen, to Cole, 1773: "Mr. Gough wants to be introduced to me. He is so dull, that he would only be troublesome; and besides you know I shun authors, and would never have been one myself, if it obliged me to keep such bad company. *They are always in earnest*, and think their profession serious, and dwell upon trifles, and reverence learning. I laugh at all these things, and write only to laugh at them and divert myself. . . . . Mr. Gough is very welcome to see Strawberry Hill, or I would help him to any scraps in my possession that would assist his publication; though he is one of those industrious who are only reburying the dead; but I cannot be acquainted with him. It is contrary to my system and my humour. . . . . I have no thirst to know the rest of my contemporaries, from the absurd bombast of Dr. Johnson down to the silly Dr. Goldsmith; though the latter changeling has had bright gleams of parts, and the former had sense till he changed it for words, and sold it for a pension. Don't think me scornful. Recollect that I have seen Pope, and lived with Gray."

Now it cannot be questioned that Walpole's letters are ever fresh and delightful; but it seems to us to be a grave doubt whether we do not err in looking upon them as possessing any other kind of truth than that of their reflecting the mind of the writer. Of what authority should be that judgment upon the true characters of men whom we do not very well know, when we find how ridiculously prejudiced they are upon those we are perfectly familiar with? "Silly Dr. Goldsmith!" In the same sense we might say "Wise Horace Walpole!"

If Walpole had no love nor respect for his literary contemporaries—no personal sympathy with their difficulties, of which Chatterton's memorable case will for ever remain an example, and a terrible reproach—if, above all, he kept himself most jealously aloof from their society, these traits all belonged to the individual, and not to the class. Nothing can be more delightful than to see how the custom begun by Shakspere and his contemporaries, at the Falcon and the Mermaid and the Devil Taverns, was kept up during the present period by the eminent men of the day, at "Will's" and "Button's," and the other coffee-houses, that have obtained so wide reputation. Indeed, the eighteenth century was especially the era of clubs. They existed for all classes of society, and in every part of the kingdom. As one evidence of their popularity, it may be noticed that Addison's and Steele's famous periodical, the 'Spectator,' is based as it were upon the idea of an imaginary club of persons who are accustomed to meet together, among whom Sir Roger de Coverley, and the Spectator himself, are the most conspicuous personages. In that same work we learn of the existence of clubs for the most fantastical purposes, such as, for instance—the Ugly Club, into which none but members of the most downright outrageous ugliness were admitted. Even the ladies had their clubs: one became very fashionable under the name of the Blue Stocking Club, in which it was intended "The fair sex might participate in conversation with literary and ingenious men, animated by a desire to please." There were also street clubs, where the inhabitants of any particular street might meet together nightly. But the most important of them all were the clubs or coffee-house societies (for the one partook very closely of the nature of the other, by not allowing indiscriminate intrusion), where the chief literary, and other eminent intellectual men of the time met together. Will's, in Covent Garden, at the end of Bow Street, on the north side of Russell Street, was Dryden's (Figs. 2428, 2431) favourite spot. Every day after dinner the poet entered and took the principal seat, and became for the evening the undisputed Jupiter of that little Olympus; and we are enabled from various sources to see his person, hear the style of his conversation, and mark the character of the persons around him almost as well as if we had actually seen him in the place with our own eyes. Thus, with regard to his dress, "I remember," says a correspondent of the 'Gentleman's Magazine' in 1745, "plain John Dryden, before he paid his court with success to the great, in one uniform clothing of Norwich drugget. I have eat tarts with him and Madame Reeve at the Mulberry Garden, when our author advanced to a sword and a Chadreux wig." The poet himself has described his manners in society. He says, "My conversation is slow and dull, my humour saturnine, and reserved. In short, I am not one of those who endeavour to break jests in company, or make repartees." Elsewhere he writes—

> Nor wine nor love could ever see me gay;
> To writing bred, I knew not what to say.

Yet it is not the less certain, we think, that he had much to say at such times, and that he said it well, or he could never have drawn around him such a brilliant circle. If we take a period towards the close of the seventeenth century, we find among the attenders at Will's, the great Duke of Ormond, the witty Earls of Dorset and Rochester, with other noblemen, Sedley, Cowley, Waller, Denham, and Davenant (Fig. 2426). It was when all these were his intimates, that "Dryden," writes Sir Walter Scott, "enjoyed those genial nights described in the dedication of the 'Assignation,' when discourse was neither too serious nor too light, but always pleasant, and for the most part instructive: the raillery neither too sharp upon the present, nor too censorious upon the absent: and the cups such only as raised the conversation of the night, without disturbing the business of the morrow."

The same writer has observed in illustration of the poet's supremacy at Will's, that "a pinch out of Dryden's snuff-box was equal to taking a degree in that academy of wit;" and many there were who have left records of their desire to be so honoured. The dean of Peterborough, who came to London about seventeen, tells us, "In spite of my bashfulness and [youthful] appearance, I used now and then to thrust myself into Will's, to have the pleasure of seeing the most celebrated wits of that time. The second time that ever I was there, Mr. Dryden was speaking of his own things, as he frequently did, especially of such as had been lately published." Cibber has also left particulars of his first visit to Will's. But the most memorable of all these youthful aspirants for the notice of the literary veteran was Pope. When he was twelve years old he prevailed upon a friend to introduce him to Will's, that he might have the pleasure of seeing an author whom he then probably admired beyond any other poet, ancient or modern. Johnson has given us an additional bit or two of pleasant gossip relating to Dryden and Will's. He remarked once to Boswell, "When I was a young fellow I wanted to write the life of Dryden, and in order to get materials, I applied to the only two persons then alive who had seen him: these were old Swiney and old Cibber. Swiney's information was no more than this, 'that at Will's coffee-house Dryden had a particular chair for himself, which was set by the fire in winter, and was then called his winter-chair; and that it was carried out for him to the balcony in summer, and was then called his summer-chair.' Cibber could tell no more but 'that he remembered him a decent old man, arbiter of critical disputes at Will's.'" Davenant, we may observe, was the poet-laureate of his day, as Rowe (Fig. 2430) was of his.

Not all Will's titled and intellectual visitors, however, seem to have made the house flourish; unless, indeed, Master Will was one of those persons whom no amount of success ever enables to succeed, whose pockets are but so many sieves through which everything passes—no matter what the amount or quantities poured in.

Dennis, the critic (Fig. 2435), with whom Dryden had so many tough battles, describes Will, or in other words, William Erwin, or Urwin, who kept the house, as taking refuge in Whitefriars, then a place of asylum, to escape the clutches of his creditors. 'For since the law," says the critic, "thought it just to put Will out of its protection, Will thought it but prudent to put himself out of its power."

The original sign of Will's had been a cow, but in Dryden's time the rose was substituted, and eventually the establishment was known as the Rose. And here, as we learn from Swift's verses on his own death, the wits of his time were accustomed to assemble, including, most probably, the set to which he himself belonged, namely, Pope, Bishop Berkeley (Fig. 2429), Gay, Arbuthnot, and others. In one passage of the poem he writes—

> Suppose me dead, and then suppose
> A club assembled at the Rose,
> Where from discourse of this and that,
> I grow the subject of their chat.
> "The Dean, if we believe report,
> Was never ill received at court,
> Although ironically grave,
> He shamed the fool, and lashed the knave,
> To steal a hint was never known,
> But what he writ was all his own."
> " Sir, I have heard another story;
> He was a most confounded Tory,
> And grew, or he is much belied,
> Extremely dull before he died."
> "Can we the Drapier then forget?
> Is not our nation in his debt?
> 'Twas he that writ the Drapier's letters."
> " He should have left them for his betters,
> We had a hundred abler men,
> Nor need depend upon his pen," &c.

The letters here referred to demand a few passing words of explanation. There was a scarcity of copper coin in Ireland, in the early part of the century, and—ostensibly—in consequence, a patent was granted to William Wood to coin farthings and halfpence to the amount of 108,000l. But it soon became known that the grant had been obtained solely through the influence of the king's mistress, the Duchess of Kendal, who was to have a share of the profits, and that the lord lieutenant of Ireland had not even been consulted upon the matter. There was a general sentiment of disgust and indignation. The Irish Parliament remonstrated, but was treated with contemptuous silence. Then stepped forth Swift, under the anonymous disguise of a Drapier, and published several letters on the subject, that so completely obtained possession of the mind of the Irish people, that if every one of Wood's Irish halfpence, &c. (Fig. 2190) had issued from the pockets of persons smitten with the plague, they could not have more universally shunned or dreaded their slightest touch. When the fourth letter appeared, a reward of 300l. was offered for the discovery of the author. That failing of success, the printer was to be prosecuted. A bill against him was about to be presented to the grand jury, when Swift wrote 'Some Seasonable Advice,' which had the effect desired; the grand jury ignored the bill, to the exceeding rage of the presiding judge, Whitehead. At last, completely defeated, the government was obliged to withdraw the Wood coppers, and compensate him. The popularity of Swift (Fig. 2420), who was soon known as the author of the 'Drapier's Letters,' was perfectly boundless. The Drapier's head was painted on public-house and other signs, woven in pocket-handkerchiefs, engraved on medals and copper-plates.

Between Swift, Pope, Gay, and Arbuthnot, much deeper feeling prevailed than sufficed merely to give a genial tone to the coffee-house assemblings. Their letters to each other are full of passages of the warmest affection. It is quite refreshing to see every now and then a gush of feeling welling up that serves to sweep away in an instant the thousand little incrustations that their respective literary quarrels—and other sources of annoyance—had gathered around their hearts. We speak not merely of their relations to each other, but generally of that desire they all more or less evidence for the enjoyment of true friendship. Thus Pope (Fig. 2434) (we quote from the invaluable collection of letters written by or to him), on one occasion writes—"I have for some years been employed much like children that build houses with cards, endeavouring very busily and eagerly to raise a friendship, which the first breath of any ill-natured bystander could puff away." In another letter we find Gay and Pope writing in the same sheet to Swift. Gay begins, and the concluding portion of his share of the correspondence relates to a most interesting subject—his 'Beggar's Opera.' He says—"You remember you were advising me to go into Newgate to finish my scenes the more correctly. I now think I shall, for I

2462.—Viaduct over the Upper Avon.

2463.—Birmingham Terminus of North-Western Railway.

2464.—London Bridge Railway Station.

2465.—Blackwall Railway Station.

2466.—London and Greenwich Railway.

2467.—Benjamin Franklin

2463.—Gas Factory.

have no attendance to hinder me ; but my opera is already finished. I leave the rest of this paper to Mr. Pope." And then Pope begins : —" Gay is a free man, and I writ him a long congratulatory letter upon it. Do you the same : it will mend him, and make him a better man than a Court could do. Horace might keep his coach in Augustus's time, if he pleased, but I won't in the time of our Augustus. My poem—(which it grieves me that I dare not send you a copy of for fear of the Curlls and Dennises of Ireland, and still more for fear of the worst of traytors, our friends and admirers)— my poem, I say, will show what a distinguishing age we lived in. Your name is in it with some others, under a mark of such ignominy as you will not much grieve to wear in that company. Adieu, and God bless you, and give you health and spirits,

> Whether thou choose Cervantes' serious air,
> Or laugh and shake in Rab'lais's easy chair,
> Or in the graver gown instruct mankind,
> Or silent let thy morals tell thy mind.

These two verses are over and above what I've said of you in the poem. Adieu." The most touching feature of this correspondence is the lamentation of the friends for the death of Gay, whose simple, guileless nature, combined with his high talents, won the love and respect of all who knew him. Pope, in relating the circumstances to Swift, observes, " *Good God! how often are we to die before we quite go off this stage?*—In every friend we lose a part of ourselves, and the best part. God keep those we have left ! Few are worth praying for, and oneself the least of all." On the back of this letter of Pope's was subsequently discovered the following remarkable memorandum by Swift :—" On my dear friend Mr. Gay's death : Received December 15, *but not read till the 20th, by an impulse foreboding some misfortune.*"

Swift's desire for friendship, though no less ardent than those felt by his friends, took occasionally a wider scope, and was connected with loftier and less personal objects. He somewhere says, " I have often endeavoured to establish a friendship among all men of genius, and would fain have done it. They are seldom above three or four contemporaries, and if they could be united, would drive the world before them." Of Swift's zeal in the cause of his friends, the coffee-houses could bear witness. Johnson states, on the authority of Kennet, that on the 2nd of November, 1713—

" Dr. Swift came into the coffee-house, and had a bow from everybody but me, who, I confess, could not but despise him. When I came to the ante-chamber to wait, before prayers, Dr. Swift was the principal man of talk and business, and acted as master of requests. Then he instructed a young nobleman that the *best poet in England* was Mr. Pope (a papist), who had begun a translation of Homer into English verse, for which *he must have them all subscribe*; for, says he, the author shall not begin to print till I have a thousand guineas for him."

Button, the owner of the coffee-house that bore his name, had been a servant of the Countess of Warwick, Addison's wife, and he enjoyed, therefore, Addison's special patronage. This was the continual resort of Addison (Figs. 2416—2421) himself, Steele, Philips, Carey, Davenant, and Colonel Brett. It was here that Pope was to have been thrashed by Ambrose Philips, when he had offended that gentleman by an ironical paper in the ' Guardian,' which Pope had been incited to write by Tickell's absurd praise of Philips's ' Pastorals,' as the finest in the language, and which annoyed Pope the more, inasmuch as that his own pastorals appeared in the pages of the same publication. Pope does not mention this threat—it was hardly to be expected he should—except in the following very modified form :—" Philips seemed to have been encouraged to abuse me in coffee-houses and conversation." And so he in revenge abused Philips, by holding him up to ridicule, as—

> The bard whom pilfered pastorals renown,
> Who turns a Persian tale for half a crown,
> Just writes to make his barrenness appear,
> And strains from hide-bound brains eight lines a year.

Of course there is little or no truth in the lines ; Pope did not write them to express any truth, but simply to express his own feelings of rage and jealousy.

In another passage, he speaks in a much more dignified spirit of their quarrel, in which Addison became engaged as the friend of Tickell and Philips. It appears that in the controversy that now raged, the critics and poets were divided into factions, led by the respective leaders. Pope says—" I have the town, that is, the mob, on my side ; but it is not uncommon for the smaller party to supply by industry what it wants in numbers—I appeal to the people as my rightful judges, and while they are not inclined to condemn me, shall not fear the high-flyers at Button's."

One of the most striking of Pope's personal traits was his own sensitiveness when the weapon that he was so fond of using against others was turned upon himself—namely, ridicule. The critic, Dennis, was like a perpetual blister at his side. Cibber, too, was by no means unwilling or unable to return his attacks, and, as far as the effect was concerned, with interest. Speaking of one of Cibber's pamphlets, Pope said it would be as good as a dose of hartshorn to him, but " his tongue and his heart were at variance." " I have heard," says Johnson, " Mr. Richardson state, that he attended his father, the painter, on a visit, when one of Cibber's pamphlets came into the hands of Pope, who said, ' These things are my diversion.' They sat by him while he perused it, and saw his features writhing with anguish ; and young Richardson said to his father, when they returned, ' that he hoped to be preserved from such diversions as had been that day the lot of Pope.' "

In his youth Pope resided in Windsor Forest. There was the paternal cell—

> A little house with trees a-row,
> And, like its master, very low.

About half a mile distant was—possibly still is—the tree shown in our engraving (Fig. 2437), and known as his favourite tree.

And let us now again glance at Twickenham—in order to notice Pope's residence there. Here the poet had purchased a house and grounds, and, like Horace Walpole, found a great pleasure afterwards in enlarging, altering, and improving. But the poet was much more successful than the noble letter-writer. Walpole's Gothic has taught nothing of any permanent value to any one ; but the laying out of Pope's grounds marks an era in landscape gardening, so superior did he make them to anything of the kind previously known in England. The house, since his time, has been for the most part pulled down, and the surface of the ground so completely dug about, that the fashionable Vandals who had possession of it would not even allow a monument that he erected to the memory of his beloved mother to remain undisturbed. Of one feature—the grotto (Fig. 2436)—he has left us his own description. In a letter to Edward Blount, Esq., he writes :—" I have put the last hand to my works of this kind, in happily finishing the subterraneous way and grotto : I there found a spring of the clearest water, which falls in a perpetual rill, that echoes through the cavern day and night. From the river Thames, you see through my arch up a walk of the wilderness, to a kind of open temple, wholly composed of shell in the rustic manner ; and from that distance under the temple you look down through a sloping arcade of trees, and see the sails on the river passing suddenly and vanishing as through a perspective glass. When you shut the doors of this grotto, it becomes on the instant, from a luminous room, a camera obscura ; on the walls of which all the objects of the river, hills, woods, and boats, are forming a moving picture in their visible radiations ; and when you have a mind to light it up, it affords you a very different scene ; it is finished with shells interspersed with pieces of looking-glass in angular forms ; and in the ceiling is a star of the same material, at which, when a lamp (of an orbicular figure of thin alabaster) is hung in the middle, a thousand pointed rays glitter and are reflected over the place. There are connected to this grotto by a narrower passage two porches, one towards the river of smooth stones full of light and open ; the other towards the garden shadowed with trees, rough with shells, flints, and iron-ore. The bottom is paved with simple pebble, as is also the adjoining walk up the wilderness to the temple, in the natural taste, agreeing not ill with the little dripping murmur, and the aquatic idea of the whole place. It wants nothing to complete it but a good statue with an inscription like that beautiful antique one which you know I am so fond of—

> Nymph of the grot, these sacred springs I keep,
> And to the murmur of these waters sleep ;
> Ah, spare my slumbers, gently tread the cave !
> And drink in silence, or in silence lave !

You'll think I have been very poetical in this description, but it is pretty near the truth. I wish you were here to bear testimony how little it owes to art, either the place itself, or the image I give of it."

Pope has compared himself to a " spider ;" and it is in the extreme constitutional debility of his frame, as well as in its deformity, that we must look for the sources of the irritability that had so often poisoned his own enjoyment, and made him so unjust, when angry, to others. Of his habits many little particulars have been recorded that help to show us the man—as he lived and moved. One of his constant demands from his attendants was coffee in the night. Of course, then, he could not sleep well at the proper period for sleep. So when he really wanted a little repose in the day-time, he was not unfrequently to be seen nodding in company. At the table he was anything but abstemious; though his love for highly-seasoned dishes, and the extent to which he allowed himself to gratify his love, must, we should think, have been but too much calculated to oppress the powers of Nature, already too constitutionally feeble in him. As for the rest of his personal characteristics, Johnson has summed up a world of shrewd insight into Pope's mental habits in their less exalted manifestations, when he says, " he hardly drank tea without a stratagem."

As his bodily powers, such as they were, began to decline, the mind partially sank too. One day, when Dodsley was with him, he asked " What arm it was that came out from the wall ?" He was also heard to say that his greatest inconvenience was inability to think. The touching picture of his death, with Lord Boling-broke weeping over him, is familiar to most readers. Johnson says, that on the noble lord's being told by Spence, that Pope, at the intermission of his deliriousness, was *always saying something kind*, either of his present or absent friends, and that his humanity seemed to have survived his understanding, answered, " It was so;" and added, " I never in my life knew a man that had so tender a heart, for his particular friends, or more general friendship for mankind." At another time he said, " I have known Pope these thirty years, and value myself more in his friendship than————:" his grief then suppressed his voice. There had been for some time before Pope's death a coolness existing between him and Bolingbroke, on account of the intimacy formed with Bishop Warburton (Fig. 2438), who first attacked, and then defended Pope, and thus became his friend instead of his enemy.

Between the eminent men of the earlier, and those of the later part of the century who made the Society of Club and Coffee-houses a more brilliant thing than we now-a-days have any practical conception of, let us interpose a group of booksellers. And first, we may relate, on the authority of Lord Bolingbroke, an anecdote illustrative of the personal relations of Dryden, and Tonson (Fig. 2452), his bookseller. The noble lord told Dr. King, of Oxford, that one day in his youth when he visited Dryden, they heard as they were conversing, another person entering the house. " This," said Dryden, " is Tonson. You will take care not to depart before he goes away: for I have not completed the sheet which I promised him; and if you leave me unprotected I must suffer all the rudeness to which his resentment can prompt his tongue." Tonson, it appears, had a high reputation with his brother booksellers, not only for his judgment but for his impartiality, and above all for his readiness to speak " his mind upon all occasions;" he " will flatter nobody," says Dunton (Fig. 2453); a man who has been " characterised as a sort of wild Defoe, a coarser mind cast in somewhat a like mould." (London, vol. v., p. 234.)

Dunton published his ' Life and Errors,' from which the foregoing words are taken, in 1705; he had been then twenty years in business, and printed no less than six hundred works. Guy (Fig. 2454), the founder of the well-known Hospital, was also a bookseller: his shop was in Lombard Street. The name of Cave (Fig. 2455) has obtained an honourable celebrity in connexion with the early efforts of Johnson. He it was who broke up the pamphlet system that reigned so pre-eminent before, and substituted in its place regular periodical publications to receive all such occasional papers, by the establishment of the ' Gentleman's Magazine' in 1731. Curll has obtained an infamous notoriety for the disreputable practices that he resorted to in the prosecution of his trade. Some of his tricks brought him into the pillory on one occasion; others have established him permanently in a pillory of another kind: nothing will ever extricate him from the ' Dunciad.' Tonson, and Jacob Lintot his great rival, have also been immortalized in that publication; but their offences were of a more venial kind, and we can enjoy a hearty laugh at their expense, without feeling our respect for them to any noticeable degree diminished. Among the multiplicity of books that now regularly issued from the press, we may mention the respective voyages round the world by Anson and Dampier (Fig. 2456) as belonging to a class that greatly interested our forefathers.

Towards the latter part of the century, the numerous Clubs and Coffee-house Societies of a literary and an artistical character grew more numerous than ever. And not content with one, the eminent men of the day belonged to several. Thus the chief members of the Pandemonium Club that met in Clarges Street, May Fair—of the Club held at the Blenheim Tavern, in Bond Street—of the famous Kit-cat and Beefsteak Clubs—and numerous others, seem to have also belonged to the Club held at the Mitre, in Essex Street in the Strand; which was founded by Johnson, and no

doubt on the principle so satisfactorily stated in his Dictionary, where he defines a Club to be an assembly of good fellows, meeting under certain conditions. The Mitre was kept by one who had been a servant to Thrale, Johnson's friend. The same set of personages appear also to have occasionally met at the St. James's Coffee House: and a truly honourable record of the men who assembled there, and of the tone of their society, has been left us by Goldsmith in his ' Retaliation,' the most brilliant and at the same time the most weighty of all personally descriptive poems. But before we speak of his portraiture, let us take a preliminary glance of himself, and of one of the localities — Green Arbour Court, Old Bailey (Fig. 2440)—that he has made famous.

Few men have been more misunderstood than Oliver Goldsmith. Not all the deep and serene wisdom that prevails through his works could prevent Walpole, who only echoed the opinion of some of the men who moved in the poet's own circle, from calling him " silly." Not all his searching penetration into the most hidden springs of human character and motives could teach those who were familiar with the writings in question, to study his character and motives with humility and that deep respect which could alone enable them to arrive at any worthy conclusion. Not all the acknowledged wit or humour with which such works as the ' Citizen of the World,' and the ' Vicar of Wakefield,' his Essays, &c., are full, could prevent some among his associates from making him the butt of their ridicule; and which they were enabled to do with impunity, partly because his nature was too unsuspicious as well as too lofty to allow him to be ever on the watch to see that his dignity was not attacked, partly because of his genial love for every kind of sport and enjoyment, whether at his own or at others' expense, and partly, because he had no spirit of malice, or hate, or revengefulness in his whole composition, that could suggest the putting down of attacks by making them too painful and hazardous to the assailants, to be persisted in, as was Pope's method. Yet could Boswell and his whole tribe (Fig. 2441)—as they made merry with Goldsmith's gait, clothes, habits, life, and conversation, have known what was sometimes probably on such occasions passing in his mind—could they have seen how in an intellectual sense they were but the merest puppets in his hand—that he could have pulled them to pieces—and often no doubt was doing so to analyse what this little movement of theirs meant, and why that little thought—thought as it did—they would never again have ventured to open their mouths, hardly to have held up their heads in his company. But with such profound knowledge of human nature as Goldsmith possessed, there is ever—and wise and beneficial indeed is the provision—as profound a sense of the responsibility that the knowledge involves. Men like Shakspere are never found to use their weapons to the pain or injury of any one—hardly ever against the wicked, unless for reformatory purpose: so is it, in a lesser degree, with Goldsmith. The moths, therefore, buzz safely around the greatest intellectual luminaries; a power, not of their own, preserves them from the *singeing* they so wantonly provoke.

The particular incidents that produced ' The Retaliation' were these. One day, at the St. James's Coffee-house, it was proposed to write epitaphs upon Goldsmith. Of course the compositions produced took considerable liberties with his country, dialect, mind, and so on. He was then expressly challenged to retaliation, and at the next meeting produced the poem. Nowhere do his good humour and brotherly feeling appear more delightful, even whilst nowhere is his wit more keen, or his sagacious insight into the mysteries of human character, in its very highest development, more perfect. We learn from the poem who were the chief men constituting the society. These were the Dean of Derry; Burke, and his relatives William and Richard; Cumberland, the author of the comedy of ' The West Indian,' and a great number of other dramatic pieces; Dr. Douglas, subsequently Bishop of Salisbury, who distinguished himself by his critical sagacity in detecting Lauder's forgeries relating to Milton; Garrick (Fig. 2444), Reynolds (Fig. 2443), and many others. Let us observe, in passing, that neither Burke, nor Reynolds, nor Garrick, were among the men who esteemed Goldsmith too lightly, as Johnson certainly was, though of course his views are not to be confounded with the views of Boswell and his class. Put any particular work of Goldsmith's before Johnson, and he was literally sure to speak of it as favourably as any one; but the common error of dissociating a man from his writings was clearly one of Johnson's errors, in weighing the character and productions even of so dear a friend as Goldsmith.

The portraits of Burke and Garrick especially are beyond all praise. As to the statesman, it is but the literal truth to say that nothing has ever been written since Goldsmith's time, even in the most laboured volumes, that has added anything essential to the

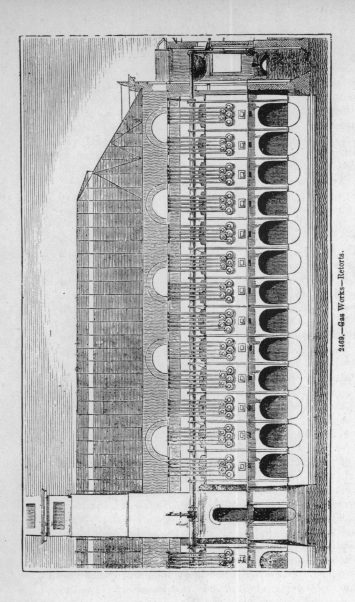

2469.—Gas Works—Retorts.

2471.—Gas Works—Gasometers.

2470.—Gas Works—Purifiers and Condensers.

2472.—Gas Works—Turning On.

2473.—Gas Works—Gas Meter.

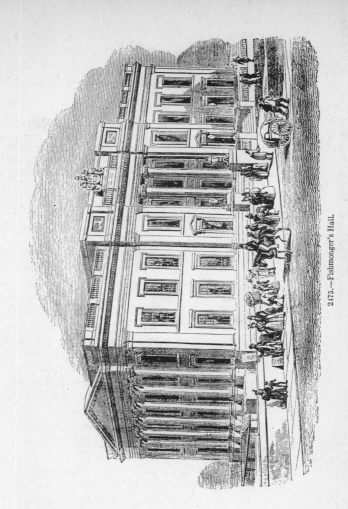

2175.—Fishmonger's Hall.

2474.—Steam Printing Machine.

truth or to the moral of the wonderful portraiture, or rendered it necessary to wish that a single line or word could be taken away. Of Burke we read, that his

> Genius was such,
> We scarcely can praise it or blame it too much;
> Who, born for the universe, narrowed his mind,
> *And to party gave up what was meant for mankind;*
> Though fraught with all learning, yet straining his throat
> To persuade Tommy Townsend to lend him a vote;
> Who, too deep for his hearers, still went on refining,
> And thought of convincing, while they thought of dining;
> Though equal to all things, for all things unfit;
> Too nice for a statesman, too proud for a wit;
> For a patriot too cool; for a drudge disobedient;
> And too fond of the *right* to pursue the expedient.
> In short, 't was his fate, unemploy'd, or in place, Sir,
> To eat mutton cold, and cut blocks with a razor.

Cumberland's was a name of high note in his own period, but time has allowed it to sink very considerably in popular as well as in critical estimation. His papers in the 'Observer' on the Greek poets, and some of his dramatic essays, are however still sufficient to preserve him a respectable rank in literature; and there are several among the numerous plays he wrote that are still and deservedly admired, the comedy of 'The West Indian' especially. Truly charming for its truth, as well as for the delightful mode in which he has made that truth palatable, is Goldsmith's portrait of Richard Cumberland :—

> A flattering painter, who made it his care
> To draw men as they ought to be, not as they are;

but—

> Quite sick of pursuing each troublesome elf,
> He grew lazy at last, and drew from himself?

One of the most interesting incidents in the history of the friendships of eminent men is that between Johnson and Garrick, notwithstanding the dissimilarity, in many respects, between their minds and views. Garrick was Johnson's pupil at Lichfield, when neither were as yet in the slightest degree known to fame. They set out for the metropolis together; and though their paths for a time diverged, they ultimately became reunited when both had obtained very high success and distinction, and from that time until death enjoyed the continual society of each other. Johnson's success was a work of time, and only obtained after long adversity; Garrick, when his thoughts and ambition were turned into the right direction, almost instantly sprang up to the very highest pinnacle of histrionic reputation. He first appeared, under an assumed name, at Ipswich, and played all kinds of characters, not even excepting that of Harlequin, in which he was admired for his grace, humour, and agility. The manager of the Ipswich theatre was also the manager of a petty London theatre situated in Goodman's Fields; and there Garrick appeared as Richard III., in October 1741. Not many nights elapsed before the new actor was the common town's-talk. Pope went to see his Richard III. His emphatic statement of the result of his visit was conveyed in these words to Lord Orrery :— "That young man never had his equal as an actor, and will never have a rival." Goldsmith says of David Garrick,—

> Describe him who can?
> An abridgment of all that is pleasant in man.
> As an actor, confess'd without rival to shine;
> As a wit, if not first, in the very first line;
> Yet with talents like these, and an excellent heart,
> The man had his failings—a dupe to his art :
> Like an ill-judging beauty, his colours he spread,
> And beplastered with rouge his own natural red.

> On the stage he was natural, simple, affecting;
> 'T was only that when he was off he was acting.
> With no reason on earth to go out of his way,
> He turned and he varied full ten times a day;
> Though secure of our hearts, yet confoundedly sick
> If they were not his own by finessing and trick :
> He cast off his friends as a huntsman his pack,
> For he knew when he pleased he could whistle them back.
> Of praise a mere glutton, he swallowed what came,
> And the puff of a dunce he mistook it for fame ;
> Till, his relish grown callous almost to disease,
> Who peppered the highest was surest to please.
> But let us be candid, and speak out our mind ;
> If dunces applauded, he paid them in kind.
> Ye Kenricks, ye Kellys, and Woodfalls so grave,
> What a commerce was yours, while you got and you gave !
> How did Grub Street re-echo the shouts that you raised,
> While he was be-Rosciused, and you were be-praised !
> But peace to his spirit, wherever it flies,
> To act as an angel, and mix with the skies :
> Those poets who owe their best fame to his skill
> Shall still be his flatterers, go where he will;
> Old Shakspere receive him with praise and with love,
> And Beaumonts and Bens be his Kellys above.

Garrick, like the other characters of 'Retaliation,' is represented as dead, in order that their epitaphs might be written with propriety. When Garrick really died, Johnson—the stern moralist Johnson—said the gaiety of nations was eclipsed.

Unhappily the 'Retaliation' was not finished, and Johnson's portrait did not get into it : it was reserved probably by Goldsmith to be one of the last, as requiring the greatest care and delicacy (Fig. 2439). His intellectual characteristics would then have been brought out as we must now never hope to see them, and with these we should have had some intimation of his extraordinary personal characteristics.

And whether it be a fancy suggested by the consideration of Johnson's character, at the conclusion of the work through which our readers have so long, and, we trust, patiently and considerately —on account of its various peculiar difficulties—accompanied us, or whether it be that Johnson really does form a very felicitous personification of the spirit of Old England, we cannot but please ourselves, in these our last lines, by briefly following out such a parallel. He had all the solid sense, with a sprinkling of the determined prejudices of Old England. He had its independence and love of freedom, purchased, as were the freedom and independence of Old England, at the cost of many and sharp and bitter struggles; and like that, for the most part his love of liberty did not run into any dangerous excesses; both were, on the whole, decided conservatives. He had all the devout feeling that was so pre-eminent a characteristic of Old England—he had also the superstitions that accompanied the faith of our forefathers; witness—but let us in respect to his memory utter the words in a whisper—the Cock Lane Ghost. He could do, and did, great things, but he also liked to be flattered and told so—to be worshipped, in short, as Boswell worshipped him : and has it not been so with Old England? He gloried in the chief glories of his country—its Shakspere and Milton; he enjoyed their writings, but he did not always very well understand them—neither did Old England. He had the ponderous learning of Old England; he had much of its poetry. Lastly, he had the genuine Old English love for argumentation, ending, when necessary, in some sort of knock-down blow :—the Old English bearishness when out of temper,—the hearty Old English love of good fellowship in his better moods—the unwearying Old English philanthropy when any called for the aid that he had the means of affording. Honour to both !

BOOK VIII.

A GLANCE AT THE PROGRESS OF SOCIETY FOR THE LAST HUNDRED YEARS.

CHAPTER I.—DISCOVERY AND INVENTION.

HE reader who has perused with ordinary attention the foregoing books of this discursive treatise upon all that is memorable and noteworthy in Old England, will have gained a tolerably correct notion, not merely of the things which are worth seeing and the events which are worth knowing in connection with our social and national history, but of the gradual growth of the national character up to the death of the second George. It is a fact, however, that the Englishman of a century back was in many respects a very different being from the Englishman of the present day. With the same patriotism, the same love of home and of order, the same religious faith, and, to a great extent, the same political predilections as our forefathers,—we have no longer the same modes of life, the same habits of thought and sympathy, and the same bigoted adherence to old and established customs which characterised them. The generation of to-day lives ten or twelve years longer in the world than the generation of a century back, and it lives more in a single year than some generations who have been long dead and gone lived in their whole lives. England has wellnigh quadrupled her population since the dawn of the eighteenth century. The population, as it has grown more numerous, has in the ratio of its increase become more capable and efficient in all the arts of living; because with increase of numbers came the necessity for increased exertion and for co-operation and competition in the various branches of industry that sustain life. Science, arts, manufactures, invention and discovery, have each and all made such prodigious strides since the day when George the Third ascended the throne—and have effected such wonderful changes both in the face of the country and the habits of the people, that, at a superficial glance, all verisimilitude between the soil and the race of our time and those of a century back would seem to have vanished; and we must look deeper than the surface of things to recognise the identity of principle and purpose which proclaims them of one common stock. The impossibilities of our forefathers are the matter-of-fact of to-day. We live in a world of wonders which habit has familiarised to us, but which, barely to have foretold a hundred, or even fifty years ago, would have drawn down upon the rash prophet the ridicule and mockery of his fellow-men, and have subjected him to public scorn, if not to the compassionate care of a lunatic asylum.

It is difficult at the present moment to realise anything like a true picture of private and domestic life and manners, among the trading and lower classes especially, during the middle and latter part of the last century. The narratives and illustrations which abound in this volume supply the best aids to the realization of such a picture which literature, so far as we are aware, has to offer in one view; but it is only by contrast with the present condition of society that a satisfactory estimate can be formed of the real difference between the peoples, their pursuits, plans, and purposes, of the two epochs. Viewed socially, the chasm is broader and deeper between the present date and that of a century back than would be found to exist in any period of five times the duration in our past history. It is our intention, with a view of bringing the interest of this work down to our own day—and thus affording our readers something like a panorama of English life and manners—to attempt, as far as our limits will allow, to bridge over this chasm, and connect as closely as may be the present era with the past. We are necessarily restricted, by the small space that remains open for the purpose, from any comprehensive view of the subject, and must therefore resort to a somewhat summary process. Of matters political and legislative we can take but small notice; and there is in fact no need that we should trench upon the functions of the historian in this department, seeing that there is no lack of popular works on such subjects. What we propose doing in the following pages, is to narrate briefly the rise, progress, and application of the great inventions and discoveries of this latter era, which, themselves the offspring of human necessities, have proved the grand means of social amelioration and advancement—to glance at the progress of art and literature, and the means available for their universal diffusion—and to suggest the connection and correspondence which ever must exist between the progress of science and invention, the spread of letters and the fine arts, and the progress towards the complete civilization and happiness of the human family.

Foremost in the list of inventions by which mankind has profited stands the STEAM-ENGINE. It is the one invention which has given birth to a thousand others; it is the vital principle of our machinery and manufactures; and is at once the Titanic power which achieves the mightiest labours, and the docile servant obedient to the feeblest hand. By steam we plough the stormy billows in the teeth of opposing winds, and bring together the uttermost parts of the earth —by steam we delve the mine, raise the hidden ore to the surface, blast it in the furnace, and weld the glowing masses to purposes of utility—and by steam, if need be, we grind a pin or polish a needle's point. There is hardly a purpose in the domain of industry to which it may not be applied, and there is scarcely a spot to be found, where labour is the business of life, in which the steam-engine in some form or other is not the motive power. Let us glance briefly at the birth and parentage of this wonderful servant of man.

Hero of Alexandria, who lived about two thousand years ago, was the first man who pointed out the efficiency of steam as a mechanical force. It seems doubtful whether he proceeded further than merely making known the principle upon which an engine of great power might be constructed; he was fond of mechanical puzzles, and of the contriving of curious instruments capitally adapted for playing off practical jokes, or producing effects calculated to astonish the uninitiated, but which were for the most part not applicable to any useful purpose; and we are of opinion that his steam-engine, notwithstanding all that has been said to the contrary, never existed save in his own illustrative diagrams. The invention of the steam-engine has been claimed by a Spaniard for one Blasco de Garay, who is stated to have made a successful experiment in steam-navigation in the harbour of Barcelona as early as the year 1543, and to have been rewarded by Philip II. for his invention with the gift of two hundred thousand maravedis—a statement which smacks too much of the improbable to be generally received. Arago, the distinguished French philosopher, makes a much more modest claim on behalf of Solomon de Caus, who, by a work which he published in Frankfort in 1615, shows that he was at least aware of the expansive force of steam, and suggests a mode of applying it to the propulsion of a column of water to a great height. Some years after the appearance of De Caus's book an Italian engineer, named Branca, published a work, in which he pointed out several novel applications to which steam-power might be directed. The first Englishman who turned his attention to the

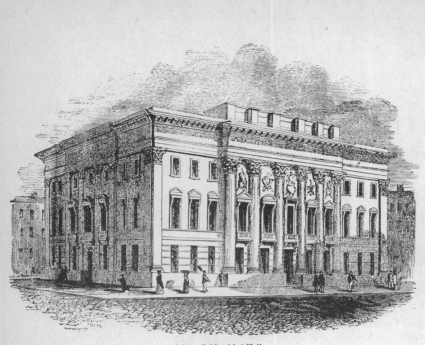

2476.—Goldsmiths' Hall.

2477.—Goldsmiths' Hall.

2478.—Front of National Gallery.

2479.—Royal Exchange.

2480.—Corn Exchange, Mark Lane.

2481.—Mansion House.

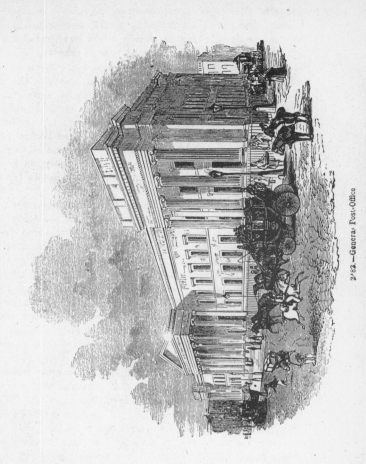

2482.—General Post-Office.

2483.—Hall of General Post-Office.

power of steam appears to have been the royalist Marquis of Worcester. The story goes that while he was imprisoned in the Tower he was one day cooking his dinner, when he observed that the lid of the pot was repeatedly forced upwards by the vapour of the boiling water. It occurred to him that the same power which raised the pot's lid might be applied to other uses. On recovering his liberty he set to work to test his idea by experiments, which proved perfectly succes ful. According to other accounts, the Marquis owed his first idea of steam force to the unfortunate De Caus, whom he found among the lunatics in the Bicêtre, whither he had been sent by Cardinal Richelieu for pertinaciously haunting him with his invention. Allowing this account to be true, the Marquis has still the merit of first demonstrating how the agency of steam could be used for mechanical purposes.

Various causes combined to render the engine of the marquis of no practical use, and it remained in abeyance for many years. In the meanwhile a Frenchman named Papin discovered the means of producing a moving power by a piston working in a cylinder, the motion to be effected by the condensation of steam into water. This was a most important discovery, but Papin tooks no steps to carry it out. The idea of a working steam-engine seemed now for a time abandoned, and the subject might have remained longer in neglect than it did, had it not been that the water got into the Cornish mines faster than it could possibly be pumped out, and as one of them had been abandoned after another, the mining interest was fast going to ruin. The ordinary pumps proving of no avail, Captain Thomas Savery turned his attention once more to steam, and in 1698 devised a machine that answered the purpose. This was a combination of the invention of Worcester and the discovery of Papin, and was the germ of the steam-engine as it now exists. It was a rude contrivance, however, and so expensive and wasteful in operation as to be only of very limited use. It was subsequently much improved by Newcomen, a Cornish agent, and though still costly in its working, became extensively used in the mining districts.

The engine of Newcomen, with improvements of various kinds by Smeaton, Brindley, and others, continued in use for a considerable part of the last century; but it was employed for few other purposes than the pumping of water, and probably, so imperfect and expensive was the machinery, would not have been employed for that, could the same service have been accomplished by other means.

But the man who was to make the steam-engine the monarch of mechanical forces now came upon the scene, and to him we must turn our attention. James Watt (Fig. 2457), a native of Greenock in Scotland, was born in 1736. From his infancy he showed a fondness for mechanics and mathematics. His father had the sense to foster his natural bent, and the lad grew up amid the studies and pursuits he loved best. At the age of nineteen he was apprenticed to a mathematical instrument-maker in Cornhill. On returning to Scotland he obtained the appointment of mathematical instrument-maker to the University of Glasgow, and he here gained the friendship of the scientific men of his day, to whom his shop became a common resort, and by whom he was held in the highest esteem for his remarkable genius and candid simplicity of character. Watt was about twenty-six years of age when his attention was first turned to the principles of the steam-engine. There was in the College a model of Newcomen's engine, which was used by the professors for the sake of illustration; it had got out of working condition, and Watt was employed to put it in order. In discharging this task he discovered that the principal cause of the waste of steam and fuel was the injection of cold water into the cylinder, for the sake of producing a vacuum, and he conceived the idea of obviating this grand defect by the use of a separate condenser. He had completed this invention by the summer of 1765, and the result was a vast and immediate saving in the cost of fuel. Another improvement effected by him about the same time was the use of steam instead of atmospheric air for the propulsion of the piston, which he accomplished by admitting steam from the boiler above and below the piston alternately. These were immense discoveries; but some years elapsed before Watt was enabled to bring them fairly before the public. An introduction to Dr. Roebuck at length enabled him to take out a patent, and to construct an experimental engine on a large scale, the success of which at once established the truth and value of the principles he had adopted, and placed him fairly on the road to fame and fortune.

Dr. Roebuck becoming embarrassed in his affairs, Watt, in 1773, entered into partnership with Matthew Boulton, of Soho, near Birmingham, and commenced the manufacture of his engines. An application to Parliament obtained for him an extension of his patent up to the year 1800, and he now applied himself vigorously in reaping the reward of his labours and in carrying out further improvements. One of the most remarkable of these was the invention of the shuttle-valve, by the opening and partial closing of which the supply of steam is increased or diminished as it is required. That the purpose for which the shuttle-valve was designed should not be defeated by want of vigilance on the part of the men in charge of the engine, Watt connected the lever by which its motions were regulated with an apparatus constructed on the principle of the regulator employed in windmills, to which he gave the name of the governor. By this means the motion of the engine could be regulated with perfect nicety, and with ordinary care, security from accident was obtained.

The steam-engine had now been brought by the energy and intelligence of Watt to a state of high perfection; but still several years passed away before the parties most interested in its use could be made aware of the advantages to be reaped from the new improvements. The men of the mining interest, who should at least have appreciated the enormous saving in fuel, continued to employ their old and wasteful engines, and it was only by making large sacrifices that Watt and Boulton were enabled to supplant them by their own superior machines. This they effected in the end by compounding for a portion of the savings accruing from the substitution of the new engines of Watt for the old ones of Newcomen. The portion agreed upon was one-third of the savings; and in order that there might be no dispute as to the amount, Watt invented an apparatus for counting and registering the strokes made by the great beam of the engine, and thus making manifest the labour it had performed: this apparatus was lodged in a box with two locks, of which the miner retained one and the patentee the other—opening it in each other's presence once in three months to ascertain the rent due. Ultimately this *pro ratâ* payment was commuted into a rent-charge, which varied throughout the mining districts from 100*l.* up to 800*l.* a-year for a single engine, according to the amount of horse-power.

With less regard for mere wealth than most men, Watt grew rich before the patent right granted to him and his partner expired in the year 1800. At that period he retired from the firm, leaving his two sons with his late partner to reap the further harvest of wealth which his own genius had secured. At the age of sixty-four he withdrew to his estate of Heathfield in Staffordshire, where for nearly twenty years he enjoyed the society of a large circle of friends, the pleasures of intellectual pursuits, and the recollections of a well-spent life. He died in 1819.

The history of the steam-engine during the last half-century—its various modifications, improvements, and applications, would occupy and indeed has occupied, several volumes—and even a glance at that history would necessitate the entering into details foreign to our purpose. The steam-engine exists at present in every variety of form, and does the chief part of the work of the world; but in whatever shape it is found, its construction is based upon the principles which the genius of Watt eliminated and brought into practical working. Let us now turn to

Steam Navigation.—(Fig. 2458.)

We have alluded above to the somewhat apocryphal exploits of the Spanish naval captain, Blasco de Garay, who was said to have succeeded in propelling a vessel by steam in 1543. Passing over that exploit, as at present wanting authentication, we find in the Marquis of Worcester's 'Century of Inventions,' an obscure statement relative to a vessel moved by steam, "which should, if need be , pass London Bridge against the current, at low water." Some twenty years after the publication of this book, Captain Savery attempted to realize the idea, but failed. Fifty years later, Jonathan Hulls took out a patent for running vessels by steam, which, with other attempts in the same direction, also came to nothing. It was not until the year 1774 that a French nobleman, the Comte D'Auxeron, launched a boat upon the Seine, which actually moved against the stream, though at a slow rate; but his experiment failed, as did that of his countryman Perier, who repeated the attempt in the following year. Three years afterwards the Marquis de Jouffroy made attempts on a larger scale on the Saone at Lyons. The breaking out of the Revolution put a stop to his efforts and forced him into exile. On his return in 1796 he found his inventions pilfered and patented by a watchmaker named Des Blancs, and could obtain no redress. Fulton was at that time in France, and experimenting with the same view; he fell in with Des Blancs, and proposed a partnership, but no arrangement was made between them.

In America experiments were made in steam navigation by

Rumsay and Fitch, as early as 1783. Rumsay, in 1784, succeeded in attaining a rate of speed equal to three miles an hour; and he afterwards came to England, where he launched a vessel on the Thames in 1793, which progressed against tide at four miles an hour. Though these essays were not successful, they yet showed the possibility of success, and experiments began to multiply in various quarters. Among the most remarkable were those made by Patrick Miller, on Dalswinton Lake, in Dumfriesshire, in which he was mainly assisted by William Symington. By these experiments a speed of seven miles an hour was obtained and the possibility of steam navigation established. But the merit of an invention is due, not to the man who first discovers the principle, but to him who brings it first into practical use—and it is therefore to Fulton, the American, that in this instance the merit must be awarded. It appears that Fulton, while on a visit to this country, learned much from Symington, who made no secret of his knowledge, but explained everything without reserve. On his return to America, Fulton found a capitalist in Chancellor Livingston, and, obtaining engineers from the works of Boulton and Watt, at Birmingham, commenced the building of his steam-boat at New York. His fellow-countrymen laughed at his plans, and nicknamed his boat 'Fulton's Folly;' his personal friends were civil, but they were shy of being seen in his company; and if they listened to his explanations, it was with a cast of incredulity on their countenances. The rabble mocked and jeered him, and waited to crush him with their scorn on the bursting of the bubble. But he held on his way in tranquil confidence as to the result. In January, 1808, came the long-expected trial. In the presence of a vast crowd of spectators the boat glided from the wharf, "and the minds of the incredulous were changed in a moment." Before she had run a quarter of a mile the greatest unbeliever was converted; the jeers of the mob died away, at first into bewildered astonishment, and the next moment were succeeded by shouts of acclamation and applause. The progress of the boat up the Hudson was one continued triumph, and the success was complete. This, the first steam-boat on the Hudson, was called the 'Clermont,' from the name of Mr. Livingston's country residence, and she continued to run up and down the river during the season.

Within a few weeks after the triumph of the 'Clermont,' Mr. Stevens, of Hoboken, launched a steam-vessel, which he took round to the Delaware, and which was the first steamer that braved the tides of the ocean. From that moment steamers multiplied rapidly in all the American rivers, and soon became the ordinary means of communication. It was not until four years after (1812) that Mr. Henry Bell, of Glasgow, launched the 'Comet,' the first British steam-vessel on the Clyde, which he employed to transport passengers across the river. In the following year a second and larger vessel appeared on the Clyde, built at the cost of Mr. Hutchison, of Glasgow. She ran between Greenock and that city, and performed the distance (twenty-seven miles) twice in the day, often traversing the whole route in three hours, and carrying a hundred passengers. This decided success on the Clyde led to new projects in other quarters. In 1814 a small pleasure-boat began to ply between London and Richmond; another, built in Bristol, was sent up to London for the Gravesend station, but had to be withdrawn owing to the opposition of the watermen. In 1815, the 'Margory,' a steamer of seventy tons, was sent from the Clyde, also intended for the transport between London and Gravesend: she maintained her ground in spite of the watermen, and continued to run between the two places. The 'Margory' was followed by the 'Thames,' which, sailing from the Clyde to Dublin, was mistaken by the Irish pilots for a vessel on fire, and they swarmed off to rescue her with a view to salvage. From Dublin she went round to Portsmouth, where her appearance created the strangest excitement in the harbour. From Portsmouth she proceeded to Margate, and thence to London, outstripping the quickest sailing-vessels in her passage.

By this time all doubt as to the practicability and advantages of steam navigation had vanished from every mind, and capital without stint began to be invested in the construction of steam-vessels. By the year 1818, besides a considerable number plying on the Thames, there were steamers on all the principal rivers of England and Scotland—two intended to run between Holyhead and Dublin; and several in Russia, France, Spain, and the Netherlands. The two which crossed the Irish Sea were the 'Ivanhoe' and the 'Talbot,' which were employed in the mail service. Their complete success established the possibility of ocean navigation by steamers, which now came rapidly into use in the coasting service. Regular lines of communication were organised, not only between our home ports, but between those and such foreign harbours as were conceived to lie within the limits of steam-navigation. As the vessels improved in construction, these limits were found capable of

indefinite extension, and embraced not only the coasts of France, Belgium, and Holland, but those of Spain and Portugal and the Island of Madeira, as well as the Scandinavian ports in the north.

The spirit of enterprise, fortunately for the general weal, is never satisfied, and it now began to be rumoured about that it would be possible to cross the Atlantic itself in an ocean steamer, and thus to abridge, by at least one half, the distance between England and America. The people generally believed the thing was practicable enough; but the men of science, almost to a man, set their faces against it, and demonstrated the absurdity of the idea. At length some bold spirits determined to settle the disputed question by a trial. The 'Sirius,' a vessel of seven hundred tons, sailed from Cork on the 4th of April 1838, and struck at once across the Atlantic for New York; and but a few days later the 'Great Western' started from Bristol for the same destination. The voyages of both ships were brilliant triumphs; neither of them stopped at any port for assistance or supplies of fuel, but steamed right on towards America; and both—the 'Sirius' first, and the 'Great Western' a few hours later—entered the harbour of New York on the same day, the 23rd of the month. "Long before their arrival, notice of their coming had been given, and when the ships approached the shores of the greatest commercial city of the New World, they were greeted with flags and banners, and with music and ringing of bells, and the acclamations and applause of unnumbered multitudes. Half the width of the Atlantic had been annihilated, the year had been doubled in its length, and three-fourths of the causes of strife and discord had been destroyed for ever; for ten thousand avenues had been opened of mutual advantage and regard between the two great branches of the most wealthy, the most enterprising, and the most powerful among the nations of the world."

Two years after the Atlantic had been thus bridged by steam, the Oriental Steam Packet Company placed their floating towns in the waters of the Mediterranean, and brought the vast empire of India within thirty days' distance of home.

Since that period fifteen years have elapsed, and every year has been marked by an extension of steam navigation, an increase in the number and size of the vessels, the power of the engines employed, and their rate of speed. The passenger-traffic across the Atlantic has been well-nigh monopolised by the various lines of steamers which, competing with each other, traverse the broad ocean in an average period of ten or eleven days, keeping time with a precision hardly excelled by wheel-carriage on land. We have mail-packets to the West Indies and the Cape running regularly by steam; and by steam we transport thousands of emigrants to the antipodes, abridging the perils and inconveniences of the voyage by one-half of its former duration.

But this is not all. The application of steam to ships-of-war was naturally desired so soon as it was found to answer for passenger-vessels. The government were not slow in enlisting the new power in the service of the navy, and numbers of war-vessels were built, uniting the qualities of strength and speed, and mounting pivot-guns of large calibre in lieu of the usual broadside, which had in a great measure to be dispensed with on account of the position occupied by the paddles on either side. This arrangement of the paddles was fatal to the use of steam in men-of-war armed with heavy batteries for close conflict; and it was felt that, unless some other means than paddles above water could be devised for propulsion, the larger vessels of the fleet would profit little by the use of steam. While the naval authorities were pondering on this desideratum, a private gentleman was experimenting at home on a new mode of propulsion by means of a screw situated under the water. He had conceived the idea that if the worm of a screw were broadened and flattened into a spiral flange, offering a large surface to the water, and set revolving, it would draw a considerable weight after it in the direction towards which it wormed its way. A series of experiments confirmed the notion, and was further attended by the discovery that a complete screw was not required but that less than one turn of the screw did the business more effectually than a coil of many turns. In actual working, the screw of a screw-steamer is nothing more than a broad, flat vane, curved in opposite directions, and revolving rapidly on a pivot. Its comparatively small size enables it to be conveniently placed between the rudder of a ship and her after-run, where it is at once out of the way, interfering in no respect with the working of the ship, and out of danger at all times from hostile shot. This invaluable invention, the merit of which is due to Mr. F. P. Smith, rendered the application of steam-power to men-of-war easily available, and it has consequently been largely adopted by the Government. We have now war-steamers of one thousand to four thousand tons burthen, and

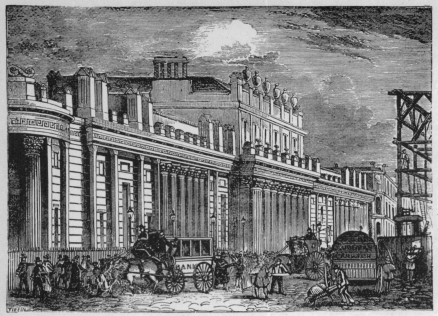

2484.—Bank of England.

2485.—College of Surgeons.

2486.—John Hunter.

2487.—Royal College of Physicians.

2488.—University College.

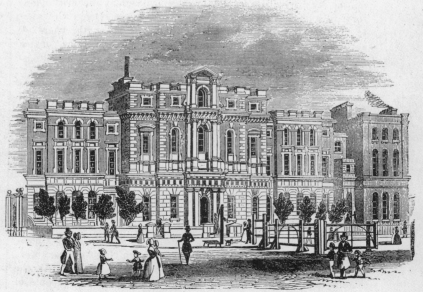

2489.—British and Foreign Schools, Borough Road.

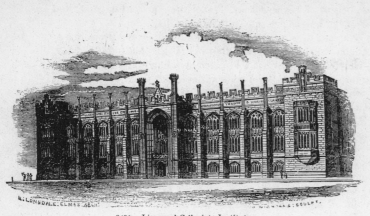

2491.—Liverpool Collegiate Institute.

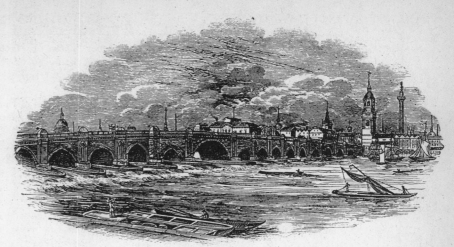

2492.—Old London Bridge.

2490.—Proprietary College, Cheltenham.

2493.—Vauxhall Bridge.

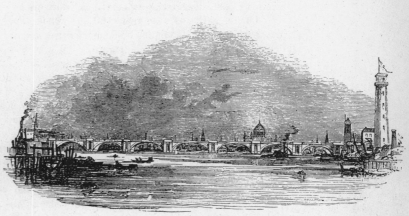

2494.—Waterloo Bridge.

carrying from ten to a hundred and thirty guns. These are facts, however, upon which we need scarcely enlarge, as the events of the late war, and the part enacted in it by our war and transport steamers, must be fresh in the recollection of the reader.

But the triumph of steam navigation has yet to reach its climax. While we write, there is building on the banks of the Thames a monster steam-vessel, of such enormous capacity as dwarfs in comparison even the leviathans of the navy. The 'Great Eastern' steam-ship is over the eighth of a mile in length, and between eighty and ninety feet in width in the widest part. She is built entirely of iron, in eleven distinct, water-tight compartments, and has a double hull, or outer framework, far above the water-line, also divided into numerous water-tight chambers. She will have promenades on deck a furlong in length, and saloons and sleeping accommodation for four thousand passengers. She will carry coal enough for a voyage out and home of twenty-five thousand miles, and have stowage-room for five thousand tons of merchandise in addition. With her entire burthen on board she will weigh twenty-seven thousand tons, and yet, owing to her enormous length, will draw but twenty-eight feet of water. She will be propelled through the waves at the rate of twenty miles an hour, by a screw twenty-four feet in diameter, moved by engines of two thousand horse-power, and by paddles fifty-six feet across, driven by two engines of a thousand horse-power each—and, in addition, will have the means of spreading from six to seven thousand square feet of canvas, upon seven masts, to catch the breeze. Her anchors will weigh fifty-five tons, and there will be two hundred tons of capstans, cables, and warps : these immense appliances will be handled by steam-engines, stationed at convenient points; and, owing to this provision, it is calculated that a crew of four hundred men will be sufficient to manage and control the motions of the prodigious fabric. It is estimated that her vast weight will effectually resist the attacks of storm and wind, and that sea-sickness will be a thing unknown in her experience. For long-boat she will carry a steamer a hundred feet in length—about as large as one of the Gravesend pleasure-boats, or of the gun-boat flotilla. The captain will have to use a telescope to watch the manœuvres of his crew, and to telegraph his orders by signals ; and the compasses will be raised forty feet above the deck to remove them from the disturbing influence of the mass of iron below. This stupendous experiment will cost, ere the first trial is completed, nearly a million sterling ; and if successful, as in all respects it promises to be, will return a round profit upon the capital thus daringly invested. Her success, if she does succeed, will inaugurate a new epoch in the history of steam navigation.

Railways.

The earliest form in which the railway existed in England was that of the tram-roads used as approaches to mines, quarries, and collieries. The first tram-roads were merely planks of wood laid upon sleepers, in order to keep the wheels of carts and waggons out of the soft mud : these were followed, at first, by sheets of iron, then by a species of iron gutter made to receive the wheels and retain them in the right track, and then by raised iron rails, having a flange on one side to confine the wheel. The flange was afterwards transferred from the rail to the wheel of the carriage, an improvement which was first adopted at the Penrhyn slate quarries in Wales, about the year 1801, and has continued in use ever since. The first railway, or rather tramway carriages, were drawn by animal power; but so early as the year 1802, Captain Trevithick, of Cornwall, took out a patent for a steam carriage, and in 1805 exhibited one on a tramway at Merthyr Tydvil, which drew a train containing ten tons of iron and several passengers. Trevithick's invention did not, however recommend itself to the public, and the idea of steam locomotives appears to have slept for a time. The success of the Stockton and Darlington Railway, which was completed in 1825, aroused the emulation of the inhabitants of Manchester and Liverpool, who resolved to connect these towns by the same species of road. They applied for and obtained an Act of Parliament, and in spite of engineering difficulties of no ordinary kind, owing to the seeming impossibility of consolidating a way over Chat Moss, they completed the iron roads in the year 1830. The question was yet undecided whether they should use steam or animal power for the draught ; but as the directors wished to obtain a high rate of speed, they offered a reward of 500l. for the best steam locomotive that could be produced. On the day of trial four competing engines (Fig. 2459) made their appearance, and the prize was gained by the 'Rocket,' built by Mr. Robert Stephenson. The line was opened shortly afterwards, and exceeded in regularity and speed the most sanguine expectations formed of it—to the

immense benefit of Liverpool and Manchester, notwithstanding that the cost of the line had been a million and a half.

The example thus set was speedily followed by the projection of the London and Birmingham Railway (Figs. 2460, 2461, 2462, 2463), which had to traverse a distance of a hundred and ten miles, to bore through hills, to span wide valleys, and to cross rivers—for all of which the necessary capital and talent were found, and the work completed in due time, at the expense of seven and a quarter millions. Next came the design of uniting London with Bristol ; and the Great Western line was planned and accomplished by Brunel, on a scale of magnificence and expense hitherto unheard of. This was followed by the completion of the line from London to Southampton ; which latter place has become, since its connection by railway with London, the third port of the kingdom, and the principal point of departure for the ports of the Mediterranean and the East. Simultaneously with the above important undertakings were commenced others of a similar nature ; and as year after year passed away, that vast reticulation of railways which now overspreads the whole face of the land like a net, came gradually into being. Their construction gave birth to a new class of officials, of working labourers, and of manufactured material, and at the same time tended more to modify the manners and customs of Englishmen than any other event of modern times. The facilities of intercourse have multiplied the amount of travelling nearly a hundredfold within the last thirty years, and the result has been a general diffusion of that species of information and knowledge of the world which travelling universally imparts. Old prejudices have been swept away, a liberal and cosmopolitan spirit has to a large extent displaced the old local jealousies—freedom of intermixture has broken down the ancient bigotries, and the way is left clear for the march of improvement.

At the present moment the capital invested in railways in this country amounts to little less than a hundred and twenty millions. In return for this vast outlay we have advantages not to be estimated by pecuniary values. We can traverse the kingdom from one end to the other in a day ; we can transact business in an unlimited market ; we can visit all that is worthy of observation at a low cost both of money and time, and can renew as often as we please the pleasures of social intercourse with absent friends. London, as the grand centre of railway communication, is, so to speak, in contact with the uttermost limits of the land. From Euston Square (Fig. 2460) we can reach the Birmingham Terminus (Fig. 2463) in three or four hours, or any city or town of note, with corresponding celerity, as far as Aberdeen in the north of Scotland. From King's Cross we may fly to York, and thence again to the northernmost limits of the island. By the Great Western, at Paddington, we are borne to Bristol, and down through Devonshire and Cornwall to the verge of the Land's End. From the Waterloo Station we are shot down to the Southampton Docks, and break-fasting in the Strand, may dine in the British Channel. From Shoreditch we are whirled through the eastern counties to the shores of the German Ocean ; and from the London Bridge Station (Fig. 2464) we may reach the south coast in two or three hours, or be wafted into the heart of Paris in time for dinner. Again we have the railway as a domestic convenience, taking us to and fro from our homes to the scenes of our daily labour. From Fenchurch-street, in half an hour, we may reach Blackwall (Fig. 2465) or any suburb to the east or north of the City ; and on all the lines short and cheap trains are constantly running at intervals of but a few minutes up to a late hour of the day. The first line open to the London public was that between London and Greenwich (Fig. 2466), and within twenty years from its opening the whole of the above important undertakings, have been planned and completed.

We say not a word here on railway interests, railway speculation, railway panics, railway manias, and railway morals : such things would lead to endless animadversions which, happily for us, lie beyond our province.

The Electric Telegraph.

Of all the advantages derived from a knowledge of the subtle electric medium, there is none that will bear any comparison with the Electric Telegraph. That a man should be able to converse instantaneously with a friend, at a hundred or a thousand miles', distance, and separated from him by barren wastes or rolling seas, seems at the first blush a notion so absurd as to harmonise only with the dreams of a lunatic. Yet this seeming impossibility is actually taking place in numberless instances even while we write—for the electric telegraph has become a common medium of communication, and among commercial men is already regarded but as a quicker and rather more expensive kind of post-office.

The first idea of supplanting the old semaphore by an adaptation of electricity to telegraph purposes was entertained almost from the earliest dawn of electrical science, which may be said to have had its birth with Franklin's discoveries. (Fig. 2467.) Lomond, in 1787, by his suggestive remarks, paved the way for actual experiment. Reizer, in 1794, made a small apparatus in his own house, by means of which he was able to communicate from room to room by momentarily illuminating pieces of tinfoil, inscribed with letters, by the electric spark. Volta's discovery of the direction of an electric current, and the battery which he contrived, gave a new impetus to the project; and, in 1807, Sömmering constructed a telegraph, worked by means of that battery, by which signals could be transmitted to short distances. In 1819 Professor Oërsted, of Copenhagen, made the discovery that a needle balanced on its centre could be deflected on either side by a galvanic current, according to the direction in which the current was transmitted. It is upon the discovery of Oërsted that the principle of the electric telegraphs now in use is based, though the contrivance of the apparatus and the application of the principle are due to others.

Mr. Cooke, having closely watched some interesting experiments in Germany, resolved if possible to turn them to a practical account. In 1836 he made trials with telegraphic instruments of his own devising, with a view to their use on the railway lines. In the following year he became acquainted with Professor Wheatstone, who had been for some time engaged in the same pursuit, and with whom conjointly he took out a patent for a telegraph. In this first essay five needles were employed, the movements of which stood in lieu of the letters of the alphabet. In 1838 they took out a second patent for an improved plan, in which the five needles were reduced to two, and provision was made for communicating, not only between the two termini, but with any of the intermediate stations. The improved telegraph was tried in 1839 on the Great Western Railway, and was perfectly successful. Various other improvements now followed in rapid succession, the merits of some of which were claimed exclusively both by Cooke and Wheatstone, and led to a fierce quarrel between the quondam partners, and no end of controversy. Meanwhile the telegraph made rapid way with the general public, and loud demands were heard for its universal adoption by the railway companies. Mr. Bain stepped into the arena with some most important inventions and improvements, which promised the fullest efficiency to the telegraphic system, and gave a fresh spur to enterprise. In 1843 Cooke matured and adopted a new plan, of suspending the electric wires on poles instead of burying them in the ground—a plan which at once reduced the expense of the entire apparatus to one-half, by allowing the substitution of iron wires for copper ones. From this time the connexion of the electric telegraph with the railway was deemed a matter of course, and its absence was considered a reasonable ground of complaint. Regarded as an element of safety, the telegraph was certainly the greatest possible boon to travellers, as by it was secured to every station on every part of the line the knowledge, when such knowledge was needed, of what was going on elsewhere. At the present moment there is hardly a railway in the United Kingdom without its attendant train of electric wires running along the line.

As might have been expected, the advantages to commerce of rapid, or rather of instantaneous, communication were readily appreciated. Electric-telegraph companies rose into being; and by capital and enterprise, communications were speedily opened with every place of note in the kingdom. Next arose the wish to traverse the seas and to connect the Continent with England by a bond of instant intercourse. The newly-discovered material, gutta percha, arrived just at this critical juncture, and furnished the means of isolating the wires, and protecting them from the action of the brine. The first ocean telegraph was sunk in the British Channel, and by its complete success gave an impetus to further undertakings of the same kind. The Irish Sea was the scene of the second trial, which also succeeded, and connected the Green Isle with Great Britain. Subsequent enterprises of greater extent and difficulty have been crowned with equal triumphs; and at the present moment communications are made from London to most of the capitals of Europe—to the shores of the Mediterranean, and even to the Black Sea. It was by means of the electric telegraph that, during the Crimean war, we received the earliest information of its progress, and the sufferings and exploits of our troops: information which a few hours sufficed to convey to us, but which, under similar circumstances to those prevailing during the wars of the first Napoleon, would have taken as many months to have reached our shores.

From the past triumphs which have been achieved in this direction, things which, to hear them spoken of, smack of the absurd and impossible, may almost be predicated with confidence. At the moment while we write measures are actively afoot for joining the New World to the Old by the electric wire. Already is Newfoundland connected with America; and it may come to pass that, before these lines are through the press, New York and London may be reciprocating hourly intercourse across the broad Atlantic. When that grand link in the chain of communication is completed, we shall be able to talk in the same hour with the Far West, with the shores of southern Europe, and with the Scandinavian ports of the North; and we shall have accomplished the larger half of the boast of the fairy Puck, who offered to

"put a girdle round about the earth
In forty minutes."

In America the electric telegraph was brought into popular use much earlier than with us, and was constructed on a much cheaper and more simple plan, principally by the energies and under the direction of Professor Morse. Single wires were made to traverse vast prairies and boundless forests, joining the most distant territories with each other, and working quite independent of the railway lines. It is by means of these far-stretching wires that, so soon as the Atlantic wire is successfully submerged, London will be united with the shores of Mexico and the Pacific.

Though the cost of an electric telegraph traversing a long distance is necessarily great, yet, from the rapidity with which its work is accomplished when the apparatus is complete, the charge for the transmission of messages or news is so moderate as to be within the reach of all classes. A despatch of a few words may be sent a hundred miles for a shilling, and every day in the year thousands of such despatches flash along the wires. At a still cheaper rate, proportionally, is the telegraph available for reports of a more lengthy nature; so that, during the sessions of Parliament, the proceedings of the Houses in London are sent flying along the wires as fast as they take place, and are published to the extent of whole columns in the far northern counties simultaneously with their publication in the columns of the 'Times.'

As yet the electric telegraphs are for the most part, if not all, the property of joint-stock companies, who work them for the benefit of the shareholders; but there is no reason (the permission of the patentees being first obtained, or their rights expired) why they should not become the mediums of private convenience and luxury. Once substantially constructed, the cost of maintaining them in working condition is comparatively trifling, and it may be that the time is not far distant when additional discoveries shall supply additional facilities, and electric communication for purposes of general intercourse shall become as common as the water-supply, or the supply of any of the daily necessities of life.

Gas Light.

A hundred years ago the streets of London were lighted for the most part by the individual efforts of the housekeepers, kept up to the duty by the night watchmen, who, when the dark nights of winter set in, called for a "whole candle" to be set up in a front window, and thundered at the door of any house that was slow to display it, threatening fine and penalty in case of non-compliance. In 1760, or thereabouts, began the system of lighting with oil lamps, a plan which endured until 1815 and after, and which most Londoners approaching the age of fifty must remember perfectly well. These lamps exhibited only a minute spark suspended in a round glass pot, and barely served the purpose of defining the outlines of the several streets. Experiments with gas had been made more than a century before by Dr. Hales, and subsequently by Dr. Clayton; but the idea of using it for the purpose of lighting seems to have first originated with Mr. Murdoch, of Redruth, in Cornwall, who had contrived an apparatus with that view in his own house and offices. Public attention was first attracted to the subject in the year 1802, when, on the occasion of the rejoicings on account of the Peace of Amiens, the same gentleman made use of coal-gas for illuminating the extensive factories of Messrs. Boulton and Watt, near Birmingham.

Not long after this, a German named Winsor drew popular attention to the same subject in London, where, in 1804, he obtained a patent as inventor of gas, and showed its efficacy by lighting up with it the Lyceum Theatre: but Winsor was an uneducated and unscientific man, and his attempts ended in commercial loss and practical failure. In 1810 a company was formed, who, on obtaining their charter, purchased large premises in Westminster, and commenced business on a large scale. They wrought for some years without profit; but as the utility of gas became more apparent, they obtained power to increase their capital and extend their works, which at length became amply remunerative. Between the years 1815 and 1820 the old oil lamps almost entirely disappeared from the streets of London, and in lieu of

2495.—John Rennie.

2496.—Southwark Bridge.

2499.—Menai Bridge.

2497.—Arch of London Bridge.

2498.—Thames Tunnel.

2500.—Interior of St. George's Hall, Liverpool.

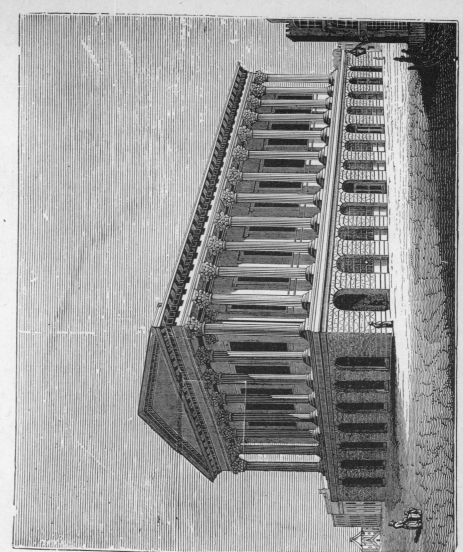

2501.—Town Hall, Birmingham.

2502.—Glasgow Exchange.

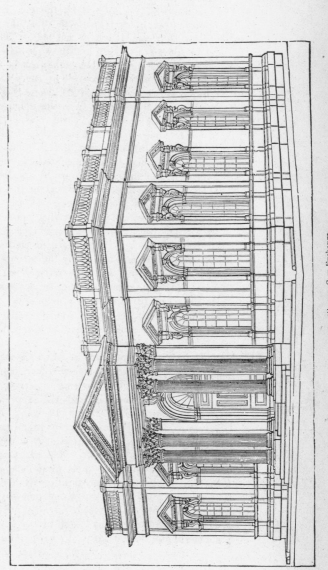

2503.—Glasgow Corn Exchange.

the blinking darkness of the old days, a brilliant light sufficient for all the purposes of traffic illumined the public ways. The introduction of gas in private houses and shops was not so rapid. Owing to inexperience in applying the necessary fittings, and carelessness in the management, numerous accidents and some fatal explosions took place, which had the effect of retarding its general spread: these obstacles to its usefulness were however removed when the nature of the subtle material became better understood, and the demand for more gas was heard on all sides. New companies arose, and as competition came into play, the gas fell in price, and, from its superior cheapness and excellence as an illuminating power, gradually made its way wherever there was the means of its introduction.

Since the first gas-pipes were laid down, London has more than doubled itself in extent, but the gas-mains have kept pace with its enormous growth, and in all directions stretch beyond the limits of the farthest suburbs. It would be difficult to estimate precisely either the quantity of gas consumed, or the mileage of pipes employed in the metropolis at the present moment. There are now above a dozen gas-light and coke-companies within the limits of the capital; some of them consume as much as a hundred thousand chaldrons of coal each, yearly; and their united mains buried in the ground are said to exceed a thousand miles in length, while the aggregate of the service-pipes and the smaller pipes above ground, if laid in one continuous line, would extend to twenty times that distance. Gas is now used for almost every purpose to which fire can be applied; it not only lights our streets, dwellings, theatres, churches, chapels, and workshops, but it melts our precious metals, warms our apartments, cooks our food, and enters largely as an implement of labour into numberless branches of our industrial operations.

A very brief glance at the mode in which gas is manufactured and distributed will not be uninteresting to the reader. A gas-factory is an assemblage of buildings (Fig. 2468) constructed for carrying out the following operations. The coal to be converted into gas and coke is first put into a series of retorts, which are closed iron vessels arranged side by side in groups of five or seven (Fig. 2469). Each retort holds about two bushels of coal loosely thrown in, and they all lie horizontally over furnaces glowing at a red heat sufficiently fierce to decompose the contained coal. From each retort a pipe, as shown in the engraving, leads above and dips again into the large horizontal pipe, called the hydraulic main. The liberated gas ascends by the pipe from each retort into the hydraulic main, carrying with it various impurities which would unfit it for combustion in that state. The chief part of these impurities, the tar, the oil, and the aqueous vapour are left by gravitation in the main, from whence they can be drawn off at pleasure, and the gas 's conducted forwards by pipes to the purifying and condensing apparatus (Fig. 2470), where it is freed from its remaining impurities, and especially from the offensive sulphuretted hydrogen with which it abounds, and which would render its use deleterious if not fatal to health. This is accomplished by forcing the gas through a mixture of lime and water contained in cylinders, as shown in the engraving. The lime has an affinity with the carburetted hydrogen, and abstracts it from the gas, leaving the latter pure. In order to effect a thorough purification, the process is repeated several times by the gas passing through several of these lime-containing vessels in succession: the engraving shows three, but more are often used. To insure the complete efficiency of the lime, and prevent its waste, it is kept in a state of constant agitation during the process, and when saturated with the carburetted hydrogen is replaced by a fresh supply. The lime may be used for this purpose in either a wet or dry state, and is in fact employed at different establishments in either condition. In this manner the gas can be thoroughly purified, and as its purity can be tested at any moment by the simplest and speediest means, it is never knowingly dispensed to the public in an impure state.

The gas, being purified, is led on through the meters, which are ingeniously-contrived instruments for measuring the quantity manufactured, into huge cylindrical reservoirs of enormous capacity, usually made of iron sheeting, and inappropriately called gasometers. A gasometer (Fig. 2471) may be compared to a huge diving-bell suspended, its orifice downward, over and partly in a correspondingly huge circular tank, just large enough to permit of its sliding up and down, and filled with water. The gas, as fast as it is manufactured is led through one large pipe, which emerges above the surface of the water, into the vast air-tight cavity, its retreat by the same pipe being prevented by a valve. As new gas is manufactured its entrance forces up the huge inverted vessel in which it is stored: when wanted for use it is led off by another pipe of equal or greater diameter into the underground mains, along which it is forced by the pressure of the superincumbent mass of the inverted cylinder, and

which pressure can be increased or diminished to the greatest nicety at any moment. Some of these gasometers are of anomalous size, containing as much as sixty thousand cubic feet of gas; they will retain their invisible stores unwasted for months, if need be, but are observed to sink and empty themselves rapidly when turned on to supply the far-stretching mains of the metropolis. (Fig. 2472.)

The introduction of gas, while it has prolonged the working hours of the day—a doubtful benefit perhaps—and banished for ever the impenetrable darkness of our towns and cities at night, has given employment to hundreds of thousands of the industrial classes. At its first appearance it imparted a new impulse to the iron trade, and set multitudes at work in digging fresh ore and casting leagues of the iron-piping. Later it has given rise to the ornamental arts of the brazier and gas-fitter, and the introduction of artistic designs in the form of gaseliers and burners—and, owing to these elegant appliances and the light they are the means of disseminating, has done more towards the increase of home luxuries and comforts than any other invention or discovery thus domestically applicable.

When gas was first burned in private houses, shops, offices, &c., it was paid for according to the size and description of the burner used, at so much for each burner. This plan was unsatisfactory to all parties, from the impossibility of justly apportioning the payment to the quantity consumed. The invention of the meter and its general introduction arose out of the necessity for it—and now, and for many years past, gas has been burned by meter at a charge of so much per thousand feet. The gas meter is a contrivance by which the quantity of gas passing through it is made to exercise a pressure proportioned to its volume upon a surface of water, and causes a cylinder contained within it to revolve. The quantity of gas which must pass through the meter to effect one revolution of the cylinder being known, and the number of revolutions registered by an apparatus of simple clock-work, it is easy at any time to see the amount of gas which has passed through since the last inspection, by simply referring to the dial-plate. In some of the gas manufactories meters of a most complex kind have been erected at a great cost, contrived to show, not only the quantity of gas consumed daily and consuming every hour, but also the quantity made and constantly making—and thus to exhibit at one view, and at any moment, a debtor and creditor account, as it were, betwixt the coal and the gas—a standing, correct, and perennial balance-sheet of the business on hand. (Fig. 2473.)

It is when looked at in a commercial point of view that the advantage of using gas in preference to any other known means of lighting is most conspicuous. From calculations carefully made, it is shown that, compared with wax (the light produced being equal), the cost of gas is but one-tenth—compared with oil it is but one-fourth—and compared with tallow one-third: these ratios, however, are by no means fixed, but vary considerably with the quantities of either material consumed—gas being much cheaper when consumed in large than in small quantities.

COTTON MANUFACTURES.

Twenty years ago it was calculated that the cotton manufactures of this country furnished employment for nearly a quarter of a million of the population, taking into account the numbers not only engaged in spinning, weaving, dyeing, printing, and variously preparing and finishing the material, but also those occupied in fabricating the necessary machinery—those navigating the seas to import the raw material, and those who were the dispensers of the finished goods to the public. Such a manufacture, which has risen from the simplest beginnings within little more than a century, must naturally have exercised a vast influence both upon the commerce of the country and the condition of the population. We must endeavour therefore, though all too briefly, to take a rapid survey of its early rise and progress—seeing that, next to agriculture, it forms the most important branch of our national industry.

Time was when the yarn from which our ancestors formed their clothing was spun by their wives and daughters with the wheel and distaff—and we are old enough to remember well the use of these humble implements in the cottages of the poor people of the provinces—for though cotton fabrics have been common enough during the present century, there is a vitality in old customs—and the hand-spinning of woollen yarn to be woven for household use died out slowly. The introduction of cotton, which furnished the material for a more cheap and convenient fabric, gradually displaced the ancient industry; but the cotton yarn during the infancy of the manufacture had itself to be spun by hand with the same ancient implements; and the weavers found themselves and their looms often at a standstill for want of yarn from the spinsters. With these hindrances to production, it is no marvel that the demand for cotton goods increased far beyond the power of supply, and that the value of the goods grew higher and higher in the market. This state of things always acts as a stimulus to enterprise and invention—and now various machines were contrived with a view to accelerate the production of cotton yarn. The first that was patented was the invention of Lewis Paul, a foreigner, but it failed in the working and came to nothing. Thirty years later, in 1768, M. De Gennes published an account of a machine to make cloth without the hands of the workman, but by water-power: it is remarkable that the description of this machine comprises the very principles of the power-loom subsequently brought to such perfection. De Gennes' machine, however, failed in his hands, as did also further experiments in the same direction made by Dolignon and Vaucanson. An Englishman named Austin met with more success, and completed a power-loom, which was put up in a factory near Glasgow, but which also had to be abandoned after working a short time.

It was while these experiments were making with the loom, and which were destined to wait for their success until success of another kind had been achieved, that Richard Arkwright was pursuing the lowly occupation of a country barber. Born at Preston in 1732, his childhood was passed in indigence and privation. As a boy he was apprenticed to a barber, and when he had served his time he set up for himself in Bolton, where he flourished the razor up to his twenty-ninth year. In 1760 he closed his barber's shop and began roaming the country in quest of human hair, which he bought from the heads of the peasant girls and sold to the makers of wigs; and it is surmised that he was possessed of some nostrum for dyeing the hair, which increased the profits of his curious trade. His first effort at mechanics was an attempt to discover the perpetual motion, in which he met with the usual reward of such enthusiasts. Abandoning that hopeless pursuit, he next turned his attention to the means of supplying the demand for spun cotton, now daily becoming more loud and urgent. It was at Preston, 1767, that the rudiments of his design began to assume shape, and inspired him with the determination to bring his machine into use. Fearful, however, of coming into collision with Hargreaves, who had taken out a patent for a similar purpose, he removed to Nottingham, where he hoped to find friends who would advance the pecuniary supplies. These, after some trouble, he obtained from the Messrs. Wright, bankers, of that town; but they grew weary of getting no cash returns, and turned him over to a stocking-maker of the name of Need; Need also got tired of him, and again turned him over to Mr. Jedediah Strutt. Mr. Strutt was a good practical mechanic, and he pointed out several deficiences in Arkwright's machine, and by his suggestions enabled him to supply what was wanting. Messrs. Strutt and Need subsequently joined Arkwright in partnership, and built their first mill, which was moved by horse-power, in Nottingham. It was entirely successful as to working, and was followed by the speedy erection of another at Cromford, turned by water-power. From various causes, it happened that for a period of five years these mills were wrought without a profit; still the partners persevered, and having effected important improvements in their machinery, began at length to reap their reward. When the tide of prosperity *did set* in it flowed unceasingly, and the firm accumulated wealth with a rapidity unexampled till then. Arkwright, the barber's apprentice, rose into honour—extended his operations into other countries, and was knighted by George the Third. He died in 1792, universally respected, and left to his heirs a fortune of half a million sterling.

Let us now glance cursorily at the process by which cotton is transformed into calico. Cotton, as our readers know, is the white woolly fibre contained in the pod of the cotton-plant, and enveloping the seed. The best for manufacturing purposes is the *Sea Island* cotton, which comes principally from Georgia, Florida, and South Carolina. The cotton is imported in bags, in a state too foul for use. The first operation is that of cleaning, and for this purpose it is exposed to the action of machines, of infernal nomenclature, in which it is variously tormented, being torn by revolving spikes, blown and blasted by revolving fans, and beaten and buffeted by metallic blades, until it is purged of its impurities, and the fine wool separated from the waste. It is then prepared for carding—a process by which the filaments of the wool are drawn parallel to each other. The cotton leaves the carding-machine in the form of a soft, thick thread, and from thence it is passed into the drawing-frame, the invention of Arkwright, through which it is often made to pass hundreds of times, until it is of one uniform thinness and texture. The cotton, now one continuous cord, is next passed to the mule-room, where, by means of a machine originally called a fly-frame, and which, by repeated improvements has been brought to an astonishing state of perfection, it is at one and the same time stretched out to a uniform thinness, twisted into the form of twine, and wound upon bobbins attached to rods to receive it. The yarn

is now complete, and ready either for home use or exportation—that which is intended for warp being first wound into hanks of a uniform and definite length.

The next process is the weaving; and it is clear that if invention in this direction had not kept pace with Arkwright's machinery for the production of yarn, the cotton trade would have gained comparatively little by his endeavours. This apprehension was in fact at one time seriously entertained; and it was owing to a conversation on this subject which took place in 1784, that the Rev. Dr. Cartwright commenced experiments in weaving by machinery. He spent 40,000*l.* in these experiments and in patenting his contrivances, and yet had finally to give up the hope of success. Some Manchester firms who made similar attempts similarly failed. The main obstacles these experimenters had to contend with was the frequent breakage of the warp, which compelled them to stop the machinery. This was at last obviated by the invention of the dressing-machine by Mr. Radcliffe, of Stockport, by which the yarn used for he warp was strengthened by passing through a reservoir of thin paste or starch. Radcliffe's invention showed the perfect practicability of the power-loom, which was subsequently brought, by the improvements of Mr. Roberts, of Manchester, to a condition of working completeness; and being moved by steam-power, which at about the same period came into general use in factories, has proved sufficient to meet all demands both as to the quantity and quality of the fabrics produced.

But the calico when woven is nothing more than a mere white sheet: we must see how it becomes covered with elegant patterns, and adapted for the gratification of female vanity. About the middle of last century there lived in the village of Blackburn, in Lancashire, a small farmer, a man of vigour and observation, who cared nothing for labour so that good were to come out of it. He formed the design, and kept it secret, of printing patterns in calico —well knowing that if he could succeed, a large reward would follow. He gave up his farm, and set to work at a new trade. With his own hands he cut out on blocks of wood the figure of a parsley-leaf; he fixed a handle on the back of each block, and drove a pin in each of the corners in the front. He mixed his colours with alum, stretched his calico on his table-top, applied his blocks to the colours first, then to the calico, and striking the back of the block sharply with a mallet, printed the coloured impression of the leaf on the cloth. The pins at the corners enabled him to repeat the operation in the right place, until the whole of the cloth was covered. When it was dry his wife and daughters ironed out the piece with the flat-iron; but as this took more of their time than he liked to bestow on it, the farmer set to work again to contrive a machine to supersede their labour, and in quick time had invented the mangle, which answered the purpose equally well, and which the world then saw for the first time.

The farmer, whose name was Robert Peel, worked on heartily, and his goods became much sought after. As ne was prudent enough to keep his secret to himself, he secured a monopoly of the trade, and grew rich very fast. His eldest son, also a Robert, joined him in the business, and grew so rich that he could afford to raise a regiment of horse for the service of the Government, and was made a baronet for his loyalty. He sent *his* son, a third Robert, to college; and the grandson of the farming cotton-printer of Blackburn became, as all the world knows, the triumphant consummator of free trade and the prime minister of the empire.

The wealth of the Peels was not, however, won by block-printing. That process was found all too slow, and had to be abandoned. Mr. Peel had recourse to cylinders instead of blocks, engraving the pattern on the face of the cylinder, which he made to revolve with half its surface in a box containing the colouring matter—the colour being shaved off, save in the hollows formed by the pattern, by a blade of soft steel. The cloth, passing between the two cylinders, receives the impression of the pattern, and then passing over another cylinder filled with hot steam, is almost immediately dried. There must be, of course, as many cylinders used as there are colours in the pattern; yet so rapid is the process, that a piece of calico twenty-eight yards in length, and of several colours, which it would have taken a week to print by the block method, may be done by the cylinder machines in two minutes. The first printed cottons were of an indifferent colour, being imperfectly bleached by exposure to the air; but chemistry came to the aid of industry, and by the application of chlorine a perfect white was obtained, much enhancing the beauty and brilliancy of the patterns. Again, the first printed goods would not wash without discharging their colour. This defect was obviated by the use of mordants, which bind the colours effectually, and prints now retain their hues to the last.

2501.—Broomielaw Bridge, Glasgow.

2505.—Stockwell Bridge, Glasgow.

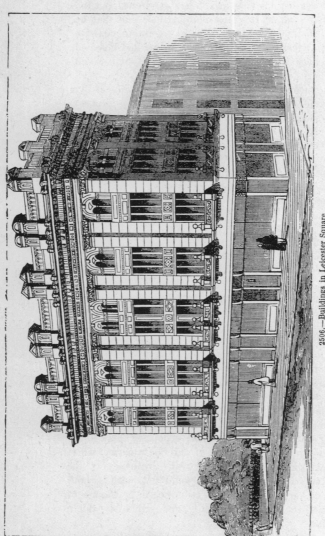

2506.—Buildings in Leicester Square

2507.—Tavern, corner of Long Acre.

2506.—Exeter Hall.

2511.—Seven Dials.

2510.—London, from York Column.

2509.—Suburb of Knightsbridge.

We need not pursue the history of cotton fabrics any farther. Were we to do so we should have to enter upon a field of inquiry of such vast extent as would only perplex and bewilder us, looking to the mere span of space we could devote to it. Let it suffice to say, that talents of the highest order, capital without limit, and unceasing energy, have been employed in this department of commerce for the last fifty years—that all that art and ingenuity can effect in the production of the most exquisite fabrics and designs is constantly effected, and that the markets of the whole world are supplied from the cotton-factories of Lancashire.

Contemporaneously with the cotton manufactures, those of silks, woollens, and linens have advanced, if not in a corresponding ratio as to quantity, yet with equal strides as to excellence in production. The textile fabrics of England, whatever be the material employed, take rank among the first in the world for excellence of workmanship, for strength and durability. In design, it must be confessed, they yield to those of France and the southern nations; but of this defect the home manufactures are fully aware, and are sparing neither pains nor expense to repair it. A new spirit has been latterly aroused in reference to this subject, and it may be confidently anticipated that a few years will suffice to connect the fine arts as closely with the manufactures of Great Britain as they are connected with those of any people on the globe.

Machine Printing (Fig. 2474).

In the days of Addison and Johnson, when the former published his 'Spectator' weekly, and the latter invented reports of Parliamentary proceedings for the gratification of the public, the press was thought a wonderful engine of reform, and was supposed to be doing the work of enlightenment, of which it is the destined instrument. Yet in those days it was but a rude, unwieldy contrivance of wood, manageable only with great labour, and capable of producing but two or three hundred copies of a single small sheet per hour—and that printed on one side by the united exertions of two strong men. The press of the printer had in fact improved but little from the days of Caxton to those of Benjamin Franklin, who, as a journeyman printer, handled the clumsy contrivance in London during some part of the third decade of the last century. The first person who made any important improvement in the printing-press was the late Earl Stanhope, who made the whole of his machine of iron, and by substituting the action of the lever for that of the screw reduced the labour of the workman by at least one-half. Further improvements in iron presses were made by Clymer, an American, by Cope, Hopkinson, and others; but these iron presses, though they saved the muscular toils of the workman, did not contribute very much to accelerate his movements, and the rate of production of printed sheets still continued at two to three hundred copies per hour.

In the year 1791 Mr. Nicholson projected an improved press, and took out a patent for affixing types to a revolving cylinder, but failed in his attempts to execute his purpose. In 1804, Herr Kœnig came from Saxony to London, and obtained a patent for working the common press with power—a plan which he had ultimately to renounce. He then made trial of the cylinder instead of a flat surface, and constructed in 1811 the first steam-press successfully worked in Britain. On the 28th of November 1814 the 'Times' newspaper was printed by a machine of this kind, and with steam-power, for the first time. This was a grand success, as a thousand impressions were producible in the hour—a rate which by after improvements was increased to eighteen hundred. In 1815, Kœnig set up a new machine for printing the sheet on both sides, which worked at the rate of eight hundred copies per hour. Not long afterwards, Messrs. Cowper and Applegath produced a machine of much more simple construction than Kœnig's, which perfected a thousand copies within the hour—a machine which, with various modifications and improvements, has continued in use to the present time throughout the kingdom. But ere many years had elapsed, the improved circulation of the 'Times' newspaper demanded a corresponding acceleration in the production of copies—a demand which was met by Mr. Applegath, who, by ingeniously combining in one leviathan machine four of the single machines, was able to supply impressions at the rate of four thousand five hundred an hour, printed on one side. But even this rate of production, great as it was, did not long continue to satisfy the exigencies of the 'Times,' whose circulation, amounting to forty thousands copies a-day, demanded a producing power of ten thousand copies an hour. "To meet this demand required the abandonment of the reciprocating motion of the type form, and so to arrange it as to make the motion continuous, for which only the circular

motion would do. Accordingly, a large central vertical drum, or cylinder (in the 'Times' printing machine this is two hundred inches, and sixty-four inches in diameter) was set up, to which the columns of type were fixed. This drum is surrounded by eight cylinders, also placed with their axes vertically, upon which the paper is carried by tapes. Thus in every revolution of the drum the type form is successively pressed against each of the eight cylinders, and the type being successively inked, and each of the eight cylinders supplied with paper, eight sheets of paper will be printed in one revolution of the drum." By this machine fifty thousand copies have been taken without a moment's stoppage in less than five hours; and the principle is indeed capable of still greater extension. Shortly after it was set to work, Mr. Applegath offered to the Royal Commissioners of the Great Exhibition, to make a machine which, with a rate of motion no greater than that of the 'Times,' should print forty thousand sheets per hour, or eleven sheets between every two ticks of the clock; and to have effected this he would have required only to have enlarged his central drum so as to have afforded space for the necessary number of additional cylinders around it.

The application of machinery to the printer's art has been, as was foreseen, productive of a complete revolution in the literary calling, in the bookselling and publishing trade, and in the position and patronage of both. A century back, authors and publishers looked for encouragement from the ranks of the upper classes, who alone were regarded as the intelligent and educated orders. A writer sought out a patron, who was to receive his dedication, and to introduce him to his peculiar circle, as naturally as he sought out a publisher; and if by this humiliating procedure he managed to sell four or five hundred copies of his book, he thought himself tolerably successful. That state of things has passed away for ever. The judges and patrons of literature are now not the few but the many. The first and most finished authors of the day address themselves to the masses and millions, not to limited cliques and circles. The expensive volumes, and the editions of a few hundreds, have given place to the cheap serial and the weekly impressions of hundreds of thousands. We purchase for pence more and better literature than our grandfathers bought for shillings—better in point of authorship, of morality, of practical sense and educational value; and the poor man's periodical, which he gets for a penny, is often better worth, intellectually considered, than the half-crown volume of even fifty years ago, and contains as much matter.

Contemporaneously with improved means of letter-press printing have arisen various arts, tending to adorn and illustrate the works of literary men. The art of wood-engraving, which may be said to have commenced in England with Bewick, and which enables the artist to multiply indefinitely copies of his drawings, has expanded under the fostering hand of the multitude, until its exercise has become almost as common as that of a handicraft trade, and has further arrived at such a degree of perfection in the hands of its most skilful professors as to leave further improvement impossible, and little more to be desired in that direction. It is by the wood-engraver's skill that the illustrated periodicals of the day are rendered producible at the low price at which they are disseminated, and it is to him we owe the major part of the illustrations which render modern works doubly instructive by appealing to the eye as well as to the mind.

Again, by the art of lithography, of which our forefathers knew nothing, works of art are reproducible on the largest scale, to stock our portfolios, adorn our dwellings, or illustrate our books. This art was the discovery of a German, and from the lowest and apparently most hopeless beginnings has become one of the greatest triumphs of artistic ingenuity and perseverance. By modifications and improvements on its earlier processes, and the application of new ones, its professors now produce fac-similes of the works of the best artists, glowing in brilliant colour, and tastefully graduated with the most delicate tintings of the pencil—thus spreading an appreciation of the higher qualities of art among the multitude.

A further aid to the illustration of books and the dissemination of works of art is found in the electrotype process, by which duplicates or repetitions to any amount, either of wood-engravings or copper-plates, are obtainable at small expense. The process, which is very popularly known, was discovered not many years ago, and is based upon the fact that the metal contained in the crystals of sulphate of copper may be precipitated upon a given surface by means of a galvanic current. This process is largely used in the multiplication of engraved plates, the impressions from which it has rendered much cheaper, as by it any number of copies, instead of the twelve or fifteen hundred which a single plate would produce, are procurable.

We are bound to add, that the process of electrotyping is applicable to an infinite variety of purposes besides those of pictorial art. In Birmingham and the manufacturing districts are large establishments for the production of jewellery, plate, busts, statuettes, and numberless articles of luxury and taste, in the formation of which silver and gold are precipitated from metallic solutions, instead of copper, and the most superb and magnificent results are produced, distinguishable in no way from the triumphs of the working goldsmith and jeweller, save by the lowness of their price.

The foregoing columns, according to our notion, record, though but briefly, the chief facts connected with these inventions and discoveries, the operation of which has been productive of the most influence upon the condition of society in the present day, and contributed most to bring about the existing contrast between the present race of Englishmen and the race of a century back. There are doubtless other inventions which have had their share in the result, but not, it is believed, in so great a degree. Many of these, however, are too important to be passed over, even in this sketch, and we shall therefore add a brief notice of those which appear to have the strongest claim to attention.

The improvement on time-pieces, from its bearing on navigation and astronomy, is deserving of especial notice. It is now nearly a hundred years since Harrison perfected his time-piece for obtaining the longitude at sea, and claimed and received from the Government the reward of 20,000l. for so doing. Since his time the chronometer has been improved by various hands to a degree of perfection that throws the success of Harrison far into the shade. Instruments are now made whose variation is less than the twentieth part of a second a month; and they are sometimes known, after traversing the globe for a period of four or five years, to have returned with hardly any perceptible variation at all. At the same time, corresponding advance has been made both in the manufacture and the cheapening of clocks and watches—so that the humblest artisan of our time may suspend in his room, or carry in his pocket a time-piece, whose correct performance would have been a marvel to the horologist of a century back. The business of common clock-making, especially, has been so simplified that the whole works of a clock can now be struck with a single blow from a brass plate, and the complete fabric in working order sold for a crown-piece.

The telescope, the ultimate capabilities of which were rather conjectured than proved in Newton's time, has in our day arrived at a state of excellency and efficiency of which that great philosopher never dreamed. Sir William Herschel, about 1783, commenced the construction of his great reflecting telescope upon the principle followed by Newton, and by 1789 had completed his famous instrument, which in the hands of himself and his son has added so much to the stock of astronomical knowledge. In the meantime, by the researches and experiments of Dollond and others, the portable dioptric instruments were freed from the prismatic rays which rendered them comparatively useless, and were improved in penetrating and defining power. This great improvement was due to the combination of different kinds of glass in the formation or arrangement of the lenses. But by far the greatest triumph in this department of mechanics and science has been accomplished in our own day by Lord Rosse, whose monster telescopes, built on his own estate in Ireland, have opened a new universe to the investigations of the astronomers—have dispelled errors entertained by the mightiest intellects of past and present times, and discovered truth at a distance which the rays of light would fail to travel in millions of years.

What the improved telescope has done for the astronomer and the navigator, the improved microscope has done for the naturalist and the minute observer. In the hands of our forefathers the microscope was little more [than an expensive toy; in the hands of the investigator of to-day it is the revealer of new worlds, teeming with wonders, and yet contained in a pinch of dust or a globule of water. More than that, its small illuminated field is the ultimate court of appeal in all cases of disputed identity of matter, and settles the question definitively. It has taught us, among other things, that every department of Nature teems with animal and vegetable life, and that these living forms are of the last importance in the economy of the world. Even our own organisms—our eyes, heart, brain, muscles, and skin—are the realms of animalcule existence, and every creature that runs or flies swarms with countless multitudes of these invisible tribes. Beings are found so small that five hundred millions of them could be shut up in a single drop of water; and the solid earth we tread upon, when it is examined, is seen to be formed of their dead bodies.

The art of photography, an art unknown by the British public twenty years ago, and which consists in delineating natural objects upon metal plates, glass, or paper, by the action of light, appears to have been simultaneously discovered by Daguerre in France, and Talbot in England. The principle of the processes adopted by either was the same, though the results were obtained by different means. By both the figure of the object to be represented is first thrown by a lens upon a surface rendered by chemical solutions sensitive to the action of light; and the impression thus obtained is fixed in a dark chamber by other chemical applications. The art has been enthusiastically received and practised both here and on the Continent, and has at length been brought to a state of almost magical perfection. Scenes of beauty and of such intricacy and perplexity as would defeat the endeavours of the pencil are transferred instantaneously to the sensitive surface with the utmost fidelity—and we have thus the means of obtaining faithful transcripts of every natural object, whether at home or abroad, "in the heavens above or in the earth beneath;" and we may add, "or in the waters under the earth"—for the lens of the photographer works faithfully at the bottom of the sea, of which a minute, but well-defined portion photographed at the depth of five fathoms, lies before us as we write. There probably never was an art which became so suddenly popular, or which is likely to retain its popularity so steadily. Already photographic portraits are to be numbered by millions—and as they cannot fail in point of resemblance, and may be obtained at merely a nominal price, the demand for them seems likely to be ever increasing and permanent. What will be the ultimate effect of photography on either the arts or the manufactures of this country, it would be as yet rash to pronounce; almost daily new agencies are tried and new wonders produced, and we can only pause and wait in silent expectation.

The improvements in agriculture demand especial notice. Our grandfathers were content to "plough and sow, and reap and mow," on the old routine principle which had sufficed to feed the population of England for a thousand years. We have grown so numerous that we should starve if we acted on that principle. Our additional millions want additional food, and must have it; and though we derive a large quantity from foreign markets, we are, and ever shall be, mainly dependent on our home growth. To increase the home produce, therefore, is now, and has been for many years past, the grand aim of the agriculturist. The introduction of guano (the dung of birds imported from the coasts and islands of the Atlantic and Pacific) showed the possibility of stimulating production to a point it had never yet reached; and this conviction once fairly entertained, there was no lack of energy on the part of those whose interest it was to make the most of their land, in the prosecution of new systems of cultivation. Draining, sub-soiling, levelling of fences, and the enclosure or tillage of wastes, brought fresh land under the plough, and the introduction of new implements of husbandry, and steam machinery, and additional capital, has made or is making the whole soil of the country doubly productive. The abolition of protective duties, which threw the English farmer on his own resources, has taught him to know the true value of them, and he is richer and more independent at the present moment than he was in the days of the sliding scale or a fixed duty; and for the wealth he now enjoys, he is indebted to his own industry—not to an obnoxious law. He has invested his gains cheerfully in the mechanical means for largely increasing them, and has now at hand every appliance which the mechanical arts can afford him for abbreviating labour and rendering it more profitable.

Within the last fifty years immense improvements have been effected in the manufacturing of iron in all its branches and departments. Without these, indeed, it would have been impossible to meet the demands excited by the exigencies of steam machinery, steam navigation, and the railroad. In digging the ore, in smelting and casting it, in welding and rolling huge masses, and in forging them by steam hammers, miracles of mechanical skill have been accomplished, each of which is a triumph of human industry and enterprise. They are all eclipsed, however, by the late discovery of Mr. Bessemer, now undergoing its experimental tests, and which promises, if successful, to reduce the cost of iron by two-thirds, and at the same time to accelerate the processes of manufacture, so as to render building with iron at once cheaper and more rapid than with the combustible materials at present employed.

The improvements in the manufacture of glass of all kinds, and which followed closely on the abolition of the glass duty, have had the effect of cheapening that material by more than one-half, while they

2512.—Royal Arcade, Newcastle.

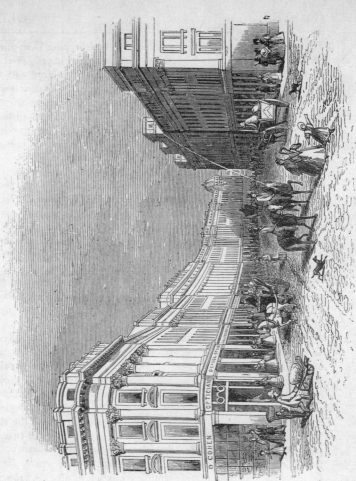
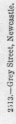

2513.—Grey Street, Newcastle.

2514.—Grainger Street, Newcastle.

2521.—John Howard, the Philanthropist.

2516.—Nelson's Monument at Yarmouth.

2515.—Nelson.

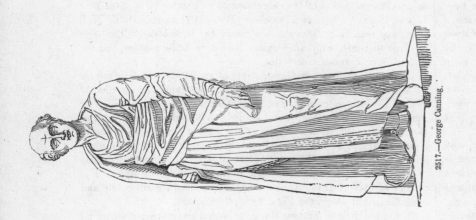

2517.—George Canning.

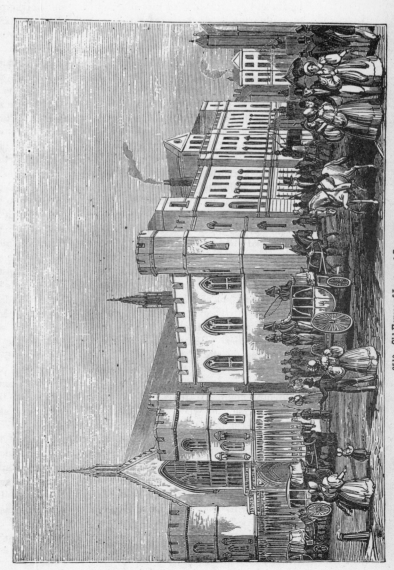

2518.—Old Houses of Lords and Commons.

nave added light to our dwellings and splendour to our apartments. Plate glass is now as common with shopkeepers, who can insure it against mischief or accident, as the crown glass and green bull's eyes were in the reign of the Georges—and in the house of every tradesman we now see mirrors in common use which a century ago would have been the marvels of a palace. In the ceramic arts a corresponding advance has also been made. The potteries of Staffordshire now rival in elegance and excel in the durability of their wares the productions of Dresden or of Sevres, and their commerce has increased since the days of Wedgwood to such a prodigious extent as to exceed in amount the aggregate of that of all the continental potteries united. In machinery of every kind the advance has been greater than the most sanguine mind could have predicted at the beginning of this century. For many years Great Britain produced the machines and engines of well-nigh all Europe, and there is scarcely any department of labour, from stitching a shirt with a needle to elevating the monster tube of the Britannia Bridge, which is not to be performed with machines of British manufacture. Again, in the adaptation of new material to purposes either old or new, most remarkable things have been accomplished. Wood and iron have been superseded by mixtures of India-rubber and gutta-percha, and with coal-tar and caoutchouc in variable proportions, everything that is useful, as well as all that is tasteful and elegant, is moulded in forms of beautiful design and lasting durability. In the manufacture of arms and weapons of war, also, has the present race of Englishmen left their predecessors far in the rear. From the revolving pistol to the Paixhans gun—from the accoutrements of a single soldier to the armaments of a fleet, our resources are equal to all, and ready at any moment. In a word, there is nothing possible within the whole range of industrial enterprise and skill which we have not triumphantly achieved within the memory of living man, while a multitude of supposed impossibilities have surrendered to the incredible pertinacity of the Saxon vigour and determination. We shall conclude this chapter with a few remarks on

Building and Architecture.

The eighteenth century was not distinguished by many remarkable works of architectural merit in this country; on the contrary, that century has been regarded as a period of decline in architecture. The style of building generally adopted was the Italianized Grecian, a tame and spiritless style, as much opposed to our naturally robust habits and predilections as it is adapted to our northern climate. The unfortunate preference for this pseudo-classical mixture continued to prevail in this country to a large and mischievous extent down almost to our own day, and to its prevalence we may attribute the existence of such discreditable erections as Buckingham Palace, the National Gallery, and other expensive failures of the kind, which the foreign visitor criticises only with a compassionate shrug of the shoulders. Happily, the partisans of a better taste and more correct style have never been quite extinct, and their influence has latterly taken the lead in reference especially to our newer ecclesiastical edifices. The Gothic style, corrupted it is true by the admixture of modern prettinesses, to mask the absence of true artistic skill, has revived, and bids fair again to supplant all other modes of architecture for religious purposes : and this revival has not been without its effect even upon the fanatics for Grecian pillars and pediments, who have latterly been led to adopt a model more correctly Grecian, yet modified to meet the necessities of our climate.

We shall notice a few of the public buildings of later years, which may serve to show the direction which architecture has taken among us; and we shall confine our remarks for the most part to London and its neighbourhood. Some of the most notable buildings of the metropolis are the halls of the City guilds, which have been erected at a vast expense, and which are, especially when viewed interiorly, monuments of the lavish luxury and expenditure of these wealthy bodies. Fishmongers' Hall (Fig. 2475) was built by Roberts, on the site of the old hall in 1830. The river-front is in the Grecian style, and the entrance front is enriched with bas-reliefs and pilasters. It has a magnificent banqueting-hall, and boasts some rare municipal relics. Among the members of the Fishmongers' Company were Sir William Walworth, who slew Wat Tyler, and Doggett, of coat-and-badge notoriety.

Goldsmiths' Hall, of which Fig. 2476 shows the exterior, and Fig. 2477 the vestibule, stands in Foster-lane, Cheapside, and is the most superb of all the City halls. It was built by Hardwick in 1832—35, and is in the Italian style. The interior is sumptuous and brilliant beyond description, and, as far as that is possible, compensates by its gorgeous magnificence and expensiveness for the absence of refined taste.

The halls of the several guilds are too numerous to be separately noticed here, and there are none of greater pretensions than the two above mentioned. Let us look further a-field. The National Gallery (Fig. 2478) stands in Trafalgar-square, and was built from the designs of W. Wilkins, R.A., who formed the portico shown in the engraving from the columns of Carlton House. The building is handsome in parts but ugly as a whole, principally owing to the puny dome and absurd cupolas sticking out of the roof. As a depository for the national pictures it proved of little use, and may be regarded on the whole as a practical blunder, by which the Royal Academy alone has profited at the public expense.

The New Royal Exchange (Fig. 2479), in Cornhill, stands on the site of two former buildings appropriated to the same purpose, and which were successively destroyed by fire. It is without exception the finest commercial edifice in London, and was built by Tite in 1842–44. The style is perhaps less chaste than it is florid and exuberant, but is appropriate to the purpose of such a structure : the plan is based upon that of the Pantheon at Rome. The Exchange, unlike most of the public buildings of the metropolis, stands on a site which permits it to be seen and judged in all its proportions.

The Corn Exchange, in Mark-lane, has been compared interiorly to the *atrium* of a Pompeian house : the colonnades within are occupied by the corn-dealers with their samples; but the whole has latterly been roofed in with glass, and the resemblance to the old Roman *impluvium* no longer exists. The front shown in Fig. 2480, with its Grecian Doric portico, was built by Smith in 1827–8, when the corn-market had to be enlarged.

The Mansion House (Fig. 2481), the residence of the Lord Mayor during his year of office, stands nearly facing the arena of the Royal Exchange. The building was begun in 1739, but was not completed until 1753. The elder Dance was the architect, and the style is that of Palladio. The principal front has a fine Corinthian portico, with six fluted columns, supporting a pediment filled with allegorical sculptures. On each side a flight of steps, balustraded, ascends to the entrance beneath the portico; and in the rusticated basement is the entrance to the offices. The grand banqueting-hall within was designed by the Earl of Burlington, and is called the Egyptian Hall, from its accordance with the Egyptian Hall described by Vitruvius. It is sufficiently capacious to dine four hundred guests, and here the Lord Mayor gives his state banquets.

The General Post-office (Fig. 2482), in St. Martin's-le-Grand, was built by Sir R. Smirke, in 1825–29. A hundred and thirty-one houses were pulled down to clear the site for this building. The grand façade has three Ionic porticoes, one at each end and one at the centre. The central one is surmounted by a pediment, and on the frieze is an inscription marking the date of the building. Below are entrances to the grand public hall (Fig. 2483), which is eighty feet long by sixty wide, and divided by Ionic columns into a centre and two aisles.

The Bank of England, in Threadneedle-street (Fig. 2484), stands upon four acres of ground, and has occupied its present site since 1734. The west wings were added by Taylor between 1766 and 1786. Sir John Soane subsequently became the architect to the Bank ; and it is to his extensive alterations and reconstructions that the present edifice owes its existing form. There is not much to admire in it beyond its fitness for the purpose for which it was intended. The Corinthian style prevails, but it is rendered heavy and dull by the ponderous appearance of the masses, and is overloaded with ornament.

The College of Surgeons (Fig. 2485), in Lincoln's Inn Fields, was originally built by Dance in 1800, but was almost entirely rebuilt by Barry in 1835–37, who added the stone front shown in the engraving, and the noble Ionic entablature. Here is the famous anatomical collection of the celebrated John Hunter (Fig. 2486).

The Royal College of Physicians (Fig. 2487) stands in Pall Mall East, and was built from the designs of Sir R. Smirke. The style is Grecian Ionic, with an elegant hexastyle Ionic portico, and the interior is sumptuously designed.

University College, in Gower-street (Fig. 2488), was designed by Wilkins, and built in 1827–8. It has a bold and rich portico of twelve Corinthian columns, and a pediment raised on a plinth of nineteen feet, and is approached by a handsome flight of steps. Behind the pediment is a cupola with a lantern light, in imitation of a peripteral temple. The building is four hundred feet in length—and in its rear stands University Hall (where the students breakfast and dine) an erection of red brick in the Elizabethan style. For further specimens of the style of architecture used for collegiate and educational buildings, see Figs. 2489, 2490, 2491.

In the building of bridges the English have been surpassed by no people either ancient or modern. The number of these erections which have been reared within the last fourscore years attests both the enterprise and success of the men of later generations. We must briefly notice those which span the Thames in or near London. The old London Bridge (Fig. 2492), with its waterworks beneath it, and which is familiar to our readers, was, up to the year 1750, the only bridge over the Thames in London. In that year Westminster Bridge was opened to the public: it was built by Labeyle, a Swiss, is twelve hundred and twenty-tree feet long by forty-four wide, and stands on fifteen arches. Its erection, together with its approaches, cost the nation nearly 400,000*l.*; but it was built on so defective a principle, the piers having no solid foundation, that it has cost a much larger sum to repair it within a period of forty years. It is now about to be replaced by a new one in harmony with the designs of the new Houses of Parliament.

Blackfriars Bridge was built in 1760–68, from the designs of Robert Mylne. It was originally a toll-bridge, but in the riots of 1780 the mob burnt the toll-house and destroyed the books of accounts. The cost of building was 260,000*l.* Repairs were completed in 1840 at a cost of 70,000*l.*, when the balustrades were removed, and a plain parapet substituted, to the destruction of the architectural effect.

Vauxhall Bridge (Fig. 2493), connecting Vauxhall-road with Millbank, was the work of four different engineers, and was finally finished by Walker at the expense of a public company. The bridge is of cast-iron, but was originally intended to be of stone. The first stone was laid in 1811, but, owing to a suspension of the works, the whole was not completed till 1816. The cost of the erection was 300,000*l.*, and the tolls do not yield one per cent. per annum on that outlay.

Waterloo Bridge (Fig. 2494), undoubtedly the finest in London, and which was said by Canova to be the finest bridge in the world, was designed by Linnell Bond, but was built for a public company by John Rennie (Fig. 2495). It was commenced in 1811, and opened in June, 1817. The cost, together with that of the approaches, was nearly a million sterling—more than the cost of St. Paul's, the Monument, and seven churches to boot. The entire length of the bridge is two thousand four hundred and fifty-six feet (not much short of half a mile): it crosses the river on nine semi-elliptic arches of one hundred and twenty feet span each, and the roadway is on a perfect level throughout. It is built of granite, and has Grecian-Doric columns between the piers. As a speculation it proved utterly ruinous to the company, who can return to the shareholders but a nominal dividend on their investments.

Southwark Bridge (Fig. 2496), designed by John Rennie, was built by a public company at a cost of 800,000*l.* It consists of three cast-iron arches, the centre of two hundred and forty feet span, and the two side ones of two hundred and ten feet each, raised above forty feet over the highest tides. The piers and abutments are of stone, founded upon timber platforms resting on piles driven below the bed of the river. The iron-work weighs five thousand seven hundred tons, and was supplied by Walker, of Rotherham. From experiments made to ascertain the rate of expansion and contraction, it is shown that the centre arch rises in summer above an inch. The bridge was commenced in 1813, and opened on March 24th 1819, at the stroke of midnight.

The old London Bridge had long been a cause of accident and a source of anxiety, and a new one was eagerly desired in its place. In March 1824 a new structure was commenced on a spot one hundred feet westward of the old bridge. The design was by John Rennie, who died in 1821, and the work had to be executed by his sons. The first arch was keyed in August 1827, the last in November 1829, and the bridge was opened in state by William IV. in August 1831. This bridge is said to be unrivalled in simplicity and justness of proportion, and is perhaps equalled by none in solidity of structure. It consists of five arches, the centre one, one hundred and fifty-two feet span, is thought to be the largest elliptical arch ever attempted. The material is Scotch and Devonshire granite; and the cost to the city, including the approaches, was little less than a million and a half sterling. It was over seven years in building, and forty of the labourers lost their lives in the progress of the works. The engraving (Fig. 2497) shows one of the dry arches crossing Thames-street.

Hungerford Suspension Bridge, leading from Hungerford Market to Lambeth, was constructed by I. K. Brunel. It consists of two lofty brick piers or towers in the Italian style, to suspend the chains, which are secured in tunnels at the abutments. There are three spans, the central one being six hundred and seventy-six feet. The entire length of the bridge is one thousand three hundred and fifty-two feet, and the roadway is in the centre thirty-two feet above the high-water mark. It was begun in 1841, and was opened in 1845, having been built without scaffolding or impediment to the navigation.

The iron-work weighs nearly eleven thousand tons, and the entire cost was but 110,000*l.*

In connection with the Thames bridges, we are bound to notice the Thames Tunnel (Fig. 2498). This extraordinary work, which connects Rotherhithe with Wapping at a point two miles below London Bridge, was designed and executed by Sir I. Brunel. It was commenced in March 1825—was closed for seven years by an irruption of the river into the works in 1828—was resumed in 1835, and opened for traffic in 1843. It could only have been accomplished by means of the shield, of Brunel's invention. This contrivance consisted of twelve separate parts, each containing three cells. In these cells the miners worked, protected by the shield above and in front, and backed by the bricklayers behind, who built up as fast as the miners advanced. Government lent 247,000*l.* to advance the works, and the total cost was 614,000*l.* The tolls bring in under 5,000*l.* annually, which is barely sufficient to keep the subaqueous thoroughfare dry and in a traversable state. The approaches are by shafts on each side of the river, descending a hundred steps each.

Vast as are the above enterprises in bridge-building in London, they have yet been exceeded in some respects by undertakings of provincial notoriety. To say nothing of the immense railway viaducts, which are bridges over valleys instead of rivers, there is the Menai Bridge which crosses the Menai Straits (Fig. 2499) near the sea at a height sufficiently lofty to permit the tallest ships to pass beneath it; and there is the Britannia Bridge which carries the Chester and Holyhead Railway across the same firth at an equal elevation. Both of these are justly regarded as engineering triumphs unparalleled in the history of the science.

In the provinces, too, and especially in the great manufacturing cities of the empire, we shall find public buildings which vie with the finest in the capital. Thus, the Exchange in Manchester will accommodate three thousand merchants at once; and even this noble edifice is exceeded by the magnificence and splendour of the Manchester warehouses, structures raised solely for commercial purposes, yet vying with, and even surpassing in grandeur and extent, the palaces of the sovereign. Again in Liverpool, we have in St. George's Hall (Fig. 2500) the finest structure in the Corinthian style of architecture in the kingdom, and, what is almost as much to the purpose, a noble building on a noble site. This remarkable temple of justice and the arts was erected from the designs of Lonsdale Elmes, Esq., between the years 1841 and 1851. In Birmingham, too, we have a Town Hall (Fig. 2501) of extraordinary magnificence, constructed not only for municipal purposes, but as a place of amusement and recreation for the inhabitants, and capable of containing about 3000 persons. It is a Grecian design of most imposing aspect, having a splendid series of Corinthian columns which run completely round the walls upon a rustic arcade: the architects were the Messrs. Hanson and Welsh, of Liverpool. Again, in Glasgow, which has more than doubled in size and importance since the birth of the living generation, we find Exchanges (Figs. 2502, 2503) worthy to rank in design with the first commercial piles in the kingdom, and bridges over the Clyde (Figs. 2504, 2505) inferior only in magnitude to those which span the Thames in London.

But the most remarkable building of modern times of which this country has to boast is the New Palace of Westminster, containing the Houses of Lords and Commons, the old Westminster Hall and Law Courts, innumerable committee-rooms, offices and official dwellings, and galleries of sculpture and art, occupying altogether an area of nearly eight acres. This prodigious undertaking was commenced by Barry in April, 1840, and though it has been actively advancing in progress for nearly seventeen years, is yet many years distant from its completion. In style and character it resembles the old town-halls of the Low Countries. Externally it has four points, that on the side of the river being 900 feet in length and divided into five principal compartments panelled with tracery and decorated with rows of statues and shields of arms of the sovereigns of England from the time of the Conquest. The land, or western front, it is said, will even surpass this in elegance. There are three principal towers, of the height respectively of 340, of 320, and of 310 feet, and various subordinate towers will break the line of view. It is impossible, in the narrow space to which we are limited, for us to convey to the reader any adequate idea of the magnificence and profuse splendour which characterises this national building either within or without. It would require a ponderous volume to write down the bare details of the multitudinous pomp and sumptuous ornament which meet the eye at every turn; and to be comprehended, either in its vastness or minutiæ, it must be personally seen and deliberately studied.

2520.—Oliver Goldsmith.

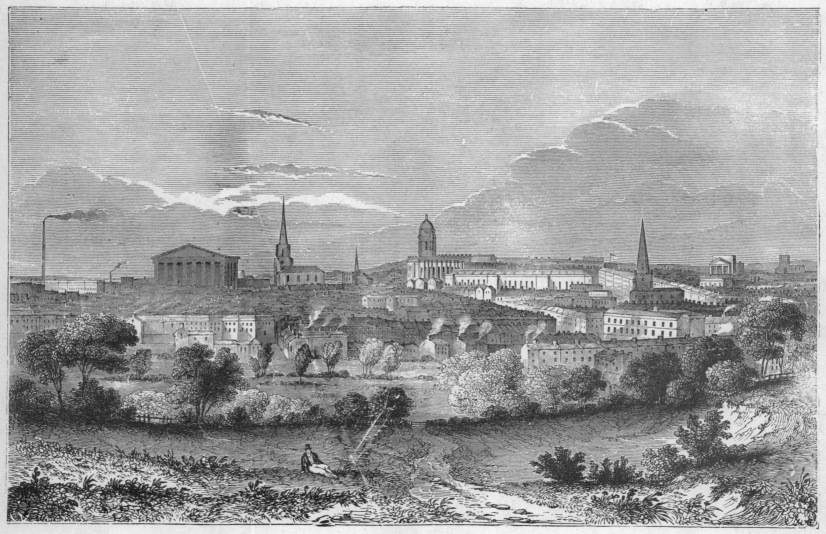

2519.—View of Birmingham.

2525.—Robert Burns.

2522. Edmund Burke.

2523.—John Wesley.

2524.—Edward Gibbon.

We must say one word on the street architecture of London, a subject that cannot be entirely passed over. Owing to the vicious system of letting land for building on short leases, which for a long time prevailed and to a large extent yet prevails, the streets of London were doomed to present the shabbiest, ugliest, and filthiest aspect producible by brick and mortar—for the plain reason, that a man who had but a few years' property in land could not be induced to lay out much money in building on it. To some not inconsiderable extent this evil has been remedied, and in consequence we have had of late years a very remarkable, though by no means a general, revolution in the aspect of new street buildings and shops. Architecture has, in fact, descended to the consideration of shop-fronts, in the design of which talent of no ordinary kind has been displayed. From shops to public offices was but a step; but it has proved in the course of years a step of such magnitude that it is almost doubtful whether the public offices and warehouses in the city are not at the present moment the finest models of a mingled style of architecture to be found in the kingdom. This lavish luxury in brick and stone, in connection with commercial purposes, is a suggestive subject, but we cannot here pause to speculate about it. Some specimens of what we refer to are shown in Figs. 2506, 2507, 2508, and the visitor in London may see more for himself in the neighbourhood of the Exchange and of St. Paul's. But it is in the west end of London that street architecture has taken the most extraordinary strides. The club-houses, those centres of luxury and isolation, are among the most finished specimens of the architect's art, standing as a class pre-eminent in point of expensiveness and magnificence, and only rivalled, if rivalled at all, by the town mansions of the nobility in Belgravia. We may add that in the outlying suburbs of London, and more especially in the west (Fig. 2509), important improvements have taken place in the style of the numberless villas and small cottages with which the land in all directions is everywhere dotted and covered. A better notion of convenience and a more practical regard to health are beginning to prevail, and the result is advantageous to the public in every way. Some idea of the improved aspect of a part of western London may be derived from the engraving Fig. 2510. What is yet wanted is a more considerate regard to the wants of the poor, and a substitution of healthful abodes for the miserable garrets, cellars, closes and undrained courts debouching in such vortices of vice and filth as the Seven Dials (Fig. 2511), to which their degradation and demoralization, each reacting on the other, at present consign them. In this direction Newcastle (see Figs. 2512, 2513, 2514,) has made as much progress, comparatively, as any city in the kingdom

CHAPTER II.—HISTORY AND BIOGRAPHY.

WE have now briefly to review some of the principal events of our history which have marked the lapse of the last hundred years. In so doing, however, we are debarred by space as well as other considerations, from attempting anything like a connected narrative, which would be foreign to our purpose while it would necessarily prove but unsatisfactory to the reader. All we can do is to select such of those events, with whatever causes they may have been connected, and irrespective of their political character, as appear to us to have been pregnant with results and influences bearing upon the social condition and social progress of the English people. Of the tactics of party and the intrigues of cabinets, the people in the mass know little or nothing, and though their interests may be seriously affected by both, their character is influenced by neither, unless and until the results of such secret agencies are brought home to them in some practical way. For this reason we shall glance only at such historical facts as, being of popular importance at the time when they transpired, may be fairly supposed to have had a share in the formation of the popular character; and we may be compelled to confine our remarks to but a few of the most prominent even of them.

George the Second died, at nearly fourscore years of age, in 1760. He left the world in the height of his military glory, and just when the nation was beginning to be sated with conquest. The war was continued under George the Third for a few years with still greater triumphs by land and sea, and, having in the course of its duration brought twelve millions of plunder to the nation, was terminated by an advantageous peace in February 1763.

In 1767 arose the first differences, on a paltry question of victualling the king's troops, between Great Britain and her American colonies. The English Parliament, instead of trying

means of conciliation, chose to carry things with a high hand, and in return for the just complaints of the colonists, decreed a tariff of customs upon goods imported from England. The Americans resisted the tariff, and threw the goods into the sea. War followed as a matter of course, and was maintained for many years with unflinching bravery on both sides. But the land forces of the British, under rash and incompetent commanders, suffered bloody defeats, uncompensated by a few partial successes, and two entire armies had to be surrendered prisoners of war to the enemy through the blind ignorance of their leaders. At home the war was unpopular, and the people neither rejoiced at the few successes nor mourned the many defeats: they looked on it rather as an affair of the king's than as their own business, and for the most part sympathised with the bold patriotism of the Americans. In 1776 the British troops were disgracefully ejected from Boston, and the rebels declared their independence. That independence was first acknowledged by France, and subsequently by Spain—events which drew on a war with both those countries; and we contrived to get embroiled with the Dutch soon after. The capture of Lord Cornwallis and his army by the forces of France and America under Washington in 1782, virtually finished the war, by which the Americans secured their independence, to the immense and undying advantage of freedom throughout the world.

In 1780 London was the scene of terrible riots, and was for many days at the mercy of a savage mob, who, meeting in St. George's Fields, at the instigation of Lord George Gordon, with the ostensible object of petitioning Parliament against the Catholic Disabilities Bill, proceeded to acts of plunder and devastation. They reduced all the Romish chapels to ruins, sacked and fired the dwellings of persons supposed to be favourable to Popery, and burned to the ground the prisons of Newgate, the Fleet, and the King's Bench. Advancing, at length, to attack the Bank, they were encountered by a force of armed citizens and a body of the regular troops, by whom upwards of two hundred of them were killed or mortally wounded, and the ringleaders secured. Lord George was tried for having originated the outrage, but nothing was proved against him. He was some years afterwards committed to prison for libel, and died in Newgate in 1793.

The years 1780–81–82 were rendered remarkable by the famous siege of Gibraltar, in which the Spaniards brought all the forces they could command, and exhausted all their resources, against the heroic garrison under General Elliot. In the course of the whole three years' siege, the garrison lost but a thousand men by the united plagues of famine and the sword, while an unnumbered host of the Spaniards perished. Their enormous battering ships, which were roofed in to protect them from the shot of the garrison, were set on fire by red-hot balls, then used in warfare for the first time—and the naval force of Spain melted away before the steady hardihood of the British soldier.

In 1789 a revolution burst out in France, which was destined to put a new aspect upon the political affairs of all Europe. The oppression of the poor by the exactions and monopolies of the rich was the originating cause of an event which, whether regarded as a disaster, or a blessing, was unequalled in the annals of the world. It deluged France with blood and crime, while it sowed the seeds of liberty, and taught to rulers the rights of the ruled. It transferred the reins of government from the monarch to the mob—brought the king and queen of France to the scaffold—exiled the nobility and overthrew the priesthood of the realm. At the same time it aroused a spirit of patriotism strong enough to withstand the banded forces of all Europe—to turn back their invading armies, and to carry the victorious arms of the Republic triumphant over the aggressors in every quarter. From the fiery bed of this revolution sprung the man who was to reconstruct the map of Europe, and apportion and distribute empires at his will. The rise and twenty years' career of Napoleon, during which he overturned nearly every throne in Europe, and made their potentates the puppets of his daring drama, constitute a series of facts too well known to all readers to allow of our recapitulating them here. Britain alone, whose sailors, under the immortal Nelson, swept his navies from the seas, effectually withstood him on the land, and was the final cause of his overthrow. The star of Napoleon, triumphing in the face of all other antagonists, waned before that of Wellington. The Iron Duke dashed the myriad hosts of France across the Spanish peninsula, crushing them in successive battles, and urging the defeated battalions to fly ignominiously from the arena of their own disgraces. It was the deadly blows of Wellington in the south, together with the icy shafts of the frozen North, that scattered to the winds the colossal preponderance of the son of the Revolution, and brought him to bay, on something like equal terms, amidst his exasperated foes, and it was at the hands of British endurance and British valour that he reaped his final defeat on the field of Waterloo —a defeat which transformed the despotic dictator of the nations into a whining, grumbling captive on a solitary rock.

On the 21st of October 1805, the battle of Trafalgar was fought off Cadiz—a battle which annihilated the combined navies of France and Spain, and virtually cleared the seas of the enemies of Britain. But in that battle Nelson (Fig. 2515) closed his long career of victory, and fell mortally wounded on his own deck. He survived the fatal shot but three hours, living long enough to witness the total ruin of the enemy, and solemnizing with his last breath the greatest triumph ever achieved on the ocean. When the glorious and gloomy tidings reached England they threw the nation into a transport at once of joy and exultation—of admiration and regret: for Nelson, the most staunch and daring viking that ever roamed the wave, had for years been the darling idol of the nation, and they held that glory dear which was purchased at the sacrifice of a life so costly. To this hour the name of Nelson is dearer to our island patriots than any other enrolled among the records of their history, and shall continue a beacon-light to the brave as long as British blood shall circulate in human veins. See Fig. 2516.

In January 1807 Lord Granville brought in a bill for the abolition of the slave trade. The king's sons, the Dukes of Clarence, Sussex, York, and Cumberland, eternally disgraced themselves by a violent and pertinacious opposition to a measure dictated by the merest humanity, and due to the self-respect of a free people. But the hearty convictions of Englishmen were, for this once, seconded by a determination as hearty; and in spite of the ceaseless efforts of the slave faction, headed by the royal princes, the Bill passed triumphantly with a majority of 100 to 36. In the Commons the majority in favour of abolition was 238 to 16; and the Bill finally received the royal assent on the 25th of March, the same day on which the ministers delivered up the seals of office—Lord Grenville before retiring congratulating the House on having performed one of the most glorious acts that had ever been done by any assembly of any nation in the world. From that hour the slave trade was finally condemned and prohibited.

On the 11th of May 1812, Mr. Perceval, then first lord of the treasury, was shot through the heart on entering the lobby of the House of Commons, and died in a few minutes. The assassin, who had mistaken him for Lord George Leveson Gower, coolly walked to the fireplace and surrendered himself. He was an unfortunate merchant of Liverpool, by name Bellingham, and was well known to be insane. The hatred of Perceval and his measures which was entertained by the mob, urged them to applaud the assassination, and it was feared that they would attempt to rescue the prisoner. It was partly from this cause, and from a determination to spite the popular faction, that the trial of Bellingham was hurried forward with indecent haste—so that he was condemned and executed within a week of the deed—before there was time, in those days of tardy locomotion and postal conveyance, for collecting and submitting to the jury evidence the most irrefragable of his insanity—and thus one insane murder was avenged by another.

In 1812, also, the Americans declared war against England. The following year saw them attempting the conquest of Canada, in which, however, they met with no success. They were more successful by sea, having the advantage in several encounters. The capture of Washington by the British, who destroyed the stores and public buildings, paved the way for a treaty of peace, which was signed at Ghent in 1814. But the news of this treaty did not reach America in time to prevent the disastrous expedition to New Orleans, where the English army, fighting in open field with an enemy strongly entrenched and shielded, lost three thousand men, and was compelled to retreat.

On the 27th of August 1816, Lord Exmouth bombarded the town of Algiers from three o'clock in the afternoon till near midnight, and wellnigh laid that nest of pirates in ruins, and utterly destroyed their fleet. This act of severity was but too richly merited by the barbarians upon whom it fell. For centuries the Algerines had been the corsairs of the Mediterranean, and had enriched themselves by piratical expeditions and the traffic in Christian slaves. The blow dealt them by Lord Exmouth crippled their resources, and reduced them, for a time at least, to good behaviour. The immediate result of the bombardment was the release and delivery to the care of the English of more than a thousand Christian slaves, who within three days arrived from the interior and were conveyed to their respective countries.

The year 1817 is memorable only for the death of the Princess Charlotte, an event which plunged the whole nation in gloom and sorrow. She was a princess whose character was in all respects

admirable; she was the darling of the populace, who looked forward to the hour when she should occupy the throne; and she merited the homage paid to her rank by the depth and sincerity of her benevolence. She died in giving birth to a dead child, and it was indignantly affirmed, with too much truth, that she died the victim of neglect in the hour of need. The public odium was directed chiefly against Sir Richard Croft, who a few months afterwards put a period to his own existence.

In 1818 died Queen Charlotte, who for fifty-seven years had been the wife of George the Third. This year was disgraced by riots in Manchester arising out of distress, itself the consequence of a strike among the cotton-spinners. The rioters were charged by the soldiery, one man was killed and several were wounded. This affair was nothing, however, in comparison with the so-called massacre of Peterloo, which drew the eyes of the whole nation upon Manchester in the following year. Orator Hunt, a well-known thick-headed demagogue, had, in despite of the magistrates of the town, got up a crowded meeting in St. Peter's Field, to discuss the public grievances, and exercise the right of petition. The magistrates, who had not made up their minds how to act, suddenly ordered the arrest of the orator while the proceedings were going quietly on. The military, receiving orders to support the civil officers in their duty, charged the crowd, when a scene of most horrible confusion ensued. Thousands of both sexes were thrown down, crushed and trampled under foot—many were ruthlessly cut down by the yeomanry, and others shot by the infantry. The number of the killed was never accurately ascertained, and though it was probably small, hundreds if not thousands were severely injured. The magistrates received the thanks of the Prince Regent for their conduct—a return for their huge blunder which probably astonished them as much as it enraged and disgusted the humbler classes of the people.

In 1820 the blood-thirsty conspiracy of Cato-street alarmed the entire kingdom. There is nothing improbable in the supposition that this most murderous plot was the offspring of the Manchester massacre, as the affair of St. Peter's Field was then termed. The contempt manifested in that affair, and its sequences, for the lives and liberties of the populace, had aroused a thirst for vengeance, and had served to reorganise the associations of the malcontents. The conspiracy in question would perhaps have ended in nothing had it been left to take its own course; but it was artfully fomented, and nursed to a head by the machinations of a Government spy, who acted with the knowledge of ministers, and reported every movement of the conspirators. The design of the gang was nothing less than the assassination of the whole of the Cabinet, and the capture of the Bank and the Tower. The ministers were to be slaughtered while assembled at a Cabinet dinner at Lord Harrowby's on Wednesday the 23rd of January, and everything was arranged for the execution of the plot. The ministers, of course, did not meet at Lord Harrowby's, but dined at home, and then assembled at Lord Liverpool's, to await the issue of the counter-plot they had prepared. They had arranged for the capture of the whole gang on their assembling for the murderous exploit; but, owing either to the tardiness of the military or the precipitation of the police, these two parties did not act together. One of the police-officers was stabbed to the heart by Thistlewood, the contriver of the plot, who then blew out the light, and escaped with fourteen of the party in the darkness. Nine were taken prisoners on the arrival of the soldiers; and of that number four suffered death for high treason; the remaining five being transported for life. The spy Edwards, and another of the name of Hidon, were not punished; on the contrary, both received a reward for their treachery—to the immense disgust of the people at large.

In this year the good old King, George III., died, after a reign of sixty years; and the Regent, who had long been virtually sovereign, ascended the throne. This event, which was agreeable to nobody, was followed by one of the most infamous exhibitions of unmanly persecution of which history has any record. The King, who hated his wife, and had driven her from his side to seek peace and quiet elsewhere, and had surrounded her with spies during her long absence abroad, now, upon her claiming to share the allegiance of the people, prosecuted her on a charge of incontinence, with a view to divorce. The dastardly act roused the indignation of the whole realm, and everywhere the people threw the shield of their sympathies over the persecuted Queen and woman. After a trial, which lasted the whole summer, and filled the entire country with the elements of bitterness and mortification, the prosecution had to be abandoned for want of evidence. The triumph of the Queen was the triumph of humanity throughout the country: but it was of no avail to her that her innocence was established by the abandonment of the prosecution. She was not restored to her rights, which she

2526.—Cowper.

2528.—Sir Walter Scott

2529.—Lord Byron.

2530.—Robert Hall.

2527.—Dr. Jenner.

2531.—Sir J. Reynolds

2532.—Benjamin West.

2533.—West's Death of General Wolfe.

2535.—Covent Garden Market.

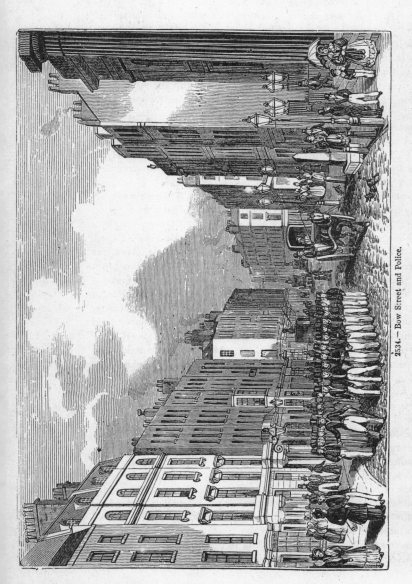

2534.—Bow Street and Police.

2536.—Hungerford Market.

was unfortunately weak enough to claim—was ignominiously turned away from the Abbey-doors on the day of the coronation, and died a month later, declaring that she quitted life without regret.

For some years following the accession of George IV. the industrial enterprise of England prospered, favoured as it was by the peace and by the consequent increase of her commerce in all parts of the world—favoured also by the spirit of invention and discovery, whose triumphs we have recorded in the previous chapter. The agricultural interest was satisfied because corn maintained, amidst constant fluctuations, a price which, on the average, was more than remunerative: the manufacturing interest was buoyant because, although the power of supply was rapidly increasing with every year and every month, it yet failed to overtake the demand, and prices remained steady under a rate of production which had no parallel in former eras : and the populace were satisfied, or at least were prevented from insisting on their grievances, by the fact that employment was plentiful at a fair rate of wages. The continued prosperity, as is always the case with a commercial community, stimulated enterprise, which, not finding for itself a sufficient sphere of action in the old and beaten paths, began to diverge into wide and unknown spheres of speculation. Men not knowing what to do with their capital, and in a hurry to increase its amount, devised new schemes and plunged into them with a recklessness which shut out calculation and reflection. Joint-stock companies grew and multiplied like mushrooms, and associations of sober individuals were seen unitedly prosecuting the maddest projects, which either one of them singly would have denounced as hopelessly absurd. Rogues, knaves, and swindlers, who had nothing, not even character, to lose, wormed or crushed themselves into the management of the new concerns, and they alone profited by them in the end. The banks and the government stock offered but a low rate of interest—the new companies offered more than double, and professed to guarantee the dividends: the consequence was, that thousands invested their whole fortunes in these fallacious bubbles, which were to burst too soon, and involve their credulous victims in ruin. The inevitable result of all this insanity came at last in the panic and crash of 1825-6. The catastrophe first announced itself by the failure of a few commercial houses supposed to be backed by capital without limit; then the failures increased in number; and soon spread consternation in all directions; and in the midst of the general alarm the banks began to stop payment. Everybody who had money in the bankers' hands now ran panic-stricken to draw it out—the panic spread like the plague, only faster—the run on the banks became general, and the crash came in the simultaneous ruin of a multitude of deluded victims, who saw with terror the old establishments on which they had relied with security for their dividends, stopping payment to the number of twelve or fifteen a-week for months together. The misery which resulted from the combined folly and villany of this memorable period will never be fully known. The most painful of the visible effects of the panic and the crash was the awful distress which ensued to the poor and labouring classes. Hundreds of thousands were thrown out of employment, and had to fight the dreary battle with cold and starvation throughout the winter. But for the humanity of those who had escaped or but partially suffered from the storm, multitudes of the industrious poor must have perished. As it was, the most fearful riots, under the aggravated pressure of want, broke out in various parts of the country, and were renewed at intervals during the whole of the year 1826.

In August 1827 died the Right Hon. George Canning (Fig. 2517). His death inflicted an irreparable loss upon the country, and was sincerely mourned by the liberal party, with whom he was immensely and deservedly popular. Like Peel, in later times, he had seen fit to revise his political opinions, and embrace a truly liberal policy, and had thus exposed himself to the rancorous abuse of the opponents of progress. The immediate cause of his death was supposed to be a chill caught while attending the midnight funeral of the Duke of York, which brought on an inflammatory attack, subsequently aggravated and rendered fatal by over-exertion and anxiety of mind. As a scholar and an orator Canning had no equal in his day.

In October of the same year was fought the battle of Navarino— a battle which ended in the destruction of the Turkish fleet by the combined navies of England, France, and Russia, but which brought no honour to either of the allies, and profited only Russia. The affair was in truth nothing better than a sad and melancholy blunder, which a little sagacity on the part of ministers at home would have prevented.

In April 1829 the Catholic Relief Bill—a measure which had been for many years a fruitful source of agitation and ill-blood, passed into a law. The purport of the Bill was to admit Catholics to the enjoyment of all municipal advantages—to the exercise of all corporate offices and of legislative functions, and to the administration of civil and criminal justice. The No-Popery party prophesied the most fatal consequences from this measure; but the experience of a quarter of a century has failed to produce them.

The grand event of 1830 was the revolution in France, brought about by the obstinacy of Polignac and the stupid imbecility of Charles X. The people, incensed by the promulgation of the infamous ordonnances, rose in insurrection, and after three days of barricades and fighting, overpowered the troops in every quarter. The silly, priest-ridden king had to run for his life; but more fortunate than Louis XVI., was allowed to make his escape and seek a refuge in England. The success of the French in thus getting rid of an obnoxious and despotic ruler awoke the slumbering embers of revolt in Belgium, where, not long afterwards, a similar drama was rehearsed; and it had the effect also, there can be little doubt, of encouraging the advocates of reform at home to a prompt and decisive struggle, which was destined ere long to be successful.

In this same year George IV. died, in the sixty-eighth year of his age and the eleventh of his reign. The court went into mourning; but the death of the modern Vitellius was received by the nation with an indifference which could be interpreted only as an expression of their unanimous consent to bury the demerits of the royal obstructive in his own grave.

At this period distress was general throughout the country, and a growing spirit of dissatisfaction goaded the oppressed to acts of barbarism. Machines were broken, factories were burned down, starving gangs perambulated the country, and the incendiary exploits of the mysterious Captain Swing spread alarm on every side. With corn scarce and dear, thousands of ricks were wantonly set on fire, and night after night the homesteads of the farmer were seen blazing in the distance. Worse than this, the system of poisoning for the sake of a paltry gain sprung up among the miserable poor—and the climax to these barbarities appeared at last in the discovery of a traffic carried on by gangs rivalling in cold-blooded atrocity the Thugs of Hindostan—wretches who murdered their fellows for the sake of the price obtainable for the dead bodies of their victims. One man, when the crime was brought home to him, confessed to fifteen of these murders.

The year 1831 was one of general excitement and commotion, especially among the lower orders, who imagined that the passing of the Reform Bill would prove a panacea for all the grievances of their lot. Political unions had sprung up all over the kingdom, and kept the popular attention on the alert in every town and almost every village. Alarming riots broke out at Derby, at Nottingham, and at various other places: these, however, were thrown into the shade by the atrocious proceedings at Bristol, which threatened at one time to end in the sacking of a whole city by a furious mob. Owing to the indecision of the magistrates, and the fatuity of Colonel Brereton, who at the head of a powerful body of troops forebore all interference, the city was for thirty hours a prey to the drunken rabble, who burned down the Mansion House, the gaols, and a large number of private dwellings. The riot was ultimately quelled and the city saved only by the slaughter of a round number of the mob, a calamity which might have been avoided by a mere show of severity at the commencement of the outbreak.

In June 1832 the Reform Bill became law, and the event was received with enthusiastic joy, testified by a general illumination throughout the kingdom. The universal satisfaction on this account was, however, dismally checked by the ravages of the cholera, a disease till then almost unknown in England, and which, appearing first in Sunderland, spread rapidly, carrying with it terror and sudden death to all parts of the kingdom. In London it slew between five and six thousand persons, chiefly of the squalid and intemperate poor; but of the number of victims throughout the kingdom no account was taken.

In August 1833 the Negro Emancipation Act—an Act by which slavery was finally abolished in the British dominions—passed the House of Lords. The Act came into operation on the first of August in the following year, on which day the name and much of the substance of slavery expired, a short term of apprenticeship only remaining. This inestimable boon to the African race was purchased for them by the free people of Britain, at the cost of twenty millions of hard cash paid over to the planters: a deed of generosity and pure principle unparalleled in the history of nations, and which won for England the admiration of the world. Wilberforce, who had devoted his life to the cause of the Negro, lived long enough to see the dawn of this final triumph, and to rejoice in the assurance of its achivement, dying at the close of 1833.

Early in 1834 a Bill was brought in to amend the Poor Law. The old law placed a premium upon the vice and immorality of the most worthless class, and operated more powerfully in debasing and degrading the labourer than all the other deteriorating influences to which he was subject. It was in fact a machinery for transforming the honest citizen of the state into a swindling pauper, and could not have accomplished such a purpose better had it been devised expressly with that view. The new bill became law on the 14th of August, and in less than two years from that date had wrought a reformation in the habits of the poor which the most sanguine had not dared to expect. It had relieved the workhouses, had changed crowds of bullying beggars into steady workers, had decreased the number of illegitimate births by ten thousand, and had reduced the poor's-rate by over a million sterling.

In October 1834 the Houses of Lords and Commons (Fig. 2518) were destroyed by fire, through the carelessness of some workmen who were employed to burn a vast accumulation of Exchequer tallies which were wanted out of the way. The law-courts were saved, and a part of the library, but a store of valuable documents and relics were consumed. The king offered the use of Buckingham Palace for the members; but it was judged better to fit up temporary accommodation for both houses on the old site, which was done at a cost of 30,000l. In 1836, above ninety plans having been sent in for consideration by the committee for rebuilding the Houses of Parliament, Mr. Barry's was chosen, and that gentleman appointed architect. The building was commenced in the year 1837 by the formation of an embankment on piles along the river side.

On the 5th of June, 1835, Lord John Russell introduced the Municipal Reform Bill into the House of Commons. Municipal law and justice had long been a mere farce when this bill was brought in, and there is nothing wonderful in the fact that it passed with astonishing rapidity through the lower house. The Peers did what they could to nullify the measure; but the pressure of opinion was too strong for them, and having succeeded in effecting some damaging modifications, they too passed the bill early in September, and it immediately became law. This same year, 1835, was marked by a serious amount of agricultural distress, and the farmers clamoured loudly for a reduction of taxation. The principles of free trade began now to be generally discussed both in this country and in France, and it was seen by those best qualified to judge, that in the abolition of all restrictions upon trade and commerce lay the only permanent cure for industrial grievances.

In 1836 Louis Napoleon made his first attempt to overthrow the government of Louis Philippe, by a quixotic appeal to the soldiery at Strasburg, whom he expected to rise in his favour at the sight of the "eagle of France." The attempt failed ludicrously, and the author of it was contemptuously shipped off to America in a French frigate. The whole world laughed at the affair,—but the laughter was misapplied.

On the 20th of June, 1837, King William IV. died after a short illness, and her present Majesty Queen Victoria succeeded to the throne. One of the first events of social import in her Majesty's reign was the popular spread of Chartism among the lower ranks. It was in the north, chiefly, that the Chartists in their periodical meetings disgraced the purity of their cause by wild speeches and violent demonstrations. Lord John Russell, anxious to prevent turbulence and the appearance of persecution on the part of the government, acted with the utmost lenity towards the misguided offenders. This was stupidly attributed to wrong motives, and only led to aggravated offences. Infatuated demagogues began openly to preach rebellion; and torch-light meetings of an alarming character spread dismay on all sides. Feargus O'Connor placed himself at the head of the movement in the north, and ignorantly fanned the flame of disaffection, which extended to all parts of the country. Fearful riots broke out in Birmingham (Fig. 2519), and for many days the town was in a state of uproar and commotion: in Sheffield the matter was still worse; robbery walked the streets, and malcontents sought the lives of employers. Newport, in Wales, became the scene of open rebellion: under the leadership of Frost, a traitorous magistrate, seven thousand men attacked the military, and were put to the rout with the loss of twenty lives. Frost, with two of his followers, was subsequently transported, in lieu of being hanged—an act of sovereign mercy, which did not prevent Frost, on being pardoned and restored to his country seventeen years afterwards, from returning to his old inflammatory practices.

It was at a public dinner given to Dr. Bowring, in Manchester, in 1838, that the persons present agreed to form themselves into an association for promoting the principles of free trade. This was the origin of the Anti-Corn-Law League, an association which was destined to effect a revolution in the commercial policy not only of

this but of surrounding nations. Sneered at and derided at first, it grew and grew until its shadow darkened the land, and until it had enlisted beneath its banners nearly the whole mass of the intelligence and patriotism of the realm. By the aid of the press, of an activity which knew no pause, of unlimited capital, and by the persuasive eloquence of its leaders, it ran a triumphant course of seven years, during which it bore down all opposition, and having first convinced the nation of the truth and value of its principles, finished by converting the prime minister to the faith he had formerly ridiculed, and by receiving at his hands the consummation of its final success. It is to Richard Cobden that the nation owes its convictions of the fallacy of restrictive systems; and it is to the eternal honour of Sir Robert Peel that, receiving such convictions himself, he had the manliness to carry them out in practice by abolishing the corn-laws. The League, when it had done its work, was dissolved in 1846.

In the latter part of 1839, the House of Commons, at the instigation of Mr. Rowland Hill, decreed the trial of a new system of postage, by which the old rates of 6d., 9d., 1s. and so on per letter, were reduced to an uniform charge of one penny. To give the Post Office time to prepare for so great a change, a fourpenny rate was charged for a few weeks; but on the 10th of January, 1840, the penny scheme was tried. How complete has been the success of this plan we all know, and what a boon it has proved to every individual in the country. It is, we think, undeniable that this single measure, in regard to its social importance, outweighs any other, we might almost say all others, that have been adopted in our time. It has certainly done more for commerce than anything commerce has been able to achieve for itself: it has probably done more for education than ten thousand schools would have accomplished in the same time; and, by cementing and increasing social and friendly relations, it has had a moral effect upon the whole population which has raised them prodigiously in the moral scale. It was the one thing wanting to make of our island home one vast domestic institution, and in connection with the rapid transition by railways, and the instantaneous communication by the electric wires, for which it prepared the way, has done all that could be done towards combining in one family the entire British race.

On the 10th of February, 1840, Her Majesty was married to Prince Albert of Saxe Coburg and Gotha, a union which was as acceptable to the English people as it was gratifying to the royal pair themselves, who formed a rare exception to the rule of princely contracts by making a marriage of affection arising out of previous intercourse often renewed.

In 1840 Louis Napoleon repeated at Boulogne the experiment made at Strasburg in 1836, and which also, was the source of as much ridicule and sarcasm at the time, but which has since assumed a significance then not dreamed of. The exploit was rewarded by six years' imprisonment in the fortress of Ham, a seclusion which has not been without its fruits. In the same year the remains of the first Napoleon were brought from St. Helena, and in the presence of all Paris were solemnly interred in the Hotel des Invalides. In this year our government commenced a war upon the helpless and unoffending Chinese. The step was cruelly tyrannous and despicable in the last degree, having for its object the forcing of opium upon the Chinese merchants, which, on moral grounds, they were unwilling to receive. The island of Chusan was taken without a blow. Canton soon after lay at the mercy of the British, and would have been taken but for the interference of the superintendent of the Indian trade. Sir Henry Pottinger took the town of Amoy and the large city of Ningpo fifteen miles inland, where the British inflicted a terrible slaughter on the enemy without suffering any loss. In the summer of 1842, Pottinger appeared before Nankin, and at last terrified the Chinese into a treaty of Peace. By this treaty they were to pay the British 27,000,000 of dollars and to grant them a free-trade at four ports besides Canton. Hong Kong was to be ceded to them; and Chusan was to be held in pledge until the conditions of the treaty were fulfilled. The Chinese tribute was all duly paid, arriving at intervals in the form of "Sycee silver" until no more was due. This war, with its sequences, is in all the details so radically infamous, that we blush to record it even thus briefly.

While the British force in China was playing the bully and the dastard by demolishing forts and towns and slaughtering timid Chinese, a force far more numerous was melting away beneath the sharp shot of the Affghans and the icy horrors of the Cabul pass. Of 17,000 men who set out on the 6th of January, all were felled by frost, bullet, or bayonet, before the dawning of the seventh day from that of their flight, and one man only escaped to tell the miserable tale. "Except the burying of Cambyses army in the African

2538.—Zoological Gardens, Regent's Park.

2539.—Paternoster Row.

2537.—Billingsgate.

2540.—Fish Street Hill, and Fire-brigade.

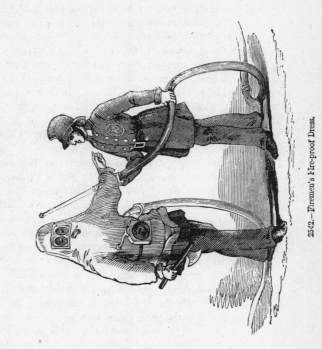

2542.—Fireman's Fire-proof Dress.

2541.—Thames Fire Engine.

2543.—Highgate Cemetery.

desert, such a destruction has perhaps never been heard of in the world."

The winter of 1842–43 was a season of terrible distress to the poor and labouring classes, and, as usual, was signalized by riots and disturbances in the manufacturing districts, and risings among the Chartists. The most remarkable of these riots, however, were those which originated in Wales among Rebecca and her children. These mysterious outbreaks took place solely in the dead of night, and at first had for their single object the destruction of the toll-gates throughout an extensive district. In one county alone eighty gates were destroyed; and in others not a gate was left standing. The success of these movements among the Welsh enticed the Chartists to visit them, and these stump orators soon inflamed the Welsh blood to acts of more daring outrage. A strong force of the military was despatched to the scene of action, and peace was produced by the usual means of severity. Rebecca's daughters (sturdy fellows in petticoats) were captured, and transported by sentence of a special commission; but the movement led to a revision of the turnpike-trusts in South Wales, and thus Rebecca's insurrection accomplished its original object.

For some years following these outbreaks the tide of commercial prosperity seemed to flow with almost unbroken current. There was employment for labour throughout the whole kingdom, and, owing to the continual projection and formation of new railways, there was ample scope for the investment of capital. The general prosperity revived the old spirit of speculation: keen and unscrupulous speculators made large and rapid fortunes, and the multitude rushed eagerly in their track, hungering for the same result. Legitimate trade gave place to a gambling traffic as delusive and fallacious as it was immoral; the whole country seemed bitten with the railway mania; the maddest schemes found favour, and enriched the projectors, to the ruin of the shareholders, who were victimised to the amount of near a hundred millions. At length came a season of scarcity and high prices, when the bubble burst, and the panic of 1825–6 was re-enacted before the eyes of the same generation. Again the greed of the many had wrought their ruin and misery, and thousands had to mourn in poverty and privation the loss of that competence of which their own covetousness had deprived them. On reviewing the course of such events it would appear that prosperity and panic revolve in cycles, and that the fatuity of mankind has decreed that the one should follow the other as regularly as night succeeds to day.

On the 15th of May 1847 died Daniel O'Connell, a man whose name for many years literally filled the three kingdoms. He was the model of an agitator, and was most in his element when contending with his adversaries. As a speaker no man ever swayed the ignorant multitude more completely, or exercised a greater mastery over their sympathies; but he was accused of wanting the instinct of honour and generosity which marks the truly great, and of seeking his own aggrandisement rather than the welfare of his worshippers. He lived to witness the wane of his popularity, and had he lived a few years longer would have seen it inherited by his opponents. It would be hard to find a parallel to such a career as O'Connell's: perhaps there never lived a man who rose to such a height in popular estimation, who yet accomplished so little for the people.

In February 1848 a revolution broke out in Paris, which in three days ended in driving the citizen king from the throne he had occupied for seventeen years. The real cause of the revolution was the corruption of the public offices and the hateful policy of the government. The people demanded the reform of these abuses, and sought to obtain it by the usual means of meetings and discussions. The government forbade the meetings and resolved to suppress them, and the people rose in arms; they were successful in every quarter, and, to their credit, used their victory with moderation. The king and his family fled to England, where Louis Philippe died a few years later. France was now a republic, and socialist principles for a time swayed the public measures. The experiment of national workshops, by which the state undertook to find employ-ment for workmen, and pay their wages, was tried and failed miserably, satisfying none but those who received the wages without caring to do the work. When the failure became evident the work-shops were abolished, and the workmen rose in insurrection, in defence of their imaginary privileges; they were subdued after a bloody butchery of four days' duration, with terrible loss of life on both sides. The revolution of '48 and the domestic troubles it brought in its train, gave the opportunity which Louis Napoleon had been waiting for all his life, and he made them the first steps in the ladder by which he ultimately ascended to the supreme power.

While these things had been going on in France, America had

annexed California (conquered from the Mexicans by Fremont) to the United States, and had almost simultaneously discovered that a large proportion of the territory was one vast gold-field, abounding in inexhaustible wealth. The wildest reports were circulated, and, to the astonishment of the whole world, were verified by the quantities of the precious metal which began to flow from the valley of the Sacramento. A golden age had at last dawned, and all eyes were turned towards the Far West.

In 1850 Sir Robert Peel died, in consequence of a fall from his horse, and the nation had to mourn an irreparable loss. In this year, also, the news arrived in this country that gold fields, equal in productiveness and superior in extent to those in California, had been discovered in the British colonies in Australia. The news was followed by vouchers in the shape of gold grains and nuggets of enormous size; and immediately there set in towards Melbourne and the diggings a tide of emigration which still continues to flow, not only from Britain but from all the nations of the civilized world. The effect of this discovery will be not merely to provide abundance of the circulating medium for the commerce of the globe, but to develop the resources of the boundless territory of Aus-tralasia, and to transform that illimitable waste into a populous and powerful empire.

The year 1851, the first of the new half-century, was signalised by an event renowned throughout the world, and which brought together in London the representatives of all civilised peoples. The Great Exhibition in Hyde Park, which opened in May, displayed such an assemblage of wealth and magnificence as mankind had never witnessed before—all classified and arranged under one crystal roof, in a building capable of accommodating a hundred thousand spectators at a time. That memorable summer was the glorious carnival of industry and the arts; and it was as notably a season of universal intercourse and brotherhood. As the treasures of all nations were piled in generous rivalry beneath the same roof—so pilgrims from all countries met in peace and good fellowship, and London became the common home of the repre-sentatives of the whole industrial world. The original idea of the Great Exhibition is ascribed to the Prince Consort: it was eminently a want of the epoch, and it aroused the enthusiastic energies of labour throughout Europe; it was successful beyond the most sanguine hopes, not merely in the accumulation of untold treasures, but in the spread of generous emulation, and the diffusion of artistic and constructive knowledge to an inappreciable amount. Paxton, the architect of the building, won a lasting reputation; and numbers of ingenious and talented men, unknown before, emerged from obscurity and took their proper place in the estimation of their fellows. Of the multitudinous treasures exhibited, the catalogue alone fills a couple of large volumes.

The close of this memorable year was marked by the explosion of the dark thunder-cloud which had been gathering in France. On the night between the 1st and 2nd of December Louis Napoleon struck his tremendous *coup d'état*. Having adroitly managed to remove the chiefs of the army and replace them by his own creatures; having won over the common soldiers as well as their leaders to his interests—he placed them in battle array in the streets of Paris in the dead of night—arrested his stanchest opponents in their beds, dragging them off to prison—and Paris awoke in the morning with fifty thousand drawn daggers at its throat, to find the Assembly dissolved, the ignorant mob endowed with universal suffrage, and the lives and liberties of France at the mercy of an unscrupulous despot. The people, stunned and paralysed at the suddenness and audacity of the stroke, remained in a state of stupor for that day; on the next they began to look around and think of resistance; and in the night barricades arose in the streets wherever the means of erecting them could be found. The morning of the 4th dawned on battle and carnage. The soldiery, acting according to orders, shot down the people indiscriminately in quarters where there was no resistance, and piled the streets with the slain bodies of the innocent—men, women, and children. Napoleon had resolved to overcome opposition by terror, and to secure the submission of the citizens at whatever cost. The price paid for it was the blood of thousands of innocent persons, shed to cement and consolidate the power of despotism. From that hour France has been despotically ruled by the will of one man: she has accepted the iron sceptre as a safeguard from the horrors of revolution; and she has been so far fortunate in her degradation as to purchase internal quiet at the expense of freedom.

In 1853 the Emperor of Russia commenced those aggressions upon Turkey which led to the formation of the alliance between England and France for the protection of the Ottoman empire. How honourably, thus far, that alliance has been maintained on both sides—how nobly the armies of both countries have fought side by side in the Crimean war—the reader is sufficiently aware; and we shall be excused in a survey of this brief nature from recapitulating events so well known. The fields of Alma, of Balaclava, of Inkermann, and of Sebastopol, which witnessed the triumphs of the allies, also combined to pave the way for an honourable peace, the sole real impediment to which was removed by the death of Nicholas. How long that peace is to last, or with whom and under what combinations grim war shall next arise, we are not sagacious enough to foresee. Meanwhile the political horizon, both in the old world and the new, is dark with cloudy portents, and warns us to stand prepared for the possible bursting of the storm.

———

A review, however brief, of the course of the last hundred years must necessarily contain some notice of its literary history, and some account of those benefactors of society who by their writings have contributed to inform the public mind, to purify the morals and manners of the age, and to elevate the general taste. The number of writers of both sexes who, during the period of which we treat, have conferred inestimable benefits on mankind is far too great even to be catalogued in the limited space we can allot to this part of our subject, and we must be satisfied, therefore, with a brief glance at the foremost few of the honoured names by which the lofty position of literature in our day was mainly achieved.

Dr. Samuel Johnson, who, a hundred years back, was undisputed sovereign of the literary kingdom, was not only the first writer but the first talker at an era when the art of conversation was emulously cultivated by the master-spirits of the time. Fortunately for us, his conversation, as well as his writings, has been faithfully transmitted; and the burly, testy moralist, and sound, sympathising, hearty man, lives and breathes among us almost as vividly and vigorously—thanks to the retentive Bozzy—as though the tomb had not yet closed over his remains. Johnson died in 1784, at the age of seventy-five. Fielding, Sterne, and Smollett—the three great novelists whose works, while they represent in living pictures the manners and peculiarities of their age, are so replete with wit, humour, and sentiment, as to command the admiration of all times, had all passed away while Johnson was yet living. Oliver Goldsmith (Fig. 2520), Johnson's friend and companion, the most tender, simple-hearted, witty, and genial of all writers of English fiction, had died in Johnson's lifetime, leaving, in the 'Vicar of Wakefield,' a legacy which the world has learned to value above all the ponderous productions of the great lexicographer. Chatterton, "the marvellous boy who perished in his pride," who was precocious in intellect, in independence, and in rashness, beyond all recorded parallel, had perished by his own hand, at seventeen years of age, in 1770.

David Hume, the celebrated historian and the leader of the modern philosophical sceptics, died in 1776. His friend and apologist, Dr. Adam Smith, the author of the 'Wealth of Nations,' the work which laid the foundation of the modern system of political economy, died in 1790. In the same year died Howard the philanthropist (Fig. 2521). Edmund Burke (Fig. 2522), the most polished writer of the last century, the author of the 'Essay on the Sublime and Beautiful,' and the 'Letters on the French Revolution,' and who to the reputation of a finished writer added that of a consummate statesman, died in 1797. John Wesley (Fig. 2523), the founder of the Wesleyan denomination, who for threescore years led a life of ceaseless activity in the cause of religion, and yet published numerous volumes of sermons and journals, died in 1791, at the age of 88. Three years later, in 1794, died Edward Gibbon (Fig. 2524), the author of the 'Decline and Fall of the Roman Empire,' a work to which the best judges have allotted the first place in historic literature.

In 1786 a ploughman of Ayrshire, in Scotland, published a small volume of poems. Their singular naturalness, beauty, and musical rhythm recommended them at once to the best judges; but the countrymen of Robert Burns (Fig. 2525) were slow in recognising in their humble bard the transcendant genius which was destined to assert itself so triumphantly in after times, and to win for the obscure driver of the plough the title of the Shakspere of Scotland. The songs of Burns, having made their way among the people, were soon followed by poems of greater length, though hardly excelling them in beauty or value. The patrons of the rural genius took him from the plough, and made him—an exciseman! The rollicking, jovial disposition of the young poet peculiarly exposed him to the temptations which at that period beset the life of the gauger, and he unfortunately succumbed to them, and fell into difficulties and perplexities which shortened his life. He

died in 1796, in the thirty-seventh year of his age. It was not until after his death that Scotland learned to estimate aright either the poet or the man. As a lyrist, Burns has never been excelled; while his merits as a humorist are almost as great: again, his pathos is irresistibly touching; and whether it is his aim to melt the listener to tenderness and to tears, to excite him to laughter, or to rouse him to patriotism, his mastery of the human sympathies is despotic and complete.

Dr. John Wolcot, better known as Peter Pindar, wrote towards the close of the last century a series of social and political satires, which gained immense popularity from their jocose and ridiculous humour, and their audacious sarcasms, levelled at the most distinguished personages of the realm. King George III. was Peter's favourite butt, and his shafts flew thick and fast at the royal quarry. Wolcot lived to a great age, dying in 1819 at fourscore. His works are little read at the present day, and would be hardly understood by the present generation, owing to the allusions they contain to matters now obsolete and forgotten.

William Cowper (Fig. 2526), the most domestically popular of modern English poets, was born in 1731, of a good family, by whose interest he might have obtained an eminent position. His temperament, however, was morbidly nervous, and would not allow of his mingling in the ordinary business of the world. Leading a retired life, chequered with seasons of fearful suffering, of religious despair, and of mental alienation—he yet laboured industriously with his pen, and exercised, by the harmonious expression of his thoughtful, just, and wholesome philosophy, a more profound and subtle influence upon his contemporaries than any other moral teacher of his day. His chief work, 'The Task,' is a model of fine sense expressed in truthful, classical verse; and his translation of Homer is perhaps the most faithful and conscientious performance in existence in that department of literature. He died in 1800.

Dr. Jenner (Fig. 2527), to whose discovery of the principle of vaccination we owe our release from the plague of small-pox, died in 1823.

In the year 1798 the Rev. T. R. Malthus published his celebrated 'Essay on the Principles of Population,' in which he asserted, and professed to prove, that it is the law of population to increase in a geometrical ratio, while the sustaining food can only increase in an arithmetical ratio—and that therefore, unless population be prevented from increase by the operation of artificial checks, famine and misery (which he assumed to be the natural checks) must ensue. Of all modern writings, this single essay has been probably most fruitful of important results—because, from the apparently demonstrated truth of the theory, legislators embraced it, and from it legislation has taken a tone which has not tended to humanize its measures. The principle, however, was not without its opponents in Malthus's day, and was the occasion of no end of controversy, political and philosophical: later it has met with severe handling from writers of acknowledged reputation, and appears on close investigation to be nothing more than a plausible fallacy. Malthus died in his seventy-sixth year in 1835.

The Rev. George Crabbe was a poet of peculiarly English character, both as to style and sentiment. He was patronised in youth by Burke and Johnson, who both saw the sterling merit and the stern uncompromising fidelity of his delineations. The subject of his poems is invariably the trials, the hardships, the temptations, and the misery of the poor; and these he has painted with a vigour and truth not to be surpassed. His works have operated largely in the instigation of private charity, and the originating of public institutions of benevolence. Crabbe was the most modest and unassuming of men, and spent a long life in labouring quietly among the poor of his parish in Trowbridge, Wilts, and in vindicating the claims of poverty with his pen. He died at an advanced age in 1832.

Samuel Rogers was a poet of a different stamp. Born in 1762, and living to the age of ninety and upwards, he connects the era of Johnson with our own. He was a banker, and the son of a banker, and passed his life surrounded with the appliances of wealth and luxury, and in intimate association with all the genius and talent of three generations. His chief work is 'The Pleasures of Memory,' which, like all his writings, is characterized by classical elegance, and a too careful simplicity of style, united with extreme polish and finish. Rogers was a man of refined and educated taste, which he was enabled to gratify by the most lavish expenditure; and he filled his dwelling with the most exquisite productions of ancient and modern art, gathered from the stores of all Europe. His habits were eccentric, and his sarcasm more biting and bitter than it was just or discriminating. He died in 1856.

Of all the poets of our own day, William Wordsworth seem

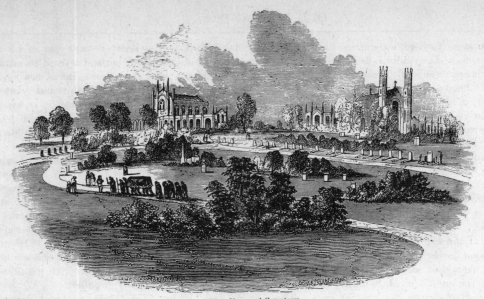

2545.—Norwood Cemetery.

2544.—Catacombs at Highgate Cemetery.

2546.—Kensall Green Cemetery.

destined to exercise the most lasting influence upon the minds of his countrymen. Born in 1770, he had lived to a mature age before the world had perceived or would acknowledge his rare merit. No writer was ever the cause of so much derision, laughter, and ridicule, or for so long a time was held by reviewers in such supreme contempt. His literal adherence to Nature offended their classical prejudices, and his obstinate persistence in his own course provoked their resentment. Eventually he gained the public approval in spite of their hostility, and turned the tide of opinion against them. He died in 1850, full of age and honours.

Samuel Taylor Coleridge, the friend of Wordsworth and Southey, was, perhaps, the man of the present century who united the largest intellectual capacity, with an almost equal amount of list-lessness, laziness, and indecision. In his youth he enlisted as a private soldier under the name of Comberbach, and astonished his officers by his erudition. In his manhood he electrified the world by the production of the "Ancient Mariner," and "Christabel," —rich promises of a golden harvest, which were never realised. In his maturer age he melted down into a mere talker—discoursing poetry, metaphysics, and art, in a style of incomprehensible inspira-tion,—but doing nothing. With his vast talents, he neglected to make any provision for his family, and with the power of achieving independence by comparatively slight exertion, he existed on the benevolence of others, and died in 1834 at Highgate—a pensioner on the bounty of a friend with whom he was domesticated.

Robert Southey, a man in most respects the contrast of Coleridge, and yet his warmest friend, was born in 1774. As a youth he published "Wat Tyler," a feeble drama of demagogic tendency, which he subsequently tried to suppress. His first earnest work was "Joan of Arc," which was followed by a series of other epics of amazing length and remarkable power, but too wire-drawn and wearisome for popular favour. Southey stands in higher estimation as a historian, biographer, and reviewer, than as a poet. His industry was amazing, and unparalleled, save by the exertions of Walter Scott; he lived among books, and wrote more than average men read in the course of a life. It is sad to be obliged to add, that his assiduity brought on disease of the brain, and that the last years of his life were consumed in hopeless insanity. He died in 1843.

Charles Lamb, the friend of Southey and Coleridge, was born in 1775. He was a man of rare powers, uniting the racy wit of the old English humorists, with a refined, delicate simplicity peculiar to himself. His most charming productions are the famous "Essays of Elia," which have formed the model of most writers of sketches and magazine article since his time. He was not dependent on literature for support, as he held a lucrative office in the East India House, and was allowed to retire before age came upon him, on a handsome pension. To this cause, perhaps, may be attributed the perfection of his compositions, which are, for the most part, master-pieces of style. Lamb was the darling of the literary circles of his day, and is the object of affectionate admiration to all lovers of genuine harmless humour. He died in 1834.

Thomas Moore, who was born in Dublin in 1780, came first into general notice as the modern Anacreon, a title he obtained by a volume of not over-delicate verse, published under the pseudonym of Thomas Little. His reputation rests, however, on his Irish Melodies; the publication of which began in 1813, and which deservedly ranked him high among the poets of the day. Perhaps, no man ever lived who made more money by writing verse than Moore. He had 3000l. for a single poem, and he drew a round income from publishers during the greater part of his life. But Tom was the favourite of the great world, and as a general rule, his expenses outran his means; he had, however, an inexhaustible fund of spirits, and though in difficulties often, was rarely in serious perplexity; and laughed his troubles away with a philosophy quite as surprising as it was creditable. He had the best wife in the world, and the sense to value such a treasure—and to her, more than to all his good fortune and aristocratic favour, he owed the happiness of his lot. In his later years he enjoyed a pension of 300l. from government, and was thus spared the penalties of poverty.

Thomas Campbell, the author of "The Pleasures of Hope," was born in Glasgow in 1777. He was a man of remarkable genius, and enriched our literature with a small but invaluable collection of the finest odes ever penned, and which will endure as long as the English tongue. We need mention only "The Battle of the Baltic," "Hohenlinden," "Ye Mariners of England," "Lochiel," and "The Last Man"—the strains of which will recur to the recollection of our readers. The exquisite poem "Gertrude of Wyoming" is accounted Campbell's masterpiece, and, like all his finest works, bids defiance to the arts of correction and amendment.

Campbell lived to reap the honours due to his exalted merit, and was justly prized by his Scottish countrymen.

Sir Walter Scott (Fig. 2528), born in 1771, obtained a world-wide reputation, and doubtless exercised more influence on the literature and literary tastes of all Europe than any other man of his time. As a poet he was unrivalled in his original and peculiar walk long before the Waverly Novels had won for their unknown author the admiration of all lovers of fiction. The rapidity with which these marvellous creations followed each other amazed and delighted the world, who waited for them with eagerness, and received them with rapture. Scott realized enormous sums by his pen; but unfortunately involving himself with the commercial trans-actions of his publisher, was dragged with him to ruin in the panic of 1825–26—and reduced to poverty, with a vast debt upon his shoulders. His high sense of integrity would not allow him to compound with his creditors; and he spent the remaining years of his life in Herculean labours to pay off the heavy debt. Many of his magnificent fictions were produced in this sublime endeavour to preserve his honour unstained; but, alas! the superhuman exertion prematurely prostrated his powers, and he sank beneath it after six years of incessant application—dying of paralysis and delirium in 1832. The history of literature, while it can produce no grander success, affords no more magnanimous instance of lofty principle and glorious self-sacrifice.

Lord Byron (Fig. 2529), whose popularity for ten years preceding his decease, and about as long a period after, approached almost to idolatry, was born in 1788. His first production, published at the age of nineteen, was the "Hours of Idleness," which, being merci-lessly assailed by Jeffrey in the Edinburgh Review, provoked as merciless a satire from the young lord, under the title of "English Bards and Scotch Reviewers." The whole scribbling tribe winced under the cutting lash of this satire, and suddenly learned becoming respect for the wielder of such a weapon. The subsequent pro-ductions of the bard met with a favourable reception, and were in the highest degree worthy of it, though they were all deeply tinged with a morbid contempt for the blessings of life and a gloomy sceptical spirit. The bold imagery, the exquisite tenderness, and the sensuous phraseology which ran through all his works fascinated the reader, and especially captivated the youth of the whole realm. The name of Byron was in every mouth, his verse were household words; and to utter a syllable in his dispraise was thought little short of blasphemy. It is impossible at this time of day to describe the enthusiastic worship of this marvellous man as it prevailed thirty years ago—the world has seen nothing like it since. But, with all his fame, Byron was a miserable being: disappointed in early life he had become the victim of passions which he cared not to control, and whose indulgence ruined his domestic happiness, and drove him into exile. Most of his famous works—his Childe Harold, Don Juan, and the Dramas—were written abroad; and they were all to some extent the reflex either of his morbid disgust with life, or of the dissipations with which he sought to dispel the gloom of his spirit. In 1824 he repaired to Missolonghi, to aid, with his for-tune and his sword, the Greeks in their assertion of their independence. He had, however, but the wreck of a short life to offer them, and died in April of the same year.

Percy Bysshe Shelley, the friend of Byron, was born in 1792. He was a man of brilliant genius, and of the purest principle; but he was subject in early life to the senseless tyrannies of blockheads in office, and driven from the pale of society by men whose bigotry blinded them to the virtues of honesty and sincerity. Their bar-barity made of the young thinker a daring infidel and a vigorous assailant of the religion they professed. His first work, "Queen Mab" is an atheistical production, and all his works are more or less full of the sceptical spirit. They abound in beauties of a dreamy and metaphysical kind, but are too abstruse and philosophical ever to become generally popular. Shelley believed in the perfectibility of man without the aid of religion, and set an example of charity and active benevolence in his own life. He was drowned in 1822 while crossing the Bay of Spezzia in a boat.

Among the other poets of our day of whom death has deprived us, we may mention John Keats, the author of "Endymion" and "Zamia," who died at Rome in 1824, and who wanted but a longer life to have ranked with the first poets of any age; James Mont-gomery, the religious poet of Sheffield, author of "William Tell," "The World before the Flood," and a host of minor poems of a serious tendency; and Thomas Hood, at once the funniest of all modern writers and the most profoundly touching and pathetic; who, in "Miss Killmansegg and her Golden Leg," makes us laugh till laughter exhausts itself, and in the "Song of the Shirt," and "Bridge of Sighs" stirs the lowest depths of grief and sorrowful indignation.

Among the living poets, whose name is legion, we may point to Walter Savage Landor, the author of "Gebir" and the "Imaginary Conversations;" to Robert Browning, whose "Bells and Pomegranates" deserve the laurels they have won; to Bailey, whose "Festus" stands alone in the profuseness of it simagery and the comprehensiveness of its grasp, and to Alfred Tennyson the laureate, and incomparably the deepest thinker, the keenest observer, the most harmonious versifier, and in all respects the most powerful *vates* of his time.

Among the divines who have reflected most honour on the present century, Robert Hall (Fig. 2530), John Foster, and Dr. Thomas Chalmers occupy the foremost rank. Among historians, Macaulay, who unites in one pen the diversified powers of Hume and Gibbon; and Alison, to whose astonishing industry and research we are indebted for the history of Europe, with all its wars, politics, literature, and social progress, from the antecedents of the French Revolution down to the present day—are the chief. The novelists of our time are a tribe which may be numbered by the hundred, and so voracious is the appetite for fiction that tolerable employment is found for them all. At the head of them stand Sir Lytton Bulwer, whose works comprise delineations from every class of society, and are greedily read by multitudes, who have the advantage of purchasing them at a nominal cost; Douglas Jerrold, whose caustic satire withers and shrivels up the shams and seemings of official pretence; Thackeray, who with remorseless pen probes and lays bare the sores and ulcers of our social body, and trots out the skeleton that is in every house, and puts him to his ghastly paces for the amusement of the million; and Dickens, ever genial and gentle, shedding sunshine on dark and dreary places, and exposing but to heal the wounds and bruises of poor struggling and stricken humanity. At the head of our miscellaneous writers must be placed De Quincey, the author of the "Confessions of an Opium Eater," and Thomas Carlyle, whose marvellous histories, essays, and biographies—pictures painted in words of fire, and thoughts uttered in thunder-claps—have thrilled through the world and made him an idol and a mystery to the thinkers of the earth.

To the above meagre sketch of the literature we must add one word on the arts and their progress during the past hundred years. It might have been thought that the age which produced Hogarth and Reynolds (Fig. 2531) would have appreciated such labours as theirs. It did so, however, but imperfectly, and Hogarth lived by his prints, not his paintings. During his day, and for some time later, it was only by portrait-painting that the artist found remuneration. Historical paintings came slightly into vogue when Benjamin West (Figs. 2532, 2533) made his appearance, but the fancy for that soon subsided, and the best painters of the last century found small encouragement save from aristocratic sitters. Wilson starved on bread and cheese. Barry did the same. Later, when Wilkie came to London, he laboured for long years before he could earn a decent livelihood; and the same tale might be told of a hundred other painters. It was not until some years after the peace of 1815 that any enthusiasm for art became general in this country. Foreign travel then taught the English what to admire, and they were not long of discovering that their own painters were equal to any living. The taste, once generated, grew apace, and English artists began to thrive, and, as a matter of course, to improve. Turner, the father of English landscape painting, led the way in his department, and, before he died, saw the English school the first in the world in landscape art. The progress in other branches, if not commensurate, has been great—in pictures of the genre species, such as Wilkie painted, and Paton, Faed, Frith, and Goodall paint now, the English, if rivalled are not surpassed; and in the delineation of animals no artists of ancient or modern times have excelled the productions of Landseer and Cowper. In water-colour art the English painters are pre-eminent and unapproachable; and indeed the palm in this delicate and fascinating style of painting is universally awarded to them throughout the Continent. Within the last few years art has been rendered increasingly popular through the means of the press; and the best results have ensued and are ensuing to the popular taste by the universal dissemination of well-executed engravings at a low price in the form of illustrations to books and periodicals.

In conclusion let us now, in a few brief words, draw the reader's attention to the most salient points of contrast between the state of society in our own day and that of a century back. We need not look beyond London for the elements of comparison, which are sufficiently obvious whichever way we turn. Our forefathers in this famous old city came into the world in a scene of riotous hubbub; they were brought up in the midst of a noisy mob, who made the narrow, miry streets the arena of their quarrels and diversions, and held, when they pleased, exclusive possession of the public ways. When sober people went abroad at night they needed the link-boy for a guide, and their men-servants for a bodyguard; *we*, on the other hand, have clean and orderly thoroughfares, tranquil by day under charge of the police (Fig. 2534), brilliantly illuminated by night, and safe from violence and tumult at all hours of the twenty-four. When our forefathers travelled, it was by slow and painful stages, over rough, sloughy roads, which made the journey a real peril, independent of the assaults of the highwayman who watched for their coming; *we* fly along the iron road on the wings of steam, and traverse the whole kingdom in a day without a thought of interruption. When they corresponded, they waited the tardy return of the post, whom floods or bad roads delayed, or the knights of the road plundered; and they paid a high price for postage, which acted as a prohibition to intercourse: *we* send letters five hundred miles for a penny, and get a reply on the morrow; or, not choosing to wait so long as that, communicate instantaneously by the electric wire. When their wives went to market, they had to chaffer in the rain and mire for provisions tumbled in heaps on the ground: *we* make palaces of our markets (Figs. 2535, 2536, 2537), and purchase at leisure from plentiful stores, garnered in galleries and arcades. If our grandsires saw a lion or an elephant, the sight was food for wonder to the end of their days: *we* walk at leisure in zoological gardens (Fig. 2538), amid specimens of natural history from all parts of the globe, and may be familiar, if we choose, with everything that crawls, runs, swims, or flies. When they wanted books they paid for them, to the few publishers of the day, a price which made literature almost a forbidden luxury: *we* find in the competition of the Row (Fig. 2539) a guarantee for cheapness, and can enjoy the luxury without anxiety about the cost. If their dwellings caught fire, they involved their neighbours in the calamity, and whole districts were often desolated by a single accident: *we* are watched over by a brigade of flame-quellers (Figs. 2540, 2541, 2542), who wrestle with the fire and subdue it without disturbing the economy of next door. When they fell under the hands of the surgeon they writhed in anguish beneath the knife: *we* dispel pain by chloroform, and escape the agony of surgical operations. When they died they were buried in heaps in back-street churchyards, amid the roar of traffic and the tramp of the multitude: *we* carry our dead to cemeteries (Figs. 2543, 2544, 2545, 2546) in suburban gardens, and lay them to rest beneath pendant foliage and amidst the sweet odours of flowers. Thus, from the cradle to the grave, the march of social amelioration has compassed us around—and, so far as the material elements of happiness and enjoyment are concerned, we are infinitely richer than they. Are we really happier, wiser, and better? That, after all, is the grand question—which we shall leave each of our readers to ponder for himself.

INDEX

TO THE

ENGRAVINGS OF VOLUME II.

GENERAL INDEX.